EUROPEAN COMMUNITY
COMPETITION PROCEDURE

EUROPEAN COMMUNITY COMPETITION PROCEDURE

SECOND EDITION

Edited by

LUIS ORTIZ BLANCO

With contributions by Luis Ortiz Blanco and Konstantin J Jörgens,
Marcos Araujo Boyd, José Luis Buendía Sierra,
Jean-Paul Keppenne and Kieron Beal

English revision by Andrew Read

OXFORD
UNIVERSITY PRESS

OXFORD
UNIVERSITY PRESS

Great Clarendon Street, Oxford OX2 6DP

Oxford University Press is a department of the University of Oxford.
It furthers the University's objective of excellence in research, scholarship,
and education by publishing worldwide in

Oxford New York

Auckland Cape Town Dar es Salaam Hong Kong Karachi
Kuala Lumpur Madrid Melbourne Mexico City Nairobi
New Delhi Shanghai Taipei Toronto

With offices in

Argentina Austria Brazil Chile Czech Republic France Greece
Guatemala Hungary Italy Japan Poland Portugal Singapore
South Korea Switzerland Thailand Turkey Ukraine Vietnam

Oxford is a registered trade mark of Oxford University Press
in the UK and in certain other countries

Published in the United States
by Oxford University Press Inc., New York

British Library Cataloguing in Publication Data

Data available

Library of Congress Cataloging in Publication Data

Data available

Typeset by RefineCatch Limited, Bungay, Suffolk
Printed in Great Britain
on acid-free paper by
Antony Rowe Ltd., Chippenham, Wiltshire

ISBN 0–19–826889–0   978–0–19–826889–5

3 5 7 9 10 8 6 4 2

FOREWORD TO PREVIOUS EDITION

A good legal text book should have several characteristics. It should be accurate, thorough and clear. It should be as concise and readable as the technicality of the subject-matter permits. It should, if possible, be practical, so that it is useful to practitioners, and at the same time it should raise issues of principle of which everyone needs to be aware even though they may not be frequently debated. It should cover regular practice even when indeed, in particular when—that practice is not embodied in regulations or case law. It should synthesize and state the up-to-date law, while summarizing its development and history as far as may be necessary to make the current law, and the leading cases in it, intelligible. It should avoid irrelevancies and extraneous material, while not failing to mention facts or rules of which, though they are outside the strict terms of reference of the book, the reader may need to be reminded for completeness, or because of gaps in his or her knowledge.

Judged by these standards, Luis Ortiz Blanco has written a valuable book. He has done so at a particularly good time. The importance of procedural principles and rules in the competition law of the European Community is now generally recognized. The law is still developing, for several reasons. This is still a young legal system, and case law is adding to the growing but still relatively small body of legislative and near-legislative rules. The Court of First Instance has now been in operation for several years, and it has done much, in long and detailed judgments, to clarify procedural rules and substantive law. The Commission is improving its procedures, and finding solutions to practical problems. New situations are arising, and with them new legal issues. The implications of the 'general principles of law', proportionality, legal certainty, the rights of the defence, and so on, are still being worked out. Lawyers are being forced to think about questions which they have apparently taken for granted, such as their duty of professional ethics not to mislead the Commission when it is exercising its powers in competition matters. National courts and national authorities, when they are applying Community competition law, are bound by some of these general principles of law. The respective rights of complainants and interveners in different kinds of proceedings are still being clarified. Some of the procedural rules, in particular those on transport and the Merger Regulation, are relatively new, and not all their implications have yet been explored. The apparently different categories of confidential information are still being defined, or at least seen more clearly. National legislatures in a majority of the

Member States of the Community have now adopted (with little or no urging from the Community institutions) competition laws based very closely on that of the Community, and they are giving rise to legal issues similar or identical to those arising under Community law itself. Rules which involve the way national courts think of their own roles are being raised like the duty of a court to raise questions of Community law on its own initiative, and the duty of national courts to give remedies sufficient to protect rights given by Community law, even if national law does not already provide such remedies. The symbiotic relationship between national courts and competition authorities and the Commission is being strengthened and elaborated.

To all this wealth of problems and precedents Luis Ortiz Blanco has brought a wealth of knowledge and experience, the results of great industry, considerable scholarship, and practical experience inside the Commission. He rightly gives as much attention to 'informal' resolution of cases as to the formal decisions originally envisaged by those responsible for Regulation 17/62. He stresses the usefulness and the frequency of informal discussions between lawyers and the Commission before notifications or complaints are filed. He gives the reasons for rules when their purpose may not be obvious. And he does not hesitate to criticize when he considers criticism is appropriate. He also draws attention to points even experienced lawyers sometimes forget—for example, tat nothing whatever is achieved by a complainant giving the Commission information which it insists is confidential, and which therefore the Commission cannot use or rely on in any way. And throughout all the procedural technicalities he keeps a firm grip on the underlying general principles of law and fundamental procedural rights. The views he states may not all be universally accepted, but they are without eccentricity, and seem to me to be essentially sound even when he expresses views on hitherto unresolved questions.

John Temple Lang

FOREWORD

Since the first edition of this book was published in 1996, a radical reform of European Community competition law enforcement has been carried out by the decentralisation Regulation, 1/2003, changes in the law on mergers, and a series of related measures. As the first person to suggest this reform publicly, I was in favour of it. But the reform was so radical that it has a great variety of consequences, for companies, for practising lawyers, for competition authorities and for national courts. So an entirely new version of this book was needed. Luis and his collaborators, indefatigably, have written it.

The reform has led to changes in emphasis. The activities of national competition authorities are more important than they were. A new kind of decision, making companies' commitments legally binding, has been introduced, and is already being more frequently used than had been expected. A series of new procedural issues have arisen, and have to be discussed, even if they have not yet been resolved. A variety of questions, not caused by decentralisation but increased in importance because of it, have arisen. Some issues have arisen because the reforms did not go so far as to involve any harmonisation of the procedures or fining policies of national competition authorities. Some in fact may not be satisfactorily solved without some degree of harmonisation. This book is not primarily concerned with the need for future reforms, but the alert reader will notice that some of the perennial controversies about the Commission's procedure, most obviously concerning access to the Commission's file, could be solved only by separating fully the responsibilities for making the case against the agreement or practice and for decision-making. Similar controversies will arise with national competition authorities which do not adopt more satisfactory procedures than the Commission in this respect.

Readers will also notice how often the activities of national competition authorities and national courts are likely in practice to involve their legal duties of cooperation with the Commission under Article 10 EC, and their duties under that Article to provide effective protection for rights given or guaranteed by Community law. Regulation 1/2003 was well drafted, but its consequences are so many and so far-reaching that it will give rise to many legal issues which it could not have been expected to anticipate and resolve. In dealing with all these issues, and in particular until the Commission publishes a Notice on the interpretation of Article 10, Luis' second edition will be immensely useful, as the first edition has been.

Once again Luis has brought to bear his combination of academic knowledge and practical experience in the Commission, with the Spanish competition authority and as a practitioner, with the knowledge of his colleagues. This book is important and valuable, and I recommend the second edition as strongly as I recommended the first.

John Temple Lang[1]

---

[1] Cleary Gottlieb Steen and Hamilton LLP, Brussels and London; Professor of Law, Trinity College Dublin; Visiting Senior Research Fellow, Oxford University.

PREFACE

Ten years on, this book has finally come to terms with its title, since it now covers all areas of EC competition law. 'Second edition' is something of a misnomer because so many things have changed in the application of Articles 81 and 82 EC that only a tiny part of the first edition has stood the passage of time. In addition, there are completely new sections on mergers, public undertakings and State aid.

This book is the result of the efforts of a prestigious team of lawyers which I have had the honour to coordinate. I am indebted to everyone in the team, but most particularly to Konstantin Jörgens, who has shown enormous patience in working head-to-head with me on this project over the last year.

The team of authors itself has been supported by several assistants: Ángel Givaja Sanz, Carlos Vérgez Muñoz, Crisanto Pérez Abad, Jonathan Entrena Rovers, Mariarosaria Ganino, Alberto Escudero Puente, Juan Andrés García Alonso and Patricia Goicoechea García, to name but a few. Our thanks go to all of them.

We hope that this book proves helpful for practitioners and undertakings. I hesitate to say 'for the Commission too', although it may find here some ideas for a General Procedural Code, and not necessarily only as regards competition matters. This would be an interesting topic for a third edition. In the meantime, we hope that we have been able to make these intricate procedures more understandable for all those interested in issues relating to EC competition law.

Luis Ortiz Blanco
Madrid, 15 December 2005

Note: On 28 June 2006 the European Commission adopted new Guidelines on the method of setting fines. A revised chapter 11 "Infringement Decisions and Penalties" which considers the new Guidelines will be made available at Oxford University Press' website in due course, at http://www.oup.com/uk/booksites/content/0198268590.

CONTENTS—SUMMARY

I ANTITRUST RULES (ARTICLES 81 AND 82 EC)
Luis Ortiz Blanco and Konstantin J Jörgens

II CONTROL OF CONCENTRATIONS
(REGULATION 139/2004)
Marcos Araujo Boyd

III PUBLIC UNDERTAKINGS AND EXCLUSIVE
OR SPECIAL RIGHTS (ARTICLE 86(3) EC)
Jose Luis Buendía Sierra

IV STATE AID (ARTICLES 87 AND 88 EC)
Jean-Paul Keppenne

V COMPETITION LAW AND PROCEDURE IN THE
EUROPEAN ECONOMIC AREA
Kieron Beal

APPENDICES

CONTENTS

I ANTITRUST RULES (ARTICLES 81 AND 82 EC)
Luis Ortiz Blanco and Konstantin J Jörgens

1. The Institutional Framework

xiii

9. Investigation of Cases (IV): Penalties, Confidentiality

10. Infringement Procedures

II CONTROL OF CONCENTRATIONS
(REGULATION (EC) 139/2004)
Marcos Araujo Boyd

III PUBLIC UNDERTAKINGS AND EXCLUSIVE OR SPECIAL RIGHTS (ARTICLE 86(3) EC)

José Luis Buendía Sierra

IV STATE AID (ARTICLES 87 AND 88 EC)

Jean-Paul Keppenne

22. Prior Control of New Notified Aid

23. Unlawful Aid

V COMPETITION LAW AND PROCEDURE
IN THE EUROPEAN ECONOMIC AREA

Kieron Beal

APPENDICES

TABLE OF CASES

TABLE OF TREATIES AND AGREEMENTS

TABLE OF REGULATIONS

TABLE OF DIRECTIVES

PART I

ANTITRUST RULES
(ARTICLES 81 AND 82 EC)

1

THE INSTITUTIONAL FRAMEWORK

I. Sources of procedure

A. Substantive Provisions

The basic Community competition provisions applicable to businesses or under-   **1.01**
takings are Articles 81 and 82 of the EC Treaty (Treaty of Rome as amended,
'*EC* ').[1] Both provisions are an important part of the Community legal order
and pursue one of the EC Treaty's main objectives namely that of achieving 'a
system ensuring that competition in the internal market is not distorted'.[2] Such
a system is in turn important with a view to promoting the goals as set out in
Article 2 EC, in particular 'a high degree of competitiveness and convergence of
economic performance.' Article 81(1) EC prohibits agreements and arrangements between undertakings that affect trade between Member States and
which have as their object or effect the prevention, restriction, or distortion of
competition within the European Union (EU).[3] Article 82 EC prohibits abuses
of a dominant position within the common market by one or more undertakings. Apart from various actions listed in Article 82(2) EC, abuses may take
the form of any conduct by a dominant undertaking that appreciably distorts
competition or exploits customers in the market in question.

---

[1] See the more detailed overview in A Jones and B Sufrin, *EC Competition Law* (2nd edn, 2004)
80–100; R Whish, *Competition Law* (5th edn, 2003) 49–60; C Bellamy and G Child, *European
Community Law of Competition* (5th edn, 2001) paras 1–041 to 1–051; see also CS Kerse and
N Khan, *EC Antitrust Procedure* (5th edn, 2005) paras 1–011 to 1–069; J Schwarze and
A Weitbrecht, *Grundzüge des europäischen Kartellverfahrensrechts* (2004) §§ 1 and 2.

[2] Art 3(g) EC. Arts 3(a)(1) and 102(a) EC reinforce the 'principle of an open market economy
with free competition', and Arts 53 and 54 EEA have reproduced, for implementation throughout the territory of the contracting parties, the provisions of Arts 81 and 82 EC.

[3] The importance of Art 3(g) EC led the drafters of the EC Treaty to provide expressly, in Art
81(2) EC, that *any* agreements or decisions prohibited pursuant to that provision are to be
automatically void. (Case C-126/97 *Eco Swiss* [1999] ECR I-3055 para 36) unless it meets the
requirements of Art 81(3) EC Commission Notice—Guidelines on the application of Art 81(3)
of the Treaty [2004] OJ C101/97.

1.02 The assessment of the effect of agreements and conduct on competition often involves a complex analysis of facts, and the conclusions derived from these facts may differ significantly depending on the underlying economic theory and model employed. Establishing the most basic concepts in competition law, such as the relevant market, are often challenges and require very specific data and sophisticated analytical tools.[4] Competition authorities are increasingly confronted with the need to investigate such complex cases, which require in-depth fact-finding and rigorous economic and empirical analysis.[5] The shift from the formalistic regulatory approach towards a more economic-oriented assessment to ensure quality and the influence of economic advice in enforcement and policy making has been a key objective of the EC Commission in recent years.[6]

---

[4] See also JS Venit, 'Private Practice in the Wake of the Commission's Modernization Program' [2005] Legal Issues of Economic Integration 147–59 (151–52).

[5] Case C-234/89 *Stergios Delimitis v Henninger Bräu AG* [1991] ECR I-935 para 44 noted that it is for the Commission to adopt, subject to review by the Court of First Instance ('CFI') and the European Court of Justice ('ECJ'), individual decisions in accordance with the procedural rules in force and to adopt exemption regulations. The performance of that task would necessarily entail complex economic assessments, in particular in order to assess whether an agreement falls under Art 81 EC. See also Opinion of AG Cosmas in Case C-344/98 *Masterfoods* [2000] ECR I-11369 para 44. The review of the Community courts is necessarily limited to verifying whether the relevant rules on procedure and on the statement of reasons have been complied with, whether the facts have been accurately stated and whether there has been any manifest error of appraisal or misuse of powers. Case 42/84 *Remia and others v EC Commission* [1985] ECR 2545 para 34, and Joined Cases 142/84 and 156/84 *BAT and Reynolds v EC Commission* [1987] ECR 4487 para 62; C-194/99 *Thyssen Stahl AG v EC Commission* [2003] ECR I-10821 para 78. For more details on the aspects of judicial review, see ch 15 'Steps following the adoption of a formal decision' para 15.26 *et seq.*

[6] A series of judgments of the CFI in 2002, particularly in the field of merger control (Case T-342/99 *Airtours v EC Commission* [2002] ECR II-2585, Case T-310/01 *Schneider Electric SA v EC Commission* [2002] ECR II-4071) have also drawn attention to the issue of the burden of proof incumbent on the Commission in adopting negative decisions. This has led the Commission '[. . .] to review and strengthen internal procedures to ensure the rigour and objectivity of the legal and economic analysis as the basis of its decisions as well as to guarantee respect for "due process" [. . .]'. EC Commission press release IP/03/603 of 30 April 2003 'Commission reorganises its Competition Department in advance of Enlargement' and IP/03/1027 of 16 July 2003 'Commission appoints Chief Competition Economist'. The Chief Competition Economist is assisted by a team of specialized economists and should offer an independent economic viewpoint for policy development and provide guidance in individual cases throughout the investigation process. In 2004, the Chief Economist Team (CET) was involved in 15 antitrust cases which are selected in agreement with the Director-General on the basis of the need for more sophisticated economic analysis. In such cases, a member of the CET is placed on the case team, having access to all information and participating in all meetings with out side experts and parties. Within the case team the members seconded from the CET have specific and independent status and report directly to the Chief Competition Economist on the line they take. The Chief Economist also coordinates the activities of the Economic Advisiory Group in Competition Policy (EAGCP). Commission Report on Competition Policy SEC (2004) 805 final 9. See also M Monti, 'EU Competition Policy after May 2004' ch 16 403–13 (406) in BE Hawk (ed), International Antitrust Law Policy, Fordham Corporate Law Institute (2003) and M Bloom, 'The Great Reformer: Mario Monti's Legacy in Article 81 and Cartel Policy' [2005] 1(1) Competition Policy International 55–78 (63–64).

Further, competition law procedures often make it necessary for the public authorities to take economic policy decisions based on considerations of public interest and objectives of social welfare which fall outside the traditional sphere of activity of national courts, better placed to dealing with private actions for damages for breaches of antitrust rules.[7] Unlike a normal commercial dispute, where the parties can determine somehow the rules of the game, the parties in a dispute involving Articles 81 and 82 EC are bound by the public interest aim of these provisions with a view to guaranteeing the maintenance of a system that ensures that competition is not distorted.[8] Furthermore, EC competition law extends beyond the interests of any one Member State and seeks to attain specific economic objectives on a much greater scale.[9] All these features, together with the principle of limited intervention laid down in Article 83 EC and the principle that the Commission's administrative practice must be appropriate to the prevailing circumstances, are reflected in the rules and procedural practices according to which the Commission and the Community courts have applied substantive competition law.[10]

[7] Commission Notice on cooperation between the Commission and the courts of the EU Member States in the application of Arts 81 and 82 EC [2004] OJ C101/54 ('National Courts Cooperation Notice') para 6 'Where an individual asks the national court to safeguard his subjective rights, national courts play a specific role in the enforcement of Arts 81 and 82 EC, which is different from the enforcement in the public interest by the Commission or by national competition authorities.' Case C-94/00 *Roquette Frères SA v Directeur général de la concurrence, de la consommation et de la répression des frauds, and EC Commission* ('*Roquette Frères*') [2002] ECR I-9011 para 42: '[. . . .] the powers conferred on the Commission by Art 14(1) of Reg No 17 [Article 20 of Reg 1/2003] are designed to enable it to perform its task of ensuring that the competition rules are applied in the common market, the function of those rules being to prevent competition from being distorted to the detriment of the public interest, individual undertakings and consumers, thereby ensuring economic well-being in the Community.'

[8] White Paper on modernization of the rules implementing Arts 85 and 86 [now 81 and 82] of the EC Treaty [1999] OJ C132/1 para 91. See also Case T-528/93 *Métropole Télévision v EC Commission* [1996] ECR II-649 para 118 in which the Court held that, for the purposes of an overall assessment, the Commission could base its decisions to grant an exemption under Art 85(3) on considerations relating to the pursuit of the public interest.

[9] Case T-31/99 *ABB Asea Brown Boveri Ltd v EC Commission* [2002] ECR-II 1881 para 116: '[. . .] [the] task [of the Commission] certainly includes the duty to investigate and punish individual infringements, but it also encompasses the duty to pursue a general policy designed to apply, in competition matters, the principles laid down by the Treaty and to guide the conduct of undertakings in the light of those principles [. . .]'

[10] WPJ Wils, 'Should Private Antitrust Enforcement Be Encouraged' [2003] World Competition 473–488 (480–484) argues that if the goal of antitrust enforcement is to ensure that antitrust prohibitions are not violated, public enforcement is inherently superior to private enforcement. By contrast, see CA Jones, 'Private Antitrust Enforcement in Europe: A Policy Analysis and Reality Check' [2004] World Competition 13–24. See also on this debate A Riley, 'Beyond Leniency: Enhancing Enforcement in EC Antitrust Law' [2005] World Competition 377–400 (381 et seq).

B. Procedural Rules

1.03 Article 83 EC empowers the EC Council to adopt regulations and directives in order, in particular,

(a) to ensure compliance with the prohibitions laid down in Articles 81(1) and 82 by making provision for fines and periodic penalty payments;

(b) to lay down detailed rules for the application of Article 85(3), taking into account the need to ensure effective supervision on the one hand, and to simplify administration to the greatest possible extent on the other;

(c) to define, if need be, in the various branches of the economy, the scope of the provisions of Articles 85 and 86;

(d) to define the respective functions of the Commission and the ECJ in applying the provisions laid down in this paragraph;

(e) to determine the relationship between national laws and the provisions contained in this Section or adopted pursuant to this Article.

On the basis of that provision, the Council has adopted a series of regulations which define in detail the procedure applicable to competition matters, and has entrusted the application of that procedure to the Commission. The Council has also authorized the Commission to adopt supplementary procedural rules.

1. General regime

1.04 In 1962 the EC Council adopted the 'First Regulation implementing Articles 81 and 82 of the Treaty', commonly known as Regulation 17.[11] This Regulation laid down the system of supervision and enforcement procedures, which the EC Commission applied for over forty years without any significant change. Under Regulation 17, the Council authorized the Commission to undertake investigations and ensure compliance with the Community competition rules, imposing penalties on offenders if necessary ('infringement procedure'). The Commission was thus able to order the termination of restrictive agreements and abuses of dominant positions in the common market and prevent their proliferation. While under Regulation 17, Articles [81(1)] and [82] were directly applicable and therefore could be applied not only by the Commission but also by national

---

[11] Council Reg (EEC) 17 implementing Arts 85 and 86 of the Treaty, as amended [1962] JO 13/204, [1959–62] OJ Spec Ed 87; See for a detailed overview on the historical perspective, A Jones and B Sufrin', *EC Competition Law* (2nd edn, 2004) 1041–54; R Whish, *Competition Law* (5th edn, 2003) 246–51; WPJ Wils, 'Community Report' in D Cahill (ed), *The Modernization of EU Competition Law Enforcement in the EU*, FIDE 2004 National Reports, 661–736, paras 13–16; CS Kerse and N Khan, *EC Antitrust Procedure* (5th edn, 2005) paras 1–007–1–008.

courts in private litigation,[12] the Council gave the Commission exclusive power to apply Article 85(3) [now 81(3)] EC, i.e. to grant individual exemptions from the prohibition of restrictive agreements contained in Article [85(1)] ('the notification procedure'). The Member States participated in Commission procedures by virtue of the provisions for cooperation between the Commission and national administrations contained in Regulation 17. In addition, Regulation 17 also allowed interested parties to submit complaints, provided for hearings of undertakings against which proceedings were brought, and required the Commission to hear the latter's submissions and publish its decisions. The Commission was also empowered to adopt regulations for the implementation of Regulation 17 relating to the form and content of applications and notifications[13] and regarding the hearing of the persons concerned.[14]

On 1 May 2004, Regulation 17 was replaced by Regulation 1/2003, which was **1.05** the result of a reform process that the Commission started with the adoption of the White Paper on modernization of the rules implementing Articles 81 and 82 EC.[15] The starting point of the reform was a threefold finding: enlargement would take place in the near future, the notification system was no longer an effective tool for enforcing competition rules,[16] and Community competition law would be sufficiently developed to allow companies to assess the legality of

---

[12] Art 1 of Reg 17; Case 127/73 *BRT v SABAM* [1974] ECR 51 para 16; Case C-234/89 *Stergios Delimitis v Henninger Bräu AG* [1991] ECR I-935 para 45.

[13] Antitrust Procedure (Applications and Notifications) Reg (EC) 3385/94 [1994] OJ L377/28, replacing Reg 27/62 [1959–62] OJ Spec Ed 132 as amended, in respect notifications under Reg 17, Reg 2843/98 [1998] OJ L354/22 adopted a single form for notification of agreements within the transport sector. Notification had to be made in the format prescribed by Form A/B, which required extensive information.

[14] Commission Reg (EC) 2842/98 on the hearing of parties in certain proceedings under Articles 85 and 86 of the EC Treaty [1998] OJ L354/18 which is now replaced by Reg (EC) 773/2004 of 7 April 2004 relating to the conduct of proceedings by the Commission pursuant to Arts 81 and 82 of the EC Treaty [2004] OJ L123/18, Art 18.

[15] White Paper on modernization of the rules implementing Arts 85 and 86 [now 81 and 82] of the EC Treaty ('White Paper') [1999] OJ C132/1. The White Paper sought to deal with the enforcement problems which had arisen since the adoption of Reg 17 in 1962. In September 2000, the Commission presented a first proposal to amend the system of enforcement of Arts 81 and 82 of the EC. See EC Commission IP/00/1064 of 27 September 2000 'Competition: Commission proposes Regulation that extensively amends system for implementing Arts 81 and 82 EC'. It went on to initiate a broad debate, in which all the interested parties—companies, associations, jurists, economists, lawyers, members of the judiciary, and national governments—were offered an opportunity to express their views, both positive and negative, to make proposals, and to look further into the issues at stake. See also summary of the Observations submitted, DG COMP Document, 29 February 2000, available on DG COMP website.

[16] The fact that only a small number of agreements was covered by the block exemptions adopted by the Commission had led to an enormous number of cases pending before the Commission. Due to its limited resources it was practically impossible for the Commission to deal with all these notifications in the way foreseen by Reg 17. The Commission was no longer able to deal properly with these cases and had therefore started the practice of sending so-called 'comfort letters' to the parties.

their agreements themselves. Regulation 1/2003 entered into force on the same date as ten new Member States acceded to the EU. It has eliminated the possibility of notifying restrictive agreements to the Commission for exemption under Article 81(3) EC. It declares Article 81(3) EC directly applicable, thus empowering national competition authorities ('NCA') and national courts to examine restrictive agreements under that provision.[17] Companies and their advisers will have to perform competition law analyses themselves, based on applicable Court precedents and Commission decisions and practice. Regulation 1/2003 is intended to free up Commission resources previously occupied with reviewing notifications under Article 81(3) EC, enabling the Commission to focus on EU-wide cartels and abuses of dominance and to raise new policy issues where appropriate.[18] In order to complement Regulation 1/2003, following extensive consultations the Commission adopted the 'Modernization Package' which, with respect to procedural matters, includes the following:[19]

• *Commission Regulation 773/2004 of 7 April 2004 relating to the conduct of proceedings by the Commission pursuant to Articles 81 and 82 EC.*[20] Regulation 773/2004 contains detailed rules regarding, in particular, the initiation of

---

[17] Art 1(2) of Reg 1/2003 is based on the Commission's position that Art 81(3) EC is suitable for direct application. While leaving a certain margin of discretion as to its interpretation, Art 81(3) does not imply discretionary powers that could only be exercised by an administrative body. WPJ Wils, 'Community Report' in D Cahill (ed), *The Modernization of EU Competition Law Enforcement in the EU*, FIDE 2004 National Reports, 661–736, paras 21–22.

[18] C Gauer, L Kjolbye, D Dalheimer, E de Smijter, D Schnichels, and M Laurila, 'Regulation 1/2003 and the Modernization Package Fully Applicable since 1 May 2004' [2004] Competition Policy Newsletter Number 2, Summer, 1–6 (3–6). See also in regard to the policy behind the modernization programme, R Whish, *Competition Law* (5th edn, 2004) 246–51; DG Comp Director-General Philip Lowe, 'Current Issues of EU Competition Law—The New Competition Enforcement Regime' [2003] North Western Journal of International Law and Business, available at http://europa.eu.int/comm/competition/speeches/index_theme.html; WPJ Wils, 'Community Report' in D Cahill (ed), *The Modernization of EU Competition Law Enforcement in the EU*, FIDE 2004 National Reports, 661–736, paras 13–16. JS Venit, 'Private Practice in the Wake of the Commission's Modernization Program' [2005] Legal Issues of Economic Integration 147–59 (147, fn 3) questions whether the most efficient approach is to decentralize enforcement partially in the manner chosen by the Commission. With twenty-five enforcement authorities to deal with, it would remain to be seen whether the administrative burden of reviewing in advance proposed enforcement actions will be less than under the old system.

[19] The Commission also adopted guidelines on the effect on trade concept contained in Arts 81 and 82 EC ([2004] OJ C101/81) and guidelines on the application of Article 81(3) EC ([2004] OJ C101/97). C Gauer, L Kjolbye, D Dalheimer, E de Smijter, D Schnichels, and M Laurila, 'Modernization Package Fully Applicable since 1 May 2004' [2004] Competition Policy Newsletter Number 2, Summer 1–6 (1–3). As regards the question whether the notices have a binding effect upon NCAs and national courts, M Schwela, 'Die Bindungswirkung von Bekanntmachungen and Leitlinien der Europäischen Kommission' [2004] Wirtschaft und Wettbewerb 1133–43 and reply of P Pohlmann, 'Keine Bindungswirkung von Bekanntmachungen and Leitlinien der Europäischen Kommission' [2005] Wirtschaft und Wettbewerb 1105–09. The modernization package is available at http://europa.eu.int/comm/competition/antitrust/legislation/.

[20] [2004] OJ L123/18.

proceedings, oral statements, complaints, hearings of parties, access to the file, and the handling of confidential information in antitrust procedures conducted by the Commission.

- *Commission Notice on cooperation within the network of competition authorities ('ECN Cooperation Notice').*[21] The ECN Cooperation Notice sets out the main pillars of cooperation between the Commission and the competition authorities of the Member States in the European Competition Network (ECN). The notice sets out the principles for sharing case work between the members of the network. In this respect the ECN Cooperation notice follows the Joint Statement of the Council and the Commission which was issued on the day when Regulation 1/2003 was adopted.[22] It provides for particular arrangements regarding the interface between exchanges of information between authorities pursuant to Articles 11(2) and (3) as well as Article 12 of Regulation 1/2003 and the operation of leniency programmes. The NCAs have signed a statement in which they declare that they will abide by the principles set out in the Commission Notice.[23]

- *Commission Notice on the cooperation between the Commission and the courts of the EU Member States in the application of Articles 81 and 82 EC ('National Courts Cooperation Notice').*[24] The notice is intended to serve as a practical tool for national judges who apply Articles 81 and 82 EC in accordance with Regulation 1/2003. It brings together the relevant case law of the ECJ, thus clarifying the procedural context in which national judges are operating. Particular attention is given to the situation where the national court deals with a case at the same time or after the Commission. Regulation 1/2003 establishes a legal basis for national judges to ask the Commission for an opinion or to supply information it holds. In addition, it created the possibility for the Commission to submit written and oral observations to the national courts in the interest of coherent application. The National Courts Cooperation Notice spells out the modalities of those cooperation mechanisms.

- *Commission Notice on the handling of complaints by the Commission under Articles 81 and 82 of the EC.*[25] This Notice starts by providing general

---

[21] [2004] OJ C101/43.

[22] Joint Statement of the Council and the Commission on the functioning of the network of competition authorities. Council Document 15435/02 ADD 1 of 10 December 2002.

[23] Each NCA of the twenty-five Member States has signed the statement regarding the ECN Cooperation Notice. The list is available at http://europa.eu.int/comm/competition/antitrust/legislation/. The ECN Cooperation Notice may thus create legitimate expectations as regards not only the Commission but also the national competition authorities. C Gauer, L Kjolbye, D Dalheimer, E de Smijter, D Schnichels, and M Laurila, 'Regulation 1/2003 and the Modernization Package Fully Applicable since 1 May 2004' [2004] Competition Policy Newsletter Number 2, Summer 1–6 (5).

[24] [2004] OJ C101/54.   [25] [2004] OJ C101/65.

information on the work sharing of the different enforcers and invites potential complainants to make an informed choice of the authority where they lodge their complaint or file their claim (whether the Commission, a national court, or national competition authority) in light of the criteria for allocation of cases. The bulk of the notice contains explanations on the Commission's assessment of complaints in the field of antitrust, and the procedures applicable. The notice also includes an indicative deadline of four months, within which the Commission endeavours to inform complainants of its intention to conduct a full investigation on a complaint or not.

• *Commission Notice on informal guidance relating to novel questions concerning Articles 81 and 82 of the EC that arise in individual cases (Guidance Letters).*[26] Regulation 1/2003 pursues the objective that the Commission refocus its enforcement action on the detection of serious infringements. The abolition of the notification system is a crucial element in this context. However, it also seems reasonable that in a limited number of cases, where a genuinely novel question concerning Articles 81 or 82 arises, the Commission may, subject to its other enforcement priorities, provide guidance to undertakings in writing (guidance letter). The notice sets out details about this instrument.

1.06 It should be noted that the Modernization Package did not affect the existing enabling block exemption regulations which remain in force: Council Regulations 19/65/EEC,[27] (EEC) 2821/71,[28] (EEC) 3976/87,[29] (EEC) 1534/91,[30] or (EEC) 479/92[31] all empower the Commission to apply Article 81(3) EC by Regulation to certain categories of agreements, decisions taken by associations of undertakings, and concerted practices. In the areas defined by such Regulations, the Commission has adopted and may continue to adopt so called 'block' exemption regulations by which it declares Article 81(1) of the Treaty

---

[26] [2004] OJ C101/78.

[27] Council Reg 19/65/EEC of 2 March 1965 on the application of Art 81(3) of the Treaty to certain categories of agreements and concerted practices [1965] OJ L36/533, as amended.

[28] Council Reg (EEC) 2821/71 of 20 December 1971 on the application of Art 81(3) of the Treaty to categories of agreements, decisions and concerted practices [1971] OJ L285/46, as amended.

[29] Council Reg (EEC) 3976/87 of 14 December 1987 on the application of Art 81(3) of the Treaty to certain categories of agreements and concerted practices in the air transport sector [1987] OJ L374/9, as amended.

[30] Council Reg (EEC) 1534/91 on the application of Art 81(3) of the Treaty to certain categories of agreements, decisions and concerted practices in the insurance sector [1991] OJ L143/1, as amended.

[31] Council Reg (EEC) 479/92 on the application of Art 81(3) of the Treaty to certain categories of agreements, decisions and concerted practices between liner shipping companies (Consortia) [1992] OJ L55/3, as amended.

inapplicable to categories of agreements, decisions, and concerted practices. In addition, a number of Commission notices, and guidelines retain their full usefulness alongside Regulation 1/2003. A list of these block exemptions regulations, notices, and guidelines can be found in the Annex to the National Courts Cooperation Notice.[32]

Under the system introduced by Regulation 1/2003, the Commission shares the competence to apply Article 81 and 82 EC with the NCAs, unless it initiates proceedings for the adoption of a Commission decision under Regulation 1/2003.[33] By enabling NCAs and national courts to apply Articles 81 and 82 EC in full, Regulation 1/2003 has removed the principal obstacles to the prosecution of infringements of Articles 81 and 82 EC at the Member State level. On the one hand, Article 35 of Regulation 1/2003 obliges the Member States to designate the competition authority or authorities responsible for the application of Articles 81 and 82 EC and to take the measures necessary to empower those authorities to apply those Articles. On the other hand, the Member States remain free to organize their system of public enforcement. In this regard, Regulation 1/2003 recognizes the wide variation which exists in the public enforcement systems of Member States[34] as long as the Member States can ensure that their NCAs have the necessary resources to be represented in the Advisory Committee,[35] to provide assistance in inspections conducted by the Commission on their territory,[36] and undertake inspections requested by the Commission.[37]   **1.07**

Article 3(1) of Regulation 1/2003 provides that where a NCA or national court applies national competition law to agreements, decisions of undertakings, or concerted practices within the meaning of Article 81(1) EC which may affect trade between Member States or to any abuse prohibited by Article 82, they shall apply Article 81 or 82 EC. When dealing with an agreement, decision, or practice within the meaning of Article 81(1) EC which may affect trade between Member States or an abuse prohibited by Article 82 EC, NCAs will thus have the choice of either applying just Articles 81 or 82 EC, or applying both   **1.08**

---

[32] See the Annex of the National Courts Cooperation Notice [2004] OJ C101/54. An up-to-date list of the block exemption is available at http://europa.eu.int/comm/competition/antitrust/legislation/.

[33] See Art 11(6) of Reg 1/2003. However, the Commission is expected to apply Art 11(6) of Reg 1/2003 in a limited number of special situations. WPJ Wils, 'Community Report' in D Cahill (ed), *The Modernization of EU Competition Law Enforcement in the EU*, FIDE 2004 National Reports, 661–736, para 46. See ch 3 'National Competition Authorities' para 3.08 *et seq*.

[34] Recital 35 and Art 35(2) of Reg 1/2003. WPJ Wils, 'Community Report' in D Cahill (ed), *The Modernization of EU Competition Law Enforcement in the EU*, FIDE 2004 National Reports, 661–736, paras 178 *et seq*.

[35] Art 14 of Reg 1/2003; see ch 3 'National Competition Authorities' paras 3.45 *et seq*.

[36] Art 20(5) and (6) of Reg 1/2003; see ch 8 'Inspections' para 8.59.

[37] Art 22 of Reg 1/2003; see ch 8 'Inspections' para 8.64.

national competition law and Articles 81 or 82 EC.[38] When NCAs of the Member States rule on agreements, decisions, or practices under Article 81 or Article 82 EC which are already the subject of a Commission decision, they cannot take decisions which would run counter to the decision adopted by the Commission.[39] In the same vein, when national courts rule on agreements, decisions, or practices under Article 81 or 82 EC which are already the subject of a Commission decision, they cannot take decisions running counter to that decision.[40] The NCAs' powers to take decisions are circumscribed by Regulation 1/2003. They may require that an infringement be brought to an end, order interim measures, accept commitments, and impose fines but they do not have the power to adopt non-infringement decisions similar to the decisions which the Commission may adopt under Article 10 of Regulation 1/2003.[41] The underlying idea is that the Commission and the NCAs have parallel competences and that they should form together a network of authorities applying Articles 81 and 82 EC in close cooperation.

1.09 In fact NCAs could have stronger powers than the Commission under Regulation 1/2003. Indeed, whereas Regulation 1/2003 only empowers the Commission to impose fines on undertakings for infringements of Articles 81 or 82 EC, Article 5 of the Regulation also allows NCAs to impose 'any other penalty provided for in their national law', including imprisonment or criminal sanctions on natural persons. With regard to the application of national competition law, the obligation to apply Articles 81 and 82 EC does not exist where the NCAs and national courts apply national merger control rules. Nor does Regulation 1/2003 preclude the application of provisions of national law that predominantly pursue an objective different from that pursued by Articles 81 and 82 EC.[42] Member States can apply national legislation that protects legitimate

---

[38] In both cases, under Reg 1/2003 they will have to inform the Commission at the beginning of their proceedings pursuant to Art 11(3) and inform the Commission of their envisaged decision at the latest thirty days before its adoption in accordance with Art 11(4). In both cases the Commission can remove the case from them by opening proceedings under Art 11(6). Indeed, it follows from Art 11(6) in conjunction with Art 3(1) that an initiation of proceedings by the Commission relieves NCAs not only of their competence to apply Arts 81 or 82 EC, but also of their competence to apply national competition law in the same case.

[39] Art 16 of Reg 1/2003.

[40] The national court may assess whether it is necessary to stay its proceedings.

[41] Art 5 of Reg 1/2003.

[42] Art 3(3) of Reg 1/2003. See also Recital 8 which states that Reg 1/2003 does not apply to national laws which impose criminal sanctions on natural persons except to the extent that such sanctions are the means whereby competition rules applying to undertakings are enforced. WPJ Wils, 'Community Report' in D Cahill (ed), *The Modernization of EU Competition Law Enforcement in the EU*, FIDE 2004 National Reports, 661–738 para 161 notes that Recital 8 merely specifies what already follows from Art 3(3), namely that Arts 1 and 2 do not preclude the application of the provisions of national law that predominantly pursue an objective other than that pursued by Arts 81 and 82 EC.

interests other than the protection of competition on the market, provided that such legislation is compatible with general principles and other provisions of Community law.[43]

2. Special regimes[44]

The powers of the Commission to enforce the competition rules conferred by **1.10** Regulation 17 did not apply to the transport sector, as a result of Council Regulation 141, which excluded the transport sector from the application of the procedural rules retroactively.[45] Over the years, the Council adopted rules for the application of Articles 81 [85] and 82 [86] EC to road, rail and inland waterway transport,[46] maritime transport,[47] and air transport[48] ('Council Transport Regulations'). In 1998, the Commission adopted a regulation on the form and content of applications and notifications provided for in the relevant Council Transport Regulations which replaced three separate Transport Regulations and forms that previously contained the rules for notifying agreements in the inland transport, maritime transport, and air transport sectors, respectively.[49] In addition, the Commission modernized and simplified the rules in relation to hearings in competition procedures.[50] Commission Regulation (EEC) 99/63 related to hearings in competition procedures, including the transport sector.

---

[43] Recital 9 of Reg 1/2003 specifically states that legislation intended to prevent undertakings from imposing on their trading partners terms and conditions that are unjustified, disproportionate, and without consideration could be applied by Member States.

[44] For an overview of the reform of the transport block exemption regulations see: Commission Report on Competition Policy SEC (2005) 805 final para 16 and what follows.

[45] Council Reg (EEC) 141/62 exempting transport from the application of Council Reg 17, [1962] JO 124/2753, as amended [1959–62] OJ Spec Ed 291. The Regulation is no longer in force, see below. The reason for this exclusion were doubts as to whether EC competition rules were applicable to the transport sector. See however, Joined Cases 209 to 213/84 *Ministère public v Asjes (Nouvelles Fontieres)* [1986] ECR 1425 para 42 stating that competition rules are applicable to transport; L Ortiz Blanco and B van der Haute, *EC Competition Law in the Transport Sector* (1996) ch 2; A Klees, *Europäisches Kartellverfahrensrecht* (2005) § 1 para 49.

[46] Council Reg (EEC) 1017/68 applying rules of competition to transport by rail, road, and inland waterway [1968] OJ L175/1 [1968] OJ Spec Ed 302. The entry into force of Reg 1/2003 required certain amendments to Reg 1017/68.

[47] Council Reg (EEC) 4056/86 laying down detailed rules for the application of Arts 85 and 86 of the Treaty to maritime transport, [1986] OJ L378/4, as amended by Reg 1/2003.

[48] Council Reg (EEC) 3975/87 laying down the procedure for the application of the rules on competition to undertakings in the air transport sector [1987] OJ 1987 L374/1, as amended latest by Reg 1/2003.

[49] Commission Reg (EC) 2843/98 on the form, content and other details of applications and notifications provided for in Council Regs (EEC) 1017/68, (EEC) 4056/86 and (EEC) 3975/87 applying the rules on competition to the transport sector [1998] OJ L354/22. See Commission press release IP/98/1177 'Commission simplifies the legislative framework for examining competition cases'.

[50] Reg 99/63 [1963–64] OJ Spec Ed 47 was replaced by Commission Reg 2842/98 [1998] OJ L354/18 which was in turn replaced by Commission Reg 773/2004.

Land and air transport

1.11 Regulation 1/2003 brought about a highly desirable simplification of a previously somewhat confused situation.[51] Transport will no longer be different, at least from a procedural point of view. In essence, only two forms of maritime transport continue to be excluded from the application of Regulation 1/2003, whilst the inland and air transport sectors are now governed entirely by Regulation 1/2003. However, unlike the Council Transport Regulations in relation to the air sector, the Council Transport Regulations relating to the land and maritime sector are not entirely repealed; in fact, Articles 36 and 38 of Regulation 1/2003 just repeal the specific procedural provisions that they contained. Council Regulation 411/2004 repealed the Regulation on air transport and deleted the provision in Regulation 1/2003 which excluded from its scope air transport between the EU and third countries, with the result that all enforcement rules in Regulation 1/2003 will also apply to these routes.[52]

Maritime transport

1.12 Recital 36 of Regulation 1/2003 explains that Regulation 141 should be repealed;[53] and that the transport sector should be subject to its procedural provisions. In particular, the Regulation subjects land transport and maritime transport to the same procedural rules as under Articles 81 and 82 EC.[54] Apart from air transport between Community airports and third countries,[55] two forms of maritime transport were excluded from the earlier Transport Regulations and Article 32 of Regulation 1/2003 maintains these exclusions: these are

---

[51] R Whish, *Competition Law* (5th edn, 2003) 273; see generally, L Ortiz Blanco and B van Haute, *EC Competition Law in the Transport Sector* (1996) ch 6.

[52] Council Reg (EC) 411/2004 of 26 February 2004 repealing Reg (EEC) 3975/87 and amending Reg (EEC) 397/87 and Reg (EC) 1/2003, in connection with air transport between the Community and third countries [2004] OJ L68/1. See Commission press release IP/03/284, 'Air transport: Commission proposes clear rules to handle alliances between EU and non-EU carriers'. In addition to amending Art 32 of Reg 1/2003, Reg 411/2004 extends the powers of the Commission under Reg 3976/87 to make block exemptions in the air transport sector in respect of traffic services between the Community and third countries as well in respect of traffic within the Community. See A Klees, *Europäisches Kartellverfahrensrecht* (2005) § 1 paras 56–57.

[53] Art 43(2) of Reg 1/2003.

[54] In regard to Reg 1017/68 (land transport) see in particular Art 36(4) which repeals Arts 5 to 29, including the special procedural rules contained in Arts 10 to 25 of Reg 1017/68 with the exception of Art 13(3) which continues to apply to decisions adopted pursuant to Art 81(3) EC prior to the date of application of Reg 1/2003 until the date of expiration of these decisions. Art 38(4) of Reg 1/2003 applies the same principle to Reg 4056/86 (maritime transport). See A Klees, *Europäisches Kartellverfahrensrecht* (2005) § 1 paras 51–55.

[55] As indicated, neither Council Reg (EEC) 3975/87 laying down the procedure for the application of the rules on competition to undertakings in the air transport sector, nor Reg 1/2003 itself would apply to air transport between the Community and third countries.

international tramp vessel services in the maritime sector[56] and a maritime service that takes place between ports belonging to the same Member State (cabotage).[57] It follows that in relation to these sectors Member States may exercise the powers conferred on them by Article 84 (ex Article 88) and that the Commission may proceed only on the basis of Article 85 (ex Article 89).[58] Article 85 enables the Commission to adopt decisions establishing infringement of the competition rules, address them directly to the Member States, and authorize the Member States to take the measures needed to bring such infringements to an end. It is a transitional provision that relates only to situations in which there are no provisions of the kind contained in Regulation 1/2003 for the implementation of Articles 81 and 82 EC.

EC Merger Control Regulation

Another special regime was introduced by Regulation 4064/89 on the control of **1.13** concentrations between undertakings, 'the Merger Regulation',[59] which was replaced by Regulation 139/2004.[60] Regulation 1/2003 does not apply to concentrations as defined in Article 3 of Regulation 139/2004, except in relation to joint ventures that do not have a Community dimension and which have as their object or effect the coordination of the competitive behaviour of

---

[56] Art 32(a) of Reg 1/2003. Pursuant to Art 1(3)(a) of Reg 4045/86, tramp vessel services are the transport of goods in bulk in vessels chartered on request. See Case T-86/95 *Compagnie de Maritime v EC Commission* [2002] ECR II-1011 para 2.

[57] Art 32(b) of Reg 1/2003. Reg 1/2003 does not change the substantive rules applying Arts 81 and 82 to maritime transport. In particular it does not seem to change the scope of Reg 4056/86 nor does it affect the block exemption for liner shipping conferences. But it does do away with Arts 10 through 25 of Reg 4056/86 replacing them with a single set of procedural rules applicable to all cases, whether transport related or not, falling under Arts 81 and 82 EC. However, it would seem that Reg 1/2003 could apply to maritime transport between ports located outside the EU which would not fall into the scope of Reg 4056/88 (see Art 1(2)). For more details on the reform package regarding the maritime sector see F Benini, 'Current and future competition policy issues in the maritime sector' [2003] Lovells Seminar on EU competition law and maritime transport, and J Stragier, 'The Review of the EU Competition Reg for Maritime Transport' [2004] 10th Annual EMLO Conference International Maritime Competition Law facing up to Regulatory Change. On 14 December, the Commission proposed to repeal the block exemption. See Commission MEMO/05/480 of 14 December 2005 'proposal to repeal block exemption for shipping conferences—FAQ'.

[58] On 13 October 2004, the Commission published its White Paper on the review of Reg 4056/86 in which it also reached the conclusion that no credible considerations would have been put forward to justify why cabotage and tramp vessel services need to benefit from different enforcement rules from those in Reg 1/2003 and proposed to bring these services within the scope of Reg 1/2003. White Paper on the review of Reg 4056/86, applying the EC competition rules to maritime transport Commission programme (2003/COMP/18).

[59] [1989] OJ L395/1. Corrected version in [1990] OJ L257/13. Reg as last amended by Reg (EC) 1310/97 ([1997] OJ L1801). Corrigendum in [1998] OJ L40/17.

[60] Council Reg (EC) 139/2004 of 20 January 2004 on the control of concentrations between undertakings [2004] OJ L24/1. See chs 16 and 17 of this book on EC merger control procedure.

undertakings that remain independent.[61] Regulation 1/2003 provides for the prior notification of concentrations with a Community dimension and is particularly rigorous from the procedural point of view, laying down very strict time limits to be observed by the Commission. The Council Regulation is supplemented by very detailed rules on notifications and hearings.[62]

Other procedures for the application of Articles 81 and 82 EC

1.14 **Article 84 EC** Article 84 EC requires Member States' authorities to apply Articles 81 (in particular paragraph three) and 82 EC where the EU Council has not made Regulations under Article 83 giving effect to Articles 81 and 82 of the EC. These powers are limited, transitional, and cease to exist on the entry into force of the implementing provisions adopted under Article 83 EC. The adoption of Regulation 17 already curtailed the scope of this provision considerably; Regulation 1/2003 has further reduced the relevance of Article 84 EC,[63] although it did not remove from the authorities of the Member States the powers derived from Article 83 to enforce Articles 81 and 82 EC. As indicated, no implementing Regulation has been made under Article 83 in respect of international tramp vessel services and maritime transport services taking place exclusively between ports in one and the same Member State. The Treaty does not, in any event, regulate the manner in which proceedings of this kind are to be conducted by the Member States.

1.15 **Article 85 EC** Article 85(1) EC confers upon the Commission a general supervisory role for competition matters.[64] Although Article 85(2) EC could be

---

[61] This applies also to Regs 1017/68 (land transport) and 4056/86 (maritime transport). See Art 21(1) of Reg 139/2004. It is to note that Art 81 EC may be applied under Reg 139/2004 to spill-over effects between parent companies resulting from the formation of full-function joint ventures that have a Community dimension (Art 2(4)) and to restrictive covenants that comprise part of a notification, but which are not ancillary to that transaction. See Part II on merger control ch 16 'General Issues. Scope of Control' para 16.80.

[62] Commission Reg (EC) 802/2004 of 7 April 2004 implementing Council Reg (EC) 139/2004 on the control of concentrations between undertakings [2004] OJ L133/1. See Part II on merger control, ch 17 'Procedures' paras 17.06 and what follows.

[63] C Bellamy and G Child, *European Community Law of Competition* (5th edn, 2001) para 1–048, speaks of '*little significance*' of Art 84 EC.

[64] Joined Cases T-305/94 to T-307/94, T-313/94 to T-316/94, T-318/94, T-325/94, T-328/94, T-329/94 and T-335/94 *Limburgse Vinyl Maatschappij NV et al v EC Commission* [1999] ECR II-931 paras 148, 149: '[. . .] The supervisory role conferred upon the Commission in competition matters includes the duty to investigate and penalise individual infringements, but it also encompasses the duty to pursue a general policy designed to apply, in competition matters, the principles laid down by the Treaty and to guide the conduct of undertakings in the light of those principles [. . .]'; Case T-54/99 *Max.mobil Telekommunikation Service GmbH v EC Commission* [2002] ECR-II 313 para 52; Opinion of AG Ruiz-Jarabo Colomer in Case C-119/97 P *Union française de l'express (Ufex), formerly Syndicat français de l'express international (SFEI), DHL International and Service CRIE v EC Commission* [1999] ECR I-1341 para 63; T-110/95 *International Express Carriers Conference (IECC) v EC Commission* [1998] ECR II-3605 para 54; CS Kerse and N Khan, *EC Anitrust Procedure* (5th edn, 2005) para 1–002 referring to T-77/92 *Parker Pen v Commission* [1994] ECR II-549 para 63.

construed as limiting the effectiveness of the power granted to the Commission by stating that if the infringement is not brought to a end, the Commission may merely record such infringement in a reasoned decision which it may publish and authorize Member States to take the measures needed to remedy the situation. Nevertheless, the Commission has acted in a number of proceedings on the basis of Article 85, in particular in proceedings involving airline alliances.[65]

Article 10, second paragraph EC in connection with Articles 81 and 82 EC[66]   **1.16**
Although it is true that Articles 81 and 82 EC are primarily directed at undertakings and do not cover measures adopted by Member States by legislation or regulations, Member States may require or give encouragement to undertakings to adopt restrictive agreements or concerted practices banned by Article 81 EC or to engage in abusive practices contrary to Article 82 EC. They may do so, for, example, by imposing minimum or maximum prices for goods or services; by adopting discriminatory taxation measures; by imposing regulatory rules that make it difficult for undertakings to enter markets; or by operating restrictive licensing regimes for particular economic activities.[67] The Community Courts have consistently held that Article 10, second paragraph EC imposes a duty on Member States not to maintain or to adopt measures, which deprive these provisions of their effectiveness.[68] Member States may not enact measures

---

[65] The Commission has investigated in particular a number of alliance agreements between Community and US airlines, regarding their compatibility under the EC competition rules. In 1996, the Commission initiated proceedings in various air alliance cases, focussing on the transatlantic routes covered by those alliances. In the absence of a specific enforcement Regulation for the application of the EC competition rules on transport between the Community and third countries, the legal basis for these proceedings was Art 85 (ex-Art 89). In 2002, the Commission decided to end its proceedings with regard to the alliance agreements between *KLM/NorthWest* ([2002] OJ C181/6) and *Lufthansa/SAS/United* ([2002] OJ C264/5) respectively, in the latter case after the parties had proposed certain remedies addressing the identified competition issues. See also *British Airways/American Airlines* [1998] OJ C239/10. The Commission has always argued that the extension of the competition enforcement rules to include international air transport to and from the Community would afford airlines the clear benefit of a common EU-wide enforcement system as to the legality of their agreements under the Community competition rules according to a much less ponderous and more direct procedure than that of Art 85 EC.

[66] R Whish *Competition Law* (5th edn 2003) 212–17.

[67] R Whish *Competition Law* (5th edn 2003) 212–13 notes that the case law has been predominantly concerned with the liability of Member States for infringements of Art 81 EC by undertakings whereas issues in relation to abusive behaviour usually arise in the context of Art 86(1) EC which applies to public undertakings and undertakings to which Member States grant special or exclusive rights. See also J Temple Lang, 'Developments, Issues and New Remedies—The Duties of National Authorities and Courts under Article 10 of the EC Treaty' [2004] Fordham International Law Journal 1904–39 (1924 et seq) on Community Courts case law on the duties of national non-judicial authorities under Art 10 EC.

[68] Case 13/77 *SA GB-INNO-BM v Association des détaillants en tabac (ATAB)* [1977] ECR 2115 para 31; Case C-185/91 *Bundesanstalt für den Güterverkehr v Reiff* [1993] ECR I-5801 para 14; Case C-401/92 *Criminal proceedings against Tankstation 't Heukske vof and JBE Boermans* [1992] ECR I-2199 para 16; Case C-332/89 *Marchandise and others* [1991] ECR I-1027 para 22.

enabling private undertakings to escape from the constraints imposed by Articles 81 and 82 EC. In the current state of the case law, the Court considers that a State measure is liable to negate the effectiveness of the competition rules in three situations: (1) where a Member State requires, or favours, the adoption of agreements, decisions of associations of undertakings, or concerted practices contrary to Article 81 EC; (2) where a Member State reinforces the effects of such conduct; and (3) where a Member State deprives its own rules of their legislative character by delegating to private economic operators the responsibility for taking decisions affecting the economic sphere.[69]

1.17 In procedural terms, Community law does not provide for a particular procedure against Member States for not fulfilling their obligations under Article 10, second paragraph EC in connection with Articles 81 and/or 82 EC. A complainant could request the EC Commission to direct a request to the Member State to comply with its obligations under the EC Treaty and if need be, to initiate infringement proceedings against it.[70] In this case, the relationship between the complainant and the Commission are governed by the Commission Communication on relations with the complainant in respect of infringements of Community law.[71] To what extent a complainant is able to challenge a refusal to initiate proceedings before the Community Courts is subject to debate. The ECJ stated that the Commission has the right but no obligation to commence proceedings under Article 226 EC; it would have a discretionary power precluding the right of individuals to require it to adopt a particular position and to bring an action for annulment against its refusal to

---

See also Commissioner for Competition Policy N Kroes, 'The Competition Principle as a Guideline for Legislation and State Action—the Responsibility of Politicians and the Role of Competition Authorities', 12th International Conference on Competition, Bonn, 6 June 2005, stating that '[. . .] States are subject to obligations under Article 10 of the EC Treaty, combined with Articles 81 or 82. Article 10 obliges Member States to abstain from any measure that could jeopardise the attainment of the objectives of the Treaty, one of which is to ensure that competition is not distorted. The European Court of Justice has concluded from this that Member States are prohibited from introducing State measures which may deprive Articles 81 and 82 of their useful effect [. . .]'.

[69] Case 267/86 *Van Eycke v ASPA, NV* [1989] ECR 4769 para 16. The issue was whether Belgian legislation which restricts the benefit of an exemption from income tax solely to certain deposits was compatible with the EC Treaty. Case C-2/91 *Criminal proceedings against Wolf W Meng* [1993] ECR I-5751 paras 14–15; in Opinion of AG Léger Case C-35/99 *Criminal proceedings against Manuele Arduino*, [2002] ECR I-1529 para 37.

[70] Art 226 EC: 'If the Commission considers that a Member State has failed to fulfil an obligation under this Treaty, it shall deliver a reasoned opinion on the matter after giving the *State* concerned the opportunity to submit its observations. If the State concerned does not comply with the opinion within the period laid down by the Commission, the latter may bring the matter before the Court of Justice.'

[71] Commission Communication to the European Parliament and the European Ombudsman on relations with the Complainant in respect of Infringements of Community Law [2002] COM 141 final.

take action.[72] If the Commission considers that a Member State has failed to fulfil an obligation under this Treaty, it delivers a reasoned opinion on the matter after giving the State concerned the opportunity to submit its observations. In the event that the Member State does not comply with the opinion within the time allowed, the Commission would have the right, but not the obligation, to apply to the ECJ for a declaration establishing the failure the Member State is accused of.[73] The Community Courts are also likely to reject an action under Article 232 EC in respect of the failure to act. It would be possible to challenge a failure to take a decision or to define a position, but not the adoption of a measure different from that desired or considered necessary by the persons concerned. In this context, the CFI has noted that the action for failure to act under Article 232 EC is contingent on the institution concerned being under an obligation to act, so that its alleged failure to act is contrary to the Treaty. Yet this is not the case here, since the Commission has a discretion as to whether it initiates the procedure in question.[74]

However, it is questionable whether from the outset the discretionary power **1.18** of the Commission shall be excluded from any judicial review. A refusal by the Commission to act against a Member State contains a legal assessment, which is capable of producing legal effects in the sense of Article 230 EC. It terminates a proceeding governed by a Communication of the Commission and it may contain an assessment of the Commission on the compatibility of national law with Community law. The purpose of the legal challenge would probably not aim to oblige the Commission to initiate proceedings which is considered as being the province of the Commission's discretionary power,[75] but

---

[72] Case C-87/89 *Société nationale interprofessionelle de la tomate and others v EC Commission* [1990] ECR I-1981 para 6.

[73] Case C-87/89 *Société nationale interprofessionnelle de la tomate and others v EC Commission* [1990] ECR I-1981 paras 6 and 7; T-126/95 *Dumez v EC Commission* [1995] ECR II-2863 para 33 '[. . .] It has consistently been held that individuals are not entitled to contest a refusal by the Commission to take action under Article [232] against a Member State [. . .] The case-law of the Community judicature concerning the non-actionable nature of a refusal by the Commission to initiate the procedure under Article [232] of the Treaty is based not only on the discretionary power conferred on the Commission by Article [232] itself, but also on the principle that, where the Commission's decision is negative, it must be appraised in the light of the nature of the request to which it constitutes a reply [. . .] It is clear from the scheme of Article [232] of the Treaty that the reasoned opinion is merely a preliminary stage following which an action may be brought before the Court of Justice for failure to fulfil obligations, and cannot therefore be regarded as an act which could form the subject-matter of proceedings for annulment. Consequently, the Commission's refusal to initiate the Art [223] procedure also constitutes an act which is not open to challenge, and there is no need to determine whether it was of direct and individual concern to the applicant.[. . .]'. See also Order in Case T-182/97 *Smanor v EC Commission* [1998] ECR II-271 para 27 stating that under Art 232 EC the only act which could be refused would be a reasoned opinion, which itself cannot form the subject-matter of proceedings for annulment.

[74] Case T-126/95 *Dumez v EC Commission* [1995] ECR II-2863 paras 43–44.

[75] Case C-212/98 *EC Commission v Ireland* [1999] ECR I-8571 para 12; Case C-317/92 *EC Commission v Germany* [1994] ECR I-2039 para 4.

rather to annul the legal assessment of the Commission not to investigate the complaint.[76]

3. Limitation periods[77]

1.19 Article 25 of Regulation 1/2003 replaces the rules formerly contained in Regulation 2988/74,[78] which laid down limitation periods both for proceedings and for the enforcement of sanctions under Community competition rules. It establishes limitation periods for action on the part of the Commission against competition law infringements: the period is three years in the case of provisions concerning requests for information or the conduct of inspections and five years in the case of all other infringements. Article 26 of Regulation 1/2003 provides that the limitation period for enforcing fines and periodic penalty payments is five years.[79]

C. General Principles and Case Law

1.20 Case law is an important source of Community law. The sometimes imprecise, incomplete, or excessively general nature of the EC Treaty provisions and the often flawed nature of the instruments containing secondary legislation, aided and abetted by political compromise and the linguistic and legal diversity of the EU, provides an opportunity for the Community courts to establish what the law is. It fills gaps where neither primary nor secondary law provide an adequate solution to the problems arising from the development of the Community. This quasi-legislative task undertaken by the Court uses very dynamic interpretative methods and resorts extensively to general principles of law. The Court has thus, for example, recognized that although the Commission is not a 'tribunal' within the meaning of Article 6 of the Convention of Human Rights, the observance of fundamental rights forms part of the Community

---

[76] See in this context K Lenaerts, 'In the Union We Trust: Trust-Enhancing Principles of Community Law' (2004) CML Rev 317–43 (339) states that the Commission is under the obligation to undertake a diligent and impartial examination of the complaints addressed to it and that the fulfilment of that obligation should be amenable to judicial review. K Lenaerts takes the view that the decisions taken by the Commission subsequent to a complaint by an individual based on Article 226 EC are not amenable to judicial review.

[77] See ch 9 'Penalties and confidentiality' paras 9.19 and what follows; ch 11 'Infringement decisions and penalties' para 11.17.

[78] Council Reg 2988/74 concerning limitation periods in proceedings and the enforcement of sanctions under the rules of the European Economic Community relating to transport and competition [1974] OJ L319/1.

[79] See recently, Joined Cases T-22/02 and T-23/02 *Sumitomo Chemical v EC Commission* not yet reported. The CFI judgment of 6 October 2005 dismissed the claim that limitation periods should also be applicable to merely declatory prohibition decisions.

legal order.[80] Regulation 1/2003 specifically states that it respects the fundamental rights and observes the principles recognized in particular by the Charter
of Fundamental Rights of the European Union. Accordingly, Regulation 1/
2003 must be interpreted and applied with respect to those rights and principles.[81] Whereas Regulation 17 contained very few provisions relating to the
rights of defence of undertakings, Regulation 1/2003 is much more explicit and
spells out a number of guarantees on which undertakings may rely during the
investigation stage.[82] The case law of the Community Courts has also developed
a series of general principles inspired by the legal traditions of the Member
States,[83] which must be applied together with the Treaty provisions and secondary legislation. Community competition procedure takes account of all these
principles, which guide the conduct of authorities responsible for ensuring
compliance with the Treaty competition rules.[84] It should, however, be noted
that not every procedural irregularity will be sufficient to vitiate a decision. As a
general principle of Community law, a person seeking the annulment of an
administrative decision on the grounds of procedural irregularity must be able
to show at least a possibility that the outcome would have been different but for
the irregularity complained of.[85] Set out below is a description of some of the
main principles.

---

[80] Case T-9/99 *HFB Holding für Fernwärmetechnik Beteiligungsgesellschaft mbH & Co KG and
others v EC Commission* [2002] ECR II-1487 para 377; Case T-112/98 *Mannesmannröhren-
Werke v EC Commission* [2001] ECR II-729 para 60; Case C-94/00 *Roquette Frères* (see n 6 above)
para 35; Opinion 2/94 [1996] ECR I-1759 para 33; T-83/96 *Van der Wal* [1998] ECR II-545
para 46; Case C-299/95 *Kremzow v Austria* [1997] ECR I-2629 para 14; Case T-11/89 *Shell v EC
Commission* [1992] ECR II-757 para 39; Joined Cases 209/78 to 215/78 and 218/78 *Van
Landewyck v EC Commission* [1980] ECR 3125 para 81; Joined Cases 100/80 to 103/80 *Musique
Diffusion Française and others v EC Commission* [1983] ECR 1825 para 7.
[81] Recital 37 of Reg 1/2003.
[82] Art 19 of Reg 17 protected the right to be heard and Arts 11(5) and 14(3) provided for
the obligatory mention of the right to appeal before the ECJ. In contrast, Reg 1/2003 refers to the
right not to incriminate oneself in Recital 23 or the control exercised by national courts regarding
assistance during inspections (Arts 20 and 21).
[83] Joined Cases C-238/99, C-244/99, C-245/99, C-247/99, C-250/99 to C-252/99 and
C-254/99 *Limburgse Vinyl Maatschappij (LVM) and others v EC Commission* [2002] ECR I-8375
para 217; see also WPJ Wils, 'Powers of Investigation and Procedural Rights and Guarantees in
EU Antitrust Enforcement', First Lisbon Conference on Competition Law and Economics,
Belém 3–4 November 2005, paras 53–54.
[84] These principles will be considered below in greater detail, each in the context in which it
has been dealt with in the case law. Thus, for example, proportionality will be considered in the
context of fines; the rights of the defence in the context of observations from the parties and so on.
[85] Case T-44/00 *Mannesmannröhren-Werke AG v EC Commission* [2004] OJ C239/12 para
55: '[. . .] the rights of the defence are infringed by virtue of a procedural irregularity only in so far
as that irregularity had a definite impact on the possibilities for the undertakings implicated to
defend themselves [. . .]'. In Case T-62/98 *Volkswagen v EC Commission* [2000] ECJ II-2707
paras 279–283 the CFI found that the Commission infringed the principle of good administration as a result of its disclosure of the likely level of the fine to the press prior to the decision but

1.21 *The principle of proportionality* The principle of proportionality means that the acts of Community institutions should not be unnecessarily burdensome for those to whom they are addressed, and must be limited to that which is strictly necessary in order to attain the objectives pursued.[86] The principle is of particular relevance in the context of Commission investigations where the coercive measures must be proportional to the subject matter of the investigation and must not constitute a disproportionate and intolerable interference.[87] In this respect, in *Roquette*[88] the ECJ confirmed its previous decision in *Hoechst*[89] and held that the Commission must respect national law procedures when exercising its investigative powers, and at the same time national authorities must respect general principles of EC law, notably the principle of proportionality.[90] As regards the imposition of fines, the amount of the fine must be proportionate in relation to the factors taken into account in the assessment of the gravity of the infringement.[91] However, fines do not have to be in direct proportion to the size

considered that the decision's content would not have differed in the absence of this irregularity. K Lenaerts and J Masetis, 'Procedural Rights and Issues in the Enforcement of Articles 81 and 82 of the EC Treaty' [2001] Fordham International Law Journal 1615–54 (1637) See also ch 15 'Steps following the adoption of a formal decision' para 15.36.

[86] This principle is of particular relevance to the imposition of fines: defendants often claim that the amount of the fines imposed must be in proportion to the impact of the infringement. It is nevertheless for the Court to verify whether the amount of the fine imposed is in proportion to the duration and gravity of the infringement: Case T-31/99 *ABB Asea Brown Boveri Ltd v EC Commission* [2002] ECR II-1881 paras 137–172; Opinion of Mischo in Case C-283/98 *Mo och Domsjö AB v EC Commission* [2000] ECR I-9855; Case T-62/98 *Volkswagen AG v EC Commission* [2000] ECR II-2707 paras 335–348.

[87] C-94/00 *Roquette Frères* [2002] ECR I-9011 paras 53 and 73; Case C-331/88 *Fedesa and others* [1990] ECR I-4023 para 13; Joined Cases C-143/88 and C-92/89 *Zuckerfabrik Süderdithmarschen and Zuckerfabrik Soest* [1991] ECR I-415 para 73; Case C-233/94 *Germany v Parliament and Council* [1997] ECR I-2405 para 57; and Case C-200/96 *Metronome Musik* [1998] ECR I-1953 paras 21 and 26; Case C-233/94 *Germany v Parliament and Council* [1997] ECR I-2405 para 57. Article 21(3) of Reg 1/2003 states that the national judicial authority shall ensure that the Commission decision is authentic and that the coercive measures envisaged are neither arbitrary nor excessive having regard to the subject matter of the inspection. In this sense, the ECJ has held that review of the proportionality of the coercive measures envisaged to the subject-matter of the investigation involves establishing that such measures do not constitute, in relation to the aim pursued by the investigation in question, a disproportionate and intolerable interference.

[88] Case C-94/00 *Roquete Frères SA* [2002] ECR I-9011 para 27.

[89] Cases 46/87 and 227/88 *Hoechst AG v Commission* [1989] ECR 2859 para 19.

[90] Case C-94/00 *Roquete Frères SA* [2002] ECR I-9011 paras 34, 81: '[. . .] . . . in order for the competent national court to be able to carry out the review of proportionality which it is required to undertake, the Commission must in principle inform that court of the essential features of the suspected infringement, so as to enable it to assess their seriousness, by indicating the market thought to be affected, the nature of the suspected restrictions of competition and the supposed degree of involvement of the undertaking concerned [. . .]'.

[91] Joined Cases T-202/98, T-204/98 and T-207/98 *Tate & Lyle and others v EC Commission* [2001] ECR II-2035 para 106. See also recently, T-38/02 *Groupe Danone v EC Commission*, not yet reported paras 50 and 51. See for more details ch 11, 'Infringement decisions and penalties' paras 11.10 *et seq.*

of the market affected, that factor being just one amongst others. The fine imposed on an undertaking for an infringement of the competition rules must be proportionate to the infringement as a whole and, in particular, to the gravity of that infringement.[92] Regard must be had to a large number of factors, the nature and importance of which vary according to the type of infringement in question and the particular circumstances of the case.[93] While the Commission has a margin of discretion when fixing the amount of each fine and cannot be considered obliged to apply a precise mathematical formula for that purpose, it is nevertheless for the Community judicature to review whether the amount of the fine imposed is proportionate in relation to the duration of the infringement and the other factors capable of entering into the assessment of the seriousness of the infringement.[94]

The principle of observance of the right to a fair hearing[95] The right to a fair hearing includes different aspects and notably comprises the threefold right of individuals to: **1.22**

• be assisted by lawyers and enjoy confidentiality in respect of correspondence with them.[96] Article 6 ECHR grants the right of the accused to participate in an effective manner in a criminal or administrative-sanctioning procedure. It includes not only the right to be physically present but also the right to be assisted by a lawyer.[97] The ECJ has recognized the role of the lawyer as collaborating in the administration of justice by the courts and as being

---

[92] Case T-229/94 *Deutsche Bahn v EC Commission* [1997] ECR II-1689 para 127.

[93] Joined Cases 100/80 to 103/80 *Musique Diffusion Française and others v EC Commission* [1983] ECR 1825 para 120; Case T-50/00 *Dalmine SpA v EC Commission* [2004] OJ C239/13 para 259.

[94] Case C-359/01 P *British Sugar plc v EC Commission* [2004] ECR I-4933 paras 105–106; Case T-150/89 *Martinelli v EC Commission* [1995] ECR II-1165 para 59; Case T-352/94 *Mo och Domsjö v EC Commission* [1998] ECR II-1989 para 268, confirmed on appeal in Case C-283/98 P *Mo och Domsjö v EC Commission* [2000] ECR I-9855 para 45.

[95] Joined Cases 100/80 to 103/80 *Musique Diffusion Française and others v Commission* [1983] ECR 1825 paras 10 and 14.

[96] Case C-94/00 *Roquette Frères* [2002] ECR I-9011 para 46: '[. . .] without prejudice to the guarantees under domestic law governing the implementation of coercive measures, undertakings under investigation are protected by various Community guarantees, including, in particular, the right to legal representation and the privileged nature of correspondence between lawyer and client [. . .].' K Dekeyser and C Gauer, 'The New Enforcement System for Articles 81 and 82 and the Rights of Defence', ch 26 in BE Hawk (ed) Annual Proceedings of the Fordham Institute [2005] 549–86, 565 and what follows.

[97] Joined Cases 100/80 to 103/80 *Musique Diffusion Française and others v EC Commission* [1983] ECR 1825 para 8. Cases T-213/95 and T-18/96 *SCK and FNK v EC Commission* [1997] ECR II-1739 para 56; Joined Cases T-305/94 to T-307/94, T-313/94 to T-316/94, T-318/94, T-325/94, T-328/94, T-329/94 and T-335/94 *Limburgse Vinyl Maatschappij and others v Commission* [1999] ECR II-931 ('PVC II') paras 120 *et seq.* and Case T-228/97 *Irish Sugar v EC Commission* [1999] ECR II-2969 paras 276 and what follows.

required to provide, in full independence and without constraints, the legal assistance that the client needs.[98] In competition cases, lawyers may assist their clients in answering written requests for information.[99] They may also be present when an interview is carried out in accordance with Article 19 of Regulation 1/2003. Legal assistance during inspections pursuant to Article 20 of Regulation 1/2003 is not regulated either in Regulation 1/2003 or in Regulation 773/2004. It is, however, consistent Commission practice to allow undertakings to consult their lawyer and to ask them to be present, although the presence of a lawyer is not a legal condition for the validity of the inspection;

- be allowed the same knowledge of the file used in the Commission's proceedings as the Commission itself, which presupposes that in a competition case the knowledge which the undertaking concerned has of the file used in the proceeding is the same as that of the Commission, including both the incriminating and potentially exculpatory documents (principle of 'equality of arms'). This principle was established in the *Soda Ash* cases which related to a concerted practice between Solvay and ICI and abuses of a dominant position by both parties.[100] The CFI ruled that in the case of illegal non-disclosure of exculpatory documents the only remedy is for the decision as a whole to be annulled, since it cannot be known what the result of the proceedings would have been, should exculpatory documents have been shown

---

[98] Case 155/79 *AM & S Europe Limited v EC Commission* [1982] ECR 1575 paras 18 and 24.

[99] Art 18(4) of Reg 1/2003.

[100] In the course of the administrative proceedings the parties were unable to have access to the files related to one another: Case T-36/91 *Imperial Chemical Industries plc v EC Commission* [1995] ECR II-1847 paras 93 and 111; Case T-30/91 *Solvay SA v EC Commission* [1995] ECR II-1775 paras 83 and 101. See K Lenaerts, 'In the Union We Trust: Trust-Enhancing Principles of Community Law' (2004) CML Rev 317–43 (325); T-175/95 *BASF Lacke+Farben AG v EC Commission* [1999] ECR II-1581 para 46; Case T-23/99 *LR AF 1998 A/S, formerly Løgstør Rør A/S v EC Commission* [2002] ECR II-1705 para 171 '[. . .] Having regard to the general principle of equality of arms, it is not acceptable for the Commission to be able to decide on its own whether or not to use documents against the undertakings, when the undertakings had no access to them and were therefore unable to decide whether or not to use them in their defence. [. . .] the Commission is to deal, in its decisions, only with those objections in respect of which the undertakings have been afforded the opportunity of making known their views. [. . .]'. Art 27(2) of Reg 1/2003 is inspired by the principle of equality of arms and provides that the parties involved shall be entitled to have access to the Commission's file subject to the classic exceptions relating to business secrets, other confidential information and internal documents of the Commission. The arrangements to give access to all relevant files are contained in the new Commission Notice on Access to the file [2005] OJ C325/7 which shall ensure compatibility with the requirements of the *Soda Ash* cases. See CS Kerse and N Khan, *EC Antitrust Procedure* (5th edn, 2005) para 4–030. As regards the new Notice on Access to the file adopted on 13 December 2005, see ch 10 'Infringement procedures' paras 10.28 and what follows.

to the companies.[101] The CFI stated that the Commission had failed to respect the rights of the defence by not allowing the companies to have access to specific documents. In particular, the Commission had not prepared a list of all the documents in the *Soda Ash* file because it considered it of no use in this case[102] and had not shown to ICI and Solvay certain allegedly confidential documents belonging to the other party.[103] Nor did the Commission provide the companies with a non-confidential summary of such documents because it considered it could not be done in this case.[104] However, the CFI took the view that by deleting their confidential parts, or by summarizing them, all documents including both incriminating evidence and exculpatory evidence could have been made available to the other party and it would not be for the Commission to decide which documents are useful for the defence. In *Hercules*, the CFI defined the limits of access to the file stating that 'the Commission has an obligation to make available to the companies involved in Article 85(1) [now Article 81(1) EC] proceedings all documents, whether in their favour or otherwise, which it has obtained during the course of the investigation, save where the business secrets of other undertakings, the internal documents of the Commission or other confidential information are involved'.[105] In *Cimenteries CBR*, the CFI dismissed an application brought against the refusal of the Commission to disclose certain documents of the SO, stating that before the decision on the existence of an infringement the Commission can still rectify procedural irregularities by granting access to the file but also emphasized that the infringement of a right of full access can lead to the annulment of the contested Commission's decision.[106] It would seem that 'access to the file' is an integral part of the right to be

---

[101] Case T-30/91 *Solvay SA v EC Commission* [1995] ECR II-1775 paras 58, 97, and 98.

[102] See Case T-36/91 *ICI* [1995] ECR II-1847 paras 60, last indent, 61, 63, and 64. The Commission had actually joined all the documents that it considered could be shown to the Statement of Objections.

[103] See Case T-36/91 *ICI v EC Commission* [1995] ECR II-1847 paras 8, 56, 61, and 100; T-30/91 *Solvay SA v Commission* [1995] ECR II-1775 paras 8 and 90.

[104] According to the Commission, what the undertakings wanted to have access to was, precisely, the other party's business secrets. See Case T-36/91 *ICI v EC Commission* [1995] ECR II-1847 para 56. K Lenaerts and J Masetis, 'Procedural Rights and Issues in the Enforcement of Articles 81 and 82 of the EC Treaty' [2001] Fordham International Law Journal 1615–1654 (1634).

[105] Case T-7/89 *Hercules v EC Commission* [1991] ECR II-1711 para 54.

[106] Joined Cases T-10/92 to T-12/92 and T-15/92 *Cimenteries CBR, SA and others v EC Commission* [1992] ECR II-2667 paras 39–42, 47. See also Case T-7/89 *Hercules v EC Commission* [1991] ECR II-1711 para 38.

heard and not a right in itself.[107] The right of access to the file is set out in Article 27(2) of Regulation 1/2003 and expanded upon in Articles 15 and 16 of Regulation 773/2004.[108] Additionally, it is also included in the EU Charter of Fundamental Rights that form Part II of the proposed Constitutional Treaty.[109]

- be granted a hearing and make submissions before any public authority takes measures which might affect their interests; a person against whom the Commission has initiated administrative proceedings must have been afforded the opportunity, during those proceedings, to make known his or her views on the truth and relevance of the facts and circumstances alleged and on the documents used by the Commission to support its claim that there has been an infringement of Community law.[110] The right to be heard is normally exercised in writing by way of reply containing observations on the accuracy of the facts and the validity of the arguments. The undertaking may also adduce evidence of its own in support of its defence.[111] In this respect, in *Transocean Marine Paint Association v EC Commission*,[112] the ECJ reiterated the general principle of Community law which requires that a person whose interests are appreciably affected by a decision taken by a public authority

---

[107] Case C-51/92 P *Hercules Chemicals NV v EC Commission* [1999] ECR I-4235 para 75: '[. . .] access to the file in competition cases is intended in particular to enable the addressees of statements of objections to acquaint themselves with the evidence in the Commission's file so that on the basis of that evidence they can express their views effectively on the conclusions reached by the Commission in its statement of objections[. . .]'.

[108] The Commission Notice of 13 December 2005 on the rules for access to the Commission file in cases pursuant to Arts 81 and 82 EC, Arts 53, 54 and 57 of the EEA Agreement, and Council Regulation (EC) 139/2004 provides the framework for the exercise of the right set out in these provisions [2005] OJ C325/7. The notice has replaced the 1997 notice on the internal rules of procedure for processing requests for access to the file.

[109] Art 41(2)(b). See regarding the relationship between the ECHR and EU Charter of Fundamental Rights, ch 4 'Organization of EC Commission proceedings' paras 4.17 and what follows.

[110] Art 27(1) of Reg 1/2003 provides that, before taking its decision, the Commission is to give the undertakings 'the opportunity of being heard on the matters to which the Commission has taken objection'. This is reiterated in Art 11(2) of Reg 773/2004. See also opinion of AG Mischo in C-254/99 *ICI v EC Commission* [2002] ECR I-8375 para 133; Case 234/84 *Belgium v EC Commission* [1986] ECR 2263 para 27.

[111] CS Kerse and N Kahn, *EC Antitrust Procedure* (5th edn, 2005) para 1–043.

[112] Case 17/74 *Transocean Marine Paint Association v EC Commission* [1974] ECR 1063 para 15: '[. . .] this rules requires that an undertaking be clearly informed, in good time, of the essence of conditions to which the Commisison intends to subject an exemption [under Article 83(3) EC] and it must have the opportunity to submit its observations to the Commisison. This is especially so in the case of conditions which [. .] impose considerable obligations having far-reaching effects [. . .].'

must be given the opportunity to make his point of view known.[113] This requirement also applies where the relevant regulation does not explicitly provide for this opportunity.[114]

The principle of presumption of innocence[115] Given the nature of the infringe- **1.23** ments in question and the nature and degree of severity of the ensuing penalties, the principle of the presumption of innocence applies to the procedures relating to infringements of the competition rules that may result in the imposition of fines or periodic penalty payments.[116] Under this principle, the Commission is required to produce sufficiently precise and consistent evidence to support the firm conviction that the alleged competition infringement has taken place.[117] However, it is important to emphasize that it is not necessary for every item of evidence produced by the Commission to satisfy those criteria in relation to every aspect of the infringement. It is sufficient if the body of evidence relied on by the institution, viewed as a whole, meets that requirement.[118] In this respect, the principle is closely connected with the principle of '*in dubio pro reo*' and with the duty to comply with the legally required standard to demonstrate the

---

[113] See also Case T-79/00 *Rewe Zentral AG v OAMI* [2002] ECR II-705 para 14.

[114] See also Case C-269/90 *Technische Universitat München v Hauptzollant* [1991] ECR I-5469 paras 23–25.

[115] See '*Soda Ash*': Case T-36/91 *Imperial Chemical Industries plc v EC Commission* [1995] ECR II-1847 paras 82 and 83 and Case T-30/91 *Solvay SA v EC Commission* [1995] ECR II-1775 paras 72 and 73; Case C-199/92 *Hüls AG v EC Commission* [1999] ECR I-4287 para 150; Case T-62/98 *Volkswagen AG v EC Commission* [2000] ECR II-2707 para 281: '[. . .] it should be borne in mind that the principle of the presumption of innocence applies to the procedures relating to infringements of the competition rules by undertakings that may result in the imposition of fines or periodic penalty payments [. . .] That presumption of innocence is clearly not respected by the Commission where, prior to formally imposing a penalty on the undertaking charged, it informs the press of the proposed finding which has been submitted to the Advisory Committee and the College of Commissioners for deliberation [. . .]'

[116] Case C-199/92 P *Hüls v EC Commission* [1999] ECR I-4287 paras 149 and 150, where the Court observed that the presumption of innocence resulting in particular from Art 6(2) of the ECHR is one of the fundamental rights which, according to the Court's settled case law, reaffirmed in the preamble to the Single European Act and in Art F(2) of the Treaty on European Union, are protected in the Community legal order; Case C-235/92 P *Montecatini v EC Commission* [1999] ECR I-4539 paras 175 and 176.

[117] See, to that effect, Joined Cases 29/83 and 30/83 *CRAM and Rheinzink v EC Commission* [1984] ECR 1679 para 20; Joined Cases C-89/85, C-104/85, C-114/85, C-116/85, C-117/85 and C-125/85 to C-129/85 *A Ahlström Osakeyhtiö and others v EC Commission* ('*Woodpulp II*') [1993] ECR I-1307 para 157; Joined Cases T-68/89, T-77/89 and T-78/89 *SIV and others v EC Commission* [1992] ECR II-1403 paras 193 to 195, 198 to 202, 205 to 210, 220 to 232, 249, 250 and 322 to 328; and Case T-62/98 *Volkswagen v EC Commission* [2000] ECR II-2707 paras 43 and 72.

[118] See, to that effect, Joined Cases T-305/94 to T-307/94, T-313/94 to T-316/94, T-318/94, T-325/94, T-328/94, T-329/94 and T-335/94 *Limburgse Vinyl Maatschaapij and others v EC Commission* ('*PVC II*') [1999] ECR II-931 paras 768 to 778, and in particular para 777, confirmed on the relevant point by the ECJ, on appeal, in its judgment in Joined Cases C-238/99 P, C-244/99 P, C-245/99 P, C-247/99 P, C-250/99 P to C-252/99 P and C-254/99 P, *LVM and others v EC Commission* [2002] ECR I-8375 paras 513 to 523.

existence of the circumstances constituting an infringement.[119] The Court examines whether 'the Commission gathered sufficiently precise and consistent evidence to give grounds for a firm conviction that the alleged infringement took place.'[120] The Court is expected not to conclude that the Commission has established the existence of the infringement at issue to the requisite legal standard if it still entertains doubts on whether the evidence and other information relied on by the Commission are sufficient to establish the existence of the alleged infringement, in particular in proceedings for the annulment of a decision imposing a fine.[121]

1.24 *The principle that administrative measures must be lawful* The lawfulness of administrative measures comes into play as regards the obligation to state the reasons on which Community measures are based (Article 253 EC) so that the addressees are informed of the reasons for their adoption and the Court is able to undertake judicial review as to the legality of those decisions and to provide the party concerned with the necessary information so that it may establish whether they are well founded.[122] The extent of that obligation depends on the circumstances of each particular case, in particular the content of the measure in question, the nature of the reasons given, and the interest which the addressees

---

[119] The principle of '*in dubio pro reo*' is laid down in Art 48 of the Charter of Fundamental Rights and Art 6 ECHR. It is one of the fundamental principles which are protected by Community law. See in particular ECJ, Case C-199/92 P *Hüls v EC Commission* [1999] ECR I-4287 para 149; see also Joined Cases T-5/00 and T-6/00 *Nederlandse Federatieve Vereniging voor de Groothandel op Elektrotechnisch Gebied and Technische Unie BV v EC Commission* [2003] ECR II-5761, para 210 rejecting that the Commission failed to demonstrate to a sufficient legal standard that its findings regarding the gentlemen's agreement were vitiated or contain material inaccuracies of such a kind as to render them invalid. It also rejected the allegation that certain documents adverse to the applicant were ambiguous and that the applicant should be granted the benefit of the doubt pursuant to the maxim '*in dubio pro reo*'. For a critical view of the Commission's approach, see F Montag, 'The case for a radical reform of the infringement procedure under Reg 17' [1996] ECLR 428–37 (429); F Montag and A Rosenfeld, 'A solution to the Problem: Reg 1/2003 and the modernization of competition procedure' [2003] Zeitschrift für Wettbewerbsrecht 107–35 (109).

[120] Joined Cases T-185/96, T-189/96 and T-190/96 *Riviera Auto Service and others v EC Commission* [1999] ECR II-93 para 47; Case T-62/98 *Volkswagen v EC Commission* [2000] ECR II-2707 para 43. The Community courts seem to take the view that this is less stringent than the criminal law standard of 'beyond reasonable doubt'. In *Woodpulp II*, AG Darmon's interpretation to that effect of the concept of sufficiently precise and coherent evidence was not adopted by the Court. Opinion of AG Darmon in Joined Cases C-89/85, C-104/85, C-114/85, C116/85, C-117/85 and C-125/85 to C-129/85 *Ahlström Osakeyhtiö and others v EC Commission* ('*Woodpulp II*') [1993] ECR I-1307 para 195. See ch 4 'Organization of EC Commission proceedings' para 4.20 and what follows.

[121] Joined Cases T-67/00, T-68/00, T-71/00 and T-78/00 *JFE Engineering Corp and others v EC Commission* [2004] OJ C239/13 para 177; T-56/02 *Bayerische Hypo- und Vereinsbank AG v EC Commission* [2004] OJ 239/13 paras 92–119 in which the Commission found the evidence adduced by the Commission 'debatable' or 'not convincing'.

[122] See e.g. Case T-44/90 *La Cinq v EC Commission* [1992] ECR II-1 para 42, and Case T-7/92 *Asia Motor France and others v EC Commission* [1993] ECR II-669 para 30.

of the measure, or other parties to whom it is of direct and individual concern, may have in obtaining explanations,[123] but the Commission must disclose in a clear and unequivocal fashion its reasoning so that the persons concerned know the reasons for the measure and can defend their rights and enable the Community courts to carry out their review.[124] In the context of the Commission's investigation powers, the Commission is required to state the reasons for the decision ordering an investigation by specifying its subject-matter and purpose. The Community Courts have held that this is a fundamental requirement, designed to enable the undertakings to assess the scope of their duty to cooperate whilst at the same time safeguarding their rights of defence.[125] Where the Commission finds in a decision that there has been an infringement of the competition rules and imposes fines on the undertakings participating in it, the Commission must, if it systematically took into account certain basic factors in order to fix the amount of fines, set out those factors in the body of the decision in order to enable the addressees of the decision to verify that the level of the fine is correct.[126] It is not necessary for the reasoning to go into all the relevant facts and points of law, since the question whether the statement of reasons meets the requirements of Article 253 EC must be assessed with regard not only to its wording but also to its context and to all the legal rules governing the matter in question.[127] It is sufficient if the Commission sets out the facts and the legal considerations having decisive importance in the context of the decision.[128] Lack of reasoning in a decision amounts to an infringement of an essential procedural requirement.[129]

The principle of sound administration   The principle of sound administration **1.25** encompasses a range of different aspects. It presupposes, *inter alia*, that the Commission must act within a reasonable time in adopting decisions following administrative proceedings relating to competition policy[130] and that it must adopt the behaviour of an administrative authority exercising ordinary care, diligence, and good faith[131] in dealing with the information obtained. In

---

[123] Joined Cases C-121/91 and C-122/91 *CT Control (Rotterdam) and JCT Benelux v EC Commission* [1993] ECR I-3873 para 31; Case C-56/93 *Belgium v EC Commission* [1996] ECR I-723 para 86; Joined Cases C-329/93, C-62/95 and C-63/95 *Germany and others v EC Commission* [1996] ECR I-5151 para 31.

[124] Case T-171/97 *Swedish Match Philippines v Council* [1999] ECR II-3241 para 82, and the case law cited there, and Joined Cases T-12/99 and T-63/99 *UK Coal v EC Commission* [2001] ECR II-2153 para 196.

[125] Case T-66/99 *Minoan Lines SA v EC Commission* [2003] ECR II-5515 paras 54 and 55.

[126] Case C-291/98 P *Sarrió SA v EC Commission* [2000] ECR I-9991 para 352.

[127] Case T-150/89 *GB Martinelly v EC Commission* [1995] ECR-II-1165 para 65.

[128] Case T-44/90 *La Cinq v EC Commission* [1992] ECR II-1 para 35, and Case T-7/92 *Asia Motor France and others v EC Commission* [1993] ECR II-669 para 31.

[129] See ch 15 'Steps following the adoption of a formal decision' para 15.28.

[130] Joined Cases T-213/95 and T-18/96 *SCK and FNK v EC Commission* [1997] ECR II-1739 paras 55 and 56.

[131] See Case T-62/98 *Volkswagen AG v EC Commission* [2000] ECR II-2707 paras 269–270.

particular, the Commission has the duty to examine carefully and impartially all the relevant aspects of the individual case and the right of the person concerned to make his or her views known and to have an adequately reasoned decision.[132] The principle is often invoked when the Commission fails to divulge, divulges partially or fails to take into account certain evidence in the applicant's favour, takes a decision public before notifying it to the addressees,[133] takes excessive time to take a decision,[134] discloses matters under deliberation to the press,[135] or does not comply with its duties to thorough and impartial examination.[136] The Community courts have stated that irregularities of this kind might lead to annulment of the decision in question if it is established that the content of that decision would have differed if that irregularity had not occurred.[137] For example, a failure to act within a reasonable time can constitute a ground for annulment only in the case of a decision finding infringements, where it has been proved that infringement of that principle has adversely affected the ability of the undertakings concerned to defend themselves. That apart, failure to comply with the principle that a decision must be adopted within a reasonable

---

[132] Case C-269/90 *Technische Universität München* [1991] ECR I-5469 paras 14 and 26 where the ECJ held that this also applies where the Commission has large power of appraisal, and Case C-367/95 P *EC Commission v Sytraval and Brink's France* [1998] ECR I-1719 para 62; Case T-44/90 *La Cinq v EC Commission* [1992] ECR II-1 para 86; and Joined Cases T-528/93, T-542/93, T-543/93 and T-546/93 *Métropole Télévision and others v EC Commission* [1996] ECR II-649 para 93. In the event of an action brought against an administrative decision, it must also be observed in the judicial proceedings before the Community judicature: Case C-185/95 P *Baustahlgewebe GmbH v EC Commission* [1998] ECR I-8417 para 21. K Lenaerts, 'In the Union We Trust: Trust-Enhancing Principles of Community Law' (2004) CML Rev 317–43 (337) suggests that it would be more appropriate to refer to the principles of sound administrations, encompassing standards of (i) administrative care and diligence, (ii) administrative fairness, and (iii) legal certainty. See also Art 41(1) of the Charter, which recognizes every person's right 'to have his or her affairs handled impartially, fairly and within a reasonable time by the institutions and bodies of the Union'.

[133] Joined Cases 96–102, 104/82, 105/82, 108/82 and 110/82 *IAZ v EC Commission* [1983] ECR 3369 para 16.

[134] Joined Cases T-213/95 and T-18/96 *SCK and FNK v EC Commission* [1997] ECR II-1739 para 56, and Case T-127/98 *UPS Europe v EC Commission* [1999] ECR II-2633 para 37; T-213/00 *CMA CGM and others v EC Commission* [2003] ECR-913 II para 317.

[135] Case T-62/98 *Volkswagen v EC Commission* [2000] ECR II-2707 para 281.

[136] In Case C-170/02 P *Schlüsselverlag JS Moser v EC Commission* [2003] ECR I-9889 para 29, the Commission said that there was no obligation to take a position with respect to complaints lodged by competitors in the context of merger control proceedings; the Court stated that the Commission 'cannot refrain from taking account of complaints from undertakings which are not party to a concentration [. . .] likely to bring about an immediate change in the complainants' situation on the market or markets concerned [. . .]' and 'that nothing justifies the Commission in avoiding its obligation to undertake, in the interests of sound administration, a thorough and impartial examination of the complaints which are made to it.'

[137] Joined Cases 40/73 to 48/73, 50/73, 54/73 to 56/73, 111/73, 113/73 and 114/73, *Suiker Unie and others v EC Commission* [1975] ECR 1663 para 91; Case T-43/92 *Dunlop Slazenger v EC Commission* para 29; Case T-62/98 *Volkswagen v EC Commission* [2000] ECR II-2707 para 283.

time cannot affect the validity of the administrative procedure under Regulation 1/2003.[138] In most cases the infringement is not of sufficient magnitude as to lead the Court to annul the decisions.[139] In *JFE*,[140] the Commission could not produce the relevant documentation relating to the EC-Japanese voluntary restraint agreement which was crucial to the determination of the duration of the infringement. Referring to the principle of sound administration, the CFI found that the Commission's 'inexplicable inability' to produce evidence should not be borne by the undertakings to which the infringement was addressed, which, unlike the Commission, were not in a position to provide the missing evidence (in particular, on the duration of the infringement). Therefore, the CFI limited the length of the infraction as to the duration that the Commission had effectively been able to prove.[141]

The principle that undertakings' business secrets must be protected It is legitimate **1.26** for an undertaking to request confidential treatment of its business secrets to prevent substantial damage to its commercial interests.[142] According to a general principle which applies during the course of the administrative procedure, undertakings have a right to the protection of their business secrets.[143] However,

---

[138] Case T-62/99 *Sodima v EC Commission* [2001] ECR II-655 para 94, and Case T-26/99 *Trabisco v EC Commission* [2001] ECR II-633 para 52; see, to that effect, the Opinion of AG Mischo in Joined Cases C-238/99 P, C-244/99 P, C-245/99 P, C-247/99 P, C-250/99 P to C-252/99 P and C-254/99 P *Limburgse Vinyl Maatschappij and others v EC Commission* [2002] ECR I-8375, in particular points 75 to 86 of the Opinion in Case C-250/99 P. K Lenaerts and J Masetis, 'Procedural Rights and Issues in the Enforcement of Articles 81 and 82 of the EC Treaty '[2001] Fordham International Law Journal 1615–1654 (1650).

[139] In Case T-62/98 *Volkswagen v EC Commission* [2000] ECR II-2707 para 270, the CFI stated that 'the material nature of an infringement which has actually been proved at the end of an administrative procedure cannot be called in question by evidence of the Commission's premature display, during that procedure, of its belief as to the existence of that infringement.' The CFI considered that the company failed to show that the Commission did in fact pre-judge the contested decision or lacked objectivity in its investigation (para 272). See also Case T-31/99 *ABB Asea Brown Boveri Ltd v EC Commission* [2002] ECR II-1881 paras 102–104, in this respect the '*regrettable conduct*' on the part of a member of the team dealing, within the Commission, with a case of infringement of the competition rules did not in itself vitiate the legality of the decision adopted in that case. Even if that official did infringe the principle of sound administration, the contested decision was not adopted by the official in question but by the College of Commissioners.

[140] Cases T-67/00, T-68/00, T-71/00 and T-78/00 *JFE Engineering Corp v EC Commission* [2004] OJ C239/13 paras 341–343.

[141] See also, Case C-137/92 P *EC Commission v BASF and others* [1994] ECR I-2555, where the Commission had to pay the costs of the court proceedings leading to the annulment of a initial decision due to the failure to authenticate it according to its own procedural rules.

[142] See Art 28 of Reg 1/2003 which imposed the obligation to respect professional secrecy on the Commission and the NCAs. As regards the unauthorized disclosure of confidential information to third parties, see Case 209/78 *FEDETAB* [1980] ECR 3125 paras 41–47.

[143] Case T-36/91 *ICI v EC Commission* [1995] ECR II-1847 para 98; Case C-36/92 P *SEP v EC Commission* [1994] ECR I-1911 para 36. The Court indicated in *ICI v EC Commission* that the Commission could either annex to the Statement of Objections all the documents which it wished to use to demonstrate the objections raised, including evidence which might 'clearly' be

the right must be balanced against safeguarding the rights of the defence. This cannot therefore justify the Commission's refusal to make disclosure to an undertaking, even in the form of non-confidential versions or by sending a list of documents gathered by the Commission, of evidence in the case file which it might use in its defence. The Commission could protect these secrets by deleting the sensitive passages from the copies of the documents in accordance with DG COMP's general practice in this area, by either sending copies of these documents right away or by granting access to these documents with the business secrets deleted. In *Imperial Chemical Industries*, the Court reasoned that if during the administrative procedure the applicant had been able to rely on documents which might exculpate it, it might have been able to influence the assessment of the College of Commissioners, at least with regard to the conclusiveness of the evidence of its alleged passive and parallel conduct as regards the beginning and therefore the duration of the infringement.[144]

1.27 *The principle of the protection of legitimate expectations* By virtue of this principle the authorities should act in accordance with measures already adopted by them and with their own prior conduct.[145] The concept of legitimate expectations presupposes that the person concerned entertains hopes based on specific assurances given to him or her by the Community administration.[146] By virtue of this principle therefore the authorities should act in conformity with measures already adopted by them and with their own prior conduct.[147] The principle extends to any individual who is in a situation in which it is apparent that the Community administration has led him to entertain

---

considered to be evidence in favour of exculpating the undertaking concerned, or send that undertaking a list of relevant documents and grant it access 'to the file', that is to say, allow it to inspect the documents at the Commission's premises.

[144] Case T-36/91 *ICI v EC Commission* [1995] ECR II-1847 para 108; Cases T-10/92, T-11/92, T-12/92 and T-15/92 *Cimenteries CBR and others v EC Commission* [1992] ECR II-2667 para 47.

[145] Case T-465/93 *Murgia Messapica v EC Commission* [1994] ECR II-361, para 67, and Order in Case T-195/95 *Guérin Automobiles v EC Commission* [1996] ECR II-171 para 20. There is nothing to prevent the Commission, however, from reconsidering its decisions or departing *from* its earlier interpretation of competition provisions. This principle must be seen, therefore, not as an obligation arising from *res judicata* but as an obligation of consistency *rebus sic stantibus*. See Case 245/81 *Edeka* [1982] ECR 2745 para 27, and Case 350/88 *Delacre and others v EC Commission* [1990] ECR I-395 para 33 and Case C-1/98 P *British Steel v EC Commission* [2000] ECR I-10349 para 52.

[146] Case T-465/93 *Murgia Messapica v EC Commission* [1994] ECR II-361 para 67 and Case T-195/95 *Guérin Automobiles v EC Commission* [1996] ECR II-171 para 20.

[147] See also Case T-115/94 *Opel Austria GmbH v Council* [1997] ECR II-39 para 93 noting that the *principle* of good faith is the corollary in public international law of the principle of protection of legitimate expectations which, according to the case law, forms part of the Community legal order.

reasonable expectations by giving him '*precise* assurances'.[148] In this respect, individuals cannot claim the violation of the principle on the basis of beliefs deduced from informal contacts or vague or general statements made by the Commission officials or even the Commissioner.[149] Similarly, when lodging a complaint before the Commission, parties should know that they had no right to obtain a decision finding an infringement of the Treaty.[150] As regards fines, the Commission may not depart from rules which it has imposed on itself. In particular, whenever the Commission adopts guidelines for the purpose of specifying, in accordance with the Treaty, the criteria which it proposes to apply in the exercise of its discretion, there arises a self-imposed limitation of that discretion inasmuch as it must then follow those guidelines. Further, undertakings cannot have a legitimate expectation that an existing situation that is capable of being altered by the Community institutions in the exercise of their discretion will be maintained forever.[151] This is the case, for instance, when the Commission adopts preliminary positions that are capable of being modified.[152] The Community Courts have recognized that the Leniency Notice[153] may lead a company to entertain legitimate expectations, but this does not automatically justify a reduction in the amount of the fine.[154] In the field of competition law,

---

[148] Case T-266/97 *Vlaamse Televisie Maatschappij v EC Commission* [1999] ECR II-2329 para 71; Joined Cases T-485/93, T-491/93, T-494/93 and T-61/98 *Dreyfus and others v EC Commission* [2000] ECR II-3659 para 85; Case T-195/95 P *Guérin Automobiles v EC Commission* [1996] ECR II-679 para 14; Case T-465/93 *Consorzio Gruppo di Azione Locale Murgia Messapica v EC Commission* [1994] ECR II-361 para 67; Case T-65/98 *Van den Bergh Foods v EC Commission* [2003] ECR II-4653 para 192; Case T-220/00 *Cheil Jedang Corporation v EC Commission* [2003] ECR II-2473 para 40; Case T-191/98 *Atlantic Container Line and others v EC Commission* [2003] ECR II-3275 paras 1565 *et seq.*

[149] Cases T-190/95 and T-45/96 *Sodima v EC Commission* [1999] ECR II-3617 para 25; Case T-195/95 P *Guérin Automobiles v EC Commission* [1996] ECR II-679 para 20; Cases T-18/96 and T-213/95 *SCK & FNK v EC Commission* [1997] ECR II-1739 para 83. See also in this respect, the possibility to allege legitimate expectations obtained from NCAs in EC competition proceedings as a mitigating circumstance (Case T-203/01 *Michelin v EC Commission* [2003] ECR II-4071 para 305 *et seq*).

[150] Case T-5/93 *Roger Tremblay and others v EC Commission* [1995] ECR II-185 para 79; Case T-24/90 *Automec v EC Commisison* [1992] ECR II-2223 para 75.

[151] See Case 245/81 *Edeka v Germany* [1982] ECR 2745 para 27; Case C-350/88 *Delacre and others v EC Commission* [1990] ECR I-395 para 33; Case T-191/98 *Atlantic Container Line and others v EC Commission* [2003] ECR II-3275 para 1567; and Case C-1/98 P *British Steel v EC Commission* [2000] ECR I-10349 para 52.

[152] Case T-65/98 *Van den Bergh Foods v EC Commission* [2003] ECR II-4653 para 194, as regards a preliminary position of the Commission as published in a notice taking into account observations of interested third parties, on the basis of Art 19(3) of Reg 17.

[153] Commission Notice on the non-imposition or reduction of fines in cartel cases ([1996] OJ C207/4–6), currently replaced by the Commission notice on immunity from fines and reduction of fines in cartel cases ([2002] OJ C45/3–5).

[154] Case T-48/00 *Corus UK v EC Commission* [2004] OJ C239/12 para 193 noting that it would not be sufficient for an undertaking to state in general terms that it does not contest the facts alleged, in accordance with that Leniency Notice, if, in the circumstances of the case, that statement is not of any help to the Commission at all. See also Case T-23/99 *LR AF 1998 v EC Commission* [2002] ECR II-1705 para 245.

the principle of legitimate expectations is often linked to the level of fines,[155] the reduction of fines under the Leniency Notice,[156] the weight given to attenuating circumstances,[157] and so on. In this respect, the CFI has stated that undertakings involved in administrative proceedings which may lead to a fine cannot entertain legitimate expectations that the Commission will not exceed the level of fines previously applied[158] nor apply the same considerations as in previous similar cases.[159] Moreover, the Commission is not bound to mention, in the Statement of Objections, the possibility of a change in its policy as regards the general level of fines, because that possibility is dependent on general considerations of competition policy that have no direct relationship with the particular circumstances of the case at hand.[160]

1.28   *The requirement of legal certainty*[161]   This principle requires any legal measure adopted to be clear and precise in order to ensure that 'situations and legal

---

[155] See Cases T-191/98 *Atlantic Container Line and others v EC Commission* [2003] ECR II-3275 para 1571; T-23/99 *LR AF 1998 v EC Commission* [2002] ECR II-1705 para 241, and T-220/00 *Cheil Jedang Corporation v EC Commission* [2003] ECR II-2473 para 35. In that case, Cheil relying on previous cases and the 1996 Leniency Notice, exposed itself to a fine by cooperating with the Commission. The application in the case at hand of the Guidelines to set fines of 1998 resulted in a fine more than seven times greater than the fine calculated under the precedent method. The CFI stated that the effective application of competition rules requires that the Commission may at any time adjust the level of fines to match the needs of Community competition policy. Consequently, the fact that, in the past, the Commission imposed fines at a certain level for certain types of infringements does not preclude it from raising that level, subject to the limits indicated in Reg 17 (or current Reg 1/2003). In this respect, the Commission would be neither bound to announce or to mention in the Statement of Objections the possibility to change its policy as regard the general level of fines. According to the Court, the only legitimate expectation which the applicant was entitled to entertain was one relating to the conditions under which a reduction would be allowed in recognition of its cooperation, not to the amount of the fine which would otherwise have been imposed upon [it] or to the calculation method that might be used to that end.

[156] Case T-48/00 *Corus UK v EC Commission* [2003] OJ C239/12 paras 192–200.

[157] Cases T-347/94 *Mayr-Melnhof v EC Commission* [1998] ECR II-1751 para 368; T-23/99 *LR AF 1998 v EC Commission* [2002] ECR II-1705 para 244.

[158] Case T-23/99 *LR AF 1998 v EC Commission* [2002] ECR II-1705 para 243. See also Case C-189/02 P, C-205/02 P, C-206/02 P, C-207/02 P, C-208/02 P, C-213/02 P *Dansk Rørindustri A/S v EC Commission* [2005] OJ C205/1 paras 169 and what follows and Opinion of AG Antonio Tizzano of 8 July 2004 paras 134 to 155.

[159] Case T-23/99 *LR AF 1998 v EC Commission* [2002] ECR II-1705 para 244.

[160] Joined Cases 100/80 to 103/80 *Musique Diffusion Française and others v EC Commission* [1983] ECR 1825 para 22.

[161] Case C-234/89 *Stergios Delimitis v Henninger Bräu AG* [1991] ECR I-935 para 47: '[. . .] Account should here be taken of the risk of national courts taking decisions which conflict with those taken or envisaged by the Commission in the implementation of Arts 85(1) [81(1)] and 86 [82], and also of Art 85(3) [81(3)]. Such conflicting decisions would be contrary to the general principle of legal certainty and must, therefore, be avoided when national courts give decisions on agreements or practices which may subsequently be the subject of a decision by the Commission. [. . .]'.

relationships governed by Community law remain foreseeable'.[162] The legal measure must be brought to the notice of the person concerned in such a way that he can ascertain exactly the time at which the measure comes into being and starts to have legal effects.[163] It is therefore essential that the Community institutions observe the principle that they may not alter measures which they have adopted and which affect the legal and factual position of persons. Accordingly, those acts may only be amended in accordance with the rules on competence and procedure.[164]

II. The authorities empowered to apply competition rules

A. Antitrust Law and Decentralization[165]

The fundamental change introduced by Regulation 1/2003 does not relate **1.29** to the substantive law but rather to the procedure and the allocation of responsibility for applying competition rules. It became increasingly clear that

---

[162] Case C-63/93 *Duff and others v Minister for Agriculture and Food and Attorney General* [1996] ECR I-569 para 20. See also recently Joined Cases T-22/02 and T-23/02 *Sunitomo Chemical v EC Commission*, CFI judgment of 6 October 2005, paras 80–91.

[163] K Lenaerts, 'In the Union We Trust: Trust-Enhancing Principles of Community Law' (2004) CML Rev 317–43 (340).

[164] Joined Cases T-79/89, T-84/89, T-85/89, T-86/89, T-89/89, T-91/89, T-92/89, T-94/89, T-96/89, T-98/89, T-102/89 and T-104/89 *BASF and others v EC Commission* [1992] ECR II-315 para 35, and Joined Cases T-80/89, etc *BASF and others v EC Commission* [1995] ECR II-729 para 73. In *Opel Austria*, the EU Council adopted a regulation establishing an import duty on gearboxes in December 1993 when it knew with certainty that the EEA Agreement would enter into force on 1 January 1994. The CFI found that the Council knowingly created a situation in which, with effect from January 1994, two contradictory rules of law would co-exist, namely the contested regulation, which was directly applicable in the national legal systems and re-established a 4.9 per cent import duty on F-15 gearboxes produced by the applicant; and Art 10 of the EEA Agreement, which had direct effect and prohibited customs duties on imports and any charges having equivalent effect. Consequently, the contested regulation could not be regarded as Community legislation which was certain and its operation could not be regarded as foreseeable by those subject to it. Thus, the Council also infringed the principle of legal certainty. See T-115/94 *Opel Austria GmbH v EC Commission* [1997] ECR II-39 para 125. The Court also held that another infringement of the same principle was the fact that the Council deliberately backdated the issue of the OJ in which the contested regulation was published. The issue was dated 31 December 1993. According to Art 2, the Regulation is to enter into force on the day of its publication in the OJ. However, according to written replies from the Publications Office to questions put by the Court, the OJ of 31 December 1993 was not made available to the public at the head office of the Publications Office in all the official languages of the Community until 11 January 1994.

[165] The first edition of this book discussed these aspects under the heading of 'Antitrust Law and Subsidiarity'. Given that the notion of subsidiarity could arguably give rise to some confusion (C-91/95 *Tremblay and others v EC Commission* [1995] ECR I-5547, Opinion of AG Jacobs, the

the system of Regulation 17 based on administrative control of the Commission in which the Commission bore almost all the responsibility for enforcing Community competition rules would not be appropriate in an enlarged Community of twenty-five Member States. Instead, the Commission took the view that ensuring the efficient protection of competition rules would require new forms of enforcing the rules which would maintain the traditional responsibility of the Commission for defining competition policy and apply the rules in individual cases while involving national bodies more in this process. As far as public enforcement is concerned, Regulation 1/2003 empowers NCAs to apply Articles 81 and 82 EC in their entirety and makes it compulsory to apply Community law whenever it is applicable, i.e. whenever the agreement or practice under review may affect trade between Member States.[166] Under the new system, not only the Commission but also the NCAs will be responsible for enforcing Community competition rules. NCAs will apply their own procedural rules and are empowered to order the infringement to be brought to an end, take interim measures, accept commitments from the infringing parties, and impose fines or other penalties provided for in their national laws.[167] Decentralization inevitably involves the risk that EC competition rules are applied inconsistently in Member States' different jurisdictions. A network of NCAs called the European competition network (ECN) will serve as the framework for the cooperation required to ensure correct case allocation and a consistent application of the rules. However, the Commission retains an important role: in particular, it may take up cases on its own initiative or following complaints made directly to it. It can deal with a case allocated to it in

term 'decentralization' is now widely used in this context and may better encapsulate the essence of the process, i.e. the application of Community competition law by the Member States. A Schaub, *EC Competition System—Proposals for Reform* (1998) Fordham Corporate Law Institute, ch 1 refers in the same context to *subsidiarity* and *proportionality*, as regards decentralization see Philip Lowe, 'The Role of the Commission in the Modernisation of EC Competition Law' [2004] Address at the UKAEL Conference on Modernisation of EC Competition Law: Uncertainties and Opportunities available at http://europa.eu.int/comm/competition/speeches/index_2004.html; PJ Slot, 'A view from the Mountain: 40 years of developments in EC competition law' (2004) CML Rev 41, 443–73 (468); CD Ehlermann and I Aranasiu, 'The Modernization of EC Antitrust Law: Consequences for the Future Role and Function of the EC Courts' [2002] ECLR 72–80. K Pijetlovic, 'Reform of EC Antitrust Enforcement: Criticism of the New System is Highly exaggerated' [2004] ECLR 356–69.

[166] For more details on the effect on trade concept, Commission Notice—Guidelines on the effect on trade concept contained in Arts 81 and 82 of the Treaty [2004] OJ C101/81 paras 19 and what follows. The guidelines are designed to assist NCAs and NCs to decide whether an agreement or practice 'may affect trade between Member States' and is thus caught by Arts 81 and 82 EC: while the guidelines for the most part contain a restatement of the Community Courts' case law, they also introduce a new rule (the non-appreciable affectation of trade rule or NAAT-rule) that attempts to link the absence of an effect on trade to specified market and revenue ceilings.

[167] Art 5 of Reg 1/2003.

the ECN because it is best placed to act.[168] In addition, it may also provide a guidance letter at the request of the parties and has a key consultative role in NCA proceedings.[169]

Regulation 1/2003 provides for a greater involvement of national courts by making Article 81 EC as a whole directly applicable. Thus, the decentralization of the enforcement of Community competition law set in place by Regulation 1/2003 envisages enforcement not only by the competition authorities of the Member States, but also a complementary role for enforcement through litigation between private parties before the national courts.[170] When drafting its proposal for the Regulation, the Commission was aware that its monopoly on Article 81(3) EC represented a major obstacle to more extensive application of the competition rules by national courts. For example, a defendant could delay an action for breach of Article 81 EC by notifying the offending agreement, rule or practice for exemption and/or clearance. In practice, the national judge had little option but to stay proceedings until the Commission had ruled on the application of Article 81, and any appeal rights on that decision to the Community courts had been exhausted. This process could take many years and deter all but the most determined litigants.[171] Conversely, under Regulation 17, Article 81 EC was often used as a means that permitted escaping the performance of a contract and potentially the payment of damages if the agreement at stake had not been properly notified to and cleared by the Commission.[172]

1.30

---

[168] This includes the possibility of clawing back a case from an NCA, for example to prevent conflicting decisions or because of the need for effective Community-wide enforcement. See Art 11(6) of Reg 1/2003. For more details, see ch 3 'National competition authorities' paras 3.08 and what follows.

[169] Recital 38 of Reg 1/2003. Commission Notice on informal guidance relating to novel questions concerning Arts 81 and 82 of the EC Treaty that arise in individual cases [2004] OJ C101/78.

[170] As regards the role of the national courts regarding private enforcement, see paras 1.40 and what follows below and ch 2 'The National Judicial Authorities' paras 2.04 and what follows. The Commission's frustration relating to the difficulties in advancing private enforcement was epitomized by the fact that in 2004 it commissioned for the third time a study into the questions of whether private actions for damages can be brought under the laws of the Member States. PJ Slot 'A view from the mountain: 40 Years of Developments in EC Competition Law' (2004) CML Rev 443–73 (467). See Ashurst, 'Study on the conditions of claims for damages in case of infringement of EC competition rules' Comparative Report, 31 August 2004, Executive Summary: 'The picture that emerges from the present study on damages actions for breach of competition law in the enlarged EU is one of astonishing diversity and total underdevelopment' available at the website of DG COMP.

[171] See, for example, T Woodgate and J Jellis, 'EU private antitrust litigation' in *The European Antitrust Review 2006* Special report, Global Competition Law Review, 53-56 (53). Further, the extent of damages resulting from anticompetitive conduct and the causal link between conduct and the amount of damages are often difficult to define and thus to prove in practice.

[172] K Lenaerts and D Gerard, 'Decentralisation of EC Competition Law Enforcement: Judges in the Frontline' [2004] World Competition Law and Economics 313–49 (315).

1.31 Regulation 1/2003 eliminates the Commission's monopoly on granting the exemption, and national judges can now rule on whether Article 81(3) EC is applicable. Article 6 states that national courts shall have the power to apply Articles 81 and 82 EC (in their entirety). The elimination of the monopoly on granting the exemption and the related abolition of the notification system may encourage private parties to bring more actions for damages before national courts. Moreover, Article 3 of Regulation 1/2003 provides that national courts shall apply Community competition law to anticompetitive behaviour which may affect trade between Member States where they apply national competition law to such behaviour. Although Regulation 1/2003 does not specifically address the issue of private remedies, it contains a number of provisions which may tend to support private actions in national courts. It may be expected that private enforcement will thus increase as a result of Regulation 1/2003.[173]

1.32 By the same token, it can be assumed that the decentralization process will also affect Community courts. Whereas the CFI is in charge of direct actions against the Commission by natural persons relating to the implementation of the competition rules applicable to undertakings, the ECJ, besides its appellate jurisdiction, addresses competition law issues mainly through preliminary rulings requested by national courts pursuant to Article 234 EC. If, due to the decentralized implementation of Articles 81 and 82 EC, the Commission can focus more on tackling the most serious antitrust infringements, the Commission is likely to adopt more prohibitions and impose fines, which may give rise to an increase in requests for review of those decisions by the CFI.[174] In turn, the

---

[173] D Woods, A Sinclair, and D Ashton, 'Private enforcement of Community Competition Law: Modernization and the Road Ahead', Competition Policy Newsletter, Number 2 Summer 2004, 31. As regards private enforcement in general: CA Jones, 'Private Antitrust Enforcement in Europe: A Policy Analysis and Reality Check' [2004] World Competition—Law and Economics Review 13–24 (14). For a more critical view of private enforcement of antitrust law, WPJ Wils, 'Should Private Antitrust Enforcement Be Encouraged in Europe' [2003] World Competition—Law and Economics Review 1–13. GS Curdy, 'The Impact of Modernisation of the EU Competition Law System on the Courts and Private Enforcement of the Competition Laws: a Comparative Perspective' [2004] ECLR 509–17, with a discussion of the Reg 1/2003 against the background of the US experience in this field.

[174] Where an action for annulment is brought against a decision of the Commission finding an infringement of Arts 81 and 82 EC, the CFI thoroughly examines the facts on which the decision is based and the Commission's legal appraisal of those facts to assess whether the latter has not committed a 'manifest error of appraisal' and whether the relevant rules on procedure and in the statement of reasons have been complied with. Joined Cases T-25/95 etc *Cimetries CBR and others v EC Commission* [2000] ECR II-491 para 719; T-65/98 *Van den Bergh Foods v EC Commission* [2003] ECR II-4653 para 60. Given the significant financial interests addressees of Commission cartel decisions have in challenging these decisions, the existing uncertainty about some procedural rights for companies and obligations for the Commission is likely to lead to appeals on almost all Commission decisions. See comment of Rein Wessling on Joined Cases C-238/99 P, C-244/99 P, C-245/99 P, C-247/99 P, C-250/99 P to C-252/99 P and C-254/99 P *Limburgse Vinyl Maatschappij NV (LVM) and others v EC Commission* [2002] ECR I-8375,

ECJ may have to deal with more appeals against CFI judgments in the field of competition law.[175] Although it is not certain whether decentralization will trigger a surge of direct cases before national courts, it is also foreseeable that the complex application of Article 81(3) EC by these courts will raise important interpretative problems. Rather than using the—arguably sometimes more informal—possibilities of cooperation afforded by Regulation 1/2003 and the Commission's communications, national courts may be prompted to request a binding preliminary ruling under Article 234 EC which would thus entail a shift of the workload from the Commission to the ECJ.[176]

B. The National Judicial Authorities

1. Role of the national courts

Regulation 1/2003 expressly provides that NCAs and national courts, in add- **1.33** ition to the Commission, can (and indeed must) apply Articles 81 and 82 EC in their entirety, including the application of Article 81(3) EC which had hitherto been the exclusive preserve of the Commission. Article 81 and 82 may become relevant in proceedings before national courts in various ways and in different types of cases, for example where a party challenges the enforceability of contracts on the basis that their provisions are contrary to Article 81(1) and void under Article 81(2) EC. National courts may also award damages for loss suffered as a result of the infringement of Article 81 and 82 EC. Thus, the antitrust prohibitions could then be used as a shield when they are invoked as defence against a contractual claim for performance or for damages or conversely as a sword to obtain an injunction to restrain unlawful conduct and/or to obtain damages. While in the past a defendant could delay an action for breach of Article 81 EC by notifying the offending agreement for exemption and/or clearance which led in most cases the national court to stay proceedings until the Commission had ruled on the application of Article 81 EC, Regulation 1/2003 has done away with this impossibility of national courts applying Article 81(3) EC themselves. Whether however, the modernization package succeeds in

---

[2004] CMLR 1141–55. K Lenaerts and D Gerard, 'Decentralisation of EC Competition Law Enforcement: Judges in the Frontline' [2004] World Competition Law and Economics, 313–47 (340).

[175] K Lenaerts and D Gerard, 'Decentralisation of EC Competition Law Enforcement: Judges in the Frontline' [2004] World Competition Law and Economics 313–49 (317).

[176] K Lenaerts and D Gerard, 'Decentralisation of EC Competition Law Enforcement: Judges in the Frontline' [2004] World Competition Law and Economics 313–49 (341), noting that the more frequent use of Art 234 EC may give rise to a similar situation as in 1989 when the CFI was created in part to alleviate the burden on the ECJ.

putting national courts 'in the frontline of EC competition law',[177] and whether these changes will result in an increase in the number of cases in which Article 81 is invoked in contractual litigation before national courts remains to be seen. While it is true that Regulation 1/2003 cannot be said to be a private remedies' charter, there is agreement that it contains a number of provisions which may support private actions in national courts.[178] The provision of direct applicability of Article 81(3) EC is complemented by rules on the burden of proof of meeting the conditions of Article 81(3) EC on the party claiming its benefit and provisions empowering the Commission to make written submissions in cases pending in national courts. At the same time, national courts may continue to seek assistance from the Commission in a specific case. It is hoped by the Commission that the new regime of cooperation embodied in Article 15 of Regulation 1/2003 will establish a more fertile climate for private actions.[179] The case for increased private enforcement received a significant boost from the ECJ preliminary ruling in *Courage Ltd v Crehan*, where the ECJ decided that individuals must have the opportunity and the right to claim damages for losses caused by any kind of behaviour liable to restrict or distort competition. The Court stated that '[. . .] the full effectiveness of Article 81 of the Treaty and, in particular, the practical effect of the prohibition laid down in Article 81(1) would be put at risk if it were not open to any individual to claim damages for loss caused to him by a contract or by conduct liable to restrict or distort competition [. . .] the existence of such a right strengthens the working of the Community competition rules and discourages agreements or practices, which are frequently covert, which are liable to restrict or distort competition. From that point of view, actions for damages before the national courts can make a significant contribution to the maintenance of effective competition in the Community [. . .].'[180]

2. Actions before national courts

1.34 Providing that national courts can also apply Articles 81 and 82 EC in their entirety, Regulation 1/2003 envisages a complementary role for enforcement

---

[177] K Lenaerts and D Gerard, 'Decentralisation of EC Competition Law Enforcement: Judges in the Frontline' [2004] World Competition Law and Economies 313–49 (314). See also Recital 7 of Reg 1/2003 stating that national courts have an essential part to play in applying the Community competition rules.

[178] CA Jones, 'Private Antitrust Enforcement in Europe: A Policy Analysis and Reality Check' [2004] World Competition 13–24 (14).

[179] See Recital 7 of Reg 1/2003.

[180] Case C-453/99 *Courage Ltd v Bernard Crehan and Bernard Crehan v Courage Ltd and others* [2001] ECR I-6297 paras 26–27. See also S Norberg 'Some elements to enhance damages actions for breach of the competition rules in Arts 81 and 82 EC', 32nd Annual International Antitrust Law & Policy Conference Fordham Corporate Law Institute, 22–23 September 2005 (forthcoming). On 19 December 2005, the Commission adopted a Green Paper and a Commission Staff Working Document on Damages for Breach of the EC antitrust rules.

through litigation between private parties before the national courts. It eliminates the exemption system and the monopoly of the Commission to apply Article 81(3) EC and as a result national judges will be able to rule on whether this provision applies. Together with the abolition of the notification system, the elimination of the exemption monopoly may encourage private parties to have more frequent recourse to national courts in actions for damages.

Request to the Court for a preliminary ruling

Decentralization brings with it the possibility of divergent decisions where national courts of the Member States have the power to hear direct actions under Articles 81 and 82 EC or actions against decisions of the NCAs.[181] Where the law is unclear, the national court can request assistance from the Commission in specific cases.[182] The only method of accessing the Community courts is through the preliminary ruling procedure under Article 234 EC, which provides that the ECJ has jurisdiction to give preliminary rulings on questions concerning, *inter alia*, the interpretation of the Treaty and the validity and interpretation of Community legislation. A national court or tribunal[183] can make a request for a preliminary ruling where such a question is raised before it and the court considers that a decision is necessary to enable it to give judgment. A preliminary ruling from the ECJ on the legality of a Commission decision is the only way for a national court to actually *bypass* such a decision in the application of EC competition law to the case before it: if a national court intends to take a decision that runs counter to that of the Commission, it must refer the a question to the ECJ for a preliminary ruling.[184]

1.35

---

[181] L Sevón, 'The National Courts and the Uniform Application of EC Competition Rules, Preliminary Observations on Council Regulation 1/2003' in *A True European—Essays for Judge David Edward* (2003) 145–53, distinguishes four methods to diminish the risk of diverging case law: (i) Application of Arts 81 and 82 by national courts, (ii) national courts may ask the Commission to transmit to them information in its possession or its opinion on questions concerning the application of the EC competition rules (Art 15(1) of Reg 1/2003), (iii) Member States shall forward to the Commission a copy of any written judgment on the application of Arts 81 and 82 EC and the Commission may submit written observations to national courts, and (iv) the request for preliminary rulings.

[182] See Art 15 of Reg 1/2003.

[183] For the criteria used to determine which entities can be regarded as courts or tribunals within the meaning of Art 234 EC, see, e.g. Case C-516/99 *Schmid* [2002] ECR I-4573 para 34: '[. . .] The Court takes account of a number of factors, such as whether the body is established by law, whether it is permanent, whether its jurisdiction is compulsory, whether its procedure is inter partes, whether it applies rules of law and whether it is independent [. . .]'. The ECJ declined jurisdiction in a reference for preliminary ruling from the Greek Competition Commission is not a court or tribunal within the meaning of Art 234 EC in C-53/03 *Syfait and others v Glaxo SmithKline* [2005] ECR I-4609.

[184] Art 16 of Reg 1/2003 codifies the ECJ ruling in *Masterfoods* (Case C-344/98 [2000] ECR I-11369) which brought into sharp relief the problem of parallel jurisdiction of national courts

Procedure for cooperation between national courts and the Commission

1.36 Given the central role of the national judges, the success of the decentralized competition law enforcement depends to a large extent on the national courts' ability to apply the law accurately and consistently. This requires that arrangements exist for cooperation between the national courts and the Commission. This is relevant to all courts of the Member States that apply Articles 81 and 82 EC, whether they apply these rules in actions between private parties or hear judicial review cases.[185] Regulation 1/2003 sets out the areas of co-operation between the Commission and the national courts. In particular, Article 15 of Regulation 1/2003 deals, among other things, with the transmission of information by the Commission and of the Commission's opinions both at the request of a national court. It also includes the possibility for the Commission to submit written observations on its own initiative and oral observations with the permission of the court. Observations may relate to the economic analysis of the case as well as legal issues. It should be noted that the Commission may request copies of all documents relevant to the case in order to prepare its observations. While these observations are not legally binding on the national courts, they will certainly carry a great deal of weight.[186] Under the former system, mechanism for facilitating the cooperation between the Commission and national courts—as well as between the Commission and NCAs—already existed but was rarely applied.[187] While it is settled law that national courts cannot disregard the Community competition rules, it has been also well established that the Commission is under a general duty to cooperate with national courts to ensure that Community law is applied and respected.[188] Article 15 of Regulation

---

and the Commission, in particular where each of them reaches opposite conclusions in concurrent proceedings. Where the outcome of the dispute before the national court of appeal depends on the validity of a Commisison decision that is being appealed before the Community courts, the obligation of sincere cooperation under Art 10 EC means that the national court of appeal should stay the proceedings pending the judgment by the Community Courts in the appeal proceedings against the Commission decision, unless a reference to the ECJ for a preliminary ruling is warranted. Thus, national courts are bound in a specific case by any previous Commission decision subject to any contrary ruling by the Community courts, either on Art 230 appeal or following an Art 234 reference. See National Courts Cooperation Notice [2004] OJ C101/54 para 13. See ch 2 'The national judicial authorities' paras 2.15 and what follows.

[185] See Recital 21 of Reg 1/2003.

[186] T Woodgate and J Jellis, 'EU private antitrust litigation' in *The European Antitrust Review 2006*, Special report, Global Competition Law Review, 53–56.

[187] Notice on cooperation between national courts and the Commission in applying Arts 85 and 86 of the EEC Treaty [1993] OJ C39/6 which is now replaced by the National Courts Cooperation Notice, at para 43. Commission Notice on cooperation between national competition authorities and the Commission in handling cases falling within the scope of Arts 85 or 86 of the EC Treaty [1997] OJ C313/3 which is now replaced by the ECN Cooperation Notice [2004] OJ C101/43 para 71.

[188] Case C-234/89 *Stergios Delimitis v Henninger Bräu AG* [1991] ECR I-935 para 53: '[. . .] It should be noted in this context that it is always open to a national court, within the limits of the

1/2003 and its implementation under the National Courts Cooperation Notice has taken this further and is intended to serve as a practical tool for national judges who apply Articles 81 and 82 EC in accordance with Regulation 1/2003. The National Courts Cooperation Notice covers, among other things, the competence of national courts to apply EC competition rules, procedural aspects of the application of EC competition rules by national courts, parallel or consecutive application of EC competition rules by the Commission and national courts, the Commission as *amicus curiae*, transmission of national courts' judgments to the Commission, and the role of national courts in the context of a Commission inspection. This is considered in more detail in Chapter 2.

The National Courts Cooperation Notice is aimed at those courts and tribunals **1.37** of the EU Member States which are entitled to refer a question for preliminary ruling to the ECJ pursuant to Article 234 EC.[189] In addition, it includes the national courts designated as national competition authorities pursuant to Article 35(1) of Regulation 1/2003. The National Courts Cooperation Notice applies where national courts are called upon to apply Articles 81 and 82 EC in actions between private parties. To the extent they act as public enforcers, they will be subject to the Notice on the Cooperation within the network of competition authorities. National courts also play a role in Commission investigations, where national legislation requires authorization from a court to allow national enforcement authorities to assist the Commission in its inspection at a company's premises. Further, pursuant to Article 21 of Regulation 1/2003, a prior authorization from the national judicial authority is needed for inspection of other premises than the undertakings themselves.[190]

---

applicable national procedural rules and subject to Art [287 EC], to seek information from the Commission on the state of any procedure which the Commission may have set in motion and as to the likelihood of its giving an official ruling on the agreement in issue pursuant to [Reg] 17. Under the same conditions, the national court may contact the Commission where the concrete application of [Art 81(1)] or of [Art 82] raises particular difficulties, in order to obtain the economic and legal information which that institution can supply to it. Under Art [10 EC], the Commission is bound by a duty of sincere cooperation with the judicial authorities of the Member State, who are responsible for ensuring that Community law is applied and respected in the national legal system. [. . .]'.

[189] National Courts Cooperation Notice [2004] OJ C101/54 para 1; as indicated, the ECJ rejected a preliminary reference in Case C-53/03 *Synetairismos Farmakopoion Aitolias & Akarnanias (Syfait) and others v GlaxoSmithKline plc and others*, [2005] ECR I-4609. The ECJ found that it has no jurisdiction to answer the questions referred by the Greek NCA (Epitropi Antagonismou) since that body is not a *'court or tribunal'* within the meaning of Article 234 EC—the provision which allows national courts or tribunals to refer questions to the Court for a preliminary ruling—because it does not have certain of the characteristics necessary for it to be classified as such, namely independence and the fact of being called upon to give judgment in proceedings intended to lead to a decision of a judicial nature.

[190] In this regard, Arts 20 and 21 of Reg 1/2003 and paras 38 to 41 of the National Courts Cooperation Notice have codified the case law in *Roquette Frères* Case C-94/00 [2002] ECR I-9011.

C. National Authorities for Upholding Competition

1. Substantive powers

1.38   The system under Regulation 17 was based on an administrative control of agreements in which the Commission bore almost sole responsibility for enforcing Community competition rules. NCAs rarely dealt with infringements of Articles 81 and 82 EC.[191] In the new system, not only the Commission but also the NCAs are responsible for enforcing Community competition rules. The NCAs have been assigned a much more significant role in the public enforcement of the EC competition rules. Regulation 1/003 creates a system of parallel competences in which the competition rules are enforced by a network of competition authorities as well as by the national courts. Provided trade between Member States is affected, Regulation 1/2003 allows NCAs to apply Articles 81 and 82 EC but leaves the Member State to determine which body will enforce the rules and which mechanism for investigating infringements and enforcing decisions will apply.[192] It is true that Regulation 1/2003 still provides that if the Commission decides to start proceedings for the adoption of a decision, this automatically ends the NCAs' jurisdiction to apply Articles 81 and 82 EC. Yet a central feature of Regulation 1/2003 is that NCAs have the

---

[191] See WPJ Wils, 'Community Report' in D Cahill (ed), *The Modernization of EU Competition Law Enforcement in the EU*, FIDE 2004 National Reports, 661–736, para 45. Among the reasons was the fact that national law empowered NCAs to apply Arts 85 and 86 EC (now Arts 81(1) and 82 EC) in only half of the Member States, or that where national law provided for this possibility, the Commission's power to grant exemptions under Art 85(3) combined with Art 9(3) of Reg 17 discouraged NCAs from taking up Art 85(1) cases. WPJ Wils, 'The EU Network of Competition Authorities, the European Convention on Human Rights and the Charter of Human Rights of the EU', European University Institute, Robert Schuman Centre for Advanced Studies, The Annual EU Competition Law and Policy Workshops, 2002, 9.

[192] Under Art 35 of Reg 1/2003, the designation of the bodies responsible for the application of the rules is left to the Member States. In practice, the nature of those bodies varies from country to country: a single administrative authority may be in charge of investigation, prosecution, and decision (e.g. Bundeskartellamt in Germany), but most often a dual structure has been set up where a section of the Ministry for Economic Affairs is responsible for investigating a particular conduct, whilst an independent administrative authority or court is endowed with the power to adjudicate on infringement and the imposition of sanctions (e.g. Austria, Finland, Ireland, Spain, and—in part—Sweden). Various Member States have chosen to give the status of administrative or judicial court to the body endowed with the power to decide in competition matters. Hence, whether it was expressly provided for or not under national law, some of these specialized courts have considered that their capacity entitled them to request preliminary rulings from the ECJ on the interpretation of EC competition provisions. See, e.g. Spain and the preliminary ruling requested by the Tribunal de Defensa de la Competencia in Case C-67/91 *Asociación Española de Banca Privada (AEB)* [1992] ECR I-4785. K Lenaerts and D Gerard, 'Decentralisation of EC Competition Law Enforcement: Judges in the Frontline' [2004] World Competition Law and Economics 313–49 (315). JD Cooke, 'General Report' in *The Modernization of EU Competition Law Enforcement in the EU*, FIDE 2004 National Reports, 630–60 (634).

power to apply Article 81 and 82 EC in individual cases and the Commission has pointed out that it would only start proceedings in a limited number of circumstances.[193]

One of the objectives of Regulation 1/2003 is to encourage the consistent **1.39** application of EC competition rules by the NCAs.[194] NCAs must give priority to the enforcement of Community law over national competition laws. It provides that where the NCAs apply national competition law to agreements, decisions by associations of undertakings, or concerted practices within the meaning of Article 81 EC which may affect trade between Member States, NCAs shall apply Article 81 EC.[195] In addition, where the NCAs apply national competition law to any abuse prohibited by Article 82 EC, they shall apply Article 82 EC. Thus, Regulation 1/2003 has an impact on the powers of NCAs only to the extent that they apply Community law and to ensure a sufficient uniformity of application throughout the Union. In the event that national competition law would lead to a stricter outcome than the position under EC competition law is different according to whether Article 81 or Article 82 EC applies. In relation to conduct which may affect trade between Member States, Article 3(2) of Regulation 1/2003 permits the application of stricter national law than Article 82 to prohibit or sanction unilateral conduct. Regulation 1/2003 does not, however, lay down the procedures to be followed by NCAs in applying Articles 81 and 82 EC. Neither does Regulation 1/2003 harmonize powers of enforcement or procedures between Member States. Instead, it limits itself to setting out the type of decisions that NCAs can take, namely, requiring that an infringement be brought to an end; ordering interim measures; accepting commitments; imposing fines, periodic penalty payments, or any other penalty provided for in their national law.[196] The latter may also include imprisonment

---

[193] ECN Cooperation Notice [2004] OJ C101/43 para 54.

[194] See F Montag and A Rosenfeld, 'A solution to the Problem: Reg 1/2003 and the modernization of competition procedure' [2003] Zeitschrift für Wettbewerbsrecht 107–35 (125). '[. . .] Since there is practically no more room for the independent application of national law in cases where EC law also applies, Art 3(2) represents a powerful incentive for Member States to harmonize their national competition rules with EC competition law. [. . .]'.

[195] National law may be applied if the agreement does not affect trade between Member States or because there is no agreement (unilateral conduct). CS Kerse and N Khan, *EC Antitrust Procedure* (5th edn, 2003) para 1–051.

[196] Art 5 of Reg 1/2003. Under Art 29(2) NCAs are also empowered to withdraw the benefit of a block exemption regulation under certain conditions. Where in any particular case, agreements, decisions by associations of undertakings or concerted practices to which a block exemption applies have effects which are incompatible with Art 81(3) EC in the territory of a Member State or in part thereof, which has all the characteristics of a distinct market, the NCA of that Member State may withdraw the benefit of the block exemption in question in respect of that territory.

or criminal sanctions on natural persons.[197] At the same time, NCAs remain entitled to establish their own enforcement priorities, including the right to decide which agreements and conduct to investigate.

2. Cooperation between the Commission and the national authorities and the European Network of Competition Authorities

1.40 Under the system of parallel competence, the Commission and the NCAs shall apply the Community competition rules in close cooperation.[198] Together the NCAs and the Commission form a network of European competition authorities (European Competition Network (ECN)), which serves as a forum for discussion and cooperation in the application of Articles 81 and 82 EC.[199] Essentially, the ECN is an informal network which is aimed at ensuring both an efficient division of labour and the consistent application of EC competition rules. The ECN provides the framework for the sharing of work between the Commission and the NCAs, on the one hand, and between the NCAs, on the other, through mutual information about new cases, especially in order to ensure efficient allocation of cases, and the possibility of exchanging information and giving assistance.[200] The fact that a case under Articles 81 or 82 EC affecting trade between Member States can be dealt with by either the Commission, or a single national authority or various national authorities acting in parallel, could lead to an increased enforcement of European competition law. Although Regulation 1/2003 has spelled out the objective that each competition case should be handled by a single authority, the ECN as such does however not take any decisions on the division of work between the enforcers; it cannot compel its Member States to act in a certain way. Nor do the Commission or the NCAs take 'referral' decisions, referring cases from one to another. The ECN Cooperation Notice sets out the principles for sharing the cases.

---

[197] This could mean that the NCAs could have stronger powers than the Commission under Regulation 1/2003. The Commission can only impose fines on undertakings for infringements of Art 81 or 82 EC while Art 23(5) of Reg 1/2003 clarifies that fines 'shall not be of a criminal law nature'.

[198] Art 11(1) of Reg 1/2003. See for more details ch 3 'The role of National Competition Authorities' paras 3.04 *et seq.*

[199] Recital 15 of Reg 1/2003.

[200] While it has been possible in the past to pass on information to the Commission (*British Sugar* [1999] OJ L76/1; *Nathan-Bricolux* [2001] OJ L54/1), Reg 1/2003 has made significant changes in this respect.

D. The Commission

1. The Commission's monitoring powers

Article 211 EC entrusts the Commission with the task of ensuring that provi-   **1.41**
sions of the Treaty, and measures adopted by the Community institutions for
their implementation, are observed. This obligation is reflected in the description of the Commission as 'the guardian of the Treaty'.[201] Its task includes the
duty to investigate and punish individual infringements, but it also encompasses
the duty to pursue a general policy designed to apply, in competition matters,
the principles laid down by the Treaty and to guide the conduct of undertakings
in light of those principles.[202] While the decentralization of the enforcement of
competition policy is at the core of the modernization process, the Commission
is determined to retain its major enforcement role.[203] By abolishing the notification system, the Commission has been able to redefine its enforcement priorities
and to concentrate its resources on the most serious infringements.[204] The detection, prosecution, and punishment of serious violations have become the core
task of all parts of the Competition Directorate ('DG COMP'), which is
responsible for Community competition policy.[205] The shift in enforcement

---

[201] See Case C-431/92 *EC Commission v Germany* [1995] ECR I-2189 para 22.
[202] Case T-228/97 *Irish Sugar v EC Commission* [1999] ECR II-2969 para 245; Case T-31/99
ABB Asea Brown Boveri v EC Commission [2002] ECR II-1881 para 166; Joined Cases T-202/98,
T204/98 and T-207/98 *Tate & Lyle plc / British Sugar/ Napier Brown & Co Ltd v EC Commission*
[2001] ECR II-2035 para 100. There has been some debate on the role of the Commission as an
investigator, prosecutor, judge, and jury. While this combination of powers is a common feature of
a number of administrative systems in Europe, the real issue should be whether the Commission's
decisions are subject to effective checks and balances. See President of the CFI Judge Bo
Vesterdorf, 'Judicial Review and Competition Law—Reflections on the Role of the Community
Courts in the EC system of Competition Law Enforcement', Speech at the International Forum
on EC Competition Law, Brussels, 8 April 2005. See also the published and edited paper version
of the speech in [2005] Competition Policy International Vol 1 Number 2, 6–7.
[203] See Commissioner for Competition Policy N Kroes 'The First Hundred Days', Speech at
40th Anniversary of the Studienvereinigung Kartellrecht 1965–2005, International Forum on
European Competition Law, Brussels, 7 April 2005 noting that in just four years since mid-2001,
the Commission has adopted thirty-one new decisions against hard-core cartels and imposed fines
of nearly 4 billion euros. That amounts to some 35 per cent of all anti-cartel decisions taken since
the first one in 1969 which bears witness to the Commission's vigour in enforcing EC competition law. See also DG COMP Director-General P Lowe, 'The Role of the Commission in the
Modernisation of EC Competition Law', Speech at the UKAEL Conference on Modernisation of
EC Competition Law: Uncertainties and Opportunities, London, 23 January 2004, noting that
this also includes intellectual leadership by taking up, among other things, cases involving new
issues.
[204] WPJ Wils, 'Community Report' in D Cahill (ed), *The Modernization of EU Competition
Law Enforcement in the EU* [2004] FIDE National Reports 661–736 (677). The notification-
related work consumed about half of the resources of the DG COMP not dealing with mergers or
State aid.
[205] Competence over State aid is sometimes shared with other DGs concerned.

powers was accompanied by a reorganization of DG COMP based on integration of both merger control and antitrust enforcement on directorates responsible for various sectors of the economy. It aims to enhance sector specific knowledge in view of the change of the antitrust enforcement culture.[206] The leniency programme, unannounced visits, or on-the-spot investigations, and server sanctions (i.e. high fines) are the three pillars of the Commission's deterrence policy.[207]

1.42 In addition to its primary task of prosecuting the most serious infringements, the Commission should deal with those cases which raise concerns in more than three Member States or which raise new issues calling for the development of competition policy. While the Commission does not fulfil the function of a 'clearing house', it recognizes its role of a *'primus inter pares'* within the ECN with a view to ensuring the consistent application of competition law.[208] Member States must inform the Commission before or without delay after commencing the first formal investigative measures and at least thirty days before a decision is taken of the intended course of action.[209] It is true that Regulation 1/2003 does not require NCAs to consult formally the Commission before a decision is taken; the NCA in question can therefore take the envisaged decision once the thirty days' deadline has expired. On the other hand, the Commission can make written observations on the decision prior to its adoption and can thus influence the findings where it deems fit. In exceptional cases, particularly when the consistent application of EC competition law is at stake, it can also relieve NCAs of their competence to apply Articles 81 and 82 EC.[210]

---

[206] See M Monti 'EU Competition Policy after *May 2004*', ch 16, 403–13 (406) in BE Hawk (ed), *International Antitrust Law Policy* (2004) Fordham Corporate Law Institute. In July 2003 the Commission's DG COMP announced the abolition of the specific cartel units as part of the internal reform associated with the implementation of Reg 1/2003. On the other hand, the Merger Task Force staff has been re-deployed to merger units within the five sectoral antitrust directorates that are organized along industry lines, being Energy, Water, Food and Pharmaceuticals; Information, Communication and Media; Services; Industry and Consumer goods. In June 2005, cartel work was again re-organized in DG COMP by grouping together some sixty specialized staff members in a single Directorate dedicated to prosecuting cartels. See P Lowe, 'Enforcement Antitrust Roundtable' 32nd Annual International Antitrust Law & Policy Conference Fordham Corporate Law Institute, 22–23 September 2005 (forthcoming); A Saarlea and P Malrick-Smith, 'Reorganization of Cartel work in DG COMP', Competition Policy Newsletter [2005] Number 2, 43.

[207] CS Kerse and N Khan, *EC Antitrust Procedure* (5th edn, 2003) para 1.035. See Communication from the Commission 'A Proactive Competition Policy for a Competitive Europe' COM (2004) 213 final, point 4.1.

[208] DG COMP Director-General Philip Lowe, 'The Role of the Commission in the Modernisation of EC Competition Law' (n 203 above).

[209] Art 11(3) and (4) of Reg 1/2003.

[210] The tool can be found in Art 11(6) of Reg 1/2003, which allows the Commission to initiate formal proceedings. However before making use of this crude instrument the Commission will discuss the matter with the NCA concerned.

The second tool enabling the Commission to maintain the consistent applica- **1.43** tion of EC competition law is intellectual leadership when it comes to formulat- ing competition law policy. In this respect the Commission can make use of a number of instruments, such as taking up cases raising new issues or issues of particular interest.[211] Another possibility is the adoption and subsequent publi- cation of a guidance letter, in which important points of law are clarified. As the Community courts have made clear, the powers vested in the Commission, particularly those deriving earlier from Regulation 17 and now from Regulation 1/2003, are intended to enable it to carry out its duty under the EC Treaty of ensuring that the rules on competition are applied in the common market. The function of those rules, as is apparent from the fourth recital in the preamble to the Treaty, Article 3(g) and Articles 81 and 82 EC, is to prevent competition from being distorted to the detriment of public interest, individual undertak- ings and consumers. The exercise of these powers given to the Commission shall contribute to the maintenance of the system of competition intended by the Treaty which undertakings have an absolute duty to comply with.[212] Article 211 EC provides that, in order to ensure the proper functioning and development of the common market, the Commission is to 'have its own power of decision' and 'exercise the powers conferred on it by the Council for the implementation of the rules laid down by the latter'. Articles 249 to 252 EC describe the principal features of decisions. Decisions may be classified as true administrative measures for the implementation of primary and secondary Community law. In this respect, Regulation 1/2003 empowers the Commission to adopt decisions in order to ensure compliance with the EC competition rules of the Treaty. Thus, the Commission, when dealing itself with an individual case combines investigative, prosecutorial and adjudicative functions.[213]

2. The internal procedure for the adoption of decisions

General procedure

The functioning of the Commission is governed by the principle of collegiality **1.44** under Article 217 EC.[214] The principle of collegiality is based on equality

---

[211] Art 10 of Reg 1/2003.

[212] Case 374/87 *Orkem v EC Commission* [1989] ECR 3283 para 19, which in turn cites Case 136/79 *National Panasonic v EC Commission* [1980] ECR 2033. See also Case C-94/00 *Roquette Frères* [2002] ECR I-9011 para 42; T-59/99 *Ventouris v EC Commission* [2003] ECR II-5257 para 120.

[213] As to whether this system is compatible with Art 6(1) ECHR, see WPJ Wils, 'Community Report' in D Cahill (ed), *The Modernization of EU Competition Law Enforcement in the EU* [2004] FIDE National Reports paras 174–177.

[214] Art 219 EC provides that the Commission shall act by a majority of the number of members provided for in Art 213. A meeting of the Commission shall be valid only if the number of members laid down in its rules of procedure is present. Currently, the Commission has

between the members of the Commission in decision taking, and means, in particular, that decisions should be discussed and adopted jointly, and also that all the members of the Commission are politically responsible for all decisions adopted.[215] All formal Commission measures must be approved by a majority of its members, at present thirteen out of a total of twenty-five members.[216] The steps leading to the formal adoption of decisions are taken by the Secretariat General of the Commission, which, among other things, prepares and records the minutes of Commission meetings. More routine decisions are often adopted by what is known as the 'written procedure' under Article 12 of the Rules of the Procedure, whereby the draft decision is circulated amongst all the members of the Commission and is approved and becomes a final decision of the Commission if no member either opposes it before a specified date or requests discussion of the matter by the full Commission.

1.45 Decisions of any significance are normally discussed at the weekly meetings of Commission members, having previously been the subject of very detailed preparation at a meeting of the Chefs de Cabinet. Commission decisions on competition matters fall within this general framework. Any action involving exercise of the Commission's authority and having legal repercussions on undertakings must be decided on directly by the Commission. Accordingly, the majority of formal Commission measures must be adopted by the members of the Commission employing either of the two methods described. Other measures are viewed as merely preparatory to future action by the Commission. Their adoption does not require a Commission decision and they are left to the discretion of the administration. Thus, in particular cases, DG COMP may, on its own authority, undertake preliminary investigative measures (such as, for example, the sending of a request for information to undertakings) under what

---

twenty-five members, including its President. Art 4 of the Protocol on the enlargement of the European Union, annexed to the Treaty of Nice, specified that as of 1 January 2005 the Commission should include only one national of each of the Member States. The Treaty of Accession, signed in Athens on 16 April 2003, amended this provision because the Commission took up its duties on 1 November 2004 and now includes, as stipulated, one national of each Member State. The Protocol on enlargement also provided that, when the EU consists of twenty-seven Member States (twenty-five current Member States plus Bulgaria and Rumania), the number of Members of the Commission shall be less than the number of Member States. The exact number of Members of the Commission is to be set by the Council.

[215] Case 5/85 *AKZO v EC Commission II* [1986] ECR 2585, and Case C-137/92 P *EC Commission v BASF and others (PVC II)* [1994] ECR I-2555 paras 62 and 63. K Lenaerts and J Maselis, 'Procedural Rights and Issues in the Enforcement of Articles 81 and 82 of the EC Treaty' [2001] Fordham International Law Journal 1615–54 (1646–47)

[216] Art 8 of the Rules of Procedure of the Commission [2000] OJ L308/26 (last amendment [2003] OJ 2003 L92/14).

is known as the 'delegation' procedure.[217] In order to expedite the procedure for the adoption of decisions, the Commission, in accordance with its own procedural rules,[218] has delegated power to take particular 'management or administrative measures' to the member of the Commission responsible for competition policy.[219] Such decisions are adopted by means of the delegation procedure. The aim of the delegation procedure is to relieve the full meeting of Commission members of the burden of adopting decisions which, in view of their routine or preliminary nature, involve the exercise of only very limited discretion and raise no difficulties of any other kind.[220]

In turn, the member of the Commission responsible for competition matters delegates many of his or her powers to the Director-General of DG COMP,[221] but he has reserved the power to initiate formal procedures for the adoption of decisions and the power to determine the content of the Statements of

1.46

---

[217] Case 5/85 *AKZO Chemie v EC Commission* [1986] ECR 2585 para 38: '[. . .] A decision ordering an undertaking to submit to an investigation is a form of preparatory inquiry and as such must be regarded as a straightforward measure of management [. . .]'.

[218] See Art 13 of the Rules of Procedure of the Commission [2000] OJ L308/26 (last amendment [2003] OJ 2003 L92/14) stating that the Commission may empower one or more of its Member States to take management or administrative measures on its behalf and subject to such restrictions and conditions as it shall impose. The Commission may also instruct one or more of its Members to adopt the definitive text of any instrument or of any proposal to be presented which has already been determined. These powers may be sub-delegated to the Director-General and Heads of Service.

[219] See Art 13(1) of the Commission's Rules of Procedure ([2000] OJ L308/26 (last amendment [2003] OJ 2003 L92/14)): '[t]he Commission may also, provided the principle of collective responsibility is fully respected, empower one or more of its Members to take management or administrative measures on its behalf and subject to such restrictions and conditions as it shall impose.' See, e.g. Case 9/56 *Meroni v High Authority* [1957–58] ECR 133. CS Kerse and N Khan, *EC Antitrust Procedure* (5th edn, 2003) para 6–002.

[220] Commission decisions delegating the adoption of certain kinds of decisions in proceedings for the application of Community competition law have not been published. In Case 5/85 *AKZO Chemie v EC Commission II* [1986] ECR 2585 paras 35–39, the Court upheld the principle of delegating the adoption of merely administrative decisions to individual members of the Commission, subject to review by the Commission, but recommended that the decisions delegating such powers be published. Similarly, see Joined Cases 46/87 and 227/88 *Hoechst v EC Commission III* [1989] ECR 2859 paras 44–46. Case T-275/94 *Carte Bleu v EC Commission II* [1995] ECR II-2169 paras 69–71, and the case law cited therein. Regarding the public access to documents, see Reg (EC) 1049/2001 of the European Parliament and of the Council of 30 May 2001 regarding public access to European Parliament, Council and Commission documents [2001] OJ L145/43 and Commission Decision of 5 December 2001 amending its rules of procedure [2001] OJ L345/94 by which Reg 1049/2003 are annexed to these rules of procedure. See also K Lenaerts, 'In the Union We Trust: Trust-Enhancing Principles of Community Law' (2004) CML Rev 317–43 (324) who notes that it is highly likely that in the future Community institutions will no longer be able to refer to an excessive administrative burden in order to decline a reasonable request for access to documents on the basis of Art 255 EC.

[221] Art 13(3) of the Commission's Rules of Procedure ([2000] OJ L308/26 (last amendment [2003] OJ 2003 L92/14) stating that Powers conferred in this way may be sub-delegated to the Directors-General and Heads of Service unless this is expressly prohibited in the empowering decision.

Objections sent to undertakings and of draft decisions submitted to the Advisory Committee for a report. Although the member of the Commission exercises those powers himself, he may authorize the Director-General of DG COMP to inform the parties of his decision. Thus, for example, the Statement of Objections will normally be signed by the Director-General for competition.[222] Powers relating to the organization of hearings of undertakings and of interested third parties have been delegated to the Hearing Officer.[223] More important decisions cannot be delegated and are discussed by the full Commission. This applies in particular to infringement decisions taken under Articles 81 and 82 (Article 7 of Regulation 1/2003),[224] and would also include interim measures (Article 8), acceptance of commitments (Article 9), findings of inapplicability (Article 10), and the imposition of fines and penalties (Article 23 and 24).[225] The member of the Commission responsible for competition policy then places before his or her colleagues a summary of the essential points of the case and a draft of the decision which, if appropriate, will be adopted. The above comments relate to the adoption of decisions and the delegation of powers under Regulation 1/2003. The procedures for concentrations and mergers follow a very similar pattern.

Procedure for the adoption of non-routine decisions

1.47   The procedures for the adoption of decisions applying Community competition law go through a first 'external phase', which involves contacts with the undertakings concerned. Having opened a file, the Commission carries out an investigation and allows the undertakings to submit observations on their activities which allegedly infringe the Community competition rules. Once this phase is

---

[222] Case T-305/94, etc *Limburgse Vinyl Maatschappij and others v EC Commission* [1999] ECR II-931 paras 329–330 '[. . .] Such delegation constitutes the normal method by which the Commission exercises its powers [. . .]'; Joined Cases 43/82 and 63/82 *VBVB and VBBB v EC Commission* [1984] ECR 19 para 52.

[223] See Commission Decision of 23 May 2001 on the terms of reference of hearing officers in certain competition proceedings [2001] OJ L162/21; see ch 10 'Infringement procedures' paras 10.07 and what follows.

[224] Adoption of such decisions by other than the full Commission would infringe the principle of collegiate responsibility. See Joined Cases T-79/89, etc *BASF AG and others v EC Commission* [1992] ECR II-315 para 71. On the other hand, a decision by which the Commission requires default interest to be paid following a judgment of the CFI upholding in part a decision imposing a fine subject to accrual of default interest must, in so far as it is a measure giving effect to the original decision setting the fine and the rate of interest, be regarded as no more than a management and administrative measure. This has been the view taken by the CFI in Case T-275/94 *Groupement des Cartes Bancaires 'CB' v EC Commission* [1995] ECR II-2169 paras 70 and 71 in which the CFI stated that '[. . .] measures which create rights and obligations for individuals amount to decisions which must be deliberated upon by the members of the Commission together' and 'measures which merely ratify those decisions constitute accessory measures of management which may be taken pursuant to a delegation of authority [. . .]'.

[225] CS Kerse and N Khan, *EC Antitrust Procedure* (5th edn, 2003) para 6–003.

complete, another 'internal phase' commences, with no undertakings involved, in which the Member States are consulted and the appropriate decision is adopted. Specifically, after consultation with the Advisory Committee,[226] it is incumbent on the Commission to revise its draft decision in the light of the Committee's report. Although it is worth repeating that the report is not binding, the Commission always takes careful note of the observations made by the Member States on the proposed draft decision. Once the appropriate Commission departments have been consulted about any changes made to the draft following the Advisory Committee meeting—including, in particular, the Legal Service—DG COMP submits its final draft decision to the member of the Commission responsible for competition matters. He or she may initially approve it and, subsequently, submit it for consideration by the full Commission, which will have been previously briefed on the details of the case. If the member of the Commission agrees and the decision is submitted to the full Commission, both the member of the Commission and the full Commission may make changes to the drafts prepared by DG COMP.

The Commission must ensure that once a draft decision has been discussed and **1.48** perhaps amended, the final text is approved by the full Commission, in accordance with the principle of collegiality. It must also be authenticated in the applicable languages, in the manner laid down in the first paragraph of Article 16 of the Commission's rules of procedure.[227] In order to guarantee legal certainty, no subsequent amendments may be made to it, unless they are of a purely orthographical or grammatical nature. It must be possible to verify that the text of the decision adopted by the Commission exactly conforms with the text notified to the parties and published in the Official Journal. Decisions must be adopted by the full Commission in each of the languages in which they are binding, to make authentication possible. Failure by the Commission to observe these formalities constitutes a breach of an essential procedural requirement and may well render the decision void if an action is brought under Article 230 EC. In the *PVC* case the full Commission had only agreed the supposed authentic text of a decision imposing fines in languages which were not the languages of certain of the undertakings to whom the decision was addressed (Italian and Dutch). The decision, with some modifications, was later adopted in these other languages by the Commissioner responsible for Competition. The CFI held

---

[226] For a summary of the procedures for the adoption of non-routine decisions, see ch 4 'The organization of EC Commission proceedings' paras 4.03 and what follows.

[227] The manner in which the Advisory Committee on restrictive practices and dominant positions participates in Commission procedures is described in ch 3 'The role of National competition authorities' paras 3.45 and what follows. Details are also given there of the measures which must be referred to that committee for a report (such as, for example, decisions finding an infringement) and of those which need not be referred.

that the adoption of a decision was not a measure of management which could be delegated within the terms of the Commission's Rules of Procedure.[228] The case law suggests that certain matters cannot be delegated and must be dealt with by the Commissioners. This would concern decisions under Article 7 (termination of infringement), Article 8 (interim measures), Article 9 (acceptance of commitments), Article 10 (findings of inapplicability), and Articles 23 and 24 (fines and penalties).[229] It should be noted that the applicant must produce evidence and specific facts to rebut the presumption that Community acts are valid[230] before the Court will order the supply of the relevant internal Community documents. In *British Airways v Virgin*, BA argued that the Commission had acted ultra vires by adopting the contested decision in July 1999, since the members of the Santer Commission, who had resigned on 16 March 1999 in order to avoid a motion of censure by the Parliament, only had the

---

[228] See Case C-137/92 P *EC Commission v BASF AG and others* [1994] ECR I-2555 paras 62 and what follows. That judgment dealt with an appeal by the Commission against the judgment Joined Cases T-79/89, T-84 to 86/89, T-89/89, T-91 and 92/89, T-94/89, T-96/89, T-98/89, T-102/89 and T-104/89, *BASF AG and others v EC Commission* [1992] ECR II-315 by which the CFI declared to be non-existent Commission Decision of 21 December 1988 in the PVC cartel case, [1989] OJ L74/1. The CFI considered that there had been a breach of the principle of the inalterability of measures adopted by the Commission and that the member of the Commission responsible for competition matters lacked powers *ratione materiae* and *ratione temporis*. On appeal, the Court concluded that, although not sufficient for a decision of non-existence, one of the irregularities pointed out by the CFI (specifically, failure to comply with Art [18] of the Commission's Rules of Procedure concerning *authentification* of its measures) constituted an essential procedural requirement under Art 230 EC, so that the *PVC* decision had to be annulled. The Court rejected the Commission's view that the Commissioners' decision-making process may be confined to expressing their will to act in a particular way, without having to take part in the drafting of the measure containing the decision or in giving it its final written form. According to the Court, the intellectual aspect and the formal aspect are wholly inseparable and the record of the measure in written form necessarily expresses the views of the authority adopting it. The *PVC II* judgment has been followed in Joined Cases T-80/89, T-81/89, T-87/89, T-88/89, T-90/89, T-93/89, T-95/89, T-97/89, T-99/89, T-100/89, T-101/89, T-103/89, T-105/89, T-107/89 and T-112/89 *BASF AG and others v EC Commission (LdPE)* [1995] ECR II-729 relating to the Commission Decision on the *LdPE* case [1989] OJ L74/21. The *LdPE* decision was adopted at the same time and contained more or less the same irregularities that led to the *PVC* decision being annulled. In particular, it was not adopted by the full Commission in all the languages in which it was binding. According to the CFI, the Commission may delegate authority to one of its Members to adopt decisions only in those official languages in which the text is not authentic for the parties to the proceedings. See Case T-80/89, etc *BASF AG and others v EC Commission (LdPE)* [1995] ECR II-729 paras 96–102. C-287/95 and C-288/95 *EC Commission v Solvay* [2000] ECR I-2391 on the failure to authenticate decisions adopted by the college of Commissioners.

[229] See CS Kerse and N Khan, *EC Antitrust Procedure* (5th edn, 2003) para 6–003 who also note that the Commissioners need to have read the complete case file before they can adopt a valid decision. The Court would consider it sufficient that the Commissioners had received complete and detailed information regarding the essential points of the case and had access to the entire file. Cases 41, 44 and 45/69 *ACF Chemiefarma v EC Commission* [1970] ECR 661 paras 21–23.

[230] Case T-43/92 *Dunlop Slazenger International Ltd v EC Commission* [1994] ECR II-441 para 24.

authority to deal with current business within the meaning of Article 201 EC (applied by analogy) until the appointment of the members of the new Commission. The CFI disagreed and took the view that the Treaty would not prohibit Commissioners who have resigned from exercising their normal powers until their resignation took effect on the date of their actual replacement in September 1999. Until this time, they retained their full powers.[231]

The importance of the Commission's internal decision-making procedure for ensuring a system of checks and balances should not be underestimated. It is certainly true that where the Commission feels it has jurisdiction to act, it has the power to investigate, prosecute and decide a case, which could make it prone to some sort of '*prosecutorial bias*' against the undertakings being investigated However, draft decisions are scrutinized by a large number of people inside the Commission, including the Legal Service, and, following the recent changes, the newly established Chief Economist and the newly created Peer Review Panels— which have a particular importance in merger proceedings and which reflects the efforts of the commission to increase the procedural informal safeguards. These internal checks and balances are complemented by external review, in the shape of judicial control by the Community Courts.[232]   **1.49**

E. The Community Courts

1. The Community judicature

At present, the judicial function in the European Communities is discharged by two courts: the European Court of Justice (ECJ) and the Court of First Instance of the European Communities (CFI), which was added by Article [225] EC.[233] The CFI is attached to the ECJ and its jurisdiction has gradually increased with successive Treaty amendments (i.e. Maastricht, Amsterdam, Nice). The functions of the CFI are identical to those of the ECJ, i.e. to review the legality of the   **1.50**

---

[231] Case T-219/99 *British Airways plc v EC Commission* [2003] ECR II-5917 paras 46–57.

[232] President of the CFI Judge Bo Vesterdorf 'Judicial Review and Competition Law— Reflections on the Role of the Community Courts in the EC System of Competition Law Enforcement', Speech at the International Forum on EC Competition Law, Studienvereinigung Kartellrecht, Brussels 8 April 2005. See also the edited paper version of the speech in [2005] Competition Policy International Vol 1 No 2.7.

[233] This Article was added by Art 11 of the Single European Act [1987] OJ L169/1. See also Council Decision 88/591 [1988] OJ L319/1 which is the enabling provision for establishing the new court. The objective was to improve judicial protection of individual interests, particularly in cases requiring the examination of complex facts while at the same time reducing the workload of the ECJ. CS Kerse and N Khan, *EC Antitrust Procedure* (5th edn, 2003) para 1–058.

acts of the Community institutions—but are limited in terms of the matters on which it may adjudicate.

1.51 One of the CFI's main areas of jurisdiction is judicial review actions brought by private persons against Community institutions, including against Commission decisions in competition cases.[234] The CFI reviews the Commission's findings both as regards the facts and the law.[235] The CFI is the principal forum for competition cases, i.e. challenges to Commission decisions applying Articles 81 and 82 EC, but remains subordinated to the ECJ. Its creation was also due to the need for judicial control which reviews comprehensively and rigorously the factually complex decisions that the Commission adopts in competition cases.[236] Appeals (on a point of law only) seeking to set aside decisions of the CFI may be brought before the ECJ.[237] Community case law has clarified which acts of the Commission can be challenged and who are entitled to bring such challenges.

2. Main types of proceedings

Actions in general

1.52 Article 220 EC provides that 'the Court of Justice shall ensure observance of the law in the interpretation and application of the Treaty'. Its jurisdiction includes competence to deal with questions concerning the interpretation and application of Articles 81 and 82 EC by the judicial authorities of Member States. The courts have been extremely active not only in the interpretation but also in the creation of Community competition law by extending gradually the scope of judicial review in the field of competition law as regards both the acts that can be challenged and the persons who can attack. As a general rule, all decisions producing legal effects such as to affect the interest of an applicant by bringing

---

[234] The initial jurisdiction of the CFI encompassed (i) staff cases, (ii) certain cases under the ECSC Treaty, (iii) actions against the Commission relating to the enforcement of the EC competition rules and damages claims (Art 288 EC) arising from an act or failure to act which is the subject of an action under any of the first three matters. In 1993, the CFI's jurisdiction was extended to cover all direct actions brought by natural or legal persons.

[235] CS Kerse and N Khan, *EC Antitrust Procedure* (5th edn, 2003) para 1–058 citing Judge Vesterdorf as the then Advocate General in Case T-7/89 *Hercules SA v EC Commission* [1991] ECR II-867: '[. . .] the very creation of the Court of First Instance as a court of both first and last instance for the examination of facts in the cases brought before it is an invitation to undertake an intensive review in order to ascertain whether the evidence on which the Commission relies in adopting a contested decision is sound [. . .]'.

[236] Case C-185/95 P *Baustahlgewebe* [1998] ECR I-8417 para 41: '[. . .] the purpose of attaching the Court of First Instance to the Court of Justice and of introducing two levels of jurisdiction was, first, to improve the judicial protection of individual interests, in particular in proceedings necessitating close examination of complex facts, and, second, to maintain the quality and effectiveness of judicial review in the Community legal order. [. . .]'.

[237] Arts 49–54 of the Statute of the Court of Justice, inserted by Art 7 of Council Decision 88/591 [1988] OJ L319/1. A consolidated version of the ECJ Statute is available at http://curia.eu.int/fr/plan/index.htm.

about a distinct change in his or her legal position may be subject to an action for annulment.[238] Additionally, by way of preliminary rulings in response to questions submitted by the national courts under Article 234 EC and by giving judgment in proceedings brought before it concerning Commission decisions, the Court has developed a substantial body of case law and Community precedents. As has been seen, these have facilitated the development of legal principles for the defense of the free market and for the attainment of economic integration of the Member States. In many cases, this goes far beyond what the Commission and the Council, because of timidity and lack of political will, respectively, could have proposed or accepted.

In statistical terms, it seems that the system of judicial review is working fairly well. The President of the CFI, Judge Vesterdorf, reported in April 2005 that all in all more than two thousand (2,173) cases involving application of competition rules, including antitrust, mergers and state aid, have been lodged before the Community Courts since the beginning. One third (741) of these cases have been lodged before the Courts in the last five years. Since its creation in 1989, the CFI has dealt with more than one thousand (1,116) competition cases, including state aid, with almost 50 per cent of those started (506) within the last five years. Since 1989, the CFI has given 372 judgments in cases relating to the annulment of decisions in the field of competition law. Of those 28 per cent resulted in full or partial annulment, i.e. the Commission has lost the case at least partially.[239] While these figures may certainly require a closer look on the areas involved and the grounds of annulment, they demonstrate that judicial review has been gaining steadily in importance and that the Community Courts have succeeded in deepening and strengthening judicial review of Commission decisions. The fact that more than one in four cases annulment actions have actually led to partial or full rectification is a sign that the Community system for judicial protection produces tangible results for applicants.[240]

1.53

---

[238] Joined Cases T-125/97 and T-127/97 *Coca-Cola v EC Commission* [2000] ECR II-1733 para 77; Case T-87/96 *Assicurazioni Generali and Unicredito v EC Commission* [1999] ECR II-203 para 37.

[239] President of the CFI Judge Bo Vesterdorf 'Judicial Review and Competition Law—Reflections on the Role of the Community Courts in the EC system of Competition Law Enforcement' (period from January 1995 until July 2004; for period before July 1993, n 232 above). See also the edited paper version of the speech in [2005] Competition Policy International Vol 1 No 2 and statistics (as of 1 July 2005) 17.

[240] Another way of looking in more detail at the activity of the Community Courts is offered by C Harding and A Gibbs, 'Why go to court in Europe? An analysis of cartel cases 1995–2004' [2005] EL Rev 349–69 who take a critical approach towards the methodology applied by F Montag ('The case for a radical reform of the infringement procedure under Reg 17' [1996] ECCR 428–37) by examining the 1995–2004 sample of cartel cases before the Community Courts. The authors conclude that a review of the case law reveals a low rate of success for cartel appellants—apart from a sometimes reduced fine—both in terms of legal argument and reversal of the Commissions decisions.

Direct actions available to undertakings

1.54 Proceedings under Articles 234 and 226 EC fall to be instituted, respectively, by the national courts and the EC Commission. Actions under the second paragraph of Article 288, in conjunction with Article 235, raise general questions of non-contractual liability which in general fall outside the sphere of competition law.[241] However, two types of direct action procedures are of particular interest with regard to competition procedure. First, the CFI has jurisdiction to review decisions of the Commission under Article 229 EC and may cancel, reduce, or increase the fine or penalty payment imposed. Secondly, it also has jurisdiction to review the legality of all decisions taken by the Commission under Article 230 EC. Proceedings may be brought by any natural or legal person to whom the decision is addressed.[242] Direct actions against Commission decisions or against the Commission's failure to act are brought under Article 232(3) EC. As well as actions under those two provisions, proceedings may also be brought under Articles 242 and 243 EC. Notwithstanding the fact that the Court may order suspension of enforcement of a contested measure, actions brought before the Court do not have suspensive effect, pursuant to Article 242 EC.[243] Similarly to Regulation 17, Regulation 1/2003 expressly provides that particular acts of the Commission are to be in the form of decisions which makes them amenable to review under Article 230 EC.[244]

1.55 The court that has jurisdiction for proceedings of this kind is the CFI, which, pursuant to Article 225 has jurisdiction to hear and determine at first instance actions or proceedings referred to in Articles 230, 232, 235, 236, and 238 EC.[245] Applications lodged at the same time as the main actions, such as applications for suspension of enforcement or for interim measures under Articles 242 and 243 EC, are also dealt with by the CFI. The CFI pays more attention to factual issues underlying Commission decisions than the ECJ, which is mainly

---

[241] See, however, Case 145/83 *Stanley Adams v EC Commission* [1985] ECR 3539 in which the Commission was found liable under Art 288 EC for the unauthorized disclosure of confidential information by Commission staff. The Commission might have the duty to take reasonable steps to avoid any disclosure (e.g. identity of an informant) that might cause a party harm.

[242] They may also be brought by any natural or legal person against a decision which although addressed to another person is of direct and individual concern to the applicant. Art 10 of Reg 1/2003 still entitles the Commission in exceptional cases 'where the Community public interest [. . .] so requires' to find by decision that Art 81 EC is not applicable to a specific agreement or practice. One might imagine that competitors could be entitled to attack such decision before the CFI on the basis of Art 230 EC like they used to challenge the legality of authorization decisions of the Commission under the previous regime.

[243] A more detailed description of these applications is given in ch 15 'Steps following the adoption of a formal decision' paras 15.14 and what follows.

[244] Ch III of Reg 1/2003.

[245] Note that according to Art 51 of the ECJ Statute jurisdiction shall be reserved to the ECJ in certain actions referred to in Arts 230 and 232 EC when they are brought by a Member State.

concerned with legal issues.[246] Historically, and for reasons of 'institutional balance',[247] the Community courts have in fact declined to substitute their own analysis of complex economic data for that of the Commission and have tended to review the decisions of the Commission with a degree of self-restraint,[248] accepting that the Commission has some discretion when making complex and technical assessments. An act or decision will not be annulled on matters of substance unless the Commission has manifestly erred in its assessment. However, within the limits of the review to which it is entitled the CFI has increasingly conducted its review in a comprehensive manner as to whether the Commission provided adequate reasoning, based on accurate and persuasive evidence.[249] The intensity of control varies depending on whether the CFI reviews the correctness of the facts or the correct application of the law, both of

---

[246] See also Judge H Legal, 'Standards of Proof and Standards of Judicial Review in EU Competition Law' 32nd Annual International Antitrust Law & Policy Conference Fordham Corporate Law Institute, September 2005 (forthcoming) 22–23 with a discussion on the fact analysis by the CFI. Opinion of AG Tizzano in C-12/03 *EC Commission v Tetra Laval BV* [2005] OJ C82/1 para 60: '[. . .] when the [CFI] has established or assessed the facts the [ECJ] has jurisdiction under [Article 225 EC] to review the legal characterisation of those facts by the CFI and the legal conclusions it has drawn from item [. . .]' See also Judge JD Cooke 'Application of EC Competition Rules by National Courts' Antitrust Reform in Europe: A Year in Practice, 9–11 March 2005, Brussels, International Bar Association (IBA) 2–3.

[247] President of the CFI Judge Bo Vesterdorf 'Judicial Review and Competition Law—Reflections on the Role of the Community Courts in the EC system of Competition Law Enforcement' (note 232 above) noting that the Commission and courts should stick to what they do best, competition policy and enforcement and judicial review, respectively. In this context see also Opinion of AG Tizzano in Case C-12/03 *EC Commission v Tetra Laval BV* [2005] ECR I-987, para 89: '[. . .] The rules on the division of powers between the Commission and the Community judicature, which are fundamental to the Community institutional system, do not however allow the judicature to go further, and particularly—as I have just said—to enter into the merits of the Commission's complex economic assessments or to substitute its own point of view for that of the institution [. . .].'

[248] In its order in Joined Cases 142 and 156/84 R *BAT and Reynolds v EC Commission* [1986] ECR 1899 para 11, e.g. the ECJ stated 'examination by the Court of the Commission's internal file [. .·.] would constitute an exceptional measure of inquiry'. From the beginning, the CFI's practice has been different. See *inter alia*, Case T-19/91 *Société d'Hygiène Dermatologique de Vichy v EC Commission* [1992] ECR II-415 para 7 where the Court requested that the Commission produce a copy of a study which was undertaken for the Commission; in particular Joined Cases T-79/89, T-84–86/89, T-91 and 92/89, T-94/89, T-98/89 and T-104/89 *BAS and others v EC Commission (PVC)* [1992] ECR II-315 para 25 and what follows in which the Commission submitted a series of documents to the Court's review. Note that according to Art 51 of the ECJ Statute jurisdiction shall be reserved to the ECJ on certain actions referred to in Arts 230 and 232 EC when they are brought by a Member State. See ch 15 'Steps following the adoption of a formal decision'.

[249] Case T-342/99 *Airtours v EC Commission* [2002] ECR II 2585; Case T-310/01 *Schneider Electric SA v EC Commission* [2002] ECR II-4071; Case T-5/02 *Tetra Laval v EC Commission* [2002] ECR II-4381, confirmed on appeal in Joined Cases C-12/03 and C-13/03 P *EC Commission v Tetra Laval* [2005] ECR I-987. In both cases the CFI engaged in an exhaustive review of the substantive and procedural issues and annulled the decision.

which are subject to full control, and the correctness of the Commission's assessment of complex economic matters where control is more restrained.[250]

Accelerated procedures

1.56 Competition cases before the CFI are complex cases with lengthy pleadings and an enormous amount of evidence which require a significant effort on the part of the Court to ascertain all the arguments at stake. Given this, it is hardly surprising that the normal CFI procedure takes around thirty months. With a view to expediting the review procedure, the Community courts have adopted two types of fast track procedures:

(i) The '*accelerated procedure*' enables the CFI to expedite the hearing and determination of appeals.[251] On 1 February 2001, the CFI's Rules of Procedure were amended to allow it to use a special accelerated or 'fast track' procedure. Under that procedure, particularly urgent cases may be dealt with immediately whereas under the normal procedure they would be held up until earlier cases had been heard. Given the Court's limited resources, that procedure can only be used in cases where there is a genuine and pressing need for the Court to come to a decision speedily. To date, this procedure has been in particular used for the review of merger decisions and helped reduce the average time required to less than ten months[252].

(ii) Pursuant to the amendments to the Rules of Procedure of the ECJ which entered into force on 1 July 2000, the President may decide to apply the accelerated procedure to a reference for a preliminary ruling where the circumstances referred to establish that a ruling on the question put to the Court is a matter of exceptional urgency.[253]

1.57 In practice, however, the accelerated procedures have had little impact on the judicial review of antitrust cases.[254] Unlike merger cases, there seems to be less

---

[250] See Joined Cases C-204/00 P, C-205/00 P, C-211/00 P, C-213/00 P, C-217/00 P and C-219/00 P *Aalborg Portland and others v EC Commisison* [2004] ECR I-123 para 279.

[251] Art 76a of the Rules of Procedure of the Court of First Instance of the European Communities, last amendment [2004] OJ L298/1, available at http://curia.eu.int/fr/plan/index.htm. See Amendments to the Rules of Procedure of 6 December 2000 [2000] OJ L322/4. The accelerated procedure entered into force on 1 February 2001 but is rarely applicable in cartel cases.

[252] Case T-310/01 *Schneider Electric v EC Commission* [2002] ECR II-4071; Case T-5/02 *Tetra Laval v EC Commission* [2002] ECR II-4381, confirmed on appeal in Case C-12/03 P and C-13/03 P *EC Commission v Tetra Laval* [2005] ECR I-987.

[253] Art 104a of the Rules of Procedure, as amended. See Amendments to the Rules of Procedure of the Court of Justice of 16 May 2000 [2000] OJ L122/43.

[254] A Jones and B Sufrin, *EC Competition Law* (2nd edn, 2004) 1145. In T-313/02 *Meca Medina v EC Commission* [2004] OJ C300/39, the CFI refused to grant use of the expedited procedure in an appeal against a rejection of a complaint filed under Arts 81 and 82 EC. See also D Geradin and N Petit, 'Judicial Remedies under EC Competition Law: Complex Issues Arising

urgency in antitrust cases because the judicial actions involve past events and where this could lead to serious and irreparable damage, a company may resort to the possibility of applying for interim relief. To streamline the procedure, one possibility would be to switch to a more US-style *prosecutorial system*, in which the CFI could not only annul a decision and but also take a final decision on the merits. This would mean abandoning the concept of restricted jurisdiction, apart from the full jurisdiction that the CFI enjoys to review fines. However, such a reform would have a significant effect on how the CFI reviews cases and may even require a change to the EC Treaty rules. The President of the CFI has recently floated the idea of releasing the CFI's resources to enable it to hear more competition cases by removing from its jurisdiction a number of other specific cases such as those relating to Commission staff and trade marks which could be dealt with by judicial panels under Article 225a EC. It is estimated that this could reduce the current work load by almost 50 per cent.[255]

---

from the *"Modernization Process"*? 32nd Annual International Antitrust Law & Policy Conference, Fordham Corporate Law Institute, 22–23 September 2005 (forthcoming) regarding the alternatives to the current system of judicial review 32–35.

[255] President of the CFI Judge Bo Vesterdorf, 'Judicial Review and Competition Law—Reflections on the Role of the Community Courts in the EC system of Competition Law Enforcement', speech at the International Forum on EC Competition Law, Brussels 8 April 2005. See also the edited paper version of the speech in Competition Policy International [2005] Vol 1 No 2 and statistics (as of 1 July 2005) page 26 in which Judge Vesterdorf stated that the removal of civil service cases would reduce 20 per cent of the current work load.

2

THE ROLE OF NATIONAL
JUDICIAL AUTHORITIES

A. Jurisdiction of National Courts

National courts' involvement in EC competition rules occurs at three different **2.01** levels. First, a specific court can be designated by a Member State as its national competition authority, thereby becoming a specialized body.[1] Second, particular courts may be vested with the power to review on appeal the decisions of the national competition authority, whether of an administrative or judicial nature. Finally, national courts are those which, in the exercise of their general jurisdiction, may be called upon to apply Articles 81 and 82 EC in claims between private parties at first instance or at the appeal stage. It is the latter function that this chapter concentrates on. Under the old system, the Commission handled the vast majority of all antitrust cases. Its decisions were subject to judicial review by the CFI and the ECJ under Article 230 EC. As indicated, Regulation 1/2003 has decentralized the enforcement of the Community competition rules. More responsibility for the enforcement of the antitrust rules are not only given to national competition authorities ('NCAs') but also to national courts. Both have the power to apply Articles 81 and 82 EC in individual cases. Therefore, national courts have the power to apply the rules directly and, additionally, the jurisdiction to hear appeals against decisions of the NCAs.[2]

---

[1] In this situation, while keeping its judicial nature, the court will be subject to all obligations related to its position within the European network of competition authorities ('ECN'). Commission Notice on cooperation within the Network of Competition Authorities [2004] OJ C101/43. See ch 3 'The role of national competition authorities'.

[2] Note that the Commission Notice on the cooperation between the Commission and the courts of the EU Member States in the application of Arts 81 and 82 EC ('National Courts Cooperation Notice') [2004] OJ C101/54 para 7 extends the competence to apply EC competition law also to acts adopted by EU institutions in accordance with the EC Treaty or in accordance with the measures adopted to give the EC Treaty effect provided that these acts have direct effect, i.e. national courts may have to enforce Commission decisions or Commission regulations applying Art 81(3) EC. When applying these EC competition rules, national courts act within the framework of Community law and are bound to observe general EC law principles.

1. Jurisdiction of national courts under Regulation 44/2001

2.02 Whether the ordinary courts of the Member States[3] are competent to deal with a case is determined according to national, EU, and international rules.[4] Of particular relevance for determining the jurisdiction of national courts at the EU level is Council Regulation 44/2001, which unifies the rules of conflict of jurisdiction in civil and commercial matters and aims to simplify the formalities with a view to rapid and simple recognition and enforcement of judgments from Member States.[5] According to Regulation 44/2001, a dispute involving a tort or contractual liability claim can be brought before the court territorially competent in the Member State where the defending party is domiciled.[6] In addition, contractual liability proceedings may be brought before the competent court for the 'place of performance' of the obligation in question and tort proceedings in the court for the place where the harmful event occurred or may occur (special jurisdiction).[7] Although Regulation 44/2001 gives some indications on the definition of the 'place of performance of the obligation' in contractual disputes, this notion nevertheless may give rise to different interpretations and may not be easily determined in pan-European agreements, or networks of agreements.

---

[3] In the discussion that followed the publication of the White Paper on the Modernisation of the Rules Implementing Arts 81 and 82 ('White Paper') [1999] OJ C132/1, it was suggested that the application of EC competition rules be entrusted to specialized courts. This was the view of the European Parliament that considered it necessary to ensure consistency and legal certainty. Of the same opinion was the ECOSOC—which went even further, suggesting a system of appeal to supranational courts—as well as other commentators from the industry and the legal profession. However, only three Member States supported this proposal. White Paper on Reform of Reg 17, Summary of Observations, COMP DG Document, 29 February 2000, available at http://europa.eu.int/comm/competition/antitrust/others/.

[4] CS Kerse and N Khan, *EC Antitrust Procedure* (5th edn 2005) para 5–055. As regards the relevant rules under the Act against Restraints of Competition in Germany, see J Schwarze and A Weitbrecht, *Grundzüge des europäischen Kartellverfahrensrechts* (2004) § 11 paras 12, 13. T Woodgate and J Jellis, 'EU private antitrust litigation' in *The European Antitrust Review 2006*, Special report Global Competition Law Review 53–56.

[5] Council Reg (EC) 44/2001 of 22 December 2000 on jurisdiction and the recognition and enforcement of judgments in civil and commercial matters [2001] OJ L12/1. Reg 44/2001 binds all Member States but Denmark (note: however, there is a proposal for a Council Decision (COM(2005) 145 final) which would extend the application of Reg 44/2001 also to Denmark). As for a necessary nexus, this will be established if (i) the defendant is domiciled in a Regulation State; (ii) a court of a Member State has exclusive jurisdiction pursuant to Art 22 (which is expanded on below); or (iii) where, in accordance with Art 23, the defendant is a party to an agreement that provides that the courts of a Member State are to have exclusive jurisdiction to settle any dispute which has arisen in connection with a particular legal relationship (usually with the aid of a choice of forum/jurisdiction clause).

[6] Art 2 of Reg. 44/2001.

[7] Art 5(1) and (3) of Reg 44/2001. In Case 21/76 *Bier v Mines de Potasse d'Alsace* [1976] ECR 1735 the ECJ has construed this as meaning either the place of the event causing the loss or the place where the loss occurred. Later cases, however, restricted this wide interpretation by stating that Art 5(3) cannot mean any place where the adverse consequences of an event which has already caused actual loss elsewhere are felt. See CS Kerse and N Khan, *EC Antitrust Procedure* (5th edn, 2005) para 1–065.

Varying interpretations may cause parallel and thus possibly inconsistent procedures and may lead to 'forum shopping', where claimants bring actions for damages against transnational cartels involving multinational defendants.[8] Claimants may prefer to bring their cases before common law jurisdictions with wide-reaching discovery rules which include the production of documents adverse to a party's own case. Civil law countries do not always have any automatic disclosure requirements. This problem also encompasses the claim for damages that may be joined to a contractual dispute. If the dispute arises out of the operations of a branch, agency, or other establishments of the defendant, the defendant may be sued where it is situated.[9] The rules on *lis pendens* and related actions aim at minimizing the possibility of concurrent proceedings and preventing contradictory decisions, since they provide that 'any court other than the court first seized' should stay its proceedings and decline jurisdiction 'in favour of that court' either in proceedings involving the same cause of action and between the same parties or in related actions.[10] However, taken together, it remains to be seen whether these rules provide a clear and effective mechanism and prevent parties from forum shopping in relation to national courts.[11] In

---

[8] See, e.g. the case before the UK courts, *Provimi Ltd v Roche Products Ltd and others* [2003] EWHC 961 (Comm), which interpreted Reg 44/2001 on jurisdiction and domestic English procedural rules in a way that greatly facilitated damages actions in European courts. In *Provimi*, the court allowed consolidation of EU actions in English courts, even where neither the claimant nor the defendant was English and where the contract contained a jurisdiction clause in favour of the German courts. The proceedings arose out of an investigation into the vitamins and pigment markets by the Commission which found that two companies, Roche and Aventis, among others, had participated in the operation of cartels contrary to Art 81 EC in relation to the sale of vitamins in the EU (the *vitamins cartel* case). The *Provimi* case has allowed damages claims against *Roche* and *Aventis* to proceed to trial. The importance of the case is that it clears potential jurisdictional hurdles for damages claims against cartel members and shows how an English court can assert jurisdiction over claims between entities from other Member States in respect of products purchased at inflated cartel prices across Europe. T Woodgate and J Jellis, 'Private EC Antitrust Enforcement' in *The European Antitrust Review 2005* Special report, Global Competition Law Review, 61–64 (63): and see update in 'EU private antitrust litigation' in *The European Antitrust Review 2006* Special report, Global Competition Law Review, 53–56 (54); CE Koob, DE Vann, and AY Oruc, 'Developments in private enforcement of competition laws—introduction' in *Private Antitrust Litigation 2005* Getting the Deal Through—Global Competition Review 3–8 (5) noting that the UK may become the forum of choice for private actions under the competition laws considering that the UK courts have asserted broad jurisdictions, requiring a 'relatively modest jurisdictional nexus'. See also update of the authority in *Private Antitrust Litigation 2006* Getting the Deal Through – Global Competition Review [2006] 3–7 (5)

[9] Art 5(5) of Reg 44/2001 (special jurisdiction)

[10] Chapter II, section 9 of Reg 44/2001. Thus, it is not possible to have an action 'reallocated' as this may occur between NCAs: once a first court is seized and its jurisdiction to rule on the action is established, any court in other member State will decline jurisdiction to rule on the same action. JS Venit, 'Private Practice in the Wake of the Commission's Modernization Program' [2005] Legal Issues of Economic Integration 147–59 (157).

[11] K Lenaerts and D Gerard, 'Decentralisation of EC Competition Law Enforcement: Judges in the Frontline' [2004] World Competition Law and Economics 313–49 (327). See also RM Steur, 'Standards of Proof and Judicial Review: A US Perspective', 32nd Annual International

conclusion, it is difficult to predict how Regulation 44/2001 will interact with the role assigned to national courts under Regulation 1/2003 in the future.

2.03 Another area of potential conflict relates to the recognition of foreign judgments and decisions of competition authorities in proceedings pending before a national court. Regulation 44/2001 provides that judgments given in a Member State must be recognized in all others 'without any special procedure being required', except, among other things, 'if such recognition is manifestly contrary to the public policy in the Member State in which recognition is sought'.[12] Problems may arise in regard to the notion of recognition. A judgment is *res judicata* between the parties to the dispute; the principle *non bis in idem* therefore prevents the same issues between the same parties being brought before another competent court. However, recognition of a foreign court's decision that clearly violates EC competition law may well be refused if it entails a manifest infringement of the *ordre public* of the Member State where such recognition is sought.[13] Determining whether the foreign judgment violates the *ordre public* might also require a thorough analysis of the case by the competent court, which could partly invalidate the automatism of recognition under Regulation 44/2001. A second concern relates to the existence of networks of identical contracts between, for instance, a party A—a supplier—and parties B, C, D, and E—dealers.[14] From a legal point of view, each contract entails a separate relationship that may be subject to a separate legal review. Yet, from an economic point of view, however, competition is affected by the network of agreements as a whole. If a national court reaches the conclusion that one of the contracts, e.g. a contract between A and B, or even the entire network of contracts, is contrary to Article 81 or even 82 EC, and annuls it, it remains to be determined what the effects of that judgment are on the same or similar disputes between A and C, D, or E since they do not involve exactly the same parties. In the absence of any specific provision dealing with that issue in Regulation 1/2003, one may conclude that the outcome of the judgment between A and B may only

---

Antitrust Law & Policy Conference Fordham Corporate Law Institute, 22–23 September 2005, (forthcoming) on the different standards of proof and review at the international level.

[12] Arts 33 and 34 of Reg 44/2001.

[13] The Community Courts have repeatedly emphasized the public order nature of Arts 81 and 82 EC, see Joined Cases C-430/93 and C-431/93 *Jeroen van Schijndel and Johannes Nicolaas Cornelis van Veen v Stichting Pensioenfonds voor Fysiotherapeuten* [1995] ECR I-4705 para 21; Case C-126/97 *Eco Swiss China Time Ltd v Benetton International NV* [1999] ECR I-3055 para 39. This may, however, be different at the Member State and national competition law level. M Dolmans and J Greisens, 'Arbitration and the Modernization of EC Antitrust Law: New Opportunities and New Responsibilities' [2003] ICC International Court of Arbitration Vol 14 No 2 37–51, 43 pointing to the Netherlands.

[14] Example used by K Lenaerts and D Gerard, 'Decentralisation of EC Competition Law Enforcement: Judges in the Frontline' [2004] World Competition Law and Economics 313–49 (327).

qualify as an indisputable fact in the other proceedings. It could be considered as strong evidential value and may even result in a reversal of the burden of proof. Where the Commission does not seize the matter, multiple and burdensome cases may thus be necessary to dismantle the anticompetitive network of agreements.[15] It is also conceivable that additional problems may arise where the same facts are not before the national courts involved. Markets evolve and the effects of an agreement may vary over time. A third issue has to do with the authority before a national court of an administrative decision given by a foreign competition authority; such a decision would not be covered by the recognition afforded under the terms of Regulation 44/2001, which only addresses the recognition of judgments. The jurisdiction of an NCA is limited to the territory of the Member State it belongs to and it would be difficult for the ECJ to extend by analogy Article 16(1) of Regulation 1/2003 to these NCA's decisions.[16]

2. Actions before national courts

The Commission has continuously stressed that the application of Articles 81 and 82 EC by national courts has many advantages for individuals.[17] In the first place, national courts may award compensation for loss suffered as a result of a restrictive practice or agreement, a possibility not open to the Commission.[18] Secondly, national courts may adopt interim or protective measures more rapidly than the Commission. Thirdly, a national court may be seized simultaneously of actions under national law and actions under Community law; the same cannot

2.04

---

[15] K Lenaerts and D Gerard, 'Decentralisation of EC Competition Law Enforcement: Judges in the Frontline' [2004] World Competition Law and Economics 313–49 (328).

[16] It seems that in the United States, in situations where the government obtains a civil or a criminal judgment against a defendant to the effect that he or she has violated the antitrust laws, the decision of an NCA could be granted the status of prima facie evidence of a violation of EC competition law in any other court proceedings between the defendant to the administrative procedure and third parties. K Lenaerts and D Gerard, 'Decentralisation of EC Competition Law Enforcement: Judges in the Frontline' [2004] World Competition Law and Economics 313–49 (328).

[17] Member of the Commission in charge of Competition Policy N Kroes, 'Damages Actions for Breaches of EU Competition Rules: Realities and Potentials', opening speech at the conference 'La reparation du prejudice cause for the protique anti-concurrentialle en France et à L'étranger: bilan et perspectives' Cour de Cessation, Paris 17 October 2005; S Norberg, 'Some elements to enhance damages actions for breach of the competition rules in Arts 81 and 82 EC', 32nd Annual International Antitrust Law & Policy Conference, Fordham Corporate Law Institute, 22–23 September 2005 (forthcoming); Speech by former commissioner for competition by M Monti, 'Private litigation as a key complement to public enforcement of competition rules and the first conclusions on the implementation of the new Merger Regulation' [2004] Fiesole, Italy IBA—8th Annual Competition Conference; for the contrary view, see WPJ Wils, 'Should Private Antitrust Enforcement Be Encouraged in Europe' [2003] World Competition—Law and Economics Review 1–13.

[18] Application of those Articles by the courts would have the additional advan encouraging compliance with Community law on the part of undertakings, which, findir selves directly threatened by such actions by individuals, would be more careful not to Community competition rules.

be said of the Commission. Fourthly, national courts may award costs against the unsuccessful party, including lawyers' fees, a course of action not available in an administrative procedure. Besides, it would seem that national courts constitute the logical forum for commercial litigation and are in a better position than the Commission to resolve conflicts between private interests. The parties and their lawyers are also more familiar with the procedure to be followed before national courts and benefit from the fact that the latter are near at hand. Finally, administrative authorities—the Community authorities at least—are not in general obliged to deal with specific cases or to process every request made to them. They can choose those which they consider most important,[19] whereas national courts are obliged to deal with all matters brought before them.[20]

2.05   Articles 81 and 82 EC may arise in a variety of contexts before national courts. National courts may be called upon to apply such rules in administrative, civil, or criminal proceedings.[21] While the National Courts Cooperation Notice makes reference to Article 6 of Regulation 1/2003 as the principal source of the ability of the national courts to apply Articles 81 and 82 EC in those disputes, such power already flows from the direct effect of these rules.[22] In this way, the role of the national courts in relation to Community competition rules was somehow defined by the Treaty itself.[23] Article 81(2) EC provides that any

---

[19] See Notice on handling of complaints [2004] C101/65 para 8. See below ch 12 'Rejection of complaints' para 12.03.

[20] In this context, it is to note that in the United States, the real deterrent factor for companies in conducting their business is not so much public actions by competition authorities and the possible resulting fines, but rather the fear of private claims for damages, which can force undertakings to pay out huge amounts of money to settle the disputes.

[21] Reg 1/2003 does not apply to national laws which impose criminal sanctions on natural persons, except to the extent that such sanctions are the means whereby competition rules applying to undertakings are enforced; however, it gives no indication as to the circumstances where Reg 1/2003 would indeed apply to criminal proceedings. See Recital 8 of Reg 1/2003, last sentence. For an interpretation of Recital 8 see WPJ Wils, 'Community Report' in D Cahill (ed), *The Modernization of EU Competition Law Enforcement in the EU*, FIDE 2004 National Reports 661–736 paras 160–161, and A Riley, 'EC Antitrust Modernisation: The Commission Does Very Nicely—Thank You! Part One: Reg 1 and the Notification Burden' [2003] ECLR 604–14 (607), fn 11.

[22] National Courts Cooperation Notice [2004] OJ C101/54 para 3 fn 5. See Case 127/73 *BRT v Sabam* [1974] ECR 51 paras 15 and 16. The ECJ has drawn a distinction between national courts applying Arts 81 and 82 EC by virtue of their direct effect and those courts especially entrusted to apply domestic competition law which apply Arts 81 and 82 qua authorities deriving competence from Art 84 EC. CS Kerse and N Khan, *EC Antitrust Procedure* (5th edn, 2003) para 1–066.

[23] The Community legal order is thus already rooted in a decentralized enforcement system in which each national court effectively acts as a Community Court. To that extent, decentralization of EC competition law and its application 'in full' by national courts is nothing more than a 'return to normal' for an area of law which was subject for an important part—the application of Art 81(3) EC—to exclusive enforcement by the Commission. K Lenaerts and D Gerard, 'Decentralisation of EC Competition Law Enforcement: Judges in the Frontline' [2004] World Competition Law and Economics 313–49 (318).

agreement which infringes Article 81(1) EC is automatically void. Given that it falls to national courts to enforce lawful agreements, the nullity—and, therefore, the inapplicability of agreements—is a matter primarily for the national courts, which are under an obligation to apply that sanction.[24] Consequently, the parties to a restrictive agreement which is caught by Article 81(1) EC cannot ask the judicial authorities to ensure that the agreement is performed. Since that provision is concerned with a matter of public policy, national courts are under an obligation to declare of their own motion that restrictive agreements are void if they find them to be in breach of Article 81(1) EC.[25] Thus, it is not only that national courts having jurisdiction are entitled to apply Articles 81 and 82 EC, since in particular circumstances they can apply such rules of their own motion and even be obliged to do so. Under the terms of the ECJ ruling in *van Schijndel*,[26] national courts are obliged to apply of their own motion binding Community rules where under national law they are obliged to apply of their own motion binding national rules. In the same vein, where national courts have discretion to apply national binding rules, the same discretion shall exist in relation to the application of binding Community law. However, national courts are not required to apply such rules of their own motion when that would oblige them to depart from the situation of judicial passivity imposed on them by national law, by going beyond the dispute as defined by the parties and relying on facts or circumstances not raised by the parties.[27] Conversely, the parties to a restrictive agreement may contend that it is void if they wish to escape a mandatory injunction to perform a contractual obligation or damages in an action for breach of the agreement in question.[28]

---

[24] In Case T-24/90 *Automec v Commission* [1992] ECR II-2223 para 93, the CFI stated that '[. . .] the Treaty presupposes that national law gives the national courts the power to safeguard the rights of undertakings which have been subjected to anti-competitive practices [. . .]'. On this aspect of nullity in Art 81(2) EC, see J Schwarze and A Weitbrecht, *Grundzüge des europäischen Kartellverfahrensrechts* (2004) § 11 paras 8, 9.

[25] cf the Commission, which can decide not to proceed with a complaint on the grounds that there is a lack of sufficient Community interest. See ch 12 on 'Rejection of complaints' paras 12.10 and what follows.

[26] Joined Cases C-430/93 and C-431/93 *Van Schijndel/Stichting Pensioenfonds voor Fysiotherapeuten* [1995] ECR I-4705 paras 20–22.

[27] In *Peterbroeck* however, the ECJ held that there was an obligation to raise an issue of Community law of its own motion where the effect of the national procedure would be to preclude any national court from considering an issue of Community law. Case C-312/93 *Peterbroeck v Belgian State* [1995] ECR I-4599, para 21. See C Bellamy and G Child. *European Community Law of Competition* (5th edn, 2001) para 10–012, referring to the Opinion of AG Jacobs who suggested in *Schijndel* that where an agreement was manifestly illegal under Art 81(1) EC the national court could and should raise the point of its own motion, since it would do the same under domestic law.

[28] Thus, for example, distributors who fail to comply with an exclusive dealing clause or licensees of a patent subject to territorial restrictions who do not wish to pay royalties for using the patented invention could plead—and have done so in similar cases—a breach of Art 81(1) EC in order to escape their contractual obligations.

2.06 The task of national courts, however, goes much further than merely applying the penalty of nullity. Even in its earliest case law, the ECJ made it clear that, since the prohibitions laid down by Article 81(1) and 82 EC are inherently capable of producing direct effects between individuals, these Articles create rights in favour of the persons concerned which the national courts must uphold.[29] This means that, in addition to the penalty of nullity, which derives directly from the EC Treaty, the national courts are obliged to provide adequate legal remedies or rights of action to enable individuals and undertakings to take action against restrictive or abusive practices. Such remedies may take many forms: striking down certain clauses of agreements as void, or indeed the agreement as a whole if the clauses in question are not severable from the whole; injunctions or orders to take or refrain from particular action; the award of compensation for loss and damage suffered through infringements of Articles 81 and 82 EC or the recovery of sums unduly paid. If necessary, such remedies may be accompanied by protective or interim measures. Undertakings and individuals are therefore entitled to use Articles 81 and 82 EC both as a 'shield' and as a 'sword'.[30] The means employed to ensure that individuals have at their disposal adequate ways of enforcing their rights under Community law vary from one Member State to another. It is a matter for national law, following any guidelines laid down by Community law, to say how Community law is to be applied. The relevant principle is that the exercise of all rights of action under Community law must be available in order to ensure observance of Community provisions having direct effect, under the same conditions as those which apply to ensure compliance with national law.[31] However, this may not be sufficient. The ECJ has held that if the national law of a Member State lacks adequate legal remedies for an infringement of national law and such remedies are necessary to enable an individual to enforce Community provisions, the national legislature is obliged to create *ex novo* the requisite remedies for the exercise of such rights of action. Consequently, if it were not possible to prescribe protective or interim

---

[29] Case 127/73 *BRT v Sabam II* [1974] ECR 313 para 16. It is precisely 'because Art [81] (1) [and Art 86] of the Treaty is directly applicable, [that] the Commission and the national court have in fact concurrent jurisdiction to apply' those provisions: Case T-24/90 *Automec v EC Commission II* [1992] ECR II-2223 para 60, citing *BRT* and *Lauder* (judgment in Case 37/79 *Marty v Estée Lauder* [1980] ECR 2481).

[30] The terms are repeatedly used in the doctrine: L Ritter and WD Braun, *European Competition Law: A Practitioner's Guide* (3rd edn, 2004) 1170; A Riley, 'Beyond Leniency: Enhancing Enforcement in EC Antitrust Law' [2005] World Competition 377–400 (382); see also ch 1 'The institutional framework' para 1.33.

[31] See, among others, Case 158/80 *REWE v Hauptzollamt Kiel* [1981] ECR 1805, and Case 199/82 *San Giorgio* [1983] ECR 3595 para 12. Similarly in Case 106/77 *Simmenthal (II)* [1978] ECR 629 the Court held that when giving effect to Community rights in national courts, the latter must, if necessary, refuse to apply any conflicting provision of national law. The implementation of rights through the conduit of national remedies cannot render the exercise of such rights overly difficult.

measures or if no action for damages were available on such grounds, the national legislature would have to create the remedies needed to safeguard the individual rights and claims of private persons under Community law.[32]

The recent case law of the Community courts has also emphasized the **2.07** importance of enforcement by private parties of Community competition law. In its ruling in *Courage v Crehan*,[33] the ECJ held that damages can be claimed before national courts for breaches of Article 81 EC and parties to agreements violating Article 81 EC cannot be barred from claiming damages against co-contractors before national courts.[34] The ECJ reaffirmed that it is for national law to provide procedural rules, including remedies, for breaches of EC law as long as the remedy must not be less favourable than that available for domestic claims and the remedy must not render ineffective the right under EC law. National rules may prevent unjust enrichment to litigants and may consequently prevent a party from benefiting from its own unlawful conduct by denying damages. Yet damages may only be denied to parties who bear 'significant responsibility' for the distortion of competition caused by the agreement.[35] The ruling reflects the view that actions for damages before the national courts are considered as making a significant contribution to the maintenance of effective

---

[32] See Case 158/80 *REWE v Hauptzollamt Kiel* [1981] ECR 1805 para 44, where the Court stated that while '[. . .] the Treaty has made it possible in a number of instances for private persons to bring a direct action, where appropriate, before the ECJ, it was not intended to create new remedies in the national courts to ensure the observance of Community law other than those already laid down by national law. On the other hand the system of legal protection established by the Treaty, as set out in Art 177 [234 EC] in particular, implies that it must be possible for every type of action provided for by national law to be available for the purpose of ensuring observance of Community provisions having direct effect, on the same conditions concerning the admissibility and procedure as would apply were it a question of ensuring observance of national law. [. . .]'.

[33] Note that the overwhelming majority of judgments received by the Commission under Art 15(2) of Reg 1/2003 and being posted on the DG COMP website, the overwhelming majority (twenty-nine) resulted from private enforcement actions, in most cases aimed at the annulment of an agreement on the ground of its incompatibility with the EU competition rules. The non-confidential versions of these judgments are listed in this database, in their original language, classified according to the Member State of origin. Within every Member State, the judgments are in a chronological order. See http://europa.eu.int/comm/competition/antitrust/national_courts/index_en.html.

[34] Case C-453/99 *Courage v Crehan* [2001] ECR I-6297 para 11 the ECJ overturned the principle of English law that a party to an illegal act may not benefit from its own wrongdoing and therefore may not recover damages from other parties to an illegal agreement.

[35] Case C-453/99 *Courage v Crehan* [2001] ECR I-6297 paras 32 and what follows where the ECJ identified two main factors to be taken into account: (i) the economic and legal context and (ii) the respective bargaining power of the parties, in particular where the party seeking damages was in a 'markedly weaker position' than the other party so as to seriously call into question that party's freedom to negotiate the terms of the contract and capacity to avoid or reduce the losses suffered.

competition in the Community.[36] It must be recognized, however, that not every aspect of proceedings before national courts is advantageous. In practice, proceedings before national courts may be as slow, complicated, and expensive (even where the unsuccessful party is ordered to pay the successful party's costs) as those before the Commission. Furthermore, many national courts may experience difficulties in making extremely complicated economic evaluations. Since proceedings before national courts are adversarial, the parties must produce evidence to support their claims. They cannot rely on evidence being obtained by the judicial authorities, as in the case of inquisitorial proceedings. Therefore, it remains to be seen how soon private enforcement becomes decoupled from parallel investigation by the Commission and/or the newly empowered NCAs, especially in those Member States where claimants have substantial difficulties in proving an infringement in certain cases.[37] These considerations continue to carry considerable weight and may prompt parties to turn to administrative authorities rather than to courts, at either Community or national level.[38]

2.08 It should be noted that national courts act in their capacity as ordinary jurisdictional bodies, i.e. not as competition authorities; thus, they are not part of the ECN and not bound to give up a case because the Commission has started proceedings at the same time. Such a situation could conflict with the necessary independence of the judiciary, and with the different tasks assigned to courts and public authorities in charge of competition enforcement. Accordingly, parallel procedures are thus possible between national courts and competition

---

[36] The central role of private enforcement in modernization, in particular in its complementary role to public enforcement, was highlighted by former Commissioner M Monti in his interview in the special edition of the Competition Policy Newsletter 'The EU gets new competition powers for the 21st century'—Interview with Mario Monti (2004/04) and his speech at the European Competition Day at Dublin in April 2004. The Commissioner emphasized that the possibility for victims of anticompetitive behaviour, including consumers, to claim compensation for losses caused by such behaviour would strengthen the deterrent effect of the competition rules and help to create a stronger culture of compliance with, and enforcement of, those rules. The lack of private enforcement in Europe has been identified by commentators as a main weakness in the EU competition enforcement system. M Monti, then European Commissioner for competition matters, 'Private litigation as a key complement to public enforcement of competition rules and the first conclusions on the implementation of the new Merger Reg' Speech at IBA—8th Annual Competition Conference, Fiesole, 17 September 2004.

[37] See JS Venit, 'Private Practice in the Wake of the Commission's Modernization' [2005] Legal Issues of Economic Integration 147–59 (151) suggests that the elimination of 'illogical procedural consequence' that an exemptible agreement could be declared void by a national court merely because it had not been notified might even reduce litigation at the national level. In cases where there is not a prior Commission decision upheld by the Community courts such analysis will require more detailed factual, economic and legal analysis than 'the more straightforward path to victory provided by the English defence.'

[38] See Ashurst, 'Study on the conditions of claims for damages in cases of infringement of EC competition rules' Comparative Report, 31 August 2004, Executive Summary.

authorities, even if they are not desired or desirable.[39] A breach of Articles 81 or 82 EC may be pleaded and the national court may apply the prohibition of Article 81 EC before or at the same time as the Commission or a NCA, as the case may be, is carrying out its own investigation. While Regulation 1/2003 seeks to diminish the potential for divergent views, there the possibility of conflicts still exists and may even have increased as the result of the changes made by Regulation 1/2003.[40]

B. The Application of Articles 81 and 82 by National Courts

1. General principles

Coherent enforcement of Community competition rules throughout the EU does not only mean the uniform application of such rules in substantive terms but also an equally effective application independently of the national court which is called on to apply them. In this respect, different national procedures may indeed result in a *de facto* different enforcement of Community competition rules, e.g. due to different rules on the standard of proof,[41] investigative powers, criminal versus civil enforcement, access to file, interim measures, etc.[42] Furthermore, the two limbs of coherent application—uniformity and effectiveness—are interrelated. In fact, it may well happen that a system of procedural autonomy between different jurisdictions may jeopardize uniform application, e.g. where a national court is unable to make a specific finding—for example the existence of a cartel due to lack of necessary investigative powers—while

2.09

---

[39] K. Lenaerts and D Gerard, 'Decentralisation of EC Competition Law Enforcement: Judges in the Frontline' [2004] World Competition Law and Economics 313–49 (315).

[40] CS Kerse and N Khan, *EC Antitrust Procedure* (5th edn, 2005) para 5–055.

[41] While Art 2 of Reg 1/2003 harmonizes rules on the burden of proof, Recital 5 makes clear that the Regulation does not affect national rules on standard of proof or the obligations of the national court to ascertain the relevant facts of the case, subject to compliance with the general principles of Community law. See, for example, regarding the UK Cases 1021/1/1/03 and 1022/1/1/2003 *JJB Sport/OFT, Allsports Limited/OFT* 1 October 2004.

[42] The relevant differences refer broadly to national procedures which would apply to litigation based on Arts 81 and 82. These may include not only differences in procedural rules *stricto sensu* (i.e. rules on investigative powers) but also differences in substantive rules which are nevertheless capable of affecting the application of Arts 81 and 82 in national proceedings (e.g. rules on fault as a condition of liability, causation, etc). 'Study on the conditions of claims for damages in case of infringement of EC competition rules,' Ashurst, Comparative Report, 31 August 2004, Executive Summary. S Norberg, 'Some elements to enhance damages actions for breach of the competition rules in Arts 81 and 82 EC', 32nd Annual International Antitrust Law & Policy Conference, Fordham Corporate Law Institute, 22–23 September 2005 (forthcoming); see also M Dougan, 'National Remedies before the Court of Justice—Issues of Harmonization and Differentiation' (2004) 368–78 on harmonization of remedies and procedural rules in Competition cases pre and past—*Courage v Grehan*.

another national court (or the Commission) enjoying different procedural powers might indeed be able to make such a finding in the same case.

2.10   While Member States are mainly free to elect their procedural conditions for the enforcement of EC competition rules, national courts need to take note of certain Community rules that determine the relationship between the Commission and the national courts. Procedural autonomy is also circumscribed by general principles of Community law, including, *inter alia*, the following:

(a) the requirement that national law provide effective, proportionate, and dissuasive sanctions for breaches of Community law;

(b) the availability, under certain circumstances, of damages for breaches of Community law;

(c) the principles of effectiveness and equivalence which require, respectively, that national procedural rules should not make excessively difficult or practically impossible the enforcement of Community law (effectiveness) nor should they be less favourable than the rules applicable to the enforcement of equivalent national law (equivalence).[43]

2.11   The National Courts Cooperation Notice seems to rate effectiveness higher than equivalence, which is consistent with the case law of the Community courts.[44] Indeed, the ECJ has established that effectiveness prevails over equivalence, i.e. even if national procedural rules ensure equal treatment to a claim based on Community law and a similar national cause of action, that might not be enough if it does not ensure the effective application of Community law.[45]

---

[43] The clearest recent statement of such principles may be found in Joined Cases C-279/96, C-280/96 and C-281/96 *Ansaldo Energia SpA v Amministrazione delle Finanze dello Stato, Amministrazione delle Finanze dello Stato v Marine Insurance Consultants Srl and GMB Srl and others v Amministrazione delle Finanze dello Stato* [1998] ECR I-5025 para 27, where the Court stated that '[. . .] in the absence of Community legislation governing a matter, it is for the domestic legal system of each Member State to designate the national courts and tribunals having jurisdiction and to lay down the detailed procedural rules governing actions for safeguarding rights which individuals derive from Community law. However, such rules must not be less favourable than those governing similar domestic actions (principle of equivalence) and they must not render virtually impossible or excessively difficult the exercise of rights conferred by Community law (principle of effectiveness). [. . .]' National Courts Cooperation Notice [2004] OJ 101/54. See also CS Kerse and N Khan, *EC Antitrust Procedure* (5th edn, 2005) para 1–065.

[44] See also J Temple Lang, 'Developments, Issues and New Remedies—The Duties of National Authorities and Courts under Art 10 of the EC Treaty' [2004] Fordham International Law Journal 1904–39 (1908) indicating that the effectiveness principle has more potential than the equivalence principle.

[45] See, e.g. Case C-199/82 *Amministrazione delle Finanze dello Stato v SpA San Giorgio* [1983] ECR I-3595 para 17. In the field of competition law, the ECJ ruling in C-126/97 *Eco Swiss* [1999] ECR I-3055 might be read as an application of this rule of effectiveness taking precedence over equivalence, although the ECJ actually based its ruling on the very nature and purpose of Art 81 as a 'fundamental provision which is essential for the accomplishment of the tasks entrusted to the Community and, in particular, for the functioning of the internal market'. On the other hand,

The ECJ established these two principles as general limits on national pro-cedural autonomy, but it has also increasingly imposed specific restraints on national courts' autonomy, including the requirement that national law provide for specific remedies, such as damages or effective sanctions.[46]

2. Application of EC and national competition rules by national courts

To avoid the risk of inconsistency in the parallel application of national and Community competition rules, Regulation 1/2003 states that where the national courts apply national competition law to agreements, decisions by associations of undertakings, or concerted practices within the meaning of Article 81(1) EC which may affect trade between Member States within the meaning of that provision, they shall also apply Article 81 EC to such agree-ments, decisions, or concerted practices. Where the competition authorities of the Member States or national courts apply national competition law to any abuse prohibited by Article 82 EC, they shall also apply Article 82 EC.[47] Regula-tion 1/2003 requires that parallel application of national law should not lead to a different outcome than that which would result from the application of Article 81 EC. Under Article 3(2) of Regulation 1/2003, agreements which are permit-ted under Article 81 EC cannot be prohibited under national law,[48] nor can agreements which are prohibited under Article 81 EC be permitted under national law.[49] In particular, this convergence obligation applies in respect of

2.12

---

another interpretation of the Court's ruling in *Eco Swiss* might be that the proper way to establish whether Dutch law was in fact ensuring equal treatment to claims based on Art 81 EC was not the corresponding provision of Dutch competition law. Instead, the comparison should be between Dutch public policy provisions on the one hand and Community public policy provisions on the other hand, the latter including Art 81 EC.

[46] In Case C-453/99 *Courage v Crehan* [2001] ECR I-6297 paras 26–27. As regards sanctions, see for instance, in the field of employment, Case C-271/91 *M Helen Marshall v Southampton and South-West Hampshire Area Health Authority* [1993] ECR I-4367 paras 36–37.

[47] Art 3 of the earlier draft Reg 1/2003 provided for the exclusive application of EC competi-tion law where applicable: 'Relationship between Arts 81 and 82 and national competition laws. Where an agreement, a decision by an association of undertakings or a concerted practice within the meaning of Art 81 of the Treaty or the abuse of a dominant position within the meaning of Art 82 may affect trade between Member States, Community competition law shall apply to the exclusion of national competition laws.'

[48] Art 3(2) of Reg 1/2003. It would appear that national law may also not be applied where the agreement serves some other legitimate purpose. In its preliminary ruling in Case C-309/99 *Wouters* [2002] ECR I-1577 the ECJ ruled that although a regulation concerning partnerships between members of the Bar and members of other liberal professions may fall within the scope of Art 81 EC, it may not amount to an infringement of the prohibition on anti-competitive agree-ment because despite the restrictive effects on competition that are inherent in them, the Bar rules may be considered as necessary for the proper practice of the legal profession, as organized in the Member State concerned.

[49] Case 14/68 *Walt Wilhelm* [1969] ECR 1. In this case, the Berliner Kammergericht sought guidance under Art [234] EC on how far the German authorities could continue with national cartel proceedings when the same case was being investigated by the Commission.

'agreements, decisions by associations of undertakings or concerted practices within the meaning of Article 81(1) [EC] which may affect trade between Member States within the meaning of that provision.' Thus, national courts will have to determine whether the agreement in question is capable of affecting trade between Member States.[50] They also have to establish whether the agreement in question is an 'agreement [. . .] within the meaning of Article 81(1) [EC]'. Such requirement will have to be construed as not only referring exclusively to the need of establishing whether the conduct in question constitutes an agreement, as opposed, for instance, to unilateral conduct[51] or whether it is an agreement between 'undertakings'. It also requires national courts to establish whether the agreement in question comes within the scope of Article 81(1) EC because it appreciably restricts competition.[52] Should the national court find that the agreement in question does not appreciably restrict competition, it would not have to apply Article 81 EC. Thus, the obligation to apply Article 81 EC in parallel with national competition law would not extend to agreements that, while affecting interstate trade, do not have an appreciable effect on competition.[53]

2.13 In regard to Article 82 EC, the Commission takes the view that Article 3(2) of Regulation 1/2003 does not require a similar convergence between national and

---

[50] See Commission Notice—Guidelines on the effect on trade concept contained in Arts 81 and 82 of the Treaty [2004] OJ C101/81 paras 6 and what follows.

[51] See on this discussion Joined Cases C-2/01 P and C-3/01 P *Bundesverband der Arzneimittel-Importeure eV and EC Commission v Bayer AG* [2004] ECR I-23; T-208/01 *Volkswagen AG v EC Commission* [2003] ECR II-5141.

[52] This conclusion is supported by a systematic interpretation of the first and second sentences of Art 3(1), which refer to the parallel application of Arts 81 and 82 EC, respectively. In particular, the last sentence of Art 3(1), dealing with Art 82, requires national courts to apply Community competition law in parallel with national competition law to 'any abuse prohibited by Art 82'. Thus, if National courts are required to establish whether the conduct in question is 'prohibited' in Art 82 cases in order to establish whether they should apply such Article in parallel with their national competition law, it seems that a similar requirement would apply in Art 81 cases, i.e. national courts would not only have to establish that the agreement in question is an 'agreement' for the purposes of Art 81, but also that Art 81 applies to that specific agreement, because it appreciably restricts competition.

[53] See on this point C Fellenius-Omnell, C Landström, and J Coyet, 'Modernizing EC competition law—Will a system of parallel application of EC and national competition laws ensure convergence?' ch 7, 111 in BE Hawk (ed), *International Antitrust Law & Policy*, Fordham Corporate Law Institute (2002). The authors suggest that Art 3(1) might not apply to agreements which are *de minimis* under the Commission De Minimis Notice ([2001] OJ C368/13), although Art 3(2) of Reg 1/2003 would still apply, thus preventing national courts from prohibiting under national law agreements which can be considered as *de minimis* under Community competition law. However, one might wonder whether, in order to establish if an agreement is *de minimis*, i.e. does not appreciably restrict competition, national courts should apply the thresholds in the Commission's De Minimis Notice or whether they would have some discretion.

Community law with respect to unilateral conduct.[54] However, it adds that the principle of primacy of Community law requires national courts to disapply those provisions of national law that contravene Community rules.[55] In this context, it is important to note that when a national court is in doubt about whether or not national legislation is incompatible with Community law, it can refer the matter to the ECJ for clarification within the preliminary ruling procedure.[56] It should be noted that Article 3(2) of Regulation 1/2003 itself expressly provides that Member States may adopt and apply on their territory *stricter* national laws which prohibit or sanction unilateral conduct. Thus, Member States are indeed entitled to prohibit under national law abusive conduct that would not be prohibited under Article 82 EC. However, Members States cannot permit under national law abusive conduct which would be prohibited under Article 82 EC. The Commission has reminded national courts that they might also have to apply other Community acts having direct effect, such as Commission's decisions or block exemption regulations. It does not, however, mention the last provision of Article 3(2) of Regulation 1/2003, providing that the national courts' duties under Article 3(1) and (2)—including the

---

[54] For criticism of the exclusion of convergence with respect to unilateral conduct, see C Fellenius-Omnell, C Landström and J Coyet, 'Modernizing EC competition law—Will a system of parallel application of EC and national competition laws ensure convergence?' ch 7 p 111 in BE Hawk (ed) *International Antitrust Law & Policy*, Fordham Corporate Law Institute (2002). 106. The authors wonder why dominant undertakings should not be granted the same legal certainty and level playing field as other companies and further point out that non-convergence will also affect other players, where, for instance a refusal to supply is prohibited in certain Member States but not in others. It seems that the exception was added to accommodate existing special rules in Germany that apply to companies with market 'strength'. In practice, the Commission's interpretation is often stricter than that under national rules. The exception is sometimes called '*Belgian compromise*' because it was achieved under the Belgium Presidency of the European Union in December 2002.

[55] Case C-198/01 *Consorzio Industrie Fiammiferi (CIF) v Autorità Garante della Concorrenza e del Mercato* [2003] ECR I-8055 para 49. In this preliminary ruling, the ECJ was asked whether in the event of an agreement between undertakings which adversely affects Community trade and which is required or facilitated by national legislation, Art 81 EC requires or permits the national competition authority (NCA) to disapply national law and to penalize the anti-competitive conduct. The ECJ ruled that Arts 81 and 82 in conjunction with Art 10 EC require that any provision which breaches Community law must be disapplied. It follows from this judgment that an NCA is bound to disapply national law incompatible with Community law. The consequences of the declaration of inapplicability is that all national courts and administrative bodies involved in the application of the national legislation incompatible with Community law were obliged to disapply it and the undertakings concerned had to terminate conflicting conduct required by such national legislation. See also J Temple Lang, 'Developments, Issues and New remedies—The Duties of National Authorities and Courts under Art 10 of the EC Treaty' [2004] Fordham International Law Journal 1904–39 (1906).

[56] A Kaczorowska, 'The Power of a National Competition Authority to disapply National Law Incompatible with EC law—and its practical consequences' [2004] ECLR 591–99 (595) which also points out that when a national court establishes the incompatibility of national legislation with Community law its judgment removes all doubts in this area and provides the parties with a high degree of certainty given that judgments are known to have binding force.

convergence duty—do not preclude the application of national law pursuing predominantly an objective different from that of Articles 81 and 82 EC, '[w]ithout prejudice to the general principles and other provisions of Community law'. Regulation 1/2003 indicates as an example of such laws national legislation which imposes sanctions on unfair trading practices, including both unilateral and bilateral acts.[57]

3. Parallel or subsequent application of Community competition rules

2.14 While concurrent application of Community competition law (i.e. application of such rules to the same case) by the Commission and the NCAs is excluded by Regulation 1/2003 in the event that the Commission initiates a proceeding,[58] this does not apply to a situation where national courts and the Commission examine a case at the same time. The National Courts Cooperation Notice sets out the principles governing such concurrent application of Community competition rules. The problem resides particularly in timing.[59] Where the Commission and the national courts can both apply Article 81 and/or Article 82 EC, the Commission Notice attempts to avoid the risk of conflicting decision in the event that either the national courts or the Commission come to a decision first.

- *If the national court comes to a decision first, it has the obligation to avoid taking a decision that would conflict with the decision contemplated by the Commission.* The National Courts Cooperation Notice has outlined a number of avenues available to national courts to ensure the consistency of their rulings with Commission practice.[60] The national court may seek information from the Commission as to whether the Commission has started proceedings, on the status of any such proceedings, and the likelihood of a decision. Such possibility was already envisaged by the 1993 Notice on cooperation between national courts and the Commission in applying Articles 81 and 82 EC,[61] based on the ECJ ruling in *Delimitis*, although it was made dependent on the national procedural rules of the requesting court,[62] while now it is expressly provided for in Article 15 of

---

[57] Recital 9 of Reg 1/2003.

[58] Under Art 11(6) of Reg 1/2003 the initiation of proceedings by the Commission relieves NCAs of their competence to apply EC competition rules.

[59] There are also some national courts that have not shied away from taking positions that may not be shared by the Commisison. In theory the Commission could adopt an individual position on the agreement that is being examined by the national court and use Art 16 of Reg 1/2003 to challenge the consistency of the national court ruling. See JS Venit, 'Private Practice in the Wake of the Commission's Modernization' [2005] Legal Issues of Economic Integration 147–59 (155).

[60] National Courts Cooperation Notice [2004] OJ C101/54 para 12. [61] [1993] OJ C39/6.

[62] See Commission Notice on cooperation with national courts [1993] OJ C39/6 ('1993 NC Notice') para 37; Case C-234/89 *Stergios Delimitis v Henninger Bräu AG* [1991] ECR I-935 para 53, where the Court states that the possibility for national courts to seek information from the Commission is 'always open to a national court, within the limits of the applicable national procedural rules'.

Regulation 1/2003.[63] Moreover, the national court may decide to stay proceedings until the Commission has reached a decision. The National Courts Cooperation Notice restates the Court's case law in *Delimitis* and confirms the Commission's commitment to give priority to cases suspended in this way as already undertaken under the 1993 National Courts Notice.[64] Where the national court cannot reasonably have any doubt in regard to the Commission's contemplated decision or where the Commission has already decided on a similar case, the national court may decide on the case pending before it 'without it being necessary' to ask the Commission for the information mentioned above or to await the Commission's decision. Strictly speaking, however, whether it is 'necessary' to either ask the Commission for procedural information or to stay the proceedings is left to the national court's choice and discretion. Indeed, the national court might instead decide to refer a preliminary ruling to the ECJ.[65]

- *If the Commission comes to a decision first, under Article 16 of Regulation 1/ 2003, the NC cannot take a decision running counter to the decision adopted by the Commission.*[66] Based on the ECJ judgments in *Foto–Frost*[67] and *Masterfoods*,[68] the Commission recalls that in view of the binding nature of Commission decisions, national courts cannot hold a Commission's decision invalid and cannot take a decision that runs counter to that of the Commission.

---

[63] A different issue is whether a national court may request information from the Commission in respect of proceedings concerning purely domestic competition law. Case C-275/00 *European Community v First NV and Franex NV* [2002] ECR I-10943 para 49 may be read as meaning that the ECJ did not limit the Commission's duty to cooperate with the national court to cases where the national court was applying EC law. C Brown and D Hardiman, 'The Extent of the Community Institutions Duty to Cooperate with National Courts—Zwartfeld revisited' [2004] ECLR 299.

[64] See 1993 National Courts Notice [1993] OJ C93/6 para 37.

[65] Note that the Commission mentioned in the White Paper on the Modernisation of the Rules Implementing Arts 81 and 82 [1999] OJ C132/1 para 102, that it could still intervene and adopt a prohibition decision—subject only to the principle of *res judicata* that applies to the dispute between the parties themselves, which has been decided once and for all by the national court after a NC had delivered a positive judgment (for example, rejecting an action on the ground that a restrictive practice satisfied the test of Art 81(3) EC, when the latter is either no longer open to appeal or has been confirmed on appeal. The argument of the Commission is that *res judicata* is valid only between the parties and that considering the different mission of the competition authorities—acting in the public interest—nothing precludes it to act afterwards in order to ensure consistency in the application of Arts 81 and 82 EC. Lately, the Commission seems to take the view that the ECJ should have the final word on this issue. K Lenaerts and D Gerard, 'Decentralisation of EC Competition Law Enforcement: Judges in the Frontline' [2004] World Competition Law and Economics 313–49 (326).

[66] This rule is not without exceptions. Recitals 13 and 22 of Reg 1/2003 indicate that it would not apply to commitments decisions under Art 9, NC Cooperation Notice [2004] OJ 101/54 para 13.

[67] Case 314/85 *Foto-Frost v Hauptzollamt Lübeck-Ost* [1987] ECR I-4199.

[68] Case C-344/98 *Masterfoods Ltd v HB Ice Cream Ltd* [2000] ECR I-11369.

Instead, it should refer the matter to the ECJ, which has exclusive jurisdiction on that matter. Where the Commission's decision is the subject of an application for annulment under Article 230[69] and the dispute before the national courts depends on the validity of the Commission decision, the national court should stay proceedings or, where it thinks this is appropriate, submit its question to the ECJ for a preliminary ruling on the validity of the Commission's decision.[70] The obligation for national courts not to adopt a decision conflicting with a prior decision of the Commission could play a role not only in avoiding conflicting decisions but also in resolving conflicts which have already arisen. In particular, if a national court's judgment found that Article 81 EC does not apply, the Commission might still prohibit the agreement in question with effect *erga omnes*. In such a case, if the national court's judgment were appealed, the appeal court would be bound by the Commission's decision.[71]

Request to the ECJ for a preliminary ruling

2.15 As indicated, decentralization brings with it the possibility of divergent decisions where national courts of the Member States have jurisdiction to hear direct actions under Articles 81 and 82 EC or actions against decisions of the NCAs. Where the law is unclear, the national courts can request assistance from the Commission in specific cases,[72] or else they can request a preliminary ruling from the ECJ pursuant to Article 234 EC.[73] In particular, national courts may

---

[69] It is often claimed that the CFI applies a 'self-imposed limited control' over the legality of Commission decisions on competition cases. Despite the language of Art 230 EC, however, the 'manifest error of appraisal' standard for reviewing the application by the Commission of Art 81(3) EC has considerably evolved over time towards a full review standard and does not *a priori* preclude the CFI from undertaking a full and exhaustive review of the facts of the case and of the Commission's legal and economic analysis in the application of the four conditions required to declare Art 81 (1) EC inapplicable. K. Lenaerts and D Gerard, 'Decentralisation of EC Competition Law Enforcement: Judges in the Frontline' [2004] World Competition Law and Economics 313–49 (326). Note that the CFI was established in order particularly to improve the judicial protection of individual interests in respect of actions requiring close examination of complex facts. As regards the Community Courts review standard, ch 15 'Steps following the adoption of a formal decision' paras 15.17 and what follows.

[70] See Art 16(1) of Reg 1/2003; Case C-344/98 *Masterfoods Ltd v HB Ice Cream Ltd* [2000] ECR I-11369 paras 52–59.

[71] See also Case T-65/98 *Van den Berg Foods v EC Commission* [2003] ECR II-4653 para 199 stating that the Commission is at any time entitled to adopt a decision under Arts 81 and 82 EC even though this may conflict with an earlier national court decision.

[72] See Art 15 of Reg 1/2003.

[73] This is particularly relevant if there is the risk of national courts taking a decision which might conflict with those taken by the Commission in applying Arts 81 and 82 EC, Case C-234/89 *Delimitis v Henninger Brau AG* [1991] ECR I-935 para 54. If the national court doubts the legality of the Commission's decision and intend to take a decision that runs counter to that of the Commission, it must refer a question to the ECJ. See National Courts Cooperation Notice [2004] OJ C101/54 para 54. In view of the binding effect of the Commission decisions under

require guidance where they apply Article 81(3) EC. Note that the Community courts have often granted the Commission some discretion when applying Article 81(3) EC, in particular where this involves 'complex economic' assessments. However, the arguments that have been put forward to justify the type of restricted jurisdiction exercised by the Community courts, e.g. '*institutional balance*' between the Commisison and the Community courts, or the prime responsibility of the Commission for conducting competition policy,[74] are difficult to use in the context of the review conducted by the national court. A national first instance court may not limit itself to a review of legality, but needs to examine the merits of the case. It applies Article 81 in its entirety, including the prohibition in Article 81(1) as well as the exception to the prohibition in Article 81(3) EC.[75] Thus, the judge must carry out this assessment, however complicated it may be. Given that the case law of the Community Court gives at best little guidance on this point, a national court may consider requesting the ECJ for orientation on how it should conduct its assessment where it believes that the Commission Guidelines on the application of Article 81(3) EC does not give him or her sufficient guidance.[76]

Any court or tribunal of a Member State may ask the ECJ to interpret a rule of Community law, whether contained in the Treaties or in acts of secondary law, if it considers that this is necessary for it to give judgment in a case before it. Courts against whose decisions there is no judicial remedy under national law must refer questions of interpretation arising before them to the ECJ, unless the latter court has already ruled on the point or the correct application of the rule of Community law is obvious. It should be noted that questions referred for a preliminary ruling must concern the interpretation or validity of a provision of Community law only, since the ECJ does not have jurisdiction to interpret **2.16**

Art 16(1) of Reg 1/2003, a preliminary ruling from the ECJ on the compatibility of a Commission decision with Community law is the only way for a national court to actually *bypass* such a decision in the application of EC competition law to the case before it.

[74] President of the CFI Judge Bo Vesterdorf, 'Judicial Review and Competition Law—Reflections on the Role of the Community Courts in the EC system of Competition Law Enforcement', speech at the International Forum on EC Competition Law, Brussels 8 April 2005, and the edited paper version of the speech in Competition Policy International [2005] Vol 1 No 2, 6–8.

[75] The finding of an infringement represents only one side of the equation. Before a finding of illegality can be made, the Art 81(3) EC analysis must be carried out and it must be concluded that on balance the agreement is anti-competitive. See L Kjolbye, 'The New Commission Guidelines on the Application of Article 81(3): An Economic Approach to Article 81' [2004] ECLR 566–77 (566). See ch 15 'Steps following the adoption of a formal decision' para 15.18.

[76] F Montag and S Cameron, 'Effective Enforcement: The Practitioner's View of Recent Experiences under Regulation 1/2003', Antitrust Reform in Europe: A Year in Practice, 1–11 March 2005, Brussels, International Bar Association (IBA), 3, see a need for guidance in particular with regard to Art 81(3) EC.

national law or assess its validity.[77] The decision by which a national court or tribunal refers a question to the ECJ for a preliminary ruling may be in any form allowed by national procedural law. The reference of a question or questions to the ECJ generally causes the national proceedings to be stayed until the Court gives its ruling, but the decision to stay proceedings is one which the national court alone must take in accordance with its own national law. A national court or tribunal may refer a question to the ECJ for a preliminary ruling as soon as it finds that a ruling on the point or points of interpretation or validity is necessary to enable it to give judgment. It must be stressed, however, that it is not for the ECJ to decide issues of fact or differences of opinion as to the interpretation or application of rules of national law. It is therefore desirable that a decision to make a reference should not be taken until the national proceedings have reached a stage where the national court is able to define, if only hypothetically, the factual and legal context of the question.[78] Thus, it is solely for the national court before which the dispute has been brought, and which must assume responsibility for the subsequent judicial decision, to determine in the light of the particular circumstances of the case both the need for a preliminary ruling in order to enable it to deliver judgment and the relevance of the questions which it submits to the Court. Consequently, where the questions submitted by the national court concern the interpretation of Community law, the ECJ is, in principle, bound to give a ruling. The ECJ may refuse to rule on a question referred for a preliminary ruling by a national court only where it is quite obvious that the interpretation of, or assessment of the validity of, a provision of Community law that is sought by the court making the reference bears no relation to the actual facts of the main action or its purpose, where the problem is hypothetical, or where the Court does not have before it the factual or legal material necessary to give a useful answer to the questions submitted to it.[79]

2.17 On average, the ECJ takes two to two and a half years to pass judgment in preliminary ruling cases. This relatively time-consuming process is perceived as

---

[77] See C-7/97 *Oscar Bronner GmbH & Co KG* [1997] ECR I-7791 para 17 stating that Art 234 EC is based on '[. . .] a clear separation of functions between national courts and this court [and] does not allow this court to review the reasons for which a reference is made. Consequently, a request from a national court may be rejected only if it is quite obvious that the interpretation of community law or review of the validity of a rule of Community Law sought by that court bears no relation to the actual facts of the case or to the subject-matter of the main action.'

[78] The administration of justice may well be best served by waiting to refer a question for a preliminary ruling until both sides have been heard in the national court.

[79] Joined Cases C-480/00 to C-482/00, C-484/00, C-489/00 to C-491/00 and C-497/00 to C-499/00 *Azienda Agricola Ettore Ribaldi and others* [2004] ECR I-2943 para 72.

being a major problem[80] which is likely to worsen if the expected higher number of requests of preliminary rulings materializes. Arguably, a second drawback is the limitation inherent in the preliminary ruling mechanism, in that the ECJ only answers abstract questions regarding the interpretation of the law, while leaving the application of the law to the referring court. The ECJ has to give its answers based on the facts described by the referring court and by the parties and does not examine the evidence.[81] Besides, although the ECJ is not competent to decide upon the materiality of the disputed facts, including those of an economic nature, it can nevertheless qualify the facts reported in the referral request with regard to Community law, and it is entitled to determine whether a specific fact is relevant or not for the determination of the antitrust offences covered by Articles 81 or 82 EC. Thus, although the rulings of the ECJ in competition cases appear short and abstract, they are still very much based on an evaluation of the facts[82] as presented by the referring

---

[80] This is in contrast to the time frame envisaged for the opinions provided by the Commission under Art 15 of Reg 1/2003. The Commission has stated its willingness to answer requests for opinion in a period of four months. See National Courts Cooperation Notice para 28. A Commission opinion, however, is a non-binding clarification of aspects of an 'economic, factual or legal nature' whereas an ECJ preliminary ruling is a binding interpretation of EC law as applicable to the facts of the case. The former is thus arguably much broader in terms of the scope of the request that may be formulated, albeit not incontestable.

[81] Case C-198/01 *Consorzio Industrie Fiammiferi (CIF) v Autorità Garante della Concorrenza e del Mercato* [2003] ECR I-8055 para 62: '[. . .] for the purposes of the procedure set out in Art 234 EC, which is based on a clear separation of functions between the national courts and the Court of Justice, the latter, when ruling on the interpretation or validity of Community provisions, is empowered to do so only on the basis of the facts which the national court puts before it [. . .]. It is not for the Court of Justice to apply Community law to the dispute before the national court [. . .] or to assess the facts in the main proceedings.' For example, the nature and geographical extent of the markets in issue or the possible justification for alleged abusive conduct are matters for the national court to decide. Case 311/84 *CBM v CLT and IPB* [1985] ECR 3261. C Bellamy and G Child, *European Community Law of Competition* (5th edn, 2001) para 10–009.

There is no second-guessing of the facts before the ECJ. C Baudenbacher, 'Judicialization of European Competition Policy' in BE Hawk (ed), *International Antitrust Law and Policy—* Fordham Corporate Law Institute [2002] 353–67 (359) citing President of the CFI Vesterdorf 'This is not precisely a very nice situation if we have to go into an intensive evaluation of Art 81(3) if we cannot really deal with the facts, if we have no influence on the facts.' Baudenbacher believes that a certain weakening of the protection of individual rights appears to be an inevitable consequence of decentralization.

[82] K Lenaerts and D Gerard, 'Decentralisation of EC Competition Law Enforcement: Judges in the Frontline' [2004] World Competition Law and Economics 313–49 (339) referring to Joined Cases C-264/01, C-306/01, C-354/01 and C-355/01 *AOK Bundesverband et al* [2004] ECR I-2493 in which the ECJ thoroughly examined the question of whether groups of sickness funds, such as the fund associations, constitute undertakings or associations of undertakings within the meaning of Art 81 EC. It is to note that in this respect the Court's jurisdiction under Art 230 EC is more limited to the extent that the Court will review a decision of the Commisison which has already formed a view on the ancillary nature or otherwise of a restriction. In so doing, the Court must take into account the Commission's powers, especially when they involve complex evaluations on economic matters. D Bailey, 'Scope of judicial Review under Art 81' (2004) CML Rev 1327–60 (1346).

judge. In this way, preliminary rulings constitute a valid source of guidance for national courts.[83]

C. Cooperation between National Courts and the Commission

2.18 Because Regulation 1/2003 assumes that Article 81(3) EC will have direct effect, the cooperation between the Commission and Member States' courts has acquired more importance. Given the central role of national courts, the success of decentralized competition law enforcement depends to a large extent on the national courts' ability to apply the law accurately and consistently. This requires that arrangements be established for cooperation between the courts of the Member States and the Commission. Article 15 of Regulation 1/2003 sets out the areas of co-operation between the Commission and the national courts. It refers to the transmission by the Commission both of information and its opinions at the request of a national court and the possibility of the Commission submitting written observations on its own initiative and oral observations with the permission of the court.[84] The National Courts Cooperation Notice has further implemented the means of cooperation, which will be considered in more detail below.

2.19 These possibilities of cooperation gain a particular relevance where the principles governing the concurrent application of Community competition law by national courts and the Commission under Article 16 of Regulation 1/2003 are not applicable since the Commission has not or is not going to take a decision on the same matter. Two of the co-operation mechanisms established by Regulation 1/2003 operate at the request of national courts—transmission of information (Article 15(1)) and request for a Commission's opinion (Article 15(1))—while the third—Commission's observations (Article 15(3))—is left to the Commission's own initiative. The Commission has indicated that assistance to the national courts' will be carried out in such a way as to respect the national courts' independence and ensure the Commission's own neutrality, adding

---

[83] President of the CFI Judge Bo Vesterdorf, 'Judicial Review and Competition Law—Reflections on the Role of the Community Courts in the EC system of Competition Law Enforcement', speech at the International Forum on EC Competition Law, Brussels 8 April 2005 has asked whether for coherence reasons it may not be better to allow the CFI as the main body for dealing with competition cases the power to deal with preliminary rulings in this area as it is possible under Art 225(3) EC. See also the edited paper version of the speech in Competition Policy International [2005] Vol 1, No 2, 27.

[84] Art 15(1) and (3) of Reg 1/2003. Pursuant to Art 15(2) Member States shall forward to the Commission a copy of any written judgments that deal with the application of Arts 81 and 82 EC. Commission Report on Competition Policy (2005) 805 final para 114 noting that the Commisison had received thirty-six judgments since May 2004 which were put on the website of DG COMP to the extent that the transmitting authority did not classify them as confidential.

that it understands that its neutral role as defendant of the public interest requires that it should not hear the parties about its assistance to the national courts.

While the Commission does not rule out making contact with the parties,[85] the general rule of not hearing the parties has attracted some criticism. The critique pointed to the usefulness of a hearing which would enhance the effectiveness of the Commission's intervention—by allowing it to make a 'useful objective intervention'[86] and ensure that the parties' defence rights are respected.[87] In addition, the neutrality of the Commission in this respect would neither be feasible nor desirable.[88] Overall, it seems that hearing the parties is in no way incompatible with the Commission's impartiality. The fact that the Commission obtains information from the parties does not mean that it is prevented from objectively assessing such information and then making an independent intervention before the national courts. In other words, hearing the parties does not mean that the Commission must share their views. The real reason for there being no hearing might well be avoiding further administrative burdens and delays, but this is not a sufficiently good reason if the parties' rights of defence are harmed as a result. **2.20**

Since the Commission has indicated that it will inform the parties of any such contact whether it took place before or after the national courts' request for information, it might well be that the parties will seek to use this channel to make their position known to the Commission. In fact, while the Commission cannot take the initiative to hear the parties, it is unlikely to refuse to listen to the parties if contacted by them. Thus, while allowing parties to make their views known to the Commission might enhance their defence rights, this could **2.21**

---

[85] At least with respect to national courts' requests for information, the Commission indicates that it may have to consult those affected by the transmission of information (NC Cooperation Notice para 22). Furthermore, the Commission indicates that it will inform the national court in case it has been contacted by the parties (ibid para 19).

[86] See National Courts Cooperation Notice [2004] OJ C101/54 paras 28–33 which refer to the Commission being able to submit 'useful' opinions and observations.

[87] See, *inter alia*, the comments to the Commission draft Notice submitted by American Bar Association (ABA), Cleary, Gottlieb, Steen and Hamilton, American Chamber of Commerce (AMCHAM), Clifford Chance and Latham & Watkins LLP, December 2003, available at the DG competition website.

[88] See H Gilliams, 'Modernization: from policy to practice' (2003) 28 EL Rev 451–74 (461). According to the author, where the Commission has already taken or is going to take some form of action against the practice on which the national court seeks assistance, it seems difficult for such assistance to be impartial. The author suggests that a better way for national courts to obtain the factual or legal information they need would be for the parties to ask the Commission for a reasoned opinion, which could then be introduced into the proceedings as evidence. This solution would have the double advantage of allowing the Commission to hear the parties before issuing its opinion and making such an opinion available to the general public, thus in turn contributing to reducing the risk of inconsistent decisions.

give rise to concerns if only one of the parties has made use of this possibility. In the same vein, it is somehow unfortunate that the Commission did not maintain its commitment in the earlier 1993 Notice to 'ensure that its answer reaches all the parties to the proceedings'.[89] In essence, the Commission leaves it to the national courts to guarantee the parties' access to the information, opinions or observations submitted by it. When dealing with the Commission's opinion in accordance with national procedural rules, the Commission obliges national courts to respect the general principles of Community law, which in turn should be understood as requiring the national courts to give the parties access to any such opinion and permit them to submit observations.

2.22 Lastly, it should be noted, however, that the National Courts Cooperation Notice is aimed at those courts and tribunals of the EU Member States which are entitled to refer a question for preliminary ruling to the ECJ pursuant to Article 234 EC.[90] Accordingly, the Commission did not extend the scope of the National Courts Cooperation Notice to cover arbitration panels or arbitrators.[91] Although they are not entitled to ask the ECJ for a preliminary ruling,[92] they are also bound to apply Articles 81 and 82 EC as public order provisions and their awards may be annulled for failure to do so.[93] Although practical considerations would have made it desirable to include arbitrators, it may have played a role that the legal

---

[89] 1993 National Courts Cooperation Notice para 42.

[90] As indicated above, a national court or tribunal may refer a question to the ECJ for a preliminary ruling as soon as it finds that a ruling on the point or points of interpretation or validity is necessary to enable it to give judgment. The Notice applies where national courts are called upon to apply Arts 81 and 82 EC in lawsuits between private parties. To the extent they act as a public enforcer, they will be subject to the National Courts Cooperation Notice.

[91] Note also that the ECJ has made it clear that an arbitration tribunal constituted pursuant to an arbitration agreement which is an expression of party autonomy is not a court or tribunal of a Member State within the meaning of Art 234 EC: in Case 102/81 *Nordsee v Reederei Mond* [1982] ECR 1095, the Court applied the test of whether the Member State had entrusted or left to the arbitration tribunal the duty of ensuring compliance with the State's obligations under Community law. The Court found that the arbitration tribunal was purely private in nature because its authority derived solely from party autonomy. Given that the arbitration tribunal is not a public authority, the duty of cooperation under Art 10 EC cannot be applied to those tribunals. On the other hand, national courts have the duty to ensure the uniform and effective application of EC competition law and policy exercising jurisdiction in respect of any matters arising out of arbitration proceedings ('second look' doctrine). For a review of the relevant EU case law, see Renato Nazzini, 'International Arbitration and Public Enforcement of Competition Law' [2004] ECLR 153–62.

[92] Case 102/81 *Nordsee v Reederei Mond* [1982] ECR 1095 para 13. M Dolmans and J Greisens, 'Arbitration and the Modernization of EC Antitrust Law: New Opportunities and new Responsibilities' [2003] ICC International Court of Arbitration Vol 14 No 2, 37–51 (42).

[93] Case C-126/97 *Eco Swiss China Time v Benetton International* [1999] ECR I-3055 paras 37 and 41. Note that the ruling related to Art 81(1) EC, although the reasoning may be extended to Art 81(3) EC.

basis of the National Courts Cooperation Notice, i.e. Article 10 EC,[94] which enshrines the principle of mutual loyal and constant cooperation between the Commission and the Member States, does not include arbitration panels formed by private parties.[95] Although nothing prevents the Commission from providing assistance to arbitrators by means of any other informal procedure,[96] it is likely that the lack of any rules in this respect may make it more difficult to institutionalize a similar exchange between the Commission and arbitration panels.[97]

1. Transmission of information

The National Courts Cooperation Notice suggests that the Commission's duty **2.23** of assistance to the national courts mainly consists in its obligation to transmit information to national courts.[98] The Notice does not give any indication as to the form a request for information should take; it simply states that any request for assistance can be sent in writing or electronically to the addresses indicated

---

[94] Art 10 reads as follows: 'Member States shall take all appropriate measures, whether general or particular, to ensure fulfilment of the obligations arising out of this Treaty or resulting from action taken by the institutions of the Community. They shall facilitate the achievement of the Community's tasks—They shall abstain from any measure which could jeopardise the attainment of the objectives of this Treaty.' See also J Temple Lang, 'Developments, Issues and New Remedies—The Duties of National Authorities and Courts under Art 10 of the EC Treaty' [2004] Fordham International Law Journal 1904–39.

[95] At the very least, such co-operation might have been addressed in the Regulation, based on Art 83(2)(e), which allegedly would cover the establishment of procedural rules for the application of Arts 81 and 82 not only by the Commission and national courts and NCAs but by any body called on to apply such provisions.

[96] Arbitration bodies could ask the Commission for an opinion or specific information pursuant to Art 15 of Reg 1/2003; see also M Dolmans and J Greisens, 'Arbitration and the Modernization of EC Antitrust Law: New Opportunities and New Responsibilities' [2003] ICC International Court of Arbitration Vol 14 No 2, 37–51 (50) on the interaction between the Commission and arbitrator panels under Art 15 of Reg 1/2003. Nothing prevents an arbiter from asking a 'supporting judge' to request on his behalf the information or opinion necessary to settle the matter. In addition, considering that the ECJ has held that Arts 81 and 82 EC were provisions of *ordre public*, a losing party to an arbitration award claiming an erroneous application of Art 81(3) EC, should in principle be allowed to obtain the *reformation* of the award by a judicial court. See also R Nazzini, 'International Arbitration and Public Enforcement of Competition Law' [2004] ECLR 153–62.

[97] The definition of the relevant market, the weighing of anti-competitive and positive effects of the agreements and the quantification of damages are as difficult before an arbitral tribunal as they are before a court. A national court, however, may avail itself of some procedural devices in order to save time and expenses and avoid handing down a judgment that may conflict with a Commission decision. It may stay the civil proceedings awaiting the outcome of the administrative investigation.

[98] There is, however, some scepticism as to the willingness of national courts to actually make use of this possibility—which was not much used under the 1993 Notice—both because they are not used to taking inquiry measures themselves and because they might feel that co-operation with an administrative authority might impinge on their independence. See H Gilliams, 'Modernization: from policy to practice' (2003) 28 EL Rev 451–74 (461).

therein. Parties may try to participate in the formulation of the request for information. Before a national court submits a request for information, it is expected that it will hear the parties.[99] Article 15 of Regulation 1/2003 refers to the possibility of asking the Commission for 'information in its possession'. The National Courts Cooperation Notice specifies that national courts may request to the Commission transmission of 'documents in its possession' or 'information of a procedural nature', the latter including information on whether a case is pending before the Commission, whether the Commission has initiated a procedure or whether it has already taken a position, as well as whether a decision is likely to be taken. The ECJ case law also refers to 'legal and economic information',[100] possibly included in the category of 'documents' mentioned in Article 15. Thus, the type of information requested is not restricted to information of a general nature. In *Postbank*, the ECJ has already upheld the transmission to national courts of documents relating to the position or conduct of the parties, such as a Statement of Objections.[101] The ruling in *Postbank* seems also to suggest that documents obtained by the Commission might also be produced in proceedings between parties other than the parties to the Commission's proceedings from which such documents originate.[102] The actual limits on the scope of a request for information are difficult to establish in abstract terms, but at least two general ones seem quite clear. First, such requests for information should relate to information 'in possession' of the Commission,[103] which might

---

[99] A similar provision is contained in the ECJ Guidelines on References under Art 234 EC, in which the ECJ states that without prejudice to the national court's discretion as to when to make a reference, it is advisable first to hear the parties. Information Note on References by National Courts for Preliminary Rulings para 7, available at the Community Courts' website.

[100] See Case C-234/89 *Delimitis v Henninger Bräu AG* [1991] ECR I-935 para 53; Joined Cases C-319/93, C-40/94 and C-224/94 *Hendrik Evert Dijkstra v Friesland (Frico Domo)* [1995] ECR I-4471 para 34.

[101] Case T-353/94 *Postbank NV v EC Commission* [1996] ECR II-921. The fact that in this case the Statement of Objections was in fact forwarded to the NC not directly by the Commission but by a third party which had in turn received it from the Commission does not seem to preclude a direct transmission of such a document from the Commission to the national courts, always subject to the procedural safeguards required by the Court. Thus, when relying on the information received by the Commission, the national courts have to protect the rights of defence of the parties concerned.

[102] In Case T-353/94 *Postbank NV v EC Commission* [1996] ECR II-921 the Commission claimed that the action brought by Postbank against disclosure of the statement of objections sent to it in NC proceedings was inadmissible for lack of interest, on the grounds that such a document had been produced in national proceedings to which Postbank was not a party. The Court ruled that this circumstance (production in proceedings to which Postbank was not a party) was irrelevant in order to establish Postbank's interest to bring an action, to the extent that Postbank had an interest in protecting its confidential and business secret information in the same way as in proceedings to which it was a party. Thus, the Court indirectly admitted the possibility of producing information concerning an undertaking in proceedings to which such undertaking is not a party.

[103] A Klees, *Europäisches Kartellverfahrenrecht* (2005) §8 para 52.

also be a criterion to distinguish a mere request for information from a request for an opinion. Second, in no event should the Commission's reply concern the merits of the case pending before the national court, in line with what the Commission's position with respect to opinions and as a guarantee of the parties' defence rights. Whether or not the information supplied by the Commission will be publicly available will depend on the content of the document in question.[104]

The National Courts Cooperation Notice restates the principles established by the Community Courts' case law as to disclosure to national courts of information covered by professional secrecy, including both confidential information and business secrets.[105] The general principle established in the case law is that the combined reading of Articles 10 and 287 EC does not prevent the disclosure of such information to national courts, provided that this does not undermine the guarantees given to the undertakings concerned by Community provisions on professional secrecy. This safeguard has two aspects.[106] On the one hand, it requires the Commission to adopt all precautions to ensure that the right of the undertaking concerned to protection of such information is not undermined, including, in particular, informing the latter of the documents or the passage of documents covered by professional secrecy. On the other hand, it requires national courts to guarantee protection of the confidentiality of such information. The principle that information covered by professional secrecy may be disclosed to national courts is however, subject to at least two sets of exceptions.[107] **2.24**

- *First, the Commission is entitled to refuse transmission of such information where national courts cannot ensure the protection of the confidential information.* The Commission indicates that it will not transmit such information to the national court if, after asking whether it can and will guarantee protection of such information, the national court cannot offer such a

---

[104] Reg 1049/2001 regarding public access to European Parliament, Council and Commission documents [2001] OJ L145/43. The Commission has also said that it may make its opinions and observations available on its website. NC Cooperation Notice para 20.

[105] National Courts Cooperation Notice [2004] OJ C101/54 para 23.

[106] See Case T-353/94 *Postbank NV v EC Commission* [1996] ECR II-921 paras 90 and 69, where the Court indicates that 'there is a presumption that the national courts will guarantee the protection of confidential information'.

[107] See National Courts Cooperation Notice [2004] OJ C101/54 paras 25–26; see also Case T-353/94 *Postbank NV v EC Commission* [1996] ECR II-921 para 93, where the Court states that '[s]uch a refusal [to provide national courts with information covered by professional secrecy] is justified only where it is the only way of ensuring "protection of the rights of third parties", which in principle is a matter for the national courts, or "where the disclosure of that information would be capable of interfering with the functioning and independence of the Community", which, in contrast, is a matter exclusively for the Community institutions concerned'.

guarantee.[108] However, the Commission has not given any indication as to what type of safeguards is required. In adversarial proceedings, a court will not be able to use information which is not in the file, i.e. which has not been disclosed to the parties. Thus, if the national court were required to maintain the confidentiality of the documents transmitted by the Commission by not disclosing them to the parties, either the court might be unable to give such a guarantee if national law requires that the parties have access to all information available to the court or the transmission of information would be deprived of all purpose, in the sense that it would be useless for the national courts to request and obtain information which it cannot use.[109]

- *The second set of exceptions refers to the need to safeguard the interests of the Community or to avoid interfering with its functioning and independence.* In this respect, one should welcome the Commission's amendment of the original draft National Courts Cooperation Notice to introduce into the final version an express commitment not to transmit to national courts information voluntarily submitted by leniency applicants without the consent of the latter.[110] This was indeed one of the main concerns of the business and legal communities, reflected in several comments submitted to the Commission's draft National Courts Cooperation Notice. It should be pointed out, however, that such a limited guarantee is by no way equivalent to the one provided by Article 12 of the Regulation in relation to exchange of information between the Commission and the national courts, since it does not address the use that national courts are entitled to make of the information received from the Commission.

2.25 Article 12 of Regulation 1/2003 states expressly that the information exchanged

---

[108] In Case T-39/90 *NV Samenwerkende Elektriciteits-Produktiebedrijven v Commission* [1991] ECR II-1497 paras 27–30, it could not be expected that the Netherlands Ministry of Industry (which at the time also dealt with Community competition matters in the Netherlands) should, when deciding on the commercial strategy of a State undertaking controlled by that Ministry (Gasunie) ignore the information provided to it by the Commission concerning relations between one of the latter's clients (SEP) and a competing supplier (Statoil). Mere knowledge of the contract entered into between SEP and Statoil might be taken into account in deciding the commercial policy of Gasunie, since the Netherlands Ministry of Industry is not required to disregard information transmitted to it.

[109] See also J Temple Lang, 'Developments, Issues and New Remedies—The Duties of National Authorities and Courts under Art 10 of the EC Treaty' [2004] Fordham International Law Journal 1904–39 (1922) who notes that when companies receive information from the Commission and when the Commission has advised them that they are not free to use it for any other purpose than the Commission's procedure, a national court should enjoin them from using it in any other way and if appropriate order compensation for the owners of the documents. This obligation would result from Art 10 EC.

[110] National Courts Cooperation Notice [2004] OJ C101/54 para 26.

between the Commission and national courts may be used in evidence, subject to the restrictions established in the same provision. Regulation 1/2003 does not contain a similar provision in relation to information transmitted to national courts, nor does the National Courts Cooperation Notice give any indications in this respect. However, in light of the Community Court's case law, it seems that national courts are equally entitled to use the information received from the Commission as evidence. Indeed, even in a situation where national courts were not allowed to use the information received by the Commission as evidence (but only for the purposes of deciding whether or not to initiate national proceedings), the Court held, in *Postbank*, that the same limitation did not apply to national courts.[111] In the same case, the Court indicated some ways whereby the national court could guarantee that the use of such information respected the parties' right of defence in the particular circumstances of the case (which was concerned with disclosure of a statement of objections), namely by taking account of the provisional nature of the opinion expressed by the Commission in a statement of objections and of the possibility of suspending proceedings pending the adoption of the final Commission decision. Since national courts can therefore use the information received by the Commission as evidence, it might have been appropriate to remind them that they must do so in accordance with the general principles of Community law, which should include the parties' right to have access to such information.[112] As indicated, the National Courts Cooperation Notice does so in relation with opinions and observations without explicitly indicating, however, the general principles of Community law it refers to. On the other hand, unlike with opinions and observations, the Notice does envisage the possibility of 'consulting those who are directly affected by the transmission of the information'.[113]

2. Opinions

Article 15 of Regulation 1/2003 entitles national courts to request from **2.26** the Commission an 'opinion on questions concerning the application of the

---

[111] See Case T-353/94 *Postbank NV v EC Commission* [1996] ECR II-921 para 71. Also, in *Zwartveld*, the Court ruled that the Commission was required to authorize its officials to give evidence in national proceedings, namely by being examined as witnesses. See Case 2/88 *Imm J J Zwartveld and others* [1990] ECR I-3365.

[112] On the one hand, the CFI clearly assumed in *Postbank* that the national courts must indeed guarantee the protection of confidential information pursuant to the principle of effective judicial protection. On the other hand, the CFI recognized that a refusal by the Commission to disclose remains the only way of ensuring the protection of the rights of third parties. The Commission has given this the making that where national rules fail to make adequate provisions for the protection of confidential information, the Commission is not obliged under Art 10 EC to supply documents requested by national judges. M Dougan, *National Remedies Before the Court of Justice— Issues of Harmonization and Differentiation* (2004) 364–365.

[113] 1993 National Courts Notice [1993] OJ C39/6 para 22.

Community competition rules'.[114] Apart from recalling that such an opinion is, of course, not binding on the national court and without prejudice to the possibility or obligation to make an Article 234 reference to the ECJ, the Commission Notice does not say much more about either the scope or the procedural aspects of such an opinion. The Notice merely indicates that the opinion may concern economic, factual and legal matters and not 'the merits of the case pending before the national court'.[115] It adds that for the purpose of providing a 'useful opinion', the Commission may request further information from the national court, but will not hear the parties, who will have to 'deal with the Commission's opinion in accordance with the relevant national procedural rules, which have to respect the general principles of Community law'.[116]

2.27 Thus, as a result of the Commission providing scant description of how the relevant provision in Article 15 is meant to work, a number of issues arise in relation to the scope of the Commission's opinion, as regards its relation to references under Article 234 EC, and its use in national proceedings. A first question is the difference in scope between a transmission of information and an opinion.[117] A second relates to the actual scope of an opinion. The dividing line between transmission of information and delivering an opinion, though not completely clear-cut, was somehow clearer under the 1993 National Courts Notice. While referring generally to 'information' which national courts may request from the Commission, the 1993 Notice further specified the scope of the national courts' request, by indicating that '[f]irst, they may ask for information of a procedural nature', '[n]ext, national courts may consult the Commission on points of law', and '[l]astly, national courts can obtain information from the Commission regarding factual data: statistics, market studies and economic analysis'. Thus, it appears that under the 1993 Notice one could distinguish between three categories of requests: a request for information *stricto sensu*, relating to information of a procedural nature; a request for an opinion, relating

---

[114] 'Q&A on modernization with Kris Dekeyser' Global Competition Review, Vol 8, Issue 3, April 2005 11–16 (12) reports that during the first year of the application of Reg 1/2003 the Commisison has received ten requests for an opinion. Commissioner Report on Competition Policy [2004] 805 final para 112 mentions nine requests of which six came from Spanish courts and all dealt with a similar type of distribution agreement in the energy sector. The Commission's replies to these six requests were largely based on its preliminary assessment in *Repsol CPP* [2004] OJ C258/7. The remaining three requests came from Belgian courts which are obliged to make a reference to the Brussels Court of Appeal for a preliminary ruling whenever they have doubts as to the application of competition rules. The Court of Appeal forwarded these request to the Commission.

[115] National Courts Cooperation Notice [2004] OJ 101/54.

[116] National Courts Cooperation Notice para 30.

[117] Although it may not be necessary to distinguish between opinion and information for the purposes of Art 15 of Reg 1/2003 because Art 15 treats them on equal terms. A Kless, *Europäisches Kartellverfahrensrecht* §8 para 52.

to points of law; and a request for specific documents. Furthermore, the 1993 Notice defined in greater detail the scope of an opinion on points of law, clarifying that it would have as its object the Commission's customary practice in relation to the principle of Community law at issue and, in particular, questions such as effect on interstate trade and the appreciable effect of a restriction of competition, as well as eligibility for an individual exemption.

Under the applicable Cooperation Notice, a request for information to the Commission may relate both to 'documents in its possession' and 'information of a procedural nature', whilst an opinion may deal not only with points of law but also with 'economic, factual and legal matters' and, in particular, include both 'factual information' and 'economic or legal clarification'. Moreover, while Article 15, when referring to requests for information, expressly states that such requests should relate to information 'in possession' of the Commission, there is no similar provision in relation to opinions. Thus, it seems that when replying to a request for information, the Commission will limit itself to 'transmit' data it already has, while in the context of an opinion the Commission might possibly take into account additional data specifically obtained *ex novo* in relation to the national court's request. As to the actual scope of an opinion, as indicated, the Notice does not give much guidance. However, based on the ECJ's judgment in *Van der Wal*, it is possible to distinguish two types. First, the Commission may limit itself to expressing an opinion of a general nature independent of the data relating to the case pending before the national court, or secondly, provide a legal or economic analysis on the basis of the data supplied by the national court.[118] It seems that such a distinction could still apply under the current Commission Notice. However, the question remains open as to how far the Commission can go in opinions of the second kind, taking into account that such opinions should not in any event address the merits of the case pending before the national court. **2.28**

In sum, it would have been useful if the Commission had expanded more on the scope of an opinion, maybe simply by reproducing the relevant explanation in the 1993 Notice as to opinions on legal matters. The scope of a Commission's opinion could have been more clearly defined also by distinguishing it from that of an Article 234 EC request for a preliminary ruling. By explaining, for example, in more detail the differences in scope between both procedures, the Commission could have helped the national court to decide when, in a particular case, it could be more helpful to ask the Commission rather than the Court or **2.29**

---

[118] Joined Cases C-174/98 P and C-189/98 P *Van der Wal v EC Commission* [2000] ECR I-1 paras 24 and 25.

vice versa.[119] In this respect, a first distinction between the two procedures is that, unlike an Article 234 reference, a request for an opinion may not only relate to points of law, but also to factual and economic matters. This broader scope of the Commission's opinion might possibly lead the national court to consider whether to ask the Commission rather than the Court where, for instance, its doubts concern factual and/or economic matters in addition to legal issues. Furthermore, even where the national court's question specifically relates to a point of law, there might be reasons for preferring a request to the Commission rather than going to the ECJ. In particular, while the Article 234 EC procedure relates to the interpretation of Community law provisions (in addition, to the separate issue of their validity), it seems that the scope of a Commission opinion under Article 15 of the Regulation may well go further, subject to the limit of not considering the merit of the case. Indeed, under Article 15 such an opinion concerns the 'application' of Community competition law. Thus, it cannot be excluded that under certain circumstances, it might be more helpful to ask the Commission rather than the Court. For instance, an opinion on the 'customary practice of the Commission', i.e. the application of the law in question to similar situations, could on occasions be sufficient for the national court to be able to decide how to apply the law to the case before it, without the need to make a reference to the ECJ. On the other hand, it has been anticipated that national courts will prefer to rely on Article 234 EC and that the absence of a specific procedure for making a request to the Commission would further discourage them from using this latter procedure.[120]

2.30 Article 15 of Regulation 1/2003 does not give any indication as to the procedure for requesting an opinion from the Commission. First, for the purposes of being able to give a 'useful opinion', the Commission may request the national court further information. Secondly, the Commission will not hear the parties before formulating its opinion. Possibly, the Commission could have given some broad indications as to, at least, the minimal information that a request for an opinion should contain. Not only would this have helped the national court in formulating its request but it could also have reduced the need for the Commission to have to request further information from the national court. In line with ECJ guidelines on Article 234 EC references, such minimal information to be provided by the national courts could have included, for instance, the factual and legal background, the reasons which prompted the request and

---

[119] The longer duration of an Art 234 EC procedure is one of the elements that the national courts could possibly take into account in deciding whether to ask for an opinion from the Commission instead of making a reference for a preliminary ruling.

[120] See A Riley, 'EC Antitrust Modernisation: The Commission Does Very Nicely—Thank You! Part Two: Between the Idea and the Reality: Decentralisation under Reg. 1' [2003] ECLR 657–72 (666).

possibly a summary of the arguments of the parties. In particular, the need to include a summary of the arguments of the parties could have been particularly important in the light of the Commission's position not to hear the parties before submitting its opinion. More generally, one might wonder whether the parties may play any role in formulating the request for an opinion. In this respect, the 1993 Notice seemed to envisage some indirect involvement of the parties.[121] The new Notice is silent on this point. It may be assumed that, as with other points, the Commission understands that national procedural rules should apply. Indeed, the Notice states that the Commission's opinion should be 'dealt with' in accordance with national procedural rules, subject to the general principles of Community law. This leads to the thorny issue of the use a national court can make of the Commission's opinion. All the Notice says is that the Commission's opinion is not binding and then makes reference to national procedural rules, which in turn have to respect the general principles of Community law. However, there is no indication as to how such an opinion may be used, and in particular, whether it may be used in evidence. In *Van der Wal*,[122] the ECJ assimilated the Commission's opinions (of the second kind, i.e. providing a legal or economic analysis on the basis of data supplied by the national court) to expert reports and ruled that they should be subject to national procedural rules applying to expert reports, including rules on disclosure. Thus, the Court first clarified the 'status' of Commission's opinions and then the treatment which should be given to them. While that case was concerned with the conditions for disclosure of such opinions to third parties, it seems that the same principles would apply to disclosure of a Commission's opinion to the parties in the proceedings, i.e. such disclosure will depend on the relevant national procedural rules. However, as indicated in the Commission's Notice, such rules must respect the general principles of Community law. It seems that such principles include a right for the parties to be heard (and/or submit observations on the Commission's opinion), whatever the use the national courts might give to the Commission's opinion.

---

[121] The 1993 Notice provided that 'As amicus curiae, the Commission is obliged to respect legal neutrality and objectivity. Consequently, it will not accede to requests for information unless they come from a national court, either directly, or indirectly through parties which have been ordered by the court concerned to provide certain information. In the latter case, the Commission will ensure that its answer reaches all the parties to the proceedings' (para 42). Taking into account that a request for 'information' under the 1993 Notice could be construed as also covering a request for an opinion (see above), one might argue that such direct involvement of the parties would be possible in all of the three possible requests for 'information' envisaged therein, including requests for an opinion.

[122] Joined Cases C-174/98 P and C-189/98 P *van der Wal v EC Commission* [2000] ECR I-1 para 25.

3. Observations

2.31 A genuinely new feature of cooperation introduced by Regulation 1/2003 is the possibility for the Commission (and the NCAs) to submit observations before national courts on issues relating to the application of Articles 81 and 82 EC.[123] While the transmission of information and the opinions provided for in Article 15(1) of Regulation 1/2003 are instruments of co-operation at the initiative of national courts, the observations pursuant to Article 15(3) are submitted by the Commission on its own motion, although it needs the permission of the national court if it wishes to submit them orally. Thus, compared to the other two instruments of cooperation, here the actual purpose of this instrument—to ensure the coherent application of Community competition law—emerges even more clearly. Indeed, the very text of Article 15(3) envisages the submission of observations '[w]here the coherent application of Article 81 or 82 of the Treaty so requires'.[124] Unlike the other two instruments of cooperation, Regulation 1/ 2003 touches on some procedural aspects of the submission of observations. Apart from requiring the national court's permission in case of oral observations, Article 15(3) envisages the possibility of the Commission requesting the national court transmission of any documents necessary for the assessment of the case. The Commission's Notice adds that, while it is for the Member States to establish the relevant procedural framework, in its absence, the procedure for submission of observations should be determined by the national courts which is dealing with the case, subject to the principles of Community law, including respecting the fundamental rights of the parties (here mentioned expressly unlike in paragraph 30 in relation to opinions). As with the other two instruments of cooperation, a number of issues arise in relation to both the scope, the use and the procedure for the submission of observations. The Commission states that it will limit its observations to 'an economic and legal analysis of the facts underlying the case pending before the national court' and links this limitation of the scope of its observations to the fact that their purpose, pursuant to Article 15, is to ensure the coherent application of Article 81 and 82 EC.

---

[123] 'Q&A on modernization with Kris Dekeyser' Global Competition Review, Vol 8, Issue 3, April 2005 reports that the Commission has not submitted *amicus curiae* briefs during the first year of application of Reg 1/2003 because it has not identified any problem of coherence in the application of Arts 81 and 82 EC by national courts.

[124] The scope of the Commission's intervention seems to be narrower than originally envisaged in the draft Regulation which provided that the Commission would be entitled to submit written (and oral) observations '[f]or reasons of the Community public interest'. See Proposal for a Council Regulation on the implementation of the rules on competition laid down in Arts 81 and 82 of the Treaty and amending Regs (EEC) 1017/68, (EEC) 2988/74, (EEC) 4056/86 and (EEC) 3975/87 ('Reg implementing Arts 81 and 82 of the Treaty'), COM(2000) 582 final [2000] OJ C365E/284. On the other hand, the scope of the Commission's intervention seems also narrower than that of the NCAs, since Art 15(3) of Reg 1/2003 does not provide for any limit on the latter's intervention.

The relation is not self-evident. In any event, it leaves open the question of whether the Commission may address the merits of the case. It is worth noting that, unlike with opinions, this is not expressly excluded. Indeed, it may well be that the very purpose of ensuring that Articles 81 or 82 are applied coherently can only be achieved by actually considering and commenting on the merits of the case.[125] In such circumstances, the questions as to the parties' defence rights and the national courts' use of the Commission's observations arise.

Both Regulation 1/2003 and the Cooperation Notice are silent as to the actual use the national court is entitled to make of the Commission's observations. However, in relation to the national procedural rules governing the submission of observations, the Notice states that those rules should be compatible with the fundamental rights of the parties involved in the case. Although the Commission might have been more explicit, this seems to indicate that the parties should be allowed not only to have access to the Commission's observations, but also to submit their own observations on the same.[126] This is even more important if, as it seems, the Commission's observations may in fact address the merits of the case. A problem may arise in connection with the considerable weight that the Commission's or NCAs' observations inevitably carry in front of a national judge, with the risks it entails for the protection of the rights of defence of the parties to the national proceedings and of the principle of 'equality of arms'. Those observations should thus be communicated to the parties and aired before the court. In this respect, the stage of the proceedings when such observations are submitted may also be important. In the absence of any indication in the Regulation or the Notice, it seems that the Commission has some discretion as to the moment when to submit its observations, subject to any national procedural law requirements, which, in turn, are likely to differ not only between Member States but also between different proceedings within the same Member State. It is submitted that if the Commission intervenes too early, it might not have all elements required to make a 'useful' intervention (without prejudice to the possibility of requesting any necessary documents to the national court), while if it intervenes too late, it may delay the proceedings precisely because of the need to ensure that the parties are given an opportunity

2.32

---

[125] On the scope of the Commission's observations and opinions, see JHJ Bourgeois and C Humpe, 'The Commission's "New Regulation 17"' [2002] ECLR 43–51 (46). According to these authors, the Commission acting as *amicus curiae* is entitled to make 'observations directly related to the dispute' and give 'its legal appraisal of disputes pending before national courts'.

[126] However, that is not the only possible interpretation of Art 15 and para 35 of the Notice. See H Gilliams, 'Modernization: from policy to practice' (2003) 28 EL Rev 451–74 (461), who doubts that national courts are required to communicate the Commission's observations to the parties and claims that the Commission (and the NCAs) should have been allowed to intervene as parties instead, applying for leaving to intervene in accordance with national law and not as 'interveners with special rights'.

to reply.[127] A different but related issue is when the Commission will actually be in a position to intervene. Indeed, the Commission should first of all be aware that proceedings are pending before the national court. Regulation 1/2003 only provides that the Commission should be notified of national courts' judgments deciding on the application of Community competition law, but not of the initiation of the corresponding proceedings. The Cooperation Notice indicates that the purpose of such obligation is primarily to enable the Commission to be aware of the cases for which it might want to submit observations on appeal. Thus, it seems that the Commission is envisaging intervention mainly on appeal. This might make sense if one considers that a decision being subject to review of a first instance court should not represent a real risk for the coherent application of Community competition law. However, that might not always be so. In fact, it may well happen that such first instance judgment is not appealed (or that the parties are not granted leave to appeal, in systems which so require), in which case the judgment of the first instance court would become final without the Commission having had a real opportunity to intervene. In such circumstances, it might have been desirable that, as proposed in the White Paper,[128] Regulation 1/2003 had provided that the Commission be informed upon commencement of the relevant national proceedings. Under the current regime, the Commission thus needs to rely on the benevolence of national judges and their registrar offices—and on the national Ministries of Justice—to be informed and intervene in national proceedings only at the appellate stage. The examination of judgments in a multitude of languages sent from across the Union is moreover likely to be a heavy burden for the Commission. If the Commission is serious in its determination to devote more means and time to the curbing of serious antitrust infringements, intervention in national proceedings is likely to remain exceptional.

2.33 Finally, a tension may also exist between the principle of direct effect and the respect for Member States' procedural autonomy. Article 15(3) of Regulation 1/2003 grants the Commission a directly applicable right to submit observations to national courts on its own initiative, but the Cooperation Notice adds that in the absence of a specific and uniform procedural framework for such submission, Member States' procedural rules and practices determine the relevant procedural framework. National courts have thus to provide within their system for the possibility of the Commission intervening, while they have to ensure at the same time respect for the fundamental rights of the parties and for the

---

[127] See comments to the draft National Courts Cooperation Notice submitted, *inter alia*, by Freshfields Bruckhaus Deringer, 10 December 2003, available at the DG COMP website.
[128] White Paper on the Modernisation of the Rules Implementing Arts 81 and 82 [1999] OJ C132/1 para 107.

general principles of Community law, such as the principles of effectiveness and equivalence.[129] Under the principle of effectiveness, the submission of observations may not be excessively (i.e. disproportionately) difficult or practically impossible. The principle of equivalence would require that the submission of observations by the Commission might not be subject to a more restrictive procedure than any other similar submission provided by national law. As a result, it may be that the Commission will in fact be granted the status of a non-party intervener with sufficient interest to submit observations to the court in proceedings in which issues of EC competition law arise.[130]

D. National Courts' Assistance to the Commission

Regulation 1/2003 not only provides for Commission's assistance to national **2.34** courts but also for national courts' assistance to the Commission. Such assistance is dealt with in Part B of Section III of the Commission's Notice. Apart from the transmission of documents necessary for the submission of observations (Article 15(3) and written copy of the judgments applying Community competition law (Article 15(2)), such assistance basically takes place in the context of Commission's inspections.[131] The Commission Notice reproduces the provisions of Regulation 1/2003 on the national courts' intervention in the context of an inspection of the undertakings' premises as well as in the context of an inspection of other premises, adding only that the national court shall provide its assistance in an appropriate timeframe as established by ECJ case law.[132] As provided for in Articles 20 and 21 of Regulation 1/2003, while in the first case judicial assistance will only be required, if national law so provides, where the undertaking concerned opposes the Commission's inspection (although it might indeed be requested on a precautionary basis), in the second case prior authorisation from the national court is required by the Regulation itself.

In both cases, the national court is entitled to a limited control—as to the **2.35** authenticity and the proportionality of the Commission's decision—but cannot call into question its necessity or validity, the latter being a matter exclusively for the ECJ. Nor can the national court, for the purposes of carrying out such control, request information in the Commission's file. However, with respect to

---

[129] See, e.g. Case C-147/01 *Weber's Wines World et al* [2003] ECR I-11365 paras 38–45.

[130] K. Lenaerts and D Gerard, 'Decentralisation of EC Competition Law Enforcement: Judges in the Frontline' [2004] World Competition Law and Economics 313–49 (334).

[131] See ch 8 'Inspections' paras 8.60 and what follows.

[132] See also M Dougan, *National Remedies Before the Court of Justice—Issues of Harmonization and Differentiation* (2004) 365–67. Case C-94/00 *Roquette Frères* [2002] ECR I-9011 para 92.

inspections of other premises, the scope of control is somehow broader than with respect to inspections of the premises of the undertaking concerned. In particular, as regards inspections of other premises, in its assessment of the proportionality of the Commission's decision, the national court may have regard not only to the seriousness of the suspected infringement and the involvement of the undertaking concerned, but also to the importance of the particular evidence sought and the reasonable likelihood that the documents the Commission is seeking are kept in the premises for which authorisation is requested. Furthermore, it may request explanations on (all) those elements necessary to allow its control of proportionality (i.e. not only on the grounds for suspecting an infringement—which should in any event be expressly stated in the decision pursuant to Article 21(2)—and the nature of the involvement of the undertaking concerned).[133]

---

[133] Case C-94/00 *Roquette Frères* [2002] ECR I-9011 para 92.

3

THE ROLE OF NATIONAL
COMPETITION AUTHORITIES[1]

A. Introduction

Regulation 17 provided for a system of administrative control of agreements **3.01**
where, in practice, the Commission had almost sole responsibility for enforcing
Community competition rules and the NCAs only rarely dealt with infringements of Articles 81 and 82 EC.[2] Under Regulation 1/2003, not only the
Commission but also the NCAs are now responsible for enforcing Community
competition rules. Since 1 May 2004 the NCAs have been assigned a much more
significant role in the enforcement of the EC competition rules.[3] Regulation
1/2003 has created a system of parallel competences in which the competition
rules are enforced by a network of competition authorities as well as by the
national courts. Provided trade between Member States is affected, Regulation
1/2003 allows NCAs to apply Articles 81 and 82 EC but leaves the Member
State to determine which body will enforce the rules and what mechanism for

---

[1] See in general D Cahill (ed), *The Modernization of EU Competition Law Enforcement in the
EU*, FIDE 2004, National Reports 630–660; CS Kerse and N Khan, *EC Antitrust Procedure* (5th
edn, 2005) paras 5–002 to 5–038; J Schwarze and A Weitbrecht, *Grundzüge des Europäischen
Kartellrechtsverfahren* (2004) §§ 8, 9; A Klees, *Europäisches Kartellverfahrensrecht* (2005) § 7.

[2] See WPJ Wils, 'Community Report' in D Cahill (ed), *The Modernization of EU Competition
Law Enforcement in the EU*, FIDE 2004, National Reports 661–736 para 45. Among the reasons
was the fact that national law empowered NCAs to apply Arts 81(1) and 82 EC in only half of the
Member States, or that where national law provided for this possibility, the Commission's power
to grant exemptions under Art 81(3) combined with Art 9(3) of Reg 17 discouraged NCAs from
taking up Art 81 EC cases.

[3] K Dekeyser, 'Reg 1/2003: First Experiences', IBC Conference London, 27 and 28 April 2005
describes as 'very encouraging' the first eleven months or so (May 2004 to March 2005) and notes
a clear increase of enforcement by ECN members of EC competition rules: between May 2004
and March 2005, the Commission was informed of fifty envisaged decisions, most of which related
to horizontal price-fixing and/or market sharing cartels.

investigating infringements and enforcing decisions will apply.[4] Article 11(6) of Regulation 1/2003 provides that if the Commission initiates proceedings for the adoption of a decision, the NCAs no longer have jurisdiction to apply Articles 81 and 82 EC. Yet a central feature of Regulation 1/2003 is that NCAs shall have the power to apply Articles 81 and 82 EC in individual cases, and the Commission has pointed out that it would only initiate proceedings in a limited number of circumstances.[5]

3.02 One of the objectives of Regulation 1/2003 is to encourage the consistent application of the EC competition rules by the NCAs.[6] In the same way as for national courts, Regulation 1/2003 provides that where NCAs apply national competition law to agreements, decisions by associations of undertakings, or concerted practices within the meaning of Article 81 EC which may affect trade between Member States, NCAs shall apply Article 81 EC.[7] Similarly, where NCAs apply national competition law to any abuse prohibited by Article 82 EC, they shall apply Article 82 EC. The original draft Regulation provided for the exclusive application of Community law in all cases where Articles 81 and 82 EC would be applicable,[8] yet Article 3 of Regulation 1/2003 does not

---

[4] Under Art 35 of Reg 1/2003, the designation of the bodies responsible for the application of the rules is left to the Member States. In practice, the nature of those bodies varies from country to country: a single administrative authority may be in charge of investigation, prosecution, and decision (e.g. *Bundeskartellamt* in Germany), but most often a dual structure has been set up where a section of the Ministry for Economic Affairs is responsible for investigating a particular conduct, whilst an independent administrative authority or court is endowed with the power to adjudicate on infringement and the imposition of sanctions (e.g. Austria, Finland, Ireland, Spain, and, in part, Sweden). Various Member States have chosen to give the status of administrative or judicial court to the body endowed with the power to decide in competition matters. Hence, whether it was expressly provided for or not under national law, some of these specialized courts have considered that their capacity entitled them to request preliminary rulings from the ECJ on the interpretation of EC competition provisions. See, e.g. Spain and the preliminary ruling requested by the *Tribunal de Defensa de la Competencia* in Case C-67/91, *Asociación Española de Barca Privada (AEB)* [1992] ECR I-4785. K Lenaerts and D Gerard, 'Decentralisation of EC Competition Law Enforcement: Judges in the Frontline' [2004] World Competition Law and Economics 313–49 (320); JD Cook, 'General Report' in *The Modernization of EU Competition Law Enforcement in the EU*, FIDE 2004, National Reports 630–66 (634).

[5] Notice on cooperation within the Network of Competition Authorities ('ECN Cooperation Notice') [2004] OJ C101/43 para 54.

[6] See F Montag and A Rosenfeld, 'A solution to the Problem? Reg 1/2003 and modernization of competition procedure' [2003] Zeitschrift für Wettbewerbsrecht 107–35 (125). '[. . .] Since there is practically no more room for the independent application of national law in cases where EC law also applies, Art 3(2) represents a powerful incentive for Member States to harmonize their national competition rules with EC competition law'.

[7] See also ch 2 'The national judicial authorities' paras 2.12 and what follows.

[8] However, this proposal was not welcomed by the Member States which criticized that the exclusive application of Community competition law unduly restricted the application of national competition law contrary to the Community principle of subsidiarity. Moreover, taken in connection with Art 11(6) of Reg 1/2003, according to which the Commission can relieve NCAs of their competence to apply either Art 81 or 82 EC by initiating proceedings itself, it was feared that the proposal for the exclusive application of Community competition law would have rendered these

provide for the exclusive application of EC law. While the obligation on NCAs (and national courts) to apply Articles 81 and 82 EC in all cases that may affect trade between Member State remains, national law may also be applied at the same time. Furthermore, NCAs retain the right to apply national rules that are stricter than Article 82 EC in cases of unilateral conduct.[9] The application of national competition law may not lead to the prohibition of agreements, decisions by associations of undertakings, or concerted practices which may affect trade between Member States but which do not restrict competition within the meaning of Article 81(1) EC, or which fulfil the conditions of Article 81(3) EC or which are covered by a regulation for the application of Article 81(3) EC. Conversely, an agreement or concerted practice which is prohibited under Article 81 EC cannot be considered as permissible under Article 81 EC: if the prohibition in Article 81(1) EC does not apply because competition is not restricted or Article 81(3) EC applies,[10] then national law cannot be applied. Article 3(2) of Regulation 1/2003 may thus be viewed as eliminating the last possibility of differing results of the application of national and EC law in a situation where Article 81 EC applies.[11] In any event, Article 3

---

national authorities overly subject to the Commission's control. See F Montag and A Rosenfeld, 'A solution to the Problem? Reg. 1/2003 and the modernization of competition procedure' [2003] Zeitschrift für Wettbewerbsrecht 107–35 (124).

[9] See Recital 8 of Reg 1/2003: '[. . .] Member States should not under this Regulation be precluded from adopting and applying on their territory stricter national competition laws which prohibit or impose sanctions on unilateral conduct engaged in by undertakings. These stricter national laws may include provisions which prohibit or impose sanctions on abusive behaviour toward economically dependent undertakings. Furthermore, this Regulation does not apply to national laws which impose criminal sanctions on natural persons except to the extent that such sanctions are the means whereby competition rules applying to undertakings are enforced. J Temple Lang, 'Developments, Issues and New Remedies—The Duties of National Authorities and Courts under Art 10 of the EC Treaty' [2004] Fordham International Law Journal 1904–39 (1929) notes that conflicts may arise under Art 10 EC and the NCA's obligation of sincere cooperation. This could be the case where national laws seem to protect competitors from competition, for example by non-discrimination rules. A national decision which in fact protected a competitor against competition even if was based on national law would be contrary to Art 3 EC which states that competition is a Community objective. Temple Lang takes the view that such a national decision would be contrary to the duties of the competition authority under Art 10 and would be open to challenge in national administrative courts.

[10] See also Case C-309/99 *Wouters* [2002] ECR I-1577 paras 97 *et seq*. Art 81(1) EC may also not apply where the agreement serves a legitimate purpose. See ch 2 'National Judicial Authorities' para 2.12 fn 47.

[11] F Montag and A Rosenfeld, 'A solution to the Problem? Reg 1/2003 and the modernization of competition procedure' [2003] Zeitschrift für Wettbewerbsrecht 107–35 (124). The authors take the view that under the terms of *Walt Wilhelm* where an explicit positive Commission decision that an agreement is exempted from the application of Art 81 EC does not exist and is not forthcoming because an agreement has not been notified and a block exemption does not apply, national law could prohibit the conduct despite the fact that it may potentially qualify for the exemption under Art 81(3) EC. See also M Siragusa, 'The Commission's Position Within the Network: The Perspective of the Legal Practitioners' (European University Institute, Robert Schuman Centre for Advanced Studies, 2002 EU Competition Law and Policy Workshop/

of Regulation 1/2003 only deals with substantive law and does not concern the application of procedural rules.

3.03 Regulation 1/2003 sets out the powers of NCAs by defining the types of decisions that can be taken. The NCAs shall have the power to apply Articles 81 and 82 EC in individual cases. For this purpose, acting on their own initiative or on a complaint, NCAs may require that an infringement be brought to an end, order interim measures, accept commitments, impose fines, periodic penalty payments, or any other penalty provided for in their national law.[12] The latter may also include imprisonment or criminal sanctions on natural persons.[13] The sanctions regimes of the Commission and NCAs are not, therefore, harmonized by Regulation 1/2003. In the case of NCAs this is left to be determined by the national laws of the relevant Member State. At the same time, NCAs remain entitled to establish their own enforcement priorities, including the right to decide which agreements and conduct to investigate. The Commission, however, retains its specific role in clarifying the law and NCAs do not have the power to adopt non-infringement decisions similar to the decisions which the Commission may adopt, acting on its own initiative and where the Community public interest relating to the application of Articles 81 and 82 EC so requires.[14]

Proceedings 3) stating that the obligation to apply EC law somehow counterbalances the 'loss' suffered by the Commission in terms of its exclusive power to apply Art 81(3) EC, by guaranteeing that such provision and also the rest of Arts 81 and 82 EC will be effectively applied.

[12] Art 5 of Reg 1/2003. Under Art 29(2) NCAs are also empowered to withdraw the benefit of a block exemption regulation under certain conditions and provides that where in any particular case, agreements, decisions by associations of undertakings or concerted practices to which a block exemption applies have effects which are incompatible with Art 81(3) EC in the territory of a Member State or part thereof, which has all the characteristics of a distinct market, the NCA of that Member State may withdraw the benefit of the block exemption in question in respect of that territory.

[13] This could mean that the NCAs have stronger powers than the Commission under Reg 1/2003. The Commission can only impose fines on undertakings for infringements of Art 81 or 82 EC while Art 23(5) of Reg 1/2003 clarifies that fines 'shall not be of a criminal law nature'. The German Federal Cartel Office (*Bundeskartellamt*) can impose fines on individuals such as directors or officers and the OFT in the UK may impose criminal sanctions which means that individuals may be sent to jail. C Canenbley and M Rosenthal, 'Cooperation between Antitrust Authorities In-and Outside the EU: What does it mean for Multinational Corporations?—Part 1' [2005] ECLR 106–14 (108) consider the existence of different procedural rules as problematic in light of the general principle of equal treatment.

[14] Art 10 of Reg 1/2003. WP Wils, 'Community Report' The Modernisation of EU Competition Law Enforcement in the EU FIDE 2004 National Reports 661–736 paras 49 and 50. In any event, if the Commission does not take up the case, companies may contact the NCAs whose territory is affected by the agreement in question for a decision that there is 'no ground for action on their part' (Art 6(3) of Reg 1/2003). Despite the fact that such a decision would only bind the issuing authority, it would provide a high degree of legal certainty in that it would be unlikely that other authorities, including the Commission, would subsequently impose fines on a company. C Canenbley and M Rosenthal, 'Cooperation between Antitrust Authorities In-and Outside the EU: What does it mean for Multinational Corporations?—Part 1' [2005] ECLR 106–14 (107).

The intention not to give NCAs the possibility of adopting decisions of inapplicability seems to be to prevent NCAs from taking decisions, in particular finding Article 81 inapplicable, which might be binding on national courts.[15] Moreover, the Commission is able to relieve the NCAs of their competence to deal with cases in certain circumstances, and NCAs cannot take decisions which would run counter to an earlier decision by the Commission regarding the same agreement or practice.[16] These are the main differences between the position of the Commission and that of the NCAs.[17]

B. Cooperation between the Commission and the NCAs

Under the system of parallel competence, the Commission and the NCAs must apply the Community competition rules in close cooperation.[18] Together the NCAs and the Commission form a network of European competition authorities ('European Competition Network' or 'ECN'), which serves as a forum for discussion and cooperation in the application of Articles 81 and 82 EC.[19] Essentially, the ECN is aimed at ensuring both an efficient division of work and an effective consistent application of the EC competition rules. The fact that a

3.04

---

[15] CS Kerse and N Khan, *EC Antitrust Procedure* (5th edn, 2005) para 5–004 point out that it may be unavoidable that NCAs will take decisions finding Art 81(1) EC inapplicable even if not expressly empowered to do so under Reg 1/2003. Such a decision may emerge as a result of the investigation of a complaint and the complainant should be entitled to a reasoned decision setting out the grounds for the rejection (scarcity of resources, lack of priority to pursue the complaint, etc). A rejection may occur on a variety of reasons, one of which may also be that the conditions of Art 81(1) EC may not be fulfilled or that Art 81(3) EC may be satisfied. See also Judge JD Cooke, 'Application of EC Competition Rules by National Courts', Antitrust Reform in Europe: A Year in Practice, 9–11 March 2005, Brussels, International Bar Association (IBA) 6 also notes that NCAs seem to be entitled to decisions that there are no grounds for action but not to decisions of inapplicability. However, JD Cooke believes this might give rise to some problems before national courts, particularly in those Member States where under the arrangements for implementing Reg 1/2003, the investigating and prosecuting functions of an NCA have been separated from the deciding function. Where a court has been designated under Art 35 of Reg 1/2003 to decide upon infringements it is presumably arguable that a judgment of the court dismissing the NCA prosecution case against defendant undertakings has precisely the effect of a decision that no infringement has taken place.

[16] Art 16(2) of Reg 1/2003.

[17] P Lowe, 'The Role of the Commission in the Modernisation of EC Competition Law', [2004] Speech at UKAEL Conference on Modernization of EC Competition Law: Uncertainties and Opportunities, suggests that the role of the Commission would be of a 'primus inter pares'.

[18] Art 11(1) of Reg 1/2003.

[19] Apart from the cooperation mechanism described below, an important development is the creation of working groups and sectoral subgroups in the ECN which allow for case and policy related exchanges between experts of certain sectors. K Dekeyser, 'Reg 1/2003: First Experiences' (n 3 above) who points to the importance of sharing information and experience in this regard. Commission Report on Competition Policy SEC (2004) 805 final para 104.

case under Articles 81 or 82 EC affecting trade between Member States can be dealt with by either the Commission, or a single national authority or various national authorities acting in parallel, could lead to an increased enforcement of European competition law. However, because Regulation 1/2003 has also spelled out the objective that each competition case should be handled by a single authority, there was broad agreement that a series of rules or orientations was needed to organize information and consultation between the entities involved.

1. The European Competition Network (ECN)

3.05   Regulation 1/2003 has not established strict rules for the allocation of cases between the Commission and the NCAs, but has only provided a series of instruments to allow a flexible and consensual allocation of cases within the ECN.[20] The European Commission has sought to give guidance through its Notice on cooperation within the Network of Competition Authorities[21] ('the ECN Cooperation Notice'). One very important issue dealt with in the ECN Cooperation Notice concerns the principles governing the division of work between the members of the network.[22] This is required to enable an undertaking to carry out its self-assessment because this must be based not only on the Commission's practice but also on the decision-taking practice of the NCAs and national courts.[23] Regulation 1/2003 has established a system of parallel competences whereby both the Commission and Member States' competition authorities are competent to apply Articles 81 and 82 EC. This approach was

---

[20] This is in sharp contrast to the allocation mechanism provided in the merger control rules where the Commission and the Member States do not have concurrent jurisdiction so that a clear division of competence is established.

[21] [2004] OJ C101/43. The ECN Cooperation Notice is based to a significant extent on the Joint Statement of the Council and the Commission on the functioning of the network of competition authorities, entered in the Council Minutes at the time of the adoption of Reg 1/2003. Council Document 15435/02 ADD 1 of 10 December 2002. Given that the Joint Statement is a political declaration, whose details were to be set out in the ECN Cooperation Notice, the analysis may therefore be limited to principles spelled out in the Notice. This notice replaces the earlier 'Commission notice on cooperation between national competition authorities and the Commission in handling cases falling within the scope of Arts 81 and 82 of the EC Treaty' [1997] OJ C313/3.

[22] In this respect the notice follows the Joint Statement of the Council and the Commission which was issued on the day when Reg 1/2003 was adopted. C Gauer, L Kjolbye, D Dalheimer, E de Smijter, D Schnichels, and M Laurila, 'Reg 1/2003 and the Modernization Package fully applicable since 1 May 2004', Competition Policy Newsletter, Number 2, Summer 2004 1–6.

[23] C Canenbley and M Rosenthal, 'Cooperation between Antitrust Authorities In-and Outside the EU: What does it mean for Multinational Corporations?—Part 1' [2005] ECLR 106–14 (108–9) indicating that in multi-jurisdictional cases multinational companies will try to establish the jurisdiction of the Commission in order to benefit from a 'one-stop shop' and thus eliminate the risk of diverging decisions by NCAs.

taken to ensure efficient work sharing for all cases, including complex ones, without burdening the system with a rigid division of competences.[24]

Principles of case allocation

The competence of the NCAs   In principle, cases under Articles 81 and/or   **3.06**
82 EC will be dealt with by (i) a single NCA, with the assistance or not of NCAs of other Member States, (ii) several NCAs acting in parallel, or (iii) the Commission.[25] The ECN Cooperation Notice sets out the criteria which should determine which NCA is the best placed to handle the case. An authority can be considered to be well placed to deal with a case if the following three cumulative conditions are met:

(i)   The agreement or practice has substantial direct actual or foreseeable effects on competition within its territory, is implemented within, or originates from its territory. This will often coincide with the centre of gravity of the case, i.e. the Member State(s) where competition is substantially affected by the infringement.

(ii)   The authority is able to effectively bring to an end the entire infringement, i.e. it can adopt a cease-and-desist order, the effect of which will be sufficient to bring an end to the infringement and it can, where appropriate, sanction the infringement adequately;[26]

(iii)   The authority can gather, possibly with the assistance of other authorities, the evidence required to prove the infringement.

Conditions (ii) and (iii) are related to the investigation and enforcement capabil-   **3.07**
ities of the authority so selected. These criteria suggest that a material link between the infringement and the territory of a Member State must exist in order for that Member State's competition authority to be considered well placed. In most cases the NCAs of those Member States will be well placed where competition is substantially affected by an infringement provided the NCA in question is capable of effectively bringing the infringement to an end through either single or parallel action—together with another NCA—unless the Commission is better placed to act.[27] The Commission takes the view that in most

---

[24] K Dekeyser, 'Reg 1/2003: First Experiences' IBC Conference London 27 and 28 April 2005 notes that the system is built on the assumption that parallel competences serve effective enforcement. In a system of exclusive competences the victims of infringements would depend on a single enforcer which sets different priorities. See also C Gauer, 'Due Process in the Face of Divergent National Procedures and Sanctions', Antitrust Reform in Europe: A Year in Practice, 9–11 March 2005, Brussels International Bar Association (IBA) 2–3.
[25] ECN Cooperation Notice [2004] OJ C101/43 para 5.
[26] The question whether an infringement having effects in several Member States can be adequately sanctioned by one NCA is a question which remains unanswered. CS Kerse and N Khan, *EC Antitrust Procedure* (5th edn, 2005) para 2–006.
[27] ECN Cooperation Notice [2004] OJ C101/43 para 9.

instances the NCA that receives a complaint or starts an *ex-officio* procedure will remain in charge of the case and provides some practical examples explaining when it could be considered that one or various authorities are well placed to deal with a case;[28] in particular, parallel action by two or three NCAs may be appropriate where an agreement or practice has substantial effects on competition in their respective territories and the action of only one NCA would not be sufficient to bring the infringement to an end or to issue adequate sanctions. Conversely, where the action of a single NCA is sufficient to bring the entire infringement to an end, this may be appropriate although more than one NCA can be regarded as well placed. A good example of this scenario is the case of a joint venture operating a maritime transport service between two Member States.[29] The prohibition of the joint venture by one of the two authorities is sufficient to bring an end to the agreement. The Commission emphasizes that each NCA retains full discretion in deciding whether or not to investigate a case.[30]

3.08 **The competence of the Commission** As regards the competence of the Commission, the ECN Cooperation Notice establishes that the Commission is particularly well placed if one or several agreement(s) or practice(s), including networks of similar agreements or practices, have effects on competition in more than three Member States (cross-border markets covering more than three Member States or several national markets). In addition, the Commission is particularly well placed to deal with a case if it is closely linked to other Community provisions which may be exclusively or more effectively applied by the Commission, if the Community interest requires the adoption of a Commission decision to develop Community competition policy when a new competition issue arises or to ensure effective enforcement.[31] Article 11(6) of Regulation

---

[28] ECN Cooperation Notice [2004] OJ C101/45 paras 10–15.

[29] K Dekeyser and C Gauer, 'The New Enforcement System for Arts 81 and 82 and the Rights of Defence' ch 23 in BE Hawk (ed), *International Antitrust Law & Policy*, Annual Proceedings of the Fordham Institute [2004] 549–85 (75, n 91).

[30] ECN Cooperation Notice [2004] OJ C101/43 para 5. See C Gauer, L Kjolbye, D Dalheimer, E de Smijter, D Schnichels, and M Laurila, 'Reg. 1/2003 and the Modernization Package fully applicable since 1 May 2004', Competition Policy Newsletter, Number 2, Summer 2004, 1–6 (3): '[. . . .] From a practical point of view this means that [. . .] the Finnish authority would not seize itself with an infringement that happens in Greece, as there are already no effects in the Finnish market, not to mention the difficulty of gathering the relevant information and bringing the infringement to an end. On the other hand, if an infringement concerned for instance a shipping line between Italy and Greece, the Greek as well as the Italian competition authority might be well placed to deal with the case, depending on the circumstances. [. . . .]'.

[31] ECN Cooperation Notice [2004] OJ C101/43 para 15. K Dekeyser and C Gauer, 'The New Enforcement System for Articles 81 and 82 and the Rights of Defence' ch 23 in BE Hawk (ed), *International Antitrust Law & Policy*, Annual Proceedings of the Fordham Institute [2004] 549–85 (75, n 91) note that the allocation criteria are drafted in such a way that the

1/2003 states that the initiation by the Commission of proceedings shall relieve all NCAs of their competence to apply Articles 81 and 82 EC.[32]

This provision can come into play in two main situations. First, once the Commission has started proceedings, NCAs cannot act on the same legal grounds against the same agreement(s) or practice(s) by the same undertaking(s) on the same relevant geographic and product market. Secondly, the Commission can also relieve the NCA of their competence to deal with a particular case.[33] During the initial allocation period (indicative time period of two months, the Commission can initiate proceedings with the effects of Article 11(6) of Regulation 1/2003 after having consulted the NCAs concerned. After the two-month allocation stage, the Commission will in principle only apply Article 11(6) of Regulation 1/2003 and disable the NCAs if one of the following situations arises:

(i)   Network members envisage conflicting decisions in the same case;
(ii) Network members envisage a decision which is obviously in conflict with consolidated case law; the standards defined in the judgments of the Community courts and in previous decisions and regulations of the Commission should serve as a yardstick; concerning the assessment of the facts (e.g. market definition), only a significant divergence will trigger an intervention of the Commission;
(iii) Network member(s) is (are) unduly drawing out proceedings in the case;

Commission is always well placed to act and that there would be 'no idea of subsidiarity' in Reg 1/2003: action by an NCA is, as a matter of principle, preferred to action by the Commission. See also C Gauer, 'Due Process in the Face of Divergent National Procedures and Sanctions' Antitrust Reform in Europe: A Year in Practice, 9–11 March 2005, Brussels, International Bar Association (IBA) 2–4.

[32] The proceedings for the adoption of a decision under Chapter III concern decisions finding an infringement and/or ordering its termination, decisions ordering interim measures, decisions making commitments binding, and decisions finding that Arts 81 or 82 EC are not applicable to an agreement or practice. The case law of the ECJ with regard to the similarly worded Art 9(3) of Reg 17 lays down that the initiation of a procedure requires an 'authoritative act of the Commission evidencing its intention of taking a decision'. See Case 48/72 *Brasserie de Haecht v Wilkin-Janssen* [1972] ECR 88 para 16. Wils notes that the effect of Art 11(6) is amplified by Art 3 of Reg 1/2003 which obliges NCAs also to apply Arts 81 or 82 EC when they apply national competition law. The initiation of proceedings by the Commission thus in fact relieves NCAs not only of their competence to apply Arts 81 and 82 EC but also of their competence to apply national competition law. WPJ Wils, 'The Principle of Ne bis in idem in EC Antitrust Enforcement: A Legal and Economic Analysis' [2004] World Competition—Law and Economics Review 134 (144) fn 44.

[33] Art 11(6) of Reg 1/2003; ECN Cooperation Notice [2004] OJ C101/43 para 54. This possibility should be used as an exception to the rule according to which EC competition law is uniformly and consistently applied by different NCAs and national courts. M Siragusa, 'The Commission's Position Within the Network: The Perspective of the Legal Practitioners', European University Institute, Robert Schuman Centre for Advanced Studies, 2002 EU Competition Law and Policy Workshop/Proceedings 9.

(iv) There is a need to adopt a Commission decision to develop Community competition policy in particular when a similar competition issue arises in several Member States or to ensure effective enforcement;

(v) The NCA(s) concerned do not object.

3.09 It follows that the Commission will only intervene where: (i) more than three Member States are involved; or (ii) there are Community provisions which may be exclusively or more effectively applied by the Commission; or (iii) if the Community interest requires the adoption of a Commission decision to develop Community competition policy when a new competition issue arises or to ensure effective enforcement. Issues of case allocation are bound to arise in the grey area where it is difficult to localize the effects of the infringement or where a single NCA appears unable to investigate the case properly or to bring the infringement to an end. However, in the first year of Regulation 1/2003, the Commission has yet to apply Article 11(6).[34]

3.10 It is important to note that neither Regulation 1/2003 nor the ECN Cooperation Notice confer jurisdiction over Articles 81 or 82 EC cases. Any competition authority wishing or requested to investigate a matter must have jurisdiction. Regulation 1/2003 does not express any direct or indirect preference for enforcement by the NCAs or—for that matter—by the Commission. While it has been argued that the ECN Cooperation Notice creates legitimate expectations, it is also true that it does not state that one single authority will be well placed to deal with a given case. It stresses that all authorities retain full discretion in deciding whether or not to investigate a case.[35] The case must fall within the scope of Articles 81 or 82 EC and there must be an effect on competition in the affected Member State's territory. If, for example, the Belgian or the Luxembourg competition authorities were not to have sufficient resources to deal with a case for which the relevant geographic market is the Benelux, the case could be dealt with by the Dutch competition authority or by the Commission. Thus, the NCA has no wider powers than it already had under its national laws to impose fines or to order remedies. One may argue that the limitations inherent

---

[34] K Dekeyser, 'Reg 1/2003: First Experiences' (IBC Conference London 27 and 28 April 2005) notes that there was no case in which the Commission considered the initiation of proceedings pursuant to Art 11(6) with a view to de-seizing an NCA for reason of coherent application; though 'certain reactions' had been given in informal ways which in some cases arguably led the NCA to re-consider its approach.

[35] ECN Cooperation Notice [2004] OJ C101/43 para 5. C Gauer, 'Due Process in the Face of Divergent National Procedures and Sanctions', Antitrust Reform in Europe: A Year in Practice, 9–11 March 2005, Brussels, International Bar Association (IBA) 3. Footnote 10 notes that it might be more appropriate to talk about re-allocation instead of case allocation. Complainants choose the authority where they want to lodge their complaint etc. (Re)-allocation only comes into play when an authority seized with a case does not want to deal with it or another authority wants to deal with it.

in public law which prohibits a sovereign State to exercise its powers outside its territory have not been addressed by Regulation 1/2003. Therefore, an NCA can only order the termination and sanction the effects of infringements on its own territory.[36] Their decisions do not have a Community-wide effect and may normally not be enforced outside their borders. One may also conclude from a combined reading of Article 10 EC, which requires the Member States to make penalties effective, proportionate, and dissuasive,[37] and Regulation 1/2003 that when sanctioning an infringement in the territory of other Member States, NCAs take into account the effects of the infringement in the territory of the Member State.[38] For example, the OFT in the UK has declared that if a penalty or fine has been imposed by the European Commission, or by a court or other body in another Member State in respect of an agreement or conduct, it will take that penalty or fine into account when setting the amount of a penalty in relation to that agreement or conduct.[39]

So far, it appears that the situations where cases have changed hands are rare in comparison with the overall number of cases treated by the network members. **3.11**

---

[36] See E Paulis and C Gauer, 'La reforme de règles d'application des Arts 81 y 82 du Traité' [2003] 11 Journal de tribunaux droit européen 35–37. An example of this system of restricted enforcement was the sanctioning of infringements of Art 81 EC in the shrimp industry in the Netherlands, Germany, and Denmark by the Dutch NCA. This was the first time that the Dutch authorities imposed a fine for an infringement of Community competition rules and in view of the restricted jurisdiction to impose fines for conduct affecting commerce elsewhere than in the Netherlands, it decided to limit the fines for the parties involved to the effect that their behaviour had had on the Dutch part of the market. See R Wesseling report The Netherlands in *The Modernization of EU Competition Law Enforcement in the EU*, FIDE 2004 National Reports 407–37 (416). R Smits, 'The European Competition Network' [2005] Legal Issues of Economic Integration 175–92 (185) takes the view that had this case arisen later and therefore been allocated under Reg 1/2003 to a single rather than three co-operating NCAs, the NCAs concerned would have had to agree on a mechanism under which the findings of one of them would be followed up by the others imposing fines on the undertakings involved for the effects of the infringement on their part of the market.

[37] Case 68/88 *EC Commission v Greece* [1989] ECR 2965 paras 23 and 24; Case C-354/99 *EC Commission v Ireland* [2001] ECR I-7657 para 46.

[38] WPJ Wils, 'Community Report' in *The Modernisation of EU Competition Law Enforcement*, FIDE 2004 National Reports 661-736 para 134; see also T-102/96 *Glencour/Lonrho* [1999] ECR II-753 para 90. See also OFT's Guidance as to the appropriate amount of a penalty—'Understanding Competition Law' [2004] at 2.6: '[. . .] In cases concerning infringements of Art 81 and/or Art 82, the OFT may, in determining the starting point, take into account effects in another Member State of the agreement or conduct concerned. The OFT will take into account effects in another Member State through its assessment of relevant turnover; the OFT may consider turnover generated in another Member State if the relevant geographic market for the relevant product is wider than the United Kingdom and the express consent of the relevant Member State or NCA, as appropriate, is given in each particular case. [. . .].'

[39] This is to ensure that where an anticompetitive agreement or conduct is subject to proceedings resulting in a penalty or fine in another Member State, an undertaking will not be penalized again in the UK for the same anticompetitive effect. See OFT's Guidance as to the appropriate amount of a penalty—'Understanding Competition Law' [2004] para 2.6. For more details on the problem of *ne bis in idem* or double jeopardy, see below para 3.16.

In 2004, a total of 298 cases were submitted to the network: ninety-nine by the Commission and 199 by the NCAs.[40] There were two principal areas in which work sharing in the network has been an issue. In cartel cases involving the flat glass sector, several NCAs had received complaints or leads from customers. The NCAs concerned 'put the pieces of the puzzle together' and discovered that the suspected scope might call for action by the Commission, i.e. to organize the inspections.[41] As a matter of fact the action of the Commission and that of a Member State competition authority can often complement each other. One concrete example is the handling of the simultaneous complaints against Deutsche Post received by both the Commission and the German *Bundeskartellamt*.[42]

Reallocation

3.12 Reallocation can occur between the NCAs or from the NCAs to the Commission. Among NCAs, a case reallocation would only be envisaged at the outset of a procedure where either that authority considers that it was not well placed to act or where other authorities informed about the fact that an authority has started to act in a certain case, express an interest in dealing with it. In order to detect multiple procedures and to ensure that a well-placed NCA deals with cases, network members have to be informed at an early stage of the cases pending before the various competition authorities. Where re-allocation issues arise, they should be resolved swiftly within a period of two months starting from the date of the first information sent to the network.[43] Once this initial allocation period of two months has elapsed, re-allocation of a case should only occur where the facts known about the case change materially during the investigation.

3.13 The reallocation principles devised by the Commission met some criticism on

---

[40] Report from the Commission—Report on Competition Policy SEC (2005) 805 final para 105. The Commission reported the following aggregated figures for the period of 1 May 2005 until 31 October 2005: 473 investigations and 97 envisaged decisions available at http://europa.eu.int/comm/competition/index_en.html. With a detailed overview on the first year under Reg 1/2003 see also E Paulis and E de Smitjer, 'Enhanced Enforcement of the EC Competition Rules since 1 May 2004 by the Commission and the NCAs'. Anti-trust reform in Europe: a year in practice, 9–11 March 2005, Brussels, International Bar Association (IBA).

[41] K Dekeyser, 'Reg. 1/2003: First Experiences' (n 3 above); Commissioner for Competition Policy N Kroes 'Taking Competition Seriously—Anti-Trust Reform in Europe', International Bar Association/European Commission Conference, Antitrust Reform in Europe: A Year in Practice, 10 March 2005.

[42] Commissioner for Competition Policy N Kroes, 'Taking Competition Seriously—Anti-Trust Reform in Europe' International Bar Association/European Commission Conference, Antitrust Reform in Europe: A Year in Practice, 9–11 March. Deutsche Post's actions were based on a provision of the German postal legislation which was already the subject of a Commission procedure under Art 86 EC. In this case, it was agreed that the most effective and efficient way forward would be for the Commission to continue its Art 86 procedure and for the *Bundeskartellamt* to continue the antitrust complaint. The combined efforts enabled both the Commission and the *Bundeskartellamt* to take their respective decisions within a very short time frame.

[43] Art 11 of Reg 1/2003.

the grounds that the rules might not be clear enough to avoid possible parallel proceedings in the same matter. It appears that in those cases where various NCAs regard themselves as well placed to act, they might actually do so in parallel in the same proceeding. The ECN Cooperation Notice provides that 'where reallocation is found to be necessary [. . .] network members *will endeavour* to reallocate cases to a single well placed competition authority as often as possible'[44] (emphasis added), but it does not provide for a proceeding to resolve disputes on allocation within the ECN. It only establishes that the Advisory Committee could serve as a forum for discussion in important cases, but the Advisory Committee does not have the legal mandate to ultimately settle disputes in a binding manner.[45] While this is deliberately conceived to leave room for flexible and pragmatic solutions, it is clear that the rather informal way of resolving disputes presupposes the will of the NCAs to cooperate and to solve disputes amicably in a significant number of cases involving agreements or practices that affect more than one Member State. In any event, if the members of the network were not to reach an agreement as to which of them should deal with a case, or if an NCA happens to disregard the principles of allocation set out in the ECN Cooperation Notice, the Commission can initiate proceedings itself, thus relieving NCAs of their competence to deal with the case.[46] During the public consultation of the modernization package, the Commission was asked to grant the parties the right to be heard before a matter is re-allocated from one NCA to another NCA which is considered as being better placed to deal with it. In more general terms, the question arises as to whether an undertaking or a person being investigated is dissatisfied with the reallocation could bring an application for judicial review against any decision. The ECN Cooperation Notice states that in a system of parallel competences, case allocation is considered as a mere division of labour and therefore it does not confer a right on the parties that their case is decided by a particular NCA.[47] Accordingly, the

---

[44] ECN Cooperation Notice para 7.

[45] ECN Cooperation Notice para 62. C Gauer, 'Due Process in the Face of Divergent National Procedures and Sanctions', Antitrust Reform in Europe: A Year in Practice, 9–11 March 2005, Brussels, International Bar Association (IBA).

[46] Art 11(6) of Reg 1/2003. Regarding the risk of parallel application of Art 81 EC by the Commission and one or more NCAs, N Levy and R O'Donoghue, 'The EU Leniency Programme Comes of Age' [2004] World Competition—Law and Economics Review, Vol 27, 75–99 (93). See also 'Leniency Programmes: An Anaemic Carrot for Cartels in France, Germany and the UK?' [2005] ECLR 13–23 (22) stating the example of a cartel member who applies for leniency in the UK and receives immunity there but abstains from applying for leniency to France and Germany for fear of criminal sanctions and argues that there would always exist the risk that these jurisdictions will be tipped off about competition violations by other sources (competitors, etc).

[47] This is also why the Commission does not consider the allocation of cases as a 'decision'. Case allocation is mainly a work sharing exercise between authorities. 'Q&A on modernization with Kris Dekeyser' Global Competition Review, Vol 8, Issue 3, April 2005 11–16 (12).

ECN Cooperation Notice merely provides that if a case is reallocated within the network, the undertakings concerned and the complainant(s) are informed as soon as possible by the competition authorities involved.[48]

3.14 Although this view is not without its merits, it is also true that in the absence of Community harmonization, the procedural rights, sanctions, and scope of judicial review vary substantially between Member States. Consequently, re-allocation might affect severely the parties' legal position, which raises the question of how a reallocation can be challenged. There is the suggestion that case-allocation does not affect the procedural rights of the undertakings.[49] The following distinction may be appropriate: if the case is reallocated from one NCA to another, up to four decisions could be envisaged: (i) a decision by the first NCA to terminate its proceedings; (ii) a decision by the second NCA to open proceedings; (iii) possibly, a decision by the first authority to transfer to the second authority the information in its file; (iv) the decision by the second authority to include into its file the information received from the first authority. Whether decision (i) and decision (iii) are challengeable acts depends on the national law of the Member State of the first NCA,[50] whereas whether decisions under (ii) and (iv) are challengeable depends on the national law of the second Member State.[51] In *Wanadoo*, the CFI will have the opportunity

---

[48] ECN Cooperation Notice para 34. It should be noted that Reg 1/2003 does not provide for an obligation of ECN members to inform the undertakings concerned of information taking place. D Reichelt, 'To what extent does the cooperation within the European Competition Network protect the rights of the undertakings?' (2005) CML Rev 745–82 (754) indicates that given the almost automatic exchange of certain information at particular procedural stages, the undertaking will, however, be able to learn what information will be transmitted.

[49] C Gauer, 'Due Process in the Face of Divergent National Procedures and Sanctions', Antitrust Reform in Europe: A Year in Practice, 9–11 March 2005, Brussels, International Bar Association (IBA), argues that, leaving aside the peculiar issue of leniency applications in no system would the subject of an investigation have a right to choose its investigator or its judge. C Gauer maintains that the rights of the complaints also remain unaltered. It may well be that they are entitled to a decision by the competition authority that no longer deals with the case.

[50] See also J Temple Lang, 'Developments, Issues and New Remedies—The Duties of National Authorities and Courts under Art 10 of the EC Treaty' [2004] Fordham International Law Journal 1904–39 (1929) states that it is not clear whether an NCA to which the Commission transfers a complaint under Reg 1/2003 has a duty to give the parties all the same procedural rights as they would have in a competition procedure. If there is no such duty, the transfer substantially alters the rights of the parties and must be open to challenge under Art 230 EC.

[51] The question whether these decisions are reviewable is subject to debate. WPJ Wils, 'Community Report' in *The Modernization of EU Competition Law Enforcement in the EU*, FIDE 2004 National Reports 661–736 paras 116–120 notes that it would seem unlikely that such appeals, if admissible under national law, could be successful. Decision (i) does not harm the undertakings concerned, given that the harm consisting of the sanctions possibly later imposed by the second authority does not result from the decision by the first NCA to terminate its proceedings. Decision (ii) does not appear in any relevant sense different from any other opening of proceedings by a competition authority. Decisions (iii) and (iv) are covered by Art 12(1) of Reg 1/2003. See also JS Venit, 'Private Practice in the Wake of the Commission's Modernization Program' [2005] Legal Issues of Economic Integration 147–59 (157) who takes the view that the actual decision suspending proceedings may be appealable under national law given their crucial

to give its view on the question whether reallocation decisions are reviewable before the Community Courts: the applicant submitted applicant submits that the French competition authority should have remained in charge of the case and that consequently the Commission should not have intervened in it.[52] Where a case is reallocated to the Commission, there will be a decision by the Commission to open proceedings, which relieves the NCA of its competence. While arguably the Member State could bring an action for annulment of this decision before the ECJ,[53] an action by a company or other person being investigated would probably not be possible, because the decision is simply a preliminary step in the Commission's procedure.[54]

The Commission reported for 2004 that the reallocation of cases notified to the network was extremely rare (less than 1 per cent of 298 cases). The vast majority of cases remain with the authority which started to investigate them.[55] In *Coca-Cola*, reallocation from the various NCAs which were already active occurred at a late stage; essentially, the Commission started proceedings in order to accept commitments that were binding for the whole of the Community.[56] **3.15**

---

influence of the case. He also suggests that general principles of due process and Art 6 ECHR provide arguments for the reviewability of these decisions at the EC level. See also D Geradin and N Petit, 'Judicial remedies under EC Competition Law: Complex issues arising from the Modernization Process' 32nd Annual International Antitrust Law & Policy Conference Fordham Corporate Law Institute, 22–23 September 2005 (forthcoming) who also discuss the reviewability of these decisions.

[52] Case T-339/04 *Wanadoo v EC Commission* [2004] OJ C262/53, appeal pending against the inspection decision adopted by the Commisison. Both the Conseil de la concurrence and the Commission had been seized with a complaint; the former limited itself to dealing with the complainant's request for interim measures.

[53] J Schwarze and A Weitbrecht, *Grundzüge des Europäischen Kartellverfahrensrechts* (2004) § 11 para 11.

[54] WPJ Wils, 'Community Report' in *The Modernization of EU Competition Law Enforcement in the EU*, FIDE 2004 National Reports 661–736 para 120. See also Case 60/81 *IBM v EC Commission* [1981] ECR 2639 in which the ECJ denied the admissibility of a judicial challenge of the initiation of a procedure indicating that those measures could be reviewed in the context of an appeal against the final decision. See also J Schwarze and A Weitbrecht, *Grundzüge des Europäischen Kartellverfahrensrechts* (2004) § 10 paras 28–41. See also D Geradin and N Petit, 'Judicial remedies under EC Competition Law: Complex issues arising from the modernization process' 32nd Annual International Antitrust Law & Policy Conference Fordham Corporate Law Institute, 22–23 September 2005 (forthcoming) argue that the reading of *IBM v EC Commission* would permit to challenge Commission decisions under Art 11(6) of Reg 1/2003 on the ground that it constitutes the end of a special procedure and that these Commissions would have legally binding effects for the undertakings involved.

[55] Commission Report on Competition Policy SEC (2004) 805 final para 105.

[56] See Commission Press Release IP/05/775 of 22 June 2005 'Competition: Commission makes commitments from Coca-Cola legally binding, increasing consumer choice'.

Principle of ne bis in idem[57]

3.16 Even before the entry into force of Regulation 1/2003, the parallel application of Article 81 and national competition laws to the same matter has been consistent with the division of responsibilities between the Commission and Member States.[58] Potential conflicts did not arise under Regulation 17, maybe also because NCAs have only recently strengthened their enforcement efforts, for example including leniency programmes of their own.[59] While it is true that Regulation 1/2003 sets out the objective that each case should be handled by a single authority, the ECN Cooperation Notice does not rule out the possibility of parallel action by several national competition authorities,[60] unless the Commission has taken up the case under the claw-back mechanism of Article 11(6) of Regulation 1/2003. The Community Courts have had to rule on several occasions on the application of the *ne bis in idem* principle in competition cases.[61] They defined the principle in competition cases as precluding an undertaking from being found liable or proceedings from being brought against it a second time on the grounds of anti-competitive conduct in respect of which

---

[57] Although the concept is broadly similar to the common law principle of 'double jeopardy', the latter also covers the requirement to set off the first penalty imposed for the same offence in a previous case. This requirement is known in EC law as a requirement of natural justice. K Dekeyser and C Gauer, 'The New Enforcement System for Arts 81 and 82 and the Rights of Defence' (n 29 above) 25. E Paulis and C Gauer 'Le règlement n° 1/2003 et le principe du *ne bis in idem*' [2005] Revue des droit de la concurrence 32–40. J Schwarze and A Weitbrecht, *Grundzüge des Europäischen Kartellverfahrensrechts* (2004) § 7 paras 24–31; C Canenbley and M Rosenthal, 'Cooperation between Antitrust Authorities In-and Outside the EU: What does it mean for Multinational Corporations?—Part 2' [2005] ECLR 179–87 (181–83). C Gauer, 'Due Process in the Face of Divergence National Procedures and Sanctions', Antitrust Reform in Europe: A Year in Practice, 9–11 March 2005, Brussels, International Bar Association (IBA) 7–8.

[58] Case 14/68 *Walt Wilhelm v Bundeskartellamt* [1969] ECR 1 paras 3 and 11. The ECJ decided that the application of national law and EC competition law to the same infringement does not raise a *ne bis in idem* issue because the interests protected by the two sets of rules are different. However, it considered that natural justice requires the fine set by the national authority for the infringement of national law to be taken into account by the Commission before imposing a fine for the infringement of EC competition law. See also Case T-141/89 *Trefileurope v EC Commission* [1995] ECR II-791 in which the Commission took into account a fine imposed by the French authority under French law.

[59] See N Levy and R O'Donoghue 'The EU Leniency Programme Comes of Age' [2004] World Competition—Law and Economics Review 75–99 (92). The authors also indicate that in comparison to the level of enforcement activity today, Commission fines in respect of antitrust violations were relatively modest and that the Commission's Notices on cooperation with NCAs and national courts might have limited potential conflicts.

[60] Joint Statement of the Council and the Commission on the functioning of the network, at 16 and 18; ECN Cooperation Notice, at 12 and 13. See also Recital 18 of Reg 1/2003 stating that the objective should be that each case is handled by a single authority. E Paulis and C Gauer, 'Le règlement n° 1/2003 et le principe du *ne bis in idem*' (E Paulis and C Gauer 'Le règlement n° 1/2003 et le principe du *nebis in idem*' [2005] Revue des droit de la Concurrence 32–40) paras 11–15.

[61] E Paulis and C Gauer, 'Le règlement n° 1/2003 et le principe du *ne bis in idem*' [2005] Revue des droit de la Concurrence 32–40 paras 27–33.

it has been penalized or declared not liable by a previous decision which is no longer subject to an appeal.[62] (In *Italcementi*, the Court stated that the application of *ne bis in idem* is subject to the threefold condition of identity of the facts, unity of offender and unity of the legal interest protected. Under that principle, the same person cannot be sanctioned more than once for a single unlawful course of conduct designed to protect the same legal asset.[63]

In its judgment relating to the *PVC II* decision,[64] the ECJ examined the question of whether the fact that the Commission had already ruled on the facts central to the case in its *PVC I* decision and the subsequent annulment of that decision by the ECJ would be compatible with the principle of *ne bis in idem*. In its judgment relating to the *PVC II* decision, the CFI had concluded that the *ne bis in idem* principle applies in Community law proceedings. According to the ECJ, the application of that principle presupposes that a ruling has been given on the question of whether an offence has in fact been committed or that the legality of the assessment thereof has been reviewed. The principle therefore merely prohibits a fresh assessment in depth of the alleged commission of an act

3.17

---

[62] Joined Cases C-238/99 P, C-244/99 P, C-245/99 P, C-247/99 P, C-250/99 P to C-252/99 P and C-254/99 P *Limburgse Vinyl Maatschappij and Others v EC Commission* [2002] ECR I-8375 paras 59, 62, and 96.

[63] Case C-213/00 P *Italcementi v EC Commission* [2003] ECR I-123 para 338 and Opinion of AG Ruiz-Jarabo Colomer paras 88–89. AG Colomer distanced himself from the ruling in *Walt Wilhelm* arguing that both national and Community competition laws pursue the same objective, i.e. the protection of competition within the EU. The ECJ did not need to rule on this point because there was no identity of facts in that case. E Paulis and C Gauer, 'Le règlement n° 1/2003 et le principe du *ne bis in idem*' [2005] Revue des droit de la Concurrence 32–40 paras 29–30 noting that under Reg 1/2003 the issue raised in *Walt Wilhelm* has lost much of its relevance given that the Commission and the NCAs apply the same set of rules although the Court refers to this consideration when it comes to international cartels where the Court has argued that an undertaking may be made the defendant to two parallel sets of proceedings concerning the same infringement and thus incur a double penalty, one imposed by the competent authority of a third country concerned and the other a Community penalty given that the possibility of concurrent sanctions is justified where the two sets of proceedings pursue different ends. Joined Cases T-236/01, T-239/01, T-244/01 to T-246/01, T-251/01 and T-252/01 *Tokai Carbon Co Ltd and others v EC Commission* (Case T-236/01 [2004] ECR II-1181 paras 130–134). T-224/00 *Archer Daniels Midland Company and Archer Daniels Midland Ingredients Ltd v EC Commission* [2003] ECR II-2597 paras 85–94.

[64] Joined Cases C-238/99 P, C-244/99 P, C-245/99 P, C-247/99 P, C-250/99 P to C-252/99 P and C-254/99 P *Limburgse Vinyl Maatschappij NV LVM and others v EC Commission* [2002] ECR 2002 I-8375 paras 59–62. The *PVC* proceedings should be seen against the background of the end of the *PVC I* procedure. In *PVC I*, the Commission investigated the behaviour of fourteen undertakings active in the PVC industry and fined all of them for infringement of Art 81 EC. On appeal, the CFI held the decision to be non-existent and dismissed the application as inadmissible. The Commission appealed to the ECJ, which set aside the CFI judgment and found the decision to be existent, but annulled it on procedural grounds. The Commission thereafter adopted a new decision which was addressed to almost all addressees of the original decision and which imposed fines of the same amounts. The *PVC* decision was again appealed. The CFI dismissed almost all of the applications.

which would result in the imposition of either a second penalty or first penalty in the event that a liability not established by the first decision is established by the second. However, the principle does not preclude the resumption of proceedings in respect of the same anti-competitive conduct where the first decision was annulled for procedural reasons without any ruling having been given on the substance of the facts alleged. The ECJ considers that in such circumstances the annulment cannot be regarded as an 'acquittal' within the meaning given to that expression in criminal law.[65] Since the decision of the Commission had been annulled for purely procedural reasons and the Court did not pronounce on the substance of the case, it did not therefore preclude the Commission from reaching another decision. If the decision had been annulled because a given conduct had been considered unproven by the Court, further proceedings could not have been brought by the Commission.[66] In a preliminary ruling on the interpretation of Article 54 of the Convention implementing the Schengen Agreement of 4 June 1985, the Court ruled that the *ne bis in idem* principle laid down in this provision would also apply to procedures whereby further prosecution is barred by way of a decision of the prosecuting authority of a Member State. The fact that no court would be involved in such a procedure and that the decision in which the procedure culminates would not take the form of a judicial decision would not alter this interpretation.[67]

3.18 **Acquittal and convictions in the enforcement system**   The prohibition of double prosecution and punishment does not exclude the possibility of parallel

---

[65] In such a case, the penalties imposed by the new decision are not added to those imposed by the annulled decision but replace them. Joined Cases C-238/99 P, C-244/99 P, C-245/99 P, C-247/99 P, C-250/99 P to C-252/99 P and C-254/99 P *LVM v EC Commission* [2002] ECR I-8375 para 62.

[66] K Dekeyser and C Gauer, 'The New Enforcement System for Arts 81 and 82 and the Rights of Defence', ch 23 in BE Hawk (ed), International Antitrust Law & Policy, Annual Proceedings of the Fordham Institute [2004] 549–85 (579); WPJ Wils, 'Ne Bis In Idem in EC Antitrust Enforcement: A Legal and Economic Analysis' [2004] World Competition—Law and Economics Review 131 (142). Wils takes the view that for example, in a case in which the main producers of some product for which the relevant geographic market is Europe had held a meeting on a certain date during which they had decided a concerted price increase and where this violation of Art 81 EC happens to be prosecuted first by the competition authority of a Member State, the Commission or the NCAs of the second Member State cannot bring a second prosecution even if either the national law of the first Member State or the practice of that competition authority lead that authority, when deciding on the amount of the fines, only to take into account the effects of the violation on its own national territory, and/or that the national law of that Member State only provides for low fines for violations of Art 81 EC. He asserts that the offence constituted by the main producers of a product for which the relevant geographic market is Europe, having held a meeting on a certain date during which they have decided a concerted price increase, constitutes a single violation of Art 81 EC, irrespective of any effect it may have had or not have had in any part of the Community. The principle of *ne bis in idem* prohibits multiple prosecution or punishments for the same offence, not merely for the same effects of an offence.

[67] Joined Cases C-187/01 and C-385/01 *Criminal proceedings against Hüseyin Gözütok and Klaus Brügge* [2003] ECR I-1345 paras 25–34.

proceedings being conducted by several members of the network of competition authorities at the same time against the same defendants, as long as none of these proceedings has already reached the stage of final acquittal or conviction. This means that at a preliminary stage, when it may not yet be clear which member of the network is best placed to deal with the case; several competition authorities may investigate the same agreement or practice. However, no later than the moment when the first proceeding is ended by a final acquittal or conviction, the other authorities have to discontinue their proceedings with regard to the same defendants.[68] The question is only which decisions constitute an acquittal or a conviction for the application of the principle of *ne bis in idem*.[69] All competition authorities can adopt cease and desist orders, decisions imposing fines, decisions accepting commitments, decisions rejecting complaints, and termination proceedings. While a decision imposing a fine for an infringement in regard to a certain market would prevent another authority from taking a decision concerning the effects in the same market,[70] the other types of decisions

---

[68] The principle of *ne bis in idem* enshrined in Art II–110 (Right not to be tried or punished twice in criminal proceedings for the same criminal offence) of the Charter of Fundamental Rights of the European Union [2004] OJ C310/41 applies not only within the jurisdiction of one Member State but also between the jurisdictions of several Member States. It thus forms part of those principles and fundamental rights which should also govern the interpretation and application of Reg 1/2003. See Reg 1/2003, Recital 37. Multiple prosecutions can be largely avoided on the ground that, when imposing fines in cases allocated to them, NCAs not only have the power, but are also obliged to take account of the effects of the infringement within the European Union. In such cases, the principle of double jeopardy would prevent a subsequent prosecution and fine for the same offence by another EU competition law authority. See WPJ Wils, 'The Principle of Ne Bis In Idem in EC Antitrust Enforcement: A Legal and Economic Analysis' (n 66 above) 134–48. However, it is questionable whether the EU's intention was to grant new and extensive extra-territorial powers to the NCAs. See N Levy and R O'Donoghue 'The EU Leniency Programme Comes of Age' [2004] World Competition—Law and Economics Review 75–99 (95), fn 84.

[69] Following a Greek initiative (Initiative of the Hellenic Republic with a view to adopting a Council Framework Decision concerning the application of the *ne bis in idem* principle [2003] OJ C100/24), a framework decision is under discussion which would require that whoever has been prosecuted and finally judged in one Member State cannot be prosecuted for the same acts in another Member State if either acquitted or convicted serving or having served the sentence, subject to some restrictions. The draft decision contains in its definition of 'criminal offences' the following (Art 1): 'acts which constitute administrative offences or breaches of order that are punished by an administrative authority by a fine [. . .] provided that they fall within the jurisdiction of the administrative authority and the person concerned is able to bring the matter before a criminal court.' Where administrative proceedings leading to the imposition of a fine for competition law infringement would be covered by this definition, the decision, if it becomes law, may affect the decentralized system of competition law enforcement. R Smits, 'The European Competition Network' [2005] Legal Issues of Economic Integration 175–92 (187).

[70] This would also hold true for 'leniency' decisions: where the Commission granted immunity or reduced the fine in Community-wide cartel proceedings, an NCA would be prevented from taking action in regard to the same conduct. This may be the consequence of a combined reading of the principle of *ne bis in idem* and Art 10 EC which obliges the NCAs and the cooperation to 'sincere cooperation'. See below at para 3.20.

would require a closer analysis. Decisions accepting commitments do not take a position either on the existence of an infringement prior to the commitments or on the absence of infringement after the commitments.[71] In addition, Regulation 1/2003 allows NCAs and national courts to act against the infringement after a commitment decision.[72] In the same vein, decisions rejecting complaints may not be regarded as acquittals either.[73] They are not addressed to the undertaking subject to the proceeding and merely settle the relationship between the authority and the complainant. The Commission may always act against an infringement even if one or several NCAs have rejected a complaint against that same infringement. Conversely, NCAs may act against an infringement even if the Commission rejected a complaint against that same infringement.[74] More complicated are decisions ordering that an infringement is brought to an end without imposing a fine. While they contain a finding of an infringement, they do not impose a sanction on the undertaking for past infringement and may be considered as an acquittal as far as the imposition of fines are concerned.[75] Similar reasoning may apply to declarations of inapplicability under Article 10 of Regulation 1/2003.[76]

---

[71] Art 9 of Reg 1/2003. E Paulis and C Gauer, 'Le règlement n° 1/2003 et le principe du *ne bis in idem*' [2005] Revue des droit de la Concurrence 32–40 para 61.

[72] Recital 13 of Reg 1/2003. K Dekeyser and C Gauer, 'The New Enforcement System for Arts 81 and 82 and the Rights of Defence', ch 23 in BE Hawk (ed), International Antitrust Law & Policy, Annual Proceedings of the Fordham Institute [2004] 549–85 (579) Hawk at 549–85 (82) points out that the preliminary ruling in *Brügge/Gözütok* might be construed as meaning that a settlement with a public prosecutor would trigger the application of the *ne bis in idem* principle and that commitment decisions are a kind of settlement with the competition authorities (Joined Cases C-187/01 and C-385/01 *Gözütok and Klaus Brügge* [2003] ECR I-1345. However, these decisions would not constitute a sanction of the infringement and they do not exclude any further prosecution. In the same sense, see E Paulis and C Gauer, 'Le règlement n° 1/2003 et le principe du *ne bis in idem*' para 61.

[73] K Dekeyser and C Gauer, 'The New Enforcement System for Arts 81 and 82 and the Rights of Defence', ch 23 in BE Hawk (ed), International Antitrust Law & Policy, Annual Proceedings of the Fordham Institute [2004] 549–85 (579) take the view that this applies to all types of rejection of complaints, be it for lack of Community interest or for lack of substantiation etc. E Paulis and C Gauer, 'Le règlement n° 1/2003 et le principe du *ne bis in idem*' paras 62–64.

[74] Commission Notice on the handling of complaints by the Commission under Arts 81 and 82 EC ('Notice on Handling of Complaints') para 79. E Paulis and C Gauer, 'Le règlement n° 1/2003 et le principe du *ne bis in idem*' [2005] Revue des droit de la Concurrence 32–40 para 64 indicates that the rejection of complaints would not require prior consultation between the Commission and the NCAs.

[75] K Dekeyser and C Gauer, 'The New Enforcement System for Arts 81 and 83 and the Rights of Defence', ch 23 in BE Hawk (ed), International Antitrust Law & Policy, Annual Proceedings of the Fordham Institute [2004] 549–85 (579). E Paulis and C Gauer, 'Le règlement n° 1/2003 et le principe du *ne bis in idem*' [2005] Revue des droit de la Concurrence 32–40 para 66 suggest that the application of *ne bis in idem* should also be extended to cases where the Commission announced its intention to impose a fine but abstained from doing so in light of the arguments put forward by the undertaking in question.

[76] E Paulis and C Gauer, 'Le règlement n° 1/2003 et le principe du *ne bis in idem*' [2005] Revue des droit de la Concurrence 32–40 para 67.

Sanctions imposed by third-country authorities The Community Courts **3.19** have also decided on the application of the principle in cases where a third country competition authority and the Commission adopt decisions relating to a worldwide cartel. As indicated, in these cases, they have always rejected the application of the *ne bis in idem* principle arguing that the two laws pursue obviously different ends. The Courts also rejected the idea that natural justice would require that the sanction imposed for a worldwide cartel by third country authorities have to be deducted from the sanction that may be imposed by the Commission.[77] There is the suggestion that the Commission should be bound, at least, by a 'general requirement of natural justice' flowing from the general principle of proportionality and requiring the Commission to consider the amount of a first sanction imposed in non-EU Member States by reducing the amount of the (second) sanction. The objective of avoiding over-punishment should also apply outside the EU.[78]

2. The ECN and the cooperation mechanism

In order to find out about possible parallel proceedings and to ensure consistency, **3.20** Regulation 1/2003 sets out a number of obligations for NCAs to provide information in regard to the opening of cases and the decisions that they intend

---

[77] Case 7/72 *Boehringer v EC Commission* [1972] ECR 1281 paras 3–6; Case T-224/00 *Archer Daniels Midland and Archer Daniels Midlands Ingredients v EC Commission* [2003] ECR II-2597 para 103, stating that 'has in no way been shown that the penalty imposed in the United States related to application of the cartel or its effects other than in the United States [. . .]. It continued and stated that an extension to the EEA would have *clearly encroached on the territorial jurisdiction of the Commission*'. See also Case T-71/03 *Tokai Carbon v EC Commission* [2005] OJ C205/18 para 116: '[. . .] In so far as SGL claims that that agreement entails the application of the principle of ne bis in idem in relations between the United States and the Community, the applicant's argument is based on an erroneous reading of that agreement. It is clear from Art I(2)(b) and Art III of that agreement that the legal interests protected by the Community authorities and the US authorities are not the same and that the purpose of the agreement is not the principle of ne bis in idem but solely to enable the authorities of one of the contracting parties to take advantage of the practical effects of a procedure initiated by the authorities of the other. [. . .]' In this case, the CFI considered that the penalties imposed in the US for SGL's participation in the graphite electrodes cartel concerned a distinct market and involved different members. Note that SGL filed an appeal against the decision. Case C328/05 P *SGL Carbon AG v EC Commission* (pending).

[78] C Canenbley and M Rosenthal, 'Cooperation between Antitrust Authorities In-and Outside the EU: What does it mean for Multinational Corporations?—Part 2' [2005] ECLR 179–87 (183) noting that pursuant to Art 23 of Reg 1/2003, the Commission is entitled to set fines on the basis of the *total* (worldwide) turnover of the companies found in violation of Arts 81 and 82 EC who also ask whether the Commission in Microsoft (Case COMP/37.792 *Microsoft*. See Commission Press release IP/04/382 'Commission concludes on Microsoft investigation, imposes conduct remedies and a fine') could impose such far-reaching remedies after the US Consent Decree had already redressed the anti-competitive behaviour.

to adopt. The exchange of information between the Commission and NCA's can occur through various channels.[79] Furthermore, Regulation 1/2003 provides for a suspension mechanism with respect to parallel proceedings, which could lead an NCA to suspend a proceeding or reject a complaint where another NCA is already investigating the same agreement, decision of an association or practice.[80] Both provisions are described in more detail below. In order to guarantee the consistency of the system, Article 11 of the Regulation 1/2003 provides that NCAs should inform other members of the network of the cases they are dealing with.[81] In particular:

- The Commission is required to provide NCAs with the most important documents related to, *inter alia*, the following: the application of EC law, the adoption of interim measures; investigations in possible infringements; the acceptance of commitments; the adoption of decisions of inapplicability; and decisions to withdraw the benefits of block exemption to agreements.[82] The exchange of information under Article 11(2) of Regulation 1/2003 covers only such documents which the Commission currently has in its possession.[83]

---

[79] Under Art 10(1) of Reg 17, the Commission was required to provide to the NCAs copies of the most important documents lodged with the Commission for purposes of establishing an infringement of Arts 81 or 82, or when it issues a negative clearance or decision applying of Art 81(3).

[80] Art 13 of Reg 1/2003.

[81] The Director-General of DG COMP, P Lowe found that '[. . .] [Reg 17] created a star-like scheme that involves in particular considerable flows of information from the Commission to the national competition authorities about Commission cases and the opportunity for the national enforcers to comment collectively—through the Advisory Committee. Reg 1/2003 turns the beams of this star-like system into two-way streets as Member States authorities will now also inform the Commission about their cases and consult the Commission on their draft decisions. The Reg moreover provides for the involvement of the other national competition authorities in the overall context of close co-operation as provided for in Art 11(1) of the new Reg. Thus, the ultimate structure of the network is no longer that of a star but that of a web. [. . .]'. P Lowe, 'Implications of the Recent Reforms in the Antitrust Enforcement in Europe For National Competition authorities, Address at the Italian Competition Consumer Day', Rome, 9 December 2003.

[82] Art 11(2) Reg 1/22003. Therefore, the term 'most important' may generally refer to documents which the Commission collected when applying the (first) investigative measures under Chapter V of Reg 1/2003, leaving aside the withdrawal of block exemptions. It may be assumed that the Commission has the exclusive power to determine which are the most important documents. See D Reichelt, 'To what extent does the cooperation within the European Competition Network protect the rights of the undertakings?' (2005) CML Rev 745–82 (758/59). See also Judge JD Cooke, 'Application of EC Competition Rules by National Courts', Antitrust Reform in Europe: A Year in Practice, 9–11 March 2005, Brussels, International Bar Association (IBA) takes the view that there would not appear to be any reason why a decision to transmit taken by the Commission should not be justifiable by direct action before the CFI.

[83] There is no possibility of the undertaking examining whether all relevant documents have been transmitted as the correspondence between the ECN members is not accessible to undertakings. See D Reichelt, 'To what extent does the cooperation within the European Competition

- NCAs shall inform the Commission when they start a proceeding under Article 81 or 82 EC. This information may be available to other NCAs.[84] In practice, this will be done in each case by means of the completion of a standard form containing limited details of the case, such as the authority dealing with the case, the product, territories and parties concerned, the nature and suspected duration of the alleged infringement and the origin of the case.[85]

- NCAs shall supply the Commission, no later than thirty days prior to the adoption of a decision, with a summary of the case and a copy of the draft decision or, in the absence thereof, any other document indicating the proposed course of action.[86] This prior consultation duty applies to: (i) prohibition decisions; (ii) acceptance of commitments; and (iii) withdrawal of block exemptions; but not to (i) rejections of complaints; or (ii) decisions to take no action.[87] The obligation to consult may serve as a check on concerns that NCAs could feel tempted to prohibit or punish particularly the behaviour of a foreign undertaking. If such bias exists, the Commission could remove the case from the acting national authority. As far as the exchange of information

---

Network protect the rights of the undertakings?' (2005) CML Rev 745–82 (758–59). See also Judge JD Cooke, 'Application of EC Competition Rules by National Courts', Antitrust Reform in Europe: A Year in Practice, 9–11 March 2005, Brussels, International Bar Association (IBA) raises the question whether an undertaking may challenge the transfer of documents in situations where the Commission's acquisition derived from an illegal act.

[84] As a rule the information will be made available to all members of the network. This can be deduced from para 10 of the Joint Statement of the Council and the Commission on the functioning of the network.

[85] Art 11(3) of Reg 1/2003. The undertaking subject to investigative measures by an NCA can expect that this minimum information is transmitted to all other ECN members, also because the Commission has stated that it forwards the information on first investigative measures automatically. D Reichelt, 'To what extent does the cooperation within the European Competition Network protect the rights of the undertakings?' (2005) CML Rev 745–82 (760).

[86] In the period from 1 May 2004 until 31 December 2004, the Commission was informed of thirty-three competition cases where an NCA envisaged adopting a decision pursuant to Art 81 and/or Art 82. Of these cases nineteen related to Art 91, thirteen to Art 82 and two to both provisions. In some of these cases the Commission provided the NCA with comments, but in none of them did it start proceedings under Art 11(6) with the effect of relieving the NCA of its competence. Commission Report on Competition Policy SEC (2004) 805 final para 110. The obligation to provide the information can also extend to, if the Commission requests so, to other documents 'which are necessary for the assessment of the case'. See D Reichelt, 'To what extent does the cooperation within the European Competition Network protect the rights of the undertakings?' (2005) CML Rev 745–82, 761.

[87] When comparing the list of types of decisions in the first sentence of Art 11(4) with the list of decisions in Art 5 of Reg 1/2003, it appears that there is no obligation for NCAs to consult the Commission on decisions imposing fines or other penalties unless these decisions also include an order requiring the infringement to be brought to an end (which may not be the case in decisions regarding past infringements). However, the understanding within the ECN network is that consultation will take place on all decisions imposing fines or other penalties. K Dekeyser, 'Reg 1/2003: First Experiences' (IBC Conference London, 27 and 28 April 2005) reported that the Commission had been informed of fifty envisaged decisions during the first eleven months.

with other NCAs is concerned, the information may be shared with other NCAs.[88]

3.21 The mechanisms to ensure consistency do not appear to be very robust. An NCA planning to adopt a decision is not required to take the Commission's comments into account, and the only way for the Commission to intervene is by taking over the case, a rather drastic measure that might have a significant impact on the companies under investigation. The Commission is also under a duty to advise or consult the authorities in the Member States when it intends to carry out investigations in their territory. The NCAs must assist the Commission during such investigations. The Commission may further request NCAs to undertake investigations in their own territory to obtain information for the Commission.[89] Member States are entitled to take part in hearings at which undertakings submit their observations. Finally, the authorities in the Member States may be called on to co-operate in the enforcement of decisions imposing fines, in accordance with the procedure contained in Article 256 EC. Regulation 1/2003 provides that one NCA may ask another NCA for assistance in order to collect information on its behalf.

Exchange of information

3.22 The question of gathering information has become more important in recent years. Recent ECJ judgments[90] suggest that the amount of information that the Commission should gather from undertakings in order to prove the existence of an anticompetitive practice is critical to the validity of its assessment. The ECN Cooperation Notice suggests that the functioning of the system is based to a large extent on exchange of information between the NCAs, and in some respect on the voluntary submission of information from undertakings to either the Commission or an NCA. Article 12 of Regulation 1/2003 states that the Commission and the NCAs shall have the power to provide one another with and use in evidence any matter of fact or law, including confidential

---

[88] It may be argued that the transmission referred to in Art 11(4) is limited to NCAs *dealing with the case* because the transmission of this information occurs no longer for the purpose of case allocation but concerns the procedural stage before the adoption of a decision. D Reichelt, 'To what extent does the cooperation within the European Competition Network protect the rights of the undertakings?' (2005) CML Rev 745–82 (758–59).

[89] Under Art 22(2) of Reg 1/2003, the Commission can ask an NCA to carry out an inspection on its behalf. Commission Report on Competition Policy SEC (2004) 805 final para 108 stating that Art 22 was used eleven times in eight months.

[90] See, e.g. Case T-56/02 *Bayerische Hypo- und Vereinsbank AG v EC Commission* [2004] OJ C314/14 para 119: '[. . .] All of the evidence just examined permits the conclusion that the Commission has not adduced to the requisite legal standard proof of the existence of the agreement which it claimed to exist, relating both to the fixing of the prices for currency exchange services of the euro-zone currencies and also to the ways of charging those prices. [. . .]'.

information.[91] The information transferred would not only cover the information collected under Article 22 (inspection) but presumably also information received and acquired from any party (including a complainant) without any need for the NCA to exercise powers of inquiry.[92] This means that exchange of information is not only taking place between an NCA and the Commission but also between and amongst NCAs. While this is an enabling power in that there is no duty on an ECN member to transmit information to another member,[93] it is the variety in the types of penalties, which can be imposed by the different members of the network of NCAs that could raise concerns with regard to the exchange of evidence within the network. However, Regulation 1/2003 contains certain safeguards with respect to the use of confidential information exchanged within the network, which the ECN Cooperation Notice expands on in more detail.[94]

Information supplied under Article 12 is supplied principally for the purpose of applying the Community rules and may only be used 'in respect of the subject matter for which it was collected'.[95] Regulation 1/2003 does not go into further detail about what is meant by 'subject matter' but it may be reasonably construed as meaning more than simply that both the transmitting and receiving NCA are pursuing the same parties in relation to the same infringement.[96] This **3.23**

---

[91] CS Kerse and N Khan, *EC Antitrust Procedure* (5th edn, 2005) para 5–012 indicate that the wording of Art 12 is designed to overcome any problems caused by restrictions on use and confidentiality whether under Community or national law. However, there is no express obligation to transfer relevant information under Art 12 with the only exception being Art 22 (the exchange and use of any information collected by one NCA in carrying out an inspection on behalf of another must be carried out under Art 12(2). D Reichelt, 'To what extent does the cooperation within the European Competition Network protect the rights of the undertakings?' (2005) CML Rev 745–82 (754) regarding the question whether Art 11 and Art 12 of Reg 1/2003 provide for the obligation to exchange information or the possibility of a voluntary exchange, respectively.

[92] CS Kerse and N Khan, *EC Antitrust Procedure* (5th edn, 2005) para 5–013 who also note that this should also include information pulled together from the domestic files of an NCA. The objective of Art 12 would be frustrated if an NCA were unable to transfer all the information on its file following upon a reallocation decision within the Network.

[93] K Dekeyser and E De Smijter, 'The Exchange of Evidence Within the ECN' [2005] Legal Issues of Economic Integration 161–74 (164–65) point to the question of how the option of Art 12 relates to the duty of loyal co-operation under Art 10 EC. The combined reading of both provisions may lead to an obligation for ECN members to exchange information between them.

[94] ECN Cooperation Notice para 26.

[95] The purpose restriction may stand in contrast to Arts 11, 13 and 22 of Reg 1/2003 which contain a broad variety of specific situations in which rights and obligations of the ECN members to exchange information exist. D Reichelt, 'To what extent does the cooperation within the European Competition Network protect the rights of the undertakings?' (2005) CML Rev 745–82 (754).

[96] CS Kerse and N Khan, *EC Antitrust Procedure* (5th edn, 2005) para 5–015. The Commission refers to the ECJ ruling in Case 85/87 *Dow Benelux v EC Commission* [1989] ECR 3137 para 20.

would mean that information collected in the context of an investigation of a suspected cartel in a given product market (e.g. widgets) could not be used as evidence against a cartel involving all or a number of the same parties in another product market (e.g. blodgets).[97] Thus, this would amount to a restriction of the use of information. Where the NCA wishes to use the information in the context of its own proceedings, Regulation 1/2003 is based on the premise that the enforcement of Community rules prevails over the enforcement of domestic law. The information can be used where national competition law is applied in the same case and in parallel to Community competition law and does not lead to a different outcome. Possibly, a different outcome would mean that national law would authorize conduct prohibited under Community law and prohibit under national law conduct that is authorized under EC law. Regulation 1/2003 does not specify what would happen if an NCA ceases to apply Community law because there is no effect on inter-State trade. While it seems that the application of national law may be excluded because it would not apply 'in the same case and in parallel', it is also true that the limitation on the use of information in Article 12(2) restricts the use of evidence in national proceedings.

3.24 There is some debate about how the option of Article 12 of Regulation 1/2003 relates to the duty of loyal cooperation as laid down in Article 10 EC. The ECJ has ruled that Article 10 imposes on the European institutions and the EU Member States mutual duties of sincere cooperation with a view to attaining the objective of the EC, which may also include the duty of the Commission to transmit information it holds to national courts.[98] Conversely, an NCA may be under a duty to provide the Commission or another NCA with the information it holds. This interpretation would reflect the need that Community institutions and NCAs have to assist one another in the application of competition rules and Article 12 of Regulation 1/2003 may thus turn into an obligation.[99] If this is true, the obligation would not be unlimited: based on the ECJ's case law, the Commission may refuse to transmit information for overriding reasons relating to the need to safeguard

---

[97] Example used by Kerse and Khan para 5–015.

[98] See, e.g. Case 2/88 *Imm JJ Zwartfeld and others* [1990] ECR I-3365 para 17: '[. . .] *relations between the Member States and the Community institutions are governed, according to [Art 10EC] of the EEC Treaty, by a principle of sincere cooperation*'. See also Case C-275/00 *European Community v First NV and Franex NV* [2002] ECR I-10943 para 49 in relation to the duties of national courts. See also regarding the duty to disapply national legislation which contravenes Community law not only for national courts but also to all organs of the State, including administrative authorities Case C-198/01 *Consorzio Industrie Fiammiferi (CIF) v Autorità Garante della Concorrenza e del Mercato* [2003] ECR I-8055. See also J Temple Lang, 'Developments, Issues and New Remedies—The Duties of National Authorities and Courts under Art 10 of the EC Treaty' [2004] Fordham International Law Journal 1904–39 (1928).

[99] K Dekeyser and E De Smijter, 'The Exchange of Evidence Within the ECN' [2005] Legal Issues of Economic Integration 161–74 (164–165).

the interest of the Community or to avoid any interference with its functioning and independence, in particular by jeopardizing the accomplishment of the tasks entrusted to it.[100] The safeguards relating to, for example, the protection of confidential information and leniency application may thus be read in this sense. For example, where the Commission has granted immunity to an undertaking under its Leniency programme, an NCA may have the duty not to impose full fines under national law using information disclosed to the Commission.[101]

Professional secrecy Article 28(1) of Regulation 1/2003 provides that information obtained pursuant to Articles 17 and 22 can only be used for the purpose for which it was acquired. Accordingly, such information is generally not available for use by NCAs under their own competition laws or other national laws.[102] In addition, Article 28(2) EC imposes an obligation not to disclose information covered by professional secrecy, which includes business secrets and other confidential information.[103] Nevertheless, this obligation is without prejudice to the exchange of necessary information in order to prove an infringement of Articles 81 and 82 EC. The term 'professional secrecy' is a Community law concept that aims to create a common minimum level of protection throughout the Community.[104] Because of the primacy of EC law, NCAs cannot rely on national law provisions in order not to send the confidential information to other ECN members[105] but they need to have an effective procedure in place in order to ensure that information which circulates within the ECN remains within the ECN.   **3.25**

Before transmitting confidential information the Commission may have to consider carefully the implications of the possibility of 'information leaks'   **3.26**

---

[100] Case C-275/00 *European Community v First NV and Franex NV* [2002] ECR I-1043 para 49; Case C-2/88 *Zwartveld* [1990] ECR I-3365 para 17.

[101] See also J Temple Lang, 'Developments, Issues and New Remedies—The Duties of National Authorities and Courts under Art 10 of the EC Treaty' [2004] Fordham International Law Journal 1904–39 (1929) who bases this duty on Art 10 EC. Otherwise, if an NCA would be able to use the information disclosed to impose a full fine for violation of *national* competition law, this would defeat the aims of the Leniency Notice.

[102] CS Kerse and N Khan (5th edn, 2005) indicate that the restriction of use offsets the broad power of enquiry in Arts 17 and 22 and is necessary to ensure the undertaking's defence rights were the Commission able to rely on evidence obtained during an investigation not related to the subject matter of the proceedings.

[103] Art 28 of Reg 1/2003. See ch 9 'Penalties, Confidentiality' paras 9.24 and what follows.

[104] ECN Cooperation Notice ([2004] C101/43) para 28.

[105] In those cases where the transmitting ECN member before or after transmission has classified information as confidential on the basis of national legislation, such classification would not be binding for the receiving ECN member, although the latter may take this qualification into account as much as possible. K Dekeyser and E De Smijter, 'The Exchange of Evidence Within the ECN' [2005] Legal Issues of Economic Integration 161–74 (68) and fn 14.

from the competition authorities.[106] In *SEP*, the ECJ acknowledged that the prohibition on disclosure does not guarantee that information contained in the documents sent to national authorities will not be taken into consideration by them or by their officials for other purposes.[107] The obligation of the Commission to provide information to NCAs would have to be read in light of the general principles of the right of undertakings to the protection of their business secrets.[108] However, this does not of course result in an automatic ban on the exchange of confidential information, where the relevant undertaking would have to invoke before the Commission the confidential nature of a document vis-à-vis the competent NCAs .[109] The general principle of the protection of business secrets, referred to above, may limit the Commission's obligation under Article 12(1) of Regulation 1/2003—together with Article 10 EC—to transmit the document to the competent national authorities. Whether the *SEP* issue—i.e. parties raising the confidentiality of the material supplied—continues to be of particular relevance under Regulation 1/2003 remains to be seen. In any event, there is nothing in Regulation 1/2003 or the accompanying notices which would limit the freedom to transfer information or which would provide for the possibility of a party to contest such a transfer.[110] The

---

[106] See Case T-39/90 *NV Samenwerkende Elektriciteits-Produktiebedrijven v EC Commission* [1991] ECR II-1497 para 25: '[. . .] Commission is entitled to require the disclosure only of information which may enable it to investigate putative infringements which justify the conduct of the inquiry and are set out in the request for information. [. . .]'.

[107] On appeal the ECJ disagreed with the CFI and stated that the restriction imposed by Art 20(1) of Reg 11 (Art 28 of Reg 1/2003) would ensure that the Dutch authorities and officials who had received confidential information from the Commission could not effectively be required to disregard the relevant information regarding a competitor when it fell to them to determine the commercial policy of a public enterprise under their supervision. Case C-36/92 P *Samenwerkende Elektriciteits-Produktiebedrijven (SEP) NV v EC Commission* [1994] ECR I-1911 para 30. See CS Kerse and N Khan, *EC Antitrust Procedure* (5th edn, 2005) para 5–010.

[108] Case C-36/92 P *Samenwerkende Elektriciteits-Produktiebedrijven (SEP) NV v EC Commission* [1994] ECR I-1911 para 36.

[109] Parties supplying information to the Commission should clearly indicate relevant sensitive material and that the 'SEP proviso' has been invoked. CS Kerse and N Khan, *EC Antitrust Procedure* (5th edn, 2005) para 5–010.

[110] Kerse and Khan at para 5–010 note that the *SEP* situation has lost some of its relevance in that many Member States have independent competition authorities. Further, Art 35 of Reg 1/ 2003 imposes the obligation to designate competition authorities that are capable of 'effectively' complying with the requirements under Reg 1/2003. D Reichelt, 'To what extent does the cooperation within the European Competition Network protect the rights of the undertakings?' (2005) CML Rev 745–82 (771) takes the view that the 'SEP proviso' may still be good law but is only applicable in particular set of circumstances. It seems that the disclosure of business secrets within the ECN only affects the right to protect business secrets only if one or more ECN members acts or act as *economic entities*. Then, an exchange of the information can be objected to for reasons of confidentiality where one of the NCA has to be classified as 'third party'. C Gauer, 'Due Process in the Face of Divergent National Procedures and Sanctions', Antitrust Reform in Europe: A Year in Practice, 9–11 March 2005, Brussels, International Bar Association (IBA) 12–13 believes that the SEP situation would not exist anymore. Member States have set up competition authorities which are not linked to State-owned companies and the risk has therefore

Commission has been at pains to point out that the same strict standard already applied under the old enforcement system, where the competition authorities of the Member States were fully informed about the cases dealt with by the Commission, including business secrets and other confidential information. Similarly, the Commission had the power to obtain all types of information from the Member States. This system never created any substantial problems. Regulation 1/2003 introduces the additional possibility of exchanging information between national competition authorities. This information also comes within the common standard of professional secrecy.[111]

Evidence Regulation 1/2003 draws a distinction between the use of information against legal and natural persons. Recital 16 provides that when the information is used by the receiving authority to impose sanctions on undertakings, there should be no other limit to the use of the information than the obligation to use it for the purpose for which it was collected. This is justified by the fact that the sanctions imposed on undertakings are of the same type in all systems and consequently the defence rights enjoyed by undertakings can be considered as sufficiently equivalent.[112] Article 12(2) of Regulation 1/2003 states that the exchanged information can only be used in evidence for the purpose of applying Article 81 or 82 EC and respecting the subject matter for which it was collected by the transmitting authority. It adds that where national competition law is applied in the same case and in parallel to Community competition law and does not lead to a different outcome, information exchanged may also be used for the application of national competition law. **3.27**

This limitation on the application of EC law is consistent with the overall scope and purpose of Regulation 1/2003, which is limited to the application of Articles 81 and 82 EC. The reference to 'national competition laws' must be read in light of Article 3 of Regulation 1/2003, which contemplates the cumulative application of EC and national competition laws in given cases. The expression 'in the same case and in parallel' in Article 12 should restrict the recipient authorities' powers to the cumulative application governed by Article 3(1). There is no scope for the use of the information exchanged in the application of 'stricter national laws which prohibit or sanction unilateral conduct' under the **3.28**

---

disappeared. She points out that there is no decision of transmission of the information which the undertaking could challenge but they may challenge the collection of the evidence.

[111] In practice, the transmission of confidential information between authorities will take place on the basis of encrypted mail or other secure ways of transmission. C Gauer, L Kjolbye, D Dalheimer, E de Smijter, D Schnichels, and M Laurila, 'Reg 1/2003 and the Modernisation Package fully applicable since 1 May 2004', Competition Policy Newsletter, Number 2, Summer 2004 4.

[112] See JS Venit and T Louko, 'The Commission's New Power to Question and its implications on Human Rights' ch 26 in BE Hawk (ed), International Antitrust Law & Policy, Annual Proceedings of the Fordham Institute [2004] 675–700 (679).

second paragraph of the same Article nor to cases where competition authorities apply 'merger control laws' or 'provisions of national law that predominantly pursue an objective different from that pursued by Articles 81 and 82' under Article 3(3) of Regulation 1/2003.[113] For any such situations, the recipient NCA will remain bound by the 'acute amnesia' rule in *Spanish Banks*.[114] On the other hand, it is not entirely clear whether evidence received from another NCA can be used as the basis for an infringement of the national provision that is equivalent to Article 81, even if the application of Community law is abandoned at the outset because there is no evidence of effect upon inter-State trade.[115]

3.29 As far as the restriction on the subject matter is concerned, it aims to ensure that the functioning of the ECN will not jeopardize the procedural guarantees in relation to the use of evidence in Articles 20(3) and (4) and 28(1) of Regulation 1/2003. The parallel provision in Regulation 17 was interpreted by the ECJ in *Dow Benelux* as preventing 'that information obtained during investigations' may eventually be 'used for purposes other than those indicated in the order or decision under which the investigation is carried out.'[116] It is not entirely clear what is meant by 'subject matter' in this context. It could refer to the specific complaint, which was being investigated by the transmitting authority so that its use would be confined to the undertakings identified in that complaint. It could also imply that the receiving authority would be entitled to make use of it in the course of an investigation into different undertakings suspected of a different practice, but in respect of the same reference market.[117]

3.30 *Sanctions* Article 12(3) of Regulation 1/2003 regulates the circumstances under which the exchanged information can be used for imposing sanctions on individuals. Regulation 1/2003 distinguishes between custodial sanctions and

---

[113] M Araujo, 'The Respect of Fundamental Rights within the European Network of Competition Authorities' ch 21 in BE Hawk (ed), International Antitrust Law & Policy, Annual Proceedings of the Fordham Institute [2004] 511–31 (527). See also ch 9 'Penalties, Confidentiality' para 9.28 regarding the issue of whether Art 12 is a legislative modification of the ECJ case law in Spanish Banks. See also D Reichelt 'To what extent does the cooperation within the European Competition Network protect the rights of the undertakings?' (2005) CML Rev 745–82 (777–78).

[114] C-67/91 *Dirección General de Defensa de la Competencia v Asociación Española de Banca Privada* [1992] ECR I- 4785 paras 35–39. In this case the ECJ was not persuaded that the absence from Art 20 of Reg 17 of references to other provisions under which the Commission obtained information necessarily meant that information obtained otherwise under the Regulation could be freely used by national authorities as evidence in their national law procedures. NCAS were not however required to suffer 'acute amnesia'. They can consider the information in deciding whether to initiate national proceedings. CS Kerse and N Khan (5th edn, 2005) para 5–009.

[115] JD Cooke, 'General Report' in *The Modernization of EU Competition Law Enforcement in the EU*, FIDE 2004 National Reports 630–60 (655).

[116] Case 85/87 *Dow Benelux v EC Commission* [1989] ECR 3137 para 17.

[117] JD Cooke, 'General Report' in *The Modernization of EU Competition Law Enforcement in the EU*, FIDE 2004 National Reports 630–60 (655).

other types of sanctions such as fines. The exchange of information for the purpose of applying Articles 81 and 82 EC is precluded unless both the laws of the transmitting and the receiving authorities provide sanctions of a similar kind in respect of individuals. In the event that the two legal systems involved do not provide sanctions of a similar kind, the exchange of information can only take place if the same level of protection of the individual rights is given in both countries. In this latter case, however, the information cannot be used by the receiving authority in order to impose custodial sanctions. This provision should ensure that to the extent that differences in procedural rights and guarantees result from differences in the kind of sanctions which can be imposed by the different members of the network, the exchange of information within the network cannot lead to any procedural right or guarantee being weakened or undermined.[118]

This system gives rise to a various questions: when the members of the network **3.31** assists each other in collecting evidence, it may well occur that one member of the network, either of its own initiative or at the second NCA's request, collects, in accordance with the law governing the investigative powers of the first NCA, evidence[119] which the second NCA could not have lawfully collected under its own law, and transfers this evidence to the second NCA so as to allow it to use the evidence. In Ireland, for example, where Articles 81 and 82 EC have been made part of criminal law, a person interrogated in connection with a potentially criminal offence is entitled to be cautioned that any information given may be used in evidence against him. For example, if the Dutch NCA obtained information from interviews in the course of investigating a suspected infringement by Dutch and Irish undertakings, the question arises whether that information

---

[118] For example, this would prevent the Commission from transmitting information to NCA in relation to the questioning of an individual because Art 12(3) of Reg 1/2003 states that the information can only be used against the individual if it has been collected by an authority which has similar sanctions for individuals. K Dekeyser, 'Session IV, Rights, Privileges and Ethics in Competition Cases' ch 28 in BE Hawk (ed), International Antitrust Law & Policy Annual Proceedings of the Fordham Institute [2004] 731–79 (741). C Gauer, 'Due Process in the Face of Divergent National Procedures and Sanctions', Antitrust Reform in Europe: A Year in Practice, 9–11 March 2005, Brussels, International Bar Association (IBA) 15 notes that, for example, the commercial manager of a company could be asked to mention the meetings with the competitors he attended on behalf of the undertaking and that information could be used to establish his own role in the infringement. The undertaking is under an obligation to answer but the individual speaking on behalf of the undertaking does not run any personal risk: his or her statements cannot be used against him in any proceedings because if he or she had been the target of the investigation he or she would have had a right to remain silent. See also ch 7 'Formal Investigation Measures' paras 7.49 *et seq.*

[119] D Reichelt, 'To what extent does the cooperation within the European Competition Network protect the rights of the undertakings?' (2005) CML Rev 745–82 (752) raises the issue that it may not be always obvious to the transmitting authority whether the information gathering was in compliance with all the relevant provisions of domestic law. Only the transmitting authority can exercise an effective control over what information is posted on the ECN.

could be used if transmitted to the Irish NCA for the purpose of prosecuting the Irish company if it had been obtained without any caution being given in the Netherlands.[120]

3.32 This issue was raised in the UK consultation on the new OFT competition law guidelines during which concern was expressed about the possibility that the OFT could use in evidence documents which might have benefited from legal professional privilege if they had been collected by the OFT in the UK but which do not benefit from legal professional privilege in the Member State where the documents were actually collected. The OFT stated that when it receives information from another competition authority it is the law of the Member State of the transmitting authority that governs whether the information was lawfully collected, not the relevant provisions of UK law.[121] Whether this would also be the case where an NCA, being aware of the existence of in-house counsel documentation concerning a given conduct (potentially as a result of a failed request for information or investigation) and unable to request it under national law, invites another authority able under its national rules to request that same documentation and transmit it under Regulation 1/2003, is subject to debate. In this situation, irrespective of whether this may be allowed under Community law, it may happen that national law would prevent the use of information so collected. Assuming the receiving authority should not be able to use evidence so obtained, the next question may be whether evidence not complying with national standards may be accepted at all. Regulation 1/2003 does not seem to distinguish between information received under a lower standard and information required specifically from another authority in the knowledge of such lower standards.[122]

---

[120] JD Cooke, 'General Report' in *The Modernization of EU Competition Law Enforcement in the EU*, FIDE 2004 National Reports 630–660 (655). See also CS Kerse and N Khan (5th edn, 2005) para 5–013 noting that Art 12 of Reg 1/2003 does not provide clear or precise answers to these questions. K Dekeyser and E De Smijter, 'The Exchange of Evidence Within the ECN' [2005] Legal Issues of Economic Integration 161–74 note that the mutual recognition of a common minimum standard of fundamental rights, these differences should not prevent the receiving NCA from using information legally collected by the transmitting ECN.

[121] Response to the points raised during the consultation on the competition law guidelines, guidance and the OFT's Rules, December 2004, at points 2.22 to 2.27. See also in regard to the example of legal privilege to documents established by in-house lawyers, K Dekeyser and E De Smijter, 'The Exchange of Evidence Within the ECN' [2005] Legal Issues of Economic Integration 161–74.

[122] In order to overcome these difficulties, when discussing the draft Reg 1/2003, Marc van der Woude had proposed three principles that these exchanges should respect, as well as appropriate procedural mechanism for their enforcement. These principles are: (i) the right to the highest standard of confidentiality; (ii) the right to the most favourable conditions, and (iii) the right to a complete transfer. These rights would essentially require a cumulative application of the procedural rights of the transmitting and receiving authorities. M van der Woude, 'Exchange of Information within the European Competition Network: Scope and Limits', in *European*

Article 12 of Regulation 1/2003, however, does depart from the principle that **3.33** evidence should be collected lawfully in accordance with the rules and procedures in the transmitting State if it is to be used in evidence by NCAs and recognized in the courts of the receiving State. Accordingly, under Article 12(1) of Regulation 1/2003 the receiving NCA could use the evidence which was collected by the first NCA and transmitted to it, even if it could not itself lawfully have collected this evidence, or could not have used it if it had collected it itself.[123] If the Commission is the receiving authority and Community law grants the protection (e.g. privilege against self-incrimination) it could be argued that protection will not be lost in proceedings before the Commission merely because the privileged information was collected in circumstances where that protection did not apply.[124] However, additional problems may arise where the law of the receiving State provides greater protection than the transmitting State. The example indicated above would suggest that it would probably matter how this information was obtained. Where the NCA has deliberately chosen to have the information collected where similar protection did not exist, this would mean a breach of fundamental rights or the general principles of Community law.[125] Where the NCA did not seek to circumvent the defence rights afforded under the law of the receiving State, the receiving NCA would be free to use the information except in the specific situation of the imposition of sanctions on natural persons. As indicated, the receiving Member State can only impose those sanctions if the law of the transmitting authority foresees sanctions of a similar kind and where an equivalent level of protection exits in the transmitting as in the receiving State.[126]

Competition Law Annual 2002: Constructing the EU Network of Competition Authorities 14–16. As Reg 1/2003 stands today it seems difficult to affirm those principles on the basis of the Regulation alone. If these principles are to be respected, it will probably be on the basis of national laws. In contrast, the ECN Cooperation Notice (para 27) suggests that Art 12 should override any national laws on the basis of the principle of primacy.

[123] Art 12 of Reg 1/2003 takes precedence over any contrary law of a Member State. The question whether information was gathered in a legal manner by the transmitting authority is governed on the basis of the law applicable to this authority. It is to be noted that in the ECN Cooperation Notice, the Commission states that the 'question whether information was gathered in a legal manner by the transmitting authority is governed on the basis of the law applicable to this authority.'

[124] CS Kerse and N Khan, *EC Antitrust Procedure* (5th edn, 2005) para 5–013 submit based on the ECJ ruling in *Otto v Postbank* that even where the right or protection is not one recognized by Community law, such right may need to be respected by the receiving NCA.

[125] cf by analogy the Court's doctrine on circumvention of national laws by individuals. See Case C-212/97 *Centros Ltd v Erhvervs- og Selskabsstyrelsen* [1999] ECR I-1459 para 24; regarding freedom to supply services, Case 33/74 *Van Binsbergen v Bedrijfsvereniging Metaalnijverheid* [1974] ECR 1299 para 13. CS Kerse and N Khan, *EC Antitrust Procedure* (5th edn, 2005) para 5–014 note that in this case the receiving authority would be prevented from using the information in 'evidence' but Art 11(4) of Reg 1/2003 might still apply.

[126] Art 12(3) of Reg 1/2003.

3.34 While the normal flow of information within the network is essential for the whole system to work, it is arguable whether the safeguards will prove sufficient. For example, in the first place, it is not even clear whether the affected companies would be informed of the exchange of information within the network before disclosure. Without such knowledge, companies cannot take legal action to safeguard their rights in those cases where they might wish to object to the exchanging of confidential information. In addition, it is unquestionable that the rules concerning the protection of confidential information differ among Member States. Therefore, one may ask from the outset whether the classification as 'confidential' of any document by one NCA could be overruled by another NCA that has obtained the document through the ECN. That could be the case when a document is transmitted from an NCA with high protection standards to another NCA whose national law is less strict when it comes to confidentiality protection. Yet it seems that Regulation 1/2003 contains a common minimum standard for the protection of confidential information in the form of Article 28(2). By replacing national guarantees for the protection of confidential information, this provision aims to release somehow ECN members from a duty that might exist under their home provisions to verify and ascertain the confidential nature of the information they have obtained and intend to send to another member.[127] Nevertheless, it is also true that this may not be sufficient to remove the reluctance of companies to provide NCAs with confidential information if they are unable to assess the scope of distribution within the ECN.[128]

3.35 In addition, differences in procedural rights and guarantees exist today between Member States, or between Member States and the EU, which do not result from different types of sanctions. The mere fact that there are differences in the procedural rules of the Member States should not prevent the exchange for the purpose of applying the common rules on competition. Procedural rules of all Member States and at Community level respect high standards of protection of the rights of defence under the control of independent courts. They are thus mutually compatible and Regulation 1/2003 takes a clear stance that in light of an implicit mutual recognition of standards of fundamental rights the remaining divergences should not stand in the way of closer cooperation between authorities in the internal market. Nevertheless, some concerns remain. As a matter of principle, parallel application of national law may not make

---

[127] K Dekeyser and E De Smijter, 'The Exchange of Evidence Within the ECN' [2005] Legal Issues of Economic Integration 161–74 (172).

[128] See in this respect, the comments received by the EC Commission during the consultation on the Modernization Package from the law firms Latham & Watkins, 5 December 2003, and Clifford Chance and Freshfields, available at http://europa.eu.int/comm/competition/antitrust/legislation/procedural_rules/comments/.

possible the use of evidence where Regulation 1/2003 would not so permit. In this regard, it is clear that national rules could not provide for the use of evidence gathered in one procedure for a 'subject matter' different to that for which it was collected by the transmitting authority. However, it is more questionable whether national laws may limit the use of information in cases not contemplated by Regulation 1/2003.[129] In addition to the examples mentioned above, there may be national rules limiting the use by the recipient authority of confidential information in light of extensive rights of access to the file. National rules may also differ on the relative weight of evidence attaching low probative value to certain documents or testimonies. This suggests that inevitably the national law of the recipient authority will influence the use of evidence received under Article 12 of Regulation 1/2003. It is also apparent that these national provisions may be based on considerations concerning the protection of fundamental rights, thus resulting in a layer of protection additional to that provided for by Regulation 1/2003. Indeed, these mechanisms may never make redundant the possibility that the recipient authority may use evidence received under Article 12, but the extent of their influence is unclear in this regard.

Leniency programmes   The Commission and a number of NCAs have leniency **3.36** programmes, under which they offer, subject to varying conditions, full immunity or a significant reduction in the penalties which they would otherwise impose or seek to have imposed on participants in cartels in exchange for the freely volunteered disclosure of information on the cartel which satisfies specific criteria prior to or during the investigative stage of proceedings.[130] The ECN Cooperation Notice deals also with the impact of the new decentralized system on the leniency process, namely regarding information exchange.[131] The Commission considers that the leniency programme has helped detect cartel activity by competition authorities and that it has acted as a deterrent for companies to participate in unlawful cartels. In fact, the Commission has

---

[129] JS Venit, 'Private Practice in the Wake of the Commission's Modernization Program' [2005] Legal Issues of Economic Integration 147–59 (157) suggests that private counsel should work on the assumption that all information provided to one competition authority will be promptly shared with the other competition authorities and that even if they cannot directly use this information they will be aware of the issue and will know where to look for the necessary information by members.

[130] See for more details ch 6 'Leniency policy'. Consistent with the approach taken under Art 23 of Reg 1/2003, the decision as to whether or not to adopt a leniency programme, together with the precise terms of any such programme, is also left to each ECN member, acting within the limits of the laws to which it is subject. Thus, whilst leniency programmes have been adopted both by the Commission and in a significant number of Member States, this is not universally the case. The Commission's website identifies fifteen Member States operating leniency programmes. S Blake and D Schnichels, 'Leniency following Modernisation: safeguarding Europe's leniency programmes' [2004] Competition Newsletter, Number 2 7–13.

[131] ECN Cooperation Notice [2004] OJ C101/43 paras 37 to 42; see also ch 6 'Leniency policy'.

acknowledged several times that most of the last major cartel cases which it has recently investigated were initiated as result of a leniency application.

3.37 The decentralized system has changed the situation for leniency applicants. Prior to the entry into force of the new system, an undertaking could expect that its application for leniency would remain in the possession of the NCA to which it was submitted. With the new system, some information regarding leniency applications may flow between NCAs. Under the ECN, the application of the allocation principles may give rise to uncertainties. These conflicts arise where it turns out that within the ECN it is decided that the authority to which the leniency application was addressed is not competent. For example, where a leniency applicant approaches the Commission in the belief that the Commission is best placed to act, but it later transpires that an NCA, or a number of NCAs, assume jurisdiction under the case reallocation procedures, the applicant may be faced with the risk of fines by these NCAs unless it has made a further application to them. Therefore, companies must not rely on a 'one-stop shop' proceeding in the EU, and this would include the situation where they apply to the Commission and another cartel member blows the whistle at the national level. The Commission has been at pains to point out that the allocation rules are not rules of jurisdiction and would not create legitimate expectations on which companies can rely.[132] Conversely, where a leniency applicant believes that a cartel is confined to one or two Member States and makes applications at the national level, but later it turns out that the Commission assumes exclusive jurisdiction on the grounds that the cartel affected more than three Member States the applicant may face the risk of substantial fines at the EU level.[133]

3.38 The ECN Notice suggests that a leniency applicant should present its application before all the NCAs which have competence to apply Article 81 of the Treaty in the territory which is affected by the infringement.[134] However, where those effects are difficult to determine, an applicant should presumably apply for leniency in all Member States.[135] In a Community comprising twenty-five

---

[132] C Canenbley and M Rosenthal, 'Cooperation between Antitrust Authorities In-and Outside the EU: What does it mean for Multinational Corporations?—Part 1' [2005] ECLR 106–14 (110–11) suggesting that the whistle blower who submits leniency applications with the Commission should also ask the Commission for formal confirmation that it will deal with the case. S Blake and D Schnichels, 'Leniency following Modernisation: safeguarding Europe's leniency programmes' [2004] Competition Newsletter, Number 2, 7–13 (10) indicate that the network notice may create legitimate expectations in so far as the Commission is concerned.

[133] N Levy and R O'Donoghue, 'The EU Leniency Programme Comes of Age' [2004] World Competition—Law and Economics Review' 75–99 (95).

[134] ECN Cooperation Notice [2004] OJ C101/43 paras 37 to 42.

[135] The Commission seems to have taken note of the fact that the present system of multiple filings with all relevant authorities within the ECN costs time and money and that differences

Member States, seeking leniency simultaneously in several Member States may be burdensome and complicated. The ECN Cooperation Network addresses two possible concerns. The first potential concern is that as a result of the cooperation provisions in Article 11 of Regulation 1/2003 a leniency application to one authority within the ECN might trigger an investigation by another ECN member to which the applicant has not also applied for leniency. The second potential concern is that the information which a leniency applicant has volunteered to one authority within the ECN, together with any information which that authority may obtain as a consequence, might be transmitted to another ECN member under Article 12 of Regulation 1/2003 and used as evidence to impose sanctions on the applicant.

Regarding the publicity that should be given to a leniency application within the ECN, the ECN Cooperation Notice establishes that an authority receiving a leniency application should inform the Commission and the other members of the network following Article 11(3) of Regulation 1/2003.[136] It is not clear whether this information should include the name of the applicant.[137] Moreover, the Notice makes clear that this information cannot be used by the NCA to start an investigation *ex officio* whether under the EC competition rules or under their national competition law. Notwithstanding the above, although an NCA is prevented from using the information obtained from a leniency application filed with a different NCA to open an investigation on its own behalf, Regulation 1/2003 also establishes that an NCA can open an investigation on the basis of information received from other sources.[138] On the other hand, transmission of the information obtained through a leniency application between NCAs pursuant to Article 12 of Regulation 1/2003 would need the **3.39**

---

between programmes might dissuade potential applicants from applying. N Kroes, 'Taking Competition Seriously—Anti-Trust Reform in Europe', International Bar Association/European Commission Conference 'Antitrust Reform in Europe: A Year in Practice', 10 March 2005, Brussels. D Schroeder, 'Leniency – Issues from a Private Practioner's Perspective' ibid also notes that the Commission advises to make filings simultaneously, but the applicant might have to ask him or herself whether he or she can afford to wait until he or she would be ready in all relevant Member States.

[136] ECN Cooperation Notice [2004] OJ C101/43 para 39.

[137] It could be argued that the competition authority which receives a leniency application is obliged to forward the minimum information contained in the standard from to the other ECN members without any consent being required. This would imply that the authority has to indicate whether it is a leniency case, whether the identity must not be disclosed and who the applicant is. The consent requirement would then only apply to nay further information. See D Reichelt, 'To what extent does the cooperation within the European Competition Network protect the rights of the undertakings?' (2005) CML Rev 745–82 (752).

[138] ECN Cooperation Notice [2004] OJ C101/43 para 40.

prior consent of the applicant.[139] This consent requirement also applies to information that has been obtained as a result of investigative measures 'which could not have been carried out except as a result of the leniency application.' Nevertheless, there are some circumstances in which the consent of the applicant is not required for the transmission of information to another NCA pursuant to Article 12 of the Regulation, namely:[140]

- *When the same applicant has presented another leniency application on the same infringement before the receiving authority, provided that he is not allowed to withdraw the provided information.* Once a leniency applicant has made the decision to apply to more than one ECN member, it must accept that the authorities to which it has applied will no longer require its consent in order to exchange information amongst themselves. The one proviso to this is that at the time the information is transmitted it must not be open to the applicant to withdraw its leniency application from the authority to which the information is to be transmitted.

- *When the receiving authority has presented a written commitment stating that it or another authority will not use the received information in order to impose sanctions either on the leniency applicant, any other legal or natural person which is covered by the favourable treatment related to the leniency application or on any employee of any of the persons mentioned before.* The authority requesting transmission of the information must guarantee that not only the information transmitted to it but also any other information that it may subsequently obtain, will not be used either by it or by any other authority to which the information is subsequently transmitted to impose sanctions on any of the following: the leniency applicant; any other person covered by the transmitting authority's leniency programme (for example, the subsidiaries of the applicant); or any employee or former employee of either of the former two. It

---

[139] ECN Cooperation Notice para 40. K Dekeyser and E De Smijter, 'The Exchange of Evidence Within the ECC' [2005] Legal Issues of Economic Integration 161–74 (166) note that although these principles guarantee the required adequate protection of the leniency applicant, they might have the effect that not only the leniency applicant but also other participants to the competition rules infringing behaviour will escape from effective sanctioning. This is because the would-be transmitting ECN member cannot or can only partially sanction the infringement, but the information being exchanged may not be of much use given the leniency applicant is expected to give only its consent when he does not risk any sanction imposed by the would-be receiving authority.

[140] ECN Cooperation Notice para 41. K Dekeyser and E De Smijter, 'The Exchange of Evidence Within the ECC' (n 127 above) 167 add one further situation where consent is not required: if the ECN member that received the leniency application asks an NCA to do inspections on its territory, the latter NCA may send the information obtained to the ECN member that initially asked for this assistance. Commission Report on Competition Policy SEC (2004) 805 final para 109 stating that in 2004 in at least two instances information was exchanged in leniency cases with the consent of the leniency applicant.

follows from this that, unless the receiving authority was already in possession of sufficient evidence to impose a sanction on the transmitting authority's leniency applicant, the guarantee will *de facto* confer on the latter immunity from any fine which the receiving authority might otherwise have imposed on it.

For the avoidance of doubt, the ECN Cooperation Notice also expressly states **3.40** that where information has been collected by an ECN member under Article 22(1) of Regulation 1/2003 on behalf of the ECN member to which the leniency application was made, such information may be transmitted to the latter authority, notwithstanding that the information might otherwise technically be covered by the restriction on the transmission of information obtained during or by means of an inspection or other fact-finding measure that could not have been carried out except as a result of the leniency application. However, it remains to be seen whether this complex system will work in practice and whether leniency applicants are well protected against investigations from other authorities. The Commission has made clear that '*an application for leniency to a given authority is not to be considered as an application for leniency to any other authority*'.[141] Given that until this date not all Member States have actual or draft leniency programmes and they all act on the basis of different rules, it is still doubtful that the safeguards foreseen by the Commission in the ECN Cooperation Notice will overcome the risks that companies would reasonably like to avoid before presenting a leniency application. Actual or potential leniency applicants are understandably sensitive about the subsequent disclosure of both the information which they have volunteered and that which the authority's investigation later uncovers and which, but for the leniency application, would not have come to light.

The ECN Cooperation Notice foresees that information exchanged within the **3.41** network on newly opened cases will not be used by other ECN members to start their own proceedings. The Commission also points out that NCAs have signed a statement in which they declare that they will abide by the principles set out in the Commission Notice.[142] The mutual information in the network is organized in such a way that only those authorities that have committed to these principles receive information on leniency cases. In order to obtain detailed information contained in a leniency application, the receiving authority will have to sign a declaration that it will not use the information transmitted or any other

---

[141] ECN Cooperation Notice para 38.
[142] For the list of NCAs that have signed the statement, which includes in particular a reference to the principles 'relating to the protection of applicants claiming the benefit of a leniency programme, in any case in which [they are] acting or act and to which those principles apply' http://europa.eu.int/comm/competition/antitrust/legislation/list_of_authorities_joint_statement.pdf.

information gathered thereafter to impose sanctions on the leniency applicant. In this respect it should also be noted that the competition authorities that operate leniency programmes have a clear interest not to undermine the functioning of their programmes by circulating the leniency information without appropriate guarantees for their leniency applicant.

3.42　Whilst prior to 1 May 2004 NCAs would not necessarily have applied EC competition law, cartel members, then as now, nevertheless risked being sanctioned by the NCAs whose territories were affected by the infringement, either under EC competition rules or under national competition law. Another ECN member will not be precluded from investigating the case altogether. It will still be free to open an investigation if it receives sufficient information to enable it to do so from another source, such as a complainant, an informant or another leniency applicant. Moreover, it is important to note that the risk to the leniency applicant of another authority independently receiving information and initiating an investigation on its own behalf does not arise as a consequence of Regulation 1/2003.

3. Suspension or termination of proceedings (Article 13 of Council Regulation 1/2003)

3.43　Article 13 of Regulation 1/2003 provides that the NCAs and the Commission have the right to suspend a proceeding or reject a complaint if the same case is or has been dealt with by another NCA. The ECN Cooperation Notice points out that the possibility of suspending or rejecting a complaint is only a possibility for the NCAs and for the Commission and not a duty. In the event of a disagreement over the allocation of a case with sufficient Community interest, relying on Article 11(6) of Regulation 1/2003, the Commission may itself initiate proceedings which will automatically relieve the NCAs of their competence to proceed with the case.

3.44　Where an authority terminates or suspends proceedings because another authority is dealing with the case, it may transfer—in accordance with Article 12 of the Council Regulation—the information provided by the complainant to the authority which is to deal with the case.[143] The possibility of suspending or terminating proceedings can also be applied to part of a complaint or to part of the proceedings in a case. It may be that only part of a complaint or of an

---

[143] It should be noted that Art 13(1) does not provide expressly for an exchange of information subsequent to the termination or suspension. However effective enforcement would be jeopardized if the information gathered by the terminating or suspending authority could not be transmitted to the other ECN member which continues to deal with the case. See D Reichelt, 'To what extent does the cooperation within the European Competition Network protect the rights of the undertakings?' (2005) CML Rev 745–82 (752).

ex-officio procedure overlaps with a case already dealt with or being dealt with by another competition authority. In that case, the competition authority to which the complaint is brought is entitled to reject part of the complaint on the basis of Article 13 and to deal with the rest of the complaint in an appropriate manner. The same principle applies to the termination of proceedings.[144] The provision reflects the principle that the allocation of cases is meant to be deliberately flexible. There is no obligation to terminate or suspend proceedings on the ground that another authority is investigating the case and there is no indication as to which authority is supposed to suspend or to terminate. This shows that the system is designed as a system of parallel competences in which each authority decides for itself if it wants to act or not against a given infringement.[145] If a complaint was rejected by an authority following an investigation of the substance of the case, another authority may not want to re-examine the case. On the other hand, if a complaint was rejected for other reasons (e.g. the authority was unable to collect the evidence necessary to prove the infringement), another authority may wish to carry out its own investigation and deal with the case. This flexibility is also reflected, for pending cases, in the choice open to each NCA as to whether it terminates or suspends its proceedings. An authority may be unwilling to terminate a case before the outcome of another authority's proceedings is clear.[146]

4. The role and the functioning of the Advisory Committee on Restrictive Practices and Monopolies

The Advisory Committee on Restrictive Practices and Monopolies ('Advisory Committee') has been described in the Commission's ECN Notice as being the forum where officials from the different NCAs meet to discuss specific cases and general issues of Community competition law. The Advisory Committee should be composed of representatives of the NCAs whereby each Member State has one representative. Yet, for meetings in which general issues are being discussed, Member States should be able to appoint an additional representative.[147] The Advisory Committee is consulted prior to the Commission taking decisions on

3.45

---

[144] ECN Cooperation Notice paras 23 and 24.

[145] K Dekeyser and C Gauer, 'The New Enforcement System for Articles 81 and 82 and the Rights of Defence' ch 26 in BE Hawk (ed), Annual Proceedings of the Fordham Institute [2005] 676–700.

[146] D Geradu and N Petit,'Judicial remedies under EC Competition Law: Complex issues arising from the modernization process', 32nd Annual International Antitrust Law & Policy Conference Fordham Corporate Law Institute, 22–23 September 2005 (forthcoming) notes that in legal terms Art 230 does not allow decisions by NCAs to reallocate a case to be challenged as only decisions taken by a Community institution fall within this Article. See also para 3.14 above.

[147] Recital 20 of Reg 1/2003. This is without prejudice to members of the Committee being assisted by other experts from the Member States.

infringement findings,[148] interim measures,[149] commitments,[150] findings of inapplicability of Articles 81 or 82 EC,[151] fines[152] or withdrawal of the benefit granted under any exemption Regulation. The requirement of consultation applies similarly in the context of sector inquiries.[153] Furthermore, the Commission or any Member State can request that a specific case dealt with by an NCA be put on the agenda of the Advisory Committee. In either case, the Commission will put the case on the agenda after having informed the NCA concerned.[154] However, this discussion will not lead to a formal opinion. The ECN Notice establishes that the Advisory Committee can be used as a forum for the discussion of case allocation. On the other hand, the Advisory Committee will also be consulted by the Commission on draft regulations and on the adoption of notices and guidelines.[155]

3.46 The Commission must fully heed the opinion of the Advisory Committee and inform the Committee of the manner in which its opinion has been taken into account.[156] Under the normal procedural rules, the consultation may take place at a meeting convened and chaired by the Commission, held not earlier than 14 days after the invitation to the meeting is sent by the Commission, together with a summary of the case, an indication of the most important documents and a preliminary draft decision.[157] The decisions are sent to each Member State in its own official language (or languages). Accompanying those documents, the Commission gives an indication of the most important documents in the case file. In respect of interim decisions, the meeting may be held seven days after the dispatch of the operative part of a draft decision.[158] Where the Commission dispatches a notice convening the meeting which gives a shorter period of notice than those specified above, the meeting may take place on the proposed date provided no Member State objects. The Advisory Committee shall deliver a written opinion on the Commission's preliminary draft decision. It may deliver an opinion even if some members are absent and are not

---

[148] Art 7 in connection with Art 14(1) of Reg 1/2003.

[149] Art 8 in connection with Art 14(1) of Reg 1/2003.

[150] Art 9 in connection with Art 14(1) of Reg 1/2003.

[151] Art 10 in connection with Art 14(1) of Reg 1/2003.

[152] Arts 23 (Fines) and 24(2) of Reg 1/2003 which allows the Commission to fix the amount of the periodic penalty payment at a figure lower than that would arise under the original decision in case that the undertaking has satisfied the obligation which the periodic payment was intended to enforce. Accordingly, the obligation to consult does not concern the decision to impose periodic payments.

[153] Art 17 of Reg 1/2003.   [154] Art 14(7) of Reg 1/2003.

[155] ECN Cooperation Notice para 66.

[156] Art 14(5) of Reg 1/2003; ECN Cooperation Notice [2004] C101/43 para 59.

[157] Art 14(3) of Reg 1/2003. ECN Cooperation Notice [2004] C101/43 para 65.

[158] ECN Cooperation Notice [2004] C101/43 para 60 states that for decisions adopting interim measures, the procedure shall be swifter and lighter and that the Advisory Committee must provided with a short explanatory note and the operative part of the decision.

represented. At the request of one or several members, the positions stated in the opinion shall be reasoned. Where the Advisory Committee delivers a written opinion, the opinion shall be appended to the draft decision. If the Advisory Committee recommends publication of the opinion, the Commission shall carry out such publication taking into account the legitimate interest of undertakings in the protection of their business secrets.[159]

3.47 The consultation may also occur by way of a written procedure unless one Member State objects and requests that the Commission convene a meeting. Under the written procedure, the Commission shall determine a time limit of not less than fourteen days within which the Member States are to put forward their observations for circulation to all other Member States.[160] In the case of interim decisions, the time limit of fourteen days is replaced by seven days. Where the Commission determines a time limit for the written procedure which is shorter than fourteen days, the proposed time-limit shall be applicable unless a Member State objects. Outside the scope of Articles 81 and 82 EC and pecuniary penalties, liaison with the Committee takes place prior to the adoption of decisions to initiate inquiries into sectors of the economy, under Article 17(2) of Regulation 1/2003. Furthermore, at the request of an NCA, the Commission shall include on the agenda of the Advisory Committee cases that are being dealt with by an NCA under Articles 81 and 82 EC. The Commission may do so on its own initiative. In either case, the Commission shall inform the NCA informed.[161] Such a request can in particular be made where the Commission intends to initiate proceedings under Article 11(6) which relieves the NCAs of their competence.[162] It should be noted that the Advisory Committee is allowed to discuss general issues of competition law but cannot issue opinions on cases dealt with by NCAs.[163]

---

[159] Art 14(6) of Reg 1/2003 and ECN Cooperation Notice [2004] C101/43 para 68. Although not binding, the opinions expressed by the Member States in the reports and at the Committee meetings are scrutinized carefully by Commission officials in order to ensure that decisions are of a high quality. See also CS Kerse and N Khan, *EC Antitrust Procedure* (5th edn, 2005) para 5–048 who consider that making the Committee's opinion public is a significant change although this does not include opinions of the Committee on cases referred to it by an NCA. Under Reg 17, any opinion of the Committee was not revealed to the undertakings concerned. In *Pioneer*, the Court rejected the view that Reg 17 should be construed as meaning the Committee's opinion need to be disclosed to the undertakings. Whatever might be the Court's opinion, the Commission would be required to base its decisions only on facts about which the undertaking have had the chance of making known their views. Cases 100 and 100/80 *Musique Diffusion Francaise v EC Commission* [1983] ECR 1823 paras 34–36.
[160] Art 14(4) of Reg 1/2003. ECN Cooperation Notice para 67. In *RTE*, the CFI held that the fourteen-day notice period under Reg 17 is a purely internal procedural rule, the failure to comply with it would not render ineffective by itself a subsequent decision by the Commission Case T-69/89 *Radio Telefis Eireann v EC Commission* [1991] ECR II-485 para 27.
[161] Art 14(7) of Reg 1/2003.   [162] Art 14(7) second para of Reg 1/2003.
[163] Art 14(7) third para of Reg 1/2003.

3.48 While the opinion of the Advisory Committee is to be published where the Committee recommends its publication, the meetings of the Advisory Committee are not public and only the Member States and the Commission take part. Undertakings have no right to participate in Advisory Committee meetings. One of the representatives, appointed on a rotating basis from among the members of the Advisory Committee, acts as rapporteur. In order to keep the proceedings to the point, the rapporteur informs the other representatives of the main issues involved and usually submits a number of questions to be considered by them. Those questions, which usually refer to the applicability of Arts 81 and 82 EC to the case in question, the appropriateness or otherwise of imposing fines, and the amount of any fines, are dealt with in turn by each country's representative, in alphabetical order. The members of the Advisory Committee may address questions to and seek clarifications from the Commission. After discussion, each question is answered succinctly by the representatives of the Member States. The report reflects the views of all the delegations, first the majority opinion and then the minority opinions.[164] However, no particular majority is required for the adoption of the report and there is no provision for individual views. Failure to consult the Advisory Committee may constitute an infringement of a procedural requirement in the application of the competition rules and could vitiate the Commission's decision.[165] However, it is not regarded, in itself, as undermining the fundamental rights of undertakings or their defence rights.[166] The Community courts are unlikely to quash a decision of the Commission for procedural irregularity unless it is sufficiently substantial and would have a harmful effect on the legal and factual situation of the party alleging the procedural irregularity.[167]

---

[164] See e.g. in relation to merger control. Opinion of the Advisory Committee on concentrations given at its 113th meeting on 20 March 2003 concerning a draft decision relating to Case COMP/M.2876 – *Newscorp/Telepiù* [2004] OJ C102/25.

[165] See Opinion of AG Gand in Case 41/69 *ACF Chemiefarma v EC Commission* [1970] ECR 661 paras 709–711.

[166] Case T-19/91 *Vichy v Commission* [1992] ECR II-415 para 38. Where not all available information is disclosed to the members of the Advisory Committee, the legality of the Commission's decisions will only be affected if it is shown that failure to forward that information to the Committee did not allow the Committee to deliver its opinion in full knowledge of the affects, that is to say, without being misled in material respect by inaccuracies or ommissions. Joined Cases T-25/95, T-26/95 etc. *Cimenteries CBR SA and others v EC Commission* [2000] ECR II-491 para 742, see also K Lenaerts and J Maselis, 'Procedural Rights and Issues in the Enforcement of Articles 81 and 82 of the EC Treaty' [2001] Fordham International Law Journal 1615–54 (1646).

[167] Case T-290/94 *Kaysersberg SA v EC Commission* [1997] ECR II-2247 para 88; CS Kerse and N Khan, *EC Antitrust Procedure* (5th edn, 2005) para 5–051. In *PVC II*, the ECJ held that there was no need to consult the Advisory Committee where a second decision, the purpose of which was to correct an illegal measure in the original decision, contained no substantial amendments to the first decision. Cases C-238, 244, 245, 247, 252 and 254/99 *Limburgse Vinyl Maarschappij v EC Commission (PVC II)* [2002] ECR I-8375 para 118.

4

THE ORGANIZATION OF EC COMMISSION PROCEEDINGS

A. Outline of the Main Types of Procedure

1. Informal guidance[1]

The enforcement scheme set out in Regulation 1/2003 is based on the premise **4.01** that undertakings are best placed to take an informed decision on whether an agreement or concerted practice is compatible with Article 81 or Article 82 EC. However, industry and practitioners alike expressed some concern that the abolition of the notification system would inject an element of uncertainty, particularly in relation to complex agreements. The Commission has repeatedly emphasized that any kind of notification/clearance procedure would run counter to the Commission's key objective of dedicating its resources to tackling major cartels and other serious anti-competitive practices.[2] However, the Commission has acknowledged that there may be cases which could give rise to genuine uncertainty because they present novel or unresolved questions for the undertakings involved.[3] In these situations, the Commission is generally ready to issue informal guidance to aid the consistent application of the competition rules in a decentralized system, as long as this is compatible with its enforcement priorities.[4]

Aware that an over generous system of acceding to requests for assistance and **4.02**

---

[1] See ch 5 'Opening of the file' paras 5.25–5.35.

[2] CS Kerse and N Khan, *EC Antitrust Procedure* (5th edn, 2005) para 2–053; see also J Schwarze and A Weitbrecht, *Grundzüge des Europäischen Kartellverfahrensrecht* (2004) § 6 para 97 in relation to Art 10 of Reg 1/2003; A Klees, *Europäisches Kartellverfahrensrecht* (2005) § 6 paras 38 and 39.

[3] Commission Notice on informal guidance relating to novel questions concerning Arts 81 and 82 of the EC Treaty that arise in individual cases (guidance letters) [2004] OJ C101/78 para 6.

[4] Reg 1/2003, Recital 38. See also A Jones and B Sufrin, *EC Competition Law* (2nd edn, 2004) 1055.

informal guidance could jeopardize the essence of the modernized enforcement of EC competition rules, the Commission has made guidance letters conditional on three cumulative requirements being met. First, the question must be novel. The problems must be real and identifiable ones. The Commission will not consider hypothetical questions and will not issue guidance letters on agreements or practices that are no longer being implemented by the parties. Where the parties present a request on an agreement, the implementation must have reached a sufficiently advanced stage. Secondly, the guidance letter should be appropriate and useful having regard to the economic implications of the transaction. Finally, expending the resources of the Commission must be compatible with the enforcement priorities of the Commission. In particular, this would mean that no further fact-finding is required.[5] During the first year of application of Regulation 1/2003, the Commission has not issued any guidance letters and very few submissions have been made to this effect.[6] The Commission seems to rule out the possibility of introducing an annulment decision against guidance letters by making it clear that guidance letters are not Commission decisions.[7]

2. Infringement proceedings[8]

4.03 Infringement of the competition rules laid down in Articles 81 and 82 EC exposes undertakings to the risk of infringement proceedings being initiated against them, with the possibility of severe fines. Where it appears to the Commission—as a result of complaints from individuals, information from the undertakings themselves, or from its own sources—that an infringement may exist, it initiates a procedure. The procedure has two successive stages.[9] In the

---

[5] Informal Guidance Notice [2004] OJ C101/78 paras 8,11. See also E Paulis and E De Smitjer, 'Enhanced Enforcement of the EC Competition Rules Since 1 May 2004 by the Commission and the NCAs', Antitrust Reform in Europe: A Year in Practice, 9–11 March 2005, Brussels, International Bar Association (IBA) 15, who point to the exceptional character of guidance letters.

[6] 'Q&A on modernization with Kris Dekeyser' Global Competition Review, Vol 8, Issue 3, April 2005, 11–16 (12). Dekyser notes that these submissions turned out to be old-style notifications and did not identify novel issues as foreseen in the Notice.

[7] Informal Guidance Notice [2004] OJ C101/78 para 25. D Geradin and N Petit, 'Judicial Remedies under EC Competition Law: Complex Issues Arising from the Modernization Process', 32nd Annual International Antitrust Law & Policy Conference, Fordham Corporate Law Institute, 22–23 September 2005 (forthcoming), 9 take the view that this solution is justified as long as these guidance letters do not '[. . .] disguise texts which are in reality prescriptive in nature imposing detailed legal obligations [. . .]' on undertakings.

[8] See in more detail ch 10 'Infringement procedures' paras 10.01 *et seq.*

[9] See, e.g. Joined Cases C-238/99, C-244–245/99, C-247/99, C250-252/99 and C-254/99 *Limburgse Vinyl Maatwschappij and others v EC Commission* [2002] ECR I-8375 paras 181–183; Case T-241/97 *Stork Amsterdam v EC Commission* [2000] ECR II-309 para 51.

first stage, the Commission investigates the facts: for this purpose it is entitled to send requests for information to undertakings and to carry out inspections at their premises. Once it has gathered sufficient evidence of an infringement, the Commission gives the undertakings an opportunity to submit observations regarding the facts and objections on the basis of which the Commission intends to take a decision against them. To that end, it sends them a Statement of Objections setting out the infringements of which they are accused and the Commission's intentions, which will simply be to declare the existence of an infringement and, if necessary, impose a fine on the undertakings involved. The undertakings are informed that they may make such submissions in writing and, in some cases, orally. In order to enable them better to prepare their defence, the Commission allows undertakings access to the case file. They will then be able to reply to the objections in writing, and it is at this time that, if they wish, they must ask for an administrative hearing. At hearings, undertakings have an opportunity to make such oral submissions to the Commission as they consider relevant to their defence. After the hearing, the Commission prepares a draft decision which is submitted to the Advisory Committee for a non-binding report to be given. The Advisory Committee is made up of the national authorities of the Member States responsible for competition matters. Commission officials (at DG COMP) amend the draft as they consider necessary. It then becomes the final draft and is presented as such to the full meeting of the Commission. The decision may then be adopted by the Commission, which notifies it to the undertakings and publishes it in the Official Journal. It may be challenged before the CFI.

The Commission may commence proceedings following a complaint, on a **4.04** request or transfer from a NCA or by simply acting on its own initiative. This mirrors the different ways by which information relating to a suspected infringement of the EC competition rules may be brought to the knowledge of the Commission. As regards complaints, there is a formal complaint procedure through which a third party may make known evidence of a possible violation of Articles 81 or 82 EC in a complaint.[10] The Commission may also receive information from a variety of other sources, e.g. monitoring of public information or through its discussions with other antitrust authorities. Sector inquiries

---

[10] Commission Notice on the handling of complaints by the Commission under Arts 81 and 82 of the EC Treaty ('Notice on Complaints') [2004] OJ C101/65. In its White Paper on modernization of the rules implementing Arts 81 and 82 of the EC Treaty [1999] OJ C132/1 para 117 the Commission estimated that almost 30 per cent of new cases it deals with stem from complaints and that many of its own-initiative investigations begin with information sent to the Commission informally. See also A Jones and B Sufrin, *EC Competition Law* (2nd edn, 2004) 1175.

may extend to a particular sector of the economy or a particular type of agreement across various sectors.[11]

3. Interim measures[12]

4.05 Regulation 17 did not specify whether the Commission had the power to adopt interim measures in relation to suspected infringements of Articles 81 and 82 EC. The existence of this power was, however, confirmed by the ECJ,[13] which set out the basic criteria in *Camera Care*.[14] Pursuant to Article 8 of Regulation 1/2003, in cases of urgency the Commission acting on its own initiative is empowered to adopt interim measures where there is a risk of serious and irreparable harm to competition and there is prima facie evidence of an infringement. It is further stipulated that interim measures may be adopted for no more than one year, with a possibility of renewal. The exceptional character of this power has led to the adoption of less than a dozen decisions ordering interim measures which were partly annulled by the Community Courts.

4.06 Regulation 1/2003 specifically stipulates that interim measures may be ordered by the Commission 'acting on its own initiative'. In its practice under Regulation 17, the Commission had accepted that a complainant could request the Commission to issue interim measures in the same way as a litigant would seek an injunction from a court.[15] It seems that this will no longer be possible under

---

[11] Recent examples concern in particular the telecommunications sector: 'EC Commission: Concluding Report on the Sector Inquiry into the Provision of Sports Content over Third Generation Mobile Networks', published in accordance with Art 17(1) of Reg 1/2003, 21 September 2005. The European Commission launched inquiries into competition in financial services and the energy sector on 13 June 2005. See the relevant Press Releases IP/05/716 'Competition: Commission opens sector inquiry into gas and electricity' and IP/05/719 'Competition: Commission opens sector inquiries into retail banking and business insurance'. Until recently, sector inquiries have rarely been used and were limited to a few inquiries in the beer brewing sector in 1969/1970. The requirements under Art 17 of Reg 1/2003 are slightly less strict and allow conducting an inquiry where certain circumstances (trend of trade, price rigidity, etc) suggest competition may be restricted or distorted. The previous wording referred to circumstances that suggest that competition is being restricted or distorted. See J Schwarze and A Weitbrecht, *Grundzüge des Europäischen Kartellverfahrensrecht* (n 1 above) § 4 para 5. The Commission is committed to a more frequent use of sector inquiries in the future. See for more details ch 5 'Opening of the file' paras 5.04 *et seq*.

[12] See ch 14 'Special procedures' paras 14.01 to 14.15.

[13] See also Reg 1/2003, Recital 11.

[14] Case 792/79 *Camera Care v EC Commission* [1980] ECR 119.

[15] Case 792/79 *Camera Care v EC Commission* [1980] ECR 119 paras 20 *et seq*; Case T-23/90 *Peugeot v EC Commission* [1991] ECR II-653 para 19; Case T-44/90 *La Cinq v Commission* [1992] ECR II-1 paras 1, 13, and 27; J Schwarze and A Weitbrecht, '*Grundzüge des Europäischen Kartellverfahrensrecht*' (2004) § 6 para 47; CS Kerse and N Khan, *EC Antitrust Procedure* (5th edn, 2005) para 6–032. In the case the application was rejected, the applicant could have the refusal reviewed by the Community Courts.

Article 8, since the Commission considers that it acts in the public interest and not in the interest of individual operators.[16] Companies could always have recourse to national courts, the very function of which is to protect the rights of individuals.[17] Article 8(1) follows the requirements laid down in *Camera Care* in requiring that the Commission show a prima facie case.[18] In *Peugeot* and *La Cinq* the CFI condemned the Commission for applying a too stringent test.[19] The requirement of certainty demanded of a final decision was not needed to satisfy the condition relating to the probable existence of an infringement in interim measures proceedings. In regard to the harm justifying intervention, in *Camera Care* the ECJ treated damage to other undertakings and jeopardizing the Competition's policy as separate criteria for adopting interim measures.[20] Article 8(1) refers to 'damage to competition' which could encompass damage to undertakings and to competition policy.

---

[16] Proposal for a Council Reg on the implementation of the rules on competition laid down in Arts 81 and 82 (EC) and amending Regs (EEC) 1017/68, (EEC) 2988/74, (EEC) 4056/86, and (EEC) 3975/87 ('Draft Regulation implementing Arts 81 and 82 EC' [2000] OJ C365E/284) [2000] OJ Explanatory Memorandum Art 8; Notice on Complaints [2004] OJ C101/65 para 80. Art 8 decisions may now be similar to decisions under former Art 15(6) of Reg 17 relating to the withdrawal of immunity from fines, where the CFI ruled that third-party complaints have no legitimate interests in having immunity withdrawn. CS Kerse and N Khan, *EC Antitrust Procedure* (5th edn, 2005) para 6–032 express doubts as to whether the Court will accept that the adoption of interim measures will be removed from the scope of judicially reviewable acts. D Geradin and N Petit, 'Judicial Remedies under EC Competition Law: Complex Issues Arising from the Modernization Process', 32nd Annual International Antitrust Law & Policy Conference, Fordham Corporate Law Institute, 22–23 September 2005 (forthcoming), 12 note that the formulation of Art 8 of Reg 1/2003 would be open to criticism and difficult to reconcile with the case law of the Community Courts which have acknowledged under certain conditions a right to interim relief by economic operators. See ch 14 'Special procedures' para 14.09.

[17] J Schwarze and A Weitbrecht, *Grundzüge des Europäischen Kartellverfahrensrecht* (2004) § 6 paras 48, 49 indicate that this does not need to entail a restriction of the legal protection given the increased role of national courts and that the assessment of the notion of public interest will also embrace the interests of individual companies.

[18] In this case, Camera Care sold and repaired cameras. It complained to the Commission that it would be denied supplies of Hasselblad cameras by Hasselblad and its distributors. It requested the Commission to take interim measures to protect its position while the matter was being investigated, but the Commission refused the request on the grounds that it had no power to do so. On appeal, the Court held that the Commission had the power to take interim measures. Case 792/79 *Camera Care v EC Commission* [1980] ECR 119 paras 19–20.

[19] Case T-23/90 *Peugeot v EC Commission* [1980] ECR 119 paras 59, 61; Case T-44/90 *La Cinq v EC Commission* [1992] ECR-II-1 paras 61 and 62. Essentially, in proceedings relating to the legality of a Commission decision concerning the adoption of interim measures, the requirement of a finding of a prima facie infringement cannot be placed on the same footing as the requirement of certainty that a final decision must satisfy. The Commission is wrong to identify the requirement of a 'prima facie infringement' with the requirement of a finding of a 'clear and flagrant infringement' at the stage of interim measures.

[20] Case 792/79 *Camera Care v EC Commission* [1980] ECR 119 para 19.

4. Rejection of complaints and finding of inapplicability

Rejection of complaints[21]

4.07 Proceedings commenced by a complaint may conclude with a decision declaring and penalizing an infringement of Articles 81 and 82 EC or else with the rejection of the complaint. While the Commission has the duty 'to examine carefully the facts and points of law brought to its notice by the complainant in order to establish whether they disclose conduct liable to distort competition in a given area',[22] the Commission is not obliged to carry out an investigation of every compliant submitted with a view to establishing whether the infringement has been committed.[23] During the first stage, the Commission examines the complaint and may collect further information in order to decide what action it will take.[24] In the second stage, the Commission may investigate the case further with a view to initiating proceedings pursuant to Article 7(1) of Regulation 1/2003. Where the Commission has investigated a complaint and intends not to pursue it, it must inform the complainant of this. The complainant, who in many cases will have actively participated during the investigation, is given the opportunity to submit any further comments within a fixed time-limit before the Commission decides formally to reject a compliant. Article 7 of Regulation 773/2004 states that 'where the Commission considers that on the basis of the information in its possession there are insufficient grounds for acting on a complaint . . . [and] set a time-limit' within which the complainant must submit his or her views. 'Article 7 letters' are similar to 'Article 6 letters' under Regulation 99/63 and seek to safeguard the rights of the complainant.[25]

4.08 It is important to note that an 'Article 7' letter does not imply that the Commission will not change its position in the future.[26] It is the result of a preliminary

---

[21] Ch 12 'Rejection of complaints'.

[22] eg Case T-575/93 *Koelman v EC Commission* [1996] ECR II-1 para 39.

[23] Notice on Complaints [2004] OJ C101/65 para 53.

[24] This stage may include an informal exchange of views between the Commission and the complainant in order to establish the factual and legal basis of the complaint. Notice on Complaints [2004] OJ C101/65 para 54.

[25] The Commission notes that this procedure between the complainant and the companies which are subject to the investigation is not adversarial. Consequently, these rights would be less far-reaching than the rights of the companies under investigation. Notice on Complaints [2004] OJ C101/65 para 59. K Lenaerts and J Maselis, 'Procedural Rights and Issues in the Enforcement of Articles 81 and 82 of the EC Treaty' [2001] Fordham International Law Journal 1615–54 (1648–49) noting that the rights of complainants would be limited to the right to 'participate' in the administrative procedure. See also L Ritter and WD Brown, *European Competition Law: A Practitioner's Guide* (3rd edn, 2004) 1102.

[26] Case 125/78 *GEMA v EC Commission* [1979] ECR 3173 para 17: '[. . .] Such a communication implies the discontinuance of the proceedings without, however, preventing the Commission from reopening the file if it considers it advisable, in particular where, within the period allowed by the Commission for that purpose in accordance with the provisions of Article 7 the

examination of the information to which the complainant has a right of access.[27] Such access is normally provided by annexing to the letter a copy of the relevant documents.[28] If the complainant does not respond within the time limit set, the complaint is deemed to have been withdrawn pursuant to Article 7(3) of Regulation 773/2004.[29] In all other cases, in the third procedural phase, the Commission takes cognisance of the observations submitted by the complainant and either initiates a procedure against the company under investigation or adopts a definitive decision rejecting the complaint stating that on the basis of the facts and information in its possession the complaint is unjustified or does not merit further action by the Commission.[30] Regulation 773/2004 makes it clear that the complainant is entitled to a decision from the Commission on the matter of its complaint.[31]

As regards the grounds for rejecting a complaint, the Commission has from the outset discretion in the choice of cases it will pursue. As the CFI recognized in *Automec II*, the Commission is entitled to give different degrees of priority to complaints made to it. In this sense, it may refer to the Community interest in order to give priority to a particular case.[32] The Commission may reject a **4.09**

---

applicant puts forward fresh elements of law or of fact [...]'. The Art 7 letter does not itself constitute a decision challengeable before the Court in an action for annulment under Art 230 EC. See Case T-186/94 *Guérin Automobiles v EC Commission* [1995] ECR II-1753 para 32, confirmed on appeal C-282/95 *Guérin Automobiles v EC Commission* [1997] ECR I-1503 para 34. It constitutes, however, a definition of the position within the meaning of Art 232, second paragraph EC and cannot therefore be challenged on the basis of that provision. However, if the Commission fails either to initiate a proceeding against the subject of the complaint or to adopt a definitive decision within a reasonable time the complainant may rely on Art [232] EC in order to bring an action for failure to act.

[27] Art 8(1) of Reg 773/2004. It is to be noted that the Commission draft Notice on Access to the file provides that access will be granted on a 'single occasion' after the issuance of the Art 7 letter [2005] OJ C325/7, para 27.

[28] Commission Notice on the handling of complaints by the Commission under Arts 81 and 82 of the EC Treaty [2004] OJ C101/65 para 69.

[29] This would mean that the Commission is not required to take a decision formally rejecting the complaint. On the other hand, this should prevent the complainant from reviving the complaint and the Commission from reassessing its position in light of any further information provided by the complainant. CS Kerse and N Khan, *EC Antitrust Procedure* (5th edn, 2005) para 3–036.

[30] This decision can be challenged before the Court. In the context of such an action the complainant may rely on any legal defects in the provisional measures prior to the definitive decision. Case C-282/95 *Guérin Automobiles v EC Commission* [1995] ECR I-1503 para 38. If the Commission fails either to initiate proceedings against the undertaking complained of or to adopt a definitive decision within a reasonable time the complainant may rely on Art 232 EC in order to bring an action for failure to act.

[31] Art 7(2) of Reg 773/2004.

[32] Case T-24/90 *Automec v EC Commission* [1992] ECR II-2223 para 85. Automec was a distributor of BMW vehicles in Italy. On the expiry of its dealership, Automec brought proceedings before the national courts to compel BMW to continue the contractual relationship and subsequently lodged a complaint. The Commission sent Automec a letter stating that it had no

complaint where it considers that the case does not display a sufficient Community interest to justify further examination.[33] While the Commission's Notice on complaints sums up the case law as to when the Commission may be justified on refusing a complaint on grounds of insufficient Community interest, the Community Courts have made it clear that there is not an exhaustive list of factors to which the Commission can or should have regard.[34] Having a wide margin of discretion, the Commission is nevertheless required to state reasons if it declines to pursue a complaint.[35] In addition, the Commission cannot exclude certain types of cases from the investigation.[36] Accordingly there is no short cut for the Commission: the Commission cannot consider certain situations as excluded in principle.[37]

Declarations of inapplicability[38]

4.10 Article 10 of Regulation 1/2003 enables the Commission acting on its own initiative to adopt a decision finding that Article 81 EC is not applicable to an agreement either because the conditions of Article 81(1) EC are not fulfilled or because the conditions of Article 81(3) EC are satisfied. Article 10 further states that the Commission may also make the same finding with reference to Article 82 EC.[39] While the Commission issued a detailed Notice on Informal Guidance, there is no similar communication on the declarations of inapplicability. There

---

power to grant its application. Automec brought the matter before the CFI seeking annulment of the letter and damages for the Commission's failure to commence proceedings against BMW (Case T-64/89 *Automec v Commission* [1990] ECR II-367). Automec and the Commission continued their correspondence. In 1990 the Commission rejected Automec's complaint stating that there was not a sufficient Community interest to justify an investigation. Automec appealed to the CFI which gave rise to *Automec II*.

[33] Notice on Complaints [2004] OJ C101/65 para 28.

[34] Case C-119/97 *Ufex and v EC Commission* [1999] ECR I-1341 para 79: '[. . .] the number of criteria of assessment the Commission may refer to should not be limited, nor conversely should it be required to have recourse exclusively to certain criteria [. . .]'; Case C-450/98 *IECC v EC Commission* [2001] ECR I-3947 para 58.

[35] The Commission is under an obligation to state reasons if it declines to continue with the examination of a complaint and those reasons must be sufficiently precise and detailed to enable the Court effectively to review the Commission's use of its discretion to define priorities. Case C-119/97 *Ufex v EC Commission* [1999] ECR I-1341 paras 89–95; Case T-26/99 *Trabisco v EC Commission* [2001] ECR II-633 para 31; Case T-115/99 *SEP v EC Commission* [2001] ECR II-691 para 31.

[36] Case C-119/97 *Ufex v EC Commission* [1999] ECR I-1341 paras 90–92.

[37] CS Kerse and N Khan, *EC Antitrust Procedure* (5th edn, 2005) para 2–045.

[38] ch 5 'Opening of the file' paras 5.32 *et seq.*

[39] CS Kerse and N Khan, *EC Antitrust Procedure* (5th edn, 2005) para 2–065 take the view this type of decision covers the old 'negative clearance' and 'exemption' although a declaration under Art 10 would appear '*to be something more than the former but less than the latter*'. The declaration of inapplicability may contain a statement as to whether Art 81(3) EC is satisfied (unlike 'negative decisions') but it would not apply for a fixed period of time (unlike exemptions).

is no prescribed form.[40] This demonstrates that the Commission is determined not to allow Article 10 to be used as a backdoor route for notifications which could jeopardize the main objective of Regulation 1/2003.[41] Article 10 of Regulation 1/2003 shows its exceptional character by stating that such decisions may be taken where 'the Community interest so requires'.[42] For this reason, and given that the Commission is under no obligation to make inapplicability declarations at the request of the parties, it is very likely that the Commission will only rarely make use of this possibility of issuing inapplicability decisions and will limit this to situations where for example the Commission desires to make quasi-legislative statements in regard to new types of agreements or practices.[43]

In contrast to NCAs, which can decide that there are no grounds for an action, **4.11** the Commission may state that Articles 81 and 82 EC are not applicable.[44] As regards findings under Article 81(3) EC, the scope of Article 10 decisions may be weaker compared to exemption decisions under former Regulation 17. Where those decisions granted exemption for a fixed period of time and could only be withdrawn in limited circumstances, a decision under Article 10 does not protect the agreement in question for a specified period of time and in principle the Commission would be free at any time to reopen the case. Where the Commission intends to adopt a decision of inapplicability, it shall publish a concise summary of the case and the main content of the proposed course of action. Interested parties may submit their observations within a time limit fixed

---

[40] It seems that a letter would suffice in order to apply for a declaratory decision. CS Kerse and N Khan, *EC Antitrust Procedure* (5th edn, 2005) suggest that given the similarity between a decision under Art 10 of Reg 1/2003 and the former negative clearance or exemption under Reg 17 the Commission may demand the amount of information it would have required under Form A/B.

[41] See Draft Regulation Implementing Articles 81 and 82 EC [2000] OJ C365E/284, Explanatory Memorandum Art 10: '[. . .] Such a possibility would seriously undermine the principal aim of the reform, which is to focus the activities of all competition authorities on what is prohibited. [. . ..]'.

[42] See also Reg 1/2003, Recital 14, stating that '[. . .] in exceptional cases where the public interest of the Community so requires, it may also be expedient for the Commission to adopt a decision of a declaratory nature [. . .]'.

[43] J Schwarze and A Weitbrecht, *Grundzüge des Europäischen Kartellverfahrensrecht* (2004) § 6 para 100 indicate that this situation may occur where an NCA has prohibited a certain agreement or concerted practice (or where such prohibition is forthcoming), which the Commission considers as permitted. Once the Commission has issued a decision, this would be binding for national courts and NCAs alike—see Art 16 of Reg 1/2003—although it would be questionable whether this would always be in line with the exceptional character of Art 10 and whether it would not be preferable for the Commission to apply Art 11(6) of Reg 1/2003 in these cases. F Montag and S Cameron, 'Effective Enforcement: The Practitioner's View of Recent Experiences under Regulation 1/2003', Antitrust Reform in Europe: A Year in Practice, 9–11 March 2005, Brussels, International Bar Association (IBA), 6, also note that the Commission is expected to use Art 10, *in extremis*, to make pronouncements to protect the consistent application of EU Law.

[44] Reg 1/2003, Art 5.

by the Commission.[45] Before the Commission issues its decision, it will consult with the Advisory Committee. Decisions under Article 10 must be published.

5. Commitments and informal settlements[46]

4.12 Article 9(1) of Regulation 1/2003 provides that where the Commission intends to adopt a decision requiring that an infringement be brought to an end and the undertakings concerned offer commitments to meet the competition concerns, the Commission may make those commitments binding on the undertakings. Such a decision can only be adopted after the Commission has begun proceedings.[47] Thus, after having made a preliminary assessment, the Commission would find that 'there are no longer grounds for action by the Commission without concluding whether or not there has been an infringement'.[48] In

---

[45] J Schwarze and A Weitbrecht, *Grundzüge des Europäischen Kartellverfahrensrecht* (2004) § 6 paras 102–105 point out that Art 27(1) and (2) and (3) of Reg 1/2003 which expand on sub-paragraph (1) do not refer to Art 10. Although the wording of Art 27 might suggest that defence rights are limited to the right to submit observations on the summary published in the OJ (see Art 27(4) of Reg 1/2003), Schwarze and Weitbrecht take the view that the defence rights referred to in Art 27(1) through (3) should also apply to proceedings under Arts 10 and 9. They argue that third parties should also be granted the right to challenge the decision under Art 10 of Reg 1/2003 on the basis of Art 230 fourth paragraph EC where (i) they have been heard; (ii) they submitted their observations and where the decision impairs their rights and interests; and (iii) the third party. See in this regard, J Schwarze and A Weitbrecht, *Grundzüge des Europäischen Kartell-verfahrensrecht* (2004) § 6 para 120. D Geradin and N Petit, 'Judicial Remedies under EC Competition Law: Complex Issues Arising from the Modernization Process', 32nd Annual International Antitrust Law & Policy Conference Fordham Corporate Law Institute, 22–23 September 2005 (forthcoming), 11 also take the view that these decisions show features of challengeable acts, also because they are binding upon NCAs and national courts.

[46] See ch 13 'Commitments, Voluntary Adjustments, Conclusion of the Procedure without a Formal Decision'.

[47] Undertakings do not have to wait until a statement of objections is sent to offer commitments and have them accepted. In some of the early cases where Art 9(1) was applied, the preliminary assessment of the Commission was expressed in a simple letter addressed to the affected undertakings, following which the undertakings concerned have offered commitments. C Fernández Vicién, 'Commitment Decisions under EC Regulation 1/2003', Antitrust Reform in Europe: A Year in Practice, 9–11 March 2005, Brussels, International Bar Association (IBA), 3–4.

[48] Reg 1/2003, Recital 13. The meaning of this stipulation remains unclear: it could mean that the Commission may decide that it no longer wishes to pursue the case or that the Commission can state that provided the commitments are complied with there is no longer an infringement. See A Jones and B Sufrin, *EC Competition Law* (2nd edn, 2004) 1115. It is to note that under the original Commission proposal Art 9(2) provided that the [commitment] decision makes no finding as to the existence of an infringement prior to the commitments or as to the absence of an infringement following the commitments. See Proposal for a Reg implementing Arts 81 and 82 EC (n 16 above). This provision was not maintained in Reg 1/2003 but now appears in Recitals 13 and 22. The latter stipulates that commitment decisions adopted by the Commission do not affect the power of the courts and NCAs to apply Arts 81 and 82 EC. Thus, the same companies may still face enforcement action before NCAs and national courts, 'provided that the uniform application of the competition rules throughout the EU is not jeopardised'. See Commission Memo/04/217 of 17 September 2004 'Commitment decisions (Art 9 of Council Regulation

addition, commitments are not appropriate where the Commission contemplates imposing a fine.[49] Prior to Regulation 1/2003, commitments offered by the parties aimed at terminating the infringement of EC competition rules,[50] whilst the Commission could require the undertaking to submit proposals with a view to bringing the infringement to an end,[51] with the difference being that the Commission could not make those commitments binding on the undertakings.

The Commission has a wide discretion in relation to the acceptance of commitments.[52] Commitments may be behavioural or structural, may be limited in time and varied or withdrawn if the facts change. In contrast to merger control proceedings where the Commission prefers the imposition of structural remedies,[53] in antitrust cases they might primarily be behavioural given that they aim to terminate infringements.[54] In deciding whether or not to accept commitments the Commission can take into consideration, together with the facts of **4.13**

1/2003 providing for a modernized framework for antitrust scrutiny of company behaviour)'. Conversely, a customer or a competitor possibly seeking private enforcement in national courts still needs to prove the illegality of the former behaviour to obtain compensation for damages.

[49] Reg 1/2003, Recital 13. J Temple Lang, 'Commitments under Regulation 1/2003: Legal Aspects of a new Kind of Competition Decision' [2003] ECLR 347–56 (347) suggests that there would be no reason why a commitment decision could not be adopted in a case in which the Commission intended to impose a fine when it sent the statement of objections, but later decided that a fine was not necessary or justified. See also Commission Memo/04/217 (n 48 above) stating that commitment decisions would be excluded in hard core cartel cases.

[50] Joined Cases 89/85, 104/85, 114/85, 116/85, 117/85 and 125/85 to 129/85 *Ahlström Osakeyhtiö and others v EC Commission 'Woodpulp II'* [1993] ECR I-1307 para 117. See also M Busse and A Leopold, 'Entscheidungen über Verpflichtungszusagen nach Article 9 VO (EG) Nr. 1/2003' [2004] Wirtschaft und Wettbewerb 146–55 (147); J Schwarze and A Weitbrecht, *Grundzüge des Europäischen Kartellverfahrensrecht* (2004), § 6 para 69. J Temple Lang, 'Commitment Decisions and Settlements with Antitrust Authorities and Private Parties under European Antitrust Law', 32nd Annual International Antitrust Law & Policy Conference Fordham Corporate Law Institute, 22–23 September 2005 (forthcoming), Part I with more references on case law.

[51] Cases 6/73 and 7/73 *Istituto Chemioterapico Italiano and Commercial Solvents v EC Commission* [1974] ECR 223 para 45.

[52] The Commission has described in its Commission Memo/04/217 commitment decisions as '[. . .] a formal settlement solicited by a company under investigation and agreed by the Commission where its enforcement priorities justify this choice. [. . .].' J Temple Lang 'Commitment Decisions and Settlements with Antitrust Authorities and Private Parties under European Antitrust Law', 32nd Annual International Antitrust Law & Policy Conference Fordham Corporate Law Institute, 22–23 September 2005 (forthcoming), 10–11 offering a detailed analysis on the situation where the Commission may consider imposing commitment decisions.

[53] Commission Notice on remedies acceptable under Council Reg (EEC) 4064/89 and under Commission Reg (EC) 447/98 [2001] OJ C68/3 paras 9, 26.

[54] M Busse and A Leopold, 'Entscheidungen über Verpflichtungszusagen nach Article 9 VO (EG) Nr. 1/2003' [2004] Wirtschaft und Wettbewerb 146–55 (148). Note that pursuant to Recital 12 of Reg 1/2003, structural remedies should only be imposed either where there is no equally effective behavioural remedy or where any equally effective behavioural remedy would be more burdensome for the undertaking concerned that the structural changes.

the case, any breach of a previous commitment given by the undertaking in question. A decision under Article 9 would not constitute proof that there has been an infringement or the opposite. Article 9(2) stipulates that the Commission is entitled to reopen the procedure only if the facts on the basis of which the Commission accepted the commitments have materially changed, if the undertaking offering the commitments has supplied incorrect, incomplete, or misleading information, or if the undertaking breaches the commitments. In accordance with Articles 23(2)(c) and 24(1)(c) of Regulation 1/2003 fines or periodic penalties may therefore be imposed for breach of a commitment. Where the Commission has evidence of a negligent or intentional non-compliance with an interim or commitment decision, it may impose a fine to sanction the 'bad faith' conduct of a company, independently of whether this infringement involved a breach of Articles 81 or 82 EC.[55] Pursuant to Article 27(4) of Regulation 1/2003, where the acceptance of commitments is envisaged a summary of the case and the main content of the offered commitments must be published, inviting comments by interested parties. In addition, the Commission publishes the full text of the commitments in their original language on the Internet,[56] giving interested parties one month within which to make comments. If this so-called market test reveals any weaknesses of the proposed course of action, the Commission can renegotiate or abandon the settlement option and revert to the prohibition scenario if appropriate.[57] The first Article 9 proceedings were initiated in relation to the liberalization of the centralized marketing of the German Football League.[58]

Informal settlements

4.14 The Community administrative procedure provides undertakings with an opportunity to adjust their agreements, practices, or conduct so as to comply with

---

[55] See ch 11 'Infringement decisions and penalties' para 11.10.
[56] See, e.g. *Joint selling of the media rights to the German Bundesliga* [2004] OJ C229/13 which was the first commitment decision under Reg 1/2003.
[57] CS Kerse and N Khan, *EC Antitrust Procedure* (5th edn, 2005) para 6–053.
[58] Commission Press Release IP/05/62 'Competition: German Football League commitments to liberalise joint selling of Bundesliga media rights made legally binding by Commission decision'. In August 1998, the German Football Federation applied for an individual exemption under Art 81(3) of the EC Treaty in respect of the joint selling of television and radio broadcasting rights and rights to other forms of exploitation for matches in the first and second national football divisions. In 2003, the parties submitted an amended version of the Agreement after the Commission had informed that the originally notified agreement was incompatible with Art 81 of the EC Treaty. By letter dated June 2004, the Commission informed the German Football Federation and the German Football League of its preliminary assessment in the sense of Art 9(1) of Reg 1/2003 and the parties subsequently confirmed the commitments offered during the notification procedure. The European Commission finally adopted a decision in January 2005 rendering such commitments legally binding. S Wilbert, 'Joint selling of Bundesliga media rights—first Commission decision pursuant to Article 9 of Regulation 1/2003', Competition Policy Newsletter, Number 2, Summer 2005, 44–46.

competition law. In principle, it is open to undertakings to secure a favourable decision from the Commission on their case—either formally or informally—if they voluntarily agree to comply with the requirements of Articles 81 and 82 EC.[59] In general, the Commission may resolve cases of any kind either formally or informally. Although it does not appear that Article 9 would prevent the Commission from settling a case by any means other than a formal decision, there is the suggestion that the Commission might no longer pursue informal settlements, given the possibility of imposing commitments under Article 9. Moreover, having recourse to informal settlements could undermine interested parties' rights of due process.[60] While informal settlements necessarily imply less transparency and the number of old-style informal settlements may decrease significantly given the procedure laid down in Article 9, the Commission cannot be understood as having waived its right to reach an amicable informal settlement with the parties during the preliminary investigation stage.[61] While the Commission is expected to focus its resources on high-profile cases, it should not be automatically forced to adopt a commitment decision under Article 9 of Regulation 1/2003 where the Commission and the parties agree on that the latter will behave in a given manner in order to avoid infringing EC competition rules, at least when no statement of objections has been issued yet. It would then be a commitment, but not one which is formally binding.[62] Unlike the US system, under Regulation 1/2003 there is no arrangement for a simplified handling of cases whereby the parties to the cartel and enforcer concur as to the nature and scope of the illegal activity undertaken and the appropriate penalty to be imposed. The Commission has indicated that if it is unable to deliver swift enforcement with timely punishment, it may look at the possible advantages of introducing some form of plea bargaining system in the context of European competition law.[63]

---

[59] See C Bellamy and G Child, *EC Law of Competition* (5th edn, 2001) 12.074; A Riley, 'EC Antitrust modernization: the Commission does very nicely—thank you!' [2003] ECLR 604–7; J Schwarze and A Weitbrecht, *Grundzüge des Europäischen Kartellverfahrensrecht* (n 1 above) § 6 para 69.

[60] CS Kerse and N Khan, *EC Antitrust Procedure* (5th edn, 2005) para 6–055.

[61] L Ritter and WD Brown, *European Competition Law: A Practitioner's Guide* (3rd edn, 2004) 1041, also note that the vast majority of cases are closed without reaching the stage of formal decision and point out that in the years 1996–2001 the number of formal decisions annually was limited to 21–68, whereas 300–500 cases were closed without formal decision. XXXI Report on Competition Policy after para 243.

[62] J Temple Lang 'Commitments under Regulation 1/2003: Legal Aspects of a new Kind of Competition Decision' [2003] ECLR 347–56 (347).

[63] Commissioner for Competition Policy, N Kroes, 'The First Hundred Days', Speech at 40th Anniversary of the Studienvereinigung Kartellrecht 1965–2005, International Forum on European Competition Law, Brussels, 7 April 2005. P Lowe, 'Enforcement Antitrust Roundtable' 32nd Annual International Antitrust Law & Policy Conference Fordham Corporate Law Institute, 22–23 September 2005 (forthcoming).

B. Use of Languages and Calculation of Time-Limits

4.15 Complainants can address themselves to the Commission in any of the twenty official languages, and have the right to be answered in the same language.[64] Pursuant to Article 3 of Regulation 1, documents which the Community institutions send to persons subject to the jurisdiction of a Member State are to be drawn up in the language of that State.[65] Complaints shall be submitted in one of the official languages of the Community.[66] This also applies to oral communications between officials of the Community institutions and individuals. For written communications, some undertakings and their lawyers prefer in certain cases—particularly where the official in charge of the case does not speak the language of the undertaking—to lodge their submissions in their own language together with a translation into French or English. They then conduct correspondence with the Commission in one of the latter languages, which are the two most common working languages used in the Commission. This does not imply any waiver of undertakings' 'linguistic rights' but may sometimes be conducive to a faster determination of cases, by avoiding the delay involved in translating the undertakings' submissions. Where the Commission relies on documentary evidence in support, for example, of the statement of objections, the original version should be made available to the undertakings

---

[64] Council Reg No 1 determining the languages to be used by the EEC [1958] OJ Spec Ed 59 last modified by Annex II, ch 22, para 1, of the Accession Act [2003] OJ L236/791.

[65] This provision has been invoked against the Commission's practice of sending the records of hearings in infringement procedures in the languages in which the various participants express themselves, without a translation. See Case T-77/92 *Parker Pen v EC Commission* [1994] ECR II-549 paras 72–75. The CFI dismissed that case because the undertaking had had an opportunity to follow the hearings in its own language through simultaneous interpretation and because the undertaking had not alleged 'substantial inaccuracies or omissions which [might] have adverse legal consequences such as to vitiate the administrative procedure as a result of the fact that there was no translation of the parts drawn up in German'. Art 3 of Reg 1 has also been invoked against the practice of sending the annexes of statements of objections in their original language to the undertakings. The CFI has differentiated between the statement of objections as such, which must be considered a 'text' within the meaning of the Art and which must therefore be sent to addressees in their own language, and its annexes. Annexes coming from the Commission are viewed as exhibits on which the Commission relies as evidence. They must therefore be brought to the attention of the addressee in their original state. This is so that the latter can see how the Commission has interpreted the evidence on which not only the statement of objections, but also the formal decision itself is based. Moreover, as the CFI has pointed out, statements of objections generally quote the most important parts of the annexes in the language of the addressees. See Case T-148/89 *Trefilunion v EC Commission* [1995] ECR II-1063 paras 19–21. See also K Lenaerts and J Maselis, 'Procedural Rights and Issues in the Enforcement of Articles 81 and 82 of the EC Treaty' [2001] Fordham International Law Journal 1615–54 (1651–52).

[66] See Art 5(3) of Reg 773/2004.

concerned.[67] The parties must be able to evaluate the interpretation that the Commission has adopted.[68]

With respect to the calculation of the time-limits applied by the Commission in Community antitrust procedure (which are generally fixed in terms of days, weeks, or months), Articles 2 and 3 of Regulation 1182/71, which apply to all Commission measures by virtue of the EC Treaty, lay down rules similar to those contained in the national laws of the Member States.[69]   **4.16**

C. General Characteristics of Proceedings

1. The nature of the Commission and its proceedings

The Commission is an administrative authority which plays several different roles at the same time. Its functions are legislative, administrative, and, consequently, political. The Commission not only enforces competition law but also creates it, and, by so creating and applying it, develops competition policy. The ECJ has stated, with regard to the Commission's administrative function, that, in applying Community competition law, it is not to be regarded as a 'tribunal' within the meaning of Article 6 of the ECHR.[70] This Article provides that every person is entitled to have his or her case fairly tried by an independent and impartial tribunal.[71] The Commission is, on the contrary, an administrative body responsible for ensuring compliance with certain rules in the public interest of the Community. Like any administrative authority, the Commission undertakes preliminary inquiries, hears submissions of the parties, and then adopts the appropriate decision, imposing fines if   **4.17**

---

[67] While the observance of defence rights therefore requires that addressees of the statement of objections should have access during the administrative procedure to all the incriminating documents in their original versions, the Commission, in communicating those annexes in their original language, does not infringe the right to be heard of the undertakings concerned. Case T-25/95 *Cimenteries CBR v EC Commission* [2000] ECR II-491 para 635.

[68] Case T-148/89 *Tréfilunion v EC Commission* [1995] ECR II-1063 para 21; Case T-338/94 *Finnboard v EC Commission* [1998] ECR II-1617 para 53; Case T-9/99 *HFB v EC Commission* [2002] ECR II-1487, para 327.

[69] See Council Reg (EEC, Euratom) 1182/71 determining the rules applicable to periods, dates, and time limits [1971] OJ L124/1. Articles 2 and 3 are contained in the Appendices of this book.

[70] Convention for the Protection of Human Rights and Fundamental Freedoms (the European Human Rights Convention) (Rome, 4 November 1950; TS 71 (1953); Cmnd 8969).

[71] Joined Cases 209–215/78 and 218/78 *Van Landewyck v EC Commission* [1980] ECR 3125 para 81; Joined Cases 100/80 and 103/80 *Musique Diffusion Française v EC Commission* [1983] ECR 1825 para 7; Case T-11/89 *Shell v EC Commission* [1992] ECR II-757 para 39. K Lenaerts and J Maselis, 'Procedural Rights and Issues in the Enforcement of Articles 81 and 82 of the EC Treaty' [2001] Fordham International Law Journal 1615–54 (1616–17).

necessary.[72] As the Court has held in competition cases, '[s]uch an investigation [. . .] does not constitute adversary proceedings between the companies concerned; it is a procedure commenced by the Commission, upon its own initiative or upon application [complaint], in fulfilment of its duty to ensure that the rules on competition are observed.'[73]

4.18 The Commission should not be viewed as a neutral civil authority in proceedings *inter partes*, adopting its decision in favour of what it considers to be the more legitimate of two opposing positions put to it. Its conduct of proceedings is governed by the principle *audi alteram partem* and by the aim of establishing the objective truth by means of an inquisitorial procedure. The Commission must allow all possible addressees of a decision and third parties with an interest in it to make submissions and be heard impartially. Thereafter, it adopts its decision on the basis of the evidence before it and the submissions made. The criticism levelled at the Commission that it is both a judge and a party to its own proceedings is thus no better founded than the objections made against administrative proceedings in general.[74]

---

[72] Fines under Art 23 of Reg 1/2003 are administrative and not criminal in nature as is made clear by Art 15(4). In practice undertakings may, however, perceive little difference between Commission fines and criminal law fines. This is particularly so in the light of the evolution of ECtHR case law. In *Societé Stenuit v France* [1992] 14 EHRR 509 the European Commission of Human Rights considered the imposition of fines under French competition law as criminal for the purposes of the European Convention. See CS Kerse and N Khan, *EC Antitrust Procedure* (5th edn, 2005) para 7–008. Article 24 does not contain a similar disclaimer regarding the criminal nature of periodic penalties.

[73] See Joined Cases 142/84 and 156/84 *BAT and Reynolds v EC Commission* [1987] ECR 4487 para 19 and Case T-65/96 *Kish Glass v EC Commission* [2000] ECR II-1885 para 33. On the basis of this feature of the procedure, the Court classified the different procedural situations of undertakings involved in the proceedings as either subjects of complaints, on the one hand, or as complainants, on the other.

[74] See, e.g. Case T-11/89 *Shell v EC Commission* [1992] ECR II-757 paras 31 *et seq.* Shell accused the Commission of bias, in that it was possible for the same officials to investigate the case and report on it to the Commission. In fact, with effect from 1985, DG COMP ceased to have a Directorate with special responsibility for carrying out inspections, and the rapporteurs themselves began to carry out inspection duties. The CFI rejected that submission, considering that the procedural safeguards provided by Community law do not require the Commission to adopt a form of internal organization which prevents the same official from acting in the same case both as investigator and as rapporteur. Judge B Vesterdorf, 'Judicial Review in EC Competition Law: Reflections on the Role of the Community Courts in the EC System of Competition Law Enforcement', [2005] Vol 1, No 2 Competition Policy International 6 noting that a concentration of investigative, prosecutorial, and decision-making powers in the hands of a single body is not an unusual feature of administrative systems. Durande and K Williams, 'The practical impact of the exercise of the right to be heard: A special focus on the effect of Oral Hearings and the role of the Hearing Officers' EC Competition Newsletter, No 2—Summer 2005, 22–28 (24–25) who also point to the adversarial aspects in the Commission's procedure. For example, the Commission must give the defendant an opportunity to comment in writing on the objections and together with the oral hearing reinforce the quasi-adversarial nature of the stage of the procedure where the Commission is no longer the sole master and where the role of the Hearing Officer is to protect the

However, although the proceedings are administrative, in competition matters **4.19** they incorporate—as a result of the particular manner in which the Commission observes the principle that the parties must be heard—safeguards similar to those available in judicial proceedings. The administrative nature of the proceedings is evident in the preparatory phase, in which evidence is gathered.[75] Its quasi-judicial character is evident at the stage when submissions are made and the parties are heard, and is reflected by the procedural safeguards accorded to undertakings.[76] This particularity of the proceedings has prompted the Court to state that, with regard to infringements, Regulation 17 (now Regulation 1/2003) lays down two successive but clearly separate procedures. First, a preparatory investigation procedure, the purpose of which is to enable the Commission to obtain the information necessary to check the actual existence and scope of a specific factual and legal situation, and which includes the possibility of requesting information and carrying out inspections at the premises of undertakings. A second procedure, *inter partes*, commences with the statement of objections that the Commission sends to the undertakings when it has sufficient evidence of an infringement. It is covered by Article 27(1) and (2) of Regulation 1/2003 and Regulation 773/2004. In this second procedure, the undertakings have an opportunity to submit written and oral observations on the objections made against them. The Commission may only take a decision on objections about which the undertakings have had an opportunity to make their views known.[77] The Court thus refers to two procedures within the procedure for the application of competition rules, the second of which is an 'administrative procedure inter partes' of a quasi judicial nature (rather than a 'civil procedure inter partes', as explained above). Accordingly, the term 'procedure' will be used here in general to cover both of the procedures described; in other words to cover the whole sequence of measures and steps taken by the Commission from the initiation of a procedure until the adoption of a decision, and even thereafter. It must nevertheless be pointed out that the proceedings in the strict sense, or the proceedings for the adoption of a decision, is initiated only by means of an express measure of the Commission. It coincides with the second *inter partes*

---

requirements of due process. There are a number of persons, whether consultative—such as Member States or the Hearing Officer—or decisive—Commission services and the Commissioners in the college—that may take account of the result of the hearing.

[75] Regarding the means of investigation available to the Commission, see below, chs 7 'Formal investigative measures' and 8 'Inspections'.

[76] The rights and procedural guarantees available to undertakings and participants in Commission procedures will be studied in the sections dealing with each of the procedural phases.

[77] See Case 374/87 *Orkem v EC Commission* [1989] ECR 3283 paras 19–25; Case 27/88 *Solvay v EC Commission* [1989] ECR 3355 paras 16–22; Joined Cases T-10/92 to T-12/92 and T-15/92 *Cimenteries CBR and others v EC Commission* [1992] ECR II-2667 para 45; and Joined Cases T-191/98, T-212/98 to T-214/98 *Atlantic Container Line and others v EC Commission* [2003] II-3275 para 110.

procedure referred to by the Court in *Orkem*, which extends from the issue of a statement of objections to the adoption of a formal decision. For this phase, the term 'formal proceedings' or 'proceedings for the adoption of a decision' will be used.[78]

2. The burden of proof

4.20 Regulation 17 did not address the problem of proving infringements of Articles 81 and 82 EC. Nevertheless, it was well established that when the Commission accuses undertakings of infringing Community competition rules it bears the burden of proving the infringement.[79] Observance of the principles of evidence common to the administrative laws of the Member States and Community law, as interpreted by the Court, precludes the Commission from requiring undertakings to prove their innocence or else be presumed guilty. Once the Commission has produced evidence as to the existence of an infringement, it will be for the undertakings to show that such evidence is inadequate or the conclusions drawn from it are incorrect.[80] Even if it is accepted that in Community administrative law that the rules of evidence are not as strict as in criminal law—where the principle in *dubio pro reo* prevails—the Commission must still adequately prove the factual basis of its decisions.[81]

4.21 Article 2 of Regulation 1/2003 codifies the established practice that the burden

---

[78] This distinction will also be made later, in relation to the initiation of proceedings properly so called. See ch 5 'Opening of the file' paras 5.08 *et seq.*

[79] Opinion of AG Slynn in Joined Cases 100/80 and 103/80 *Musique Diffusion française v EC Commission* [1983] ECR 1825; Case C-185/95 P *Baustahlgewebe v EC Commission* [1998] ECR I-8417 para 58; Case C-49/92 P *EC Commission v Anic Partecipazioni SpA* [1999] ECR I-4125 para 86.

[80] Opinion of AG Slynn in Case 100/80 and 103/80 *Musique Diffussion Françiase v EC Commission* [1983] ECR 1825.

[81] See Joined Cases 40/73 to 48/73, 50/73, 54/73 to 56/73, 111/73, 113/73 and 114/73 *Suiker Unie v Commission* [1975] ECR 1663 paras 199–210. See also Case 41/69 *ACF Chemiefarma v EC Commission* [1970] ECR 661 paras 145–153, and Case 6/72 *Continental Can v EC Commission* [1973] ECR 215 paras 35–37. The criminal standard of 'beyond reasonable doubt' was suggested by AG Darmon in his Opinion in Joined Cases 89/85, 104/85, 114/85, 116/85, 117/85 and 125/85 to 129/85 *Ahlström Osakeyhtiö and others v EC Commission* [1993] ECR I-1307, but was not adopted by the Court. See also for the UK *Napp v Director-General of Fair Trading* [2002] CAT 1 [2002] Comp AR 13 paras 98 to 109. In *JJB Sports plc v Office of Fair Trading and Allsports* [2004] CAT 17 paras 164–209 it is also stated that while the proceedings may be classified as criminal for the purposes of the ECHR this would not in itself lead to the conclusion that these proceedings must be subject to the procedures and rules that apply to the investigation and trial of offences classified as criminal offences for the purposes of domestic law. the applicable standard of proof in such case would be the civil standard of proof—i.e. the infringement must be established on a preponderance of probabilities. The evidence must however be sufficient to convince the tribunal in the circumstances of the particular case, and to overcome the presumption of innocence to which the undertaking concerned is entitled. See also B Louveaux and P Gilbert, 'The Standard of Proof under the Competition Act' [2005] ECLR 173–77.

of proving an infringement of Article 81(1) or of Article 82 EC rests on the party or the authority alleging the infringement. Conversely, the undertakings claiming the benefit of Article 81(3) EC shall bear the burden of proving that the conditions are fulfilled.[82] From the undertakings' point of view, the Commission must produce sufficient reliable evidence to support its allegation that an infringement took place,[83] since, if it did not do so, the undertakings' only obligation would be to show that the evidence was inadequate.[84] All the elements of an infringement have to be proved, in particular the identity of the parties and their involvement in the infringement,[85] the products and services involved,[86] the restrictions agreed by the parties,[87] and the duration of the infringement.[88] If the Commission's reasoning is based on suppositions based on specific evidence, the fact that an undertaking can give a plausible explanation different from that relied on by the Commission would be a good ground

---

[82] Case T-66/89 *Publishers Association v EC Commission* [1992] ECR II-1995 paras 5–6 (this judgment has been quashed for reasons unrelated to the burden of proof in exemption proceedings; see Case C-360/92 *Publishers Association v Commission* [1995] ECR I-23. See the Joined Cases T-39/92 and T-40/92 *Groupement des Cartes Bancaires 'CB' and Europay International v EC Commission* [1994], ECR II-49 para 114 (which cites Case 258/78 *Nungesser v EC Commission* [1982] ECR 2015, and Case 45/85 *Verband der Sachversicherer v EC Commission* [1987] ECR 405, and also its own judgment in the *Publishers Association* case, cited above) and Case T-17/93 *Matra Hachette v EC Commission* [1994] ECR II-595 para 104 (which cites, *inter alia*, Joined Cases 43/82 and 63/82 *VBVB and VBBB v EC Commission* [1984] ECR 19). Case T-35/92 *John Deere v EC Commission* [1994] ECR II-957 para 105; Case T-29/92 *SPO and others v EC Commission* [1995] ECR II-289 para 262; Case T-86/95 *Compagnie Générale Maritime and others v EC Commission* [2002] ECR II-1011 para 381.

[83] Joined Cases 29/83 and 30/83 *CRAM v EC Commission* [1984] ECR 1679 para 20. See also Joined Cases 89/85, 104/85, 114/85, 116/85, 117/85 and 125/85 to 129/85 *Ahlström Osakeyhtiö and others v EC Commission* [1993] ECR I-1307 para 127; Joined Cases T-68/89, T-77/89 and T-78/89 *SIV and others v EC Commission* [1992] ECR II-1403 paras 193–195, 198–202, 205–210, 220–232, 249, 250, and 322–328; Case T-62/98 *Volkswagen v EC Commission* [2000] ECR II-2707 paras 43 and 72; and Joined Cases T-67/00, T-68/00, T-71/00 and T-78/00 *JFE Engineering v EC Commission* [2004] OJ C239/13 para 58.

[84] The CFI has referred expressly to the necessary 'standard of proof' or 'requisite legal standard' in its judgment in the *Italian Flat Glass* case, Joined Cases T-68/89, T-77/89, T-78/89 *SIV v EC Commission* [1992] ECR II-1403 paras 223–275. If that standard is not attained, no finding should be made against undertakings. See also Case T-6/89 *Enichem v EC Commission* [1991] ECR II-1623 paras 69 *et seq.*, and Case T-43/92 *Dunlop v EC Commission* [1994] ECR II-441 para 84; Joined Cases 29/83 and 30/83 *CRAM v EC Commission* [1984] ECR 1679 paras 16 *et seq.*, and Joined Cases T-185/96, T-189/96 and T-190/96 *Riviera Auto Service v EC Commission* [1999] ECR II-93 para 47. These cases demonstrate how the CFI is prepared to examine thoroughly and critically the evidence on which the Commission has based its decision.

[85] Joined Cases T-67/00, T-68/00, T-71/00 and T-78/00 *JFE Engineering v EC* [2004] OJ C239/13 para 58; Joined Cases T-68/89, T-77/89, T-78/89 *SIV v EC Commission* [1992] ECR II-1403 paras 175–194 and 324; Joined Cases 40/73 to 48/73, 50/73, 54/73 to 56/73, 111/73, 113/73 and 114/73 *Suiker Unie v EC Commission* [1975] ECR 1663 paras 301–304.

[86] Case T-68/89, etc *SIV and others v EC Commission* [1992] ECR II-1403 paras 175–194 and 324; Joined Cases 40/73 *Suiker Unie* [1975] ECR 1663 paras 301–304.

[87] Case T-295/94 *Enso-Gutzeit OY v EC Commission* [1998] ECR II-1571 paras 102–150.

[88] Case T-43/92 *Dunlop v EC Commission* [1994] ECR II-441 para 79; Case T-67/00, etc *JFE Engineering v EC Commission* [2004] OJ C239/13 paras 341–344.

for seeking to have the decision annulled.[89] This seems to be justified in situations where the Commission's evidence on unlawful anticompetitive conduct, such as the minutes of a meeting, is only fragmentary and sparse, so that it is often necessary to reconstitute certain details by deduction and to infer the existence of an anticompetitive agreement or concerted practice from a number of indicia and coincidences.[90] This seems all the more obvious as cartels are by their very nature hidden and secret and little or nothing will be in writing.[91] Conversely, the evidential burden may shift to the applicant if the decision invokes evidence capable of substantiating the infringement; it would then appear insufficient that the applicant could merely deny the infringement.[92]

4.22 Where it can be established that Article 81(1) EC applies, the question arises

[89] See Joined Cases 29/83 and 30/83 *CRAM v EC Commission* [1984] ECR 1679 para 16. To similar effect, Joined Cases 40/73 to 48/73, 50/73, 54/73 to 56/73, 111/73, 113/73 and 114/73 *Suiker Unie v EC Commission* [1975] ECR 1663 para 354. See also Joined Cases 89/85, 104/85, 114/85, 116/85, 117/85 and 125/85 to 129/85 *Ahlström Osakeyhtiö and others v EC Commission* [1993] ECR I-1307 para 126 and 127; Case C-53/92 *Hilti v EC Commission* [1994] ECR I-667 paras 33 *et seq.* and Case T-185/96 *Riviera AutoService v EC Commission* [1999] ECR II-93 para 47.

[90] Joined Cases C-204/00, C-205/00, C-211/00, C-213/00, C-217/00 and C-219/00 *Aalborg Portland v EC Commission* [2004] ECR I-123 paras 55–57, 81; Case T-23/99 *LR AF 1998 v EC Commission* [2002] ECR II-1705 para 39 stating that it is settled case law that where an undertaking participates, even if not actively, in meetings between undertakings with an anti-competitive object and does not publicly distance itself from what occurred at them, thus giving the impression to the other participants that it subscribes to the results of the meetings and will act in acordance with them, it may be concluded that it is participating in the cartel resulting from those meetings; see Case C-199/92 *Hüls v EC Commission* [1999] ECR I-4287 para 155; Case C-49/92 *EC Commission v Anic* [1999] ECR I-4125 para 96; Case T-7/89 *Hercules Chemicals v EC Commission* [1991] ECR II-1711 para 232; Case T-12/89 *Solvay v EC Commission* [1992] ECR II-907 para 98, and Case T-141/89 *Tréfileurope v EC Commission* [1995] ECR II-791 paras 85–86.

[91] In relation to the UK see also B Louveaux and P Gilbert, 'The Standard of Proof under the Competition Act' [2005] ECLR 173–77.

[92] Joined Cases T-67/00, T-68/00, T-71/00 and T-78/00 *JFE Engineering* [2004] OJ C239/13 para 203: '[. . .] it must also be pointed out that, in practice, the Commission is often obliged to prove the existence of an infringement under conditions which are hardly conducive to that task, in that several years may have elapsed since the time of the events constituting the infringement and a number of the undertakings covered by the investigation have not actively cooperated therein. Whilst it is necessarily incumbent upon the Commission to establish that an illegal market-sharing agreement was concluded [. . .], it would be excessive also to require it to produce evidence of the specific mechanism by which that object was attained [. . .]. Indeed, it would be too easy for an undertaking guilty of an infringement to escape any penalty if it was entitled to base its argument on the vagueness of the information produced regarding the operation of an illegal agreement in circumstances in which the existence and anticompetitive purpose of the agreement had nevertheless been sufficiently established'. See also Joined Cases C-204/00, C-205/00, C-211/00, C-213/00, C-217/00 and C-219/00 *Aalborg Portland v EC Commission* [2004] ECR I-123 para 79 in regard to burden of proof under Reg 17 and Reg 1/2003 para 79: '[. . .] Although according to those principles the legal burden of proof is borne either by the Commission or by the undertaking or association concerned, the factual evidence on which a party relies may be of such a kind as to require the other party to provide an explanation or justification, failing which it is permissible to conclude that the burden of proof has been discharged [. . .].'

whether Article 2 of Regulation 1/2003 requiring an undertaking to prove that an agreement benefits from the exemption under Article 81(3) is qualified by general principles of EC law and in particular the principle of in *dubio pro reo*. Some authors argue that when the undertaking establishes a prima facie case that Article 81(3) EC applies, it is up to the Commission or to the relevant NCA to investigate the facts further and a situation of *non liquet* at the end of such investigation would have to be decided in favour of the undertaking.[93] Given that the administrative procedure before the Commission might result in the imposition of a fine for the infringement of Article 81 EC, such proceedings could be regarded as equivalent to criminal proceedings where the presumption of innocence would apply. Consequently, it is argued that the burden of proof rule under Article 2 of Regulation 1/2003 could not be applied in the context of an infringement procedure leading to the imposition of a fine where the under-taking cannot adequately prove that Article 81 (3) EC applies, nor does the Commission succeed in demonstrating that it does not apply.[94] Others view Article 81(3) EC as an affirmative defence to an infringement of Article 81(1) EC which is admitted or established. If a prima facie case of such defence being invoked by the undertaking were rebutted, the burden of proof would lie with the undertaking. If it does not meet the burden, the Article 81(3) EC defence would fail and the infringement of Article 81(1) EC stands. In *dubio pro reo* might be of relevance when it comes to weighing up the conflicting evidence in the context of Article 81(3) EC.[95] It appears that before a finding of illegality can be made, the Article 81(3) EC assessment must be carried out by the competition authority or court and it must be concluded that *on balance* the agreement is *anti-competitive*,[96] meaning that its redeeming factors are

---

[93] This may be the case where the facts of the case could not be adequately substantiated.

[94] F Montag and A Rosenfeld, 'A solution to the Problem? Reg 1/2003 and modernization of competition procedure' [2003] Zeitschrift für Wettbewerbsrecht 107–35 (120). The authors submit that contrary to what the wording of Art 2 of Reg 1/2003 may suggest, a situation of *non liquet* at the end of a Commission investigation would have to be decided in favour of the undertakings concerned. Although the last sentence of Recital 5 of Reg 1/2003 explains that this provision 'affects neither national rules on the standard of proof nor obligations of competition authorities and courts of the Member States to ascertain the relevant facts of the case, provided that such rules and obligations are compatible with general principles of Community law', there was concern among Member States that the distribution of the burden of proof might lead to conflicts with the presumption of innocence. For example, at the time of the adoption of Reg 1/2003 Germany entered in the Council Minutes a statement that should enable the Cartel Authorities to prove the absence of the conditions under Art 81(3) EC in criminal proceedings and proceedings equivalent to criminal proceedings, http://www.bmwa.bund.de/Redaktion/Inhalte/Downloads/protokollerklaerung-vo–1–2003,property=pdf.pdf. See also J Schwarze and A Weitbrecht, *Grundzüge des Europäischen Kartellverfahrensrecht* (2004) § 11 paras 35–38.

[95] J Bourgeois and T Baumé, 'Decentralisation of EC Competition Law Enforcement and General Principles of Community Law' College of Europe, Research Papers in Law 4/2004 8.

[96] L Kjolbye, 'The New Commission Guidelines on the Application of Article 81(3): An Economic Approach to Article 81' [2004] ECLR 566–77 (566). This would require that the party can put forward some evidence for so-called pro-competitive (or positive) effects.

insufficient for the legal exception to apply. Where an undertaking or association of undertakings reasonably invokes the benefit of a defence against a finding of an infringement to demonstrate that the conditions for applying such defence are satisfied, the authority will then have to resort to other evidence.[97]

4.23 Apart from the issue of which party has the burden of proof, there may be questions as to what *standard of proof* will be required to apply Article 81(3) EC before the Commission or a national court. Especially, under Regulation 17, the Commission exercised a certain measure of discretion when deciding whether to exempt an agreement.[98] It remains to be seen the extent to which Article 81 (3) EC will allow the relevant competition authority or court to exercise a similar measure of discretion.[99] Arguably, there may be less room for discretion in the context of a legal exception; the consequence of the removal of the Commission's monopoly to apply Article 81(3) EC may well be that the requisite standard of proof under Article 81 (1) and 81(3) EC may end up being quite similar.[100] In the context of the application of both Article 81(1) and (3) EC, it may be expected that the Community courts will review thoroughly the probative value of the evidence taken into consideration by the Commission to see whether it reveals inaccuracies or errors.[101] What is a fact and what falls within an assessment of the facts is often far from easy to distinguish. At a national level, where Article 81(3) EC is now subject to a wide range of national procedural rules both as regards the way in which an appellate court reviews a decision of an NCA and the way a national court handles private litigation

---

[97] Joined Cases C-204/00, C-205/00, C-211/00, C-213/00, C-217/00 and C-219/00 *Aalborg Portland v EC Commission* [2004] ECR I-123 para 79.

[98] Opinion of AG Lenz in Case 42/84 *Remia v EC Commission* [1985] ECR 2545 section B.4 : 'since the conditions for an exemption are outlined in a general matter, the Commission enjoys a wide discretion even in the case of a straightforward application of Article [81(3) EC]'.

[99] CS Kerse and N Khan, *EC Antitrust Procedure* (5th edn, 2005) para 1–017.

[100] Note that the Guidelines on the application of Art 81(3) EC ([2004] OJ C101/97) try to develop an exclusively economic approach towards Art 81(3) EC. It particularly states that '[. . .] goals pursued by other Treaty provisions can be taken into account to the extent that they can be subsumed under the four conditions of Article 81(3) [. . .]' (para 43). This may lead to conflicts where the Commission seeks to use discretion to take into account other policies under Art 81(3) EC. See generally regarding the application of the Art 81(3) EC guidelines L Kjolbye, 'The New Commission Guidelines on the Application of Article 81(3): An economic Approach to Article 81' [2004] ECLR 566–77.

[101] See Case C-360/92 P *Publishers Association v EC Commission* [1995] ECR I-23 para 39: '[. . .] decisions must state the reasons on which they are based. It has consistently been held that while the Commission is not required to discuss all the issues of fact and law raised by undertakings seeking an exemption, the statement of reasons in any adverse decision must enable the Court to review its lawfulness and make clear to the Member State and the persons concerned the circumstances in which the Commission has applied the Treaty [. . .]'. The ECJ set aside both the judgment of the CFI and the Commission's decision. The CFI had committed an error of law by not considering the indispensability of the restrictions for objectives by the Association within the single language area comprising the UK and the Irish market.

matters, it may be that where a national court or tribunal has doubts on this issue, it will attempt to seek guidance on the application of Article 81(3) EC from the ECJ through a preliminary ruling.[102]

3. Choice of priorities

While Regulation 1/2003 provides the basis for the Commission's enforcement procedure and gives it the power to investigate and take decisions requiring the termination of infringements, it has led to a change of focus of DG COMP's activities. As the Commission is an administrative authority which must act in the public interest and since it is responsible not only for the application of competition rules but also for the shaping of competition policy,[103] a fundamental task inherent in the exercise of the Commission's administrative activity by which it directs its policy is 'setting priorities within the limits laid down by the law.'[104] It will no longer have to deal with notifications of agreements or have the power by administrative decision to exempt agreements under Article 81(3) EC. Under Regulation 1/2003, like under Regulation 17, the Commission does not investigate all the matters brought to its attention.[105] Nor does it observe the same degree of formality in every case it deals with, since that is not its function and, in any event, it does not have the material resources to do so. A fundamental criterion applied by the Commission in determining whether a case is sufficiently important, is the extent to which it involves a Community interest. That may be assessed, in the case of complaints, by reference, *inter alia*, to the impact of the alleged infringements on the functioning of the common market and the probability of establishing the infringement by a level of investigative activity commensurate with the importance of the case.[106] In other instances, regard is had to the novelty of the problems raised and the economic significance of cases. Under the new regime, DG COMP will be mainly involved with cases that are liable to result in prohibition decisions and decisions imposing fines. It is expected to focus on investigations in sectors where there are only a few players and where cartel activity is recurrent or where abuses of market power are generic.[107] Tackling cartels will remain a clear priority.

4.24

---

[102] D Baily, 'Scope of Judicial Review under Article 81 EC' (2004) CML Rev 1327–60 (1356, fn 150) notes that this would be in the interest of the uniform and coherent application of Community law, but it is not clear whether this would be a question of Community law upon which the ECJ could give a preliminary ruling.

[103] Case T-24/90 *Automec v EC Commission* [1992] ECR II-2223 para 73, citing Case C-234/89 *Delimitis v Henninger Bräu* [1991] ECR I-935.

[104] See Case T-24/90 *Automec* [1992] ECR II-2223 para 77.

[105] Regarding the treatment of complaints, see ch 12.

[106] See Case T-24/90 *Automec* [1992] ECR II-2223 para 86.

[107] Communication from the Commission—A pro-active Competition Policy for a Competitive Europe, COM (2004) final 20 April 2004.

D. Commission Decisions

1. General characteristics of decisions

4.25 During the procedures described above, or at their culmination, the Commission adopts various types of decisions which, pursuant to Article 249, fourth paragraph, EC, are binding in all respects on their addressees. As is apparent from the European Court case law on measures which may be challenged under Article 230 EC, Commission decisions are measures which produce legal effects and are liable to have a considerable impact on the legal situation of their addressees—and other interested parties—and thus affect their interests.[108] The vast majority of Commission decisions in competition matters are addressed to undertakings[109] and apply Community competition rules in a specific manner to specific cases. In that sense, its decisions may be regarded as equivalent to administrative measures under national law and constitute a means of administrative enforcement of Community law available to the Commission. All in all, decisions often have a value which goes beyond the mere determination of specific cases with which the Commission has to deal. The particular way in which the Commission—and more particularly DG COMP—works, dictated by the impossibility of dealing formally with all cases, makes it necessary to select those cases which will be brought to a formal conclusion and to some extent makes these decisions precedents for the future.[110]

4.26 Article 253 EC also provides that Commission decisions must state the reasons on which they are based and must refer to the proposals or opinions required to be obtained pursuant to the EC Treaty. The case law of the Court interprets the obligation to state reasons as a requirement that the Commission state clearly and unequivocally the reasoning followed for the adoption of its decisions. The reasons must disclose the Commission's arguments to the addressees, thus

---

[108] See, among others, Case 53/85 *AKZO v EC Commission* [1986] ECR 1965 para 16. A statement of objections cannot, therefore, be regarded as a decision against which proceedings may be brought: Case 60/81 *IBM v Commission* [1981] ECR 2639 para 11. D Geradin and N Petit, 'Judicial remedies under EC Competition Law: Complex Issues arising from the Modernization Process', 32nd Annual International Antitrust Law & Policy Conference Fordham Corporate Law Institute, 22–23 September 2005 (forthcoming) 5–6 suggest that the ruling in *IBM* permits an exception to the principle that the act must be of a definitive nature where the acts fall within a phase which can be separated from the course of proceedings leading to the definitive act. This point will be considered in greater detail in ch 10.

[109] However, a decision rejecting a complaint may be addressed to an individual. Regarding the main types of decision, see below.

[110] This does not mean that the Commission is unable to re-orientate its policy regarding specific restrictive agreements and conduct, as has been already seen. The value as a precedent does not go as far as the common law concept of *stare decisis*.

enabling them to judge whether or not the decision is well founded and, ultimately, properly to defend their rights. The obligation to state reasons also serves to enable the Court to carry out its task of judicial review.[111] The obligation to state reasons is highly important and must be fulfilled with particular care where a Commission decision goes significantly further than previous decisions.[112] A contradiction in the statement of reasons on which a decision is based constitutes a breach of Article 253. If the reasons are not stated adequately, or at all, the decision will be rendered void.[113]

2. Types of decision

The Commission may take a final decision ordering the termination of the **4.27** infringements of the competition rules and may take procedural decisions during the course of its investigation. As indicated, it may also take interim measures in order to prevent irreparable damage before it can come to a final decision. In addition, it has two new powers provided under Regulation 1/2003: firstly, it may take a decision subject to binding commitments but without finding an infringement, and secondly it may reach a 'positive' decision finding that Article 81 or 82 EC is inapplicable.

Under Article 7(1) of Regulation 1/2003, a decision finding an infringement **4.28** may therefore order undertakings to bring the infringement to an end to the extent that it has not been definitely terminated already. These are 'cease-and-desist' orders. The decision may also contain a 'like effects order' whereby the parties are prohibited from entering into similar arrangements.[114] While the corresponding Article 3 under Regulation 17 did not state whether the Commission could take decisions ordering the parties to take positive steps in order

---

[111] For the interpretation of Art 253 EC in the context of competition law proceedings, see Joined Cases 142/84 and 156/84 *BAT and Reynolds v EC Commission* [1987] ECR 4487 para 72; Case T-76/89 *ITP v EC Commission* [1991] ECR II-575; Case T-44/90 *La Cinq v EC Commission* [1992] ECR II-1 para 42; Case T-16/91 *Rendo v EC Commission* [1992] ECR II-2417 para 124; Case T-7/92 *Asia Motor France and others v EC Commission* [1993] ECR II-669 para 80; Case T-102/92 *Viho Europe BV v EC Commission* [1995] ECR II-17 paras 75–76; and Case T-114/92 *BEMIM v EC Commission* [1995] ECR II-147 para 41. The Commission is not required, however, to deal with all matters of fact and law which may have arisen in the course of the procedure. It suffices that the Commission refers to it in general terms: Joined Cases 43/82 and 63/82 *VBVB and VBBB v EC Commission* [1984] ECR 19 para 22. It has to be noted that recent practice has been to provide extensive citation of the evidence relied on. See *Austrian Banks* [2004] OJ L56/1.

[112] If the Commission's decision breaks new ground, it must give more extensive legal reasoning. See Case 73/74 *Papiers Peints v EC Commission* [1975] ECR 1491 para 31 and Joined Cases 142/84 and 156/84 *BAT and Reynolds v EC Commission* [1987] ECR 4487 para 71.

[113] Reasoning ex post such as during proceedings before the Court cannot salvage an inadequately reasoned decision. Joined Cases T-236/01, T-239/01, T-244/01 to T-246/01, T-251/01 and T-252/01 *Tokai Carbon v EC Commission* [2004] ECR II-1181 para 415.

[114] *Welded Steel Mesh* [1989] OJ L260/1.

to bring an infringement to an end,[115] Regulation 1/2003 now expressly gives the Commission power to make orders by stating that it may impose 'any behavioural [. . .] remedies which are proportionate to the infringement committed and necessary to bring the infringement effectively to an end'. As regards infringements of Article 81 EC, however, the CFI has ruled that the Commission does not have the power to order a party to enter into a contractual relationship where there are other ways of making the party end the infringement.[116]

3. Notification of decisions and information to the Member States

Notification

4.29 Pursuant to Article 254 EC, decisions 'shall be notified to those to whom they are addressed and shall take effect upon such notification.' The Court has made it clear that a decision is deemed to be duly notified when received by its addressee and the latter has an opportunity to take note of its content.[117] The Court takes an objective approach. If the document containing the notification has been presented to an undertaking, the latter cannot allege lack of notification merely because it refuses to admit that it has been notified. Irregularities affecting the method of notification do not constitute a defect affecting the legality or propriety of the notified measure in itself.[118] The Articles of the decisions (or operative part) are normally communicated to undertakings by fax[119] immediately after being adopted, in order to ensure that undertakings are made aware of decisions before details appear in the press,[120] since as a general

---

[115] Note however Case 6/73 and 7/73 *Istituto Chemioterapico Italiano and Commercial Solvents v EC Commission* [1974] ECR 223 para 252: '[. . .] [Article 3] must be applied in relation to the infringement which has been established and may include an order to do certain acts or provide certain advantages which have been wrongfully withheld as well as prohibiting the continuation of certain actions, practices or situations which are contrary to the Treaty.'

[116] Case T-24/90 *Automec v EC Commission* [1992] ECR II-2223 paras 51–54.

[117] See Case 48/69 *ICI v EC Commission* [1972] ECR 619 and Case 6/72 *Europemballage Corp and Continental Can Co v EC Commission* [1973] ECR 215 para 10, both cited in Case 374/87 *Orkem v EC Commission* [1989] ECR 3283, para 6.

[118] See Case 48/69 *ICI v EC Commission* [1972] ECR 619 paras 39–40, and Case 52/69 *Geigy AG v EC Commission* [1972] ECR 787 para 18, cited in Case T-43/92 *Dunlop Slazenger v EC Commission* [1994] ECR-II 441 para 25. It does not seem to matter whether the addressee is situated outside the Community. See also CS Kerse and N Khan, *EC Antitrust Procedure* (5th edn, 2005) para 6–013. K Lenaerts and J Maselis, 'Procedural Rights and Issues in the Enforcement of Articles 81 and 82 of the EC Treaty' [2001] Fordham International Law Journal 1615–54 (1648) noting that an irregularity in the notification may sometimes prevent the period within which an application must be lodged from starting to run.

[119] See Case T-46/92 *Scottish Football v EC Commission* [1994] ECR II-1039 para 4, which seems to indicate that notification of a decision by fax does not constitute formal notification.

[120] There have been some occurrences of this. The Court has stated that, although it is regrettable, the fact that a decision is made public before it is notified to its addressee is not a formal defect such as to invalidate it (Joined Cases 96/82–102/82, 104/82, 105/82, 108/82 and 110/82 *IAZ v EC Commission* [1983] ECR 3369 para 16). See also Case T-43/92 *Dunlop Slazenger v EC Commission* [1994] ECR-II 441 paras 27–29.

rule a press release is issued on the day of adoption of the decision.[121] The Secretariat General of the Commission deals with the despatch of notifications.[122] The full text of the decision, in the form of a copy certified by the Secretary General of the Commission, is sent by registered post with acknowledgement of receipt and notification takes place on receipt by the undertaking.[123] The only exception to the rule just described concerns the notification of inspection decisions, which takes place upon commencement of inspections by the officials responsible for performing them. The date of formal notification of the decision as a whole—which will generally be the date on which the addressees sign the postal form for acknowledgement of receipt[124]—marks the start of the time-limit for commencing proceedings before the CFI. Traditionally, decisions have been signed by the member of the Commission responsible for competition matters or by the senior official of DG COMP (normally the Director-General) to whom the Commission and the relevant member of the Commission have delegated that authority.[125] The judgment in the *PVC* cartel has prompted the Commission to redouble its precautions regarding signature and completion of other formalities.[126] In any event, no provision requires the

---

[121] Regarding Press Releases, see immediately below.

[122] The Commission has notified some decisions by using courier services.

[123] If there is no serious indication of any irregularity, this copy is conclusive as to the content of a decision. See Joined Cases 97/87, 98/87 and 99/87 *Dow Chemical Ibérica and others v EC Commission* [1989] ECR 3165 para 59, and the judgments of the CFI in Case T-43/92 *Dunlop Slazenger v EC Commission* [1994] ECR II-441 paras 24 and 25, Case T-34/92 *Fiatagri UK and New Holland Ford v EC Commission* [1994] ECR II-905 para 27, and Case T-35/92 *John Deere v EC Commission* [1994] ECR II-957 para 31.

[124] See Case T-12/90 *Bayer v EC Commission* [1991] ECR II-219 (in particular para 20), in which the CFI held that postal receipt provides conclusive evidence of the date of notification and takes precedence over other acknowledgements of receipt which, although sent by the Commission to the parties, are of subsidiary status. The subsequent appeal against this decision was rejected by the Court: see Case C-195/91 *Bayer v EC Commission* [1994] ECR I-5619. The Court at para 21 confirmed that an undertaking is taken to have notice of a Commission decision from the time when the form containing the decision (sent by registered post) arrived at the undertaking's registered office. The CFI, however, has accepted that when it has been established that the information contained in the postal record of delivery is incorrect, it must be disregarded. See Joined Cases T-80/89, T-81/89, T-87/89, T-88/89, T-90/89, T-93/89, T-95/89, T-97/89, T-99/89, T-100/89, T-100/89, T-101/89, T-103/89, T-105/89, T-107/89 and T-112/89 *BASF and others v Commission* [1995] ECR II-729 paras 58–61.

[125] In accordance with the procedure for delegation of powers. Regarding delegation of authority to sign, in general, see Commission Decision 73/2 on delegation of signature [1973] OJ L7/2.

[126] In its judgment in Joined Cases T-79/89, T-84 to 86/89, T-89/89, T-91 and 92/89, T-94/89, T-96/89, T-98/89, T-102/89 and T-104/89 *BASF and others v EC Commission* [1992] ECR II-315, the CFI declared the Commission Decision in *PVC Cartel* [1988] OJ L/74/1 non-existent because of a number of formal defects. By its judgment in Case C-137/92 *EC Commission v BASF and others* [1994] ECR I-2555, the Court set aside the judgment of the CFI, taking the view that the formal defects in the Commission's Decision were such that it should be declared void rather than non-existent.

copy of the decision notified to be signed by the competent member of the Commission.[127]

Information concerning adopted decisions

4.30 The Member States have decisions notified to them, in the same way as the direct addressees of decisions, whenever the decision has been the subject of a report by the Advisory Committee. The operative part of the decision is communicated by fax and the full text is subsequently sent by post.

4. Publication of decisions and other measures

The Official Journal (OJ)

4.31 Similar to its corresponding provision under Regulation 17 (Article 21) Article 30 of Regulation 1/2003 requires the Commission to publish its decisions (finding and termination of infringement, interim measures, Commitments, finding of inapplicability and penalties). Decisions in competition matters are published in the L series (legislation) of the OJ, Part II: 'measures whose publication is not a precondition for their applicability'. Decisions other than those mentioned in Article 30 may also be published if the Commission considers them sufficiently important to the development of competition policy. Thus, for example, there may be publication of decisions to inspect, those rejecting complaints and others.[128]

4.32 As published, the decisions in many cases do not contain all the information included in the decisions notified to the undertakings.[129] The reason for this is to safeguard the business secrets of undertakings, in accordance with Article 28 of Regulation 1/2003. The Commission considers, however, that undertakings are not entitled to request confidentiality for information establishing or proving the existence or seriousness of an infringement. Sometimes, differences of opinion between the Commission and undertakings may delay the publication of decisions.[130] If the Commission wished to publish information contained in

---

[127] Joined Cases 97/87, 98/87 and 99/87 *Dow Chemical Ibérica and others v EC Commission* [1989] ECR 3165 para 59. Cited in the judgment of the CFI in Case T-43/92 *Dunlop Slazenger* [1994] ECR-II 441 para 25.

[128] In the relevant sections, reference is made to certain decisions of this kind which have been published in the OJ.

[129] Case T-198/03 *Bank Austria Creditanstalt v EC Commission* [2003] ECR II-4879 para 39 in which the CFI identified an ambiguity in Art 9(3) of the Mandate of the Hearing Officer, questioning whether the Hearing Officer has to decide also whether or not parts of a Commission decision, being not part of the decision's 'main content', should be published under Art 21 of Reg 17 (now Art 30 of Reg 1/2003).

[130] For example, the Commission decision in COMP/38.096—*PO/Clearstream* (Clearing and settlement of 2 June 2004 was published ten months later on DG COMP's website. A non-confidential version may be published on DG COMP's website before its publication in the OJ.

its decisions which undertakings regarded as constituting business secrets, it would have to give them an opportunity to submit arguments and adopt a formal decision which could be challenged before publishing the decision containing such information.[131] All texts published in the Official Journal are translated into the twenty working languages of the Community and revised by the lawyer-linguists in the Commission's Legal Service.

Press releases

The Commission always issues a press release when it adopts a formal decision under Articles 81 and 82 EC. Press releases (or Commission 'Memos') are not usually issued regarding measures or decisions of a procedural nature, unless the cases involved are already public knowledge and the Commission wishes to clarify some aspect of the situation.[132] It seems that commitment decisions under Article 9 of Regulation 1/2003 are the subject of press releases[133] while this will not apply to informal settlements outside this framework. The Commission may nevertheless consider it appropriate to rely on a press release to clarify matters relating to its policy or to make undertakings or consumers aware of the more interesting points in their decisions where the case in question may be a source of useful information. Generally, there is no publication in respect of intermediate steps such as the statement of objections. Sometimes, if the issue involved is of sufficient importance, being novel or likely to affect other cases, the Commission may put out a press release concerning measures adopted by other institutions or national authorities and courts. Releases of that kind are fairly frequent in cases heard by the Court under Article 234 EC (preliminary rulings). Press releases may also be issued in respect of CFI cases.[134] Press releases can be obtained from the Commission Press Offices and may be consulted on the Commission's Rapid Database.[135]

4.33

---

[131] The procedure would be the same as that followed for granting access to information purportedly constituting business secrets, in other words the *AKZO* procedure. See ch 9 'Penalties, confidentiality' para 9.33.

[132] See Commission Memo/05/63 'Anti-trust: Commission investigation in the flat and car glass sector', 24 February 2005 in which the Commission confirmed that Commission officials carried out unannounced inspections at the premises of several European manufacturers of flat and car glass in several European countries; see also Commission Press Release IP/04/134 'Commission launches sector inquiry into the sale of sports rights to Internet and 3G mobile operators', 30 January 2004.

[133] See only recently, Commission Press Release IP/05/664 'Competition: Commission seeks interested parties' comments on ALROSA and De Beers commitments' 3 June 2005; Commission Press Release IP/04/1247 'Commission close to settle antitrust probe into Coca-Cola practices in Europe', 19 October 2004. See for a more detailed discussion ch 13 'Commitments, voluntary adjustments, conclusion of the procedure without a formal decision' paras 13.03 *et seq*.

[134] It should be borne in mind that both the European Court and the CFI publish their own Press Releases.

[135] http://europa.eu.int/rapid/.

Periodical publications

4.34 Undertakings and individuals can periodically familiarize themselves with the Commission's activities in competition matters through a number of publications of the European Commission. The *Bulletin of the European Union* provides a monthly insight into the activities of the Commission and of the other Community institutions. It is published by the Secretariat-General of the Commission and appears ten times a year in all the Community languages and informs about the Commission activities, including competition policy.[136] In the field of competition policy, the annual report contains general information on the development of Community competition policy and comments on the decisions of the Commission and the Community Courts on competition matters. Finally, the Commission has prepared a number of information leaflets on competition policy,[137] and issues a regular EC Competition Policy Newsletter in electronic format to keep undertakings and practitioners informed of the latest developments in competition matters.[138]

Europe Direct, European Documentation Centres, and the Internet

4.35 In addition to the formal requirements in Regulation 1/2003 to publish notices and decisions, the Commission has been constantly trying to improve the transparency of Community policy and its application in practice. The Commission has created *Europe Direct* which encompasses an extensive network of information centres and contact points set up by the European Union for the public.[139] Official publications can be consulted at a large number of European Documentation Centres. The DG COMP Internet homepage contains material on all the main areas of Community competition policy. Under each heading (antitrust, mergers, etc) the user can search an increasing number of sections containing a variety of documents, including press releases, Community legislation, and case law.

---

[136] http://europa.eu.int/abc/doc/off/bull/en/welcome.htm. The Bulletin is supplemented by the General Report on the activities of the European Union which provides an overview of the activities of the previous year.

[137] Most of them can be downloaded from DG COMP's website.

[138] The three yearly newsletters may be complemented by special editions. See in particular the special edition 'The EU gets new competition powers for the 21st century'. All issues of the Competition Policy Newsletter are available on-line.

[139] *Europe Direct* can be contacted by a single freephone number from the twenty-five Member States and by e-mail.

E. The Compatibility of the EC Competition Procedure with the ECHR

1. Introduction

In recent years, fundamental rights, invoked under the European Convention **4.36** for the Protection of Human Rights ('ECHR'),[140] have steadily grown in importance.[141] This has caused the Courts to pay increasing regard to the case law of the European Court of Human Rights ('ECtHR'). More recently parties have had recourse to the EU Charter of Fundamental Rights ('CFR').[142] The provisions of the EU Charter and ECHR most relevant to investigations are the following:

• The right to a fair trial: Article 47 of the CFR and Article 6 of the ECHR;
• The principle of *ne bis in idem* or double jeopardy, restricting the possibility of a defendant being prosecuted or punished more than once for the same offence: Article 50 of the EU Charter and Article 4 of Protocol No 7 to the ECHR.
• The right to respect for private and family life, home, and correspondence: Articles 7 and 8 of the Charter and Article 8 of the ECHR.

Whilst the Member States are all part of the ECHR, the EC has not acceded **4.37** to the ECHR due to lack of competence under the Treaties. That is the reason why in the past the Community courts have alleged that they had no jurisdiction to apply the ECHR because it was not part of Community law.[143] This

---

[140] Convention for the Protection of Human Rights and Fundamental Freedoms (The European Human Rights Convention) (Rome, 4 November 1950; TS 71 (1053); Cmd 8969).

[141] EM Ameye, 'The Interplay between Human Rights and Competition Law' [2004] ECLR 332–41 (333), stating that since 1995 there have been more than thirty cases before the Community courts in which the applicants relied upon human rights with respect to competition law.

[142] The CFR was solemnly proclaimed by the European Parliament, the Council and the Commission on 7 December 2000 (Charter of fundamental rights of the European Union [2000] OJ C364/1). See also M Araujo, 'The Respect of Fundamental Rights within the European Network of Competition Authorities' ch 21 in BE Hawk (ed), International Antitrust Law & Policy, Annual Proceedings of the Fordham Institute [2005] 511–31 (517) who notes that it would be remarkable that a charter guaranteeing fundamental rights appear in the C series of the OJ (where only non-binding legislative acts such as communications and information are published). The EU Charter is planned to be incorporated in Part II of the Treaty Establishing a Constitution for Europe [2004] OJ C310/41, which essentially reflects the ECHR in most relevant aspects. The Charter contains an extensive repertory of fundamental rights and so-called rights of defence. The Constitution was scheduled to come into force on 1 November 2006, but it is unlikely that the requisite ratification instruments have been deposited by then after two Member States (France, the Netherlands) rejected in referendums the Draft Constitution.

[143] Case T-347/94 *Mayr-Melnhof Kartongesellschaft v EC Commission* [1998] ECR II-1751 para 31. Also Case T-112/98 *Mannesmannröhren-Werke AG v EC Commission* [2001] ECR II-729

situation has made it difficult for litigants to invoke infringements of the
ECHR before the ECJ. The ECJ ruled in 1996 that the Community lacked
competence under the Treaties to accede to the Convention.[144] This ruling
also makes reference to the limited application that the ECHR and the jurisprudence of the ECtHR may have before the ECJ. While the rights guaranteed
by the ECHR are a source of inspiration for the unwritten general principles
of European law, the ECJ has ruled that the validity of EC law can only
be judged in the light of Community law,[145] even though following its
judgment in *Stauder* the ECJ responded more positively to claims of infringement of the ECHR.[146] The attempts of applicants to plead particular fundamental human rights enshrined in the ECHR have been especially important
in competition procedures. While the ECHR is not a formal part of EC
law, it is the most common source of reference for fundamental rights of

---

para 59. For a more detailed discussion see M Araujo, 'The Respect of Fundamental Rights within
the European Network of Competition Authorities' ch 21 in BE Hawk (ed) Annual Proceedings of
the Fordham Institute [2004] 511–31.

[144] For a detailed discussion on the difficulties of an incorporation of the ECHR into the
Community legal order see Opinion C-2/94 *Accession of the Community to the ECHR* [1996] ECR
I-1759.

[145] Case 11/70 *Internationale Handelsgesellschaft GmbH v Einfuhr- und Vorratsstelle für Getreide
und Futtermittel* [1970] ECR 1125 para 3, where the ECJ affirmed that constitutionally protected
rights at a national level should not stand in the way of the effectiveness of EU Law. See also
Opinion of AG Darmon in Case 374/87 *Orkem v EC Commission* [1989] ECR 3283 paras
139–140: '[T]he existence in Community law of fundamental rights drawn from the [ECHR]
does not derive from the wholly straightforward application of that instrument as interpreted by
the Strasbourg authorities [. . .]. This Court may [. . .] adopt, with respect to provisions of the
[ECHR], an interpretation which does not coincide exactly with that given by the Strasbourg
authorities, in particular the [ECtHR]. It is not bound, in so far as it does not have systematically
to take into account, as regards fundamental rights under Community law, the interpretation of
the Convention given by the Strasbourg authorities [. . .]'.

[146] The suggestion that fundamental rights should be respected was formulated in 1969 in
Case 29/69 *Stauder v Stadt Ulm* [1969] ECR 419. It was however in Case 4/73 *Nold v EC
Commission* [1974] ECR 491 that the principle was further developed under the 'principles
common to the constitutional traditions of Member States' formula. In the *Nold* case, the ECJ
ruled that fundamental rights formed an integral part of the general principles of law, the observance of which the ECJ ensures, in accordance with the constitutional traditions common to the
Member States; and with international treaties regarding which Member States have collaborated or of which they are signatories. See Case C-29/69 *Stauder v Stadt Ulm* [1969] ECR 419
paras 4–7; and Case 4/73 *Nold v EC Commission* [1974] ECR 491 para 13. The ECHR has
special significance in that respect, cf Case 222/84 *Johnston v Chief Constable of the Royal Ulster
Constabulary* [1986] ECR 1651 para 18. Later judgments include a reference to the Treaty on the
European Union: Joined Cases T-305/94 to T-307/94, T-313/94 to T-316/94, T-318/94,
T-325/94, T-328/94, T-329/94, and T-335/94 *Limburgse Vinyl Maatschappij (LVM) and others v
EC Commission* [1999] ECR II-931 para 120: '[. . .] Moreover, Article F.2 [Article 6(2)] of the
Treaty on European Union states that "[t]he Union shall respect fundamental rights, as guaran-
teed by the [ECHR] and as they result from the constitutional traditions common to the Member
States, as general principles of Community law" '.

defence.[147] The ECHR and the jurisprudence of the ECtHR may be regarded as an 'indirect source' of the Community's general principles of law, due to the fact that they represent basic principles and common values to which all of the Member State signatories have committed themselves.[148] Regulation 1/2003 expressly mentions the respect of the fundamental rights and the observation of the principles recognized in particular by the CFR.[149] The question of the CFR's legal status may be solved by its incorporation in the European Constitution if this is finally ratified.[150] This would make Community institutions subject to the review jurisdiction of the ECtHR and the ECJ would no longer be the final arbiter of the lawfulness of EC action. As far as the relationship between the CFR and the ECHR is concerned, Article 52 (or Article II-112(3)

---

[147] The ECJ developed a doctrine on the protection of fundamental rights as 'principles common to the constitutional traditions of the Member States which form an integral part of European Community law' and 'whose observance is guaranteed by [EU] Law'. In Case C-185/95 *Baustahlgewebe v EC Commission* [1998] ECR I-8417 paras 26–47, the ECJ endorsed the claimant's request for a finding of excessive duration of a CFI procedure (thirty-two months between the end of the written procedure and the decision to open the oral procedure and of twenty-two months between the end of the oral procedure and judgment) on the basis of the ECHR. But it is probably most clear in the *PVC II* appeal, in which the Court assumed clearly that it needed to examine whether the CFI had applied correctly the doctrine of the ECtHR on the privilege against self-incrimination: Joined Cases C-238/99, C-244–245/99, C-247/99, C250–252/99 and C-254/99 *Limburgse Vinyl Maatwschappij (LVM) and others v EC Commission* [2002] ECR I-8375 paras 258–293. In Case C-94/00 *Roquette Frères* [2002] ECR I-9011 paras 22–29, the ECJ considered the *Hoechst* case law on the inviolability of corporate domicile and assessed how much regard it should have to the ECHR and the jurisprudence of the ECtHR. See also Joined Cases T-236/01, T-239/01, T-244/01 to T-246/01, T-251/01 and T-252/01 *Tokai Carbon v EC Commission* [2004] ECR II-1181 paras 130 *et seq.* regarding *ne bis in idem*; Joined Cases T-67/00, etc *JFE Engineering v EC Commission* [2004] OJ C239/13 paras 178 *et seq.* regarding the presumption of innocence:

> In the latter situation, it is necessary to take account of the principle of the presumption of innocence resulting in particular from Article 6(2) of the European Convention for the Protection of Human Rights (ECHR), which is one of the fundamental rights which, according to the case-law of the Court of Justice and as reaffirmed in the preamble to the Single European Act, by Article 6(2) of the Treaty on European Union and by Article 47 of the Charter of Fundamental Rights of the European Union proclaimed on 7 December 2000 in Nice, are protected in the Community legal order. Given the nature of the infringements in question and the nature and degree of severity of the ensuing penalties, the principle of the presumption of innocence applies in particular to the procedures relating to infringements of the competition rules applicable to undertakings that may result in the imposition of fines or periodic penalty payments (see, to that effect, in particular the judgments of the European Court of Human Rights of 21 February 1984 in Öztürk, Series A No 73, and of 25 August 1987 in Lutz, Series A No 123-A, and of the Court of Justice in Case C-199/92 P *Hüls v Commission* [1999] ECR I-4287, paras 149–150, and Case C-235/92 P *Montecatini v Commission* [1999] ECR I-4539, paras 175–176).

[148] Art 6(2) of the Treaty on European Union approved this mechanism. This Article provided that the Union would respect the fundamental rights guaranteed by the ECHR. The major change introduced by the Amsterdam Treaty was to amend Art 6, which now declares that the Union 'is founded on' the principles of liberty, democracy, and respect for human rights and fundamental freedoms.

[149] Recital 37 of Reg 1/2003.

[150] It seems that the Community Courts take a quite pragmatic approach: Case T-54/99 *max.mobil Telekommunikation Service GmbH v EC Commission* [2002] ECR II-313 para 48.

of the draft Constitution) provides that where the Charter contains rights which correspond to rights guaranteed by the ECHR, the meaning and scope of those rights shall be the same as those laid down by the ECHR.

2. Human rights capable of constituting a defence in competition law cases

The right to a fair trial

4.38 The ECtHR has interpreted the right to a fair hearing before an independent and impartial tribunal in a liberal manner,[151] regardless of whether the matter is to be classified as civil or criminal. The provision is applicable to administrative procedures as well as to disciplinary procedures.[152] Article 6 ECHR is applied in a more or less strict fashion depending on whether the offence is of criminal or non-criminal nature.[153] Although national law may not necessarily classify a matter as 'criminal', the ECtHR may do so taking into account the nature of the offence and the severity of the penalty. Where a penalty is liable to be imposed on all persons infringing a rule and is imposed to deter and to punish infringements and where those penalties are substantial, the matter would be classified as criminal.[154] The fact that Regulation 1/2003 states the fines being imposed 'shall not be of a criminal law nature' would not bind the ECtHR.[155] In *Société Stenuit v France* the ECtHR considered a matter of French administrative law which concerned the imposition of a fine under French competition law for participation in a cartel as a criminal proceedings, notwithstanding the non-criminal charge of the penalty under French law.[156] The Community courts have accepted this interpretation and do not seem to contest the criminal nature of the Commission's decisions in which it imposes fines.[157]

---

[151] Case No 8692/79 *Piersack v Belgium* judgment of 1 October 1982 Series A Vol 5 No 53 167 paras 28–32.

[152] Cases Nos 6878/75 and 7238/75 *Le Compte, Van Leuven and De Meyère* judgment of 23 June 1981 Series A No 43 paras 41–48.

[153] M Ameye, 'The Interplay between Human Rights and Competition Law' [2004] ECLR 332–41 (333). Art 6(1) ECHR applies in civil matters as well as in the criminal sphere.

[154] Case No 12547/86 *Bendemoun v France* judgment of 24 February 1994 Series A No 284 para 47 [1994] 18 EHRR 54.

[155] Art 23(5) of Reg 1/2003.

[156] The fine imposed was not large but the law allowed a fine of up to 5 per cent of turnover. The ECtHR held that the criminal nature of the case was 'revealed unambiguously' by the possibility of severe and deterrent maximum fines in the event of a breach. Case No 11598/85 *Société Stenuit v France* judgment of 27 February 1992 Series A No 232-A. It further observed that penalties were levied against undertakings that committed acts constituting 'infractions', and that the maximum fine that could be imposed (5 per cent of the undertaking's annual turnover) 'shows quite clearly that the penalty in question was intended to be deterrent' (paras 62–64). See, however, Case No 69042/01 *OOO Neste St. Petersburg v Russia* judgment of 3 June 2004, in which penalties under Russian competition law were not considered of being of criminal nature.

[157] CS Kerse and N Khan, *EC Antitrust Procedure* (5th edn, 2005) para 3–004. C Bellamy and G Child, *EC Law of Competition* (5th edn, 2001) para 12–120.

The rights of the accused

The principle of the presumption of innocence Article 6(2) ECHR enshrines **4.39**
the presumption of innocence. The indictment or formal charge against any
person is not evidence of guilt. The law does not require a person to prove his
innocence or produce any evidence at all. The prosecution has the burden of
proving a person guilty beyond a reasonable doubt, and if it fails to do so the
person is (so far as the law is concerned) not guilty.[158] The ECtHR states that
Article 6 (2) ECHR governs criminal proceedings in their entirety, irrespective
of the outcome of the prosecution. In its case law, the presumption of innocence
is violated if, without the accused having previously been proved guilty according to law and, notably, without having had the opportunity of exercising his or
her rights to a fair defence, a judicial decision concerning him or her reflects
a guilty verdict.[159] The Community courts have also recognized that the
principle of the presumption of innocence applies to the procedures relating to
infringements of the competition rules by undertakings that may result in the
imposition of fines or periodic penalty payments.[160]

Privilege against self-incrimination The privilege against self-incrimination **4.40**
means that no one can be compelled to produce evidence against oneself. This
includes the right of silence and the right not to answer questions. Although not
expressly mentioned in Article 6 ECHR, the ECtHR has held that this privilege
is part of the notion of the right to a fair procedure provided by Article 6
ECHR.[161] The EctHR has not yet heard a case where a legal entity sought to
invoke the right of silence. Its case law solely relates to situations where a natural
person was questioned and refused to answer.[162] The first step in recognizing the
privilege against self-incrimination was taken in *Funke*.[163] That case was based

---

[158] Case No 8660/79 *Minelli v Switzerland* judgment of 25 March 1983 Series A No 62
para 37.
[159] Case No 10590/83 *Barberà, Mesegué and Jabardo v Spain* judgment of 6 December 1988
Series A No 146 para 91.
[160] Case T-62/98 *Volkswagen v EC Commission* [2000] ECR II-2707 para 281: '[The] presumption of innocence is clearly not respected by the Commission where, prior to formally
imposing a penalty on the undertaking charged, it informs the press of the proposed finding
which has been submitted to the Advisory Committee and the College of Commissioners for
deliberation.' See also Joined Cases T-67/00, T-68/00, T-71/00 and T-78/00, *JFE Engineering
Corp v EC Commission* [2004] OJ C239/13 para 178.
[161] Case No 18731/91 *John Murray v United Kingdom* judgment of 8 February 1996 Reports
of Judgments and Decisions 1996-I para 45.
[162] K Dekeyser and C Gauer, 'The New Enforcement System For Articles 81 and 82 and
the Rights of Defence' ch 23 in BE Hawk (ed), International Antitrust Law & Policy, Annual
Proceedings of the Fordham Institute [2005] 549–85 (562).
[163] Case No 10828/84 *Funke v France* judgment of 25 February 1993 Series A No 256-A. In
Orkem the ECJ seemed to take the view that neither the wording of Art 6 ECHR nor the decisions
of the ECtHR indicated that it upheld the right not to give evidence against oneself. Case 374/87
Orkem v EC Commission [1989] ECR 3283 para 30.

on a complaint by a French citizen against France. French custom officers had searched Mr Funke's home and requested him to produce statements concerning foreign bank accounts and financial information by customs authorities. Mr Funke was fined, pursuant to the French Customs Code, for refusing to provide the statements. The ECtHR considered that '[. . .] the customs secured Mr Funke's conviction in order to obtain certain documents which they believed must exist, although they were not certain of the fact. Being unable or unwilling to procure them by some other means, they attempted to compel the applicant himself to provide the evidence of offences he had allegedly committed'.[164] The ECtHR concluded that '[t]he special features of customs law [. . .] cannot justify such an infringement of the right of anyone "charged with a criminal offence", within the autonomous meaning of this expression in Article 6 [ECHR], to remain silent and not contribute to incriminating himself'.[165] This interpretation was further developed in the *John Murray* and *Saunders* judgments,[166] although the latter seems to circumscribe the privilege more narrowly by excluding documents from the scope of Article 6 ECHR.[167] In *Saunders*, the ECtHR ruled that the right not to incriminate oneself 'cannot reasonably be confined to statements of admission of wrongdoing or to remarks that are directly incriminating'. On the other hand, the Court also stated that '[. . .] [t]he right not to incriminate oneself is primarily concerned [. . .] with respecting the will of an accused person to remain silent'. Therefore, 'it does not extend to the use in criminal proceedings of material which may be obtained from the accused through the use of compulsory powers but which has an existence independent of the will of the suspect such as, inter alia, documents acquired pursuant to a warrant, breath, blood and urine samples and bodily tissue for the purpose of DNA testing'.[168] The ECtHR further noted that '[t]estimony obtained under compulsion which appears on its face to be of a non-incriminating nature—such as exculpatory remarks or mere information on questions of fact—may later be deployed in criminal proceedings in support of the prosecution case, for example to contradict or cast doubt upon other statements of the accused or evidence given by

---

[164] Case No 10828/84 *Funke v France* judgment of 25 February 1993 Series A No 256-A para 44.

[165] Case No 10828/84 *Funke v France* judgment of 25 February 1993 Series A No 256-A para 44.

[166] Case No 18731/91 *John Murray v United Kingdom* judgment of 8 February 1996, Reports of Judgments and Decisions 1996-I para 45; Case No 19187/91 *Saunders v United Kingdom* judgment of 17 December 1996, Reports of Judgments and Decisions 1996-IV para 71.

[167] C Bellamy and G Child, *EC Law of Competition* (5th edn, 2001) para 12–121, suggesting that the *Saunders* case overruled the *Funke* case.

[168] Case No 19187/91 *Saunders v United Kingdom* judgment of 17 December 1996, Reports of Judgments and Decisions 1996-VI para 69.

him during the trial or to otherwise undermine his credibility'.[169] In contrast to documents acquired pursuant to a warrant, the latter suggests a broad approach to the nature of statements made by the accused which benefit from the privilege.[170]

This interpretation went beyond the protection against actual admissions, but the CFI seemed to take the view in *Mannesmannröhren-Werke*[171] that interpretations of certain rights in competition proceedings did not have to coincide exactly with those of the ECtHR when the latter deals with criminal procedures involving natural persons.[172] However, later the ECJ explained in *PVC II* in very explicit terms that it was ready to analyse the privilege against self-incrimination based on the ECtHR case law[173] and even found that there had been considerable evolutions in the case-law of the ECtHR since *Orkem* 'which the Community judicature must take into account when interpreting the fundamental rights'.[174] This stance contrasts with previous statements to the effect that the interpretations of fundamental rights by the Community courts did not have to coincide exactly with those of the ECtHR, and fits in with a more general trend of the Community courts of relying extensively on the case-law of the ECtHR[175] and the express reference by the Charter of Fundamental Rights to the case-law of the ECtHR.[176]

4.41

---

[169] Case No 19187/91 *Saunders v United Kingdom* judgment of 17 December 1996, Reports of Judgments and Decisions 1996-VI para 71 (emphasis added). Joined Cases C-204/00 P, C-205/00 P, C-211/00 P, C-213/00 P, C-217/00 P and C-219/00 P *Aalborg Portland and others v EC Commission* [2004] ECR I-123 para 64.

[170] CS Kerse and N Khan, *EC Antitrust Procedure* (5th edn, 2005) para 3–018.

[171] Case T-112/98 *Mannesmannröhren-Werke v EC Commission* [2001] ECR II-729.

[172] Judge B Vesterdorf, 'Legal Professional Privilege and the Privilege Against Self-Incrimination in EC Law: Recent Developments and Current Issues' ch 27 in BE Hawk (ed), International Antitrust Law & Policy, Annual Proceedings of the Fordham Institute [2004] 701–30 (713).

[173] Joined Cases C-238/99, C-244–245/99, C-247/99, C250–252/99 and C-254/99 *Limburgse Vinyl Maatwschappij (LVM) and others v EC Commission* [2002] ECR I-8375.

[174] Joined Cases C-238/99, C-244–245/99, C-247/99, C250–252/99, and C-254/99 *Limburgse Vinyl Maatwschappij (LVM) and others v EC Commission* [2002] ECR I-8375 para 274.

[175] For example, the ECJ interpreted a directive mainly exclusively in light of the ECtHR case law on Art 8 ECHR (Joined Cases C-465/00, C-138/01 and C-139/01 *Österreichischer Rundfunk and others* [2003] ECR I-4989).

[176] See Recital 5 of the Charter of fundamental rights of the European Union [2000] OJ 364/1: '[t]his Charter reaffirms, with due regard for the powers and tasks of the Community and the Union and the principle of subsidiarity, the rights as they result, in particular, from [. . .] *the case-law of* the Court of Justice of the European Communities and of *the European Court of Human Rights*' (emphasis added). Article I-7 of the draft Treaty establishing a Constitution for Europe provides that '[t]he Union shall recognise the rights, freedoms and principles set out in the Charter of Fundamental Rights'. Pursuant to the same provision, it is planned that the Union will accede to the ECHR.

Defence rights

4.42   **The principle of equality of arms**   The principle of equality of arms is one of the elements of the broader concept of the right to a fair trial.[177] Closely linked to this principle is the right to have access to the file and the right to an adversarial procedure. The Commission must give the undertaking concerned the opportunity to examine all the documents in the investigation file which may be relevant for its defence.[178] Access to the file is one of the procedural safeguards intended to protect the rights of the defence. These principles imply that all parties involved in a case are awarded the same knowledge in order to secure the observance of their defence rights.[179] The ECtHR has emphasized the need to respect the right to adversarial procedure, noting that this entails the parties' right to have knowledge of and comment on all evidence adduced or observations filed.[180] Recognizing these procedural safeguards, the ECJ has indicated that nonetheless the ECtHR has held that, just like the observance of the other procedural safeguards enshrined in Article 6(1) of the ECHR, compliance with the adversarial principle relates only to judicial proceedings before a 'tribunal' and that there is no general, abstract principle that the parties must in all instances have the opportunity to attend the interviews carried out or to receive copies of all the documents taken into account in the case of other persons.[181] The failure to communicate a document would constitute a breach of the rights of the defence only if the undertaking concerned shows, first, that the Commission relied on that document to support its objection concerning the existence of an infringement.[182] If there were other documentary evidence of which the parties were aware during the administrative procedure that specifically supported the Commission's findings, the fact that an incriminating document not communicated to the person concerned was inadmissible as evidence would not affect the validity of the objections upheld in the contested decision.[183]

---

[177] Case No 39594/94 *Kress v France* [GC] judgment of 7 June 2001, Reports of Judgments and Decisions 2001-VI para 72.

[178] Case No 22209/93 *Foucher v France* judgment of 18 March 1997, Reports of Judgments and Decisions 1997-II para 36.

[179] Case No 18990/91 *Niederöst-Hube v Switzerland* judgment of 18 February 1997, Reports of Judgments and Decisions 1997-II para 24.

[180] Cases Nos 11170/84, 12876/87 and 13468/87 *Branstetter v Austria* judgment of 28 August 1991 Series A No 211 para 67.

[181] *Kerojärvi v Finland* judgment of 19 July 1995 Series A No 322 para 42, and *Mantovanelli v France* judgment of 18 March 1997, Reports of Judgments and Decisions 1997-II para 33.

[182] Case 322/81 *Michelin v EC Commission* [1983] ECR 3461 paras 7, 9; Case 107/82 *AEG v EC Commission* [1983] ECR 3151 paras 24–30.

[183] Joined Cases C-204/00 P, C-205/00 P, C-211/00 P, C-213/00 P, C-217/00 P and C-219/00 P *Aalborg Portland and others v EC Commisison* [2004] ECR I-123 para 70.

Reasonableness of the length of the proceedings   The ECHR establishes in   **4.43**
Article 6(1) that every person has the right to have his or hers affairs handled
impartially, fairly and within a reasonable time. The reasonableness of the length
of proceedings is to be assessed in the light of the circumstances of the case and
having regard to the criteria laid down in the Court's case law, in particular the
complexity of the case[184] and the conduct of the applicant and of the relevant
authorities. On the latter point, what is at stake for the applicant in the litigation
has to be taken into account, but in any case, the applicant must not slow down
the proceedings with a dilatory intention. The judicial authorities have to be
prompt in rendering their decisions. The ECtHR has pointed out that the ECHR
places a duty on the Member States to organize their legal systems so as to allow
the courts to comply with the requirements of Article 6(1) including that of trial
within a 'reasonable time'. On a number of occasions, the CFI has had regard to
the case law on delays under Article 6 ECHR in considering whether or not the
Commission had taken a more than reasonable time to reach its decision.[185]

Principles in criminal procedures

The principle of *ne bis in idem* or double jeopardy   This principle can be   **4.44**
found in Article 4 of Protocol No 7 to the ECHR. We have seen that the
ECtHR applies a wide interpretation of the concept of 'criminal offences'. On
the other hand, the scope of Article 4 of Protocol No 7 to the ECHR is
restricted to acts within the same jurisdiction and does not prevent a person
from being convicted for the same offence in a different jurisdiction.[186] Article 50

---

[184] Case No 22121/93 *Vallée v France* judgment of 26 April 1991 Series A No 289-A para 34.
[185] Joined Cases T-213/95 and T-18/96 *SCK and FNK v EC Commission* [1997] ECR II-1739
para 56; Joined Cases T-305/94 to T-307/94, T-313/94 to T-316/94, T-318/94, T-325/94,
T-328/94, T-329/94 and T-335/94 *Limburgse Vinyl Maatschappij and others v EC Commission*
[1999] ECR II-931 paras 120 *et seq*; Case T-228/97 *Irish Sugar v Commission* [1999] ECR
II-2969 paras 276 *et seq*, and Joined Cases T-5/00 and T-6/00 *Nederlandse Federatieve Vereniging
voor de Groothandel op Elektrotechnisch Gebied v EC Commission* [2003] ECR II-5761 paras 73
et seq. In that connection, it must be observed, first, that, in criminal matters the reasonable time
referred to in Art 6(1) ECHR runs from the time at which a person is charged (see Case No 8304/
78 *Coriglianov Italy* judgment of 10 December 1982 Series A No 57 para 34) and, secondly,
that the fundamental rights guaranteed by the ECHR are protected as general principles of
Community law. In a procedure relating to Community competition policy, of the kind at issue in
this case, the persons concerned are not the subject of any formal accusation until they receive the
statement of objections. Accordingly, the prolongation of this stage of the procedure alone is not
in itself capable of adversely affecting the rights of the defence.
[186] Joined Cases T-236/01, T-239/01, T-244/01 to T-246/01, T-251/01 and T-252/01 *Tokai
Carbon v EC Commission* [2004] ECR II-1181 para 130; Joined Cases 18/65 and 35/65 *Gutmann
v EC Commission* [1966] ECR 75 paras 103, 119; Joined Cases C-238/99 P, C-244/99 P, C-245/
99 P, C-247/99 P, C-250/99 P to C-252/99 P and C-254/99 P *Limburgse Vinyl Maatschappij NV
(LVM) and others v EC Commission* [2002] ECR I-8375 paras 59, 131; Case T-224/00 *Archer
Daniels Midland Co and Archer Daniels Midland Ingredients v EC Commission* [2003] ECR
II-2597 paras 85–86; Case T-223/00 *Kyowa Hakko Kogyo v EC Commission* [2003] ECR II-2553
para 96.

CFR prohibits double prosecution within the Union and thus also covers the situation of parallel prosecutions by the Commission and a national competition authority or by the competition authorities of several Member States. There is little guidance from the ECtHR on the application of the principle: most of the cases decided by the Court relate to road traffic infringement where a person drives under the influence of alcohol and injures someone and seem to be of little relevance to the application of the principle in competition cases.[187]

The right to respect for private and family life, home, and correspondence

4.45 Article 8 of the ECHR states that everyone has the right to respect for his private and family life, his home, and his correspondence. Even though the ECtHR has been willing to extend the right to respect for a home to business premises, it does not recognize Article 8 as an absolute right. Interferences are allowed as long as they are in accordance with the law, pursue a legitimate aim, and are necessary. These exceptions are to be interpreted narrowly,[188] and are easier to justify where business premises are involved than where a case concerns wholly domestic premises. In *Roquette Frères*, which concerned a request for a preliminary ruling requesting clarification on how should the *Hoechst* case on the inviolability of corporate domicile be interpreted the ECJ examined how much regard it should have to the ECHR and the jurisprudence of the ECtHR.[189] In addition to laying down an entirely new standard for the division of functions between national courts and the Community courts in these matters,[190] the Court considered whether the applicable national rules for order-

---

[187] K Dekeyser and C Gauer, 'The New Enforcement System for Arts 81 and 82 and the Rights of Defence' ch 23 in BE Hawk (ed) International Antitrust Law & Policy, Annual Proceedings of the Fordham Institute [2004] 549–85 (556).

[188] Case No 37971/97 *Colas Est and others v France* judgment of 16 April 2002, Reports of Judgments and Decisions 2002-III, in which the ECtHR ruled for the first time that in certain situations the rights guaranteed by Art 8 apply to a company's head office, branch office, or place of business. In this case, the investigators entered the applicant's premises without a prior judicial warrant and without a police officer with judicial investigation powers being present. The ECtHR ruled that the inspections were disproportionate to the legitimate purposes pursued. See also J Temple Lang and C Rizza, 'The Ste Colas Est and others v France case European Court of Human Rights Judgment of April 16, 2002' [2002] ECLR 413–16 who question the compatibility of the Commission inspections with the *Colas* judgment. See also K Dekeyser and C Gauer, 'The New Enforcement System for Arts 81 and 82 and the Rights of Defence' ch 23 in BE Hawk (ed), International Antitrust Law & Policy, Annual Proceedings of the Fordham Institute [2004] 549–85 (556).

[189] See Case C-94/00 *Roquette Frères* [2002] ECR I-9011 paras 22–29. In Joined Cases T-305/94, T-306/94, T-307/94, T-313/94 to T-316/94, T-318/94, T-325/94, T-328/94, T-329/94 and T-335/94 *Limburgse Vinyl Maatschappij NV (LVM) and others v EC Commission* [1999] ECR II-931 paras 419–420, the CFI rejected an invitation to qualify Hoechst in the light of Case No 13710/88 *Niemietz v Germany* judgment of 16 December 1992 Series A No 251-B, (1993) 16 EHRR 97. See C Bellamy and G Child, *EC Law of Competition* (5th edn, 2001) para 12–124.

[190] See ch 8 on 'Inspections' paras 8.61 *et seq*.

ing entry upon premises and seizures are compatible with Community law, including, as the case may be, the rights established by the ECHR as general principles of law, observance of which is to be ensured by the ECJ.[191] The ECJ went on and stated that to determine the scope of the protection against arbitrary or disproportionate intervention by public authorities in the sphere of the private activities of any person in relation to the protection of business premises, regard must be had to the case law of the ECtHR subsequent to the judgment in *Hoechst*. According to that case law, the ECJ concluded that the protection of the home provided for in Article 8 ECHR may in certain circumstances be extended to cover business premises and, second, that the right of interference established by Article 8(2) ECHR might well be more far-reaching where professional or business activities or premises were involved than would otherwise be the case.[192]

---

[191] Case C-94/00, *Roquette Frères* [2002] ECR I-9011 para 26.
[192] Case C-94/00 *Roquette Frères* [2002] ECR I-9011 para 29 which expressly refers to the *Colas* judgment.

5

OPENING OF THE FILE

A. Action Taken by the Commission before a File is Opened

1. Sources of information

Instead of spending its time processing notifications of largely benign agree-   **5.01**
ments, Regulation 1/2003 should enable the Commission to use its limited
resources to crack down on serious infringements, such as cartels. In line with its
enforcement priorities, it is expected that the Commission will only open an
investigation if there is a realistic chance of uncovering sufficient evidence to
prove a cartel or an abuse of a dominant position. The widening of the Commission's investigatory powers was precisely aimed at enhancing methods of
discovering cartel activity at all levels of enforcement.[1] Notwithstanding, in so
doing it is dependent on receiving information from third parties, both informally or through formal complaints. In essence, cartels can come to light
either directly, through whistleblowers[2] and complaints by third parties or
indirectly, through other regulatory activities, such as sector inquiries or merger

---

[1] As regards the Commission's enlarged investigative powers, see ch 7 on 'Formal investigative
measures' and ch 8 'Inspections'.

[2] See also former Commissioner for Competition Policy M Monti, 'Proactive Competition
Policy and the role of the Consumer', Speech at the European Competition Day Dublin, 29 April
2004: '[. . .] The leniency programme has proved to be a formidable tool for encouraging firms
which have infringed competition rules to cooperate with the Commission. Not only does this
allow cartels to be uncovered, but more generally the risk that a member of the cartel might go to
the authorities to secure immunity tends to destabilise the activity of the cartel itself and to
discourage the formation of cartels in the first place.' P Lowe, 'Enforcement Antitrust Roundtable' 32nd Annual International Antitrust Law & Policy Conference Fordham Corporate Law
Institute, 22–23 September 2005 (forthcoming) stating that the leniency programme has proved
to be an efficient and successful tool for uncovering cartels: in 2004, twenty-nine companies, and
so far in 2005, ten companies have requested leniency. WPJ Wils, 'Powers of Investigation
and Procedural rights and Guarantees in EU Antitrust Enforcement', First Lisbon Conference on
Competition Law and Economics, Belém 3–4 November 2005, paras 2 *et seq*.

investigations. The Commission strongly encourages citizens and undertakings to address themselves to the public enforcers to inform them about suspected infringements of the competition rules as complainants.[3] Thus, to supplement formal complaint proceedings, the Commission also seeks to collect information which does not need to be submitted pursuant to the requirements for complaints under Regulation 1/2003 and Regulation 773/2004[4] but which may nevertheless be relevant with a view to detecting competition law violations. For this purpose, the Commission has created a special web site to collect information from citizens and undertakings and their associations who wish to inform the Commission about suspected infringements of Articles 81 and 82 EC.[5] Further, the 'Consumer Liaison Officer' within the Commission's COMP DG provides a direct point of contact for disenchanted consumers.[6]

---

[3] The Commission Notice on the handling of complaints by the Commission under Arts 81 and 82 of the EC Treaty ('Notice on Handling of Complaints') [2004] OJ C101/65 has set out a detailed procedure for lodging a complaint with the Commission. See also M Monti 'Proactive Competition Policy and the role of the Consumer' Speech at the European Competition Day Dublin, 29 April 2004: '[. . .] The abolition of the notification system under the antitrust rules will mean that the Commission is even more eager to learn about breaches of competition law from external sources [. . .] it is of crucial importance that we have active consumers and consumer associations which provide the competition authorities with market information, given that it is consumers who are usually on the receiving end of anti-competitive practices. While a simple letter from one consumer is rarely enough, a series of complaints or a complaint submitted by a consumer association, where the conduct complained of is likely to affect the interests of its members, can normally provide the Commission with a basis to open an investigation [. . .]' See Case C-119/97 *Ufex v EC Commission* [1999] ECR I-01341 para 74, Opinion of AG Ruiz-Jarabo Colomer in Case C-119/97 *Ufex v EC Commission* [1999] ECR I-1341 para 7: '[. . .] Undertakings which complain of anti-competitive practices perform an activating function or, so to speak, act as catalysts for measures by the Commission involving two orders of interests—the interests of the undertakings themselves in averting commercial damage as a result of the unlawful practices of their competitors, and the general interest that the competition rules should be observed, an interest which is safeguarded by Community law and must be protected by the Commission[. . .]'.

[4] Art 7(2) of Reg 1/2003 and Art 5 (admissibility of complaints) of Reg 773/2004.

[5] Complainants may also come to the Commission's notice informally. Given the limited nature of informal contacts, they are not in principle treated as necessarily constituting the basis for an investigation, since at this stage it is still not known whether a procedure will ultimately be initiated. This phase is preparatory and exploratory and in many cases does not automatically culminate in the initiation of a procedure, although some informal contacts of this kind may in fact produce that result. The Commission has created a mailbox that can be used by citizens and undertakings and their associations who wish to inform the Commission about suspected infringements (COMP-MARKET-INFORMATION@cec.eu.int). Any initiation of a procedure will be either at the request of the complainant, when the purpose of the informal contact has been to complain—and when he or she may need guidance to file a complaint (see below), or on the Commission's own initiative, when, as 'guardian of the Treaty' and authority responsible for ensuring the observance of Community law, it considers such a course to be necessary.

[6] The task of this officer is to be 'a primary contact point for consumer organizations' and to alert 'consumer groups to competition cases where their input might be useful. Commission appoints Consumer Liaison Officer', Commission Press Release IP/03/1679 of 9 December 2003.

Such information can be the starting point for an investigation by the Commission.[7]

The Commission also relies on the monitoring of the specialized press or may **5.02** also receive information from internal sources. It may also use information contained in a request for a guidance letter[8] or information gathered in the context of a sector inquiry under Article 17 of Regulation 1/2003.[9] Requests for information under Article 18 of Regulation 1/2003[10] and investigations under Articles 19 (Power to take statements),[11] 20 (inspections), and 21 (inspections of other premises),[12] which have been carried out in the market for a given product may reveal prohibited practices in other markets and affecting other products. The ECJ interpreted Article 20(1) of former Regulation 17, which provided—in the same sense as Article 28 of Regulation 1/2003—that 'information acquired as a result of the application of Articles 11, 12, 13, and 14[13] shall be used only for the purpose of the relevant request or investigation', as not preventing the Commission from relying on information concerning markets or products not directly investigated initially, in order to commence a new and separate investigation into them.[14] In such cases, the ECJ ruled that Article 28(1) merely obliged the Commission to obtain the necessary information as part of a new procedure separate from the one in which evidence emerged of a

---

[7] Notice on Handling of Complaints [2004] OJ C101/65 paras 3–4. In practice, complaints have tended not to be the starting point for Commission cartel investigations, although they have been the norm for NCAs in some Member States. Complaints rarely provide as much evidence as leniency applications, as the innate secrecy of a cartel prevents third parties from possessing sufficient information. The Commission will only open an investigation if there is a realistic chance of uncovering sufficient evidence to prove a cartel.

[8] The information remains with the Commission and can be used in subsequent procedures under Reg 1/2003. A request for a guidance letter is without prejudice to the power of the Commission to open proceedings in accordance with Reg 1/2003. Commission Notice on informal guidance relating to novel questions concerning Arts 81 and 82 of the EC Treaty that arise in individual cases ('Notice on Informal Guidance') [2004] OJ C101/78 paras 11, 18.

[9] See below paras 5.04 *et seq.*

[10] See ch 8 on 'Information requests' below paras 7.21 *et seq.*

[11] See ch 7 'Formal investigative measures in general. Interviews and requests for information' on paras 7.51 *et seq.*

[12] See ch 8 on 'Inspections' paras 8.06 *et seq.* and 8.54 *et seq.*

[13] Arts 11, 12, 13, and 14 of former Reg 17 are equivalent to Arts 18, 17, 22, and 20, respectively, of Reg 1/2003.

[14] See Case 85/87 *Dow Benelux v EC Commission* [1989] ECR 3137 para 19. To interpret that provision otherwise would be tantamount to granting impunity for restrictive practices which come to the notice of Commission officials accidentally or incidentally. In the Court's view, this would prevent the Commission from effectively upholding the Community legal order. Indeed, if the fact that such information became known informally prevented the initiation of proceedings and the imposition of penalties, undertakings themselves would have an interest in letting information slip out regarding other possible restrictive practices on their part affecting markets or products not directly under investigation, in order to obtain immunity from penalties in those other areas.

different infringement. However, the Commission is not entitled to use—even as a basis for the commencement of an investigation—the information obtained in national civil proceedings where the applicability of Articles 81 and 82 EC is in issue and one of the parties has been called on to admit an infringement of those provisions, provided that the Commission could not have obtained that information using its powers under Regulation 1/2003.[15]

5.03   Information may also be received from other competition enforcement authorities. It has been a core element of the modernization of competition rules that the Commission and the NCAs should form a network and work closely together in the application of Articles 81 and 82 EC. This network provides an infrastructure for mutual exchange of information, including confidential information, and assistance, thereby expanding considerably the scope for each member of the network to enforce Articles 81 and 82 effectively.[16] In addition, the Commission is member of the International Competition Network (ICN) and has agreements with a number of other antitrust authorities outside the EU under which information may be passed.

2. Inquiries into sectors of the economy

5.04   The Commission constantly monitors the Community economy. Direct observation of the various industrial and commercial sectors enables it to detect and then investigate both abuses and agreements infringing competition law. Against these, the Commission will initiate a procedure on its own initiative with a view to imposing a penalty. Article 17 of Regulation 1/2003 has substituted Article 12 of Regulation 17 and enables the Commission to undertake inquiries into sectors of the economy where there are indications to suggest that competition is being restricted or distorted in an economic sector of the

---

[15] This applies to both the Commission and NCAs. See Case C-60/92 *Otto v Postbank* [1993] ECR I-5683 paras 16–20. The Court so held in answering a preliminary question as to whether a party to civil proceedings could shield itself by reliance on the judgment of the Court in Case 374/87 *Orkem v EC Commission* [1989] ECR 3283 and thereby decline to answer certain questions which might have caused it to admit an infringement of Arts 81 and 82 EC. The Court held that Community law did not allow an undertaking in such circumstances to refuse to answer. The quid pro quo for the disclosure to the Commission of such information was that the latter could not rely on it as proof or possible evidence of an infringement. It thus seems that the Commission will, although to a very limited extent, be obliged to suffer 'acute amnesia' (see Case C-67/91 *Dirección General de Defensa de la Competencia (DGDC) v Asociación Española de Banca Privada (AEB) and others* [1992] ECR I-4785 para 39), if anyone supplies it with information from civil proceedings in which a party has been compelled to admit an infringement of the competition rules. As a result, the infringement would necessarily go unpunished, although, if Community infringement proceedings were initiated on the basis of the same facts, the Commission could be called on to indicate the evidence on which it relied in order to commence its investigations, if the *Otto* judgment were invoked against it.

[16] See ch 2 'National competition authorities' paras 3.04 *et seq.*

Common Market.[17] Inquiries into sectors of the economy may thus serve to pave the way for individual procedures under Regulation 1/2003. Their main purpose remains, however, to discover possible and emerging restrictions and distortions of competition in a given sector, enabling the Commission better to apprehend the underlying economic situation and take the appropriate remedial action. Data collection undertaken in a sector inquiry covers the legal environment as well as business practices, contracts, technical elements, and financial conditions which help to define which competition law principles should apply to a given sector.[18] Where the Commission has focused its resources on investigating serious infringements, awareness of market dynamics and performance, sector particularities and obstacles to competition have become increasingly important, in particular in emerging and technology-based markets.[19] In this regard, in the view of the Commission, sector inquiries provide a particularly appropriate tool for investigating crossborder market concerns and examining sector wide practices that do not normally fall within the scope of an individual case.[20] In assessing markets to be reviewed, DG COMP will focus on sectors where there are only a few players, where cartel activity is recurrent or where abuses of market power are generic.[21] At one time, this instrument seemed to fall into disuse, or even abandonment.[22] However, sector inquiries are now making

---

[17] See D Wood and N Baverez 'Sector inquiries under EU competition law' [2005] Competition Law Insight, February Issue, 3–5.

[18] A Crawford and P Adamopoulos, 'Using the instrument of sector-wide inquiries: inquiry into content for 3G services' [2004] Competition Newsletter, Number 2, 63–65 (64).

[19] See D Wood and N Baverez, 'Sector inquiries under EU competition law' [2005] Competition Law Insight, 3–5 (4); A Crawford and P Adamopoulos, 'Using the instrument of sector-wide inquiries: inquiry into content for 3G services' [2004] Competition Newsletter, Number 2, 63–65 (64) with respect to 3rd generation mobile telecommunications networks.

[20] Commission Press Release IP/04/134 of 30 January 2004 'Commission launches sector inquiry into the sale of sports rights to Internet ad 3G mobile operators'. Whistleblowers may be induced to come forward more readily if they believe that a sector inquiry is likely.

[21] Commission Communication 'A Pro Active Competition Policy for a Competitive Europe' [2004] COM (204) 293 Final; Commissioner for Competition Policy, N Kroes, 'Taking Competition Seriously—Anti-Trust Reform in Europe' International Bar Association/European Commission Conference 'Antitrust Reform in Europe: A Year in Practice', 10 March 2005, Brussels, identifying the sector of financial services and energy as particularly apt for sector inquiries in the future: '[. . .] both markets [. . .] are key to the EU's overall competitiveness. In that context I would encourage you to let us know when you find that regulatory barriers—at both Community and national level—unnecessarily, and often unintentionally, hold back competition in these areas [. . .]'; see also N Kroes 'The Competition Principle as a Guideline for Legislation and State Action—the Responsibility of Politicians and the Role of Competition Authorities', 12th International Conference on Competition, Bonn, 6 June 2005: '[. . .] We [. . .] intend to use these sectoral investigations to identify any significant barriers to competition, including regulatory barriers. In a first stage, we will focus work on financial services and the energy sector, more specifically gas and electricity. These are both areas which are key to the efficient operation of many other economic activities [. . .]'. As regards the inquiries launched by the Commission into this sectors, see para 5.07 below.

[22] See earlier inquiries in the beer brewing sector *Alba* [1971] OJ L161/2; *Union des Brasseries* [1971] OJ L161/6; *Maes* [1971] OJ L161/10.

a reappearance as one of the key investigatory tools for DG COMP and its increased focus on major infringements.[23] Such inquiries are aimed to allow the Commission to analyse allegedly anticompetitive practices in a systematic and transparent manner, and to give the NCAs the opportunity of launching their own parallel national investigations on the basis of the Commission's findings.

5.05 The opening of an investigation enquiring into a sector of the economy presupposes, under Article 17(1) of Regulation 1/2003, the adoption of a decision to that effect by the Commission. Since it is not a purely routine decision—despite not being one whose publication is required pursuant to Article 30 of Regulation 1/2003—it must be adopted by the full Commission, after the opinion of the Advisory Committee has been obtained.[24] The decision will define the economic sector concerned and identify the undertakings which will be required to provide information. Decisions under Article 17 of Regulation 1/2003 enable the Commission fully to exercise its investigative powers under Articles 18,[25] 19, 20,[26] and 22[27] of Regulation 1/2003 without having first opened an individual procedure in which specific investigative measures may be decided upon and without having to prove the need for such measures.[28] This means that, in its requests for information and its inspections, the Commission need refer only to the decision to open an investigation enquiring into a particular economic sector in order to justify the specific investigative measure vis-à-vis the undertakings concerned. Thus, the Commission may ask undertakings to supply information necessary to carry out its inquiry. Undertakings concerned are obliged to answer the Commission's questionnaires and even to provide documents, if they are so required.[29] Later, the Commission may publish a report on the results of its inquiry and invite comments from interested parties.[30]

---

[23] See D Wood and N Baverez, 'Sector inquiries under EU competition law' [2005] Competition Law Insight 3–5 (5). Sector inquiries came into focus again in the telecommunications sector in 1999.

[24] See Art 17(2) of Reg 1/2003.

[25] Regarding requests for information, see ch 7 'Investigative measures' below paras 7.21 *et seq.*

[26] Regarding inspections, see ch 8 'Inspections' below paras 8.06 *et seq.*

[27] See ch 7 'Investigative measures' paras 7.51 *et seq.*

[28] As will be seen, the exercise of the Commission's investigative powers is based, in general terms, on the existence of evidence showing the involvement of the undertakings investigated. See below ch 7 'Investigative measures'.

[29] Art 23 allows the Commission to impose fines on undertakings and associations of undertakings which, in response to a request for information either supply incorrect or misleading information or do not supply it at all. Such fines may reach 1 per cent of the total turnover in the preceding business year. Pursuant to Art 24 periodic penalties may also be imposed, up to 5 per cent of the average daily turnover of the firm.

[30] Art 17, third subparagraph. Public presentation of the preliminary findings of the New Media (3G) Sector Inquiry, Brussels 27 May 2005. EC Commission: 'Concluding report on the Sector Inquiry into the provision of sports content over third generation mobile Networks', published in accordance with Art 17(1) of Reg 1/2003, 21 September 2005.

The main advantage of inquiries into sectors of the economy for the Commis-   **5.06**
sion thus lies in the breadth of the powers available to it, unlimited by
the requirement to prove the need for investigative measures which applies in
individual cases. Recent examples of sector inquiries include the following:

- *Telecoms sector:* on interconnected tariffs applied between fixed and mobile
  telecoms operators and prices for calls from fixed to mobile networks, in
  1998; on provision and prices of leased lines, in 1999;[31] on national and
  international mobile roaming services, in 2000;[32] on the provision of access to
  and use of the residential local loop, in 2000.[33]
- *Music sector:* on the vertical relationships between the five major record companies and their retailers;[34] on the compatibility of the DVD regional coding
  system with the EC competition rules, in 2001.[35]
- *Sale of sports rights to providers of third generation mobile phones services*: this
  has been the first sector inquiry conducted by the Commission under Regulation 1/2003, launched in 2004.[36]
- *Energy and financial service sectors:* the inquiry into competition in the energy,
  retail banking, and insurance sectors shows the Commission's determination
  to use sector inquiries in order to improve its knowledge about a particular
  sector and in view of better identifying obstacles to competition.[37]

---

[31] Commission Press Release IP/99/786 of 22 October 1999, 'Commission launches first
phase of sectoral inquiry: leased line tariffs'; Commission Press Release IP/02/1852 of 11 December 2002 'Price decreases of up to 40 per cent lead Commission to close telecom leased line
inquiry'. The sector inquiry into telecom leased lines produced, or at least coincided with, a
significant decrease in the price for international telecom-leased lines across the EU (prices have
decreased, on average, 30 per cent to 40 per cent). Moreover, the inquiry led to a pro-active stance
on the part of the national regulatory authorities (NRAs) with respect to both pricing and
providing of leased lines. The NRAs adopted a number of measures, such as wholesale offers to
competitors, that enhance and maintain competition at the retail level. D Wood and N Baverez,
'Sector inquiries under EU competition law' [2005] Competition Law Insight 3–5.
[32] Commission Press Release IP/00/111 of 4 February 2000 'Commission launches second
phase of telecommunications sector inquiry under the competition rules: mobile roaming';
Commission MEMO/01/262 of 11 July 2001 'Statement on inquiry regarding mobile roaming'.
[33] Commission Press Release IP/02/686 of 8 May 2002 'Commission suspects Deutsche Telekom of charging anti-competitive tariffs for access to its local network'.
[34] Commission Press Release IP/01/1212 of 17 August 2001 'Commission closes inquiry into
CD prices after changes to business practices'.
[35] Commission Press Release IP/01/1212 of 17 August 2001 'Commission closes inquiry into
CD prices after changes to business practices' stating that the inquiry in the DVD regional
coding system would continue.
[36] Commission press release IP/04/134 of 30 January 2004 'Commission launches sector
inquiry into the sale of sports rights to Internet and 3G mobile operators'; see also A Crawford
and P Adamopoulos, 'Using the instrument of sector-wide inquiries: inquiry into content for 3G
services' [2004] Competition Newsletter, Number 2, 63–65.
[37] Commission Press Release IP/05/716 of 13 June, 2005 'Commission opens sector inquiry
into gas and electricity'; see also Commission MEMO/05/203 of 13 June 2005 'Energy sector

B. Initiating Proceedings

5.07 Proceedings conducted by the Commission in competition matters may be commenced by the Commission on its own initiative, or in response to a complaint. Article 2 of Regulation 774/2004 provides that the Commission may decide to initiate proceedings with a view to adopting a decision pursuant to Articles 7–10 of Regulation 1/2003.[38] There is no specified time or moment for the initiation of proceedings and it can occur at any stage in the investigation of a case. In particular, the initiation of proceedings is not necessary before the Commission can exercise its powers of investigation.[39] However the formal step must be taken no later than the issuing of the statement of objections to the undertakings concerned in infringement proceedings or the publication of the notice under Article 27(4) of Regulation 1/2003 prior to a decision making commitments binding or declaring inapplicability.[40] The Commission may publish the initiation of proceedings in the Official Journal (but it is not obliged to)[41] or to make it public in any other appropriate way, e.g. on DG COMP website. Before the Commission publishes the initiation of the proceedings, it shall inform the parties but there is no requirement that the parties should be immediately informed when the proceedings have been commenced.[42]

5.08 Regardless of whether there is a complaint or a procedure commenced on the Commission's own initiative, each case receives a Registry number and name

---

inquiry—frequently asked questions'; Commission MEMO/05/204 of 13 June 2005 'Financial service sector inquiry—frequently asked questions'; Commission press release IP/05/719 of 13 June 2005 'Competition: Commission opens sector inquiries into retail banking and business insurance'.

[38] Finding and termination of infringement (Art 7), interim measures (Art 8), commitments (Art 9) and finding of inapplicability (Art 10). Under Art 2(4) of Reg 774/2004 proceedings have not to be commenced for rejecting a complaint.

[39] Article 2(3) of Reg 1/2003.

[40] In practice, proceedings will not be formally initiated until just before the statement of objections is served on the parties.

[41] Article 2(2) of Reg 1/2003.

[42] In *Dyestuffs* it was argued that the Commission had violated the procedural rules then contained in Reg 17 by communicating to the parties its statement of objections at the same time as it announced the initiation of proceedings to determine whether any infringements had taken place. The ECJ rejected this argument emphasizing that the statement of objections was the crucial document in this regard. See Case 57/69 *Azienda Colori Nazionali—ACNA SpA v EC Commission* [1972] ECR 933 paras 10 and 11: '[. . .] neither the provisions in force nor the general principles of law require notice of the decision to initiate the procedure to establish an infringement to be given prior to the notification of the objections adopted against the interested parties in the context of such proceedings [. . .] It is the notice of objections alone and not the decision to commence proceedings which is the measure stating the final attitude of the Commission concerning undertakings against which proceedings for infringement of the rules on competition have been commenced [. . .].' CS Kerse and N Khan, *EC Antitrust Procedure* (5th edn, 2005) para 2–080.

when it is commenced. The number and name serve to identify the case in DG COMP files and appear in all subsequent correspondence as a reference both for the undertakings concerned and for the Commission itself. When the file thus opened relates to another procedure already at the investigative stage, the Registry still gives it its own number, even though the processing of the cases, and the final decision, may be the same for the original procedure and for subsequent procedures if combined with the first one. There are no formal rules for the joining of procedures. In general, a decision must relate to at least one infringement. In view of the fact that a procedure may relate to several infringements and several procedures may relate to a single infringement, a procedure may result in one decision or several, as the case may be. Given the possibility of joining procedures, a single decision may deal with several infringements and several procedures. The ECJ has confirmed the Commission's authority to deal with several infringement procedures in a single decision, provided that the decision enables each addressee to determine precisely what conduct has been imputed to it.[43] When the Commission considers that there is evidence of an unlawful agreement or abuse of a dominant position in a particular market or economic sector and that action should be taken against the offending undertakings, it initiates a procedure of its own motion and undertakes investigations. This can happen without the need for any action by the persons concerned. However, the fact that an infringement is public and notorious does not impose a duty on the Commission to initiate a procedure under Articles 81(1) or 82 EC, at least in the absence of a formal complaint.[44]

The communication of the initiation of the proceedings to an undertaking may produce effects in relation to the interruption of the limitation period under Article 25 of Regulation 1/2003. This may be of relevance where the Commission may have to demonstrate that it acted in a timely fashion. The risk of being time barred does not appear to be particularly significant given that it is most likely that the Commission will have undertaken one of the other acts which interrupts the running of time under Article 25(3) before it reaches the stage of deciding to initiate proceedings.[45] The main consequence of the initiation of the formal proceedings by the Commission, however, is laid down in Article 11(6) of Regulation 1/2003 which states that the initiation by the Commission of

5.09

---

[43] See Joined Cases 40–48/73, 50/73, 54–56/73, 111/73, 113/73 and 114–73 *Suiker Unie and others v EC Commission* [1975] ECR 1663 para 111; and Joined Cases 209–15/78 and 218/78 *Van Landewyck v EC Commission (FEDETAB)* [1980] ECR 3125 para 77; Opinion of AG General Ruiz-Jarabo Colomer in Joined Cases C-204/00 P *Aalborg Portland v EC Commision* [2003] ECR I-123 para 86: '[. . .] That approach is legitimate and is based on the Commission's power to adopt a single decision covering several infringements [. . .].'

[44] Case T-29/92 *Vereniging van Samenwerkende Prijsregelende Organisatie in de Bouwnijverheid (SPO) and others v EC Commission* [1995] ECR II-289 para 360.

[45] CS Kerse and N Khan, *EC Antitrust Procedure* (5th edn, 2005) para 2–074.

proceedings for the adoption of a decision under Chapter III[46] shall relieve all NCAs of their competence to apply Articles 81 and 82 EC. Consequently, once the Commission has started proceedings, NCAs cannot act under the same legal basis against the same agreement(s) or practice(s) by the same undertaking(s) on the same relevant geographic and product market.[47] Two situations could be distinguished:

5.10 First, where the Commission is the first competition authority to initiate proceedings in a case for the adoption of a decision, NCAs may no longer deal with the case. Article 11(6) provides that once the Commission has initiated proceedings, the NCAs can no longer start their own procedure with a view to applying Articles 81 and 82 EC to the same agreement(s) or practice(s) by the same undertaking(s) on the same relevant geographic and product market. Secondly, where one or more NCAs have informed the network pursuant to Article 11(3) of Regulation 1/2003 that they are acting on a given case. During the initial allocation period of two months,[48] the Commission can initiate proceedings with the effects of Article 11(6) after having consulted the authorities concerned.

5.11 After the allocation phase, the Commission will in principle only apply Article 11(6) if there is a risk of inconsistency or if network members are unduly delaying proceedings in a given case. The ECN Cooperation Notice acknowledges in particular the possibility for the Commission to use its power under Article 11(6) when 'network members envisage conflicting decisions' or when 'network members envisage a decision which is obviously in conflict with consolidated case law; the standards defined in the judgments of the Community courts and in previous decisions and regulations of the Commission should serve as a yardstick'.[49] In addition, the Commission may intervene where there is a need to adopt a Commission decision to develop Community competition policy in particular when a similar competition issue arises in several Member States or to ensure effective enforcement. If an NCA is already acting on a case,

---

[46] Art 7 to 10 of Reg 1/2003.

[47] It is to note that the application of Art 11(6) of the Regulation is limited and modulated by Art 35(3) of Reg 1/2003, which states that the effects of Art 11(6) shall not extend to courts insofar as they act as review courts in respect of the types of decisions foreseen in Art 5 of Reg 1/2003. According to Art 35(4), where, for the adoption of certain decisions foreseen in Art 5, 'an authority in a Member State brings an action before a judicial authority that is separate and different from the prosecuting authority and provided that the terms of this paragraph are complied with, the effects of Article 11(6) shall be limited to the authority prosecuting the case which shall withdraw its claim before the judicial authority when the Commission opens proceedings and this withdrawal shall bring the national proceedings effectively to an end.'

[48] ECN Cooperation Notice [2004] OJ C101/43 para 18.

[49] WPJ Wils, 'Community Report' in *The Modernization of EU Competition Law Enforcement in the EU*, FIDE 2004 National Reports 661–736 para 1.68.

the Commission will explain the reasons for the application of Article 11(6) in writing to the NCA concerned and to the other ECN members. The Commission will announce to the network its intention of applying Article 11(6) in due time, so that network members will have the possibility of asking for a meeting of the Advisory Committee on the matter before the Commission initiates proceedings. The Commission will probably not—and to the extent that Community interest is not at stake—adopt a decision which is in conflict with an NCA's decision after the NCA has properly informed the Commission pursuant to both Articles 11(3) and (4) of Regulation 1/2003 and the Commission has not deemed it necessary to invoke Article 11(6).

In *IBM*, the ECJ held that the initiation of proceedings was merely a procedural **5.12** measure adopted preparatory to the decision which represents its culmination.[50] By the same token, the initiation of proceedings under Regulation 1/2003 is not a challengeable act within the meaning of Article 230 EC. The initiation of proceedings is made with a view to adopting a definitive or final measure under Articles 7 to 10 of Regulation 1/2003. Accordingly it is only those measures which definitively determine the position of the Commission upon the conclusion of that procedure which are open to challenge and not intermediate measures whose purpose is to pave the way for the final decision, which would arguably exclude also decisions by the Commission under Article 11(6) of Regulation 1/2003 from the scope of challengeable acts.[51] Any legal defects

---

[50] Case 60/81 *IBM v EC Commission* [1981] ECR 2639 para 21; this also applies to the statement of objections, Joined Cases T-191/98, T-212/98–T-214/98 *Atlantic Container Line and others v EC Commission* [2003] ECR I-3275 para 114.

[51] Case 60/81 *IBM v EC Commission* [1981] ECR 2639 paras 9–10; Case T-95/99 *Satellimages TV 5 SA v EC Commission* [2002] ECR II-1425 para 32. D Geradin and N Petit, 'Judicial remedies under EC Competition Law: Complex Issues arising from the Modernization Process', 32nd Annual International Antitrust Law & Policy Conference Fordham Corporate Law Institute, 22–23 September 2005 (forthcoming) acknowledge that the *IBM* case law, which excludes decisions to initiate a procedure from the scope of challengeable acts on the grounds that these acts are a preparatory step towards a final decision, could also be transposed to Art 11(6) decisions, maintains, however, that Commission decisions recalling cases from the national level deserve special treatment and may be considered as 'challengeable' within the meaning of Art 230 EC, also because—by way of analogy—the CFI has held that the decision to refer a case under Art 9 of the Merger Control Regulation (Reg 139/2004) and affects the legal situation of the parties to the concentration and could therefore be the subject of an action for annulment (Case T-119/02 *Royal Philips Electronics BV v EC Commission* [2003] ECR II-1433 para 281). See also Judge JD Cooke, 'Application of EC Competition Rules by National Courts' Antitrust Reform in Europe: A Year in Practice, 9–11 March 2005, Brussels, International Bar Association (IBA) 7, also indicates that the parties may have invested considerable time and money in defending themselves, and are then faced with the prospect of having to start all over again in a different forum.

therein may be relied upon in an action directed against the definitive act for which they represent a preparatory step.[52]

5.13 The Commission may also wish to reopen an investigation which it had shelved previously. In this event, it needs, however, to set out the reasons for having changed its opinion. In *Storck Amsterdam*, the Commission informed by decision the parties to an agreement that it would not take any further action on the matter because of its limited economic importance at Community level. Later, the Commission went back on its previous position regarding the economic importance of the agreement at Community level. The Court found that the reasons for that change of position were not explained by the Commission. Nor could they be inferred from the context of the decision. In particular, the decision to re-examine the case was not based on the presence or awareness of new points of fact or law warranting re-examination of the matter. Because the parties were not in a position to ascertain the reasons for the contested decision which implied that the Commission, in taking the view that the matter was of sufficient economic importance to warrant its staff conducting a thoroughgoing examination, the CFI annulled the decision to reopen the investigation on the grounds of the inadequacy of the statement of reasons.[53]

C. Complaints

1. Introduction

5.14 Under Article 7(2) of Regulation 1/2003, the Member States and any natural or legal persons who claim a legitimate interest are entitled to apply to the Commission for a finding of an infringement of Articles 81 or 82 EC. Under Regulation 17, the ECJ and the CFI held that the fact of lodging a complaint under Article 3 of Regulation 17 did not confer upon the complainant the right to obtain from the Commission a decision within the meaning of Article 249 EC, regarding the existence or otherwise of an infringement of Article 81 or 82 EC, or both.[54] Rather, the Commission is entitled to give different degrees of

---

[52] Case 60/81 *IBM v EC Commission* [1981] ECR 2639 para 12; Case T-241/97 *Storck v EC Commission* [2000] ECR II-309 para 49; Case T-189/95 *SGA v EC Commission* [1999] ECR II-3587 para 26; Order of the President of the CFI in Case T-213/01 *Österreichische Postparkasse v EC Commission* [2001] ECR II-3963 para 46; Case T-95/99 *Satellimages TV 5 SA v EC Commission* [2002] ECR II-1425 para 32.

[53] Case T-241/97 *Storck Amsterdam BV v EC Commission* [2000] ECR II-309 paras 70–83.

[54] Case 125/78 *GEMA v EC Commission* [1979] ECR 3173 para 17 and Case T-16/91 *Rendo v EC Commission* [1994] ECR II-2417 para 98; Case T-24/90 *Automec v EC Commission II* [1992] ECR II-2223 paras 75–76; and Case T-114/92 *BEMIM v EC Commission* [1995] ECRII-147 para 62.

priority and may decide on the order in which they are to be examined.[55] The new decentralized enforcement system requires potential complainants and their advisers to consider most carefully the appropriate authority to which a complaint shall be addressed. The Commission is not the first and not necessarily the only authority which will receive complaints. Nor does the Commission have the role of a case allocation agency.[56] For this reason, the complainant is therefore well advised to identify the competition authority or authorities best placed to handle the complaints, also in order to reduce the risk of any delay caused by a possible reallocation. A complainant may consider the legal powers and procedural rules available to a given NCA in addition to its reputation for effectiveness.

Of particular importance for the complainant, however, are the rules which the **5.15** Commission and the NCAs themselves apply with a view to determining which authority shall deal with a complaint. Guidance for the work sharing between the Commission and the NCAs are laid down in the ECN Cooperation Notice[57] which should help complainants to determine the authority most likely to be well placed to deal with their case. In principle, a case may be dealt with by one NCA, several NCAs acting in parallel, or the Commission. In essence, the Commission considers an authority as being well placed to deal with a case if there is a *material link* between the infringement and the territory of that Member State.[58] In most cases the authorities of those Member States where

---

[55] See, e.g. Case T-26/99 *Trabisco SA v EC Commission* [2001] ECR II-633 para 30 also noting that the Commission is not required to join the procedures for examining different complaints concerning the conduct of a particular undertaking, since the conduct of an investigation falls within the scope of its discretion. In particular, the fact that there are a number of complaints from operators belonging to different categories such as, in the context of this case, independent resellers, authorized intermediaries and dealers cannot preclude the dismissal of such of those complaints as appear, according to the evidence available to the Commission, to be unfounded or lacking in Community interest. See also Case T-5/93 *Tremblay and others v EC Commission* [1995] ECR II-185 para 60. The position is different only if the complaint comes within the exclusive remit of the Commission, as in the case of withdrawal of an exemption granted under Art 81(3) EC. Notice on the Handling of Complaints by the Commission [2004] OJ C101/65 para 41.

[56] Director-General DG COMP P Lowe, 'The Role of the Commission in the Modernisation of EC Competition Law', Speech at the UKAEL Conference on Modernisation of EC Competition Law: Uncertainties and Opportunities, 23 January 2004: '[. . .] The Commission cannot and will not act as a clearing house between independent national authorities, but will leave it to the authorities to agree on the appropriate case allocation. The Commission will also not undermine the parallel application of European competition law—the very aim of the modernisation exercise. And it will finally not go against the political compromise reached in the Council as regards the number of countries that need to be concerned before the Commission is considered to be best placed to deal with a case. In the case allocation process the Commission is thus merely a primus inter pares [. . .]'.

[57] ECN Cooperation Notice [2004] OJ C101/43 paras 5–15; Notice on the Handling of Complaints by the Commission [2004] OJ C101/65 paras 19–25.

[58] For more details, see ch 3 'National competition authorities' paras 3.06 *et seq.*

competition is substantially affected by an infringement are expected to be well placed—either through single or parallel action—unless the Commission is better placed to act. A single NCA is usually well placed to deal with agreements or practices that substantially affect competition mainly within its territory. Parallel action by two or three NCAs may be appropriate where an agreement or practice has substantial effects on competition mainly in their respective territories and the action of only one NCA would not be sufficient to bring the entire infringement to an end and/or where the evidence is most likely to be found in more than one Member State. Conversely, the Commission is 'particularly well placed' if one or several agreement(s) or practice(s), including networks of similar agreements or practices, have effects on competition in more than three Member States (cross-border markets covering more than three Member States or several national markets). Moreover, the Commission feels to be well placed to deal with a case if it is closely linked to other Community provisions which may be exclusively or more effectively applied by the Commission, if the Community interest requires the adoption of a Commission decision to develop Community competition policy when a new competition issue arises or to ensure effective enforcement. Within the ECN, information on cases that are being investigated following a complaint will be made available to the other members of the network before or without delay after commencing the first formal investigative measure.[59] Where the same complaint has been lodged with several authorities or where a case has not been lodged with an authority that is well placed, the members of the network will endeavour to determine within an indicative time limit of two months which authority or authorities should be in charge of the case. In conclusion, complainants themselves have an important role to play in reducing the potential need for reallocation of a case originating from their complaint when deciding on where to lodge their complaint. If nonetheless a case is reallocated within the network, the undertakings concerned and the complainant(s) are informed as soon as possible by the competition authorities involved.[60] The Commission may reject a complaint in accordance with Article 13 of Regulation 1/2003, on the grounds that a Member State competition authority is dealing with or has dealt with a given case. When doing so, the Commission must, in accordance with Article 9 of Regulation 773/2004, inform the complainant without delay which is the NCA concerned.

5.16 Apart from approaching public enforcers, a complainant may also envisage bringing matters before national courts. It may be easier to obtain interim relief in a national court or to receive damages for loss suffered as a result of the

---

[59] ECN Cooperation Notice [2004] OJ C101/43 para 17.
[60] Notice on Handling of Complaints [2004] OJ C101/65 para 24.

infringement.[61] In addition, the complainant may better control the proceedings, for example, if it wishes it may simply withdraw a complaint, whereas a public enforcer could investigate a case on its own motion. A complainant may be reluctant to take action before national courts because litigating the matter may involve more costs. Further, the complainant may be faced with a myriad of different and often burdensome rules of civil procedure in Member States.[62] While the Commission is at pains to stress the complementary role of private and public enforcement, the decision whether to turn to the Commission, an NCA or a national court hinges on various factors which must be carefully weighed up in each individual case.

2. Informal or unofficial complaints

Complaints can comprise several types, namely formal complaints, informal, or unofficial complaints. As regards the latter, complaints of this kind do not formally rank as complaints; the identity of the persons who make them is not disclosed, either because they are made anonymously or because the complainants ask the Commission to keep their identity secret. In the latter case, the Commission is careful at all times to maintain the anonymity of the complainant[63]—who in reality is merely an informant—in order to obviate problems of the kind which gave rise to the judgment of the Court in *Stanley Adams v Commission*. In *Stanley Adams* the ECJ held that where information is supplied on a voluntary basis and accompanied by a request for confidentiality in order to protect the informant's anonymity the Commission is legally bound to comply with that condition.[64] Informal complaints may be made orally or in writing and do not constitute 'formal applications' or formal complaints, and for that reason those who make them do not enjoy the legal and procedural safeguards available to other complainants.[65] The Commission is under no obligation to investigate informal complaints and they are acted upon only if the person in charge of the relevant sectoral unit or other DG COMP senior officials decide

5.17

---

[61] Art 8 of Reg 1/2003 provides that the Commission may adopt interim measures only on its own initiative.

[62] C Kerse and N Khan, *EC Antitrust Procedure* (5th edn, 2005) para 2–014; see also the advantages of private action before national courts highlighted by the Notice on Handling of Complaints by the Commission [2004] OJ C101/5 para 6.

[63] Notice on the Handling of Complaints [2004] OJ C101/05 para 81.

[64] Case 145/83 *Stanley Adams v EC Commission* [1985] ECR 3539. Stanley Adams was an informant whose identity was disclosed by the Commission during the investigation of restrictive practices in the vitamins market (Commission Decision of 9 June 1976 [1976] OJ L223/27), with serious consequences. The informant, employed by the Swiss multinational Hoffmann-La Roche, was tried and imprisoned in Switzerland, where any person who divulges business secrets of his employer is liable to imprisonment. Judgment was given against the Commission in proceedings for non-contractual liability.

[65] See ch 12 'Rejection of complaints'.

to do so. In such cases, the informal complaint will serve as a factual basis for the commencement of a procedure on the Commission's own initiative. The Commission takes care to ensure that the documents and submissions supporting informal complaints are not shown to the undertakings whose conduct is criticized except where there is no risk whatever that the anonymity of the complainants might be breached—otherwise they could not be used.[66] Where it is impossible to show the documents to the undertakings concerned so that the latter can verify them, the Commission prefers to take a more adventurous approach and use its own investigative facilities to gather evidence of the infringement (and perhaps not find the documents or information sought) rather than jeopardize the interests of informal complainants.

3. Formal complaints

5.18   Complaints under Article 7 of Regulation 1/2003 are subject to the formalities laid down in Article 5 of Regulation 773/2004. Under Regulation 17 old Form C was the standard form for complaints,[67] but in practice no particular or special form was required, in sharp contrast with applications for negative clearance and notifications for exemption, which required Form A/B to be used. The only formal requirement was the disclosure of the identity of the complainant or that of its authorized representative. At present, any person having a legitimate interest—and not only undertakings—is empowered to lodge them and Article 5(1) of Regulation 773/2004 provides that complaints shall contain the information required by Form C. Nevertheless, in the past, the Commission has rarely rejected a complaint because of formal defects. In practice, it was sufficient for complaints to be submitted in writing and signed by the complainant, who, as

---

[66] In *Plasterboard*, the ECJ acknowledged the need to provide for protection to customers of the firm being investigated. Case C-310/93 P *BPB Industries and British Gypsum v EC Commission* [1995] ECR I-865 paras 26–27; see also Case T-9/99 *HFB v EC Commission* [2002] ECR II-1487 para 225 and Joined Cases T-191/98, T-212/98–T-214/98 *Atlantic Container Line v EC Commission* [2003] ECR II-3275 para 393: '[. . .] the Commission may in any event refuse access to the correspondence with third parties by reason of its confidential nature, since an undertaking to which a statement of objections has been addressed, and which occupies a dominant position in the market, may adopt retaliatory measures against a competing undertaking, a supplier or a customer who has collaborated in the investigation carried out by the Commission [. . .]' However, there is no absolute guarantee of confidentiality. Art 15(3) of Reg 773/2004 states that 'nothing in this Regulation prevents the Commission from disclosing and using information necessary to prove an infringement of Article 81 or 82 EC'. Circumstances where the disclosure of the identity of the complainant would become indispensable to proving an infringement are likely to be rare, but nevertheless in some cases, e.g. infringements of Art 82 by a refusal to supply, the identity of the complainant is likely to be obvious to the addressee of such a decision. CS Kerse and N Khan, *EC Antitrust Procedure* (5th edn, 2005) para 2–020.

[67] Form C was annexed to the original version of Reg 27 (OJ 1118/62, [1959–62] OJ Spec Ed 132) and was updated by Reg 3666/93 ([1993] OJ L336/1).

stated above, may not request anonymity if he or she wishes to enjoy the procedural rights of a formal complainant.

New Form C

Complaints should be in one of the official EU languages and in order to **5.19** be admissible they must contain the information requested in Form C.[68] Correspondence to the Commission that does not comply with the formal requirements set out in Article 5 of Regulation 773/2004 does not constitute a complaint within the meaning of Article 7(2) of Regulation 1/2003 and will be considered as general information which may lead to an investigation at its own motion.[69] Form C requires complainants to submit comprehensive information in relation to their complaint and to use their best efforts to complete it as fully as possible. If the complainant believes any detail asked for to be unavailable, a reasoned explanation should be given. The Commission may waive the obligation to provide any particular information, including documents, where it considers that such information is not necessary for the examination of the case.[70] This may enable, where appropriate, a complaint to be tailored to the particular case so that the key information strictly needed for the Commission's preliminary examination is provided. Where a complainant is uncertain how to complete Form C or wishes further explanation he or she may contact DG COMP to obtain guidance from Commission officials. Preliminary contacts can help to identify what DG COMP regards as necessary in a particular commercial or industry context. Such contacts may facilitate completion of the form and serve to speed up things later in the process. Any material which the complainant considers to be confidential or contains business secrets should be clearly marked and the Commission's attention drawn to any restrictions on its use. It is common practice for parties to submit documents where each page is marked with the term that it contains 'Business Secrets', but it may sometimes be worth indicating specifically the confidential items in a given document. Where Form C contains confidential information it is necessary to attach a non-confidential version.[71] The reason for this is that the full complaint, subject to the exclusion of business secrets, will eventually be shown to the undertaking the subject of the complaint. The complainant should follow the style and order of the Form and make clear at the outset, using the headings given in Regulation 773/2004

---

[68] Form C is available at the DG COMP website and is also annexed to the Notice on the Handling of Complaints [2004] OJ C101/65.

[69] Notice on the Handling of Complaints [2004] OJ C101/65 para 32.

[70] Art 5(1) of Reg 773/2004; Notice on the Handling of Complaints [2004] OJ C101/65 para 31 where the Commission states that this possibility can play a role in facilitating complaints by consumer associations which will not have access to the relevant information held by the undertakings concerned.

[71] Art 5(2) of Reg 773/2004.

that the document is a complaint on Form C. A complainant should expressly refer to Regulation 1/2003 and Form C in making its complaint in order to demonstrate clearly that reliance is also being placed on the provisions of the Regulation.[72]

5.20 **Information regarding the parties**   Section I of Form C requires the identification of the complainant. Where the complainant is an undertaking, information is required of any group to which it belongs. The complaint must also give the names and addresses of the undertaking or undertakings the subject of the complaint as well as the nature and scope of their business activities. The relationship (e.g. competitor, customer) should also be given and could be further expanded in Section III where the complainant has to demonstrate its legitimate interest.

5.21 **Details of alleged infringement**   Section II requires a description of the arrangements or behaviour in question. The details will largely depend on the circumstances of the particular case. The substance of the complaint should be set out as clearly as possible: copies of all relevant correspondence and other documents, if any, should be attached. A description of the relevant products or services should be given, particularly where they have a specialized or technical nature: where appropriate, photographs, diagrams, catalogues, price lists, etc might be supplied. Some indication should be given of the nature and structure of the relevant market and position of the undertakings concerned in relation to it: any available statistical information and other published reports and materials might be referred to or copies or extracts supplied. Where the contents of agreements or practices in question are not, or are only partially, available in writing or documents are not available to the complainant the fullest description should be given. Details should be given of provisions restricting or perceived to restrict parties in their freedom to take independent commercial decisions in relation to a variety of matters, such as prices, choice of markets, and sources of supply. Section II is also the place to give the names and addresses of any other relevant persons, e.g. of persons who may be able to corroborate any statements made by the complainant or who can provide other information or assistance in the matter. Although the Commission will not necessarily adopt the complainant's legal analysis and arguments, the complainant should nevertheless indicate how Article 81 or 82 EC and/or Article 53 or 54 EEA is

---

[72] As the CFI has indicated, the nature of a complaint may be determined by reference to is purpose and not only its form. Case T-117/96 *Intertronic F Cornelis GmbH v EC Commission* [1997] ECR II-141 (Summary Publication): 'Mere reference to [Art 7 of Reg 1/2003], without further observation, in a letter to the Commission cannot serve to give that letter the character of a complaint under that article when it is apparent that its purpose is to obtain a declaration that a Member State has failed to fulfil its obligations under the Treaty.'

thought to apply in the circumstances. Where the complainant wants the Commission to investigate the alleged infringement under both Articles 81 and 82 EC the complainant should indicate so and to substantiate its allegations with facts and data. The complainant may need to show how the agreements in question affect competition to an appreciable extent. Information must be given on how the agreement affects trade between Member States and/or EFTA States trade.

Finding sought from the Commission This section of the complaint **5.22** addressees two distinct issues. First, the complainant should state exactly what 'finding or action' is being sought by making it. As mentioned above, if it alleges the infringement of a number of Treaty Articles the complaint must specify them all in the complaint and in calling on the Commission to act. The introduction of a specific invitation to the complainant to identify the relief sought might appear as somehow surprising given that Article 8 of Regulation 1/2003 seems to deny complainants any standing to seek interim measures. Since the question is nevertheless raised by Form C, complainants need not be inhibited about requesting interim measures, even if Article 8 does prove to constitute a barrier to obtaining relief against a refusal to order interim measures. Where specific relief is sought the complainant should be careful to identify the type of relief which the Commission can, and should, in the circumstances grant.[73] The applicant might usefully summarize any reasons for any claim that the case involves an issue of exceptional urgency. In addition, the complainant should adduce evidence to show that he or she has a 'legitimate interest' within the meaning of Article 7(2) of Regulation 1/2003.

Proceedings before NCAs or national courts Section IV is especially import- **5.23** ant in the context of the new enforcement regime. If a similar complaint (i.e. one concerning the same or a closely related subject matter) has been made to any other authority (e.g. the NCA of a Member State or to the EFTA Surveillance Authority) or is the subject of proceedings in a national court, the current position of such complaint or action should be made known to the Commission. The authority or court must be identified and details given of submissions made. It may also be relevant to explain, if it is the case, why no national remedies are available or why they would be inadequate. Finally under this section, the applicant is asked to say whether it intends to produce further

---

[73] In *Automec II*, the complainant unsuccessfully sought injunctive relief requiring supply of vehicles to it for resale. The CFI held that although the Commission could have granted alternative forms of relief which might in fact have had the same result of resuming supply to the complainant it was not the Commission's duty to redefine the complainant's application. Case T-24/90 *Automec II v EC Commission* [1992] ECR II-2223 paras 52–54. CS Kerse and N Khan, *EC Antitrust Procedure* (5th edn, 2005) para 2–026.

supporting facts or arguments not yet available and, if so, to identify the relevant points.

5.24 **Other formal requirements** The complaint must be signed by the complainant, under a formal declaration that the information given in the form has been given in good faith. Where a representative signs the complaint, written proof of the representative's authority to act should be supplied. For these purposes, a notification signed by an officer of the company or companies concerned is not considered one signed by a representative. The complaint must be submitted in three paper copies as well as, if possible, an electronic copy.

D. Request for Informal Guidance and Finding of Inapplicability

1. Informal guidance

5.25 As indicated, Regulation 1/2003 places a burden of complete self-reliance upon companies and their legal advisors to determine whether their arrangements satisfy the criteria for exemption. Undertakings can rely on the existing Commission decision-making practice, Community Court case law, and the Commission's guidance, including block exemptions and Commission notices. One of the main concerns of businesses when this reform was announced was that there would be reduced legal certainty, in particular because agreements and commercial arrangements would no longer be able to be notified to the Commission and receive either a positive exemption decision, or an informal 'comfort letter'. The Commission has taken this concern into account and has recognized that there may be cases where assistance is effectively needed. These novel questions require a greater legal certainty than the explanations of the existing rules can provide. The Commission has adopted a Notice on Informal Guidance relating to unresolved questions concerning Articles 81 and 82 EC,[74] which offers undertakings the possibility to request from the Commission an assessment regarding the compatibility of their conduct with the EC Competition rules.

5.26 The other avenue which the Commission may use to issue guidance regarding its approach to certain restrictions and where it is prepared to alleviate the burden of undertakings to perform a self-assessment is laid out in Article 10 of Regulation 1/2003. Where the Community public interest relating to the application of Articles 81 and 82 EC so requires, the Commission, acting on its own

---

[74] Commission Notice on informal guidance relating to novel questions concerning Arts 81 and 82 of the EC Treaty that arise in individual cases (guidance letters) 'Notice on Informal Guidance' [2004] OJ C101/78.

initiative, may by decision find that Article 81 EC is not applicable to an agreement, a decision by an association of undertakings, or a concerted practice, either because the conditions of Article 81(1) EC are not fulfilled, or because the conditions of Article 81(3) EC are satisfied. Declarations of inapplicability may be compared to the old 'negative clearance' and 'exemption' decisions;[75] together with the guidance letter, declarations of inapplicability figure as an exception to the system of self-assessment and provide guidance on which undertakings can rely to some extent. These are therefore discussed in the same context.

Guidance letters

As stated in Recital 3 of Regulation 1/2003, one of the primary objectives of the new system is to allow the Commission to concentrate its resources on curbing the most serious infringements. For this reason, the possibility of requesting informal guidance should not lead to some kind of notification/clearance procedure, which would interfere with the Commission's main task of ensuring effective enforcement of the competition rules. Regulation 1/2003 does not make express provision for guidance letters, but limits itself to stating that where cases give rise to genuine uncertainty because they present novel or unresolved questions, individual undertakings may wish to seek informal guidance from the Commission.[76] The Commission has indicated that during the first year of the application of Regulation 1/2003, it has received very few requests for guidance letters which turned out to be more 'old-style notifications' than requests for guidance on novel issues.[77] Accordingly, the Commission has not issued any guidance letters in this period.

5.27

The three cumulative conditions   The Commission may only consider issuing a guidance letter if the nature of the question being considered is not hypothetical and where the transaction has reached a sufficiently advanced stage. Conversely, it will not consider the issue if the agreement or practice is no longer implemented. In addition, the Notice on Informal Guidance stipulates that three positive cumulative conditions must be fulfilled.

5.28

• Firstly, the assessment of conduct with regard to Articles 81 and/or 82 EC, should pose a question for which the existing EC legal framework does not

---

[75] CS Kerse and N Khan, *EC Antitrust Procedure* (5th edn, 2005) para 2–065.

[76] Recital 38 of Reg 1/2003. J Schwarze and A Weitbrecht, *Grundzüge des europäischen Kartellrechts* (2004) § 6 para 135.

[77] 'Q&A on modernization with Kris Dekeyser' Global Competition Review, Vol 8, Issue 3, April 2005 11–16 (12). F Montag and S Cameron, 'Effective Enforcement: The Practioners View of Recent Experiences under Regulation 1/2003', Antitrust Reform in Europe: A Year in Practice, 9–11 March 2005, Brussels, International Bar Association (IBA) 5 raise the question whether it may be too difficult for companies to qualify for guidance in light of the cumulative conditions that need to be met.

provide any answer or clarification. This means that the question raised is so original that no case of the Community courts can be found on the point, nor is there any general guidance, precedent in decision-making practice, or previous guidance letters.[78]

- Secondly, after a preliminary evaluation of the characteristics and background of the case, the Commission will estimate whether or not the issuance of a guidance letter will help find the adequate answer to the question raised. The Commission will have to appraise the usefulness of a guidance letter considering:

  —the economic importance from the point of view of the consumer of the goods or services concerned by the agreement or practice;

  —the extent to which the agreement corresponds or is liable to correspond to a more widely spread economic usage in the market place;

  —the size of investments regarding the transaction taking into account the size of the companies concerned and the extent to which the transaction affects a structural operation such as the creation of a non-full function joint venture.[79]

- Finally, the Commission will only issue a guidance letter using the information provided by the applicant(s). Thus, it will not enter into a fact-finding process.[80] However, the Commission is free to use any other public or private source available and may ask the applicant(s) to provide supplementary information.[81]

5.29   In addition, the Notice on Informal Guidance establishes certain negative circumstances in which the Commission will not consider a request for guidance where (i) there are similar if not identical issues raised in cases before the Community courts or (ii) the agreement is subject to proceedings pending with the Commission, national courts or the NCA's.

5.30   **Procedure**   Either one undertaking or a group of them can present a request for guidance in order to clarify the questions raised by an agreement or practice into which they have entered that could fall within the scope of Articles 81 and/ or 82 EC. There is no specific request form to fill out but the requests should be accompanied by a memorandum which contains the relevant information. The

---

[78] Notice on Informal Guidance [2004] OJ C101/78 para 88(a).
[79] Notice on Informal Guidance Guidance [2004] OJ C101/78 para 8(b).
[80] Notice on Informal Guidance Guidance [2004] OJ C101/78 para 8(c).
[81] Notice on Informal Guidance Guidance [2004] OJ C101/78 para 15. F Montag and S Cameron, 'Effective Enforcement: The Practioners View of Recent Experiences under Regulation 1/2003', Antitrust Reform in Europe: A Year in Practice, 9–11 March 2005, Brussels, International Bar Association (IBA) argue that the lack of guidance letters might have to do with the fact that a guidance letter will only be issued if it is possible to do so on the basis of the information provided. This requirement could potentially reduce the value of guidance letters.

memorandum shall be addressed to DG COMP, and include the following items:[82]

(i) identity and addresses of the parties involved;
(ii) questions on which the parties are seeking guidance;
(iii) complete information about all the relevant questions raised;
(iv) a detailed reasoning why the issue raises a novel question;
(v) all other relevant information for the evaluation of the case and a declaration that states that the agreement or practice is not subject to proceedings pending before a Member State Court or NCA; and,
(vi) clear identification of the elements which represent business secrets.

As stated above, the Commission will essentially evaluate the request for guidance taking into account the information provided by the applicant and if appropriate, any additional data from public sources, former proceedings and any other kind of sources. In addition the Commission may ask the applicant(s) to provide supplementary information. In any case, the information supplied by the applicant(s) will be governed by the rules of professional secrecy.[83] The Commission can share all this information with the NCAs through the European Competition Network ('ECN'),[84] which will allow it to receive information from the ECN as well as to discuss the substance of the request with the NCAs before issuing a guidance letter. Where the Commission ultimately decides not to issue a guidance letter, it will inform the applicant accordingly. The Notice on Informal Guidance contains no rules on time periods in this respect. Given the wide discretion of the Commission to issue guidance letters, one may not expect that the Commission will need to explain in great detail the reasons for its refusal to consider the request. The applicants may withdraw their request for guidance at any point in time. Nevertheless, in any case all the supplied information will remain with the Commission which can initiate proceedings in accordance with Regulation 1/2003 with regard to the facts stated in the request. **5.31**

Content of the guidance letter Guidance letters will include a summary description of the facts on which the request is based. They will also contain the principal legal grounds underlying the understanding of the Commission of the novel question relating to Articles 81 and/or 82 EC raised by the request. The Commission is free to extend the content of the guidance letter not just to the novel question raised, but also to additional related aspects that are not mentioned in the applicant's request. The Commission will publish guidance **5.32**

---

[82] Notice on Informal Guidance Guidance [2004] OJ C101/78 para 14.
[83] Notice on Informal Guidance Guidance [2004] OJ C101/78 para 15.
[84] Notice on Informal Guidance Guidance [2004] OJ C101/78 para 16.

letters on its website with due regard to business secrets. Similar to other proceedings, the parties are invited to agree on a non-confidential version.

5.33 **Effects of a guidance letter** The main purpose of a guidance letter is to help undertakings make an informed assessment of their agreements or practices, but it is not a formal decision of the Commission. It cannot prejudge the assessment of the same question by the Community courts, nor does it bind national courts or NCAs.[85] In addition, the issue of a guidance letter will not preclude the subsequent examination of the same agreement or practice by the Commission in a procedure under Regulation 1/2003, and in particular after a complaint. In that event, the Commission is expected to take the previous guidance letter into account, adapting it to any change relating to the facts, any development of the Community case law or change in the Commission's policy.[86] While guidance letters are non-binding, NCAs and courts are free to take these guidance letters into account as they feel fit in the context of a case. This may lead to the paradoxical situation of an undertaking being fined by an NCA or a national court for having followed the guidance received by the Commission, although this is unlikely to occur where the undertaking can allege that it followed in good faith the guidance by the Commission. As a result, guidance letters may lead to controversy until the Community courts decide the matter.[87]

2. Finding of inapplicability

Policy objective

5.34 Article 10 of Regulation 1/2003 regulates decisions where the Commission finds that Articles 81 and/or 82 EC do not apply. It provides that where the Community public interest relating to the application of Articles 81 and 82 of the Treaty so requires, the Commission, acting on its own initiative, may by decision find that Article 81 EC is not applicable to an agreement, a decision by an association of undertakings or a concerted practice, either because the conditions of Article 81(1) EC are not fulfilled, or because the conditions of Article 81(3) of the Treaty are satisfied. A similar finding may be made with respect to Article 82 EC. These 'findings of inapplicability' were first proposed in the White Paper on the Modernization of the Rules Implementing Articles [81] and [82] EC which considered as a key element of the new and more efficient

---

[85] Notice on Informal Guidance Guidance [2004] OJ C101/78 para 15.

[86] Recital 38 of Reg 1/2003. J Schwarze and A Weitbrecht, *Grundzüge des europäischen Kartellrechts* (2004) § 6 para 134. F Montag and S Cameron, 'Effective Enforcement: The Practioners View of Recent Experiences under Regulation 1/2003' Antitrust Reform in Europe: A Year in Practice, 9–11 March 2005, Brussels, International Bar Association (IBA) take the view that guidance letters are less likely to have statutes similar to that of comfort letters in the absence of an investigation of the underlying facts by the Commission.

[87] CS Kerse and N Khan, *EC Antitrust Procedure* (5th edn, 2005) para 2–064.

enforcement system that the Commission would not be able to adopt exemption decisions under Article 81(3) EC.[88] Nevertheless, it went on and proposed that it should be able to adopt 'individual decisions that are not prohibition decisions' provided that the case in point gave rise to a new issue, in order to 'provide the market with guidance regarding the Commission's approach to certain restrictions in it. Positive decisions of this kind would therefore be taken in exceptional cases, on grounds of general interest' and would be limited 'to finding that an agreement is compatible with Article 85 as a whole, whether because it falls outside Article [81](1), or because it satisfies the tests of Article [81](3). They would be of a declaratory nature, and would have the same legal effect as negative clearance decisions have at present.' This approach was somehow controversial, since, as was noted in the observations accompanying the White Paper, the idea of inapplicability decisions was contrary to the directly applicable legal exception system.[89] Similarly, the views of Member States about inapplicability decisions were sometimes at odds. One group of Member States accepted that 'only the Commission should take positive decisions on its own initiative and only in exceptional circumstances as stated in the White Paper' although it recognized that 'there is a risk that such positive decisions will pave the way for a reintroduction of the notification system' since 'positive decisions are difficult to reconcile with a legal exception system'. A second group expressed some fears that an exclusive power for the Commission to adopt positive decisions would restore the monopoly over the application of Article 81(3) EC, and therefore suggested that NCAs should also be empowered to take positive decisions. They also declared that it would be difficult to distinguish positive decisions from other types of decisions such as rejection of complaints that might be based on Article 81(3).[90]

In response to these issues, the Explanatory Memorandum of the draft Regulation 1/2003 justified inapplicability decisions on the grounds that after modernization the Commission must 'promote consistent application of the rules by means of general measures such as block exemption regulations and guidelines'. It also stated that inapplicability decisions:

5.35

---

[88] White Paper on modernization of the rules implementing Articles 85 and 86 [now 81 and 82] of the EC Treaty [1999] OJ C132/1 para 88.

[89] CS Kerse and N Khan, *EC Antitrust Procedure* (5th edn, 2005) para 2–066; J Schwarze and A Weitbrecht, *Grundzüge des europäischen Kartellverfahrensrechts* (2004) § 6 para 97. During the consultation the EU's Economic and Social Committee declared that 'there is a need to clarify when they must be adopted, under what conditions and what their legal effect will be. Such decisions should be subject to brief procedures and have an effect erga omnes'. Further, this Committee suggested that they could become a complement (or a step before the adoption) of Block Exemption Regulations. White Paper on Reform of Regulation 17, Summary of Observation, DG COMP Document, 29 February 2000, para 4.4., also available at DG COMP website.

[90] White Paper on Reform of Reg 17, Summary of Observations, DG COMP Document 29 February 2000 para 4.4.

[C]an be adopted only at the Commission's own initiative and in the Community public interest. These conditions ensure that decisions making a finding of inapplicability cannot be obtained on demand by companies. Such a possibility would seriously undermine the principal aim of the reform, which is to focus the activities of all competition authorities on what is prohibited. In the decentralised system the Commission, as the guardian of the Treaty and the centrally placed authority, has a special role to play in setting competition policy and in ensuring that Articles 81 and 82 are applied consistently throughout the single market. To that end it is necessary to empower the Commission to adopt positive decisions if the Community public interest so requires. This power allows the Commission to adopt a decision making a finding of inapplicability, in particular in respect of new types of agreements or practices or issues that have not been settled in the existing case-law and administrative practice.[91]

5.36 In this sense, Recital 14 of Regulation 1/2003 indicates the Commission's intention that only in exceptional cases where the public interest of the Community so requires, it could be expedient for the Commission to adopt a decision finding that the prohibition in Article 81 or Article 82 EC does not apply. This could help clarify the law and ensure its consistent application throughout the Community. Together with Article 11(6) of Regulation 1/2003, under which the Commission may relieve NCAs of their competence to deal with the same case, and the rule laid down in Article 16(2) of the Regulation, according to which NCAs cannot take decisions which would run counter to an earlier decision by the Commission concerning the same agreement or practice, the possibility of adopting inapplicability decisions differentiates the position of the Commission from that of the NCAs.[92]

Legal nature

5.37 The legal nature of inapplicability decisions is open to debate.[93] In the first place, it is not easy to differentiate them for a decision to reject a complaint; and secondly they are both declaratory and binding in nature. As regards the difference with the rejection of complaints, the Commission Notice on the handling of complaints under Articles 81 and 82 EC ('Notice on Complaints') states that the decision to reject a complaint does not involve a definitive declaration regarding the existence or not of a breach of Articles 81 and 82, even where the

---

[91] Draft Regulation implementing Arts 81 and 82 of the Treaty COM (2000) 582 final [2000] OJ C365E/284, Explanatory Memorandum Art 10.

[92] WPJ Wils, 'Community Report' in D Cahill (ed), *The Modernization of EU Competition Law Enforcement in the EU*, [2004] FIDE National Reports 661–736 para 50.

[93] CS Kerse and N Khan, *EC Antitrust Procedure* (5th edn, 2005) para 2–065 take the view that the new decision covers the old 'negative clearance' and 'exemption' decisions, though declarations under Art 10 appear to be something more than the former but less than the latter.

Commission has evaluated the facts on the basis of these Articles.[94] This differentiates these acts from the findings of inapplicability. The assessments carried out by the Commission in a decision rejecting a complaint cannot prevent the national judge or competition authority from applying Articles 81 and 82 EC to the agreements and practices in issue, which again differs from the situation pertaining to decisions under Article 10. The Commission's assessments in a decision rejecting a complaint are factual matters that the national courts or competition authorities may take into account when examining whether the agreements or practices in question comply with Articles 81 and 82. In addition, the Notice on Complaints clarifies that '[w]here the Commission rejects a complaint in a case that also gives rise to a decision pursuant to Article 10 of Regulation 1/2003 (Finding of inapplicability of Articles 81 or 82) or Article 9 of Regulation 1/2003 (Commitments), the decision rejecting a complaint may refer to that other decision adopted on the basis of the provisions mentioned'. From this it seems clear that Article 10 declarations and acts where complaints are rejected are two different ways of ending proceedings. The Commission can choose between a simple rejection, or alternatively it can adopt an Article 10 decision. If it opts for this second course of action, its decision will bind national courts and competition authorities. By contrast, the national authorities cannot adopt Article 10 decisions, although obviously in a decision closing the file, they could find that there are no grounds for it to act. This statement will have no binding effect on other public enforcers or on national courts.[95]

Further, a decision under Article 10 is by nature declaratory but binding for the NCAs and courts of the Member States.[96] Certain authors doubted that they would be binding.[97] Others limited themselves to highlighting their declaratory nature without drawing any conclusions as to whether or not they were binding.[98]   **5.38**

---

[94] Commission Notice on the handling of complaints by the Commission under Arts 81 and 82 of the EC Treaty ('Notice on Complaints') [2004] OJ C101/65 para 79.

[95] C Gauer, D Dalheimer, L Kjolbyek, and E De Smitjer, [Spring 2003], 'Reg 1/2003: a modernized application of EC competition rules' [2003] Competition Policy Newsletter No 1, 3–8 (5–6). WPJ Wils, 'Community Report' in D Cahill (ed), *The Modernization of EU Competition Law Enforcement in the EU* [2004] FIDE National Reports 661–736 para 49. It remains to be seen whether in practice, NCAs will not also adopt decisions which are quite similar to decisions under Art 10. See in this respect, CS Kerse and N Khan, *EC Antitrust Procedure* (5th edn, 2005) para 5–004 and ch 3 'National competition authorities' para 3.03.

[96] Art 16(1) and (2) of Reg 1/2003.

[97] M Siragua, 'A Critical Review of the White Paper on the Reform of the EC Competition law Enforcement Rules,' ch 15 in BE Hawk (ed), International Antitrust and Policy, Annual Proceedings of the Fordham Institute [1999] 273–306 (282).

[98] A Riley, 'EC Antitrust Modernisation: The Commission does very nicely—Thank you! Part one: Regulation 1 and the notification burden' Riley [2003] ECL 604–15 (608) stating that the provision should be of a declaratory nature and would not be intended to provide a back door notification procedure. H Gilliams, 'Modernization: From Policy to Practice' [2003] EL Rev

In this regard, during the process to approve the Regulation, the Commission made it clear that inapplicability decisions were declaratory in nature in the sense that they do not 'create' rights, unlike the former exemption decisions under Article 81(3) EC. For this reason, their 'declaratory' nature, defined in such terms, is compatible with their binding nature with respect to national courts and national competition authorities.

5.39 This is reflected in the justifications of the Commission contained in the proposed Regulation.[99] Decisions under Article 10 of Regulation 1/2003 thus differ significantly from the exemption decisions adopted under Article 81(3) EC, which create rights with effect *erga omnes* for the duration of the decision regardless of any material change in the facts.[100] Non-infringement decisions will have the effects of Community acts. Article 16 has created a general obligation for NCAs and national courts to make every effort to avoid decisions conflicting with decisions adopted by the Commission. A finding of inapplicability by the Commission pursuant to Article 10 can therefore make an important contribution to the uniform application of Community competition law.[101] These decisions would have the effects laid down in Article 16, i.e. national courts and NCAs may not adopt decisions that would run counter to a decision of the Commission. Accordingly, such decisions would thus not be intended as a replacement for the exemption decisions of the old system or to function as an instrument to 'bless' individual agreements in the absence of any issue of coherent application or policy. In short the declaratory nature of inapplicability decisions does not prevent them from having binding effect for national courts and NCAs (under Article 16 of Regulation 1/2003). They would be similar to qualified guidance letters, although unlike the latter, they would have binding effect.

The application of Article 10 of Regulation 1/2003 in practice

5.40 It is expected that the Commission will use these decisions as a means of steering the way in which Community competition law is applied to (i) new situations;

451–74 (461) put emphasis on the aspect that the Commission has reserved the power to adopt decisions 'acting on its own initiative', i.e. not pursuant to a notification or complaint, for certain landmark cases.

[99] Draft Regulation implementing Arts 81 and 82 EC, COM (2000)582 final [2000] OJ C365E/284, Explanatory Memorandum.

[100] Unlike an exemption decision under Reg 17 which granted exemption for a fixed period of time (often as long as ten years) and could be withdrawn in limited circumstances, a decision under Art 10 does not protect the agreement in question for a specified time. CS Kerse and N Kahn, *EC Antitrust Procedure* (5th edn, 2005) para 2–067.

[101] C Gauer, D Dalheimer, L Kjolbyek, and E De Smitjer [Spring 2003], 'Reg 1/2003: a modernized application of EC competition rules' [2003] Competition Policy Newsletter Number 1, 3–8 (5–6).

or (ii) cases where Community competition law has been applied inconsistently by national courts or competition authorities. It could also use them to put a brake on what it sees as an excessively rigorous application of Community competition law by national courts or competition authorities. More specifically, the Commission may proceed to adopt a decision under Article 10 where it has occurred that an NCA has prohibited an agreement or practice which the Commission deemed to be lawful. In short, they will only be used in exceptional circumstances and in order to clarify or unify the application of Community competition law. The inclusion of the words 'in the application of Articles 81 and 82' clarifies that 'the Community public interest' is strictly linked to the public interest of effective and coherent implementation of the competition rules; it cannot be construed as relating to wider 'public policy' goals. At the same time, the adjective 'public' is not without meaning. It must be seen in conjunction with the fact that the Commission adopts Article 10 decisions on its own initiative only. By this, the regulation intends to exclude that a 'private interest' could trigger the adoption of an Article 10 decision.[102]

It is clear that this instrument limits the powers of NCAs. For example, it may **5.41** prevent them from withdrawing the benefit of the exemption of a block exemption regulation as regards a particular agreement. It may also be used by the Commission to limit the powers of NCAs where a national authority intends to prohibit certain behaviour under Articles 81 or 82 EC but the Commission feels that the national authority's interpretation of Community law is too strict.[103] Applying Article 11(6), the Commission takes the matter out of the national authority's hands before it can take a decision, and adopts a decision under Article 10. However, the effect of these decisions on the application of Article 82 by the national authorities will be more limited. Under Article 3(2) *in fine*, an Article 10 decision declaring behaviour to be compatible with Article 82 does not prevent a national court or authority from holding that the same conduct amounts to an abuse of a dominant position under its national competition law.

Procedural issues The Commission is the only body with the power to take **5.42** inapplicability decisions but it has not issued any guidance on the procedure to be followed. As regards the national authorities, Article 5 *in fine* states that they can only decide that 'there are no grounds for action on their part' because the information at their disposal does not show that the conditions for a prohibition

---

[102] C Gauer, D Dalheimer, L Kjolbyek, and E De Smitjer, [Spring 2003], 'Reg 1/2003: a modernized application of EC competition rules' [2003] Competition Policy Newsletter No 1, 3–8 (5–6).

[103] J Schwarze and A Weitbrecht, *Grundzüge des europäischen Kartellverfahrensrechts* (2004) § 6 para 100 noting whether this may be contrary to the exceptional character of the provision if the Commission would intervene this way in proceedings before NCAs.

exist, but it does not give them the power to end a procedure with an Article 10 decision. The Commission commences the Article 10 procedure on its own initiative. It is submitted that on the one hand this means that the filing of a request for a letter of guidance or an 'informal' request for a declaration of the Commission under Article 10 of Regulation 1/2003 will not give the party making the request any right to obtain a declaration from the Commission under Article 10. On the other hand this will not prevent the Commission from adopting an Article 10 decision on the basis of the facts described in the request, if the Commission's view is that the Community's public interest with respect to the application of Articles 81 and 82 EC is affected. Obviously, although a request has not been filed, the Commission may also commence this procedure. It also seems that the Commission can adopt a decision under Article 10 based on the facts stated in a complaint. Regulation 1/2003 does not require there to be any hearings in these procedures; it only obliges the Commission to publish a brief summary of the matter and the proposed course of action. Interested third parties can file submissions within a period to be fixed by the Commission when it publishes the summary, which will be no more than one month from the date of publication.[104]

5.43 The publication will respect the legitimate interest of undertakings to protect their commercial secrets.[105] Article 2(1) of Regulation 773/2004 obliges the Commission to commence the proceedings no later than the date on which it publishes a notice pursuant to Article 27(4) of Regulation 1/2003. The Commission will send to the competition authorities of all Member States a copy of the most important documentation which it has compiled with a view to adopting its decision. Following a request from a Member State's competition authority, the Commission will send it copies of other existing documents that are necessary for the assessment of the matter (Article 11(2)). Before adopting a decision, it will consult the Advisory Committee.[106] The decision of the Commission adopted under Article 10 will be published.[107] As regards whether a decision under Article 10 could be challenged under Article 230(4) EC, there is the suggestion that a decision under Article 10 can be challenged before the Community Courts. The beneficiary of a declaration under Article 10 will have no

---

[104] It seems that in regard to Art 10 (declarations of inapplicability) and Art 9 (commitments) Art 27(4) of Reg 1/2003 limits the participation of third parties to submit observations. Art 27 (1)–(3) which contains a more detailed description of defence rights does not seem to apply to decisions under Art 10. J Schwarze and A Weitbrecht, *Grundzüge des europäischen Kartellverfahrensrechts* (2004) § 6 paras 102–105 take the view that competitors should also enjoy the same defence rights as third parties in other proceedings before the Commission, given that declarations under Art 10 of Reg 1/2003 could also affect the legal position of third parties.
[105] Art 27(4) of Reg 1/2003.   [106] Art 14(1) of Reg 1/2003.
[107] Art 30(1) of Reg 1/2003.

interest in contesting the decision but a competitor may do so provided the declaration is of direct and individual concern to it.[108] This may be the case in two situations. First, where the competitor participated in the proceedings and was heard as an affected third party although this might need to go beyond the mere submission of observations under Article 27(4) of Regulation 1/2003. Secondly, where the competitor did not participate in the administrative procedure and claims rights that might be available to it before the Court. In this latter case, the competitor must show that it is individually affected in accordance with the general rules established by the ECJ.[109]

---

[108] See Art 230 fourth paragraph EC.

[109] See in respect to the possibility of third parties challenging a decision under Art 10: J Schwarze and A Weitbrecht, *Grundzüge des europäischen Kartellverfahrensrechts* (2004) § 6 paras 108–121 referring to the ECJ case law in C-263/02P *Jégo-Quéré* [2004] ECR I-3425 paras 44 *et seq*. The ECJ reiterated that a natural or legal person is to be regarded as individually concerned by a Community measure of general application that concerns him or her directly if the measure in question affects his or her legal position, in a manner which is both definite and immediate. A person would be affected by reason of certain attributes peculiar to them, or by reason of a factual situation which differentiates them from all other persons and distinguishes them individually in the same way as an addressee.

6

INVESTIGATION OF CASES (I): LENIENCY POLICY

A. Policy and Objectives

Nowadays, competition authorities around the world encourage companies to **6.01** report their own antitrust violations in exchange for 'amnesty' or 'leniency' from fines.[1] Simply put, leniency programmes offer companies incentives to 'blow the whistle' on cartels, making cartel participation riskier and creating a 'race to confess' in order to obtain full immunity. Such policy is based on the recognition that while cartels rank among the most serious violations of competition rules, the collection of evidence to prosecute them is increasingly difficult. Already in earlier decisions, the Commission had taken account of the existence or absence of cooperation on the part of undertakings.[2] Encouraged by the experiences of the operation of a leniency programme by the US Department of Justice, the Commission adopted in 1996 the Notice on the non-imposition or reduction of fines in cartel cases (the '1996 Notice').[3] The 1996 Notice was replaced in February 2002 by the '2002 Notice'[4] that changed the earlier system, and was largely modelled on the US 'amnesty' programme.

---

[1] See overview in OECD 'Fighting Hardcore Cartels: Harm, Effective Sanctions, and Leniency Programmes' 2002. The OECD has identified an increasingly successful 'carrot-and-stick' approach—applying stiffer punishment for cartel operators and enhancing programmes aimed at rewarding cartel members who decide to defect and co-operate with the authorities. At the EU level, the first Member States that have adopted leniency programmes were Germany, France, Ireland, The Netherlands, and the United Kingdom. The Commission has published in its website a list of the eighteen authorities in EU Member States which operate a leniency programme: Belgium, Cyprus, the Czech Republic, Estonia, Finland, France, Germany, Greece, Hungary, Ireland, Latvia, Lithuania, Luxembourg, the Netherlands, Poland, Slovakia, Sweden, and the United Kingdom, available at http://europa.eu.int/comm/competition/antitrust/legislation/authorities_with_leniency_programme.pdf. See also DJ Arp and CRA Swaak, 'A Tempting Offer: Immunity from Fines for Cartel Conduct under the European Commission's New Leniency Notice' [2003] ECLR 9–18 (9).

[2] e.g. *National Panasonic* [1982] OJ L354/28. [3] [1996] OJ C207/4.

[4] [2002] OJ C45/3.

6.02 Under the 1996 Notice, the first company to provide 'decisive evidence' of a cartel could gain between a 75 per cent reduction to full immunity from fines. Besides, where the Commission had already begun an investigation, a company providing 'decisive evidence' could obtain a reduction of 50–75 per cent. Finally, those companies not satisfying the latter conditions that nevertheless cooperated with the Commission could benefit from a reduction in fines from 10 to 50 per cent. The Commission applied the 1996 Notice in sixteen formal decisions with fines, out of a total of eighteen cartel decisions adopted from 1998 to June 2002,[5] notwithstanding that in most cases leniency was granted for not substantially contesting the facts established in the statement of objections.[6] The 1996 Notice was subject to criticism because it was considered as providing insufficient incentive for a whistleblower to approach the Commission about a cartel unknown to it. Companies that 'confessed' were given little or no indication until the very end of the administrative process of the reduction in fines, if any, that they would receive in return for their cooperation.[7] Under the 1996 Notice, the decision on the granting of immunity would not be taken until the adoption of the final decision imposing fines, which can take place several years after the application. Further, the 'decisive evidence' criterion was

---

[5] F Arbault and F Peiró, 'The Commission's new notice on immunity and reduction of fines in cartel cases: building on success', Competition Policy Newsletter, Number 2, June 2002, 15–22; see also B Van Barlingen, 'The European Commission's 2002 Leniency Notice after one year of operation', Competition Policy Newsletter, Number 2, Summer 2003, 16–22.

[6] *British Sugar* [1999] OJ L76/1, *Pre-insulated Pipes* [1999] OJ L24/1; *Seamless Steel Tubes* [2003] OJ L140/1; *Aminoacids* [2001] OJ L152 /24; *Graphite Electrodes* [2002] OJ L100/1; *SAS-Maersk* [2001] OJ L265/15; Commission press release IP/01/1355 of 2 October in *Sodium Gluconate* (Case COMP/37.756, note: this is a revised version of the original press release following the adoption of a new Commission decision on 19 March 2002 withdrawing the decision of 2 October 2001 to the extent that it was addressed and notified to one of the addressees of that earlier decision); *Vitamins* OJ [2003] OJ 6/1; *Interbrew—Alken-Maes/Danone* [2003] OJ L200/1; *Citric Acid* [2002] OJ L239/18; *Zinc Phosphate* [2003] OJ L153/1; *Carbonless Paper* [2004] OJ L115/1; *Industrial Tubes* [2004] OJ L/125/50; Commission press release IP/03/ 1700 in *Peroxides Cartel* (COMP/37.857, non-confidential version available at DG COMP's wewbsite). *Electrical and Mechanical Carbon Graphite* [2004] OJ L125/45; Commission press release IP/02/1744 of 27 November 2002 in *Plasterboard* (Case COMP/37.152, non-confidential version available at DG COMP's web site); *Methionine* [2003] OJ L255/1. M Jephcott, 'The European Commission's New Leniency Notice—Whistling the Right Tune' [2002] ECLR 378– 85 (378) indicated that the programme was only implemented in earnest during the last year of the existence of the 1996 Notice in which ten decisions were made. The first time that a significant reduction was granted was in mid-2001 (*Graphite Electrodes*) and the first non-imposition (*Vitamins*) was granted at the very end of 2001. D Geradin and D Henry, 'The EC fining policy for violation of competition law: An empirical review of the Commission decisional practice and the Community's courts' judgments', Paper prepared for the Conference Remedies and Sanctions in EC Competition Policy, 17–18 February 2005, Amsterdam University, giving a detailed overview of the application of the Leniency Notice under the review of the CFI.

[7] M Jephcott, 'The European Commission's New Leniency Notice—Whistling the Right Tune' [2002] ECLR 378–85 (378); DJ Arp and CRA Swaak, 'A Tempting Offer: Immunity from Fines for Cartel Conduct under the European Commission's New Leniency Notice' [2003] ECLR 9–18 (11).

unclear and necessarily subjective.[8] The requirement that a company could not have acted as a ringleader could easily disqualify a whistleblower from the 'very substantial reduction or non-imposition'.

In response to the shortcomings of the 1996 Notice, the Commission adopted **6.03** the 2002 Notice, mainly for two reasons: first, the leniency programme's effectiveness would be improved by increasing the transparency and certainty of the conditions on which any reduction of fines will be granted. The Commission considered it necessary to ensure greater coherence between the level of reduction of fines and the value of a company's contribution to establishing the infringement. Secondly, the 1996 Notice excluded from immunity those companies that had played 'a determining role in the illegal activity'.[9] Such a concept was not considered as insufficiently precise and it was thought that it could not deter companies from informing the Commission of their participation in illegal cartels. Like its US counterpart, the 2002 Notice continues to be an important case generator.[10] The leniency policy has seriously affected legal

---

[8] F Arbault and F Peiró, 'The Commission's new notice on immunity and reduction of fines in cartel cases: building on success' Competition Policy Newsletter, Number 2, June 2002, 15–22 (22). JM Joshua and PD Camesasca, 'Where angels fear to tread: the Commission's new leniency policy revisited', The European Antitrust Review 2005, Global Competition Review 10–13 (10) taking the view that the 1996 Notice—in essence—called for the production of the 'smoking gun'. Though the element of subjectivity seems to continue to be present in the 2002 Notice which provides that the information must be satisfactory 'in the Commission's view'. CS Kerse and N Khan, *EC Antitrust Procedure* (5th edn, 2005) para 7–060. See paras 6.05 *et seq.*

[9] DJ Arp and CRA Swaak, 'A Tempting Offer: Immunity from Fines for Cartel Conduct under the European Commission's New Leniency Notice' [2003] ECLR 9–18 (13).

[10] As a result of the 2002 Notice, there has been an increase in the number of cases in the last few of years. XXXIII Report on Competition Policy (2003) paras 29 and 30: '[. . .] the Commission has received 34 applications for immunity dealing with at least 30 separate alleged infringements. Conditional immunity has been granted in 27 cases. Almost all of these have been investigated by the Commission, most through inspections [. . .].' See also Commissioner for Competition Policy N Kroes, 'The First Hundred' 40th Anniversary of the Studienvereinigung Kartellrecht 1965–2005, International Forum on European Competition Law, Brussels, 7 April 2005. According to P Lowe, 'Enforcement Antitrust Roundtable' 32nd Annual Conference Fordham Corporate Law Institute, 22–23 September 2005 (forthcoming), until September 2005, there have been ten companies requesting leniency in 2005. B Van Barlingen and M Barennes, 'The European Commission's Leniency Notice in Practice' Competition Policy Newsletter, Number 3, Autumn 2005, 6–16 (6 and notes 6 and 7) have counted a total of eighty applications for immunity and seventy-nine applications for a reduction of fine as from the entry into force of the 2002 Notice until the end of September 2005; for statistical purposes where several immunity applications have been received for the same alleged infringement, the first application is counted as an immunity application and the subsequent ones as applications for a reduction of fine, if the applicant so requests. They point out that the most interesting aspect is not so much the high number of leniency applications under the 2002 Notice (compared to a total of eighty leniency applications under the 1996 Notice), than the fact that the large majority of leniency applications under the 1996 Notice were made only after the Commission had undertaken inspections and resulted in a reduction of fines. Under the 2002 Notice more than half of all the leniency applications have been made before any inspection took place. A senior US DoJ official hailed the Commission's 2002 Notice as the single most important contribution to US anti-cartel

strategies in cartel cases. The system's logic tends to create a race between cartel members where the last company to confess will face difficulties in avoiding the imposition of heavy fines, not only because this company will probably not benefit from the leniency notice, but also because by then the Commission will dispose of all the necessary information to built a strong case.[11]

B. Procedures

6.04 According to the 2002 Notice, leniency is applied for and granted to single and separate undertakings. Given that prohibitions decisions with fines are addressed to legal persons,[12] it is important to determine which legal persons are meant to be covered by a leniency application and which may ultimately benefit from immunity of fines or a reduction of fines. This is of particular relevance to groups of undertakings in which case leniency application may be made for example, by either the subsidiary that is involved in the infringement or the

---

enforcement of 2002 highlighting the interdependence of leniency programmes across multiple jurisdictions. See oral remarks of Scott Hammond, Director of Criminal Enforcement, ABA Section of Antitrust Spring Meeting, Washington DC, 2 April 2003. See also K Nordlander, 'Discovering Discovery—US Discovery of EC Leniency Statements' [2004] ECLR 646–59 (646–47).

[11] B Van Barlingen, 'The European Commission's 2002 Leniency Notice after one year of operation', Competition Policy Newsletter, Number 2, Summer 2003, takes the view that looking at the number of applications the 2002 Notice is a success. See also the follow-up analysis of B Van Barlingen and M Barennes, 'The European Commission's Leniency Notice in practice' Competition Policy Newsletter, Number 3, Autumn 2005, 6–16 (16) in which the authors confirm this appraisal and praise the key role of the 2002 Notice in revealing secret cartels. JM Joshua and PD Camesasca, 'Where angels fear to tread: the Commission's new leniency policy revisited', The European Antitrust Review 2005, Global Competition Review 10–14 (13) however, lament the fact that the Commission has done nothing to speed up the efficient disposition of cases. The Commission would often grant leniency or a fine reduction to all the participants in a cartel and would still go through the lengthy and time-consuming process of issuing a full statement of objections.

[12] WPJ Wils, 'Powers of Investigation and Procedural Rights and Guarantees in EU Antitrust Enforcement', First Lisbon Conference on Competition Law and Economics, Belém 3–4 November 2005, note 31 states that as regards the choice of the person or persons to whom a violation is to be imputed, the general rule formulated by the Community Courts is that 'when [. . .] a violation is to have been committed, it is necessary to identify the natural or legal person who was responsible for the operation of the undertaking at the time when the violation was committed, so that it can answer for it' (C-279/98 P *Cascades v EC Commission* [2000] ECR I-9709 para 78). If the undertaking found to have committed a violation were found to consist of an unincorporated business (e.g. several natural persons operating a single business) the Commission would necessarily have to address its fining decision to the natural persons operating the business. However, under Reg 17 and Reg 1/2003 up to now, this situation has not yet occurred. All fines have been imposed on companies or other legal persons. WPJ Wils refers to *Pre-Insulated Pipes* [1999] OJ L24/1 paras 157–160 where the Commission appears to have made an effort to avoid imposing the fine on a natural person (Dr W Henss) who managed and controlled one of the undertakings concerned. See also Case T-9/99 *HFB v EC Commission* [2002] ECR II-1487 para 105.

parent company. The Commission seems to prefer that leniency applications are made by the legal person that manages or controls the behaviour of the undertaking that is involved in the infringement with a view to ensuring that all potentially liable legal entities that are under the direct or indirect control of the applicant may benefit from lenient treatment in any prohibition decision.[13]

1. Immunity from fines

Conditions for the grant of complete immunity

The 2002 Notice takes a more generous approach and makes it easier for companies to obtain full immunity[14] or obtain a reduction of fine.[15] In particular, it offers two alternative thresholds. Complete immunity from fines may be obtained where an undertaking is the first to submit evidence which in the Commission's view may enable: **6.05**

(i)   either an on-the-spot investigation to be carried out provided the Commission does not already have sufficient evidence to launch such an inspection (paragraph 8(a)); or

(ii) to establish an infringement of Article 81 EC with an alleged cartel that affects the Community, provided that the Commission does not already have sufficient evidence to reach such a finding (paragraph 8(b)).

These options are mutually exclusive, and therefore only one undertaking can qualify for full immunity. In the first case where the existence of the cartel is still unknown to the Commission the undertaking should provide the Commission with 'concrete and reliable' information in order to launch a 'dawn raid'. The 2002 Notice[16] stipulates that 'sufficient evidence' given by the undertaking demanding immunity will have to allow the Commission to adopt a decision to start up the investigation. In the second case, in which a company reports its **6.06**

---

[13] B Van Barlingen and M Barennes, 'The European Commission's Leniency Notice in practice' Competition Policy Newsletter, Number 3, Autumn 2005, 6–16 (8) indicate that the filing of an application by the parent company is not interpreted by the Commission as an admission that it had been involved in the infringement or is liable for the breach of competition rules. In case of joint ventures, applicants are requested to discuss with the Commission the possible association of their parents companies to the applications as quickly as possible.

[14] 2002 Notice [2002] OJ C45/3 paras 8–9. B Van Barlingen and M Barennes, 'The European Commission's Leniency Notice in practice' Competition Policy Newsletter, Number 3, Autumn 2005, 6–16 (6–7) state that by the end of September 2005, the Commission had granted conditional immunity decisions in forty-nine cases, forty-five of these conditional immunity decisions were granted under para 8(a) of the 2002 Notice (see below). Most of these decisions were indeed followed up by surprise inspections or requests for information after conditional immunity was granted. The remaining four were granted under para 8(b) of the 2002 Notice (see below).

[15] 2002 Notice [2002] OJ C45/3 paras 20–27.

[16] 2002 Notice s 9.

own antitrust violation, the Commission will have already conducted an investigation or be in a position to do so, but does not have enough evidence to establish the infringement. This requirement is more demanding because the evidence has to be very concrete and direct, which means that the applicant for immunity must volunteer clear information suggesting the existence of an infringement.[17] Of course, at the pre-dawn raid stage there is nothing to stop an applicant providing conclusive evidence of the violation to meet the higher threshold instead of the other but lower standard when requires the submission of sufficient evidence to enable the Commission to carry out a surprise inspection.[18] The undertaking will only be granted immunity if the Commission did not have, at the time of the submission, sufficient evidence to find an infringement of Article 81 EC in connection with the alleged cartel.[19] It is therefore in the interest of applicants to provide as much evidence as possible immediately.

6.07 Inevitably, the Commission retains some discretion to determine whether the information supplied by the applicant is enough to carry out an investigation as shown by the expressions 'in the Commission's view' or 'may enable it to find an infringement'.[20] In addition, the 2002 Notice requires all undertakings to

---

[17] See e.g. Commission Press Release IP/04/1313 of 26 October 2004 'Commission fines Coats and Prym for a cartel in the needle market and other haberdashery products', when fining Coats and Prym for a cartel in the needle market and other haberdashery products. Entaco benefited from full immunity of fines because it came forward and disclosed information which enabled the Commission to take this decision; see also Commission Press Release IP/05/61 of 19 January 2005 'Antitrust: Commission imposes €216.91 million in fines on MCAA chemicals cartel' in which Clariant received full immunity for being the first to provide evidence of the existence of the cartel to the Commission. B Van Barlingen and M Barennes, 'The European Commission's Leniency Notice in practice' Competition Policy Newsletter, Number 3, Autumn 2005, 6–16 (7, n 1) explain that the Commission policy is to use the lower of the two thresholds for conditional immunity whenever both options have been applied for because the legal position of the applicant would not be different under para 8(a) and para 8(b) of the 2002 Notice. The Commission would be able to grant conditional immunity more quickly than if it had first to make a definitive analysis of whether the evidence provide for is sufficient to establish an infringement of Art 81 EC.

[18] JM Joshua and PD Camesasca, 'Where angels fear to tread: the Commission's new leniency policy revisited' The European Antitrust Review 2005, Global Competition Review 10–14 (10). B Van Barlingen and M Barennes, 'The European Commission's Leniency Notice in practice' Competition Policy Newsletter, Number 3, Autumn 2005, 6–16 (6 and notes 6 and 7) state that para 8(b) of the 2002 Notice is in practice primarily used to deal with immunity applications that are made after an inspection has taken place.

[19] 2002 Notice [2002] OJ C45/3 para 9.

[20] DJ Arp and CRA Swaak, 'A Tempting Offer: Immunity from Fines for Cartel Conduct under the European Commission's New Leniency Notice' [2003] ECLR 9–18 (14), noting that even with the reduced evidentiary hurdle, the EC approach continues to chart something of different course from US policy which does not incorporate an explicit evidentiary standard in its leniency criteria.

meet three further cumulative conditions in order to be granted immunity.[21] Thus, the undertaking must:

(i) fully cooperate with the Commission on a continuous basis, including providing all evidence that comes into its possession relating to the suspected infringement;[22]

(ii) end its involvement in the cartel no later than the time when it submits evidence;[23]

(iii) not have coerced other undertakings to participate in the infringement.[24]

In view of the voluntary nature of the leniency programme, the issue is not **6.08** whether the cooperation from undertakings that is required may trigger conflicts with the privilege against self-incrimination,[25] but rather maintaining confidentiality in the initial stages in order to be able to carry out a 'dawn raid' based on the information obtained. The Commission is expected to maintain confidentiality until it has undertaken a surprise inspection and shows reluctance to accept regulatory requirements that might exist to disclose matters (e.g. publication obligations of companies listed on the US stock exchange in relation to potential liability for antitrust infringement) but which could adversely affect the success of the inspection[26] Where the 2002 Notice requires the applicant to end their involvement immediately, the Commission does not seem to take into account the fact that if the undertaking stops its activity in the cartel without good reason, this may put the other participants in the cartel on notice, removing

---

[21] Because full immunity will not be granted only by satisfying the conditions set out in paras 8(a) and (b) of the 2002 Notice [2002] OJ C45/3.

[22] 2002 Notice [2002] OJ C45/3 para 11(a).

[23] 2002 Notice [2002] OJ C45/3 para 11(b). In *Italian Raw Tobacco*, Deltafina had been granted conditional immunity at the beginning of the procedure under the terms of the Leniency Notice, but the Commission decision withheld final immunity 'due to a serious breach by Deltafina of its co-operation obligations': having received conditional immunity, Deltafina revealed to its main competitors that it had applied for leniency with the Commission. This occurred before the Commission could carry out surprise inspections, so that when these took place, most companies concerned were already aware of the existence of the Commission investigation. See Commission press release IP/05/1315 of 20 October 2005 'Competition: Commission fines companies €56 million for cartel in Italian raw tobacco market'.

[24] 2002 Notice [2002] OJ C45/3 para 11(c).

[25] CS Kerse and N Khan (5th edn, 2005) para 7–061 note that cooperation will probably not go so far as to require the undertaking to acquire information by acting as a covert agent of the Commisison. See also U Soltész, 'Der "Kronzeuge" im Labyrinth des ECN' [2005] Wirtschaft und Wettbewerb 616–24 (617) who criticizes the fact that undertakings may have less incentive to invoke their rights of defence because they can only obtain a reduction if they cooperate.

[26] See also B Van Barlingen, 'The European Commission's 2002 Leniency Notice after one year of operation', Competition Policy Newsletter, Number 2, Summer 2003, 16–22 (19) notes that those surprise inspections will be carried out within weeks after the reception of the application. Violation of the obligation to cooperate fully with the Commission, i.e. to abstain from any publication without the Commisison permission before the inspection has been carried out, may result in the loss of leniency. See also CS Kerse and N Khan *EC Antitrust Procedure* (5th edn, 2005) para 7–061. As regards surprise inspections, see also ch 8 'Inspections' paras 8.19 *et seq*.

the surprise factor from the investigation. Commission officials have, however acknowledged that the application of this condition requires a delicate balancing act: it will not allow active participation in the cartel but it may allow passive participation where it is ensured that the applicant does not actively seek for information from the cartel and acts upon the information obtained. Conversely, passing on information may be permitted.[27]

6.09 The Commission mentions as the last requirement not having coerced another undertaking to participate in the cartel. By this 'prohibition of coercing' the Commission seeks to put an end to a debate under the 1996 Notice which established that applicants for reduction of fines qualified only if the undertaking had 'not compelled another enterprise to take part in the cartel and not acted as an instigator or played a determining role in the illegal activity'. The Commission concluded that the notion of 'instigator' is vague and to some extent jeopardizes the effectiveness of the programme.[28] The term 'played a determining role' was extended to almost any actor of the cartel, which ended up giving the Commission greater discretion and reducing predictability for leniency applicants. Arguably, the 2002 Notice has not fully resolved the difficulties of interpretation in that 'coercing' other undertakings could also include forms of instigation. Actual evidence of coercion will be needed to consider an undertaking responsible for instigating the infringement. Where undertakings race to be the first one to confess, those undertakings that are 'queuing' to confess might declare to the Commission that the first one confessing has actually instigated the others to participate in the infringements. This could create a 'battle' between applicants to prove who has actually instigated other parties, creating a lack of legal certainty for the applicants and little transparency in the leniency programme.

6.10 The exposure to civil actions is extremely important for undertakings when applying for leniency. Companies that apply for leniency may manage private litigation in a way that minimizes the damage but may be less inclined to do so if this involves the risk of incurring treble-damage lawsuits as this could occur in the US.[29]

---

[27] See also B Van Barlingen, 'The European Commission's 2002 Leniency Notice after one year of operation', Competition Policy Newsletter, Number 2—Summer 2003, 16–22 (19); see D Schroeder, 'Leniency from a Private Practitioner's Perspective' Antitrust Reform in Europe: A Year in Practice, 9–11 March 2005, Brussels, International Bar Association (IBA) draws the attention to differences with other jurisdictions. Following the US approach, some Member States believe that it may be useful to allow continued attendance at for example trade associations meetings, so as not to arouse suspicion while the agency is preparing its dawn raids.

[28] Commission Memo/02/23 of 13 February 2002 'Questions and Answers on the Leniency Policy'.

[29] See K Nordlander, 'Discovering Discovery—US Discovery of EC Leniency Statements [2004] ECLR 646–59 (647). Note that in the US, the disincentive effect of private actions on cartel leniency has been addressed in the Antitrust Criminal Penalty Enhancement and Reform Act 2004, which provides for the detrebling of damages for whistleblowers who cooperate with the plaintiffs in private damages actions.

In contrast to most European countries, the far-reaching US discovery rules whereby courts can order one party to produce documents for another party and particularly the availability of treble damages before US courts provide private plaintiffs with stronger tools and incentives to litigate antitrust infringements.[30]

The procedure to obtain immunity

As we have seen, the procedures introduced by the 2002 Notice intended to **6.11** address weaknesses of the 1996 Notice, in particular in regard to the uncertainty as to whether full or partial immunity will be granted.[31] Under the 2002 Notice, the applicant will be immediately informed about its situation upon receipt by the Commission of evidence satisfying the Notice's criteria.[32] If immunity is still available, the Commission sends a written acknowledgement.[33] The Commission will not consider other applications for immunity from fines before it has taken a position on the pending application in relation to the same suspected infringement. A first applicant cannot dictate the speed at which its application is considered. It may somehow reserve its place in the queue by producing a sufficient but not yet complete application. Unless the application is substantiated in due course, there is the possibility that another applicant will appear in which case the first application will be assessed on the basis of the evidence submitted by the date of the second application.[34] Once the Commission has received evidence that fulfils the various criteria, it grants the company conditional immunity from fines in writing. Note that an undertaking which fails to meet the conditions set out in paragraph 8(a) and (b), as appropriate, may withdraw the evidence disclosed for the purposes of its immunity application or request the Commission to consider it under Section B of the 2002 Notice.[35]

---

[30] As regards the situation in the EU, A Riley, 'Beyond Leniency: Enhancing Enforcement in EC Antitrust Law' [2005] World Competition 377–400 (389) sees 'glimmerings of [an] antitrust litigation culture' emerging by referring to *Provimi Limited v Roche Products Ltd and others* (see ch 2 'The National Judicial Authorities' para 2.02) and takes the view that the publication of prohibition decisions based largely on leniency evidence will further encourage plaintiffs to sue. However, similar to the US, this may have a disincentive effect for potential whistle blowers. As regards the importance of private actions in antitrust enforcement, see ch 2, paras 2.04 *et seq.*
[31] 2002 Notice [2002] OJ C45/3 paras 12–19.
[32] The company can contact DG COMP via dedicated and secure fax and phone numbers. When making contact with the Commission, potential applicants must comply with the necessary verification process set out in the 2002 Notice; the Commission will not respond to informal telephone enquiries as to whether or not full leniency is still available.
[33] 2002 Notice [2002] OJ C45/3 para 14.
[34] 2002 Notice [2002] OJ C45/3 para 18. B Van Barlingen, 'The European Commission's 2002 Leniency Notice after one year of operation', Competition Policy Newsletter, Number 2, Summer 2003, 18.
[35] 2002 Notice [2002] OJ C45/3 paras 15 and 17. B Van Barlingen and M Barennes, 'The European Commission's Leniency Notice in practice' Competition Policy Newsletter, Number 3, Autumn 2005, 6–16 (13 n 2) indicate that the possibility of switching to an application for a reduction of the fine or withdrawing the evidence is however not afforded to undertakings that

This does not prevent the Commission from using its normal powers of investigation in order to obtain the information.

6.12   An undertaking may initially present this evidence in hypothetical terms,[36] in which case it must present a descriptive list of the evidence it proposes to disclose at a later agreed date. If these conditions are not satisfied, the undertaking may withdraw the evidence disclosed. Withdrawal of the application may only be a viable option where an application has not gone beyond the hypothetical stage. While the Commission would be required to use its ordinary investigative powers to obtain the relevant information outside the framework of the immunity application, it may not be expected to adopt a position of 'acute amnesia' towards the existence of the infringement has been brought to its attention.[37] The fall back option is to request the Commission to consider it to proceed to a reduction of the fine.[38] Once the administrative procedure is finished, the Commission will check the undertaking has met the cumulative conditions[39] and, if so, the Commission will grant the undertaking the immunity in the relevant decision.

6.13   Commission officials have highlighted that applications for immunity[40] should ideally include a 'corporate statement', specially prepared for and addressed to the Commission, in which the company formally applies for immunity from fines and describes its participation in a cartel.[41] Based on the information in the

---

have qualified for conditional immunity but have subsequently violated their obligations under the 2002 Notice, namely to fully cooperate with the Commission under para 11 of the Notice.

[36] Through this hypothetical offer companies are able to discuss with the Commission officials anonymously if they are in position to seek leniency without making admissions or revealing incriminating documents. See 'Hypothetical applications' para 6.18 below.

[37] The principles set out in '*Spanish Banks*', Case C–67/91 *Dirección General de Defensa de la Competencia (DGDC) v Asociacion Española de Banca Privada (AEB) and others* [1992] ECR I–4785 may prevent the Commission from using directly as evidence the information obtained earlier, but it may still be able to initiate its own inquiry; CS Kerse and N Khan, *EC Antitrust Procedure* (5th edn, 2005) para 7–060.

[38] JM Joshua and PD Camesasca, 'Where angels fear to tread: the Commission's new leniency policy revisited', The European Antitrust Review 2005, Global Competition Review 10–14 (12) noting that in practice the Commission will not entertain any approach unless the applicant commits in advance to converting the application on the spot to one for a fine reduction rather than walk out.

[39] 2002 Notice [2002] OJ C45/3 para 11. B Van Barlingen and M Barennes, 'The European Commission's Leniency Notice in Practice' Competition Policy Newsletter, Number 3, Autumn 2005, 6–16.

[40] 2002 Notice [2002] OJ C45/3 paras 8(a) and (b).

[41] B Van Barlingen, 'The European Commission's 2002 Leniency Notice after one year of operation', Competition Policy Newsletter, Number 2, Summer 2003, 16–22. B Van Barlingen and M Barennes, 'The European Commission's Leniency Notice in Practice' Competition Policy Newsletter, Number 3, Autumn 2005, 6–16 (10) in relation to the access to corporate statements in the administrative procedure. See 'Oral Applications' below para 6.19 where generally the same principles apply.

applicant's possession at the time of the statement, it should describe the product or service concerned, the production process, the market, the customers, and, in particular, the precise functioning of the cartel, including its membership, period of functioning, geographic area covered, activities, internal rules, meetings, and other contacts. This synthesis should be supported by copies of previously existing documents, whenever such documents are available to the applicant. All written evidence that can be found should be submitted. The written evidence may be supplemented by written statements of company employees or former employees on behalf of the corporate applicant, describing their participation in the cartel. It is particularly important for the Commission's purposes that, under paragraph 8(a) of the Notice, the application should include precise information about the names, functions, and office locations of the participants of other companies in the cartel. If the company is represented by counsel, the application should include a power of attorney.

2. Reduction of a fine

Conditions for the grant of fine reduction

As regards the situations where the Commission does not grant immunity, the practice of the Commission under the 2002 Notice seems to have given rise to a distinction between different scenarios. First, it may be that the facts reported are simply not covered by the material scope of 2002 Notice because they do not relate to secret cartel arrangements. In these cases, the Commison services so-called 'non-eligibility letters' which is a short standard letter at the administrative level indicating that—without prejudice to the compatibility of the reported arrangements with EC competition rules—those arrangements do not fall within the scope of the 2002 Notice and the applicant may withdraw the evidence disclosed.[42] Secondly, immunity applications may not meet the substantive conditions for conditional immunity under paragraph 8(a) of the 2002 Notice. This means that carrying out an inspection would not be possible on the basis of the information provided. The Commission adopts a 'rejection decision' whereby it denies conditional immunity. In instances where the application for immunity cannot be granted, the undertakings usually

6.14

---

[42] See generally, B Van Barlingen and M Barennes, 'The European Commission's Leniency Notice in practice' Competition Policy Newsletter, Number 3, Autumn 2005, 6–16 (11) who refer to applications for immunity which concern the review of clauses in business contracts. Those may raise issues under Art 81 EC but would certainly not reflect secret cartel arrangements. When asking for immunity, the companies would attempt to create something similar to the previous but abolished notification system.

opt for a reduction of fine rather than withdraw the evidence. The application for a reduction of fine then remains on the record but only becomes active if the Commisison decides to investigate the matter further.[43] Thirdly, it may occur that *prima facie*, not all of the conditions of the 2002 Notice are met (e.g. the effects of the infringement are geographically limited) and the case is not suitable for further investigation in accordance with the priorities that the Commisison has established for its enforcement policy. It appears that the Commission will then send a so-called 'no action letter' stating that the Commission does not have the intention to investigate the matter further without prejudice to the power of the Commission to take position on the application for immunity at a later stage. The decision on the initial immunity is somehow put on hold in case the applicant does not withdraw its application.[44] Lastly, as indicated, a loss of lenience may occur where the company does not cooperate fully with the Commisison throughout the procedure (e.g. the applicant does not terminate its involvement in the cartel or reveals that it may face liability for an antitrust infringement under the rules of the US Securities and Exchange Commission). Rather than withdrawing the conditional immunity it had granted, the Commission will decide in its prohibition decisions not to grant immunity.[45] All these four scenarios involve provisional decisions. Accordingly, it would appear that ultimately only the Commission's prohibition decision can be successfully appealed before the Community Courts.

6.15 Companies that are unable to obtain full immunity may still obtain a reduction of the fine according to a decreasing scale. The 2002 Notice requires those undertakings requesting a reduction to contribute with evidence of the suspected infringement that has 'significant added value' ('SAV') with respect to the evidence already in the Commission's possession.[46] The 2002 Notice describes the concept of SAV by referring to the extent to which the evidence provided strengthens, by its very nature and/or its level of detail, the

---

[43] See B Van Barlingen and M Barennes, 'The European Commission's Leniency Notice in Practice' Competition Policy Newsletter, Number 3, Autumn 2005, 6–16 (11–12).

[44] See B Van Barlingen and M Barennes, 'The European Commission's Leniency Notice in Practice' Competition Policy Newsletter, Number 3, Autumn 2005, 6–16 (11).

[45] See B Van Barlingen and M Barennes, 'The European Commission's Leniency Notice in Practice' Competition Policy Newsletter, Number 3, Autumn 2005, 6–16 (13) notes that before taking the decision, the Commission will inform the applicant that no reduction of fines will be granted and provide it with an opportunity to respond. In any event, if conditional immunity is denied, this will also imply that no reduction of fines will be granted.

[46] 2002 Notice [2002] OJ C45/3 para 21.

Commission's ability to prove the facts in question.[47] The Commission, in order to assess the evidence, generally prefers written evidence originating from the period of time to which the facts pertain rather than evidence subsequently established. In the same way, evidence that is directly relevant to the facts (for instance, the minutes of cartel meetings) in question will have a greater value than that with only indirect relevance. The final decision of the Commission will determine whether the evidence submitted has provided SAV or not. The Commission fixes in the same decision the level of reduction of the undertaking. The 2002 Notice also provides an incentive to confess participation in a cartel as early as possible by linking the order in which competing applicants cooperate with the Commission with the level of reduction. Thus, three bands are established to determine the level of reduction of fines for companies presenting evidence:

(i)   30 to 50 per cent for the first undertaking providing SAV;[48]

(ii) 20 to 30 per cent for the second undertaking providing SAV; and

(iii) 0 to 20 per cent for any subsequent undertaking providing SAV.[49]

The actual amount fixed depends in particular upon the point in time at which the undertakings started to cooperate, the quality of the evidence submitted, and the extent of cooperation throughout the proceedings. Furthermore, if the undertaking reveals facts unknown previously by the Commission that have a direct repercussion on the gravity or duration of the cartel under investigation, the Commission will not take these facts into consideration when setting the fine for the undertaking that provided them. For instance, if a leniency applicant discloses facts by which the Commission can determine that the cartel lasted longer than the Commission was aware, the company will not be fined for the extended duration of the cartel. As indicated the fact that the Commisison has granted a reduction to an undertaking does not protect the latter from the civil law consequences of its participation in an infringement of Article 81 EC. **6.16**

---

[47] B Van Barlingen and M Barennes, 'The European Commission's Leniency Notice in Practice' *Competition Policy Newsletter*, Number 3, Autumn 2005, 6–16 (13) describe the situations where it is only through the second applicant that the Commisison was able to find an infringement. Where the Commission has already granted immunity under para 8(a) of the 2992 Notice but is not yet be able to prove the infringement, a leniency applicant that submits sufficient new evidence to allow the Commission to prove the infringement will be considered as having provided significant added value. The same applies where a leniency applicant does not necessarily bring new evidence, but confirms existing evidence where such confirmation is needed to prove the infringement.

[48] 2002 Notice [2002] OJ C45/3 para 21 stipulates that 'an undertaking must provide the Commission with evidence of the suspected infringement which represents significant added value'.

[49] 2002 Notice [2002] OJ C45/3 para 23(b).

The procedure for obtaining the reduction

6.17 Undertakings that wish to obtain a reduction in their fines must contact DG COMP.[50] As indicated, the Commission only considers other applications for reduction once it has formed its opinion on the existing application regarding the same infringement. Similar to applications for immunity, the Commission will initially take a conditional decision, the definitive one being reserved for the adoption of the final decision. The applying undertakings will receive an acknowledgement of receipt from DG COMP recording the date on which the relevant evidence was submitted. When the Commission comes to the pre-liminary conclusion that the evidence qualifies as SAV, it will inform the under-taking in writing no later than the day, on which the statement of objection is notified.[51] As with applications for immunity, this preliminary conclusion is conditional. It appears that the letters assigning bands of reduction are not yet decisions that are challengeable before the Community Courts. At the end of the administrative procedure the Commission will adopt a decision where the Commission will definitively evaluate the level of reduction of the fine.

3. Hypothetical applications

6.18 The 2002 Notice establishes the possibility of making an alternative application by providing the evidence not directly in the first instance but by presenting the evidence in hypothetical terms.[52] This option, colloquially branded as 'putting down a marker' to save a company's place in the queue,[53] affords the under-

---

[50] 2002 Notice [2002] OJ C45/3 paras 24–27. The Commission notes that such applications often take the form of a string of submissions over time, each one of them being made as soon as the evidence is ready to be presented. It recognizes that undertakings are in a virtual race against one another to be the first to voluntarily provide the Commission with evidence of significant added value. B Van Barlingen and M Barennes, 'The European Commission's Leniency Notice in Practice' Competition Policy Newsletter, Number 3, Autumn 2005, 6–16 (14–15).

[51] The notification of the statement of objections thus seem to mark the end of availability of leniency; yet where an undertaking reveals another dimension to a cartel which would result in issuing a further statement of objections, a fine reduction might still be available. CS Kerse and N Khan, *EC Antitrust Procedure* (5th edn, 2005) para 7–060. B Van Barlingen and M Barennes, 'The European Commission's Leniency Notice in Practice' Competition Policy Newsletter, Number 3, Autumn 2005, 6–16 (15) on procedural issues.

[52] 2002 Notice [2002] OJ C45/3 para 13(b).

[53] See also B Van Barlingen, 'The European Commission's 2002 Leniency Notice after one year of operation', Competition Policy Newsletter, Number 2, Summer 2003, 16–22 (18) notes that the expression is somewhat misleading in that the Commission will not consider another application for immunity before it has taken a position on an existing application. See 2002 Notice s 18. In some cases where the applicant is in a great hurry to apply, the Commission may well grant the applicant the possibility of supplementing its file within one or two weeks. The date of the application will be taken as the first date. See also B Van Barlingen and M Barennes, 'The European Commission's Leniency Notice in Practice' Competition Policy Newsletter, Number 3, Autumn 2005, 6–16 (6 and nn 6 and 7) note that of the eighty applications for immunity under the 2002 Notice (until 30 September 2005) eleven of them were hypothetical applications.

taking the chance to form an idea of whether or not it will satisfy the conditions required. The legal advisers can approach the Commission to discuss with Commisison officials whether a leniency application could be successful without making admissions or disclosing the identity of the undertaking to the Commission.[54] The undertaking is required to submit a list that accurately reflects the nature and content of the evidence, whilst safeguarding the hypothetical nature of its disclosure. Expurgated copies of documents, from which sensitive parts have been removed, may be used to illustrate the nature and context of the evidence.[55] It will also be required to reveal the industrial sector in which the cartel is operating. The possibility of 'presenting evidence in hypothetical terms' permits the undertakings to assess whether full immunity would be available or not on the basis of the quality of evidence provided.[56] The 2002 Notice is silent on the possibility of using the hypothetical offer for both total and partial leniency, or just total. The 2002 Notice establishes that companies applying for a reduction are required to 'provide the Commission with evidence of the cartel in question',[57] and if this is taken literally, it suggests that there can be no reductions for hypothetical approaches. Nevertheless, in practice, the Commission will not prohibit hypothetical offers from applying for a reduction of the fine.

4. Oral applications

Under the 1996 Notice applicants were required to present documentary evidence of an infringement. Oral evidence was not permitted. This point is particularly important where applicants face the possibility that a written corporate statement might have to be disclosed in civil litigation, either in a Member State or outside the EU.[58] Being aware that written admissions might

6.19

---

[54] While it is not necessary for the applicant to identify itself in a first inquiry, it must at least identify the larger product sector (e.g. construction, chemical, or transport sector) in order to allow the Commission a meaningful assessment. See also B Van Barlingen, 'The European Commission's 2002 Leniency Notice after one year of operation', Competition Policy Newsletter, Number 2, Summer 2003, pp 16–22 (17).

[55] 2002 Notice [2002] OJ C45/3 para 13(b).

[56] N Levy and R O'Donoghue, 'The EU Leniency Programme Comes of Age' [2004] World Competition 75–99 (83) point out that it may be difficult to determine with certainty whether full immunity can be obtained, but hypothetical offers can be employed to obtain comfort as to whether the quality of evidence available would be sufficient to obtain leniency under the EU programme.

[57] 2002 Notice [2002] OJ C45/3 para 24.

[58] Most major cartels operate on a global basis, and parallel or consecutive enforcement action by several jurisdictions is the norm. N Levy and R O'Donoghue, 'The EU Leniency Programme Comes of Age' [2004] World Competition 75–99 (86) point out that the risk of disclosure is not only limited to those corporate statements and is particularly pertinent before US courts. K Nordlander, 'Discovering Discovery—US Discovery of EC Leniency Statements' [2004] ECLR 646–59 (655 *et seq.*) proposes measures how to avoid US discovery of EU corporate statements.

be discoverable in national civil proceedings, the Commission has begun to accept oral applications.[59] While the 2002 Notice continues to stipulate a preference for 'written evidence originating from the period of time to which the facts pertain'[60] over any oral evidence, Commission officials have in practice been flexible as regards allowing more oral applications.[61] In *Citric Acid*, for the first time, a reduction of the fine of 90 per cent was granted on the basis of the oral evidence of a cartel revealed during a meeting with the Commission.[62] The Commission staff is expected to take minutes of an applicant's oral corporate statement. Similar to written statements, which form part of the Commission

---

[59] Joined Cases T-236/01, T-239/01, T-244/01 to T-246/01, T-251/01 and T-252/01 *Tokai Carbon v EC Commission (Graphite Electrodes)* [2004] OJ C251/13 para 431 where the CFI states that not only 'documents' but also information may serve as evidence which materially contributes to establishing the existence of the infringement. The Commission also intervenes in pending US civil proceedings as *amicus curiae* where discovery of a leniency corporate statement is at stake. See K Nordlander, 'Discovering Discovery—US Discovery of EC Leniency Statements' [2004] ECLR 646–59 (650); B Van Barlingen, 'The European Commission's 2002 Leniency Notice after one year of operation', Competition Policy Newsletter, Number 2, Summer 2003, 16–22 (19 n 1) and B Van Barlingen and M Barennes, 'The European Commission's Leniency Notice in Practice' Competition Policy Newsletter, Number 3, Autumn 2005, 6–16 (7–9) indicate that the value to the Commission of (oral) corporate statements is considerable with a view to providing sufficient evidence for a prohibition decision and for the imposition of fines because nothing would convince more than a cartel participant's own admission of misbehaviour. As regards the problem of civil discovery rules, see P Lowe, 'What's the future for cartel enforcement' Conference Understanding Global Cartel Enforcement, Brussels, 11 February 2003; JM Joshua, 'Oral Statements in EC competition proceedings: a due process short-cut?' Competition Law insight, Issue 26 December 2004, 1–7 (1). See again Joined Cases T-236/01, T-239/01, T-244/01 to T-246/01, T-251/01 and T-252/01 *Tokai Carbon v EC Commission (Graphite Electrodes)* [2004] ECR I-1181para 108: '[. . .] where [the undertaking] explicitly admits during the administrative procedure the substantive truth of the facts which the Commission alleges against it in the statement of objections, those facts must thereafter be regarded as established and the undertaking estopped in principle from disputing them during the procedure before the Court [. . .]'.

[60] The preference for documentary evidence may also be borne out by the fact that no complex cartel can operate without the most detailed records being kept, if only because it allows the ring leaders to keep track of exactly what was agreed. JM Joshua, 'Oral Statements in EC competition proceedings: a due process short-cut?' Competition Law Insight Issue 26, December 2004, 1–7 (3).

[61] B Van Barlingen, 'The European Commission's 2002 Leniency Notice after one year of operation', Competition Policy Newsletter, Number 2, Summer 2003, 16–22 (20). See also the follow-up review—B Van Barlingen and M Barennes, 'The European Commission's Leniency Notice in Practice, Competition Policy Newsletter, Number 3, Autumn 2005, 6–16 (10) where the authors point out that it is up to the applicant to submit directly evidence in the meetings with the Commission which could be arranged on very short notice as proposed by the applicant provided it falls within normal working hours (or the applicant may already send in advance relevant documents in its possession). If the Commisison receives evidence from another undertaking before the scheduled meeting takes place or before it is resumed during normal working hours, the second application would take priority of place.

[62] *Citric Acid* [2001] L239/18. The undertaking granted the reduction was Cerestar Bioproducts, even though another member of the cartel met the Commission first and also contributed with documentary evidence. Yet the Commission considered that Cerestar Bioproducts provided the decisive information.

file and may not be disclosed or used by the Commission for any other purpose than the enforcement of Article 81 EC,[63] the minutes become part of the Commission file and the applicant does not retain a copy: it seems that it would have the character of an internal document, which may remove it from the scope of disclosure procedures.[64] As an internal document, the minutes would not be included in the CD-ROM sent to parties being granted access to the Commission's file. Instead, the document may be available for consultation at the Commission's premises, and no copies may be made.[65] Conversely, where the applicant has agreed the minutes—such as in the context of Article 19 of

---

[63] 2002 Notice [2002] OJ C45/3 para 33. The Commission also emphasizes that normally documents it receives in the context of the 2002 Notice will not be disclosed under Reg 1049/2001 [2001] OJ L145/43 regarding public access to European Parliament, Council, and Commission documents. However, this was challenged by a national consumer association that requested access to the file in Case C-2/03 *Verein für Konsumenteninformation v EC Commission* [2005] OJ C155/14. The Commission argued that third parties access to those documents obtained in the context of a leniency application (in this case, *Austrian Banks* [2004] OJ C56/1) would deter undertakings from cooperating with the Commission and would be detrimental to inspections and investigations in future cases. On these grounds, the Commission denied the applicant access to any of the documents falling into different categories. The CFI took the view that the Commisison is required, in principle, to carry out a concrete, individual assessment of the content of the documents referred to in the request with a view to determining whether any of the exceptions referred to in Reg 1049/2001 are applicable to the documents in question, unless it is obvious that access can be denied. The Court added that it is only in exceptional cases, and only where the administrative burden entailed by a concrete, individual examination of the documents proves to be particularly heavy, exceeding the limits of what may reasonably be required, that a derogation from that obligation to examine the documents may be permissible.

[64] CS Kerse and N Khan, *EC Antitrust Procedure* (5th edn, 2005) para 7–063 and n 26 indicates that the fact that the document is created by the Commission rather than the leniency applicant would not necessary remove the document from the scope of disclosure procedures. They point out that in this context the applicant's obligation to disclose contemporaneous documentary evidence which exists independently of the immunity application, will always apply. K Nordlander, 'Discovering Discovery—US Discovery of EC Leniency Statements' [2004] ECLR 646–59 (655, 557–659) notes that while the Commission may assert the *investigatory privilege* to avoid for example US discovery given that the oral statement is under the Commission control, this may in practice face some hurdles as seen in the *Vitamins* litigation in the US. See also T Reeves, H Albers, and R Hunter, 'A Closer Look at *Intel v AMD*' in light of the EU Complaints Procedure, Antitrust magazine, Fall 2004, ABA section of Antitrust Law 72–78. In *Intel v AMD*, the US Supreme Court of appeals affirmed a US Court of appeals ruling allowing discovery on aid of proceedings before the Commission, although the information sought was not discoverable under the Commission's own rules.

[65] N Levy and R O'Donoghue, 'The EU Leniency Programme Comes of Age' [2004] World Competition 75–99 (90). B Van Barlingen and M Barennes, 'The European Commission's Leniency Notice in Practice', Competition Policy Newsletter, Number 3, Autumn 2005, 6–16 (10) indicate that parties may read written corporate statements and transcripts of corporate statements and make their own notes. They could also request access to a copy of the tape recording of an oral corporate statement and make their own notes. But they are not allowed to make copies in any mechanic copies of corporate statements or of transcripts thereof. See also Communication from the Commission relating to the revision of the 1997 Notice on the internal rules of procedure for processing requests for access to the file [2004] OJ C259/8 para 12. The new rules (not yet published in the OJ) were adopted on 13 December 2005. See Commission

Regulation 1/2003 which enables the Commission to interview any natural or legal person who consents to be interviewed for the purpose of collecting information relating to the subject matter of the investigation—the minutes will be considered as part of the evidence on which the Commission can rely in its assessment of a case.[66] There is the suggestion that unless the applicant has signed them, they may not be made accessible because they would remain internal documents.[67] Where the applicant makes an oral leniency statement, the decision to grant immunity is communicated orally to the applicant's lawyer who will sign for (oral) notification. The certificate showing that the applicant is applying for leniency may itself also be kept by the Commission in its file.[68]

C. Implications of Regulation 1/2003 on Leniency Programmes[69]

6.20 As noted above, leniency applicants report their own antitrust violations to the Commission, thus providing the latter with information to enable it to start or continue its investigation, in return for which they obtain full immunity or a reduction of the fine. At this point applicants are very concerned with the information they have disclosed to the Commission in exchange for immunity or reduction of the fine, and they need assurances that it will remain confiden-

---

press release IP/05/1581 'Competition: Commission improves rules for access to the file in merger and antitrust procedures'. JM Joshua 'Oral Statements in EC competition proceedings: a due process short-cut?', Competition Law Insight Issue 26, December 2004, 1–7 (3–4) takes the view that the 'oral testimony' procedure in which the Commission currently relies heavily on in leniency cases to prove serious breaches of the competition rules raises serious due process issues.

[66] Commission Notice relating to the revision of the 1997 Notice on the internal rules of procedure for processing requests for access to the file [2005] OJ C325/7 para 12. The new rules (not yet published in the OJ) were adopted on 13 December 2005. See Commission press release IP/05/1581.

[67] JM Joshua, 'Oral Statements in EC competition proceedings: a due process short-cut?' Competition Law Insight Issue 26, December 2004, 1–7 (5) is of the view that this procedure may presumably ensure that oral-only applications under the new Access to the File Notice will not be disclosed with the statement of objections and hence may not be made subject to immediate discovery in the US unless the maker has 'imprudently' signed them.

[68] K Nordlander, 'Discovering Discovery—US Discovery of EC Leniency Statements' [2004] ECLR 646–59 (647) with a description of the oral leniency statement referring to O Guersent, 'Cartels and Leniency: EC leniency and US discovery proceedings' IBC's 9th Annual Advanced EC Competition Law Conference, 21 November 2002. On 22 February 2006, the European Commission published for consultation draft amendments it proposes to make to its Notice on immunity from fines and reduction of fines in cartel cases. The amendments reflect concerns about the risk of discovery in civil damage proceedings, in particular in third country jurisdictions, of corporate statements made to the Commission in the context of its leniency program. The Commission proposed adding an annex to the 2002 Notice regarding the 'Procedure for corporate statements made for the purpose of obtaining immunity from fines or reduction of fines in cartel cases'.

[69] See ch 3 'National competition authorities' paras 3.34 *et seq.*

tial, also for fear that the authorities receiving information obtained from leniency applicants use this information to bring proceedings against the applicant. The NCAs and the Commission have sought to address these concerns via the Commission's ECN Cooperation Notice[70] by putting in place two safeguards: the first one relates to the exchange of information under Article 11 and the second one to Article 12 of Regulation 1/2003. The mechanisms are aimed at ensuring that there is no disincentive to go lenient under the existing leniency programmes and create legitimate expectations vis-à-vis the Commission and the NCAs, which have committed themselves to respecting the principles set out in the ECN Cooperation Notice.[71]

1. Article 11 of Regulation 1/2003

Under Article 11(3) of Regulation 1/2003 the NCAs must, when acting under **6.21** Article 81 EC (or Article 82), inform the Commission in writing before or without delay after commencing the first formal investigative measure. This information may also be made available to the competition authorities of the other Member States. In cases that have been initiated as a result of a leniency application the ECN Cooperation Notice specifies that the information provided to one ECN member may not be used by another ECN member as the basis for starting an investigation on its behalf.[72] Anyway, it will be free to open an investigation if it receives sufficient information to enable it to do so from another source, such as a complaint.[73] These provisions apply equally to cases that have been initiated as a result of a leniency application.

2. Article 12 of Regulation 1/2003

Under Article 12 of Regulation 1/2003 the Commission and the NCAs shall **6.22** have the power to provide one another with and use in evidence any matter of

---

[70] The risk of parallel application of Art 81 EC is reduced but not eliminated through the application of the case allocation criteria, simply because there may be a number of NCAs that are well placed to investigate. Commission Notice on cooperation within the network of competition authorities ('ECN Cooperation Notice') [2004] OJ C101/43. See also N Levy and R O'Donoghue, 'The EU Leniency Programme Comes of Age' [2004] World Competition 75–99 (93). D Schroeder, 'Leniency from a Private Practitioner's Perspective' Antitrust Reform in Europe: A Year in Practice, 9–11 March 2005, Brussels, International Bar Association (IBA).

[71] K Dekeyser, 'Regulation 1/2003: First Experiences', IBC Conference London, 27 and 28 April 2005, D Reichelt, 'To what extent does the cooperation within the European Competition Network protect the rights of the undertakings?' (2005) CML Rev 745–82 (767–70).

[72] ECN Cooperation Notice [2004] C101/43 para 39.

[73] The approach taken in Reg 1/2003 is to limit further the scope of the use of information by NCAs developed under Reg 17 in '*Spanish Banks*', Case C-67/91 *Dirección General de Defensa de la Competencia (DGDC) v Asociacion Española de Banca Privada (AEB) and others* [1992] ECR I-4785 in which the ECJ ruled that one cannot exclude the possibility that such information may prompt an NCA to start its own investigation into the matter.

fact or law, including confidential information for the purpose of applying Articles 81 and 82 EC. Nevertheless, the ECN Cooperation Notice sets out the way the members of the ECN will handle the information submitted in the context of leniency programmes. The information may be twofold. On the one hand, it could include all the information that has been voluntarily disclosed by the leniency applicant and the second category covers information that has been obtained during or following an inspection or it could also encompass the information that has been found by means of or following any other fact-finding measures which, in each case, could not have been carried out except as a result of the leniency application. Also in the latter case, if there was a free exchange of information, the leniency applicant could still suffer from a sanction by another ECN member which could be able to prove an infringement of the competition rules on the basis of evidence that was obtained. Accordingly, in both cases, the information should not be used against the applicant without the consent of the applicant.[74] Where the leniency applicant has consented to the exchange of the information which it has voluntarily submitted as part of its leniency application, this information may be transmitted.[75] Further, the consent of the applicant for the transmission of information to another authority pursuant to Article 12 of Regulation 1/2003 is not required in any of the following circumstances:[76]

(i) if the receiving authority has also received a leniency application relating to the same infringement from the same applicant as the transmitting authority, provided that at the time the information is transmitted it is not open to the applicant to withdraw the information which it has submitted to that receiving authority;

(ii) if the receiving authority has provided a written commitment that neither the information transmitted to it nor any other information it may obtain following the date and time of transmission as noted by the

---

[74] K Dekeyser and E De Smijter, 'The Exchange of Evidence Within the ECN' [2005] Legal Issues of Economic Integration 161–74 (166).

[75] D Reichelt, 'To what extent does the cooperation within the European Competition Network protect the rights of the undertakings?' (2005) CML Rev 745–82 (767) indicating that the transmission of the (minimum) information to other ECN members using the ECN interactive form does not require the consent of the leniency applicant. The consent requirement would only apply further information. See ch 3 'National competition authorities' paras 3.36 *et seq.*

[76] ECN Cooperation Notice [2004] C101/43 para 4. K Dekeyser and E De Smijter, 'The Exchange of Evidence Within the ECN' [2005] Legal Issues of Economic Integration 161–74 (166) maintain that the exceptions intend to avoid an 'unwanted scenario of structural underpunishment' because not only the leniency applicant but also other participants in the competition rules infringing behaviour will escape any effective sanction. See also C Gauer, 'Due Process in the Face of Divergent National Procedures', Antitrust Reform in Europe: A Year in Practice, 9–11 March 2005, Brussels, International Bar Association (IBA) 15.

transmitting authority, will be used by it or by any other authority to which the information is subsequently transmitted to impose sanctions:[77]

(a) on the leniency applicant;

(b) on any other legal or natural person covered by the favourable treatment offered by the transmitting authority as a result of the application made by the applicant under its leniency programme;

(c) on any employee or former employee of any of the persons covered by (a) or (b).

A copy of the receiving authority's written commitment will be provided to the applicant.

In the case of information collected by a network member in the context of an inspection under Article 22(1) of Regulation 1/2003 on behalf of and for the account of the network member to whom the leniency application was made, such information may be transmitted to, and used by, the network member to whom the application was made. In the case of an international cartel, the applicant may decide to apply for leniency to antitrust authorities in other jurisdictions.[78] In these cases the applicant should provide a waiver to the Commission in order to discuss the case and share information, as well allowing for simultaneous dawn raids in different parts of the world.

6.23

3. Parallel leniency applications

In the absence of an EU-wide system of fully harmonized leniency programmes,[79] an application for leniency to a given authority is not to be considered as an application for leniency to any other authority. It is therefore in the interest of the applicant to apply for leniency to all of the competition authorities, which have competence to apply Article 81 EC in the territory

6.24

---

[77] 'Q&A on modernization with Kris Dekeyser' Global Competition Review, Vol 8, Issue 3, April 2005, 11–16 (14) notes that this may lead to a situation where the company obtains immunity in a Member State that does not have a leniency programme.

[78] USA, Australia, Canada, and Japan.

[79] While the leniency programmes of the Member States have a lot in common, they also differ in certain aspects. Its seems that under all programmes it is possible to 'go lenient' only in respect of horizontal cartels, whereas some Member States polices also cover vertical arrangements. The 2002 Notice requires the company to terminate involvement in the cartel as a precondition, whereas some Member States actually seem to require the opposite so as to not jeopardize the investigation (e.g. France). See discussion of these issues in 'Q&A on modernization with Kris Dekeyser' Global Competition Review, Vol 8, Issue 3, April 2005, 11–16 (15); see also D Henry, 'Leniency Programmes: An Anaemic Carrot for Cartels in France, Germany and the UK' [2005] ECLR 13–23. The Commission is testing the possibility of introducing a one-stop shop for leniency; Commissioner for Competition Policy N Kroes, 'The First Hundred' 40th Anniversary of the Studienvereinigung Kartellrecht 1965–2005, International Forum on European Competition Law Brussels, 7 April 2005.

which is affected by the infringement and which may be considered well placed to act against the infringement in question.[80] An application under the 2002 Notice does not exclude the simultaneous application of national competition laws by one or more NCAs. Regulation 1/2003 increases the incidence of the parallel application by the Commission and the NCAs. The ECN Cooperation Notice clarifies which authority must take over the competence for the leniency application, but it does not take into consideration the real risk of the simultaneous application of Article 81 EC by the Commission and one or more NCAs. Applicants are aware that from May 2004 NCAs are more encouraged than ever to begin investigations regarding infringements of Articles 81 and 82 EC. The point in time at which an application is made is therefore of great importance, because it will determine where the applicant is 'in the queue'. In fact situations may arise where one of the applicants applies to the Commission and the other one to the NCAs.

6.25   For this reason, it is very important to measure the size of the cartel. The scope of a case may not be obvious from the outset: this applies both to ECN members and the leniency applicant itself.[81] Where a cartel covers different jurisdictions, an undertaking should be aware of the possibility of someone else applying for leniency at the relevant NCA. If it is a worldwide or a European cartel, the Commission is expected to deal with it under Article 11(6) of Regulation 1/2003.[82] In other cases, if the Commission does not take up the case, there could be the risk that the party which has applied directly to an NCA might already have provided that NCA with sufficient evidence which would make it redundant that this NCA needs to resort to the information provided by another applicant in order to uncover a cartel. Thus, if single applications for immunity are made by different parties to different authorities, the decision on case allocation will be crucial in deciding who enjoys immunity from fines. Given that applying for leniency does not entitle the applicant to have the case dealt with by a given authority, the best way forward is to seek immunity simultaneously before several authorities.[83] If a company decides to apply for

---

[80] As regards the criteria for case allocation under the ECN Cooperation Notice, see ch 3 paras 3.06 *et seq.*

[81] See also U Soltész, 'Der "Kronzeuge" im Labyrinth des ECN' [2005] Wirtschaft und Wettbewerb 616–24 (620) noting that smaller cases may be more problematic because for larger cases the Commission may offer the 'one-stop shop'.

[82] The Commission is particularly well placed to deal with a case if more than three Member States are substantially affected by a practice or an agreement. If the Commisison takes up the case, this will relieve NCAs of their competence. ECN Cooperation Notice [2004] OJ C101/43 para 14.

[83] S Blake and D Schichels, 'Leniency Modernization: safeguarding Europe's leniency programmes' Competition Policy Newsletter No 2, Summer 2004, 7–13 (11); U Soltész, 'Der "Kronzeuge" im Labyrinth des ECN' [2005] Wirtschaft und Wettbewerb 616–24 (619) criticizes the fact that this would require substantial efforts on the part of the undertaking and would defeat the purpose of efficient allocation of resources.

leniency, it is therefore of interest not only to apply to all competent ECN members but to do so as quickly as possible.

4. Judicial review

With respect to the 1996 Notice, a number of companies alleged that the Commission did not apply properly the criteria for granting a lower fine,[84] and asked the CFI to appraise the cooperation shown to obtain a reduction of a fine arguing—among other things—an infringement of the principle of equal treatment where other cartels benefited from a larger reduction.[85] The CFI has ruled that in the context of a leniency application, a reduction in the amount of the fine on the grounds of cooperation is justified only if the conduct made it easier for the Commission to establish infringements of the Community competition rules and to put an end to them. The Commission is entitled to grant leniency applicants different reductions of fines, in accordance with the difference in the value of their cooperation[86] In *ABB*, the CFI ruled that cooperation by an undertaking before the Commission has issued a request for information may make the Commission's investigation easier. Given this, it was perfectly

6.26

---

[84] e.g. '*Seamless steel tube*' cases: Case T-44/00 *Mannesmannröhren-Werke AG v EC Commission* [2004] OJ C239/12 paras 295 *et seq.*; Case T-50/00 *Dalmine SpA v EC Commission* [2004] OJ C239/13 paras 340 *et seq.*; Joined Cases T-67/00, T-68/00, T-71/00, and T-78/00 *JFE Engineering Corp and others v EC Commission* [2004] C239/13 paras 497 *et seq.*; see also '*Stainless steel*' cases Case T-45/98 *Krupp Thyssen Stainless v EC Commission* [2001] ECR II-3757 paras 232 *et seq.* and Case T- 48/98 *Acerinox v EC Commission* [2001] ECR II-3859 paras 126 *et seq.*; Case T-202/98 *Tate & Lyle v EC Commission* [2001] ECR II-2035 paras 157 *et seq.*; Case T-230/00, *Daesang Corp and Sewon Europe v EC Commission* [2003] ECR II-2733 paras 121 *et seq.*; Case T-31/99 *ABB Asea Brown Boveri Ltd v EC Commission* [2002] ECR II-1881 paras 234 *et seq.*; Joined Cases T-236/01, T-239/01, T-244/01 to T-246/01, T-251/01 and T-252/01 *Tokai Carbon Co Ltd and others v EC Commission* [2004] ECR I-1181 paras 273 *et seq.* See finally F Arbault and F Peiró, 'The Commission's new notice on immunity and reduction of fines in cartel cases: building on success' Competition Policy Newsletter, Number 2, June 2002, 15–22 (22). D Geradin and D Henry, 'The EC fining policy for violation of competition law: An empirical review of the Commission decisional practice and the Community's courts judgments' [2005] European Competition Law Journal 401–73 (465) have counted eleven cases since the introduction of the 1998 Guidelines until the end of 2004 in which the fine was reduced for incorrect application of the Leniency Notice.

[85] As regards the application of this principle in the context of cooperation, see Case T-45/98 *Krupp Thyssen Stainless GmbH and Acciai speciali Terni SpA v EC Commission* [2001] ECR II-3757 para 237: '[...] As regards appraisal of the cooperation shown by undertakings, the Commission is not entitled to disregard the principle of equal treatment, a general principle of Community law which is infringed only where comparable situations are treated differently or different situations are treated in the same way, unless such difference of treatment is objectively justified. [...]'. In this case, the CFI found that the two undertakings in question provided the Commission with similar information at the same stage of administrative procedure and in similar circumstances.

[86] Case T-347/94 *Mayr-Melnhof v EC Commission* [1998] ECR II-1751 para 309 '[...] an undertaking which expressly states that it is not contesting the factual allegations on which the Commission bases its objections may be regarded as having facilitated the Commission's task of finding and bringing to an end infringements of the Community competition rules [...]'.

permissible for the Commission not to grant the maximum reduction envisaged to the applicant, which did not declare its willingness to cooperate until after receiving a first request for information.[87] The mere fact that one of those undertakings was the first to acknowledge the contested facts in response to the questions put by the Commission cannot constitute an objective reason for treating them differently. The appraisal of the extent of the cooperation shown by undertakings cannot depend on purely random factors, such as the order in which they are questioned by the Commission.[88] The Commission may not take into account the cooperation of a company as a mitigating factor where this cooperation falls under the leniency notice. The 1998 Guidelines on fines clearly set out that the effective co-operation of an undertaking may be taken into account as a mitigating factor in proceedings 'outside the scope of the [leniency] notice'.[89]

D. Amnesty Plus

6.27 Undertakings often operate in a worldwide context which makes it more likely that the same undertaking colludes in different product or geographical markets. Under the 'Amnesty Plus' programme an undertaking involved in an illegal cartel has the chance to report its own involvement in a second cartel in exchange for immunity or a substantial reduction of any fine. In the United States, 'Amnesty Plus' was implemented in 1999, and since then leniency applications have increased enormously.[90] 'Amnesty Plus' operates on the same basis as the conventional leniency programmes but essentially seeks to encourage cartel members to disclose their participation in cartels that operate in distinct

---

[87] Case T-31/99 *ABB Asea Brown Boveri Ltd v EC Commission* [2002] ECR II-1881 paras 181–182; Case T-17/99 *KE KELLIT Kuntstoffwerk GmbH v EC Commission* [2002] ECR II-1647 paras 181–182.

[88] Case T-45/98 *Krupp Thyssen Stainless GmbH and others v EC Commission* [2001] ECR II-3757 paras 243–247. See in particular: '[. . .] an undertaking cannot be regarded as having been the first to cooperate with the Commission where it has provided the Commission, at the same stage of the administrative procedure as the other undertakings questioned and in similar circumstances, with information identical to that provided by the latter [. . .]'. Case T-48/98 *Acerinox v EC Commission* ECR II-3859 paras 139–140: '[. . .] the extent of the cooperation provided by the applicant and Usinor must be regarded as comparable, in so far as those undertakings provided the Commission, at the same stage of the administrative procedure and in similar circumstances, with similar information concerning the conduct imputed to them [. . .] Accordingly, the mere fact that one of those undertakings was the first to acknowledge the contested facts in response to the questions put by the Commission cannot constitute an objective reason for treating them differently. The appraisal of the extent of the cooperation shown by undertakings cannot depend on purely random factors, such as the order in which they are questioned by the Commission.'

[89] Case T-9/99 *HFB and others v EC Commission* [2002] ECR II-1487 paras 608–610.

[90] It is said that the DOJ receives three applications per month. Within the EU, only the OFT formally offers 'leniency plus'.

product and geographic markets. The 2002 Leniency Notice does not expressly establish the possibility of such an immunity or reduction in the fine when disclosing information about a second cartel, it merely provides for the possibility of obtaining a reduction in the fine under the 'aggravating and mitigating' circumstances used by the Commission when setting fines.[91] At present in Europe, only one undertaking[92] has disclosed its involvement in a second cartel. This cooperation was not granted with a reduction of the fine. The omission of an express 'Amnesty Plus' proviso in the 2002 Notice was lamented,[93] as it could have brought more certainty for undertakings when calculating the amount of the supposed fine if they ever decide to make leniency applications.

---

[91] 1998 Guidelines on the method of setting fines [1998] OJ C9/3 para 10.

[92] Interbrew in the Decisions *Interbrew and Malken-Maes* [2003] OJ L200/1 and *Luxemburg Brewers* [2002] OJ L253/21.

[93] e.g. D McElwee, 'Should the European Commission adopt "Amnesty Plus" in its Fight Against Hard-Core Cartels?' [2004] ECLR 558–65 (559).

7

INVESTIGATION OF CASES (II): FORMAL INVESTIGATIVE MEASURES IN GENERAL. INTERVIEWS AND REQUESTS FOR INFORMATION

A. Formal Investigative Measures in General[1]

1. Principles applicable in the initial investigative phase

The Commission is entitled to investigate possible infringements of Articles 81 and 82 EC and, where appropriate, impose penalties on undertakings and associations of undertakings. In this regard, it performs the activities both of fact-finding and legal evaluation.[2] Once proceedings have been initiated, the Commission needs, in many cases, to take steps to establish with certainty the existence of the alleged infringements. Although Regulation 1/2003 has put an end to the Commission's monopoly to grant exemptions under Article 81(3) EC, the Commission has preserved its central role in the application of the principles laid down in Articles 81 and 82 EC[3] and maintains the powers of investigation it had under Regulation 17. The two principal avenues that were available to the Commission were the powers to receive information and to

7.01

---

[1] K Dekeyser and C Gauer, 'The New Enforcement System for Arts 81 & 82 and the Rights of Defence' ch 23 in BE Hawk (ed), *International Antitrust Law and Policy*, Annual Proceedings of the Fordham Institute (2004) 545–89. J Schwarze and A Weitbrecht, *Grundzüge des Europäischen Kartellverfahrensrechts* (2004) § 4; CS Kerse and N Khan, *Antitrust Competition Procedure* (5th edn, 2005) paras 3–001 *et seq.*; A Jones and B Sufrin, *EC Competition Law* (2nd edn, 2004) 1059–83. K Lenaerts and J Maselis, 'Procedural Rights and Issues in the Enforcement of Articles 81 and 82 of the EC Treaty' [2001] Fordham International Law Journal 1615–54.

[2] The role of the Commission as an investigator, prosecutor, and judge has long been subject to criticism, but this combination of powers was not changed by the modernization package. See WPJ Wils, 'The Combination of the Investigative and Prosecutorial Function in EC Antitrust Enforcement, A Legal and Economic Analysis' [2004] World Competition 201–24. F Montag, 'The Case for Radical Reform of the Infringement Procedure under Regulation 17' [1998] ECLR 428. For a more detailed discussion see ch 4.

[3] See ch 3 on 'The role of national competition authorities' paras 3.05 *et seq.*

conduct on-site inspections. These powers have remained. As was the case under Regulation 17, the investigative powers set out in Regulation 1/2003 apply only to the Commission. Whenever NCAs and national courts are required to apply Articles 81 and 82 EC, their powers of investigation and procedures are governed by national law.[4]

7.02 Chapter V of Regulation 1/2003 and its implementing Regulation 773/2004[5] lay down the conditions for the exercise by the Commission of its formal powers for the investigation of cases, in their various forms. Generally, its powers have increased in several aspects, particularly as regards the collection of information and for fines attached to a breach of the duties triggered by these powers.[6] By extending the scope of the investigative powers afforded to the Commission under Regulation 17, the Commission hopes to be more able to detect infringements of competition rules, which the Commission considers as being more and more difficult.[7] Whereas the Commission may exercise its powers of investigation pursuant to Chapter V of Regulation 1/2003 before initiating proceedings,[8] its powers are not limited by reference to time or the stage reached in the case, so that they can be used after completion of the investigation, during the observations phase, between the latter phase and the adoption of a decision, and even afterwards.[9]

---

[4] It is to note that apart from obtaining assistance from the Member States for the inspections it conducts itself, under Art 22 of Reg 1/2003 the Commission can also request the NCAs to conduct inspections on its behalf. The officials of the NCA who are responsible for conducting these inspections as well as those authorized or appointed by them shall exercise their powers in accordance with national law. WPJ Wils, 'Powers of Investigation and Procedural Rights and Guarantees in EU Antitrust Enforcement', First Lisbon Conference on Competition Law and Economics, Belém 3–4 November 2005, para 26 notes that it would follow from the principles of effectiveness and equivalence that these powers must be effective, and at least equivalent to what the Member State would provide for in comparable situations of enforcement of its own national law.

[5] Commission Reg (EC) 773/2004 relating to the proceedings by the Commission pursuant to Arts 81 and 82 of the EC Treaty [2004] OJ L123/18. Reg 773/2004 was adopted pursuant to Art 33 of Reg 1/2003.

[6] K Dekeyser and C Gauer, 'The New Enforcement System for Arts 81 & 82 and the Rights of Defence' ch 23 in BE Hawk (ed), *International Antitrust Law and Policy*, Annual Proceedings of the Fordham Institute [2004] 545–89 (550). WPJ Wils, 'Powers of Investigation and Procedural Rights and Guarantees in EU Antitrust Enforcement', First Lisbon Conference on Competition Law and Economics, Belém, 3–4 November 2005, paras 32–33 indicates that the powers of some NCAs appear to be stronger than those of the Commission under Reg 1/2003. Art 5 of Reg 1/2003 allows NCAs to impose any other penalty provided for in their national law, which would include prison sanctions for directors or managers responsible for their companies' behaviour.

[7] Recitals 23 and 25 of Reg 1/2003; Schwarze and Weitbrecht, *Grundzüge des Europäischen Kartellverfahrensrechts* (2004) § 4 para 3.

[8] Art 2(3) of Reg 773/2004.

[9] According to the CFI, '[t]he Commission cannot be deprived of its powers of investigation into facts subsequent to those penalized in a decision, even if such facts are identical to those on which that decision is based.' Case T-34/93 *Société Générale v EC Commission* [1995] ECR II-545 para 77. The power may be used to obtain clarification after the oral hearing, e.g. *Glaxo Wellcome* [2001] OJ L302/1; CS Kerse and N Khan, *Antitrust Competition Procedure* (5th edn, 2005)

Articles 18 ('Requests for information'), 19 ('Power to take statements') and **7.03**
20 ('The Commission's powers of inspection') of Regulation 1/2003 empower
the Commission to require such information to be supplied as is necessary
to detect any agreement, decision, or concerted practice prohibited by Article
81 EC or any abuse of a dominant position prohibited by Article 82 EC.[10]
The Community Courts have repeatedly ruled that, as regards the needs
of information, the Commission enjoys considerable latitude. Even if the
Commission already has evidence, or indeed proof, of the existence of an
infringement, the Commission may legitimately take the view that it is necessary to order further investigations enabling it to better define the scope of the
infringement, to determine its duration, or to identify the circle of undertakings
involved.[11] In the same vein, the Courts have also held that the Commission
enjoys a margin of discretion to set priorities in enforcing competition
rules.[12] However, in using its investigative powers under Regulation 1/2003, the
Commission is required to observe the general principles and rights prescribed
by EC law.[13] Of particular relevance in the context of regulatory investigations

---

para 3–005. 'Dealing with the Commission—Notification, complaints, inspections and fact-
finding powers under Arts [81] and [82] of the EEC Treaty' (1997 edn) point 4.1.

[10] Arts 18 and 20 of Reg 1/2003 correspond to Arts 11 and 14 of Reg 17, respectively.

[11] Case C-94/00 *Roquette Frères SA v Directeur Général de la Concurrence, de la Consommation
et de la Répression des Fraudes* ('*Roquette Frères*') [2002] ECR I-9011 para 78: '[. . .] it is in
principle for the Commission to decide whether a particular item of information is necessary to
enable it to bring to light an infringement of the competition rules. [. . .]'. In relation to requests
for additional information: Case 374/87 *Orkem v EC Commission* [1989] ECR 3283 para 15;
Case 27/88 *Solvay v EC Commission* [1989] ECR 3355 para 12; Case 155/79 *AM & S Europe v
Commission* [1982] ECR 1575 para 17; Case 136/79 *National Panasonic v EC Commission*
[1980] ECR 2033 para 13; and Case T-39/90 *Samenwerkende Elektriciteits-produktiebedrijven
(SEP) v EC Commission I* [1991] ECR II-1497 para 30. See also CS Kerse and N Khan, *Antitrust
Competition Procedure* (5th edn, 2005) para 3–006.

[12] Case T-24/90 *Automec Srl v EC Commission (Automec II)* [1992] ECR II-2223 para 77:
'[. . .] In that connection, it should be observed that, in the case of an authority entrusted with a
public service task, the power to take all the organizational measures necessary for the performance of that task, including setting priorities within the limits prescribed by the law [. . .] This
must be the case in particular where an authority has been entrusted with a supervisory and
regulatory task as extensive and general as that which has been assigned to the Commission in the
field of competition. Consequently, the fact that the Commission applies different degrees of
priority to the cases submitted to it in the field of competition is compatible with the obligations
imposed on it by Community law. [. . .]' In Case T-219/99 *British Airways v EC Commission*
[2003] ECR II-6917 paras 65–71, the CFI dismissed claims that the Commission had infringed
the principle of non-discrimination by bringing Art 82 EC against British Airways but not against
others. Case C-119/97 P *Ufex and others v EC Commission* [1999] ECR I-1341 para 88.

[13] Opinion of AG Ruiz-Jarabo in Joined Cases C-204/00, C-205/00, C-211/00, C-213/00,
C-217/00 and C-219/00 *Aalborg Portland and others v EC Commission* [2004] ECR I-123
para 26: '[. . .] the Commission has wide powers of investigation and inquiry but, precisely
because of that nature and because one and the same body is invested with the power to conduct
investigations and the power to take decisions, the rights of defence of those subject to the
procedure must be recognised without reservation and respected. [. . .]'. 'Dealing with the Commission—Notification, complaints, inspections and fact-finding powers under Articles [81] and
[82] of the EEC Treaty' (1997 edn) point 3.1.

is the principle of proportionality and the protection against arbitrary investigations.[14]

7.04 In its preliminary ruling in *Roquette Frères*, the ECJ clarified the application of these two principles where the ECJ was asked to consider the scope of review to be undertaken by a national court on an application for assistance made under Article 14(6) of Regulation 17, the equivalent of Article 20(6) of Regulation 1/2003.[15] Although the ruling concerned the national courts' scope of review of Commission's decision, the ECJ took the opportunity to spell out the general principles which govern the exercise of the Commission's powers of investigation. Confirming its previous ruling in *Hoechst*, the Court held that the powers conferred on the Commission are designed to enable it to perform its task of ensuring that the competition rules are applied.[16] Without prejudice to the guarantees under domestic law governing the implementation of coercive measures, undertakings under investigation would be protected by various guarantees under Community law, including, in particular, the right to legal representation and the privileged nature of correspondence between lawyer and client.[17] The ECJ also pointed out that the Commission would be required to state reasons for the decision ordering an investigation by specifying its subject matter and purpose. As the ECJ held, this would be a fundamental requirement, designed not merely to show that the proposed entry onto the premises of the undertakings concerned is justified but also to enable those undertakings to assess the scope of their duty to cooperate whilst at the same time safeguarding

---

[14] See, e.g. Case C-331/88 *Fedesa* [1990] ECR 4023 para 13.

[15] When an inspection is ordered by decision of the Commission it is current practice in certain Member States that the competent authority asks for the preventive delivery of a judicial order in case the undertaking concerned refuses to submit to the investigation. In Case C-94/00 *Roquette Frères SA* [2002] ECR I-9011 the judicial order had been issued against Roquette Frères by a regional French court in the course of the Commission's investigation into the sodium gluconate cartel and had been challenged before the French Appeal Court by its addressee. The Appeal Court had subsequently asked the ECJ to clarify the scope of the review by national courts of the requests submitted to them pursuant to Art 14(6) of Reg 17. Art 14 of Reg 17 empowered the Commission to undertake all necessary investigations into undertakings and associations of undertakings, including (a) examine the books and other business records (b) to take copies of or extracts from the books and business records; (c) to ask for oral explanation on the spot; (d) to enter any premises, land and means of transport of undertakings. For more details on the powers of inspection under Art 20 of Reg 1/2003, see ch 8 'Inspections' paras 8.06 *et seq*.

[16] Case C-94/00 *Roquette Frères SA* [2002] ECR I-9011 para 42; Joined Cases 46/87 and 227/88 *Hoechst AG v EC Commission* [1989] ECR 2859 para 25; Joined Cases C-204/00, C-205/00, C-211/00, C-213/00, C-217/00 and C-219/00 *Aalborg Portland and others v EC Commission* [2004] ECR I-123 para 54.

[17] Case 155/79 *AM & S Europe v EC Commission* [1982] ECR 1575 paras 18 to 27 which stated that communications concerning legal advice with lawyers in private practice in the then Member States were entitled to confidentiality; Joined Cases 46/87 and 227/88 *Hoechst AG v EC Commission* [1989] ECR 2859 para 16; Case 85/87 *Dow Benelux v EC Commission* [1989] ECR 3137 para 27.

their rights of defence.[18] The possibility of judicial review of the Commission's exercise of its investigative powers and defence rights exist to protect undertakings against arbitrary measures and to keep such measures within the limits of what is necessary in order to perform its task of ensuring that the competition rules are applied.[19] Thus, when exercising its powers of investigation, the Commission must observe some principles in substance and others in form: substantively, the principles of necessity, appropriateness regarding the surrounding circumstances and the means deployed, proportionality, and observance of the rights of the defence;[20] and formally, the obligation to inform the undertakings concerned of the reasons justifying its action. However, this does not detract from the Commission's relatively wide discretion in carrying out its investigative duties. Ultimately, whether these principles are complied with depends on how investigations under Regulation 1/2003 are conducted by the investigating authorities.

2. The obligations of undertakings

Regulation 17 required undertakings to co-operate actively with the Commission,[21] which meant making available to the Commission all information concerning the subject matter of the investigation. This principle applies both to requests for information—the answers to which must not be evasive—and to investigations—in which the representatives of undertakings are required **7.05**

---

[18] Case C-94/00 *Roquette Frères* [2002] ECR I-9011 para 47; Joined Cases 46/87 and 227/88 *Hoechst v EC Commission* [1989] ECR 2859 para 29.

[19] Case C-94/00 *Roquette Frères* [2002] ECR I-9011 paras 42 and 50. J Schwarze and A Weitbrecht, *Grundzüge des Europäischen Kartellverfahrensrechts* (2004) § 4 para 21.

[20] Unlike Reg 17, Reg 1/2003 is more explicit and spells out a number of guarantees. See, for example, the right not to incriminate oneself in Recital 23 or the control exercised by national courts over assistance during inspections as provided in Arts 20 and 21 of Reg 1/2003. K Dekeyser and C Gauer, 'The New Enforcement System for Articles 81 & 82 and the Rights of Defence' ch 23 in BE Hawk (ed), *International Antitrust Law and Policy*, Annual Proceedings of the Fordham Institute International Antitrust Law and Policy (2005) 549–85 (551).

[21] See Case T-46/92 *Scottish Football Association v EC Commission* [1994] ECR II-1039 para 31; T-9/99 *HFB and others v EC Commission* [2002] ECR II-1487 para 561: '[. . .] Regulation 17 places the undertaking being investigated under a duty of active cooperation, which means that it must be prepared to make any information relating to the object of the inquiry available to the Commission. [. . .]'. Joined Cases C-204/00, C-205/00, C-211/00, C-213/00, C-217/00 and C-219/00 *Aalborg Portland and others v EC Commission* [2004] ECR I-123 paras 61–62. Note that the obligation to provide the relevant information also applies to governments and NCAs under the terms of Art 18(6) (former Art 11 of Reg 17) of Reg 1/2003. The provision has been of little practical relevance. *Cast iron and steel rolls* [1983] OJ L317/1 in which an information request was directed to the German *Bundeskartellamt*. J Schwarze and A Weitbrecht, *Grundzüge des Europäischen Kartellverfahrensrechts* (2004) § 4 para 6; CS Kerse and N Khan, *Antitrust Competition Procedure* (5th edn, 2005) para 3–001. However, in the light of the stronger role given to NCAs by Reg 1/2003, it is likely that Commission investigations will in future rely more heavily on information obtained from NCAs. Kerse and Khan para 3–008.

actively to cooperate with the Commission, not merely allow the inspectors access to the undertaking's premises. The Commission stated in *Fabricca Pisana* that the company must do more than merely give the inspectors access to information they require: it should actually produce the specific documents required.[22] The company's argument that the Commission inspectors chose not to examine the business records which were kept in the company's administration department was rejected, because the inspectors had not been told that the documents requested were, or might have been, kept in that department and there was otherwise no reason to suppose that documents of that nature might have been found there.

7.06 The fact that an undertaking considers that the Commission has no grounds for action under Article 81 EC does not entitle it to resist a request.[23] In the course of the preliminary inquiry procedure, Regulation 17 was construed as not giving an undertaking under investigation any right to refuse to comply with an investigative measure on the ground that evidence that it had infringed the rules on competition might thereby be obtained.[24] In *CSM NV*, the Commission imposed a fine because CSM refused to hand over documents which it regarded as irrelevant; providing these documents later did not mitigate the fine. The Commission took the view that it should decide what lies within the scope of the investigation, although it did concede that there might be circumstances where production can be refused. The decision stated that inspectors are not entitled to examine business records if they are obviously, or in the Commission officials' opinion, not related to the subject matter of the investigation.[25] Companies, however, cannot enforce this on their own initiative. On the contrary, the Community Courts ruled that Regulation 17 would place the undertaking under a duty of active cooperation, which means that it must be prepared to make any information relating to the object of the inquiry available to the

---

[22] *Fabricca Pisana* [1980] OJ L75/30. K Lenaerts and J Maselis, 'Procedural Rights and Issues in the Enforcement of Articles 81 and 82 of the EC Treaty' [2001] Fordham International Law Journal 1615–54 (1622–23).

[23] See, e.g. *Fire Insurance* [1982] OJ L80/36 paras 4 and 5; *Deutsche Castrol Vertriebsgesellschaft mbH* [1983] OJ L114/26 paras 4–7.

[24] The refusal to cooperate with or attempts to obstruct the Commission in carrying out its investigation may constitute an aggravating circumstance leading to an increased fine for the antitrust violations found following the investigation. See the Commission's guidelines on the method of setting fines imposed under Art 15(2) of Reg 17 and Art 65(5) of the ECSC Treaty [1998] OJ C9/3, point 2 second indent. Pursuant to Art 43(3) of Reg 1/2003, these guidelines continue to apply to fines imposed under Art 23(2) of Reg 1/2003.

[25] *CSM NV* [1992] OJ L305/16 at section II. 1.: '[. . .] The obligation incumbent on an undertaking to submit to an investigation ordered by a decision adopted pursuant to Article 14(3) of Reg 17 [20(4) of Reg 1/2003] is not satisfied even if the undertaking's refusal to let officials charged with the investigation by the Commission to exercise their powers is only temporary. Any other interpretation would jeopardize the effectiveness of the investigation. [. . .]'

Commission.[26] On the other hand, the Community Courts have also pointed out that defence rights should not be irremediably impaired during preliminary investigation procedures which may be decisive in providing evidence of the unlawful nature of conduct engaged in by undertakings. Although like Regulation 17, Regulation 1/2003 does not provide for an absolute right to silence in competition proceedings; it is necessary to reconcile the Commission's powers to investigate during the preliminary stage with the need to safeguard the undertakings' defence rights.[27] In *Mannesmannröhren-Werke*, the CFI stated that the Commission is entitled to compel an undertaking to provide all necessary information concerning such facts as may be known to it and to disclose to the Commission, if necessary, such documents relating thereto as are in its possession, even if the latter may be used to establish, against it or another undertaking, the existence of anti-competitive conduct.[28]

3. Probative value of the documents and information obtained

The ECJ held that the purpose of a request for information addressed to an undertaking on the basis of [Article 18 of Regulation 2003] is to provide the Commission with the factual or legal information needed to enable it to exercise its powers. The probative value of the information thus communicated and the conditions under which such information may be relied on against undertakings are, therefore, defined by Community law and confined exclusively to proceedings governed by [Regulation 1/2003].[29] The prevailing

7.07

---

[26] Case 374/87 *Orkem v EC Commission* [1989] ECR 3283 paras 27, 34; Case T-34/93 *Société Générale v EC Commission* [1995] ECR II-545 para 72. The privilege against self-incrimination will be further discussed below at paras 7.49 *et seq*.

[27] Joined Cases C-238/99 P, C-244/99 P, C-245/99 P, C-247/99 P, C-250/99 P to C-252/99 P and C-254/99 P *Limburgse Vinyl Maatschappij and others v EC Commission* [2002] ECR I-8375 para 272; Case 374/87 *Orkem v EC Commission* [1989] ECR 3283 para 32; Case T-112/98 *Mannesmannröhren-Werke v EC Commission* [2001] ECR II-729 para 63.

[28] The CFI held that some of the questions asked by the Commission went further than permitted under the earlier ruling in *Orkem*. These were the request for a description of the object of the meetings and of decisions adopted during those meetings. They were not purely factual questions and effectively required Mannesmann to admit participation in a cartel. Case T-112/98 *Mannesmannröhren-Werke v EC Commission* [2001] ECR II–729 para 65. See PR Willis, 'You have the right to remain silent . . . or do you? The privilege against self incrimination following *Mannesmannröhren-Werke* and other recent decisions' [2001] ECLR 313–21; Case 374/87 *Orkem v EC Commission* [1989] ECR 3283 para 34, and Case 27/88 *Solvay & Cie v EC Commission* [1989] ECR 3355, summary publication and Case T-34/93 *Société Générale v EC Commission* [1995] ECR-II 545 para 74. See also Recital 23 of Reg 1/2003.

[29] Case C-67/91 *Dirección General de Defensa de la Competencia v Asociación Española de Banca Privada* [1992] ECR I-4785 paras 31–39. The Court stated that Reg 17 would not govern proceedings conducted by the NCAs which would be distinct from those conducted by the Commission. The gathering of evidence by those authorities would be in conformity with the provisions of national law, provided that Community law is complied with. Even in cases where Member States would apply substantive EC competition law, it would be incumbent upon the

principle of Community law is the unfettered evaluation of evidence and the sole criterion relevant in that evaluation is the reliability of the evidence.[30] The burden of proof[31] in infringement procedures falls on the Commission, which, although fulfilling a role different from that of a public prosecutor or investigating judge, who must present a preliminary indictment to a court, is required to prove its allegations against undertakings before making a finding against them. In the same way, undertakings claiming the benefit of Article 81(3) EC shall bear the burden of proving that the conditions of that paragraph are fulfilled.[32]

7.08 In proceedings before NCAs and the Commission, Article 2 of Regulation 1/2003 has codified the existing rules. Under Regulation 17, it was essentially for the Commission to decide whether there was a breach of Article 81(1) EC.[33] If the Commission found that there was an infringement, then the burden of proof shifted to the undertaking claiming the benefit of an exemption under

---

NCAs to implement it in accordance with national rules. The Court concluded that the probative value of the information and the conditions under which such information might be relied on against undertakings are confined exclusively to proceedings governed by Reg 17. While the purpose of the request for information is not to furnish evidence to be used by the Member States in proceedings governed by national law, the Member States would, however, not be required to ignore the information disclosed to them and thereby undergo some type of 'acute amnesia'. That information provides *circumstantial evidence* which might be taken into account to justify initiation of a national procedure. Regarding the use by the Commission of information provided by the national authorities, see Case C-60/92 *Otto v Postbank* [1993] ECR I-5683 para 20: '[. . .] Information obtained in the course of such national proceedings may indeed be brought to the attention of the Commission, in particular by an interested party. However, it follows from the Orkem judgment that the Commission—or for that matter a national authority—cannot use that information to establish an infringement of the competition rules in proceedings which may result in the imposition of penalties, or as evidence justifying the initiation of an investigation prior to such proceedings [. . .].'

[30] Opinion of Judge B Vesterdorf acting as AG in Case T-1/89 *Rhône-Poulenc v EC Commission* [1991] ECR II-867; see also, to that effect, Joined Cases C-310/98 and C-406/98 *Met-Trans and Sagpol* [2000] ECR I-1797 para 29, and Joined Cases T-141/99, T-142/99, T-150/99 and T151/99 *Vela and Tecnagrind v EC Commission* [2002] ECR II-4547 para 223. It may be necessary for the Commission to protect the anonymity of its informants (see, to that effect, Case T-50/00 *Dalmine v EC Commission* [2004] OJ C239/13 para 72; Case 145/83 *Stanley Adams v EC Commission* [1985] ECR 3539 para 34) but that fact alone would not require the Commission to set aside evidence in its possession. Thus, the anonymity of informants may be a factor in evaluating the reliability, but not the admissibility of the evidence.

[31] See Art 2(2) of Reg 1/2003. See also ch 4 'Organization of EC Commission proceedings' paras 4.20 *et seq.*

[32] On the one hand, there was the concern that NCAs or claimants using Art 81 EC as a sword in private litigation would have to shoulder the burden of proof as to the conditions of Art 81(3) EC not being fulfilled. WPJ Wils, 'Community Report' in *The Modernization of EU Competition Law Enforcement in the EU* [2004] FIDE National Reports 661–736 para 80.

[33] Under Reg 17, the NCAs have only rarely prosecuted infringements of Arts 81 or 82 EC. As regards the reasons, WPJ Wils, 'Community Report' in *The Modernization of EU Competition Law Enforcement in the EU* [2004] FIDE National Reports 661–736 para 45.

Article 81(3) EC.[34] As far as civil proceedings in national courts are concerned, the onus was on the party alleging an infringement of Article 81(1) EC to prove the facts supporting such a conclusion. The defendant in turn had to show either that it held or had applied for an individual exemption under Article 81(3) EC or that the agreement satisfied the requirements of a block exemption. This continues to be the case under Regulation 1/2003. According to Recital 5 of Regulation 1/2003, the application of Article 2 will not affect the obligation of a competition authority to ascertain the relevant facts of the case. The burden of proving an infringement of Articles 81(1) or 82 EC shall rest on the authority alleging the infringement. Undertakings have to show that Article 81(3) EC could reasonably apply. It is then for the Commission or the NCA to investigate whether the conditions of Article 81(3) EC are met.[35]

A good example of the probative force of documents and the assessment of evidence is the ECJ ruling in *Hüls* which concerned the Commission decision fining fifteen producers of polypropylene for infringing Article 81(1) EC. The only evidence put forward by the Commission to prove Hüls' participation in the meetings during the period in question and which had the purpose of fixing target prices and sale volumes was that adduced by one participant, Imperial Chemical Industries (ICI), in reply to a request for information.[36] While stating that the value of the evidence forms part of the assessment to be carried out by the CFI, the ECJ stated that given the nature of the infringements in question and the nature and degree of severity of the ensuing penalties, the principle of the presumption of innocence applies to the procedures relating to infringements of the competition rules applicable to undertakings that may result in the imposition of fines or periodic penalty payments. If there were a dispute as to the existence of an infringement of the competition rules, it is incumbent on the Commission to prove the infringements found by it and to adduce evidence capable of demonstrating to the requisite legal standard the existence of the

7.09

---

[34] Case T-67/01 *JCB Service v EC Commission* [2004] ECR II-49 para 162: '[. . .] It is incumbent on the applicant undertaking to submit all the evidence necessary to substantiate the economic justification for an exemption and to prove that it satisfies each of the four conditions laid down in Article 81(3) EC, which are cumulative [. . .] Similarly, it is for that undertaking to show that the restrictions of competition in question meet the objectives referred to by Article 81(3) EC and that those objectives could not be attained without the introduction of those restrictions [. . .]'.

[35] F Montag and A Rosenfeld, 'A solution to the Problem? Reg 1/2003 and the modernization of competition procedure' [2003] Zeitschrift für Wettbewerbsrecht 107–35 (120) who also discuss how the burden-of-proof rule applies to a situation in which the Commission is unable to reach a definitive conclusion on an infringement (non-liquet). See ch 4 'Organization of EC Commission proceedings' para 4.20.

[36] See Case T-9/89 *Hüls AG v EC Commission* [1992] ECR II-499 para 96; confirming Case C-199/92 P, *Hüls AG v EC Commission* [1999] ECR I-4287 paras 149–156. Other examples include, e.g. the Commission Decisions in the European '*Sugar Cartel Cases*': *European Sugar Industry* [1973] OJ L140/17; *Zinc Producer Group* [1984] OJ L220/27; *Polypropylene* [1986] OJ L230/1.

circumstances constituting an infringement. Since the Commission was able to establish that *Hüls* had participated in meetings between undertakings of a manifestly anti-competitive nature, it was for *Hüls* to put forward evidence to establish that its participation in those meetings was without any anti-competitive intention by demonstrating that it had indicated to its competitors that it was participating in those meetings in a spirit that was different from theirs.[37] As regards the proof of knowledge of the activities of a cartel as proof of participation in the infringement, it appears that provided that it is clear that the meetings attended or notes circulated were for the purposes of committing an infringement, a party's failure to distance itself from the activities in question may be accepted as a proof of its participation in the infringement.[38] In *German Banks*, the CFI questioned the probative value of documents on which the Commission based its case. The Court noted that the document on which the Commission relied to prove the existence of an agreement to use a percentage commission as the method for charging for the exchange of national currencies into euros could lend itself to other plausible interpretations in light of the evidence that the applicants adduced to call into question the validity of the conclusions drawn by the Commission. Another document also 'cast serious doubts or, indeed [. . .] contradict directly the Commission's interpretation.'[39]

7.10 While in most cases Commission decisions are based on documentary evidence,[40]

---

[37] See Case T-9/89 *Hüls AG v EC Commission* [1992] ECR II–499 paras 96, 126; see also Case T-348/94 *ENSO Española v EC Commission* [1998] ECR II-1875 paras 160 to 171 stating that the Commission must rely on actual proof and not just assertions of the content and object of the meetings which the parties to the alleged agreement supposedly attended.

[38] See CS Kerse and N Khan, *EC Antitrust Procedure* (5th edn, 2005) para 8–040 pointing to Case T-141/89 *Tréfileurope v EC Commission* [1995] ECR II-791 para 85 in which the applicant had chaired the meetings in question; in Case T-56/99 *Marlines v EC Commission* [2003] ECR II-5225 para 41 where the Court found that the applicant had received communications the content of which showed that their authors believed the applicant to be party to the agreement.

[39] Case T-56/02 *Bayrische Hypovereinsbank v EC Commission* [2004] OJ C314/13 paras 73 and 77. The Court concluded that the applicant succeeded in demonstrating that the Commission has not established to the requisite legal standard that there was an agreement on the way of charging for currency exchange services. It is to note that owing to a fax error the Commission had not submitted its defence in time. Without taking into account the Commission defence, the Court assessed the applicant's arguments against those in the Commission's decision, but without the Commission defence.

[40] 'Dealing with the Commission—Notification, complaints, inspections and fact-finding powers under Arts [81] and [82] of the EEC Treaty' (1997 edn) point 3.1. Undertakings should bear in mind that the Commission has found that an infringement committed by specified undertakings has been proved on the basis of documents and information found at the head-quarters of other undertakings. This may suggest in practice that the larger a cartel, the easier it is to prove its existence, and the greater the vulnerability of the infringing undertakings. See also JM Joshua, 'Oral Statements in EC competition proceedings: a due process short-cut?' [2004] Competition Law Insight, Issue 26, 1–7 (3) who maintains that no complex cartel could operate without the most detailed records being kept, if only to allow ringleaders to keep track of exactly

oral statements taken in the context of inspections may also have great probative value and may become more important. In the *Seamless Steel Tubes* cases, the Commission had relied heavily on the written statements made by an executive of Vallourec during the dawn raid in response to oral requests for explanations. On appeal, the CFI recognized that there were certain concerns relating to the corroborative effects of a few of the documents on the written statements, but the CFI accepted that his statement was intrinsically of particularly great probative value.[41]

4. Undertakings which may be investigated

It is not only undertakings which are parties to agreements or are involved in   **7.11**
conduct restrictive of competition that are subject to the Commission's investigative powers. As with Regulation 17, by referring to undertakings or associations of undertakings Regulation 1/2003 enables the Commission to request and obtain information from 'third-party undertakings'.[42] Thus, whenever necessary, the Commission is empowered to request information from customers, suppliers, competitors, distributors, or any other undertakings having any relationship with the undertakings involved.[43] Under Regulation 1/2003, the Commission is entitled to approach—otherwise than informally—individuals or bodies which are not 'undertakings' in the economic sense of the

what has been agreed and to be able to confront 'cheaters' at the next meeting. A Riley, 'Beyond Leniency: Enhancing Enforcement in EC Antitrust Law' [2005] World Competition 377–400 (386 n 68) who points out that documents are vital in antitrust cases. Undertakings would go to great lengths to ensure victims of the cartel and authorities do not obtain any evidence.

[41] In Case T-50/00 *Dalmine SpA v EC Commission* [2004] OJ 239/13 paras 342 *et seq*, the CFI considered that the answers given on behalf of the company carry more weight than those given in an individual capacity. In addition, the author was under a professional obligation to act in the interest of the company, he was a direct witness speaking from personal knowledge of the facts; the statements were made deliberately and after mature reflection, and he supplemented and confirmed the statement at a later stage in the investigation. See JM Joshua, 'Oral Statements in EC competition proceedings: a due process short-cut?' [2004] Competition Law Insight Issue 26, 1–7 (5–6) regrets however that interviews are not conducted by an independent examiner, but the case team and the absence of meaningful opportunity for cross-examination. Joshua argues that this kind of oral testimony should always be secondary to contemporaneous documentary evidence.

[42] See Art 18(4) of Reg 1/2003. The owners of the undertakings or their representatives and, in the case of legal persons, companies or firms, or associations having no legal personality, the persons authorised to represent them by law or by their constitution shall supply the information requested on behalf of the undertaking or the association of undertakings concerned. See e.g. *Austrian Banks* [2004] OJ L56/1 para 18; CS Kerse and N Khan, *Antitrust Competition Procedure* (5th edn, 2005) para 3–007 who raise the question whether and if so, to what extent 'secondary' sources such as lawyers, accountants, bankers which act for an undertaking may be obliged to supply information.

[43] The Commission Decision *Fides* [1979] OJ L57/33 is a good example of how third-party undertakings are also subject to the Commission's powers. Fides was a company entrusted with the management of a cartel in which it did not participate directly. In order to obtain information about the cartel, the Commission compelled Fides, by means of a decision, to submit to an inspection.

term. Article 18(4) of Regulation 1/2003 explains who should provide the information: an innovation is that authorized lawyers can supply information on behalf of a client, although the client remains responsible for incomplete, incorrect, or misleading information.[44]

7.12   Undertakings in EFTA-countries which are parties to the agreement on the 'European Economic Area (EEA)', are also subject to the Commission's investigative powers, albeit subject to certain conditions.[45] The ECJ has not been called upon to consider the extent to which the Commission may require information from or conduct investigations of undertakings that have no business establishment in any EU or EFTA States.[46] In relation to undertakings outside the EU and EFTA area, there would seem to be little objection to the Commission simply asking for information,[47] there being no compulsion to comply with such a request; in practice the Commission does send mere requests to non-EU undertakings.[48] The Commission could not require information under Article 18(3) of Regulation 1/2003.[49] By the same token, it is inconceivable that Article 20 entitles the Commission to carry out an investigation abroad, unless it has the authority of the State concerned. Thus, there is no 'enforceable' set of supranational rules for cooperation.[50] However, the fact that

---

[44] Lawyers duly authorized to act may supply the information on behalf of their clients. The latter shall remain fully responsible if the information supplied is incomplete, incorrect or misleading. Individuals normally enjoy more extensive defence rights, e.g. a right to remain silent compared to undertakings which may only refuse to answer questions which would lead them to admit that they have committed an infringement. This is so because individuals may be subject to criminal sanctions in Member States.

[45] Regarding the exercise of the investigative powers conferred by the competition provisions of the EEA Agreement, see Part V of this book.

[46] To avoid jurisdictional complications; the information request is normally served on a business establishment within the EU/EFTA, such as a sales office, branch, or subsidiary. If the firm has no office or subsidiary in an EU or EFTA State, the Commission writes directly to the head office of the foreign companies. See L Ritter and WD Braun, *European Competition Law: A Practitioner's Guide* (3rd edn, 2004) 1062–63.

[47] Art 18(2) of Reg 1/2003.

[48] *Seamless Tubes* [2003] OJ L140/1 in which a number of Japanese steel producers were accused of operating a market sharing cartel with European producers.

[49] See in relation to Reg 17 'Dealing with the Commission—Notification, complaints, inspections and fact-finding powers under Arts [81] and [82] of the EEC Treaty' (1997 edn) point 3.1.

[50] See OECD Recommendation Concerning Cooperation between Member Countries on Restrictive Business Practices Affecting International Trade, 27–28 July 1995, C(95)130 final. See also P Lowe, 'Enforcement Antitrust Roundtable' 32nd Annual International Antitrust Law & Policy Conference Fordham Corporate Law Institute, 22–23 September 2005 (forthcoming), who sees a need for enhanced international cooperation in the field of cartels (evidence gathering and evidence exchange). In this respect see the recent adoption by the OECD of 'Best Practices for the formal exchange of information between competition authorities in hard core cartel investigations' October 2005. C Canenbley and M Rosenthal, 'Cooperation between Antitrust Authorities In- and Outside the EU: What does it mean for Multinational Corporations?—Part 2' [2005] ECLR 178–87 (178) indicating there are currently more than forty-five bilateral cooperation agreements in force.

the Commission intends to investigate a trade association within the EC which represents non-EC undertakings does not entitle that association to refuse to submit to the investigation.[51] If the Commission carries out an investigation in a new Member State of the EC and discovers information relating to an infringement committed by undertakings prior to that State's accession to the Community, the Commission is entitled to take that information into account.[52]

Irrespective of the limited possibilities under Regulation 1/2003 of obtaining information from undertakings outside the EC jurisdiction, in recent years competition authorities have become increasingly aware that since national systems of competition law are not always adequate to deal with cartels and anti-competitive practices that cross national boundaries, international cooperation between them may increase the chances of achieving a successful solution. The recent establishment of the International Competition Network (ICN) bears testimony to these efforts. The ICN's work is complementary to that of UNCTAD, the OECD,[53] and the WTO and operates as an informal, virtual network that seeks to facilitate cooperation between competition authorities and to promote procedural and substantive convergence of competition laws.[54] As the ICN is a network of competition authorities it has no rule-making power but is limited to increasing convergence in the administrative practice of ICN members. **7.13**

International cooperation between competition authorities has also been advanced by the adoption of several bilateral agreements.[55] Most notably, US and EU antitrust enforcement authorities remain committed to cooperating in the detection and punishment of international cartel activities. Cooperation and **7.14**

---

[51] *Ukwal* [1992] OJ L121/45; R Whish, *Competition Law* (5th edn, 2003) 438.

[52] Cases 97–99/87 *Dow Chemical Ibérica SA v EC Commission* [1989] ECR 3165 paras 61–65.

[53] See the Commission Report on Competition Policy SEC (2005) 805 final paras 680–683.

[54] The ICN's website is a valuable source of material, including links to the sites of its member competition authorities. The ICN, established in October 2001, seeks by enhancing convergence and co-operation to promote more efficient, effective antitrust enforcement worldwide. Unlike the ECN, it is not a vehicle for exchanging detailed information on individual cases. The ICN Cartel Working Group is aimed at addressing the challenges of repression of cartels at national and international levels. It reviews the necessity and benefits of combating cartels with a view to reaching an international consensus on the justification for intervention in such cases. See Commission Report on Competition Policy SEC (2005) 805 final paras 666–670 and for more information in general http://www.internationalcompetitionnetwork. org/.

[55] See the list of bilateral agreements on the DG COMP website at http://europa.eu.int/ comm/competition/international/bilateral/bilateral.html. Report from the Commission on Competition Policy SEC (2005) 805 final paras 639 *et seq.* and the 2004 update on bilateral activities between DG COMP and antitrust authorities in United States, Canada, Japan, Australia, China, and Korea.

convergence in cartel enforcement provide powerful incentives for participants to avail themselves of effective leniency programmes and to expose illegal activity in all jurisdictions where they have exposure. The most profound boost to cooperation in cartel enforcement resulted from collaboration between US and EU officials on the convergence of the two jurisdictions' corporate amnesty programmes.[56] According to US antitrust officials, the Commission's revised programme 'has led to a surge in parallel amnesty applications to both the Commission and the Division.'[57] Similarly, the level of cooperation has risen as a result of the revised programme.

7.15 More specifically, the US and the Commission have entered into two agreements controlling cooperation on antitrust matters in which the governments' interests overlap. The first agreement, entered into in 1991, regarding the application of their competition laws demonstrates the effort being made to co-ordinate an international approach to competition policy.[58] The Commission and the Antitrust Division of the US Justice Department ('DoJ') will now notify each other whenever they become aware that their enforcement activities may affect important interests of the other, exchange information, and coordinate and cooperate in enforcement activities to the extent that their respective laws allow.[59] In particular, one agency may ask the other to take action in order to remedy anti-competitive behaviour in the former's territory.[60] This Agreement was complemented by the agreement on the application of positive comity

---

[56] Based in part on shared insights and experiences with US antitrust authorities in fighting the increasing 'internationalization' of cartel activity, the European Commission revised its leniency programme in 2002 to provide more transparency for applicants and less discretion for enforcers in administering the programme. The Commission's revised leniency programme now substantially mirrors the US Department of Justice corporate amnesty policy. See BMB Newman and M Delgado Echevarría, 'Gaps and Bridges: Transatlantic Cooperation' in *The European Antitrust Review 2005*, Global Competition Review 26–31 (26).

[57] R Hewitt Pate, 'Antitrust in a Transatlantic Context—from the Cicada's Perspective' address at the Antitrust in a Transatlantic Context Conference, 7 June 2004, cited by BMB Newman and M Delgado Echevarría, 'Gaps and Bridges: Transatlantic Cooperation' in *The European Antitrust Review 2005*, Global Competition Review 26–31 (29).

[58] The Agreement was approved on behalf of the EC by Decision 95/145/EC, ECSC, Decision of the Council and Commission of 10 April 1995 concerning the conclusion of the Agreement between the EC and the USA regarding the application of their competition laws [1995] OJ L95/45. The text of the Agreement is annexed to the Decision. The prototype to this agreement, (*published in Competition Law in the European Communities*, Vol 14, Issue 12, Dec 1991 312–18) was annulled by the Court in Case C-327/91 *France v EC Commission* [1994] ECR I-3641 after the French Government successfully challenged the legal basis on which the Commission had proceeded, since the Council of Ministers should have been involved in the adoption of the Agreement. The direct result of this judgment is the Council Decision cited above. The text is also accompanied by a letter with two interpretative statements, the first dealing with the type of information that may be exchanged under the Agreement, and the second confirming that the respective authorities should keep confidential any information received pursuant to the system.

[59] See Arts II–IV of the Agreement.   [60] See Art IV of the Agreement.

principles in the enforcement of competition laws in both jurisdictions, which develops further the principle of positive comity in Article V of the first agreement. The EU or US antitrust authorities may request the other competition authorities to investigate and, if warranted, to remedy anticompetitive activities in accordance with the requested party's competition laws.[61] The 1998 Agreement clarifies both the mechanics of the positive comity cooperation instrument, and the circumstances in which it can be availed of. In particular, it describes the conditions under which the requesting party should normally suspend its own enforcement actions and make a referral.[62] The timing of an investigation is increasingly being influenced by cooperation efforts between cartel agencies worldwide due to the growing number of cases with an international dimension. One example is the *Heat Stabilisers and Impact Modifiers* case, where in 2003 the Commission and the antitrust authorities in the US, Canada, and Japan closely coordinated their investigative actions and undertook near-simultaneous inspections or other investigative measures. Another example is the *Industrial Copper Tubes* case decided in December 2003, where much of the evidence on which the decision relied resulted from inspections that were coordinated with the US antitrust authorities.[63] Another example is the *Bulk Liquids Shipping* case, where the Commission, in a joint effort with the EFTA Surveillance Authority and the Norwegian authorities, undertook inspections simultaneously with the DoJ. In May 2004, the US and the EU made known their joint investigations of alleged price fixing among leading European paper and pulp manufacturers, which authorities in Europe based on the confession of a participant in the alleged cartel activities.

In spite of the remarkable level of coordination that antitrust authorities in the US and the EU have achieved in their cartel enforcement efforts, practical impediments to cooperation remain. Antitrust agencies are more limited in their willingness and ability to share information in this area than in the merger control context, due primarily to local laws prohibiting the sharing of information obtained in the course of investigations.[64] The US and the EU both

7.16

---

[61] Agreement between the European Communities and the Government of the United States of America on the application of positive comity principles in the enforcement of their competition laws, [1998] OJ L173/28; the first case to be initiated on the basis of positive comity was *Sabre*: see XXX Report on Competition Policy [2000] para 453.

[62] Agreement between the European Communities and the Government of the United States of America on the application of positive comity principles in the enforcement of their competition laws [1998] OJ L173/28.

[63] XXXIII Report on Competition Policy [2003] paras 32, 684; Commission Report on Competition Policy [2004] SEC (2005) 805 final paras 640, 646.

[64] The agencies strive to obtain waivers from private parties, but frequently are hindered by the spectre of exposure to private civil damages actions. Documents given by the applicant to the authorities have in some cases been used by claimants in private civil litigation before US or Member State courts, a fact that dissuades potential applicants from exposing illegal activity under

maintain policies of not disclosing an amnesty applicant's identity, or any information obtained from the applicant, to foreign authorities without the applicant's consent. Policy convergence has begun to break down these barriers as well, however, and information sharing to the extent that it is permitted happens routinely. The decentralization of EU competition law may be a new source of divergence in competition matters. Existing agreements between the US and each Member State will be of increasing importance, since the 1991 and 1998 agreements between the EU and the US are not binding on national jurisdictions.[65] In the absence of 'a second generation' cooperation agreement providing for the exchange of such information, the Commission and NCAs (if the latter have the authority to enter into such an agreement) cannot share information obtained, for example, through the questioning of an employee with non-EU antitrust authorities who could use it to prosecute antitrust violations outside the EU.[66] Article 28 of Regulation 1/2003 prevents the Commission and also the NCAs from disclosing confidential information obtained from companies during the course of their investigations outside the EU. Accordingly confidential information will not automatically find its way to third country authorities.[67]

5. Retroactivity of the Commission's investigative powers

7.17 In an action for the annulment of an investigation decision put into effect in Spain one year after accession, it was pleaded that Spanish undertakings could not be subjected to an investigation relating to action taken prior to accession, since at that time the undertakings in question were not subject to the Commission's powers. In other words, it was pleaded that the Commission's power could not be exercised retroactively.[68] The ECJ held, first, that since no

---

the leniency programmes. Philip Lowe, DG Comp Director, has pointed this out with respect to EU cases in 'What's the future for cartel enforcement', Brussels, 11 February 2003 cited in 'Cicada's Perspective' address at the Antitrust in a Transatlantic Context Conference, 7 June 2004, cited by BMB Newman and M Delgado Echevarría, 'Gaps and Bridges: Transatlantic Cooperation' in *The European Antitrust Review 2005*, Global Competition Review 26–31 (30); see also C Canenbley and M Rosenthal, 'Cooperation between Antitrust Authorities In- and Outside the EU: What does it mean for Multinational Corporations?—Part 2' [2005] ECLR 179–87 (178–79).

[65] BMB Newman and M Delgado Echevarría, 'Gaps and Bridges: Transatlantic Cooperation' in *The European Antitrust Review 2005*, Global Competition Review 26–31 (28).

[66] See JS Venit and T Louko, 'The Commission's New Power to Question and its Implications on Human Rights' ch 26 in BE Hawk (ed), Annual Proceedings of the Fordham Institute [2005] 675–700 (682).

[67] C Canenbley and M Rosenthal, 'Cooperation between Antitrust Authorities In- and Outside the EU: What does it mean for Multinational Corporations?—Part 2' [2005] ECLR 178–87 (179).

[68] See Joined Cases 97/87 to 99/87 *Dow Chemical Ibérica v EC Commission* [1989] ECR 3165 para 61.

derogation whatsoever to Regulation 17 was incorporated into the Act of Accession of Spain to the European Communities, undertakings established in Spain could be the subject of Commission investigations as from 1 January 1986. Secondly, it held that the subject matter of the investigations could only be limited by the scope of the Community competition rules. The Court concluded that, since there was no Community provision limiting the Commission's investigative powers to conduct occurring after accession, the applicants' argument that there was no retroactive effect had to be rejected.[69] The same applies to the ten new Member States which have recently joined the European Union, given that no restrictions in relation to the Commission's powers were established under Regulation 1/2003.[70]

6. The choice of investigative measures

Subject to the principle of proportionality—which, as already stated, often **7.18** operates in conjunction with the principle of administrative simplicity—the Commission may choose to send requests and undertake investigations, and is not bound to any particular chronological order. Thus, an investigation may precede a request for information, and vice versa, the information obtained at the first stage, whatever it might be, being used to clarify the information obtained at the next stage. In relation to Regulation 17, the ECJ made it clear that Articles 11 (requests for information) and 14 (inspections) provided for two entirely independent procedures.[71] The fact that an investigation under Article 14 had already taken place did not in any way diminish the Commission's powers to issue a request for information, so that it is entitled to request the disclosure of documents of which it was unable to take a copy or extract during an investigation at an earlier stage.[72] Under Regulation 1/2003, the Commission may also opt for a simple request or a request by decision, or for an (ordinary) investigation, to which the undertakings consent, or a compulsory investigation (by decision). The ECJ has held that in respect of investigations— and this very principle could extend to requests—the Commission's choice

---

[69] Joined Cases 97/87 to 99/87 *Dow Chemical Ibérica v EC Commission* [1989] ECR 3165 paras 62–63. Companies in countries seeking accession may infringe Community antitrust law prior to their accession to the Communities, for which reason it would seem logical for their earlier activities to be open to investigation and even the imposition of penalties, if the limitation period has not expired.

[70] Unlike the State aid sector which has been subject to a number of transitional arrangements, antitrust/abuse of dominance elements of EU competition law apply from 1 May 2004 and will be jointly implemented by NCAs and the European Commission.

[71] K Lenaerts and J Maselis, 'Procedural Rights and Issues in the Enforcement of Articles 81 and 82 of the EC Treaty' [2001] Fordham International Law Journal 1615–54 (1616–20) with references to the Courts' case law.

[72] Case 374/87 *Orkem v EC Commission* [1989] ECR 3283 para 14 and Case 27/88 *Solvay v EC Commission* [1989] ECR 3355 para 11.

between an investigation by straightforward authorisation and an investigation ordered by a decision does not depend on matters such as the particular seriousness of the situation, extreme urgency or the need for absolute discretion, but rather on the need for an appropriate inquiry, having regard to the special features of the case. In particular, the Court has concluded in that regard that, where an investigation decision is solely intended to enable the Commission to gather the information needed to assess whether the competition rules have been infringed, such a decision is not contrary to the principle of proportionality.[73]

7. Cooperation with Member States' authorities

7.19 Article 20(5) of Regulation 1/2003 provides that NCA officials must actively assist the Commission's officials with their inspections at the request of the Commission. Where an undertaking refuses to submit to an inspection, Article 20(6) requires the Member State concerned to afford the Commission the necessary assistance to enable the inspections to take place: this may require the involvement of the police or an equivalent enforcement authority. Article 20(7) states that if judicial authorization is required, for example, to obtain entry to premises, this must be applied for. Article 20(8) gives expression to the ECJ's judgment in *Roquette Frères* and sets out the role of the judicial authority in circumstances where it is asked, for example, to issue a warrant ordering entry into premises.[74] The national court should ensure that the Commission's decision is authentic and that the coercive measures sought are neither arbitrary nor excessive; for this purpose, the court may address questions to the Commission. However the court may not call into question the necessity for the inspection, nor require that it be provided with all the information in the Commission's file.[75]

7.20 As regards inspections, if these are carried out by NCAs under Article 22(2) of Regulation 1/2003, there is full interaction between the Commission and the

---

[73] Case C-94/00 *Roquette Frères* [2002] ECR I-9011 para 77; Case 136/79 *National Panasonic v EC Commission* [1980] ECR 2033 paras 28–30.

[74] Case C-94/00 *Roquette Frères* [2002] ECR I-9011 paras 36–47.

[75] Roquette submitted that the court might refuse to make an order authorizing entry and seizure where no information or evidence has been put before it. The ECJ stated that for the purposes of enabling the competent national court to satisfy itself that the coercive measures sought are not arbitrary, the Commission is required to provide that court with explanations showing, in a properly substantiated manner, that the Commission is in possession of information and evidence providing reasonable grounds for suspecting an infringement of the competition rules by the undertaking concerned. On the other hand, the competent national court may not demand that it be provided with the information and evidence in the Commission's file on which the latter's suspicions are based. Case C-94/00 *Roquette Frères* [2002] ECR I-9011 paras 61–62. Joined Cases 46/87 and 227/88 *Hoechst AG v EC Commission* [1989] ECR 2859 para 35. See ch 8 'Inspections' paras 8.62 *et seq.*

national authority. If carried out by the Commission, it must inform the NCAs '[i]n good time before the inspection' (Article 20(3)). Further, it must specify the subject matter and purpose of the investigation, although a change from Regulation 17 is that it no longer has to give the identity of the authorized officials (see last sentence of Article 14(2) of Regulation 17), and it must also consult the NCAs before adopting a decision to investigate (Article 20(4)). The Commission may also request the NCAs' assistance for the actual investigation (Article 20(5)) and where undertakings refuse to submit to an investigation (Article 20(6)).

B. Requests for Information

1. Introduction

Pursuant to Article 18 of Regulation 1/2003, the Commission may request **7.21** undertakings or associations of undertakings to provide it with all information it deems necessary. Undertakings are required to provide the Commission with all the information specified in the request, being therefore compelled to hand over existing documents or to provide answers to questions within the time limit fixed.[76] This power may be seen as a specific example of its general investigative power—including 'checks'—conferred on the Commission by Article 284 EC. Written requests for information constitute the method most commonly used by the Commission in its investigations, and the number of such requests far exceeds the number of inspections. Requests for information—as stated above—may be made at any stage of proceedings, from the opening of the file until delivery of the decision, and even afterwards. Thus, the Commission has a discretion whether it is necessary to employ them.[77] It is not unusual for one and the same undertaking to receive several requests in the course of the same procedure. The term 'information' must be interpreted as including specific documents, so that the Commission may request such business records[78] as it considers appropriate, by means of a written request.

---

[76] Art 18(6) of Reg 1/2003, like Art 11 of Reg 17, also includes the possibility of obtaining information from the governments and competent authorities of the Member States. Under Reg 17, the vast majority of requests for information were sent to undertakings, Art 12 of Reg 1/2003 also provides for the possibility of exchanging information between the Commission and the NCAs and the NCAs among themselves.

[77] Case 27/88 *Solvay v EC Commission* [1989] ECR 3355 paras 12–13; Case 374/87 *Orkem v EC Commission* [1989] ECR 3283 paras 15–16; Joined Cases 46/87 and 227/88 *Hoechst AG v EC Commission* [1989] ECR 2859 para 25; L Ritter, WD Braun, *European Competition Law: A Practitioner's Guide* (3rd edn, 2004) 1063.

[78] See below ch 9 'Penalties, Confidentiality' paras 9.23 *et seq.* regarding the term 'business records'.

7.22 The power to obtain information has been strengthened in comparison with the power as it existed under Regulation 17.[79] Article 11 of Regulation 17 laid down a procedure for requests for information comprising of two successive phases which the Commission had to follow. In the first phase, the Commission had to send an ordinary request for information to the undertakings. Only if a complete reply had not been given by the undertakings within the time limit prescribed for that purpose might the Commission proceed to the second phase and sent a request for information by binding decision. This could give rise to pecuniary penalties if the undertakings refused to reply a second time.[80] Under Regulation 1/2003, the Commission has a choice: the Commission may decide to issue either a simple request or it may proceed immediately to a decision requiring that information be provided. Having regard to the Commission's traditional practice, the Commission is expected to start by issuing a request addressed to the undertakings, unless it has any reasons to believe that they will be uncooperative. If the Commission issues a simple request, undertakings are not compelled to respond, as they incur no penalization if they decide not to surrender the information required, except that they may be deemed uncooperative by the Commission. However, the provision of misleading information may lead to the imposition of a fine of up to 1 per cent of the undertaking's turnover in the previous year, pursuant to Article 23(1)(a) of Regulation1/2003.[81]

7.23 Under Article 3 of Regulation 1,[82] undertakings are entitled to receive requests for information in the official Community language or languages[83] of the country in which they are situated. However, as a matter of practice, the Commission sometimes writes its requests in English or another widely used language in order to deal with them more swiftly. If the undertaking(s) accept(s)

---

[79] A Riley, 'EC Antitrust Modernisation: The Commission Does Very Nicely—Thank You! Part One: Reg 1 and the Notification Burden' [2003] ECLR 604 (608).

[80] See Case 136/79 *National Panasonic v EC Commission* [1980] ECR 2033 para 10. This was repeatedly confirmed, in Case T-39/90 *Samenwerkende Elektriciteits-produktiebedrijven (SEP) v EC Commission* [1991] ECR II-1497 para 26; in Case T-46/92 *The Scottish Football Association v EC Commission* [1994] ECR II-1039 para 30; and in Case T-34/93 *Société Générale v EC Commission* [1995] ECR-II 545 para 38.

[81] Regarding the possibility of imposing fines in these situations, see ch 9 'Penalties, Confidentiality' paras 9.03 *et seq.*

[82] Council Reg 1 of 25 April 1958 determining the languages to be used by the EEC ([1952–58] OJ Spec Ed 59), last modified by Annex II, ch 22, para 1, of the Accession Act [2003] OJ L236/791. Art 3 of Reg 1 provides: 'Documents which an institution of the Community sends to a Member State or to a person subject to the jurisdiction of a Member State shall be drafted in the language of such State'. Neither the EC Treaty nor Reg 1/2003 contains any express provisions determining the languages to be used by the Commission or by the NCAs.

[83] Regarding official languages, see above, ch 4 'The Organization of EC Commission Proceedings' paras 4.15 *et seq.*

this correspondence, the Commission will continue addressing them in this language. The companies may either reply in English or whichever language the request is written in, or in their own language. On the other hand, at the request of undertakings, the Commission may agree to send requests and other correspondence in a Community language other than that of the place where the undertaking is established.[84] Requests for information are made in writing and are sent to the undertakings by registered letter with a form for acknowledgement of receipt. It is also possible, in urgent cases, to send them by telex, fax, e-mail, or any other means, provided that the Commission is able to satisfy itself, on a basis that cannot be challenged, that the undertakings receive the request on a particular date. Even then, the Commission always sends the original request by registered post at the same time. The period within which a reply must be given starts to run from the day following the date of receipt. In order to avoid argument as to whether a means of transmission such as fax provides conclusive evidence of receipt of a letter, the Commission usually calculates its time-limits by reference to the date on the acknowledgement of receipt returned by the postal authorities, even where it has sent the letter first by fax. Requests for information are always sent to undertakings as such, and not personally to their directors, managers, or representatives. Nor are they sent to lawyers acting for them, unless they are authorized to provide the information on behalf of their clients.[85]

As regards the type of information which the Commisison may demand from an **7.24** undertaking, the Community Courts have upheld the Commission's prerogatives as to the appropriateness and content of its requests for information in most cases—*inter alia* in its judgments in the *Orkem, Solvay,* and *SEP* cases.[86] The Commission is well-advised to ensure that its questions are as precise as possible, in order to enable undertakings to reply to them clearly and completely. Despite the latitude which it enjoys in asking questions, the Commission is required scrupulously to observe undertakings' defence rights when formulating them. It may not frame its questions in such a manner that an undertaking cannot reply without admitting that it has infringed the competition rules or pursued objectives which would in themselves be regarded as

---

[84] An example might be an undertaking with a US parent company whose branch in the EC is located in Germany. A US undertaking might prefer to receive correspondence in English and would make a request to the Commission to that effect; the Commission would, in general, agree.

[85] In contrast to Art 11 of Reg 17, note that Art 18(4) of Reg 1/2003 expressly refers to this possibility.

[86] Case 374/87 *Orkem v EC Commission* [1989] ECR 3283 paras 14–17; Case 27/88 *Solvay v EC Commission* [1989] ECR 3355 para 8 and Case T-39/90 *Samenverkende Elektriciteits-produktiebedrijven (SEP) v EC Commission* [1991] ECR II-1497, paras 25–28.

constituting an infringement.[87] It is incumbent upon the Commission to prove the infringement by reconstructing the facts. The Commission is not authorized to ask undertakings simply to admit guilt—if it did so, the relevant question or questions in its request would be void.[88] Purely factual questions cannot be regarded as capable of requiring the applicant to admit the existence of an infringement of the competition rules. The Commission approach was best illustrated in *Orkem* and later in *Mannesmannröhren*. In *Orkem*, the applicant was an undertaking that challenged a request for information made pursuant to Article 11 of Regulation17. The undertaking contended that a series of questions asked by the Commission infringed 'the general principle that no one may be compelled to give evidence against himself'. The Court concluded that the principles laid down in *Orkem* protected undertakings against self-incrimination to the extent that replying would result in an actual admission of guilt.[89] It considered that the following questions were not permitted:[90]

- Questions relating to the purpose of the action taken and the objectives pursued.
- A request for clarification on every step or concerted measure which may have been envisaged or adopted to support the price initiatives.
- A request for details of any system or method which made it possible to attribute sales targets or quotas to the participants.
- A request for details of any method facilitating annual monitoring of compliance with any system of targets in terms of volume or quotas.

These questions related to the purpose and objective of the measures or were aimed at obtaining from the undertakings an acknowledgement of their

---

[87] However, the fact that an undertaking is not entitled to base a refusal to reply on the grounds that the objective information or documents requested by the Commission could be used as evidence against it, is far from being unproblematic. By contrast with the position under criminal law in the Member States, Community competition law provides no protection against self-incrimination in this respect. The right not to give evidence against oneself or to confess guilt relates only to persons accused of a criminal offence in court proceedings and thus has no bearings on proceedings against firms. Under EC law, unlike e.g. German antitrust laws (see s 59(5) of the German Act Against Restrictions of Competition), only firms (not their individual executives or officials) are liable to penalties for antitrust infringements.

[88] In its judgments in Case 374/87 *Orkem v EC Commission* [1989] ECR 3283 and Case 27/88 *Solvay v EC Commission* [1989] ECR 3355, the Court annulled certain questions put by the Commission to these two undertakings on the ground that they required them to admit an infringement of former Art 85 [now 81] of the EC Treaty. The Commission had thereby infringed their defence rights and disregarded the rules concerning burden of proof (paras 41 and 37 respectively). Regarding the interpretation of the *Orkem* judgment and its inapplicability to civil proceedings on the basis of Arts 81 and 82 EC, see Case C-60/92 *Otto v Postbank* [1993] ECR I-5683, paras 11 *et seq*.

[89] See also Case T-34/93 *Société Générale v EC Commission* [1995] ECR II-545 para 75.

[90] PR Willis, 'You have the right to remain silent? The privilege against self-incrimination following Mannesmannröhren-Werke and other recent decisions' [2001] ECLR 313 (317).

involvement in what was referred to as a market-sharing arrangement. Yet, it may require the parties to provide information concerning, for example, the dates of certain meetings, the persons who attended these meetings, the capacity in which the participants attended, the subjects discussed during the meetings.[91]

In *PVC II*, the CFI found that the questions contained in the decisions requiring information and which were challenged by the applicants were identical to those annulled by the ECJ in *Orkem* and that they were therefore unlawful.[92] The CFI added, however, that simple requests for information did not contain any element of compulsion (in contrast to a request for information by means of a binding decision) and therefore could not warrant a claim of the privilege against self-incrimination.[93] In *Mannesmannröhren*, the CFI held that some of the questions asked by the Commission went further than permitted under *Orkem*.[94] These were requests for a description of the object of the meetings and of decisions adopted during those meetings, where Mannesmann was unable to

7.25

---

[91] K Lenaerts and J Maselis, 'Procedural Rights and Issues in the Enforcement of Articles 81 and 82 of the EC Treaty' [2001] Fordham International Law Journal 1615–54 (1622) with references to the Courts' case law.

[92] However, the CFI indicated that the undertakings had either refused to answer those questions or denied the facts on which they were being questioned, which meant that the illegality of the questions could not affect the legality of the decision by which the Commission had fined them. Joined Cases T-305/94 to T-307/94, T-313/94 to T-316/94, T-318/94, T-325/94, T-328/94, T-329/94 and T-335/94 *Limburgse Vinyl Maatschappij and others v EC Commission* [1999] ECR II-931 paras 439–453.

[93] On appeal, the ECJ considered that the CFI had correctly drawn the distinction between a mere simple request for information, which left the undertaking the possibility to reply and a decision requiring information with the possibility of imposing a penalty in the event of a refusal to reply. In this case, the Commission established that the investigation took place on the basis of an authorization in the sense of Art 14(2) of Reg 17, which is a measure that does not permit recourse to coercive action in the event of a refusal of an undertaking to submit to such an investigation. Thus, the privilege against self-incrimination depends on an element of compulsion. The ECJ thus dismissed the allegation of an infringement of the privilege against self-incrimination. Joined Cases C-238/99 P, C-244/99 P, C-245/99 P, C-247/99 P, C-250/99 P to C-252/99 P and C-254/99 P *Limburgse Vinyl Maatschappij and others v EC Commission* [2002] ECR I-8375 paras 236–344.

[94] In *Mannesmannröhren*, the applicant submitted that based on the ECtHR ruling in *Funke* the scope of privilege against self-incrimination as laid down by the ECJ in *Orkem* had to be broadened. The CFI recalled that it had no jurisdiction to apply the ECHR when reviewing an investigation under competition law. The CFI took the view that the privilege against self-incrimination was not absolute; as such a solution 'would go beyond what is necessary in order to preserve the rights of defence of undertakings, and would constitute an unjustified hindrance to the Commission's performance of its duty'. As a consequence, an undertaking in receipt of a request for information pursuant to Art 11(5) of Reg 17 [Art 18(3) of Reg 1/2003] could be recognized as having a right to silence 'only to the extent that it would be compelled to provide answers which might involve an admission on its part of the existence of an infringement which it is incumbent upon the Commission to prove'. Case T-112/98 *Mannesmannröhren-Werke v EC Commission* [2001] ECR II-729 paras 60, 66, and 67. See for more details on the influence of the ECtHR case law, ch 4 paras 4.36 *et seq.* 'The compatibility of the EC competition procedure with the ECHR'.

provide written evidence such as minutes. They were not purely factual questions, and effectively required this company to admit participation in a cartel. Similarly, the Commission's request for a description of the relationship between a series of agreements and the decisions adopted at the various meetings went further than the merely factual, and required an analysis of the nature of the agreements and therefore contravened the *Orkem* principles.[95]

7.26 It is interesting to note that the Commission always allows undertakings to supply unsolicited information or documents which they consider to be important to the investigation of the case, which they may use in their defence at a later stage. Further, where the Commission has received a formal complaint, the sending of a request for information may be an opportunity to ask the undertakings for their views on the action attributed to them by the complainants.[96] Such views are not covered by the rules in Article 18 of Regulation 1/2003, which means that the Commission cannot insist on receiving them, and therefore can only set recommended time limits. Undertakings give their views on complaints forwarded to them only if they wish to do so.

2. Simple requests

7.27 Simple requests for information usually incorporate two distinct parts. First, an accompanying letter which contains the necessary formal and substantive clarifications to enable the undertakings to reply to the request. Secondly, as an attached annex to the letter, a questionnaire specifying in detail the information and documents requested. A request for information must be regarded as comprising all the documents sent to undertakings under Article 18 of Regulation 1/2003, not merely the questions contained in the questionnaire. The ECJ's case law has established that the Commission must specify 'with reasonable precision' the suspected infringement of Articles 81 or 82 EC[97] when sending

---

[95] Joined Cases T-236/01, T-239/01, T-244/01 to T-462/01, T-251/01 and T-252/01 *Tokai Carbon and others v EC Commission* [2004] ECR II-1181. On appeal, Case C-301/04 P *EC Commission v SGL Carbon AG*, pending application [2004] OJ C262/13. In regard to the appeal filed by SGL, WPJ Wils, 'Powers of Investigation and Procedural rights and Guarantees in EU Antitrust Enforcement', First Lisbon Conference on Competition Law and Economics, Belém 3–4 November 2005, para 60 takes the view that if the Community Courts were come to the view that fundamental rights of defence would require a broader right not to give evidence against oneself than recognized under *Orkem*, the fact that Recital 23 of Reg 1/2003 reflects the current case law should not prevent the Community Courts from reaching such conclusion. In the hierarchy of norms general principles of Community law would take precedence over legislative acts and it would be the Courts task to find and, interpret and apply these principles. As regards the problem of self-incrimination, see para 7.49 below.

[96] See ch 5 'Opening of the file' paras 5.15 *et seq.* and generally, ch 12 'Rejection of complaints'.

[97] See Opinion of AG Jacobs in Case C-36/92 P *SEP v EC Commission* [1994] ECR I-1911 para 30; endorsed by Case C-36/92 P *SEP v EC Commission* [1994] ECR I-1932 para 21. CS Kerse and N Khan, *Antitrust Competition Procedure* (5th edn, 2005) para 3–011.

the request. In *Société Générale*, the ECJ held that in order to show that it acted within the limits of its powers under both Article 11 and Article 14 of Regulation 17, the Commission had to demonstrate that it was entitled to require the disclosure of information which might enable it to investigate putative infringements which justify the conduct of the enquiry and are set out in the request for information.[98] The Commission must therefore reasonably suppose that the information requested would help it to determine whether the alleged infringement had taken place. While the Commission must clearly indicate the alleged facts which it intends to investigate, it is not obliged to disclose all the facts known. It must give a concise indication of the suspected infringement of the competition rules and of how the firm concerned is believed to be involved although it does not need to recite at length the facts and grounds for infringement.[99] Article 18 of Regulation 1/2003 has codified these requirements and states that in simple requests, the Commission is obliged to indicate:

- the legal basis of the request;
- the purpose of the request, being a brief description of the type of activity investigated, allegedly constituting an infringement of the competition rules;[100]
- specification of the information to be provided;
- time-limit within which the information is to be provided.[101]
- the penalties for providing incorrect information. The provision of misleading information may lead to the imposition of a fine of up to 1 per cent of the undertaking's turnover in the previous year, pursuant to Article 23(1)(a) of Regulation 1/2003. This provision is usually reproduced on the reverse of the first page of the accompanying letter.

---

[98] Case T-34/93 *Société Générale v EC Commission* [1995] ECR-II 545 para 40 (as regards requests for information).

[99] Joined Cases 46/87 and 227/88 *Hoechst AG v EC Commission* [1989] ECR 2859 paras 39–43; Case 136/79 *National Panasonic v EC Commission* [1980] ECR 2033 paras 24–27; Case 85/87 *Dow Benelux v EC Commission* [1989] ECR 3137 paras 6–11; CS Kerse and N Khan, *Antitrust Competition Procedure* (5th edn, 2005) para 3–011.

[100] The description of the subject-matter of the investigation does not constitute a statement of objections (see ch 10 'Infringement procedures' paras 10.12 *et seq.*). As the Court has held: 'By disclosing its suspicion of the existence of agreements contrary to Article 85(1) of the Treaty [81(1) EC], the Commission merely complied with the obligations imposed on it by Article 11(3) to state the purpose of its request'—see Case 374/87 *Orkem v EC Commission* [1989] ECR 3283 para 11 and Case 27/88 *Solvay v EC Commission* [1989] ECR 3355 para 8.

[101] Art 11(3) of Reg 17 did not refer to a time-limit for a reply. It may be several days or weeks as from receipt, or a date may be specified. The Commission sets the time limit for answers at its own discretion, according to the complexity of the questions. The most usual time-limits are between two and four weeks. If the time is insufficient to prepare a proper answer, this should be explained to the Commisison. Reasonable requests for extra-time are usually granted. See CS Kerse and N Khan, *Antitrust Competition Procedure* (5th edn, 2005) para 3–011. Regarding the set-up of time-limits in Community law, see ch 4 'Organization of EC Commission proceedings' para 4.15.

7.28 In addition to the above, ordinary requests for information always contain a statement that both the questions and the replies are covered by professional secrecy under Article 28 of Regulation 1/2003. In view of the fact that, notwithstanding that general protection, the Commission is under an obligation to disclose the file to specified third parties, mainly the complainants, who may be customers or competitors of the undertaking responding to a request,[102] the Commission asks the undertakings, when replying, clearly to identify what they regard as constituting business secrets which must not be disclosed to third parties or published.[103] The Commission also usually indicates in the last paragraph of the accompanying letter the name and telephone number of the investigating official, case handler, or rapporteur so that the undertakings may contact him or her if they have any doubts about the content of the request or the procedure to be followed in answering the questions. The undertakings may contact him or her for advice of any kind concerning their cases. The official concerned will endeavour to communicate with them in a language which they both understand or, if necessary, will seek the assistance of an official who speaks the language of the undertaking's representative.

7.29 Article 18 of Regulation 1/2003 empowers the Commission not only to request explanations, figures, or statistical tables, but also to request specific documents in the possession of undertakings, containing information needed for the purposes of the investigation. For example, the Commission, having notice of the existence of an allegedly restrictive agreement, quite frequently asks the parties to it to provide a copy. The Commission enjoys considerable discretion in determining what information is necessary for its inquiries. The information demanded need not be confined to the firm's own business, but may extend to questions about the background of the industry and the market as far as the requested information is available to, or can be estimated by, the addressee.[104] The Court merely exercises a limited review in that regard. The meaning of 'necessary information' was considered by the Court in *SEP*.[105] The CFI stated that the term 'necessary information' must be interpreted by reference to the purposes for which the powers of investigation in question were conferred upon the Commission. The requirement for a correlation between the request for information and the presumed infringement is met if, at this stage of the procedure, the request can be legitimately considered to be related to the presumed infringement. The ECJ upheld this interpretation. Although it is not easy,

---

[102] See ch 9 'Penalties and confidentiality' paras 9.27 *et seq.*

[103] Regarding the difference between professional secrecy and business secrets, see ch 9 'Penalties and confidentiality' paras 9.24 *et seq.*

[104] L Ritter and WD Braun, *European Competition Law: A Practitioner's Guide* (3rd edn, 2004) 1063.

[105] Case T-39/90 *SEP v EC Commission* [1991] ECR II-1497.

therefore, to show that the information requested is outside the leeway allowed to the Commission, it does mean that the Commission cannot go on a complete 'fishing expedition' and that the Court would be prepared to hold in an appropriate case that it had exceeded its powers.[106]

The Commission may request information from undertakings not directly **7.30** involved either in the proceedings or in the infringements under investigation. The Commission may indeed approach third-party undertakings or associations of undertakings if they possess information needed for the investigation.[107] It may also approach any undertaking directly or indirectly affected by the agreements or conduct under investigation. The Commission must observe the generally applicable rules in such cases and give reasons for its request, indicating its legal basis and purpose. The undertakings concerned will also be informed that the procedure is not directed against them (for the time being, at least). However, it does not appear that, in principle, the Commission is required to reveal the identity of the undertakings allegedly involved in the infringement under investigation, above all in the initial phase of the investigation, when discretion is more important. The ECJ indicated that the information obtained under Article 11 of Regulation 17 might not be used for purposes other than that for which it was requested and requires both the Commission and the competent authorities of the Member States and their officials and other servants to observe professional secrecy.[108] Defence rights, which must be respected in the preliminary investigation procedure, require, on the one hand, that, when the request for information is made, undertakings be informed, in accordance with Article 11(3) of Regulation 17 (now Article 18(3) of Regulation 1/2003), of the purposes pursued by the Commission and of the legal basis of the request and, on the other, that the information thus obtained should not subsequently be

---

[106] B Sufrin and L Jones, *EC Competition Law* (2nd edn, 2004) 1061; see also Case 155/79 *AM&S Ltd v EC Commission* [1982] ECR 1575 paras 14–16; Case 374/87 *Orkem v EC Commission* [1989] ECR 3283 para 15.

[107] In *Fides* [1979] OJ L57/33 the Commission compelled a management company to produce documentation regarding various undertakings for which it worked. The inspection in that case was carried out pursuant to a decision, but the principle also applies to requests for information.

[108] Case C-67/91 *Dirección General de Defensa de la Competencia v Asociación Española de Banca Privada ('Spanish Banks')* [1992] ECR I-4785 para 34: '[. . .] The information thus obtained by the Commission is transmitted to the competent authorities of the Member States, on the basis of Article 10(1) of Reg No 17, in order to meet two concerns. One is the concern to inform Member States of Community proceedings relating to undertakings situated within their territories and the other is to enhance the provision of information to the Commission by enabling it to compare the particulars given by the undertakings with such indications and observations as may be made to it by the Member State concerned. The mere disclosure of such information to the Member States does not, of itself, mean that they may use it under conditions which would undermine the application of Reg No 17 and the fundamental rights of undertakings [. . .]'.

used outside the legal context in which the request was made.[109] That information provides circumstantial evidence which may, if necessary, be taken into account to justify initiation of a national procedure.[110] As has been seen,[111] the Commission may send requests for information to undertakings established in non-Community countries, although its powers are limited in such cases. In general, the Commission will only send requests for information outside the Community where an undertaking whose principal office is in a non-member country has no subsidiaries or branches within EU territory.[112] In such cases, the Commission usually writes directly to the head of the foreign company and may choose to send a formal request for information under Article 18 or to send an unofficial request for information in which reference will not be made to either Article 18 or to the penalties provided for in Article 23(1)(a) of Regulation 1/2003.[113] As regards the European Economic Area (EEA), the procedural rules applicable to competition cases enable the Commission to send requests for information to undertakings in the territory of the EFTA (except Switzerland) under conditions very similar to those applicable to companies in the Community. If an agreement exists with other non-Community competition

---

[109] Recital 16 of Reg 1/2003.

[110] Case C-67/91 *Dirección General de Defensa de la Competencia v Asociación Española de Banca Privada ('Spanish Banks')*, [1992] ECR I-4785 para 39: '[. . .] The Member States are not required to ignore the information disclosed to them and thereby undergo to echo the expression used by the Commission and the national court "acute amnesia". That information provides circumstantial evidence which may, if necessary, be taken into account to justify initiation of a national procedure [. . .]'. Note that under Art 12 of the Reg 1/2003, the information may be used only 'for the purposes of applying Arts 81 and 82 of the Treaty', although it may also be used to apply national competition laws 'in the same case and in parallel' to EC rules. The expression 'in the same case and in parallel' in Art 12 should restrict the recipient authorities' powers to the cumulative application governed by Art 3(1) of the Regulation. There is no scope for the use of the information exchanged in the application of 'stricter national laws which prohibit or sanction unilateral conduct' under the second paragraph of the same provision nor to cases where competition authorities apply 'merger control laws' or 'provisions of national law that predominantly pursue an objective different from that pursued by Arts 81 and 82 of the Treaty' under the third paragraph of Art 3. For any such situations, the recipient NCA will remain bound by the 'acute amnesia' rule in *Spanish Banks*. M Araujo, 'The Respect of Fundamental Rights within the European Network of Competition Authorities', ch 21 in BE Hawk (ed), *International Antitrust Law and Policy*, Annual Proceedings of the Fordham Institute [2005] 511–30 (527).

[111] See above 'Undertakings which may be investigated' paras 7.11 *et seq.*

[112] It will either send the request to the business establishment alone, or to it and the registered office of the foreign company. Service of procedural documents such as statements of objections and decisions has been judged by the ECJ to have been properly effected both when it was made through branches or subsidiaries in the EC (Case 48/69 *ICI v EC Commission* [1972] ECR 619 paras 34–44. See L Ritter and WD Braun, *European Competition Law: A Practitioner's Guide* (3rd edn, 2004) 1063, n 252.

[113] In accordance with *OECD Council Recommendation Concerning Cooperation between Member Countries on Restrictive Practices Affecting International Trade*, 27–28 July 1995 C (95) 130/final, the government of the foreign company's country and those of other non-EC countries affected would be informed. See L Ritter and WD Braun, *European Competition Law: A Practitioner's Guide* (3rd edn, 2004) 1063.

authorities,[114] or there is an arrangement concerning the application of competition rules, the Commission will inform the authorities in the non-member country of the despatch of the request for information.[115]

It is important to note that with respect to a simple request, the Commission 7.31
cannot insist that an undertaking replies to the questions. If, however, undertakings do give answers, they must be correct. Otherwise the Commission may very well impose fines.[116] The fact that ultimately the Commission can demand the information by adopting a decision under Article 18(3) may be an incentive to comply with a simple request. The ruling in *Scottish Football Association* demonstrates how undertakings served with a request are expected to co-operate if the Commission is not to proceed to a decision. In that case, the Commission had received a complaint from the European Sports Network that the Scottish Football Association (SFA) was intending to prevent it from broadcasting Argentinean football matches in Scotland. The Commission asked the SFA certain specific questions about its correspondence with the Argentinean FA and communications with FIFA. The SFA wrote back expressing 'some surprise' at the letter, explaining in general terms its policy about broadcasts, and saying it was 'happy to meet you at any time to explain our views'. The Court did not think that this amounted to the required 'active co-operation' and considered that SFA's comment 'we honestly think that as to the Argentinian matter, the Commission need not be troubled about an exchange of correspondence between two fraternal associations' 'a polite but explicit refusal' to co-operate with the Commission in the matter.[117]

When undertakings do not reply to an initial request or reply incompletely or 7.32

---

[114] This might occur, for example, with the US under Art III of the Agreement between the US and the European Commission regarding the application of their competition laws, see para 7.11 above ('Undertakings which may be investigated'). This Article provides, *inter alia*, for the exchange of information between the Justice Department and the Commission, meetings at least twice a year and the establishment of a mutual request procedure on enforcement activities.

[115] This would be the case with OECD countries. See, e.g. *OECD Council Recommendation concerning Cooperation between Member Countries on Anticompetitive Practices affecting International Trade*, 27 July 1995—C(95)130/final and Recommendation of the Council concerning Effective Action Against Hard Core Cartels 25 March 1998—C(98)35/final. The non-EU members of the OECD are Australia, Canada, US, Iceland, Japan, New Zealand, Norway, Switzerland, Turkey, and South Korea.

[116] For an example of the supply of incorrect information: *Comptoir commercial d'importation* [1982] OJ L27/31, at II. It follows, therefore, that for the purposes of Art 15(1)(b) of Reg 17 (and it can be assumed, for the purposes of Art 23(1)(a) of Reg 1/2003), a response to a request for information must be taken to include not only the answers to the actual questions asked by the Commission, but also to information supplied which goes beyond the particular scope of those questions, as well as information supplied by the undertaking on its own initiative which does not directly relate to any specific question asked by the Commission.

[117] Example mentioned by A Jones and B Sufrin, *EC Competition Law* (2nd edn, 2004) 1061. Case T-46/92 *The Scottish Football Association v EC Commission* [1994] ECR II-1039.

incorrectly, the Commission may, on expiry of the time-limit, send an administrative letter containing a formal reminder before requesting the information by binding decision. In it the Commission reminds the undertakings of its earlier communication and grants them an additional period (which is shorter and ends on a specified date) for them to reply to the request for information. Whenever requested to do so by the undertakings, provided sound reasons are given, the Commission willingly grants a reasonable extension to the time-limit for replying. It is important to note that at this first stage the Commission cannot impose a penalty for total failure to reply or partial failure (incomplete answers). In both cases, the Commission has no alternative but to request the information not supplied, wholly or in part, by means of a binding decision. Lack of co-operation from undertakings may be conducive to an increase of such fines as may be imposed.[118]

3. Requests for information by means of a binding decision

7.33   As seen, the Commission has a choice: it can issue a simple request for information or it can proceed by decision to demand the information. Requests by means of a decision differ from simple requests in that the addressee is compelled to respond. In case the Commission requests the information by decision, fines may be imposed either if the information provided is intentionally or negligently incorrect, incomplete, or misleading, or if the information is not provided within the time limit set by the Commission.[119] The Commission is also entitled to impose periodic penalty payments which may amount up to 5 per cent of the undertaking's average daily turnover in the preceding year, in order to compel it to supply the information requested by decision in a complete and correct manner.[120] Accordingly, where the Commission requires undertakings and associations of undertakings to supply information by

---

[118] Certainly the opposite is true. In the Commission Decision in the *Cartonboard* cartel [1994] OJ L243/1, early cooperation with the Commission led to fines being substantially reduced for certain participating undertakings. See Press Release IP/94/642 of 13 July 1994 'The Commission condemns a cartel of European Cartonboard Producers and imposes substantial fines'. T-48/02 *Brouwerij Haacht NV v EC Commission*, CFI judgment of 6 December 2005 (not yet published), para 106: '[. . .] an undertaking's cooperation in the investigation does not entitle it to a reduction in its fine where that cooperation did not go further than that which it was required to provide under Article 11(4) and (5) of Regulation No 17 [Art 18(2) and (3) of Reg 1/2003]. On the other hand, where an undertaking, in response to a request for information under Article 11 [18 of Reg 1/2003], supplies information going much further than that which the Commission may require under that article, the undertakings in question may receive a reduction in its fine. [. . .]'. See also ch 9 'Penalties, Confidentiality' paras 9.03 *et seq.*

[119] Art 23(1)(b) of Reg 1/2003.

[120] Codification of the Community Courts case law in Case 374/87 *Orkem v EC Commission* [1989] ECR 3283 and Case T-112/98 *Mannesmannröhren-Werke AG v EC Commission* [2001] ECR II-729.

decisions, it must state the legal basis and the purpose of the request, specify what information is required and fix the time-limit within which it is to be provided. In addition, the Commission must also indicate the penalties which may be imposed under Article 24 should the undertaking in question fail to comply with the decision. In addition, the Commission must indicate the right to have the decision reviewed by the ECJ. Decisions of this kind are adopted by the Commissioner responsible for competition matters, who is authorized for that purpose by the Commission. They do not need to be published or reported on by the Advisory Committee, even where they give notice of a periodic penalty payment.[121] In all cases, the national authorities in the Member State in whose territory the undertaking is located will receive a copy of the decision.

C. The Reply

In its requests for information, the Commission lays down a time limit within **7.34** which a reply must be given. Under Regulation 17, in order for the second phase to be initiated, that is to say for a request for information of the second type (by decision) to be sent, the undertakings concerned ought to have failed to reply, or replied incompletely, 'within the time-limit fixed by the Commission'. However, Article 18(2) of Regulation 1/2003 simply provides that the Commission must 'fix the time-limit within which the information is to be provided' but no longer makes reference to the two-stage-procedure required previously under Article 11 of Regulation 17. Regulation 1/2003 does not determine what constitutes an appropriate or reasonable time-limit, or even a minimum time limit for replies. Once again, the Commission enjoys discretion but must ensure that the rights of undertakings are not undermined by excessively short time-limits. The most common time-limits imposed are between three weeks and two months, but they may be shorter or longer. The period decided on by the Commission will depend on the circumstances of the case. The circumstances of the undertakings and the quantity and complexity of the information requested are among the factors to be taken into account. Despite its efforts to allow an adequate time-limit, the Commission may not be aware of all the circumstances which sometimes complicate the task of seeking and compiling information in specific undertakings, or the time required in each case. For that reason—as already stated—the Commission usually agrees to extend the period for replying

---

[121] In such circumstances, this will be the first phase of the imposition of a periodic penalty payment. Only in the second phase, when the final amount of the penalty is fixed, will the Advisory Committee have to be consulted. See ch 3 above paras 3.45 *et seq.* ('The role and the functioning of the Advisory Committee on Restrictive Practices and Monopolies'.)

if undertakings submit a reasoned request in writing before the expiry of the first time-limit notified to them.

1. Persons authorized to supply information

7.35   According to Article 18(4) of Regulation 1/2003, the owners of the undertakings or their representatives and, in the case of legal persons, companies or firms or associations having no legal personality, the persons authorized to represent them by law or by their constitution, are to supply the information requested. The aim of this provision is to ensure that replies to requests are made by persons with sufficient seniority to reply on undertakings' behalf. This guarantees that the replies legally bind the undertakings and, as a practical matter, that those replying enjoy access to sources of information within the undertaking under investigation. However, it is not necessary for the executives or directors of undertakings to sign replies to requests. It is sufficient for replies to be signed by someone who is entitled to act on behalf of the undertaking, giving proof to that effect.[122] Regardless of who is instructed to sign, undertakings will be responsible for the content of the replies and will be liable to the prescribed penalties if incorrect information is provided and not the individuals concerned.[123] This means that even where executives or directors are unaware of the content of the replies, the latter will be binding on the undertakings if another authorized person within the undertaking has replied on its behalf.

7.36   Given that in practice the management of undertakings usually entrusts the drafting of replies to in-house lawyers or independent law firms, or both, within their respective areas of responsibility, Article 18(4) has provided for the possibility that lawyers duly authorized may supply the information of their clients. Nevertheless, the undertakings remain fully responsible if the information is incomplete, incorrect, or misleading. Where the information is correct, complete and in time but is provided by a person who is not authorized to do so, the information is considered as having been provided by the undertaking. No liability to penalty under Article 23 of Regulation 1/2003 would arise and the person who is competent for the purposes of Article 18(4) could simply ratify the acts of the individual who supplied the information.[124]

---

[122] Sometimes, when the reply is signed by a person whose level of responsibility in the undertaking is unknown, the Commission makes a written request for confirmation that the person concerned had authority to provide a reply.

[123] CS Kerse and N Khan, *Antitrust Competition Procedure* (5th edn, 2005) para 3–008.

[124] Ibid.

2. Content of the replies

It is not for undertakings to judge whether or not a request for information or **7.37** documents is justified or whether the details of an infringement have been correctly established by the Commission.[125] At this stage, undertakings should merely give their replies, since they will be entitled subsequently, in the observations phase, to put forward arguments on those points and on any other matters.[126] When replies are given to requests for information, it is important to bear in mind that the Commission may request the documents in which the requisite information is contained, whether they be agreements, balance-sheets, statistical tables or any other kind of document. Undertakings may not decline to supply them on the pretext that they are confidential,[127] because Article 28 of Regulation 1/2003 guarantees confidential treatment of the information obtained during investigations.[128]

The Commission may sometimes request information or documents not in the **7.38** possession of the undertakings or not immediately available to them or available in a form other than that requested by the Commission. If what is requested is absolutely unavailable to them and they have no way of obtaining it, their reply to the Commission must say so. If the information is not immediately available and the time limit allowed is insufficient for them to obtain it, undertakings must, before the expiry of the time-limit, write to the Commission requesting an extension. If they have information similar to, but not exactly the same as, the information requested, the undertakings should make direct contact with the official in DG COMP responsible for the conduct of the case and ask him whether it would be possible to substitute the information available for that requested. This may facilitate the preparation of their reply and they may

---

[125] *Fédération Chaussure de France* [1983] OJ L319/12.

[126] In the case of a decision requesting information, undertakings could, however, endeavour not to reply by applying to the CFI for interim measures under Arts 242 and 243 of the Treaty, with a view to having the Court suspend the operation of the Commission Decision.

[127] *Fédération Chaussure de France* [1983] OJ L319/12.

[128] Even where the production of documents is prohibited and gives rise to penalties imposed by non-Community authorities (for example, the Swiss legislation which gave rise to Case 145/83 *Stanley Adams v EC Commission* [1985] ECR 3539), it seems unlikely that the Commission (with the support of the Court) would agree not to use this investigative measure. This is because limitations on the use of documents and the principle of professional secrecy guarantee to undertakings (except where there are errors, as in the *Adams* case) that the information supplied to the Commission will remain confidential. In other words where the information is supplied on a voluntary basis and accompanied by a request for confidentiality to protect anonymity and if the Commission accepts such request, it is bound to comply with such a condition. See CS Kerse and N Khan, *Antitrust Competition Procedure* (5th edn, 2005) para 2–071. The European system is considered more rigorous regarding the production of documents than systems in other countries, such as the US, which allows undertakings to invoke the fact that third countries prohibit, and impose penalties for, the production of documents in order to resist requests for information from the US authorities.

also receive more favourable treatment in the event of fines being imposed for substantive infringements if the Commission takes into account their cooperation in the investigation.[129]

7.39   It is advisable for undertakings to examine the Commission's requests for information in their entirety, and provide such information as may help to clarify the facts to which the investigation relates, even if such information is not directly requested from them by the Commission. The Commission, in turn, assesses and evaluates the replies from undertakings in their entirety. It does not confine itself to the literal terms of the replies to the specific questions contained in the questionnaire forming part of the request for information. It also takes account of any information which goes further than the specific terms of the questions and any information given by undertakings on a voluntary basis, even though it may not relate directly to the headings in the questionnaire.[130] The provision of complete and detailed information on a voluntary basis may not only obviate recourse by the Commission to more coercive methods of investigation (for example, surprise inspections pursuant to decisions), but may also— as just indicated—be taken into account by the Commission so as to reduce a possible fine for infringement of Articles 81 and 82 EC.

7.40   Articles 23(1) and 24(1) of Regulation 1/2003 restore the deterrent power of the Commission's procedural system of fines. This may well encourage the Commission to make greater use of its new power to issue Article 18(3) decisions requiring information to be provided. Where it knows that the information is available, an Article 18(3) decision backed up by significant financial consequences may well save the Commission the time and resources of organizing an inspection under Article 20. The Commission can also impose more than one obligation on an undertaking and attach a periodic penalty to each obligation.[131] In *Commercial Solvents*, the Commission imposed two obligations on Commercial Solvents and its subsidiaries, first to resupply the alleged victim of the supposed abusive practices, and secondly to submit within two months proposals for continued supplies to the alleged victim. In each case, the

---

[129] For the calculation of fines and 'mitigating' circumstances, see ch 11 'Infringement decisions and penalties' para 11.35.

[130] In practice, the questionnaires may contain an invitation to undertakings to provide any other unsolicited information which they consider relevant. However, this information shall not mislead the Commission (see Art 23(1)(a) of Reg 1/2003) in an attempt to divert it from its enquiry. The inclusion of information intended to set the Commission on a false trail may attract a fine. CS Kerse and N Khan, *Antitrust Competition Procedure* (5th edn, 2005) para 3–012.

[131] A Riley, 'EC Antitrust Modernisation: The Commission Does Very Nicely—Thank You! Part One: Reg 1 and the Notification Burden' [2003] ECLR 604–15 (609).

Commission imposed a periodic penalty payment of one thousand euros per day. The ECJ upheld this practice, albeit *sub silentio*.[132]

3. The problem of self-incrimination[133]

According to the case law of the Community Courts,[134] during the preliminary **7.41** investigation procedure Community law incorporates certain specific guarantees which must be observed by the Commission. However, as with Regulation 17, Regulation 1/2003 does not grant an undertaking subject to investigation any express right to refuse to comply with a measure on the grounds that it might thereby provide evidence of its participation in an infringement of Community competition rules. Regulation 1/2003 contains a 'catch-all' Recital 37, which states that it 'respects the fundamental rights and observes the principles recognised in particular by the Charter of Fundamental Rights of the European Union. Accordingly, this Regulation should be interpreted and applied with respect to those rights and principles.' Additionally, Recital 23 codifies the principles defined in *Mannesmannröhren-Werke*, stating that an undertaking cannot be forced to admit that it has committed an infringement. However, this right has to be contrasted with the obligation to cooperate actively, i.e. to answer factual questions and to provide documents, even if this information could be used to establish the existence of an infringement.[135]

In the absence of a 'right of silence' expressly enshrined in Regulation 17, the **7.42** Community courts have gone a long way to considering to what extent general principles of law, including fundamental rights which must underlie the interpretation of Community law, imply recognition of an undertaking's right not to provide information that might be used to incriminate it.[136] The applicant in *Orkem* was an undertaking that challenged a request for information made pursuant to Article [18] of Regulation [1/2003]. The undertaking asserted that several questions asked by the Commission infringed 'the general principle that

---

[132] Joined Cases 6/73 and 7/73 *Istituto Chemioterapico Italiano S.p.A. and Commercial Solvents Corporation v EC Commission* [1974] ECR 223.

[133] See in relation to the problem in the context of Reg 1/2003, WPJ Wils, 'Self-Incrimination in EC Antitrust Enforcement, A Legal and Economic Analysis', [1994] World Competition, 567–88 (574); Judge B Vesterdorf, 'Legal Professional Privilege and the Privilege against self-incrimination in EC Law: Recent developments and Current Issues' ch 27 in BE Hawk (ed), *International Antitrust Law & Policy*, Annual Proceedings of the Fordham Institute [2004] 701–30 (709–18).

[134] See Case 374/87 *Orkem v EC Commission* [1989] ECR 3283 and Case 27/88 *Solvay v EC Commission* [1989] ECR 3355 paras 26–41 and 23–37 respectively.

[135] See above paras 7.31 *et seq.*

[136] See also ch 4 'Organization of EC Commission proceedings' para 4.36.

no one may be compelled to give evidence against himself'.[137] In response, the ECJ noted that, in general, the laws of the Member States afforded the right not to give evidence against oneself only to a *natural person* charged with an offence *in criminal proceedings*. By contrast, there was no principle common to the laws of the Member States which allowed *legal entities* to claim a right against self-incrimination in the context of alleged infringements *in the economic sphere*.[138] Further, the ECJ considered that, although Article 6 ECHR may be invoked by an undertaking subject to an investigation relating to competition law, neither the wording of that provision nor the decisions of the ECtHR indicated that it upheld the right not to give evidence against oneself.[139] Accordingly, the ECJ ruled that none of the legal bases relied upon by the applicant was appropriate for the right invoked, examining further whether certain limitations on the Commission's powers of investigation were 'implied by the need to safeguard the rights of the defence which the [ECJ] has held to be a fundamental principle of the Community legal order'.[140] In that regard, the ECJ found that the Commission was entitled to compel an undertaking to provide all necessary information concerning such *facts* as may be known to it and to disclose to the Commission, if necessary, such *documents* relating thereto as are in its possession, even if the latter may be used to establish the existence of anti-competitive conduct.

7.43 The ECJ also took the view that the Commission may not, by means of a decision calling for information, undermine the defence rights of the undertaking concerned.[141] The ECJ further stated that 'the Commission may not compel an undertaking to provide it with answers which might involve an admission on its part of the existence of an infringement which it is incumbent upon the Commission to prove'.[142] Accordingly, the principles laid down in *Orkem* protected undertakings against self-incrimination only to the extent that replying to questions would result in an actual recognition.[143] The scope of the principle was further delimited three years later in *Otto*, a case in which the ECJ ruled that

---

[137] The applicant submitted that the principle was supported by three different legal bases: (i) the laws of the Member States; (ii) the ECHR, and (iii) the International Covenant on Civil and Political Rights of 19 December 1966 (the 'International Covenant'). The ECJ considered that the right not to give evidence against oneself or to confess guilt upheld by Art 14(3)(g) of the International Covenant related only to persons accused of a criminal offence in court proceedings and thus had no bearing on investigations in the field of competition law. Case 374/87 *Orkem v EC Commission* [1989] ECR 3283 para 31 (see also opinion of AG Darmon, in the same case, para 127).

[138] Case 374/87 *Orkem v EC Commission* [1989] ECR 3283 para 29 (see also opinion of AG Darmon in the same case, paras 98–121).

[139] Case 374/87 *Orkem v EC Commission* [1989] ECR 3283 para 30.

[140] Case 374/87 *Orkem v EC Commission* [1989] ECR 3283 paras 32–33.

[141] Case 374/87 *Orkem v EC Commission* [1989] ECR 3283 para 34.

[142] Case 374/87 *Orkem v EC Commission* [1989] ECR 3283 para 35.

[143] See also Case T-34/93 *Société Générale v EC Commission* [1995] ECR II-545 para 75.

the privilege against self-incrimination could not be claimed in the context of national civil proceedings applying Articles 81 EC and 82 EC before a court on the grounds that civil proceedings cannot lead, directly or indirectly, to the imposition of a penalty by a public authority.[144] In *Mannesmannröhren-Werke*, however, the CFI begun to take a more critical stance on this issue.[145] In this case, the applicant submitted, *inter alia*, that based on the ECtHR ruling in *Funke* the scope of the privilege against self-incrimination as laid down by the ECJ in *Orkem* had to be widened. The CFI recalled that it had no jurisdiction to apply the ECHR when reviewing an investigation under competition law, because the ECHR as such is not part of EC law.[146] However, the Court went on to reiterate its previous findings that first the Community Courts would draw inspiration from the constitutional traditions common to the Member States and from the guidelines supplied by international treaties for the protection of human rights on which the Member States have collaborated and to which they are signatories; and secondly, it highlighted the special significance of the ECHR in that respect.[147] The CFI considered that the privilege against self-incrimination was not absolute, because such a solution 'would go beyond what is necessary in order to preserve the rights of defence of undertakings, and would constitute an unjustified hindrance to the Commission's performance of its duty'.[148] As a result, an undertaking in receipt of a request for information pursuant to a binding decision could be granted a right to silence 'only to the

---

[144] Case C-60/92 *Otto v Postbank* [1993] ECR I-5683. In this case, Postbank contended in its defence that, in so far as the Dutch procedural rules compelled it to produce the information requested, they were incompatible with Community law. The question was where the *Orkem* principles applied, by virtue of Community law, as part of the rights of the defence, in national civil proceedings. It stated at paras 15–17 that '[. . .] The guarantees necessary to ensure respect for the right of the defence of an individual in the course of an administrative procedure such as that at issue in the *Orkem* case are different from those which are necessary to safeguard the rights of the defence of a party involved in civil proceedings. Where, as in the main proceedings, a procedure is involved which concerns exclusively private relations between individuals and cannot lead directly or indirectly to the imposition of a penalty by a public authority, Community law does not require a party to be granted the right not to give answers which might entail admission of the existence of an infringement of the competition rules. That guarantee is essentially intended to protect an individual against measures of investigation ordered by public authorities to obtain his admission of the existence of conduct laying him open to administrative or criminal penalties. It follows that the limitation on the Commission's power of investigation under Reg No 17 with regard to an undertaking's obligation to reply to questions, which the Court deduced from the principle of respect for the rights of the defence in the *Orkem* case, cannot be transposed to national civil proceedings involving the application of Art 85 and 86 of the Treaty which exclusively concern private relations between individuals, since such proceedings cannot lead, directly or indirectly, to the imposition of a penalty by a public authority [. . .]'.
[145] Case T-112/98 *Mannesmannröhren-Werke v EC Commission* [2001] ECR II-729.
[146] Case T-112/98 *Mannesmannröhren-Werke v EC Commission* [2001] ECR II-729 paras 59 and 75, citing Case T-347/94 *Mayr-Melnhof v EC Commission* [1998] ECR II-1751 para 311.
[147] Case T-112/98 *Mannesmannröhren-Werke v EC Commission* [2001] ECR II-729 para 60.
[148] Case T-112/98 *Mannesmannröhren-Werke v EC Commission* [2001] ECR II-729 para 66.

extent that it would be compelled to provide answers which might involve an admission on its part of the existence of an infringement which it is incumbent upon the Commission to prove'.[149] In this regard, *Mannesmannröhren-Werke* builds on the ruling in *Orkem*.[150]

7.44 In the *PVC II* appeal, the ECJ explained very clearly that it was ready to assess the privilege against self-incrimination based on the ECtHR case law.[151] In the case before the CFI,[152] the applicants had submitted that the Commission should not have used allegedly incriminating answers given by *any* of the undertakings fined by the Commission (and not only their own answers) under *any* legal basis (i.e. either under Article [18(1)] or under Article [18(3)] of Regulation [1/2003].[153] The CFI found that the questions contained in the decisions requiring information and which were challenged by the applicants were identical to those annulled by the ECJ in *Orkem* and that they were therefore unlawful.[154] Yet, the CFI also indicated out that the undertakings had either refused to answer those questions or denied the facts on which they were being questioned, which meant that the illegality of the questions could not affect the legality of the decision by which the Commission had fined them.[155] As indicated, the

---

[149] Case T-112/98 *Mannesmannröhren-Werke v EC Commission* [2001] ECR II-729 para 67.

[150] Judge Bo Vesterdorf has indicated that *Mannesmannröhren-Werke* could be interpreted as a signal to the effect that the Community Courts' interpretations of certain rights in competition proceedings did not have to coincide exactly with those of the ECtHR when the latter deals with criminal procedures involving natural persons, although noting that more recently the Community Courts have made an effort to make these interpretations converge. Judge B Vesterdorf, 'Legal Professional Privilege and the Privilege against self-incrimination in EC Law: Recent developments and Current Issues' ch 27 in BE Hawk (ed), Annual Proceedings of the Fordham Institute [2005] 701–30 (713–14).

[151] Joined Cases C-238/99 P, C-244/99 P, C-245/99 P, C-247/99 P, C-250/99 P to C-252/99 P and C-254/99 P *Limburgse Vinyl Maatschappij and others v EC Commission* [2002] ECR I-8375.

[152] Joined Cases T-305/94 to T-307/94, T-313/94 to T-316/94, T-318/94, T-325/94, T-328/94, T-329/94 and T-335/94 *Limburgse Vinyl Maatschappij and others v EC Commission* [1999] ECR II-931.

[153] LVM (Limburgse Vinyl Maatschappij) and DSM (DSM NV and DSM Kunststoffen BV) contended that Art 6 ECHR, as interpreted by the ECtHR (relying on *Funke* and *Saunders*), laid down a right to remain silent and in no way to contribute to one's own incrimination, without any distinction being made according to the type of information requested (including documentary forms). Joined Cases T-305/94 to T-307/94, T-313/94 to T-316/94, T-318/94, T-325/94, T-328/94, T-329/94 and T-335/94 *Limburgse Vinyl Maatschappij and others v EC Commission* [1999] ECR II-931 para 429.

[154] Joined Cases T-305/94 to T-307/94, T-313/94 to T-316/94, T-318/94, T-325/94, T-328/94, T-329/94 and T-335/94 *Limburgse Vinyl Maatschappij and others v EC Commission* [1999] ECR II-931 para 451.

[155] Joined Cases T-305/94 to T-307/94, T-313/94 to T-316/94, T-318/94, T-325/94, T-328/94, T-329/94 and T-335/94 *Limburgse Vinyl Maatschappij and others v EC Commission* [1999] ECR II-931 paras 452–453; Judge B Vesterdorf, 'Legal Professional Privilege and the Privilege against self-incrimination in EC Law: Recent developments and Current Issues' ch 27 in BE Hawk (ed), *International Antitrust Law & Policy*, Annual Proceedings of the Fordham Institute [2004] 701–730 (714).

CFI added that simple requests for information did not contain any element of compulsion and therefore could not warrant a claim of the privilege against self-incrimination.[156]

On appeal, the ECJ first noted that the CFI had not followed one of the **7.45** findings of the *Orkem* judgment, namely that neither the wording of Article 6 ECHR nor the decisions of the ECtHR indicate that that Article recognizes any privilege against self-incrimination.[157] On the other hand, however, the CFI had upheld other principles laid down in *Orkem*.[158] Having summarized the main findings of the CFI, the ECJ found that there had been further developments in the case-law of the ECtHR since *Orkem* 'which the Community judicature must take into account when interpreting the fundamental rights'.[159] However, the ECJ concluded that both the *Orkem* judgment and the recent case law of the ECtHR would require, first, the exercise of coercion against the suspect in order to obtain information from him and, second, 'establishment of the existence of an actual interference with the right which they define'.[160] Having defined these two conditions, the ECJ considered that, examined in light of that finding

---

[156] Joined Cases T-305/94 to T-307/94, T-313/94 to T-316/94, T-318/94, T-325/94, T-328/94, T-329/94 and T-335/94 *Limburgse Vinyl Maatschappij and others v EC Commission* [1999] ECR II-931 paras 455–457. See also Joined Cases T-25/95, T-26/95, T-30/95 to T-39/95, T-42/95 to T-46/95, T-48/95, T-50/95 to T-65/95, T-68/95 to T-71/95, T-87/95, T-88/95, T-103/95 and T-104/95 *Cimenteries CBR SA and others v EC Commission* [2000] ECR II-491 para 731–736 where the CFI pointed out that the parties are free to decide whether or not to reply to such request for information. In addition, only the undertakings that have given the relevant answers have grounds, if at all, for claiming that during the course of the administrative procedure have infringed the right not to give evidence against themselves. See also K Lenaerts and J Maselis, 'Procedural Rights and Issues in the Enforcement of Articles 81 and 82 of the EC Treaty' [2001] Fordham International Law Journal 1615–54 (1621). *Austrian Banks* ([2004] OJ L56/1 paras 485 *et seq.* and paras 544 *et seq.*) discusses extensively whether companies which give more than they have to in response to requests for information should receive cooperation credit for so doing. The Commission considered that the banks were required to give the material facts of their involvement in meetings, and existing documents (the Commission stated that here it relied entirely on pre-existing documents). The banks argued that insofar as this involves direct admissions they do not have to answer such request and if they do, it is a voluntary act deserving reduction in fine. See also J Ratliff, 'Major Events and Policy Issues in EC Competition Law, 2003–2004 (Part 2)' [2005] ICCLR 109–28 (112–13).

[157] Joined Cases T-305/94 to T-307/94, T-313/94 to T-316/94, T-318/94, T-325/94, T-328/94, T-329/94 and T-335/94 *Limburgse Vinyl Maatschappij and others v EC Commission* [1999] ECR II-931 para 271.

[158] Joined Cases T-305/94 to T-307/94, T-313/94 to T-316/94, T-318/94, T-325/94, T-328/94, T-329/94 and T-335/94 *Limburgse Vinyl Maatschappij and others v EC Commission* [1999] ECR II-931 para 272 referring to the principles set out at paras 27, 28, and 32 to 35 of *Orkem*.

[159] Joined Cases T-305/94 to T-307/94, T-313/94 to T-316/94, T-318/94, T-325/94, T-328/94, T-329/94, and T-335/94 *Limburgse Vinyl Maatschappij and others v EC Commission* [1999] ECR II-931 para 274.

[160] Joined Cases T-305/94 to T-307/94, T-313/94 to T-316/94, T-318/94, T-325/94, T-328/94, T-329/94, and T-335/94 *Limburgse Vinyl Maatschappij and others v EC Commission* [1999] ECR II-931 para 275.

and the specific circumstances of the case, the ground of appeal raised by the applicants did not permit annulment of the contested judgment on the basis of the developments in the case law of the ECtHR. The ECJ first considered that the CFI had correctly drawn the appropriate distinction between (i) a simple request for information, which left the undertaking the possibility not to reply; and (ii) a decision requiring information, which additionally subjected an undertaking to a penalty in the event of a refusal to reply: only the latter exerts actual compulsion on the recipient undertaking.[161] Second, as regards requests pursuant to a binding decision, for which an element of compulsion exists, the ECJ observed that the applicants did not indicate any aspects of those answers which were *in fact* used to incriminate them or the addressees of the requests. The ECJ therefore concluded that it was to rule on the question of whether the CFI had erred in law in holding, by reference to the *Orkem* judgment, that such decisions are illegal only in so far as a question obliges an undertaking to supply answers leading it to admit that there has been an infringement.

7.46   The Community courts in *PVC II* broke new ground by expressly making the privilege against self-incrimination dependent on an element of compulsion or coercion.[162] Furthermore, the ECJ very clearly emphasized the relevance of the case law of the ECtHR for the purpose of interpreting fundamental rights. As Judge Vesterdorf noted, this stance contrasts with previous statements to the effect that the interpretations of fundamental rights by the Community Courts did not have to coincide exactly with those of the ECtHR.[163] Later in *Tokai*

---

[161] Joined Cases T-305/94 to T-307/94, T-313/94 to T-316/94, T-318/94, T-325/94, T-328/94, T-329/94, and T-335/94 *Limburgse Vinyl Maatschappij and others v EC Commission* [1999] ECR II-931 para 279.

[162] Voluntary statements given under Art 19 and arguably statements given to the Commission under Art 20(2)(e) of Reg 1/2003 are made free of state coercion. Thus, it would seem that no privilege could be asserted by the individual or legal entity concerned. K Dekeyser and C Gauer, 'The New Enforcement System for Arts 81 & 82 and the Rights of Defence', ch 23 in BE Hawk (ed), Annual Proceedings of the Fordham Institute [2005] 549–85 (562) submit that the reasoning behind the right to silence in the ECHR case law is to protect the accused against improper psychological or even physical pressure of the authorities and to avoid miscarriages of justice. This would not apply to undertakings.

[163] See, e.g. opinion of AG Darmon in Case 374/87 *Orkem v EC Commission*, [1989] ECR 3283 paras 139–140 ('the existence in Community law of fundamental rights drawn from the [ECHR] does not derive from the wholly straightforward application of that instrument as interpreted by the Strasbourg authorities. [. . .] This Court may [. . .] adopt, with respect to provisions of the [ECHR], an interpretation which does not coincide exactly with that given by the Strasbourg authorities, in particular the [ECtHR]. It is not bound, in so far as it does not have systematically to take into account, as regards fundamental rights under Community law, the interpretation of the Convention given by the Strasbourg authorities.'). Judge B Vesterdorf, 'Legal Professional Privilege and the Privilege against self-incrimination in EC Law: Recent developments and Current Issues' ch 27 in BE Hawk (ed), *International Antitrust Law & Policy*, Annual Proceedings of the Fordham Institute (2004) 701–30 (716).

Carbon,[164] the CFI confirmed its previous finding in *Mannesmannröhren-Werke* that '[a] right to silence can be recognised only to the extent that the undertaking concerned would be compelled to provide answers which might involve an admission on its part of the existence of an infringement which it is incumbent upon the Commission to prove'.[165] The CFI also reiterated its previous finding that the Commission 'is entitled to compel the undertakings to provide all necessary information concerning such facts as may be known to them and to disclose to the Commission, if necessary, such documents relating thereto as are in their possession, even if the latter may be used to establish the existence of anti-competitive conduct'.[166] Further, the CFI considered that this power did not fall foul of either Article 6(1) and (2) ECHR or the case law of the ECtHR, noting that in *PVC II* the Court had not reversed its previous case law in spite of *Funke* and *Saunders*.[167]

---

[164] Joined Cases T-236/01, T-239/01, T-244/01 to T-246/01, T-251/01 and T-252/01, *Tokai Carbon and others v EC Commission* [2004] OJ C251/13. The question of the privilege against self-incrimination came up in the specific context of the assessment of the reduction of the fine from which SGL should have benefited due to its cooperation with the Commission (see paras 401–411). SGL argued that it had provided the Commission with information that it could have withheld (because it was covered by the privilege against self-incrimination) and that accordingly it should have benefited from an additional reduction of the fine imposed on it.

[165] Joined Cases T-236/01, T-239/01, T-244/01 to T-246/01, T-251/01 and T-252/01, *Tokai Carbon and others v EC Commission* [2004] OJ C251/13 para 402, citing Case T-112/98 *Mannesmannröhren-Werke v EC Commission* [2001] ECR II-729 paras 66 and 67.

[166] Joined Cases T-236/01, T-239/01, T-244/01 to T-246/01, T-251/01 and T-252/01 *Tokai Carbon and others v EC Commission* [2004] ECR II-1181, citing again Case T-112/98 *Mannesmannröhren-Werke v EC Commission* [2001] ECR II-729 para 65. While this seems to suggest that as far as pre-existing documents are concerned, undertakings are always under an obligation to provide them, even if the documents may be used to establish against them the existence of anti-competitive conduct, the CFI stated later in the same judgment that requests for the protocols of certain meetings, the working documents and the preparatory documents concerning them, the handwritten notes relating to them, the notes and the conclusions pertaining to the meetings, the planning and discussion documents would have required SGL to admit its participation in the infringement of competition rules (para 408). The CFI appeared to have failed to distinguish between documents on the one hand and answers to questions on the other. K Dekeyser and C Gauer, 'The New Enforcement System for Arts 81 & 82 and the Rights of Defence', ch 23 in BE Hawk (ed), *International Antitrust Law & Policy*, Annual Proceedings of the Fordham Institute (2004) 549–85 (561) take the view that the CFI ruling would suffer from an 'internal contradiction'. Similarly, CS Kerse and N Khan, *EC Antitrust Procedure* (5th edn, 2005) para 3–019 also note that there might be a contradiction between that finding, i.e. the suggested extension of the privilege to protocols, etc and the CIF's acceptance that the privilege against self-incrimination did not extend to pre-existing documents since the materials it referred to as also being privileged would by their very nature have been 'documents already in existence'. The Commission has appealed the judgment and has requested clarification whether it can without restriction insist that documents that already exist and relate to the subject matter of the investigations be handed over. Case C-301/04 *EC Commission v SGL Carbon AG*, appeal pending, application in [2005] OJ C262/13.

[167] Joined Cases T-236/01, T-239/01, T-244/01 to T-246/01, T-251/01 and T-252/01 *Tokai Carbon and others v EC Commission* [2004] OJ C251/13 para 404. The CFI further considered that 'the mere fact of being obliged to answer purely factual questions put by the Commission and to

7.47 While in *Tokai Carbon* the CFI expressly restated the principles laid down in *Mannesmannröhren-Werke*, when applying these principles to the facts the Court seemed to take a broader view of the scope of the privilege against self-incrimination. The CFI first considered that the privilege applied to requests to describe the purpose of, and what actually occurred at, those meetings. More controversially, the CFI also considered that the privilege applied to certain types of pre-existing *documents* related to these meetings (e.g. protocols, working documents and preparatory documents, handwritten notes, notes and conclusions, planning and discussion documents), but fell short of explicitly overturning previous case law.[168] If the Commission would not be empowered to request the production of those documents, its enforcement powers would become dependent on either voluntary cooperation or on the use of other means of coercion (dawn raids). As case law stands now the ECJ has emphasized that the application of the privilege against self-incrimination closely depends on the existence of an element of compulsion. Arguably, simple requests for information lack this element of compulsion because the undertaking is not obliged to answer and no fine is possible. Therefore, the invocation of the privilege against self-incrimination seems to be limited to requests made by decision (sector inquiries and formal requests) on the grounds that there exists coercion resulting from the possibility that fines may be imposed. While this element helps distinguish between the two types of information requests under Article 18 of Regulation 1/2003, the situation seems more problematic in regard to questions asked to representatives and members of staff in the context of inspections.[169] It is difficult to ascertain to what extent the person questioned is compelled to answer and whether he or she may or may not speak on behalf of the

comply with its requests for the production of documents already in existence cannot constitute a breach of the principle of respect for the rights of defence or impair the right to fair legal process, which offer, in the specific field of competition law, protection equivalent to that guaranteed by Article 6 [ECHR].' The CFI explained this stance on the grounds that '[t]here is nothing to prevent the addressee of a request for information from showing, whether later during the administrative procedure or in proceedings before the Community Courts, when exercising his rights of defence, that the facts set out in his replies or the documents produced by him have a different meaning from that ascribed to them by the Commission' (citing Case T-112/98 *Mannesmannröhren-Werke v EC Commission* [2001] ECR II-729 paras 77 and 78).

[168] Case C-301/04 *EC Commission v SGL Carbon AG*, pending, application [2004] OJ C262/13 para 408. As indicated, the Commission has appealed the judgment, also in order to seek clarification on this alleged contradiction. Case C-301/04 *EC Commission v SGL Carbon AG*, appeal pending, application in [2005] OJ C262/13. It would seem that the right not to make self-incriminatory statements would not extend to information which exists independently of the will of the suspect, such as documents. CS Kerse and N Khan, *EC Antitrust Procedure* (5th edn, 2005) para 3–020 also note while the ECtHR ruling in *Saunders* may be construed as being broader than direct admissions and might extend to a wider range of statements, the CFI's extension to pre-existing documents would be difficult to reconcile with the case law of the ECtHR and the Community Courts.

[169] Art 20(2)(e) of Reg 1/2003.

undertaking.[170] Although questions are put to representatives and members of staff, procedural fines can only be imposed on undertakings and not on individuals. Thus, the issue is when an undertaking can be considered to have given an incorrect or misleading answer through a representative or a member of staff. A possible approach would be attributing the employee's acts to the undertaking if the former were authorized to act on behalf of the latter.[171] As a consequence, the undertaking would be liable for incorrect or misleading answers where the person asked was authorized to speak on its behalf.[172] Facing the risk of a fine, the undertaking is exposed to an element of compulsion, which would result the privilege against self-incrimination being recognized as available to it.[173] Conversely, where the person questioned is not authorized to speak on behalf of the undertaking, acknowledging the existence of the privilege would be more problematic due to the absence of an element of compulsion weighing on the undertaking itself. Neither could a penalty be imposed on this person for lack of cooperation. On the other hand, if coercion is the decisive factor for the application of the privilege against self-incrimination, it is arguable that representatives

---

[170] The employer's coercion through threats of losing employment may not qualify since the employer is not a State or alternatively, because national labour law does not allow the termination of employment on the grounds that the employee has failed to cooperate with an antitrust investigation. See JS Venit and T Louko, 'The Commission's New Power to Question and its Implications on Human Rights' ch 26 in BE Hawk (ed), *International Antitrust Law & Policy*, Annual Proceedings of the Fordham Institute [2004] 675–700 (678 *et seq.*).

[171] See Judge B Vesterdorf, 'Legal Professional Privilege and the Privilege against self-incrimination in EC Law: Recent developments and Current Issues' ch 27 in BE Hawk (ed), *International Antitrust Law & Policy*, Annual Proceedings of the Fordham Institute (2004) 701–30 (728–29) See in regard to the principles applicable to impute an employee's acts to an undertaking in the context of a violation of Arts 81 and/or 82 EC, Joined Cases 100–103/80 *Musique Diffusion Française v Commission* [1983] ECR 1825 para 97; Case T-9/99 *HFB and others v Commission* [2002] ECR II-1487 para 275.

[172] Judge Bo Vesterdorf notes that this principle seems to be reflected in Art 4(3) of Reg 773/2004 which grants the undertaking under investigation the possibility of rectifying, amending, or supplementing the explanations during inspections given by persons who are not authorized to provide explanations on behalf of the undertaking. The undertaking does not have this possibility where explanations are given by its 'representatives'. Judge B Vesterdorf, 'Legal Professional Privilege and the Privilege against self-incrimination in EC Law: Recent developments and Current Issues' ch 27 in BE Hawk (ed), *International Antitrust Law & Policy*, Annual Proceedings of the Fordham Institute (2004) 701–30 (727–29). See nevertheless that Art 3(3) of Reg 773/2004 which provides that statements taken by the Commission under Art 19 of Reg 1/2003 may be corrected by the persons interviewed whether authorized by the undertakings for which they may work or not. Note, however, that Art 23 of Reg 1/2003 does not foresee any sanction for providing incorrect or misleading information in this case.

[173] The question arises whether the person questioned could claim privilege for himself or herself when he or she is requested to make statements that would incriminate him or her under certain national laws while *not* incriminating the undertaking. However, it seems doubtful that such a situation will often arise in practice: an admission by a person who is authorised to speak in the name of an undertaking to the effect that he or she personally participated in a breach of Arts 81 and/or 82 EC will in most instances incriminate the company itself (and therefore be covered by the latter's potential privilege).

or members of staff questioned in the course of an inspection could refrain from making statements incriminating the undertaking.[174]

4. Cooperation with the authorities of the Member States

7.48   The Commission is obliged to forward copies of all simple requests and requests by decision to the competent authorities in the Member States in whose territory the headquarters of the undertaking or association of undertakings under investigation is situated, and the NCA whose territory is affected.[175] In practice, the Commission tends to send copy requests to all the Member States when it seems likely that the case will lead to a formal decision and will therefore be dealt with in the future by the Advisory Committee. The Court has made it clear, however, that the obligation of the Commission to transmit to the competent authorities of the Member States copies of the most important documents it has collected with a view to, *inter alia*, finding an infringement, does not require the Commission automatically to forward to NCAs all documents received by it from undertakings, and that the provision itself empowers the Commission to determine which documents are most important in that regard.[176] Furthermore, the obligation to transmit the most important documents to the Member States must be interpreted in the light of the general principle that undertakings are entitled to protection of their business secrets.[177]

7.49   In *SEP II*, the Court concluded that where an undertaking has expressly raised before the Commission the confidential nature of a document as against the competent national authorities on the ground that it contains business secrets, and where that argument is not irrelevant, the general principle of the protection of business secrets may limit the Commission's obligation to transmit the document to the competent national authorities.[178] Accordingly, after referring to its judgment in *AKZO II*,[179] the Court stated that, for similar reasons, if the

---

[174] For more details on Art 20(2)(e), see ch 8 'Inspections' paras 8.50 *et seq.* Judge B Vesterdorf, 'Legal Professional Privilege and the Privilege against self-incrimination in EC Law: Recent developments and Current Issues' ch 27 in BE Hawk (ed), *International Antitrust Law & Policy*, Annual Proceedings of the Fordham Institute [2004] 701–30 (729).

[175] Art 18(5) of Reg 1/2003. As regards the competition authority of the Member State whose territory is affected, the Commission used to send a copy of the requests to all the Community countries concerned, for one reason or another, with the case, although Reg 17 did not expressly provide for this requirement.

[176] As regards Art 10(1) of Reg 11/62, see T-39/90 *NV Samenwerkende ElektriciteitsProduktiebedrijven (SEP) v EC Commission* [1991] ECR II-1497 paras 34 and 35.

[177] A principle which Art 287 EC and various provisions of Reg 1/2003, such as Arts 28(2) and 30(2) embody. Regarding the treatment by the Commission and the NCAs of the information provided by undertakings, see below ch 9 'Penalties and confidentiality' paras 9.24 *et seq.*

[178] See T-39/90 *NV Samenwerkende Elektriciteits-Produktiebedrijven (SEP) v EC Commission* [1991] ECR II-1497 para 37.

[179] See Case C-53/85 *AKZO v EC Commission II* [1986] ECR I-1965 para 29. For a more detailed consideration of this judgment, see ch 9 'Penalties and confidentiality' para 9.32.

Commission wishes to transmit a document to the competent national authorities, notwithstanding the claim that in the particular circumstances of the case that document is of a confidential nature with respect to those authorities, [it must] adopt a properly reasoned decision capable of being subject to judicial review by means of an action for annulment. It is in an action for the annulment of such a decision that an undertaking might effectively rely on its right to protection of its business secrets.[180] In practice therefore, provided that, (1) undertakings expressly claim confidentiality for a document as against NCAs, and, (2) their argument is not entirely irrelevant,[181] the Commission will first have to give the undertakings an opportunity of expressing their views and secondly adopt a reasoned decision, before proceeding to forward those documents which it considers important for the purposes of transmission to NCAs and which allegedly contain business secrets.[182] The procedure to be followed in practice will be the same as the procedure for disclosure to complainants of documents which undertakings consider contain business secrets.[183]

Once it has received a formal complaint and decided to investigate it, the Commission must disclose its content to the alleged offenders for them to submit their observations. To that end, the Commission may, before carrying out any inquiries whatsoever, send them a separate letter together with a copy of the complaint or else treat the sending of a request for information as an opportunity to ask the undertakings for their views on the action attributed to them by the complainants. Otherwise it may wait until the stage at which access to the file is granted. In any of these three cases, in view of the fact that the complainants may have disclosed business secrets in their complaint which warrant protection, the Commission must obtain a non-confidential version, stripped of the information and documents regarded by the complainants as secret.[184] In **7.50**

---

[180] See T-39/90 *NV Samenwerkende Elektriciteits-Produktiebedrijven (SEP) v EC Commission* [1991] ECR II-1497 paras 39–40, which referred to Art 10(1) of Reg 17, now replaced by Art 11(2) of Reg 1/2003.

[181] It may be difficult for the Commission to invoke this requirement, since if it refuses to block the forwarding of a document because the request is not based on relevant grounds, it will probably have to adopt a reasoned decision for that purpose and observe a prudent waiting period, without forwarding the documents, until after the owner of the document has had the opportunity to challenge such decision the CFI rules whether or not the request for confidentiality 'is entirely irrelevant'. The result would thus be the same as if the Commission adopted directly a decision to the effect that, first, the request was irrelevant and, second that the documents did not qualify for confidentiality as against the national authorities.

[182] Although *SEP II* does not say so expressly, it seems to emerge from the reasoning of the Court that the limitations on the forwarding of documents to the NCAs on these grounds relate only to those authorities as against which the confidentiality of those documents might be invoked, and not to all NCAs in general, if several have a direct interest in the procedure.

[183] Regarding the *AKZO* procedure, see Case 53/85 *AKZO v EC Commission I* [1986] ECR 1965.

[184] Art 5(2) of Reg 773/2004.

that connection, formal complainants must bear in mind that it will not be possible to regard their complaints as formal if their fundamental elements—without which they would be meaningless—are confidential and consequently cannot be used by the Commission in dealing with the case. Accordingly, the Commission can disclose and use information necessary to prove an infringement of Articles 81 and 82 EC[185] The level of fine for providing incorrect or misleading information used to be low but has been raised by Article 23(1) of Regulation 1/2003 to a maximum of 1 per cent of the undertaking's total turnover in the preceding business year. A desire to co-operate with the Commission and not to make the situation worse is often also a spur to accuracy in the provision of information.

D. Interviews and Oral Statements

7.51　Under Article 19 of Regulation 1/2003, the Commission now has a general power to take statements from individuals and company representatives for the purpose of collecting information relevant to an investigation. This investigation technique was not available under Regulation 17.[186] Rather than merely recording unilateral statements, the Commission may use this power to conduct interviews at its own premises in Brussels after an inspection which implies that questions may be asked by the Commission. However, unlike other investigative techniques, the Commission is not entitled to adopt a decision to compel a person to give a statement; the relevant individual or company must consent to the interview taking place. Article 19 is not restricted to officers or employees of undertakings suspected of infringements. There is the suggestion that the Commission would not be required to inform the undertaking under investigation that the statements are being taken, even where the interviewee is also an employee of that undertaking.[187] However, while there is no explicit requirement to do so, basic procedural principles would require the Commission to inform the undertaking under investigation where the interviewed person is an

---

[185] Art 15(3) of Reg 773/2004.

[186] Art 19 of Reg 1/2003. Proposal for a Council Regulation ('Regulation implementing Articles 81 and 82 of the Treaty') COM (2000) 582 final—CNS 2000/0243 Explanatory Memorandum Art 19. The provision aimed to fill a gap in the Commission's powers by allowing for oral submissions to be recorded and used as evidence in proceedings. CS Kerse and N Khan, *EC Antitrust Procedure* (5th edn, 2005) para 3–069 and n 63 at 184 indicate that the absence of such power in Reg 17 did not prevent the Commission from using statements outside the framework of inspections. *Pre-insulated Pipes* [1999] OJ L24/1 para 24; *Zinc Phosphate* [2003] OJ L153/1 paras 57 and 59 referring to undertakings which voluntarily provided information and to oral accounts record of which was taken outside inspections.

[187] L Garzaniti, 'Dawn of a New Era—Powers of Investigation and Enforcement under Regulation 1/2003', May 2004, 10, available at www.freshfields.com.

employee of that undertaking and offers to be interviewed without the undertaking's authorization.[188] Because of its voluntary nature, no penalties apply to a refusal to grant an interview nor do penalties apply to the supply of incorrect information. However, giving incorrect or false statements may expose a witness to criminal and/or civil penalties under national law.[189]

The power to take statements may assume great importance within the context **7.52** of leniency proceedings, as it favours the provision of evidence without requiring too many explanations or the need to submit to Commission inspections.[190] Commission Regulation 773/2004 requires the Commission to state the legal basis and purpose of the interview and to recall its voluntary nature. The Commission shall also inform the person interviewed of its intention to make a record of the interview.[191] The interview may be conducted by any means, including by telephone or electronic means,[192] and concern any 'information relating to the subject-matter of an investigation' and thus might have a potentially wider scope than Article 20(2)(e), which refers to the subject matter and purpose of an investigation.[193] Article 19 is silent as regards an individual's right to be accompanied by a lawyer during the interview. While the Commission is

---

[188] As a matter of principle, it appears that in this case the Commission should not undermine loyalty obligations of the employee towards his or her company, which is subject to a Commission investigation, which thus should be informed when the Commission will take a statement. For the same reason, the obligation to inform the undertaking may then not apply to employees of other undertakings (which are not under investigation) or to ex-employees of the undertaking under investigation.

[189] JM Joshua, 'Oral Statements in EC competition proceedings: a due process short-cut?' [2004] Competition Law Insight, Issue 26, 1–7 (6) criticizes the fact that the interviews are not conducted by an independent examiner, but by the Commission's case team. He raises the point that the process of taking statements would be entirely within the control of the Commission and that undertakings are not given any meaningful opportunity for cross-examination. This could have the effect that sometimes critical points in the testimony on which the Commission will base its case are accepted at face value without allowing some kind of probing from the parties under attack with a view to uncovering inconsistencies and contradictions or exposing bias or incentives to dissimulate.

[190] The power would appear to be aimed at allowing the Commission to take statements from people like ex-employees of the undertaking or competitors without exposing them to the risks of Commission sanctions. At the same time, this may have an adverse effect on the probative value of the evidence. A Jones and B Sufrin, *EC Competition Law* (2nd edn, 2004) 1083. JM Joshua, 'Oral Statements in EC competition proceedings: a due process short-cut?' [2004] Competition Law Insight, Issue 26, 1–7 (5–6).

[191] Art 3(1) of Reg 773/2004.

[192] Art 3(2) of Reg 773/2004. The Commission may record the statements made by the persons interviewed in any form. A copy of any recording shall be made available to the person interviewed for approval. Where necessary, the Commission shall set a time-limit within which the person interviewed may communicate to it any correction to be made to the statement. Art 3(3) of Reg 773/2004.

[193] CS Kerse and N Khan, *EC Antitrust Procedure* (5th edn, 2005) para 3–070 question the utility of Art 19(2) given that the territory in which the interview takes place will not necessarily be a territory in which an infringement was committed.

allowed to record the interview, it must first inform the interviewee of its intention to do so. A copy of the record must be provided to interviewee. Further, the Commission must set a time limit within which the interviewee can correct his or her statement, although no sanctions follow from an incorrect statement. During the consultations regarding the modernization package, various submissions were made asking that the recordings of statements be made available to the undertakings concerned in order to ensure the defence rights of the parties.[194] Indeed, as a matter of fairness, it would be desirable for the Commission to adopt clear guidance that would oblige it to inform a witness that he or she is not required to consent to an interview, is entitled to retain legal counsel and that counsel has the right to be present during the interview. This approach would reflect the principle that a witness shall be given all possible information necessary to make an informed decision and to safeguard his or her rights. Given that the Community Courts have indicated that a central element to the privilege of self-incrimination is the existence of compulsion,[195] it would appear that no privilege could be asserted by the individual or legal entity concerned, since there must be consent to be interviewed.[196] Article 19(2) gives the NCA of the territory in which the interview takes place the right to be present if the interview takes place on the premises of the undertaking. The provision has been supplemented by Regulation 773/2004, which specifies the above formalities for conducting an interview.[197]

---

[194] Responses to European Commission Consultation on the Modernization Package: submissions by Baker and McKenzie, 23 December 2003, point 7.1 and Cleary, Gottlieb, Steen, and Hamilton, 5 December 2003, point VIII.1.

[195] Joined Cases T-305/94 to T-307/94, T-313/94 to T-316/94, T-318/94, T-325/94, T-328/94, T-329/94 and T-335/94 *Limburgse Vinyl Maatschappij and others v EC Commission, PVC II* [1999] ECR II-931 para 275.

[196] Judge B Vesterdorf indicated that the protection of those persons is enhanced by Art 3(1) of Reg 773/2004 which provides that: '[w]here the Commission interviews a person with his consent in accordance with Article 19 of Reg (EC) No 1/2003, it shall, at the beginning of the interview, state the legal basis and the purpose of the interview, and recall its voluntary nature. It shall also inform the person interviewed of its intention to make a record of the interview'. See also Recital 3 of Reg No 773/2004. One may argue that the Commission shall also inform the individual that before he answers the question, he should be aware that the Commission has the right to transmit the information. Further, that information could be used by NCAs in evidence against the individual concerned. See Judge Vesterdorf, 'Rights, Privileges and Ethics in Competition Cases Roundtable' in BE Hawk (ed), Annual Proceedings of the Fordham Institute [2005] 731–79 (739).

[197] Art 3 of Reg 773/2004.

8

INVESTIGATION OF CASES (III): INSPECTIONS[1]

A. Overview

The powers to require information or documents and to send inspectors into firms to gather evidence directly are used for different purposes and in different circumstances. Whereas written discovery of information is typically employed to elicit particulars of contractual arrangements and firms' market position, on-the-spot investigations are usually conducted to obtain direct evidence of hard-core infringement such as cartels.[2] Unannounced inspections are an important instrument to detect the existence of hardcore cartels or abuses of a dominant position.[3] By way of an example, in 2003 the Commission carried out cartel

8.01

---

[1] A Riley, 'EC Antitrust Modernisation: The Commission Does Very Nicely—Thank You! Part One: Regulation 1 and the Notification Burden' [2003] ECLR 604–15; JHJ Bourgeois and C Humpe, 'The Commission's "New Regulation 17"' [2002] ECLR 43–51; K Dekeyser and C Gauer, 'The New Enforcement System for Articles 81 & 82 and the Rights of Defence', ch 23 in BE Hawk (ed), *International Antitrust Law & Policy*, Annual Proceedings of the Fordham Institute (2004) 549–86; CS Kerse and N Khan, *EC Antitrust Procedure* (5th edn, 2005) paras 3–034 to 3–070; A Jones and B Sufrin, *EC Competition Law* (2nd edn, 2004) 1062–83; J Schwarze and A Weitbrecht, *Grundzüge des europäischen Kartellverfahrensrechts* (2004) § 4 paras 16–33; A Klees, *Europäisches Kartellverfahrensrecht* (2005) § 9 paras 53–145.

[2] L Ritter and WD Braun, *European Competition Law: A Practitioner's Guide* (3rd edn, 2004) 1069–70. See also Case T-59/99 *Ventouris v EC Commission* [2003] ECR II–5257 para 121: '[. . .] the Court has expressly ruled that the right to enter any premises, land and means of transport of undertakings is of particular importance inasmuch as it is intended to permit the Commission to obtain evidence of infringements of the competition rules in the places in which such evidence is normally to be found, that is to say, on the business premises of undertakings [. . .]'. See also Case T-65/99 *Strintzis Lines Shipping SA v EC Commission* [2003] ECR II-5433, para 41; Case T-66/99 *Minoan Lines SA v EC Commission* [2003] ECR II-5515 para 51.

[3] Antitrust enforcers often call cartel activities the 'supreme evil of antitrust' and the 'scourge of the economy'. See XXXIII Report on Competition Policy [2003] para 717. See also Commissioner N Kroes, 'The First Hundred Days' 40th Anniversary of the Studienvereinigung Kartellrecht 1965–2005, International Forum on European Competition Law Brussels, 7 April 2005: '[. . .] Cartel behaviour is illegal, unjustified and unjustifiable—whatever the size, nature or scope of the business affected. [. . .].' The rise in cartel decisions is accompanied by a considerable surge in the number of unannounced inspections. See Speech by Director-General of COMP DG, P Lowe,

inspections in cases covering no less than twenty-one products or services.[4] The Commission takes the view that the carrying out of inspections is of value, not only as a means of uncovering unlawful conduct, but also in itself, as companies usually stop their illegal behaviour immediately after the Commission's intervention.[5]

8.02 Article 20(1) gives the Commission powers to carry out 'all necessary inspections' of undertakings and associations of undertakings. This means investigations at the undertaking's premises. Although the power of inspection contained in Article 20 of Regulation 1/2003 is very similar to that contained in the equivalent provision found in Article 14 of Regulation 17, there are a number of significant extensions, including the power to carry out investigations on domestic property. In addition, Regulation 1/2003 incorporates some of the case law developed under Regulation 17. Article 20(2) inspections also involve the power to examine the books and other records related to the business, irrespective of the medium on which they are stored. The inclusion of any form of powers 'to take or obtain in any form copies of, or extracts' of all kinds of records provides the Commission with a legal basis allowing it to obtain all electronically held information. Besides, of the five powers listed in Article 20(2), the power to seal any business premises or records did not appear in Regulation 17, and the power to ask for explanations on facts or documents could be considered wider than the power to ask for 'oral explanations on the spot' under Article 14(1) of Regulation 17/62:

- The Commission has been given the power to seal any business premises and books or records for the period and to the extent necessary for the inspection. This power serves to ensure the efficiency of inspections, in particular in cases where an inspection is carried out over more than one day and where the officials have to leave the premises of the company before they have finished. Although an informal seal procedure existed before, the recognition of a formal power to seal is expected to provide a much more secure basis

---

'What the future for Cartel Enforcement, Understanding Global Cartel Enforcement', Brussels, 11 February 2003. In the four years from 2000 to 2003 the Commission took twenty-six cartel decisions with fines totalling 3,330 million euros, compared with eight decisions (552 million euros) in the previous four years, 1996 to 1999, and eleven decisions (393 million euros) from 1992 to 1995, Margaret Bloom 'The Great Reformer: Mario Monti's Legacy in Article 81 and Cartel Policy' [2005] Competition Policy International 54–78 (65). During 2004, the Commission maintained its emphasis on anti-cartel activity established during the previous three years by issuing another six decisions against unlawful horizontal agreements, involving some thirty companies. Fines totalling over 390 million euros were imposed in these decisions. See Commission Report on Competition Policy [2004], 2/SEC(2005)805 final 29.

[4] It should be borne in mind that each case/inspection usually involves visits to a number of different companies.

[5] XXXIII Report on Competition Policy [2003] para 28.

for the procedure and probably encourage the Commission to use it more often.[6]

- The Commission is also entitled to ask any representative or member of staff of the undertaking or association of undertakings for explanations on facts or documents relating to the subject matter and purpose of the inspection and to record the answers.[7] The former Article 14 of Regulation 17 was unclear whether the Commission had the possibility to ask questions during inspections. The ECJ stated in *National Panasonic*[8] that Commission officials conducting on the spot investigations are allowed to ask questions regarding the books and business records being examined. The new legal framework seemingly goes further and allows inspectors to ask for explanations regarding either the facts or the documents related to the subject matter and purpose of the inspection. Regulation 773/2004 which implements Regulation 1/2003 dealing with the conduct of Commission proceedings in its application of competition rules addresses specifically oral inquiries during inspections and sets out the Commission's power to ask representatives or members of the staff of the undertakings under inspection for explanations, which may be recorded.[9]

Under Article 20(3) of Regulation 1/2003 the Commission can carry out the **8.03** inspection at the premises simply on production of a 'written authorization'.[10] The officials may either give advance notice of their arrival or come without warning (although they have to give notice 'in good time before the inspection' to the NCA of the Member State in whose territory the inspection is conducted). If they only have the Article 20(3) 'authorization', an undertaking is under no legal obligation to submit to the inspection.[11] Under Article 20(4), however,

---

[6] A Riley, 'EC Antitrust Modernisation: The Commission Does Very Nicely—Thank You! Part One: Regulation 1 and the Notification Burden' [2003] ECLR 604 (608 n 20).

[7] Art 20(2)(e) of Reg 1/2003.

[8] Case 136/79 *National Panasonic v EC Commission* [1980] ECR 2033 paras 2 and 15. Case T-59/99 *Ventouris v EC Commission* [2003] ECR II-5257 para 122: '[. . .] right of access would serve no useful purpose if the Commission's officials could do no more than ask for documents or files which they could identify precisely in advance. On the contrary, such a right implies the power to search for various items of information which are not already known or fully identified [. . .]'.

[9] See Art 4(1) of Reg 773/2004: '[. . .] When, pursuant to Article 20(2)(e) of Reg (EC) No 1/2003, officials or other accompanying persons authorised by the Commission ask representatives or members of staff of an undertaking or of an association of undertakings for explanations, the explanations given may be recorded in any form. [. . .]'.

[10] This must contain the same or equivalent matters as required in respect of requests for information under Art 18(2) of Reg 1/2003.

[11] However, where a undertaking voluntarily submits to the inspection, it is under the obligation to cooperate with the inspectors. E.g. if the required books are produced in an incomplete form the undertaking may be liable to fines. See below ch 9 'Penalties and Confidentiality' para 9.07. K Lenaerts and J Maselis, 'Procedural Rights and Issues in the Enforcement of Articles 81 and 82 of the EC Treaty' [2001] Fordham International Law Journal 1615–54 (1622–23); A Klees, *Europäisches Kartellverfahrensrecht* (2005) § 9 para 61.

undertakings *must* submit to procedures ordered by decision of the Commission[12] and actively co-operate. Article 20(4) further requires the Commission to consult with the NCA of the Member State in whose territory the inspection is to take place before adopting a decision to proceed with an inspection.

8.04   Unlike Article 14 of Regulation 17, Article 20(8) provides for additional rights for undertakings subject to Commission's inspections, which have been in part granted by the ECJ in its rulings in *Hoechst*[13] and in *Roquette Frères SA.*[14] Where the assistance by national police authorities or equivalent enforcement authorities is dependent upon the authorization from a judicial authority pursuant to national law or where the Commission considers this to be appropriate, the Commission will seek authorizations from national courts. The reviewing national judicial authority must limit its review to ensuring that the Commission's decision is authentic and that the measures are neither arbitrary nor excessive. The national judicial authority is not entitled, however, to question the necessity of the inspection or to request access to the information in the Commission's files.[15] The national court can ask for detailed explanations where necessary, to ensure that the inspection and coercive measures required are neither arbitrary nor disproportionate.[16]

---

[12] For example as regards Reg 17, *Vereinigung deutscher Freiformschmieden* [1978] OJ L10/32; see for the similar obligation under Reg 4056/86 on the application of Arts [81] and [82] EC to maritime transport *Ukwal* [1992] OJ L121/45 and *Mewac* [1993] OJ L20/6. Case 5/85 *AKZO v EC Commission* [1986] ECR 2585 para 27; Cases 46/87 and 227/88 *Hoechst AG v EC Commission* [1989] ECR 2859 paras 22 *et seq.*

[13] See regarding Reg 17: Joined Cases 46/87 and 227/88 *Hoechst AG v EC Commission* [1989] ECR 2859 paras 22 and 31. Where the undertaking cooperates voluntarily with the Commission, the authorization also has to specify the subject matter and the purpose of the investigation.

[14] Case C-94/00 *Roquette Frères SA v Directeur Général de la Concurrence, de la Conommation et de la Répression des Fraudes* [2002] ECR I-9011.

[15] Art 20(8) of Reg 1/2003. In case of opposition of an undertaking, there is some kind of double judicial control insofar as a judicial authorization is required under national law to use public force: a control on the proportionality between the coercive measures and the seriousness of the infringement on the one hand exercised by the national judge and a full control over the legality of the Commission exercised by the Community Courts on the other hand. See K Dekeyser and C Gauer, 'The New Enforcement System for Articles 81 & 82 and the Rights of Defence', ch 23 in BE Hawk (ed), *International Antitrust Law & Policy*, Annual Proceedings of the Fordham Institute [2005] 549–86 (555). Joined Cases 97/87 to 99/87 *Dow Chemical Ibérica and others v EC Commission* [1989] ECR 3165 para 52 pointing out that there is 'no fundamental difference' between the review of the national court and the review which the Community judicature may be called upon to carry out for ensuring that the investigation decision itself is in no way arbitrary. J Schwarze and A Weitbrecht, *Grundzüge des europäischen Kartellverfahrensrechts* (2004) § 4 para 24 criticize that the national courts do not have access to the Commission file, but have to rely on *second hand* explanations by the Commission which can decide on the nature and scope of the information provided. A Klees, *Europäisches Kartellverfahrensrecht* (2005) § 6 paras 75–80.

[16] The national judge is empowered to check the authenticity of the decision and to assess whether the measures of constraint envisaged are neither arbitrary nor excessive having regard in

As indicated earlier, the exercise of the power of inspection is not conditional **8.05**
upon the exercise of the 'power to request information in writing'. It is not
necessary to make a prior request for information and undertakings do not have
to refuse to provide such information before an inspection can be carried out. In
practice, the Commission is entitled to exercise both powers independently, so
that on some occasions inspections will follow requests for information (e.g.
where the reply given by the undertakings is unsatisfactory) and in other cases the
position will be reversed (e.g. where the Commission seeks clarifications concerning documents and information obtained during an inspection). Apart from this,
Article 20 of Regulation 1/2003 does not define the types of undertakings which
the Commission can approach, with the result that it is entitled—as in the case of
requests—to order inspections not only at the premises of undertakings allegedly
implicated in an infringement but also at those of all undertakings in possession
of information regarding the restrictive agreements or conduct under investigation.[17] The Commission also has the power to search premises, land, or means of
transport other than those of an undertaking or association of undertakings,
where reasonable suspicion exists that books and records related to the business
are kept there. Article 21(1) of Regulation 1/2003 describes these premises as
including the homes of directors, managers and other members of staff of the
undertakings and associations of undertakings concerned. This power can only
be exercised by decision, and such decisions can only be taken after the
Commission has consulted the NCA of the Member State in whose territory the
inspection is to be conducted. Article 21(3) provides that the national judicial
authority must give prior authorisation for the execution of the Commission's
decision.

---

particular to the seriousness of the suspected infringement, the importance of the evidence
sought, and the involvement of the undertaking concerned. Case T-66/99 *Minoan Lines SA v EC
Commission* [2003] ECR II-5515 para 49: '[. . .] The Court has held that, in all the legal systems
of the Member States, any intervention by the public authorities in the sphere of private activities
of any person, whether natural or legal, must have a legal basis and be justified on the grounds laid
down by law, and, consequently, that those systems provide, albeit in different forms, protection
against arbitrary or disproportionate intervention [. . .]'. K Dekeyser and C Gauer, 'The New
Enforcement System for Articles 81 & 82 and the Rights of Defence', ch 23 in BE Hawk
(ed), *International Antitrust Law & Policy*, Annual Proceedings of the Fordham Institute [2005]
549–86 (554–58) noting that the more intrusive the measures of constraint, the stricter is likely to
be the proportionality test carried out by the national judge.

[17] This possibility, however, has been used rarely. In such cases, the Commission prefers to
request information by letter. See, however, *Fides* [1979] OJ L57/33.

B. Types of Inspections

1. Alternatives

8.06   Article 20 of Regulation 1/2003 describes two types of inspection: straight-forward inspections based on a written authorization and inspections ordered by decision of the Commission. The two types of inspections constitute alternatives. The Commission is entitled at its discretion to decide which type is most appropriate to each case.[18] Thus, as with the requests for information under Article 18 of Regulation 1/2003, the exercise of the power to inspect does not provide for a two-stage process but offers two options. The Commission may decide in a particular case to proceed immediately with an inspection based on a binding decision without having previously tried an ordinary inspection or even made a request for information. Like Regulation 17 before, Regulation 1/2003 recognizes that the Commission may wish to carry out a surprise visit, whether it has previously encountered resistance on the part of the firm where it wishes to carry out the inspection or not. Thus, Regulation 1/2003 does not provide that inspection decisions are to be preceded by an unsuccessful ordinary inspection.[19] Under Article 20(3) of Regulation 1/2003 the Commission can carry out the inspection at the premises simply on production of a 'written authorization'. As stated, the officials may either give advance notice of their arrival or come without warning (although they have to give notice 'in good time before the inspection' to the NCA of the Member State in whose territory the inspection is carried out).

8.07   The ECJ considered the different nature of requests for information under Article 18 (former Article 11 of Regulation 17) and inspections under Article 20 (former Article 14 of Regulation 17) in *National Panasonic*. The applicant challenged the validity of the decision ordering the inspection at Panasonic's offices where the officials arrived without warning, armed with a decision. The ECJ held that the Commission was entitled to do so under Article 14(3) of Regulation 17, the precursor equivalent to Article 20(3) of Regulation, 1/2003, without going through the voluntary procedure first. The Court made it clear that whilst the information which the Commission seeks by a request for

---

[18] See Case 136/79 *National Panasonic v EC Commission* [1980] ECR 2033 para 12: '[. . .] two procedures do not necessarily overlap but constitute two alternative checks the choice of which depends upon the special features of each case [. . .]'.

[19] See regarding Reg 17 Case 136/79 *National Panasonic v EC Commission* [1980] ECR 2033 para 11. See also Cases 46/87 and 227/88 *Hoechst v EC Commission* [1989] ECR 2859 para 22, Case 85/87 *Dow Benelux v EC Commission* [1989] ECR 3137 para 33, and Cases 97–99/87 *Dow Ibérica v EC Commission* [1989] ECR 3165 para 19.

information cannot generally be obtained without the cooperation of the undertakings possessing it, inspections are not subject to any such restrictions. The purpose of inspections is different, namely to verify the actual existence and scope of the information already in the Commission's possession. For that reason, the Commission would not need the prior cooperation of undertakings and, accordingly, the Commission's discretion in choosing between an ordinary inspection and an inspection based on a decision is entirely justified.[20]

2. Ordinary inspections

Content of the authorization

Article 20(3) of Regulation 1/2003 provides that officials of the Commission **8.08** authorized for the purpose of this kind (inspectors) are to exercise their powers upon authorization of a written authorization. The authorization to inspect must specify:

(1) the name or trading name of the undertaking or association of undertakings under investigation;
(2) the name of the Commission officials authorized to undertake the inspection;[21]
(3) the subject-matter and purpose of the inspection; and
(4) the penalty provided for in Article 23 of Regulation 1/2003 in cases where the required books or other business records are produced in incomplete form or where the answers to questions asked under Article 20(2) are incorrect or misleading.

Name or trading name of the undertakings

The address of the undertaking is usually included in this section. It is import- **8.09** ant to note that, since the Commission is empowered to 'enter any premises, land and means of transport of undertakings',[22] the address included in the authorization does not limit what might be termed the 'geographical scope' of the inspection. In other words, it does not prevent inspectors from entering, if their search for information makes this necessary, buildings, premises, or offices owned by undertakings and located at a place other than that indicated in the authorization.[23] The essential component, therefore, is the name of the undertaking

---

[20] See Case 136/79 *National Panasonic v EC Commission* [1980] ECR 2033 para 13.
[21] It is to note that under former Art 14(2) of Reg 17, the Commission was explictely required to indicate the identity of the Commission officials. Art 20(3) of Reg 1/2003 no longer contains this requirement. Nevertheless, there is no reason why this should not continue to apply.
[22] Art 20(2)(b) of Reg 1/2003.
[23] In Case T-66/99 *Minoan Lines SA v EC Commission* [2003] ECR II-5515 paras 69 *et seq*. The Commission conducted the investigation not on the premises of Minoan Lines to whom the inspection decision was addressed but on the premises of the European Trust Agency (ETA), a

and not any address as may be given in the authorization, which is more than anything a further means of identifying the undertaking. Regardless of what is stated in the authorization, it is reasonable to infer that all the premises of the undertaking identified by its name or trading name, wherever they are located, are in principle liable to be inspected.[24]

Officials authorized to carry out inspections

8.10 On site inspections are carried out by Commission officials as well as by 'other accompanying persons' authorized for that purpose by the Commission.[25] The persons in charge of the case file (*rapporteurs*) are currently the persons authorized to prepare for and supervise inspections. In some cases, other *rapporteurs* not involved in the case may take part in inspections. Thus, for example, where it is necessary to carry out several inspections simultaneously in undertakings located in different Member States, there may be ten or more inspectors. The official in charge of the case will provide his colleagues with information regarding the evidence available to the Commission and the conclusions drawn from it, and the subject matter and purpose of the inspection, so that they can perform their duties efficiently. Instructions will also be given for all the inspectors to obtain the documentation necessary for the accomplishment of their task. Regulation 1/2003 does not specify who can be appointed as 'other accompanying persons'. An obvious example would be IT experts who can assist with gaining access to information stored electronically.[26] Regulation 1/2003

---

different legal entity from that mentioned in the investigation decision. During the inspection the Commission obtained copies of a large number of documents which it subsequently treated as evidence in relation to the various companies into which it was inquiring. ETA had no parent/subsidiary relationship with Minoan but was merely Minoan's agent. The Court held that in carrying out its work as agent and representative of Minoan, ETA had authority to present itself to the public at large and to the Commission as Minoan, its identity, when conducting the commercial matters in question, being practically one with that of Minoan. Minoan had also delegated the conduct of its business to ETA to the point that this agency housed in fact the real centre of Minoan's commercial activities and was therefore the place where the books and business records relating to the activities in question were held. Whilst ETA was legally a separate entity from Minoan, in its role as Minoan's representative and sole manager of those of Minoan's affairs which were the subject-matter of the investigation, its identity merged with that of its principal. Consequently, it would have fallen under the same obligation to cooperate as that incumbent on its principal. The Court found that the Commission acted diligently and amply fulfilled its duty to make as sure as possible, before the investigation began, that the premises which it proposed to inspect indeed belonged to the legal entity which it wished to investigate. See also Case T-65/99 *Strintzis Lines Shipping SA v EC Commission* [2003] ECR II-5433 paras 53 *et seq.*

[24] Confirming this view, see in regard of an inspection decision against *AKZO*, XXIV Report on Competition Policy [1994] 376–77.

[25] Art 20(2) of Reg 1/2003. Former Art 14 of Reg 17 did not mention 'other accompanying persons'.

[26] This reflects the reality that inspections are no longer just about going through drawers of paper files, but increasingly involve a high-tech search of computer systems for information. CS Kerse and N Khan, *EC Antitrust Procedure* (5th edn, 2005) para 3–053.

does not specify any limits on the activities that 'other accompanying persons' can engage in.

Subject-matter and purpose of inspections

The subject-matter of inspections encompasses the specific agreements, prac- **8.11** tices, or conduct of the undertakings under investigation in the marketplace in relation to specified products.[27] The aim of the inspection will in all cases be to verify or determine the existence of an infringement of Articles 81 and/or 82 EC and establish its legal and economic context for the purpose of proceedings. The Commission's obligation to indicate those two points in its authorizations[28] will be fulfilled if it describes, even succinctly, the nature of the alleged infringement which it is sought to uncover.[29] The ECJ has declared that the requirement that the Commission inform the undertakings of the subject-matter and purpose of the inspection constitutes a fundamental safeguard of the rights of the defence of undertakings under investigation.[30] The obligation to state reasons cannot therefore be limited by virtue of considerations affecting the effectiveness of the investigation. It is fair to acknowledge that to date the Community Courts have been quite lenient regarding the extent of the reasoning that the Commission must give.[31] Under the new regime, there is the suggestion that Regulation 1/2003 may provoke a substantial change regarding the level of detail that the

---

[27] As the Commission's jurisdiction covers the EU and Member States jurisdictions' their respective national territories, it seems clear that any inspection under Reg 1/2003 can only be used to prosecute antitrust violations in the EU because the 'subject-matter' of an investigation in the EU cannot cover non-EU territories. Accordingly, in the absence of a cooperation agreement providing for the exchange of information collected, the Commission and the NCAs cannot share information obtained, e.g. through questioning of an employee with non-EU antitrust authorities who could use it to prosecute anti-trust violations outside the EU. See JS Venit and T Louko, 'The Commission's New Power to Question and its implications on Human Rights' ch 26 in BE Hawk (ed), *International Antitrust Law & Policy*, Annual Proceedings of the Fordham Institute (2004) 675–700 (682 *et seq*).

[28] This must contain the same or equivalent matters as required in respect of requests for information. The same requirement applies to inspection decisions.

[29] Case T-66/99 *Minoan Lines SA v EC Commission* [2003] ECR II-5515 para 55: '[. . .] The Commission is likewise obliged to state in that decision, as precisely as possible, what it is looking for and the matters to which the investigation must relate. As the Court has held, that requirement is intended to protect the rights of defence of the undertakings concerned, which would be seriously compromised if the Commission could rely on evidence against undertakings which was obtained during an investigation but was not related to the subject-matter or purpose thereof. [. . .]'.

[30] Case 85/87 *Dow Benelux v EC Commission* [1989] ECR 3137 para 18; Case 136/79 *National Panasonic v EC Commission* [1980] ECR 2033 paras 26 and 27.

[31] Early on, the Community courts took the view that the Commission cannot know in advance which documents it expects to find. Case 31/59 *Brescia v High Authority* [1960] ECR 153 paras 80 and 81: '[..] it is only the object in view which must serve as the criterion and not an a priori statement of the results expected which drawn up unilaterally and without knowledge of the facts, may change by reasons of the checks when they are carried out [. . .]' CS Kerse and N Khan, *EC Antitrust Procedure* (5th edn, 2005) para 3–043.

Commission may need to put forward.[32] Consequently, although the Commission is not required to inform undertakings of all the evidence in its possession concerning the presumed infringements,[33] or to describe the latter in strictly legal terms, it is under an obligation to set out clearly the allegations that it seeks to prove. Provided the essential information is given there may be no need to specify precisely the relevant market, the exact legal nature of the presumed infringements, nor the period during which the infringements were committed.[34] However, the Commission takes particular care to ensure that the subject-matter and purpose of the inspection are sufficiently clear and that the undertakings concerned are fully appraised of them. The degree of clarity depends not so much on the Commission as on the quantity and quality of the evidence and presumptions which prompted it to open the file and order an inspection.[35] The clarity of the authorization is of fundamental importance in enabling undertakings to satisfy themselves that the information requested and the evidence gathered are relevant to the subject-matter of the inspection.

Clear details of possible sanctions

8.12 Article 23(1) of Regulation 1/2003 empowers the Commission to impose fines on undertakings which, having submitted to an ordinary inspection under an authorization, produce the required books or other business records in incomplete form. In obvious parallel with ordinary requests for information, ordinary inspections are not compulsory and undertakings must decide voluntarily whether or not to submit to them. However, once they have allowed an

---

[32] The Commission may be required to provide complementary explanations to national judicial authorities under Art 20(8) of Reg 1/2003, which calls for '[. . .] detailed explanations in particular on the grounds the Commission has for suspecting infringement of Articles 81 and 82 of the Treaty, as well as on the seriousness of the suspected infringement and on the nature of the involvement of the undertaking concerned.'

[33] The question of whether or not the company under investigation should have access to that very material already at the time of the inspection is a live issue. While Reg 1/2003 does not require that these explanations should be included in the inspection decisions notified to the undertaking subject to an investigation, it does not prohibit that either. Accordingly, it has been submitted that there is no valid reason why it should be elsewhere but in the inspection decisions and it would strengthen materially the defence rights. M Araujo, 'The Respect of Fundamental Rights within the European Network of Competition Authorities' ch 21 in BE Hawk (ed), *International Antitrust Law & Policy*, Annual Proceedings of the Fordham Institute (2004) 511–53 (514).

[34] See Cases 46/87 and 227/88 *Hoechst AG v EC Commission* [1989] ECR 2859 paras 40 and 41; Case 85/87 *Dow Benelux v EC Commission* [1989] ECR 3137 paras 7–10, and Cases 97–99/87 *Dow Ibérica v EC Commission* [1989] ECR 3165 paras 44–46. CS Kerse and N Khan, *EC Antitrust Procedure* (5th edn, 2005) para 3–044.

[35] Case C-94/00 *Roquette Frères* [2002] ECR I-9011 para 78. '[. . .] Even if it already has evidence, or indeed proof, of the existence of an infringement, the Commission may legitimately take the view that it is necessary to order further investigations enabling it to better define the scope of the infringement, to determine its duration or to identify the circle of undertakings involved. [. . .]'.

inspection to commence, undertakings may not place any barriers in the way of the investigative work of the Commission inspectors or withhold full information about their activities from them by any means. Thus, ordinary inspections, once agreed to voluntarily by undertakings, proceed in exactly the same way as inspections undertaken pursuant to decisions.[36]

Explanatory memorandum

In order to inform undertakings of all their rights and obligations during inspections, the Commission has prepared an explanatory memorandum setting out the powers of inspectors and the limits to which their investigative powers are subject.[37] In accordance with consistent administrative practice, the officials carrying out the inspection deliver a copy of the memorandum to undertakings together with the authorization. The explanatory memorandum is an informal document, which does not affect the powers of the inspectors, but explains how the inspection will proceed and sets out the basic rights of the firm being inspected. **8.13**

3. Inspections pursuant to a binding decision

Content of the decision

Article 20(4) of Regulation 1/2003 provides that 'undertakings and associations of undertakings shall submit to investigations ordered by decision of the Commission'. By contrast with ordinary inspections, which undertakings may oppose without thereby committing any infringement, inspections pursuant to a decision are of a mandatory nature and undertakings must submit to them.[38] As stated earlier, the choice between methods of investigation and types of inspection is a matter for the Commission and will in general depend on the circumstances of the case, in particular the attitude displayed by undertakings at **8.14**

---

[36] Just as the reply to a request for information of either type must be correct, inspections must be complete. The fact that they are submitted to voluntarily does not mean that they will be less rigorous. Doubts may exist, however, as to whether it is appropriate to seek enforcement measures for an ordinary inspection which has already been commenced. Like Art 14(6) of Reg 17, Art 20(6) of Reg 1/2003 appears to require the national authorities to provide assistance in such cases as well, although in practice the authorization given to the inspectors and the wording of that provision may not be sufficient for a judge to order enforcement, in the absence of a Commission decision.

[37] There is another explanatory memorandum, but not another form of authorization, for inspections pursuant to a binding decision.

[38] Undertakings could, in theory, attempt to paralyse the conduct of an inspection by applying to the CFI for interim measures under Arts 242 and 243 EC. In view of the possibility of recourse to enforcement measures to implement inspection decisions, it would seem unrealistic to consider that such an application would be dealt with by the CFI before the inspection was carried out. The party concerned will, however, be able to seek judicial redress before the CFI *ex post* by lodging an action for annulment against the decision ordering an investigation. See para 8.16 below.

an earlier stage. Thus, for example, the Commission will tend to opt for mandatory inspections where undertakings have declined to respond to a request for
information or, having responded, have provided inexact or incomplete information; or if they have refused to agree to an ordinary inspection or, having
agreed, have impeded the inspection, failing to provide complete information;
or again, if there are sufficient indications for the Commission to believe that the
evidence or documents sought are liable not to be traceable if some other investigation procedure is adopted; or if it suspects the existence of particularly serious
infringements, for the investigation of which it would be naive to seek the
cooperation of the undertakings involved. Furthermore, the Commission must
consult with an NCA before carrying out such an inspection in its territory,
although this can be done in an informal manner, by telephone if necessary.[39]

8.15 The Commission is expected to take particular care in drafting binding inspection decisions and in stating the reasons on which they are based.[40] Besides
subject matter and purpose, the decision must specify the date on which the
inspection is to begin and needs to indicate the penalties provided for in Article
23 (fixed fine of up to 1 per cent of the total turnover in the preceding business
year of the company) and Article 24 (daily periodic penalty of up to 5 per cent
of the average daily turnover of the undertaking concerned). In addition, the
decision shall also specify the right to have the decision reviewed by the Community Courts. A decision ordering an inspection is open to judicial review,
independently of any final decision on the substantive issue of an infringement
which might be adopted at the conclusion of the investigation. The Commission has indicated that the decision may be the subject of an application for
annulment under Article 230 EC and that such actions do not have suspensive
effect, as provided in Article 242 EC.[41] The question arises whether the lawfulness of this decision can be later challenged as part of an appeal against the final
decision. Where the undertaking has not sought its annulment, it will be fore-
closed from pleading the illegality of the decision ordering the investigation in

---

[39] Case 5/85 *AKZO Chemie BV v EC Commission II* [1986] ECR 2585 para 24.

[40] CS Kerse and N Khan, *EC Antitrust Procedure* (5th edn, 2005) para 3–043 point out that the
degree of detail may vary from case to case. In *Roquette Frères*, the ECJ did not criticize the
operative part of the decision which referred to the product scope of the suspected infringement
and then merely required the undertaking 'to submit for inspection the books and other business
records required by the said officials'. Case C-94/00 *Roquette Frères* [2002] ECR I-9011 paras
88–89.

[41] An undertaking against which the Commission has ordered an investigation may bring an
action against that decision before the Community Courts under the fourth paragraph of Art 230
EC within two months. Case T-59/99 *Ventouris v EC Commission* [2003] ECR II-5257 para 126;
Case 46/87 R *Hoechst v EC Commission* [1987] ECR 1549 para 34 indicating that in the event of
annulment of the inspection decision, the Commission would be prevented from using the
evidence obtained in the course of the inspection; Case 85/87 R *Dow Chemical Nederland v EC
Commission* [1987] ECR 4367 para 17, and Case C-94/00 *Roquette Frères* [2002] ECR I-9011 para

any subsequent action for annulment of the Commisison decision finding an infringement. An undertaking may not challenge the legality of the manner in which investigation procedures are carried out in the context of an action for the annulment of the measure on the basis of which the Commission carries out that investigation. Judicial review of the conditions in which an investigation was conducted falls within the scope of an action which may, in an appropriate case, be brought for the annulment of the final decision adopted by the Commission.[42] Although appeals against inspection decisions will not prevent inspections from being carried out, the Commission may be ordered by the Court not to use the information obtained if the decision is annulled. The possibility that Commission inspectors may have acted discourteously in carrying out an inspection will not in any circumstances undermine the validity of the inspection decision.[43]

A detail overlooked in Article 20(4), probably because it is obvious, is the name   **8.16**
or trading name of the company, to which may be added its address in a particular city. This detail is important, since the Commission's powers relate to the undertaking as defined in the decision. The information concerning its address serves to identify the undertaking, not to limit the Commission's powers to the place given as the undertaking's address. Indeed, Community inspections are carried out on an *ad personam* basis. Although in these cases the Commission is likewise under no obligation to disclose the evidence in its

---

49. It will not have any suspensory effect but a separate application for a stay of execution of the Commission's decision may be made under Art 242 EC. It is however very unlikely if not unconceivable that, e.g. in the circumstances of a surprise investigation, an appeal with an application for a stay could be made and an order from the CFI be obtained to prevent the inspection from being carried out. CS Kerse and N Khan, *EC Antitrust Procedure* (5th edn, 2005) para 3–062 indicating that weighing up the possibility of serious and irreparable damage to the undertaking and the risk of evidence disappearing, the latter prevails. If the decision in question is annulled by the Community judicature, the Commission will in that event be prevented from using, for the purposes of proceedings in respect of an infringement of the Community competition rules, any documents or evidence which it might have obtained in the course of that investigation, as otherwise the decision on the infringement might, in so far as it was based on such evidence, be annulled by the Community judicature. As regards the exclusion of evidence improperly obtained, see J Schwarze and A Weitbrecht, *Grundzüge des europäischen Kartellverfahrens* (2004) § 4 para 21.

[42] Joined Cases T-305/94 to T-307/94, T-313/94 to T-316/94, T-318/94, T-325/94, T-328/94, T-329/94 and T-335/94 *Limburgse Vinyl Maatschappij and others v EC Commission* [1999] ECR II-931 paras 408–415; Case T-66/99 *Minoan Lines v EC Commission* [2003] ECR II-5515 para 93; Case T-65/99 *Strintzis Lines Shipping SA v EC Commission* [2003] ECR II-5433 para 81 in which the CFI alluded to the right of the undertakings to ask for judicial review of the 'intrinsic lawfulness' of the investigation. When filing an appeal against the final decision, the allegation that the inspection impinged upon the right of self-incrimination may also be contested, see CS Kerse and N Khan, *EC Antitrust Procedure* (5th edn 2005) para 3–063. See also K Lenaerts and J Maselis, 'Procedural Rights and Issues in the Enforcement of Articles 81 and 82 of the EC Treaty' [2001] Fordham International Law Journal 1615–54 (1624).

[43] See Case 85/87 *Dow Benelux v EC Commission* [1989] ECR 3137 para 49.

possession, the Court held in its judgment in *Hoechst III* that the Commission must clearly indicate in its decision the allegations it intends to substantiate through the inspection.[44] The date on which the inspection is to begin is indicated in the decision and refers to the time as from which inspections may begin rather than the actual time of commencement (and this is how it is indicated in the decisions). It may in fact happen that inspections do not begin on the first day indicated but one or more days later. Commencement of the inspection on a date later than that indicated does not invalidate the Commission's powers, provided that the inspection takes place within a reasonable time, meaning few days following the date indicated in the decision. As regards penalties, the decision indicates the fines which may be imposed in the event of the required books or other business records being produced in incomplete form or refusal to submit to an inspection.[45] It also details the periodic penalty payments which may be applied for refusal to submit to an inspection.[46]

Procedure

8.17 For the adoption of inspection decisions there is no need for undertakings to be allowed to submit observations, or for a report to be obtained from the Advisory Committee, or for the decision to be published. Any decision is adopted by the member of the Commission responsible for competition policy under the delegation procedure and on behalf of the Commission.[47] Inspection decisions which impose periodic penalty payments are subject to the general rules governing such penalties.[48]

Other documents

8.18 Together with the inspection decision in the strict sense, the inspectors deliver to the undertakings both the authorization empowering them personally to carry out the inspection,[49] and an explanatory memorandum setting out the rights and duties of undertakings and the powers of the inspectors.[50] When a copy of the decision is delivered, the inspectors make a formal note of the notification.

---

[44] Joined Cases 46/87 and 227/88 *Hoechst v EC Commission* [1989] ECR 2859 para 41.
[45] Art 23(1)(c) of Reg 1/2003.   [46] Art 24(1)(e) of Reg 1/2003.
[47] The copy does not have to be signed by the Commissioner. It is sufficient if it is duly certified as authentic by signature of the Secretary-General of the Commission. The Court confirmed this procedure in its judgments in Case 5/85 *AKZO v EC Commission II* [1986] ECR 2585 paras 29–40, Joined Cases 46/87 and 227/88 *Hoechst v EC Commission* [1989] ECR 2859 paras 44–46, and Joined Cases 97–99/87 *Dow Chemical Ibérica v EC Commission* [1989] ECR 3165 para 58.
[48] See ch 9 'Penalties and confidentiality' para 9.14.
[49] The authorization is the same for ordinary inspections and inspection decisions and the identity of the authorized official must be correctly given. See below.
[50] As seen earlier, this explanatory memorandum is different from that used in ordinary inspections.

4. Surprise inspections

As indicated, Article 20 of Regulation 1/2003 does not require the Commission **8.19** to give undertakings prior notice of inspections. Prior notice is required to be given only to the competent authorities of the Member States, not to undertakings. Whether or not to give notice is a matter for the Commission. Ordinary inspections are usually announced in advance. The officials responsible may in such cases speak directly by telephone with the executives of undertakings to explain the purpose of the inspection and set a date for it to be carried out. However, if the Commission believes that there is a risk that documents will be destroyed if the company is alerted in advance, it will not issue an advanced notice. Inspections pursuant to a binding decision may either be announced or carried out without notice, and in fact most are surprise inspections.[51] In the early days, the Commission resorted very rarely to surprise inspections, often referred to as 'dawn raids'.[52] The toughening of Community competition policy in the 1990s gave rise—in addition to increased fines for infringements of Articles 81 and 82 EC[53]—to more intensive investigations into alleged infringements, represented by the use of more coercive and efficient methods, such as unannounced inspections.

Today, the Commission resorts with more frequency to surprise inspections.[54] If **8.20** it were unable to do so, it would be deprived of a particularly effective method of precisely establishing the facts on which it bases its decisions, and its position in actions brought by undertakings before the Court against its infringement decisions would be considerably weakened. The number of unannounced inspections also surged considerably. This drive stems from the top priority given by the Commission to stopping illegal cartel activity, and to do so swiftly. In this regard it should be noted that according to the Commission, once there is awareness of an illegal cartel, time for reaction is very brief, between four and six weeks.[55] In

---

[51] *Graphite Electrodes* [2002] OJ L100/1 para 33: '[. . .] by the time the investigation started, all the relevant files had been "reviewed" and incriminating documents destroyed or moved to a safe location away from offices and private homes. [. . . .].' The Commission does not need to set out whether it is concerned that an undertaking might conceal or destroy evidence. CS Kerse and N Khan, *EC Antitrust Procedure* (5th edn, 2005) para 3–044.

[52] 'Dealing with the Commission—Notification, complaints, inspections and fact-finding powers under Articles [81] and [82] of the EEC Treaty' (1997 edn) point 5.6. The scope of the powers of investigation.

[53] See ch 11 'Infringement decisions' paras 11.38 *et seq.*

[54] CS Kerse and N Khan, *EC Antitrust Procedure* (5th edn, 2005) para 3–039.

[55] XXXII Report on Competition Policy [2002] para 32 indicating that '[E]xperience so far shows that, following an inspection, cartels generally collapse and hence stop their illegal activities. [. . .]' e.g. in *Pre-insulated Pipes* [1999] OJ L24/1; *Seamless Tubes* [2003] OJ L140/1 and *Industrial and Medical Gases* [2003] OJ L84/1 the Commission's first step was an inspection by decision carried out simultaneously. See CS Kerse and N Khan, *EC Antitrust Procedure* (5th edn, 2005) para 3–044.

National Panasonic, an undertaking subjected to the first unannounced Regulation 17, Article 14(3) investigation claimed that the procedure infringed its fundamental rights.[56] Panasonic challenged the validity of the decision ordering the inspection. It relied in particular on Article 8 of the European Convention on Human Rights ('ECHR').[57] It also claimed that in this case the principle of proportionality was infringed. The Court confirmed the legality of surprise inspections. In its opinion, the carrying out of inspections pursuant to decisions and by surprise does not infringe the fundamental rights of undertakings. It considers such inspections to be justified as an exception to the principle of non-interference by public authorities in the exercise of individual rights, which is properly regulated and is necessary to defend the public interest. The Court's view is that the exercise of the investigative powers vested in the Commission contributes to maintenance of the competitive conditions upheld by the EC Treaty, which undertakings must observe without fail. In those circumstances, it would not seem that, by giving the Commission powers to undertake inspections without prior notice, Regulation 17 (or Regulation 1/2003) in any way would violate the private rights, domicile or correspondence of undertakings.[58]

8.21   Moreover, the unannounced inspection would also not infringe the right to be heard. The Commission's inspection would not aim at terminating an infringement or declaring that an agreement, decision or concerted practice is incompatible with Article 81 EC where such right of defence would be applicable. Its sole objective is to enable the Commission to gather the necessary information to check the actual existence and scope of a given factual and legal situation. As regards the violation of the principle of proportionality, the Court stated that this aimed solely at enabling the Commission to collect the necessary information to appraise whether there was any infringement of the Treaty. It does not therefore appear that the Commission's action in this instance was disproportionate to the objective pursued and infringed the principle of proportionality. The ECJ therefore rejected National Panasonic's claims and

---

[56] See A Jones and B Sufrin, *EC Competition Law* (2nd edn, 2004) 1064 noting that Commission officials arrived at Panasonic's offices in Slough at 10.00 a.m. The directors asked if the inspection could be delayed to await the arrival of their solicitor, who was in Norwich. The officials waited until 10.45 a.m. and then began. The solicitor did not arrive until 1.45 p.m. and the inspection finished at 5.30 p.m.

[57] Art 8 ECHR reads as follows: 'Right to respect for private and family life (1) Everyone has the right to respect for his private and family life, his home and his correspondence. (2) There shall be no interference by a public authority with the exercise of this right except such as is in accordance with the law and is necessary in a democratic society in the interests of national security, public safety or the economic well-being of the country, for the prevention of disorder or crime, for the protection of health or morals, or for the protection of the rights and freedoms of others.'

[58] See Case 136/79 *National Panasonic v EC Commission* [1980] ECR 2033 para 20.

held that an unannounced inspection does not infringe the rights of an undertaking.

The application of Article 8(1) of the ECHR was considered again in *Hoechst*. **8.22** The position of undertakings faced with unannounced inspections under Article 14(3) of Regulation 17 (the equivalent of Article 20(4) of Regulation 1/2003) and the powers of the Commission in respect thereof were considered at length by the Court. The case arose from an unannounced investigation in the course of the Commission's investigations into the PVC and polyethylene cartels. Hoechst refused to admit the Commission inspectors when they arrived.[59] The Court held that the Commission's officials might, without the cooperation of the undertakings, search for any information necessary for the investigation with the assistance of the national authorities, which are required to afford them the assistance necessary for the performance of their duties. Although such assistance is required only if the undertaking expresses its opposition, it may also be requested as a precautionary measure, in order to overcome any opposition on the part of the undertaking.

C. Representation of Undertakings during Inspections

1. Persons allowed to represent undertakings

Article 20 of Regulation 1/2003, unlike Article 18(4) in relation to requests **8.23** for information, does not specify who is permitted to represent undertakings during inspections. In such cases, it is for the undertakings, and not the Commission, to designate the person or persons who will represent them. The Commission and its inspectors have no authority to make any judgment as to the competence or knowledge of the persons designated by the undertakings— they are designated by the undertakings, at their own risk[60]—and merely seek a proper interlocutor so that they can discharge their duties. It is just as beneficial to undertakings as to the Commission—or even more so—for their representatives on such occasions to be responsible and well informed. It should

---

[59] The ECJ's response to the application of Art 8 ECHR has been that the provision is directed at individuals and therefore had no application to dawn raids on business premises. Joined Cases 46/87 and 227/88 *Hoechst v EC Commission* [1989] ECR 2859 para 18. CS Kerse and N Khan, *EC Antitrust Procedure* (5th edn, 2005) para 3–037. Note that the issue of compatibility of inspections with Art 8 ECHR was again considered in C-94/00 *Roquette Frères* [2002] ECR I-9011.

[60] In *Fabbrica Pisana* [1980] OJ L75/30 the Commission explained that it is not permissible for an undertaking which has not produced certain documents requested by the inspectors to argue that its failure to do so was caused by the absence of its general manager and that the commercial manager was unaware of the whereabouts of the documents concerned.

be noted that the officials and other accompanying persons authorized by the Commission to conduct an inspection have the power to ask any representative or member of staff of the undertaking or association of undertakings for explanations on facts and documents relating to the subject-matter and purpose of the inspection and to record the answers. The corresponding provision in Regulation 17 (Article 14(1)(c)) empowered the inspectors 'to ask for oral explanations on the spot' and there was a surprising lack of authority on what this meant. The generally accepted view was that it encompassed asking questions directly arising from the books and records being examined and asking for explanations of such matters as the references, terms, and abbreviations appearing in them, but that it did not authorize a general interrogation of officers or employees of the undertaking. Article 14 of Regulation 17 did not specify who should answer the oral questions put to the undertaking but a failure by the undertaking to put forward a suitable person could be construed as a refusal to cooperate. These uncertainties have been remedied by Article 20(2)(e) of Regulation 1/2003, which seems to have expanded the Commission's powers to ask questions. The inspectors may now ask 'any representative or member of staff' for explanations on *facts* and documents relating to *the subject-matter and purpose* of the inspection. The answers can be recorded.[61]

8.24   Article 23(1)(d) provides that the Commission may fine the undertaking up to 1 per cent of total turnover of the previous business year if, in response to a question asked in accordance with Article 20(2)(e):

- they give an incorrect or misleading answer;
- they fail to rectify within a time-limit set by the Commission an incorrect, incomplete or misleading answer given by a member of staff; or
- they fail or refuse to provide a complete answer on facts relating to the subject matter and purpose of an inspection ordered by a decision adopted pursuant to Article 20(4).

8.25   The term 'they' in this provision refers to the undertakings in question, not to the individual members of staff. Unlike in a number of Member States, there are no powers under Regulation 1/2003 to impose fines on individuals. It will be noted, however, that as regards members of staff the fine is to be imposed on undertakings for failure or refusal to rectify any incomplete, incorrect, or misleading answers given by their employees. Under Regulation 773/2004 relating

---

[61] Art 4(3) of Reg 773/2004 permits an undertaking to rectify an employee's responses, but Recital 4 to that Reg nevertheless specifies that the answer given by a member of the staff should remain in the Commission file as recorded during the inspection. This may be construed as meaning that the original answer, albeit rectified, may be used as evidence to corroborate another party's evidence. CS Kerse and N Khan, *EC Antitrust Procedure* (5th edn, 2005) para 3–059.

to the conduct of proceedings by the Commission, in cases where a member of staff of an undertaking or of an association of undertakings who is not or was not authorized by the undertaking or by the association of undertakings to provide explanations on behalf of the undertaking or association of undertakings has been asked for explanations, the Commission shall set a time-limit within which the undertaking or the association of undertakings may communicate to the Commission any rectification, amendment, or supplement to the explanations given by such member of staff.[62] The rectification, amendment, or supplement shall be added to the explanations as recorded pursuant to paragraph 1.

The possibility of rectification is only granted in regard to staff 'not authorized by the undertaking to provide explanations'. Undertakings might also wish, however, to rectify or supplement answers given by staff being 'authorized', all the more as there is no definition of an 'authorized' member of staff. It would appear only fair that the Commission would allow the undertakings to do this without a fine, unless there was some evidence of bad faith on the part of the undertaking at the time that an incorrect or misleading answer was given.[63] **8.26**

2. Assistance from a lawyer or legal adviser

Assistance of a lawyer during inspections is regulated neither in Regulation 1/2003 nor in the Implementing Regulation 773/2004. It is, however, consistent Commission practice to allow undertakings to be assisted by their own legal advisers or by independent lawyers. This results from the general principle that undertakings under investigation are protected by various Community guarantees, including, in particular, the right to legal representation.[64] However, that right does not imply any limitation on the investigative powers of Commission officials. The Court has confirmed that an inspection carried out without awaiting the arrival of an undertaking's legal adviser is lawful.[65] Thus, the presence of a lawyer is not required. **8.27**

---

[62] Art 4(3) of Reg 773/2004.

[63] A Jones and B Sufrin, *EC Competition Law* (2nd edn, 2004) 1071. See also Comments on Modernization Package, by the law firm Cleary, Gottlieb, Steen & Hamilton, 3 December 2003, available at http://europa.eu.int/comm/competition/antitrust/legislation/procedural_rules/comments/.

[64] Case C-94/00 *Roquette Frères* [2002] ECR I-9011 para 46; Case 155/79 *AM & S Europe Limited v EC Commission* [1982] ECR 1575 paras 18 to 27; Joined Cases 46/87 and 227/88 *Hoechst v EC Commission* [1989] ECR 2859 para 16; Case 85/87 *Dow Benelux v EC Commission* [1989] ECR 3137 para 27.

[65] Case 136/79 *National Panasonic v EC Commission* [1980] ECR 2033 para 19. Note that asking for a postponement until a particular designated representative of the firm or a particular lawyer can be present can also constitute a refusal to submit, leading to the imposition of a fine.

8.28 When conducting the unannounced investigation in *National Panasonic*, however, the Commission was prepared to wait for some time for the undertakings' legal advisers to arrive, but after a while proceeded in their absence. The Court held that National Panasonic's fundamental rights had not been infringed in the investigation, although it did not expressly consider the legal adviser point. The Commission has a policy of allowing firms a reasonable time to secure the services of an in-house legal adviser or lawyer of its choice although it will not permit undue delay.[66] During any wait the undertaking's management has to ensure that business records remain as they were on the officials' arrival and the officials have to be allowed to enter and remain in the offices of their choice. In other words, there must be no opportunity for the operation of the paper-shredder or the wiping of the hard-drive. The new power of the Commission to designate a member of staff for answering a given oral question raises the question whether it would be necessary that such members of staff be also assisted by their own lawyer. There is the view that the member of staff is not the real subject of the questioning and for this reason it would not be strictly necessary to be assisted by a lawyer. He or she is only questioned as an employee of the undertaking and no incrimination of that individual may occur under EC competition law.[67] However, the individual may be liable under national rules, which could allow sanctions to be imposed on individuals.[68]

---

[66] The inspectors allow the company to call its external lawyers to attend the inspection. However, the inspectors are not obliged to wait until the lawyers arrive and in practice are unlikely to wait for more than a few minutes before proceeding with the investigation. A Klees, *Europäisches Kartellverfahrensrecht* (2005) § 9 para 92.

[67] He or she would not face any personal sanction, neither for incomplete, incorrect or misleading answers nor for the infringement as such. Art 23(2)(d) of Reg 1/2003 indicates that the fines may only be imposed on the undertaking. K Dekeyser and C Gauer, 'The New Enforcement System for Arts 81 & 82 and the Rights of Defence', ch 23 in BE Hawk (ed), *International Antitrust Law of Policy*, Annual Proceedings of the Fordham Institute (2004) 549–85 (559–64). However, if the individual in question refuses to answer the question and the company does not provide the answer by other means, the company may then be liable. If the employee is represented by a lawyer, the question arises whether a counsel can represent employees under investigation as well as their employer. This may be a problem where the employee is subject to disciplinary measures pursuant to his or her contract of employment or in the event of possible criminal proceedings under relevant legislation. See HJ Niemeyer, D Stockhausen, J Boyce and D Loukas, 'European Union' [2004] *Cartel Regulation*, Global Competition Review 55.

[68] While national sanctions may be envisaged, Art 12(3) of Reg 1/2003 contains limits on the possibility that the information can be used by a national authority to impose sanctions on natural persons and excludes custodial sanctions. If an individual provides evidence in a Commission investigation or refuses to answer, a Member State should not be permitted to use the statements or the fact of his or her silence in subsequent national criminal proceedings targeting that individual or other individuals incriminated by the individual's testimony. E Gippini-Fournier, 'Legal Professional Privilege in Competition Proceedings before the European Commission: Beyond the Cursory Glance' ch 24 in BE Hawk (ed), *International Antitrust Law & Policy*, Annual Proceedings of the Fordham Institute (2004) 24, 587–658 (643).

D. The Commission's Ordinary Powers during Inspections

The powers of the Commission during inspections are the same for ordinary **8.29** inspections, under Article 20(2), or those pursuant to a binding decision under Article 20(3). The only difference lies in the fact that undertakings may object to the former but not to the latter. Undertakings are required to submit to inspection decisions and may be fined and forced to comply if they do not voluntarily undergo inspection. Undertakings are entitled to object to an ordinary inspection in its entirety; but if they agree to submit to it, the Commission's view is that they are required to enable its inspectors to exercise all their powers and must present all documentation requested in complete form, as if the inspection were being carried out pursuant to a decision. Under Article 20(2) the Commission powers include:

(a) to enter any premises, land, and means of transport of undertakings and associations of undertakings;
(b) to examine the books and other records related to the business, irrespective of the medium on which they are stored;
(c) to take or obtain in any form copies of or extracts from such books or records;
(d) to seal any business premises and books or records for the period and to the extent necessary for the inspection;
(e) to ask any representative or member of staff of the undertaking or association of undertakings for explanations on facts or documents relating to the subject-matter and purpose of the inspection and to record the answers

The five subparagraphs of Article 20(2) will now be dealt with in turn and the practical implications of each will be considered.

1. Access to premises, land, means of transport of undertakings, and associations of undertakings

Commission inspectors are entitled to free access to all buildings, land, and **8.30** vehicles of undertakings. This extends to access to all offices containing documents and files which relate to the investigation. Undertakings may not prevent Commission officials from entering any of their premises or means of transport by claiming inviolability of their premises.[69] Regulation 1/2003 does not speak exclusively of administrative premises or in any way limit inspectors' access. They have overriding powers to select the premises, dwellings, land,

---

[69] See Cases 46/87 and 227/88 *Hoechst v EC Commission* [1989] ECR 2859 paras 26–27.

or vehicles in which they wish to commence, continue and complete their task.[70] The Commission takes the view that its powers of inspection are not limited to premises owned, leased, or otherwise formally occupied by the undertaking.[71] However, this power does not extend to premises of external lawyers or accountants used by the undertaking even if such persons may well hold 'books or other business records' belonging to the undertaking being investigated.[72]

8.31 The extent of this power was explained in *Hoechst*.[73] If the undertakings are willing to co-operate, the Commission officials have power to have shown to them the documents they request, and to enter such premises they choose and have shown to them the contents of particular furniture they indicate. They are *not* entitled forcibly to enter premises or furniture or carry out searches without the undertaking's consent. If the undertaking does not submit to the investigation, Article 20(6) of Regulation 1/2003 comes into play and the Commission has to rely on the assistance of the Member State.[74]

8.32 The Commission is also entitled to investigate businesses which are suspected of any infringement of the competition rules. It may wish to see the documents of third party complainants or of customers or suppliers. In such cases, the Commission is unlikely to carry out an unannounced dawn raid and will instead warn the relevant business in advance. Usually, this power is rarely used because the Commission tends to request such information by letter instead. The power of entry under Regulation 17 did not extend to a director's private home. Nor did it automatically extend to the premises of the company's external lawyers, bankers or accountants (although these could be subject to a separate inspection authorized by the Commission. In practice, if documents were located outside the company's premises, the inspectors could require the company to produce them. Under Regulation 1/2003, the Commission has been granted an express

---

[70] If no particular premises are specified in the substantive Art of the decision, there is no limitation of the scope of the decision geographically. *Akzo Chemicals BV* [1994] OJ L294/31 para 17. CS Kerse and N Khan, *EC Antitrust Procedure* (5th edn, 2005) para 3–052.

[71] In *Akzo Chemicals*, the Commission said that 'offices' were 'premises' if and to the extent that the business of the undertaking was carried out in them. *Akzo Chemicals BV* [1994] OJ L294/31 para 19.

[72] CS Kerse and N Khan, *EC Antitrust Procedure* (5th edn, 2005) para 3–052. The Commission must require the undertaking to produce the relevant documents unless a decision is adopted which allows it to enter the premises of these other undertakings.

[73] Cases 46/87 and 227/88 *Hoechst v EC Commission* [1989] ECR 2859 paras 31 and 32.

[74] Where a company refuses entry, the Commission can impose fines and can obtain appropriate assistance such as an injunction from the NCAs. In some countries (see, for example, s 22 of the UK Competition Act 1998), national competition law may authorize the local competition authorities and Commission officials to use force to enter the premises and to search them to assist with a Commission investigation.

power to inspect the private homes of directors and other member of staff as well as other premises.[75]

2. Examination of books and other business records

Business records in general

The term 'business records' embraces all documentation, in writing or otherwise **8.33** relating to the undertaking's business.[76] Business documents include correspondence, accounting records and financial documents (invoices, balance sheets, and others), photographs, transparencies, films, magnetic tapes, cassettes, computer programs (and their content), microfilms, videocassettes, CDs, DVDs, and so on. In other words, Commission inspectors' investigations extend to all possible physical materials for the recording of information, not only written documents.[77] The only requirement is that they should relate to the economic activity of the undertaking.[78] The ECJ has also stressed how important it is to preserve the effectiveness of investigations as a necessary tool for the Commission in carrying out its role as guardian of the Treaty in competition matters, ruling that that right of access would serve no useful purpose if the Commission's officials could do no more than ask for documents or files which they could identify precisely in advance. On the contrary, such a right implies the power to search for various items of information which are not already known or fully identified. Without such a power, it would be impossible for the Commission to obtain the information necessary to carry out the investigation.[79]

The business nature of a document cannot be determined until after the officials **8.34** responsible have examined it. As a rule, the principle is that a document is deemed to be a business record if it is found on the premises and in the files of an undertaking. If, after examination, a document proves in fact to be entirely private, the inspectors will not examine it in greater detail or take copies. In the

---

[75] Art 21 of Reg 1/2003. For more details, see para 8.54 below

[76] See *FNICF* [1982] OJ L319/12 para 5: correspondence, internal memoranda and records of meetings with various other trade organizations, minutes or records of meetings of the management organ of the association.

[77] Art 20(2)(b) of Reg 1/2003 specifies that the Commission may examine records 'irrespective of the medium on which they are stored'. This encompasses all forms of information technology. It is thought likely that the Community Courts would construe the words 'examine' so as to include the right of reasonable access and use of necessary facilities for the examination and copying of the records. CS Kerse and N Khan, *EC Antitrust Procedure* (5th edn, 2005) para 3–053.

[78] Case 155/79 *AM & S Europe v EC Commission* [1982] ECR 1575 para 16: '[. . .] the scope of the Commission's investigatory powers does not extend to cover, in particular, documents of a non-business nature, that is to say, documents not relating to the market activities of the undertaking. [. . .].'

[79] Case T-59/99 *Ventouris v EC Commission* [2003] ECR II-5257 para 122.

case of written documents, the inspectors may work both on final documents which have been used by undertakings for formal purposes (for example, correspondence) and unofficial or informal documents (internal memoranda and minutes of meetings, hand-written notes and drafts of documents not yet finalized, and so on). Regulation 1/2003 does not limit the powers of inspectors regarding the type of document to be investigated. In view of the fact that many restrictive agreements—or at least, some of the most seriously restrictive ones—are secret or take the form of concerted practices, it would be impractical to require the Commission to find a public or formal physical record of them—which often does not exist—otherwise it would be prevented from exercising its powers specifically against the most reprehensible conduct from the point of view of competition law.

8.35 In the case of information stored in electronic-data systems (computers), the inspectors may request, and undertakings are required to provide, a printed copy of all or any part of such information, or a list if they prefer in order to examine it.[80] It appears that the limitation of the inspection to the 'premises' in Article 20(2) (a) does not necessarily mean that the records susceptible to inspection under Article 20(2)(b) have to be on the premises if they are accessible from there. This would apply to information stored in a computer system: where undertakings use computers to access information stored on a server situated elsewhere that information would also be considered as coming within the scope of the inspection.[81] Failure to cooperate in this respect—on the pretext, for example, that no one is available on the premises who is able to operate the electronic system—would be regarded as incomplete production of the requisite business records, liable to a penalty under Article 23(1)(c) of Regulation 1/2003.[82] All the business documents described above are liable to be examined by Commission inspectors.

8.36 The logical basis for this extremely wide power of examination is the fact that it is impossible for the Commission precisely to specify the documents which it is

---

[80] Although this seems to be in many instances the current practice of the Commission, it is questionable whether the Commission should be allowed to copy the hard disc drives of computers on the undertaking's premises. Granting this right comes close to enabling the Commission to conduct a 'fishing expedition' which does not come within its powers. The right to examine necessarily relates to all relevant documents that the Commission identifies during the inspection, but the right to copy should be limited to documents which are related—directly or indirectly—with the investigation.

[81] CS Kerse and N Khan, *EC Antitrust Procedure* (5th edn, 2005) para 3–053 pointing to the UK Competition Act 1998 which includes the power for inspectors to take possession of 'information' which is held in a computer and is accessible from the premises. This would suggest that information stored on a server even outside the jurisdiction could be obtained within the framework of an inspection at the company's premises provided those have links to the server.

[82] See ch 9 'Penalties and confidentiality' paras 9.06 *et seq.*

looking for, although in exceptional cases it can do so.[83] Under normal conditions, the Commission has no way of determining in advance which documents may be of interest to it. Its interest in any particular document will normally become apparent during the inspection.

Limitations

Despite the power of Commission inspectors to examine all business records, **8.37** they are authorized to take away (by making copies or extracts for use in their procedures) only those that relate directly or indirectly to the subject matter and purpose of the inspection. Moreover, the subject-matter of the inspection must coincide wholly or partly with the subject matter of the procedure.[84] The fact that the Commission, through its inspectors, must observe certain limits in collecting information from undertakings does not mean that those limits apply to what the inspectors may *see or examine*. In fact, without this preliminary phase it would be impossible to determine which documents are relevant to the subject matter of the investigation and which are not. Furthermore, undertakings could impede inspections if it were left to them to decide what inspectors might and might not be allowed to see. The limits on inspections thus relate not to accessibility and unrestricted examination of business records—which is essential to establish the relevance of documents to the investigation—but to removal and subsequent use of them by the Commission in its procedures. Similarly, the Commission's power to take away documents is not limited to those that are directly and closely related to the subject-matter of the investigation. In order to arrive at a more informed judgment as to the existence of an alleged infringement, it may be necessary to obtain documents of a general nature relating to the business of the undertaking in the relevant economic sector.

Thus, Commission inspectors may have access to all documents concerning the **8.38** *whole* business of undertakings, although they will take away (by making extracts or copies) only those directly or indirectly relating to the subject matter of the inspection. The Commission has acknowledged that its investigative powers are accompanied by 'an obligation not to examine business records, or to stop examining such records, if they are obviously or in the Commission officials' opinion not related to the subject matter of the investigation'.[85] The

---

[83] Thus, e.g. the Commission will know exactly what documents it seeks when it has been informed about them in an anonymous, informal, unofficial complaint or within a request of leniency. Even in such cases, the Commission is not obliged to specify them, if it does not wish to do so, in the authorization or inspection decision.

[84] The observations made earlier regarding 'fishing expeditions' should be borne in mind. See ch 7 'Investigative measures' para 7.28.

[85] *CSM* [1992] OJ L305/16.

Commission will confine its activities to business records relating directly or indirectly to the suspected infringement being investigated, the latter having been described in the authorization or decision by reference to the subject matter and purpose of the inspection. The inspection will be limited to the product or service and market and the alleged infringement affecting them. In practice, the scope of the investigation may be very broadly defined because of the Commission's own lack of knowledge of the business under investigation, so that attempts to avoid handing over certain material could be seen as obstructive and lead to the company being penalized. If they consider it appropriate to do so, on the ground that the documents collected by the inspectors fall outside the scope of the authorization or decision, not being related to the subject matter and purpose thereof, undertakings may register their protest in the record of the inspection. However, they may not prevent inspectors from taking copies or extracts, and if they do so will be liable to fines and periodic penalty payments. Such a protest is not a formal precondition for an action for annulment of the decision to inspect.[86] Undertakings may also subsequently request the return of copies which in their view have no bearing on the subject matter of the inspection decision.[87] Furthermore, the Commission can not use evidence, which it had obtained unlawfully if a finding of unlawfulness is made by the CFI.[88] In conclusion, undertakings may not substitute their interpretation of the inspection decision for that of the Commission, since only the CFI 'is competent to supervise the Commission's conduct'.[89]

Correspondence with lawyers

8.39 The general power of examination enjoyed by Commission inspectors is subject to one exception; it does not extend to correspondence between undertakings and their lawyers.[90] Although neither Regulation 17 nor Regulation 1/2003 contain a special provision dealing with the position of lawyer–client communications, in *AM & S v Commission*,[91] the ECJ held that Regulation 17 must be interpreted as providing protection for such correspondence and defined the

---

[86] Certain firms of lawyers specializing in Community law nevertheless protest in this way as a matter of routine.

[87] To that effect, see the Decision in *CSM* [1992] OJ L305/6.

[88] Order of the Court in Case 46/87 R *Hoechst v EC Commission II* [1987] ECR 1549 para 34, and Order of the Court in Case 85/87 R *Dow Chemical Nederland v EC Commission* [1987] ECR 4367 para 17.

[89] *CSM* [1992] OJ L305/16.

[90] Obviously, having no power of examination, in these cases the Commission lacks, even more so than in respect of documents not relating to the subject matter of the inspection, the power to take copies or extracts.

[91] Case 155/79 *AM & S Europe Limited v EC Commission* [1982] ECR 1575. The case originated in a dispute about the confidentiality of a series of documents found at the premises of AM & S during an inspection into a cartel among zinc producers. The company claimed these

conditions under which such protection is available, and the manner in which undertakings and the Commission must behave in such cases.[92]

Taking as a starting point the fact that correspondence between an undertaking **8.40** and a lawyer forms part of the business records referred to in Article 14 of the former Regulation 17 (and in Article 18 of Reg 1/2003), and that the Commission may require production of the business records of undertakings, and has the sole right—not enjoyed by the undertakings or any third party—to decide whether or not a document should be produced to it, the Court upheld the possibility that, within the system of procedural rules, certain business records, specifically correspondence between undertakings and lawyers, may be recognized as confidential. That right to confidentiality—the Court held—reflects the requirement, the importance of which is recognized in all the Member States, that every person must be entirely free to consult his or her lawyer. The ECJ acknowledged that a person must be able without constraint to consult a lawyer whose profession entails the giving of independent legal advice to all those in need of it.[93] Confidentiality can be recognized, however, only where two conditions are fulfilled: first, the correspondence must have been sent for the purposes and in the interests of the client's rights of defence; secondly, it must be correspondence with independent lawyers, that is to say lawyers not linked to their client (the undertaking) by an employment relationship. However, the ECJ did not define the exact scope of the privilege.

In administrative proceedings before the Commission, the protection of con- **8.41** fidentiality must be seen as extending *ipso jure* to all correspondence exchanged after initiation of proceedings under Regulation 1/2003, and all prior correspondence connected with the subject matter of that procedure. The existence of the protection is not dependent on there being an inspection under Article 20, nor is the extent of the protection necessarily limited to the scope of any such inspection.[94] Since the formal initiation of proceedings usually takes place after the preliminary investigation, in which inspections play an important part, it

---

were privileged written communications between lawyer and client and related documents, and refused to show them to the Commission. The Commission issued a decision requiring AM & S to produce the documents. See also E Gippini-Fournier, 'Legal Professional Privilege in Competition Proceedings before the European Commission: Beyond the Cursory Glance' ch 24 in BE Hawk (ed.) *International Antitrust Law & Policy*, Annual Proceedings of the Fordham Institute (2004) 587–658 (621–26); J Temple Lang, 'The AM & S Judgment' ch 12 in M Hoskins and W Robinson, *A True European—Essays for Judge David Edward* (2003) 153–60; J Joshua, 'Privilege in multi-jurisdictional cartel investigations: are European courts missing the point', Global Competition Review, February 2004, 39–41.

[92] The CFI followed its ruling in Case 155/79 *AM & S Europe Limited v EC Commission* in Case T-30/89 *Hilti v EC Commission* [1991] ECR II-1439 paras 13 and 14.

[93] Case 155/79 *AM & S Europe Limited v EC Commission* [1982] ECR 1675 para 18.

[94] CS Kerse and N Khan, *EC Antitrust Procedure* (5th edn, 2005) para 3–024.

must be considered that, when it refers to initiating proceedings, the Court is referring to what has been called here opening the file.[95] According to that interpretation, previous correspondence which is protected may include, for example, letters to and from undertakings and lawyers concerning matters dealt with informally by the Commission before a file came into physical existence, at meetings or in contacts prior to a notification. If such communications are reproduced in internal notes which merely report their text or content, those notes must also be regarded as confidential.[96]

8.42 The immunity described above is enjoyed generally by correspondence from all lawyers entitled to practise before a court[97] in any of the Member States, regardless of the Member State in which the undertaking is located. Correspondence between an undertaking and its non-EU lawyers does not therefore enjoy the immunity established by the *AM & S* judgment.[98] The same benefit is available to lawyers in EFTA countries which are parties to the EEA agreement.[99] Finally, the immunity granted to such correspondence does not prevent undertakings, if they see fit, from revealing its contents to Commission inspectors. If differences arise as to the immunity of allegedly confidential correspondence, in view of the fact that as a rule all business records must be produced to the Commission inspectors, it is incumbent on undertakings to prove that the correspondence at issue meets the conditions justifying its legal protection. However, undertakings are not required for that purpose to disclose its contents. Undertakings may, for example, disclose certain passages of the document concerned, produce other documents which refer to that document, make a formal statement as to its subject-matter (lawyer-client relationship), give a written description of its general content, and so on. The inspectors will

[95] CS Kerse and N Khan, *EC Antitrust Procedure* (5th edn, 2005) para 3–023 noting that the protection must extend to earlier written communications which have a relationship to the subject-matter of the procedure under the Reg because inquiries, formal and informal may be made by the Commission before such initiation proceedings and there should be no discouragement from taking legal advice at the earliest opportunity.

[96] Case T-30/89 *Hilti v EC Commission* [1991] ECR II-1439 paras 13–18.

[97] The French text says '*inscrits au barreau*'.

[98] The position may well be re-considered if it were to come before the Court in a new case. See J Joshua, 'Privilege in multi-jurisdictional cartel investigations: are European courts missing the point' Global Competition Review, February 2004, 39–41 (40); J Temple Lang, 'The AM & S Judgment' ch 12 in M Hoskins and W Robinson, *'A True European' Essays for Judge David Edward* (2003) 153–60.

[99] Individuals and undertakings have the right to be represented, before the CFI and ECJ as well as before the EFTA Court, by lawyers entitled to practice either before the EC or EFTA national courts. Lawyers from EFTA/EEA States further enjoy rights as to legal privilege, whether the proceeding is conducted by the EC Commission or the ESA. *EEA Agreement* [1994] OJ L1/3. See also ch 28 'European Economic Area Competition Procedure' para 28.51. J Temple Lang 'The AM & S Judgment' ch 12 in M Hoskins and W Robinson, *A True European—Essays for Judge David Edward* (2003) 157.

have to judge whether the evidence produced is sufficient for them to accept that the document is confidential. If they consider it insufficient, they will ask for further evidence. If the undertakings decline to provide it, or if the new evidence fails to convince them, the inspectors will make a record of the disagreement, which must be signed by the undertakings, the inspectors and, if they are present, the representatives of the NCAs. The undertakings will receive a copy of the record.[100]

Moreover, the Court has held that it is for the Commission to request delivery **8.43** of the contested correspondence, imposing pecuniary penalties if necessary where undertakings fail to hand over the documents or provide sufficient evidence of their confidentiality. The Court has stated that judicial review ensures that neither the interests of the Commission nor those of the undertakings themselves are affected by this procedure since, firstly, the Commission may apply for immediate enforcement of the decision and, secondly, undertakings may apply to the Court for its suspension. It will ultimately be the Court which decides whether or not the document must be produced for examination. As indicated, legal advice of a general nature unrelated to the particular investigation will not be privileged (but equally it will not be relevant to the inspection). More significantly, as the law currently stands, advice and correspondence originating from in-house lawyers will not be privileged.[101] In principle, privilege will not be available to written advice given by the in-house lawyer to the company or a written request from the company to its in-house lawyer for legal advice, even if the request is subsequently passed on to an external lawyer). The CFI held that internal notes which merely report the text or comments of communications from an external layer that would have

---

[100] See Joined Cases T-125/03 R and T-253/03 R *Akzo Nobel Chemicals Ltd/Akcros Chemicals Ltd v EC Commission* [2003] ECR II-4771 para 132: '[. . . .] Where the Commission is not satisfied that such evidence has been supplied, it is for the latter to order production of the communications in question and, if necessary, to impose on the undertaking fines or periodic penalty payments under that Regulation as a penalty for the undertaking's refusal either to supply such additional evidence as the Commission considers necessary or to produce the communications in question whose confidentiality, in the Commission's view, is not protected by law [. . .] It is then open to the undertaking subject to the investigation to lodge an application for annulment of the Commission's decision, together where appropriate with an application for interim measures, under Arts 242 EC and 243 EC. [. . . .]'. 'Dealing with the Commission—Notification, complaints, inspections and fact-finding powers under Arts [81] and [82] of the EEC Treaty' (edn 1997), at point 6.7.

[101] The Commission rejected the staff of Audi's legal department's claim of 'attorneys' privilege' in *Volkswagen* [1998] OJ L124/60 paras 198–199. See also *Opel* [2000] OJ L59/1. Opel Nederland BV claimed that an internal document which included *inter alia* guidance on how dealers verify whether sales are compatible with the dealer contract should be protected by legal privilege as it was based on written advice from an independent legal adviser and oral advice from an outside legal counsel. The Commission rejected this argument, as the document in question is not confined to reporting the text or the content of legal counsel's communication, and the legal considerations contained therein are not used as evidence.

attracted privilege if received in writing from the external lawyer will themselves be privileged.[102]

8.44 However, in a recent case, the President of the CFI decided, in an interim hearing, that the parties' arguments, i.e. that legal privilege should attach to memos prepared for the purpose of a telephone conversation with an independent lawyer, raised such significant questions about the possible need to extend the scope of professional privilege in EC law that it had to be considered by the CFI in the main application. In particular, the President noted that a number of changes have occurred in Member States since the ECJ's ruling in *AM & S*. Today, a majority of Member States recognize privilege for properly qualified in-house lawyers subject to ethical rules and disciplinary proceedings. In procedural terms, the President considered that 'it is not precluded at this stage that, in the context of an investigation under Article 14(3) of Regulation 17, the Commission's officials must refrain from casting even a cursory glance over the documents which an undertaking claims to be protected by professional privilege, at least if the undertaking has not given its consent.'[103] The President was cautious to put the burden so heavily on the undertaking to demonstrate that the communications fulfil the conditions for being granted legal protection. Specifically, as regards the procedure to be adopted, the President found that the procedural principles of AM & S tended to demonstrate that, in the event of a dispute regarding a particular document where the undertaking has provided evidence to suggest that the document is privileged but the Commission is not satisfied by such evidence, 'the Commission is not *prima facie* entitled to examine the document concerned before it has adopted a decision allowing the undertaking under investigation to bring the matter before the [CFI] and, where appropriate, the judge with jurisdiction to order interim measures'. Responding to the contention of the Commission that an undertaking could challenge the decision ordering the inspection pursuant to Article [20(4) of Regulation 1/2003], the President noted that a challenge to the investigation decision does not provide a basis for challenging the Commission's conduct

---

[102] Case T-30/89 *Hilti v EC Commission* [1991] ECR II-1439.

[103] Joined Cases T-125/03 R and T-253/03 R *Akzo Nobel Chemicals Ltd/Akcros Chemicals Ltd v EC Commission* [2003] ECR II-4771 para 139. The action arose as a result of a dawn raid executed by the Commission and the OFT who were seeking evidence of possible anti-competitive practices at the premises of Akzo and Akcros. During the course of the investigation, Commission officials were advised that certain documents contained in a file might be covered by legal professional privilege. The Commission representatives responded by stating that they needed to take a quick glance at the documents in question, without examining them in detail, in order to satisfy themselves on the question of privilege. See also G Murphy, 'CFI signals Possible Extension of Professional Privilege to In-house Lawyers' [2004] ECLR 447–54. A Burnside and H Crossley, 'AM & S and Beyond: Legal Professional Privilege in the Wake of Modernization' Antitrust Reform in Europe: A Year in Practice, 9–11 March 2005, Brussels, International Bar Association (IBA) 10–11.

during the investigation.[104] He took the view that the risk of a breach of privilege could be avoided if copies of the disputed documents are placed in a sealed envelope with a view to a subsequent resolution of the dispute by the competent court.[105] However, the President of the ECJ annulled the suspension, holding that there was no urgency about keeping any of the documents from the Commission.[106] The case shows that companies wishing to assert the professional privilege in these circumstances may face a dilemma. If they refuse to let Commission officials have sight of documents, and refuse to hand documents over, they may face a decision requiring such documents to be produced, and may be liable to daily fines if they fail to comply. Instituting proceedings before the Community Court does not suspend the application of such penalties unless and until a judgment to that effect is adopted by the Court. However, if documents are handed over, and the Commission does have the opportunity to review them then chances of obtaining interim measures at the Court appear remote. The documents would therefore remain with the Commission and, whilst the Commission may ultimately be prevented from using them as evidence if the Court rules that they are privileged, even a cursory glance at the documents may give the Commission valuable insight that would have otherwise been unavailable.[107]

For the time being, whether or not a document is privileged will depend on the parties to the communication and the purpose for which the document came into existence. The current rules can be summarized as follows:[108]   **8.45**

---

[104] Joined Cases T-125/03 R and T-253/03 R *Akzo Nobel Chemicals Ltd/Akcros Chemicals Ltd v EC Commission* [2003] ECR II-4771 para 146.

[105] Joined Cases T-125/03 R and T-253/03 R *Akzo Nobel Chemicals Ltd/Akcros Chemicals Ltd v EC Commission* [2003] ECR II-4771 para 138. The President rejected the argument that a subsequent annulment of the investigation decision would be sufficient because the reduction of professional privilege to a mere guarantee that the information entrusted by a litigant will not be used against him dilutes the essence of this right.

[106] Given the far-reaching negative implications of such a change for day-to-day enforcement work in antitrust cases, the Commission considered it necessary to appeal this order with a view to obtaining legal certainty as regards applicability of the established case law. Order of the President of the ECJ in Case C-7/04 P *EC Commission v Akzo Nobel* [2004] ECR I-8739. The President of the Court ruled that '[t]he harm which might possibly result from a more detailed reading of those documents is not sufficient to establish the existence of serious and irreparable harm, since the Commission is prevented from using the information thus obtained. [. . .]' (paras 42–43).

[107] This scenario has been described by A Burnside and H Crossley, 'AM & S and Beyond: Legal Professional Privilege in the Wake of Modernization', Antitrust Reform in Europe: A Year in Practice, 9–11 March 2005, Brussels, International Bar Association (IBA) 11 who suggest that one solution might be to allow an independent third person, such as a court or other type of arbitrator, to review documents in full (without allowing the investigating officials to look at them) to determine whether they are privileged.

[108] See distinction made by PLC Competition and L Ainsworth, 'Competition Regime: EC Legal Privilege' Practice Note—Practical Law Company, available at http://www.practical-law.com/main.jsp. (accessed in December 2005). It is to note that Art 12 of Reg 1/2003 permits

- *Communications between the company and an in-house lawyer.* Communications between an in-house lawyer and the company are not privileged under EC law.[109] Thus privilege will not be available in the case of (i) written advice given by the in-house lawyer to the company; or (ii) a written request from the company to its in-house lawyer for legal advice. This would also be the case even if the request were subsequently passed on to an external lawyer.

- *Communications between the company and an external lawyer.* Correspondence between a company and an external lawyer for the purpose of obtaining legal advice will be granted privilege as long as (i) the correspondence is made for the purposes and in the interest of the client's defence rights; and (ii) the external lawyer is qualified to practice in an EEA country. If these conditions are satisfied, protection extends to all written communications exchanged after the Commission has started a formal investigation which may lead to a decision under Articles 81 or 82 EC, or to a decision imposing a fine. In addition, it covers earlier written communications relating to the same subject matter.[110]

- *Internal reports of advice received from external lawyers, prepared by an in-house lawyer or other employee.* In *Hilti v Commission*, the CFI has held that internal notes which merely report the text or content of communications from an external lawyer that would have enjoyed privilege if received in writing from the external lawyer will themselves be privileged. However, it does not appear that this would permit in-house lawyers or other employees to re-state advice from external lawyers indiscriminately.[111] For example, a summary which

---

the Commission and NCAs to 'provide one another with and use in evidence any matter of fact or of law, including confidential information'. Thus, if for example OFT officials in the UK carry out an inspection, they must apply UK rules of procedure, and could not therefore seize documents that would be privileged under UK law, even if such documents would likely not be privileged under EU law. However, the OFT could be sent the communications of in-house lawyers, or lawyers qualified outside the EU, by an NCA from another Member State where the communications of such lawyers are not privileged. In turn, the Commission would not be prevented from using materials that would be privileged under national rules, but do not attract privilege under EU rules. See ch 3 'The national judicial authorities' para 3.38.

[109] Case 155/79 *AM & S v EC Commission* [1982] ECR 1575 paras 18 *et seq.*; J Temple Lang, 'The AM & S Judgment' ch 12 in M Hoskins and W Robinson, *A True European – Essays for Judge David Edward* (2003) 155 submits that this runs counter to the policy of Reg 1/2003 which puts emphasis on the voluntary compliance with Community competition law because it discourages consultation of employed lawyers.

[110] Case 155/79 *AM & S v EC Commission* [1982] ECR 1575 para 23.

[111] Order in Case T-30/89 *Hilti v EC Commission* [1990] ECR II-163 para 18: '[. . .] the principle of the protection of written communications between lawyer and client may not be frustrated on the sole ground that the content of those communications and of that legal advice was reported in documents internal to the undertaking. Thus the principle of the protection of written communications between lawyer and client must, in view of its purpose, be regarded

includes an expression of opinion or amendments made by the in-house lawyer or other employee will not be privileged insofar as the expression of that opinion, or those amendments, are concerned.

- *Requests for information from the in-house lawyer to the company for the purpose of instructing an external lawyer, and responses to such requests.* The status of such requests and responses is not entirely clear. In the *AM & S* case, the ECJ made it clear that the limited privilege available in competition investigations did not extend to communications between in-house lawyers and their employing companies. It is therefore likely that internal communications between an in-house lawyer and the company, even when seeking information to enable external lawyers to advise, will also not be privileged. If the communications are to enable the company to exercise its rights of defence, the communications will be privileged if they pass between the external lawyer and the in-house lawyer or directly between the external lawyer and the company. If the in-house lawyer is the first recipient of the request or communication from the external lawyer, and the request is passed on without written amendment, the communication will remain privileged, as will the response from the company which is addressed to the external lawyer. The question arises whether under the principles established in *Hilti*, the privilege will no longer apply if the communication is amended by the in-house lawyer or any other person within the company. While it is unlikely to be the case that any amendment may necessarily entail the loss of privilege, it may be difficult to agree on an operative criteria and enable the Commission to distinguish between the amended parts and those which were not amended. In any event, legal advice which is circulated widely within the company may well lose its privilege.

- *Communication by the in-house lawyer or other employee to the company of advice which has been received from professional advisers other than an external lawyer qualified to practise in the EEA.* Requests from the company to the in-house lawyer to obtain advice from professional advisers other than an external lawyer qualified to practise in the EEA and requests from the in-house lawyer or other employee to professional advisers other than an external lawyer qualified to practise in the EEA for information or advice will not be privileged under EC law.

---

as extending also to the internal notes which are confined to reporting the text or the content of those communications [. . .].' PLC Competition and L Ainsworth, 'Competition Regime: EC Legal Privilege' Practice Note—Practical Law Company available at http://www.practicallaw.com (accessed in December 2005).

- *File notes.* File notes prepared by an in-house lawyer or other employee will not be privileged. The only possible exception is where the note records advice received from the external legal advisers, and no comment or modification has been added. As indicated above, the question arises as to whether any in-house comment or amendment will be sufficient to remove legal privilege and to what extent the distinction is operative in practice.

8.46 Where legal privilege is claimed, a difficult situation arises, because the Commission officials at the scene will require to be convinced that the documentation meets the criteria for privilege set out above, but the company under investigation will not wish to disclose the contents. The procedure to be followed in such circumstances was set out by the ECJ in *AM & S*. The company must initially be able to satisfy the Commission inspector that a particular document qualifies for privilege. There is no specified procedure, but the company might, for example:[112]

- disclose certain passages of the document, for example, external lawyers' headed notepaper
- produce other documents referring to the document in question, which show that it is from or to external lawyers
- make a formal statement as to the nature and contents of the document
- give a written description of the general content of the document

If the inspector is not convinced by the company's argument, he can ask for further evidence to be produced. If the company refuses to produce further evidence, or the inspector remains unconvinced, a formal record should be made of the disagreement, signed by the inspector and on behalf of the company. The disputed document should then be placed in a sealed envelope. At this stage, the Commission may make a separate decision demanding the delivery of the contested document, and indicating that it may impose a fine if the company fails to comply. It is then open to the company to appeal the Commission's decision to the CFI, which will decide whether or not the document is privileged, subject to any appeal to the ECJ. Depending on the precise circumstances of the dispute, there may in practice be a more substantial exchange of views and arguments between the company, its lawyers and the Commission before a decision is adopted. If possible, it may be desirable to involve the Hearing Officer in DG COMP (who is responsible for resolving certain procedural issues during Commission competition investigations). This might help to resolve the dispute by agreement, without recourse to legal proceedings.

---

[112] PLC Competition and L Ainsworth, 'Competition Regime: EC Legal Privilege' Practice Note—Practical Law Company, available at http://www.practicallaw.com (accessed in December 2005).

3. Copies and extracts

The main aim of inspections is to obtain documents concerning the restrictions **8.47** described in the authorization or decision to inspect. Since the Commission is not entitled to retain undertakings' documents, it copies them in most cases (extracts are taken very infrequently). As stated earlier, the information copied must have a direct or indirect bearing on the subject matter and purpose of the inspection, the criteria by which the scope of the inspection is delimited. Practical arrangements for the identification and copying of documents will vary from one investigation to another. Sometimes the inspectors will take charge of copying arrangements, and on other occasions the company itself will undertake the copying on their behalf. As most businesses now communicate internally and often externally primarily electronically, access to e-mail systems and computer systems generally form an increasingly important part of an on-site investigation.

Whatever the practical arrangements in place, the company is well advised to **8.48** ensure that it maintains an inventory and has its own copy of every document copied by the inspectors. A note should be kept of the names and location of the files from which copies were taken. Those documents which, in the opinion of the undertakings, contain business secrets must be specified as confidential to ensure that copies of them are not shown to third parties.[113] The Commission has acknowledged that where inspectors take copies of records which in the opinion of the undertaking concerned are not related to the subject-matter of the investigation the undertaking can ask the Commission to return the copies taken,[114] although the Commission is unlikely to return them if their relevance remains in issue.[115]

4. The power to seal any business premises and books or records for the period to the extent necessary for the inspection (Article 20(2)(d))

This is a new power in Regulation 1/2003, although the Commission already **8.49** made use of this practice if it thought it necessary. The difference is that the power is now expressly conferred on the Commission and the undertaking can be fined under Article 23(1)(e) for breaking the seals. Recital (25) says that seals should not normally be affixed for more than seventy-two hours. It is not

---

[113] In particular at the access-to-file stage. Ch 10 'Infringement procedures' para 10.27.
[114] *CSM* [1992] OJ L305/16.
[115] Commission Notice on access to file [1997] OJ C23/3 para II.A.1. already specified that documents which turn out to be irrelevant to the case in question may be returned to the parties from whom they were obtained. See also new Commission Notice on the internal rules of procedure for processing requests for access to the file ([2005] OJ C325/7) para 9. The new rules were adopted on 13 December 2005. See Commission press release IP/05/1581 'Competition: Commission improves rules for access to the file in merger and antitrust procedures'.

entirely clear whether the seal should not be continuously affixed for more than seventy-two hours or that seals should not be affixed overnight for more than three nights.[116] The Commission considers this possibility as a logical extension of its powers which follows from the limitation imposed on the Commission not to extend its presence in a company beyond normal business hours and concern to ensure that during an inspection no evidence disappears overnight. Until now, 'dawn raids' have tended to last only a day or two, which meant that there was a risk that incriminating documents might be removed. Unless appropriate safeguards are put in place, longer inspections appeared somewhat pointless.[117] Up to now, the Commission has relied on the powers of NCAs to seal cupboards or offices.[118]

5. Oral explanations

8.50   For the better performance of their tasks and to obtain additional relevant information, inspectors often ask for oral explanations from the representatives of undertakings. The primary aim of seeking oral explanations is to facilitate the conduct of inspections, the most important aspect of which is not the gathering of information which could be obtained by writing to undertakings but to obtain business documents useful to the investigation. In that connection, the Commission recognized that this right was, 'if anything, an ancillary right', at least under Regulation 17.[119] The company has a duty to cooperate actively and it should therefore ensure that the most appropriate staff of sufficient seniority and knowledge of operations are available to deal with the inspectors' enquiries. It is generally advisable to identify one member of staff to act as a central point of contact for all queries.

8.51   The ECJ held that, under Regulation 17, inspectors have the power to request information on specific questions arising from the books and business records which they examine.[120] Such questions could relate, for example, to practical matters, including the location, organization, and layout of offices or files. They

---

[116] CS Kerse and N Khan, *Antitrust Competition Procedure* (5th edn, 2005) para 3–057.

[117] ibid.

[118] See Speech by Director-General of DG Competition, Philip Lowe, *What's the Future for Cartel Enforcement*, Understanding Global Cartel Enforcement, Brussels, 11 February 2003, available at http://europa.eu.int/comm/competition/speeches.

[119] 'Dealing with the Commission—Notification, complaints, inspections and fact-finding powers under Articles [81] and [82] of the EEC Treaty' (1997 edn), point 5.6 'The scope of the powers of investigation [under Reg 17]' available at http://europa.eu.int/comm/competition/pub-lications/dealen1_en.pdf.

[120] Case 136/79 *National Panasonic v EC Commission* [1980] ECR 2033 para 15: '[. . .] Panasonic Officials authorized by the Commission, in carrying out an investigation, have the power to request during that investigation information on specific questions arising from the books and business records which they examine [. . .]'. A Riley, 'EC Antitrust Modernisation: The Commission Does Very Nicely—Thank You! Part One: Regulation 1 and the Notification Burden' [2003] ECLR 604–14 (608).

may also arise as a direct result of the contents of the documents or files investigated, such as the job description and broad responsibilities of individuals, or an explanation of internal reporting structures. However, in *National Panasonic* the ECJ did not deal directly with the question whether inspectors could ask questions which are related with the investigation in progress and its subject matter. Accordingly, there was however some uncertainty as to the extent of the Commission's powers under the old Regulation 17 to question individual employees about wider issues and whether inspectors could also address individuals other than those identified by the company. On the face of it, the powers of the Commission under Article 20(2)(e) of Regulation 1/2003 only seem to codify existing powers that the Community courts arguably attributed to the Commission.[121] But these powers have always been an issue for intense debate. The wording of the provision suggests that inspectors may not be simply restricted to asking questions arising from the books and business records that they examine. On the contrary, the provision may also permit inspectors to ask for explanations on any facts or documents relevant to the inspection. Whether inspectors should be entitled to question any member of staff or representatives of the company, and to question staff other than those identified by the company as the most appropriate to respond to questions, is even more debatable. The risk that this power could be used to conduct general interrogations cannot entirely be ruled out.[122] While the Commission has previously indicated that it is aware of the implications of an extensive interpretation of this power,[123] the provision that questions may be asked about facts or documents relating to the subject-matter and purpose of the inspection is not capable of resolving ambiguities. It seems that a fact or document can 'relate' to the subject matter or purpose of an inspection even if it is not disclosed by the undertaking under inspection or a document of that undertaking.[124] Whenever

---

[121] Although the Commission itself has indicated that the extent of the inspectors' powers to request on-the-spot oral explanations has never been fully clarified by the Community Courts. See in relation to Reg 17, 'Dealing with the Commission—Notification, complaints, inspections and fact-finding powers under Arts [81] and [82] of the EEC Treaty', at point 5.6.

[122] L Jones and B Sufrin, *EC Competition Law* (2004) 1070; see also CS Kerse and N Khan, *EC Antitrust Procedure* (5th edn, 2005) para 3–058. See also on this discussion: A Klees, *Europäisches Kartellverfahrensrecht* (2005) § 9 paras 101–105.

[123] As regards Reg 17, 'Dealing with the Commission—Notification, complaints, inspections and fact-finding powers under Arts [81] and [82] of the EEC Treaty', at point 5.6. indicating that the inspectors would be certainly entitled to demand oral explanations where these arise directly out of the documents produced (or not produced), and they may ask for more extensive explanations. However, this power would have to be read in the light of Art 11 of Reg 17 and the safeguards it contains for firms requested to provide information. 'In particular, the power should not be used to pressure the officials of a firm into making oral admissions which they would not make if they had the time for reflection afforded them by a written request under Art [11].'

[124] CS Kerse and N Khan, *EC Antitrust Procedure* (5th edn, 2005) para 3–059 also indicate that Art 19 (power to take statements) uses a wider term—'the subject matter of an investigation'—while Art 20(2)(e) refers to the subject matter and purpose of the inspection.

the Commission's inspectors see a certain employee's name in relevant documents, they may put their questions to that employee. There is the suggestion that any question asked pursuant to Article 20(2)(e) should be such that it can be reasonably answered in the circumstances of the inspection. Exposing the undertaking to the risk of fines for incorrect answers to question which require reflection and internal investigation would appear too severe and not justified.[125]

8.52   The Commission may record the explanations given in any form, a copy of which shall be made available to the company.[126] The recorded explanations are subject to rectification, amendment, or additional explanations by the members of the staff. Under Article 4(3) of the Implementing Regulation, however, the possibility of rectification is only granted in regard to staff 'not authorized by the undertaking to provide explanations'.[127] While an undertaking may rectify an employee's responses, Recital (4) to that Regulation nevertheless specifies that the answer given by a member of the staff should remain in the Commission file as recorded during the inspection. This may be construed as meaning that the original answer, albeit rectified, may be used as evidence to corroborate another party's evidence.[128]

8.53   Any refusal by undertakings to provide explanations is regarded by the Commission as opposition to the inspection. In an ordinary inspection, such a refusal might lead to suspension of the inspection. In an inspection under a decision, it might give rise to fines and periodic penalty payments.[129] Where for any reason, it is not possible to give an immediate answer, the inspectors may agree to receive the requested explanations subsequently in writing, in the same way that, if certain documents requested are not available, they may accept an offer

---

[125] CS Kerse and N Khan, *EC Antitrust Procedure* (5th edn, 2005) para 3–059.

[126] Art 20(2)(e) of Reg 1/2003 in conjunction with Art 4(2) of Reg 773/2004.

[127] See para 8.25 above.

[128] CS Kerse and N Khan, *EC Antitrust Procedure* (5th edn, 2005) para 3–060.

[129] It is not entirely clear which fine provision applies to a situation where, e.g. a company employee refuses to answer to Commission officials questioning because of fear that the information could be used against him or her to establish a personal liability in some other jurisdiction. Would this be construed as (i) the company not submitting to the inspection and subject to fines under Art 24.1; (ii) or the company failing to provide a complete answer and subject to a fine under Art 23; or (iii) the company cooperating with the Commission especially if it tries to compel the employee to answer? However, Art 24.1 makes no mention of Art 20(2)(e) in its enumeration of situations in which periodic penalty payments may be imposed, which suggests that the 5 per cent periodic penalty payment would not apply to a refusal to answer questions under Art 20(2)(e). See JS Venit and T Louko, 'The Commission's New Power to Question and its implications on Human Rights', ch 26 in BE Hawk (ed), *International Antitrust Law and Policy,* Annual Proceedings of the Fordham Institute (2004) 675–700 (678 n 8).

by the undertaking to send them to the Commission after completion of the inspections. This does not affect the Commission's power to request such explanation (or documents) under Article 18 of Regulation 1/2003. However, the Commission has no powers to compel the representatives of undertakings to respond to its questions during inspections: compulsion is inappropriate in such cases. National competition laws, which, by contrast with Community law, incorporate powers of enforcement exercisable not only against undertakings but also against their representatives, usually provide for criminal or administrative penalties for executives guilty of this type of conduct.[130]

E. The Commission's Power to Inspect other Premises

One of the most remarkable extensions to the Commission's investigative 8.54 powers is its right to conduct inspections of non-business premises, including private homes of directors, managers, and other company staff members. The use of this new power is restricted to investigations related to breaches of Article 81 and 82 EC. The provision has been introduced because the Commission's experience has shown that there are cases where business records are kept in the homes of directors or other people working for an undertaking[131] and the Commission is determined that its efforts to crack down on hard-core cartels are not frustrated by this practice.[132] The Commission's original proposal for Regulation 1/2003 provided for an extension of its powers of inspection to include private homes within Article 20, with the difference that a judicial warrant was needed for such an inspection. The fact that Regulation 1/2003 now devotes a separate provision to the inspection of other premises also indicates the importance of this new power.[133]

Article 21 specifies that 'if a reasonable suspicion exists that books or other 8.55 records related to the business and to the subject matter of the inspection, which may be relevant to prove a serious violation of Article 81 or Article 82 EC, are being kept in any other premises, land and means of transport, including the homes of directors, managers and other members of staff of the undertakings and associations of undertakings concerned, the Commission can by decision

---

[130] See JD Cooke, 'General Report' in *The Modernization of EU Competition Law Enforcement in the EU*, FIDE 2004 National Reports 630–60 (645–46).

[131] See Recital (26) of Reg 1/2003.

[132] A Jones and B Sufrin, *EC Competition Law* (2004) 1081 citing *SAS/Maersk Air* [2001] OJ L265/15 at para 89 in which a note of one meeting recorded a Maersk representative as saying that 'all material on price agreements, market-sharing agreements and the like had to be destroyed before going home today. Anything that might be needed had to be taken home.'

[133] CS Kerse and N Khan, *EC Antitrust Procedure* (5th edn, 2005) para 3–065.

order an inspection to be conducted in such other premises, and means of transport'. The reference to other 'premises' is to be understood to refer to Article 20(2)(a), which permits inspections of premises etc of undertakings. Regulation 1/2003 provides that inspections of private premises are only allowed if there exists a reasonable suspicion that books and other records related to the business and to the scope of this inspection are being kept in private premises, and if such documents may be relevant to prove a serious violation of Articles 81 or 82 EC. Regulation 1/2003 does not provide any guidance on what is meant by a 'serious' infringement. Typically the search of private premises will be carried out in the context of cartels as the most serious infringement of competition law rules where evidence might be kept at a director's home.[134] In any event, it may be expected that inspections of private premises will be limited, at least for an initial period of time, to cases where the Commission has clear indications that incriminating evidence is being kept in private homes. While conducting inspections of private premises, officials will have the right to examine documents and take copies thereof but they will not have the right to conduct interviews or to seal up cupboards, rooms, or premises.[135] It is worth noting that neither Article 21 nor Articles 23 or 24 refer to any Commission power to impose fines in relation to inspections under Article 21. Where the inspection is resisted and recourse to national police powers seem to be required, the reasoning is that the individual's conduct cannot be attributed to the undertaking through the imposition of a procedural fine.[136]

8.56 Finally the Commission's decision to conduct an inspection at non-corporate premises cannot be executed without prior authorization from the national judiciary authority of the Member State concerned. The national judicial authority will ensure that the Commission decision is authentic and that the coercive measures envisaged are neither arbitrary nor excessive having regard in particular to the seriousness of the suspected infringement, to the importance of the evidence sought, to the involvement of the undertaking concerned and to the reasonable likelihood that business books and records relating to the subject matter of the inspection are kept in the premises for which the authorization is requested. The national judicial authority may ask the Commission, directly or through the Member State competition authority, for detailed explanations about these elements, which are necessary to allow its control of the proportionality of the coercive measures envisaged. The wording suggests that the intensity

---

[134] ibid.

[135] K Dekeyser and C Gauer, 'The New Enforcement System for Arts 81 & 82 and the Rights of Defence' ch 23 in BE Hawk (ed), *International Antitrust Law and Policy*, Annual Proceedings of the Fordham Institute International Antitrust Law and Policy (2004) 545–89 (557).

[136] CS Kerse and N Khan, *EC Antitrust Procedure* (5th edn, 2005) para 3–068.

of judicial scrutiny is more intense than under Article 20(8). Article 21(2) requires the decision to state why the Commission considers the basic conditions of Article 21(1) are met. Article 21(3) states that the national court shall not merely assess the proportionality of the interference with the undertakings' rights by reference to the subject matter. The appraisal shall be made with due regard to the importance of the evidence sought, the involvement of the undertaking concerned and the reasonable likelihood that evidence will be on the premises. However, it is not entirely clear whether the national court will not examine in practice the same requirements. In some countries rules on inspections of corporate premises may be less strict on this point.

F. Cooperation between the Commission and the NCAs

1. Involvement of the NCAs

Prior notice or consultation

In the case of ordinary inspections under an authorization, Article 20(3) **8.57** requires the Commission 'in good time before the investigation, . . . [to] inform the competent authority of the Member State in whose territory the same is to be made of the investigation and of the identity of the authorized officials'. In general, the Commission gives the NCAs two weeks' notice. However, there are no formal rules requiring it to observe that time limit or give notice in any particular form. The Commission may thus inform them in writing or orally, or even by telephone. The ECJ has stated that it is of little importance if the consultation took place informally or by telephone, without any record of it being made. Since the purpose of that provision is to enable the Commission to carry out surprise inspections at the premises of undertakings suspected of infringements of Community competition provisions, the Commission must be in a position to take a decision without being bound by formal conditions which would delay its adoption.[137] In the case of inspections pursuant to a binding decision, Article 20(4) provides that 'the Commission shall take decisions after consultation with the competent authority of the Member State in whose territory the investigation is to be made.'

Thus, the cooperation between the Commission and the NCA is more or **8.58** less formal depending on whether the inspections are by authorization or decision. In the former case, the Commission 'informs' the authorities that it intends to carry out an inspection, without resorting to more effective powers of

---

[137] Case 5/85 *Akzo Chemie BV v EC Commission II* [1986] ECR 2585 para 24. R Whish, *Competition Law* (5th edn, 2003) 5 265.

investigation—an inspection which may not take place, since it depends upon the willingness of the undertakings concerned. In the second case, there is 'consultation' on the part of the Commission concerning a decision which, if necessary, the competent NCA will have to implement and enforce. According to the logic of Article 20, where enforcement by action on the part of the NCAs is not feasible or is extremely unlikely,[138] the formal requirements to be observed by the Commission are less rigorous. It is important to note that assistance may be requested as a precautionary measure, in order to overcome any opposition on the part of the undertaking[139] or if there are grounds for apprehending attempts at concealing or disposing of evidence in the event that an investigation ordered pursuant to Article [20(4) of Regulation 1/2003] is notified to the undertaking concerned.[140]

Assistance and inspection work by national officials alongside Commission inspectors

8.59 When inspections are carried out, whether ordinarily or under a decision, the NCAs are not only present but also, as a general rule, participate actively in the inspection work. They help Commission officials to locate, read, and copy or take extracts from business records. Although it is theoretically possible for the NCAs not to be present—if they have no interest in being present and the European Commission has no interest in their being present—the Commission always seeks their assistance, and in practice they never fail to assist. As stated, the role of national officials accompanying Community officials is not generally limited to their physical presence but extends to providing direct assistance to Commission inspectors. They do not, therefore, operate as arbiters or neutral observers. The inspection work carried out by national officials is also based on Article 20(5) of Regulation 1/2003 according to which 'officials of the competent authority of the Member State in whose territory the investigation is to be made may, at the request of such authority or of the Commission, assist the officials of the Commission in carrying out their duties'.[141]

---

[138] It is debatable whether, in the event of opposition to an ordinary inspection already embarked upon, the Commission would be entitled to take enforcement proceedings.

[139] Case Joined Cases 46/87 and 227/88 *Hoechst AG v EC Commission* [1989] ECR 2859 para 32.

[140] Case C-94/00 *Roquette Frères* [2002] ECR I-9011 paras 74 and 75. It is for the Commission to provide the competent national court with the explanations needed by that court to satisfy itself that, if the Commission were unable to obtain, as a precautionary measure, the requisite assistance in order to overcome any opposition on the part of the undertaking, it would be impossible, or very difficult, to establish the facts amounting to the infringement.

[141] Although the NCAs sometimes do not take an active part in the inspection and search for documents, they usually do so. This sometimes causes surprise on the part of undertakings, some of which may think that, because the inspection is one ordered by a supranational institution, the national authorities should be on their side or at least refrain from assisting Commission officials during the inspections.

Inspections facilitated by measures of constraint

The role of the Member States becomes more important if the undertakings do   **8.60**
not submit to the investigation. The duty to submit to a decision ordering an
inspection is a continuing one, entailing both allowing the inspection to begin
and cooperating thereafter, but the limited nature of the Commission's officials'
powers, and their reliance on NCAs and national procedures was demonstrated
in *Hoechst*. In this case, the ECJ has stated that where the Commission seeks to
carry out an inspection pursuant to a decision without the cooperation of the
undertakings concerned, it is obliged to call on NCAs to assist in overcoming
any opposition and to observe the procedural safeguards and, by extension, the
procedures laid down for that purpose by national law.[142] Article 20(6),
replacing Article 14(6) of Regulation 17, provides that where the officials and
other accompanying persons authorized by the Commission find that an undertaking opposes an inspection ordered pursuant to this Article, the Member State
concerned shall afford them the necessary assistance, requesting where
appropriate the assistance of the police or of an equivalent enforcement authority, so as to enable them to conduct their inspection.[142a] If the 'assistance'
requires authorization, under national law, from a judicial authority (i.e. because
national law requires a court to sanction coercive measures such as forcible
entry) that must be applied for. The powers and duties of the national court in
this situation, which were not expressly mentioned under Regulation 17 but were
spelt out in *Hoechst*, as seen above, were examined again in *Roquette Frères SA*.

Article 20(8) of Regulation 1/2003 sets out the role of the national court. The   **8.61**
provision enacts, in effect, the judgment of the Court in *Roquette Frères* in which
the ECJ confirmed and clarified the permitted scope of national courts' review
of requests for search warrants in the context of surprise inspections by the
Commisison at corporate premises. In this case, in September 1998 the Commission requested the assistance of the French administrative authorities with
respect to an inspection it wished to conduct at the premises of *Roquette Frères*
in connection with the investigation of a cartel in the sodium gluconate sector.
The French administrative authorities applied to the *Tribunal de grande instance
de Lille* for authorization pursuant to the relevant French legislation and

---

[142] Case Joined Cases 46/87 and 227/88 *Hoechst AG v EC Commission* [1989] ECR 2859
para 34; 85/87 *Dow Benelux* [1989] ECR 3165 para 45, and Joined Cases 97/87, 98/87 and
99/87 *Dow Chemical Ibérica* [1989] ECR 1369 para 31. 'Dealing with the Commission—
Notification, complaints, inspections and fact-finding powers under Arts [81] and [82] of the
EEC Treaty' (1997 edn) at point 5.4.1.

[142a] If a Member State were to fail to provide the necessary assistance to Commission inspections, the Commission could bring an action against that Member State before the ECJ under Art
226 EC. WPJ Wils 'Powers of investigation and procedural rights and guarantees in EU antitrust
enforcement', First Lisbon Conference on Competition Law and Economics, November 2005,
para 23 and note 28.

attached to the application a copy of the Commission decision ordering the investigation and a text of the *Hoechst* judgment. The *Tribunal* granted the authorization. Roquette Frères submitted to the inspection, but later claimed in the French courts that the authorization should not have been made on the limited information placed before the *Tribunal.* Roquette asserted that it was impossible for the judge to verify whether the application was justified and in particular whether there were reasonable grounds for suspecting the existence of anti-competitive measures that would warrant the coercive measures. The *Cour de Cassation* referred to the ECJ questions about the scope of the review to be carried out by the national court in this situation, and the information which the Commission should be required to produce. The ECJ held that the national court could not review the need for the Commission's investigation.[143] This task is reserved to the Community Courts. However, it stated that the national court could examine that there is nothing arbitrary about a coercive measure or disproportionate relative to the subject matter of the investigation. The competent national court is required, in essence, to satisfy itself that there exist reasonable grounds for suspecting an infringement of the competition rules by the undertaking concerned.[144]

8.62 Such an examination of possible arbitrariness cannot be precluded on the ground that, in satisfying itself as to the existence of reasonable grounds for suspecting an infringement of the competition rules, the competent national body might substitute its own assessment of the need for the investigations ordered for that of the Commission and call into question the latter's assessments of fact and law. The national court may not demand the information and evidence on which the Commission's suspicions are based, such as the Commission's file because this could make the Commission's action ineffective, especially where simultaneous investigations are carried out in several Member States. However, for the purposes of enabling the competent national court to satisfy itself that the coercive measures sought are not arbitrary, the Commission is required to provide that court with '[. . .] explanations showing, in a properly

---

[143] Control over the legality of a Community act may only be exercised by Community Courts. There is the suggestion that the system of double control (control on the proportionality between the coercive measures and the seriousness of infringement exercised by the national judge and a full control by the Community Courts over the legality of the Community act is confusing for applicants who often do not always clearly know which ground they may invoke before which court. In addition, where the Commission conducts inspections simultaneously in various Member States it must seek numerous court warrants before various national courts. Also for these reasons in his opinion in *Hoechst* AG Mischo has argued in favour of a system of prior control in the hands of the Community Courts. Joined opinions of AG Mischo in Joined Cases 46/87 and 227/88 *Hoechst AG and others v EC Commission* [1989] ECR 2859 paras 149 *et seq.* K Dekeyser and C Gauer, 'The New Enforcement System for Articles 81 & 82 and the Rights of Defence' ch 23 in BE Hawk (ed), *International Antitrust Law & Policy*, Annual Proceedings of the Fordham Institute International Antitrust Law and Policy [2005] 549–85 (559).

[144] The ECJ refers to Art 14(1) of Reg 17, but the same is applicable to Art 18 of Reg 1/2003.

substantiated manner, that the Commission is in possession of information and evidence providing reasonable grounds for suspecting infringement of the competition rules by the undertaking concerned [. . .].'[145] In regard to the proportionality of the coercive measures to the subject-matter of the investigation and the information which the Commission may be required to provide to that end, the Court states that this involves establishing that such measures are appropriate to ensure that the investigation can be carried out. The Commission shall inform the national court about the '[. . .] essential features of the suspected infringement, so as to enable it to assess their seriousness, by indicating the market thought to be affected, the nature of the suspected restrictions of competition and the proposed degree of the involvement of the undertaking concerned [. . .]'.[146] The Commission is required to indicate as precisely as possible the evidence sought and the matters to which the investigation relates. However, it does not need to identify specific documents or files given that the Commission is entitled to search for items not already known or identified in advance. The Commission cannot be required to limit its investigation to requesting the production of documents or files which it is able to identify precisely in advance. That would significantly impede its right of access to such documents or files. Coercive measures may be so requested on a precautionary basis only in so far as there are grounds for apprehending opposition to the investigation and/or attempts at concealing or disposing of evidence in the event that an investigation ordered by decision is notified to the undertaking concerned. Consequently, it is for the Commission to provide the competent national court with the explanations needed by that court to satisfy itself that, if the Commission were unable to obtain, as a precautionary measure, the requisite assistance in order to overcome any opposition on the part of the undertaking, it would be impossible, or very difficult, to establish the facts amounting to the infringement. The Court held that the Commission's choice between an investigation by straightforward authorization and an investigation ordered by a decision does not depend on matters such as the particular seriousness of the situation, extreme urgency or the need for absolute discretion, but rather on the need for an appropriate inquiry, having regard to the special features of the case.

The competent national court can refuse to grant the coercive measures applied for where the suspected impairment of competition is so minimal, the extent of the likely involvement of the undertaking concerned so limited, or the evidence sought so peripheral, that the intervention in the sphere of the private activities of a legal person which a search using law enforcement authorities **8.63**

---

[145] Case C-94/00 *Roquette Frères* [2002] ECR I-9011 para 61.
[146] Case C-94/00 *Roquette Frères* [2002] ECR I-9011 para 81.

entails necessarily appears manifestly disproportionate and intolerable in the light of the objectives pursued by the investigation. However, the Court ruled that a national court cannot simply dismiss an application for coercive measures in this circumstance. Before rejecting such application, it must as rapidly as possible inform the Commission or the national authority assisting the Commission and where necessary request additional information required to conduct its review. The Commission may respond and provide such clarification orally. The national court cannot give its final ruling on the coercive measures until it obtains the requested clarifications or the Commission does not respond to such requests.[147] It should be noted that the fact of having finally gained access to the premises of undertakings and carried out the inspection does not prevent the Commission from imposing the pecuniary penalties available for cases where inspections are impeded. On the contrary, the Commission does not hesitate to impose penalties in such cases.[148] Similarly—and this has a greater impact from the economic point of view—a refusal by undertakings to cooperate with the Commission may be taken into account in the calculation of the fines which may be imposed on undertakings for infringements of Community competition provisions.

2. Inspections carried out under Article 22 of Regulation 1/2003

8.64 This Article is based on Article 13 of the Regulation 17, adapted to the new implementing system. While continuing to allow Member States to conduct investigations on their territory on behalf of the Commission, it also enables them to carry out fact-finding measures on behalf of a competition authority of another Member State. This provision is necessary in order to allow effective cooperation between the competition authorities of the Member States. Such cooperation enables NCAs to deal with cases where some evidence is to be found in other Member States. Without such mechanisms a real decentralization of the application of Community competition rules could be hampered.

---

[147] It appears that not all Member States require prior judicial authorization for the search of corporate premises. According to the White Paper on modernization of the rules implementing Arts 85 and 86 [now 81 and 82] of the EC Treaty [1999] OJ C132/1 para 110 a prior judicial authorization was at that time not required in Austria, Finland, Italy the Netherlands, and Sweden. In its judgment *Société Colas Est and others v France* Case No 37971/97, ECHR 2002-I, in which the inspections had been carried out on the basis of an *Ordonance* of 1945 which empowered the inspectors to seize documents without a court warrant, the ECtHR however held that Art 8 ECHR includes the right that corporate premises are respected and determined that those premises cannot be searched without a prior judicial warrant. Where national law does not (yet) provide for the requirement of a search warrant, the Commission inspection which includes the forcible entry of corporate premises might be declared illegal for failure to comply with *Colas East*.

[148] See, e.g. the Decisions in *CSM* [1992] OJ L305/16 and *MEWAC* [1993] OJ L20/6 applying the procedural rules of the Reg concerning maritime transport.

G. The Conduct of Inspections

1. Arrival of inspectors

The Commission inspectors, accompanied if appropriate by national officials **8.65** assisting them, always arrive at undertakings during office hours.[149] The first thing they do is inform the employees who receive them that they are Community officials and ask to speak with those in charge of the business. Only the latter will be informed of the officials' intentions in surprise inspections. The company should ensure that a senior member of the legal department (if there is one on-site) or an appropriately senior company representative is immediately alerted on the arrival of the inspectors. The inspectors will also allow the company to call its external lawyers to attend the inspection. However, the inspectors are not obliged to wait until the lawyers arrive and in practice are unlikely to wait before starting the investigation, particularly where the company has in-house lawyers available. Legal advice may in any event be obtained by telephone until the lawyers arrive. To ensure that the investigation is appropriately managed and supervised, the company is well advised to establish a team of three employees, headed by a senior company representative who will take overall responsibility. Other relevant staff should be informed that an investigation is under way. The company may want to set aside a meeting room as a base for the place where files can be examined and any necessary discussions with inspectors can be held.

2. Designated representatives

The Community officials may not be aware in advance of the exact identity of **8.66** those to whom they will speak on the day of the inspection. They will know whom they are dealing with when they have informed undertakings of the inspection before carrying it out, since by their very nature such prior contacts will enable them to identify the appropriate people. But in the case of surprise inspections, the officials' first task will be to discover, without delay, who is to represent the undertakings during the inspection. In practice, the Commission officials ask to be received by directors, commercial managers, company secretaries, heads of the relevant departments, and in general those people who, by reason of their office, seem most appropriate both to represent the interests of the undertakings and to answer the questions and requests for clarification from the inspectors. However, it is for the undertakings, not the Commission, to designate their representatives.[150]

---

[149] 'Dealing with the Commission—Notification, complaints, inspections and fact-finding powers under Arts [81] and [82] of the EEC Treaty' (1997 edn) point 5.1.

[150] See paras 8.23 *et seq.*

3. Identification and documentation

8.67   Once the undertakings have decided who is to represent them, the officials proceed to identify themselves, Community officials by means of their 'service cards', which incorporate their photographs, and national officials by means of an equivalent identity document. They then hand to the undertaking's representatives the documentation necessary for the exercise of their powers of inspection and inform the undertakings of their rights. Thus, respectively, they will hand over:

(1)   In ordinary inspections:
    (a)   the authority to inspect;[151] and
    (b)   the explanatory memorandum concerning ordinary inspections;[152]

(2)   In inspections pursuant to a binding decision:
    (a)   the authority to inspect;
    (b)   the explanatory memorandum concerning inspections pursuant to a decision;
    (c)   an authenticated copy of the decision itself.

8.68   When the copy of the decision is handed over, the inspectors draw up a formal minute of notification testifying to the fact that the representatives of the undertaking have received the copy. The fact of signing the record does not imply that the undertaking accepts the decision or agrees to undergo the inspection. The minute of notification is, therefore, a simple acknowledgement of receipt.[153]

4. Clarifications and legal representation

8.69   The inspectors then ask the representatives of the undertakings to read the appropriate explanatory note and, if so requested, they explain particular aspects of the inspection. In ordinary inspections, the Community officials may give explanations regarding both the subject-matter and purpose of the inspection and matters of procedure, including questions of confidentiality and the use of documents,[154] the presence of a lawyer,[155] the voluntary nature of the inspection and, notwithstanding such voluntary nature, the obligation to produce

---

[151] Regarding the content of the authorization, see para 8.08 above. The authorization is the same regardless of the type of inspection involved. If the identity of any official does not coincide with the particulars given in his authorization, the undertakings may request that the official concerned refrain from taking part in the inspection.

[152] Regarding the content of the memorandum, see para 8.13 above.

[153] CS Kerse and N Khan, *EC Competition Procedure* (5th edn, 2005) para 3–045 noting that the minutes merely serve as a proof of notification, but do not have a prejudicial effect. It would not prevent a later challenge to the validity of the decision or the way in which it has been implemented.

[154] See paras 8.39 *et seq.*   [155] See paras 8.27 *et seq.*

complete information once an undertaking has decided to submit to it,[156] and so on. In the case of inspections pursuant to a decision, there is no need to ask Community officials to explain the subject-matter and purpose of the inspection or the reasons for which the decision to inspect was taken. The decision itself deals with all those points in detail. However, the inspectors may clarify points of procedure (for example the confidential treatment and limited use of the information obtained), indicate the consequences of opposition to the inspection and the production of documents in incomplete form, and mention the right of undertakings to be assisted by a lawyer or legal adviser. The explanations given may not in any circumstances take the place of the authority or decision to inspect, or the accompanying explanatory memorandum. The time spent on such explanations will be as short as possible, so as not to hamper the conduct of the inspection.

In the case of a surprise inspection, if the undertaking has no legal advisers of its own, the inspectors may not agree to wait until a lawyer arrives. If they did they might require that the undertakings guarantee, first, that all the business documents will remain in the same place as when the officials arrived and, secondly, that they will not be prevented from entering and remaining on such premises as they may choose. If advance notice has been given of the inspection, inspectors will not await the arrival of the undertaking's lawyer. Nor will the start of the inspection be delayed if undertakings have their own legal advisers but wish to be assisted by independent lawyers—the Commission will not await the arrival of the latter. **8.70**

5. Submission to inspections

After being given explanations, undertakings have to decide whether or not to agree to an ordinary inspection. The Commission will not accept partial or conditional submission to an inspection. Although this point has not been dealt with in the case law, the Commission's view is that if undertakings agree to the commencement of an inspection they must agree to its being carried through as if it were an inspection pursuant to a decision.[157] Any interruption caused by the undertaking might give rise to a penalty for failure to produce complete information.[158] In the event of initial opposition to an ordinary inspection, the Commission officials prepare an official note or record, of which **8.71**

---

[156] Regarding pecuniary penalties for providing incomplete information, see below ch 9 'Penalties and confidentiality' para 9.06.

[157] As stated earlier on several occasions, the literal wording of Art 14(6) of Reg 17 and Art 20(6) of Reg 1/2003 appears to empower the Commission to seek the assistance of NCAs for all kinds of inspections. This might be interpreted as meaning that enforcement measures are available in respect of ordinary inspections commencing with the express consent of undertakings.

[158] See *FNICF* [1982] OJ L319/12.

the undertaking may be given a copy, if it wishes, and leave the premises of the undertaking. The Commission will then be obliged (if it wishes to continue the investigation) to adopt a decision to compel the undertaking to undergo an inspection. Experience shows that the Commission can act extremely rapidly in such cases. Undertakings should not therefore hope to gain much time by opposing an ordinary inspection. There is no doubt, however, that the Commission runs the risk, in ordinary inspections, that certain compromising documents may not be found on the premises of undertakings when inspections are subsequently carried out pursuant to a decision.

6. Enforcement

8.72 If undertakings oppose an inspection decision, it is incumbent on NCAs of the Member States to enforce an inspection, in accordance with Article 20(6) of Regulation 1/2003. Community officials are not entitled to enter the premises of undertakings by force. They merely document the opposition and request the assistance of NCAs. The forms which such assistance take are determined by the various national laws. Opposition must not be interpreted as being confined to an outright refusal to allow inspectors to enter an undertaking's premises or to allow them to examine business records. It includes any action taken by undertakings to hamper the inspectors' work once an inspection pursuant to a decision has commenced. It does not appear that the principle of primacy of Community law enables safeguards provided for in the national laws of Member States to be overridden; for example, if leave must be obtained from the judicial authorities for forced entry into the premises of an undertaking. As stated, it should be noted, however, that, as the Court has held, the judicial authority is not empowered in such cases to substitute its own assessment of the necessity or otherwise of inspections for that of the Commission, the latter's assessment being subject only to review of legality by the Court.[159] This means that the national judicial authority will be authorized only to verify the authenticity of the inspection decision, ensure that the measures of constraint envisaged are not arbitrary or disproportionate in relation to the subject matter of the inspection and guarantee that the provisions of national law are observed during the inspection.

8.73 In practice, national officials may always apply for a court order to gain access to the premises of undertakings which oppose Community inspections, so that fundamental rights and guarantees upheld by Member States' and the Community legal order are always safeguarded. Assistance in executing the court order allowing inspection will be provided by national law-enforcement

---

[159] Case C-94/00 *Roquette Frères* [2002] ECR I-9011 para 39.

authorities. Up to the time of actual entry and inspection, the Commission officials may, where authorized by national law (or where the undertakings agree) request that the national authorities seal the premises, accommodation and files and cupboards where documents relating to the subject-matter of the inspection may be located, in order to ensure that they are not removed from the premises or furniture in which they are located. For the conduct of inspections in such cases—and only in such cases—the Commission inspectors may, if the companies persist in their refusal to co-operate, search the premises of the undertaking, in accordance with Article 20(6) of Regulation 1/2003, and, with the assistance of the officials of the national authorities, endeavour to locate any business records.[160] In normal circumstances, the Commission is entitled to require that the documents requested by it be produced, but not to undertake a search. By contrast with other inspections, it does not appear feasible in such circumstances to insist on obtaining oral explanations from the representatives of undertakings. Once the inspection has been carried out, a record will be drawn up to which will be annexed, if appropriate, a list of the documents copied, or from which extracts have been taken.[161] The Commission does not normally resort to enforcement except where it conducts surprise inspections or where, during an inspection pursuant to a decision, the undertaking refuses to allow it access to certain parts of the premises or to permit it to examine or copy documents as requested. If an inspection pursuant to a decision is carried out after an unsuccessful ordinary inspection (after which it seems sensible to assume that the documentation which the undertakings wished to hide will have disappeared), the Commission may prefer in the event of non-submission to impose periodical penalty payments when adopting the inspection decision, rather than resort to a procedure which—in this particular case—is liable to produce results of dubious value.

7. Examination of business records

Once undertakings have consented to an ordinary inspection or have complied **8.74** with an inspection decision—whether or not enforcement was necessary—both types of inspection follow the same pattern. The inspectors usually ask for details of the layout of the offices and the location of the cupboards or files which are of interest to them. The Commission officials may 'ask any representative or member of staff [. . .] for explanations on facts or documents relating to the subject matter and purpose of the investigation and [. . .] record the answers.

---

[160] Joined Cases 46/87 and 227/88 *Hoechst AG v EC Commission* [1989] ECR 2859 paras 30–35; Case 85/87 *Dow Benelux* [1989] ECR 3137 paras 41–46 and Joined Cases 97/87 to 99/87 *Dow Chemical Ibérica* [1989] ECR 3165 paras 27–28.

[161] Regarding the preparation of final records and document lists, see para 8.76 below.

They may also ask undertakings to produce specific documents and the undertakings must make them available.' The representatives of the undertakings must open the cupboards and filing cabinets and hand the documents to the inspectors who, except in cases of enforcement, may not themselves remove them from their location, unless the undertakings prefer that they do so and voluntarily give their authority for that purpose.[162] In practice, undertakings prefer that the inspectors themselves look through cupboards, filing cabinets, and so on, rather than being obliged to allocate one or more people to the task of producing documents for a day or more. Similarly, the Commission is not authorized—in contrast with certain national administrations—to retain original documents, and therefore inspectors merely take copies of them. The Commission officials may ask undertakings to produce specific documents and the undertakings must make them available. It is not sufficient for them generally to make the premises, archives, and all documents available to the inspectors. Article 20 of Regulation 1/2003 requires the active participation of undertakings, and the latter do not fulfil their obligation to produce in complete form the documents requested by the Commission staff unless those documents are actually delivered to the inspectors. This implies that it is the undertakings which must locate them and remove them from the filing cabinets. Any 'go slow' attitude on the part of the representatives and employees of the undertakings will thus be penalized as being tantamount to breach of the obligation to provide complete information.[163] In short, this means that the representatives of the undertakings must accompany the inspectors throughout the inspection or be available at all times.

8.75 If any of the documents or information is not available when requested by the inspectors, undertakings may send it to the Commission later. The officials will include in the final record of the inspection both their request and the commitment given to send the documents to it once they have been prepared or completed. Where undertakings decline to produce specific documents, the inspectors will record that refusal. The Commission may penalize the undertaking for failure to produce the business records in complete form.[164] Quite apart from any such penalty, the Community inspectors may request measures of enforcement to secure the production of particular documents.[165] Where

---

[162] See Case 85/87 *Dow Benelux* [1989] ECR 3137 para 42, and Joined Cases 97/87 to 99/87 *Dow Chemical Ibérica* [1989] ECR 3165 para 28. As explained, inspectors may carry out a search for themselves without authorization from the undertakings only in the case of enforced inspections.

[163] See the Commission Decision *Fabbrica Pisana* [1980] OJ L75/30.

[164] See ch 9 'Penalties and confidentiality' para 9.07.

[165] The Commission could also choose to impose periodic penalty payments if the documents were not submitted subsequently. See the Decision in *CSM* [1992] OJ L305/16.

undertakings claim that documents are confidential, comprising correspondence with their lawyers, they must provide evidence that the documents requested qualify for confidential treatment, failing which they will be obliged to produce them in due course in accordance with a specific procedure.[166] Further, undertakings may draw the attention of inspectors to particular documents relating to the subject-matter of the inspection which are favourable to them and have not been examined by the inspectors, this being indicated in the explanatory memoranda concerning inspections. These documents will be placed with the others, if the undertakings so wish, and will be used with the others to complete the investigation of the case.

8. The taking of copies or of extracts from documents

Inspectors are also entitled to take photocopies of information required. **8.76** Practical arrangements for the identification and copying of documents will vary from one investigation to another. Sometimes the inspectors will take charge of copying arrangements, and on other occasions the company itself will undertake the copying on their behalf. The inspectors, on their own initiative or at the request of undertakings, prepare on completion of the inspection an inventory, or list, of the documents of which photocopies or extracts have been taken. The list will be signed by all those present, who will receive a copy.

9. The completion record

Once the inspection is completed, a record is made of the matters which did **8.77** not merit a separate record—some examples were seen earlier[167]—and copies of the documents and a list or inventory of them are handed over and a receipt is given for them. At this stage, provided that the inspectors consider it appropriate and the undertakings agree, the latter may make any statement which they consider appropriate, which will be incorporated in the record. All those present sign and receive a copy of the closing record which, together with any other minutes, the list of documents and photocopies of them, thereupon form part of the Commission's administrative file. After the inspection is completed, the officials prepare a report on the conduct of the inspection. This is an internal document. Nevertheless, the Commission may agree to disclose it to

---

[166] See ch 9 'Penalties and confidentiality' paras 9.24 *et seq.*

[167] It is in the interests of undertakings progressively to obtain, as they are produced and before the final record is prepared, copies of the records mentioning specific events occurring during the inspection and copies of any documents, inventories, etc, so that on completion of the inspection their documentation will be complete and the same as that produced by the Commission during the inspection. See also on the completion record, A Klees, *Europäisches Kartellverfahrensrecht* (2005) § 9 para 66.

any undertakings suspected of involvement in an infringement, at the stage when access to the file is granted.[168]

10. Duration and timing of inspections

8.78 The period from the arrival of the inspectors at the undertaking's premises until their departure will not normally exceed forty-eight hours. In most cases, inspections last one day. Inspections may last more than two days—and they sometimes do—although the Commission endeavours to keep them as short as possible in order not to disrupt the normal running of the undertaking. The Commission is required to carry out its inspections at times when the premises and buildings of the undertakings are normally open. When premises have to be closed, Community officials may ask the undertakings to provide them with a place (a cupboard or filing cabinet) in which documents to be photocopied can be sealed and kept under lock and key.

---

[168] As regards the difference between accessible and internal documents, see Communication from the Commission relating to the revision of the 1997 notice on the internal rules of procedure for processing requests for access to the file (the 'Notice on Access to File') [2005] OJ C325/7 paras 10 *et seq*. The new rules were adopted on 13 December 2005. See Commission press release IP/05/1581 'Competition: Commission improves rules for access to the file in merger and antitrust procedures'. See ch 10 'Infringement procedures' para 10.27.

9

INVESTIGATION OF CASES (IV): PENALTIES, CONFIDENTIALITY

I. Pecuniary penalties

A. Introduction

Undertakings which fail to fulfil their procedural obligations may be liable to pecuniary penalties. Community competition law provides for two types of financial penalties. Firstly, fines which are very similar to those which may be imposed by the National Competition Authorities (NCAs). Secondly, periodic penalty payments, which are re-imposed daily as from a particular date; the final amount is calculated once the acts or omissions which the Commission seeks to penalize have occurred or been brought to an end, the daily amount being multiplied by the number of days elapsed. The aim and purpose of such penalties is threefold. They are designed (i) to penalize infringements (the punitive aspect); (ii) to ensure that undertakings refrain in general (the exemplary or dissuasive aspect) or specifically (the coercive aspect) from hampering investigations and inspections by the Commission; and (iii) to induce undertakings to take or refrain from taking certain action.   **9.01**

Article 23(1) of Regulation 1/2003 largely follows Article 15(1) of Regulation 17,[1] save in one important respect: the level of fines that may be imposed. Whereas fines under Article 15(1) were limited to a range of between 100 and 5,000 euros, under Article 23(1) the Commission may by decision impose on undertakings fines of up to 1 per cent of total turnover (based on the previous year's turnover). This modification, together with that made to the scale of periodic penalties under Article 24 was triggered by the consideration that the   **9.02**

---

[1] Although notifications no longer form part of the system, the case law in the context of Art 15(1)(a) of Reg 17 remains relevant as to the general approach to Art 23(1) of Reg 1/2003.

previous amounts did not have any deterrent effect[2] and should thus allow for a substantial increase in the level of fines on undertakings which obstruct the investigation of substantive infringements. As with substantive infringements under Article 23(2), Article 23(1) requires that the infringement be committed 'intentionally or negligently'. It is to note that there can be an infringement under Article 23(1) even if there is no proven infringement of Articles 81 or 82 EC. All undertakings are required in the same way as those which are implicated to submit to Commission investigations and inquiries and are therefore liable to a pecuniary penalty if they do not cooperate with the Commission. But whether to proceed under Article 23(1) is a matter of discretion for the Commission.

B. Fines

1. In relation to requests for information

9.03 Under Article 23(1) of Regulation 1/2003, the Commission may by decision impose on undertakings and associations of undertakings fines not exceeding 1 per cent of the total turnover in the preceding business year where, intentionally or negligently:

(a) they supply incorrect or misleading information in response to a request made pursuant to Article 17 or Article 18(2);

(b) in response to a request made by decision adopted pursuant to Article 17 or Article 18(3), they supply incorrect, incomplete, or misleading information or do not supply information within the required time-limit.

9.04 Article 23(1)(a) and (b) is thus similar to the wording of Article 15(1)(b) of Regulation 17, but extends the scope to cover not only information that is 'incorrect' but also 'incomplete or misleading'. Under Regulation 17, however, the Commission considered that incorrect information had been supplied when the information was false or so incomplete that the reply as a whole might be misleading.[3] In fact, therefore, this extension simply codifies a former practice. When replying to a request for information, undertakings must reply correctly and comprehensively to all of the Commission's questions. Firms must give an extensive response to the request which is sent to them; they must carefully interpret the question posed in the light of the objective pursued and the spirit

---

[2] Art 22 of the proposed Regulation ('Draft Regulation implementing Articles 81 and 82 of the Treaty') COM(2000)582 final—CNS 2000/0243, Explanatory Memorandum. Given the inflation of the last thirty years, any deterrent effect had clearly been eroded. See A Riley, 'EC Antitrust Modernization: The Commission Does Very Nicely—Thank you! Part One: Regulation 1 and the Notification Burden' [2003] ECLR 604–14 (609).

[3] *Telos* [1982] OJ L58/19; *National Panasonic* [1982] OJ L113/18.

and purpose of the investigation.[4] The correctness of the information supplied also depends on the context in which it is requested. Thus, for example, if the Commission makes clear in a request for information that the relationship between two undertakings may constitute an infringement of Article 81 EC and asks one of the undertakings to provide a copy of the documents in its possession defining the nature of its relationship with the other, the first undertaking does not provide a correct answer if it merely states that it has no written contract with the other undertaking, and it is then established that a clearly defined commercial relationship existed between them which was prohibited by Article 81(1) EC.[5] The falsity or incompleteness of the information supplied can be assessed by comparing facts or figures clearly established by other means. Alternatively, it may be apparent from a deliberately misleading presentation of reality which is liable to lead the Commission into error. In conclusion, any information which gives a distorted view of the circumstances under investigation, beyond the literal terms of a particular question, constitutes incorrect information. Undertakings may be fined when they refuse to supply the Commission with information which it requests by decision within the time limit laid down in the decision. The fine is the same as for incorrect information.

The Commission fined undertakings for supplying incorrect information in **9.05** reply to Article 11(3) requests for information under Regulation 17 in approximately half a dozen occasions, most recently in *Anheuser-Busch/Scottish & Newcastle*,[6] although most date back to the mid-eighties. In principle, the Commission has not shied away from imposing the maximum amount (5,000 euros) although it is ready to consider specific circumstances. In *Peugeot*, the Commission seemed to have considered in Peugeot's favour that two consecutive requests for information constituted only one single request because they put a series of questions in a single context, and because the second letter made reference to the first. The Commission also took into account that the infringement had been committed partly intentionally and partly negligently. The persons who drafted the replies were not fully acquainted with the facts. Nevertheless the Commission found that the company did not exercise sufficient supervision within the group to prevent false statements being made and

---

[4] 'Dealing with the Commission—Notification, complaints, inspections and fact-finding powers under Articles [81] and [82] of the EEC Treaty' (1997 edn) point 4.5.

[5] *Comptoir d'importation* [1982] OJ L27/31; see also Case 28/77 *Tepea BV v EC Commission* [1978] ECR 1391 para 69 in which the Court took the view that the notification form clearly drew the attention of Theal to the duty to inform the Commission of the provisions of the agreement and to state whether it involved market sharing.

[6] *Anheuser/Busch/Scottish Newcastle* [2000] OJ L49/37. See M Van der Woude and C Jones, *EC Competition Law Handbook* (2004/2005 edn) 197 which includes a comprehensive list of cases in which fines were imposed for infringement of procedural rules. See also for a maritime transport case under Reg 4056/86 *Secrétama* [1991] OJ L35/23.

imposed a slightly lower fine (4,000 euros).[7] Similarly, in *Anheuser-Busch/ Scottish & Newcastle*, the Commission accepted that there was no intention to provide incorrect information and that the infringement only subsisted for a short time. The relatively small number of cases should not be taken as a sign that the Commission may not always be willing to use the power granted by Regulation 1/2003. On the contrary, the Commission has shown a determination to penalize companies found to have frustrated competition law investigations by providing false or incomplete information. The increase in fines under Regulation 1/2003 may give this determination additional impetus. The Commission may follow a similar approach as under the corresponding provision of Regulation 139/2004 (the EC Merger Regulation) which is indicative of a firm line against infringements of the obligation to supply accurate information.[8]

2. In relation to inspections

9.06 According to Article 23(1)(c) of Regulation 1/2003, fines may be imposed on undertakings where 'they produce the required books or other records related to the business in incomplete form during inspections under Article 20 or refuse to submit to inspections ordered by a decision adopted pursuant to Article 20(4).' Fines may thus be imposed following inspections in two cases. First, where the documents produced by the undertakings are incomplete; secondly, where the undertakings refuse to comply with inspection decisions. It is important to note that the provisions cited above relate to all types of fines and are applicable both as a result of inspections carried out by the authorities of the Member States on behalf of the Commission (ordinary inspections or inspection decisions under Article 22 in conjunction with Article 20(3) and (4)) and as a result of inspections carried out by Community officials (inspections under Article 20(3) and (4)). Article 23(1)(c) thus specifies two separate types of infringement. Because they are alternatives (note the second 'or') it is on the one hand arguable that the incomplete production of books does not amount to a refusal to submit to an investigation where ordered by decision. On the other hand, an undertaking's

---

[7] *Peugeot* [1986] OJ L295/19 para 52.

[8] See *Sanofi/Synthélabo* [2000] OJ L95/34; see also Commission Press Release IP/04/863 of 7 July 2004, 'Commission fines Tetra Laval for providing incorrect information in Sidel acquisition'. The Commission imposed a fine of 90,000 euros for the infringements ([2005] OJ L98/27). The fines in question were imposed under the former EC Merger Control Regulation. In view of the importance of full disclosure of relevant information in merger cases, the new Merger Control Regulation adopted by the Council and in force since 1 May 2004 has increased the maximum penalty for each infringement from 50,000 euros to a maximum of 1 per cent of aggregate turnover. Commission Press Release IP/02/897 of 19 June 2002, 'Commission fines Deutsche BP for supplying incorrect information in notification of Erdölchemie purchase'; Commission Press Release IP/00/764 of 12 July 2000 'Commission fines Mitsubishi for failing to supply information on Kvaerner/Ahlström joint venture'.

refusal to hand over a document during an inspection pursuant to a decision would in principle fall within both categories. In *CSM*, the undertaking's refusal to hand over documents for inspection which it considered as not relevant was treated as a refusal to submit to the investigation.[9]

Production of business records in incomplete form

Article 23(1)(c) of Regulation 1/2003 is substantively identical to its predeces- **9.07** sor Article 15(1)(c) of Regulation 17 and earlier practice therefore remains directly relevant. The incompleteness of the documents may be attributable not so much to the objective fact that the documentation produced is incomplete as to the attitude of undertakings during an inspection. Reference was made earlier to the possibility that information requested but not available for any reason could be forwarded to the Commission subsequently by undertakings. It was also stated that the obligation to provide the requested information calls for active cooperation on the part of undertakings and that a 'go slow' attitude might be regarded by the Commission as equivalent to the production of incomplete documentation. For example, during its investigation of the glass market in Italy, the Commission fined two undertakings which voluntarily submitted to the Commission's inspection for producing books, etc in incomplete form. In *Fabbrica Sciarra*, the Commission's inspectors asked specific questions about the relation of the company with Fides, the exact date when these relations were entered into, their precise objectives requested pro- ductions of all correspondence with it or other glass manufacturers. In response, *Fabbrica Sciarra* presented documentation which was incomplete. Taking the view that *Fabbrica Sciarra* had ample opportunity to demonstrate its good faith by informing the Commission that it intended to produce all the documents which had been requested, the Commission considered the infringement as intentional.[10] A similar reasoning led to the imposition of a fine on *Fabbrica Pisana* because the Commission considered that *Fabbrica Pisana* could not have been unaware of the extent of the Commission's power of investigation or of the exact nature of three documents sought.[11] Failure to produce a document requested by the Commission or interruption of an ordinary inspection will be regarded as constituting incomplete production of records. It must be remem- bered that once an ordinary inspection has been agreed to and has commenced, it follows exactly the same course as an inspection pursuant to a decision.

---

[9] *CSM* [1992] OJ L305/16. Providing the documents later did not mitigate the fine. The undertaking's obligation to cooperate in the investigation is not limited to supplying those documents it considers relevant. See also *FNICF* [1982] OJ L319/12 in which FNICF's Federal Council refused to produce the minutes of its meetings alleging that the documents were confidential and related to matters which had no bearing on the subject of the investigation.

[10] *Fabbrica Sciarra* [1980] OJ L75/35. See also in this respect *Fides* [1979] OJ L57/33.

[11] *Fabbrica Pisana* [1980] OJ L75/30.

Undertakings may not therefore either interrupt an inspection that has begun or refuse to produce a document or information on the pretext that, if they are entitled to refuse outright to submit to an inspection, they are entitled to the lesser option of refusing to hand over a document or interrupting an inspection.

Opposition to an inspection conducted pursuant to a decision

9.08 By contrast with the position concerning ordinary inspections—where the Commission's only reaction to opposition on the part of undertakings can be the very moderate measure of drawing up a record of what has happened and, if appropriate, seeking to carry out the inspection pursuant to a decision—the Commission may also impose fines where undertakings refuse to submit to an inspection pursuant to a binding decision of the Commission. The concept of opposition is not limited simply to cases where inspectors are denied access to undertakings' premises or to all their installations, property and furniture which may contain business records on the subject-matter of the inspection. Dissimulated opposition, that is to say any subterfuge intended to delay and hamper the inspection, on various pretexts, is also regarded as opposition to an inspection. Unduly delaying the commencement of an inspection will be treated as a refusal to submit to the investigation. In *MEWAC*, the Commission stated that the liner conference *MEWAC* held up matters for what was manifestly an unreasonablly long period.[12] It would not be for the undertaking concerned to decide the date and time of the investigation.[13] Asking for a postponement until a particular designed representative of the firm or a particular lawyer can be present can also constitute a refusal to submit.[14] Finally, it must again be pointed out that the fact that enforcement measures have been taken to implement a decision does not prevent the Commission from imposing a fine for opposition on the part of undertakings.

Incorrect and misleading answers

9.09 Pursuant to Article 23(1)(d) of Regulation 1/2003, fines may be imposed on undertakings where, in response to a question asked in accordance with Article 20(2)(e):

(a) they give an incorrect or misleading answer;

---

[12] *MEWAC* [1993] OJ L20/06 para 7. In this case, the police sealed the premises until the inspection could begin the following day.

[13] *MEWAC* [1993] OJ L20/06 para 7; *UKWAL* [1992] OJ L121/45 para 9 in which the Commission found that the infringement was very serious. UKWAL's refusal jeopardized the effectiveness of the investigation by preventing the Commission from carrying out the inspection on the envisaged date. Both *MEWAC* and *UKWAL* are maritime cases under Reg 4056/86.

[14] 'Dealing with the Commission—Notification, complaints, inspections and fact-finding powers under Articles [81] and [82] of the EEC Treaty' (1997 edn) point 4.5.

(b) they fail to rectify within a time-limit set by the Commission an incorrect, incomplete, or misleading answer given by a member of staff; or

(c) they fail or refuse to provide a complete answer on facts relating to the subject-matter and purpose of an inspection ordered by a decision adopted pursuant to Article 20(4).

This new provision supplements Article 20(1)(b) and should resolve the linger-   **9.10**
ing uncertainty under Article 15(1)(c) of Regulation 17 as to whether it was wide enough to deal with at least some cases where an undertaking either refused to give oral explanations or gave a false explanation.[15] In *Akzo Chemicals*, the Commission imposed the maximum fine where the surprise effect of its unannounced inspection was frustrated by the undertaking giving incorrect information as to where it had offices and by denying access to the office of one of its directors.[16] Whilst the latter clearly fell within Article 15(1)(c) of Regulation 17, it might have been argued that Article 15(1)(c) did not suffice to penalize false explanations. By virtue of Article 23(1)(d), the issue could not now arise.

Seals broken

Fines may be imposed on undertakings where 'seals affixed by authorised offi-   **9.11**
cials of the Commission in accordance with Article 20(2)(e) have been broken.' The Commission has not yet imposed a fine for breaking seals affixed in the course of an inspection, but it seems that the prohibition is straightforward to apply and should not give rise to major problems of interpretation.

C. Periodic Penalty Payments

Article 24(1) of Regulation 1/2003 empowers the Commission to impose peri-   **9.12**
odic penalty payments not exceeding 5 per cent of the average daily turnover in the preceding business year per day to ensure compliance with both procedural rules and substantive decisions. As regards procedural rules, periodic penalty payments may be imposed for delay in supplying the information requested by the Commission, or for each day of non-compliance in the case of inspections. With respect to substantive decisions, they may be imposed in order to compel undertakings (i) to comply with a decision ordering to put an end to an infringement of Articles 81 or 82 EC or (ii) to comply with a decision ordering interim measures pursuant to Article 8 or (iii) to comply with a commitment made binding by a decision pursuant to Article 9.

Periodic penalty payments, being punitive, are principally coercive, and play a   **9.13**

---

[15] See paras 9.04 *et seq.*   [16] *Akzo Chemicals* [1994] OJ L294/31.

supporting role. The Commission resorts to them mainly to ensure that obstacles to its investigative work, when encountered, are removed, or where there are sufficient grounds for doubting that undertakings are co-operating. Periodic penalty payments may follow, or even in certain circumstances accompany, decisions requesting information or decisions to inspect. In the first case, the Commission will adopt a specific decision imposing the periodic penalty payment.[17] In the second case, the decision in question will provide for a periodic penalty payment to be imposed in the event of an infringement by the undertakings. There is nothing to prevent the Commission, provided it observes the principle of proportionality, from deciding to request information or undertake an inspection and at the same time impose periodic penalty payments in the event of a failure to reply or opposition.[18] The particular aim of periodic penalty payments makes them independent from, yet capable of accompanying, fines. Thus, for example, an incorrect reply to a request for information based on a decision is liable to give rise not only to a fine but also to a periodic penalty payment until such time as correct answers are given to the questions. The Commission does not hesitate to impose both penalties on recalcitrant undertakings.

1. In relation to requests for information

9.14 Under Article 24(1)(d) of Regulation 1/2003, the Commission may impose on undertakings or associations of undertakings periodic penalty payments in order to compel them 'to supply complete and correct information which it has requested by decision taken pursuant to Article 17 or Article 18(3).' Periodic penalty payments may therefore be imposed not only when no or only partial answers are given, but also when the answers are incorrect, in the sense that the information given is not what was asked for or the answers are vague or unclear. What is certain is that under Regulation 17, as far as requests for information are concerned, the Commission did not in most cases go so far as to adopt a decision. Only in such circumstances could it also decide to impose periodic penalty payments on undertakings. Undertakings invariably co-operated with the Commission at the stage of ordinary requests, which meant that in nearly every case it was unnecessary to adopt a decision to request information or impose periodic penalty payments. Under Regulation 1/2003, the Commission

---

[17] A periodic penalty payment may not have retroactive effect in such cases since it is primarily intended to operate in the future (ensuring that undertakings follow a particular course of conduct) and does not take effect until it has been notified.

[18] An example might be a decision to request information, following an unsuccessful ordinary request for information, or else a decision to inspect following an ordinary inspection which the undertakings have resisted.

may directly proceed to a decision requiring the disclosure of information under Regulation 1/2003.[19] Thus, it may well be that the alteration of the Commission's powers may also lead to more cases in which the Commission will impose periodic penalties.

2. In relation to inspections

Article 24(1)(d) of Regulation 1/2003 also enables the Commission to impose **9.15** periodic penalty payments per day in order to compel undertakings 'to submit to an inspection which it has ordered by decision taken pursuant to Article 20(4).' Normally, the Commission makes no provision in its inspection decisions for the imposition of periodic penalty payments in the event of opposition on the part of undertakings. Nevertheless, if there were grounds for believing that the undertakings would resist (because they had done so on other occasions or had failed to respond to an earlier request for information, for example), the Commission could resort to a single decision in order to obtain documents more rapidly, without prejudice to the possibility of resorting to enforcement as well.[20] However, in practice it is not usual to resort to periodic penalty payments and enforcement measures at the same time, since the success of the latter precludes the former.

D. Procedure

1. General

Procedural infringements on the part of undertakings make it necessary for **9.16** the Commission to initiate new penalty proceedings, ancillary to the main procedure. Despite their obligation to cooperate with Community inspectors, undertakings might refuse to allow them to enter their premises in order to undertake an inspection pursuant to a decision. The Commission would be empowered to impose a fine in respect of that action and also to impose a periodic penalty payment if for any reason enforcement measures were unsuccessful.[21] The following procedures would thus be pending before the Commission:

---

[19] Art 18(3) of Reg 1/2003 stipulates the same formalities as for a simple request under Art 18(2) of Reg 1/2003 with the additional requirements that the Commission 'indicate or impose the penalties provided for in Art 24'.

[20] As stated earlier, the Commission must ensure that the principle of proportionality is observed in such cases.

[21] That was what happened in Joined Cases 46/87 and 227/88 *Hoechst v EC Commission* [1989] ECR 2859 paras 3–8.

(i)   a main procedure for infringement of Article 81(1) EC;

(ii) a procedure for infringement of Article 20(4), under Article 23(1) c of Regulation 1/2003, with a view to the imposition of fines for opposition to an inspection;

(iii) a procedure under Article 24(1)(e) of Regulation 1/2003, intended to compel the undertakings to submit to the inspection.

9.17 Each procedure would be self-sufficient. Each of them would follow its own independent course—although in parallel—until the adoption of three final decisions. One which may not entail pecuniary penalties (the main procedure, a matter of substantive law), and the two other procedures which would necessarily—that being their specific purpose—lead to the imposition of penalties. The new procedures would be dealt with within DG COMP itself by the same officials dealing with the substantive case. As stated, it should not be thought, however, that procedures concerning infringements of Regulation 1/2003 are possible only when undertakings are the subject of a procedure for infringement of Treaty competition provisions. All undertakings, including 'third-party undertakings',[22] are required, in the same way as those which are implicated, to submit to Commission investigations and inquiries. All, therefore, are liable to a pecuniary penalty if they do not cooperate with the Commission.

2. Procedure for the imposition of fines

9.18 Article 27(1) of Regulation 1/2003 provides that before adopting the decisions provided for, *inter alia*, in Articles 23 and 24(2), the Commission will give undertakings and associations of undertakings an opportunity to submit their observations on the objections or charges made by the Commission against them. Article 14(1) of Regulation 1/2003 provides that the Advisory Committee on Restrictive Practices and Monopolies is also to be consulted.[23]

9.19 From the Commission's point of view, the imposition of a periodic penalty payment comprises two phases, in each of which there is a decision. In the first phase—either in parallel with another decision, or by an independent decision—the Commission determines the amount of the periodic penalty payment per day's delay. In this first phase, the Commission is not required to send a statement of objections or to allow undertakings to submit observations. Nor is it necessary for it to submit a draft decision to the Advisory Committee. If the undertakings comply with the order made, there are no adverse consequences for them. If they do not do so within the time-limit set, the Commission as a

---

[22] e.g. undertakings which, without having been parties to a restrictive agreement, practice, or conduct, are in possession of information which they refuse to disclose to the Commission.

[23] See ch 3 'The role of national competition authorities' paras 3.45 *et seq.*

rule sends a brief reminder letter advising them of the financial consequences of their conduct, namely that, for each day that passes without the undertakings complying with the order made by the Commission, the amount they will have to pay will increase. When the undertakings finally comply, and this takes place after expiry of the 'voluntary' time-limit, the second phase commences. In the second phase the Commission determines by decision—in this case it is always an independent decision—the definitive amount of the periodic penalty payment. Pursuant to Article 24(2) of Regulation 1/2003, 'where the undertakings or associations of undertakings have satisfied the obligation which it was the purpose of the periodic penalty payment to enforce, the Commission may fix the total amount of the periodic penalty payment at a lower figure than that which would arise under the original decision.' This second decision is adopted after a statement of objections is sent and the undertakings submit observations, as a rule exclusively in writing. The draft decision is reported on by the Advisory Committee. By virtue of Article 30(1) of Regulation 1/2003, the decisions under Articles 23 and 24 have to be published. The two-decision procedure was approved by the Court in its judgment in *Hoechst III*.[24]

E. Limitation Period

Since the adoption of Regulation 2988/74,[25] the Commission's power to **9.20** impose penalties for infringements of Community competition law is subject to limitation periods. The relevant provisions of Regulation 1/2003 fix two types of limitation period, those relating to the Commission's powers to impose fines and penalties ('limitation period in proceedings') and those relating to the enforcement of the collection of fines and penalties ('limitation period for the enforcement of sanction'). Regulation 1/2003 has taken over the rules contained in Regulation 2988/74 with some minor changes in order to adapt the enforcement system to the new decentralized application of competition rules.[26] Pursuant to Article 25 of Regulation 1/2003, the limitation period for procedural infringements is three years. Time begins to run on the day on which the infringement is committed. However, in the case of continuing or repeated

---

[24] See Joined Cases 46/87 and 227/88 *Hoechst v EC Commission* [1989] ECR 2859 paras 51–57.

[25] Council Reg 2988/74 concerning limitation periods in proceedings and the enforcement of sanctions under the rules of the European Economic Community relating to transport and competition [1974] OJ L319/1, as amended.

[26] Pursuant to Art 37 of Reg 1/2003, Reg 2988/74 has been amended so that it does not apply to measures taken under Reg 1/2003.

infringements, time begins to run on the day on which the infringement ceases.[27]

9.21 Under Regulation 2988/74 the limitation period was suspended by steps taken by the Member States only if they acted at the Commission's request. The latter condition is now removed, so that the limitation period is also interrupted by measures taken by NCAs applying Articles 81 or 82 EC, irrespective of any request from the Commission. Any action taken by the Commission or by an NCA for the purpose of the investigation or proceedings in respect of an infringement interrupts the limitation period for the imposition of fines or periodic penalty payments. The limitation period is interrupted with effect from the date on which the action is notified to at least one undertaking or association of undertakings which has participated in the infringement. Actions which interrupt the running of the period shall include in particular the following:

(a) written requests for information by the Commission or by an NCA;

(b) written authorizations to conduct inspections issued to its officials by the Commission or by an NCA;

(c) the initiation of proceedings by the Commission or by an NCA;

(d) notification of the statement of objections of the Commission or of an NCA.

9.22 The Commission is not prevented from taking action in relation to any agreements or practices after these periods have elapsed but is merely prohibited from imposing fines.[28] Thus, the Commission may adopt a decision declaring that an infringement has taken place which may have consequences for the liability of the parties before a national court.[29] For limitation purposes time starts running afresh after each interruption.[30] Moreover, the time bar will take effect in any

---

[27] For a case in which the CFI, having taken the view that insufficient evidence had been given of the existence of a continuous infringement between two dates on which there had indeed been specific instances of infringements, declared the first infringement time-barred, see Case T-43/92 *Dunlop v EC Commission* [1994] ECR II-441 para 84.

[28] In *Sumitomo Chemical*, the CFI reaffirmed that the five-year limitation period only applies to the Commission's ability to impose a fine, not to its ability to address infringement decisions to undertakings and so making findings that violations of Arts 81 and 82 EC have occurred. However, in this case, the Commission decision was annulled because the Commission failed to establish a legitimate interest in addressing such decision to the undertaking. Joined Cases T-22/02 and T-23/02 *Sumitomo Chemical v EC Commission*, CFI judgment of 6 October 2005 (not yet published).

[29] This naturally is subject to national procedural rules (*res judicata* etc). CS Kerse and N Khan, *EC Antitrust Procedure* (5th edn, 2005) para 7–082, n 81.

[30] See, however, Case T-213/00 *CMA CGM v EC Commission* [2003] II-913 para 488 in which the CFI held that the interruption of the limitation period has to be interpreted restrictively and the Commission cannot make a request for information for the sole purpose of prolonging the limitation.

event after six years (for procedural infringements) if the Commission fails to impose a fine or other penalty.[31] This time-limit will be extended by the period during which the limitation period was suspended as a result of an action being brought against the Commission decision before the CFI or ECJ.[32]

Article 26 of Regulation 1/2003 specifies a limitation period of five years in respect of the Commission's power to enforce any decision imposing a fine and/ or periodic penalty payment under Articles 23 and 24 of Regulation 1/2003. Time begins to run on the day on which the decision becomes final. The limitation period for the enforcement of penalties is interrupted (i) by notification of a decision varying the original amount of the fine or periodic penalty payment or refusing an application for variation and (ii) by any action of the Commission or of a Member State, acting at the request of the Commission, designed to enforce payment of the fine or periodic penalty payment. The limitation period for the enforcement of penalties is suspended for so long as (i) time to pay is allowed and (ii) enforcement of payment is suspended pursuant to a decision of the Community Courts. There is no case law on these provisions, but in practice the far-reaching possibilities of interrupting actions will make it unlikely that limitation periods will prevent the Commission from recovering a fine.[33]

9.23

II. Confidentiality and use of information

A. Professional Secrecy and Business Secrets

Undertakings dealing with the Commission will naturally wish to ensure that confidential information given to the Commission is protected from disclosure. The information covered by professional secrecy may be both confidential information and business secrets and is thus not limited to the latter. Article 287 EC applies to 'information of the kind covered by professional secrecy'. It applies in particular to 'information about undertakings, their business relations

9.24

---

[31] Art 25(5) of Reg 1/2003: '[. . .] the limitation period shall expire at the latest on the day on which a period equal to twice the limitation period has elapsed without the Commission having imposed a fine or a periodic penalty payment [. . .]'.

[32] Art 25(6) of Reg 1/2003: 'The limitation period for the imposition of fines or periodic penalty payments shall be suspended for as long as the decision of the Commission is the subject of proceedings pending before the Court of Justice.' See *PVC* [1994] OJ L239/14, in particular paras 47 and 56–58. That decision followed the annulment of the first *PVC* decision by the ECJ, after the CFI had declared it non-existent.

[33] CS Kerse and N Khan, *EC Antitrust Procedure* (5th edn, 2005) para 7–087.

or their cost components'. It thus expressly refers to information which, in principle, falls, by reason of its content, within the category of business secrets, as defined by the ECJ.[34] Business secrets are information of which not only disclosure to the public but also mere transmission to a person other than the one that provided the information may seriously harm the latter's interests.[35]

9.25   Article 28 of Regulation 1/2003 extends this concept to the enforcement of competition rules and provides that the Commission and NCAs, their officials, servants, and other persons working under the supervision of these authorities as well as officials and civil servants of other authorities of the Member States shall not disclose information acquired or exchanged by them pursuant to Regulation 1/2003 and of the kind covered by the obligation of professional secrecy. This obligation also applies to all representatives and experts of Member States attending meetings of the Advisory Committee. In this connection, the CFI has stated: '. . .[I]nformation obtained during investigations must not be used for purposes other than those indicated in the order or decision pursuant to which the investigation is carried out [. . .] That requirement is intended to protect, in addition to the professional secrecy expressly referred to in Article [28(1) of Regulation 1/2003], the undertakings' defence rights, which not only form part of the fundamental principles of Community law but are also enshrined in Article 6 of the ECHR'.[36] The protection provided for by Article 28 is consequently twofold. First, paragraph 2 of that provision prohibits the disclosure of information acquired as a result of the application of Regulation 1/2003 and of the kind covered by the obligation of professional secrecy. Secondly, Article 28(1) prohibits the use of information acquired as a result of the application of Articles 17–22 of Regulation1/2003 for any purpose other than that for which it has been requested.[37] As the CFI has said, those two safeguards, which are of a complementary nature, apply not only to the Community administration but also to national administrations. This means that the requirement of confidential treatment also applies to information transmitted to Member States as a result of cooperation between authorities as provided in Article 12 of Regulation

---

[34]   See Case 145/83 *Stanley Adams v EC Commission* [1985] ECR 3539 para 34; Case T-353/94 *Postbank v EC Commission* [1996] ECR II-921 para 86 and more recently T-62/98 *Volkswagen v EC Commission* [2000] ECR II-2707 para 279.

[35]   Case T-353/94 *Postbank v EC Commission* [1996] ECR II-921 paras 86–87.

[36]   Case 85/87 *Dow Benelux v EC Commisison* [1989] ECR 3137 paras 17–18; Joined Cases C-238/99, C-245/99, C-247/99, C-250/99, C-252/99 and C-254/99 *Limburgse Vinyl Maatschappij NV and others v EC Commission* [2002] ECR I-8375 paras 298–299.

[37]   See Case T-39/90 *Samenwerkende Elektriciteitsproduktiebedrijven (SEP) v EC Commission* [1991] ECR II-1497 para 55. See, to the same effect, 'Spanish Banks' Case C-67/91 *Dirección General de Defensa de la Competencia (DGDC) v Asociación Española de Banca Privada (AEB) and others* [1992] ECR I-4785 para 37. As regards the question whether the 'SEP-scenario' still applies, see ch 3 'The role of national competition authorities' para 3.26.

1/2003.[38] The general principle of the protection of business secrets is also reflected in other provisions: Article 30(2) of Regulation 1/2003 provides that publication of decisions under Article 21 'shall have regard to the legitimate interest of undertakings in the protection of their business secrets.'[39] By virtue of this principle, in certain circumstances the Commission is required not to disclose—even to the competent authorities in Member States—certain documents which contain business secrets.[40]

While professional secrecy is an obligation of Community or national officials **9.26** and other employees who are involved in proceedings, and covers all information obtained, business secrets relate to the activities of undertakings. Business secrets relate to particular items of information among those which may have been used in the investigation, the confidential nature of which is apparent from the possible consequences for undertakings in the event of its disclosure to third parties.[41]

B. Use of the Information

Article 28(1) of Regulation 1/2003 provides that 'information acquired as a **9.27** result of the application of Articles 17 to 22 shall be used only for the purpose of

---

[38] See Case T-39/90 *Samenwerkende Elektriciteitsproduktiebedrijven (SEP) v EC Commission* [1991] ECR II-1497 para 55, *in fine*. Case C-60/92 *Otto v Postbank* [1993] ECR I-5683 para 20. That obligation may not be sufficient to safeguard the general principle that undertakings are entitled to protection of their business secrets in certain cases. See Case C-36/92 P *Samenverkende Elektriciteits-produktiebedrijven (SEP) v EC Commission II* [1994] ECR I-1911 para 31.

[39] See also Arts 8, 14(6) and (8), and 16 of Reg 773/2004.

[40] The reason is that it is not possible to require those authorities to disregard the information transmitted to them. In the *SEP II* (Case C-36/92 P [1994] ECR I-1911) it could not be expected that the Netherlands Ministry of Industry (which at the time dealt with Community competition rules in the Netherlands) should, when deciding on the commercial strategy of a State undertaking controlled by that Ministry (Gasunie), ignore the information provided to it by DG COMP (DG IV at the time) concerning relations between one of the latter's clients (SEP) and a competing supplier (Statoil). Mere knowledge of the contract entered into between SEP and Statoil might be taken into account in deciding the commercial policy of Gasunie, since the Netherlands Ministry of Industry is not required to disregard information transmitted to it. See *SEP II* [1994] ECR I-1911 paras 27–30, citing Case C-67/91 'Spanish Banks' [1992] ECR I-4785. The requirement imposed by *SEP I* (Case T-39/90 [1991] ECR II-1497 paras 56–57) that NCAs should not divulge information received to other national administrative departments, in particular those responsible for managing public undertakings or mixed-economy companies controlled by the Member State whose competition authorities might receive information from the Commission regarding other undertakings, seems therefore to have been regarded by the Court as insufficient to guarantee observance of the principle of protection of business secrets.

[41] See Case T-353/94 *Postbank v EC Commission* [1996] ECR II-921 para 87. See examples in Draft Commission Notice on the rules for access to the Commission File in cases pursuant to Arts 81 and 82 of the EC Treaty, Arts 53, 54, and 57 of the EEA Agreement and Council Reg 139/2004 para 17. As regards the Draft Notice on Access to the File, ch 10 'Infringement procedures' paras 10.28 *et seq*.

the relevant request or investigation'. In other words, the information and documents obtained by the Commission as a result of requests for information and inspections may be used only to determine whether or not the EC competition rules have been infringed in the specific case under investigation. In fact, the Court held that the limitation on the use of the information obtained by the Commission in its procedures extend to the information contained in old applications and notifications for individual clearance or exemption, even though they were not covered by provisions analogous to Article 28(1) of Regulation 1/2003.[42] However, Article 28(1) should not be construed as meaning 'that the Commission is barred from initiating an inquiry in order to verify or supplement information which it happened to obtain during a previous investigation if that information indicates the existence of conduct contrary to the competition rules in the Treaty. Such a bar would go beyond what is necessary to protect professional secrecy and the rights of the defence and would thus constitute an unjustified hindrance to the performance by the Commission of its task of ensuring compliance with the competition rules in the Common Market and bringing to light infringements of Articles [81] and [82] [. . .].'[43] For the rest, undertakings need not fear that the information and documents used for the investigation of their case by the Commission might be used at the same time or subsequently in some other kind of Community or national proceedings, such as, for example, for the application of national tax, criminal, or customs law by administrations in Member States.[44] As regards the application of national competition law, it has to be noted that Regulation 1/2003 has provided for the possibility that the Commission and NCAs 'provide one another with and use in evidence any matter of fact or of law, including confidential information'. The Court had held that the information received by NCAs in the context of Regulation 17 'constituted circumstantial evidence which might, if necessary, be taken into account to justify the initiation of a national procedure.' Therefore, NCAs are not obliged to suffer 'acute amnesia' in respect of such information.[45] The Court has made clear, however, that facts

---

[42] In particular, Art 20(1) of Reg 17. See Case C-67/91 *Direccion General de Defensa de la Competencia (DGDC) v Asociacion Española de Banca Privada (AEB) and others ('Spanish Banks')* [1992] ECR I-4785 paras 44–55.

[43] See Case 85/87 *Dow Benelux v Commission* [1989] ECR 3137 para 19. However, there is nothing to prevent the Commission from asking for the same documents in connection with another procedure.

[44] Regarding the confidentiality of information showing the existence of an offence, the question arises as to whether the Commission, rather than observing confidentiality in respect of that particular 'business secret', thereby overriding national criminal law, should in fact report the offence. That does not seem to be the case, with the result that, even where the documents requested by the Commission are capable of being used as evidence in criminal proceedings against their management, undertakings may not refuse to produce them.

[45] Case C-67/91 *Direccion General de Defensa de la Competencia (DGDC) v Asociación Española de Banca Privada (AEB) and others ('Spanish Banks')* [1992] ECR I-4785 para 39.

coming to the notice of NCAs through the Commission 'may validly be the subject-matter of a national procedure, provided that the evidence of their existence derives not from documents and information obtained by the Commission but from forms of evidence provided for by national law, in compliance with the safeguards provided by the latter'.[46]

Article 12 of Regulation 1/2003 gives a wide power to the Commission and the NCAs to exchange information which can be used in evidence for the purposes of applying Articles 81 and 82 EC. It arguably implies leaving behind the 'acute amnesia' principle laid down in *Spanish Banks*.[47] The limitations under Article 12 can be summarized as follows: **9.28**

(a) The information may be used only '[. . .] for the purposes of applying Articles 81 and 82 of the Treaty [. . .]', although it may also be used to apply national competition law 'in the same case and in parallel' to EC rules.

(b) Information shall only be used in respect of the subject matter for which it was collected.

(c) Information can only be used as evidence to impose sanctions on natural persons where (i) the law of the transmitting authority foresees sanction of a similar kind in relation to an infringement of Articles 81 or 82 EC; or the information has been collected in a way which respects the same level of protection of the defence rights of natural persons as provided for under the national rules of the receiving authority. In the latter case, the receiving authority may not use the information exchanged to impose custodial sanctions.[48]

---

[46] Case C-67/91 *Direccion General de Defensa de la Competencia (DGDC) v Asociación Española de Banca Privada (AEB) and others ('Spanish Banks')* [1992] ECR I-4785 para 43.

[47] Case C-67/91 *Direccion General de Defensa de la Competencia (DGDC) v Asociación Española de Banca Privada (AEB) and others ('Spanish Banks')* [1992] ECR I-4785. However, the modification has been criticized to some extent due to the fact that after the implementation of this exchange system, information handled by the Commission and NCAs will now be subject to both national and EC law, with different standards and guarantees. See also CS Kerse and N Khan, *EC Antitrust Procedure* (5th edn, 2005) para 5–008; M Araujo, 'The Respect of Fundamental Rights within the European Network of Competition Authorities' ch 21 in BE Hawk (ed), *International Antitrust Law & Policy*, Annual Proceedings of the Fordham Institute (2004) 511–53 (526–27 and n 61) regarding the compatibility of Art 12 with the ruling in 'Spanish Banks'. D Reichelt, 'To what extent does the cooperation within the European Competition Network protect the rights of the undertakings?' (2005) CML Rev 745–82 (777–78).

[48] Note that it has been said that 'the rights of defence enjoyed by undertakings in the various systems can be considered as sufficiently equivalent' (Recital 16 of Reg 1/2003). However, this statement may nevertheless be challenged when looking at the apparent differences among EU countries. Belgium and the UK deem as eligible for non-disclosure lawyer-client communications with in-house legal counsel, while other Members exclude in-house lawyers' correspondence from the mentioned privilege either completely (Spain, France, Sweden, or the European Commission itself) or partially (as in the Netherlands, where legal privilege merely applies to correspondence between undertakings and lawyers admitted to the bar, in-house lawyers seldom being admitted to

9.29   Article 287 EC and Article 28(2) of Regulation 1/2003 do not require the Commission to prohibit third parties from producing, in national legal proceedings, documents received in the procedure before the Commission which contain confidential information and business secrets. These provisions, even if they prevent undertakings from transmitting such documents to third parties, do not in any way prevent their disclosure to the national courts. The CFI has ruled that Article 20(2) of Regulation 17 (the corresponding provision of Article 28(2) of Regulation 1/2003) would be inapplicable to the exchange between national courts and the Commission. Secondly, Article 287 EC, which prohibits all officials and employees of the institutions from disclosing confidential information and business secrets to third parties, could not be interpreted as meaning that, by virtue of its obligation to observe professional secrecy, the Commission is required to prohibit undertakings from producing to national courts any documents received in the course of the administrative procedure.[49] Such an interpretation might compromise cooperation between the national judicial authorities and the Community institutions and above all detract from the right of economic agents to effective judicial protection.[50] More specifically, it would deprive certain undertakings of the protection, afforded by national courts, of the rights conferred on them by virtue of the direct effect of Articles 81 and 82 EC. The Commission may not in any circumstances undermine the guarantees given to individuals by the Community provisions concerning professional secrecy.[51] The upholding of such guarantees requires

---

the bar). See M Araujo, 'The Respect of Fundamental Rights within the European Network of Competition Authorities' ch 21 in BE Hawk (ed), *International Antitrust Law & Policy*, Annual Proceedings of the Fordham Institute (2004) 511–53 (523); see also M van der Woude, 'Exchange of Information within the European Competition Network: Scope and Limits' in *European Competition Law Annual 2002: Constructing the EU Network of Competition Authorities* (2002) 13. See K Dekeyser and E De Smijter, 'The Exchange of Evidence Within the ECN' [2005] Legal Issues of Economic Integration 161–74 (171) stating that because of mutual recognition, such a difference in standards cannot prevent the receiving ECN member from using in evidence information exchanged to the extent that it was legally collected by the transmitting ECN member according to its home rules. At the time when the draft Reg 1/2003 was still being discussed, van der Woude proposed a number of principles that should be cumulatively respected by exchanges and indicated several procedural mechanism for their enforcement. These principles would include: (i) the right to the highest standard of confidentiality; (ii) the right to the most favourable conditions, and (iii) the right to a complete transfer. While these principles may not result from Reg 1/2003, national law could help to implement them.

[49] Case T-353/94 *Postbank v EC Commission* [1996] ECR II-921 para 90.

[50] However, for national courts there may be a duty under Art 10 EC prevent misuse of documents obtained in competition cases. When the Commission has advised to undertakings that they are not free to use information for any other purpose than the Commission's proceedings, the national court may be required to enjoin them from using this information in any other way and if appropriate order compensation for the owners of the documents. See also J Temple Lang, 'Developments, Issues and New remedies—The Duties of National Authorities and Courts under Art 10 of the EC Treaty' [2004] Fordham International Law Journal 1904–39 (1922).

[51] Case C-234/89 *Stergios Delimitis v Henninger Bräu AG* [1991] ECR I-935 para 53.

the Commission, faced with a request from an undertaking for authority to produce to those courts documents containing confidential information and business secrets, to take all necessary precautions to ensure that the entitlement of the undertakings concerned to protection of that information is not undermined by or during the transmission of the documents to the national courts. Such precautions may include, in particular, informing the latter of the documents or passages of documents which contain confidential information or business secrets. It is nevertheless for the national court to guarantee, on the basis of national rules of procedure, that such undertakings' defence rights are protected.[52]

C. Protection of Information

Requests for confidentiality are quite common in practice. Article 16 of Regulation 773/2004 provides for a procedure for the identification and protection of confidential information.[53] Article 16(1) of Regulation 773/04 sets out the principle that the Commission is obliged not to communicate or make accessible information, in so far as it contains business secrets or other confidential information. Therefore, any person which makes known its views, including but not limited to the participation of complainants—pursuant to Article 6(1)— rejection of complaints—Article 7(1)—reply to statement of objections— Article 10(2)—and Hearing of other parties—Article 13(1) and (3),[54] Hearing of other parties—or subsequently submits further information to the Commission in the course of the same procedure, must clearly identify any material which it considers to be confidential, giving reasons, and provide a separate non-confidential version by the date set by the Commission for making its views known. **9.30**

Where the Commission may require undertakings and associations of undertakings which produce documents or statements pursuant to Regulation 1/2003 to identify the documents or parts of documents which they consider to contain business secrets or other confidential information, it may set a time-limit within which the undertakings and associations of undertakings are to: **9.31**

(a) substantiate their claim for confidentiality with regard to each individual document or part of document, statement or part of statement;

---

[52] Case T-353/94 *Postbank v Commission* [1996] ECR II-921 para 90.

[53] See also Draft Commission Notice on the rules for access to the Commision file in cases pursuant to Arts 81 and 82 of the EC Treaty, Arts 53, 54, and 57 of the EEA Agreement, and Council Reg 139/2004 para 20.

[54] There may other parties or circumstances in which the Commission receives confidential information. CS Kerse and N Khan, *EC Antitrust Procedure* (5th edn, 2005) para 2–073.

(b) provide the Commission with a non-confidential version of the documents or statements, in which the confidential passages are deleted;

(c) provide a concise description of each piece of deleted information.

9.32 Similarly, the Commission may likewise require undertakings or associations of undertakings within a time limit to identify any part of a statement of objections, a case summary drawn up pursuant to Article 27(4) of Regulation 1/2003 or a decision adopted by the Commission which in their view contains business secrets. Pursuant to Article 16(4) in connection with Article 16(2) and (3) of Regulation 773/2004, if a party fails to comply with these requirements, for example where a party does not respond within the specified time limit, the Commission may assume that the documents do not contain confidential information.

9.33 Where the Commission does not agree with the confidentiality claim from the outset or where it takes the view that the provisional acceptance of the confidentiality claim should be reversed, and thus intends to disclose information, it will grant the person or undertaking in question an opportunity to express its views. In such cases, DG COMP will inform the person or undertaking in writing of its intention to disclose information, give its reasons and set a time limit within which such undertaking may inform it in writing of its views.[55] If, following submission of those views, a disagreement on the confidentiality claim persists, the matter will be dealt with by the Hearing Officer according to the applicable Commission terms of reference of Hearing Officers. Under Article 9(2) of the Hearing Officer Mandate,[56] where the undertaking concerned objects to the disclosure of the information but it is found that the information is not protected and may therefore be disclosed, that finding must be stated in a reasoned decision which must be notified to the undertaking concerned.[57] The

---

[55] Note that an applicant cannot (yet) taken action against letters of the Commission informing the applicant first that the Commission does not share the applicant's point of view that the information in question would be protected by business secrecy and secondly, that the Commission is ready to communicate to the complainants more information than the applicant wishes. In this context, the Commission grants the applicant a time period in which he or she can submit its comments to the Hearing Officer. Case T-90/96 *Automobiles Peugeot SA v EC Commission* [1997] ECR II-663 paras 34–36; Case T-213/01 R *Österreichische Postsparkasse AG v EC Commission* [2001] ECR I-3963 para 46.

[56] Commission Decision 2001/462/EC on the terms of reference of hearing officers in certain competition proceedings [2001] OJ L162/21. See also Commission Notice of 13 December 2005 on the rules for access to the Commission file pursuant to Arts 81 and 82 EC Treaty, available at DG COMP's website para 41. As regards the new Notice on Access to the File see 'Infringement Procedures' paras 10.28 *et seq.*

[57] See a similar provision in the Draft Commission Regulation relating to proceedings by the Commission pursuant to Art 81 and 82 of the EC Treaty [2000] OJ C 243/3 which provided in Art 17 that where the Commission intends to disclose information provided by an undertaking or by an association of undertakings, which the undertaking and/or association of undertakings

decision must specify the date after which the information will be disclosed, which cannot be less than one week from the date of notification. The basic features of this procedure were essentially established in *Akzo*.[58] The decision on disclosure may be attacked 'before the Court of First Instance within a period of two months after its notification, in accordance with Article 230 of the EC Treaty. Since the application in such proceedings may have suspensory effect, if the CFI so decides, pursuant to the last sentence of Article 242 of the Treaty, undertakings will be able to avoid disclosure if they make a request to that effect to the CFI and the latter grants it. The CFI thus has an opportunity to examine the merits of the Commission's intention to disclose the document or information at issue to third parties. It is empowered to disallow such disclosure, having regard to the fact that complainants are not entitled in any circumstances to receive documents which contain business secrets. It should be noted that these formal decisions on the disclosure of business secrets, which are taken by the Hearing Officer on the Commission's behalf, have been challenged before the Court in only a very small number of cases.[59]

---

considers to be confidential, it shall inform them in writing of its intention and of its reasons. If the undertaking and/or association of undertakings continues to object to the disclosure, the Commission shall adopt a decision on the disclosure of the given piece of information which should be notified to the undertaking concerned. Reg 773/2004 does not contain this provision. See also CS Kerse and N Khan, *EC Antitrust Procedure* (5th edn, 2005) para 2–073.

[58] Case 53/85 *Akzo v EC Commission II* [1986] ECR 1965; see also Case T-219/01 *Commerzbank AG v EC Commission* [2003] ECR II-2843 paras 69 and 70.

[59] In this context, the CFI addressed in its order in Case T-198/03 *Bank Austria Creditanstalt v EC Commission* [2003] ECR II-4879, an ambiguity in Art 9(3) of the Mandate of the Hearing Officer, questioning whether the Hearing Officer has to decide also whether or not parts of a Commission decision, being not part of the decision's 'main content', should be published under Art 21 of Reg 17 (now Art 30 of Reg 1/2003).

10

INFRINGEMENT PROCEDURES

I. Introduction

A. Formal Initiation and Conclusion of the Procedure: Infringement Decisions

Where, after examination of the case and having regard—where appropriate— **10.01**
to the information obtained during the preliminary investigation on the basis of
requests for information and inspections, the Commission considers that there
is clear evidence of a breach of competition rules, it initiates the procedure for
the formal adoption of a decision on the substance of the case. So far, reference
has been made to processing of the case and to 'procedure' in the broad sense.
Any procedural step or measure taken by the Commission with a view to
applying Articles 81 and 82 EC in a particular case—from the opening of the
file until the adoption of a formal decision—falls into that category. The 'procedure' in the strict sense usually commences after a preliminary investigation of
the case, but not later than the date (i) on which the Commission issues a
preliminary assessment, as referred to in Article 9(1) of Regulation 1/2003
regarding commitments offered by the undertakings before a formal decision is
taken; or (ii) when the Commission issues a statement of objections; or (iii)
when it issues a notice pursuant to Article 27(4) of Regulation 1/2003 summarizing the case and the main content of the commitments or the proposed course
of action, whichever date is the earlier.[1]

The formal initiation of the procedure for the adoption of a decision itself takes **10.02**
the form of a *sui generis* Commission decision. It is a purely internal administrative decision which, as a general rule, is adopted immediately before a statement

---

[1] Art 2(1) of Reg 773/2004 which refers to the catalogue of formal decisions adopted by the
Commission under Chapter III of Reg 1/2003 (Art 7 – finding and termination of infringement,
Art 8 – interim measures, Art 9 – commitment decisions, and Art 10 – finding of inapplicability).
The notice mentioned in Art 27(4) of Reg 1/003 refers to Arts 9 and 10 of Reg 1/2003.

of objections is served in infringement procedures. Decisions to initiate the procedure cannot be challenged under Article 230 EC. The Community Courts have defined them as 'procedural measures adopted preparatory to the decision which represents their culmination'.[2] As the Commission may decide to initiate proceedings at any point in time, it may well decide to do so prior to the statement of objections, quite independently.[3] In such case, the Commission is not required immediately to inform undertakings suspected of being implicated in the infringement. The main effect of formal initiation of proceedings is that the Commission becomes the sole *administrative* authority competent to apply Articles 81 and 82 EC to the matter in question thereby relieving NCAs of their jurisdiction to apply Articles 81 and 82 EC.[4]

10.03 Undertakings are usually informed of the initiation of proceedings when they receive the statement of objections or the notice pursuant to Article 27(4) of Regulation 1/2003 summarizing the case and the main content of the commitments or the proposed course of action. Where the procedure is initiated before that stage (as for instance, in case of a preliminary assessment pursuant to Article 9(1) of Regulation 1/2003), the undertakings are informed by letter. In any event, they should be informed before the Commission makes public the initiation of proceedings.[5] Complainants and other natural or legal persons with a 'sufficient interest' may also be informed by the Commission of the initiation of the proceedings.[6] Regulation 773/2004 seems to draw a distinction between 'complainants' and 'other third parties': complainants having demonstrated a legitimate interest in bringing complaints are presumed to have a 'sufficient

---

[2] See Case 60/81 *IBM v EC Commission* [1981] ECR 2639 para 21. Case T-241/97 *Stork Amsterdam v EC Commission* [2000] ECR II-309 para 49. The initiation of proceedings remains a preparatory step and is made 'with a view to adopting' a definitive or final measure under Arts 7 to 10 of Reg 1/2003. D Geradin and N Petit, 'Judicial remedies under EC Competition Law: Complex Issues Arising from the Modernization Process', *32rd Annual International Antitrust Law & Policy Conference Fordham Corporate Law Institute*, 22–23 September 2005, (forthcoming) take the view that the initiation of proceedings under Art 11(6) of Reg 1/2003 may nevertheless be challengeable. See also on this discussion on whether (re-) allocation decisions within the ECN are challengeable ch 3 'Role of the national competition authorities' paras 3.14 *et seq.*

[3] The Commission may in its discretion choose the time for formal initiation of the procedure, which usually follows—but may precede specific investigative measures. See Case 107/82 *AEG v EC Commission* [1983] ECR 3151 paras 19–20.

[4] Art 11(6) of Reg 1/2003. This relates to the application of competition law by NCAs, in administrative proceedings, in order to bring to an end conduct contrary to Arts 81 and 82 EC. It does not concern the application of competition provisions by national courts or judges in civil proceedings with a view, *inter alia*, to the annulment of agreements or the award of damages. National courts may continue to apply the EC competition law in that way, even after exclusive competence has become vested in the Commission.

[5] Art 2(2) of Reg 773/2004. It appears that where the Commission initiates the procedure with a view to adopting a declaration of inapplicability, a prior notification of this to the parties will also be made.

[6] Arts 5, 7, and 11 of Reg 773/2004.

interest' whereas other third parties must demonstrate this interest if they wish to be informed of the nature and subject-matter of the procedure. The Member States are also informed of the initiation of a procedure immediately after it has been decided upon, so as to make it clear to them that the Commission now has jurisdiction under Article 11(6) of Regulation 1/2003. The letter by which the Member States are informed[7] stipulates that the Commission has decided to initiate a procedure and that it intends adopting a decision of the kind provided for in Articles 7, 8, 9, or 10 of Regulation 1/2003.

B. Procedural Guarantees

The initiation of an infringement procedure by the Commission implies the **10.04** need to put into place and observe a set of procedural guarantees aiming at protecting the parties' defence rights. Notwithstanding the Commission's lack of a judicial role, the conduct of its administrative infringement procedures must respect certain guarantees that constitute general principles of Community law.[8] As the Community Courts have repeatedly made it clear, fundamental rights—defence rights included—form part of the Community legal order and are to be respected by the European Union institutions according to Member States' common constitutional traditions and the European Convention of Human Rights.[9] These rights must be respected despite the absence of an express provision recognizing them in the procedural rules or where the existing provisions do not in themselves take account of them.[10]

Regulation 1/2003 specifically states that it respects fundamental rights **10.05** and follows the principles enshrined in the EU Charter of Fundamental

---

[7] In accordance with Case 48/72 *Brasseries de Haecht v Wilkin-Janssen* [1973] ECR 77 para 16: '[. . .] the initiation of a procedure [. . .] obviously concerns an authoritative act of the Commission, evidencing its intention to take a decision [. . .]'.

[8] e.g. recently, T-9/99 *HFB Holding für Fernwärmetechnik Beteiligungsgesellschaft mbH & Co. KG (HFB) and others v EC Commission* [2002] ECR II-1487 para 391 (on appeal mostly confirmed in Joined Cases C-189/02 P, C-202/02 P, C-205/02 P to C-208/02 P and C-213/02 P *Dansk Rørindustri and others v EC Commission* [2005] OJ C205/1). See also C Kerse and N Khan, *EC Antitrust Procedure* (5th edn, 2005) para 4–001.

[9] See, e.g. Case T-112/98 *Mannesmannröhren-Werke v EC Commission* [2001] ECR II-729 para 60. Joined Cases T-67/00, T-68/00, T-71/00 and T-78/00 *JFE Engineering Corp and others v EC Commission* [2004] OJ C239/1 para 178. According to the case law, fundamental rights are protected in the Community legal order as reaffirmed in the preamble to the Single European Act, by Art 6(2) of the EU Treaty and by Art 47 of the Charter of Fundamental Rights of the European Union proclaimed on 7 December 2000 in Nice [2000] OJ 2000 C364/1.

[10] See Case C-32/95 P *EC Commission v Lisrestal* [1996] ECR I-5373 para 21; Case C-135/92 *Fiskano v EC Commission* [1994] ECR I-2885 para 39.

Rights.[11] Furthermore, both Regulation 1/2003 (Article 27) and Regulation 773/2004 (Article 11) provide that the Commission must respect undertakings' defence rights by requiring it to base its decisions on objections and arguments on which the parties concerned have been able to comment. Neither Regulation limits defence rights but rather explains what these are in relation to the Commission's procedure. The Community Courts have recognized that the rights of the defence include, among others, the right to be heard, the right of access to the file, the right against self-incrimination, the right to be assisted by a lawyer, the legal professional privilege, and the principle of good administration.[12] The right to be heard—right to a fair hearing—during the Commission proceedings comprises:

- the right to obtain a precise and complete statement of objections against the party concerned;
- the opportunity for the party to submit its observations on the documents and information on which the Commission bases its objections and arguments to reach a decision. Observance of the defence rights requires that once the administrative procedure has started the undertaking concerned be afforded the opportunity to put forward its view as to the truth and relevance of the facts and circumstances alleged and objections raised by the Commission.[13] In particular, the statement of objections must supply the undertaking with all the information necessary to enable it properly to defend itself before the Commission adopts a final decision.[14] Article 27 of Regulation 1/2003 draws a distinction between parties who must be given the opportunity to be heard and those who may be given such an opportunity if the Commission

---

[11] Recital 37 of Reg 1/2003. The Charter of Fundamental Rights adopted in 2000 in Nice and now included in Part II of the Treaty establishing a Constitution for Europe [2004] OJ C310/1 which has codified these rights in Art II-101. For more details see ch 4 'Organization of EC Commission proceedings' paras 4.36 *et seq.*

[12] See, e.g. President of the CFI Judge Bo Vesterdorf, 'Judicial Review and Competition Law—Reflections on the Role of the Community Courts in the EC system of Competition Law Enforcement', Speech at the International Forum on EC Competition Law, Brussels 8 April 2005 noting that important due process rights include the requirement for the Commisison to address its objections in writing, the right of the parties to respond in writing or orally to those objections and to have access to the Commission's file, see also published and edited paper version in Competition Policy International [2005] Vol 1, Number 2, page 7. See also S Durande and K Williams, 'The practical impact of the exercise of the right to be heard: A special focus on the effect of Oral Hearings and the role of the Hearing Officers' EC Competition Newsletter, Number 2, Summer 2005, 22–28 (22). See ch 1 'The institutional framework' paras 1.20 *et seq.*

[13] T-228/97 *Irish Sugar v EC Commission* [1999] ECR II-2969 para 35.

[14] Case 45/69 *Boehringer Mannheim v EC Commission* [1970] ECR 769 para 9; Case 52/69 *Geigy v EC Commission* [1972] ECR 787 para 11; Case 27/76 *United Brands v EC Commission* [1978] ECR 207 paras 274 and 277; Joined Cases C-89/85, C-104/85, C-114/85, C-116/85, C-117/85 and C-125/85 to C-129/85 *Ahlström Osakeyhtiö and others v EC Commission* ('Woodpulp II') [1993] ECR I-1307 para 42.

considers it necessary or NCAs so request. Such other persons must be heard where they show a sufficient interest;

- the right to be allowed the same case knowledge used by the Commission in the proceedings, what implies access to the Commission's file on the same terms as the latter. This is also referred to as the principle of equality of arms, which means that, when adopting a decision, it is impossible for the Commission to take into account information not disclosed to the undertaking concerned on the grounds that it is covered by the principle of confidentiality. In *Hercules*, the CFI defined the limits of access to the file stating that 'the Commission has an obligation to make available to the companies involved in Article 85(1) [now Article 81(1) EC] proceedings all documents, whether in their favour or otherwise, which it has obtained during the course of the investigation, save where the business secrets of other undertakings, the internal documents of the Commission or other confidential information are involved'.[15] It appears from this judgment that 'access to the file' is an integral part of the right to be heard and not a right in itself because it would be intended to enable the addressees to acquaint themselves with the evidence in the Commission's file so that on the basis of their evidence they can express their views effectively on the conclusions reached by the Commission.[16] The right of access to the file is now set out in Article 27(2) of Regulation 1/2003 and expanded upon in Regulation 773/2004. It is worth noting that the Community Courts have ruled that the breach of an undertaking's defence rights as regards access to the Commission's administrative file does not warrant annulment of a decision finding that there has been an infringement unless the ability of that undertaking to defend itself has been affected by the conditions in which it had access to the Commission's administrative file. However, in that respect, it would be sufficient for a finding of infringement of defence rights for it to be established that non-disclosure of the documents in question might have influenced the course of the procedure and the content of the decision to the applicant's detriment.[17]

---

[15] e.g. Case T-7/89 *SA Hercules Chemicals NV v EC Commission* [1991] ECR II-1711 para 54.

[16] e.g. Case T-7/89 *SA Hercules Chemicals NV v EC Commission* [1991] ECR II-1711 paras 51–53; Joined Cases T-10/92 to T-12/92, T-14/92 and T-15/92 *Cimentieries CBR SA v EC Commisison* [1992] ECR II-2667 para 38.

[17] e.g. Joined Cases T-25/95, T-26/95, T-30/95 to T-39/95, T-42/95 to T-46/95, T-48/95, T-50/95 to T-65/95, T-68/95 to T-71/95, T-87/95, T-88/95, T-103/95 and T-104/95 *Cimenteries CBR SA and others v EC Commission* [2000] ECR II-491 paras 240–241 stating that there will be an infringement of the defence rights if there was even a small chance that the outcome of the administrative procedure might have been different if the applicant could have relied on the document during that procedure (with references to Case T-30/91 *Solvay v EC Commission* [1995] ECR II-1775 and Case T-36/91 *ICI v EC Commission* [1995] ECR II-1775).

10.06 As regards the principle of good administration,[18] this refers firstly to the obligation of public authorities to ensure that third parties do not have access to the information collected by public authorities, such obligation not being absolute in all circumstances. Secondly, it requires the Commission to adopt decisions in administrative proceedings within a reasonable time and to exercise its authority with ordinary care and diligence by carefully and impartially examining all the relevant aspects of the cases at hand. Finally, it implies that the parties to the administrative proceedings are given the opportunity to make their views known and to obtain from the Commission an adequately reasoned decision.

C. The Role of the Hearing Officer[19]

10.07 In order to make the oral observations phase more objective and impartial, the Commission decided in 1982 to create the post of Hearing Officer,[20] under whose chairmanship hearings are held.[21] The Hearing Officer was originally a senior Community official in the Directorate General for Competition (DG COMP), who had been granted certain autonomous powers in order to guarantee his independence of action.[22] The Hearing Officer not only conducts the

---

[18] See ch 1 'The institutional framework' para 1.32.

[19] See also J Gilchrist, 'Rights of defence and the role of the Hearing Officer in EU merger cases' [2000–2001] Global Competition Review 19–24; House of Lords, Select Committee on the European Union, 'Strengthening the Role of the Hearing Officer in EC Competition Cases, Report with Evidence'. House of Lords, Session 1999–2000, 19th Report (Stationery Office, London, November 2000); M van der Woude, 'Hearing Officers and EC Antitrust Procedures; the Art of Making Subjective Procedures more Objective' (1996) CML Rev and T Giannakopoulos, 'The Right to be Orally Heard by the Commission in Antitrust, Merger, Anti-dumping/Anti-subsidies and State Aid Community Procedures' [2001] World Competition 541–69. See also, Commission Press Release IP/01/736 of 23 May 2001, 'European Commission strengthens the role of the Hearing Officer in competition proceedings'. S Durande and K Williams, 'The practical impact of the exercise of the right to be heard: A special focus on the effect of Oral Hearings and the role of the Hearing Officers' EC Competition Newsletter, Number 2, Summer 2005, 22–28.

[20] See XII Report on Competition Policy [1982] para 36.

[21] The Hearing Officer's terms of reference are set out principally in Arts 2 to 12 of Decision 2001/462/EC of 23 May 2001 on the terms of reference of hearing officers in certain competition proceedings ('Mandate') [2001] OJ L162/21. This Decision repeals Decision 94/810/ECSC/EC of 12 December 1994 on the terms of reference of hearing officers in competition procedures before the Commission [1994] OJ L330/67 which, in turn, adapted and consolidated the original 1982 mandate in light of subsequent developments in Community law.

[22] Art 1(3) of the repealed Decision 94/810/ECSC/EC of 12 December 1994 provided that administratively the Hearing Officer belonged to the Directorate-General for Competition. To ensure the independence of the Hearing Officer in the performance of his duties, he had the right of direct access to the Member of the Commission with special responsibility for competition. Under the former regime, if the Hearing Officer was unable to act, the Director-General after consultation with the Hearing Officer (if appropriate) had to designate another senior

discussions but also makes all the arrangements for the hearings (e.g. he serves the summonses to attend) and supervises the subsequent stages (e.g. transcription of the statements made and dispatch of them to the participants, under Article 14 of Regulation 773/2004). The role of the Hearing Officer is not that of a judge.[23] He or she has the task of ensuring the proper and effective exercise of the right to be heard in competition proceedings under Articles 81 and 82 EC and the Merger Control Regulation 139/2004. His function is to chair the hearings fairly, maintaining good order, allowing the parties to exercise their right to make observations in the most appropriate manner, and at the same time making certain that the Commission takes due note of what is said and prepares an accurate record of the proceedings.[24] However, the Hearing Officer does not merely ensure the proper conduct of the hearings[25] without dealing at all with matters of fact or arguments put forward during them.[26] While the Commission is not bound to follow the arguments of the Hearing Officer(s) when it comes to the substance of the case, their opinion is likely to be carefully taken into consideration, particularly in the framework of the ongoing

---

official not involved in the case to carry out the same duties. See Art 1(4) of the repealed Decision. Art 2(2) of the Mandate [2001] OJ 2001 L162/21 provides that 'the hearing officer shall be attached, for administrative purposes, to the member of the Commission with special responsibility for competition'. If the Hearing Officer is unable to act, the competent member of the Commission, where appropriate after consultation with the hearing officer, shall designate another official, who is not involved in the case in question, to carry out the hearing officer's duties (See Art 2(3) of the Mandate).

[23] S Durande and K Williams, 'The practical impact of the exercise of the right to be heard: A special focus on the effect of Oral Hearings and the role of the Hearing Officers' EC Competition Newsletter, Number 2, Summer 2005, 22–28 (26) note that while the Hearing Officers have decisive power in some merely purely procedural matters, they cannot impose any new view on the Commission as to the other procedural guarantees of the defendants or as to the substance of a case. Note that at the time of the writing Serge Durand and Karen Williams are the two Hearing Officers that are attached to the Cabinet of the Commissioner.

[24] Arts 5 and 12 of the Mandate [2001] OJ L162/21. In particular, Art 12 gives the Hearing Officer basically free reign to decide when, where, for how long and in what manner any hearing will be conducted. The Hearing Officer has been described as a 'guardian of basic procedural rights'. CS Kerse and N Khan, *EC Antitrust Procedure* (5th edn, 2005) para 4–014.

[25] As part of this task to make the hearings run as smoothly as possible, the Hearing Officer may supply in advance to participating undertakings, a list of questions to be answered at the hearing, or hold a pre-hearing meeting between the parties and Commission staff to prepare for the main hearing itself. The Hearing Officer may also ask for a form of written 'witness statement' covering what the participant intends to say at the hearing. See Art 11 of the Mandate [2001] OJ 2001 L162/21.

[26] On the contrary, according to Art 3(3) of the Mandate [2001] OJ L162/21, the Hearing Officer may present observations on any matter arising out of any Commission competition proceedings to the competent member of the Commission. This provision may be clearly interpreted as allowing the Hearing Officer to give its opinion on the substance of the case. It must be pointed out that, in fact, such a provision merely constitutes the express recognition of a power that the Hearing Officer already held in practice even before the new Decision was adopted by the Commission. See earlier edn of CS Kerse and N Khan, *EC Antitrust Procedure* (3rd edn, 1994) para 4.26 163. See also Report on Competition Policy [2004], SEC (2005) 805 final, 12.

reinforcement of the Commission's checks and balances through the appoint-ment of a Chief Economist and the introduction of scrutiny panels.[27] The Commission hoped that entrusting the organization and conduct of the administrative procedures, designed to protect the right to be heard, to an independent person experienced in competition matters would further the objectivity, transparency, and efficiency of the Commission's competition pro-ceedings.[28] In this spirit, Article 2 of the Mandate foresees that Commission decisions on the appointment, termination of appointment, or transfer of Hearing Officers will be published in the Official Journal.

10.08 The Hearing Officer also draws up a general report on the conclusions drawn from the hearing and on the conduct of the procedure in the case.[29] This interim—or first—report is subsequently complemented with a final report prepared by the Hearing Officer on the basis of the draft decision to be submit-ted to the Advisory Committee in the case in question.[30] Under the former terms of reference, none of these reports were disclosed to the parties.[31] The Hearing Officer had then only the power[32] of proposing the Commissioner for Competition Policy to forward the final report to the full meeting of the Commission together with the draft decision that the Competition Commissioner submits for approval by the remainder of the members.[33] The

---

[27] S Durande and K Williams, 'The practical impact of the exercise of the right to be heard: A special focus on the effect of Oral Hearings and the role of the Hearing Officers' EC Competition Newsletter, Number 2, Summer 2005, 22–28 (27–28) who admit that arguments related to other than procedural questions may or may not be endorsed, but they would be accorded the attention that deserves the opinion of a fresh pair of eyes with special responsibility over the defendants' rights of defence and direct knowledge of the case.

[28] See Art 5 and Recital 3 to the preamble of the Mandate [2001] OJ L162/21. Report on Competition Policy [2004] SEC (2005) 805 final, 10.

[29] Art 13 of the Mandate ([2001] OJ 2001 L162/21). Under this Art, the Hearing Officer may also make observations on the further progress of the proceedings, including, for example, the need for further information, the withdrawal of certain objections or the formulation of further objections. As referred to above, these observations and observations on any other matter may, under Art 3(3), be referred directly to the Competition Commissioner by the Hearing Officer.

[30] Art 15 of the Mandate [2001] OJ L162/21. This report will consider whether the draft decision deals only with objections in respect of which the parties have been afforded the opportunity to make known their views.

[31] Although recommendations had been made that the report be published and sent to all the participants in the procedure. See House of Lords, Select Committee on the European Com-munities, 'Enforcement of Community Competition Rules', Report with Evidence. House of Lords, Session 1993–94, 1st Report (HMSO London, 1993). See also and in particular, House of Lords, Select Committee on the European Union, 'Strengthening the Role of the Hearing Officer in EC Competition Cases', Report with Evidence. House of Lords, Session 1999–2000, 19th Report (2000).

[32] Art 10 of the old Mandate [1994] OJ L330/67.

[33] According to the case law prior to the new terms of reference, the Hearing Officer's report has the status of an opinion and the Commission is not required to follow it. In those circum-stances, the report does not constitute a decisive factor which the Community judicature has to

new Mandate has reformed this situation. In order to improve transparency in the competition decision-making process, the Hearing Officer's final report on the respect of procedural rights of the parties is now:

• submitted to the Competition Commissioner, the Director-General for Competition and the director responsible;
• communicated to the Member States;
• attached systematically to the draft Commission decision submitted to the College; and
• disclosed to the parties and published in the Official Journal together with the final decision.[34]

The functions of the Hearing Officer have been progressively widened since 1982 by the attribution of the power to adopt decisions concerning the rights of the defence.[35] The College of Commissioners has delegated the power of decision for matters of this kind to the Commissioner responsible for competition, who in turn has delegated it to the Hearing Officer.[36] In fact, the new Mandate strengthens this relationship: the Hearing Officer will no longer belong to the DG COMP but will be directly attached to the office of the Commissioner in charge of competition policy to further reinforce his or her independence. The Hearing Officer's role in Commission procedures is now therefore significantly more relevant. In particular, the tasks of the Hearing Officer include the following: **10.09**

• deciding, after consultation with the Director responsible for investigating the case, on applications from third parties to participate in procedures

---

take into account in performing its judicial review (Case T-13/89 *ICI v EC Commission* [1992] ECR II-1021 para 40). Even if the new Decision establishes now the obligation to publish the final report of the Hearing Officer, the latter precedents may still be considered applicable, although the importance of the final report has undoubtedly been enhanced.

[34] Arts 15 and 16(1) of the Mandate [2001] OJ L162/21 stipulate the obligation to attach the Hearing Officer's final report to the draft decision submitted to the Commission, in order to ensure that, when it reaches a decision on an individual case, the Commission is fully apprised of all relevant information as regards the course of the procedure and respect of the right to be heard. The two Hearing Officers take the view that it would be difficult to see how the Commission could attach to one of its decisions a negative final report of a Hearing Officer stating that the procedure followed was not correct and has led to the violation of the right to be heard. Such procedural shortcomings have to be corrected in the course of the investigation before the final report is attached to the draft decision of the College. S Durande and K Williams, 'The practical impact of the exercise of the right to be heard: A special focus on the effect of Oral Hearings and the role of the Hearing Officers' EC Competition Newsletter, Number 2, Summer 2005, 22–28 (26).

[35] Art 2(2) of the repealed Decision 94/810/ECSC/EC of 12 December 1994 required the Hearing Officer in performing his or her duties to see to it that the rights of the defence are respected. Article 1 of the new Mandate refers more specifically to the 'right to be heard' instead of the 'rights of the defence'.

[36] See XXIII Annual Report on Competition Policy [1993] para 204.

concerning other persons, undertakings or associations of undertakings. The third party must submit an application to be heard in writing, together with a written statement explaining his or her interest in the outcome of the procedure. If the Hearing Officer finds that no sufficient interest exists, he or she gives written reasons for this decision and lays down a time-limit within which any further written comments may be submitted;[37]

- deciding, after consultation with the Director responsible for investigating the case, whether persons are to be heard orally. Applications for an oral hearing must be made in the written reply of the undertaking or person concerned to a letter from the Commission which either: (a) contains a statement of objections; (b) invites the written comments of a third party who has shown sufficient interest to be heard; or (c) informs a complainant that there are insufficient grounds for finding an infringement of the EC Treaty and inviting further written submissions.[38]

- deciding on applications for extensions of time from undertakings that consider that the time-limit given to them for responding to the statement of objections or any of the other letters mentioned in Article 7(2) is insufficient. The Hearing Officer informs the applicant in writing whether such a request for an extension has been granted;[39]

- deciding, in response to a reasoned application, whether the undertakings are entitled to have access to additional documents which the undertaking has reason to believe that the Commission has in its possession and that are necessary for the proper exercise of the right to be heard and which, although in the file, were not disclosed to them with the statement of objections or other letter identified in Article 7(2). The Hearing Officer's reasoned response to such a request may also be sent to any party concerned by the procedure;[40]

- finally—and this is of the utmost importance—the Hearing Officer will have to decide on what information in the file obtained from undertakings may be disclosed to other undertakings upon their request or be published, for which

---

[37] Art 6(3) of the Mandate [2001] OJ L162/21.

[38] Arts 6(1) and 7 of the Mandate [2001] OJ L162/21. Interestingly, the list in Art 7(2) (a)–(c) of the Mandate dealing with applications to be heard orally no longer includes the written reply to the Art 6(3) letter informing a person that in the Commission's view that person has not shown sufficient interest to be heard as a third party (former Art 4(3)(d)). The reason for its removal may be that a person must have shown a sufficient interest under Art 6 before he or she can apply to be heard orally. The reply to the Art 6(3) letter must demonstrate that this interest exists, which is the requirement for being afforded the possibility of being heard either orally or in writing.

[39] Art 10 of the Mandate [2001] OJ L162/21.

[40] Art 8(1) and (2) of the Mandate [2001] OJ L162/21.

purpose he will follow a procedure equivalent to that described by the Court in its judgment in *Akzo I*.[41]

In the interim report, or more generally when he or she reports to the Commissioner, with special reference to the content of the hearing, the Hearing Officer may make use of his or her ability to alert the Commissioner on a substantive issue raised by the case where they consider this would enhance the quality of the final decision. The Hearing Officer may make observations in cases, to help improve the decision-making process and ultimately the quality of the final decisions. The Hearing Officer also acts as an advisor to the Commissioner for competition policy discussing policy issues with DG COMP, among other things, the reform of the Notice on access to the file or certain aspects of the Commission's leniency programme.[42]   **10.10**

II. Infringement procedure: Observations and the formal adoption of decisions

The general principle of observance of the rights of the defence, which the Court has held to be a fundamental principle of the Community legal order,[43] requires the Commission and all Community institutions in all circumstances,   **10.11**

---

[41] See Art 9 of the Mandate. Such a procedure—'*Akzo Procedure*'—was set out by the Court in Case 53/85 *Akzo Chemie v EC Commission* [1986] ECR 1965 para 29. Firstly, the undertaking must be given an opportunity to state its views. Then, the Commission is required to adopt a decision in that connection containing an adequate statement of the reasons on which it is based and which must be notified to the undertaking concerned. Taking into account the serious damage which could result from improper communication of documents to a competitor, the Commission must, before implementing its decision, give the undertaking an opportunity to bring an action before the Court with a view to having the assessments made reviewed by it and to preventing disclosure of the documents in question. See ch 9 'Penalties and confidentialities' para 9.32.

[42] Commission Report on Competition Policy [2004], SEC (2005) 805 final, 12. S Durande and K Williams, 'The practical impact of the exercise of the right to be heard: A special focus on the effect of Oral Hearings and the role of the Hearing Officers' EC Competition Newsletter, Number 2, Summer 2005, 22–28 (27) note that the Hearing Officers have an obligation to use their best efforts to ensure that the best possible decision is taken, although their opinions are not compulsory and are not published. They admit that the absence of publicity may be lamented but also indicate that the informal character of these consultations can also enhance their freedom to express internally their views.

[43] See already Case 322/81 *Nederlandsche Banden Industrie NV Michelin v EC Commission* [1983] ECR 3461 para 7; for a discussion of the rights of the defence in Community competition law, see M Araujo, 'The Respect of Fundamental Rights within the European Network of Competition Authorities', ch 21 and K Dekeyser and C Gauer, The New Enforcement System for Arts 81 & 82 and the Rights of Defence, ch 26 in BE Hawk (ed), *International Antitrust Law & Policy*, Annual Proceedings of the Fordham Institute (2004) 549–85 (551).

to allow persons to make observations and be heard before the Community institutions adopt any measures which might adversely affect them despite the fact that proceedings are of an administrative nature.[44] Similarly, they may not irreversibly compromise the future exercise of such rights during the conduct of the administrative procedure.[45] With respect to infringement procedures, Article 27(2) of Regulation 1/2003 expressly provides that the rights of defence of the parties concerned will be fully respected in the proceedings. For such purposes, when the Commission intends to adopt a decision against the interests of undertakings, it will draw up a statement of objections on which the undertakings will be given the opportunity of being heard in writing and orally. Also, the parties will be enabled to obtain information about the most important documents in the file.[46] Those steps together constitute the 'right to be heard' phase in infringement procedures, after which, following the report from the Advisory Committee, the Commission will adopt its decision. In most cases nearly one year will have elapsed between the end of the investigation and the adoption of the final decision.

A. The Statement of Objections

1. Introduction

10.12 The legal basis for the statement of objections is provided by Article 27(1) of Regulation 1/2003 and by Article 10 of Commission Regulation 773/2004. The statement of objections serves to inform undertakings of the Commission's objections against them with a view to enabling them to exercise efficiently their defence.[47] The principle of respect for the rights of the defence requires that an

---

[44] See Cases 100–103/80 *Musique Diffusion Française v EC Commission (Pioneer)* [1983] ECR 1825 para 10; Case 85/76 *Hoffmann-La Roche v EC Commission* [1979] ECR 461 para 9; Joined Cases T-305/94, T-306/94, T-307/94, T-313/94 to T-316/94, T-318/94, T-325/94, T-328/94, T-329/94 and T-335/94 *Limburgse Vinyl Maatschappij and others v EC Commission* [1999] ECR II-931 para 246; T-308/94 *Cascades v EC Commission* [1998] ECR II-925 para 39; Case T-348/94 *Enso Española v EC Commission* [1998] ECR II-1875 para 80. See also Joined Cases T-5/00 and T-6/00 *Nederlandse Federatieve Vereniging voor de Groothandel op Elektrotechnisch Gebied and Technische Unie BV v EC Commission* [2003] ECR II-4121 para 32.

[45] See, e.g. Joined Cases 46/87 and 227/88 *Hoechst v EC Commission III* [1989] ECR 2859 para 15; Joined Cases C-204/00 P, C-205/00 P, C-211/00 P, C-213/00, P, C-217/00 P and C-219/00 P *Aarlborg et al v EC Commission* [2004] ECR II-123 para 63.

[46] In accordance with Art 27(1) of Reg 1/2003 and Arts 10 and 11 of Reg 773/2004. See also, Joined Cases T-236/01, T-239/01, T-244/01 to T-246/01, T-251/01 and T-252/01 *Tokai Carbon Co Ltd and others v EC Commission* [2004] ECR II-1181 para 38.

[47] See Joined Cases 142–156/84 *BAT and Reynolds Industries v Commission* [1987] ECR 4487 para 14 *et seq.*; Case T-19/91 *Vichy v EC Commission* [1992] ECR II-415 para 121; Case T-10/92 *Cement Industries v EC Commission* [1992] ECR II-2667 para 33; Joined Cases T-39/92 and T-40/92 *Europay v EC Commission* [1994] ECR II-49 para 48; Joined Cases C-89/85, C-104/85,

exact and complete statement of the objections which the Commission intends to raise against the addressee of the decision should be sent to that person before the decision is finally adopted.[48] They then have an opportunity to reply to the Commission setting out all the facts known to them which are relevant to their defence against the objections raised: whether the facts are correctly stated, whether the legal reasoning relied on against them by the Commission is well founded, and whether the Commission's conclusions fit the facts and the legal provisions relied on by it.[49] The sending of the statement of objections may also be an occasion for undertakings to modify their agreements and practices and bring them in line with Community competition law. Yet, the statement of objections does not in itself place undertakings under an obligation to modify or reconsider their commercial practices.[50] The provisions applicable to the statement of objections clearly indicate that it is provisional.[51] It carries with it due protection of the rights of the defence in Commission procedures,[52] in that the undertakings are entitled to know the objections made against them, and they have the right to respond to the Commission; in other words, the right to show that the Commission's assessments are incorrect.[53] They also have the right to have their observations taken into account by the Commission—that is to say,

---

C-114/85, C-116/85, C-117/85 and C-125/85 to C-129/85 *Ahlström Osakeyhtiö and others v EC Commission* [1993] ECR I-1307 para 42, and Case T-352/94 *Mo och Domsjö v EC Commission* [1998] ECR II-1989 para 63; J Schwarze and A Weitbrecht, *Grundzüge des europäischen Kartellrechts* (2004) § 5 para 8. K Lenaerts and J Maselis, 'Procedural Rights and Issues in the Enforcement of Articles 81 and 82 of the EC Treaty' [2001] Fordham International Law Journal 1615–54 (1626–29).

[48] Joined Cases T-305/94, T-306/94, T-307/94, T-313/94 to T-316/94, T-318/94, T-325/94, T-328/94, T-329/94 and T-335/94 *Limburgse Vinyl Maatschappij (LVM) and others v EC Commission* [1999] ECR II-931 para 263. Note that in 2004 statements of objections were issues in twenty-eight cases compared to thirty-two in 2003. S Durande and K Williams, 'The practical impact of the exercise of the right to be heard: A special focus on the effect of Oral Hearings and the role of the Hearing Officers' EC Competition Newsletter, Number 2, Summer 2005, 22–28 (23).

[49] The statement of objections must clearly set out the facts on which the Commission relies, and the legal inferences to be drawn from them. See Case C-62/86 *Akzo v EC Commission III* [1991] ECR I-3359 para 29; and Joined Cases T-5/00 and T-6/00 *Nederlandse Federatieve Vereniging voor de Groothandel op Elektrotechnisch Gebied and Technische Unie BV v EC Commission* [2003] ECR II-5761 para 33.

[50] Case 60/81 *IBM v EC Commission* [1981] ECR 2639 para 19.

[51] The statement of objections is not a final decision that is subject to appeal. See Case 60/81 *IBM v EC Commission* [1981] ECR 2639 para 21.

[52] See Case 85/76 *Hoffmann-La Roche v EC Commission* [1979] ECR 461 paras 9 *et seq.*

[53] Case T-213/00 *CMA CGM and others v EC Commission (FETTCSA)* [2003] ECR II-913 para 109: '[. . .] the statement of objections must allow those concerned to have effective knowledge of the conduct in respect of which they are accused by the Commission. That requirement is met when the final decision does not find that the undertakings concerned have committed infringements different from those referred to in the statement of objections and establishes only facts on which the persons concerned have had the opportunity to explain themselves [. . .]'; Case T-352/94 *Mo och Domsjö v EC Commission* [1998] ECR II-1989 para 63; and Case T-348/94 *Enso Española v EC Commission* [1998] ECR II-1875 para 83.

the right to expect that their cases will not be prejudged. Finally they have the right not to have any finding made against them in the final decision otherwise than in respect of the objections on which they have had a chance to give their views.[54] Because it is a procedural and preparatory document, the Commission is not prevented from withdrawing the statement of objections, either in whole or part, or from dropping or amending specific objections.[55] For the same reason, the statement of objections is not a decision or other act which may be challenged before the Court under Article 230 EC.[56]

10.13 The statement of objections—as stated earlier—must be used in procedures in which the Commission intends to adopt a decision adverse to the interests of undertakings. In particular:

- in procedures in which the Commission, acting on a complaint or on its own initiative, finds in its preliminary assessment that there is an infringement of Article 81 or Article 82 of the Treaty, under Article 7(1) of Regulation 1/2003.
- in procedures for the adoption of interim measures based on Article 8 of Regulation 1/2003.[57]
- in procedures for the withdrawal in an individual case of the benefit of a block exemption under Article 29(1) of Regulation 1/2003.[58]
- whenever, for any reason, the Commission intends imposing fines or periodic penalty payments under Articles 23 and 24(2) of Regulation 1/2003.

10.14 Article 27(1) of Regulation 1/2003 provides that the Commission must base its decisions only on objections on which the parties concerned have been able to comment, otherwise the decision will be void.[59] For that reason, the Commission must set out in the statement of objections exhaustively—but not

---

[54] See Joined Cases C-238/99 P, C-244/99 P, C-245/99 P, C-247/99 P, C-250/99 P to C-252/99 P and C-254/99 P *Limburgse Vinyl Maatschappij (LVM) and others v EC Commission* [2002] ECR I-8375 para 103. See also, Joined Cases T-236/01, etc *Tokai Carbon Co Ltd and others v EC Commission* [2004] ECR II-1181 para 47.

[55] Final Report of the Hearing Officer in *GVG/FS* [2004] OJ C12/2 and in *Brasseries Kronenbourg Brasseries Heineken* [2005] OJ C175/4.

[56] Case 60/81 *IBM v EC Commission* [1981] ECR 2639 para 21. Case T-10/92 *Cimenteries CBR v EC Commission* [1992] ECR II-2667 para 47.

[57] See ch 14 'Special procedures' paras 14.01 *et seq.*

[58] ibid.

[59] See the Joined Cases C-89/85, C-104/85, C-114/85, C-116/85, C-117/85 and C-125/85 to C-129/85 *Ahlström Osakeyhtiö and others v EC Commission* [1993] ECR I-1307 paras 40–54 and 148–154 in which the Court partially annulled the decision which the Commission had adopted on the merits. The portion annulled concerned certain conduct objected to and the participation of certain undertakings therein, about which the objections were not sufficiently clear or were silent. As a result, the undertakings were not able to defend themselves properly in the administrative procedure. See also Case T-213/00 *CMA CGM and others v EC Commission* [2003] ECR II-913 para 109.

necessarily at great length[60] each and every instance of conduct and each and every legal argument on which it proposes to rely for its decision. That is why it is only at the end of the investigation—which may last several months or several years—that the Commission decides to take this measure. If, despite all its efforts, certain objections were not included in the statement of objections—because the events occurred, or came to the notice of the Commission, after the statement of objections was sent—the Commission would have to send a supplementary statement of objections.[61] The final decision adopted by the Commission does not necessarily have to be a copy of the statement of objections.[62] The Commission may and must withdraw its objections against undertakings wholly or in part, amend them or correct them, or supplement them, having regard to the action taken during the 'the right to be heard' phase. The latter possibility does not conflict with the principle of the right to a fair hearing laid down in Article 11 of Regulation 773/2004.[63] Partial withdrawal of

---

[60] The length of the statement of objections is very variable and depends on the complexity and novelty of the matter. The statement of objections fulfils its function by being clear and informing the undertakings of the essential facts and arguments relied on against them, albeit succinctly. See Case 27/76 *United Brands v EC Commission* [1978] ECR 207 para 274. See also, Case T-50/00 *Dalmine SpA v EC Commission* [2004] OJ C239/13 para 145; Case T-213/00 *CMA CGM v EC Commission* [2003] ECR II-347 para 109; and Case T-5/00 R *Nederlandse Federatieve Vereniging voor de Groothandel op Elektrotechnisch Gebied and Technische Unie BV v EC Commission* [2003] ECR II-5761 para 33. The Commission is not required to set out or recite at great length in the statement of objections every fact or matter on which it may rely. See also CS Kerse and N Khan, *EC Antitrust Procedure* (5th edn, 2005) para 4–020.

[61] See Case T-67/01 *JCB Service v EC Commission* [2004] ECR II-49 para 52.

[62] See Case T-48/00 *Corus UK Ltd v EC Commission* [2004] OJ C239/12 paras 100–101; Case T-228/97 *Irish Sugar* [1999] ECR II-2969 para 35.

[63] See Joined Cases 209 and 218/78 *Van Landewyck v EC Commission (FEDETAB)* [1980] ECR 3125 para 68. See also Case 41/69 *ACF Chemiefarma v EC Commission* [1970] ECR 661 paras 91–93; Joined Cases 142 and 156/84 *BAT and Reynolds v EC Commission* [1986] ECR 189 paras 13 and 14, and the judgment of the CFI in Case T-66/89 *Publishers Association v EC Commission* [1992] ECR II-1995 para 65. (This judgment has been quashed by the ECJ; see Case C-360/92 P *The Publishers Association v EC Commission II* [1995] ECR I-23). See, more recently, the judgments concerning the polypropylene cartel, those of the CFI in Case T-9/89 *Hüls v EC Commission* [1992] ECR II-499 paras 59 *et seq.*, Case T-11/89 *Shell v EC Commission* [1992] ECR II-757 paras 59 *et seq.* and Case T-15/89 *Chemie Linz v EC Commission* [1992] ECR II-1275 at para 36. See also Joined Cases T-10/92, T-11/92, T-12/92 and T-15/92 *Cimenteries CBR SA v EC Commission* [1992] ECR II-2667 para 47 '[. . .] until a final decision has been adopted, the Commission may, in view, in particular, of the written and oral observations of the parties, abandon some or even all of the objections initially made against them. [. . . .]..' In this case, the Commission rejected the attempt by the undertakings to use inseparability of the SO as a ground for arguing that their defence rights were infringed by the failure to send the chapters relating to the national agreements and concerted practices other than the chapter relating to the Member State in which the particular addressee of the SO was established where the Commission had dropped some of the charges in relation to certain agreements. See also Joined Cases T-67/00, T-68/00, T-71/00 and T-78/00 *JFE Engineering Corp and others v EC Commission* [2004] OJ C239/1 para 429: '. . .[ ] the rights of the defence are not breached by an inconsistency between the SO and the final decision unless a criticism contained in the latter had not been set out in the former sufficiently clearly to enable the addressees to defend themselves [. . .]'.

objections is quite frequent, although it is rare for objections to be completely withdrawn.[64]

2. Layout and general scheme of the statement of objections

10.15 The Commission's practice is to produce statements of objections comprising three parts. With the statement of objections in the strict sense an accompanying letter is sent, containing a number of statements—most of which are of a mandatory nature—together with any annexes referred to in the statement of objections or the letter.

The statement of objections strictly speaking

10.16 In general terms, the structure of the statement of objections is very similar to that of a Commission decision applying Articles 81(1) and 82 EC, which in turn are similar—formally, and only in part—to a judicial decision. The content of decisions will be examined in detail in due course, but in the statement of objections there are two distinct parts. These are the descriptive part (the facts) and the legal conclusions drawn from the evidence (the legal grounds) regarding the infringement. They are accompanied by certain statements from the Commission concerning its conclusions and intentions, for example to prohibit an agreement or practice, impose a fine, etc. The statement of objections is therefore, in appearance, a decision in embryo.[65]

---

[64] A Commission case in which the objections were withdrawn in their entirety was *BAT and Reynolds v Phillip Morris*. See Joined Cases 142 and 156/84 *BAT and Reynolds v EC Commission* [1987] ECR 4487 paras 26 and 27. Regarding the need to take account of the action taken when withdrawing or amending objections, see also Case 60/81 *IBM v EC Commission* [1981] ECR 2639 paras 18 and 21, and Joined Cases 100 to 103/80 *Musique Diffusion Française v EC Commission (Pioneer)* [1983] ECR 1825 paras 13–14. In the ruling on the 'Cement Cartel', Joined Cases C-204/00 P, C-205/00 P, C-211/00 P, C-213/00 P, C-217/00 P and C-219/00 P *Aarlborg et al v EC Commission* [2004] ECR II-123 para 192, the ECJ found that an interested party is not entitled to be informed by the Commission if the latter drops certain objections (in the that case, in relation to certain conduct on the Italian market). The ECJ reiterated that it would be only necessary to inform a would-be addressee of such decision if there would be a material alteration in the evidence relied on in a decisions ore if new evidence would be taken into account.

[65] As indicated, the subsequent decision does not, however, have to be a copy of the statement of objections. The Commission may withdraw its objections in whole or in part, or lessen their severity, as stated above. Not only must the statement of objections contain a description of the contested practices, it must also indicate the duration of the infringement that the Commission provisionally intends to find in its decision. The withdrawal of objections is precisely the objective that their addressee hopes to achieve by replying to them. See Final Report of the Hearing Officer in *Food Flavour Enhancers* [2004] OJ C64/4.

The letter accompanying the statement of objections—time-limit for a reply

Together with the statement of objections strictly speaking, the Commission **10.17**
sends a letter which is also of great importance. It should indicate clearly:

(1) The nature of the letter, the statement of objections and the annexes
thereto. In other words, it is made clear that the communication constitutes a statement of objections issued pursuant to Article 27 of Regulation
1/2003 in respect of an infringement of the Community competition
provisions.

(2) The commencement of the procedure (whether it commenced when the
Commission decided to send the statement of objections or at an earlier
stage), and the legal consequences provided for in Article 7 of Regulation
1/2003.

(3) The time-limit within which observations may be submitted in response to
the statement of objections. The period allowed might not be less than four
weeks, pursuant to Article 17(2) of Regulation 773/2004. In practice,
depending on the complexity of the matter and the time of year (Christ-
mas, Easter or summer holidays), the Commission sets a period of between
eight and sixteen weeks. However, for proceedings initiated with a view to
adopting interim measures pursuant to Article 8 of Regulation 1/2003, the
time-limit may be shortened to one week. The period will not, in principle,
be extended. Nevertheless, Article 17(3) of Regulation 773/2004 provides
that where appropriate and upon request made before the expiry of the
original time-limit, time-limits may be extended.

(4) The fact that, in response to the statement of objections, undertakings are
entitled to make any submissions and raise any matters relevant to their
defence. To substantiate facts, the undertakings may, if they wish, append
documents of any kind. The Commission requests that in such cases
the undertakings clearly identify—preferably in a separate annex—the
documents which contain business secrets.[66] Undertakings may, when lodging written observations, ask to give oral arguments at an administrative
hearing, under Article 12 of Regulation 773/2004. They may also request,
pursuant to Article 13 of Regulation 773/2004, that other persons
(witnesses or experts) be heard and be allowed to appear and participate in
the administrative hearing, in order to make oral observations confirming
the facts on which they rely in their defence.

(5) That the undertakings may orally expound their views at an administrative
hearing which, if requested, would be arranged by the Commission (Articles
12 *et seq* of Regulation 773/2004).

---

[66] For examples of how the term 'business secrets' may be interpreted, see below regarding
access to the file, paras 10.29 *et seq.*

(6) That access to the file is granted when the statement of objections is sent and that the right of access to the file is not extended to confidential information and internal documents of the Commission and Member States, under Article 27(2) of Regulation 1/2003 and Articles 15 and 16 of Regulation 773/2004.

The annexes to the statement of objections

10.18 Together with the accompanying letter and the statement of objections itself, and with a view to expediting the procedure as much as possible, the Commission encloses, a list of annexes. Those annexes are documents that do not emanate from the Commission and must be regarded as supporting documentation on which the Commission relies and must therefore be brought to the attention of the addressee in their original language, so that the addressee can apprise himself of the interpretation of them which the Commission has adopted and on which it has based its statement of objections.[67] However, the Commission will not annex all other documents which the parties may be entitled to inspect under the access to the file procedure. For the purpose of access to the file, the Commission provides a CD-ROM containing a list of all the documents of the file, giving both the number of each document, the nature of it[68] and its content when it is not confidential. This includes the documentary evidence on which it relied in drawing up the statement of objections, and even evidence which is already well known to the undertakings.[69] The Commission must not conceal exculpatory evidence and must cooperate in order to enable the parties concerned to exercise their defence rights. It is

---

[67] See Case T-148/89 *Tréfilunion SA v EC Commission* [1995] ECR II-1063 para 21. For a detailed description of the summary list of documents annexed to a statement of objections, see Case T-65/89 *BPB v EC Commission* [1993] ECR II-389 para 31; Joined Cases T-305/94, T-306/94, T-307/94, T-313/94 to T-316/94, T-318/94, T-325/94, T-328/94, T-329/94 and T-335/94 *Limburgse Vinyl Maatschappij (LVM) and others v EC Commission* [1999] ECR II-931 paras 337–338. T-338/94 *Finnboard v EC Commission* [1998] ECR II-1617 para 53; T-9/99 *HFB v EC Commission* [2002] ECR II-1487 para 327.

[68] In general terms, the Commission classifies them as disclosable (A), partially disclosable (B or AP) or non-disclosable (N or NA). The classification of a document may vary according to the persons who are to have access to the file: a company whose business secrets are contained in the Commission's documentation may see its own documents, but that right is not available to competitors also implicated in the procedure or to complainants.

[69] See Case 107/82 *AEG v EC Commission* [1983] ECR 3151 para 26 where the ECJ pointed out that it is not the documents themselves that are important but the conclusions drawn from them by the Commission. The Court held that if documents were not mentioned in the statement of objections, AEG could reasonably conclude that they were not important for the case.

important that the Commission identify and undertakings be able to consider the material on which the Commission is relying.[70]

3. Formal conditions

The statement of objections, as described above, must be formally sent to the undertakings so that they are able to exercise their defence rights.[71] Article 10(1) of Regulation 773/2004 simply provides that the statement of objections must be notified to each of the undertakings and/or associations of undertakings concerned. In principle, every single undertaking implicated in restrictive agreements or practices will have received a copy of the statement of objections.[72] In the case of associations of undertakings, however, in order to comply with the principle of observing the defence rights, it is sufficient if the Commission sends a single statement to the association. In *Industrial and Medical Gases*, the Hearing Officer took the view that where one party member of a group of companies accepts service and assumes responsibility for the defence of the company or companies to whom the statement of objections should otherwise have been notified, this latter company is considered as having waived its right to be notified.[73] Statements of objections do not have to be sent to an association's members; at least if it appears from their internal rules that the members

---

[70] Nevertheless, in certain circumstances the Commission takes the view that it may be able to use a document as evidence without disclosing its source, date or authorship. *Seamless Steel Tubes* [2003] OJ L140/1 para 121. CS Kerse and N Khan, *EC Antitrust Procedure* (5th edn, 2005) para 4–021.

[71] If the statement of objections is sent to the undertakings only for their information and without a time-limit for a response, the defence rights are infringed, since the possibility cannot be excluded that the result of the procedure would have been different if the undertakings had had an opportunity to give their views on the statement. See Joined Cases T-39 and T-40/92 *Carte Bleu v EC Commission* [1994] ECR II-49 paras 46 *et seq.*, in particular paras 58 and 60. In this case, the Commission had sent a supplementary statement of objections, solely for information, to one of the undertakings involved, which had in fact had the first statement notified to it formally.

[72] In Cases T-24/93, T-26/93 and T-28/93 *Compagnie Maritime Belge Transports v EC Commission* [1996] ECR II-1201 para 35 the CFI adopted the view that a party cannot complain if the statement of objections does not properly name it where it is otherwise clear that it is the intended addressee and has the opportunity to exercise its defence rights. However, on appeal, the ECJ disagreed and annulled the fines for the appellants. It ruled that '[. . .] It is clear that a statement of objections which merely identifies as the perpetrator of an infringement a collective entity, such as Cewal, does not make the companies forming that entity sufficiently aware that fines will be imposed on them individually if the infringement is made out. Contrary to what the [CFI] held, the fact that Cewal does not have legal personality is not relevant in this regard. [. . .] Similarly, a statement of objections in those terms is not sufficient to warn the companies concerned that the amount of the fines imposed will be fixed in accordance with an assessment of the participation of each company in the conduct constituting the alleged infringement.' Joined Cases C-395/96 P and C-396/96 P *Compagnie Maritime Belge Transports SA v EC Commission* [1996] ECR I-1365 paras 144–145.

[73] Final Report of the Hearing Officer in *Industrial and Medical Gases* [2003] OJ C78/4.

are liable for the debts of the association.[74] However, in certain cases the Commission may not be entitled to separate the evidence regarding several related infringements in the statement of objections—with the result that separate decisions are adopted—if by so doing it prevents the undertakings from examining relevant documents for their defence which may have been placed in other files, thus infringing the undertakings' defence rights.[75]

10.20　Statements of objections do not have to be limited to dealing with a single infringement—they may refer to several, although these must be connected. It is normal for them to be addressed to several undertakings at the same time and for them to relate to different undertakings and to varying extents. The Commission may also bring together in one statement of objections facts which have been the subject of separate complaints. It is not required to draw up a separate statement of objections for each complaint and it is entitled to join related cases without any formal requirement to adopt a reasoned decision for that purpose.[76]

10.21　Statements of objections are sent in the Community language of the country where the addressee undertakings are situated. The Commission may agree to send statements of objections in another Community language, if undertakings so argue or request.[77]

4. Substantive conditions—evidential documents

10.22　The Commission must establish clearly and exhaustively in the statement of objections the accusations—administrative, not criminal—made against the undertakings suspected of infringing Community competition law. Regardless of whether they have knowledge of facts and documents mentioned in the statement of objections, the undertakings must be informed of all the conduct and documents on which the Commission intends to rely for its decision. As stated, pursuant to Article 27(1) of Regulation 1/2003 the final decision may be based only on the objections and the documents in respect of which the undertakings have had an opportunity to give their views or version of events. Community competition procedure is essentially a written procedure and where necessary the Commission cites the documents which lead it to think that there

---

[74] In Joined Cases T-39/92 and T-40/92 *Carte Bleu v EC Commission* [1994] ECR II-49 the CFI considered that it was lawful, by implication, for the Commission to send the statement of objections to two associations and not to its members (paras 22 and 25) and held that the Commission had not infringed the principle of the individual nature of penalties by imposing on the association a fine exceeding ECU 1 million (para 139).

[75] See Case T-36/91 *Imperial Chemical Industries plc (ICI) v EC Commission* [1995] ECR II-1847 para 94; and Case T-30/91 *Solvay SA v Commission* [1995] ECR II-1775 para 84.

[76] See Joined Cases 209/78 and 218/78 *Van Landewyck v EC Commission (FEDETAB)* [1980] ECR 3125 paras 29 and 32.

[77] Regarding Community languages, see ch 4 'Organization of EC Commission Proceedings' paras 4.15 *et seq.*

has been an infringement of the Treaty provisions. Nevertheless, as it has been already said, what is important in the statement of objections is not the documents themselves but the conclusion arrived at by the Commission on the basis of them.[78] As regards documents, if the Commission failed to give the undertakings information identifying those which would be used in the decision, it would prevent the latter from giving their views on their evidential value and infringe the rights of the defence, with the result that such documents could not be regarded as valid evidence against them.[79] The Commission must therefore take care to indicate in its statement of objections the evidential documents on which it relies. As regards annexed documents which have not been referred to in the statement, they may be used in the final decision only to the extent to which the addressees could reasonably have drawn from the statement of objections the same conclusions as the Commission drew from those documents.[80] In certain cases, the Commission may, even after sending the statement of objections, forward evidential documents to undertakings so that they may make their observations on them.[81] As in the case of facts and evidential documents, undertakings must be given an opportunity to contest the legal conclusions concerning the alleged infringements adopted by the Commission, and its assessments as to their gravity, whether they were committed deliberately, and their duration. The importance of the latter requirement lies in the fact that such circumstances will serve as the basis for calculating the fines in those cases where the statement of objections indicates that they will be imposed.

---

[78] See Case 107/82 *AEG v EC Commission* [1983] ECR 3151 paras 24–28, in particular para 27. See also C-62/86 *Akzo v EC Commission III* [1991] ECR I-3359 para 21, and the polypropylene cartel cases, *inter alia*, Case T-9/89 *Hüls v EC Commission* [1992] ECR II-499 para 38; Case T-11/89 *Shell v EC Commission* [1992] ECR II-757 para 55; and Case T-15/89 *Chemie Linz v EC Commission* [1992] ECR II-1275 para 36. K Lenaerts and J Maselis, 'Procedural Rights and Issues in the Enforcement of Articles 81 and 82 of the EC Treaty' [2001] Fordham International Law Journal 1615–54 (1632).

[79] See, *inter alia*, Case 107/82 *AEG v EC Commission* [1983] ECR 3151 para 27, and Case C-62/86 *Akzo v EC Commission III* [1991] ECR I-3359 paras 18–24. See also Case T-9/89 *Hüls v EC Commission* [1992] ECR II-499 para 38; Case T-11/89 *Shell v EC Commission* [1992] ECR II-757 para 55; and Case T-15/89 *Chemie Linz v EC Commission* [1992] ECR II-1275 para 36. See Case T-148/89 *Tréfilunion SA v EC Commission* [1995] ECR II-1063 para 25. Here the CFI stated that: '[t]he Court finds that the documents mentioned by the applicant were not disclosed to it when the statement of objections was sent. It follows that the applicant was entitled to consider that they were not important to the case. It follows that they cannot be regarded as admissible evidence as far as it is concerned [. . .]' referring to Case C-62/86 *Akzo v EC Commission III* [1991] ECR I-3359 para 21, and Case T-8/89 *DSM NV v EC Commission* [1991] ECR II-1833 para 37.

[80] See Case T-9/89 *Hüls v EC Commission* [1992] ECR II-499 para 39; Case T-11/89 *Shell v EC Commission* [1992] ECR II-757 para 56; and Case T-15/89 *Chemie Linz v EC Commission* [1992] ECR II-1275 para 37. See also Case T-4/89 *BASF v EC Commission* [1991] ECR II-1523 at paras 36 and 37.

[81] Joined Cases T-236/01, T-239/01, T-244/01 to T-246/01, T-251/01 and T-252/01 *Tokai Carbon Co Ltd and others v EC Commission* [2004] ECR II-1181 para 45.

The main legal arguments relied on by the Commission must be based on Article 81—prohibition of agreements and practices restrictive of competition—and Article 82—prohibition of the abuse of a dominant position.

5. Publicity of the statement of objections

10.23 Article 2(2) of Regulation 773/2004 states that, after having informed the undertakings concerned,[82] the Commission may decide to make public the initiation of proceedings in 'any appropriate way'. However, the Regulation does not specify where the Commission might decide to make public (rather than publish) the statement of objections nor the grounds on which the Commission might opt to do so.[83] It is frequent that the Commission, for the sake of promoting the implementation of competition policy, issues a press release or refers to the issue of a statement of objections in a particular case in its annual report on competition policy. The obligation of professional secrecy imposed on the Commission by Article 28 of Regulation 1/2003 does not prevent it from making a public announcement as to the issue of a statement of objections. Article 28 deals with the use of information obtained in the investigation of cases by the Commission. Such information may not be divulged.[84] Except in the case of specific information obtained under Regulation 1/2003, there is no principle or rule whatsoever preventing the Commission from releasing 'information relating to particular undertakings' involved in procedures being conducted by it. The Commission must take care, in any event, that there is no confusion on the part of readers of a Press notice between a statement of objections and a final decision finding an infringement and that the notice is not made public before the statement of objections reaches its addressees.

6. Cases where a financial penalty is envisaged

10.24 If the Commission plans to impose a fine or fix the amount of a periodic penalty payment, the statement of objections must indicate equally clearly that it has such an intention and, referring to the evidence available to it,[85] must specify the duration, and gravity of the infringement, together with the culpability of the

---

[82] Under Art 10(1) of Reg 773/2004 the Commission shall inform the parties concerned in writing of the objections raised against them. The statement of objections must be notified to each of the undertakings concerned.

[83] Interestingly, former Art 2(2) of Reg 99/63 expressly provided that the Commission could decide to publish the statement of objections in the OJ, although in practice this seemed to be limited to exceptional circumstances.

[84] See ch 9 'Penalties and confidentiality' paras 9.25 *et seq.*

[85] e.g. Case C-176/99 P *ARBED SA v EC Commission* [2003] ECR I-10687 para 21.

undertakings concerned.[86] However, undertakings are not entitled to require the Commission to inform them in the course of the procedure of the amount of the fines or the basis on which it intends to calculate them.[87] At this stage the Commission does not—and is not required to—anticipate the amount of the fine, not even provisionally and approximately. Where the Commission indicates the main factual and legal criteria capable of giving rise to a fine, such as the gravity and the duration of the alleged infringement and whether that infringement was committed intentionally or negligently, the Commission is considered as having fulfilled its obligation to respect the undertakings' right to be heard. In doing so, it provides them with the necessary means to defend themselves not only against the finding of an infringement but also against the imposition of fines.[88]

If the fines are for procedural infringements in connection with requests for   **10.25**

---

[86] Joined Cases T-25/95, T-26/95, T-30/95 to T-39/95, T-42/95 to T-46/95, T-48/95, T-50/95 to T-65/95, T-68/95 to T-71/95, T-87/95, T-88/95, T-103/95 and T-104/95 *Cimenteries CBR SA and others v EC Commission* [2000] ECR II-491 para 480; A failing in this respect will not necessarily make impossible any subsequent decision imposing fines. Case T-48/00 *Corus UK v EC Commission* [2004] OJ C239/12 para 155; note, however, that in Joined Cases C-395/96 and C-396/96 P *Compagnie Maritime Belge Transports SA v Commission* [2000] ECR I-1365 paras 144–145 the ECJ held, as indicated, that it is not sufficient that the statement of objections merely identifies as the perpetrator of an infringement a collective entity (in the case at hand, a liner conference made up of shipping companies, CEWAL) because this does not make the companies forming that entity sufficiently aware that fines will be imposed on them individually if the alleged infringement is shown to exist. The fact that CEWAL did not have legal personality would be irrelevant. By the same token, a statement of objections in those terms is not sufficient to warn the companies concerned that the amount of the fines imposed will be fixed in accordance with an assessment of the participation of each company in the conduct constituting the alleged infringement.

[87] See Cases 100–103/80 *Musique Diffusion v EC Commission (Pioneer)* [1983] ECR I-1825 paras 21 *et seq.* While following this judgment, the CFI has indicated that 'it is desirable for undertakings in order to be able to define their position in full knowledge of the facts to be able to determine in detail, in accordance with any system which the Commission might consider appropriate, the method of calculation of the fine imposed upon them, without being obliged, in order to do so, to bring court proceedings against the Commission decision which would be contrary to the principle of good administration.' The CFI appears to have addressed a recommendation to the Commission, without imposing new obligations different from those in *Pioneer*. See Case T-148/89 *Tréfilunion SA v EC Commission* [1995] ECR II-1063 para 142; see also Case T-31/99 *ABB Asea Brown Boveri v EC Commission* [2002] ECR II-1881 paras 85–89; Case T-23/99 *LR af 1998 v EC Commission* [2002] ECR II-1705 paras 199–209.

[88] Case T-23/99 *LR af 1998 v EC Commission* [2002] ECR II-1705 para 199 emphasizing that the Commission is under no obligation to explain the way in which it would use each of those elements in determining the level of the fine. To give indications as regards the level of the fines envisaged, before the undertaking has been invited to submit its observations on the allegations against it, would be to anticipate the Commission's decision and would thus be inappropriate. See also Opinion of AG Antonio Tizzano in Joined Cases C-189/02 P, C-202/02 P, C-205/02 P to C-208/02 P and C-213/02 P *Dansk Rørindustri and others v EC Commission* [2005] OJ C205/1 para 171.

information[89] or inspections[90] the Commission is also obliged to inform the undertakings of its objections. The period allowed for written observations is also usually between fifteen days and one month. If the Commission envisages imposing periodic penalty payments, the statement of objections is sent after the amount thereof is calculated, that is to say before the adoption of the decision as an enforceable measure, not before the adoption of the decision in which the periodic penalty payment merely plays a contributory role, serving to penalize certain conduct.[91] The procedure for the imposition of fines for the infringement of procedural rules is different from the main procedure. It follows its own course separately from the latter, the result of which has no bearing on any finding of procedural infringements committed by the undertakings involved in the procedure. Where, after a first phase of resistance or opposition to the Commission's action, the undertakings modify their agreements or practices in order to make them conform with Community requirements or reach an amicable settlement with the Commission under Article 9 of Regulation 1/2003, those facts do not release the undertakings from their liability for infringing the provisions of Regulation 1/2003 (for example, by giving incorrect information or opposing an inspection). The Commission's consistent practice shows that even in cases with a 'happy ending', infringements which offend against the Commission's investigative powers do not go unpunished.

7. New objections and new evidence

10.26 Despite the Commission's scrupulous care not to omit any important aspect of the case from the statement of objections, it may happen that new matters come to light on which the undertakings have not had an opportunity to express their views. This may be as a result of a fresh complaint or from the observations of the undertakings accused of restrictive practices at this stage of the procedure or information obtained by the Commission in the exercise of its investigative powers. In such circumstances, the Commission may be required to send a supplementary statement of objections and to give the parties the necessary time to submit their views on the new material. Three situations may arise. Firstly, the new facts and the legal conclusions drawn from them may differ substantially from those previously described and detailed by the Commission in the statement of objections so that, even if the undertakings are the same, the new information may not be sufficiently related to the Commission's actual proceedings. In such cases, the Commission may choose to initiate a new substantive

---

[89] Art 23(1)(a) and (b) of Reg 1/2003. See ch 9 'Penalties and confidentiality' paras 9.03 *et seq.*
[90] Art 23(1) (c), (d), and (e) of Reg 1/2003. See ch 9 'Penalties and confidentiality' paras 9.06 *et seq.*
[91] Regarding the procedure for the imposition of periodic penalty payments, see ch 9 'Penalties and confidentiality'.

infringement procedure or else may deal with both infringements in the same decision.[92] The second situation which may arise is that, despite the emergence of new information in the case which might give rise to new objections, the legal conclusions about the incriminated agreements, practices, or conduct is basically the same. There are no new infringements but there are new objections in respect of the same infringements. The Commission will be required to send a new statement of objections, but the same proceedings will continue, and there will be only one substantive decision, which will set out both the original and the new objections and will refer to the infringements indicated originally. The third situation which may arise is that the Commission has obtained new evidence corroborating the objections previously notified to the undertakings. There will be no new objections, but there will be factual information over and above that already known to the undertakings. Narrowing down the date of an agreement does not constitute an additional objection. In *Plasterboard*, the statement of objections was relatively imprecise as to the exact date on which Lafarge was deemed to be a party to the agreement ('after the London meeting'). The Commission is able to make its information more explicit during the course of the investigation.[93]

In the first two situations, where new facts are to be used against the undertakings and/or where there is a material change in the evidence of the contested infringements, the Commission should send an additional statement of objections to the undertakings concerned. In the third, the Commission will choose to communicate to the undertakings involved the new information confirming and extending the objections, in a letter asking the parties to submit observations on the new evidence within a specified time-limit.[94] It appears that the Commission sends so-called 'letter of facts' to the parties by which they are informed of additional information which will be taken into account in the final decision.[95] **10.27**

---

[92] In both cases, the Commission would be required to send a new and different statement of objections which will, if appropriate, give rise to a new substantive decision or else the treatment of several infringements in a single decision. This latter situation is quite normal.

[93] Final Report of the Hearing Officer, *Plasterboard* [2005] OJ C156/6.

[94] See *Sperry New Holland* [1985] OJ L376/21. In that case, the Commission sent to the undertakings, for them to submit their observations, additional documents which referred to objections already discussed at the hearing. If the undertakings were unable to give their views after the statement of objections was sent, the rights of the defence would be infringed and the Commission's decision would be annulled. See Joined Cases C-89/85, C-104/85, C-114/85, C116/85, C-117/85 and C-125/85 to C129/85 *Ahlström Osakeyhtiö and others v Commission* (*'Woodpulp II'*) [1993] ECR I-1307 para 138; Joined Cases C-238/99 P, C-244/99 P, C-245/99 P, C-247/99 P, C-250/99 P to C-252/99 P and C-254/99 P *Limburgse Vinyl Maatschappij (LVM) and others v EC Commission* [2002] ECR I-8375 para 497 and Case T-23/99 *LR af 1998 v Commission* [2002] ECR II-1705 paras 188–190, where the CFI held that the Commission did not introduce fresh objections but that the Commission letters cited certain documents constituting further evidence in support of the objections set out in the statement of objections.

[95] e.g. Commission Report on Competition Policy [2004], SEC (2005) 805 final, 10. Access to the file was granted five times to Microsoft throughout the procedure, which included access to documents not mentioned in the Statement of Objections but to which the conclusions of the

This information does not alter the conclusions drawn earlier in the statement of objections being sent earlier.[96] This step will not give rise to a hearing but the parties will be given access to the file. The letter will not reproduce the objections—they having been notified previously—nor will new reasoning be called for (still less a repetition of that already set out). The Court has accepted this practice in the case of a new complaint being made in the course of the procedure without any change being made to the original objections.[97] A supplementary statement of objections may however be issued in order to clarify the Commission's position regarding the material and reasoning contained in the undertaking's reply to the original statement of objections.[98] In any event, the Commission cannot use against undertakings evidence on which they have not had an opportunity to express their views[99] in accordance with Article 27(1) of Regulation 1/2003 and Article 11(2) of Regulation 773/2004.

B. The Granting of Access to the File

1. Introduction

10.28 Once informed of the objections, the undertakings involved have an opportunity to submit observations. To enable them to do so in full knowledge of the facts, undertakings are allowed, at the time of the statement of objections, to obtain information regarding the non-confidential parts of the files relating to them. Access to the Commission's file is one of the procedural guarantees intended to apply the principle of equality of arms and to protect the rights of

---

Commission referred in its 'letter of facts'. Commission Decision COMP/C-3/37.792 *Microsoft* (non-confidential version) of 24 March 2004, para 15. See also Commission Decision COMP/38.096—*Clearstream* (non-confidential version) of 2 June 2004, para 15.

[96] A straightforward example may be that the Commisison has gathered further evidence for meetings that the parties to a cartel held. This would not affect as such the finding on the duration of the infringement contained in the statement of objections and would thus not amount to material alteration in the evidence.

[97] See Joined Cases 209/78 and 218/78 *Van Landewyck v EC Commission (FEDETAB)* [1980] ECR 3125 para 36. Case 107/82 *AEG v EC Commission* [1983] ECR 3151 para 29; Case T-23/99 *LR af 1998 v EC Commission* [2002] ECR II-1705 para 190. In *PVC II* the ECJ found that a second statement of objections was not necessary where the purpose of the new proceedings was to correct a procedural illegality in the taking of the original decision. Joined Cases C-238/99 P, C-244/99 P, C-245/99 P, C-247/99 P, C-250/99 P to C-252/99 P and C-254/99 P *Limburgse Vinyl Maatschappij (LVM) and others v EC Commission* [2002] ECR I-8375 para 98.

[98] *Deutsche Telekom AG*, Final report of the Hearing Officer [2003] OJ C227/2. This can be done by letter, there is no requirement for a formal document entitled 'supplementary statement of objection'.

[99] See Case T-2/89 *Petrofina v EC Commission* [1991] ECR II-1087 para 39, and Case T-43/92 *Dunlop v EC Commission* [1994] ECR II-441 para 33. See in particular the *Soda Ash* cases (Case T-30/91 *Solvay v EC Commission* [1995] ECR II-1775 para 55, Case T-31/91 *Solvay v EC Commission* [1995] ECR II-1821, Case T-32/91 *Solvay v EC Commission* [1995] ECR II-1825,

the defence.[100] This is a procedural requirement deriving from case law[101] with which the Commission has complied with good grace[102] and which has now a legal basis in Article 27(1) and (2) of Regulation 1/2003. While it is true that initially the Commission imposed on itself certain rules and patterns of action as regards granting access to the file, as the ECJ recognized, it now forms part of the EU Charter of Fundamental Rights,[103] which is not dependent upon a self-imposed obligation by the Commission. Article 15(1) of Regulation 773/2004 provides that the Commission shall grant access to the file to the parties to whom it has addressed a statement of objections. Pursuant to Article 15(2) of Regulation 773/2004 the right of access to the file shall not extend to business secrets, other confidential information, and internal documents of the Commission or of the competition authorities of the Member States.[104] Article 16(2) establishes the right of the parties to indicate, explaining the main reasons, the material they consider as confidential and to facilitate a non-confidential version. It should be borne in mind that access to the file is not a special procedure distinct from the infringement procedure but a procedural stage in contentious competition cases.[105]

Case T-36/91 *ICI v EC Commission* [1995] ECR II-1847, and Case T-37/91 *ICI v EC Commission* [1995] ECR II-1901) in which the CFI criticized the Commission for having carried out additional investigations into a case after the hearing of the undertaking without giving it the opportunity to state its views on those findings before the decision was adopted.

[100] The Notice was adopted on 13 December 2005, see Commission press release IP/05/1581 'Competition: Commission improves rules for access to the file in merger and antitrust procedures'. See also Commission Notice of 13 December 2005 on the rules for access to the Commission file pursuant to Art 81 and 82 EC Treaty [2005] OJ C252/7 para 1.

[101] See the Joined Cases 56/64 and 58/64 *Consten & Grundig v EC Commission* [1966] ECR 299 para 5, and Case 85/76 *Hoffmann-La Roche v EC Commission* [1979] ECR 461 para 11.

[102] Joined Cases T-10/92, T-11/92, T-12/92 and T-15/92 *Cimenteries CBR v EC Commission* [1992] ECR II-1571 para 38; Case T-7/89 *SA Hercules Chemicals NV v EC Commission* [1991] ECR II-1711 para 53, established that the Commission may not depart from the rules imposed by it on itself, in that specific case those concerning access to the file. To the same effect, see also the judgments of the CFI in all the polypropylene cartel cases—e.g. Case T-9/89 *Hüls v EC Commission* [1992] ECR II-499 paras 42 *et seq.*

[103] See Art 41(2)b of the Charter of Fundamental Rights of the European Union, adopted in Nice on 7 December 2000 ([2000] OJ C364/1). In fact, the ECJ has already referred to the EU Charter in various cases (see, e.g. Joined Cases C-204/00 P, C-205/00 P, C-211/00 P, C-213/00 P, C-217/00 P and C-219/00 P *Aalborg et al v EC Commission* [2004] ECR II-123 para 94). The principle has also been already recognized by the case law of the European Court of Human Rights when interpreting Art 6(1) of the European Convention of Human Rights, to which refers Art 6(2) of the EU Treaty.

[104] As the case law had already recognized: Case T-7/89 *SA Hercules Chemicals NV v EC Commission* [1991] ECR II-1711 para 54.

[105] Joined Cases C-204/00 P, C-205/00 P, C-211/00 P, C-213/00 P, C-217/00 P and C-219/00 P *Aalborg et al v EC Commission* [2004] ECR II-123 para 68: '[. . .] A corollary of the principle of respect for the rights of the defence, the right of access to the file means that the Commission must give the undertaking concerned the opportunity to examine all the documents in the investigation file which may be relevant for its defence [. . .]' However, it continues and explains that the rights of the defence are not infringed for limiting access to certain documents (para 70):

10.29   The meaning of the term 'file' has been generally interpreted by the Commission to mean the documents upon which the decision was to be taken, i e 'the statement of objections, the documents upon which the Commission relied in order to support the allegations against the undertaking in the statement of objections and anything on which the Commission did not rely but which was clearly exculpatory.' The Commission had considered that '[all] other material [. . .] obtained in the course of its investigation but which did not fall within one of those categories was not part of the file, so that it was not necessary to enquire whether the party had had access to it.'[106] The Commission maintained that even if a wider interpretation of the term 'file' was accepted, once confidential and other non-accessible documents were excluded, the practical consequence was that the undertaking had access to the same documents as under the first approach.[107] The Notice on Access to File[108] which has replaced the 1997 Notice on Access to File, establishes that the term 'Commission file' in a competition investigation consists of all documents '[. . .] which have been obtained, produced and/or assembled by [DG COMP], during the investigation [. . .].'[109] The term 'access to the file' is used here exclusively to mean access granted to those parties to whom the Commission has addressed a statement of objections.[110] The CFI has interpreted the expression 'file' more widely,

'[. . .] The ECHR has nonetheless held that, just like observance of the other procedural safeguards enshrined in Art 6(1) of the ECHR, compliance with the adversarial principle relates only to judicial proceedings before a "tribunal" and that there is no general, abstract principle that the parties must in all instances have the opportunity to attend the interviews carried out or to receive copies of all the documents taken into account in the case of other persons [. . .]' with references to ECHR case law.

[106] Case T-36/91 *ICI v EC Commission* [1995] ECR II-1847 para 59. See also Notice on Access to File, adopted on 13 December 2005, [2005] OJ C325/7 paras 3 and 12 *et seq.* Replies to the Statement of Objections as such are not accessible. It is only when the Commission intends to use a reply of one undertaking as incriminating evidence against another undertaking or as exonerating evidence of another undertaking that this information is passed to the undertaking concerned, Final Report of the Hearing Officer [2005] OJ C173/5. See also *Vitamins* [2003] OJ L106/1 para 147. At the oral hearing the undertakings were given the opportunity to comment on the written replies of the other parties.

[107] See Case T-36/91 *ICI v EC Commission* [1995] ECR II-1847 para 59.

[108] The new Access Notice (see [2005] OJ C325/7 para 24) takes account of experience gained in applying the 1997 Notice and recent case law, in particular in Joined Cases T-25/95, T-26/95, T-30/95 to T-39/95, T-42/95 to T-46/95, T-48/95, T-50/95 to T-65/95, T-68/95 to T-71/95, T-87/95, T-88/95, T-103/95 and T-104/95 *Cimenteries CBR SA and others v EC Commission* [2000] ECR II-491.

[109] Commission Notice on the rules for access to the Commission file pursuant to Arts 81 and 82 EC [2005] OJ C325/7 para 8. Interestingly the earlier draft ([2004] OJ C259/8, para 7) contained the qualification that the file consisted of documents obtained the 'during the investigation *that has led the Commission to raise its objections*' (emphasis added).

[110] Commission Notice on the rules for access to the Commission file pursuant to Arts 81 and 82 EC [2005] OJ C325/7 para 3 noting that '[. . .] The same term, or the term access to documents, is also used in the above-mentioned regulations [e.g., Reg 1/2003 and Reg 773/2004] in respect of complainants or other involved parties. These situations are, however, distinct from

to include not only incriminatory documents on which the objections are based and clearly exculpatory documents, but also any possibly exculpatory documents which might help the undertakings defend themselves against the Commission's objections, even if they are confidential.[111] In specific circumstances the file may even include documents that are physically contained in folders relating to other infringements. In the case of documents that are confidential but possibly aid the defence, the Commission may be obliged to provide non-confidential summaries.

2. Limits on access to the file

By virtue of its obligation to respect defence rights, the Commission must grant undertakings allegedly implicated in an infringement access to the evidence and documents on which it relies for its objections, as set out in the statement of objections or the annexes to it,[112] and on which it may finally base its decision, so that they can submit their observations on them.[113] However, the Commission is under no obligation to disclose its entire file to the undertakings[114] and, in practice, not all the documents contained in the file are shown to the undertakings. There are several reasons for this.[115] **10.30**

First, there are documents in the file that contain business secrets of the undertakings involved in the procedure, which must be kept confidential. Those secrets may emanate from a complainant company, which may legitimately object **10.31**

---

that of the addressees of a statement of objections and therefore do not fall under the definition of access to the file for the purposes of this notice. These related situations are dealt with in a separate section of the notice.[. . .]'

[111] In Case T-36/91 *ICI v EC Commission* [1995] ECR II-1775 para 91 the CFI stated that it is not for the Commission exclusively to rule upon the documents which may be deemed as suitable for the undertakings' defence; undertakings must be given the chance to assess their probative value.

[112] See Case 322/82 *Michelin v EC Commission* [1983] ECR 3461 para 7.

[113] Documents not shown to the undertakings will not be available as evidence against them in the Commission's final decision.

[114] See Joined Cases 43/82 and 63/82 *VBVB and VBBB v EC Commission* [1984] ECR 1984 para 25, cited in Case C-62/86 *Akzo v EC Commission III* [1991] ECR I-3359 para 16. According to AG Warner in his Opinion in Case 30/78 *Distillers v EC Commission* [1980] ECR 2229 it is sufficient if the parties are able to apprise themselves of the content of all the important documents.

[115] See Art 27(2) of Reg 1/2003, Arts 15(2) and 16(1) of Reg 773/2004. Those exceptions are also mentioned in Case T-7/89 *SA Hercules Chemicals NV v EC Commission* [1991] ECR II-1711 para 54. Note, however, that the Court has ruled that it does not belong to the Commission alone to decide which documents in the file may be useful for the purposes of the defence (see Case T-30/91 *Solvay v EC Commission* [1995] ECR II-1775 paras 81–86, and Case T-36/91 *ICI v EC Commission* [1995] ECR II-1847 paras 91–96). However, the Commission is allowed to preclude evidence which has no relation to the allegation of fact and of law in the SO. Joined Cases C-204/00 P etc, *P. Aalborg Portland v EC Commission* [2004] ECR I-123 para 126.

to any access to its confidential documents[116] by the undertaking complained against, or vice versa. The same position may arise where two undertakings are the subject of the same complaint. In such cases, access to the file must not enable the undertakings—which in many cases will be competitors, in theory at least—to exchange information that in any other circumstances would in itself be contrary to the competition rules.

10.32 The Court has on numerous occasions ruled as to the scope of 'business secrets',[117] and has opted for the broadest possible definition.[118] In general, any document or information supplied by an undertaking, which contains strategic information as to its business activities, must be regarded as constituting business secrets.[119] Documents capable of providing evidence of infringements by one party are not to be disclosed to other parties.[120] The new Notice on Access to the File also puts forward some examples of business secrets in order to provide some guidance.[121]

---

[116] It should be borne in mind that when complaints contain business secrets, described as such by the complainant, the Commission may not disclose any copy until it has deleted all confidential information from them—if the complainant did not place the confidential documents and information in special annexes. Art 16(2) of Reg 773/2004 establishes that any party which makes known its views shall clearly identify any material which it considers to be confidential, giving reasons, and provide a separate non-confidential version by the date set by the Commission for making its views known. If it does not do so by the set date, the Commission may assume that the submission does not contain such materials.

[117] See, among others, Order of the ECJ in Case 236/81 *Celanese Corp v EC Commission* [1982] ECR 1183 paras 9–13; Case C-62/86 *Akzo v EC Commission III* [1991] ECR I-3359; Case 142/84 and 156/84 *BAT and Reynolds Industries v EC Commission* [1987] ECR 4487 paras 18–21.

[118] e.g. Case T-353/94 *Postbank NV v EC Commission* [1996] ECR II-921 para 87 states that '[. . .] in so far as disclosure of information about an undertaking's business activity could result in a serious harm to the same undertaking, such information constitutes business secrets [. . .]'. See also CD Ehlermann and BJ Drijber, 'Legal Protection of Enterprises: Administrative Procedure, in particular Access to Files and Confidentiality' [1996] ECLR 375 (382) noting that whilst the concept of business secrets may include very different types of information, its essential trait is the fact that its disclosure negatively affects the interests of the undertaking which owns the document in question.

[119] In different judgments, the Community Courts and the Commission have given examples of types of information constituting business secrets. See in particular Case T-9/89 *Hüls v EC Commission* [1992] ECR II-499 paras 127 and 294; Case C-7/95 P *John Deere* [1998] ECR I-3111 para 89; T-353/94 *Postbank v EC Commission* [1996] ECR II-9 para 86; or Case T-9/99 *HBF Holding v EC Commission* [2002] ECR II-1487 para 367 and *Polypropylene* [1986] OJ L230/1, regarding sales volumes, selling prices, deliveries, profitability thresholds, stock levels, cost components, or the commercial strategy.

[120] See Case C-310/93 P *BPB Industries Plc and British Gypsum Ltd v EC Commission II* [1995] ECR I-865 para 28. The Court referred in particular to the reports of verifications relating to inspections carried out in third-party undertakings.

[121] Commission Notice on the rules for access to the Commission file pursuant to Arts 81 and 82 EC [2005] OJ C325/7, para 18: '[. . .] Examples of information that may qualify as business secrets include: technical and/or financial information relating to an undertaking's knowhow, methods of assessing costs, production secrets and processes, supply sources,

Second, internal Commission documents are not part of the Commission file. If   **10.33**
the Commission chooses to make notes of meetings with any persons or undertakings, such documents constitute the Commission's own interpretation of
what transpired at the meeting (unless the person or undertaking has agreed the
minutes).[122] A particular case of internal documents is the Commission correspondence between it and the authorities of the Member States, are regarded
as confidential by virtue of Article 287 EC, since as a general rule they fall
within the exceptions to the principle of general access to documents provided
for in Regulation 1049/2001 of the European Parliament and of the Council
regarding public access to European Parliament, Council and Commission
documents.[123] The new Notice on Access to the File establishes as examples of
internal documents four different types of Commission's correspondence with
other public authorities:[124]

- correspondence between the Commission and the competition authorities of
  the Member States [NCAs], or between the latter, referring to Article 27(2) of
  Regulation 1/2003 and Article 15(2) of Regulation 773/2004;

---

quantities produced and sold, market shares, customer and distributor lists, marketing plans, cost
and price structure and sales strategy. [. . .]'. The Notice on Access to the File also sets out the
criteria according to which the Commission will accede to requests for confidential treatment
(paras 21–25).

[122] Commission Notice on the rules for access to the Commission file pursuant to Arts 81 and
82 EC, para 13. Studies commissioned as part of the investigation will be disclosed, para 11; see
qualification in para 14. In *Sorbates*, the Hearing Officers considered the notes of telephone
conversations between the parties and Commission officials are internal documents of the Commission and thus, in principle, non-accessible. Final Report of the Hearing Officer in *Sorbates*
[2003] OJ C173/5.

[123] [2001] OJ L145/43. The right of access to the file in antitrust and merger proceedings is
distinct from the general right of access to documents under Reg 1049/2001 which is subject to
different criteria and pursues a different purpose. Note that in Case T-2/03 *Verein für Konsumenteninformation (VKI) v EC Commission* [2005] OJ C155/14 the Court annulled a Commission
decision rejecting in its entirety access to the administrative file. In this case, an Austrian consumer association requested access to the administrative file of the proceedings in *Austrian Banks*
[2004] OJ L56/1. When the Commission rejected that request in its entirety, maintaining that
the documents were covered by the exception to the right of access, the *VKI* brought an action for
annulment of that rejection before the CFI. The CFI held that where the Commission receives
such a request it is required, in principle, to carry out a concrete, individual assessment of the
content of the documents referred to in the request. However, this does not mean that such an
examination is required in all circumstances. Since the purpose of the concrete, individual examination which the institution must in principle undertake in response to a request for access is to
enable the institution in question to assess, on the one hand, the extent to which an exception to
the right of access is applicable and, on the other, the possibility of partial access, such an
examination may not be necessary where, due to the particular circumstances of the individual
case, it is obvious that access must be refused or, on the contrary, granted. Only in exceptional
cases and only where the administrative burden entailed by a concrete, individual examination of
the documents proves to be particularly heavy, thereby exceeding the limits of what may reasonably be required, may derogation from that obligation to examine the documents be permissible.

[124] Commission Notice on the rules for access to the Commission file pursuant to Arts 81 and
82 EC [2005] OJ C325/7 para 15. This is not an exhaustive enumeration, but merely examples.

- correspondence between the Commission and other public authorities of the Member States;[125]
- correspondence between the Commission, the EFTA Surveillance Authority and public authorities of EFTA States;
- correspondence between the Commission and public authorities of non-member countries, including their competition authorities, in particular where the Community and a third country have concluded an agreement governing the confidentiality of the information exchanged.

10.34 However, the new Notice states that in certain exceptional circumstances access is granted to documents originating from Member States, or the EFTA Surveillance Authority of EFTA States, after deletion of any business secrets or other confidential information.[126]

10.35 Finally, 'other confidential information', such as details that might make it possible to identify the complainants (in the case of an informal complaint) or information disclosed on the condition that the Commission keeps it confidential.[127] The Commission seeks to ensure that documents of which disclosure might have serious consequences for the people who made them available to the Commission are not shown to people who might guess their origin and the identity of the Commission's informant.[128] That is not a purely hypothetical concern.[129] An important action to establish non-contractual

---

[125] See Order of the in Joined Cases T-134/94, T-136/94, T-137/94, T-138/94, T-141/94, T-145/94, T-147/94, T-148/94, T-151/94, T-156/94 and T-157/94 *NMH Stahlwerke and others v EC Commission* [1997] ECR II-2293 para 36, and Case T-65/89 *BPB Industries and British Gypsum v EC Commission* [1993] ECR II-389 para 33 (correspondence with Member States).

[126] See Commission Notice on the rules for access to the Commission file pursuant to Arts 81 and 82 EC [2005] OJ C325/7, para 16.

[127] Commission Notice on the rules for access to the Commission file pursuant to Arts 81 and 82 EC para 19 defines other confidential information as '[. . .] information other that business secrets, which may be considered as confidential, insofar as its disclosure would significantly harm a person or undertaking [. . .]'. Therefore the notion of other confidential information may include information that would enable the parties to identify complainants or other third parties where those wish to remain anonymous.

[128] As regards the correspondence and other documents provided by third-party undertakings during the Commission's investigations, the Court has stated that it is clear that third parties which submit such documents and consider that reprisals might be taken against them as a result can do so only if they know that account will be taken of their request for confidentiality. See Notice on the rules for access, para 19. Case C-310/93 P *BPB Industries Plc and British Gypsum Ltd v EC Commission II* [1995] ECR I-865 paras 29–35. In practice the Commission is extremely cautious about disclosing third-party documents in all the circumstances, even if it has not received a formal request for confidentiality.

[129] The Community Courts have pronounced upon this question both in cases of alleged abuse of a dominant position (Art 82 EC): Case T-65/89 *BPB Industries and British Gypsum v EC Commission* [1993] ECR II-389 para 33; and Case C-310/93P *BPB Industries and British Gypsum v EC Commission* [1995] ECR I-865 para 26; and in merger cases: Case T-221/95 *Endemol v EC Commission* [1999] ECR II-1299 para 69, and Case T-5/02 *Tetra Laval v EC Commission* [2002] ECR II-4381 paras 98 *et seq.*

liability[130] in which judgment was given against the Commission arose from just such a case of carelessness on the part of the Commission.[131] The category of other confidential information also includes military secrets.[132]

Subject to the three exceptions mentioned above, all the other documents, **10.36** whether imposing or removing obligations, and whether favourable or unfavourable, must be made available to the parties to the procedure.[133] Access to the file thus represents a necessary exception to the obligation of professional secrecy attaching to the Commission and its officials under Article 28 of Regulation 1/2003.[134] That obligation extends to all the documents in the file—even those that are disclosed to the undertakings—and not merely to those containing business secrets. Only the need to enable the parties to exercise their defence rights, in accordance with Article 27 of Regulation 1/2003, justifies an exception to the strict rules of confidentiality by which the Commission is bound.[135]

The limits on access to the file are even stricter for complainants before formal **10.37** rejection of their complaint and for complainants and other third parties involved in infringement procedures against other undertakings. This is due to the fact that the right of such persons to obtain information from the file derives not from the right to defend themselves but from the right to give their views on agreements or restrictive conduct in which they have a sufficient

---

[130] See the second para of Art 288 of the Treaty.

[131] See Case 145/83 *Stanley Adams v EC Commission* [1985] ECR 3539 para 44. Hoffmann-La Roche had been able to identify Adams as the informant as a result of carelessness by the Commission and although he had left the company he was arrested for economic espionage in Switzerland.

[132] Commission Notice on the rules for access to the Commission file pursuant to Arts 81 and 82 EC [2005] OJ C325/7, para 20.

[133] See Case T-7/89 *SA Hercules Chemicals NV v EC Commission* [1991] ECR II-1711 para 54. In that case, the Hercules company accused the Commission of selecting the documents disclosed in such a way as to prevent it from proving that it had not participated in the infringement. To the same effect, see the Joined Cases T-10/92 to T-12/92 and T-15/92 *Cimenteries and others v EC Commission* [1992] ECR II-2667 paras 38–41 (that judgment was preceded by the order of 23 March 1992 in Joined Cases T-10/92 to T-12/92 and T-15/92 R *Cimenteries v Commission III (interim measures)* [1992] ECR II-1571 and Case T-65/89 *BPB Industries and British Gypsum* [1993] ECR II-389 paras 29 *et seq*. The Court has implicitly rejected that the criterion for non-disclosure should not be whether the Commission relies on a document but whether the document is truly confidential. See Case C-310/93 P *BPB Industries and British Gypsum v EC Commission* [1995] ECR I-865 especially paras 23–24, in which the appellants criticize para 22 of the judgment in Case T-65/89 *BPB v EC Commission* I [1993] ECR II-389. For an action based on incomplete disclosure of the file to be successful, the undertakings should prove that the documents to which they have been granted access were insufficient, given that other documents would have been necessary for their defence. See Case T-145/89 *Baustahlgewebe GmbH v EC Commission* [1995] ECR II-987 para 35.

[134] See Case 53/85 *Akzo v EC Commission I* [1986] ECR 1965 paras 26–28.

[135] As is apparent, the concept of professional secrecy is different from and broader than that of business secrets. The first is an obligation attaching to the Community administration and the second is a right enjoyed by undertakings. The first covers the entire file whilst the second applies only to parts of it. This distinction has been, and will be, emphasized elsewhere in this book.

interest, provided for by Article 27(3) of Regulation 1/2003 and by Article 13 of Regulation 773/2004.

3. Access to the file and confidential documents

10.38 The application of the rules mentioned above might lead to disagreements between the participants in the procedure and the Commission as to whether or not access to certain documents may be granted. Since access to the file has been granted by systematically sending with the statement of objections all the disclosable documents (not only those mentioned in the statement) and the list of documents making up the file (more numerous than the disclosable documents) the most noteworthy source of disagreement is the view taken by some undertakings that they are entitled to see documents which the Commission has not shown to them. In such cases, the undertakings must make a reasoned request to the Commission. They must call on it to reconsider the list of disclosable documents and to send them a larger number of documents, or a specific document.[136]

10.39 A second example is where the undertaking to which the document belongs has raised no objection to its disclosure to other participants in the procedure but the Commission considers that it should not be shown to the other parties. The primary reason for preventing the information contained in a document from being divulged to other undertakings is that the Commission must take care to ensure in all cases that no restriction of competition comes into being between the parties. If the Commission considers that the information in question may have an adverse impact on competition between the undertakings, it is not only empowered but also obliged to ensure that no such veiled exchange of information between undertakings occurs.

10.40 A third example is the opposite case. The participating undertakings refuse to allow disclosure of documents which the Commission regards as essential to this phase of access to information, prior to the observations phase, in order to ensure that the procedure as a whole is conducted in the most appropriate—and productive—manner. The most significant case is where the documents or information in question establish an infringement of the Community competition rules. The Commission is then under an obligation to enable the parties to

---

[136] In the *Graphite Electrodes* case, SGL claimed before the CFI that the Commission should have communicated to it at least a list or a non-confidential summary of the documents containing secret or confidential matters. The Commission had provided it with a list of the documents that could be consulted, although SGL did not submit a request to this effect. In these circumstances, the Commission was not under an obligation to make available, of its own initiative, the lists and summaries. Joined Cases T-236/01, T-239/01, T-244/01 to T-246/01, T-251/01 and T-252/01 *Tokai Carbon Co Ltd and others v EC Commission* [2004] ECR II-1181 para 39; Joined Cases T-25/95, T-26/95, T-30/95 to T-39/95, T-42/95 to T-46/95, T-48/95, T-50/95 to T-65/95, T-68/95 to T-71/95, T-87/95, T-88/95, T-103/95 and T-104/95 *Cimenteries CBR SA and others v EC Commission* [2000] ECR II-491 para 383.

the procedure to determine the contents of the documents or information that demonstrate that the action taken by the Commission is well founded.

As stated, even where the Commission must observe its obligation to maintain **10.41** professional secrecy, laid down in Article 28 of Regulation 1/2003, that obligation must be interpreted without prejudice to the right of the parties to be heard in accordance with Article 27.[137] The Commission is thus obliged to disclose the essential parts of the file to the participants in the procedure so that they are in a position to give their views. If the Commission did not show certain evidence to the undertakings to which the procedure relates, it must disregard it for the purposes of its decision. In its judgment in *AEG v EC Commission*,[138] the ECJ held that the Commission was precluded from using as evidence in its decision a document which it had not disclosed to *AEG* for reasons of professional secrecy and that it had no probative value in the proceedings before the Court. The Commission will decide whether or not a document contains business secrets[139] It should be noted, however, that the Commission is not authorized to disclose documents containing such secrets and that if it declines to disclose documents to the undertakings involved, its decision will not, otherwise than in exceptional cases (as, for example, where its refusal is patently unlawful) be appealable, although if, as a result, the rights of the defence have been encroached upon, the Commission's final decision could be annulled by the CFI.[140] In this respect, where an infringement of the right of access to the file has taken place during administrative proceedings, such an infringement is not remedied by the mere fact that access was made possible during the judicial proceedings relating to an action in which annulment of the contested decision is sought. Where access has been granted at that stage, the undertaking concerned does not have to show that, if it had had access to the non-disclosed documents, the Commission decision would have been different in content, but only that it would have been able to use those documents for its defence.[141]

However, it must be stated that not every failure to disclose documents will lead **10.42** to an outright annulment of the Commission's decision, as this will rest on the

---

[137] See Case 85/76 *Hoffmann-La Roche v EC Commission* [1979] ECR 461 para 13.

[138] Case 107/82 *AEG v EC Commission* [1983] ECR 3151 paras 22–25.

[139] See Case 53/85 *Akzo v EC Commission I* [1986] ECR 1965 paras 29 and 30. As it has been already explained in ch 9 'Penalties and Confidentiality' para 9.33, provision is made for such matters to be settled by the Hearing Officer, by delegation from the Commission, acting through the member of the Commission responsible for competition.

[140] Case 60/81 *IBM v EC Commission* [1981] ECR 2639 para 23: see also Joined Cases T-10/92 to T-12/92 and T-15/92 *Cimenteries and others v EC Commission* [1992] ECR II-2667 paras 42, 47, 48, and 53. The concept of 'exceptional circumstances' in which such decisions may be amenable to judicial recourse may give rise to room for interpretation in practice.

[141] See Joined Cases C-238/99 P, C-244/99 P, C-245/99 P, C-247/99 P, C-250/99 P to C-252/99 P and C-254/99 P *Limburgse Vinyl Maatschappij (LVM) and others v EC Commission* [2002] ECR I-8375 para 318, and Case T-67/01 *JCB Service v EC Commission* [2004] ECR II-49 para 64.

content, weight, and significance of the non-disclosed documents and the objections raised by the Commission in the particular case. In this line, the distinction between incriminatory and exculpatory documents established by the Court[142] shows that non-disclosure of certain documents may not have any influence on defence rights. Thus, for instance, if an incriminatory document has not been disclosed, the undertaking concerned cannot allege a breach of its rights of defence when there are other documents disclosed on which the Commission has equally relied upon to base an infringement.[143]

10.43   The Community Courts appear to have established a quasi-absolute prohibition of disclosing the business secrets of undertakings.[144] The question arises, however, what would happen in the event of a conflict between the principle of the protection of business secrets and the principle of upholding defence rights.[145] Since undertakings are entitled to obtain information regarding both favourable and unfavourable documents, and since the documents in a case may—and in fact usually do—belong to third-party undertakings involved in the same infringement procedure, situations may arise in which a document discharging one of the undertakings previously regarded as implicated in an infringement contains genuine business secrets of third-party undertakings. In such cases, the Commission would probably endeavour, first, to resolve the conflict indirectly (authorized summaries, omission of the part of the document containing business secrets). If that proved impossible, and in light of the possibility of contravening a general principle of Community law, it is logical to conclude that the Commission would first allow the undertakings involved to make observations,

---

[142] Joined Cases T-25/95, T-26/95, T-30/95 to T-39/95, T-42/95 to T-46/95, T-48/95, T-50/95 to T-65/95, T-68/95 to T-71/95, T-87/95, T-88/95, T-103/95 and T-104/95 *Cimenteries CBR SA and others v EC Commission* [2000] ECR II-491 paras 248 and 284. See also Commission Notice on rules for access to the Commission file [2005] OJ C325/7 para 24.

[143] However, in the same case ('Cement Cartel'), certain applicants succeeded in demonstrating that documents which had not been disclosed to them shed a different light on the documentary evidence which had been used by the Commission to prove their participation in the cartel. The CFI was of the view that there was a chance that the outcome could have been different if they had access to these documents. The Court annulled therefore the decision as regards those applicants (e.g. Joined Cases T-25/95 etc *Cimenteries CBR SA and others v EC Commission* [2000] ECR II-491 paras 2205–2212, 2224, 2225, 2284–2290 etc).

[144] See Case 53/85 *Akzo v EC Commission I* [1986] ECR 1965 para 28. This interpretation appears to be confirmed both by Joined Cases T-10–12 and T-15/92 *Cimenteries and others v EC Commission III* [1992] ECR II-2667 and by Case C-36/92 P *Samenverkende Elektriciteitsproduktiebedrijven (SEP) v EC Commission II* [1994] ECR I-1911 paras 28 *et seq*.

[145] It should be noted that a conflict would arise in practice only if the Commission accepted that the document contained business secrets and believed that not disclosing it to the undertakings implicated in the infringement might adversely affect the latter's defence rights. If the Commission considered that the documents did not contain business secrets, it would adopt a decision under the *Akzo procedure* (Case 53/85 [1986] ECR 1965) so that the CFI could decide as to the confidentiality of the document before it was disclosed to the undertakings involved.

and then would weigh up their respective and opposing interests: the undertakings accused would rely on their defence rights whereas third-party undertakings would claim that their business secrets should not be disclosed. Finally, the Commission would have to decide in favour of one or the other, giving both the opportunity to contest its decision before the CFI, without disclosing the document to the undertakings involved until a final decision has been given by the CFI or the ECJ. A balance must be established between safeguarding defence rights and the right to protection of business secrets.[146] In *Belgian Architects Associations*, the danger of retaliation led the Hearing Officer to refuse access to a document in the file which would have allowed the parties to identify the informant.[147] It seems, nevertheless, that there will be cases where the Commission will have to disclose confidential information (business secrets included) in order to support its case. This seems to be the consequence of the terms of new Article 27(2) of Regulation 1/2003 and 15(3) of Regulation 773/2004, which provide that the Commission will be able to disclose or use the information necessary to prove an infringement of Articles 81 and 82 EC.

Finally, a reference should be made to the specific cases in which the parties to an antitrust procedure before the Commission have been capable of exchanging information and documents among themselves. This may happen more easily depending on the number of parties involved. In *Soda Ash* some documents had been in fact exchanged between the parties. However, this possibility of 'self-help by the undertakings concerned,'[148] which may lend itself also to problems under Article 81(1) EC,[149] may not relieve the Commission from fully complying with its obligations regarding access to the file. The fact that the parties could have access to certain documents by means of cooperation and exchanges with other parties to the proceedings cannot be an argument for lessening the Commission's duty to ensure that the parties' defence rights are respected.[150] It

10.44

---

[146] See Case T-36/91 *ICI v EC Commission* [1995] ECR II-1847 para 98.

[147] Final report of the hearing officer in Case COMP/38.549—*Architects' Association* [2005] OJ C3/4. The anonymity of a person who supplies information must be respected if that person so requests and may otherwise be open to reprisals (Case 143/83 *Stanley Adams v EC Commission* [1985] ECR 3539 para 34.

[148] CS Kerse and N Khan *EC Antitrust Procedure* (5th edn, 2005) para 4–034.

[149] As stated, in certain cases such an exchange of information may even constitute an infringement of the competition rules.

[150] Case T-23/99 *LR af 1998 v EC Commission* [2002] ECR II-1705 para 184: '[. . .] by suggesting that the undertakings concerned facilitate access to the documents by exchanging documents among themselves, and at the same time itself ensuring the right of access to the entire investigation file, the Commission had due regard to the requirements laid down in the case-law of the Court of First Instance, namely that an exchange of documents between the undertakings cannot in any event eliminate the Commission's own duty to ensure that during the investigation of an infringement of competition law the rights of defence of the undertakings concerned are respected.' See also Case T-30/91 *Solvay v EC Commission* [1995] ECR II-1775 paras 85–86, and Case T-36/91 *ICI v EC Commission* [1995] ECR II-1847 paras 95–96.

cannot be expected in all circumstances that such an exchange will take place, particularly when the parties involved are competitors.

4. Forms of access to the file

10.45 In antitrust proceedings[151] access to the file will be granted upon request and, normally, on a single occasion, following the notification of the Commission's objections to the parties. However, a party will be granted access to documents received after notification of the objections at later stages of the administrative procedure, prior to the adoption of a formal decision, where such documents may constitute new evidence pertaining to the allegations against that party in the Commission's statement of objections. The CFI has stated that complainants do not have the same rights as the parties under investigation.[152] Consequently, complainants cannot claim a right of access to the file as established for the parties.[153]

10.46 As a general rule, disclosure is now effected by means of one or more CD-ROMs while sending the statement of objections (in the case of undertakings implicated in an infringement), while sending an 'Article 7 letter'[154] or by means of a letter in which, having recognized that the complainants have a sufficient interest in giving their views in an infringement procedure against other undertakings, the Commission invites the complainants or other interested third parties to submit observations.[155] However, the possibility cannot be excluded that, where it is advisable to do so in the circumstances of the case, the Commission might resort to the procedure of convening the undertakings and their lawyers to a meeting at the offices of DG COMP to familiarize themselves with the administrative file.

---

[151] In merger proceedings the notifying parties will be given access to the Commission's file upon request at every stage of the procedure following the notification of the Commission's objections up to the Advisory Committee consultation process. Access to the file must be given as well, upon request, to other involved parties who have been informed of the objections in so far as this is necessary for the purposes of preparing their comments. See ch 17 'Procedures' paras 17.16 *et seq.*

[152] See Case T-17/93 *Matra-Hachette SA v EC Commission* [1994] ECR II-595 para 34. The Court ruled that the rights of third parties, as laid down by Art 19 of Reg 17 (now replaced by Art 27 of Reg 1/2003), were limited to the right to participate in the administrative procedure.

[153] Commission Notice on the rules for access to the Commission file pursuant to Arts 81 and 82 EC [2005] OJ C325/7, paras 3 and 7.

[154] Under Reg 17 it was called 'Article 6 letter' [of Reg 99/63].

[155] The Commission will also forward the non-confidential documents which it considers appropriate to those persons whom, under Art 13(3) of Reg 773/2004 it has invited to the administrative hearings on its own initiative.

C. The Reply to the Statement of Objections

1. Introduction

Pursuant to Article 27(1) of Regulation 1/2003, the Commission is required to **10.47**
give the undertakings and associations of undertakings concerned—those which
are implicated in the alleged infringements to which the procedure relates—the
opportunity of making known their views on the objections against them. This
is a fundamental right of the parties to be heard. However, there is no legal
obligation to reply to the Commission's statement of objections. Undertakings
are entitled in their written comments to set out 'all facts relevant [. . .] to their
defence. [. . .]'[156] This means that in principle the undertaking can include in its
defence such factual, legal, and economic arguments and material as it considers
necessary. Where it is necessary to rectify any factual information supplied
previously to the Commission, the correction should be explained in detail.[157]
As regards the question of whether a party is able to contest on appeal to the
Community courts something which it has admitted during the administrative
procedure, the CFI has ruled that this hinges on the nature of the admission. In
Tokai Carbon, the CFI reiterated that where a party does not expressly acknowledge the facts during the administrative proceedings, the Commission must
prove the facts and the undertaking is free to put forward, in the procedure
before the Court, any plea in its defence which it deems appropriate.[158] However, this would not be the case where the undertaking expressly, clearly, and
specifically acknowledges the facts: where it expressly admits during the
administrative procedure the substantive truth of the facts which the Commission alleges against it in the statement of objections, those facts must thereafter
be regarded as established and the undertaking stopped in principle from
disputing them during the court proceedings.[159]

The principle of good administration requires that parties must be given a **10.48**
reasonable time to respond bearing in mind both the time required for

---

[156] Art 10(3) of Reg 774/2003. In practice, only a very limited number of defendants prefer
not to make use of their right to be heard in writing and this is usually in the context of statements
of objections addressed to several defendants. S Durande and K Williams, 'The practical impact
of the exercise of the right to be heard: A special focus on the effect of Oral Hearings and the
role of the Hearing Officers' EC Competition Newsletter, Number 2, Summer 2005, 22–28
(23).

[157] Case T-334/94 *Sarrio SA v EC Commission* [1998] II-1439 paras 380–381.

[158] Joined Cases T-236/01, T-239/01, T-244/01 to T-246/01, T-251/01 and T-252/01 *Tokai
Carbon and others v EC Commission* [2004] ECR II-1181 para 108; Case C-297/98 P *SCA
Holding v EC Commission* [2000] ECR I-10101 para 37.

[159] Joined Cases T-236/01, T-239/01, T-244/01 to T-246/01, T-251/01 and T-252/01 *Tokai
Carbon and others v EC Commission* [2004] ECR II-1181 para 108.

preparation of comments and the urgency of the case, for example, where there is a complainant who may be suffering immediate loss as a result of the alleged breach of Articles 81 and 82 EC.[160] The Community Courts have held, in a number of cases involving voluminous documentation, that a two-month period was sufficient for submission of observations on the statement of objections.[161] The minimum time-limit allowed is four weeks, except where interim measures are being proposed when it may be reduced to one week.[162] The Hearing Officer can extend the time-limit where the parties make a reasoned request.[163]

10.49 Article 27(3), first sentence of Regulation 1/2003 makes provision for the participation of other persons at this stage of proceedings stating that where the Commission or the competent authorities of the Member States consider it necessary, other natural or legal persons may also express their views. The Commission and the Member States (acting, by implication, through the Commission, which has the conduct of the procedure) are thus empowered to invite persons other than the allegedly infringing undertakings to submit observations on the statement of objections. The observations of third parties— which for these purposes include the complainants, who are parties to the procedure only in a loose sense—may also be allowed by the Commission at their request. If the third parties demonstrate a sufficient interest, the Commission cannot prevent them from submitting observations. Its discretion to invite third parties to submit observations then becomes an obligation. Third parties with a sufficient interest who ask to be heard must, therefore, be heard (second sentence of Article 27(3)).

10.50 Observations by the parties are submitted in two quite separate stages, only one of which is mandatory and occurs in all cases. The mandatory phase is that of

---

[160] Note also that the sending of the relevant requests should not impose a disproportionate burden on the parties. In Case T-191/98 *Atlantic Container and others v EC Commission* [2003] ECR II-3275 para 418: '[. . .] The sending of a large number of requests for information after the adoption of the statement of objections may affect the effective exercise by the undertakings concerned of their right to comment on the complaints made against them. According to the case-law [. . .] it is for the Commission to ensure that the administrative procedure is conducted with due care. It has been held that the Commission's requests for information must comply with the principle of proportionality and the obligation imposed on an undertaking to supply information should not be a burden on that undertaking which is disproportionate to the needs of the inquiry [. . .]'.

[161] Case 27/76 *United Brands v EC Commission* [1978] ECR 207 paras 272 and 273; Joined Cases 40/73 to 48/73, 50/73, 54/73 to 56/73, 111/73, 113/73 and 114/73 *Suiker Unie and others v EC Commission* [1975] ECR 1663 paras 94–99; see also Case T-9/99 *HFB v EC Commission* [2002] ECR II-1487 para 344 (fourteen weeks). Regarding the guidelines used by the Commission in this context see also CS Kerse and N Khan, *EC Antitrust Procedure* (5th edn, 2005) para 4–055.

[162] Art 17(2) in conjunction with Art 10(2) of Reg 773/2004.

[163] Art 10 of the Mandate of the Hearing Officer. e.g. Final Report of the Hearing Officer in *Deutsche Telekom* [2003] OJ C288/2 and in *Compagnie Maritime Belge* [2005] OJ C162/2 (four-week extension due to Easter holiday).

the written observations, which may be followed by an oral phase. As stated earlier, Community competition procedures are principally written procedures. However, under Article 12 of Regulation 773/2004 the Commission must give the parties to whom it has addressed a statement of objections the opportunity to develop their arguments at an oral hearing, if they so request in their written submissions. In effect, pursuant to the same provision, the first precondition for a hearing is a request to that effect from the interested parties (undertakings involved, complainants, or third parties), who must ensure that their wish to be heard *viva voce* is put forward in their written observations on the statement of objections (in other words, during the written phase). It is essential for the undertakings—and, by extension, the other interested parties—to reply in writing to the objections within the time-limit laid down by the Commission for them to be entitled to be heard orally.[164] Third parties, natural, or legal persons that apply to be heard, have to show sufficient interest. The Commission will set a time limit within which they may make known their views in writing or orally if they request so.

Apart from the *right* of the undertakings and interested parties to be heard orally **10.51** in certain cases, the Commission has the *power* to allow any other person—not merely the undertakings involved, the complainants, or third parties that show sufficient interest who have made a request to that effect—the opportunity to give their views in writing or to attend and express their views at the oral hearing (Article 13(3) of Regulation 773/2004 in conjunction with the first sentence of Article 27(3) of Regulation 1/2003). In such cases, it is not necessary for such persons to submit written observations before the oral phase. Normally, the Commission exercises this power only when a hearing has already been arranged at the request of the interested parties.[165] There may be doubts as to whether the persons recognized by the Commission as having a sufficient interest are always required to submit written observations in order to take part in the administrative hearings, even where the Commission considers their participation necessary and invites them on its own initiative, under Article 13(2) of Regulation 773/2004. It is clear that it is advantageous for the undertakings involved to know in advance what will be stated by the other participants in the hearings. However, it is not similarly clear that the absence of an advance written text in which the participants give details of the oral observations they

---

[164] See Joined Cases 209/78 and 218/78 *Van Landewyck v EC Commission (FEDETAB)* [1980] ECR 3125 para 24.

[165] If it allows third parties to submit written observations, the Commission must allow them to consult the necessary documents in the file to enable them to support their views adequately—in other words, it must disclose the file to them, on the more limited basis provided for in the case of third parties.

will make[166] contravenes undertakings' defence rights, in view of the fact that, if they contain new facts or accusations, the Commission will be obliged either to give the undertakings an opportunity to express their views separately on the observations of third parties—if they had not already had an opportunity to do so adequately at the hearings[167]—or to disregard the information concerned or else to use it in a supplementary statement of objections.[168]

2. Written observations

10.52　With respect to written observations, the position can be summarized as follows:

(i)　The Commission is always automatically obliged to allow them to be submitted by the undertakings more directly involved: parties and complainants.

(ii)　The Commission is under a conditional obligation to allow them to be submitted by third parties (if they ask to do so and demonstrate a sufficient interest).

(iii)　The Commission may also allow any person to submit written observations if it considers it necessary.

10.53　The Commission may reject applications by third parties to submit observations, on the grounds that they lack a sufficient interest. However, the Commission must inform them in advance of its reasons for rejecting their observations and allow them to make comments in this regard. The Commission must provide these third parties with sufficient information to enable them to express their views adequately, and only after such views have been expressed may the Commission adopt a decision disallowing their participation.[169]

10.54　The written reply submitted by the undertakings within the period allowed by the Commission becomes part of the file and serves as a reference for the parties in the subsequent stages of the administrative procedure and, if appropriate, for proceedings before the CFI after the administrative phase is completed. The

---

[166] Under Art 11(3) of the Hearing Officer's Mandate, ([2001] OJ L162/21), the Hearing Officer may ask for prior written notification of the essential contents of the intended statement of persons whom the parties invited to the hearing propose give evidence.

[167] The Commission would invite the undertakings to reply in writing to the observations of the third parties if the latter had put forward new facts or evidence not already relied on by the Commission, without making further objections.

[168] If they disclosed the existence of new objections and the Commission wished to use them in the same procedure.

[169] The Hearing Officer decides whether or not to admit third parties to the written procedure, after consulting the director responsible. The Hearing Officer will inform in writing to third parties where he or she disallows their participation in written procedures due to the lack of sufficient interest.

parties' observations are notified to the competition authorities in the Member States and the relevant Commission departments. The Hearing Officer[170] and the Legal Service also receive a copy of the document containing them.

3. Oral observations

As regards oral observations:

10.55

(i) The Commission is required to arrange for them to be made if the undertaking to whom the statement of objections has been addressed requests an oral hearing (Article 12 of Regulation 773/2004).[171]

(ii) The Commission may discretionally arrange for them to be made when those who ask to make them—whether they be complainants or other third parties—show a sufficient interest in giving their views orally, over and above their interest in submitting written observations (Article 13(2) of Regulation 773/2004).

(iii) The right to make oral observations is conditional upon previous submission of written observations, without which the Commission may decline to hear oral submissions from the person concerned.

(iv) The Commission may in any case invite any person to make oral observations, without it being necessary in such cases for written observations to be submitted beforehand (Article 13(3) of Regulation 773/2004).

When an application to be heard orally has been made in the applicant's written comments on letters which the Commission has addressed to him,[172] the Hearing Officer, after consulting the director responsible, will decide

---

[170] See as regards the tasks of the Hearing Officer para 10.09 above.

[171] S Durande and K Williams, 'The practical impact of the exercise of the right to be heard: A special focus on the effect of Oral Hearings and the role of the Hearing Officers' EC Competition Newsletter, Number 2, Summer 2005, 22–28 (23) note that defendants are often reluctant to make use of their right to express their views at an oral hearing. They often fear that oral hearings would give third parties an opportunity to present their views and that secondly, given that the Commission is unlikely to change its opinion, they would unlikely reverse the orientation of the case. Accordingly, the general perception would be that the value of those hearings is at best limited. However, Durande and Williams (currently, the two Hearing Officers) take the view that oral hearings would provide defendants with the widest possible audience they can reach in the Commission's proceedings. More importantly, the strength of the Commission's case would be tested and the really significant issues could be more easily identified than in the written comments. It would not be too bold to argue that oral hearings circumscribe the genuine object of the debate. Experience would show that in a number of instances the orientations of cases have been altered quite dramatically subsequent to the explanations given in oral hearings, even leading the Commission to drop entirely its objections, i.e. to abandon the case.

[172] The letters referred to are those quoted in Art 7(2) of the Hearing Officer Mandate: (a) communicating a statement of objections; (b) inviting the written comments of a third party having shown sufficient interest to be heard; (c) informing a complainant that in the Commission's view there are insufficient grounds for finding an infringement and inviting him to submit any further written comments.

whether the applicant—undertakings involved, complainant, or third party—has a sufficient interest in the holding of administrative hearings (Article 7(3) of the Hearing Officer's Mandate).

10.57 The procedure for hearings is governed by Regulation 773/2004, in particular, Articles 12–14 thereof, and the Commission Decision on the Mandate of the Hearing Officer. The hearing always takes place after the end of the period set for a reply to the statement of objections and before a meeting of the Advisory Committee on Restrictive Practices and Dominant Positions is convened.[173]

Preparation for the hearing

10.58 Whenever it is foreseeable that the parties will ask for and be granted a hearing, the Commission will, at the outset, indicate in the statement of objections an approximate date for it to be held.[174] The final date, determined by the Hearing Officer after consulting the director responsible,[175] will be notified later, but always allowing sufficient time to make due preparations for the hearing. However, the Commission is not obliged to observe a minimum period between the date of the summons and that of the hearing, by contrast with the position regarding convening of the Advisory Committee.[176] Undertakings may request that the date for the hearing be set back, but the Commission is rather less compliant in such cases than where a similar request is made regarding the period for replying to the statement of objections. The physical arrangements for the hearing are so complex that there is little room for a flexible approach, and only in rare cases will the Commission agree to a deferment. For that reason, if, having received the statement of objections, undertakings foresee some difficulty in attending the hearing on the dates suggested provisionally, or on dates on which it is foreseeable that hearings might be held, it is advisable for them to inform the Hearing Officer and suggest a time convenient to them before the dates are fixed definitively. The Hearing Officer will endeavour as far as possible to strike a balance between the interests of the undertakings and the need to ensure the proper conduct of the procedure.

---

[173] Regarding this Committee, see ch 3 'National competition authorities' paras 3.45 *et seq.*

[174] There seems to be somehow contradictory information on the number of cases in which the parties requested an oral meeting. The Commisison reported in 2003, the vast majority of undertakings took advantage of their right to defend their case in an oral hearing. Only approximately one-fifth of the addressees of a statement of objections would have waived this right to an oral hearing. XXXIII Report on Competition Policy [2003] para 23. S Durande and K Williams, 'The practical impact of the exercise of the right to be heard: A special focus on the effect of Oral Hearings and the role of the Hearing Officers' EC Competition Newsletter, Number 2, Summer 2005, 22–28 (23) note, however, while only a very limited number of defendants preferred not to make use of their right to be heard in writing, in ten of those thirty-two cases in which statement of objections were issued, all the defendants waived their right to an oral hearing.

[175] See Art 12(1) of the Mandate of the Hearing Officer [2001] OJ L162/21.

[176] See Art 10(5) of Reg 17.

As stated earlier, the Commission does not usually query the interest of the **10.59** undertakings implicated in the infringement, even where it has no intention of imposing a fine on them. As regards other interested parties not directly implicated in an infringement, the Commission likewise does not query the interest of the complainants (Article 27(1) of Regulation 1/2003 read in conjunction with Article 6(2) of Regulation 773/2004) or even that of other persons who might contribute new information or arguments to the procedure.[177] As the Commission itself is empowered to seek their assistance in hearings (Article 13(3) of Regulation 773/2004), it is unlikely that the Commission will decline to receive written or oral observations from those who ask to submit them.[178] Although according to Article 13(1) of Regulation 773/2004, a 'sufficient interest' is to be shown by natural or legal persons other than complainants, paragraph (3) of the same provision allows the Commission to hear any other person to express its views, thus allowing the possibility of summoning persons capable of providing useful and relevant information even in the absence of a 'sufficient interest'.

In practice, when the undertakings wish to have evidence given by experts or **10.60** witnesses—whose status in this administrative procedure is hybrid and is not precisely the same as in civil proceedings in the Member States—they should mention the fact in their written reply to the statement of objections. The undertakings may annex to their submissions such opinions or reports as they consider appropriate, send them to the Commission after lodging their reply but before the hearing, or hand them to the Commission at the start of the hearing. When information of this kind from experts or special witnesses is to be given orally—regardless of whether or not it has been submitted in writing earlier or at the same time—the Hearing Officer must be given advance notice of that fact by the undertakings. The Hearing Officer may then ask for a summary of the draft of the contribution to be made by such persons, if he has not previously received one from the undertakings (which will enable him to consider whether or not their participation is relevant), and define the limits of that contribution in the context of the hearing. The preparatory meetings

---

[177] See CS Kerse and N Khan, *EC Antitrust Procedure* (5th edn, 2005) para 194.
[178] Nevertheless, the Commission has on occasions not allowed persons who had previously submitted written observations to take part in a hearing. See in that connection Case 8/71 *Deutscher Komponisterverband v EC Commission* [1971] ECR 705. In that case, the Court dismissed an action brought on the basis of Art 232 EC—for failure to act—against the Commission for not holding a hearing and inviting the German Composers' Association to such a hearing in the *GEMA I* [1971] OJ L134/15. The German Composers' Association had previously submitted written observations in that case. The Court took the view that the Commission had in fact acted under Art 5 of Reg 99/63 by sending a letter to the Association giving it a period of one month to submit written observations, and that it was therefore inappropriate to uphold the action for failure to act.

mentioned below are used for this purpose.[179] The Commission does not usually object to the participation of such persons in hearings and in the rare cases in which it limits the duration of the statements or determines their subject-matter, its intention is principally to concentrate discussions within a limited time-frame; hearings do not usually last more than two or three days and a large number of people have to take part in them.[180] That said, the Commission has no alternative in most cases but to accede to the undertakings' wishes. The hearings are held at the request of the undertakings and it is the undertakings which have to make the observations. Other contributions to hearings, both from the Commission and from the complainants, are less important.

10.61　As regards the category of persons whose involvement is considered useful or necessary by the Commission in accordance with Article 13(2) of Regulation 773/2004, it may also include other experts or witnesses whose participation is desired by the Commission. The summonses to hearings are sent by the Commission to the persons named by the undertakings for that purpose. They may contain certain information from the Hearing Officer concerning the central issues and the matters about which the Commission would like to hear in more detail from the undertakings. The competition authorities of the Member States are invited to attend the hearing, pursuant to Article 14(3) of Regulation 773/ 2004. Officials and civil servants of other authorities of the Member States may also be invited to the hearing. The summonses sent to undertakings are, strictly speaking, nothing more than invitations. The position cannot be otherwise since it is incumbent on those persons who have a sufficient interest to request a hearing, which would not take place if not requested. In that respect, hearings are a step in the procedure to which the right may be waived.

10.62　The Commission cannot compel the undertakings or specific officers of them to attend, nor may it impose any penalty for non-attendance. According to Article 14(4) and (5) of Regulation 773/2004, '[p]ersons invited to attend shall either appear in person or be represented by legal representatives or by representatives authorised by their constitution as appropriate. Undertakings and associations of undertakings may also be represented by a duly authorised agent appointed from among their permanent staff. Persons heard by the Commission may be assisted by their lawyers or other qualified persons admitted by the Hearing Officer.' This provision corresponds to former Article 12(1) and (2) of Regulation 2842/1998 on the hearing of parties. It must be interpreted primarily as meaning that it allows the undertakings involved to be represented at the

---

[179] See Art 11 of the Mandate of the Hearing Officer.

[180] In addition to the undertakings and the Commission, the representatives of the Member States, and sometimes the complainants, interested third parties, and witnesses or experts will also participate.

hearings both by their management or by persons whose offices normally enable them to represent the undertakings in all kinds of proceedings, and by members of their staff who have been appointed and empowered by the undertakings specifically in order to participate in this stage of the procedure. The 'duly authorised agent' must therefore have sufficient powers to speak on behalf of the undertaking or undertakings represented by him at hearings. The requirement that the persons representing the undertakings which are to present observations are to be members of their permanent staff is intended to make the hearings more fruitful as regards the information or clarifications which may be given to the Commission during them. The advantage of having representatives directly involved in the management of the undertakings lies in the fact that they may have more detailed or far-reaching knowledge than the lawyers or other legal advisers, of technical details or economic or commercial information about the products and services concerned and their markets.

Secondly, Regulation 773/2004 provides for the participation of lawyers, or **10.63** 'other qualified persons', who may assist those who are to be heard (Article 14(5) of Regulation 773/2004). As regards the participation of lawyers and other legal specialists, the criteria for appearing before the Commission are the same as those for appearing before the ECJ, as set out in Article 19 of the Protocol on the Statute of the Court of Justice.[181] By requiring that the 'advisers' or 'lawyers' be 'entitled to practise before a court of a Member State', the Protocol and Regulation 773/2004 itself leave the matter to national legislation. Membership of a Bar—(*inscription au barreau*)—or Law Society in any part of the Community territory may prove, therefore, to be an essential precondition for graduates or those with higher degrees in law to be able to take part in DG COMP procedures as lawyers or legal advisers. The Commission, however, interprets this rule very flexibly. Thus, lawyers of non-member countries may

---

[181] Treaty establishing the European Community (Nice consolidated version) Protocol on the Statute of the Court of Justice [2002] OJ C325/167, Art 19: 'The Member States and the institutions of the Communities shall be represented before the Court by an agent appointed for each case; the agent may be assisted by an adviser or by a lawyer.

The States, other than the Member States, which are parties to the Agreement on the European Economic Area and also the EFTA Surveillance Authority referred to in that Agreement shall be represented in same manner. Other parties must be represented by a lawyer.

Only a lawyer authorised to practise before a court of a Member State or of another State which is a party to the Agreement on the European Economic Area may represent or assist a party before the Court.

Such agents, advisers and lawyers shall, when they appear before the Court, enjoy the rights and immunities necessary to the independent exercise of their duties, under conditions laid down in the Rules of Procedure.

As regards such advisers and lawyers who appear before it, the Court shall have the powers normally accorded to courts of law, under conditions laid down in the Rules of Procedure.

University teachers being nationals of a Member State whose law accords them a right of audience shall have the same rights before the Court as are accorded by this article to lawyers.'

generally take part in hearings, even where there is no reciprocal arrangement and the countries of origin of those lawyers do not allow Community lawyers to take part in similar proceedings. The lawyers or legal advisers should not in such cases be regarded as representatives of the undertakings, except for the purpose of defending them in legal proceedings. If the undertakings were represented solely by independent lawyers, that would—quite apart from matters relating to rights of the defence—to some extent frustrate the Commission's expectations regarding hearings, at which—as will be seen below—the Commission has an opportunity of putting questions to the representatives of the undertakings, and would render the procedure less helpful to it. The phrase 'other qualified persons' also seems to leave the door open for non-lawyers to defend the interests of participants in hearings.[182]

10.64 It is the prerogative of the Hearing Officer in certain cases to request the attendance of undertakings to a meeting prior to the hearing in order to focus the debate on the aspects of the case which in its view call for most attention.[183] Such meetings are attended both by the undertakings and by the officials of DG COMP who are directly conducting the case. They also provide an opportunity to make preparations as to how exactly the hearing is to be conducted. Thus, for example, arrangements may be made regarding the order in which the participants are to be heard in those cases where several wish to put their views forward (for example, several undertakings involved in the procedure and several complainants and third parties); the arrangements for the participation of persons involved in the defence of the undertakings (usually witnesses and experts) in accordance with Article 10(3) of Regulation 773/2004, the maximum time allowed for speaking according to the time available, and so on.

The conduct of the hearing

10.65 Administrative hearings are not public.[184] Only persons duly summoned to attend may do so. Neither of the procedural Regulations, nor even the Decision on hearings, lays down detailed rules for the manner in which they are to be conducted. In the event, the Commission's consistent administrative practice has led to the emergence of a general pattern that, with slight variations, is followed by the Community administration in all cases. The Commission provides simultaneous interpretation into all the Community languages that are to be used by the participants. It is quite normal for hearings to involve persons from several Member States, who in general express themselves in their own

---

[182] This could give rise to an unusual problem of professional encroachment if it were intended that such persons should act mainly in order to provide legal defence.
[183] Art 11(2) of the Hearing Officer's Mandate.
[184] Art 14(6) Reg 773/2004.

languages.[185] Undertakings established in non-Community countries have to follow the proceedings in one of the Community languages. In view of the limited time available, and having regard to the number of participants, the Hearing Officer will grant each a period in which to present oral observations. The speaking time is always flexible, the intention being that no participant should not be heard as a result of insufficient time. The speaking time varies according to the nature of the participants. In most cases, the presentation of oral observations by the undertakings involved in the procedure—the period granted to them is usually the longest—does not take longer than three hours.

The Hearing Officer opens the session and calls on the investigating official or **10.66** the head of the Unit dealing with the case to speak. The DG COMP officials briefly set out the facts and state the alleged infringement. The summary thus given is useful because it allows the undertakings to focus discussion on the points which most concern, or are of most interest to, the Commission. Furthermore, the Commission's account may give the undertakings a first inkling of how their written arguments (reply to the statement of objections) have been received by the Commission. The undertakings involved then present their observations. These do not necessarily have to be limited to what has already been touched on in writing, but may cover new points not previously raised. Since there is little point in repeating aloud arguments already set out in the reply to the statement of objections, the Commission has made it clear that the advantage of a hearing lies in the opportunity thereby given to undertakings to clarify anything not properly dealt with in their written submissions and to lay down the main lines of their defence. This is the appropriate time for the persons who are able to confirm the facts set out in the reply to the statement of objections (the above-mentioned *sui generis* witnesses or experts) to speak. If its contribution has been properly prepared, the Commission will already have available at the start of the meeting a sufficient number of copies of the report, opinion or evidence[186] which will be appended to the file.[187] This does not mean that such documents cannot be produced at the hearing. In this way, the oral observations can concentrate on the most important specific details, or on the general outlines of the document—merely repetitive reading thus being avoided. Any members of the management of the undertaking who wish to do so may also make their observations at this stage. Those who take part in the administrative hearing do not do so under oath. Nor are they even formally

---

[185] This also applies to the *rapporteur*, case handler or investigating official, although in many cases the language chosen for his participation is one of the two usual working languages of the Commission, namely English or French.

[186] Numerous persons may be involved in hearings and will each require a copy.

[187] The appropriate stage in the procedure for this may be the reply to the statement of objections, or between the end of the period allowed for a reply and the date of the hearings.

called upon to state the truth. As regards the experts, witnesses and other persons involved in defending the undertakings, their statements must be regarded as reflecting the best of their knowledge and belief. Their reliability and objectivity—despite the fact that they are brought in by the undertakings involved—will be appraised by the Commission. The undertakings usually give the Commission information as to the standing and professional competence of their experts and witnesses. The statements made by undertakings at the hearing are not covered by the same obligations as those imposed by Articles 18 and 20 of Regulation 1/2003 (requests for information and inspections) as regards the truth of the information given to the Commission, and undertakings cannot be fined if for any reason they give incorrect information or particulars that do not reflect the true position. Neither Article 23(1) of Regulation 1/2003—relative to fines—nor Regulation 773/2004 provide for such a possibility.

10.67 By contrast with the investigation phase, in which the undertakings are obliged to give true and accurate information to the Commission, in the knowledge that if they do so they might incriminate themselves,[188] the hearing is a phase of the procedure in which the rights of the defence prevail over all other considerations. This does not mean that the Commission has no interest in whether the information given at this stage reflects the true situation. Although it may subsequently check such information, the position is that in order to ensure that the rights of the defence are fully safeguarded, the Commission simply has no powers, in this phase of the procedure, to impose penalties of the kind described above.[189] As regards written reports and evidence, they and any other documents should be forwarded to the Commission with the minimum delay, if possible well before the hearings—although they can in fact be produced at the hearing.[190] If they contain business secrets, the Commission must be informed. It is important to note that under Article 14(6) of Regulation 773/2004 the undertakings and the Commission may ask the Hearing Officer—who will give a decision on the matter—that, in order to safeguard the business secrets of the undertakings making oral statements, the other undertakings should leave the room for a short time so that the speakers will not be heard by the other undertakings present at the hearing.[191] Since the complainants—who are usually customers or competitors—often take part in the hearings, this situation arises quite frequently.

---

[188] Regarding the problem of self-incrimination, or the right to remain silent, in relation to the Commission's investigative powers, see ch 7 'Investigative Measures' para 7.39 *et seq.*

[189] See ch 9 'Penalties and confidentiality' paras 9.01 *et seq.*

[190] The Hearing Officer may in any event 'ask for prior written notification of the essential contents of the intended statement of persons whom the undertakings concerned have proposed for hearing' (Art 11(3) of the Mandate of the Hearing Officer).

[191] Art 14(6) of Reg 773/2004.

The complainants may be heard after the undertakings involved. Practice varies **10.68** regarding the order in which they take part. Sometimes the complainants give their observations orally immediately after the Commission *rapporteur* has summarized the case. On other occasions, they speak after the undertakings involved. In each case, the order depends largely on what has been previously agreed between the undertakings and the Hearing Officer. After the undertakings have spoken, the Commission may ask questions if it wishes to do so. It is under no obligation to ask questions and the fact of not putting questions to the undertakings cannot be regarded as an indication that it has prejudged the case. When it decides to ask questions, the Commission must confine itself to those facts or arguments, whether oral or written, put forward in the observations phase that call for clarification. It is important to note that, for the Commission, this step in the procedure is not investigative; the facts on which it seeks to rely must already have been set out in the statement of objections and any request for clarification must be specifically directed towards those facts. The hearing cannot be treated by the Commission as a means of obtaining particulars and information that could be satisfactorily obtained by the exercise of its investigative powers under Articles 18 and 20 of Regulation 1/2003.

It is also important to note that the hearing cannot operate as a substitute for a **10.69** statement of objections. If the Commission advances new allegations of infringements or new essential facts, different from those contained in the statement of objections, it has to issue a supplementary statement of objections and conduct a new hearing.[192] Conversely, if the undertakings agree to discuss facts and arguments not contained in the statement of objections—and which do not materially differ from those raised in the statement of objections[193]—and have an opportunity to give their views on them at the hearing and produce evidence relating to them, they cannot later contend that the decision is vitiated because it does not correspond precisely to the statement of objections.[194] Just as the undertakings involved are not under a specific obligation to tell the truth and are not liable to fines in the event that the particulars or information they

---

[192] Art 12(3) of the Mandate of the Hearing Officer stating that fresh documents may be produced only with the Hearing Officer's consent. The admission of those documents would seem appropriate where they may shed light on some points of law or fact on which the Commison has not reached a clear understanding. S Durande and K Williams, 'The practical impact of the exercise of the right to be heard: A special focus on the effect of Oral Hearings and the role of the Hearing Officers' EC Competition Newsletter, Number 2, Summer 2005, 22–28 (25).

[193] As regards the question of fresh evidence and the requirement to issue a new statement of objections, para 10.26 above.

[194] See Cases 100–103/80 *Musique Diffusion (Pioneer) v EC Commission* [1983] ECR 1825 paras 18–19.

give in their oral observations are incomplete, misleading, or false, the Commission has no procedural means of making the undertakings answer its questions or of making them give true and complete answers if they do not wish to do so. In practice, the undertakings decline only very rarely to answer the Commission's questions, and only then in cases where it is not possible to give replies—not even approximate replies—on the spot. In such cases, the undertakings may reply in writing after the hearing to the Commission's questions that were left unanswered. The details regarding the time-limit for such replies can be settled at the end of the hearing between the Hearing Officer and the undertakings. The written replies are likewise not covered by Article 18 and do not appear to allow the Commission to fine undertakings when the information provided is incorrect. Quite apart from this possibility, the Commission is in all cases entitled, after the hearing, formally to call for more precise details and information to supplement the statements made by the participants at this stage.[195]

10.70 It is then the turn of the national competition authorities of the Member States, who, like the Commission, may put questions to the undertakings in the person of their lawyers, those supporting them, or their executives. In view of the fact that the NCAs will have an opportunity to question the Commission at meetings of the Advisory Committee, it is better for them to defer putting questions to the Commission until then. Finally, before the hearing ends, the undertakings have a further opportunity to speak, briefly. The undertakings involved may thereby respond to the comments made by the complainants. It is the appropriate point in the procedure for them to request measures which they consider appropriate; for example, that the infringement procedure be suspended or that fines should not be imposed or should be reduced, and so forth. The Hearing Officer, who will have chaired the proceedings throughout, intervening when necessary, then closes the hearing.

Record of the hearings

10.71 The statements made by each person heard will be recorded. Upon request, the audio recording of the hearing will be made available to the persons who attended the hearing. While this sets out a record of the entire proceedings, regard must be had to the legitimate interest of the parties in the protection of

---

[195] The Commisison can always issue formal information requests under Art 18 of Reg 1/2003. The Commission powers are not limited by reference to time or the stage reached in the case, so that they can be used after completion of the investigation, during the observations phase, between the latter phase and the adoption of a decision, and even afterwards. See ch 7 'Investigative measures' para 7.02 and the possibility of the Commission sanctioning the supply of incorrect or misleading information ch 9 'Penalties and confidentiality' paras 9.03 *et seq.*

their business secrets and other confidential information'.[196] In practice, the Commission makes a recording of and formerly used to transcribe everything said by the participants, in the language used by each of them[197] or in the English translation.

Participation of the complainants and of other third parties

Status of complainants Procedures for the application of Community com-   **10.72**
petition law conducted by the European Commission are administrative procedures which are commenced on the initiative of the Commission.[198] This is
due to the fact that the Community competition rules form part of Community
public policy and their implementation by administrative authorities is not a
matter where private initiative should prevail. In that respect, private individuals
are above all, as far as the Commission is concerned, informants and not always
parties to procedures in the strict sense, even when they may in fact have
prompted the Commission to take action. Regardless of the starting-point of
procedures, it is always the Commission that decides how and when the various
stages of the procedure are to take place once the Community machinery has
been put into action. The limitations on the Commission's discretionary powers
on procedural issues derive solely from the procedural regulations themselves
and do not result from requests from those involved, except of course to the
extent to which they reflect the procedural rules.

From the procedural point of view, this has an important practical consequence: **10.73**
the only necessary parties to infringement procedures are the undertakings
implicated in the agreements, practices, or abuses contrary to Articles 81 and 82
of the EC Treaty. Other 'parties' rank as such only in the sense that they 'take
part' and even then their participation is to a large extent a matter for the

---

[196] Art 14(8) of Reg 773/2004. Note that formerly written minutes were prepared and submitted to the parties for their approval in order to enable them to check what they said at the hearing to ensure that they contained a true record of the substance of what they had said. See Case T-9/99 *HFB Holding für Fernwärmetechnik Beteiligungsgesellschaft mbH & Co. KG (HFB) and others v EC Commission* [2002] ECR II-1487 paras 408–411 where the parties challenged the decision of the Commission because of alleged failings in the production of the minutes. See also Case 44/69 *Buchler v EC Commission* [1970] ECR 733 para 17. Cited, *inter alia*, in Case T-9/89 *Hüls v EC Commission* [1992] ECR II-499 para 77, and Case T-15/89 *Chemie Linz v EC Commission* [1992] ECR II-1275 para 74. For a case in which there was an—unsuccessful—challenge regarding the procedure followed by the Commission in forwarding the minutes of the hearing, see Case T-34/92 *Fiatagri UK and another v EC Commission* [1994] ECR II-905 paras 28–31, which cited, *inter alia*, the above-mentioned judgments.

[197] This administrative practice has been attacked on the ground that it is contrary to Council Reg 1 of 25 April 1958 determining the languages to be used by the EEC ([1952–58] OJ Spec Ed 59). See Case T-77/92 *Parker Pen v EC Commission* [1994] ECR II-549, in which that contention was rejected.

[198] For more detailed treatment of this point, see ch 5 'Opening of the file' paras 5.08 *et seq.*

Commission's discretion.[199] Complainants—formal complaints, not those who lodge informal or unofficial complaints, who are treated differently from the procedural point of view—fall into that category and are third parties in a more limited sense than other possible participants (whether or not directly interested). In the same manner remarks concerning the participation of complainants in the written observations phase of infringement procedures also apply to other third parties who, like the complainants themselves, demonstrate a legitimate interest in having their *written* views on the objections considered (Article 27(3) of Regulation 1/2003 in conjunction with Article 13(1) of Regulation 773/2004). The following remarks on the participation of the complainants in the *oral* observations phase (hearings) may also apply to other persons with a sufficient interest (Article 27(3) of Regulation 1/2003 in conjunction with Article 13(2) of Regulation 773/2004) and to other third parties with or without a direct interest who are called on by the Commission to express their views (Article 13(3) of Regulation 773/2004).

10.74 The Commission's interest in the participation of the complainants in procedures lies in the fact that, through their first-hand knowledge of the market and of the infringements which constitute the factual basis of the procedure— the most usual complainants are customers or competitors of the undertakings involved—they provide enormous help to the Commission in proving infringements of Articles 81 and 82 EC. The Commission is also obliged to examine the matters of fact and law which the complainants have brought to its notice and to allow them to defend their legitimate interests during the administrative procedure.[200] However, despite their considerable usefulness, complainants do not enjoy the same rights and procedural safeguards as the undertakings implicated in an infringement.[201]

10.75 **Participation of complainants** Regulation 773/2004—in a similar line to previous Regulation 2842/1998 on the hearing of parties in certain proceedings under Articles 85 and 86 of the EC Treaty—establishes a different level of protection regarding the right to be heard depending on whether the person to

---

[199] The Commission may even be willing to hold such a hearing even when the defendants have waived this right. Defendants cannot be forced to attend, but nothing in the law or in the Community Courts' case law would seem to prevent the Commission from organizing a meeting with complainants and third parties where this could enhance the correct understanding of the facts of the case. S Durande and K Williams, 'The practical impact of the exercise of the right to be heard: A special focus on the effect of Oral Hearings and the role of the Hearing Officers' EC Competition Newsletter, Number 2, Summer 2005, 22–28 (23).

[200] See Case 298/83 *CICCE v EC Commission* [1985] ECR 1105, cited in Joined Cases 142/84 and 156/84 *BAT and Reynolds Industries v EC Commission* [1987] ECR 4487 para 20.

[201] See Joined Cases 209/78 and 218/78 *Van Landewyck v EC Commission ('FEDETAB')* [1980] ECR 3125 para 18, and Joined Cases 142/84 and 156/84 *BAT and Reynolds Industries v Commission* [1987] ECR 4487 paras 19–20.

be heard is a party subject of the proceedings, a complainant or a third party. In infringement procedures the role of the complainant has primarily been that of an informant.[202] The lodging of a complaint causes the procedure to be set in motion but—important though that step may be—the complainant was not previously *de jure* in a more privileged position than other third parties as regards the right to be heard in the observations phase, since the requirement of demonstrating a sufficient interest applied to complainants and other third parties alike. It should be noted that an interest in being heard differs from an interest in lodging a complaint. *De facto*, however, a complainant—at least, one making a formal complaint[203]—was considered to play a rather more active role than that of mere instigator. As a consequence, in the vast majority of cases, the Commission considered it advisable to allow complainants to participate actively in the procedure following the filing of the initial complaint, so that they could give their views, in writing or orally, on the statement of objections and even on the defence put forward by the undertakings implicated in the infringements.

Modernization rules (both Regulation 1/2003 and Regulation 773/2004) have **10.76** enshrined such a *de facto* position of complainants by conferring them a specific status in the proceedings.[204] Thus, first, according to Article 27(1) of Regulation 1/2003, 'complainants shall be associated closely with the proceedings'. Secondly, Regulation 773/2004, while establishing a clear distinction between complainants and other third parties, does not require complainants to prove a 'sufficient interest' after having shown a 'legitimate interest' in lodging a complaint—as required by Article 5(1). It is obvious therefore that complainants have been legally recognized the special position that they were previously afforded in the Commission's practice.[205] Regarding the rights of the complainant, where the Commission considers that there are insufficient grounds for acting on the complaint it will inform the complainant of its reasons setting a time-limit for the complainant to make known its views in writing.[206] If the Commission raises objections relating to a matter in respect of which a complaint has been lodged, it will provide the complainant with a copy of the non-confidential version of the statement of objections and will set a time-limit within which the complainant may make known its views in

---

[202] In the words of AG Lenz, '[T]he complainant is limited to a role which corresponds to the position, under criminal procedure, of a person who reports a matter to the authorities'. Opinion in *Akzo I* Case 53/85 *Akzo v EC Commission I* [1986] ECR 1965.

[203] Regarding the difference between formal and unofficial or informal complainants, see ch 5 'Opening of the file' para 5.15.

[204] It must be pointed out, however, that Reg 2842/1998—repealed by Reg 773/2004— already foresaw the recognition of the specific status of complainants.

[205] According to CS Kerse and N Khan, *EC Antitrust Procedure* (5th edn, 2005) para 193, such special position is somewhere between the undertakings to whom the Commission has addressed a statement of objections and other third parties.

[206] Art 7(1) of Reg 773/2004.

writing.[207] However, the presence of the complainant during the hearing will be decided by the Commission where appropriate.[208]

10.77   During the investigation phase, the Commission may inform the complainants both of the content of the requests for information sent to the undertakings involved in the alleged infringement of the competition provisions of which they complain, and of the answers given by the undertakings to such requests and to the complaints themselves if copies were forwarded to the undertakings. Three comments are called for at this stage. The first is that the Commission has a discretion as to whether or not the complainants should receive those documents. In many cases the Commission waits until the hearing before asking for the opinion of the complainants on the information given and the defence put forward by the undertakings against which the complaints are directed. The second is that while respecting the safeguards contained in Article 28 (1) and (2) of Regulation 1/2003 the Commission may make non-confidential information available to the complainant or to other third parties.[209] Finally, while Article 15(1) of Regulation 773/2004 establishes that access to the file is to be granted to the parties after the notification of the statement of objections, it might be argued that the Commission may rely on Article 15(3) to make the information available to the complainant provided it relates to the subject matter for which it was acquired and is not covered by the obligation of professional secrecy and confidentiality.[210]

10.78   At this stage, the complainants receive a copy of the statement of objections, from which all business secrets have been duly deleted, and have an opportunity to examine the non-confidential documents in the file. However, complainants do not have the same rights as the undertakings involved regarding access to the administrative file. Complainants and other third parties are entitled to take part and be heard in Commission procedures, but—unlike undertakings allegedly

---

[207] Art 6(1) of Reg 773/2004.   [208] Art 6(2) of Reg 773/2004.

[209] Complainants cannot claim a right of access to the file as established for parties. In any event they neither have a right of access to business secrets or other confidential information which the Commission has obtained in the course of its investigation. Commission Notice on the rules for access to the Commission file pursuant to Arts 81 and 82 EC [2005] OJ C325/7, para 30.

[210] See also Commission Notice on the rules for access to the Commission file pursuant to Arts 81 and 82 EC, para 31: '[. . .] a complainant who, pursuant to Art 7(1) of the Implementing Regulation [Reg 773/2004] has been informed of the Commission's intention to reject its complaint [. . .], may request access to the documents on which the Commission has based its provisional assessment [. . .]. The complainant will be provided access to such documents on a single occasion, following the issuance of the letter informing the complainant of the Commission's intention to reject its complaint.' The CFI has held that a complainant may not in any circumstances be given access to documents containing business secrets. See Case T-5/97 *Industrie des poudres sphériques v EC Commission* [2000] ECR II-3755 para 229.

implicated in an infringement, by reason of their defence rights—their rights are not unlimited when it comes to obtaining information about the file.[211] It should be noted that, in any case, there are certain limits to access to the file which are common to the undertakings involved and complainants—for example, regarding internal documents of the Commission,[212] and that the documents available may vary according to who is being given information from the file, by virtue of the principle of protection of the business secrets of undertakings.

In order to safeguard the rights of the defence, the opinions expressed by the complainants and other third parties concerning the statement of objections must be communicated to the undertakings directly involved in the alleged infringements. The forwarding of a copy may be sufficient in those cases where the statements from such persons do not contain new matters of fact to be added to the statement of objections, or else contain new facts which corroborate those contained in the statement of objections. In those cases where facts are mentioned which have not previously been brought to the notice of the Commission or of the undertakings against which the objections are directed, and they do not fundamentally affect the overall assessment of the matter—if they did and the Commission wanted to use them in its final decision it would be necessary to send a supplementary statement of objections—the Commission will observe the rights of the defence by allowing the undertakings concerned to submit observations on the comments made by the complainants. For that purpose, it will set a (usually short) period for them to be submitted, if they are to be in writing. **10.79**

The possibility cannot be excluded, however, that both the observations of the complainants and of third parties concerning the statement of objections and **10.80**

---

[211] For a summary of the relevant case law, see Case T-17/93 *Matra v EC Commission* [1994] ECR II-595 paras 34–36. That judgment cites those in Case 53/85 *Akzo v EC Commission I* [1986] ECR 1965 and Joined Cases 142/84 and 156/84 *BAT and Reynolds Industries v EC Commission* [1987] ECR 4487 paras 19 and 20, and Case T-64/89 *Automec v EC Commission I* [1990] ECR II-367 para 46. See also the judgment in Joined Cases 209/78 and 218/78 *Van Landewyck v EC Commission* ('*FEDETAB*') [1980] ECR 3125 para 18. See also Final report of the Hearing Officer in Case COMP/36.571—*Austrian Banks* [2004] OJ C162/1.

[212] Case T-17/93 *Matra v EC Commission* [1994] ECR II-595 paras 34 and 36, appears to have overlooked this fact stating that the undertakings involved in a procedure are entitled to 'full disclosure' of the file. However, Art 15(2) of Reg 773/2004 provides that the right of access to the file shall not extend to business secrets, other confidential information, internal documents of the Commission and of the competition authorities of the Member States and the correspondence between the Commission and those authorities or between the latter when such correspondence is contained in the Commission's file. See, e.g. Joined Cases T-236/01, T-239/01, T-244/01 to T-246/01, T-251/01 and T-252/01 *Tokai Carbon and others v EC Commission* [2004] OJ C251/13 para 40: '[. . .] [I]nternal documents can be made available only if the exceptional circumstances of the case so require, on the basis of serious evidence which it is for the party concerned to provide, both before the Community Court and in the administrative procedure conducted by the Commission [. . .]'.

the defence put forward in response to those observations by the undertakings involved may be expressed orally at the hearing, and even in writing subsequently. This procedure is not—not even by analogy—one of replies and rejoinders of the kind typical of civil proceedings.[213] The Commission's intention is to observe scrupulously undertakings' defence rights and ensure that the right to a fair hearing is upheld, and it does not, in principle, consider it appropriate to allow an exchange of mutual accusations between undertakings. However, in certain cases there is no option but to accept the inherent consequences of the written phase of the procedure. The Commission tries to ensure that the written phase does not become too protracted. The participation of complainants in hearings is based on Article 6(2) of Regulation 773/2004. When having submitted observations on the statement of objections, complainants request to express their views orally,[214] it is for the Commission to decide whether or not it is appropriate to afford them such an opportunity. Therefore, the Commission enjoys considerable discretion as to who is to be invited to attend. The likelihood of the complainants participating in the hearing depends largely on the interest which the Commission has in their contribution or its probative value.[215] Complainants take part in the hearings either after the undertakings concerned or, once the session has been opened by the Hearing Officer, after the Commission has given a summary of the case. The undertakings concerned will have an opportunity to reply at the end of the hearing, in their closing observations.

10.81 **Other third parties** Firstly, it must be established that third parties must show a 'sufficient interest' in order to be heard by the Commission in competition proceedings (Article 13(1) of Regulation 773/2004). It may therefore be affirmed that third parties are not accorded a status similar to that of complainants,[216] let alone to that of the parties to whom the Commission has

---

[213] The Community administrative procedure in competition matters is not a civil adversarial procedure. See also the judgment in Joined Cases 142/84 and 156/84 *BAT and Reynolds Industries v Commission* [1987] ECR 4487 para 19. Nevertheless, the Court itself has described the procedure following a statement of objections as contentious proceedings. See Joined Cases 46/87 and 227/88 *Hoechst v EC Commission III* [1989] ECR 2859 para 16; Case 27/88 *Solvay v EC Commission* [1989] ECR 3355 paras 17, 21–22; and Case 374/87 *Orkem v EC Commission* [1989] ECR 3283 paras 20, 24, and 25. In those cases, the Court makes it clear that the opposing parties are the undertakings involved and the Commission, and that there is no adversarial litigation between complainants and undertakings, in the civil procedural sense.

[214] According to Art 6(2) of Reg 773/2004, complainants must apply to be heard orally in their written comments. See also Case 43/85 *ANCIDES v EC Commission* [1987] ECR 3131 para 8, where an express request by the undertaking is required.

[215] The Commission enjoys a 'reasonable margin of discretion' in deciding which persons are to be heard, according to the relevance of their participation in the investigation of the case. See Joined Cases 43/82 and 63/82 *VBVB and VBBB v EC Commission* [1984] ECR 1984 para 18.

[216] As stated, complainants are supposed to have a sufficient interest once they have shown a legitimate interest to be entitled to lodge a complaint.

addressed a statement of objections. Furthermore, according to that very provision, third parties showing a sufficient interest shall be informed in writing of the 'nature and subject matter of the procedure'. Therefore, it is not foreseen in principle by the applicable rules that third parties might be sent the statement of objections to comment on it (even in a non-confidential version) as in the case of complainants, but only to be informed of the type of procedure and its main aspects. This could also be seen as an additional sign of the secondary or less important status of third parties in terms of possibilities to be heard. However, in practice, the Commission usually sends a non-confidential version of the statement of objections to interested third parties.[217] In fact, the above-mentioned expression 'nature and subject matter of the procedure' has been interpreted by the Hearing Officer as implying the communication of a non-confidential version of the statement of objections just as in the case of complainants. Thus, in *Deutsche Telekom AG* the Hearing Officer reported that a company that had been admitted as an interested third party '[. . .] was informed of the nature and subject-matter of the procedure in this case by means of a non-confidential version of the Statement of Objections [. . .]'.[218]

While it is not completely clear what 'sufficient interest' means—and no ruling of the Community courts has yet been given on the matter—it must be pointed out that in any event the Commission has a wide margin of discretion as to the persons to be heard, apart from the parties to the proceedings and complainants, since Article 13(3) of Regulation 773/2004 recognizes the power of the Commission to hear 'any other person' to express its views in writing and to attend the oral hearing. Once a third party is capable of showing a sufficient interest and is informed of the nature and subject matter of the procedure, Article 13(1) provides that the Commission shall set a time-limit in order to allow such third party to make observations in writing. Finally, and regarding the possibility of attending the oral hearing and developing arguments, third parties must make such a request in their written comments, the Commission having the last word on the matter (Article 13(2) of Regulation 733/2004). **10.82**

D. The Remaining Stages of the Procedure Until the Adoption of a Decision

The further procedural stages, following the observations under Article 27(1) of Regulation 1/2003, have been considered in general terms in Chapter 1 dealing **10.83**

---

[217] See Final reports of the Hearing Officer in *UEFA Champions League* [2003] OJ C269/22 and *Deutsche Telekom AG* [2003] OJ C288/2.
[218] Final report of the Hearing Officer in *Deutsche Telekom AG* [2003] OJ C288/2.

with the manner in which the Commission adopts decisions in competition matters.[219] In short, once the observations phase is completed, DG COMP prepares, in all cases with the approval of the Legal Service and, in some cases, of the other departments involved,[220] a draft decision which is referred to the Advisory Committee, made up of the representatives of NCAs, for its opinion.[221] DG COMP, taking into account that opinion, then prepares a final draft which is again approved by its Legal Service and the departments associated with DG COMP, if any. The full Commission then approves the draft, with or without amendments, notifies its decision to the undertakings and publishes it in the Official Journal together with the Final Report of the Hearing Officer (Article 16(3) of the Mandate of Hearing Officers).

---

[219] See ch 1 'Institutional framework' paras 1.44 *et seq.*

[220] Only the report of the Legal Service is required in cases dealt with under Reg 1/2003, but the Commission may obtain the opinion of other Directorates General in individual cases.

[221] See ch 2 'The role of national competition authorities' para 2.45.

11

INFRINGEMENT DECISIONS
AND PENALTIES

I. General content of infringement decisions

A. Layout

There is no specific structure for competition decisions issued by the Commis- **11.01**
sion, but they must meet the requirements contained in Article 253 EC. The
basic layout of decisions applying Articles 81 and 82 EC consists of (1) a title,
(2) a preamble in the form of Recitals which provide a structured narrative
of the matter, (3) an account of the facts, (4) a legal assessment of the facts
and (5) the Articles of the decision, known as the operative part or simply the
'decision' which sets out the finding of an infringement and its duration, the
identity of the undertaking(s) concerned, and where appropriate the amounts of
the fines and the arrangements of the payment of the fines and the remedy
required by the Commission.[1] It should be borne in mind that the Commission
may and must withdraw its objections against undertakings wholly or in part,
amend or correct them, or supplement them, taking into account the action
taken during the observations phase. Decisions are not, therefore, a copy of the
statement of objections.[2] It should also be remembered that although decisions
must specify the evidence on which the Commission's opinion is based, they do
not have to enumerate exhaustively every available item of evidence.[3] As regards

---

[1] Note that infringement decisions make no reference to the right of undertakings to contest
the decision before the European Court—within a period of two months from the day following
the date of notification, under the fourth paragraph of Art 230 EC. That formal requirement
applies only to procedural decisions adopted under the Commission's investigative powers
pursuant to Arts 18(4) (decisions to request information) and 20(3) (inspection decisions) of
Reg 1/2003.

[2] e.g. Case T-191/98 *Atlantic Container Line and others v EC Commission* [2003] ECR-II
3275 para 191.

[3] See Case T-2/89 *Petrofina v EC Commission* [1991] ECR II-1087 para 39; Case T-43/92
Dunlop v EC Commission [1994] ECR II-441 para 34. Case T-48/00 *Corus UK v EC Commission*

the reasoning on which its decisions are based, it is true that, under Article 253 EC, the Commission is required to give a statement of the reasons for its decisions, indicating the matters of fact and of law on which it relied in adopting them.[4] But the Commission cannot be required to discuss each and every one of the points of fact and law submitted by each of the parties involved in the course of the administrative procedure.[5] This chapter will focus on infringement decisions as such. Particular attention will be paid to the operative part, comparable to a judicial decision, although it is drafted as a series of Articles (as if it were a piece of legislation). The last part will deal principally with declaratory decisions, enforcement decisions (ie orders), obligations, and fines, and periodic penalty payments imposed on undertakings for infringements of the substantive provisions of Articles 81 and 82 EC.

B. Declarations and Orders or Notices

11.02 Commission decisions in competition matters contain both declaratory components and enforcing components in the operative part. Here, the first are referred to as declaratory decisions and the second, which are strictly speaking 'orders' as enforcement decisions.[6]

[2003] OJ C239/12 para 101: '[. . .] the assessment appearing in a statement of objections is often more succinct than that contained in the final decision as adopted, since it only represents the Commission's provisional view. Divergences of wording between a statement of objections and a final decision, deriving from the difference between the respective purposes of those two documents, are not, in principle, capable of infringing the rights of the defence. [. . .]' For more details on the required degree of similarity of the statement of objections and the final decision, see ch 10 'Infringement procedures' paras 10.12 *et seq.*

[4] See Joined Cases T-80/89, T-81/89, T-87/89, T-88/89, T-90/89, T-93/89, T-95/89, T-97/89, T-99/89, T-100/89, T-101/89, T-103/89, T-105/89, T-107/89, and T-112/89 *BASF AG and others v EC Commission* [1995] ECR II-729 para 76: '[. . .] The [ECJ] also made it clear that the operative part of a decision under the competition rules can be understood, and its full effect ascertained, only in the light of the statement of reasons. [. . .]' This is of particular importance where, for example in *Vitamins* [2003] OJ L6/1, the Articles of the decision simply refer to the undertakings having infringed Arts 81 EC by participating in agreements affecting the Community. As far as the operative part is concerned, the Community Courts do not seem to require more than the identity of the undertakings concerned and the duration of the infringement. See Art 2 of Commission decision in *Seamless Steel Tubes* [2003] OJ L140/1, upheld in this respect by Case T-48/00 *Corus UK v EC Commission* [2003] OJ C239/12 para 87. CS Kerse and N Khan, *EC Antitrust Procedure* (5th edn, 2005) para 6–028.

[5] Case T-8/89 *DSM v EC Commission* [1991] ECR II-1833 para 257; Case T-2/93 *Air France v EC Commission II* [1994] ECR II-323 para 92; Case C-367/95 P *EC Commission v Sytraval and Brink's France* [1998] ECR I-1719 para 63: '[. . .] It is not necessary for the reasoning to go into all the relevant facts and points of law, since the question whether the statement of reasons meets the requirements of Article [253] of the Treaty must be assessed with regard not only to its wording but also to its context and to all the legal rules governing the matter in question [. . .]'. Case T-198/98 *Micro Leader Business v EC Commission* [1999] ECR II-3989 para 40.

[6] The term used in French is '*injonction*'.

1. Declaratory decisions

Commission infringement decisions always contain a statement to the effect **11.03** that the agreements or conduct to which the procedure relates constitute an infringement of Article 81(1), Article 82 EC, or both (abuse of a collective dominant position deriving from an agreement or restrictive practice).[7] Although Article 7 of Regulation 1/2003 which states that the Commission may by 'decision require the undertakings or associations of undertakings concerned to bring such infringement to an end', the Community Courts have always taken the view in the context of Regulation 17 that this power implies the possibility of giving a decision as to the existence of an infringement, also on the grounds that the Commission has a legitimate interest to clarify its position in law and to prevent any future infringement of the same or a similar kind.[8] In certain cases where undertakings have brought the infringement to an end during the course of the procedure, the Commission may confine itself to declaring that the conduct to which the procedure relates constituted an infringement of the Community competition rules. The Commission has adopted declaratory decisions of this kind relatively frequently not only because they give guidance but also because they are meant to have dissuasive effect.[9] A legitimate interest in establishing an infringement may also be established on the basis of the policy inherent in Regulation 1/2003 of using national courts to enforce and sanction infringements of the competition rules.[10] Accordingly, if the infringement

---

[7] An example of the simultaneous application of both Articles is the second *Italian Flat Glass case* [1989] OJ L33/44. That decision was partially annulled by the CFI in what is known as the '*Flat Glass judgment*' of 10 March 1992 in Joined Cases T-68/89, T-77/89 and T-78/89 *Società Italiana Vetro (SIV) v EC Commission* [1992] ECR II-1403. See also Cases C-395/96 P and 396/96 P *Compagnie Maritine Belge Transports v EC Commission* [2000] ECR I-1365 stating that because a practice is exempted under Art 81(3) EC this would not mean that the same practice may not be challenged under Art 82 EC.

[8] See Case 7/82 *GVL v EC Commission* [1983] ECR 483 paras 16–28; *Bayer Dental* [1990] OJ L351/46 (para 20 of the decision cites Case 7/82 *GVL v EC Commission*); *World Cup Tours* [1992] OJ L326/31, which cites Case 7/82 *GVL v EC Commission* (para 126 of the decision). See Case T-347/94 *Mayr-Melnhof Kartongesellschaft mbH v EC Commission* [1998] ECR II-1751 para 180 '[. . .] also it is sufficient to point out that the applicant disputes the substantive scope of the directions in Art 2 of the Decision, which demonstrates the Commission's legitimate interest in specifying the extent of the obligations on the undertakings [. . .]'.

[9] See also Recital 11 of Reg 1/2003. Case 8/72 *Vereeniging van Cementhanelaren v EC Commission* [1972] ECR 977; See also CS Kerse and N Khan, *EC Antitrust Procedure* (5th edn, 2005) para 6–020 referring to Case T-175/95 *BASF Coatings AG v EC Commission* [1999] ECR II-1581 para 156 in which the Court stated that a decision might be needed: '[. . .]. Even if the Court were unable to find that such a clause was implemented, the fact remains that its mere existence was capable of creating a 'visual and psychological' effect which contributed to a partitioning of the market [. . .]'; Case T-66/92 *Herlitz v EC Commission* [1994] ECR II-531 para 40.

[10] CS Kerse and N Khan, *EC Antitrust Procedure* (5th edn, 2005) para 6–019 pointing to Case C-453/99 *Courage v Crehan* [2001] ECR I-6297. In Joined Cases T-22/02 and T-23/02

procedure was prompted by a complaint, and the complainants wish to bring an action for damages based on the illegality of action prohibited by the Treaty, the Commission might also consider it appropriate to adopt a purely declaratory decision. The Commission is not empowered to give a decision on such claims in the Community administrative procedure. A separate action would be necessary before a competent civil court, one basis for which could be a formal decision finding an infringement.[11]

2. Enforcement decisions: remedies

11.04 This category includes both orders to bring infringements to an end and orders to carry out specific acts, and the obligations that the Commission may attach to such orders. Sometimes, it may be decided to impose a periodic penalty payment in addition to such obligations.[12]

Orders to bring infringements to an end

11.05 Article 7(1) of Regulation 1/2003 establishes that where the Commission, acting on a complaint or on its own initiative, finds an infringement of Article 81 or of Article 82 EC, it may by decision require the said infringement to be brought to an end.[13] The Commission adopts these 'cease and desist' decisions where the undertakings have not co-operated with the Commission by cancelling their restrictive agreements or desisting from their unlawful conduct prior to the decision, or in those cases where the Community administration is not sure that the undertakings have in fact brought to an end the infringement to which the procedure relates or infringements having similar effects.[14] These decisions may also include a 'like effects order' whereby the parties are prohibited from entering into similar arrangements which may have the same effect or object.[15]

Sumitomo Chemical v EC Commission, [2005] OJ C296/20, the Commission decision was annulled because the Commission failed to establish a legitimate interest in addressing a merely declaratory decision to the undertaking.

[11] Regarding actions for damages, and others in which Community competition law is applied directly by national courts, see ch 2 'National courts' paras 2.04 *et seq.*

[12] This is the first phase of the imposition of a periodic penalty payment. Regarding the procedure for the imposition of periodic penalty payments, see ch 9 'Penalties and confidentiality' paras 9.12 *et seq.*

[13] This is the most straightforward type of decision. See para 1 of *Frankfurt Airport* [1998] OJ L72/30; para 3 of *Irish Sugar plc* [1997] OJ L258/1. See also J Schwarze and A Weitbrecht, *Grundzüge des europäischen Kartellverfahrensrechts* (2004) § 6 para 19.

[14] See para 2 of *Industrial and medical gases* [2003] OJ L84/1; para 2 in *Food Flavour Enhancers* [2004] OJ L75/1; para 2 of *Opel* [2001] OJ L59/1.

[15] A Jones and B Sufrin, *EC Competition Law* (2nd edn, 2004) 1110 pointing to para 2 of the Commission decision *Welded Steel Mesh* [1989] OJ L260/1; see also *Methionine* [2003] OJ L255/1. However, it is to note that in *Langnese-Iglo* (Cases T-7/93 and T-9/93 *Langnese-Iglo & Schöller Lebensmittel v EC Commission* [1995] ECR II-1533 paras 205–209 upheld by the ECJ in Case C-279/95P *Langnese Iglo v EC Commission* [1998] ECR I-5609 para 74) the ECJ held that

Orders to take specific action[16]

In addition, Article 7(1) of Regulation 1/2003 empowers the Commission to **11.06**
impose on undertakings that have infringed Article 81 or 82 EC all remedies
necessary to bring the infringement to an end, including (i) behavioural or
(ii) structural remedies. As regards behavioural remedies, the ECJ had already
interpreted Article 3 of Regulation 17 (the equivalent provision to Article 7(1)
of Regulation 1/2003) as enabling the Commission not only to order an end to
certain acts, practices, or situations which are contrary to the Treaty (restraining
orders), but also to order undertakings to do certain acts or take certain courses
of action which, unlawfully, have not been done.[17] However, it is not for the
Commission to impose on the parties its own choice from among all the various
potential courses of action which are in accordance with the Treaty.[18] In practice,
the Commission does not hesitate to use such 'mandatory injunctions' where it
is necessary to remedy the consequences of an abuse of a dominant position,[19]

---

the Commission was not entitled to forbid undertakings from entering into exclusive purchasing
agreements in the *future*. Whether or not an exclusive purchasing agreement is restrictive of
competition and satisfies Art 81(3) EC depends on the circumstances and the context. Case T-34/
92 *Fiatagri UK Ltd and New Holland Ford Ltd v EC Commission* [1994] ECR II-905 para 39 in
which the CFI held that parts of Commission decisions, according to which undertakings are to
refrain from entering into any information exchange system having an object identical or similar
to the agreement, are purely declaratory because Art 81(1) EC would apply in any event.

[16] J Schwarze and A Weitbrecht, *Grundzüge des Europäischen Kartellverfahrensrechts* (2004) § 6
para 21 propose the distinction between the following obligations: (i) obligation to report; (ii)
modification of discount and price policy; (iii) modifications of terms and conditions of sale; (iv)
grant of access to infrastructure, licenses; (v) obligation to supply; and (vi) divestiture or sale of
shareholdings or businesses. See also A Klees, *Europäisches Kartellverfahrensrecht* (2005) § 6 paras
70 *et seq.*

[17] Joined Cases C-241/91 P and C-242/91 P *Radio Telefis Eireann and Independent Television
Publications Ltd (ITP) v EC Commission ('RTE')* [1995] ECR I-743 para 90, citing Joint Cases 6/
73 and 7/73 *Istituto Chimioterapico Italiano and Commercial Solvents Corp v EC Commission*
[1974] ECR 223 para 45 in which the dominant undertaking was ordered to supply a certain
amount of raw material to the complainant which involved the parties entering into contractual
relations; Case T-9/93 *Schöller v EC Commission* [1995] ECR II-1611 para 159; T-228/97 *Irish
Sugar v EC Commission* [1999] ECR II-2969 para 298. See also Commission decision of
24 March 2004 in COMP/37.792 *Microsoft* in which the Commission ordered Microsoft to offer
versions of Window's without Window's Media Player incorporated and to make available certain
interoperability information, see Commission Press Release IP/04/382 'Commission concludes
Microsoft investigation, imposes conduct remedies and a fine'.

[18] Case T-24/90 *Automec v Commission II* [1992] ECR II-2223 para 52. The CFI stated that
infringements arising out of the application of an illegal distribution system could also be eliminated by the abandonment or amendment of the distribution system instead of imposing the
obligation to allow the use of certain trade marks. The Commission could not order the party to
enter into a contractual relationship because this would constitute a disproportionate restriction
of the freedom of contract. Case T-7/93 *Langnese-Iglo v EC Commission* [1995] ECR II-1533
paras 205–209.

[19] See Case C-242/91 P *Radio Telefis Eireann and Independent Television Publications Ltd (ITP)
v EC Commission ('RTE')* [1995] ECR I-743 para 90, citing Joint Cases 6/73 and 7/73 *Istituto
Chimioterapico Italiano and Commercial Solvents Corp v EC Commission* [1974] ECR 223 para 19.

although it takes a more prudent stance with regard to agreements and restrictive practices caught by Article 81(1) EC.[20] In any event, in light of the Courts' interpretation of Article 3 of Regulation 17, Article 7(1) of Regulation 1/2003 is thus deemed to imply the right of the Commission to address certain orders to undertakings, requiring them to take or refrain from certain action, with a view to bringing the infringement to an end in order to ensure the effective application of its decisions,[21] as long as the measures adopted by Community institutions do not exceed what is appropriate and necessary to attain the objective pursued.[22]

11.07 As regards the implementation of structural remedies, Regulation 17 did not specifically provide for such a possibility. Yet Article 7(1) of Regulation 1/2003 expressly empowers the Commission to impose on undertakings structural remedies 'provided that there is no equally effective behavioural remedy or that any equally effective behavioural remedy would be more burdensome for the undertaking concerned than the structural remedy'.[23] This may in particular be the case with regard to cooperation agreements and abuses of a dominant position, where divestiture of certain assets may be necessary.[24] Under the Community Courts' case law, the Commission's discretion in this area neverthe-less remains bounded by the principle of proportionality, which implies that '[t]he burdens imposed on undertakings in order to bring an infringement of competition law to an end must not exceed what is appropriate and necessary to attain the objective sought, namely re-establishment of compliance with the

---

[20] See e.g., para 3 of *Astra* [1993] OJ L20/23, which provided that customer contracts should be renegotiated and readjusted. *Volkswagen* [1998] OJ L124/60 para 203: '[. . .] In order to bring the infringements established in this case to an end, taking into account the fact that they still persist today [. . .], the Italian authorised dealers must be informed that the warnings, instructions and penalties have been declared invalid. Furthermore, the contracts with the Italian dealers must be amended with respect to the bonus and margins schemes. All authorised dealers within the Community must be told that cross-deliveries within the Community are allowed and not to be penalised in any way [. . .].' See however, Case T-395/94 *Atlantic Container Line AB v EC Commission* [2002] ECR II-875 paras 410–420 in which the obligation imposed by the Commission to inform customers that they are entitled, if they so wish, to renegotiate the terms of those contracts or to terminate them, was considered as being not necessary, because the Commission could not explain why this obligation would be required.

[21] Joined Cases C-89/85, C-104/85, C-114/85, C-116/85, C-117/85 and C-125/85 to C-129/85 *A. Ahlström Osakeyhtiö and others v EC Commission ('Woodpulp II')* [1993] ECR I-1307 para 181.

[22] See Case T-9/93 *Schöller Lebensmittel GmbH & Co KG v EC Commission* [1995] ECR II-1611 para 192. The Commission has no power to prohibit an undertaking which it orders to dismantle the network of exclusive purchasing agreements established by that undertaking to conclude new agreements of that kind in the future.

[23] A Klees, *Europäisches Kartellverfahrensrecht* (2005) § 6 paras 80 and 81 suggests that it would be more adequate to require that structural remedies should only be taken if behavioural remedies are not '*sufficiently* effective.'

[24] Draft Reg implementing Arts 81 and 82 of the Treaty COM (2000) 582 final, [2000] OJ C365E/284, Explanatory Memorandum, Art 7.

rules infringed.'[25] The imposition of divestiture would only in exceptional circumstances stand the proportionality test.[26] Where there is an abuse of a dominant position by, for example, a refusal to supply, it may be difficult to contemplate any other remedy other than an order to supply.[27]

Additional obligations

Sometimes, the Commission requires undertakings to grant access to certain **11.08** information or infrastructure.[28] Together with the foregoing, the Commission may impose obligations which enable it to ascertain whether or not the undertakings are changing their conduct to conform with the positive or negative requirement imposed by the Commission.[29] In general, such obligations consist in giving to the Commission or to third parties specific information indicated in the decisions,[30] although the Commission is required not to be overly intrusive in this respect given that the consequences in civil law attaching to an infringement of Article 81 EC, such as the obligation to make good the damage

---

[25] See Case T-151/01 R *Duales System Deutschland v EC Commission* [2001] ECR II-3295 para 169; Case T-7/93 *Langnese-Iglo v EC Commission* [1995] ECR II-1533 para 209; and Case T-9/93 *Schöller v EC Commission* [1995] ECR II-1611 para 163; Joined Cases C-241/91 P and C-242/91 P *Radio Telefis Eireann and Independent Television Publications Ltd (ITP) v EC Commission ('RTE')* [1995] ECR I-743 para 93, confirming Case T-76/89 *ITP v EC Commission* [1991] ECR II-575 para 80.

[26] See, e.g. Case T-311/94 *BPB de Eendracht NV, formerly Kartonfabriek de Eendracht NV v EC Commission* [1998] ECR II-1129 para 272. *Continental Can* [1972] OJ L7/25; *Warner-Lambert/ Gillette and Others* and *BIC/Gillette and Others* [1993] OJ L116/21. These operations might have come within merger control rules but the investigations were initiated before the entry into force of the former EC Merger Control Reg 4069/89. J Schwarze and A Weitbrecht, *Grundzüge des Europäischen Kartellverfahrensrechts* (2004) § 6 para 41.

[27] In Joint Cases 6/73 and 7/73 *Istituto Chimioterapico Italiano and Commercial Solvents Corp v EC Commission* [1974] ECR 223 the dominant undertaking was ordered to supply a certain amount of raw material to the complainant which involved the parties entering into contractual relations. Many subsequent Art 82 cases on refusal to supply and essential facilities have involved ordering a dominant undertaking to supply or share facilities. In *Magill TV Guide* the Court upheld the Commission's decision ordering compulsory licensing of the applicants television programme listings. Joined Cases C-241/91 P and C-242/91 P *Radio Telefis Eireann and Independent Television Publications Ltd (ITP) v EC Commission ('RTE')* [1991] ECR I-743.

[28] *Magill TV Guide/ITP, BBC and RTE* [1989] OJ L78/43 confirmed in T-69/89 *Radio Telefis Eireann* ECR II-485 and Joined Cases C-241/91 P and C-242/91 P *Radio Telefis Eireann and Independent Television Publications Ltd (ITP) v EC Commission ('RTE')* [1991] ECR I-743 imposing the requirement to supply each other and third parties on request and on a non-discriminatory basis with their individual advance weekly programme listings and to permit reproduction of those listings by such parties.

[29] In Commission decision of 24 March 2004 in *Microsoft* (COMP/37.792 non-confidential version available on DG COMP's website) with a view to ensuring effective and timely compliance, the Commission provided for a Monitoring Trustee to ensure Microsoft's interface disclosures were complete and accurate and that the version of Windows which does not contain the Windows Media Player is equivalent in terms of performance to the version available.

[30] See, e.g. to that effect paras 4 and 5 of *ECS/Akzo* [1985] OJ L374/1; *Tetra Pak* [1992] OJ L72/1; Case T-83/91 *Tetra Pak v EC Commission II* [1994] ECR-II 755 and Case C-333/94 P *Tetra Pak v EC Commission II* [1996] ECR I-5951; See also para 4 of *VBBB/VBVB* [1982] OJ L54/36.

caused to a third party or a possible obligation to enter into a contract, are generally to be determined under national law.[31] In *JCB*[32] the Commission required the parties to inform dealers of the changes in their agreements and that they may carry out passive sales to end-users and other authorized distributors.

Decision to impose a periodic penalty payment

11.09 Sometimes, particularly where the Commission fears open opposition or reluctance on the part of undertakings to comply with the orders to be given to them or the obligations to be attached to a decision, the Commission also decides, as a measure of constraint, to impose a periodic penalty payment in the event of refusal to comply or delay in complying.[33] The penalty payment must not exceed 5 per cent of the average daily turnover in the preceding business year per day. The undertakings do not have to pay anything, merely comply with the Commission's requirements in order to avoid the imposition of a fine.[34]

II. Penalties

A. Introduction

11.10 The following paragraphs will deal only with the pecuniary penalties which the Commission may impose for infringements of Articles 81 and 82 EC—

---

[31] Case T-395/94 *Atlantic Container Line AB and others v EC Commission* [2002] ECR II-875 para 414.

[32] Art 3 of the Commission Decision in *JCB* [2002] OJ L69/1. See also *Mercedes* [2002] OJ L257/1. In regard to these additional obligations, the CFI has ruled that such obligations on the part of the undertakings might not exceed what is appropriate and necessary to attain the objective sought, namely to restore compliance with the rules infringed. See *Cartonboard* cases: T-310/94 *Gruber & Weber GmbH & Co KG v EC Commission* [1998] II-1043 para 178: '[. . .] Such a prohibition [restriction on the exchange of not only individual commercial information] exceeds what is necessary in order to bring the conduct in question into line with what is lawful because it seeks to prevent the exchange of purely statistical information which is not in, or capable of being put into, the form of individual information on the ground that the information exchanged might be used for anti-competitive purposes [. . .].' Case T-311/94 *BPB de Eendracht NV, formerly Kartonfabriek de Eendracht NV v EC Commission* [1998] ECR II-1192 para 286; Case T-317/94 *Moritz J Weig GmbH & Co KG v EC Commission* [1998] ECR II-1235 para 172; see also Case T-7/93 *Langnese-Iglo v EC Commission* [1995] ECR II-1533 para 209, and Case T-9/93 *Schöller v EC Commission* [1995] ECR II-1611 para 163.

[33] Art 24(1)(a) of Reg 1/2003. See Section II C of this chapter. Unlike Reg 17, Art 24(1)(b) and (c) provides that periodic penalty payments may also be imposed to compel undertakings to comply with interim measures (Art 8) and commitment decisions (Art 9), respectively. In practice, the Commission has attached a periodic penalty payment to compel performance of interim measures, e.g. *Ford Werke* [1982] OJ L256/20.

[34] See Art 6 of the Commission decision in *ECS/Akzo* [1985] OJ L374/1 in which the Commission imposed a periodic penalty payment of 1,000 ECUs for each day's delay in fulfilling

Article 23(2)(a) of Reg 1/2003—to the exclusion of pecuniary penalties for infringements of decisions adopted pursuant to Article 8—interim measures[35]—and Article 9—commitments[36]—and for infringements of procedural rules (Articles 17 to 22 of Regulation 1/2003, concerning requests for information, power to take statements, and inspections).[37] Fines for substantial infringements represent the principal tool in the enforcement of EC competition law. The high level of fines over the last years conveys the Commission's determination to strike at cartel activity. Add to this that the new regulatory framework under Regulation 1/2003 which provides for a reinforcement of investigation powers is expected to intensify this activity. This trend is however not only found in the case of cartels, but also extends to other types of Article 81 and Article 82 EC infringements.[38] This chapter will only focus on the imposition of fines for infringing Article 81 or 82 EC under Article 23(2)(a) of Regulation 1/2003.

1. Nature of the penalties and persons on whom they may be imposed

The pecuniary penalties imposed by the Commission in competition matters,   **11.11** like other measures adopted by the Commission, are imposed exclusively on undertakings,[39] and not individuals. European Community competition law—by contrast with that of the United States and a small number of EU

---

each of the obligations which it imposed on AKZO in Arts 4 and 5. See also para 5 of *Irish Sugar* [1997] OJ L258/1; para 5 of *Volkswagen* [1998] OJ L124/60.

[35] See below 'Imposition of financial penalties' para 14.15.

[36] See below 'Reopening Proceedings. Financial Penalties' paras 13.13 *et seq.*

[37] See ch 9 'Penalties and confidentiality' paras 9.03 *et seq.*

[38] D Geradin and D Henry, 'The EC fining policy for violation of competition law: An empirical review of the Commission decisional practice and the Community's courts' judgments' [2005] European Competition Law Journal 401–73 pointing to on the one hand *Volkswagen* [1998] OJ L124/60 and *Nintendo/Video Games* [2003] OJ L255/33 which concerned anti-competitive distribution agreements and in which the parties were fined 102 million euros and 168 million euros, respectively, and on the other hand, to *TACA* [1999] OJ L95/1 and Commission decision of 24 March 2004 in COMP/37.792 *Microsoft* (non-confidential version available on DG COMP's website) which included the imposition of fines of 102 million euros and 168 million euros, respectively, for the abuse of a dominant position.

[39] Arts 81 and 82 EC apply to 'undertakings'. In competition law, the concept of undertaking is more an economic and functional concept than a legal one, i.e. an economic unit which participates in commercial dealings is an undertaking, regardless of its legal structure and status. Case T-352/94 *Mo Och Domsjo v EC Commission* [1998] ECR II-1989 para 87. Certain natural persons may be regarded as undertakings, for example, inventors, artists, and athletes, independent entrepreneurs, and so on where they commercially exploit the product of their talent. Non-profit-making organizations or entities may also be regarded as undertakings if they have any commercial dealings. Furthermore, one and the same economic unit may include several legal persons, such as a parent or holding company which owns or controls a number of subsidiaries. If the undertaking found to have committed a violation would consist of an 'unincorporated' business, the Commission would have to address its fining decision to the natural persons operating the business. So far this has not occurred. See as regards this issue para 6.04 n 12.

Member States[40]—does not allow criminal or administrative proceedings to be taken against persons such as chief executives or employees of undertakings or any other persons directly responsible for conduct contrary to Articles 81 and 82 EC. Only undertakings as such may have a penalty imposed on them.[41] Such penalties are considered as not having a criminal-law nature, but instead are seen as administrative, as are all proceedings before the Commission.[42]

---

[40] In the US, the Antitrust Criminal Penalty and Reform Act 2004 raised the statutory maximum fine for corporations to 100 million US Dollars (from 10 million US Dollars) and for individuals to 1 million US Dollars (from 350,000 US Dollars). In a addition, the Act increased the maximum prison term to ten years per violation (from three years). As regards the EU, JD Cook, 'General Report' in 'The Modernization of EU Competition Law Enforcement in the EU' [2004] FIDE 2004 National Reports 635 notes that criminal sanctions appear to play a relatively limited role in the enforcement of NCAs. Ireland appears to be the only one of the old Member States which has provided criminal sanctions in the form of both fines and imprisonment for infringement of both Arts 81 and 82 EC and the corresponding rules of national law (in minor cases, undertakings accused of breaching either rule are prosecuted by the NCA before the criminal courts: in more serious cases, the NCA passes its file to the public prosecutor who prosecutes the offences before the higher criminal courts). In Denmark, criminal fines for infringement of competition rules can be imposed by the criminal courts, but sanctions in the form of prison sentence are not provided for. On the other hand, in two Member States, criminal sanctions for competition infringements which had existed under earlier laws have been removed (Austria and France). In all Member States, of course, it is recognized that some activities may at the same time infringe competition rules and constitute criminal offences under the Penal Code, for example the manipulation of auctions or collusive tendering (e.g. Germany). The UK Enterprise Act 2002 establishes a 'cartel offence' punishable by imprisonment of up to five years and/or an unlimited fine. The arrangements covered by the offence include 'bid-rigging' and also a series of acts based closely on the wording of sub-paras (a) to (e) of Art 81(1) EC. In addition, infringement of Arts 81 and 82 EC and the corresponding provisions of the national rules can lead to the disqualification of the directors of corporate undertakings by the court.

[41] Art 23(1) and (2) of Reg 1/2003.

[42] According to Art 23(5) of Reg 1/2003, decisions imposing such fines 'shall not be of a criminal nature'. The provision may have some importance as to the status of such fines under national law, e.g. whether they are tax deductible in some Member States. In any event, the Commission's assessment will depart from the premise that the fine will not be tax deductible (see Case T-10/89 *Hoechst v EC Commission* [1992] ECR-II 629 para 369. (As regards, e.g. German law, see the ruling of the *Finanzgericht Rheinland-Pfalz*, judgment of 15 July 2003 Case 2K 2377/01 stating that a Commission fine was not deductible for tax purposes, except in so far as it represented the refund of profits which themselves had been taxed. Further, the Commission does not need to take into account differences relating to the tax treatment of fines under national revenue law. See Case 44/69 *Buchler & Co v EC Commission* [1970] ECR 733 paras 50 and 51). J Temple Lang, 'Developments, Issues and New Remedies—The Duties of National Authorities and Courts under Art 10 of the EC Treaty' [2004] Fordham International Law Journal 1904–39 (1910) states that it would be contrary to Art 10 EC for a Member State to reduce the effect of a Commission fine by allowing it to be deducted for tax purposes, or otherwise to reduce the costs of the infringement.). In practice fines under Art 23 of Reg 1/2003 may be likened to criminal or penal sanctions. The Council may also have considered that it had some relevance as to the necessary legal basis under the EC Treaty (see Arts 29 and 47 EU; Case C-176/03 *EC Commission v Council*, currently pending before the ECJ, application in [2003] OJ C135/21). In any event, the provision has not prevented such fines from being qualified as 'criminal' within the meaning of the European Convention of Human Rights and the Charter of Fundamental Rights of the EU (see Opinion of Judge Vesterdorf acting as AG in Case T-1/89 *Rhône-Poulenc v EC Commission* [1991] ECR II-867 para 885, Opinion of AG Léger in Case C-185/95 P *Baustahlgewebe v EC*

In the case of a group of undertakings, the Commission's starting point is that **11.12** the competition rules are addressed to undertakings as 'economic units which consist of a unitary organisation of personal, tangible and intangible elements, which pursue a specific economic aim on a long-term basis.'[43] Thus, parent companies may be held liable for the actions of their subsidiaries where the parent companies have had decisive influence over the conduct of the subsidiary. In this context, the Community Courts have stated that the fact that a subsidiary has a separate legal personality is not sufficient to exclude the possibility of its conduct being imputed to the parent company, especially where the subsidiary does not independently decide its own conduct on the market, but carries out, in all material respects, the instructions given to it by the parent company, having regard in particular to the economic and legal links between them.[44] In *ThyssenKrupp*,[45] TKS (jointly controlled by Thyssen and Krupp) and ATS (owned by TKS) argued that the amount of fine should not have been applied separately, but rather to the entire group acting as one single economic entity. The ECJ, however, confirmed the Commission decision and the ruling of the CFI finding that TKS and ATS had never denied acting autonomously throughout the duration of the infringement of the competition rules.[46] Without mentioning any specific circumstances, the Commission earlier had

---

Commission [1998] ECR I-8417 para 31; Joined Cases T-213/95 and T-18/96 *Stichting Certificatie Kraanverhuurbedrijf (SCK) and Federatie van Nederlandse Kraanbedrijven (FNK) v EC Commission* [1997] ECR II-1739 para 56; Case C-199/92 P *Hüls v EC Commission* [1999] ECR I-4287 paras 149–150; CS Kerse and N Khan, EC *Antitrust Procedure* (5th edn, 2005) para 7–008.

[43] Case T-11/89 *Shell v EC Commission* [1992] ECR II-757 para 311, and Case T-352/94 *Mo och Domsjö v EC Commission* [1998] ECR II-1989 para 87.

[44] Case 6/72 *Europemballage and Continental Can v EC Commission* [1973] ECR 215 para 15; Case C-294/98 P *Metsä-Serla and others v EC Commission* [2000] ECR I-10065 para 27. Where a subsidiary is wholly owned, there is a rebuttable presumption that the parent company was in a position to exert a decisive influence over the conduct of the subsidiary. Case C-286/98 *Stora Koppabergs v EC Commission* [2000] ECR I-9925 paras 26–29. But see also Joined Cases T-236/01, T-239/01, T-244/01 to T-246/01, T-251/01 and T-252/01 *Tokai Carbon and others v EC Commission* [2004] ECR II-1181 para 279 in which the CFI rejected the objection that the responsibility for the infringement should have been attributed to the parent company of the offender. The Court stated that the issue whether the unlawful conduct could have been attributed to another undertaking did not arise given that the Commission addressed itself in *Graphite Electrodes* ([2002] OJ L100/1) only to the company which committed the infringement, i.e. UCAR International Inc, and not to the parent companies. CS Kerse and N Khan, *EC Antitrust Procedure* (5th edn, 2005) para 7–004. Some (older) judgments suggest that in order to impute the infringement to the parent company, the Commission would not only have to establish that the parent company was able to exercise decisive influence over the policy of the subsidiary but also that in fact it used this power. Case 107/82 *AEG-Telefunken v EC Commission* [1983] ECR 3151 para 50. WPJ Wils, *The Optimal Enforcement of EC Antitrust Law* (2002) 184 with more references.

[45] Joined Cases C-65/02 P and C-73/02 *ThyssenKrupp Stainless GmbH v EC Commission* [2005] OJ C217/3.

[46] ibid paras 66–70.

imputed to *Siderúrgica Aristrain Madrid* (SAM) the conduct of its sister company *José Maria Aristrain SA*, which both belonged to the Aristrain group whose shares were held by members of the Aristrain family. The ECJ stated that 'the simple fact that the share capital of two separate commercial companies is held by the same person or the same family is insufficient, in itself, to establish that those two companies are an economic unit with the result that, under Community competition law, the actions of one company can be attributed to the other and that one can be held liable to pay a fine for the other'.[47] Where there is no legal or natural person at the head of a group of companies, as the person responsible for coordinating the group's activities and for the infringements committed by the various component companies of the group, the Commission may hold the component companies jointly and severally responsible for all the acts of the group.[48]

11.13　A change in the legal form and name of an undertaking as such does not exonerate the new undertaking from its liability for the anti-competitive behaviour of its predecessor.[49] By the same token, where a party transfers its business activities to another undertaking, the transferor undertaking continuing in existence remains liable.[50] In the event that the business has been transferred or merged with that of another undertaking with the result that the original undertaking has ceased to exist, the responsibility may lie with the new (or merged) entity.[51] In this context, the question is whether in line with the

---

[47] Case C-196/99 P *Siderúrgica Aristrain Madrid SL v EC Commission* [2003] ECR I-11005 paras 96–99; Joined Cases C-189/02 P, C-202/02 P, C-205/02 P to C-208/02 P and C-213/02 P *Dansk Rørindustri A/S and others v EC Commission* [2005] OJ C205/1 para 118.

[48] Case T-9/99 *HFB and others v EC Commission* [2002] ECR-II 1487 para 66 noting that in this case the Commission was entitled to hold the component companies jointly and severally responsible for all the acts of the group. The formal separation between those companies, resulting from their separate legal personality could not prevent a finding that they had acted jointly on the market for the purposes of applying the rules on competition; on appeal confirmed in Joined Cases C-189/02 P, C-202/02 P, C 205/02 P to C-208/02 P, and C-213/02 P *Dansk Rørindustri A/S and others v EC Commission* [2005] OJ C205/1 paras 117–130.

[49] CS Kerse and N Khan, *EC Antitrust Procedure* (5th edn, 2005) para 7–005 pointing to Cases 40–48/73, 50/73, 54–56/73, 111/73, 113/73 and 114/73 *Coöperative Vereniging 'Suiker Unie' UA v EC Commission* [1975] ECR 1663 paras 75–88.

[50] Case C-49/92 P *EC Commission v Anic* [1999] ECR I-4125 para 145; Case T-327/94 *SCA Holding Ltd v EC Commission* [1998] ECR II-1373 para 63. Case C-286/98 P *Stora Kopparbergs Bergslags AB v EC Commission* [2000] ECR I-9925 paras 37–39 stating that the fact that an acquirer is aware that the undertakings acquired participated in an infringement before their acquisition does not suffice to impute to it the unlawful conduct prior to that acquisition.

[51] *Food Flavour Enhancers* [2004] OJ L75/1 para 192: '[. . .] Miwon Corporation Limited's full merger with Sewon Co. Ltd to form Daesang Corporation means that responsibility passes to the new entity. There is an obvious continuity between Miwon and the new entity into which it has been subsumed. Miwon ceased to exist in law and its legal personality as well as all its assets and staff were transferred to Daesang Corporation. [. . .]'; *Amino Acids* [2001] OJ L152/24 para 444; *Cartonboard* [1994] OJ L243/1; Joined Cases T-305/94 to T-307/94, T-313/94 to T-316/94, T-318/94, T-325/94, T-328/94, T-329/94, and T-335/94 *Limburgse Vinyl Maatschappij and others v EC Commission* [1999] ECR II-931 para 953.

concept of undertaking there is an economic and functional continuity between the original undertaking and its successor.[52] Where between the commission of the infringement and the time when the undertaking in question must answer for it the person responsible for the operation of that undertaking has ceased to exist in law, it is necessary 'to find the combination of physical and human elements which contributed to the commission of the infringement and then to identify the person who has become responsible for their operation,' so as to avoid the result that because of the disappearance of the person responsible for its operation when the infringement was committed the undertaking may fail to answer for it.[53] Where the Commission's decision seeks to attribute liability for an infringement to the purchaser or other successor of an undertaking alleged to have committed the infringement, the Commission must clearly identify the identity of the legal entity which is the legal successor and the reality of the continuance by that entity, through the relevant undertaking, of the activity in question.[54]

11.14 As with Regulation 17, Regulation 1/2003 does not expressly state whether an undertaking which has not been specifically and formally held liable for an infringement found by the Commission may be declared jointly and severally liable with another undertaking for payment of a fine imposed on that other undertaking, which has committed and been penalized for the infringement. However, the Community courts interpreted Article 15(2) of Regulation 17 as meaning that an undertaking may be declared jointly and severally liable with another undertaking for payment of a fine imposed on the latter undertaking, which has committed an infringement intentionally or negligently, provided that the Commission demonstrates, in the same decision, that the infringement could also have been found to have been committed by the undertaking held jointly and severally liable.[55] Crucial to this assessment is whether there are

---

[52] *Welded Steel Mesh* [1989] OJ L260/1 paras 194–195; *Cartonboard* [1994] OJ L243/1 para 145. The 'economic continuity' test is to be applied exclusively where the entity which committed the infringement has ceased to exist in law. When such an entity is still in existence, it must be held liable for the infringement, irrespective of the nature of its current activities in the market: see *Zinc Phosphate* [2003] OJ L153/1.

[53] Case T-6/89 *Enichem Anic v EC Commission* [1991] ECR II-1623 paras 236–238; Opinion of AG Mischo in C-297/98 *SCA Holding Ltd v EC Commission* [2000] ECR I-10101 para 13.

[54] CS Kerse and N Khan, *EC Antitrust Procedure* (5th edn, 2004) para 7–006 referring to Joined Cases 29/83 and 30/83 *Compagnie Royale Asturrienne (CRA) v EC Commission* [1984] ECR 1679 paras 6–9. Where imputation of liability is disputed, the Commission decision should contain a more detailed account of the grounds for holding the legal entity liable for the infringement.

[55] In *Commercial Solvents*: Joined Cases 6/73 and 7/73 *Istituto Chemioterapico and Commercial Solvents Corp v EC Commission* [1974] ECR 223, the Court accepted that the parent company and its subsidiary had infringed the competition rules together and were therefore jointly and severally liable for the infringement.

sufficient economic and legal links between the undertakings that they can be considered to be one economic unit.[56] It is important to remember that the Commission is required to specify unequivocally in the statement of objections the persons on whom fines may be imposed. In *Compagnie Maritime Belge*, the ECJ ruled that a statement of objections which merely identifies a collective entity as the perpetrator of an infringement does not make the companies forming that entity sufficiently aware that fines will be imposed on them individually.[57]

11.15 The Commission decision in *Organic Peroxides* sets out the Commission's views on the liability of consultancy companies which provided services to a price-fixing and market-sharing cartel agreement but did not produce the products. The Commission found that AC Treuhand, a Swiss based consultancy company, played an important role in the organization and implementation of the infringement. Among other things, it had a key role in determining the methods of implementing the cartel by carrying out auditing of the cartel members. The relatively modest fine of 1,000 euros may be attributable to the fact that this seems to be the first time that the Commission has imposed a fine on a third party in these circumstances.[58]

2. Purpose of the penalties

11.16 In imposing fines and periodic penalty payments, the Commission's main aim is to ensure that the prohibited conduct does not recur.[59] Thus, the essential purpose of both types of penalty is, in the main, to deter and persuade. In the specific case of fines, the Community Courts have recognized their twofold character, in that they punish past acts and have a general deterrent effect for the

---

[56] *Cartonboard* [1994] OJ L243/1 upheld in T-339/94 *Metsä-Serla and others v EC Commission* [1998] ECR II-1727 paras 45–58 expanding on the connection between a trade association and its members: '[. . .] the economic and legal links between Finnboard and each of the applicants [Finish cartonboard producers] were thus such that, in marketing cartonboard for the benefit of the applicants, Finnboard merely acted as an auxiliary organ of each of those companies. In the light of those links and the fact that it was bound to follow the instructions issued by each of the applicants and could not adopt conduct on the market independently of any of them, Finnboard in practice formed an economic unit with each of its cartonboard-producing member companies. [. . .].' T-9/99 *HFB v EC Commission* [2002] ECR-II 1487 para 527.

[57] Joined Cases C-395/96 and C-396/96 *Compagnie Maritime Belge v EC Commission* [2000] ECR I-1365 para 144.

[58] Commission Decision of 10 December 2003 in *PO/Organic peroxyde* (Case COMP/E-2/37.857), non-confidential version available at DG COMP's website, in particular para 454.

[59] Case T-18/97 *Atlantic Container Line AB and others v EC Commission* [2002] ECR II-1125 para 50; Joined Cases 41/69, 44/69 and 51–57/69 *ACF Chemiefarma v EC Commission* [1970] ECR 661 para 173; Case 45/69 *Boehringer Mannheim GmbH v EC Commission* [1970] ECR 769 para 53.

future,[60] and this applies not only to the undertakings involved but also to others who might be tempted to engage in the same type of conduct. The Commission often explicitly justifies a high fine of being imposed to exclude, by its deterrent effect, any repetition of the behaviour in question.[61] The focus on the 'deterrent effect' of fines is of particular relevance where the infringement involves large undertakings which are presumed to have the legal and economic knowledge and internal structures that will enable them more easily to recognize that their conduct constitutes an infringement.[62] The Commission may also impose fines where the infringement has already come to an end[63] and is not precluded from imposing a fine by the fact that no fine was imposed in other cases.[64] Periodic penalty payments, for their part, are mainly coercive and are intended to prevent specific conduct contrary to the competition provisions or to compel undertakings to comply with Commission decisions for the application of those provisions.

3. Intentional or negligent infringement

Article 23(2) of Regulation 1/2003 states that the infringement must have been committed 'intentionally or negligently'. The ECJ has made clear that this requirement applies independently of the question of gravity of the infringement. Indeed, Article 23(2) deals with two distinct issues: Article 23(2) sets out that the infringement must be intentional or negligent in order that a fine may be imposed ('initial conditions'). In addition, the provision governs the

11.17

---

[60] Joined Cases 100–103/80 *Musique Diffusion Française v EC Commission (Pioneer)* [1983] ECR 1825 para 106. See also Case 49/69 *BASF v EC Commission* [1972] ECR 713 paras 38 *et seq.*; See Case T-203/01 *Michelin v EC Commission* [2003] ECR-II 4071 para 293. See also Joined Cases T-202/98, T-204/98 and T-207/98 *Tate & Lyle plc, British Sugar plc and Napier Brown & Co Ltd v EC Commission* [2001] ECR II-2035 paras 133 *et seq.* The Commission repeatedly emphasizes the importance of 'credible deterrence' for potential offenders. See, e.g. XXXIII Report on Competition Policy [2003] paras 722 and 725.

[61] See *Opel* [2001] OJ L59/1 para 194; *Far East Trade Tariff Charges and Surcharges Agreement (FETTCSA)* [2000] OJ L268/1 para 178: '[. . .] Only a fine is both punitive and preventive [. . .]'; the decision in *1998 Football World Cup* somehow figures as an exception. The Commission restated that every abuse of a dominant position should normally be penalized by a fine varying in accordance with the gravity and duration of the infringement, but it acknowledged that measures were implemented to respond to competition concerns and imposed only a token fine of 1,000 euros ([2000] OJ L5/55 para 125).

[62] *Methylglucamine* [2004] OJ L38/18 para 239. *Pre-Insulated Pipes* [1999] L24/1 para 169: '[. . .]It is abundantly clear that ABB systematically used its economic power and resources as a major multinational company to reinforce the effectiveness of the cartel and to ensure that other undertakings complied with its wishes. [. . .]'

[63] Joined Cases 41/69, 44/69 and 51–57/69 and *ACF Chemiefarma v EC Commission* [1970] ECR 661 paras 170–175.

[64] Case 32/78 *BMW Belgium v EC Commission* [1979] ECR 2435 paras 52 and 53.

determination of the fine which depends on the gravity of the infringement.[65] Gravity in turn has to be determined by reference to numerous factors, such as the particular circumstances of the case, its context, and the dissuasive effect of fines.[66] When ascertaining the gravity of an infringement, it is not required to distinguish between the two alternatives. Infringements committed negligently are not, from the point of view of competition, less serious than those committed intentionally,[67] and the amount of the fine is not affected. While the reference to an 'intentional' or 'negligent' infringement reflects some degree of culpability on the part of the undertakings concerned, it is clear that an undertaking acts through human agency and the intentions and negligence in issue are in effect those of its directors and employees. In EC law the undertaking is responsible for the conduct of its directors and employees and does not concern itself with the imputation of the employees' conduct to the companies.[68] In *Volkswagen*, the ECJ held that it was not necessary for the Commisison to identify the persons whose conduct was indicative of the intentional or negligent nature of the infringement,[69] but is correct in carrying out an 'objective assessment of the facts'.[70] It appears that an intentional infringement requires at least the deliberate commission of an act which is designed to achieve anti-competitive ends or which is committed in the knowledge that anti-competitive effects would ensue. Thus intentional means an intention to restrict competition and not an intention to infringe the rules.[71] Negligence would imply that the

---

[65] Case C-137/95 P *Vereniging van Samenwerkende Prijsregelende Organisaties in de Bouwnijverheid (SPO) and others v EC Commission* [1996] ECR I-1611 para 53. See also Case T-28/99 *Sigma Tecnologie di rivestimento Srlv EC Commission* [2002] ECR II-1845 paras 79–94; Case T-368/00 *General Motors Nederland BV and Opel Nederland BV v EC Commission* [2003] ECR II-4491 paras 190–200.

[66] Case C-219/95 P *Ferriere Nord v EC Commission* [1997] ECR I-4411 para 33; see also Case T-295/94 *Buchmann v EC Commission* [1998] ECR II-813 para 163.

[67] Case C-137/95 P *Vereniging van Samenwerkende Prijsregelende Organisaties in de Bouwnijverheid (SPO) and others v EC Commission* [1996] ECR I-1611 para 57.

[68] This is why undertakings should have in place and enforce compliance programmes to prevent infractions of rules. A Jones and B Sufrin, *EC Competition Law* (2nd edn, 2004) 1122.

[69] Case C-338/00 *Volkswagen v EC Commisison* [2003] ECR I-9189 paras 94–98.

[70] See in this respect, *Nederlandse Federative Vereniging voor de Groothandel op Elektrotechnisch Gebied and Technische Unie (FEG and TU)* [2000] OJ L39/1 paras 131–135, confirmed in Joined Cases T-5/00 and T-6/00 *Nederlandse Federatieve Vereniging voor de Groothandel op Elektrotechnisch Gebied v EC Commission* [2003] ECR II-5761, in particular paras 396–397.

[71] Joined Cases 100 to 103/80 *Musique Diffusion Française v EC Commisison* [1983] ECR 1825 para 49; C Bellamy and G Child, *European Community Law of Competition* (5th edn, 2001) para 12–080; A Jones and B Sufrin, *EC Competition Law* (2nd edn, 2004) 1122. See recently, Case T-52/02 *Société nouvelle des couleurs zinciques SA (SNCZ) v EC Commission*, CFI judgment of 29 November 2005 (not yet published) para 83; D Geradin and D Henry, 'The EC fining policy for violation of competition law: An empirical review of the Commission decisional practice and the Community's courts' judgments' [2005] European Competition Law Journal 401–73 (404).

undertaking concerned could reasonably foresee that its conduct would have anti-competitive effects.[72] Since both intention and negligence trigger liability to fines it is usually unnecessary to decide into which category the infringement falls. More recently, the Commission has begun not to dwell on the interpretation of intentional or negligent infringements. Instead, it now qualifies a hard-core infringement, such as price-fixing cartels, as a *deliberate* infringement, which would come within the scope of Article 23(2).[73] Sometimes, however, the Commission seems to take note of the existence of grey areas where issues are less settled. Following up a complaint filed by the *UK Post Office*, the Commisison decided that *Deutsche Post AG* had abused its dominant position in the German letter market by intercepting, surcharging and delaying incoming international mail which it erroneously classified as circumvented domestic mail. However, owing to the legal uncertainty that prevailed at the time of the infringement, the fine was set at the token figure of 1,000 euros.[74] Similarly, where the Commission believes that dealers forming part of a distribution agreement were forced into restrictive arrangements imposed by the supplier, it

---

[72] Opinion of AG Mayras in Case C-26/75 *General Motors v EC Commission* [1975] ECR 1367 stating that '[. . .] the concept of negligence must be applied where the author of the infringement, although acting without any intention to perform an unlawful act, has not foreseen the consequences of his action in circumstances where a person who is normally informed and sufficiently attentive could not have failed to foresee them [. . .]'. Case T-66/92 *Herlitz v EC Commission* [1994] ECR II-531 para 45; Case T-176/95 *Accinauto v EC Commission* [1999] ECR II-1635 para 119: '[. .] For an infringement of the competition rules of the Treaty to be considered to have been committed intentionally, it is not necessary for the undertaking to have been aware that it was infringing a prohibition laid down by those rules; it is sufficient that it was aware that the object of the offending conduct was to restrict competition [. . .]'. Case T-143/89 *Ferriere Nord v EC Commission* [1995] ECR II-917 para 41; *British Sugar* [1999] OJ L76/1 para 191; *BASF/Accinauto* [1995] OJ L272/16 para 6. In particular, in view of their size and sophistication large companies cannot rely on this defence, e.g. *Methyglucamine* [2004] OJ L38/18 para 239. Undertakings from new Member States cannot invoke the lack of knowledge about Community law to escape Art 23 of Reg 1/2003, see, e.g. *Austrian Banks* [2004] OJ L56/1 paras 494–500. See *Bayer Dental* [1990] OJ L351/46 as one of the few cases in which alleged ignorance did not lead to the imposition of a fine.

[73] *Methylglucamine* [2004] OJ L38/18 para 224; *Nintendo* [2003] OJ L255/33 para 371; *Greek Ferries* [1999] OJ L109/24 para 145; Case T-229/94 *Deutsche Bahn v EC Commission* [1997] ECR II-1689 para 128. See also *Michelin* [2002] OJ L143/1 para 352 in which the Commission considered the infringement as being intentional given that Michelin has been subject of previous finding of the breach of EC competition rules for the same practices, which added to the fact that the company had a large legal department which could not have been unaware that the practices constituted an infringement.

[74] *Deutsche Post/British Post Office* [2001] OJ L331/40 para 193: '[. . .] in accordance with the case law of German courts. Despite the fact that the Commission considers that DPAG's behaviour in some respects goes beyond what can be determined with certainty from German case law, it must be concluded that the said case law resulted in a situation where the legal situation was unclear. Moreover, at the time when the majority of the interceptions, surcharging and delays in the present case took place, no Community case law existed that concerned the specific context of cross-border letter mail services [. . .]'.

does not consider whether the infringement was committed intentionally or negligently by those dealers.[75]

4. Compatibility of fines and periodic penalty payments

11.18 Although it looks as if Article 23 of Regulation 1/2003 (Penalties) seeks to punish past infringement and Article 24 of Regulation 1/2003 (Periodic Penalties) deals with continuing and future infringements, there is nothing to prevent the Commission from imposing fines and periodic penalty payments on undertakings at the same time. Similar to Regulation 17, Regulation 1/2003 does not limit the Commission's recourse to either penalty, or exclude the imposition of both at the same time. Although each penalty pursues different aims, it has been argued that by imposing both at the same time the Commission is imposing two penalties for the same conduct.[76]

5. Limitation periods

11.19 As indicated, the Commission's power to impose penalties for infringements of Community competition law is subject to limitation periods. The relevant provisions of Regulation 1/2003 fix two types of limitation period, those relating to the Commission's powers to impose fines and penalties ('limitation periods in proceedings') and those relating to the enforcement of the collection of fines and penalties ('limitation period for the enforcement of sanction').[77] Regulation 1/2003 has taken over the rules contained in Regulation 2988/74 with some minor changes in order to adapt the enforcement system to the new decentralized application of competition rules.[78] Pursuant to Article 25 of Regulation 1/2003,

---

[75] *Opel* [2001] OJ L59/1 para 174: '[. . .] The Dutch Opel dealers, as participants together with Opel Nederland BV through agreements to prevent or limit exports, are victims of the restrictive policy decided by their contracting party, to which they had to agree under pressure. The dealers did not participate actively. The Commission is therefore of the opinion that no fine should be imposed on them. [. . .]'.

[76] In *Sumitomo Chemical*, the CFI reaffirmed that the five-year limitation period only applies to the Commission's ability to impose a fine, not to its ability to address infringement decisions to undertakings and so making findings that violations of Arts 81 and 82 EC have occurred. Joined Cases T-22/02 and T-23/02 *Sumitomo Chemical v EC Commission*, CFI judgment of 6 October 2005 (not yet published).

[77] See CS Kerse and N Khan, *EC Antitrust Procedure* (5th edn, 2005) para 7–080 noting the example that if an undertaking refuses to admit inspectors to its premises to carry out an inspection ordered by decision under Art 20(4), it may be liable to a fine of up to 1 per cent of turnover pursuant to Art 23(1)(c) but it may also be liable to a fine of up to 5 per cent of its daily turnover pursuant to Art 24(1)(e). The same conduct would, therefore, be subject to two different fines which would lead to a conflict with Art 50 of the EU Charter of Fundamental Rights and general principles of law.

[78] Council Reg 2988/74 concerning limitation periods in proceedings and the enforcement of sanctions under the rules of the European Economic Community relating to transport and competition [1974] OJ L319/1, as amended. Pursuant to Art 37 of Reg 1/2003, Reg 2988/74 has been amended in that it does not apply to measures taken under Reg 1/2003.

the imposition of penalties is limited to a period of five years for substantive infringements. Time shall begin to run on the day on which the infringement is committed. However, in the case of continuing or repeated infringements, time shall begin to run on the day on which the infringement ceases.[79] The Commission often takes the view that a complex cartel may be viewed as a single continuing infringement for the period of time in which it existed.[80]

As regards the running of time, any action taken by the Commission or by **11.20** the competition authority of a Member State for the purpose of the investigation or proceedings in respect of an infringement will interrupt the limitation period for the imposition of fines or periodic penalty payments in relation to both procedural and substantive infringements. The limitation period is interrupted with effect from the date on which the action is notified to at least one undertaking or association of undertakings which has participated in the infringement. The Commission is not prevented from taking action in relation to any agreements or practices after these periods have elapsed but is merely prohibited from imposing fines. Thus, the Commission may adopt a decision declaring that an infringement has taken place which may have consequences for the liability of the parties before a national court.[81] For limitation purposes, time starts to run again after each interruption has ended.[82] In *FETTSCA*, the CFI made it clear that the interruption of the five-year limitation period is an exception to the rule and must be interpreted narrowly. Moreover, written requests for information must be for the purpose of the preliminary investigation or proceedings in respect of an infringement and they must be necessary in the sense that they must legitimately be regarded as having a connection with the putative infringement. Thus, requests for information aimed at artificially prolonging the limitation period cannot be considered as necessary in this regard.[83] Moreover, the time bar

---

[79] For a case in which the CFI, having taken the view that insufficient evidence had been given of the existence of a continuous infringement between two dates on which there had indeed been specific instances of infringements, declared the first infringement time-barred, see Case T-43/92 *Dunlop v EC Commission* [1994] ECR II-441 para 84.

[80] e.g. Case T-7/89 *SA Hercules Chemicals NV v EC Commission* [1991] ECR II-1711 para 310: '[. . .] the applicant participated in a single infringement which began in November 1977, when it subscribed to an agreement fixing a target price for 1 December 1977, and continued until November 1983. In this regard, it should be noted that the continuity of the infringement between the conclusion of that agreement and the agreements and concerted practices found from 1979 onwards is borne out by the contacts with other producers which the applicant maintained without interruption beginning in 1977 [. . .].' *Carbonless paper* [2004] OJ L115/1 para 323; *Flood flavour enhancers* [2004] OJ L75/1 para 162.

[81] This is naturally subject to national procedural rules (*res judicata*, etc). CS Kerse and N Khan, EC Antitrust Procedure (5th edn, 2005) para 7–082, n 81.

[82] Art 25(5) of Reg 1/2003.

[83] See Case T-213/00 *CMA CGM v EC Commission* [2003] ECR II-913 para 488: in which the CFI held that the interruption of the limitation period would have to be interpreted narrowly

will take effect in any event after six years (for procedural infringements) or ten years (for substantive infringements) if the Commission fails to impose a fine or other penalty.[84] This time-limit will be extended by the period during which time stopped running as a result of an action being brought against the Commission decision before the CFI or ECJ.[85]

6. Procedure

11.21 Fines and periodic penalty payments for breach of decisions under Article 8—interim measures—and Article 9—commitments—of Regulation 1/2003, those for substantive infringements—of Articles 81 and 82 EC—and those for procedural infringements—of Articles 18 to 22 of Regulation 1/2003—must be preceded by a statement of objections. In order to comply with the defence rights, the Commission is required to include in the statement of objections addressed to an undertaking on which it intends to impose a penalty for infringement of competition rules the essential factors taken into consideration against that undertaking, such as the facts alleged, the classification of those facts and the evidence on which the Commission relies, so that the undertaking may submit its arguments effectively during the administrative procedure brought against it, although it does not need to explain how it uses each element to determine the fine.[86] Given its importance, the statement of objections must specify unequivocally the legal person on whom fines may be imposed and be addressed to that person.[87] Throughout the procedure, the Commission must

---

and the Commission cannot make a request for information for the sole purpose of prolonging the period. The Court considered that two requests for turnover information did not interrupt the limitation period.

[84] Art 25(5) of Reg 1/2003.

[85] Art 25 (6) of Reg 1/2003. See *PVC* [1994] OJ L239/14, in particular paras 47 and 56–58. That decision followed the annulment of the first *PVC* decision by the ECJ, after the CFI had declared it non-existent.

[86] Case 41/69 *ACF Chemiefarma v EC Commission* [1970] ECR 661 para 26; Case 62/86 *AKzo v EC Commission* [1991] ECR I-3359 para 29; and Joined Cases 89/85, 104/85, 114/85, 116/85, 117/85 and 125/85 to 129/85 *Ahlström Osakeyhtiö and others v EC Commission* [1993] ECR I-1307 para 135; Joined Cases C-189/02P etc *Dansk Rørindustri and others v EC Commission* [2005] OJ C205/1, CFI judgment of 28 June 2005 para 428.

[87] Case C-176/99 *Arbed and others v EC Commission* [2003] ECR I-10687 paras 19–24. The Court set aside the finding of the CFI that the failure to address a statement of objections to the appellant was not such as to entail annulment of the contested decision. The Court held that although the applicant was aware of the statement of objections addressed to its subsidiary TradeARBED and of the procedure which had been initiated against that subsidiary, it cannot be concluded from that fact that the appellant's rights of defence were not infringed. Ambiguity as to the legal entity to whom the fines would be imposed, which could have been dispelled only by properly addressing a fresh statement of objections to the appellant, persisted up to the end of the administrative procedure. See also Joined Cases C-395/96 P and C-396/96 P *Compagnie Maritime Belge Transports SA v EC Commission* [2000] ECR I-1365 para 144: '[. . .] It is clear that a statement of objections which merely identifies as the perpetrator of an infringement a collective

respect the fundamental rights developed by the case law of the Community Courts.[88] The procedure for the imposition of fines for infringements of Articles 81 and 82 EC is the same as the substantive procedure in every respect. The fines are dealt with in a specific section of the statement of objections. During the hearing the undertakings must give their views not only on the infringements of which the Commission accuses them, but also on the seriousness and estimated duration of the infringements, matters which the Commission will take account in determining the amount of the fine. The final decision also deals with the matter of fines. In practice, therefore, there is no separate procedure for the imposition of fines for substantive infringements. On the other hand, there is a separate procedure for infringement of interim measures and commitments decisions and fines for infringement of a procedural nature. The procedure for the imposition of periodic penalty payments displays certain particular features, as already indicated in the section dealing with procedural infringements, even though it forms part of main or substantive proceedings. The procedure for the imposition of periodic penalty payments, specifically in proceedings for infringements of Articles 81 and 82 EC, will be examined below, after the next section on fines.

B. Fines

1. Quantitative limits

Pursuant to Article 23(2) of Regulation 1/2003, 'the Commission may by decision impose fines on undertakings or associations of undertakings [. . .] [which] shall not exceed 10% of its total turnover in the preceding business year.[89]   **11.22**

---

entity, such as Cewal, does not make the companies forming that entity sufficiently aware that fines will be imposed on them individually if the infringement is made out. Contrary to what the Court of First Instance held, the fact that Cewal does not have legal personality is not relevant in this regard [. . .]'.

[88] Joined Cases T-67/00, T-68/00, T-71/00 and T-78/00 *JFE Engineering Corp and others v EC Commission* [2004] OJ C239/1 para 178: '[. . .] Given the nature of the infringements in question and the nature and degree of severity of the ensuing penalties, the principle of the presumption of innocence applies in particular to the procedures relating to infringements of the competition rules applicable to undertakings that may result in the imposition of fines or periodic penalty payments [. . .]'. See 'General principles and case law' paras 1.20 *et seq.* and 'Procedural guarantees' paras 10.04 *et seq.*

[89] In one of the judgment on the 'zinc phosphate' cartel, Case T-33/02 *Britannia Alloys & Chemicals Ltd v EC Commission*, CFI judgment of 29 November 2005 (not yet published), Britannia challenged that the Commission had not used the turnover of the business year preceding the decision—when its turnover was nil because it was a non-trading company at that time after having sold its business in the zinc sector to another company. The Commission relied instead on the 1996 turnover (55.7 million euros) as 'the last available figure reflecting an entire

Where the infringement of an association relates to activities of its members, the fine shall not exceed 10% of the sum of the total turnover of each member'. The discussion regarding the required identification of the addressees of decisions imposing fines is also relevant to the determination which turnover of what company has to be considered, for example whether it is justified to depart from the turnover of the parent company or whether the Commission should only consider the turnover of the subsidiary. The implication of attributing responsibility to a parent company would be to increase the ceiling of the potential fine.[90] As indicated, conduct of one undertaking may only be attributed to another where it has not acted independently on the market but in all material respects carried out the instructions given to it by the second undertaking, in particular considering the economic and legal links between them.[91]

11.23 According to the ECJ, the quantitative limits determined by Regulation [1/2003] for fines for infringements of Articles 81 and 82 EC seek to ensure that the fines

---

year of economic activity' given that after 1996 the company was continuously running down its activities. Britannia alleged that the Commission was not entitled to impose a fine of more than 1 million euros instead of 3.37 million euros actually imposed. In response, the CFI stated that it would be true that the 'preceding business year' refers in principle to the last full business year of each of the undertakings concerned at the date of adoption of the contested decision. However both from the objectives of the system of which [Art 23(2) of Reg 1/2003] part and from the case-law that the application of the 10 per cent upper limit presupposes, it would be clear, first, that the Commission has at its disposal the turnover for the last business year preceding the date of adoption of the decision and, second, that those data represent a 'full year of normal economic activity over a period of 12 months'. In conclusion, the Commission would therefore be entitled to rely on the turnover achieved in an earlier year, if appropriate.

[90] See, for an example, *Industrial and Medical Gases* [2003] OJ L84/1, in particular nn 20 and 282. The Commission fined seven companies in a Dutch industrial gases price-fixing cartel between 1993 and 1997 which included AGA Gas BV. Following the liquidation of AGA Gas BV in 2000 to 2001, AGA AB accepted liability for the acts of its subsidiary and is the addressee of the decision. As AGA AB was held liable for its former subsidiary AGA Gas BV, the amount has been reduced to 10 per cent of the last turnover of the subsidiary. Generally, the implications for attributing responsibility within groups of companies may be far-reaching and disturbing for multi-national conglomerates. The issue whether they may be fined more *just because they are built that way* is also raised by J Ratliff Major, 'Events and Policy Issues in EC Competition Law, 2002–2003 (Part 1)' [2004] ICCLR 19–41 (37) who questions—commenting on the CFI rulings on the 'Lysine Cartel'—whether the total worldwide turnover of a company should be taken into account in determining the amount of the fine and suggests that fine levels should be adjusted in relation to involvement in infringements and markets affected. Under the current rules, and in respect to the issue of attributing responsibility within groups of companies, it is reasonable to require the Commission to assess in each case with great care to what extent the parent companies were involved in the infringements (instructions, knowledge etc). Conversely, similar problems may also later arise in the context of leniency applications, where relevant. Only if the legal person which manages and controls the undertaking that is involved in the infringement has filed the application, the Commission will assume that all legal persons under the direct or indirect control of the parent company are also covered by the application. See 'Leniency' para 6.04.

[91] See above at paras 11.12 *et seq.*

are not disproportionate to the size of the undertakings.[92] The practice followed by the Commission itself has recognized that the imposition of fines must be guided by the principle of proportionality. The Commission may thus bear in mind, in specific cases, that even within the limits laid down by Regulation 1/2003 the fines which it is empowered to impose may be disproportionate and therefore moderate their amount. As regards the interpretation of the notion of 'turnover', the Community Courts have confirmed that it refers to the total turnover of the undertaking in question, not its volume of sales in the European Community or its turnover in respect of the products in whose market the infringements of Articles 81 and 82 EC were committed.[93] The latter basis may, as will be seen, be used to determine the effects of the infringement and the profit obtained by the undertaking as a result of the infringement, and thereby be taken into account in determining the amount of the fine.[94] The importance of these two turnover figures should not be overstated by comparison with the other points of reference. Consequently, the determination of an appropriate fine cannot be the result of a mere calculation based on overall turnover.[95] Turnover

---

[92] Joined Cases 100–103/80 *Musique Diffusion Française v Commission ('Pioneer')* [1983] ECR 1825 paras 119 and 120; Joined Cases T-67/00, T-68/00, T-71/00 and T-78/00 *JFE Engineering Corp and others v EC Commission* [2004] OJ C239/13 para 533.

[93] See recently the ruling in the 'Zinc phosphate' cartel, Case T-62/02 *Union Pigments v EC Commission*, CFI judgment of 29 November 2005 (not yet published) paras 148 *et seq.*; Joined Cases 100–103/80 *Musique Diffusion Française v EC Commission ('Pioneer')* [1983] ECR 1825 para 119; for confirmation that the 10 per cent refers to world-wide turnover, see Case C-279/87 *Tipp-Ex v EC Commission* [1990] ECR I-261 para 39. See also Case T-148/89 *Tréfilunion SA v EC Commission* [1995] ERC II-1063 para 140; Case C-199/92 *Hüls v EC Commission* [1999] ECR I-4287 para 195: '[. . .] in determining the fine, account may be taken both of the overall turnover of the undertaking, which gives some indication, however approximate and imperfect it may be, of the size and economic strength of that undertaking, and of the part of that turnover represented by the goods concerned in the infringement which therefore serves to provide an indication of the extent of that infringement [. . .]'; in Joined Cases T-236/01, T-239/01, T-244/01 to T-246/01, T-251/01 and T-252/01 *Tokai Carbon v EC Commission* [2004] ECR II-1181 para 369 the CFI stated that provided that the limits set by Art 15(2) of Reg 17 [Art 23(2) of Reg 1/2003] are respected, the Commission may in principle choose which turnover to take in terms of territory and products in order to determine the fine.

[94] A valid question is whether in specified cases the Commission might be able to use other criteria more appropriate to the type of undertaking or association of undertakings in question than turnover, in the same way that Art 5(3) of Council Reg (EEC) 139/2004 of 20 January 2004 on the control of concentrations between undertakings [2004] OJ L24/1 lays down criteria to be used in place of turnover in order to determine the economic importance of the operations of concentrations of certain types of undertakings (banks and insurance companies). See also in Commission Notice, on calculation of turnover under the Merger Control Reg ([1998] OJ L66/25) which aims to give guidance on how to calculate turnover, taking into account any geographical or operational idiosyncrasies in order to ensure that the figures supplied are a better and more accurate reflection of the economic strength of the undertakings involved in a transaction.

[95] Case T-77/92 *Parker Pen v EC Commission* [1994] ECR II-549 para 94, citing *Pioneer* (Joined Cases 100–103/80 *Musique Diffusion Française v EC Commission* [1983] ECR 1825 para 121, and Case 183/83 *Krupp v EC Commission* [1985] ECR 3609 para 40. In Case

may still be a relevant factor in assessing the 'effective economic capacity' and size of the undertakings,[96] but gravity and duration are now the key elements[97] of the calculation.

11.24 Following the Commission's practice, the 10 per cent limit only applies to the final amount of the fine, after the consideration of the aggravating and mitigating factors and before the application of any reduction granted under the Commission Notice on the non-imposition or reduction of fines in cartel cases ('*Leniency Notice*').[98] The Court has stated that this limit does not prohibit the Commission from using an intermediate amount in its calculations higher than 10 per cent of the turnover of the affected undertaking, provided that the ultimate fine imposed does not exceed this maximum limit.[99] With respect to

T-224/00 *Archer Daniels Midland and others v EC Commission* [2003] ECR II-2597 the Court accepted that global turnover is an imprecise guide for purposes of assessing an offender's effective capacity to cause significant damage: '[. . .] It is of course possible for a powerful undertaking with a multitude of different business activities to have only a very limited presence in certain specific markets, such as the lysine market. Similarly, an undertaking with a strong position in a geographical market outside the Community may have only a weak position in the Community or EEA market. In such cases, the mere fact that the undertaking in question has a high total turnover does not necessarily mean that it has a decisive influence on the market affected by the infringement'. In Case T-241/01 *Scandinavian Airlines System v EC Commission* [2005] OJ C229/12 paras 158–170 the CFI confirmed that the CFI has some flexibility when choosing the turnover to be used as a point of reference when calculating the fine to be imposed on a company, provided this is not unreasonable in circumstances. The Court held that the Commission was entitled to ignore the total turnover the AP Møller Group because the other members were active in sectors clearly distinct from air transport, such as maritime transport and energy. Even if the Commission had erred in Maersk Air's favour by forgetting to take account of its belonging to the AP Møller Group, that fact could not constitute a valid reason for reducing the fine imposed on SAS—which appeared to challenge the approach of the Commisison—since no one might rely on an unlawfulness committed in favour of another party.

[96] See the rulings on the 'Zinc phosphate' cartel: Case T-62/02 *Union Pigments v EC Commission*, CFI judgment of 29 November 2005 (not yet published) paras 152 in which the CFI confirmed that the Commission approach to take account of both market shares and the turnovers of the undertakings with a view to determining the relative importance of the undertakings in the relevant market and Case T-52/02 *Société nouvelle des couleurs zinciques SA (SNCZ) v EC Commission*, CFI judgment of 29 November 2005 (not yet published) para 65.

[97] The 1998 Guidelines may be considered as a manifestation of the fact that the Commission has moved away from its reliance on turnover figures to set the fine. D Geradin and D Henry, 'The EC fining policy for violation of competition law: An empirical review of the Commission decisional practice and the Community's courts' judgments' [2005] European Competition Law Journal, 401–73 (409).

[98] [2002] OJ C45/3.

[99] See Case T-52/02 *Société nouvelle des couleurs zinciques SA (SNCZ) v EC Commission*, CFI judgment of 29 November 2005 (not yet published) para 38; Case T-23/99 *LR af 1998 v EC Commission* [2002] ERC II-1705 para 288. Nevertheless, AG Tizzano has stated in his Opinion in Case C-189/02 *Dansk Rørindustri v EC Commission* [2005] OJ L205/1 paras 129–133, that in some cases a calculation method which does not take into account at all this maximum limit of 10 per cent in calculating the initial amount may violate the proportionality, equity and transparency principles. The system would be liable to hit small-and medium-sized undertakings making it questionable whether it would be in conformity with the principles of reasonableness

the imposition of fines on associations of undertakings, Regulation 1/2003 codifies the CFI's case law and establishes that associations can be fined an amount of up to 10 per cent of the joint turnover of their members.[100] Furthermore, Article 23(4) of Regulation 1/2003 provides for new rules in cases where the association of undertakings is insolvent. Article 15 of Regulation 17 did not provide that the members were jointly and severally liable and this could prevent the collection of fines.[101] Under Regulation 1/2003, in the event of insolvency, the association is obliged to call for contributions from its members to cover the amount of the fine. If such contributions have not been made to the association within the time limit fixed by the Commission, the Commission may require payment of the fine directly by any of the undertakings whose representatives were members of the decision-making bodies of the association. If such payments are not sufficient as to ensure full payment of the fine, the Commission may require payment of the balance by any of the members of the association which were active on the market on which the infringement occurred.[102]

---

and fairness. In one of the judgments in the 'Zinc phosphate' cartel, Case T-64/02 *Dr Hans Heubach GmbH & Co KG v EC Commission*, CFI judgment of 29 November 2005 (not yet published) para 39, the CFI indicated that the 1998 Guidelines would enable the Commission to take into consideration, where circumstances so require, the particular circumstances of SME in comparison with undertakings which have a higher turnover in the relevant market and overall turnover.

[100] The CFI established in Joined Cases T-39/92 and T-40/92 *Groupement des Cartes Bancaires 'CB' and Europay International SA v EC Commission* [1994] ECR II-49 paras 136 *et seq.* that the maximum limit of 10 per cent of turnover must be calculated in relation to the turnover achieved by each of the undertakings participating in the agreements or concerted practices or by all the members of the association, 'at least where, by virtue of its internal rules, the association is able to bind its members'. This case law was confirmed and developed in e.g. Case T-29/92 *Vereniging van Samenwerkende Prijsregelende Organisaties in de Bouwnijverheid (SPO) and others v EC Commission* [1995] ECR II-289 para 385 : '[. . .] setting fines, regard may be had, inter alia, to the influence which an association of undertakings has been able to exert on the market, which does not depend on its own turnover, which discloses neither its size nor its economic power, but rather on the turnover of its members, which constitutes an indication of its size and economic power [. . .]'. Case T-9/99 *HFB Holding für Fernwärmetechnik Beteiligungsgesellschaft mbH & Co. KG (HFB) and others v EC Commission* [2002] ECR II-1487 para 529.

[101] Commission's White Paper on Modernization [1999] OJ C132/1 paras 127–128 referring to Joined Cases T-213/95 and T-18/96 *Stichting Certificatie Kraanverhuurbedrijf (SCK) and Federatie van Nederlandse Kraanbedrijven (FNK) v EC Commission* [1997] ECR I-1739 where the problem came up.

[102] From the procedural point of view, the Commission is not obliged to send a statement of objections to the member undertakings of an association where it intended to impose a fine on the association. The CFI has considered that it is implicitly lawful for the Commission to have sent the statement of objections to the association and not to its members and held that the Commission had not breached the principle of the individual nature of penalties. Joined Cases T-39/42 and T-40/92 *Groupement des Cartes Bancaires ('CB') and Europay International SA v EC Commission* [1992] ECR II-49 paras 22, 25, and 139.

2. Calculation: the Commission's guidelines

11.25 Regulation 1/2003 lays down certain maximum figures, but does not determine intermediate levels according to the type of infringement. Similar to Regulation 17, it merely restates that in fixing the fine the Commission shall have regard to both duration and gravity of the infringement.[103] Until 1998, it had been the practice of the Commission to take account of the gravity and duration in each specific case, and—*albeit* subject to the unlimited jurisdiction of the Court[104]— to determine freely the amount of fines.[105] The CFI voiced some mild criticism over this practice under the perspective that the addressees of the decision should be able to assess whether the level of the fine is correct and if there has been any discrimination.[106] Thus, in order to ensure the transparency of its decision-making processes, the Commission adopted in 1998 its 'Guidelines on the Method of Setting Fines' ('the 1998 Guidelines').[107] The system set out by the Commission in the 1998 Guidelines responded to the criticism that the Commission should not have unfettered discretion in relation to the level of fines.[108] Yet, the 1998 Guidelines neither indicate the level at which the Commission sets fines nor do they refer to a specific overall amount; far from surrendering the Commission's discretion,[109] it establishes the methodology to calculate the amount of fines which is based on determining the basic amount in accordance with gravity and duration of the infringement. In its ruling on the appeal against the judgment of the CFI in the 'Pre-insulated pipes' cartel, the ECJ confirmed

---

[103] Art 23(3) of Reg 1/2003, see also Art 15(2) of former Reg 17.

[104] Art 229 EC and Art 17 of Reg 17 (now Art 31 of Reg 1/2003).

[105] The CFI said in Case T-150/89 *Martinelli v EC Commission* [1995] ECR II-1165 para 69 that the Commission could not be expected to apply a precise mathematical formula to a fining calculation.

[106] See Case T-347/94 *Mayr-Melnhof Kartongesellschaft mbH v EC Commission* [1998] ECR II-1751 para 285 referring to Case T-148/89 *Tréfilunion v EC Commission* [1995] ECR II-1063 para 142: '[. . .] it is desirable for undertakings to be able to ascertain in detail the method used for calculating the fine imposed without having to bring court proceedings against the Commission's decision in order to do so [. . .]'.; Case T-147/89 *Société Métallurgique de Normandie v EC Commission* [1995] ECR II-1057, summary publication, and Case T-151/89 *Société des Treillis et Panneaux Soudés v EC Commission* [1995] ECR II-1191, summary publication.

[107] Guidelines on the method of setting fines imposed pursuant Art 15(2) of Reg 17 and Art 65(5) of the ECSC Treaty [1998] OJ C9/03. The 1998 Guidelines will now be applied to fines imposed under Reg 1/2003.

[108] R Whish, *Competition Law* (5th edn, 2003) 268; A Jones and B Sufrin, *EC Competition Law* (2nd edn, 2004) 1127. However, the Court has always acknowledged that the Commission has a margin of discretion when fixing the amount of each fine and cannot be considered obliged to apply a precise mathematical formula for that purpose. Case T-150/89 *Martinelli v EC Commission* [1995] ECR II-1165 para 59; Case T-352/94 *Mo och Domsjö v EC Commission* [1998] ECR II-1989 para 268, confirmed on appeal in Case C-283/98 P *Mo och Domsjö v EC Commission* [2000] ECR I-9855, in particular para 45.

[109] It is still difficult, if not impossible, for undertakings to compute the fine they are incurring. The 1998 Guidelines contain a large number of variables and many matters continue to fall within the scope of discretionary assessment by the Commission.

for the first time the legality of the 1998 Guidelines and in particular the application of the method of calculating the amount of fines and underlined the wide discretion of the Commisison in the field of competition policy.[110] The ECJ takes the view that the Commission remained within the legal framework laid down by Article 15(2) of Regulation 17 [now Article 23(2) of Regulation 1/2003] and did not exceed the discretion conferred on it by the legislature.[111]

The determination of the basic amount

The determination of the basic amount is the core element of the Commission's **11.26** fining policy. It determines to a great extent the final amount. For each infringement a starting amount is fixed by reference to the gravity of the infringement without taking into account the degree of responsibility of the infringing undertakings. In assessing the gravity, account must be taken of its nature, its actual impact on the market—where this can be measured—and the size of the relevant geographic market. Secondly, the Commission groups the undertakings involved in the infringement by reference to their market share in the relevant market and sets differential basic amounts for each of them. Furthermore, the level of the basic amount can be increased taking into account the undertaking's size and their economic capacity to cause damage to other operators to ensure that the fine has a sufficiently deterrent effect (deterence multiplier).[112] Additional amounts are added to the starting amount in view of the duration of the infringement, which may be, as applicable, of short, medium, and long duration. Finally a number of aggravating and attenuating circumstances can lead to an increase or decrease of the basic amount.[113] This

---

[110] Joined Cases C-189/02 P, C-202/02 P, C-205/02 P to C-208/02 P and C-213/02 P *Dansk Rørindustri A/S and others v EC Commission* [2005] OJ C205/1 paras 169 *et seq.*

[111] Joined Cases C-189/02 P, C-202/02 P, C-205/02 P to C-208/02 P and C-213/02 P *Dansk Rørindustri A/S and others v EC Commission* [2005] OJ C205/1 para 252. The Commission welcomed the judgment as a confirmation of the method of calculating the fines which it has been using in its decisions since 1998. I Breit, 'The "Pre-insulated pipes" judgment: the European Court of Justice confirms the legality of the Commission's Guidelines on fines' Competition Newsletter, Number 3, Autumn 2005, 78–79. P Lowe, 'Enforcement Antitrust Roundtable' 32rd Annual Conference Fordham Corporate Law Institute, 22–23 September 2005 (forthcoming).

[112] See Case T-23/99 *LR af 1998 A/S v EC Commission* [2002] ECR II-1705 paras 224–331; Case C-189/02 *Dansk Rørindustri v EC Commission* [2005] OJ 205/1 paras 225–230.

[113] JM Joshua and PD Comesasca, 'EC fining policy against cartels after the Lysine ruling: the subtle secrets of x' [2004] The European Antitrust Review, Global Competition Review 5–10 (6–7) distinguish between (i) an elective stage in which the start point for the calculation has to be chosen, (ii) 'arithmetical exercise' in which the start point is adjusted to reflect duration and aggravating circumstances, and (iii) a third stage in which final adjustments have to be made. The authors take the view that there would be no indication in the 1998 Guidelines of what the start point for the calculation is or should be given that the Commission had abandoned its practice by which it determined the amount of the fine based on turnover. Crucial to the assessment of fines

methodology demonstrates that fixing fines is no longer principally based on turnover in the relevant market but on range of parameters.

Classifying the infringement (gravity)

11.27 The Community Courts have consistently stated that in assessing the gravity of an infringement '[. . .] regard must be had to a large number of factors, the nature and importance of which vary according to the type of infringement in question and the particular circumstances of the case. Those factors may, depending on the circumstances, include the volume and value of the goods in respect of which the infringement was committed and the size and economic power of the undertaking and, consequently, the influence which the undertaking was able to exert on the market [. . .]'. The 1998 Guidelines defines three main criteria to assess the gravity of the infringement: (i) the nature of the infringement, (ii) the impact on the market and (iii) the geographical scope of the market concerned.[114] The CFI has consistently stated that in assessing the gravity of an infringement '[. . .] regard must be had to a large number of factors, the nature and importance of which vary according to the type of infringement in question and the particular circumstances of the case, those factors may, depending on the circumstances, include the volume and value of the goods in respect of which the infringement was committed and the size and economic power of the undertaking and, consequently, the influence which the undertaking was able to exert on the market [. . .]'.[115]

11.28 As regards the importance of each of these criteria, the Commission attaches most importance to the nature of the infringement, which is the first factor listed in the 1998 Guidelines. The Commission distinguishes three categories of infringements:[116]

---

on a particular participant would be the relationship between its assigned start point and that of the largest producer.

[114] 1998 Guidelines Section 1.A; e.g. Case T-23/99 *LR af 1998 A/S v EC Commission* [2002] ECR II-1705 para 225; Case T-220/00 *Cheil Jedang Corp v EC Commission* [2003] ECR II-2473 para 49.

[115] See Joined Cases 100–103/80 *Musique Diffusion Francaise and others v EC Commission* [1983] ECR 1825 paras 120 and 121; Case C-219/95 *Ferriere Nord v EC Commission* [1996] ECR I-4411 para 33; and Case C-137/95 *Vereniging van Samenwerkende Prijsregelende Organisaties in de Bouwnijverheid (SPO) and others v EC Commission* [1995] ECR I-1611 para 54; Case T-28/99 *Sigma Tecnologie di rivestimento Srl v EC Commission* [2002] ECR II-1845 para 86; AG Dámaso Ruiz-Jarabo Colomer in his Opinion in Joined Cases C-204/00 P etc *Aalborg Portland A/S v EC Commission* [2004] ECR I-123 para 100 stated that these criteria must be considered both from an objective perspective, that of the infringement itself, and from a subjective perspective, that of the undertaking responsible.

[116] 1998 Guidelines Section 1.A which states that the basic amounts provided for are merely 'likely'. See Case T-64/02 *Dr Hans Heubach GmbH & Co KG v EC Commission*, CFI judgment of 29 November 2005 (not yet published) para 44 in which the CFI stated that the 'flat-rate'

(i) *Minor infringements*: Pursuant to the guidelines, these will usually represent restrictions of a vertical nature with a limited market impact. For this type of infringements the 1998 Guidelines foresee fines ranging from 1,000–1 million euros.[117]

(ii) *Serious infringements*: This category includes horizontal or vertical restrictions with a wider market impact. There might also be abuses of a dominant position such as a refusal to supply, price discrimination, exclusion, or loyalty discounts[118] made by dominant firms in order to shut competitors out of the market, etc. Fines may range from 1 million–20 million euros.[119]

(iii) *Very serious infringements*: Represented generally by horizontal restrictions including price cartels and market-sharing quotas, which jeopardize the functioning of the single market, such as the partitioning of the national markets and clear-cut abuse of a dominant position by undertakings holding a virtual monopoly. In these cases the imposed fines will be above 20 million euros.[120]

---

amounts are merely indicative and therefore cannot in themselves give rise to a breach of the principle of proportionality.

[117] The only time the Commission has qualified an infringement as minor was in *Nathan Bricolux* [2000] OJ L54/01 para 131 indicating that although the infringement could be considered as serious, the restrictions in question were not implemented systematically in French-speaking Belgium and France. In *Deutsche Telekom AG* [2003] OJ L263/9 para 207 the Commission found that Deutsche Telekom (DT) had charged its competitors and end-users unfair monthly and one-off charges for access to the local network which it considered a serious infringement which became a minor infringement when DT reduced the margin squeeze.

[118] *Michelin* [2002] OJ L143/1, confirmed in Case T-203/01 *Michelin v EC Commission* [2003] ECR II-4071; *Virgin/British Airways* [2000] OJ L30/1 confirmed in T-219/99 *British Airways v EC Commission* [2003] ECR II-5917. See also *Deutsche Post AG* [2001] OJ L125/27. D Geradin and D Henry, 'The EC fining policy for violation of competition law: An empirical review of the Commission decisional practice and the Community's courts' judgments' [2005] European Competition Law Journal 401–73 (434) indicate that it would not have been clear that the fine imposed varied significantly in each of these cases (*Michelin* 8 million euros, *British Airways* 4 million euros, and *Deutsche Post* 12 million euros) while it concerned the same conduct.

[119] See, e.g. *Greek Ferries* [1999] OJ L109/24, in which the Commission asserted that the relevant market of ferry transport in question was small compared to the cross-Baltic and cross-Channel markets and therefore qualified the the price-fixing agreement as a 'serious' infringement. *Far East Trade Tariff Charges and Surcharges Agreement (FETTCSA)* [2000] OJ L268/1 also concerned a price-fixing agreement which was classified as a serious infringement on account of the fact that it had no evidence of the effects of the infringement on the level of prices even though horizontal price agreements are normally regarded as very serious infringements. On appeal, in Case T-213/00 *CMA CGM* [2003] ECR II-913, the Court found that where the Commission relies on the 1998 Guidelines for calculating fines, it must provide express reasons justifying any departure from them. In the decision appealed the Commission set the basic level for the largest company at 1.3 million euros instead of 1 million euros which is the lowest amount laid down by the Guidelines for serious infringements.

[120] See e.g. *Carbonless paper* [2004] OJ L115/1 para 378 (price fixing/market sharing); *Nintendo* [2003] OJ L255/33 para 374 (market partitioning); *Methionine* [2003] OJ L255/1 para 273 (market sharing/price fixing); in *Volkswagen* [1998] OJ L124/60, the Commission stated that the steps taken by VW to prevent its Italian dealers from supplying the German and Austrian

11.29   Classical competition infringements such as price-fixing or market-sharing agreements will almost always be classified as 'very serious' even if the market is limited to the territory of one or two Member States and no specific impact has been shown by the Commission.[121] In practice, however, the distinction between the two last categories of infringements is sometimes blurred. In many cases, the Commission has qualified infringements as only 'serious' because the infringements occurred in a small number of Member States or even in only one Member State—even though on the face of it they would fall within the category of 'very serious'.[122] Furthermore, the Commission does not always

---

markets were contrary to the Common Market and therefore the infringement was qualified as 'very serious'. In Case T-62/98 *Volkswagen v EC Commission* [2000] ECR II-2707, the CFI partly upheld an application for annulment of this decision and confirmed it to a very large extent, but reduced the fine from 102 million euros to 90 million euros, in particular because the Commission failed to establish that the infringement had been committed throughout the period found in the decision. In Case C-338/00 *Volkswagen v EC Commission* [2003] ECR I-9189, the ECJ dismissed the appeal of VW against the judgment of the CFI. See other examples of serious infringements in connection with the alleged obstruction of parallel imports *Opel* [2001] OJ L59/1 and *Mercedes* [2002] OJ L257/44. D Geradin and D Henry, 'The EC fining policy for violation of competition law: An empirical review of the Commission decisional practice and the Community's courts' judgments' [2005] European Competition Law Journal 401–73 (434–35).

[121] See e.g. *Methylglucamine* [2004] OJ L38/18 para 227: '[. . .] The present infringement consisted of market-sharing and price-fixing practices, which are by their very nature the worst kind of violation of Art 81(1) of the Treaty and 53(1) of the EEA Agreement.[. . .]'; *Flood flavour enhancers* [2004] OJ L75/1 paras 222–224 (market-sharing and price-fixing); *SAS/Maersk Air* [2001] OJ L265/15 paras 88–89 (market-sharing practices), confirmed in T-241/01 *Scandinavian Airlines System v EC Commission* [2005] OJ C229/12; *Amino acids* [2001] OJ L152/24 para 258 (price cartels and market-sharing quotas); *Graphite electrodes* [2002] OJ L100/1 para 131–134 (market-sharing and price-fixing).

[122] See, e.g. *Bank charges for exchanging euro-zone currency-Germany* [2003] OJ L15/1; *PO/Luxembourg brewing industry* [2002] OJ L253/21; *Industrial and medical gases* [2003] OJ L84/1; *British Sugar* [1999] OJ L76/01 and *Greek Ferries* [1999] OJ L109/24; Commission decision of 22 December 2004 in *Brasseries Kronenbourg, Brasseries Heineken* (COMP/C.37.750/B2), non-confidential version available on DG COMP's website, paras 83 and 87: '[. . .] The objectives of the armistice agreement were to control the cost of acquiring wholesalers and to establish equilibrium in the on-trade between the two leading brewery groups in France. The agreement was therefore a horizontal agreement designed to restrict competition between undertakings holding large market shares. However, an agreement designed to bring wholesaler acquisition costs under control in the short term by putting an end to an acquisition war cannot be regarded as a clear infringement on a par with a price-fixing agreement [. . .]. Taking into account the nature of the armistice agreement, the lack of any actual impact on the market and the fact that the agreement was confined to the on-trade in mainland France, it must be concluded that the relevant undertakings committed a serious infringement of Art 81 of the Treaty [. . .]. However, in *Austrian Banks* ([2004] OJ L56/1), the sophistication of the price-fixing agreements and the importance of the sector for the consumer led the Commission to qualify the infringements as very serious despite its limitation to the Austrian bank sector. In Case T-241/01 *Scandinavian Airlines System v EC Commission* [2005] OJ C229/12 the Court noted that market sharing constituted a very serious infringement even though it only affected a small number of air routes. It distinguished the case from *Greek Ferries* in which the market sharing represented exceptionally only a 'serious' infringement because that earlier case had only been partially implemented and its impact had been affected by the actions of the Greek government. D Geradin and D Henry, 'The EC fining

apply the minimum fine of 20 million euros to cartels that commit 'very serious' infringements. In several cases, although the participation in a cartel is automatically considered a 'very serious' infringement (which would merit the imposition of fines equal or superior to 20 million euros), some undertakings were granted a lower initial amount due to their modest portion of the market or because of the reduced size of the market in question. For instance, in *Spanish Raw Tobacco* the Commission found that several undertakings active in the Spanish raw tobacco processing market had entered into a price-fixing agreement. The Commission considered such conduct as a very serious infringement and fixed as starting point fines between 200,000 and 8 million euros given that the product market had a relatively small size of 25 million euros.[123] In the same sense, in *Seamless Steel Tubes*,[124] which concerned an international market-sharing agreement between Japanese and European producers, the Commission fixed the basic amount of the fine at 10 million euros in view of the reduced size of the market of the product in question and of the total turnover in the four countries involved for that product, which amounted to 73 million euros.

As to the importance of the size of the market, a distinction has to be made **11.30** between the size of the relevant product market and the impact on the market in which the infringement took place.[125] As far as the size of the relevant product market is concerned, the Commission emphasizes that the size of the market is not considered to be a relevant factor in assessing gravity.[126] However, the fact

---

policy for violation of competition law: An empirical review of the Commission decisional practice and the Community's courts' judgments' [2005] European Competition Law Journal 401–73 (439) who conclude that there is no clear demarcation between serious and very serious infringements.

[123] Commission Press Release IP/04/1256 'Commission fines companies in Spanish raw tobacco market'. COMP/38.238 *Spanish Raw Tobacco* [2004] non-confidential version, para 409, See also the Commission decision in *Italian Raw Tabacco* (COMP/38.281), Commission press release IP/05/1315 of 20 October 2005 'Competition: Commission fines companies €56 million for cartel in Italian raw tobacco market' where the fines were higher, also because Italy is the largest raw tobacco producer in Europe.

[124] *Seamless steel tubes* [2003] OJ L140/1 paras 162–163.

[125] See, e.g. *Amministrazione Autonoma dei Monopoli di Stato* [1998] OJ L252/47 para 70: '[. . .] the behaviour in question can be regarded, on the one hand, as constituting infringements of a nature and with a purpose that are markedly anti-competitive and, on the other hand, as having had effects on the market that are in practical terms relatively minor and limited to a single Member State [. . .].'

[126] CS Kerse and N Khan, *EC Antitrust Procedure* (5th edn, 2005) para 7–028 referring to *Zinc Phosphate* [2003] OJ L153/1 para 302, although the Commission went on and stated that without prejudice to the very serious nature of an infringement, it had in that case taken into consideration the limited size of the product market (para 303). The decision of the Commission was confirmed in Joined Cases T-33/02, T-52/02, T-62/02 and T-64/02 *Britannia Alloys & Chemicals Ltd, Société nouvelle des couleurs zinciques SA (SNCZ), Union Pigments AS and Dr Hans Heubach GmbH & CO KG v EC Commission*, CFI judgments of 29 November 2005 (not yet published).

that the relevant product market is a minor one could be taken into consideration by the Commission when setting the amount of the fine.[127] In regard to the company's total turnover, the Commission stated in *Interbrew/Alken Maes* that '[. . .] there is no reason why the fine for Haacht should reflect the fact that the company's sales of private-label beer account for a small proportion of its total turnover' and recalls that '[. . .] the starting points for calculating the amount of the fine are the gravity and duration of the infringements [. . .]'.[128] Nevertheless, the Commission added that '[. . .] the Commission took due account of the economic importance of the specific activity to which the infringement related when it assessed the gravity of the infringement [. . .]'.[129] In *Flood Flavour Enhancers* the Commission confirmed that 'a clear distinction must be made between the question of the size of the product market and that of the actual impact of the infringement on this product market', and added that 'it is not the practice of the Commission to consider the size of the product market as a relevant factor to assess gravity'.[130] Thus, it asserted that '[. . .] it is clear that price and market-sharing cartels by their very nature jeopardize the proper functioning of the single market. It would be erroneous to conclude on the basis of the small size of the market that their infringement was not very serious [. . .]'.[131] Yet, without prejudice to the very serious nature of an infringement, the Commission stated that in this case it would take into consideration the limited size of the product market.[132] In *Dutch Association of Electrotechnical Equipment Wholesalers*, the Commission uncovered two infringements of competition law, a collective exclusive dealing arrangement and a price-fixing agreement, which would have fit within the 1998 Guidelines description of serious infringements, but the limited size of the geographic market (the Netherlands) also led the Commission to consider these infringements as only serious.[133]

11.31 The relevance of the actual effects on the market is described in the 1998

---

[127] e.g. *PO/Interbrew/Alken-Maes* [2003] OJ L200/1 para 338. *Luxemburg Brewers* [2002] OJ L253/21 para 92: '[. . .] the Agreement applies only to Luxembourg. The territory of this Member State is relatively small and it is the smallest market in the Community in terms of total beer consumption [. . .]', confirmed in Joined Cases T-49/02 to T-51/02 *Brasserie nationale SA and others v EC Commission* [2005] OJ C229/13. See also D Geradin and D Henry, 'The EC fining policy for violation of competition law: An empirical review of the Commission decisional practice and the Community's courts' judgments' [2005] European Competition Law Journal 401–73 (437–38).

[128] *PO/Interbrew/Alken-Maes* [2003] OJ L200/1 para 351. Confirmed in T-48/02 *Brouwerij Haacht NV v EC Commission*, CFI judgment of 6 December (not yet published).

[129] *PO/Interbrew/Alken-Maes* [2003] OJ L200/1 para 351 *in fine*; *De Post–La Poste* [2002] OJ L61/32 para 87.

[130] *Flood Flavour enhancers* [2004] OJ L75/1 para 242.

[131] *Flood flavour enhancers* [2004] OJ L75/1 para 226.

[132] *Flood flavour enhancers* [2004] OJ L75/1 para 243.   [133] [2000] OJ L39/1.

Guidelines by the qualification that those effects will be taken into account to the extent that they can be measured. Sometimes the Commission seems to accept that infringements have only a limited impact[134] but usually it is reluctant to give a precise measurement of the actual impact where this is difficult to establish.[135] Instead, it looks at the object of the agreement or practices which is to restrict competition and how vigorously the parties pursue it, rather than at its effects.[136] In *FETTCSA* one of the applicants claimed that the Commission did not take into account that it had not derived any benefit from the agreement. The CFI replied that while the Commission might consider the amount of profit an undertaking has derived from an infringement, it is not prevented from imposing a fine where the undertaking has made no profit. The Court added that the Commission had already reduced the fine across the board on the grounds that the agreement in question had no discernible effects on price levels.[137]

Separate treatment and size of the undertakings involved

When a case involves several undertakings committing the same infringements, **11.32** the Commission considers that it is necessary to apply weightings in order to take account of the specific weight and impact of the conduct of each of them.[138] This may be the case where there is a considerable disparity, either between the sizes of the undertakings involved, or the nature of their specific roles in the offending activity.[139] When setting fines in cartel cases, the Commission has dealt with undertakings of different sizes and has tried to consider their specific weight and the impact of each undertaking's offending conduct on competition. Where an infringement involves several undertakings, the Commission applies a differential treatment dividing them in various groups

---

[134] *Greek Ferries* [1999] OJ L109/24 para 148.

[135] In *SAS/Maersk Air* [2001] OJ L265/15 para 92, the Commission could establish that the parties withdrew from or reduced their frequencies on certain routes.

[136] *British Sugar* [1999] OJ L76/1 para 192. CS Kerse and N Khan, *EC Antitrust Procedure* (5th edn, 2005) para 7–029 referring to *Amino Acids* [2001] OJ L152/24 para 286 ('[. . .] The Commission considers that the findings of the parties themselves are eloquent on the impact of this cartel. It is inconceivable that the parties would have repeatedly agreed to meet in locations across the world to fix prices and share markets over such a long period without there being an impact on the lysine market. [. . .]') and contrasting it with *Seamless tubes* [2003] OJ L140/1 in which the Commission took the view that the serious nature of the infringement was mitigated by the limited market impact.

[137] Case T-213/00 *CMA CGM and others v EC Commission (FETTCSA)* [2003] ECR II-913 para 340.

[138] A different issue is whether the Commission may impose a single fine on an undertaking which has committed several infringements without being required to break down the amount of the fine by reference to each infringement. See Case T-25/95 *Cimenteries CBR SA & others v EC Commission* [2000] ECR II-491 para 476.

[139] The ECJ endorsed this policy in Case 246/86 *Belasco v EC Commission* [1989] ECR 2117.

regarding their respective market shares[140] and imposing a set basic amount for each group.[141] For example in *Electrical and Mechanical Carbon Graphite*,[142] the Commission divided the undertakings involved into three different groups, establishing a comparison between their total turnover and the turnover in the product market in question. The basic amount assessed for the first group of undertakings was 6 million euros for the first, 21 million euros for the second, and 35 million euros for the third group. In general terms, the CFI has endorsed on numerous occasions the general approach of the Commission of dividing undertakings into different groups including *Conduites précalorifugées*,[143] *British Sugar*,[144] *FETTCSA*,[145] and *Greek Ferries*.[146] In *Greek Ferries*, the CFI found that since the Commission had, in its decision, sanctioned two distinct infringements—in terms of the various shipping routes involved—it could not, for reasons of equity and proportionality, penalize with the same severity the

---

[140] e.g. *British Sugar* [1999] OJ L76/1 paras 195–198; Sometimes market shares may not be the appropriate criterion. In *French Beef* [2003] OJ L209/12 para 169: '[. . .] Market shares do not provide an appropriate criterion. First, as the parties are federations, they have not got market shares properly so called. Second, in the case of the farmers' federations even the market shares of the members do not provide a basis for a comparison between the federations themselves. [. . .]'. See also Case T-48/98 *Acerinox v EC Commission* [2001] ECR II-3859 para 88: '[. . .] It is true that an undertaking's market shares may be relevant in order to determine what influence it may exert on the market but they cannot be a decisive factor in concluding that an undertaking belongs to a powerful economic entity [. . .].'

[141] In Case T-23/99 *LR af 1998 v EC Commission* [2002] ECR II-1705 paras 278 and 298, the CFI stated that the Commission was not obliged to assess the calculation of the fine regarding the turnovers of the involved undertakings nor differentiate them regarding their global turnover or the turnover in the product market in question.

[142] *Electrical and Mechanical Carbon Graphite* [2004] OJ L125/45 in which the first category of undertakings had EEA market shares of more than 20 per cent, the second category included companies with market shares between 10 per cent and 20 per cent and undertakings with market shares below 10 per cent were placed in the third category. See also B Van Baumgarten, 'Commission fines five companies in carbon and graphite products cartel' Competition Policy Newsletter Number 1, Spring 2004 44–45.

[143] Case T-9/99 *HFB Holding and others v EC Commission* [1999] ECR II-2429.

[144] See Joined Cases T-202–204/98 and C-207/98 *Tate & Lyle and others v Commission* [2001] ECR II-2035.

[145] Case T-213/00 *CMA CGM and others v EC Commission (FETTCSA)* [2003] ECR II-913 para 385.

[146] Five of the companies fined in *Greek Ferries* subsequently brought actions before the CFI seeking annulment of the decision and reductions in the fines: Cases T-56/99 *Marlines SA v EC Commission* [2003] ECR II-5225; Case T-59/99 *Ventouris Group Enterprises SA V EC Commission* [2003] ECR II-5257; Case T-61/99 *Adriatica di Navigazione SpA v EC Commission* [2003] ECR II-5349; Case T-65/99 *Strintzis Lines Shipping SA v EC Commission* [2003] ECR II-5433; Case T-66/99 *Minoan Lines SA v Commission* [2003] ECR II-5515. The CFI reduced the fine imposed by the Commission on two shipping companies, Ventouris (from 1,01 million euros to 252,000 euros) and Adriatica (from 1,01 million euros to 24,000 euros). The Commission had treated the infringement as a single continuous one whereas in fact the infringement should have been divided into two, one related to passenger services and another related to cargo services. Ventouris had only been involved in the cargo infringement, which only concerned a smaller market on specific routes.

undertakings which were found to have been involved in only one infringement and those which had participated in both cartels. The Court took account of the size of those undertakings and the relative volume of trade on each of the routes concerned.[147] In the *CMA CGM*, the CFI stated that for the application of the equal treatment principle, the delimitation of the undertakings in categories needs to be based on objective criteria and have a certain degree of internal coherence.[148] Generally, fines are imposed on all undertakings found to have participated in an infringement.[149] The 1998 Guidelines also indicate that account may also be taken of the resources at the disposal of the offending undertaking.[150] This means that large undertakings may be dealt with more severe fines than smaller firms or firms with fewer resources in similar circumstances. There is an assumption that the former will be better equipped to ensure that their activities comply with Community competition law and therefore more likely to commit an offence intentionally. This has been done so far by means of applying a multiplying factor to the base amount applicable to a given undertaking.[151]

Duration of the infringement

As indicated, under Article 23(2) of Regulation 1/2003, when fixing the **11.33** amount of the fine the Commission is required to take into account not only

---

[147] T-59/99 *Ventouris Group Enterprises SA v EC Commission* [2003] ECR II-5257 paras 217–222.

[148] Case T-213/00 *CMA CGM and others v EC Commission (FETTCSA)* [2003] ECR II-913 paras 405–426 where the division was based on the applicants' worldwide 1994 shipping turnovers relative to the largest company. The Court found that the division, although not contrary to the principle of individual assessment, was discriminatory and lacked adequate reasoning. The Commission decision did not explain how the dividing line was drawn between the groups in question. During the judicial proceedings, the Commission argued that the distinction was drawn where there was the greatest differences in relative terms between the size of two consecutive companies. The Court accepted that using relative rather than absolute differences was correct but ruled that the division did not in fact reflect the greatest relative size differences; Case T-236/01 etc *Tokai Carbon v EC Commission* [2004] ECR II-1181, paras 219–237.

[149] In *Austrian Banks* hundreds of banks were found to be involved in the infringement, but the decision was only addressed to eight of the most significant banking groups. The argument that this infringed the principle of equal treatment was rejected by the Commission asserting that it could select a sample 'on the basis of objective criteria' [2004] OJ L56/1 para 472.

[150] 1998 Guidelines, Section 1.A, fifth paragraph: '[. . .] Generally speaking, account may also be taken of the fact that large undertakings usually have legal and economic knowledge and infrastructures which enable them more easily to recognize that their conduct constitutes an infringement and be aware of the consequences stemming from it under competition law. [. . .]'. See also Case T-48/98 *Acerinox v EC Commission* [2001] ECR-II 3859 para 79.

[151] In this context, the Commission often refers to the necessity that the fine should ensure sufficient deterrent effect. This was first applied in the *Pre-Insulated Pipe Cartel* [1999] OJ L24/1 para 166, where ABB's starting amount was increased by 250 per cent. See also *Graphite Electrodes* [2002] OJ L100/1 paras 153–154; *Vitamins* [2003] OJ L6/1 para 698; *Citric Acid* [2002] OJ L239/18 para 246; *Carbonless Paper* [2004] OJ L115/1 para 412.

the gravity but also the duration of the infringement. The 1998 Guidelines draw a threefold distinction which may lead the Commission to put an additional sum on top of that calculated on the basis of gravity:[152]

(i) *Short duration infringements* (less than one year): Usually there will be no increase in the amount indicated in the gravity criteria.[153]

(ii) *Medium duration infringements* (one to five years): An increase of up to 50 per cent in the amount determined for gravity can be determined.[154]

(iii) *Long duration infringements* (more than five years): In these cases an increase up to 10 per cent per annum in the amount determined for gravity can be imposed.[155]

11.34 Although this is not an automatic or fixed rule applicable to every infringement, it has been general practice that for infringements that lasted over twelve months, the Commission applied a 10 per cent increase every year plus 5 per cent for any period less than a year but six months or more.[156] In *Luxemburg Brewers*, the Commission applied a limit of 100 per cent for infringements that lasted fourteen years.[157] In *Organic Peroxides*, the Commission calculated an increase of 10 per cent per year for the last twenty years of the infringement (1980–1999) and an increase of 5 per cent per year for the part of the infringement which took place before that period (1971–1979).[158] The Commission justified this

---

[152] Case T-48/98 *Acerinox v EC Commission* [2001] ECR II-3859 para 78.

[153] *French Beef* [2003] OJ L209/12 para 171.

[154] *British Sugar* [1999] OJ L76/1 paras 199–200 (10 per cent increase per year); *Seamless Steel Tubes* [2003] OJ L140/1 paras 166–167 (10 per cent increase per year). In *Opel* [2001] OJ L59/1 the infringements in place varied in intensity during the seventeen months. The fine was increased by 7.5 per cent instead of 10 per cent.

[155] e.g. *Virgin/British Airways* [2000] OJ L30/1 para 122 (7 years = 70 per cent). The 10 per cent per year increase has not been applied consistently to infringements of long duration. In *Amministrazione Autonoma dei Monopoli di Stato* [1998] OJ L252/47 paras 72–73 the infringement had persisted for at least thirteen years but the fine was only increased by 100 per cent for this reason. In *Methionine* [2003] OJ L255/1 para 311 the infringement lasted for twelve years and ten months, but the fine was increased by 125 per cent. In *JCB* [2002] OJ L69/1 para 253, the Commission applied a rate of increase of 55 per cent for an infringement that lasted eleven years. However, not all elements were implemented. The CFI later reduced the fine from 39,614,000 euros to 300,000 euros: Case T-67/01 *JCB v EC Commission* [2004] OJ C85/23 para 193.

[156] e.g. *Carbonless Paper* [2004] OJ L115/1 paras 413–416; *Zinc phosphate* [2003] OJ L153/1 paras 310–311.

[157] *Luxemburg Brewers* [2002] OJ L253/21 para 97.

[158] Commission decision of 10 December 2003 in *Organic Peroxides* (Case COMP/E-2/37.857), non-confidential version available at DG COMP's website, para 466. The 245 per cent increase has been the maximum increase imposed since the introduction of the 1998 Guidelines. See also D Geradin and D Henry, 'The EC fining policy for violation of competition law: An empirical review of the Commission decisional practice and the Community's courts' judgments' [2005] European Competition Law Journal 401–73 (440).

method on the basis of the less strict approach of competition policy in the 1970s when companies were less aware that their behaviour infringed competition laws and fine were lower.

Aggravating and mitigating factors

The addition of the starting amount and the increase resulting from duration **11.35** constitutes the basic amount of the fine, which can be increased or reduced if any aggravating or mitigating circumstances apply. Whereas gravity and duration refer mainly to the infringement as such, aggravating and mitigating circumstances deal with the specific role performed by each firm participating in the infringement. The 1998 Guidelines provide an illustrative but not exhaustive list of mitigating and aggravating factors. It is to be noted that this is not an area where clear precedents can always be found. The CFI held that '[. . . .] any percentage increases or reductions decided upon to reflect aggravating or mitigating circumstances must be applied to the basic amount of the fine set by reference to the gravity and duration of the infringement, not to the amount of any increase already applied for the duration of the infringement or to the figure resulting from any initial increase or reduction to reflect aggravating or mitigating circumstances. [. . .]'[159] Cases are inevitably fact-specific and reflect how the Commission exercises its discretion in certain circumstances. In addition, before considering the aggravating or mitigating factors themselves the CFI has insisted on a rigorous approach towards the methodology of calculating the consequences of these factors on the final amount of the fine.[160]

Aggravating circumstances The 1998 Guidelines indicate five specific forms **11.36** of aggravating factors.[161] A further reference to 'other' aggravating circumstances leaves scope for the development of new additional categories:

(i) *Repeated infringement of the same type by the same undertaking(s).* The Commission may apply an increase of 50 per cent for repeated infringements. In *British Sugar* the defendant had previously been found to infringe the competition rules in the same relevant market.[162] In *Pre-Insulated*

---

[159] Case T-220/00 *Cheil Jedang v EC Commission* [2003] ECR II-2473 para 229; see also Case C-359/01 P *British Sugar plc v EC Commission* [2004] ECR I-4933 paras 108–109.

[160] CS Kerse and N Khan, *EC Antitrust Procedure* (5th edn, 2005) paras 7–034 to 7–035.

[161] 1998 Guidelines Section 2 'Aggravating Circumstances'. See also D Geradin and D Henry, 'The EC fining policy for violation of competition law: An empirical review of the Commission decisional practice and the Community's courts' judgments' [2005] European Competition Law Journal 401–73 (443–48). Paper prepared for the Conference Remedies and Sanctions in EC Competition Policy, 17–18 February 2005, Amsterdam University, 33–42.

[162] *British Sugar* [1999] OJ L76/01. The accumulation of all aggravating circumstances increased British Sugar's fine by 75 per cent.

Pipes[163] the Commission took this factor into account to increase the amount of the fine by 50 per cent.[164] In *Interbrew*,[165] the Commission stated that Danone had already been found to have committed similar infringements in two occasions before.[166] Additional examples can be found in *Concrete Reinforcing Bars*,[167] *Plasterboard*,[168] *Industrial Tubes*,[169] and *Organic Peroxides*.[170] The CFI has made clear that repeated infringement might be considered an aggravating factor where the subsequent infringement occurs after a decision or at least a clear warning in relation to the earlier infringement.[171] In *Kronenbourg, Brasseries Heineken*, Danone argued that an increase in its fine for recidivism (it had been already fined in 1984 for market sharing infringement) would breach the principle of proportionality and legal certainty where the previous violation occurred long time ago. The Commission responded that recidivism is not subject to any prescription period.[172]

---

[163] *Pre-Insulated Pipes* [1999] OJ L24/1. This was only one of the factors considered by the Commission when increasing the amount of the fine by 50 per cent. The Commission took into account 'its continuation of such a clear-cut and indisputable infringement after the investigations despite having been warned at high level by the Directorate-General for Competition of the consequences of such conduct.'

[164] See also *Michelin* [2002] OJ L143/1 paras 361–363 '[. . .] The Commission takes the view, however, that when a dominant undertaking has been censured by the Commission it has a responsibility not only to put an end to the abusive practices on the relevant market but also to ensure that its commercial policy throughout the Community conforms to the individual Decision notified to it; Michelin did not do this, quite the reverse. [. . .] It must be concluded that the abuses committed by Michelin on the defined relevant markets are aggravated by the fact that this was a repeated infringement, which justifies an increase of 50% in the basic amount of the fine [. . .]'. Upheld in Case T-203/01 *Michelin v EC Commission* [2003] ECR II-4071 paras 282–283.

[165] *PO/Interbrew Alken Maes* [2003] OJ L200/1 para 314.

[166] The Commission pointed out that it considered as relevant the fact that the same person occupied the post of chairman and chief executive during the period in which the three infringements were committed. *PO/Interbrew Alken Maes* [2003] OJ L200/1 para 314.

[167] Commission Press Release IP/02/1908 of 17 December 2002 'Commission fines eight firms for taking part in a concrete reinforcing bar cartel in Italy'.

[168] Commission Press Release IP/02/1744 of 27 November 2002 'Commission imposes heavy fines on four companies involved in plasterboard cartel' (COMP/37.152—*PO/Plasterboard*).

[169] *Industrial Tubes* [2004] OJ L125/50.

[170] Commission Press Release IP/03/1700 of 10 December 2003 'Commission fines members of organic peroxides cartel'.

[171] Case T-141/94 *Thyssen Stahl v EC Commission* [1999] ECR II-347 para 617. In turn, the absence of any previous infringement is a normal circumstance which the Commission does not have to take into account as a mitigating factor. Case T-8/89 *DSM v EC Commission* [1991] ECR II-1833 para 317.

[172] Commission decision of 29 September 2004 in *Kronenbourg, Brasseries Heineken* (COMP/C37.750) non-confidential version available on the website of DG COMP, para 93: '[. . .] since a repeated infringement demonstrates that the penalty previously imposed was not a sufficient deterrent (see also paragraph (94)), increasing the fine to take account of a repeated infringement is not disproportionate' (10 per cent increase). See also *Nintendo/Video Games* [2003] OJ L255/33 (20 per cent increase for adducing false information).

(ii) *Refusal to cooperate or attempts to obstruct the Commission in carrying out its investigation.* In *Pre-Insulated Pipes*,[173] two of the undertakings involved in the cartel attempted to mislead the Commission about its corporate structure and received a higher fine. The same reasoning was applied in *Greek Ferries*,[174] where Minoan proposed to restructure the cartel after the beginning of the investigation. In *Bayo-n-ox*,[175] an attempt to coordinate responses to the Commission's inquiries was considered an obstruction. In *Graphite Electrodes*, fines were increased for obstruction by 25 per cent on the grounds that warning other participants of 'impending' inspections was an aggravating factor.[176]

(iii) *Ring leader or instigator of the infringement.* In *Cartonboard*, the CFI approved the distinction between 'instigators' or 'ringleaders' of a cartel and 'ordinary members'.[177] In *Pre-Insulated Pipes*,[178] ABB was held to be the instigator and to have put pressure on other companies to join. This contributed to an increase of 50 per cent on the basic amount. In *Greek Ferries*,[179] Minoan was considered to be the instigator because it proposed ways in which the cartel could be disguised from the Commission's scope. The Commission may punish the role of instigator with substantial increases for example, of up to 85 per cent in the case of SGL in *Graphite Electrodes*[180] and 50 per cent for Roche in *Vitamins*,[181] Nintendo in *Nintendo*,[182] and AWA in *Carbonless Paper*.[183]

(iv) *Retaliatory measures against other undertakings with a view to enforcing practices, which constitute an infringement.* In the *ABB* judgment,[184] the CFI has stated that it is legitimate for the Commission to take account of the pressure exerted by one party on others to participate or concur to an

---

[173] *Pre-Insulated Pipes* [1999] OJ L24/1.   [174] *Greek Ferries* [1999] OJ L109/29.
[175] *Bayo-n-ox* [1990] OJ L21/71.
[176] *Graphite Electrodes* [2002] OJ L100/1 and the CFI judgment in Joined Cases T-236/01, T-239/01, T-244/01 to T-246/01, T-251/01 and T-252/01 *Tokai Carbon v EC Commission* [2004] ECR II-1181 paras 312–314.
[177] Case T-311/94 *BPB de Endracht NV v EC Commission* [1998] ECR II-1129 paras 307–308; Case T-319/94 *Fiskey Board AB v EC Commission* [1998] ECR II-1331 para 97 and Case C-352/94 *Mo och Domsjo AB v EC Commission* [1998] ECR II-1989 para 375.
[178] *Pre-Insulated Pipes* [1999] OJ L24/1.   [179] *Greek Ferries* [1999] OJ L109/29.
[180] *Graphite Electrodes* [2002] OJ L100/1.
[181] *Vitamins* [2003] OJ L6/1. *BSAF* received a milder increase as the Commission found Roche to be the prime mover. It took the view that Roche stood to gain most from the arrangements.
[182] *Nintendo* [2003] OJ L255/33. Nintendo was found to be the ringleader and instigator of anti-competitive distribution agreements involving the monitoring of parallel trade imports.
[183] *Carbonless Paper* [2004] OJ L115/1 paras 418–424.
[184] Case T-31/99 *ABB Asea Brown Boveri v EC Commission* [2002] ECR II-1881 para 208; on appeal mostly confirmed in Joined Cases C-189/02 P, C-202/02 P, C-205/02 P to C-208/02 P and C-213/02 P *Dansk Rørindustri A/S and others v EC Commission* [2005] OJ C205/1.

unlawful agreement. In *Volkswagen*,[185] VW's fine was increased by 20 per cent resulting from two aggravating circumstances: (i) taking advantage of its power over its dealers to enforce the measures adopted to impede sales of its cars in Italy for foreigners and (ii) terminating several dealership contracts and threatening many other dealers. In *PO/Interbrew and Alken Maes*[186] the threatening of such measures resulted in an increase in the fine of 50 per cent. In *JCB*,[187] the Commission decided to increase the basic amount of the fine imposed on JCB by twice the amount of the sanction which JCB had imposed on a distributor for not complying with the agreement. In *Pre-insulated Pipes*,[188] the fact that ABB put pressure on the other parties in order to participate in the infringement was regarded as an aggravating factor and the basic amount was increased by 50 per cent.

(v) *Need to increase the penalty in order to exceed the amount of gains improperly made as a result of the infringement when it is objectively possible to estimate the amount.* Before the adoption of the 1998 Guidelines, the Commission took into account in its assessment of the gravity the benefits generated for the participating undertakings by the infringement. However, the Commission was criticized on the basis that the deterring effect of fines can only be produced if their amount systematically exceeds the benefit to the undertakings.[189] Under the new guidelines this factor only becomes relevant if the calculation based on other factors produces a result that is less than the benefit derived by the undertakings from the infringement in cases where the benefit can be assessed properly. The Commission refers to the duration and intensity of the cartel's activities as an indication that the parties considered the cartel to be beneficial to them.[190] In *Gosme/Martell*,[191] the

---

[185] *Volkswagen* [2001] OJ L262/14. The Commission found that circulars and individual letters were not just intended to restrict the freedom of dealers to set their prices, but warnings were given and legal action was threatened unless dealers demonstrated greater price discipline.

[186] *PO/Interbrew and Alken-Maes* [2003] OJ L200/1. The Commission held that Danone's threat to destroy Interbrew on the French market if a significant amount of beer was not transferred to Alken-Maes led to an extension of the duration of the cartel. In T-38/02 *Group Danone v EC Commisison*, CFI judgment of 25 October 2005 (not yet published), however, the CFI found that the Commission did not prove to the required legal standard that there was a causal link between the threat that was made by Danone with a view to forcing Interbrew to extend their collaboration and the extension of the cartel. The causes of that extension cannot be reduced to a threat but derive from the aim of eliminating competition pursued together by both parties to the cartel. Consequently, the Commission was wrong to find that aggravating circumstance proved against Danone which fine was thereby reduced.

[187] *JCB* [2002] OJ L69/1 para 255.   [188] *Pre-Insulated Pipes* [1999] OJ L24/1.

[189] See WPJ Wils, 'The Commission's New Method for Calculating Fines in Antitrust Cases' (1998) 23 EL Rev 252–63 (259).

[190] See CS Kerse and N Khan, *EC Antitrust Procedure* (5th edn, 2005) para 7–043.

[191] *Gosme/Martell-DMP* [1991] OJ L185/23: The Commission stated that Martell was the primary beneficiary from the collusion and imposed a much higher fine than the other undertaking involved.

Commission took into account the extent to which one party may have derived more benefits than another, judging the different levels of fine for parties involved in the same infringement.

Apart from these, one of the other most common aggravating factors is continu- **11.37** ing the agreement after intervention by the Commission.[192] Continuing an infringement after the Commission has initiated even preliminary inquiries can be an aggravating factor. It is, however, necessary to assess whether the undertaking in question continued the infringement in the knowledge that it was subject to a Commission inquiry.[193] In *Graphite Electrodes*,[194] the Commission increased the amount of the fine by 10 per cent considering that '[. . .] for Tokai, SEC and Nippon the Commission must take into account one aggravating circumstance, namely their continuation of this clear-cut and indisputable infringement after the Commission had carried out its investigations [. . .].' In *Volkswagen*[195] and *French Beef*,[196] the undertakings involved persisted with their behaviour after receiving notice of the starting of the investigation. In these two cases, the Commission imposed a 20 per cent increase.

Mitigating circumstances[197]   The 1998 Guidelines also mention six specific **11.38** forms of mitigating circumstances. Similarly, a reference to 'other' mitigating circumstances leaves scope for the development of further categories. Whilst it is for the Commission to identify any aggravating circumstances, undertakings wishing to invoke the benefit of mitigating circumstances should ensure that they draw the Commission's attention to the merits of the case as early as possible during the course of the investigation, and no later than their reply to the statement of objections.

(i)   *An exclusively passive or 'follow my leader' role in the infringement.* In *Pre-Insulated Pipes*, two of the involved undertakings (Ke-Kelit and Sigma) received a 66 per cent reduction of the fine for their minor role in the cartel and the fact that their participation was confined to Austria and Italy, both relatively small markets for district heating.[198] In the *Cheil Jedang*, the CFI emphasized that the undertaking must have adopted a 'low profile', characterized by no active participation in the creation of the anti-competitive agreements. The Court confirmed a reduction of 10 per cent of the basic amount of the fine because the undertaking's passive role in

---

[192] See CS Kerse and N Kahn, *EC Antitrust Procedure* (5th edn, 2005) para 7–044.
[193] Case T-28/99 *Sigma Tecnologie v EC Commission* [2002] ECR II-1845 para 102.
[194] *Graphite Electrodes* [2002] OJ L100/1.   [195] *Volkswagen* [2001] OJ L262/14.
[196] *French Beef* [2003] OJ L209/12 para 408.   [197] 1998 Guidelines para 3.
[198] *Pre-Insulated Pipes* [1999] OJ L24/1.

the alleged cartel arrangements relating to sales volume.[199] In *Greek Ferries*, the Commission stated that four of the involved lines played a 'follow my leader' role and applied a reduction of 15 per cent. Further, in *Industrial and Medical Gases*,[200] the Commission assessed that Westfalen had played an exclusively passive role in the infringement and granted a decrease of 15 per cent. Even though in some cases, the Commission did not contemplate playing minor role as a mitigating circumstance like in *Citric Acid*.[201]

(ii) *Non-implementation in practice of the offending agreements or practices.* The Commission has interpreted the concept of 'non-implementation' in a very restrictive way, stating that the fact that the parties may have regularly not complied with the agreements does not necessarily represent evidence of non-implementation.[202] Sometimes, however, the Commission recognized this as a mitigating circumstance like in *Alloy Surcharge*,[203] where the basic amount of the fine was reduced by 20 per cent for late implementation of the agreement. In *Amino Acids*,[204] the CFI rejected the interpretation of the Commission by which this circumstance only applied where the cartel as a whole was not implemented. The Court stated that the aggravating and mitigating factors set out in the Guidelines made reference to the individual circumstances of each undertaking involved.[205] In several cases, the

---

[199] Case T-220/00 *Cheil Jedang v EC Commission* [2003] ECR II-2473 paras 165–183. The Commission had granted Sewon a reduction of 20 per cent of the increase applied on account of duration on the ground that it had played a passive role in connection with the agreements on sales quotas for a period of six months out of the five years during which it was involved in the cartel. Therefore, the CFI considered a reduction of 10 per cent of the basic amount of the fine applied to Cheil Jedang as being justified because for half of the time during which it participated in the cartel, Cheil played a passive role in the arrangements relating to sales volumes. See also T-48/02 *Brouwerij Haacht NV v EC Commission*, CFI judgment of 6 December 2005 (not yet published), paras 74–83, where the Court concluded that the applicant that by attending all the cartel meetings and exchanging information on prices and customer-sharing during these meetings, the applicant demonstrated a degree of active participation in the cartel.

[200] *Industrial and Medical Gases* [2003] OJ L84/1 paras 442 and 351.

[201] *Citric Acid* [2002] OJ L239/18 para 283: 'The fact that Cerestar Bioproducts was a small player in the citric acid market and that it may have been worried about the consequences of not joining the cartel does not relieve it of its own corporate responsibility. For instance, Cerestar Bioproducts could have reported the cartel to the Commission'. In this sense see also *Methionine* [2003] OJ L255/1.

[202] *Food Flavour enhancers* [2004] OJ L75/1 para 270; see also Commission decision of 9 December 2004 in *Choline Chloride* (Case COMP/37.533), non-confidential version available at DG COMP's website para 211.

[203] *Alloy Surcharge* [1998] OJ L100/55.   [204] *Amino Acids* [2001] OJ L152/24 para 364.

[205] Case T-224/00 *Archer Daniels Midland v EC Commission* [2003] ECR II-2597 paras 260–271, indicating that it would be necessary to ascertain the circumstances which the applicants put forward to show that during the period in which they were party to the infringing agreements, they actually avoided applying them by adopting competitive conduct in the market (para 268).

Commission has decided that cheating or lack of discipline in the cartel is not a mitigating factor.[206]

(iii) *Termination of the infringement as soon as the Commission intervenes.* The Commission's practice shows that when the infringement ceases following its intervention, this will be a mitigating circumstance as in *Vitamins.*[207] In *FETTCSA,*[208] all shipping lines were granted a 20 per cent reduction for terminating the infringement as soon as the Commission sent a warning letter. In *Nathan Bricolux,*[209] Nathan was granted a reduction for modifying its distribution agreements just after receiving the statement of objections from the Commission. In *Austrian Banks*[210] on the contrary, the Commission assessed that the termination following the inspections should not be regarded as a mitigating circumstance because of the 'manifest character' of the infringement.

(iv) *Existence of reasonable doubt on the part of the undertaking as to whether the restrictive conduct does indeed constitute an infringement.* It was common practice of the Commission to reduce fines when they were the first ones imposed in a particular sector.[211] Nevertheless, this was not taken into account when the undertaking had been informed by the Commission or by its own lawyers that its behaviour constituted a competition infringement.[212] Only if there is a reasonable doubt about the application of competition rules this can constitute a mitigating circumstance. In *Greek Ferries,*[213] all companies were granted a 15 per cent discount for the confusion created by the Greek Government, which had been promoting agreements for domestic ferry routes within Greece that were similar to the cartel agreement (relating to Italy/Greece services) that was prohibited in the decision. In *Akzo,*[214] the ECJ reduced the fine stating that: 'abuses of this kind come within the field of law in which the rules of competition have never been determined precisely'. In *Deutsche Post,*[215] the Commission came to the conclusion that there was no Community case law concerning the specific context of cross-border letter mail services and imposed a token fine of 1,000 euros. In other cases, such as *Deutsche*

---

[206] In Case T-308/94 *Cascades SA v EC Commission* [1998] ECR II-925 para 230. The CFI stated that an undertaking which despite colluding with its competitors follows a more or less independent policy on the market may simply be trying to exploit the cartel for its own benefit. See also *Austrian Banks* [2004] OJ L56/1.

[207] *Vitamins* [2003] OJ L6/1 para 732.   [208] *FETTCSA* [2000] OJ L268/00.

[209] *Nathan-Bricolux* [2001] OJ L54/00.   [210] *Austrian Bank* [2004] OJ L56/1 para 529.

[211] *Eurocheque: Helsinki Agreement* [1992] OJ L95/50.

[212] *London European/Sabena* [1988] OJ L317/47.   [213] *Greek Ferries* [1999] OJ L109/29.

[214] Case 62/86 *Akzo v EC Commission* [1996] ECR I-3359 para 163.

[215] *Deutsche Post AG-Interception of Cross-Border Mail* [2001] OJ L331/40.

Telekom,[216] the Commission took this circumstance into account when assessing the gravity of the infringement as a mitigating circumstance. In the same way, in *GVG/FS*[217] the novelty of the case prevented the Commission from imposing a fine. On the contrary, in the *Tetra Pak,*[218] the ECJ upheld the CFI's judgment stating that because of the manifest nature and particular gravity of the restrictions on competition, the undertaking could not have been unaware that its practices were infringing the competition rules.

(v) *Infringements committed as a result of negligence or unintentionally.* The existence of a compliance system has been held to be a potential mitigating factor, but not if it is ineffective or disobeyed by the managers of the undertaking. That is why in *British Sugar,*[219] the fact that the conduct contravened its own compliance programme that had been assessed as a mitigating factor in a previous case was declared to be an aggravating circumstance.

(vi) *Effective cooperation by the undertaking in the proceedings (outside the scope of Notice of 18 July 1996 on the non-imposition or reduction of fines in cartel cases).* The Notice of 18 July 1996 on the non-imposition or reduction of fines in cartel cases was replaced in 2002 by the Notice on immunity from fines and reduction of fines in cartel cases (the 'Leniency Notice').[220] In *Nathan/Bricolux,*[221] the Commission reduced the fine imposed on Nathan because of its cooperation with the Commission by providing at its request fundamental pieces of evidence without which the infringement could not have been established. Similarly, Bricolux cooperated with the Commission during the investigation by providing on request or spontaneously a number of relevant documents. In *Spanish Raw Tobacco,*[222] the Commission reduced the fine imposed on a group of undertakings active in the Spanish raw tobacco processing market, which participated in a cartel of raw tobacco purchase, by 20–40 per cent, taking into account the different

---

[216] *Deutsche Telekom* [2003] OJ L263/9 paras 201–206: the Commission stated that the fact that the weighted method applied in this decision to determine the margin squeeze had not previously been the subject of a formal decision. This and other factors were taken into account in order to treat the infringement as 'serious', resulting in a much lower fine.

[217] *GVG/FSO* [2003] OJ L11/17.

[218] Case C-333/94 *Tetra Pak v EC Commission* [1996] ECR I-5951 paras 46–49.

[219] *British Sugar* [1999] OJ L76/1 (75 per cent increase).

[220] Commission Notice on immunity from fines and reduction of fines in cartel cases [2002] OJ C45/3.

[221] *Nathan-Bricolux* [2001] OJ L54/01 para 130. Bricolux was only imposed a symbolic fine of 1,000 euros.

[222] Commission Press Release IP/04/1256 'Commission fines companies in Spanish raw tobacco market' inn *Spanish Raw Tobacco* (COMP/38.238), non-confidential version available at DG COMP's website.

ways of cooperating and the utility of the documents presented by each of the undertakings. The CFI has held that any percentage increases or reductions decided upon to reflect aggravating or mitigating circumstances must be applied to the basic amount of the fine set by reference to the gravity and duration of the infringement, not to any increase already applied for the duration of the infringement or to the figure resulting from any initial increase or reduction to reflect aggravating or mitigating circumstances. This would ensure equal treatment between the various undertakings participating in one and the same cartel. Since the Commission had failed to do so, the Court applied this method and adjusted the level of fines in *Archer Daniels Midlands* and *Dewang Sewon Europe*.[223]

Depending on the circumstances of each case, the Commission has treated **11.39** various factors as mitigating circumstances. These include:

(i) *The effects of the domestic legislative or administrative context.* The Commission considered the fact that the German central authority authorized the foundation of a structural crisis cartel in Germany as a mitigating factor in *Welded Steel Mesh*.[224] A similar circumstance was also applied among other cases: *Luxembourg Brewers*,[225] *Deutsche Telekom*,[226] *Dutch Building and Construction Industry*,[227] *Greek Ferries*,[228] *French Beef*,[229] and *Spanish Raw Tobacco*.[230] In other cases, the knowledge of national governments of the infringements did not represent a valid defence for example in *Zinc Producers Group*,[231] although, in *Building and Constructing Industry*

---

[223] See the CFI judgments in the Lysine cartel, in which the CFI found that the Commission did not apply the reductions granted on account of mitigating circumstances in the same way to all the undertakings concerned. Case T-220/00 *Cheil Jedang Corporation v EC Commission* [2003] ECR II-2473 para 229; Case T-224/00 *Archer Daniels Midland v EC Commission* [2003] ECR II-2597 para 378; Case T-230/00 *Daesang Corporation and Sewon Europe GmbH v EC Commission* [2003] ECR II-2733 para 152.

[224] *Welded Steel Mesh* [1989] OJ L260/1.

[225] *Luxembourg Brewers* [2002] OJ L253/21 para 100.

[226] *Deutsche Telekom* [2003] OJ L263/9 para 212.

[227] *Building and Construction Industry in the Netherlands* [1992] OJ L92/1 para 141: '[. . .] In determining the general order of magnitude of the fines to be imposed, the Commission has also taken account of the following considerations: [. . .] The intervention by the Dutch authorities, in adopting the Royal Decree of 29 December 1986, may be considered to have created a certain ambiguity on the part of the building and construction undertakings as well as on its associations as to the compatibility of the concertation with the competition rules of the Treaty [. . .]'.

[228] *Greek Ferries* [1999] OJ L109/24 paras 147, 148 and 150.

[229] *French Beef* [2003] OJ L209/12 para 150.

[230] Commission Press Release IP/04/1256 'Commission fines companies in Spanish raw tobacco market'. COMP/38.238 *Spanish Raw Tobacco* [2004] non-confidential version, available at DG COMP's website para 409.

[231] *Zinc Producer Group* [1984] OJ L220/27.

in the Netherlands,[232] the Commission considered this to be a mitigating factor.

(ii) *Being 'victims' of the infringement.* The Commission has stated that the parties which are pressed by others to participate in an infringement still have the possibility of informing about the situation as happened in *French West African Shipowners Committees,*[233] *Lysine,*[234] and *Carbonless Paper.*[235] In *Citric Acid,*[236] the Commission did not take into account the fact that the infringement constituted a defence against some other anticompetitive behaviour.

(iii) *Implementation of legal advice or compliance programme.* The practice of the Commission shows that neither of these two circumstances is considered as a mitigating factor. On the contrary, legal advice was considered an aggravating factor, as in *BMW.*[237] As regards the existence of a compliance programme, the Commission is reluctant to apply any reduction in fines.[238]

(iv) *Commission investigation exceeds reasonable period of time.* In this respect, in *Commercial Solvents*[239] the ECJ reduced the imposed fine by half. In *FEG,*[240] a reduction of 100,000 euros was granted for both parties given that the Commission did not take a decision within a period of eight years.

---

[232] *Building and Construction Industry in the Netherlands* [1992] OJ L92/1 paras 141 *et seq.*

[233] *French-West African Shipowners Committees* OJ [1992] L134/1.

[234] *Amino Acids* [2001] OJ L152/24.   [235] *Carbonless Paper* [2004] OJ L115/1.

[236] *Citric Acid* [2002] OJ L239/18.

[237] Case 32/78 *BMW Belgium v EC Commission* [1979] ECR 2435.

[238] e.g. the Commission has taken into consideration the introduction of a compliance policy by the involved undertakings, the effect of national law or that the Commission did not take any decision within a reasonable period of time. *Zinc Phosphate* [2003] OJ L153/1; Case T-352/94 *Mo och Domsjö AB v EC Commission* [1998] ECR II-1989 para 417: '[. . .] Consequently, although the implementation of a compliance programme demonstrates the intention of the undertaking in question to prevent future infringements and thus better enables the Commission to accomplish its task of applying the principles laid down by the Treaty in competition matters and of influencing undertakings in that direction, the mere fact that in certain of its previous decisions the Commission took the implementation of a compliance programme into consideration as a mitigating factor does not mean that it is obliged to act in the same manner in this case. [. . .]'. See also Commission decision of 9 December 2004 in *Choline Chloride* (Case COMP/37.533), non-confidential version available at DG COMP's website para 217: '[. . .] While the Commission welcome measures taken by undertakings to avoid cartel infringements in the future, such measures cannot change the reality of the infringement and the need to sanction it [. . .]'.

[239] Joined Cases 6/73 and 7/73 *Istituto Chimioterapico Italiano and Commercial Solvents Corp v EC Commission* [1974] ECR 223.

[240] *Nederlandse Federative Vereniging voor de Groothandel op Elektrotechnisch Gebied and Technische Unie (FEG and TU)* [2000] OJ L39/1 para 152: '[. . .] The Commission acknowledges that the duration of the proceedings in the present case, which started in 1991, is considerable. There are various reasons for this, some of which can be attributed to the Commission itself and some to the parties. In so far as the Commission is to blame in this respect, it acknowledges its responsibility.[. . .]'

In *BMW Belgium*,[241] however, the ECJ rejected the contention that the duration of the infringement could have been considerably shortened if the Commission had notified its objections earlier.

(v) *Poor financial situation of the undertaking.* The Commission is not required, when determining the amount of the fine, to take into account the poor financial situation of an undertaking concerned, since recognition of such an obligation would be tantamount to giving an unjustified competitive advantage to undertakings least well adapted to market conditions.[242]

The result is an individual modification to the basic amount of the fine that will **11.40** be compared with the maximum threshold the Commission may impose as a fine pursuant to Regulation 1/2003. Once these calculations have been made, the Notice provides that the final amount cannot exceed 10 per cent of the worldwide turnover or the undertaking.[243] If this would be the case, the Commission will apply a reduction so as no longer to exceed the maximum fine.[244]

3. Amount

The Commission Policy on fines. After the adoption of Regulation 17, whereby it **11.41** was empowered to impose fines on undertakings which had infringed EC competition rules, the Commission maintained an extremely discreet attitude regarding fines.[245] So much so that between 1962 and 1969 no fines at all were imposed, and when finally one was imposed—in *Quinine*[246]—the fines were of an almost token amount. The turning point in the Commission's policy on fines was marked by its decision in *Pioneer*, which was confirmed later by the ECJ.

---

[241] Joined Cases 32/78, 36/78 to 82/78 *BMW Belgium v EC Commission* [1979] ECR 2435 para 45.

[242] Joined Cases 96/82 to 102/82, 104/82, 105/82, 108/82 and 110/82 *IAZ and others v EC Commission* [1983] ECR 3369 paras 54 and 55; Case T-319/94 *Fiskeby Board v EC Commission* [1998] ECR II-1331 paras 75 and 76; and Case C-282/98 P *Enso Española v EC Commission* [2000] ECR I-9817 para 316; Commission decision of 9 December 2004 in *Choline Chloride* (Case COMP/37.533), non-confidential version available at DG COMP's website paras 215–216 referring to Joined Cases T-236/01, T-239/01, T-244/01 to T-246/01, T-251/01 and T-252/01 *Tokai Carbon v EC Commission* [2004] ECR II-1181 para 343.

[243] 1998 Guidelines para 5.

[244] Case T-31/99 *ABB Asea Brown Boveri v EC Commission* [2002] ECR II-1881 para 184: '[. . .] Art [23(2)] of Reg [1/2003] does not prohibit the Commission from referring, during its calculation, to an intermediate amount exceeding 10% of the turnover of the undertaking concerned, provided that the amount of the fine eventually imposed on the undertaking does not exceed that maximum limit [. . .]'

[245] D Geradin and D Henry, 'The EC fining policy for violation of competition law: An empirical review of the Commission decisional practice and the Community's courts' judgments' [2005] European Competition law Journal 401–73 (404–08).

[246] *Quinine* [1969] OJ L192/5. Although the fine was 500,000 ECUs, the gravity and duration of the infringements in this case would indicate that if the case were to be considered now, the fines would have been much higher.

In this case, the Commission first went so far as to impose fines equivalent to around 4 per cent of the total turnover of the offending undertakings. In its judgment, the Court, although reducing the amount of the fines, gave clear support for the Commission's new policy of attempting to discourage restrictive conduct on the part of undertakings by fines of an exemplary nature. The Court stated that it was indeed appropriate to raise the level of fines in order to increase their dissuasive or deterrent effect.[247] As a result of that judgment, the Commission made it known in 1984, in its *Thirteenth Report on Competition Policy*, that in the future it would continue to impose high fines in order to achieve the dissuasive effect which so far had not been achieved by the Commission's pecuniary penalties.[248] From the mid-1980s onwards the size of the fines increased considerably. In 1992, a fine of 75 million euros was imposed on Tetra Pak for abuse of a dominant position. This amounted to almost 2.5 per cent of its overall turnover. Forty-one participants were fined in the Cement Cartel, with a total fine of 248 million euros in 1994.[249]

11.42 The 1998 Guidelines on setting fines introduced a new method: the basic amount is determined in absolute terms according to the intrinsic gravity of the infringement. The same year, the Commission imposed a fine of 272,940 million euros on the *Trans-Atlantic Conference Agreement* (TACA),[250] a group of shipping companies, which provided scheduled container transport for freight between ports in northern Europe and the United States. In 2001 the Commission imposed fines on fifty-six companies, totalling 1,836 billion euros, nearly half of which was imposed in the Vitamins[251] cartel case. *Hoffmann-La Roche AG*, one of the laboratories involved in this case, was fined 462 million euros because of its participation in a price fixing cartel for eight different vitamins, which was considered as constituting eight separate infringements. One year later, the largest cartel fine for a vertical agreement was imposed on *Nintendo* totalling an amount of 167.9 million euros.[252] In the same year, one single undertaking, the French company Lafarge was fined 249.6 million

---

[247] Cases 100–103/80 *Musique Diffusion Française v EC Commission* ('Pioneer') [1983] ECR 1825 para 106.

[248] XIII Report on Competition Policy [1983] paras 62–66. The Commission said that the purpose was twofold '[. . .] to impose a pecuniary sanction on undertaking for the infringement and prevent a repetition of the offence, and to make the prohibition in the Treaty more effective [. . .]'.

[249] Some of these fines were reduced on appeal since the Commission had not proved the length of the infringement: Some of these fines were reduced on appeal since the Commission had not proved the length of the infringement: Joined Cases T-25/95, T-26/95, T-30/95 to T-39/95, T-42/95 to T-46/95, T-48/95, T-50/95 to T-65/95, T-68/95 to T-71/95, T-87/95, T-88/95, T-103/95 and T-104/95 *Cimenteries CBR SA and others v EC Commission* [2000] ECR II-491.

[250] *Trans-Atlantic Conference Agreement* [1999] OJ L95/01.

[251] *Vitamins* [2003] OJ L6/01.   [252] *Nintendo* [2003] OJ L255/33.

euros.[253] Taking together, in the four years from 2000 to 2003 the Commission took twenty-six cartel decisions with fines totalling 3,330 million euros, compared with eight decisions (552 million euros) in the 1996 to 1999 period, and eleven decisions (393 million euros) from 1992 to 1995.[254] In early 2004, the Commission imposed the largest fine ever on an individual undertaking in its *Microsoft* decision,[255] with a total amount of 497.2 million euros relating to a proceeding under Article 82 EC.[256] A factor that undoubtedly caused the substantial growth in cartel decisions and the increasing fines is the determination of the Commission to focus on seriously damaging anticompetitive behaviour.[257] In this respect the modernization process has already borne its fruits. Another key issue was the adoption of the Leniency Notice and the actual implementation of the Leniency Program since then.[258]

Review of the fine. In the event of court proceedings, the CFI and the ECJ are   **11.43** empowered to decide on the appropriateness of the amounts of fines, having regard to the circumstances of the case. The Court then decides in the exercise of the unlimited jurisdiction conferred on it by Article 229 EC and Article 31 of Regulation 1/2003. The Court has the power to assess whether the amount of the fine imposed by the Commission is reasonable and to determine the

---

[253] Commission Press Release IP/02/1744 of 27 November 2004 'Commission imposes heavy fines on four companies involved in plasterboard cartel'.

[254] M Bloom, 'The Great Reformer: Mario Monti's Legacy in Art 81 and Cartel Policy' [2005] Competition Policy International 55–78 (69).

[255] Commission decision of 24 March 2004 in *Microsoft* (Case COMP/37.792), non-confidential version available at DG COMP's website; Case T-201/04 *Microsoft v EC Commission* (appeal pending) application in [2004] OJ C179/18. Note that Commission Memo 05/454/2005 of 30 November 2005 'Competition: Commission action against cartels – Questions and answers' includes two tables, one relating to the largest fines imposed by the Commission in cartel cases, the other relating to fines imposed by the Commission in the last three years.

[256] Although nearly 500 million euros might seem a significant amount, at the time of the decision Microsoft had approximately 50 billion euros in cash reserves. The fine imposed by the Commission amounted to not more than 1 per cent of its worldwide turnover. This may lead one to question whether the deterrent effect of the fine will be sufficient. It seems that from Microsoft's perspective, rather than the fine, the real problem of the decision is the remedies required by the Commission.

[257] A dedicated cartel unit central to the overall process of enhancing the Commission's efficiency in its fight against cartels was created in 1998 and brought together in one place the existing Commission skills in investigating cartels. In 2002, a further increase of resources was achieved by the creation of a second cartel unit, which was later decentralized throughout DG COMP. M Bloom, 'The Great Reformer: Mario Monti's Legacy in Art 81 and the Cartel Policy' [2005] Competition Policy International 55–78 (71–73). JM Joshua and PD Comesasca, 'EC fining policy against cartels after the Lysine ruling the subtle secrets of x' [2004] The European Antitrust Review, Global Competition Review, 5–10. In June 2005, however, an entire directorate (Directorate F, with a staff of around sixty) in DG COMP has been involved exclusively in detecting and combating cartels. See Commission Memo 05/454/2005 of 30 November 2005 'Competition: Commission action against cartels—Questions and answers.'

[258] See ch 6 'Leniency policy'.

appropriate amount of the fine.[259] Thus, unlike actions brought under the limited review provided for in Article 230 EC, the Court examines how in each particular case the Commission appraised the gravity and duration of unlawful conduct and then is entitled to substitute its own opinion for that of the Commission. That assessment may justify the production and taking into account of additional information which the duty to state reasons does not require to be set out in the decision.[260] In so doing, the Court has often annulled or reduced the fines imposed by the Commission.

11.44 *Non bis in idem.* As indicated earlier,[261] undertakings involved in international cartels that also extend to non-Member States cannot argue that they were already fined in another jurisdiction. The CFI held that the principle of *non bis in idem*, according to which a person who has already been tried may not be prosecuted or fined for the same conduct, cannot be applied where the proceedings initiated and fines imposed by the Commission, on the one hand, and by the authorities of a non-Member State on the other, do not pursue the same objectives. Furthermore, although fairness requires the Commission to take account, when fixing the amount of a fine, of penalties already imposed on the undertaking in question for infringements of the cartel law of a Member State, the CFI considers that there would be no such obligation on the Commission where the previous fines were imposed by authorities or courts of a non-Member State.[262]

4. The payment of fines

11.45 Infringement decisions contain a number of provisions in their operative part regarding the payment of fines. In the first place, the decision determines the amount of the fine in euros. Secondly, decisions set a time limit for payment,

---

[259] See Case T-220/00 *Cheil Jedang v EC Commission* [2003] ECR-II-2473 para 215. See also JM Joshua and PD Comesasca, 'EC fining policy against cartels after the Lysine ruling: the subtle secrets of x' [2004] The European Antitrust Review Global Competition Review 5–10 (5) who take the view that the Courts are reluctant to scrutinize the exercise of the Commission's discretion and seem to be far more concerned with second-guessing its sums: provided the Commission sufficiently explains its rationale in the final decision, it is free to determine the factual importance attached to the various factors used to set the fines.

[260] See, *inter alia*, Case C-248/98 P *NV Koninklijke KNP BP v EC Commission* [2000] ECR I-9641 para 38–40.

[261] See ch 3 'National competition authorities' paras 3.16 *et seq.* on *ne bis in idem*.

[262] In the Lysine cartel for example, searches were carried out in the US at the premises of several companies operating in the lysine market. Following those investigations, Archer Daniels Midland, Kyowa Hakko Kogyo, Sewon, Cheil Jedang, and Ajinomoto were charged by the US authorities with having formed a cartel to fix lysine prices and to allocate sales of lysine between June 1992 and June 1995. Case T-223/00 *Kyowa Hakko Kogyo Co. Ltd and others v EC Commission* [2003] ECR II-2553 paras 38–40.

usually three months. Payment must be made before the end of that period, unless the undertaking has lodged an appeal against the decision or has furnished a bank guarantee covering the principal amount of the fine and interest on it until judgment.[263] This is an administrative practice based on the case law of the Court where in several cases undertakings requested suspension of the enforcement of Commission decisions, under Article 242 EC.[264] Proceedings before the Court and the CFI do not have suspensive effect.

If the undertakings do not pay before the expiry of the period for voluntary payment of the fine, or bring an appeal and do not lodge a bank guarantee,[265] the Commission will start execution to secure payment, even while proceedings are pending. However, in line with its administrative practice, where undertakings request an interim order suspending a Commission decision, the Commission will not enforce such decision pursuant to Article 256 EC until the Court has decided on the merits of such action. Exceptionally the CFI has allowed the suspension of the execution of decisions imposing fines without lodging a bank guarantee when the undertaking faces serious difficulties in order to obtain the **11.46**

---

[263] After the adoption of a decision applying Arts 81 and 82 EC and imposing a fine, the letter notifying the decision always includes a form of a bank guarantee which must be duly completed and delivered to the Commission by any undertaking which institutes proceedings before the CFI with a view to preventing the Commission from implementing its decision. While the bank guarantee must usually cover the full amount of the fine, the President of the CFI has some times ordered the suspension of an obligation to provide bank guarantees for the amount of the fine, like in *Cartonboard*. In this case, the undertaking was ordered to guarantee 30 per cent of the fine immediately and the remainder to be guaranteed within six months, while its appeal was pending. See Case T-308/94 R *Cascades SA v EC Commission* [1995] ECR II-265.

[264] XII Report on Competition Policy [1982] paras 60–61; Case 107/82 *EG v EC Commission* [1983] ECR 3151 para 141 and XIII Report on Competition Policy [1983] para 66.

[265] The costs incurred in providing guarantees have sometimes been claimed by undertakings before the Community judicature in proceedings brought by them against Commission decisions imposing financial penalties, in addition to the costs of the proceedings properly so-called – but unsuccessfully. See Case 183/83 *Krupp v EC Commission* [1987] ECR 4611; Case T-43/92 *Dunlop v EC Commission* [1994] ECR II-441 paras 180 *et seq.*, and Case T-77/92 *Parker Pen v EC Commission* [1994] ECR II-549 paras 99–101. In *Parker Pen* (para 101), the CFI stated, citing the Order in *Krupp v EC Commission*, that the costs incurred by the applicants in guaranteeing payment of a fine are not recoverable costs under Art [91(b)] of the Rules of Procedure of the CFI (last amendment, [2005] OJ L298/1), since they cannot be regarded as costs incurred 'for the purpose of the proceedings'. A claim for reimbursement of the damage resulting from the obligation to provide a guarantee was also made, unsuccessfully, by Montedison, one of the companies involved in the *LdPE* case. See Joined Cases T-80/89, T-81/89, T-87/89, T-88/89, T-90/89, T-93/89, T-95/89, T-97/89, T-99/89, T-100/89, T-100/89, T-101/89, T-103/89, T-105/89, T-107/89 and T-112/89 *BASF AG and others v EC Commission* ('*LdPE*') [1995] ECR II-729 paras 127–128. Recently, in *Holcim*, the CFI dismissed Holcim's request for reimbursement of its costs providing a bank guarantee instead of paying the fine. The Court held that the illegality of a Commission decisions fining Holcim for its participation in a cartel in the cement sector (which was earlier annulled by the CFI) does not necessarily constitute a sufficiently breach to trigger liability, also taking into account that the case was extremely complex and required intensive legal and factual analysis. Case T-28/03 *Holcim v EC Commission* [2005] OJ C155/14.

guarantee or if its cost would produce a serious and irreparable damage.[266] The CFI has also stated that the allowance of this type of suspension is exceptional and that there is a need to present objective and reliable evidence in order to prove that the undertaking is unable to lodge a bank guarantee.[267] Exceptional circumstances may exist, in particular, where the undertaking is unable to lodge the required bank guarantee; where its own survival would be at risk, should a bank guarantee be lodged; where it risks bankruptcy; or where pleas made in the context of the main appeal raise, at first sight, particularly serious doubts as to the legality of the fine.[268] In order to assess the ability of the undertakings to give a guarantee, account must be taken of the group of companies on whom they are directly or indirectly dependent.[269]

11.47 Payment may also be deferred if the undertakings have requested and obtained from the Commission an extension of the time limit or relaxed payment

---

[266] In *Trans-Atlantic Conference Agreement* ([1999] OJ L95/1), Senator Lines GmbH was imposed a fine of 13.75 million euros by the Commission for an infringement of Arts 81 and 82 EC. Requests by Senator Lines for payment of the fine to be suspended pending the outcome of the appeal were rejected by the CFI (Order of the President of the CFI in Case T-191/98 R *DSR-Senator Lines v EC Commission* [1999] ECR II-2531) and on appeal by the ECJ (Order of the President of the Court in Case C-364/99 P(R) *DSR-Senator Lines v EC Commission* [1999] ECR I-8733). It was required to pay the fine before a decision was taken in the substantive proceedings before the ECJ. Senator Lines asserted then before the ECtHR that the requirement to pay the fine before a decision was taken in the substantive proceedings was a violation of Art 6 ECHR. The hearing in this case was cancelled in the light of the judgment of the CFI setting aside the fine imposed by the Commission on Senator Lines (Joined Cases T-191/98, T-212/98 to T-214/98 *Atlantic Container Line and others v EC Commission* [2003] ECR II-3275. See ECtHR press release of 16 October 2003 'Cancellation of hearing in the case Senator Lines GmbH v the 15 Member States of the European Union', available at the ECtHR website.

[267] Order of the President of the CFI in Case T-245/03 *FNSEA and others v EC Commission* [2004] ECR II-271, in particular paras 119–130 in which the CFI suspended the obligation on certain agricultural syndicates to make a bank guarantee under very strict conditions in order to avoid the enforcement of the fine. See also Order of the President in Case T-301/94 *Laakman Karton v EC Commission* [1994] ECR II-1279 paras 26–27 which held that difficulties in obtaining a bank guarantee cannot be regarded as insurmountable on the sole ground that the grant of the bank guarantee is subject to the involvement of other companies in the group to which the applicant belongs, in the absence of evidence that those companies are economically or legally prevented from providing the necessary support. Case T-104/95 *Tsimenta Chakidos v EC Commission* [1995] ECR II-2235 paras 21–25; Order of the President of the CFI in Case T-9/99 *HFB Holding für Fernwärmetechnik Beteiligungsgesellschaft mbH & Co KG and others v EC Commission* [1999] ECR II-2429 para 38 stating that the mere risk that the parties concerned might be obliged to apply for winding-up proceedings as a consequence of the obligation to provide a bank guarantee covering the outstanding amount of the fine, as a condition for the recovery of that amount not being immediately pursued, cannot constitute serious and irreversible damage.

[268] Order of the President of the CFI in Case T-295/94 R *Buchmann GmbH v EC Commission* [1994] ECR II-1265 para 23 and Order of the President of the CFI in Case T-301/94 R *Laakmann Karton GmbH v EC Commission* [1994] ECR II-1279 para 22.

[269] Case T-301/94 *Laakman Karton v EC Commission* [1994] ECR II-1279 para 26; see also Case 86/82 R *Hasselblad v EC Commission* [1982] ECR 1555 para 4, and Case T-156/94 R *Aristrain v EC Commission* [1994] ECR II-715 para 33; cited in Case T-295/94 R *Buchmann GmbH v EC Commission* [1994] ECR II-1265 para 26.

terms (payment by instalments). For that purpose, they will have to claim and demonstrate economic difficulties justifying their request. The Commission will in its discretion decide whether in each particular case such a request may be entertained.[270] Decisions give the details of the Commission bank account into which the undertakings must pay the fine. Further, the decision will determine the rate of interest payable in the event of failure to pay within the stated period.[271] This rate will be that applied by the European Central Bank to its main refinancing operations on the first day of the month in which this decision was adopted, plus 3.5 per cent.[272] As a general rule, decisions determine the

---

[270] In *CEWAL*, for example, the Commission granted payment facilities when adopting its decision. See Commission press release IP/92/1110 'Commission fine shipping companies for abusing dominant position on shipping trade between Northern Europe and Zaire' concerning the Commission Decision in *CEWAL* [1993] OJ L34/20. Compagnie Maritime Belge had four years within which to pay the fine.

[271] According to Case T-275/94 *Groupement des Cartes Bancaires 'CB' v EC Commission II* [1995] ECR II-2169 para 47: [. . .] The power conferred on the Commission [Art 22(2) of Reg 1/2003] covers the power to determine the date on which the fine is payable and that on which default interest begins to accrue, the power to set the rate of such interest and to determine the detailed arrangements for implementing its decision by requiring, where appropriate, the provision of a bank guarantee covering the principal amount of the fine imposed plus interest.[. . .]'

The Commission 'also has the power to decide how payments made in relation to those fines are to be applied, provided it does not infringe general rules or principles of Community law.' The Commission's decisions in this regard, 'must, in so far as [they are] measure[s] giving effect to the original decision setting the fine and the rate of interest, be regarded as no more than [ ] management and administrative measure[s].' See Case T-275/94 *Groupement des Cartes Bancaires 'CB' v EC Commission II* [1995] ECR II-2169 paras 94 and 71.

[272] The legality of interest being charged by the Commission in the event of delay in paying a fine or an application to the Court has been upheld by the Court itself – judgment in Case 107/82 *AEG v EC Commission* [1983] ECR 3151 para 143. The same rate applies in case an action is brought before the CFI or the ECJ. The CFI has established, referring to the formerly applied increase of the interest rate (1. 5 per cent), that the Commission was entitled 'to adopt a higher rate than that charged by the European Monetary Cooperation Fund in the event of late payment and in any event, as far as proceedings are concerned, to discourage manifestly unfounded actions brought with the sole object of delaying payment of the fine'. Case T-142/89 *Usines Gustave Boël SA v EC Commission* [1995] ECR II-867 para 138. The rate increase applied at present (3.5 per cent) has been upheld by the CFI for the same reasons. Although the interest rate must not be so high as to oblige undertakings to pay fines even though they consider that they have reason to challenge the validity of the Commission decision, the Commission may adopt a reference point above the market rate offered to the average borrower. Case T-23/99 *LR af 1998 A/S v EC Commission* [2002] ECR II-1705 para 398. See Art 5 of *Mercedes* [2002] OJ L257/1 (interest rate 7.26 per cent), decision partly annulled in T-325/01 *DaimlerChrysler AG v EC Commission*, CFI judgment of 15 September 2005.

The CFI has also confirmed the legality of the Commission's practice of applying a higher interest rate in case the undertakings do not actually bring an action before the Court (see also, Case T-275/94 *Groupement des Cartes Bancaires 'CB' v EC Commission II* [1995] ECR II-2169 para 83). The CFI observed '[. . .] that the accompanying letter [sent by the Commission] provided not for an increase in the rate of interest in the event of proceedings being brought but for a reduction, in such circumstances, to a rate below that which would apply in the event of late payment. It follows that, contrary to the applicant's assertion, the Commission did not seek to discourage applications to the Court. See Case T-142/89 *Usines Gustave Boël SA v EC Commission* [1995] ECR II-867 paras 139–140.

amount of the fine payable by each undertaking for its participation in the infringements covered by the procedure. The Commission may in specific cases declare the offending undertakings to be jointly and severally liable.[273] But where possible, it attempts to apply differential treatment to undertakings in order to take account of the effective economic capacity of the offenders. This particularly applies to cases in which considerable disparity exists regarding the size of the undertakings participating in the infringement.[274] The amount of the fines forms part of the income of the Commission and is included in its general budget.[275]

C. Periodic Penalty Payments

11.48 In accordance with Article 24(1) of Regulation 1/2003, the Commission may, by decision, impose on undertakings periodic penalty payments not exceeding 5 per cent of the average daily turnover in the preceding business year per day. There are two stages in the imposition of periodic penalty payments, in each of which the Commission adopts a decision. The first stage may coincide both with decisions intended to ensure compliance with procedural rules (periodic penalty payments in the event of delay in supplying the information requested by the Commission, or for each day of non-compliance in the case of inspections) and with substantive decisions (periodic penalty payments imposed in order to compel undertakings (i) to comply with a decision ordering to put to an end to an infringement of Article 81 or 82 EC, or (ii) to comply with a decision ordering interim measures or (iii) to comply with a commitment made binding by a decision pursuant to Article 9.

11.49 The Commission may also, in the case of both procedural and substantive infringements, initiate proceedings for the imposition of periodic penalty payments separately from, and at a later stage than, the decisions with which they

---

[273] This particularly applies to associations of undertakings. See, e.g. Case T-9/99 *HFB Holding für Fernwärmetechnik Beteiligungsgesellschaft mbH & Co. KG and others v EC Commission* [2002] ECR II-1487 para 526: '[. . .] there was no person at the head of all the companies belonging to the [. . . .] group to which, as the person responsible for the acts of the group, responsibility for the infringement could have been imputed. In that regard, the Court of First Instance has held that, in a situation in which, owing to the family composition of the group and the dispersal of its shareholders, it may be impossible or exceedingly difficult to identify the person at its head to which, as the person responsible for coordinating the group's activities, responsibility for the infringements committed by its various component companies may be imputed, the Commission is entitled, to hold the subsidiaries jointly and severally responsible for all the acts of the group [. . .]'.

[274] e.g. *Graphite Electrodes* [2002] OJ L100/1 paras 146 *et seq.*; *Amino Acids* [2001] OJ L152/24 paras 303 *et seq.*

[275] Answer to European Parliament written Question No 715/80 [1980] OJ C245/15.

are associated. Situations may arise where no periodic penalty payments are mentioned in an inspection decision, and the Commission's investigative action is obstructed, or where a Commission decision requires an infringement to be brought to an end without periodic penalty payments being imposed in the event of non-compliance, and the undertakings fail to bring the infringement to an end. In such cases, the Commission may decide separately as to the amount of the periodic penalty payments and the date on which they will start to be payable if the undertakings fail to comply with the directions addressed to them by the Commission. Unlike the situation with fines, with periodic penalty payments, the Commission does not have to show that undertakings acted deliberately or negligently. In determining the periodic penalty payment, the Commission is not required to apply criteria such as seriousness and duration, although in practice it decides on the daily amount according to the circumstances. Although there are no precedents yet under Regulation 1/2003, under Regulation 17, due to the low amounts involved and the very nature of periodic penalty payments—which are imposed almost always in cases where undertakings are obstructive towards the Commission—the amount was frequently the maximum daily figure. Where obligations are attached to an infringement decision, the Commission may impose periodic penalty payments for each obligation of which it seeks to ensure fulfilment, as long as it complies with the principle of proportionality.[276]

---

[276] In *Commercial Solvents* [1972] OJ L299/51 and in *ECS/Akzo* [1985] OJ L374/1 the Commission imposed the then maximum periodic penalty under Reg 17 (1,000 ECUs) for the eventual breach of each one of the obligations.

12

REJECTION OF COMPLAINTS

A. Introduction

Procedures commenced by formal complaint[1] may conclude as requested by the **12.01**
complainants with a decision declaring and penalizing an infringement of
Articles 81 and 82 EC, or else with rejection of the complaint.[2] In some cases,
an infringement procedure following a complaint may give rise to a formal
settlement under Article 9 of Regulation 1/2003 or possibly an informal settlement between the undertakings criticized and the Commission, as a result of
which the complainant may—in some ways—be doubly discontent if the
settlements do not respond to his concerns. Not only will his complaint have
been rejected, but it also will have had more or less the opposite of the desired
effect.[3] In such situations, the Commission is required to inform the complainants—who will in many cases have actively participated during the investigation
throughout the proceedings leading to the adoption of the decision—of its
reasons for not considering it appropriate to take action against the undertak-

---

[1] For the difference between unofficial or informal and official or formal complaints, see ch 5
'Opening the file' para 5.18. The term complainants is used only for formal complainants, since
proceedings initiated in response to an unofficial or informal complaint are, for administrative
purposes, deemed to be procedures commenced on the Commission's own initiative in which the
complainants do not play the role or have the rights of a formal complainant.

[2] The Commission must define its position regarding all the alleged infringements that the
complainants have referred to it. The Commission may determine which legal basis for a complaint is best suited for resolving a competition matter but if a complainant relies both on Arts 81
and 82 the Commission cannot be regarded as having satisfied its demands when it acts on the
basis of only one of those provisions. See Case T-74/92 *Ladbroke Racing (Deutschland) GmbH v
EC Commission* [1995] ECR II-115 paras 60–61, replying to the arguments of the Commission in
paras 50–51. See also Case T-548/93 *Ladbroke Racing Limited v EC Commission* [1995] ECR
II-2565 paras 50–51.

[3] A clear example is the amicable settlement between Philip Morris and Rothmans, on the one
hand, and the Commission, on the other, following the complaint by British American Tobacco
(BAT) and Reynolds against them. The former agreed to make specific changes to their agreements and the Commission closed the file by means of a comfort letter, formally rejecting the
complaint. The rejection of the complaint gave rise to Joined Cases 142/84 and 156/84 *BAT and
Reynolds v EC Commission* [1987] ECR 4487.

485

ings concerned and for rejecting their complaint (Article 7 of Regulation 773/2004).

12.02 In line with the case law of the CFI,[4] upon receipt of a complaint the Commission, 'within its terms of reference as the upholder of undistorted competition in the Community',[5] can choose one of the following options:

(i) to initiate proceedings for establishing a breach of Article 81(1) and/or Article 82 EC, so that a decision confirming such a breach can be adopted; or

(ii) to take a duly-reasoned decision not to pursue the complaint on the ground of lack of Community interest; or[6]

(iii) to dismiss the complaint after having sent the complainant a letter under Article 7 of Regulation 773/2004[7] with or without a formal decision.[8]

B. The Treatment of Complaints

12.03 The Commission is required to 'examine carefully the factual and legal particulars brought to its notice by the complainant in order to decide whether they disclose conduct of such a kind as to distort competition in the Common Market and affect trade between Member States'.[9] Nevertheless, the Commission is not obliged to investigate all complaints which it receives.[10] The CFI considers that 'setting priorities within the limits prescribed by the law' is 'an inherent feature of administrative activity',[11] so that the Commission may give priority to certain complaints, which will indeed be investigated, and reject others without having taken any specific investigative measures. This results

---

[4] See Case T-74/92 *Ladbroke Racing (Deutschland) GmbH v EC Commission* [1993] ECR II-115 paras 58, 59, and 69; the Commission has expanded on these principles in its Commission Notice on the handling of complaints by the Commission under Arts 81 and 82 EC [2004] OJ C101/05; Opinion of AG Ruiz-Jarabo Colomer in Joined Cases C-449/98 P and C-450/98 P *International Express Carriers Conference (IECC) v EC Commission* [2001] ECR I-3875 para 56.

[5] Opinion of AG Ruiz-Jarabo Colomer in Joined Cases C-449/98 P and C-450/98 P *International Express Carriers Conference (IECC) v EC Commission* [2001] ECR I-3875 para 56.

[6] See paras 12.10 *et seq.* below.

[7] This is the equivalent of former Art 6 of Reg 99/63 and of Reg 2842/98 (repealed).

[8] See para 12.14 below.

[9] See Case T-24/90 *Automec v EC Commission II* [1992] ECR II-2223, para 79; Joined Cases T-189/95, T-39/96 and T-123/96 *Service pour le groupement d'acquisitions (SGA) v EC Commission* [1999] ECR II-3587 para 53; Case T-575/93 *Koelman v EC Commission* [1996] ECR II-1 para 39, confirmed on appeal by Case C-59/96 P *Koelman v EC Commission* [1997] ECR I-4809.

[10] Case T-24/90 *Automec v EC Commission II* [1992] ECR II-2223 para 79.

[11] See Case T-24/90 *Automec v EC Commission II* [1992] ECR II-2223 para 77; Case C-119/97 P *Ufex and others v EC Commission* [1999] ECR I-1341 para 88; Case T-219/99 *British Airways v EC Commission* [2003] ECR II-5917, para 68.

from the task assigned to the Commission of ensuring application of Articles 81 and 82 EC and its responsibility for defining and implementing effectively the orientation of Community competition policy.[12] Of the complaints examined, some will also ultimately be rejected. The Commission may thus reject a complaint both after undertaking a detailed examination of the content of the complaint—which it must do—and after investigating the case by, for example, making requests for information and carrying out inspections. Although the Commission is not required to examine all the complaints it receives, once it has decided to investigate it must do so carefully, seriously, and diligently so as to enable it to appraise, in full knowledge of the circumstances, the matters of fact and of law which the complainants have referred to it for consideration.[13]

The Commission is required, where appropriate, to inform the complainants of **12.04** the reasons why it considers that the information gathered by it does not justify upholding the complaint and to allow them a period within which to submit any observations in writing, in accordance with Article 7 of Regulation 773/ 2004. The notice on the handling of complaints establishes that the statement of reasons must disclose in a clear and unequivocal fashion the reasoning followed by the Commission in such a way as to enable the complainant to ascertain the reasons for the decision and to enable the competent Community court to exercise its power of review. However, the Commission is not obliged to adopt a position on all the arguments relied on by the complainant in support of its complaint. It only needs to set out the facts and legal considerations, which are of decisive importance in the context of the decision.[14]

Until the early 1990s the ECJ did not seem to require the Commission to adopt **12.05** a decision as to the existence of the infringements complained of, except where

---

[12] Case T-77/95 RV *Union française de l'express (Ufex) and others v EC Commission* [2000] ECR II-2167 para 39.

[13] In the absence of the requisite care, integrity, and diligence, a rejection decision following an investigation carried out incorrectly would be annulled. See Case T-7/92 *Asia Motor France v EC Commission II* [1993] ECR II-669. However, see also Case T-319/99 *Federación Nacional de Empresas de Instrumentación Científica, Médica, Técnica y Dental (FENIN) v EC Commission* [2003] ECR II-357 para 43: '[. . .] the Commission is not required, when considering a complaint, to examine facts which have not been brought to its notice by the complainant before rejecting a complaint on the ground that the practices complained of do not infringe Community competition rules or do not fall within the scope of the Community competition rules '[. . .] An applicant bringing an action against a decision of the Commission rejecting its complaint in a competition matter cannot, therefore, criticise the Commission for failing to take account of facts which it has not brought to the Commission's attention and which the Commission could only have discovered by investigation. [. . .]'.

[14] Notice on the handling of complaints [2004] OJ C101/65 para 75.

the subject matter of the complaint fell within its exclusive remit.[15] Today the CFI has made clear that having followed the rejection procedure, the complainant is entitled to obtain a formal decision from the Commission on its complaint.[16] However, the Commission is not required to adopt a decision compelling undertakings to bring an infringement to an end, once it has been found to exist, since Article 7 of Regulation 1/2003 indicates that the Commission *may* adopt such a decision.[17]

C. Reasons for Rejecting Complaints

12.06 The main reasons for which the Commission may reject a complaint after the prescribed detailed examination of its content are: (i) lack of a legitimate interest on the part of the complainant;[18] (ii) lack of any connection with Articles 81 and 82 EC; (ii) the applicability of an individual[19] or block exemption; and— most importantly—(iv) the lack of any Community interest in the matter complained of.[20] Another obvious reason for rejecting a complaint after a preliminary examination, which will not be considered in detail here, is the fact that the complainant has again raised the same issue without adducing fresh evidence,

---

[15] See Case T-16/91 *Rendo v EC Commission I* [1992] ECR II-2417 paras 52, 58, and 59. (This judgment of the CFI was quashed by the ECJ in Case C-19/93 P *Rendo v EC Commission II* [1995] ECR I-3319. See also Case 26/76 *Metro v EC Commission I* [1977] ECR 1875; Case 125/ 78 *GEMA v EC Commission II* [1979] ECR 3173, and Case T-64/89 *Automec v EC Commission I* [1990] ECR II-367. The Commission is obliged to carry out an investigation or take a final decision on the existence or otherwise of the alleged infringement only if the complaint is within its exclusive jurisdiction. Regarding the Commission's obligations deriving from its exclusive powers, see Case T-24/90 *Automec v EC Commission II* [1992] ECR II-2223 para 75.

[16] See also Notice on the handling of complaints [2004] OJ C101/65 para 28. Case T-77/95 RV *Union française de l'express (Ufex) and others v EC Commission* [2000] ECR II-2167 para 37: '[. . .] complainants are entitled to have the fate of their complaint settled by a decision of the Commission against which an action may be brought [. . .]'; T-127/98 *UPS Europe SA v EC Commission* [1999] ECR II-2633 para 36: '[. . .] when a complainant has submitted his observations on the notification under [Art 7 of Reg 773/2004], the Commission is required either to initiate a procedure against the person who is the subject of the complaint or to adopt a definitive decision rejecting the complaint, which may be the subject of an action for annulment before the Community judicature [. . .]'; Case C-282/95 P *Guérin Automobiles v EC Commission* [1997] ECR I-1503 para 36.

[17] Case C-449/98 *International Express Carriers Conference (IECC) v EC Commission* [2001] ECR I-3875 para 35 in which the ECJ states that Art 3 of Reg 17 (now Art 7 of Reg 1/2003) does not give a person making an application under that Art the right to insist that the Commission take a final decision as to the existence or non-existence of the alleged infringement and does not oblige the Commission to continue the proceedings, whatever the circumstances, right up to the stage of a final decision.

[18] See also Notice on the handling of complaints [2004] OJ C101/65 paras 33–40.

[19] Decisions adopted pursuant to Art 81(3) EC remain valid until they expire. See Art 43(1) of Reg 1/2003.

[20] See also Notice on the handling of complaints [2004] OJ C101/65 paras 41–45.

after its first complaint was definitively rejected.[21] Once the investigation has been carried out, the Commission may finally take the view that a complaint is unfounded.

1. Lack of a legitimate interest[22]

Pursuant to Article 5 of Regulation 773/2004, natural and legal persons shall show a 'legitimate interest' in order to be entitled to lodge a complaint for the purposes of Article 7 of Regulation 1/2003. Where a natural person or legal entity lodging a complaint is unable to demonstrate a legitimate interest, the Commission is entitled, without prejudice to its right to initiate proceedings of its own initiative, not to pursue the complaint.[23] Member States are deemed to have legitimate interest for all complaints they choose to lodge.[24] Neither Regulation 1/2003 nor Regulation 773/2004 define this concept; however, the Notice on the handling of complaints[25] sets out a number of situations where the condition of legitimate interest needs to be assessed in more detail. In the case of an association of undertakings, the CFI has stated that it does not necessarily have to be directly concerned but needs to be entitled to represent the interests of its members and that the conduct complained of is liable to adversely affect their interests.[26] Therefore, the Commission does not pursue the complaint of an association whose members were not involved in the type of business transactions that is being complained of.[27] Thus, a legitimate interest can be claimed either by the parties of the complained practice or agreement, by competitors whose interests have been affected or by undertakings which were excluded from a distribution system. In the same manner, a consumer

12.07

---

[21] Notice on the handling of complaints [2004] OJ C101/65 para 79. Opinion of AG Alber in Joined Cases C-172/01 P, C-175/01 P, C-176/01 P and C-180/01 P *International Power plc, British Coal Corporation, PowerGen (UK) plc and EC Commission v National Association of Licensed Opencast Operators* [2003] ECR I-11421 para 99: '[. . .] If the complainant then lodges a fresh complaint which does not contain any significant new facts, the Commission is not obliged to re-examine the matter. Its rejection of the complaint on that ground is merely confirmation of the earlier decision and cannot be challenged [. . .]'.

[22] As will be seen below, in the Community competition law context, the terms 'interest' and 'legitimate interest' are *sui generis* and may have little in common with similar expressions used in any of the national laws of the Member States.

[23] Notice on the handling of complaints [2004] OJ C101/65 para 40.

[24] Notice on the handling of complaints [2004] OJ C101/65 para 33.

[25] Notice on the handling of complaints [2004] OJ C101/65 paras 34–40.

[26] Case T-114/92 *Bureau Européen des Médias et de l'Industrie Musicale (BEMIM) v EC Commission* [1995] ECR II-147 para 28. Associations of undertakings were also the complainants in the cases underlying the judgments in Case 298/83 *Comité des industries cinématographiques des Communautés européennes (CICCE) v EC Commission* [1985] ECR 1105 and Case T-319/99 *Federación Nacional de Empresas de Instrumentacion Científica, Médica, Técnica y Dental (FENIN) v EC Commission* [2003] ECR II-357.

[27] Joined Cases T-133/95 and T-204/95 *International Express Carriers Conference (IECC) v EC Commission* [1998] ECR II-3645 paras 79–83.

association[28] is able to lodge complaints as well as individual consumers[29] whose economic interests are affected where they are the buyers of goods or services that is the subject matter of the infringement. However, the Commission does not consider that persons or organizations that have a general interest without being directly and adversely affected have a sufficient legitimate interest to present formal complaints under Article 7(2) of Regulation 1/2003. Finally, the Notice mentions that local or regional public authorities can also show a legitimate interest where there are buyers or users of goods or services, that are affected by the conduct complained of. The Court has also drawn attention to the relationship between Article 7(2) of Regulation [1/2003] and Article 230 EC, taking the view that a complainant may, under the fourth paragraph of Article 230 EC, bring an action for the annulment of an individual exemption decision in favour of agreements complained of by him.[30]

12.08 The Commission has interpreted the concept of 'legitimate interest' referred to in Article 3(2)(b) of Regulation 17 (now Article 7(2) of Regulation 1/2003) using roughly the same approach as that adopted by the Court in interpreting the expression 'direct and individual' concern in the fourth paragraph of Article 230 EC, where the latter refers to persons who, although not the addressees of a decision, may bring an action for annulment. Thus, for the Commission, the complainant must be adversely affected by the alleged infringement, since otherwise its legitimate interests would not be affected, as required by Article 7(2). The complainant must set out in its written complaint the reasons justifying its legitimate interest. It is not sufficient to make a general allegation that the person concerned considers itself adversely affected by the alleged infringement, despite the literal wording of the provision, which appears to indicate that a

---

[28] Case T-37/92 *Bureau Européen des Unions des Consommateurs (BEUC) v EC Commission* [1994] ECR II-285 para 36.

[29] This question has been raised in a pending procedure before the CFI regarding the legitimate interest of a political party whose members might be affected in the *Austrian Banks* case (Joined Cases T-213/01 and T-214/01 *Österreichische Postsparkasse AG v EC Commission*, pending). The Commission has also accepted as complainant an individual consumer in *Greek Ferries* [1999] OJ L109/24 para 1.

[30] See Case 26/76 *Metro v EC Commission I* [1977] ECR 1875 para 13; In Case 75/84 *Metro v EC Commission II* [1986] ECR 3021 paras 20–23, the Court went even further and established a link between the fourth para of Art 230 EC (then the second para of Art 173 EC) and Art 19(3) of Reg 17, placing on the same footing the 'interested third parties' referred to in the latter provision and the 'natural or legal persons who claim a legitimate interest' referred to in Art 3(2)(b) of Reg 17 (now Art 7(2) of Reg 1/2003). In the Court's opinion, proof that Metro was a person 'directly and individually' concerned by a decision by which the Commission renewed an individual exemption for SABA derived from the fact that Metro had submitted observations after the publication prescribed by Art 19(3) of Reg 17. The Court stated that: '[. . .] The Commission recognized that Metro had a legitimate interest in submitting its observations in accordance with Article 19(3) of Regulation 17. [. . .]', thereby assimilating 'interested third parties' to 'natural or legal persons who claim a legitimate interest'.

mere 'claim' would be a sufficient basis for the requisite legitimate interest. The Commission may ascertain whether this condition is met at any stage of the investigation.[31] It should not be concluded, however, that a decision finding an infringement under Article 7(1) of Regulation 1/2003 would be unfounded if the procedure had been initiated in response to a complaint from a person lacking a legitimate interest within the meaning of Article 7(2), since the Commission, under Article 7(1), is entitled to commence infringement proceedings on its own initiative, without any outside intervention.[32] It could use information obtained from a complainant without a legitimate interest in order to initiate proceedings. If a complainant does not have a legitimate interest, it would nevertheless be regarded as an informant or possibly, an informal complainant with limited procedural rights. In practice, the Commission has rejected complaints for this reason very rarely.

2. Complaints having no connection with Articles 81 and 82 EC

Sometimes DG COMP receives complaints from individuals which relate to conduct unconnected with Articles 81 and 82 EC. Thus, e.g. complaints may be made concerning particular situations which are not the responsibility of the undertakings,[33] or one undertaking may complain about another on the ground that the latter is taking action which is more properly described as unfair competition[34] and is in principle a matter for the competent national courts or authorities, rather than the Commission.[35] Alternatively, an undertaking may incorrectly approach DG COMP to raise a matter which should be dealt with by other departments of the Commission, using different legal instruments

12.09

---

[31] Joined Cases T-133/95 and T-204/95 *International Express Carriers Conference (IECC) v EC Commission* [1998] ECR II-3645 para 79.

[32] See Joined Cases 32/78 and 36/78 to 82/78 *BMW Belgium v EC Commission* [1979] ECR 2435 para 18.

[33] Such as, e.g. national regulations on prices, entry into the market, etc. in particular sectors. See, for a rejection of a complaint based on the existence of national restrictive rules, *Ijsselcentrale and others* [1991] OJ L28/32; and Case T-16/91 *Rendo v EC Commission I* [1992] ECR II-2417 paras 42 *et seq.* It should be borne in mind, however, that Community law does not allow national rules which reinforce pre-existing restrictive agreements between undertakings, even though such agreements may appear in principle to pursue laudable aims such as combating unfair competition. See in that connection, among others, Case 311/85 *Vlaamse Reisbureaus (VVR) v Sociale Dienst* [1987] ECR 3801.

[34] Regarding 'unfair competition', it is interesting to observe that sometimes agreements between undertakings designed to eliminate such competition may simply be disguised cartels—as in the case of the agreements between Flemish travel agents which gave rise to *Vlaamse Reisbureaus (VVR) v Sociale Dienst*, cited in the foregoing footnote. Allegedly unfair competition on the part of two German agencies also gave rise to the judgment in Case 66/86 *Ahmed Saeed and another v ZBW* [1989] ECR 803.

[35] An example might be misleading advertising or any other typical act of unfair competition. The fact that EC competition law does not in principle deal with such issues does not mean that, in particular circumstances, certain unfair conduct cannot be dealt with under Arts 81 and 82 EC.

from those used by DG COMP. In this case DG COMP will on its own initiative refer the matter to the Secretariat General of the Commission for allocation, or else directly to the competent department of the Commission, informing the complainants that it has done so. More generally there may be complaints concerning matters clearly outside the scope of the Community antitrust provisions, which strictly speaking cannot be regarded as complaints within the meaning of Article 7(2) of Regulation 1/2003.[36] Since the Commission has no power to act upon this type of complaint, the communication to the complainant informing it of the steps taken on the complaint does not constitute a decision which may be subject to an action before the CFI. If a matter brought before the Commission falls outside the terms of reference of the Community competition authorities, in that it does not fulfil the requirements of Articles 81 and 82 EC (in particular as regards effects on trade between Member States), the Commission may raise the issue within the ECN[37] and advise the complainants to invoke national competition law and to approach the relevant authorities for its application.

3. Exempt agreements

12.10 The Commission may also receive a complaint concerning an agreement or a practice which has been authorized individually under Regulation 17 or under a block exemption regulation. Unless the complainants refer to conduct not covered by the exempting decision or regulation, or request withdrawal of the exemption on substantive grounds (breach of the decision or of Article 81(3) EC[38]), the Commission will also reject complaints in such cases. For the Commission to withdraw the benefit of the block exemption pursuant to Article 29 of Regulation 1/2003, it must find that upon individual assessment an agreement to which the exemption regulation applies has certain effects which are incompatible with Article 81(3) EC.

4. Lack of Community interest

12.11 The concept of Community interest or, more properly, lack of a Community interest, as such does not appear in the EC Treaties nor could it be inferred from any provision of Regulation 17. Having previously been used more or less sporadically by the Commission, it was incorporated into legal jargon at the

---

[36] Not even when they have been submitted on the legal basis of the Community competition provisions concerning State aid. See the order of the CFI in Case T-36/92 *SFEI v Commission I* [1992] ECR II-2479.

[37] See ch 3 'The role of the national competition authorities' para 3.05.

[38] Regarding the procedure for withdrawal of a block exemption on an individual basis, see below, ch 14.

time of the *Automec II* judgment, in which the existence of a sufficient Community interest was seen only as a criterion for the attribution, by the Commission, of varying degrees of priority when investigating a complaint.[39] The concept relates exclusively to the Commission's obligations regarding the investigation of conduct complained of. As regards the authority to adopt or not adopt a decision, the CFI takes the view that the Commission is under no obligation to rule on the existence or otherwise of an infringement.[40]

In *BEMIM*, the CFI made it clear that the Commission might take a decision to **12.12** shelve a complaint for lack of a sufficient Community interest not only before commencing an investigation of the case but also after taking investigative measures, if that course seems appropriate to it at that stage of the proceedings.[41] It pointed out that to conclude otherwise would be tantamount to placing the Commission under an obligation, once it had taken investigative measures following the submission of an application under Article 7 of Regulation 1/2003, to adopt a decision as to whether or not either Articles 81 and 82 EC, or both, had been infringed, which would be contrary not only to the very wording of Article 7 of Regulation 1/2003, according to which the Commission '*may*' adopt a decision concerning the existence of the alleged infringement, but would also conflict with the settled case law according to which a complainant has no right to obtain from the Commission a decision on the existence or otherwise of an infringement.[42] The Notice on the handling of complaints establishes that '[. . .] the Commission is entitled to give different degrees of priority to complaints made to it and may refer to the Community interest presented by a case as a criterion of priority. The Commission may reject a complaint when it considers that the case does not display a sufficient

---

[39] Opinion of AG Ruiz-Jarabo Colomer in Joined Cases in C-449/98 P and C-450/98 P *International Express Carriers Conference (IECC) v EC Commission* [2001] ECR I-3875 para 57: '[. . .] It is no more than an abbreviated formula, a shortcut, to describe, succinctly, the discretion—neither unfettered nor arbitrary, since it is subject to judicial review—which the Treaties confer on the Commission for its examination of a complaint alleging the existence of anti-competitive practices. The substance of that concept varies very considerably, to the same extent as the widely differing circumstances which surround cases involving infringements of the competition rules [. . .]'.

[40] See Case T-24/90 *Automec v EC Commission II* [1992] ECR II-2223 para 84.

[41] See Case T-114/92 *Bureau Européen des Médias et de l'Industrie Musicale (BEMIM) v EC Commission* [1995] ECR II-147 para 81 and Case C-449/98 P *International Express Carriers (IECC) v EC Commission* [2001] ECR I-3875 para 37: '[. . .] The existence of that discretion does not depend on the more or less advanced stage of the investigation of a case. However, that element forms part of the circumstances of the case which the Commission is required to take into consideration when exercising its discretion [. . .]'.

[42] Case C-449/98 P *International Express Carriers (IECC) v EC Commission and others* [2001] ECR I-3875 para 35.

Community interest to justify further examination'.[43] In this respect, the Commission differs from a civil court, which must uphold the subjective rights of private individuals in their reciprocal relations.[44] The Commission's power to reject a complaint on these grounds is nevertheless conditional on the availability of appropriate remedies at national level.[45]

12.13 The CFI considers, however, that the Commission may not confine itself to referring abstractly to the Community interest but must specifically indicate the factual and legal considerations which prompted it to conclude that there was no Community interest, in accordance with Article 253 EC. Thus it is obliged to state reasons if it declines to continue with the examination of a complaint, and the reasons stated must be sufficiently precise and detailed to enable the CFI effectively to review the Commission's exercise of its discretion to define priorities. The purpose of that review is to ascertain whether or not the contested decision is based on materially incorrect facts, or is vitiated by an error of law, a manifest error of appraisal or misuse of powers. This is the only way to ensure that action by the Commission does not escape review of legality by the Court.[46] Accordingly, if the Commission decides not to pursue a complaint on the ground of lack of a Community interest, it must first adopt a formal decision against which an action may be brought.[47] In this specific case the CFI does not seem to require that the Commission follows the standard three-stage procedure for the rejection of complaints described below. In practice the Commission may want to send a brief letter to the complainants relying on Article 7(2) of Regulation 773/2004, allowing them to make their views known

---

[43] The Court said the Commission 'is entitled to give differing degrees of priority to the complaints brought before it'. Case C-119/97 *Union française de l'express (Ufex) and others v EC Commission* [1999] ECR I-1341 paras 88 and 89 and Case C-449/98 P *International Express Carriers Conference (IECC) v EC Commission* [2001] ECR I-3875 para 3.

[44] See Case T-24/90 *Automec v EC Commission II* [1992] ECR II-2223 para 85.

[45] According to the CFI in Case T-5/93 *Roger Tremblay and others v Syndicat des Exploitants de Lieux de Loisirs (SELL)* [1995] ECR II-185 paras 65 and 68: '[. . .] the Commission is entitled to reject the complaint . . . provided however that the rights of the complainant or of its members can be adequately safeguarded, in particular by the national courts.' In particular, 'the rights of a complainant could not be regarded as sufficiently protected before the national court if that court were not reasonably able, in view of the complexity of the case, to gather the factual information necessary in order to determine whether the practices criticized in the complaint constituted an infringement of [Article 81] or [Article 82] of the Treaty or of both [. . .]', citing the judgment of Case T-24/90 *Automec v EC Commission* [1992] ECR II-2223 paras 89–96.

[46] Case T-77/95 RV *Union française de l'express (Ufex) and others v EC Commission* [2000] ECR II-2167 para 42; Case T-198/98 *Micro Leader Business v EC Commission* [1999] ECR II-3989 para 27; Case T-24/90 *Automec v EC Commission II* [1992] ECR II-2223 para 80; and Case T-114/92 *BEMIM v EC Commission* [1995] ECR II-147 para 72.

[47] See Case T-37/92 *BEUC and others v EC Commission* [1994] ECR II-285 para 47. The *BEUC* judgment has been confirmed in Case T-114/92 *Bureau Européen des Médias et de l'Industrie Musicale (BEMIM) v EC Commission* [1995] ECR II-147.

before a decision not to pursue the complaint is adopted.[48] In order to assess the Community interest in further investigation of a case, the Commission must take account of the circumstances of the case, and must in particular balance the significance of the damage which the alleged infringement may cause to the functioning of the common market against the probability of its being able to establish the existence of the infringement and the extent of the investigative measures required for it to perform, under the best possible conditions, its task of ensuring that Articles 81 and 82 EC are complied with.[49] The Commission has provided some guidance for assessing the Community interest of a case in its Notice on the handling of complaints.[50] The criteria pointed out by the Commission are based on the case law of the Community courts. These include:

- the fact that the complainant can bring an action to assert its rights before national courts;[51]
- the impact on trade between Member States and the duration and the extent of the infringements complained of;[52]
- the significance of the alleged infringement as regards the functioning of the Common Market, the probability of establishing the existence of the infringement and the scope of the investigation;[53]
- the more or less advanced stage of the investigation of a case;[54]
- the fact that the practices in question have ceased;[55]

---

[48] Whenever the Commission invokes the Community interest, the CFI seems to have established an obligation for the Commission to react formally. In spite of this, and for reasons of good administration, it seems logical to believe that if the complainant did not insist in having a formal decision the Commission would not be obliged to adopt such a decision.

[49] Joined Cases T-189/95, T-39/96 and T-123/96 *SGA v EC Commission* [1999] ECR II-3587, para 52; Joined Cases T-185/96, T-189/96 and T-190/96 *Riviera Auto Service and others v EC Commission* [1999] ECR II-93 para 46.

[50] Notice on the handling of complaints [2004] OJ C101/65 para 44.

[51] Case T-24/90 *Automec v EC Commission II* [1992] ECR II-2223 paras 88 *et seq.*; Case T-5/93 *Roger Tremblay and others v EC Commission* [1995] ECR II-185 paras 65 *et seq.*; Case T-575/93 *Casper Koelman v EC Commission* [1996] ECR II-1 paras 75–80.

[52] Case C-119/97 P *Union Française de l'Express (Ufex) and others v EC Commission* [1999] ECR I-1341 paras 92–93.

[53] Case T-24/90 *Automec v EC Commission* [1992] ECR II-2223 para 86.

[54] Case C-449/98 P *International Express Carriers Conference (IECC) v EC Commission* [2001] ECR I-3875 para 37.

[55] Case T-77/95 *Syndicat Français de l'Express International and others v EC Commission* [1997] ECR II-1 para 57; Case C-119/97 P *Union Française de l'Express (Ufex) and others v EC Commission* [1999] ECR I-1341 in which the Commission assessed the seriousness and duration of the infringements complained of and whether their effects were continuing. The ECJ stated that '[. . .] the Commission [. . .] cannot rely solely on the fact that practices alleged to be contrary to the Treaty have ceased, without having ascertained that anti-competitive effects no longer continue and, if appropriate, that the seriousness of the alleged interferences with competition or the persistence of their consequences has not been such as to give the complaint a Community interest [. . .]' (para 95); see also CFI judgment following the referral of the case back to the CFI, Case T-77/95 *Ufex v EC Commission* [2000] ECR II-2167 paras 43 *et seq.*, in which the CFI

- the acceptance by the undertakings concerned to change their conduct in such a way that it can consider that there is no longer a sufficient interest warranting intervention.[56]

5. Unfounded complaints

12.14 A complaint may be rejected as unfounded where, during the investigation, insufficient evidence has been obtained to substantiate it. Where an infringement has not been proved, there is no alternative but to reject the complaint (rejection on factual grounds). Similarly, a complaint may be rejected where, after sufficient evidence has been obtained, the conduct is found not to be contrary to Articles 81 and 82 EC.[57] In the absence of an infringement, the complaint must be rejected (rejection on legal grounds).

D. Rejection Procedure[58]

1. First stage

12.15 The rejection of complaints may involve three stages. In those cases where it is appropriate to reject a complaint, the Commission contacts the complainants

---

concluded that the Commission did not assess the seriousness and duration of the infringements complained of and whether their effects were continuing: '[. . .] By considering, finally, that it was not obliged to investigate past infringements if the sole purpose or effect of such an investigation was to serve the individual interests of the parties, the Commission misunderstood its task in the field of competition, which was not indeed to apply itself to establishing the conditions for compensation for the pecuniary loss said to have been suffered by one or more undertakings, but to ensure, following the complaint brought by an organisation representing almost all the French private operators active in the market in question, a state of undistorted competition. [. . .]'. See also the rejection decision in *UFEX* (COMP/38.663) which notes that the practices complained of—which had not in any event been duly established—were brought to an end more than ten years ago and that, since then, no lasting anti-competitive effects attributable to them had been apparent in the relevant market, cited in Commission Report on Competition Policy [2004], SEC (2005) 805 final para 102.

[56] Case T-110/95 *International Express Carriers (IECC) v EC Commission and others* [1998] ECR II-3605 para 57, upheld by Case C-449/98 P *International Express Carriers (IECC) v EC Commission and others* [2001] ECR I-3875 paras 44–47. See ch 13 'Commitments, voluntary adjustments' paras 13.01 *et seq.*

[57] e.g. in Case COMP/A36.568 *Scandlines v Port of Helsingborg* and Case COMP/A36.570 *Sundbusserne v Port of Helsingborg*, the Commission came to the conclusion that the available evidence was insufficient to demonstrate to the requisite legal standard that the prices at issue were excessive. These two parallel complaints related to alleged abuses within the meaning of Art 82 EC involving excessive port fees.

[58] The procedure for the rejection of complaints has been described by the CFI in Case T-64/89 *Automec v EC Commission I* [1990] ECR II-367 paras 45–47, and developed in the XX Report on Competition Policy [1990] paras 163–165. Similar descriptions are to be found in the Order of the CFI in T-36/92 *Syndicat Français de l'Express international (SFEI) and others v EC Commission* [1992] ECR II-2479 paras 38 *et seq.* and the judgment Case T-37/92 *BEUC and*

and informally explains the reasons why it is not possible to uphold their complaint or ascertain the existence of an infringement of the EC competition rules. It will usually be the head of the competent administrative unit of DG COMP who informs the complainants, by letter, of the provisional and informal conclusions reached by the department responsible for dealing with the complaint. It is possible as well to hold a meeting with the complainant.[59] Where the complaints are not adequately supported, the Commission official will ask the complainant for additional factual information or legal considerations which might enable the Commission to conclude that there has been an infringement. This is an informal step in the procedure prior to formal rejection of the complaint; it does not constitute a decision and as such does not bind the Commission. Letters of this kind are purely preliminary and are without prejudice to the rights of the complainants, and therefore they are not actionable.[60] The Commission uses them to allow complainants to put forward new information and arguments, without which it would be impossible to ascertain an infringement. In practice, if, after a considerable lapse of time, the complainants have not supplied any new information or arguments and they have not expressly asked for a more detailed explanation of the Commission's reasoning, the latter will close the file.

2. Second stage

In cases where the complainants express interest in receiving a more detailed 12.16 explanation, the Commission sends a formal letter before rejecting the complaint, as provided for in Article 7 of Regulation 773/2004 (former Article 6 of Regulation 99/63). The obligation to deliver this type of letters is one of the most important procedural guarantees for complainants.[61] Previously known as

---

others v EC Commission [1994] ECR II-285 para 29 (less clearly in the latter case than in *Automec I*, since it appears to confuse the second and third stages).

[59] See Joined Cases T-191/98 and T-212/98 to T-214/98 *Atlantic Container Line v EC Commission* [2003] ECR II-3275 para 351: '[. . .] There is by contrast no general duty on the part of the Commission to draw up minutes of discussions in meetings or telephone conversations with the complainants which take place in the course of the application of the Treaty's competition rules [. . .]'.

[60] Case T-64/89 *Automec v EC Commission I* [1990] ECR II-367 para 45.

[61] The disappearance of the restriction of competition which was the subject-matter of the complaint 'could not entitle the Commission to dispense with the requirement of defining its position on the applicant's complaint, in conformity with the procedural guarantees provided for in Article [7] of Regulation [1/2003] and Article [7] of Regulation [773/2004]'. Case T-74/92 *Ladbroke Racing (Deutschland) GmbH v EC Commission* [1995] ECR II-115 para 67. Case C-282/95 P *Guérin Automobiles v EC Commission* [1997] ECR I-1503 para 35: '[. . .] The purpose of that intermediate phase in the administrative procedure before the Commission is, in fact, to safeguard the rights of the complainant, to whom an unfavourable decision should not be addressed without first giving him the opportunity to submit observations on the grounds upon which the Commission intends to rely [. . .]'.

'Article 6 letters', these letters are normally complex and lengthy, their main aim being to provide the reasoning of the Commission in relation to the object of the complaint.[62] National courts are not bound by the Commission's appraisals contained in such letters regarding the applicability or otherwise of Articles 81 and 82 EC.[63] Their content corresponds to that of a statement of objections in an infringement procedure (in a way, they are statements of objections, but in reverse) and, like statements of objections, they are not measures against which proceedings may be brought.[64] A statement of objections also serves to define the position of the Commission regarding a complaint and substitutes an 'Article 7 letter' when the Commission intends to act against the alleged infringements.[65][66] These letters contain a factual part and a legal part, which are both generally very detailed. They are Commission acts, *albeit* in practice signed by the Director-General for Competition, after consultation with the Legal Service.[67] Formally, the letters contain an express reference to Article 7 of Regulation 773/2004, an invitation to the complainants to submit their observations on the letter in writing, generally within a period of at least four

---

[62] As the CFI has stated, the only purpose of an 'Article 6 [now 7] letter' is to enable a complainant under Art 3 of Reg 17 [now Art 7 of Reg 1/2003] to be informed of the reasons which have led the Commission to conclude that there are insufficient grounds for granting the complainant's application. Case 125/78 *GEMA v EC Commission II* [1979] ECR 3173 para 17.

[63] See Case T-114/92 *Bureau Européen des Médias et de l'Industrie Musicale (BEMIM) v EC Commission* [1995] ECR II-147 para 65 and Case T-575/93 *Casper Koelman v EC Commission* [1996] ECR II-1 paras 41–43.

[64] See Case T-64/89 *Automec v EC Commission I* [1990] ECR II-367 para 46, and in Case T-28/90 *Asia Motor France v EC Commission I* [1992] ECR II-2285 para 42. Both judgments cite Case 125/78 *GEMA v EC Commission II* [1979] ECR 3173. See also Case T-17/93 *Matra v EC Commission* [1994] ECR II-595 para 35, which cites *Automec I*. See further T-186/94 *Guérin Automobiles v EC Commission* [1995] ECR II-1753 para 34 (confirmed by Case C-282/95 P *Guérin Automobiles v EC Commission* [1997] ECR I-1503); Case T-37/92 *Bureau Européen des Unions des Consommateurs (BEUC) and others v EC Commission* [1994] ECR II-285 paras 27 and 30 and Case T-241/97 *Stork Amsterdam BV v EC Commission* [2000] ECR II-309 para 52.

[65] The Commission will not send an 'Article 7 letter' if it does not have the intention to reject a complaint, and is actually pursuing the procedure for investigating the alleged breaches of the competition rules. See Case T-74/92 *Ladbroke Racing (Deutschland) GmbH v EC Commission* [1995] ECR II-115 para 44.

[66] The Commission maintained in the *Ladbroke* case (para 33) that a communication pursuant to Art 19(3) of Reg 17 (removed in Art 27 of Reg 1/2003) acts as an 'Article 6 letter' in defining the position of the Commission when it intended to exempt the relevant agreements or practices. The CFI does not seem to have replied to this question in *Ladbroke* (paras 65 and 72). Traditionally, in its administrative practice the Commission sought to address 'Article 6 letters' whenever it had disregarded all or part of the elements of a complaint, regardless of whether an exemption had been granted or not. For an example of this, see Joined Cases 142/84 and 156/84 *BAT and Reynolds v EC Commission* [1987] ECR 4487. Under Reg 1/2003 the question remains whether a publication under Art 27(4)—before commitments and findings of inapplicability decisions—may act as an 'Article 7 letter'.

[67] However, briefer and less detailed 'Article 7 letters' may be considered to satisfy all the formal requirements in that provision. See Case T-186/94 *Guérin Automobiles v EC Commission* [1995] ECR II-1753 paras 8 (which contains the text of a short Art 7 letter), 28 and 29.

weeks,[68] and, as an annex, the documents from the file to which they are entitled to have access.[69] Failure to respond in the time specified in the letter may be detrimental to the interests of complainants. As will be apparent, this procedure is very similar to the one considered in connection with the statement of objections. In these cases, however, it is not usual to hold an administrative hearing, and access to the file is not necessarily as comprehensive as that granted to the undertakings involved.[70]

3. Third stage

If the complainant does not respond to the statement submitted by the Commission in the 'Article 7 letter', the rejection procedure will end. However, if the complainants have submitted written observations responding to the 'Article 7 letter' and insisted on obtaining a formal decision, the third stage will start and the Commission will continue the procedure up to the point of adoption of a decision rejecting the complaint or further investigation of the case. When responding to an 'Article 7 letter', the complainant has the right to request access to documents on which the Commission has based its provisional assessment but which have not been provided.[71] Failure to respond in the time specified in the letter may be critical.[72] Regulation 773/2004 establishes that 'if the complainant fails to make known its views within the time-limit set by the Commission, the complainant shall be deemed to have been withdrawn'.[73]

12.17

The rejection decision will be adopted and signed, by virtue of a delegation of powers from the Commission, by the member of the Commission responsible for competition. It will not require to be reported on by the Advisory Committee, nor will it necessarily be published in the Official Journal—although a non-confidential version is usually made available on the DG COMP website.[74] The complainants will have a period of two months after notification of the decision

12.18

---

[68] Art 17(2) of Reg 773/2004 establishes at least a four-week period to submit observations to the letter.

[69] The Notice on the handling of complaints [2004] OJ C101/65 para 69 provides that access is normally provided by annexing to the letter a copy of the relevant documents.

[70] See ch 10 paras 10.28 *et seq.* above ('Access to the File').

[71] Art 8(1) of Reg 773/2004. As stated, access is normally provided by annexing to the letter a copy of the relevant documents; for example, in a CD-ROM if need be.

[72] Art 7(1) of Reg 773/2004 specifies that 'the Commission shall not be obliged to take into account any further written submission received after that date'.

[73] Art 7(3) of Reg 773/2004.

[74] Decisions of this type, when published, form part of a Commission Communication in Series C of the OJ. An example of a decision rejecting a complaint is to be found in Commission Communication in Case IV/33.018 *GEC-Siemens/Plessey* [1990] OJ C239/2. The rejection of the complaint in *Automec II* was also made public in the CFI judgment in that case, cited above, para 13.

to commence proceedings before the CFI.[75] The CFI has established that having submitted, within the time stipulated, comments in response to an 'Article 6' [now Article 7] letter, the complainant is henceforth entitled to obtain a definitive decision from the Commission on its complaint.[76] As regards the content and the effects of such decisions, the European Court[77] and the CFI[78] have stated that they have the following features: they bring the investigation to an end, they contain an assessment of the agreements or practices in question, and they prevent the complainants from requiring reopening of the investigation, unless they put forward new evidence. The Commission must give adequate reasons for its decision, but if it sets out the decisive facts and legal considerations this will be sufficient.[79]

---

[75] See, e.g. the judgments in Case 210/81 *Demo Studio Schmidt v EC Commission* [1983] ECR 3045; and Case 298/83 *CICCE v EC Commission* [1985] ECR 1105. See also Joined Cases 142/84 and 156/84 *BAT and Reynolds v EC Commission* [1987] ECR 4487.

[76] See Case T-186/94 *Guérin Automobiles v EC Commission* [1995] ECR II-1753 paras 23 and 34. Interestingly, it was the Commission itself which proposed this solution (see para 16 of the judgment). Relying on the Opinion of Judge Edward acting as Advocate General in *Automec II*, Case T-24/90 *Automec v EC Commission II* [1992] ECR II-2223 paras 22 and 22, and citing Case 377/87 *Parliament v Council* [1988] ECR 4017 paras 7 and 10 and Case 302/87 *Parliament v Council* [1988] ECR 5615 para 16, the CFI considered 'Article 6 letters' as acts which are the prerequisite for the next step in a procedure which culminates in a legal act which is itself open to an action for annulment under the conditions laid down in Art 230 EC. Referring to the previous case law—in particular, Case 125/78 *GEMA v EC Commission* [1979] ECR 3173 para 17; Case T-24/90 *Automec v EC Commission II* [1992] ECR II-2223 paras 75 and 76; and Case T-16/91 *Rendo and Others v EC Commission* [1992] ECR II-2417 para 98—and citing the judgments in Case 222/84 *Johnston v Chief Constable of the Royal Ulster Constabulary* [1986] ECR 1651 para 18, and Case C-249/88 *EC Commission v Belgium* [1991] ECR I-1275 para 25, the CFI stated that there is nothing in the approach taken in these judgments to prevent a complainant from obtaining 'a Commission decision on its complaint capable of forming the subject-matter of an action for annulment, in accordance with the general principle that there is a right of access to judicial review.' Accordingly, the CFI concluded that there is an obligation for the Commission to adopt such a rejection decision, or risk an action for failure to act under Art 232 EC.

[77] See Joined Cases 142/84 and 156/84 *BAT and Reynolds v EC Commission* [1987] ECR 4487 para 12.

[78] See Case T-64/89 *Automec v EC Commission I* [1990] ECR II-367 para 57; Case T-116/89 *Prodifarma v EC Commission* [1990] ECR II-843 para 70; Case T-16/91 *Rendo and others v EC Commission* [1992] ECR II-2417 para 49; and Order of the CFI in T-36/92 *SFEI v EC Commission I* [1992] ECR II-2479 para 29. All these CFI decisions cite Joined Cases 142/84 and 156/84 *BAT and Reynolds v EC Commission* [1987] ECR 4487. See also Case 210/81 *Demo-Studio Schmidt v EC Commission* [1983] ECR 3045 and Case 298/83 *CICCE v EC Commission* [1985] 1105.

[79] Case T-387/94 *Asia Motor France SA v EC Commission* [1996] ECR II-961 para 104; Case T-111/96 *ITT Promedia v EC Commission* [1998] ECR II-2937 para 79.

13

COMMITMENTS, VOLUNTARY ADJUSTMENTS, CONCLUSION OF THE PROCEDURE WITHOUT A FORMAL DECISION

I. Voluntary adjustments

A. The Administrative Procedure as an Opportunity for Adjustment

Under Regulation 17 undertakings could reach an amicable agreement with the **13.01** Commission from the very commencement of the case if they agreed to bring their activities into line with Community competition law.[1] The Annual Reports of the Commission showed that a high number of cases were indeed resolved by way of a settlement.[2] In some cases, the terms of the settlement were published in the Annual Report or even in the Official Journal which is indicative of the Commission's flexible and quite pragmatic approach in this regard. Where the companies have made enough concessions to satisfy the Commission and where the Commission has considered nothing may be gained by pursuing

[1] The administrative procedure specifically gives undertakings an opportunity to explain their conduct and adjust their agreements to the requirements of Community law. See Joined Cases 142/84 and 156/84 *BAT and Reynolds v EC Commission* [1987] ECR 448 para 23; A Jones and B Sufrin, *EC Competition Law* (2nd edn, 2004) 1143.

[2] Some of these cases also related to notified agreements which have enjoyed immunity from fines, and where therefore a formal decision would have served little purpose. For example, see recently European Commission, Report on the Application of Competition Rules in conjunction with XXXIII Report on Competition Policy [2003] 203 *et seq*. See also 'Dealing with the Commission—Notification, complaints, inspections and fact-finding powers under Arts 81 and 82 of the EEC Treaty' (edn 1997) point 8.3: '[. . .] In numerical terms, the informal settlements the Commission makes are of much greater significance than formal decisions. [. . .]'. L Ritter and WD Brown, *European Competition Law: A Practitioner's Guide* (3rd edn, 2004) 1041 also note that the vast majority of cases are closed without reaching the stage of formal decision.

formal proceedings further, an informal settlement has often appeared as the most expedient way to terminate the matter.[3]

13.02 There is some discussion as to whether the Commission will continue to end cases by informal settlements given that Article 9 of Regulation 1/2003 now empowers the Commission to adopt decisions accepting commitments offered by undertakings in the course of proceedings.[4] While the Commission is expected to terminate its proceedings by relying on this new power to take decisions which make commitments offered by companies binding on them, it is not obliged to do so.[5] Nor is the Commission obliged to adopt any other formal decision provided by Regulation 1/2003.[6] Thus, it is submitted that Regulation 1/2003 will not prevent the Commission from settling cases by way of informal arrangements.[7] The Commission has itself stated that in the future more formal decisions might be taken in those cases which it will investigate with a view to providing additional legal certainty and allowing the Commission to clarify its policy formally. For example, in *Microsoft* the Commission indicated that the parties had been close to a settlement, but finally believed that it was essential to establish clear principles for the future conduct of a company with such a strong dominant position in the market.[8] It should be noted that the Commission may also pass a file to a better placed NCA: such

---

[3] A Jones and B Sufrin, *EC Competition Law* (2nd edn, 2004) 1143.

[4] CS Kerse and N Khan, *EC Antitrust Procedure* (5th edn, 2004) para 6–055 argue that although Art 9 of Reg 1/2003 would not prevent the Commission from settling a matter other than by formal commitments imposed on the parties, it would be surprising if the Commission were to continue to use informal settlements rather than commitment decisions. The provision would confer procedural rights on third parties and recourse to an informal settlement could be open to criticism as circumventing third parties' procedural rights. See also J Schwarze and A Weitbrecht, *Grundzüge des europäischen Kartellverfahrensrechts* (2004) § 6 para 16 who expect that informal settlements will be limited to exceptional cases when problematic issues are directly discussed with the companies concerned.

[5] J Temple Lang, 'Commitment Decisions and Settlements with Antitrust Authorities and Private Parties under European Antitrust Law', 32nd Annual International Antitrust Law & Policy Conference Fordham Corporate Law Institute, 22–23 September 2005 (forthcoming), 8 elaborates on the reasons why the Commission may consider imposing commitment decisions. Commitment decisions are unlikely to be used when the Commission seeks to establish a clear precedent. See below ch 13 on 'Commitment Decisions' paras 13.08 *et seq.*

[6] Note, however, that this principle requires a qualification: where subject-matter falls within its exclusive purview of the Commission, the Commission may be required to give a decision as in the case of the withdrawal of an exemption granted under Art 81(3) EC. See Case T-24/90 *Automec v EC Commission* [1992] ECR II-2223 para 75; see paras 14.20 *et seq.*

[7] Commission Report on Competition Policy [2004], SEC (2005) 805 final 57 stating that out of 391 cases closed in 2004, 363 were solved informally (called 'Informal Procedure') and only twenty-eight of them by formal decision.

[8] European Commission Memo/04/70 of 24 March 2004 'Microsoft—Questions and Answers on Commission Decision'. See also 'Q&A on modernization with Kris Dekeyser' Global Competition Review, Vol 8, Issue 3, April 2005, 11–16 (14) stating that commitment decisions are a 'very important instruments' for the Commission. If the Commission would think that it could remove or substantially reduce the competition concerns rather quickly with this instrument, it would do so.

reallocation of the file to an NCA in accordance with the ECN Network Notice should not be considered a settlement as it is for that NCA to decide on the future course of action in the case.[9] At the same time, the Commission has also made clear that it would continue to accept requests for settlements if it considers that through a settlement a real change in the marketplace could be better achieved.[10] All things considered, it is unlikely that informal settlements will disappear: there will be fewer cases solved this way but there will also be fewer cases the Commission will investigate due to its focus on serious infringements of competition rules and the fact that the work will be shared with other 'well-placed' ECN members having enforcement powers parallel to those of the Commission. As regards the application of Article 9 of Regulation 1/2003, It may turn out that the Commisison prefers to adopt a commitment decision where it has followed through the procedure up to a point, for example where it has taken investigation measures or where it has sent a statement of objections, whereas it may be more open to the possibility of 'informal settlements' at an earlier stage.

The Commission usually informs undertakings of the investigations which it has commenced concerning them at the earliest stage of the inquiries and, in particular, always sends the undertakings a copy of the formal complaints received against them, usually before, but certainly no later than, the sending of the statement of objections. Moreover, the Commission is open to all kinds of direct contact, which enable undertakings to gain better knowledge both of the procedures and of the substantive rules of competition law. This means that in many cases the undertakings themselves, aware of the Commission's critical view of particular agreements, conduct, or practices, change their own behaviour appropriately, thus avoiding the initiation of an infringement procedure or the adoption of a formal decision against them. Voluntary adjustments would thus appear possible at any time, and the undertaking is itself responsible for assessing whether they suffice to comply with Articles 81 and 82 EC. In principle, the Commission does not formally approve any such voluntary adjustments. **13.03**

There are various moments when a voluntary adjustment may be possible, from the moment the file is opened and even before, and coming to an end immediately before the formal decision declaring the infringement. Thus, formalities such as the transmission of the complaint to the undertakings to which they relate (where this is done separately), a request for information or an inspection, **13.04**

---

[9] See ch 3 'National competition authorities' paras 3.12 *et seq.*
[10] XXXIII Report on Competition Policy [2003] Part I para 97. See also Part II 206 *et seq.* which describes the cases which the Commission closed by way of settlements in 2003.

a statement of objections[11] or even the administrative hearings may prompt the undertakings to reflect and facilitate the adjustment of their agreements, practices and conduct in order to comply with Community law. A unilateral declaration made in the course of proceedings that the agreements criticized in the statement of objections will cease to be applied wholly or in part may, in practice, be insufficient to avoid continuation of the infringement procedure and, in appropriate cases, the imposition of fines.[12] It may also be that from time to time the Commission considers it as convenient to hold a 'stay of play' meeting with the parties. However, at the same time, the Commission will avoid issuing any communication which could be compared to the instruments used under Regulation 17 (exemption, negative clearance, or comfort letter). Thus, the Commission takes care that these informal contacts will not lead to a notification procedure through the back door. Nothing should be construed as altering the principle that companies should perform their self-assessment under EC competition rules.[13] Undertakings are generally considered as being well placed to assess the legality of their actions in such a way as to enable them to take an informed decision on whether to go ahead with an agreement or practice in whatever form.

---

[11] Nevertheless, the statement of objections does not in itself impose an obligation on undertakings to modify or reconsider their commercial practices. See Case 60/81 *IBM v EC Commission* [1981] ECR 2639 para 21. When the Commission sends a statement of objections concerning agreements or practices which require modification for the legal exception in Art 81(3) EC to be applied, the Commission may, but is not obliged to, give guidance to the undertakings as to possible alternative solutions, in other words regarding the specific changes to be made. See Joined Cases 43/82 and 63/82 *VBVB and VBBB v EC Commission* [1984] ECR 19 para 19.

[12] The scope of a procedure is not automatically changed just because the undertakings unilaterally announce in the course of the procedure that they will cease in part to apply the agreements covered by the statement of objections, particularly if that intention has not been notified to the Commission or verified in practice. See Case T-66/89 *The Publishers' Association v EC Commission* [1992] ECR II-1995 para 53, citing Cases 142/84 and 156/84 *BAT and Reynolds v EC Commission* [1987] ECR 4487 para 22. The judgment of the CFI was quashed in Case C-360/92 P *The Publishers Association v EC Commission II* [1995] ECR I-23, but the above dicta remain valid.

[13] Recital 38 of Reg 1/2003 states that where cases give rise to genuine uncertainty because they present novel or unresolved questions for the companies, they may wish to seek guidance from the Commission. According to JS Venit, 'Private Practice in the Wake of the Commission's Modernization Program' [2005] Legal Issues of Economic Integration 147–59 (148–49) the significance of this 'loss' needs to be qualified: under the old system, where an agreement was highly questionable it would have been seldom notified and if it was, it brought with it the risk of forceful Commission intervention. Besides, the need for self-assessment would hardly be new; in the past responsible firms would also have been unlikely to negotiate an agreement or enter into it without having first concluded that it would fall outside the scope of Art 81(1) EC or, if caught by the prohibition, could prove exemptable under Art 81(3) EC. What is genuinely new is the increasing sophistication of this assessment considering the economically oriented approach of the regulator and courts.

B. Procedure after Voluntary Adjustment

Once they comply with the competition rules, the undertakings' agreements, **13.05** conduct, and practices may be dealt with by the Commission either formally or informally. One example might be a case where, despite termination of the infringement, the Commission considered it necessary to adopt a formal decision covering the period before the undertakings brought their behaviour into line with the Community rules.[14] It would then have to send a statement of objections and go through the entire infringement procedure, if it had not already done so. The Commission's reasons for adopting such a stringent approach are various. It may doubt that the agreement, practice or conduct objected to will actually be abandoned by the undertakings. Or else the complainants may have asked the Commission for a formal decision to enable them to seek damages with confidence before a national court.[15] The Commission may also wish to set a precedent[16] or penalize particularly serious infringements (for example in cases of abuse of a dominant position).[17] Informal abandonment of the procedure after voluntary adjustments will be due either to the fact that the case has low priority or is of little relevance to competition policy, or to the impossibility of dealing with the case formally by means of a favourable decision. An example would be a procedure commenced on the basis of a complaint or on the Commission's own initiative, in the course of which the undertakings change their agreements to the satisfaction of the Commission.

---

[14] Note that under Art 7 of Reg 1/2003 in conjunction with Recital 11 the Commission is empowered to adopt a decision finding an infringement not only when it orders the termination of an infringement or imposes a fine, but also where the infringement has already come to an end and no fine is imposed. The power of the Commission to adopt an infringement decision in such circumstances is limited to cases where it has a legitimate interest to do so. This may be the case where there is a danger that the addressee might re-offend, or where the case raises new issues, the clarification of which is in the public interest.

[15] There appears to be a clear public interest in establishing an infringement by a Commission decision in the light of *Courage and Crehan* (Case C-453/99 [2001] ECR I-6297) and the policy objective inherent in Reg 1/2003 of using national courts to enforce EC competition rules. CS Kerse and N Khan EC *Antitrust Procedure* (5th edn, 2005) para 6–019.

[16] Thus, e.g. in *London European Airways/SABENA* [1988] OJ L317/47 the Commission imposed a token fine on Sabena for an abuse of a dominant position which had already ceased, insofar as the Belgian airline gave certain undertakings regarding its future conduct in the Belgian computer flight reservation market. See also *PO Video Games/PO Nintendo Distribution/ Omega-Nintendo* [2003] OJ L255/33 para 371: '[. . .] However, the Commission has wide discretionary powers when determining the amount of fines to be imposed, including the power not to impose a fine at all or merely a symbolic fine [. . .]'.

[17] See *Tetra Pak II* [1992] OJ L72/1. As is clear from Annex 7 to the decision, Tetra Pak's undertakings did not enable it to avoid the imposition of a fine of 75 millions.

II. Commitments

A. Introduction

13.06 For a long time, the Commission has been using accepted commitments to settle antitrust proceedings on an informal basis. A number of cases have been resolved through informal commitments, called 'undertakings', offered by the undertaking concerned and considered by the Commission as acceptable[18] but it was not until Regulation 1/2003 that this practice was given an express legal basis. Article 9 of Regulation 1/2003 empowers the Commission to adopt decisions accepting commitments offered by undertakings in the course of proceedings in which the Commission intends to adopt a decision that orders termination of an alleged infringement.[19] Such commitments must constitute an appropriate remedy to the competition concerns identified by the Commission during the proceedings, and are binding upon the undertaking to which they are addressed.

13.07 Under Article 9 of Regulation 1/2003, the Commission is never obliged to terminate its proceedings by adopting a commitment decision, but it can consider such a decision if and when (i) the companies under investigation are willing to offer commitments which remove the Commission's initial competition concerns as expressed in a preliminary assessment; (ii) the case is not one where a fine would be appropriate (this therefore excludes commitment decision in hard core cartels cases); (iii) efficiency reasons justify that the Commission limits itself to making the commitments binding, and does not issue a formal prohibition decision.[20] In the event of multi-party infringements,

---

[18] A review of the Commission's informal practice prior to Reg 1/2003 shows that the informal decisions where undertakings or commitments were given most frequently concerned high technology industries where the implementation of undertakings by the parties was a rapid and effective form of resolving the specific problems of constantly changing markets for which there was no solution under Reg 17: *IBM* [1985] OJ L118/24; COMP/30.566 *United International Pictures BV (UIP)*, Commission press release IP/99/681 of 14 September 1999 'Commission renews UIP authorisation for five years'; *Irish Distillers Group* (XVIII Competition Report [1988]); *Coca-Cola* (XIX Competition Report [1989]); *Microsoft I* (XXIV Competition Report [1994]), *Digital* (XXVII Report on Competition Policy [1997]). See also with more references to the case law. J Temple Lang, 'Commitment Decisions and Settlements with Antitrust Authorities and Private Parties under European Antitrust Law, 32nd Annual International Antitrust Law & Policy Conference Fordham Corporate Law Institute, 22–23 September 2005 (forthcoming), 3.

[19] Art 9 of Reg 1/2003 should be read together with Recital 13. By virtue of Art 5 of Reg 1/2003 NCAs will also be entitled to adopt commitment decisions.

[20] Commission Memo/04/217 of 17 September 2004 'Commitment decisions (Art 9 of Council Reg 1/2003 providing for a modernised framework for antitrust scrutiny of company behaviour)'. It seems that at the time two consecutive Commission memos have been issued, both surprisingly with the same reference and the same date but with different headings and content. The other one is entitled 'New cartel procedure under Art 9 of Reg 1/2003' (which, however, seems to have been removed from DG COMP's website). We will therefore refer to them by their title.

this instrument may also be used vis-à-vis one undertaking whereas the Commission may at the same time continue its infringement procedure against the others.[21] To date, under Regulation 1/2003 there have been only a few, albeit steadily increasing number of cases, in which Article 9 has been applied. The fact that the Commission resorts to this instrument in a rising number of cases is already indicative of a certain popularity of commitment decisions.[22] In most of these cases, the Commission has raised objections as regards practices that could infringe Article 81 EC, particularly as regards vertical agreements (*German Bundesliga, Repsol CPP SA, Premier League,* and *Alrosa-De Beers*), there being one case involving both Articles 81 and 82 EC (*Alrosa-De Beers*) and one case under Article 82 EC (*Coca-Cola*). Further, three of the cases were originally petitions for individual authorization which the Commission, with the coming into force of Regulation 1/2003, turned into commitment decisions (e.g. *German Bundesliga, Repsol CPP SA, Premier League, BUMA and SABAM, Austrian Airlines/SAS*). While it seems premature to draw any conclusions about the Commission's practice, it seems safe to assume, therefore, that the situations where the Commission will use a commitment decision

---

[21] M Busse and A Leopold, 'Entscheidungen über Verpflichtungszusagen nach Art 9 VO (EG) Nr. 1/2003' [2004] Wirtschaft und Wettbewerb (WuW) 146–55 (152) do not see a conflict with the principle of equal treatment where the Commission communicates its objections to all undertakings concerned, thus giving them the opportunity of submitting a proposal for commitments. See also J Temple Lang, 'Commitment Decisions and Settlements with Antitrust Authorities and Private Parties under European Antitrust Law', 32nd Annual International Antitrust Law & Policy Conference Fordham Corporate Law Institute, 22–23 September 2005 (forthcoming), 16.

[22] *German Bundesliga* (Art 27(4) notice in [2004] OJ C229/13 and summary in [2005] OJ L134/46), is the first case in which the Commission has applied Art 9 and the only one in which it has adopted a final commitment decision. This procedure resulted from the request of the German Football Federation (DFB) for a negative clearance decision, or alternatively an individual exemption under Art 81(3) EC, for the centralized marketing of the TV and radio broadcasting rights. See also T Körber, 'Die erstmalige Anwendung der Verpflichtungszusage gemäss Art 9 VO 1/2003' [2005] Wettbewerb in Recht und Praxis 463–7. The Case *Repsol CPP SA* (Art 27(4) notice in [2004] OJ C258/7 COMP/38.348) arose following a request for an individual authorization or a declaration of compliance with Art 81 EC with regard to eight standard contracts which set out the manner in which Repsol CPP carries out the distribution of petrol products. In *Coca-Cola* (Case COMP/39.116) the Commission began an investigation concerning Coca-Cola in 1999, which ended on 19 October 2004. On that day, Coca-Cola presented a series of commitments to the Commission, which, in principle, eliminated the Commission's vis-à-vis concerning certain clauses in its distribution contracts and their effects on competition. The Commission adopted the commitment decision on 22 June 2005. See Commission Press Release of 22 June 2005, 'Competition: Commission makes commitments from Coca-Cola legally binding, increasing consumer choice.' See also Case COMP/38.453 *Premier League*, Commission press release IP 05/1441/2005 of 17 November 2005 'Competition: Commission receives improved commitments from FAPL over sale of media rights' and Case COMP/38.381 *De Beers Alrosa*, Art 27(4) notice available at DG COMP's website; *BUMA and SABAM–Santiago Agreement* [2005] OJ C200/11; *Austrian Airlines/SAS* [2005] OJ C233/18.

have changed following the systematization of these decisions under Article 9 of Regulation 1/2003.[23]

B. Main Aspects of Commitment Decisions

1. Scope of the Commission's assessment

13.08 One of the unique features of commitment decisions—which fundamentally differentiates them from finding and termination of infringement decisions, or inapplicability decisions—is the scope of the assessment that the Commission carries out. Article 9 provides that commitment decisions will only state that there are no reasons for the Commission to intervene. Further, Recital 13 provides that such decisions will not declare whether or not the infraction has been produced or whether it exists. Therefore, the Commission does not carry out an in-depth assessment of the matter, and instead simply decides whether the commitments offered are sufficient to remove its concerns about the case in question. This has been seen[24] as one of the advantages of commitment decisions, since it maintains a balance between the interests of the undertakings, which see how their practices are accepted without being declared unlawful (which should encourage undertakings to submit commitments) and the interests of interested third parties, which are free to bring an action for damages before national courts. Nevertheless, allowing the NCAs to examine cases which have already been decided by the Commission could present a problem, since this may seriously undermine the legal certainty provided by the decision, which would in turn dissuade companies from using this mechanism.

---

[23] J Temple Lang, 'Commitment Decisions and Settlements with Antitrust Authorities and Private Parties under European Antitrust Law', 32nd Annual International Antitrust Law & Policy Conference Fordham Corporate Law Institute, 22–23 September 2005 (forthcoming), 6, notes that the Commission itself has been rather surprised that there have been so many cases involving commitment decisions.

[24] C Fernandez Vicién, 'Commitment Decisions under Reg 1/2003', Antitrust Reform in Europe: A Year in Practice, 9–11 March 2005, Brussels, International Bar Association (IBA), 4. J Temple Lang, 'Commitment Decisions and Settlements with Antitrust Authorities and Private Parties under European Antitrust Law', 32nd Annual International Antitrust Law & Policy Conference Fordham Corporate Law Institute, 22–23 September 2005 (forthcoming), 8, gives an ample overview on the reasons why companies may be interested in obtaining commitment decisions.

2. Type of commitments

The Commission has a wide discretion in relation to the acceptance of **13.09**
commitments.[25] Commitments can be behavioural or structural;[26] as opposed
to merger control proceedings, they might be primarily behavioural given that
they aim to terminate infringements.[27] To date, a number of (envisaged or
adopted) commitment decisions have been published (*Bundesliga, Repsol, Coca-
Cola,* and *De Beers-Alrosa, BUMA and SABAM – Santiago Agreement, Austrian
Airlines/SAS*). Of these, it can be concluded that, in general, the Commission
will look favourably on those commitments that aim to ensure that there is
no foreclosure of the market: (i) by ending or limiting exclusivity agreements;
(ii) by offering the product in question to the greatest number of possible
purchasers (*Bundesliga* and *De Beers-Alrosa*); (iii) by opening as far as possible
distribution networks so that suppliers can have access to these and thus distribute their products (*Repsol*); (iv) by ending practices such as tying or discounts
for bulk purchase that oblige clients to buy only that company's products
(*Coca-Cola*); (v) by offering contracts through transparent procedures
(*Bundesliga*); and (vi) where they enable competition on affected air routes by
surrendering take-off and landing slots (*Austrian Airlines/SAS*).

3. Procedural aspects

Time when commitments may be offered

Article 9 clearly states that undertakings will be able to offer commitments once **13.10**
the Commission has carried out its 'preliminary assessment', so that the undertaking is able to offer commitments in order to meet the Commission's concerns. It is clear therefore that a commitment decision can only be adopted after
the Commission has begun proceedings. The difficulty resides in establishing at
which stage of the procedure the preliminary assessment can be considered to

---

[25] The Commission has described commitment decisions as '[. . .] a formal settlement solicited
by a company under investigation and agreed by the Commission where its enforcement priorities
justify this choice. [. . .]'. Commission Memo/04/217 of 17 September 2004 'Commitment
decisions (Art 9 of Council Reg 1/2003 providing for a modernised framework for antitrust
scrutiny of company behaviour').

[26] Commission Memo/04/217 of 17 September 2004 'Commitment decisions (Art 9 of
Council Reg 1/2003 providing for a modernised framework for antitrust scrutiny of company
behaviour'). J Temple Lang, 'Commitment Decisions and Settlements with Antitrust Authorities
and Private Parties under European Antitrust Law', 32nd Annual International Antitrust Law &
Policy Conference Fordham Corporate Law Institute, 22–23 September 2005 (forthcoming),
18–19.

[27] M Busse and A Leopold, 'Entscheidungen über Verpflichtungszusagen nach Art 9 VO (EG)
Nr. 1/2003' [2004] Wirtschaft und Wettbewerb (WuW) 146–55 (148). Note that pursuant to
Recital 12 of Reg 1/2003 structural remedies should only be imposed either where there is no
equally effective behavioural remedy or where any equally effective behavioural remedy would be
more burdensome for the undertaking concerned than the structural changes.

be satisfied. It has been said that the need of a preliminary assessment means in practice that the Commission must have sent a statement of objections, since there is no other formal kind of preliminary assessment in Commission procedures under Regulation 1/2003.[28] Although it is true that during Article 9's short life so far a statement of objections has been issued in a couple of cases (*Premier League, Santiago Agreement*) before the undertakings had offered commitments, in most cases a simple letter sent by the Commission explaining its concerns has been considered sufficient to provide a preliminary assessment of the Commission's concerns following which the undertakings concerned have offered commitments (*German Bundesliga*).[29] This interpretation is supported by the reading of Article 2(1) of Regulation 773/2004,[30] which distinguishes between the statement of objections and the preliminary assessment of Article 9(1) as being two different procedural stages. This solution appears more appropriate since preparing a statement of objections entails a great deal of work by the Commission and, depending on the specific cases, it may not be necessary for undertakings to be aware of the Commission's concerns.[31]

Duration of commitments

13.11 Under Article 9 of Regulation 1/2003, commitment decisions may be either for a fixed period, or indefinite. Fixed period decisions will be more appropriate for cases where the Commission expects the factual situation to change, and such change will either make the commitments unnecessary, or mean that they must be updated. From this it can be deduced that decisions for a fixed period of time will be more common when the undertakings making the commitments in question are operating in markets undergoing rapid change.[32] In the decisions

---

[28] J Temple Lang, 'Commitments under Reg 1/2003: Legal Aspects of a New Kind of Competition Decision' [2003] ECLR 347–56 (347).

[29] M Sousa Ferro, 'Committing to Commitment-Unanswered Questions on Article 9 Decisions' [2005] ECLR 451–59 (458); J Temple Lang, 'Commitment Decisions and Settlements with Antitrust Authorities and Private Parties under European Antitrust Law', 32nd Annual International Antitrust Law & Policy Conference Fordham Corporate Law Institute, 22–23 September 2005 (forthcoming), 12. See 'Scope of the Commission's assessment' para 13.08 above.

[30] Art 2(1) of Reg 773/2004 states that '[. . .] Commission may decide to initiate proceedings with a view to adopting a decision pursuant to Chapter III of Reg (EC) No 1/2003 at any point in time, but no later than the date on which it issues a preliminary assessment as referred to in Art 9(1) of that Reg or a statement of objections or the date on which a notice pursuant to Art 27(4) of that Reg is published, whichever is the earlier [. . .]'.

[31] However, this may have repercussions for third parties: it is certainly easier for a third party interested in pursuing a private claim to obtain a copy of the statement of objections. Art 6 of Reg 773/2004 provides that complainants are to be provided with a copy of the non-confidential statement of objections whereas there is no such provision regarding the preliminary assessment. See S Eibl, 'Commitment Decisions: An Australian Perspective' [2005] ECLR 328–37 (331).

[32] This will be particularly important in high technology and starting industries. J Temple Lang, 'Commitments under Reg 1/2003: Legal aspects of a new Kind of Competition Decision' [2003] ECLR 347–56 (354).

taken to date, commitments have been imposed for a period of four and of five and a half years.[33] In addition, the time-limit for commitment decisions was supported in the proposed Regulation, since it makes it possible to re-examine the agreement or practice in question and, where appropriate, the effectiveness of such commitments.[34] Support has also been expressed for time limits, indicating that an initial period of five years may be appropriate.[35] Everything therefore suggests that commitment decisions will be for a specific period of time.

Publicity and content of the decision

One of the points which the Commission has placed most emphasis on has been the importance of publicizing both the proposed commitments and the final decision.[36] Article 27(4)[37] of Regulation 1/2003 obliges the Commission to publish a brief summary of the case and the essential content of the commitments or the line of action proposed, giving interested third parties one month within which to submit their observations.[38] Further, under Article 30 of Regulation 1/2003 the final decision in which commitments are accepted must

13.12

---

[33] In *Bundesliga* the commitments were made binding taking effect on 9 January 2005 until June 2009. See Commission Press Release IP/05/62 of 19 January 2005 'Competition: German Football League commitments to liberalise joint selling of Bundesliga media rights made legally binding by Commission decision'. See also summary of the commitment decision in [2005] OJ L134/46. In *Coca-Cola*, the commitment will be binding until December 2010. Commission press release IP/05/775 of 22 June 2005 'Competition: Commission makes commitments from Coca-Cola legally binding, increasing consumer choice', see also summary of the commitment decision in [2005] OJ L253/21.

[34] Proposal for a Council Regulation implementing Arts 81 and 82 of the Treaty, COM (2000) 582 final—CNS 2000/0243, Explanatory Memorandum, Art 9.

[35] White Paper on Reform of Regulation 17, Summary of Observations, COMP DG Document, 29 February 2000, para 4.5, also available at DG COMP's website.

[36] Commission Memo/04/217 of 17 September 2004 'Commitment decisions (Art 9 of Council Reg 1/2003 providing for a modernised framework for antitrust scrutiny of company behaviour)'.

[37] The Commission needs to allow interested companies to comment on the terms of commitments offered by the undertakings. Article 27(4) of Reg 1/2003 reads as follows: 'where the Commission intends to adopt a commitment decision, it shall publish a concise summary of the facts of the case and the main content of the commitments and any interested third parties may submit their observations within a time limit which is fixed by the Commission in its publication and which may not be less than one month [. . .]'. As indicated, as regards Art 9 (commitments) Art 27(4) of Reg 1/2003 limits the participation of third parties to submit observations. Art 27(1)–(3) which contains a more detailed description of defence rights does not seem to apply to decisions under Art 9. J Schwarze and A Weitbrecht, *Grundzüge des europäischen Kartellverfahrensrechts* (2004) § 6 paras 102–105 take the view that competitors should also enjoy the same defence rights as third parties in other proceedings before the Commission given that decisions under Art 9 of Reg 1/2003 (similar to declarations under Art 10) could also affect their legal position.

[38] Commission Memo/04/217 of 17 September 2004. 'New cartel procedure under Art 9 of Regulation 1/2003' noting that in particular 'associations, media firms and consumer organizations' are therefore free to notify the Commission of their observations on the proposed commitments.

be published by the Commission. In both cases the publication must take into account the legitimate business interests of companies and avoid revealing their commercial secrets. Failure to publicize will be a ground for annulment via the procedure contained in Article 230 EC. In order for publicity to be correct, the commitment decision must state the material facts of the case and the prima facie evidence of the suspected infringement, and incorporate the accepted commitments.[39]

Reopening proceedings. Financial penalties

13.13 Article 9(2) of Regulation 1/2003 sets out the three situations where the Commission may, either following a request or of its own initiative, reopen proceedings. Article 9(2)(a) provides that, where the facts with respect to an essential element of the decision have materially changed, the Commission can decide to reopen proceedings. This means that the Commission must give sufficient detail in the commitment decision of the most relevant facts, so that it can evaluate whether at any given moment such facts have changed. In turn, a change in circumstances may also lead the Commission to reassess whether the commitments are still necessary. The company concerned will have the right to ask the Commission to lift a commitment that is no longer appropriate.[40] As well as the above, Article 9(2)(b) and (c) refers to two other situations in which the Commission has the right to reopen proceedings. This would occur where the undertakings concerned do not comply with their commitments or if the decision was based on 'incomplete, incorrect or misleading information provided by the parties'.[41] In such cases, the undertakings that are in breach of their obligations or that have omitted information or furnished incorrect information may be fined.[42]

13.14 Indeed, Article 23(2)(c) of Regulation 1/2003 enables the Commission to impose on undertakings fines where they fail to comply with a commitment made binding by a decision pursuant to Article 9. In this case, the Commisison may impose a fine of up to 10 per cent of the undertaking's total turnover in the preceding business year.[43] However, it is not clear which specific criteria the Commission will apply when it imposes fines for non-compliance with

---

[39] Proposal for a Council Regulation implementing Arts 81 and 82 of the Treaty, COM (2000) 582 final—CNS 2000/0243 Explanatory Memorandum Art 8.

[40] Commission Memo/04/217 of 17 September 2004 'Commitment decisions (Art 9 of Council Reg 1/2003 providing for a modernised framework for antitrust scrutiny of company behaviour)'.

[41] Art 92(b) and (c) of Reg 1/2003.   [42] Art 24 1(c) of Reg 1/2003.

[43] Note that in its press release in *Coca-Cola* (IP/05/775 of 22 June 2005 'Competition: Commission makes commitments from Coca-Cola legally binding, increasing consumer choice'), the Commission emphasized that it would have the power to impose a a fine amounting to 10 per cent of Coca-Cola's total worldwide turnover if Coca-Cola breaks its commitments.

commitments decisions. The Commission 'Guidelines on the method of setting fines'[44] do not seem to provide any clear guidance on this point. Previously, the Commission could take account of circumstances that fall now into the scope of Article 23(2)(c) as an aggravating factor when it sanctioned the infringement of Article 81 or 82 EC.[45]

The imposition of fines for breach of a commitment decision represents how- **13.15** ever a new category for which it seems this case law will only give limited guidance. While the Commission has reserved the right to impose the same type of fines of up to 10 per cent of the company's total turnover to two different types of infringement, on the one hand the infringement of Article 9 of Regulation 1/2003, and on the other hand the substantial infringement of Article 81 and/or Article 82 EC, the issue arises whether the Commission would have the right to impose in both cases the maximum amount of up to 10 per cent of the company's total turnover as the wording of Article 23(2) of Regulation 1/2003 may suggest. This discussion is closely related to the principle of proportionality and leads to the twofold question, under which circumstances the Commission is entitled to impose a fine for a breach of a commitment decision and if so what amount will be appropriate and proportionate. Where the Commission has evidence of a negligent or intentional non-compliance with a commitment decision, the Commission may impose a fine to sanction the 'bad faith' conduct of the company, independently of whether this infringement involved a breach of Article 81 or 82 EC.[46]

Yet, the fact that the Commisison does not need to show that there has been an **13.16** infringement of Articles 81 and 82 EC where it fines a company for non-compliance with Article 9 may lead to the assumption that in these cases the Commission will not exhaust the maximum limit of 10 per cent of the company's turnover which could be as high as the fine which the Commission

---

[44] [1998] OJ C9/3. Note that the same questions arise in respect to the breach of interim decisions under Art 8 of Reg 1/2003. As regards the application of Art 23(2)(b), see ch 14 'Special Procedures' para 14.15.

[45] See the example given by CS Kerse and N Khan, *EC Antitrust Procedure* (5th edn, 2005) para 65: *Napier Brown* [1988] OJ L284/41 where British sugar promised to introduce a compliance programme which the Commission considered as a mitigating factor. Later, the Commission treated as an aggravating factor the fact that the infringement had occurred despite British Sugar's commitment ([1999] OJ L76/1 para 208: '[. . .] British Sugar acted in a manner contrary to the clear wording contained in its compliance programme, which it announced to the Commission in October 1986 and introduced in December 1986 [. . .].').

[46] As indicated, it is already sufficient that the Commission has identified concerns during a preliminary assessment. M Busse and A Leopold, 'Entscheidungen über Verpflichtungszusagen nach Art 9 VO (EG) Nr. 1/2003' [2005] Wirtschaft und Wettbewerb (WuW) 146–55 (152); A Klees, *Europäisches Kartellverfahrensrecht* (2005) § 10 para 44 proposes that minor forms of non-compliance, to be judged by their gravity and duration, may not be sanctioned if this appears disproportionate.

would impose to sanction an actual infringement which has been proven. There may be different ways to circumscribe the power of the Commission to impose a double fine in these circumstances. There is the suggestion—although the wording of Article 23(2) provides otherwise—to put *a priori* a limit of 1 per cent of the company's turnover when the Commision sanctions the non-compliance with a commitment decision. This is the maximum amount under Article 23(1) of Regulation 1/2003 with which to sanction procedural infringements and may thus also be used as guidance where an infringement of Articles 81 and 82 EC has not been proven. Where the Commission wishes to impose a higher fine, it should prove the infringement of Articles 81 and 82 EC.[47]

13.17 Generally, the Commission is also required to act in a proportionate manner when it imposes a fine for non-compliance with commitment decisions.[48] This is of particular relevance where for example the Commission has imposed a fine for the breach of a commitment decision and subsequently, seeks to sanction the substantive infringement of Articles 81 and/or 82 EC where it has reopened the proceedings. Although the Commission may *a priori* impose in an extreme case twice the amount of 10 per cent of the company's turnover, the general principle of proportionality would require the Commission to take the prior fine under Article 23(2)(c) into account when setting the amount of the fine in relation to the substantive infringement. Ultimately, it is reasonable to assume that the amount of the double fine should not exceed 10 per cent of the turnover.[49]

13.18 Where the Commission reopens the proceedings, it appears that there are two types of decisions being involved: (i) the decision to reopen the proceedings as such; and (ii) where relevant, the decision on the infringement or the lifting of the commitments. Given that only those measures which definitively determine the position of the Commission or any other institution upon the conclusion of that procedure which may be open to challenge and not intermediate measures

---

[47] A Klees, *Europäisches Kartellverfahrensrecht* (2005) § 10 para 43 who also indicates that a fine of up to 10 per cent of the company's turnover applies typically to hardcore cartels for which commitment decisions do not provide an appropriate remedy (see Recital 13 of Regulation 1/2003).

[48] The Commission has proved to conduct a careful assessment when it has sanctioned infringement of procedural rules. The amounts imposed varied before Reg 1/2003 were relatively minor and varied between 100 euros and 5,000 euros. e.g. *Anheuser-Busch Incorporated—Scottish & Newcastle* [2000] OJ L49/37 paras 75–83. See ch 9 'Penalties and Confidentiality'.

[49] See also A Klees, *Europäisches Kartellverfahrensrecht* (2005) § 10 para 46 who suggests that where the Commission reopens the proceedings, it should refrain from imposing a fine under Art 23(2)(c) of Reg 1/2003 and should consider the breach of the commitment decision when setting the fine in relation to the substantive infringement.

whose purpose is to prepare for the final decision,[50] only the second decision would be subject to judicial review. This decision constitutes a measure the legal effects of which are binding on, and capable of affecting the interests of, the undertaking in question by bringing about a distinct change in its legal position.

Review of commitment decisions

Regulation 1/2003 does not provide any specific mechanism for the review of **13.19** commitment decisions. Nevertheless, as with any other decision, nothing prevents a commitment decision from being challenged under Article 230 EC by any company to which it is of direct and individual concern.[51] However, given the nature of these decisions, where the Commission has a great degree of discretion, it might be difficult to appeal successfully. There is more chance of an appeal being successful if it is based on formal grounds, for example, if the Commission has not given the parties concerned the opportunity of making submissions on the proposed commitments, or if it has not made available their content.[52] It also remains to be seen whether an undertaking that had a proposed commitment rejected will be able to use this fact as the basis of an appeal against any final infringement decision. The company on which the commitment has been made binding may challenge a Commission refusal to lift a commitment that the company considers no longer appropriate.

Other safeguards

Regulation 1/2003 does not place any limit on the powers that the Commission **13.20** has to negotiate commitments. The limit should be based on the Commission's powers under Article 81 EC, the need of a connection with the subject matter of

---

[50] Case 60/81 *IBM v EC Commission* [1981] ECR 2639 para 9; Joined Cases C-68/94 and C-30/95 *France and others v EC Commission* [1998] ECR I-1375 para 62; Case T-241/97 *Storck Amsterdam BV v EC Commission* [2000] ECR II-309 para 49. J Temple Lang, 'Commitment Decisions and Settlements with Antitrust Authorities and Private Parties under European Antitrust Law', 32nd Annual International Antitrust Law & Policy Conference Fordham Corporate Law Institute, 22–23 September 2005 (forthcoming), 29 noting that the terms of a commitment can be altered only through a second formal commitment decision.

[51] This could also include third parties that may assert that the commitment decisions are not apt to eliminate the risk of an infringement of Art 81 or 82 EC.

[52] M Busse and A Leopold, 'Entscheidungen über Verpflichtungszusagen nach Art 9 VO (EG) Nr. 1/2003' [2005] Wirtschaft und Wettbewerb 146–55 (153) pointing out that an addressee is unlikely to prevail with the assertion that the Commission forced it to accept the undertakings, given that Art 9 is based on the premise that the undertaking *offers* the commitments. J Temple Lang, 'Commitment Decisions and Settlements with Antitrust Authorities and Private Parties under European Antitrust Law', 32nd Annual International Antitrust Law & Policy Conference Fordham Corporate Law Institute, 22–23 September 2005 (forthcoming), 28 notes that a company may challenge the way in which the decision is drafted as this could give rise to private claims for infringements, however also takes the view that companies cannot challenge incidental findings where they cannot or do not do challenge the operative part.

the case and the fundamental prohibition on abuse of authority.[53] Nevertheless, concern has been expressed about the possibility of the Commission abusing its position, as it might be tempted to encourage undertakings to offer commitments which produce results that it would find hard to impose through the usual enforcement procedure, and which might not be judicially tested. It is interesting to note that in the US proceedings in which consent decrees are adopted are regulated in greater detail. Compared to commitment decisions, consent decrees are a mechanism in which the competition authority enjoys considerable discretion.[54]

Effects of commitment decisions

13.21   From the scope of commitment decisions it is clear that the effects of such decisions will differ, according to whether they are effective with respect to: (i) undertakings; (ii) the Commission; (iii) national courts; or (iv) NCAs.

13.22   **With respect to undertakings**   Article 9 and Recital 13 of Regulation 1/2003 provide that through the adoption of a commitment decision, the Commission converts such commitments into obligations for undertakings. Consequently, the company to whom the decision is addressed must respect the conditions of the settlement,[55] and if it fails to do so, the Commission will be able to impose fines and periodic penalty payments.[56] The fine could amount up to 10 per cent of the turnover and it could also consist of a periodic penalty payment, to force the company to fulfil the commitments.[57] Non-compliance with the commitments is as such sufficient to justify the fine whereas the presence of negligence or intent on the part of the undertaking will probably be relevant when setting the amount of the fine.[58] The possibility of large fines may give undertakings even more reason to consider the implications of the commitments. Moreover,

---

[53] White Paper on Reform of Reg 17, Summary of Observations COMP DG Document, 29 February 2000, para 4.5, also available at COMP DG website, para 4.5. J Temple Lang, 'Commitment Decisions and Settlements with Antitrust Authorities and Private Parties under European Antitrust Law', 32nd Annual International Antitrust Law & Policy Conference Fordham Corporate Law Institute, 22–23 September 2005 (forthcoming), 15 lamenting the absence of effective internal safeguards within the Commission.

[54] M Furse, 'The Decision to Commit: Some pointers from the US' [2004] ECLR 5–10 (10); in regard to Australia, see S Eibl, 'Commitment Decisions: An Australian Perspective' [2005] ECLR 328–37 (332–37).

[55] Commission Memo/04/217 'Commitment decisions (Art 9 of Council Reg 1/2003 providing for a modernised framework for antitrust scrutiny of company behaviour)' (n 20 above) as regards the scope of the effects of a commitment decision.

[56] Arts 23(2)(c) and 24(1)(c) of Reg 1/2003. In this case, the Commission can take two decisions imposing a fine amounting of up to 10 per cent of the company's turnover, one for failure to respect the conditions of the settlement and the other for the infringement of Art 81 or 82 EC.

[57] See above 'Reopening of the Proceedings. Financial Penalties' para 13.13.

[58] M Busse and A Leopold, 'Entscheidungen über Verpflichtungszusagen nach Art 9 VO (EG) Nr. 1/2003' [2004] Wirtschaft und Wettbewerb 146–55 (152).

national courts must enforce the commitments by any means provided for by national law, including the adoption of interim measures. That means that if a commitment is not carried out in full, the Commission, an NCA, or a national court may take steps to enforce the commitment without having to prove that the conduct was unlawful, or to prove anything except that the undertaking had behaved in a way contrary to the commitment.[59] The case law, although limited, affirms the binding nature of the commitments once their viability is confirmed and the Commission has adopted them.[60] Under Regulation 17, the Commission gave undertakings the possibility of terminating a commitment if there are '[. . .] relevant, material or objective circumstances that justify such a termination [. . .]'.[61] There is no reason why this practice might not be maintained under Regulation 1/2003 as long as the possibility of termination is expressly provided for in the commitment decision.[62]

With respect to the Commission   The Commission decision must state that   **13.23**
there are no grounds for the Commission intervening and that the Commission will not impose a fine as regards the conduct in question. Thus, vis-à-vis the Commission, commitment decisions will be binding, which provides legal certainty for undertakings, that the Commission will not review the case and impose any fine.[63] This is, of course, without prejudice to the Commission's right to reopen proceedings in any of the situations covered by Article 9(2) of Regulation 1/2003.

With respect to national courts (third parties' rights)   Recital 13 states that   **13.24**
the commitment decisions are without prejudice to the powers of competition authorities and the courts of the Member States to make such a finding of infringement of Articles 81 or 82 EC and decide upon the case. It is clear from

---

[59] J Temple Lang, 'Commitments under Reg 1/2003: Legal aspects of a new Kind of Competition Decision' [2003] ECLR 347–56 (349).

[60] e.g. see Commission press release IP/04/1247 of 19 October 2004 in *Coca-Cola* 'Commission close to settle antitrust probe into Coca-Cola practices in Europe', Commission press release IP/04/1513 of 20 December 2004 in *De Beers-Alrosa* of 20 December 2004 'Alrosa and De Beers offer diamond trade commitments'. See for a detailed analysis on the binding nature of commitment decisions J Davies and M Das, 'Private Enforcement of commitment decisions: a steep climb not a gently stroll' 32nd Annual International Antitrust Law & Policy Conference Fordham Corporate Law Institute (forthcoming).

[61] See, e.g. *La Poste/Swift GUF* [1997] OJ L335/3 para 3(3).

[62] M Busse and A Leopold, 'Entscheidungen über Verpflichtungszusagen nach Art 9 VO (EG) Nr. 1/2003' [2004] Wirtschaft und Wettbewerb (WuW) 146–55 (153).

[63] J Temple Lang, 'Commitment Decisions and Settlements with Antitrust Authorities and Private Parties under European Antitrust Law', 32nd Annual International Antitrust Law & Policy Conference Fordham Corporate Law Institute, 30 notes that this conclusion is reinforced by the EU principle of legitimate expectations which entitles a company to rely on a precise and specific assurance given in the individual case. See in this connection ch 1 'Institutional Framework' para 1.27.

this that both the NCAs and national courts can reassess matters which have already been the subject of a Commission decision and decide whether or not there has been a breach of Articles 81 and 82 EC or whether such a breach still exists. The possibility of national courts judging a case that has already been decided by the Commission is logical, since the former have the task of defending a different legal interest from that which is protected by the Commission; the Commission is entrusted with defending the public interest, whereas the national courts protect private interests; in other words, they will hear cases concerning the possible harm caused to third parties and, where appropriate, will award damages. Since the national courts are the only ones which can award damages for breach of Articles 81 and 82 EC,[64] it is essential that their powers in this regard are not limited. Further, it should not be forgotten that commitment decisions do not resolve any substantive issues and, in principle, do not decide whether or not there is a breach of Articles 81 and/or 82. This has three consequences. The first is that commitment decisions cannot protect undertakings which were parties to agreements or carried out practices capable of being contrary to Article 81 and/or Article 82 from private third party actions. The second is that a customer or a competitor possibly seeking private enforcement in national courts still needs to prove the illegality of the former behaviour to obtain compensation for damages.[65] Finally, it is questionable whether an Article 9 decision is on its own actionable by third parties claiming such compensation.[66] In any event, national courts can request copies of information in the Commission's possession.

13.25 **With respect to NCAs** The possibility of NCAs adopting a decision on the

---

[64] Art 6 of Reg 1/2003.

[65] Commission Memo/04/217 of 17 September 2004 'Commitment decisions (Art 9 of Council Reg 1/2003 providing for a modernised framework for antitrust scrutiny of company behaviour)'. Therefore, in order to seek private enforcement a commitment decision is substantially less valuable for the claimant than a Commission decision finding that an infringement has been committed, which leaves a claimant only with the task of proving causation and quantum of damage. J Temple Lang 'Commitments under Reg 1/2003: Legal Aspects of a new Kind of Competition Decision' [2003] ECLR 347–56 (350). See also J Davies and M Das, 'Private Enforcement of commitment decisions: a steep climb not a gently stroll' 32nd Annual International Antitrust Law & Policy Conference Fordham Corporate Law Institute (forthcoming) note that a national court will need to determine on each occasion whether the particular claimant seeking enforcement benefits from any rights under the commitments in question.

[66] Art 15(1) of Reg 1/2003. Note that while it is clear that the Commission's decisions are binding on their addressees (Art 249 EC), it may be more difficult to ascertain to what extent third parties can rely on the binding effect of a commitment decision under Community law. F Montag and S Cameron, 'Effective Enforcement: The Practitioner's View of Recent Experiences under Regulation 1/2003', Antitrust Reform in Europe: A Year in Practice, 9–11 March 2005, Brussels, International Bar Association (IBA), 12–13; 'Q&A on modernization with Kris Dekeyser' Global Competition Review, Vol 8, Issue 3 April 2005, 11–16 (12) noting that if a complainant can prove that the company has not respected the commitments, national courts must enforce them by the means provided by national law.

basis of the same facts as the Commission is the aspect that has encountered most opposition. The conclusions that can be reached from a reading of Recitals 13 and 22 are as clear as they are surprising. NCAs may decide whether or not there has been a breach of Articles 81 and 82 EC or whether this still exists, and therefore impose a fine. In addition, it is specifically stated that the decisions of the Commission where commitments are imposed do not affect the powers of the courts and competition authorities of the Member States to apply Articles 81 and 82 EC.[67] Although the principles stated above are unambiguous, the decision-making practice is at a very early stage, and these rules—which to some extent clash with the general principles laid down in Regulation 1/2003—have proved very controversial. This has led to various theories concerning the scope and legal effect of commitment decisions vis-à-vis NCAs. It has been suggested that the Commission, through a commitment decision, decides that the Community interest—within the meaning laid down in *Automec II*[68]—makes it advisable to end the proceedings and, therefore, will not carry out any assessment as to whether or not there has been an infringement. This approach would fit in perfectly with the provisions that regulate commitment decisions, which limit their scope to 'finding' that there are no longer grounds for action by the Commission.[69] It has also been argued that an Article 9 decision reflects the implicit finding that the Commission has assessed the factual situation and has concluded that the agreement or practice as modified by the commitments is in line with EC competition law.[70] This theory, which would restrict NCAs' freedom to take a decision about a given matter, gains credence taking into account the following:

(i)   the task of both the Commission and NCAs is to protect the public interest;
(ii) certain provisions of Regulation 1/2003; and
(iii) the Commission's declarations concerning Article 9.

As noted, both the NCAs and the Commission must act in the public interest. **13.26** It therefore follows that if, on the basis of the agreed commitments, the Commission has already decided that the public interest is safeguarded, there

---

[67] Recital 22 of Reg 1/2003.

[68] Case T-24/90 *Automec Srl v EC Commission* [1992] ECR II-2223. J Temple Lang 'Commitments under Reg 1/2003: Legal Aspects of a New Kind of Competition Decision' [2003] ECLR 347–56 (348–49).

[69] Recital 13 of Reg 1/2003.

[70] See F Montag and S Cameron, 'Effective Enforcement: The Practioner's View of Recent Experiences under Regulation 1/2003', Antitrust Reform in Europe: A Year in Practice, 9–11 March 2005, Brussels, International Bar Association (IBA), 14 noting that NCAs are unlikely to pursue behaviour which has been subject of a negotiated settlement between a company and the Commission unless there are important national peculiarities which have not been taken into account by the Commission's investigation.

is no reason for the NCA to reach a different decision. The possibility that a Commission decision may be reviewed by a NCA contradicts (i) Article 13(2) of the Regulation 1/2003, as regards the principles that govern the way cases are to be allocated between the Commission and NCAs[71]; (ii) Article 11(6) of Regulation 1/2003;[72] and (iii) Article 16(2), which concerns the uniform application of Community competition law.[73] These three provisions clearly show that if the Commission has reached a decision concerning a case the NCAs must either reject the claim brought against the agreement in question or reach the same decision as the Commission. Under no circumstances can it contradict the Commission's decision.[74] Although it is true that Recital 22 provides a derogation to these principles (especially as regards the rule on conflicting decisions contained in Article 16) for commitment decisions, it will be interesting to see how this plays out in practice. In fact, the first cracks have already appeared following the publication of the Commission's memorandum, in which the Commission made the application by national courts and NCAs of Articles 81 and 82 EC subject to the condition that 'the uniform application (of Articles 81 and 82) throughout the EU is not jeopardised'.[75] This statement, which is not to be found in either Article 9 or Recital 13, introduces the first limitation on the free rein that Recital 22 appears to give NCAs when applying Articles 81 and 82. Further, by imposing this limit the Commission has circumscribed the power of NCAs, and it is possible that it will continue to interpret and arguably, narrow down the extent of this unprecedented freedom, which flies in the face of the general principles governing relations

---

[71] '[. . .] Where a competition authority of a Member State or the Commission has received a complaint against an agreement, decision of association or practice which has already been dealt with by another competition authority, it may reject it [. . .]'.

[72] '[. . .] the initiation by the Commission of proceedings for the adoption of a decision under Chapter III shall relieve the competition authorities of the Member States to apply Arts 81 and 82 of the Treaty [. . .]'.

[73] '[. . .] When competition authorities of the member states rule on agreements, decisions or practices under Art 81 or 82 of the Treaty which are already the subject of Commission decisions, they cannot take decisions which would run counter to the decision adopted by the Commission [. . .]'.

[74] M Sousa Ferro, 'Committing to Commitment—Unanswered Questions on Article 9 Decisions' [2005] ECLR 451–59 (455–56) indicates that Art 10 EC imposes on NCAs a duty to closely cooperate with the Commission in applying Community competition law. This may also give additional support to the view that companies who accept commitments will be protected from further investigation into the same practices; see also J Temple Lang, 'Commitment Decisions and Settlements with Antitrust Authorities and Private Parties under European Antitrust Law', 32nd Annual International Antitrust Law & Policy Conference Fordham Corporate Law Institute, 32–33 who notes that this obligation also extends to national courts, which for example would be prevented from saying that a commitment decision gave rise to a presumption that the conduct in question had been illegal under EU law in the past.

[75] See Commission Memo/04/217 of 17 September 2004 'Commitment decisions (Art 9 of Council Regulation 1/2003 providing for a modernized framework for antitrust scrutiny of company behaviour)'.

between the NCAs and the Commission. Nevertheless, a communication like the Commission Memorandum has limited legal effect, whereas Article 9 and Recitals 13 and 22 clearly provide for the possibility of revision by the NCAs. Thus, the Commission or ultimately the ECJ may clarify this issue, which will largely define the degree of legal certainty that undertakings can obtain from such decisions and the extent to which undertakings will use this mechanism.

III. Conclusion of the procedure without a formal decision

A. Introduction

As regards cases where Commission procedures are brought to an end infor- **13.27** mally, several points must be emphasized. First, that when the Commission decides in the broad sense to terminate a procedure, it may do so without having to adopt a decision in the strict sense, which would require the formal initiation of a procedure. In other words, the Commission may decide to close a procedure without ever having decided to open it. This apparent contradiction stems from the twofold sense of the word 'procedure': a broad sense, which includes all procedural measures taken by the Commission in applying Articles 81 and 82 EC, and a narrow sense, which limits its scope to the steps necessary for the adoption of a formal decision applying those provisions, commencing only after an internal administrative decision to that effect. As stated above, after the investigation—which in general terms may and must be treated as part of the procedure in the broad sense—the procedure in the strict sense is initiated by a formal Commission decision which often coincides with the statement of objections. But that is not always the sequence of events after the investigation. The investigative phase, where in most cases the procedure in the strict sense has not yet been formally opened—although the Commission may already use its investigative powers—is sometimes followed by a phase in which the case is dealt with informally. In these cases the formal initiation of a procedure is likewise unnecessary. Under Regulation 17 informal solutions were the most frequent outcome of Commission procedures. It is expected that the Commission reserves the right to determine which cases should be dealt with by means of a decision, having regard to a number of factors, including the significance of each case for the development of competition policy.

B. Type of Letters Sent by the Commission to Close a File

13.28   The Commission may continue to use letters of this kind to inform undertakings that their cases are to be closed. There are various reasons for closing files, relating mainly to the limited importance of certain cases, usually because of the minimal restrictive effects of the agreements, practices and conduct at issue.[76] In infringement procedures commenced on the Commission's own initiative, the Commission may use letters of this kind to inform the undertakings concerned of its intention to close the file where it is unable to prove the infringement and the undertakings have been the subject of investigative measures such as requests for information and inspections. Finally, these letters may also be used where, with the passage of time, a case has ceased to be of importance or interest. The Commission used letters of this kind to dispose of cases which had been pending a long time and have become devoid of purpose ('the backlog'). Normally, the Commission will inform undertakings that it is in favour of closing the file, and will set a time limit for them to produce further information and submit comments. If the undertakings have not submitted observations by the end of the period allowed, the Commission will close the file. In general, letters giving notice that a file is to be closed should not be regarded as expressing the definitive position adopted by the Commission, producing legal effects as against their addressees, and therefore constituting actionable measures, but rather as provisional, preliminary or preparatory opinions, pending the submission of observations from the addressees. Only if they do not clearly display their preparatory or preliminary nature, in that it is not made clear that the validity of the Commission's conclusions is subject to the observations received from the addressees, should such letters be regarded as actionable measures.[77]

---

[76] The position regarding agreements of minor importance (*de minimis*) should be borne in mind. Commission Notice on Agreements of Minor Importance [2001] OJ C368/13. It was adopted in January 2001 and had four key features. The *de minimis* thresholds (above which the notice does not apply) were raised to 10 per cent market share for agreements between competitors and 15 per cent for agreements between non-competitors, compared with the previous 5 per cent and 10 per cent respectively. The notice introduced a new *de minimis* threshold of 5 per cent for markets where networks of agreements can produce a cumulative anticompetitive effect. The previous notice excluded markets where 'competition is restricted by the cumulative effects of parallel networks of similar agreements established by several manufacturers or dealers.' The current notice contained the same list of hard-core restrictions as in the new vertical and horizontal block exemption regulations. It also stated that agreements between small and medium-sized enterprises are rarely capable of appreciably affecting trade between Member States and, hence, would generally fall outside the scope of Art 81(1). See Margaret Bloom, 'The Great Reformer: Mario Monti's Legacy in Art 81 and Cartel Policy' [2005] Competition Policy International 54–78 (69–70).

[77] See Case C-39/93P *SFEI v EC Commission* [1994] ECR II-2681 paras 30 and 32.

C. Comfort Letters, Pending Notifications, Individual Exemptions, and Negative Clearance Decisions under Regulation 1/2003

One consequence of the modernization process is that the Commission will no **13.29** longer adopt negative clearance or individual exemption decisions, or comfort letters.[78] The question is how this will affect exemption decisions or comfort letters that existed before Regulation 1/2003 came into force on 1 May 2004 or what will happen to agreements and practices notified under Regulation 17, but on which the Commission has not taken a decision before this date. The White Paper proposed that pending notifications filed by companies in an attempt to benefit from Article 81(3) EC should lapse when the new Regulation came into force.[79] Nevertheless, it went on to state that during the period between the publication of the White Paper and the coming into force of the new Regulation, the Commission should continue with its activity of granting exemptions at the same rate and in the same way as it had done until then. It did not mention, however, the question of the validity of negative clearance or exemption decisions, or of comfort letters, after the new Regulation came into force. As regards pending notifications, Regulation 1/2003 reflects the proposal contained in the White Paper: these will lapse when the Regulation comes into force.[80] However, Regulation 1/2003 appears to be more flexible than the draft Regulation[81] as regards the validity of individual exemption decisions, since

---

[78] Under Reg 17, it was possible to notify an agreement to the Commission in order to seek a ruling either that the agreement or practice did not come within the terms of Art 81(1) EC at all (negative clearance) or that the agreement was subject to the prohibition in Art 81(1) EC but that the agreement should be exempted by virtue of Art 81(3) (exemption). In practice, however, very few agreements received a formal decision but were subject to so-called informal arrangements by way of 'comfort letters' issued by the Commission.

[79] White Paper on the Modernisation of the Rules Implementing Arts 85 and 86 of the EC Treaty [1999] OJ C132/1 para 129.

[80] Art 34 of Reg 1/2003.

[81] Art 35(1) of the Draft Regulation implementing Arts 81 and 82 of the Treaty COM (2000) 582 final—CNS 2000/0243, ([2000] OJ L365/284) stated that '[t]he validity of decisions applying Art 81(3) [. . .] adopted by the Commission under those Regulations shall come to an end no later than the date of application of this Regulation'. As a connected issue, it should be noted that the proposed Reg also contained a curious obligation to register with the Commission certain agreements capable of restricting competition, although this was not included in the final version of Reg 1/2003. Recital 10 of the proposed Reg justified this obligation as follows: '[a]s the system of notification will now come to an end, it may be expedient, in order to improve transparency, to require registration of certain types of agreement. The Commission should accordingly be empowered to require registration of certain types of agreement. If any such requirement is introduced, it must not confer any entitlement to a decision on the compatibility with the Treaty of the agreement registered, and must not be prejudicial to effective action against infringements.' Article 4(2) of the draft Reg stated that '[t]he Commission may, by regulation,

these are still valid after the Regulation came into force until their expiry date. For this reason, Article 43 of Regulation 1/2003 also provides that Article 8(3) of Regulation 17, which regulates the circumstances in which the Commission may revoke or amend such decisions, will remain in force. On the other hand, Regulation 1/2003 is silent as regards comfort letters. The Commission tried to clarify the outstanding issues regarding the legal situation of negative clearance or individual exemption decisions, as well as comfort letters existing prior to 1 May 2004, following the coming into force of Regulation 1/2003.[82] Based on the premise that neither exemption decisions nor comfort letters could have any place in the new system, and that there will be neither formal exemption decisions nor new comfort letters, nor will existing ones be prolonged, the current situation of these types of formal and informal arrangements under Regulation 17 can be summarized as follows:

1. Comfort letters

13.30   Comfort letters issued before 1 May 2004 may remain useful for undertakings or associations of undertakings as a starting point for the assessment of their legal situation under Articles 81 and 82 EC, taking account of the extent to which factual or legal circumstances relevant for their case may have evolved in the meantime. National courts, when assessing a case under Articles 81 or 82 EC, could still take a comfort letter into account. This is for the national court in question to decide.[83] Thus comfort letters do not bind legally the competition authorities and courts of Member States but they are an important factual element to be taken into account in the assessment; and it is very unlikely that a fine will be imposed on any undertaking which operates under the umbrella of a valid (i.e. recent) comfort letter.[84] It is possible that, both for the Commission and national competition authorities and courts, they will have a factual weight similar to that of a Commission decision rejecting a complaint, or a letter providing informal guidance. Once again, if there is a significant change in the case law or the factual circumstances (market share, etc) they will cease to be an

---

determine types of agreements, decisions of associations of undertakings and concerted practices caught by Art 81(1) of the Treaty which must be registered by undertakings. In that event, it shall also determine the procedures for such registration and the penalties applicable in the event of failure to comply with the obligation. Registration of an agreement, a decision of an association or a concerted practice shall confer no entitlement on the registering undertakings or associations of undertakings and shall not form an obstacle to the application of this Regulation.'

[82] C Gauer, L Kjolbye, D Dalheimer, E De Smitjer, D Schnichels, and M Laurila, 'Regulation 1/2003 and the Modernisation Package fully applicable since May 2004' Competition Policy Newsletter, Number 2, Summer 2004, 1–6 (5–6).

[83] C Gauer, L Kjolbye, D Dalheimer, E De Smitjer, D Schnichels, and M Laurila, 'Regulation 1/2003 and the Modernisation Package fully applicable since May 2004' Competition Policy Newsletter, Number 2 – Summer 2004, 1–6 (6).

[84] See ch 14 'Special Procedures' paras 14.20 *et seq.*

important factual element. The *de facto* binding effect of a comfort letter will lessen over time. It is submitted that, as with exemption decisions, comfort letters also have some explicit or implicit 'expiry date' or reasonable period of validity depending on the case in question. With the Commission's focus on investigating the most serious restrictions on competition, it is unlikely that it will take action with respect to behaviour covered by a comfort letter which was issued shortly before the entry into force of Regulation 1/2003, although the situation may be different for comfort letters issued many years ago under totally different market conditions. However, any Commission action will be considered in accordance with the general criteria which the Commisison applies to decide whether it will investigate a case or not. NCAs may take a similar approach. Addressees of a comfort letter who feel unsure about their position may request the Commission to give informal guidance regarding the behaviour in question. At least, the Notice on informal guidance does not seem to exclude the possibility that behaviour which has been subject to assessment in a comfort letter could also be covered by an informal guidance letter.[85] The parties may allege that comfort letters do not appear to be the 'publicly available guidance' in whose absence the Commission in fact accedes to the request for guidance.

2. Pending notifications

The transitional provisions in Regulation 1/2003 provide that notifications still pending on 1 May 2004 would lapse as from that date. Regulation 1/2003 also provides that Commission proceedings started under the old regime could continue under Regulation 1/2003. For pending cases based on a notification, this implies that the Commission simply might have closed the file following the lapsing of the notification. It might however also have considered that a case should be further investigated. In that case, it has continued the file as an *ex officio* investigation. The outcome would depend on the circumstances of the individual case, the gravity of any competition problem involved and the Commission's enforcement priorities.[86] Accordingly, pending notifications can

13.31

---

[85] Commission Notice on informal guidance relating to novel questions concerning Art 81 and 82 of the EC Treaty that arise in individual cases (guidance letters) ('Informal Guidance Notice') [2004] OJ C101/6 para 8: '[. . .] the Commission, seized of a request for a guidance letter, will consider whether it is appropriate to process it. Issuing a guidance letter may only be considered if the following cumulative conditions are fulfilled: (a) The substantive assessment of an agreement or practice with regard to Arts 81 and/or 82 of the Treaty, poses a question of application of the law for which there is no clarification in the existing EC legal framework including the case law of the Community Courts, nor publicly available general guidance or precedent in decision-making practice or previous guidance letters [. . .].'

[86] C Gauer, L Kjolbye, D Dalheimer, E De Smitjer, D Schnichels, and M Laurila, 'Regulation 1/2003 and the Modernisation Package fully applicable since May 2004' Competition Policy Newsletter, Number 2, Summer 2004, 1–6 (6).

be used as a basis for a procedure applying Articles 81 and 82 EC, should the Commission consider this to be appropriate. The question arises as to whether the parties to notified agreement or practice could be subject to sanctions. Two contrasting ways of interpreting this situation would appear to be possible:

- A fine cannot be imposed for the following reasons: (i) Article 34 of Regulation 1/2003 does not expressly allow this possibility; (ii) Regulation 17 only permitted immunity from fines to be removed through the procedure contained in Article 15(6); and (iii) principles of legal certainty and legitimate expectations.
- A fine should be imposed because: (i) the notification cannot have the effect of perpetual immunity; and (ii) otherwise, competition law would not be applied in the same way to all undertakings (those that had not notified under Regulation 17 would be discriminated against).

Again, the approach of the Commission may vary on a case-by-case basis, but it seems unlikely that the Commission will go ahead and impose a fine in these cases. Rather, the Commission is expected to try to resolve the matter with the parties either informally or through commitment decisions.[87]

3. Exemption decisions and negative clearance decisions

13.32 Regulation 1/2003 provides that existing exemption decisions will remain in force until their expiry. More specifically, on the basis of Articles 16 and 43 of Regulation 1/2003, it appears that such decisions enjoy immunity from fines and have binding force vis-à-vis the Commission, and the national courts and NCAs until they expire.[88] However, Regulation 1/2003 also maintains the legal mechanism by which the Commission may withdraw an exemption if the facts change fundamentally and the exemption is no longer merited.[89] Once they expire they are no longer legally binding. However, they will be a very important factual element to be taken into account when assessing the compatibility of

---

[87] As indicated, three of the first series of commitments decisions under Art 9 (*German Bundesliga, Repsol CPP SA*, and *Premier League*) came before the Commission as notifications for individual exemption. When Reg 1/2003 came into force, the Commission pursued the cases under the procedure of Art 9 of Reg 1/2003. See also F Montag and S Cameron, 'Effective Enforcement: The Practioner's View of Recent Experiences under Regulation 1/2003', Antitrust Reform in Europe: A Year in Practice, 9–11 March 2005, Brussels, International Bar Association (IBA), 14. See above para 13.09.

[88] As indicated, the draft Regulation proposed that they would cease to be valid on 1 May 2004.

[89] See Art 8(3) of Reg 17 which will remain in force. The Commission may revoke or amend its decision or prohibit specified acts by the parties: (a) where there has been a change in any of the facts which were basic to the making of the decision; (b) where the parties commit a breach of any obligation attached to the decision; (c) where the decision is based on incorrect information or was induced by deceit; (d) where the parties abuse the exemption from the provisions of Art 85(1) of the Treaty granted to them by the decision. See ch 14.

behaviour with Articles 81 and 82 EC; further, it is very unlikely that fines will be imposed or that there will be a declaration of incompatibility with Article 81 EC. It is possible that as a factual element they have greater weight for the Commission, national courts and competition authorities than, for example, a Commission decision rejecting a complaint[90] and a letter providing informal guidance.[91] However, should there be a significant change in the case law or the factual circumstances they might cease to be an important factual element and become irrelevant. The validity of negative clearance decisions will also depend on whether there will be a significant change in the case law or the factual circumstances. Before Regulation 1/2003, the Commission issued decisions declaring that there were no grounds for action to be taken. As with comfort letters, the underlying assessment at the time of the adoption may no longer be correct where there has been a significant change. However, whether the Commission (or the NCAs) will take action will involve taking into account a number of factors, which include, among other things, enforcement actions against hardcore cartels.

---

[90] Notice on the handling of complaints by the Commission under Arts 81 and 82 [2004] OJ C101/5 para 79: 'A decision to reject a complaint does not definitively rule on the question of whether or not there is an infringement of Arts 81 or 82, even where the Commission has assessed the facts on the basis of Arts 81 and 82. The assessments made by the Commission in a decision rejecting a complaint therefore do not prevent a Member State court or competition authority from applying Arts 81 and 82 to agreements and practices brought before it. The assessments made by the Commission in a decision rejecting a complaint constitute facts which Member States' courts or competition authorities may take into account in examining whether the agreements or conduct in question are in conformity with Arts 81 and 82(69).'

[91] Notice on Informal Guidance [2004] OJ C101/78 paras 24–25: 'Where an agreement or practice has formed the factual basis for a guidance letter, the Commission is not precluded from subsequently examining that same agreement or practice in a procedure under Reg 1/2003, in particular following a complaint. In that case, the Commission will take the previous guidance letter into account, subject in particular to changes in the underlying facts, to any new aspects raised by a complaint, to developments in the case law of the European Courts or wider changes of the Commission's policy. Guidance letters are not Commission decisions and do not bind Member States' competition authorities or courts that have the power to apply Arts 81 and 82. However, it is open to Member States' competition authorities and courts to take account of guidance letters issued by the Commission as they see fit in the context of a case.'

14

SPECIAL PROCEDURES

A. Interim Measures[1]

1. Origin and legal basis[2]

Article 8 of Regulation 1/2003 entitles the Commission, 'in cases of urgency **14.01** due to the risk of serious and irreparable damage to competition, [. . .] acting on its own initiative', to take a decision ordering interim measures 'on the basis of a prima facie finding of infringement'. Such decisions are adopted for a specified period of time and may be renewed in so far as it is necessary and appropriate.[3] Former Regulation 17 did not expressly grant the Commission such a power but in *Camera Care v EC Commission*,[4] the ECJ ruled that in certain circumstances the Commission was entitled to adopt interim measures under Article 3 of Regulation 17. That provision—which did not expressly refer to measures of

---

[1] The 'interim measures' referred to here should not be confused with those granted under Art 243 EC. Regarding those, see below ch 15 'Steps following the adoption of a formal decision' paras 15.57 *et seq.*

[2] See e.g. J Schwarze and A Weitbrecht, *Grundzüge des Europäischen Kartellverfahrensrechts* (2004) § 6 para 47; CS Kerse and N Khan, *EC Antitrust Procedure* (5th edn, 2005) para 6–032; A Klees *Europäisches Kartellverfahrensrecht* (2005) § 6 paras 95 and 96.

[3] Art 8(2) of Reg 1/2003.

[4] That case arose when a complainant applied for interim measures, which the Commission refused, on the grounds that Reg 17 did not empower it to adopt them. In that case, as in many others, the Court went much further than the Commission in defining the latter's powers. See Case 792/79 R *Camera Care v EC Commission* [1980] ECR 119 paras 17 and 19: '[. . .] it is essential that it should be exercised in the most efficacious manner best suited to the circumstances of each given situation. To this end the possibility cannot be excluded that the exercise of the right to take decisions conferred upon the Commission should comprise successive stages so that a decision finding that there is an infringement may be preceded by any preliminary measures which may appear necessary at any given moment [. . .] The powers which the Commission holds under Article 3(1) of Regulation No 17 therefore include the power to take interim measures which are indispensable for the effective exercise of its functions and, in particular, for ensuring the effectiveness of any decisions requiring undertakings to bring to an end infringements which it has found to exist [. . .]' Joined Cases 228/82 and 229/82 *Ford v EC Commission* [1984] ECR 1129 paras 18 and 19; Case T-23/90 *Peugeot v EC Commission* [1991] ECR II-653 paras 19–20 and Case T-44/90 *La Cinq v EC Commission* [1992] ECR II-1 paras 27 and 28.

529

that kind, merely mentioning decisions and recommendations—was interpreted by the Court as empowering the Commission to adopt interim measures being considered as indispensable for the effective exercise of its functions.[5] In practice, the Commission has made relatively limited use of this power since *Camera Care*, although it has been extended to cover positive measures rather than just prohibitory orders.[6]

14.02   The main difference between the situation under Regulation 17 and Article 8 of Regulation 1/2003 is that interim measures may be ordered by the Commission 'on its own initiative'. The draft proposal of Regulation1/2003 referred to the conditions under the *Camara Case* line of case law requiring the Commission to show a prima facie case, but the Commission also emphasized that it would act in the public interest and not in the interest of individual operators. While companies could always have recourse to national courts to seek interim relief, it would therefore be appropriate to ensure that the Commission may adopt interim measures only in cases where there is a risk of serious and irreparable harm to *competition*.[7] At that point in time, however, it did not yet contain the

---

[5] e.g. Case T-184/01 *IMS Health v EC Commission* [2001] ECR II-3193 para 49.

[6] One of the most recent examples of a positive measure is *IMS Health* in which the Commission granted interim relief ordering IMS Health to license its '1860 brick structure' for data collection to its then competitors in the market for German regional pharmaceutical sales data services. IMS, in return, was entitled to royalties. This decision was suspended by the President of the CFI and the suspension was later confirmed by the ECJ. The interim measure was subsequently withdrawn by the Commission on the grounds that IMS's competitors no longer needed a licence to compete with IMS. *NDC Health/IMS Health—Interim Measures*, [2002] OJ L59/18; Orders of the President of the CFI in Case T-184/01 *IMS Health v EC Commission* [2001] ECR II-2349 and ECR II-3193; Case C-481/01 P(R) *NDC Health v IMS Health and EC Commission* [2002] ECR 1-3401; earlier examples include *Ford Werke—Interim Measures* [1982] OJ L256/20 annulled by Joined Cases 228/82 and 229/82 *Ford v EC Commission* [1984] ECR 1129; *ECS/AKZO—Interim Measures* [1983] OJ L252/13; *BBI/Boosey and Hawkes— Interim Measures* [1987] OJ L286/36; *Ecosystem/Peugeot—Interim Measures* (Case IV/33.157), not published, Commission Press Release IP/90/233 of 27 March 1990; *Lagnese/Iglo GmbH* (Case IV/ 34.072) not published, Commission Press Release IP/92/1109 of 25 March 1992; *B and I/Sealink* Press Release IP/92/478 of 11 June 1992. The decision, which was unofficially published [1992] 5 CMLR 255, was adopted on the basis of Art 10 of Reg 4056/86, the equivalent for maritime purposes of Art 3 of Reg 17; *Mars* [1993] OJ L183/1 suspended by Joined Cases T-24/92 R and T-28/92 R *Langnese-Iglo and Schöller v EC Commission* [1992] ECR II-1839. On other occasions, the Commission interrupted the procedure before adopting a formal decision, either because the undertakings ceased their activities in breach of the EC Competition rules (e.g. in the *IGR Stereo Television I* case, XI Commission Report on Competition Policy (1981) para 94; and in *Amicon/ Fortia*, ibid, para 112); or because an amicable settlement was reached with the undertakings complained of in the form of commitments given by them (e.g. in the *Hilti* case, XV Report on Competition Policy (1985) para 49; *Napier Brown/British Sugar* XVI Report on Competition Policy (1986) para 74; *Eurofix-Bauco/Hilti* [1988] OJ L65/19; *Napier Brown/British Sugar* [1988] OJ L284/41 and *MTV Europe RMC Records (UK) Ltd* [1995] 1 CMLR 437 para 13. See finally Case T-23/90 *Peugeot v EC Commission* [1991] ECR II-653 and Case T-44/90 *La Cinq v EC Commission* [1992] ECR II-1.

[7] Draft Reg implementing Arts 81 and 82 of the Treaty COM (2000) 582 final—CNS 2000/ 0243 Explanatory Memorandum, Art 8.

qualification that the Commission 'acting on its initiative' may take interim decisions, which encapsulates the intention of the Commission to use the widest margin of discretion when it grants interim measures. Relying on the complementary role of private action in regard to public enforcement, the Commission has been at pains to reiterate in its notices that national courts are better placed to grant interim relief at the request of complainants and that Article 8 of Regulation 1/2003 shall be construed as meaning that interim measures cannot be applied for by complainants under Article 7(2) of Regulation 1/2003.[8] Therefore, the Commission is unlikely to change its practice, and it will reserve the adoption of interim measures to exceptional circumstances where the public interest so requires.[9] While this will shift the focus to national court remedies, the Commission also indicates that in a decentralized enforcement system, not only national courts but also NCAs may order interim measures at the request of complainants to the extent that their national rules give them this possibility.[10]

2. Conditions for the grant of interim measures

Article 8 of Regulation 1/2003 describes the conditions that must be satisfied in order for the Commission to order interim measures: **14.03**

- there is a reasonably strong prima facie case establishing an infringement; and
- there is an urgent need for protective measures because of the likelihood of serious and irreparable harm to competition unless the measures are ordered.[11]

As noted above, under Regulation 17, in the absence of a legal basis for interim measures, such conditions were established and expanded upon by the Community Courts. In *Camera Care*, the ECJ laid down the two conditions which must both be fulfilled for interim measures to be granted, namely the prima facie existence of an infringement of the competition rules and the probability that there will be serious and irreparable damage to individuals or intolerable damage to the public interest, justifying the urgent adoption of measures.[12] **14.04**

---

[8] Notice on Handling of Complaints [2004] OJ C101/65 para 80. See also Commission Notice on the co-operation between the Commission and the courts of the EU Member States in the application of Arts 81 and 82 EC [2004] OJ C101/4 para 14 stating that it is incumbent on the national court whether it was necessary to order interim measures to safeguard the interests of the parties.

[9] J Schwarze and A Weitbrecht, *Grundzüge des Europäischen Kartellverfahrensrechts* (2004) § 6 paras 48–50; see below at paras 14.03 *et seq.*

[10] Notice on Handling of Complaints [2004] OJ C101/65 n 70.

[11] See also T-184/01 *IMS Health Inc v EC Commission* [2001] ECR II-3193 para 52.

[12] See Case T-44/90 *La Cinq v EC Commission* [1992] ECR II-1 para 32.

Until *La Cinq*, the Commission had maintained that urgency constituted a third condition for the grant of interim measures,[13] a view which was corrected by the CFI,[14] which considered it to be an inextricably linked aspect of the second condition, since if a risk of serious and irreparable harm exists urgency is simultaneously established.[15] Since the two conditions for ordering interim measures are cumulative, failure to fulfil either of them will suffice to prevent the Commission from exercising its power to adopt interim measures.[16]

Prima facie case of an infringement

14.05 In *Peugeot* and *La Cinq* the CFI has made it clear that, contrary to the interpretation adopted by the Commission which, in *La Cinq*, had treated that condition as requiring the existence of a 'clear and flagrant' infringement, the case law of the Community Courts itself only required the probability or appearance of a prima facie or *a priori* infringement.[17] The CFI observed that the Commission's interpretation would be tantamount to requiring, for the adoption of interim measures, a degree of certainty as to the existence of an infringement which would be sufficient for the adoption of a final decision in the case as a whole,

---

[13] ibid. Regarding the Commission's traditional approach, see paras 14 and 25. The CFI itself, in its judgment in Case T-23/90 *Peugeot v EC Commission* [1991] ECR II-653, had not clearly rejected the applicants' contention that urgency was a further condition to be fulfilled.

[14] See Case T-44/90 *La Cinq v EC Commission* [1992] ECR II-1 para 29.

[15] Case T-184/01 R *IMS Health Inc v EC Commission* [2001] ECR II-3193 paras 53–54: '[. . .] the condition concerning urgency, which, in the decision at issue in that case, just as in the contested decision, the Commission had regarded as a third condition for ordering interim measures, was, however, in reality but one aspect of the condition concerning the risk of serious and irreparable damage. It follows, since if a risk of serious and irreparable harm exists urgency is inevitably simultaneously established, that the three conditions enumerated by the Commission in the contested decision fall correctly to be characterised as constituting effectively two conditions.' Regarding the calculation of interests, in *Carte Bleu II* the CFI agreed with the Commission that 'where the Community judicature reduces the amount of fine imposed by the Commission by upholding the action in part, the interest charge calculated at the reduced rate borne by the undertaking is reduced in proportion to the amount thus set.' Case C-275/94, *Carte Bleu v EC Commission II* [1996] ECR I-1393 para 81. Carte Bleu had argued that taking into account that the fine had been reduced by the CFI (from 5 million euros to 2 million euros), no interest was due for the period between the decision and the judgment, because the fine set by the CFI was legally different from that which the Commission imposed, a point which the CFI did not accept (see previous note). The Commission had applied the payment made by the undertakings (2 million euros) against interest first and then against principal—a method generally accepted in national legal systems and upheld by the CFI (para 93)—and required further payment of the remainder of the principal as set by the CFI plus interests from the date of the partial payment. See paras 8–13 of the judgment.

[16] Case T-184/01 R *IMS Health Inc v EC Commission* [2001] ECR II-3193 para 55; Case T-44/90 *La Cinq v EC Commission* [1992] ECR II-1 para 30.

[17] In the French text, the CFI uses both expressions in the same way.

and would render interim measures procedures unnecessary and pointless.[18] Thus, ascertaining *a priori* or prima facie an infringement does not involve going so far as to finding a 'clear and flagrant' infringement;[19] the Commission only needs to show the appearance or probability of an infringement, which results in a less detailed analysis both as regards the underlying facts and the legal arguments.[20]

Urgency due to the risk of serious and irreparable harm to competition

Article 8(1) refers to damage to *competition*. It is submitted that this may **14.06** include damage to undertakings or to competition policy or both. Under Regulation 17, the Commission was required to 'take account of all the relevant facts in the case in order to determine whether there was a risk of serious and irreparable damage to the applicant, establishing an urgent need to adopt the measures requested'.[21] Due to the shift to a regime under which complainants no longer seem to be able to apply for interim measures solely on the basis of the damage inflicted on them, the focus will rest on the other limb to show urgency under the previous case law, namely the need to avoid a situation which causes 'intolerable damage to the public interest'.[22] The prevention of a situation in which serious and irreparable damage to a *competitor* arises will only be of relevance under Article 8 of Regulation 1/2003 to the extent that the Commission reasonably believes that this is tantamount to damage of *competition* as a whole.[23] This may indicate that the Commission is expected to adopt interim measures where public interests are at stake which may be the case where there is a threat to the objectives of the Community's competition policy. By contrast with the position regarding damage to individual competitors, the case law of the Community Courts concerning Articles 242 and 243 EC (applications for

---

[18] Case T-44/90 *La Cinq v EC Commission* [1992] ECR II-1 para 61. See also Case T-184/01 *IMS Health Inc v EC Commission* [2001] ECR II-3193 para 106: '[. . .] there is, at the very least, a serious dispute regarding the correctness of the fundamental legal conclusion underpinning the contested decision, i.e. that exceptional circumstances exist in the present case capable of justifying the imposition of a compulsory-licence obligation, the applicant has clearly established a prima facie case justifying the interim relief sought [. . .]'.

[19] Case T-44/90 *La Cinq v EC Commission* [1992] ECR II-1 para 62.

[20] See Case T-44/90 *La Cinq v EC Commission* [1992] ECR II-1 para 41; Case T-23/90 *Peugeot v EC Commission* [1990] ECR II-195 para 61; T-184/01 R *IMS Health Inc v EC Commission* [2001] ECR II-3193 para 67 referring to Case T-23/90 *Peugeot v EC Commission*: 'in proceedings relating to the legality of a Commission decision imposing provisional measures, the requirement of a finding of a prima facie infringement cannot be placed on the same footing as the requirement of certainty that a final decision must satisfy'.

[21] Case T-44/90 *La Cinq v EC Commission* [1992] ECR II-1 para 94.

[22] T-184/01 R *IMS Health Inc v EC Commission* [2001] ECR II-3193 para 53 referring to Case T-44/90 *La Cinq v EC Commission* [1992] ECR II-1 para 28 and Joined Cases 228/82 and 229/82 *Ford v EC Commission* [1984] ECR 1129.

[23] See also A Klees, *Europäisches Kartellverfahrensrecht* (2005) § 6 para 98.

suspension of enforcement and for interim measures) gives little guidance on this notion. The case law relates to cases of applicants seeking interim measures and, therefore, may again be of limited use to identify the situations of serious and irreparable harm to competition. Only the order in *Camera Care* gives certain indications regarding the meaning of 'public interest'.[24] At least in part, but not exclusively, it may involve protection of the interests of the Member States and their citizens, or the objectives of competition policy.[25] However, the Commission's practice does not make clear what 'intolerable' means in this context.[26] It may signal a certain degree of magnitude, seriousness, or severity that justifies the taking of exceptional measures.[27] The seriousness of the damage must be judged according to the circumstances of the case. The elimination from the market of undertakings is likely to be regarded by the Commission as serious damage only where this results in damage to competition.[28] Conversely, the Commission is less likely to intervene where there is an identifiable victim that could seek relief before national courts or NCAs. Where the Commission has a wide discretion to decide whether it will intervene, it may also consider other possibilities of relief, which are available to a competitor. It is also possible that the number of cases before the Commission may even decrease further in the future because the Commission tended to use its powers in the past to issue interim measures in 'local' cases involving a suspected infringement in one Member State.[29] These cases would follow the principles of case allocation amongst the members of the ECN and could thus be handled by NCAs or national courts.[30]

14.07   As regards 'irreparability', the Court regarded as irreparable any damage which cannot be remedied by the decision which the Commission might adopt on conclusion of the administrative procedure.[31] The decision in question had been specifically the main decision dealing with the substance of the case, and not 'any decision'.[32] In its judgment in *La Cinq*, again in the context of an

---

[24] See Case 792/79 R *Camera Care v EC Commission* [1980] ECR 119 paras 14 and 19.

[25] CS Kerse and N Khan, *EC Antitrust Procedure* (5th edn, 2005) para 6–035.

[26] No decision ordering interim measures has so far been adopted purely on the Commission's own initiative.

[27] See CS Kerse and N Khan, *EC Antitrust Procedure* (5th edn, 2005) para 6–035.

[28] That view was taken, e.g. in *BBI/Boosey and Hawkes—Interim Measures* [1987] OJ L286/36 para 22: 'An eventual finding in the main decision that B&H had abused its dominant position under Art [82] would be illusory if meanwhile BBI and the other undertakings had been put out of business [. . .]'. The seasonal nature of ice cream triggered the intervention in *Mars* (XXII Report on Competition Policy (1992) para 195 and [1998] OJ L246/1). CS Kerse and N Khan, *EC Antitrust Procedure* (5th edn, 2005) para 6–036.

[29] *NDC Health/IMS Health—Interim Measures*, [2002] OJ L59/18 (Germany).

[30] CS Kerse and N Khan, *EC Antitrust Procedure* (5th edn, 2005) para 6–038.

[31] Case 792/79 R *Camera Care v EC Commission* [1980] ECR 119 para 19.

[32] Case T-44/90 *La Cinq v Commission* [1992] ECR II-1 para 79.

application for interim measures, the CFI rejected the view that damage must be regarded as irreparable only where those applying for the interim measures are unable to claim damages before a national court on the basis of a possible future infringement decision. The CFI held that the Commission had interpreted the notion of 'irreparable' as meaning that it could not be remedied by any subsequent decision—and not merely the decision which represents the culmination of the administrative process carried out by the Commission—to the detriment of the French television channel, since such an approach would make it impossible to verify whether the damage is irreparable.[33]

According to the CFI, 'the condition concerning urgency, which [. . .] the Commission regarded as a third condition for ordering interim measures, is in reality but one aspect of the condition concerning the risk of serious and irreparable damage'.[34] In *La Cinq*, the Commission had denied that there was any urgency, which it interpreted as an independent condition. However, in *Peugeot*, the Commission itself stated that 'such urgency may derive from a risk likely to cause serious and irreparable damage'.[35] The CFI, going even further, perceived urgency not as a possibility stemming from the risk of serious and irreparable damage but rather as a natural and necessary consequence of that situation.[36] **14.08**

3. Procedure for rejection or adoption

As indicated, the main difference between the former practice under Regulation 17 and Article 8 of Regulation 1/2003 is that the Commission may 'acting on its own initiative' order interim measures. Under the previous regime, the Commission appeared to accept the view that complainants could request the Commission to issue interim measures based on the Commission powers under Article 3 of Regulation 17. The codification of the power to adopt interim measures in Article 8 of Regulation 1/2003 and the accompanying Commission statements on this issue[37] reflect the latter's determination to remove the complainant's right to apply for interim relief, or at least to be the addressee of a challengeable act. Ironically, the express codification of this power has curtailed the rights of third-party complainants. If this holds true, decisions rejecting the adoption of interim measures would fall outside the scope of judicially reviewable acts under Article 232 EC. At present, they may be similar to decisions under former Article 15(6) of Regulation 17 relating to the withdrawal of **14.09**

---

[33] ibid.   [34] See Case T-44/90 *La Cinq v EC Commission* [1992] ECR II-1 para 29.
[35] See Case T-23/96 *Peugeot v EC Commission* [1990] ECR II-195 para 67, in which those statements of the Commission are set out.
[36] Case T-184/01 R *IMS Health Inc v EC Commission* [2001] ECR II-3193 para 54.
[37] ibid.

immunity from fines, where the CFI ruled that third-party complaints had no legitimate interest in having immunity withdrawn.[38] The CFI indicated that a decision withdrawing immunity on the basis of 'expediency' and the 'general interest' does not seek to protect the interests of third-party market participants.[39] While this may contradict somewhat the ruling in *Camera Care*, where the Court considered that the power to adopt interim measures was inherent to the power to adopt decisions against infringements by a public enforcer which is entrusted with the task of receiving complaints by governments and individuals,[40] it is plain that the Council gave the Commission an explicit legal base for adopting interim measures. The power to adopt interim measures will thus no longer emanate from the Commission's powers contained in Article 7 of Regulation 1/2003 (formerly, Article 3 of Regulation 11) but must be judged on the basis of this mandate (Article 8 of Regulation 1/2003). There may be some doubts about whether the shift under Regulation 1/2003 will ultimately survive the test of the Community courts in view of the earlier case law,[41] but it looks as if the adoption of interim measures now constitute the culmination of a special procedure which is distinct from the procedure under Article 7 of Regulation 1/2003, in which third-party complainants retain their full rights.[42]

14.10   Where the Commission proceeds to issue interim measures, it is also required to observe the basic procedural safeguards provided for by Regulation 1/2003, in particular Article 27 thereof (observations from the parties in response to the

---

[38] As regards Art 15(6) of Reg 17, Case T-3/90 *Prodifarma v EC Commission* [1991] ECR II-1 para 43. See also CFI Order in Case T-18/97 *Atlantic Container Line AB and others v EC Commission* [1998] ECR II-589 para 15.

[39] Case T-18/97 *Atlantic Container Line AB and others v EC Commission*, ibid.

[40] Case 792/79 R *Camera Care v EC Commission* [1980] ECR 119 paras 17–19.

[41] CS Kerse and N Khan, *EC Antitrust Procedure* (5th edn, 2005) para 8–032 submit that although Art 8 of Reg 1/2003 seems to preclude the reviewability of refusals by providing that interim measures are taken by the Commission acting on its own initiative, this may not prevent judicial review of inaction on the part of the Commission in the face of request for interim measures from complainants. D Geradin and N Petit, 'Judicial remedies under EC Competition Law: Complex Issues arising from the Modernization Process', 32nd Annual International Antitrust Law & Policy Conference Fordham Corporate Law Institute, 22–23 September 2005 (forthcoming), 12, also take the view that the refusal to give access to interim relief before the Community Courts would raise objections 'within the meaning of Article 230 EC'.

[42] This is the description used for Art 15(6) decisions under Reg 17 in Case T-18/97 *Atlantic Container Line AB and others v EC Commission* [1998] ECR II-589 para 15. Note that from the complainants' perspective, they may try to request the adoption of interim measures, but maybe with no avail. See also A Klees, *Europäisches Kartellverfahrensrecht* (2005) § 6 para 99. Indeed, Form C does not prevent them from formulating such a request and thus complainants can indicate which measures or action they want the Commission to take. See Section III 6 of Form C, Annex to Commission Notice on the handling of complaints [2004] OJ C101/65. For an example of measures applied for, see Case T-44/90 *La Cinq v EC Commission* [1992] ECR II-1 para 13, which gives details of the relief sought in the second application for interim measures made by the private French television channel.

Commission's objections, hearing, and so on).[43] As a first measure, in the pre-liminary investigation stage the Commission may send a letter to the allegedly offending undertakings informing them of the possibility of interim measures being adopted if the conduct regarded as contrary to the competition rules does not cease. The interim measures procedure is commenced at the same time as the substantive or ordinary procedure. The Commission is required to inform the undertakings of its objections against them when it intends to take a deci-sion unfavourable to their interests. The adoption of interim measures under Article 8 of Regulation 1/2003 is no exception and thus, despite the urgency in such cases, undertakings have an opportunity to submit their observations in procedures of this kind as well. The statement of objections indicates the meas-ures which the Commission intends to adopt. Where it considers this necessary, the Commission makes provision for periodic penalty payments in order to enforce compliance with the measures ordered, in case the undertakings do not voluntarily observe the decision prescribing interim measures. Access to the file is granted by including the documents which may be disclosed to the undertakings as an annex to the statement of objections, in electronic format or otherwise. If appropriate, it is accompanied by a copy of the complaint and the request for interim measures, from which business secrets have been duly deleted.

According to Article 17(2) of Regulation 773/2004, the period for responding to the statement of objections is at least four weeks. However, Article 17(2) also provides that the time-limit for proceedings initiated with a view to adopting interim measures pursuant to Article 8 of Regulation 1/2003 may be shortened to one week. The date of the administrative hearing may already be fixed by the Commission in the statement of objections, immediately following the end of the time-limit for submitting observations. As in ordinary procedures, third parties who show a sufficient interest and ask to be heard may take part in the hearing. After the observations phase, the Commission draws up a draft decision and consults the Advisory Committee. Under Regulation 17 the CFI confirmed that since procedures for the adoption of interim measures were procedures under Article 3 of Regulation 17, that step had to be taken before any decision was adopted.[44] Article 14(1) of Regulation 1/2003 provides expressly for the Advisory Committee to be consulted on draft interim decisions. This consultation takes place immediately after the hearing, and the decision on interim measures is then adopted by the full Commission. Article 30 of Regulation 1/2003 does not include decisions on interim measures among

14.11

---

[43] See Case 792/79 R *Camera Care v EC Commission* [1980] ECR 119 para 19 interpreting Reg 17.

[44] See Case T-19/91 *Vichy v EC Commission* [1992] ECR II-415 para 37.

those for which publication is required. Despite this, they have been published in the past and this practice is likely to continue.

4. Content of the decisions

General structure

14.12 Interim measures have to be adopted in such a way that the undertakings affected may challenge them before the CFI.[45] Decisions granting interim measures are decisions within the meaning of Article 249 EC and do not differ as regards their general layout from substantive decisions, although they are usually more concise. Under Article 253, the grounds for such decisions must be stated, failing which they will be void, and under Article 254, they take effect as from notification. By contrast with formal infringement decisions, they are essentially concerned not with the infringement itself, which will be the subject of the substantive decision at a later stage, but with proof of the fulfilment of the two conditions necessary for its adoption.

Nature of interim measures

14.13 The operative part of the decision will contain the specific measures adopted by the Commission. As regards their nature, it can be stated in general that, first, the measures must be limited in time and scope and, secondly, that they must fall within the scope of the subject matter of the main procedure. Concerning the limitations in time, Article 8(2) of Regulation 1/2003 states that 'a decision under paragraph 1 shall apply for a specified period of time and may be renewed in so far as this is necessary and appropriate'. The measures must be temporary or interim and will only be valid until a substantive decision is adopted or they are annulled by the CFI, whichever occurs earlier.[46] The measures must keep within the limits of what is strictly necessary to remedy a particular situation,[47] and may go no further. This means that they will be purely protective. As emphasized, under Regulation 1/2003, they must safeguard competition and not the individual interests, maintaining the position as it was before the commission of the alleged infringement, without prejudicing the merits of the case,

---

[45] See Case 792/79 R *Camera Care v EC Commission* [1980] ECR 119 paras 19–20. CS Kerse and N Khan, *EC Antitrust Procedure* (5th edn, 2005) para 6–032 submit that in light of the earlier case law, according to which the power to adopt interim measures was inherent to the power to adopt decisions against infringements, it might be that the Court will continue to apply *Automec* to enable complainants to challenge failures by the Commission to adopt interim measures under Art 232 EC: Case T-64/80 *Automec v EC Commission* [1990] ECR II-367.

[46] In *Ford*, the Commission adopted the substantive decision (*Ford Werke AG* [1983] OJ L327/31) before the annulment of the interim measures decision.

[47] Regarding the principle of proportionality, see Case T-76/89 *ITP v EC Commission* [1991] ECR II-575 para 80, citing Case 181/84 *The Queen, ex parte E.D. & F. Man (Sugar Ltd v Intervention Board for Agricultural Produce) (IBAP)* [1985] ECR 2889 para 20.

which will be dealt with in the final decision. Finally, from the range of measures available to remedy a given situation, the Commission must choose those which create the least difficulties for the undertakings to which they are to apply. Consequently, interim measures must also be the least burdensome possible.[48]

In *Ford*, the Commission's interim measures were annulled because, since the **14.14** main procedure was concerned with the dealer agreement between Ford and its concessionaires, the measures ordered by the Commission—which related to a refusal to supply that the Commission agreed was not an infringement of Articles 81 and 82—did not fall within the framework of a possible substantive decision.[49] By contrast with the position in *Ford*, in *Peugeot* (which was concerned with a Commission decision on a circular sent by Peugeot to its concessionaires to the effect that they should not supply new vehicles to the company Ecosystem), the CFI held that both the interim measures procedure and the main procedure were concerned with the same issues (namely, the legality of the circular under Article 81(1) EC) and that there was no reason for the decision to be annulled on that ground.[50] In conclusion, the measures laid down by the Commission will not be acceptable where it has gone outside the scope of the main procedure and adopted measures whose subject matter is different.[51]

5. Imposition of financial penalties

The Commission can impose pecuniary penalties in order to compel undertak- **14.15** ings to comply with the measures adopted. Article 23(2)(b) expressly empowers the Commission to impose fines on undertakings where they contravene a decision ordering interim measures under Article 8 of Regulation 1/2003, which are based on a prima facie infringement of Article 81 and/or Article 82 EC. Given that the Commission has reserved the right to impose the same type of fines of up to 10 per cent of the company's total turnover to two different types of infringement, on the one hand the infringement of Article 8, and on the other hand the substantial infringement of Articles 81 and/or Article 82 EC, the issue arises—similar to the discussion relating to the imposition of fines for a breach of a commitment decision under Article 9[52]—whether the Commission

---

[48] Otherwise, they could be annulled, as occurred in *Ford*. Regarding the need for the measures not to cause more harm than they remedy, see Joined Cases 228/82 and 229/82 R *Ford v EC Commission* [1982] ECR 3091 paras 11 and 14. To the same effect, see Case T-23/90 R *Peugeot v EC Commission* [1990] ECR II-195 para 24 and Joined Cases T-24/92 R and T-28/92 R *Langnese-Iglo and Schöller v EC Commission* [1992] ECR II-1839 paras 28–30. In the latter case, the CFI partially annulled the interim measures decision on the ground that, prima facie, the possibility that the applicants' claims were well founded could not be ruled out (para 27).

[49] Joined Cases 228 and 229/82R *Ford v EC Commission* [1982] ECR I-3091, paras 20 and 21.

[50] See Case T-23/90 R *Peugeot v EC Commission* [1990] ECR II-195, para 56.

[51] See Case T-23/90 R *Peugeot v EC Commission* [1990] ECR II-195 para 57.

[52] See ch 13 'Reopening of Proceedings, Financial Penalties' paras 13.13 *et seq.*

would have the right to impose in both cases the maximum amount of up to 10 per cent of the company's total turnover as the joint reading of Article 23(2)(a) and (c) of Regulation 1/2003 may suggest. Similar to the suggestion in the context of fines for infringements of commitment decisions, it is fair to assume that the cumulative imposition of fines under Article 23(2)(a) and (b) should not exceed 10 per cent of the company's turnover. While it is true that each fine aims to sanction a different conduct of the company, the Commission is expected to take into account a fine imposed under Article 23(2)(b) when it will subsequently set the fine for a substantial infringement of Articles 81 and/or 82 EC.[53] The Commission may also impose periodic penalty payments under Article 24(1)(b) of Regulation 1/2003 in order to ensure that undertakings comply with its decision.

B. Withdrawal of the Benefit of a Block Exemption[54]

14.16 The Commission may revoke a block exemption in individual cases, without the need to modify the Regulation under which that exemption was granted. The procedure for this is laid down in Article 29(1) of Regulation 1/2003 which empowers the Commission, acting on its own initiative or on a complaint, to withdraw the benefit of an exemption Regulation when it finds that in any particular case an agreement, decision or concerted practice to which the exemption Regulation applies has certain effects which are incompatible with Article 81(3) EC. Additionally, when such practices to which a Commission block exemption applies have effects which are incompatible with Article 81(3) EC in the territory of a given Member State, or in a part thereof, and which has all the characteristics of a distinct geographic market, the NCA of that Member State may also withdraw the benefit of the Regulation in question in respect of that territory.

14.17 The reason for withdrawing the exemption has thus to do with the effects of the exempt agreements and practices in specific cases. The exemption is granted because the Community institutions consider that in certain circumstances

---

[53] See also A Klees, *Europäisches Kartellverfahrensrecht* (2005) § 10 paras 35–38 who also suggests that independently of the fact that the fines relate to a different conduct—breach of a interim measure on the one hand, and substantial infringement of competition rules on the other hand—the basis for both sanctions continues to be to the same infringement of competition rules, although in the former case it is the repeated infringement despite a interim measure of the Commission aimed at providing a remedy against the suspected breach. Klees believes that the Commission will refrain from imposing a fine under Art 23(2)(b) in the first place when it seeks to impose subsequently a fine for the substantial infringement. When setting the fine, the Commission may then consider the breech of the interim decision an aggravating factor under Guidelines on the method of setting fines ([1998] OJ C9/3).

[54] Guidelines on the application of Art 81(3) of the Treaty [2004] OJ C101/97 para 36.

certain categories (or types) of agreements in general fulfil the conditions for exemption from the effects of the prohibition contained in Article 81(1) EC. However, that view is subject to effective, and not merely presumed, fulfilment of the conditions of Article 81(3) EC. It is for that reason that, without undermining legal certainty, the Commission may revoke the exemption in those cases in which a formally exempt agreement does not in practice meet the exemption criteria.

The procedure may be commenced on the Commission's own initiative or in response to a complaint from natural or legal persons claiming a legitimate interest.[124] In the latter case, since the withdrawal of a block exemption on an individual basis is one of its exclusive prerogatives,[55] the Commission may be obliged to adopt a formal decision withdrawing the exemption or rejecting the complaint.[56] The Commission, when dealing with specific exempt agreements which in practice appear not to satisfy the requirements of Article 81(3) EC, would simply revoke them. As a result of revocation, the generally exempt agreements or conduct are prohibited in that specific case by virtue of Article 81(1) since they no longer enjoy the benefit of Article 81(3) anymore. The Commission is required to withdraw the benefit of the block exemption, and to initiate a procedure of the kind usual in cases of infringement. Thus, Article 14(1) of Regulation 1/2003 provides that the Advisory Committee shall be consulted prior to the taking of any decision under Article 29(1). This provision indicates the applicability of Regulation 773/2004 to the proceedings for the withdrawal of a block exemption which means that the parties have to be heard.[57] In *Langnese-Iglo*, the Commission withdrew a block exemption on an individual basis in respect of certain exclusive dealing agreements covered by Regulation 1984/93, without at the same time granting an individual exemption.[58] The Commission also threatened to withdraw a block exemption enjoyed by the Peugeot vehicle distribution network.[59] **14.18**

Article 29(2) of Regulation 1/2003 gives the NCAs—but not national **14.19**

---

[55] As regards the possibility for Member States of withdrawing the benefit of a block exemption under Art 29(2) of Reg 1/2003, see ch 3 'The Role of NCAs' para 3.03.

[56] See Case T-24/90 *Automec v Commission II* [1992] ECR II-2223 para 75.

[57] It is true that Art 29(1) of Reg 1/2003 does not form part of chapter III of Reg 1/2003 which contains the list of formal decisions which the Commission can adopt respecting a series of procedural requirements. However, Art 11 of Reg 773/2004 also provides that the parties have a right to be heard before the Advisory Committee is consulted. Thus, the general principle of the right to be heard applies also in this context. CS Kerse and N Khan, *EC Antitrust Procedure* (5th edn, 2005) para 6–046. For the hearing, the parties in this type of cases, see below, paras 14.20 *et seq*.

[58] *Langnese-Iglo* [1993] OJ L183/19.

[59] *Ecosystem/Peugeot* [1992] OJ L66/1. The block exemption in that case was the one granted by Commission Reg (EEC) 123/85 on the distribution of motor vehicles [1985] OJ L15/16.

courts—the power to withdraw the benefit of block exemptions for their own territory, provided that this constitutes a distinct relevant geographic market. Before Regulation 1/2003 came into force, NCAs had such a power only in respect of vertical agreements.[60] To ensure consistency in the application of block exemption regulations, which are Community acts, Regulation 1/2003 provides for prior consultation with the Commission in respect of national decisions withdrawing the benefit of a block exemption.[61] The NCA must demonstrate that the agreement infringes Article 81(1) EC and that it does not satisfy the conditions laid down in Article 81(3) EC before it can withdraw the block exemption. In practice, NCAs are expected to use this power only rarely. It is expected that the NCAs will also observe the standard procedural safeguards, i.e. they will give written notice to the parties to that agreement and give them the opportunity to make representations.[62] As regards national courts, they have no power to withdraw the benefit of block exemption regulations. Moreover, when applying block exemption regulations, they may not modify their scope by extending their sphere of application to include agreements not covered by the block exemption regulation in question.[63]

C. Revocation or Amendment of an Individual Exemption Adopted under Regulation 17

14.20   The Commission may also revoke or even amend an individual exemption adopted pursuant to Regulation 17. According to Article 43(1) of Regulation 1/ 2003,' 'Regulation No 17 is repealed with the exception of Article 8(3) which continues to apply to decisions adopted pursuant to Article 81(3) of the Treaty prior to the date of application of this Regulation until the date of expiration of those decisions'. Article 8(3) of Regulation 17 provides that '[t]he Commission may revoke or amend its decision or prohibit specified acts by the parties: (a) where there has been a change in any of the facts which were basic to the making of the decision; (b) where the parties commit a breach of any obligation attached to the decision; (c) where the decision is based on incorrect information or was induced by deceit; [or] (d) where the parties abuse the

---

[60] See Art 1(4) of Council Reg (EC) 1215/1999 ([1999] OJ L48/1) amending Reg 19/65/ EEC on the application of Art 81(3) EC to certain categories of agreements and concerted practices.

[61] Art 11(4) of Reg 1/2003.

[62] See UK Office of Fair Trading, Guidelines 'Vertical Agreements–Understanding Competition Law' (2004) paras 3.31 and 3.32 also stating that the withdrawal of the benefit of the Block Exemption establishes at the same time that the agreement infringes Art 81 but it will only have effect from the date of the withdrawal.

[63] Guidelines on the application of Art 81(3) of the Treaty [2004] OJ C101/97 para 39.

exemption from the provisions of Article [81](1) of the Treaty granted to them by the decision. In cases to which subparagraphs (b), (c) or (d) apply, the decision may be revoked with retroactive effect' Article 29(1) of Regulation 1/2003 which governs the withdrawal of block exemption in individual cases does not apply in this case.

Regulation 17, Article 8(3) has never been used to date, at least not to the **14.21** extent of adopting a formal decision of revocation. Article 8(3) enables the Commission not only to revoke its own decision in its entirety but also, in general, to alter its content and, more specifically, 'prohibit specified acts by the parties', which may in practice mean that new conditions subsequently are imposed. Since in all three cases the decisions are unfavourable to their interests, the undertakings are entitled to make observations and the revocation or amendment must be by formal decision, in accordance with the general rules applicable to Commission infringement procedures.

After modernization, it is unlikely that the Commission might want to modify **14.22** —but not revoke—an existing individual exception in any way. Although Article 8(3) of Regulation 17 provides for such a possibility, it is arguable that once Regulation 1/2003 was adopted, the Commission lost its powers to except individual agreements from the prohibition of Article 81(1) EC; even more so the power to attach conditions and/or obligations to an individual exception.

1. Grounds for revocation

The list of grounds in Article 8(3) of Regulation 17 is exhaustive and the **14.23** Commission must necessarily base its action on the existence of one of the following four situations:

(i) *The factual situation changes in relation to an essential element of the decision.* The reference to a 'factual situation' clearly shows that a circumstance brought into being by the undertakings, intentionally or negligently is not required. A change in the market situation to which the undertakings did not contribute in any way might also justify revocation. As regards the expression 'essential element of the decision', this refers both to the conditions for the grant of the exemption under Article 81(3)—the last of which refers specifically to the competitive situation in the market for the product in question—and to possible changes in the content and field of application of the agreements. Regarding the latter point, any change in the originally exempted agreements could endanger continuation of the exemption. If such changes went further than matters of form, the exemption decision might not extend to them.

(ii) *The parties concerned infringe an obligation attached to the decision.*[64] Under Regulation 17, where an obligation was breached not only could an exemption be withdrawn but also—in addition, or in isolation—a fine could be imposed under Article 15(2)(b). Article 23 of Regulation 1/2003 does not provide any authority to impose fines in this case, so at present any breach of an obligation would go unpunished.

(iii) *The decision was based on incorrect information or was obtained by fraud.* In the case of revocation on the ground that the exemption was based on incorrect information, it is not necessary—as in the case of the first ground of revocation—for the information to have been supplied by the undertakings seeking the exemption. If the incorrect information came from another source, the Commission could still revoke the exemption.

(iv) *The persons concerned abuse the exemption from the provisions of Article 81(1) of the Treaty accorded to them by the decision.* Article 8(3) does not go into detail regarding the kind of abuse referred to, but in any event the concept of abuse of an exemption is different from that of abuse of a dominant position, with the result that it is unnecessary for undertakings to occupy a dominant position for an abuse of the exemption to occur. Since there is no precedent of any revocation on this ground—or on any other—it is impossible to anticipate how the Commission will interpret that provision if and when the times comes.

14.24 The consequences of the situations described in paragraphs (b), (c), and (d) of Article 8(3) are more serious than those described in paragraph (a), in that the revocation decision may take effect retroactively.

2. Procedure

14.25 As already indicated, the revocation procedure should be similar in every respect to the infringement procedure. It commences in response to a complaint[65] or on the Commission's own initiative. The parties receive a statement of objections and are allowed a period within which to respond, and during that period the file is disclosed to them. If they so request, a hearing may be held. The Advisory Committee is consulted regarding the preliminary draft decision. The latter is adopted by the Commission in accordance with the internal procedure described already; it is published in the Official Journal and may be challenged before the Court.

---

[64] For the consequences of the infringement of an obligation under Reg 17, in general, see the first edition of this book, ch 9.II.B and ch 12.I.B.

[65] Revocation of an individual exemption is also an exclusive prerogative of the Commission; accordingly, it may be forced to adopt a formal decision either revoking the exemption or rejecting the request for revocation. See Case T-24/90 *Automec v EC Commission II* [1992] ECR II-2223 para 75.

The Commission's decision must be based on one of the grounds mentioned **14.26**
above—(a) to (d)—and must show that circumstances justifying the revocation
have in fact arisen. In that connection, there is a reversal of the burden of proof,
it now being incumbent on the Commission to show that at least one of those
grounds of revocation is present, just as, previously, it was incumbent on the
undertakings to show that each and every one of the conditions in Article 81(3)
was satisfied.

If an 'exemption' comfort letter were revoked,[66] the Commission, in view of the **14.27**
fact that it has undertaken to treat such letters as if they constituted formal
exemption decisions in the strict sense,[67] would be obliged to observe procedural
safeguards similar to those applicable to the formal revocation procedure, and
would therefore have to send a statement of objections, allow the undertakings
to submit observations and, if necessary, adopt a formal infringement decision
(not, in reality, a revocation) in which it would be necessary to set out the
reasons for which the comfort letter was revoked. In such circumstances it
would be inappropriate to impose fines during the period of validity contemplated by the letter, if any. If the relevant comfort letter did not contain a clear
time-limit, undertakings could not rely on its protection after some time, unless
perhaps in the very unlikely event that market circumstances would not at all
have changed.

---

[66] Regarding letters of this type, see the first edition of this book, ch 10.II.B.2.c.

[67] That view was expressed by Sir Leon Brittan, the Member of the Commission responsible
for competition until 1992 and Vice-president of the European Commission, in an address
entitled 'The future of EEC competition policy', given in Brussels on 7 December 1992 at the
Centre of European Policy Studies, summarized in Commission Press Release IP/92/009 of 8
December 1992.

15

STEPS FOLLOWING THE ADOPTION
OF A FORMAL DECISION.
JUDICIAL REVIEW

I. Monitoring of formal decisions

The Commission's activity does not cease with the adoption of formal decisions **15.01**
in matters referred to it for examination. In all such cases, the Commission
monitors developments in order to ensure that the requirements of its decisions
are complied with. In the case of infringement decisions—with the exception of
purely declaratory decisions without pecuniary penalties—the Commission
collects the fines and checks that its notices and orders, and the undertakings'
obligations under its decision, are complied with.

A. Infringement Decisions

1. Collection of fines and periodic penalty payments

The CFI has made clear that the Commission has 'the power to determine the **15.02**
date on which the fine is payable and that on which default interest begins to
accrue, the power to set the rate of such interest and to determine the detailed
arrangements for implementing its decision by requiring, where appropriate,
the provision of a bank guarantee covering the principal amount of the fine
imposed plus interest'.[1] The CFI considers that if the Commission had no such
power, the advantage which undertakings might be able to derive from late
payment of fines would weaken the effect of penalties imposed by the Commission. In the Court's view, the charging of default interest on fines is not only

---

[1] Case T-257/94 *Groupement des Cartes Bancaires 'CB' v EC Commission* [1995] ECR II-2169
para 47; Joined Cases T-236/01, T-239/01, T-244/01 to T-246/01, T-251/01 and T-252/01
Tokai Carbon and others v EC Commission ('Graphite Electrodes') [2004] ECR II-1181 para 475.

justified by the need to ensure that the enforcement of competition rules is not rendered ineffective by practices applied unilaterally by undertakings which delay paying fines imposed on them, but also to ensure that those undertakings do not enjoy an advantage over those which pay their fines within the stipulated period.[2] Therefore, an undertaking which challenges a Commisison decision imposing a fine can choose one of three options: it can pay the fine together with any default interest, if applicable, it can apply for suspension of the decision, or it can provide a bank guarantee as security for the payment.[3]

Voluntary payment

15.03 Details were given in chapter 11 in connection with the content and structure of infringement decisions, and fines and periodic penalty payments imposed by the Commission, of how the Commission describes in minute detail in its decisions the way in which such pecuniary penalties are to be paid. The Commission not only fixes a sum in euros[4] but also indicates the bank account into which the payment is to be made. A former practice of the Commission consisted in providing the account number in the country where payment would be easier for the undertaking in question, but currently it is most common to indicate a nominated account in Brussels.[5] As indicated, if undertakings apply for payment facilities the Commission may, in exceptional cases, grant them. Such facilities basically consist in the deferred payment of one or more instalments of the fine (against payment of interests) or in the scheduling of the periodic penalty payment.[6] Further, the appeal against the decision does not automatically lead the Commission to defer enforcement of the fine. But if the undertakings give security or a bank guarantee covering payment of the principal amount and interest, the Commission may agree to defer its collection of the fine until determination of the action.[7]

---

[2] Joined Cases T-236/01, T-239/01, T-244/01 to T-246/01, T-251/01 and T-252/01 *Tokai Carbon and others v EC Commission*, ibid.

[3] Case T-23/99 *LR af 1998 v EC Commission* [2002] ECR II-1705 paras 395–398.

[4] Since 1 January 1999 fines have been fixed in euros. In looking at past cases and decisions, the units of account and ECUs in which the fines and penalties were expressed can be taken as equivalent to the sum in euros. See Art 2(1) of Council Reg 1103/97 on certain provisions relating to the introduction of the euro [1997] OJ L162/1, under which every reference in a legal instrument to the ECU, as referred to in Art 118 EC and as defined in Council Reg (EC) 3320/94 of 22 December 1994 on the consolidation of the existing Community legislation on the definition of the ECU following the entry into force of the Treaty on European Union [1994] OJ L350/27, is to be replaced by a reference to the euro at a rate of one euro to one ECU.

[5] e.g. Art 2 of *De Post -La Poste* [2002] OJ L61/32.

[6] Joined Cases T-213/95, T-18/96 R *Kraanverhuurbedrijf v EC Commission* [1996] ECR II-407 para 31.

[7] See answer to written question 1406/81 [1982] OJ C47/28 and Orders of the President of the Court in Case 107/82 R *AEG-Telefunken v EC Commission* [1982] ECR 1179; Case T-191/98 R *DSR-Senator Lines v EC Commission* [1999] ECR II-2531 and on appeal Order in Case C-364/99 P(R) *DSR-Senator Lines v EC Commission* [1999] ECR I-8733. The costs of providing a

A request for dispensation from the obligation to provide a bank guarantee, **15.04** where that guarantee is the condition imposed in return for staying enforcement of a fine imposed by the Commission for infringement of the competition rules, cannot be granted unless there are exceptional circumstances, such as where the provision of a guarantee would threaten the very existence of the undertaking or where the grounds of challenge advanced in the main application against the decisions which imposed the fine reveal particularly serious doubts as to the legality of the decision.[8] The Community Courts seem to take a rigorous approach to evidence intended to make a showing of an undertaking's poor financial situation, which requires the undertakings concerned to produce actual proof of its inability to obtain a bank guarantee, i.e. adducing its rejected application to the bank.[9] The mere risk that the undertaking concerned might be obliged to commence winding-up proceedings as a consequence of the obligation to provide a bank guarantee may not necessarily constitute serious and irreversible damage, but has to be assessed on a case-by-case basis.[10] When assessing the ability of undertakings to furnish a bank guarantee, the Community Courts also look at the group of undertakings to which the applicant belongs and, in particular, to the resources available to that group as a whole on the premise that objective interests of the undertaking concerned are not independent of those of the natural or legal persons with a controlling interest in it. Consequently, the serious and irreparable nature of the damage alleged must be assessed at the level of the group comprising those persons. In particular, given that the interests at stake overlap, the undertaking's interest in its own survival must not be viewed in isolation from the interest of those controlling it in prolonging its life indefinitely. In that connection a simple unilateral refusal of assistance by the principal shareholder cannot be enough to preclude the financial situation of the group as a whole from being taken into account.[11]

---

guarantee or security have not been regarded by the CFI as recoverable procedural costs. In the main proceeding the CFI set aside a fine imposed by the European Commission on Senator Lines GmbH and other companies.

[8] '*Cartonboard*' Cases: Case T-295/94 R *Buchmann v EC Commisison* [1994] ECR II-1265 paras 22, 24, 27; Case T-301/94 R *Laakmann Karton GmbH v EC Commission* [1994] ECR II-1279 paras 22 *et seq.* and Case T-308/94 R *Cascades SA v EC Commission* [1995] ECR II-265 paras 43 *et seq*; see also *TACA* Cases: e.g. Case T-191/98 R II *Cho Yang Shipping v EC Commission* [2000] ECR II-2551 paras 42 *et seq.*, on appeal confirmed in Case C-361/00 *Cho Yang Shipping Co Ltd v EC Commission* [2000] ECR I-11657 paras 88–93.

[9] Joined Cases T-236/01, T-239/01, T-244/01 to T-246/01, T-251/01 and T-252/01 *Tokai Carbon and others v EC Commission* ('*Graphite Electrodes*') [2004] ECR II-1181 para 480.

[10] Order of the President of the CFI in Case T-9/99 R *HFB Holding v EC Commisison* [1999] ECR II-2429 para 28; on appeal Order of the President of the Court in Case C-335/99 P (R) *HFB Holding v EC Commission* [1999] ECR I-8705 paras 55 *et seq.*

[11] Case C-364/99 P (R) *DSR-Senator Lines GmbH v EC Commission* [1999] ECR I-8733 paras 53 and 54. Accordingly, the extent of the damage cannot flow from the unilateral intent of the majority shareholder of the undertaking seeking suspension.

15.05 Except in cases where security or a bank guarantee are given, undertakings are required to make payment in accordance with the instructions set out by the Commission in the operative part of the infringement decision. Even then, deferment is subject to the conditions laid down by the Commission. Failure to pay voluntarily within the prescribed time limits—whether imposed in the decision itself or in connection with the payment facilities or judgments—triggers the execution machinery.

Enforcement procedure

15.06 The collection of fines is not administered directly by DG COMP but by the Commission's Budget Directorate-General (DG Budget).[12] DG COMP, however, retains the right to grant an extension of the time-limit for voluntary payment. In such circumstances, it informs the above-mentioned Commission departments, which must take account of the new time-limit granted. Failure to pay within the time-limit (usually three months from the date of notification to the undertaking) has two main consequences. First, most decisions provide that interest must be directly paid at 3.5 per cent above the rate charged by the ECB on the first working day of each month. The CFI has upheld the right to charge default interest, stating that '[. . ..] if the Commission did not have the power to charge default interest on fines, undertakings which delayed paying their fines would enjoy an advantage over those which paid their fines within the period laid down [. . .]'.[13] Second, DG Budget will write to the undertakings in question requiring payment. In the absence of a satisfactory response to its letter—and the only satisfactory response is payment, no deferment having been granted—DG Budget forwards the file to the Commission's Legal Service, which undertakes enforcement of the decision by approaching the competent national authorities or courts. The usual practice is for the Legal Service to entrust enforcement proceedings to independent lawyers practising in the country in question. The Legal Service does not become directly involved, as such, in proceedings of this kind. DG COMP is merely informed of non-payment within the time limit, the forwarding of the demand for payment and the stage reached in the enforcement proceedings—if any—commenced before a national authority or court.

15.07 The implementing provisions in such cases are Article 256 EC and the rules adopted by the Member States to give effect to it. It may be stated in general, with regard to procedures under Article 256, that, although the Community

---

[12] The functions of 'Financial Control' — which in the past were attributed to former Directory-General XX that also participated in the collection of fines (see 1st edn of this book ch 12.(A)1.(b)) — have now been decentralized to and within the Commission's various Directorate Generals.

[13] Case T-275/94 *Groupement des Cartes Bancaires v EC Commission* [1995] ECR II-2169 paras 48 and 49. Case T-23/99 *LR af 1998 v EC Commission* [2002] ECR II-1705 para 395.

authorities (in particular the Commission) may impose pecuniary penalties, the enforcement of such penalties is a matter solely for the Member States, which are required to grant the Community authorities direct access to national civil proceedings for enforcement under a simplified procedure, without the need for any *exequatur*. Article 256 in fact provides that Commission decisions are enforceable measures. Enforcement is governed by the rules of civil procedure in force in the Member State where the addressees of the decisions are located. The only precondition for ordinary enforcement is verification by the national authorities designated for that purpose that the decision is genuine. On completion of that formality, the Commission may proceed to enforcement in accordance with national law by bringing the matter directly before the competent authority. The national authority empowered to verify the authenticity of the document varies from Member State to Member State. In practice, the Commission would ask the Permanent Representation of the country concerned to the European Communities to verify the authenticity of the decision. It would take the necessary steps in the country concerned and return the decision to the Commission now in a form fully enforceable under domestic law. The application for enforcement of the Commission's independent lawyers entrusted with the collection of the sums due would be processed by the ordinary civil court which would be required to treat the decision as if it were a final judgment of a civil court.[14] It will be recalled that the European Community has legal personality (Article 281 EC) and may be a party to legal proceedings in order to uphold its rights under the same conditions as an individual. Finally, enforcement may be suspended only by a decision of the ECJ. However, the courts of the country concerned shall have jurisdiction over complaints that enforcement is being carried out in an irregular manner.[15]

---

[14] In the UK, the European Communities ('Enforcement of Community Judgments') Order enables the Commission's decisions imposing fines to be registered in the High Court and be given the same treatment as if they had been issued by the High Court itself. The European Communities (Enforcement of Community Judgments) Order 1972, S.I. 1972/1590, as amended by S.I. 1998/1259 and by S.I. 2003/3204. CS Kerse and N Khan, *EC Antitrust Procedure* (5th edn, 2005) para 7–091; C Bellamy and G Child, *European Community Law of Competition* (5th edn, 2001) para 12–116.

[15] In *Pioneer* [1980] OJ L60/21 and Joined Cases 100–103/80 *Musique Diffusion Française v EC Commission* [1983] ECR 1825, one of the undertakings, the German company C Melchers & Co, which was fined 400,000 ECUs, applied to the European Commission of Human Rights for a finding against the Federal Republic of Germany on the ground that its Ministry of Justice had issued an order under Art 256 EC at the request of the European Commission of the European Communities. Melcher claimed that its fundamental rights had not been observed during the Community procedure. See the decision of the European Commission of Human Rights of 9 February 1990 on the admissibility of Application No 13258/87 of *C Melchers & Co v Germany*, D.R. 64, 138.

2. Monitoring of compliance with 'injunctions'

15.08   Pursuant to Article 7(1) of Regulation 1/2003, the Commission may include whatever is necessary to bring to an end the infringements of the competition rules which have been ascertained. The Commission is empowered not only to require the cessation of specific conduct (earlier referred to as 'negative injunctions', which literally reflect the content of that provision), but also to require certain conduct by undertakings (earlier referred to as 'positive injunctions' or orders to take—as opposed to refrain from—action, in respect of which the Commission's powers have been upheld by the Court).[16]

15.09   In its decision, the Commission may confine itself to prohibiting or requiring a particular conduct, without further details being given. If no time limit is set for compliance and no express penalty is imposed for non-compliance, the position is deemed to be that the orders contained in the Commission decisions must be complied with immediately and that the requirements or orders will be enforced—to put it bluntly—by the imposition of periodic penalty payments in the event of delay.[17] The Commission has no other means of requiring undertakings to comply with its decisions. In other cases, the decision itself may provide for the manner in which the operative part of the decision, as regards cessation of the infringement, is to be monitored. The Commission may attach obligations to its decisions which facilitate monitoring. Thus, for example, an undertaking in a dominant position may be required to inform the Commission periodically of its prices, to allow it to verify that the infringement—a discriminatory or 'predatory' pricing policy destroying competition—has in fact been brought to an end,[18] or to notify to the Commission those contracts in which prohibited clauses were found in the course of the procedure, so that the Commission can determine whether those clauses are no longer being applied. In such cases, the Commission may provide for periodic penalty payments in the infringement decision itself, which will be applied if the undertakings do not fulfil the obligation.[19]

15.10   To date, the Commission itself has always tried to monitor compliance with its

---

[16] See ch 11 'Declarations and Orders or Notices' paras 11.02 *et seq.*

[17] The Commission may, however, where immediate cessation is not possible for objective reasons, grant a limited period—as short as possible—to undertakings in order to bring the infringement to an end.

[18] See Art 5 of Commission Decision in *ECS/Akzo II* [1985] OJ L374/1; see also Case T-128/98 *Aérports de Paris v EC Commission* [2000] ECR II-3929 paras 82–83 regarding the obligation to apply a non-discriminatory scheme of commercial fees at the airport of Paris.

[19] Art 6 of Commission Decision in *ECS/Akzo II* [1985] OJ L374/1; see also e.g. Art 5 of *Mercedes* [2002] OJ L257/1.

antitrust decisions.[20] Unlike to the Commission's practice in the merger control area where the Commission has developed *Best Practice Guidelines for Divestiture Commitments and Trustee Mandate*,[21] the Commission does not use a similar set of rules for monitoring commitments imposed in proceedings under Articles 81 and 82 EC. One reason may be that most of Commission's decisions in this field have involved mere reporting duties or less complex remedies than in the field of mergers. Not only because Article 7 of Regulation 1/2003 makes explicit provision for the Commission's power to impose any remedy, whether behavioural or structural, which is necessary to bring the infringement effectively to an end, but also because proceedings may become increasingly complex, Regulation 1/2003 calls for a more sophisticated monitoring mechanism in the future and maybe also some guidelines from the Commission.[22] In *Microsoft*, the Commission was concerned that a mere reporting mechanism would not be sufficient to ensure compliance with its decision and the remedies imposed. Therefore, it required Microsoft to submit within thirty days a proposal to the Commission for a suitable monitoring regime, including the appointment of a monitoring trustee whose primary responsibility would be '[. . .] to issue opinions, upon application by a third party or by the Commission or sua sponte, on whether Microsoft has, in a specific instance, failed to comply with this Decision, or on any issue that may be of interest with respect to the effective enforcement of this Decision [. . . .]'.[23] After lengthy discussion, the Commission appointed in October 2005 a Trustee providing technical advice to the Commission on issues relating to Microsoft's compliance with the decision.[24]

---

[20] Art 7 of *DSD* [2001] OJ L166/1: 'DSD shall inform the Commission, within three months of notification of this Decision, of the fulfilment of the commitments under Arts 3 to 6'.

[21] Commission Press Release IP/03/614 of 2 May 2003. 'Commission publishes best practice guidelines for divestiture commitments in merger cases'. Explanatory Note on the Commission's Model Texts for Divestiture Commitments and the Trustee Mandate under the EC Merger Control Reg and the Standard Models available at DG COMP's website.

[22] The Commission seems to have recognized this. 'Q&A on modernization with Kris Dekeyser' Global Competition Review, Vol 8, Issue 3 April 2005, 11–16.

[23] Commission decision of 24 March 2004 in Microsoft (Case COMP/C-3/37.792) paras 1043 *et seq.* and Art 6 of the Commission decision, available as non-confidential version, at DG COMP's website. Case T-201/04 *Microsoft v EC Commission* (appeal pending) application in [2004] OJ C179/18.

[24] On 22 December 2004, the President of the CFI rejected Microsoft's request for the suspension of the remedies. During the proceedings, the Commission had, in deference to the CFI, suspended the Decision pending that order. See Commission Memo/04/305 'Questions and answers—Order of the President of the Court of First Instance in Case T-201/04 R, *Microsoft Corp v EC Commission* [2005] OJ C69/16. Commission Press Release IP/05/673 'Competition: Commission to market test new proposals from Microsoft on interoperability', 6 June 2005. Commission press release IP/05/1215 of 5 October 2005 'Competition: Commission appoints Trustee to advise on Microsoft's compliance with 2004 Decision'. See also Commission press release IP/05/1695 of 22 December 2005 'Competition: Commission warns Microsoft of daily penalty for failure to comply with 2004 decision'.

II. Closing or shelving of the file

15.11 Files may be closed either because the matter has been disposed of formally by means of a decision or because the matter at issue is regarded by the Commission as no longer of importance at any stage of the procedure.[25] The Commission may also take a decision to shelve a complaint for lack of a sufficient Community interest not only before commencing an investigation of the case but also after taking investigative measures, if that course seems appropriate to it at that stage of the procedure.[26] All files disposed of are closed, unless:

(i) the formal decision contains obligations or undertakings fulfilment of which must be monitored by the Commission, in which case the *rapporteur* or monitoring trustee responsible will follow developments during the period prescribed or necessary to verify fulfilment of the requirements imposed by the Commission. This situation may result for example from infringement decisions[27] or commitments;[28]

(ii) the formal decision bringing the procedure to an end is challenged before the Community Courts, in which case the file may be forwarded to the Legal Service and to the Court itself.[29]

---

[25] As regards the possibility of re-allocating the file to an NCA, see 'Principles of Case Allocation' paras 3.06 *et seq.*

[26] See Opinion of AG Ruiz-Jarabo Colomer in Joined Cases C-449/98 P and C-450/98 P *International Express Carriers Conference (IECC) v EC Commission* [2001] ECR I-3875 paras 54–56, who stated, alluding to the CFI case law, that '[t]o conclude otherwise would be tantamount to placing the Commission under an obligation, once it had taken investigative measures following the submission of an application under Article 3(2) of Regulation No 17, to adopt a decision as to whether or not either Article [81] or Article [82] of the Treaty, or both, had been infringed, which would be contrary not only to the very wording of Article 3(1) of Regulation No 17, according to which the Commission may adopt a decision concerning the existence of the alleged infringement, but would also conflict with the settled case-law [. . .] according to which a complainant has no right to obtain from the Commission a decision within the meaning of Article [249] of the Treaty.' See Joined Cases T-133/95 and T-204/95 *International Express Carriers Conference (IECC) v EC Commission* [1998] ECR II-3645 paras 146–147.

[27] An example might be an obligation to inform the Commission annually, over a specified period, of the conditions under which a product is sold (Art 6 of Commission Decision in *ECS/Akzo II* [1985] OJ L374/1).

[28] Thus, e.g. if need be the *rapporteur* responsible for the case verifies, on a day-to-day basis, fulfilment of the undertakings' commitments under Art 9 of Reg 1/2003.

[29] Before the creation of the CFI, the ECJ as a rule asked only for the complaints or notifications, the statement of objections and the reply from the undertakings, the minutes of administrative hearings, the opinion of the Advisory Committee and the decision itself, but it had access, if it wished, to the entire file. The Court itself expressed the view in its order in Joined Cases 142/84 and 156/84 *BAT and Reynolds v EC Commission* [1986] ECR 1899 para 11, that the examination of the Commission's file was an exceptional measure of inquiry which could be contemplated if there was any suspicion of misuse of powers on the part of the Commission. The CFI seemingly has departed from the earlier practice and examines the administrative file in detail.

Files which for any reason cease to have any purpose or interest are also closed **15.12** and shelved. This may be the case, for example, because the complaints which gave rise to them have been withdrawn; because the undertakings to which the file relates no longer exist, or for other reasons. In such cases, whenever formal investigative measures have been taken, such as requests for information or inspections, the Commission may close the file and will not reopen it unless new evidence is submitted which would justify this. If the file to be closed has been initiated under Article 11(6) of Regulation 1/2003, the Commission is also expected to inform the Member States of the end of its investigation in the same way as it previously announced its intention to apply Article 11(6). NCAs should then no longer be barred from applying Articles 81 and 82 EC to the same case. It may be recalled that in those cases where, pursuant to Article 9 of Regulation 1/2003, the Commission has opted for a decision by virtue of which commitments are made binding upon the undertaking(s) concerned, the proceedings are not closed. Proceedings may be reopened in the following circumstances: (i) a material change in the facts on which the decision was based takes place; (ii) undertakings fail to comply with their commitments; or (iii) the decision is proven to have been based on incomplete, incorrect, or misleading information provided by the parties.[30]

The ECJ considered that a letter sent in the course of an administrative pro- **15.13** cedure in which the Commission stated that it was ending the investigation without offering the parties the opportunity to submit their observations was a definitive act, and as such could be challenged. Indeed in *SFEI*, the Court stated that '[. . .] a letter closing the file may be analysed as a preliminary or preparatory statement only if the Commission has clearly indicated that its conclusion is valid only subject to submission by the parties of supplementary observations. [. . .]'[31] Later, the ECJ further explained that letters definitely '[c]losing the file may be the subject of an action, since they have the content and effect of a decision, inasmuch as they close the investigation, contain an assessment of the agreements in question and prevent the applicants from requiring the reopening of the investigation unless they put forward new evidence [. . .]'.[32]

---

[30] For more details on commitment decisions, see ch 13 'Voluntary adjustments' paras 13.06 *et seq.*
[31] This did not apply in Case C-39/93 P *Syndicat Français de l'Express international (SFEI) v EC Commission* [1994] ECR I-2681 para 30; Opinion of AG Saggio in Case C-265/97 P *Coöperatieve Vereniging De Verenigde Bloemenveilingen Aalsmeer BV (VBA) v EC Commission* [2000] ECR I-2061 para 34.
[32] Case T-241/97 *Stork Amsterdam BV v EC Commission* [2000] ECR II-309 para 53; Case 210/81 *Demo-Studio Schmidt v EC Commission* [1983] ECR 3045 paras 14–15; Case 298/83 *CICCE v EC Commission* [1985] ECR 1105 para 18, and Joined Cases 142/84 and 156/84 *BAT and Reynolds v EC Commission* [1987] ECR 4487 para 12.

III. Court proceedings concerning the application of Community competition law

15.14 Commission decisions in antitrust cases are subject to judicial review by the Community Courts. The CFI, created in 1989, was only competent to hear actions in competition (and staff) cases but its jurisdiction has been subsequently enlarged to cover all direct actions brought by private parties. A recent amendment to Article 51 of the Protocol on the Statute of the Court of Justice means that even a challenge by a Member State to a competition decision will now be dealt with by the CFI.[33] It has jurisdiction at first instance to hear applications for annulment and for failure to act, while any appeal on its rulings will go to the ECJ. For the time being, the ECJ has retained jurisdiction over all requests for preliminary references under Article 234 EC from national courts.

A. Application for Annulment

15.15 In a given case, the Commission may choose the evidence upon which it wishes to rely and decide whether it supports the finding of an infringement under Articles 81 and 82 EC. The CFI may then be asked to undertake an exhaustive review of both the Commission's substantive findings of fact and its legal appraisal of those facts and to assess whether the evidence and other information relied on by the Commission in its decision are sufficient to establish the existence of the alleged infringement.[34] The provisions applicable to requests for annulment are Articles 230, 231, and 233 EC. In actions under Article 230, the CFI exercises a supervisory jurisdiction to the extent that it has to satisfy itself that the Commission's findings of fact and legal conclusions drawn from those facts are correct. In general terms, it is not concerned with the merits of a decision, but rather whether the Commission's findings regarding the facts and its legal assessment satisfy the requisite legal standard.[35] Under Article 229 EC in conjunction with Article 31 of Regulation 1/2003, the Court has unlimited

---

[33] *Council Decision* 2004/407 [2004] OJ L132/5.

[34] See Joined Cases T-25/95, T-26/95, T-30/95 to T-39/95, T-42/95 to T-46/95, T-48/95, T-50/95 to T-65/95, T-68/95 to T-71/95, T-87/95, T-88/95, T-103/95 and T-104/95 *Cimenteries CBR SA and others v EC Commission* [2000] ECR II-491 para 719; Joined Cases T-67/00, T-68/00, T-71/00 and T-78/00 *JFE Engineering Corp and others v EC Commission* [2004] OJ C239/1 para 175.

[35] D Bailey, 'Scope of Judicial Review under Article 81 EC' (2004) CML Rev 1327–60 (1331). Joined Cases C-2/01 P and C-3/01 P *Bundesverband der Arzneimittel-Importeure eV (BAI) and EC Commission v Bayer* [2004] ECR I-23 para 62; T Joined Cases T-67/00, T-68/00, T-71/00 and T-78/00 *JFE Engineering Corp v EC Commission* [2004] OJ C239/1 para 175: '[. . .] Thus,

jurisdiction in respect of fines and penalties. This enables the CFI and the ECJ to adjudicate on the amount of the pecuniary penalties imposed by the Commission in its infringement decisions. Unlike actions brought under the limited head of review contained in Article 230 EC, the Court examines in each particular case whether the amount of the fine imposed by the Commission is reasonable and determines the appropriateness of the fine.[36] That assessment may justify the production and taking into account of additional information which is not as such required, by virtue of the duty to state reasons under Article 253 EC, to be set out in the decision.[37]

In most cases, addressees of fines seek above all the annulment of the Commission decision in regard to the penalties or at least a reduction of the fine.[38] The Community Courts have not limited themselves to reviewing legal and procedural issues and have tested the accuracy of the Commission's economic and market analysis. The CFI has demonstrated its willingness to resolve issues of economic importance and its commitment to a 'comprehensive judicial review' which will cause the Court to review a decision to the maximum extent possible.[39] The ECJ has stated that the CFI has exclusive jurisdiction '[. . .] first,

15.16

---

the role of a Court hearing an application for annulment brought against a Commission decision finding the existence of an infringement of the competition rules and imposing fines on the addressees consists in assessing whether the evidence and other information relied on by the Commission in its decision are sufficient to establish the existence of the alleged infringement [. . .]'.

[36] Case T-317/94 *Moritz J Weig v EC Commission* [1998] ECR II-1235 para 194: '[. . .] It follows that, when it finds in a decision that there has been an infringement of the competition rules and imposes fines on the undertakings participating in it, the Commission must, if it systematically took into account certain basic factors in order to fix the amount of fines, set out those factors in the body of the decision in order to enable the addressees of the decision to verify that the level of the fine is correct and to assess whether there has been any discrimination. [. . .]'.

[37] Case C-248/98 *KNP BT v EC Commission* [2000] ECR I-9641 para 40.

[38] Sometimes the principal interest of the undertaking may be to challenge the remedies imposed and not the fine. After having filed appeal against the Commission's decision with the CFI, Microsoft has also lodged an application for suspension of the Commission decision imposing the obligation for Microsoft to offer an unbundled version of Windows and the obligation for Microsoft to make available to its competitors certain technical interface information necessary to allow non-Microsoft work group servers to achieve full interoperability with Windows PCs. This application for interim relief was rejected in the Order of the President of the CFI. Case T-201/04 *Microsoft v EC Commission* [2005] OJ C69/16. The fine was already paid in full to the Commission on 29 June 2004.

[39] D Bailey, 'Scope of judicial Review under Article 81 EC' (2004) CML Rev 1327–62 (1332); Opinion of AG Cosmas in Case C-83/98 P *France v Ladbroke Racing v EC Commission* [2000] ECR I-3271 para 15; Opinion of Judge Vesterdorf acting as AG in Case T-7/89 *Hercules v EC Commission* [1992] II-1711 noting that the review is 'governed by the principle of the unfettered evaluation of evidence, unrestrained by the various rules laid down in national legal systems'. See also in cases related to State aid: T-198/01 *Technische Glaswerke Ilmenau v EC Commission*, CFI judgment of 8 July 2004 (not yet published), para 79 indicating that comprehensive judicial review and discretion of the Commission go hand in hand: '[. . .] Where the Commission adopts a

to establish the facts except where the substantive inaccuracy of its [Commission] findings is apparent from the documents submitted to it and, second, to assess those facts.[40] On appeal, the ECJ's task is limited to examining whether, in exercising its power of review, the CFI made an error of law. Under Article 225 EC and Article 51, first paragraph, of the Statute of the ECJ, an appeal must be limited to points of law and must lie on grounds of lack of competence of the CFI, a breach of procedure before it which adversely affects the interests of the applicant or an infringement of Community law by the CFI. Essentially, the ECJ reviews the legality of the way in which the CFI reviewed the Commission's decision but does not substitute its own view for that of the CFI on the evidence of the case and thus will have regard to the role played and the policy conducted by the Commission.[41]

1. Jurisdiction of the courts

15.17 Pursuant to Article 229, '[r]egulations made by the Council pursuant to the provisions of this Treaty may give the Court of Justice unlimited jurisdiction in regard to the penalties provided for in such regulations'. In the context of competition proceedings, Article 31 of Regulation 1/2003 specifies that '[t]he Court of Justice shall have unlimited jurisdiction to review decisions whereby the Commission has fixed a fine or periodic penalty payment; it may cancel, reduce or increase the fine or periodic penalty payment imposed' by the Commission. It is important to bear in mind that Article 229 does not provide for an unlimited judicial review in the sense that it restricts the extent and exercise of the review to the consideration of the fine or other penalty imposed by the Commission.[42] It would not permit the applicant to seek annulment on wider

---

measure involving such an appraisal [private operator in market economy], it enjoys a wide discretion and, even though judicial review is in principle a comprehensive review of whether a measure falls within the scope of Article 87(1) EC, review of that measure is limited to establishing whether there has been compliance with the rules governing procedure and the statement of reasons, whether any error in law has been made, whether the facts on which the contested finding was based have been accurately stated and whether there has been any manifest error of assessment or a misuse of powers. In particular, the Court is not entitled to substitute its own economic assessment for that of the author of the decision [. . .].' See however, 'Dealing with the Commission—Notification, complaints, inspections and fact-finding powers under Articles 81 and 82 of the EEC Treaty' (1997 edn) point 8.4: The work of the CFI to date has shown that it is prepared to take a more proactive attitude in its factual examination of the cases brought before it.

[40] Case C-7/95 P *John Deere v EC Commission* [1998] ECR I-3111 para 21.

[41] Joined Cases C-204/00 P, C-205/00 P, C-211/00 P, C-213/00 P, C-217/00 P and C-219/00 P *Aalborg Portland A/S and others v EC Commission* [2004] ECR I-123 para 47.

[42] Note that the Court is only entitled to 'cancel', 'reduce', or 'increase' the fine imposed by the Commission, but it cannot impose a fine where none was imposed by the Commission in the first place. As regards the interpretation of Art 229 EC, see Case C-275/94 *Carte Bleu v EC Commission II* [1996] ECR I-1393 paras 57–65, in which the CFI concludes that the fines it sets are not legally different from those imposed by the Commission.

grounds, although in practice, the distinct scope of review is mitigated by the fact that applicants bring their action under both Articles 229 and 230 EC. In addition, both Articles 229 and 230 EC give the Commission a degree of discretion in the exercise of its powers.[43] The review undertaken by the CFI under Article 230 EC does not involve reassessing the facts of a case afresh.[44] The possibilities for challenging the Commission's appraisal are often limited because of the discretion that it enjoys. A decision will be overturned if the Commission has manifestly erred in its judgment which is to be decided on the basis of the persuasive evidence in each case; this involves the CFI verifying objectively and materially the accuracy of certain facts and the correctness of the conclusions drawn.[45]

While in the past the review under Article 81(3) EC seemed to be less intense,[46] **15.18**

[43] D Bailey, 'Scope of Judicial Review under Article 81 EC' (2004) CML Rev 1337–39 distinguishes between discretion (which tends to restrict the scope of judicial review by allowing the Commission to choose the criteria by which a decision is reached) and power of appraisal in regard to Art 81 which is subject to comprehensive judicial review but which may be limited in cases involving complex economic assessment. See, e.g. Case T-112/99 *Métropole Television v EC Commission* [2001] ECR II-2459 para 114.

[44] Case T-342/00 *Petrolessence v EC Commission* [2003] ECR II-1161 para 103: '[. . .] it must be observed that the applicants have not established that the Commission's appraisal of those points is clearly mistaken and it must be concluded that the applicants' present arguments consist in inviting the Court of First Instance to substitute a different appraisal of their candidacy for that of the Commission [. . .]'.

[45] President of the CFI Judge Bo Vesterdorf, 'Judicial Review and Competition Law—Reflections on the Role of the Community Courts in the EC System of Competition Law Enforcement', Speech at the International Forum on EC Competition Law, Brussels 8 April 2005 takes the view that the case law (e.g. Case T-44/02 *German Banks v EC Commission* [2004] OJ C314/13, Case T-67/01 *JCB Service v EC Commisison* [2004] ECR II-49, Case T-208/01 *Volkswagen v EC Commission* [2003] ECR II-5141) shows that the CFI does not shy away from examining closely and without restraint whether the Commission had got the core facts right. See also the published and edited paper version of the Vesterdorf's speech in Competition Policy International [2005] Vol 1, Number 2, page 15.

[46] See CD Ehlermann and I Atanasiu, 'The Modernization of EC Antitrust Law: Consequences for the Future Role and Functions of the EC Courts' [2002] ECLR 72–80 (74) stating that the Community Courts have exercised a self-imposed limited control over Commission decisions under Art 81(3) EC referring to Case T-29/92 *Vereniging van Samenwerkende Prijsregelende Organisaties in de Bouwnijverheid and others v EC Commission* [1995] ECR II-289 para 288. (upheld on appeal in Case C-137/95 P *Vereniging van Samenwerkende Prijsregelende Organisaties in de Bouwnijverheid and others v EC Commission* [1996] ECR I-1611). The CFI made the classic point that the review under Art 81(3) EC 'must be limited to ascertaining whether the procedural rules have been complied with, whether proper reasons have been provided, whether the facts have been accurately stated and whether there has been any manifest error of appraisal or misuse of powers.' See also Case T-65/98 *Van den Bergh Foods Ltd v EC Commission* [2003] ECR II-4653 para 135 and D Bailey, 'Scope of Judicial Review under Article 81 EC' (2004) CML Rev 1327–60 (1347) pointing to the relatively few Commission's Art 81(3) EC decisions which have been overturned: Case 17/74 *Transocean Marine Paint Association v EC Commission* [1974] ECR 1063 (procedural error); in Case T-79/95 R *SNCF and BRB v EC Commission* [1996] ECR II-1491; and Joined Cases T-374/94, T-375/94, T-384/94 and T-388/94 *European Night Services v EC Commission* [1998] ECR II-3141 paras 180–189 the CFI considered the

it may be expected that the direct applicability of Article 81(3) EC will require the CFI to take a similar approach as with Article 81(1) EC. The CFI may review the probative value of the evidence taken into consideration by the Commission, in particular whether the efficiency gains flowing from an agreement outweighs its anti-competitive nature.[47] What is fact and what comes within an assessment of facts will not always be easy to decide. Where an issue involves a complex assessment which may lead two reasonable persons to a disagreement on the conclusions to be drawn, this may already fall outside the ambit of pure facts and could amount to an assessment of the facts. In any event, this does not relieve the Commission from the obligation to provide adequate reasons for its decision which the Community Courts consider as material to exercising their power of judicial review. Whether this opens the way to a 'normal' standard of judicial review remains to be seen.[48] While the CFI remains bound by its duty to control the legality of the Commission's decision, the Community Courts are unlikely to 'replace' the Commission's assessment of the four conditions of Article 81(3) but the Court will review the facts of the case and the interpretation of those facts by the Commission with due regard to economic theory.[49] In *Tetra Laval,* a merger case, the ECJ summarized the scope of judicial review in competition cases as follows: 'Whilst the Court recognises that the Commission has a margin of discretion with regard to economic matters, that does not mean that the Community Courts must refrain from reviewing the Commission's interpretation of information of an economic nature. Not only must the Community Courts, inter alia, establish whether the evidence

---

Commission was wrong to conclude that the agreement was restrictive of competition within the meaning of Art 81(1). See also Joined Cases T-185/00, T-216/00, T-299/00 and T-300/00 *Métropole télévision SA (M6) and others v EC Commission* [2002] ECR II-3805 in which the Court disagreed with the Commission's conclusion that the fourth condition of Art 81(3) (that the exempted agreement should not enable the undertakings concerned eliminate condition) was satisfied because non EBU members have sufficient access to live TV rights that EBU members do not use.

[47] Case T-65/98 *Van den Bergh Foods Ltd v EC Commission* [2003] ECR II-4653 para 74 (appeal pending): '[. . .] It is only within the specific framework of that provision that the pro and anti-competitive aspects of a restriction may be weighed [. . .]'. See, to that effect, Case 161/84 *Pronuptia* [1986] ECR 353 para 24; Case T-17/93 *Matra Hachette v EC Commission* [1994] ECR II-595 para 48, and Joined Cases T-374/94, T-375/94, T-384/94 and T-388/94 *European Night Services v EC Commission* [1998] ECR II-3141 para 136.

[48] Interestingly, the CFI sometimes seems to consider that under both Art 81(1) and (3) EC the judicial appraisal of complex matters is limited to examining whether procedural rules have been applied with, whether the Commission has accurately stated the reasons and whether there has been any manifest error of assessment. Case T-65/98 *Van den Bergh Foods Ltd v EC Commission* [2003] ECR II-4653 paras 80 and 135.

[49] K Lenaerts and D Gerard, 'Decentralisation of EC Competition Law Enforcement: Judges in the Frontline' [2004] World Competition 27(3) 313–49 (327, n 128). See L Parret, 'Judicial Protection after Modernization of Competition Law' [2005] Legal Issues of Economic Integration 339–68 (363–64).

relied on is factually accurate, reliable and consistent but also whether that evidence contains all the information which must be taken into account in order to assess a complex situation and whether it is capable of substantiating the conclusions drawn from it. [. . .]'.[50] The CFI would need to check whether other factors not mentioned by the Commission or mentioned but to which the Commission did not pay proper attention should be considered or whether there other obvious elements should be taken into account.[51] Based on the premise that the right to a fair defence is a fundamental requirement of Community law, the Community Courts thus constantly scrutinize the observance of procedural rules and the parties' defence rights.

When fixing fines, for example, the Community Courts have been mindful that   **15.19** fines are an instrument of competition policy and the level of fines may need to be adjusted to ensure compliance with EC competition law.[52] Although the CFI has full jurisdiction as a matter of law in determining the appropriate level of

---

[50] Cases C-12/03 *EC Commission v Tetra Laval* [2005] ECR I-987 para 39. See also T-210/01 *General Electric v EC Commission*, judgment of 14 December 2005 (not yet published) para 63. Judge H Legal 'Standards of Proof and Standards of Judicial Review in EU Competition Law' 32nd Annual International Antitrust Law & Policy Conference Fordham Corporate Law Institute, 22–23 September 2005 (forthcoming), 4–5 notes that this reasoning applies not only to merger cases but to all decisions involving interpretation of information of economic nature. He suggests that the Court's review aims to assess whether the material evidence is irrelevant, unreliable or otherwise insufficient to prove the point the Commission is trying to make. T Reeves and N Dodoo, 'Standards of Proof of Judicial Review in EC Merger Law' 32nd Annual International Antitrust Law & Policy Conference Fordham Corporate Law Institute, 22–23 September 2005 (forthcoming), 15, note in the same context that in antitrust cases which often span several years with intensive fact-finding there might be less room for speculation than in a merger investigation which is by its very nature forward-looking.

[51] President of the CFI Judge Bo Vesterdorf 'Judicial Review and Competition Law— Reflections on the Role of the Community Courts in the EC system of Competition Law Enforcement', Speech at the International Forum on EC Competition Law, Brussels 8 April 2005 argues that this may be considered as a 'slight tightening of the manifest error test.' See also the published and edited paper version of the speech in Competition Policy International [2005] Vol 1, Number 2, page 16.

[52] Case T-311/94 *BPB de Eendracht NV, formerly Kartonfabriek de Eendracht NV v EC Commission* [1998] ECR II-1129 para 303. D Geradin and D Henry, 'The EC fining policy for violation of competition law: An empirical review of the Commission decisional practice and the Community's courts' judgments' [2005] European Competition Law Journal 401–73 (457 *et seq*) note that since the introduction of the 1998 Guidelines, the CFI has reduced fines which the Commission has imposed in thirty-two cases. From the empirical evidence it can be deduced that in over 50 per cent of the judgments rendered where the CFI has lowered the fine, the fine has been reduced by between 7 per cent and 25 per cent. Geradin and Henry have identified the following grounds for granting a reduction (459–71): (i) incorrect assessment of the duration of the infringement (seven cases); (ii) incorrect assessment of gravity of the infringement (eight cases); (iii) expiry of limitation period for the imposition of fines (one case); (iv) incorrect application of the leniency notice (eleven cases); (v) incorrect assessment of mitigating and attenuating circumstances (four cases); (vi) wrongful imputation of unlawful conduct (two cases); (vii) failure to establish infringement (one case); and (viii) incorrect method employed in calculating fines (seven cases).

fine and to verify whether the amount of the fine imposed is in proportion to the duration and gravity of the infringement,[53] the CFI is at pains not to usurp a role which the Treaty has conferred on the Commission.[54] Where the Commission has not proved all of its case or where there has been some defect in reasoning in the Commission's decision which is not sufficient to justify complete annulment, the Court is ready to reduce fines.[55] The essential procedural requirement to state reasons is satisfied where the Commission indicates in its decision the factors which enabled it to determine the gravity of the infringement and its duration. If those factors are not stated, the decision is vitiated by failure to state adequate reasons.[56] This reluctance is even more pronounced when it comes to increasing the fines.[57] As regards the ECJ, the purpose of its review is, first, to examine to what extent the CFI took into consideration, in a legally correct manner, all the essential factors to assess the gravity of particular conduct in the light of Article 81 EC and Article 23 of Regulation 1/2003 and, second, to consider whether the CFI responded to a sufficient legal standard to

---

[53] Case T-229/94 *Deutsche Bahn v EC Commission* [1997] ECR II-1689 para 127.

[54] Case T-150/89 *Martinelli v EC Commission* [1995] ECR II-1165 para 59 stating that the Commission has a margin of discretion and cannot be considered obliged to apply a precise mathematical formula when imposing a fine.

[55] See Case T-311/94 *BPB de Eendracht NV, formerly Kartonfabriek de Eendracht NV v EC Commission* [1998] ECR II-1129 paras 341 *et seq.*: '[. . .] applicant's participation in the meetings of the JMC is proven only in regard to two of the 17 meetings of that body held during the period in which it is proved that the applicant committed an infringement of Art [81(1)] [. . .] As it is apparent [. . .] the applicant's participation in the meetings of that body was significantly more sporadic than that of the other undertakings regarded as "ordinary members" of the cartel [. . .] Having regard to those factors, the applicant should have been regarded as having played a less significant role in the alleged cartel than that of the other undertakings considered to be "ordinary members" of it. [. . .] Taking those factors into account, the Court, exercising its unlimited jurisdiction, will reduce the amount of the fine. [. . .]'; Case 86/82 *Hasselblad (GB) Limited v EC Commission* [1984] ECR 883 para 57; Case T-59/99 *Ventouris v EC Commission* [2003] ECR II-5257 paras 215–222.

[56] Case C-248/98 P *KNP BT v EC Commission* [2000] ECR I-9641 paras 42 and 45–46 which read: '[. . .] Admittedly, the Commission cannot, by a mechanical recourse to arithmetical formulae alone, divest itself of its own power of assessment. However, it may in its decision give reasons going beyond the requirements, in particular by indicating the figures which, especially in regard to the desired deterrent effect, influenced the exercise of its discretion when setting the fines imposed on a number of undertakings which participated, in different degrees, in the infringement. [. . .] It may indeed be desirable for the Commission to make use of that possibility in order to enable undertakings to acquire a detailed knowledge of the method of calculating the fine imposed on them. More generally, such a course of action may serve to render the administrative act more transparent and facilitate the exercise by the Court of First Instance of its unlimited jurisdiction, which enables it to review not only the legality of the contested decision but also the appropriateness of the fine imposed. However, [. . .] the availability of that possibility is not such as to alter the scope of the requirements resulting from the duty to state reasons. [. . .].'

[57] Case T-354/94 *Stora Kopparbergs Bergslags v EC Commission* [2002] ECR II-843 para 85; see para 15.21 below.

all the arguments raised by the appellant with a view to having the fine cancelled or reduced.[58]

Where the Commission uses the calculation method that it has imposed on itself in the 1998 Guidelines, it may not depart from those rules. In this regard, a self-imposed limitation of that discretion arises inasmuch as it must then follow those guidelines.[59] While in exercising its jurisdiction the Court would not be bound by the Commission's Guidelines on the imposition of fines,[60] the Court has nevertheless followed the suggested approach of the 1998 Guidelines.[61] In the event that the applicant could successfully demonstrate that the Commission did not comply with the methodology set out in the 1998 Guidelines, this does not necessarily result in a reduction of fine which might have been the outcome where the Court had applied the 1998 Guidelines. The Court is entitled to conduct its own assessment which may justify the production and taking into account of additional information[62] but in most cases this does not lead to a significant reduction of a fine. In *Archer Daniels Midland*, the CFI found that the Commission did not take account of the turnover of each undertaking from sales in the market concerned by the infringement, namely the lysine market in the EEA, but concluded that this failure to adhere to the Guidelines did not lead to breach of the principle of proportionality in setting the fine.[63] In the same case, however, the CFI found that the Commission did not apply the reductions granted on account of mitigating circumstances in the same way to all the undertakings concerned. It stated that the percentage increases or reductions adopted on account of aggravating or mitigating circumstances must be applied to the basic amount of the fine, determined by reference to the gravity and duration of the infringement, and not to the amount of an increase previously applied in respect of the duration of the infringement or to the figure resulting from the first increase or reduction adopted to reflect an aggravating or a mitigating circumstance. That method of calculating the fines should ensure equal treatment between the various undertakings participating

15.20

---

[58] C-185/95 P *Baustahlgewebe v EC Commission* [1998] ECR I-8417 para 128.

[59] Case T-380/94 *AIUFFASS and AKT v EC Commission* [1996] ECR II-2169 para 57, and Case T-214/95 *Vlaams Gewest v EC Commission* [1998] ECR II-717 para 89.

[60] See, e.g. Case C-338/00 P *Volkswagen AG v EC Commission* [2003] ECR I-9189 para 147; Case 322/81 *Michelin v EC Commission* [1983] ECR 3461 para 111; Case T-148/94 *Preussag Stahl v EC Commission* [1999] ECR II-613 para 728.

[61] Case T-220/00 *Cheil Jedang v EC Commission* [2003] ECR II-2473 paras 48–60 in which the CFI sets out the methodology used by the Commission under the 1998 Guidelines.

[62] Case C-297/98 P *SCA Holding v EC Commission* [2000] ECR I-10101 paras 53–55.

[63] Case T-224/00 *Archer Daniels Midland Company v EC Commission* [2003] ECR II-2597 paras 197–206.

in one and the same cartel.[64] In *Volkswagen*, the Court reduced the fine imposed on Volkswagen from 120 million ECUs to 90 million euros, in particular because it found that the infringement had lasted for only three years (from 1993 to 1996), but the reduction granted was less than it could have been using the method set out in the 1998 Guidelines.[65] Thus, the reduction of the fine did not necessarily have to be proportionate to the reduction in the infringement period which the Commission had taken into account or correspond to the method of calculation which it had used. The ruling in *Dalmine* is an example where the CFI effectively reduced the fine using the Commission method to take account of the fact that the duration of the infringement found was erroneously fixed at four years instead of five.[66] Where the Court reviews the imposition of fines on several undertakings, it needs to give reasons if it departs from the methodology applied by the Commission in regard to any of the undertakings concerned.[67] These cases show that an applicant may be in a better position if it is able to obtain a reduction of a fine where it can be demonstrated that the infringement has not occurred to the extent alleged by the Commission (e.g., with regard to duration).[68] Conversely, it may be more difficult to have the fine reduced on grounds that the infringement did not have the gravity alleged by the Commission.[69]

---

[64] See the 'Lysine cartel' cases: Case T-220/00 *Cheil Jedang v EC Commission* [2003] ECR II-2473 para 229; see also Case T-224/00 *Archer Daniels Midland v EC Commission* [2003] ECR II-2597 para 378; Case T-230/00 *Daesang Corporation and Sewon Europe GmbH v EC Commission* [2003] ECR II-2733 para 152.

[65] Case T-62/98 *Volkswagen v EC Commission* [2000] ECR II-2707 para 347; confirmed by the ECJ in Case C-338/00 P *Volkswagen v EC Commission* [2003] ECR I-9189 para 149, although noting that when ruling on questions of law in the context of an appeal, the ECJ cannot substitute, on grounds of fairness, its own assessment for that of the CFI to rule on the amount of fines imposed on undertakings for infringements of Community law. The Court cannot therefore, at the appeal stage, examine whether the amount of the fine fixed by the CFI, in the exercise of its unlimited jurisdiction, is proportionate in relation to the gravity and duration of the infringement as established by the CFI on completion of its appraisal of the facts (para 151). See also Case C-310/93 P *BPB Industries Plc and British Gypsum Ltd v EC Commission* [1995] ECR I-865 para 34.

[66] See the 'Seamless Steal Tube cartel' cases: Case T-50/00 *Dalmine v EC Commission* [2004] OJ C239/13 paras 347–349; T-44/00 *Mannesmann v EC Commission* [2004] OJ C239/12 paras 314–316; Case T-48/00 *Corus UK Ltd, formerly British Steel plc v Commission* [2004] OJ C239/12 paras 219–221; Joined Cases T-67/00, T-68/00, T-71/00 and T-78/00 *JFE Engineering Corp and others v EC Commission* [2004] OJ C239/1 paras 588–590.

[67] Case C-291/98 P *Sarrió v EC Commission* [2000] ECR I-9991 para 98.

[68] Case T-44/00 *Mannesmannröhren-Werke AG v EC Commission* [2004] OJ C239/12 paras 259–270 in which the CFI concluded that the correct duration of the infringement found was four years. The fine imposed on Mannesmann had therefore to be reduced accordingly.

[69] Case T-59/99 *Ventouris v EC Commission* [2003] ECR II-5257, ECJ judgment of 11 December 2003 para 219 punished in like manner the undertakings which participated in two infringements and those which participated in only one of them, in disregard of the principle of proportionality. However, for reasons of equity and proportionality, the Court held that it is important that the companies whose involvement is limited to a single cartel are punished less

Where the Commission asks the Court to exercise its unlimited discretion **15.21** under Article 229 EC and increase the fine on an undertaking, the Court seems generally less inclined to accede to such requests. In this regard, increase often means the withdrawal of a reduction which the Commisison granted to an undertaking for not contesting the facts during the administrative procedure. The underlying issue which arises in this context is whether an undertaking which received a reduction under the Leniency Notice during the administrative procedure may be estopped from contesting before the Courts the fact that it did not dispute or acknowledged before the Commission, or whether this should open the way for a removal of the reduction. In *Stora Kopparbergs Bergslags* (*Cartonboard*) the CFI held that the risk that an undertaking which has been granted a reduction in its fine in recognition of its cooperation will subsequently seek annulment of the decision finding the infringement of the competition rules and imposing a penalty on the undertaking responsible for the infringement, and will succeed before the Community Courts on appeal, is a normal consequence of the exercise of the remedies.[70] The mere fact that an undertaking has been successful before the Community judicature should not justify fresh review of the size of the reduction granted to it. The issue whether an undertaking can go back on its cooperation under the Leniency Notice and claim before the Court that it had not participated in an infringement came before the Court again in *Tokai Carbon*. In this case, the Commission requested the CFI to increase by 10 per cent the fine imposed on Nippon which challenged the findings in respect of the duration of its infringement after having obtained a reduction of the same amount under the Leniency Notice. During the administrative procedure, Nippon had not disputed the facts on which the Commission based its allegations in the statement of objections but it did not expressly accept them either. Referring to its earlier ruling in *SCA Holding*,[71] the

severely than the companies which participated in all the agreements in issue. The Commission cannot punish with the same degree of severity the companies which the Decision charges with two infringements and those which, like the applicant, are charged with only one. In Joined Cases T-67/00, T-68/00, T-71/00 and T-78/00 *JFE Engineering Corp and others v EC Commission* [2004] OJ C239/1 paras 566–588, the Court found that the Commission violated the principle of equal treatment by omitting to take account of the European producers' second infringement (the contracts relating to the UK market) in determining the amount of the fine. Recognizing that the appropriate way of restoring a fair balance between the addressees of its decision would have been to increase the amount of the fine imposed on each of the European producers, it finally decided for procedural reasons to reduce the amount decided on by the Commission in respect of the gravity of the infringement: in view of the fact that the Commission had not pleaded in its arguments that the amount of the fine should be revised upwards in this case, the Court held that the most suitable way of remedying the unequal treatment as between the European and Japanese producers was to reduce the amount of the fine imposed on each of the Japanese producers by 10 per cent.

[70] Case T-354/94 *Stora Kopparbergs Bergslags v EC Commission* [2002] ECR II-843 para 67.
[71] Case C-297/98 P *SCA Holding v EC Commission* [2000] ECR I-10101 para 37.

Court held that where the undertaking does not expressly accept the facts, the Commission must prove the facts and the undertaking would be free to put forward any plea in its defence it deems adequate.[72] Since Nippon did not 'expressly', 'clearly', and 'specifically' acknowledge its participation in the cartel during the procedure before the Commission, it was not prevented from contesting the evidence put forward by the Commission.[73] However, the Court stated that the Commission could take the view on the basis of the facts presented during the administrative procedure that Nippon participated in the cartel, irrespective of Nippon challenging certain facts. The CFI partially allowed the request of the Commission to withdraw the reduction of the fine initially granted by the Commission to Nippon. The Court increased Nippon's fine by 2 per cent: it stated that the Commission could establish that Nippon participated in the cartel during the relevant period and secondly, Nippon's challenge made it necessary that the Commission drafted a defence dealing specifically with Nippon's challenge of facts which it considered that Nippon would no longer question.[74] The Court did not see a conflict with its earlier ruling in *Stora Kopparbergs Bergslags* because the latter did not deal with the issue of fine reduction. Thus, the CFI reiterated its right to increase the amount of the fine imposed on an undertaking which, after having the benefit of a reduction in its fine in return for not having disputed the substantive truth of the facts established previously by the Commission, calls into question the accuracy of those facts for the first time before the CFI.[75]

---

[72] Joined Cases T-236/01, T-239/01, T-244/01 to T-246/01, T-251/01 and T-252/01 *Tokai Carbon v EC Commission (Graphite Electrodes)* [2004] ECR II-1181 para 108.

[73] Joined Cases T-236/01, T-239/01, T-244/01 to T-246/01, T-251/01 and T-252/01 *Tokai Carbon v EC Commission (Graphite Electrodes)* [2004] ECR II-1181 para 109: '[. . .] Nippon's participation in the cartel between May 1992 and March 1993 was inferred by the Commission not from a clear and precise statement made by Nippon, referring expressly to that period, but from a range of evidence such as its conduct towards the Commission during the administrative procedure and its rather general no-contest statements. In those circumstances, Nippon cannot be prevented from pleading before the Court that that range of evidence was misinterpreted as proving its participation during the abovementioned period [. . .]'.

[74] Joined Cases T-236/01, T-239/01, T-244/01 to T-246/01, T-251/01 and T-252/01 *Tokai Carbon v EC Commission (Graphite Electrodes)* [2004] ECR II-1181 para 112.

[75] Joined Cases T-236/01, T-239/01, T-244/01 to T-246/01, T-251/01 and T-252/01 *Tokai Carbon v EC Commission (Graphite Electrodes)* [2004] OJ C251/13 para 113: '[. . .] It should be pointed out, in that regard, that the judgment [in Stora Kopparbergs Bergslags] against which the appeal had been brought, had not adjudicated on the appropriateness or otherwise of the reduction of the fine granted to the undertaking in return for its cooperation and that the judgment of the [CFI in Stora Kopparbergs Bergslags] which set aside in part the judgment of the [CFI], had likewise not dealt with the problem of the reduction of the fine. Having regard to that particular procedural situation, the fact that the [CFI] refused [. . .] to embark upon a fresh review of the size of the reduction granted to the applicant in that case must not be interpreted as meaning that the [CFI] cannot in any circumstances, in the exercise of its unlimited jurisdiction, increase the amount of the fine imposed on an undertaking which, after having the benefit of a reduction in its fine in return for not having disputed the substantive truth of the facts established by the

As regards the nullity of measures, the Community Courts always allowed the **15.22** Commission considerable discretion and confined themselves to verifying that the limits of such discretion had not been exceeded and that an error of law has not occurred. In various judgments,[76] the Courts has justified the latitude available to the Commission by referring to the complex nature of the economic assessments which the Commission is required to undertake in competition matters. Nevertheless, where the Commission has a power of assessment in order to carry out its duties, respect for the rights guaranteed by the Community legal order in administrative procedures is of even more fundamental importance. Those guarantees include, in particular, the duty of the competent institution to examine carefully and impartially all the relevant aspects of the individual case.[77]

In cases where the legal assessment is not straightforward and is related with **15.23** economic analysis, the Courts normally confine their scope of review. Where, for example, the object of an agreement is not to restrict competition, it must be considered whether it has an anti-competitive effect. The effect of an agreement must be appraised in the legal and economic context in which it operates. In *Van den Bergh Foods*, the CFI acknowledged that this might require the exercise of judgment as to the existence and extent of market foreclosure. In such cases, judicial review of Commission measures involving an appraisal of complex economic matters must be limited to verifying whether the relevant rules on procedure and on the statement of reasons have been complied with, whether the facts have been accurately stated and whether there has been any manifest error of assessment or a misuse of powers.[78] As stated previously, the CFI seems much more inclined than the ECJ to examine in detail the facts on which the

---

Commission during the administrative procedure, calls in question the veracity of those facts for the first time before the [CFI] [. . .]'.

[76] Case C-194/99 P *Thyssen Stahl v EC Commission* [2003] ECR I-10821 para 78; Case T-17/93 *Matra Hachette SA v EC Commission* [1994] ECR II-595 para 104 and Case 42/84 *Remia and others v EC Commission* [1985] ECR 2545 para 34.

[77] Case T-154/98 *Asia Motor France SA, Jean-Michel Cesbron, Monin Automobiles SA and Europe Auto Service SA v EC Commission* [2000] ECR II-3453 para 54 and Case C-269/90 *Technische Universität München* [1991] ECR I-5469 para 14.

[78] Case T-65/98 *Van den Bergh Foods Ltd v EC Commission* [1998] ECR II-2641 paras 80 and 135. Interestingly, in this case, the CFI has used similar language to describe the review under Art 81(1) and (3) EC—which may be indicative of similar standards—and states that the review carried out by the Court of the complex economic assessments undertaken by the Commission in the exercise of the discretion conferred on it by Art [81(3)] EC in relation to each of the four conditions laid down therein, must be limited to ascertaining whether the procedural rules have been complied with, whether proper reasons have been provided, whether the facts have been accurately stated and whether there has been any manifest error of appraisal or misuse of powers.

Commission relied in adopting its decisions and has departed from the previous practice of the Courts.[79]

2. Measures against which actions may be brought. *Locus standi*

Actionable measures

15.24 Article 230 EC provides that '[t]he Court of Justice shall review the legality of acts of the [. . . .] Commission other than recommendations or opinions'. The ECJ has made clear that '[a]s far as individuals are concerned, such measures must be in the nature of decisions and capable of affecting the applicant's interests by bringing about a significant change in his legal position'.[80] The Court has adopted a broad interpretation of the nature of Commission measures against which actions may be brought, which is not confined to final formal decisions but extends to certain decisions cloaked in administrative letters,[81] 'certain regulations',[82] and even 'other acts'.[83]

15.25 Regulation 1/2003 requires the Commission to adopt a formal decision in a number of circumstances, in particular where a fine is being imposed, but does not expressly provide for a similar requirement in all situations that may arise, although the Commission's act may affect the legal position of the parties to whom it is addressed. Thus, there may be measures that the Commission may take which may be decisions, though neither Regulation 1/2003 nor Regulation 773/2004 explicitly refer to them. The important question in deciding whether a measure constitutes a decision actionable under Article 230 EC is not the form but rather whether the content or substance of the measure itself is of direct and individual concern to an individual.[84] According to the Courts, the two main

---

[79] Including in cases in which it has relied on *Remia* to justify a summary examination of the facts. See Case T-17/93 *Matra v EC Commission* [1994] ECR II-595 paras 104 *et seq.*

[80] Case 60/81 *IBM v EC Commission* [1981] ECR 2639 para 9.

[81] However, it is not sufficient for a letter to have been sent by a Community institution to its addressee in response to a request from the latter for such a letter to be classifiable as a decision within the meaning of Art 230 of the Treaty. See Case C-25/92 *Miethke v Parliament* [1993] ECR I-473, and Case T-83/92 *Zunis Holdings and others v EC Commission* [1993] ECR II-1169 para 30.

[82] See, e.g. outside the context of competition rules, Case 101/76 *Koninklijke Scholten Honig NV v EC Council and Commission* [1977] ECR 797 concerning an action for the annulment of an article of an agricultural Regulation. By virtue of Art 241 it would be possible for an undertaking to challenge an act which affects it individually if it is understood to have been adopted on the basis of an unlawful provision of a regulation.

[83] As stated in Case 60/81 *IBM v EC Commission* [1981] ECR 2639 para 9, and, even more explicitly, outside the sphere of competition rules, in its judgment in Case 22/70 *EC Commission v Council (ERTA)* [1971] ECR 263 paras 39–42, in which the delimitation of the external powers of each of those institutions was in issue.

[84] See Case T-37/92 *BEUC and another v EC Commission* [1994] ECR II-285 para 38. In its defence, the Commission had contended that the letter at issue could not constitute a decision because it had been signed by a Director of DG Competition. The CFI held that the argument

criteria for a measure to constitute a decision capable of being challenged under Article 230 EC are: (i) that it must constitute the Commission's final position—an aspect which is particularly important in the case of measures or decisions which go through various stages—and; (ii) that it produces binding legal effects capable of affecting the interests of the parties and clearly altering their legal position.[85] The particular form in which acts and decisions are adopted is, in principle, immaterial as regards the possibility of their being challenged by an action for annulment.[86] In accordance with those two criteria, various forms of administrative letters have been regarded as decisions capable of being subject to judicial review: administrative letters originally sent by the Commission under former Article 15(6) of Regulation 17—so-called 'provisional decisions';[87] a letter in which a Commission official declined to adopt interim measures because in his view the Commission had no powers to do so;[88] letters sent by the Commission announcing closure of the file or the rejection of complaints.[89]

The Court also held that an undertaking imposed in conjunction with a Commission decision is a measure that may be challenged under Article 230. The Commission had contended that the commitment in question constituted a **15.26**

---

was not relevant to the examination of the admissibility of the action against that letter. See L Parret, 'Judicial Protection after Modernization of Competition Law' [2005] Legal Issues of Economic Integration 339–68 (357) takes the view that the decisive criterion should be whether the decisions of the Commisison contains an assessment of the factual and legal position of a party in such a way that this has consequences not only for the parties but possibly for third parties' rights.

[85] See Case 60/81 *IBM v EC Commission* [1981] ECR 2639; Case T-64/89 *Automec Srl v EC Commission I* [1990] ECR II-367 para 42; Joined Cases T-10/92 to T-12/92 and T-15/92 *Cimenteries v EC Commission III* [1992] ECR II-2667 para 28; and Case T-2/92 *Rendo v EC Commission* [1994] ECR II-2417 para 40. See also Case T-83/92 *Zunis Holdings v EC Commission* [1993] ECR II-1169 para 30; Case T-186/94 *Guérin Automobiles v EC Commission* [1995] ECR II-1753 para 39; Case T-241/97 *Stork Amsterdam BV v EC Commission* [2000] ECR II-309 para 49; and Joined Cases C-68/94 and C-30/95 *France and others v EC Commission* [1998] ECR I-1375 para 62.

[86] Case T-241/97 *Stork Amsterdam BV v EC Commission* [2000] ECR II-309 para 49; Case T-64/89 *Automec Srl v EC Commission I* [1990] ECR II-367 para 42; Case 60/81 *IBM v EC Commission* [1981] ECR 2639 para 9.

[87] See Joined Cases 8–11/66 *Cimenteries v EC Commission I* [1967] ECR 75. See ch 11.I.A of the 1st edn of this book.

[88] See Case 792/79R *Camera Care v EC Commission* [1980] ECR 119. Note that Art 8 of Reg 1/2003 now gives the Commission the express power to taken interim measures, but it remains to be seen the extent to which refusals to take interim measures can be subject to judicial review, given that such measures shall be taken by the Commission 'acting on its own initiative'. See ch 14 'Special procedures' para 14.09.

[89] See Case T-64/89 *Automec Srl v EC Commission I* [1990] ECR II-367 paras 52–58 and Case 142/84 *BAT and Reynolds v EC Commission* [1986] ECR 1899 para 2. The CFI also treated as constituting an actionable decision, statements made by the Commission spokesman concerning a concentration between air transport undertakings. See Case T-3/93 *Air France v EC Commission I* [1994] ECR II-121 paras 44 *et seq*. The CFI cites Joined Cases 316/82 and 40/83 *Kohler v Court of Auditors* [1984] ECR 641, in which an action brought against a purely oral decision was considered admissible.

unilateral act on the part of the undertakings which could not therefore be the subject of an action. The Court rejected the Commission's view outright and declared that the obligations resulting from the undertaking were to be assimilated to orders requiring infringements to be brought to an end of the kind provided for in Article 3 of Regulation 17 (Article 7 of Regulation 1/2003). Pursuing that particular course of conduct, the undertakings had, for personal reasons, agreed to acquiesce in a decision which the Commission could have adopted unilaterally.[90] The list is by no means exhaustive and the Community Courts may add to it if they consider it appropriate without the need of acting according to a restrictive interpretation. In regard to the rejection of complaints, the Commission's decision will usually take the form of a letter signed by a senior official. The ECJ considers those rejections as 'decisions' for the purpose of Article 230 EC: they have the content and effect of a decision, inasmuch as they end the investigation, contain an assessment of the agreements in question and prevent the applicants from requiring the reopening of the investigation unless they put forward new evidence.[91]

15.27 By virtue of the two above-mentioned criteria, none of the following have been regarded as decisions for the purposes of Article 230 EC: the formal commencement of the procedure and the forwarding of a statement of objections;[92] a refusal by the Commission to disclose certain documents contained in its files;[93] letters from the Commission asking complainants for submissions;[94] certain administrative letters sent by the member of the Commission responsible for competition and DG COMP's staff during the investigation of a case, suggesting amendments to a notified agreement.[95]

15.28 In cases of acts or decisions drawn up in a procedure involving several stages like the one for rejecting a complaint, and particularly at the end of an internal procedure, it is generally only those measures which definitively determine the position of the institution upon the conclusion of that procedure which are

---

[90] See Joined Cases C-89/85, C-104/85, C-114/85, C-116/85, C-117/85 and C-125/85 to C-129/85 *Ahlström, Osakeyhtiö and others v EC Commission ('Woodpulp II')* [1993] ECR I-1307 paras 180–182, citing the judgment in Joined Cases 6/73 and 7/73 *Istituto Chimioterapico Italiano and Commercial Solvents Corporation v EC Commission* [1974] ECR 223.

[91] Case 210/81 *Demo-Studio Schmidt v EC Commission* [1983] ECR 3045 paras 14–15; Case 298/83 *CICCE v EC Commission* [1985] ECR 1105 para 18, and Joined Cases 142/84 and 156/84 *BAT and Reynolds v EC Commission* [1987] ECR 4487 para 12.

[92] See Case 60/81 *IBM v EC Commission* [1981] ECR 2639 para 21. Regarding the nature of the measure formally initiating the procedure and the nature of the statement of objections, see above, ch 10 'Infringement procedures' paras 10.01 *et seq.*

[93] See Joined Cases T-10/92, T-11/92, T-12/92 and T-15/92 *Cimenteries CBR SA v EC Commission* [1992] ECR II-2667 paras 42–48 and 53.

[94] Case C-282/95 P *Guérin Automobiles v EC Commission* [1997] ECR I-1503 paras 33 *et seq.*

[95] See Case T-113/89 *Nefarma v EC Commission* [1990] ECR II-797 paras 66–81 and Case T-116/89 *Prodifarma v EC Commission* [1990] ECR II-843 paras 75–87.

open to challenge and not intermediate measures whose purpose is to prepare for the final decision.[96] As explained,[97] during the first stage, following the lodging of the complaint, the Commission collects the information which it needs to enable it to decide how to deal with the complaint. That stage may include an informal exchange of views between the Commission and the complainant with a view to clarifying the factual and legal issues with which the complaint is concerned and to allowing the complainant an opportunity to expand on its allegations in the light of any initial reaction from Commission officials. These preliminary observations cannot be regarded as a measure which is open to challenge.[98] In the same vein, the existence of an internal Commission report which was used as a basis for discussion in an effort to reach a settlement with the parties involved does not confer on a provisional statement of the Commission[99] the nature of a final position adopted by the Commission in relation to the complaint lodged by the applicant. The Commission is required to make a fresh analysis of the competition conditions, which will not necessarily be based on the same considerations as those underlying its previous internal report.[100] During the second stage, the Commission may indicate, in a notification to the complainant, the reasons why it does not propose to pursue the complaint, in which case it must offer the complainant the opportunity to submit any comments it may have within a time-limit which it fixes for that purpose. In the third stage of the procedure, the Commission takes cognisance of the observations submitted by the complainant and adopts a formal decision.

Letters setting out the Commission's views as to whether a document is pro- **15.29** tected by business secrecy and sent prior to a decision of the Hearing Officer on the matter are not actionable measures because they do not affect the undertaking's position immediately and irreversibly.[101] The refusal to give access to the

---

[96] Note that D Geradin and N Petit, 'Judicial remedies under EC Competition Law: Complex Issues Arising from the Modernization Process', 32rd Annual International Antitrust Law & Policy Conference Fordham Corporate Law Institute, 22–23 September 2005 (forthcoming) point out that in accordance with the *IBM* case law acts must not always be of definitive natures for them to be challenged if they fall within a phase that can be separated from the course of the proceedings leading to the definitive act. See L Parret, 'Judicial Protection after Modernization of Competition Law' [2005] Legal Issues of Economic Integration 339–68 (359–61) who also argues that inter-network decisions should not be excluded a priori from judicial review.

[97] See ch 12 'Rejection of complaints' paras 12.14 *et seq*.

[98] Case T-64/89 *Automec v Commission I* [1990] ECR II-367 paras 45–46.

[99] Case T-95/99 *Satellimages TV 5 SA v EC Commission* [2002] ECR II-1425 paras 12–13: '[. . .] the Director in charge of the matter sent the applicant the letter . . . and stress[ed] that the [. . .] comments are provisional and based on the information available to [the] department at present. They do not constitute a final position of the European Commission and are subject to any further comments you or your client may wish to make. [. . .]'.

[100] Case T-95/99 *Satellimages TV 5 SA v EC Commission* [2002] ECR II-1425 paras 34–41.

[101] Case T-90/96 *Automobiles Peugeot SA v EC Commission* [1997] ECR II-663. The letter merely stated that the Commission did not share the undertaking's point of view regarding

Commission's file is not a reviewable act because it is a preparatory measure forming part of a preliminary administrative procedure. The Court takes the view that the Commission could rectify any procedural irregularities by subsequently granting access to the file. Thus it could afford the undertakings concerned another opportunity to consult the file and to express their view.[102] Similarly, an action for annulment will not be allowed against a decision which has not been challenged in good time and which merely confirms an earlier decision, contains no new factors as compared with the measure and is not preceded by any re-examination of the situation of the addressee of the earlier measure.[103]

15.30 A decision under Article 24(1) of Regulation 1/2003 imposing a periodic penalty payment does not produce binding legal effects and does not therefore constitute a challengeable measure. That decision constitutes only a procedural step before the Commission adopts, where appropriate, a decision definitively fixing the total amount of the periodic penalty payment which thus becomes enforceable.[104] By abolishing the notification system, Regulation 1/2003 has removed from controversy the legal status of acts whose judicial reviewability was discussed under Regulation 17, such as comfort letters.[105] Other uncertainties may arise where undertakings seek to challenge the re-allocation of cases under Regulation 1/2003; whether decisions may be subject to review will often depend on national law. For example, the lawfulness of the transmission to the Commission by a national prosecutor or the authorities competent in competition matters of information obtained in application of national criminal law and its subsequent use by the Commission are in principle questions covered by the national law governing the conduct of investigations by those NCAs, and also, in the case of court proceedings, by the jurisdiction of the national courts. In an

---

the information which the latter maintained was protected by business secrecy, and that the Commission was prepared to communicate to the complainants more information than the applicant wished, and to allow the applicant time in which to submit its comments to the Hearing Officer.

[102] Case T-216/01 R *Reisebank AG v EC Commission* [2001] ECR II-3481 paras 46–48 referring to Cases T-10/92 to T-12/92 and T-14–15/92 *Cimenteries CBR SA v EC Commission* [1992] ECR II-2667 para 42.

[103] Opinion of AG Jacobs in Case C-123/03 P *EC Commission v Greencore* [2004] ECR I-11647 para 18 referring to Joined Cases T-83/99, T-84/99 and T-85/99 *Ripa di Meana v EC Commission* [2000] ECR II-3493 para 33.

[104] Case T-596/97 *Dalmine v EC Commission* [1998] ECR II-2383 in reference to decisions issued under Art 16(1) of Reg 17: '[. . .] Consequently, in a decision adopted on the basis of Arts 11(5) and 16(1) of Reg No 17, a provision such as Art 2 of the contested decision is only preliminary in nature, serving as a warning for the undertaking concerned [. . .]'.

[105] This question was dealt with by the Court in its judgments in the 'Perfume' cases. See specifically Joined Cases 253/78 and 1–3/79 *Procureur de la République v Guérlain* [1980] ECR 2327 paras 11–13 and Case 99/79 *Lancôme v Etos* [1980] ECR 2511 para 18.

action brought under Article 230 EC, the Community courts would have no jurisdiction to rule on the lawfulness, as a matter of national law, of a measure adopted by a national authority.[106] A possible, albeit non-exhaustive, list of actionable measures may be as follows:[107]

- decisions ordering the cessation of an infringement under Article 7 of Regulation 1/2003;
- decisions adopting interim measures under Article 8 of Regulation 1/2003 (although it appears that this does not apply to the refusal to take interim measures);[108]
- decisions adopting commitments under Article 9 of Regulation 1/2003;
- finding of inapplicability under Article 10 of Regulation 1/2003;
- decisions rejecting a complaint under Article 7 of Regulation 773/2004; and
- refusal to accept the confidential nature of information supplied to the Commission.

These decisions are notified to the addressee. The date of notification constitutes the starting point from which the two-month period laid down in Article 230 fifth paragraph EC for the initiation of annulment proceedings begins to run.

Locus standi

Actions of this kind may be brought not only by Member States, the Council, the Commission, and other Institutions, but also by natural or legal persons to whom the contested decision is addressed and persons who, although not directly addressed, are directly and individually concerned by a decision addressed to another person (fourth paragraph of Article 230 EC).[109] As regards

15.31

---

[106] Case T-50/00 *Dalmine v EC Commission* [2004] OJ C239/13 para 86 referring 'by analogy' to Case C-97/91 *Oleificio Borelli v EC Commission* [1992] ECR I-6313 para 9 and Case T-22/97 *Kesko v EC Commission* [1999] ECR II-3775 para 83. See above ch 3 'The role of the NCAs' paras 3.14 *et seq.*

[107] D Geradin and N Petit, 'Judicial Remedies under EC Competition Law: Complex Issues Arising from the Modernization Process', 32rd Annual International Antitrust Law & Policy Conference Fordham Corporate Law Institute, 22–23 September 2005 (forthcoming) 8–9 argue that for example Commission decisions under Art 11(6) of Reg. 1/2003 to recall cases from NCAs should also be challengeable on the ground that they constitute the end of a special procedure.

[108] See ch 14 'Special procedure' para 14.09. As explained, the Commission may want the refusal to take interim measures to fall outside the category of reviewable acts.

[109] In *Jégo-Quéré* the CFI undertook a review the existing case law on the possibility of private parties attacking Community measures of a general nature and proposed a new criterion for analyzing 'individual concern'. Case T-177/01 *EC Commission v Jégo Quéré & Cie SA* [2002] ECR II-2365. The reasoning was mainly based on the principle of effective judicial review based on the ECHR. On appeal, Case C-263/02 P *EC Commission v Jégo Quéré & Cie SA* [2004] ECR I-3425 the ECJ, however, refused to depart from the settled case law to allow more actions by private parties to be brought under Art 230 EC. The Court seemed to indicate that a more flexible interpretation of 'individual concern' in cases where there is no effective judicial review for parties

non-addressees of a decision, they may not claim that a decision affects them individually unless it does so by reason of certain attributes which are peculiar to them or by reason of circumstances in which they differentiated from all other persons, with the result that it distinguishes them individually just as in the case of the person addressed.[110] The mere fact that a measure may exercise an influence on the competitive relationships existing in the market in question is not sufficient to allow any trader in any competitive relationship whatsoever with the addressee of the measure to be regarded as directly and individually concerned by the measure.[111] The Court first allowed legal standing to a non-addressee in *Metro I* in respect of a party who had complained under Article 3(2)(b) of Regulation 17—the equivalent of Article 7(2) of Regulation 1/2003—and who objected to the granting of an exemption.[112] A complainant who is entitled to bring a complaint under Article 7(2) of Regulation 1/2003 and Article 5 of Regulation 773/2004 may sue under Article 230 EC. As regards complainants in the Commission's administrative procedure, the CFI has established that the fact that applicants (in the procedure before the CFI) have been identified in the contested decision as complainants, is not sufficient for them to be considered as individually concerned by those parts of the contested decision which do not deal with the issues raised in their complaint.[113] In *Metro II*, the Court widened the complainant category to cover a party who had not formally complained but who had taken part in the Commission's proceedings and been

---

goes further than the text of the EC treaty would allow. See L Parret, 'Judicial Protection after Modernization of Competition Law' [2005] Legal Issues of Economic Integration 339–68 (342–43).

[110] See Case C-25/62 *Plaumann v EC Commission* [1963] ECR 199; cited in the CFI judgments in Case T-2/93 *Air France v EC Commission II* [1994] ECR II-323 para 42. See also Case T-32/93 *Ladbroke v EC Commission* [1994] ECR II-1015 paras 41 and 42; Joined Cases T-447/93, T-448/93 and T-449/93 *AITEC and others v EC Commission* [1995] ECR II-1971 para 34; Case C-321/95 P *Stichting Greenpeace Council v EC Commission* [1998] ECR I-1651, and Case C-50/00 P *Unión de Pequeños Agricultores v Council* [2002] ECR I-6677.

[111] Despite the dictum in *Plaumann* to the effect that the provisions concerning individual entitlement to bring an action should not be interpreted restrictively (para 106); see also Case T-113/89 *Nefarma v EC Commission* [1990] ECR II-797 para 98, citing *Plaumann*.

[112] The Community Courts have held that complainants should be able, if their request is not complied with either wholly or in part, to institute proceedings in order to protect their legitimate interests. See Case 26/76 *Metro v EC Commission I* [1977] ECR 1875 para 13; Case 210/81 *Demo-Studio Schmidt v EC Commission* [1983] ECR 3045 para 14; Case T-37/92 *BEUC and NCC v EC Commission* [1994] ECJ II-285 para 36 and Case T-114/92 *BEMIM v EC Commission* [1995] ECR II-147.

[113] See Case T-16/91 *Rendo v EC Commission I* [1994] ECR II-2417 para 74. *Rendo* (para 72) relied on the case law of the Court whereby undertakings which have been identified in the act that they mean to contest or involved in preparatory inquiries may be directly and individually concerned by the said act. Joined Cases 239/82 and 275/82 *Allied Corporation v EC Commission* [1984] ECR 1005 para 12.

recognized by the Commission as having a legitimate interest.[114] Conversely, the question arises as to whether the fact of having made adverse comments on Commission publications prior to the adoption of positive decisions, is an essential precondition for the Community Courts to treat third parties purporting to contest a decision of this kind as being directly and individually concerned. On one occasion, the Commission appears to have taken that view, in connection with the monitoring of concentrations between undertakings.[115] In either case, however, it might be thought that, in analysing the interest of third parties in bringing proceedings, regard should be had rather to the applicant's circumstances as a whole, without including or excluding anything absolutely. If that were the case, and if the Court took that view, a person who had commented on a publication might be regarded as not being directly and individually concerned by a positive decision and a person who had not made such comments might be regarded as qualified to bring an action for the annulment of a decision which he or she had not opposed previously.

In *Métropole Television*, Antena 3, a TV service provider, was refused admission **15.32** to the European Broadcasting Union ('EBU') as an active member before the Commission adopted a decision exempting EBU's rules. Antena 3 brought an action to have the decision annulled. The Commission argued that it was not individually and directly concerned and had not submitted observations. The CFI, however, held that taking part in the administrative proceedings was not a prerequisite for being accorded legal standing and its application to join the EBU distinguished Antena 3 in the same way as if it were an addressee of the decision.[116]

In any event, it seems that where an applicant was actually denied access to the **15.33** market, this party is likely to be accorded legal standing.[117] In *Kruidvat* the Commission denied legal standing to a retailer who wished to challenge the Article 81(3) EC exemption of Givenchy's selective distribution system. It had

---

[114] The applicant in both *Metro* cases was a retailer who was excluded by the provisions of SABA's exempted selective distribution system from distributing SABA products. See Case 75/84 *Metro v EC Commission II* [1986] ECR 3021 para 20. See also Case 191/83 *FEDIOL v EC Commission* [1983] ECR 2913 paras 28 *et seq.*; Case 169/84 *COFAZ v EC Commission* [1986] ECR 391 and Case 43/85 *ANCIDES v EC Commission* [1987] ECR 3131 para 8. See also Case T-96/92R *Grandes Sources v EC Commission (Perrier)* [1992] ECR II-2579 paras 32–33, citing some of the above judgments.

[115] Case T-3/93 *Air France v Commission II* [1994] ECR II-121 para 34.

[116] Joined Cases T-528/93, T-542/93, T-543/93 and T-546/93 *Métropole Télévision v EC Commission* [1996] ECR II-649 para 67. Nevertheless, L Parret, 'Judicial Protection after Modernization of Competition Law' [2005] Legal Issues of Economic Integration 339–68 (355) takes the view that it would seem advisable that interested parties make sure they have clearly manifested themselves in an early stage of a Commission investigation to have stronger case at the Courts in terms of admissibility.

[117] CS Kerse and N Khan, *EC Antitrust Procedure* (5th edn, 2005) para 8–030.

not taken part in the Commission's proceedings, complained to the Commission or applied to become member of Givenchy's network, nor did it seek to be one. The Commission declared that to grant Kruidvat legal standing would be to allow a practically limitless number of actions from unforeseeable sources to be brought. The CFI agreed and stated that individual concern could not be established on the basis that the legality of the decision might affect indirectly related national proceedings.[118] As regards the addressees of a decision, the CFI has held that even they must prove a 'vested and continuing' interest in the annulment of the contested measure. In the absence of such an interest, an action by an addressee of a decision may also be regarded as inadmissible.[119] However, in the case of a decision requesting information (and, by extension, ordering an inspection), the addressees always, by definition, have a substantiated and real interest in obtaining its annulment.[120]

3. Pleas in law

15.34 Article 230 provides for four pleas on which actions under it may be based, although they appear to be encompassed in the third one, the infringement of the Treaty or any rule of law relating to its application. Given the large degree of overlap, the Community Courts usually do not specify under which heading the reasons for an annulment fall. The fourth ground, misuse of powers, means that the Community institution had used its powers other than for the purpose for which they were conferred.

Lack of competence

15.35 The concept of lack of competence covers different situations, which includes notably the lack of competence of the particular institution or official to take the challenged act. In such cases, parties allege that the power to take decisions was unlawfully delegated.[121] The delegation to the Commissioner responsible for competition of the power to take decisions ordering 'dawn raid' inspections

---

[118] Case T-87/92 *Kruidvat v EC Commission* [1996] ECR II-1931 paras 69–77.

[119] See Case T-138/89 *Nederlandse Bankiersvereniging and Nederlandse Vereniging van Banken v EC Commission (Dutch Banks)* [1992] ECR II-2181 paras 33–34. The Court considered that there was no vested (or 'present') interest in the annulment of the legal grounds of the Commission's negative clearance decision, since: (i) the banks' interest related to a future and uncertain legal situation (the possible action of the Netherlands' authorities, if they disagreed with the Commission and considered that the Dutch Banks' agreements were liable to affect intra-Community trade); and (ii) if the circumstances changed, so that intra-Community trade was affected, the applicant banks would have an opportunity to challenge a new Commission decision, if and when one was adopted.

[120] See Case T-46/92 *Scottish Football Association v EC Commission* [1994] ECR II-1039 paras 13 and 14.

[121] See, e.g. in Joined Cases 46/87 and 227/88 *Hoechst v EC Commission III* [1989] ECR 2859, in particular, paras 44 and 47.

under Regulation 17 was unsuccessfully challenged in *Akzo*.[122] Yet a challenge on both accounts (i.e., competence and infringement of an essential procedural requirement) of the infringement decision adopted by a single Commissioner succeeded in the *PVC* cartel case. The ECJ had however recognized a distinction between a delegation of powers and a delegation of signature, and acknowledged that the delegation of authority to sign is the normal means by which the Commission exercises its powers.[123] The plea of lack of competence has also been relied on in relation to allegedly extra-territorial action by the Commission, directed against non-Community undertakings or relating to agreements or action theoretically put into effect outside the Community frontiers.[124] The ECJ rejected the plea that the Commission had no jurisdiction to apply Community competition law in *Woodpulp*.[125] The case involved the anti-competitive conduct of forty-one producers and two trade associations having their registered offices outside the EC. The ECJ based the Community's jurisdiction to apply its competition rules to such conduct on the territoriality principle in public law. The issue of lack of competence is a matter of public interest and should therefore be raised by the Court of its own motion.[126]

Infringement of an essential procedural requirement

Not every procedural irregularity will be sufficient to vitiate a Commission **15.36** decision. The ECJ has classified the Commission's procedure in competition cases as administrative and non-judicial. As a general principle of Community law, a person seeking the annulment of an administrative decision on the grounds of irregularity must be able to show at least a possibility that the outcome would have been different *but for the irregularity complained of.*[127] The Court has treated as infringements of essential procedural requirements, *inter alia*:

- the failure to hear the views of the undertakings concerned regarding the

---

[122] Case 5/85 *Akzo Chemie BV v EC Commission* [1986] ECR 2585.

[123] *'Dutch Books'* Joined Cases 43/82 and 63/82 *Vereniging ter Bevordering van het Vlaamse Boekwezen, VBVB, and Vereniging ter Bevordering van de Belangen des Boekhandels, VBBB v EC Commission* [1984] ECR 19 para 14.

[124] e.g. in Case 57/69 *Azienda Colori Nazionali–ACNA SpA v EC Commission* [1972] ECR 933; Case 6/72 *Europemballage and Continental Can v EC Commission* [1973] ECR 215; and Joined Cases 6/73 and 7/73 *Istituto Chimioterapico Italiano and Commercial Solvents Corporation v EC Commission* [1974] ECR 223 among others.

[125] See Joined Cases 89/85, 104/85, 114/85, 116/85, 117/85 and 125–129/85, *A. Ahlström Osakeyhtio and Others v EC Commission (Woodpulp-I)* [1988] ECR I-5193 paras 11–23.

[126] Joined Cases T-79/89, T-84/89, T-85/89, T-86/89, T-89/89, T-91/89, T-92/89, T-94/89, T-96/89, T-98/89, T-102/89 and T-104/89 *BASF and others v EC Commission* [1992] ECR II-315 para 31.

[127] See e.g. 30/78 *Distillers v EC Commission* [1980] ECR 2229 para 26.

conditions and obligations which the Commission intended to attach to the renewal of an individual exemption;[128]

- the failure to give an adequate statement of the reasons for Commission decisions, in breach of Article 253 EC.[129] For example, in an early judgment in *Cimenteries* the Court took the view that a letter from a senior Commission official (in DG COMP) which presupposed an 'evaluation of facts and law' constituted a disguised decision.[130] The fact that the letter did not sufficiently state the reasons on which it was based for the purposes of Article 253 EC constituted grounds for the annulment of the decision. As regards third party applicants, the fact that they are not addressees of the contested decision does not prevent them from alleging infringement of Article 253 of the Treaty, since such interest as third parties directly and individually affected by a decision may have in receiving explanations must also be taken into account in evaluating the scope of the Commission's obligation to state the reasons for its decision;[131]

- the lack of sufficient evidence of the infringement;[132] and

- defects in the internal procedure for the adoption of the decision, such as the irregular authentication of the decision.[133]

15.37 Infringements of essential procedural requirements may be brought to the attention of the Community judicature by the parties involved in Commission proceedings, but may also be examined by the Community Courts of their own

---

[128] See Case 17/74 *Transocean Marine Paint Association v EC Commission* [1974] ECR 1063.

[129] Case T-241/97 *Storck Amsterdam v EC Commission* [2000] ECR II-309 para 82.

[130] Joined Cases 8–11/66 *Cimenteries v EC Commission I* [1967] ECR 93 para 92.

[131] See Case T-16/91 *Rendo v EC Commission* [1994] ECR II-2417 para 122, citing Case 41/83 *Italy v EC Commission* [1985] ECR 873 and Case 294/81 *Control Data v EC Commission* [1983] ECR 911.

[132] See recently, e.g. Case T-56/02 *Bayerische Hypo- und Vereinsbank AG v EC Commission* [2004] OJ C314/14 para 119: '[. . .] All of the evidence just examined permits the conclusion that the Commission has not adduced to the requisite legal standard proof of the existence of the agreement which it claimed to exist, relating both to the fixing of the prices for currency exchange services of the euro-zone currencies and also to the ways of charging those prices. It follows that the pleas alleging that those findings of fact are incorrect and that the inculpatory evidence is not probative must be declared founded [. . .]'. On the facts, the Court found accordingly for the applicant and annulled the decision. This occurred by way of a ruling on judgment in default; owing to fax error the Commission had not submitted its defense in time. Without taking into account the Commission defence, the Court assessed the applicant's arguments against those in the Commission's decision, but without the Commission defence and concluded that the Commission's decision was not founded on sufficiently cogent evidence. See also J Ratliff, 'Major Events and Policy Issues in EC Competition Law, 2003–2004 (Part 1)' [2005] ICCLR 47–66 (66).

[133] When the Commission adopts an infringement decision, therefore, the Commissioner responsible for competition lays the draft before the whole College at one of its meetings and the measure is adopted by the College. The ECJ confirmed that the failure of the College to adopt an authenticated version of the decision was one reason for the annulment of the *PVC* decision in Case C-137/92 P *EC Commission v BASF AG and others* [1994] ECR I-2555.

motion.[134] The Court has not taken an excessively rigorous approach in inter-preting the formal conditions relating to Commission procedures and decisions, and in general has taken the view that formal defects are not a basis for annul-ling the decision, except where the parties' defence rights are undermined or where, had there been no irregularities, a different result might have been arrived at in the administrative procedure.[135]

Procedural grounds may nevertheless give rise to annulment. In *PVC*, certain **15.38** irregularities of competence and form prompted the CFI not to annul a decision but to go so far as to declare it non-existent.[136] The CFI found differences in both the statement of reasons and the operative part of the decision between the version adopted by the College of Commissioners at its relevant meeting and the version notified to the parties concerned. On appeal, the ECJ considered that the absence of an authenticated original was not of such obvious gravity that the decision must be treated as legally non-existent, but would nonetheless constitute an infringement of an essential procedural requirement and hence a ground for annulment under Article 230 EC.[137] As the CFI has said 'it is

---

[134] See Case T-31/91 *Solvay SA v EC Commission (Soda Ash—Art 81: Germany)* [1995] ECR II-1821 para 37 and Case T-32/91 *Solvay SA v EC Commission (Soda Ash—Art 82)* [1995] ECR II-1825 para 43. Case T-241/97 *Storck Amsterdam v EC Commission* [2000] ECR II-309 para 74: '[. . .] The obligation to state the reasons for a measure with sufficient precision, enshrined in Art 190 of the Treaty, is one of the fundamental principles of Community law which the Court has to ensure are observed, if necessary by considering of its own motion a plea of failure to fulfil that obligation [. . .]' Case C-265/97 *VBA v Florimex and others* [2000] ECR I-2061 para 93.

[135] See Case 30/78 *Distillers v EC Commission* [1980] ECR 2229 para 26. See also the Opinion of AG Warner in that case (2267). For the AG Warner, Community law is distinct from French administrative law in that, under the French system, procedural defects in all cases render subsequent administrative decisions invalid. In Community law, those who attack the validity of an administrative decision are not entitled to rely on a procedural irregularity preceding the adoption of that decision unless they can demonstrate at least the possibility that, in the absence of that irregularity, the decision would have been different. This rule has been applied by the CFI in both staff cases and in competition cases. Amongst the latter, AG Warner cited the cases on the *Quinine* cartel: Case 41/69 *ACF v EC Commission* [1970] ECR 661 paras 47–53; Case 44/69 *Buchler v EC Commission* [1970] ECR 733 paras 15, 35 and 36; and Case 45/69 *Boehringer Mannheim v EC Commission* [1970] ECR 769 paras 15, 39, and 40.

[136] Case C-200/92 P *Imperial Chemical Industries plc (ICI) v EC Commission* [1999] ECR I-4399 paras 70 and 71: '[. . .] acts tainted by an irregularity whose gravity is so obvious that it cannot be tolerated by the Community legal order must be treated as having no legal effect, even provisional, that is to say they must be regarded as legally non-existent. The purpose of this exception is to maintain a balance between two fundamental, but sometimes conflicting, requirements with which a legal order must comply, namely stability of legal relations and respect for legality. [. . .] From the gravity of the consequences attaching to a finding that an act of a Community institution is non-existent it is self-evident that, for reasons of legal certainty, such a finding is reserved for quite extreme situations [. . .]'.

[137] In Case C-137/92 P *EC Commission v BASF AG and others* [1994] ECR I-2555, the Court upheld as part of Community law the theory of the non-existence of administrative acts which prevails in various Community countries—led by France—but confined declarations of non-existence to extreme cases. The Court heard an appeal brought by the Commission against the judgment of the CFI in Joined Cases T-79/89, T-84/89 to T-86/89, T-89/89, T-91 and 92/89,

essential that the Community institutions observe the principle that they may not alter measures which they have adopted and which affect the legal and factual situations of persons, so that they amend those acts only in accordance with its rule on competence and procedure.'[138] However, the Court has also

---

T-94/89, T-96/89, T-98/89, T-102/89 and T-104/89 *BASF AG and others v EC Commission* (*'PVC'*) [1992] ECR II-315, in which the CFI declared non-existent the Commission Decision concerning the *PVC* cartel [1989] OJ L74/1. The grounds for that finding were, *inter alia*, the lack of an original decision validly signed and duly authenticated, discrepancies between the decision adopted and the version notified to the parties and published in the OJ (which indicated, in the view of the CFI, a breach of the principle of the inalterability of Commission measures) and certain differences between the language versions. The Court considered that the irregularities concerning powers and form highlighted by the CFI, which related to the procedure for the adoption of the Commission decision, were not clearly serious enough for the decision to be declared non-existent, and set aside the judgment of the CFI. However, the Court did not refer the case back to the CFI but, giving judgment on the substantive issues, also annulled the Commission decision. It concluded that one of the irregularities referred to by the CFI (specifically, the failure to comply with Art 12 of the Commission's Rules of Procedure regarding the authentication of its measures) constituted an infringement of an essential procedural requirement of the kind referred to in Art 230 of the Treaty, for which reason the *PVC* decision should also be annulled. Once the Court ruled that its first *PVC* decision, albeit existent, was to be annulled, the Commission adopted a new *PVC* decision rectifying its past internal procedural errors. See [1994] OJ L239/14, IP, which was again subject to an appeal. Joined Cases T-305/94 to T-307/94, T-313/94 to T-316/94, T-318/94, T-325/94, T-328/94, T-329/94 and T-335/94 *Limburgse Vinyl Maatschaapij (LVM) and others v EC Commission* (*'PVC II'*) [1999] ECR II-931 on appeal partly annulled in Joined Cases C-238/99 P, C-244/99 P, C-245/99 P, C-247/99 P, C-250/99 P to C-252/99 P and C-254/99 P *LVM and others v EC Commission* [2002] ECR I-8375). The undertakings claimed that this would breach the principle of double jeopardy, or *non bis in idem*, and that the Commission had denied them the right to be heard by not sending a new statement of objections and holding hearings. The ECJ held that *non bis in idem* did not apply when the annulment was only on procedural grounds and that given that the Court had not found any defects in the preliminary stages, there was no need to repeat those stages (paras 54 *et seq.*).

[138] Case T-229/94 *Deutsche Bahn AG v EC Commission* [1997] ECR II-1689 para 113 and Joined Cases T-79/89, T-84/89 to T-86/89, T-89/89, T-91/89, T-92/89, T-94/89, T-96/89, T-98/89, T-102/89 and T-104/89 *BASF and others v EC Commission* [1992] ECR II-315 para 35. The CFI has followed the *PVC II* judgment in Joined Cases T-80/89, T-81/89, T-87/89, T-88/89, T-90/89, T-93/89, T-95/89, T-97/89, T-99/89, T-100/89, T-101/89, T-103/89, T-105/89, T-107/89 and T-112/89 *BASF AG and others v EC Commission (LdPE)* [1995] ECR II-729 (see especially para 73), relating to the Commission decision concerning *LdPE* [1989] OJ L74/21. The irregularities that made the *LdPE* decision be annulled were very similar to those of the *PVC* decision, which was adopted by the Commission at the same time. The *PVC II* judgment has also been followed by the CFI in its *Soda Ash* judgments. In three of them, Case T-31/91 *Solvay SA v EC Commission (Soda Ash—Art 81: Germany)* [2000] ECR II-1821; Case T-37/91 *Imperial Chemical Industries plc (ICI) v EC Commission (Soda Ash—Art 82)* [1995] ECR II-1901 and Case T-32/91 *Solvay SA v EC Commission (Soda Ash—Art 82)* [2000] ECR I-2391, the Commission's decisions were quashed for lack of appropriate authentication. The annulment was upheld by the ECJ in C-287/95 P and C-288/95 P *EC Commission v Solvay* [2000] ECR I-2391. In the other two, Case T-36/91 *Imperial Chemical Industries plc (ICI) v EC Commission (Soda Ash—Art 81: UK-Continent)* and Case T-30/91 *Solvay SA v EC Commission (Soda Ash—Art 81: UK-Continent)* the CFI clearly suggested that it would have quashed the Commission's decisions for the same reasons, were it not because it found other grounds for annulment. See, in particular in Case T-36/91 *Imperial Chemical Industries plc (ICI) v EC Commission (Soda Ash—Art 81: UK-Continent)* [1995] ECR II-1847 paras 21 and 26 and in Case T-30/91 *Solvay SA v EC Commission (Soda Ash—Art 81: UK-Continent)* [1995] ECR II-1775 paras 20 and 25.

stated that a measure which has been notified and published must be presumed to be valid. It would be thus for a person who seeks to allege the lack of formal validity or the non-existence of a measure to provide the Court with grounds enabling it to look behind the apparent validity of the measure which has been formally notified and published. Thus, the applicants should put forward any evidence to suggest that the measure notified and published has not been approved or adopted by the members of the Commission acting as a college. In particular, the applicant would have to adduce evidence that the principle of the inalterability of the adopted measure—leaving aside minor corrections of spelling and grammar—was infringed by a change to the text of the decision after the meeting of the College of Commissioners at which it was adopted.[139]

Where a Community institution is required to consult another prior to the adoption of an act, failure to comply with this requirement may be challenged by means of an application of annulment.[140] Thus, the failure to consult the Advisory Committee would most likely represent an infringement of an essential procedural requirement.[141] **15.39**

As regards the lack of reasoning, the extent of the obligation to state reasons depends on the nature of the measure in question and on the context in which it was adopted. The statement of reasons must disclose in a clear and unequivocal **15.40**

On the basis that the CFI held the *PVC* decision to be non-existent for the reasons indicated, undertakings have claimed on various occasions in actions for annulment that irregularity of the internal procedure for the adoption of decisions constituted a breach of an essential procedural requirement, but so far without success. See Case T-43/92 *Dunlop v EC Commission* [1994] ECR II-441 paras 22–26, and Case T-77/92 *Parker Pen v EC Commission* [1994] ECR II-549 paras 22 and 23; in Case T-34/92 *Fiatagri UK and another v EC Commission* [1994] ECR II-905 paras 25–27; and Case T-35/92 *John Deere v EC Commission* [1994] ECR II-957 paras 28–31. More recently, see in Case T-29/92 *Vereniging van Samenwerkende Prijsregelende Organisatie in de Bouwnijverhe (SPO) and others v EC Commission* [1995] ECR II-289, in which the CFI called on the Commission to produce the decision authenticated at the time of its adoption in the language in which it was binding. The CFI had detected some evidence that the principles set down in *PVC II* might not have been respected—the undertakings had been consecutively notified of two different versions of the decision—but finally agreed that the text adopted by the Commission was the one notified to the undertakings in second place, and that there was no irregularity that made the Commission's decision non-existent or void. See also Case T-106/89 REV *Norsk Hydro v EC Commission* [1994] ECR II-419, in which, relying on *PVC II*, and in view of the fact that the Commission *PVC* decision was not non-existent but had merely been annulled, the CFI dismissed the application for revision brought by *Norsk Hydro*, an undertaking involved in the *PVC* cartel which did not contest the above-mentioned decision within the prescribed period and therefore had to pay the fine which the Commission had imposed on it.

[139] Case C-200/92 P *Imperial Chemical Industries plc (ICI) v EC Commission* [1999] ECR I-4399 paras 66–68.

[140] See Case C-21/94 *Parliament v EC Commission* [1995] ECR I-1827.

[141] 'Quinine Cartel', see Case 41/69 *ACF Chemiefarma v EC Commission* [1970] ECR 661 cited by AG Warner in Case 30/78 *Distillers v EC Commission* [1980] ECR 2229. Warner also considered that the failure of the Advisory Committee itself to observe procedural requirements might be sufficient to vitiate the Commission's decision.

fashion the reasoning of the institution, in such a way as to give the persons concerned sufficient information to enable them to ascertain whether the decision is well founded or whether it is vitiated by a defect which may permit its legality to be contested, and to enable the Community judicature to carry out its review of the legality of the measure.[142] In this regard, it is not necessary for the reasoning to go into all the relevant facts and points of law, since the requirements of Article 253 EC must be assessed with regard not only to its wording, but also to its context and to all the legal rules governing the matter in question.[143]

15.41 In many cases, the applicants invoke the excessive duration of the administrative proceedings which is not in itself such as to impair the undertaking's defence of rights. For the purposes of applying the principle of good administration which involves a reasonable length of time to decide, the Community Courts distinguish between the investigative phase prior to the statement of objections and the remainder of the administrative procedure.[144] In a procedure relating to Community competition policy, the persons concerned are not the subjects of any formal accusation until they receive the statement of objections. Accordingly, the prolongation of this stage of the procedure alone is not in itself capable of adversely affecting defence rights.[145] In addition, in *FETTSCA* the CFI acknowledged that whilst the unreasonable length of the procedure, particularly where it infringes the parties' defence rights, justifies the annulment of a decision establishing an infringement of the competition rules, the same does not apply where the amount of the fines imposed by that decision is in dispute. The Commission's power to impose fines is governed by the rules on limitation periods which cover in detail the periods within which the Commission is entitled, without undermining the fundamental requirement of legal certainty, to impose fines on undertakings which are the subject of procedures under the Community competition rules. Thus the Commission could not put off a decision on fines indefinitely without incurring the risk of the limitation period expiring. In the light of those rules, there is no room for consideration of the

---

[142] Joined Cases T-213/95 and T-18/96 *Stichting Certificatie Kraanverhuurbedrijf (SCK) and Federatie van Nederlandse Kraanbedrijven (FNK) v EC Commission* [1997] ECR II-1739 para 226; T-241/97 *Storck Amsterdam v EC Commission* [2000] ECR II-309 para 73; Case C-278/95 P *Siemens v EC Commission* [1997] ECR I-2507 para 17; Case T-150/89 *Martinelli v EC Commission* [1995] ECR II-1165 para 65.

[143] Case C-367/95 P *EC Commission v Sytraval and Brink's France* [1998] ECR I-1719 para 63.

[144] AG Mischo in points 40 to 53 of his Opinion in Case C-250/99 P *Limburgse Vinyl Maatschappij and others v EC Commission*, followed by the judgment [2002] ECR I-8375 paras 178 *et seq.*

[145] Joined Cases T-5/00 and T-6/00 *Nederlandse Federatieve Vereniging voor de Groothandel op Elektrotechnisch Gebied and Technische Unie BV v EC Commission* [2003] ECR II-5761 paras 78–79.

Commission's duty to exercise its power to impose fines within a reasonable period.[146]

Infringement of the Treaty or of any provision of secondary law

This plea is put forward principally in connection with the Commission's inter- **15.42** pretation of the competition rules and of general principles of Community law in its decisions. Viewed broadly, this plea could encompass the other three grounds on which proceedings may be brought.[147] The CFI will annul a decision where the Commission has misinterpreted the law or failed to abide by general principles of law such as proportionality, non-discrimination, legitimate expectations, the presumption of innocence or legal certainty. However, this would go beyond misinterpreting or misapplying the law. It would also cover the Court finding that the Commission committed 'a manifest error of appraisal' and that the evidence relied on by the Commission do not support the finding. The clearest cases of infringement of the Treaty may arise where the Commission has interpreted as restrictive or abusive a clearly defined course of action of which there is sufficient evidence and the Court interprets it as not being restrictive or abusive, which means that the Commission has incorrectly applied Articles 81 and 82 EC.[148]

Misuse of powers

Community law does not diverge significantly from the administrative law of **15.43** Member States regarding the concept of misuse of powers. A decision is vitiated by misuse of powers only if it appears, on the basis of objective, relevant and consistent factors, to have been taken for the purpose of achieving ends other than those stated or of evading a procedure specifically prescribed by the Treaty for dealing with the circumstances of the case.[149] This ground has not so far

---

[146] Case T-213/00 *CMA CGM and others v EC Commission ('FETTSCA')* [2003] ECR II-913 paras 321–324 in regard to Reg 2988/74 which is now replaced by the limitation periods of Arts 25 and 26 of Reg 1/2003. See also Case 48/69 *ICI v EC Commission* [1972] ECR 619 paras 46–49; Case 52/69 *Geigy v EC Commission* [1972] ECR 787 paras 20–22, and Joined Cases C-74/00 P and C-75/00 P *Falck v EC Commission* [2002] ECR I-7869 paras 139–141.

[147] See CS Kerse and N Khan, *EC Antitrust Procedure* (5th end, 2005) para 8–050.

[148] Thus, e.g. in its judgment on the *Sugar* cartel (in Joined Cases 40–48, 50, 54–56, 111, 113 and 114/73 *Suiker Unie and others v EC Commission* [1975] ECR 1663, the Court considered that certain conduct regarded as improper by the Commission did not constitute an abuse of a dominant position within the meaning of Art 82 of the Treaty, and therefore partially annulled the decision and reduced the fines which had been imposed on some of the members of the cartel for that reason. See in particular paras 492 and 493 of the judgment. Another example is 'Adalat', Cases C-2/01 P and C-3/01 P *Bundesverband der Arzneimittel–Importeure and EC Commission v Bayer* [2004] ECR I-23, which confirmed Case T-41/96 *Bayer v EC Commission* [2000] ECR II-3383. The CFI had found that the Commission had not proved that there was an agreement within the meaning of Art 81(1) EC between Bayer and its Spanish and French wholesalers to limit parallel exports of Adalat to the UK.

[149] Case T-110/95 *IECC v EC Commission* [1998] ECR II-3605 para 83.

been successfully relied upon before the CFI in competition cases and the case law shows the exceptional character of this concept.[150] For example, in *European Beams Producers*, one applicant alleged that the Commission had abused its powers by holding negotiations with the steel industry with a view to bringing about a thorough restructuring of the industry, negotiations which it broke off just a day before DG COMP imposed a penalty on various steel operators in the sector for competition law infringement. Neither the co-existence of parallel negotiations between the Commission and the industry on restructuring the European steel industry, dating back to the 1980s, or even the 1970s, nor the 'coincidence' between the failure of those negotiations and the adoption of the infringement decision, constituted per se evidence of abuse of powers. The ECJ dismissed the claim that the administrative procedure was used for the purpose of forcing the steel industry to restructure itself or to penalize its lack of cooperation in that regard.[151]

4. Annulment of the contested measure

Partial nullity

15.44 The first paragraph of Article 231 EC provides that '[i]f the action is well founded, the Court of Justice shall declare the act concerned to be void'. However, the ECJ has consistently held that the nullity of measures of the other Community institutions may be partial, contrary to what might be thought if that provision were interpreted literally. Partial nullity of a measure will depend on whether the void part of the contested decision can be severed from the whole. If that is not the case, the result reached will be precisely as envisaged in Article 231 EC: total nullity of the decision. There is a relatively large number of examples in which Commission decisions in competition matters have been declared partially void.[152] If the Court opts for annulment, the Commission may restart the investigation at the point at which the error occurred.[153] Partial annulment must respect the principle according to which the Court cannot remake a decision; while it may remove elements from the decision which may

---

[150] For examples in which that ground was relied on and rejected by the CFI, see Case T-24/90 *Automec v EC Commission II* [1992] ECR II-2223 paras 102–108; Case T-5/93 *Roger Tremblay v EC Commission* [1995] ECR II-185 paras 85–93; see Case C-84/94 *United Kingdom v EC Council* [1996] ECR I-5755 para 69; and Case T-77/95 *SFEI and others v EC Commission* [1997] ECR II-1 para 116.

[151] Case C-196/99 P *Siderúrgica Aristrain Madrid SL v EC Commission* [2003] ECR I-11005 paras 526–532.

[152] Decisions of this kind may, e.g. lead to reduction of the fines imposed by the Commission.

[153] See for example Commission decision of 30 April 2004 in *Compagnie Maritime Belge* (COMP/32.448 and 32/450), adopted after the ECJ annulled fines imposed in the original decision ([1993] OJ L34/20) in Joined Cases C-395/1996 P and C-396/1996 P *Compagnie Maritime Belge Transports SA v EC Commission* [2000] ECR I-1365.

entail that the Court rewrites the decision to a certain extent, it abstains from adding new findings.[154] Typically, the Court might find that an infringement was only proved to exist for a shorter period of time than found by the decision.

The commission's obligations. Claims for compensation

The annulment of a Commission decision takes effect *ex tunc* and thus has the effect of retroactively eliminating the annulled measure from the legal system.[155] The first paragraph of Article 233 EC provides that '[t]he institution whose act has been declared void [. . .] shall be required to take the necessary measures to comply with the judgment of the Court.' The defendant is thus required to take the necessary measures to reverse the effects of the illegalities as found in the judgment of annulment. In the case of an act that has already been executed, this may take the form of restoring the applicant to the position he was in prior to that act.[156] However, it is not for the Court to issue directions to the Commission or to substitute itself for it.[157] This is particularly the case in the context of judicial review, where the administration concerned is under a duty to take the necessary measures to comply with the judgment of the Court, which applies to both actions for annulment and actions for failure to act.[158] Accordingly, the Court may not in judicial review proceedings under Article 230 EC order the Commission to adopt specific measures to replace the contested measure.[159] From a procedural point of view it may be more effective if ending the litigation would be achieved by allowing the CFI to take a final decision on

15.45

---

[154] Joined Cases T-68/89, T-77/89 and T-78/89 *Societa Italiano Vetro SpA v EC Commission* [1992] ECR II-1403 para 319.

[155] See Joined Cases 97/86, 99/86, 193/86 and 215/86 *Asteris and others v EC Commission* [1988] ECR 2181 para 30; Joined Cases T-481/93 and T-484/93 *Exporteurs in Levende Varkens and others v EC Commission* [1995] ECR II-2941 para 46; Opinion of AG Léger in Case C-127/94 *The Queen v Ministry of Agriculture, Fisheries and Food, ex parte H. & R. Ecroyd Holdings Ltd and John Rupert Ecroyd* [1996] ECR I-2731 point 74.

[156] Case 22/70 *EC Commission v EC Council* [1971] ECR 263 para 60; Case 92/78 *Simmenthal v EC Commission* [1979] ECR 777 para 32; Case 21/86 *Samara v EC Commission* [1987] ECR 795 para 7; Joined Cases T-480/93 and T-483/93 *Antillean Rice Mills and others v EC Commission* [1995] ECR II-2305 paras 59 and 60.

[157] See Joined Cases T-374/94, T-375/94, T-384/94 and T-388/94 *European Night Services and others v EC Commission* [1998] ECR II-3141 in which the CFI refused to annul conditions which the Commission had attached to Art 81(3) exemption and leave the applicants with an unconditional decision. Instead, it annulled the decision completely.

[158] Case T-74/92 *Ladbroke Racing (Deutschland) GmbH v EC Commission* [1995] ECR II-115 para 75. Annulling judgments thus require the Commission to amend or apply its decisions in the manner indicated by the Court. One of the clearest cases is the judgment in Case 17/74 *Transocean Marine Paint Association*, already referred to frequently [1974] ECR 1063, which gave rise to the Commission decision *Transocean III* [1975] OJ L286/24 (after the Commission had amended its Decision *Transocean II* [1974] OJ L19/18) and completed the procedural steps the absence of which had given rise to the proceedings.

[159] See Joined Cases 142/84, and 156/84 *BAT and Reynolds v Commission* [1987] ECR 4487; Case T-191/98 *Atlantic Container Line v EC Commission* [2003] ECR II-3275 para 1643.

the merits, especially in those cases where it is not clear for the Commission which measures it should take.[160]

15.46 In *Corus*, the ECJ held that in the case of a judgment annulling or reducing the fine imposed on an undertaking for infringement of the EC competition rules, it is the Commission's obligation to repay all or part of the fine paid by the undertaking in question, in so far as that payment must be described as a sum unduly paid following the annulment ruling.[161] The ECJ considers that the payment of default interest on the amount overpaid would seem to be an essential component of the Commission's obligation to restore the applicant to his original position following an annulment judgment, or a judgment exercising the Court's unlimited jurisdiction, since complete reimbursement of a fine unduly paid cannot ignore certain factors, such as the lapse of time, which may in fact reduce its value and during which the applicant did not have the use of the sums it had unduly paid. A failure to reimburse interest could result in the unjust enrichment of the Community, which would be contrary to the general principles of Community law. It follows that the Commission is required to reimburse not only the principal amount of the fine unduly paid, but also the amount of any enrichment or benefit it has obtained as a result of such payment.

15.47 In *Greencore*, the applicant also requested the Commission to pay interest on the amount of the fine overpaid after the CFI reduced the fine on Irish Sugar for breach of Article 82 EC. The Commission, however, transferred the principal amount due without interest. Following the ECJ ruling in *Corus*, the applicant repeated its request. In a letter to Greencore the Commission indicated that payment of the principal sum without interest was tantamount to a refusal to pay any interest, of which Greencore sought annulment before the Court. Before the CFI the Commission raised an objection of inadmissibility on the basis that the letter merely provided information and did not change Greencore's legal position and argued that the applicant should have brought an appeal when the Commission paid the principal amount. The CFI dismissed the Commission's objection of inadmissibility,[162] and its ruling was confirmed by the ECJ, which stated that the Commission's silence could not be placed on

---

[160] President of the CFI Judge Bo Vesterdorf 'Judicial Review and Competition Law—Reflections on the Role of the Community Courts in the EC system of Competition Law Enforcement', Speech at the International Forum on EC Competition Law, Brussels 8 April 2005. See also the published and edited paper version of the Vesterdorf's speech in Competition Policy International [2005] Vol 1, Number 2, 21.

[161] Case T-171/99 *Corus UK Ltd v EC Commission* [2001] ECR II-2967 paras 54, 55.

[162] Case T-135/02 *Greencore Group v EC Commission*, Order of the CFI of 7 January 2003 (not yet published).

the same footing as an implied refusal.[163] The letter therefore contained a refusal to pay interests and did not merely repeat an earlier refusal.[164]

The second paragraph of Article 233 also provides that the obligation to adopt a new measure complying with the judgment of the Court is not to affect any obligation deriving from the second paragraph of Article 288 EC. This means that the subsequent adjustment of the contested measure to meet the requirements of Community law does not release the Community institutions from any non-contractual liability which they may have incurred as a result of the adoption of the measure in its original form. **15.48**

If a Commission decision was annulled for formal defects, the Commission would not be required to terminate the proceedings and could rectify the errors and adopt a new decision in due form, on the basis of the same facts.[165] The reopening of the file in order to rectify errors and adopt a second decision on the same matter is also possible in the case of an infringement of defence rights.[166] Apart from that, it is more and more common for undertakings to claim damages from the Commission where its decisions are annulled.[167] The CFI has held that even if a decision were annulled, the Commission would not incur liability unless it had committed a sufficiently serious breach of a superior rule of law for the protection of the individual or had manifestly and gravely disregarded the **15.49**

---

[163] Case C-123/03 P *EC Commission v Greencore* [2004] ECR I-11647 para 45.

[164] It added that Greencore's failure to bring an action under Art 232 EC for failure to act to oblige the Commission to pay interest had no bearing on the question of admissibility of its action. Case C-123/03 P *EC Commission v Greencore Group* [2004] ECR I-11647 para 46. See T-135/02 *Greencore Group v EC Commission*, CFI judgment of 14 December 2005 (not yet published) in which the Court annulled the decision by which the Commisison refused to grant Greencore the right to claim payment of default interest.

[165] See, e.g. Joined Cases T-305/94 to T-307/94, T-313/94 to T-316/94, T-318/94, T-325/94, T-328/94, T-329/94 and T-335/94 *Limburgse Vinyl Maatschaappij NV and others v EC Commission* [1999] ECR II-931 paras 151, 257, and 266. See *PVC II* [1994] OJ L239/14. The Commission relied on Art 3 of Reg 2988/74.

[166] See e.g. Case T-37/91 *Imperial Chemical Industries plc (ICI) v EC Commission (Soda Ash—Art 82)* [1995] ECR II-1901 para 72; Commission decision of 30 April 2004 in *Compagnie Maritime Belge* (COMP/32.448 and 32/450), adopted after the ECJ annulled fines imposed in the original decision ([1993] OJ L34/20) in Joined Cases C-395/96 P and C-396/96 P *Compagnie Maritime Belge Transports SA v EC Commission* [2000] ECR I-1365.

[167] See Case 183/83 *Krupp v EC Commission* [1988] ECR 4611, and Case T-43/92 *Dunlop v EC Commission* [1994] ECR II-441 paras 180 *et seq.* (expenses incurred in providing security for payment of the fine) and Case T-77/92 *Parker Pen v EC Commission* [1994] ECR II-549 paras 99–101 (claim for reimbursement of the expenses of providing the bank guarantee); Case T-387/94 *Asia Motor France SA v EC Commission* [1996] ECR II-961 paras 106–111; see also claims for damages pending in the merger area Case T-212/03 *My Travel v EC Commission* (pending) application in [2003] OJ C200/28 and Case T-351/03 *Schneider Electric v EC Commission* (pending) application in [2003] OJ C71/37. In the past, these claims often failed because the applicant could not prove the unlawfulness of the alleged conduct of the institution concerned, actual damage and the existence of a causal link between that conduct and the damage pleaded.

limits imposed on its powers.[168] Thus, the mere reversal of a decision is usually insufficient to establish fault. Fault has been found by the Community Courts in cases of 'inexcusable mistakes' and 'grave neglect of the duties of supervision and obvious lack of care.'[169] In *Holcim*, the Court dismissed a request for reimbursement of its costs providing a bank guarantee instead of paying the fine. The Court held that the illegality of a Commission decisions fining Holcim for its participation in a cartel in the cement sector (which was earlier annulled by the CFI) does not necessarily constitute a sufficient breach to trigger liability, also taking into account that the case was extremely complex and required intensive legal and factual analysis.[170]

5. Enforceability

15.50   Article 244 EC provides that '[t]he judgments of the Court of Justice shall be enforceable under the conditions laid down in Article 256'. Article 256 EC gives detailed provision for the enforcement of financial obligations in accordance with the rules of civil procedure in the relevant EU Member State.[171] Such enforcement shall be governed by the rules of civil procedure of the State where it is carried out.

B. Proceedings for Failure to Act

15.51   Article 232 EC enables action to be taken against the Commission's failure to act.[172] The Court's approach in dealing with actions of this kind in competition

---

[168] Case T-120/89 *Stahlwerke Peine-Salzgitter v EC Commission* [1991] ECR II-279 para 74, cited in its defence by the Commission in Case T-34/93 *Société Générale v EC Commission* [1995] ECR II-545, note on judgment in [1995] OJ C87/10 para 81. See also Case C-63/89 *Assurances du Crédit v Council and EC Commission* [1991] ECR I-1799 para 28, relied on in Case T-34/93 *Société Général* [1995] ECR II-545 para 82. In Joined Cases T-80/89, T-81/89, T-83/89, T-87/89, T-88/89, T-90/89, T-93/89, T-95/89, T-97/89, T-99/89, T-100/89, T-101/89, T-103/89, T-105/89, T-107/89 and T-112/89 *BASF and others v EC Commission (LdPE)* [1995] ECR II-729 paras 127–128, the CFI dismissed the claim for damages of one of the undertakings because it was not supported by any argument or by any evaluation of the alleged damage so as to enable the CFI to adjudicate on it.

[169] Case T-171/99 *Corus UK Ltd v EC Commission* [2001] ECR I-2967 para 45 citing the case law in regard to Art 34 CS which is similar to Art 233 EC.

[170] Case T-28/03 *Holcim v EC Commission* [2005] OJ C155/14.

[171] Note that when the Court decides that a Community act does not comply with the treaties or when it provides interpretation of Community law, this decision has binding force and is applicable in all the courts of the Member States. Thus, the national courts are bound by the interpretation of the Court. This is also the case for public authorities.

[172] As it has been seen, Art 233 refers both to actions for annulment and actions for failure to act.

matters is laid out in the judgment in *Lord Bethell v EC Commission*[173] and *GEMA II*.[174]

1. Actionable omissions

Nature of the action not taken

Article 232 EC provides that natural or legal persons may bring an action for failure to act where the Community institutions have failed to address to that person 'any act other than a recommendation or opinion'. The measures typically likely to be adopted by the Community institutions are mentioned in Article 249 EC. Once recommendations and opinions are eliminated, as expressly required by Article 232, and regulations and directives are also ruled out because they are of general application, the only measures whose non-adoption can be the subject of proceedings by individuals are decisions. However, in administrative proceedings before the Commission under competition law there may be acts that fall short of formal decisions yet that can be subject to an action by individuals for failure to act, namely letters sent pursuant to Article 7 of Regulation 773/2004.[175]

15.52

The failure to act must involve 'an infringement of the Treaty'. This requirement has been interpreted as allowing proceedings not only where the Treaty has been infringed but also where secondary Community law—including therefore Regulation 1/2003—has been infringed. Moreover, according to the Court, the term infringement implies that the Commission must be under a specific obligation to take action in the circumstances concerned.[176] Since the Commission can decide not to continue the proceedings whatever the circumstances, the Commission is not under such an obligation vis-à-vis complainants under Article 7(1) of Regulation 1/2003 (former Article 3 of Regulation 17), in so far as complainants may not require the Commission to adopt a formal infringement decision in cases which they have brought to its attention.[177] Nevertheless, complainants may require the Commission to take action in two successive

15.53

---

[173] See Case 246/81 *Lord Bethell v EC Commission* [1982] ECR 2277.

[174] See Case 125/78 *GEMA v Commission II* [1979] ECR 3173. See also the judgment in Case 8/71 *Deutsche Kompanistenverband v EC Commission* [1971] ECR 705.

[175] See Case T-28/90 *Asia Motor France v EC Commission* [1992] ECR II-2285 para 42 referring to Case T-64/89 *Automec v EC Commission* [1990] ECR II-367 and Case 125/78 *GEMA v EC Commission* [1979] ECR 3173 para 21 stating that communications by which the Commission rules provisionally, under the conditions set out in Art 6 of Reg 99/63 (now Art 7 of Reg 1/2003), on a complaint referred to it under Art 3 of Reg 17 (now Art 7 of Reg 1/2003) are not in the nature of decisions capable of having adverse effects and are not therefore open to challenge by means of an annulment action under Art [230] EC.

[176] See Case 48/65 *Lutticke v EC Commission* [1966] ECR 27, in particular paras 24 and 25 and the Opinion of AG Gand in the same case.

[177] See Case 125/78 *GEMA v EC Commission II* [1979] ECR 3173 para 18.

stages in proceedings for the rejection of their complaints. Firstly, under Article 7 of Regulation 773/2004—as under Article 6 of Reg 99/63—complainants have traditionally been entitled to be informed as to the lack of any grounds for their complaint to be acted upon, and therefore they are entitled to receive an explanation from the Commission. Secondly, although in the past complainants did not seem to be clearly entitled to require a formal rejection decision, the case law of the CFI has established that having submitted comments in response to an [Article 7] letter the complainant is entitled to obtain a definitive decision from the Commission on its complaint[178] and this element might have been picked up by Regulation 773/2004, Article 7(2). Accordingly, although the Commission is not obliged to adopt an infringement decision, it shall not refuse to adopt formal decisions rejecting complaints provided the complainant requests so. If no answer is received within two months, the complainant can bring an action for failure to act.[179]

The need for the applicants to be direct addressees

15.54 The third paragraph of Article 232 EC provides that any natural or legal person may bring an action on the ground that 'an institution of the Community has failed to address to that person any act other than a recommendation or an opinion'. In a first place the applicant had to be a person to whom the unadopted legal measure, which the Commission should have adopted without fail, might potentially have been addressed.[180] That requirement was not fulfilled, for example, in the case of *Lord Bethell v EC Commission*[181] in which Lord Bethell complained that the Commission had not adopted measures under Article [81] EC against infringements of the Community competition provisions committed by airlines. However, a decision under Article [81] EC would have been addressed to the airlines, not to Lord Bethell. Nevertheless, the Court later changed the direction of its case law when it held that '[t]he possibility for individuals to assert their rights should not depend upon whether the institution concerned has acted or failed to act',[182] a statement that made it possible for undertakings to bring an action against a failure to act provided that the omitted act is regarded as being of 'direct and individual concern' to them (in

---

[178] See Case T-186/94 *Guérin Automobiles v EC Commission* [1995] ECR II-1753 paras 23 and 34.

[179] Case T-28/90 *Asia Motor France v EC Commission* [1992] ECR II-2285 para 28.

[180] See Case 246/81 *Lord Bethell v EC Commission* [1982] ECR 2277. See also Case C-371/89 *Emrich v EC Commission* [1990] ECR I-1555 paras 5 and 6; Case C-72/90 *Asia Motor France v EC Commission* [1990] ECR I-2181 paras 10–12; and Case T-3/90 *Prodifarma v EC Commission* [1991] ECR II-1 para 35, all of which are cited in T-471/93 *Ladbroke v EC Commission* [1995] ECR II-2537 para 40.

[181] See Case 246/81 *Lord Bethell v EC Commission* [1982] ECR 2277.

[182] Case C-68/95 *T. Port GmbH & Co KG v Bundesanstalt fur Landwirtschaft und Ernahrung* [1996] ECR I-6065 para 59.

the sense previously explained), even in those cases where the addressee of the act would have been another party. For analogous reasons, complainants in proceedings for the application of the competition rules may not bring actions under Article 232 EC where the Commission takes a measure having the contrary or a different effect from that sought by them, since the Commission is not obliged to take a decision on the terms sought by the complainants—Article 7(1) of Regulation 1/2003 allows it, but does not compel it to do so, as has been seen. The only remedy available to a complainant in such circumstances is therefore an action for annulment under Article 230.

2. Preconditions

The second paragraph of Article 232 lays down as a precondition for proceedings of this kind the fact that the Community institution against which an action for failure to act has been brought before the Community Courts[183] has been called upon by the applicant to act. This call must follow a reasonable period of time that will depend on the matter concerned[184] and clearly on the act required that it must indicate the intention of the party to start proceedings if a failure to act finally occurs. Only upon the expiry of two months after the Community institution has been called on to act without it having defined its position may an action be brought, within a further period of two months. 'Defining their position' means that the Community institutions must adopt a formal measure—in this case, a decision on the issue raised, but not necessarily the decision sought by the applicant—or a clear and express view concerning that measure. This means, for example, a provisional communication under Article 7 of Regulation 773/2004 to the effect that with the information in its possession there are no grounds to conclude that the agreement complained of infringes Article 81 or 82 EC, the complainant being informed in both cases that it is inappropriate to adopt an infringement decision, and being allowed to submit observations.[185] The fact that the Commission informs the person seeking the measure that it is considering the question is not sufficient to prevent that person from bringing an action for failure to act. If the Commission were to define its position in the manner described above after the two month time-limit and the person seeking the measure had already commenced proceedings within the further period of two months, the CFI could halt the proceedings and order the Commission to pay the applicant's costs.[186]

15.55

---

[183] In proceedings for failure to act in competition matters, the Community institution will be the Commission and the judicial authority the CFI.

[184] Case T-127/98 *UPS Europe v EC Commission* [1999] ECR II-2633 para 38.

[185] See Case C-282/95 P *Guérin Automobiles v EC Commission* [1997] ECR I-1503 para 31.

[186] See, e.g. Case 75/69 *Ernest Hake & Co v EC Commission* [1970] ECR 535, and more recently, Case T-186/94 *Guérin Automobiles v EC Commission* [1995] ECR II-1753.

3. Consequences of the action

15.56 Where an action for failure to act in competition matters is upheld by the CFI, the Commission will be found to be at fault and will be obliged to adopt the measures necessary to comply with the judgment (first paragraph of Article 233 EC). Since judgments in actions for failure to act are basically declaratory, the CFI will merely state that the failure to act is contrary to the Treaty. The CFI will not take any steps to rectify the omission or even require the Commission to adopt specific measures, although the measures which the CFI considers appropriate may be inferred from the terms of the judgment. As in the case of actions for annulment, the fulfilment of the obligations stemming from judgments given in proceedings for the failure of Community institutions to act does not exclude non-contractual liability resulting from omissions declared by the CFI to be contrary to the Treaty (second paragraph of Article 233). The judgments of the CFI in actions for failure to act are also 'enforceable under the conditions laid down in Article 256' (Article 244 EC).

C. Applications to the Courts for Interim or Protective Measures

15.57 Where an applicant challenges a decision of the Commission under Article 229 or 230, the application does not automatically stay the operation and effect of the decision in question. Pursuant to Article 242 EC, actions brought before the Community Courts shall not have suspensive effect. However, Article 242 goes on to give the Community Courts the possibility of suspending the application of the contested act, where circumstances so require. In addition, Article 243 EC provides that the Community Courts may in any cases before it prescribe any necessary interim measures. The nature of the measures which may be adopted by the Community courts under either provision is basically the same, for which reason they are both described here in general terms as interim measures. In any event, it is very common in practice for actions to be brought jointly on the basis of both provisions. Applications of this kind are always related and subordinate to a main action—either under Article 230 EC (annulment) or Article 232 EC (failure to act)—and may be submitted only after or at the same time as the main action is brought.[187] In any event—and this is very important—submission must be by means of a separate document, in which reasons must be set out justifying the urgent need for interim measures. Applications for suspension of the operation of the contested measure under Article 242 may be brought concerning procedural decisions based on Article 18 and

---

[187] If the main action is manifestly inadmissible, the application for interim relief must also fail. Case C-117/91 R *Jean-Marc Bosnan v EC Commission* [1991] ECR I-3353 para 7.

Article 20 of Regulation 1/2003 (i.e. requests for information and inspections) and substantive decisions, principally under Article 7 of Regulation 1/2003 (i.e. infringement of Articles 81 and 82 EC). In the past, undertakings have requested (and sometimes secured) both suspension of the operation of Commission decisions imposing fines,[188] prescribing certain conduct or prohibiting other conduct,[189] and the suspension of inspection decisions (although in such cases no undertaking has so far been successful).[190]

Article 104(1) of the CFI Rules of Procedure spells out the requirements for **15.58** undertakings that seek to apply to the Court with a view to obtaining the suspension of an act or decision or any other interim relief stating that '[a]n application [to suspend the operation of measure or for any other interim measure] shall state the subject-matter of the proceedings, the circumstances giving rise to urgency and the pleas of fact and law establishing a prima facie case for the interim measures applied for.'[191] The President of the CFI may grant the application even before the observations of the opposite party have been submitted.[192] This decision may be varied or cancelled even without any application being made by any party. The suspension may be partial and in practice is usually limited to certain parts of the contested decision, which in all other

---

[188] The Community Courts take a very strict approach to this issue. For this reason it has become extremely difficult to be granted a suspension without a bank guarantee. See, e.g. Cases T-104/95 R *Tsimenta Chalkidos v EC Commission* [1995] ECR II-2235 or T-18/96R *SCK & NCK v EC Commission* [1996] ECR II-407; see also Case T-191/98 R II *Cho Yang Shipping v EC Commission* [2000] ECR II-2551 and on appeal Case C-361/00 P(R) *Cho Yang Shipping v EC Commission* [2000] ECR I-11657. See also paras 15.04 *et seq.* above.

[189] See, e.g. Case 27/76 R *United Brands v EC Commission* [1976] ECR 425 where the Court suspended part of the Commission's decision requiring United Brands to refrain from charging discriminatory and unfair selling prices for bananas; Cases 76–77/89 and 91/89 R *Radio Telefis Eireann v EC Commission (Magill)* [1989] ECR 1141 in which the Court suspended part of the Commission's decision which would have required the broadcasters to grant compulsory licence of their programme schedules, admitting that the case raised delicate questions concerning the scope of Art 82; Case C-56/89 R *Publishers' Association v EC Commission* [1989] ECR I-1693 in which the Court suspended part of the Commission's decision requiring substantial amendments to the agreements in question.

[190] Thus, e.g. *Hoechst* unsuccessfully sought suspension of a Commission inspection decision adopted in 1988. Case 46/87 R *Hoechst AG v EC Commission* [1987] ECR 1549. See also Case 85/87 R *Dow Chemical v EC Commission* [1987] ECR 4367. Nevertheless, the Court's view seems to have changed. In an Order issued recently in *Akzo Nobel*, the President of the CFI pointed out this tendency when assuring that except in 'very special circumstances' defence rights prevail over 'considerations of administrative efficiency and of resource allocation'. Order of the President of the CFI in Cases T-125/03 R and T-253/03 R *Akzo Nobel Chemicals v EC Commission* [2003] ECR II-4771 para 186, annulled in Case C-7/04 P(R) *EC Commisison v Akzo Nobel* [2004] ECR I-8739.

[191] As amended, last amendment [2005] OJ L298/1. See also the similar provision, Art 83(1) of the ECJ Rules of Procedure, as amended, last amendment [2005] L288/51, available of http://curia.eu.int.

[192] Art 105(2) of the CFI Rules of Procedure. See Case T-184/01 R *IMS Health v EC Commission* [2001] ECR II-3193.

respects remains directly enforceable. The primary aim of interim measures in general is to guarantee the full effectiveness of the definitive future decision, in order to ensure that there is no lacuna in the legal protection provided by the Community Courts.[193] An application under Article 243 EC to suspend the operation of a measure adopted by an institution is admissible only if the applicant is challenging that measure in proceedings before the Court. In addition, an application for the adoption of any other interim measure referred to in Article 243 EC is admissible only if it is made by a party to a case before the CFI and relates to that case. In order for a decision to be suspended, the applicants must state the circumstances giving rise to urgency and the pleas of fact and law establishing a prima facie case for the interim measures sought. The measures sought must be necessary in order to avoid serious and irreparable damage to the applicant's interests arising before a decision is reached in the main action and provisional in that they must not prejudge that decision or neutralize in advance its effects.[194] Those conditions are cumulative, so that an application for interim measures must be dismissed if any one of them is absent.[195] It is for the party seeking suspension of the operation of an act to prove that it cannot wait for the outcome of the main proceedings without suffering damage of that kind.[196] In the context of that overall examination, the judge dealing with the application must exercise the broad discretion which he or she enjoys when determining the manner in which those various conditions are to be examined in the light of the specific circumstances of each case.[197] Article 107 (1) of the CFI Rules of Procedure states that '[t]he decision on the application shall take the form of a reasoned order'.[198] It has, however, been held that a judge dealing with an application for interim relief cannot be required to reply expressly to all the points of fact and law raised in the course of the interim proceedings. In particular, it is sufficient that the reasons given by the judge dealing with the application at first

---

[193] Order of the President of the ECJ Case C-7/04 *EC Commission v Akzo Nobel* [2004] ECR I-8739 para 36.

[194] Order of the President of the CFI in Case T-184/01 R *IMS Health v EC Commission* [2002] ECR-II 3193 para 47; Case T-65/98 R *Van den Berg-Foods Ltd v EC Commisison* [1998] ECR II-4653; orders in Joined Cases 76/89 R, 77/89 R and 91/89 R *RTE and others v EC Commission* [1989] ECR 1141 para 12; Case C-149/95 P(R) *EC Commission v Atlantic Container Line and others* [1995] ECR I-2165 para 22 and Case C-268/96 P(R) *SCK and FNK v EC Commission* [1996] ECR I-4971 para 30.

[195] Order of the President of the ECJ Case C-7/04 P(R) *EC Commission v Akzo Nobel* [2004] ECR I-8739 para. 28.

[196] Order of the President of the CFI in Joined Cases T-38/99 R to T-42/99 R, T-45/99 R and T-48/99 R *Sociedade Agrícola dos Arinhos and others v EC Commission* [1999] ECR II-2567 para 42.

[197] Case T-201/04 R *Microsoft v EC Commission* [2005] OJ C69/16 para 72.

[198] As amended, last amendment [2005] OJ L298/1; see also Art 86(1) of the ECJ Rules of Procedure, as amemded, last amendment [2005] OJ L288/51, available at http://curia.eu.int.

instance validly justify his order in the light of the circumstances of the case and enable the ECJ to exercise its powers of review.[199]

The Court hearing the application evaluates whether the arguments put forward **15.59** by the applicant cannot be dismissed at that stage of the procedure without a more detailed examination.[200] In particular, where the applicant seeks interim relief against an interim decision, the applicant is not required to demonstrate a particularly strong or serious stateable case against the validity of what constitutes a prima facie evaluation by the Commission of the existence of an infringement of Community competition law.[201] The urgency of an application for interim relief must be assessed in the light of the need for an interlocutory order in order to avoid serious and irreparable damage to the party seeking the relief.[202] It is sufficient for the harm, particularly where it depends on the occurrence of a number of factors, to be foreseeable with a sufficient degree of probability.[203]

Commonly, the Court has taken the view that damage of a purely financial **15.60** nature cannot, save in exceptional circumstances, be regarded as irreparable, or even as being reparable only with difficulty, if it can ultimately be the subject of financial compensation.[204] Interim relief is generally not granted in respect of financial damage unless the applicant is in a position to adduce evidence that would justify a prima facie finding that, failing the relief sought, the losses alleged would be such as to threaten its survival on the relevant market.

However, in *IMS Health* the CFI stated that the case law on the interpretation of **15.61** the notion of damage is mainly based on the '[. . .] premise that damage of

---

[199] Order of the President of the Court of Justice in Case C-159/98 P(R) *Netherlands Antilles v EC Council* [1998] ECR I-4147 para 70.

[200] Case T-395/94 R *Atlantic Container Line and others v EC Commission* [1995] ECR II-595 para 26; Case T-184/01 *IMS Health Inc v EC Commission* [2001] II-3193 paras 59 and 60; Case T-41/96 R *Bayer AG v EC Commission* [1996] ECR II-381 para 42: '[. . .] the applicant's arguments do not appear prima facie to be manifestly lacking foundation [. . .]'; Order of the President of the CFI in Case T-201/04 R *Microsoft v EC Commission* [2005] OJ C69/16 paras 204–225 stating that arguments which Microsoft put forward concerning the issues raised in the main case could not be regarded as prima facie unfounded in the interim-relief proceedings.

[201] Case T-184/01 *IMS Health Inc v EC Commission* [2001] II-3193 para 66.

[202] Orders in Case C-268/96 P(R) *Stichting Certificatie Kraanverhuurbedrijf (SCK) and Federatie van Nederlandse Kraanverhuurbedrijven (FNK) v EC Commission* [1996] ECR I-4971 para 30; Case C-329/99 P(R) *Pfizer Animal Health v EC Council* [1999] ECR I-8343 para 94; and Case C-471/00 P(R) *EC Commission v Cambridge Healthcare Supplies* [2001] ECR I-2865 para 107.

[203] Case C-335/99 P(R) *HFB and others v EC Commission* [1999] ECR I-8705 para 67; Case T-237/99 R BP *Nederland and others v EC Commission* [2000] ECR II-3849 para 49; Case T-201/04 R *Microsoft v EC Commission* [2005] OJ C69/16 para 241.

[204] Orders in C-213/91 *Abertal SAT Ltda and others v EC Commission* [1991] ECR I-5109 para 24; Case T-230/97 R *Comafrica and Dole v EC Commission* [1997] ECR II-1589 para 32; Case T-137/00 *Cambridge Healthcare Supplies Ltd v EC Commission* [2002] ECR II-4945 para 113; Case T-339/00 R *Bactria v EC Commission* [2002] ECR II-2287 para 94.

a financial nature that is not eliminated by the implementation of the judgment in the main proceedings constitutes an economic loss which may be made good by the means of redress provided for in the Treaty, in particular Articles 235 EC and 288 EC [. . .]'.[205] It stated however that prospects for an adequate redress would be difficult to ascertain where the applicant is basically limited to seeking redress before national courts. Having regard to the broad discretion enjoyed by the Commission in deciding whether it is appropriate to adopt interim decisions, it would seem unlikely that the applicant could succeed in any action for damages brought against the Commission on the grounds that the Commission had manifestly and gravely disregarded the limits on its discretion.[206] While these factors as such did not threaten the survival of IMS Health in the market, the President of the CFI concluded that there would be a real and tangible risk that execution of the Commission decision could, before judgment in the main action, cause serious and irreparable harm to IMS Health because it might trigger market developments that would be very difficult, if not impossible, later to reverse[207] and imposed significant restrictions on the freedom to define its business policy.[208]

15.62 Similarly, the President of the CFI in *Adalat* took the view that the immediate implementation of the prohibition imposed by the Commission to refuse supplies to wholesalers in order to prevent an increase in parallel exports might deprive *Bayer* of its independence in defining its business policy. The risk of serious damage would stem from price disparities in Member States over which Bayer had no control which might cause Bayer to lower prices in those countries to which wholesalers might export the drug.[209]

15.63 In *Van den Bergh Foods*, the Commission adopted a decision in which an exclusivity requirement applicable to freezer cabinets and contained in distribution agreements was held to constitute an infringement of the EC competition rules. When assessing the degree of urgency resulting from the application to suspend the immediate revocation of the exclusivity requirement provided for in the Commission decision, the CFI considered that this could have immediate serious and irreparable effects: competitors would make every effort to sell their

---

[205] Case T-184/01 *IMS Health Inc v EC Commission* [2001] ECR II-3193 para 119 referring to the Orders in Case T-230/97 R *Comafrica and Dole v EC Commission* [1997] ECR II-1589 para 38 and in Case T-169/00 R *Esedra v EC Commission* [2000] ECR II-2951 para 47.

[206] Case T-184/01 *IMS Health Inc v EC Commission* [2001] ECR II-3193 paras ECR 119–120; see also Case C-352/98 P *Bergaderm and Goupil v EC Commission* [2000] ECR I-5291 paras 41–44, Joined Cases T-198/95, T-171/96, T-230/97, T-174/98 and T-225/99 *Comafrica and Dole v Commission* [1997] ECR II-1589 para 134.

[207] See also Cases C-76/89, C-77/89 and C-91/89 R *Radio Telefis Eireann v EC Commission* [1989] ECR I-1141.

[208] Case T-184/01 *IMS Health Inc v EC Commission* [2001] ECR II-3193 paras 128–132.

[209] Case T-41/96 R *Bayer v EC Commission* [1996] ECR II-381 paras 53–56.

products through outlets which had previously been less readily accessible to which adds the seasonal nature of sales of the products in question, which are purchased largely during the summer months.[210] In such a situation, if the decision in question were to be annulled, the financial losses would have been extremely difficult to quantify for the purposes of making reparation, in the light of unpredictable variations in sales of such products. Moreover, there were serious grounds for believing that the market developments which immediate execution of the decision was likely to cause would be very difficult, if not impossible, to reverse if the application in the main action were subsequently successful.[211] The President of the CFI therefore ordered the suspension of the Commission decision.

Previously, in *Atlantic Container Lines*, the Court found that the immediate effect of the Commission decision would have been to preventing the applicants from pursuing a practice which had been current in Europe since the early 1970s, i.e., the joint fixing of rates by shipping lines in respect of the inland portions of through-intermodal transport services in the maritime sector. The President of the CFI agreed that the interruption of that practice might entail a risk for the operation of the transport market since the applicants could put forward credible evidence that if they were unable to jointly fix rates for that type of transport, a general collapse of maritime transport rates would be likely to ensue.[212] **15.64**

Ultimately, the Court's assessment hinges on striking a balance between the harm to the applicant from non-suspension—foreseeable with a sufficient degree of probability—with any harm which will be suffered by other parties if the suspension is granted.[213] In *IMS Health*, the President of the CFI did not agree with the Commission decision which had seemed to equate the interests of IMS' competitors with the interests of competition, thereby ignoring the primary purpose of Article 82 EC, which is to prevent the distortion of competition, and especially to safeguard the interests of consumers, rather than to protect the position of particular competitors.[214] In *Adalat*, the President weighed up the risk of major and irrevocable losses of profit faced by Bayer against the interests of wholesalers in Spain and France in increasing the volume of their exports to the UK and concluded that the risk of damage to which Bayer **15.65**

---

[210] Case T-65/98 *Van den Bergh Foods Ltd v EC Commission* [1998] ECR II-2641 paras 62 and 63.
[211] Case T-65/98 *Van den Bergh Foods Ltd v EC Commission* [1998] ECR II-2641 paras 65–67.
[212] Case T-395/94 R *Atlantic Container Line AB and others v EC Commission* [1995] ECR II-595 paras 51–57.
[213] Case C-445/00 R *Austria v EC Council* [2001] ECR I-1461 para 73; Case T-308/94 R *Cascades v EC Commission* [1995] ECR II-265.
[214] Case T-184/01 *IMS Health Inc v EC Commission* [2001] II-3193 para 145.

would be exposed would be disproportionate.[215] In *Van den Bergh Foods*, the Court not only weighed up the risk of damage to the applicant, but also noted a reduction of legal certainty as a result of a contradiction between the views of the Commission and those of the national courts in their application of EC competition law which earlier ruled that Van den Bergh's distribution system did not infringe Articles 81 and 82 EC.[216] In *Microsoft*, however, the CFI found that Microsoft had not adduced evidence that disclosure of the information previously kept secret would cause serious and irreparable damage. Following a factual examination of the actual consequences of disclosure as alleged by Microsoft, the President concluded that the required disclosure of information previously kept secret did not necessarily entail serious and irreparable damage and that, in the light of the circumstances of the case, such damage had not been demonstrated. Microsoft could not prove any of the following four points, namely that (i) the use by its competitors of the information disclosed would lead to its 'dilution'; (ii) the fact that the competing products would remain in the distribution channel after the decision had been annulled would constitute serious and irreparable damage; (iii) it would be required to make a fundamental change in its business policy; or (iv) the decision would cause an irreversible development on the market.

[215] Case T-41/96 R *Bayer v EC Commission* [1996] ECR II-381 paras 59–60.
[216] Case T-65/98 *Van den Bergh Foods Ltd v EC Commission* [1998] ECR II-2641 paras 70–74. The President took the view that the fact that Van den Bergh's competitors on the market found it difficult to distribute their products as a result of alleged structural barriers could not take precedence over the risks thus identified.

Part II

CONTROL OF CONCENTRATIONS (REGULATION (EC) 139/2004)

16

GENERAL ISSUES. SCOPE OF CONTROL

A. Introduction

Council Regulation (EC) 139/2004 on the control of concentrations between **16.01** undertakings[1] (hereinafter 'the Merger Control Regulation' or 'MCR') was published on 29 January 2004 and applies to the twenty-five Member States of the European Union. Like former Regulation (EEC) 4064/89,[2] the Merger Control Regulation is based on the recognition of the fact that achieving a single market involves the transnational restructuring of companies whose aim is to improve competitiveness and strengthen European industry in a globalized economy. In this context, the purpose of the EU rules for the control of concentrations is to avoid obstacles that prevent greater European integration, ensuring a level playing field between undertakings operating in the different Member States.[3] This equal treatment requires the application of common criteria and procedures that provide the necessary legal certainty under the exclusive control of the Commission, and the obligatory nature of the notification of concentrations with a Community dimension.

The Merger Control Regulation contains new substantive and procedural **16.02** features with respect to the Regulation it replaces, former Regulation 4064/89. The substantive assessment is no longer limited to analysing whether the operation creates or reinforces a dominant position, being now extended to all significant impediments of effective competition in the common market or a

---

[1] Council Reg (EC) 139/2004 of 20 January 2004 [2004] OJ L24/1.

[2] Council Reg (EC) 4064/89 of 21 December 1989 on the control of concentrations between undertakings [1989] OJ L395/1, amended by Council Reg (EC) 1310/97 of 30 June 1997 [1997] OJ L180/1.

[3] Recitals 2–5 of the Merger Control Reg. The Commission has published on the webpage for the Directorate-General for Competition (DG COMP) a memorandum containing the FAQs (Frequently Asked Questions) concerning concentration operations which explain various aspects of the Merger Control Reg in brief notes. This memorandum can be found at http://europa.-eu.int/rapid/pressReleasesAction.do?reference=MEMO/04/9&format=HTML&aged=-0&language=EN&guiLanguage=en.

substantial part thereof.[4] As to procedural matters, the new Merger Control Regulation reinforces the European *one-stop shop* principle for those concentrations that reach certain thresholds as well as the system of fixed periods—that are widened in general terms—for the assessment of the operation. Of particular significance are the changes with regard to the referral mechanism of concentration cases, so that each case is dealt with by the competition authority that is best placed to do so, limiting as far as possible the notification of the same operation to various competition authorities. Further, in line with the reform of the sanctions rules approved in the context of Regulation 1/2003 applying Articles 81 and 82 of the EC Treaty,[5] the Merger Control Regulation widens the Commission's investigative powers.

B. Basic Principles of Procedure under the MCR

1. Prior notification of concentrations

16.03 A fundamental principle of the Merger Control Regulation system is that undertakings must notify concentrations prior to their implementation once an agreement has been reached, a public bid has been announced or a controlling

---

[4] Art 2, paras 2 and 3 of the Merger Control Regulation, in relation with Recital 25. The Merger Control Reg extends its application to 'non-coordinated effects' or unilateral anticompetitive effects that may arise from concentration operations that take place in oligopolistic markets, that is, those effects that result from behaviour that is not coordinated between undertakings that do not have a dominant position on the relevant market. Thus, as Recital 25 suggests, the Reg makes possible the prohibition of operations that do not create or reinforce a dominant position, whether sole or joint, widening the scope of the examination of legality. The Merger Control Reg also expressly includes the assessment of the efficiencies that a concentration leads to, which could offset the negative effects of an operation. In order to give greater transparency to undertakings regarding the assessment of the impact of the operation on competition, the Merger Control Reg is accompanied by 'Guidelines on the assessment of horizontal mergers under the Council Regulation on the control of concentrations between undertakings' [2004] OJ C31/5. The package also comprises a Code of Best Practices on procedures in the control of concentrations, available to the public online at: europa.eu.int/comm/competition/mergers/legislation/regulation/best_practices.pdf.

[5] See Recital 38 of the Merger Control Reg. This alignment is clear from a simple comparison of the powers contained in Arts 11–15 of the Merger Control Reg and Arts 18–24 of Reg 1/2003. Both systems recognize the power of the Commission to send requests for information, carry out inspections on the premises of undertakings, check books, and other materials stored on any medium whatever, take copies, seal premises, interview and request explanations, as well as record answers, impose fines and periodic penalty payments. However, the Merger Control Regulation says nothing about carrying out inspections at the private residence of the directors and other members of staff of the undertakings concerned, unlike Art 21 of Reg 1/2003. On this point, see the comments of Mr Monti, Speech/02/252 of 4 June 2002. Further, there is a fundamental difference between both systems; as regards concentrations with a Community dimension the Commission has exclusive jurisdiction to investigate (although the national authority must assist the Commission), while with restrictive practices, the Commission and the NCAs share jurisdiction.

interest has been attained.[6] Breach of the obligation to notify may lead to sanctions being imposed.[7] In the initial years following the adoption of former Regulation 4064/89, the Commission was lenient with companies that did not notify or notified late, in particular when the operations concerned were complicated, it was not clear whether or not notification was necessary, and where there was no evidence that the companies concerned deliberately intended to breach the Regulation.[8] The Commission now takes a stricter line and has confirmed its intention to impose fines, not only where breaches are intentional but also where breaches are the result of negligence, contacting the companies concerned and taking the appropriate measures when it considers that an operation must be notified.[9] In 1998, a fine was imposed for the first time on a company for non-notification of a concentration in a case where deciding whether or not notification was necessary did not involve a complicated assessment of the relevant facts.[10] In practice, it is worth contacting the Commission,

---

[6] Art 4(1) of the Merger Control Reg and Recital 34. Reference to the need to notify the operation within one week of reaching an agreement has been removed. Further, the need for a binding agreement before notification is possible has also been removed. It is now possible to notify on the basis that the parties merely intend to reach an agreement. Recital 34 of the Reg requires that in such a case the parties must show the Commission that any such plan is sufficiently specific, 'for example on the basis of an agreement in principle, a memorandum of agreement or a letter of intent signed by all undertakings concerned'.

[7] Under Art 14(2)(a) Merger Control Regulation, the fine could reach 10 per cent of the aggregate turnover of the undertakings concerned.

[8] *Air France/Sabena* (Case IV/M.157) [1992] OJ C272/5 para 21; *Torras/Sarrió* (Case IV/M.166) [1992] OJ C58/20 para 3, in which the Commission abstained from imposing a fine in the light of the problems experienced by the parties when calculating turnover; *Hutchison/RCPM/ECT* (COMP/JV.55) [2003] OJ C223/1 para 6, Commission Press Release of 26 October 2000, IP/00/199 in which the parties had notified the transaction in accordance with Reg 17 as a cooperation agreement. The Commission declared in the Statement of Objections that it was a concentration and threatened to impose a fine for breach of the duty to notify under former Reg 4064/89. Finally, the parties duly notified the concentration which was approved by the Commission. See Competition Law of the European Community: N Levy, *The Control of Concentrations between Undertakings* (Matthew Bender, 2002) Ch 5 Section 5.13 [3][c].

[9] *Skanska/Scancem* (Case IV/M.1157) [1999] OJ L183/1 para 9: '[. . .] Skanska and Aker, however, did not share that view [note: a change in control that required notification] and thus maintained that the transaction did not have a Community dimension and should therefore not be notified to the Commission. In view of the parties' unwillingness to notify the transaction, they were informed that the Commission would carefully monitor Scancem to see whether appropriate proceedings were warranted. [. . .]'. In *Telefónica/Sogecable/Cablevisión* (Case IV/ M.709) (1996), the Commission sent a Statement of Objections to Telefónica and Sogecable declaring that Cablevisión had not notified the Commission and had carried out the operation after the Spanish government had authorized the concentration as having a national dimension. The parties ultimately filed the notification, but subsequently announced a termination of the deal. See Commission Press Release dated 22 July 1996, IP/96/677.

[10] Commission Decision of 18 February 1998 imposing fines for failing to notify and for putting into effect a concentration in breach of Arts 4(1) and 7(1) of Council Reg (EEC) 4064/89 (Case IV/M.920—*Samsung/AST*) [1999] OJ L225/12 para 29. The imposition of a fine for failure to notify included an even higher fine—33,000 euros—due to the fact that the parties

and, if appropriate, notifying an operation, even if the parties disagree about the need for this.[11] In this way, the parties may defend their position within the context of the Merger Control Regulation and they avoid the risk of being fined. Although the Merger Control Regulation has abolished the period of one week in which it was necessary to notify the operation, it is normally in undertakings' interests to notify as soon as possible, in order to advance approval of the concentration with the resulting lifting on the suspension of the operation.

2. Mandatory suspension

16.04 Article 7(1) of the Merger Control Regulation provides that the execution of a concentration that comes within the scope of the Merger Control Regulation must be suspended until a definitive decision is adopted or the presumption contained in Article 10(6) applies.[12] The Regulation does not elaborate on what may constitute implementation of a concentration. This may indeed be a critical point in many transactions. Given the purpose of this mechanism, the acquisition of the capacity to influence the activities of the target under-taking is unlikely to be permitted.[13] 'Gun jumping', as the breach of the obligation to suspend implementation is known, may result in the Commission imposing heavy fines (up to 10 per cent of the turnover of the business group of

---

executed the operation without the authorization of the Commission. As mitigating factors justifying a reduced fine, the Commission considered that the failure to notify did not damage competition, the operation had ultimately been notified, the breach did not appear to have been committed intentionally and Samsung recognized its failure before the Commission and cooper-ated with the latter during the proceedings. In Commission Decision of 10 February 1999 imposing fines for failing to notify and for putting into effect three concentrations in breach of Arts 4 and 7(1) of Council Reg (EEC) 4064/89 (Case IV/M.969—*AP Møller*) [1999] OJ L183/29 para 12, the Commission underlined the importance of Arts 4(1) and 7(1) in order for former Reg 4064/89 to work effectively. The size of the fine imposed on the Danish company AP Møller for failure to notify and execute three concentrations without prior approval amounted to 219,000 euros. Despite the token nature of the fines, the Commission Decisions *Samsung/AST* and *AP Møller* are still important since they show that the Commission was determined to use its powers to impose sanctions which it had under former Reg 4064/89. It is expected that under the Merger Control Reg the Commission will continue in this line, thus confirming its stated inten-tion to impose fines in this area.

[11] Recital 11 of Commission Reg (EC) 802/2004 dated 7 April 2004 applying the Merger Control Reg [2004] OJ L133/1, (hereinafter 'the Implementing Reg') provides that the Commis-sion must give the notifying parties the opportunity to discuss the proposed concentration in an informal and strictly confidential manner prior to notification. Reg 802/2004 replaces Commis-sion Reg 447/98 on the notifications, time limits and hearings provided for in Reg 4064/89 [1998] OJ L61/1.

[12] Art 10(6) provides that '[w]here the Commission has not taken a decision in accordance with Article 6(1)(b), (c) or Article 8 (1), (2), or (3) within the time limits set in paragraph 1 and 3 respectively, the concentration shall be deemed to have been declared compatible with the common market, without prejudice to Article 9.'

[13] For a brief elaboration on this point see Case T-3/93 *Air France v EC Commission* [1994] ECR II-121 para 80.

the company involved). When the parties ignore the prohibition on implementation and carry out an operation without obtaining authorization, national
courts may intervene in order to ensure compliance with the prohibition.[14]

There are three important exceptions to the prohibition on implementation: **16.05**

(i)   with respect to public bids and operations concerning a series of trans-
      actions 'in securities admitted to trading on a market such as a stock
      exchange';
(ii) when the Commission grants a derogation from the suspension obligations
      in accordance with Article 7(3) of the Merger Control Regulation; and
(iii) concentrations referred by Member States, that may have been imple-
      mented provided that, in accordance with Article 22(4) of the Merger
      Control Regulation. In this case, the obligation only applies if the concen-
      tration has not been implemented by the date on which the Commission
      informs the undertakings concerned that a referral request has been filed by
      one or more Member States.

Public bids and other transactions involving securities

The Merger Control Regulation provides that the suspension obligation does   **16.06**
not prevent a public bid or a series of transactions in securities admitted to
trading on a market such as a stock exchange which has been notified without
delay to the Commission, provided that 'the acquirer does not exercise the
voting rights attached to the securities in question or does so only to maintain
the full value of its investments.'[15] The new Merger Control Regulation has
extended this possibility, so far reserved to public bids, to cover a series of
transactions in securities admitted to trading on a market such as a stock
exchange and on the basis of a derogation granted by the Commission.[16] The

---

[14] As regards the civil consequences of implementation without authorization, see L Ritter,
WD Braun, and F Rawlinson, *European Competition Law: A Practitioner's Guide* (Kluwer Law
International, 2000) 519, who argue that the prohibition on implementing an operation without
authorization would have direct effect in national law and could therefore give rise to claims for
damages; they refer to a judgment of the Landgericht Düsseldorf of 16 April 1997, Zeitschrift für
Wirtschaft und Wettbewerb (WuW) 1998, July/August at 78, which discussed the implementation of a joint venture in the telecommunications area before fulfilling the undertakings requested
in the Commission's exemption decision. Note that the case was decided under Art 85 (now 81)
of the EC Treaty.

[15] Art 7(2) of the Merger Control Reg. If it is intended to exercise voting rights attached to the
securities in question in order to maintain the full value of the investments the undertakings must
first request a derogation from the Commission in accordance with the procedure set out in Art
7(3).

[16] The reference is to what the Commission has called 'creeping takeovers via the stock
exchange' (Green Paper on the review of Reg 4064/89, s 134). These are concentrations carried
out through multiple transactions that involve a certain number of acquisitions of legally separate
rights which, in economic terms, make up a unit, where the objective is to acquire the control of

content of this provision essentially safeguards the objective pursued by the prohibition on implementation, since it prevents the acquirer from exercising effective control without the final authorization of the Commission since it cannot exercise voting rights to determine the competitive strategy of the undertaking acquired.

The derogation: removing the suspension

16.07 The Commission may grant a derogation with regard to the obligation to suspend the implementation of the operation, including the obligation to refrain from using voting rights as discussed above.[17] There are basically two factors which the Commission must take into account when examining a reasoned request for a derogation. The first relates to the potential damage to private interests, while the second refers to the public interest:

(i)   the potential damage or negative effect of the suspension for one or more undertakings concerned or for a third party;

(ii) the extent of the threat to competition caused by the concentration, arising from the need to prevent the operation having adverse affects on the market.

16.08 Conditions and obligations aimed at guaranteeing effective competition could be attached to the derogation.[18] The breach of the conditions or obligations may result in the imposition of fines of up to 10 per cent of the total turnover of the undertaking concerned[19] or periodic penalty payments of a maximum of 5 per cent of the average daily aggregate turnover of the undertakings concerned for each working day of delay, from the day laid down in the decision.[20]

16.09 The Merger Control Regulation does not require any special procedure for these decisions, providing expressly that the request can be made and the derogation granted at any time, even before the notification.[21] In the event the

---

the undertaking being absorbed. The Commission's view is that such operations can range from direct and relatively straightforward share purchases from various previous shareholders to more complicated transactions which involve any number of financial intermediaries and a variety of different financial instruments. Despite the fact that normally such acquisitions on the Stock Exchange are not, unlike public bids, subject to mandatory rules that oblige the undertaking making the offer to carry out the transaction by a given date, Art 7(2) of the Merger Control Reg was drafted to include these operations, it being considered that, for practical reasons, Art 7(1) should not be allowed to impede such transactions being carried out if the conditions contained in Art 7(3) were fulfilled. (See ss 187–189 of the Green Paper.)

[17] Art 7(3) of the Merger Control Reg.

[18] For example, in *Eurostar* (Case IV/M.1305) [1999] OJ C256/3 para 5, the derogation was linked to the condition that British Airways would not be involved in the preparation and approval of Eurostar's budget and the business plan.

[19] Art 14(2)(d) of the Merger Control Reg.   [20] Art 15(1)(d) of the Merger Control Reg.

[21] Art 7(3) *in fine* of the Merger Control Reg. For example, see *FCC/Vivendi* (Case IV/M.1365) [1999] OJ C120/20 paras 1 and 2; *ING/Barings* (Case IV/M.573) [1995] OJ C114/6 para 7.

need of a derogation is anticipated, it is advisable to make the request as early as possible. Article 12 of the Implementing Regulation however sets some rules for cases where adverse effects are anticipated. In these situations, the Commission will take a formal provisional decision and invite the notifying and other interested parties to express their point of view, communicating the provisional decision and fixing a time period within which they can make known their views in writing.[22] Once this is completed, the Commission will adopt a final decision in which it will revoke, modify, or confirm its provisional decision. If within the period laid down neither the notifying parties nor other interested parties have made known their points of view, the provisional decision of the Commission will automatically become final on expiry of the said period.

In practice, the Commission is careful to ensure that the granting of the deroga- **16.10** tion is the exception rather than the rule. It therefore carries out an in-depth analysis to establish whether the circumstances really justify a derogation of the suspensive effect.[23]

The following examples illustrate the current practice of the Commission[24]

(i) *Urgent interim measures to ensure the success of the operation.* In *BT/Airtel*, the Commission granted a derogation to enable the parties to take certain measures to ensure the success of the operation.[25] Even as regards operations that consist in a simple restructuring, it is not sufficient to show that the operation does not damage competition. The parties must show the extent to which its situation is different from that of any other party

---

[22] Art 12 of the Implementing Reg.

[23] XXXIII Report on Competition Policy [2003], 'Statistics', 301: in 2003, the Commission granted eight derogations out of 212 notifications; in 2002, fourteen derogations out of 277 notifications. Note, however, that the information does not state the number of petitions.

[24] See also the categories in 'Competition Law of the European Community', N Levy, *The Control of Concentrations between Undertakings* (Matthew Bender 2002) Ch 5, 5.13[3][a][*ii*], with examples of derogations with suspensive effect awarded in situations in which the Commission had already started a second-phase investigation in *Nestlé/Perrier* (Case IV/M.190) [1992] OJ L356/1, and in *Mercedes-Benz/Kässbohrer* [1995] OJ L211/1. Some derogations were granted under Art 7(4) in the original (and stricter) wording of former Reg 4064/89 ('[. . .] to prevent serious damage to one or more undertakings concerned by a concentration or to a third party') whereas the wording of the Merger Control Regulation, which was the wording introduced into the former Reg 4064/89 following Reg 1310/97, appears to allow the Commission greater leeway ('[. . .] the Commission shall take into account inter alia the effects of the suspension on one or more undertakings concerned by a concentration or on a third party and the threat to competition posed by the concentration'.

[25] *BT/Airtel* (Case COMP/JV.3) (1998) para 6. The interim measures included the reduction in the number of Advisory Committee members, determining the special duties of the Managing Director and the creation of a committee to investigate technical areas in accordance with the agreement between the parties.

that has acquired a new business and wishes to exercise control over that business as soon as possible.[26]

(ii) *No negative effect on competition.* The Commission has shown itself to be prepared to grant a derogation provided that the impact on competition has been examined first, and it has been concluded that there are no competition problems. For example, in *Philips/Lucent*[27] and *Matra Marconi*,[28] the Commission had already examined the relevant product and geographic market for satellites in two earlier decisions involving the same parties.

(iii) *Fulfilment of prior commitments.* The purpose of the Mobil/JV operation (dissolution) was the cessation of Mobil's participation in a joint venture which was the fulfilment of a commitment made by the parties in *Exxon/Mobil.*[29]

(iv) *Threat of serious damage for the parties and third parties.* In *Kelt/American Express,* the Commission granted the derogation because it was 'convinced of the need to swiftly effect the restructuring operation in order to prevent serious damage to one or more undertakings concerned by the concentration.'[30] Similarly, in *ING/Barings* the derogation was granted because of the need to carry out the operation rapidly so that Barings and third parties did not suffer serious harm while Barings Holding was subject to insolvency proceedings.[31]

(v) *The need to fulfil legal requirements.* The Commission can grant a derogation if it considers this to be necessary for the parties to enable them, for example, to comply with the time periods stated in licences to build a telecommunications network.[32]

---

[26] *France Telecom/Global One* (Case COMP/M.1865) (2000) para 7. The operation did not give rise to any competition law problems. However, the Commission rejected France Telecom's request to take certain preliminary decisions such as the appointment of executives, considering that FT had not demonstrated the relevance and the negative impact involved in waiting for a period of three or four weeks to restructure Global One.

[27] *Philips/Lucent Technologies* (Case IV/M.1358) (1999) para 7.

[28] *Matra Marconi Space/Satcoms* (Case IV/M.497) (1994) paras 1 and 9.

[29] See *Mobil/JV Dissolution* (Case IV/M.1822) (2000) para 2; see also *Groupe Cofinoga/BNP* (Case IV/M.1419) (1999) para 2 (where it appears that there is little or no overlapping between the parties' activities). See also Competition Law of the European Community: N Levy, *The Control of Concentrations between Undertakings* (Matthew Bender, 2002), Ch 5, 5.13[3][a][*ii*] referring to *Rhodia/Donau Chemie/Albright & Wilson* (Case IV/M.1517) [1999] OJ C248/10 in which the Commission rejected the derogation request on the grounds that the operation had given rise to competition problems and therefore the parties failed to show that any serious damage would result from the standstill period. See Competition Policy Newsletter [1999] Number 3—October 44.

[30] *Kelt/American Express* (Case IV/M.116) (1991) para 7.

[31] *ING/Barings* (Case IV/M.573) (1995) para 7. See also *Siemens/Alstom Gas and Steam Turbines* (Case IV/M.3148) (2003) para 7.

[32] *ENEL/FT/DT* (Case IV/JV.2) (1998) para 8: 'derogation was granted in order to facilitate Wind's meeting the deadlines and obligations imposed by the licences granted in the fixed line sector and in order to enable Wind to start building its networks.' See Commission Decision in *Omnitel* (Case IV/M.538) (1995) para 6: 'This was necessary for OPI to be in a position to meet

(vi) *The need to comply with certain conditions of a bid.* In *Cinven Limited/Angel Street Holdings*, the Commission granted a derogation in order to facilitate a bid for a purchase of assets the sale of which had to be completed unconditionally on a given date. In the absence of the derogation, the parties would have been effectively excluded from the auction.[33]

Article 22(4) of the Merger Control Regulation

Another exception to the principle of suspension of concentrations subject to **16.11** the Merger Control Regulation is found where a referral of a case takes place. As explained in further detail below,[34] Article 22 of the Merger Control Regulation, also known as 'Dutch clause', provides for the possibility of referral by national authorities to the European Commission of concentrations that do not have a Community dimension that affect trade between Member States and threaten to affect competition in a significant way in the Member State or States making the request to the Commission. Cases referred by Member States under this mechanism may, insofar as permitted under national law, already have been implemented. That has happened already several times.[35]

Article 22(4) provides for a limited application of the principle of suspension to **16.12** these transactions. The obligation laid down in Article 7 to suspend implementation will operate as long as the concentration has not been implemented as at the date when the Commission notified the undertakings concerned that a request has been made. If the concentration has already been implemented at that date, the Article 7 prohibition will not apply. If the transaction is finally prohibited, divestiture under Article 8(4) of the Regulation may be ordered.

3. Prohibition on multiple filings (the *one-stop shop* principle)

Unlike the system of shared competences introduced by Regulation 1/2003 **16.13** with respect to prohibited practices, concentrations which meet the thresholds that define Community dimension are examined under the Merger Control Regulation alone. This is known as the *one-stop shop* principle.[36] Conversely,

---

the deadlines established by the licence and to operate in competition with Telecom Italia, which has already built its GSM network and has a significant presence in the market for analogue mobile telephony in Italy.'

[33] *Cinven Limited/Angel Street Holdings* (Case IV/M.2777) (2002) para 2. See also *FCC/Vivendi* (Case IV/M.1365) (1999) para 2.

[34] See Section D of this Chapter.

[35] *Veronica/Endemol* (Case IV/M.553) (1995); *Kesko/Tuko* (Case IV/M.784) (1996); *Blokker/Toys 'R' Us* (Case IV/M.890) (1997).

[36] Recital 8 of the Merger Control Reg provides that '[s]uch concentrations should, as a general rule, be reviewed exclusively at Community level, in application of a *one-stop shop* system and in compliance with the principle of subsidiarity. Concentrations not covered by this Reg come, in principle, within the jurisdiction of the Member States.'

the Commission has no jurisdiction with respect to concentrations that lack a Community dimension. This is consistent with the overall policy goal of establishing uniform conditions and guaranteeing the same notification requirements, procedure, and legal rules for all concentrations with significant cross-border effects through a single, centralized system of control.

16.14 By exception, Member States may take appropriate measures to protect certain legitimate interests affected by transactions caught by the Merger Control Regulation. These legitimate interests must abide by various limitations. Firstly, these must be other than those protected by the Merger Control Regulation (essentially, the protection of competition), and must be compatible with the general and other provisions of Community law.[37] The Regulation expressly mentions certain of these legitimate interests: public security,[38] plurality of media,[39] and prudential rules, such as those applying in the insurance sector.[40] The Commission considers that these interests expressly listed should be subject to uniform interpretation, guided, where possible, by Community law in the field.[41]

16.15 Any other public interest must be notified by the Member State in question to the Commission, who must recognize it, having first tested its compatibility with general principles (including the principles of necessity, effectiveness, and proportionality) and other provisions of Community law. A case where the Commission also recognized interests that went outside these categories is *Lyonnaise des Eaux/Northumbrian Water*,[42] where the Commission accepted that the UK would take certain measures for the protection of consumer interests. It is noted that the legitimate interest exception is interpreted strictly, the Commission being careful to prevent concentrations with a Community

---

[37] Art 21(4) of the Merger Control Reg.

[38] See Recital 19 of the Merger Control Reg. The scope of public security as a public interest that naturally involves questions concerning national defence must be understood without prejudice to the provisions of Art 296 EC. However, the concept of public security also includes maintaining the supplies of those products or services that are considered to be vitally important in order to protect the health of the population. *IBM France/CGI* (Case IV/M.336) (1993) concerning measures concerning two subsidiaries of CGI which previously worked for the French Ministry of Defence.

[39] *Newspaper Publishing* (Case IV/M.423) (1994) paras 22–23: in the UK, mergers that concern newspapers are subject to specific rules that involve reviewing specific aspects of the media industry (concerning the way news is presented or freedom of expression). As regards the annex to former Reg 4064/89 and in particular as regards the proportionality principle, in its authorization decision, the Commission imposed on the British authorities to be informed about any condition which they considered it appropriate to attach to the concentration.

[40] *Sun Alliance/Royal Insurance* (Case IV/M.759) (1996) paras 16–17: the Commission accepted that the UK was entitled to apply legislation concerning the authorization and supervision of insurance companies operating in the UK.

[41] See *Sampo/Storebrand* (Case IV/M.2491) (2001) para 39.

[42] *Lyonnaise des Eaux/Northumbrian Water* (Case IV/M.567) (1995) para 8.

dimension from being blocked by Member States for reasons other than those laid down in the Merger Control Regulation.[43]

Article 21 of the Merger Control Regulation has been enforced by the Commission to oppose actions by Member States seeking to oppose the implementation of concentrations that have already been approved by the Commission for various reasons. The *Champalimaud/BSCH* case was the first time that the Commission used Article 21 in order to prevent a Member State—Portugal—from blocking a concentration with a Community dimension. The transaction in question had been notified on 30 June 1999 and authorized by the Commission on 3 August 1999.[44] Already during the procedure, the Portuguese Government issued two decisions against the transaction, which forced the Commission to adopt an initial decision ordering the suspension of the national measures on 20 July 1999[45] even before the Commission gave formal approval. On 20 October 1999, the Commission adopted a decision declaring that the Portuguese Government's actions did not protect any legitimate interest admissible under Article 21(4) of the Merger Control Regulation and were an attempt to protect national strategic interests in a way that contravened that provision.[46] On 3 November 1999 it was made public that the Commission would bring an action before the ECJ under Article 226 EC against the Portuguese Republic for failure to suspend the measures in issue. Finally, Portugal withdrew the measures and the Commission did not bring any action.[47]

16.16

The Commission followed a similar approach when the Portuguese Government blocked the purchase by Secil Companhia Geral de Cal e Cimentos SA and Holderbank of the Portuguese company Cimpor Cimentos de Portugal SGPS.[48] In contrast with the *Champalimaud/BSCH* case, however, there was never a decision of the Commission on the transaction, given that the operation (and notification under the MCR) was abandoned following the actions of the

16.17

---

[43] Commission Decision of 27 January 1999 in *Edf/London Electricity* (Case IV/M.1346) (1999): the British authorities argued that the UK had a public interest in maintaining the legal system in the electricity sector and proposed changes to London Electricity's licence. However, the Commission concluded that it was not necessary to recognize a legitimate interest since the changes proposed to the said licence amounted to the application of provisions of national law. Further, the changes did not refer to the concentration in itself, but rather to the management of the merged entities after the concentration, in order to guarantee that the regulatory body was capable of carrying out its tasks. XXIXth Report on Competition Policy [1999] 66–67.

[44] *BSCH/Champalimaud* (Case IV/M.1616) (1999).

[45] Commission Decision of 20 July 1999. The text may be found at www.europa.eu.int/comm/competition/mergers/cases/decisions/m1724_19990720_1290_en.pdf.

[46] Commission Decision of 20 October 1999. The text may be found at www.europa.eu.int/comm/competition/mergers/cases/decisions/m1724_19991020_1290_pt.pdf (Portuguese only).

[47] See for additional information on this interesting case Commission Press Releases IP/99/610, IP/99/669, IP/99/749, IP/99/774, IP/00/296.

[48] *Secil/Holderbank/Cimpor*, (COMP/M.2054) (2000) withdrawn.

Portuguese Government. The Commission did in any event adopt a decision under Article 21 of the Merger Control Regulation, which was challenged by the Portuguese Government before the Court of Justice. In its Judgment of 22 June 2004, the Court confirmed the validity of the Commission decision,[49] endorsing its interpretation of the *one-stop shop* principle.

16.18 The single authority principle applies without prejudice to Article 296 (former Article 223) EC, which allows Member States to 'take such measures as it considers necessary for the protection of the essential interests of its security which are connected with the production of or trade in arms, munitions and war material; such measures shall not adversely affect the conditions of competition in the common market regarding products which are not intended for specifically military purposes.' Some Member States have relied on this provision vis-à-vis concentrations in the defence industry, instructing the notifying parties not to notify certain aspects of the concentration for national security reasons. For its part, the Commission has laid down certain conditions to enable the exemption to be invoked.[50]

C. Competent Authorities in the Merger Control Area

1. The Competition Directorate-General of the European Commission and the former 'Merger Task Force'

16.19 As explained earlier in this book, the European Commission is divided into a series of Directorates-General or 'DGs', including the Competition DG (also

---

[49] Case C-42/01 *Portuguese Republic v EC Commission* [2004].

[50] Commission Decision in *British Aerospace/GEC Marconi* (Case IV/M.1438) (1999) para 2: 'The United Kingdom, relying upon Article 296(1)(b) of the EC Treaty, has instructed BAe not to notify the military aspects of this operation. The notification therefore relates only to the non-military aspects of the transaction.'; para 8 '[. . .] [t]he Commission has considered the applicability of Article 296(1)(b) of the EC Treaty in the present case. In this context it has noted, on the basis of the information provided by the government of the United Kingdom, that the part of the concentration which has not been notified only relates to the production of or trade in arms, munitions and war material which are mentioned in the list referred to in Article 296(2) EC; the measures taken by the United Kingdom are necessary for the protection of the essential interests of its security; the measures taken will have no spillover effects on the non-military products of BAe and MES.' Para 9 continues '[t]herefore, the Commission is satisfied that the measures taken by the United Kingdom fall within the scope of Article 296(1)b of the EC Treaty.' cf Commission Decision in *Saab/Celsius* (Case IV/1797) (2000) para 2. In *GEC Marconi/Alenia* (Case IV/M.1258) (1998) para 15 the Commission declared that 'the merger will have no significant impact on suppliers and sub-contractors of the undertakings concerned and on Ministries of Defence of other Member States [. . .]'. For more on this point, see Competition Law of the European Community: N Levy, *The Control of Concentrations between Undertakings* (Matthew Bender, 2002), Ch 5, S 5.05[5]. L Ritter, W D Braun, and F Rawlinson, *European Competition Law: A Practioner's Guide* (Kluwer Law International, 2000), Ch VI, 436.

known as 'DG COMP'). Below the Commissioner in charge of Competition Policy stands the Director-General of the DG COMP and three Deputy Directors General, one of whom has special responsibilities for concentrations. The DG COMP is further divided into Directorates that are organized into three main areas (concentrations, prohibited practices, and State aid) which are in turn divided into Units which contain various teams of instructors. Until May 2004 there was a Directorate known as the Merger Task Force ('MTF') within the Competition DG, but this no longer exists.[51]

The current structure of DG COMP is the result of the period of reflection **16.20** which began after the extensive debate which began at the end of the century and was furthered by the annulment of three concentration decisions by the Court of First Instance.[52] Following this debate, the Commission announced various internal changes in order to improve the investigation procedure.[53] The internal reorganization led to the units of the MTF no longer forming part of the same Directorate; instead, the MTF has been transformed into six units that are located in six different Directorates. With the exception of Directorate A, which focuses on general competition policy, directorates and units of the Commission analyse the impact of the concentrations that have been notified in each of its sectors. The six Directorates with Units that focus on the control of concentrations are: A (policy), B (energy, basic industries—food, water— chemicals and pharmaceutical products), C (information, communication and media), D (services) and E (industry, consumer goods, and manufacturing). Each possesses a unit which deals exclusively with concentrations.

The above services reorganization was complemented by various initiatives **16.21** aimed at reinforcing the capacity and role of economic analysis in the Commission's decision making.[54] One of such initiatives was the creation of groups of

---

[51] See European Commission Press Release of 30 April 2003 (IP/03/603).

[52] Case T-342/99 *Airtours plc v EC Commission* [2002] ECR II-2585; Case T-310/01 *Schneider Electric SA v EC Commission* [2002] ECR II-4071; Case T-80/02 *Tetra Laval v EC Commission* [2002] ECR II-4381.

[53] M Monti, Speech on 'Merger control in the European Union: a radical reform', Conference of the European Commission/IBA concerning the EU control of mergers, 7 November 2002, Brussels, online at http://europa.eu.int/comm/competition/speeches/index_2002.html. The objective was to publish various Best Practice guidelines regarding various aspects of the day-to-day handling of a merger. Other important measures referred to by Monti included the appointment of a Chief Economist directly attached to the Director-General of DG COMP and the recruitment of more economists in order to improve the economic analysis of cases; the introduction of peer review groups in the second phase (i.e. a type of round-table with experts from other DG COMP units) in order to review the conclusions of the case team that had carried out the first-phase investigations; allowing the parties to have access to the file as soon as the second phase started, including the submissions of third parties against the merger; and strengthening of the role of Hearing Officers.

[54] Speech/02/252, Monti, 4 June 2002.

experts to evaluate, afresh, the conclusions of the case team ('peer review').[55] Civil servants with recognized experience in the field of concentrations conduct these evaluations. Their conclusions on given cases are then compared with those of the case team. This method of internal review is part of the organizational reform of DG COMP, in particular as regards the second-phase review.[56] Other new features concerning the internal organization and functioning of the Commission are the appointment of a Chief Economist who depends directly on the Director-General of the Commission and whose role is to provide the Commission services with an economic analysis that is independent of that carried out by the case team.[57] To all of the above must be added the formalization of best practices in the conduct of merger proceedings,[58] which have been instrumental in providing a clearer procedural framework in the conduction of the procedure.

2. The role of National Competition Authorities ('NCAs')

16.22   The Merger Control Regulation provides for a framework of close cooperation between the Commission and National Competition Authorities. This encompasses two distinct possibilities. One is the active participation of NCAs in the procedures run by the Commission, and is discussed here. The other takes place through referral mechanisms, either by national authorities in favour of the Commission or conversely by the Commission in favour of national authorities. That is discussed in Section D below.

Cooperation with the NCAs (Article 19 of the Merger Control Regulation)

16.23   The Merger Control Regulation requires the Commission to deal with cases 'in close and constant liaison with the competent authorities of the Member States'.[59] The importance of a close relationship is obvious given that there are

---

[55]   Commission Press Release 20 January 2004, IP/04/70.

[56]   P Lowe referred to 'a panel composed of experienced officials would be appointed for all in-depth investigations, and would have the task of scrutinising the case team's conclusions with a fresh pair of eyes at key moments of the enquiry.' European Lawyers, April 2003 where Mr. Lowe explains the way ahead, and his speech of 17 February 2003 for the RBB/FIPRA seminar, online at http://europa.eu.int/comm/competition/speeches/text/sp2003_045_en.pdf.

[57]   In particular, the functions are those of a general assessment as regards economic and econometric analysis in the application of competition law and general competition policy, general advice on specific matters, in-depth analysis in those cases which give rise to the most complicated economic questions, such as those requiring sophisticated quantitative analysis. As for resources, the objective is for the Chief Economist to have at his or her disposal approximately ten specialist economists with exclusive dedication, of whom half would be permanent and half temporary civil servants.

[58]   The Best Practice Guidelines, available at DG COMP's website, are discussed later.

[59]   Recital 13 and Art 19(2) of the Merger Control Reg. Recital 14 alludes to the creation of a network of competition authorities, as well as to the principles of single authority, subsidiarity and the one-stop shop. As the Recital says, 'the Commission and the competent authorities of the Member States should form together a network of public authorities, applying their respective

many cases where a given Member State has a given interest and therefore maintains close contact with the Commission. The involvement of Member States enables them to be kept informed and make their views known. This is made possible through various procedural mechanisms.

For a start, during first-phase investigations,[60] the Commission must send to **16.24** NCAs a copy of the notifications within three working days, together with the most important documents that have been sent to it or that it has issued with respect to the notification.[61] The NCAs are free to express their views at any time of the procedure, in particular as regards commitments that have been proposed to resolve competition issues. In addition, when the Commission sends a request for information to an undertaking, it will send immediately a copy of such a petition to the NCAs of the Member State where the headquarters of the undertaking or group of undertakings is located.[62] Further, the Commission will notify the NCAs of the said Member State in question that it has decided to carry out an inspection.[63] At the behest of the Commission, the NCAs of the Member States will proceed to carry out such verifications[64] or they may cooperate with the Commission's agents.[65]

Cooperation is even more intense in the second phase. Before adopting certain **16.25** decisions, in particular those ordering a second-phase investigation, the Commission must consult with the Advisory Committee on concentrations.[66] The Advisory Committee is made up of one or two representatives of the NCAs of each Member State, at least one of whom must be an expert in restrictive practices and dominant positions.[67] The Merger Control Regulation reinforces the role of the Advisory Committee whose influence should not be underestimated, in particular as regards those matters that involve markets with a national scope.[68]

competences in close cooperation, using efficient arrangements for information-sharing and consultation, with a view to ensuring that a case is dealt with by the most appropriate authority, in the light of the principle of subsidiarity and with a view to ensuring that multiple notifications of a given concentration are avoided to the greatest extent possible.'

[60] See s 6 below.   [61] Art 19(1) of the Merger Control Reg.
[62] Art 11(5) of the Merger Control Reg.   [63] Art 13(3)–(6) of the Merger Control Reg.
[64] Art 12(1) of the Merger Control Reg.   [65] Art 12(2) of the Merger Control Reg.
[66] Art 19(3) of the Merger Control Reg. See ch 17.0.5.
[67] Art 19(4) of the Merger Control Reg.
[68] Commission Decision of 30 October 2001, *Tetra Laval/Sidel* (COMP/M.2416) [2001] OJ L43/13, n 168 referring to the previous comments of the Advisory Committee. See also 'Competition Law of the European Community': N Levy, *The Control of Concentrations between Undertakings* (Matthew Bender, 2002) Ch 5, S 5.13[7], Green Paper on the review of Regulation 4064/89, COM (2001) 745 final, of 11 December 2001, para 246: 'the fact that the Commission attaches significant importance to the Committee's opinion is verifiable, as the opinion is published.' By Art 19(7) of the Merger Control Reg, 'the Commission shall communicate the opinion of the Advisory Committee, together with the decision, to the addresses of the decision. It shall make the opinion public together with the decision, having regard to the legitimate interest of undertakings in the protection of their business secrets.'

D. Referral of Concentrations

1. Basic principles

16.26 The system for the attribution of jurisdiction under the Merger Control Regulation is based on three basic principles: the one-stop shop, legal certainty, and subsidiarity.[69] The Merger Control Regulation rests in the first place on the *one-stop shop* principle, according to which a single authority should examine a given operation. Referral to a different authority is the exception to this general principle. For reasons of legal certainty, referrals are limited to those cases where the principle of subsidiarity makes it advisable that another authority which is better placed to investigate is entrusted with the case. This may result in either the Commission or NCAs obtaining jurisdiction over a concentration in circumstances other than those provided for in Article 1 of the Merger Control Regulation, which define a Community dimension.

16.27 The Merger Control Regulation sets out two procedural moments in which referrals may take place. One initial possibility is before a notification has taken place, and serves to avoid a double filing. The second moment in time is after a notification has been placed. These two alternatives are discussed below.

2. Referral prior to notification of the operation (Article 4(4) and (5) of the Merger Control Regulation)

Referral to National Competition Authorities

16.28 Article 4(4) of the Merger Control Regulation introduces the possibility, that was absent in former Regulation 4064/89, for parties to a concentration with a Community dimension to submit a reasoned request for the operation to be referred to one or more Member States before formally notifying the operation to the Commission. Such a request must be based on the possibility of the concentration affecting significantly competition in one or more markets within a Member State which has all the features of a distinct market. The parties must justify the fact that the operation may have an effect on competition in a distinct market in the Member State in question.[70] This latter requirement aims to limit referrals to cases that cause competition problems, since otherwise there is no reason to make an exception to the general Community competition rules.

---

[69] Commission Notice on Case Referral in respect of Concentrations [2005] OJ C56/2, (hereinafter 'the Case Referral Notice') also refers to a network of NCAs (paras 53–54), underlining the importance of cooperation and dialogue between the Commission and the NCAs in the case of concentrations that are the object of the referral system contained in the Reg.

[70] See Case Referral Notice at para 17.

Although the parties are not required to show a negative affect on competition, they must point to factors that normally suggest the existence of potential problems such as, for example, the existence of affected markets.[71] In addition, the parties have to certify that the scope of the geographic market where the potential competition problem exists is national (or smaller).

This request must be made in the Form 'RS' (Reasoned Submission) in accordance with Article 4(4) and (5) of the Merger Control Regulation. Form RS is contained in Annex III of Regulation 802/2004 ('the Implementing Regulation'). Although the Commission will accept Form RS in any official EU language, the Case Referral Notice recommends that the undertakings file it in a language that will be understood by all of those to whom it is addressed to make it easier for the NCAs in question to deal with the request. The information that the parties include in the form has to be correct and complete. In the event of incorrect information, the Commission could impose fines in accordance with Article 14(1)(a) of the Merger Control Regulation.[72] The Commission could also request additional information. In an effort to prevent any problem concerning the possibility that the information is incomplete, prior contacts with the Commission and the NCAs are encouraged. The Commission undertakes to offer help in this regard.[73]   **16.29**

Once the request has been received, the Commission will transmit it to the 'affected' Member States, that is, those to whom the case would be referred in the event that the request is authorized. The Commission has pledged in the Case Referral Notice to 'endeavour to transmit' the reasoned requests—by e-mail, fax, surface mail within a period of one working day of being received. Confidential information is sent by protected means of communication, e.g. secure e-mail.[74] The Member State(s) in question must agree or disagree within a maximum period of fifteen working days from receipt of the request. If a Member State is silent within this period it is deemed to accept the referral. But in the event any, even just one affected Member State, states its disagreement, the referral will not take place. Even if there is agreement—express or implied—from all Member States affected, the Commission retains discretion in referring the matter Member States.   **16.30**

The Commission will adopt its decision to proceed or not with the referral within a period of twenty-five working days from its receipt of Form RS. The decision to refer will depend on whether the Commission considers that the   **16.31**

---

[71] Section 6.III of Form CO (Annex I of Reg 802/2004) defines markets affected as those where the joint market share of the parties to the concentration is over 15 per cent.
[72] Case Referral Notice para 60.   [73] Case Referral Notice para 64.
[74] Case Referral Notice para 56.

NCA is the most appropriate authority to carry out the investigation bearing in mind the effects of the operation; for example, it would normally make the referral if the effects of the proposed concentration were confined to a single Member State and national or infranational markets that did not constitute a substantial part of the common market. These are the same factors that are taken into account in cases of referral of a notified concentration under Article 9 of the Merger Control Regulation, as discussed below. If an expressly negative decision is not adopted it is presumed that the Commission has decided to refer. As with referrals under Article 9(3), any referral may be in whole or in part.[75] The Commission will inform the Member States and the undertakings concerned of this decision.[76] If the Commission decides to refer part of the operation to the relevant NCA, the latter must begin to examine the part that has been referred in accordance with national competition law without delay.[77] The Merger Control Regulation will be applied to the part of the operation not referred to the NCA. Total referral frees the parties of the obligation to notify the Commission in accordance with Article 1 of the Merger Control Regulation. The relevant national competition rules must be applied in accordance with the provisions of Article 9(6)–(9) of the Merger Control Regulation. These provisions require that the relevant NCA decides on the case in question without undue delay. It must, in turn, inform the undertakings concerned of its preliminary analysis and what it intends to do within a period of forty-five working days from the referral. It must also respect the principle of proportionality.

Prior referral to the European Commission

16.32 Under Article 4(5) of the Merger Control Regulation, the parties to a concentration without Community dimension—and therefore, not capable of being notified to the Commission—may request that the Commission examine the operation under the Merger Control Regulation. This possibility is reserved for cases where the operation is capable of being analysed by virtue of the national competition rules of, at least, three Member States.[78] The request has to be made before making any notification to the competent NCAs.[79]

---

[75] Unlike Art 4(5), Art 4(4) para 3 allows a partial referral of the operation to the Commission. However, neither the Commission nor the Member States can modify the scope of the request for total or partial referral.

[76] As stated, the decision whether or not to refer will be made within a period of twenty-five working days from receipt of the Commission's request.

[77] As required by Art 9(6) of Reg 139/2004, which Art 4(4) refers to.

[78] The Case Referral Notice confirms that it is not necessary for national law to require the operation to be notified; the fact that an operation comes within the jurisdiction of a Member State in accordance with its national competition law is sufficient (para 71).

[79] The referral mechanism under Art 4(5) can only be used if no national notification has been filed yet. See Case Referral Notice at para 69.

As with Article 4(4), the referral request has to be made on Form RS. The **16.33**
Commission will transfer the request to all Member States within one working
day. The affected Member States, that is, those competent to examine the
concentration under national rules, must be clearly identified in Form RS,[80] and
they may oppose the referral request within fifteen working days from receipt
of the request. If any of the affected Member States opposes the referral, it
will not take place.[81] The Commission will inform without delay all Member
States and the undertakings concerned of any disagreement of this nature, with
the result that the parties will need to fulfil the applicable national rules regarding notifications. If however none of the affected Member States disagrees, the
Commission will gain jurisdiction over the matter and the parties will notify
the operation under the Merger Control Regulation. Unlike referrals under
Article 4(4), partial referral is not possible; the whole operation has to be
referred.

In analysing the chances of the referral request being accepted, the parties must **16.34**
consider whether, as well as the notification requirements that the operation
must satisfy under each system of national law, the Commission will be the most
appropriate authority to investigate the matter. This will be so when the effects
of the concentration are not limited to the territory of a single Member State, or
the case involves geographical markets which go beyond the national scope.
Another important factor is the powers of investigation required in the case at
hand. The Commission will also be seen as the most appropriate authority
to assess operations that create competition problems in national geographic
markets or even those that are smaller, but which overlap different Member
States.[82]

3. Post-notification referral of the operation

The Merger Control Regulation contemplates also referrals following a notifica- **16.35**
tion. In fact, this was the only possibility in the original Regulation 4064/89,
and assumes a decision following an initial examination by Member States. It is
noted that, in contrast with the pre-notification referrals regulated by Article
4(4) and (5) of the Regulation, post-notification referral requests are made at

---

[80] If any Member State does not agree with being identified as 'competent' to examine the
operation referred to in Form RS, it may inform the Commission of this within fifteen working
days following receipt of the request (Case Referral Notice [2005] OJ C56/2 para 75). If, due to
incorrect information in Form RS, a Member State subsequently takes the view that, in contrast
to the parties' submissions, it is competent to review the concentration, it could request that the
Commission make a post-notification referral under Art 9 (Case Referral Notice [2005] OJ C56/
2 para 77).

[81] This would not prevent the Member States to later make a post-notification referral to the
Commission under Art 22 MCR.

[82] Case Referral Notice [2005] OJ C56/2 para 20.

the initiative of either Member States or the European Commission, and not of the parties.

Referral to National Competition Authorities

16.36 In accordance with Article 9 of the Merger Control Regulation, at the request of one or more Member States, whether of its own motion or upon the invitation of the Commission,[83] the Commission can refer to the authorities of the requesting Member State(s) a duly notified concentration with a Community dimension. In the event the referral takes place, the operation will be assessed in accordance with that Member State's national competition law.[84]

16.37 Article 9 was included in former Regulation 4064/89 at the request of, among others, Germany. It is frequently referred to as 'the German clause', and reflects a certain reluctance of Member States to abandon completely their competences and sovereignty and therefore an interest to examine certain cases notwithstanding the European Commission's exclusive jurisdiction to examine all concentrations with a Community dimension.

16.38 For an operation to be totally or partially referred to a National Competition Authority, two elements are required. First, the operation must have significant effects on competition in a given market. Second, the market in question must come within the requesting Member State and have all the features of a distinct market.[85]

16.39 Article 9(2)(a) and (b) of the Merger Control Regulation distinguishes the following two scenarios:

---

[83] In its Green Paper, the Commission suggested that '[i]n line with the objective of facilitating the referral of cases which, due to a lack of significant cross-border effects, would be most appropriately assessed at national level, it would be reasonable to provide the Commission with the possibility to refer such cases on its own initiative.' (para 80).

[84] The CFI confirmed in Case T-119/02 *Royal Philips Electronics NV v EC Commission* [2003] ECR II-1433 para 381, and Joined Cases T-346/02 and T-347/02 *Cableuropa and others v EC Commission* [2003] ECR II-451 para 217, that the NCAs are completely free to apply their national law and to achieve a completely independent result from that of the European Commission. This is so, even when, in the case of a partial referral, the results obtained by the Commission and the NCA are irreconcilable. The CFI specifically stated that: 'However, provided they comply with those obligations [referring to Art 9 of Reg 4064/89 and Art 10 EC] the French competition authorities are free to rule on the substance of the concentration referred to them on the basis of a proper examination conducted in accordance with national competition law'. [. . .] In Joined Cases T-346/02 and T-347/02 *Cableuropa and others v EC Commission* [2003] ECR II-451 para 217: '[. . .] Consequently, as matters currently stand, the Court of First Instance cannot but find that, in the event of a partial referral to the national authorities, the risk that their decision will be inconsistent, or even irreconcilable, with the decision adopted by the Commission is inherent in the referral system established by Article 9 of Regulation No 4064/89 [. . .]'.

[85] See N Lacalle, 'La repatriación de las operaciones de concentración de dimensión comunitaria', in L Ortiz Blanco and R León (eds), *Derecho de la Competencia Europeo y Español*, Vol III, (Dykinson, Madrid, 2002) 339–57 (342).

(a) When a concentration threatens to affect significantly competition in a market within a Member State that *constitutes a substantial part of the common market*, the said Member State may request to examine these effects if it can be demonstrated in accordance with Article 9(2)(a), following a preliminary examination, that:

   (i) There is a real risk that the operation will have a significant negative effect on competition, and

   (ii) The geographic market or markets in which the competition will be affected have a national or infra-national dimension.

   In this case, the Commission retains a certain degree of discretion to decide whether or not it will refer the operation. If the Commission takes the view that Member States cannot safeguard or restore effective competition in the market concerned it will not refer the case.[86]

(b) When a concentration affects a market within a Member State that *does not constitute a substantial part of the common market*, in accordance with Article 9(2)(b) the Commission is under an obligation to refer the operation.[87] 'Distinct market' means an area that constitutes a separate geographic market within a Member State.[88] The concept of 'a substantial part of the common market' is not clearly defined. The Commission has considered that markets which in principle could appear local have amounted to a substantial part of the common market, in particular in circumstances where an interaction exists between certain local markets which produce regional or national effects.[89]

---

[86] See Case T-119/02 *Royal Philips Electronics N v EC Commission* [2003] ECR II-1433 paras 342–43; and Joined Cases T-346/02 and T-347/02 *Cableuropa and others v EC Commission* [2003] ECR II-451 para 175.

[87] Art 9(2)(b) was introduced into former Reg 4064/89 to facilitate referral requests, establishing less rigorous rules.

[88] *Alcatel/AEG Kabel* (Case IV/M.165) (1992) paras 9 and 10: the Commission considered that there was no distinct German market for telecommunications cables and that although there was a German market for electrical cables, the concentration did not threaten to create or reinforce a dominant position in that market. The Case Referral Notice states that when defining the geographic market, one has to take into account the typical factors that arise in national (or smaller) markets, such as reduced transport costs, demand that is supplied in places close to its centres of activity, significant change in prices and market shares in different countries or the existence of legal barriers or other factors delimiting markets.

[89] *Blokker/Toys 'R' Us* (Case IV/M.890) [1998] OJ L316/1 para 38: retail sale is local in nature but it could have wider effects: '[a]lthough the catchment area of a retail outlet, which can be based on the distance the consumer is willing to travel to reach it, is of a local or regional scale, the catchment area does not necessarily determine the geographic market. In a situation where several retail chains operate networks of stores on a national scale, the important parameters of competition are determined on a national scale [. . .]'. Commission Decision *Kesko/Tuko* (Case IV/M.784) (1997) OJ L110/53 paras 21–23. The ECJ confirmed that geographically limited monopolies within a Member State which taken together covered the whole territory thereof, could make up a substantial part of the common market when assessing a restriction on competition in that territory. Case C-323/93 *La Crespelle* [1994] ECR I-5889.

16.40 Prior to the changes introduced by the Merger Control Regulation, it was considered that the referrals to Member States under Article 9 of the Regulation could create procedural problems and a lack of legal certainty for the parties to a concentration.[90] The Commission was criticized for not having published any guidance describing the functioning of the referral mechanism as regards its procedure and, above all, with respect to the notifying parties in each case.[91] The new Case Referrals Notice was published in response to these criticisms.

16.41 The Commission's decision-making practice shows that concentrations have been referred to NCAs on relatively few occasions although in recent years more requests have been received and the Commission has been more ready to make referrals. Between 1990 and 1996, only six cases were referred to NCAs, while fifty-nine were referred between 1997 and 2004, of which approximately half came within the period 2001/2004.[92] One reason for this increase in referrals is the increase in cooperation experience between the NCAs and the Commission, principally via the Advisory Committee; this has created a greater degree of trust between the different NCAs and their improved ability to carry out the analysis of these operations. This development must be seen in the context of the Commission's new policy of the decentralized application of Community competition law, which has made it more flexible when deciding whether or not to refer a case.[93] This tendency towards more referrals to NCAs reflects a greater acceptance of the principle of subsidiarity and greater trust in the capacity of Member States to apply the competition rules rigorously.[94]

---

[90] Normally, the parties hold informal weekly or even monthly meetings prior to the notification with civil servants of the European Commission and filled out the notification Form CO as per what has been agreed in those meetings. One of the criticisms of the system prior to the Merger Control Reg was that when the Commission accepted the request for partial or total referral, the advantages of any pre-notification efforts and adjustments made to the CO by the parties were totally lost. The parties had to rewrite the form to adjust it to the information of the Member State and even change the language, which involved additional costs. The Merger Control Reg resolves these problems through the possibility of making pre-notification requests (Article 4(4)) and relaxing the old requirement that there must be a previous binding agreement between the parties before notification can be made.

[91] See N Lacalle, 'La repatriación de las operaciones de concentración de dimensión comunitaria', in L Ortíz Blanco and R León (eds), *Derecho de la Competencia Europeo y Español*, Vol III, (Dykinson, Madrid, 2002) 339–57 (341).

[92] European Commission figures as at 31 December 2004, online at www.europa.eu.int/web;.

[93] A Schaub, Speech on 'Developments of competition law and policy—European and National Perspective', Conference of the Hellenic Competition Commission, 19 April 2002, online at http://europa.eu.int/comm/competition/speeches/text/sp2002_014_en.pdf/web;.

[94] Art 5 EC requires intervention to take place at the most adequate level to enable the objectives to be achieved in a sufficient manner. According to the Commission Report to the European Council on adapting Community legislation to the principle of subsidiarity (COM(93)545 final, of 24 November 1993), actions will take place at the most appropriate

The main principles on which the referral policy has been based until the entry **16.42** of the MCR in May 2004 may be summarized as follows:[95]

(i) When it was a local market, the Commission was always more prepared to make the referral.[96]

(ii) When the geographic market affected was national or constituted a significant part of the Common Market, the Commission indicated that the referral should only take place in exceptional circumstances.[97] However, in recent times the Commission seemed more willing to refer cases.[98]

(iii) The Commission also assessed the presence or otherwise of foreign companies that competed with national companies, for example in the case of military products. In *Krauss-Maffei/Wegmann*,[99] the Commission decided to refer to the German NCA the part of the operation concerning military armoured vehicles.

(iv) When the geographic market went beyond the limits of a Member State, the Commission often rejected the referral request. In *Alcatel/AEG Kabel*,[100] the Commission concluded that there was no distinct German market for telecommunications cables and although there was a distinct German market for electrical cables, the notified operation did not threaten to create or reinforce a dominant position in that market.

In the limited time since the coming into force of the Merger Control Regula- **16.43** tion on 1 May 2004, the Commission's approach has become more flexible; in particular:

---

jurisdictional level, taking into account the objectives to be achieved and the means available to the Community and Member States. Green Paper on the review of Reg 4064/89 COM(2001)745 final, of 11 December 2001 para 16. As has been mentioned above, the Merger Control Reg— and on numerous occasions the Case Referral Notice—stresses the importance of the principle of subsidiarity.

[95] Distinction established in Competition Law of the European Community: N Levy, *The Control of Concentrations between Undertakings* (Matthew Bender, 2002), Ch 5, S 5.05[2](b).

[96] e.g. *Carrefour/Promodes* (Case IV/M.1684) (2000) paras 3 and 19. See also 'Competition Law of the European Community': N Levy, *The Control of Concentrations between Undertakings* (Matthew Bender, 2002), Ch 5, S 5.05 [2].

[97] M Waelbroeck, A Frignani, *Derecho de la Competencia* (Bosch, Barcelona, 1998) Vol II, para 925. Competition Law of the European Community: N Levy *The Control of Concentrations between Undertakings* (Matthew Bender, 2002), Ch 5, S 5.05 [2] b(1)–(2).

[98] Commission Decision, *Danish Crown/Steff-Houlberg* (Case COMP/M.2662) (2002), Commission Decision, *Interbrew/Bass* (Case COMP/M.2044) (2000) para 38, where the Commission 'concluded that the relevant geographic markets for the supply [of beer] to both the "on-trade" and the "off-trade" are no wider than the UK and therefore the UK presents all the characteristics of a distinct market, thereby satisfying the geographic criteria for referral to the competent UK authorities under Article 9(2)(a) [. . .]'.

[99] *Krauss-Maffei/Wegmann* (Case IV/M.1153) (1998) para 2.

[100] *Alcatel/AEG Kabel* (Case IV/M.165) (1991) paras 9–10.

- The Commission has continued to authorize referrals in cases where markets have a local dimension.[101]

- The fact that the NCAs have investigated or are investigating operations that affect the same companies and/or raise the same competition concerns in the same markets underlines the need for a referral to enable matters to be dealt with in a uniform way by the competent authority, provided that it is not a question of local markets in the Member State in question.[102]

- In addition to the local dimension of markets, the Commission will refer the operation if there are significant competition problems. As regards whether the market in question constitutes a substantial part of the common market, the Commission will leave this point open if the result of its analysis, in the light of the markets and the competition problems, is that the conditions for referral under Article 9 are fulfilled in any event, by applying either letter (a) or letter (b) of Article 9(2).[103]

Partial referrals

16.44 When a concentration involves two or more products, it is possible that the conditions for a referral are fulfilled with respect to one product but not in relation to the other(s). In such cases, Article 9 of the Merger Control Regulation expressly contemplates the possibility of a partial referral of the case. This enables the Commission to refer to an NCA the part of the transaction related to given markets and retain jurisdiction over other aspects of the concentration.[104] In the event that an NCA is investigating another concentration in the same market or in a related market, or has previously done so, the Commission will consider referring a concentration to this NCA.[105] Similarly, when a concentration involves two concurrent offers concerning the same undertaking one of which is already being investigated by the requesting authority, the Commission

---

[101] *Accor/Colony/Barrière* (Case IV/M.3373) (2004); see Commission Press Release IP/04/716; *Shell/Cepsa* (Case COMP/M.3275) (2004) See Commission Press Release IP/04/1397. Commission Decision in *Blackstone/NHP* (Case COMP/M.3669) (2005).

[102] *Kabel Deutschland/Ish* (Case COMP/M.3271) (2004). See Commission Press Release IP/04/717. Commission Decision in *Iesy Repositor/ISH* (Case COMP/M.3674) (2004).

[103] Commission Decision *Shell España/CEPSA/SIS JV* (Case COMP/M.3275) (2004).

[104] See for example *Carrefour/Promodes* (Case IV/M.1684) (2000), *BP/E.ON* (Case COMP/M.2533) [2002] OJ L276/31 para 9, Commission Decision *Shell/Dea* (Case COMP/M.2389) [2003] OJ L15/35 para 13.

[105] Commission Press Release IP/01/1247 dated 6 September 2001 in *BP/E.ON* (Case COMP/M.2533), cited above; Commission Press Release IP/01/1222 dated 24 August 2001 in *Shell/Dea* (Case COMP/M.2389).

will refer the case given the administrative advantages of the second offer being examined by the same authority.[106]

Referral request

Within a period of fifteen working days, which begin to run after receipt of **16.45** the copy of Form CO, Member States having interest in seeking referral of a case must notify the Commission of their request.[107] This means that, in a relatively short period of time, the Member State has to carry out an analysis that, in certain cases, may be complicated. As well as the problem posed by this short period of time, a post-notification referral request generally creates difficulties for the parties. During the period of time available for this assessment, Member States may only carry out the necessary investigation and take adequate measures for the application of Article 9(2) (and Article 4(4)).[108]

Effects on the time periods for deciding on the substance of the operation

The referral request automatically involves an extension of time in the first **16.46** phase of ten working days, so that the period increases from twenty-five to thirty-five working days. Therefore, when a Member State files a referral request, the Commission will inform the notifying parties and extend the period within which the Commission can examine a notification. The fact that the period for the request is fifteen working days and that this does not start to run until receipt of Form CO by the NCAs means that, in certain cases,[109] the end of that period almost coincides with the final of the period corresponding to the first phase of the procedure before the Commission. Prior to the coming into force of the Merger Control Regulation, criticism was levied at the fact that the process of verifying the fulfilment of the requirements to which reference has been made takes a significant period of time, and the implementation of the operation on the agreed terms could be seriously affected if, only a few days before the first-phase period ended and without the operation apparently raising any competition concerns, the position were complicated by the receipt of a referral request.[110] The new Merger Control Regulation has tried to alleviate this

---

[106] Commission Press Release IP/96/254 dated 22 March 1996 in *GEHE/Lloyds* (Case IV/ M.716) (1996). The investigation of a national authority in relation to an offer in concurrent proceedings is a legitimate matter to be taken into account in a referral request.

[107] Art 9(2) of the Merger Control Reg and Case Referral Notice para 40.

[108] Art 21(3) of the Merger Control Reg.

[109] e.g. where holidays do not coincide for the European Commission and the NCAs, which may delay the filing of the copy of Form CO or the referral request of the relevant NCA because the civil servant in charge of the matter is not available.

[110] N Lacalle, 'La repatriación de las operaciones de concentración de dimensión comunitaria', in L Ortiz Blanco and R León (eds.), *Derecho de la Competencia Europeo y Español*, Vol III, (Dykinson, Madrid, 2002) 339–57 (345): With respect to former Reg 4064/89, '[. . .] the procedure may become even more complicated if commitments have also been offered during the

situation, by introducing the possibility of making pre-notification requests. At the same time, it also tries to limit the effects of this situation by encouraging pre-notification contacts with the Commission.[111]

Referral decision

16.47 The Commission generally reaches a referral decision within a period of thirty-five working days from the day after receipt of notification. When the Commission has set second phase proceedings in motion, it will take a decision on referral within sixty-five working days from the date of notification. When the Commission fails to take a referral decision within the period of sixty-five days despite the request of the Member State in question having been repeated, it will be deemed to have adopted a decision referring the matter to the said Member State. When the Commission considers that the conditions for a referral are not fulfilled, it will adopt a decision to that effect addressed to the Member State in question.[112] As has already been mentioned, there is a substantial difference in the discretion enjoyed by the Commission to make a referral depending on whether the case concerns an effect on competition in a market that constitutes a substantial part of the common market (Article 9(2)(a)) or not (Article 9(2)(b)). In the former case, if the Commission considers that 'a concentration threatens to affect significantly competition' in a distinct market, it will either deal with the case itself in accordance with the Merger Control Regulation, or it will refer the operation—wholly or in part—to the NCAs. If the Commission considers that there is no distinct market or no such threat exists, it will adopt a decision addressed to the Member State in question and deal with the matter itself. In the latter case, if the Commission considers that the operation affects competition in a distinct market that does not constitute a significant part of the common market, the Commission will proceed to refer the whole matter or that part which is related to the distinct market.[113]

16.48 When the Commission refers a concentration to an NCA, that authority may only apply national competition rules and can only take the measures that are strictly necessary to preserve or re-establish effective competition in the market in question.[114] Although the NCA has some discretion as to how it will fulfil this

---

first phase to resolve the concerns that the proposed concentration may raise. If this occurs the time period is extended by two weeks, if a referral request is also made, the Commission and the national authorities will have to resolve within a potentially very short period of time both the validity of the commitments offered and the opportunity or need to grant the referral to the requesting Member State [. . .].' [Author's own translation].

[111] See the Best Practice Guidelines and the Case Referral Notice.
[112] Art 9(3) of the Merger Control Reg.
[113] Art 9(3)(b) of the Merger Control Reg last para.
[114] Art 9(8) of the Merger Control Reg.

obligation, it must comply with the principle of proportionality which is now contained in Article 9(8). National courts can review the use by Member States of this discretionary power.[115]

In accordance with Article 9(6) of the Merger Control Regulation, the NCA **16.49** in question must inform the undertakings concerned of the results of its preliminary analysis and, where appropriate, the steps it intends to take, within a maximum period of forty-five working days from the referral by the Commission or receipt of a complete notification by the NCA. This provision involves a preliminary decision within the said period of forty-five working days from the referral of the operation, or, where appropriate, from the subsequent notification of the operation to the NCA. The wording of Article 9(6) of the former Merger Regulation offered the NCA a time period of four months for 'the announcement of the findings of the examination', a longer period than that which the European Commission had to decide the matter if it had been entrusted with the examination. The new wording of Article 9(6) therefore appears to reduce the period, although it should be noted that the Merger Control Regulation only requires the NCA to inform the undertakings concerned of the result of its preliminary analysis, rather than reach a final decision on whether or not to authorise an operation. As a result, the Green Paper's more

---

[115] There are at least three cases where the Commission referred the matter to the NCAs and then the latter's final decisions were appealed before national courts. Commission Decision *Interbrew/Bass* (Case COMP/M.2044) (2000) concerned an operation that was referred to the UK in 2000. Once the British competition authorities had carried out an in-depth investigation, the Secretary of State for Trade and Industry reached a decision requiring the complete divestments of the brewing activity of Bass, which effectively meant that the deal was prohibited. Interbrew sought judicial review of this decision alleging that it was neither reasonable nor proportional, and was based on an abuse of due process. The High Court found against Interbrew as regards their first (and main) allegation but agreed that the procedures of the British competition authorities were unfair since Interbrew had not had a fair chance to resolve the fundamental problems relevant to assessing an alternative and less onerous solution. The second case concerned the supply of electricity in Commission Decision *Enel/FT/Wind/Infostrada* (Case COMP/M.2216) (2001), which was referred to the Italian competition authorities. After a detailed investigation, the Italian authorities approved the proposed merger, imposing on ENEL various conditions. ENEL and CODACONS, the Italian consumer protection association, both appealed against the decision and, in a judgment on both appeals, the competent Italian regional administrative tribunal (TAR, 'Tribunale Amministrativo Regionale') concluded that ENEL did not have a dominant position in the electricity supply market and also annulled the decision of the Italian competition authorities regarding the conditions imposed. The third case was the Commission Decision in *Sogecable/Canalsatélite Digital/Vía Digital* (Case COMP/M.2845) (2002), involving a concentration operation that was referred to the Spanish authorities under Art 9(2) of Reg 4064/89. The Spanish cabinet approved the operation subject to various conditions in its Resolution of 29 December 2002 (BOE 14 January 2003, No 12, 1707), and various competitors have brought judicial review proceedings before the Spanish Supreme Court challenging these conditions. Judgment is still pending before the Spanish Supreme Court.

ambitious idea of introducing a maximum period within which the NCAs must adopt a final decision has not seen the light of day.[116]

16.50 Article 9(6) of the Merger Control Regulation does however oblige NCAs to reach a decision according to their national law 'without undue delay'. This reference could be interpreted as meaning that the final decision on the concentration must be taken within the periods laid down in national law without any additional time being given on the grounds that it is a referral from the Commission.

Referral by the NCAs to the European Commission under Article 22 of the Merger Control Regulation

16.51 Originally, the possibility of a referral to the European Commission was conceived of for the benefit of those Member States which lacked the necessary instruments to investigate mergers at a national level. The idea was to allow Member States to request the Commission to act in their stead and assess the effects of concentrations that did not reach the thresholds of former Regulation 4064/89. At the time of the adoption of former Regulation 4064/89, this was known as the Dutch clause, since it was introduced at the request of the Netherlands, which lacked its own system for the control of concentrations. In its original wording, Article 22 had a very limited scope.[117]

16.52 The amendments that came into force in 1998 aimed to give the provision a new function as a means of allowing two or more Member States to make joint referrals to the Commission when they considered that the latter was best placed to evaluate an operation. The declared intention was to consolidate both the

---

[116] In the Green Paper on the review of Reg 4064/89 the Commission stated that: '[. . .] referred cases should arguably be treated on an equal footing to all cases subject to a merger control procedure within the specific reviewing authority. Nevertheless, there may be some merit in seeking to harmonise the timeframe in which the final decision is taken. A possibility would be to clarify the current rule in Article 9(6) so that a decision of a definitive nature comparable to an Article 8 decision under the Merger Regulation would have to be adopted within the same timeframe as would have applied for the Commission. Another more far-reaching possibility would be to provide, in the Merger Regulation, that any national authority dealing with a case that has been referred to it should do so under the procedure indicated in the Merger Regulation.' (para 82).

[117] Until 30 June 2005 only four concentrations have been referred to the Commission by a single Member State (as opposed to joint referral) under Art 22: *British Airways/Dan Air* (Case IV/M.278) [1993] OJ C68/5 (air transport market), in which the first-phase investigation period started to run from the date of the submission of additional information by the Belgian authorities because the Commission considered itself unable to investigate the merger on the basis of previously submitted information; *RTL/Verónica/Endemol* (Case IV/M.553) [1996] OJ L134/32 (Dutch TV market); *Kesko/Tuko* (Case IV/M.784) [1997] OJ L110/53 (retail market in daily consumer goods in Finland); *Blokker/Toys 'R' Us* (Case IV/M.890) [1998] OJ L316/1 (retail toy market in the Netherlands).

application of Community competition law to crossborder cases and the single authority principle, and to resolve the problem of multiple filings.[118] These amendments had little effect despite the fact that in 2001 for the first time two joint requests filed by various Member States were filed asking for the Commission to intervene in their stead.[119]

The recent amendments to the former Article 22 made by the Merger Control **16.53** Regulation have not affected its main features. Article 22(1) allows one or more Member States[120] to request the Commission to carry out the analysis of an operation that lacks a Community dimension if the two cumulative requirements (that also existed under former Regulation 4056/89) are fulfilled. These are as follows:

• It affects trade between Member States (that is, it can have an appreciable influence on trade flows between Member States)[121] and;
• It threatens to affect in a significant manner competition in the Member State(s) requesting referral. This requirement involves showing that there is a real risk of the operation having a significant negative effect on competition.

The new version of Article 22 is an attempt to resolve the previous procedural **16.54** and operational failings so that it can function as a generally applicable corrective mechanism to the problem of multiple filings. This amendment has to be seen in conjunction with the new feature of pre-notification referral contained

---

[118] In the Green Paper on the review of Reg 4064/89 para 84 the Commission points out that this amendment was to some extent seen as complementary to the simultaneous introduction of the thresholds of Art 1(3) which in principle was aimed at resolving the same problems.

[119] Until 30 June 2005 there were four joint referrals of various Member States to the Commission. In the case of the acquisition authorized by the Commission of Unison Industries by a subsidiary of General Electric, this was originally notified to various Member States (the UK, Germany, France, Italy, Spain, Austria, and Greece. These Member States decided to make a request to the Commission under Art 22 of Reg 4064/89. See Commission Press Release 17 April 2002, IP/02/578. The Commission recognized that '[t]his was only the second joint referral of a merger to the Commission by Member States in the almost eleven years that the Merger Regulation has been in place. The first such case was the *Promotech/Sulzer Textil* merger, on which the Commission started an in-depth investigation this week'. In *Unison Industries* the requests by Member States contained prima facie indicators to suggest that the concentration would create or consolidate a dominant position which would enable it to obstruct significantly competition in the territory of the Member States concerned, as well as the crossborder trade concerned. See Commission Press Release 24 July 2002, IP/02/1140. The third joint referral occurred in *GE/Agfa* by the NCAs in Germany, Austria, Greece, Ireland, Spain, Portugal, and Italy (see Commission Press Release dated 5 December 2003, IP/03/1666). The fourth joint referral of a concentration operation was *Areva/Urenco*, which was referred by France, Sweden, and Germany (see Commission Press Release dated 22 June 2004, IP/04/777).

[120] Art 22 also allows the Commission to invite one or more Member States to present a referral request if the requirements for referral are fulfilled.

[121] On this point the Case Referrals Notice refers to the Guidelines on the effect on trade concept contained in Arts 81 and 82 of the EC Treaty [2004] OJ C101/81.

in Article 4(5). The greater speed in assigning matters as a result of a general reduction in time periods is worthy of note. The suspension of the implementation of concentrations contained in Article 7 of the Merger Control Regulation will apply if the concentration has not been implemented by the date on which the Commission informs the undertakings affected that a request has been filed.[122]

16.55 Paragraph 2 of Article 22(1) of the Merger Control Regulation reduces the one-month period for filing the request contained in former Regulation 4064/89 to fifteen working days from 'the date on which the concentration was notified,'[123] or if no notification is required, otherwise made known to the Member State concerned'. Once it has received the request, the Commission will notify all the Member States and undertakings concerned. Any Member State may join in the request within fifteen working days of receipt of the initial request (even if the operation has been notified in various Member States[124]). During this period, national time limits for assessing the concentration are suspended until the Commission adopts a decision on jurisdiction. This suspension will end with respect to any Member State from the moment that such State informs the Commission and the undertakings concerned that it does not wish to join the request.[125] After this period of fifteen days, the Commission has ten working days to decide and duly inform all Member States and the undertakings concerned of its decision. If it does not expressly state its position within this time, it is deemed to have decided to examine the concentration in accordance with the request.

16.56 With regard to the effects of the referral decision, if the Commission accepts its competence to analyse the impact of the operation, the national control proceedings end and the Commission can require the parties to file a notification using Form CO. With respect to the scope of the investigation, the Commission will not assess the effects of the concentration in the territory of those Member States that have not joined the request unless such an examination is necessary to evaluate the effects of the concentration within the territory of the requesting Member States (e.g., if the geographic market extends beyond the territory of

---

[122] Art 22(4) of the Merger Control Reg.

[123] The Notice clarifies that notification of a Member State must be interpreted here as meaning the notification of sufficient information to carry out a preliminary analysis in order to determine whether the criteria for requesting a referral under Art 22 are fulfilled (para 50).

[124] The Case Referral Notice encourages the parties to notify the operation simultaneously in all Member States so that all of the NCAs involved have the necessary information about the operation and can join in the request on a properly informed basis (para 50).

[125] It is observed that, in contrast with pre-notification filings under Art 4(5) of the Merger Control Reg, some Member States may retain the case and that would not prevent the Commission from accepting a referral.

the requesting Member States).[126] Once the operation has been referred to the Commission, the Member State cannot control the direction and scope of the Commission's investigation. The Commission can examine all of the relevant aspects of the concentration, independently of the scope of the request, with the exception mentioned before that, in principle, it will limit itself to examining the impact of the concentration in the territory or territories of the Member State(s) who made the referral request. In *Endemol Entertainment Holding*, the parties considered that the Commission's investigation should be limited to the market for TV advertising since the Dutch government had only asked the Commission to examine whether the operation would create or reinforce a dominant position that would obstruct significantly effective competition in the Dutch TV advertising market. Since the Dutch government considered that there were no competition problems in other markets, in the opinion of the parties any investigation of other markets would go beyond the request made by the Dutch authorities.[127]

Unlike referrals under Article 9 of the Merger Control Regulation, Article 22 **16.57** of the Merger Control Regulation does not permit partial referral and therefore the Commission's investigations must be made in relation to the whole operation rather than just specific aspects of it, such as a particular product market. In practice, Article 22 results in an identical procedure to that applicable to concentrations with a Community dimension. Consequently, the CFI affirmed that:

> Article 22(3) in no way allows a Member State to submit only one particular aspect of a concentration for consideration by the Commission; on the contrary, it necessitates consideration of the concentration *in toto*. Following such a request, the Commission must examine the concentration as if it had a Community dimension. The powers which it has in that regard would be inappropriate if it were expected that the Member State concerned should already have identified in its request the competition problem requiring a solution.[128]

Member States having referred the case lose the power to apply national law to **16.58** the concentration. In the event that the transaction is being examined by various NCAs, the Commission will decide the operation on behalf of those Member States who have filed the referral request with respect to their territory, while those Member States who have not requested referral will continue to apply national law. In the procedure, the Commission will apply the provisions of the Merger Control Regulation only, including any of the substantive decisions contemplated, *inter alia*, in Articles 6 and 8 thereof.[129] In particular, given that

---

[126] Case Referral Notice para 50 and n 46.

[127] Case T-221/95 *Endemol Entertainment Holding v EC Commission* [1999] ECR II-1229 para 37.

[128] Case T-221/95 *Endemol Entertainment Holding v EC Commission* [1999] ECR II-1229 para 40.

[129] Case Referral Notice n 45.

the transaction may have already been carried out, if the outcome of the procedure is a prohibition decision the Commission may order a separation under Article 8.4 of the Regulation.[130]

E. Scope of the Merger Control Regulation: Concentrations with a Community Dimension

16.59 The Merger Control Regulation applies solely to concentrations (as defined in its Article 3) that have a Community dimension as defined in Article 1(2) and (3).

1. Concentrations as defined in Article 3

16.60 A concentration within the meaning of Article 3 of the Merger Control Regulation occurs when a single undertaking or two or more undertakings together acquire the control of another undertaking, of a group of assets or in the case of a merger of previously independent undertakings. The concept is limited to changes in the structure of control over undertakings. Control is attained[131] through a given concentration if the possibility of exercising a decisive influence over an economic entity (hereinafter the 'acquired entity') is obtained through rights, contracts or other means. Decisive influence can refer to a part or the whole of the undertaking in question, or over a whole group of undertakings.

16.61 The Regulation distinguishes three types of concentration: mergers of undertakings, acquisition of sole control, and acquisition of joint control over full-function undertakings. These three situations are examined below.

Merger of two formerly independent entities

16.62 A concentration arises, according to the Regulation, where two or more previously independent undertakings or parts of undertakings merge. As explained in the Notice on the Concept of Concentration, this may also occur where, in the absence of a legal merger, the combining of the activities of previously independent undertakings results in the creation of a single economic unit, such as where two or more undertakings, while retaining their individual legal personalities, establish contractually a common economic management. If this leads to a *de*

---

[130] This has happened in the following cases: *RTL/Verónica/Endemol* (Case IV/M.553) [1996] OJ L134/32; *Kesko/Tuko* (Case IV/M.784) [1997] OJ L110/53; *Blokker/Toys 'R' Us* (Case IV/M.890) [1998] OJ L316/1.

[131] The Commission Notice on the concept of concentration under Council Reg (EEC) 4064/89 on the control of concentrations between undertakings [1998] OJ C66/2 (hereinafter 'Notice on the Concept of Concentration') para 17 provides that 'the concept of control under the Merger Regulation may be different from that applied in specific areas of legislation concerning, for example, prudential rules, taxation, air transport or the media.'

facto amalgamation of the undertakings concerned into a genuine common economic unit, the operation is considered to be a merger. A prerequisite for the determination of a common economic unit is the existence of a permanent, single economic management. Other relevant factors may include internal profit and loss compensation as between the various undertakings within the group, and their joint liability externally. The *de facto* amalgamation may be reinforced by cross shareholdings between the undertakings forming the economic unit.

Sole control

Sole control arises when a single undertaking acquires control over the acquired **16.63** entity through rights, contracts or other means and can thus determine the latter's commercial strategy. Article 3(1) of the Merger Control Regulation describes this as follows:

(b) the acquisition, by one or more persons already controlling at least one undertaking, or by one or more undertakings, whether by purchase of securities or assets, by contract or by any other means, of direct or indirect control of the whole or parts of one or more other undertakings.

The acquired entity may be a pre-existing undertaking or a part thereof that **16.64** could be labelled as an undertaking and, as such, one to which a given turnover can be clearly attributed. The Merger Control Regulation provides that a concentration does not arise—and thus there is no obligation to notify—with respect to financial or credit entities or insurance companies whose normal activities include transactions and dealings in securities on their own account or on behalf of others which they have acquired solely in order to resell them. This is subject to the caveat that the acquirers do not exercise the voting rights in respect of the shares they hold, or they only exercise those rights to prepare the resale of the undertaking or its assets provided that the said resale occurs within a year of the date of purchase.[132]

Article 3(5)(b) provides that a concentration will not exist either if 'control is **16.65** acquired by an off-holder according to the law of a Member States relating to liquidation, winding up, insolvency, cessation of payments, compositions or analogous proceedings'. Finally, Article 3(5)(c) provides that there is no concentration when the acquiring party is a financial holding company referred to in the Fourth Council Directive 78/660/EEC, provided that the voting rights in respect of the holding are only used to maintain the full value of the investment.

---

[132] Art 3(5)(a) of the Merger Control Reg and paras 41–42 of the Notice on the concept of concentration. The Reg provides for the possibility of the Commission extending the one-year period if the acquiring entities so request, provided that they can show that it was not 'reasonably possible' to make the disposal within the said period. Other acquisitions that do not amount to a concentration fall under (sub) provisions (b) and (c) of Art 2(5).

16.66 Sole control may have a legal or a *de facto* basis. The elements that must be taken into account in the acquisition of sole control are as follows:

- The stake acquired: 51 per cent of the share capital normally gives legal control.
- The percentage of voting rights that can be exercised in the shareholders' Annual General Meeting (AGM); the ability to exercise more than half of the voting rights normally confers legal control.
- The number of directors appointed in the Board of Directors of the acquired entity: the power to appoint more than half of the directors normally confers legal control, since with the support of such directors, resolutions can be approved and therefore the competitive strategy of the acquired entity can be determined.

16.67 These aspects are often directly related, so that when an undertaking acquires most of the share capital in another company it normally also acquires most of the voting rights, and has the right to appoint more than half of the directors. Although this is the rule, in practice there are exceptions. The first aspect, then, which must be analysed is the proportion of share capital acquired, bearing in mind that normally a stake of more than 50 per cent of the capital often confers control in the absence of other factors. It is, however, possible for minority shareholdings (below 50 per cent) to confer legal control if such shares have specific rights attached to them. These inherent rights may consist in preferential shares that give most of the voting rights or that allow the minority shareholder to determine exclusively the competitive strategy of the company in question. Among such rights, the power to appoint more than half of the members of the Board of Directors or the supervisory Board is seen as being very important.[133]

16.68 A minority shareholder may also exercise *de facto* sole control. Take, for example, a minority shareholder without a majority of voting rights or the ability to appoint the majority of directors. If the other shares are widely dispersed, it is unlikely that all of the small shareholders will attend or be represented at the shareholders' AGM. If the average attendance at previous AGMs is observed, it may be that only half of the voting shares are represented. In such a situation, it is possible that with a stake of less than 50 per cent and using the same percentage of votes in the AGM, a company may be able to obtain approval of its resolutions. This would amount to an acquisition of control.[134]

---

[133] Commission Notice on the concept of concentration para 14.

[134] Commission Notice on the concept of concentration para 14. In *Arjomari/Wiggins Teape* (Case M25) (1990), the Commission found that Arjomari had sole control with a minority stake of 39 per cent of WTA bearing in mind that none of WTA's remaining 107,000 shareholders owned more than 4 per cent of the company and only three shareholders had stakes of more than 3 per cent.

To determine whether control exists, a forecast or prediction will have to be made in each case, in which the extent of dispersion of shares as well as attendance at AGMs in the previous three years will be analysed, before deciding whether or not a given minority shareholder is capable of systematically obtaining the approval of its resolutions.[135] In addition, a situation of economic dependence may, in certain exceptional situations, result in the *de facto* acquisition of control when there are very substantial long-term supply agreements or credits granted by suppliers or clients, together with structural links that allow the latter to exercise a decisive influence over the acquired entity.[136]

An option to purchase or convert shares will give the acquirer sole control if the purchase is made through legally binding agreements.[137] If the exercise of the option in question is only probable, its existence will be treated as merely another factor to be taken into account in assessing the existence of control. If the operation creates joint control for an initial period of time or on start up but legally binding agreements provide that this will subsequently become sole control, the acquisition will be treated as one of sole control.[138]

16.69

---

[135] See n 4 of the Notice on the concept of concentration. An example of such forecasting arose in *Societé General de Belgique/Générale de Banque* (Case IV/M.343) [1993], where Societé General de Belgique (SGB) increased its stake in General de Banque (GB) from 21 per cent to 26 per cent. The Commission considered that the 21 per cent stake which SGB had held was not enough to give it control, since although the other shareholders were quite dispersed, Groupe AG held almost 15 per cent of GB's share capital. The prediction of SGB's vote, taking into account attendance at the last three AGMs, gave it more than 40 per cent of the votes, but the Commission concluded that this did not amount to control. However, with the additional 5 per cent, giving it a total stake of 26 per cent, SGB was predicted to have almost 56 per cent of the votes in the AGM, and, therefore, the purchase of this additional stake was considered to be a *de facto* acquisition of control.

[136] *CCIE/GTE* (Case IV/M.258) (1992).

[137] Commission Decision IV/M.259 *British Airways/TAT* (1992) and Case T-2/93 *Air France v EC Commission* [1994] ECR II-323. In this case, the Commission concluded that BA acquired joint rather than sole control, despite acquiring 49 per cent of TATEA and an option to purchase the remaining 51 per cent of the shares held by TAT, on the grounds that it was not definite that the option to purchase would be exercised. The Commission Decision was appealed to the CFI by Air France, one of BA's competitors. In its judgment, the CFI confirmed the Commission's assessment, holding that the exercise by BA of its option to purchase was a hypothetical factor, and when the Decision was adopted it had not been proved that BA had the intention to exercise it (para 71). The Commission's reasoning is that the intention to exercise an option would be easy to corroborate through the existence of a legally binding agreement between the parties in this regard.

[138] Commission Decision *British Telecom/Banco Santander* (Case IV/M.425) (1994) para 21. The Commission concluded that since Banco Santander could exercise a decisive influence over the joint venture BTSA only within the first three years of BTSA's existence and that the investment was long term, the three-year period was insufficient to create a permanent change in the structure of the undertakings concerned. Accordingly, Banco Santander did not acquire joint control over BTSA and British Telecom had sole control. See also paras 37–38 of the Notice on the concept of concentration.

Acquisition of joint control over full-function joint ventures

16.70 **Joint control** When more than one independent entity acquires control over another previously independent entity in the sense referred to above, a joint venture emerges.[139] The most common transactions resulting in joint control are:

- two or more independent entities decide to create an entity that they will jointly control

- one or more undertakings takes controlling stakes in the share capital of another company controlled until that moment exclusively by a single undertaking

- a *de facto* merger or combination of the activities of previously independent undertakings which, without amounting a legal merger, results in the creation if a sole economic entity.[140] This occurs, for example, when joint economic management is established.

16.71 Joint control exists when the parent companies must reach an agreement on most decisions from a commercial point of view which affect the undertaking controlled. Unlike exclusive power, which gives a shareholder the power to determine the strategic decisions of an undertaking, joint control is typified by the possibility of a deadlock situation, derived from the power held by the parent companies of the joint venture to reject the strategic decisions proposed by one or other of the parties. Joint control may therefore be defined in this negative way as the power to block actions that determine the competitive strategy of an undertaking.[141] Joint control is obvious when the parent companies hold the same number of shares, or the same amount of voting rights needed to approve resolutions at the Shareholders' AGM of the joint venture. There may also be a formal agreement between the parent companies concerning the number of representatives that each may appoint to the administrative or

---

[139] See para 3 of the Commission Notice on the concept of full-function joint venture under Council Reg (EEC) 4064/89 on the control of concentrations between undertakings [1998] OJ C66/1 (hereinafter 'the Notice on the concept of full-function joint ventures').

[140] Notice on the concept of concentration, para 6. See Commission Decision *Alitalia/KLM* (Case JV.19) (1999) [2000] OJ C96/5, Commission Press Release IP/ 99/628. In this case, despite the fact that the parties did not merge or create a joint venture as a separate legal entity, the Commission examined the operation in accordance with former Reg 4064/89. Both undertakings continued to operate activities outside of the alliance as well as independent decision-making bodies. However, the Commission considered that the parties had, through contractual means, achieved such a high level of integration that the operation amounted to a full-function joint venture. This was the first time the Commission established that there was a contractual joint venture or '*de facto* integration of the undertakings concerned'. See Enrico Maria Armani, DG COMP-D-2, 'Alitalia-KLM: A new trend in assessing airline alliances?' EC Competition Policy Newsletter No 3, October 1999, 19.

[141] Notice on the concept of concentration, para 19.

decision-making bodies, or deciding who has a casting vote (normally held by the Chairman of the Board of Directors). In order for joint control to exist, this agreement must provide that both parent companies have the right to appoint the same number of directors and that none of them has the right to exercise a casting vote. If this is not the case, it may be that one of the parent companies holds sole control.

Although two or more parent companies in a joint venture are not equally represented in the decision-making bodies of the company, joint control may also exist when there are veto rights. For this purposes, the mere possibility conferred by the power to exercise the right is sufficient, even though in practice it is not executed. Veto rights that confer control must be more than just rights that protect the interests of minority shareholders, that is, those rights that protect their investment. The latter category of rights protect the shareholder with respect to decisions that create a risk for the very essence of the joint venture, such as, *inter alia*, significant changes in the Articles, increases or reductions in the share capital, the sale or liquidation of the undertaking, etc.[142] Veto rights must refer to questions such as the budget, the business plan, major investments or the appointment of senior executives. To obtain control it is not necessary to have veto rights over each and every one of these aspects; sometimes, a veto right over only one may give control. Priority is given to veto rights over the budget or the business plan, which, in general, give control. In other cases, the acquisition of control will depend on both the nature and number of veto rights, which will be assessed as a whole.[143] Even if there are no veto rights, it is also possible for two or more undertakings that are minority shareholders to exercise joint control. This would be the case if the minority shareholders jointly possessed and exercised most voting rights. This situation may arise when there is a legally binding agreement in this regard between the minority shareholders, if they create a holding company to which they transfer their rights, or if there is *de facto* concerted action between them. As regards this last point, the Commission may consider that *de facto* concerted action could exceptionally be carried out if the minority shareholders held significant interests in common, which would create a disincentive to adopt conflicting agreements within the joint venture.[144] Examples of facts suggesting the existence of common interest would be the prior existence of links between such shareholders or the acquisition of shares through concerted action.

16.72

---

[142] *Eridania/ISI* (Case IV/M.62) (1991). The Commission considered that the rights of certain shareholders to oppose the ISI being taken over by another company, to closure, to changes to its share capital or to the transfer of its headquarters did not confer control since they did not amount to veto rights but rather the rights to protect the interests of minority shareholders.

[143] Notice on the concept of concentration para 29.

[144] *Hutchison/RCPM/ECT* (Case COMP/JV.55) [2003] OJ L 223/1, para 15.

16.73 Joint control will also exist where there are various minority shareholders that make an essential contribution to the functioning of the joint venture, for example in terms of technology, know-how or important supply agreements. The reason that such contributions can give control is that the only way that the undertaking can be viable is if the contributors to such activities agree on the most important strategic decisions.[145] If one of the parent companies makes an essential contribution in this regard, while another parent company's role is limited, even to the point of playing no part in the day-to-day running of the company, the latter may still exercise joint control with the former, but only if there exists a real possibility of challenging or opposing the decisions adopted by the other parent company.

16.74 A casting vote in favour of a director appointed by a given undertaking normally confers sole control to that undertaking. However, there may not be sole control if the right can only be exercised after a series of arbitration procedures and attempts at reconciliation have been exhausted or its scope is very limited.[146]

16.75 It must be stressed that in order for there to be an acquisition of joint control, the undertakings that have the possibility of exercising control have to be the same with respect to all decisions that confer control. In other words, joint control will not exist in situations where taking into account the majorities required for the approval of strategic agreements, it is possible that different combinations or coalitions of shareholders may approve specific agreements in certain circumstances, without there being a fixed majority (known as shifting alliances).

16.76 It is not unusual for the parties to allege that a situation of shifting alliances exists and, therefore, there is no acquisition of control and the operation does not constitute a concentration that requires notification. In such cases, the Commission will take into account whether it is more reasonable for the shareholders in question to act by exercising joint control in a permanent fashion instead of looking for occasional alliances with other minority shareholders.[147]

---

[145] Notice on the concept of concentration, para 34.

[146] *British Telecom/Banco Santander* (Case IV/M.425) (1994) (Case IV/M.425) (1994), para 7 which suggested that the existence of a casting vote in favour of the Chairman appointed by BT did not in itself give the latter sole control because it only applied for a limited period of time and to a limited number of questions (three years and not with respect to certain strategic questions). The Commission concluded that BT had sole control for different reasons.

[147] *Skanska/Scancem* (Case IV/M.1157) [1999] OJ L183/1 where the parties alleged that there was a lack of joint control because they were in a situation of variable alliances. The factors that the Commission took into account when reaching the decision that Skanska and Aker exercised joint control over Scancem prior to the operation were, *inter alia*, that the prior acquisition of Scancem had taken place through the concerted action of both undertakings and that these had entered into a detailed shareholders' agreement which would have included an agreement with respect to the *Scancem* agreement.

The Commission will analyse whether the possible convergence of commercial interests or incentives of the different shareholders means that they always vote in the same way, rather than there being a situation of shifting alliances.[148]

Full function

In accordance with Article 3(4) of the Merger Control Regulation, in order for a **16.77** concentration to exist a joint venture has to carry out 'on a lasting basis all of the functions of an autonomous economic entity'. This means that it has to carry out all of the functions that are carried out by undertakings operating in the same activities. The Notice on the concept of full function joint ventures[149] provides that for this to take place, the joint venture will require management dedicated to the day-to-day running of the company, and have access to financial and human resources and assets (both tangible and intangible) in such a way that it carries out a business activity in a lasting manner. The specific functions that a joint venture must carry out will depend on the particular market but generally it must be active in all of the typical functions such as production, distribution, and sales, thus enjoying access to the market. If the joint venture only carries out one of these functions, for example, it is only engaged in R&D, or it only manufactures products or distributes those made by its parent companies, it will be considered as an undertaking that is ancillary to the activities of its parent companies.[150] Such cases do not amount to notifiable concentrations within the Merger Control Regulation, although their impact on competition under Articles 81 and 82 must be appraised.

In assessing whether a joint venture has full functionality, it is necessary to **16.78** consider the presence of the parent companies in upstream or downstream markets vis-à-vis the market where the joint venture is present. In particular, the level of sales made by the joint venture to the parent companies or vice versa will have to be assessed to see whether it is a high proportion of total production. It

---

[148] *Deutsche Telekom/BetaResearch* (Case IV/M.1027) [1999] OJ L53/31 para 78, with respect to the commitments offered by the parties to avoid competition problems. See also the arguments that led the Commission to conclude the existence of joint control in *Hutchison/RCPM/ECT* (Case COMP JV.55) [2003] OJ L223/1 para 15.

[149] Commission Notice on the concept of full-function joint ventures under Council Regulation (EEC) 4064/89 on the control of concentrations between undertakings [1998] OJ C66/1 (hereinafter, 'Notice on the concept of full-function joint ventures').

[150] The Notice specifies that if a joint venture uses the distribution or sales networks of one or more of the parent companies, this does not mean that it automatically lacks full functions, provided that the parent companies act exclusively as agents. In Commission Decision IV/M.102 *TNT/Canada Post* (1991) (paras 13–14), the Commission found that there was a full-function joint venture because it carried out all of the operational and administrative functions despite the fact that some operations could be contracted out to the post offices of its parent companies. The Commission considered that such access did not mean that the joint venture lacked full functions since this was a normal market practice and, in addition, it was an agency contract, and therefore the joint venture would bear the full commercial risk of such operations.

may be concluded, for example, that the joint venture lacks full functions because it is ancillary to the parent companies, since it supplies them almost exclusively and therefore depends on them. Nevertheless, if the joint venture has an initial start-up period during which time the parent companies acquire a substantial amount of its production, this will not prevent it being concluded that there is a full-function joint venture, provided that this start-up period does not exceed three years.[151] If the substantial sales of the joint venture to the parent companies is not of final but rather of secondary products that are seen as being less important for the joint venture, such sales will not be considered to indicate a lack of full functions.[152] Another relevant criterion in this assessment is whether or not the sales from the joint venture to the parent companies are carried out in normal market conditions; if, on the contrary, sales are on more favourable terms (including prices) this suggests that the joint venture lacks full functionality. If the joint venture acquires a large part of its supplies from one or more parent companies, whether or not it has full functions will depend on the added value which the joint venture contributes to the products or the services supplied by the parent company.[153] If the amount of this added value is low the joint venture may be nothing more than a sales agencies for the parent companies.

The difference between concentrative and cooperative joint ventures

16.79 The original wording of Article 3(2) of former Regulation 4064/89 excluded from the scope of the Regulation those joint ventures that were called 'cooperative'.[154] In this way, a line was drawn between concentrative and cooperative joint ventures, the latter being defined as those which had as their object or effect the coordination of the competitive behaviour of undertakings that would remain independent. In accordance with this system, only concentrative joint ventures had to be notified to the European Commission under former Regulation

---

[151] Notice on the concept of full-function joint ventures, para 13.

[152] *Union Carbide/Enichem* (Case IV/M.550) (1995). The Commission found that the products which the joint venture sold to its parent company, Enichem, were of little importance to the former: 'Enichem will also enter into long-term agreements to buy from Polimeri Europa all the ethylene by-products [. . .] currently produced by the two ethylene steam crackers that will be contributed to the venture. These purchases of ethylene by-products do not call into question the autonomy of the joint venture, because these by-products are of minor interest for the joint venture.'

[153] In *Union Carbide/Enichem*, ibid, there were also supply agreements from the parent company Enichem to the joint venture *Polimeri Europa*. The Commission found that '[t]hese supply agreements do not call into question the functioning of the joint venture as an autonomous economic entity. Given the significant added value between the raw material, ethylene, and the product manufactured, PE, Polimeri Europa cannot be considered as a commercial agency of Enichem.' (para 15).

[154] See Commission Notice on the difference between cooperative and concentrative joint ventures of 31 December 1994 [1994] OJ C385/1 which substituted the Commission Notice on the same matter of 25 July 1990 [1990] OJ C20/10.

4064/89, while cooperative joint ventures were subject to the competitive analysis under Article 81(1) and (3) and could be notified to the Commission or be investigated in accordance with the rules contained in Regulation 17.[155] Following the amendment in 1997 to former Regulation 4064/89,[156] both types of joint ventures came within the scope of the Regulation, provided they had full functionality. Nevertheless, the distinction between the two types of joint venture continues to be relevant, since concentrative joint ventures must be assessed according to whether they entail a significant impediment to effective competition, in particular, because they create or reinforce a dominant position, under Article 2(3) of the Merger Control Regulation, while the criteria contained in Article 81(3) of the Treaty will be applied to cooperative joint ventures.

In accordance with Article 2(4) and (5) of the Merger Control Regulation, the Commission must assess whether the creation of the joint venture has as its object or effect coordination. In order to carry out this assessment, the Commission must assess whether: i) the parent companies retain a significant level of activity on the same market; (ii) the creation of the joint venture directly causes coordination; and iii) the coordination would allow the elimination of competition 'in respect of a substantial part of the products or services in question'. If, in accordance with this test, it is clear that the joint venture has as its object or effect coordination, the Commission will apply Article 81.   **16.80**

The practice of the Commission shows that, in the first place, the markets where coordination could take place must be identified. This means those markets where at least two parent companies retain activities to a significant degree in the same geographic market, whether the same market of the joint venture, or in an upstream, downstream, or neighbouring market. Sometimes in its assessment the Commission considers the position of the parent companies in the same market to see whether their presence is significant.[157] The next step is to see whether the creation of the joint venture will mean that the parent companies acquire certain   **16.81**

---

[155] Council Regulation (EEC) 17/62: First Regulation implementing Arts 85 and 86 of the Treaty [1962] OJ 13/204.

[156] Reg 1310/97 ([1997] OJ L180/1) amended former Reg 4064/89 through the introduction of para 4 into Art 2, which represented an examination of coordination under Art 81 of the EC Treaty within the Reg 4064/89 with respect to undertakings in cooperative joint ventures. Following this amendment, the Notice on the concept of full function joint ventures was adopted. This 1998 Notice stated that it was the Commission's intention to adopt guidelines concerning the application of the said Art 2(4) that have yet to be adopted. The Notice provided that until such guidelines are adopted, the interested parties should refer to the principles laid down in paras 17–20 of the 1994 Notice on the difference between concentrative and cooperative joint ventures.

[157] *BT/AT&T* (Case IV/JV.15) (1998) para 170, *Lazard/Intesabci/JV* (Case IV/M.2982) (2003) para 28, *Intracom/Siemens/Sti* (Case IV/M.2851) (2003) para 41, *Danapak/Teich/JV* (Case IV/M.2840) (2002) para 26, *Rwe Gas/Lattice International/JV* (Case IV/M.2744) (2002) para 34, abovementioned; *Sampo/Varma Sampo/If Holding/JV* (Case IV/M.2676) (2002) paras 34 and 37, *Mannesmann/Bell Atlantic/Opi* (Case IV/JV.17) (1999) para 20.

incentives to coordinate their competitive behaviour, thus giving rise to an appreciable restriction on competition.[158] Here, the Commission assesses whether coordination provides the parent companies with sufficient market power to eliminate competition in a substantial part of those markets where coordination could occur. The Commission must also take into account whether the restriction on competition would have an effect on intra-Community trade.[159]

16.82 The factors that the Commission must take into account when carrying out the competitive analysis are, *inter alia*, the joint market share of the parent companies,[160] the market structure,[161] asymmetry in the size of the parent companies,[162] the existence of barriers to entry,[163] the buying power of clients,[164] the nature of the product (whether homogeneous or heterogeneous[165]), the price of the intermediate product which the joint venture manufactures in relation to the price of the final product,[166] whether each parent company will have access to the confidential information of the other parent company or companies,[167] the geographic scope of the activities of the parent companies,[168] the limited

---

[158] *Newhouse/Júpiter/Scudder/M&G/JV* (Case IV/M.2075) (2000) para 19.

[159] *BT/AT&T* cited above paras 176 and 191.

[160] An analysis of the Commission's practice reveals that if the joint market share of parent companies in markets where coordination could occur is less than 40 per cent, this usually means that there are no coordination problems. See *Cementbouw/Enci/JV* (Case IV/M.3141) (2003) para 21, *Intracom/Siemens/Sti* (Case IV/M.2851) (2003) paras 41 and 42, *Starcore Llc* (Case IV/M.2874) (2002) para 16, *Sampo/Varma Sampo/If Holding/JV* (Case IV/M.2676) (2002) *Norske Skog/Abitibi/Papco* (Case IV/M.2493) (2001) para 8, *Universal Studio Networks/De Facto 829 (Ntl)/Studio Channel Limited* (Case IV/M.2211) (2000) para 38, *BP Chemicals/Solvay/Hdpe JV* (Case IV/M.2299) (2001) para 30. If the parent companies possess high market shares, it is very likely that the Commission will consider that the parent companies have an incentive to avoid competition and it is more likely that the restriction is considered as being appreciable: *BT/AT&T* (Case IV/JV.15) (1999) para 175, *Elf/Texaco/Antifreeze JV* (1998) paras 16–17, *Asahi Glass/Mitsubishi/F2 Chemicals* (Case IV/JV.42) (2000) paras 21 and 23.

[161] The presence of strong competitors in markets where coordination is possible suggests a lack of incentive to coordinate. *Rwe Gas/Lattice International/JV* (Case IV/M.2744) (2002) para 34, *Intracom/Siemens/Sti* above, para 43, *Sampo/Varma Sampo/If Holding/JV* above, para 37, *Asahi Glass/Mitsubishi/F2 Chemicals*, cited above, para 22.

[162] *Intracom/Siemens/Sti* above, para 44.

[163] *Panagora/Dg Bank* (Case IV/JV.14) (1998) para 32.

[164] *Intracom/Siemens/Sti* above, para 43, *Asahi Glass/Mitsubishi/F2 Chemicals*, para 22.

[165] *Starcore Llc* above, para 16.

[166] If the price of the intermediate product is relatively low cf total cost of the final product, the Commission may consider that the parties cannot use those prices as a means of coordinating the prices of the final product in which the parent companies are active. *Ericsson/Nokia/Psion* (Case COMP/JV.6) (1998) para 31.

[167] If this is so, it would help possible coordination. See *Accor/Hilton/Six Continents/JV* (Case IV/M.3101) (2003), para 2. *Newhouse/Júpiter/Scudder/M&G/JV* (Case IV/M.2075) (2000) cited above, para 21.

[168] If a parent company is only present in one Member State whereas the other parent company is present throughout the EU, it is probable that the Commission will consider that it makes no sense for the parent companies to coordinate their behaviour. *Intracom/Siemens/Sti*, cited above, para 44.

importance of the activities of the joint venture for the parent companies,[169] or the importance of innovation in the market in question.[170]

2. Community dimension

Only those concentrations with a Community dimension within the meaning **16.83** of Article 1 of the Merger Control Regulation must be notified to the European Commission, with the exception of those referral cases described above and which are covered by Articles 4(5) and 22 of the Merger Control Regulation.

Thresholds in Article 1 of the Merger Control Regulation

Article 1(2) and (3) states the criteria used to determine whether a concentra- **16.84** tion has a Community dimension. Each paragraph states a series of thresholds, based on the turnovers of the parties in different geographic areas.

The turnover must refer to the participants in the operation that are considered **16.85** to be 'undertakings concerned', a concept which is described in the Commission's Notice on the subject.[171] In summary, a distinction is drawn between undertakings concerned in the cases of merger, acquisitions of sole control and acquisitions of joint control as follows:

- As regards a merger between companies, the parties concerned will be those that merge, including the whole of the respective business groups in a broad sense, which means direct subsidiaries and parent companies, together with the latter's parent companies and subsidiaries.

- As regards an acquisition, the undertakings concerned will be the acquiring and the acquired or target company. In the case of the purchaser, the turnover of the purchasing company together with the whole of its business group in the sense indicated above will be taken into account. The turnover established in Article 1 is therefore the global figure of the acquiring undertaking plus the whole of its business group. As regards the acquired entity, only its turnover will be taken into account, that is, the acquired entity and its subsidiaries if these are transferred in the same operation, but not the selling undertaking(s). On this point, the Notice lays down that from the moment that control is no longer exercised over the undertaking, the selling undertaking's links with it

---

[169] *Intracom/Siemens/Sti* (Case IV/M.2851) (2003) para 44, where the Commission considered the reduced size of the joint venture, which amounted to 0–10 per cent of the sales of the parent company Siemens in the EEA. See also *Accor/Hilton/Six Continents* (Case IV/M.3101) (2003) (para 28) and *Norske Skog/Abitibi/Papco*, (Case IV/M.2493) (2002) para 10 both cited above. *Telia/Sonera/Lithuanian Telecommunications* (Case IV/JV.7) (1998) para 31.

[170] *Starcore Llc* cited above, para 16, *Intracom/Siemens/Sti* cited above, para 43.

[171] Commission Notice on the concept of undertakings concerned [1998] OJ C66/14.

extinguish. If the purchase refers to part of an undertaking, with respect to the vendor, only the part transferred which is the object of the transaction will be taken into account.

- If the case in question involves the acquisition of joint control over a joint venture, the undertakings concerned will be the parent companies and their respective business groups. If the joint venture already existed, then the joint venture itself would also be considered to be an undertaking concerned. In the same way, in the change from joint to sole control, the undertakings concerned will be the acquiring shareholder company which gains sole control and the joint venture.

16.86 When the case involves a joint venture where there are changes in shareholdings, a concentration will exist when there is a change in the nature of control. If a new shareholder acquires control, it becomes an undertaking concerned, while those shareholders that do not exercise control are not considered to be undertakings concerned. The Notice provides that the date on which turnover has to be calculated is that which is closest in time to the fact which triggered the obligation to notify (e.g. entering into the purchase agreement).[172] If the acquiring party is a joint venture, it will be an undertaking concerned itself if it has the necessary financial and other resources to carry on a lasting business activity, or if the joint venture is merely a vehicle of the parent companies in order to affect the acquisition its parent companies will be undertakings concerned.[173]

16.87 Article 5(2) of the Merger Control Regulation contains special rules for what the Notice has labelled 'staggered operations or follow-up deals'. These are a series of operations between the same parties that take place within a two-year period. Such operations will be considered as a concentration carried out on the date of the last such operation. Thus, if an operation between two parties—for example, the purchase of an entity—does not have to be notified, but then in the next two years another purchase takes place between the same parties, the turnovers of the entities acquired must be added together in order to assess whether the operation needs to be notified.

16.88 If certain undertakings purchase jointly a target undertaking in order to partition immediately the assets, despite the fact that there is a single operation, then each of the acquiring undertakings will be considered to be an undertaking concerned, as will the part of the target company that each has acquired as if there had been a series of independent operations.

---

[172] Thus, turnover attributable to any part of the undertaking concerned that has recently been sold off must not be counted. As will be seen, the annual accounts must be adjusted to reflect this.

[173] Notice on the concept of undertakings concerned paras 26 *et seq.*

Thresholds in Article 1(2) of the Merger Control Regulation The threshold   **16.89**
described in Article 1(2) refers to the worldwide and Community-wide turnover
of the undertakings concerned. In order for a Community dimension to exist,
Article 1(2) provides that the following two criteria must be fulfilled on a
cumulative basis:

(a) The combined aggregate worldwide turnover of all the undertakings concerned
     is more than 5,000 million euros; and
(b) The aggregate Community-wide turnover of each of at least two of the under-
     takings concerned is more than 250 million euros.

The worldwide threshold aims to establish the global dimension of the under-   **16.90**
takings concerned while the objective of the Community-wide threshold is
to determine whether the concentration involves a minimal level of activity in
the EU.

At the same time, in order for a Community dimension to exist, a negative   **16.91**
criterion known as the 'two-thirds rule' has to be fulfilled. This rule refers to the
situation where each and every of the undertakings concerned obtain more than
two-thirds of its aggregate EU turnover in the same Member State; if this
occurs, the concentration is seen as having an essentially national impact and
therefore it will not be of Community dimension. This two-thirds rule also
applies to the threshold contained in paragraph 3.

Thresholds contained in Article 1(3) of the Merger Control Regulation The   **16.92**
Article 1(3) threshold will only apply if the Article 1(2) threshold does not. This
second threshold reduces the turnover figure established in the worldwide and
Community thresholds of paragraph 2 to 2,500 and 100 million euros respectively and introduces and combines two thresholds with a national scope. These
provide that at least two of the undertakings concerned must have at least a
certain level of activity in at least three Member States.[174] Thus, for an operation
to be notifiable, in addition to fulfilling the worldwide and Community
thresholds the following conditions must be met:

(1) The turnover of all of the undertakings concerned must be more than 100
     million euros in each of at least three Member States and
(2) the total turnover achieved individually by at least two of the undertakings
     concerned in at least three of the relevant Member States in (1)—i.e. those

---

[174] The Notice on the calculation of turnover states that para 3 is aimed at dealing with
operations that 'would need to be notified under national competition rules in at least three
Member States'. This is not correct. While this is a new criterion for the referral of concentrations
to the Commission under Art 4(5) of the Merger Control Regulation, in the previous system it
was possible for operations to exist that fell below the scope of the second threshold of Art 1 of
Reg 4064/89 and which should, therefore, be notified to the Commission despite not having to
be notified in three Member States; e.g. in Spain, a turnover of more than €25 million has never
created any obligation to notify (the minimum is €60 million).

Member States where turnover is above 100 million euros—is more than 25 million euros.

As mentioned, in order to have a Community dimension with this second threshold, the 'two-thirds rule' must not apply.

Calculating the level of turnover

16.93 **General rules** In addition to determining the undertakings concerned, in order to evaluate whether or not a concentration has a Community dimension and must be notified to the European Commission, it is necessary to calculate their turnover and see whether the thresholds established in Article 1 of the Merger Control Regulation are reached. This matter is regulated in Articles 1 and 5 and in the Commission Notice on the calculation of turnover.[175] Article 1 of the Merger Control Regulation regulates the thresholds that give an operation a Community dimension. The general rule under Article 5 is that turnover will include the amounts resulting from the sales of products and the provision of services by the undertakings concerned during the preceding financial year relating to its ordinary activities after sales rebates,[176] VAT and other directly related taxes have been deducted.[177]

16.94 The turnover must refer to the preceding tax year. If the information for the preceding year is not available, the figures from the year immediately before that will be used. The Commission considers that the most reliable and exact information will come from company accounts that have been audited in accordance with Community accounting rules. In line with the principle of assessing the undertaking's situation with the greatest possible rigour, the audited turnover must be adjusted if, prior to the concentration, purchases or sales of businesses have taken place. That said, the amount will not be adjusted to reflect purely temporary factors such as a fall in orders. The turnover must include the sales figures not only of the specific acquiring entity or participant in the operation, but also all sales made by its business group. This aspect should not be confused with the fact that Article 5 excludes from the calculation of turnover sales between undertakings of the same business group, in order to avoid double accounting. The sales to be taken into account for this calculation are therefore limited to sales to third parties.

16.95 Article 5(2) excludes the turnover of the seller, since it is not an undertaking

---

[175] Commission Notice on calculation of turnover under Council Regulation (EEC) 4064/89 on the control of concentrations between undertakings [1998] OJ C66/25.

[176] The Notice on calculation of turnover (para 20) describes 'sales rebates' as all rebates or discounts granted by undertakings to their clients.

[177] This would cover all indirect taxes that have an impact on the turnover, such as taxes on alcoholic drinks.

concerned unless it retains control. The target undertaking or part thereof will be considered to be an undertaking concerned regardless of whether or not it has legal personality, and therefore the turnover which it generates must be taken into account, without including that of undertakings that are connected through a relationship of control that are neither the target company nor retain control over it.

As already stated, under Article 5(2) paragraph two, when two or more oper-   **16.96**
ations between the same persons—natural or legal—are carried out in a staggered manner within a period of two years, they will be considered as a single
concentration carried out on the date of the last operation. The purpose of this
provision is to prevent concentrations from being fragmented into different
parts to avoid having to notify, since no individual operation reaches the thresholds contained in Article 1 of the Merger Control Regulation. This provision
appears to encourage undertakings not to notify fragmented operations until
the moment when they carry out the last in the series of operations, although
there is nothing to prevent an undertaking from notifying each time that an
operation is carried out if the said thresholds are reached.

The amount of aid granted by State bodies must be included in the turnover   **16.97**
if the undertaking is the beneficiary and the aid is directly linked to supporting the sale of that undertaking's products and is therefore reflected in the
price.[178]

In the event that the undertakings concerned are the parent companies of a joint   **16.98**
venture, the sales of the latter to its parent companies will not be included to
avoid double accounting. The sales of the joint venture to third parties, however, will be imputed in equal shares to the parent companies.[179] With regard to
the calculation of the turnover of State-owned companies or holding companies, the fundamental principle is to identify the undertakings that constitute
an independent economic entity equipped with autonomous decision-making
power. Having identified this group and included its turnover, that of other
State-owned groups must not be included.

In order to apply the thresholds contained in Article 1, it is necessary to apportion   **16.99**

---

[178] The Notice gives the example of aid granted towards the consumption of the product which would allow the manufacturer to sell it at a higher price than that actually paid by consumers.

[179] Note that the percentage of the share capital held by each parent company in the joint venture is not important; the only relevant factor is that they share control. For example, if there are two parent companies, they will each be attributed with 50 per cent of the joint venture's sales, even if one has a 60 per cent stake and the other a 40 per cent stake; in the same way, if there were three parent companies, each would be attributed with 33.3 per cent of the sales. This method of imputing sales is also applicable to joint ventures between an undertaking concerned and third parties.

the turnover for different geographic areas, in particular, in the European Union and in each Member State where the undertaking concerned has activities. With respect to the geographic distribution of the turnover, this will be determined by the location of the client at the time of the transaction. Thus, Article 5 refers to the place where the sale takes place or where the service was provided. This is taken as the place where the client is located, since frequently it will coincide with the place where the transaction was carried out and where the undertaking has competed. The place where the goods or service are consumed will not be taken into account.[180]

16.100 **Credit institutions** Article 5(3)(a) of the Merger Control Regulation sets forth special provisions for calculating the turnover of credit and other financial entities. The turnover will be substituted for the total obtained by adding together a series of income items (interest and other similar income, income from securities, commissions, net profits on financial operations and other operating income) less VAT and other taxes that are directly related to these items. Paragraph 51 of the Notice refers to the definitions contained in the First and Second Banking Directives, thus confirming that the term 'credit institution' means an undertaking whose activity consists in receiving deposits or other repayable funds from the public granting credits for its own account. 'Financial entity' means any undertaking other than a credit entity whose main activity consists in acquiring holdings or in exercising one or more of the activities listed in points 2 to 12 in the Annex to the Second Banking Directive.[181] The territorial attribution of each amount of income will be on the basis of the location of the branch or division of the corresponding entity.

16.101 **Insurance companies** Article 5(3)(b) provides that with respect to insurance companies, turnover is to be substituted by the value of gross premiums written[182] which will comprise all amounts received and receivable in respect of insurance contracts, including outgoing reinsurance premiums and parafiscal

---

[180] Notice on the calculation of turnover paras 45–48.

[181] Para 52 of the Notice on the calculation of turnover explains that the term 'financial entity' covers both holding companies and those undertakings whose regular main activity is one of those contained in the list annexed to the Directive: lending, financial leasing, money transmission services, issuing and managing instruments of payment, giving guarantees, trading on own account or on account of clients in money market instruments, foreign exchange, financial futures and options, exchange and interest rate instruments, and transferable securities, participation in share issues, advice to undertakings on capital structure, industrial strategy etc, money broking, and others. As regards holding companies, paras 59–61 of the Notice contain a specific method of calculating turnover.

[182] All premiums received, including outgoing reinsurance premiums, i.e. all amounts paid or payable by the undertaking concerned to obtain reinsurance cover. Both premiums paid for new insurance contracts entered into in the accounting year in question and those relating to contracts from previous years but which are still in force are counted.

contributions applied to the total volume of such premiums. Such income will be attributed to the territory of the Member State where the client paying the premium resides. If an insurance company acquires an investment stake in another company without acquiring control, the sales of the latter company will not be taken into account when calculating turnover.

17

PROCEDURES

A. Notification

1. General aspects of notification

The Notifying parties

The Merger Control Regulation provides that concentrations that consist in the **17.01**
merger or acquisition of joint control must be notified jointly by the parties
involved in the merger or acquisition of joint control.[1] In all other cases the
notification must be made by the person or undertaking that acquires control of
all or part of one or more undertakings. When the case concerns a public bid to
acquire the shares of an undertaking, it is the bidder who must notify.[2]

Mergers and acquisitions of sole control do not normally raise great difficulties of **17.02**
interpretation. The obligation to notify rests respectively with the undertakings
to the merger or the party acquiring control. However, in the case of acquisitions
of joint control in a joint venture, all the undertakings that participate in the
joint control—the parent companies—must notify. This includes not only the
undertakings which acquire control as a result of the operation, but also eventually companies that may not have participated in any transaction but will enjoy
joint control following the concentration. A clear example is that of the replacement of one parent company in a joint venture. Irrespectively of the fact that
the other parent company (or companies) of the joint venture may not have
intervened in the deal in any manner, they will have to participate in the filing.

When the notifications are made by representatives of the undertakings con- **17.03**
cerned, they must provide written proof that they are authorized to act.[3] Joint
notifications must be filed through a representative appointed jointly by the
parties who is empowered to transfer and receive documents on behalf of all

---

[1] Art 4(2).
[2] Annex I Implementing Reg (section 1.2).
[3] Art 2(2) of the Implementing Reg.

notifying parties.[4] In a joint notification, the Commission may address its requests for information separately to each party.

Time of notification

17.04 Article 4(1) of former Regulation 4064/89 gave the parties one week within which to notify concentrations with a Community dimension to the Commission, although in practice this period was systematically exceeded. Article 4(1) of the Merger Control Regulation provides that concentrations must be notified to the Commission 'prior to their implementation and following the conclusion of the agreement' in question, the announcement of the public bid, or the acquisition of a controlling interest. While there is no longer a specific period within which notification must take place, there remains a general duty to file the notification as quickly as possible, coupled with the prohibition on implementation before authorization.[5] Besides, undertakings have every incentive to notify so as to obtain clearance as soon as possible. In any event, significant and unjustifiable delays will not be accepted, although in very complicated cases it is normal for notification to be made several weeks or even months after the date on which the parties have entered into the agreement that gave rise to notification.

17.05 The earlier wording of Article 4(1) did not permit notifying parties to file in the absence of a definitive agreement. The new text makes it possible to notify proposed concentrations when the undertakings involved can show the Commission that their intention in good faith is to enter into an agreement, or when they have publicly announced their intention to make a bid, provided that the agreement or bid in question gives rise to a concentration of a Community dimension. Recital 34 of the Merger Control Regulation clarifies that undertakings will comply with Article 4(1) if they can show that their plan for the proposed concentration is 'sufficiently concrete, for example on the basis of an agreement in principle, a memorandum of understanding, or a letter of intent signed by all undertakings concerned'.

2. The notification form

Standard notification: The ordinary form or Form CO

17.06 The rules concerning notification are contained in the Implementing Regulation. The notification is made using Form CO, which is contained in Annex I of the Implementing Regulation. In the event of joint notification, a single form is

---

[4] Art 2(3) of the Implementing Reg.

[5] It is noted that the Spanish version of the Merger Control Reg reads 'en cuanto se haya concluido el acuerdo [. . .]' (as soon as the agreement has been entered into). The other linguistic versions however read more like the English version.

used.[6] The form contains a series of questions about different aspects of the proposed concentration, which will be used to carry out the Commission's subsequent in-depth analysis. The parties must fill in Form CO in full and also provide all of the required documentation, unless the Commission considers that certain data or documents are not necessary to evaluate the concentration, in which case it may dispense with the need for them to be filed.[7]

The notification must be made in one of the official languages of the European Union, which will then be the language to be used in the proceedings for the notifying parties. If notifications are made in accordance with Article 12 of Protocol 24 of the EEA Agreement in an official language of an EFTA States the notification must be accompanied simultaneously with a translation into an official Community language.[8] Supporting documents must be submitted in their original language, and if this is not one of the official Community languages, the documents must be translated into the language used in the proceedings.[9] Supporting documents must be originals or copies of originals, in which case the notifying party will confirm that they are authentic and complete.[10] The original and thirty-five copies of Form CO and all the supporting documents must be filed with the Commission. **17.07**

Form CO requires the filing of detailed information and to complete it properly generally takes a considerable length of time (from two weeks to several months) and involves the joint effort of lawyers and notifying parties. The following categories of information must be initially supplied: **17.08**

(1) Business and financial information concerning the notifying parties,[11] including personal and economic links between undertakings and previous acquisitions.[12]

(2) Detailed information concerning the nature of the transaction, where a joint venture is concerned, since determining whether or not the Merger Control Regulation applies may not always be straightforward.[13]

(3) Supporting documents, copies of the final or most recent versions of all documents bringing about the concentration, copies of the most recent annual reports, and accounts of all the parties to the concentration. Further, copies of all analyses, reports, studies and surveys prepared by or for any member or members of the board of directors or the supervisory board or the shareholders' meeting, for the purposes of assessing or analysing the

---

[6] Art 3(1).   [7] Art 4(2).
[8] Art 3(5) of the Implementing Reg. See also para E, Form CO.
[9] Art 3(4) of the Implementing Reg.   [10] Art 3(3) of the Implementing Reg.
[11] ss 2, 3 and 4.   [12] s 4.2.3.   [13] ss 1 and 3.

concentration with respect to market share, competition conditions, actual or potential competitors, the rationale for the operation, the potential for sales growth or the expansion into other product or geographic markets, and the general market conditions.[14]

(4) A description of the relevant markets, both product and geographic, which will determine the scope of the assessment of the concentration.[15]

(5) With respect to each of the product markets affected and each of the last three financial years, extensive information on sales (volume and amount).[16]

(6) General conditions of the affected markets (defined as those where the parties have a joint share of 15 per cent where there is horizontal overlapping or 25 per cent if a vertical relationship exists), the structure of supply and demand of the affected markets, market access, information on research and development, cooperation agreements, and the lists of the parties' main independent suppliers, clients and competitors.[17]

(7) Cooperative effects of a joint venture, particularly if its creation may give rise to coordination between independent undertakings that restricts competition in the sense of Article 2(4) of the Merger Control Regulation.[18]

(8) The worldwide context of the proposed concentration, and the effects that this may have on the interests of intermediate and final consumers and on technical and economic development.[19]

17.09 Form CO is more a report than just a form. It gives the parties the chance to make submissions regarding the relevant market, the competitive context of the operation and the effects on the notified operation. In preparing the form, the parties must take into account the fact that the Commission generally considers the approach it has taken in previous cases, particularly with respect to the definition of market. For example, in *Airtours/First Choice*, the Commission stated that 'in previous decisions on cases in this area, the Commission has distinguished certain distinct product markets and these are used as the starting point for establishing the relevant markets here.'[20] However, the Commission is not bound by any previous decision and it is prepared to modify its approach to

---

[14] s 5.   [15] s 6.   [16] s 7.   [17] s 8.   [18] s 10.   [19] s 9.

[20] Commission Decision *Airtours/First Choice* (Case IV/M.1524) [1999] OJ L93/01 para 4, annulled by the CFI on 6 June 2002, in Case T-342/99. The judgment of the CFI did not deal with the Commission's approach of taking as its starting point the analysis of the relevant precedents. See also Commission Decision *Conoco/Philipps Petroleum* (Case COMP/2681) (2000) para 10: '[. . .] Consistent with previous Commission decisions [. . .] the following markets are relevant . . .'. Commission Decision *Magneti Marelli/MM Automotive Lighting JV* (Case COMP/M.2102) (2000) para 15. See also 'Competition Law of the European Community': N Levy, *The Control of Concentrations between Undertakings* (Matthew Bender, 2002), ch 5, s 5.13 [3] [e].

a particular market when it feels this to be necessary.[21] In addition, given that the Commission tries to confirm the situation stated in the form by contacting the main operators in the industry in question, it is crucial that economic evidence be provided to back up the observations contained in the form, in particular, with regard to the definition of relevant market. All internal documentation should be thoroughly revised to assess whether these contain incorrect and/or damaging observations and if these need any additional explanation.

Notifications must contain all the information, including the documents, **17.10** requested in Form CO.[22] This information must be correct and complete.[23] The parties may request the Commission to accept the notification despite not having provided the information requested in the form, if that information is either partially or totally unavailable.[24] Further, the Commission may be requested to accept that the notification is complete and, therefore, valid despite a party not having made available the information required in the form if it is considered that some of the information required, whether in its full or abbreviated version, is not necessary for the Commission's analysis.[25] In general, the European Commission is prepared to alleviate the notifying parties' obligation to complete certain parts of the form, in particular in cases where there is no significant overlapping or where the market shares are marginal.[26]

Simplified notification: the short form

A short-form notification also exists.[27] This can be used for filing those concen- **17.11** trations that prima facie do not pose any significant competition concerns, and

---

[21] 'Competition Law of the European Community': N Levy, *The Control of Concentrations between Undertakings* (Matthew Bender, 2002), ch 5, s 5.13 [3] [e] with references: Commission Decision *Allied Signal/Honeywell* (Case COMP/M.1601) [1999] OJ L4/31 Commission Decision *General Electric/Honeywell* (Case IV/M.2220) (2001). In *Allied Signal/Honeywell*, the Commission considered it unlikely that bundling would damage competition. By contrast, in *General Electric/Honeywell*, the concern about bundling was the main reason for prohibiting the transaction.

[22] Art 4(1) of the Implementing Reg.

[23] s 1.3 of Form CO.

[24] Implementing Reg Annex I Form CO s 1(3)(f): 'The Commission will consider such a request, provided that you give reasons for the unavailability of that information, and provide your best estimates for missing data together with the sources for the estimates.'

[25] Implementing Reg, Annex I Form CO, s 1(3)(g): 'You may request in writing that the Commission accept that the notification is complete notwithstanding the failure to provide information required by this Form, if you consider that any particular information required, in the full or short form version, may not be necessary for the Commission's examination of the case.'

[26] See DG COMP Best Practices on the conduct of EC Merger Control Proceedings, paras 6 and 19 and Art 3(2) of the Implementing Reg.

[27] See Art 3(1) of the Implementing Reg. The form is contained in Annex II of the Implementing Reg.

which are generally authorized. The Commission has adopted a Notice which sets out the general aspects of this procedure.[28]

17.12 The simplified procedure—and the short form—will apply when:[29]

(a) two or more undertakings acquire joint control of a joint venture provided that the latter does not operate nor is it expected to operate within the European Economic Area (EEA), or when such activities are 'negligible'. Here, 'negligible' means that: i) the turnover of the joint venture or the turnover of the activities contributed (by the parent companies) is less than 100 million euros within the EEA territory; and ii) the total value of the assets transferred to the joint venture is less than 100 million euros within the EEA territory;

(b) two or more undertakings merge, or one or more undertakings acquires sole or joint control of another undertaking, provided that none of the parties to the concentration carries out business activities in the same product and geographic market or in a product market that is upstream or downstream from a product market in which any other party to the concentration operates;

(c) two or more undertakings merge, or one or more undertakings acquire sole or joint control of another undertaking and: i) two or more of the parties to the concentration exercise business activities in the same product and geographic market (horizontal relationships) provided that their combined market share is less than 15 per cent or ii) one or more parties to the concentration carries out business activities in a product market which is upstream or downstream from a product market in which any other party to the concentration operates (vertical relationships) provided that none of their individual or combined market shares reaches 25 per cent;

(d) a party to a concentration is to acquire sole control of an undertaking over which it already has joint control. This procedure is not appropriate for cases where the parties request an express assessment of the restrictions directly related to and necessary for the implementation.

17.13 The short form limits considerably the information that must be provided in sections 7 and 10 of the form and therefore the efforts that the notifying parties must make. In particular, they only have to submit market share data for the last

---

[28] Commission's Notice on a simplified procedure for treatment of certain concentrations under Council Reg (EC) 139/2004 [2005] OJ C56/32 (hereinafter, 'the Simplified Procedure Notice'), which substitutes the previous Notice of 2000.

[29] See point 19 of the Simplified Procedure Notice and s 1.1 of Annex II of the Implementing Reg.

year instead of the last three years,[30] and it is not necessary to offer all the detailed market information that is required in section 8 of the standard form. Notification on the short form, as with those cases notified on the normal form but which do not give rise to competition problems, will end in an abbreviated decision, which will be adopted within twenty-five working days of the date of notification.

Despite having initiated the simplified procedure, the Commission will, on **17.14** occasion,[31] require a full investigation and, therefore, a normal decision. The Commission will also adopt a normal decision if a Member State expresses 'substantiated [competition] concerns' about the concentration within a period of fifteen working days from the date of receipt of the copy of the notification, or if a third party does the same within the time period laid down for such observations.[32]

The Simplified Procedure Notice does not allow the simplified procedure to be **17.15** used when a Member State requests the referral of a concentration under Article 9 of the Merger Control Regulation. Short-form notification is, however, possible despite the fact that the Commission had considered a referral on the basis of a Member State's request under Article 4(4) or when a concentration is referred to it under Article 4(5) of the Merger Control Regulation. The decision taken by the Commission in these cases is also an abbreviated decision. It is adopted within a period of twenty-five days (and the Commission will attempt to adopt it as soon as possible once the fifteen day period has expired) from the date of the notification. These abbreviated decisions are limited to identifying the parties and the general features of the business but they do not analyse the definition of the markets or the position of the parties in detail.

---

[30] The Notice requires market shares for relevant markets, both products and geographic, as well as all the plausible definitions of alternative relevant markets, both product and geographic, in which two or more parties develop business activities (regardless of their market share) or at least carry on activities in a market that is upstream or downstream from a market in which any other party to the concentration operates and in which its individual or combined market shares exceed 25 per cent.

[31] e.g. in situations which combine technological financial or other resources or those of another kind for parties that do not operate in the same market; in concentrations when any of the parties holds individually a market share equal to or higher than 25 per cent in any product market in which there is no horizontal or vertical relationship between the parties but it is a neighbouring market to another in which another party operates; in new or little developed markets where it is not possible to determine exactly what the market shares of the parties are; or in markets with high barriers to entry, a high degree of concentration or other known competition problems (para 8). The Notice excludes from the procedure cases where it is difficult to define the relevant markets or determine the market shares of the parties as well as concentrations that involve new legal aspects of a general interest (para 6).

[32] Para 12 of the Simplified Procedure Notice.

3. Notification of sensitive or confidential information

17.16 The Commission must respect undertakings' legitimate interest in protecting their business secrets and other confidential information.[33] This information will not be divulged nor will access be given to it, including documents, provided that it contains the business secrets of any person or undertaking, in particular the notifying parties, other interested parties and third parties, as well as no other confidential information which the Commission does not consider it necessary to divulge for the purpose of the proceedings.[34] This covers any internal document of the Member States.[35] The Commission has largely been able to maintain the confidentiality of business secrets, although in some specific situations there have been complaints that its representatives have divulged confidential information to the press.[36]

17.17 According to the Implementing Regulation, in order to ensure the protection of confidential information, any person (notifying, interested, or third party[37]) who makes known her point of view through an invitation to submit observations on the text of a provisional decision to waive the obligation to suspend implementation of the concentration[38] or a statement of objections,[39] or in the oral hearing,[40] or a request for information[41] should indicate clearly which elements it considers confidential and why. In addition, it will have to provide a separate non-confidential version of the document within the period laid down by the Commission.[42] The Commission could require the notifying parties and the undertakings that have filed documents in the proceeding to identify—and justify—the documents or parts thereof which they consider contain business secrets or other confidential information which belongs to them, and to identify as well the undertakings with respect to which the documents in question must be considered confidential.[43] This applies to confidential information contained

---

[33] Art 287 EC: 'The members of the institutions of the Community, the members of committees, and the officials and other servants of the Community shall be required, even after their duties have ceased, not to disclose information of the kind covered by the obligation of professional secrecy, in particular information about undertakings, their business relations or their cost components.'

[34] Art 18 of the Implementing Reg.   [35] Art 17 of the Implementing Reg.

[36] 'Competition Law of the European Community': N Levy, *The Control of Concentrations between Undertakings* (Matthew Bender, 2002), ch 5, s 5.13 [10] referring to *Financial Times*, 'GE lost interest in Honeywell bid in early June—EU officials', 5 July 2001.

[37] Art 11 refers to the parties with the right to be heard and distinguishes between notifying parties, other involved parties (such as the seller or the target company), and third parties (clients, suppliers and competitors, provided that a sufficient interest is justified). Under Art 11, all will have the right to be heard in the proceedings.

[38] Art 12.   [39] Art 13.   [40] Art 14.

[41] Art 11 of the Merger Control Reg.   [42] Art 18(2).   [43] Art 18(3).

in the statement of objections or in a decision.[44] Whenever the Commission receives a request for access to the file, it must carry out a specific assessment in relation to each document.[45] It is considered that the interests of those parties would be prejudiced if the information provided to the Commission were published or divulged in any other form. Whenever the Commission is provided with information it is recommended sending any confidential information separately, clearly marking each page 'Business secret'. It is also necessary to state why the information should not be divulged or made public. When the case involves a merger or a joint acquisition, or when notification has been made by more than one of the parties, the documents protected by business secrets could be sent in a separate envelope, stating on the notification form that it is a confidential annex.

B. Overview of Key Deadlines

One of the most important procedural features of the Merger Control Regulation is the strict adherence to mandatory deadlines. This adherence is reinforced by the mechanism provided in Article 10(6) of the Merger Control Regulation, which provides that where the Commission has not taken a decision at the end of either the first phase or the second phase within the applicable deadlines, the operation shall be deemed to have been declared compatible with the common market.[46] The originality of the Merger Control Regulation when read against former Regulation 4064/89 in the way it approaches calculation of deadlines is that the Merger Control Regulation has substituted the reference to months for working days and has made the time periods more flexible in a number of ways. The most important periods can be summarized as follows:

17.18

---

[44] Art 18(3) second para.

[45] The CFI has established that the Commission cannot reject access to the whole file without having carried out a specific assessment and an individual examination of each document requested in order to determine whether access (even partial) is possible. The CFI did add, however, that an individual examination may not be necessary in cases where it is obvious that access must be rejected or granted (Case T-2/03 *Verein Für Konsumenteninformation v EC Commission* [2005] OJ C155/13 para 75).

[46] As the Commission itself recognised at the time of adoption of the Merger Control Reg, '(t)he legally-binding review timetable is unquestionably the most appreciated feature of the current Merger Regulation. The Commission's and Council's objective has been to change this only to the extent necessary to avoid even the perception that a merger may have to be blocked because there was no time left to discuss remedies to the competition problems. Allowing more time in a clearly defined and controlled way may also be essential for the Commission as it is held to high standards to prove both the existence and non-existence of competition problems.' New Merger Reg Frequently Asked Questions, at http://europa.eu.int/rapid/pressReleasesAction.do?reference=MEMO/04/9&format=HTML&aged=0&language=EN&guiLanguage=en.

1. Time periods in the first phase

17.19 The first phase should normally be cleared in twenty-five working days from the working day following effective notification. This period can be extended by ten working days (to thirty-five working days) if there exists a request for referral to a Member State (Article 9(2) of the Merger Control Regulation) or if the parties put forward commitments.[47] In the latter case, the commitments must be filed within a maximum period of twenty days following receipt of notification.[48]

2. Time periods in the second phase

17.20 The maximum duration of the second phase is, in principle, ninety working days from the date on which it is formally initiated. This period may be extended by fifteen working days (giving a total of 105 working days) if the parties concerned propose commitments at least fifty-five days after the start of the second phase.[49] Commitments must be proposed within sixty-five working days from the date that second-phase proceedings are initiated.[50] However, if the period for adopting a decision is extended, the sixty-five day period for filing commitments will automatically be extended by the same number of working days. The period for adopting a second-phase decision will exceptionally be suspended if, due to circumstances for which one of the undertakings involved in the concentration is responsible, the Commission has been forced to request information in accordance with Article 11 or to order an inspection by decision pursuant to Article 13 of the Merger Control Regulation.[51]

3. 'Stop the clock' provisions

17.21 The Merger Control Regulation has introduced limited flexibility in the deadlines in second phase procedures. Within the first fifteen working days of the initiation of a procedure under an Article 6(1)(c) of the Regulation, the parties may request an extension. Alternatively, at any subsequent moment (provided the parties agree) the Commission may grant an extension of its own initiative. Any extension or extensions cannot exceed a maximum of twenty working days.[52]

---

[47] Art 10(1) of the Merger Control Reg. [48] Art 19(1) of the Merger Control Reg.
[49] Art 10(3) of the Merger Control Reg. [50] Art 19(2) of the Merger Control Reg.
[51] Art 10(4) of the Merger Control Reg.
[52] Art 10(3) of the Merger Control Reg second para.

C. Pre-Notification and First Phase

1. Pre-notification and waivers

Before an actual filing is made, informal contacts with the Commission usually **17.22** take place. This practice was in the early days of the Regulation rather informal. Currently however, pre-notification meetings between the parties and the Commission are described in detail in the 'Best Practice Guidelines' issued by the Commission[53] and formally regarded as a most important aspect of notification procedures under the Merger Control Regulation,[54] recognized by the ECJ as an example of the principle of good administration.[55]

Pre-notification is based on the mutual interest of both the parties and the **17.23** Commission. On the one hand, it allows the Commission's services to find out about an operation in advance, which enables them to examine the case before notification actually takes place and the various time periods apply. Further, the

---

[53] Commission Best Practice Guidelines 2004, online at: http://europa.eu.int/comm/competition/mergers/legislation/regulation/best_practices.pdf: '[. . .] DG Competition finds it useful to have pre-notifying contacts with notifying parties even in seemingly non-problematic cases [. . .] Pre-notification contacts should preferably be initiated at least two weeks before the expected date of notification. The extent and format of these pre-notification contacts will depend on the complexity of the individual cases in question. In more complex cases a more extended pre-notification period may be appropriate and in the interests of the notifying parties. In all cases it is advisable to make contact with DG Competition as soon as possible as this will facilitate planning of the case. Pre-notification contacts should be launched with a submission that allows the selection of an appropriate DG Competition case team. This memorandum should provide a brief background to the transaction, a brief description of the relevant sector(s) and market(s) involved and the likely impact of the transaction on competition in general terms [. . .] In straightforward cases, the parties may choose to submit a draft Form CO as a basis for further discussions with DG Competition [. . .] Any submission sent to DG Competition should be provided sufficiently ahead of meetings or other contacts in order to allow for well prepared and fruitful discussions. In this regard, preparatory briefing memoranda/draft Form COs sent in preparation of meetings should be filed in good time before the meeting (at least three working days) unless agreed otherwise with the case team [. . .] DG Competition would normally require five working days to review the draft before being asked to comment, at a meeting or on the telephone, on the adequacy of the draft.' Paras 5, 10, 11, 14, and 15.

[54] See Recital 11 of the Implementing Reg: 'The Commission should give the notifying parties and other parties involved in the proposed concentration, if they so request, an opportunity before notification to discuss the intended concentration informally and in strict confidence.'

[55] Case T-3/93 *Air France v EC Commission* [1994] ECR II-121 para 67. Götz Drauz has explained the value of such meetings as follows: 'Before any formal steps are taken, the members of the Merger Task Force are always prepared to discuss with the parties to mergers proposed transactions which may be notifiable informally and in confidence. Such prior contact is, in the Commission's experience, generally regarded as beneficial to all concerned. In particular, it can reduce or remove the risk of delay or other inconvenience arising from submissions of an incomplete notification or of notifying a transaction to which the Regulation does not apply'. European Commission, *Merger Control Law in the European Union: Situation in March 1998*, Introduction, 13. Quoted in 'Competition Law of the European Community': N Levy, *The Control of Concentrations between Undertakings* (Matthew Bender, 2002), ch 5 s 5.10 [2].

notifying parties will obtain an initial idea of the Commission's view of the matter and can avoid the risk that the notification is declared incomplete.[56]

17.24 Contacts with the Commission often start a few days before notification, although in more complex cases greater time should be allowed to enable more detailed discussions to take place. In particular, the following matters will be dealt with:

(1) The obligation to notify the operation under the Merger Control Regulation: it is not uncommon for the parties to consult the Commission on aspects, *inter alia*, related with the acquisition of control, the identification of affected undertakings and the turnover thresholds contained in Article 1 of the Merger Control Regulation. If the Commission considers that it does not have jurisdiction to deal with the case, it may issue a letter confirming this.

(2) Procedural matters such as the possibility of requesting a derogation under Article 7(3) Merger Control Regulation of the obligation to suspend implementation of the concentration or jurisdictional aspects, such as whether it is convenient to notify NCAs or use the prior referral mechanism.

(3) Waivers related to the information required: Form CO requires the parties to supply from the outset a significant amount of information. In many cases, a waiver can be requested with respect to certain sections or aspects of Form CO.[57] The waiver must be requested by the parties in a reasoned manner, justifying that the information in question is not necessary for the Commission's assessment of the concentration. Experience has shown that pre-notification meetings are extremely valuable, both for the notifying party or parties and the Commission, in order to determine the precise volume of information required in a notification; in addition, in the vast majority of cases, they allow a significant reduction in the amount of information that must be filed.[58] In this way, the Commission

---

[56] Best Practice Guidelines para 20 and Art 5(4) of the Implementing Reg.

[57] Art 4(2) Implementing Reg: 'The Commission may dispense with the obligation to provide any particular information in the notification, including documents, or with any other requirement specified in Annexes I and II where the Commission considers that compliance with those obligations or requirements is not necessary for the examination of the case.'

[58] Annex I of the Implementing Reg states: 'It is recognised that the information requested in this Form is substantial. However, experience has shown that, depending on the specific characteristics of the case, not all information is always necessary for an adequate examination of the proposed concentration. Accordingly, if you consider that any particular information requested by this Form may not be necessary for the Commission's examination of the case, you are encouraged to ask the Commission to dispense with the obligation to provide certain information ("waiver").' Section 1.3.(g) of the Annex provides that: 'You may request in writing that the Commission accept that the notification is complete notwithstanding the failure to provide information required by this Form, if you consider that any particular information required, in

applies the proportionality principle to the information which must be supplied.[59]

(4) Whether the concentration qualifies for short-form notification if it does not cause any competition problems: as the Simplified Procedure Notice states, even with respect to cases where there may be complications although they appear to be straightforward, it is worth resolving these problems in the pre-notification phase, contacting the Commission two weeks before the date of notification.

(5) A preliminary examination of competition law questions: in these meetings potential difficulties related to the transaction can be identified in the light of the Commission's practice and previous experience in relevant markets. This may include reaching an agreement on the correct definition of markets, the methodology used to calculate market shares, possible markets affected, potential competition problems and possible solutions. To increase the usefulness of these conversations, it is recommended that as much information as possible is provided. In practice, the Commission's services will request a memorandum which explains the most important features of the concentration, which will then form the basis of discussions in pre-notification meetings. These contacts can therefore highlight potential problems which can be resolved without entering into a more detailed analysis. In fact, without contacts in the pre-notification phase, it may be difficult to determine the need and the scope of the possible commitments to be made in the first phase of the investigation.

(6) Contacts between the Commission and other NCAs: if the transaction must be notified in other countries, contacts may be established with other NCAs, since the Commission always tries to coordinate its investigations with other authorities.

2. The first phase

Proceedings under the Merger Control Regulation have two phases, known **17.25** as phase 1 and phase 2. This two-stage technique, imported from the US Hart-Scott-Rodino Act of 1976, reserves a more in-depth analysis for more

---

the full or short form version, may not be necessary for the Commission's examination of the case.—The Commission will consider such a request, provided that you give adequate reasons why that information is not relevant and necessary to its inquiry into the notified operation. You should explain this during your pre-notification contacts with the Commission and, submit a written request for a waiver, asking the Commission to dispense with the obligation to provide that information, pursuant to Article 4(2) of the Implementing Regulation.'

[59] E Navarro, A Font, J Folguera, and J Briones, *Merger Control in the EU* (OUP, 2002) para 12.2.2.

complicated cases, thus enabling those matters less liable to damage competition to be dealt with speedily.

17.26 The first phase is limited to confirming whether there are serious doubts about the operation that justify initiating the second phase. This involves an analysis of the markets affected. At the same time, other tasks are carried out, such as verifying that the notification is complete, contacting NCAs and competitors, and where appropriate, drafting and signing the decision. Within the first phase the following main stages can be identified:

Filing

17.27 After the pre-notification contacts, one original and thirty-five copies of the notification are filed with DG COMP to the Commission. The supporting documents must be originals or certified copies. It is convenient for the contact details required by Form CO (for clients, suppliers and competitors) to be facilitated to the Commission in an electronic version.[60] Notifications start to have effect on the date that they are received by the Commission.[61] The Commission will send to the notifying parties or their representatives an acknowledgement of receipt without delay.[62]

17.28 Information that is either incorrect or misleading will be considered incomplete information.[63] If the information contained in the notification, including the documents, is incomplete in relation to an essential point, the Commission will inform the notifying parties or their representatives in writing without delay and will a fix an adequate period so that it can be completed. In these cases, a notification will have effect from the date on which the Commission receives the complete information.[64]

17.29 All essential amendments to the information contained in the notification which the notifying parties are or should be aware of must be notified to the Commission without delay. If such a modification could have a significant effect on the assessment of the operation, the Commission could consider that the notification takes effect from the date of receipt of the information concerning the essential change. The Commission will inform the parties or the representatives of this in writing and without delay.[65]

---

[60] Best Practice Guidelines on the conduct of EC merger control proceedings, para 21.

[61] Art 5(1) of the Implementing Regulation. See also Annex I Introduction, s 1.3. 'a) In accordance with Article 10(1) of the EC Merger Regulation and Article 5(2) and (4) of the Implementing Regulation, the time-limits of the EC Merger Regulation linked to the notification will not begin to run until all the information that has to be supplied with the notification has been received by the Commission. This requirement is to ensure that the Commission is able to assess the notified concentration within the strict time-limits provided by the EC Merger Regulation'.

[62] Art 4(3) of the Implementing Reg.   [63] Art 5(4) of the Implementing Reg.

[64] Art 5(2) of the Implementing Reg.   [65] Art 5(3) of the Implementing Reg.

There are many reasons why a notification can be declared incomplete. However, **17.30** three main categories can be clearly identified.[66]

(i) Breach of certain formal requirements, for example failure to include all of the parties concerned;

(ii) The information requested in the notification is insufficient, for example, with respect to markets that are affected by the merger and the shares of the parties and competitors in those markets, or they are not filed with sufficient clarity to enable an adequate assessment of competition to be carried out. This latter aspect can be particularly important in the relatively frequent cases where the supporting documentation is voluminous and the possible markets affected both numerous and complicated;

(iii) Cases where the Commission's investigations reveals the existence of potentially affected markets that have not been mentioned by the notifying parties, and about which more information is needed, information that cannot be provided or assessed within the time available.

In the first few years of the application of former Regulation 4064/89, the **17.31** number of notifications declared to be incomplete was relatively few. By the end of the 1990s a significant increase in such declarations took place, partly because of the growing number of notifications and the pressure on the Commission's resources. However, following the adoption of the first Guidelines in 1999, this trend was reversed, and fewer declarations of incomplete notifications have been made. The increase in pre-notification contacts between undertakings and the Commission in recent years, encouraged in the Guidelines, is one of the main reasons for this positive change.[67]

The declaration on an incomplete notification may have important implications **17.32** to the extent that the process must be restarted through the presentation of a new notification that is subsequently judged to be complete.[68]

---

[66] XXVIII [1998] Report on Competition Policy SEC/1999/0743 final para 173.

[67] The immediate effect of the Guidelines was to reduce the proportion of notifications declared incomplete from 10–11 per cent in 1997–1999 to 6 per cent in 2000 and 2001. Green Paper, 'The Review of Regulation 4064/89' COM(2001)745 final 11 December 2001 para 199.

[68] CW Bellamy, G Child, and P Roth (eds), *European Community Law of Competition* (Sweet & Maxwell, 2001) para 6–191 points out that the declarations about an incomplete notification could delay the start of the first phase given that the Commission may issue the declaration of an incomplete notification just before the end of said phase. e.g.: *Vodafone Airtouch/Mannesmann* (Case COMP/M.1795) [2000] OJ C19/3 paras 1–2: notification of 14 January 2000 and declaration of incomplete notification of 22 February 2000; Commission Decision in *Gerronics/ Hagemeyer/JV* (Case COMP/M.2223) [2001] OJ C15/3 para 1: notification of 22 December 2000 and declaration of incomplete notification of 23 January 2001.

Appointment of case team

17.33 After receipt of notification, the unit entrusted with the matter[69] will appoint a 'case team' unless this had already been done in the pre-notification phase. The case-team is normally made up of at least three people, an attempt being made to choose both lawyers and economists that are capable of working in the case language; experience in the relevant market(s) is also an important factor.

Market analysis. The 'market test'

17.34 One of the first initiatives of the case team is to carry out a global study of competition conditions. Normally, the notification form is a useful starting point that the Commission completes with its own means of investigation.

17.35 After fifteen years controlling concentrations and after adopting more than 2,700 decisions, the Commission has amassed a vast array of information on various markets. In addition, the Commission addresses requests for information to interested parties (competitors, clients, suppliers, business associations) to obtain their preliminary observations.[70] The replies of these undertakings are frequently decisive; if there is no opposition to the proposed concentration, it is unlikely that the Commission will continue with its assessment. Conversely, if significant opposition is noted and especially if it is felt that this may result in a complaint or proceedings before the Community Courts, the first phase will be more complicated for the notifying party.

17.36 Contact with interested parties is possible as a result of the publicity given to the notification and the ensuing investigation. This occurs through the publication of a short notice in the Official Journal noting the names of the undertakings concerned, their country of origin, the nature of the concentration, and the economic sectors affected, as well as the date of receipt of the notification.[71] In addition, the Commission enters into direct contact with possible interested parties, whose contact details must be supplied in the form, and are subject to the express warning that possible mistakes in addresses and phone numbers may result in the notification being declared incomplete.[72]

---

[69] At present there are five specialist units in the analysis of concentrations that are focused on different areas of activity (Units B-3, C-4, D-4 and E-3). One unit also forms part of the Directorate for general policy and strategic support, A-2, concerned with preparing general policy regarding concentrations. See ch 16.c.

[70] Best Practice Guidelines, para 27.

[71] Art 4(3) of the Merger Control Reg and Art 5(5) of the Implementing Reg.

[72] Best Practice Guidelines on the conduct of EC merger control proceedings, para 20.

Meetings—State of Play Meetings, meetings with competitors, and triangular meetings

The Best Practice Guidelines refer to the need to give all the interested parties **17.37** in the proceedings the opportunity to maintain free and frank channels of communication through various types of meetings in order to make known to the Commission its points of view. Three different types of meetings can be distinguished.

First, there are the 'State of Play Meetings' between the Commission and the **17.38** notifying parties that can take place at crucial moments throughout the proceedings with respect to notifications that create competition problems, or at least potential problems. Thus, holding these meetings takes place during the second phase, or possibly in the first phase but in relation to cases where, if the parties do not put forward a clear solution to the problem, the second phase will be initiated. These meetings may take place at the Commission, or alternatively by telephone or video conference, and the agenda to be followed must be prepared well in advance. Although there are five crucial moments when these meetings can be held, the parties can notify to the Commission important aspects at any time such as a commitments proposal or the development of any other question already discussed in one such meeting.

The five different occasions during the proceedings when a bilateral meeting **17.39** between the parties and the Commission can take place under the Best Practice Guidelines are as follows:

(i) In the first phase before the end of the three-week period from notification if there are serious doubts about the compatibility of the operation with the common market within the meaning of Article 6(1)(c) of the Merger Control Regulation. The objective of this meeting is for the parties to be aware of the Commission's concerns and for them to have the opportunity to propose an acceptable solution in order that the operation is authorized without the second phase starting.

(ii) In the second phase, in the two-week period after a decision under Article 6(1)(c) has been taken. In this meeting, the parties must provide the Commission with a written explanation of their position with respect to the competition concerns set out in the Article 6(1)(c) decision. The Commission will tell the parties whether or not they have properly understood its reasoning and they could also discuss what should be the scope of the investigation, the definition of markets, and competition problems. They could also discuss the need to extend the second-phase time limit by twenty days.[73]

---

[73] Art 10(3) of the Merger Control Reg second para.

(iii) Before adopting the statement of objections once the second-phase investigation has ended, in order to give the parties the opportunity to understand the Commission's preliminary point of view.

(iv) After the statement of objections and the hearing. This meeting gives the parties a clear idea of the Commission's position after the latter has had the opportunity to consider their reply to the statement of objections and its position in the hearing. It can also be used to discuss the scope and the timing for proposing remedies.

(v) Before the meeting of the Advisory Committee in order to discuss with the Commission the proposed commitments, improvements made to these proposals and, where appropriate, the results of the market test of such commitments.

17.40 A second type of bilateral meetings are those which take place between the Commission and third parties and which show sufficient interest in the proceedings, such as clients, suppliers, competitors, members of managing bodies of undertakings concerned, or representatives of such undertakings. These mainly participate in the 'market test' through their answers to the request for information send by the Commission, but they may also be invited by the Commission to attend meetings. In appropriate cases, the Commission may offer these third parties a copy of the statement of objections in order that they make submissions about its content. Third parties may call attention to a possible competition concern, or give a point of view that does not coincide with that presented to the Commission by the parties, but they must provide the Commission with proof of their submissions (examples, documents, any proof of the facts) as soon as possible.

17.41 Finally, triangular meetings between the Commission, the notifying parties, and other third parties are voluntary meetings that may take place if the Commission considers that in the interests of the investigation it could hear the opinions of all of them in a single forum. These occur in cases where there are different points of view as regards the key market information or the effects of the concentration on competition. These meetings do not replace the oral hearing. Both this type of meetings and the bilateral meetings between the Commission and third parties must take place as soon as possible to allow the Commission to reach the most detailed conclusions it can as regards the nature of the relevant market, and to clarify substantive aspects.[74] Triangular meetings will normally be preceded by an exchange of information filed by the notifying parties and third parties in sufficient time before the meeting, and will be chaired by a senior member of DG COMP.

---

[74] Best Practice Guidelines, para 39.

First phase decisions

After the internal consultation process in the Commission, a draft decision that **17.42**
ends the first phase will be presented to the Commissioner for Competition or his
or her substitute, authorized to take internal decisions on behalf of the College
of Commissioners. One of three decisions is possible: a declaration of lack of
competence (Article 6(1)(a) of the Merger Control Regulation), a definitive
authorization declaring the compatibility of the concentration with the common market (Article 6(1)(b) of the Regulation), or a declaration that there are
serious doubts about the compatibility of the concentration with the common
market, which initiates the second phase (Article 6(1)(c) of the Regulation).

Article 6(1)(a) decision   The Commission will declare that the Merger Con-   **17.43**
trol Regulation is inapplicable when it reaches the conclusion that the notified
operation is not a 'concentration' as defined in Article 3 of the Merger Control
Regulation or that it does not have a Community dimension. Generally, less
than 1 per cent of notifications come within this category.[75]

Article 6(1)(b) decision   When the Commission establishes that the notified   **17.44**
concentration comes within the scope of Regulation but does not raise serious
doubts about its compatibility with the common market, the Commission will
decide not to oppose it and will declare its compatibility with the common
market. The Commission may also take the initial view that the operation raises
serious doubts, but the changes that the undertakings have made to the concentration enable it to declare its compatibility with the common market under
Article 6(1)(b).

The CFI has concluded that although the Commission has no discretion as   **17.45**
regards initiating the second phase when it has serious doubts about the compatibility of a concentration with the common market, it does enjoy a degree
of discretion in the investigation and the examination of the circumstances of
each specific case to determine whether these raise serious doubts or when
commitments have been proposed or continue to be proposed.[76]

---

[75] Under Reg 4064/89, fifty decisions of this type were adopted between 1989 to 1998. From
1999 to June 2005, however, only four such decisions were adopted. See Statistics at DG COMP
web page hhttp://europa.eu.int/comm/competition/mergers/cases/stats.html. Although not necessarily under formal Art 6(1)(a) decisions, but with similar legal effects, the Commission responds
frequently to requests by interested parties to confirm whether a given transaction falls within the
scope of the Merger Control Reg. In Case C-170/02 P *Schlüsselverlag JS Moser GmbH et al v
EC Commission* [2003] ECR I-9889 paras 26–30 the Court stressed that the Commission has a
legal duty to respond to these requests.

[76] Case T-119/02 *Royal Philips Electronics NV v EC Commission* [2003] ECR II-1433. Thus,
even when the concept of serious doubts has an objective nature, the investigation of the existence
of such doubts necessarily obliges the Commission to carry out complex economic appraisals,
specifically when the question of whether the commitments proposed by the parties to the

17.46 In the five-year period to May 2005, about 95 per cent of final concentration decisions come within this category[77] and about 5 per cent of these were made subject to commitments.

17.47 **Article 6(1)(c) decision**   When the Commission finds that the notified concentration comes within the scope of the Merger Control Regulation and there are serious doubts about its compatibility with the common market, it will state that it is necessary to start second-phase proceedings. Such decisions involve a preliminary examination of the operation, justifying the opinion of the Commission that the operation is capable of being prohibited. In 2002, 2003 and 2004 the number of decisions of this type that were adopted were seven, nine, and eight respectively. This number is often roughly the same as the number of final decisions adopted at the end of the second phase, although some proposed concentrations are withdrawn by the parties during the second phase in order to avoid the bad publicity that a prohibition decision would entail.[78]

Publication of decisions

17.48 Once the decision has been signed by the Commissioner, it will be sent by the General Secretariat of the Commission to the undertakings concerned, through the person appointed in the notification as legal representative for the receipt of all notices. The Commission is under a duty to inform both the undertakings concerned and the NCAs of its decision without delay.[79]

17.49 Article 20 of the Merger Control Regulation obliges the Commission to publish decisions ending the second phase.[80] However, there is no requirement to publish decisions ending the first phase, which only have to be notified to the parties to the concentration and the Member States.[81] In practice, the Commission publishes those decisions where concentrations are authorized at the end of the second phase in the Official Journal, as well as giving a brief summary of its decisions in press releases. As regards first-phase decisions approving concentrations, the Commission makes them available to the public on its web site.[82]

---

concentration are sufficient to deal with such doubts. Where the Commission has approved a concentration without initiating phase two in the light of the commitments given, it must have found that such commitments provided a direct and satisfactory answer to the concerns raised, unless there is a manifest error in its appraisal.

[77] See Statistics at DG COMP webpage hhtp://europa.eu.int/comm/competition/mergers/cases/stats.html.

[78] On withdrawal of notifications, see paras 17.51 *et seq.* below.

[79] Art 6(5) of the Merger Control Reg.

[80] Decisions adopted under Art 8(1)–(6) of the Merger Control Reg. As regards the obligation to publish these decisions, see Art 20(1) of the Merger Control Reg.

[81] Art 6(5) of the Merger Control Reg.

[82] http://europa.eu.int/comm/competition/mergers/cases/.

Revocation or amendments of a first-phase decision

The Commission can only revoke or amend a first-phase decision in the following **17.50**
situations:

(i) When the decision is based on incorrect information for which one of the
undertakings is responsible or which has been obtained by fraudulent
means.[83]

(ii) When the undertakings concerned have breached an obligation attached
to the decision.[84] In this case, the Commission could reach a new decision
without being subject to the normal first-phase time periods.[85]

(iii) When it is concluded that the decision is illegal after its adoption. This
extraordinary possibility of revision is open only within a reasonable period
of time and must take into account the legitimate expectations of the
beneficiary of the decision, which may have trusted its legality.[86]

Withdrawal of the notification. The right to a new notification

The notifying parties are free to withdraw their notification at any moment.[87] In **17.51**
numerous cases, notifications have been withdrawn before the end of the first

---

[83] Art 6(3)(a) for the first phase and Art 8(6)(a) for the second phase. For a practical example,
see Commission Decision *Sanofi/Synthélabo* (Case IV/M.1397) (1999) para 2: in this case, the
Commission revoked its previous authorization when, following complaints made by third parties
which led the Commission to question the compatibility of the operation, it was shown that the
parties were not supplying the information required concerning a sector where their subsidiaries
were active. Specifically, the breach committed by both Sanofi and Synthélabo consisted in the
omission of information and in the notification of manifestly incorrect data with regard to the
relevant markets. This led the Commission to impose a maximum fine on each of the undertakings for the inexact nature of the information given: Commission Decision of 28 July 1999
imposing fines for having supplied incorrect information in a notification submitted pursuant to
Art 4 of Council Reg 4064/89, *Sanofi/Synthélabo* (Case IV/M.1543) (1999). See CW Bellamy,
G Child, and P Roth (eds), *European Community Law of Competition* (Sweet & Maxwell, 2001)
para 6–213 and at n 37. The authors point out that the Commission and some Member States
exert much more pressure to increase the level of fines for these infringements (para 6–242).

[84] The Merger Control Reg and the Acceptable Remedies Notice differentiate between
conditions and obligations, aimed at guaranteeing that the undertakings concerned fulfil the
obligations entered into with the Commission. The carrying out of each measure that leads to
structural market change is a condition; for example, the transfer of an activity. The means to
achieve this result are, in general, obligations imposed on the parties; for example, the appointment of an administrator with the irrevocable power to sell that activity. If the parties breach an
obligation, the Commission may revoke the decision of compatibility, and also impose periodic
penalty payments. If the parties breach a condition, the compatibility decision will no longer be
valid and, therefore, the Commission can take any measure to re-establish or maintain effective
competition conditions, including divestments. See Part E of this chapter on commitments.

[85] Art 6(4) of the Merger Control Reg.

[86] Case T-251/00 *Lagardére SCA and Canal+ SA v EC Commission* [2002] ECR II-4825
paras 139–141.

[87] Commission Press Release 19 September 2001 IP/01/1290. The Commission stated that it
accepted with 'surprise' the decision of the two Swedish banks, Skandinaviska Enskilda Banken

phase, amended to resolve the problems identified by the Commission and then notified again in order to avoid second-phase proceedings.[88]

17.52   In cases where notifications are withdrawn, the Commission's practice has been to issue a press release,[89] but without taking a formal decision. However, in June 2000 the Commission adopted a negative decision in *MCIWorldCom/ Sprint*[90] one day after the parties had informed them of their intention to withdraw the notification, and that they no longer intended to implement the proposed concentration in the way that it had been filed. The Commission took this decision on the basis that the undertakings involved had not formally abandoned the proposed concentration, since they had not withdrawn the merger agreement. In a Judgment delivered on 28 September 2004 the CFI annulled the Commission's decision, on the understanding that the distinction between the 'mere withdrawal of the notification' that the parties had entered into and the 'withdrawal of the merger agreement' which, according to the Commission should have taken place, was excessively formalistic.[91] According to the CFI, the Commission could not adopt a prohibitive decision once the parties had notified by fax (signed by the lawyers) their intention to withdraw the notification and that they did not intend to implement the proposed concentration in the manner filed in the notification. The CFI held that at the very least the Commission should previously warn the parties that its notice was insufficient, and concluded that the parties could legitimately expect, in accordance with the Commission's previous administrative practice, that its communication would be enough to bring the file to a close. The Court further held that in adopting its decision, the Commission had departed from

---

(SEB) and FöreningsSparbanken (FSB), to annul their concentration agreement. The Commission pointed out that it was not common for parties to withdraw their notification at such an early stage of the proceedings. The parties withdrew their notification after the Commission had issued its Statement of Objections.

[88] e.g. *Procter & Gamble/VP Schickedanz (I)*, (Case V/M.398) (withdrawn) and *Procter & Gamble/VP Schickedanz (II)* (Case IV/M.430) [1994] OJ L354/32 and Commission Press Release of 19 January 1994 IP/94/35: on 17 January, Procter & Gamble withdrew its initial notification sent to the Commission in compliance with former Reg 4064/89, regarding its intention to acquire the German company Vereinigte Papierwerke Schickedanz AG (part of Gustav & Grete Schickedanz Holding KG). Once this notification was withdrawn, Procter & Gamble re-notified an amended operation in which they established not only a simultaneous separation of the whole of VPS's nappy business, but also part of the business concerning VPS's feminine hygiene products associated with three of its brands (Blümia, Femina, and Tampona) and its own-brand activity. See also *Tractebel/ Distrigaz (II)* (Case IV/M.493) (1994); *Unilever France/Ortiz Miko (II)* (Case IV/M.422) (1994).

[89] See, e.g. Commission Press Release of 24 June 1999 in *KLM/Martinair* (Case IV/M.1328), IP/99/421; Commission Press Release of 8 September 1999 in *Ahlström/Kvaerner* (Case IV.M.1431), IP/99/665; Commission Press Release of 14 March 2000 in *Alcan/Pechiney* (Case IV/M.1715) IP/00/258. This last notification was withdrawn.

[90] Case COMP/M.1741 (2000) [2003] OJ L300/1.

[91] Case T-310/00 *MCI v EC Commission* paras 83, 107, and 108.

its standard administrative practice, which was clearly known to the public through the various previous cases in which the Commission had closed the file without adopting any decision at all on the day that the parties had communicated their decision to withdrawn the notification. In November 2005, the Commission published a Notice on withdrawal of notifications.[92]

D. The Second Phase

1. Initiating proceedings: Article 6(1)(c) proceedings and fixing the timetable

Article 6(1)(c) of the Merger Control Regulation provides that 'where the Commission finds that the concentration notified falls within the scope of this Regulation and raises serious doubts as to its compatibility with the common market, it shall decide to initiate proceedings.' These decisions, which bring an end to the first phase and initiate the second, normally contain a lengthy statement of the Commission's doubts. In addition, the Commission often publishes a brief note referring to its decisions in a Press Release, as well as a note in the Official Journal.   **17.53**

The Commission decision to start the second phase appears to be an intermediate act in the proceedings, and it is therefore questionable that it may be the object of an appeal before the Community Courts in accordance with the principles laid down in *IBM*.[93]   **17.54**

Once this decision has been adopted, the Commission will invite the notifying parties to discuss the timetable, with a view to making the investigation more effective, reduce the burden on the notifying parties and third parties, and increase transparency in the procedure.[94] While this aspect is often discussed in the pre-notification phase, in cases where the level of contacts or information supplied in that phase is limited, the agenda will be fixed when the second phase starts.   **17.55**

2. The statement of objections and the parties' observations

At the end of the investigation and independently of thee statements contained in the decision initiating the second phase, the Commission must send to the   **17.56**

---

[92] DG Competition Information note on Art 6(1)c 2nd sentence of Reg 139/2004 (abandonment of concentrations), available online at: http://europa.eu.int/comm/competition/mergers/legislation/regulation/notice_on_simplyfied_procedure_en.pdf

[93] See Case 60/81 *IBM v EC Commission* [1981] ECR 2639 para 19. This point is further discussed in ch 18 below.

[94] Best Practice Guidelines para 25.

parties a statement of objections so that they know exactly the issues that they must deal with in their defence.[95] The objective of the statement of objections is to set out all of the grounds on which the Commission intends to base its final decision. The Commission can only base its decisions on objections on which the interested parties have had the opportunity to make submissions. Neither the Merger Control Regulation nor the Implementing Regulation lay down any time period for adoption and sending to the parties of the statement of objections.

17.57   In the statement of objections, the Commission will fix the period within which the notifying parties—or other interested parties—must file their observations concerning the issues and it will not be obliged to deal with the submissions received until after this period has ended.[96] In practice, the parties generally have two weeks within which to reply, which is often a very tight timeframe for the undertakings and their lawyers.[97]

17.58   The parties to whom the Commission has addressed the statement of objections may make known in writing their viewpoints about the Commission's position. In the written observations that they file, they can make the submissions which they consider appropriate and attach all relevant documentation to prove the truth of the facts alleged. In order that they can reply effectively to the objections raised, the undertakings must be allowed to comment on the documents on which the Commission based its statement of objections.

3. Access to the file

17.59   The notifying parties have the right of access to the Commission's file once the statement of objections has been adopted.[98] This right extends to documentation received after the statement of objections has been adopted and until consultations take place with the Advisory Committee. The right of access to the file is justified by the need to guarantee undertakings' rights to a fair defence

---

[95] Art 13(2) of the Implementing Reg. The second phase of the procedure will have a more contradictory nature than the first, which is where the procedural guarantees are incorporated into the system in a more solid and express manner. See Green Paper, 'The Review of Regulation 4064/89', COM(2001)745 final, 11 December 2001 para 240.

[96] Art 13(2) of the Implementing Reg.

[97] A frequent problem is that the period for replying to the statement of objections coincides with the end of the period for filing commitments (now sixty-five days from the start of the second phase). This creates problems for the parties, given the importance of preparing with sufficient time the observations on the statement of objections in the context of an administrative authorization proceeding. Further, the Commission hardly has time to study the reply to the statement of objections before having to deal with commitments.

[98] Art 18(3) of the Merger Control Reg and Art 13(3) of the Implementing Reg. Best Practice Guidelines on the conduct of EC merger control proceedings, paras 42 *et seq.*

against the allegations contained in the statement of objections.[99] The Community Courts have confirmed that the Commission may refuse access to certain types of documents, including the business secrets[100] of other undertakings, the Commission's internal documents, and other confidential information.[101]

A particular problem in this regard is access to observations made by third **17.60** parties within the course of proceedings, whether of a formal or informal nature, (telephone conversations, e-mails, etc). There is no consistent approach on this point, although it seems that the right to a fair defence should mean that the parties have access to such observations. Recently the Commission has been more willing to allow access to the file, including such third party comments.[102]

Once they have consulted the file, the parties will draft their observations. One **17.61**

---

[99] Art 18(3) of the Merger Control Reg and Art 13(3) of the Implementing Reg: 'The Commission shall base its decisions only on objections on which the parties have been able to submit their observations. The rights of the defence shall be fully respected in the proceedings. Access to the file shall be open at least to the parties directly involved, subject to the legitimate interest of undertakings in the protection of their business secrets.' See also the Commission Notice on the internal rules of procedure for processing requests for access to file in cases under Arts 85 and 86 of the EC Treaty, Arts 65 and 66 of the ECSC Treaty and Council Regulation (EEC) 4064/89 [1997] OJ C23/3.

[100] 'Business secret' is not defined in the EC Treaty or any of the implementing regulations. The ECJ has stated its position regarding the scope of this concept, adopting a wide definition, but without ever identifying a homogenous class of information. A common feature of information classified by the ECJ as business secrets is that its divulgation may negatively affect the interests of the owners of the information. See V Sopeña Blanco, 'El Derecho de Acceso al Expediente en el Derecho Comunitario de la Competencia' in L Ortiz Blanco and V Sopeña Blanco (eds), *Derecho de la Competencia Europeo y Español*, Vol II (Universidad Rey Juan Carlos, Madrid, 2000) 323–47 (329). Commission Notice on the internal rules of procedure for processing requests for access to file, following the judgment in Case 53/85 *Akzo v EC Commission* [1986] ECR 1965 paras 24–28, defines them as 'strategic information on their essential interests and on the operation or development of their business' not known by third parties.

[101] For an analysis of the right of access to the file enjoyed by undertakings involved in proceedings involving the application of Arts 81 and 82 EC, see ch 10. The CFI has considered that the same principles are applicable in concentration cases examined under the Merger Control Reg. See Case T-290/94 *Kaysersberg v EC Commission* [1997] ECR II-2137 para 113; Case T-221/95 *Endemol Entertainment Holding BV v EC Commission* [1999] ECR II-1299, particularly para 68: 'The Court considers that the same principles are applicable to access to the files in concentration cases examined under Regulation No 4064/89, even though their application may reasonably be adapted to the need for speed, which characterises the general scheme of that regulation'; and para 66: '[. . .] the case-law also makes it clear that access to certain documents may be refused, in particular in the case of documents or parts thereof containing other undertakings' business secrets, internal Commission documents, information enabling complainants to be identified where they wish to remain anonymous and information disclosed to the Commission subject to an obligation of confidentiality.' Accordingly, 'the fact that the applicant had access only to non-confidential summaries of the replies to the questionnaires sent to the independent producers does not amount to an infringement of its rights of defence'.

[102] M Monti, Speech on 'Merger Control Policy in the European Union: a radical reform', European Commission/IBA Conference on EU Merger Control, 7 November 2002, Brussels, who also refers to the possibility that the notifying parties and third parties hold meetings before the hearing.

original and thirty-five copies of these must be sent to the Commission, addressed to DG COMP, as well as one electronic version. The Commission will then send copies to the different NCAs.

4. The right to be heard. The formal hearing

17.62 In their written submissions on the statement of objections, the notifying parties have the right to request an oral hearing in order to present their arguments more fully. The parties to whom the Commission has addressed its objections may also propose that the Commission hears those persons who can corroborate the truth of the facts on which the defence is based.[103]

17.63 Normally, the hearing takes place after the parties have filed their written observations in reply to the statement of objections. The Commission must give the persons, undertakings, and associations of undertakings involved the right to be heard with regard to the objections raised against them at all stages of the proceedings prior to consultations with the Advisory Committee.[104] The hearing normally takes one day, although in very complicated cases two or more days may be necessary, and it will be organized and presided over by the Hearing Officer in a totally neutral manner.[105]

17.64 The Commission is normally represented at the public hearing by a team of civil servants that usually includes the Head of Unit, and the 'case team' that has carried out most of the investigation (including the peer review panel, composed of EU civil servants with lengthy experience in concentration cases, that in the second phase compares the conclusions reached by the case team in the first phase)[106] and other civil servants of other Directorates General as well as the Legal Service.

---

[103] Art 13(3) of the Implementing Reg.

[104] Art 13(1) of the Implementing Reg in conjunction with Art 18(1) of the Merger Control Reg. Note that Art 18 of the Merger Control Reg provides that those with a right to be heard can exercise it 'at every stage of the procedure up to the consultation of the Advisory Committee'.

[105] Art 15(1) of the Implementing Reg and Art 4 of Decision 2001/462/EC ECSC of the Commission of 23 May 2001 concerning the powers of Hearing Officers in certain competition procedures [2001] OJ L162/21. The Hearing Officer will file his report on the hearing directly to the competent Commissioner, which generally covers the questions of procedural guarantees, divulging documents and access to the file, the time period for replies to the statement of objections and what happened in the hearing, as well as possible oral observations regarding the future developments of the case (e.g. withdrawal of certain objections). His final report (which will be notified to Member States, attached to the draft final decision and published with the final decision in the OJ), will also consider whether the draft decision covers more than just the objections with respect to which the parties have had the opportunity to express their positions, and, where appropriate, the objective nature of any investigation with regard to the impact of commitments from the perspective of competition. See ch 10.

[106] Note that the welcome idea of setting up review panels in the second phase has yet to be reflected in any rule. See ch 16.C.1.

Those invited to attend can either appear in person or with a legal or other **17.65** representative as allowed by their constitution. Undertakings or business associations may be represented by a duly authorized agent. Those whom the Commission hears may be assisted by lawyers or other duly 'qualified and duly authorised persons admitted by the Hearing Officer.'[107]

In addition, representatives of the NCAs of Member States may also attend.[108] **17.66** The importance of a Member State's opinion, particularly with a view to the next procedural stage (the participation of the Advisory Committee on concentrations), is clearly recognized by the parties, which often enter into bilateral contacts with the NCAs about the case.

Confidential information will be protected in the hearing. No disclosure or access **17.67** will be allowed to business secrets or other confidential information which the Commission does not consider it necessary to divulge for the purposes of the case in hand, or the internal documents of either the Commission or the NCAs.[109] A record will be kept of the statements made by all those giving evidence at the hearing, and on request the record will be made available to all those attending.[110]

Apart from the notifying parties, the Commission may, in other phases of the **17.68** proceedings, offer the notifying parties and any other interested party (for example, the seller and the target company) the chance to express their opinions orally.[111] The Merger Control Regulation and the Implementing Regulation provide for the possibility of hearing third parties that are defined as those natural or legal persons, including clients, suppliers, and competitors provided that they can show a sufficient interest.[112]

The parties which the Commission proposes to fine also have the same rights of **17.69** audience.[113]

---

[107] Art 15(4) and (5) of the Implementing Reg.   [108] Art 15(3) of the Implementing Reg.
[109] Arts 15(8), 17, and 18 of the Implementing Reg.
[110] Art 15(8) of the Implementing Reg. At present, the record is in the form of a CD-ROM. See ch 10.
[111] Arts 11 and 14 of the Implementing Reg.
[112] Art 18 of the Merger Control Reg and Art 11 of the Implementing Reg which particularly refers to members of the administrative or management bodies of the undertakings concerned, employees' representatives and consumers' associations. In Case C-170/02 P *Schlüsselverlag JS Moser and others v EC Commission* [2003] ECR I-9889, the ECJ has confirmed that it is the Commission's duty to hear third parties, in this case competitors, with respect to their complaints concerning the breach of the obligation to notify to the Commission all operations with a Community dimension. With respect to Art 18 of the Merger Control Reg, the ECJ stated that: '[. . .] the Commission cannot refrain from taking account of complaints from undertakings which are not party to a concentration capable of having a Community dimension. Indeed, the implementation of such a transaction for the benefit of undertakings in competition with the complainants is likely to bring about an immediate change in the complainants' situation on the market or markets concerned' (para 27).
[113] Art 11(d) of the Implementing Reg.

5. Consultation with the Member States: the Advisory Committee

17.70 Throughout the procedure from the time of the notification, the Commission handles the case in close and constant contact with the NCAs of Member States, as is required by Article 19(2) of the Merger Control Regulation.[114] This cooperation mainly takes place in the Advisory Committee for the control of concentrations between undertakings, which was first set up under former Regulation 4064/89 and is maintained under the new Merger Control Regulation.

17.71 The Advisory Committee is composed of representatives of the Member States' NCAs.[115] They are normally specialists in their respective authorities dealing with concentrations with national dimensions, which allows a comparative debate to take place about the competition issues at stake in any given case. The Merger Control Regulation requires each Member State to appoint one or more representatives, and at least one of these must be a specialist in Competition law.

17.72 In the first phase, the Commission will refer to the NCAs within three days a copy of the notifications and the most important documents (including commitments) that have been sent to them, or have been issued in application of the Merger Control Regulation. In the same way, the Member States have the right to make observations with respect to the proceedings.[116] However, the Commission is not obliged to consult Member States before adopting a first-phase decision. It should be noted that this communication takes place outside of the Advisory Committee.

17.73 Throughout the second phase, however, the function of the Member States is much more formalized within the Advisory Committee. The Commission is obliged to consult the Committee before adopting one of the decisions referred to in Article 8(1)–(6) of the Merger Control Regulation, that is, the decisions bringing an end to second phase proceedings (authorizing—whether or not subject to conditions—or prohibiting the concentration), as well as the decisions on revocation, interim measures, or orders to dissolve the concentration and those that impose sanctions under Articles 14 and 15 of the Merger Control Regulation.

17.74 Meetings of the Advisory Committee are called and chaired by a representative of the Commission and take place in Brussels (normally they are chaired by the Director in charge of coordination within DG COMP). In accordance with Article 19 of Merger Control Regulation, the meeting cannot take place

---

[114] See ch 16, C.2 of this book.   [115] Arts 19(4) and 23(2) of the Merger Control Reg.
[116] Art 19(2) of the Merger Control Reg.

before ten working days have passed from the date when the meeting was called, although in exceptional circumstances the Commission may reduce this period in order to prevent one or more undertakings affected by the operation from being seriously prejudiced. In practice, this ten-day period cannot always be respected for two main reasons. First, in the second phase the Commission is under extreme time pressure in cases where it will try to avoid a prohibition if the last-minute commitments offered by the parties resolve the competition problem in issue. Secondly, minimal logistical needs related to the convening of the meeting (presentation of an explanatory note on the points to discuss, translations, etc) must be ensured. The Community Courts have held that a failure to observe the notice period when calling a meeting of the Advisory Committee, even in the event that there are no exceptional circumstances related to the risk of a serious prejudice, is not in itself enough to make the final Commission decision illegal. A breach of this type can only make the final decision illegal when it is sufficiently substantial and it has a harmful effect on the legal and factual situation of the party alleging a procedural irregularity.[117]

In meetings called to discuss a draft decision under Article 8 of the Merger **17.75** Control Regulation, the representative of one of the Member States will act as *rapporteur* and will inform the representatives from the other Member States about the matter. After a debate about the content of the Commission's draft, this may be subjected to a vote and the Committee will issue an opinion either in favour or against the draft decision as a whole or with regard to certain aspects of it (for example, disagreement about the Commission's finding of a significant impediment to effective competition or the creation or reinforcement of a dominant position in a given market affected by the concentration and agreement with regard to the analysis in other markets, or disagreement about the case coming within the legal definition of concentration or as a concentration with a Community dimension). The Committee may give its opinion even when some of its members are not present or represented in the meeting. The Committee's meetings take place in private, and neither interested parties nor third parties may attend.

The Merger Control Regulation provides that a written opinion will be delivered **17.76** and will be annexed to the draft decision. The Advisory Committee's opinions

---

[117] See Case T-290/94 *Kaysersberg SA v EC Commission* [1997] ECR II-2137 para 88. Here, the CFI, in a flexible interpretation that favoured the Commission's view of the procedural requirements in the Community control of concentrations, rejected one of the grounds for appeal against the Commission Decision in *Procter & Gamble/VP Schickedanz* (Case IV/M.430) [1994] OJ L354/32 which was based on failure to comply with the notice period for convening the Advisory Committee.

are not binding on the Commission,[118] which is in line with the latter's exclusive competence in this field, although the Commissioner for Competition and the Commission's services will take them account before proposing a definitive decision to the College of Commissioners. The Merger Control Regulation requires the Commission to take 'the utmost account' of the Committee's opinion as well as the latter's report explaining the manner in which it has reached its opinion.[119] Under the previous system, the Committee could only recommend the publication of its opinion and the Commission was free to decide whether or not to publish. At present the Commission must notify the opinion, together with the decision, to its addressees and publish it together with the decision, taking into account the legitimate interest of undertakings in protecting their commercial secrets.[120]

6. Decisions at the end of the second phase. Publication

Article 8(1) and (2) decisions

17.77 When the Commission finds that a notified concentration does not significantly obstruct competition in the common market, either as notified (Article 8(1) of the Merger Control Regulation) or following the changes that the undertakings concerned may have made to it (Article 8(2) of the Regulation), it must take a decision declaring that the concentration is compatible with the common market. The Commission may attach to its decisions conditions and agree specific commitments aimed at guaranteeing that the undertakings comply with the obligations that they have entered into with the Commission in order to make the concentration compatible with the common market. As already noted, second-phase decisions do not reach 4 per cent of the total number of notified operations. Out of this figure, nearly all of them are decisions approving concentrations under Article 8(1) or (2), although those including commitments are more frequent.

Article 8(3) decisions

17.78 By contrast, if the Commission concludes that a proposed concentration will 'significantly impede effective competition in the common market or in a substantial part of it', it must adopt a decision declaring that the concentration is incompatible with the common market.[121] The parties run the risk of being

---

[118] Arts 19(3) and 23(2)(c).
[119] Arts 19(6) and 23(2)(c).
[120] Art 19(7).
[121] While five concentrations were prohibited in 2001, in the 2002–2004 period only one was prohibited. To 31 July 2005, there have been nineteen prohibitions out of a total of 2,800 notified operations. See http://europa.eu.int/comm/competition/mergers/cases/stats.html.

fined if they implement an operation that has been declared incompatible with the common market in a decision adopted under Article 8(3).[122]

Article 8(4) decisions

If a concentration which has been declared incompatible with the common market has been implemented,[123] the Commission is empowered to force the undertakings concerned to dissolve it, in particular through the dissolution of the merger or the disposal of all the shares or assets acquired, so as to restore the situation prevailing prior to the implementation of the concentration. Alternatively, the Commission may order any other appropriate measure to achieve restoration of the *status quo ante*.

17.79

Article 8(5) decisions

The Commission may take interim measures to restore or maintain effective competition when a concentration is implemented in breach of the obligation to suspend until a decision over the compatibility of the operation with the common market is adopted. Further, such measures could be taken when a concentration has been implemented in breach of one of the conditions attached to a first-phase decision.

17.80

Publication

The Commission will publish in the Official Journal of the European Union the decisions adopted in accordance with Article 8 as well as those imposing sanctions under Articles 14 and 15, together with the report of the Advisory Committee.[124] The published decision will mention the undertakings concerned and all the relevant elements of the case, but not the undertakings' business secrets. To this end, it is a common practice of the Commission to make available to the undertakings concerned the draft decision to enable them to request that those aspects which they consider to be business secrets be treated as confidential (such as market share, prices, clients, suppliers, etc).

17.81

Revocation or amendment of Article 8 decisions

Article 8(6) of the Merger Control Regulation provides for the revocation by the Commission of its decisions where (i) the declaration of compatibility

17.82

---

[122] Art 14(2)(c) of the Merger Control Reg.

[123] Implementation of a concentration may be either the result of a breach of Art 7 of the Merger Control Reg or a case in which there was no obligation to suspend implementation. See ch 16.A.2 for a discussion on these exceptions. Significant examples of Art 8(4) decisions are *Kesko/Tuko* (Case IV/M.784) [1997] OJ L110/53 and the Decision of 30 January 2002 in *Tetra Laval/Sidel* (Case COMP/M.2416) (2002). This latter decision would remain ineffective as a result of the annulment by the CFI and later confirmation by the Court of Justice of the Commission decision prohibiting the concentration.

[124] Art 20 of the Merger Control Reg.

with the common market is the result of incorrect or fraudulent information or (ii) where an obligation included in the decision is not complied with. These provisions are similar to those provided for in respect of decisions at the end of the first phase under Article 6(3) of the Merger Control Regulation, as discussed elsewhere in this Chapter.[125] The Commission may also amend its decisions for reasons of legality under the doctrine established by the CFI in *Lagardère/Canal+*.[126]

E. The Negotiation of Commitments: Acceptable Solutions that Remedy the Competition Concerns

1. Introduction

17.83   Commitments are, in general, solutions proposed by the parties to the Commission while the latter is examining a proposed concentration in an attempt to eliminate any competition problem and thus obtain authorization. Normally, this involves reducing the market share of the parties to the concentration. Despite the fact that the decisions where commitments are offered are less than 5 per cent of all notifications received annually by the Commission, this is an area where the Commission has published a significant number of documents that provide assistance to the notifying parties.

17.84   The original wording of former Regulation 4064/89 only covered the Commission's power to negotiate, where appropriate, the acceptance of commitments from the parties to a concentration in the second phase. In practice, however, the Commission negotiated and accepted commitments during the first phase as a prior condition to adopting a decision permitting the concentration under Article 6(1)(b), thus avoiding the initiation of second-phase proceedings.

17.85   Following the 1997 amendments, the acceptance of commitments in the first phase was expressly included in the Regulation.[127] The Commission noted that '[t]he formalization of phase I undertakings has proved of interest and benefit to merging parties and the Commission alike. It enables the delay and consequent

---

[125] See para 17.50.
[126] Case T-251/2000 *Lagardère SCA and Canal+ SA v EC Commission* [2002] ECR II-4825.
[127] Recital 8 of Reg 1310/97 amending Reg 4064/89 [1997] OJ L180/1, provided that the Commission has the power to declare a concentration to be compatible with the common market in the second phase, once the parties have presented commitments 'that are proportional to and would entirely eliminate the competition problem [. . .]'. Recital 8 also states that 'it is also appropriate to accept commitments in the first phase of the procedure when the competition problem is readily identifiable and can easily be remedied' and that 'transparency and effective consultation of Member States and interested third parties should be ensured in both phases of the procedure'.

uncertainty over the outcome of a notified transaction to be reduced, and avoids the need to deploy some of the substantial extra resources (at the Commission as well as by the parties) required for a full phase II investigation and decision. Experience with the new power shows clearly that the revised system is able to deal both quickly—in a matter of weeks, rather than several months—and efficaciously with mergers where a potential dominant position may be created.'[128]

Recitals 30 and 31 of the new Merger Control Regulation tackle the question of commitments, establishing that these must be proportional to the competition problem in question and completely eliminate it. In accordance with Article 6(2) of the Merger Control Regulation, the Commission may declare a concentration to be compatible with the common market when it can show that, once modified, it does not give rise to serious doubts about competition. Article 8(2) of the Merger Control Regulation uses the same terms in relation to concentrations that are subject to second-phase proceedings.   **17.86**

In the first phase, the notifying parties can offer commitments within a maximum period of twenty working days from the date of receipt of notification.[129] The period for filing commitments in the second phase is twenty days from the date when the second phase commences. If commitments are filed this automatically extends the period available to the Commission to decide the approval of the concentration in the first and second phase to thirty-five and 105 days respectively (except where second-phase commitments are proposed within less than fifty-five days, in which case no time extension will be allowed).[130]   **17.87**

The time periods are short, and it is difficult for both the parties and the Commission to determine precisely the most appropriate type of commitments to propose. What the parties may consider to be the most acceptable proposal for the Commission after negotiations have taken place may be insufficient in light of the Commission's definition of the market or technical difficulties identified by the Commission once it has examined in detail the specific solutions proposed by the parties. In cases where the parties suspect that the transaction may cause competition problems they should contact the Commission as soon as possible, but especially before formal notification takes place.   **17.88**

---

[128] XXVIII Report on Competition Policy [1998] para 142 insert 6.
[129] Art 19(1) of the Implementing Regulation. One of the widest commitments negotiated in first-phase proceedings was the subject-matter of the Commission Decision of 9 August 1999 in *Hoechst/Rhône-Poulenc* (Case IV/M.1378). See XXIX Report on Competition Policy 1999 paras 182–183: the commitments included the divestiture of the chemical divisions of Rhodia and Celanese, as well as the veterinary division of Hoechst, HR Vet. In addition, commitments were given in answer to the competition problems in various pharmaceutical and agrochemical markets that the Commission identified during its investigation.
[130] Art 10(1) and (3) of the Merger Control Reg.

Further, a new feature of the Merger Control Regulation makes it important for the parties to evaluate whether they will need to request an extension of time within fifteen working days from the commencement of second-phase proceedings. Any such extension cannot exceed twenty days, during which time the 'clock stops' with respect to the time periods of general authorization.[131]

2. The acceptable remedies notice

17.89 In December 2000, the Commission adopted a Notice on remedies acceptable to resolve competition problems that arise in concentrations ('the Acceptable Remedies Notice'),[132] aimed at giving guidance about amendments to concentrations, including commitments, based on the Commission's experience. The importance of this matter for the Commission was shown again in the creation in 2001 of an 'enforcement unit', whose task was to develop a consistent policy of assessment, acceptance and implementation of the commitments.[133] Subsequently, the Commission adopted its 'Best Practice Guidelines for Divestiture Commitments' which contain model texts for divestiture commitments and the trustee's mandate, which will be looked at below.[134] In October 2005, the Commission published a study evaluating the experience gathered so far in merger cases.[135]

3. Types of commitments

17.90 Commitments are often classified as either 'structural' (that is, those that modify the market structure through the sale or transfer of assets or undertakings) or 'behavioural'. The Commission generally prefers structural remedies to eliminate competition problems, the most typical one being divestiture or sale of a subsidiary company.[136] The subject matter of the transfer may be a combination

---

[131] Art 10(3) of the Merger Control Reg.

[132] Commission Notice on remedies acceptable under Council Reg (EEC) 4064/89 and Reg (EC) 447/98 [2001] OJ C68/3. This Notice has not been adapted to the new Merger Control Regulation and therefore continues to refer to the previous test, i.e. that of the creation or reinforcement of a dominant position. At the time of writing discussion on a new Notice is under way.

[133] See M Monti, Speech on 'The Commission notice on merger remedies—one year after', 18 January 2002, CERNA (Centre d'économie industrielle, École Nationale Supérieure de mines) Paris, online at http://europa.eu.int/rapid/start/cgi/guesten.ksh?p_action.gettxt=gt&-doc=SPEECH/02/10 0 RAPID&lg=EN

[134] These models are available at: http://europa.eu.int/comm/competition/mergers/legislation/divestiture_commitments.

[135] This study is available at: http://europa.eu.int/comm/competition/mergers/others/remedies_study.pdf

[136] In Case T-102/86 *Gencor v EC Commission* [1999] ECR II-753 para 316, the CFI laid down that structural commitments such as the sale of a subsidiary, are preferable to behavioural commitments, in that they eliminate the root of the competition problem and, in addition,

of tangible and intangible assets; this may be a pre-existing undertaking or group of undertakings or an economic activity that does not constitute an undertaking. The transfer of a viable business is seen as the best means of restoring effective competition. A viable business is defined as an existing activity that could be operated on a lasting basis independently of the parties to a notification as regards, for example, the supply of consumables, or the purchase of products that it manufactures or the services that it provides (except during a start-up period). The objective is to create, through the divestiture, an entity that will be a stable competitor in the market in question. Normally, the commitment will be accepted only if the identity of the acquiring party is made known.

As regards commitments other than divestiture, the Notice refers to the elimin- **17.91** ation of structural links with a competitor in a market affected by the operation. This may involve the sale of a stake that gives joint control in a joint venture or of a minority holding if it is felt that such a holding creates disincentives to compete.[137]

There are other acceptable solutions apart from the permanent transfer of **17.92** businesses, such as facilitating market entry through giving access to consumables, or to the distribution network or certain infrastructures that are necessary to compete. This will include remedies such as terminating exclusivity agreements or guaranteeing that competitors have access to key technologies (including patents, know-how, and other intellectual property rights).

The parties can offer a package of solutions combining a number of different **17.93** remedies, but the onus is on the parties to propose remedies that satisfy the Commission.[138]

4. Requirements for the filing of commitments

It is for the notifying parties to file commitments in the form that they consider **17.94** to be appropriate, since the Merger Control Regulation does not fix any specific

---

they do not need supervision in the medium or long term. In *Gencor*, the CFI held that the commitments which consisted in mere promises to behave in a certain way, such as the promise not to abuse a dominant position created by the concentration, would not in itself be considered enough to make the operation compatible with the common market. In the context of the application of Arts 81 and 82 under Reg 1/2003, for the first time express mention is made of the possibility of the Commission imposing any structural or behaviour commitment in order to produce the effective ending of the breach of such provisions (Art 7(1)). See paras 11.04 *et seq*.

[137] Notice on Acceptable Remedies, paras 24 and 25, citing, *inter alia*, Commission Decision in *Totalfina/Elf* (COMP/M.1628) [2000] OJ L143/01.
[138] Notice on Acceptable Remedies, para 6.

method for this. However, bearing in mind the short time limits involved, the Commission has published guidelines and model texts concerning (i) divestiture commitments and (ii) the mandate of the trustee of the undertaking to be divested in order to assist undertakings when drawing up their proposed remedies and the said mandate.[139] These model texts aid the uniform treatment of different matters, helping to increase the level of transparency and legal certainty.[140]

17.95 According to these models, the proposed commitments must contain the following elements:[141]

- In the case of a divestiture,[142] a clear definition and description of its object including all of the elements of the activity being transferred: tangible assets (production plants, real property, distribution premises, sales offices, and others), intangible assets (intellectual or industrial property rights, goodwill), personnel and key personnel, supply or sales agreements, client lists, technical assistance, etc.

- A description of the responsibilities of the parties vis-à-vis the Commission, the trustee and the business to be transferred such as the commitment of the parties to preserve the full economic viability of the business until divestiture actually takes place, provide all of the assistance required by the trustee, or the parties' commitments not to take on employees that are part of the business to be divested.

- The possibility that the proposed purchaser can carry out a due diligence inspection of a corporation (process of examining the financial underpinnings of a corporation).

- The obligation of the parties to appoint an independent trustee,[143] the requirements that the latter must fulfil, the procedure for election, the period within which it is to be elected, duties and obligations and remuneration.

---

[139] These documents are found at http://www.europa.eu.int/comm/competition/mergers/legislation/ divestiture_commitments/.

[140] However, it is open to debate whether the negative effect of the legislative rigidity is outweighed by these benefits. In practice, it is difficult to propose solutions that differ from the Commission's model texts.

[141] See Best Practice Guidelines on model texts for divestiture commitments and the trustee's mandate.

[142] In other cases, the details of the commitment in question (e.g. as regards the termination of exclusivity of the supply contract, all of its terms) must be clearly defined.

[143] The Notice distinguishes between the administrator or 'Hold Separate Manager', who is responsible for running the business (and maintaining its viability until divestiture as per the commitment) and a trustee of the divestiture (who supervises the implementation of the commitments and periodically informs the Commission of any incident). Both functions can be carried out by the same person.

Both the actual trustee and the mandate must be approved by the Commission.[144]

- The criteria for the approval of the purchaser by the Commission (*inter alia*, being independent of the parties, or ensuring that the purchase will not create any competition concerns). If the purchase amounted to a concentration with a Community dimension, the new operation must be notified in accordance with the Merger Control Regulation in the usual way.

In broad terms, the commitments presented to the Commission in the first phase have to be sufficient to remove the doubts concerning the compatibility of the operation with the common market, because there is no detailed investigation (this only occurs in the second phase) and the period within which the decision must be adopted is very short.[145] Accordingly, remedies are acceptable where there are readily identifiable concerns.[146] These commitments must fulfil the following requirements: **17.96**

(a) they must be presented within the prescribed time-limit;
(b) they will specify the commitment entered into by the parties in sufficient detail to allow a complete evaluation;
(c) they will explain how the commitments offered resolve the competition problems that have been defined by the Commission.

Following Article 20 of the Implementing Regulation, one original and ten copies of the proposed commitments must be sent to the Commission, together with an electronic version. The Commission will then send copies to the NCAs without delay. When presenting these commitments, the parties will give reasons why any information should be treated as confidential and they will supply a non-confidential version of the commitments for market testing.[147]   **17.97**

The Commission will evaluate the parties' proposals in light of the above   **17.98**

---

[144] It is necessary to file the trustee's mandate with the Commission. The mandate will state the appointment and approval of the trustee, clarify the relation between the Commission, the trustee, and the parties and set out the duties of the trustees, in order that they fulfil the obligations to implement the commitments. The commitments establish the main points that the mandate must cover. The guidelines establish that the mandate is the basis of a triangular relationship between the Commission, the trustee, and the parties. Despite the fact that the mandate puts the trustee in a contractual relationship with the parties, the latter cannot give instructions to the trustee (para 9).

[145] Notice on Acceptable Remedies para 11.

[146] Notice on Acceptable Remedies para 37.

[147] Art 20 provides that the Commission will be sent one original and ten copies of the commitments proposed by the undertakings concerned, whether in the first or second phase, an electronic copy thereof, while indicating clearly any information that they consider to be confidential on the reasons for this, and supplying a non-confidential version.

requirements, in consultation with the NCAs and, if it considers it appropriate, with third parties as well as through a market test. When the Commission's assessment confirms that the proposed remedies remove the grounds for serious doubts, it will declare that the concentration is compatible, and duly inform the parties of this.

17.99 Given that the object of the remedies proposed in the first phase is to obtain a direct solution to a clearly determinable competition problem, only limited modifications to the proposed commitments can be accepted. These modifications, presented immediately after the results of the consultations, will include clarifications, refinements and other improvements that guarantee that the commitments are 'workable and effective'.[148] If the parties have not removed the doubts, the Commission will publish an Article 6(1)(c) decision and start second-phase proceedings.

17.100 The requirements and procedure are similar in relation to commitments proposed in the second phase, apart from the time periods (twenty days from the initiation of the second phase[149]) and that the proposed commitments must tackle all of the competition concerns raised in the statement of objections which have not subsequently been abandoned by the Commission. The Commission is prepared to discuss the appropriateness of the commitments at any stage of the proceedings.

5. The implementation of commitments

17.101 Designing commitments and assessing their viability is an exercise that is not free of difficulties, particularly because, by their nature, commitments can only be put into practice once the Commission has approved the proposed concentration. The Commission will assess the future impact of the commitments, and must also establish mechanisms that guarantee that the parties effectively implement them. The Commission will attach to its decision a series of conditions and obligations aimed at guaranteeing the implementation of the commitments. After this, the Commission must ensure that:

- the parties are doing everything necessary to implement correctly the commitments agreed with the Commission, including ensuring that the divestiture takes place within the agreed time period. The Commission carries out this supervisory task on the basis of the reports supplied to it by the trustee;

- the business to be divested is kept independent of the activities retained by the

---

[148] Notice on Acceptable Remedies paras 35–37.
[149] This period substitutes the three-month period from the day on which proceedings are commenced as per the Notice on Acceptable Remedies para 39.

parties and is managed as a distinct and saleable business. Since the Commission cannot participate in the day-to-day running of the business, this task is entrusted to the Hold Separate Manager,[150] who is chosen by the parties and approved by the Commission, as is the Hold Separate Manager's mandate.

• the viable business will be transferred to an appropriate purchaser within a specific period of time. The Commission will have to approve the potential purchaser and the purchase agreement, confirming that it is in line with the contents of the commitments offered. The purchaser must be an existing or potential competitor, and not have any connection whatsoever with the parties.

The trustee has special responsibility for vetting possible purchasers and must **17.102** propose the most adequate one to the Commission in accordance with the commitments given. Within the first period, when it is the parties' sole responsibility to find the right purchaser and they commit themselves to divesting the business (normally within a period of six months), the business may be divested for the price which the parties consider to be appropriate. The parties are free to add of their own accord other assets to the deal in order to make a more attractive package. However, if at the end of this period they have not found an adequate purchaser, the trustee is empowered to carry out the divestiture at any price within what is known as the Extended Divestiture Period, which normally lasts for three months.[151]

6. Consequences of breach of the commitments

The Commission must ensure that the commitments offered by the parties **17.103** are honoured and that they have the effect of making the operation compatible with the common market. Commitments take the form of conditions and obligations which must be met by the undertakings.[152]

The consequences of failure to comply by the undertakings concerned differ **17.104** depending on whether the decision to authorize the operation is taken in the first or second phase and whether the infringement relates to conditions

---

[150] The Notice on Acceptable Remedies provides that the trustee is the general supervisor of the implementation of the commitments. He can normally propose or even impose measures to guarantee the fulfilment of the commitments as well as the presentation of periodical reports. He also oversees the parties' efforts to find an acceptable purchaser within the period established in the commitments; if they fail in this regard, the trustee will receive an irrevocable mandate to sell off the business within a specific time period at any price, subject to the Commission's prior approval.

[151] Best Practice Guidelines on Divestiture Commitments para 15.

[152] See the Merger Control Reg, Recital 31. For a distinction between conditions and obligations, see para 12 of the Notice on Acceptable Remedies.

(e.g. the divestiture of an activity) or obligations arising from the decision (e.g. the appointment of a trustee).

In the first phase

17.105 In the case of non-compliance with a condition, the Commission may:

- take appropriate provisional measures for the re-establishment or maintenance of effective competition conditions;[153] and/or
- adopt a decision (which may be to approve or prohibit the operation) but this shall not be subject to the time-limit laid down in Article 10(1) of the Merger Control Regulation;[154] and/or
- decide to impose a fine of up to 10 per cent of the total turnover of the undertaking concerned.[155]

17.106 In the case of non-compliance with an obligation, the Commission may:

- revoke the decision to authorize the operation;[156] and
- if revocation takes place, adopt a decision in the first phase—of approval or prohibition—subsequent to a new examination of the operation but this shall not be subject to the time-limit laid down in Article 10(1) of the Merger Control Regulation for first phase decisions;[157] and/or
- by means of a decision, impose a fine of up to 10 per cent of the total turnover of the undertaking concerned; and/or
- impose a periodic penalty payment of up to 5 per cent of the average daily aggregate turnover of the undertakings for each working day of delay starting from the date laid down in the decision, in order that they comply with the obligation imposed in the first phase authorisation decision.[158]

In the second phase

17.107 In the case of non-compliance with a condition, the Commission may:

- demand, by means of a decision, that the concentration be dissolved, i.e. that the undertakings dissolve the concentration in such a manner that, by means of divestiture of acquired assets, the situation prior to the implementation of the concentration is re-established, or demand any other appropriate measure to guarantee the re-establishment of the prior situation;[159] and/or

---

[153] Art 8(5)(b) of the Merger Control Reg.   [154] Art 8(7)(a)(i) of the Merger Control Reg.
[155] Art (14)(2)(d) of the Merger Control Reg.   [156] Art (6)(3) of the Merger Control Reg.
[157] Art 6(4) of the Merger Control Reg.   [158] Art (15)(1)(c) of the Merger Control Reg.
[159] Art (8)(4)(b) of the Merger Control Reg. This provision refers to the case that the compatibility of the concentration under Art 2(3) and (4) of the Merger Control Reg depends on the fulfilment of the conditions attached to its authorization.

- take appropriate provisional measures for the re-establishment or maintenance of effective competition conditions;[160] and

- adopt a decision (be it to approve or prohibit the operation) but without being subject to the time-limit laid down in Article 10(3) of the Merger Control Regulation for the second phase;[161] and/or

- by means of a decision, impose a fine of up to 10 per cent of the total turnover of the undertaking concerned.

In the case of failure to comply with an obligation, the Commission may: **17.108**

- revoke the decision to authorize the operation;[162] and

- if revocation takes place, adopt a decision in the second phase but without being subject to the time limit laid down in Article 10(3); and/or

- by means of a decision, impose a fine of up to 10 per cent of the total turnover of the undertaking concerned and/or

- impose a periodic penalty payment of up to 5 per cent of the average daily aggregate turnover of the undertakings for each working day of delay starting from the date laid down in the decision, in order that they comply with the obligation imposed in the first phase authorization decision.[163]

If a concentration is implemented and a condition has not being complied with   **17.109**
(whether attached to a first or second-phase decision), it is not necessary for the Commission to adopt a decision revoking the one which authorised the operation. It is considered that, having failed to comply with the condition, the situation which gave rise to the concentration being declared compatible with the common market does not materialize. The concentration is therefore deemed to be 'non-notified' and implemented without authorization. Furthermore, Recital 31 of the Merger Control Regulation provides that if the Commission has concluded that, given the failure to comply with the condition in question, the concentration would be incompatible with the common market, the Commission may order the dissolution of the concentration on the grounds of non-compliance. The Merger Control Regulation reserves the right to order the dissolution of the concentration to second-phase decisions, which, unlike the first phase, would probably be the only procedure where the Commission would have sufficient time to reach such a conclusion.

If a decision is revoked for reasons of non-compliance with an obligation,   **17.110**
the Commission may subsequently adopt a new decision, but this shall not be subject to the usual time-limits governing the first and second phases. The absence of time-limits—something which is generally detrimental to the

---

[160] Art (8)(5)(b) of the Merger Control Reg.   [161] Art (8)(7) of the Merger Control Reg.
[162] Art (8)(6) of the Merger Control Reg.   [163] Art (15)(1)(c) of the Merger Control Reg.

undertakings—would be justifiable, on the one hand, by the complexity of the relevant operation (shown by the fact that the undertakings have had to offer commitments) and also by a certain lack of trust on the Commission's part with respect to undertakings who have failed to comply with commitments that they themselves have given.

17.111 In the case of non-compliance with obligations, a combination of fines and periodic penalty payments can be imposed, and, at the same time, the undertakings can be ordered to adjust their behaviour so that they fulfil the commitment. The capacity to impose periodic penalty payments to obtain (belated) compliance following non-implementation is only possible with respect to the non-compliance of obligations and not conditions, where non-compliance gives rise to the revocation of a decision or an order of dissolution. The imposition of periodic penalty payments implies that the decision approving the operation is not revoked, since the Commission is primarily interested in compliance with the commitments given.

17.112 Provisional measures for the re-establishment or maintenance of effective competition conditions are only possible in the case of non-compliance with conditions. In these cases, while revocation is not required, it may be necessary for reasons of legal certainty to adopt a decision whereby appropriate measures are taken for the re-establishment of effective competition.[164]

F. Investigative Powers of the Commission

17.113 The Merger Control Regulation grants a number of prerogatives to the Commission for the purposes of carrying out investigations during the proceedings. These powers of investigation include the power to request information and, as will be seen, the power to inspect the premises of undertakings. The Commission's investigative powers exist in both the first and second phases.

17.114 In general, the provisions in relation to investigative powers in the Merger Control Regulation are similar to those in Regulation 1/2003 for the application of Articles 81 and 82 EC. These provisions are primarily related to requests for information and inspections carried out by the Commission. The remit of this part is limited to highlighting those matters that relate to concentrations, while Chapters 7 and 8 of this book offer a more detailed analysis of the relevant issues.

---

[164] Green Paper on the review of Reg 4064/89 para 223.

1. Requests for information

Article 11 of the Merger Control Regulation gives the Commission the right to request information, in a broad sense of the word, from undertakings. This covers individuals, undertakings, or groups of undertakings whether acquiring or acquirer, as well as other undertakings and business groups.[165] Similarly to requests under Regulation 1/2003, the request may be either a 'simple request for information' or a 'decision'. Unlike Regulation 1/2003 however, the Commission is not obliged to furnish the respective NCAs with a copy of all simple requests and decisions of this nature unless there is a specific request from the NCA in question.[166]

17.115

Former Regulation 4064/89 had established a two-phase procedure whereby decisions to request information could only be adopted if the undertakings failed to furnish requested information within the period stipulated in a simple request.[167] However like Regulation 1/2003, the new Merger Control Regulation enables, from the very outset and at the discretion of the Commission, the adoption of a decision to request information without there being any prior need for a simple request.[168] Article 11(7) of the Merger Control Regulation has also incorporated the possibility for the Commission to obtain information by means of interviews with any natural or legal person that agrees to be interviewed for the purposes of obtaining information for the investigation, in parallel with Article 19 of Regulation 1/2003.

17.116

Simple requests for information do not normally suspend calculation of the tight deadlines provided for in the Merger Control Regulation for the adoption of final decisions under the Regulation, including decisions on whether to refer concentration cases to the NCAs. By exception however, Article 9 of the Implementing Regulation contemplates a suspension of these terms under for the following circumstances:

17.117

- Information sought by the Commission by means of a simple request to

---

[165] When the Commission requires information of other market participants, it places particular importance on information furnished by clients and competitors with respect to the relevant market and the transaction under investigation.

[166] Art (11)(5) of the Merger Control Reg.

[167] Art 11(5) of Reg 4064/89 stated that 'where a person, undertaking or an association of undertakings does not provide the information requested within the period fixed by the Commission or provides incomplete information, the Commission shall by decision require the information to be provided.' That was in line with the procedural tools existing at the time for Arts 81 and 82 EC infringements under Art 11 of Reg 17/62.

[168] This is the literal interpretation of the new rule. Although it can be inferred from reading Art 9 of the Implementing Reg that decisions will be adopted if information is not furnished within the time limit established in a simple request, there is nothing to prevent the adoption of a decision even if non-compliance with a previously issued simple request has not occurred.

one of the notifying parties or another interested party[169] which has not been furnished within the period stipulated by the Commission or said information is incomplete; or

- Information sought by the Commission by means of a simple request to a third party[170] that has not been furnished within the period stipulated by the Commission or said information is incomplete for reasons that can be attributed to one of the notifying parties or any other interested party.[171]

17.118 In the event of a suspension of time-limits operate during the period from the elapsing of the period stipulated in the simple request for information or the decision and receipt of the correct and complete information.[172]

17.119 As concerns information requested through a formal decision, Article 9(2) of the Implementing Regulation provides that the time-limits for final decisions, including referral decisions will automatically be when the Commission, for reasons attributable to one of the undertakings participating in the concentration, has to take a decision to request information without proceeding first by way of a simple request.

2. Inspections

17.120 In general terms, the powers of the Commission concerning investigations are similar to those under Regulation 1/2003.[173] There is a marked exception however: the Commission may not carry out inspections in the private residences of directors and persons related to the undertakings, such as those contemplated in Article 21 of Regulation 1/2003.[174]

---

[169] Art 9(1)(a) which refers to the interested parties of Art 11(2) of the Merger Control Reg. The reference in this provision to 'interested parties' seems to encompass parties to the concentration other than the notifying parties, such as the seller or the undertaking which is the object of the concentration.

[170] Art 9(1)(b) which refers to 'third parties' in the sense of Art 11(c) of the Implementing Reg, i.e. parties with the right to be heard in the proceedings apart from notifying parties and other interested parties such as clients, suppliers and competitors provided they show a sufficient interest.

[171] Art 9(1) of the Implementing Reg.

[172] Art 9(3)(a) of the Implementing Reg. Art 10(4) of the Merger Control Reg provides for an exceptional indefinite suspension of time-limits if, for circumstances that can be attributed to one of the undertakings participating in the concentration, the Commission is obliged to request information by means of a decision under Art 11 or order an inspection by means of a decision adopted under Art 13 of the Merger Control Reg.

[173] See ch 8.

[174] Former Competition Commissioner, Mario Monti, stated that certain powers were more necessary and appropriate for the discovery of cartels than for the enforcement of the Merger Control Regulation: 'For that reason, I remain unconvinced of the need and therefore, will not propose, that the Commission will be given the power to conduct home searches under the Merger Control Regulation'. Speech/02/252 of Mario Monti 4 June 2002 on the 'Roadmap for

Therefore, Commission officials may verify books and other professional **17.121**
documents irrespective of the medium in which they may be stored, make or
demand copies of books and professional documents in any format whatsoever,
request any representative or member of staff to provide verbal explanations,[175]
have access to any premises, land, or means of transport pertaining to the
undertaking and seal off[176] all premises and books belonging to the undertaking
for the period necessary and to the degree necessary for the investigation to be
carried out. The Commission may carry out an inspection through the use of a
written authorization or by means of a decision. The two forms are alternatives,
and the Commission has the discretion to choose what it considers to be the
most appropriate method for a given case.

Again, the time-limits set out in the Merger Control Regulation to decide on the **17.122**
substance of the matter or as regards referral cases under Article 9(4) may be
affected by reasons attributable to the notifying parties or another interested
party. In particular that is the case where any of these has refused to be the
subject of a verification deemed necessary by the Commission, or has refused to
cooperate with the Commission in accordance with the relevant provisions.[177]
The period of suspension will span the period between the date of the failed
attempt to carry out the verification and the date when the inspection, ordered
by means of a decision, is deemed to have concluded.[178]

3. Infringements and sanctions

Articles 14 and 15 of the Merger Control Regulation lay down two types **17.123**
of administrative sanctions of an economic nature. The first—set out in
Article 14—sanctions infringements that have already taken place, such as failure to notify, early implementation, implementation of a concentration that has
been declared incompatible with the common market, failure to comply with
obligations and conditions imposed by the Commission, and conduct obstruct-
ing the investigation of the Commission. In these cases, a fixed fine is imposed.

---

the reform project Conference on Reform of European Merger Control', British Chamber of
Commerce the review of the Merger Control Reg, available at http://europa.eu.int/rapid/
pressReleasesAction.do?reference=SPEECH/02/252&format=HTML&aged=0&language=
EN&guiLanguage=en.

[175] Art 13(2)(e) of the Merger Control Reg establishes that explanations must be limited to
facts or documents related to the objective and purpose of the inspection. Recital 38 provides that
it is particularly important that the Commission has the power to interview all persons who may
have useful information at their disposal and to make a record of their statements.

[176] Recital (39) of the Merger Control Reg limits the use of seals to exceptional circumstances
and for the time that is strictly necessary for the inspection, which is not more than forty-eight
hours.

[177] Art 9(1)(c) of the Implementing Reg. Up to the present date, inspections have only been
used in exceptional cases under the Merger Control Reg.

[178] Art 9(3)(b) of the Implementing Reg.

Article 15, in turn, contains periodic penalties aimed at forcing the undertakings to comply with obligations such as responding to a request for information, agreeing to and cooperating with an inspection, and complying with the obligations imposed on the concentration. These latter vary according to the number of days undertakings take to comply.

17.124 The potentially most severe sanctions, reflecting greater seriousness of infringement, are those laid down in Article 14(2) and can be as high as 10 per cent of the total turnover of the undertaking concerned.[179] This provision seems to have been drawn up along the lines of Article 23(2) of Regulation 1/2003.[180] In setting the exact amounts of the fines, the Commission should take into account the nature, gravity, and duration of the infringement.[181]

17.125 Sanctions can be classified into three principal groups: (i) for infringements related to investigation, (ii) for infringements related to improper implementation of the concentration, and (iii) periodic penalty payments.

Sanctions for infringements related to the investigation

17.126 The notifying parties must make known to the Commission, in a full and honest manner, the relevant facts and circumstances[182] for the adoption of a decision on the notified concentration.[183] The Commission places considerable importance on its duty to defend this essential principle in the exercising of its mission to monitor concentration operations with a Community dimension.[184]

---

[179] This provision refers the interpretation of the concept of 'undertaking concerned' to Art 5 of the Merger Control Reg which, in conjunction with Art 3(1), should be understood to refer to the parties who merge or the acquirer or acquirers in their totality—the entire group of enterprises where relevant—and the acquired party—be it a group of undertakings, an undertaking or part of an undertaking—in the concentration. The concept of group refers to undertakings controlled as defined in Art 3 of the Merger Control Reg; see ch 16.

[180] However, the nature of the two types of infringement is quite different in terms of gravity and impact on competition. Whereas infringements of Reg 1/2003 are clear infringements of basic competition rules (set out in Arts 81 and 82 EC) such as the creation of a cartel or the abuse of a dominant position, breaches of Art 14 of the Merger Control Reg seem to be mainly procedural infringements (except as regards complying with conditions and obligations). In any case, failing to break down the sanctions into different groups plus the general reference to a maximum sanction which seems exorbitant is a valid ground for criticism, particularly for infringements relating to concentrations.

[181] Art 14(3) of the Merger Control Reg. Nonetheless, unlike Reg 1/2003, there is no Notice giving guidance on this point (such as the Guidelines for the calculation of fines imposed under Art 15(2) of Reg 17 and Art 65(5) of the ECSC Treaty [1998] OJ C9/3.

[182] The Merger Control Reg does not provide for a *de minimis* exception to its application, and therefore the fact that the turnover in a given market is not very significant cannot justify the exclusion of these activities from the notification form.

[183] Recital 5 and Art 4(1) of the Implementing Reg.

[184] As stated in the Commission's Green Paper on the review of Reg 4064/89, Document COM (2001) 745/6 final, December 11, paras 197–202. See also Commission Press Release of 18 February 1998, IP/98/66 (Samsung); and Commission Press Release of 10 February 1999, IP/99/100 (*AP Møller*).

Failure to comply with this obligation, whether intentional or negligent, will give rise to a fine of up to 1 per cent of the total turnover of the relevant undertaking.[185] This fine, set out in Article 14(1) of the Merger Control Regulation, will also apply if the parties furnish incorrect or misleading information[186] in response to a request for information, whether required through a simple request or by means of decision; in the latter case, the sanction will also be applicable if the information is incomplete or is not furnished within the period stipulated. Third parties to which the Commission has addressed a request for information may be sanctioned under these provisions as well.[187]

---

[185] Art 14(1) of the Merger Control Reg. Para 225 of the Green Paper referred to reviewing the calculation of fines as follows: 'It would be appropriate [. . .] to switch to a percentage-based calculation of fines for procedural rules (up to 1% of annual turnover). Moreover, it would be appropriate to add the violation of failing to comply with an obligation imposed by decision pursuant to Article 6(2) of the Merger Control Regulation to the list in Article 14(2)(a) [. . .]. It would be appropriate [. . .] to switch to a percentage-based calculation of periodic penalty payments (up to 5% of average daily turnover). Again, it would be appropriate to add the violation of failing to comply with an obligation imposed by decision pursuant to Article 6(2) of the Merger Regulation to the list in Article 15(2)(a) [. . .].'

[186] In December 1999, the Commission imposed a fine of 50,000 euros on Deutsche Post for its notification in February 1999 of the proposed acquisition of a high speed delivery service, trans-o-flex GmbH. Although Deutsche Post withdrew the notification in the second phase, the Commission held that Deutsche Post had deliberately given incorrect information in its notification and had subsequently failed to divulge information regarding a previous transaction (*Deutsche Post/trans-o-flex*, Case IV/M.1447). Also in December 1999, the Commission imposed a fine on KLM (40,000 euros), because KLM had furnished incorrect, incomplete, and misleading information. The Commission concluded that the conduct of KLM had been negligent, at the very least (*KLM/Martinair*, Case IV/M.1128 and *KLM/Martinair (II)* Case IV/M.1328). In announcing the decisions for both cases, former Competition Commissioner Mario Monti pointed out that an essential condition for the purposes of the application of competition rules was that the companies provided exact and complete information: '[t]hese decisions underline the Commission's determination to ensure that firms comply fully with their legal obligations. Firms which fail to do so—whether deliberately or through a failure to take proper care—should not expect to escape sanction in future'. Commission Press Release of 14 December 1999, IP/99/985. In *Sanofi/Synthélabo* in 1999, the Commission decided to impose a fine on the grounds of incorrect information furnished by the notifying parties. Following allegations made by third parties, the Commission reviewed the information provided by the notifying parties and revoked its initial authorization because it was based on incorrect information and manifestly incorrect statements. The Commission imposed the maximum fine of 50,000 euros and emphasized that the parties could not have been ignorant of the monopolies enjoyed by each of them. Furthermore, the Commission considered that the fact that the initial notification had been declared incomplete should have drawn the attention of the parties and their representatives to the shortcomings in their preparatory work. Actually, the parties were given an additional period of eight days to check that their notification complied with the requirements of the Reg. The most recent example is the decision adopted by the Commission on 7 July 2004 [2005] OJ L98/27 imposing a fine of 90,000 euros against *Tetra Laval* for supplying misleading and incorrect information in the context of the *Tetra Laval/Sidel* notification. It is interesting to note that the Commission became aware of this failure in the context of the appeal brought by *Tetra Laval* against the Commission decision prohibiting that merger.

[187] The Commission fined Mitsubishi for providing incomplete information in response to a request for information under Art 11 of Reg 4064/89 with respect to the *Ahlstrom/Kvaerner*

17.127   The above fines apply to the following cases, which represent obstacles to a Commission investigation:

- if the undertaking in question presents incomplete information in the context of an inspection;
- if it refuses to be made subject to an inspection required by decision;
- if it refuses to answer an oral question or answers it in an incomplete, incorrect or misleading manner;[188] or
- if it breaks the seals placed on the premises of the undertaking by agents of the Commission or their assistants.

Sanctions for infringements related to the improper implementation of the concentration

17.128   As mentioned, Article 14(2) gives the Commission the power to impose fines of up to 10 per cent of the total turnover of the relevant undertaking. Infringements which may give rise to this sanction are the following:

- omission of the duty to notify prior to implementation;[189] or
- omission of the duty not to implement a concentration prior to notification and approval; or
- implementation of a concentration declared to be incompatible with the common market; or
- failure to comply with measures imposed by the Commission in order to guarantee the dissolution of the concentration under the terms of Article 8(4) or appropriate provisional measures for the re-establishment or maintenance of effective competition conditions under the terms of Article 8(5); or

---

concentration (Case IV/M.1471), withdrawn. The Commission noted that it had been forced to estimate the market size for boilers and that the information was important in ensuring correct decisions. This is the first case of an undertaking being fined, with the exception of a notifying party, in merger control proceedings. Commission Press Release of 12 July 2000, IP/00/764.

[188] Art 14(1)(e), second para of the Merger Control Reg provides that the person who has given incorrect or misleading information in response to requests for oral explanations can rectify the situation within the time period prescribed by the Commission for the purposes of avoiding a sanction.

[189] Commission Decision of 5 October 1992 in *Samsung/AST* (Case IV/M.920) [1999] OJ L225/12 para 29. The imposition of a fine included a (heavier) fine for the implementation of the operation without the authorization of the Commission. As mitigating factors, the Commission considered that omitting to notify did not have an impact on competition and that Samsung made its omission known to the Commission and cooperated during the proceeding. Commission decision of 10 February 1999 in IV/M.969 (*AP Møller*) para 12 where the Commission highlighted the importance of Arts 4(1) and 7(1) for the effectiveness of the Reg. In spite of the imposition of token fines the *Samsung/AST* and *AP Møller* decisions are not insignificant since they indicate the determination of the Commission to use, when appropriate, the sanctioning powers it has under the Merger Control Reg.

- failure to comply with conditions or obligations imposed on the undertakings with a view to making the concentration compatible with the common market.[190]

When the Commission foresees the adoption of a decision under the terms **17.129** of Article 14 or 15 of Regulation 4064/89, before consulting the Advisory Committee on matters of concentration operations, it will grant a hearing to the undertakings to be affected by the said decision. The Commission will offer the undertakings on which it proposes to impose a fine or a periodic penalty payment, the opportunity to verbally present their arguments in a formal hearing, if the undertakings have requested this in their written observations.[191]

Periodic penalty payments

Periodic penalty payments are aimed at obliging the undertakings to take **17.130** certain action, whether this be furnishing information or complying with an obligation.[192] Their amount increases as time passes and the undertaking fails to take the action that has been required of it, and they end when compliance takes place. Article 15 of the Merger Control Regulation lays down that the Commission may impose periodic penalty payments of up to 5 per cent of the aggregate average turnover of the relevant undertakings or groups of undertakings concerned within the meaning of Article 5 for each working day of delay starting from the date stipulated in the decision, in order to oblige them to:

- supply in complete and correct form the information requested by Commission decision; or
- agree to an inspection ordered by Commission decision; or
- comply with an obligation imposed via decision or comply with measures ordered by Commission decision adopted under Articles 8(4) (breach of the obligation not to implement unauthorized concentrations, or breach of the conditions for authorization) or 8(5) (interim measures).

Judicial review

The undertaking(s) fined may appeal to the CFI by challenging the legality **17.131** of the Commission's decision by means of an action for annulment under Article 230 EC. The Community Courts have full jurisdictional competence

---

[190] As stated, the Notice on Acceptable Remedies refers to the difference between conditions and obligations.

[191] Arts 13(4) and 14(3) of the Implementing Reg.

[192] See paras 9.14, 11.18, and 11.48.

under Article 229 EC to review both fines and periodic penalty payments, which means that it can annul, reduce or increase them.[193]

17.132 As already stated, undertakings on which the Commission proposes to impose a periodic penalty payment shall be heard before the final amount they must pay is set.[194]

---

[193] Recital (43) and Art 16 of the Merger Control Reg.
[194] Arts 13(4) and 14(3) of Reg 802/2004. Regarding the procedure for the imposition of periodic penalty payments, see paras 9.16 and 11.21.

18

JUDICIAL REVIEW OF COMMISSION DECISIONS REGARDING CONCENTRATIONS

A. Introduction

The review by Community Courts of Commission decisions in the field of concentrations has become a major issue in the recent times. The annulment of various decisions in the merger control field, to some extent unexpected, has touched may aspects of the Commission's practice, raising questions as to where the balance of discretion from the Commission and intensity of the review should lie; in fact, in a recent case the Commission went as far as to appeal to the ECJ with the confessed intention of limiting the CFI's judicial review capacity[1] and, as said at the time, to recover the inter-institutional equilibrium, which the Commission argued had been lost. As discussed further below, this appeal would ultimately be dismissed by the ECJ.[2] In any event, and quite independently of this healthy institutional tension, the important body of case law dictated on the Merger Control Regulation must be hailed as a driving force that has been instrumental in the review and improvement of the working methods of the Commission and played a major instigating role in the reform process that the DG COMP and the Merger Regulation itself have recently undergone.

This chapter discusses some of the principles that can be extracted from the case law of the Community Courts regarding judicial review. The emphasis is placed on revision on matters of procedure, in line with the aims of this publication.

18.01

18.02

---

[1] Press Release IP/02/1952 of 20 December 2002 'Commission appeals CFI ruling on Tetra Laval/Sidel to the European Court of Justice'.
[2] See Case C-12/03 *EC Commission v Tetra Laval*, not yet reported.

B. Reviewable Acts

18.03   Article 21(2) of the Merger Control Regulation provides for the review of decisions adopted by the Commission by the Community Courts. This control naturally extends to decisions on the merits adopted by the Commission under Article 8 of the Merger Regulation. Article 16 also provides for judicial review of decisions imposing sanctions. There are however many other acts of the Commission open for judicial review, as described below.

1. Form of the act not relevant

18.04   Article 230 EC provides that private persons may initiate actions for annulment as regards decisions addressed at the applicant or against a decision which, although in the form of a regulation or a decision addressed to another person, is of direct and individual concern to the former.[3] According to the case law, those acts whose legal effects affect the interests of the applicants by bringing about a distinct change in their legal position may be challenged.[4] In principle, therefore, the form of such acts or decisions is irrelevant to the question of whether they can be reviewed under Article 230 EC.

18.05   *Dan Air*[5] is a good example of the judicial review of an informal decision of the Commission in the field of merger control. In this case, the CFI accepted as admissible an annulment action brought by Air France against an oral statement made by the Competition Commissioner's spokesman stating that the acquisition of Dan Air by British Airways was not notifiable under the Merger Regulation. The Court considered that the announcement had the same legal effects[6]

---

[3] Although this is the only action that exists to attack the validity of a concentration decision, there is another appeal procedure which has been explored following the first annulment judgments. By virtue of Arts 235 and 288(2) EC, the ECJ is competent to hear actions for damages arising from claims for non-contractual liability against the EU Institutions. To date, there have been two such cases. Case T-212/03 *MyTravel Group plc v EC Commission* [2005], pending, and Case T-351/03 *Schneider Electric SA v EC Commission* [2002], pending, where, after having obtained a judgment in their favour, the parties decided to sue for damages caused by the Commission's decision. Both cases are currently awaiting judgment before the Court of First Instance. The actions brought have been published: Case T-212/03 in [2003] OJ 200/51 and Case T-351/03 in [2004] OJ C7/68.

[4] See Case 60/81 *IBM v EC Commission* [1981] ECR I-2639 para 9; Joined Cases C-68/94 and C-30/95 *France and others v EC Commission* [1998] ECR I-1375 para 62; Case T-87/96 *Assicurazioni Generali and Unicredito v EC Commission* [1999] ECR II-203 para 37; and Joined Cases T-125/97 and T-127/97 *Coca-Cola Company v EC Commission* [2000] ECR II-1733 para 77.

[5] Case T-3/93 *Air France v EC Commission* [1994] ECR II-121.

[6] In that case, the effect of the statement by the Commissioner responsible for competition matters, by which he publicly declared the MCR to be inapplicable to the transaction in issue, was to confirm beyond all doubt the competence of the Member States whose territory was more particularly affected—the UK and France—to appraise the concentration in light of their own national laws on the review of such concentrations. *Dan Air*, para 45.

as a formal decision since it was not material that the decision took the unusual form of a verbal communication to the public at large.[7]

2. Article 6 decisions

Article 6 of the Merger Control Regulation lists the different types of decisions **18.06** that may be adopted at the end of the first phase of the procedure. These are (i) declarations that the Merger Regulation does not apply to a given transaction under Article 6(1)(a); (ii) clearance decisions at the end of the first phase under Article 6(1)(b); and (iii) decisions to initiate second-phase proceedings under Article 6(1)(c). There is no question that Article 6(1)(b) decisions are open to review, since these are final clearance decisions. Whether or not the other two types of decision can be reviewed is, however, less straightforward.

As regards Article 6(1)(a) decisions, these are definitive acts of the Commission **18.07** whose effect is the termination of merger control procedures that open the door for potential action by the Commission or Member States under other competition rules. This was found sufficient by the CFI in *Dan Air* when granting Air France leave to appeal against an informal declaration of the Commission that it was not competent to examine a transaction under the Merger Control Regulation.

Subsequently, *Generali/Unicredito*[8] gave the CFI an occasion to respond to that **18.08** same question, albeit this time with respect to a formal Article 6(1)(a) decision. Not surprisingly, the Court again affirmed that these decisions can be reviewed by the Courts.

More recently, the *Austrian Newspapers* case has given both Community Courts **18.09** an occasion to review yet another case involving letters from the Commission rejecting jurisdiction over a case.[9] In this case, the proposed concentration had been notified to and authorized by the relevant NCAs, but the applicant argued that it had a Community dimension and filed a complaint to that effect. The Commission disagreed. Instead of challenging that decision, the applicants

---

[7] A similar situation occurred in *Sogecable-Cablevisión*. Again, the challenged acts of the Commission were contained in certain letters and public declarations. Their content, however, was the exact opposite of that in *Dan Air*, since in the letters, the Commission affirmed its jurisdiction under former Regulation 4064/89 regarding a concentration that had been notified to the Spanish competition authorities. In disagreement with the Commission over the issue of Community dimension, the parties appealed against the letters and declarations. The case was later withdrawn. Case T-52/96 R *Sogecable v EC Commission* [1994] ECR II-797.

[8] Case T-87/96 *Assicurazioni Generali SpA and Unicredito SpA v EC Commission* [1999] ECR II-203.

[9] Case T-3/02 *Schlüsselverlag JS Moser GmbH et al v EC Commission* [2002] ECR II-1473. On appeal, Case C-170/02 P [2003] ECR I-9889.

requested the Commission to act under Article 232 EC and subsequently brought an action for failure to act.

18.10 The CFI rejected the application as inadmissible. Applying *Dan Air*, it held that the Commission had indeed acted through a decision, which the applicants could have challenged under Article 230 EC. Interestingly, the ECJ took on appeal a slightly different view. In its judgment, it avoided examining whether the letters in issue amounted to 'decisions', and instead found against the applicant on the basis of the lateness of its request to the Commission.[10]

18.11 Finally, the question of whether Article 6(1)(c) decisions initiating second-phase proceedings may be reviewed has yet to be decided. It is submitted that, unlike Article 6(1)(a) decisions, they do not express the Commission's final position, but rather initiate a procedure that, following the very wording of Article 6(1)(c), is to be concluded with a decision. They would therefore be acts of a preparatory nature within the meaning of the *IBM* doctrine and therefore not open for review.[11]

3. Review of decisions imposing sanctions under the Merger Control Regulation

18.12 Article 16 expressly provides that Commission decisions imposing sanctions on undertakings are capable of being reviewed. Although not expressly mentioned, it is understood that other procedural decisions, including formal requests for information under Article 11 and decisions ordering investigations under Article 13, should also be capable of being reviewed along similar lines to the equivalent procedural decisions under Regulation 1/2003, which are discussed elsewhere in the book.

4. Referral decisions

18.13 Article 9, concerning referral decisions, does not expressly provide for judicial review by the Community Courts. However, in *Philips Electronics*[12] the CFI rejected the request of inadmissibility put forward by the Commission, concluding that the partial referral decision, however not addressed at the applicant but to the relevant Member State, affected in a relevant manner the applicant's legal situation since it had the effect of excluding the application of the Merger

---

[10] The ECJ also took the chance to reject firmly the Commission's arguments that it was under no duty to take a position on requests by complainants to decide the applicability of the Merger Reg to given cases. See paras 26–30.

[11] See Case 60/81 *IBM v EC Commission* [1981] ECR 2639. That solution would however clearly underestimate the modification of the position of the parties that undoubtedly arises from these decisions in practice.

[12] Case T-119/02 *Royal Philips Electronics v EC Commission* [2003] ECR II-1433 para 280.

Regulation to the part of the concentration which had been referred and to make that part of the concentration subject to exclusive review by the NCAs under their national competition law. As a result, the partial referral altered the criteria for the assessment of the lawfulness of the concentration and the procedure and possible sanctions applicable to it. The applicant would therefore be deprived of the opportunity to have the Commission review the lawfulness of the concentration from the point of view of the Merger Regulation.[13]

This principle was later confirmed by the CFI in the context of a full referral to a **18.14** national authority in *Cableuropa*.[14] This time the Court developed the argument further, stressing that the review of a concentration under the laws of a Member State cannot be considered, as regards its scope and effects, to be comparable with that carried out by the Commission under the Merger Regulation. Therefore, contrary to what the Commission had argued, referral decisions were capable of producing legally binding effects. The outcome of the transactions considered in both *Philips Electronics* and *Cableuropa* would later show that the referral of a merger might have a crucial impact on the chances of securing the approval.

5. Article 8 decisions

Clearance (whether conditional or unconditional) and prohibition decisions **18.15** under Article 8 of the Merger Regulation are reviewable acts and as such have been challenged on various occasions by the notifying parties.[15] The discussion has, however, emerged concerning appeals brought by persons other than addressees of the decisions of the Commission. This is discussed in Section C below.

There may, however, be aspects within a decision that may not be capable of **18.16** producing legal effects; the question would therefore arise as to whether those elements may be challenged. This is what happened in *Coca-Cola*,[16] where the CFI did not allow *Coca-Cola* to challenge a finding of dominance in a decision clearing the company's acquisition of its UK bottler. The Court held that none of the contested findings had any influence on the conclusions reached by the Commission in the operative part of the decision. As regards the concern that the contested findings might prejudice Coca-Cola's in future cases, it held that

---

[13] *Royal Philips Electronics*, para 282. See also, by analogy, Case T-87/96 *Assicurazioni Generali and Unicredito v EC Commission* [1999] ECR II-203 paras 37–44.

[14] Joined Cases T-346/02 and T-347/02 *Cableuropa and others v EC Commission* [2003] ECR II-4251.

[15] See Case T-342/99 *Airtours v EC Commission* [2002] ECR II-2585; Case T-310/01 *Schneider Electric SA v EC Commission* [2002] ECR II-4071; Case T-5/02 *Tetra Laval v EC Commission* [2002] ECR II-4381; and Case T-310/00 *MCI v EC Commission* [2004–5] OJ C300/38.

[16] See Joined Cases T-125/97 and T-127/97 *Coca-Cola Company v EC Commission* [2000] ECR II-1733.

any such findings did not constitute a legally binding precedent either for the Commission or for national authorities and courts.

18.17 Similarly to final decisions by the Commission, eventual amendments to these should be open to challenge in the same manner as the original decision. That was the situation in *Lagardère-Canal+* France.[17] In this case however the Commission argued that the amendment did not produce legal effects and therefore the challenge should not be admitted. The Commission relied particularly in the fact that the operative part of the decision had not been amended. The Court however affirmed that the measure in question, affecting the treatment of ancillary restrictions, would produce significant effects in the legal sphere of the applicant.

6. Acts adopted in the implementation of merger clearance decisions

18.18 Conditional clearance decisions frequently require the Commission to take various initiatives after the decision itself. There is a great variety of such initiatives, especially with regard to the management of the divestiture process. Some of these actions may give rise to reviewable acts.

18.19 One example of such acts is found in *Petrolessence*,[18] concerning the implementation of certain conditions for the approval of the *Total Fina/Elf* concentration[19] was made. In that case, the compatibility of a concentration with the common market was conditional upon the execution of commitments consisting in divesting assets to third parties, provided that such third parties had the ability to compete effectively on the relevant market.[20] Through a subsequent decision addressed to *TotalFina Elf*, the Commission indicated that the transfer of service stations to Petrolessence and Société de gestion de restauration routière SA did not allow the continuation and development of effective competition, and therefore did not meet the conditions contained in the commitments. The said undertakings brought an action for annulment against that decision addressed at *Total Fina Elf* before the CFI. In marked contrast to the doubts expressed by the Commission, the CFI stated that 'it follows that the contested decision constitutes a refusal by the Commission to approve the applicants' candidacy, thus bringing about a significant change in their legal position'.[21] The CFI also emphasized the definitive nature of the decision, since the rejection of the claimants as proposed acquirers did not require the

---

[17] Case T-251/00 *Lagardère and Canal+ v EC Commission* [2002] ECR II-4825 para 110.
[18] Case T-342/00 *Petrolessence and SG2R v EC Commission* [2003] ECR II-1161.
[19] Commission Decision in *TotalFina/Elf* (Case COMP/M.1628) (2000) OJ L143/1.
[20] The case involved divesting seventy service stations owned by Elf, Total, and Fina located along French motorways.
[21] Case T-342/00 *Petrolessence and SG2R v EC Commission* [2003] ECR II-1161 para 38.

Commission to take any further act and would automatically take effect if TotalFina Elf did not submit any observations,[22] as well as the fact that the claimants were excluded from the subsequent commercial negotiations that TotalFina Elf held at the time.[23]

C. *Locus Standi*

Article 230 EC differentiates between two categories of applicants. First, there are 'privileged' applicants, namely Member States, the Commission, the Council, the European Parliament, the Court of Auditors and the ECB. These institutions may bring an annulment action without having to show any special interest, the ECJ being the competent court to hear their claims. Claims for judicial review concerning the control of concentrations are, however, normally brought by non-privileged plaintiffs, with some rare exceptions.[24]

18.20

As regards non-privileged applicants, Article 230 EC provides that any individual or undertaking can bring an action for judicial review against a decision which is addressed to them, and also against decisions which, although in the form of a regulation or a decision addressed to another person, affect them directly and individually. The situation of the different possible applicants will now be examined in detail below.

18.21

1. The notifying party

In general, the party notifying a concentration will be the person, or one of the persons, to which the decision is addressed. Under Article 230 EC, the addressees of a decision have *locus standi* to initiate an annulment action in the Community courts. In these cases, the direct and individual interest is obvious and there is therefore no need for it to be established.[25]

18.22

The notifying party may, however, not be the addressee of the various acts capable of being reviewed, such as referral decisions. In such cases, their position will be the same as that of a third party.

18.23

---

[22] *Petrolessence and SG2R v EC Commission* para 39.

[23] *Petrolessence and SG2R v EC Commission* para 41.

[24] Case C-42/01 *Portugal v EC Commission* [2004] ECR I-6079 and Case C-68/94 *France and Société comerciale des potasses et de l'azote v EC Commission* ECR I-1375 [1998]. Nevertheless the Member States and the Commission have supported certain undertakings, e.g. in Case T-342/00 *Petrolessence and SG2R v EC Commission* [2003] ECR II-1161 and Case T-310/00 *MCI v EC Commission* [2004–5], not yet reported.

[25] D Simon, *Le système juridique communautaire* (2nd edn, 1997) 378.

2. *Locus standi* of third parties

18.24 Third parties in the sense of those that are not addressees of decisions may, in certain circumstances, bring actions for the review of such decisions. The current criterion is based on the rule laid down in *Plaumann*,[26] where the ECJ imposed on the claimants a very high standard, based on the definition of 'individual interest'.[27]

18.25 It is, however, fair to say that in merger cases this standard is, in practice, applied quite flexibly. The mere fact that the claimant has been more or less directly associated with the procedure leading to the decision is normally considered to be sufficient.[28] In fact, actions brought by those participating in the procedure are generally accepted.[29]

18.26 Besides participation in the procedure the courts have given weight to the general principle that any competitor will be affected by the decision in question. Thus, in *TAT*,[30] the CFI found that an individual interest of Air France existed not only because of said company's participation in the procedure through the submission of observations throughout the same (submissions which had even been taken into account by the Commission) but also because Air France was BA's main competitor in the two markets identified in the concentration[31] and it had been obliged to divest in full its stake in TAT four months prior to the notification.

---

[26] Case 25/62 *Plaumann v EC Commission* [1963] ECR 95 para 107 confirmed recently in Case C-50/00 P *Unión de Pequeños Agricultores v Council* [2002] ECR I-6677 para 36.

[27] Establishing that an undertaking is 'individually concerned': 'if that decision affects them by reason of certain attributes which are peculiar to them to or by reason of the circumstances in which they are differentiated from all other persons and by virtue of these factors distinguishes them individually just as in the case of the person addressed'. This standard has been seen as a barrier preventing EU citizens from having access to justice, and various Advocates General and the CFI have tried to lower it. E.g. Opinion of AG Jacobs in *Unión de Pequeños Agricultores* (UPA), establishing a more straightforward test granting *locus standi* to third parties whose interests are substantially prejudiced by the decision. So far, the ECJ has not (Case C-50/00 *Unión de Pequeños Agricultores* [2002] ECR I-6677; Case C-263/02 P *Jego Quéré*).

[28] D Simon, *Le système juridique communautaire* (2nd edn, 1997) 380.

[29] The importance of participating in the procedure was made clear in the first sentence of Case T-3/93 *Air France v EC Commission* [1994] ECR II-121, where the possibility of acting in the proceedings in the event that the Commission had already initiated them was stated by the CFI as one of the elements on which it would base a finding that an applicant had *locus standi*.

[30] Case T-2/93 *Air France v EC Commission* [1994] ECR II-323.

[31] In the same sense, Case T-3/93 *Air France v EC Commission* [1994] ECR II-121 paras 80 and 81. Case T-119/02 *Royal Philips Electronics v EC Commission* [2003] ECR II-1433 para 292. 'The parties agree that the applicant is one of the principal current competitors of the parties to the concentration on the relevant markets. In recital 32 of the Approval Decision, the applicant is thus mentioned as one of the operators which, like SEB, Moulinex, Bosch, Braun and De'Longhi, offer a wide range of products in the small electrical household appliances sector and have a pan-European presence.'

These principles were developed by the CFI in *Babyliss*,[32] a case where doubts as **18.27** to whether the claimant was even a competitor were raised. In this case, the Court began by recalling that mere participation in the administrative procedure is in itself not sufficient to show that the decision is of individual concern to the applicant. After examining the case law in competition matters, including the more specific area of the control of concentrations, the Court concluded that participation in the administrative procedure is a factor regularly taken into account when establishing, in conjunction with other specific circumstances, the *locus standi* of the applicant.[33]

The CFI went on to verify whether there were other specific circumstances that **18.28** meant that the applicant was 'individually concerned'. As regard the applicant's status as a competitor, the CFI stated that although the applicant's market presence was limited to only one of the markets in which SEB was active at the date of adoption of the contested decision, Babyliss was found to be at least a potential competitor.[34] That was judged sufficient to grant *locus standi*.

This definition was further broadened in *ARD v EC Commission*.[35] In this case, **18.29** the CFI considered that the fact that the applicant was not a competitor or even a potential competitor of KirchPayTV on the pay-TV market did not necessarily mean that it was not individually concerned by the decision. The CFI considered that an action brought by an operator present only in the neighbouring upstream or downstream markets may be admissible under certain circumstances. The CFI based its decision on five main arguments: (i) the existence of some level of competition between free television and pay-TV; (ii) the future convergence between free television and pay-TV due to digitalisation; (iii) the effect of the merger on digital interactive television services; (iv) the applicant's participation in the FUN project; and (v) the acquisition of broadcasting rights.[36]

---

[32] Case T-114/02 *BaByliss v EC Commission* [2003] ECR II-1279 the CFI examined whether the Commission's decision to clear the concentration between *SEB* and *Moulinex* was open to challenge by *Babyliss*, a third party who had taken part in the Commission's procedure.

[33] *BaByliss v EC Commission* para 95, with references to Case T-169/84 *Cofaz and others v EC Commission* [1986] ECR II-391 paras 24–25; Joined Cases C-68/94 and C-30/95 *France v EC Commission* [1998] ECR I-1375 para 54, and Case T-2/93 *Air France v EC Commission* [1994] ECR II-121 para 44.

[34] *BaByliss v EC Commission* para 99 'in so far as it is entering the European market for small electrical household appliances and that the oligopolistic market is characterized by substantial barriers to entry arising from strong brand loyalty and by the difficulty of access to retail trading'.

[35] Case T-158/00 *ARD v EC Commission* [2003] ECR II-3825. In this case ARD, a company providing free-to-air TV services in Germany, appealed the Commission's decision to clear a concentration between Kirch Pay TV and BSkyB involving the markets for pay TV, digital interactive services and the acquisition of broadcasting rights.

[36] Case T-158/00 *ARD v EC Commission* [2003] ECR II-3825 para 79.

3. Shareholders as applicants—the *Zunis* case

18.30 The admissibility of appeals brought by shareholders against decisions deserves a special mention. In *Zunis Holding*,[37] three minority shareholders of Generali, each of which had a shareholding of less than 0.5 per cent, contested the Commission's decision that Mediobanca's increased shareholding in Generali was not sufficient to confer control over Generali. The CFI held that the decision was not in itself sufficient to affect the substance or the extent of the rights of the shareholders, and that it did not affect the applicants individually, by virtue of any special attributes which differentiated them from other minority shareholders. Nevertheless, the Court left open the question of whether shareholders with larger stakes may be able to establish a direct and individual concern.[38]

4. Trade unions

18.31 Article 18(4) of the Merger Control Regulation grants to recognized representatives of their employees the right to be heard by the Commission but that right does not confer automatic *locus standi* under Article 230 EC to appeal against a Commission decision.

18.32 In *Nestlé/Perrier*[39] it was ruled *in casu* that express and specific reference to the employee representatives among third persons showing a sufficient interest to submit their observations to the Commission was enough to differentiate them from all other persons, whether or not they have made use of their rights during the administrative procedure. The CFI held, however, that they were not directly concerned, because any redundancies or changes in social benefits that could possibly arise following the merger were not an inevitable or direct consequence of the Commission's decision.

D. Scope of Revision and Discretion of the Commission

18.33 The scope and extent of judicial review under the Merger Control Regulation has been a much debated issue in the last few years. This should hardly come as a surprise, given the impact that Commission decisions have on mergers and other forms of corporate reorganization. Indeed, the Regulation grants the

---

[37] Case T-83/92 *Zunis Holding, Finan and Massinvest v EC Commission* [1993] ECR II-116 paras 34–37. See also on appeal Case C-480/93 P [1996] ECR I-1, although decided on other grounds.

[38] M Siragusa, 'Judicial Review of competition decisions under EC Law' 1–9 (2), available at http://www.competition-commission.org.uk.

[39] Case T-96/92 *Comité Central d'Entreprise de la Société Générale des Grandes Sources and others v EC Commission* [1995] ECR II-1213.

Commission significant powers to review and investigate mergers but also to conclude this investigation by adopting final, binding decisions and to impose fines. These powers are set against an institutional framework where the Commission acts as investigator, prosecutor, and as it has been widely suggested, even judge and jury.[40] This means that the checks and balances, whether internal[41] (within the Commission itself) or external (by the Community courts) are of particular importance to ensure that the system works fairly.

In addition to the impact that these decisions may have, and to some extent in contrast with decisions based on Articles 81 and 82 EC, the Commission enjoys exclusive powers under the Merger Regulation. It is therefore not surprising that the traditional self-restraint of the Community Courts in competition cases in recognition of the Commission's wide margin of discretion has been tested in actions for judicial review of decisions adopted under the Merger Regulation. The current view is that the discretion enjoyed by the Commission should be regarded as a limited operational discretion, confined to a certain latitude or margin of appraisal in its determination of the facts and its economic assessment of the proposed concentration.[42] As such, it is more limited than the broad discretion that the Commission enjoys in the exercise of its legislative, policy-making function. **18.34**

In addition, this discretion will vary according to the type of assessment being carried out. Concerning matters of law (both procedural and substantive) and facts, the Commission has no discretion at all as regards what legal criteria are to apply and the way the facts should be appraised.[43] In the same way, the constantly increasing process of codification through guidelines and notices relating to concentrations has meant that the Commission has less room to manoeuvre when adopting decisions. **18.35**

---

[40] B Vesterdorf, 'Judicial Review and Competition Law—Reflections on the role of the Community Courts in the EC System of Competition Law Enforcement', Competition Policy International, Vol 1, no 2, Autumn 2005, 2–27 (6), See also M Hoskins and W Robinson (eds), *A True European, Essays for Judge David Edward*, Oxford and Portland, Oregon, 2003.

[41] In particular the procedural rights, the Legal Service, the Chief Economist office and the Peer Review Panels. See para 16.19.

[42] B Mckenna, 'The scope of review of merger decisions under Community law' European Competition Journal, March 2005, 123–52 (148).

[43] In this sense, Opinion of AG Teasuro in *France v EC Commission*, para 21 '[a review of legality] appears all the more necessary if it is borne in mind that the twofold nature of the Commission's functions—a power of inquiry and investigation, coupled with a decision-making power—should impose on it an even stricter obligation to respect the right to a fair hearing'. See also, B Vesterdorf, Judicial Review and Competition Law—Reflections on the role of the Community Courts in the EC System of Competition Law Enforcement Competition Policy International, Vol 1, no 2, Autumn 2005, 2–27 (12), and B Vesterdorf, 'Standard of Proof in Marger Cases: Reflections in the Light of Recent Case Law of the Community Courts' European Competition Journal Vol 1, March 2005, 3–33 (12–16).

18.36 In contrast, the Commission has a certain degree of discretion when carrying out complex economic assessments. Nevertheless, the degree of discretion allowed to the Commission seems to vary according to the novelty and contro-versial or contested nature of the economic theories upon which it bases its assessment.[44]

18.37 A recent and important example of the above can be found in *Tetra Laval*.[45] In this case, the CFI held that the Commission's analysis regarding concentrations with a conglomerate effect is subject to analogous requirements to those laid down in the case law as regards the creation of a collective dominant position,[46] and, therefore, this analysis requires an examination that is particularly sensitive to the relevant circumstances, and must be backed up by 'convincing evi-dence'.[47] The CFI went however one step further, adding that when a dominant position is not created or reinforced immediately it will be necessary to be able to show that 'in all likelihood' it will be created in the future.[48]

18.38 Faced with these statements, the Commission considered that the CFI had imposed a disproportionate standard of proof on merger prohibition decisions and had exceeded its role, which is to review the administrative decision of the

---

[44] In this sense, see B Vesterdorf, 'Certain Reflections on Recent Judgments Reviewing Com-mission Merger Control Decision' in M Hoskins and W Robinson (eds), *A True European, Essays for Judge David Edward* (Oxford and Portland, Oregon, 2003) 117–44 (142) 'when new theories advanced by the Commission in the context of the exercise of its merger control function are contested before the Community judicature, it is, in my view, the duty and responsibility of the CFI, so as to ensure effective judicial review, closely to scrutinize the convincing nature of the evidence relied upon in the contested decision in support of such theories'. Also B Vesterdorf, 'Standard of Proof in Marger Cases: Reflections in the Light of Recent Case Law of the Com-munity Courts' European Competition Journal Vol 1, March 2005, 3–33 (17–25).

[45] Case T-5/02 *Tetra Laval v EC Commission* [2002] ECR II-4381 para 155.

[46] Joined Cases C-68/94 and C-30/95 *France and others v EC Commission* (*Kali and Salz*) [1998] ECR I-1375 para 222, and Case T-342/99 *Airtours v EC Commission* [2002] ECR II-2585 para 63.

[47] B Vesterdorf, 'Certain Reflections on Recent Judgments Reviewing Commission Merger Control Decision' in M Hoskins and W Robinson (eds), *A True European, Essays for Judge David Edward* (Oxford and Portland, Oregon, 2003) 117–44 (140), 'when the CFI refers, as it has done in particularly in the Airtours, Tetra Laval and Babyliss cases to the Commission's not having proved a claim to a sufficient legal standard or to the absence of "convincing evidence" it is quite clear that the CFI means that, having regard to primary facts and the direct inferences made therefrom, the particular prospective positive or negative analysis if the Commission decision at issue is so uncertain as to amount to, or form part of what amounts overall to, a manifest error of appreciation'.

[48] Case T-5/02 *Tetra Laval v EC Commission* [2002] ECR II-4381 para 148 'It is necessary first to determine whether a merger transaction creating a competitive structure which does not immediately confer on the merged entity a dominant position may nevertheless be prohibited under Article 2(3) of the Regulation, when in all likelihood it will allow that entity, as a result of leveraging by the acquiring party from a market in which it is already dominant, to obtain in the relatively near future a dominant position on another market in which the party acquired currently holds a leading position, and when the acquisition in question has significant anti-competitive effects on the relevant markets'.

Commission for clear errors of fact or reasoning, and not to substitute its view of the case for that of the Commission.[49] As a result, it decided for the first time with respect to the field of concentrations to appeal to the ECJ, which gave rise to the judgment that laid down the parameters for the judicial review of concentration decisions.

In its appeal judgment, the Court removed the doubts about the scope of the **18.39** review that the Courts could carry out in economic cases, declaring that '[w]hilst the Court recognises that the Commission has a margin of discretion with regard to economic matters, that does not mean that the Community Courts must refrain from reviewing the Commission's interpretation of information of an economic nature. Not only must the Community Courts, *inter alia*, establish whether the evidence relied on is factually accurate, reliable and consistent but also whether that evidence contains all the information which must be taken into account in order to assess a complex situation and whether it is capable of substantiating the conclusions drawn from it [. . .]'.[50]

Some authors have argued that the Court may have 'trespassed the limits of its **18.40** judicial review, by stepping into the Commission's shoes',[51] at least with regard to the concentrations that do not immediately affect the market structure, such as those what could have a conglomerate effect on a neighbouring market[52] since they involved cause-effect relations that are not clearly perceptible, and

---

[49] Press Release, IP/02/1952, of 20 December 2002 'Commission appeals CFI ruling on Tetra Laval/Sidel to the European Court of Justice'.

[50] Judgment of 15 February 2005 '[. . .] such a review is all the more necessary in the case of a prospective analysis required when examining a planned merger with conglomerate effect'. Case C-12/03 *EC Commission v Tetra Laval*.

[51] M Siragusa, 'Judicial Review of competition decisions under EC Law' 1–8 (7–8), available at Competition Commission web page: http://www.competition-commission.org.uk. See also, J Temple Lang 'Two important Merger Regulation judgements: the implications of Schneider-Legrand and Tetra Laval-Sidel' (2003) 28 EL Rev 259–72 (268), 'The Court sets a new burden of proof. The transaction must 'in all likelihood' create or strengthen a dominant position 'in the relatively near future' and this will call for a particularly close examination of the circumstances. Analyses of effects which would occur only after a significant lapse of time must 'whilst allowing for certain margin of discretion, be particularly plausible'. See also D Drauz 'Conglomerate and vertical mergers in the light of the Tetra Judgment' Competition Policy Newsletter, number 2-summer 2005 35–39.

[52] Case C-12/03 *EC Commission v Tetra Laval*, not yet reported, para 44: 'The analysis of a conglomerate-type' concentration is a prospective analysis in which, first, the consideration of a lengthy period of time in the future and, secondly, the leveraging necessary to give rise to a significant impediment to effective competition mean that the chains of cause and effect are dimly discernible, uncertain and difficult to establish. That being so, the quality of the evidence produced by the Commission in order to establish that it is necessary to adopt a decision declaring the concentration incompatible with the common market is particularly important, since that evidence must support the Commission's conclusion that, if such a decision were not adopted, the economic development envisaged by it would be plausible'.

that are uncertain and difficult to determine. In such cases, the Commission will analyse prospective effects that must be proved through 'convincing evidence'[53] as to how and why it is considered that competition will be significantly impeded, in particular, through the creation or reinforcement of a dominant position.

E. Interim Measures

18.41 Interim measures are very important in appeal procedures in general. This is even more so in merger control cases, where action often has to be taken immediately. Article 243 EC provides that '[t]he Court of Justice may in any cases before it prescribe any necessary interim measures'. This provision neither establishes what kind of interim measures might be granted nor what conditions are required for them to be granted. The possibility of suspending the application of a contested decision is hinted at in Article 242 EC, which provides that '[t]he Court of Justice may, however, if it considers that circumstances so require, order that application of the contested act be suspended'. There is no list of possible interim measures that may be sought, so the parties might apply not only for the suspension of the effects of a Commission's decision but also for 'any other interim measure', as per the wording of Article 60 of the Statute of the Court of Justice.[54]

18.42 Article 39 of the Statute of the Court of Justice provides that the President of the Court may, by way of summary procedure, 'adjudicate upon applications to suspend execution, as provided for in Article 242 of the EC Treaty and Article 157 of the EAEC Treaty, or to prescribe interim measures in pursuance of Article 243 of the EC Treaty or Article 158 of the EAEC Treaty'. In connection with applications for the adoption of interim measures, the President of the Court is supported by Assistant Rapporteurs.[55]

---

[53] ECJ *Tetra Laval* para 155, Case T-342/99 *Airtours v EC Commission* [2002] ECR II-2585 para 63, Joined Cases C-68/94 and C-30/95 *France and others v EC Commission (Kali and Salz)* ECR I-1375 para 222. Confirmed by judgment of 14 December 2005 in *General Electric v EC Commission*, para 69, not yet reported.

[54] Protocol on the Statute of the Court of Justice annexed to the Treaty on the European Union, to the Treaty establishing the European Community and to the Treaty establishing the European Atomic Energy Community, in accordance with Art 7 of the Treaty of Nice, amending the Treaty on European Union, the Treaties establishing the European Communities and certain related acts, signed at Nice on 26 February 2001 [2001] OJ C80, as amended by decisions of the Council of 15 July 2003 [2003] OJ L188/1 and 19 April 2004 [2004] OJ L132/1, 5.

[55] Art 24 of the Rules of Procedure of the Court of Justice of the European Communities of 19 June 1991 [1991] OJ L176/7, and [1992] OJ L383/04 (corrigenda).

A successful application of interim measures requires a number of elements. On **18.43** the one hand, the main action should have been validly lodged. Second, there has to be a sound prima facie case (*fumus boni iuris*). The applicant has to specify the circumstances of law and fact upon which the plea of urgency is based. Furthermore, it has to be proven that there is a serious risk of causing irreparable harm to the applicant (*periculum in mora*). The measures applied for have to be necessary in order to avoid this serious damage, which has to be directly linked with the implementation of the contested decision.

Ultimately, the decision requires a balancing of two conflicting interests: a **18.44** public interest in ensuring an immediate application of the Commission decision, and the private interests of affected companies. In practice it is frequent that the request is limited to the specific mandates included in the decision causing the irreparable harm.

The *Nestlé/Perrier* cases[56] initiated by workers representatives gave the President **18.45** of the CFI the occasion to decide on interim measures in connection with disposals of businesses. The two Orders interpreted strictly the requirements for the granting of interim measures in cases where the interests of persons not party to the procedure may be affected. Citing *Simmenthal v EC Commission*,[57] it was recalled that in these situations interim measures could only be granted if there was a risk of disappearance of the requesting parties. That was not found to be the case in *Nestlé/Perrier*. In addition, the President took the view that the allegedly irreparable effect that the transfer may have had on the level of employment had not been sufficiently established and the requests were dismissed.

Some months later, limited interim protection was granted to the applicant in **18.46** *Kali and Salz*.[58] In its decision, the Commission had, *inter alia*, imposed on the notifying parties a condition that they withdraw from a marketing joint venture (entered into with a competitor), which was active in third countries. The other shareholder in the joint venture, SCPA and its parent company EMC asked the President of the Court to suspend that part of the decision pending judicial review. The request was granted given the irreparable harm that the dissolution of the joint venture would cause to SCPA, an undertaking which was not a party to the procedure. It was also observed that the joint venture had existed for many years, and there was no good reason to dismantle it prior to the judicial review of the decision.

---

[56] Case T-96/92 R *Comité Central d'Entreprise de la Société des Grandes Sources v EC Commission* [1992] ECR II-2579 and Case T-12/93 R *Comité Central d'Entreprise de la SA Vittel et Comité d' Etablissement de Pierval v EC Commission* [1993] ECR II-785.
[57] Case 92/78 R *Simmenthal v EC Commission* [1978] ECR 1129.
[58] Case T-88/94 R *SCPA and EMC v EC Commission* [1994] ECR II-401.

18.47 The application for interim relief in *Union Carbide*,[59] decided later in 1994, also failed. The applicant had a joint venture with Shell, and opposed the conditional clearance granted by the Commission in *Shell/Montecatini*.[60] The applicant claimed, *inter alia*, that certain commitments offered by Shell would damage the business of the existing UCC/Shell joint venture. The President of the CFI dismissed these claims, considering that the causal link between the damage and the commitments had not been sufficiently well established.

18.48 A particular type of interim measure was requested in *Sogecable*,[61] where the measure sought was aimed at preventing the Commission from adopting any act within a merger control procedure. In the applicant's view, the case lacked a Community dimension and for this reason had been notified to the Spanish competition authorities. However, the Commission took the view that the case did have a Community dimension, and had therefore initiated proceedings under the Merger Regulation. The President of the CFI rejected the request for interim measures, noting that the judge should not be empowered to grant such an open ended measure that would prevent the Commission from adopting any conceivable measure, without prejudice to the review of the potentially actionable measures that the Commission may actually adopt within the said procedure.

18.49 One more recent example of interim measures in special circumstances is found in *Petrolessence*,[62] which concerned the rejection by the Commission of the applicants as potential purchasers of a business that had to be divested following *TotalFina/Elf*.[63] Again, based on the particularly strict test to be followed where the request may affect third parties not party to the procedure, the President of the Court rejected the request.

18.50 Finally, it is worth mentioning that interim measures were requested in *Schneider/Legrand* and *Tetra Laval/Sidel*.[64] However, these applications were withdrawn after the Commission agreed to postpone enforcement of its decisions until the end of the judicial review. This suggests that the Commission may take a flexible approach as regards enforcement in the context of appeals brought under the fast-track procedure.

---

[59] Case T-322/94 R *Union Carbide v EC Commission* [1994] ECR II-1159.
[60] *Shell/Montecatini* (Case IV/M.269) [1996] OJ L332/48.
[61] Case T-52/96 R *Sogecable v EC Commission* [1996] ECR II-797.
[62] Case T-342/00 R *Petrolessence and SG2R v EC Commission* [2001] ECR II-67.
[63] *TotalFina/Elf* (Case COMP/M.1628) [2001] OJ L143/1.
[64] M Siragusa, 'Judicial Review of competition decisions under EC Law' 1-9 (2), available at http://www.competition-commission.org.uk

F. Procedure before European Courts

The judicial review of Commission decisions under the Merger Control Regula- **18.51**
tion is governed by the Rules of Procedure of the Community Courts. With the
obvious and rather infrequent exception of cases brought by Member States
and institutions, these cases are heard by the CFI and, on appeal, by the ECJ.
The main features of these procedures are summarized below.

1. Ordinary procedure

The ordinary procedure, which is conducted in the language chosen by the **18.52**
applicant, consists of a written and an oral phase.

The written phase begins with the filing of the application, which is composed **18.53**
of a pleading together with all of the schedules mentioned therein, and the
supporting documents.[65] The defendant must file a defence within one month
of notification of the application, although this period may be extended if
grounds are given. The supporting documents could be supplemented by way of
further pleadings (a reply from the applicant and a rejoinder from the defendant), unless the Court considers this to be unnecessary. During the proceedings,
new documents cannot be adduced, except if new factual or legal reasons that
have come to light during the proceedings. Evidence can be proposed by both
parties in the application or defence, and the Court can order the procedural
steps or evidence which it considers necessary. Once the evidential stage or any
measures of procedural organization have taken place, the President will fix a
date for opening the oral phase.

At the end of the written phase, and, where appropriate, the steps relating to the **18.54**
evidence to be adduced, the oral submissions will be made in a public hearing.
Oral submissions are translated simultaneously, where necessary. The President
may put questions to the agents, advisers or lawyers. The oral phase will be
declared to have ended once the hearing has finished. Finally, the judges will
deliberate the matter and pass judgment in public.

The large number of procedural steps together with the backlog of cases in the **18.55**
CFI[66] are ill-suited for the review of concentrations. The effectiveness and speed
of the notification procedure before the Commission, necessary in all concentration operations, is in marked contrast to the slowness of the procedure before

---

[65] The application must contain the matters listed in Art 44 of the Procedural Regulation of
the CFI.
[66] The *Kali and Salz* judgment (C-68/94) was given four years after the Commission decision,
and the *Airtours* judgment (T-342/99) three years after the Commission decision.

the Community Courts, which has regularly frustrated the aspirations of the parties to concentrations. The system became so slow and ineffective that the CFI would often pass judgment in judicial review cases when it was no longer feasible to carry out the transaction that was the subject matter of the appeal. Ultimately, the severe criticism of this situation led to the expedited or 'fast-track' procedure being introduced.

2. The fast-track procedure

18.56   The expedited or 'fast-track' procedure in the CFI was introduced in February 2001. This procedure has radically changed the position of the judicial review of Commission merger control decisions where fast-evolving markets mean that time is of the essence.

18.57   When introducing the fast-track procedure, the CFI took into account the need to offer a rapid reply in actions for the judicial review of concentrations. Undertakings have clearly seen the benefits of this new procedure in concentration cases; witness the fact that eleven of the fourteen requests to use the fast-track procedure have been with regard to Commission decisions in the field of the control of concentrations.[67]

18.58   To date, seven[68] cases have been reviewed under the fast-track procedure, and none has taken more than one year. *Schneider* and *Tetra Laval* were resolved within ten months from the time that the action began and in seven months from the moment that the applicability of the fast-track procedure was accepted. In *Babyliss* and *Philips*, judgment was given one year after the appeal started and nine months after the fast-track procedure commenced.[69] In *EDP*, judgment was delivered in a record time of seven months. In fact, it seems that the fast-track procedure may not take much longer than the time required for the Commission investigations.[70]

18.59   Access to the fast track is not automatic. A series of requirements must be

---

[67] B Vesterdorf, 'Certain Reflections on Recent Judgments Reviewing Commission Merger Control Decision', 117–44 (118) in M Hoskins and W Robinson (eds), *A True European, Essays for Judge David Edward* (Oxford and Portland, Oregon, 2003).

[68] Case T-310/01 *Schneider Electric v EC Commission* [2002] ECR II-4071, Case T-77/02 *Schneider Electric v EC Commission* [2002] ECR II-4201, Case T-5/02 *Tetra Laval v EC Commission* [2002] ECR II-4381, Case T-80/02 *Tetra Laval v EC Commission* [2002] ECR II-4519, Case T-114/02 *BaByliss v EC Commission* [2003] ECR II-1279, Case T-119/02 *Royal Philips NV v EC Commission* [2003] ECR II-1433 and Case T-87/05 *EDP v EC Commission* [2005], not yet reported.

[69] B Vesterdorf, 'Certain Reflections on Recent Judgments Reviewing Commission Merger Control Decision', 117–44 (118) in M Hoskins and W Robinson (eds), *A True European, Essays for Judge David Edward* (Oxford and Portland, Oregon, 2003).

[70] For instance, in *Schneider/Legrand* the Commission investigation lasted eight months and the procedure before the CFI took slightly over ten months. In *EDP* the Commission investigation lasted five months and the procedure before the CFI took seven months.

fulfilled, since only those cases that are particularly urgent and which have special circumstances will be allowed to proceed in this way. The request must be filed by either of the parties and made on a separate document at the same time as the application or defence is filed, depending on who is making the request.[71] The President of the CFI will hear the parties and decide whether or not a case qualifies for the fast track.[72]

It appears that, in general, cases concerning the judicial review of the Commission's decisions on concentrations fulfil the requirements needed to qualify for the fast track procedure, since, in most cases, special urgency will exist. However, there will be cases where due to the peculiar circumstances of the appeal, for example where the application is based on a large number of grounds or is especially complicated, the fast-track procedure will not be appropriate.[73] **18.60**

Although it could be thought that the speed of this procedure would mean that judgments would be shorter and less detailed, those fast-track judgments given to date are of the same quality as ordinary procedure judgments, both with respect to the grounds given and the detail of the examination and explanation of the Court's findings.[74] The fast track has been lauded by both academics and practitioners, but above all by undertakings; the latter have particularly welcomed this new system which has enabled the CFI to review decisions with a real sense of urgency, thus providing a convincing response to the criticism of the Commission's current role of investigator, prosecutor, and decision-maker.[75] **18.61**

G. Appeals to the ECJ

CFI rulings that terminate proceedings, as well as those that partially resolve a substantive issue or decide a procedural issue concerning a plea of lack of competence or inadmissibility, can be appealed against to the ECJ within two months from the date of notification of the challenged decision.[76] Any appeal to **18.62**

---

[71] Art 76 bis of the Rules of Procedure of the CFI.

[72] ibid.

[73] e.g. in T-103/02 *Ineos Phenol* the CFI refused the fast-track procedure because the issues were too complicated. In *EDP* it was necessary that the applicant withdrew its procedural pleas, which were unrelated to the Commission Competitive assessment of the transaction, to be reviewed under the fast-track procedure.

[74] In this sense, J Temple Lang, 'Two important Merger Regulation judgments: the implications of Schneider-Legrand and Tetra Laval-Sidel', (2003) 28 EL Rev 259–72 (259).

[75] B Vesterdorf, 'Certain Reflections on Recent Judgments Reviewing Commission Merger Control Decision', 117–44 (118) in M Hoskins and W Robinson (eds), *A True European, Essays for Judge David Edward*.

[76] Art 56 of the Statute of the ECJ.

the ECJ must be limited to questions of law and must be based on one or more of the following grounds: (i) the lack of competence of the CFI; (ii) procedural irregularities before the CFI that damage the interests of the appellant; and (iii) breach of Community law by the CFI.[77] This division of labour between the CFI and the ECJ in the review of concentration decisions has been recently summarized by AG Tizzano in his Opinion in *Tetra Laval*.[78]

18.63 Appeal proceedings may be started by filing a written appeal with the Registrar of the ECJ or CFI[79] by any parties whose submissions have been totally or partially dismissed by the CFI. The procedure before the ECJ concerning an appeal against a CFI ruling will consist of a written part and an oral part. After hearing the Advocate General and the parties, the ECJ can make declarations in accordance with the conditions laid down in the Rules of Procedure.[80] The purpose of the appeal must be the total or partial annulment of the declarations made at first instance; the appeal cannot modify the subject matter of the case brought before the CFI.

18.64 In the very few cases where an appeal has taken place to date,[81] the ECJ has always confirmed the CFI's rulings.

H. Consequences of Judicial Review

18.65 The general rule concerning the consequences of Court decisions is set out in the Treaty itself. Under Article 233 EC, '(t)he institution or institutions whose act has been declared void or whose failure to act has been declared contrary to this Treaty shall be required to take the necessary measures to comply with the judgment of the Court of Justice'. The necessary measures may, depending on the judgment, require the adoption of a new decision in accordance with the Merger Control Regulation.

---

[77] Art 58 of the Statute of the ECJ.

[78] Opinion of AG Tizzano delivered 25 May 2004 in Case C-12/03 *Commission v Tetra Laval BV*, (para 60) 'that the Court of First Instance has exclusive jurisdiction, first, to establish the facts except where the substantive inaccuracy of its findings is apparent from the documents submitted to it and, second, to assess those facts. When the Court of First Instance has established or assessed the facts, the Court of Justice has jurisdiction under Article 168a of the Treaty [now Article 225 EC] to review the legal characterisation of those facts by the Court of First Instance and the legal conclusions it has drawn from them. The Court of Justice thus has no jurisdiction to establish the facts or, in principle, to examine the evidence which the Court of First Instance accepted in support of those facts. Provided that the evidence has been properly obtained [. . .]'.

[79] Art 56 Statute of the ECJ.   [80] Art 59 Statute of the ECJ.

[81] Case C-480/93 *Zunis Holding and others v EC* Commission [1996] ECR I-1 and Case C-170/02 P *Schlüsselverlag JS Moser GmbH et al v EC Commission* [2003] ECR I-9889. These appeals are limited to the question of admissibility. For a full appeal before the Court see Case C-12/03 *EC Commission v Tetra Laval* [2005] OJ C82/2.

Originally, Regulation 4064/89 regulated the effects of Court decisions on mer-   **18.66** gers rather cryptically. Article 10(5) stated that the periods laid down in the Regulation would start to run as from the date of the Court's judgment. The Regulation did not specify how these terms should be calculated, nor whether the analysis should be carried out having regard to the circumstances prevailing at the time of the original notification or the later date where the decision was to be adopted.

In *Kali and Salz*,[82] the first case where the Community Courts reviewed the   **18.67** substance of a decision adopted under the Regulation, the Commission was confronted with the need to adopt the measures necessary to comply with the ECJ's judgment. In order to make a new examination, the Commission requested additional information to the parties in order to update the information on file.[83] Only following the receipt of this information, more than two months after the Court's judgment, did the Commission consider that the term had started to run. As to whether the analysis should be carried out having regard to current market conditions or those prevailing at the time of the initial case, the Commission seemingly adopted a mixed interpretation. As regards determining its competence over the concentration, it relied on data provided in the original notification to ascertain that the transaction had a Community dimension; however, concerning its assessment of competition, the Commission relied on the then-current situation since any decision made on the basis of five-year-old data risked identifying competitive concerns that no longer existed. By way of exception, the possible availability of a 'failing firm defence' had to rely on the previous situation since at the time of the re-examination the failing company no longer existed.[84]

A similar approach would be followed in *Tetra Laval/Sidel* following the annul-   **18.68** ment of the first prohibition decision by the CFI.[85] As the decision adopted by the Commission in the second procedure explains,[86] the Commission relied on Article 4(2) of the then implementing Regulation 447/98 and declared the notification incomplete in a material respect. Only following the receipt of that information did the time-limits start running again. The Commission finally cleared the transaction with conditions, noting however that its decision may

---

[82] Joined Cases C-68/94 and C-30/95 *France and others v EC Commission* (*Kali and Salz*) [1998] ECR I-1375.

[83] See Commission Decision of 9 July 1998, *Kali and Salz/MDK/Treuhand* (Case M.308) (1998), para 3.

[84] See on this point N Hacker, 'The Kali and Salz case—the re-examination of a merger after an annulment by the Court' Competition Policy Newsletter, 1998, number 3 (October), 40.

[85] Case T-5/02 *Tetra Laval v EC Commission* [2002] ECR II-4381.

[86] Decision of 13 January 2003, *Tetra Laval/Sidel* (Case COMP/M.2416) (2003), available at http://www.europa.eu.int/comm/competition/mergers/cases/decisions/m2416_62_en.pdf.

depend on the outcome of the appeal that had been made before the Court of Justice.[87]

18.69 The above precedents have shaped the new text of Article 10(5) of the Merger Control Regulation, which now explains that, following a judgment that affects any decision subject to the time-limits provided for in said Article 10,[88] a new examination will be made. The notifying parties will be required to either file a new notification or complete the notification originally filed in the event that market changes have taken place, or certify otherwise that no such changes have occurred. The time periods laid down in the Merger Regulation will start to run once the new notification, supplemented notification or certification as the case may be have been delivered to the Commission.

18.70 As regards the scope of the examination that the Commission would initiate, Article 10(5) paragraph 2 provides that '[t]he concentration shall be re-examined in the light of current market conditions', which must be understood as meaning those existing at the time a new decision is adopted. That again is consistent with the Commission's practice in *Kali and Salz* and *Tetra Laval/ Sidel*; actually, both cases resulted in a clearance of the transactions that in the initial assessment had been declared incompatible with the common market. In both cases, the new circumstances were instrumental for the new assessment.[89]

---

[87] Decision cited above, para 3. In its Judgment of 18 March 2005 the Court dismissed the appeal made by the Commission. See Case C-12/03 *EC Commission v Tetra Laval* [2005] OJ C82/2.

[88] Or the time-limits contained in Arts 6(4) and 8(7).

[89] In contrast, the review of the *Schneider/Legrand* case following the annulment by the CFI of the initial prohibition decision resulted in second stage proceedings being opened. The notification was later withdrawn and a claim for damages filed with the CFI (Case T-351/03, action brought on 10 October 2003 [2004] OJ C7/68, pending case).

Part III

PUBLIC UNDERTAKINGS AND EXCLUSIVE OR SPECIAL RIGHTS (ARTICLE 86(3) EC)

19

PROCEDURE ON STATE MEASURES—
DECISIONS UNDER ARTICLE 86(3) EC

A. Introduction

This chapter will concentrate on the procedure for the application of rules **19.01**
regarding public undertakings and special and exclusive rights in Community
law, a question which is much more complicated and of greater scope than may
first appear. In fact, Article 86(3) EC provides a special procedure intended not
only to *bring an end to* infringements of Article 86(1) EC committed by Member States, but also to adopt general measures designed to *define* the scope of the
obligations under Article 86(1) and/or to *prevent* future infringements of those
obligations[1] Thus, Article 86(3) grants to the Commission, on the one hand,
the power to adopt *decisions* declaring that Member States have infringed the
obligations under Article 86(1) and obliging the Member State to put an end to
the infringement. This procedure constitutes an exception to the general procedure contained in Article 226 EC, in which it is up to the ECJ to declare that
the Treaty has been infringed, but it is not a revolutionary idea. Indeed, the
Commission has similar powers as regards the anti-competitive behaviour of
undertakings (Articles 81 and 82 EC) and State Aid (Articles 87 and 88 EC).
This suggests a system giving the Commission similar powers to react quickly
against all restrictions of competition, irrespective of their public or private

---

[1] See JL Buendía Sierra, *Exclusive Rights and State Monopolies in EC Law* (OUP, 1999) ch 10; F
Blum and A Logue, *State Monopolies under EC Law* (Wiley, 1998), ch 3; C Hocepied, 'Les
directives Article 90, paragraphe 3. Une espèce juridique en voie de disparition?' [1994] RAE ii
49–63; A Pappalardo, 'State Measures and Public Undertakings: Article 90 of the ECC Treaty
Revisited' [1991] 1 ECLR 29–39; M Kerf, 'The Policy of the Comisión of EEC Toward Nacional
Monopolies. An analysis of the Measures Adopted on the Basis of Article 90(3) of the EEC Treaty'
(1993) 17(1) World Competition 73–111; LM Pais Antunes, 'L'Article 86 du Traité CEE—
Obligations des Etats Membres et pouvoirs de la Commission' [1991] RTDE ii 187 *et seq*.; F
Melin-Soucramanien, 'Les pouvoirs spéciaux conférés à la Commission en matière de concurrence
par l'Article 86.3 du Traité de Rome' [1994] 382 RMCUE 601–10.

origin. Article 86(3) also provides the Commission with the power to adopt obligatory directives aimed at Member States, designed to define the scope of the rules under Article 86(1) and (2) and/or prevent future infractions of these rules. These two aspects of Article 86(3) raise some difficult questions of interpretation and delimitation with respect to other procedures provided for in the Treaty.

B. Procedures for the Application of the Community Rules

19.02 The Community legal system consists of a set of rules which are addressed to Member States and/or individuals.

1. Procedure regarding the behaviour of undertakings

19.03 Articles 81 and 82 EC are rules addressed to undertakings. These rules may be applied either by the national courts, by the competent national authorities, or by the European Commission. Naturally, in the exercise of these functions the Commission is subject to the jurisdictional control of the CFI and the ECJ. The application procedures of these provisions are currently contained in the so-called 'Modernisation' Regulation 1/2003 which is the object of other chapters of this book.[2]

2. Procedures regarding State measures

19.04 The normal procedure for the general application of the rules of the Treaty addressed to Member States is proceedings for failure to fulfil an obligation provided for in Article 226 EC. Apart from this general procedure, the Treaty has provided certain special procedures for the application of specific provisions. Thus, Article 88 provides a special procedure for the application of Article 87, which is a rule regarding State aid. In the same way, Article 86(3) provides a special procedure for the application of Article 86(1), a rule which concerns, *inter alia*, exclusive rights. Much of this chapter will be dedicated to this last mentioned procedure.

Application by the national courts and preliminary rulings (Article 234 EC)

19.05 It should be remembered that, apart from these procedures reserved to the Community institutions, individuals may bring an action before the *national* courts for the application of Community rules which have *direct effect*. The ECJ

---

[2] Reg 1/2003 on the implementation of the rules on competition laid down in Arts 81 and 82 of the Treaty [2003] OJ L1/1.

has recognized the direct effect of practically all of the rules regarding matters of exclusive rights, such as Articles 28, 29, 30, 31(1), 31(2), 43, 49, or 86(1). This means that the national courts are competent to judge the compatibility of exclusive rights with these provisions. Within this context, under Article 234 of the Treaty national courts have the possibility (or the obligation if the national court's decision can not be appealed) of referring a matter to the ECJ for a *preliminary ruling* on the interpretation of the Community provisions mentioned above.[3] The importance of Article 234 must not be underestimated. It is true that in the context of a preliminary ruling, the Court of Justice is in theory limited to offering an interpretation of the Treaty provisions. It is not competent to judge on the legality or illegality of the State measure in question, since this is within the national courts' competence. In practice, however, the dividing line between 'interpret' the rules and 'apply' the rules is fairly unclear. The 'interpretation' of a rule makes no sense if it is not in reference to some facts.[4] Frequently, the interpretation given by the ECJ to a national court makes it absolutely clear as regards the legality or illegality of the national measure. In such cases the decision of the ECJ therefore determines beforehand the resolution of the proceedings.[5] However, there are many cases in which the ECJ prefers to limit itself to giving a general interpretation whose use by the national courts for resolving and settling proceedings is somewhat doubtful.[6] In any case, it should be taken into account that most of the judgments regarding Articles 31 and above all Article 86 have been given within the framework of preliminary rulings. The considerable changes experienced in the way that these provisions have been interpreted have almost always been as a result of individuals bringing legal proceedings before the national courts which have been referred for preliminary rulings. For this reason, it would be a serious mistake to perceive Article 234 as being of secondary importance in the application of Community rules concerning public undertakings and special and exclusive rights.

Proceedings for failure to fulfil an obligation (Article 226 EC)

Irrespective of the possible actions open to individuals, Article 211 of the Treaty entrusts to the Commission the task of acting as the Community guardian, thereby ensuring 'that the provisions of this Treaty [. . .] are applied'. The **19.06**

---

[3] For a detailed study of the procedure for preliminary rulings under Art 234, see G Isaac, *Droit communautaire général* (4th edn, 1994) 291–309. M Waelbroeck and D Waelbroeck, 'La Cour de Justice' in Various, *Commentaire Megret, Le Droit de la CEE* (2nd edn Vol 10, 1993) 197–278.

[4] M Waelbroeck and D Waelbroeck, 'La Cour de Justice' in Various, *Commentaire Megret, Le Droit de la CEE* (2nd edn Vol 10, 1993) 197–278 (243).

[5] G Isaac, *Droit communautaire général* (4th edn, 1994) 295.

[6] M Waelbroeck and D Waelbroeck, 'La Cour de Justice' in Various, *Commentaire Megret, Le Droit de la CEE* (2nd edn Vol 10, 1993) 197–278 (243 n 266).

Commission's main instrument for carrying out this task is to bring an enforcement action for a Member State's failure to fulfil a Treaty obligation under Article 226:

> If the Commission considers that a Member State has failed to fulfil an obligation under this Treaty, it shall deliver a reasoned opinion on this matter after giving the State concerned the opportunity to submit its observations.
>
> If the State does not comply with the opinion within the period laid down by the Commission, the latter may bring the matter before the Court of Justice.

19.07 A detailed examination of Article 226 goes beyond the limits of this book.[7] The principal features will now be highlighted so that the originality of the special procedure of Article 86(3) of the Treaty can be appreciated. Following actions brought by individuals or by any other means, the Commission may conclude that a Member State is in breach of certain of its obligations under Community law. If it does so conclude, Article 226 confers upon it the power to bring proceedings before the ECJ for a declaration that the Member State is in breach of the obligation in question. Prior to bringing proceedings before the court, Article 226 provides for an obligatory informal or pre-contentious stage.[8] This initial stage of the procedure officially begins with the Commission sending a *letter of formal notice* to the Member State in which all the State measures that are considered to be incompatible with the Treaty are identified. The Commission sets out the arguments in support of its opinion and the Member State is invited to submit its observations. If a satisfactory solution is not found the Commission will proceed to issue a 'reasoned opinion' in which the Member State is required to take action to end the infringement, normally within a specified time limit. Most of the cases are settled during this first conciliation stage. However, when the matter is not resolved and the Member State does not agree or comply with the requirements of the reasoned opinion, the Commission has the possibility of bringing proceedings for the failure to fulfil an obligation before the Court. This is the beginning of the formal or contentious stage. It is necessary to emphasize that Article 226 provides the Commission with wide discretionary powers. The Commission is not obliged to commence proceedings or to follow them up once they have been started. It may therefore decide to begin or to continue proceedings not only for legal but also for tactical reasons.

---

[7] For a detailed study of Art 226, see JV Louis, 'Le rôle de la Commission dans la procédure en manquement selon la jurisprudence de la Cour de justice' in Various, *Du droit international au droit de l'intégration—Liber Amicorum Pierre Pescatore* (Nomos Verlagsgesellschaft, 1987) 387–409; G Isaac, *Droit communautaire général* (4th edn, 1994) 278–90; M Waelbroeck and D Waelbroeck, 'Article 169' in Various, *Commentaire Megret, Le Droit de la CEE* (2nd edn Vol 10, 1993) 57–78.

[8] For a detailed description of the pre-contentious stage, see A Mattera, *Le marché unique européen. Ses règles, son fonctionnement* (Jupiter, 1988) 569–93.

The Commission may, for example, favour using negotiations in order to elim-inate a certain type of breach. From this it follows that individuals can not bring a direct action under Article 230 for the annulment of a Commission decision not to institute infringement proceedings nor may they bring an action under Article 232 against the inactivity of the Commission.[9] The purpose of Article 226 is not then to protect the rights that the Community rules give to individuals. This protection has to be primarily sought before the national courts.

Proceedings for failure to fulfil an obligation of the ECSC Treaty

From an institutional point of view, Article 226 EC establishes a system **19.08** whereby disagreements between the Commission and Member States concern-ing the scope of the latter's obligations are determined by the ECJ. This is not the only possible approach. In fact, proceedings for the infringement of the EC Treaty are based on a very different rationale from proceedings for infringement of the old ECSC (European Coal and Steel Community) Treaty.[10] Proceedings under this latter treaty gave a much greater role to the Commission as can be clearly seen from Article 88 of the ECSC Treaty:

> If the Commission considers that a State has failed to fulfil an obligation under this Treaty, it shall record this failure in a reasoned decision after giving the State concerned the opportunity to submit its comments. It shall set the State a time limit for the fulfilment of its obligation.
>
> The State may institute proceedings before the Court within two months of notification of the decision [. . .]

From an institutional point of view, the Commission's position in relation to Member States under the ECSC Treaty was much stronger than under the EC Treaty. In the procedure under Article 88 of the ECSC Treaty the Commission established the existence of a breach and adopted a decision which required the Member State to bring the breach to an end. If the Member State did not agree with this decision, it had no other remedy but to bring an action against this decision before the Court within two months. By contrast, under Article 226 EC the 'reasoned opinion' of the Commission is not binding upon the Member State and thus the Commission has no choice but to request the ECJ for a declaration of incompatibility.[11]

---

[9] Case T-84/94 *German Accountants* [1995] ECR II-101 paras 21–26, upheld on appeal, Case C-107/95 P *Bundesverband der Bilanzbuchhalter e.V. v EC Commission (German Accountants (appeal))* [1997] ECR I-947 paras 17–19.

[10] The ECSC Treaty expired on 23 July 2002. Since then the coal and steel sectors are subject to the EC Treaty.

[11] On the procedure of Art 88 of the ECSC Treaty, see G Isaac, *Droit communautaire général* (4th edn, 1994) 282–83; M Waelbroeck and D Waelbroeck, 'Article 169' in Various, *Commentaire Megret, Le Droit de la CEE* (2nd edn Vol 10, 1993) 58–59.

Special procedures of the EC Treaty

19.09   Nevertheless, it should not be forgotten that although Article 226 contains the general procedure for rectifying infringements of Treaty provisions there are certain procedures applicable to specific Treaty rules which are closer to the approach taken under Article 88 of the ECSC Treaty than to Article 226. This is the case of the procedure laid down in Article 88(2) EC regarding State aids and of the procedure under Article 86(3) which is applicable, amongst other matters, to exclusive rights.

19.10   **Special procedure regarding State aids (Article 88(2) EC)**   The special procedure for State aids contained in Article 88(2) EC is an exception to the normal procedure under Article 226.[12] By virtue of Article 88(2), the Commission may order a Member State to suspend and to recover aid that is incompatible with Article. If the Member State does not agree with this decision it must appeal under Article 230, requesting the Court to annul the decision within two months. If the Member State does not act within this given time-limit, the legality of the decision may not be questioned. If the Member State does not comply with or enforce the decision within the time-limit stated by the Commission, Article 88(2), paragraph 2 authorizes the Commission to bring the matter directly before the Court for a declaration that the Member State has fulfilled its obligations. This special procedure of Article 88(2) is, therefore, fairly different from the general procedure under Article 226 of the EC Treaty and quite similar to the procedure under Article 88 of the ECSC Treaty.

19.11   **Special procedure relating to exclusive rights and other State measures concerning public or privileged undertakings (Article 86(3) EC)**   As will now be explained in detail, Article 86(3) EC also provides a special procedure for the application of the remaining provisions of Article 86:

> The Commission shall ensure the application of the provisions of this Article and shall, where necessary, address appropriate directives or decisions to Member States.

Thus, the procedure under Article 86(3) may be applicable when it is a question of ensuring that an exclusive right or any other State measure regarding public or privileged undertakings complies with Article 86(1) and (2).[13] Like the

---

[12] For a description and examination of the procedure of Art 88, see L Hancher, T Ottervanger, and PJ Slot, *EC State Aids* (Chancery Law Publishing, 1993) 261–62; M Waelbroeck and D Waelbroeck, 'Article 169' in Various, *Commentaire Megret, Le Droit de la CEE* (2nd edn Vol 10, 1993), 60–61.

[13] Article 86(2) is applicable both to State measures and to the behaviour of undertakings. The application of Art 86(2) to justify the behaviour of undertakings which is contrary to Arts 81 and 82 may be carried out under Reg 1/2003. The application of Art 86(2) to justify State aid may be carried out in the context of an Art 88 procedure. In these cases, the Commission applies Art 86(2) without using the procedure under Art 86(3).

procedures under Article 88 of the old ECSC Treaty and Article 88(2) of the EC Treaty (and unlike the procedure under Article 226 of the EC Treaty), Article 86(3) allows the Commission itself to establish, through a binding decision, the non-compliance by a Member State with its obligations. If a Member State disagrees with the Commission's decision it must bring an action before the Court requesting the annulment of the decision within two months. (It should be remembered that under the general procedure of Article 226, the Commission's reasoned opinion is not binding upon the Member State and the onus is upon the Commission to bring an action before the ECJ to seek a declaration of incompatibility.) Article 86(3) thus provides a procedure for adopting *individual decisions* in order to end the specific breaches by Member States of their obligations. Although this procedure is different from the one provided for in Article 226, it is very similar to other Community procedures and contains nothing new or revolutionary. A detailed examination of this matter is dealt with in the second section of this chapter. What is much more original and controversial is the other facet of Article 86(3): the power conferred upon the Commission to adopt directives. This matter will be dealt with in the third section of this chapter.

C. Decisions under Article 86(3) EC

1. General points

The Commission has adopted sixteen individual decisions based on Article 86(3) of the Treaty: **19.12**

- Commission Decision (EEC) 85/276 [1985] OJ L152/25 regarding the insurance in Greece of public goods and of loans granted by Greek public banks;
- Commission Decision (EEC) 87/359 [1987] OJ L194/28 regarding the tariff reductions in air and shipping transport reserved exclusively to Spanish residents in the Canary and Balearic islands;
- Commission Decision (EEC) 90/16 [1990] OJ L10/47 regarding the provision in the Netherlands of courier postal services;
- Commission Decision (EEC) 90/456 [1990] OJ L233/19 regarding the provision in Spain of international courier postal services;
- Commission Decision (CE) 94/119 [1994] OJ L55/52 regarding the refusal of access to the installations of the port of Rødby (Denmark);
- Commission Decision (EC) 95/364 [1995] OJ L216/8 regarding the discount system in the landing tariffs in the national airport of Brussels;
- Commission Decision (EC) 95/489 [1995] OJ L280/49 regarding the conditions imposed upon the second operator of radio-telephonic GSM services in Italy;

- Commission Decision (EC) 97/181 [1997] OJ L76/19 regarding the conditions imposed upon the second operator of radio-telephonic services GSM in Spain;
- Commission Decision (EC) 97/606 [1997] OJ L244/18 on the exclusive right to broadcast television advertising in Flanders;
- Commission Decision (EC) 97/744 [1997] OJ L301/17 on the provisions of Italian ports legislation relating to employment;
- Commission Decision (EC) 97/745 [1997] OJ L301/27 regarding the tariffs for piloting in the Port of Genoa;
- Commission Decision (EC) 99/199 [1999] OJ L69/31 Portuguese airports;
- Commission Decision (EC) 2000/521 [2000] OJ L208/36 Spanish airports;
- Commission Decision (EC) 2001/176 [2001] OJ L63/59 in relation to the provision of certain new postal services with a guaranteed day- or time-certain delivery in Italy;
- Commission Decision (EC) 2002/344 [2002] OJ L120/19 on the lack of exhaustive and independent scrutiny of the scales of charges and technical conditions applied by La Poste to mail preparation firms for access to its reserved services;
- An Article 86(3) Decision was adopted on 20/10/2004 but is not yet published in the OJ (Press release IP/04/1254 of 'The Commission acts against the discrimination of mail preparation service providers in Germany').

These sixteen decisions only constitute the tip of the iceberg.[14] Most of the cases dealt with by the Commission based on Article 86 are settled without the need to resort to a formal decision. The most significant cases are recorded in the annual reports on competition policy. Another decision which should be added to the decisions of the Commission mentioned above concerns the gaming machines sector, which was adopted by EFTA on the basis of Article 59(3) of the European Economic Area Treaty, which is a rule similar to 86(3) of the EC Treaty.[15]

Application to the grant or maintenance of exclusive rights

19.13 The procedure under Article 86(3) only applies to State measures that infringe Article 86(1). Accordingly, State measures relating to public undertakings or

---

[14] C Hocepied, 'Les directives articles 90, paragraphe 3. Une espèce juridique en voie de disparition?' [1994] RAE ii 52.

[15] Decision 336/94/COL of the EFTA Surveillance Authority of 30 December 1994, on exclusive rights regarding gaming machines in Finland.

undertakings holding exclusive or special rights come within its scope. Thus, the grant or maintenance of an exclusive right which is incompatible with Article 86(1) together with another provision of the Treaty, can always be subject to the procedure under Article 86(3). In principle the procedure under Article 86(3) does not allow the Commission to adopt decisions which are directly addressed to public undertakings or to undertakings holding exclusive or special rights.[16] To the extent that the autonomous behaviour of these undertakings infringes Articles 81 and 82 it must be dealt with under the Regulation 1/2003 procedure. This is clearly shown from the position taken by the ECJ in the context of Article 86(3) directives, a position which is also applicable to the individual decisions adopted on that legal basis:[17]

> [I]t should be noted that Article 90 (now Article 86) of the Treaty confers powers on the Commission only in relation to State measures [. . .] and that anti-competitive conduct engaged in by undertakings on their own initiative can be called in question only by individual decisions adopted under Articles 85 and 86 of the Treaty (now Articles 81 and 82).

Nevertheless, there will be cases where, by virtue of Article 86(1), the veil will be lifted and certain behaviour of these undertakings will be attributed to the Member State. In these cases, at least, use of the Article 86(3) procedure will be fully justified.[18] Generally, the dividing line between the conduct of undertakings and State measures is rather blurred, which is an argument in favour of greater flexibility when delimiting the respective areas of Article 86(3) and Regulation 1/2003. Certain behaviour of public or private undertakings is likely to come within both areas when it is the result of 'incitement' by the authorities. In such cases the Commission should be able to proceed under either Article 86(3) or Regulation 1/2003.[19] This possibility seems to be accepted implicitly in the case law. Thus, the Court has only excluded from the scope of Article 86(3) anti-competitive behaviour which the undertakings have adopted 'on their own initiative'. It has also suggested that the behaviour of undertakings resulting from them being 'obliged or incited' by the State to behave in that way would

19.14

---

[16] A Bercovitz, 'Normas sobre la competencia del Tratado de la AELC' in E Garcia de Enterria, JD Gonzalez Campos and S Muñoz Machado (ed), *Tratado de Derecho comunitario*, Vol II, (Civitas, 1986) 437.

[17] Case C-202/88 *French Republic v EC Commission (Telecommunications Terminal Equipment)* [1991] ECR I-1272 paras 24 and 55. See also Joined Cases C-271/90, C-281/90 and C-289/90 *Spain, Belgium and Italy v EC Commission (Telecommunications Services)* [1992] ECR I-5866 para 24.

[18] See the reference to the *Transmediterránea* case in XVIII Report on Competition Policy (1988) para 309.

[19] This position was suggested by J Temple Lang, 'Community Antitrust Law and Government Measures relating to Public and Privileged Entreprises: Article 90 EEC Treaty' [1984] FCLI 550 (564–65).

come within the scope of Article 86(3).[20] In short, it is a question of proving the autonomous or non-autonomous character of the decisions of undertakings.

Justification for a special procedure

19.15 The justification for the existence of the special procedure under Article 86(3) is controversial. The reason that is generally put forward is the existence of particularly close relations between Member States and public or privileged undertakings in addition to the difficulty of detecting the influence that those Member States may exercise over such undertakings.[21] However, this reasoning can only be used to justify the adoption of preventive measures through directives under Article 86(3). It cannot be used to justify the adoption of decisions under Article 86(3) whose scope is limited to declaring the existence of an infringement and ordering that it be brought to an end. Indeed, the probability that Article 86(1) is infringed and that such infringements are detected is the same irrespective of whether they are prevented by using Article 226 or Article 86(3) of the Treaty. It is submitted that the reason why the Treaty provided a procedure for adopting decisions under Article 86(3) is probably connected with the need to ensure that there is consistency in the removal of distortions in competition, whether such distortions are caused by the private or public sector.[22] Thus, the powers of rapid intervention that the Treaty gives to the Commission with respect to the behaviour of undertakings (Articles 81 and 82) are echoed in the field of State measures, whether they are State aids (Articles 87 and 88), special or exclusive rights, or other restrictive measures (Article 86(3)). Thus, in any event the Commission itself has the power to find that an illegal restriction of the competition rules has occurred and the power to order that the restriction in question is ended, without having to bring proceedings before the ECJ. It is the responsibility of the party to whom the decision is addressed, whether an undertaking or a Member State, to appeal against the decision to the ECJ. As the ECJ has pointed out, the Treaty tries to grant to the Commission the adequate and appropriate instruments to guarantee that the competition rules are respected both by undertakings and by Member States.[23]

---

[20] Case C-202/88 *Telecommunications Terminal Equipment* [1991] ECR I-1272 paras 55–56; Joined Cases C-271/90, C-281/90 and C-289/90 *Telecommunications Services* [1992] ECR I-5866 paras 24–25.

[21] A Pappalardo, 'State measures and Public Undertakings: Article 90 of the EEC Treaty Revisited' [1991] ECLR i 35; M Kerf, 'The policy of the Commission of the EEC Toward National Monopolies. An Analysis of the Measures Adopted on the Basis of Article 90.3 of the EEC Treaty' World Competition Vol 17, September 1993, No 1, 77.

[22] This is the position advocated by H Papaconstantinou, *Free Trade and Competition in the EEC. Law, Policy and Practice* (Routledge, 1988) 102–4.

[23] Joined Cases C-48/90 and C-66/90 *Netherlands and Koninklijke PTT Nederland NV and PTT Post BV v EC Commission (PTT)* [1992] ECR I-635 para 30.

Procedural sources

The procedure of Article 86(3) is not regulated in detail by the Treaty nor by **19.16** secondary Community legislation. There is no supplementary text that specifies Article 86(3) procedure in greater detail. As a result, analogies with other procedures acquire great importance, the obvious ones being the antitrust procedure,[24] the State aids procedure,[25] or the Article 226 procedure.[26] However, these analogies have to be handled with care, and due account must be taken of the differences between these rules and Article 86.

Competent authority

The only authority competent to adopt decisions based on 86(3) is the European **19.17** Commission. It does not make any difference that Article 86(1) is of direct effect.[27] The national courts and the ECJ may of course apply these substantive provisions but may not adopt decisions under 86(3), as this power is expressly reserved to the European Commission.

The discretionary nature of the decision to initiate infringement proceedings

Article 211 of the Treaty entrusts the Commission with the task of ensuring the **19.18** application of the Treaty and Article 86(3) entrusts it with a similar task as regards Article 86(1) but even if the Commission always has the ability to act (*ex officio* or following a complaint), it is not automatically obliged to initiate infringement proceedings whenever a breach of Article 86(1) comes to light. The infringement procedure is only one of the instruments that the Commission has at its disposal to carry out its function as the 'guardian of the Treaty'. Other more flexible instruments, such as recommendations or legislative proposals, may in certain cases effectively contribute towards ensuring that this function is carried out. The text of Article 86(3) only provides for the adoption of decisions or directives 'where necessary'. In this sense, the ECJ has held that the Commission enjoys a wide margin of discretion when deciding whether to initiate proceedings against a Member State for breach of Article 86(1) of the Treaty.[28] A

---

[24] Rejected by the CFI in Case T-32/93 *Ladbroke I* [1994] ECR II-1015 para 38.
[25] Case C-18/88 *RTT* [1991] ECR I-5941 para 31; Opinion of AG La Pergola, Case C-107/95 P *Expert Accountants* [1996] ECR I-957 paras 14–21.
[26] Opinion of AG Van Gerven, Case C-18/88 *RTT* [1991] ECR I-5941 para 8.
[27] Case 66/86 *Ahmed Saeed Flugreisen and Silver Line Reisebüro GmbH v Zentrale zur Bekämpfung Unlauteren Wettbewerbs eV (Ahmed Saeed)* [1989] ECR 852 para 53.
[28] Case C-163/99 *Portuguese Airports* [2001] ECR I-2613 para 20; Case T-266/97 *VTM* [1999] ECR II-2329 para 75; Case T-111/96 *ITT Promedia* [1998] ECR II-2937 para 97; Case T-575/93 *Koelman* [1996] ECR II-1 paras 70–73, confirmed by Case C-59/96 P *Koelman (appeal)* [1997] ECR I-4809 paras 57–58; Case T-32/93 *Ladbroke I* [1994] ECR II-1031 paras 37–38; Case T-548/93 *Ladbroke II* [1995] ECR II-2584 para 45; Case T-84/94 *Expert Accountants* [1995] ECR II-101 para 31 upheld by the ECJ on appeal, Case C-107/95 P *Expert Accountants (appeal)* [1997] ECR I-965 para 27.

2002 judgement of the CFI in the *max.mobil* case put into jeopardy this well-established line of authority.[29] In this judgment, the CFI seemed to narrow the margin of discretion of the Commission by making it clear that the Commission was obliged to examine complaints based on Article 86 EC in a diligent and objective way as a consequence of the general principle of good administration. This implied on the one hand that, after an analysis of the complaint, the Commission should at least give grounds explaining why it considered that there is (or there is not) an infringement and whether it considered it necessary to intervene. On the other hand, judicial review on these two points (and in particular on the opportunity to intervene) would in any case be minimal and limited to manifest errors.[30] However on appeal,[31] the ECJ overruled the CFI on the grounds that, contrary to the position in cases involving Articles 81 and 82 EC, the Commission's refusal to act under Article 86 is not susceptible of judicial review under Article 230 EC, especially because that particular act could not be regarded as producing legal effects. This confirms that the Commission enjoys a wide margin of discretion when deciding whether to initiate proceedings against a Member State for breach of Article 86(1) of the Treaty. As will be explained later, this discretion greatly limits the possibilities of the individuals who are complaining of such infringements successfully appealing against the Commission's decision.

Optional nature of the procedure under Article 86(3)

19.19 It must be determined whether the Commission can choose between various infringement procedures when it decides in a particular case to act against an infringement of Article 86(1). Thus, while it is clear that the Commission *can* always use the special procedure under Article 86(3) in order to end infringements of Article 86(1), it is less clear whether the Commission *must* use the special procedure or not. In other words, if the Commission decides to intervene to end an infringement of Article 86(1), is it obliged to use the special procedure under Article 86(3) or may it opt for the general procedure under Article 226? Although this question has not been expressly dealt with by the ECJ, it is submitted that the Commission has the discretionary power to opt for either of the procedures.[32] This is also suggested in the text of Article 86(3),

---

[29] Case T-54/99 *max.mobil* [2002] ECR II-313
[30] Case T-54/99 *max.mobil* [2002] ECR II-313 paras 56–59.
[31] Case C-141/02 P *max.mobil (appeal)* [2005] (not yet reported) paras 68–73.
[32] Case T-266/97 *VTM* [1999] ECR II-2329 para 75. This question has hardly been dealt with by academics. In favour of the optional nature of Art 86(3) was Papaconstantinou (n 30 above) 113; J Flynn and E Turnbull 'Joined Cases C-48/90 and C-66/90, (the 'Dutch Couriers' case)' [1993] 30 CML Rev 402 and C Hocepied, 'Les directives Article 90, paragraphe 3. Une espèce juridique en voie de disparition?' [1994] RAE ii 55. However, this author highlights the advantages of Art 86(3) and considers that the Commission should opt, whenever possible, for this procedure.

which provides for the adoption of decisions only 'where necessary'. A clear parallel can be drawn with the situation affecting State aids, where the Court has held that bringing proceedings under Article 88 does not prevent proceedings being brought under Article 226.[33] In conclusion, the possibility of using the Article 226 procedure always remains open, although the nature of Article 86(3) would normally make it the more probable choice.

Commencing proceedings ex officio

The Commission may at any time commence proceedings of its own motion under Article 86(3).[34] It is sufficient for the Commission to have obtained information regarding a possible infringement of 86(1) by a Member State and for it to consider that it is necessary to act. The information may have been obtained from any source; from the press, from questionnaires carried out by civil servants, from sector studies, from parliamentary questions, and so on. **19.20**

2. The processing of complaints and 'own initiative' proceedings

Commencing proceedings on the basis of a complaint

In many cases the Commission acts following complaints submitted by individuals or undertakings. These complaints constitute a very important source of information for the Commission enabling it, for example, to go beyond the legal texts and to understand how the law is applied in practice by national authorities. The complaints are examined during the processing stage, following which the Commission decides whether or not to commence infringement proceedings by sending the letter of formal notice to the Member State. The processing stage of complaints (or where files are opened on the Commission's own initiative) should not be confused with the infringement procedure. **19.21**

The processing of complaints

There are no particular formalities for the submission of a complaint for the breach of Article 86(1). It is sufficient to send a letter which clearly identifies who the complainant is, fully describes the facts or measures of a Member State which are alleged to have breached Article 86(1), and requests the Commission to act. It is advisable, although not essential, to attach to the complaint the legal grounds for stating that a breach of Article 86(1) has been committed. There is no particular application form which must be used, although the Commission has published in the Official Journal a model form that may be **19.22**

---

[33] M Waelbroeck and D Waelbroeck, 'Article 169' in Various, *Commentaire Megret, Le Droit de la CEE* 2nd edn Vol 10, 1993, 61.

[34] e.g. Cases C-157/94 to C-160/94 *Gas and Electricity Monopolies* [1997] ECR I-5699, 5789, 5815, and 5851.

used for submitting complaints.[35] The complaint has to be submitted before the Commission. It may be sent to the postal address of the Commission,[36] to its General Secretary, to the Directorate-General which is in principal competent, or to the offices of the Commission in the Member States. The complaints are registered at a central registry which is part of the General Secretary of the Commission. There they are attributed to the competent Directorate-General or Directorates-General for processing. Normally the complaints based on Article 86 are processed by the Directorate-General of Competition (DG COMP). However, very often the complaints are simultaneously directed against the behaviour of undertakings (Articles 81 and 82), against State aids (Articles 87 and 88), and/or against other State measures (Article 86). For that reason, many of these complaints are only initially registered at the special registries for State aids and for the behaviour of undertakings, although subsequently those aspects concerning Article 86 are separated from other aspects of the complaint and registered at the central registry.

19.23 The Commission notifies the complainant by letter of the registration of his complaint who is further informed that a copy of his complaint will be sent to the Member State in order that it may submit its observations. If the complainant does not wish the Member State to be aware that he has brought the complaint he has to clearly state this in the actual complaint. In such cases the Commission may, if it considers it appropriate, use the information thus obtained to act of its own motion. The complaint is examined by the Commission, which proceeds if necessary to request additional reports from the complainant. Normally, a copy of the complaint is transferred to the Member State in question to allow it to submit its observations. The Commission may also request additional information from the Member State in order to clarify the situation. In such a case, Article 10 obliges the Member State to cooperate with the Commission, by providing it with the information that it has in its possession. If the Member State does not cooperate this may give rise to a breach of Article 10. This may result in proceedings under Article 226, such proceedings being separate from the main proceedings. The Commission then decides whether to commence infringement proceedings against the Member State, having analysed the facts and the law. If it decides to proceed it sends the Member State a letter of formal notice. This decision is discretionary. Even in the case of a formal complaint, the complainant cannot force the Commission to commence proceedings.[37] The Commission informs each complainant,

---

[35] The official form can be found at [1989] OJ C26/07.
[36] European Commission, Rue de la Loi, 200, B-1049 Brussels.
[37] This, at least, is the position adopted by the CFI in Case T-32/93 *Ladbroke I* [1994] ECR II-1031 paras 37 and 38, and Case T-548/93 *Ladbroke II* [1995] ECR II-2584 para 45, as well as in Case T-84/94 *German Accountants* [1995] ECR II-101 para 31. Similarly, although less

normally within one year of receiving the complaint, of the steps taken against the Member State and the possible decision to commence proceedings.

Processing 'own initiative' cases

The Commission may also investigate of its own initiative facts which seem to it **19.24** capable of constituting an infringement of the Treaty. The processing of these claims is similar to that for complaints. At the end of the processing stage the Commission has to decide whether to proceed by beginning infringement proceedings or whether the case should be closed.

Dismissal of complaints or inactivity of the Commission

The Commission may, in principle, dismiss a complaint based on Article 86 **19.25** for legal or tactical reasons. If the complaint is dismissed for legal reasons, the Commission informs the complainant by letter why it considers that there has not been a breach of Community law. If the complaint is dismissed because this is considered opportune, the Commission limits itself to informing the complainant that the complaint does not have sufficient interest to justify the Commission's intervention and recommends that the complainant seek redress in a national court. The CFI considered in *max.mobil* that the Commission may react to a complaint based on Article 86 EC by adopting a decision refusing to take action and that an action for annulment by the complainant against such a decision may be admissible. On appeal, however, the ECJ rejected this approach in its 2005 judgment. According to this judgment, such letters cannot be regarded as producing legal effects and cannot be subject of an action for annulment.[38] Of course, persons and undertakings wishing to complaint about an alleged infringement of Article 86(1) EC still have the right to invoke the direct effect of this provision before national courts. This right is totally independent from the possibility of filing a complaint with the Commission and—legally speaking—it is not affected by the outcome of such complaint. The possibilities for complainants reacting to an implicit or explicit refusal by the Commission are much more limited. Traditionally it was considered that complainants did not have *locus standi* to either bring an Article 230 annulment action against the Commission's refusal to initiate proceedings[39] or bring an Article 232 action against the Commission's failure to act following a complaint

---

emphatically, the ECJ, in Case C-107/95 P *German Accountants (appeal)* [1997] ECR I-965 para 27, did not completely exclude the possibility that, in exceptional circumstances, the Commission may be obliged to act under Art 86(3). See paras 19.25 to 19.30 for a detailed discussion of this point.

[38] Case C-141/02 P *max.mobil (appeal)*, [2005] (not yet reported) para 70.

[39] Case T-84/94 *Expert Accountants* [1995] ECR II-101 para 31, confirmed by Case C-107/95 P *Expert Accountants (appeal)* [1996] ECR I-957 para 27.

based on Article 86.[40] According to the ECJ, such actions could only be introduced in 'exceptional situations'.[41]

19.26 In *max.mobil* the CFI tried to interpret these 'exceptional situations' very widely, declaring that a complainant could attack the Commission's refusal to act or its lack of action if the complaint refers not to measures in general but to specific measures favouring a competitor.[42] This distinction was, however, hardly relevant to cases under Article 86(1) EC. Indeed, one of the necessary conditions for this provision to apply is precisely that the measure at stake is not general but specific to public or privileged undertakings and therefore the 'specificity' criteria will—by definition—be automatically fulfilled in all Article 86(1) EC cases. On appeal in the *max.mobil* case,[43] the ECJ reversed the CFI ruling on the basis that the Commission's refusal to act under Article 86 cannot be the subject of judicial review proceedings under Article 230 EC. This confirms that the Commission enjoys a wide margin of discretion when deciding whether to initiate proceedings against a Member State for breach of Article 86(1) of the Treaty. Since the Commission is not obliged to initiate infringement proceedings, the ECJ has held that the complainant has no grounds for an action of annulment under Article 230 against a decision to dismiss the complaint.[44] In the same way, in the event that the Commission does not make a decision regarding the complaint, the complainant has no grounds for bringing proceedings for failure to act under Article 232 of the Treaty.[45]

19.27 The fact that the complainant cannot bring actions against the Commission's decision not to act or against its inactivity under Article 86(3) derives from the analogical application of the doctrine applicable to the procedure under Article 226. In fact, this analogy seems to dominate the conception that the

---

[40] Case T-32/93 *Ladbroke I* [1994] ECR II-1015 paras 34–36.

[41] Case C-141/02P *max.mobil (appeal)* [2002] OJ C169/15. See also Opinion of AG Poiares Maduro of 21 October 2004.

[42] Case T-17/96 TF 1 [1999] ECR II-1757 paras 52–57; Case T-54/99 *max.mobil* [2002] ECR II-313 paras 64–72.

[43] Case C-141/02 P *max.mobil (appeal)* [2005] (not yet reported) paras 68–73.

[44] See Case C-141/02 P *max.mobil (appeal)* [2005] (not yet reported) paras 68–73; Case T-84/94 *German Accountants* [1995] ECR II-0101 para 31 and the more qualified judgment of the ECJ in Case C-107/95 P *German Accountants (appeal)* [1997] ECR I-965 para 27. Against this position, see the Opinion of AG La Pergola in the same case paras 14–22. See para 462 for a detailed discussion of this point. For a detailed study of annulment proceedings see G Isaac, *Droit communautaire général* (4th edn, 1994) 245–57; M Waelbroeck and D Waelbroeck, 'Article 173' in Various, *Commentaire Megret, Le Droit de la CEE* (2nd edn Vol 10, 1993) 97–170.

[45] Case T-32/93 *Ladbroke I* [1994] ECR II-1030 paras 34–46. The exceptional circumstances that according to the ECJ in *German Accountants (appeal)* would allow annulment proceedings to be brought should, logically, open the door to possible proceedings for failure to act. For a detailed study of proceedings for failure to act see G Isaac, *Droit communautaire général* (4th edn, 1994) 257–59; M Waelbroeck and D Waelbroeck, 'La Cour de Justice' in Various, *Commentaire Megret, Le Droit de la CEE* (2nd edn Vol 10, 1993) 177–92.

Commission, the CFI, and the ECJ have of the procedure under Article 86(3). However, other more flexible possibilities might have been conceived of, such as the application by analogy of the remedies applicable in the field of State aids[46] or under Regulation 1/2003. The question was raised for the first time in 1989 in *Ladbroke*. In this case the undertaking Ladbroke submitted a complaint before the Commission, based, *inter alia*, on former Article 90 (now Article 86), against the organization of the betting system for horse racing in France. In 1992, Ladbroke demanded that the Commission adopt a final and definite decision concerning the complaint. The mandatory time limit of two months had elapsed without the Commission having taken any decision, therefore Ladbroke started proceedings for the Commission's failure to act in the Court of First Instance. Ladbroke argued that an analogy should be drawn between Article 86(3) and the rights that complainants are recognized in the antitrust field.[47] The Commission did not accept this analogy and submitted that the closest analogy to Article 86(3) was Article 226, and that therefore the complainants did not have any such rights. Accordingly, the Commission requested that the proceedings be declared inadmissible. In *Ladbroke I* the Court of First Instance fully supported the Commission's position and confirmed the wide discretionary margin that the Commission enjoys. It rejected the analogy with antitrust procedures, held that Ladbroke was not a party who was directly and individually interested and affected, and declared that the proceedings were inadmissible.[48]

This approach, whereby the rights of the complainant are excluded under Article 86(3), was followed to the letter by the Court of First Instance in *German Accountants*.[49] In this case, proceedings were brought by a German accountancy association against the Commission, who had rejected a complaint submitted by the German association. The complaint, based in particular on Article 86, had required the Commission to act against Germany because of legislation that reserved the exercise of tax consultancy services to certain professions, which did not include the complainant association. The President of the Court of First Instance declared the proceedings for annulment to be inadmissible. The complainant association appealed to the ECJ. In his Opinion, Advocate General La Pergola rejected the analogy between the procedures under Articles 86(3) and 226. Instead, the Advocate General advocated, on the basis of the case law regarding State aids, the right of individuals to appeal against Commission

19.28

---

[46] Opinion of AG Poiares Maduro, Case C-141/02P *max.mobil (appeal)* [2005] (not yet reported).
[47] Case T-32/93 *Ladbroke I* [1994] ECR II-1222 para 7.
[48] Case T-32/93 *Ladbroke I* [1994] ECR II-1030 paras 34–46.
[49] Case T-84/94 *German Accountants* [1995] ECR II-101 paras 27–32.

decisions for failure to act on the basis of Article 86(3).[50] According to the Advocate General, however wide the Commission's discretion this does not exclude the possibility of jurisdictional control.[51] On this basis, the Advocate General recommended that the ECJ quash the judgment of the Court of First Instance.

19.29 In *German Accountants* the ECJ did not follow this recommendation and upheld the judgment of the Court of First Instance. However, it distanced itself from the restrictive conception of third party rights that the Court of First Instance had favoured, by making the following exception:[52]

> The possibility cannot be ruled out that exceptional situations might exist where an individual or, possibly, an association constituted for the defence of the collect- ive interests of a class of individuals has standing to bring proceedings against a refusal by the Commission to adopt a decision pursuant to its supervisory functions under Article 90(1) and (3) [now Article 86].

After having left open this possibility for when some as yet undefined 'exceptional situations' arise, the ECJ returned to the well-known argument of the 'wide discretion'[53] of the Commission and it added another more original argument:[54]

> Moreover, an individual may not, by means of an action against the Commission's refusal to take a decision against a Member State under Article 90(1) and (3) [now Article 86], indirectly compel that Member State to adopt legislation of general application.

The clear impression which this judgment gives is that the ECJ is against comparing complainants under Article 86(3) with complainants in questions of State aids. The reason for this is probably because of the different consequences that arise from the different procedures for the Member State involved. While, with respect to aid, the most that the Member State normally risks is having to require that the aid granted be refunded, as regards Article 86 the result would, in many cases, entail substantial legislative change in areas which are particularly politically sensitive. Recognizing the right of individuals to appeal against the inactivity of the Commission is the same as obliging it to act almost automatic- ally. Such an automatic obligation is to a certain extent logical in cases of specific

---

[50] Opinion of Advocate General La Pergola in Case C-107/95 P *German Accountants (appeal)* [1997] ECR I-953 paras 14–22.

[51] Opinion of Advocate General La Pergola in Case C-107/95 P *German Accountants (appeal)* [1997] ECR I-954 para 18.

[52] Case C-107/95 P *German Accountants (appeal)* [1997] ECR I-964 para 25.

[53] Case C-107/95 P *German Accountants (appeal)* [1997] ECR I-965 para 27.

[54] Case C-107/95 P *German Accountants (appeal)* [1997] ECR I-965 para 28.

intervention, such as aid.[55] However, it is more risky with respect to such delicate matters as exclusive rights, where sensitive issues of a legal, political, and economic nature come into play.

In *max.mobil*, the CFI tried to extend the possibilities of complainants to appeal **19.30** against a refusal by the Commission to act under Article 86.[56] The judgment seemed to reduce the Commission's margin of discretion by making it clear that the Commission was obliged to examine complaints based on Article 86 EC in a diligent and objective way. This implied on the one hand that the Commission should at least give its reasons for considering that there is (or there is not) an infringement and whether it is considered necessary to intervene. On the other hand judicial review regarding these two issues (particularly with respect to the need to intervene) would in any case be minimal and limited to manifest errors.[57] On appeal in *max.mobil*,[58] the ECJ reversed the CFI judgment on the basis that the Commission's refusal to act under Article 86 is not susceptible to judicial review under Article 230 EC. This judgment has confirmed the traditional interpretation that the Commission enjoys a wide margin of discretion when deciding whether to initiate proceedings against a Member State for breach of Article 86(1) of the Treaty. Therefore, the current position is that individuals cannot in principle appeal against the Commission's refusal to take action under Article 86(3) as regards State measures. It remains to be seen whether the case law evolves further in the future.

3. Infringement proceedings

Commencement of infringement proceedings

Normally infringement proceedings are commenced by the Commission send- **19.31** ing to the Member State a letter of formal notice. In certain cases, however, the letter could be preceded by the adoption of interim measures.

Interim measures

It is submitted that by analogy with the approach of the ECJ in the field of **19.32** antitrust cases[59] the Commission may, when necessary, order specific measures which enable it to fulfil effectively the task that it is entrusted with under Article

---

[55] Certain kinds of aid schemes, like fiscal aid, may however be as politically sensitive as exclusive rights.
[56] Case T-54/99 *max.mobil* [2002] ECR II-313.
[57] Case T-54/99 *max.mobil* [2002] ECR II-313 paras 56–59.
[58] Case C-141/02 P *max.mobil (appeal)* [2005] (not yet reported) paras 68–73.
[59] Case 792/79 R *Camera Care Ltd v EC Commission* [1980] ECR 119.

86(3).[60] Thus, while Article 86(3) does not expressly say anything about interim measures, by taking this approach it is possible for the Commission to adopt such measures under this provision. In any event, interim measures can only be adopted where an emergency situation exists and where if they were not adopted this would seriously and irreparably prejudice the interested party or the general interest. The Commission may only order provisional measures after having heard the observations of the Member State[61] and the objective of the measures thus adopted can only be to maintain the existing situation until the main proceedings are resolved.

The letter of formal notice

19.33   Article 86(3) is silent with respect to the letter of notice. However, in *PTT* the ECJ held that the rights of defence of a Member State require the Commission to inform it in an exact and complete manner, before adopting the decision, of the charges against it and of the legal reasoning upon which the charges are based. This is necessary in order to give the Member State the opportunity to submit its observations.[62] This information is normally given in the form of a letter of formal notice sent by the Commission to the government of the Member State in question. In *PTT* the Court examined two actions for annulment under Article 230 brought by the Dutch government and the public undertaking PTT Nederland NV against a decision adopted in 1989 by the Commission under Article 86(3) concerning courier mail services in the Netherlands.[63] In its decision, the Commission considered that the grant of exclusive rights by the State to the public undertaking PTT Nederland NV for the activities of courier mail services constituted a breach of the Treaty. The ECJ found that there was a case to answer in both actions: the action brought by the government of the Netherlands in its capacity as addressee of the decision and the action brought by the beneficiary undertaking, as a directly interested party in the proceedings.

19.34   The ECJ annulled the decision of the Commission, holding that neither the Member State's right to a fair defence nor the beneficiary undertaking's right to be heard had been respected during the proceedings. The right to a fair defence of the Member State includes in particular the right to 'receive an exact and complete statement of the objections which the Commission intends to raise against it.'[64] This implies that the letter of formal notice must contain the

---

[60] This is implied in the Opinion of AG Reischl in Joined Cases C-188–190/80 *Transparency Directive* [1982] ECR I-2587.
[61] Joined Cases C-48/90 and C-66/90 *PTT* [1992] ECR I-639 para 44.
[62] Joined Cases C-48/90 and C-66/90 *PTT* [1992] ECR I-639 para 45.
[63] Commission Decision (EEC) 90/16 *Courier Postal Services—The Netherlands* [1990] OJ L10/50.
[64] Joined Cases C-48/90 and C-66/90 *PTT* [1992] ECR I-639 para 45.

following information: a statement of the State measure that is the object of the proceedings, the Treaty provisions which are considered to be breached by the Member State, and the reasons why the Commission considers that an infringement has occurred. The letter of formal notice sets a time-limit within which the Member State must inform the Commission of the measures adopted in order to correct the position or notify the Commission of the reasons why the Member State disagrees with the Commission's position. The letter concludes by stating that the Commission may adopt a decision under Article 86(3) of the Treaty.[65] The object of the proceedings is set out in the letter of formal notice in such a way that any subsequent decision cannot be based on legal grounds that have not been stated in the letter. In addition, the Commission cannot require measures that are not referred to in the letter to be modified. If the Commission considers that it is necessary to modify the object of the proceedings, it must offer the Member State an opportunity to submit its own observations, normally by sending an additional letter of formal notice. In general, the Commission does not publicise the fact that it has sent a letter of formal notice to a Member State: only the Member State is notified. Nevertheless, in certain cases the Commission may decide to give some publicity to its actions.

The rights of the Member State, the beneficiary undertaking, and the complainant

In *PTT* the ECJ held that although the procedure under Article 86(3) is only **19.35** directed against the Member State, which is the only party that enjoys the right to a fair defence,[66] the undertaking that benefits from the State measure in question has a right to be heard under the infringement procedure.[67] This means that there is a right to be informed of the Commission's position and a right to make comments to the Commission. However, the undertaking does not have a right to know the comments made by the Member State nor a right to obtain a copy of the complaint.[68] As has already been explained, the case law has given the complainant limited rights, since he is considered as a third party without any direct and individual rights, and therefore he is not legally able to bring proceedings for failure to act or for annulment.[69] Accordingly, the complainant has no right to participate in the proceedings, although the Commission may, if it considers it appropriate, notify the complainant of the nature of

---

[65] Normally in the letter of formal notice the Commission states whether it intends to proceed under Art 86(3) or Art 226. However, it is submitted that there is nothing to prevent the letter leaving both options open.

[66] Joined Cases C-48/90 and C-66/90 *PTT* [1992] ECR I-640 para 49. See also Case T-226/97 *VTM* [1999] ECR II-2329 paras 32–37.

[67] Joined Cases C-48/90 and C-66/90 *PTT* [1992] ECR I-640 para 49.

[68] Case T-226/97 *VTM* [1999] ECR II-2329 para 37.

[69] Case C-141/02 P *max.mobil (appeal)* [2005] (not yet reported) para 70; Case T-32/93 *Ladbroke I* [1994] ECR II-1032 paras 40–42.

the response to the letter of formal notice and ask for the complainant's opinion as well as any additional information. However this level of participation does not make the complainant a party directly and individually concerned for the purpose of Articles 230 and 232.[70] In the event that the complainant or any other third party provides his opinion the Commission would have to notify the Member State concerned before a decision is adopted.[71]

The termination of proceedings without a final decision being given

19.36 Decisions which have been formally adopted by the Commission on the basis of Article 86(3) only constitute the tip of the iceberg.[72] In numerous cases, infringement proceedings end without a formal decision being adopted, either because the Member State accepts the Commission's requirements or because the Commission modifies its position in light of the Member State's observations. If the case is sufficiently important the settlement reached is given a degree of publicity.[73] However, the Commission is not bound under Article 86 EC to adopt a formal decision stating that this provision has not been infringed. So, contrary to what happens with regard to State Aid cases, there are normally no 'positive' Article 86 decisions.

4. The formal decision and its effects

Formal decisions under Article 86(3)

19.37 If the matter is not settled following the letter of formal notice, the Commission may proceed to adopt a formal decision under Article 86(3). The Commission retains a wide margin of discretion to decide whether or not to adopt such a decision, and to date it has adopted sixteen decisions of this kind.[74] Decisions adopted by the Commission under Article 86(3) are normal 'decisions', as provided by Article 249 of the Treaty.[75] By virtue of Article 253, decisions must 'state the reasons on which they are based'. In the recitals the legal reasoning is described which led the Commission to the conclusion that the State measure in question breached Article 86(1) in conjunction with one or more Articles of the

---

[70] Case C-141/02 P *max.mobil (appeal)* [2005] (not yet reported) paras 70–73; Case T-32/93 *Ladbroke I* [1994] ECR II-1033 para 43.

[71] The fact that the Commission did not inform the Member State of the observations submitted by the courier undertakings was one of the reasons which led the Court to annul the decision in *PTT* (Joined Cases C-48/90 and C-66/90 *PTT* [1992] ECR I-639 para 46).

[72] C Hocepied, 'Les directives articles 90, paragraphe 3. Une espèce juridique en voie de disparition?' [1994] RAE ii 52.

[73] Through press releases, the Reports on Competition Policy, and the Commission's periodic publications.

[74] See above, para 19.12.

[75] For an analysis of the concept of 'decision' in the EC Treaty see R Greaves, 'The Nature and Binding Effect of Decisions under Article 189 EC' [1996] ELR 3–16.

Treaty. The decision declares that the State measure is incompatible with the provisions referred to and states the measures that the Member State must adopt in order to comply with its obligations under Community law.[76] In addition, the Member State is given a specific time limit within which it must notify the Commission that it has adopted the necessary measures. Thus, decisions adopted under Article 86(3) enable the Commission not only to declare that the Member State has committed a breach but also to specify the particular measures that it must adopt to remedy the situation. This means that although the breach may, in principle, be eliminated in different ways, the Commission can require the Member State to proceed in the way that the Commission prefers.[77] According to Article 191(3) of the Treaty, the decision is notified to the Member State in question and takes effect from the date of its notification. Normally, decisions adopted under Article 86(3) are subsequently published in the Official Journal of the Community.

The obligatory nature of Article 86(3) decisions

Decisions adopted under Article 86(3) are normal decisions, as provided for in **19.38** Article 249 of the EC Treaty, and therefore are obligatory for the Member State to whom they are addressed.[78] Despite the wording of Article 86(3), there were some authors who initially doubted that Article 86(3) 'decisions' were truly binding decisions within the meaning of Article 249, and who maintained that they were in fact more similar to recommendations.[79] Such authors viewed Article 86(3) as being a derogation from the normal procedure under Article 226. According to them, the Commission cannot itself declare the existence of a breach by a Member State, nor is the Member State obliged to comply with a decision that is addressed to it by the Commission under Article 86(3). Such effects may only be obtained from a judgment of the ECJ in which the Court declares, in proceedings brought under Article 226, that the Member State had breached the Treaty. The fact that Article 86(3), unlike Article 88(2), does not expressly exclude Article 226 supports this argument.

---

[76] Joined Cases C-48/90 and C-66/90 *PTT* [1992] ECR I-635 para 28; Case C-107/95 P *German Accountants (appeal)* [1997] ECR I-964 para 23.

[77] Joined Cases C-48/90 and C-66/90 *PTT* [1992] ECR I-635 para 28; Case C-107/95 P *German Accountants (appeal)* [1997] ECR I-964.

[78] Case C-136/99 *Portuguese Airports* [2001] ECR I-2613 paras 19–20; Case C-226/87 *EC Commission v Greece (Greek Insurance)* [1988] ECR I-3623 para 12.

[79] A Pappalardo, 'Régime de l'article 90 du Traité CEE: les aspects juridiques' in Various, *L'entreprise publique et la concurrence. Les articles 90 et 37 du Traité CEE et leurs relations avec la concurrence* (Semaine de Bruges, 1968, De Temple, Bruges, 1969) 81; G Marenco, 'Public Sector and Community Law' [1983] 20 CML Rev 522–23.

19.39 This interpretation was defended by the Greek government in *Greek Insurance*,[80] a case that perfectly illustrates this issue. In 1985 the Commission adopted a decision based on Article 86(3) in which Greece was stated to have breached its obligations under Article 86(1) in conjunction with Articles 43 (former Article 52), 53 (now derogated), 10 (former Article 5), and 3 of the Treaty, by adopting legislation which obliged State banks to recommend to their clients that they obtain insurance from State insurers.[81] The Commission decision ordering Greece to stop the breach was ignored by the Greek authorities, which neither complied with the decision nor appealed against it within the given time-limits. The Commission therefore brought infringement proceedings under Article 226 against Greece, based not on the breach of Article 86(1) together with Articles [52], [53], [5], and 3 of the Treaty but on Greece's failure to respect the Commission's decision. These proceedings led to the judgment of the ECJ in *Greek Insurance*. In this judgment, the Court confirmed that the Greek republic was obliged to execute the decision of the Commission unless the ECJ suspended or annulled it.[82] Given that the Greek republic had not appealed within the time limit of two months, nor had it applied for the suspension of the measure,[83] the decision had automatically become final. This meant that once the time limit had elapsed, the Greek government could no longer bring proceedings before the ECJ challenging the legality of the decision: it was obliged to comply with it.[84] The exception of illegality may only be adduced when the decision is so seriously defective that it could be classified as non-existent.[85] The *Greek Insurance* and *Portuguese Airports* judgments confirmed that decisions under Articles 86(3) bind the Member States to whom they are addressed.[86] The obligatory nature also affects the judicial organs of the Member State.[87] To the extent that the decision imposes clear and unconditional obligations upon the Member State, the decision will probably have direct effect and may be invoked by individuals before the national courts once the deadline has expired without the measures being implemented.[88] For example, an undertaking wishes

---

[80] Case 226/87 *Greek Insurance* [1988] ECR 3611–3625.

[81] Commission Decision (CEE) 85/276 concerning the insurance in Greece of public property and loans granted by Greek State-owned banks [1985] OJ L152/25.

[82] Case 226/87 *Greek Insurance* [1988] ECR 3623 para 12.

[83] Case T-23/01 R *Poste Italiane* [2001] ECR II-1479.

[84] Case 226/87 *Greek Insurance* [1988] ECR 3623–3624 paras 13–14.

[85] Case 226/87 *Greek Insurance* [1988] ECR 3624 para 16.

[86] Case C-163/99 *Portuguese Airports* [2001] ECR I-2613 paras 19–20.

[87] R Greaves, 'The Nature and Binding Effect of Decisions under Article 189 EC' [1996] ELR xxi 13.

[88] LM Pais Antunes, 'L'article 90 du Traité CEE—Obligations des Etats Membres et pouvoirs de la Commission' [1991] RTDE ii 205–6; C Hocepied, 'Les directives Article 90, paragraphe 3. Une espèce juridique en voie de disparition?' [1994] RAE ii 55. The direct effect of decisions in general was recognized by the Court in Case 9/70 *Franz Grad v Finanzamt Traunstein (Grad)* [1970] ECR 838 para 5; Case 249/85 *Albako Margarinefabrik Maria von der Linde GmbH &*

to operate an activity which is subject to an exclusive right may base its case on a decision declaring an exclusive right to be contrary to the Treaty. As will be explained later, the decision could also serve as the basis for a claim for damages against the Member State under the rule in *Francovitch*.[89]

Proceedings for annulment against a formal decision under Article 86(3)

The Member State to whom the decision is addressed has two months from the date of notification of the decision to bring proceedings for annulment before the ECJ under Article 230 of the Treaty.[90] Article 242 provides that the proceedings do not have, in principle, suspensory effect, but the Member State may request the Court to adopt an interim suspension.[91] The suspension would only be granted if the usual conditions for interim measures (prima facie good case, urgency and balance of public and private interest) are fulfilled. As regards the beneficiary undertaking of the State measure challenged, although the decision is not addressed to it, it is directly and individually affected by the decision. Therefore it has the right to bring an action for annulment under Article 230 of the Treaty.[92] In addition, other third parties which can show a direct and individual interest in the decision might be able to bring proceedings.[93] If after the time-limit of two months has expired proceedings for annulment have not been brought, or having been brought the proceedings have been dismissed by the ECJ, the decision becomes final and its legality cannot be further questioned, unless it is so seriously defective that it should be declared inexistent.[94]

19.40

Proceedings in the event of non-compliance with the decision by the Member State

Once the time limit stated in the decision has elapsed, and assuming that the Court has not suspended its execution under Article 242, if the decision has not

19.41

Co. KG v Bundesanstalt für landwirtschaftliche Marktordnung—'Berlin butter' (Albako) [1987] ECR 2345 para 17. See also G Isaac, *Droit communautaire général* (4th edn, 1994) 129, 172–73; R Greaves, 'The Nature and Binding Effect of Decisions under Article 189 EC' [1996] ELR xxi 13–14.

[89] Joined Cases C-6/90 and C-9/90 *Francovich* [1991] ECR I-5357 paras 36–37.

[90] An action of this type was what gave rise to the *RTT* judgment (Case C-18/88 *Régie des télégraphes et des téléphones v GB-Inno-BM SA (RTT)* [1991] ECR I-5941). For a detailed study of actions for annulment see G Isaac, *Droit communautaire général* (4th edn, 1994) 245–57; M Waelbroeck and D Waelbroeck, 'Article 173' in Various, *Commentaire Megret, Le Droit de la CEE* (2nd edn Vol 10, 1993, 97–170).

[91] See, e.g. Case T-53/01 R *Poste Italiane* [2001] ECR II-1479.

[92] This is clear from Joined Cases C-48 and 66/90 *PTT* [1992] ECR I-640 para 50 and from the Opinion of AG van Gerven in the same case (ECR I-593 para 5). See also Case C-107/95 P *German Accountants (appeal)* [1997] ECR I-947 para 24 '[. . .] individuals may, in some circumstances, be entitled to bring an action for annulment [. . .]'.

[93] The language of the Court appears deliberately loose in Case C-107/95 P *German Accountants (appeal)* [1997] ECR I-947 para 24.

[94] Case C-226/87 *Greek Insurance* [1988] ECR I-3623 paras 12–16.

been enforced by the Member State to whom it is addressed the Commission may bring proceedings under Article 226 asking the Court to make a declaration that the Member State has failed to comply with the decision.[95] Whereas under Article 88(2) paragraph 2 concerning State aid cases, the Commission can bring an action directly to the ECJ without having to go through the pre-contentious stage as laid down in Article 226, Article 86(3) does not allow this 'fast-track' procedure. The Commission must send a letter of formal notice and subsequently a reasoned opinion to the Member State before it can commence proceedings under Article 226. It is important to emphasize that if proceedings are brought under Article 226 this does not mean a re-examination of the merits of the case. The ECJ will limit itself to examining whether the State has complied with the decision, without questioning its legality, unless it contains defects which are so serious that the decision is held to be non-existent.[96] If a Member State persists in refusing to comply with the decision after having been found by the ECJ to have failed to fulfil its obligations, Article 228(2) of the Treaty allows the Commission to initiate proceedings which can result in the ECJ imposing fines upon the Member State in question.

Liability of Member States for failure to fulfil their Community obligations

19.42   Apart from the actions of the Commission and the Court, following *Francovich* individuals and undertakings that have suffered loss as a result of a Member State's failure to fulfil its obligations under Article 86 can sue the Member State in question for damages.[97]

---

[95] Case C-226/87 *Greek Insurance* [1988] ECR I-3623 paras 11–17; Joined Cases C-48/90 and C-66/90 *PTT* [1992] ECR I-637 para 36. The main features of Art 226 were examined in the previous section.

[96] Case C-226/87 *Greek Insurance* [1988] ECR I-3623 paras 13–16.

[97] Joined Cases C-6/90 and C-9/90 *Andrea Francovich and Danila Bonifaci and others v Italy (Francovich)* [1991] ECR I-5337 paras 36–37.

20

DIRECTIVES UNDER ARTICLE 86(3) EC

A. Functions of Directive under Article 86(3) EC

In order to fulfil the task of Community guardian that Article 86(3) of the **20.01**
Treaty entrusts to the Commission, this institution has the power to address,
'where necessary', not only decisions but also directives to Member States. This
power to adopt directives which Article 86(3) grants to the Commission gives
rise to sensitive problems of a legal and particularly of a political nature. A
full understanding of paragraphs 1 and 2 of Article 86 requires taking into
consideration the institutional dimension implicit in Article 86(3). Thus, the
interpretation given to the substantive rules contained in Article 86(1) and (2)
becomes more important given the Commission's power to adopt directives
under paragraph 3. In the same way, the significance, in terms of the Community institutional structure, of the rule-making power enjoyed by the Commission under Article 86(3) is largely due to the politically sensitive nature of
the rules applied.

The relationship between the substantive and procedural rules in the field of **20.02**
exclusive rights is particularly close. This particular closeness arises from certain
fundamental differences in the nature of the Community legal system as compared with national legal systems. Thus, unlike most national constitutional
rules regarding State intervention in the economy, which establish a programme
of general goals to be attained (but which are nevertheless legally unenforceable), the Treaty rules directly impose legal obligations on Member States that
they are obliged to respect and that individuals can invoke before the courts.[1]
The primary function of Article 86(1) and (2) of the Treaty is not therefore to

---

[1] A Alonso Ureba, 'El marco constitucional económico español y la adhesión a las Comuni-
dades europeas' in E Garcia de Enterria, JD Gonzalez Campos and S Muñoz Machado (ed),
Tratado de Derecho comunitario europeo, Vol I, (Civitas, 1986) 253–74.

provide the Community legislator with a programme of general goals but to impose obligations upon Member States. In turn, within their respective areas of competence the ECJ, the national courts, and the Commission have to ensure that these obligations are observed. Some of the implications of this system are not always fully taken on board by everyone. In the Community legal system, unlike in other legal systems, the abolition of exclusive rights is not a question left to the free discretion of the legislator of the moment. Rather, it is a fundamental choice largely put into effect by the signatory States to the Treaty of Rome,[2] accepted by the new Member States, and ratified each time that the Treaties have been revised. It is important not to lose sight of this point, since this characteristic of Community law in general and Article 86 in particular blurs the dividing line between what is 'creating law' and what is 'applying the law in force'.[3]

20.03 In addition, in the words of Advocate General Reischl, 'Montesquieu's principle is only partially put into effect in the Community' and it is not possible simply to identify the Commission with the executive and the Council with the legislature.[4] In the Community legal system, the three classic functions cannot be perfectly identified with the institutions that exist.[5] Legislative power is currently shared by the Council and by the European Parliament, with the important qualification that the Commission has a monopoly over legislative initiative. Executive power tends to be identified with the Commission, but two facts must be borne in mind: first, the power of Member States exercised through extensive use of the 'comitology' and second, the fact that many Community policies are

---

[2] This was explained by Baron Snoy et D'Oppuers, member of the Belgian delegation during the *travaux preperatoires* for the Treaty, in an interesting article, 'La notion de l'intérêt de la Communauté à l'article 90 du Traité de Rome sur le marché Commun—rapport international' in *Concorrenza tra settore pubblico e privato nella CEE*, Colloquio di Bruxelles della 'Ligue Internationale contre la concurrence déloyale' 5–6 March [1963] RDI anno XII 252.

[3] In fields such as Community law, where the legal instruments available do not match the traditional legal methods, the words of Hans Kelsen make complete sense: 'Is interpretation an act of applying knowledge or is it instead an act of free will? There is no essential difference between, on the one hand, the preparation of a court judgment or an administrative act carried out in accordance with a statute and, on the other hand, the drafting of a statute in accordance with the Constitution . . . There is however a qualitative difference between these two cases, as the freedom of the legislator is, from a substantive point of view, greater than that of a judge. Nevertheless, a judge is also called on to create legal rules and enjoys a degree of freedom in his activity, since the creation of an individual rule [the judgment] is an act of will to the extent that it consists in completing the framework provided by one or more general rules.' *Théorie pure du droit*, Author's translation of French translation by H Thévenaz (Ed. de la Baconnière, 1988) 153.

[4] Opinion of AG Reischl in Cases 188–190/80 *Transparency Directive* [1982] ECR 2585.

[5] Neither do classifications other than that of Montesquieu fit, such as the distinction between functions of coordination, of policy-making, of administration and of control, proposed by N Emiliou 'Treading a slippery slope: the Commission's original legislative powers' [1993] 18(4) ELR 309.

put into practice by national authorities. The debate about the 'democratic deficit' adds another complicated dimension to the question of directives under Article 86(3) of the Treaty. The lack of sufficient democratic legitimacy is a structural problem that affects the Community as a whole. However, traditionally the Commission, the 'technocratic' institution par excellence, has been considered in the past to be less 'democratic' than both the Council of Ministers, which represents the 'democratically elected' governments of Member States, and the European Parliament, which is elected by citizens through direct universal suffrage.[6] This then provides a brief outline of the political-institutional situation which provides the backdrop to any consideration of the two main schools of thought as regards the application of Article 86. On the one hand, there is the Commission's interpretation of the Treaty, repeatedly confirmed by the Court. This view sees the abolition of exclusive rights, at least in theory, as an obligation derived from the Treaty. As such it has an 'automatic' quality, and is therefore largely beyond the reach of the discretionary power of Member States and/or the Community legislator. The second approach is based on an invocation of the principles of the separation of powers and of democratic legitimacy to resist this 'automatic' quality. Its supporters not only attempt to avoid the application of the Treaty but also to modify the Treaty itself.

Two political debates are thus confused in the discussions over Article 86: the **20.04** debate on the limits of State intervention in the economy (free competition versus monopoly) and the debate on the principle of 'subsidiarity' (Community institutions versus national institutions). It is necessary to stress that these are two different, although related, debates. While it is true that most supporters of large scale State intervention in the economy perceive this intervention as a national competence and invoke in support of their position the 'subsidiarity' argument, it would be quite feasible to carry out intervention at the Community level. It is also clear that some of the most fervent supporters of liberalization at any price are somewhat hostile to the idea of accepting any Community competence that affects 'national sovereignty'. The myth of the Commission's 'unbridled liberalism' therefore co-exists with the myth of the 'omnipresent intervention' of the Brussels bureaucrats, while the logical incompatibility between the two propositions goes largely unnoticed. In such a context, it would be impossible to try to present a 'politically neutral' interpretation of Article 86 of the Treaty.[7] The interpretation expressed here is neither

---

[6] The innovation of the investiture of the Commission by the European Parliament (and the possibility of this latter organ bringing down the Commission through a vote of no confidence) brings a new dimension to the debate, by providing the Commission with an added dose of democratic legitimacy.

[7] C Hocepied, 'Les directives Article 90, paragraphe 3. Une espèce juridique en voie de disparition?' [1994] RAE ii 53.

politically neutral, nor is it the only interpretation legally possible. It is however submitted that it is a logical interpretation, one consistent with the status quo. With the above comments in mind, the law relating to directives under Article 86(3) of the Treaty will now be examined.

B. Directives Adopted on the Basis of Article 86(3) EC

20.05 The Commission has made use on twelve occasions of the power that Article 86(3) confers upon it to adopt directives. These nine directives can be divided into two groups. In the first group is the Transparency Directive[8] originally adopted in 1980 and subsequently modified in 1985, 1993 and 2000.[9] In the second group are the directives relating to telecommunications. Thus, in 1988 the Commission adopted the Terminals Directive,[10] in 1990 the Services Directive,[11] in 1994 the Satellites Directive[12] that amends the two former directives, and from 1994 onwards, the Cable Directive (1995),[13] the Mobile Communications Directive (1996),[14] the Full Competition Directive (1996)[15] and a directive requiring that cable television networks and telecommunication networks owned by a single operator are separate legal entities.[16] The last four directives modified the Services Directive.

---

[8] Commission Dir (EEC) 80/723 on the transparency of financial relations between Member States and public undertakings [1980] OJ L195/35–37.

[9] Commission Dir (EEC) 80/723 concerning the transparency of financial relations between Member States and their public undertakings [1980] OJ L195/35. This Dir has been modified by the following directives:
- Commission Dir (EEC) 85/413 [1985] OJ L229/20;
- Commission Dir (EEC) 93/84 [1993] OJ L254/16;
- Commission Dir (EC) 2000/52 [2000] OJ L193/75;

A consolidated version of the transparency dir can be found at the following internet address: http://europa.eu.int/eur-lex/en/consleg/main/1980/en_1980L0723_index.html. A new Dir amending this Dir was adopted on 15 July 2005 but has not yet been published in the OJ.

[10] Commission Dir (EEC) 88/301 on competition in the markets in telecommunications terminals equipment [1988] OJ L131/73–77.

[11] Commission Dir (EEC) 90/388 on competition in the markets for telecommunications services [1990] OJ L192/10–16.

[12] Commission Dir (EC) 94/46 amending Dir (EEC) 88/301 and Dir (EEC) 90/388 in particular with regard to satellite communications [1994] OJ L268/15–21.

[13] Commission Dir (EC) 95/51 amending Commission Dir (EEC) 90/388 with regard to the abolition of the restrictions on the use of cable television networks for the provision of already liberalized telecommunications services [1995] OJ L256/49–54.

[14] Commission Dir (EC) 96/2 amending Dir (EEC) 90/388 with regard to mobile and personal communications [1996] OJ L20/59–66.

[15] Commission Dir (EC) 96/19 amending Dir (EEC) 90/388 with regard to the implementation of full competition in telecommunications markets [1996] OJ L74/13–24.

[16] Commission Dir (EC) 99/64 [1999] OJ L175/39 amending Dir 90/388/EEC in order to ensure that telecommunications networks and cable TV networks owned by a single operator are separate legal entities.

In 2002 the Commission consolidated all these instruments in a single text which, together with the Terminal Equipment Directive, is the one currently in force: Commission Directive (EC) 2002/77 on competition in the markets for electronic communications networks and services.[17]

1. Preventive function of directives under Article 86(3) EC

Article 86(3) states as follows:

20.06

> The Commission shall ensure the application of the provisions of this Article and shall, where necessary, address appropriate directives or decisions to Member States.

This provision therefore entrusts the Commission with the task of ensuring that Member States fulfil their obligations under Article 86. In order to achieve this aim Article 86(3) gives the Commission the possibility of using two legal instruments: decisions and directives. The role of Article 86(3) decisions as instruments designed to eliminate infringements has been looked at in the previous section of this chapter. The next step is therefore to examine the function or functions that Article 86(3) reserves to directives. Logically the functions of the directives of Article 86(3) are going to be defined in light of the role of Community guardian which this provision gives to the Commission. Article 86(3) EC does not refer to 'regulations'. However, in theory the Commission may also adopt decisions under Article 86(3) that are addressed not to one individual Member State but to all Member States.[18] The nature of such 'horizontal' decisions would be very similar to that of directives, both having binding effects on Member States. The main difference would be that decisions automatically have a 'direct effect', while directives only have such an effect in certain circumstances. The references made in this chapter to 'directives' may be understood to also apply to such kind of 'horizontal decisions'.

The two possible functions of directives under Article 86(3) of the Treaty are the **20.07** creation of additional but accessory obligations and the 'specifying' of the obligations under the Treaty. The former function means that directives under Article 86(3) may impose upon Member States certain additional obligations to the extent that these are intended to make easier the Commission's task of

---

[17] Commission Dir (EC) 2002/77 [2002] OJ L249/21 on competition in the markets for electronic communications networks and services.

[18] The Commission adopted on 15 July 2005 a horizontal decision under Art 86(3) to deal with public service compensations (i.e. aid granted by Member States to compensate undertakings in charge of services of general economic interest for the additional costs resulting from these missions). This instrument specifies that certain compensations (those below a certain threshold and fulfilling certain conditions) are considered compatible with Art 86(2) and are exempted from the obligation to notify under Art 88 EC. The text of the decision is not yet published in the OJ.

ensuring Article 86(1) is respected. The other possible function of the Article 86(3) directives is that of specifying the obligations under the Treaty. These two dimensions mean that the Commission enjoys a certain degree of rule-making power, although as will be seen, this is subject to strict limits.[19] The two recognized functions of the directives under Article 86(3) are to *prevent* future infringements. Tackling infringements which have been committed is not a function of these directives.[20] As has previously been explained, within the scope of Article 86(3) this latter function corresponds to individual decisions. The prevention of infringements through Article 86(3) directives is done in two ways: first, by creating the necessary mechanisms to enable the Commission to detect infringements in the event that they occur, and second by specifying the meaning and scope of the obligations that already exist under Article 86(1) and/ or the exception under Article 86(2) of the Treaty so that legal certainty is increased and the risk of unintentional infringements is reduced. The first aspect was dealt with in the 'Transparency' Directive, the second in the different directives regarding the liberalization of the telecommunications sector.

The 'Transparency' Directive and the creation of additional accessory
obligations through directives under Article 86(3)

20.08 Today it seems paradoxical to state that it was initially the Parliament which persistently asked the Commission to adopt directives under Article 86(3) designed to eliminate distortions in competition between public and private undertakings. In its annual reports on competition policy in the 1970's, the Commission announced that it was studying different directives under Article 86(3). Thus, in 1972, the Commission stated:[21]

> the possibility of demanding (by appropriate directives or decisions under Article 90(3) [now Article 86(3)] that the Member States, in certain fields where the risk of such behaviour is apparent, should take the necessary steps to stop the undertakings referred to in Article 90(1) [now Article 86(1)] from excluding all or some of the products or services of the other Member States when placing their contracts.

This aborted directive under former Article 90(3) provided a precedent for the subsequent Council directives concerning public procurement.

In 1975, it recommended an even more ambitious plan:[22]

---

[19] M Kerf, 'The policy of the Commission of the EEC Toward National Monopolies. An Analysis of the Measures Adopted on the Basis of Article 90.3 of the EEC Treaty' World Competition Vol 17, September 1993, No 1, 106.

[20] Case C-202/88 *Terminal equipment for telecommunications* [1991] ECR I-1223 para 17.

[21] III Report on Competition Policy (1972) para 129.

[22] V Report on Competition Policy (1975) para 159.

[A] directive based on Article 90(3) [now Article 86 EC] of the EEC Treaty with the three-fold aim of clarifying for Member States their responsibilities under Article 90 [now Article 86 EC] introducing rules which will put the Commission in a better position to check on compliance with the Treaty by Member States operating through public undertakings and by the undertakings themselves, and finally making the financial links between governments and public undertakings more transparent.

In 1976 the Commission clearly expressed the idea that directives under Article 86(3) could be merely preventive in nature and added:[23]

This means that the Commission can have procedures and approaches initiated which are not necessarily linked to specific departures from the Treaty but which will serve generally to prevent them happening.

By 1977, the ambitious initial plans had been reduced to a draft directive under Article 86(3), which only concerned the transparency of financial relations between Member States and public undertakings. Despite Article 86(3) providing it with the power to adopt such a directive itself, the Commission commenced prior consultations with the Member States, the European Parliament, and the Economic and Social Committee. These consultations lasted for several years and finally led to the adoption of the 'Transparency' Directive by the Commission in 1980.[24]

In its original version, the 'Transparency' Directive[25] obliged Member States to **20.09** guarantee the transparency of financial relations between public authorities and public undertakings so that the different types of financial transfers made from public authorities to public undertakings or from some public undertakings to others could be clearly followed. Amongst these transactions are compensation for operating losses, capital contributions, grants, loans on favourable terms, and so on. In particular, Member States were required to ensure the necessary transparency of these transactions and to keep records at the disposal of the Commission for a five year period. In order for the directive to be applied a definition of the term 'public undertaking' was given, based on the dominant influence of public authorities. In its original version, the directive did not apply to public undertakings which were active in a series of important sectors: water, energy, postal services, telecommunications, transport, banks, and a good number of different services.[26] Following subsequent modifications, the 'Transparency' Directive currently obliges Member States to guarantee not only the

---

[23] VI Report on Competition Policy (1975) para 275.
[24] VII Report on Competition Policy (1975) para 271; VIII Report (1978) para 253; IX Report (1979) paras 207–208; X Report (1980) paras 235–239.
[25] See n 9 above.
[26] These 'excluded sectors' were mostly subject to the dir as amended by Dir 85/413.

transparency of financial relations between public authorities and public undertakings but also the transparency of the costs and revenues that are imputable to the different activities performed by the undertakings.

20.10 It is important to stress that the 'Transparency' Directive did not itself prohibit any of the above mentioned transactions from being carried out. The legality of these transactions had to be examined only in light of Articles 87 and 88 of the Treaty, the rules concerning State aids. The only thing that the directive did was to create an additional but related obligation for Members States: the obligation to ensure transparent accounting systems and to make information regarding its financial relations available to the Commission. It is a necessary obligation to enable the Commission to fulfil its task of Community guardian as regards State aids granted to public undertakings. The modest objectives pursued by the directive did not prevent several Member States from bringing proceedings for annulment. These States were probably concerned by the institutional implications of the adoption of a directive by the Commission.

20.11 In *Transparency Directive*[27] the ECJ, following the opinion of Advocate General Reischl, confirmed the validity of the directive and hence the power of the Commission to adopt directives of a preventive nature.[28] The Court first dealt with the arguments according to which the Commission had breached the division of powers provided for in the Treaty, according to which legislative powers was exclusively reserved to the Council. The Court pointed out that in Community law there was no general principle enshrining such a division of power[29] and that according to Article 249(1) both the Commission and the Council could adopt directives within the conditions laid down in the Treaty. Accordingly, it was a question of having regard to what the provisions of the different Articles stated. Since Article 86(3) expressly established that directives could be adopted by the Commission, it had to be concluded that the Commission was competent in principle to adopt them.[30] According to the Court, the fact that the rules of the directive could have been adopted by the Council on the basis of Article 89 of the Treaty in no way prevented the use of Article 86(3). The two provisions have different areas of application and different conditions as regards execution. Article 89 allows the Council to adopt all the regulations that are considered useful for the application of Articles 87 and 88 in general. On the other hand, under Article 86(3) the Commission's powers are limited to

---

[27] Joined Cases 188–190/80 *France, Italy, and the United Kingdom v EC Commission (Transparency Directive)* [1982] ECR 2545.
[28] The expression appears in the Opinion of AG Reischl in Joined Cases 188–190/80 *Transparency Directive* [1982] ECR 2587.
[29] It is worth adding that former Art 96(2) was not the only Treaty provision which authorized the Commission to adopt directives. See, e.g. former Arts 33 and 97.
[30] Joined Cases 188–190/80 *Transparency Directive* [1982] ECR 2572 paras 4–7.

adopting measures which are necessary for it to fulfil effectively its role of Community guardian which this particular provision imposes on it as regards public and private undertakings. The competence of the Commission is limited to a specific area and is subject to very precise conditions, but it is not a residual competence, since it may exercise it even in areas in which the Council can act. In short, the Court admitted that there may be a certain amount of overlapping between directives adopted by the Commission under Article 86(3) and those adopted by the Council on other legal bases.[31]

The Court recognized that the obligations established by the directives were **20.12** necessary in order for the Commission to fulfil effectively its task of controlling State aids granted to public undertakings. By virtue of Article 86(3) the Commission had the power of appraisal to specify what information was necessary for the above purpose as regards State aids. The Court held that the Member States contesting the directive had not proved that it had exceeded or abused its authority by requesting unnecessary information. Further, the Court held that the directive did not breach the principal of equal treatment of public and private undertakings since the situations of the two groups of undertakings as regards relations with public authorities were not comparable. In summary, the 'Transparency' Directive confirmed that the Commission has its own power to adopt directives under Article 86(3) and that it can use this power, in a preventive way, to create related obligations that are necessary to enable it to carry out its task of Community guardian. However, it remained to be clarified whether the Commission's power to adopt directives under Article 86(3) allowed it to 'specify' the obligations derived under the Treaty and/or to declare that specific infringements exist.[32]

The Telecommunications Terminals Directive and the specification of Treaty obligations through directives under Article 86(3) EC

Subsequent judgements made clear that Article 86(3) directives may also be **20.13** used to 'specify' the meaning and extent of the obligations that already exist under Article 86(1) of the Treaty.[33] The first example of this approach was the 'Telecom Terminals' Directive, adopted by the Commission in 1988 the

---

[31] Joined Cases 188–190/80 *Transparency Directive* [1982] ECR 2574 paras 8–14.
[32] LM Pais Antunes, 'L'Article 86 du Traité CEE- Obligations des Etats Membres et pouvoirs de la Commission' [1991] RTDE ii 203 argued that if the Commission could create instrumental obligations necessary for its Community guardian role, a fortiori it should be able to create rules that were limited to specifying obligations that already existed in the Treaty. Similar reasoning is employed by A Deringer, 'Equal treatment of public and private enterprises. General report' in Various, *Equal treatment of public and private enterprises,* 1978 FIDE Congress in Copenhagen [1978] FIDE Copenhagen Vol 2 1.33 para 92.
[33] Case C-163/99 *Portuguese Airports* [2001] ECR I-2613 paras 26 and 28.

Commission adopted on the basis of Article 86.[34] Unlike the 'Transparency' Directive, this directive was not limited to creating related obligations aimed at facilitating the supervisory tasks of the Commission. Instead, its objective was to 'specify' the obligations that Article 86(1) imposed upon Member States as regards telecommunication terminals. However, these 'specifications' of the Commission were not simply a non-binding interpretation of Treaty provisions but were directly imposed upon Member States as new obligations. Thus, the Commission considered that the exclusive rights for the import, marketing, connection, bringing into service, and maintenance of telecommunication terminals were incompatible with Article 86(1) in conjunction with Articles 28, 31, 49, and 82 of the Treaty. Accordingly, the directive ordered Member States to abolish such rights. France brought an action for annulment of this directive, based, *inter alia*, on arguments regarding the alleged lack of competence of the Commission.

20.14　In his Opinion, Advocate General Tesauro considered that to 'define the obligations incumbent on the Member States' was a task that went beyond the limits of Article 86(3) and was therefore reserved to the Council.[35] The preventive function of Article 86(3) directives can only justify related obligations of the type contained in the 'Transparency' Directive, designed to make possible the supervisory tasks of the Commission. However, it did not authorize, under the pretext of preventing future infringements, the detailed regulation of the sector through the creation of substantive obligations for the Member States.[36] According to the Advocate General:[37]

> Certainly, the preventive effect will be achieved on a satisfactory and permanent basis by abolishing the legal situation which is liable to give rise to infringements of the Treaty, but whether doing so is a merely preventive action is very doubtful [. . .] [T]he Commission, unlike the Council, is not empowered to adopt all *appropriate* measures for the application of Article 90(1) [now Article 86(1)] [. . .] but only such measures as are *necessary* for the more effective performance of the duty of supervision. [Author's emphasis added]

Advocate General Tesauro therefore rejected the argument that Article 86 conferred upon the Commission the power to adopt directives designed to 'specify' the obligations derived from Article 86(1) of the Treaty.

---

[34] Commission Dir (EEC) 88/301 on competition in the markets in telecommunications terminals equipment [1988] OJ L131/73.
[35] Opinion of AG Tesauro in Case C-202/88 *Telecommunications Terminal Equipment* [1991] ECR I-1255 para 48.
[36] Opinion of AG Tesauro in Case C-202/88 *Telecommunications Terminal Equipment* [1991] ECR I-1258 para 54.
[37] Opinion of AG Tesauro in Case C-202/88 *Telecommunications Terminal Equipment* [1991] ECR I-1256 paras 49, 51.

In his Opinion, the Advocate General also examined another possible justifica-   **20.15**
tion of the directive; that it was an example of the 'repressive' function underlying Article 86(3). According to this idea, the directive was simply a 'bundle' of
decisions under Article 86(3). The Commission may, through a decision under
Article 90(3), declare that a Member State has breached Article 86(1) and may
order and impose upon it certain measures to bring the infringement to an end.
In the same way, it can achieve the same end as regards all Member States
through adopting a directive under Article 86(3). Advocate General Tesauro
rejected the idea that a directive could be used to declare the existence of specific
breaches and added that the general reasoning employed by the Commission
may not serve as the basis for establishing specific infringements of the Treaty
rules.[38] The ECJ, in its historical judgment *Telecommunications Terminals*,[39] also
rejected the argument that a directive under Article 86(3) can be used as a
repressive instrument (to declare the existence of specific infringements and to
require their elimination). Nevertheless, it gave a wide interpretation to the
preventive function of directives under Article 86(3) and recognized that they
could be used to specify the obligations that are derived from the Treaty. In the
words of the Court:[40]

> Article 90(3) [now Article 86(3)] of the Treaty empowers the Commission to
> specify in general terms the obligations arising under Article 90(1) [now Article
> 86(1)] by adopting directives. The Commission exercises that power where, with-
> out taking into consideration the particular situation existing in the various
> Member States, it defines in concrete terms the obligations imposed on them
> under the Treaty. In view of its very nature, such a power cannot be used to make a
> finding that a Member State has failed to fulfil a particular obligation under the
> Treaty.

The Court repeated the rule established in *Transparency Directive* that the
adoption by the Commission of a directive based on Article 86(3) was compatible with the existence of the legislative powers of the Council, such as those
derived from Articles 83 and 95 of the Treaty.[41]

The judgment in *Telecommunications Terminal Equipment* was fully approved   **20.16**
by the ECJ in *Telecommunications Services*.[42] In this case various Member
States brought annulment proceedings against the Telecommunications Services
Directive, adopted in 1990 by the Commission on the basis of Article 86(3),

---

[38] Opinion of AG Tesauro in Case C-202/88 *Telecommunications Terminal Equipment* [1991]
ECR I-1250–1253 paras 32–40.
[39] Case C-202/88 *Telecommunications Terminal Equipment* [1991] ECR I-1264.
[40] Case C-202/88 *Telecommunications Terminal Equipment* [1991] ECR I-1264 para 17.
[41] Case C-202/88 *Telecommunications Terminal Equipment* [1991] ECR I-1265 paras 23–26.
[42] Joined Cases C-271/90, C-281/90 and C-289/90 *Telecommunications Services* [1992] ECR
I-5833.

which required the abolition of certain exclusive rights in the supply of telecommunications services.[43]

The Court confirmed once again that the scope of Article 86(3) directives was not limited to 'preventive' measures, stating as follows:

> The Commission's power is not, therefore, limited to mere surveillance to ensure the application of the existing Community rules.

Instead, it also had the power 'to lay down general rules specifying the obligations arising from the Treaty which are binding on the Member States'.[44] The Court, following the Opinion of Advocate General Jacobs,[45] rejected the submissions of the Belgium government that the Commission's recognized power of 'specification' should be limited to areas where the scope of Member States' obligations had been previously specified through Council directives. The judgment pointed out, quite logically, that such an interpretation would have deprived Article 86(3) of its *effet utile*.[46] What would be the sense of the power of 'specification' only being applied to situations which have been previously specified? The main use of Article 86(3) is precisely to specify the meaning of general rules whose specific scope is somewhat uncertain.

20.17 The 'specification' function of Article 86(3) is of course not restricted to 'obligations' imposed on Member States. It may also be used to 'specify' the meaning and extent of the exception foreseen in Article 86(2) EC for services of general economic interest.[47] This arises from the wording of Article 86(3), which expressly refers to 'the application of the provisions of this Article', thus clearly including the application of Article 86(2) EC. In this respect the Commission adopted on 15 July 2005 a horizontal decision under Article 86(3) to deal with public service compensations (i.e. aid granted by Member States to compensate undertakings in charge of services of general economic interest for the additional costs resulting from these missions). This instrument specifies that certain compensations (those below a certain threshold and fulfilling certain conditions) are considered compatible with Article 86(2) and are exempted from the obligation to notify under Article 88 EC.[48]

---

[43] Commission Dir (EEC) 90/388 on competition in the markets for telecommunications services [1990] OJ L192/10.

[44] Joined Cases C-271/90, C-281/90 and C-289/90 *Telecommunications Services* [1992] ECR I-5863 para 12.

[45] Opinion of AG Jacobs in Joined Cases C-271/90, C-281/90 and C-289/90 *Telecommunications Services* [1992] ECR I-5853 paras 39–41.

[46] Joined Cases C-271/90, C-281/90 and C-289/90 *Telecommunications Services* [1992] ECR I-5865 para 21.

[47] For an example see Commission Dir (EEC) 90/388 [1990] OJ L192/10–16 on competition in the markets for telecommunications services paras 18–20.

[48] The text is not yet published on the OJ.

2. The rules concerning directives under Article 86(3) EC

The approach laid down by the ECJ in the three cases mentioned above, **20.18** concerning the Transparency, Telecommunications Terminals, and Telecommunications Services Directives, provided the basis for the rules concerning directives under Article 86(3). In the following pages these rules will be carefully analysed, with an examination not only of these three judgments, but also of other subsequent judgments and the practice of the Commission.

Preparation of Article 86(3) directives

The Commission has sole competence for adopting directives under Article **20.19** 86(3). The Treaty does not require the participation of any other institution in the preparation process. In practice, however, the Commission normally consults the other institutions, in particular the European Parliament, Member States, and even undertakings and interested individuals. The normal procedure for the preparation of Article 86(3) directives was explained by the Commission in its *XXV Report on Competition Policy*.[49] The initiative for preparing an Article 86(3) directive belongs to the Commission, which enjoys total discretion in deciding the necessity and the timing of the initiative.[50] Naturally, the European Parliament, Member States, associations, undertakings, and individuals are free to request the Commission to adopt a directive under Article 86(3) if they consider it necessary. However, it is the Commission alone who decides whether it will take action and whether such action must take the form of an Article 86(3) directive. It must not be forgotten that apart from this instrument the Commission possesses various alternatives, such as adopting individual decisions under Article 86(3), bringing proceedings under Article 226, recommendations, proposed harmonization directives, and so on.

The Commission normally has recourse to Article 86(3) directives to deal with **20.20** two principal situations. First, situations where the Commission cannot properly carry out its controlling function (as occurred with the control of State aids to public undertakings before the Transparency Directive) and second, situations where the Commission receives a large number of complaints concerning a sector. The decision to boost liberalization in a given sector often underlies the use of directives under Article 86(3). In cases where the reason for the directive is based on the liberalization of a sector, before preparing the draft proposal the

---

[49] XXV Report on Competition Policy (1995) COM (96) 126 final para 100.

[50] In light of the judgments of both Courts in *Ladbroke* and *German Accountants* the opinion of C Hocepied, 'Les directives articles 90, paragraphe 3. Une espèce juridique en voie de disparition?' [1994] RAE ii 60, that the Commission is obliged to act under Art 90(3) and could be sued if it did not act, no longer appears sustainable. See the section in this chapter concerning decisions under Art 90(3).

Commission often proceeds to carry out a previous consultation process about the general direction of this liberalization process or about certain aspects of it. This consultation can take the form of a 'Green Paper' or of a 'Consultation Document', which is discussed with the interested parties (undertakings in the sector concerned, representatives of consumers associations, etc), with experts in the sector, with Member States, and/or with the other Community institutions.

20.21 The next step is for the Commission to prepare a draft directive, taking into particular account the results of the consultation process. The text is then adopted 'at first reading' by the Commission as a 'draft directive under Article 86(3)' and is sent for observation to the European Parliament, the Economic and Social Committee, the Committee of the Regions, and the Member States. The text is also published in the Official Journal as a draft directive in order to give interested parties the opportunity to formulate any observations they may have about it. The Commission has committed itself to consider attentively the comments received (particularly those of the European Parliament, the Economic and Social Committee, the Committee of the Regions, and the Member States) before finally adopting the directive. In any event, it is clear that the opinions received by the Commission do not legally bind it. Despite that, the importance of this consultation process is considerable from a political point of view. Although the Commission has its own rule-making powers under Article 86(3), it will still attempt to reach the greatest degree of consensus possible on its proposals before adopting them. The adoption of a directive under Article 86(3) against the will of the majority of Member States and against the opinion of Parliament is a most unlikely scenario.

Adoption of the directive

20.22 In any event, the adoption of directives based on Article 86(3) of the Treaty corresponds exclusively to the Commission. The ECJ has laid down the precise limits of the Commission's rule-making power under this provision and accordingly it is possible to state what those limits are in some detail.

Limits on the rule-making power of the Commission

20.23 As is clear from the case law mentioned above, Article 86(3) does not provide the Commission with a general legal basis to adopt legislation. In fact, the situation is quite the reverse, since Article 86(3) confers on the Commission specific competence to adopt rules which specify Member States' obligations under Article 86(1) and (2). The limited nature of the Commission's competence gives rise to a series of consequences. The obligations which can be 'specified' by means of an Article 86(3) directive are solely those obligations that for Member States derive from Article 86(1) and (2) of the Treaty. Of course, given the character of Article 86(1) as a 'reference rule' this process of specifying

Member States' obligations may also relate to other Treaty provisions, to the extent that they apply in conjunction with Article 86(1). It should be recalled that in order for Article 86(1) to apply the State measures in question must concern public undertakings or undertakings which enjoy special or exclusive rights. More specifically, the grant or maintenance of exclusive rights is a State measure which comes within the scope of Article 86(1). For this reason it is perfectly possible for the objective of a directive under Article 86(3) to be the abolition of exclusive rights. Other State measures which are not specifically related either to public undertakings or to special or exclusive rights cannot in principle be the object of a directive under Article 86(3).

Article 86(3) directives and the behaviour of undertakings

Article 86(3) only confers powers on the Commission as regards State measures. **20.24** This means that the behaviour of an undertaking cannot, in principle, be the object of an Article 86(3) directive if such behaviour was due to the undertaking acting of its own free will. In the Telecommunications Terminals Directive and the Telecommunications Services Directive the Commission obliged Member States, in addition to eliminating certain exclusive rights, to ensure that traditional telecommunications operators allowed that clients to rescind their contracts concerning goods or services affected by the liberalization process whose duration was greater than one year. Clearly, the objective was to prevent the existence of long-term contractual obligations between these operators and their clients from turning the elimination of exclusive rights into a pointless exercise. Nevertheless, the ECJ annulled this part of both directives on the following basis:[51]

> [I]t should be noted that Article 90 [now Article 86] of the Treaty confers powers on the Commission only in relation to State measures [. . .] and that anti-competitive conduct engaged in by undertakings *on their own initiative* can be called in question only by individual decisions adopted under Articles 85 and 86 (now Articles 81 and 82) of the Treaty.

It does not appear either from the provisions of the directive or from the preamble thereto that the holders of special or exclusive rights were *compelled or encouraged by State regulations* to conclude long-term contracts.

> Article [86] cannot therefore be regarded as an appropriate basis for dealing with the obstacles to competition which are purportedly created by the long-term contracts referred to in the directive. [Author's emphasis added]

Nevertheless, it would be an error to interpret these judgments in a simplistic **20.25**

---

[51] Case C-202/88 *Telecommunications Terminal Equipment* [1991] ECR I-1272 paras 55–57. Similar reasoning appeared in Joined Cases C-271/90, C-281/90 and C-289/90 *Telecommunications Services* [1992] ECR I-5866 paras 24–26.

manner and conclude that directives under Article 86(3) can never be aimed at the behaviour of undertakings. In the public sector, the boundaries between the behaviour of undertakings and State measures are blurred and Article 86 was included in the Treaty precisely in order to tackle this type of problem. A careful reading of these judgments reveals that the behaviour of public or privileged undertakings only escapes from the scope of Article 86(1) to the extent that it has been decided by the undertaking acting on its own initiative. The Court has recognized that the behaviour of public or privileged undertakings which are obliged or incited by a State rule to behave in that way can be the object of directives under Article 86(3). The same reasoning should be applied with respect to behaviour which is the result of the State obliging or inciting the undertaking to behave in a given way not through a rule but through less obvious but equally effective measures. This last category clearly causes evidential problems. How can it be proved that the apparently independent behaviour of an undertaking is in reality the result of the influence of public powers? The answer is 'with extreme difficulty'. Nevertheless, it is necessary to remember that one of the legal effects of Article 86(1) is to attribute to the State certain behaviour apparently carried out by public or privileged undertakings. Accordingly there are no good reasons for excluding on principle these situations from the scope of directives under Article 86(3) of the Treaty.[52]

20.26   Article 86(3) authorizes the Commission to specify the scope of the obligations derived from Article 86(1) and the exception contained in Article 86(2). The Commission will therefore jointly examine both sections in the light of the circumstances of the sector in question. The directive does not have to limit itself to prohibiting exclusive rights; it can also conclude that an exclusive right or another measure is justified, even in a transitional manner, on the basis of Article 86(2).[53] Directives under Article 86(3) can be employed to specify the scope of the exception contained in Article 86(2). Since this exception is applicable to both State measures and the behaviour of undertakings, an Article 86(3) directive could probably be used to specify the application of Article 86(2) to the behaviour of undertakings.

---

[52] Prior to the judgment in *Telecommunications Terminal Equipment* academics took a more flexible approach to this question; see A Deringer, 'Equal treatment of public and private enterprises. General report' in Various, *Equal treatment of public and private enterprises*, 1978 FIDE Congress in Copenhagen [1978] FIDE Copenhagen Vol 2 1.33 1.32–1.33 paras 92–93.

[53] For an example see Commission Dir (EEC) 90/388 [1990] OJ L192/10–16 on competition in the markets for telecommunications services, paras 18–20. Moreover the Commission announced in 2004 its intention to adopt a horizontal decision under Art 86(3) to deal with public service compensations (online at: http://europa.eu.int/comm/competition/state_aid/others/interest/en.pdf).

Clear and obscure acts

The power under Article 86(3) to specify Treaty obligations is not limited to **20.27** those provisions whose interpretation is particularly difficult.[54] It is even less correct to say that the power is limited only to those provisions whose interpretation is unproblematic.[55] Article 86(3) allows the meaning of general rules whose specific scope is uncertain to be clarified and also to remind Member States that they must fulfil the obligations contained in the Treaty whose interpretation is not in doubt.

How specific can directives under Article 86(3) be?

The function of specifying the obligations under the Treaty includes that of **20.28** indicating to Member States what specific measures have to be adopted in order to comply with those obligations. However, there are obligations in the Treaty whose general character allows Member States various ways of fulfilling them, at least in the absence of directives under Article 86(3). The question which arises is whether directives under Article 86(3) can reduce this room for manoeuvre which, in principle, Member States enjoy, and impose on them a particular way of fulfilling Treaty obligations. The question of how specific directives can be in laying down obligations does not only arise in the field of Article 86(3): rather, it affects all directives. It must not be forgotten that according to paragraph 3 of Article 249:

> A directive shall be binding, as to the result to be achieved, upon each Member State to which it is addressed, but shall leave to the national authorities the choice of form and methods.

Although the decision as to the form that national acts of transposition take without doubt corresponds to Member States, the boundary between 'the result to be achieved' and 'the methods' to achieve it is not easy to draw. The choice of methods used will depend heavily on the end pursued by the directive. The more specific the end of the directive the less freedom Member States will have in their choice of means. In practice, the trend is for directives to be increasingly precise.[56]

In the context of Article 86(3) the question of how specific directives can be **20.29**

---

[54] LM Pais Antunes, 'L'article 90 du Traité CEE—Obligations des Etats Membres et pouvoirs de la Commission' [1991] RTDE ii 208; on the other hand, Marenco, G, 'Public Sector and Community Law' [1983] CMLRev xx 522 was in favour of confining the use of Art 86(3) to situations whose compatibility with the Treaty was doubtful.

[55] Joined Cases C-271/90, C-281/90, and C-289/90 *Telecommunications Services* [1992] ECR I-5865 para 21.

[56] JV Louis, 'Les actes des institutions' in Various, *Commentaire Megret, Le Droit de la CEE*, 2nd edn Vol 10, 1993, 500–1; G Isaac, *Droit communautaire general* (4th edn) (Edition Masson, 1994) 127–28.

was raised by the Belgian government in its action against the Telecommunications Services Directive. In this action, the Belgian government criticised the Commission for having drastically reduced Member States' room for manoeuvre under the Treaty to fulfil their obligations in various ways. According to the Belgian government, the Commission lacked, as regards Article 86(3) directives, the right to impose on Member States a particular means of fulfilling its obligations.[57] The Court rejected this argument, pointing out that contrary to what was alleged by the Belgian government the directive concerned had not specified in an exhaustive manner the methods open to Member States to fulfil their obligations.[58] This reasoning appeared to suggest that the Commission therefore does not have complete freedom to choose the methods which Member States had to use. Some authors have even suggested that the Commission would exceed its powers if it were to impose on Member States the use of certain methods to fulfil their obligations in cases where the Treaty permitted them to choose freely the method they preferred in order to achieve the desired result.[59] Nevertheless, when the Commission has specified a method it has in fact been guilty more of being excessively prudent than excessively zealous, to the extent that many of the provisions contained in the directives are dangerously ambiguous and could jeopardize the effectiveness of the liberalization process. It is submitted that more detailed rules should be adopted in the future.[60]

20.30 It is submitted that the function of specifying the obligations contained in the Treaty can include that of selecting from among the methods in principle available to Member States those that the Commission considers most appropriate. This principle has already been recognized by the case law as regards Article 86(3) individual decisions.[61] It should also apply as regards Directives. The limits of this particular power of 'specification' are, on the one hand, respect for the principle of proportionality and, on the other hand, the inherent legal flexibility of directives.[62] Within these limits, an Article 86(3) directive can reduce the degree of freedom which Member States have and oblige them to use specific methods to comply with the Treaty. This appears to be clear from the *Taillandier, Lagauche,* and *Decoster* judgments, all given on 27 October

---

[57] Joined Cases C-271/90, C-281/90 and C-289/90 *Telecommunications Services* [1992] ECR I-5864 para 17.

[58] Joined Cases C-271/90, C-281/90 and C-289/90 *Telecommunications Services* [1992] ECR I-5865 para 22.

[59] M Kerf, 'The policy of the Commission of the EEC Toward National Monopolies. An Analysis of the Measures Adopted on the Basis of Article 90.3 of the EEC Treaty' World Competition Vol 17, September 1993, No 1, 90.

[60] C Hocepied, 'Les directives Article 90, paragraphe 3. Une espèce juridique en voie de disparition?' [1994] RAE ii 56–58.

[61] Joined Cases C-48/90 and C-66/90 *Dutch PTT* [1992] ECR I-565, para 28; Case C-107/95 P *Expert Accountants (appeal)* [1996] ECR I-947 para 23.

[62] Art 249 para 3 EC.

1993.[63] These cases concerned Article 6 of the Terminals Directive, which established an obligation on Member States to attribute the functions of the regulation of the telecommunications sector to a public entity, 'independent' from the public or private undertakings in that sector. The situations examined in the three cases were almost identical: criminal proceedings against people who had marketed non-approved terminals, thus breaching the Belgian (*Lagauche*) and French (*Taillandier* and *Decoster*) legislation. In the three cases the submissions of the interested parties made it clear that the legislative provisions in question were incompatible with Community law, given that the entities entrusted with the type-approval process were at the same time active in the telecommunications market. The Court proceeded to examine whether this situation was compatible with Articles 86(1) and 82 of the Treaty (for the period prior to the coming into force of Article 6 of the directive, 1 July 1989) and with Article 6 of the directive (for the period after Article 6 came into force).

It is clear that the Court wished to differentiate between two standards: while a **20.31** degree of independence between the regulator and the operator is a general requirement directly derived from Articles 86(1) and 82, the level of independence required is much higher as regards Article 6 of the directive. Thus, the Court appeared to suggest that where a public undertaking were given the functions of *monitoring* and *type-approval* this would not be incompatible with Articles 86(1) and 82 as long as the specifications concerned were *fixed* by the public authority.[64] It should be recalled that in the field of Article 6 of the directive the attribution of any regulatory functions to an operator, whether these relate to drawing up specifications, type-approval, or simply monitoring activities, is prohibited. From this it appears clear that the function attributed to directives under Article 86(3) to specify the Treaty obligations implies the power to specify those means that Member States have to employ to fulfil their obligations. The obligations of Member States become more precise than they were before the directive as a consequence of the directive.

Directives under Article 86(3) are not a repressive instrument of specific infringements

If Article 86(3) confers on the Commission the power to repress specific **20.32** infringements this power can only be exercised through individual decisions and

---

[63] Joined Cases C-46/90 and C-93/91 *Procureur du Roi v Jean-Marie Lagauche and others (Lagauche)* [1993] ECR I-5267; Case C-69/91 *Criminal proceedings against Francine Gillon, née Decoster (Decoster)* [1993] ECR I-5335; Case C-92/91 *Criminal proceedings against Annick Neny, née Taillandier (Taillandier)* [1993] ECR I-5383.

[64] In this regard *Lagauche* clearly modifies the rule established in *RTT* (para 26) despite the claims of the Court that the two judgments are consistent. See L Hancher, 'Judgments of the Court Lagauche, Decoster and Taillandier', (1994) CML Rev xxxi 857–73.

not through directives. Thus, even in the context of Article 86(3) directives are regulatory not repressive instruments. As the ECJ recognized in *Telecommunications Terminal Equipment*, a directive under Article 86(3) cannot be used to declare the existence of specific infringements and require their elimination:[65]

> Article 90(3) [now Article 86(3)] of the Treaty empowers the Commission to specify in general terms the obligations arising under Article 90(1) [now Article 86(1)] by adopting directives. The Commission exercises that power where, *without taking into consideration the particular situation existing in the various Member States*, it defines in concrete terms the obligations imposed on them under the Treaty. *In view of its very nature, such a power cannot be used to make a finding that a Member States has failed to fulfil a particular obligation under the Treaty.* [Author's emphasis added]

Accordingly, there are no grounds for interpreting Article 86(3) directives as 'bundles' of decisions under Article 86(3). The reasoning used to justify directives under Article 86(3) is both abstract and general. This would, in many cases, provide an inadequate basis on which to found a declaration that a specific infringement has been committed by a Member State.[66] A directive under Article 86(3) is therefore not a particular application of the Treaty to a given case, but rather a rule-making act which specifies the scope of the Treaty in a general and abstract way.

The principles of 'necessity' and 'proportionality'

20.33 In addition, Article 86(3) directives, in their preventive guise, can impose obligations on Member States which do not directly derive from the Treaty but which are necessary for the Commission to be able to fulfil its role as Community guardian. For example, obligations of accounting transparency do not directly derive from the Treaty but they are necessary to enable the Commission to ensure that Articles 87 and 88 of the Treaty, regarding State aids to public undertakings, are respected. In the Transparency Directive, the Commission did not specify the scope of the pre-existing Treaty rules. Instead, it created fresh obligations which were necessary for the fulfilment of the Community guardian role conferred on it by Article 86(3).

> It is not sufficient for an obligation to be 'useful' for the fulfilment of the task of overseeing: it must be 'necessary'. Nevertheless, the ECJ has recognized that the Commission has some discretion when judging which measures are necessary. Only the establishment of obligations that are clearly disproportionate will be considered to be a breach of the inherent limits contained in Article 86(3) of the

---

[65] Case C-202/88 *Telecommunications Terminal Equipment* [1991] ECR I-1264 para 17.
[66] Opinion of AG Tesauro in Case C-202/88 *Telecommunications Terminal Equipment* [1991] ECR I-1250 paras 32–40.

Treaty. The proportionality principle therefore constitutes a limit on the rule-making actions of the Commission in the context of Article 86(3) of the Treaty.[67]

Form of directives under Article 86(3)

The general principle of legal certainty requires that all acts destined to produce **20.34** legal effects expressly indicate the legal basis that authorizes their adoption and the legal form that they take. The legal effects of 'specifying the Treaty rules' or of 'creating preventive rules' can only be achieved validly through acts which take the legal form of directives or decisions and which expressly invoke the legal basis of Article 86(3) of the Treaty. This question was debated in 1991 when the Commission adopted a communication concerning the application of the rules of State aid contained in the Treaty and the application of the Transparency Directive in relation to public undertakings in the manufacturing sector.[68] The communication presented, on the one hand, the Commission's interpretation of the case law of the Court concerning public undertakings as well as the approach which it intended to adopt on the question of the control of State aids. The communication then went on to point out that Article 5 of the Transparency Directive obliged Member States to maintain certain accountancy information for five years and to present such information to the Commission should they request it. This information would allow financial flows between the different undertakings and public authorities to be identified. The communication concluded by 'inviting' Member States to present in advance to the Commission an annual declaration as regards undertakings which exceeded a given volume of business and that included an amount of information which was not expressly provided for in the directive. The French government appealed against the communication, arguing that its aim was to create new obligations (filing of annual reports, additional information) without respecting the formalities of Article 86(3).

In *Transparency Communication* the ECJ, following the Opinion of Advocate **20.35** General Tesauro, found in favour of the French government and annulled the Commission communication. The Court held that the object of the communication was to produce, in a general and abstract mode, its own legal effects distinct from those of Article 5 of the Transparency Directive. For this reason it effectively purported to be an amendment of that directive and as such an

---

[67] LM Pais Antunes, 'L'Article 86 du Traité CEE—Obligations des Etats Membres et pouvoirs de la Commission' [1991] RTDE ii 203; F Melin-Soucramanien 'Les pouvoirs spéciaux conférés à la Commission en matière de concurrence par l'article 90.3 du Traité de Rome' [1994] RMCUE No 382, 606.

[68] Commission Communication to the Member States on the application of Art 92–93 [now Art 87 and 88] of the EEC Treaty and of Art 5 of Commission Directive 80/723 (EEC) to public undertakings in the manufacturing sector [1991] OJ C273/2–17.

amendment could only be properly affected through the adoption of another directive under Article 86(3) the communication was annulled.[69] As a result of this judgment, in 1993 the Commission adopted a directive under Article 86(3) which amended the Transparency Directive, introducing the obligations contained in the annulled communication.[70] No action was brought against this new directive. Accordingly, the use of communications and other instruments of 'soft law' is limited to cases where the intention is not to create new obligations for Member States.[71]

Reasons for adopting directives under Article 86(3)

20.36   By virtue of Article 253 of the Treaty, the reasons for adopting directives under Article 86(3) must be expressed. The Commission must explain sufficiently clearly its interpretation of the Treaty rules and/or the reasons that it considers the measures contained in the directive to be necessary. It should be recalled, however, that the reasons in a directive must be general and abstract, with no intention of showing the existence of specific infringements. The ECJ annulled two of the articles contained in the Terminals and Services Directives for failure to contain sufficient reasoning. In both cases the Commission was criticised for having required the abolition of special rights without previously having differentiated this category with respect to exclusive rights, and without having explained why special rights breached the Treaty.[72] The reasons concerning exclusive rights were considered, by contrast, sufficiently clear.[73]

Publication and entering into force of directives under Article 86(3)

20.37   Article 254(2) of the Treaty[74] provides that directives which are addressed to all Member States are to be published in the Official Journal of the Community and 'shall enter into force on the date specified in them or, in the absence thereof, on the twentieth day following that of their publication.' This provision

---

[69] Case C-325/91 *France v EC Commission (Transparency Communication)* [1993] ECR I-3283–3313.

[70] Commission Dir (EEC) 93/84 amending Directive (EEC) 80/723 on the transparency of financial relations between Member States and public undertakings [1993] OJ L254/16–18.

[71] A Papaioannou, 'Case C-325/91, France v Commission (Transparency communication)' (1994) CML Rev xxxi 161.

[72] Case C-202/88 *Telecommunications Terminal Equipment* [1991] ECR I-1270 paras 45–47; Joined Cases C-271/90, C-281/90, and C-289/90 *Telecommunications Services* [1992] ECR I-5866 paras 28–31. It is interesting to note that, years later, the ECJ ended up endorsing the approach considering 'exclusive rights' and 'special rights' as synonyms in Case C-475/99 *Ambulanz Glöckner* [2001] ECR I-8089 para 24.

[73] Case C-202/88 *Telecommunications Terminal Equipment* [1991] ECR I-1272 para 61.

[74] The text of the current Art 254(2) of the Treaty was introduced by Art G point 63 of the TEU. Previously, Art 254 did not require publication of directives (although the usual practice was to publish them), did not speak of 'coming into force', and provided that they took effect from the moment of notification.

also applies to directives adopted under Article 86(3) of the Treaty. Initially, however, some authors doubted that directives under Article 86(3) could 'enter into force'. These doubts were based on a misconception of such directives being 'bundles' of decisions which were limited to declaring infringements of the Treaty rules, rules which had been in force since the entering into force of the Treaty itself. This approach probably explains the fact that in the 1988 Terminals and Services 1990 Directives the expression 'entering into force' was not used, but instead Member States were required to notify the Commission of the measures they had taken before the dates established in the directives. Subsequently, the ECJ has repeatedly confirmed that Article 86(3) directives can have their own legal effect, distinct from that of the Treaty rules on which they are based. It is therefore quite correct to use the expression 'entering into force' and this wording has been used in all the recent Article 86(3) directives. Nevertheless, to the extent that the content of the directive corresponds with the content of obligations derived from the Treaty, the entering into force of the directive will not affect the existing legal situation, and it will therefore be superfluous.[75]

Binding nature of directives under Article 86(3)

Once in force, directives adopted under Article 86(3) will bind Member States in accordance with Article 249(3) of the Treaty. It is important to emphasize that directives under Article 86(3) have *their own legally binding, independent effect* from those Treaty rules whose scope they determined or whose observation they help to ensure.[76] If a Member State does not respect a directive, this could in itself lead to infringement proceedings, regardless of whether this failure to fulfil an obligation is, in many cases, also an infringement of the Treaty rules.[77] **20.38**

Direct effect of Article 86(3) directives

In principle, directives are not directly applicable, but instead need to be transposed through acts of national law. However, the ECJ has recognized that provisions contained in directives, as long as they are sufficiently precise and unconditional, can have a degree of direct effect. In order for direct effect to exist the time limit within which Member States must take measures to transpose them into national law must have expired or the measures taken by the **20.39**

---

[75] See the Opinion of AG Tesauro in Case C-69/91 *Decoster* [1993] ECR I-5364 n 13.

[76] D Edward and M Hoskins, 'Article 90: deregulation and EC Law. Reflections arising from the XVI FIDE Conference' (1995) CML Rev xxxii 184.

[77] LM Pais Antunes, 'L'Article 86 du Traité CEE—Obligations des Etats Membres et pouvoirs de la Commission' [1991] RTDE ii 203.

Member States must be inconsistent with the directive.[78] Thus, in these cases, the case law recognizes the 'vertical' direct effect of directives: the right of individuals to invoke *against Member States* in the national courts provisions of a directive which is in force. This right can be invoked to oppose the application of national rules which contravene the directive or to require the State to fulfil the obligations which the directive imposes on it. While the ECJ has recognized the 'vertical' direct effect of directives it has refused to admit the possibility of directives having so-called 'horizontal' direct effect. This is the right of individuals to invoke *against another individual* in the national courts provisions of a directive in force which have not been transposed (or which have been incorrectly transposed) by the Member State. From this it can be deduced that before being transposed a directive in force can bind the authorities of a Member State, but it cannot bind individuals. The absence of direct horizontal effect must be, however, qualified in the light of the wide interpretation that the ECJ gave to the concept of 'authority of a Member State'. For the purposes of delimiting the entities which are obliged to respect a directive even before it has been transposed into national law, all entities subject to the control or influence of public authorities or that possess exorbitant powers have to be included in this category.[79] This means that not only public authorities but also public undertakings and private undertakings that enjoy exclusive or special rights will be subject to the 'vertical' direct effect of directives.[80]

20.40 As far as specific directives under Article 86(3) are concerned, there is no doubt that once the time limit for transposing the directive has expired individuals can invoke the direct effect of its provisions before the national courts. This they can do not only against Member States,[81] but also against public undertakings and private undertakings which enjoy exclusive or special rights. For example, if a directive obliged a Member State to abolish a particular exclusive right, an

---

[78] JV Louis, 'Le rôle de la Commission dans la procédure en manquement selon la jurisprudence de la Cour de justice' in Various, *Du droit international au droit de l'intégration—Liber Amicorum Pierre Pescatore,* (Nomos Verlagsgesellschaft, 1987) 505–12; G Isaac, '*Droit communautaire général,*' (4th edn) (Edition Masson, 1994) 128.

[79] Case 152/84 *M H Marshall v Southampton and South-West Hampshire Area Health Authority (Teaching) (Marshall)* [1986] ECR 723 *et seq;* Case C-188/89 *A Foster and others v British Gas plc (Foster)* [1990] ECR I-3313 para 18. See also JV Louis, 'Le rôle de la Commission dans la procédure en manquement selon la jurisprudence de la Cour de justice' in Various, *Du droit international au droit de l'intégration—Liber Amicorum Pierre Pescatore,* (Nomos Verlagsgesellschaft, 1987) 509–10; D Curtin, 'The Province of Government: Delimiting the Direct Effect of Directives in the Common Law Context' (1990) 15(3) ELR 195–223; M Hecquart-Theron, 'La notion d'Etat en Droit communautaire' [1990] RTDE xxvi (iv) 693–711.

[80] As is explained in JL Buendía Sierra, *Exclusive Rights and State Monopolies in EC Law* (OUP, 1999) ch 6 para 229 one of the legal effects of Art 86 EC is to subject public and privileged undertakings to certain obligations that EC law imposes on Member States.

[81] N Emiliou, 'Treading a slippery slope: the Commission's original legislative powers' (1993) 18(4) ELR 311–12.

individual could begin to operate the activity in question legally once the period for transposing the directive had expired. If the individual were faced with legal action for breach of the exclusive right, he could invoke the incompatibility of such exclusive rights with the directive in question before the national courts. The direct effect of directives under Article 86(3) has been recognized on various occasions by the ECJ. The question arose in various criminal proceedings brought against undertakings which had imported into France and Belgium telephones which had not been approved in accordance with the legislation of those countries. The accused parties alleged that the legislation in question empowered the respective State telecommunications undertakings with approving the terminals and these undertakings were also importers of such products. This situation created a conflict of interests and was incompatible with Article 6 of the Terminals Directive, which required that the regulatory and type-approval functions be carried out by entities independent from the State telecommunications undertakings.

The question of the direct effect of Article 6 of the Terminals Directive was examined by Advocates General Lenz and Tesauro. Both accepted that in principle Article 86(3) was capable of having direct effect; however they differed in their Opinions as to whether Article 6 in particular had direct effect. Advocate General Lenz considered that Article 6 was not sufficiently specific to have direct effect.[82] Against this, Advocate General Tesauro recognized 'without any hesitation' the existence of direct effect; his view was that Article 6 specified the precise nature of Treaty rules which had already been recognized as having direct effect and it was a 'clear, precise and unconditional prohibition'.[83] The ECJ favoured Advocate General Tesauro's approach and in all the cases examined held that this provision had direct effect.[84] It is submitted that contrary to what Advocate General Tesauro suggested the direct effect of directives under Article 86(3) should not be limited to cases where the directive provides precise detail of the meaning of Treaty rules which themselves have direct effect. Indeed, if a Treaty rule lacks direct effect this may be due precisely to its lack of precision. If this is the case, the intervention of the Commission under Article 86(3) can remedy the lack of precision of the provision in question, thus giving it direct

20.41

---

[82] Opinion of AG Lenz in Joined Cases C-46/90 and C-93/91 *Lagauche* [1993] ECR I-5317 paras 13–19.

[83] Opinion of AG Tesauro in Case C-69/91 *Decoster* [1993] ECR I-5363.

[84] *Lagauche, Decoster and Taillandier*, Case C-314/93 *Criminal proceedings against François Rouffeteau and Robert Badia (Rouffeteau)* [1994] ECR I-3257; Case C-91/94 *Criminal Proceedings against Thierry Tranchant and Telephone Store SARL, Party Liable In Civil Law (Tranchart)* [1995] ECR I-3911.

effect.[85] The doubts concerning the limits to the direct effect of Article 86(3) Directives do not apply to Article 86(3) decisions. Decisions are normally considered as having direct effect.[86] This effect does not depend on whether they are addressed to one Member State or all of them.

3. Relations between directives under Article 86(3) EC and harmonization directives

20.42   One of the main arguments against directives under Article 86(3) was that the rules contained in them could have been adopted by the Council on other legal bases. The rules of the Transparency Directive could probably have been the object of a Council regulation based on Article 89. In the same way, the rules relating to the liberalization of telecommunications contained in the Terminals and Services Directives could probably have been adopted by the Council on the basis of Articles 83 and/or 95 of the Treaty. In the opinion of the Member States who have brought proceedings on this ground, the existence of legal bases such as Articles 83, 89, and 95, which recognize the competence of the Council to regulate an area, exclude the competence of the Commission to adopt directives under Article 86 concerning the same subject. According to this view, the rule-making power which Article 86(3) recognized the Commission as having would, in any event, be merely residual with respect to the legislative competence of the Council. In *Transparency Directive, Telecommunications Terminal Equipment*, and *Telecommunications Services* the ECJ totally rejected this argument. According to the Court, the fact that the provisions of a directive adopted under 86(3) could have been adopted by the Council on other legal bases such as Articles 83, 89, or 95 of the Treaty in no way affected the legitimacy of using Article 86(3), given the different objects of these provisions.[87] Thus, Article 86(3) has a different and more specific object than that of the other Articles mentioned. The object of Article 83 is the adoption of appropriate regulations or directives for the application of the principles contained in Articles 81 and 82, that is, the competition rules applicable to all undertakings.[88] Article 89 forms part of a group of provisions which regulate the field of State aid, irrespective of the forms and recipients of such aid.[89] Article 95 refers to the

---

[85] This position is fully supported by M Kerf, 'The policy of the Commission of the EEC Toward National Monopolies. An Analysis of the Measures Adopted on the Basis of Article 90.3 of the EEC Treaty' World Competition Vol 17, September 1993, No 1, 89.

[86] Case C-156/91 *Hansa Fleisch* [1992] ECR I-5567; Case C-249/85 *Albako* [1987] ECR I-2345 paras 17–18.

[87] Joined Cases 188–190/80 *Transparency Directive* [1982] ECR 2575 paras 11–14; Case C-202/88 *Telecommunications Terminal Equipment* [1991] ECR I-1265 paras 23–26; Joined Cases C-271/90, C-281/90 and C-289/90 *Telecommunications Services* [1992] ECR I-5863 para 14.

[88] Case C-202/88 *Telecommunications Terminal Equipment* [1991] ECR I-1266 para 24.

[89] Cases 188–190/80 *Transparency Directive* [1982] ECR 2575 para 12.

adoption of measures concerning the harmonization of legal, regulatory, and administrative provisions of Member States whose object is the establishment and functioning of the internal market.[90] The competence of the Commission under Article 86(3) is limited to taking the necessary measures for the effective fulfilment of the Community guardian role with regard to public and privileged undertakings which this provision imposes on it.

It should be added that to the extent that directives under Article 86(3) substantially coincide with obligations under the Treaty that are directly applicable their object cannot, in theory, coincide with the object of harmonization directives. Thus, by definition, harmonization only occurs with respect to measures which despite being *compatible* with the Treaty produce difficulties for the common market.[91] On the contrary, directives under Article 86(3), to the extent that they specify the obligations under the Treaty, only eliminate measures which are *incompatible* with the Treaty. As a result, theoretically there should not be any overlapping between the object of the two sets of directives.[92] Of course in practice things are not that simple and harmonization directives are employed in certain cases to liberalize exclusive rights whose compatibility with the Treaty is, at the very least, doubtful (at the same time allowing for exceptions and transitional periods not provided for in the Treaty). Regardless of the possible legal actions against such provisions the truth is that in practice there is overlapping between liberalization directives under Article 86(3) and harmonization directives. As well as differences of object, there are also differences in the conditions necessary for the employment of the two types of directives. As the Court stated in *Transparency Directive*, while Article 89 permits the Council to adopt all regulations which are useful for the application of Articles 87 and 88, Article 86(3) only allows the Commission to adopt the 'necessary' measures.[93] Although the Court has not emphasized this point in subsequent judgments, it appears clear that the room for manoeuvre which the Community legislator enjoys by virtue of Articles 83, 89, and 95 is greater than that enjoyed by the Commission under Article 86(3). The legislator 'creates' rules and therefore the scope of his decision-making is largely conditioned by considerations of opportunity, whereas the Commission has to limit itself to specifying what the existing law is, and therefore the limits on its discretion are much greater.

20.43

---

[90] Case C-202/88 *Telecommunications Terminal Equipment* [1991] ECR I-1265 para 24.

[91] PJ Slot, 'Harmonisation' [1996] ELR xxi 379–80.

[92] A Abate, 'Droit Communautaire, privatisations, déréglementations—rapport communautaire' in Various, *Le processus de libéralisation d'activités économiques et de privatisation d'entreprises face au Droit de la concurrence*, XVI Congrès de la FIDE [1994] FIDE Rome iii 82 (text also published in [1994] RMUE iii 11–73).

[93] Joined Cases 188–190/80 *Transparency Directive* [1982] ECR 2575 para 13.

20.44   On the basis of these differences in the object and the conditions of application, the ECJ reached the following conclusion:[94]

> It follows that the Commission's power to issue the contested directive depends on the needs inherent in its duty of surveillance provided for in Article 90 [now 86] and that the possibility that rules might be laid down by the Council, by virtue of its general power under Article 94 [now 89], containing provisions impinging upon the specific sphere of aids granted to public undertakings does not preclude the exercise of that power by the Commission.

The rule-making competence that the Commission has under Article 86(3) is therefore *concurrent* with the legislative competences of the Council. In other words, the Court recognizes that there is a certain degree of overlapping between the object of Article 86(3) and the legislative competences of the Council. Certain areas can be regulated by both a directive of the Commission or of the Council. This concurrent nature of the competences of the Commission and the Council also means that a directive adopted by the Commission under Article 86(3) could modify, within its own field of competence, the provisions of a directive previously adopted by the Council.[95] This overlapping between the competences of the Council and the Commission is found primarily in questions of liberalization. Thus, when the Commission considers that it is necessary to tackle the question of liberalization in a given sector, it will be faced with a delicate question: whether to opt for adopting a directive itself based on Article 86(3) or to propose to the Council a draft directive on a different legal basis. From a strictly legal point of view, the decision to choose one or other instrument rests with the Commission, since the Council cannot adopt any legislation which has not been first proposed by the Commission. Nevertheless, it would be totally unrealistic to ignore the political context in which such decisions are taken.

20.45   An essential aspect of this question is the participation of the European Parliament in the legislative process. Thus, Article 95 of the Treaty gives to the European Parliament a prominent role in the legislative process. Following the Maastricht Treaty the Parliament can even reject, by simple majority, a proposed directive based on Article 95. Thus, directives under Article 95 enjoy reinforced democratic legitimacy which directives adopted under Article 86(3) do not have.[96] As would be expected, the European Parliament exerts political pressure on the Commission in the hope that it will choose to act, whenever possible, under Article 95 instead of Article 86(3), given that the latter provision does not

---

[94] Joined Cases 188–190/80 *Transparency Directive* [1982] ECR 2575 para 14; Case C-202/88 *Telecommunications Terminal Equipment* [1991] ECR I-1266 para 26; Joined Cases C-271/90, C-281/90 and C-289/90 *Telecommunications Services* [1992] ECR I-5863 para 14.

[95] C Hocepied, 'Les directives articles 90, paragraphe 3. Une espèce juridique en voie de disparition?' [1994] RAE ii 54.

[96] C Hocepied, 'Les directives Article 90, paragraphe 3. Une espèce juridique en voie de disparition?' [1994] RAE ii 60.

provide for the intervention of Parliament.[97] It is clear that in such a context the room for manoeuvre which the Commission theoretically enjoys when choosing which legal basis to proceed under is, from a political point of view, in fact very limited. This explains the fact that despite enjoying the power to adopt directives under Article 86(3), the Commission has used this power very sparingly. Leaving on one side the Transparency Directive and its amendments, applicable to all sectors although of a very limited scope, all the other directives adopted under Article 86(3) relate to the telecommunications sector, a sector where there is almost complete agreement in favour of liberalization. In other monopolized sectors, where unanimity in favour of liberalization is a long way off, the Commission has in general opted for proposing directives under Article 95 (or other legal bases under which the Council has competence) despite in many cases considering it possible to take action through adopting directives under Article 86(3).[98] The prudence of the Commission is seen by many to be clearly excessive.[99] Apart from the telecommunications sector, the majority of Community liberalization programmes have been carried out on the basis of directives or regulations adopted by the Council and, in some cases, also by the European Parliament. This has been the case with air transport,[100] airport ground handling services,[101] rail transport,[102] exploration and operation activities concerning hydrocarbons,[103] electricity,[104] gas,[105] and postal services.[106]

---

[97] This fact probably helps explain the common practice of the Commission of consulting the European Parliament informally before adopting directives under Art 86(3).

[98] This was declared by the Commission in relation to energy in its document 'The internal market in energy' COM (90) 124 final, 12–13. As regards airport assistance services see XXI Report on Competition Policy (1992) para 519.

[99] C Hocepied, 'Les directives Article 90, paragraphe 3. Une espèce juridique en voie de disparition?' [1994] RAE ii 60.

[100] Council Reg (EEC) 92/2407 on licensing of air carriers [1992] OJ L240/1–7; Council Reg (EEC) 2408/92 on access of Community air carriers to intra-Community air routes [1992] OJ L240/8.

[101] Council Dir (EC) 96/67 on access to the ground handling market at Community airports [1996] OJ L272/36–45.

[102] Council Dir (EC) 95/18 on the licensing of railway undertakings [1995] OJ L143/70–74; Council Dir (EC) 95/19 on the allocation of railway infrastructure capacity and the charging of infrastructure fees [1995] OJ L143/75.

[103] European Parliament and Council Dir (EC) 94/22 on the conditions for granting and using authorizations for the prospection, exploration and production of hydrocarbons [1994] OJ L164/3–8.

[104] European Parliament and Council Dir (EC) 96/92 concerning common rules for the internal market in electricity [1996] OJ L27/20–29. This directive has been repealed by Dir 2003/54/EC of the European Parliament and of the Council concerning common rules for the internal market in electricity [2003] OJ L176/37–56.

[105] Directive of the European Parliament and the Council (EC) 98/30 concerning common rules for the internal market in natural gas [1998] OJ L204/1–12.

[106] Directive of the European Parliament and the Council (EC) 97/67 on common rules for the development of the internal market in Community postal services and the improvement of quality of service [1998] OJ L15/14–25.

20.46 If these facts appear to qualify the role of directives under Article 86(3) as instruments of liberalization, it would be wrong to think that such rule-making powers play no part outside the telecommunications sector. Nothing could be further from the truth. The simple fact that within the Commission's armaments is the *possibility* of adopting a directive under Article 86(3) without doubt influences the attitude of the different actors in the legal process. The mere existence of Article 86(3) is enough to prevent Member States and the Parliament from blocking *sine die* draft directives presented by the Commission on the basis of Article 95.[107] In the context of long and difficult negotiations concerning the liberalization of the electricity and postal service sectors, the Commission has evoked, on various occasions, the possibility of having recourse to Article 86(3) if the situation remained locked in a stalemate. Probably partly because of these timely reminders, it has been possible to conclude both processes with specific, albeit modest, results.

20.47 In this way, Article 86(3) plays a 'dissuasive' role against excessive resistance to liberalization found in certain sectors. While it is necessary for the liberalization process to enjoy broad support, it must not be forgotten that the choice of a system of free competition is part of the basic principles of the Community legal system. In this respect, unlike the situation pertaining in other legal systems, the abolition of exclusive rights is not a question which is simply left to the legislator of the moment. Rather, it is a fundamental choice which has largely carried out by the signatory States to the Treaty of Rome, agreed to by new Member States and ratified whenever the treaties have been revised. It is submitted that the system of concurrent rule-making powers currently provided for in the Treaty allows the fundamental choices enshrined in the Treaty to co-exist reasonably with the position of the legislator of the moment.

20.48 The Community legislator enjoys great discretion in reaching decisions and therefore can take into account a wider range of considerations. However, it should not be forgotten that he is also limited to some extent by the need to respect the Treaty provisions, which play a similar role to the constitution in national legal systems. Given that the European Community is a 'legal community' the Community legislator is obliged to respect, in the exercise of his legislative powers, the limits set out in the Treaty. The substantive content of Community legislation cannot ignore the substantive rules derived from the Treaty.[108] In principle, a Council directive could not, therefore, come into direct

---

[107] M Kerf, 'The policy of the Commission of the EEC Toward National Monopolies. An Analysis of the Measures Adopted on the Basis of Article 90.3 of the EEC Treaty' World Competition Vol 17, September 1993, No 1, 111.

[108] G Isaac, *Droit communautaire généra*, (4th edn) (Edition Masson, 1994) 130.

conflict with the principle of free competition derived from Articles 4 and 86 of the Treaty.[109] Faced with such a case, the ECJ could, in theory, declare the directive to be incompatible with the Treaty.

---

[109] G Marenco in 'Le Traité CEE interdit-il aux Etats membres de restreindre la concurrence?' [1986] CDE année XXII, iii–iv 285–86 n 2 interprets the Court's case law in this way although without being in favour of the Court's approach. See Case 114/76 *Bela-Mühle Josef Bergmann KG v Grows-Farm GmbH & CO. KG (Bela-Mühle)* [1977] ECR 1211; Case 139/79 *Maizena GmbH v Council (Maizena)* [1980] ECR 3393 paras 22–23; Case 172/82 *Syndicat national des fabricants raffineurs d'huile de graissage and others v Groupement d'intérêt économique 'Inter-Huiles' and others (Used Oils)* [1983] ECR 565 paras 9 and 15; Case 66/86 *Ahmed Saeed* [1989] ECR 852 para 51. See the Opinion of AG Rozes in Case 172/82 *Used Oils* [1983] ECR 571.

Part IV

STATE AID
(ARTICLES 87 AND 88 EC)

21

GENERAL QUESTIONS ON PROCEDURE. CONTROL OF STATE AID COMPATIBILITY. COUNCIL'S DECISION-MAKING POWER

I. Introduction

Article 88 EC provides for a special control system to check on the compatibility **21.01** of aid. This comes largely under the control of the Commission, which not only decides beforehand on the compatibility of new aid (Article 88(2) and (3)) but also permanently reviews existing aid schemes (Article 88(1) and (2)). As part of this latter role, the Commission, in cooperation with Member States, decides whether or not the smooth running of the common market calls for these schemes to be altered or abolished. If so, the Commission has to follow the procedure laid down in paragraphs 1 and 2 of Article 88 when ordering the Member State(s) concerned to alter or abolish their schemes, with future effect. As regards new aid, the Commission is empowered to rule directly on its compatibility. To enable the Commission to carry out this task, Member States are bound to notify it of their aid plans before putting them into effect. Aid declared to be incompatible with the common market by the Commission cannot be granted; if it has already been paid unlawfully the Commission would in principle ask the Member State in question to recover it from the undertaking that has benefited from it. National courts, moreover, have the power to enforce the previous obligation to notify as regards new aid.

Article 88 EC lays down the fundamental rules governing the procedure for the **21.02** control of State aid. The detailed terms of these rules have been progressively fleshed out by the ECJ and finally set out in Council Regulation (EC) 659/1999 of 22 March 1999 laying down detailed rules for the application of Article 93 of the EC Treaty (hereinafter 'the Procedural Regulation').[1] As well as systematizing the practice to date, the Regulation also introduces some new rules: the concept of 'existing aid' is extended to include measures that become aid due to the evolution of the common market, a limitation period is established for the recovery of unlawful aid, etc. The provisions of the Regulation deal successively with notified aid, unlawful aid, misuse of aid, existing aid and monitoring methods. Although it does introduce some new features, this Regulation does not fundamentally change the aid review procedure. Its principal merit resides in its binding legal nature, thereby confirming and clarifying the rules established in the case law of the ECJ and from the texts and practice of the Commission. Also worthy of note is the fact that the Commission and Council have confirmed the traditional approach according to which the control of State aid is part and parcel of a bilateral dialogue between the Commission and the Member State concerned. Certain complementary arrangements were established in a recent Commission Regulation.[2]

21.03 The Regulation came into force on 16 April 1999. Its provisions are procedural in nature and as such are applicable, unless a transitional provision expressly states otherwise, to all administrative State aid procedures that were pending before the Commission at the time the Regulation came into force.[3]

II. Classification of measures as State aid

21.04 Article 88 EC, which deals with the procedure for checking on the compatibility of State aid, says nothing about the procedure to follow for ascertaining whether or not a given measure falls within the scope of Article 87(1) EC and, if so, whether it is new or existing aid.[4] But this has been shown in practice to be potentially a contentious issue.

21.05 The competence for determining measures as State aid and also for ascertaining whether it is new or existing in character is shared between the Commission and the national authorities, especially the judicial authorities.

---

[1] [1999] OJ L83/1.

[2] Case T-366/00 *Scott v EC Commission* [2003] ECR II-1763 para 52; Case T-369/00 *Département de Loiret v EC Commission* [2003] ECR II-1789 para 50 and Case T-274/01 *Valmont Nederland v EC Commission* not yet reported, para 56.

[3] Commission Reg (EC) 794/2004 of 21 April 2004 implementing Council Reg (EC) 659/1999 laying down detailed rules for the application of Art 93 of the EC Treaty [2004] OJ L140/1.

[4] On this second question see also below, ch 24.

A. Powers of the Commission

1. Characteristics

Principle

Endowed with exclusive powers for deciding on the compatibility of State aid **21.06**
with the common market, the Commission should also be considered as
empowered to determine beforehand whether the measures under examination
really do constitute State aid under Article 87(1) EC.[5] This power is not
exclusive, however, since it is also enjoyed by national courts.[6]

Discretionary power

In cases of application of Article 87(1) involving complex questions of an eco- **21.07**
nomic or legal nature that have to be implemented in a Community context,
there would be some grounds for considering the Commission to have some
discretionary power,[7] which would amount to a limited jurisdictional control.
For instance, where the Commission needs to apply the test of a prudent private
investor's normal conduct when deciding whether or not a measure constitutes
aid, this normally entails a complex economic appraisal.[8] On the other hand,
given that aid is an objective concept, defining a measure as State aid cannot
in principle justify the Commission having a broad discretion, except in particular circumstances owing to the complex nature of the State intervention in
question.[9]

Any discretionary power exercised by the Commission in deciding whether or not **21.08**
a measure constitutes aid is thus qualitatively different from—and less than—the
broad discretionary power it has when reviewing the compatibility of aid.[10]

---

[5] Case 323/82 *Intermills v EC Commission* [1984] ECR 3809 para 32 and Case C-301/87
France v EC Commission [1990] ECR I-307 para 13.

[6] See below, ch 26. The fact that the Commission does not have exclusive powers for deciding
on the existence of aid does not exempt it from the obligation of dealing with all measures
submitted to it within a reasonable time.

[7] Case C-409/00 *Spain v EC Commission* [2003] ECR I-1487 para 69. For an account of
the Commission's limits of discretion within the context of the Common Agricultural Policy,
see the Opinion of AG Cosmas in the Joined Cases C-329/93, C-62/95 and C-63/95 [1996]
ECR I-5151 para 20.

[8] In particular Case C-56/93 *Belgium v EC Commission* [1996] ECR I-723 para 11 and Case
T-358/94 *Air France v EC Commission* [1996] ECR II-2109 para 71–72.

[9] Case T-67/94 *Ladbroke v EC Commission* [1998] ECR II-1 para 52.

[10] The CFI has clearly pointed to this difference in Case T-95/94 *Sytraval v EC Commission*
[1995] ECR II-2651 para 54 and Case T-67/94 *Ladbroke v EC Commission* para 52. It has
however sometimes employed the term 'a discretion' in speaking of the Commission's finding of
the existence of aid (Case T-358/94 *Air France v EC Commission* para 72).

Obligation to give reasoned decisions

21.09   The Commission must explain its grounds for considering that the measure in question comes within Article 87(1).[11] The scope of this obligation is more limited, however, when dealing with the conditions of distortion of competition and effect on trade. Further, the Commission does not have to give its opinion on all submissions made by the interested parties; its remit extends only to setting out the facts of the case and the legal considerations upon which the decision was largely based.[12] In particular it is not bound to state its position on an aspect which is manifestly immaterial to the classification of the contested measures as State aid.[13]

21.10   The Commission's obligation to give grounds for its decisions is less strict when it is able to base its case on facts that have not been contested by the Member State involved (for example when the Member State concerned formally acknowledges that the measure under examination does come within Article 87(1),[14] or when it has itself supplied details of a rate of return on which the decision was subsequently based).[15]

2. Terms

21.11   The EC Treaty does not provide any particular procedure for classifying a measure as State aid. It takes it for granted that this previous stage, before compatibility is examined, will be carried out without problems.

Procedure for examining the nature of a measure

21.12   In view of the Treaty's silence, the Commission has considered that the set of procedures for checking the compatibility of new and existing aid, as laid down in Article 88 of the Treaty, could be used for ascertaining whether or not the disputed measures do actually come within the scope of Article 87(1). As regards 'new measures', the Commission adheres to the procedure laid down in Article 88(2) to verify whether a state measure constitutes State aid. To deal with 'existing measures' (by analogy with existing aid) the Commission likewise makes use of the procedure laid down in paragraphs 1 and 2 of Article 88. This practice has been borne out by the Community Courts. Certain subsequent

---

[11] Case T-16/96 *Cityflyer Express v EC Commission* [1998] ECR II-757 para 66; Joined Cases T-228/99 and T-233/99 *WestLB and others v EC Commission* [2003] ECR II-435 para 281 and Case T-109/01 *Fleuren Compost v EC Commission* not yet reported, para 120.

[12] Case T-214/95 *Vlaams Gewest v EC Commission* [1998] ECR II-717 para 63 and Case T-16/96 *Cityflyer Express v EC Commission* para 65.

[13] Case C-5/01 *Belgium v EC Commission* [2002] ECR I-11991 para 71.

[14] See especially the Decision of 9 June 1999 [1999] OJ L227/27 para 14.

[15] Joined Cases T-228/99 and T-233/99 *WestLB and others v EC Commission* para 345.

developments concerning the Commission's examination of aid compatibility hence apply *mutatis mutandis* to the procedure followed by the Commission for classifying a measure as State aid. Witness in particular the developments concerning the nature of the examination procedure, the interlocutors of the Commission and the internal operation of the latter.

Whereas the Commission is bound to cooperate on an ongoing basis with Member States in vetting the compatibility of existing aid, the same cooperation obligation is not incumbent upon it when ascertaining whether a measure classifies as aid. In theory it could forge its own completely independent method of evaluation, subject to the control of the Community Courts. In practice, however, the Commission takes care to obtain the Member States' backing or at least present its evaluation to them beforehand. **21.13**

Prior notification

The Commission has sometimes sought to extend the Member States' notification obligations by informing them that they must still notify even when they deem that the measure in question does not have all the characteristics of Article 87(1).[16] According to this approach, the notification obligation would extend to measures 'which may involve aid within the meaning of Article [87](1) of the Treaty'[17] and the scope of Article 88(3) would to some extent be broader than that of Article 87(1). It would nonetheless seem more correct to consider the notification obligation to be applicable at the very most when the Member State is not sure that all the criteria of Article 87(1) are in fact met. **21.14**

The Commission has likewise sought to make sure that it has all the information necessary by making use of its power under Article 86(3) to force Member States to provide it with certain information about their financial relations with their public undertakings.[18] **21.15**

External expertise

The Commission has sometimes resorted to outside help from consultants in deciding whether or not it is dealing with a case of State aid. The Community Courts have held that the Commission is entitled but not bound to avail itself of outside help but it is not thereby exempted from the duty of appraising their work.[19] **21.16**

---

[16] Commission Communication [1983] OJ C318/3, or *Competition Law in the European Communities*, Vol IIA, 1999, 59.

[17] Notice on cooperation between national courts and the Commission in the State aid field [1995] OJ C312/8, s 15.

[18] See the Transparency Directive mentioned below at point 21–19.

[19] Case T-106/95 *FFSA and others v EC Commission* [1997] ECR II-229 para 102, and Case T-274/01 *Valmont Nederland v EC Commission* para 72.

3. Quasi-regulations of the Commission

21.17 The Commission has approved texts of a general nature relating to the scope of Article 87(1). These deal with the classification of certain financial transactions vis-à-vis Article 87(1) and lay down the criteria for the Commission's evaluation of capital investments, state guarantees and other types of financial transfers in favour of undertakings. These texts represent a sort of systemization of the Commission's action, backed up as need be by certain case law decisions.

21.18 The ECJ has accepted that the Commission is entitled to take the view, in the notices and guidelines it draws up, that certain aid do not come within Article 87 but it can do so only 'in accordance with the Treaty'.[20] These texts therefore express an interpretation of Article 87(1) that is always, in the last resort, subject to judicial control. Moreover, the Commission does not have the exclusive right to interpret Article 87(1).

4. 'Transparency' Directive

21.19 The sheer complexity of the financial relations of the national public authorities with public undertakings is enough to jeopardize the Commission's task of reviewing aid. The Commission has therefore obliged Member States to ensure the transparency of their financial relations with public undertakings through its Directive 80/723/EEC of 25 June 1980.[21] Member States must keep a record of certain financial information and produce this to the Commission when so requested; they must also supply annually certain information on each public undertaking operating in the manufacturing sector.

21.20 The ECJ has confirmed the validity of this Directive after having in particular ruled that the financial relations obtaining between public undertakings and the public authorities are of a particular type, very different from those existing between public authorities and private undertakings.[22] As Advocate General Reischl pointed out in the context of this case, the Commission must be aware of the financial relations existing between the public authority and public undertakings for two reasons: firstly because it cannot be left up to the Member States to decide whether a particular case constitutes aid and, secondly, because this question needs to be settled in a uniform way by all Member States, the Commission, and, finally, the Court.[23]

---

[20] Case C-409/00 *Spain v EC Commission* [2003] ECR I-1487 para 69.
[21] [1980] OJ L195/35, thereafter amended by Dir 2000/52/EC [2000] OJ L193/75.
[22] Joined Cases 188/80 to 190/80 *French Republic and others v EC Commission* [1982] ECR 2545.
[23] Opinion ibid para 7.

B. Powers of the National Courts

Following the procedure of the Commission, a national court may have cause **21.21**
to pronounce on the application of Article 87(1) and on the new or existing
nature of the aid in question. This subject is dealt with in more detail in
Chapter 26.

III. Control of State aid compatibility

A. Introduction

The procedure for controlling the compatibility of State aid is regulated by **21.22**
Article 88 EC, the Procedural Regulation of the Council, the case law of the
Community courts, and the practice of the Commission.[24] Many informal texts
of the Commission on certain procedural questions have been declared obsolete
since April 2004.[25] Moreover, many particular procedural rules only apply to
certain aid categories or economic sectors (reinforced notification obligations,
accelerated examination procedures, specific notification forms, etc).

B. General Principles

Article 88 lays down a special procedure for the constant review and control of **21.23**
State aid by the Commission.[26] The competent authority is in principle the
Commission, which exerts its control in the context of a special administrative
procedure, the main interlocutor being the Member State concerned.

1. Exclusive powers of the Commission

Exclusivity principle

Competence of the Commission The Treaty establishes certain derogations **21.24**
from the general principle that aid is prohibited. It is therefore necessary
to establish which authority is invested with this competence: the Treaty

---

[24] For more information on how far this procedure can be used by the Commission for
examining whether a measure can be classified as aid in the sense of Art 87(1), see above.

[25] Commission Communication concerning the obsolescence of certain State aid policy
documents [2004] OJ C115/1.

[26] Case C-367/95 P *EC Commission v Sytraval* [1998] ECR I-1719 para 35.

provides that the Commission is responsible for implementing the aid control procedure.[27]

21.25 This competence of the Commission extends first and foremost to new aid that Member States wish to grant and which has to be previously authorized before it can be granted, pursuant to paragraphs 2 and 3 of Article 88. It then extends to existing aid, which the Commission is bound to keep under constant review and, where necessary, alter or abolish it.[28]

21.26 **Exclusivity** The Commission's competence, subject to certain exceptions and reductions, is 'exclusive'.[29] To ensure the consistency of the aid authorization policy, the Treaty has in effect given the Commission the sole responsibility for pronouncing on the compatibility of aid.

21.27 **Control obligation** The Commission's remit is to ensure that no aid that conflicts with the common interest is granted. As a result of the exclusive and obligatory character of the Commission's authorization it is bound to carry out its remit fully.[30] In other words, in the absence of any other authority entitled to pronounce on the compatibility of an aid project, the Commission has to pronounce on each case that comes to its notice[31] and is also bound to act within a reasonable time period.[32] Unlike the situation under Articles 81 and 82 EC, therefore, it would seem difficult to argue that it is entitled to waive its responsibility in the absence of any 'Community interest'.[33]

21.28 This obligation to review the compatibility of aid takes the following forms:

- Vis-à-vis the Member State granting the aid and the beneficiary thereof in

---

[27] Case 78/76 *Steinike and Weinlig* [1977] ECR 595 para 9; Case C-301/87 *France v EC Commission* [1990] ECR I-307 para 16; Case C-354/90 *French Salmon* [1991] ECR I-5505 para 9, and Case C-387/92 *Banco Exterior de España* [1994] ECR I-877 para 16.

[28] The distinction between existing aid and new aid is equally valid for State aid granted to undertakings under Art 86(2) (Case C-387/92 *Banco Exterior de España* para 18).

[29] Case C-354/90 *French Salmon* para 14; Case C-44/93 *Namur-Les assurances du crédit* [1994] ECR I-3829 para 17; Case T-95/94 *Sytraval and others v EC Commission* para 54 and Case T-95/96 *Gestevisión Telecinco v EC Commission* [1998] ECR II-3407 para 54.

[30] According to the ECJ, 'the Commission, for its part, is bound to enforce the provisions of [Article 88]; this obliges it to keep existing aid schemes under constant review, together with the Member States' (Case 6/64 *Costa* [1964] ECR 585 para 6–64). According to AG Tesauro 'in aid matters the Commission has the *obligation* to rule on the compatibility of any aid as soon as the granting thereof comes to its notice (by means of a notification, a complaint or by any other means)' (Opinion in Case C-198/91 [1993] ECR I-2487 para 32).

[31] Case T-95/96 *Gestevisión Telecinco v EC Commission* [1998] ECR II-3407 paras 54–55 and 71 *et seq*.

[32] Case T-182/98 *UPS Europe v EC Commission* [1999] ECR II-2857 para 46.

[33] See in this regard Opinion of AG Tesauro in Case C-142/87 *Belgium v EC Commission* [1990] ECR I-59 para 20.

the case of new aid: If it is established that the measure in question does indeed come within the scope of Article 87, the Commission is the only authority that can validate the grant of aid. In other words, in default of Commission control the aid in question cannot lawfully be granted and its status will remain challengeable. The Commission's responsibility is, therefore, onerous since it must carefully examine and determine its position as regards all new aid that comes to its notice.

• Vis-à-vis the competitors of the beneficiary in the case of unlawful aid.

Nonetheless, the obligation to determine its position does not necessarily imply the need to take a decision with legal effects. Thus, the Commission is probably entitled to inform a complainant that there are no grounds for making a declaration since the aid paid out is covered by an exemption regulation. **21.29**

As for existing aid, although the Commission's responsibility might appear at first sight to be just as important, its binding character is less immediate. In effect, any failure by the Commission in exercising its permanent power of review does not prevent Member States from granting aid in application of their existing schemes. It is rather in the interests of the beneficiaries' competitor undertakings to ensure that the Commission enforces the compatibility requisites on existing schemes. The vetting power over existing schemes is therefore exercised more broadly at the Commission's discretion. **21.30**

Control of the Community Courts   The Commission exercises its powers subject to the control of the Community Courts. Its action can be censored by the ECJ or the CFI. These courts, however, are not entitled to replace the Commission's assessment with their own, whether in terms of the determination of the existence of aid or its compatibility with the common market. **21.31**

Attenuations of the exclusivity principle

Role of the Council and Member States   In exercising its power of control over the compatibility of State aid, the Commission has to liase mainly with the Council on the one hand and Member States on the other. **21.32**

The Council is invested with several powers. First and foremost it possesses powers of a regulatory nature.[34] Under Article 87(3)(e) it is entitled to determine the supplementary categories of aid that can be considered to be compatible by the Commission. Article 89 also authorizes it to make any appropriate regulations for application of Articles 87 and 88, in particular to determine the conditions under which Article 88(3) shall apply and the categories of aid exempted from this procedure. Thus, in authorizing the Council to lay down **21.33**

---

[34] The Council has specific powers in the farming and transport sectors.

the general derogations from the prior aid-notification obligation, Article 89 allows it to remove these categories of aid from the control of the Commission. This might involve a significant limitation on the Commission's exclusive control powers.

21.34 Besides its regulatory powers, in certain cases the Council, instead of the Commission, is also entitled to pronounce directly on the compatibility of particular aid. This power is conferred on it under the third and fourth subparagraphs of Article 88(2). This provision allows the Commission's normal powers on new aid to be, to some extent, short-circuited, each Member State being entitled to request the Council for a ruling on whether an aid project 'should' be considered to be compatible.[35]

21.35 A priori, the Member States hardly seem eligible for taking part in the aid control procedure since it is their own measures that are under review.[36] They do however play an important role in the field of aid control. Article 88 does indeed impose on Member States 'clear-cut obligations designed to facilitate the task of the Commission and to prevent the latter from being confronted with a fait accompli'.[37]

21.36 Firstly, the Commission is bound to cooperate closely with Member States in its constant review of existing aid under Article 88(1). Secondly they are also the Commission's main interlocutors in the control of new aid; each Member State notifies it of its aid plans, cooperates with it in providing all appropriate information and the Member States are also the only addressees of all decisions adopted. An Advisory Committee on State Aid has also been set up by the Procedural Regulation (Article 28) to involve Member States in the procedure for adopting the implementing provisions of this Regulation.

21.37 Their cooperation is therefore essential in the aid control procedure, for the Commission itself has hardly any direct investigative authority over the undertakings concerned[38] and its only official interlocutors are the Member States. This apparent weakness in the Commission's position is hardly a handicap, however, since if the Member State concerned does not cooperate, the Commission is authorized to exercise its powers on the basis of the information to hand. It is hence possible to say that Member States have a real 'duty to cooperate' with the Commission, so that they must supply the Commission with all the

---

[35] This power of the Council is examined in more detail below, paras 21.100 to 21.114.

[36] See, however, the proposal for a procedural regulation, which provides for the setting up of an independent control authority in each Member State. This idea was not taken up by the Council in the final version of the regulation.

[37] Case 171/83 R *EC Commission v France* [1983] ECR 2621 para 10.

[38] See however the on-site monitoring provision contained in Art 22 of the Procedural Regulation.

information it needs to check that the conditions of the derogation claimed are in fact met.[39] This duty to cooperate is a by-product of Member States' general duty to cooperate fully with the Commission as laid down in Article 10 EC.[40]

2. Nature of the examination procedure

The examination procedure is special and administrative in nature

Special nature of the aid examination procedure   Article 88 of the Treaty lays **21.38** down a 'special procedure'[41] for reviewing the compatibility of State aid; this procedure is different from the general procedures designed to ensure respect for community law. According to the ECJ, 'the intention of the Treaty, in providing for a permanent aid vetting procedure by the Commission in Article 88 EC, is that the finding that an aid may be incompatible with the common market is to be determined, subject to review by the Court, by means of an appropriate procedure that it is the Commission's responsibility to set in motion'.[42] The Commission's 'specific duty of supervision'[43] therefore implies a particular procedure, albeit as part and parcel of the Commission's general mission as 'guardian of the Treaty' under Article 211 first indent of the Treaty.

This particular procedure bears witness to the singular nature of State aid super- **21.39** vision as laid down in the Treaty. First and foremost it exists to 'ensure the efficacy' of aid prohibition.[44] Secondly it aims to reconcile, on the one hand 'the general interest of the Communities' at work particularly in the context of the preliminary aid examination procedure laid down in Article 88(3) and, on the other, 'the interests of the private parties concerned', assured in the context of the formal examination procedure of Article 88(2).[45] Indeed, the procedure laid down in Article 88(2) grants to the interested parties guarantees that go well beyond those granted by the preliminary procedure laid down in Article 226 EC, involving the participation only of the Commission and the Member State concerned.[46] The existence of this special procedure implies that the Commission is duty bound to use it to supervise the aid granted by the

---

[39] Case C-364/90 *Italy v EC Commission* [1993] ECR I-2097 para 20 and Case C-372/97 *Italy v EC Commission* not yet reported, para 81.

[40] Case C-382/99 *Netherlands v EC Commission* [2002] ECR I-5163 para 48.

[41] Case C-256/97 *DM Transport* [1999] ECR I-3913 para 14.

[42] Case 74/76 *Iannelli* [1977] ECR 557 para 12; Case C-354/90 *French Salmon* para 9 and Case C-256/97 *DM Transport* para 16.

[43] Case 171/83 R *EC Commission v France* para 10.

[44] Case C-404/00 *EC Commission v Spain* [2003] ECR I-6695 para 20.

[45] On these two aspects see Joined Cases 91/83 and 127/83 *Heineken Brouwerijen* [1984] ECR 3435 para 14. As regards the taking into account the general interest of the Communities, see also Case C-301/87 *France v EC Commission* [1990] ECR I-307 para 17 and para 19 of the Opinion of AG Tesauro in Case C-142/87 [1990] ECR I-959.

[46] Case 290/83 *EC Commission v France* [1985] ECR 439 para 17.

Member States and may not replace it by a simple action for failure to fulfil an obligation except under certain particular circumstances.

21.40 When implementing this procedure, the Commission is essentially bound to make a diligent and impartial examination of the facts. This obligation is associated with the right to sound administration, which is one of the general principles that are observed in a State governed by the rule of law and are common to the constitutional traditions of the different Member States.[47]

21.41 **Derogations** This special procedure constitutes the general rule from which derogations may be laid down by the Council, on the basis of Article 89 or any other Treaty provision. Thus:

21.42 First and foremost—and this is the most important derogation—the Council regulation on block exemptions derogates from the normal application of the control mechanisms of Article 88.[48]

21.43 Second, in the agricultural sector, Articles 87 and 88 are applicable only by virtue of secondary legislation and sometimes in derogation from the normal application of the control procedure. Thus, only the provisions of Article 88(1) and (3), first sentence, are applicable to State aid granted in favour of the production and marketing of agricultural products for which no common organisation of the markets has been adopted.

21.44 Third, in the transport sector, regarding road, rail or navigable waterway transport, some Council regulations have also limited the application of Article 88.

21.45 **Administrative nature of the examination procedure** The assessment procedure laid down in Article 88 is administrative in nature,[49] rather than judicial, penal, etc. It culminates in decisions that authorize or prohibit State aid, on a provisional or definitive basis, but involving no penalties against the States or undertakings concerned.

3. The Member State concerned as the Commission's main interlocutor

Principle

21.46 **Member State as the addressee of the decision** State aid decisions adopted by the Commission are addressed to the Member State concerned.[50]

---

[47] Joined Cases T-228/99 and T-233/99 *WestLB and others v EC Commission* para 167.
[48] See below, in this section.
[49] Case T-366/00 *Scott v EC Commission* [2003] ECR II-1763 paras 52 and 59 and Case T-369/00 *Département de Loiret v EC Commission* [2003] ECR II-1789 paras 50 and 84.
[50] Case C-367/95 P *EC Commission v Sytraval and Brink's France* [1998] ECR I-1719 para 45 and Case T-82/96 *ARAP and others v EC Commission* [1999] ECR II-1889 para 28. With the same purport see Art 25 of the Procedural Reg.

Bilateral dialogue   In principle the Member State granting the aid is the   **21.47**
Commission's sole interlocutor, the only party with whom a truly *inter partes*
procedure exists. It is the Member State that informs the Commission of the aid
project; it is the Member State the Commission contacts to obtain information;
and it is the Member State that is the addressee of the decision adopted. The
supervision of aid should therefore always take the form of a series of bilateral
dialogues between the Commission and each Member State. The procedure for
reviewing State aid, therefore, is, in view of its general scheme, a procedure
initiated in respect of the Member State responsible under its Community
obligations for granting the aid.[51]

This idea, as set out in the Treaty, is based on the premise (which often does not   **21.48**
apply in practice) that the control of State aid is pre-emptive in the sense that
Member States cannot grant the aid before receiving authorization from the
Commission. The control procedure at Community level therefore precedes in
principle the effective implementation of aid at national level and is independent thereof. In this context neither the situation of the designated aid recipient
nor that of its competitors would seem to be directly influenced by the particular dialogue between the Member State and the Commission, for at the time
that this dialogue takes place the recipient has not yet in principle acquired any
rights vis-à-vis the Member State. Normally it is only after the Commission's
authorization has been given that any binding legal relationships are likely to be
formed between the Member State and the recipient of the aid.

The particular situation of infrastate entities   The general trend towards   **21.49**
regionalization and decentralization in Member States has generated new aid-
supervision problems. In the Community system, the central government
authorities of the Member States are the only direct interlocutors with the
Community institutions. It is they, through their Permanent Representation in
the European Communities, to whom the institutions' acts are addressed. This
general rule also applies to State aid supervision matters. The control procedure
therefore does not vary according to the government level of the national body
effectively granting the aid, whether it be the central State, a region, a district,
a municipality, etc. It is therefore up to the national authorities to organize
themselves: should the central government of a Member State fail to meet its
prior-notification obligations, for example, to the detriment of an aid-paying
territorial group, this is an internal problem for the Member State involved and
cannot be blamed on the Commission.[52]

---

[51] Case T-198/01 *TGI v EC Commission* para 191.
[52] Case T-369/00 *Département de Loiret v EC Commission* para 58.

Reduction of the Member State's role as main interlocutor

21.50   Even though Member States remain the sole addressees of the Commission's decisions, their role as its main interlocutor, under the terms of the Treaty, has been reduced over time both by the actual practice of the Commission and the case law of the Community Courts. The other parties involved are essentially three in number: beneficiary undertakings, competitor undertakings, and associations of undertakings.

21.51   **Role of beneficiary undertakings**   In practice, the undertakings benefiting from the aid that is controlled by the Commission play a role that goes beyond that of a mere third party. In fact, it seems clear that they are often directly and individually concerned by the Commission's decisions. Moreover, they are obviously in a position to be able to furnish useful information for assessing the compatibility of the measures examined. They therefore play an important role vis-à-vis the Commission during the examination of the measures in question; they directly furnish information, take part in working meetings with the services of the Commission, etc. Moreover, they benefit from privileged treatment in terms of access to the Community Courts. Formally, however, they are not in a different procedural situation from that of competitor undertakings.

21.52   **Role of competitor undertakings**   Directly interested in the content of the Commission's decisions, those Community undertakings that are in competition with a beneficiary of State aid have progressively come to have a role as private interlocutors vis-à-vis the Commission. They often play the role of complainants, reporting the existence of unlawful aid, and are in contact with the Commission in its initial investigations. They are also authorized to put forward their observations in the formal examination procedure of Article 88(2) and also, under certain conditions, to contest the Commission's decisions before the Community courts.

21.53   **Role of associations of undertakings**   Associations of undertakings have come to play a twofold role, firstly as interlocutors with the Commission in the examination of the compatibility of national measures and secondly as claimants before Community jurisdictions. They are also closely associated with the process of drawing up the general aid-compatibility criteria, laid down by the Commission.

Dealing with complaints

21.54   **Status of complainant**   The Commission's State aid decisions are addressed to the Member States concerned in each case. This applies equally to cases where the Commission, acting on a complaint about State measures claimed to be State aid in breach of the Treaty, declines to open the procedure laid down in Article 88(2), either because it deems the reported measures not be State aid within the meaning of Article 87 or because they are considered to be compatible with the common market. If the Commission adopts such decisions and, in due accordance with the duty of good administration, informs the complainants of this, any action for annulment which the complainant wishes to bring must be against the Decision addressed to the Member State rather than the letter addressed to the latter informing it of the Commission's decision.[53]

The complainant therefore plays a restricted role in the procedure for controlling State aid.[54]   **21.55**

Procedural rights of complainants   It follows from the above that complainants have only the same procedural rights as any other interested party in the examination of a measure by the Commission. The ECJ has thus found that there are no grounds for imposing on the Commission an obligation to engage in adversarial proceedings with the complainant.[55] The Commission therefore has no obligation to hear the complainants during the preliminary phase for the examination of aid under Article 88(3). Moreover, after the formal phase of Article 88(2), the Commission is only obliged to serve notice on the interested parties, including the complainants, to present their observations.[56]   **21.56**

Neither is the Commission under any obligation to examine of its own motion objections that the complainant would undoubtedly have lodged if it had been given the opportunity to become fully aware of the information obtained by the Commission in the course of its enquiry. According to the ECJ, this criterion, which requires the Commission to place itself in the complainant's shoes, is not an appropriate criterion for defining the scope of the Commission's obligation of investigation.[57]   **21.57**

In practice, despite this case law, the Commission does in fact often liase closely with certain complainants, both in the preliminary examination procedures and the formal examination procedures. Moreover, the existence of a complaint obliges the Commission to examine the matter and also impinges on its obligation to give reasons for its decisions.   **21.58**

Form for the submission of complaints   The Commission has published in all Community languages a 'Form for the submission of complaints concerning   **21.59**

---

[53] Case C-367/95 P *EC Commission v Sytraval* paras 44 and 45 and Case T-82/96 *ARAP and others v EC Commission* para 28; Case T-182/98 *UPS Europe v EC Commission* [1999] ECR II-2857 paras 37 and 38.
[54] Case C-367/95 P *EC Commission v Sytraval* and Case T-188/95 *Waterleiding v EC Commission* [1998] ECR II-3713 para 144.
[55] Procedural Reg, Art 20(2).
[56] Case C-367/95 P *EC Commission v Sytraval* paras 58 and 59.
[57] ibid paras 60 and 61.

alleged unlawful State aid' which indicates the information it needs to be able to look into a complaint.[58]

Power of investigation

21.60   Under Article 88 the Commission does not have a power of investigation in its own right for controlling State aid; it needs to fall back on the information given by Member States and, as the case may be, by third parties.[59] On the other hand, Member States are duty bound, under Article 10 EC, to cooperate with the Commission. The confidential nature of the economic, accounting or other information of the undertakings concerned cannot be invoked as grounds for not supplying this information to the Commission, since the latter is bound by an obligation of professional secrecy under Article 287 of the Treaty.[60] More-over, as regard notified aid, the Commission is entitled to refrain from giving its approval until such time as it is in possession of all necessary information; as far as unlawful aid is concerned it is even authorized to base its decision on the only information to hand if the Member State does not fully fulfil its duty to cooperate and fails to furnish all necessary information.

21.61   Article 22 of the Procedural Regulation has in any case invested the Commission with the power to make 'on-site monitoring visits' in the undertakings.

4. Internal workings of the Commission

21.62   Each year, the Commission is responsible for making declarations on the compatibility of hundreds of aid or aid-scheme files. This requires a great deal in terms of human and technical resources and internal organization.

The principle of collegiality

21.63   The Commission in the strict sense, i.e. the College of Commissioners, is bound to adopt all decisions itself, subject to the possibility of delegating certain matters. Indeed, the operation of the Commission is governed by the principle of collegiality,[61] which means that the members of the Commission are all equally

---

[58] [2003] OJ C116/3.

[59] See especially the Opinion of AG Darmon in Joined Cases C-324/90 and C-342/90 *Germany and Pleuger Worthington v EC Commission* [1994] ECR I-1173 paras 31 and 35.

[60] Case T-86/96 R *Arbeitsgemeinschaft Deutscher Luftfahrt-Unternehmen and others v EC Commission* [1998] ECR II-641 para 69.

[61] This also implies that the Commission has to be properly constituted (for the decisions adopted during the 'leave of absence' of Mr Bangemann see Case C-334/99 *Germany v EC Commission* [2003] ECR I-1139 paras 17 to 28 and Joined Cases T-227/99 and T-134/00 *Kvaerner Warnow Werft v EC Commission* [2002] ECR II-1205 paras 57 *et seq.*, in which, after Mr Bangemann was asked to take leave of absence, the CFI ruled that the legality of a Commission decision, taken in the presence of and by a majority of its members, pursuant to Art 219(2), (3) EC and the provisions it refers to, is not called into question by the granting of a leave of absence to one of its members).

entitled to take part in the decision-making process. It also means, even more importantly, not only that all decisions should be deliberated in common but also that all college members are to be held collectively liable, in political terms, for the whole series of decisions taken. The delegation procedure is hence compatible with the collegiality principle only as regards the adoption of managerial or administrative measures.[62]

In view of the broad discretionary power at play in the State aid control procedure, the College should in principle adopt all decisions itself.[63] This is also clear from the judgment of the CFI in *Italgrani*, where a State aid supervision decision made solely on the basis of a limited check to see that the conditions of a former decision of the Commission to approve the corresponding aid scheme was in fact being observed in the case of this individual aid does not necessarily constitute a management or administrative measure.[64] This collegiality principle is also essential in terms of giving reasons for decisions; these reasons cannot therefore be tagged on afterwards.[65] Only in deciding whether aid is existing or new, in cases of simple administrative acts, would it be possible for the Commission's services to speak on behalf of the latter. **21.64**

Commission limited to dealing only with current business

According to the CFI, where the Commission can only deal with the management of current business, in the sense of Article 201, paragraph 2, second sentence, of the EC Treaty, it is authorized to adopt individual decisions only if, in doing so, it restricts itself to implementing a legal system composed of longstanding rules and principles.[66] **21.65**

Internal organization

It is the Commissioner with special responsibility for competition who presents his/her proposals to the College. The service he/she is in charge of (DG COMP) **21.66**

---

[62] Case 5/85 *AKZO Chemie v EC Commission* [1986] ECR 2585; Case C-137/92 P *Commission v BASF and others* (*PVC*) and Case T-435/93 *ASPEC and others v EC Commission* [1995] ECR II-1281 paras 101 and 102.

[63] Decision to initiate the formal investigation procedure, decision to raise no objection, final decision (see Case T-435/93 *ASPEC and others v EC Commission* paras 118 to 124), suspension injunction, etc.

[64] ibid paras 105 to 114.

[65] Joined Cases T-371/94 and T-394/94 *British Airways and others v EC Commission* [1998] ECR II-2405 paras 117 and 279, and Case T-157/01 *Danske Busvognmænd v EC Commission* not yet reported, para 115.

[66] Joined Cases T-228/99 and T-233/99 *WestLB and others v EC Commission* [2003] ECR II-435 paras 94–105; for information on the caretaker Santer Commission that dealt with current business, see Case T-219/99 *British Airways v EC Commission* not yet reported, paras 46–57.

is in charge of the files in this area, except as regards aid files that concern common Community policies, namely agriculture, fishery, energy and transport. These files are the direct responsibility of the respective Commissioners.

21.67 The same distribution of tasks is found at the level of Commission services. The Directorate-General of Competition (DG COMP) deals with State aid files, except for the sectors of agriculture, fishery, energy, and transport. All proposals brought before the College are subjected to a preliminary consultation procedure to elicit the opinion of the main services concerned, notably the Legal Service, which issues an opinion on each file.

C. Regulatory Framework

21.68 The regulatory framework of the State aid control procedure is governed by a diversity of texts.For a long time the matter was governed only by Commission texts of a quasi-regulatory scope, plus some Council regulations of a limited scope. For some years now, the Council has been making proper use of its own regulatory powers.

1. Quasi-regulations of the Commission

21.69 Due to the lack of Council intervention, the Commission was forced to draw up a regulatory framework. It soon became aware that a case-by-case treatment of the files had serious drawbacks: it took too long, given the sheer number of cases to be dealt with, it ran the risk of introducing discrimination into the treatment of the files and it generated a lack of legal certainty. The Commission has therefore progressively fleshed out a varied and complex range of guidelines that aim to help it, first of all, to decide when a measure can be classified as State aid, when such aid can be declared to be compatible with the common market, and, finally, to lay down the procedure to be followed for that purpose.

21.70 The Court has endorsed the Commission's right to produce these guidelines.[67] These documents contain indicative rules that cannot derogate from the Treaty provisions.[68]

21.71 The Commission is bound by the guidelines or notices that it adopts in the field

---

[67] Case C-382/99 *Netherlands v EC Commission* [2002] ECR I-5163 para 24 and Case C-242/00 *Germany v EC Commission* [2002] ECR I-5603 para 27.

[68] Case 310/85 *Deufil v EC Commission* [1987] ECR 901 para 22; Case T-214/95 *Vlaams Gewest v EC Commission* [1998] ECR II-717 para 79; Case T-110/97 *Kneissl Dachstein Sportartikel v EC Commission* [1999] ECR II-2881 para 51, and Case C-382/99 *Netherlands v EC Commission* para 24.

of State aid control and may not go outside them in individual cases[69] unless there is good reason for doing so, otherwise it will be in breach of the principle of equal treatment.[70] When the Commission adopts guidelines which are consistent with the Treaty and are designed to specify the criteria which it intends to apply in the exercise of its discretion, it itself limits that discretion in that it must comply with the indicative rules which it has imposed upon itself.[71] The parties concerned are therefore entitled to rely on these self-imposed rules and the Court will check to see whether the Commission has abided by them in adopting the contested decision.[72]

In the absence of a clear legal base, these texts have mushroomed in a disorderly **21.72** fashion, without any attempt being made to clarify or harmonize them.[73]

Legal certainty and equal treatment

The adoption of general rules for deciding on the compatibility of aid helps to **21.73** ensure that the principles of legal certainty and equal treatment are complied with. In terms of legal certainty, the Commission endeavours to adopt rules that allow Member States and the beneficiaries of aid to predict its decisions with sufficient certainty, even when aid plans are being examined on a case-by-case basis.[74] Rules of a general scope also help to ensure equal treatment throughout the whole Community, at least in so far as the Commission ensures that its rules apply both to notified aid and existing aid schemes through appropriate measures.

These texts published by the Commission have a special status, which varies **21.74** according to the measures they refer to. The rules they lay down have a twofold purpose, firstly vis-à-vis new aid and secondly vis-à-vis existing aid: 'They constitute first and foremost "appropriate measures" within the meaning of Article [88], paragraph 1 and secondly they follow from the specific

---

[69] Case C-313/90 *CIRFS and others v EC Commission* [1993] ECR I-1125 para 44; Case C-351/98 *Spain v EC Commission* [2002] ECR I-8031 para 53, and Case C-409/00 *Spain v EC Commission* [2003] ECR I-1487 para 95.

[70] For more general information on Commission communications, see the Opinion of AG Ruiz-Jarabo in Case C-387/97 *EC Commission v Greece* [2000] ECR I-5047 paras 12 and 100, and AG Jacobs in Case C-91/01 *Italy v EC Commission* not yet reported, para 38.

[71] Case T-27/02 *Kronofrance v EC Commission* not yet reported, para 79.

[72] Case T-35/99 *Keller and Keller Meccanica v EC Commission* [2002] ECR II-261 paras 74 and 77 and Case T-176/01 *Ferriere Nord v EC Commission* not yet reported, para 134.

[73] The sheer diversity of the vocabulary used is in itself an indication of this disorderliness: communication, guidelines, disciplines, letters, circulars, working documents, etc. The dissemination of these texts is also very variable: publication in the Official Journal, in the Commission reports or a simple letter to the Member States.

[74] As regards the multi-sectoral framework, see, for example, the Communication concerning Germany's refusal to accept the introduction of this framework [1998] OJ C171/4–5.

exercising [of] [the Commission's] power of discretion under Article [87], paragraph 3.'[75]

Assessment criteria for new aid

21.75 As regards new aid dealt with in Article 88(3), the notices or guidelines in force contain the criteria on the basis of which the Commission takes its individual decisions about the compatibility or incompatibility of the aid. Although they lack any legal value in their own right vis-à-vis the Member States and parties concerned, these texts nonetheless do acquire such a validity insofar as the Member States are bound to abide by them as a formal condition of the Commission's decisions to approve a given aid or scheme. By way of example, when a Member State notifies the Commission of a new regional aid scheme, the Commission makes sure in principle that the State concerned expressly accepts that, once the scheme has been put into effect, it will be bound to observe not only the general regional-aid criteria but also any other existing rules for governing certain individual cases of application of the scheme (for example stricter rules pertaining to certain sectors). If it does not obtain the express commitment of the Member State, the Commission will then resort to the Article 88(2) procedure for enforcing such rules by way of formal conditions laid down in the final decision.[76]

21.76 The Community Courts have often had to take into account these quasi regulations of the Commission. The CFI has ruled in particular that the power to make all appropriate regulations conferred on the Council under Article 89 EC is in no way called into question by the fact that the Commission uses such 'pre-established operational criteria'.[77] Quite on the contrary, the court decisions have sometimes even seemed to make the adoption of such general criteria a prior condition of the exercising of the Commission's control power.[78] The Commission is therefore entitled to impose guidance rules on itself for exercising its discretion, in the form of guidelines or notices, insofar as they contain rules indicating the course to be followed by the Commission and do not stray

---

[75] Para 15 of the Opinion of AG Lenz in Case C-311/94 *IJssel-Vliet Combinatie* [1996] ECR I-5023.

[76] cf para 49 of the Opinion of AG Lenz in Case C-311/94 *IJssel-Vliet Combinatie* [1996] ECR I-5023 according to which by accepting the appropriate measures the Member State also accepts them for all future new aid. The Commission would hence not be bound to expressly impose the obligation to observe these rules after the approval of each individual aid or each scheme. This opinion has not been supported by others.

[77] Joined Cases T-132/96 and T-143/96 *Freistaat Sachsen and others v EC Commission* [1999] ECR II-3663 para 241.

[78] In Joined Cases C-278/92 to C-280/92 *Spain v EC Commission* [1994] ECR I-4103 the ECJ declared, with respect to a 'loophole' in the rules adopted by the Commission, that the latter is bound 'beforehand [i.e. before adopting the case of application] to specify the criteria according to which it considers aid *ad hoc* to have exceptionally a regional character' (para 49).

from the rules of the Treaty.[79] According to the CFI, the adoption by the Commission of such guidelines is an example of the exercising of its discretion and requires only a self-imposed limitation of that power in the examination of aid to which these guidelines apply, in accordance with the principle of equal treatment. By assessing specific aid in the light of such guidelines, which it has previously adopted, the Commission cannot be said to have overstepped the limits of its discretion or waived its right thereto. On the one hand, it reserves the right to repeal or amend the guidelines if circumstances so dictate. On the other, the guidelines concern a specific sector and are based on the desire to follow a policy determined by the Commission itself.[80]

Appropriate measures vis-à-vis existing aid

The general texts adopted by the Commission also represent a regular and periodical cooperation arrangement whereby the Commission permanently reviews existing aid schemes together with the Member States.[81] Indeed these schemes are generally approved by the Commission for long periods of time, so whenever it decides to make stricter its criteria for authorizing new aid, it also has to make sure that no new individual cases of application of existing schemes now slip through the more rigorous net that it has seen fit to introduce.[82] To keep track of this situation, the Commission, whenever it adopts new guidelines that are stricter than the previous ones, addresses them in principle by way of 'appropriate measures' to all the Member States and asks them to confirm that all their existing aid schemes will henceforth abide by the content of the new text. After these appropriate measures have been sent out, two scenarios are possible with regard to each Member State. In the first scenario, the Member State accepts them and expresses its conformity within the deadline for doing so;[83] in this case the procedure stops with regard to this Member State, on which the appropriate measures now have a binding effect, and it is hence bound to

21.77

---

[79] Case C-313/90 *CIRFS and others v EC Commission* paras 34 and 36; Case T-380/94 *AIUF-FASS and AKT v EC Commission* [1996] ECR II-2169 para 57; Case T-149/95 *Établissement R. Ducros v EC Commission* [1997] ECR II-2031 para 61; Case T-214/95 *Vlaams Gewest v EC Commission* para 79, and Case T-16/96 *Cityflyer Express v EC Commission* [1998] ECR II-757 para 57. Obviously it is a question only of 'clarifications given to the Member States and not an invitation to grant such aid' (answer to the written question P-3945/97 [1998] OJ C187/187).

[80] Case T-214/95 *Vlaams Gewest v EC Commission* para 89.

[81] Case C-242/00 *Germany v EC Commission* para 28.

[82] It is a question of implementing a general rule whereby, in due accordance with the principle of non-discrimination, 'a new rule applies immediately to the future effects of a situation which arose under the earlier rules' (in particular Case 278/84 *Germany v EC Commission* [1987] ECR 1 para 36 and Case T-176/01 *Ferriere Nord v EC Commission* paras 138 ff).

[83] This is the most frequent situation, since the Commission endeavours to prepare its communications in agreement with the Member States.

make sure the implementation conditions of its aid schemes are brought into line with the appropriate measures it has accepted. In the second scenario the State refuses to accept them, whereupon the Commission normally initiates the formal examination procedure vis-à-vis all the existing schemes in that Member State and enforces these new rules by means of a final decision that is binding on the addressee Member State.[84]

21.78 In principle all Commission texts making its previous practice stricter should be addressed to Member States in the form of appropriate measures, since they might well be applicable to existing schemes and contain new rules that render these schemes incompatible. Indeed, without the appropriate measures the Commission would create a situation where there would be discrimination between the operators of different Member States, whereby some of them would only be able to benefit from aid conforming to the new, stricter criteria laid down by the Commission, while others would be entitled to more generous aid on the basis of an existing scheme. Certain notices and guidelines of the Commission, however, have not been drawn up as appropriate measures, even though they do contain new, stricter rules.[85]

Horizontal and sectoral regulations

21.79 An overall distinction can be made between two types of rules in the communications, notices and guidelines adopted by the Commission: on the one hand, the regulations of a horizontal type that examine the compatibility of certain types of aid regardless of the sectors concerned; and on the other, sectoral regulations, which determine the compatibility of aid in terms of the particular characteristics of the sector in question. The cumulative application of several communications might therefore give rise to conflicting rules, which are usually solved in an ad hoc manner.

2. Regulations of the Council

21.80 The draftspersons of the Treaty of Rome allowed the basic provisions of Articles 87 and 88 to be developed by secondary regulations. To this end a very generally worded provision, Article 89, has been added to the essential principles laid down in Articles 87 and 88, allowing the Council to legislate in this field. It stipulates that the Council 'may make any appropriate regulations for the

---

[84] See e.g. Decision 90/381/EEC of 21 February 1990 on all the German aid schemes applicable to the automobile sector [1990] OJ L188/55.

[85] Instead of proposing to the Member States that they directly modify their existing schemes, the Commission sometimes establishes a transition period of several years during which it reviews all existing schemes in each Member State, demanding that the new rules be phased in while this review is being carried out (see, e.g. para 6.3 of the old framework of aid to SMEs of 1992).

application of Articles 87 and 88 and may in particular determine the conditions in which Article 88(3) shall apply and the categories of aid exempted from this procedure'. This legislative power offered by the Treaty was hardly used for some time. Barring a Commission proposal for a regulation in 1966, which came to nothing,[86] only certain specific rules of a very limited scope were adopted on the basis of Article 89 pertaining to particular economic sectors, namely transport and shipbuilding. Otherwise, the legislative loophole persisted for forty-odd years.

The sheer number of files to be dealt with and the rapid proliferation of liti- **21.81** gation finally convinced legislators of the need to make use of the legislative potential of Article 89. The Council has thus exercised its power in adopting, first of all, the regulation on block exemptions,[87] the Procedural Regulation based on Article 89 and also certain procedural rules applicable to particular sectors (for example the coal industry.)[88]

Regulation 994/98

Council Regulation (EC) 994/98 on the application of Articles 92 and 93 of the **21.82** Treaty establishing the European Community to certain categories of horizontal State aid was adopted on 7 May 1998.[89] It marked a turning point in the way the control of State aid was dealt with. The essential provisions of the Regulation are twofold. First, it authorizes the Commission to decide, by means of a Regulation, that aid not exceeding a certain fixed amount per undertaking does not meet all the criteria of Article 87(1) and are hence exempted from the notification procedure (Article 2—the *de minimis* provision); secondly, the Commission may also declare that certain categories of aid, if they meet certain criteria, are automatically compatible with the common market and, by derogation from Article 88(3), are also exempt from the notification requirement (Article 1).

The Regulation constitutes a solid base for shoring up the Commission's com- **21.83** patibility criteria, clearing up some of the uncertainties about the legal scope of its guidelines and notices. It also takes a heavy workload off the Commission, which is transferred to national courts as regards aid not involving any undue risk of distorting the free play of competition. The Regulation is implemented through Commission enabling regulations.

The de minimis rule

Article 2 of the Council Regulation entitles the Commission, by means of a **21.84** regulation, to decide that, having regard to the development and functioning of

---

[86] COM(66) 95 def. of 30 March 1966 (amended by COM(66) 457 of 10 November 1966).
[87] See below.   [88] Reg 1407/2002.   [89] [1998] OJ L142/1.

the common market, certain aid does not meet all of the Article 87(1) criteria and that they are therefore exempted from the notification procedure contained in Article 88(3), provided that aid granted to the same undertaking over a given period of time does not exceed a certain fixed amount.

21.85 As regards the *de minimis* rule, Article 2 seeks to give a more solid legal base than was provided by the Commission's previous practice. This practice was in fact beset by certain doubts; there was no provision expressly authorizing the Commission to exclude certain aid from the scope of Article 87(1). This official recognition of a *de minimis* aid category aimed above all to release the Commission services from the obligation of examining aid of lesser amounts. The content of the Commission's *de minimis* regulation is very similar to the Commission's previous communication on the same subject.

21.86 Two regulations have been adopted.[90] Paradoxically, the Commission's *de minimis* regulations and its exemption regulations work in opposite directions: the latter's effect is to increase the powers of the national courts (which now have certain power, albeit limited, for monitoring compatibility) whereas the former restricts these powers. Beforehand, indeed, the competence for establishing whether or not a measure came within the scope of Article 87(1) belonged both to the Commission and the national courts, each dealing with a different part. Thus, the Commission had to decide whether or not a measure constituted aid under this provision before being able to assess its compatibility. For their part, the national courts, before penalizing any infringement of the previous notification obligation contained in the last sentence of Article 88(3), had to ensure that the measure in dispute effectively came under Article 87(1). But the *de minimis* regulation has increased the powers of the Commission at the expense of the national courts. The latter are indeed bound by the Regulation due to the supremacy of Community law[91] and are entitled only to verify that the measure in dispute comes within its scope. If it does, they must then take note of this and recognize the non-application of Article 87(1) and *ipso facto* the absence of any infringement of the last sentence of Article 88(3).

---

[90] Commission Reg (EC) 69/2001 of 12 January 2001, which applies until 31 December 2006. It establishes a ceiling of 100,000 euros as the total that can be granted to the same undertaking in any three-year period. Certain sectors as well as certain categories of aid are excluded (Art 1). Art 3 of the Regulation lays down the monitoring arrangements that Member States have to make to ensure observance of the *de minimis* ceiling when granting such aid. Commission Reg (EC) 1860/2004 on the *de minimis* aid in the agriculture and fisheries sectors lays down stricter conditions (3,000 euros per undertaking in a three-year period; the cumulative amount granted to various undertakings in the agriculture or fisheries sector may not exceed a set value per Member State).

[91] Subject to referral to the ECJ for a preliminary ruling on validity.

Exemption by category of certain horizontal aid

Article 1 of the Regulation authorizes the Commission, through regulations, to **21.87** declare certain categories of aid to be compatible with the common market and hence exempt from the notification obligation laid down in Article 88(3). The categories concerned are:

- first, aid in favour of small and medium-sized undertakings, research and development, protection of the environment, employment and training, and
- secondly, aid that complies with the map approved by the Commission for each Member State for the grant of regional aid.

As regards the material scope of the authorization, it applies only to certain **21.88** categories of 'horizontal' (as opposed to 'sectoral') aid.[92] The Regulation does not refer specifically to paragraph 3 of Article 87 when it enumerates the categories of horizontal aid eligible to be declared compatible by the Commission regulation. These categories, however, would seem to be inferable only through those mentioned in paragraph 3, to the exclusion of the very specific categories of paragraph 2.[93]

The scope of the authorization conferred on the Commission is very broad: **21.89** within the various categories identified by the Regulation, the Commission has carte blanche for determining the compatibility criteria that make aid eligible for exemption from the preliminary notification obligation. The Commission already had such a *de facto* power, since it exercised its control powers in the absence of all legislation in this field. The Regulation has nonetheless changed the scope of these powers by permitting the Commission to authorize exemptions from the previous notification obligation laid down in Article 88(3). Such an authority would seem to be in keeping with the idea of the Commission's 'exclusive' powers in aid compatibility assessment, as laid down in the Treaty.

As for the rest, the Regulation is characterized by an absence of any radical **21.90** change of the ground rules; the aid categories mentioned were already well known and had already been dealt with in Commission guidelines or notices.

By allowing the adoption of exemption regulations for certain aid categories, the **21.91** Regulation profoundly alters the aid control procedure: Article 1 stipulates that the aid categories determined by the Commission are not subject to the notification obligation laid down in Article 88(3). It is therefore no longer necessary for the measure to pass through the Commission beforehand.

---

[92] 'Sectoral aid' means aid paid to undertakings operating in sectors covered by specific Commission regulations.
[93] In this sense, see Art 3(1) of Reg 1/2004.

21.92 As regards the schemes that Member States will implement directly on the basis of a Commission exemption regulation, without being subject to previous approval by the Commission, Article 4(1) of the Council Regulation states that they are exempt 'for the period of validity of that regulation [of exemption]'. Each time the Commission alters or abolishes an exemption regulation, all existing schemes which were exempted by it are therefore directly affected.[94]

21.93 The Commission in principle expressly states that aid granted before the entry into force of an exemption regulation is nonetheless covered by the said exemption.[95]

21.94 The Commission's exemption regulations have only a 'positive direct effect' and not a 'negative direct effect'. This presumably means that the effect of the regulations is to automatically confer compatibility on national aid meeting the criteria they lay down and exempting them from the Commission's preliminary control procedure, but they cannot on the other hand serve as the basis for automatically establishing the incompatibility of State aid coming within their scope and not meeting the criteria laid down therein. The Commission's exemption regulations are therefore not in principle exhaustive, in the sense that horizontal aid coming within the scope of one of these regulations is not automatically incompatible on the sole grounds that it does not meet the criteria laid down in that regulation. This limit restricts the scope of the group exemption regulation. Indeed the Commission remains always exclusively responsible for examining the compatibility of all aid brought to its knowledge and not covered by an exemption regulation. This means that it cannot merely refer any complaint to the national court but must continue to examine all complaints with due diligence, just as in the past. Moreover, in principle, the exemption regulations do not prevent the Member State's from notifying aid coming under these regulations if they so wish.[96]

21.95 The essential provision of the Regulation is that the Commission is not bound to carry out a preliminary review of new aid (individual aid and aid schemes) that meets the criteria laid down by the exemption regulations. The latter have a direct effect that allows Member States themselves to review the compatibility of their aid plans, under the control of national courts. The Regulation thus enshrines a power that was envisaged by the ECJ as early as 1973.[97]

---

[94] The exemption regulations sometimes provide that aid schemes exempted thereunder shall remain exempt for a six-month adjustment period after the exemption regulation itself has run its term (Art 20(3) of Reg 1/2004).

[95] See, e.g. Art 7 bis of Reg 68/2001 (training aid), introduced by Reg 363/2004.

[96] See in particular preamble Recital (4) of Reg 1/2004.

[97] Case 77/72 *Capolongo* [1973] ECR 611 para 6.

This development has led to a change in the distribution of powers between the **21.96** Commission and the national courts: when a case is brought before them by a disgruntled competitor, the national courts may now check directly whether the public aid meets the compatibility criteria laid down by the Commission and can thus be granted without previous notification to the latter. This new competence of the national courts remains limited however in terms of the examination of the compatibility. They can find that the aid meets the conditions laid down by one of the Commission's exemption regulations and can therefore be granted directly; in this case, however, it is always the lawfulness of the aid grant that is the central object of the control; observance of the compatibility conditions is only a prerequisite and the national court has no discretionary power in this context. If on the other hand a court finds that aid paid out directly does not satisfy the compatibility conditions laid down by the Commission, it cannot declare the aid to be incompatible (absence of negative direct effect) and is entitled only to penalize the unlawful nature of its granting (non-compliance with the Commission's previous notification obligation). Outside the scope of the group exemption regulations the distribution of powers is the traditional situation of the Commission monitoring compatibility and the national courts monitoring lawfulness.

Diverse provisions of the regulation

As regards the arrangements for drawing up the Commission regulations, the **21.97** Council Regulation makes provision, on the one hand, for the publication of the draft regulation to enable all interested parties to submit their comments on it (Article 6) and, on the other, for previous liaison of the Commission with an Advisory Committee on State Aid made up by representatives of the Member States (Article 8).

Article 3 of the Regulation contains numerous publication and transparency **21.98** rules, with the aim of obtaining information similar to that which is currently obtained by the preliminary control procedure. The information is addressed as the case may be to the Commission (paragraph 3), to the Member States (paragraph 4) or to all interested parties (paragraph 2).

In default of any transitory provision in the Regulation itself, the Commission's **21.99** guidelines and notices remain applicable until otherwise decided.

IV. Council's decision-making power

A. Principles

21.100 The third and fourth subparagraphs of Article 88(2) state as follows :

'On application by a Member State, the Council may, acting unanimously, decide that aid which that State is granting or intends to grant shall be considered to be compatible with the common market, in derogation from the provisions of Article 87 or from the regulations provided for in Article 89, if such a decision is justified by exceptional circumstances. If, as regards the aid in question, the Commission has already initiated the procedure provided for in the first subparagraph of this paragraph, the fact that the State concerned has made its application to the Council shall have the effect of suspending that procedure until the Council has made its attitude known.

If, however, the Council has not made its attitude known within three months of the said application being made, the Commission shall give its decision on the case.'

21.101 This is, therefore, a derogation procedure under which, in exceptional circumstances, the Council can replace the Commission's assessment of aid compatibility with its own. This procedure represents a sort of 'safety valve',[98] an 'exceptional and particular case'[99] with the object of allowing Member States to override the Commission's point of view, for political reasons.

21.102 The decisions that the Council can adopt on this basis have an individual rather than a regulatory character. Unlike the powers conferred on the Council under Article 87(3)(e), and Article 89, which aim to set up general measures, this is a power enabling the specific authorization of a special aid measure in a particular case.[100] These Council decisions deal with the compatibility of aid as laid down in Article 87(1). It would not seem possible, however, for the Council to use this power as the Commission does regularly to decide that a measure does not come under Article 87(1).

21.103 Furthermore, the place where this provision is inserted suggests that this power of the Council under the third and fourth subparagraph of Article 88(2) to make its own declaration on the compatibility of certain aid in exceptional circumstances can be exercised not only in relation to new aid but also in

---

[98] According to the expression used by AG Cosmas in his Opinion in the Case C-122/94 *EC Commission v EC Council* [1996] ECR I-881 para 62.

[99] Case 156/77 *EC Commission v Belgium* [1978] ECR 1881 para 16 and Case C-110/02 *EC Commission v EC Council* para 30.

[100] Opinion of AG Cosmas in Case C-122/94 *EC Commission v EC Council* [1996] ECR I-881 para 58.

relation to existing aid.[101] It is therefore possible to imagine a case in which a Member State that has rejected the appropriate measures proposed by the Commission against one of its existing schemes then turns to the Council on the day the Commission initiates the procedure, seeking confirmation of the compatibility of its scheme.[102]

Article 88(2)(3) is used on a regular but discrete basis by the Council, which **21.104** approves some cases every year under this rule. The decisions are mainly related to the agricultural sector.

This power of the Council is bound by no condition whatsoever as regards the form of its decisions. It adopts simple decisions of principle, the content of which is then immediately sent on to the Member State concerned in the form of a simple letter. The Commission is also informed by post to avoid the possibility of its conducting its own examination of the compatibility of the aid concerned.

Previously there was no system for publishing the Council's decisions in the **21.105** Official Journal.[103] The Procedural Regulation has only partly plugged this loophole by providing that the Council may decide to publish its decisions in the Official Journal.[104]

B. Scope of the Council's Power

The power conferred on the Council is clearly exceptional in character.[105] **21.106** Nonetheless the Council does have a wide margin of discretion in terms of assessing the appropriateness of taking certain measures ('the Council [. . .] may decide').[106] This textual interpretation is borne out by the case law of the ECJ, according to which the Council is invested with 'extensive power' or a 'wide discretion' in terms of accepting State aid by derogation from the general prohibition laid down in Article 87(1).[107] In a 1996 judgment, concerning the

---

[101] The first sentence of the third subparagraph of Art 88(2) speaks of 'aid which that State is granting or intends to grant'.

[102] In the same sense, see the Opinion of AG Mayras in Case 70/72 *EC Commission v Germany* [1973] ECR 813.

[103] If the Commission has already initiated the formal examination procedure, it nonetheless makes mention of the Council's intervention in the termination of the procedure adopted consecutively by the Commission, which is then published in Series C of the Official Journal (see for example the termination in [1999] OJ C120/16).

[104] Art 26(5).

[105] Case C-110/02 *EC Commission v EC Council* para 31.

[106] See the Opinion of AG Cosmas in Case C-122/94 *EC Commission v EC Council* [1996] ECR I-881 para 75. An action for failure to comply with its obligations cannot in principle, therefore, be lodged against the Council if it decides to take no measures.

[107] See, respectively, Case 74/76 *Iannelli* [1977] ECR 557 para 11 and Case 78/76 *Steinike & Weinlig* [1977] ECR 595 para 8, and Case C-225/91 *Matra v EC Commission* [1993] ECR I-3203 para 41.

assessment of a complex economic situation to do with the Council's implementation of the Community's agricultural policy, the Court even came to the conclusion that the Council's discretion extends not only to the nature and scope of the measures to be taken but also, to some extent, to the finding of the basic facts.[108]

21.107 In the case of aid to the wine sector, which concerned agriculture,[109] the Commission brought an action before the ECJ for annulment of a Council decision declaring wine-sector aid paid by France and Italy to be compatible.[110] The Commission argued that when the Council makes use of its powers under the third subparagraph of Article 88(2) it can derogate only from the provisions of Article 87 or regulations provided for by Article 89 of the Treaty and not from other rules of Community law. In this particular case it considered the Council to have derogated from the agricultural legislation. After brief reflection, the ECJ rejected this line of argument on the following grounds: under Article 36 EC the Council had made Articles 87 to 89 applicable to the production of and trade in wines and musts; it followed that the power conferred on the Council by the third subparagraph of Article 88(2) is to apply in the wine sector, within the limits indicated by that provision, namely the existence of exceptional circumstances.[111] Since these exceptional circumstances in fact existed, the Council was entitled in its individual decisions to derogate from the rules of common organisation of the sector in question.[112]

C. Existence of Exceptional Circumstances

21.108 The Council's powers apply only if it can establish the existence of 'exceptional circumstances'. According to Advocate General Cosmas, this term has to be understood as 'the idea of the extraordinary, the unforeseen or, at least, the non permanent, non-continuous and, obviously, something that strays beyond the boundaries of the normal'.[113] According to the Advocate General, 'exceptional circumstances' are facts or situations that might depend on a particular sector or

---

[108] Case C-122/94 *EC Commission v EC Council* [1996] ECR I-881 paras 18 and 19.

[109] Case C-122/94 *EC Commission v EC Council* [1996] ECR I-881.

[110] The considerations made by the Court on this occasion should nonetheless be treated with some caution, given the very specific nature of the case being dealt with. Indeed, Art 88 is applicable only by virtue of secondary Community legislation, namely the Council Regulation on the common organization of the market concerned. It cannot therefore be ruled out that this particular regulatory framework influenced the Court, given the predominance of common agricultural policy objectives over those of competition policy.

[111] Case C-122/94 *EC Commission v EC Council* paras 12 and 13.

[112] Along the same lines, see the Opinion of AG Slynn in Case 253/84 *GAEC de la Ségaude v EC Council and Commission* [1987] ECR I-123.

[113] Opinion in Case C-122/94 *EC Commission v EC Council* [1996] ECR I-881 para 83.

the economy in general but which, assessed in each particular case in a reasonable manner, within the context of a specific Member State and specific sector, show that an alteration of such magnitude has occurred, viewed in relation to situations hitherto considered to be normal, or at least non-extraordinary, that it becomes obvious that the situations existing up to that moment have changed, that new situations have been created and that it was also necessary to take corrective measures, the adoption of which is not provided for by the existing regulations governing the sector concerned.[114]

The ECJ checks whether the exceptional circumstances in fact exist in each particular case. This is therefore a binding limit to be met by the Council. In the light of the political nature of the Council's intervention, however, the Court has been careful in fact to set a wide margin to this limit. It has therefore ruled that, even if the situation of the market concerned was similar to that of previous years, this does not preclude the Council from considering the situation as exceptional.[115]   **21.109**

On the other hand, in the *GAEC de la Ségaude* case, Advocate General Slynn   **21.110**
concluded that a Council decision authorizing aid with the goal of offsetting the loss of revenue suffered by German farmers as a result of the phasing out of the system of monetary compensatory amounts represented an exceeding of its powers insofar as it had not demonstrated that the action was justified on the grounds of the existence of exceptional circumstances.[116] The ECJ has not had the occasion to examine this point.

D. Procedure

Application to the Council by a Member State suspends the examination   **21.111**
underway in the Commission for up to three months. Once this deadline has passed without the Council having defined its position, the Commission can make its own ruling.According to the ECJ, once the three-month deadline has passed, the Council is no longer competent to adopt a decision. The taking of decisions which contradict each other is thereby avoided.[117] The Court has also judged the Council to be no longer competent if the Member State concerned has made no application to the Council before the Commission declares the aid in question to be incompatible.[118]

---

[114] ibid para 85.
[115] Case C-122/94 *EC Commission v EC Council* para 21.
[116] Opinion in Case 253/84 *GAEC de la Ségaude v EC Council and Commission* above.
[117] Case C-110/02 *EC Commission v EC Council* not yet reported, para 32.
[118] ibid para 33. According to AG Mayras, if an application could be made to the Council after the Commission had produced its final decision, the intervention of the Council, 'essentially a

21.112   The Council is not empowered to rule on an aid measure whose aim is to allocate to beneficiaries of the illegal aid previously declared incompatible by a Commission decision an amount designed to compensate for the repayments which they are obliged to make pursuant to that decision. Accepting such a competence would indeed be tantamount to undermining the effectiveness of the decisions taken by the Commission. The aid granted in the second instance is in effect so indissolubly linked to that previously found by the Commission to be incompatible with the common market that it appears largely artificial to claim to make a distinction between those aids for the purposes of applying Article 88(2).[119]

21.113   The fact that the aid has already been implemented does not seem to prevent the case from being brought before the Council. Where the aid has been granted unlawfully, however, there is some doubt about the effect of the Council's involvement on the unlawful character of the aid's implementation. The procedure initiated by the Commission is certainly suspended but the last sentence of Article 88(3) continues to apply, so the aid should still be considered for all intents and purposes as unlawful. A competitor could still bring the matter before a national court, therefore, despite the application made to the Council by the Member State. Applying the principles established in *French Salmon*, there would even be grounds for considering the unlawfulness to persist after the Council's decision declaring it compatible.

21.114   Finally, the Council's declaration of an aid scheme's compatability no doubt rules out any immediate attempt by the Commission to initiate a procedure of appropriate measures under Article 88(1), where the latter has doubts about the compatibility of this scheme. Such a possibility would not be precluded in the medium term, however, if there is any change in the circumstances upon which the Council's decision was based.

---

question of opportuneness', could not then be reconciled with the Commission's acknowledged right of applying to the Court for an action for failure to fulfil an obligation (Opinion in Case 70/72 *EC Commission v Germany* [1973] ECR 813). In the case of an aid scheme, however, it is not at all clear whether a Member State could invite the Council to deal with a file even if the Commission has already adopted a decision, by hypothesis negative. In such a case, the Council could declare the scheme to be compatible, if only with future effect, to avoid directly contradicting the Commission's decision (See the Opinion of AG Mayras in Case 156/77 *EC Commission v Belgium* [1978] ECR 1881, who seems to accept that the effect of a negative decision by the Commission could 'be called into question for the future, [. . .] by a new act of the Commission or Council').

[119] Case C-110/02 *EC Commission v EC Council* paras 37 *et seq.*

22

PRIOR CONTROL OF NEW
NOTIFIED AID

A 'preventive' control procedure has been set up to deal with any new aid (and **22.01**
alterations to existing aid) that the Member States might intend to grant. Only
after having been reviewed under this procedure can the aid be considered to
have been lawfully granted.[1]

Part A gives a definition of what is meant by 'new aid'. The scope of the **22.02**
Member States' previous notification obligation is examined in Part B, while
the subsequent stages of the procedure are dealt with in Parts C (preliminary
procedure) and D (formal procedure). Part E deals with the final decision that
closes the whole procedure.

A. Concept of New Aid

Article 1(c) of the Procedural Regulation defines new aid as 'all aid that is not **22.03**
existing aid, including alterations to existing aid'. All measures to grant or alter
aid must therefore be considered to be new aid[2] and their compatibility with the
common market should be checked by the Commission before they can be
granted. As Advocate General Lenz pointed out, 'The expression "grant or
alteration of aid" refers to [. . .] an event that, by virtue of its potential effects on
the common market, needs to be looked at systematically to check whether the
advantage afforded to the undertaking is compatible with the principles set out
in Article [87](1)'.[3]

New aid has to be notified to the Commission before being granted (notified aid). **22.04**

---

[1] Case C-44/93 *Namur-Les assurances de crédit* [1994] ECR I-3829 para 12, and Case C-367/
95 P *EC Commission v Sytraval* [1998] ECR I-1719 para 35.
[2] Case C-44/93 *Namur-Les assurances du crédit* para 13.
[3] Opinion in Case C-44/93 *Namur-Les Assurances du Crédit* para 59.

Should the public authorities grant the aid before having received authorization from the Commission, the aid is then unlawful (or unlawfully granted).

22.05 The Member States are also bound to submit any 'plans to alter aid' for a preliminary review by the Commission. This concept of the alteration of existing aid is not defined in the Treaty. Its scope has to be interpreted in functional terms and is determined in accordance with the object of the Commission's control procedure.[4]

22.06 According to Article 4 of Regulation 794/2004[5] 'an alteration to existing aid shall mean any change, other than alterations of a purely formal or administrative nature which cannot affect the evaluation of the compatibility of the aid measure with the common market. However an increase in the original budget of an existing aid scheme by up to 20% shall not be considered an alteration to existing aid'.

22.07 Thus, the fact that the legal basis of an aid scheme is altered, without changing the characteristics of the aid itself, should not be construed as an alteration of aid.[6] On the other hand, an extension of time for a measure that was approved for a set period does constitute an alteration, and it therefore has to be approved by the Commission.[7] This is particularly so when the temporary character of the measure was apparently an essential factor in the Commission's decision to declare it compatible; in such a case the extension is tantamount to a substantial alteration of the aid.[8]

22.08 If an alteration affects the very substance of an existing scheme the whole scheme becomes a new aid scheme. Conversely, if the new feature is clearly severable from the initial scheme (for example the extension to new categories of

---

[4] AG Warner has called for a strict interpretation of this concept, otherwise the object of Art 88(3) may be frustrated. He admits, however, under the legal principle of *de minimis non curat lex*, that any amendment that may justly be defined as negligible can be ignored (Opinion in Case 177/78).

[5] Commission Reg (EC) 794/2004 of 21 April 2004 implementing Council Reg (EC) 659/1999 laying down detailed rules for the application of Art 93 of the EC Treaty [2004] OJ L140/1.

[6] See however the strict and somewhat formal stance taken by the ECJ in *Commission v Italy* Case 169/82, paras 9 and 10, where it declares that Art 88(3) applies to laws that are merely a 'single simplifying procedure connected with the establishment of the budget by means of the substantial renewal of existing provisions which are well known and are not contested at Community level'.

[7] See Case 70/72 *EC Commission v Germany* [1973] ECR 813 in which the ECJ considered in para 3 that Germany, under the terms of Art 88(3), had to notify a two-year extension of an aid-establishing law originally approved by the Commission.

[8] Opinion of AG Mayras in Case 70/72 *EC Commission v Germany* [1973] ECR 813. See, for example, the communication on a toll exemption system on the Tauern motorway for undertakings set up in the district of Lungau [1998] OJ C198/6 para 20.

measures or beneficiaries) the procedure can be initiated only to deal with the alteration properly speaking.[9]

The definition of what is an alteration to aid is important, for this will deter- **22.09** mine when there is a need for a new notification to be made to the Commission, pursuant to Article 88(3).[10]

With respect to a 'pre-accession' existing aid scheme, the ECJ has declared that, **22.10** by application of paragraphs 1 and 3 of Article 88, the emergence of new aid or the alteration of existing aid cannot be assessed according to the scale of the aid or, in particular, its amount in financial terms at any moment in the life of the undertaking concerned when the aid is provided under earlier statutory provisions that remain unaltered. According to the Court, the aid can be qualified as new or an alteration to existing aid only in reference to the provisions providing for it, the arrangements and limits thereof.[11] Nonetheless, this judgment should not be construed as meaning that Member States can freely vary the budgets of all of their existing aid schemes.[12]

In principle, when an aid scheme has been approved by the Commission, **22.11** this approval covers future applications of that scheme, which do not therefore have to be examined afresh by the Commission (except, in cases of doubt, to verify that they in fact comply with the conditions under which the scheme was approved). In its scheme approval decision, however, the Commission is entitled to make an exception to that rule and expressly lay it down that certain cases of application should still be notified individually on the basis of Article 88(3). The cases of application in question might concern certain sectors where specific guidelines have been adopted, cases of application exceeding a threshold or even, sometimes, all cases of application of the scheme without distinction.

This prior notification obligation with respect to certain individual cases should **22.12**

---

[9] Joined Cases T-195/01 and T-207/01 *Gibraltar v EC Commission* [2002] ECR II-2309 paras 111–115.

[10] Note however that the alterations of existing schemes are in principle for notification by the simplified procedure (see Art 4(2) of the aforementioned Regulation 794/2004).

[11] Case C-44/93 *Namur-Les assurances du crédit* para 28 (The Court wanted to avoid imposing a notification obligation on all measures that affect the activity of the undertaking and which may have an impact on the functioning of the common market, on competition or simply on the actual amount, over a specific period, of aid which is available in principle but which varies in amount according to the undertaking's turnover).

[12] In this case the Court was dealing with a pre-accession scheme and could not ascertain which characteristics of the scheme would have had decisive importance compatibility-wise in the Commission's eyes. It is therefore logical for it to have chosen to define existing pre-accession aid in terms of the only legal provisions that have established it and defined the scope thereof. The situation would therefore be different for aid that the Commission would have approved in the light, in particular, of its budget.

be considered as a reservation to the scheme approval.[13] This implies that these cases of application are in principle wholly submitted to the new-aid control procedure, despite the scheme being originally approved in principle.[14] In such a case the Commission cannot limit itself to checking that the individual aid in question meets the terms laid down in the scheme approval decision, which would be only a partial examination, but is bound to conduct a complete examination of its compatibility with the terms of Article 87.[15]

B. Prior Notification Obligation for New Aid[16]

1. Prior notification obligation

22.13 According to Article 88(3), the Commission has to be informed of any plans to grant or alter aid in sufficient time to enable it to present its comments. This obligation affects Member States, which are bound to notify their aid projects before putting them into practice, rather than the undertakings that benefit from the aid.[17] This prior notification obligation is the key to the Treaty's whole system of supervision, for it enables the Commission to carry out a pre-emptive examination of all aid plans.[18]

Scope of the notification obligation

22.14 Although the wording of Article 88(3) is not very clear on this matter, the Procedural Regulation has confirmed that the notification obligation applies only to aid fulfilling all of the conditions of Article 87(1).[19] Member States are therefore not systematically bound to notify the Commission of the numerous cases of aid that do not fall within the scope of this provision, either because they do not affect trade between the Member States or because they do not threaten to distort competition (this covers in particular the numerous

---

[13] Joined Cases T-447/93, T-448/93 and T-449/93 *AITEC and others v EC Commission* [1996] ECR II-1631 para 129.

[14] In the *AITEC* case, the CFI considered that this principle applied equally to a case of application of a scheme predating the Commission's approval of the scheme (Joined Cases T-447/93, T-448/93 and T-449/93 *AITEC and others v EC Commission* para 130).

[15] ibid paras 135 and 137.

[16] See Arts 2 *et seq.* of the Procedural Reg.

[17] See Case C-39/94 *SFEI* [1996] ECR I-3547 para 73.

[18] The Commission has often drawn Member States' attention to this obligation (see the communications published in [1980] OJ C252/2, and [1983] OJ C318/3).

[19] See Arts 1(a) and 2(1) of the Procedural Reg and Joined Cases 91 and 127/83 *Heineken Brouwerijen* [1984] ECR 3435 para 11, according to which individuals may invoke a breach of Art 88(3) before a national court 'only if the national measures in question constitute aid within the meaning of Article 92', and Case C-345/02 *Pearle* not yet reported para 31.

subsidies of lesser amounts granted to small local and handicraft undertakings).[20] *De minimis* aid in particular is exempted from the prior notification obligation.

Notification in case of doubt?

It is a moot point whether Member States can themselves determine whether **22.15** the conditions of Article 87(1) are complied with or whether they must necessarily notify all measures where they have any doubts about them. The Commission has sometimes advocated the latter approach,[21] which would seem reasonable[22] and in keeping with the philosophy of a system based on a priori control.

The Member State's obligation will, however, largely depend on the facts of **22.16** the particular case. Thus, according to the ECJ, if the Commission has previously decided that a certain type of measure does constitute aid, a new measure of the same type can only be put into effect if it is clear that it does not constitute aid.[23]

Notification in cases of presumption of aid

The Commission also considers that, when certain conditions are met, notifica- **22.17** tion is required in the case of a 'presumption of aid' pertaining to those circumstances. Such is the case, for example, in any sale of land by a Member

---

[20] cf AG Slynn has claimed in the past that the scope of Art 88 is broader than that of Art 87(1) in that Art 88 would not limit the scope of the notification obligation to aid that distorts or threatens to distort the free play of competition and affects trade between Member States. Those are matters to be examined by the Commission during its review of the aid plan (Opinion in Joined Cases 67, 68 and 70/85 *Van der Kooy v EC Commission* [1988] ECR 219).

[21] See the Communication published in [1983] OJ C318/3: 'As there is no provision for any exception concerning the obligation to inform the Commission "in sufficient time", Member States cannot evade this obligation, even if they consider that the measures they plan do not have all the characteristics described in Article [88](1) [. . .]' Along the same lines, see para 13 of Case C-301/87 *France v EC Commission* [1990] ECR I-307 according to which 'the provisions of Articles 92, 93 and 94 lay down procedures which imply that the Commission is in a position to determine, on the basis of the material at its disposal, whether the disputed financial assistance constitutes aid within the meaning of those Articles'.

[22] According to AG Lenz, 'The very wording of Article 93(3) sentence 1 of the EEC Treaty [. . .] as well as the object and goal of this provision plead in favour of a wide-ranging information obligation incumbent on the Member States, since it is desirable as far as possible to head off any differences of opinion between the Commission and the Member States on the lawfulness of aid. The information obligation laid down in Article 93(3) of the EEC Treaty thus concerns not only the aid cases where it suffices to vet the compatibility with the EEC Treaty but also the measures whose classification as aid might appear doubtful' (Opinion in Case 40/85 *Belgium v EC Commission* [1986] ECR 2321).

[23] Joined Cases 67, 68 and 70/85 R *Van der Kooy v EC Commission* [1985] ECR 1315 para 43.

State that was not concluded on the basis of an open and unconditional tendering procedure or without any independent expert valuation.[24]

22.18 As regards public authorities' holdings with characteristics that give rise to a presumption of aid, the Commission asks the Member States to send it 'preliminary information' and reserves the right to decide within fifteen days whether or not there are grounds for considering this information to be a notification within the meaning of Article 88(3).[25]

22.19 It should be noted, finally, that the obligation notification also applies to aid likely to benefit from an authorization under Article 87(2), for the Commission has to check that it meets the requisite conditions; also worthy of note is that fact that, to reinforce its control, the Commission permanently vets transfers from public funds to undertakings in the public or private sector.[26]

Notification of an individual case of application of aid schemes

22.20 Once a general aid scheme has been approved by the Commission, the individual cases of application represent the implementation of an existing scheme and do not have to be notified unless a reservation to this effect was made by the Commission in its approval decision. Indeed, since the individual grants of aid are merely measures implementing the general aid scheme, the factors to be taken into account by the Commission in its assessment would be the same as those applied in the examination of the scheme. In principle, therefore, there is no need to submit individual grants of aid for examination by the Commission.[27]

Purpose, contents, and arrangements of the notification

22.21 The purpose of the notification is to give the Commission the chance to exert its control over all plans to grant or alter aid, doing so in the appropriate time and in the general interest of the Communities.[28]

22.22 The content of the notification is important because it is on the basis thereof

---

[24] Communication on State aid elements in sales of land and buildings by public authorities [1997] OJ C209/3 para 3.

[25] Section 4.4 of the Communication on the application of Arts 92 and 93 of the EEC Treaty to public authorities' holdings, *EC Bull.*, 9, 1984.

[26] 'Transparency Directive' of 25 June 1980 and Communication on the application of Arts 92 and 93 of the EEC Treaty to public authorities' holdings, *EC Bull.*, 9, 1984 (By virtue of this text, Member States are in particular bound to furnish *a posteriori* annual reports on certain public authority holdings).

[27] Case C-47/91 *Italy v EC Commission* [1994] ECR I-4635 para 21.

[28] Case C-301/87 *France v EC Commission* [1990] ECR I-307 para 17, and Joined Cases T-126/96 and T-127/97 *Breda Fucine Meridionali and others v EC Commission* [1998] ECR II-3437 para 46.

that any necessary clarification of the scope of the Commission's decision will be made.[29]

The notification therefore needs to be sufficiently clear and complete to enable the Commission to reach a decision. As pointed out by Advocate General Jacobs, 'the obligation to notify proposed aids is of such manifest importance for the functioning of the common market that, in the absence of any Council regulations on the matter, it is plain that the obligation must be rigorously observed both as to content and as to form, and it is essential, in particular, that the notification should make it clear beyond doubt that its purpose is to enable the Commission to submit its comments under Article 93(3) and if necessary to initiate the procedure provided for in Article 93(2) before the proposed aid is implemented'.[30]   **22.23**

The notification has to be complete.[31] The notification is 'considered as complete' if the Commission does not ask for further information within a given time period.[32]   **22.24**

The State is bound in particular to indicate the compatibility criterion serving as grounds for its claim, failing which the Commission cannot be held liable for having failed to examine it.[33]   **22.25**

The Commission has indicated to Member States the information that needs to be included in their notification for it to be considered as complete.[34]   **22.26**

When the aid financing method is an integral part of the measure, the notification must also cover this financing method so that the Commission can conduct its examination on the basis of all the facts.[35]   **22.27**

Subsequent alterations

If subsequent alterations are made to an initial aid plan these alterations also have to be brought to the Commission's notice: **22.28**

- If the Commission has not yet ruled on the initial notification, such information may be supplied to the Commission in the course of the consultations

---

[29] The ECJ has ruled, on the basis of a notification by Germany, that the Commission's decision has neither the purpose nor the effect of rejecting an additional request of that Member State (Case C-242/00 *Germany v EC Commission*).

[30] Para 19 of the Opinion in Case C-301/87 *France v EC Commission* [1990] ECR I-307.

[31] See Art 2(2) of the Procedural Reg.

[32] Art 4(5) of the Procedural Reg.

[33] Case C-382/99 *Netherlands v EC Commission* [2002] ECR I-5163 para 84.

[34] Regulation 794/2004.

[35] Case C-345/02 *Pearle* para 30.

which take place between the Commission and the Member State concerned following the initial notification.[36]

- On the contrary, if these alterations take place after the Commission's decision, a new notification of them has to be made under the terms of Article 88(3). In particular no Member State will be entitled to unilaterally extend the scope of an initial aid-scheme authorization by means of a post-authorization alteration thereof.[37]

22.29 The CFI seems to have confirmed the Commission's requirement to the effect that, for a notification to be accepted as valid, a communication from the national authorities to the Commission must make an express reference to Article 88(3) and be presented to the Commission's Secretariat General.[38]

Publicizing the notification

22.30 The notification of an aid plan made to the Commission by a Member State does not have to be brought to the notice of all interested parties, whether by the notifying State or the Commission, unless the Commission decides to open the procedure under Article 88(2).[39]

Withdrawal of the notification

22.31 Should the Member State decide not to grant the aid after having notified the Commission, it is entitled to withdraw its notification.

Exemption from the notification obligation

22.32 The Council is authorized under Article 89 to exempt certain categories of aid from the previous notification obligation. It has made use of this authority in the block exemption regulation.[40]

2. Suspension obligation

22.33 According to the last sentence of Article 88(3), the Member State concerned cannot put the planned measures into effect until the procedure has run its

---

[36] Joined Cases 91/83 and 127/83 *Heineken Brouwerijen* [1984] ECR 3435 para 17. These alterations to an aid plan notified during the investigation phase do not therefore have to be formally notified to the Commission by means of a new and separate notification (see however the ambiguously worded last sentence of para 13 of Case C-44/93 *Namur-Les assurances du crédit*, which would seem to call for a formal notification of the said alterations).

[37] Case T-109/01 *Fleuren Compost v EC Commission* para 80.

[38] Joined Cases T-126/96 and T-127/96 *Breda Fucine Meridionali and others v EC Commission* para 47.

[39] *Heineken Brouwerijen*, above para 15.

[40] See paras 21.82 *et seq.*

course. The Member State is hence bound to suspend the implementation of the aid until such time as the Commission has pronounced on its compatibility with the common market, failing which it is unlawful to grant the aid. This standstill arrangement for new aid is intended to ensure that the aid measures do not come into effect before the Commission has had a reasonable time to examine the aid plan in detail and, if need be, initiate the formal examination procedure.[41] The standstill lasts throughout the preliminary phase, during which the Member State concerned cannot implement the aid plan.[42] Should the examination procedure provided for in Article 88(2) be initiated, this standstill will last until such time as the Commission gives its final decision.[43] Compliance with this standstill obligation, which has direct effect, determines the lawfulness of the aid being implemented.

According to the ECJ, the final sentence of Article 88 is the means of safeguarding the review machinery laid down by that Article, which, in turn, is essential for ensuring the proper functioning of the common market. It therefore follows that even if the Member State deems the aid measure to be compatible with the common market, this does not entitle it to defy the clear provisions of Article 88.[44]   **22.34**

Should a Member State make any alterations to a previously approved aid scheme without informing the Commission, the Court has held that the final sentence of Article 88(3) precludes the implementation of the aid scheme in its entirety, unless the alteration in question is in fact a different aid measure that should be assessed separately and therefore does not impinge on the Commission's initial assessment of the plan.[45]   **22.35**

Concept of putting aid into effect

To ascertain the scope of the standstill obligation incumbent on Member States it is necessary first of all to determine what is to be understood by the 'putting into effect' or implementation of aid. In principle, aid is considered to have been implemented from the moment that a responsible authority has entered into a legally binding agreement to that effect.[46] The Commission thus refers to   **22.36**

---

[41] *Heineken Brouwerijen* para 20 and Case C-301/87 *France v EC Commission* para 17.
[42] In particular Joined Cases C-278/92, C-279/92 and C-280/92 *Spain v EC Commission* para 14.
[43] Case 120/73 *Lorenz* [1973] ECR 1471 para 4; Case 171/83 R *EC Commission v France* [1983] ECR 2621 para 13; Case 310/85 *Deufil v EC Commission* para 24 and Case C-367/95 P *EC Commission v Sytraval* para 37.
[44] Joined Cases 31/77 R and 53/77 R *EC Commission v United Kingdom* [1977] ECR 921 and Case 171/83 R *EC Commission v France* para 12.
[45] Joined Cases 91/83 and 127/83 *Heineken Brouwerijen* para 21.
[46] Case T-109/01 *Fleuren Compost v EC Commission* para 74.

the act of implementing or instituting the aid at a legislative level and according to the constitutional rules of the Member State concerned. Aid is therefore deemed to have been put into effect as soon as the legislative machinery enabling it to be granted, without the need for any further formalities, has been set up.[47] Aid can therefore be considered to have been put into effect even if the actual money has not yet been granted to the beneficiary. A Member State will therefore be in breach of its obligations under Article 88(3) if it fails to notify the Commission of any draft legislation instituting aid schemes until after they have passed as legislation.[48]

22.37 This definition implies that aid measures should be notified to the Commission when they are still at the draft stage, i.e. before being put into effect and while they can still be modified in line with any observations the Commission might like to make. Given that Article 88(3) contains no formal criteria, the onus is on each Member State to determine at which stage of the procedure, legislative or otherwise, it should submit the plan for the Commission's examination, always on condition that the plan is not put into effect before the Commission has pronounced on its compatibility with the common market.[49]

22.38 When a decision in principle to grant aid has been made subject to a reservation (standstill clause) linked with the Commission's declaration of compatibility, the latter considers that the aid in question has not been put into effect nor has it been granted unlawfully.[50] Conversely, once the aid has effectively been paid out to its beneficiary, there is automatically a breach of the final sentence of Article 88(3), and it is not then possible to remedy this breach simply by providing for a revision clause to bring it into line with the Community rules or any similar sort of clause. In other words, such clauses do not cancel the unlawful character of the aid[51] for the aid has already produced its economic effects.

C. Preliminary Examination Procedure for Notified Aid

22.39 At the end of a common preliminary procedure, the procedure then followed by the Commission for pronouncing on aid compatibility can take two different

---

[47] Letter to Member States SG (89) D/5521 of 27 April 1989, in: *EC Competition Law*, Vol IIA, 1999, 64.
[48] Case 169/82 *EC Commission v Italy* [1984] ECR 1603 para 11.
[49] Case T-188/95 *Waterleiding v EC Commission* [1998] ECR II-3713 para 118.
[50] Decision of 15 November 2000 on the State aid that Italy is planning to grant to Solar Tech [2001] OJ L292/45 para 3.2.1.
[51] Decision of 30 April 1997 concerning aid granted by Spain to the undertaking Casa [1997] OJ L331/10 para VIII.

paths: sometimes the aid can be declared to be compatible straightaway, by means of a 'decision not to raise objections'; on other occasions the Commission resorts to the more complex arrangements of the formal examination procedure contained in Article 88(2).

As regards the procedure laid down in Article 88, a distinction has to be made **22.40** between the preliminary examination phase and the formal examination procedure. The preliminary examination phase laid down in Article 88(3) has the sole object of allowing the Commission to form a prima facie opinion on the partial or total conformity of the aid in question (and, previously, on whether it does in fact qualify as aid).[52] The purpose of the formal examination procedure of Article 88(2) is to allow the Commission to be fully informed of all the facts of the case.[53]

1. Preliminary examination procedure

When the Commission learns of any new aid plan, it must carry out immedi- **22.41** ately a preliminary evaluation of its compatibility. The Member State cannot put the measure into effect before having notified the Commission; this prohibition is effective throughout the whole of the preliminary stage.[54]

The fact that it is a preliminary examination does not, however, prevent the **22.42** Commission from carrying out enquiries in this period and gathering supplementary information. It is not necessarily bound to limit itself to examining the notified aid plan.[55]

2. Commission examination deadline

'Lorenz' time-limit

The Commission has an initial time period of two months for reacting to **22.43** the notification made by the Member State. By setting this time-limit in its Article 4, the Procedural Regulation has endorsed the so-called *Lorenz* time-limit, the name 'Lorenz' being taken from the case of that name. In 1973, the Court ruled that in stating that the Commission shall be informed of plans to grant new or alter existing aid 'in sufficient time to enable it to submit its comments', the intention of the Treaty was to provide this institution with

---

[52] Case 84/82 *Germany v EC Commission* [1984] ECR 1451 para 11, and Case C-198/91 *Cook v EC Commission* [1993] ECR I-2487 para 22.

[53] Case C-198/91 *Cook v EC Commission* para 22; Case C-225/91 *Matra v EC Commission* [1993] ECR I-3203 para 16 and Case C-367/95 P *EC Commission v Sytraval* [1998] ECR I-1719 para 38.

[54] Case 84/82 *Germany v EC Commission* para 11.

[55] See the Opinion of AG Slynn in Case 84/82 *Germany v EC Commission* [1984] ECR 1451.

sufficient time for consideration and investigation to form a prima facie opinion on the partial or complete conformity with the Treaty of the plans notified to it. It is only after being put in a position to form this opinion that the Commission is bound, if it considers the plan incompatible with the common market, to initiate without delay the formal examination procedure.[56] The Commission must act with due expedition in order to take account of the Member States' interest in obtaining clarification in cases in which there may be an urgent need to take action.[57] It therefore has a time limit for carrying out this preliminary examination, a time-limit set by the Court at two months in keeping with Articles 230 and 232 of the Treaty.[58] This is a mandatory time-limit.[59] The Commission has set itself a shorter time limit for certain types of aid.

22.44 If the Commission fails to come to a decision or has not asked for any further information from the Member State concerned by the end of this two-month time period, this Member State can then make the necessary arrangements to implement its aid plan. It must however first notify the Commission,[60] if need be simply by fax.[61] The Commission then has an additional period of fifteen days to take a decision[62] and notify the Member State;[63] once this period has ended, the aid becomes existing.

Consequence of inaction by the Commission

22.45 When the aid has been put into effect at the end of the *Lorenz* time-limit without any ruling from the Commission, this cannot be construed to mean that the aid is in fact compatible with the Treaty. At most it becomes existing aid. In principle it is then governed by the provisions of Article 88(1) and (3)[64] (but aid granted as a lump sum cannot then be made the object of appropriate measures).

---

[56] Case 120/73 *Lorenz* [1973] ECR 1471 para 3.

[57] Case 84/82 *Germany v EC Commission* para 11.

[58] Case 171/83 R *EC Commission v France* para 13.

[59] Case C-334/99 *Germany v EC Commission* [2003] ECR I-1139 para 49.

[60] On this matter the Procedural Regulation has confirmed the case law of the ECJ, whereby the demands of legal certainty mean that the Member State, after the two month period has run its course, should give previous notice to the Commission before putting its aid plans into effect (Case 171/83 R *EC Commission v France* para 14 and *Lorenz* para 4; Case 84/82 *Germany v EC Commission* para 11 and Case C-312/90 *Spain v EC Commission* [1992] ECR I-4117 para 18).

[61] Case C-398/00 *Spain v EC Commission* para 23.

[62] Art 4(6) Procedural Reg.

[63] According to the strict interpretation of Case C-398/00 *Spain v EC Commission* [2002] ECR I-5643 para 32.

[64] Case 120/73 *Lorenz* [1973] ECR 1471 para 5. The silence of the Commission should not therefore be seen as a legitimate way of approving notified aid. In view of the Commission's examination obligation, it would be anomalous for potentially incompatible aid to become existing aid due to an oversight of the Commission.

Extension of the Lorenz time-limit

In practice the two-month time-limit is often extended by mutual agreement; **22.46** this is not possible without the State's express consent thereto.[65] Nonetheless, a long extension might be a sign that the Commission has run into difficulties which should have prompted it to initiate the formal examination procedure.[66]

This two-month time-limit does not start to run until the Commission is in **22.47** possession of a complete notification.[67]

3. Decision not to lodge an objection

At the end of its preliminary examination of the aid, the Commission can **22.48** either adopt a decision not to raise objections or alternatively decide to open the formal examination procedure of Article 88(2). The decision not to raise objections brings the procedure to an end and authorises the aid to be put into effect.

Content

'Decision not to raise objections' means the Commission's decision addressed to **22.49** the Member State in question declaring without further ado either that the measure in question does not constitute aid or that it constitutes aid that is compatible with the Treaty (Article 4 of the Procedural Regulation). In particular, if the Commission declares that the aid is compatible, then the aid in question, granted after the Commission's approval, becomes 'existing aid' and is subject to the permanent review laid down in Article 88(1). In practice, the Commission can also reach the conclusion that it is an individual application of an existing aid scheme.

Decisions not to classify the measure as aid

Even though the Treaty only lays down the review procedure with reference to **22.50** the compatibility of measures, it follows from the practice of the Commission,

---

[65] Art 4(5) of the Procedural Reg. Case C-334/99 *Germany v EC Commission* para 50.

[66] See Case 84/82 *Germany v EC Commission* para 15, in which the Court rules that a sixteen-month time period from the initial notification to the decision not to raise objections 'well exceeds the period normally required for a preliminary examination under Article [88](3).'

[67] AG Tesauro shares this opinion on condition that it does not entail a *de facto* transfer during the preliminary phase of examinations and assessments that should rightly take place only under the procedure laid down in Article 88(2) and with the full guarantees thereof (Opinion in Case C-198/91 *Cook v EC Commission* [1993] ECR I-2487 para 11). cf AG Slynn does not accept the argument that a request for information stops time running until the answer is received as otherwise the 'administration' could in all cases and more than once extend time by asking for information (Opinion in Case 223/85 *RSV v EC Commission* [1987] ECR 4617).

case law and the Procedural Regulation (Article 4(2)) that decisions not to raise objections can also have the object of deciding that a measure cannot be classified as aid.

22.51   To declassify a measure as aid the Commission often issues comfort letters to the requesting Member States, setting forth its informal point of view on the basis of the information that the Member State has furnished.

Procedural arrangements

22.52   One of the main traits distinguishing the formal examination procedure of Article 88(2) from the preliminary phase of Article 88(3) is that the Commission is under no obligation whatsoever at the preliminary stage to give notice to the parties concerned to submit their comments before taking its decision.[68] In the preliminary phase third parties are therefore totally excluded from the examination procedure; they receive no information and have no right to present information, much less to be heard. In the case of unlawful aid the same goes for any complainant who has reported the allegedly unlawful aid to the Commission.

Conditions

22.53   The Commission may restrict itself to the preliminary examination under Article 88(3) when taking a decision in favour of a plan to grant aid only if it is convinced after the preliminary examination that the plan is compatible with the Treaty.[69] In it has any doubts, however, it must initiate the formal examination procedure.

Appeal procedures

22.54   A decision not to raise objections is in principle favourable to the Member State concerned, so it should by rights give rise to no appeal by the latter or the beneficiary undertaking.[70] Third parties, for their part, are entirely excluded from the preliminary procedure, so their only possibility of contesting the decision is to assert before the Community Court that the Commission has made a mistake or should have initiated the formal examination procedure. The ECJ has therefore recognized that such a decision by the Commission was an

---

[68] Case 84/82 *Germany v EC Commission* para 13; Case C-198/91 *Cook v EC Commission* para 22; Case C-225/91 *Matra v EC Commission* para 53 and Case T-266/94 *Skibsværftsforeningen and others v EC Commission* [1996] ECR II-1399 para 257.

[69] Case 84/82 *Germany v EC Commission* para 13.

[70] See however the appeal lodged by the French Republic in Case C-241/94 *France v EC Commission* [1996] ECR I-4551 against the Commission's decision not to raise objections. France considered that the measure in question was not aid and should not therefore have given rise to a declaration of compatibility.

adversely affecting act against which it is possible to bring an action for annulment.

Publication

Summaries of decisions not to raise objections are published in the Official **22.55** Journal series C. This publication takes the form of an 'information box', which sums up the main characteristics of the aid (amount, beneficiaries, etc). This publication, however, does not always allow provide details of the scope of the Commission's decisions.[71]

D. Formal Examination Procedure for Notified Aid[72]

If the Commission is not in a position to decide outright to raise no objection **22.56** to the aid, it has to resort to the formal examination procedure laid down in Article 88(2) EC.

1. Opening of the procedure

Doubts about the compatibility of the aid (Article 4 of the Procedural Regulation)

As soon as the Commission encounters difficulties in deciding whether an aid **22.57** plan is compatible with the common market, it is bound to initiate the formal examination procedure laid down in Article 88(2). Indeed, if the preliminary phase has convinced the Commission that the aid is incompatible, or has not (objectively[73]) enabled it to overcome all the difficulties raised by the assessment of the compatibility of the State measure in question with the common market, it is duty bound to obtain all necessary opinions.[74]

Doubts about the existence of aid

Although neither Article 88 EC nor the Procedural Regulation makes any express **22.58** provision on this point, it is generally accepted that the formal examination

---

[71] Art 26(1) of the Procedural Reg.

[72] Besides the case of notified aid, the formal examination procedure can be opened to cover three other situations, namely the examination of any unlawful aid (see para 23.13), misuse of aid (see para 25.13) and when a Member State rejects the appropriate measures proposed by the Commission concerning an existing aid scheme (see para 24.44).

[73] Case T-114/00 *ARE v EC Commission* [2002] ECR II-5121 para 48.

[74] Case 84/82 *Germany v EC Commission* para 13; Case C-198/91 *Cook v EC Commission* para 29; Case C-225/91 *Matra v EC Commission* para 33; Case T-49/93 *SIDE v EC Commission* [1995] ECR II-2501 para 58; Joined Cases T-126/96 and T-127/96 *Breda Fucine Meridionali and others v EC Commission* [1998] ECR II-3437 para 44 and Joined Cases T-195/01 and T-207/01 *Government of Gibraltar v EC Commission* [2002] ECR II-2309 para 72.

procedure can and, if need be, must be opened to solve any doubts about whether a measure does in fact constitute aid coming within the scope of Article 87(1).[75] In this case, however, according to the CFI, the Commission is only bound to initiate the procedure when its initial examination has not enabled it to overcome all doubts about whether the measure concerned, assuming that this measure does in fact constitute aid, is in any case compatible with the common market.[76] This implies, in principle, that the State cannot put the measure into effect until the Commission has closed the procedure. The Commission brings this procedure to an end in classic fashion, by adopting a final decision.[77]

Control

22.59 The need to initiate the procedure has to be determined by the Commission, subject to the control of the Community Courts, depending on the factual and legal circumstances involved in the case.[78] The existence of any difficulties is evaluated by the Community Courts in an objective manner, comparing the grounds of the decision with the information available to the Commission when it took a decision on the compatibility of the disputed aid with the common market.[79] Signs of the fact that the Commission should initiate the procedure are the length of its discussions with the Member State and the fact that the initial plan has to be altered to be able to be declared compatible,[80] the link existing between the measure under examination and other measures for which a procedure has been initiated,[81] the Commission's inability to produce the clear calculations made at the time of the preliminary examination,[82] etc.

22.60 On the other hand the obligation to initiate the procedure does not depend on the aid's implementation conditions (notified aid or unlawful aid) or the provision of Article 87 that is applied.[83] Moreover, again according to the ECJ, the amount of the investment or aid in question cannot in itself constitute a serious difficulty, as otherwise the Commission would be obliged to initiate

---

[75] See, implicitly, Case T-95/94 *Sytraval v EC Commission* [1995] ECR II-2651 para 79 *in fine*, and, explicitly, Case T-11/95 *BP Chemicals v EC Commission* [1998] ECR II-3235 para 166.

[76] Case T-11/95 *BP Chemicals v EC Commission* para 166 and Joined Cases T-269/99, T-271/99 and T-272/99 *Territorio Histórico de Guipúzcoa and others v EC Commission* [2002] ECR II-4217 para 45 and Joined Cases T-346/99, T-347/99 and T-348/99 *Territorio Histórico de Álava and others v EC Commission* [2002] ECR II-4259 para 41.

[77] For a closure decision of this type, see the Communication concerning the aid granted to the undertaking Gildemeister [1998] OJ C181/4.

[78] Case C-198/91 *Cook v EC Commission* para 30.

[79] Case T-49/93 *SIDE v EC Commission* para 60.

[80] Case 84/82 *Germany v EC Commission* paras 14–17.

[81] Case T-11/95 *BP Chemicals v EC Commission* paras 170 *et seq.*

[82] ibid para 193.

[83] Case C-198/91 *Cook v EC Commission* para 30.

the procedure under Article 88(2) whenever the investment or aid exceeded a certain level, which would moreover have to be defined.[84] Likewise, supplementation of the original scheme by the Member State with additional information and detail cannot be considered to be significant alterations complying with the conditions laid down by the Commission and justifying the initiation of the procedure. Finally, the obligation imposed on the Member State to produce an annual assessment report cannot be considered to be proof of the existence of serious assessment difficulties.[85]

Purpose of the formal examination procedure

The goal of this procedure is twofold: firstly, to oblige the Commission to **22.61** ensure that all persons who may be concerned, including other Member States, are notified and given an opportunity of putting forward their arguments;[86] secondly it enables the Commission to obtain all necessary opinions and become completely clear about all the facts of the case before taking its definitive decision on whether the measure can be classified as aid and, if so, if it is compatible with the common market.[87]

Contents and scope of the decision to initiate the procedure

The formal examination procedure can be initiated only by a 'decision' within **22.62** the meaning of Article 249(4) EC.[88] According to Article 6 of the Procedural Regulation, the decision to initiate the procedure summarizes the relevant issues of fact and law, including a 'preliminary assessment' of the measure and also gives the grounds for any doubts about its compatibility. The nature of the information to be furnished is determined by the need of permitting the interested parties to participate effectively in the procedure.

Assessment of the nature of the aid

Given that the decision to initiate the procedure represents only a 'preliminary **22.63** assessment' of the nature of the aid, the CFI considers that the classification of

---

[84] Case C-225/91 *Matra v EC Commission* para 36.
[85] ibid para 38.
[86] Case 323/82 *Intermills v EC Commission* para 17. In the particular case of an aid beneficiary concerned in the initiation of the procedure, the Commission in principle asks the Member State to inform it of the opening of the procedure as soon as possible.
[87] Case 84/82 *Germany v EC Commission* para 13; Case T-266/94 *Skibsværftsforeningen and others v EC Commission* para 256; Joined Cases T-371/94 and T-394/94 *British Airways and others v EC Commission* [1998] ECR 11-2405 para 58, and Joined Cases T-269/99, T-271/99 and T-272/99 *Territorio Histórico de Guipúzcoa and others v EC Commission* paras 47 and 93, and Joined Cases T-346/99, T-347/99 and T-348/99 *Territorio Histórico de Álava and others v EC Commission* paras 43 and 89.
[88] Joined Cases T-195/01 and T-207/01 *Government of Gibraltar v EC Commission* para 74.

the measure as State aid does not have a definitive character: this decision is necessarily provisional, as is the assessment of its compatibility with the common market.[89] According to the CFI, the fact that the Commission does not expressly state any doubts in the decision to initiate the procedure about the classification of the measure in dispute as State aid does not in any way show that this classification is not provisional; it considers in effect that, in a decision to initiate the procedure, the Commission is only bound to state expressly its doubts about the compatibility of the measure with the common market.[90]

Assessment of the nature of new aid

22.64 The initiation of the procedure also has the effect of confirming the Commission's classification as new aid (or misuse of existing aid) of the measure under examination, which is thenceforth subjected to the standstill effect contained in the last sentence of Article 88(3). The classification of the measure as new aid is equally provisional, limited in time until the conclusion of the formal procedure.[91] This implies that an initiation decision is a contestable act, inasmuch as it could, in particular, be used before a national court for proving the breach of the previous notification obligation.

Assessment of the compatibility

22.65 The Commission can only set forth its 'doubts' which does not prejudge its final decision.

Penalizing of the failure to initiate the procedure

22.66 Wrongful omission by the Commission to initiate the formal examination procedure before ruling on the existence and compatibility of aid constitutes an essential procedural infringement which, in the event of litigation, automatically renders null and void the decision not to raise objections.[92] Indeed, in so acting the Commission infringes the procedural rights of the applicant as a party concerned within the meaning of Article 88(2).[93]

---

[89] Joined Cases T-269/99, T-271/99 and T-272/99 *Territorio Histórico de Guipúzcoa and others v EC Commission* paras 47 and 82, and Joined Cases T-346/99, T-347/99 and T-348/99 *Territorio Histórico de Álava and others v EC Commission* paras 43, 75 and 78, and Case T-190/00 *Regione Siciliana v EC Commission* not yet reported para 48.

[90] *Territorio Histórico de Guipúzcoa and others v EC Commission* para 84 and *Territorio Histórico de Álava and others v EC Commission* para 77.

[91] Case T-190/00 *Regione Siciliana v EC Commission* para 46.

[92] Case 84/82 *Germany v EC Commission* para 19.

[93] Case T-11/95 *BP Chemicals v EC Commission* para 200.

Cases in which the Commission is not empowered to initiate the procedure

For certain aid in favour of agriculture, the Commission, even if it judges the aid **22.67** to be incompatible with the common market, is not entitled to initiate the procedure laid down in Article 88(2) but only to give its recommendations.

2. Extension of the procedure

The Commission will extend the procedure when new facts come to light after **22.68** the initiation of the procedure and these new facts might affect the final decision. These facts are usually either ones that the Commission discovers during the procedure or alterations to the aid under examination, proposed by the State concerned to facilitate the Commission's approval. On the contrary, when any alterations do not change the main elements of the aid and therefore seem unlikely to affect the contents of the final decision, the Commission considers that it is authorized not to extend the procedure, so as not to lengthen the examination of the file unduly.[94]

A particular case arises when, during the examination of aid that is to be granted **22.69** to an undertaking, the Commission is informed of the existence of other aid, whether notified or unlawful, in favour of the same beneficiary, which was not taken into account at the time of initiating the procedure. In this case the Commission will either deal with the aids in separate procedures or in an overall manner, particularly when they mutually affect each other, in extending the initial procedure to aid that has subsequently come to light.[95] The danger of this second approach, when public authorities proceed to pay out aid regularly to an undertaking in breach of Article 88(3), is that it might postpone the adoption of a final decision almost indefinitely.[96]

---

[94] The Commission has thus declined to extend the procedure when it is notified of a cost overrun of limited importance that does not modify the characteristics of the aid (see, for example, the Decisions of 1 February 1995 concerning State aid to Georgsmarienhütte [1995] OJ L257/37 s VI 44, and of 4 April 1995 concerning aid to Neue Mahütte Stahlwerke, Sulzbag-Rosenberg and Lech-Stahlwerke [1995] OJ L253/22), which would seem to be reasonable, or when a Member State renounces the privatisation procedure that formed part of the restructuring plan described in the initiation of the procedure (Decision of 21 January 1998 granting provisional approval to the aid that France has decided to grant to Société Française de Production [1998] OJ L205/68 s 4), which would seem to be more doubtful.

[95] See, e.g. the extension of the procedure concerning the aid that the German government intends to grant to Dieselmotorenwerk Rostock [1998] OJ C169/8.

[96] See the procedure initiated in September 1994 and extended in 1998 to cover additional aid paid out in the meantime (Communication on the subject of aid granted by Italy to Seleco [1998] OJ C155/24).

3. Suspensive effect

22.70 The initiation of the formal examination procedure has the effect of extending the standstill situation arising under Article 88(3), last sentence.[97] As far as new aid is concerned, this standstill effect associated with the initiation of the procedure cannot be broken unless the Member State obtains an approval decision from the Council on the basis of the third subparagraph of Article 88(2),[98] which sometimes occurs, or when the Member State has lodged an action for annulment against the decision to initiate the procedure on the grounds, for example, that the measure manifestly cannot be classified as aid and it requests and obtains provisional measures from the ECJ;[99] this has never actually happened in practice.

4. Procedural arrangements

Burden of proof

22.71 When the Commission decides to open the formal procedure, the onus is on the Member State and the potential recipient of aid to put forward the arguments in which they seek to show that the planned aid corresponds to the exceptions provided for in the application of the Treaty. Although the Commission is required to express its doubts clearly, the fact remains that it is for the aid applicant to dispel those doubts.[100]

Participation of the Member State concerned

22.72 The procedure laid down by Article 88(2) takes place primarily between the Commission and the Member State concerned.[101] Indeed, by virtue of its very structure, the administrative procedure is opened only against the Member State concerned in terms of its Community aid-granting obligations.[102] It is also the Member State that is the addressee of the Commission's final decision. All this justifies the Member States' privileged status in terms of contacts with the Commission[103] and in particular their rights to a fair defence.[104]

---

[97] Case 120/73 *Lorenz* para 8.

[98] For more information on this procedure see para 21.100.

[99] See the Opinion of AG Mayras in Case 156/77 *EC Commission v Belgium* [1978] ECR 1881.

[100] Case T-176/01 *Ferriere Nord v EC Commission* paras 93–94.

[101] Case T-366/00 *Scott v EC Commission* [2003] ECR II-1763 para 59 and Case T-369/00 *Département de Loiret v EC Commission* [2003] ECR II-1789 para 84.

[102] Joined Cases T-228/99 and T-233/99 *WestLB and others v EC Commission* [2003] ECR II-435 para 122; Case T-109/01 *Fleuren Compost v EC Commission* para 42 and Case T-198/01 *TGI v EC Commission* not yet reported para 191.

[103] Case T-198/01 *TGI v EC Commission* para 61. On this matter see Art 6(2) of the Procedural Reg.

[104] Case T-176/01 *Ferriere Nord v EC Commission* not yet reported para 74.

According to settled case law, the right to be heard is, in all proceedings initiated **22.73** against a person that are liable to culminate in a measure adversely affecting that person, a fundamental principle of Community law.[105] This principle means that the Member State involved in the process has to be allowed to make effectively known its point of view on the observations made by third parties pursuant to Article 88(2), upon which the Commission intends to base its decision. The Commission's decision may therefore be based only on information that the Member State was previously afforded the opportunity of commenting on.[106]

Penalty for failure to give a Member State a proper hearing Should the **22.74** Commission base its decision on documents to which the Member State has not been afforded access, the Community Courts do not take a dogmatic stance, but rather examine the importance of access to those documents in the context of the administrative procedure as a whole, analysing whether this has prevented the Member State from effectively making known its point of view on the situation and the pertinence of the facts, grievances and circumstances alleged by the Commission.[107]

In practice As a general rule, the Commission services' consultations with the **22.75** Member State concerned are made in successive stages. First of all the Member State reacts to the Commission' letter on the initiating of the procedure, addressed to the former and informing it of the measures in dispute.[108] At this point, the Commission often chooses to initiate the procedure as a means of requesting from the Member State certain information or documents it deems to be essential for carrying out its examination properly.[109] The State then receives a copy of any third-party comments received by the Commission and is given the opportunity to make its own comments on these texts, doing so within a set time-limit that does not normally exceed one month (Article 6(2) of the Procedural Regulation). The contacts made thereafter with the Member State vary according to the particular case. Meetings are frequently held between the Commission services and the State representatives to clarify their respective positions. The discussions between the Member State and the Commission are

---

[105] Joined Cases T-228/99 and T-233/99 *WestLB and others v EC Commission* [2003] ECR II-435 para 121.

[106] Case 234/84 *Belgium v EC Commission* [1986] ECR 2263 para 30 and Case 40/85 para 30; Case 259/85 *France v EC Commission* [1987] ECR 4393 para 12; Case C-301/87 *France v EC Commission* paras 29 and 30; Case C-142/87 *Belgium v EC Commission* paras 46 and 47, and Case T-198/01 *TGI v EC Commission* para 201.

[107] Joined Cases T-228/99 and T-233/99 *WestLB and others v EC Commission* paras 150 *et seq.*

[108] Case T-323/99 *INMA and Itainvest v EC Commission* [2002] ECR II-545 para 91.

[109] See, e.g. the many documents and copious information requested in the initiation of procedure relating to State aid granted to Crédit Mutuel [1998] OJ C146/6.

necessarily more thorough than those conducted with the interested parties in terms of such factors as the details of the aid plan, the economic, financial, and competitive situation of the beneficiary undertaking and its internal operation.[110]

22.76 The Commission expects the Member State to take responsibility for its submissions made during the procedure,[111] since the final decision is based on these submissions, which, if they turn out to be incorrect, could throw the decision itself into doubt.

Consultation with the parties concerned

22.77 When the procedure is initiated, the Commission is required to give notice to the parties concerned to present their comments.[112]

22.78 **The notion of 'parties concerned'** The parties concerned represent an indeterminate group of persons to whom notice must be given.[113] This concept covers not only the undertaking(s) receiving aid,[114] but equally the persons, undertakings, or associations whose interests might be affected by the granting of the State aid concerned.[115] According to the CFI, to be considered as a 'party concerned', it is necessary to be able to show a 'legitimate interest' in whether or not the aid measures in dispute are actually put into effect or maintained when they have already been agreed.[116]

22.79 Besides the recipients of the aid, the notion of 'parties concerned' covers the following:

- the competitor undertakings[117] and trade associations.[118] As regards under-

---

[110] Joined Cases T-371/94 and T-394/94 *British Airways and others v EC Commission* [1998] ECR II-2405 para 62.

[111] Thus, in cases where a Member State passes on to the Commission a document drawn up by a third party for simple information purposes, without implicitly or explicitly taking responsibility for it, the Commission has considered that it cannot take this document to be observations made by the State in the context of the procedure and has declined to take them into account (Decision of 30 July 1996 concerning State aid granted by Germany to Werkstoff-Union [1997] OJ L48/31 s I *in fine*).

[112] Joined Cases T-228/99 and T-233/99 *WestLB and others v EC Commission* para 123.

[113] Case 323/82 *Intermills v EC Commission* [1984] ECR 3809 para 16 and Case T-189/97 *Comité d'entreprise de la Société française de production and others v EC Commission* [1998] ECR II-335 para 42.

[114] Joined Cases T-228/99 and T-233/99 *WestLB and others v EC Commission* para 122.

[115] Case T-41/01 *Rafael Pérez Escolar v EC Commission* [2003] ECR II-2157 para 34.

[116] ibid para 35.

[117] Their legitimate interest consists in the safeguarding of their competitive position in the market (ibid para 35).

[118] See Art 1(h), of the Procedural Reg. Case 323/82 *Intermills v EC Commission* para 16; Case C-198/91 *Cook v EC Commission* paras 24–26; Case C-225/91 *Matra v EC Commission* [1993] ECR I-3203 para 18 and Joined Cases T-371/94 and T-394/94 *British Airways and others v EC Commission* para 91 and Case T-189/97 *Comité d'entreprise de la Société française de production and others v EC Commission* [1998] ECR II-335 para 42.

takings, the CFI has ruled in many judgments that any undertaking other than the aid beneficiary needs to show that its competitive position is affected by the granting of the aid before it can be considered as a party concerned.[119] In the case of an association it is necessary in principle that it has been set up to promote the collective interest of its members and that at least some of the latter can themselves be considered to be parties concerned or that it claims a specific legal interest in bringing proceedings because its negotiating position is affected by the contested decision.[120]

- infrastate regional entities granting the aid;[121]

- Member States other than the State concerned;[122]

- workers' representative bodies of the aid-receiving undertaking, insofar as they are concerned parties within the meaning of Article 88(2), may be entitled to present to the Commission their observations on matters of a social order that might, in the context, be taken into consideration by the latter;[123]

- the purchasers or suppliers of the aid-receiving undertaking.[124]

Although the group of 'parties concerned' is indeterminate, this does not mean that it is infinite. Thus, according to the CFI, it is not enough to have a purely general or indirect interest.[125] In particular the notion of 'parties concerned' cannot be construed to mean that any taxpayer is a party concerned within the meaning of Article 88(2) of the Treaty in relation to aid financed through the general tax resources of a Member State.[126]   **22.80**

The notion of 'parties concerned' is ambiguous because it serves a twofold purpose: **22.81**

- it determines the persons who are entitled to take part in the formal examination procedure;

---

[119] Case T-188/95 *Waterleiding Maatschappij v EC Commission* [1998] ECR II-3713 para 62; Case T-69/96 *Hamburger Hafen- und Lagerhaus and others v EC Commission* [2001] ECR II-1037 para 41 and Case T-114/00 *ARE v EC Commission* [2002] ECR II-5121 para 51.

[120] Case T-114/00 *ARE v EC Commission* paras 53 and 65.

[121] Joined Cases T-228/99 and T-233/99 *WestLB and others v EC Commission* para 122.

[122] See para 22.85.

[123] Case T-189/97 *Comité d'entreprise de la Société française de production and others v EC Commission* para 41.

[124] Opinion of AG Verloren van Themaat in Case 323/82 *Intermills v EC Commission* [1984] ECR I-3809 para 2.1.

[125] Case T-41/01 *Rafael Pérez Escolar v EC Commission* [2003] ECR II-2157 para 36.

[126] Case T-188/95 *Waterleiding v EC Commission* para 68. In this respect the situation of a person who finances an aid-implementing parafiscal charge is without any doubt specific.

- it is used in the *Cook* and *Matra* case law for determining which persons are entitled to lodge an action for annulment against a Commission decision not to initiate the formal examination procedure, claiming an infringement of their procedural rights. Recent case law of the CFI has shown this second question to be the most important because it involves the determination of whether a person is a party concerned.[127]

22.82 Consultations with the parties concerned aim only to obtain from them all the necessary information so that the Commission can base its future decision on all relevant facts.[128] The essential role of the parties concerned for the Commission is therefore one of 'sources of information'.[129] It follows therefore that they can lay claim to no right to be heard in the procedure, an entitlement recognized for persons against whom the procedure has been initiated;[130] their only right is to be associated with the administrative procedure as far as is necessary for the particular circumstances of the case in hand.[131] This latter right is respected insofar as the concerned parties are able to put forward their arguments in presenting their opinion in writing, in the supporting documents, and to discuss aspects of the case at meetings with representatives of the Commission, etc.[132]

---

[127] Indeed, the CFI quickly realized in applying the *Cook* judgment that using the concept of 'concerned party' in its widest sense might well deprive of all legal sense the concept of 'person individually concerned' within the meaning of the fourth subparagraph of Art 230 of the Treaty (Case T-398/94 *Kahn Scheepvaart v EC Commission* [1996] ECR II-477 para 50 and Case T-188/95 *Waterleiding v EC Commission* [1998] ECR II-3713 para 68). To avoid this danger it went off down two different paths. Firstly, in an isolated judgment, *Kahn Scheepvaart*, it purely and simply rejected *Cook* and considered that the simple fact of being a 'party concerned' in the sense of Art 88(2) was not enough to be individually concerned. Later, the CFI moved the goalposts again and instead of rejecting *Cook* interpreted the notion of 'concerned party' more restrictively to bring it within subparagraph 4 of Art 230 of the Treaty (*Waterleiding* mentioned above, and Case T-41/01 *Rafael Pérez Escolar v EC Commission* para 36).

[128] Case 70/72 *EC Commission v Germany* para 19; Joined Cases T-371/94 and T-394/94 *British Airways and others v EC Commission* para 59; Joined Cases T-126/96 and T-127/96 *Breda Fucine Meridionali and others v EC Commission* para 45; Joined Cases T-228/99 and T-233/99 *WestLB and others v EC Commission* para 124, and Case T-109/01 *Fleuren Compost v EC Commission* para 41.

[129] Case T-266/94 *Skibsværftsforeningen and others v EC Commission* para 256; Joined Cases T-371/94 and T-394/94 *British Airways and others v EC Commission* para 59; Joined Cases T-228/99 and T-233/99 *WestLB and others v EC Commission* para 125, and Case T-366/00 *Scott v EC Commission* para 59 and Case T-369/00 *Département de Loiret v EC Commission* para 84 and Case T-198/01 *TGI v EC Commission* para 192.

[130] Case T-176/01 *Ferriere Nord v EC Commission* para 74. In particular they can claim no right to debate the issues with the Commission (Case T-198/01 *TGI v EC Commission* para 192).

[131] Joined Cases T-371/94 and T-394/94 *British Airways and others v EC Commission* para 60 and Joined Cases T-228/99 and T-233/99 *WestLB and others v EC Commission* para 125.

[132] Joined Cases T-228/99 and T-233/99 *WestLB and others v EC Commission* para 129.

According to the CFI, the Community Court cannot, on the basis of general **22.83** legal principles such as those of the right to due process, the right to be heard, sound administration or equal treatment, extend the procedural rights conferred on interested parties in State aid review procedures by the Treaty and secondary legislation.[133] The Article 88(2) procedure is therefore an *inter partes* procedure only in relation to the Member State concerned and not in relation to the parties concerned.[134] Nonetheless, there is a certain tendency in some case law decisions to extend the right of an *inter partes* procedure in particular to the aid recipient.[135] The restricted nature of the concerned parties' rights impinges on the content of the information they have to be furnished with.[136] Finally, it should be noted that the restricted nature of the concerned parties' rights does not affect the Commission's duty of giving sufficient grounds for its final decision.[137]

Status of the aid recipient None of the provisions on the procedure for **22.84** reviewing State aid reserves a special role, among the interested parties, for the aid recipient. Moreover, this procedure is not a procedure initiated 'against the aid recipient' that gives rise to rights on which it may rely and which are as extensive as the rights to a fair defence as such.[138]

Status of the Member States other than the granter of the aid The Member **22.85** States other than the Member State concerned have no particular rights vis-à-vis the other concerned parties. They are therefore only entitled to put forward their comments. In particular, the Commission is not bound to pass on to them the observations it has received from the government of the Member State seeking authorization to grant the aid. The other Member States are therefore involved in a specific case of aid only where, in application of subparagraph three

---

[133] Case T-198/01 *TGI v EC Commission* para 194.

[134] Joined Cases T-228/99 and T-233/99 *WestLB and others v EC Commission* para 168; Case T-109/01 *Fleuren Compost v EC Commission* para 43 and Case T-198/01 *TGI v EC Commission* para 61.

[135] See Case T-198/01 R *TGI v EC Commission* [2002] ECR II-2153 para 85, in which the President of the CFI obliged the Commission to pass on to the aid recipient a comment containing the specific observations it had expressly requested from a competitor in answer to the comments initially lodged by the aid recipient. On appeal, the President of the ECJ was somewhat loath to accept this approach, declaring that such a procedural obligation on the Commission was not contained either in the regulations or the case law (Case C-232/02 P(R) *EC Commission v TGI* [2002] ECR I-8977 para 76).

[136] See para 22.87.

[137] Joined Cases T-228/99 and T-233/99 *WestLB and others v EC Commission* para 132. For more information on the obligation to give the grounds for decisions, see para 22.106.

[138] Case T-109/01 *Fleuren Compost v EC Commission* para 44 and Case T-198/01 *TGI v Commission* para 193.

of Article 88(2), that case has, at the request of the Member State concerned, been submitted to the Council.[139]

22.86 **Method of giving information to parties concerned**   Article 88(2) does not require individual notice to be given to particular persons. Its sole purpose is to oblige the Commission to take steps to ensure that all persons who may be concerned are notified and given an opportunity of putting forward their arguments. Under those circumstances, the publication of a notice in the Official Journal of the European Union, series C, is an appropriate means of informing all the parties concerned that a procedure has been initiated.[140] Since the entry into force of the Procedural Regulation, only a summary of the procedure initiated is published in all Community languages, with the entire text being made available in the authentic language version.[141] Under no circumstances may the Commission be held liable for any omission by the Member State concerned in notifying the aid recipient of the letter communicating the initiation of the procedure.[142]

Information to be communicated to the parties concerned[143]

22.87 The content of the information to be included in the notification of the initiation of the procedure should be determined on a case-by-case basis. The information given to the parties concerned should in the first place be sufficient to allow them to realize that they are involved in the enquiry as addressees or as competitors of the addressees.[144] It should then allow them to put forward effectively their arguments on the aspects about which the Commission entertains doubts. The notice does not therefore have to mention matters about which the Commission entertains no doubts.[145] On the other hand, if the Commission intends to base its decision on new principles or assessment criteria, not mentioned in the initiation decision, it should ask the concerned parties for

---

[139] Joined Cases T-371/94 and T-394/94 *British Airways and others v EC Commission* para 76. For more information on Council intervention, see para 21.100.

[140] Case 323/82 *Intermills v EC Commission* para 17; Joined Cases T-371/94 and T-394/94 *British Airways and others v EC Commission* para 59; Joined Cases T-228/99 and T-233/99 *WestLB and others v EC Commission* para 124 and Case T-109/01 *Fleuren Compost v EC Commission* para 41.

[141] See Art 26(2) of the Procedural Reg.

[142] Case T-109/01 *Fleuren Compost v EC Commission* para 47.

[143] See Art 6(1) of the Procedural Reg.

[144] Case 323/82 *Intermills v EC Commission* para 18.

[145] This incomplete character of the communication does not however prevent the concerned parties from arguing before the Community Court that the Commission's final decision is insufficiently reasoned or contains manifest errors of assessment or law in regard to these matters, even if they have not been mentioned in the communication (Joined Cases T-371/94 and T-394/94 *British Airways and others v EC Commission* paras 66 and 67).

their observations on this matter.[146] It suffices for the concerned parties to know the grounds that have led the Commission to consider provisionally that the measure in question constitutes new aid that is incompatible with the common market.[147]

According to the CFI, there may be two reasons for restricting the extent of the concerned parties' right to be given information during this procedure: **22.88**

- On the one hand, after having carried out a thorough discussion with the Member State concerned, the Commission is entitled to limit its notice in the Official Journal to the points of the aid plan that it still entertains doubts about.

- On the other, the Commission is bound under Article 287 of the Treaty not to furnish concerned parties with information of the kind covered by the obligation of professional secrecy.[148] To meet this obligation the Commission asks the Member State concerned to inform it of by way of a reasoned request which information in the letter communicating the initiation decision it considers to be confidential, doing so within fifteen days of receiving the said letter, so that this confidential information can then be omitted from the publication in the Official Journal.[149]

The sufficient character of the information contained in the notice of initiation should also be assessed in the light of the Member State's degree of cooperation with the Commission. Thus the aid recipient cannot criticize the Commission for the vague and imprecise character of the information contained in the notice of the initiation of the procedure, if this is the result of the national authorities' failure to furnish the Commission with the information asked for; moreover, as the aid recipient itself, it can hardly have been unaware of the State aid it has received over previous years.[150] **22.89**

The information communicated does not need to be limited to a simple description of the measure. The Commission is fully entitled to make known its **22.90**

---

[146] Case T-176/01 *Ferriere Nord v EC Commission* paras 75 and 80.

[147] Joined Cases T-269/99, T-271/99 and T-272/99 *Territorio Histórico de Guipúzcoa and others v EC Commission* [2002] ECR II-4217 para 105 and Joined Cases T-346/99, T-347/99 and T-348/99 *Territorio Histórico de Álava and others v EC Commission* [2002] ECR II-4259 para 100.

[148] Joined Cases T-371/94 and T-394/94 *British Airways and others v EC Commission* [1998] ECR II-2405 paras 61 to 63. See also Art 24 of the Procedural Reg.

[149] If the Commission does not receive any reasoned request within the deadline, it considers the Member State to be in agreement with the publication of the notice of initiation in its entirety.

[150] Joined Cases T-126/96 and T-127/96 *Breda Fucine Meridionali and others v EC Commission* [1998] ECR II-3437 paras 48–53.

reservations about the plan that has come to its attention, so as to notify all the parties concerned of its initial reaction and thus permit the undertakings concerned to ensure that their interests are defended.[151] The information, however, can have no other effect than to make known the initiation of the formal examination procedure[152] and not to give any definitive ruling on certain elements of the file before the adoption of the final decision.[153]

Processing the information received. The time-limit for presenting observations

22.91 The Commission sets a time-limit, usually one month, within which the parties concerned can make their observations; this time period usually runs from the date of publication of the initiation of the procedure in the Official Journal.[154] It enforces this deadline fairly strictly and seems to consider that it is not authorized to take information that is submitted late into consideration.[155]

22.92 The Commission is bound to take due consideration of the information received and give grounds for its decision accordingly. The absence of such observations, however, does not prohibit it from concluding that the aid is incompatible. Moreover, the Commission cannot be held to blame for not having taking into consideration any issues of fact or law that could have been but were not in fact presented during the administrative procedure, since the Commission is not bound to examine *ex officio* and on the basis of supposition the information that might have been submitted.[156]

22.93 When the Commission draws up its decisions it is not in principle either obliged to turn to external experts[157] or prohibited from doing so.[158]

Deadline for the formal examination procedure

22.94 Before the entry into force of the Procedural Regulation the Commission was not bound to adopt its final decision within a given deadline, whether minimum or maximum; no text stated that State aid decisions adopted under

---

[151] Case 323/82 *Intermills v EC Commission* para 21.

[152] ibid.

[153] Nothing prevents the Commission, however, from adopting in one single act a decision to initiate the procedure against certain elements of aid *and* a decision not to raise objections with regard to other measures in favour of the same recipient(s).

[154] Art 6(1) of the Procedural Reg.

[155] See the Decision of 30 July 1996 concerning State aid granted by Germany to Werkstoff-Union [1997] OJ L48/31, para I *in fine*.

[156] Case T-109/01 *Fleuren Compost v EC Commission* not yet reported paras 48–49.

[157] Joined Cases T-371/94 and T-394/94 *British Airways and others v EC Commission* para 72.

[158] Case T-106/95 *FFSA and others v EC Commission* [1997] ECR II-229 para 102.

Article 88(2) had to adhere to a fixed deadline.[159] According to the ECJ, when the Commission decided to initiate a procedure under Article 88, it then had a reasonable time limit to see this procedure through.[160] The specification of this reasonable time limit depended on the particular case in question. If the Commission took too long to give its decision and indefinitely stymied the action of the Member State concerned, an action for failure to comply with its obligations could not be ruled out. For its part, the Commission endeavoured to end the procedure within six months.[161]

At the present time the Procedural Regulation suggests a time limit of eighteen months, extendable by common agreement.[162] The CFI has confirmed that this is not a mandatory time limit.[163] When this time-limit has run its course, the Member State in question can request the Commission to adopt a decision within a final time period of two months (Article 7(6) and (7)).[164] **22.95**

The Commission is not bound to inform the Member State concerned that the adoption of a decision is imminent, for this would allow it to submit new information, a process that would be liable to create procedural delays preventing the Commission from closing the administrative procedure under way.[165] **22.96**

Finally, it should be noted that, in the case of unlawful aid, an excessively long time limit could, depending on the circumstances of the case, prevent the Commission from ordering the recovery of the aid even if it is finally declared to be incompatible. **22.97**

According to the case law of the ECJ, when the conditions justifying the initiation of the procedure are met, no alternative procedure can be pursued. It would therefore not suffice for the Commission to enter into consultations with the Member States in the form of bilateral meetings,[166] nor for it to engage **22.98**

---

[159] Joined Cases T-371/94 and T-394/94 *British Airways and others v EC Commission* para 71 (in this case the Commission had been criticised for taking its decision too quickly given the complexity of the disputed aid plan. The CFI rejected this argument, without ruling out the possibility that any undue haste by the Commission might involve a breach of specific procedural rules or the duty to give reasons, or of the internal legality of the disputed decision).

[160] Case 59/79 *Producteurs de vins de table and vins de pays v EC Commission* [1979] ECR 2425.

[161] See s 42 of the Guide to the Procedures Applicable to State aid.

[162] See Art 7(6) of the Procedural Reg.

[163] Case T-190/00 *Regione Siciliana v EC Commission* not yet reported para 139 and Case T-176/01 *Ferriere Nord v EC Commission* para 69.

[164] Note that the Commission's proposal refrains from laying down a maximum time limit at the end of which it must adopt its final decision. For an individual case of application see the Decision of 24 June 2003, see [2004] OJ L43/88 sections 11–12.

[165] Case T-198/01 *TGI v EC Commission* para 156.

[166] Case 84/82 *Germany v EC Commission* para 18.

in a simple *inter partes* dialogue with any complainant in the context of the preliminary phase laid down in Article 88(3).[167]

E. Final Decision

22.99 At the end of the examination procedure the Commission adopts in principle a final decision on the existence of aid and its compatibility or incompatibility with the common market.

1. General considerations

Form and effect

22.100 The final decision is a decision as defined in subparagraph 4 of Article 249 EC, 'binding in its entirety on those to whom it is addressed',[168] namely, the Member State concerned. This means that the Member State has the obligation to abide by a negative decision, which corresponds in essence to a ban on putting the aid into effect. A positive decision, on the other hand, constitutes a simple authorization that is in no way binding on the addressee State, which remains at liberty to decide in the end not to put the aid into effect.[169] The final decision adopted by the Commission also has direct effect.

Content

22.101 The Procedural Regulation provides for four types of final decisions (Article 7):

- The Commission can first of all decide that the measure in question 'does not constitute aid', i.e. that it does not meet all the conditions of Article 87(1). Apart from the lack of any advantage involved in the measure the Commission can also come to that decision on the grounds that the measure is not directly or indirectly funded by State resources, that it does not affect trade, or that it is not likely to impinge on competition. Moreover, according to the CFI, nothing prevents the Commission from finally deciding that the measure in question in fact constitutes existing aid.[170]
- Secondly the Commission can adopt a 'positive decision'.[171] The Procedural Regulation provides that the decision must mention which exception under the Treaty is being applied. This stands to reason, and, in fact, the

---

[167] Case C-367/95 P *EC Commission v Sytraval and others* [1998] ECR I-1719 para 59.
[168] Case 156/77 *EC Commission v Belgium* para 18.
[169] See the Opinion in Case C-6/99, paras 38–39.
[170] Case T-190/00 *Regione Siciliana v EC Commission* para 48.
[171] These are decisions that were previously adopted in the form of a simple letter.

Commission's obligations to give grounds go further than this essential point.[172]

• The Commission can also adopt a 'conditional decision'. The Regulation expressly provides that the Commission is entitled to subject its decision on the compatibility of aid to certain conditions. It certainly does not give any precise idea of the nature of these 'conditions' that can be imposed by the Commission. The Commission sometimes seeks to obtain any concession under the form of voluntary 'commitments' by the Member State if it is unable to impose it as a condition. In particular the compatibility of restructuring aid is often linked to a commitment to privatize the beneficiary public undertaking, the validity of which under Article 295 of the Treaty is somewhat dubious.

• The Commission can finally adopt a 'negative decision' declaring the aid to be incompatible and impossible to grant.

22.102 The Commission may alter the assessment made in the initiating decision.[173] On the contrary, it must be careful not to adopt decisions that lie beyond the powers conferred upon it, for example by requiring a State to extend its aid to other recipients.[174]

Withdrawal

22.103 If a Member State decides not to grant the aid under examination and withdraws its notification (or, in the case of unlawful aid, if the State recovers the whole sum on its own initiative), the Commission then sends the Member State a simple communication recording the withdrawal of the notification or the disappearance of the aid.[175] Article 8 of the Regulation formally authorizes Member States to withdraw a notification before the Commission has adopted a decision. Such a possibility would seem to be logical and is moreover in keeping with current practice. The Commission's competence is in effect always linked either to the existence of unlawfully granted aid or a notification made in the correct form. Notification of withdrawal usually occurs because the Member State concerned decides not to grant the notified aid, either due to difficulties encountered with the Commission or for independent reasons.

---

[172] See para 22.106.

[173] Case T-190/00 *Regione Siciliana v EC Commission* para 51.

[174] Case T-107/96 *Pantochim v EC Commission* [1998] ECR II-311 para 52. On the other hand it is entitled to take note of the transformation of aid into a general measure in view of its extension to all potential recipients.

[175] It would seem that the Commission, acting prudently, sometimes makes sure that the aid plan has actually been revoked under the national procedures before closing the examination procedure (see the decision terminating the procedure [1999] OJ C99/17.).

There is however a risk of this withdrawal procedure being used illegally by Member States.[176]

Information

22.104 As soon as the decision has been taken, the Commission's Secretariat General informs the Permanent Representation of the Member State concerned of the decision in a brief letter, which precedes the sending of the full text of the decision.[177] On the other hand the Commission is not required to inform the Member State concerned of its position before adopting its decision.[178]

22.105 Moreover, Article 20(1) of the Procedural Regulation provides that any interested party that has submitted comments during the formal examination procedure and any beneficiary of individual aid shall be sent a copy of the final decision.

Reasons for the decision

22.106 The Commissions decision is subject to Article 253 EC. The requirement to give reasoned decisions implies that the Commission should state the essential considerations upon which its decision is based.[179] The requirements to be satisfied by the statement of reasons depend in particular on the need for information of the undertakings to whom the measure is addressed or of other parties to whom it is of direct and individual concern within the meaning of Article 230 EC,[180] in particular, according to the CFI, when they have played an active role in the procedure prior to the adoption of the contested measure and knew the reasons of fact and law which led the Commission to take its decision.[181] The requirement to provide reasons for a decision taken in regard to State aid thus cannot be determined solely on the basis of the interest which the addressee Member State may have in obtaining information.[182] According

---

[176] When the Commission opens the formal examination procedure on an aid plan, for example, it has sometimes happened in the past that the Member State withdraws its notification and simultaneously notifies an amended plan within the meaning required by the Commission. Such a manoeuvre deprives the aid approval procedure of all transparency, for the positive decision is then a decision 'not to raise objections' which is only subject to an extremely summary publication whereas the formal examination procedure is closed by a simple letter of termination; the parties concerned do not even realise that the aid plan has been withdrawn with one hand, only to be reintroduced with another.

[177] See s 52 of Guide to Procedures in State Aid Cases.

[178] Joined Case T-198/01 *TGI v EC Commission* para 198.

[179] Joined Cases T-228/99 and T-233/99 *Westdeutsche Landesbank Girozentrale v EC Commission* [2003] ECR II-435 para 402.

[180] Joined Cases 296/82 and 318/82 *Netherlands and Leeuwarder Papierwarenfabriek v EC Commission* [1985] ECR 809 para 19 and Joined Cases T-371/94 and T-394/94 *British Airways and others v EC Commission* para 90.

[181] Joined Cases T-132/96 and T-143/96 *Freistaat Sachsen and others v EC Commission* [1999] ECR II-3663 para 268.

[182] Joined Cases T-371/94 and T-394/94 *British Airways and others v EC Commission* para 92.

to the CFI, a final aid-authorizing decision must contain sufficient reasons that address all the essential complaints which parties directly and individually concerned by that decision have made either on their own initiative or as a result of information supplied by the Commission. Thus, even on the assumption that the Commission may, in a particular case, validly prefer to use other sources of information and thereby reduce the significance of the participation of interested parties, it is not thereby released from its obligation to include an adequate statement of reasons in its decision.[183]

That said, the Commission's duty to give reasons for its decisions in rejecting an argument brought by a concerned party during the administrative procedure cannot be understood to be as extensive as its requirement to give reasons to the addressee Member State whose arguments it has rejected.[184]   **22.107**

The obligation to give grounds may be less in certain cases. Firstly, the requirement to give reasons for a final decision has to be weighed up not only in terms of its wording but also its context and also the whole set of legal rules governing the issue concerned. Any former decisions should therefore be taken into account as well as the content of the notification of the formal initiation of the examination procedure.[185] Secondly the Commission is not bound to respond to all issues of law or fact raised by the concerned parties, as long as it gives due consideration to all the relevant factors and circumstances of the particular case.[186] Lastly, the reasons cannot normally be given after the adoption of the decision itself.   **22.108**

Publication

The final decisions adopted by the Commission are published in the Official Journal,[187] series L.[188] In the case of individual decisions, pursuant to Article 254(3) of the Treaty, the publication of final decisions is not a *sine qua non* of their entry into force. They come into force upon receipt by the addressee.   **22.109**

Confidential information

The Commission can exclude from publication in the Official Journal such information as it deems to be covered by the obligation of professional secrecy,   **22.110**

---

[183] Joined Cases T-371/94 and T-394/94 *British Airways and others v EC Commission* paras 64 and 96.

[184] Case T-198/01 *TGI v EC Commission* para 64.

[185] Case C-56/93 *Belgium v EC Commission* [1996] ECR I-723 para 87.

[186] Joined Cases T-132/96 and T-143/96 *Freistaat Sachsen and others v EC Commission* [1999] ECR II-3663 para 268.

[187] See Art 26(3) of the Procedural Reg.

[188] Formerly, the positive decisions were adopted in the form of simple letters of termination addressed to the Member State and published in the OJ series C.

pursuant to Article 287 of the Treaty.[189] A defect in form as regards the giving of reasons vis-à-vis the addressee cannot therefore be justified by the obligation laid down in Article 287 of the Treaty to safeguard professional secrecy, and especially the commercial secrecy of the undertaking concerned. From this point of view the Commission's practice in certain sensitive cases, consisting in making reference in the body of its decision to unpublished side letters, is open to criticism.[190]

Revocation of decisions

22.111 A formal procedure for revoking Commission decisions is laid down in Article 9 of the Procedural Regulation. This allows the Commission to 'revoke' a decision not to raise objections or a final positive or conditional decision when this decision was based on incorrect information furnished during the procedure and this inaccuracy had a significant effect on the decision handed down. The Commission is bound to open a formal examination procedure before adopting a new final decision.

2. Decision ruling out the existence of aid

22.112 A final decision may first conclude that the notified measure does not constitute aid within the meaning of Article 87, the Commission hence finding that there is no State aid involved in the case. Decisions concluding that Article 87(1) does not apply to a notified measure may for example be based on the finding that the measure affords no advantage to the undertaking concerned because it is justifiable on the basis of the market-economy private-investor principle.

3. Positive final decision

22.113 The Commission adopts:

- either a decision that rules definitively and positively on the compatibility of the aid with the common market. In principle, the aid can then be granted;
- or the Commission could also conclude that the measure constitutes an individual application of an existing scheme.

---

[189] Joined Cases 296/82 and 318/82 *Netherlands and Leeuwarder Papierwarenfabriek v EC Commission* [1985] ECR 809 para 28.

[190] See, e.g. the enigmatic symbols '[. . .]' which mean that the scope of the Commission's conditions imposed on its approval of the (first) aid to Crédit Lyonnais cannot be fully grasped (Art 2(c)), of the 'Commission Decision of 26 July 1995 giving conditional approval to the aid granted by France to the bank Credit Lyonnais' [1995] OJ L308/92.

4. Conditional final decision

Conditional authorization

The Commission may declare the aid to be compatible while making this **22.114** decision dependent on certain conditions or reservations that are added to the notification arrangements and the commitments agreed to by the Member State.[191] The usefulness of such conditions is that, if the recipient undertaking were to fail to observe the authorization conditions, it would be for the Member State to make sure that the decision was properly carried out and, failing that, for the Commission to assess whether it was appropriate to demand that the aid be repaid.[192] If the Member State fails to enforce the Commission's aid-approval conditions, the Commission is also entitled under the second subparagraph of Article 88(2), in derogation from the provisions of Articles 226 and 227, to refer the matter directly to the ECJ.[193] In the case of aid for restructuring companies, the scope of the Commission's conditions is generally limited to the duration of the restructuring plan.[194] As regards rescue aid, the Commission sometimes inserts a formal condition of repayment at the end of the aid, this being one of the main compatibility criteria for this category of aid.[195]

In an action for annulment, a mere statement that one of the conditions on **22.115** which a decision authorising the grant of aid was based will not be complied with cannot cast doubt on the legality of the decision.[196] Only those complaints alleging that the conditions of authorization were inherently and manifestly inappropriate, and in particular legally inadequate in scope, may be capable of justifying the annulment of the contested decision.[197]

Conditional final decision approving aid divided into tranches

A particular case of a conditional decision is when the aid is approved on **22.116** condition of a timetable for paying out the aid in successive tranches or linking

---

[191] For examples of the Commission's possibility of making its decision subject to conditions or reservations, see in particular Joined Cases T-244/93 and T-486/93 *TWD v EC Commission* [1995] ECR II-2265 para 55; Joined Cases T-371/94 and T-394/94 *British Airways and others v EC Commission* para 288 and Case C-321/99 P *ARAP and others v EC Commission* [2002] ECR I-4287 para 72.

[192] Case T-380/94 *AIUFFASS and AKT v EC Commission* [1996] ECR II-2169 para 128 and Joined Cases T-371/94 and T-394/94 *British Airways and others v EC Commission* para 290.

[193] Case C-294/90 *British Aerospace and Rover v EC Commission* [1994] ECR I-5423 para 11 and Joined Cases T-371/94 and T-394/94 *British Airways and others v EC Commission* paras 290 and 348.

[194] ibid para 294.

[195] Decision of 13 November 2002 concerning the cash advance granted by France to the company Bull [2003] OJ L209/1.

[196] Case T-380/94 *AIUFFASS and AKT v EC Commission* para 128 and Joined Cases T-371/94 and T-394/94 *British Airways and others v EC Commission* para 291.

[197] ibid para 293.

its payment to the progressive compliance with certain conditions. This practice has been used in the air transport sector for long term restructuring aid.[198] A standard condition is that the Commission should be afforded the opportunity of issuing a 'comment' prior to the payment of each aid tranche. This comment can probably not be construed as an adversely affecting act since it is simply a confirmation of the original decision.[199]

22.117   Another possible situation is when the Commission, before payment of a tranche, adopts an instrument whereby it not only issues its comments on the original decision but also authorizes a limited exception to the conditions it has originally laid down. In the course of an action for annulment against such an instrument, the CFI has considered that the various parts of the decision form one whole, so that it is the whole decision that adversely affects the appellant.

Procedure to be followed for aid divided into tranches

22.118   What administrative procedure should be followed by the Commission when it has approved State aid divided into tranches under an Article 88(2) procedure, subject to compliance with a certain number of conditions, but it soon finds out that one of them has been breached? According to the CFI, the consequence of a breach of such a condition is that the subsequent tranches of aid have to be assumed to be incompatible with the common market and cannot be released without a new Commission decision granting a formal derogation from the condition in question.[200] As for the procedure to be followed for adopting such a decision, the CFI has transposed the procedure of Article 88 'by analogy'. The Commission therefore has to examine whether the derogation can be agreed, while at the same time assuring that the aid remains compatible; if need be, it has to open the formal examination procedure to assure itself of this, resulting in the suspension of the aid payment until such time as the final decision is adopted. One of the important points of this line of reasoning is therefore that the CFI accepts that the Commission is not necessarily obliged to follow a new formal examination procedure in order to make a derogation from the initial decision it had adopted after a previous formal examination procedure. It

---

[198] Para 48 of the guidelines of 2004.

[199] *A contrario*, this also means that the Commission, on pain of jeopardizing the legal certainty of the concerned parties, would not be authorized to question the payment of a tranche if all the conditions of the initial decision are met. cf Advocate General Darmon has argued that, in decisions approving the payment of aid tranches, the Commission has to ascertain whether or not the aid is still necessary and, if not, to reduce the sum accordingly (Opinion in Case C-180/88 *Wirtschaftsueseinigung Eisen—und Stablindustrie v EC Commission* [1990] ECR I-4413 paras 28 and 29).

[200] Case T-140/95 *Ryanair v EC Commission* [1998] ECR II-3327.

imposes strict conditions on this possibility, however, to prevent the Commission from avoiding the normal procedure. To be able to avoid reinitiating the procedure the Commission has to satisfy two conditions,[201] which seem to concern, first, the scope of the derogation from the initial decision and secondly the object itself of this derogation:

• The Commission is not entitled to depart from the scope of its initial decision. It follows that if one of the conditions to which approval of aid was subject is not satisfied, the Commission may normally adopt a decision derogating from that condition without re-opening the procedure under Article 88(2) of the Treaty only in the event of relatively minor deviations from the initial condition, where it has no doubt that the aid at issue is still compatible with the common market.

• The variations examined in their own right must raise no doubts about the compatibility of the aid.

In formulating these conditions the CFI has gradually established a truly general theory whereby the Commission is invested with what it calls the 'power to manage and monitor an aid divided into tranches'; since it is a case of aid already approved in principle, paid in successive tranches over a relatively long period in association with a restructuring plan, the results of which will be achieved only after a number of years, the Commission must enjoy a power to manage and monitor the implementation of such aid in order, in particular, to enable it to deal with developments which could not have been foreseen when the initial decision was adopted.[202]   **22.119**

In practice, the Commission does not tend to question the compatibility of an aid tranche when the breach of the initial conditions does not arise from the undertaking itself but from external factors.[203]   **22.120**

5. (Partially) negative final decision

In a negative final decision the Commission declares the aid under examination to be totally or partially incompatible with the common market. In this case the Member State cannot put part or all of the aid into effect. An example of partially incompatible aid is where aid is declared to be incompatible only once its intensity exceeds a maximum allowable threshold.[204]   **22.121**

---

[201] Paras 88 to 90 of the abovementioned *Ryanair* judgment.

[202] Para 89 of the abovementioned *Ryanair* judgment.

[203] See, e.g. the content of the Communication concerning the payment of the fourth tranche of aid to TAP [1997] OJ C239/7.

[204] Decision of 15 November 2000 on State Aid that Italy is planning to grant to Solar Tech [2001] OJ L292/45.

6. Implementation of final decision

22.122 In principle, the execution of final decisions on aid not yet granted raises no particular problem, the Member State being bound simply not to put the planned measures into effect. For this reason the principles governing the execution of negative final decisions are examined exclusively in Chapter 23 on unlawful aid, which is more problematic from this point of view.

22.123 The remedies to hand in the event of any breach of a Commission decision are dealt with in Chapter 25, paras 25.04 *et seq.*

23

UNLAWFUL AID

I. General matters

Aid is considered to be unlawful (or unlawfully granted) when it is put into **23.01** effect without first having been notified to the Commission or when it has been notified but then put into effect before the Commission has made a decision within the given time limit. Its unlawfulness derives from an infringement of the last sentence of Article 88(3).

The existence of unlawful aid represents a 'pathological' situation in relation to **23.02** the procedure laid down by the Treaty, thus explaining why it is not dealt with as such therein. The particular features of the unlawful aid control procedure have therefore had to be established on the basis of the Commission's practice, the case law of the ECJ, and the Council's Procedural Regulation. The general principle is one of parallelism with the review of notified aid, unless otherwise specified. Thus, the notion of existing aid serves to determine whether or not it is a case of unlawful aid. As for the procedure to be followed by the Commission in controlling unlawful aid, it also ensues from the stages laid down for the notified aid review procedure, namely the preliminary examination procedure and, if need be, the formal procedure, leading in principle to the adoption of a final decision. Three different principles, examined later, nonetheless characterise the unlawful aid control procedure: the *Lorenz* two-month time-limit does not apply; the Commission can use its powers to impose injunctions; finally, if the aid is declared to be incompatible, the Commission normally has to demand its recovery.

It is possible for initially notified aid to become subsequently unlawful if the **23.03** Member State puts it into effect without waiting for the Commission's final decision. This means that the rules for dealing with notified aid, laid down in Chapter II of the Procedural Regulation, may immediately become those of Chapter III, on unlawful aid, for dealing with the measure in question.

23.04 The case law on the consequences to be drawn from the initiation of the procedure require clarification. *Tirrenia* suggests that if the Commission initiates the procedure correctly, this implies that there was a doubt (about the nature of the aid, about whether it was new or existing aid, about its compatibility) which should have prompted the Member State to make a previous notification and suspend the measure. If the measure has already been put into effect, the initiation of the procedure would then establish its unlawfulness, since there is an obligation to notify the measure where there is a doubt about its compatibility. Confirmation of the infringement of Article 88(3), as ensuing from the initiating decision, would then be definitive, whatever the Commission's conclusion in its final decision: thus, even if the Commission eventually decides that the measure does not come within Article 87(1), the infringement of the final sentence of Article 88(3) would still be established, for the existing doubt should have prompted the Member State to suspend the measure. The CFI seems to consider, however, that the confirmation of the infringement of Article 88(3) in an initiating decision is necessarily provisional.[1]

A. Consequences of the Unlawful Implementation of Aid

1. Direct effect of the final sentence of Article 88(3) EC

23.05 The status of unlawfully granted aid is challengeable. The prohibition laid down in the final sentence of Article 88(3), which is formulated 'in unequivocal terms'[2] has direct effect; this means that the infringement can be brought before a national court for the due conclusions to be drawn under national law, in particular the annulment of the decision to grant the aid.

2. Obligation to examine the compatibility of unlawful aid

23.06 Some jurists originally argued that, in the event of the unlawful granting of aid, the Commission should prosecute the infringing Member State under Article 226 to obtain the annulment of the national measure, and hence could no longer follow the Article 88 procedure.[3] The ECJ has not reached the same conclusion. On the contrary, it has established a strict separation between the unlawfulness of the aid, arising from a breach of the procedural obligation of

---

[1] Joined Cases T-269/99, T-271/99 and T-272/99 *Territorio Histórico de Guipúzcoa and others v EC Commission* [2002] ECR II-4217 para 88, and Joined Cases T-346/99, T-347/99 and T-348/99 *Territorio Histórico de Álava and others v EC Commission* [2002] ECR II-4259 para 73.

[2] Case 171/83 R *EC Commission v France* [1983] ECR 2621 para 11.

[3] See the Opinion of AG Warner in Case 173/73 *Italy v EC Commission* [1974] ECR 709.

the final sentence of Article 88(3), and the incompatibility of the aid with the common market, pursuant to Article 87. It has deduced from this that the Commission is not entitled to prohibit the aid for irregularities of form, since this aid could turn out to be compatible with the common market.[4] The irregularity arising from the implementation of the aid before the end of the procedure laid down in Article 88(3) renders the aid in question unlawful but does not make the examination of its compatibility superfluous,[5] which is always the responsibility of the Commission.[6]

3. Obligation to deal with complaints of unlawful aid

Since the Commission has exclusive competence for pronouncing on the com- **23.07** patibility of aid, it is bound to conduct a diligent and impartial examination of all complaints received, otherwise it would run the risk of an action for failure to comply with its obligations being lodged against it. The only exception concerns matters which are manifestly irrelevant or insignificant or plainly of secondary importance.[7]

B. Examination Procedures for Unlawful Aid

1. Preliminary examination procedure

The Commission has first of all to come to a preliminary opinion on the **23.08** compatibility of the measure, on the basis of which it then adopts either a decision not to raise objections or a decision to initiate the formal examination procedure. In the case of unlawful aid, which it may learn of in various ways (late notification, a complaint, the press, etc), the two-month time-limit is not applicable.[8] Silence by the Commission of more than two months does not therefore have the effect of giving the unlawful aid the status of existing aid[9] and does not prevent the Commission from initiating a formal examination procedure as regards this aid.[10]

---

[4] Case C-301/87 *France v EC Commission* [1990] ECR I-307.
[5] Case C-142/87 *Belgium v EC Commission* [1990] ECR I-959 para 20, and Case C-91/01 *Italy v EC Commission* not yet reported para 44.
[6] Case C-409/00 *Spain v EC Commission* [2003] ECR I-1487 para 94.
[7] Case C-367/95 P *Commission v Sytraval* [1998] ECR I-1719 paras 62 and 64, and Case T-157/01 *Danske Busvognmænd v EC Commission* not yet reported paras 44 and 54.
[8] Case C-39/94 *SFEI and others* [1996] ECR I-3547 paras 46–48, and Art 13(2) of the Procedural Regulation.
[9] See the Opinion of AG Slynn in Joined Cases 296 and 318/82 *Netherlands and Leeuwarder Papierwarenfabriek v EC Commission* [1985] ECR 809.
[10] See, in particular, Case C-305/89 *Italy v EC Commission* [1991] ECR I-1603 para 30.

Action within a reasonable time period

23.09   The Commission is nonetheless bound to carry out its investigation with all due diligence,[11] in particular when dealing with complaints,[12] otherwise it again runs the risk of being appealed against for failure to act. The fundamental requirement of legal certainty in itself demands that the Commission should not be allowed to drag out the exercising of its powers indefinitely.[13] The question of whether or not the conduct of the procedure is characterized by excessive delay or lack of due diligence most certainly has to be ascertained not in terms of the time elapsed since the unlawful aid was granted but rather the date on which the Commission became aware that the aid had been granted.[14] From that moment on the Commission is bound, under Article 10 of the Procedural Regulation, to examine the information in its possession 'without delay'.

Request for information

23.10   Article 10(2) of the Procedural Regulation provides that 'If necessary [the Commission] shall request information from the Member State concerned. Article 2(2) [State's obligation to provide all necessary information] and Article 5(1) and (2) [Commission's obligation to send a reminder to a State that fails to come up with the information first time], shall apply *mutatis mutandis*'. According to the CFI, this provision imposes an immediate obligation on the Member State concerned to provide all necessary information following a request from the Commission.[15] This is a particular application of the general obligation of loyal cooperation laid down in Article 10 EC. The Member State is not entitled to refuse to furnish the information on the grounds that, in its opinion, it is not relevant.[16]

Information of third parties

23.11   According to the CFI, the Commission is not under a duty to warn potentially interested persons, including the beneficiary of the aid, of the measures it is taking in respect of unlawful aid before it initiates the formal examination procedure.[17]

---

[11] According to AG Slynn, even in the case of unlawful aid, the Commission is not entitled to drag out the case indefinitely. He argues that, by analogy with the Lorenz decision in relation to notified aid, the Commission must come to a preliminary conclusion with due diligence, in a time period that should not normally exceed two months (Opinion in Case 223/85 *RSV v EC Commission* [1987] ECR 4617).

[12] Joined Cases T-297/01 and T-298/01 *SIC v EC Commission* [2004] ECR II-743 para 56.

[13] Case T-109/01 *Fleuren Compost v EC Commission* not yet reported para 145.

[14] Case T-369/00 *Département de Loiret v EC Commission* [2003] ECR II-1789 para 56.

[15] ibid para 81.

[16] Proceedings of the restructuring of Spanish shipyards [2003] OJ C199/9 paras 20–21 of the letter.

[17] Case T-366/00 *Scott v EC Commission* [2003] ECR II-1763 para 59, and Case T-369/00 *Département de Loiret v EC Commission* para 84.

Voluntary recovery of unlawful aid

Should a Member State change its mind after having granted unlawful aid and **23.12**
then wish to prevent a formal decision thereon from the Commission, it has to
prove that the aid, including any interest, has been totally recovered and that its
effects no longer obtain. For the Commission to conclude that aid no longer
exists after such a voluntary recovery procedure by the national authorities, it is
necessary for the latter to furnish material proof of the effective recovery of the
updated amount of the aid initially paid out. The updating has to cover the
period running from the date of actual payment of the aid until its effective
repayment; the interest rate must be identical to the reference rate used for
calculating the net grant equivalent of the various types of aid in that Member
State.[18]

2. Formal examination procedure

The procedure is similar to that used for notified aid. Since it is a case of **23.13**
unlawful aid, the Commission's procedure-initiation text in principle gives
some indication of the precarious character of the aid and the consequences
deriving therefrom.

C. Final Decision

At the end of its examination procedure the Commission adopts a final decision **23.14**
on the compatibility of the measure.[19]

1. Positive decision

If the measure does not constitute aid or if the aid is declared to be compatible, **23.15**
the Commission approves it. Although the compatibility decision does not
provide a remedy for any infringement of Article 88(3), the Commission is not
then entitled to demand the recovery thereof on that grounds alone. Furthermore, the Regulation contains no provision allowing the Commission to penalise Member States for unlawful payment of aid declared thereafter to be
compatible.[20]

---

[18] Commission notice concerning aid which France plans to grant to Saab-Scania [1998] OJ
C79/10.
[19] The wording of Art 13(1) of the Procedural Reg seems to render the adoption of a decision
necessary, so the Commission could not abstain to act for lack of 'Community interest'.
[20] It would be possible to imagine, for example, that the Commission would be authorized, in
the case of compatible but unlawful aid, to impose the payment of interest covering the period
running from the payment of the aid to the Commission's final decision on the compatibility

That which is applicable to individual aid does not automatically apply to aid schemes

23.16 This at least appears to be the practice of the Commission. If an aid scheme has been put into effect before having been approved by the Commission and it is then declared to be compatible with the common market, the Commission then seems to consider that the individual cases of application executed before the scheme approval date do not benefit from the declaration of compatibility and could thereafter be examined as individual aid unlawfully granted and, as the case may be, declared incompatible.[21]

2. Negative or conditional decision

23.17 If the aid is declared to be incompatible, the Commission normally requires it to be recovered or altered in the formal decision it adopts. It is then up to the Member State concerned to enforce this decision.[22] Indeed, the Member States are bound to comply with the final decisions addressed to them, by virtue of their duty of loyal cooperation under Article 10 EC and also the supremacy of Community law. Since it is a case of aid declared to be incompatible, the role of the national authorities is merely to give effect to the Commission's decision. The authorities do not, therefore, have any discretion as regards revocation of a decision granting aid.[23]

23.18 When, despite an information injunction, the Commission considers the information received to be insufficient and bases its negative decision on the only information to hand, it is bound to put that fact on record.[24]

23.19 Should a Member State fail to observe 'with all due diligence'[25] a negative or conditional decision reached by the Commission, the latter or any other Member State concerned will be entitled, under Article 88(2)(2) to bring the matter directly before the ECJ by derogation from Articles 226 and 227.

(See the Opinion of AG Tesauro in Case 142/87 *Belgium v EC Commission* [1987] ECR 2589 and of AG Cosmas in Joined Cases C-329/93, C-62/95 and C-63/95 *Germany, Hanseatische Industrie-Beteiligungen and Bremer Vulkan Verbund v EC Commission* [1996] ECR I-2633).

[21] Thus, according to the Commission, when a guarantee in favour of a private firm has been established before authorization by the Commission of the national scheme concerned, this guarantee cannot be regarded as covered by that scheme (Commission Decision of 21 December 2000 on the State aid granted by the Federal Republic of Germany to Zeuro Möbelwerk [2002] OJ L282/1, s 39).

[22] Joined Cases T-228/99 and T-233/99 *WestLB and others v EC Commission* [2003] ECR II-435 para 140.

[23] Case C-24/95 *Alcan Deutschland* [1997] ECR I-1591 para 34.

[24] Case T-126/99 *Graphischer Maschinenbau v EC Commission* [2002] ECR II-2427 para 95.

[25] Case 173/73 *Italy v EC Commission* [1974] ECR 709 para 16.

Time-limit

No legal time-limit for execution is laid down within the framework of the **23.20** exceptional rules for bringing an action for failure to comply, based on the second subparagraph of Article 88(2) EC.[26] Unlike in the case of existing aid, when adopting a negative decision on unlawful aid the Commission is not bound to grant a time-limit to the Member State for implementing its decision, since the measure concerned should not have been put into effect.[27]

If the decision lays down a given deadline for implementing its obligations, the **23.21** Member State must abide by this deadline. More often, however, the Commission merely establishes a time-limit within which the Member State has to inform it of the measures taken to implement its obligations, without fixing a different time limit for implementation of the measures required by the decision. In one case, the ECJ concluded that the fixing of such a date for informing the Commission of the action taken clearly implies that this date was also the deadline agreed for implementing the decision.[28] Subsequently, however, the Court ruled that the State's only obligation within the Commission's deadline is to inform the Commission of the measures already taken and those which it intends to take; such a ruling would seem to leave some leeway for effective implementation.[29]

Abolition of aid

When a State is obliged to abolish aid declared to be incompatible, it has to do **23.22** so fully. This means in particular that, if the Commission has identified an aid scheme in reference to a legal act providing for same, the State infringes its obligations if it repeals that act but maintains the measure by adopting a different act.[30] Moreover, it is not enough for the State simply to stop paying the aid involved in a scheme declared to be incompatible. It is also bound in principle to formally repeal the provisions declared to be incompatible.[31]

---

[26] Case C-499/99 *Spain v EC Commission* [2002] ECR I-6031 para 42.
[27] Case 173/73 *Italy v EC Commission* para 13.
[28] Case 213/85 *EC Commission v Netherlands* [1988] ECR 281 para 19.
[29] Case C-499/99 *EC Commission v Spain* paras 28 and 42.
[30] See Case 203/82 *EC Commission v Italy* [1983] ECR 2633 in which the Court ruled against Italy for having extended by successive decree-laws an aid that Commission had demanded be abolished on the grounds of its original decree-law. As Advocate General Rozès pointed out: 'true it is that the provision that the Commission's final decision required the Italian government to abolish no longer formally exists because decree law 503 [. . .] has been repealed, but the substance thereof has been reproduced without any break in the subsequent texts [. . .]' (Opinion in Case 203/82, para V).
[31] Case 130/83 *EC Commission v Italy* [1984] ECR 2849 para 7. This formal repeal obligation is logical since it is the formal adoption of the regulation that is considered to constitute the institution of the aid under Art 88(3).

II. Recovery of incompatible aid unlawfully put into effect

A. Recovery Principle

1. Principle

23.23 The principle of recovering incompatible aid unlawfully put into effect is laid down in Article 14 of the Procedural Regulation, which provides that, in the case of a negative decision, the Commission 'shall decide' that the aid must be recovered. The words 'shall decide' shows that it is an obligation for the Commission, once unlawful aid has been declared to be incompatible.

23.24 This provision bears out previous case law.[32] Indeed, faced with a relatively high number of cases in which aid had been paid out to its recipient before being approved, the Commission had previously demanded the recovery thereof, in cases where such aid had been declared incompatible, and the Court had approved this practice. As Advocate General Jacobs pointed out, 'The most important point to bear in mind is that the question of recovery would never arise if Member States complied with their obligation to inform the Commission, in advance, of any plans to grant or alter aid, in accordance with the first sentence of Article 88(3) of the Treaty, and with their obligation to refrain from implementing plans to grant aid until the Commission has given its final decision, as required by the last sentence of Article 88(3).'[33]

23.25 According to the ECJ, since the Commission is empowered under Article 88(2) to decide whether the State should abolish or alter incompatible aid, this abolition or alteration, to be of practical effect, may involve an obligation placed on the Member State to demand repayment of the aid granted in breach of the Treaty.[34]

23.26 The recovery of unlawfully granted State aid aims to restore the situation existing prior to the payment of such aid.[35] This cannot be considered, in principle,

---

[32] Case C-404/00 *EC Commission v Spain* [2003] ECR I-6695 para 23.

[33] Opinion in Joined Cases C-278/92, C-279/92 and C-280/92 *Spain v EC Commission* [1994] ECR I-4103 para 63.

[34] Case 70/72 *EC Commission v Germany* [1973] ECR 813 para 13; Case 310/85 *Deufil v EC Commission* [1987] ECR 901 para 24; Case C-24/95 *Alcan Deutschland* para 22; Case C-209/00 *EC Commission v Germany* [2002] ECR I-11695 para 30, and Case C-404/00 *EC Commission v Spain* para 20.

[35] Case C-348/93 *EC Commission v Italy* [1995] ECR I-673 para 26, and C-350/93 [1995] ECR I-699 para 21; Case C-24/95 *Alcan Deutschland* para 23; Joined Cases C-328/99 and C-399/00 *Italy and others v EC Commission* [2003] ECR I-4035 para 66; Case C-277/00 *Germany v EC Commission* para 74, and Case C-298/00 P *Italy v EC Commission* not yet reported para 76, and Case T-198/01 *TGI v EC Commission* not yet reported para 132.

to be a measure disproportionate to the Treaty's objectives as regards State aid.[36] Quite on the contrary, 'the abolition of unlawful aid by way of recovery is the logical consequence of the finding that it is illegal.'[37] The Court has in particular refused to take into consideration any damage the recovery might cause to third parties, for example creditors.[38]

2. Recovery and form of the aid

The possibility of requiring the recovery of aid cannot be made to depend on the form in which it was granted.[39] Member States could otherwise evade the applicable State-aid rules by giving the aid a particular form.[40] **23.27**

The ECJ does not provide that any particular grounds must be given for justifying a decision requiring the recovery of aid, since its incompatibility with the common market has been established.[41] Neither is the Commission bound to establish that the aid has actually been granted before requiring the recovery thereof; in the absence of any guarantee to this effect, the Commission cannot be criticized for clearly setting out the practical consequences of its decision with the intention of creating greater legal certainty.[42] **23.28**

---

[36] Case C-142/87 *Belgium v EC Commission* [1990] ECR I-959 para 66; Joined Cases C-278/92, C-279/92 and C-280/92 *Spain v EC Commission* para 75; Case T-459/93 *Siemens v EC Commission* [1995] ECR II-1675 para 96; Case C-298/00 P *Italy v EC Commission* para 75, and Case T-198/01 *TGI v EC Commission* para 133.

[37] Case C-142/87 *Belgium v EC Commission* para 66; Case C-305/89 *Italy v EC Commission* [1991] ECR I-1603 para 41; Case C-169/95 *Spain v EC Commission* [1997] ECR I-135 para 47; Joined Cases C-328/99 and C-399/00 *Italy and others v EC Commission* para 66; Case C-404/00 *EC Commission v Spain* para 44; Case C-99/02 *EC Commission v Italy* not yet reported para 15, and Case C-298/00 P *Italy v EC Commission* para 75 ('unlawfulness' in the sense of 'incompatibility').

[38] Case C-142/87 *Belgium v EC Commission* paras 65 and 66.

[39] Case C-183/91 *EC Commission v Greece* [1993] ECR I-3131 para 16; Case C-404/97 *EC Commission v Portugal* [2000] ECR I-4897 para 38; Case C-404/00 *EC Commission v Spain* para 44; Case C-99/02 *EC Commission v Italy* para 15, and Case T-198/01 *TGI v EC Commission* para 132. The fact that the aid was granted under a private law contract, for example, is deemed to have no relevance (Case C-278/00 *Greece v EC Commission* not yet reported para 113).

[40] Case C-278/00 *Greece v EC Commission* para 113.

[41] Case C-303/88 *Italy v EC Commission* [1991] ECR I-1433 para 54, and Joined Cases C-278/92, C-279/92 and C-280/92 *Spain v EC Commission* para 78. See, in this sense, the observations of AG Darmon in Joined Cases C-324/90 and C-342/90 *Germany and Pleuger Worthington v EC Commission* [1994] ECR I-1173 paras 106 to 119; he rules in particular that a requirement of a statement of specific reasons for the repayment of aid would favour those States that, in breach of Art 88(3), did not previously notify their aid, since there is no such requirement when the Commission objects to aid which has not yet been granted.

[42] Case C-364/90 *Italy v EC Commission* [1993] ECR I-2097 paras 48 and 49. The Commission therefore regularly claims the repayment of 'any aid already paid' (see, e.g. the Commission Decision of 21 January 1998 on the tax concessions under Art 52(8) of the German Income Tax Act [1998] OJ L212/50).

23.29 The ECJ has however imposed an important limit on the recovery of aid: such a recovery can be the consequence only of the aid's incompatibility with the common market and represents the means of restoring the pre-aid situation. The Commission therefore has to establish the incompatible character of aid, by definition unlawfully granted, before being able to order its recovery.[43] The recovery of incompatible aid for the purpose of restoring the previous situation does not therefore constitute a penalty against the undertaking or Member State, even if it is implemented long after the aid itself was put into effect.[44]

3. Legitimate expectations

No grounds for legitimate expectations of the recipients

23.30 In view of the mandatory nature of the review of State aid by the Commission under Article 88 EC, undertakings to which aid has been granted may not, in principle, entertain a legitimate expectation that the aid is lawful unless it has been granted in compliance with the procedure laid down therein. A diligent businessman should normally be able to determine whether that procedure has been followed.[45] It follows that until such time as the Commission has taken an approval decision and even until such time as the deadline for lodging appeals against that decision has expired,[46] the recipient cannot be certain about the lawfulness of the proposed aid, which certainty alone is capable of giving rise to a legitimate expectation on its part.[47]

23.31 Consequently, the legitimate expectations of the recipients of unlawful aid cannot in principle be invoked as grounds for annulment by the Community Courts of the Commission's decision to demand recovery of the aid or a refusal by the national courts to order the effective restitution in execution of that decision.

---

[43] Case C-301/87 *France v EC Commission* para 11; Case T-49/93 *SIDE v EC Commission* [1995] ECR II-2501 para 84, and Case C-39/94 *SFEI and others* [1996] ECR I-3547 para 43.

[44] Case T-369/00 *Département de Loiret v EC Commission* para 57. See also para 22 of the Opinion of AG Van Gerven in Case C-305/89 *Italy v EC Commission* [1991] ECR I-1603.

[45] Case C-5/89 *EC Commission v Germany* [1990] ECR I-3437 para 17; Case C-169/95 *Spain v EC Commission* para 51; Case C-334/99, *Germany v EC Commission* [2003] ECR I-1139 para 41; Case T-366/00 *Scott v EC Commission* para 61, and Case T-369/00 *Département de Loiret v EC Commission* para 58; Case C-91/01 *Italy v EC Commission* para 65, and Joined Cases C-183/02 P and C-187/02 P *Demesa v EC Commission* not yet reported para 44.

[46] Joined Cases T-116/01 and T-118/01 *P & O European Ferries (Vizcaya) and Diputación Foral de Vizcaya v EC Commission* [2003] ECR II-2957 para 205.

[47] Case C-91/01 *Italy v EC Commission* para 66.

No grounds for legitimate expectations of third parties

As with the recipients, the third parties, including the territorial authorities **23.32** granting the aid, will not be able to rely on legitimate expectations.[48]

4. Practice

Evolution of the Commission's practice

The recovery of incompatible aid was originally a simple power that the Com- **23.33** mission used in an uneven manner. However, it soon decided to do so in a systematic way, barring justified exceptions. In a Communication of 1983, it informed 'potential recipients of State aid of the risk attached to any aid granted to them unlawfully, inasmuch as all recipients of unlawfully granted aid, i.e. without the Commission having reached a definitive solution on its compatibility, might be called upon to refund the aid.'[49] The Procedural Regulation has since borne out the systematic character of aid recovery (Article 14).

Difficulties in enforcing aid recovery decisions

If, when executing a recovery decision, the addressee Member State encounters **23.34** unforeseen or unforeseeable difficulties or perceives consequences overlooked by the Commission, it must submit those problems to the Commission for consideration, together with proposals for suitable amendments of the decision in question. In such a case the Commission and the Member State concerned must respect the principle underlying Article 10 of the Treaty, which imposes a duty of genuine cooperation on the Member States and Community institutions; accordingly, they must work together in good faith with a view to overcoming difficulties whilst fully observing the Treaty provisions, and in particular the provisions on aid.[50]

The Member State cannot therefore take the passive attitude of merely inform- **23.35** ing the Commission of the practical, political, or legal difficulties involved in implementing the decision. It is bound to take all due steps to recover the

---

[48] Case T-369/00 *Département de Loiret v EC Commission* [2003] ECR II-1789 para 58.

[49] [1983] OJ C318/3. The Court has based its arguments on the existence of this Communication to dismiss the claim of a principle of legitimate expectations on behalf of the recipients of unlawful aid (Case C-5/89 *EC Commission v Germany* para 15).

[50] Case 52/84 *EC Commission v Belgium* [1986] ECR 89 para 16; Case 94/87 *EC Commission v Germany* [1989] ECR 175 para 9; Case C-303/88 *Italy v EC Commission* para 58; Case C-183/91 *EC Commission v Greece* para 19; Case C-349/93 *EC Commission v Italy* para 13; Case C-348/93 *EC Commission v Italy* para 17, and Case C-350/93 *EC Commission v Italy* [1995] ECR I-699 para 16; Case C-499/99 *EC Commission v Spain* para 24; Case C-404/00 *EC Commission v Spain* para 46; Case C-99/02 *EC Commission v Italy* para 17, and Case C-278/00, *Greece v EC Commission* para 114.

aid from the undertaking in question and propose to the Commission any alternative arrangements that might allow those difficulties to be overcome,[51] in the interests of finding 'common ground' with the Commission.[52] Nonetheless, the State's commitment to enter into negotiations with the Commission will not be understood to exempt it from the obligation of taking all necessary measures for complying with the Commission's decision in the time-limit laid down for doing so.[53] Moreover, no procedural or other difficulties in regard to the implementation of the contested measure can have any influence on the lawfulness thereof.[54]

23.36 In the absence of sufficient details in the decision itself, the implementation obligation is not then incumbent on the Member State until such time as the Commission is in a position to specify with the necessary precision exactly what its obligations are.[55]

Agricultural sector

23.37 In the agricultural sector, instead of recovering incompatible aid, the Commission is entitled to refuse to make EAGGF advanced payments or to charge to the EAGGF budget the expenditure in relation to national measures that directly affect Community measures.[56] If it financially penalises the Member State concerned, however, this way of proceeding does not affect the aid recipients.

B. Exceptions to Recovery

23.38 What are the exceptions to the recovery of incompatible aid?

1. Recovery time-limit

Limitation period for the recovery of unlawful aid

23.39 Formerly there was no time-limit laid down in legislation for the recovery of unlawful aid. In order to fulfil their function of ensuring legal certainty, limitation periods must be fixed in advance; the fixing of their duration and the

---

[51] Case 94/87 *EC Commission v Germany* para 10; Case C-183/91 *EC Commission v Greece* para 19; Case C-349/93 *EC Commission v Italy* para 15; Case C-280/95 *EC Commission v Italy* [1998] ECR I-259 para 14; Case C-499/99 *EC Commission v Spain* para 25; Case C-404/00 *EC Commission v Spain* para 47, and Case C-99/02 *EC Commission v Italy* para 18.

[52] Case C-499/99 *EC Commission v Spain* para 27.

[53] Case 5/86 *EC Commission v Belgium* especially paras 7 and 11.

[54] Case C-142/87 *Belgium v EC Commission* para 63.

[55] Case 70/72 *EC Commission v Germany* para 23.

[56] See the Communication published in [1983] OJ C318/3.

detailed rules for their application come within the powers of the Community legislature. It followed from these two factors the Commission was not subject to any limitation period as regards the unlawfulness or incompatibility of aid.[57]

Aid that had been paid out for several years or even several decades before it **23.40** came to the Commission's notice could therefore always be examined and, as the case may be, declared incompatible and made subject to recovery. The Commission in effect considered that the effects of aid granted in the past persisted and therefore justified action on its part. It was only in exceptional circumstances, therefore, for example when the beneficiary undertaking had definitively ceased to exist, that it sometimes chose not to examine the incompatibility of the aid or not to demand its refund.

Article 15 of the Procedural Regulation

This situation changed with the introduction of a limitation period in Article 15 **23.41** of the Procedural Regulation. Article 15(1) provides that 'The Commission's powers to recover aid shall be subject to a limitation period of ten years'. Aid paid unlawfully for at least ten years should therefore be considered as existing aid and its compatibility with the common market cannot be called into question. According to the CFI, this is a single limitation period that applies in the same way to the Member State concerned, the aid recipient and third parties. The fact that the recipient or a third party was not aware of the existence of measures interrupting the limitation period is, therefore, irrelevant.[58]

According to Article 15(2) of the Procedural Regulation, 'The limitation period **23.42** shall begin on the day on which the unlawful aid is awarded to the beneficiary either as individual aid or as aid under an aid scheme. Any action taken by the Commission or by a Member State, acting at the request of the Commission, with regard to the unlawful aid shall interrupt the limitation period. Each interruption shall start time running afresh. The limitation period shall be suspended for as long as the decision of the Commission is the subject of proceedings pending before the ECJ of the European Communities'. The measures interrupting the limitation period may be adopted by the Commission or the Member State acting at the Commission's behest.

Transitional provisions

The CFI has ruled that Article 15 contains no transitional provision as regards **23.43** its application in time and hence applies to any definitive action ordering

---

[57] Joined Cases T-126/96 and T-127/96 *Breda Fucine Meridionali v EC Commission* [1998] ECR II-3437 para 67, and Case C-298/00 P *Italy v EC Commission* para 89.

[58] Case T-366/00 *Scott v EC Commission* para 58, and Case T-369/00 *Département de Loiret v EC Commission* para 83.

recovery of aid taken after the date on which the regulation entered into force, including aid granted before that date. Aid granted before the entry into force of the Regulation can therefore benefit from the limitation period. As a corollary, however, the CFI has ruled that a request for information made by the Commission before the entry into force of the Regulation, even though it did not 'then' have the effect of interrupting the limitation period, acquires such an effect in some way thereafter, thereby enabling the Commission to recover the aid after the entry into force of the Regulation. This solution, according to the CFI, does not seek to confer retrospective effect on the Articles of the Regulation but merely to ensure the uniform application of those Articles to a series of past facts or events which have been examined after the coming into force of the Regulation.[59]

2. Disappearance of the distortion-of-competition

23.44 The Commission has sometimes declined to demand the recovery of aid when the distortion-of-competition effects have disappeared, thereby terminating the infringement of Article 87(1). This might occur when the aided undertaking has definitively ceased trading before the adoption of the Commission's final decision.[60]

3. General principles of law preventing the recovery of aid

Principle

23.45 Exceptional circumstances may sometimes mean that the recovery of the aid is not demanded. The exceptional circumstances invoked often involve the legitimate expectations of the recipient (even if the recipient of unlawfully paid aid cannot, in principle, base its case for legitimate expectations on the lawfulness of the aid payment) or of the State. The Procedural Regulation confirms that the Commission will not require recovery of the aid if this would be against a general principle of Community law (Article 14). On the contrary, the simple existence of internal difficulties would not be sufficient justification.[61]

---

[59] Case T-366/00 *Scott v EC Commission*, para 57, and Case T-369/00 *Département de Loiret v EC Commission* paras 51 and 80 to 82.

[60] When the Commission considers that the real beneficiary of aid is the undertaking that has been wound up and that any effective recovery is unrealistic, it sometimes still demands that the aid be recovered within the limits of the firm's liquidation; on other occasions it waives its right to demand recovery (see, for example, the Commission Decision of 9 December 1987 on aid from the French Government to the wood processing sector [1988] OJ L119/38, p. 38, point V).

[61] Case C-298/00 P *Italy v EC Commission* para 78.

Case law

In *RSV*, the Commission had opened the formal examination procedure and **23.46** terminated it twenty-six months later with a negative decision requiring the recovery of the aid; the Court ruled that the Commission's delay in giving its decision could have established a legitimate expectation on the part of the recipient undertaking, thereby preventing the Commission from ordering the recovery of the aid.[62] This is only valid, however, in the case of 'exceptional' circumstances,[63] in particular in the case of an excessive delay by the Commission, on the understanding that such a delay may be imputed to the Commission only from the moment it became aware of the existence of the aid.[64] According to the ECJ, when a Member State that grants aid contrary to the duty of notification laid down in Article 88(3) of the Treaty subsequently displays reluctance to provide the appropriate information to the Commission, it is itself responsible for prolonging the examination procedure; it cannot therefore rely on the length of that procedure as a ground for a legitimate expectation regarding the compatibility of the aid in question with the common market.[65]

In another case the CFI decided in favour of non-recovery on the grounds that **23.47** the Commission had acted in a manner contrary to the principle of legal certainty. It had in fact itself created a situation of uncertainty and lack of clarity in implicitly and ambiguously altering over time its interpretation of certain rules. This situation, combined with the prolonged lack of reaction on the part of the Commission, despite its awareness of the aid received by the applicant, led to the creation by the Commission, in disregard of its duty of care, of an equivocal situation that the Commission was under a duty to clarify before it could take any action to order the recovery of the aid already paid.[66]

The legitimate expectation of the recipient has also been invoked in the case of **23.48** unlawfully-paid aid that the Commission had originally declared to be compatible and then, following the annulment of this first decision by the ECJ, had

---

[62] Case 223/85 *RSV v EC Commission* [1987] ECR 4617 paras 12–17.

[63] Case C-334/99 *Germany v EC Commission* [2003] ECR I-1139 para 44, and Case C-298/00 P *Italy v EC Commission* para 90.

[64] Case C-298/00 P *Italy v EC Commission* para 91. Thus in the *Boussac* and *ENI-Lanerossi* Cases the ECJ ruled that the Commission had not infringed the principle of legal certainty in requiring aid recovery, even though it had waited several months before initiating the formal examination procedures, which then lasted, respectively thirty-one and fifty-five months. In reaching this conclusion, the Court ruled that it was a lack of cooperation from the Member State concerned that was essentially to blame for the delay (Case C-301/87 *France v EC Commission* paras 26–28, and Case C-303/88 *Italy v EC Commission* paras 40–44. Along the same lines, see Case T-109/01 *Fleuren Compost v EC Commission* para 147).

[65] Case C-303/88 *Italy v EC Commission* [1991] ECR I-1933 para 43.

[66] Case T-308/00 *Salzgitter v EC Commission* not yet reported paras 167–180.

declared to be incompatible. The ECJ declared in the case that the fact that the Commission initially decided not to raise any objections to the aid in issue cannot be regarded as capable of having caused the recipient undertaking to entertain any legitimate expectation since that decision had been challenged in due time and then annulled by the Court. However regrettable it may be, the Commission's error cannot, according to the Court, erase the consequences of the unlawful conduct of the Member State.[67]

Legitimate expectations

23.49 The general principle of law most often invoked against the recovery is that of legitimate expectations, either of the Member State or the aid recipient. Except where there are 'exceptional circumstances',[68] such a claim will not succeed.

23.50 In view of their privileged negotiating position with the Commission, the national authorities are therefore less able than the recipients of aid to claim that their legitimate expectations have been prejudiced.[69] As for recipients, they cannot argue on the grounds of their small size that they were not obliged to be aware of Community law, otherwise the effectiveness of this law would be undermined.[70] Any apparent failure to act by the Commission is equally irrelevant when an aid scheme has not been notified.[71] The fact that they have not been informed by their national authorities of the progress of the administrative procedure cannot be deemed to be an exceptional circumstance serving as grounds for their legitimate expectation. The only possibly valid grounds would therefore be when the Commission had given them precise assurances of such a nature as to engender well-founded expectations of the lawfulness of the aid concerned.[72]

23.51 The mere passing of time cannot be deemed to create such a legitimate expectation if it did not exist originally.[73]

Practice of the Commission

23.52 The Commission regularly refrains from demanding the recovery of incompatible aid. The commonest reason for doing so is the attitude and good faith of the aid recipient, of the national authorities and of the Commission itself, as well as

---

[67] Case C-169/95 *Spain v EC Commission* para 53.
[68] Joined Cases C-183/02 P and C-187/02 P *Demesa v EC Commission* para 51.
[69] Case C-334/99 *Germany v EC Commission* para 45.
[70] Case C-298/00 P *Italy v EC Commission* para 88.
[71] Joined Cases C-183/02 P and C-187/02 P *Demesa v EC Commission* para 52.
[72] Case T-109/01 *Fleuren Compost v EC Commission* paras 140–142.
[73] Joined Cases T-126/96 and T-127/96 *Breda Fucine Meridionali and others v EC Commission* paras 69 and 70.

the nature and effects of the aid and the length of the examination procedure. The Commission has thus declined to demand aid recovery in the following circumstances:

- when aid is incompatible for the sole reason that it has been paid late, if the recipient has shown good faith and the delay is due to objective difficulties of powers on this matter shared between the local and central authorities of the Member State concerned;[74]

- when aid has been paid over ten years ago, the Commission has been informed of it indirectly and the authorities of the Member State may have been misled about their obligations due to the internal power-sharing problems;[75]

- because of the length of time running from the date on which the Commission learned of the aid and the date of adopting the final decision;[76]

- when there is a legitimate expectation on the part of the public authorities and recipients as to the private nature of the funds paid out because the same funds had been considered to be private in the context of Community structural funds;[77]

- as regards tax exemptions for biofuels, due to the conformity of the purpose of the aid with Community policy and the smallness of the advantage for the beneficiaries, in view of the fact that the aid offset excess production costs.[78]

Case law of the CFI

In a judgment of January 1998, the CFI ruled against the Commission's prac- **23.53** tice of not requiring the recovery of aid in certain cases.[79] It considered in fact that the invocation of exceptional circumstances serving as grounds for the

---

[74] Decision 91/176/CECA [1991] OJ L86/28.

[75] Decision of 17 July 1996 on aid granted by the Province of Bolzano to the company Acciaierie di Bolzano [1996] OJ L274/30 para IV.

[76] Decision of 25 July 1990 on aid granted by the Italian government to a manufacturer of ophthalmic products [1992] OJ L183/30 para VIII (in this case the procedure had lasted twenty months and had not however suffered any unexplained interruption).

[77] Decision of 3 June 2003 on aid Case C 87/2001—*Orkney Islands Council Track Record Scheme* [2003] OJ L211/49 paras 70–72.

[78] Decision of 18 December 1996 on tax exemptions for biofuels in France [1997] OJ L222/26 (these grounds, which could be valid for determination of aid compatibility, are hardly convincing, however, as grounds for not requiring aid recovery). In a later file the Commission considered that the conditions laid down in that decision of December 1996 were not met, despite the arguments to the contrary put forward by the recipient (Decision of 21 January 1998 on aid granted by the Netherlands to a hydrogen pyroxide works in Delfzijl [1998] OJ L171/36, para VII).

[79] Case T-67/94 *Ladbroke Racing v EC Commission* [1998] ECR II-1 paras 179 to 185.

legitimate expectations of the recipient is subject to a double limit: firstly, such exceptional circumstances can be invoked not by the Member State concerned but only by the recipient, and secondly it can be invoked only in the context of proceedings before the public authorities or the national courts.[80] This double limit seems to conflict with the case law of the ECJ. Indeed, the Court does not seem to rule out the possibility of the Member State claiming the legitimate expectations of the recipient in the context of an action for annulment against the Commission's decision[81] and above all, as that right is a direct consequence of the *RSV* judgment, the same possibility is open to the recipient before Community Courts, not only before national courts.

Non-recovery by virtue of Community law and non-recovery by virtue of national law

23.54 Apart from the case law of the CFI mentioned in the previous section, we find that there are certain elements of Community law that could serve to justify the choice not to recover incompatible aid. These are principles that the Commission has to take into account when it adopts its decision and, in default thereof, could be invoked before the Community courts as supporting grounds for the party's claim for annulment of the decision requiring aid recovery.

23.55 Even though they share many common features, a clear distinction should be made between these principles of Community law and principles of national law that, albeit not questioning the validity of a Commission decision calling for aid recovery, can nonetheless be invoked before national courts by the aid recipient to challenge the recovery demanded in the Commission's final decision.[82] At Commission level any prohibition of aid-recovery rulings is based exclusively on principles drawn directly from Community law, whereas, in national courts, it is national law that is applied, within the limits allowed by Community law. The circumstances that may be invoked might also be different. Thus, only national courts can base their arguments on the circumstances subsequent to the Commission's final decision, for example the subsequent behaviour of the latter or the national authorities.

23.56 The recipient of unlawful aid which is declared to be incompatible is therefore perfectly entitled, in our view, to lodge an action for annulment against the Commission's decision before the Community Court and demand the abolition

---

[80] This second condition was first formulated by the CFI in *Siemens v EC Commission* (Case T-459/93 para 104), on the basis of a mistaken reading, in our view, of the Court's previous case law. This was reaffirmed by Case T-109/01 *Fleuren Compost v EC Commission* para 137.

[81] A clear distinction should be made here between action for annulment and action for failure to fulfil an obligation.

[82] See para 23.71 for more information on this procedure before the national courts.

of the recovery order (*RSV*); afterwards, if this appeal is turned down, it is likewise entitled to challenge the effective recovery and lodge a new appeal against the recovery before its national courts.[83]

Recovery of incompatible aid and repayment of unlawful aid

An aid recovery requirement may also be based on the sole grounds that it has **23.57** been granted unlawfully without abiding by the procedure set out in Article 88(3) and this repayment obligation may be resisted only in 'exceptional circumstances'.[84] These 'exceptional circumstances', to be taken into account by the national courts when an infringement of the last sentence of Article 88(3) is brought before them and they have to appraise the rightfulness of an order to repay illegally paid aid, are different from the 'exceptional circumstances' serving as the grounds for blocking the recovery of aid declared to be incompatible.

C. Implementation

1. Obligations of the Member State

Under Article 249 of the EC Treaty, the Member State to which a decision **23.58** ordering the recovery of unlawful aid is addressed must take all necessary measures to ensure the implementation of the said decision.[85] A Member State fulfils its obligations as regards recovery if the measures it takes are conducive to the re-establishment of the normal conditions of competition which were distorted by the grant of the illegal aid and are consistent with the relevant provisions of Community law.[86] The refunding of aid therefore implies that the recipient no longer has effective enjoyment of it or, in other words, that it is deprived of any illicit competitive advantage deriving from it.[87] The Member State is free to choose the means by which it will execute this obligation, provided that the measures chosen do not adversely affect the scope and effectiveness of Community law.[88]

The ECJ and the Commission sometimes rule that, in order to implement a **23.59** recovery-ordering decision, the Member State is required to act like a 'private

---

[83] In such a case the national judge has to bear firmly in mind the judgment of the Community Court.

[84] See para 26.11.

[85] Case C-209/00 *EC Commission v Germany* [2002] ECR I-11695 para 31, and Case C-404/00 *EC Commission v Spain* [2003] ECR I-6695 para 21.

[86] Case C-209/00 *EC Commission v Germany* para 35.

[87] A simple provision in an undertaking's balance sheet in anticipation of a future recovery is therefore not the same as repaying the aid in question (Joined Cases T-244/93 and T-486/93 *TWD v EC Commission* [1995] ECR II-2265 para 84).

[88] Case C-209/00 *EC Commission v Germany* para 34, and Case C-404/00 *EC Commission v Spain* para 24.

creditor'.[89] It is not clear what exactly this statement covers, but, in any event, it implies that in order to act like a diligent creditor, the Member State must exhaust all the legal instruments available under its own legal system, such as those used to combat fraud against creditors in the form of acts carried out by the firm in liquidation during the suspect period prior to the bankruptcy, which would allow such acts to be declared invalid.[90]

Alternative means of recovery

23.60   Instead of a 'transfer of funds' the Member State may make arrangements for returning the aid by other measures, providing these measures have an identical, unconditional effect and are applicable without delay. When a Member State chooses to recover unlawful aid by any means other than a cash payment, it must ensure that the measures it chooses are sufficiently transparent and that it furnishes the Commission with all due information allowing it to verify that the method chosen is in fact an alternative way of achieving the decision's purpose.[91]

Liquidation of the recipient undertaking

23.61   When the undertaking's financial situation is so dire that effective recovery turns out to be impossible, the public authorities must bring about the liquidation of the undertaking concerned. According to the ECJ, the Commission's objective in abolishing the aid, could likewise be achieved from the competition point of view, in the absence of an effective recovery, by winding up the company and including the aid recovery as a creditor to be satisfied in the list of claims in the liquidation of the assets:[92] this procedure frees the market segment previously held by the wound-up undertaking, allows public creditors to enforce their claims against the assets or acquire them and reallocate them more effectively. In the absence of recoverable assets, this procedure is the only way of showing the absolute impossibility of recovering the aid.[93] The fact that insolvency proceedings have been brought against the undertaking after the adoption of the Commission's decision ordering the recovery of the aid can in any case cast no doubts on the lawfulness of the decision.[94]

---

[89] Joined Cases C-328/99 and C-399/00 *Italy and others v EC Commission* [2003] ECR I-4035 para 68.

[90] ibid para 69.

[91] Case C-209/00 *EC Commission v Germany* [2002] ECR I-11695 paras 40–44 and 57–58.

[92] Case 52/84 *EC Commission v Belgium* para 14; Case C-499/99 *Spain v EC Commission* [2002] ECR I-6031 para 38, and Case C-277/00 *Germany v EC Commission* para 85.

[93] Case C-499/99 *Spain v EC Commission* para 37, and Joined Cases C-328/99 and C-399/00 *Italy and others v EC Commission* para 69.

[94] Joined Cases C-278/92, C-279/92 and C-280/92 *Spain v EC Commission* [1994] ECR I-4175 para 80, and Case C-42/93 [1994] ECR I-4175 para 33.

2. Recovery Procedure

Procedural arrangements

The sole addressee of a Commission decision ordering the recovery of aid is the **23.62**
Member State concerned and it generates no direct payment obligation vis-à-vis
the undertaking that has benefited from the aid.[95] Community law does not
therefore require that it be enforceable in the relevant national legal system.

According to the Procedural Regulation, the recovery is effected in accordance **23.63**
with the procedures under the national law of the Member State concerned but
only 'provided that they allow the immediate and effective execution of the
Commission's decision'. The aim of this provision is to remedy the drawn-out
process and snags that the recovery procedure currently runs into.[96]

Referral to national law

Since there are no Community provisions on the procedure to be followed, the **23.64**
aid must, in principle, be recovered in accordance with the relevant procedural
provisions of national law.[97]

The Commission's decisions merely order the recovery of the aid without laying **23.65**
down the actual procedures to be followed. Providing that the provisions of the
Procedural Regulation are observed, the recovery of the aid can be effected in
accordance with the relevant procedural provisions of national law,[98] by virtue of
the principle of 'procedural autonomy'. In their arrangements to recover the aid,
national authorities have to make use of the most appropriate internal legal
instruments to hand, with due consideration being paid to the nature of the
instrument by which the aid was granted, the identity of the direct aid-paying
authority, etc. The possibility of recovering aid, however, cannot be made to
depend on the form in which the aid in question was granted.[99]

When aid was granted by way of an administrative decision, which is in fact the **23.66**
most frequent case, the national authorities generally adopt a revocation and
recovery decision on the basis of the national procedure for the revocation of

---

[95] See the Commission's explanations in para 19 of Case 310/85 R *Deufil v EC Commission*
[1986] ECR 537.
[96] The Council, on the contrary, has refused to endorse the Commission's proposal, according
to which the recourses offered by national law could no longer have a suspensive effect.
[97] Case C-404/00 *EC Commission v Spain* para 22.
[98] Case T-459/93 *Siemens v EC Commission* [1995] ECR II-1675 para 82; Case C-24/95
Alcan Deutschland [1997] ECR I-1591 para 24, and Case C-209/00 *EC Commission v Germany*
para 32.
[99] For this reason the Court rejected the Greek government's arguments that the recovery of a
tax exemption was impossible because it would necessarily have to take the form of a retrospective
tax, which would be incompatible with the Greek Constitution and the general principles of law
(Case C-183/91 *EC Commission v Greece* para 17).

unlawful administrative acts. If the undertaking has been declared bankrupt, it then suffices for the public authorities to include their claim in assets to be liquidated; in this case the recovery does not have to be carried out on a privileged basis.[100] Moreover, the undertaking in question can, in principle, challenge the recovery by lodging the appropriate appeals.

Limits on the referral to national law

23.67 The Member States' procedural autonomy, both administrative and jurisdictional, for recovering State aid declared to be incompatible is not limitless.

23.68 **Administrative procedure** No action for annulment having been lodged against the Commission's decision, the competent authorities of the addressee Member States cannot themselves refuse to execute the decision on grounds taken from their internal law. Their role is merely to give effect to the Commission's decision and they are not entitled to reach any other finding.[101] Only the undertaking receiving aid is entitled to adopt such an attitude.[102]

23.69 **Jurisdictional procedure** The Court accepts that the recovery of unlawful aid should in principle be carried out in accordance with the pertinent provisions of national law, but these provisions must be applied subject to the following two conditions: firstly, in such a way as to ensure that the recovery required by Community law is not rendered practically impossible and the interests of the Community are taken fully into consideration in the application of provisions that require the various interests involved to be weighed up before a defective administrative measure is withdrawn and, secondly, in a non-discriminatory way in relation to comparable cases governed only by national law.[103] Here again we once more come across the traditional principles of 'effectiveness' and 'equivalence'.

23.70 In this respect, although the Community legal system cannot override national legislation that ensures respect for legitimate expectations and legal certainty in the recovery process, the Court has nonetheless ruled that in view of the mandatory nature of the supervision of State aid by the Commission under Article 88 of the Treaty, undertakings to which aid has been granted may not, in principle, have a legitimate expectation that the aid is lawful unless it has been granted in compliance with the procedure laid down in that Article. Indeed, any diligent

---

[100] Case C-142/87 *Belgium v EC Commission* [1990] ECR I-959 paras 60 and 62.
[101] Case C-24/95 *Alcan Deutschland* [1997] ECR I-1591 para 34.
[102] Case C-5/89 *EC Commission v Germany* para 17.
[103] Case 94/87 *EC Commission v Germany* [1989] ECR 175 para 12; Case C-142/87 *Belgium v EC Commission* para 61; Case C-5/89 *EC Commission v Germany* [1990] ECR I-3437 para 12; Case T-459/93 *Siemens v EC Commission* [1995] ECR II-1675 para 82; Case C-24/95 *Alcan Deutschland* para 24; Case C-382/99 *Netherlands v EC Commission* [2003] ECR I-4035 para 90, and Case C-404/00 *EC Commission v Spain* [2003] ECR I-6695 para 51.

businessmen should normally be able to ensure that this procedure is observed.[104] It is therefore only in 'exceptional circumstances' that the recipient of unlawful aid may properly rely on legitimate expectation of the lawful character of that aid to challenge the recovery order. In such a case, it is for the national court, if the case comes before it, to assess the circumstances in question, if necessary after submitting to the ECJ questions for a preliminary ruling on interpretation.[105]

In the context of the preliminary procedure, the ECJ has made certain com- **23.71** ments about national jurisdictions. For the most part these comments are based on the need to avoid rendering the recovery required under Community law practically impossible. As regards the aid-recipient's legitimate expectations and the principle of legal certainty, the Court has thus declared that, from the moment the recipient is informed of the Commission's decision declaring the aid to be incompatible and demanding the recovery thereof, the recipient is no longer in a position of legal uncertainty, in view of the obligation of the national authorities to implement this decision without having any discretionary power in regard thereto. It cannot therefore claim that it does not know whether the competent authorities are going to reach a decision and will not be able to set the principle of legal certainty against the recovery of the aid on the grounds that the national authorities have taken too long to comply with the recovery decision.[106] Moreover, even if it is the authority that is responsible for the illegality of the aid decision to such a degree that revocation appears to be a breach of good faith towards the recipient, this cannot be construed as grounds for giving the recipient legitimate expectations as to the lawfulness of the aid.[107] Finally, the aid recipient cannot base its case on the fact that the benefit (of the aid) no longer exists, even in the absence of bad faith on its part. This is so because, first, it has no legitimate expectations regarding the lawfulness of the aid and, secondly, it continues in principle to reap the advantages of the aid, in terms of the retention of its place on the market, reputation, and goodwill, even if the benefit resulting from the grant of State aid no longer appears in its balance sheet.[108]

Such a restrictive account of the arguments that could be legitimately put for- **23.72** ward before a national court would seem to be even more justified in the case where the aid-benefiting undertaking had already had the chance to submit an

---

[104] Case 310/85 *Deufil v EC Commission* [1987] ECR 901 paras 20–25; Case C-5/89 *EC Commission v Germany* para 14; Joined Cases T-244/93 and T-486/93 *TWD v EC Commission* [1995] para 69 and Case C-24/95 *Alcan Deutschland* para 25.

[105] Case C-5/89 *EC Commission v Germany* para 16, and Joined Case T-244/93 and T-486/93 *TWD v EC Commission* [1995] ECR II-2265 para 69.

[106] Case C-24/95 *Alcan Deutschland* paras 27–38. Only delay caused by the Commission, therefore, could be taken into consideration.

[107] Case C-24/95 *Alcan Deutschland* paras 39–43.

[108] ibid paras 44–54.

action for annulment directly to the CFI against the Commission's decision and to bring up the question of legitimate expectations, which forms part of the fundamental rights underpinning the Community legal order.[109] It cannot be totally ruled out, however, that the recipient could claim before the national courts that it had acquired a legitimate expectation after the adoption of the Commission's decision, for example because of the behaviour of the latter.

23.73 Furthermore, Community law does not prevent national courts from deferring a preliminary question to the Court under Article 234 EC or ordering a stay of execution of the recovery requirement proceedings while the basic issue is being dealt with in the Community Court,[110] at least insofar as the conditions laid down by the Court in *Zuckerfabrik Süderdithmarschen*[111] are met.

3. Determination of the person bound to return the aid

23.74 The aid is to be recovered from the aid recipients, i.e. the persons who have actually benefited from it.[112] The implementation of this rule is not always straightforward, especially in the event of the sale of the undertaking or the part of the undertaking concerned between the moment of granting the aid and the moment the Commission's decision was taken. The implementation arrangements must always take into account that the main purpose of the reimbursement is to eliminate the distortion of competition.[113]

Recovery from third party undertakings

23.75 In certain decisions the Commission has ordered incompatible aid to be recovered not only from the direct recipient thereof but also other undertakings in whose benefit there has been a transfer of shares ('share deal') or assets ('asset deal') from the direct recipient, in particular when it suspects that this transfer had been carried out to undermine the effects of the Commission's decision.

23.76 In the case of a 'share deal', the aid-receiving undertaking continues to exist; only the ownership thereof has changed. The recovery obligation is hence still

---

[109] As the undertaking Deufil has done, for example, in Case 310/85 *Deufil v EC Commission* [1987] ECR I-537 paras 20–25. See also para 22 of the Opinion of AG Darmon in Case C-5/89 *EC Commission v Germany* [1990] ECR I-3437. cf the approach, mistaken in our view, followed by the CFI Case T-459/93 *Siemens v EC Commission* para 104.

[110] Case T-181/02 R *Neue Erba Lautex v EC Commission* [2002] ECR II-5081 para 108.

[111] Joined Cases C-143/88 and C-92/89 *Zuckerfabrik Süderdithmarschen* [1991] ECR I-415.

[112] Case C-303/88 *Italy v EC Commission* para 57, and Case C-305/89 *Italy v EC Commission* [1991] ECR I-1603 para 40; Joined Cases C-328/99 and C-399/00 *Italy and others v EC Commission* [2003] ECR I-4035 para 65, and Case C-277/00 *Germany v EC Commission* not yet reported para 75.

[113] Case C-277/00 *Germany v EC Commission* para 76.

incumbent on it, the aid following the undertaking, whatever the price fixed for the transaction.[114] Neither the seller nor the purchaser are, in principle, concerned with the obligation to return the aid.

In the case of an 'asset deal', however, the Court concentrates on the financial **23.77** conditions of these transactions. When there is a sale at a market price, it considers that the aid element has been assessed at market price and included in the purchase price, and therefore the purchaser of the assets cannot be considered to have benefited from a competitive market advantage.[115]

The ECJ acknowledges that certain circumstances can undermine the effective- **23.78** ness of the recovery decision, especially when, after the Commission's enquiry or decision, the undertaking's assets and liabilities are transferred to another company (for example a shell company[116]), controlled by the same persons at below-market prices or by way of procedures that lack transparency; the purpose of such a transaction may be to safeguard the assets from the decision and allow the economic activity in question to be continued indefinitely.[117] It then accepts that the recovery should not be restricted to the original firm but also be extended to the firm that continues the activity of the original firm, using the transferred means of production, in cases where certain elements of the transfer point to economic continuity between the two firms. The factors that have to be taken into account are the purpose of the transfer, the identity of the share-holders or owners of the acquiring firm and of the original firm, the moment at which the transfer was carried out, the economic logic and, above all, the transfer price. The Court considers this last factor to be crucial: the Commission has to be able to establish that the assignment price has been influenced (downwards) by the purchaser's risk of having to return the aid in due course; if not, the Court considers that it is the original undertaking or its shareholders that have kept the benefit of the aid received from the sale of its shares at market price.[118] In other words, in the case of a repurchase of assets at market price, the aid element would have been included in the purchase price and the purchaser cannot be regarded as having benefited from an advantage in relation to other

---

[114] Case C-277/00 *Germany v EC Commission* para 81. (This judgment has fortunately corrected the error committed by the Court in para 78 of the judgment of 20 September 2001, *Banks*, Case C-390/98, in which it had asserted that 'when a company which has benefited from aid has been sold at the market price, the purchase price reflects the consequences of the previous aid, and it is the seller of that company that keeps the benefit of the aid').

[115] Case C-390/98 *Banks* [2001] ECR I-6117 para 77, and Case C-277/00 *Germany v EC Commission* para 80.

[116] Case C-277/00 *Germany v EC Commission* para 86.

[117] Joined Cases C-328/99 and C-399/00 *Italy and others v EC Commission* para 69.

[118] ibid paras 77–85.

market operators.[119] In the case of an 'asset deal', the Commission considers that, if the assets of an aid-recipient company are transferred to undertakings belonging to the same group as the recipient company, the aid-repayment obligation will then be equally incumbent on the whole group of undertakings that, thanks to the asset transfer, have been able to profit from the favourable effects of the granting of aid. If, on the other hand, the assets are sold to third-party undertakings, separately and at market price, the Commission then considers that the purchasers will not be bound to repay the aid; if they are sold en bloc, however, allowing the subsidised activity to continue, then the purchaser will be considered to be free from the repayment obligation only if the sales procedure was unconditional and open to all competitors, as well as being a sale at market price.[120] The ECJ subsequently rectified this approach, specifying that it sufficed for the procedure to be 'sufficiently open and transparent'. The Court also attaches importance to any intervention by an official receiver under a court order, thereby reducing the risks of fraudulent behaviour.[121]

4. Determination of the body through which the aid-repayment operation is to be effected

23.79   Unless specifically indicated by the Commission, in principle it is sufficient for the recipient to repay the aid through the body from which it had originally received it. True, it cannot be ruled out that such an allocation of funds to this body could in turn be considered as new aid. But such aid is not covered by the Commission's original negative decision and it cannot therefore demand that the aid be returned into the coffers of the public authorities in the strict sense,[122] at least in the absence of any explicit indication to that effect in the decision.

5. Calculation of the sum to be recovered

23.80   As a general rule the Commission is not required to determine the sum to be reimbursed in its decision ordering the repayment of the aid.[123] It suffices for the decision to give indications enabling the addressee Member State to determine this sum itself without excessive difficulties.[124] The obligation on a Member State to calculate the exact amount of aid to be recovered—particularly where that calculation is dependent on information which that Member State has not

---

[119] Case C-390/98 *Banks* para 77, and Case C-277/00 *Germany v EC Commission* para 80.
[120] Case C-277/00 *Germany v EC Commission* paras 65–70.
[121] ibid paras 93 and 95.
[122] Case C-348/93 *EC Commission v Italy* [1995] ECR I-699 paras 28 and 29, and Case C-350/93, paras 23 and 24.
[123] Case T-67/94 *Ladbroke Racing v EC Commission* [1998] ECR II-1 para 187.
[124] Case 102/87 *France v EC Commission* [1988] ECR 4067 para 33, and Case C-480/98 *Spain v EC Commission* [2000] ECR I-8717 para 25.

provided to the Commission—forms part of the more general reciprocal obligation to cooperate in good faith in the implementation of Treaty rules concerning
State aids imposed on the Commission and the Member States.[125]

Insofar as the calculation of the amount of aid to be recovered may call for **23.81**
consideration of tax regimes where the basis of assessment, the rates and the
rules governing recovery are fixed directly by the relevant domestic legislation,
the Commission is entitled merely to make a general statement that the recipient is obliged to repay the aid in question and to leave it up to the national
authorities to calculate the exact amount of aid to be recovered.[126] The Commission is not obliged to determine the incidence of tax on the amount of aid to
be recovered, since that calculation falls within the scope of national law; it is
merely required to indicate the gross sum to be recovered. That does not prevent
the national authorities, when recovering the amount in question, from deduct-
ing certain sums, where appropriate, from the amount to be recovered pursuant
to their internal rules, provided that the application of those rules does
not make such recovery impossible in practice or discriminate in relation to
comparable cases governed by national law.[127]

Interest on the sum to be repaid

The sums to be reimbursed shall include interest calculated from the moment **23.82**
the aid was granted to the moment of its effective repayment.[128] This addition
of interest, applied by initiative of the Commission and then approved by
the Community Courts, has finally been enshrined as an official rule in the
Procedural Regulation (Article 14(2)). The Court often speaks of 'default
interest'.[129] The restoration of the situation that obtained before payment of the
unlawful aid indeed entails the elimination of all financial advantages resulting
from the aid and adversely effecting competition within the common market. It
follows that a Commission decision ordering the recovery of unlawful aid pursuant to Article 88(2) may also require interest to be recovered on the sums
granted in order to eliminate any financial advantages incidental to such aid.
This interest represents the equivalent of the financial advantage accruing from
the free provision of the capital in question for a certain period. The absence of
any claim to interest on the unlawfully granted sums at the time of their
recovery would amount to maintaining incidental financial advantages, consisting of the grant of an interest-free loan, for the undertaking concerned; this

---

[125] Case C-382/99 *Netherlands v EC Commission* [2002] ECR I-5163 para 91.
[126] Case T-67/94 *Ladbroke Racing v EC Commission* para 188, and Case C-480/98 *Spain v EC Commission* para 26.
[127] Case T-459/93 *Siemens v EC Commission* para 83.
[128] See, initially the letter of 4 March 1991, in: *EC Competition Law*, Vol IIA, 1999, 65.
[129] Case C-480/98 *Spain v EC Commission* para 35.

would in itself represent the granting of aid that would distort or jeopardize competition.[130]

Exception to the charging of interest

23.83 According to the ECJ, the Commission ought to accept any provisions under national legislation whereby interest ceases to accrue on the debts of undertakings that have been declared insolvent with effect from the date of the relevant declaration. The Court has based its position on the following factors: the objective sought by this legislation (the common interest of the creditors not to impose new obligations on the assets of the bankrupt undertaking, likely only to worsen its situation); the absence of any discrimination in its application and the fact that it applies only to interest falling due after the declaration of insolvency on aid unlawfully received before that declaration, concluding that the legislation cannot be regarded as contrary to the principle of effectiveness.[131]

Calculation of interest

23.84 To determine the interest rate to be applied, the Commission at first merely deferred to national legislation on default interest on State debts. This method soon proved unsatisfactory, so it decided to fix the interest rate. The method for fixing the interest rate is now laid down in Article 9 of the Regulation 794/2004 of 21 April 2004 implementing Regulation (EC) 659/1999.[132] The interest period runs from the date on which the aid was actually made available until the date of its effective repayment.[133]

III. Interim measures and the Commission's power to grant injunctions

A. Principle

23.85 Although the Treaty is silent on the point, the ECJ has accepted in practice that the Commission should be able to grant certain interim measures to palliate

---

[130] Case T-459/93 *Siemens v EC Commission* paras 97–102, and Case C-480/98 *Spain v EC Commission* para 35.

[131] Case C-480/98 *Spain v EC Commission* para 37.

[132] [2004] OJ L140/1 Previously the Commission had used the reference rate serving for the calculation of the net grant equivalent of regional aid within the Member State concerned (Communication to Member States of 22 February 1995 on the interest rate to be used in reimbursements of unlawful and incompatible aid, in: *EC Competition Law*, Vol IIA, 1999, 76).

[133] Case T-459/93 *Siemens v EC Commission* para 103, and Case C-169/95 *Spain v EC Commission* para 47. The interest application method is also dealt with in Art 11 of Reg 784/2004.

any infringement by a Member State of its standstill obligation on new aid.[134] It considers that the Treaty's a priori control system, if it is to be effective, presupposes that measures may be taken to counteract any infringement of the rules laid down in Article 88(3) of the Treaty and that such measures may, with a view to protecting the legitimate interests of the Member States, form the subject matter of an action.[135] Conversely, any precautionary measures that might be taken by the Commission seek only to obviate any infringement of the rules of Article 88(3), so any interim measure that does not seek such an end will be regarded as unlawful.[136]

Three types of measures are envisaged, namely decisions ordering the Member   **23.86** State to suspend payment of aid, its provisional recovery, or the provision of information.[137]

B. 'Boussac' Suspension Injunction

1. Object

This injunction is dealt with in Article 11(1) of the Procedural Regulation.   **23.87** When the Commission finds that aid has been set up or altered without preliminary notification it can carry out the examination to assess the compatibility of this measure with the common market but it is also empowered, after having afforded the Member State concerned the opportunity to make its comments, to issue an interim decision requiring it to suspend immediately the payment of the aid pending the result of the aid examination procedure (the so-called 'Boussac' injunction). The Commission has the same power in cases where it has been notified of aid but the Member State in question, instead of awaiting the outcome of the procedure provided for under Article 88(2) and (3) of the Treaty, has instead proceeded to put the aid into effect, contrary to the prohibition contained in Article 88(3).[138]

Such a suspension can be effective only if the aid concerned has not already been   **23.88**

---

[134] This possibility of taking 'immediate interim' measures if need be, within the context of Art 88(3) was first acknowledged in Case 70/72 *EC Commission v Germany* [1973] ECR 813 para 20.

[135] Case C-301/87 *France v EC Commission* [1990] ECR I-307 para 18.

[136] Case T-107/96 R *Pantochim v EC Commission* [1996] ECR II-1361 paras 40 and 41.

[137] The 'Boussac' suspension injunction as presented in Court judgments usually includes a requirement of information from the State but such a requirement does not seem to be necessarily bound up with the adoption of a suspension injunction. These two types of injunction are dealt with separately below.

[138] Case C-301/87 *France v EC Commission* paras 19 and 20, and Case C-303/88 *Italy v EC Commission* para 46.

entirely paid. It would hence seem to be a suitable measure for 'freezing' the implementation of unlawful aid schemes rather than combating the unlawful payment of individual aid.[139]

23.89 When a Member State has complied in full with the Commission's order, the Commission is obliged to examine the compatibility of the aid with the common market, in accordance with the procedure laid down in Article 88(2) and (3).[140] Conversely, if the Member State fails to suspend payment of the aid, the ECJ has recognized the Commission's right, while carrying out the substantive examination of the matter, to bring the matter directly before the Court by applying for a declaration that such payment amounts to an infringement of the Treaty. According to the Court, such a referral is justified on the grounds of urgency because there has been a decision embodying an order, taken after the Member State in question has been given an opportunity to submit its comments and thus at the conclusion of a preliminary procedure in which it has been allowed to put forward its arguments, as in the case of the means of redress provided under the second subparagraph of Article 88(2).[141]

2. Form

23.90 Suspension injunctions are sometimes adopted in the form of a formal decision published in the Official Journal series L[142] and sometimes in the form of a simple communication, often at the same time as the start of the procedure.[143]

3. Preliminary procedure

23.91 Before adopting a suspension injunction, the Commission is bound to give the Member State concerned an opportunity to submit its comments. This

---

[139] See para 39 of the Opinion of AG Jacobs in Case C-42/93 *Spain v EC Commission* [1994] ECR I-4175.

[140] Case C-301/87 *France v EC Commission* para 21, and Case C-303/88 *Italy v EC Commission* para 47.

[141] Case C-301/87 *France v EC Commission* para 23, and Case C-303/88 *Italy v EC Commission* para 48.

[142] See the Decision of 11 June 1991 requiring the French government to suspend the implementation of the aid described below in favour of PMU and introduced in breach of Art 93(3) [1992] OJ L14/35; the Decision of 26 January 1994 requiring France to suspend the payment to Groupe Bull of aid granted in breach of Art 93(3) of the EC Treaty [1994] OJ L107/61; Decision of 30 April 1996 ordering the Italian government to supply all the documentation, information and data on aid for restructuring the road haulage sector and to suspend forthwith the payment of any further aid [1996] OJ L233/20, and Decision of 30 April 1997 requiring the Portuguese government to suspend the aid in the form of a State guarantee granted to the undertaking EPAC [1997] OJ L186/25.

[143] See, e.g. the Communication on guidelines introduced by the Burgenland authorities on holdings in companies *in fine* [1998] OJ C154/7.

preliminary letter from the Commission requires the State to suspend implementation of the aid and inform the Commission of the measures taken to meet this obligation. The Commission then gives it in principle a thirty-day period to respond.[144] This letter is often enclosed with the letter communicating the initiation of the formal examination procedure.[145] The injunction properly speaking is then adopted if the Member State declines or fails to respond.[146]

4. Simple enabling power

According to the CFI, the Commission is simply empowered to resort to this   **23.92**
procedure but is by no means required automatically to order the Member State concerned to suspend the payment of aid that has not been duly notified.[147] The Commission is hence invested with a discretionary power and would not be bound to give grounds to a disgruntled competitor for its decision not to make use of this suspension procedure.

C. Provisional Recovery Injunction

Article 11(2) of the Procedural Regulation empowers the Commission to adopt   **23.93**
a provisional recovery injunction, the legality of which had previously been challenged.[148] It lays down strict eligibility conditions for resorting to this recovery injunction; there must be no doubts about the aid character of the measure concerned; there must be an urgency to act and a serious risk of substantial and irreparable damage to a competitor. The burden of proof is on

---

[144] ommunication to Member States of 4 March 1991, in: *EC Competition Law*, Vol IIA, 1999, 65.

[145] See, for example, the Communication on the guidelines of the Wirtschaftsservice Burgenland Aktiengesellschaft on holdings in companies [1998] OJ C154/7, 11.

[146] Decision of 30 April 1997 requiring the Portuguese government to suspend aid granted to EPAC [1997] OJ L186/25.

[147] Case T-49/93 *SIDE v EC Commission* [1995] ECR II-2501 para 83.

[148] On the basis of the *Boussac* judgment, the Commission had previously regarded itself as also empowered to take decisions requiring Member States to provisionally recover aid paid out in breach of the last sentence of Art 88(3), to counter this breach, this entitlement lasting until the final decision on the compatibility of the measure (Communication to Member States [1995] OJ C156/5). The compatibility of such an injunction with the case law of the Court was not certain, however: Advocate General Jacobs had requested a solution of this type in 1994 (Opinion in Case C-42/93 *Spain v EC Commission* [1994] ECR I-4175 para 39) but the Court, in para 45 of the judgment of 11 July 1996, *SFEI and others* (Case C-39/94, para 45), declared that 'the Commission can do no more than order further payments to be suspended so long as it has not adopted its final decision on the substance of the matter'. The Commission itself seemed resigned to not being able to order a provisional recovery pending the Council regulation (see the position expressed by this institution in para 26 of the Order of 21 October 1996, *Pantochim v EC Commission*, Case T-107/96 R). It is no doubt for this reason that the Commission has always seen fit since to waive the use of this power that it had always thought itself entitled to.

the Commission, so this procedure is difficult to resort to and hence rarely used. Moreover, this procedure can be applied only to unlawful aid implemented after the entry into force of the Regulation.

23.94 Under cover of a simple 'suspension', however, the Commission has sometimes imposed on the Member States measures that strongly resemble those of a provisional recovery injunction. Thus, when an undertaking has become bankrupt, the Commission has invited the Member State to include in the bankruptcy proceedings (under all reserves) all debts corresponding to aid for which recovery might be claimed.[149] Such an action seems to be equivalent *de facto* to a provisional recovery.

D. Information Injunction

23.95 The information injunction contained in Article 10(2) and (3) of the Procedural Regulation is an instrument at the disposal of the Commission when faced with a Member State that does not comply with its duty to cooperate with the Commission and fails to furnish the information requested. The failure to furnish the Commission with sufficient information hardly raises any problem when the Member State has complied with its duty of not paying the aid before receiving the Commission's approval; indeed, the Commission can refrain from authorizing the implementation of the aid until it has received all necessary information. It is therefore not necessary to resort to an information injunction. However, the same cannot be said of unlawful aid, for in this case it is in the interests of the common market for the Commission to be able to palliate the effects of any incompatibility of the measure as soon as possible.

23.96 To guarantee the effectiveness of the system, the ECJ decided that, failing the cooperation of the Member State concerned, the Commission was empowered to base its decision on the only information to hand. The Member State's silence hence played against it. In view of the exorbitant nature of this power granted to the Commission, however, the ECJ ruled that, before taking a decision, the Commission had to require the Member State to furnish all necessary information. This is therefore a procedural stage introduced by the Court in an attempt to reconcile the States' right to a defence and the need to deal with unlawful aid cases swiftly and efficiently.

23.97 Such an injunction is not systematically made use of; it is only when the Commission considers that it is not in possession of all the necessary information

---

[149] See the Communication on aid granted by the German government to *Spindelfabrik Hartha* [1998] OJ C224/6 para 4.3 *in fine*.

that it requires the Member State concerned to furnish it. It is perfectly entitled to adopt a final decision directly without doing so, on the understanding that when it has not made use of its powers to require the Member State concerned to furnish it with information, it cannot then justify its decision on the grounds of the fragmentary nature of the information to hand.[150]

23.98 The Procedural Regulation envisages the information injunction as part of the unlawful aid control procedure and obliges the Commission to address a first request for information to the State concerned (Article 10(2) and (3)) and then, if need be, a reminder. Two situations are possible according to whether the purpose of the injunction is to allow the Commission to open the examination procedure with standstill effect (*Italgrani* injunction) or to enable it to adopt a final decision (*Pleuger* injunction).

1. *Italgrani* injunction

23.99 The first case covers those situations in which individual aid or an aid scheme has been approved by the Commission and therefore constitutes in principle an existing aid, but the Commission suspects that the existing aid has been applied in an improper fashion (breaching the approval decision) or that, under cover of existing aid, entirely new aid has in fact been paid out. In such a case the Commission might be bound to send a previous information injunction to the Member State before being able to open the formal examination procedure and come to the conclusion that it in fact consists of new aid or an improper use of existing aid. This injunction, called the *Italgrani* injunction, is part of the wider picture of the vetting of existing aid and is dealt with in more detail in paragraph 24.27 below.

2. *Pleuger* injunction

23.100 The other situation arises when the Commission is conducting an enquiry into unlawfully granted aid and the Member State fails to furnish the Commission with certain information on the aid, either due to deliberate evasion or lack of organization. In this case the Commission formally asks it to furnish the information required and it is only if the Member State still fails to come up with the information sought, despite the Commission's order, that the latter is entitled to put an end to the procedure and base its final decision on the

---

[150] Case T-274/01 *Valmont Nederland v EC Commission* not yet reported paras 58 and 60.

information to hand.[151] Thus, in the *Pleuger* case, the Court held that in order for the Commission to be able to deal with the whole set of individual aid as a scheme or programme, as appears solely from the information to hand (thus permitting it to establish the application of Article 87 globally and not in relation to each individual aid) when the Member State has denied the existence of such a scheme, the Commission must first require the Member State by way of an interim decision to furnish it with all relevant information on the whole set of aid concerned.[152] In this case, the Commission's injunction is normally adopted after or concurrently with the opening of a procedure under Article 88(2) and before the final decision[153] (unlike an *Italgrani* injunction, which has to be adopted before the initiation of the procedure). The *Pleuger* injunction probably does not constitute a contestable act. Such an injunction can be adopted at the same time as a *Boussac* injunction for suspension of the part of the aid not yet granted.

23.101 A variant of this procedure concerns aid that the Commission suspects is being misused and in relation to which it has already opened the examination procedure.[154]

---

[151] Case C-301/87 *France v EC Commission* para 22; Case C-303/88 *Italy v EC Commission* para 47; Joined Cases C-324/90 and C-342/90 *Germany and Pleuger Worthington v EC Commission* para 26, and Case T-274/01 *Valmont Nederland v EC Commission* para 55.

[152] Joined Cases C-324/90 and C-342/90 *Germany and Pleuger Worthington v EC Commission*.

[153] For examples of injunctions decided at the same time as the initiation of the procedure see the Communication concerning the aid granted by the German government to Everts Erfurt [1998] OJ C37/8; the Communication on aid to firms in Venice and Chioggia by way of relief from social security contributions [1998] OJ C51/9; the Communication concerning the aid granted by the German government to Brockhausen Holze [1998] OJ C144/15, and the Communication concerning the aid granted to Ergee Textilwerk GmbH, Autriche [1998] OJ C298/2 para 9. For an example of an injunction adopted after the initiation of the procedure, see the Decision of 15 July 1997 inviting Germany to furnish all documentation, information and facts on the restructuring of of SHB Stahl—und Hartgußwerke Bösdorf AG, and on the aid granted to it ([1997] OJ L323/29). The form adopted varies accordingly: ranging from a simple communication published in the Official Journal series C, in one case, to a formal Decision published in the Official Journal L, in the other. This uneven treatment appears logical.

[154] The Commission had approved restructuring aid in favour of an undertaking. Later on it initiated the procedure in relation to, firstly, new aid unlawfully granted to the same undertaking and, secondly, aid previously approved. In view of the lack of cooperation of the Member State concerned, the Commission finally decided to require it to furnish all necessary information for assessing the compatibility of the aid (Commission Decision of 15 July 1997 ordering Germany to provide all documentation, information and data on the restructuring of Bösdorf, and on the aid granted to it [1997] OJ L323/29). In this decision the Commission considered that the principle of such an injunction 'applies equally when the Commission has already approved the aid but has initiated the procedure because it entertains doubts about the information on which its decision was based'.

24

CONTROL OF EXISTING AID SCHEMES

The existing aid schemes in the various Member States are permanently **24.01**
reviewed by the Commission under Article 88(1). It can propose or demand
that these schemes be altered or abolished when it considers that their
compatibility with the common market is not clear.

The notion of 'existing aid' is examined below in Part I and the determination **24.02**
of whether aid can be considered to be existing aid is examined in Part II. Part
III deals with the procedural arrangements for the permanent review system
exercised by the Commission in cooperation with Member States.

I. Concept of existing aid scheme

The category of existing aid takes in the whole set of aid that can be or has been **24.03**
granted by Member States. The notion of existing aid aims to ensure legal
certainty for Member States and recipient undertakings by guaranteeing the
legality of the aid concerned. Existing aid can therefore continue to be paid as
long as the Commission has not found it to be incompatible with the common
market.[1]

A. Distinction Between an Existing Aid Scheme and Existing Individual Aid

The control of existing aid properly speaking concerns only aid schemes and not **24.04**
individual aid. When an aid scheme is said to be 'existing', this means that the
individual aid can be paid to recipients in application of this scheme (individual
case of application) without the Commission needing in principle to carry out a

---

[1] Case C-387/92 *Banco Exterior de España* [1994] ECR I-877 para 20.

889

new preliminary review. Insofar as such a scheme allows the granting of a host of individual aid during a period that might be unlimited, therefore, it is important that there be a system in place for regularly reviewing and reassessing its compatibility with the common market in line with ongoing economic and regulatory trends. This is not the case, however, with existing individual aid, which has been approved on the basis of its own characteristics and can hence be paid to its recipient without being called into question any longer.

24.05 The permanent review procedure for existing aid contained in paragraphs 1 and 2 of Article 88 concerns in principle, therefore, only aid schemes. Indeed, insofar as it is a procedure that has only future effects it makes sense only in relation to measures that have not yet been paid to their recipients.

B. Categories of Existing Aid

24.06 Existing aid is grouped into five categories; there are three main ones,[2] namely approved aid, 'pre-accession' aid and *Lorenz* aid, and two subsidiary categories which were added by the Procedural Regulation.

1. Approved aid[3]

24.07 First of all, existing aid is considered to be aid that has already been approved by an express decision from the Commission declaring it to be compatible with the common market (or as the case may be by the Council on the basis of Article 88(2)(3)). This is the most important category; most of the aid granted by Member States is deemed to be in application of aid schemes whose particular arrangements have been approved by the Commission.

24.08 To qualify as existing aid it is necessary for the individual application of an approved scheme to observe completely not only the particular arrangements of the scheme such as they have been notified to the Commission but also any conditions or restrictions, sectoral or otherwise, that might have been imposed by the Commission at the moment of approving the scheme. In other words, it must be aid that represents the strict and foreseeable application of the conditions laid down in the decision approving the general aid scheme.[4]

2. Pre-accession aid

24.09 Secondly, all aid that already 'existed' on the day a given Member State joined the European Community is, in principle, considered to be existing aid. This

---

[2] Case C-44/93 *Namur-Les assurances du crédit* [1994] ECR I-3829 para 13.
[3] See Art 1(b)(ii) of the Procedural Reg.
[4] Case T-176/01 *Ferriere Nord v EC Commission* not yet reported para 51.

obviously takes in all the individual aid that had been granted to undertakings before accession but also aid schemes in force on the day of accession. The individual cases of application of these schemes can therefore continue to be legally granted after accession.[5]

Given that 'pre-accession' aid may turn out to be incompatible with existing **24.10** legislation or the Commission's practice, provision needs to be made for bringing it into line with Community interests. This can be done either at the moment the new Member State joins the Community, by inserting specific provisions in the Act of Accession, or later by following the classic *ex nunc* aid-altering procedure as laid down in paragraphs 1 and 2 of Article 88.

Although without referring to the notion of existing aid, the Commission has **24.11** sometimes decided that the preliminary control procedure contained in Article 88(3) should not be applied to aid granted after the accession of the Member State concerned to the Community but stemming from an event prior to that accession.[6]

In the case of Austria, Finland, and Sweden, consideration was given to the **24.12** fact that an EFTA aid control system already existed. Article 172 of the Act of Accession made provision for a transmission of powers from the EFTA Surveillance Authority to the Commission. In particular it stipulates that all decisions taken by the EFTA Surveillance Authority before the date of accession remain valid in regard to Article 87, but that aid granted in 1994 by the new Member States in breach of the control procedure laid down in the EEA agreement is not considered to be existing aid within the meaning of Article 88(1).[7]

---

[5] See above Case C-387/92 *Banco Exterior de España* [1994] ECR I-877 para 19.

[6] Thus the Commission considered that an exceptional payment made to honour the obligations bound up with the Amoco Cádiz accident 'should not, in the current situation (sic), be considered as State aid in the sense of the Treaty, for this accident happened in 1978, i.e. before the date of Spain's accession to the Community'. (Communication concerning aid that the Spanish government plans to grant for public-sector shipyard restructuring of the DCN [1997] OJ C354/2, 7). cf for the ex GDR, the Decision of 20 January 1999 [1999] OJ L107/35, s V.

[7] Acts of Accession [1994] OJ C241/1. For cases in which schemes not notified to the EFTA Surveillance Authority are later refused the status of existing aid under the EC Treaty, see the Commission Decision of 21 May 1997 on the proposal of Austria to award aid to Hoffmann-La Roche [1998] OJ L103/28, para II.D, and Communication on the guidelines of the Wirtschaftsservice Burgenland Aktiengesellschaft on holdings in companies, [1998] OJ C154/7. In the agricultural sector see Art 144 of the Act of Accession.

24.13   Some specific provisions have been made in the most recent Act of Accession.[8] A specific procedure has in particular been set up allowing the Commission to assess the compatibility of aid already approved by the public-aid review authority of the new Member State. Some one-off interim derogations have also been agreed to for certain new Member States.[9]

3. 'Lorenz' aid

24.14   To lessen the impact of any failing by the Commission, the ECJ had set up another category of existing aid, subsequently endorsed in the Procedural Regulation: when a Member State previously notifies new aid to the Commission but the Commission then fails to react to this notification within two months, the Member State is then authorized to pay the aid to the recipient, after having informed the Commission thereof. This aid then comes under the system of existing aid.[10] This is a category of aid whose compatibility with the common market may be problematic, but which Member States are nonetheless entitled to grant to make up for any failing by the Commission.[11]

4. Aid benefiting from the recovery limitation period

24.15   The Procedural Regulation has introduced a category of aid granted unlawfully but then benefiting from the ten-year-time limit, after which a recovery order can no longer be made.[12]

5. Measures that become aid after coming into force

24.16   The Procedural Regulation has introduced a category of aid which is deemed to be existing aid because it can be established that it did not constitute aid at the time it was implemented but subsequently became aid due to the evolution of the common market and without itself being altered.[13]

---

[8] Annex IV (List referred to in Art 22 of the Act of Accession), s 3 (Competition Policy) [2003] OJ L236/797.

[9] See annex VII, s 4 (Cyprus), annex X, s 4 (Hungary), annex XI, s 3 (Malta), annex XII, s 5 (Poland), annex XIV, s 4 (Slovakia), Protocol No 2 of the Accession Treaty on the restructuring of the Czech steel industry, Protocol No 8 of the Accession Treaty on the restructuring of the Polish steel industry.

[10] Case 120/73 *Lorenz* [1973] ECR 1971 para 4, and Case C-312/90 *Spain v EC Commission* [1992] ECR I-4117 para 18.

[11] The *Lorenz* procedure is dealt with in paras 22.43 *et seq.*   [12] See para 23.41.

[13] Procedural Reg, Art 1(b)(iv) and (v).

II. Determination of whether aid can be considered to be existing aid

As in the classification of a measure as aid, deciding whether aid is new or existing cannot be allowed to depend on a subjective assessment by the Commission; instead, it must be determined quite independently of any previous administrative practice.[14] It is sometimes difficult to decide whether or not aid should be defined as existing. This might above all be the case when a Member State wishes to pay aid to a private undertaking in application of an existing aid scheme in which it is difficult to decide whether, in this particular case, the compatibility conditions under which the aid was granted are still being met. This might also occur in the case of individual aid when there are doubts about whether the Member State is complying with the conditions subject to which aid was approved. **24.17**

There are two types of eligibility conditions to be met for aid to be able to be granted as existing aid: **24.18**

* the national rules governing the scheme or the individual aid arrangements, such as they are recorded in the notification to the Commission.

* the supplementary conditions imposed by the Commission at the time of approving the scheme or the aid. These might be specific conditions pertaining to the approved aid or general obligations arising from quasi regulatory texts adopted by the Commission. The aim of the latter, in principle, is to ensure that the aid approval provisions are met when the aid scheme is subsequently put into effect.

A. Importance of the Question

Deciding whether aid can be regarded as existing aid is crucial because only then can it be granted directly to the beneficiary undertaking without a new notification and control procedure. In the particular case of aid agreed under a scheme already approved by the Commission, the latter is entitled in principle only to verify that the aforementioned scheme conditions are still being met; if so, there **24.19**

---

[14] Case C-295/97 *Piaggio* [1999] ECR I-3735 paras 45–48; Joined Cases T-195/01 and T-207/01 *Government of Gibraltar v EC Commission* [2002] ECR II-2309 para 121, and Joined Cases T-269/99, T-271/99 and T-272/99 *Territorio Histórico de Guipúzcoa and others v EC Commission* [2002] ECR II-4217 para 80, and Joined Cases T-346/99, T-347/99 and T-348/99 *Territorio Histórico de Álava and others v EC Commission* [2002] ECR II-4259 para 84.

will be no need for a subsequent examination of the compatibility of the aid with the Treaty.

B. Procedure

24.20 There is no regulation laying down how, where there is doubt, it should be decided whether State aid is existing aid. The question arises when aid has already been granted and the Member State concerned claims that it is a particular application of an approved scheme or is being applied in a normal fashion as approved by the Commission, while the Commission itself contests this claim and believes that it might be a case of unlawful aid.[15]

1. Individual case of application of an existing scheme

24.21 The decision 'albeit on a provisional basis' on whether or not an aid should be considered as new or existing aid has to be taken before opening the formal examination procedure.[16] When the Commission has before it a specific grant of aid alleged to be made in pursuance of a previously authorized scheme, it cannot at the outset examine it directly in relation to the Treaty. Prior to the initiation of any procedure, it must first examine whether the aid is covered by the general scheme and satisfies the conditions laid down in the decision approving it. If it did not do so, the Commission could, whenever it examined individual aid, go back on its decision approving the aid scheme which already involved an examination in the light of Article 87 of the Treaty. This would jeopardize the principles of the protection of legitimate expectations and legal certainty from the point of view of both the Member States and traders since individual aid in strict conformity with the decision approving the aid scheme could at any time be called into question anew by the Commission.[17]

---

[15] On the other hand, if the Member State accepts that the aid constitutes new aid or an alteration of existing aid, the Commission may immediately treat it as such and is then a priori justified in initiating the formal examination procedure under the regime applicable to new aid (Case T-190/00 *Regione Siciliana v EC Commission* not yet reported para 65). In cases where the Member State has not pronounced clearly either way and keeps the two possibilities open, the Commission has likewise tended to treat the aid as new aid and immediately initiate the examination procedure of Art 88(2), even if it is not in a position to exclude the possibility that the aid might be covered by a previous approval (see the Communication on aid granted to Dow/Buna SOW Leuna Olefinverbund [1998] OJ C128/13, in particular paras 6.1 and 9.1).

[16] Joined Cases T-297/01 and T-298/01 *SIC v EC Commission* [2004] ECR II-743 para 49.

[17] Case C-47/91 *Italy v EC Commission* [1994] ECR I-4635 para 24; Case C-278/95 P *Siemens v EC Commission* [1997] ECR I-2507 para 31; Case C-321/99 P *ARAP and others v EC Commission* [2002] ECR I-4287 para 83, and Case T-176/01 *Ferriere Nord v EC Commission* not yet reported para 51.

Should the Commission find, after an examination in the aforementioned **24.22** limited sense, that individual aid abides by the aid-scheme approval decision, this aid should then be treated as authorized aid and *ipso facto* as existing aid. The Commission cannot then suspend such aid, because Article 88(3) empowers it to do so only in relation to new aid. Conversely, should the Commission find that the individual aid is not covered by its aid-scheme approval decision, the aid should then be considered to be new aid.[18]

According to the CFI, however, this case law can be properly invoked only when **24.23** the national authorities have clearly asserted that the aid comes under an approved scheme and not:

• when they first claimed that the aid in question was existing aid only after the initiation of the formal examination procedure;[19]
• when they themselves notified the measure to the Commission as new aid in application of Article 88(3) EC.[20]

When the Commission has already opened the formal examination procedure **24.24** laid down in Article 88(2) against aid it considers to be new, and then, while the procedure is underway, the Member State concerned proposes some amendments to the project to bring it into line with a general scheme-approval decision, the Commission should first assess whether such amendments really do bring the project into line with the aid-scheme approval decision. If so, it no longer has the right to assess the aid project's compatibility with Article 87, since this assessment has already been made in the context of the procedure culminating in the decision approving the general scheme.[21]

2. Application of individual aid

The same reasoning applies when a Member State claims that individual aid has **24.25** been implemented in due accordance with the Commission decision that approved it. The Commission should first check whether the aid has been properly applied in a normal fashion and can benefit from the initial approval before, if need be, opening a formal examination procedure if it considers there to be a misuse of aid.

---

[18] Case C-47/91 *Italy v EC Commission* paras 25 and 26.
[19] Case T-190/00 *Regione Siciliana v EC Commission* not yet reported para 78.
[20] Case T-176/01 *Ferriere Nord v EC Commission* not yet reported paras 54–56.
[21] Case T-435/93 *ASPEC and others v EC Commission* [1995] ECR II-1281 para 105, and Case T-442/93 *AAC and others v EC Commission* [1995] ECR II-1329 para 86.

3. Procedure to be followed for carrying out this preliminary check: the *Italgrani* case

24.26 If the Commission already has enough evidence to hand to cast doubts on the measure's right to be qualified as existing aid, it can immediately open the examination procedure laid down in Article 88(2).[22] The effect of opening this procedure is then to treat the aid as new aid or misuse of aid; this implies that the aid is considered to be unlawful and the payment thereof should be suspended.

24.27 On the other hand, if the Commission only entertains doubts about whether individual aid is compatible with its scheme-approval decision, it should first of all ask the Member State concerned to furnish it with all necessary information and documentation for deciding on the conformity of the aid in question with the scheme and its scheme approval decision (the so-called '*Italgrani* injunction' information), within the time period laid down by the Commission.[23] It is only if the Commission finds after this examination that the individual aid is not covered by the scheme as approved that the aid in question can be considered to be new aid and treated as such. Should the Member State fail to come up with the required information, despite the Commission's injunction, the Commission will then be entitled to order the suspension of the aid and directly assess its conformity with the Treaty as though it were a case of new aid.[24] By definition, therefore, the *Italgrani* injunction is adopted before initiating the formal procedure of Article 88(2).

24.28 A variant of this situation occurs when the Commission thinks that its initial approval decision has been tainted by false information given by the Member State and wishes to reopen the file. If the Member State contests the Commission's interpretation, it would seem that the Commission is bound, in the event of doubt, to ask the Member State to provide it with all information it needs to reach a decision before being able to initiate the examination procedure for abuse of aid, which procedure suspends the implementation of the aid.

24.29 The Commission has progressively brought its practice into line with this case law. The information injunctions it adopts have often taken the form of formal decisions, published in the Official Journal series L.[25] Nonetheless, when the injunction is decided at the same time as the initiation of the

---

[22] Case C-47/91 *Italy v EC Commission* para 31.

[23] ibid para 34. See, for example, the Communication on aid granted to the undertaking Demesa [1998] OJ C103/3, s 5.1.

[24] Case C-47/91 *Italy v EC Commission* para 35.

[25] See the Decision of 30 April 1996 requiring Spain to provide the necessary information in order to prove definitively that aid was granted under an existing aid scheme [1996] OJ L246/41.

examination procedure laid down in Article 88(2), with regard to other aid, the injunction is simply inserted in the letter commencing the procedure as published in the Official Journal series C.[26] The deadline given to the Member State to provide the information required is usually short, being only a few weeks.

4. Consequences of an error of assessment

Should the Commission realize at any stage of the procedure that it has **24.30** made a mistake in its assessment of the new or existing character of aid it should try as far as possible to obviate the consequences of this error.[27] Such an error, however, might threaten to invalidate the whole subsequent procedure. Thus, if the procedure has been opened against aid as though it were a case of new aid and if the Commission comes to realize later that it is in fact existing aid, then the Commission cannot normally adopt a final decision against it, even in terms of limiting the future effects thereof, except by previously following the cooperation procedure with the State as laid down in Article 88(1).

5. Interpretation of the scope of an existing scheme

The attempt to ascertain whether individual aid is an application of an existing **24.31** scheme might raise some questions of interpretation about the scope of the scheme in question. In such cases, the CFI, followed by the ECJ, has declared that it is necessary to interpret the national provisions concerning an authorized regime in light of the Community rules on the matter, namely, the Commission's decision to approve this scheme and the relevant provisions of the Treaty.[28]

The Commission considers that aid granted on the basis of an aid scheme **24.32** but before this scheme has been authorized by the Commission cannot be considered to be covered by such a scheme.[29]

---

[26] See, e.g. the injunction included in the Communication on the aid granted to the undertaking Demesa [1998] OJ C103/3.

[27] Thus, in cases where the Commission has come to realise that the aid it had treated as new aid when it started the procedure was in fact existing aid, it has proposed appropriate measures to the Member State concerned. If these measures are accepted by the latter it has then closed the formal examination procedure (Communication concerning the transport aid in favour of Volvo Truck Corporation [1998] OJ C215/5, and response to the written question E-0731/98 [1998] OJ C310/119).

[28] Case T-459/93 *Siemens v EC Commission* [1995] ECR II-1675 para 45, and Case C-278/95 P *Siemens v EC Commission* paras 31–33.

[29] Decision of 21 December 2000 on the State aid granted by the Federal Republic of Germany to Zeuro Möbelwerk GmbH, Thüringen [2002] OJ L82/1 s 39.

III. Permanent review of the compatibility of existing aid

24.33 In view of the fact that an aid scheme might remain in force for a long time or even indefinitely, the Treaty has made provision for a permanent review procedure whereby the Commission can prohibit or alter existing aid, doing so with future effect.

24.34 This procedure involves permanent cooperation between the Commission and the Member States. If Member States fail to meet their obligations in this regard, the Commission can alter or abolish aid as it sees fit.

A. Permanent Cooperation with Member States

24.35 To ensure the control of existing aid, the Treaty has laid down a permanent cooperation procedure between the Commission and Member States. More specifically, the ECJ considers that Article 88(1) involves an obligation of regular, periodic cooperation on the part of the Commission and Member States, from which neither the Commission nor a Member State can release itself for an indefinite period of its own volition.[30] Apart from specific obligations, the Court refers to a 'spirit of regular, periodic cooperation'[31] that has to preside over application of Article 88(1). The procedure involves three phases, dealt with below: information to be presented by the Member State concerned, proposal of appropriate measures addressed to the said Member State and finally either acceptance of these measures by the Member State or initiation of the formal examination procedure and adoption of a final decision.

1. Exchange of information

24.36 The Commission and the Member States regularly exchange views on a bilateral basis and also in the form of 'multilateral' meetings organised by the Commission. The Commission also makes sure that the Member States keep it informed of all their existing aid schemes so that it can permanently review them; this is done by means of annual reports.[32]

---

[30] Case C-135/93 *Spain v EC Commission* [1995] ECR I-1651 para 24, and Case C-311/94 *IJssel-Vliet* para 36.

[31] Case C-311/94 *IJssel-Vliet* [1998] ECR II-1129 para 37.

[32] The abovementioned Reg 794/2004.

2. Appropriate measures

Proposal of appropriate measures

When the Commission considers that an existing aid scheme does not meet the **24.37** current compatibility criteria, it sends the Member State concerned a proposal of appropriate measures, in accordance with Article 88(1). This is not a binding act producing its own legal effects, but rather a simple recommendation within the meaning of Article 249 EC, and the Member State is not obliged to abide by it.[33] It is therefore not an act against which an action for annulment can be brought.

If the Member State accepts the Commission's proposal, it has to express its **24.38** consent, in principle in writing. In the appropriate measures it is invited to express its consent.[34] The consequence of the Member State expressing its consent is that the measures are then binding upon it.[35] The Member State undertakes to alter with future effect the terms for the granting of its existing schemes, in line with the provisions laid down in the proposal of appropriate measures. The arrangement is hence of a quasi-contractual nature, committing both the Member State concerned and the Commission. The scheme's individual cases of application granted by the Member State before accepting the appropriate measures remain valid and are in no way affected by the alteration of the scheme. If, on the contrary, the Member State refuses to accept the appropriate measures proposed by the Commission or fails to give its express consent, the Commission can then follow the procedure laid down in Article 88(2) to bind the Member State to enforce them.

Apart from the straightforward abolition of the scheme, the appropriate measures **24.39** may also deal with the aid compatibility criteria (lowering of maximum intensities, limitation of activities eligible for grants, etc) or the aid-scheme control procedure arrangements (for example by requiring that certain individual cases of application of existing schemes have to be notified in the future and individually approved before being granted, or by requiring that specific information on the application of existing schemes be sent to the Commission).

---

[33] Case T-330/94 *Salt Union v EC Commission* [1996] ECR II-1475 para 35.

[34] It follows from the case law of the ECJ, however, that once guidelines been adopted in the form of appropriate measures, these guidelines containing specific provisions regarding cooperation with Member States, it is then these provisions that govern relationships with Member States, providing these provisions abide by the basic principles of Art 88(1). Thus, if the first appropriate measures make due provision for the same, the agreement of the Member States is not necessary when the Commission is merely extending guidelines for a given period without making any alteration thereto (in particular, the *a contrario* interpretation of para 30 Case C-292/95 *Spain v EC Commission* [1997] ECR I-1931).

[35] Case C-311/94 *IJssel-Vliet Combinatie* para 42, and C-242/00 *Germany v EC Commission* [2002] ECR I-5603 para 28. See Art 19 Procedural Reg.

Lack of direct effect

24.40 The provisions of Article 88(1) and (2) governing the control of existing aid schemes do not have direct effect and cannot therefore be invoked before national courts unless they have been put into specific form by acts having general application provided for by Article 89 or by decisions in particular cases envisaged by Article 88(2).[36]

Categories of appropriate measures

24.41 In practice, the appropriate measures proposed by the Commission can be broken down into two different categories depending on their addressees and purpose:

- Sometimes the appropriate measures concern a particular aid scheme that has to be brought into line with the Community rules governing the type of aid concerned.

- On other occasions the appropriate measures are directed at the whole set of existing schemes in one or several Member States and aim to implement a change in the Commission's policy. The appropriate measures then serve to apply the Commission's new guidelines or notices to all existing schemes and comprise rules of general application. If for example the Commission intends to bring in stricter rules for aid granted to recipients trading in a certain economic sector (textile, automobile sector [. . .]), it will propose to Member States that they alter the conditions for granting aid with respect to all their existing schemes affecting the sector in question.

  In this last case the alterations proposed by the Commission might come into force at different times in different Member States: in some Member States from the moment of their acceptance and in others, those that have rejected the appropriate measures, only from the moment of the adoption of a final decision. To avoid this disparity of treatment the Commission endeavours, in its appropriate measures, to establish an entry-into-force date for the new rules that is far enough ahead to be valid for all Member States.[37]

24.42 The initiative as to how to operate the control procedure thus belongs to the Commission.[38] It would seem to be a case of discretionary power, hedged in by

---

[36] Case 77/72 *Capolongo* [1973] ECR 611 para 6.

[37] Thus, the Commission proposed to Member States that the multi-sectoral guidelines should apply as from 1 September 1998. Germany rejected these appropriate measures, so the Commission had time to initiate the examination procedure in relation to all existing schemes in Germany ([1998] OJ C171/4) and then adopt a final decision that could be notified to Germany before 1 September 1998; these guidelines has therefore come into force simultaneously in all Member States on 1 September 1998.

[38] Case C-44/93 *Namur-Les assurances du crédit* [1994] ECR I-3829 para 11.

no time limit, which the Commission is not bound to use.[39] It is therefore not conceivable that actions for failure to fulfil its obligations be brought against the Commission for not having initiated the procedure under Article 88(1).

Duration of the appropriate measures

According to the ECJ, the obligation of regular periodic cooperation under **24.43** Article 88(1) of the Treaty precludes existing systems of aid from being examined according to rules established or agreed for an indefinite period depending on the unilateral will of either the Commission or the Member States.[40] It follows that the appropriate measures proposed by the Commission for altering existing schemes of the Member States can have only a limited duration, and their content must be confirmed or altered regularly, in accordance with the procedure laid down in Article 88(1).

B. Formal Examination Procedure

If the Member State concerned refuses to accept the appropriate measures **24.44** proposed by the Commission, the Procedural Regulation states that the Articles on new aid shall then apply, *mutatis mutandis*. The Commission, after having examined the arguments put forward by the Member State, can then initiate the formal procedure laid down in paragraph 2 of Article 88 to bind the Member State to alter its scheme(s). It then invites the Member State concerned and all other parties concerned to make their observations. The procedure initiated must deal with the same aid as that involved in the appropriate measures and have the same object. Thus, if the appropriate measures required alteration of all the existing schemes of a Member State, the procedure as initiated must also deal with the whole set of these schemes.[41]

Unlike the consequences when a Member State notifies new aid, there is **24.45** no question of a standstill effect here as in the examination procedure of Article 88(2). Its implementation does not aim to freeze the normal application of existing aid schemes. The Member State concerned can therefore

---

[39] As opposed to the situation with new aid, when the Commission is bound to lay down a reasonable time limit from learning of the existence of the aid in question, after a notification, complaint, etc.

[40] Case C-135/93 *Spain v EC Commission* para 38, and Case C-311/94 *IJssel-Vliet* para 36.

[41] For example, when Spain refused to adapt the whole set of existing schemes in line with the Community guidelines on State aid to the motor vehicle industry, to guarantee individual notification of aid to the automobile sector, the Commission initiated the procedure against the whole set of existing Spanish schemes (see the Commission Decision of 20 December 1995 amending Spanish aid schemes for the motor vehicle industry [1996] OJ L119/51).

continue to pay its aid on the basis of the existing scheme throughout the whole procedure.

24.46 Except for the standstill effect, the arrangements of the formal examination procedure are the same as those used for the examination of new aid, as already dealt with in above.[42]

24.47 Should the Member State voluntarily decide to accept the Commission's appropriate measures after initiation of the procedure, the Commission makes an official note thereof and closes the examination procedure,[43] otherwise the procedure follows its course and leads in principle to the adoption of a final decision.

C. Final Decision

24.48 After the State's refusal to accept the appropriate measures and the initiation of the formal examination procedure, the Commission can adopt a final decision that imposes the alterations or abolitions it considers appropriate. In the course of the examination procedure of existing aid this final decision is the first act with binding effect.[44] Its effect is only forward looking and therefore, as a general principle of law, it cannot have a retrospective effect. Such a decision hence has a constitutive rather than declaratory effect. It is as a result of the decision and the decision alone that the abolition of the aid or the obligation to alter it, as the case may be, arises.[45]

24.49 It is hence only as of the date of the Commission's decision, which date must be later than the adoption date thereof, that the aid concerned loses its status of existing aid. Individual aid can continue to be lawfully paid in application of the existing scheme throughout the whole procedure for the re-examination of the scheme, whether this be after the sending of the appropriate measures or after the initiation of the examination procedure.

24.50 According to Article 88(2), the Commission's decision can oblige the Member State to abolish or alter the aid 'within a period of time to be determined by the

---

[42] See in particular the comments on the consultation of the parties concerned (see paras 22.77 *et seq.*) and of the Member State concerned (see paras 22.72 *et seq.*). On the other hand, since it is a question of existing aid, the Commission does not seem bound to bring the procedure to an end within any deadline.

[43] See, e.g. the termination of the procedure started against Sweden for enforcing the Community guidelines on State aid to the motor vehicle industry [1998] OJ C122/4.

[44] Case T-330/94 *Salt Union v EC Commission* para 35.

[45] See the Opinion of AG Mayras in Case 70/72 *EC Commission v Germany* [1973] ECR 813.

Commission'. According to the ECJ, the idea of cooperation underpinning Article 88, in terms of the permanent review of existing aid, obliges the Commission to allow the Member State concerned a period of time within which to comply with the decision taken.[46] It is a moot point whether this means that a fixed deadline should be laid down in the decision. According to Advocate General Mayras, the Commission has to bear in mind the internal procedures necessary for implementing its decision; it could however merely require the Member State concerned to act 'without delay.'[47]

After adopting a decision, the Commission is then bound to ensure that it is **24.51** entirely and fully put into effect. To do so, it sometimes requires the Member State to send it regular reports on the execution of its decision. The Member States are also bound to send the Commission annual reports on the application of their existing schemes.[48]

---

[46] Case 173/73 *Italy v EC Commission* [1974] ECR 709. Along the same lines, Joined Cases C-182/03 R and C-217/03 R *Belgium and Forum 187 v EC Commission* [2003] ECR I-6887 para 124.

[47] See the Opinion of AG Mayras in Case 70/72 *EC Commission v Germany* [1973] ECR 813.

[48] Reg 794/2004.

25

IMPLEMENTATION OF THE COMMISSION'S DECISIONS

I. A posteriori control by the Commission

A. Annual Reports

Member States must in any event furnish the Commission with annual reports.[1]   **25.01**

B. On-site Monitoring

Breaking with precedent,[2] the Procedural Regulation lays down the principle of   **25.02**
'on-site monitoring' (Article 22). Previously, the Commission used to impose
certain control conditions addressed directly to the State: it was the latter that
was bound to furnish the Commission, where applicable with the assistance of
the undertaking concerned, with sufficient information for checking on compliance with its decision. If the Commission did not receive the necessary
information (where necessary after having served an information injunction) it
opened the examination procedure for misuse of aid and could finally adopt a
negative decision on the basis of the only information to hand. It was hence
conducive to the interests of the State and, indirectly, the recipient undertaking
to cooperate with the Commission.

On the basis of the rules laid down in Articles 85 and 86 EC and also in the   **25.03**
ECSC Treaty,[3] the Regulation on the other hand lays down direct rights of the

---

[1] Art 21 of the Procedural Reg and Reg 794/2004.
[2] On-site monitoring by the Commission had already been established in certain particular
cases, however. See Council Reg 1013/97 of 2 June 1997, whose Art 2 states as follows:
'The programme of monitoring shall include on site monitoring by the Commission'.
[3] By virtue of the last subpara of Art 86 of the ECSC Treaty 'Officials of the Commission entrusted by it with tasks of inspection shall enjoy in the territories of Member States, to the

905

Commission services vis-à-vis undertakings. This development seems to be fraught with consequences. While it is true that it facilitates enforcement of the Commission's decisions, it is now arguable whether the Commission can henceforth limit its proceedings to simply questioning the Member State concerned before taking a negative decision, or whether it is not always bound to use fully the powers invested in it by the Regulation. It would seem, moreover, that the Regulation should not be construed as having direct effects against the undertakings concerned; it is rather a case of proceedings to be adopted by Member States with binding character as regards the undertakings concerned (Article 22(6)).

II. Remedies if any of the Commission's decisions are breached

25.04 Apart from the particular case of aid broken down into tranches, for which the Commission is invested with particular powers,[4] there are several other options open to the Commission when it finds that one of its decisions has not been fully complied with. It can first of all bring the matter directly before the ECJ by applying for a declaration that such payment amounts to an infringement committed by the State. It may also initiate the formal examination procedure to examine the misuse of aid by the Member State. And finally it may decide to block all new aid to a given undertaking on the grounds of past failures to recover incompatible aid from the same undertaking.

A. Bringing the Matter before the European Court of Justice[5]

25.05 If the Member State does not comply with a Commission decision finding proposed aid to be incompatible or does not meet the conditions placed by the Commission on an aid approval decision, under the second subparagraph of Article 88(2) both the Commission and any other Member State concerned are entitled to bring the matter directly before the Court by derogation from

---

full extent required for the performance of their duties, such rights and powers as are granted by the laws of these States to their own revenue officials. Forthcoming visits of inspection and the status of the officials shall be duly notified to the State concerned. Officials of that State may, at its request or at that of the Commission, assist the Commission's officials in the performance of their task'.

[4] See paras 22.114 *et seq.*   [5] See paras 27.87 *et seq.*

Articles 226 and 227 of the Treaty.[6] This option is simply a variant of the action for a failure to comply with obligations, as adapted to the specific common-market competition problems caused by State aid (or 'the maintenance of State aid declared to be illegal'[7]).[8]

According to the CFI, this possibility of direct referral to the Court is part and **25.06** parcel of the Commission's wider remit of enforcing compliance with its decisions by the Member States. The Commission's monitoring powers over Member States that do not comply with its decisions within the prescribed period mean that the Commission has a wide margin of discretion. The Commission is not therefore under any obligation to commence the proceedings provided for in that provision. On the contrary, its wide discretion prevents any individual from requiring it to adopt a specific position.[9] Third parties therefore have no procedural rights in the context of monitoring the execution of a decision under the second subparagraph of Article 88(2).[10]

In practice, the Commission tends to resort to this option only when a Member **25.07** State fails to execute a completely negative decision (ordering the abolition or recovery of aid). In cases where a State has failed to abide fully by a conditional decision, it generally tends to initiate a new formal procedure for misuse of aid,[11] because this procedure, unlike direct referral to the Court, allows it to order recovery of the aid for breach of the conditions attached to the declaration of compatibility.

It follows from the wording of the second subparagraph of Article 88(2) that **25.08** this possibility of direct referral to the Court is limited to cases in which the Commission has adopted a final decision at the end of a formal examination procedure, on the basis of Article 88(2).[12]

---

[6] Case C-294/90 *British Aerospace and Rover v EC Commission* [1994] ECR I-5423 para 11, and Case T-277/94 *AITEC v EC Commission* [1996] ECR II-351 para 65. The Commission can also open a classic procedure for failure to comply with obligations under Art 226 (Case C-209/00 *EC Commission v Germany* [2002] ECR I-11695 para 37, and Case C-404/00 *EC Commission v Spain* [2003] ECR I-6695 para 25).

[7] Case C-209/00 *EC Commission v Germany* para 37.

[8] Case C-301/87 *France v EC Commission* [1990] ECR I-307 para 23, and Case T-358/94 *Air France v EC Commission* [1996] ECR II-2109 para 60.

[9] Case T-277/94 *AITEC v EC Commission* paras 65 and 66.

[10] ibid para 54 *in fine*.

[11] See paras 25.09 *et seq*.

[12] The problem is not posed in principle by a decision not to raise objections, adopted at the end of the preliminary examination procedure, for such a decision is by definition a positive decision and is therefore not breachable as such.

B. Procedure in the Event of Abusive Application of Existing Aid

25.09   Just as it can initiate a formal procedure against new aid where it has doubts about its compatibility, the Commission may also initiate a formal examination procedure pursuant to Article 88(2) to ascertain whether aid has been misused.[13]

25.10   Subject to the caveats laid down below, a misuse of existing aid is dealt with by means of the same procedure as that used in a formal procedure on new unlawful aid. The Commission can therefore initiate the formal examination procedure and adopt a final decision; it can require recovery of aid that has been misused; it can adopt interim measures forcing the State to suspend the improper application of the aid, etc.

25.11   The Procedural Regulation, however, gives a restrictive definition of the notion of misuse of aid, while at the same time laying down an unprecedented 'revocation' procedure. It restricts the concept of misuse of aid to those cases of misuse 'by the beneficiary' (Article 1(g)).

25.12   One of the classic conditions placed on the declaration of aid compatibility is the prohibition of granting new aid to the same undertaking, in principle over a set period. Such a prohibition is in particular imposed on undertakings in difficulty, for as long as the restructuring period lasts.

25.13   According to the ECJ, if this condition is not observed and the undertaking receives new aid, the Commission has to choose from the two following procedures:[14]

- Either it considers it to be a breach of the condition attached to the first decision, in which case it can refer the matter directly to the ECJ, under the second subparagraph of Article 88(2).

- Or it can deem it to be new aid that has not been examined under the procedure culminating in the first decision, in which case it initiates a formal examination procedure. If the Member State submits no new information during the formal examination procedure, the Commission is entitled to base its decision on the assessments it made in its previous decision and on the failure to comply with the condition it had imposed

---

[13] However if the Member State challenges the misuse-of-aid accusation, we believe that the Commission is then bound, where there is doubt about compatibility, to ask the Member State to furnish it with all information allowing it to assess the conformity of the implementation with the approval decision, before being able to initiate the procedure.

[14] Case C-294/90 *British Aerospace and Rover v EC Commission* paras 12 and 13.

therein.[15] In this case it does not therefore have to initiate a new detailed examination, provided, however, that it takes its decision at the end of a new procedure under Article 88(2).

In practice the Commission tends to choose a third option, which consists in **25.14** initiating the procedure in relation to the whole set of aid, so as to examine at the same time the misuse of the first aid and the compatibility of the new aid.[16] The investigation will result in a new decision in which the Commission gives its findings concerning both the previously approved aid and the unnotified payments and in which, if appropriate, it may demand recovery of all aid (both previously approved and subsequently discovered) which it finds to be incompatible with the common market in the light of the new information.[17]

C. Taking into Account the Non-recovery of Unlawful Aid in the Consideration of New Aid

The Commission found it to be by no means a straightforward matter to get **25.15** Member States to expedite the recovery of unlawful aid declared to be incompatible and sought ways to remedy this situation. In two decisions concerning the undertaking TWD Deggendorf, it expressly declared for the first time that notified aid in favour of an undertaking could not be declared compatible and the granting thereof should be suspended until such time as certain aid previously paid to the same undertaking and since declared to be incompatible should be recovered.

The CFI, followed by the ECJ, has borne out this practice by handing down **25.16** decisions in the sense that new aid considered in itself to be compatible with the common market may not be authorized until the cumulative effect of the old aid has been eliminated.[18] The CFI has in particular considered that the Commission can act in this way, on the grounds that the main objective sought is to ensure that competition in the common market is not distorted by the cumulative effect of the aid in question, provided that the formal examination procedure contained in Article 88(2) is followed. According to the CFI, Community law does not require the Commission, before so acting, to await the outcome

---

[15] Case C-261/89 *Italy v EC Commission* [1991] ECR I-4437 para 23.

[16] See, e.g. the Communication on the aid that the German government has decided to grant to Addinol Mineralöl and to Auffanggesellschaft [1998] OJ C186/7.

[17] This possibility had already been pointed out by AG Van Gerven in his Opinion in Case C-294/90 *British Aerospace Public and Rover v EC Commission* [1992] ECR I-5423 para 11.

[18] Joined Cases T-244/93 and T-486/93 *TWD v EC Commission* [1995] ECR II-2265 para 51, and Case C-355/95 P *TWD v EC Commission* [1997] ECR I-2549 para 22.

of national litigation dealing with the recovery of the old aid. To reach that conclusion the CFI has based its arguments on three factors: first, the fact that the old aid was not granted in accordance with the procedure laid down in Article 88(3) of the Treaty, secondly on the fact that the legitimate expectations upon which the undertaking relies in the national proceedings may be acknowledged only in exceptional circumstances and, thirdly, the fact that the national court has not made a reference to the ECJ in order to obtain a preliminary ruling on whether such exceptional circumstances exist in the present case.[19]

25.17 At first the Commission did not resort to this option systematically.[20] It has since made increasing use of it[21] in a progressively stricter sense.[22]

25.18 The suspension of new aid payment as in the *Deggendorf* case has been analysed by the CFI as an integral part of the normal analysis of aid compatibility. This would suggest that the Commission is, in principle, bound to take account of this aspect when analysing the compatibility of aid and give grounds, if need be, for its assessments in this sense.

---

[19] Joined Cases T-244/93 and T-486/93 *TWD v EC Commission* paras 70 and 71.

[20] Thus, even though an incompatible aid of 13,000 million FRF had not yet been repaid by the undertaking one year after the Commission's negative decision, the Commission nonetheless authorized new aid to the same undertaking, merely indicating in the grounds of its positive decision that 'The French authorities gave the Commission an undertaking that they would recover this aid, arising from the negative decision, as soon as possible' (Commission Decision of 21 January 1998 granting conditional approval to aid which France has decided to grant to Société française de production [1998], OJ L205/68, s 1).

[21] For example the Decision of 12 March 2002 on aid in favour of Neue Erba Lautex GmbH and Erba Lautex GmbH [2002] OJ L282/48, ss 57 to 59.

[22] See:

— point 23 of the 2004 Community guidelines on State aid for rescuing and restructuring firms in difficulty;

— the Magefesa Decision of 14 October 1998 [1999] OJ L198/15, s VII, a) in which the Commission took account of unrecovered aid, even considering that it had not in fact been repaid because the national authorities had simply included it in a list of creditors, doing so late and through an intermediary shell company.

26

ROLE OF NATIONAL COURTS

I. The enforcement of the obligation not to grant unauthorized aid

The concept of the 'lawfulness' of aid involves compliance with the procedural **26.01** obligation laid down in Article 88(3) EC, i.e. the obligation incumbent on Member States not to grant any aid before it is approved by the Commission. According to the ECJ, in the Treaty system it is, in principle, the national courts that are responsible for enforcing this obligation, in cooperation with the Community institutions.

A. Role of the National Judge

1. Direct effect of Article 88(3), last sentence

The clear and unconditional prohibition laid down in the final sentence of **26.02** Article 88(3) has direct effect,[1] for it establishes procedural criteria that national courts can appraise.[2] The direct effect of that prohibition extends to all aid that has been implemented without being notified and, in the event of notification, operates during the preliminary period, and where the Commission sets in motion the contentious procedure, up to the final decision.[3]

---

[1] Case 6/64 *Costa* [1964] ECR 585.
[2] Case 77/72 *Capolongo* [1973] ECR 611 para 6.
[3] Case 120/73 *Lorenz* [1973] ECR 1471 para 8; Case C-354/90 *French Salmon* [1991] ECR I-5505 para 11, and Case C-39/94 *SFEI and others* [1996] ECR I-3547 para 39. Case T-182/98 *UPS Europe v EC Commission* [1999] ECR II-2857 para 48.

2. Powers of the national courts

26.03   The involvement of national courts is the result of the direct effect that the last sentence of Article 88(3) is acknowledged to have.[4] This provision creates rights in favour of individuals, which national courts are bound to protect.[5] The standstill obligation incumbent on Member States can be invoked before national courts, and moreover in many different types of case. The most obvious example is when a competitor of the aid-receiving undertaking appeals to the competent court for annulment of the aid granted, and the refunding thereof. The commonest case, in practice, is when a taxpayer seeks to avoid payment of a tax resulting from an aid payment. Many other hypothetical cases might be mentioned.[6]

26.04   An examination is made below of the obligations incumbent on the national court when it is called upon to deal with an action based on the direct effect of the last sentence of Article 88(3).

Determination of the existence of a breach of Article 88(3), last sentence

26.05   The national court has to ascertain whether the State measure in dispute was set up without taking into account the preliminary control procedure of Article 88(3) and then if it should be subject thereto. Indeed the national court can intervene only 'if the national measures in question constitute aid within the meaning of Article [87] and if the procedure for review provided for in Article [88](3) has not been complied with'.[7] To do so:

- It has first of all to ascertain whether the measure in dispute does indeed come under Article 87(1),[8] which might oblige it to interpret and apply the

---

[4] Case C-354/90 *French Salmon* [1991] ECR I-5505 para 11; Case C-44/93 *Namur-Les assurances du crédit* [1994] ECR I-3829 para 16, and C-39/94 *SFEI and others* [1996] ECR I-3547 para 39.

[5] Case 120/73 *Lorenz* [1973] ECR 1471 para 8.

[6] Thus in the *Sloman Neptun* case, a Seafarers' Committee objected to the employment on more favourable terms of sailors with no fixed abode in Germany, on the grounds that the German legislation allowing such a hiring arrangement constituted a State aid. After the Seafarers' Committee's refusal to give its consent to the employment of the persons in question, the undertaking concerned applied to the competent national court to do so in lieu of the Seafarers' Committee. The national court took the view that it needed an interpretation of the concept of aid as laid down in Art 87 to ascertain whether or not the German legislation in dispute, set up without giving any consideration to the preliminary control procedure of Art 88(3), should in fact be subjected thereto (Joined Cases C-72/91 and C-73/91 *Sloman Neptun* [1993] ECR I-887).

[7] Joined Cases 91/83 and 127/83 *Heineken Brouwerijen* [1984] ECR 3435 para 11.

[8] Case 78/76 *Steinike and Weinlig* [1977] ECR 595 para 14, and Case C-189/91 *Kirsammer-Hack* [1993] ECR I-6185 para 14.

notion of aid as laid down in Article 87[9] and also to check whether the other criteria of Article 87(1) are met (effect on trade and competition and state origin).

- When a national court has to deal with an individual application of a rule that it deems to constitute an unlawful aid scheme, it is debatable whether the national court should take a position on the law as such or only the individual case in regard to Article 87(1). Called upon to rule on this question, Advocate General Fennelly argued that the court could base its case on the general characteristics of the rule to ascertain whether or not it constitutes in principle aid, but that this conclusion should be open to refutation in any given case, where the undertaking in question is in a position to demonstrate to the satisfaction of the competent court that the one-off application of the rule in its favour does not constitute aid.[10] The Court has stressed the assessment of the individual case.[11]

- Then, if it does turn out to be aid, the Court has to determine whether it has been granted in breach of Article 88(3), which might oblige it, if necessary, to examine whether it is a case of new aid or existing aid.[12]

- Where necessary, the national court has to check whether the aid comes under a block exemption regulation,[13] in which case there would be no infringement of the last sentence of Article 88(3).

If decisions have already been adopted by the Commission, the national court is **26.06** bound to take them into consideration, under the principle of the supremacy of Community law. Thus, where a formal examination procedure has been initiated to deal with the measure in question, from which examination it transpires that the Commission does not rule out the possibility of it being new aid, the national court is bound by this classification.[14] Likewise a final decision whereby the Commission confirms the aid character of the measure or, as the case

---

[9] Case C-354/90 *French Salmon* [1991] ECR I-5505 para 10; Case C-44/93 *Namur-Les assurances du crédit* [1994] ECR I-3829 para 16, and Case C-39/94 *SFEI and others* [1996] ECR I-3547 para 49.

[10] Opinion in Case C-200/97 *Ecotrade* [1998] ECR I-7907 para 31.

[11] Case C-200/97 *Ecotrade* [1998] ECR I-7907.

[12] In this sense see Case C-44/93 *Namur-Les assurances du crédit* in particular para 18.

[13] See paras 21.82 *et seq.*

[14] See, in this sense, para 23 of Case C-312/90 *Spain v EC Commission* [1992] ECR I-4117 which acts as the link between the *French Salmon* judgment and the Commission's classification of a measure as new aid. See also para 59 of Case C-400/99 *Italy v EC Commission* [2001] ECR I-7303 according to which an initiation decision could be invoked before a national court called upon to establish all the consequences arising from the infringement of the last sentence of Art 88(3).

may be, the unlawful nature of its granting,[15] binds the national court in its assessment of the existence of a breach of the final sentence of Article 88(3).

Consequences flowing from the unlawful character of aid

26.07 **General matters** If the national court finds that there has indeed been a breach of the standstill obligation incumbent on the State, it has to determine the consequences of this for the case in hand. After initially giving national authorities a certain leeway,[16] the ECJ then chose to specify the nature of these consequences in more detail. According to the consecrated formula, national courts must offer to individuals in a position to rely on such a breach the certain prospect that all the necessary inferences will be drawn, in accordance with their national law, as regards the validity of measures giving effect to the aid, the recovery of financial support granted in disregard of that provision and possible interim measures.[17] In this sense the role of the national court goes beyond that of a judge ruling on an application for interim relief. The national court is under a duty to provide protection in the final judgment it gives in such a case against the consequences of unlawful implementation of aid.[18]

26.08 The intervention of the national court is particularly important since it is the only authority that can directly penalize the unlawfulness of the aid, without detriment to such interim measures as the Commission may adopt against the unlawful aid (*Boussac* injunction, etc). It should be noted, however, that the possibility of remedying an infringement of Article 88(3) at a national level is limited by a series of factors (lack of transparency in the granting of aid, differences between the various national legal systems, difficulties for national courts

---

[15] Indeed, if the Commission cannot declare aid to be incompatible for the sole fact that it has been granted unlawfully, this does not prevent it, however, from formally recording this unlawfulness in its decision ruling on the compatibility of the aid with the common market (in this sense, see the Opinion of AG Cosmas in Joined Cases C-329/93, C-62/95 and C-63/95 *Germany, Hanseatische Industrie-Beteiligungen and Bremer Vulkan Verbund v EC Commission* [1996] ECR I-5151 para 96). Moreover, this is the constant practice of the Commission.

[16] In *Lorenz* the referring national court asked for a ruling on whether the unlawful character of an aid scheme brought in by legislation rendered the said legislation void. The Court replied that national courts are bound to apply the prohibition laid down in the last sentence of Art 88(3) but it was for the internal legal system of every Member State to determine the legal procedure leading to this result (Case 120/73 *Lorenz* para 9).

[17] Case C-354/90 *French Salmon* [1991] ECR I-5505 para 12, and Case C-39/94 *SFEI and others* [1996] ECR I-3547 para 40.

[18] Case C-39/94 *SFEI and others* para 67. A mistaken interpretation of the intervention of the national court has therefore been given by the CFI when it stated that it was an interim intervention 'while waiting for the CFI to hand down its decision in the main action' against the Commission's decision (Case T-155/96 R *Ville of Mayence v EC Commission* [1996] ECR II-1655 para 27).

in obtaining the necessary information, etc).[19] In practice, therefore, only a tiny fraction of unlawful aid is actually blocked by national courts.

The main consequences that may flow from the unlawful character of aid are set out below. **26.09**

Implementation of the aid is rendered void   First and foremost the 'validity' of the measures leading to the implementation of the aid is affected by the national authority's disregard of the last sentence of Article 88(3). The national court should therefore, in principle, annul them. **26.10**

Reimbursement of aid   According to the ECJ, a finding that aid has been granted in breach of the last sentence of Article 88(3) must, in principle, lead to its repayment in accordance with the procedural rules of domestic law.[20] A national court requested to order the repayment of aid must grant that application, unless because of exceptional circumstances repayment is inappropriate.[21] As regards the type of exceptional circumstances that the national court might take into consideration, the Advocate General in the *SFEI* case mentioned the difficulty the recipient undertaking might have had in realizing that the measure constituted aid and the slowness of the Commission in dealing with the measures in dispute.[22] **26.11**

Liability of the Member State   A breach of the final sentence of Article 88(3) may in certain cases be considered to be a sufficiently serious breach for the Member State to be held liable for any damage caused to private individuals, applying the principles contained in *Francovich* and *Brasserie du Pêcheur*.[23] **26.12**

Provisional jurisdictional protection   Where there is likely to be some delay before final judgment can be given, a national court should consider whether it **26.13**

---

[19] In this regard, see para 8 of the Opinion of AG Tesauro in Case C-142/87 *Belgium v EC Commission* [1987] ECR I-2589.

[20] Case C-39/94 *SFEI and others* [1996] ECR I-3547 para 68.

[21] ibid para 71.

[22] The slowness of the Commission is a reasonable criterion, which can only serve to encourage the Commission to deal with files more quickly. The reference to the complex nature of the measure, however, is more dangerous, for it might encourage Member States to draw up complex and obscure aid-payment measures in an attempt to elude the control of national courts. Moreover, in contrary to the Advocate General's opinion, it would seem that the 'exceptional circumstances' that might be taken into consideration by national courts in terms of compliance with Art 88(3) should not be mixed up with the exceptional circumstances that might prevent the Commission from ordering the recovery of aid declared to be incompatible (see paras 23.45 *et seq.*). The latter concept should be interpreted in a stricter sense, otherwise the effectiveness of the State aid preventive control procedure will be undermined.

[23] Joined Cases C-6/90 and C-9/90 *Francovich and others* [1991] ECR I-5357 and Joined Cases C-46/93 and C-48/93 *Brasserie du Pêcheur and Factortame* [1996] ECR I-1029. See para 77 of the Opinion of AG Jacobs in Case C-39/94 *SFEI* [1996] ECR I-3547.

is appropriate to order interim measures such as suspension of payment of the aid, in accordance with the applicable national procedural rules, in order to safeguard the interests of the parties.[24]

26.14 **Particular cases. Tax financed aid**   When national taxes are used to finance unlawful aid, should the national court order the repayment of the taxes to guarantee the full effect of the last sentence of Article 88(3)? There is no settled case law to enable this question to be answered in a straightforward way: in the *van Calster* case,[25] the Court declared that the consequences ensuing from a breach of the obligation of notifying aid plans applies equally to their mode of financing. According to Advocate General Ruiz-Jarabo, this response would always depend on the particular case in hand. He considers that a national court can only reject the demand for reimbursement of the aid-financing levies if this is not accompanied with a simultaneous reimbursement of aid; any other solution, he submits, would run counter to the provisions of the Treaty, for the benefit received would then increase by virtue of removal of the financial charges, which would further distort competition.[26]

26.15 **Extension of aid?**   According to the ECJ, persons liable to pay an obligatory contribution cannot rely on the argument that the exemption enjoyed by other persons constitutes unlawful State aid in order to avoid payment of that contribution.[27]

26.16 **Influence of the Commission's decisions on the obligations of the national judge**   The national court is bound by the Commission's assessment of the existence of aid or its character of new or existing aid. On the other hand its role cannot be made to depend on the state of the Commission's examination of the matter. Thus the opening by the Commission of a preliminary examination procedure under Article 88(3) or the formal examination procedure laid down in Article 88(2) cannot be held to exempt national courts from their obligation to safeguard the rights of individuals in the event of any breach of the previous-notification obligation.[28]

26.17 The consequences of a final decision from the Commission ruling on the compatibility of the aid are not entirely clear. In *French Salmon*, the ECJ stated that the Commission's final decision on the compatibility of the aid does not have the effect of regularising *ex post facto* the implementing measures which were invalid because they had been taken in breach of the prohibition laid down by

---

[24] Case C-39/94 *SFEI and others* para 52.
[25] Joined Cases C-261/01 and C-262/01 para 44.
[26] Opinion in Case C-345/02 *Pearle* not yet reported paras 25–44.
[27] Case C-390/98 *Banks* [2001] ECR I-6117 para 80, and Joined Cases C-430/99 and C-431/99 *Sea-Land Service and Nedlloyd Lijnen* [2002] ECR I-5235 para 47.
[28] Case C-39/94 *SFEI and others* para 44.

the last sentence of Article 88(3) of the Treaty, since otherwise the direct effect of that prohibition would be impaired and the interests of individuals, which, as stated above, are to be protected by national courts, would be disregarded.[29] It follows that, even when the Commission's final decision declares the aid to be compatible with the common market, national courts may still be called on to declare invalid the implementing measures adopted by Member State authorities that are in breach of the last sentence of Article 88(3).[30] Such a decision, however, would seem to be somewhat dogmatic and certain recent judgments tend to favour the interpretation that once the Commission's final decision has been taken, the national court needs to ensure compliance with this rather than with the last sentence of Article 88(3).[31]

The intervention of the national court cannot, in principle, be held to depend **26.18** on the lodging of an action for annulment against the Commission's decision on the compatibility of the measure. Indeed, whatever may be the fate reserved for this decision, the breach of the final sentence of Article 88(3) subsists and must be penalized.

Cumulative infringement of the last sentence of Article 88(3), and of another provision of Community law

In its examination of the lawfulness of a national measure, the national court has **26.19** to give due consideration not only to any Commission decision on the compatibility of aid or an infringement of the last sentence of Article 88(3) but also the possible direct effect of any other provision of Community law that might equally be breached by the measure under examination. In order to fully observe the principles of direct effect and the primacy of Community law, it is in principle bound to annul the measure in dispute as soon as any infringement of the three abovementioned tenets has been proven. The Court has however mitigated the full effect of this principle in the following circumstances:

---

[29] Case C-354/90 *French Salmon* [1991] ECR I-5505 para 16.
[30] Case T-49/93 *SIDE v EC Commission* [1995] ECR II-2501 para 86, and Order of 30 September 1999, *UPS Europe v EC Commission* [1999] ECR I-3829 para 48. The situation is not so clear when the Commission's final decision rules that the measures do not constitute aid under Art 87(1). In that case, two approaches are possible, according to the scope granted to the Member States' notification obligation: either it can be decided, *a posteriori*, that the measures did not have to be notified and that the last sentence of Art 88(3) has not been breached, or it can be argued that there was a doubt that justified the notification obligation, the scope of the last sentence of Art 88(3) being deemed to be broader that that of Art 87(1).
[31] See para 13 of the Order in Case T-90/99 *Salzgitter v EC Commission* [2002] ECR II-4535 according to which 'adoption by the Commission of the final decision, which stated that the measures in question constituted State aid that was incompatible with the common market and directed the German authorities to recover it, removed any grounds on which interested third parties could invoke before the national courts the decision to initiate the formal examination procedure in order to obtain an order for the recovery of aid already paid to the applicant'.

- When a national court is dealing with aid in which only one of the constituent elements which is not necessary for attaining the objective of the aid represents an infringement of a Community provision with direct effect, the ECJ has ruled that this circumstance does not entitle national courts to make a declaration to the effect that the aid scheme is incompatible 'as a whole' with the Treaty.[32]
- The Court has ruled that the procedure under Article 88, dealt with by the Commission, must be used when an infringement of any other Community law provision concerns constituent elements of the aid so indissolubly linked to the object thereof that it would be impossible to evaluate them separately.[33] In such a case the national court cannot therefore itself establish all the consequences of the breach of the provision concerned.

26.20 All in all, therefore, it would seem that a national court will not normally have cause to annul an aid measure as a whole due to the infringement of another provision of Community law.

3. Distinction between the role of the national judge and the role of the Commission

26.21 Under Article 88, 'the Commission and the national courts have different powers and responsibilities'.[34] In other words, they play complementary and different roles.[35]

26.22 According to the ECJ, the principal and exclusive role conferred on the Commission by Articles 87 and 88 of the Treaty, namely to hold aid to be incompatible with the common market where this is appropriate, is fundamentally different from the role of national courts in safeguarding rights that individuals enjoy as a result of the direct effect of the prohibition laid down in the last sentence of Article 88(3) of the Treaty. Whilst the Commission must examine the compatibility of the proposed aid with the common market, even where the Member State has acted in breach of the prohibition on giving effect to aid, national courts do no more than preserve, until the final decision of the Commission, the rights of individuals faced with a possible breach by Member State authorities of the prohibition laid down by the last sentence of Article 88(3) of the Treaty. When those courts make a ruling on such a matter, they do not thereby decide on the compatibility of the aid with the common

---

[32] Case 74/76 *Iannelli/Meroni* [1977] ECR 557 para 16 (concerning the existence within a system of aid of a measure having an effect equivalent to a quantitative restriction).

[33] Case 74/76 *Iannelli/Meroni* para 14, and Case C-225/91 *Matra v EC Commission* [1993] ECR I-3203 para 41.

[34] Case C-44/93 *Namur-Les assurances du crédit* [1994] ECR I-3829 para 14.

[35] Case C-39/94 *SFEI and others* [1996] ECR I-3547 para 41.

market; the final determination of that matter is the exclusive responsibility of the Commission, subject to the supervision of the ECJ.[36]

Individuals cannot therefore, on the basis of Article 87 alone, challenge the compatibility of aid with Community law before the national courts or ask them to decide as to any incompatibility that may be the main issue in actions before them or may arise as a subsidiary issue.[37]   **26.23**

This traditional dichotomy between the Commission (monitoring of compatibility) and national court (monitoring of lawfulness) has one exception, due to the Regulation on block exemptions:[38] the national court and the Commission may be brought to effect the same monitoring procedure, i.e. checking whether the aid in question comes under a particular exemption regulation and could hence be paid without previous notification to the Commission.   **26.24**

B. Cooperation with the ECJ and the Commission

1. Cooperation with the ECJ

Within the context of the control of the lawfulness of aid, the national court cooperates with the ECJ in the form of a reference for a preliminary ruling: **26.25**

- A national court may have cause to interpret and apply the concept of aid contained in Article 87 in order to determine whether State aid introduced without observance of the preliminary examination procedure provided for in Article 88(3) ought to have been subject to this procedure. In this context, a national court may have cause to refer a question concerning the interpretation of Article 87 of the Treaty to the ECJ if it considers that a decision thereon is necessary to enable it to pass judgment.[39]

- A national court may question the ECJ about certain aspects of the procedure under Article 88(3) to ascertain whether or not the aid involved in the main action has been lawfully granted.[40]

---

[36] Case C-354/90 *French Salmon* para 14, and Case C-44/93 *Namur-Les assurances du crédit* paras 16 and 17.

[37] Case 74/76 *Iannelli and Volpi* and Case 78/76 *Steinike and Weinlig* and Joined Cases C-78/90 to C-83/90 *Compagnie commerciale de l'Ouest* [1992] ECR I-1847 para 33.

[38] See paras 21.29 *et seq.*

[39] Case 78/76 *Steinike & Weinlig* paras 14 and 15; Joined Cases C-72/91 and C-73/91 *Sloman Neptun* [1993] ECR I-887 para 12; Case C-189/91 *Kirsammer-Hack* [1993] ECR I-6185 para 14; Case C-39/94 *SFEI and others* para 51, and Case C-256/97 *DM Transport* [1999] ECR I-3913 para 15.

[40] See, e.g. the pre-litigation questions on the scope of Art 88(3), which are answered in Joined Cases 91/83 and 127/83 *Heineken Brouwerijen* [1984] ECR 3435.

- A national court may examine the validity of a Commission decision declaring aid to be compatible with the common market. Since the power to hold a Community measure invalid is reserved to the ECJ, a national court that considers the decision in question to be invalid is required to refer a question to the ECJ for a preliminary ruling.[41]

- On the other hand, the ECJ has no jurisdiction to respond to a referral for a preliminary ruling on the compatibility of aid with the Treaty, since such an assessment would in principle be the exclusive responsibility of the Commission.[42]

2. Cooperation with the Commission

26.26   The national court may be called upon to cooperate with the Commission.[43] According to the ECJ, where the national court has doubts as to whether the measures at issue should be categorized as State aid, it may seek clarification from the Commission. As a consequence of the duty of loyal cooperation between the Community institutions and the Member States under Article 10 of the Treaty, the Commission must respond as quickly as possible to such requests from national courts.[44]

26.27   In order to encourage national courts to address questions to it, the Commission has issued a general notice dealing with cooperation between national courts and the Commission in the field of State aid, along the lines of what it had already done in terms of the implementation of Articles 81 and 82.[45] The notice provides that national courts may, within the limits of their national procedural law, ask the Commission for information of a procedural nature to enable them to discover whether a certain case is pending before the Commission, whether a case has been the subject of a notification, or whether the Commission has officially initiated a procedure or taken any other decision. National courts may also consult the Commission on the established practice concerning the application of Article 87(1), or Article 88(3), and also for

---

[41] Case T-188/95 *Waterleiding v EC Commission* [1998] ECR II-3713 para 147.

[42] Case C-256/97 *DM Transport* para 16.

[43] It was AG Lenz who first sketched out the main lines of this cooperation procedure in his Opinion in Case C-44/93 *Namur-Les Assurances du Crédit* [1994] ECR I-3829 paras 104–108. In his view it is useful in such cases for the national court to know the criteria which the Commission has employed or contemplates employing. Moreover, account must be taken of the fact that proceedings under Art 88(3) before the national court have the remit of safeguarding the Commission's prerogatives and therefore should be concluded as quickly as possible. This is why, in his opinion, it would seem to be out of the question to propose the suspension of proceedings until the Commission has taken a decision.

[44] Case C-39/94 *SFEI and others* para 50.

[45] Notice on cooperation between national courts and the Commission in the State aid field [1995] OJ C312/8.

obtaining factual data, statistics, market studies and economic analyses. In practice national courts have very rarely used this option.

II. Other litigation before the national courts

Apart from the monitoring of the legality of the granting of aid, which is linked **26.28** to the direct effect of the final sentence of Article 88(3) with regard to the application of Commission decisions, it must be stressed that the Commission's State-aid decisions in principle have a direct effect. They can be invoked in national litigation of all types, whether civil, administrative, or criminal procedures, etc.

The Commission's positive aid decisions are binding on national courts, unless **26.29** they have made a submission to the ECJ for a preliminary ruling on validity. The existence of such a decision, however, does not *a posteriori* remedy the unlawfulness of any national aid-granting act adopted in breach of the last sentence of Article 88(3).

National courts may be appealed to by public authorities seeking to recover aid **26.30** declared to be incompatible. They may also be appealed to by a competitor trying to annul the granting of aid for the same reason. Indeed, it is up to national courts to uphold the rights of those concerned, by drawing all the inferences, in accordance with their national law, as regards the validity of measures implementing the aid in question and the recovery of the financial support granted, where the Commission finds by a decision adopted under Article 88(2) EC that a measure granting aid is incompatible with the common market.[46]

The most critical case obviously concerns the situation where public authorities **26.31** seek to obtain the recovery of aid that had been paid out unlawfully, after a Commission decision declaring the aid to be incompatible and ordering them to recover it.

Further, when a national court is called upon to take a Commission decision **26.32** into consideration to deal with a case brought before it, it may come up against problems of interpretation of this decision or entertain doubts about its validity. In these circumstances it can (or must, as the case may be) ask the Court of Justice for a preliminary ruling on interpretation or validity, pursuant to Article 234 EC.

---

[46] Case C-17/91 *Lornoy* [1992] ECR I-6523 para 31, referring to Case 78/76 *Steinike and Weinlig.*

26.33   As regards negative Commission decisions, the case law of the ECJ has been careful to interpret restrictively the preliminary ruling procedure to reduce the possibility of that decision being indefinitely called into question.[47]

---

[47]   Case C-188/92 *TWD Textilwerke Deggendorf* [1994] ECR I-833 para 29.

27

STATE AID LITIGATION BEFORE THE COMMUNITY COURTS

As we will see later, State aid litigation before Community Courts can take the most varied forms. The contending parties may be Member States and Community institutions or Community Institutions and private persons, usually undertakings and associations of undertakings. As for the types of procedures, the vast majority of cases involve actions for annulment or for failure to fulfil an obligation, to which may be added some proceedings for failure to act or non contractual liability. **27.01**

The main questions raised by this litigation involve the admissibility of the appeal, due to uncertainties about determining the contestable acts, on the one hand, and the *locus standi* of the persons concerned, on the other. **27.02**

According to Article 40 of the Statute of the Court of Justice, Member States and institutions of the Communities may intervene in cases before the Court. The same right is open to any other person establishing an interest in the result of any case filed with the Court. This means that it has to establish a direct, existing interest in the grant of the order as sought by one of the parties and not a mere interest in the pleas in law put forward.[1] **27.03**

No interest in intervening will exist when the applicant shows only an indirect **27.04**

---

[1] The aid beneficiary undertaking may be given leave to intervene in support of the Commission: Case T-443/93 *Casillo Grani v EC Commission* [1995] ECR II-1375 para 2. Beneficiary undertakings may intervene in support of another beneficiary undertaking: Case 323/82 *Intermills v EC Commission* [1984] ECR 3809 para 2. The competitors of a beneficiary undertaking may intervene in support of the Commission or of an applicant demanding the annulment of a positive decision: Joined Cases 296/82 and 318/82 *Netherlands and Leeuwarder Papierwarenfabriek v EC Commission* [1985] ECR 809 para 11 and Case T-442/93 *AAC and others v EC Commission* [1995] ECR II-1329 para 30. The authority in charge of the defence of the interests of a region may also be given leave to intervene when the economic situation of the region is likely to be directly affected by the aid in question: Case C-186/02 P *Ramondín and others v EC Commission* [2003] ECR I-2415 para 9, and Case C-188/02 P *Territorio Histórico de Álava v EC Commission* para 9.

interest in the solution of the case on the grounds of similarity between its own situation and that of one of the parties.[2]

I. Procedures against the Commission

A. Scope of the Judicial Review

27.05   Considerations of two types might limit the scope of the judicial review of the merits of the Commission's decisions.

27.06   First of all a decision has to be made on whether or not the Commission has any discretion: the Community judicature is in principle bound to exert a complete control over the question of deciding whether or not a measure falls within the field of application of Article 87(1), paying due consideration to the specific elements of the case submitted to it and the technical or complex character of the appraisals made by the Commission,[3] on the other hand it is equally bound not to encroach on the Commission's wide discretion in deciding on the compatibility of aid under Article 87(3): its control on this point is therefore not as 'comprehensive' as it is under Article 87(1).[4] Thus, the CFI has found that, when appraising the Commission's assessment of a plan designed to restructure an undertaking in economic and financial difficulties, 'it is only in cases where the Commission has committed a particularly manifest and serious error when assessing such a plan that the Court may rule against the authorisation of State aid intended to finance such restructuring'.[5]

27.07   Secondly, given that the Commission's decisions in State aid control matters are usually based on complex judgments of an economic and social order, the judicial review is restricted, in the sense that the court limits itself, in principle, to verifying: (i) observance of the rules of procedure and giving reasoned decisions; (ii) the material exactness of the facts upon which the contested

---

[2] Take the example of a region of a Member State that claims that the legal questions brought up in a case are equally likely to be applicable to aid it has paid out or wishes to grant: Orders of 6 March 2003, Case C-183/02 P *Demesa v EC Commission*, Case C-186/02 P *Ramondín and others v EC Commission*, and Case C-188/02 P *Territorio Histórico de Álava v EC Commission*.

[3] Case T-98/00 *Linde v EC Commission* [2002] ECR II-3961 para 40, and Case T-274/01 *Valmont Nederland v EC Commission* not yet reported para 37.

[4] Joined Cases T-228/99 and T-233/99 *WestLB and others v EC Commission* [2003] ECR II-435 para 282.

[5] Joined Cases T-371/94 and T-394/94 *British Airways and others v EC Commission* [1998] ECR II-2405 para 447.

decision is based; (iii) absence of any manifest error in the appraisal of the facts; and (iv) absence of any misuse of power.

The above refers to both the Commission's assessments on the existence of aid[6] **27.08** and the compatibility of aid.[7] In particular the ECJ is not entitled to substitute its own assessment of the facts, especially in the economic sphere, for that of the author of the decision.[8]

The limited scope of the judicial review reinforces the burden of proof on **27.09** the applicant contesting the Commission's interpretation.[9] The applicant has to prove to the Community Courts, beyond any reasonable doubt, that the Commission made errors of fact that undermine the conclusions it finally came to.[10] It is hence bound to adduce factual evidence 'sufficient to cast serious doubt' on the elements contained in the contested decision,[11] advance figures that are 'fundamentally' different from the data taken into account by the Commission.[12]

---

[6] Case C-56/93 *Belgium v EC Commission* [1996] ECR I-723 para 11; Joined Cases T-126/96 and T-127/96 *Breda Fucine Meridionali and others v EC Commission* [1998] ECR II-3437 para 81, and Case T-274/01 *Valmont Nederland v EC Commission* para 37.

[7] Joined Cases T-244/93 and T-486/93 *TWD v EC Commission* [1995] ECR II-2265 para 82; Case T-266/94 *Skibsværftsforeningen and others v EC Commission* [1996] ECR II-1399 para 170; Joined Cases T-371/94 and T-394/94 *British Airways and others v EC Commission* para 79; Case T-110/97 *Kneissl Dachstein Sportartikel v EC Commission* [1999] ECR II-2881 para 46; Case T-152/99 *HAMSA v EC Commission* [2002] ECR II-3049 para 48, and Case C-409/00 *Spain v EC Commission* [2003] ECR I-1487 para 93.

[8] Case C-225/91 *Matra v EC Commission* [1993] ECR I-3203 para 23; Case T-266/94 *Skibsværftsforeningen and others v EC Commission* para 168; Case C-169/95 *Spain v EC Commission* [1997] ECR I-135 para 34; Case T-106/95 *FFSA and others v EC Commission* [1997] ECR II-229 para 101; Joined Cases T-371/94 and T-394/94 *British Airways and others v EC Commission* para 79; Joined Cases T-126/96 and T-127/96 *Breda Fucine Meridionali and others v EC Commission* para 81; Case T-110/97 *Kneissl Dachstein Sportartikel v EC Commission* para 46; Case T-123/97 *Salomon v EC Commission* [1999] ECR II-2925 para 47, and Case T-152/99 *HAMSA v EC Commission* para 48. As regards interim measures, Case T-107/96 R *Pantochim v EC Commission* [1996] ECR II-1361 para 44. For a case of manifest misuse of powers by the Community Court see Case T-126/99 *Graphischer Maschinenbau v EC Commission* [2002] ECR II-2427 from para 50 onwards.

[9] Case T-266/94 *Skibsværftsforeningen and others v EC Commission* para 176.

[10] See the Opinion of AG Fennelly in Case C-56/93 *Belgium v EC Commission* [1996] ECR I-723 para 29.

[11] Case T-266/94 *Skibsværftsforeningen and others v EC Commission* para 195.

[12] Case T-123/97 *Salomon v EC Commission* [1999] ECR II-2925 para 89. Nonetheless the Commission is bound to furnish all possible assistance to the Community court: see the Opinion of AG Fennelly in Case C-56/93 *Belgium v EC Commission* [1996] ECR I-723 para 30. The ECJ may also decide to obtain the assistance of independent economic experts: see Case C-169/84 *CDF Chimie AZF v EC Commission* [1990] ECR I-3083 .

27.10 In contrast to the limited character of the Community Court's review of the Commission's substantive interpretations, the Community Court exerts a strict control over the procedural rules, insofar as these rules represent the concerned parties' main guarantee of being associated with the Commission's decisions.[13] The Commission's discretion thus goes hand in hand with the obligation to observe scrupulously the procedural rules within which its decision was taken and examine with due care and impartiality all the relevant facts of the case in hand, all of which reflects on its obligation to state the reasons for its decisions.[14]

27.11 In principle, an infringement of the procedural rules by the Commission is not, however, grounds for annulling the contested decision if it is established that the decision would have been no different even in the absence of the alleged breach. In other words, in order for such an infringement to result in annulment, it must be established that, had it not been for such an irregularity, the outcome of the procedure might have been different.[15]

27.12 The lawfulness of the Commission's approach has to be interpreted:

(i) in terms of the issues of fact and law existing at the time the measure was adopted.[16] It cannot be made to depend on retrospective considerations of its effectiveness[17] nor on arguments relating to the detailed rules for implementation of the decision, claiming that they have not been or will not be completely observed;[18] moreover, the mere statement that one of

---

[13] According to the settled case law of the ECJ, respect for the rights guaranteed by the Community legal order in administrative procedures is of even more fundamental importance where the Community institutions have a power of appraisal (Case C-269/90 *Technische Universität München* [1991] ECR I-5469 para 14).

[14] Joined Cases T-371/94 and T-394/94 *British Airways and others v EC Commission* para 95.

[15] Case T-198/01 *TGI v EC Commission* not yet reported para 201. As regards an infringement of the Member State's defence right, established as such but without having any effect on the content of the contested decision, see Case 234/84 *Belgium v EC Commission* [1986] ECR 2263 para 30, and 40/85 para 30; Case 259/85 *France v EC Commission* [1987] ECR 4393 para 13; Case C-301/87 *France v EC Commission* [1990] ECR I-307 para 31, and Case C-142/87 *Belgium v EC Commission* [1990] ECR I-959 para 48. As regards the failure by the Member State concerned to produce certain documents within the time limit for doing so, see Case T-266/94 *Skibsværftsforeningen and others v EC Commission* [1996] ECR II-1399 paras 197 and 243. Nonetheless, should the Commission wrongfully refrain from starting the formal examination procedure, this infringement automatically entails annulment of the decision to raise no objection.

[16] Case T-109/01 *Fleuren Compost v EC Commission* not yet reported para 50.

[17] As regards decisions on State aid matters, see Joined Cases T-371/94 and T-394/94 *British Airways and others v EC Commission* para 81, and Case T-123/97 *Salomon v EC Commission* [1999] ECR II-2925 paras 49 and 115.

[18] Case T-380/94 *AIUFFASS and AKT v EC Commission* [1996] ECR II-2169 para 128, and Case T-67/94 *Ladbroke Racing v EC Commission* [1998] ECR II-1 para 190.

the conditions on which an aid-granting decision was based will not be complied with cannot cast doubt on the legality of the decision;

(ii) strictly in light of the information to hand, either potentially or actually when the Commission reached its decision.[19] Thus an applicant cannot rely on factual arguments which were unknown to the Commission and which it had not notified to the latter during the examination procedure.[20] This applies first and foremost to Member States, which will not be entitled to complain of the Commission's failure to take certain evidence into account if at no stage in the administrative procedure did they submit that evidence to the Commission, thereby refusing to cooperate fairly therewith.[21] This is also a fortiori the case where the Member State has refused to reply to an express request for information from the Commission.[22] In the case of an appeal brought by the State to which the decision was addressed, the ECJ has rejected certain legal pleas for the simple reason that the applicant did not make them in sufficient time, having previously refrained from contesting a Commission decision that had foreshadowed the later one. The same goes for a beneficiary undertaking that has failed to present information or documents during the administrative phase.[23] This only applies to factual matters, however. Nothing prevents the interested party from raising against the final decision a legal argument that was not made during the administrative procedure.[24]

---

[19] As regards decisions on State aid matters see Case 234/84 *Belgium v EC Commission* [1986] ECR 2263 para 16; Case C-241/94 *France v EC Commission* [1996] ECR 4551 para 33; Joined Cases T-371/94 and T-394/94 *British Airways and others v EC Commission* [1998] ECR II-2405 para 81; Cases T-110/97 *Kneissl Dachstein Sportartikel v EC Commission* para 47, and Case T-123/97 *Salomon* [1999] ECR II-2925 para 48; Case C-276/02 *Spain v EC Commission* not yet reported para 31 and Case T-274/01 *Valmont Nederland v EC Commission* not yet reported para 38. Notwithstanding the above, the Commission might still be placed under the obligation of endeavouring to obtain more information.

[20] Case T-110/97 *Kneissl Dachstein Sportartikel v EC Commission* [1999] ECR II-2881 para 102, and Case T-176/01 *Ferriere Nord v EC Commission* not yet reported para 154.

[21] Case 102/87 *France v EC Commission* [1988] ECR 4067 para 27; Joined Cases C-278/92, C-279/92 and C-280/92 *Spain v EC Commission* [1994] ECR I-4103 para 31; Case C-382/99 *Netherlands v EC Commission* [2002] ECR I-5163 paras 49 and 76; Case T-109/01 *Fleuren Compost v EC Commission* not yet reported para 51, and Case C-277/00 *Germany v EC Commission* not yet reported para 39.

[22] Case C-382/99 *Netherlands v EC Commission* para 76.

[23] Joined Cases T-126/96 and T-127/96 *Breda Fucine Meridionali and others v EC Commission* para 88, and Case T-176/01 *Ferriere Nord v EC Commission* paras 123 and 154.

[24] Case T-123/97 *Salomon v EC Commission* [1999] ECR II-2925 para 55.

B. Action for Annulment

1. General principles

Contestable act

27.13 An action for annulment can be brought against measures producing legal effects which are binding on and capable of affecting the interests of the applicant by having a significant effect on its legal position.[25]

27.14 One difficulty of annulment proceedings in State aid matters may be to determine the act of which the annulment is sought. Some cases are fairly straightforward, for example when the action for annulment is brought against the decision to initiate the formal examination procedure or against a final decision adopted at the end of a formal examination procedure. But other actions may be brought against Commission letters or its services, involving acts not specifically defined as such in the official rules: refusal to initiate the formal examination procedure, refusal to address the appropriate measures, dismissal of a complaint, decision to consider aid to be compatible with the conditions of an existing scheme, etc. The same act can sometimes be construed as implicitly encapsulating different decisions.

27.15 The act against which an action for annulment is being brought by a third party has sometimes to be ascertained in terms of the previous correspondence between that third party and the Commission and in particular the requests made therein. This seems to be paradoxical, since the Commission's decisions are always supposed to be addressed only to the Member State concerned and not the third party.[26]

27.16 In short, an ostensibly single decision might, as the case may be, have to be analysed as a bundle of different decisions (for example decisions on different items of aid granted to the same undertaking by different public entities).[27]

27.17 The letters addressed directly to third parties, in particular to complainants, have to be considered as sent for information purposes and hence do not

---

[25] In particular, in State-aid matters, Case T-190/00 *Regione Siciliana v EC Commission* not yet reported para 43.

[26] Thus, in the examination of a decision establishing the absence of aid, addressed to France, the CFI found that the Commission had acted correctly in restricting its examination to certain measures and not others, inasmuch as it might reasonably have assumed that the complainants against the original decision had abandoned their complaints in relation to these other measures (Case T-106/95 *FFSA and others v EC Commission* [1997] ECR II-229 para 38).

[27] Joined Cases T-127/99 T-129/99 and T-148/99 *Territorio Histórico de Álava and others v EC Commission* [2002] ECR II-1275 para 56.

constitute acts that may be challenged in annulment actions.[28] These letters may, however, reflect the content of a decision, even if it has not effectively been sent to the Member State concerned.[29] When the Commission addresses a letter to a third party informing it of the contents of a decision it has adopted on a State measure, this third party's action for annulment against the letter will not necessarily be inadmissible: the Community Courts have sometimes admitted the action if the Commission had adopted a decision in the contested letter addressed in fact to the Member State concerned, even if that decision had not effectively been sent to said State.[30] On the other hand, in a case where the applicant has lodged a complaint against the decision addressed to the Member State and, at the same time, the letter that had been sent to it, the CFI has dismissed the claim for annulment of the letter as inadmissible.[31]

27.18 Should the Commission fail to adopt a position on certain measures included in the complaint, without expressly rejecting the complaint in this respect and while opening the formal examination procedure to deal with other measures included in the complaint, this circumstance does not affect the lawfulness of the Commission's decision. If the complainant wishes to obtain a decision on the complaint as a whole, it behoves it to call upon the Commission to do so in accordance with Article 232 of the Treaty.[32] A letter stating that the Commission services intend to take no action against the State, without characterizing the facts or setting a deadline for the examination of the compatibility is not a challengeable act.[33] In sum, purely informative letters not in any way constituting a decision are not acts open to challenge.[34]

27.19 The principle of Community legality implies the obligation of recognizing the full efficacy of Community acts as long as they have not been declared to be invalid (presumption of legality). Moreover, under the terms of Article 242 of

---

[28] See Case C-198/91 *Cook v EC Commission* [1993] ECR I-2487 para 14 (as AG Tesauro observed in his Opinion in Case C-198/91 *Cook v EC Commission* [1993] ECR I-2487 para 32, 'in the framework of the procedure laid down in Art 93, unlike the procedures followed by application of Art 85 and 86, the only decision the Commission can make is to rule on the compatibility of aid. An autonomous and different decision involving the rejection of a complaint brought by a competitor undertaking of the beneficiary undertaking is therefore not conceivable').

[29] Case T-182/98 *UPS Europe v EC Commission* [1999] ECR II-2857 para 38.

[30] ibid paras 38 and 41.

[31] Case T-82/96 *ARAP and others v EC Commission* [1999] ECR II-1889 paras 29 and 30.

[32] Case T-67/94 *Ladbroke Racing v EC Commission* [1998] ECR II-1 para 92.

[33] Case T-182/98 *UPS Europe v EC Commission* paras 42–43.

[34] Case T-82/96 *ARAP and others v EC Commission* para 30. Thus, when the Commission, upon examining new aid, replies to an argument or a request put forward by a complainant in respect of different aid already approved, that circumstance does not in itself demonstrate that the latter has been the subject of a fresh examination by the Commission: Case T-188/95 *Waterleiding v EC Commission* [1998] ECR II-3713 para 128.

the Treaty, actions brought before the ECJ or the CFI do not have a suspensory effect. Unless an interim measure is obtained from the judge responsible for dealing with such applications, the challenged decisions have to be put into effect even if their annulment has been sought meanwhile.[35] Failing that, the Commission is entitled to bring an action for failure to fulfil an obligation before the ECJ, which is examined independently of the action for annulment brought against the decision whose breach prompted this action for failure to fulfil an obligation.[36]

27.20 Likewise, the fact that an action for annulment has been lodged against a negative decision by the Commission does not, in principle, prevent it from adopting other negative decisions with regard to supplementary aid granted to the same beneficiary.[37]

Locus standi

27.21 The Member State concerned is, in principle, the addressee of the Commission's decisions. Moreover, the Member States and the Community institutions benefit in all circumstances from a privileged access to the Community Courts, by virtue of the second subparagraph of Article 230. As regards the Member States' *locus standi*, the ECJ has ruled that even when a Member State has infringed the provisions of Article 88 it may not be deprived of the right to challenge before the Court, the legality of a Commission decision adversely affecting it, under Articles 230 *et seq.* in particular.[38]

27.22 The Commission's State aid decisions are addressed to the Member State granting the aid dealt with in the decision, whether it is a matter of a decision ruling on the absence of aid,[39] a decision ruling on the existing character of

---

[35] See Case 310/85 R *Deufil v EC Commission* [1986] ECR 537 para 13, and Case 63/87 *EC Commission v Greece* [1988] ECR 2875 paras 10 to 12.

[36] In the past the ECJ tended to deal with these two types of actions in parallel (see, for example Joined Cases 67, 68 and 70/85 *Van der Kooy v EC Commission* [1988] ECR 219, and Case 213/85 *EC Commission v Netherlands* [1988] ECR 281, and Case 57/86 *Greece v EC Commission* [1988] ECR 2855, and Case 63/87 *EC Commission v Greece*). Sometimes the ECJ now deals first of all with the action for failure to fulfil an obligation before ruling on the action for annulment. This might lead to a decision where the State is found to be remiss before a subsequent annulment of the Commission's decision.

[37] Case C-399/95 R *Germany v EC Commission* [1996] ECR I-2441 paras 71–73.

[38] Joined Cases 67, 68 and 70/85 R *Van der Kooy v EC Commission* [1988] ECR 219 para 37. The same goes, *a fortiori*, for aid beneficiary undertakings, on condition that they are directly and individually concerned (solution implicitly followed since Case 323/82 *Intermills v EC Commission* [1984] ECR 3809 which dealt with unlawfully paid aid. As AG Slynn quite rightly pointed out, the Commission cannot challenge the admissibility of the procedure on the grounds of the unlawful granting of the aid since it has a wide range of powers dealing with the illegal implementation of aid (Opinion in Cases 67, 68 and 70/85)).

[39] See para 51 of Case T-178/94 *ATM v EC Commission* [1997] ECR II-2529.

aid,[40] a decision ruling on the compatibility of aid,[41] or a decision to refuse to initiate the formal examination procedure adopted after the lodging of a complaint.[42]

The admissibility of actions brought by persons other than the addressee **27.23** Member State is therefore a thorny issue. It is usually necessary to establish, on the one hand, an interest in bringing proceedings and, on the other, a direct and individual interest as laid down in subparagraph 4 of Article 230 EC.

It is necessary for the person concerned to prove a legally protected and existing **27.24** interest or, failing that, a future and certain interest. The interest in bringing an action raises almost no doubts in the case of actions brought by the undertakings benefiting from the aid concerned or the competitors thereof (or the associations representing the latter). This applies even if the aid has not yet been paid out or if the aid scheme has not yet been implemented: where there is no doubt that the national authorities wish to act in a certain way, the possibility of their not making use of the option afforded by the Commission decision is purely theoretical, with the result that the applicant may be directly concerned.[43] Conversely, the ECJ has ruled that a third party who is not in competition with the aid beneficiary or does not represent persons in competition therewith, cannot be considered to be concerned by the contested decision, the confirmation or annulment thereof in no way affecting its interests. The case concerned an association representing undertakings that were not in competition with the aid beneficiaries but wished to benefit themselves from the contested aid.[44] The CFI has adopted the same approach in relation to an action brought by the mutual provident association of an undertaking objecting to State aid allegedly awarded to that undertaking, ruling that the confirmation or annulment of the Commission's decision was in no way liable to affect the interests of that association or its members.[45]

The interest in bringing an action may likewise not exist when the applicant **27.25** requires annulment of certain parts of a decision whose operative part is favourable to it.[46]

The concept of direct and individual interest has to be examined on a case by **27.26**

---

[40] See para 28 of Case C-313/90 *CIRFS and others v EC Commission* [1993] ECR I-1125.
[41] See para 31 of Case T-189/97 *Comité d'entreprise de la Société française de production and others v EC Commission* [1998] ECR II-335 .
[42] Case T-188/95 *Waterleiding v EC Commission* [1998] ECR II-3713 para 127.
[43] Case T-114/00 *ARE v EC Commission* [2002] ECR II-5121 para 73.
[44] Case C-295/92 *Landbouwschap v EC Commission* [1992] ECR I-5003 para 12.
[45] Case T-178/94 *ATM v EC Commission* [1997] ECR II-2529.
[46] Case T-212/00 *Nuove Industrie Molisane v EC Commission* [2002] ECR II-347.

case basis, in view of the nature of the contested act and the *locus standi* of the applicant. The main problems concern the individual interest, in particular when decisions on aid schemes are being dealt with.

27.27   The main issue here is to ascertain whether other public authorities or groups besides the central authorities of the State concerned, such as regional or local authorities, etc, are also entitled to bring actions against the Commission's aid decisions, insofar as they are the granters of such aid and have *locus standi* the standing of non-privileged applicants. The ECJ and the CFI have generally found such actions to be admissible, on the grounds that said public authorities, even if they cannot be considered to be the addressees of the Commission's decisions, were directly and individually concerned by such decisions and could lay claim to their own interests. The individual interest may arise from a set of circumstances, in particular the fact that the contested decision affects acts of which they are the authors, when it prevents them from exercising, as they see fit, their own powers, which they enjoy directly under national law or that it has the effect of obliging them to engage in the administrative aid recovery procedure, etc.[47] The direct interest arises from the fact that, even when the contested decision is addressed to the Member State, the national authorities in principle exercise no discretion in communicating it to the infra-State authority.[48] The rightful interest of these authorities ensues from the autonomy they are granted under their national law.[49]

27.28   *Locus standi* is ruled out only when the regional authority is not the grantor of the aid and lays claim only to the socio-economic knock-on effects of the contested act on its territory[50] or when there is no rightful or special interest to act against the Commission's decision because this interest is not clearly distinguishable from the Member State's.[51]

27.29   The CFI is in principle in favour of collective action brought by associations for

---

[47] See Joined Cases 62/87 and 72/87 *Exécutif Régional Wallon v EC Commission* [1988] ECR 1573; Case T-214/95 *Vlaams Gewest v EC Commission* [1998] ECR II-717 para 28; Case T-288/97 *Regione autonoma Friuli Venezia Giulia v EC Commission* [1999] ECR II-1891; Joined Cases T-132/96 and T-143/96 *Freistaat Sachsen and others v EC Commission* [1999] ECR II-3663 paras 81 to 94; Joined Cases T-127/99, T-129/99 and T-148/99 *Territorio Histórico de Álava and others v EC Commission* [2002] ECR II-1275 para 50, and Joined Cases T-269/99, T-271/99 and T-272/99 *Territorio Histórico de Guipúzcoa and others v EC Commission* [2002] ECR II-4217 para 41, and Joined Cases T-346/99, T-347/99 and T-348/99 *Territorio Histórico de Álava and others v EC Commission* [2002] ECR II-4259 para 37.
[48] Joined Cases T-132/96 and T-143/96 *Freistaat Sachsen and others v EC Commission* [1999] ECR II-3663 paras 89–90.
[49] ibid para 91.
[50] Case T-238/97 *Comunidad Autónoma de Cantabria v Council* [1998] ECR II-2271.
[51] Case 282/85 *DEFI v EC Commission* [1986] ECR 2469 para 18.

this has the procedural advantage of obviating the need for numerous separate actions against the same decision.[52]

When several applicants seek annulment of the same Commission decision, it **27.30** may turn out that only some of them are judged to have *locus standi*. In such a case, if they have brought separate actions, the Community Court checks the admissibility of each one and may declare certain of them to be inadmissible even if all the cases are joined for judgment purposes.[53] On the other hand, when a single action is involved, it is admitted if at least one of the applications is eligible for bringing it.[54]

Admissible legal pleas

As regards pleas based on illegal procedures, it is a moot point whether an **27.31** applicant is entitled to object to an illegality that has not directly had an adverse effect on it. In such a case, however, when dealing with the addressee Member State's defence rights, the CFI has judged it to be an essential requirement and that a third party may have a legitimate interest in pleading an infringement thereof where a failure to comply with the Member State's right to be heard may have a bearing on the legality of the contested measure.[55]

As regards pleas dealing with the merits of a case, a plea put forward by a **27.32** complainant is not inadmissible on the grounds that it has not been previously brought before the Commission. The CFI first applied this principle to a situation where the adoption of the Commission's decision had not been preceded by the initiation of the formal examination procedure, declaring that there did not have to be strict consistency between the complaint and the action.[56] It has subsequently applied this principle to cases where the Commission has initiated the formal examination procedure, laying it down that 'no provision in the field

---

[52] Joined Cases T-447/93 to T-449/93 *AITEC and others v EC Commission* [1996] ECR II-1631 para 60, and Case T-114/00 *ARE v EC Commission* [2002] ECR II-5121 paras 44 and 45.

[53] Joined Cases 67, 68 and 70/85 *Van der Kooy v EC Commission* [1988] ECR 219 para 16.

[54] Case C-313/90 *CIRFS and others v EC Commission* [1993] ECR I-1125 para 31; Case T-435/93 *ASPEC and others v EC Commission* [1995] ECR II-1281 para 72; Joined Cases T-447/93 to T-449/93 *AITEC and others v EC Commission* para 82; Case T-266/94 *Skibsværfts-foreningen and others v EC Commission* [1996] ECR II-1399 para 51, and Joined Cases T-127/99, T-129/99 and T-148/99 *Territorio Histórico de Álava and others v EC Commission* para 52.

[55] Joined Cases T-228/99 and T-233/99 *WestLB and others v EC Commission* [2003] ECR II-435 paras 142–143. Conversely, see the negative response given by AG Lenz in Cases 62/87 and 72/87, para 13 of the Opinion thereon. He considers therein that a third party has no legitimate interest in bringing an action in defence of the procedural rights of the Member State. The ECJ has not however followed his ruling and has rejected this plea in the merits stage of the judgment.

[56] Case T-49/93 *SIDE v EC Commission* [1995] ECR II-2501 para 73.

of State aid makes the right for a person directly and individually concerned to challenge a measure addressed to a third party conditional upon all the complaints set out in the application having been raised during the administrative procedure'.[57]

27.33 Likewise, an applicant is not prevented from putting forward certain pleas against a final decision on the grounds that it has not previously raised them when objecting to the decision to initiate proceedings.[58] The applicant therefore has the right to bring an action for the annulment of the decision in its entirety, including the classification of aid as new aid, irrespective of whether or not it challenged that aspect of the decision to start the formal investigation procedure in respect of the aid in question.[59] It is, in principle, entitled to invoke any illegality that might vitiate the preparatory acts for the final decision.[60]

27.34 The plea of legitimate expectations is often put forward: the Commission, in following the State-aid examination procedure, is bound to take account of the legitimate expectations which the parties concerned may entertain as a result of what was said in the decision opening the procedure and, consequently, not to base its final decision on the absence of elements which, in light of those indications, the parties concerned could not consider that they were bound to furnish.[61] Note that any inaction by the Commission with regard to a national measure cannot be taken as a precise assurance by the Commission that a similar measure does not constitute State aid.[62] There is also the question of whether a Member State applying for the annulment of a negative Commission decision is entitled to invoke the legitimate expectations of the beneficiaries when the State authorities have granted aid in breach of the procedural rules laid down in Article 88. Case law on this point has changed over time.

---

[57] Case T-380/94 *AIUFFASS and AKT* [1996] ECR II-2169 para 64, and Case T-16/96 *Cityflyer Express v EC Commission* [1998] ECR II-757 para 39. Along the same lines, Case T-110/97 *Kneissl Dachstein Sportartikel v EC Commission* [1999] ECR II-2881 para 102, and Case T-123/97 *Salomon* [1999] ECR II-2925 para 55, and Case T-274/01 *Valmont Nederland v EC Commission* not yet reported para 102.

[58] Joined Cases T-126/96 and T-127/96 *Breda Fucine Meridionali and others v EC Commission* [1998] ECR II-3437 para 43.

[59] Case T-190/00 *Regione Siciliana v EC Commission* not yet reported para 49. As the CFI has quite rightly pointed out in this judgment, a contrary interpretation would amount to admitting that a ruling by the Community judicature at a preliminary stage of the procedure on preparatory measures such as the decision to initiate a formal investigation procedure, and in particular on the classification of aid as new aid, would prevent the parties concerned from challenging the final decision, where the Commission may alter the assessment made in the initiating decision (ibid para 51).

[60] Case T-182/98 *UPS Europe v EC Commission* [1999] ECR II-2857 para 47.

[61] Case T-176/01 *Ferriere Nord v EC Commission* para 88.

[62] Joined Cases T-346/99, T-347/99 and T-348/99 *Territorio Histórico de Álava and others v EC Commission* [2002] ECR II-4259 para 95.

The Court at first seemed to simply transpose its case law on actions for failure to fulfil an obligation brought by the Commission against the failure to execute its decisions. This implied that the State could not put forward such a plea in support of an action for annulment brought against the Commission's decision.[63] More recently, however, the ECJ has admitted that there is a difference according to whether such a plea is put forward by the State as defendant wishing to avoid the obligation entailed in the Commission's decision, or as an appellant challenging the validity of that decision. When dealing with an action for annulment brought by a State, it has first examined to see whether the claim of the beneficiary's legitimate expectations was well founded before dismissing it when looking at the substantive issues of the case.[64] It is submitted that this is the correct approach but it does not seem to have been followed by the CFI.[65]

Pleas claiming that insufficient reasons were given for the decision are often put forward, and often with a degree of success.[66] **27.35**

A Commission decision based on factual errors or an arbitrary approach is prone to be annulled, without the Community Courts thereby prejudging the result that would have been obtained in the absence of this factual error.[67] **27.36**

Burden of proof

Acts of the Community institutions are presumed to be valid. It therefore behoves parties seeking their annulment to rebut that presumption by producing convincing evidence to cast doubt on the assessments made by the Commission.[68] **27.37**

Time-limit for bringing the action

The interested parties have to make sure they exercise their appeal rights within the requisite time-limits, which are public policy provisions. Failing that, not **27.38**

---

[63] Joined Cases C-278/92, C-279/92 and C-280/92 *Spain v EC Commission* [1994] ECR I-4103 para 76.

[64] Case C-169/95 *Spain v EC Commission* [1997] ECR I-135 paras 49 and 50. More recently, Case C-334/99 *Germany v EC Commission* [2003] ECR I-1139 comes across as ambiguous (paras 41 to 44).

[65] The CFI, for its part, seems to consider that the beneficiaries' legitimate expectations can only be pleaded in the national court and only by the aid beneficiary.

[66] See Case C-415/96 *Spain v EC Commission* [1998] ECR I-6993 and Joined Cases T-371/94 and T-394/94 *British Airways v EC Commission* [2003] ECR II-5917.

[67] For examples in the aid field see Joined Cases T-127/99, T-129/99 and T-148/99 *Territorio Histórico de Álava and others v EC Commission* [2002] ECR II-1275 para 90, and Case C-276/02 *Spain v EC Commission* not yet reported paras 31 *et seq.*

[68] Case T-110/97 *Kneiss Dachstein Sportartikel v EC Commission* [1999] ECR II-2881 para 45.

only is the annulment no longer possible[69] but they also risk forfeiting the right to challenge the legality of the decision in any later collateral proceeding. Thus, a Member State that has received a negative decision will not be able to call into question the validity of this decision in any action for failure to fulfil an obligation brought against it by the Commission for having failed to execute it. Likewise, any beneficiary undertaking of individual aid that could have brought an action for annulment against a negative Commission decision cannot later invoke the unlawfulness of this decision, whether before the national court[70] nor before the Community Courts.[71]

27.39 For the addressee to whom the decision is notified (in principle the Member State), time starts to run from the date of the notification. For others, it is the date of publication in the Official Journal that is taken into account. The criterion based on the moment that the contested act came to the knowledge of the applicant, pursuant to the wording of subparagraph five of Article 230 EC, is subsidiary to the other criteria of notification or publication. For decisions that are normally published in the EU Official Journal, therefore, it is the date of publication that marks the start of the time limit, whether the applicant is a Member State or interested third party, even if the latter learned of it earlier.[72]

2. Appeal against a decision not to raise objections/a refusal to initiate the formal examination procedure

Contestable act

27.40 The Commission may decide not to raise any objection to a measure after a preliminary examination thereof. This category of decisions takes in, on the one hand, decisions concluding that the measure concerned does not constitute aid[73] and, on the other, decisions concluding that new aid, notified or otherwise, is compatible. Such decisions also imply a refusal, implied or express (in the case of a complaint), to initiate the formal examination procedure of the measure,

---

[69] For cases of inadmissibility due to late application in the aid sector, see Orders of 29 May 2002, Case T-4/02 *Arca Delio Eredi-Ledda Battistina v EC Commission*, and Case T-21/02 *Atzeni and others v EC Commission*.

[70] Case C-188/92 *TWD* [1994] ECR I-883.

[71] Joined Cases T-244/93 and T-486/93 *TWD v EC Commission* [1995] ECR II-2265 para 103.

[72] Case T-11/95 *BP Chemicals v EC Commission* [1998] ECR II-3235 para 47; Case T-110/97 *Kneissl Dachstein Sportartikel v EC Commission* [1999] ECR II-2881 paras 40 to 43; Case T-123/97 *Salomon v EC Commission* paras 42–44; Case T-296/97 *Alitalia v EC Commission* [2000] ECR II-3871 para 61, and Case T-190/00 *Regione Siciliana v EC Commission* para 30.

[73] See, e.g. Case T-11/95 *BP Chemicals v EC Commission* paras 84 *et seq.*

for the Commission cannot declare aid to be incompatible without having previously initiated that procedure.[74] These are contestable acts. It does not matter whether they have been adopted after notification by the Member State or after a third-party complaint.

Locus standi

The refusal to initiate the formal examination procedure deprives the parties **27.41** concerned (in the sense of the first subparagraph of Article 88(2)) of their right to make their submissions to the Commission. In *Cook*, the ECJ held that the persons intending to benefit from the procedural guarantees of Article 88(2) may secure compliance therewith only if they are able to challenge that decision by the Commission before the Community Courts. To be able to challenge such a decision, therefore, it suffices to fulfil a twofold condition; namely, to be a concerned party as defined in Article 88(2) and to be seeking to safeguard the procedural rights laid down in that provision.[75] This is sufficient to be considered as directly and individually concerned within the meaning of the fourth subparagraph of Article 230 EC. This principle applies both when the ground on which the decision is taken is that the Commission regards the aid as compatible with the common market and when, in its view, the very existence of aid must be discounted.[76]

The principle established in *Cook*, based on the safeguarding of procedural **27.42** rights, is wider than that laid down in *Cofaz*,[77] which concerns the admissibility of an action for annulment of a final decision taken at the end of the formal examination procedure.[78]

---

[74] Case T-398/94 *Kahn Scheepvaart v EC Commission* [1996] ECR II-477 para 47, and Case T-11/95 *BP Chemicals v EC Commission* [1998] ECR II-3235 para 88.

[75] Case C-198/91 *Cook v EC Commission* [1993] ECR I-2487 paras 23 and 24; Case C-225/91 *Matra v EC Commission* [1993] ECR I-3203 paras 17 and 18; Orders of 21 September 1999, Case C-204/97 *Portugal v EC Commission* para 4 and Case T-182/98 *UPS Europe v EC Commission* [1999] ECR II-2857 para 47, and Case T-114/00 *ARE v EC Commission* [2002] ECR II-5121 paras 44 and 45; Case T-41/01 *Rafael Pérez Escolar v EC Commission* [2003] ECR II-2157 para 33; Case T-27/02 *Kronofrance v EC Commission* not yet reported para 33.

[76] Case T-11/95 *BP Chemicals v EC Commission* paras 89 and 165.

[77] See para 27.59.

[78] This greater flexibility for action taken against decisions adopted without initiating the procedure is justified on two grounds: first, it would seem normal for competitors not to be obliged to prove a 'substantial detriment' when they challenge a decision not to raise objections, insofar as in such a case they are usually in possession only of the information on the aid communicated by the Commission or gleaned from the summary publication in the Official Journal; secondly, it is also reasonable not to require competitors to have participated in the preliminary procedure, insofar as they might have been completely ignorant of the fact that this procedure had been initiated (see paras 41 and 43 of the Opinion of AG Tesauro in Case C-198/91 *Cook v EC Commission* [1993] ECR I-2487).

27.43 The concerned parties are any persons, undertakings or associations whose interests might have been affected by the granting of the aid, in particular the beneficiary undertakings. This concept, mainly dealt with in the Treaty in the context of the administrative procedure carried out before the Commission, finally turns out, therefore, actually more important with respect to court proceedings.[79]

27.44 As well as being a concerned party, the applicant also has to contest specifically the Commission's refusal to initiate the formal examination procedure. In other words the applicant must be seeking in its action to safeguard the procedural rights laid down in Article 88(2).[80] The CFI does not however require the applicant to expressly allege infringement by the Commission of its obligation to initiate the procedure under Article 88(2), preventing the exercise of the procedural rights provided for thereby; it suffices for the pleas for annulment put forward to be construed as seeking to establish that the measures at issue pose serious difficulties as regards their compatibility with the common market, difficulties which place the Commission under an obligation to initiate the formal procedure.[81] As for the pleas that may be put forward, the CFI has ruled that once a party has challenged the decision not to initiate the procedure in defence of its procedural rights, it may then put forward any plea for annulment, without being limited to relying on infringement of its procedural rights.[82]

27.45 If the applicant limits itself to challenging the aid approval decisions as such, putting forwards pleas based on the merits of the case but without claiming infringement of its procedural rights, the simple fact of its being eligible for consideration as a 'concerned' party within the meaning of Article 88(2) will not be sufficient to guarantee the admissibility of the action. Here, the *Cofaz* case law[83] is applied and the applicant is bound to prove that it is in a particular situation distinguishing it individually from all other businessmen.[84] An undertaking must therefore prove that its competitive position could be substantially affected by the granting of the disputed aid[85] and, where applicable, that it has intervened in the preliminary procedure. The action brought by an associ-

---

[79] See paras 22.78 *et seq.*
[80] Case T-188/95 *Waterleiding Maatschappij 'Noord-West Brabant' v EC Commission* [1998] ECR II-3713 para 53.
[81] Case T-114/00 *ARE v EC Commission* para 47.
[82] Case T-157/01 *Danske Busvognmænd v EC Commission* not yet reported para 41.
[83] See para 27.59.
[84] Case T-188/95 *Waterleiding Maatschappij v EC Commission* para 54.
[85] Case T-266/94 *Skibsværftsforeningen and others v EC Commission* [1996] ECR II-1399 para 45.

ation is therefore admissible insofar as it is acting as an agent for its members, some of whom have *locus standi* by virtue of the effect on their competitive position.[86]

As for decisions to raise no objection against aid schemes, there is as yet no settled case law.[87] **27.46**

Effects of an annulment

If the ECJ annuls a decision not to raise objections, this normally means that the Commission is bound to initiate the formal examination procedure.[88] It is nonetheless conceivable that a decision annulled due to a technical defect (failure to give reasons or infringement of the principle of collegiality in the Commission, for example) could simply be adopted anew under the form of a decision not to raise objections. **27.47**

3. Appeal against a decision considering aid to constitute existing aid

Contestable act

Without initiating the formal procedure, the Commission can adopt a decision concluding that aid is existing aid on the grounds that it constitutes an individual case of application of an existing aid scheme (hence the ensuing decision not to initiate the formal examination procedure). This type of decision is usually taken in response to a complaint. This category also takes in decisions concluding that there is no misuse of existing individual aid (hence the ensuing decision not to initiate the formal examination procedure). **27.48**

The contestable character of such acts depends on the particular circumstances. When the applicant has previously contested a disputed measure's character of existing aid in a complaint to the Commission, then the Commission's decision rejecting the complaints represents a 'statement of position' and *ipso facto* a contestable act, insofar as the refusal to initiate the formal examination procedure has a definitive character.[89] On the contrary, if the applicant has previously only asked the Commission for information without calling upon it to take any decision and without claiming that the disputed measure was covered by an **27.49**

---

[86] Case T-266/94 *Skibsværftsforeningen and others v EC Commission* para 50, and Case T-157/01 *Danske Busvognmænd v EC Commission* para 40.

[87] On this matter, see Case T-398/94 *Kahn Scheepvaart v EC Commission* [1996] ECR II-477 paras 36–46. The CFI has confirmed this distinction between decisions on individual aid and decisions on general aid schemes in para 76 of Case T-109/97 *Molkerei Großbraunshain and Bene Nahrungsmittel v EC Commission* [1998] ECR II-3533. See also the *Waterleiding* judgment. For a scheme yet to come into force, see Case T-114/00 *ARE v EC Commission* para 71.

[88] Case C-313/90 R *CIRFS and others v EC Commission* [1991] ECR I-2557 para 21.

[89] Case C-313/90 *CIRFS and others v EC Commission* [1993] ECR I-1125 para 26, and Case C-321/99 P *ARAP and others v EC Commission* [2002] ECR I-4287 para 61.

existing scheme, then the Commission's letter indicating that the disputed measure was individual aid covered by an existing scheme is not a contestable act.[90] In such a case the Commission would only 'formally record' the fact that the measures at issue were in the nature of existing aid.[91]

Locus standi

27.50   The principles governing *locus standi* in actions for annulment against a decision not to raise objections or a refusal to open the formal examination procedure would seem capable of being extrapolated to the present case, in which the decision considering the measure to be existing aid is also adopted without initiating the procedure.

Effects of annulment

27.51   If a Commission decision considering aid to be existing aid is annulled, this would normally be because the aid in fact constitutes new aid, subjected to the previous notification obligation. After such a judgment, therefore, the Commission will, in principle, be bound to treat the aid as new aid and will have to approve it after the due preliminary examination or after having opened the formal examination procedure to deal with it.

4. Appeal against a final decision

Contestable act

27.52   A final Commission decision constitutes a contestable act under Article 230. Whether it is positive, negative, modifying, or conditional, it normally has binding legal effects that are likely to affect the interests of the concerned parties, for it brings the procedure at issue to a close and gives a definitive ruling on the nature and/or compatibility of the measure examined.

Eligibility for bringing the action

27.53   As well as Member States and other institutions the other parties that could have *locus standi* for bringing an action for annulment are the beneficiary undertakings of the aid in question, the competitor firms of these beneficiaries and the associations representing these two categories of undertakings. On the other hand the associations representing the employees of the beneficiary undertakings would not seem to qualify.

27.54   The beneficiary undertaking of individual aid is considered to be directly and

---

[90] Case T-154/94 *CSF and CSME v EC Commission* [1996] ECR II-1377 paras 38 to 45. The CFI seems to go even further in paras 46 and 49 of this Judgment, where it speaks of the 'impossibility of adopting a decision'.
[91] Case C-321/99 P *ARAP and others v EC Commission* para 61.

individually concerned by the Commission's final decision on this aid. As the aid recipient it is in fact distinguished as in the case of the addressee of the decision.[92] As for its direct interest, this cannot be contested either, on two counts: in the case of unlawful aid the litigation decision has the effect of depriving it of aid it has already enjoyed;[93] in the case of notified aid the decision prevents it from receiving aid it had been assured of.[94]

An association in charge of defending the collective interests of undertakings **27.55** has, in principle, *locus standi* if the undertakings themselves are entitled to on an individual basis[95] or if it can demonstrate that it has its own functional interest in pursuing the action. An association can also claim to be affected by the Commission's final decision as the negotiator of aid schemes in the interests of its members, when it is one of the signatories of an agreement whereby the contested scheme was set up and it has been obliged to undertake new negotiations and reach a new agreement to implement the final decision. In such circumstances it is entitled to bring annulment proceedings against a final decision on an aid scheme.[96] It is therefore conceivable that associations could lay claim to have *locus standi* on the basis of different considerations.[97]

Any of the beneficiary's competitor firms that are not satisfied with a final **27.56** Commission decision are entitled to request its annulment if they are directly and individually concerned by the act. The contested decision would in principle be a positive or conditional decision.

Their direct interest can, in principle, be established in either of the following **27.57** two circumstances: first, when the aid has already been granted (or the engagement to do so made), in which case the contested decision, which allows the conservation of the aid, directly affects the competitor applying for its

---

[92] See Case 730/79 *Philip Morris v EC Commission* [1980] ECR 2671 para 5; Joined Cases 296/82 and 318/82 *Netherlands and Leeuwarder Papierwarenfabriek v EC Commission* [1985] ECR 809 para 13; Case C-188/92 *TWD Textilwerke Deggendorf* [1994] ECR I-833 para 14, and Case T-358/94 *Air France v EC Commission* [1996] ECR II-2109 para 31.

[93] Case 223/85 *RSV v EC Commission* [1987] ECR 4617 para 10.

[94] See, first of all, Case 730/79 *Philip Morris v EC Commission* para 5. See also Case 323/82 *Intermills v EC Commission* [1984] ECR 3809 para 5.

[95] Case 282/85 *DEFI v EC Commission* [1986] ECR 2469 para 16, and Case C-6/92 *Federmineraria and others v EC Commission* [1993] ECR I-6357 para 17.

[96] Joined Cases 67, 68 and 70/85 *Van der Kooy v EC Commission* paras 20–24. See also Case C-313/90 *CIRFS and others v EC Commission* [1993] ECR I-1125 para 30.

[97] The judge responsible for hearing applications for interim measures has thus not flatly ruled out the idea that an association whose raison d'être is affected by the decision might be able to claim a rightful interest in calling for the annulment (Joined Cases C-182/03 R and C-217/03 R *Belgium and Forum 187 v EC Commission* [2003] ECR I-6887 para 103).

abolition;[98] secondly, when the aid has not yet been granted at the moment of adopting the contested decision, but there is no doubt about the public authorities' will to make use of the authorization and pay out the aid.[99] A decision declaring a measure not to constitute aid likewise has direct effects vis-à-vis all concerned parties.[100]

27.58 It is somewhat harder to demonstrate individual interest. Indeed, the fact that the applicant is a party concerned within the meaning of Article 88(2) is not sufficient in itself to distinguish it as in the case of the addressee of the decision.[101]

27.59 In *Cofaz*, the ECJ ruled that establishing an undertaking's individual interest meant fulfilling a dual condition: first that it has played a role in the procedure laid down in Article 88 and, secondly, that its market position is substantially affected by the aid measure dealt with in the contested decision. To reach this decision the ECJ held that where a regulation accords applicant undertakings procedural guarantees entitling them to request the Commission to find an infringement of Community rules, those undertakings should be able to institute proceedings in order to protect their legitimate interests. Article 88(2), indeed, recognizes in general terms that concerned undertakings are entitled to submit their comments to the Commission.[102]

27.60 As regards the substantial effect on the applicant's market position, it has to be determined whether or not the latter had 'a direct competitive relationship' with the aid beneficiary/ies.[103] The substantial effect on the concerned party's market position should not necessarily be construed as a fall in profits, a reduction in its market share or the recording of operating losses; it may simply mean that it loses the opportunity to make a profit.[104]

Effects of an annulment

27.61 If the ECJ or the CFI annuls a final Commission decision, neither of them is entitled to substitute its own assessment for the Commission's. The Commission

---

[98] Case 169/84 *Cofaz v EC Commission* [1986] ECR 391 para 30; Joined Cases T-447/93, T-448/93 and T-449/93 *AITEC and others v EC Commission* [1995] ECR II-1971 para 41; Case T-149/95 *Ducros v EC Commission* [1997] ECR II-2031 para 32, and Case T-11/95 *BP Chemicals v EC Commission* [1998] ECR II-3235 para 70.

[99] Case T-435/93 *ASPEC and others v EC Commission* [1995] ECR II-1281 para 60, and Case T-442/93 *AAC and others v EC Commission* [1995] ECR II-1329 para 45, and Case T-266/94 *Skibsværftsforeningen and others v EC Commission* [1996] ECR II-1399 para 49.

[100] Case T-358/02 *Deutsche Post and DHL International v EC Commission* not yet reported para 32.

[101] Case T-11/95 *BP Chemicals v EC Commission* para 73.

[102] Case 169/84 *Cofaz v EC Commission* paras 23 *et seq.*

[103] ibid para 27.

[104] Case T-36/99 *Lenzing v EC Commission* not yet reported para 90.

therefore has to adopt a new decision in light of the findings made by the Community Courts.

The question of whether the Commission is bound to repeat the whole aid **27.62** examination process or whether it can simply and immediately adopt a new decision depends on the reasons for the annulment. When the ECJ annuls a decision due to manifest errors of appraisal, the Commission normally initiates the procedure anew before adopting a new final decision.[105] Conversely, in cases where the final decisions have been annulled due to a failure to give sufficient reasons for the decision, the Commission has been able to immediately adopt a new final decision that sets forth the reasons upon which it is based, without having to renew the preparatory procedure.[106]

Appeal against a decision to propose appropriate measures or a refusal to adopt such a decision

According to the CFI, neither a decision to propose appropriate measures to **27.63** one or several Member States nor a refusal to adopt such a decision is an act against which an action for annulment may be brought. Appropriate measures are simple propositions, which are not binding on the addressee State.[107]

Appeal against a refusal to bring an action for failure to fulfil an obligation pursuant to subparagraph 2 of Article 88(2)

If a Member State fails to enforce correctly a Commission decision, interested **27.64** third parties have hardly any means of asserting their rights. Indeed, according to the CFI, private individuals are not entitled to bring proceedings against a refusal by the Commission to institute proceedings against a Member State for failure to fulfil its obligations, on the basis of the second subparagraph of Article 88(2), which concerns failures to enforce a final decision.[108]

---

[105] Initiation published in [1992] OJ C10/3. Although the ECJ had given no indication in its Judgment annulling the first Commission decision, AG Mischo for his part ended his summing up by stating that it was incumbent on the Commission to 'reopen the procedure provided for in Article 93' (para 53 of the Opinion in Case C-169/84 *CdF Chimie azote et fertisants v EC Commission* [1990] ECR I-3083).

[106] See Case C-415/96 *Spain v EC Commission* [1998] ECR I-6993 and the Opinion of AG Jacobs. See the decision on aid to *Air France* [1999] OJ L63/66 adopted one month after Joined Cases T-371/94 and T-394/94 *British Airways and others v EC Commission* [1998] ECR II-2405 which had annulled the first decision due to a failure to give sufficient reasons.

[107] Case T-330/94 *Salt Union v EC Commission* [1996] ECR II-1475 paras 33–37.

[108] Case T-277/94 *AITEC v EC Commission* [1996] ECR II-351 paras 55 and 56.

C. Action for Failure to Act

1. General principles

27.65 Pursuant to Article 232 EC, should the Commission fail to act, in infringement of the Treaty, then an action may be brought before the ECJ to have this infringement established. This action may be brought by Member States and by other Community institutions or, under certain conditions, by any natural or legal person. The ECJ has ruled that, just as the fourth paragraph of Article 230 EC allows individuals to bring an action for annulment against a measure of an institution not addressed to them provided that the measure is of direct and individual concern to them, the third paragraph of Article 232 EC must be interpreted as also entitling them to bring an action for failure to act against an institution which they claim has failed to adopt a measure that would have concerned them in the same way.[109] All the questions of interpretation that crop up in the context of actions for annulment, concerning the direct and individual interest and, in particular, the notion of 'concerned party', also apply, *mutatis mutandis*, in the context of an action for failure to act.[110] Article 232 refers to a failure to act, not the adoption of a measure different from that desired by the applicant.[111] As long as the Commission defines its position, this will suffice.[112]

2. Appeal against a failure to adopt a decision not to raise objections

27.66 A Member State that has notified aid plans to the Commission is entitled to grant the aid at the end of the two-month *Lorenz* time-limit. It would therefore be unlikely to bring an action for failure to act against the Commission if it does not react within that time-limit. Such a possibility cannot be completely ruled out, however. The Commission is, in principle, bound to rule on all aid that comes to its knowledge and the Member State might rightfully wish to obtain certainty from the Commission about the compatibility of its aid. The same might apply to the beneficiary/ies of the aid concerned.

---

[109] Case C-68/95 *T. Port* [1996] ECR I-6065 para 59.
[110] For a ruling on the inadmissibility of an action for failure to act on the grounds that the applicant does not qualify as a 'concerned party' within the meaning of Art 88(2), see Case T-41/01 *Rafael Pérez Escolar v EC Commission* [2003] ECR II-2157.
[111] Case T-26/01 *Fiocchi* [2003] ECR II-3951 para 82.
[112] Case T-26/01 *Fiocchi* [2003] ECR II-3951 paras 90–92.

3. Appeal against a failure to rule on a complaint and/or to initiate the formal examination procedure

A Member State or a third-party competitor can, in principle, bring an action **27.67** for failure to act against the Commission if it refrains from initiating the formal examination procedure on unlawful aid. This entitlement is a useful means of forcing the Commission to deal with complaints that are brought before it. In this case the failure to act is ended by either a decision to initiate the formal examination procedure or a refusal to initiate that procedure. This refusal will normally be adopted at the same time as a decision not to raise objections.[113]

4. Appeal against a failure to bring an action for failure to fulfil an obligation under the second subparagraph of Article 88(2)

An action for failure to act brought by a third party following the Commission's **27.68** failure to institute an action for failure to fulfil an obligation under the second subparagraph of Article 88(2) is not possible; in no case would the act sought be of direct concern to the applicant and the Commission has a wide margin of discretion in terms of deciding whether or not to bring a matter directly before the ECJ.[114]

5. Appeal against a failure to take the measures involved in the execution of a judgment of the ECJ or the CFI

This possibility has been addressed in the judgment of 19 February 2004, *SIC v* **27.69** *EC Commission*.[115] The examination of such an appeal implies determining the execution measures involved in the judgment upon which the appeal is based.

D. Action for Non-contractual Liability

Under the second subparagraph of Article 288, dealing with non-contractual **27.70** liability, the Community shall, in accordance with the general principles

---

[113] See the actions for failure to act that gave rise to Joined Cases 166/86 and 220/86 *Irish Cement* [1988] ECR 6473, and Case T-95/96 *Gestevisión Telecinco v EC Commission* and Case T-41/01 *Rafael Pérez Escolar v EC Commission*.

[114] Case T-277/94 *AITEC v EC Commission* paras 63 and 65–68. Note that paras 58 to 60 of this judgment, based on the premise that it is necessary to be the potential addressee of an act to be eligible for bringing the action for failure to act, are no longer relevant after Case C-68/95 *T. Port*, whereby the ECJ has interpreted Art 232(3) as entitling private individuals to bring an action for failure to act against an institution that they claim has failed to adopt a measure which would have concerned them, even if they are not the addressees thereof.

[115] Joined Cases T-297/01 and T-298/01, para 32.

common to the laws of the Member States, 'make good any damage caused by its institutions or by its servants in the performance of their duties'.

27.71 Such actions are conceivable in the field of aid, in particular when a complainant has suffered a loss as a result of an infringement by the Commission of the reasonable time period for adopting measures involved in the execution of a previous judgment.[116] To date, however, there have been very few actions of this type, and they have never ended in the granting of damages.[117]

E. Application for Interim Measures

1. General principles

27.72 Under Articles 242 and 243, the Community Courts may order the application of a contested act to be suspended or prescribe any necessary interim measures if the requisite conditions (urgency, prima facie good case, and balance of interests) are met.

27.73 This procedure is possible in the field of State aid. In general, however, the judge dealing with the case will be reluctant to grant the measures sought if his/her intervention is likely to encroach on the Commission's wide margin of discretion in deciding on the compatibility of State aid. Such an intervention would effectively undermine the Commission's role in protecting competition as laid down in Articles 87 and 88.[118]

2. Interim measures and stay of execution of a decision to initiate the formal examination procedure

27.74 It is conceivable that a Member State or aid beneficiary may seek a stay of execution of a Commission decision to open the formal examination procedure. Conversely, a competitor undertaking of an aid beneficiary will not, in principle, be entitled to seek an order directing the Commission to require the Member State concerned to extend the aid to benefit it as well, not even on an interim basis.[119]

---

[116] Joined Cases T-297/01 and T-298/01 *SIC v EC Commission* not yet reported para 58.
[117] Case 40/75 *Société des produits Bertand v EC Commission* [1976] ECR 1; Case 114/83 *Société d'initiative et de coopération agricoles v EC Commission* [1984] ECR 2589; Case 289/83 *GAARM and others v EC Commission* [1984] ECR 4295 and T–107/96 *Pantochin v EC Commission* [1998] ECR II-311.
[118] See in particular Case T-86/96 R *Arbeitsgemeinschaft Deutscher Luftfahrt-Unternehmen and others v EC Commission* [1998] ECR II-641 para 74.
[119] Case T-107/96 R *Pantochim v EC Commission* [1996] ECR II-1361.

3. Interim measures and stay of execution of a decision to amend or abolish an existing aid scheme

When a Commission decision orders the amendment or abolition of an existing **27.75** aid scheme against which an action for annulment has been brought, a stay of execution of the decision may be sought until the validity of the decision has been definitively settled.

4. Interim measures and stay of execution of a negative decision

Negative decision on notified aid

When the Commission prohibits the grant of new aid by a State, a simple stay of **27.76** execution is pointless. Even if the negative decision is suspended the aid still cannot be granted until it has been expressly approved by the Commission. Moreover, it is not at all certain that the applicant could persuade the judge dealing with the application to authorise the granting of the aid on an interim basis, for such a measure could be seen as exceeding the object of the main claim and encroaching on the Commission's exclusive responsibility for approving aid.

Negative decision on unlawful aid

It is often the case that a stay of execution is requested on a Commission **27.77** decision declaring aid or an aid scheme to be incompatible and calling for the recovery or interruption thereof. This application can be made by the aid-granting State, the aid beneficiary or even the public authority or body that has granted the aid. The latter can in fact challenge the decision in its own right under subparagraph 4 of Article 230 and seek at the same time a suspension of implementation of the decision.[120]

The ECJ has held that even if a Member State has infringed the provisions of **27.78** Article 88 it may not be deprived of the right to challenge before the court, by means of Articles 230 *et seq.* in particular, the legality of a Commission decision adversely affecting it and consequently it must be entitled to apply for the suspension of the operation of that decision in accordance with Article 243 of the Treaty.[121] The same goes, *a fortiori*, for the beneficiary of unlawful aid.[122] The Community Courts have confirmed, in particular, that the beneficiary does not have to wait for the engagement of the recovery procedure by the national authorities, then using the internal appeal procedures that are open to it for

---

[120] Case T-155/96 R *Ville de Mayence v EC Commission* [1996] ECR II-1655.

[121] Joined Cases 67, 68 and 70/85 R *Van der Kooy v EC Commission* [1985] ECR 1315 para 37.

[122] See Case C-232/02 P(R) *EC Commission v TGI* [2002] ECR I-8977 paras 30 to 36. Earlier, the *locus standi* of the beneficiary undertaking had not been contested in Case 310/85 R *Deufil v EC Commission* [1986] ECR 537.

challenging this recovery, but is entitled to address the Community judge for dealing with applications for interim measures directly; the admissibility of an application for the stay of execution of the act of a Community institution is subordinated only to the condition that the applicant has already contested this act in an action before the Community Courts.[123] Any infringement of Article 88(3) is however taken into consideration as an unfavourable element in weighing up the interests involved and deciding whether or not to grant the requested stay of execution.[124]

27.79 When assessing the existence of serious damage to the undertaking concerned, the Community Courts take the following factors into account. First, the likelihood of the alleged damage actually occurring. In accordance with normal rules, the imminence of the damage does not have to be established with absolute certainty; it suffices for it to be foreseeable with a sufficient degree of probability. However, the applicant is required to prove the facts forming the basis of its claim that serious and irreparable damage is likely.[125] Secondly, the serious and irreparable nature of the damage. It is up to the undertaking concerned to establish the circumstances on the basis of precise, individual, and well-founded indications.[126] In this regard, an adverse effect on the rights of the persons considered to be the recipients of State aid which is incompatible with the common market forms an integral part of any Commission decision requiring the recovery of such aid and cannot be regarded as constituting in itself serious and irreparable damage.[127] Moreover, damage of a pecuniary nature cannot, save in exceptional circumstances, be regarded as irreparable, or even as being reparable only with difficulty, since it can ultimately be the subject of financial compensation.[128] An interim measure is justified only if it appears that, without that measure, the undertaking would be in a position that could imperil its existence before final judgment in the main action. The applicant undertaking therefore has to establish to the requisite legal standard that the implementation of the contested decision would inevitably cause it to go into liquidation and disappear from the market before a ruling is given in

[123] Case C-232/02 P(R) *EC Commission v TGI* paras 30–36, and Case T-181/02 R *Neue Erba Lautex v EC Commission* [2002] ECR II-5081 para 39.
[124] Joined Cases 67, 68 and 70/85 R *Van der Kooy v EC Commission* para 44.
[125] Case T-181/02 R *Neue Erba Lautex v EC Commission* para 83.
[126] Case T-86/96 R *Arbeitsgemeinschaft Deutscher Luftfahrt-Unternehmen and others v EC Commission* paras 64 *et seq.*
[127] Case T-237/99 R *BP Nederland and others v EC Commission* [2000] ECR II-3849 para 52; Case T-34/02 R *B v EC Commission* [2002] ECR II-2803 para 97, and Case T-316/04 R *Wam v EC Commission* not yet reported para 33.
[128] In particular, in the field of aid, Case T-91/02 R *Klausner Nordic Timber v EC Commission* para 30.

the main action.[129] Such an assessment must however be carried out on a case-by-case basis, having regard to the facts of each case and the legal issues involved.[130]

To assess the existence of serious and irreparable damage to a Member State, the **27.80** damage suffered by the undertakings concerned has sometimes been taken into account as such.[131] A Member State may nonetheless invoke the risk to its national economy in general due to the bankruptcy of the undertakings involved in the recovery procedure and the knock-on effects thereof.[132]

If the applicant is able to establish the urgency (serious and irreparable **27.81** damage) and the existence of a prima facie good case, the judge hearing the application for interim relief then has to weigh up, on the one hand, the applicant's interest in obtaining the interim measures sought and, on the other, the public interest in the execution of decisions taken in the framework of State-aid control. Case law on this matter has established that, in connection with an application for interim measures seeking the suspension of the obligation imposed by the Commission to repay aid which it has declared to be incompatible with the common market, the Community interest must normally, if not always, take precedence over the interest of the aid recipient in avoiding enforcement of the obligation to repay it before judgment is given in the main proceedings.[133] The applicant therefore has to fall back on exceptional circumstances.

5. Interim measures and stay of execution of a positive decision

A Member State might try to block the Commission's approval of aid notified **27.82** by another Member State. A competitor undertaking seeking annulment of a Commission decision declaring aid to be compatible can likewise seek a stay of execution of this decision. Such applications for suspension of execution rarely come to anything, however, since it is difficult to prove a serious and irreparable damage to the applicant.

---

[129] Case T-181/02 R *Neue Erba Lautex v EC Commission* paras 85 and 86
[130] ibid para 89.
[131] Case 57/86 R *Greece v EC Commission* [1986] ECR 1497 para 12.
[132] Case 303/88 R *Italy v EC Commission* [1989] ECR 801.
[133] Case T-181/02 R *Neue Erba Lautex v EC Commission* paras 112–114.

II. Procedures against Member States

27.83 Member States are often brought before the Community Courts by the Commission in an attempt to establish the infringement of their State aid obligations.

A. Distinction between the Administrative Aid-Control Procedure and the Infringement Procedure

27.84 When the Commission considers that a State has infringed the provisions of Article 87 by granting incompatible aid, it has necessarily to follow the procedure laid down in Article 88(2) if it wishes to establish the incompatibility of a measure, as aid, with the common market. The procedure laid down in Article 88(2) provides all the parties concerned with guarantees which are specifically adapted to the special problems created by State aid with regard to competition in the common market and which go much further than those provided in the preliminary procedure laid down in Article 226 of the Treaty in which only the Commission and the Member State concerned participate. The Commission cannot therefore directly bring an action for failure to fulfil an obligation on the grounds of infringement of Article 87 without first having followed the procedure laid down in Article 88, even if the aid in question has been established by a law.[134]

27.85 On the other hand the Commission can follow the procedure laid down in Article 226 to ascertain whether the Member State has failed to meet any of its procedural obligations under Article 88(3).[135] In such a case the Community Court, in order to admit the action, has to verify that the measures concerned are aid within the meaning of Article 87 and should have been previously notified under Article 88(3). The Commission could accompany such an action with an application for interim relief with a view to obtaining the recovery or suspension of the measure.

27.86 Direct recourse to the procedure of Article 226 is also possible when the Commission intends to establish the infringement of other Community law

---

[134] Case 290/83 *EC Commission v France* [1985] ECR 439 para 17, and Joined Cases C-356/90 and C-180/91 *Belgium v EC Commission* [1993] ECR I-2323 para 18.
[135] See the action for failure to fulfil an obligation in the Case 171/83, which has been withdrawn (Order of 20 September 1983, Case 171/83 R *EC Commission v France* [1983] ECR 2621 para 1) and also Case 169/82 *EC Commission v Italy* [1984] ECR 1603; Case C-35/88 *EC Commission v Greece* [1990] ECR I-3125 para 34, Case C-61/90 *EC Commission v Greece* [1992] ECR I-2407 para 25.

provisions rather than those of Article 87.[136] In particular, in the agricultural sector, when the Commission believes that a State has granted aid in breach of the provisions of a common organization of the markets (COM), it can bring an action for failure to fulfil an obligation, even if Articles 87 and 88 have been made applicable by the provisions of the COM. Likewise, when a parafiscal tax is likely to represent an infringement of either Article 90 of the Treaty or the aid prohibition, the Commission is entitled to bring an action for failure to fulfil an obligation on the grounds of infringement of Article 90.[137] It is only when the aspect related to Article 87 is inseparable from another infringement of Community law that the Commission is bound to follow the procedure contained in Article 88.

B. Direct Referral to the ECJ

1. General principles

Pursuant to subparagraph 2 of Article 88(2), should a State fail to comply, within the prescribed time, with a final Commission decision adopted at the end of a formal examination procedure, then the Commission or any other interested Member State may, in derogation from Articles 226 and 227, refer the matter directly to the ECJ.   **27.87**

Direct referral of a matter to the ECJ is justified on the grounds that the Commission has already given notice to the Member State concerned to submit its comments. The *inter partes* nature of the preliminary procedure has therefore been respected.[138] Moreover all the rules governing the standard action for failure to fulfil an obligation are applicable.[139]   **27.88**

As regards the reference date to be taken into account, Article 88(2) subparagraph 2 does not provide for a pre-litigation phase and therefore the Commission does not issue a reasoned opinion allowing Member States a certain period within which to comply with its decision, so the reference period can only be that provided for in the decision whose implementation is being contested or, where appropriate, that subsequently fixed by the Commission.[140]   **27.89**

Note that the existence of this direct referral under subparagraph 2 of Article   **27.90**

---

[136] Case 290/83 *EC Commission v France* [1985] ECR 439 para 17.

[137] See, e.g. Case 277/83 *EC Commission v Italy* [1985] ECR 2049 para 16.

[138] See the Opinion of AG Mayras in Case 70/72 *EC Commission v Germany* [1973] ECR 813.

[139] For example, the burden of proof incumbent on the Commission (Case C-404/00 *EC Commission v Spain* [2003] ECR I-6695 para 26).

[140] Case C-99/02 *EC Commission v Italy* not yet reported para 24.

88(2) does not prevent the Commission or a State from also resorting to the procedures under Articles 226 or 227.[141]

27.91 If the ECJ finds in favour of the Commissions, the Member State is then bound to take such measures as may be laid down in the judgment of the ECJ. Failing that, the Commission would be entitled to apply to the ECJ anew on the basis of Article 228 for it to impose on the State concerned a lump-sum fine or penalty payment.[142]

2. Grounds of defence that may be put forward by the Member State

Invalid grounds

27.92 **Prohibition of invoking the illegality of the decision** Once a Member State has allowed the mandatory time-limit for bringing an action for annulment against a Commission decision to expire, it will no longer be able to call in question that decision by means of Article 241 of the Treaty when an action for failure to fulfil an obligation is lodged by the Commission for failure to execute said decision.[143] Such a solution would indeed be impossible to reconcile with the principles governing the legal remedies established by the Treaty and would jeopardize the stability of that system and the principle of legal certainty upon which it is based, by allowing Community acts having legal effects to be indefinitely called into question.[144] The position could be different if the measure in question contained such particularly serious and manifest defects that it could be deemed non-existent.[145]

27.93 **Prohibition of invoking the legitimate expectations of the beneficiary** A Member State whose authorities have granted aid contrary to the procedural rules laid down in Article 88 may not rely on the legitimate expectations of recipients in order to justify a failure to comply with the obligation to take the steps necessary to implement a Commission decision instructing it to recover

---

[141] Case 70/72 *EC Commission v Germany* [1973] ECR 813 para 13; Case C-209/00 *EC Commission v Germany* [2002] ECR I-11695 para 37, and Case C-404/00 *EC Commission v Spain* para 25.

[142] See Case C-375/89 *EC Commission v Belgium* [1991] ECR I-383 for the possibility of applying Art 228 of the Treaty after a first Judgment given under the procedure of Art 88(2)(2).

[143] Case 156/77 *EC Commission v Belgium* [1978] ECR 1881 para 21; Case 52/83 *EC Commission v France* [1983] ECR 3707 para 10; Case 93/84 *EC Commission v France* [1985] ECR 829 para 9; Case 52/84 *EC Commission v Belgium* [1986] ECR 89 para 13; Case C-183/91 *EC Commission v Greece* [1993] ECR I-3131 para 10; Case C-188/92 *TWD Textilwerke Deggendorf* [1994] ECR I-833 para 15, and Case C-404/00 *EC Commission v Spain* para 40.

[144] Case 156/77 *EC Commission v Belgium* para 24, and Case C-188/92 *TWD Textilwerke Deggendorf* para 16.

[145] Case C-404/00 *EC Commission v Spain* para 41.

the aid. If it could do so, Articles 87 and 88 of the Treaty would be redundant, since national authorities would thus be able to rely on their own unlawful conduct in order to deprive decisions taken by the Commission under these provisions of their effectiveness.[146]

Prohibition on invoking the existence of a parallel action for annulment As **27.94** we have already seen, the existence of an action for annulment against the disputed decision will not be grounds for exempting the Member State from the duty of executing it, unless it has obtained an interim measure to this effect from the Community Courts..[147]

Valid grounds

Indeterminate character of the obligation laid down in the decision The **27.95** Member State can, however, claim that the obligation imposed on it by the Commission's decision is indeterminate, if it has been couched in vague and obscure terms.[148]

Absolute impossibility of implementing the decision If the Commission's **27.96** decision imposes a clear obligation on the Member State, the only grounds for defence that the Member State could put forward against an action for failure to fulfil an obligation is that it was absolutely impossible to implement the decision properly.[149] This impossibility may refer to the object of the decision or the timeframe for implementing it.[150] The ECJ interprets this concept in a restrictive way, so it is rarely pleaded.

In the event of unforeseen and unforeseeable difficulties or consequences the **27.97** ECJ invites the Member State to come to some arrangement with the Commission. However, the condition that it be absolutely impossible to implement a decision is not fulfilled where the Member State merely informs the Commission of the legal, political or practical difficulties involved in implementing the

---

[146] Case C-5/89 *EC Commission v Germany* [1990] ECR I-3437 para 17, and Case C-183/91 *EC Commission v Greece* para 18, and Case C-99/02 *EC Commission v Italy* para 21.

[147] See para 27.19.

[148] Case 70/72 *EC Commission v Germany* paras 21–23.

[149] Case 52/84 *EC Commission v Belgium* para 14; Case 213/85 *EC Commission v Netherlands* para 22; Case 94/87 *EC Commission v Germany* para 8; Case 183/91 *EC Commission v Greece* para 10; Case C-349/93 *EC Commission v Italy* para 12; Case C-348/93 *EC Commission v Italy* para 16, and C-350/93 para 15; Case C-280/95 *EC Commission v Italy* para 13; Case C-261/99 *EC Commission v France* para 23; Case C-209/00 *EC Commission v Germany* para 70; C-499/99 *EC Commission v Spain* para 21, and Case C-404/00 *EC Commission v Spain* para 45, and Case C-99/02 *EC Commission v Italy* para 16.

[150] Opinion of AG Slynn in Case 63/87 *EC Commission v Greece* [2000] ECR I-5047.

decision, without taking any real step to recover the aid from the undertakings concerned, and without proposing to the Commission any alternative arrangements for implementing the decision which could have enabled the difficulties to be overcome.[151]

27.98   It is up to the Member State concerned to prove that the necessary measures could not have been implemented within the deadline laid down in the Commission's decision.[152] It therefore has to back up such a plea with specific arguments demonstrating that the alleged absolute impossibility actually existed.[153]

C. Applications for the Adoption of Interim Measures

27.99   An action for failure to fulfil an obligation brought against a Member State could be accompanied with an application for interim measures.

III. Procedure for action against Council decisions adopted on the basis of the third subparagraph of Article 88(2) EC

27.100   Two actions are conceivable against the Council when it exercises the powers conferred on it under the third subparagraph of Article 88(2). In particular Council decisions can be appealed against by actions for annulment[154] or liability questions can be raised.[155] The questions of admissibility and *locus standi* raised by an action for annulment are essentially the same as those raised by an appeal against a Commission decision.

---

[151] Case C-499/99 *EC Commission v Spain* para 25, and Case C-404/00 *EC Commission v Spain* para 47.

[152] Case 213/85 *EC Commission v Netherlands* para 24.

[153] Case 63/87 *EC Commission v Greece* para 14.

[154] See the actions for annulment brought by the Commission in Joined Cases C-122/94 *EC Commission v EC Council* [1996] ECR I-881 and C-309/95 *EC Commission v EC Council* [1998] ECR I-655.

[155] See the action brought by GAEC in Case 253/84 *GAEC de la Ségaude v EC Council and Commission* [1987] ECR I-123 claiming compensation for the damage it alleges to have sustained as a result of a Council decision authorizing certain aid. The ECJ rejected the appeal after finding that the damage and its causal link to the disputed decision had not been proven (Judgment of 15 January 1987).

PART V

COMPETITION LAW AND PROCEDURE
IN THE EUROPEAN ECONOMIC AREA

28

EUROPEAN ECONOMIC AREA
COMPETITION PROCEDURE

I. Introduction to the Agreement on the European Economic Area

This chapter seeks to set out the general structure of the competition provisions **28.01** and procedure, together with an overview of the rules on state aid, applicable under the Agreement on the European Economic Area ('EEA Agreement'). It will briefly set out the background to the EEA Agreement, before describing its substantive competition rules, the procedure to be followed in their application and the allocation of jurisdiction between the EC Commission and the EFTA Surveillance Authority in that application. The EEA provisions corresponding to EC Merger control and state monopolies will be identified. A separate section will briefly explore EEA rules on State aids (equivalent to Articles 90 and 92–93 EC). In practical terms, the scope of application of the EEA provisions is relatively limited. Nonetheless, undertakings situated in Iceland, Liechtenstein and Norway, or undertakings doing business with those countries will need to take heed of the EEA provisions. This chapter is therefore intended to provide only a brief overview of some of the key procedural aspects and differences in EEA competition law. Practitioners in this area are referred to more detailed practitioners' texts for further information.[1]

A. Formation and General Institutional Framework

The European Free Trade Association (EFTA) was established in 1960 by **28.02** Austria, Denmark, Norway, Portugal, Sweden, Switzerland, and the United

---

[1] See, *inter alia*, S Norberg, K Hökborg, M Johansson, D Eliasson, and L Dedichen, *The European Economic Area, EEA Law: A Commentary on the EEA Agreement* (Kluwer, Deventer, 1993) and T Blanchet, R Piipponen, and M Westman-Clément, *The Agreement on the European Economic Area (EEA). A Guide to the Free Movement of Goods and Competition Rules* (Clarendon Press, Oxford, 1994).

Kingdom. Its goal was to reduce or remove import duties, quotas and other obstacles to trade in Western Europe and to uphold liberal, non-discriminatory practices in world trade. Iceland joined EFTA in 1970 while Finland became an associate member in 1961 and a full member in 1986. Liechtenstein became a member in 1991. Six members have since left EFTA to join the European Union ('EU'): the United Kingdom and Denmark in 1973; Portugal in 1986; and Austria, Finland, and Sweden in 1995. Norway completed negotiations for accession to the EU, but decided against membership in a referendum in November 1994. The present members of EFTA are therefore Iceland, Liechtenstein, Norway, and Switzerland.[2] EFTA membership served as a platform for EFTA members to negotiate a specific agreement with Member States of the European Community for an extension of the internal market to those countries. The resultant EEA Agreement came into force on 1 January 1994.[3] It was first signed on 2 May 1992 at Oporto, Portugal, between the European Community, its then twelve Member States and the seven other countries[4] of EFTA. Since that date, Austria, Finland, and Sweden have joined the EU. Switzerland is no longer a contracting party to the EEA Agreement.[5] Liechtenstein became a full member of the EEA on 1 May 1995.[6] Further, the enlargement of the EU on 1 May 2004 has been reflected in the EEA Agreement.[7] In December

---

[2] See the Model Yearbook entry for EFTA found in the EFTA Secretariat's website at www.secretariat.efta.int/Web/EFTAAtAGlance/.

[3] See Decision 94/1/ECSC, EC of the Council and Commission of 13 December 1993 on the conclusion of the Agreement on the European Economic Area, together with the Final Act [1994] OJ L1/1; and Decision 94/2/ECSC, EC of the Council and Commission of 13 December 1993 on the conclusion of the Protocol adjusting the Agreement on the European Economic Area, together with the [1994] OJ L1/671. A special edition of the *Common Market Law Reports* contains the original EEA Treaty and EFTA Surveillance Agreement, together with the relevant Notices and Guidelines. See [1994] 5 CMLR Parts 2 and 3. See also H Charlton, 'EC Competition Law: The New Regime under the EEA Agreement', *European Competition Law Review*, Vol 15, No 2, March 1994, 55–59; A Diem, 'EEA Competition Law' *European Competition Law Review*, Vol 15, No 5, November–December 1994, 263–71; M Broberg, 'The Delimitation of Jurisdiction with regard to Concentration Control under the EEA Agreement' *European Competition Law Review*, Vol 16, No 1, January–February 1995, 30–39.

[4] Austria, Finland, Iceland, Liechtenstein, Norway, Sweden, and Switzerland.

[5] In a referendum on 6 December 1992, a majority of both the Cantons and citizens voted against membership. A Protocol to the Agreement was signed on 17 March 1993, recognizing this change. Switzerland remains a party to the EFTA Convention, originally signed in 1960 in Stockholm. The original Stockholm Convention was replaced and updated in Vaduz in 2001. Article 18 of the Vaduz Convention (i.e. the updated EFTA Convention) requires Member States to recognize that conduct equivalent to that prohibited by Arts 81 and 82 EC is incompatible with the Convention.

[6] Liechtenstein was obliged initially to wait for an EEA Council resolution confirming that its customs union with Switzerland would not adversely affect the functioning of the EEA before fully taking part.

[7] Art 128 of the EEA Agreement provides that any European country becoming a member of the European Community shall also apply for membership of the EEA. Applications are submitted to the EEA Council and subject to ratification by all parties to the EEA Agreement.

2002, the ten countries acceding to the EU applied for EEA membership. Negotiations for their admission were successful. The EEA Enlargement Agreement was signed on 14 October 2003.[8] There was therefore a parallel enlargement of the EEA and EU on 1 May 2004.[9] Thus, after various modifications,[10] the EEA now encompasses the newly enlarged European Union, together with Iceland, Liechtenstein and Norway.

The EEA Agreement is an international treaty that is considered to be *sui*   **28.03**
generis and which contains a distinct legal order of its own.[11] The Agreement, whilst falling short of a customs union, has created the world's largest integrated economic area.[12] The EEA countries now represent a single market in services, capital, and manufactured goods for over 400 million people. The EEA Agreement reiterates the *acquis communautaire* in seeking to establish the 'four freedoms' of the EC Treaty in the EEA territory, as well as covering a wide range of areas linked to the achievement of the four freedoms, such as social policy, consumer protection, the environment, and competition.[13] The EEA Enlargement Agreement consists of a main agreement listing the amendments to be made to the previous text of the EEA Agreement. The Protocols and Annexes to the EEA Agreement have also been amended to take into account the changes made to the Community *acquis* by the EU Treaty of Accession. This

---

[8] The Agreement on the participation of the Czech Republic, the Republic of Estonia, the Republic of Cyprus, the Republic of Latvia, the Republic of Lithuania, the Republic of Hungary, the Republic of Malta, the Republic of Poland, the Republic of Slovenia and the Slovak Republic in the European Economic Area signed on 14 October 2003 in Luxembourg [2004] OJ L130/3. See also Decision of the EEA Joint Committee No 68/2004 of 4 May 2004 extending the application of certain Decisions of the EEA Joint Committee to the New Contracting Parties and amending certain Annexes to the EEA Agreement following the enlargement of the European Union [2004] OJ L277/187.

[9] The national parliaments of all twenty-eight contracting parties to the EEA Enlargement Agreement were expected to ratify the Instruments by the end of 2004. In the meantime, the EEA/EFTA States and the EU signed an agreement (constituted by an exchange of letters) that permitted the EEA Enlargement Agreement to enter into force provisionally on 1 May 2004. See [2004] L130/1.

[10] Some of these, as above, were brought about by the political process. Others, such as changes to the institutional structure, came as a response to a European Court of Justice ('ECJ') opinion, Opinion 1/91 of 14 December 1991 [1991] ECR I-6079 which held that the judicial system as initially established by the EEA Agreement was incompatible with the Treaty of Rome. An amended Agreement received the blessing of the ECJ in Opinion 1/92 [1992] ECR I-282 and was signed in its revised form by the parties on 2 May 1992.

[11] See the Advisory Opinion of the EFTA Court of 10 December 1998, Case E-9/97 *Erla María Sveinbjörnsdóttir v Iceland* [1999] 1 CMLR 884 para 59.

[12] See the Advisory Opinion of the EFTA Court in Case E-2/97 *Mag Instrument Inc v California Trading Company Norway* [1997] EFTA Court Report 127 para 25.

[13] For general information on the EEA Competition provisions, see the web site of the EFTA Surveillance Authority (www.eftasurv.int/about/) and the overview provided on the European Commission's website at http://europa.eu.int/comm/external_relations/eea/.

has been done by a simple cross-referencing technique.[14] A consolidated version of the EEA Agreement can be found on the EFTA Secretariat website.[15]

28.04 The EEA Agreement is founded on a 'two-pillar' approach, with each 'pillar', the EC side and the EFTA[16] side, responsible for its own share of the work. The Agreement sets up several joint institutions.[17] The EEA Council is the highest political body. The EEA Joint Parliamentary Committee and the EEA Consultative Committee are intended to coordinate at a political level with their EU counterparts. The EEA Joint Committee takes decisions and administers the Agreement. All decisions made by these institutions must meet with unanimous agreement from the relevant EU institutions. The EFTA States, through two Agreements signed on 2 May 1992,[18] have created three additional institutions to ensure the proper functioning of the EEA Agreement, which are of particular relevance to the EEA competition provisions.

- First, the EFTA Surveillance Authority ('ESA'),[19] an independent body with powers similar to those of the EC Commission, which is in charge of ensuring that the EFTA States fulfil their obligations. It is also responsible for ensuring the application of the competition rules. Based in Brussels, the ESA is led by a College of three Members, one from each EFTA State participating in the EEA.[20] College Members are appointed by common agreement of the

---

[14] See [2004] OJ L130/3 and EEA Supplement No 23, 29 April 2004 1. Art 3 of the Enlargement Agreement states that all amendments made to the Community *acquis* by the EU Act of Accession are hereby 'incorporated into and made part' of the EEA Agreement. Annex A to the Enlargement Agreement lists all the acts referred to in the Annexes of the EEA Agreement that have been amended by the EU Act of Accession and indicates where these acts are to be found in the EEA Agreement.

[15] http://secretariat.efta.int/Web/LegalCorner/.

[16] The term EFTA is used here, even though, as has been seen, only three participating countries are 'true' EFTA states for the purposes of the EEA Agreement. This terminology is sanctioned by the Protocol adjusting the Agreement on the European Economic Area, cited above (n 3).

[17] See generally C. Reymond, 'Institutions, decision-making procedure and settlement of disputes in the European Economic Area' (1993) 30 CML Rev 449–80.

[18] The Agreement between the EFTA States on the Establishment of a Surveillance Authority and a Court of Justice ('the Surveillance and Court Agreement') [1994] OJ L344/1, adjusted by the Protocol Adjusting the Agreement between the EFTA States on the Establishment of a Surveillance Authority and a Court of Justice signed in Brussels on 17 March 1993 and subsequently by the Agreement Adjusting certain Agreements between the EFTA States signed in Brussels on 29 December 1994; The Agreement on a Standing Committee of the EFTA States ('the Standing Committee Agreement'), amended by the Protocol Adjusting the Agreement on a Standing Committee of the EFTA States signed in Brussels on 17 March 1993, by the Decision No 2/94/SC of the Standing Committee of the EFTA States of 10 January 1994 [1994] OJ L85/76, and EEA Supplement No 1, 30 March 1994 14 and subsequently by the Agreement Adjusting certain Agreements between the EFTA States signed in Brussels on 29 December 1994.

[19] See Art 108(1) of the EEA Agreement.

[20] The current College members are: Einar M Bull (Norway) and Bernd Hammermann (Liechtenstein). The College heads a Competition and State Aid Directorate. At the time of writing, Hannes Hafstein, the President of the ESA, had recently passed away and no replacement had yet been appointed.

governments of the EFTA/EEA States for a period of four years. A President is appointed from among the College Members for a period of two years. The College is completely independent of other institutions, as well as of the EFTA States. It takes decisions according to the majority vote of its Members. Its working language is English.

- Secondly, the EFTA Court[21] which mainly deals with: (i) infringement actions brought by the ESA against an EFTA State with regard to the implementation, application or interpretation of an EEA rule; (ii) the settlement of disputes between two or more EFTA States; (iii) appeals concerning decisions taken by the ESA; and (iv) giving advisory opinions to courts in EFTA States on the interpretation of EEA rules. It only has jurisdiction with regard to EFTA States which are parties to the EEA Agreement. The EFTA Court consists of three Judges, one nominated by each of the EFTA States party to the EEA Agreement. The Judges are appointed by common accord of the Governments for a period of six years. The Judges elect their President for a term of three years.[22] All proceedings are in English except in cases where an advisory opinion is sought by a national court of an EFTA State party to the EEA, where the opinion of the Court will be both in English and in the national language of the requesting court.[23]

- Thirdly, the EFTA Standing Committee, composed of the EFTA States' representatives.[24] The Committee provides a forum in which the EEA/EFTA States may consult one another and arrive at a common position before meeting with the EU side in the EEA Joint Committee.[25] It consists of representatives from Iceland, Liechtenstein and Norway and observers from Switzerland and the ESA. Chairmanship of the Committee rotates between the EEA/EFTA States. The EFTA Standing Committee formally liases with the EC Commission under the auspices of the EEA Joint Committee. The main function of the EEA Joint Committee is to adopt decisions extending Community Regulations and Directives to the EEA/EFTA States. The EEA is thus managed on a day-to-day basis by the EEA Joint Committee, with

---

[21] See Art 108(2) of the EEA Agreement.

[22] The current full-time judges are Carl Baudenbacher (Liechtenstein), President; Per Tresselt (Norway); and Thorgeir Örlygsson (Iceland). A system of *ad hoc* judges has also been created in case one of the full-time judges is unable to sit.

[23] Guidance on references to the EFTA Court for advisory opinions is contained in [1999] 3 CMLR 525. Guidance for Counsel in written and oral proceedings is at [1999] 2 CMLR 883.

[24] Andreas Diem notes that 'while the EFTA institutions apply EEA law only, the Commission, the ECJ and the CFI will act partly as EC institutions and partly as EEA institutions and will apply different law in each case.' 'EEA Competition Law' *op.cit.* n 3 at 264. However he also notes that given the substantial similarity between EEA and EC provisions and the duty to interpret in the same way, any differences will have little significance.

[25] As to the nature of the EEA Joint Committee, see Case E-6/01 *CIBA Speciality Chemicals Water Treatment Ltd v Norway*, judgment of the EFTA Court dated 9 October 2002, at paras 32–33.

political direction given by the EEA Council. The EEA Council meets twice a year at ministerial level and twice a month at the level of heads of the permanent national delegations.

28.05 The institutional structure is represented in tabular form as follows:[26]

EEA bodies	Joint bodies	EU bodies
Iceland, Liechtenstein and Norway	▶ *EEA Council* Ministers of EU and EFTA/EEA Sates	◀ EU Council
EFTA Standing Committee	▶ *EEA Joint Committee* Commission and EU and EFTA Government Representatives	◀ European Commission
EFTA Secretariat		Commission Services
EFTA Surveillance Authority	◀- - - - - - - - - - - - - -▶	
EFTA Court	◀- - - - - - - - - - - - - -▶	European Court of Justice
Committee of MPs of the EFTA States	▶ *EEA Joint Parliamentary Committee* MPs from the EFTA Parliaments and MEPs	◀ European Parliament EP Secretariat
EFTA Secretariat EFTA Consultative Committee	▶ *EEA Consultative Committee*	◀ Economic and Social Committee (ECOSOC)
EFTA Secretariat		ECOSOC Secretariat

B. An Overview of the Competition Provisions of the EEA Agreement

28.06 The general aim of the EEA Agreement, as laid down in Article 1(1) EEA, is to promote a continuous and balanced strengthening of trade and economic

---

[26] Information for this table is derived from the helpful web site maintained by the Principality of Liechtenstein: www.liechtenstein.li/en/eliechtenstein_main_sites/portal_fuerstentum_liechtenstein/fl-staat-staat/fl-staat-ewr/fl-staat-ewr-instutitionelleaspekte.htm.

relations between the Contracting Parties with equal conditions of competition and the respect of the same rules, with a view to creating a homogenous European Economic Area.[27] To this end, Article 1(2)(e) EEA provides for the creation and maintenance of a system ensuring that competition is not distorted and that the corresponding rules are equally respected. The EEA competition rules may be found in Articles 53 to 60, Annex XIV and Protocols 21 to 24 of the Agreement. To all intents and purposes, these provisions adapt in their entirety the substantive rules on competition found in the original EC Treaty. They also include identical provisions to the Merger Regulation, most of the block exemptions and many of the Commission notices applicable to competition policy. Article 59 contains rules governing public undertakings or those undertakings granted special or exclusive rights by EFTA states. Chapter 2 of the EEA Agreement, incorporating Articles 61 to 64, together with Annex XV to the Agreement, set out comparable rules on State aid to those found in Community law.

One important difference relates to the range of products falling within the scope of the competition provisions. Article 8(3) of the EEA Agreement defines the products covered by the rules of the EEA by reference to the Harmonized Commodity Description and Coding System. The EEA provisions do not apply to products described in Chapters 1 to 24 of that System, save to the extent that they are brought within the remit of the Agreement by Tables I and II attached to Protocol 3 to the Agreement. In practical terms, the EEA competition provisions will not generally apply to agricultural and fisheries products, except for a limited number of processed agricultural products. The following list provides a brief overview of the main provisions of the EEA competition rules: **28.07**

- Article 53 EEA contains a general prohibition on anti-competitive agreements and practices;
- Article 54 EEA prohibits the abuse of a dominant position by undertakings;
- Article 57 EEA governs large mergers and other concentrations of undertakings;
- Article 59 EEA lays down provisions on anti-competitive behaviour by public undertakings;
- Articles 61 to 64 EEA set out comparable provisions on State aid;
- Protocol 21 to the EEA Agreement deals with the implementation of competition rules applicable to undertakings;
- Protocol 22 concerns the definition of undertaking and turnover;
- Protocol 23 addresses the cooperation between the surveillance authorities (based also on Article 58 EEA);

---

[27] See also the fourth and fifteenth recitals to the Preamble of the Agreement and Case E-9/97 *Erla María Sveinbjörnsdóttir v Iceland* (above n 11) at paras 47–51.

- Protocol 24 contains rules on cooperation in the field of control of concentrations;
- Protocol 26 stipulates that the ESA is entrusted with equivalent powers and similar functions to those of the European Commission in the field of State aid;
- Protocol 27 lays down the principles according to which the ESA and the Commission shall cooperate in order to ensure a uniform application of the State aid rules;
- Annex XIV to the EEA Agreement incorporates by reference the Community *acquis* in the competition field, subject to certain sectoral adaptations;
- Annex XV to the Agreement incorporates by reference the Community *acquis* in the field of State aid, subject to certain sectoral adaptations
- Finally, the procedural rules relevant to the application of the EEA competition rules can be found in Chapter II, Part I of Protocol 4 to the Surveillance and Court Agreement. Protocol 3 to the Surveillance and Court Agreement contains procedural rules relating to the implementation of the provisions on State aid.

28.08 The introduction or amendment of secondary Community legislation applicable in the competition field has, over the years, been given equivalent effect under the EEA Agreement through decisions of the EEA Joint Committee.[28] The EEA Joint Committee is obliged to ensure the effective implementation and operation of the EEA Agreement. Its decisions insert new pieces of Community legislation into the EEA Agreement through amendment of the twenty-two Annexes to the EEA Agreement.[29] In this way, the parallel application of EU and EEA law in parallel fields is maintained, achieving the homogeneity across the entire EEA that the EEA Agreement mandates. New pieces of Community legislation with relevance to the EEA countries are marked 'text with EEA relevance' in any Official Journal publication. Non-binding acts in the competition area, such as notices adopted by the EC Commission, have been promulgated for the EFTA/EEA States by the ESA.

28.09 Under Article 6 of the EEA Treaty, the provisions of the EEA Agreement shall, insofar as they are identical in substance to corresponding provisions of the EC Treaty, be interpreted in conformity with the relevant rulings of the Court of Justice of the European Communities given prior to the date of signature of the

---

[28] In accordance with the provisions of Chapter II, Part VII of the EEA Agreement, which sets out the decision-making procedure. If no decision is taken to transpose the Community legislation, the general structure of the EEA Agreement cannot be relied upon to fill the gap. See Case E-1/97 *Jan and Kristian Jaegar AS v Opel Norge AS* [1999] 4 CMLR 147, EFTA Court para 30.

[29] Art 7 EEA establishes the legally binding nature of secondary EC legislation incorporated into the EEA Agreement in this manner.

EEA Agreement. Article 3(2) of the Surveillance and Court Agreement also provides that 'due account' shall be paid to the relevant rulings of the ECJ given after the date of signature of the EEA Agreement. Where the EEA substantive rules are identical to the Community law rules from which they are drawn, the legal result should in practice be the same regardless of which set of rules is applied to the given facts.[30] Subject to the process of decentralization of enforcement of competition law, the competition rules in the EEA will be enforced by the EC Commission and the ESA.[31] However in accordance with a 'one-stop-shop' principle, cases are attributed either to the EC Commission or the ESA. In cases falling within the responsibility of the EC Commission,[32] the implementation of the EEA competition rules will be based on the existing Community competences, supplemented by the provisions contained in the EEA Agreement.

II. The substantive competition rules of the EEA agreement: a brief description

A. The Basic Rules

1. Article 53 (Article 81 EC)

The substantive EEA competition rules are essentially identical to the corresponding EC competition rules. The only major difference is in their geographical scope. This is widened in the EEA rules to include the EFTA States. Thus Article 53(1) EEA prohibits, as incompatible with the functioning of the EEA Agreement, agreements between undertakings, decisions by associations of undertakings and concerted practices which have as their object or effect, the prevention, restriction or distortion of competition within the territory of the contracting parties to the EEA. This provision is the exact counterpart to Article 81 EC, except that trade between the EC and one or more EFTA States or between EFTA States must be affected, if the prohibition is to apply. Article 53(1) lists five paradigmatic practices which are caught by the

28.10

---

[30] See Case E-N8/00 *Landsorganisasjonen i Norge v Norsk Kommuneforbund* [2002] 5 CMLR 5 para 39. Arts 111 *et seq.* of the EEA Agreement sets up a dispute settlement procedure for differences in interpretation of the EEA rules between EC and EFTA institutions. The dispute is first referred by either side to the EEA Joint Committee which attempts to reconcile the conflicting interpretations. If the provision in dispute is identical in substance to an EC provision, the question may after three months be referred with the consent of both sides to the CJEC for a definitive ruling.

[31] Art 55(1) EEA.

[32] For details of how jurisdiction is allocated between the EC Commission and the ESA, see paras 28.27 *et seq.*

prohibition. Articles 53(2) and 53(3) follow Articles 81(2) EC and 81(3) EC word for word.[33]

2. Article 54 (Article 82 EC)

28.11 Similarly, Article 54 EEA prohibits, as incompatible with the functioning of the EEA Agreement, any abuse by undertakings of a dominant position within the territory covered by the Agreement or a substantial part of it. As with Article 53, the only major divergence from Article 82 EC is that trade between the EC and one or more EFTA States or between EFTA States must be affected. A list of the main abusive practices specified in Article 82 EC is repeated in Article 54.

3. Article 57 (The Merger Regulation)

28.12 Article 57(1) EEA renders incompatible with the EEA Agreement, concentrations which create or strengthen a dominant position as a result of which effective competition would be significantly impeded within the territory covered by the EEA Agreement or a substantial part of it. The original EC Merger Control Regulation[34] was applied to EEA law (with appropriate modifications) by Article 57(2) EEA, Annex XIV and Protocol 24 to the EEA Agreement. The original Merger Control Regulation was replaced with a new EC Merger Regulation at Community level in early 2004, following a comprehensive review of merger control.[35] While the wording of Article 57(2) has not been up-dated, two EEA Joint Committee decisions now set out the applicability of the EC Merger Regulation to the entire EEA area.[36] The new text of Protocol 24 when read with Article 57 EEA and Article 1 of the EC Merger Regulation establishes that the EC Commission retains sole competence to rule on concentrations with a 'Community dimension.' The ESA only has competence to deal with applications to approve mergers if there is no Community dimension and an EFTA

---

[33] The full text of Art 53 and all the other major provisions of the EEA competition rules are reprinted at the end of this Chapter.

[34] Council Reg (EEC) 4064/89 of 21 December 1989 on the Control of Concentrations between Undertakings [1989] OJ L395/1—as amended by [1990] OJ L257/13.

[35] Council Reg (EC) 139/2004 of 20 January 2004 on the control of concentrations between undertakings ('the EC Merger Regulation') [2004] OJ L24/1. The EC Merger Reg is accompanied by Commission Reg (EC) 802/2004 of 7 April 2004 implementing Council Reg (EC) 139/2004 on the control of concentrations between undertakings ('the Implementing Regulation').

[36] The EEA Joint Committee adopted Decision No 78/2004 [2004] OJ L219/1 and Decision No 79/2004 [2004] OJ L219/24 on 8 June 2004. The first decision, 78/2004, entered into force on 9 June 2004. The entry into force of the second decision, 79/2004, was delayed pending notification under Art 103(1) EEA from Iceland and Norway. It finally entered into force on 1 July 2005. Decision 78/2004 establishes a new Protocol 24 which takes into account the promulgation of the new EC Merger Reg and the Implementing Reg.

dimension is established.[37] No concentrations falling within its competence have yet been notified to the ESA.

4. Article 59 EEA (cf Article 86 EC)

Article 59 EEA requires EFTA states to ensure that no anti-competitive meas- **28.13**
ures are either enacted or maintained in force for public undertakings or for undertakings to which they have granted special or exclusive rights. This provision principally affects state monopolies having a commercial character.[38] A derogation is provided under Article 59(2) for such entities which provide services in the general economic interest or which have the character of a revenue producing monopoly. The competition rules continue to apply to such entities, but only in so far as the application of the rules does 'not obstruct the performance, in law or in fact, of the particular tasks assigned to them.' The derogation is itself subject to the proviso that the 'development of trade must not be affected to such an extent as would be contrary to the interests of the Contracting Parties.'

The EEA Agreement also requires EFTA States, under Article 16 EEA, to adjust **28.14**
any State monopoly of a commercial character so that no discrimination exists between EEA nationals regarding the conditions under which goods are procured and marketed. The ESA delivered reasoned opinions to Norway in December 1994, and to Iceland in February 1995 concerning state monopolies in the importation and wholesale of alcoholic products. Both countries subsequently amended their legislation, leading to the termination of exclusive rights for the State alcohol monopolies in those countries. Annex IV to the EEA Agreement has also incorporated (with appropriate modifications) relevant Community measures which apply to public undertakings. In particular, the *acquis* incorporated into EEA law includes Commission Directive 88/301/EEC of 16 May 1988 on competition in the markets in telecommunications terminal equipment;[39] and Commission Directive 2002/77/EC of 16 September 2002 on competition in the markets for electronic communications networks and services.[40]

---

[37] The tests for establishing an EFTA dimension are set out below.

[38] See, for example, Case E-1/94 *Ravintoloitsijain Liiton Kustannus Oy Restamark* [1995] EFTA Court Rep 15 para 48, where the EFTA Court considered a state monopoly on the importation of alcohol under the free movement provisions of the EEA Agreement, but recognized that these also fell to be interpreted in light of competition considerations as well. See also Case E-6/96 *Tore Wilhelmsen AS v Oslo kommune* [1997] EFTA Court Rep 53; and Case E-9/00 *EFTA Surveillance Authority v Norway* [2002] EFTA Court Rep 72; [2002] 2 CMLR 17, which concerned in part the Norwegian State monopoly on the retail of alcoholic beverages.

[39] [1988] OJ L131/73, as amended by Commission Dir 94/96/EC of 13 October 1994 [1994] OJ L268/15.

[40] [2002] OJ L249/21.

5. Article 3 EEA (cf Article 10 EC)

28.15 Finally, Article 3 of the EEA Agreement corresponds to Article 10 EC and imposes a duty on the contracting parties to take appropriate measures to ensure the fulfilment of obligations arising from the Agreement.

B. 'Acts' Giving Effect to the Basic Rules

1. Block exemptions

28.16 The implementation of Article 53 is also subject to various block exemptions, which were either in force when the EEA Agreement was signed, or as have been updated from time to time.[41] New block exemption regulations have to be

---

[41] Article 60 and Annex XIV, s B to F and J, of the EEA Agreement. The block exemptions listed in Annex XIV to the EEA Agreement are currently:

- Commission Reg (EC) 2790/1999 of 22 December 1999 on the application of Art 81(3) of the Treaty to categories of vertical agreements and concerted practices—the Vertical Agreements Block Exemption [1999] OJ L336/21, as amended by the Act concerning the conditions of Accession of the Czech Republic, the Republic of Estonia, the Republic of Cyprus, the Republic of Latvia, the Republic of Lithuania, the Republic of Hungary, the Republic of Malta, the Republic of Poland, the Republic of Slovenia and the Slovak Republic and the adjustments to the Treaties on which the European Union is founded, adopted on 16 April 2003 ('the 2003 Act of Accession' [2002] OJ L236/33.)

- Commission Reg (EC) 1400/2002 of 31 July 2002 on the application of Art 81(3) of the Treaty to categories of vertical agreements and concerted practices in the motor vehicle sector—the Motor Vehicle Block Exemption [2002] OJ L203/30, as amended by the 2003 Act of Accession.

- Commission Reg (EC) 772/2004 of 27 April 2004 on the application of Art 81(3) of the Treaty to categories of technology transfer agreements—the Technology Transfer Block Exemption [2004] OJ L123/11, as corrected by [2004] OJ L127/158.

- Commission Reg (EC) 2658/2000 of 29 November 2000 on the application of Art 81(3) of the Treaty to categories of specialization agreements—the Specialization Agreements Block Exemption [2000] OJ L304/3, as amended by the 2003 Act of Accession.

- Commission Reg (EC) 2659/2000 of 29 November 2000 on the application of Art 81(3) of the Treaty to categories of research and development agreements—the Research and Development Block Exemption [2000] OJ L304/7, as amended by the 2003 Act of Accession.

- Commission Reg (EEC) 1617/93 of 25 June 1993 on the application of Art 85(3) of the Treaty to certain categories of agreements and concerted practices concerning joint planning and co-ordination of schedules—IATA passenger tariff conferences block exemption [1993] OJ L155/18, as amended by Commission Reg Nos 1523/96; 1083/1999; 1324/2001; 1105/2002 and the 2003 Act of Accession.

- Commission Reg (EC) 823/2000 of 19 April 2000 on the application of Art 81(3) of the Treaty to certain categories of agreements, decisions and concerted practices between liner shipping conferences (consortia)—Liner conferences block exemption [2000] OJ L100/24, as amended by the 2003 Act of Accession and Commission Reg Nos 463/2004 and 611/2005.

implemented under the rather complicated scheme contained in Articles 102 to 104 of the EEA Agreement. Annex XIV to the EEA Agreement also transposes into an EEA context two Commission Regulations applying the competition rules to the transport sector.[42]

The block exemptions have been supplemented and modified by the provisions **28.17** of Protocol 1 to the EEA Agreement ('horizontal adaptations') and by Annex XIV of the EEA Agreement ('sectoral and specific adaptations'). The original text of the EC block exemptions must therefore be read subject to these adaptations. The block exemptions thus adapted will be automatically applied by the EC Commission and the ESA when dealing with EEA competition cases within their respective jurisdictions. They will also fall to be applied directly by national courts and national competition authorities acting in accordance with the Modernization Regulation as implemented in EEA law.

Two important differences should be noted. First, the scope for withdrawing the **28.18** benefit of the exemption is expanded. Both the Commission and the ESA may now withdraw the exemption not only on their own initiative or at the request of a State or of a natural or legal person claiming a legitimate interest, but furthermore at the request of the other surveillance authority. Secondly, the provisions in any given block exemption are applied in an EEA context only through the prism of specific provisions in Protocol 21 to the EEA Agreement.[43]

2. Commission Notices and Guidelines

The Commission and the ESA are obliged, when applying the EEA competition **28.19** rules, to take into account pertinent, existing Commission Notices and Guidelines. The list of notices to be taken into account is set out in Annex XIV.[44]

• Commission Reg (EC) 358/2003 of 27 February 2003 on the application of Art 81(3) of the Treaty to certain categories of agreements, decisions and concerted practices in the insurance sector—Insurance agreements block exemption [2003] OJ L53/8.

[42] See Council Reg (EEC) 1017/68 of 19 July 1968 applying rules of competition to transport by rail, road and inland waterway—Transport by rail, road and inland waterways [1968] OJ L175/1, as amended by the Modernization Reg, Council Reg (EC) 1/2003 of 16 December 2002 [2003] OJ L/1/1; Council Reg (EEC) 4056/86 of 22 December 1986 laying down detailed rules for the application of Arts 85 and 86 of the Treaty to maritime transport—Maritime transport [1986] OJ L378/4 as amended by the 2003 Act of Accession and the Modernization Reg.

[43] Protocol 21 on the implementation of competition rules applicable to undertakings. See Part IV.B. below. Annex XIV to the EEA Agreement makes clear that where the proper application of the above block exemptions is subject to the application of the Modernisation Reg, in the EEA context this will be subject to the application of the equivalent provisions under Protocol 21.

[44] The Notices and Guidelines listed in Annex XIV are:

• Commission Notice regarding restrictions ancillary to concentrations [1990] OJ C203/5.
• Commission Notice regarding the concentrative and co-operative operations under Council

These Notices and Guidelines have not been adapted for EEA purposes. Instead the ESA is simply obliged to take due account of the principles and rules contained in them, when applying Articles 53 to 60 of the Agreement.[45] The existing Notices and Guidelines are read in light of their *effet utile* for the application of the EEA competition provisions. It is worth noting, therefore, that a number of notices are included in the list which relate to Community measures that are no longer in force. These notices will be of largely historical interest only. They represent measures adopted by the EC Commission up to 31 July 1991.

28.20 More modern notices are not included in an amended version of Annex XIV but are instead adopted by the ESA under its own competence. From the date of entry into force of the EEA Agreement, acts corresponding to measures taken by the EC Commission are adopted by the ESA under Articles 5(2)(b) and 25 of the Surveillance and Court Agreement. They are published in accordance with the exchange of letters on publication of EEA relevant information.[46] Thus, for example, a series of ten Annexes to a Decision of the ESA adopted in January 1994 contained the equivalent text of ten Commission Notices and

---

Reg (EEC) 4064/89 of 21 December 1989 on the control of concentrations between undertakings [1990] C203/10.

- Commission Notice concerning Commission Reg (EEC) 1983/83 and (EEC) 1984/83 of 22 June 1983 on the application of Art 85(3) of the Treaty to categories of exclusive distribution and exclusive purchasing agreements [1984] OJ C101/2.

- Commission Notice concerning Reg (EEC) 123/85 of 12 December 1984 on the application of Art 85(3) of the Treaty to certain categories of motor vehicle distribution and servicing agreements [1985] OJ C17/4.

- Commission Notice on exclusive dealing contracts with commercial agents [1962] OJ 139/2921/62.

- Commission Notice concerning agreements, decisions and concerted practices in the field of cooperation between enterprises 1968 OJ C75/3, as corrected by [1968[OJ C84/14.

- Commission Notice concerning imports into the Community of Japanese goods falling within the scope of the Rome Treaty [1972] OJ C111/13.

- Commission Notice of 18 December 1978 concerning its assessment of certain subcontracting agreements in relation to Art 85(1) of the EEC Treaty [1979] OJ C1/2.

- Commission Notice on agreements of minor importance which do not fall under Art 85(1) of the Treaty establishing the European Economic Community [1986] OJ C231/2.

- Guidelines on the application of EEC competition rules in the telecommunication sector [1991] OJ C233/2.

[45] See Preamble to the section headed 'Acts of which the EC Commission and the EFTA Surveillance Authority shall take due account' in Annex XIV to the Agreement.

[46] The acts adopted by the Commission will not be integrated into Annex XIV but a reference to their publication in the Official Journal of the European Communities will be made in the EEA Supplement to the Official Journal. The corresponding acts adopted by the ESA are to be published in the EEA Supplement to, and the EEA Section of, the Official Journal.

Guidelines to be applied by the ESA in an EEA context.[47] Both surveillance authorities shall take due account of these measures in cases where they have jurisdiction under the EEA Agreement.[48] The scope for divergence in application is further reduced by the obligation imposed on the EC Commission to ensure that equal conditions of competition are met in the EEA as in the Community itself. The ESA has not issued interpretative guidelines or notices in the field of merger control. Instead, it has simply indicated that it will apply the principles set out in relevant notices issued by the EC Commission.

III. The procedure for the application of the EEA competition rules

A. The Modernization of Community Competition Law

Article 55 of the EEA Agreement entrusts the enforcement of the EEA Com-   **28.21**
petition provisions to both the EC Commission and the ESA Article 55(1)
requires the 'competent surveillance authority' to investigate cases of suspected
infringement of the EEA competition rules and to take appropriate measures to
bring them to an end. It may launch an investigation of its own initiative, on the
application of an EEA state within its respective territory, or on the application
of the other surveillance authority. Investigations are required to be carried out
in cooperation with the national authorities in the respective territory and with
the other surveillance authority. Article 55 imposes an obligation on a surveillance authority to assist its counterpart in accordance with its own internal rules.
Under Article 55(2), findings in relation to infringements must be set out in a
reasoned decision, which may be published. The competent surveillance authority is also empowered to authorize States within its territory to 'take the measures, the conditions and details of which it shall determine, needed to remedy
the situation.' It may also request the other surveillance authority to authorize
States within the other respective territory to take such measures.

---

[47] Decision of the EFTA Surveillance Authority No 3/94/COL of 12 January 1994 on the issuing of 10 notices and guidelines in the field of competition [1994] OJ L153/1.

[48] Examples of such measures include Notice on Cooperation between national courts and the EFTA Surveillance Authority in applying Arts 53 and 54 of the EEA Agreement [1995] OJ C112/7; EFTA Surveillance Authority Notice on cooperation between national competition authorities and the EFTA Surveillance Authority in handling cases falling within the scope of Arts 53 or 54 of the EEA Agreement [2000] OJ C307/6; EFTA Surveillance Authority Guidelines on the applicability of Art 53 of the EEA Agreement to Horizontal Cooperation Agreements [2002] OJ C266/1; and EFTA Surveillance Authority Guidelines on Vertical Restraints [2002] OJ C122/1.

28.22 While the terms of Article 55 EEA are silent as to the detailed measures needed to ensure the enforcement of the EEA competition rules, the implicit emphasis is upon a system of centralised enforcement by the competent surveillance authorities. But such an emphasis is misplaced. The Community has reformed the centralized system of enforcement provided for by Regulation 17/62. It has implemented a system of decentralized enforcement of the competition provisions, leaving the EC Commission free to focus its resources on a limited number of significant cases. The 'Modernization Regulation'—Council Regulation 1/2003—was adopted on 16 December 2002 and entered into force on 1 May 2004.[49] It brings with it a radical shake up of the enforcement of the competition rules in the Community. Its scope and effect are examined in detail in the main body of this work. The Modernization Regulation has been accompanied by a Commission Regulation ('the Implementing Regulation') that sets out the provisions governing the exercise by the Commission of its powers in the wake of the decentralisation of enforcement of EC competition law.[50]

28.23 The cross application of the Modernization Regulation to undertakings established in, or conducting business with, the EEA/EFTA States was effected by two EEA Joint Committee Decisions. By EEA Joint Committee Decision 130/2004, the text of the Modernization Regulation has been formally applied to the EEA competition regime with effect from 19 May 2005. Further, by EEA Joint Committee Decision 178/2004, the Implementing Regulation No 773/2004 was also brought within the scope of the EEA rules with effect from 1 July 2005. Necessary amendments have been made to Annex XIV and Protocols 21 and 23 of the EEA Agreement. Indeed, the implementation of Joint Decisions 130/2004 and 178/2004 has seen Protocol 23 replaced in its entirety. In addition, changes have been made to Protocol 4 to the Surveillance and Court Agreement, which contains the procedural rules applied by the ESA for the purposes of implementing Articles 53 and 54 EEA. These changes incorporate the terms of the Modernization Regulation in Chapter II to Protocol 4 and the Implementing Regulation in Chapter III to Protocol 4. The ESA has adopted a number of Notices equivalent to those adopted by the EC Commission as part of the modernization package. Notices adopted to date include Informal Guidance to be provided by the Authority concerning the application of Articles 53 and 54 EEA; the Effect on Trade Concept contained in Articles 53 and 54 EEA; and the Application of Article 53(3) EEA. The remaining notices will be adopted in short order.

---

[49] Council Reg (EC) 1/2003 of 16 December 2002 on the implementation of the rules on competition laid down in Arts 81 and 82 of the Treaty [2003] OJ L1/1, as amended by Council Reg (EC) 411/2004 amending Reg (EC) 1/2003 [2004] OJ L68/1.

[50] Commission Reg (EC) 773/2004 of 7 April 2004 relating to the conduct of proceedings by the Commission pursuant to Arts 81 and 82 of the EC Treaty [2004] OJ L123/18.

The Joint Committee decision 130/2004 was adopted on 24 September 2004 **28.24** and entered into force on 19 May 2005. Decision 178/2004 was adopted on 3 December 2004 and entered into force on 1 July 2005. At the time of writing, neither Decision has been published in either the Official Journal or in the EEA Supplement. The entry into force of both measures was delayed pending notification from Iceland under Article 103 of the EEA Agreement. Nonetheless, the modernization regime provisionally applied to EEA competition law with effect from 24 March 2005. This is because Article 103(2) of the EEA Agreement provides that, if, upon the expiry of a period of six months after the decision of the EEA Joint Committee relevant notification under Article 103 has not taken place, the decision of the EEA Joint Committee shall be applied provisionally pending the fulfilment of the constitutional requirements. This is the case unless a Contracting Party notifies that such a provisional application cannot take place. As no such reservation was lodged by Iceland, the modernization regime in fact took effect from March 2005.

The ESA will no longer receive notifications concerning the application of **28.25** Articles 53 and 54 EEA. Instead, it will focus upon investigations conducted of its own initiative and complaints made to it by members of the public. The ESA will retain enforcement powers equivalent to those of the EC Commission. It will therefore be able to:

- issue decisions finding that an agreement or practice does not infringe Articles 53 or 54 EEA;
- close proceedings subject to commitments assumed by undertakings which will be binding upon them;
- impose structural remedies to deal with competition concerns;
- enjoy increased powers while on inspections; and
- impose higher fines when procedural rules have not been complied with.[51]

In keeping with the spirit of the Modernization Regulation, the ESA has indi- **28.26** cated that it will in the future seek to give priority (in terms of its in-depth investigations) to cases where one or more of the following conditions are met:

- The ESA has sole jurisdiction (notably in competition cases involving the potential application of Article 59 EEA to an EFTA state);
- Articles 53 and 54 may resolve a competition concern where national rules differ from EEA provisions to such an extent that they could not achieve a similar result;
- A hardcore infringement of the EEA competition rules can be established;

---

[51] EFTA Surveillance Authority, *Annual Report*, 2003, 46.

- The economic impact of a violation is significant in the relevant market;
- A case raises new points of law which will benefit from clarification.[52]

B. Division of Responsibility between the EC Commission and the EFTA Surveillance Authority

28.27 The ESA has been granted equivalent powers and similar functions to those of the Commission, to enable it to carry out the implementation of the EEA competition rules. It applies procedural rules similar to those applied in the Community itself.[53] The EC Commission continues to use its own procedural rules even when dealing with EEA cases. But the Community is obliged, under Article 1 of Protocol 21 to the EEA Agreement, to adopt any necessary provisions to ensure that the Commission is granted the necessary powers to enforce EEA competition rules under the EC pillar. This position is maintained over time by virtue of Article 2 of Protocol 21. This requires corresponding amendments to be made to the ESA's powers so that it is 'entrusted simultaneously with equivalent powers and similar functions to those of the EC Commission.' The EEA Agreement envisages close cooperation between the EC Commission and the ESA in order to achieve a uniform application of the competition rules throughout the EEA. The two authorities are obliged to exchange information and consult one another on general policy issues and in connection with individual cases.[54] A high degree of cooperation has been achieved in practice.[55]

28.28 Given the dual enforcement policy, it is essential that some method of allocating cases to the respective authorities is established. This has been achieved through Articles 56 and 57 of the EEA Agreement. These provisions remain unchanged by the Modernization Regulation. Article 56 caters for allocation of cases concerning restrictive agreements and abuses of dominant positions. Article 57 deals with allocation for merger control cases. Whilst the EEA competition system is based on 'two pillars', a 'one-stop shop' approach has been adopted

---

[52] EFTA Surveillance Authority, *Annual Report*, 2003, 55.

[53] See generally Arts 1 and 2 of Protocol 21. The powers and functions of the EC Commission for the application of the EC competition rules are reflected in the acts which are listed in Art 3 of Protocol 21 to the EEA Agreement. This refers principally to the Modernization Reg and the Implementing Reg, but also refers back to the various acts listed in Annex XIV (mentioned above). Cross-references are also made to other procedural regs in the field of merger control, transport and coal and steel.

[54] See Art 1 of Protocol 23 to the EEA Agreement.

[55] See the *Annual Reports* prepared by the ESA for the years 2001 to 2004, available on its web site.

for the convenience of undertakings involved.[56] This means that undertakings should deal either solely with the Commission or solely with the ESA in relation to any given agreement or practice.

The following rules are important in practice, as they represent the only signifi-   **28.29**
cant point of departure from the otherwise very similar substantive and procedural rules already found in EC competition law.

C. Allocation of Cases[57]

1. Article 53 cases

Where a case raises issues of agreements, decisions or concerted practices caught   **28.30**
by Article 53, Article 56 of the Agreement attributes competence between the EC Commission and the ESA as follows:

EC pure cases

These cases involve only trade between EC Member States. They are decided by   **28.31**
the EC Commission on the basis of Article 81 EC. As a matter of law, these cases do not fall within the ambit of the EEA Competition rules at all.

EFTA pure cases

Where only trade between EFTA States is implicated, the case is dealt with by   **28.32**
the ESA. Article 53 of the EEA Agreement is then the controlling, substantive provision.[58]

Mixed cases

So-called 'mixed cases' involve two situations which must be distinguished if the   **28.33**
rules on attribution of competence are to be understood. 'Mixed Cases' in the broad sense are those cases where trade between the Community and one or more EFTA States is affected by the Agreement or practice in question, regardless of whether trade between the EC Member States themselves is also affected

---

[56] Art 55 of the EEA Agreement mandates the 'competent surveillance authority' to ensure the application of Arts 53 and 54. On the application of the 'one stop shop' principle, see also Joined Cases T-67/00, T-68/00, T-71/00 and T-78/00 *JFE Engineering Corp and others v EC Commission* (not yet reported) paras 489 and 490.

[57] For a commentary on the origin of the allocation provisions, together with an explanation of their resulting nature and reasons why they are quite complicated, see Blanchet *et al,* 'The Agreement on the European Economic Area (EEA). A Guide to the free Movement of Goods and Competition Rules', *op cit* n 1 at 184–6. See also Bellamy and Child, *European Community Law of Competition* (Sweet & Maxwell, 5th edn, 2001) para 12–164ff.

[58] See Art 56(1)(a) EEA.

or not. In addition there is a sub-category of 'mixed cases' which has been referred to as '1 + 1 cases'.[59] These are cases where trade between EC Member States is not affected, only trade between the Community and one or more EFTA States. The first question to ask therefore, when considering the rules governing the attribution of cases between the two authorities, is whether trade between EC Member States is affected or not. Mixed cases where both trade between EC Member States and trade between the EC and one or more EFTA/ EEA States is involved will almost always be handled by the Commission.[60] An exception is where the agreements or practices concerned, whilst formally affecting inter-EC trade or competition within the Community, do so only to a limited extent. That is, if the effect on trade between EC Member States or on competition within the Community is not appreciable, the ESA assumes jurisdiction. It has been accepted by the contracting parties to the Agreement that for these purposes, the phrase 'appreciable' shall correlate to the definition of *de minimis* agreements found already in EC Competition law.[61] The allocation of '1 + 1 cases', where trade between EC Member States is not affected, is slightly more complicated. In such cases, jurisdiction is determined by a threshold criterion. Article 56(1)(b) of the EEA Agreement provides that if the turnover of the undertakings concerned in EFTA territories is equal to or greater than 33 per cent of their turnover in the EEA as a whole, then the ESA will handle the matter.[62] The Commission decides on all other cases where the threshold criterion is not met, regardless of the existence of any effect on competition in the EC or not. The fact that the undertakings achieve 67 per cent of their turnover within the Community will be sufficient to ground the Commission's jurisdiction. In practice though, the ESA will decide the case if the effect on competition[63] within the EC is not an appreciable one, under Article 56(3). Two particular situations deserve clarification:

---

[59] The phrase and definition comes from Blanchet *et al*, 'The Agreement on the European Economic Area (EEA). A Guide to the free Movement of Goods and Competition Rules', *op cit* note 1 at 186 *et seq*.

[60] Art 56(1)(c) EEA. See, for example, Case T-44/00 *Mannesmanröhren-Werke AG v EC Commission* (not yet reported) para 5. The fact that the ESA may already have commenced an investigation does not operate as a bar to the Commission exercising its own powers in relation to the same agreements or practices. See Joined Cases T-67/00, T-68/00, T-71/00 and T-78/00 *JFE Engineering Corp and others v EC Commission* (not yet reported) paras 459 to 493.

[61] Art 56(3) of the Agreement.

[62] This would technically encompass mixed cases generally and not just '1 + 1 cases'. Art 56(1)(b) is, however, expressed to be without prejudice to sub-para (c). Therefore, even if this threshold is met, the EC Commission retains an element of 'residual' competence. Provided that trade between EC Member States is affected to some extent, then the Commission assumes jurisdiction, relinquishing it only if the effect is not appreciable pursuant to Art 56(3). This is, in reality, simply the application of the mixed case attribution described immediately above.

[63] The effect must be on competition, not trade, since *ex hypothesi*, in a '1 + 1 case', trade between Member States is not affected.

- Article 56(1)(c) refers only to an effect on *trade* between EC Member States, not on *competition* more generally within the Community. Provided therefore that the matter qualifies as a '1 + 1 case' (trade between EC Member States not being affected) and the turnover threshold is met, the ESA will handle the case even if competition in the Community is affected to an appreciable extent.

- The ESA will also have jurisdiction over cases where the undertakings involved generate less than 33 per cent of their turnover in EFTA States, but the effect on either trade or competition within the Community is not appreciable.[64]

The allocation of jurisdiction in 'mixed cases' can therefore be seen to be based **28.34** essentially on a two-step test; a determination of whether trade between EC Member States is affected and a threshold determination of turnover, both subject to a residual 'appreciable effect' consideration. As a rough guide, it would seem that the Commission will deal with a case if either greater than two-thirds of the undertakings' turnover is achieved in the Community, or if trade between Member States or competition generally in the Community is affected to an appreciable extent. The overall process is demonstrated in Figure 1.

2. Article 54 cases

Article 56(2) provides that '[i]ndividual cases falling under Article 54 shall be **28.35** decided upon by the surveillance authority in the territory of which a dominant position is found to exist.' The only exception is where a dominant position exists within the territories of both the EC Member States and the EFTA States. Then identical rules to those for Article 53 cases apply. That is, the relevant case will be attributed to the ESA where: (i) either trade or competition within the Community is not affected to an appreciable extent; or (ii) there being no effect on trade between EC Member States and the turnover of the undertaking(s) concerned in the territory of the EFTA States equals 33 per cent or more of its (their) turnover in the territory of the EEA, even if there is an appreciable effect on competition within the Community. The Commission is competent for all other cases.

The overall process can be seen in Figure 2. **28.36**

The appreciable effect criterion used in both Articles 53 and 54 cases, may **28.37** be equated with the notion of *de minimis* thresholds already encountered in EC Competition law. The ESA's 'Notice on agreements of minor importance which do not appreciably restrict competition under Article 53(1) of the EEA

---

[64] See Art 56(3) EEA.

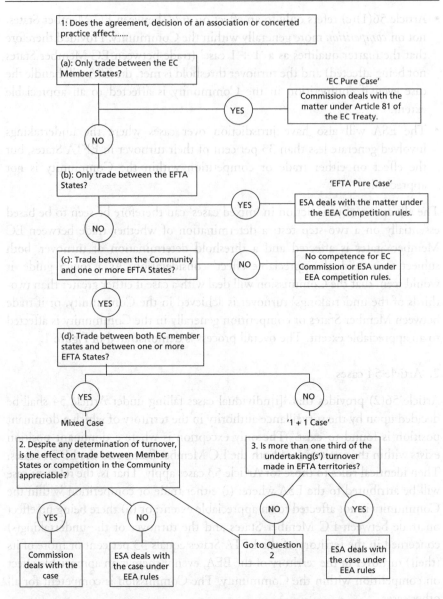

Figure 1 **Allocation of Jurisdiction between the Commission and the ESA in EEA Competition Cases falling under Article 53.**

Agreement (*de minimis*)'[65] quantifies, with the help of market share thresholds, a negative test for determining what is not an appreciable restriction of competition

---

[65] [2003] OJ C67/20; and EEA Supplement No 15, p 11, 20.3.2003. The ESA's Notice follows the terms of the Commission's Notice entitled 'Agreements of minor importance which do not appreciably restrict competition under Art 81(1) of the Treaty establishing the European Community (*de minimis*)' [2001] OJ C368/13.

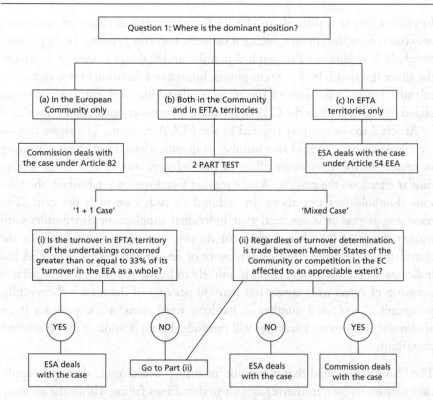

Figure 2 **The Allocation of Jurisdiction in Article 54 cases.**

for the purposes of Article 53 EEA. Paragraph 7 of the Notice sets out the ESA's view that agreements between undertakings[66] which affect trade between the Contracting Parties to the EEA Agreement do not appreciably restrict competition within the meaning of Article 53(1) EEA:

(a) If the aggregate market share held by the parties to the agreement does not exceed 10 per cent on any of the relevant markets affected by the agreement, where the agreement is made between undertakings which are actual or potential competitors on any of these markets (agreements between competitors);

(b) If the market share held by each of the parties to the agreement does not exceed 15 per cent on any of the relevant markets affected by the agreement, where the agreement is made between undertakings which are not actual or potential competitors on any of these markets (agreements between non-competitors).

---

[66] An undertaking is defined in Art 1 of Protocol 22 as 'any entity carrying out activities of a commercial or economic nature.'

28.38 In cases where it is difficult to classify the agreement as either an agreement between competitors or an agreement between non-competitors, the 10 per cent threshold is applicable. Paragraph 9 permits undertakings a 'leeway' to exceed the above thresholds by 2 per cent points, limited to a duration of two successive calendar years. Definitions of the terms 'undertaking' and 'turnover' are contained in Protocol 22 to the EEA Agreement.[67] Turnover calculation is restricted by Article 2 to the territory covered by the EEA Agreement. The above threshold classification is subject to a number of qualifications. First, there is a saving in respect of the foreclosure effect of parallel networks of agreement having similar effects on the market. Where market foreclosure is established, the relevant thresholds set out above are reduced in each case to 5 per cent. The reasoning is that it is assumed that individual suppliers or distributors with market shares of less than 5 per cent do not contribute significantly to the cumulative foreclosure effect of a network of similar agreements. The ESA has indicated that a foreclosure effect is unlikely to be found if the effect of parallel networks of agreements covers less than 30 per cent of the market.[68] Secondly, paragraph 11 sets out a number of 'hardcore restrictions' whose presence in an agreement between undertakings will preclude the application of the *de minimis* provisions.

28.39 The ESA has indicated that it will not institute proceedings (either upon application or on its own initiative) against undertakings falling within the *de minimis* Notice. Further, where undertakings assume in good faith that they fall within its terms, the ESA will not impose fines in the event of a finding of an infringement of Articles 53 or 54 EEA. Paragraph 3 to the Notice makes clear that agreements may in addition not fall under Article 53(1) EEA because they are not capable of appreciably affecting trade between the Contracting Parties to the EEA Agreement. The *de minimis* Notice does not deal with this issue. It does not quantify what amounts to 'an appreciable effect on trade'. The ESA has, however, acknowledged that agreements between small and medium-sized undertakings[69] are rarely capable of appreciably affecting trade between the Contracting Parties to the EEA Agreement. Small and medium-sized undertakings are currently defined as undertakings which have fewer than 250 employees

---

[67] Specific rules will be used for the banking and insurance sectors (Art 3 of Protocol 22) as well as for distribution and supply arrangements and transfers of technology (Art 4 of Protocol 22). Specific rules are also included to calculate the turnover of ECSC undertakings for a mixture of ECSC and EEC products (Art 5 of Protocol 22).

[68] See para 8 of the *de minimis* Notice.

[69] As defined in the EFTA Surveillance Authority Decision No 112/96/COL of 11 September 1996 [1996] OJ L42/33, and EEA Supplement No 7, 1, 13 February 1997. This decision corresponds to European Commission Recommendation 96/280/EC [1996] OJ L107/4.

and have either an annual turnover not exceeding 40 million euros or an annual balance-sheet total not exceeding 27 million euros.[70]

3. Merger cases

The decision as to whether a merger case is allocated to the EC Commission or to the ESA depends on whether or not the merger creates an 'EFTA dimension'. Article 57(2) provides that the control of concentrations falling within Article 57(1) EEA shall be carried out by the EC Commission in cases falling under the Community Merger Regulation and in accordance with Protocols 21 and 24 and Annex XIV to the EEA Agreement. In contrast, the ESA has jurisdiction in any other cases where the relevant thresholds set out in Annex XIV are fulfilled in the territory of the EFTA States, in accordance with Protocols 21 and 24 and Annex XIV to the EEA Agreement. However, that jurisdiction is expressed to be without prejudice to the competence of the EC Member States. **28.40**

The upshot of these provisions is that the EC Commission will have sole competence to rule on concentrations with a 'Community dimension', as defined in Article 1 of the EC Merger Regulation (Regulation (EEC) 139/2004). As set out in the main body of this work, the existence of a Community dimension depends on a number of thresholds being met within the EU as regards the turnover of the parties to the concentration. A 'Community dimension' will not, however, be established if each undertaking concerned achieves more than two-thirds of its aggregate Community-wide turnover within one and the same Member State of the EU. Articles 6(5) and 13 of Protocol 24 to the EEA Agreement and Article 4(5) of the EC Merger Regulation provide that where a concentration is capable of being reviewed under the national competition laws of at least three EC Member States and at least one EFTA State, the parties to the concentration can by way of a reasoned submission request the EC Commission to examine the concentration. If the competent Member States do not express their disagreement, the concentration will be deemed to have a 'Community dimension'. Should one of the competent EFTA States express its disagreement, the competent EFTA States shall retain their competence to examine the concentration. **28.41**

In contrast, an EFTA dimension is established if the turnover thresholds set out in the EC Merger Regulation are met within the EFTA pillar. That is, the combined aggregate worldwide turnover of all the undertakings involved is more than 5 billion euros and the aggregate EFTA-wide turnover of each of at **28.42**

---

[70] The ESA Notice anticipates that the European Commission will revise its recommendation to increase the annual turnover threshold from 40 million euros to 50 million euros and the annual balance-sheet total threshold from 27 million euros to 43 million euros.

least two of the undertakings is greater than 250 million euros. If, however, all the undertakings involved achieve more than two-thirds of their turnover within one and the same EFTA State, the requisite EFTA dimension would be lacking. The proposed merger would then be dealt with at a national level. Alternatively, a concentration which does not meet these thresholds will still have an EFTA dimension where: (a) the combined aggregate worldwide turnover of all of the undertakings concerned is more than 2.5 billion euros; (b) in each of at least three EFTA states, the combined aggregate turnover of all of the undertakings concerned is more than 100 million euros; (c) in each of at least three EFTA states included for the purpose of point (b), the aggregate turnover of each of at least two of the undertakings concerned is more than 25 million euros; and (d) the aggregate EFTA-wide turnover of each of at least two of the undertakings concerned is more than 100 million euros. This is subject to the same exception for each of the undertakings achieving more than two-thirds of its aggregate EFTA-wide turnover in one and the same EFTA state.[71]

4. Public undertakings

28.43 Article 59 EEA reproduces most of the text of Article 86 (ex Article 90) of the EC Treaty concerning the application of the competition rules to public undertakings or undertakings that have been granted special or exclusive rights. The difference lies in Article 59(3) EEA. This provides that responsibility for the application of the provisions of Article 59(1) and (2) EEA shall be allocated to either the EC Commission or the ESA, based on their 'respective competence.' Within its own sphere of competence, therefore, the ESA will be responsible for addressing 'appropriate measures' to states falling within its territory. This is to be contrasted with the more specific power granted to the EC Commission, under Article 86(3) EC, to address decisions or directives to Member States.

D. Cooperation between the EC Commission and the ESA

28.44 Article 58 states that through the functioning of the EEA Agreement, it is intended to develop and maintain a uniform surveillance on competition throughout the European Economic Area and 'to promote a homogeneous implementation, application and interpretation of the relevant rules.'[72] To this end, the Article further stipulates that 'the competent authorities shall

---

[71] See Art 57(1) and (2); Annex XIV, Section A, Merger Control; and Protocols 21 and 24 to the Agreement.
[72] See also Case E-1/94 *Ravintoloitsijain Liiton Kustannus Oy Restamark* [1994–1995] EFTA Court Report 15 paras 32 to 35.

cooperate in accordance with the provisions . . . [of] Protocols 23 and 24.'[73] The cooperation extends to general policy issues as well as involvement in particular cases.[74] The aim is to coordinate the method of and the policy behind the application of EEA Competition rules for both the Commission and the ESA. Thus, for example, the ESA participated in discussions with the EC Commission concerning the review of competition rules relating to vertical restraints; the review of leniency policy; the re-drafting of the *de minimis* Notice; and more recently on the need for modernization of the Community competition regime, to name but a few.

The duty of cooperation between the surveillance authorities applies, as regards **28.45** Articles 53 and 54 of the EEA Agreement, only in 'mixed cases'. In such cases, both surveillance authorities have historically supplied one another with copies of notifications, complaints and information about the opening of *ex officio* procedures. For Article 53 and 54 cases, the key aspects of cooperation are as follows:

- The EC Commission and the ESA regularly consult and inform each other at different stages of proceedings.[75] Each of the surveillance authorities and the States within the respective territories are entitled to attend any hearings or Advisory Committees held by their counterparts. Furthermore, each surveillance authority may, before the other surveillance authority takes a final decision, make any observations it considers appropriate. To this end, each surveillance authority is entitled to see copies of the important documents held by the other.

- In addition to the above exchange of information, the Commission and ESA grant each other more tangible, administrative assistance,[76] if the need arises in individual cases. For instance, each competent surveillance authority may request the other surveillance authority to undertake investigations within its territory, and may take an active part in such investigations. Thus in 1994, the ESA asked the EC Commission to carry out investigations at the premises of a number of Community undertakings as part of the ESA investigation into the supply of steel tubes to the Norwegian offshore industry.[77] Conversely, in 1998, the ESA carried out investigations at the Commission's request into undertakings in its territory operating in the zinc phosphate industry. Parallel investigations have also occurred, for example, into the telecommunications sector.[78] In practice, cooperation has tended to involve

---

[73] Protocol 23 applies to Art 53 and 54 cases and Protocol 24 relates to merger cases.
[74] See Art 109(2) EEA and Art 1 of Protocol 23 to the EEA Agreement.
[75] See para 28.53.   [76] For further details, see ibid.
[77] This culminated in the Commission's decision challenged in Joined Cases T-67/00, T-68/00, T-71/00 and T-78/00 *JFE Engineering Corp and others v Commission* (not yet reported).
[78] Commission Press Release IP/99/786; ESA Press Release PR(99)19.

the ESA assisting the EC Commission with the latter's case load. Between 1994 and 2001, the ESA was involved in assisting with or commenting on over 400 cases managed by the EC Commission. During the same period, the ESA took only two formal decisions finding infringements in competition matters.[79]

28.46 A detailed system of cooperation is also provided for in merger cases by virtue of Protocol 24. If a notification or complaint is not properly addressed to the competent authority, it will be transferred between the EC Commission and the ESA so as to reach the authority which has competence. Article 1(2) of Protocol 24 provides that the EC Commission and the ESA shall cooperate in those cases where the EC Commission has sole competence in relation to the merger, by virtue of Article 57(2)(a) of the EEA Agreement. In other words, where the EC Commission has competence in a 'mixed case', the ESA is still obliged to participate in the decision-making process. Article 2 further specifies that cooperation shall take place in one of five circumstances:

- the combined turnover of the undertakings concerned in the territory of the EFTA states equals 25 per cent or more of their total turnover within the territory covered by the Agreement;
- Each of at least two of the undertakings concerned has a turnover exceeding 250 million euros in the territory of the EFTA states;
- The concentration is liable to impede significantly effective competition in the territories of the EFTA states, or a substantial part thereof, in particular as a result of the creation or strengthening of a dominant position;
- The concentration fulfils the criteria for referral to the competent body of an EFTA state, under Article 6 of Protocol 24;
- Where an EFTA state wishes to take protective measures with regard to one of its legitimate interests, under Article 7 of Protocol 24.

28.47 Article 3 of Protocol 24 imposes a tight requirement on the EC Commission to transmit copies of the notifications to the ESA within a period of three days, but only in two situations: in cases where the 25 per cent turnover criterion is met; or where the concentration fulfils the criteria for an Article 6 referral to an EFTA state. In those two scenarios, the ESA also has a right to be represented at the hearings of the undertakings concerned, pursuant to Article 4 of Protocol 24. Close cooperation will take place with the relevant authority of the EFTA State in the case of an Article 6 referral. An Article 6 referral may take place where the concentration threatens to affect significantly competition in a market within a

[79] Both concerning the markets for round wood in Norway. See the summary given by the ESA on its website.

particular EFTA State, which presents all the characteristics of a distinct market. It may alternatively be referred where there is a lesser anti-competitive effect on such a distinct market, but that market does not constitute a substantial part of the territory covered by the Agreement.

In all other cases, the obligation on the Commission is merely to maintain 'close   **28.48** and constant liaison' with the ESA. The ESA is obliged to provide the EC Commission with administrative assistance in order to enable it to discharge its functions under Article 57 of the EEA Agreement.[80] The ESA and EFTA States are entitled to be present at meetings of the EC Advisory Committee on Concentrations and to express their views. They are not, however, given any voting rights.[81] The ESA is informed in advance of any interview by the EC Commission of a natural or legal person in the ESA's territory. The ESA has a right to attend such interviews.[82]

There has not yet been a merger case with an EFTA dimension dealt with by the   **28.49** ESA. In 2004, the ESA was involved in fourteen merger cases handled by the EC Commission. The new referral procedures contained in Article 6 of Protocol 24 were used for the first time in the *CVC Group/ANI Printing Inks* case. This was a referral to the Commission from Norway and eight Member States after a reasoned submission from the parties to the merger. The ESA acted in a liaison capacity between the EC Commission and the Norwegian national competition authorities.

E. Judicial Review

The Court of First Instance ('CFI') and the Court of Justice ('ECJ') hear appeals   **28.50** concerning decisions taken by the EC Commission in the competition field. The EFTA Court entertains appeals against competition appeals adopted by the ESA.[83] The two court systems operate in parallel and exchange information with each other on the development of their case law.

F. Rights of Lawyers

Individuals and undertakings have the right to be represented, before the CFI   **28.51** and ECJ as well as before the EFTA Court, by lawyers entitled to practice either before the EC or EFTA national courts. Lawyers of EC Member States

---

[80] Art 8 of Protocol 24 to the EEA Agreement.   [81] Art 5(3) of Protocol 24.
[82] Art 8(3) of Protocol 24.
[83] See Diem, 'EEA Competition Law' [1994] ECLR 263–71 n 3, 270.

and EFTA/EEA States further enjoy rights as to legal privilege, whether the proceeding is conducted by the EC Commission or the ESA, meaning that special protection is granted as regards their relationship with their clients.

IV. Practical procedural aspects in Articles 53 and 54 cases

A. The Former System of Notifications, Applications, and Complaints

28.52 Formerly, undertakings that wished to obtain a negative clearance or an individual exemption or partake in the 'opposition procedure' under various block exemption regulations had to notify their agreements or practices to the competent surveillance authority.[84] The ESA would be required to examine a case where an agreement was notified to it, an application was made for an individual exemption or where a complaint was received from another undertaking. It might also decide to investigate a matter on its own initiative. In fact, the ESA found that the majority of its cases were opened either as a result of complaints received or on the authority's own initiative. The ESA on average opened between ten and twelve new competition cases a year between 1994 and 2003. By the end of 2003, it had twenty-five pending cases awaiting resolution. Of these, eighteen had arisen from complaints.[85] By the end of 2004, the figure for pending cases handled by the ESA had dropped to nineteen the number of mixed antitrust cases handled by the EC Commission had risen to thirty-one.[86]

B. The New Decentralized Enforcement of the EEA Competition Rules

28.53 Neither Article 81(3) EC nor Article 53(3) EEA state who should (or could) grant exemptions from the provisions of Articles 81(1) and 53(1) respectively. The former regime[87] provided that only the competent surveillance authority, be it the Commission or the ESA, could grant individual exemptions. By 2003, however, it was considered that the centralized scheme no longer secured a

---

[84] The relevant rules were contained in the previous version of Protocol 23 to the EEA Agreement.
[85] See the Annual Report for 2003 (above n 51). 88 per cent of the ESA's cases between 1994 and 2003 related to Norway.
[86] See the Annual Report for 2004, available on the ESA's website.
[87] Under Reg 17/62 as transposed to the EEA context.

proper balance between effective supervision of the competition provisions and, as far as possible, a simplified administration. The centralized scheme for enforcement was felt to hamper the application of competition law by the courts and national competition authorities of the Member States. Further, the administrative burden of the notification scheme prevented the Commission from concentrating its resources on the most serious infringements. The Community therefore decided to decentralize the enforcement of competition law. It put in place a directly applicable 'exception system.' This permits both the national authorities and the courts of the Member States to consider Article 53 in its entirety and grant exemptions where they consider the relevant conditions are met. The system of notifications and applications for negative clearance and/or exemption has now been swept away.

C. The Main Features of the Decentralized Regime

The key features of the new regime are: 28.54

• The enforcement of Articles 53 and 54 in their entirety is now permitted by the national competition authorities and national courts of the EFTA/EEA States. Indeed, national authorities and national courts are obliged to apply these provisions to cases before them which may affect trade between EEA States when they apply national competition law. Further, they should also apply Article 54 EEA whenever they apply national competition law to any abuse prohibited by that Article. In order to ensure a level-playing field, national competition law can no longer prohibit agreements, decisions, or concerted practices which are not also prohibited by the EEA competition rules. Nonetheless, EFTA/EEA States will not be prevented from applying on their own territory stricter national laws which prohibit or sanction unilateral conduct engaged in by undertakings. Nor will EFTA/EEA States be precluded by these provisions from applying national laws which predominantly pursue an objective different from that of Articles 53 or 54 EEA.[88]

• Despite this decentralization, the Commission and the ESA retain a key role in the enforcement of the competition provisions. They will each be empowered to make a finding that there has been an infringement of the competition provisions. They may then take steps to terminate that infringement. The competent surveillance authorities are now empowered to impose

---

[88] See Art 3 of the Modernization Regulation, read together with Recitals (6)–(9) of the Preamble to the Reg; and Art 3 of Chapter II, Part I of Protocol 4 to the Surveillance and Court Agreement.

both structural and behavioural remedies where they find an infringement. Each is also empowered to impose interim measures and to accept binding commitments from an undertaking to cease its infringing behaviour. In addition, where the public interest so requires it, the ESA may, acting on its own initiative, make a finding that Articles 53 and/or 54 EEA are inapplicable to an agreement, decision, and concerted practice or to the actions or omissions of an undertaking in a dominant position.[89]

- The Commission, ESA, and national competition authorities of the EFTA/ EEA States will form a network of public authorities applying the Community and EEA competition rules. This will provide for close cooperation between the different bodies and for the exchange of information. The Modernization Regulation makes provision for the Commission to assume sole responsibility for the proceedings in a given case. Equivalent powers will be granted to the ESA. Provision is also made for determining which national competition authority should deal with a case where two or more are interested. The Advisory Committee on Restrictive Practices and Dominant Positions is retained. A network of cooperation is also envisaged between different national courts.[90]

- The Commission and ESA are permitted to carry out investigations into sectors of the economy or to specific types of agreement.[91] This enables them to investigate suspicious pricing structures across the board in a market or industry. It frees the surveillance authorities from the need to concentrate on one particular undertaking. This is a particularly valuable tool in newly liberalized sectors of the economy and emerging markets. It has been used effectively in the telecommunications sector, for example, the examination into international mobile phone roaming rates. A sector inquiry may lead to individual enforcement action in due course. The ESA retains powers to require undertakings to supply them with all necessary information. In addition, the surveillance authorities are empowered to take statements from the personnel of undertakings, carry out inspections and seek assistance from national competition authorities. This now expressly encompasses a power to carry out a search in the private homes of directors, subject to prior sanction from a national judicial authority. Officials from the competent surveillance

---

[89] See Arts 7 to 10 of the Modernization Reg, read together with Recitals (10) to (14) of the Preamble; and Arts 7–10 of Chapter II, Protocol 4.

[90] See Arts 11–16 of the Modernization Reg and Recitals (15)–(22) of the Preamble; and Arts 11–16 of Chapter II, Protocol 4.

[91] Under Art 17 of Chapter II, Protocol 4, the ESA may decide to conduct an inquiry into a particular sector of the economy or into particular types of agreements across various sectors. This will be done where the trend of trade between the EEA States, the rigidity of prices or other circumstances suggest that competition may be restricted or distorted within the territory covered by the EEA Agreement.

authority may also assist with investigations conducted by national competition authorities.[92]

• The ESA has the power to impose fines for breach of procedural requirements and for infringements of the substantive provisions of Articles 53 and 54 EEA. It is also authorized to impose periodic penalty payments on defaulters.[93]

• Provision is made for limitation periods governing both the powers exercised by the competent surveillance authority and the imposition of penalties under the Regulation.[94]

• The Modernization Regulation also provides for the rights of the defence in hearings involving parties, complainants and others. Protection is afforded for documents that are covered by obligations of professional secrecy.[95]

• The Recitals to the Preamble of the Modernization Regulation envisage the use of guidance letters by the competent surveillance authorities to ease uncertainty; and the application to the competition field of the principles contained in the Charter of Fundamental Rights of the European Union.[96]

D. Powers of the Competition Authorities and National Courts of EFTA/EEA States

The EEA Joint Committee Decision 130/2004 requires Articles 53 and 54 EEA **28.55** to be given direct effect to by both the national competition authorities of the EFTA/EEA States and by their national courts. The principle of direct effect has been recognized in the EFTA Court case law for some time.[97] Nonetheless, such domestic bodies will now be entitled to rule on whether or not agreements, decisions, or concerted practices of undertakings or associations of undertakings which otherwise fall within Article 53(1) may nonetheless be saved by the application of Article 53(3). This is not a case of the national competition authority or national court granting the undertaking in question an individual exemption. Instead, the national body will simply apply Article 53 as a whole. This change to the procedure has various consequences. First, undertakings will

---

[92] See Arts 17–22 and Recitals (23)–(28) to the Preamble; and Arts 17–22 of Chapter II, Protocol 4.

[93] Arts 23 and 24 of the Modernization Reg and Recitals (29) and (30) to the Preamble; Arts 23 and 24 of Chapter II, Protocol 4.

[94] Art 25 and 26 and Recital (31) to the Preamble; Arts 25 and 26 of Chapter II, Protocol 4.

[95] Arts 27 and 28 of the Modernization Regulation and Recital (32); Arts 27 and 28 of Chapter II, Protocol 4.

[96] Recitals (38) and (37) respectively.

[97] See Case E-1/94 *Ravintoloitsijain Liiton Kustannus Oy Restamark* (above n 72) para 78.

no longer be able to have the security blanket of an individual exemption for a particular agreement for a period of time. One can expect greater reliance on the block exemption regulations and a greater risk of multiple challenges to offending agreements, possibly across different jurisdictions. Secondly, the national competition authorities now have power to require that an infringement of Article 53 be brought to an end without waiting for a notification to the ESA to be dealt with. They also have greater powers for ordering interim measures, accepting commitments and imposing fines, periodic penalty payments and other penalties provided for under national law.

28.56 Both national competition authorities and national courts will have to pay heed to the Notices issued by the ESA. Such notices give (or will give once adopted) guidance equivalent to that found in the following Notices issued by the Commission:[98]

- Commission Notice on cooperation within the Network of Competition Authorities;[99]
- Commission Notice on the cooperation between the Commission and the courts of the EU Member States in the application of Articles 81 and 82 EC;[100]
- Commission Notice—Guidelines on the effect on trade concept contained in Articles 81 and 82 of the Treaty;[101]
- Communication from the Commission—Notice—Guidelines on the application of Article 81(3) of the Treaty.[102]

E. Powers of the ESA as a Competent Surveillance Authority under the New Regime

28.57 The ESA retains a major role in the enforcement of the competition rules in the EFTA/EEA States. This section will briefly examine the procedure likely to be adopted by the ESA during the course of a competition case under the new regime. These following procedural steps will be considered in turn:

(1) the opening of the case file;

(2) cooperation between the ESA and the Commission in the conduct of the proceedings;

(3) investigations and inquiries conducted by the ESA;

---

[98] By virtue of the provisions of Art 2 to Protocol 21 to the EEA Agreement.
[99] [2004] OJ C101/1, [2004] OJ C101/43.
[100] [2004] OJ C101/4, [2004] OJ C101/54.   [101] [2004] OJ C101/81.
[102] [2004] OJ C101/97.

(4) a formal or informal decision being taken by the ESA:

(5) the nature and extent of any remedies adopted by way of subsequent action.

1. The opening of the case

The case will be opened by the ESA upon receipt of a complaint, by the ESA of **28.58** its own initiative or upon the case being transmitted to it by the EC Commission. Historically, the majority of the cases before the ESA have arisen as a result of complaints. This trend is almost certain to continue now that the notification system has been abolished.

Complaints

Complaints may be lodged by either natural or legal persons who can show a **28.59** legitimate interest, or by one of the EEA/EFTA States (or Member States of the EU).[103] Article 11 of Protocol 23 provides that complaints may be made to either competent surveillance authority. A transfer system operates between the Commission and ESA so that any complaint should end up in the right hands even if it is technically addressed to the wrong authority.[104] A complaint may be rejected by the ESA without it formally initiating proceedings.[105]

Complaints should usually be made on the appropriate form C provided by **28.60** the competent surveillance authorities. They have to be submitted in one of the official languages of the Community or one of the official languages of the EFTA States.[106] This principle also applies as regards proceedings which are opened upon the ESA's own initiative.[107] In order to ensure a rapid and efficient procedure, undertakings have traditionally been encouraged to use one of the official or working languages of the respective surveillance authority that is responsible.[108] The address of the ESA for such complaints is 'EFTA Surveillance Authority, Competition Directorate, Rue Belliard 35, B-1040 Brussels, Belgium' and its telephone number is (+32)(0)2 286 18 11.

---

[103] See Art 7(2) of the Modernization Reg; Art 5(1) of the Implementing Reg; and Arts 5–7 of Chapter III to Protocol 4.

[104] See s IV.E.(1)(c) below.   [105] Art 2(4) of Chapter III to Protocol 4.

[106] See Art 5(3) of Chapter III to Protocol 4 and Art 12 of Protocol 23 to the EEA Agreement.

[107] Art 12 of Protocol 23 provides that this choice of language 'shall also cover all instances of a proceeding, whether it be opened following a complaint or *ex officio* by the competent surveillance authority.'

[108] It should be noted that English (an official language of the Community) is the working language of the ESA, in addition to one of the official languages of the EFTA States. In practice, therefore, it may be easier for undertakings, if not to choose English as the language of the proceedings, then at least to submit a translation of all documentation into English, which satisfies the requirements of both the Commission and the ESA.

Cases opened on the ESA's own initiative

28.61 The ESA may decide to initiate proceedings with a view to adopting one of the various decisions open to it under Section III of Chapter II of Protocol 4 to the Surveillance and Court Agreement. Such proceedings may be initiated at any stage, but no later than the earliest of the dates on which either it:[109]

    (i) issues a preliminary assessment, pursuant to Article 9(1) of Chapter II to Protocol 4;

    (ii) issues a statement of objections; or

    (iii) publishes a notice under Article 27(4) of Chapter II to Protocol 4.

28.62 Each of these stages might be considered to be already part of the 'procedure' opened by the ESA. Nonetheless, Article 2(3) of Chapter III to Protocol 4 expressly provides that the ESA may exercise its powers of investigation prior to initiating formal proceedings as such. It would seem that proceedings are initiated when the ESA forms a view that it might adopt one of the decisions set out in Section III of Chapter II to Protocol 4 (i.e. a finding of an infringement, an interim measure, an acceptance of a commitment or a finding of inapplicability). The ESA is required to inform the parties concerned that it has initiated proceedings and may then make the initiation public in an appropriate way.[110]

Transfer of cases

28.63 If a complaint is addressed to a surveillance authority that is not competent to decide on a given case under Article 56 EEA, then it must be transferred without delay to the other competent surveillance authority.[111] Similarly, if during the course of the Commission's investigation it becomes apparent that the case should properly be with the ESA, it will also be transferred.[112] In order to avoid cases being transferred several times between the authorities, such individual cases may not be re-transmitted to the initial surveillance authority once a transfer of the file has taken place.[113] Further, once a case has reached a certain point, it cannot be transferred between the two competent authorities. This cut-off arises when either:

    (i) the statement of objections has been sent to the undertaking(s) or association(s) of undertakings concerned;

    (ii) a letter has been sent to the complainant informing him that there are insufficient grounds for pursuing the complaint;

    (iii) the publication of the intention to adopt a decision declaring Article 53 or 54 not applicable, or

---

[109] Art 2(1) of Chapter III to Protocol 4.
[110] Art 2(2) of Chapter III to Protocol 4.   [111] Art 11(1) of Protocol 23.
[112] Art 11(2) of Protocol 23.   [113] See Art 11(3) of Protocol 23.

(iv) the publication of the intention to adopt a decision making commitments offered by the undertaking(s) binding on the undertaking(s).

New or transferred proceedings before the EC Commission (instigated either on the basis of complaints or on the Commission's own initiative) will take into account the EEA competition provisions where appropriate. In either event, the decision should refer to the relevant provisions.   **28.64**

2. Cooperation between the ESA and the Commission in the conduct of the proceedings

In order to make the cooperation between the surveillance authorities effective, exchange of information and consultation between the surveillance authorities takes place at different stages of the proceeding.[114] A task force consisting of representatives from the Commission and from the ESA has prepared pro-forma letters which are used in this consultation process and this should ensure an uncomplicated implementation of the cooperation procedure. The surveillance authority with initial responsibility for the conduct of the case first examines whether the case appears to have a 'mixed' nature. That is, whether it is likely to produce effects both within the common market and within the EFTA territory.[115] Each surveillance authority generally only has a right to be consulted or informed in 'mixed cases'. In practice, however, the two authorities liaise very closely with each other all the time. In relation to 'mixed cases', the ESA will inform the Commission both when it decides to open an *ex officio* procedure on its own initiative; and where it receives a complaint where it is not clear that it has also been received by the Commission.[116] It will also let the Commission know when formal investigative measures have been started by one of the national competition authorities within the ESA's territory. The Commission may present comments within thirty days of receipt of the information. This facilitates the operation of the transfer mechanism described above. In practice, this also means that the ESA will refrain from taking any definitive measures[117] within those thirty days which might pre-empt any observations that are received. Further consultation takes place when a competent surveillance authority is:[118]   **28.65**

• addressing to undertakings a statement of objections;
• publishing its intention to adopt a decision declaring Article 53 or 54 of the Agreement not applicable; or

---

[114] See Art 58 of the EEA Agreement and Protocol 23 attached thereto.
[115] A practical indication to be considered is, in particular, whether turnover is apparent in both territories.
[116] Art 2 of Protocol 23 to the EEA Agreement.
[117] Conversely, this means that urgent or provisional measures could be taken.
[118] See Art 3 to Protocol 23.

- publishing its intention to adopt a decision making commitments offered by the undertakings binding on the undertakings.

28.66 The surveillance authority which is consulted makes its comments within the same time limits as set out in the publication or in the statement of objections. Observations received from the undertakings involved or comments received from third parties as a result of the communications mentioned above are similarly transmitted between the two authorities.[119] The surveillance authorities inform each other if an individual case is settled by a formal decision. Transmission of copies of the administrative letters by which a file is closed or a complaint is rejected is also provided for.[120] More generally, in 'mixed cases', the surveillance authority not in charge of the matter may request at any stage of proceedings copies of the most important documents lodged and filed with their counterpart.[121] The authorities may also, at any stage before a final decision is made, submit any observations it considers appropriate. For the purpose of applying Articles 53 and 54 of the EEA Agreement, the ESA and the EC Commission have the power to provide one another with any matter of fact or of law, including confidential information.[122] Nonetheless, such information may only be used in evidence by the receiving surveillance authority for the purpose of procedures under Articles 53 and 54 EEA and in respect of the subject matter for which it was collected.[123] Detailed rules govern evidence obtained under the application of a leniency programme.[124] Information may also be passed on to national competition authorities.[125]

28.67 The provisions guaranteeing professional secrecy and ensuring restricted use of information apply both to information received by the surveillance authorities on the basis of their own internal rules and to the information that is received in the context of cooperation and administrative assistance between the surveillance authorities and national competition authorities. Neither the surveillance authorities nor the competent authorities of Member States and EFTA States may disclose any information covered by the obligation of professional secrecy and obtained in the course of EEA competition procedures. This limitation applies equally to officials and employees of any such authority.[126] These rules (and any national rules protecting professional secrecy) will not, however, prevent the exchange of information envisaged by the Protocol itself.[127]

---

[119] Art 3(2) and (2) of Protocol 23.   [120] See Art 4 of Protocol 23.
[121] See Art 7 of Protocol 23.   [122] Art 9(1) of Protocol 23.
[123] Art 9(2) of Protocol 23.
[124] Art 9(3) to (5) of Protocol 23; and Arts 11A and 11B of Chapter II to Protocol 4 to the Surveillance and Court Agreement.
[125] Art 10(1) of Protocol 23.
[126] See Reg 28 of the Modernization Reg and Art 10(2) of Protocol 23.
[127] Art 10(3) of Protocol 23.

Further, when the competent surveillance authority either requests or, by **28.68** decision, requires an undertaking or association of undertakings located within the territory of the other surveillance authority to supply information, it shall at the same time forward a copy of the request or decision to the other surveillance authority.[128] Cooperation between the two authorities also takes place with regard to investigations and inspections[129] and hearings[130] (both addressed below). Protocol 23 to the EEA Agreement establishes a procedure for cooperation in the context of the Advisory Committee on Restrictive Practices and Dominant Positions. Whenever an Advisory Committee is to be convened before a final decision is taken by one of the surveillance authorities, the latter is obliged to inform the other authority of the date of the Advisory Committee meeting and transmit any relevant documentation.[131] The other surveillance authority as well as representatives of the States of its territory have the right to attend the meetings and to express their views at it. There is, however, no attendant right to vote at such meetings.[132] The consultation process may be conducted as a written procedure unless a request is made for an oral hearing by the non-competent surveillance authority.[133]

3. Investigations and inquiries conducted by the ESA

As indicated above, the EC Commission and the ESA will follow the same **28.69** procedural rules,[134] namely those which are in use in the EC (listed in Article 3 of Protocol 21 to the EEA Agreement). In the context of the EEA Agreement, some more particular aspects should be observed. The ESA will be able to investigate not simply individual agreements or abuses, but also particular sectors of the economy or particular types of agreement.[135] It is open to the ESA in such circumstances to publish a report of its inquiry and simultaneously to take action against individual infringements. In the course of its inquiry, the ESA may request that undertakings supply it with all information necessary to give effect to Articles 53 and 54 EEA. It may also carry out inspections for that purpose.

The ESA also has more general powers to obtain information from undertak- **28.70** ings.[136] First, the ESA may by simple request or by decision require undertak-

---

[128] Art 8(1) of Protocol 23.   [129] Art 8(2) to (6) of Protocol 23.
[130] Art 5 of Protocol 23.
[131] See Art 6(1) of Protocol 23; and Art 14 of Chapter II to Protocol 4.
[132] See Art 6(2) and (3) of Protocol 23.   [133] Art 6(4) of Protocol 23.
[134] See Art 1 of Protocol 21. Chapters II and III to Protocol 4 to the Court and Surveillance Agreement reproduce (with adaptations for the EEA context) the procedural rules applied by the Commission in competition cases.
[135] Art 17 of Chapter II to Protocol 4.
[136] Arts 18 to 22 of Chapter II to Protocol 4.

ings to provide all necessary information to it.[137] Whichever course is adopted, the request or decision must identify the information to be provided and the time-limit within which the information is to be produced. The communication should also set out the penalties which might be levied under Article 23 of Chapter II in the event that the ESA is supplied with incorrect or misleading information. If a formal decision is taken requiring information to be supplied, the decision should additionally set out the periodic penalty payments which can be charged under Article 24 in the event that no correct information is forthcoming. The final amount of the periodic penalty payments may, where necessary, be fixed at a later date.

28.71 Secondly, the ESA may interview any natural or legal person who consents to be interviewed for the purpose of collecting information relating to the subject-matter of an investigation.[138] This may be carried out in co-operation with the authorities of the EEA/EFTA state in whose territory the interview takes place. The ESA may also interview a consenting natural or legal person in the Commission's territory. If it does so, it must inform the Commission. Both the Commission and officials from the national competition authority of the Member State concerned are entitled to be present.[139] The interviewer must state the legal basis for the interview at its inception. He or she must also reiterate its voluntary nature and inform the interviewee that a record of the interview will be taken.[140]

28.72 Thirdly, the ESA may conduct inspections of undertakings.[141] Inspections may take place of premises, land, or means of transport. Written authorization for inspections must be obtained from the ESA. The authorization stipulates the subject-matter and purpose of the inspection. The ESA may adopt a formal decision requiring an undertaking to submit to an inspection. This is adopted only after consultation by the ESA with the competition authority of the EEA/EFTA State in whose territory the inspection is to take place. The ESA may call on the assistance of the competition and police authorities of that EEA/EFTA state, if necessary with prior judicial approval from the state in question. This allows the ESA to make unannounced 'dawn raids' if there is a danger that evidence will be tampered with otherwise. Inspections may also be carried out at the premises of other third parties, such as directors, managers, and other members of staff of the undertaking concerned. This can include the homes of the persons concerned. There must be a reasonable suspicion that business books or records may be found there (which may prove a serious violation of Articles 53 and 54 EEA) before such an inspection will be permitted.[142] Furthermore, an

---

[137] See Art 18(1) of Chapter II to Protocol 4.   [138] Art 19 of Chapter II to Protocol 4.
[139] Art 8(6) of Protocol 23.   [140] Art 3(1) of Chapter III to Protocol 4.
[141] Art 20 of Chapter II to Protocol 4.   [142] Art 21 of Chapter II to Protocol 4.

additional safeguard is that prior authorization from the national judicial authority of the EFTA/EEA state concerned must be obtained.[143] Officials and other accompanying persons authorised by the ESA to conduct an inspection are empowered to:[144]

(a) enter the undertaking's premises;

(b) examine the books and records of the undertaking, in whatever medium they may be stored;

(c) take or obtain copies of the business records;

(d) seal the business premises and records for the period necessary for the inspection;

(e) ask questions of representatives of the undertaking (or members of its staff) seeking explanations for any fact or document relating to the subject-matter and purpose of the inspection and to record the answers.

Each surveillance authority informs the other of the fact that inspections have taken place and will receive upon request a note of the outcome of these investigations.[145]

Fourthly, the ESA may consider that inspections in the territory of the Commission (as the other surveillance authority) are necessary. If a request is made to this effect, an inspection must be organized and carried out by the Commission. The inspection will be conducted in accordance with the Commission's own internal rules, but the ESA will be entitled to be present.[146] Finally, the ESA may enlist the administrative assistance of the national competition authorities of the EEA/EFTA states to carry out their own inspections or fact-finding missions on behalf of the ESA or the Commission.[147] Indeed, it is relatively common for coordinated inspections to be instigated simultaneously in both the EC and EFTA territories, involving close cooperation between the Commission, the ESA and national competition authorities. **28.73**

Undertakings involved in competition procedures have the right to be heard in a certain number of instances, including the right to make written observations.[148] Such written observations—as well as observations from third parties— shall be transmitted to the other surveillance authority for information. Where an oral hearing is organized in a 'mixed case', the competent surveillance authority must invite its counterpart to be represented and extend the invitation to representatives of States of the other territory, which both have the right to **28.74**

---

[143] Art 21(3) of Chapter II to Protocol 4.

[144] Art 20(2) of Chapter II to Protocol 4.

[145] See Art 8(5) of Protocol 23 to the EEA Agreement.

[146] See Art 8(2) and (3) of Protocol 23.   [147] Art 22 of Chapter II to Protocol 4.

[148] See generally Art 27 of Chapter II to Protocol 4; and Arts 10 to 14 of Chapter III.

attend such hearings.[149] Ordinarily the right to be heard will be accompanied by a right to have access to the ESA's file of documents.[150] This ensures equality of arms. Nonetheless, when the ESA grants access to the file to recipients of a statement of objections, the right does not extend to internal documents of the Commission or of the competition authorities of the EC Member States and the EFTA States involved. Nor does the right of access to the file extend to correspondence between the surveillance authorities, between a surveillance authority and the competition authorities of the EC Member States or EFTA States or between the competition authorities of the EC Member States or EFTA States where such correspondence is contained in the file of the competent surveillance authority.[151] The EEA has made similar provision for the appointment of a hearing officer to that found in EC law. The main task of the hearing officer is to ensure that the procedural rights of the parties involved in competition proceedings are respected.[152] He or she will determine any dispute about access to the file and ensure that business secrets and professional confidentiality are maintained.[153]

28.75 In order to encourage undertakings to blow the whistle on anti-competitive practices and agreements, the ESA has adopted a leniency programme in similar terms to that adopted by the Commission.[154] The adoption of a formal programme was a response to two developments. First, the desire of the EC Commission and the ESA to concentrate their efforts on hard-core cartels that have a significant impact on competition. Secondly, the need to fight against increasingly sophisticated methods adopted by cartelists in the coordination of their behaviour. The ESA will accordingly grant total immunity from fines to the first company to submit evidence on a cartel unknown to, or unproved by, the ESA where it is competent to handle the case. This takes two forms. First, total immunity will be granted to the first member of a cartel to provide sufficient information to allow the ESA to launch an inspection on the premises of the suspected cartelists. Secondly, in cases where the existence of the cartel has already been discovered, such immunity will alternatively be afforded to the first

---

[149] See Art 5 of Protocol 23.

[150] See Arts 15 and 16 of Chapter III to Protocol 4.

[151] Art 10A of Protocol 23.

[152] Provision is made for the appointment and functions of a hearing officer in College Decision No 177/02/COL from the ESA, dated 30 October 2002, on the terms of reference of Hearing Officers in certain competition proceedings. See [2002] OJ L80/27 and EEA Supplement No 16, 27 March 2003, 2.

[153] See Art 122 EEA which imposes an obligation on both EFTA States and officials acting under the EEA Agreement not to disclose information of a kind covered by the obligation of professional secrecy or business sensitive information.

[154] See Notice on Immunity from fines and reduction of fines in cartel cases [2003] OJ C10/13, and EEA Supplement to the OJ No 3, 16 January 2003, 1.

member of a cartel to provide evidence which enables the ESA to establish an infringement of Article 53 EEA. This alternative immunity only applies where a member of the cartel has not benefited from the first type of immunity. The ESA expects full and continuous cooperation if immunity is to be awarded. The ESA also operates a rewards system falling short of full immunity. Fines may be reduced in respect of undertakings whose evidence provides 'significant added value' to the prosecution of an infringement. A tiered approach to reductions is adopted, so that the first in time to provide such evidence will be given a reduction of 30 to 50 per cent of the fine imposed, with reductions tapering down for subsequent informants. Any decision will be confirmed in a formal letter.

4. Formal and informal decisions taken by the ESA

There are a number of formal decisions which the ESA may take in respect of **28.76** agreements or abuses that fall within its jurisdiction:

- The ESA may address to undertakings or associations of undertakings decisions which bring to an end any infringement of Articles 53 or 54 EEA.[155] If a legitimate interest is served by it, the ESA may also adopt a decision finding that an infringement of the competition provisions occurred in the past. This is so even if the ESA does not proceed to impose any fines on the undertakings concerned.[156]

- The ESA is also empowered to adopt interim measures in cases of urgency. The urgency must stem from the risk of serious and irreparable damage to competition. In addition, the ESA must show that there is a prima facie finding of an infringement.[157]

- The ESA may also adopt a decision making commitments offered by the parties binding on those parties.[158]

- In exceptional circumstances, where the public interest of the Community requires it, the ESA may also make a finding of non-applicability. This consists in a declaration from the ESA that the provisions of Article 53 and/or 54 do not apply. The purpose behind this is to clarify the law and ensure the consistent application of the competition provisions throughout the EFTA territory.[159] The recital to the Modernization Regulation envisages that this will be of particular use in relation to new agreements, for which existing case law and administrative practice may provide an uncertain guide.

---

[155] Arts 5 and 7(1) of Chapter II to Protocol 4.
[156] See Recital (11) to the Modernization Regulation and Art 7(1); Art 7(1) of Chapter II.
[157] Recital (11) and Art 8 of the Modernization Regulation; Art 8 of Chapter II.
[158] Art 9 of Chapter II to Protocol 4.
[159] Recital (14) and Art 10 of the Modernization Regulation; Art 10 of Chapter II.

- Finally, the ESA may withdraw the benefit of a block exemption where the agreement, decision or concerted practice in question produces effects that are incompatible with Article 53(3) EEA.[160] This power is exercised by the ESA either on the basis of complaints made to it; or on its own initiative.

28.77 An obligation is imposed on the ESA by Article 30 of Chapter II to Protocol 4 to the Surveillance and Court Agreement to publish any such formal decisions which it takes. In addition, the ESA may decide that on the basis of the information in its possession, there are insufficient grounds for acting on a complaint.[161] If so, the ESA is required to inform the complainant of the reasons for its decision. It must also set a time-limit within which the complainant must set out its views in writing. If the further views provided do not persuade the ESA to change its proposed course of action, a decision rejecting the complaint must be taken. If no views are made known within that period, the complaint is deemed to have been withdrawn.[162] The ESA will no longer provide 'comfort' or 'discomfort' letters to undertakings within its territory. A Notice equivalent to the Commission's Notice on informal guidance relating to novel questions concerning Articles 81 and 82 of the EC Treaty that arise in individual cases (guidance letters)[163] has, however, been adopted by the ESA on 18 May 2005. The ESA may issue guidance letters to concerned undertakings.

5. The nature and extent of any remedies adopted by way of subsequent action

28.78 Once the ESA has made a finding of an infringement of Articles 53 and/or 54, it may take various steps to ensure that the infringement is effectively terminated. The power to adopt remedies is subject, however, to the requirement that any remedy proposed should be proportionate.[164] The Modernization Regulation and the equivalent provisions in Protocol 4 for the first time envisage the use by the competent competition authorities of structural as well as behavioural remedies. This is permissible only where there is no equally effective behavioural remedy or where any equally effective behavioural remedy would in fact be more burdensome on the undertaking than the structural remedy initially proposed.[165] The relevant provisions make clear that changes to the structure of the undertaking will only be proportionate where there is a substantial risk of a lasting or repeated infringement of the competition provisions that derives from the very structure of the undertaking itself. The ESA may also accept

---

[160] Art 29 of Chapter II. [161] See Art 7 of Chapter III.
[162] Art 7(3) of Chapter III. [163] [2004] OJ C101/78.
[164] Art 7(1) of Chapter II to Protocol 4.
[165] Recital (12) to and Art 7(1) of the Modernization Regulation; Art 7(1) of Chapter II to Protocol 4.

commitments offered by undertakings which meet its concerns. Protocol 4 makes provision for these commitments to be binding on the undertakings which have given them.[166] Decisions as to commitments may be specified to last for a specified period. The decision must also state that there are no longer any grounds for action by the ESA. Nonetheless, the ESA may re-open their proceedings despite commitments having been given in three situations: (i) where there has been a material change in the facts underpinning the decision; (ii) where the undertaking has acted contrary to its commitments given; or (iii) where the initial decision was based on incomplete, incorrect or misleading information given by the parties. Nonetheless, the adoption of a binding commitments decision does not preclude the competition authorities or courts of the EFTA/EEA States from making their own finding of an infringement of Articles 53 and/or 54 EEA.[167]

In respect of failures by undertakings to comply properly or at all with requests for information or disclosure of business records or for breaking seals affixed by ESA officials, the ESA has power to impose fines of up to 1 per cent of the total turnover of the undertakings concerned for the preceding business year.[168] Fines of up to 10 per cent of such turnover may be imposed for substantive infringements of the competition provisions or a failure to comply with binding commitments.[169] Periodic penalty payments may also be levied in respect of continued failures to bring infringements to an end; to comply with decisions ordering interim measures; to comply with commitments; supply complete and correct information or to submit to an inspection ordered by decision.[170] There is a limitation period of three years for imposing procedural penalties and a limit of five years for the imposition of fines for substantive infringements. **28.79**

V. Practical procedural aspects in merger cases

A. The Adoption of the Revised Merger Regulation

Procedural rules governing the control of mergers under the EEA Agreement are to be found in the amended versions of Annex XIV and Protocol 24 to the EEA Agreement, and in Part III of Protocol 4 to the Surveillance and Court **28.80**

---

[166] See Recital (13) to the Modernization Regulation and Art 9; Art 9 of Chapter II to Protocol 4.
[167] See Recital (13).
[168] Art 23(1) of the Modernization Regulation; Art 23(1) of Chapter II to Protocol 4.
[169] Art 23(2) of Chapter II to Protocol 4.
[170] Art 24(1) of Chapter II to Protocol 4.

Agreement. Part III to Protocol 4 contains two separate chapters. Chapter XIII contains rules relating to the control of concentrations between undertakings. Chapter XIV contains rules on the notifications, time-limits, and hearings in the field of the control of concentrations.

28.81 The changes introduced to the EEA Agreement in June 2004 give effect to the revised EC Merger Regulation and the Implementing Regulation. The new legislation clarifies the substantive test applied in challenging a concentration. In keeping with the changes to EU merger control, it moves the analysis from an examination solely of dominance to an examination of whether a concentration would significantly impede competition in the relevant market (albeit within which analysis dominance will continue to be highly relevant). It also elaborates on the pre-existing 'one-stop shop' principle behind merger control through the adoption of a more streamlined referral system in certain circumstances. Where a merger raises an EFTA dimension and is to be dealt with by the ESA, the application of national merger provisions is precluded.[171]

B. Pre-Notification Procedures

28.82 As with the EC Merger Regulation, certain pre-notification procedures are available to the parties to a concentration. The procedures are slightly different, depending on whether or not the concentration has an EFTA dimension.

28.83 Prior to the notification of a concentration with an EFTA dimension, the parties can send a reasoned submission requesting that their concentration be looked at in whole or in part by an EFTA State. In order to benefit from the referral, certain criteria must be met.[172] These are that the concentration must significantly affect competition in a market within an EFTA State which presents all the characteristics of a distinct market and which should therefore be examined, in whole or in part, by that EFTA State. The ESA transmits the reasoned submission to all the EFTA States. The EFTA State that is the subject-matter of the request then has a period of fifteen days within which to confirm its agreement or disagreement to the proposed referral. A failure to reply constitutes a deemed acceptance. Unless the EFTA State disagrees, the ESA must consider whether or not the criteria are met. If they are, the case can be transferred in whole or in part to the national competition authorities of the EFTA State. The ESA has a time-limit of twenty-five days in which to make its assessment from

---

[171] Art 21 of Chapter XIII, Part III, Protocol 4 to the Surveillance and Court Agreement.
[172] Art 4(4) of Part III, Chapter XIII to Protocol 4 to the Surveillance and Court Agreement.

date of receipt of the reasoned submission. A failure to respond leads to a deemed decision to refer. If a referral is made, no notification is needed and the matter is dealt with by the relevant national competition authorities. An equivalent procedure is also available to the EC Commission (who may refer the case to an EFTA state) in a concentration in a mixed case, pursuant to Article 6(4) of Protocol 24 to the EEA Agreement.

If the concentration does not have an EFTA dimension, the parties may none-   **28.84**
theless request that it be treated as if it did have an EFTA dimension and ask for it to be assessed by the ESA if certain criteria are met.[173] The concentration must be capable of being reviewed under the national competition laws of at least three EFTA states. The request is made by means of a reasoned submission. The request is transmitted to the EFTA States. The onus is then on any EFTA state within fifteen days to lodge its disagreement to the proposed transfer of competence. If disagreement is expressed, the case is not transferred. Otherwise the case is deemed to have an EFTA dimension and will be dealt with by the ESA. Again, an equivalent power is bestowed upon the Commission in a mixed case, under Article 6(5) of Protocol 24. The difference is that the merger must be capable of being reviewed under the national competition laws of at least three EC Member States and one EFTA State. This was the procedure adopted in the *CVC Group/ANI Printing Inks* case referred to above.

C. Notifications of Concentrations

Notification of a concentration with an EFTA dimension is mandatory. With   **28.85**
certain limited exceptions, it cannot be implemented before its notification or until after it has been declared compatible with the EEA Agreement.[174] Notification is now possible on the basis of a good-faith intent to merge, without the need for a formal, binding agreement.

The procedure for notifying a concentration is virtually identical to that found   **28.86**
in Community law. A Form CO is used.[175] Certain information and documents are required to be provided.[176] Notifications may be in an official language either of the EFTA States or of the Community.[177] Nonetheless, if a language is used which is not an official language of the EFTA States or the working language of the ESA (i.e. any Community language other than English), a translation into

---

[173] Art 4(5) of Part III to Protocol 4.

[174] Art 7, Part III, Chapter XIII to Protocol 4. The exceptions relate to the implementation of a public bid or a series of transactions in securities, subject to conditions laid down in Art 7.

[175] Art 2 of Chapter XIV, Part III to Protocol 4 to the Surveillance and Court Agreement.

[176] Art 3 of Chapter XIV.   [177] See also Art 12 of Protocol 24 to the EEA Agreement.

one of the official languages or into the working language of all documents must be provided. The standard requirements for documentation apply, subject to any dispensation that may be granted by the ESA.[178] The effective date of notification is the date of receipt by the ESA.[179] Copies of any notification and the important documents will be transmitted to the competent authorities of the EFTA States within three working days.

D. Procedure Once Notified

28.87 The ESA is obliged to consider the notification as soon as it is received.[180] It may take one of the following decisions:

- Make a finding (in a formal decision) that the concentration does not fall within the scope of the revised Merger Regulation as applied under EEA law.

- Make a decision not to oppose the concentration and to declare it compatible with the EEA Agreement.[181]

- Initiate proceedings (i.e. move to Phase 2) if it considers that the concentration falls within the scope of the relevant provisions and there are serious doubts as to its compatibility with the EEA Agreement.

- If a concentration is modified to the ESA's satisfaction, it is open to the ESA to make a subsequent declaration of compatibility.[182]

28.88 The ESA has the power in Phase 2 of the procedure to declare a concentration compatible with the EEA agreement if the relevant substantive criteria are fulfilled. The relevant substantive criteria are found in Article 2(2) of the Merger Regulation and, in certain other cases, the criteria contained in Article 53(3) EEA.[183] The ESA has power to attach conditions to a concentration or require commitments to be given before clearing it.[184] A decision declaring the concentration compatible with the EEA Agreement can be made once the original concentration has been modified to the ESA's satisfaction.[185] It also has the power to declare the concentration incompatible with the EEA Agreement. If the ESA finds that an incompatible concentration has been implemented or that

---

[178] Art 3 of Chapter XIV, Part III to Protocol 4.

[179] Art 4 of Chapter XIV, Part III to Protocol 4; and Arts 10 and 11 of Protocol 24.

[180] Art 6(1) of Part III, Chapter XIII to Protocol 4 of the Surveillance and Court Agreement.

[181] These first two types of decision are revocable if they were based on incorrect information. See Art 6(3) of Part III, Chapter XIII.

[182] Art 6(2) of Part III, Chapter XIII.

[183] Art 8(1) of Chapter XIII, Part III to Protocol 4.

[184] Arts 18 and 19 of Chapter XIV to Protocol 4.

[185] Art 8(2) of Chapter XIII.

a condition has not been complied with, a wide range of remedial powers are available to it.[186] These mirror the powers available to the EC Commission. They include the power to require the merger to be dissolved, restorative measures to be taken and/or any other appropriate measure. They also include the power to take appropriate interim measures.[187]

Decisions are taken after consultation with the Advisory Committee on Concentrations and in liaison with the competent authorities of the EFTA States.[188] They are published in the EEA Section of the Official Journal of the European Communities. There are strict time-limits for Phase 1 decisions and more relaxed time limits for Phase 2 decisions, in keeping with the EU approach.[189] Time-limits may be suspended in certain circumstances.[190] **28.89**

In addition, certain other referral procedures are available following notification of a concentration: **28.90**

- After notification of a concentration without a Community dimension, an EFTA State may join a request made by one or more EU States requesting that the Commission examine the concentration.

- After notification of a concentration with an EFTA dimension, an EFTA State may request a transfer to its national competition authority. The ESA may refer a notified concentration, in whole or in part, to an EFTA State in which the concentration threatens significantly to affect competition in a market within that EFTA State, which has the characteristics of a distinct market. The same procedure is also available where the concentration affects competition in a market within that EFTA State, which presents the characteristics of a distinct market and which does not constitute a substantial part of the territory of the EFTA States.[191] An equivalent power is open to the EC Commission under Article 6 of Protocol 24 to the EEA Agreement.

- After notification of a concentration, or otherwise when a concentration is made known to an EFTA State, that State may request the ESA to examine a concentration that does not have an EFTA dimension.[192] Any such request must be made within fifteen days of the concentration coming to the EFTA State's attention. It will be transmitted to the other EFTA States, who may join in the request. The ESA may decide to examine the concentration if it affects trade between EFTA States and threatens significantly to affect com-

---

[186] Art 8(4) of Chapter XIII. [187] Art 8(5) of Chapter XIII.
[188] Art 19 of Chapter XIII. [189] Art 10 of Chapter XIII.
[190] See, e.g. Arts 8(7) and 10(4) of Chapter XIII.
[191] Art 9(2) of Chapter XIII to Protocol 4;
[192] Art 22 of Chapter XIII to Protocol 4.

petition within the territory of the EFTA State or States making the request. The ESA has ten days to decide whether or not to take the case over.

E. Powers Available to the ESA in Dealing with Merger Cases

28.91 The ESA has been granted the usual range of powers to enable it to discharge its functions, including the ability to make requests for information,[193] conduct interviews,[194] organize inspections to be carried out by the national competition authorities of the EFTA States, or conduct its own inspections,[195] and impose fines and periodic penalty payments in an equivalent range of circumstances to that found under EC law.[196] Similar provision is also made for protecting professional secrecy,[197] and for the conduct of any hearings involving the merging parties and any third parties.[198]

VI. An overview of the EEA provisions on State aids

A. Introduction

28.92 The EEA Agreement follows the EC Treaty in establishing a general prohibition on measures taken by contracting parties that are likely to distort competition by favouring certain industries or enterprises. This prohibition is subject to exemption if certain conditions are met. A wide definition is given to State aid. It encompasses not merely old-style subsidies to national industries, but other forms of State intervention or assistance, such as preferential tax treatment,[199] favourable loans,[200] or trading guarantees provided by public bodies. The ESA is required to approve any new State aid measures. It also supervises and proposes appropriate measures against existing aid.[201]

---

[193] Art 11 of Chapter XIII, Part III of Protocol 4 to the Surveillance and Court Agreement.
[194] Art 11(7) of Chapter XIII.   [195] Arts 12 and 13 of Chapter XIII.
[196] Arts 14 and 15 of Chapter XIII.
[197] Art 17 of Chapter XIII; Art 17 of Chapter XIV.
[198] Art 18 of Chapter XIII; Arts 11 to 16 of Chapter XIV.
[199] See, e.g. Case E-6/98 *Norway v ESA* [1998] EFTA Court Rep 242, [1999] 2 CMLR 1033.
[200] See, e.g. Case E-4/97 *Norwegian Bankers' Association v ESA (No 2)* [1999] 4 CMLR 1292.
[201] See, in particular, the website maintained by the ESA—www.eftasurv.int/about/.

B. The Basic Provisions

The substantive provisions on State aids under the EEA Agreement are con-   **28.93**
tained in Articles 61 to 63 EEA. Article 61 EEA states that any aid granted by
EC Member States, EFTA States or through State resources in any form whatsoever which distorts or threatens to distort competition by favouring certain
undertakings or the production of certain goods is in principle incompatible
with the functioning of the EEA Agreement in so far as it affects trade between
Contracting Parties. Article 61(2) provides a list of compatible aids, which is
mandatory in its terms. Three types of aid must be declared compatible by the
ESA:

- aid having a social character, granted to individual consumers, provided that
  such aid is granted without discrimination related to the origin of the products concerned;
- aid granted to make good damage caused by natural disasters or exceptional
  occurrences;
- aid granted to the economy of certain areas of the Federal Republic of Germany affected by the division of Germany, in so far as such aid is required in
  order to compensate for the economic disadvantages caused by that division.

In contrast, Article 61(3) sets out the types of aid which may, in the discretion of   **28.94**
the ESA, be considered to be compatible with the EEA Agreement. The four
categories are:

- aid to promote the economic development of areas where the standard of
  living is abnormally low or where there is serious underemployment;
- aid to promote the execution of an important project of common European
  interest or to remedy a serious disturbance in the economy of an EC Member
  State or an EFTA State;
- aid to facilitate the development of certain economic activities or of certain
  economic areas, where such aid does not adversely affect trading conditions to
  an extent contrary to the common interest;
- such other categories of aid as may be specified by the EEA Joint Committee
  in accordance with Part VII.

Article 62 also requires the ESA to conduct a constant review of existing meas-   **28.95**
ures of aid found in EFTA States and to assess their compatibility with Article
61 EEA. For this purpose, Article 62 confers on the ESA the powers and
functions described in Protocol 26. Further, Article 62(2) provides for cooperation between the EC Commission and the ESA on matters relating to
State aid, in accordance with the provisions of Protocol 27.

28.96 The rules on State aid in an EEA context have used a similar mechanism to that adopted in the competition context to ensure homogeneity between the EC and EFTA pillars. Article 63 thus provides that Annex XV to the EEA Agreement contains specific provisions on State aid. Annex XV then sets out a detailed list of measures which form the basis of the *acquis communautaire* for State aid. Annex XV also incorporates by reference the sectoral adaptations found in the mainstream competition provisions. The procedural rules are generally found in Protocol 3 to the Surveillance and Court Agreement. The ESA has published very detailed guidelines on its State aid practice and procedure. Specific provisions are also laid down for the transport sector and coal and steel.[202]

C. Powers and Functions of the ESA

28.97 Protocol 26 confers on the ESA 'equivalent powers and similar functions' to those afforded to the EC Commission under the EU State aid regime. Protocol 26 is not very forthcoming about the specific powers conferred on the ESA. That task is left to Protocol 3 to the Surveillance and Court Agreement.

1. Examination of new aid

28.98 Article 2 of Part II of Protocol 3[203] requires any EFTA State which is planning to make an award of new State aid to notify the ESA in sufficient time. The notification must contain sufficient detail and documentation to enable the ESA to make a decision. If a notification does not contain full and complete notification, any subsequent decision based on it may be revoked.[204] An EFTA State is not permitted to give effect to a new measure of State aid without the prior approval of the ESA.[205] The ESA upon receipt of the notification will carry out a preliminary investigation.[206] Unless a notification is withdrawn under Article 8 to Protocol 3, it must then take one of several decisions within a period of two months from the date of receipt of the notification:

---

[202] See Parts III and IV of Protocol 3 to the Surveillance and Court Agreement.

[203] See also Art 1(2) and 1(3) of Part I of Protocol 3.

[204] Art 9 of Part II to Protocol 3. See also the ESA Decision 195/04/COL dated 14 July 2004 on the Implementing Provisions referred to under Art 27 in Part II of Protocol 3 to the EEA Agreement, which provides, *inter alia*, for a simplified notification procedure in relation to certain alterations to existing aid.

[205] Art 3 of Part II to Protocol 3.

[206] Art 4 of Part II to Protocol 3. In Case E-2/02 *Technologien Bau—und Wirtschaftsberatung GmbH and Bellona Foundation v EFTA Surveillance Authority* [2003] EFTA Court Rep 52 para 44, the EFTA Court stressed the preliminary nature of this investigation, in contrast to the more detailed procedure described below.

- It can decide that the proposed measure does not constitute aid for the purposes of EEA law.[207]
- It can decide not to raise any objections to the aid and take a formal decision confirming that the proposed measure is compatible with the EEA Agreement. The decision must record which of the above exceptions contained in Article 61 EEA is satisfied.[208]
- If, after a preliminary examination, it finds that doubts are raised as to the compatibility with the functioning of the EEA Agreement of a notified measure, it shall decide to initiate the formal investigation procedure.[209]

If the ESA feels that it has insufficient information to reach one of these formal decisions, it may request further information from the EFTA State concerned. If the relevant information is not provided, the notification is deemed to be withdrawn.[210]   **28.99**

The formal investigation procedure commences with the ESA producing a summary of all relevant issues of fact and law, together with a preliminary assessment of the nature of the aid granted by the proposed measure. The ESA shall also spell out its doubts as to compatibility.[211] The EFTA State is then invited to comment on this document. Unless the notification is withdrawn by the EFTA State, the ESA then reaches one of the following decisions to bring the procedure to an end. A non-binding time-limit of eighteen months is provided for such decisions.[212]   **28.100**

- It can decide, if appropriate after necessary modifications from the EFTA State concerned, that the measure does not constitute aid.[213]
- It can decide, if appropriate after necessary modifications from the EFTA State, to take a 'positive decision'. That is, to find that the aid is compatible with the EEA Agreement. The exception relied upon must be specified.[214]
- It can take a positive decision, but impose conditions to be met by the EFTA State.[215]
- It can take a 'negative decision' that the aid in question should not be implemented.[216]

---

[207] Art 4(2) of Part II to Protocol 3.   [208] Art 4(3) of Part II to Protocol 3.
[209] Art 4(4) of Part II to Protocol 3.   [210] Art 5 of Part II to Protocol 3.
[211] Art 6 of Part II to Protocol 3.
[212] Art 7(6) of Part II to Protocol 3. Once that eighteen month period has expired, an EFTA State may request that the ESA take a decision on the basis of the information then available to it within a further period of two months. If the ESA cannot resolve its doubts on compatibility, it shall take a negative decision.
[213] Art 7(2) of Part II to Protocol 3.   [214] Art 7(3) of Part II to Protocol 3.
[215] Art 7(4) of Part II to Protocol 3.   [216] Art 7(5) of Part II to Protocol 3.

2. Powers of the ESA to deal with unlawful State aid

28.101 Wide powers are available to the ESA to deal with unlawful State aid which has not been notified to the ESA in a proper fashion. The ESA is required to examine any such situation as soon as it is brought to its attention.[217] It can then take a decision to suspend or provisionally recover the aid, before it proceeds to adopt the preliminary investigation and, if necessary, the formal investigation procedures referred to above.[218] The ESA is not, however, bound by any time-limits where the aid was not notified to it. Non-compliance with any ESA injunctions against an EFTA state either to provide information or to recover aid can lead to infraction proceedings before the EFTA Court.[219]

28.102 Where negative decisions are taken in cases of unlawful aid, the ESA must issue a formal decision that the EFTA State concerned shall take all necessary measures to recover the aid from the beneficiary, referred to as a 'recovery decision', unless to do so would be contrary to a general principle of EEA law.[220] The aid to be recovered pursuant to a recovery decision shall include interest at an appropriate rate fixed by the ESA. Interest is payable from the date on which the unlawful aid was at the disposal of the beneficiary until the date of its recovery. An obligation is imposed on EFTA States to effect recovery without delay and in accordance with the procedures under the national law of the EFTA State concerned, provided that they allow the immediate and effective execution of the ESA's decision. EFTA States may be required to take interim or provisional measures where appropriate. Recovery of aid is subject to an overall limitation period of ten years.[221]

3. Review of existing aid

28.103 The ESA is obliged to liaise with EFTA States to conduct a review of their existing aid schemes.[222] Where the ESA considers that an existing aid scheme is not, or is no longer, compatible with the functioning of the EEA Agreement, it shall inform the EFTA State concerned of its preliminary view and give the EFTA State concerned the opportunity to submit its comments within a period of one month. If the ESA considers that the aid is not, or is no longer, compatible with the EEA Agreement, it shall issue a recommendation of proposed measures. This recommendation may suggest:

- the substantive amendment of the aid scheme;

---

[217] Art 10 of Part II to Protocol 3. [218] Arts 11 to 13 of Part II to Protocol 3.
[219] Art 12 of Part II to Protocol 3. See also Art 23 of Part II to Protocol 3.
[220] Art 14 of Part II to Protocol 3. [221] Art 15 of Part II to Protocol 3.
[222] Art 17 of Part II to Protocol 3.

- the introduction of procedural requirements; or
- the abolition of the scheme.

If the EFTA State accepts the recommendation, the ESA issues a binding deci- **28.104**
sion to that effect. If the recommendation is not accepted, the ESA must initiate
the preliminary investigation and, if necessary, formal investigation procedures
referred to above.[223]

D. Complaints

A complaint that a measure from an EFTA State is unlawful State aid may be **28.105**
lodged by both individuals and undertakings, or their legal representatives.[224]
The ESA's State Aid Guidelines provides information about the submission of a
complaint. To lodge a complaint, a complaint form is sent to the ESA's Competition and State Aid Directorate. Upon receipt of a complaint, the ESA will
conduct a preliminary assessment. If the ESA considers the complaint to be
unfounded or outside its competence, it will inform the complainant that it
intends to close the file without further action. Otherwise, the ESA informs the
EFTA State of the complaint and initiates the procedures set out above.[225] The
complainant may be asked to supply further information to the ESA and will be
informed of the outcome of the investigation. Article 24 to Protocol 3 requires
the ESA and its officials to respect professional secrecy. In addition, the identity
of complainants is protected unless they agree to having their names divulged.
While individuals and economic operators are entitled to address the ESA in any
of the official languages of the EFTA States or of the European Union, they are in
practice encouraged to use English to avoid delay in the handling of a complaint.

E. Cooperation between the EC Commission and the ESA

Protocol 27 provides that, in order to ensure a uniform implementation, appli- **28.106**
cation and interpretation of the rules on State aid throughout the territory of
the Contracting Parties, the EC Commission and ESA would cooperate in a
number of different ways. These include:

- exchange of information and views on general policy issues;

---

[223] Art 19 of Part II to Protocol 3.   [224] See Art 20 of Part II to Protocol 3.
[225] Depending on the level of involvement of the complainant and its status, it may have
standing to challenge any subsequent decision taken before the EFTA Court: see Case E-2/02
*Technologien Bau- und Wirtschaftsberatung GmbH and Bellona Foundation v EFTA Surveillance
Authority* [2003] EFTA Court Rep 52.

- exchange of periodic surveys on state aid in their respective territories;
- informing one another of salient decisions;
- exchange of information and views on a case by case basis.

28.107 Article 64 EEA provides for a dispute resolution mechanism where one of the surveillance authorities considers that the other's implementation of the State aid provisions is not maintaining equal conditions of competition in their respective territories.

VII. Adaptation periods

A. Article 53

28.108 Articles 8 and 10 to 13 of Protocol 21 to the EEA Agreement continue to provide for certain transitional arrangements to apply to agreements, decisions and concerted practices in existence at the date of entry into force of the EEA Agreement.[226]

1. New agreements

28.109 The EEA Agreement does not provide for transition periods for agreements between enterprises which are concluded after its entry into force.[227]

2. Existing agreements

28.110 An adaptation period was provided for existing agreements which, by virtue of the entry into force of the EEA Agreement, fell under the prohibition contained in Article 53(1).

General

28.111 Undertakings were allowed a period of six months as from the entry into force of the EEA Agreement to adapt such arrangements to or take any other steps necessary to bring them into line with the new provisions of the EEA. This period has now passed. Undertakings should either have:

---

[226] See Case E-7/01 *Hegelstad Eiendomsselskap Arvid B Hegelstad v Hydro Texaco A/S* [2003] 4 CMLR 6 para 17.

[227] This was formerly addressed under Art 4 of Protocol 21. The amendment of Protocol 21 by Decision 130/2004 has removed that provision. The proposition is now only shown by the absence of any saving provision for new agreements in the terms of Protocol 21 or in Part V, Chapter XVI to Protocol 4 to the Surveillance and Court Agreement.

- modified their agreements or practices so that they now comply with existing block exemptions, taking into account the ESA dimension;[228]

- obtained an individual exemption from the Commission which has not yet expired and in respect of which the Commission has not yet decided that it should be discontinued. Agreements which at the date of entry into force of the EEA Agreement already enjoyed a formal individual exemption granted by the EC Commission will continue to benefit from this even in relation to EEA aspects for the duration stipulated in the exemption decision, unless the Commission decides to withdraw the exemption;[229]

- modified them in such a way that they are no longer caught by the prohibition of Article 53(1) of the EEA Agreement.[230]

It remains advisable for undertakings which have not verified their agreements **28.112** but suspect that Article 53 may be applicable to them, to carry out compliance programmes to ensure that their agreements are not at risk. Agreements already the subject of an administrative letter from the Commission before the entry into force of the EEA Agreement should be brought into conformity with the new EEA provisions. Article 35 of Protocol 4 to the Surveillance and Court Agreement states that applications and notifications made under the former procedural regime (prior to modernization) shall lapse. However, certain other procedural steps which have been taken may continue to have effect. Specific provision is made under Article 39 to Protocol 4 for the duration and revocation of decisions taken by the ESA under Article 53(3) EEA.

B. Article 54

No specific transitional provisions are envisaged in respect of Article 54 EEA. **28.113**

C. The Merger Regulation

Article 14 of Protocol 24 to the EEA Agreement provides that Article 57 EEA **28.114** shall not apply to any concentration which was the subject of an agreement or announcement or where control was acquired before the date of entry into force

---

[228] See Art 11 of Protocol 21 and Art 7 of Chapter XVI to Protocol 4 to the Surveillance and Court Agreement. The corresponding rules in the EC context are contained in different block exemptions.

[229] See Art 13 of Protocol 21 and Art 9 of Chapter XVI, Protocol 4.

[230] See Art 12 of Protocol 21 and Art 8 of Chapter XVI, Protocol 4.

of the EEA Agreement. Nor shall it apply to a concentration where proceedings were initiated before that date by a national competition authority.[231]

VIII. Conclusion

28.115 The substantive EEA competition rules should not pose any particular problems for undertakings already used to the enforcement of competition policy in the EC. The substantive provisions are, to all intents and purposes, identical. The EFTA Court has shown itself willing to apply the long-established case law of the ECJ in competition matters.[232] The two most significant differences are to be found in the wider geographical scope of the rules and the system of attribution of cases and cooperation between the two surveillance authorities. In terms of the enforcement of those provisions, interesting times may lie ahead. First, the Modernization regime had a delayed entry into force, leaving EEA competition law for some time in a curious limbo. The ramifications of this hiatus may fall to be determined in due course. In Case E-4/01 *Karl Karlsson hf v. The Icelandic State*,[233] the EFTA Court held that unimplemented EEA provisions would be of persuasive, not binding, authority:

> It follows from Article 7 EEA and Protocol 35 to the EEA Agreement that EEA law does not entail a transfer of legislative powers. Therefore, EEA law does not require that individuals and economic operators can rely directly on non-implemented EEA rules before national courts. At the same time, it is inherent in the general objective of the EEA Agreement of establishing a dynamic and homogeneous market, in the ensuing emphasis on the judicial defence and enforcement of the rights of individuals, as well as in the public international law principle of effectiveness, that national courts will consider any relevant element of EEA law, whether implemented or not, when interpreting national law.

28.116 Now that the new regime has been brought into force, it remains to be seen whether there will be an increased level of domestic enforcement of EEA competition law. The ESA's experience from 1994 to 2004 indicated that companies were prepared to complain about perceived anti-competitive conduct. It remains to be seen whether this will now find voice in domestic actions based on Articles 53 and 54 EEA. Early indications from Member States in the EU do not suggest that a substantial up-turn in actions before national courts may be expected. Secondly, experience has shown that the ESA has adopted a subsidiary, but nonetheless important, enforcement role to that exercised by the EC

---

[231] See also Art 10 of Chapter XVI, Part III, Protocol 4.
[232] See, e.g. Case E-1/97 *Jan and Kristian Jaegar AS v Opel Norge AS* [1999] 4 CMLR 147.
[233] Judgment of the EFTA Court dated 30 May 2002 para 28.

Commission. It would be fair to say that the EC Commission has led the way in most of the joint EEA/EC investigations into anti-competitive behaviour. In the residual areas where primary enforcement of the competition rules falls to the competent surveillance authority, there is no reason why this trend should not continue.

Finally, the centralized system of enforcement permitted close and constant **28.117** cooperation between the EC Commission and the ESA. Further, the judicial control exercised, as appropriate, by the CFI, the ECJ, and the EFTA Court (following the jurisprudence set down by the ECJ) largely led to the 'homogeneous application' of the EEA competition rules throughout the area, as envisaged by the EEA Agreement. It remains to be seen whether the same degree of homogeneity may be expected in an era of decentralized enforcement across the twenty-eight states which now comprise the EEA territory.

APPENDICES

II. Merger Control (Regulation 139/2004)

III. Public Undertakings (Article 86 EC)

IV. State Aid (Articles 87 and 88 EC)

ANTITRUST RULES
(ARTICLES 81 AND 82 EC)

PART 1

ANTITRUST RULES
(ARTICLES 81 AND 82 EC)

APPENDIX 1

Articles 81 to 86 of the EC Treaty

Article 81 (ex Article 85)

Section 1. Rules applying to undertakings

1. The following shall be prohibited as incompatible with the common market: all agreements between undertakings, decisions by associations of undertakings and concerted practices which may affect trade between Member States and which have as their object or effect the prevention, restriction or distortion of competition within the common market, and in particular those which:

(a) directly or indirectly fix purchase or selling prices or any other trading conditions;

(b) limit or control production, markets, technical development, or investment;

(c) share markets or sources of supply;

(d) apply dissimilar conditions to equivalent transactions with other trading parties, thereby placing them at a competitive disadvantage;

(e) make the conclusion of contracts subject to acceptance by the other parties of supplementary obligations which, by their nature or according to commercial usage, have no connection with the subject of such contracts.

2. Any agreements or decisions prohibited pursuant to this Article shall be automatically void.

3. The provisions of paragraph 1 may, however, be declared inapplicable in the case of:

— any agreement or category of agreements between undertakings;

— any decision or category of decisions by associations of undertakings;

— any concerted practice or category of concerted practices,

which contributes to improving the production or distribution of goods or to promoting technical or economic progress, while allowing consumers a fair share of the resulting benefit, and which does not:

(a) impose on the undertakings concerned restrictions which are not indispensable to the attainment of these objectives;

(b) afford such undertakings the possibility of eliminating competition in respect of a substantial part of the products in question.

Article 82 (ex Article 86)

Any abuse by one or more undertakings of a dominant position within the common market or in a substantial part of it shall be prohibited as incompatible with the common market insofar as it may affect trade between Member States.

Such abuse may, in particular, consist in:

(a) directly or indirectly imposing unfair purchase or selling prices or other unfair trading conditions;

(b) limiting production, markets or technical development to the prejudice of consumers;

(c) applying dissimilar conditions to equivalent transactions with other trading parties, thereby placing them at a competitive disadvantage;

(d) making the conclusion of contracts subject to acceptance by the other parties of supplementary obligations which, by their nature or according to commercial usage, have no connection with the subject of such contracts.

1023

Article 83 (ex Article 87)

1. The appropriate regulations or directives to give effect to the principles set out in Articles 81 and 82 shall be laid down by the Council, acting by a qualified majority on a proposal from the Commission and after consulting the European Parliament.

2. The regulations or directives referred to in paragraph 1 shall be designed in particular:

(a) to ensure compliance with the prohibitions laid down in Article 81(1) and in Article 82 by making provision for fines and periodic penalty payments;

(b) to lay down detailed rules for the application of Article 81(3), taking into account the need to ensure effective supervision on the one hand, and to simplify administration to the greatest possible extent on the other;

(c) to define, if need be, in the various branches of the economy, the scope of the provisions of Articles 81 and 82

(d) to define the respective functions of the Commission and of the Court of Justice in applying the provisions laid down in this paragraph;

(e) to determine the relationship between national laws and the provisions contained in this Section or adopted pursuant to this Article.

Article 84 (ex Article 88)

Until the entry into force of the provisions adopted in pursuance of Article 83, the authorities in Member States shall rule on the admissibility of agreements, decisions and concerted practices and on abuse of a dominant position in the common market in accordance with the law of their country and with the provisions of Article 81, in particular paragraph 3, and of Article 82.

Article 85 (ex Article 89)

1. Without prejudice to Article 84, the Commission shall ensure the application of the principles laid down in Articles 81 and 82. On application by a Member State or on its own initiative, and in cooperation with the competent authorities in the Member States, who shall give it their assistance, the Commission shall investigate cases of suspected infringement of these principles. If it finds that there has been an infringement, it shall propose appropriate measures to bring it to an end.

2. If the infringement is not brought to an end, the Commission shall record such infringement of the principles in a reasoned decision. The Commission may publish its decision and authorise Member States to take the measures the conditions and details of which it shall determine, needed to remedy the situation.

Article 86 (ex Article 90)

1. In the case of public undertakings and undertakings to which Member States grant special or exclusive rights, Member States shall neither enact nor maintain in force any measure contrary to the rules contained in this Treaty in particular to those rules provided for in Article 12 and Articles 81 to 89.

2. Undertakings entrusted with the operation of services of general economic interest or having the character of a revenue-producing monopoly shall be subject to the rules contained in this Treaty, in particular to the rules on competition, insofar as the application of such rules does not obstruct the performance, in law or in fact, of the particular tasks assigned to them. The development of trade must not be affected to such an extent as would be contrary to the interests of the Community.

3. The Commission shall ensure the application of the provisions of this Article and shall, where necessary, address appropriate directives or decisions to Member States.

APPENDIX 2

Council Regulation (EC) No 1/2003 of 16 December 2002 on the implementation of the rules on competition laid down in Articles 81 and 82 of the Treaty

(Text with EEA relevance)

THE COUNCIL OF THE EUROPEAN UNION.

Having regard to the Treaty establishing the European Community, and in particular Article 83 thereof,

Having regard to the proposal from the Commission,[1]

Having regard to the opinion of the European Parliament,[2]

Having regard to the opinion of the European Economic and Social Committee,[3]

Whereas:

(1) In order to establish a system which ensures that competition in the common market is not distorted, Articles 81 and 82 of the Treaty must be applied effectively and uniformly in the Community. Council Regulation No 17 of 6 February 1962, First Regulation implementing Articles 81 and 82* of the Treaty,[4] has allowed a Community competition policy to develop that has helped to disseminate a competition culture within the Community. In light of experience, however, that Regulation should now be replaced by legislation designed to meet the challenges of an integrated market and a future enlargement of the Community.

(2) In particular, there is a need to rethink the arrangements for applying the exception from the prohibition on agreements, which restrict competition, laid down in Article 81(3) of the Treaty. Under Article 83(2)(b) of the Treaty, account must be taken in this regard of the need to ensure effective supervision, on the one hand, and to simplify administration to the greatest possible extent, on the other.

(3) The centralised scheme set up by Regulation No 17 no longer secures a balance between those two objectives. It hampers application of the Community competition rules by the courts and competition authorities of the Member States, and the system of notification it involves prevents the Commission from concentrating its resources on curbing the most serious infringements. It also imposes considerable costs on undertakings.

(4) The present system should therefore be replaced by a directly applicable exception system in which the competition authorities and courts of the Member States have the power to apply not only Article 81(1) and Article 82 of the Treaty, which have direct applicability by virtue of

---

[1] OJ C365 E, 19.12.2000, p 284.

[2] OJ C72 E, 21.3.2002, p 305.

[3] OJ C155, 29.5.2001, p 73.

* The title of Reg No 17 has been adjusted to take account of the renumbering of the Art of the EC Treaty, in accordance with Art 12 of the Treaty of Amsterdam: the original reference was to Arts 85 and 86 of the Treaty.

[4] OJ 13, 21.2.1962, p 204/62. Reg as last amended by Reg (EC) No 1216/1999 (OJ L148, 15.6.1999. p 5).

the case-law of the Court of Justice of the European Communities, but also Article 81(3) of the Treaty.

(5) In order to ensure an effective enforcement of the Community competition rules and at the same time the respect of fundamental rights of defence, this Regulation should regulate the burden of proof under Articles 81 and 82 of the Treaty. It should be for the party or the authority alleging an infringement of Article 81(1) and Article 82 of the Treaty to prove the existence thereof to the required legal standard. It should be for the undertaking or association of undertakings invoking the benefit of a defence against a finding of an infringement to demonstrate to the required legal standard that the conditions for applying such defence are satisfied. This Regulation affects neither national rules on the standard of proof nor obligations of competition authorities and courts of the Member States to ascertain the relevant facts of a case, provided that such rules and obligations are compatible with general principles of Community law.

(6) In order to ensure that the Community competition rules are applied effectively, the competition authorities of the Member States should be associated more closely with their application. To this end, they should be empowered to apply Community law.

(7) National courts have an essential part to play in applying the Community competition rules. When deciding disputes between private individuals, they protect the subjective rights under Community law, for example by awarding damages to the victims of infringements. The role of the national courts here complements that of the competition authorities of the Member States. They should therefore be allowed to apply Articles 81 and 82 of the Treaty in full.

(8) In order to ensure the effective enforcement of the Community competition rules and the proper functioning of the cooperation mechanisms contained in this Regulation, it is necessary to oblige the competition authorities and courts of the Member States to also apply Articles 81 and 82 of the Treaty where they apply national competition law to agreements and practices which may affect trade between Member States. In order to create a level playing field for agreements, decisions by associations of undertakings and concerted practices within the internal market, it is also necessary to determine pursuant to Article 83(2)(e) of the Treaty the relationship between national laws and Community competition law. To that effect it is necessary to provide that the application of national competition laws to agreements, decisions or concerted practices within the meaning of Article 81(1) of the Treaty may not lead to the prohibition of such agreements, decisions and concerted practices if they are not also prohibited under Community competition law. The notions of agreements, decisions and concerted practices are autonomous concepts of Community competition law covering the coordination of behaviour of undertakings on the market as interpreted by the Community Courts. Member States should not under this Regulation be precluded from adopting and applying on their territory stricter national competition laws which prohibit or impose sanctions on unilateral conduct engaged in by undertakings. These stricter national laws may include provisions which prohibit or impose sanctions on abusive behaviour toward economically dependent undertakings. Furthermore, this Regulation does not apply to national laws which impose criminal sanctions on natural persons except to the extent that such sanctions are the means whereby competition rules applying to undertakings are enforced.

(9) Articles 81 and 82 of the Treaty have as their objective the protection of competition on the market. This Regulation, which is adopted for the implementation of these Treaty provisions, does not preclude Member States from implementing on their territory national legislation, which protects other legitimate interests provided that such legislation is compatible with general principles and other provisions of Community law. In so far as such national legislation pursues predominantly an objective different from that of protecting competition on the market, the competition authorities and courts of the Member States may apply such legislation on their territory. Accordingly, Member States may under this Regulation implement on their territory national legislation that prohibits or imposes sanctions on acts of unfair trading

practice, be they unilateral or contractual. Such legislation pursues a specific objective, irrespective of the actual or presumed effects of such acts on competition on the market. This is particularly the case of legislation which prohibits undertakings from imposing on their trading partners, obtaining or attempting to obtain from them terms and conditions that are unjustified, disproportionate or without consideration.

(10) Regulations such as 19/65/EEC,[5] (EEC) No 2821/71,[6] (EEC) No 3976/87,[7] (EEC) No 1534/91,[8] or (EEC) No 479/92[9] empower the Commission to apply Article 81(3) of the Treaty by Regulation to certain categories of agreements, decisions by associations of undertakings and concerted practices. In the areas defined by such Regulations, the Commission has adopted and may continue to adopt so called 'block' exemption Regulations by which it declares Article 81(1) of the Treaty inapplicable to categories of agreements, decisions and concerted practices. Where agreements, decisions and concerted practices to which such Regulations apply nonetheless have effects that are incompatible with Article 81(3) of the Treaty, the Commission and the competition authorities of the Member States should have the power to withdraw in a particular case the benefit of the block exemption Regulation.

(11) For it to ensure that the provisions of the Treaty are applied, the Commission should be able to address decisions to undertakings or associations of undertakings for the purpose of bringing to an end infringements of Articles 81 and 82 of the Treaty. Provided there is a legitimate interest in doing so, the Commission should also be able to adopt decisions which find that an infringement has been committed in the past even if it does not impose a fine. This Regulation should also make explicit provision for the Commission's power to adopt decisions ordering interim measures, which has been acknowledged by the Court of Justice.

(12) This Regulation should make explicit provision for the Commission's power to impose any remedy, whether behavioural or structural, which is necessary to bring the infringement effectively to an end, having regard to the principle of proportionality. Structural remedies should only be imposed either where there is no equally effective behavioural remedy or where any equally effective behavioural remedy would be more burdensome for the

---

[5] Council Reg No 19/65/EEC of 2 March 1965 on the application of Art 81(3) (The titles of the Regulations have been adjusted to take account of the renumbering of the Arts of the EC Treaty, in accordance with Art 12 of the Treaty of Amsterdam; the original reference was to Art 85(3) of the Treaty) of the Treaty to certain categories of agreements and concerted practices (OJ 36, 6.3.1965, p 533). Reg as last amended by Reg (EC) No 1215/1999 (OJ L148, 15.6.1999, p 1).

[6] Council Reg (EEC) No 2821/71 of 20 December 1971 on the application of Art 81(3) (The titles of the Regulations have been adjusted to take account of the renumbering of the Arts of the EC Treaty, in accordance with Art 12 of the Treaty of Amsterdam; the original reference was to Art 85(3) of the Treaty) of the Treaty to categories of agreements, decisions and concerted practices (OJ L285, 29.12.1971, p 46). Reg as last amended by the Act of Accession of 1994.

[7] Council Reg (EEC) No 3976/87 of 14 December 1987 on the application of Art 81(3) (The titles of the Regulations have been adjusted to take account of the renumbering of the Arts of the EC. Treaty, in accordance with Art 12 of the Treaty of Amsterdam; the original reference was to Art 85(3) of the Treaty) of the Treaty to certain categories of agreements and concerted practices in the air transport sector (OJ L374, 31.12.1987, p 9). Reg as fast amended by the Act of Accession of 1994.

[8] Council Reg (EEC) No 1534/91 of 31 May 1991 on the application of Art 81(3) (The titles of the Regulations have been adjusted to take account of the renumbering of the Arts of the EC Treaty, in accordance with Art 12 of the Treaty of Amsterdam; the original reference was to Art 85(3) of the Treaty) of the Treaty to certain categories of agreements, decisions and concerted practices in the insurance sector (OJ L143, 7.6.1991, p 1).

[9] Council Reg (EEC) No 479/92 of 25 February 1992 on the application of Art 81(3) (The titles of the Regulations have been adjusted to take account of the renumbering of the Arts of the EC Treaty, in accordance with Art 12 of the Treaty of Amsterdam; the original reference was to Art 85(3) of the Treaty) of the Treaty to certain categories of agreements, decisions and concerted practices between liner shipping companies (Consortia) (OJ L55, 29.2.1992, p 3). Reg amended by the Act of Accession of 1994.

undertaking concerned than the structural remedy. Changes to the structure of an undertaking as it existed before the infringement was committed would only be proportionate where there is a substantial risk of a lasting or repeated infringement that derives from the very structure of the undertaking.

(13) Where, in the course of proceedings which might lead to an agreement or practice being prohibited, undertakings offer the Commission commitments such as to meet its concerns, the Commission should be able to adopt decisions which make those commitments binding on the undertakings concerned. Commitment decisions should find that there are no longer grounds for action by the Commission without concluding whether or not there has been or still is an infringement. Commitment decisions are without prejudice to the powers of competition authorities and courts of the Member States to make such a finding and decide upon the case. Commitment decisions are not appropriate in cases where the Commission intends to impose a fine.

(14) In exceptional cases where the public interest of the Community so requires, it may also be expedient for the Commission to adopt a decision of a declaratory nature finding that the prohibition in Article 81 or Article 82 of the Treaty does not apply, with a view to clarifying the law and ensuring its consistent application throughout the Community, in particular with regard to new types of agreements or practices that have not been settled in the existing case-law and administrative practice.

(15) The Commission and the competition authorities of the Member States should form together a network of public authorities applying the Community competition rules in close cooperation. For that purpose it is necessary to set up arrangements for information and consultation. Further modalities for the cooperation within the network will be laid down and revised by the Commission, in close cooperation with the Member States.

(16) Notwithstanding any national provision to the contrary, the exchange of information and the use of such information in evidence should be allowed between the members of the network even where the information is confidential. This information may be used for the application of Articles 81 and 82 of the Treaty as well as for the parallel application of national competition law, provided that the latter application relates to the same case and does not lead to a different outcome. When the information exchanged is used by the receiving authority to impose sanctions on undertakings, there should be no other limit to the use of the information than the obligation to use it for the purpose for which it was collected given the fact that the sanctions imposed on undertakings are of the same type in all systems. The rights of defence enjoyed by undertakings in the various systems can be considered as sufficiently equivalent. However, as regards natural persons, they may be subject to substantially different types of sanctions across the various systems. Where that is the case, it is necessary to ensure that information can only be used if it has been collected in a way which respects the same level of protection of the rights of defence of natural persons as provided for under the national rules of the receiving authority.

(17) If the competition rules are to be applied consistently and, at the same time, the network is to be managed in the best possible way, it is essential to retain the rule that the competition authorities of the Member States are automatically relieved of their competence if the Commission initiates its own proceedings. Where a competition authority of a Member State is already acting on a case and the Commission intends to initiate proceedings, it should endeavour to do so as soon as possible. Before initiating proceedings, the Commission should consult the national authority concerned.

(18) To ensure that cases are dealt with by the most appropriate authorities within the network, a general provision should be laid down allowing a competition authority to suspend or close a case on the ground that another authority is dealing with it or has already dealt with it, the objective being that each case should be handled by a single authority. This provision should not prevent the Commission from rejecting a complaint for lack of Community interest, as

the case-law of the Court of Justice has acknowledged it may do, even if no other competition authority has indicated its intention of dealing with the case.

(19) The Advisory Committee on Restrictive Practices and Dominant Positions set up by Regulation No 17 has functioned in a very satisfactory manner. It will fit well into the new system of decentralised application. It is necessary, therefore, to build upon the rules laid down by Regulation No 17, while improving the effectiveness of the organisational arrangements. To this end, it would be expedient to allow opinions to be delivered by written procedure. The Advisory Committee should also be able to act as a forum for discussing cases that are being handled by the competition authorities of the Member States, so as to help safeguard the consistent application of the Community competition rules.

(20) The Advisory Committee should be composed of representatives of the competition authorities of the Member States. For meetings in which general issues are being discussed, Member States should be able to appoint an additional representative. This is without prejudice to members of the Committee being assisted by other experts from the Member States.

(21) Consistency in the application of the competition rules also requires that arrangements be established for cooperation between the courts of the Member States and the Commission. This is relevant for all courts of the Member States that apply Articles 81 and 82 of the Treaty, whether applying these rules in lawsuits between private parties, acting as public enforcers or as review courts. In particular, national courts should be able to ask the Commission for information or for its opinion on points concerning the application of Community competition law. The Commission and the competition authorities of the Member States should also be able to submit written or oral observations to courts called upon to apply Article 81 or Article 82 of the Treaty. These observations should be submitted within the framework of national procedural rules and practices including those safeguarding the rights of the parties. Steps should therefore be taken to ensure that the Commission and the competition authorities of the Member States are kept sufficiently well informed of proceedings before national courts.

(22) In order to ensure compliance with the principles of legal certainty and the uniform application of the Community competition rules in a system of parallel powers, conflicting decisions must be avoided. It is therefore necessary to clarify, in accordance with the case-law of the Court of Justice, the effects of Commission decisions and proceedings on courts and competition authorities of the Member States. Commitment decisions adopted by the Commission do not affect the power of the courts and the competition authorities of the Member States to apply Articles 81 and 82 of the Treaty.

(23) The Commission should be empowered throughout the Community to require such information to be supplied as is necessary to detect any agreement, decision or concerted practice prohibited by Article 81 of the Treaty or any abuse of a dominant position prohibited by Article 82 of the Treaty. When complying with a decision of the Commission, undertakings cannot be forced to admit that they have committed an infringement, but they are in any event obliged to answer factual questions and to provide documents, even if this information may be used to establish against them or against another undertaking the existence of an infringement.

(24) The Commission should also be empowered to undertake such inspections as are necessary to detect any agreement, decision or concerted practice prohibited by Article 81 of the Treaty or any abuse of a dominant position prohibited by Article 82 of the Treaty. The competition authorities of the Member States should cooperate actively in the exercise of these powers.

(25) The detection of infringements of the competition rules is growing ever more difficult, and, in order to protect competition effectively, the Commission's powers of investigation need to be supplemented. The Commission should in particular be empowered to interview any persons who may be in possession of useful information and to record the statements

made. In the course of an inspection, officials authorized by the Commission should be empowered to affix seals for the period of time necessary for the inspection. Seals should normally not be affixed for more than 72 hours. Officials authorized by the Commission should also be empowered to ask for any information relevant to the subject matter and purpose of the inspection.

(26) Experience has shown that there are cases where business records are kept in the homes of directors or other people working for an undertaking. In order to safeguard the effectiveness of inspections, therefore, officials and other persons authorised by the Commission should be empowered to enter any premises where business records may be kept, including private homes. However, the exercise of this latter power should be subject to the authorization of the judicial authority.

(27) Without prejudice to the case-law of the Court of Justice, it is useful to set out the scope of the control that the national judicial authority may carry out when it authorizes, as foreseen by national law including as a precautionary measure, assistance from law enforcement authorities in order to overcome possible opposition on the part of the undertaking or the execution of the decision to carry out inspections in non-business premises. It results from the case-law that the national judicial authority may in particular ask the Commission for further information which it needs to carry out its control and in the absence of which it could refuse the authorization. The case-law also confirms the competence of the national courts to control the application of national rules governing the implementation of coercive measures.

(28) In order to help the competition authorities of the Member States to apply Articles 81 and 82 of the Treaty effectively, it is expedient to enable them to assist one another by carrying out inspections and other fact-finding measures.

(29) Compliance with Articles 81 and 82 of the Treaty and the fulfilment of the obligations imposed on undertakings and associations of undertakings under this Regulation should be enforceable by means of fines and periodic penalty payments. To that end, appropriate levels of fine should also be laid down for infringements of the procedural rules.

(30) In order to ensure effective recovery of fines imposed on associations of undertakings for infringements that they have committed, it is necessary to lay down the conditions on which the Commission may require payment of the fine from the members of the association where the association is not solvent. In doing so, the Commission should have regard to the relative size of the undertakings belonging to the association and in particular to the situation of small and medium-sized enterprises. Payment of the fine by one or several members of an association is without prejudice to rules of national law that provide for recovery of the amount paid from other members of the association.

(31) The rules on periods of limitation for the imposition of fines and periodic penalty payments were laid down in Council Regulation (EEC) No 2988/74,[10] which also concerns penalties in the field of transport. In a system of parallel powers, the acts, which may interrupt a limitation period, should include procedural steps taken independently by the competition authority of a Member State. To clarify the legal framework, Regulation (EEC) No 2988/74 should therefore be amended to prevent it applying to matters covered by this Regulation, and this Regulation should include provisions on periods of limitation.

(32) The undertakings concerned should be accorded the right to be heard by the Commission, third parties whose interests may be affected by a decision should be given the opportunity of submitting their observations beforehand, and the decisions taken should be widely pub- licised. While ensuring the rights of defence of the undertakings concerned, in particular, the

---

[10] Council Reg (EEC) No 2988/74 of 26 November 1974 concerning limitation periods in proceedings and the enforcement of sanctions under the rules of the European Economic Community relating to transport and competition (OJ L319, 29.11.1974, p 1).

right of access to the file, it is essential that business secrets be protected. The confidentiality of information exchanged in the network should likewise be safeguarded.

(33) Since all decisions taken by the Commission under this Regulation are subject to review by the Court of Justice in accordance with the Treaty, the Court of Justice should, in accordance with Article 229 thereof be given unlimited jurisdiction in respect of decisions by which the Commission imposes fines or periodic penalty payments.

(34) The principles laid down in Articles 81 and 82 of the Treaty, as they have been applied by Regulation No 17, have given a central role to the Community bodies. This central role should be retained, whilst associating the Member States more closely with the application of the Community competition rules. In accordance with the principles of subsidiarity and proportionality as set out in Article 5 of the Treaty, this Regulation does not go beyond what is necessary in order to achieve its objective, which is to allow the Community competition rules to be applied effectively.

(35) In order to attain a proper enforcement of Community competition law, Member States should designate and empower authorities to apply Articles 81 and 82 of the Treaty as public enforcers. They should be able to designate administrative as well as judicial authorities to carry out the various functions conferred upon competition authorities in this Regulation. This Regulation recognises the wide variation which exists in the public enforcement systems of Member States. The effects of Article 11(6) of this Regulation should apply to all competition authorities. As an exception to this general rule, where a prosecuting authority brings a case before a separate judicial authority, Article 11(6) should apply to the prosecuting authority subject to the conditions in Article 35(4) of this Regulation. Where these conditions are not fulfilled, the general rule should apply. In any case, Article 11(6) should not apply to courts insofar as they are acting as review courts.

(36) As the case-law has made it clear that the competition rules apply to transport, that sector should be made subject to the procedural provisions of this Regulation. Council Regulation No 141 of 26 November 1962 exempting transport from the application of Regulation No 17[11] should therefore be repealed and Regulations (EEC) No 1017/68,[12] (EEC) No 4056/86[13] and (EEC) No 3975/87[14] should be amended in order to delete the specific procedural provisions they contain.

(37) This Regulation respects the fundamental rights and observes the principles recognized in particular by the Charter of Fundamental Rights of the European Union. Accordingly, this Regulation should be interpreted and applied with respect to those rights and principles.

(38) Legal certainty for undertakings operating under the Community competition rules contributes to the promotion of innovation and investment. Where cases give rise to genuine uncertainty because they present novel or unresolved questions for the application of these rules, individual undertakings may wish to seek informal guidance from the Commission.

---

[11] OJ 124, 28.11.1962, p 2751/62; Reg as last amended by Reg No 1002/67/EEC (OJ 306, 16.12.1967, p 1).

[12] Council Reg (EEC) No 1017/68 of 19 July 1968 applying rules of competition to transport by rail, road and inland waterway (OJ L175, 23.7.1968, p 1). Reg as last amended by the Act of Accession of 1994.

[13] Council Reg (EEC) No 4056/86 of 22 December 1986 laying down detailed rules for the application of Arts 81 and 82 (The title of the Reg has been adjusted to take account of the renumbering of the Arts of the EC Treaty, in accordance with Art 12 of the Treaty of Amsterdam; the original reference was to Arts 85 and 86 of the Treaty) of the Treaty to maritime transport (OJ L378, 31.12.1986, p 4). Reg as last amended by the Act of Accession of 1994.

[14] Council Reg (EEC) No 3975/87 of 14 December 1987 laying down the procedure for the application of the rules on competition to undertakings in the air transport sector (OJ L374, 31.12.1987, p 1). Reg as last amended by Reg (EEC) No 2410/92 (OJ L240, 24.8.1992, p 18).

This Regulation is without prejudice to the ability of the Commission to issue such informal guidance.

HAS ADOPTED THIS REGULATION:

CHAPTER I. PRINCIPLES

Article 1
Application of Articles 81 and 82 of the Treaty

1. Agreements, decisions and concerted practices caught by Article 81(1) of the Treaty which do not satisfy the conditions of Article 81(3) of the Treaty shall be prohibited, no prior decision to that effect being required.

2. Agreements, decisions and concerted practices caught by Article 81(1) of the Treaty which satisfy the conditions of Article 81(3) of the Treaty shall not be prohibited, no prior decision to that effect being required.

3. The abuse of a dominant position referred to in Article 82 of the Treaty shall be prohibited, no prior decision to that effect being required.

Article 2
Burden of proof

In any national or Community proceedings for the application of Articles 81 and 82 of the Treaty, the burden of proving an infringement of Article 81(1) or of Article 82 of the Treaty shall rest on the party or the authority alleging the infringement. The undertaking or association of undertakings claiming the benefit of Article 81(3) of the Treaty shall bear the burden of proving that the conditions of that paragraph are fulfilled.

Article 3
Relationship between Articles 81 and 82 of the Treaty and national competition laws

1. Where the competition authorities of the Member States or national courts apply national competition law to agreements, decisions by associations of undertakings or concerted practices within the meaning of Article 81(1) of the Treaty which may affect trade between Member States within the meaning of that provision, they shall also apply Article 81 of the Treaty to such agreements, decisions or concerted practices. Where the competition authorities of the Member States or national courts apply national competition law to any abuse prohibited by Article 82 of the Treaty, they shall also apply Article 82 of the Treaty.

2. The application of national competition law may not lead to the prohibition of agreements, decisions by associations of undertakings or concerted practices which may affect trade between Member States but which do not restrict competition within the meaning of Article 81(1) of the Treaty, or which fulfil the conditions of Article 81(3) of the Treaty or which are covered by a Regulation for the application of Article 81(3) of the Treaty. Member States shall not under this Regulation be precluded from adopting and applying on their territory stricter national laws which prohibit or sanction unilateral conduct engaged in by undertakings.

3. Without prejudice to general principles and other provisions of Community law, paragraphs 1 and 2 do not apply when the competition authorities and the courts of the Member States apply national merger control laws nor do they preclude the application of provisions of national law that predominantly pursue an objective different from that pursued by Articles 81 and 82 of the Treaty.

CHAPTER II. POWERS

Article 4

Powers of the Commission

For the purpose of applying Articles 81 and 82 of the Treaty, the Commission shall have the powers provided for by this Regulation.

Article 5

Powers of the competition authorities of the Member States

The competition authorities of the Member States shall have the power to apply Articles 81 and 82 of the Treaty in individual cases. For this purpose, acting on their own initiative or on a complaint, they may take the following decisions:
— requiring that an infringement be brought to an end,
— ordering interim measures,
— accepting commitments,
— imposing fines, periodic penalty payments or any other penalty provided for in their national law.
Where on the basis of the information in their possession the conditions for prohibition are not met they may likewise decide that there are no grounds for action on their part.

Article 6

Powers of the national courts

National courts shall have the power to apply Articles 81 and 82 of the Treaty.

CHAPTER III. COMMISSION DECISIONS

Article 7

Finding and termination of infringement

1. Where the Commission, acting on a complaint or on its own initiative, finds that there is an infringement of Article 81 or of Article 82 of the Treaty, it may by decision require the undertakings and associations of undertakings concerned to bring such infringement to an end. For this purpose, it may impose on them any behavioural or structural remedies which are proportionate to the infringement committed and necessary to bring the infringement effectively to an end. Structural remedies can only be imposed either where there is no equally effective behavioural remedy or where any equally effective behavioural remedy would be more burdensome for the undertaking concerned than the structural remedy. If the Commission has a legitimate interest in doing so, it may also find that an infringement has been committed in the past.

2. Those entitled to lodge a complaint for the purposes of paragraph 1 are natural or legal persons who can show a legitimate interest and Member States.

Article 8

Interim measures

1. In cases of urgency due to the risk of serious and irreparable damage to competition, the Commission, acting on its own initiative may by decision, on the basis of a *prima facie* finding of infringement, order interim measures.

2. A decision under paragraph 1 shall apply for a specified period of time and may be renewed in so far this is necessary and appropriate.

Article 9
Commitments

1. Where the Commission intends to adopt a decision requiring that an infringement be brought to an end and the undertakings concerned offer commitments to meet the concerns expressed to them by the Commission in its preliminary assessment, the Commission may by decision make those commitments binding on the undertakings. Such a decision may be adopted for a specified period and shall conclude that there are no longer grounds for action by the Commission.

2. The Commission may, upon request or on its own initiative, reopen the proceedings:
(a) where there has been a material change in any of the facts on which the decision was based;
(b) where the undertakings concerned act contrary to their commitments; or
(c) where the decision was based on incomplete, incorrect or misleading information provided by the parties.

Article 10
Finding of inapplicability

Where the Community public interest relating to the application of Articles 81 and 82 of the Treaty so requires, the Commission, acting on its own initiative, may by decision find that Article 81 of the Treaty is not applicable to an agreement, a decision by an association of undertakings or a concerted practice, either because the conditions of Article 81(1) of the Treaty are not fulfilled, or because the conditions of Article 81(3) of the Treaty are satisfied.

The Commission may likewise make such a finding with reference to Article 82 of the Treaty.

CHAPTER IV. COOPERATION

Article 11
Cooperation between the Commission and the competition authorities of the Member States

1. The Commission and the competition authorities of the Member States shall apply the Community competition rules in close cooperation.

2. The Commission shall transmit to the competition authorities of the Member States copies of the most important documents it has collected with a view to applying Articles 7, 8, 9, 10 and Article 29(1). At the request of the competition authority of a Member State, the Commission shall provide it with a copy of other existing documents necessary for the assessment of the case.

3. The competition authorities of the Member States shall, when acting under Article 81 or Article 82 of the Treaty, inform the Commission in writing before or without delay after commencing the first formal investigative measure. This information may also be made available to the competition authorities of the other Member States.

4. No later than 30 days before the adoption of a decision requiring that an infringement be brought to an end, accepting commitments or withdrawing the benefit of a block exemption Regulation, the competition authorities of the Member States shall inform the Commission. To that effect, they shall provide the Commission with a summary of the case, the envisaged decision or, in the absence thereof, any other document indicating the proposed course of action. This information may also be made available to the competition authorities of the other Member States. At the request of the Commission, the acting competition authority shall make available to the Commission other documents it holds which are necessary for the assessment of the case. The information supplied to the Commission may be made available to the competition authorities of the other Member States. National competition authorities may also exchange between themselves information necessary for the assessment of a case that they are dealing with under Article 81 or Article 82 of the Treaty.

5. The competition authorities of the Member States may consult the Commission on any case involving the application of Community law.

6. The initiation by the Commission of proceedings for the adoption of a decision under Chapter III shall relieve the competition authorities of the Member States of their competence to apply Articles 81 and 82 of the Treaty. If a competition authority of a Member State is already acting on a case, the Commission shall only initiate proceedings after consulting with that national competition authority.

Article 12
Exchange of information

1. For the purpose of applying Articles 81 and 82 of the Treaty the Commission and the competition authorities of the Member States shall have the power to provide one another with and use in evidence any matter of fact or of law, including confidential information.

2. Information exchanged shall only be used in evidence for the purpose of applying Article 81 or Article 82 of the Treaty and in respect of the subject-matter for which it was collected by the transmitting authority. However, where national competition law is applied in the same case and in parallel to Community competition law and does not lead to a different outcome, information exchanged under this Article may also be used for the application of national competition law.

3. Information exchanged pursuant to paragraph 1 can only be used in evidence to impose sanctions on natural persons where:
— the law of the transmitting authority foresees sanctions of a similar kind in relation to an infringement of Article 81 or Article 82 of the Treaty or, in the absence thereof,
— the information has been collected in a way which respects the same level of protection of the rights of defence of natural persons as provided for under the national rules of the receiving authority. However, in this case, the information exchanged cannot be used by the receiving authority to impose cutodial sanctions.

Article 13
Suspension or termination of proceedings

1. Where competition authorities of two or more Member States have received a complaint or are acting on their own initiative under Article 81 or Article 82 of the Treaty against the same agreement, decision of an association or practice, the fact that one authority is dealing with the case shall be sufficient grounds for the others to suspend the proceedings before them or to reject the complaint. The Commission may likewise reject a complaint on the ground that a competition authority of a Member State is dealing with the case.

2. Where a competition authority of a Member State or the Commission has received a complaint against an agreement, decision of an association or practice which has already been dealt with by another competition authority, it may reject it.

Article 14
Advisory Committee

1. The Commission shall consult an Advisory Committee on Restrictive Practices and Dominant Positions prior to the taking of any decision under Articles 7, 8, 9, 10, 23, Article 24(2) and Article 29(1).

2. For the discussion of individual cases, the Advisory Committee shall be composed of representatives of the competition authorities of the Member States. For meetings in which issues other than individual cases are being discussed, an additional Member State representative competent in competition matters may be appointed. Representatives may, if unable to attend, be replaced by other representatives.

3. The consultation may take place at a meeting convened and chaired by the Commission, held not earlier than 14 days after dispatch of the notice convening it, together with a summary of the case, an indication of the most important documents and a preliminary draft decision. In respect of decisions pursuant to Article 8, the meeting may be held seven days after the dispatch of the operative part of a draft decision. Where the Commission dispatches a notice convening the meeting which gives a shorter period of notice than those specified above, the meeting may take place on the proposed date in the absence of an objection by any Member State. The Advisory Committee shall deliver a written opinion on the Commission's preliminary draft decision. It may deliver an opinion even if some members are absent and are not represented. At the request of one or several members, the positions stated in the opinion shall be reasoned.

4. Consultation may also take place by written procedure. However, if any Member State so requests, the Commission shall convene a meeting. In case of written procedure, the Commission shall determine a time-limit of not less than 14 days within which the Member States are to put forward their observations for circulation to all other Member States. In case of decisions to be taken pursuant to Article 8, the time-limit of 14 days is replaced by seven days. Where the Commission determines a time-limit for the written procedure which is shorter than those specified above, the proposed time-limit shall be applicable in the absence of an objection by any Member State.

5. The Commission shall take the utmost account of the opinion delivered by the Advisory Committee. It shall inform the Committee of the manner in which its opinion has been taken into account.

6. Where the Advisory Committee delivers a written opinion, this opinion shall be appended to the draft decision. If the Advisory Committee recommends publication of the opinion, the Commission shall carry out such publication taking into account the legitimate interest of undertakings in the protection of their business secrets.

7. At the request of competition authority of a Member State, the Commission shall include on the agenda of the Advisory Committee cases that are being dealt with by a competition authority of a Member State under Article 81 or Article 82 of the Treaty. The Commission may also do so on its own initiative. In either case, the Commission shall inform the competition authority concerned.

A request may in particular be made by a competition authority of a Member State in respect of a case where the Commission intends to initiate proceedings with the effect of Article 11(6).

The Advisory Committee shall not issue opinions on cases dealt with by competition authorities of the Member States. The Advisory Committee may also discuss general issues of Community competition law.

Article 15
Cooperation with national courts

1. In proceedings for the application of Article 81 or Article 82 of the Treaty, courts of the Member States may ask the Commission to transmit to them information in its possession or its opinion on questions concerning the application of the Community competition rules.

2. Member States shall forward to the Commission a copy of any written judgment of national courts deciding on the application of Article 81 or Article 82 of the Treaty. Such copy shall be forwarded without delay after the full written judgment is notified to the parties.

3. Competition authorities of the Member States, acting on their own initiative, may submit written observations to the national courts of their Member State on issues relating to the application of Article 81 or Article 82 of the Treaty. With the permission of the court in question, they may also submit oral observations to the national courts of their Member State. Where the coherent application of Article 81 or Article 82 of the Treaty so requires, the Commission, acting

on its own initiative, may submit written observations to courts of the Member States. With the permission of the court in question, it may also make oral observations.

For the purpose of the preparation of their observations only, the competition authorities of the Member States and the Commission may request the relevant court of the Member State to transmit or ensure the transmission to them of any documents necessary for the assessment of the case.

4. This Article is without prejudice to wider powers to make observations before courts conferred on competition authorities of the Member States under the law of their Member State.

Article 16
Uniform application of Community competition law

1. When national courts rule on agreements, decisions or practices under Article 81 or Article 82 of the Treaty which are already the subject of a Commission decision, they cannot take decisions running counter to the decision adopted by the Commission. They must also avoid giving decisions which would conflict with a decision contemplated by the Commission in proceedings it has initiated. To that effect, the national court may assess whether it is necessary to stay its proceedings. This obligation is without prejudice to the rights and obligations under Article 234 of the Treaty.

2. When competition authorities of the Member States rule on agreements, decisions or practices under Article 81 or Article 82 of the Treaty which are already the subject of a Commission decision, they cannot take decisions which would run counter to the decision adopted by the Commission.

CHAPTER V. POWERS OF INVESTIGATION

Article 17
Investigations into sectors of the economy and into types of agreements

1. Where the trend of trade between Member States, the rigidity of prices or other circumstances suggest that competition may be restricted or distorted within the common market, the Commission may conduct its inquiry into a particular sector of the economy or into a particular type of agreements across various sectors. In the course of that inquiry, the Commission may request the undertakings or associations of undertakings concerned to supply the information necessary for giving effect to Articles 81 and 82 of the Treaty and may carry out any inspections necessary for that purpose.

The Commission may in particular request the undertakings or associations of undertakings concerned to communicate to it all agreements, decisions and concerted practices.

The Commission may publish a report on the results of its inquiry into particular sectors of the economy or particular types of agreements across various sectors and invite comments from interested parties.

2. Articles 14, 18, 19, 20, 22, 23 and 24 shall apply *mutatis mutandis.*

Article 18
Requests for information

1. In order to carry out the duties assigned to it by this Regulation, the Commission may, by simple request or by decision, require undertakings and associations of undertakings to provide all necessary information.

2. When sending a simple request for information to an undertaking or association of undertakings, the Commission shall state the legal basis and the purpose of the request, specify what

information is required and fix the time-limit within which the information is to be provided, and the penalties provided for in Article 23 for supplying incorrect or misleading information.

3. Where the Commission requires undertakings and associations of undertakings to supply information by decision, it shall state the legal basis and the purpose of the request, specify what information is required and fix the time-limit within which it is to be provided. It shall also indicate the penalties provided for in Article 23 and indicate or impose the penalties provided for in Article 24. It shall further indicate the right to have the decision reviewed by the Court of Justice.

4. The owners of the undertakings or their representatives and, in the case of legal persons, companies or firms, or associations having no legal personality, the persons authorised to represent them by law or by their constitution shall supply the information requested on behalf of the undertaking or the association of undertakings concerned. Lawyers duly authorised to act may supply the information on behalf of their clients. The latter shall remain fully responsible if the information supplied is incomplete, incorrect or misleading.

5. The Commission shall without delay forward a copy of the simple request or of the decision to the competition authority of the Member State in whose territory the seat of the undertaking or association of undertakings is situated and the competition authority of the Member State whose territory is affected.

6. At the request of the Commission the governments and competition authorities of the Member States shall provide the Commission with all necessary information to carry out the duties assigned to it by this Regulation.

Article 19
Power to take statements

1. In order to carry out the duties assigned to it by this Regulation, the Commission may interview any natural or legal person who consents to be interviewed for the purpose of collecting information relating to the subject-matter of an investigation.

2. Where an interview pursuant to paragraph 1 is conducted in the premises of an undertaking, the Commission shall inform the competition authority of the Member State in whose territory the interview takes place. If so requested by the competition authority of that Member State, its officials may assist the officials and other accompanying persons authorised by the Commission to conduct the interview.

Article 20
The Commission's powers of inspection

1. In order to carry out the duties assigned to it by this Regulation, the Commission may conduct all necessary inspections of undertakings and associations of undertakings.

2. The officials and other accompanying persons authorised by the Commission to conduct an inspection are empowered:

(a) to enter any premises, land and means of transport of undertakings and associations of undertakings:

(b) to examine the books and other records related to the business, irrespective of the medium on which they are stored:

(c) to take or obtain in any form copies of or extracts from such books or records;

(d) to seal any business premises and books or records for the period and to the extent necessary for the inspection;

(e) to ask any representative or member of staff of the undertaking or association of undertakings for explanations on facts or documents relating to the subject-matter and purpose of the inspection and to record the answers.

3. The officials and other accompanying persons authorised by the Commission to conduct an inspection shall exercise their powers upon production of a written authorization specifying the subject matter and purpose of the inspection and the penalties provided for in Article 23 in case the production of the required books or other records related to the business is incomplete or where the answers to questions asked under paragraph 2 of the present Article are incorrect or misleading. In good time before the inspection, the Commission shall give notice of the inspection to the competition authority of the Member State in whose territory it is to be conducted.

4. Undertakings and associations of undertakings are required to submit to inspections ordered by decision of the Commission. The decision shall specify the subject matter and purpose of the inspection, appoint the date on which it is to begin and indicate the penalties provided for in Articles 23 and 24 and the right to have the decision reviewed by the Court of Justice. The Commission shall take such decisions after consulting the competition authority of the Member State in whose territory the inspection is to be conducted.

5. Officials of as well as those authorized or appointed by the competition authority of the Member State in whose territory the inspection is to be conducted shall, at the request of that authority or of the Commission, actively assist the officials and other accompanying persons authorized by the Commission. To this end, they shall enjoy the powers specified in paragraph 2.

6. Where the officials and other accompanying persons authorised by the Commission find that an undertaking opposes an inspection ordered pursuant to this Article, the Member State concerned shall afford them the necessary assistance, requesting where appropriate the assistance of the police or of an equivalent enforcement authority, so as to enable them to conduct their inspection.

7. If the assistance provided for in paragraph 6 requires authorization from a judicial authority according to national rules, such authorization shall be applied for. Such authorisation may also be applied for as a precautionary measure.

8. Where authorization as referred to in paragraph 7 is applied for, the national judicial authority shall control that the Commission decision is authentic and that the coercive measures envisaged are neither arbitrary nor excessive having regard to the subject matter of the inspection. In its control of the proportionality of the coercive measures, the national judicial authority may ask the Commission, directly or through the Member State competition authority, for detailed explanations in particular on the grounds the Commission has for suspecting infringement of Articles 81 and 82 of the Treaty, as well as on the seriousness of the suspected infringement and on the nature of the involvement of the undertaking concerned. However, the national judicial authority may not call into question the necessity for the inspection nor demand that it be provided with the information in the Commission's file. The lawfulness of the Commission decision shall be subject to review only by the Court of Justice.

Article 21
Inspection of other premises

1. If a reasonable suspicion exists that books or other records related to the business and to the subject-matter of the inspection, which may be relevant to prove a serious violation of Article 81 or Article 82 of the Treaty, are being kept in any other premises, land and means of transport, including the homes of directors, managers and other members of staff of the undertakings and associations of undertakings concerned, the Commission can by decision order an inspection to be conducted in such other premises, land and means of transport.

2. The decision shall specify the subject matter and purpose of the inspection, appoint the date on which it is to begin and indicate the right to have the decision reviewed by the Court of Justice. It shall in particular state the reasons that have led the Commission to conclude that a

suspicion in the sense of paragraph 1 exists. The Commission shall take such decisions after consulting the competition authority of the Member State in whose territory the inspection is to be conducted.

3. A decision adopted pursuant to paragraph 1 cannot be executed without prior authorisation from the national judicial authority of the Member State concerned. The national judicial authority shall control that the Commission decision is authentic and that the coercive measures envisaged are neither arbitrary nor excessive having regard in particular to the seriousness of the suspected infringement, to the importance of the evidence sought, to the involvement of the undertaking concerned and to the reasonable likelihood that business books and records relating to the subject matter of the inspection are kept in the premises for which the authorisation is requested. The national judicial authority may ask the Commission, directly or through the Member State competition authority, for detailed explanations on those elements which are necessary to allow its control of the proportionality of the coercive measures envisaged.

However, the national judicial authority may not call into question the necessity for the inspection nor demand that it be provided with information in the Commission's file. The lawfulness of the Commission decision shall be subject to review only by the Court of Justice.

4. The officials and other accompanying persons authorized by the Commission to conduct an inspection ordered in accordance with paragraph 1 of this Article shall have the powers set out in Article 20(2)(a), (b) and (c). Article 20(5) and (6) shall apply *mutatis mutandis*.

Article 22
Investigations by competition authorities of Member States

1. The competition authority of a Member State may in its own territory carry out any inspection or other fact-finding measure under its national law on behalf and for the account of the competition authority of another Member State in order to establish whether there has been an infringement of Article 81 or Article 82 of the Treaty. Any exchange and use of the information collected shall be carried out in accordance with Article 12.

2. At the request of the Commission, the competition authorities of the Member States shall undertake the inspections which the Commission considers to be necessary under Article 20(1) or which it has ordered by decision pursuant to Article 20(4). The officials of the competition authorities of the Member States who are responsible for conducting these inspections as well as those authorised or appointed by them shall exercise their powers in accordance with their national law.

If so requested by the Commission or by the competition authority of the Member State in whose territory the inspection is to be conducted, officials and other accompanying persons authorised by the Commission may assist the officials of the authority concerned.

CHAPTER VI. PENALTIES

Article 23
Fines

1. The Commission may by decision impose on undertakings and associations of undertakings fines not exceeding 1% of the total turnover in the preceding business year where, intentionally or negligently:

(a) they supply incorrect or misleading information in response to a request made pursuant to Article 17 or Article 18(2);

(b) in response to a request made by decision adopted pursuant to Article 17 or Article 18(3), they supply incorrect, incomplete or misleading information or do not supply information within the required time-limit;

(c) they produce the required books or other records related to the business in incomplete form during inspections under Article 20 or refuse to submit to inspections ordered by a decision adopted pursuant to Article 20(4);

(d) in response to a question asked in accordance with Article 20(2)(e),
— they give an incorrect or misleading answer,
— they fail to rectify within a time-limit set by the Commission an incorrect, incomplete or misleading answer given by a member of staff, or
— they fail or refuse to provide a complete answer on facts relating to the subject-matter and purpose of an inspection ordered by a decision adopted pursuant to Article 20(4);

(e) seals affixed in accordance with Article 20(2)(d) by officials or other accompanying persons authorised by the Commission have been broken.

2. The Commission may by decision impose fines on undertakings and associations of undertakings where, either intentionally or negligently:
(a) they infringe Article 81 or Article 82 of the Treaty; or
(b) they contravene a decision ordering interim measures under Article 8; or
(c) they fail to comply with a commitment made binding by a decision pursuant to Article 9.
For each undertaking and association of undertakings participating in the infringement, the fine shall not exceed 10% of its total turnover in the preceding business year.

Where the infringement of an association relates to the activities of its members, the fine shall not exceed 10% of the sum of the total turnover of each member active on the market affected by the infringement of the association.

3. In fixing the amount of the fine, regard shall be had both to the gravity and to the duration of the infringement.

4. When a fine is imposed on an association of undertakings taking account of the turnover of its members and the association is not solvent, the association is obliged to call for contributions from its members to cover the amount of the fine.

Where such contributions have not been made to the association within a time-limit fixed by the Commission, the Commission may require payment of the fine directly by any of the undertakings whose representatives were members of the decision-making bodies concerned of the association.

After the Commission has required payment under the second subparagraph, where necessary to ensure full payment of the fine, the Commission may require payment of the balance by any of the members of the association which were active on the market on which the infringement occurred.

However, the Commission shall not require payment under the second or the third subparagraph from undertakings which show that they have not implemented the infringing decision of the association and either were not aware of its existence or have actively distanced themselves from it before the Commission started investigating the case.

The financial liability of each undertaking in respect of the payment of the fine shall not exceed 10 % of its total turnover in the preceding business year.

5. Decisions taken pursuant to paragraphs 1 and 2 shall not be of a criminal law nature.

Article 24
Periodic penalty payments

1. The Commission may, by decision, impose on undertakings or associations of undertakings periodic penalty payments not exceeding 5% of the average daily turnover in the preceding business year per day and calculated from the date appointed by the decision, in order to compel them:

(a) to put an end to an infringement of Article 81 or Article 82 of the Treaty, in accordance with a decision taken pursuant to Article 7;

(b) to comply with a decision ordering interim measures taken pursuant to Article 8:

(c) to comply with a commitment made binding by a decision pursuant to Article 9;

(d) to supply complete and correct information which it has requested by decision taken pursuant to Article 17 or Article 18(3);

(e) to submit to an inspection which it has ordered by decision taken pursuant to Article 20(4).

2. Where the undertakings or associations of undertakings have satisfied the obligation which the periodic penalty payment was intended to enforce, the Commission may fix the definitive amount of the periodic penalty payment at a figure lower than that which would arise under the original decision. Article 23(4) shall apply correspondingly.

CHAPTER VII. LIMITATION PERIODS

Article 25
Limitation periods for the imposition of penalties

1. The powers conferred on the Commission by Articles 23 and 24 shall be subject to the following limitation periods:

(a) three years in the case of infringements of provisions concerning requests for information or the conduct of inspections;

(b) five years in the case of all other infringements.

2. Time shall begin to run on the day on which the infringement is committed. However, in the case of continuing or repeated infringements, time shall begin to run on the day on which the infringement ceases.

3. Any action taken by the Commission or by the competition authority of a Member State for the purpose of the investigation or proceedings in respect of an infringement shall interrupt the limitation period for the imposition of fines or periodic penalty payments. The limitation period shall be interrupted with effect from the date on which the action is notified to at least one undertaking or association of undertakings which has participated in the infringement. Actions which interrupt the running of the period shall include in particular the following:

(a) written requests for information by the Commission or by the competition authority of a Member State;

(b) written authorisations to conduct inspections issued to its officials by the Commission or by the competition authority of a Member State;

(c) the initiation of proceedings by the Commission or by the competition authority of a Member State;

(d) notification of the statement of objections of the Commission or of the competition authority of a Member State.

4. The interruption of the limitation period shall apply for all the undertakings or associations of undertakings which have participated in the infringement.

5. Each interruption shall start time running afresh. However, the limitation period shall expire at the latest on the day on which a period equal to twice the limitation period has elapsed without the Commission having imposed a fine or a periodic penalty payment. That period shall be extended by the time during which limitation is suspended pursuant to paragraph 6.

6. The limitation period for the imposition of fines or periodic penalty payments shall be suspended for as long as the decision of the Commission is the subject of proceedings pending before the Court of Justice.

Article 26
Limitation period for the enforcement of penalties

1. The power of the Commission to enforce decisions taken pursuant to Articles 23 and 24 shall be subject to a limitation period of five years.

2. Time shall begin to run on the day on which the decision becomes final.

3. The limitation period for the enforcement of penalties shall be interrupted:
(a) by notification of a decision varying the original amount of the fine or periodic penalty payment or refusing an application for variation;
(b) by any action of the Commission or of a Member State, acting at the request of the Commission, designed to enforce payment of the fine or periodic penalty payment.

4. Each interruption shall start time running afresh.

5. The limitation period for the enforcement of penalties shall be suspended for so long as:
(a) time to pay is allowed;
(b) enforcement of payment is suspended pursuant to a decision of the Court of Justice.

CHAPTER VIII. HEARINGS AND PROFESSIONAL SECRECY

Article 27
Hearing of the parties, complainants and others

1. Before taking decisions as provided for in Articles 7, 8, 23 and Article 24(2), the Commission shall give the undertakings or associations of undertakings which are the subject of the proceedings conducted by the Commission the opportunity of being heard on the matters to which the Commission has taken objection. The Commission shall base its decisions only on objections on which the parties concerned have been able to comment. Complainants shall be associated closely with the proceedings.

2. The rights of defence of the parties concerned shall be fully respected in the proceedings. They shall be entitled to have access to the Commission's file, subject to the legitimate interest of undertakings in the protection of their business secrets. The right of access to the file shall not extend to confidential information and internal documents of the Commission or the competition authorities of the Member States. In particular, the right of access shall not extend to correspondence between the Commission and the competition authorities of the Member States, or between the latter, including documents drawn up pursuant to Articles 11 and 14. Nothing in this paragraph shall prevent the Commission from disclosing and using information necessary to prove an infringement.

3. If the Commission considers it necessary, it may also hear other natural or legal persons. Applications to be heard on the part of such persons shall, where they show a sufficient interest, be granted. The competition authorities of the Member States may also ask the Commission to hear other natural or legal persons.

4. Where the Commission intends to adopt a decision pursuant to Article 9 or Article 10, it shall publish a concise summary of the case and the main content of the commitments or of the proposed course of action. Interested third parties may submit their observations within a time limit which is fixed by the Commission in its publication and which may not be less than one month. Publication shall have regard to the legitimate interest of undertakings in the protection of their business secrets.

Article 28
Professional secrecy

1. Without prejudice to Articles 12 and 15, information collected pursuant to Articles 17 to 22 shall be used only for the purpose for which it was acquired.

2. Without prejudice to the exchange and to the use of information foreseen in Articles 11, 12, 14, 15 and 27, the Commission and the competition authorities of the Member States, their officials, servants and other persons working under the supervision of these authorities as well as officials and civil servants of other authorities of the Member States shall not disclose information acquired or exchanged by them pursuant to this Regulation and of the kind covered by the obligation of professional secrecy. This obligation also applies to all representatives and experts of Member States attending meetings of the Advisory Committee pursuant to Article 14.

CHAPTER IX. EXEMPTION REGULATIONS

Article 29
Withdrawal in individual cases

1. Where the Commission, empowered by a Council Regulation, such as Regulations 19/65/EEC, (EEC) No 2821/71, (EEC) No 3976/87, (EEC) No 1534/91 or (EEC) No 479/92, to apply Article 81(3) of the Treaty by regulation, has declared Article 81(1) of the Treaty inapplicable to certain categories of agreements, decisions by associations of undertakings or concerted practices, it may, acting on its own initiative or on a complaint, withdraw the benefit of such an exemption Regulation when it finds that in any particular case an agreement, decision or concerted practice to which the exemption Regulation applies has certain effects which are incompatible with Article 81(3) of the Treaty.

2. Where, in any particular case, agreements, decisions by associations of undertakings or concerted practices to which a Commission Regulation referred to in paragraph 1 applies have effects which are incompatible with Article 81(3) of the Treaty in the territory of a Member State, or in a part thereof, which has all the characteristics of a distinct geographic market, the competition authority of that Member State may withdraw the benefit of the Regulation in question in respect of that territory.

CHAPTER X. GENERAL PROVISIONS

Article 30
Publication of decisions

1. The Commission shall publish the decisions, which it takes pursuant to Articles 7 to 10, 23 and 24.

2. The publication shall state the names of the parties and the main content of the decision, including any penalties imposed. It shall have regard to the legitimate interest of undertakings in the protection of their business secrets.

Article 31
Review by the Court of Justice

The Court of Justice shall have unlimited jurisdiction to review decisions whereby the Commission has fixed a fine or periodic penalty payment. It may cancel, reduce or increase the fine or periodic penalty payment imposed.

Article 32
Exclusions

This Regulation shall not apply to:

(a) international tramp vessel services as defined in Article 1(3)(a) of Regulation (EEC) No 4056/86;

(b) a maritime transport service that takes place exclusively between ports in one and the same Member State as foreseen in Article 1(2) of Regulation (EEC) No 4056/86;

(c) air transport between Community airports and third countries.

Article 33
Implementing provisions

1. The Commission shall be authorised to take such measures as may be appropriate in order to apply this Regulation. The measures may concern, *inter alia*;

(a) the form, content and other details of complaints lodged pursuant to Article 7 and the procedure for rejecting complaints;

(b) the practical arrangements for the exchange of information and consultations provided for in Article 11;

(c) the practical arrangements for the hearings provided for in Article 27.

2. Before the adoption of any measures pursuant to paragraph 1, the Commission shall publish a draft thereof and invite all interested parties to submit their comments within the time-limit it lays down, which may not be less than one month. Before publishing a draft measure and before adopting it, the Commission shall consult the Advisory Committee on Restrictive Practices and Dominant Positions.

CHAPTER XI. TRANSITIONAL, AMENDING AND FINAL PROVISIONS

Article 34
Transitional provisions

1. Applications made to the Commission under Article 2 of Regulation No 17, notifications made under Articles 4 and 5 of that Regulation and the corresponding applications and notifications made under Regulations (EEC) No 1017/68, (EEC) No 4056/86 and (EEC) No 3975/87 shall lapse as from the date of application of this Regulation.

2. Procedural steps taken under Regulation No 17 and Regulations (EEC) No 1017/68, (EEC) No 4056/86 and (EEC) No 3975/87 shall continue to have effect for the purposes of applying this Regulation.

Article 35
Designation of competition authorities of Member States

1. The Member States shall designate the competition authority or authorities responsible for the application of Articles 81 and 82 of the Treaty in such a way that the provisions of this regulation are effectively complied with. The measures necessary to empower those authorities to apply those Articles shall be taken before 1 May 2004. The authorities designated may include courts.

2. When enforcement of Community competition law is entrusted to national administrative and judicial authorities, the Member States may allocate different powers and functions to those different national authorities, whether administrative or judicial.

3. The effects of Article 11(6) apply to the authorities designated by the Member States including courts that exercise functions regarding the preparation and the adoption of the types of decisions foreseen in Article 5. The effects of Article 11(6) do not extend to courts insofar as they act as review courts in respect of the types of decisions foreseen in Article 5.

4. Notwithstanding paragraph 3, in the Member States where, for the adoption of certain types of decisions foreseen in Article 5, an authority brings an action before a judicial authority that is separate and different from the prosecuting authority and provided that the terms of this paragraph are complied with, the effects of Article 11(6) shall be limited to the authority prosecuting the case which shall withdraw its claim before the judicial authority when the

Commission opens proceedings and this withdrawal shall bring the national proceedings effectively to an end.

Article 36
Amendment of Regulation (EEC) No 1017/68

Regulation (EEC) No 1017/68 is amended as follows:

1. Article 2 is repealed;
2. in Article 3(1), the words 'The prohibition laid down in Article 2' are replaced by the words 'The prohibition in Article 81(1) of the Treaty';
3. Article 4 is amended as follows:
   (a) In paragraph 1, the words 'The agreements, decisions and concerted practices referred to in Article 2' are replaced by the words 'Agreements, decisions and concerted practices pursuant to Article 81(1) of the Treaty';
   (b) Paragraph 2 is replaced by the following:
      '2. If the implementation of any agreement, decision or concerted practice covered by paragraph 1 has, in a given case, effects which are incompatible with the requirements of Article 81(3) of the Treaty, undertakings or associations of undertakings may be required to make such effects cease.'
4. Articles 5 to 29 are repealed with the exception of Article 13(3) which continues to apply to decisions adopted pursuant to Article 5 of Regulation (EEC) No 1017/68 prior to the date of application of this Regulation until the date of expiration of those decisions;
5. in Article 30, paragraphs 2, 3 and 4 are deleted.

Article 37
Amendment of Regulation (EEC) No 2988/74

In Regulation (EEC) No 2988/74, the following Article is inserted:

'Article 7a

Exclusion

This Regulation shall not apply to measures taken under Council Regulation (EC) No 1/2003 of 16 December 2002 on the implementation of the rules on competition laid down in Articles 81 and 82 of the Treaty*.

* OJ L 1, 4.1.2003, p. 1.'

Article 38
Amendment of Regulation (EEC) No 4056/86

Regulation (EEC) No 4056/86 is amended as follows:
1. Article 7 is amended as follows:
   (a) Paragraph 1 is replaced by the following:
      '1. *Breach of an obligation*
      Where the persons concerned are in breach of an obligation which, pursuant to Article 5, attaches to the exemption provided for in Article 3, the Commission may, in order to put an end to such breach and under the conditions laid down in Council Regulation (EC) No 1/2003 of 16 December 2002 on the implementation of the rules on competition laid down in Articles 81 and 82 of the Treaty* adopt a decision that either prohibits them from carrying out or requires them to perform certain specific acts, or withdraws the benefit of the block exemption which they enjoyed.

         * OJ L 1, 4.1.2003, p. 1.
   (b) Paragraph 2 is amended as follows:

(i) In point (a), the words 'under the conditions laid down in Section II' are replaced by the words 'under the conditions laid down in Regulation (EC) No 1/2003';

(ii) The second sentence of the second subparagraph of point (c)(i) is replaced by the following:

'At the same time it shall decide, in accordance with Article 9 of Regulation (EC) No 1/2003, whether to accept commitments offered by the undertakings concerned with a view, *inter alia*, to obtaining access to the market for non-conference lines.'

2. Article 8 is amended as follows:

(a) Paragraph 1 is deleted.

(b) In paragraph 2 the words 'pursuant to Article 10' are replaced by the words 'pursuant to Regulation (EC) No 1/2003'.

(c) Paragraph 3 is deleted:

3. Article 9 is amended as follows:

(a) In paragraph 1, the words 'Advisory Committee referred to in Article 15' are replaced by the words 'Advisory Committee referred to in Article 14 of Regulation (EC) No 1/2003';

(b) In paragraph 2, the words 'Advisory Committee as referred to in Article 15' are replaced by the words 'Advisory Committee referred to in Article 14 of Regulation (EC) No 1/2003';

4. Articles 10 to 25 are repealed with the exception of Article 13(3) which continues to apply to decisions adopted pursuant to Article 81(3) of the Treaty prior to the date of application of this Regulation until the date of expiration of those decisions;

5. in Article 26, the words 'the form, content and other details of complaints pursuant to Article 10, applications pursuant to Article 12 and the hearings provided for in Article 23(1) and (2)' are deleted.

Article 39
Amendment of Regulation (EEC) No 3975/87

Articles 3 to 19 of Regulation (EEC) No 3975/87 are repealed with the exception of Article 6(3) which continues to apply to decisions adopted pursuant to Article 81(3) of the Treaty prior to the date of application of this Regulation until the date of expiration of those decisions.

Article 40
Amendment of Regulation No 19/65/EEC, (EEC) No 2821/71 and (EEC) No 1534/91

Article 7 of Regulation No 19/65/EEC, Article 7 of Regulation (EEC) No 2821/71 and Article 7 of Regulation (EEC) No 1534/91 are repealed.

Article 41
Amendment of Regulation (EEC) No 3976/87

Regulation (EEC) No 3976/87 is amended as follows:

1. Article 6 is replaced by the following:

'Article 6

The Commission shall consult the Advisory Committee referred to in Article 14 of Council Regulation (EC) No 1/2003 of 16 December 2002 on the implementation of the rules on competition laid down in Articles 81 and 82 of the Treaty* before publishing a draft Regulation and before adopting a Regulation.

* OJ L 1, 4.1.2003, p. 1.'

2. Article 7 is repealed.

Article 42
Amendment of Regulation (EEC) No 479/92

Regulation (EEC) No 479/92 is amended as follows:

1. Article 5 is replaced by the following:

   'Article 5

   Before publishing the draft Regulation and before adopting the Regulation, the Commission shall consult the Advisory Committee referred to in Article 14 of Council Regulation (EC) No 1/2003 of 16 December 2002 on the implementation of the rules on competition laid down in Articles 81 and 82 of the Treaty*.

   * OJ L 1, 4.1.2003, p. 1.'

2. Article 6 is repealed.

Article 43
Repeal of Regulations No 17 and No 141

1. Regulation No 17 is repealed with the exception of Article 8(3) which continues to apply to decisions adopted pursuant to Article 81(3) of the Treaty prior to the date of application of this Regulation until the date of expiration of those decisions.

2. Regulation No 141 is repealed.

3. References to the repealed Regulations shall be construed as references to this Regulation.

Article 44
Report on the application of the present Regulation

Five years from the date of application of this Regulation, the Commission shall report to the European Parliament and the Council on the functioning of this Regulation, in particular on the application of Article 11(6) and Article 17.

On the basis of this report, the Commission shall assess whether it is appropriate to propose to the Council a revision of this Regulation.

Article 45
Entry into force

This Regulation shall enter into force on the 20th day following that of its publication in the *Official Journal of the European Communities*.

It shall apply from 1 May 2004.

This Regulation shall be binding in its entirety and directly applicable in all Member States.

Done at Brussels, 16 December 2002.

For the Council
The President
M. FISCHER BOEL

APPENDIX 3

Commission Regulation (EC) No 773/2004 of 7 April 2004 relating to the conduct of proceedings by the Commission pursuant to Articles 81 and 82 of the EC Treaty

(Text with EEA relevance)

THE COMMISSION OF THE EUROPEAN COMMUNITIES.

Having regard to the Treaty establishing the European Community,

Having regard to the Agreement on the European Economic Area,

Having regard to Council Regulation (EC) No 1/2003 of 16 December 2002 on the implementation of the rules on competition laid down in Articles 81 and 82 of the Treaty,[1] and in particular Article 33 thereof,

After consulting the Advisory Committee on Restrictive Practices and Dominant Positions,

Whereas:

(1) Regulation (EC) No 1/2003 empowers the Commission to regulate certain aspects of proceedings for the application of Articles 81 and 82 of the Treaty. It is necessary to lay down rules concerning the initiation of proceedings by the Commission as well as the handling of complaints and the hearing of the parties concerned.

(2) According to Regulation (EC) No 1/2003, national courts are under an obligation to avoid taking decisions which could run counter to decisions envisaged by the Commission in the same case. According to Article 11(6) of that Regulation, national competition authorities are relieved from their competence once the Commission has initiated proceedings for the adoption of a decision under Chapter III of Regulation (EC) No 1/2003. In this context, it is important that courts and competition authorities of the Member States are aware of the initiation of proceedings by the Commission. The Commission should therefore be able to make public its decisions to initiate proceedings.

(3) Before taking oral statements from natural or legal persons who consent to be interviewed, the Commission should inform those persons of the legal basis of the interview and its voluntary nature. The persons interviewed should also be informed of the purpose of the interview and of any record which may be made. In order to enhance the accuracy of the statements, the persons interviewed should also be given an opportunity to correct the statements recorded. Where information gathered from oral statements is exchanged pursuant to Article 12 of Regulation (EC) No 1/2003, that information should only be used in evidence to impose sanctions on natural persons where the conditions set out in that Article are fulfilled.

(4) Pursuant to Article 23(1)(d) of Regulation (EC) No 1/2003 fines may be imposed on undertakings and associations of undertakings where they fail to rectify within the time limit fixed

---

[1] OJ L1, 4.1.2003, p 1. Reg as amended by Reg (EC) No 411/2004 (OJ L68, 6.3.2004, p 1).

by the Commission an incorrect, incomplete or misleading answer given by a member of their staff to questions in the course of inspections. It is therefore necessary to provide the undertaking concerned with a record of any explanations given and to establish a procedure enabling it to add any rectification, amendment or supplement to the explanations given by the member of staff who is not or was not authorized to provide explanations on behalf of the undertaking. The explanations given by a member of staff should remain in the Commission file as recorded during the inspection.

(5) Complaints are an essential source of information for detecting infringements of competition rules. It is important to define clear and efficient procedures for handling complaints lodged with the Commission.

(6) In order to be admissible for the purposes of Article 7 of Regulation (EC) No 1/2003, a complaint must contain certain specified information.

(7) In order to assist complainants in submitting the necessary facts to the Commission, a form should be drawn up. The submission of the information listed in that form should be a condition for a complaint to be treated as a complaint as referred to in Article 7 of Regulation (EC) No 1/2003.

(8) Natural or legal persons having chosen to lodge a complaint should be given the possibility to be associated closely with the proceedings initiated by the Commission with a view to finding an infringement. However, they should not have access to business secrets or other confidential information belonging to other parties involved in the proceedings.

(9) Complainants should be granted the opportunity of expressing their views if the Commission considers that there are insufficient grounds for acting on the complaint. Where the Commission rejects a complaint on the grounds that a competition authority of a Member State is dealing with it or has already done so, it should inform the complainant of the identity of that authority.

(10) In order to respect the rights of defence of undertakings, the Commission should give the parties concerned the right to be heard before it takes a decision.

(11) Provision should also be made for the hearing of persons who have not submitted a complaint as referred to in Article 7 of Regulation (EC) No 1/2003 and who are not parties to whom a statement of objections has been addressed but who can nevertheless show a sufficient interest. Consumer associations that apply to be heard should generally be regarded as having a sufficient interest, where the proceedings concern products or services used by the end-consumer or products or services that constitute a direct input into such products or services. Where it considers this to be useful for the proceedings, the Commission should also be able to invite other persons to express their views in writing and to attend the oral hearing of the parties to whom a statement of objections has been addressed. Where appropriate, it should also be able to invite such persons to express their views at that oral hearing.

(12) To improve the effectiveness of oral hearings, the Hearing Officer should have the power to allow the parties concerned, complainants, other persons invited to the hearing, the Commission services and the authorities of the Member States to ask questions during the hearing.

(13) When granting access to the file, the Commission should ensure the protection of business secrets and other confidential information. The category of 'other confidential information' includes information other than business secrets, which may be considered as confidential, insofar as its disclosure would significantly harm an undertaking or person. The Commission should be able to request undertakings or associations of undertakings that submit or have submitted documents or statements to identify confidential information.

(14) Where business secrets or other confidential information are necessary to prove an infringement, the Commission should assess for each individual document whether the need to disclose is greater than the harm which might result from disclosure.

(15) In the interest of legal certainty, a minimum time-limit for the various submissions provided for in this Regulation should be laid down.

(16) This Regulation replaces Commission Regulation (EC) No 2842/98 of 22 December 1998 on the hearing of parties in certain proceedings under Articles 85 and 86 of the EC Treaty,[2] which should therefore be repealed.

(17) This Regulation aligns the procedural rules in the transport sector with the general rules of procedure in all sectors. Commission Regulation (EC) No 2843/98 of 22 December 1998 on the form, content and other details of applications and notifications provided for in Council Regulations (EEC) No 1017/68, (EEC) No 4056/86 and (EEC) No 3975/87 applying the rules on competition to the transport sector[3] should therefore be repealed.

(18) Regulation (EC) No 1/2003 abolishes the notification and authorization system. Commission Regulation (EC) No 3385/94 of 21 December 1994 on the form, content and other details of applications and notifications provided for in Council Regulation No 17[4] should therefore be repealed.

HAS ADOPTED THIS REGULATION:

CHAPTER I. SCOPE

Article 1

Subject-matter and scope

This regulation applies to proceedings conducted by the Commission for the application of Articles 81 and 82 of the Treaty.

CHAPTER II. INITIATION OF PROCEEDINGS

Article 2

Initiation of proceedings

1. The Commission may decide to initiate proceedings with a view to adopting a decision pursuant to Chapter III of Regulation (EC) No 1/2003 at any point in time, but no later than the date on which it issues a preliminary assessment as referred to in Article 9(1) of that Regulation or a statement of objections or the date on which a notice pursuant to Article 27(4) of that Regulation is published, whichever is the earlier.

2. The Commission may make public the initiation of proceedings, in any appropriate way. Before doing so, it shall inform the parties concerned.

3. The Commission may exercise its powers of investigation pursuant to Chapter V of Regulation (EC) No 1/2003 before initiating proceedings.

4. The Commission may reject a complaint pursuant to Article 7 of Regulation (EC) No 1/2003 without initiating proceedings.

CHAPTER III. INVESTIGATIONS BY THE COMMISSION

Article 3

Power to take statements

1. Where the Commission interviews a person with his consent in accordance with Article 19 of Regulation (EC) No 1/2003, it shall, at the beginning of the interview, state the legal basis and

---

[2] OJ L354, 30.12.1998, p 18.   [3] OJ L354, 30.12.1998, p 22.
[4] OJ L377, 31.12.1994, p 28.

the purpose of the interview, and recall its voluntary nature. It shall also inform the person interviewed of its intention to make a record of the interview.

2. The interview may be conducted by any means including by telephone or electronic means.

3. The Commission may record the statements made by the persons interviewed in any form. A copy of any recording shall be made available to the person interviewed for approval. Where necessary, the Commission shall set a time-limit within which the person interviewed may communicate to it any correction to be made to the statement.

Article 4
Oral questions during inspections

1. When, pursuant to Article 20(2)(e) of Regulation (EC) No 1/2003, officials or other accompanying persons authorized by the Commission ask representatives or members of staff of an undertaking or of an association of undertakings for explanations, the explanations given may be recorded in any form.

2. A copy of any recording made pursuant to paragraph 1 shall be made available to the under-taking or association of undertakings concerned after the inspection.

3. In cases where a member of staff of an undertaking or of an association of undertakings who is not or was not authorized by the undertaking or by the association of undertakings to provide explanations on behalf of the undertaking or association of undertakings has been asked for explanations, the Commission shall set a time-limit within which the undertaking or the association of undertakings may communicate to the Commission any rectification, amendment or supplement to the explanations given by such member of staff. The rectification, amendment or supplement shall be added to the explanations as recorded pursuant to paragraph 1.

CHAPTER IV. HANDLING OF COMPLAINTS

Article 5
Admissibility of complaints

1. Natural and legal persons shall show a legitimate interest in order to be entitled to lodge a complaint for the purposes of Article 7 of Regulation (EC) No 1/2003.

Such complaints shall contain the information required by Form C, as set out in the Annex. The Commission may dispense with this obligation as regards part of the information, including documents, required by Form C.

2. Three paper copies as well as, if possible, an electronic copy of the complaint shall be submitted to the Commission. The complainant shall also submit a non-confidential version of the complaint, if confidentiality is claimed for any part of the complaint.

3. Complaints shall be submitted in one of the official languages of the Community.

Article 6
Participation of complainants in proceedings

1. Where the Commission issues a statement of objections relating to a matter in respect of which it has received a complaint, it shall provide the complainant with a copy of the non-confidential version of the statement of objections and set a time-limit within which the complainant may make known its views in writing.

2. The Commission may, where appropriate, afford complainants the opportunity of expressing their views at the oral hearing of the parties to which a statement of objections has been issued, if complainants so request in their written comments.

Article 7
Rejection of complaints

1. Where the Commission considers that on the basis of the information in its possession there are insufficient grounds for acting on a complaint, it shall inform the complainant of its reasons and set a time-limit within which the complainant may make known its views in writing. The Commission shall not be obliged to take into account any further written submission received after the expiry of that time-limit.

2. If the complainant makes known its views within the time-limit set by the Commission and the written submissions made by the complainant do not lead to a different assessment of the complaint, the Commission shall reject the complaint by decision.

3. If the complainant fails to make known its views within the time-limit set by the Commission, the complaint shall be deemed to have been withdrawn.

Article 8
Access to information

1. Where the Commission has informed the complainant of its intention to reject a complaint pursuant to Article 7(1) the complainant may request access to the documents on which the Commission bases its provisional assessment. For this purpose, the complainant may however not have access to business secrets and other confidential information belonging to other parties involved in the proceedings.

2. The documents to which the complainant has had access in the context of proceedings conducted by the Commission under Articles 81 and 82 of the Treaty may only be used by the complainant for the purposes of judicial or administrative proceedings for the application of those Treaty provisions.

Article 9
Rejections of complaints pursuant to Article 13 of Regulation (EC) No 1/2003

Where the Commission rejects a complaint pursuant to Article 13 of Regulation (EC) No 1/2003, it shall inform the complainant without delay of the national competition authority which is dealing or has already dealt with the case.

CHAPTER V. EXERCISE OF THE RIGHT TO BE HEARD
Article 10
Statement of objections and reply

1. The Commission shall inform the parties concerned in writing of the objections raised against them. The statement of objections shall be notified to each of them.

2. The Commission shall, when notifying the statement of objections to the parties concerned, set a time-limit within which these parties may inform it in writing of their views. The Commission shall not be obliged to take into account written submissions received after the expiry of that time-limit.

3. The parties may, in their written submissions, set out all facts known to them which are relevant to their defence against the objections raised by the Commission. They shall attach any relevant documents as proof of the facts set out. They shall provide a paper original as well as an electronic copy or, where they do not provide an electronic copy, 28 paper copies of their submission and of the documents attached to it. They may propose that the Commission hear persons who may corroborate the facts set out in their submission.

Article 11
Right to be heard

1. The Commission shall give the parties to whom it has addressed a statement of objections the opportunity to be heard before consulting the Advisory Committee referred to in Article 14(1) of Regulation (EC) No 1/2003.

2. The Commission shall, in its decisions, deal only with objections in respect of which the parties referred to in paragraph 1 have been able to comment.

Article 12
Right to an oral hearing

The Commission shall give the parties to whom it has addressed a statement of objections the opportunity to develop their arguments at an oral hearing, if they so request in their written submissions.

Article 13
Hearing of other persons

1. If natural or legal persons other than those referred to in Articles 5 and 11 apply to be heard and show a sufficient interest, the Commission shall inform them in writing of the nature and subject matter of the procedure and shall set a time-limit within which they may make known their views in writing.

2. The Commission may, where appropriate, invite persons referred to in paragraph 1 to develop their arguments at the oral hearing of the parties to whom a statement of objections has been addressed, if the persons referred to in paragraph 1 so request in their written comments.

3. The Commission may invite any other person to express its views in writing and to attend the oral hearing of the parties to whom a statement of objections has been addressed. The Commission may also invite such persons to express their views at that oral hearing.

Article 14
Conduct of oral hearings

1. Hearings shall be conducted by a Hearing Officer in full independence.

2. The Commission shall invite the persons to be heard to attend the oral hearing on such date as it shall determine.

3. The Commission shall invite the competition authorities of the Member States to take part in the oral hearing. It may likewise invite officials and civil servants of other authorities of the Member States.

4. Persons invited to attend shall either appear in person or be represented by legal representatives or by representatives authorized by their constitution as appropriate. Undertakings and associations of undertakings may also be represented by a duly authorized agent appointed from among their permanent staff.

5. Persons heard by the Commission may be assisted by their lawyers or other qualified persons admitted by the Hearing Officer.

6. Oral hearings shall not be public. Each person may be heard separately or in the presence of other persons invited to attend, having regard to the legitimate interest of the undertakings in the protection of their business secrets and other confidential information.

7. The Hearing Officer may allow the parties to whom a statement of objections has been addressed, the complainants, other persons invited to the hearing, the Commission services and the authorities of the Member States to ask questions during the hearing.

8. The statements made by each person heard shall be recorded. Upon request, the recording of the hearing shall be made available to the persons who attended the hearing. Regard shall be had to the legitimate interest of the parties in the protection of their business secrets and other confidential information.

CHAPTER VI. ACCESS TO THE FILE AND TREATMENT OF
CONFIDENTIAL INFORMATION

Article 15
Access to the file and use of documents

1. If so requested, the Commission shall grant access to the file to the parties to whom it has addressed a statement of objections. Access shall be granted after the notification of the statement of objections.

2. The right of access to the file shall not extend to business secrets, other confidential information and internal documents of the Commission or of the competition authorities of the Member States. The right of access to the file shall also not extend to correspondence between the Commission and the competition authorities of the Member States or between the latter where such correspondence is contained in the file of the Commission.

3. Nothing in this Regulation prevents the Commission from disclosing and using information necessary to prove an infringement of Articles 81 or 82 of the Treaty.

4. Documents obtained through access to the file pursuant to this Article shall only be used for the purposes of judicial or administrative proceedings for the application of Articles 81 and 82 of the Treaty.

Article 16
Identification and protection of confidential information

1. Information, including documents, shall not be communicated or made accessible by the Commission in so far as it contains business secrets or other confidential information of any person.

2. Any person which makes known its views pursuant to Article 6(1), Article 7(1), Article 10(2) and Article 13(1) and (3) or subsequently submits further information to the Commission in the course of the same procedure, shall clearly identify any material which it considers to be confidential, giving reasons, and provide a separate non-confidential version by the date set by the Commission for making its views known.

3. Without prejudice to paragraph 2 of this Article, the Commission may require undertakings and associations of undertakings which produce documents or statements pursuant to Regulation (EC) No 1/2003 to identify the documents or parts of documents which they consider to contain business secrets or other confidential information belonging to them and to identify the undertakings with regard to which such documents are to be considered confidential. The Commission may likewise require undertakings or associations of undertakings to identify any part of a statement of objections, a case summary drawn up pursuant to Article 27(4) of Regulation (EC) No 1/2003 or a decision adopted by the Commission which in their view contains business secrets.

The Commission may set a time-limit within which the undertakings and associations of undertakings are to:

(a) substantiate their claim for confidentiality with regard to each individual document or part of document, statement or part of statement;

(b) provide the Commission with a non-confidential version of the documents or statements, in which the confidential passages are deleted;

(c) provide a concise description of each piece of deleted information.

4. If undertakings or associations of undertakings fail to comply with paragraphs 2 and 3, the Commission may assume that the documents or statements concerned do not contain confidential information.

CHAPTER VII. GENERAL AND FINAL PROVISIONS

Article 17

Time-limits

1. In setting the time-limits provided for in Article 3(3), Article 4(3), Article 6(1), Article 7(1), Article 10(2) and Article 16(3), the Commission shall have regard both to the time required for preparation of the submission and to the urgency of the case.

2. The time-limits referred to in Article 6(1), Article 7(1) and Article 10(2) shall be at least four weeks. However, for proceedings initiated with a view to adopting interim measures pursuant to Article 8 of Regulation (EC) No 1/2003, the time-limit may be shortened to one week.

3. The time-limits referred to in Article 3(3), Article 4(3) and Article 16(3) shall be at least two weeks.

4. Where appropriate and upon reasoned request made before the expiry of the original time-limit, time-limits may be extended.

Article 18

Repeals

Regulations (EC) No 2842/98, (EC) No 2843/98 and (EC) No 3385/94 are repealed.

References to the repealed regulations shall be construed as references to this regulation.

Article 19

Transitional provisions

Procedural steps taken under Regulations (EC) No 2842/98 and (EC) No 2843/98 shall continue to have effect for the purpose of applying this Regulation.

Article 20

Entry into force

This Regulation shall enter into force on 1 May 2004.

This Regulation shall be binding in its entirety and directly applicable in all Member States.

Done at Brussels, 7 April 2004.

For the Commission
Mario MONTI
Member of the Commission

ANNEX

FORM C. COMPLAINT PURSUANT TO ARTICLE 7 OF REGULATION (EC) NO 1/2003

1. Information regarding the complainant and the undertaking(s) or association of undertakings giving rise to the complaint

1. Give full details on the identity of the legal or natural person submitting the complaint. Where the complainant is an undertaking, identify the corporate group to which it belongs

and provide a concise overview of the nature and scope of its business activities. Provide a contact person (with telephone number, postal and e-mail-address) from which supplementary explanations can be obtained.

2. Identify the undertaking(s) or association of undertakings whose conduct the complaint relates to, including, where applicable, all available information on the corporate group to which the undertaking(s) complained of belong and the nature and scope of the business activities pursued by them. Indicate the position of the complainant vis-à-vis the undertaking(s) or association of undertakings complained of (e.g. customer, competitor).

II. Details of the alleged infringement and evidence

3. Set out in detail the facts from which, in your opinion, it appears that there exists an infringement of Article 81 or 82 of the Treaty and/or Article 53 or 54 of the EEA agreement. Indicate in particular the nature of the products (goods or services) affected by the alleged infringements and explain, where necessary, the commercial relationships concerning these products. Provide all available details on the agreements or practices of the undertakings or associations of undertakings to which this complaint relates. Indicate, to the extent possible, the relative market positions of the undertakings concerned by the complaint.

4. Submit all documentation in your possession relating to or directly connected with the facts set out in the complaint (for example, texts of agreements, minutes of negotiations or meetings, terms of transactions, business documents, circulars, correspondence, notes of telephone conversations . . .). State the names and address of the persons able to testify to the facts set out in the complaint, and in particular of persons affected by the alleged infringement. Submit statistics or other data in your possession which relate to the facts set out, in particular where they show developments in the marketplace (for example information relating to prices and price trends, barriers to entry to the market for new suppliers etc.).

5. Set out your view about the geographical scope of the alleged infringement and explain, where that is not obvious, to what extent trade between Member States or between the Community and one or more EFTA States that are contracting parties of the EEA Agreement may be affected by the conduct complained of.

III. Finding sought from the Commission and legitimate interest

6. Explain what finding or action you are seeking as a result of proceedings brought by the Commission.

7. Set out the grounds on which you claim a legitimate interest as complainant pursuant to Article 7 of Regulation (EC) No 1/2003. State in particular how the conduct complained of affects you and explain how, in your view, intervention by the Commission would be liable to remedy the alleged grievance.

IV. Proceedings before national competition authorities or national courts

8. Provide full information about whether you have approached, concerning the same or closely related subject-matters, any other competition authority and/or whether a lawsuit has been brought before a national court. If so, provide full details about the administrative or judicial authority contacted and your submissions to such authority.

Declaration that the information given in this form and in the Annexes thereto is given entirely in good faith.

Date and signature.

APPENDIX 4

Commission Notice on cooperation within the Network of Competition Authorities

(2004/C 101/03)

(Text with EEA relevance)

1. INTRODUCTION

1. Council Regulation (EC) No 1/2003 of 16 December 2002 on the implementation of the rules on competition laid down in Articles 81 and 82 of the Treaty[1] (hereafter the 'Council Regulation') creates a system of parallel competences in which the Commission and the Member States' competition authorities (hereafter the 'NCAs')[2] can apply Article 81 and Article 82 of the EC Treaty (hereafter the 'Treaty'). Together the NCAs and the Commission form a network of public authorities: they act in the public interest and cooperate closely in order to protect competition. The network is a forum for discussion and cooperation in the application and enforcement of EC competition policy. It provides a framework for the co-operation of European competition authorities in cases where Articles 81 and 82 of the Treaty are applied and is the basis for the creation and maintenance of a common competition culture in Europe. The network is called 'European Competition Network' (ECN).

2. The structure of the NCAs varies between Member States. In some Member States, one body investigates cases and takes all types of decisions. In other Member States, the functions are divided between two bodies, one which is in charge of the investigation of the case and another, often a college, which is responsible for deciding the case. Finally, in certain Member States, prohibition decisions and/or decisions imposing a fine can only be taken by a court: another competition authority acts as a prosecutor bringing the case before that court. Subject to the general principle of effectiveness, Article 35 of the Council Regulation allows Member States to choose the body or bodies which will be designated as national competition authorities and to allocate functions between them. Under general principles of Community law, Member States are under an obligation to set up a sanctioning system providing for sanctions which are effective, proportionate and dissuasive for infringements of EC law.[3] The enforcement systems of the Member States differ but they have recognised the standards of each other's systems as a basis for cooperation.[4]

3. The network formed by the competition authorities should ensure both an efficient division of work and an effective and consistent application of EC competition rules. The Council Regulation together with the joint statement of the Council and the Commission on the

---

[1] OJ L1. 4.1.2003, p 1.

[2] In this notice, the European Commission and the NCAs are collectively referred to as 'the competition authorities'.

[3] cf ECJ case 68/88—*Commission v Greece* [1989] ECR 2965 (Recitals 23 to 25)

[4] See para 8 of the Joint Statement of the Council and the Commission on the functioning of the network available from the Council register at http://register.consilium.eu.int (document No 15435/02 ADD 1).

functioning of the European Competition Network sets out the main principles of the functioning of the network. This notice presents the details of the system.

4. Consultations and exchanges within the network are matters between public enforcers and do not alter any rights or obligations arising from Community or national law for companies. Each competition authority remains fully responsible for ensuring due process in the cases it deals with.

2. DIVISION OF WORK

2.1. Principles of allocation

5. The Council Regulation is based on a system of parallel competences in which all competition authorities have the power to apply Articles 81 or 82 of the Treaty and are responsible for an efficient division of work with respect to those cases where an investigation is deemed to be necessary. At the same time each network member retains full discretion in deciding whether or not to investigate a case. Under this system of parallel competences, cases will be dealt with by:

— a single NCA, possibly with the assistance of NCAs of other Member States; or
— several NCAs acting in parallel; or
— the Commission.

6. In most instances the authority that receives a complaint or starts an *ex-officio* procedure[5] will remain in charge of the case. Re-allocation of a case would only be envisaged at the outset of a procedure (see paragraph 18 below) where either that authority considered that it was not well placed to act or where other authorities also considered themselves well placed to act (see paragraphs 8 to 15 below).

7. Where re-allocation is found to be necessary for an effective protection of competition and of the Community interest, network members will endeavour to re-allocate cases to a single well placed competition authority as often as possible.[6] In any event, re-allocation should be a quick and efficient process and not hold up ongoing investigations.

8. An authority can be considered to be well placed to deal with a case if the following three cumulative conditions are met:

   1. the agreement or practice has substantial direct actual or foreseeable effects on competition within its territory, is implemented within or originates from its territory;
   2. the authority is able to effectively bring to an end the entire infringement, i.e. it can adopt a cease-and-desist order the effect of which will be sufficient to bring an end to the infringement and it can, where appropriate, sanction the infringement adequately;
   3. it can gather, possibly with the assistance of other authorities, the evidence required to prove the infringement.

9. The above criteria indicate that a material link between the infringement and the territory of a Member State must exist in order for that Member State's competition authority to be considered well placed. It can be expected that in most cases the authorities of those Member States where competition is substantially affected by an infringement will be well placed provided they are capable of effectively bringing the infringement to an end through either single or parallel action unless the Commission is better placed to act (see below paragraphs 14 and 15).

---

[5] In this Notice the term 'procedure' is used for investigations and/or formal proceedings for the adoption of a decision pursuant to the Council Reg conducted by an NCA or the Commission, as the case may be.
[6] See Recital 18 of the Council Reg.

10. It follows that a single NCA is usually well placed to deal with agreements or practices that substantially affect competition mainly within its territory.

Example 1: Undertakings situated in Member State A are involved in a price fixing cartel on products that are mainly sold in Member State A.
The NCA in A is well placed to deal with the case.

11. Furthermore single action of an NCA might also be appropriate where, although more than one NCA can be regarded as well placed, the action of a single NCA is sufficient to bring the entire infringement to an end.

Example 2: Two undertakings have set up a joint venture in Member State A. The joint venture provides services in Member States A and B and gives rise to a competition problem. A cease-and-desist order is considered to be sufficient to deal with the case effectively because it can bring an end to the entire infringement. Evidence is located mainly at the offices of the joint venture in Member State A.

The NCAs in A and B are both well placed to deal with the case but single action by the NCA in A would be sufficient and more efficient than single action by NCA in B or parallel action by both NCAs.

12. Parallel action by two or three NCAs may be appropriate where an agreement or practice has substantial effects on competition mainly in their respective territories and the action of only one NCA would not be sufficient to bring the entire infringement to an end and/or to sanction it adequately.

Example 3: Two undertakings agree on a market sharing agreement, restricting the activity of the company located in Member State A to Member State A and the activity of the company located in Member State B to Member State B.
The NCAs in A and B are well placed to deal with the case in parallel, each one for its respective territory.

13. The authorities dealing with a case in parallel action will endeavour to coordinate their action to the extent possible. To that effect, they may find it useful to designate one of them as a lead authority and to delegate tasks to the lead authority such as for example the coordination of investigative measures, while each authority remains responsible for conducting its own proceedings.

14. The Commission is particularly well placed if one or several agreement(s) or practice(s), including networks of similar agreements or practices, have effects on competition in more than three Member States (cross-border markets covering more than three Member States or several national markets).

Example 4: Two undertakings agree to share markets or fix prices for the whole territory of the Community. The Commission is well placed to deal with the case.

Example 5: An undertaking, dominant in four different national markets, abuses its position by imposing fidelity rebates on its distributors in all these markets. The Commission is well placed to deal with the case. It could also deal with one national market so as to create a 'leading' case and other national markets could be dealt with by NCAs, particularly if each national market requires a separate assessment.

15. Moreover, the Commission is particularly well placed to deal with a case if it is closely linked to other Community provisions which may be exclusively or more effectively applied by the Commission, if the Community interest requires the adoption of a Commission decision to develop Community competition policy when a new competition issue arises or to ensure effective enforcement.

2.2 Mechanisms of cooperation for the purpose of case allocation and assistance

2.2.1. Information at the beginning of the procedure (Article 11 of the Council Regulation)

16. In order to detect multiple procedures and to ensure that cases are dealt with by a well placed competition authority, the members of the network have to be informed at an early stage of the cases pending before the various competition authorities.[7] If a case is to be re-allocated, it is indeed in the best interest both of the network and of the undertakings concerned that the re-allocation takes place quickly.

17. The Council Regulation creates a mechanism for the competition authorities to inform each other in order to ensure an efficient and quick re-allocation of cases. Article 11(3) of the Council Regulation lays down an obligation for NCAs to inform the Commission when acting under Article 81 or 82 of the Treaty before or without delay after commencing the first formal investigative measure. It also states that the information may be made available to other NCAs.[8] The rationale of Article 11(3) of the Council Regulation is to allow the network to detect multiple procedures and address possible case re-allocation issues as soon as an authority starts investigating a case. Information should therefore be provided to NCAs and the Commission before or just after any step similar to the measures of investigation that can be undertaken by the Commission under Articles 18 to 21 of the Council Regulation. The Commission has accepted an equivalent obligation to inform NCAs under Article 11(2) of the Council Regulation. Network members will inform each other of pending cases by means of a standard form containing limited details of the case, such as the authority dealing with the case, the product, territories and parties concerned, the alleged infringement, the suspected duration of the infringement and the origin of the case. They will also provide each other with updates when a relevant change occurs.

18. Where case re-allocation issues arise, they should be resolved swiftly, normally within a period of two months, starting from the date of the first information sent to the network pursuant to Article 11 of the Council Regulation. During this period, competition authorities will endeavour to reach an agreement on a possible re-allocation and, where relevant, on the modalities for parallel action.

19. In general, the competition authority or authorities that is/are dealing with a case at the end of the re-allocation period should continue to deal with the case until the completion of the proceedings. Re-allocation of a case after the initial allocation period of two months should only occur where the facts known about the case change materially during the course of the proceedings.

2.2.2. Suspension or termination of proceedings (Article 13 of the Council Regulation)

20. If the same agreement or practice is brought before several competition authorities, be it because they have received a complaint or have opened a procedure on their own initiative, Article 13 of the Council Regulation provides a legal basis for suspending proceedings or rejecting a complaint on the grounds that another authority is dealing with the case or has dealt with the case. In Article 13 of the Council Regulation, 'dealing with the case' does not merely mean that a complaint has been lodged with another authority. It means that the other authority is investigating or has investigated the case on its own behalf.

21. Article 13 of the Council Regulation applies when another authority has dealt or is dealing with the competition issue raised by the complainant, even if the authority in question has

---

[7] For cases initiated following a leniency application see paras 37 *et subseq.*
[8] The intention of making any information exchanged pursuant to Art 11 available and easily accessible to all network members is however expressed in the Joint Statement on the functioning of the network mentioned above in n 4.

acted or acts on the basis of a complaint lodged by a different complainant or as a result of an *ex-officio* procedure. This implies that Article 13 of the Council Regulation can be invoked when the agreement or practice involves the same infringement(s) on the same relevant geographic and product markets.

22. An NCA may suspend or close its proceedings but it has no obligation to do so. Article 13 of the Council Regulation leaves scope for appreciation of the peculiarities of each individual case. This flexibility is important: if a complaint was rejected by an authority following an investigation of the substance of the case, another authority may not want to re-examine the case. On the other hand, if a complaint was rejected for other reasons (e.g. the authority was unable to collect the evidence necessary to prove the infringement), another authority may wish to carry out its own investigation and deal with the case. This flexibility is also reflected, for pending cases, in the choice open to each NCA as to whether it closes or suspends its proceedings. An authority may be unwilling to close a case before the outcome of another authority's proceedings is clear. The ability to suspend its proceedings allows the authority to retain its ability to decide at a later point whether or not to terminate its proceedings. Such flexibility also facilitates consistent application of the rules.

23. Where an authority closes or suspends proceedings because another authority is dealing with the case, it may transfer—in accordance with Article 12 of the Council Regulation—the information provided by the complainant to the authority which is to deal with the case.

24. Article 13 of the Council Regulation can also be applied to part of a complaint or to part of the proceedings in a case. It may be that only part of a complaint or of an *ex-officio* procedure overlaps with a case already dealt or being dealt with by another competition authority. In that case, the competition authority to which the complaint is brought is entitled to reject part of the complaint on the basis of Article 13 of the Council Regulation and to deal with the rest of the complaint in an appropriate manner. The same principle applies to the termination of proceedings.

25. Article 13 of the Council Regulation is not the only legal basis for suspending or closing ex-officio proceedings or rejecting complaints. NCAs may also be able to do so according to their national procedural law. The Commission may also reject a complaint for lack of Community interest or other reasons pertaining to the nature of the complaint.[9]

2.2.3. *Exchange and use of confidential information (Article 12 of the Council Regulation)*

26. A key element of the functioning of the network is the power of all the competition authorities to exchange and use information (including documents, statements and digital information) which has been collected by them for the purpose of applying Article 81 or Article 82 of the Treaty. This power is a precondition for efficient and effective allocation and handling of cases.

27. Article 12 of the Council Regulation states that for the purpose of applying Article 81 and 82 of the Treaty, the Commission and the competition authorities of the Member States shall have the power to provide one another with and use in evidence any matter of fact or of law, including confidential information. This means that exchanges of information may not only take place between an NCA and the Commission but also between and amongst NCAs. Article 12 of the Council Regulation takes precedence over any contrary law of a Member State. The question whether information was gathered in a legal manner by the transmitting authority is governed on the basis of the law applicable to this authority. When transmitting information the transmitting authority may inform the receiving authority whether the gathering of the information was contested or could still be contested.

---

[9] See Commission notice on complaints.

28. The exchange and use of information contains in particular the following safeguards for undertakings and individuals.

    (a) First, Article 28 of the Council Regulation states that 'the Commission and the competition authorities of the Member States, their officials, servants and other persons working under the supervision of these authorities (. . .) shall not disclose information acquired or exchanged by them pursuant to the' Council Regulation which is 'of the kind covered by the obligation of professional secrecy'. However, the legitimate interest of undertakings in the protection of their business secrets may not prejudice the disclosure of information necessary to prove an infringement of Articles 81 and 82 of the Treaty. The term 'professional secrecy' used in Article 28 of the Council Regulation is a Community law concept and includes in particular business secrets and other confidential information. This will create a common minimum level of protection throughout the Community.

    (b) The second safeguard given to undertakings relates to the use of information which has been exchanged within the network. Under Articles 12(2) of the Council Regulation, information so exchanged can only be used in evidence for the application of Articles 81 and 82 of the Treaty and for the subject matter for which it was collected.[10] According to Article 12(2) of the Council Regulation, the information exchanged may also be used for the purpose of applying national competition law in parallel in the same case. This is, however, only possible if the application of national law does not lead to an outcome as regards the finding of an infringement different from that under Articles 81 and 82 of the Treaty.

    (c) The third safeguard given by the Council Regulation relates to sanctions on individuals on the basis of information exchanged pursuant to Article 12(1). The Council Regulation only provides for sanctions on undertakings for violations of Articles 81 and 82 of the Treaty. Some national laws also provide for sanctions on individuals in connection with violations of Article 81 and 82 of the Treaty. Individuals normally enjoy more extensive rights of defence (e.g. a right to remain silent compared to undertakings which may only refuse to answer questions which would lead them to admit that they have committed an infringement.[11]) Article 12(3) of the Council Regulation ensures that information collected from undertakings cannot be used in a way which would circumvent the higher protection of individuals. This provision precludes sanctions being imposed on individuals on the basis of information exchanged pursuant to the Council Regulation if the laws of the transmitting and the receiving authorities do not provide for sanctions of a similar kind in respect of individuals, unless the rights of the individual concerned as regards the collection of evidence have been respected by the transmitting authority to the same standard as they are guaranteed by the receiving authority. The qualification of the sanctions by national law ('administrative' or 'criminal') is not relevant for the purpose of applying Article 12(3) of the Council Regulation. The Council Regulation intends to create a distinction between sanctions which result in custody and other types of sanctions such as fines on individuals and other personal sanctions. If both the legal system of the transmitting and that of the receiving authority provide for sanctions of a similar kind (e.g. in both Member States, fines can be imposed on a member of the staff of an undertaking who has been involved in the violation of Articles 81 or 82 of the Treaty), information exchanged pursuant to Article 12 of the Council Regulation can be used by the receiving authority. In that case, procedural safeguards in both systems are considered to be equivalent. If on the other hand, both

---

[10] See ECJ Case 85/87—*Dow Benelux*, [1989] ECR 3137 (Recitals 17–20).
[11] See ECJ Case 374/87—*Orkem* [1989] ECR 3283 and CFI, Case T-112/98—*Mannesmannröhren-Werke AG*, [2001] ECR II-729.

legal systems do not provide for sanctions of a similar kind, the information can only be used if the same level of protection of the rights of the individual has been respected in the case at hand (see Article 12(3) of the Council Regulation). In that latter case however, custodial sanctions can only be imposed where both the transmitting and the receiving authority have the power to impose such a sanction.

2.2.4. Investigations (Article 22 of the Council Regulation)

29. The Council Regulation provides that an NCA may ask another NCA for assistance in order to collect information on its behalf. An NCA can ask another NCA to carry out fact-finding measures on its behalf. Article 12 of the Council Regulation empowers the assisting NCA to transmit the information it has collected to the requesting NCA. Any exchange between or amongst NCAs and use in evidence by the requesting NCA of such information shall be carried out in accordance with Article 12 of the Council Regulation. Where an NCA acts on behalf of another NCA, it acts pursuant to its own rules of procedure, and under its own powers of investigation.

30. Under Article 22(2) of the Council Regulation, the Commission can ask an NCA to carry out an inspection on its behalf. The Commission can either adopt a decision pursuant to Article 20(4) of the Council Regulation or simply issue a request to the NCA. The NCA officials will exercise their powers in accordance with their national law. The agents of the Commission may assist the NCA during the inspection.

2.3. Position of undertakings

2.3.1. General

31. All network members will endeavour to make the allocation of cases a quick and efficient process. Given the fact that the Council Regulation has created a system of parallel competences, the allocation of cases between members of the network constitutes a mere division of labour where some authorities abstain from acting. The allocation of cases therefore does not create individual rights for the companies involved in or affected by an infringement to have the case dealt with by a particular authority.

32. If a case is re-allocated to a given competition authority, it is because the application of the allocation criteria set out above led to the conclusion that this authority is well placed to deal with the case by single or parallel action. The competition authority to which the case is re-allocated would have been in a position, in any event, to commence an *ex-officio* procedure against the infringement.

33. Furthermore, all competition authorities apply Community competition law and the Council Regulation sets out mechanisms to ensure that the rules are applied in a consistent way.

34. If a case is re-allocated within the network, the undertakings concerned and the complainant(s) are informed as soon as possible by the competition authorities involved.

2.3.2. Position of complainants

35. If a complaint is lodged with the Commission pursuant to Article 7 of the Council Regulation and if the Commission does not investigate the complaint or prohibit the agreement or practice complained of, the complainant has a right to obtain a decision rejecting his complaint. This is without prejudice to Article 7(3) of the Commission implementing regulation.[12] The rights of complainants who lodge a complaint with an NCA are governed by the applicable national law.

---

[12] Commission Reg (EC) No 773/2004, OJ L123, 27.4.2004.

36. In addition, Article 13 of the Council Regulation gives all NCAs the possibility of suspending or rejecting a complaint on the ground that another competition authority is dealing or has dealt with the same case. That provision also allows the Commission to reject a complaint on the ground that a competition authority of a Member State is dealing or has dealt with the case. Article 12 of the Council Regulation allows the transfer of information between competition authorities within the network subject to the safeguards provided in that Article (see paragraph 28 above).

2.3.3. *Position of applicants claiming the benefit of a leniency programme*

37. The Commission considers[13] that it is in the Community interest to grant favourable treatment to undertakings which co-operate with it in the investigation of cartel infringements. A number of Member States have also adopted leniency programmes[14] relating to cartel investigations. The aim of these leniency programmes is to facilitate the detection by competition authorities of cartel activity and also thereby to act as a deterrent to participation in unlawful cartels.

38. In the absence of a European Union-wide system of fully harmonized leniency programmes, an application for leniency to a given authority is not to be considered as an application for leniency to any other authority. It is therefore in the interest of the applicant to apply for leniency to all competition authorities which have competence to apply Article 81 of the Treaty in the territory which is affected by the infringement and which may be considered well placed to act against the infringement in question.[15] In view of the importance of timing in most existing leniency programmes, applicants will also need to consider whether it would be appropriate to file leniency applications with the relevant authorities simultaneously. It is for the applicant to take the steps which it considers appropriate to protect its position with respect to possible proceedings by these authorities.

39. As for all cases where Articles 81 and 82 of the Treaty are applied, where an NCA deals with a case which has been initiated as a result of a leniency application, it must inform the Commission and may make the information available to other members of the network pursuant to Article 11(3) of the Council Regulation (cf paragraphs 16 *et subseq.*). The Commission has accepted an equivalent obligation to inform NCAs under Article 11(2) of the Council Regulation. In such cases, however, information submitted to the network pursuant to Article 11 will not be used by other members of the network as the basis for starting an investigation on their own behalf whether under the competition rules of the Treaty or, in the case of NCAs, under their national competition law or other laws.[16] This is without prejudice to any power of the authority to open an investigation on the basis of information received from other sources or, subject to paragraphs 40 and 41 below, to request, be provided with and use information pursuant to Article 12 from any member of the network, including the network member to whom the leniency application was submitted.

---

[13] OJ C45, 19.2.2002, p 3 at para 3.

[14] In this Notice, the term 'leniency programme' is used to describe all programmes (including the Commission's programme) which offer either full immunity or a significant reduction in the penalties which would otherwise have been imposed on a participant in a cartel, in exchange for the freely volunteered disclosure of information on the cartel which satisfies specific criteria prior to or during the investigative stage of the case. The term does not cover reductions in the penalty granted for other reasons. The Commission will publish on its website a list of those authorities that operate a leniency programme.

[15] See paras 8 to 15 above.

[16] Similarly, information transmitted with a view to obtaining assistance from the receiving authority under Arts 20 or 21 of the Council Reg or of carrying out an investigation or other fact-finding measure under Art 22 of the Council Reg may only be used for the purpose of the application of the said Arts.

40. Save as provided under paragraph 41, information voluntarily submitted by a leniency applicant will only be transmitted to another member of the network pursuant to Article 12 of the Council Regulation with the consent of the applicant. Similarly other information that has been obtained during or following an inspection or by means of or following any other fact-finding measures which, in each case, could not have been carried out except as a result of the leniency application will only be transmitted to another authority pursuant to Article 12 of the Council Regulation if the applicant has consented to the transmission to that authority of information it has voluntarily submitted in its application for leniency. The network members will encourage leniency applicants to give such consent, in particular as regards disclosure to authorities in respect of which it would be open to the applicant to obtain lenient treatment. Once the leniency applicant has given consent to the transmission of information to another authority, that consent may not be withdrawn. This paragraph is without prejudice, however, to the responsibility of each applicant to file leniency applications to whichever authorities it may consider appropriate.

41. Notwithstanding the above, the consent of the applicant for the transmission of information to another authority pursuant to Article 12 of the Council Regulation is not required in any of the following circumstances:

    1. No consent is required where the receiving authority has also received a leniency application relating to the same infringement from the same applicant as the transmitting authority, provided that at the time the information is transmitted it is not open to the applicant to withdraw the information which it has submitted to that receiving authority.

    2. No consent is required where the receiving authority has provided a written commitment that neither the information transmitted to it nor any other information it may obtain following the date and time of transmission as noted by the transmitting authority, will be used by it or by any other authority to which the information is subsequently transmitted to impose sanctions:

       (a) on the leniency applicant;
       (b) on any other legal or natural person covered by the favourable treatment offered by the transmitting authority as a result of the application made by the applicant under its leniency programme;
       (c) on any employee or former employee of any of the persons covered by (a) or (b).

       A copy of the receiving authority's written commitment will be provided to the applicant.

    3. In the case of information collected by a network member under Article 22(1) of the Council Regulation on behalf of and for the account of the network member to whom the leniency application was made, no consent is required for the transmission of such information to, and its use by, the network member to whom the application was made.

42. Information relating to cases initiated as a result of a leniency application and which has been submitted to the Commission under Article 11(3) of the Council Regulation[17] will only be made available to those NCAs that have committed themselves to respecting the principles set out above (see paragraph 72). The same principle applies where a case has been initiated by the Commission as a result of a leniency application made to the Commission. This does not affect the power of any authority to be provided with information under Article 12 of the Council Regulation, provided however that the provisions of paragraphs 40 and 41 are respected.

---

[17] See para 17.

3. Consistent Application of EC Competition Rules[18]

3.1. Mechanism of cooperation (Article 11(4) and 11(5) of the Council Regulation)

43. The Council Regulation pursues the objective that Articles 81 and 82 of the Treaty are applied in a consistent manner throughout the Community. In this respect NCAs will respect the convergence rule contained in Article 3(2) of the Council Regulation. In line with Article 16(2) they cannot—when ruling on agreements, decisions and practices under Article 81 or Article 82 of the Treaty which are already the subject of a Commission decision—take decisions, which would run counter to the decisions adopted by the Commission. Within the network of competition authorities the Commission, as the guardian of the Treaty, has the ultimate but not the sole responsibility for developing policy and safeguarding consistency when it comes to the application of EC competition law.

44. According to Article 11(4) of the Council Regulation, no later than 30 days before the adoption of a decision applying Articles 81 or 82 of the Treaty and requiring that an infringement be brought to an end, accepting commitments or withdrawing the benefit of a block-exemption regulation, NCAs shall inform the Commission. They have to send to the Commission, at the latest 30 days before the adoption of the decision, a summary of the case, the envisaged decision or, in the absence thereof, any other document indicating the proposed course of action.

45. As under Article 11(3) of the Council Regulation, the obligation is to inform the Commission, but the information may be shared by the NCA informing the Commission with the other members of the network.

46. Where an NCA has informed the Commission pursuant to Article 11(4) of the Council Regulation and the 30 days deadline has expired, the decision can be adopted as long as the Commission has not initiated proceedings. The Commission may make written observations on the case before the adoption of the decision by the NCA. The NCA and the Commission will make the appropriate efforts to ensure the consistent application of Community law (cf. paragraph 3 above).

47. If special circumstances require that a national decision is taken in less than 30 days following the transmission of information pursuant to Article 11(4) of the Council Regulation, the NCA concerned may ask the Commission for a swifter reaction. The Commission will endeavour to react as quickly as possible.

48. Other types of decisions, i.e. decisions rejecting complaints, decisions closing an *ex-officio* procedure or decisions ordering interim measures, can also be important from a competition policy point of view, and the network members may have an interest informing each other about them and possibly discussing them. NCAs can therefore on the basis of Article 11(5) of the Council Regulation inform the Commission and thereby inform the network of any other case in which EC competition law is applied.

49. All members of the network should inform each other about the closure of their procedures which have been notified to the network pursuant to Article 11(2) and (3) of the Council Regulation.[19]

---

[18] Art 15 of the Council Reg empowers NCAs and the Commission to submit written and, with the permission of the Court, oral submissions in court proceedings for the application of Arts 81 and 82 of the Treaty. This is a very important tool for ensuring consistent application of Community rules. In exercising this power NCAs and the Commission will cooperate closely.

[19] See para 24 of the Joint Statement on the functioning of the network mentioned above in n 4.

3.2. The initiation of proceedings by the Commission under Article 11(6) of the Council Regulation

50. According to the case law of the Court of Justice, the Commission, entrusted by Article 85(1) of the Treaty with the task of ensuring the application of the principles laid down in Articles 81 and 82 of the Treaty, is responsible for defining and implementing the orientation of Community competition policy.[20] It can adopt individual decisions under Articles 81 and 82 of the Treaty at any time.

51. Article 11(6) of the Council Regulation states that the initiation by the Commission of proceedings for the adoption of a decision under the Council Regulation shall relieve all NCAs of their competence to apply Articles 81 and 82 of the Treaty. This means that once the Commission has opened proceedings, NCAs cannot act under the same legal basis against the same agreement(s) or practice(s) by the same undertaking(s) on the same relevant geographic and product market.

52. The initiation of proceedings by the Commission is a formal act[21] by which the Commission indicates its intention to adopt a decision under Chapter III of the Council Regulation. It can occur at any stage of the investigation of the case by the Commission. The mere fact that the Commission has received a complaint is not in itself sufficient to relieve NCAs of their competence.

53. Two situations can arise. First, where the Commission is the first competition authority to initiate proceedings in a case for the adoption of a decision under the Council Regulation, national competition authorities may no longer deal with the case. Article 11(6) of the Council Regulation provides that once the Commission has initiated proceedings, the NCAs can no longer start their own procedure with a view to applying Articles 81 and 82 of the Treaty to the same agreement(s) or practice(s) by the same undertaking(s) on the same relevant geographic and product market.

54. The second situation is where one or more NCAs have informed the network pursuant to Article 11(3) of the Council Regulation that they are acting on a given case. During the initial allocation period (indicative time period of two months, see paragraph 18 above), the Commission can initiate proceedings with the effect of Article 11(6) of the Council Regulation after having consulted the authorities concerned. After the allocation phase, the Commission will in principle only apply Article 11(6) of the Council Regulation if one of the following situations arises:

   (a) Network members envisage conflicting decisions in the same case.
   (b) Network members envisage a decision which is obviously in conflict with consolidated case law; the standards defined in the judgements of the Community courts and in previous decisions and regulations of the Commission should serve as a yardstick; concerning the assessment of the facts (e.g. market definition), only a significant divergence will trigger an intervention of the Commission;
   (c) Network member(s) is (are) unduly drawing out proceedings in the case;
   (d) There is a need to adopt a Commission decision to develop Community competition policy in particular when a similar competition issue arises in several Member States or to ensure effective enforcement;
   (e) The NCA(s) concerned do not object.

55. If an NCA is already acting on a case, the Commission will explain the reasons for the

---

[20] See ECJ Case C-344/98—*Masterfoods Ltd*, [2000] ECR 1-11369.

[21] The ECJ has defined that concept in the Case 48/72—*SA Brasserie de Haecht*, [1973] ECR 77: 'the initiation of a procedure within the meaning of Art 9 of Reg No 17 implies an authoritative act of the Commission, evidencing its intention of taking a decision.'

application of Article 11(6) of the Council Regulation in writing to the NCA concerned and to the other members of the Network.[22]

56. The Commission will announce to the network its intention of applying Article 11(6) of the Council Regulation in due time, so that Network members will have the possibility of asking for a meeting of the Advisory Committee on the matter before the Commission initiates proceedings.

57. The Commission will normally not – and to the extent that Community interest is not at stake—adopt a decision which is in conflict with a decision of an NCA after proper information pursuant to both Article 11(3) and (4) of the Council Regulation has taken place and the Commission has not made use of Article 11(6) of the Council Regulation.

4. THE ROLE AND THE FUNCTIONING OF THE ADVISORY COMMITTEE IN THE NEW SYSTEM

58. The Advisory Committee is the forum where experts from the various competition authorities discuss individual cases and general issues of Community competition law.[23]

4.1. Scope of the consultation

4.1.1. Decisions of the Commission

59. The Advisory Committee is consulted prior to the Commission taking any decision pursuant to Articles 7, 8, 9, 10, 23, 24(2) or 29(1) of the Council Regulation. The Commission must take the utmost account of the opinion of the Advisory Committee and inform the Committee of the manner in which its opinion has been taken into account.

60. For decisions adopting interim measures, the Advisory Committee is consulted following a swifter and lighter procedure, on the basis of a short explanatory note and the operative part of the decision.

4.1.2. Decisions of NCAs

61. It is in the interest of the network that important cases dealt with by NCAs under Articles 81 and 82 of the Treaty can be discussed in the Advisory Committee. The Council Regulation enables the Commission to put a given case being dealt with by an NCA on the agenda of the Advisory Committee. Discussion can be requested by the Commission or by any Member State. In either case, the Commission will put the case on the agenda after having informed the NCA(s) concerned. This discussion in the Advisory Committee will not lead to a formal opinion.

62. In important cases, the Advisory Committee could also serve as a forum for the discussion of case allocation. In particular, where the Commission intends to apply Article 11(6) of the Council Regulation after the initial allocation period, the case can be discussed in the Advisory Committee before the Commission initiates proceedings. The Advisory Committee may issue an informal statement on the matter.

4.1.3. Implementing measures, block-exemption regulations, guidelines and other notices (Article 33 of the Council Regulation)

63. The Advisory Committee will be consulted on draft Commission regulations as provided for in the relevant Council Regulations.

---

[22] See para 22 of the Joint Statement mentioned above in n 4.

[23] In accordance with Art 14(2) of the Council Reg, where horizontal issues such as block-exemption regulations and guidelines are being discussed, Member States can appoint an additional representative competent in competition matters and who does not necessarily belong to the competition authority.

64. Beside regulations, the Commission may also adopt notices and guidelines. These more flexible tools are very useful for explaining and announcing the Commission's policy, and for explaining its interpretation of the competition rules. The Advisory Committee will also be consulted on these notices and guidelines.

4.2. Procedure

4.2.1. Normal procedure

65. For consultation on Commission draft decisions, the meeting of the Advisory Committee takes place at the earliest 14 days after the invitation to the meeting is sent by the Commission. The Commission attaches to the invitation a summary of the case, a list of the most important documents, i.e. the documents needed to assess the case, and a draft decision. The Advisory Committee gives an opinion on the Commission draft decision. At the request of one or several members, the opinion shall be reasoned.

66. The Council Regulation allows for the possibility of the Member States agreeing upon a shorter period of time between the sending of the invitation and the meeting.

4.2.2. Written procedure

67. The Council Regulation provides for the possibility of a written consultation procedure. If no Member State objects, the Commission can consult the Member States by sending the documents to them and setting a deadline within which they can comment on the draft. This deadline would not normally be shorter than 14 days, except for decisions on interim measures pursuant to Article 8 of the Council Regulation. Where a Member State requests that a meeting takes place, the Commission will arrange for such a meeting.

4.3. Publication of the opinion of the Advisory Committee

68. The Advisory Committee can recommend the publication of its opinion. In that event, the Commission will carry out such publication simultaneously with the decision, taking into account the legitimate interest of undertakings in the protection of their business secrets.

5. FINAL REMARKS

69. This Notice is without prejudice to any interpretation of the applicable Treaty and regulatory provisions by the Court of First Instance and the Court of Justice.

70. This Notice will be the subject of periodic review carried out jointly by the NCAs and the Commission. On the basis of the experience acquired, it will be reviewed no later than at the end of the third year after its adoption.

71. This notice replaces the Commission notice on cooperation between national competition authorities and the Commission in handling cases falling within the scope of Articles 81 and 82 of the Treaty published in 1997.[24]

6. STATEMENT BY OTHER NETWORK MEMBERS

72. The principles set out in this notice will also be abided by those Member States' competition authorities which have signed a statement in the form of the Annex to this Notice. In this statement they acknowledge the principles of this notice, including the principles relating to the protection of applicants claiming the benefit of a leniency programme[25] and declare that they will abide by them. A list of these authorities is published on the website of the European Commission. It will be updated if appropriate.

---

[24] OJ C313, 15.10.1997, p 3.   [25] See paras 37 *et subseq.*

ANNEX

STATEMENT REGARDING THE COMMISSION NOTICE ON COOPERATION WITHIN THE NETWORK OF COMPETITION AUTHORITIES

In order to cooperate closely with a view to protecting competition within the European Union in the interest of consumers, the undersigned competition authority:

1. Acknowledges the principles set out in the Commission Notice on Cooperation within the Network of Competition Authorities; and
2. Declares that it will abide by those principles, which include principles relating to the protection of applicants claiming the benefit of a leniency programme, in any case in which it is acting or may act and to which those principles apply.

....
               (place)   (date)

APPENDIX 5

Commission Notice on the cooperation between the Commission and the courts of the EU Member States in the application of Articles 81 and 82 EC

(2004/C 101/04)

(Text with EEA relevance)

1. THE SCOPE OF THE NOTICE

1. The present notice addresses the cooperation between the Commission and the courts of the EU Member States, when the latter apply Articles 81 and 82 EC. For the purpose of this notice, the 'courts of the EU Member States' (hereinafter 'national courts') are those courts and tribunals within an EU Member State that can apply Articles 81 and 82 EC and that are authorized to ask a preliminary question to the Court of Justice of the European Communities pursuant to Article 234 EC.[1]

2. The national courts may be called upon to apply Articles 81 or 82 EC in lawsuits between private parties, such as actions relating to contracts or actions for damages. They may also act as public enforcer or as review court. A national court may indeed be designated as a competition authority of a Member State (hereinafter 'the national competition authority') pursuant to Article 35(1) of Regulation (EC) No 1/2003 (hereinafter 'the regulation').[2] In that case, the co-operation between the national courts and the Commission is not only covered by the present notice, but also by the notice on the cooperation within the network of competition authorities.[3]

II. THE APPLICATION OF EC COMPETITION RULES BY NATIONAL COURTS

A. The competence of national courts to apply EC competition rules

3. To the extent that national courts have jurisdiction to deal with a case,[4] they have the power

---

[1] For the criteria to determine which entities can be regarded as courts or tribunals within the meaning of Art 234 EC, see e.g. Case C-516/99 *Schmid* [2002] ECR 1–4573, 34: 'The Court takes account of a number of factors, such as whether the body is established by law, whether it is permanent, whether its jurisdiction is compulsory, whether its procedure is inter partes, whether it applies rules of law and whether it is independent'.

[2] Council Reg (EC) No 1/2003 of 16 December 2002 on the implementation of the rules on competition laid down in Arts 81 and 82 of the Treaty (O) L1, 4.1.2003, p 1).

[3] Notice on the cooperation within the network of competition authorities (O) C 101, 27.4.2004, p 43). For the purpose of this notice, a 'national competition authority' is the authority designated by a Member State in accordance with Art 35(1) of the reg.

[4] The jurisdiction of a national court depends on national, European and international rules of jurisdiction. In this context, it may be recalled that Council Reg (EC) No 44/2001 of 22 December 2000 on jurisdiction and the recognition and enforcement of judgements in civil and commercial matters (O) L12, 16.1.2001, p 1) is applicable to all competition cases of a civil or commercial nature.

to apply Articles 81 and 82 EC.[5] Moreover, it should be remembered that Articles 81 and 82 EC are a matter of public policy and are essential to the accomplishment of the tasks entrusted to the Community, and, in particular, for the functioning of the internal market.[6] According to the Court of Justice, where, by virtue of domestic law, national courts must raise of their own motion points of law based on binding domestic rules which have not been raised by the parties, such an obligation also exists where binding Community rules, such as the EC competition rules, are concerned. The position is the same if domestic law confers on national courts a discretion to apply of their own motion binding rules of law: national courts must apply the EC competition rules, even when the party with an interest in application of those provisions has not relied on them, where domestic law allows such application by the national court. However, Community law does not require national courts to raise of their own motion an issue concerning the breach of provisions of Community law where examination of that issue would oblige them to abandon the passive role assigned to them by going beyond the ambit of the dispute defined by the parties themselves and relying on facts and circumstances other than those on which the party with an interest in application of those provisions bases his claim.[7]

4. Depending on the functions attributed to them under national law, national courts may be called upon to apply Articles 81 and 82 EC in administrative, civil or criminal proceedings.[8] In particular, where a natural or legal person asks the national court to safeguard his individual rights, national courts play a specific role in the enforcement of Articles 81 and 82 EC, which is different from the enforcement in the public interest by the Commission or by national competition authorities.[9] Indeed, national courts can give effect to Articles 81 and 82 EC by finding contracts to be void or by awards of damages.

5. National courts can apply Articles 81 and 82 EC, without it being necessary to apply national competition law in parallel. However, where a national court applies national competition law to agreements, decisions by associations of undertakings or concerted practices which may affect trade between Member States within the meaning of Article 81(1) EC[10] or to any abuse prohibited by Article 82 EC, they also have to apply EC competition rules to those agreements, decisions or practices.[11]

6. The regulation does not only empower the national courts to apply EC competition law. The parallel application of national competition law to agreements, decision of associations of undertakings and concerted practices which affect trade between Member States may not lead to a different outcome from that of EC competition law. Article 3(2) of the regulation provides that agreements, decisions or concerted practices which do not infringe Article 81(1) EC or which fulfil the conditions of Article 81(3) EC cannot be prohibited either under national competition law.[12] On the other hand, the Court of Justice has ruled that agreements, decisions or concerted practices that violate Article 81(1) and do not fulfil the conditions of Article 81(3) EC cannot be upheld under national law.[13] As to the parallel

---

[5] See Art 6 of the reg.

[6] See Arts 2 and 3 EC, Case C-126/97 *Eco Swiss* [1999] ECR I–3055, 36; Case T-34/92 *Fiatagri UK and New Holland Ford* [1994] ECR II-905, 39 and Case T-128/98 *Aéroports de Paris* [2000] ECR II-3929, 241.

[7] Joined Cases C-430/93 and C-431/93 *van Schijndel* [1995] ECR 1–4705, 13 to 15 and 22.

[8] According to the last sentence of recital 8 of Reg (EC) No 1/2003, the reg does not apply to national laws which impose criminal sanctions on natural persons except to the extent that such sanctions are the means whereby competition rules applying to undertakings are enforced.

[9] Case T-24/90 *Automec* [1992] ECR II-2223, 85.

[10] For further clarification of the effect on trade concept, see the notice on this issue (O) L101, 27.4.2004, p 81).

[11] Art 3(1) of the reg.

[12] See also the notice on the application of Art 81(3) EC (O) L101, 27.4.2004, p 2).

application of national competition law and Article 82 EC in the case of unilateral conduct, Article 3 of the regulation does not provide for a similar convergence obligation. However, in case of conflicting provisions, the general principle of primacy of Community law requires national courts to disapply any provision of national law which contravenes a Community rule, regardless of whether that national law provision was adopted before or after the Community rule.[14]

7. Apart from the application of Articles 81 and 82 EC, national courts are also competent to apply acts adopted by EU institutions in accordance with the EC Treaty or in accordance with the measures adopted to give the Treaty effect, to the extent that these acts have direct effect. National courts may thus have to enforce Commission decisions[15] or regulations applying Article 81(3) EC to certain categories of agreements, decisions or concerted practices. When applying these EC competition rules, national courts act within the framework of Community law and are consequently bound to observe the general principles of Community law.[16]

8. The application of Articles 81 and 82 EC by national courts often depends on complex economic and legal assessments.[17] When applying EC competition rules, national courts are bound by the case law of the Community courts as well as by Commission regulations applying Article 81(3) EC to certain categories of agreements, decisions or concerted practices.[18] Furthermore, the application of Articles 81 and 82 EC by the Commission in a specific case binds the national courts when they apply EC competition rules in the same case in parallel with or subsequent to the Commission.[19] Finally, and without prejudice to the ultimate interpretation of the EC Treaty by the Court of Justice, national courts may find guidance in Commission regulations and decisions which present elements of analogy with the case they are dealing with, as well as in Commission notices and guidelines relating to the application of Articles 81 and 82 EC[20] and in the annual report on competition policy.[21]

B. Procedural aspects of the application of EC competition rules by national courts

9. The procedural conditions for the enforcement of EC competition rules by national courts and the sanctions they can impose in case of an infringement of those rules, are largely covered by national law. However, to some extent, Community law also determines the conditions in which EC competition rules are enforced. Those Community law provisions may provide for the faculty of national courts to avail themselves of certain instruments, e.g. to ask for the Commission's opinion on questions concerning the application of EC

---

[13] Case 14/68 *Walt Wilhelm* [1969] ECR 1 and Joined Cases 253/78 and 1 to 3/79 *Giry and Guerlain* [1980] ECR 2327, 15 to 17.

[14] Case 106/77 *Simmenthal* [1978] ECR 629, 21 and Case C-198/01, *Consorzio Industrie Fiammiferi* (CIF) [2003] 49.

[15] E.g. a national court may be asked to enforce a Commission decision taken pursuant to Arts 7 to 10, 23 and 24 of the reg.

[16] See e.g. Case 5/88 *Wachauf* [1989] ECR 2609, 19.

[17] Joined Cases C-215/96 and C-216/96 *Bagnasco* [1999] ECR I-135, 50.

[18] Case 63/75 *Fonderies Roubaix* [1976] ECR 111, 9 to 11 and Case C-234/89 *Delimitis* [1991] ECR I-935, 46.

[19] On the parallel or consecutive application of EC competition rules by national courts and the Commission, see also points 11 to 14.

[20] Case 66/86 *Ahmed Saeed Flugreisen* [1989] ECR 803, 27 and Case C-234/89 *Delimitis* [1991] ECR I-935, 50. A list of Commission guidelines, notices and regs in the field of competition policy, in particular the regs applying Art 81(3) EC to certain categories of agreements, decisions or concerted practices, are annexed to this notice. For the decisions of the Commission applying Arts 81 and 82 EC (since 1964), see http://www.europa.eu.int/comm/competition/antitrust/cases/.

[21] Joined Cases C-319/93, C-40/94 and C-224/94 *Dijkstra* [1995] ECR I-4471, 32.

competition rules[22] or they may create rules that have an obligatory impact on proceedings before them, e.g. allowing the Commission and national competition authorities to submit written observations.[23] These Community law provisions prevail over national rules. Therefore, national courts have to set aside national rules which, if applied, would conflict with these Community law provisions. Where such Community law provisions are directly applicable, they are a direct source of rights and duties for all those affected, and must be fully and uniformly applied in all the Member States from the date of their entry into force.[24]

10. In the absence of Community law provisions on procedures and sanctions related to the enforcement of EC competition rules by national courts, the latter apply national procedural law and—to the extent that they are competent to do so—impose sanctions provided for under national law. However, the application of these national provisions must be compatible with the general principles of Community law. In this regard, it is useful to recall the case law of the Court of Justice, according to which:

(a) where there is an infringement of Community law, national law must provide for sanctions which are effective, proportionate and dissuasive;[25]

(b) where the infringement of Community law causes harm to an individual, the latter should under certain conditions be able to ask the national court for damages;[26]

(c) the rules on procedures and sanctions which national courts apply to enforce Community law

— must not make such enforcement excessively difficult or practically impossible (the principle of effectiveness)[27] and they

— must not be less favourable than the rules applicable to the enforcement of equivalent national law (the principle of equivalence).[28]

On the basis of the principle of primacy of Community law, a national court may not apply national rules that are incompatible with these principles.

C. Parallel or consecutive application of EC competition rules by the Commission and by national courts

11. A national court may be applying EC competition law to an agreement, decision, concerted practice or unilateral behaviour affecting trade between Member States at the same time as the Commission or subsequent to the Commission.[29] The following points outline some of the obligations national courts have to respect in those circumstances.

---

[22] On the possibility for national courts to ask the Commission for an opinion, see further in points 27 to 30.

[23] On the submission of observations, see further in points 31 to 35.

[24] Case 106/77 *Simmenthal* [1978] ECR 629, 14 and 15.

[25] Case 68/88 *Commission v Greece* [1989] ECR 2965, 23 to 25.

[26] On damages in case of an infringement by an undertaking, see case C-453/99 *Courage and Crehan* [2001] ECR 6297, 26 and 27. On damages in case of an infringement by a Member State or by an authority which is an emanation of the State and on the conditions of such state liability, see e.g. Joined Cases C-6/90 and C-9/90 *Francovich* [1991] ECR I-5357, 33 to 36; case C-271/91 *Marshall v Southampton and South West Hampshire Area Health Authority* [1993] ECR I-4367, 30 and 34 to 35; joined cases C-46/93 and C-48/93 *Brasserie du Pêcheur and Factortame* [1996] ECR I-1029; Case C-392/93 *British Telecommunications* [1996] ECR I-1631, 39 to 46 and Joined Cases C-178/94, C-179/94 and C-188/94 to 190/94 *Dillenkofer* [1996] ECR I-4845, 22 to 26 and 72.

[27] See e.g. Case 33/76 *Rewe* [1976] ECR 1989, 5; Case 45/76 *Comet* [1976] ECR 2043, 12 and Case 79/83 *Harz* [1984] ECR 1921, 18 and 23.

[28] See e.g. Case 33/76 *Rewe* [1976] ECR 1989, 5; Case 158/80 *Rewe* [1981] ECR 1805, 44; Case 199/82 *San Giorgio* [1983] ECR 3595, 12 and Case C-231/96 *Edis* [1998] ECR I-4951, 36 and 37.

[29] Art 11(6), juncto Art 35(3) and (4) of the reg prevents a parallel application of Arts 81 or 82 EC by the Commission and a national court only when the latter has been designated as a national competition authority.

12. Where a national court comes to a decision before the Commission does, it must avoid adopting a decision that would conflict with a decision contemplated by the Commission.[30] To that effect, the national court may ask the Commission whether it has initiated proceedings regarding the same agreements, decisions or practices[31] and if so, about the progress of proceedings and the likelihood of a decision in that case.[32] The national court may, for reasons of legal certainty, also consider staying its proceedings until the Commission has reached a decision.[33] The Commission, for its part, will endeavour to give priority to cases for which it has decided to initiate proceedings within the meaning of Article 2(1) of Commission Regulation (EC) No 773/2004 and that are the subject of national proceedings stayed in this way, in particular when the outcome of a civil dispute depends on them. However, where the national court cannot reasonably doubt the Commission's contemplated decision or where the Commission has already decided on a similar case, the national court may decide on the case pending before it in accordance with that contemplated or earlier decision without it being necessary to ask the Commission for the information mentioned above or to await the Commission's decision.

13. Where the Commission reaches a decision in a particular case before the national court, the latter cannot take a decision running counter to that of the Commission. The binding effect of the Commission's decision is of course without prejudice to the interpretation of Community law by the Court of Justice. Therefore, if the national court doubts the legality of the Commission's decision, it cannot avoid the binding effects of that decision without a ruling to the contrary by the Court of Justice.[34] Consequently, if a national court intends to take a decision that runs counter to that of the Commission, it must refer a question to the Court of Justice for a preliminary ruling (Article 234 EC). The latter will then decide on the compatibility of the Commission's decision with Community law. However, if the Commission's decision is challenged before the Community courts pursuant to Article 230 EC and the outcome of the dispute before the national court depends on the validity of the Commission's decision, the national court should stay its proceedings pending final judgment in the action for annulment by the Community Courts unless it considers that, in the circumstances of the case, a reference to the Court of Justice for a preliminary ruling on the validity of the Commission decision is warranted.[35]

14. When a national court stays proceedings, e.g. awaiting the Commission's decision (situation described in point 12 of this notice) or pending final judgement by the Community Courts in an action for annulment or in a preliminary ruling procedure (situation described in point 13), it is incumbent on it to examine whether it is necessary to order interim measures in order to safeguard the interests of the parties.[36]

---

[30] Art 16(1) of the reg.

[31] The Commission makes the initiation of its proceedings with a view to adopting a decision pursuant to Arts 7 to 10 of the reg public (see Art 2(2) of Commission Reg (EC) No 773/2004 of 7 April relating to proceedings pursuant to Arts 81 and 82 of the EC Treaty (O) C 101, 27.4.2004). According to the Court of Justice, the initiation of proceedings implies an authoritative act of the Commission, evidencing its intention of taking a decision (case 48/72 *Brasserie de Haecht* [1973] ECR 77, 16).

[32] Case C-234/89 *Delimitis* [1991] ECR I-935, 53, and Joined Cases C-319/93, C-40/94 and C-224/94 *Dijkstra* [1995] ECR I-4471, 34. See further on this issue point 21 of this notice.

[33] See Art 16(1) of the reg and case C-234/89 *Delimitis* [1991] ECR I-935, 47 and Case C-344/98 *Masterfoods* [2000] ECR I-11369, 51.

[34] Case 314/85 *Foto-Frost* [1987] ECR 4199, 12 to 20.

[35] See Art 16(1) of the reg and case C-344/98 *Masterfoods* [2000] ECR 1–11369, 52 to 59.

[36] Case C-344/98 *Masterfoods* [2000] ECR I–11369, 58.

III. THE COOPERATION BETWEEN THE COMMISSION
AND NATIONAL COURTS

15. Other than the cooperation mechanism between the national courts and the Court of Justice under Article 234 EC, the EC Treaty does not explicitly provide for co-operation between the national courts and the Commission. However, in its interpretation of Article 10 EC, which obliges the Member States to facilitate the achievement of the Community's tasks, the Community courts found that this Treaty provision imposes on the European institutions and the Member States mutual duties of loyal cooperation with a view to attaining the objectives of the EC Treaty. Article 10 EC thus implies that the Commission must assist national courts when they apply Community law.[37] Equally, national courts may be obliged to assist the Commission in the fulfilment of its tasks.[38]

16. It is also appropriate to recall the co-operation between national courts and national authorities, in particular national competition authorities, for the application of Articles 81 and 82 EC. While the co-operation between these national authorities is primarily governed by national rules, Article 15(3) of the regulation provides for the possibility for national competition authorities to submit observations before the national courts of their Member State. Points 31 and 33 to 35 of this notice are *mutatis mutandis* applicable to those submissions.

A. The Commission as Amicus Curiae

17. In order to assist national courts in the application of EC competition rules, the Commission is committed to help national courts where the latter find such help necessary to be able to decide on a case. Article 15 of the regulation refers to the most frequent types of such assistance: the transmission of information (points 21 to 26) and the Commission's opinions (points 27 to 30), both at the request of a national court and the possibility for the Commission to submit observations (points 31 to 35). Since the regulation provides for these types of assistance, it cannot be limited by any Member States' rule. However, in the absence of Community procedural rules to this effect and to the extent that they are necessary to facilitate these forms of assistance, Member States must adopt the appropriate procedural rules to allow both the national courts and the Commission to make full use of the possibilities the regulation offers.[39]

18. The national court may send its request for assistance in writing to

European Commission
Directorate General for Competition
B-1049 Brussels
Belgium

or send it electronically to comp-amicus@cec.eu.int

19. It should be recalled that whatever form the co-operation with national courts takes, the Commission will respect the independence of national courts. As a consequence, the assistance offered by the Commission does not bind the national court. The Commission has also to make sure that it respects its duty of professional secrecy and that it safeguards its own functioning and independence.[40] In fulfilling its duty under Article 10 EC, of assisting national courts in the application of EC competition rules, the Commission is committed to

---

[37] Case C-2/88 *Imm Zwartveld* [1990] ECR I-3365, 16 to 22 and Case C-234/89 *Delimitis* [1991] I-935, 53.

[38] C-94/00 *Roquette Frères* [2002] ECR 9011, 31.

[39] On the compatibility of such national procedural rules with the general principles of Community law, see points 9 and 10 of this notice.

[40] On these duties, see e.g. points 23 to 26 of this notice.

remaining neutral and objective in its assistance. Indeed, the Commission's assistance to national courts is part of its duty to defend the public interest. It has therefore no intention to serve the private interests of the parties involved in the case pending before the national court. As a consequence, the Commission will not hear any of the parties about its assistance to the national court. In case the Commission has been contacted by any of the parties in the case pending before the court on issues which are raised before the national court, it will inform the national court thereof, independent of whether these contacts took place before or after the national court's request for cooperation.

20. The Commission will publish a summary concerning its cooperation with national courts pursuant to this notice in its annual Report on Competition Policy. It may also make its opinions and observations available on its website.

1. The Commission's duty to transmit information to national courts

21. The duty for the Commission to assist national courts in the application of EC competition law is mainly reflected in the obligation for the Commission to transmit information it holds to national courts. A national court may, e.g. ask the Commission for documents in its possession or for information of a procedural nature to enable it to discover whether a certain case is pending before the Commission, whether the Commission has initiated a procedure or whether it has already taken a position. A national court may also ask the Commission when a decision is likely to be taken, so as to be able to determine the conditions for any decision to stay proceedings or whether interim measures need to be adopted.[41]

22. In order to ensure the efficiency of the cooperation with national courts, the Commission will endeavour to provide the national court with the requested information within one month from the date it receives the request. Where the Commission has to ask the national court for further clarification of its request or where the Commission has to consult those who are directly affected by the transmission of the information, that period starts to run from the moment that it receives the required information.

23. In transmitting information to national courts, the Commission has to uphold the guarantees given to natural and legal persons by Article 287 EC.[42] Article 287 EC prevents members, officials and other servants of the Commission from disclosing information covered by the obligation of professional secrecy. The information covered by professional secrecy may be both confidential information and business secrets. Business secrets are information of which not only disclosure to the public but also mere transmission to a person other than the one that provided the information might seriously harm the latter's interests.[43]

24. The combined reading of Articles 10 and 287 EC does not lead to an absolute prohibition for the Commission to transmit information which is covered by the obligation of professional secrecy to national courts. The case law of the Community courts confirms that the duty of loyal cooperation requires the Commission to provide the national court with whatever information the latter asks for, even information covered by professional secrecy. However, in offering its cooperation to the national courts, the Commission may not in any circumstances undermine the guarantees laid down in Article 287 EC.

25. Consequently, before transmitting information covered by professional secrecy to a national court, the Commission will remind the court of its obligation under Community law to uphold the rights which Article 287 EC confers on natural and legal persons and it will ask the court whether it can and will guarantee protection of confidential information and

---

[41] Case C-234/89 *Delimitis* [1991] ECR I-935, 53, and joined Cases C-319/93, C-40/94 and C-224/94 *Dijkstra* [1995] ECR I-4471, 34.

[42] Case C-234/89 *Delimitis* [1991] I-935, 53.

[43] Case T-353/94 *Postbank* [1996] ECR II-921, 86 and 87 and Case 145/83 *Adams* [1985] ECR 3539, 34.

business secrets. If the national court cannot offer such guarantee, the Commission shall not transmit the information covered by professional secrecy to the national court.[44] Only when the national court has offered a guarantee that it will protect the confidential information and business secrets, will the Commission transmit the information requested, indicating those parts which are covered by professional secrecy and which parts are not and can therefore be disclosed.

26. There are further exceptions to the disclosure of information by the Commission to national courts. Particularly, the Commission may refuse to transmit information to national courts for overriding reasons relating to the need to safeguard the interests of the Community or to avoid any interference with its functioning and independence, in particular by jeopardising the accomplishment of the tasks entrusted to it.[45] Therefore, the Commission will not transmit to national courts information voluntarily submitted by a leniency applicant without the consent of that applicant.

2. Request for an opinion on questions concerning the application of EC competition rules

27. When called upon to apply EC competition rules to a case pending before it, a national court may first seek guidance in the case law of the Community Courts or in Commission regulations, decisions, notices and guidelines applying Articles 81 and 82 EC.[46] Where these tools do not offer sufficient guidance, the national court may ask the Commission for its opinion on questions concerning the application of EC competition rules. The national court may ask the Commission for its opinion on economic, factual and legal matters.[47] The latter is of course without prejudice to the possibility or the obligation for the national court to ask the Court of Justice for a preliminary ruling regarding the interpretation or the validity of Community law in accordance with Article 234 EC.

28. In order to enable the Commission to provide the national court with a useful opinion, it may request the national court for further information.[48] In order to ensure the efficiency of the co-operation with national courts, the Commission will endeavour to provide the national court with the requested opinion within four months from the date it receives the request. Where the Commission has requested the national court for further information in order to enable it to formulate its opinion, that period starts to run from the moment that it receives the additional information.

29. When giving its opinion, the Commission will limit itself to providing the national court with the factual information or the economic or legal clarification asked for, without considering the merits of the case pending before the national court. Moreover, unlike the authoritative interpretation of Community law by the Community Courts, the opinion of the Commission does not legally bind the national court.

30. In line with what has been said in point 19 of this notice, the Commission will not hear the parties before formulating its opinion to the national court. The latter will have to deal with the Commission's opinion in accordance with the relevant national procedural rules, which have to respect the general principles of Community law.

---

[44] Case C-2/88 *Zwartveld* [1990] ECR I-4405, 10 and 11 and Case T-353/94 *Postbank* [1996] ECR II-921, 93.

[45] Case C-2/88 *Zwartveld* [1990] ECR I-4405, 10 and 11; Case C-275/00 *First and Franex* [2002] ECR I-10943, 49 and Case T-353/94 *Postbank* [1996] ECR II-921, 93.

[46] See point 8 of this notice.

[47] Case C-234/89 *Delimitis* [1991] ECR I-935, 53, and joined Cases C-319/93, C-40/94 and C-224/94 *Dijkstra* [1995] ECR I-4471, 34.

[48] Compare with case 96/81 *Commission v the Netherlands* [1982] ECR 1791, 7 and Case 272/86 *Commission v Greece* [1988] ECR 4875, 30.

3. The Commission's submission of observations to the national court

31. According to Article 15(3) of the regulation, the national competition authorities and the Commission may submit observations on issues relating to the application of Articles 81 or 82 EC to a national court which is called upon to apply those provisions. The regulation distinguishes between written observations, which the national competition authorities and the Commission may submit on their own initiative, and oral observations, which can only be submitted with the permission of the national court.[49]

32. The regulation specifies that the Commission will only submit observations when the coherent application of Articles 81 or 82 EC so requires. That being the objective of its submission, the Commission will limit its observations to an economic and legal analysis of the facts underlying the case pending before the national court.

33. In order to enable the Commission to submit useful observations, national courts may be asked to transmit or ensure the transmission to the Commission of a copy of all documents that are necessary for the assessment of the case. In line with Article 15(3), second subparagraph, of the regulation, the Commission will only use those documents for the preparation of its observations.[50]

34. Since the regulation does not provide for a procedural framework within which the observations are to be submitted, Member States' procedural rules and practices determine the relevant procedural framework. Where a Member State has not yet established the relevant procedural framework, the national court has to determine which procedural rules are appropriate for the submission of observations in the case pending before it.

35. The procedural framework should respect the principles set out in point 10 of this notice. That implies amongst others that the procedural framework for the submission of observations on issues relating to the application of Articles 81 or 82 EC

   (a) has to be compatible with the general principles of Community law, in particular the fundamental rights of the parties involved in the case;
   (b) cannot make the submission of such observations excessively difficult or practically impossible (the principle of effectiveness);[51] and
   (c) cannot make the submission of such observations more difficult than the submission of observations in court proceedings where equivalent national law is applied (the principle of equivalence).

B. The national courts facilitating the role of the Commission in the enforcement of EC competition rules

36. Since the duty of loyal cooperation also implies that Member States' authorities assist the European institutions with a view to attaining the objectives of the EC Treaty,[52] the regulation provides for three examples of such assistance: (1) the transmission of documents necessary for the assessment of a case in which the Commission would like to submit observations (see point 33), (2) the transmission of judgements applying Articles 81 or 82 EC): and (3) the role of national courts in the context of a Commission inspection.

1. The transmission of judgements of national courts applying Articles 81 or 82 EC

37. According to Article 15(2) of the regulation, Member States shall send to the Commission a copy of any written judgement of national courts applying Articles 81 or 82 EC without

---

[49] According to Art 15(4) of the reg, this is without prejudice to wider powers to make observations before courts conferred on national competition authorities under national law.

[50] See also Art 28(2) of the reg, which prevents the Commission from disclosing the information it has acquired and which is covered by the obligation of professional secrecy.

[51] Joined Cases 46/87 and 227/88 *Hoechst* [1989] ECR, 2859, 33. See also Art 15(3) of the reg.

[52] Case C-69/90 *Commission v Italy* [1991] ECR 6011, 15.

delay after the full written judgement is notified to the parties. The transmission of national judgements on the application of Articles 81 or 82 EC and the resulting information on proceedings before national courts primarily enable the Commission to become aware in a timely fashion of cases for which it might be appropriate to submit observations where one of the parties lodges an appeal against the judgement.

2. The role of national courts in the context of a Commission inspection

38. Finally, national courts may play a role in the context of a Commission inspection of undertakings and associations of undertakings. The role of the national courts depends on whether the inspections are conducted in business premises or in non-business premises.

39. With regard to the inspection of business premises, national legislation may require authorisation from a national court to allow a national enforcement authority to assist the Commission in case of opposition of the undertaking concerned. Such authorisation may also be sought as a precautionary measure. When dealing with the request, the national court has the power to control that the Commission's inspection decision is authentic and that the coercive measures envisaged are neither arbitrary nor excessive having regard to the subject matter of the inspection. In its control of the proportionality of the coercive measures, the national court may ask the Commission, directly or through the national competition authority, for detailed explanations in particular on the grounds the Commission has for suspecting infringement of Articles 81 and 82 EC, as well as on the seriousness of the suspected infringement and on the nature of the involvement of the undertaking concerned.[53]

40. With regard to the inspection of non-business premises, the regulation requires the authorisation from a national court before a Commission decision ordering such an inspection can be executed. In that case, the national court may control that the Commission's inspection decision is authentic and that the coercive measures envisaged are neither arbitrary nor excessive having regard in particular to the seriousness of the suspected infringement, to the importance of the evidence sought, to the involvement of the undertaking concerned and to the reasonable likelihood that business books and records relating to the subject matter of the inspection are kept in the premises for which the authorization is requested. The national court may ask the Commission, directly or through the national competition authority, for detailed explanations on those elements that are necessary to allow its control of the proportionality of the coercive measures envisaged.[54]

41. In both cases referred to in points 39 and 40, the national court may not call into question the lawfulness of the Commission's decision or the necessity for the inspection nor can it demand that it be provided with information in the Commission's file.[55] Furthermore, the duty of loyal cooperation requires the national court to take its decision within an appropriate timeframe that allows the Commission to effectively conduct its inspection.[56]

IV. Final Provisions

42. This notice is issued in order to assist national courts in the application of Articles 81 and 82 EC. It does not bind the national courts, nor does it affect the rights and obligations of the EU Member States and natural or legal persons under Community law.

43. This notice replaces the 1993 notice on cooperation between national courts and the Commission in applying Articles 85 and 86 of the EEC Treaty.[57]

---

[53] Art 20(6) to (8) of the reg and Case C-94/00 *Roquette Frères* [2002] ECR 9011.
[54] Art 21(3) of the reg.
[55] Case C-94/00 *Roquette Frères* [2002] ECR 9011, 39 and 62 to 66.
[56] See also ibidem, 91 and 92.
[57] OJ C39, 13.2.93, p 6.

Annex

Commission Block Exemption Regulations, Notices and Guidelines

This list is also available and updated on the website of the Directorate General for Competition of the European Commission:

http://europa.eu.int/comm/competition/antitrust/legislation/

A. Non-sector specific rules

1. Notices of a general nature

— Notice on the definition of the relevant market for the purposes of Community competition law (OJ C372, 9.12.1997, p 5)
— Notice on agreements of minor importance which do not appreciably restrict competition under Article 81(1) of the Treaty establishing the European Community (de minimis) (OJ C368, 22.12.2001, p 13)
— Notice on the effect on trade concept contained in Articles 81 and 82 of the Treaty (OJ C101, 27.4.2004, p 81)
— Guidelines on the application of Article 81(3) of the Treaty (OJ C101, 27.4.2004, p 2)

2. Vertical agreements

— Regulation (EC) No 2790/1999 of 22 December 1999 on the application of Article 81(3) of the Treaty to categories of vertical agreements and concerted practices (OJ L336, 29.12.1999, p 21)
— Guidelines on Vertical Restraints (OJ C291, 13.10.2000, p 1)

3. Horizontal cooperation agreements

— Regulation (EC) No 2658/2000 of 29 November 2000 on the application of Article 81(3) of the Treaty to categories of specialization agreements (OJ L304, 5.12.2000, p 3)
— Regulation (EC) No 2659/2000 of 29 November 2000 on the application of Article 81(3) of the Treaty to categories of research and development agreements (OJ L304, 5.12.2000, p 7)
— Guidelines on the applicability of Article 81 to horizontal cooperation agreements (OJ C3, 6.1.2001, p 2)

4. Licensing agreements for the transfer of technology

— Regulation (EC) No 773/2004 of 27 April 2004 on the application of Article 81(3) of the Treaty to categories of technology transfer agreements (OJ L123, 27.4.2004)
— Guidelines on the application of Article 81 of the EC Treaty to technology transfer agreements (OJ C101, 27.4.2004, p 2)

B. Sector specific rules

1. Insurance

— Regulation (EC) No 358/2003 of 27 February 2003 on the application of Article 81(3) of the Treaty to certain categories of agreements, decisions and concerted practices in the insurance sector (OJ L53, 28.2.2003, p 8)

2. Motor vehicles

— Regulation (EC) No 1400/2002 of 31 July 2002 on the application of Article 81(3) of the Treaty to categories of vertical agreements and concerted practices in the motor vehicle sector (OJ L203, 1.8.2002, p 30)

1083

3. *Telecommunications and postal services*

— Guidelines on the application of EEC competition rules in the telecommunications sector (OJ C233, 6.9.1991, p 2)
— Notice on the application of the competition rules to the postal sector and on the assessment of certain State measures relating to postal services (OJ C39, 6.2.1998, p 2)
— Notice on the application of the competition rules to access agreements in the telecommunications sector – Framework, relevant markets and principles (OJ C265, 22.8.1998, p 2)
— Guidelines on market analysis and the assessment of significant market power under the Community regulatory framework for electronic communications networks and services (OJ C165, 11.7.2002, p 6)

4. *Transport*

— Regulation (EEC) No 1617/93 on the application of Article 81(3) of the Treaty to certain categories of agreements and concerted practices concerning joint planning and co-ordination of schedules, joint operations, consultations on passenger and cargo tariffs on scheduled air services and slot allocation at airports (OJ L155, 26.6.1993, p 18)
— Communication on clarification of the Commission recommendations on the application of the competition rules to new transport infrastructure projects (OJ C298, 30.9.1997, p 5)
— Regulation (EC) No 823/2000 of 19 April 2000 on the application of Article 81(3) of the Treaty to certain categories of agreements, decisions and concerted practices between liner shipping companies (consortia) (OJ L100, 20.4.2000, p 24)

APPENDIX 6

Commission Notice on the handling of complaints by the Commission under Articles 81 and 82 of the EC Treaty

(2004/C 101/05)

(Text with EEA relevance)

1. INTRODUCTION AND SUBJECT-MATTER OF THE NOTICE

1. Regulation 1/200[1] establishes a system of parallel competence for the application of Articles 81 and 82 of the EC Treaty by the Commission and the Member States' competition authorities and courts. The Regulation recognises in particular the complementary functions of the Commission and Member States' competition authorities acting as public enforcers and the Member States' courts that rule on private lawsuits in order to safeguard the rights of individuals deriving from Articles 81 and 8.[2]

2. Under Regulation 1/2003, the public enforces may focus their action on the investigation of serious infringements of Articles 81 and 82 which are often difficult to detect. For their enforcement activity, they benefit from information supplied by undertakings and by consumers in the market.

3. The Commission therefore wishes to encourage citizens and undertakings to address themselves to the public enforcers to inform them about suspected infringements of the competition rules. At the level of the Commission, there are two ways to do this, one is by lodging a complaint pursuant to Article 7(2) of Regulation 1/2003. Under Articles 5 to 9 of Regulation 773/200,[3] such complaints must fulfil certain requirements.

4. The other way is the provision of market information that does not have to comply with the requirements for complaints pursuant to Article 7(2) of Regulation 1/2003. For this purpose, the Commission has created a special website to collect information from citizens and undertakings and their associations who wish to inform the Commission about suspected infringements of Articles 81 and 82. Such information can be the starting point for an investigation by the Commission.[4] Information about suspected infringements can be supplied to the following address:

    http://europa.eu.int/dgcomp/info-on-anti-competitive-practices

    or to:

    Commission européenne/Europese Commissie
    Competition DG
    B-1049 Bruxelles/Brussel

---

[1] Council Reg (EC) No 1/2003 of 16 December 2002 on the implementation of the rules on competition laid down in Arts 81 and 82 of the Treaty (O) L 1, 4.1.2003, pages 1–25).

[2] cf in particular Recitals 3–7 and 35 of Reg 1/2003.

[3] Commission Reg (EC) No 773/2004 of 7 April 2004 relating to the conduct of proceedings by the Commission pursuant to Arts 81 and 82 of the EC Treaty (OJ 123, 27.4.2004).

[4] The Commission handles correspondence from informants in accordance with its principles of good administrative practice.

5. Without prejudice to the interpretation of Regulation 1/2003 and of Commission Regulation 773/2004 by the Community Courts, the present Notice intends to provide guidance to citizens and undertakings that are seeking relief from suspected infringements of the competition rules. The Notice contains two main parts:

    — Part II gives indications about the choice between complaining to the Commission or bringing a lawsuit before a national court. Moreover, it recalls the principles related to the work-sharing between the Commission and the national competition authorities in the enforcement system established by Regulation 1/2003 that are explained in the Notice on cooperation within the network of competition authorities.[5]

    — Part III explains the procedure for the treatment of complaints pursuant to Article 7(2) of Regulation 1/2003 by the Commission.

6. This Notice does not address the following situations:

    — complaints lodged by Member States pursuant to Article 7(2) of Regulation 1/2003.
    — complaints that ask the Commission to take action against a Member State pursuant to Article 86(3) in conjunction with Articles 81 or 82 of the Treaty.
    — complaints relating to Article 87 of the Treaty on state aids,
    — complaints relating to infringements by Member States that the Commission may pursue in the framework of Article 226 of the Treaty.[6]

II. DIFFERENT POSSIBILITIES FOR LODGING COMPLAINTS ABOUT SUSPECTED INFRINGEMENTS OF ARTICLES 81 OR 82

A. Complaints in the new enforcement system established by Regulation 1/2003

7. Depending on the nature of the complaint, a complainant may bring his complaint either to a national court or to a competition authority that acts as public enforcer. The present chapter of this Notice intends to help potential complainants to make an informed choice about whether to address themselves to the Commission, to one of the Member States' competition authorities or to a national court.

8. While national courts are called upon to safeguard the rights of individuals and are thus bound to rule on cases brought before them, public enforcers cannot investigate all complaints, but must set priorities in their treatment of cases. The Court of Justice has held that the Commission, entrusted by Article 85(1) of the EC Treaty with the task of ensuring application of the principles laid down in Articles 81 and 82 of the Treaty, is responsible for defining and implementing the orientation of Community competition policy and that, in order to perform that task effectively, it is entitled to give differing degrees of priority to the complaints brought before it.[7]

9. Regulation 1/2003 empowers Member States' courts and Member States' competition authorities to apply Articles 81 and 82 in their entirety alongside the Commission. Regulation 1/2003 pursues as one principal objective that Member States' courts and competition authorities should participate effectively in the enforcement of Articles 81 and 8.[8]

---

[5] Notice on cooperation within the network of competition authorities (p 43).

[6] For the handling of such complaints, cf Commission communication of 10 October 2002, COM(2002) 141.

[7] Case C-344/98, *Masterfoods v HB Ice Cream*, [2000] ECR I-11369, para 46; Case C-119/97 P, *Union française de l'express (Ufex) and Others v Commission of the European Communities*, [1999] ECR I-1341, para 88; Case T-24/90, *Automec v Commission of the European Communities*, [1992] ECR II-2223, paras 73–77.

[8] cf in particular Arts 5, 6, 11, 12, 15, 22, 29, 35 and Recitals 2 to 4 and 6 to 8 of Reg 1/2003.

10. Moreover, Article 3 of Regulation 1/2003 provides that Member States' courts and competition authorities have to apply Articles 81 and 82 to all cases of agreements or conduct that are capable of affecting trade between Member States to which they apply their national competition laws. In addition, Articles 11 and 15 of the Regulation create a range of mechanisms by which Member States' courts and competition authorities cooperate with the Commission in the enforcement of Articles 81 and 82.

11. In this new legislative framework, the Commission intends to refocus its enforcement resources along the following lines:

— enforce the EC competition rules in cases for which it is well placed to act,[9] concentrating its resources on the most serious infringements;[10]

— handle cases in relation to which the Commission should act with a view to define Community competition policy and/or to ensure coherent application of Articles 81 or 82.

B. The complementary roles of private and public enforcement

12. It has been consistently held by the Community Courts that national courts are called upon to safeguard the rights of individuals created by the direct effect of Articles 81(1) and 82.[11]

13. National courts can decide upon the nullity or validity of contracts and only national courts can grant damages to an individual in case of an infringement of Articles 81 and 82. Under the case law of the Court of Justice, any individual can claim damages for loss caused to him by a contract or by conduct which restricts or distorts competition, in order to ensure the full effectiveness of the Community competition rules. Such actions for damages before the national courts can make a significant contribution to the maintenance of effective competition in the Community as they discourage undertakings from concluding or applying restrictive agreements or practices.[12]

14. Regulation 1/2003 takes express account of the fact that national courts have an essential part to play in applying the EC competition rules.[13] By extending the power to apply Article 81(3) to national courts it removes the possibility for undertakings to delay national court proceedings by a notification to the Commission and thus eliminates an obstacle for private litigation that existed under Regulation No 17.[14]

15. Without prejudice to the right or obligation of national courts to address a preliminary question to the Court of Justice in accordance with Article 234 EC, Article 15(1) of Regulation 1/2003 provides expressly that national courts may ask for opinions or information from the Commission. This provision aims at facilitating the application of Articles 81 and 82 by national courts.[15]

---

[9] cf Notice on cooperation within the Network of Competition Authorities . . ., points 5 ss.

[10] cf Recital 3 of Reg 1/2003.

[11] Settled case law, cf Case 127/73, *Belgische Radio en Televisie (BRT) v SABAM and Fonior*, [1974] ECR 51, para 16; Case C-282/95 P, Guérin automobiles v Commission of the European Communities, [1997] ECR I-1503, para 39; Case C-453/99, *Courage v Bernhard Crehan*, [2001] ECR I-6297, para 23.

[12] Case C-453/99, *Courage v Bernhard Crehan*, [2001] ECR I-6297, paras 26 and 27; the power of national courts to grant damages is also underlined in Recital 7 of Reg 1/2003.

[13] cf Arts 1, 6 and 15 as well as Recital 7 of Reg 1/2003.

[14] Reg No 17: First Reg implementing Arts 85 and 86 of the Treaty; OJ P13 of 21 February 1962, p 204–211: English special edition: Series 1 Chapter 1959–1962 p 87. Reg No 17 is repealed by Art 43 of Reg 1/2003 with effect from 1 May 2004.

[15] For more detailed explanations of this mechanism, cf Notice on the cooperation between the Commission and the courts of the EU Member States in the application of Arts 81 and 82 EC . . .

16. Action before national courts has the following advantages for complainants:

    — National courts may award damages for loss suffered as a result of an infringement of Article 81 or 82.

    — National courts may rule on claims for payment or contractual obligations based on an agreement that they examine under Article 81.

    — It is for the national courts to apply the civil sanction of nullity of Article 81(2) in contractual relationships between individuals.[16] They can in particular assess, in the light of the applicable national law, the scope and consequences of the nullity of certain contractual provisions under Article 81(2), with particular regard to all the other matters covered by the agreement.[17]

    — National courts are usually better placed than the Commission to adopt interim measures.[18]

    — Before national courts, it is possible to combine a claim under Community competition law with other claims under national law.

    — Courts normally have the power to award legal costs to the successful applicant. This is never possible in an administrative procedure before the Commission.

17. The fact that a complainant can secure the protection of his rights by an action before a national court, is an important element that the Commission may take into account in its examination of the Community interest for investigating a complaint.[19]

18. The Commission holds the view that the new enforcement system established by Regulation 1/2003 strengthens the possibilities for complainants to seek and obtain effective relief before national courts.

C. Work-sharing between the public enforcers in the European Community

19. Regulation 1/2003 creates a system of parallel competence for the application of Articles 81 and 82 by empowering Member States' competition authorities to apply Articles 81 and 82 in their entirety (Article 5). Decentralised enforcement by Member States' competition authorities is further encouraged by the possibility to exchange information (Article 12) and to provide each other assistance with investigations (Article 22).

20. The Regulation does not regulate the work-sharing between the Commission and the Member States' competition authorities but leaves the division of case work to the co-operation of the Commission and the Member States' competition authorities inside the European Competition Network (ECN). The Regulation pursues the objective of ensuring effective enforcement of Articles 81 and 82 through a flexible division of case work between the public enforcers in the Community.

21. Orientations for the work sharing between the Commission and the Member States' competition authorities are laid down in a separate Notice.[20] The guidance contained in that Notice, which concerns the relations between the public enforcers, will be of interest to complainants as it permits them to address a complaint to the authority most likely to be well placed to deal with their case.

---

[16] Case *T-24/90, Automec v Commission of the European Communities*, [1992] ECR II-2223, para 93.

[17] Case C-230/96, *Cabour and Nord Distribution Automobile v Arnor 'SOCO'*, [1998] ECR I-2055, para 51; Joined Cases T-185/96, T-189/96 and T-190/96, *Dalmasso and Others v Commission of the European Communities*, [1999] ECR II-93, para 50.

[18] cf Art 8 of Reg 1/2003 and para 80 below. Depending on the case. Member States' competition authorities may equally be well placed to adopt interim measures.

[19] cf points 41 ss. below.

[20] Notice on cooperation within the Network of Competition Authorities (p 43).

22. The Notice on cooperation within the Network of Competition Authorities states in particular:[21]

'An authority can be considered to be well placed to deal with a case if the following three cumulative conditions are met:
— the agreement or practice has substantial direct actual or foreseeable effects on competition within its territory, is implemented within or originates from its territory;
— the authority is able effectively to bring to an end the entire infringement, i.e. it can adopt a cease-and desist order, the effect of which will be sufficient to bring an end to the infringement and it can, where appropriate, sanction the infringement adequately;
— it can gather, possibly with the assistance of other authorities, the evidence required to prove the infringement.

The above criteria indicate that a material link between the infringement and the territory of a Member State must exist in order for that Member State's competition authority to be considered well placed. It can be expected that in most cases the authorities of those Member States where competition is substantially affected by an infringement will be well placed provided they are capable of effectively bringing the infringement to an end through either single or parallel action unless the Commission is better placed to act (see below [. . .]).

It follows that a single NCA is usually well placed to deal with agreements or practices that substantially affect competition mainly within its territory [. . .]

Furthermore single action of an NCA might also be appropriate where, although more than one NCA can be regarded as well placed, the action of a single NCA is sufficient to bring the entire infringement to an end [. . .].

Parallel action by two or three NCAs may be appropriate where an agreement or practice has substantial effects on competition mainly in their respective territories and the action of only one NCA would not be sufficient to bring the entire infringement to an end and/or to sanction it adequately [. . .].

The authorities dealing with a case in parallel action will endeavour to coordinate their action to the extent possible. To that effect, they may find it useful to designate one of them as a lead authority and to delegate tasks to the lead authority such as for example the coordination of investigative measures, while each authority remains responsible for conducting its own proceedings.

The Commission is particularly well placed if one or several agreement(s) or practice(s), including networks of similar agreements or practices, have effects on competition in more than three Member States (cross-border markets covering more than three Member States or several national markets) [. . .].

Moreover, the Commission is particularly well placed to deal with a case if it is closely linked to other Community provisions which may be exclusively or more effectively applied by the Commission, if the Community interest requires the adoption of a Commission decision to develop Community competition policy when a new competition issue arises or to ensure effective enforcement.'.

23. Within the European Competition Network, information on cases that are being investigated following a complaint will be made available to the other members of the network before or without delay after commencing the first formal investigative measure.[22] Where the same complaint has been lodged with several authorities or where a case has not been lodged with an authority that is well placed, the members of the network will endeavour to determine

---

[21] Notice on cooperation within the Network of Competition Authorities . . ., points 8–15.
[22] Art 11(2) and (3) of Reg 1/2003; Notice on cooperation within the Network of Competition Authorities . . ., points 16/17.

within an indicative time-limit of two months which authority or authorities should be in charge of the case.

24. Complainants themselves have an important role to play in further reducing the potential need for reallocation of a case originating from their complaint by referring to the orientations on work sharing in the network set out in the present chapter when deciding on where to lodge their complaint. If nonetheless a case is reallocated within the network, the undertakings concerned and the complainants(s) are informed as soon as possible by the competition authorities involved.[23]

25. The Commission may reject a complaint in accordance with Article 13 of Regulation 1/2003, on the grounds that a Member State competition authority is dealing or has dealt with the case. When doing so, the Commission must, in accordance with Article 9 of Regulation 773/2004, inform the complainant without delay of the national competition authority which is dealing or has already dealt with the case.

III. The Commission's Handling of Complaints Pursuant to Article 7(2) of Regulation 1/2003

A. General

26. According to Article 7(2) of Regulation 1/2003 natural or legal persons that can show a legitimate interest[24] are entitled to lodge a complaint to ask the Commission to find an infringement of Articles 81 and 82 EC and to require that the infringement be brought to an end in accordance with Article 7(1) of Regulation 1/2003. The present part of this Notice explains the requirements applicable to complaints based on Article 7(2) of Regulation 1/2003, their assessment and the procedure followed by the Commission.

27. The Commission, unlike civil courts, whose task is to safeguard the individual rights of private persons, is an administrative authority that must act in the public interest. It is an inherent feature of the Commission's task as public enforcer that it has a margin of discretion to set priorities in its enforcement activity.[25]

28. The Commission is entitled to give different degrees of priority to complaints made to it and may refer to the Community interest presented by a case as a criterion of priority.[26] The Commission may reject a complaint when it considers that the case does not display a sufficient Community interest to justify further investigation. Where the Commission rejects a complaint, the complainant is entitled to a decision of the Commission[27] without prejudice to Article 7(3) of Regulation 773/2004.

B. Making a complaint pursuant to Article 7(2) of Regulation 1/2003

(a) Complaint form

29. A complaint pursuant to Article 7(2) of Regulation 1/2003 can only be made about an alleged infringement of Articles 81 or 82 with a view to the Commission taking action under

---

[23] Notice on cooperation within the Network of Competition Authorities . . ., point 34.

[24] For more extensive explanations on this notion in particular, cf points 33 ss. below.

[25] Case C-119/97 P, *Union française de l'express (Ufex) and Others v Commission of the European Communities*, [1999] ECR I-1341, para 88; Case T-24/90, *Automec v Commission of the European Communities*, [1992] ECR II-2223, paras 73–77 and 85.

[26] Settled case law since Case T-24/90, *Automec v Commission of the European Communities*, [1992] ECR II-2223, para 85.

[27] Case C-282/95 P, *Guérin automobiles v Commission of the European Communities*, [1997] ECR I-1503, para 36.

Article 7(1) of Regulation 1/2003. A complaint under Article 7(2) of Regulation 1/2003 has to comply with Form C mentioned in Article 5(1) of Regulation 773/2004 and annexed to that Regulation.

30. Form C is available at http://europa.eu.int/dgcomp/complaints-form and is also annexed to this Notice. The complaint must be submitted in three paper copies as well as, if possible, an electronic copy. In addition, the complainant must provide a non-confidential version of the complaint (Article 5(2) of Regulation 773/2004). Electronic transmission to the Commission is possible via the web site indicated, the paper copies should be sent to the following address:

Commission européenne/Europese Commissie
Competition DG
B-1049 Bruxelles/Brussel

31. Form C requires complainants to submit comprehensive information in relation to their complaint. They should also provide copies of relevant supporting documentation reasonably available to them and, to the extent possible, provide indications as to where relevant information and documents that are unavailable to them could be obtained by the Commission. In particular cases, the Commission may dispense with the obligation to provide information in relation to part of the information required by Form C (Article 5(1) of Regulation 773/2004). The Commission holds the view that this possibility can in particular play a role to facilitate complaints by consumer associations where they, in the context of an otherwise substantiated complaint, do not have access to specific pieces of information from the sphere of the undertakings complained of.

32. Correspondence to the Commission that does not comply with the requirements of Article 5 of Regulation 773/2004 and therefore does not constitute a complaint within the meaning of Article 7(2) of Regulation 1/2003 will be considered by the Commission as general information that, where it is useful, may lead to an own-initiative investigation (cf. point 4 above).

(b) Legitimate interest

33. The status of formal complainant under Article 7(2) of Regulation 1/2003 is reserved to legal and natural persons who can show a legitimate interest.[28] Member States are deemed to have a legitimate interest for all complaints they choose to lodge.

34. In the past practice of the Commission, the condition of legitimate interest was not often a matter of doubt as most complainants were in a position of being directly and adversely affected by the alleged infringement. However, there are situations where the condition of a 'legitimate interest' in Article 7(2) requires further analysis to conclude that it is fulfilled. Useful guidance can best be provided by a non-exhaustive set of examples.

35. The Court of First Instance has held that an association of undertakings may claim a legitimate interest in lodging a complaint regarding conduct concerning its members, even if it is not directly concerned, as an undertaking operating in the relevant market, by the conduct complained of, provided that, first, it is entitled to represent the interests of its members and secondly, the conduct complained of is liable to adversely affect the interests of its members.[29] Conversely, the Commission has been found to be entitled not to pursue the complaint of

---

[28] cf Art 5(1) of Reg 773/2004.

[29] Case T-114/92, *Bureau Européen des Médias et de l'Industrie Musicale (BEMIM) v Commission of the European Communities*, [1995] ECR II-147, para 28. Associations of undertakings were also the complainants in the cases underlying the judgments in Case 298/83, *Comité des industries cinématographiques des Communautés européennes (CICCE) v Commission of the European Communities*, [1985] ECR 1105 and Case T-319/99, *Federacion Nacional de Empress (FENIN) v Commission of the European Communities*, not yet published in [2003] ECR.

an association of undertakings whose members were not involved in the type of business transactions complained of.[30]

36. From this case law, it can be inferred that undertakings (themselves or through associations that are entitled to represent their interests) can claim a legitimate interest where they are operating in the relevant market or where the conduct complained of is liable to directly and adversely affect their interests. This confirms the established practice of the Commission which has accepted that a legitimate interest can, for instance, be claimed by the parties to the agreement or practice which is the subject of the complaint, by competitors whose interests have allegedly been damaged by the behaviour complained of or by undertakings excluded from a distribution system.

37. Consumer associations can equally lodge complaints with the Commission.[31] The Commission moreover holds the view that individual consumers whose economic interests are directly and adversely affected insofar as they are the buyers of goods or services that are the object of an infringement can be in a position to show a legitimate interest.[32]

38. However, the Commission does not consider as a legitimate interest within the meaning of Article 7(2) the interest of persons or organisations that wish to come forward on general interest considerations without showing that they or their members are liable to be directly and adversely affected by the infringement (*pro bono publico*).

39. Local or regional public authorities may be able to show a legitimate interest in their capacity as buyers or users of goods or services affected by the conduct complained of. Conversely, they cannot be considered as showing a legitimate interest within the meaning of Article 7(2) of Regulation 1/2003 to the extent that they bring to the attention of the Commission alleged infringements *pro bono publico*.

40. Complainants have to demonstrate their legitimate interest. Where a natural or legal person lodging a complaint is unable to demonstrate a legitimate interest, the Commission is entitled, without prejudice to its right to initiate proceedings of its own initiative, not to pursue the complaint. The Commission may ascertain whether this condition is met at any stage of the investigation.[33]

C. Assessment of complaints

(a) Community interest

41. Under the settled case law of the Community Courts, the Commission is not required to conduct an investigation in each case[34] or, *a fortiori*, to take a decision within the meaning of Article 249 EC on the existence or non-existence of an infringement of Articles 81 or 82,[35] but is entitled to give differing degrees of priority to the complaints brought before it and

---

[30] Joined Cases T-133/95 and T-204/95, *International Express Carriers Conference (IECC) v Commission of the European Communities*, [1998] ECR II-3645, paras 79–83.

[31] Case T-37/92, *Bureau Européen des Unions des Consommateurs (BEUC) v Commission of the European Communities*, [1994] ECR II-285, para 36.

[32] This question is currently raised in a pending procedure before the Court of First Instance (Joined cases T-213 and 214/01). The Commission has also accepted as complainant an individual consumer in its Decision of 9 December 1998 in Case IV/D-2/34,466, *Greek Ferries*, OJ L 109/24 of 27 April 1999, para 1.

[33] Joined Cases T-133/95 and T-204/95, *International Express Carriers Conference (IECC) v Commission of the European Communities*, [1998] ECR II-3645, para 79.

[34] Case T-24/90, *Automec v Commission of the European Communities*, [1992] ECR II-2223, para 76; Case C-91/95 P, *Roger Tremblay and Others v Commission of the European Communities*, [1996] ECR I-5547, para 30.

[35] Case 125/78, *GEMA v Commission of the European Communities*, [1979] ECR 3173, para 17; Case C-119/97/P, *Union française de l'express (Ufex) and Others v Commission of the European Communities*, [1999] ECR I-1341, para 87.

refer to the Community interest in order to determine the degree of priority to be applied to the various complaints it receives.[36] The position is different only if the complaint falls within the exclusive competence of the Commission.[37]

42. The Commission must however examine carefully the factual and legal elements brought to its attention by the complaint in order to assess the Community interest in further investigation of a case.[38]

43. The assessment of the Community interest raised by a complaint depends on the circumstances of each individual case. Accordingly, the number of criteria of assessment to which the Commission may refer is not limited, nor is the Commission required to have recourse exclusively to certain criteria. As the factual and legal circumstances may differ considerably from case to case, it is permissible to apply new criteria which had not before been considered.[39] Where appropriate, the Commission may give priority to a single criterion for assessing the Community interest.[40]

44. Among the criteria which have been held relevant in the case law for the assessment of the Community interest in the (further) investigation of a case are the following:

— The Commission can reject a complaint on the ground that the complainant can bring an action to assert its rights before national courts.[41]
— The Commission may not regard certain situations as excluded in principle from its purview under the task entrusted to it by the Treaty but is required to assess in each case how serious the alleged infringements are and how persistent their consequences are. This means in particular that it must take into account the duration and the extent of the infringements complained of and their effect on the competition situation in the Community.[42]
— The Commission may have to balance the significance of the alleged infringement as regards the functioning of the common market, the probability of establishing the existence of the infringement and the scope of the investigation required in order to fulfil its task of ensuring that Articles 81 and 82 of the Treaty are complied with.[43]
— While the Commission's discretion does not depend on how advanced the investigation of a case is, the stage of the investigation forms part of the circumstances of the case which the Commission may have to take into consideration.[44]

---

[36] Settled case law since the Case T-24/90, *Automec v Commission of the European Communities*, [1992] ECR II-2223, paras 77 and 85; Recital 18 of Reg 1/2003 expressly confirms this possibility.

[37] Settled case law since Case T-24/90, *Automec v Commission of the European Communities*, [1992] ECR II-2223, para 75. Under Reg 1/2003, this principle may only be relevant in the context of Art 29 of that Reg.

[38] Case 210/81, *Oswald Schmidt, trading as Demo-Studio Schmidt v Commission of the European Communities*, [1983] ECR 3045, para 19; Case C-119/97 P, *Union française de l'express (Ufex) and Others v Commission of the European Communities*, [1999] ECR I-1341, para 86.

[39] Case C-119/97 P, *Union française de l'express (Ufex) and Others v Commission of the European Communities*, [1999] ECR I-1341, paras 79–80.

[40] Case C-450/98 P, *International Express Carriers Conference (IECC) v Commission of the European Communities*, [2001] ECR I-3947, paras 57–59.

[41] Case T-24/90, *Automec v Commission of the European Communities*, [1992] ECR II-2223, paras 88ss.; Case T-5/93, *Roger Tremblay and Others v Commission of the European Communities*, [1995] ECR II-185, paras 65ss.; Case T-575/93, *Casper Koelman v Commission of the European Communities*, [1996] ECR II-1, paras 75–80; see also part II above where more detailed explanations concerning this situation are given.

[42] Case C-119/97 P, *Union française de l'express (Ufex) and Others v Commission of the European Communities*, [1999] ECR I-1341, paras 92/93.

[43] Settled case law since Case T-24/90, *Automec v Commission of the European Communities*, [1992] ECR II-2223, para 86.

[44] Case C-449/98 P, *International Express Carriers Conference (IECC) v Commission of the European Communities* [2001] ECR I-3875, para 37.

— The Commission may decide that it is not appropriate to investigate a complaint where the practices in question have ceased. However, for this purpose, the Commission will have to ascertain whether anti-competitive effects persist and if the seriousness of the infringements or the persistence of their effects does not give the complaint a Community interest.[45]

— The Commission may also decide that it is not appropriate to investigate a complaint where the undertakings concerned agree to change their conduct in such a way that it can consider that there is no longer a sufficient Community interest to intervene.[46]

45. Where it forms the view that a case does not display sufficient Community interest to justify (further) investigation, the Commission may reject the complaint on that ground. Such a decision can be taken either before commencing an investigation or after taking investigative measures.[47] However, the Commission is not obliged to set aside a complaint for lack of Community interest.[48]

(b) Assessment under Articles 81 and 82

46. The examination of a complaint under Articles 81 and 82 involves two aspects, one relating to the facts to be established to prove an infringement of Articles 81 or 82 and the other relating to the legal assessment of the conduct complained of.

47. Where the complaint, while complying with the requirements of Article 5 of Regulation 773/2004 and Form C, does not sufficiently substantiate the allegations put forward, it may be rejected on that ground.[49] In order to reject a complaint on the ground that the conduct complained of does not infringe the EC competition rules or does not fall within their scope of application, the Commission is not obliged to take into account circumstances that have not been brought to its attention by the complainant and that it could only have uncovered by the investigation of the case.[50]

48. The criteria for the legal assessment of agreements or practices under Articles 81 and 82 cannot be dealt with exhaustively in the present Notice. However, potential complainants should refer to the extensive guidance available from the Commission,[51] in addition to other sources and in particular the case law of the Community Courts and the case practice of the Commission. Four specific issues are mentioned in the following points with indications on where to find further guidance.

---

[45] Case T-77/95, *Syndicat français de l'Express International and Others v Commission of the European Communities* [1997] ECR II-1, para 57; Case C-119/97 P, *Union française de l'express (Ufex) and Others v Commission of the European Communities*, [1999] ECR I-1341, para 95. cf also Case T-37/92, *Bureau Européen des Unions des Consommateurs (BEUC) v Commission of the European Communities*, [1994] ECR II-285, para 113, where an unwritten commitment between a Member State and a third county outside the common commercial policy was held not to suffice to establish that the conduct complained of had ceased.

[46] Case T-110/95, *International Express Carriers (IECC) v Commission of the European Communities and Others*, [1998] ECR II-3605, para 57, upheld by Case 449/98 P, *International Express Carriers (IECC) v Commission of the European Communities and Others*, [2001] ECR I-3875, paras 44–47.

[47] Case C-449/98 P, *International Express Carriers (IECC) v Commission of the European Communities* e.a. [2001] ECR I-3875, para 37.

[48] cf Case T-77/92, *Parker Pen v Commission of the European Communities*, [1994] ECR II-549, paras 64/65.

[49] Case 298/83, *Comité des industries cinématographiques des Communautés européennes (CICCE) v Commission of the European Communities*, [1985] ECR 1105, paras 21–24; Case T-198/98, *Micro Leader Business v Commission of the European Communities*, [1999] ECR II-3989, paras 32–39.

[50] Case T-319/99, *Federación Nacional de Empresas (FENIN) v Commission of the European Communities*, not yet published in [2003] ECR, para 43.

[51] Extensive guidance can be found on the Commission's web site at http://europa.eu.int/comm/competition/index_en.html

49. Agreements and practices fall within the scope of application of Articles 81 and 82 where they are capable of affecting trade between Member States. Where an agreement or practice does not fulfil this condition, national competition law may apply, but not EC competition law. Extensive guidance on this subject can be found in the Notice on the effect on trade concept.[52]

50. Agreements falling within the scope of Article 81 may be agreements of minor importance which are deemed not to restrict competition appreciably. Guidance on this issue can be found in the Commission's *de minimis* Notice.[53]

51. Agreements that fulfil the conditions of a block exemption regulation are deemed to satisfy the conditions of Article 81(3).[54] For the Commission to withdraw the benefit of the block exemption pursuant to Article 29 of Regulation 1/2003, it must find that upon individual assessment an agreement to which the exemption regulation applies has certain effects which are incompatible with Article 81(3).

52. Agreements that restrict competition within the meaning of Article 81(1) EC may fulfil the conditions of Article 81(3) EC. Pursuant to Article 1(2) of Regulation 1/2003 and without a prior administrative decision being required, such agreements are not prohibited. Guidance on the conditions to be fulfilled by an agreement pursuant to Article 81(3) can be found in the Notice on Article 81(3).[55]

D. The Commission's procedures when dealing with complaints

(a) Overview

53. As recalled above, the Commission is not obliged to carry out an investigation on the basis of every complaint submitted with a view to establishing whether an infringement has been committed. However, the Commission is under a duty to consider carefully the factual and legal issues brought to its attention by the complainant, in order to assess whether those issues indicate conduct which is liable to infringe Articles 81 and 82.[56]

54. In the Commission's procedure for dealing with complaints, different stages can be distinguished.[57]

55. During the first stage, following the submission of the complaint, the Commission examines the complaint and may collect further information in order to decide what action it will take on the complaint. That stage may include an informal exchange of views between the Commission and the complainant with a view to clarifying the factual and legal issues with which the complaint is concerned. In this stage, the Commission may give an initial reaction to the complainant allowing the complainant an opportunity to expand on his allegations in the light of that initial reaction.

56. In the second stage, the Commission may investigate the case further with a view to initiating proceedings pursuant to Article 7(1) of Regulation 1/2003 against the undertakings

---

[52] Notice on the effect on trade concept contained in Arts 81 and 82 of the Treaty (p 81).

[53] Commission Notice on agreements of minor importance which do not appreciably restrict competition under Art 81(1) of the Treaty establishing the European Community (*de minimis*), OJ C368 of 22 December 2002, p 13.

[54] The texts of all block exemption regulations are available on the Commission's web site at http://europa.eu.int/comm/competition/index_en.html

[55] Commission Notice—Guidelines on the application of Art 81(3) of the Treaty (p 97).

[56] Case 210/81, *Oswald Schmidt, trading as Demo-Studio Schmidt v Commission of the European Communities*, [1983] ECR 3045, para 19: Case T-24/90, *Automec v Commission of the European Communities*, [1992] ECR II-2223, para 79.

[57] cf Case T-64/89, *Automec v Commission of the European Communities*, [1990] ECR II-367, paras 45–47; Case T-37/92 *Bureau Européen des Unions des Consommateurs (BEUC) v Commission of the European Communities*, [1994] ECR II-285, para 29.

complained of. Where the Commission considers that there are insufficient grounds for acting on the complaint, it will inform the complainant of its reasons and offer the complainant the opportunity to submit any further comments within a time-limit which it fixes (Article 7(1) of Regulation 773/2004).

57. If the complainant fails to make known its views within the time-limit set by the Commission, the complaint is deemed to have been withdrawn (Article 7(3) of Regulation 773/2004). In all other cases, in the third stage of the procedure, the Commission takes cognisance of the observations submitted by the complainant and either initiates a procedure against the subject of the complaint or adopts a decision rejecting the complaint.[58]

58. Where the Commission rejects a complaint pursuant to Article 13 of Regulation 1/2003 on the grounds that another authority is dealing or has dealt with the case, the Commission proceeds in accordance with Article 9 of Regulation 773/2004.

59. Throughout the procedure, complainants benefit from a range of rights as provided in particular in Articles 6 to 8 of Regulation 773/2004. However, proceedings of the Commission in competition cases do not constitute adversarial proceedings between the complainant on the one hand and the companies which are the subject of the investigation on the other hand. Accordingly, the procedural rights of complainants are less far-reaching than the right to a fair hearing of the companies which are the subject of an infringement procedure.[59]

(b) Indicative time limit for informing the complainant of the Commission's proposed action

60. The Commission is under an obligation to decide on complaints within a reasonable time.[60] What is a reasonable duration depends on the circumstances of each case and in particular, its context, the various procedural steps followed by the Commission, the conduct of the parties in the course of the procedure, the complexity of the case and its importance for the various parties involved.[61]

61. The Commission will in principle endeavour to inform complainants of the action that it proposes to take on a complaint within an indicative time frame of four months from the reception of the complaint. Thus, subject to the circumstances of the individual case and in particular the possible need to request complementary information from the complainant or third parties, the Commission will in principle inform the complainant within four months whether or not it intends to investigate its case further. This time-limit does not constitute a binding statutory term.

62. Accordingly, within this four month period, the Commission may communicate its proposed course of action to the complainant as an initial reaction within the first phase of the procedure (see point 55 above). The Commission may also, where the examination of the complaint has progressed to the second stage (see point 56 above), directly proceed to informing the complainant about its provisional assessment by a letter pursuant to Article 7(1) of Regulation 773/2004.

---

[58] Case C-282/95 P, *Guérin automobiles v Commission of the European Communities*, [1997] ECR I-1503, para 36.

[59] Joined Cases 142 and 156/84, *British American Tobacco Company and R. J. Reynolds Industries v Commission of the European Communities* [1987] ECR 249, para 19/20.

[60] Case C-282/95 P, *Guérin automobiles v Commission of the European Communities*, [1997] ECR I-1503, para 37.

[61] Joined Cases T-213/95 and T-18/96, *Stichting Certificatie Kraanverhuurbedrijf (SCK) and Federatie van Nederlandse Kraanbedrijven (FNK) v Commission of the European Communities*, [1997] ECR 1739, para 57.

63. To ensure the most expeditious treatment of their complaint, it is desirable that complainants cooperate diligently in the procedures,[62] for example by informing the Commission of new developments.

(c) Procedural rights of the complainant

64. Where the Commission addresses a statement of objections to the companies complained of pursuant to Article 10(1) of Regulation 773/2004, the complainant is entitled to receive a copy of this document from which business secrets and other confidential information of the companies concerned have been removed (non-confidential version of the statement of objections; cf. Article 6(1) of Regulation 773/2004). The complainant is invited to comment in writing on the statement of objections. A time-limit will be set for such written comments.

65. Furthermore, the Commission may, where appropriate, afford complainants the opportunity of expressing their views at the oral hearing of the parties to which a statement of objections has been addressed, if the complainants so request in their written comments.[63]

66. Complainants may submit, of their own initiative or following a request by the Commission, documents that contain business secrets or other confidential information. Confidential information will be protected by the Commission.[64] Under Article 16 of Regulation 773/2004, complainants are obliged to identify confidential information, give reasons why the information is considered confidential and submit a separate non-confidential version when they make their views known pursuant to Article 6(1) and 7(1) of Regulation 773/2004, as well as when they subsequently submit further information in the course of the same procedure. Moreover, the Commission may, in all other cases, request complainants which produce documents or statements to identify the documents or parts of the documents or statements which they consider to be confidential. It may in particular set a deadline for the complainant to specify why it considers a piece of information to be confidential and to provide a non-confidential version, including a concise description or non-confidential version of each piece of information deleted.

67. The qualification of information as confidential does not prevent the Commission from disclosing and using information where that is necessary to prove an infringement of Articles 81 or 82.[65] Where business secrets and confidential information are necessary to prove an infringement, the Commission must assess for each individual document whether the need to disclose is greater than the harm which might result from disclosure.

68. Where the Commission takes the view that a complaint should not be further examined, because there is no sufficient Community interest in pursuing the case further or on other grounds, it will inform the complainant in the form of a letter which indicates its legal basis (Article 7(1) of Regulation 773/2004), sets out the reasons that have led the Commission to provisionally conclude in the sense indicated and provides the complainant with the opportunity to submit supplementary information or observations within a time-limit set by the Commission. The Commission will also indicate the consequences of not replying pursuant to Article 7(3) of Regulation 773/2004, as explained below.

69. Pursuant to Article 8(1) of Regulation 773/2004, the complainant has the right to access the information on which the Commission bases its preliminary view. Such access is normally provided by annexing to the letter a copy of the relevant documents.

---

[62] The notion of 'diligence' on the part of the complainant is used by the Court of First Instance in Case T-77/94, *Vereniging van Groothandelaren in Bloemkwekerijprodukten and Others v Commission of the European Communities*, [1997] ECR II-759, para 75.

[63] Art 6(2) of Commission Reg 773/2004.

[64] Art 287 EC, Art 28 of Reg 1/2003 and Arts 15 and 16 of Reg 773/2004.

[65] Art 27(2) of Reg 1/2003.

70. The time-limit for observations by the complainant on the letter pursuant to Article 7(1) of Regulation 773/2004 will be set in accordance with the circumstances of the case. It will not be shorter than four weeks (Article 17(2) of Regulation 773/2004). If the complainant does not respond within the time-limit set, the complaint is deemed to have been withdrawn pursuant to Article 7(3) of Regulation 773/2004. Complainants are also entitled to withdraw their complaint at any time if they so wish.

71. The complainant may request an extension of the time-limit for the provision of comments. Depending on the circumstances of the case, the Commission may grant such an extension.

72. In that case, where the complainant submits supplementary observations, the Commission takes cognisance of those observations. Where they are of such a nature as to make the Commission change its previous course of action, it may initiate a procedure against the companies complained of. In this procedure, the complainant has the procedural rights explained above.

73. Where the observations of the complainant do not alter the Commission's proposed course of action, it rejects the complaint by decision.[66]

(d) The Commission decision rejecting a complaint

74. Where the Commission rejects a complaint by decision pursuant to Article 7(2) of Regulation 773/2004, it must state the reasons in accordance with Article 253 EC, i.e. in a way that is appropriate to the act at issue and takes into account the circumstances of each case.

75. The statement of reasons must disclose in a clear and unequivocal fashion the reasoning followed by the Commission in such a way as to enable the complainant to ascertain the reasons for the decision and to enable the competent Community Court to exercise its power of review. However, the Commission is not obliged to adopt a position on all the arguments relied on by the complainant in support of its complaint. It only needs to set out the facts and legal considerations which are of decisive importance in the context of the decision.[67]

76. Where the Commission rejects a complaint in a case that also gives rise to a decision pursuant to Article 10 of Regulation 1/2003 (Finding of inapplicability of Articles 81 or 82) or Article 9 of Regulation 1/2003 (Commitments), the decision rejecting a complaint may refer to that other decision adopted on the basis of the provisions mentioned.

77. A decision to reject a complaint is subject to appeal before the Community Courts.[68]

78. A decision rejecting a complaint prevents complainants from requiring the reopening of the investigation unless they put forward significant new evidence. Accordingly, further correspondence on the same alleged infringement by former complainants cannot be regarded as a new complaint unless significant new evidence is brought to the attention of the Commission. However, the Commission may re-open a file under appropriate circumstances.

79. A decision to reject a complaint does not definitively rule on the question of whether or not there is an infringement of Articles 81 or 82, even where the Commission has assessed the facts on the basis of Articles 81 and 82. The assessments made by the Commission in a decision rejecting a complaint therefore do not prevent a Member State court or competition authority from applying Articles 81 and 82 to agreements and practices brought before it.

---

[66] Art 7(2) of Reg 773/2004; Case C-282/95 P, *Guérin automobiles v Commission of the European Communities*, [1997] ECR I-1503, para 36.
[67] Settled case law, cf i.a. Case T-114/92, *Bureau Européen des Médias et de l'Industrie Musicale (BEMIM) v Commission of the European Communities*, [1995] ECR II-147, para 41.
[68] Settled case law since Case 210/81, *Oswald Schmidt, trading as Demo-Studio Schmidt v Commission of the European Communities*, [1983] ECR 3045.

The assessments made by the Commission in a decision rejecting a complaint constitute facts which Member States' courts or competition authorities may take into account in examining whether the agreements or conduct in question are in conformity with Articles 81 and 82.[69]

(e) **Specific situations**

80. According to Article 8 of Regulation 1/2003 the Commission may on its own initiative order interim measures where there is the risk of serious and irreparable damage to competition. Article 8 of Regulation 1/2003 makes it clear that interim measures cannot be applied for by complainants under Article 7(2) of Regulation 1/2003. Requests for interim measures by undertakings can be brought before Member States' courts which are well placed to decide on such measures.[70]

81. Some persons may wish to inform the Commission about suspected infringements of Articles 81 or 82 without having their identity revealed to the undertakings concerned by the allegations. These persons are welcome to contact the Commission. The Commission is bound to respect an informant's request for anonymity,[71] unless the request to remain anonymous is manifestly unjustified.

ANNEX

FORM C. COMPLAINT PURSUANT TO ARTICLE 7 OF
REGULATION (EC) No 1/2003

I. Information regarding the complainant and the undertaking(s) or association of undertakings giving rise to the complaint

1. Give full details on the identity of the legal or natural person submitting the complaint. Where the complainant is an undertaking, identify the corporate group to which it belongs and provide a concise overview of the nature and scope of its business activities. Provide a contact person (with telephone number, postal and e-mail-address) from which supplementary explanations can be obtained.

2. Identify the undertaking(s) or association of undertakings whose conduct the complaint relates to, including, where applicable, all available information on the corporate group to which the undertaking(s) complained of belong and the nature and scope of the business activities pursued by them. Indicate the position of the complainant vis-à-vis the undertaking(s) or association of undertakings complained of (e.g. customer, competitor).

II. Details of the alleged infringement and evidence

3. Set out in detail the facts from which, in your opinion, it appears that there exists an infringement of Article 81 or 82 of the Treaty and/or Article 53 or 54 of the EEA agreement. Indicate in particular the nature of the products (goods or services) affected by the alleged infringements and explain, where necessary, the commercial relationships concerning these products. Provide all available details on the agreements or practices of the undertakings or associations of undertakings to which this complaint relates. Indicate, to the extent possible, the relative market positions of the undertakings concerned by the complaint.

4. Submit all documentation in your possession relating to or directly connected with the facts set out in the complaint (for example, texts of agreements, minutes of negotiations or

---

[69] Case T-575/93, *Casper Koelman v Commission of the European Communities*, [1996] ECR II-1, paras 41–43.
[70] Depending on the case, Member States' competition authorities may equally be well placed to adopt interim measures.
[71] Case 145/83, *Stanley George Adams v Commission of the European Communities*, [1985] ECR 3539.

meetings, terms of transactions, business documents, circulars, correspondence, notes of telephone conversations . . .). State the names and address of the persons able to testify to the facts set out in the complaint, and in particular of persons affected by the alleged infringement. Submit statistics or other data in your possession which relate to the facts set out, in particular where they show developments in the marketplace (for example information relating to prices and price trends, barriers to entry to the market for new suppliers etc.).

5. Set out your view about the geographical scope of the alleged infringement and explain, where that is not obvious, to what extent trade between Member States or between the Community and one or more EFTA States that are contracting parties of the EEA Agreement may be affected by the conduct complained of.

III. Finding sought from the Commission and legitimate interest

6. Explain what finding or action you are seeking as a result of proceedings brought by the Commission.

7. Set out the grounds on which you claim a legitimate interest as complainant pursuant to Article 7 of Regulation (EC) No 1/2003. State in particular how the conduct complained of affects you and explain how, in your view, intervention by the Commission would be liable to remedy the alleged grievance.

IV. Proceedings before national competition authorities or national courts

8. Provide full information about whether you have approached, concerning the same or closely related subject-matters, any other competition authority and/or whether a lawsuit has been brought before a national court. If so, provide full details about the administrative or judicial authority contacted and your submissions to such authority.

Declaration that the information given in this form and in the Annexes thereto is given entirely in good faith.

....

Date and signature

Commission Notice on informal guidance relating to novel questions concerning Articles 81 and 82 of the EC Treaty that arise in individual cases (guidance letters)

(2004/C 101/06)

(Text with EEA relevance)

I. REGULATION 1/2003

1. Regulation 1/2003[1] sets up a new enforcement system for Articles 81 and 82 of the Treaty. While designed to restore the focus on the primary task of effective enforcement of the competition rules, the Regulation also creates legal certainty inasmuch as it provides that agreements[2] which fall under Article 81(1) but fulfil the conditions in Article 81(3) are valid and fully enforceable *ab initio* without a prior decision by a competition authority (Article 1 of Regulation 1/2003).

2. The framework of Regulation 1/2003, while introducing parallel competence of the Commission, Member States' competition authorities and Member States' courts to apply Article 81 and 82 in their entirety, limits risks of inconsistent application by a range of measures, thereby ensuring the primary aspect of legal certainty for companies as reflected in the case law of the Court of Justice, i.e. that the competition rules are applied in a consistent way throughout the Community.

3. Undertakings are generally well placed to assess the legality of their actions in such a way as to enable them to take an informed decision on whether to go ahead with an agreement or practice and in what form. They are close to the facts and have at their disposal the framework of block exemption regulations, case law and case practice as well as extensive guidance in Commission guidelines and notices.[3]

4. Alongside the reform of the rules implementing Articles 81 and 82 brought about by Regulation 1/2003, the Commission has conducted a review of block exemption regulations, Commission notices and guidelines, with a view to further assist self-assessment by economic operators. The Commission has also produced guidelines on the application of Article 81(3).[4] This allows undertakings in the vast majority of cases to reliably assess their agreements with regard to Article 81. Furthermore, it is the practice of the Commission to

---

[1] Council Reg (EC) No 1/2003 of 16 December 2002 on the implementation of the rules on competition laid down in Arts 81 and 82 of the Treaty (OJ LI, 4.1.2003, pages 1–25).

[2] In this Notice, the term 'agreement' is used for agreements, decisions by associations of undertakings and concerted practices. The term 'practices' refers to the conduct of dominant undertakings. The term 'undertakings' equally covers 'associations of undertakings'.

[3] All texts mentioned are available at: http://europa.eu.int/comm/competition/index_en.html

[4] Commission Notice – Guidelines on the application of Art 81(3) of the Treaty (p 97).

[5] Symbolic fines are normally set at 1,000 EUR, cf Commission Guidelines on the method of setting fines imposed pursuant to Art 15(2) of Reg No 17 and Art 65(5) of the ECSC Treaty, (OJ C9, 14.1.1998).

impose more than symbolic fines[5] only in cases where it is established, either in horizontal instruments or in the case law and practice that a certain behaviour constitutes an infringement.

5. Where cases, despite the above elements, give rise to genuine uncertainty because they present novel or unresolved questions for the application of Articles 81 and 82, individual undertakings may wish to seek informal guidance from the Commission.[6] Where it considers it appropriate and subject to its enforcement priorities, the Commission may provide such guidance on novel questions concerning the interpretation of Articles 81 and/or 82 in a written statement (guidance letter). The present Notice sets out details of this instrument.

II. Framework for Assessing whether to Issue a Guidance Letter

6. Regulation 1/2003 confers powers on the Commission to effectively prosecute infringements of Articles 81 and 82 and to impose sanctions.[7] One major objective of the Regulation is to ensure efficient enforcement of the EC competition rules by removing the former notification system and thus allowing the Commission to focus its enforcement policy on the most serious infringements.[8]

7. While Regulation 1/2003 is without prejudice to the ability of the Commission to issue informal guidance to individual undertakings,[9] as set out in this Notice, this ability should not interfere with the primary objective of the Regulation, which is to ensure effective enforcement. The Commission may therefore only provide informal guidance to individual undertakings in so far as this is compatible with its enforcement priorities.

8. Subject to point 7, the Commission, seized of a request for a guidance letter, will consider whether it is appropriate to process it. Issuing a guidance letter may only be considered if the following cumulative conditions are fulfilled:

   (a) The substantive assessment of an agreement or practice with regard to Articles 81 and/or 82 of the Treaty, poses a question of application of the law for which there is no clarification in the existing EC legal framework including the case law of the Community Courts, nor publicly available general guidance or precedent in decision-making practice or previous guidance letters.

   (b) A prima facie evaluation of the specificities and back-ground of the case suggests that the clarification of the novel question through a guidance letter is useful, taking into account the following elements:
   — the economic importance from the point of view of the consumer of the goods or services concerned by the agreement or practice, and/or
   — the extent to which the agreement or practice corresponds or is liable to correspond to more widely spread economic usage in the marketplace and/or
   — the extent of the investments linked to the transaction in relation to the size of the companies concerned and the extent to which the transaction relates to a structural operation such as the creation of a non-full function joint venture.

   (c) It is possible to issue a guidance letter on the basis of the information provided, i.e. no further fact-finding is required.

9. Furthermore, the Commission will not consider a request for a guidance letter in either of the following circumstances:
   — the questions raised in the request are identical or similar to issues raised in a case pending before the European Court of First Instance or the European Court of Justice;

---

[6] cf Recital 38 of Reg 1/2003.
[7] cf in particular Arts 7 to 9, 12, 17–24, 29 of Reg 1/2003.
[8] cf in particular Recital 3 of Reg 1/2003.   [9] cf Recital 38 of Reg 1/2003.

— the agreement or practice to which the request refers is subject to proceedings pending with the Commission, a Member State court or Member State competition authority.

10. The Commission will not consider hypothetical questions and will not issue guidance letters on agreements or practices that are no longer being implemented by the parties. Undertakings may however present a request for a guidance letter to the Commission in relation to questions raised by an agreement or practice that they envisage, i.e. before the implementation of that agreement or practice. In this case the transaction must have reached a sufficiently advanced stage for a request to be considered.

11. A request for a guidance letter is without prejudice to the power of the Commission to open proceedings in accordance with Regulation 1/2003 with regard to the facts presented in the request.

III. Indications on how to Request Guidance

12. A request can be presented by an undertaking or undertakings which have entered into or intend to enter into an agreement or practice that could fall within the scope of Articles 81 and/or 82 of the Treaty with regard to questions of interpretation raised by such agreement or practice.

13. A request for a guidance letter should be addressed to the following address:

Commission européenne/Europese Commissie
Competition DG
B-1049 Bruxelles/Brussel.

14. There is no form. A memorandum should be presented which clearly states:

— the identity of all undertakings concerned as well as a single address for contacts with the Commission;
— the specific questions on which guidance is sought;
— full and exhaustive information on all points relevant for an informed evaluation of the questions raised, including pertinent documentation;
— a detailed reasoning, having regard to point 8 a), why the request presents (a) novel question(s);
— all other information that permits an evaluation of the request in the light of the aspects explained in points 8–10 of this Notice, including in particular a declaration that the agreement or practice to which the request refers is not subject to proceedings pending before a Member State court or competition authority;
— where the request contains elements that are considered business secrets, a clear identification of these elements;
— any other information or documentation relevant to the individual case.

IV. Processing of the Request

15. The Commission will in principle evaluate the request on the basis of the information provided. Notwithstanding point 8 c), the Commission may use additional information at its disposal from public sources, former proceedings or any other source and may ask the applicant(s) to provide supplementary information. The normal rules on professional secrecy apply to the information supplied by the applicant(s).

16. The Commission may share the information submitted to it with the Member States' competition authorities and receive input from them. It may discuss the substance of the request with the Member States' competition authorities before issuing a guidance letter.

17. Where no guidance letter is issued, the Commission shall inform the applicant(s) accordingly.

18. An undertaking can withdraw its request at any point in time. In any case, information supplied in the context of a request for guidance remains with the Commission and can be used in subsequent procedures under Regulation 1/2003 (cf. point 11 above).

V. GUIDANCE LETTERS

19. A guidance letter sets out:
    — a summary description of the facts on which it is based;
    — the principal legal reasoning underlying the understanding of the Commission on novel questions relating to Articles 81 and/or 82 raised by the request.

20. A guidance letter may be limited to part of the questions raised in the request. It may also include additional aspects to those set out in the request.

21. Guidance letters will be posted on the Commission's web site, having regard to the legitimate interest of undertakings in the protection of their business secrets. Before issuing a guidance letter, the Commission will agree with the applicants on a public version.

VI. THE EFFECTS OF GUIDANCE LETTERS

22. Guidance letters are in the first place intended to help undertakings carry out themselves an informed assessment of their agreements and practices.

23. A guidance letter cannot prejudge the assessment of the same question by the Community Courts.

24. Where an agreement or practice has formed the factual basis for a guidance letter, the Commission is not precluded from subsequently examining that same agreement or practice in a procedure under Regulation 1/2003, in particular following a complaint. In that case, the Commission will take the previous guidance letter into account, subject in particular to changes in the underlying facts, to any new aspects raised by a complaint, to developments in the case law of the European Courts of wider changes of the Commission's policy.

25. Guidance letters are not Commission decisions and do not bind Member States' competition authorities or courts that have the power to apply Articles 81 and 82. However, it is open to Member States' competition authorities and courts to take account of guidance letters issued by the Commission as they see fit in the context of a case.

APPENDIX 8

Commission notice on immunity from fines and reduction of fines in cartel cases

(2002/C 45/03)

(Text with EEA relevance)

INTRODUCTION

1. This notice concerns secret cartels between two or more competitions aimed at fixing prices, production or sales quotas, sharing markets including bid-rigging or restricting imports or exports. Such practices are among the most serious restrictions of competition encountered by the Commission and ultimately result in increased prices and reduced choice for the consumer. They also harm European industry.

2. By artificially limiting the competition that would normally prevail between them, undertakings avoid exactly those pressures that lead them to innovate, both in terms of product development and the introduction of more efficient production methods. Such practices also lead to more expensive raw materials and components for the Community companies that purchase from such producers. In the long term, they lead to a loss of competitiveness and reduced employment opportunities.

3. The Commission is aware that certain undertakings involved in this type of illegal agreements are willing to put an end to their participation and inform it of the existence of such agreements, but are dissuaded from doing so by the high fines to which they are potentially exposed. In order to clarify its position in this type of situation, the Commission adopted a notice on the non-imposition or reduction of fines in cartel cases,[1] hereafter 'the 1996 notice'.

4. The Commission considered that it is in the Community interest to grant favourable treatment to undertakings which cooperate with it. The interests of consumers and citizens in ensuring that secret cartels are detected and punished outweigh the interest in fining those undertakings that enable the Commission to detect and prohibit such practices.

5. In the 1996 notice, the Commission announced that it would examine whether it was necessary to modify the notice once it had acquired sufficient experience in applying it. After five years of implementation, the Commission has the experience necessary to modify its policy in this matter. Whilst the validity of the principles governing the notice has been confirmed, experience has shown that its effectiveness would be improved by an increase in the transparency and certainty of the conditions on which any reduction of fines will be granted. A closer alignment between the level of reduction of fines and the value of a company's contribution to establishing the infringement could also increase this effectiveness. This notice addresses these issues.

6. The Commission considers that the collaboration of an undertaking in the detection of the existence of a cartel has an intrinsic value. A decisive contribution to the opening of an

[1] OJ C207, 18.7.1996, p 4.

investigation or to the finding of an infringement may justify the granting of immunity from any fine to the undertaking in question, on condition that certain additional requirements are fulfilled.

7. Moreover, cooperation by one or more undertakings may justify a reduction of a fine by the Commission. Any reduction of a fine must reflect an undertaking's actual contribution, in terms of quality and timing, to the Commission's establishment of the infringement. Reductions are to be limited to those undertakings that provide the Commission with evidence that adds significant value to that already in the Commission's possession.

A. IMMUNITY FROM FINES

8. The Commission will grant an undertaking immunity from any fine which would otherwise have been imposed if:

   (a) the undertaking is the first to submit evidence which in the Commission's view may enable it to adopt a decision to carry out an investigation in the sense of Article 14(3) of Regulation No 17[2] in connection with an alleged cartel affecting the Community; or

   (b) the undertaking is the first to submit evidence which in the Commission's view may enable it to find an infringement of Article 81 EC[3] in connection with an alleged cartel affecting the Community.

9. Immunity pursuant to point 8(a) will only be granted on the condition that the Commission did not have, at the time of the submission, sufficient evidence to adopt a decision to carry out an investigation in the sense of Article 14(3) of Regulation No 17 in connection with the alleged cartel.

10. Immunity pursuant to point 8(b) will only be granted on the cumulative conditions that the Commission did not have, at the time of the submission, sufficient evidence to find an infringement of Article 81 EC in connection with the alleged cartel and that no undertaking had been granted conditional immunity from fines under point 8(a) in connection with the alleged cartel.

11. In addition to the conditions set out in points 8(a) and 9 or in points 8(b) and 10, as appropriate, the following cumulative conditions must be met in any case to qualify for any immunity from a fine:

   (a) the undertaking cooperates fully, on a continuous basis and expeditiously throughout the Commission's administrative procedure and provides the Commission with all evidence that comes into its possession or is available to it relating to the suspected infringement. In particular, it remains at the Commission's disposal to answer swiftly any request that may contribute to the establishment of the facts concerned;

   (b) the undertaking ends its involvement in the suspected infringement no later than the time at which it submits evidence under points 8(a) or 8(b), as appropriate;

   (c) the undertaking did not take steps to coerce other undertakings to participate in the infringement.

Procedure

12. An undertaking wishing to apply for immunity from fines should contact the Commission's Directorate-General for Competition. Should it become apparent that the requirements set

---

[2] OJ 13, 21.2.1962, p 204/62. (Or the equivalent procedural regulations: Art 21(3) of Reg (EEC) No 1017/68 of the Council; Art 18(3) of Council Reg (EEC) No 4056/86 and Art 11(3) of Council Reg (EEC) No 3975/87).
[3] Reference in this text to Art 81 EC also covers Art 53 EEA when applied by the Commission according to the rules laid down in Art 56 of the EEA Agreement.

out in points 8 to 10, as appropriate, are not met, the undertaking will immediately be informed that immunity from fines is not available for the suspected infringement.

13. If immunity from fines is available for a suspected infringement, the undertaking may, in order to meet conditions 8(a) or 8(b), as appropriate:

   (a) immediately provide the Commission with all the evidence relating to the suspected infringement available to it at the time of the submission; or

   (b) initially present this evidence in hypothetical terms, in which case the undertaking must present a descriptive list of the evidence it proposes to disclose at a later agreed date. This list should accurately reflect the nature and content of the evidence, whilst safeguarding the hypothetical nature of its disclosure. Expurgated copies of documents, from which sensitive parts have been removed, may be used to illustrate the nature and content of the evidence.

14. The Directorate-General for Competition will provide a written acknowledgement of the undertaking's application for immunity from fines, confirming the date on which the undertaking either submitted evidence under 13(a) or presented to the Commission the descriptive list referred to in 13(b).

15. Once the Commission has received the evidence submitted by the undertaking under point 13(a) and has verified that it meets the conditions set out in points 8(a) or 8(b), as appropriate, it will grant the undertaking conditional immunity from fines in writing.

16. Alternatively, the Commission will verify that the nature and content of the evidence described in the list referred to in point 13(b) will meet the conditions set out in points 8(a) or 8(b), as appropriate, and inform the undertaking accordingly. Following the disclosure of the evidence no later than on the date agreed and having verified that it corresponds to the description made in the list, the Commission will grant the undertaking conditional immunity from fines in writing.

17. An undertaking which fails to meet the conditions set out in points 8(a) or 8(b), as appropriate, may withdraw the evidence disclosed for the purposes of its immunity application or request the Commission to consider it under section B of this notice. This does not prevent the Commission from using its normal powers of investigation in order to obtain the information.

18. The Commission will not consider other applications for immunity from fines before it has taken a position on an existing application in relation to the same suspected infringement.

19. If at the end of the administrative procedure, the undertaking has met the conditions set out in point 11, the Commission will grant it immunity from fines in the relevant decision.

B. REDUCTION OF A FINE

20. Undertakings that do not meet the conditions under section A above may be eligible to benefit from a reduction of any fine that would otherwise have been imposed.

21. In order to qualify, an undertaking must provide the Commission with evidence of the suspected infringement which represents significant added value with respect to the evidence already in the Commission's possession and must terminate its involvement in the suspected infringement no later than the time at which it submits the evidence.

22. The concept of 'added value' refers to the extent to which the evidence provided strengthens, by its very nature and/or its level of detail, the Commission's ability to prove the facts in question. In this assessment, the Commission will generally consider written evidence originating from the period of time to which the facts pertain to have a greater value than evidence subsequently established. Similarly, evidence directly relevant to the facts in question will generally be considered to have a greater value than that with only indirect relevance.

23. The Commission will determine in any final decision adopted at the end of the administrative procedure:

    (a) whether the evidence provided by an undertaking represented significant added value with respect to the evidence in the Commission's possession at that same time;

    (b) the level of reduction an undertaking will benefit from, relative to the fine which would otherwise have been imposed, as follows. For the:
        — *first* undertaking to meet point 21: a reduction of 30–50%,
        — *second* undertaking to meet point 21: a reduction of 20–30%,
        — *subsequent* undertakings that meet point 21: a reduction of up to 20%.

    In order to determine the level of reduction within each of these bands, the Commission will take into account the time at which the evidence fulfilling the condition in point 21 was submitted and the extent to which it represents added value. It may also take into account the extent and continuity of any cooperation provided by the undertaking following the date of its submission.

    In addition, if an undertaking provides evidence relating to facts previously unknown to the Commission which have a direct bearing on the gravity or duration of the suspected cartel, the Commission will not take these elements into account when setting any fine to be imposed on the undertaking which provided this evidence.

Procedure

24. An undertaking wishing to benefit from a reduction of a fine should provide the Commission with evidence of the cartel in question.

25. The undertaking will receive an acknowledgement of receipt from the Directorate-General for Competition recording the date on which the relevant evidence was submitted. The Commission will not consider any submissions of evidence by an applicant for a reduction of a fine before it has taken a position on any existing application for a conditional immunity from fines in relation to the same suspected infringement.

26. If the Commission comes to the preliminary conclusion that the evidence submitted by the undertaking constitutes added value within the meaning of point 22, it will inform the undertaking in writing, no later than the date on which a statement of objections is notified, of its intention to apply a reduction of a fine within a specified band as provided in point 23(b).

27. The Commission will evaluate the final position of each undertaking which filed an application for a reduction of a fine at the end of the administrative procedure in any decision adopted.

General Considerations

28. From 14 February 2002, this notice replaces the 1996 notice for all cases in which no undertaking has contacted the Commission in order to take advantage of the favourable treatment set out in that notice. The Commission will examine whether it is necessary to modify this notice once it has acquired sufficient experience in applying it.

29. The Commission is aware that this notice will create legitimate expectations on which undertakings may rely when disclosing the existence of a cartel to the Commission.

30. Failure to meet any of the requirements set out in sections A or B, as the case may be, at any stage of the administrative procedure may result in the loss of any favourable treatment set out therein.

31. In line with the Commission's practice, the fact that an undertaking cooperated with the Commission during its administrative procedure will be indicated in any decision, so as to

explain the reason for the immunity or reduction of the fine. The fact that immunity or reduction in respect of fines is granted cannot protect an undertaking from the civil law consequences of its participation in an infringement of Article 81 EC.

32. The Commission considers that normally disclosure, at any time, of documents received in the context of this notice would undermine the protection of the purpose of inspections and investigations within the meaning of Article 4(2) of Regulation (EC) No 1049/2001 of the European Parliament and of the Council.

33. Any written statement made vis-à-vis the Commission in relation to this notice, forms part of the Commission's file. It may not be disclosed or used for any other purpose than the enforcement of Article 81 EC.

APPENDIX 9

Guidelines on the method of setting fines imposed pursuant to Article 15(2) of Regulation No 17 and Article 65(5) of the ECSC Treaty

The principles outlined here should ensure the transparency and impartiality of the Commission's decisions, in the eyes of the undertakings and of the Court of Justice alike, whilst upholding the discretion which the Commission is granted under the relevant legislation to set fines within the limit of 10% of overall turnover. This discretion must, however, follow a coherent and non-discriminatory policy which is consistent with the objectives pursued in penalizing infringements of the competition rules.

The new method of determining the amount of a fine will adhere to the following rules, which start from a basic amount that will be increased to take account of aggravating circumstances or reduced to take account of attenuating circumstances.

(1) BASIC AMOUNT

The basic amount will be determined according to the gravity and duration of the infringement, which are the only criteria referred to in Article 15(2) of Regulation No 17.

A. Gravity

In assessing the gravity of the infringement, account must be taken of its nature, its actual impact on the market, where this can be measured, and the size of the relevant geographic market.

Infringements will thus be put into one of three categories: minor infringements, serious infringements and very serious infringements.

— Minor infringements: these might be trade restrictions, usually of a vertical nature, but with a limited market impact and affecting only a substantial but relatively limited part of the Community market.

Likely fines: ECU 1 000 to ECU 1 million

— Serious infringements: these will more often than not be horizontal or vertical restrictions of the same type as above, but more rigorously applied, with a wider market impact, and with effects in extensive areas of the common market. They might also be abuses of a dominant position (refusals to supply, discrimination, exclusion, loyalty discounts made by dominant firms in order to shut competitors out of the market, etc.).

Likely fines: ECU 1 million to ECU 20 million.

— Very serious infringements: these will generally be horizontal restrictions such as price cartels and market-sharing quotas, or other practices which jeopardize the proper functioning of the single market, such as the partitioning of national markets and clearcut abuses of a dominant position by undertakings holding a virtual monopoly (cf. Decisions 91/297/EEC, 91/298/EEC, 91/299/EEC, 91/300/EEC and 91/301/EEC—*Soda Ash*;[1] 94/815/EC—

---

[1] OJ L152, 15.6.1991, p 1.

Cement;[2] 94/601/EC—*Cartonboard;*[3] 92/163/EC—*Tetra Pak;*[4] and 94/215/ECSC—*Steel beams.*[5]

Likely fines: above ECU 20 million

Within each of these categories, and in particular as far as serious and very serious infringements are concerned, the proposed scale of fines will make it possible to apply differential treatment to undertakings according to the nature of the infringement committed.

It will also be necessary to take account of the effective economic capacity of offenders to cause significant damage to other operators—in particular consumers—and to set the fine at a level which ensures that it has a sufficiently deterrent effect.

Generally speaking, account may also be taken of the fact that large undertakings usually have legal and economic knowledge and infrastructures which enable them more easily to recognize that their conduct constitutes an infringement and be aware of the consequences stemming from it under competition law.

Where an infringement involves several undertakings (e.g. cartels), it might be necessary in some cases to apply weightings to the amounts determined within each of the three categories in order to take account of the specific weight and, therefore, the real impact of the offending conduct of each undertaking on competition, particularly where there is considerable disparity between the sizes of the undertakings committing infringements of the same type.

Thus, the principle of equal punishment for the same conduct may, if the circumstances so warrant, lead to different fines being imposed on the undertakings concerned without this differentiation being governed by arithmetic calculation.

B. Duration

A distinction should be made between the following:

— infringements of short duration (in general, less than one year): no increase in amount;
— infringements of medium duration (in general, one to five years): increase of up to 50% in the amount determined for gravity;
— infringements of long duration (in general, more than five years): increase of up to 10% per year in the amount determined for gravity.

This approach will therefore point to a possible increase in the amount of the fine.

Generally speaking, the increase in the fine for long-term infringements represents a considerable strengthening of the previous practice with a view to imposing effective sanctions on restrictions which have had a harmful impact on consumers over a long period. Moreover, this new approach is consistent with the expected effect of the notice of 18 July 1996 on the non-imposition or reduction of fines in cartel cases.[6] The risk of having to pay a much larger fine, proportionate to the duration of the infringement, will necessarily increase the incentive to denounce it or to cooperate with the Commission.

The basic amount will result from the addition of the two amounts established in accordance with the above:

x gravity + y duration = basic amount

(2) Aggravating Circumstances

The basic amount will be increased where there are aggravating circumstances such as:

— repeated infringement of the same type by the same undertaking(s);

---

[2] OJ L343, 30.12.1994, p 1.   [3] OJ L243, 19.9.1994, p 1.
[4] OJ L72, 18.3.1992, p 1.   [5] OJ L116, 6.5.1994, p 1.   [6] OJ C207, 18.7.1996, p 4.

— refused to cooperate with or attempts to obstruct the Commission in carrying out its investigations;
— role of leader in or instigator of the infringement;
— retaliatory measures against other undertakings with a view to enforcing practices which constitute an infringement;
— need to increase the penalty in order to exceed the amount of gains improperly made as a result of the infringement when it is objectively possible to estimate that amount;
— other.

(3) ATTENUATING CIRCUMSTANCES

The basic amount will be reduced where there are attenuating circumstances such as:

— an exclusively passive or 'follow-my-leader' role in the infringement;
— non-implementation in practice of the offending agreements or practices;
— termination of the infringement as soon as the Commission intervenes (in particular when it carries out checks);
— existence of reasonable doubt on the part of the undertaking as to whether the restrictive conduct does indeed constitute an infringement;
— infringements committed as a result of negligence or unintentionally;
— effective cooperation by the undertaking in the proceedings, outside the scope of the Notice of 18 July 1996 on the non-imposition or reduction of fines in cartel cases;
— other.

(4) APPLICATION OF THE NOTICE OF 18 JULY 1996 ON THE NON-IMPOSITION OR REDUCTION OF FINES[7]

(5) GENERAL COMMENTS

(a) It goes without saying that the final amount calculated according to this method (basic amount increased or reduced on a percentage basis) may not in any case exceed 10% of the world-wide turnover of the undertakings, as laid down by Article 15(2) of Regulation No 17. In the case of agreements which are illegal under the ECSC Treaty, the limit laid down by Article 65(5) is twice the turnover on the products in question, increased in certain cases to a maximum of 10% of the undertaking's turnover on ECSC products.

The accounting year on the basis of which the world-wide turnover is determined must, as far as possible, be the one preceding the year in which the decision is taken or, if figures are not available for that accounting year, the one immediately preceding it.

(b) Depending on the circumstances, account should be taken, once the above calculations have been made, of certain objective factors such as a specific economic context, any economic or financial benefit derived by the offenders (cf TwentyFirst Report on Competition Policy, point 139), the specific characteristics of the undertakings in question and their real ability to pay in a specific social context, and the fines should be adjusted accordingly.

(c) In cases involving associations of undertakings, decisions should as far as possible be addressed to and fines imposed on the individual undertakings belonging to the association. If this is not possible (e.g. where there are several thousands of affiliated undertakings), and except for cases falling within the ECSC Treaty, an overall fine should be imposed on the association, calculated according to the principles outlined above but equivalent to the total of individual fines which might have been imposed on each of the members of the association.

---

[7] See n 6.

(d) The Commission will also reserve the right, in certain cases, to impose a 'symbolic' fine of ECU 1 000, which would not involve any calculation based on the duration of the infringement or any aggravating or attenuating circumstances. The justification for imposing such a fine should be given in the text of the decision.

APPENDIX 10

Form C

Complaint pursuant to Article 7 of Regulation (EC) No 1/2003

I. Information Regarding the Complainant and the Undertaking(s) or Association of Undertakings Giving Rise to the Complaint

1. Give full details on the identity of the legal or natural person submitting the complaint. Where the complainant is an undertaking, identify the corporate group to which it belongs and provide a concise overview of the nature and scope of its business activities. Provide a contact person (with telephone number, postal and e-mail-address) from which supplementary explanations can be obtained.

2. Identify the undertaking(s) or association of undertakings whose conduct the complaint relates to, including, where applicable, all available information on the corporate group to which the undertaking(s) complained of belong and the nature and scope of the business activities pursued by them. Indicate the position of the complainant vis-à-vis the undertaking(s) or association of undertakings complained of (e.g. customer, competitor).

II. Details of the Alleged Infringement and Evidence

3. Set out in detail the facts from which, in your opinion, it appears that there exists an infringement of Articles 81 or 82 of the Treaty and/or Articles 53 or 54 of the EEA agreement. Indicate in particular the nature of the products (goods or services) affected by the alleged infringements and explain, where necessary, the commercial relationships concerning these products. Provide all available details on the agreements or practices of the undertakings or associations of undertakings to which this complaint relates. Indicate, to the extent possible, the relative market positions of the undertakings concerned by the complaint.

4. Submit all documentation in your possession relating to or directly connected with the facts set out in the complaint (for example, texts of agreements, minutes of negotiations or meetings, terms of transactions, business documents, circulars, correspondence, notes of telephone conversations?). State the names and address of the persons able to testify to the facts set out in the complaint, and in particular of persons affected by the alleged infringement. Submit statistics or other data in your possession which relate to the facts set out, in particular where they show developments in the marketplace (for example information relating to prices and price trends, barriers to entry to the market for new suppliers etc.).

5. Set out your view about the geographical scope of the alleged infringement and explain, where that is not obvious, to what extent trade between Member States or between the Community and one or more EFTA States that are contracting parties of the EEA Agreement may be affected by the conduct complained of.

III. Finding sought from the Commission and Legitimate Interest

6. Explain what finding or action you are seeking as a result of proceedings brought by the Commission.

7. Set out the grounds on which you claim a legitimate interest as complainant pursuant to Article 7 of Regulation (EC) No. 1/2003. State in particular how the conduct complained of affects you and explain how, in your view, intervention by the Commission would be liable to remedy the alleged grievance.

IV. Proceedings before National Competition Authorities or National Courts

8. Provide full information about whether you have approached, concerning the same or closely related subject-matters, any other competition authority and/or whether a lawsuit has been brought before a national court. If so, provide full details about the administrative or judicial authority contacted and your submissions to such authority.

Declaration that the information given in this form and in the Annexes thereto is given entirely in good faith.

Date and signature.

....

Send by email to Greffe Antitrust

or to:

European Commission
DG Competition, Antitrust Registry
B – 1049 – Brussels

APPENDIX 11

Commission Notice on the rules for access to the Commission file in cases pursuant to Articles 81 and 82 of the EC Treaty, Articles 53, 54 and 57 of the EEA Agreement and Council Regulation (EC) No 139/2004

(2005/C 325/07)

(Text with EEA relevance)

1. INTRODUCTION AND SUBJECT-MATTER OF THE NOTICE

1. Access to the Commission file is one of the procedural guarantees intended to apply the principle of equality of arms and to protect the rights of the defence. Access to the file is provided for in Article 27(1) and (2) of Council Regulation (EC) No 1/2003,[1] Article 15(1) of Commission Regulation (EC) No 773/2004 ('the Implementing Regulation'),[2] Article 18(1) and (3) of the Council Regulation (EC) No 139/2004 ('Merger Regulation')[3] and Article 17(1) of Commission Regulation (EC) No 802/2004 ('the Merger Implementing Regulation').[4] In accordance with these provisions, before taking decisions on the basis of Articles 7, 8, 23 and 24(2) of Regulation (EC) No 1/2003 and Articles 6(3), 7(3), 8(2) to (6), 14 and 15 of the Merger Regulation, the Commission shall give the persons, undertakings or associations of undertakings, as the case may be, an opportunity of making known their views on the objections against them and they shall be entitled to have access to the Commission's file in order to fully respect their rights of defence in the proceedings. The present notice provides the framework for the exercise of the right set out in these provisions. It does not cover the possibility of the provision of documents in the context of other proceedings. This notice is without prejudice to the interpretation of such provisions by the Community Courts. The principles set out in this Notice apply also when the Commission enforces Articles 53, 54 and 57 of the EEA Agreement.[5]

2. This specific right outlined above is distinct from the general right to access to documents under Regulation (EC) No 1049/2001,[6] which is subject to different criteria and exceptions and pursues a different purpose.

---

[1] Council Regulation (EC) No 1/2003 of 16 December 2002 on the implementation of the rules on competition laid down in Articles 81 and 82 of the Treaty, OJ L 1, 4.1.2003, p. 1–25.

[2] Commission Regulation (EC) No 773/2004 of 7 April 2004 relating to the conduct of proceedings by the Commission pursuant to Articles 81 and 82 of the EC Treaty, OJ L 123, 27.4.2004, p. 18–24.

[3] Council Regulation (EC) No 139/2004 of 20 January 2004 on the control of concentrations between undertakings, OJ L 24, 29.1.2004, p. 1–22.

[4] Commission Regulation (EC) No 802/2004 of 21 April 2004 implementing Council Regulation (EC) No 139/2004 on the control of concentrations between undertakings, OJ L 133, 30.4.2004, p. 1–39. Corrected in the OJ L 172, 6.5.2004, p. 9.

[5] References in this Notice to Articles 81 and 82 therefore apply also to Articles 53 and 54 of the EEA Agreement.

[6] Regulation (EC) No 1049/2001 of the European Parliament and of the Council of 30 May 2001

3. The term access to the file is used in this notice exclusively to mean the access granted to the persons, undertakings or association of undertakings to whom the Commission has addressed a statement of objections. This notice clarifies who has access to the file for this purpose.

4. The same term, or the term access to documents, is also used in the above-mentioned regulations in respect of complainants or other involved parties. These situations are, however, distinct from that of the addressees of a statement of objections and therefore do not fall under the definition of access to the file for the purposes of this notice. These related situations are dealt with in a separate section of the notice.

5. This notice also explains to which information access is granted, when access takes place and what are the procedures for implementing access to the file.

6. As from its publication, this notice replaces the 1997 Commission notice on access to the file.[7] The new rules take account of the legislation applicable as of 1 May 2004, namely the above referred Regulation (EC) No 1/2003, Merger Regulation, Implementing Regulation and Merger Implementing Regulation, as well as the Commission Decision of 23 May 2001 on the terms of reference of Hearing Officers in certain competition proceedings.[8] It also takes into account the recent case law of the Court of Justice and the Court of First Instance of the European Communities[9] and the practice developed by the Commission since the adoption of the 1997 notice.

II. SCOPE OF ACCESS TO THE FILE

A. Who is entitled to access to the file?

7. Access to the file pursuant to the provisions mentioned in paragraph 1 is intended to enable the effective exercise of the rights of defence against the objections brought forward by the Commission. For this purpose, both in cases under Articles 81 and 82 EC and in cases under the Merger Regulation, access is granted, upon request, to the persons, undertakings or associations of undertakings,[10] as the case may be, to which the Commission addresses its objections[11] (hereinafter, 'the parties').

---

regarding public access to European Parliament, Council and Commission documents, OJ L 145, 31.5.2001, p. 43. See for instance Case T-2/03, *Verein für Konsumenteninformation v. Commission*, judgment of 13 April 2005, not yet reported.

[7] Commission notice on the internal rules of procedure for processing requests for access to the file in cases under Articles 85 and 86 [*now 81 and 82*] of the EC Treaty, Articles 65 and 66 of the ECSC Treaty and Council Regulation (EEC) No 4064/89, OJ C 23, 23.1.1997, p. 3.

[8] OJ L 162, 19.6.2001, p. 21.

[9] In particular Joint Cases T-25/95 et al., *Cimenteries CBR SA et al. v Commission*, [2000] ECR II-0491.

[10] In the remainder of this Notice, the term 'undertaking' includes both undertakings and associations of undertakings. The term 'person' encompasses natural and legal persons. Many entities are legal persons and undertakings at the same time; in this case, they are covered by both terms. The same applies where a natural person is an undertaking within the meaning of Articles 81 and 82. In Merger proceedings, account must also be taken of persons referred to in Article 3(1)(b) of the Merger Regulation, even when they are natural persons. Where entities without legal personality which are also not undertakings become involved in Commission competition proceedings, the Commission applies, where appropriate, the principles set out in this Notice *mutatis mutandis.*

[11] Cf. Article 15(1) of the Implementing Regulation, Article 18(3) of the Merger Regulation and Article 17(1) of the Merger Implementing Regulation.

B. To which documents is access granted?

1. The content of the Commission file

8. The 'Commission file' in a competition investigation (hereinafter also referred to as 'the file') consists of all documents,[12] which have been obtained, produced and/or assembled by the Commission Directorate General for Competition, during the investigation.

9. In the course of investigation under Articles 20, 21 and 22(2) of Regulation (EC) No 1/2003 and Articles 12 and 13 of the Merger Regulation, the Commission may collect a number of documents, some of which may, following a more detailed examination, prove to be unrelated to the subject matter of the case in question. Such documents may be returned to the undertaking from which those have been obtained. Upon return, these documents will no longer constitute part of the file.

2. Accessible documents

10. The parties must be able to acquaint themselves with the information in the Commission's file, so that, on the basis of this information, they can effectively express their views on the preliminary conclusions reached by the Commission in its objections. For this purpose they will be granted access to all documents making up the Commission file, as defined in paragraph 8, with the exception of internal documents, business secrets of other undertakings, or other confidential information.[13]

11. Results of a study commissioned in connection with proceedings are accessible together with the terms of reference and the methodology of the study. Precautions may however be necessary in order to protect intellectual property rights.

3. Non-accessible documents

3.1 Internal documents

3.1.1 General principles

12. Internal documents can be neither incriminating nor exculpatory.[14] They do not constitute part of the evidence on which the Commission can rely in its assessment of a case. Thus, the parties will not be granted access to internal documents in the Commission file.[15] Given their lack of evidential value, this restriction on access to internal documents does not prejudice the proper exercise of the parties' right of defence.[16]

13. There is no obligation on the Commission departments to draft any minutes of meetings[17] with any person or undertaking. If the Commission chooses to make notes of such meetings, such documents constitute the Commission's own interpretation of what was said at the meetings, for which reason they are classified as internal documents. Where, however, the

---

[12] In this notice the term 'document' is used for all forms of information support, irrespective of the storage medium. This covers also any electronic data storage device as may be or become available.

[13] Cf. Article 27(2) of Regulation (EC) No 1/2003, Articles 15(2) and 16(1) of the Implementing Regulation, and Article 17(3) of the Merger Implementing Regulation. Those exceptions are also mentioned in Case T-7/89, *Hercules Chemicals v Commission*, [1991] ECR II-1711, paragraph 54. The Court has ruled that it does not belong to the Commission alone to decide which documents in the file may be useful for the purposes of the defence (Cf. Case T-30/91 *Solvay v. Commission*, [1995] ECR II-1775, paragraphs 81–86, and Case T-36/91 *ICI vs. Commission*, [1995] ECR II-1847, paragraphs 91–96).

[14] Examples of internal documents are drafts, opinions, memos or notes from the Commission departments or other public authorities concerned.

[15] Cf. Article 27(2) of Regulation (EC) No 1/2003, Article 15(2) of the Implementing Regulation, and Article 17(3) of the Merger Implementing Regulation.

[16] Cf. paragraph 1 above.

[17] Cf. judgement of 30.9.2003 in Joined Cases T-191/98 and T-212/98 to T-214/98 *Atlantic Container Line and others v Commission* (*TACA*), [2003] ECR II-3275, paragraphs 349–359.

person or undertaking in question has agreed the minutes, such minutes will be made accessible after deletion of any business secrets or other confidential information. Such agreed minutes constitute part of the evidence on which the Commission can rely in its assessment of a case.[18]

14. In the case of a study commissioned in connection with proceedings, correspondence between the Commission and its contractor containing evaluation of the contractor's work or relating to financial aspects of the study, are considered internal documents and will thus not be accessible.

3.1.2 *Correspondence with other public authorities*

15. A particular case of internal documents is the Commission's correspondence with other public authorities and the internal documents received from such authorities (whether from EC Member States ('the Member States') or non-member countries). Examples of such non-accessible documents include:

— correspondence between the Commission and the competition authorities of the Member States, or between the latter;[19]

— correspondence between the Commission and other public authorities of the Member States;[20]

— correspondence between the Commission, the EFTA Surveillance Authority and public authorities of EFTA States;[21]

— correspondence between the Commission and public authorities of non-member countries, including their competition authorities, in particular where the Community and a third country have concluded an agreement governing the confidentiality of the information exchanged.[22]

16. In certain exceptional circumstances, access is granted to documents originating from Member States, the EFTA Surveillance Authority or EFTA States, after deletion of any business secrets or other confidential information. The Commission will consult the entity submitting the document prior to granting access to identify business secrets or other confidential information.

This is the case where the documents originating from Member States contain allegations brought against the parties, which the Commission must examine, or form part of the evidence in the investigative process, in a way similar to documents obtained from private parties. These considerations apply, in particular, as regards:

— documents and information exchanged pursuant to Article 12 of Regulation (EC) No 1/2003, and information provided to the Commission pursuant to Article 18(6) of Regulation (EC) No 1/2003;

— complaints lodged by a Member State under Article 7(2) of Regulation (EC) No 1/2003.

Access will also be granted to documents originating from Member States or the EFTA

---

[18] Statements recorded pursuant to Article 19 or Article 20(2)(e) of Regulation 1/2003 or Article 13(2)(e) of Merger Regulation will also normally belong to the accessible documents (see paragraph 10 above).

[19] Cf. Article 27(2) of Regulation (EC) No 1/2003, Article 15(2) of the Implementing Regulation, Article 17(3) of the Merger Implementing Regulation.

[20] Cf. Order of the Court of First Instance in Cases T-134/94 et al *NMH Stahlwerke and Others v Commission* [1997] ECR II-2293, paragraph 36, and Case T-65/89, *BPB Industries and British Gypsum* [1993] ECR II-389, paragraph 33.

[21] In this notice the term 'EFTA States' includes the EFTA States that are parties to the EEA Agreement.

[22] For example, Article VIII.2 of the Agreement between the European Communities and the Government of the United States of America regarding the application of their competition laws (OJ No L 95, 27.4.1995, p. 47) stipulates that information provided to it in confidence under the Agreement must be protected 'to the fullest extent possible'. That Article creates an international-law obligation binding the Commission.

Surveillance Authority in so far as they are relevant to the parties' defence with regard to the exercise of competence by the Commission.[23]

3.2. Confidential information

17. The Commission file may also include documents containing two categories of information, namely business secrets and other confidential information, to which access may be partially or totally restricted.[24] Access will be granted, where possible, to non-confidential versions of the original information. Where confidentiality can only be assured by summarising the relevant information, access will be granted to a summary. All other documents are accessible in their original form.

3.2.1 Business secrets

18. In so far as disclosure of information about an undertaking's business activity could result in a serious harm to the same undertaking, such information constitutes business secrets.[25] Examples of information that may qualify as business secrets include: technical and/or financial information relating to an undertaking's know-how, methods of assessing costs, production secrets and processes, supply sources, quantities produced and sold, market shares, customer and distributor lists, marketing plans, cost and price structure and sales strategy.

3.2.2 Other confidential information

19. The category 'other confidential information' includes information other than business secrets, which may be considered as confidential, insofar as its disclosure would significantly harm a person or undertaking. Depending on the specific circumstances of each case, this may apply to information provided by third parties about undertakings which are able to place very considerable economic or commercial pressure on their competitors or on their trading partners, customers or suppliers. The Court of First Instance and the Court of Justice have acknowledged that it is legitimate to refuse to reveal to such undertakings certain letters received from their customers, since their disclosure might easily expose the authors to the risk of retaliatory measures.[26] Therefore the notion of other confidential information may include information that would enable the parties to identify complainants or other third parties where those have a justified wish to remain anonymous.

20. The category of other confidential information also includes military secrets.

3.2.3 Criteria for the acceptance of requests for confidential treatment

21. Information will be classified as confidential where the person or undertaking in question has made a claim to this effect and such claim has been accepted by the Commission.[27]

22. Claims for confidentiality must relate to information which is within the scope of the above descriptions of business secrets or other confidential information. The reasons for which information is claimed to be a business secret or other confidential information must be substantiated.[28] Confidentiality claims can normally only pertain to information obtained by

---

[23] In the merger control area, this may apply in particular to submissions by a Member State under Article 9(2) of the Merger Regulation with regard to a case referral.

[24] Cf. Article 16(1) of the Implementing Regulation and Article 17(3) of the Merger Implementing Regulation; Case T-7/89 *Hercules Chemicals NV v Commission*, [1991] ECR II-1711, paragraph 54; Case T-23/99, *LR AF 1998 A/S v Commission*, [2002] ECR II-1705, paragraph 170.

[25] Judgement of 18.9.1996 in Case T-353/94, *Postbank NV v Commission*, [1996] ECR II-921, paragraph 87.

[26] The Community Courts have pronounced upon this question both in cases of alleged abuse of a dominant position (Article 82 of the EC Treaty) (Case T-65/89, *BPB Industries and British Gypsum* [1993] ECR II-389; and Case C-310/93P, *BPB Industries and British Gypsum* [1995] ECR I-865), and in merger cases (Case T-221/95 *Endemol v Commission* [1999] ECR II-1299, paragraph 69, and Case T-5/02 *Laval v Commission* [2002] ECR II-4381, paragraph 98 et seq.).

[27] See paragraph 40 below.   [28] See paragraph 35 below.

the Commission from the same person or undertaking and not to information from any other source.

23. Information relating to an undertaking but which is already known outside the undertaking (in case of a group, outside the group), or outside the association to which it has been communicated by that undertaking, will not normally be considered confidential.[29] Information that has lost its commercial importance, for instance due to the passage of time, can no longer be regarded as confidential. As a general rule, the Commission presumes that information pertaining to the parties' turnover, sales, market-share data and similar information which is more than 5 years old is no longer confidential.[30]

24. In proceedings under Articles 81 and 82 of the Treaty, the qualification of a piece of information as confidential is not a bar to its disclosure if such information is necessary to prove an alleged infringement ('inculpatory document') or could be necessary to exonerate a party ('exculpatory document'). In this case, the need to safeguard the rights of the defence of the parties through the provision of the widest possible access to the Commission file may outweigh the concern to protect confidential information of other parties.[31] It is for the Commission to assess whether those circumstances apply to any specific situation. This calls for an assessment of all relevant elements, including:

— the relevance of the information in determining whether or not an infringement has been committed, and its probative value;
— whether the information is indispensable;
— the degree of sensitivity involved (to what extent would disclosure of the information harm the interests of the person or undertaking in question)
— the preliminary view of the seriousness of the alleged infringement.

Similar considerations apply to proceedings under the Merger Regulation when the disclosure of information is considered necessary by the Commission for the purpose of the procedure.[32]

25. Where the Commission intends to disclose information, the person or undertaking in question shall be granted the possibility to provide a non-confidential version of the documents where that information is contained, with the same evidential value as the original documents.[33]

C. When is access to the file granted?

26. Prior to the notification of the Commission's statement of objections pursuant to the provisions mentioned in paragraph 1, the parties have no right of access to the file.

1. In antitrust proceedings under Articles 81 and 82 of the Treaty

27. Access to the file will be granted upon request and, normally, on a single occasion, following the notification of the Commission's objections to the parties, in order to ensure the principle of equality of arms and to protect their rights of defence. As a general rule, therefore, no access will be granted to other parties' replies to the Commission's objections.

A party will, however, be granted access to documents received after notification of the objections at later stages of the administrative procedure, where such documents may

---

[29] However, business secrets or other confidential information which are given to a trade or professional association by its members do not lose their confidential nature with regard to third parties and may therefore not be passed on to complainants. Cf. Joined Cases 209 to 215 and 218/78, *Fedetab*, [1980] ECR 3125, paragraph 46.
[30] See paragraphs 35–38 below on asking undertakings to identify confidential information.
[31] Cf. Article 27(2) of Regulation (EC) No 1/2003 and Article 15(3) of the Implementing Regulation.
[32] Article 18(1) of the Merger Implementing Regulation.
[33] Cf. paragraph 42 below.

constitute new evidence — whether of an incriminating or of an exculpatory nature —, pertaining to the allegations concerning that party in the Commission's statement of objections. This is particularly the case where the Commission intends to rely on new evidence.

2. *In proceedings under the Merger Regulation*

28. In accordance with Article 18(1) and (3) of the Merger Regulation and Article 17(1) of the Merger Implementing Regulation, the notifying parties will be given access to the Commission's file upon request at every stage of the procedure following the notification of the Commission's objections up to the consultation of the Advisory Committee. In contrast, this notice does not address the possibility of the provision of documents before the Commission states its objections to undertakings under the Merger Regulation.[34]

III. Particular Questions Regarding Complainants and other Involved Parties

29. The present section relates to situations where the Commission may or has to provide access to certain documents contained in its file to the complainants in antitrust proceedings and other involved parties in merger proceedings. Irrespective of the wording used in the antitrust and merger implementing regulations,[35] these two situations are distinct — in terms of scope, timing, and rights — from access to the file, as defined in the preceding section of this notice.

A. Provision of documents to complainants in antitrust proceedings

30. The Court of First Instance has ruled[36] that complainants do not have the same rights and guarantees as the parties under investigation. Therefore complainants cannot claim a right of access to the file as established for parties.

31. However, a complainant who, pursuant to Article 7(1) of the Implementing Regulation, has been informed of the Commission's intention to reject its complaint,[37] may request access to the documents on which the Commission has based its provisional assessment.[38] The complainant will be provided access to such documents on a single occasion, following the issuance of the letter informing the complainant of the Commission's intention to reject its complaint.

32. Complainants do not have a right of access to business secrets or other confidential information which the Commission has obtained in the course of its investigation.[39]

B. Provision of documents to other involved parties in merger proceedings

33. In accordance with Article 17(2) of the Merger Implementing Regulation, access to the file in merger proceedings shall also be given, upon request, to other involved parties who have been

---

[34] This question is dealt with in the Directorate General Competition document 'DG COMP Best Practices on the conduct of EC merger control proceedings', available on the web-site of the Directorate General for Competition: http://europa.eu.int/comm/competition/index_en.html.

[35] Cf. Article 8(1) of the Implementing Regulation, which speaks about 'access to documents' to complainants and Article 17(2) of Merger Implementing Regulation which speaks about 'access to file' to other involved parties 'in so far as this is necessary for the purposes of preparing their comments'.

[36] See Case T-17/93 *Matra-Hachette SA v Commission*, [1994] ECR II-595, paragraph 34. The Court ruled that the rights of third parties, as laid down by Article 19 of the Council Regulation No 17 of 6.2.1962 (now replaced by Article 27 of Regulation (EC) No 1/2003), were limited to the right to participate in the administrative procedure.

[37] By means of a letter issued in accordance with Article 7(1) of the Implementing Regulation.

[38] Cf. Article 8(1) of the Implementing Regulation.

[39] Cf. Article 8(1) of the Implementing Regulation.

informed of the objections in so far as this is necessary for the purposes of preparing their comments.

34. Such other involved parties are parties to the proposed concentration other than the notifying parties, such as the seller and the undertaking which is the target of the concentration.[40]

IV. Procedure for Implementing Access to the File

A. Preparatory procedure

35. Any person which submits information or comments in one of the situations listed hereunder, or subsequently submits further information to the Commission in the course of the same procedures, has an obligation to clearly identify any material which it considers to be confidential, giving reasons, and provide a separate non-confidential version by the date set by the Commission for making its views known:[41]

(a) In antitrust proceedings
   — an addressee of a Commission's statement of objections making known its views on the objections;[42]
   — a complainant making known its views on a Commission statement of objections;[43]
   — any other natural or legal person, which applies to be heard and shows a sufficient interest, or which is invited by the Commission to express its views, making known its views in writing or at an oral hearing;[44]
   — a complainant making known his views on a Commission letter informing him on the Commission's intention to reject the complaint.[45]

(b) In merger proceedings
   — notifying parties or other involved parties making known their views on Commission objections adopted with a view to take a decision with regard to a request for a derogation from suspension of a concentration and which adversely affects one or more of those parties, or on a provisional decision adopted in the matter;[46]
   — notifying parties to whom the Commission has addressed a statement of objections, other involved parties who have been informed of those objections or parties to whom the Commission has addressed objections with a view to inflict a fine or a periodic penalty payment, submitting their comments on the objections;[47]
   — third persons who apply to be heard, or any other natural or legal person invited by the Commission to express their views, making known their views in writing or at an oral hearing;[48]
   — any person which supplies information pursuant to Article 11 of the Merger Regulation.

36. Moreover, the Commission may require undertakings.[49] in all cases where they produce or have produced documents, to identify the documents or parts of documents, which they

---

[40] Cf. Article 11(b) of the Merger Implementing Regulation.
[41] Cf. Article 16(2) of the Implementing Regulation and Article 18(2) of the Merger Implementing Regulation.
[42] pursuant to Article 10(2) of the Implementing Regulation.
[43] pursuant to Article 6(1) of the Implementing Regulation.
[44] pursuant to Article 13(1) and (3) of the Implementing Regulation.
[45] pursuant to Article 7(1) of the Implementing Regulation.
[46] Article 12 of the Merger Implementing Regulation.
[47] Article 13 of the Merger Implementing Regulation.
[48] pursuant to Article 16 of the Merger Implementing Regulation.
[49] In merger proceedings the principles set out in the present and subsequent paragraphs also apply to the persons referred to in Article 3(1)(b) of Merger Regulation.

consider to contain business secrets or other confidential information belonging to them, and to identify the undertakings with regard to which such documents are to be considered confidential.[50]

37. For the purposes of quickly dealing with confidentiality claims referred to in paragraph 36 above, the Commission may set a time-limit within which the undertakings shall: (i) substantiate their claim for confidentiality with regard to each individual document or part of document; (ii) provide the Commission with a non-confidential version of the documents, in which the confidential passages are deleted.[51] In antitrust proceedings the undertakings in question shall also provide within the said time-limit a concise description of each piece of deleted information.[52]

38. The non-confidential versions and the descriptions of the deleted information must be established in a manner that enables any party with access to the file to determine whether the information deleted is likely to be relevant for its defence and therefore whether there are sufficient grounds to request the Commission to grant access to the information claimed to be confidential.

B. Treatment of confidential information

39. In antitrust proceedings, if undertakings fail to comply with the provisions set out in paragraphs 35 to 37 above, the Commission may assume that the documents or statements concerned do not contain confidential information.[53] The Commission may consequently assume that the undertaking has no objections to the disclosure of the documents or statements concerned in their entirety.

40. In both antitrust proceedings and in proceedings under the Merger Regulation, should the person or undertaking in question meet the conditions set out in paragraphs 35 to 37 above, to the extent they are applicable, the Commission will either:

— provisionally accept the claims which seem justified; or
— inform the person or undertaking in question that it does not agree with the confidentiality claim in whole or in part, where it is apparent that the claim is unjustified.

41. The Commission may reverse its provisional acceptance of the confidentiality claim in whole or in part at a later stage.

42. Where the Directorate General for Competition does not agree with the confidentiality claim from the outset or where it takes the view that the provisional acceptance of the confidentiality claim should be reversed, and thus intends to disclose information, it will grant the person or undertaking in question an opportunity to express its views. In such cases, the Directorate General for Competition will inform the person or undertaking in writing of its intention to disclose information, give its reasons and set a time-limit within which such person or undertaking may inform it in writing of its views. If, following submission of those views, a disagreement on the confidentiality claim persists, the matter will be dealt with by the Hearing Officer according to the applicable Commission terms of reference of Hearing Officers.[54]

---

[50] Cf. Article 16(3) of the Implementing Regulation and Article 18(3) of the Merger Implementing Regulation. This also applies to documents gathered by the Commission in an inspection pursuant to Article 13 of the Merger Regulation and Articles 20 and 21 of Regulation (EC) No 1/2003.
[51] Cf. Article 16(3) of the Implementing Regulation and Article 18(3) of the Merger Implementing Regulation.
[52] Cf. Article 16(3) of the Implementing Regulation.
[53] Cf. Article 16 of the Implementing Regulation.
[54] Cf. Article 9 of the Commission Decision of 23.5.2001 on the terms of reference of hearing officers in certain competition proceedings, OJ L 162 19.6.2001, p. 21.

43. Where there is a risk that an undertaking which is able to place very considerable economic or commercial pressure on its competitors or on its trading partners, customers or suppliers will adopt retaliatory measures against those, as a consequence of their collaboration in the investigation carried out by the Commission,[55] the Commission will protect the anonymity of the authors by providing access to a non-confidential version or summary of the responses in question.[56] Requests for anonymity in such circumstances, as well as requests for anonymity according to point 81 of the Commission Notice on the handling of complaints[57] will be dealt with according to paragraphs 40 to 42 above.

C. Provision of access to file

44. The Commission may determine that access to the file shall be granted in one of the following ways, taking due account of the technical capabilities of the parties:

   — by means of a CD-ROM(s) or any other electronic data storage device as may become available in future;
   — through copies of the accessible file in paper form sent to them by mail;
   — by inviting them to examine the accessible file on the Commission's premises.

   The Commission may choose any combination of these methods.

45. In order to facilitate access to the file, the parties will receive an enumerative list of documents setting out the content of the Commission file, as defined in paragraph 8 above.

46. Access is granted to evidence as contained in the Commission file, in its original form: the Commission is under no obligation to provide a translation of documents in the file.[58]

47. If a party considers that, after having obtained access to the file, it requires knowledge of specific non-accessible information for its defence, it may submit a reasoned request to that end to the Commission. If the services of the Directorate General for Competition are not in a position to accept the request and if the party disagrees with that view, the matter will be resolved by the Hearing Officer, in accordance with the applicable terms of reference of Hearing Officers.[59]

48. Access to the file in accordance with this notice is granted on the condition that the information thereby obtained may only be used for the purposes of judicial or administrative proceedings for the application of the Community competition rules at issue in the related administrative proceedings.[60] Should the information be used for a different purpose, at any point in time, with the involvement of an outside counsel, the Commission may report the incident to the bar of that counsel, with a view to disciplinary action.

49. With the exception of paragraphs 45 and 47, this section C applies equally to the grant of access to documents to complainants (in antitrust proceedings) and to other involved parties (in merger proceedings).

---

[57] Commission Notice on the handling of complaints by the Commission under Articles 81 and 82 of the EC Treaty, OJ C 101, 27.4.2004, p. 65.

[55] Cf. paragraph 19 above.

[56] Cf. Case T-5/02, *Tetra Laval vs. Commission*, [2002] ECR II-4381, paragraph 98, 104 and 105.

[58] Cf. Case T-25/95 et al. *Cimenteries*, paragraph 635.

[59] Cf. Article 8 of the Commission Decision of 23.5.2001 on the terms of reference of hearing officers in certain competition proceedings, OJ L 162, 19.6.2001, p. 21.

[60] Cf. Articles 15(4) and 8(2) of the Implementing Regulation, respectively, and Article 17(4) of the Merger Implementing Regulation.

Commission Decision of 23 May 2001 on the terms of reference of hearing officers in certain competition proceedings

(notified under document number C(2001) 1461)

(Text with EEA relevance)

(2001/462/EC, ECSC)

THE COMMISSION OF THE EUROPEAN COMMUNITIES,

Having regard to the Treaty establishing the European Community,

Having regard to the Treaty establishing the European Coal and Steel Community,

Having regard to the Agreement on the European Economic Area,

Having regard to the Rules of Procedure of the Commission,[1] and in particular Article 20 thereof,

Whereas:

(1) The right of the parties concerned and of third parties to be heard before a final decision affecting their interests is taken is a fundamental principle of Community law. That right is also set out in Council Regulation (EEC) No 4064/89 of 21 December 1989 on the control of concentrations between undertakings,[2] as last amended by Regulation (EC) No 1310/97,[3] Commission Regulation (EC) No 2842/98 of 22 December 1998 on the hearing of parties in certain proceedings under Articles 85 and 86 of the EC Treaty[4] and Commission Regulation (EC) No 447/98 of 1 March 1998 on the notifications, time limits and hearings provided for in Council Regulation (EEC) No 4064/89 on the control of concentrations between undertakings.[5]

(2) The Commission must ensure that that right is guaranteed in its competition proceedings, having regard in particular to the Charter of Fundamental Rights of the European Union.[6]

(3) The conduct of administrative proceedings should therefore be entrusted to an independent person experienced in competition matters who has the integrity necessary to contribute to the objectivity, transparency and efficiency of those proceedings.

(4) The Commission created the post of hearing officer for these purposes in 1982 and last laid down the terms of reference for that post in Commission Decision 94/810/ECSC, EC of 12 December 1994 on the terms of reference of hearing officers in competition procedures before the Commission.[7]

(5) It is necessary to further strengthen the role of the hearing officer and to adapt and consolidate those terms of reference in the light of developments in competition law.

---

[1] OJ L308, 8.12.2000, p 26.

[2] OJ L395, 30.12.1989, p 1 (corrected version in OJ L257, 21.9.1990, p 13).

[3] OJ L180, 9.7.1997, p 1.

[4] OJ L354, 30.12.1998, p 18.

[5] OJ L61, 2.3.1998, p 1.

[6] OJ C364, 18.12.2000, p 1.

[7] OJ L330, 21.12.1994, p 67.

(6) In order to ensure the independence of the hearing officer, he should be attached, for administrative purposes, to the member of the Commission with special responsibility for competition. Transparency as regards the appointment, termination of appointment and transfer of hearing officers should be increased.

(7) The hearing officer should be appointed in accordance with the rules laid down in the Staff Regulations of Officials and the Conditions of Employment of Other Servants of the European Communities. In accordance with those rules, consideration may be given to candidates who are not officials of the Commission.

(8) The terms of reference of the hearing officer in competition proceedings should be framed in such a way as to safeguard the right to be heard throughout the whole procedure.

(9) When disclosing information on natural persons, particular attention should be paid to Regulation (EC) No 45/2001 of the European Parliament and of the Council of 18 December 2000 on the protection of individuals with regard to the processing of personal data by the Community institutions and bodies and on the free movement of such data.[8]

(10) This Decision should be without prejudice to the general rules granting or excluding access to Commission documents.

(11) Decision 94/810/ECSC, EC should be repealed,

HAS DECIDED AS FOLLOWS:

Article 1

The Commission shall appoint one or more hearing officers (hereinafter 'the hearing officer'), who shall ensure that the effective exercise of the right to be heard is respected in competition proceedings before the Commission under Articles 81 and 82 of the EC Treaty, Articles 65 and 66 of the ECSC Treaty, and Regulation (EEC) No 4064/89.

Article 2

1. The appointment of the hearing officer shall be published in the *Official Journal of the European Communities*. Any interruption, termination of appointment or transfer by whatever procedure, shall be the subject of a reasoned decision of the Commission. That decision shall be published in the *Official Journal of the European Communities*.

2. The hearing officer shall be attached, for administrative purposes, to the member of the Commission with special responsibility for competition (hereinafter 'the competent member of the Commission').

3. Where the hearing officer is unable to act, the competent member of the Commission, where appropriate after consultation of the hearing officer, shall designate another official, who is not involved in the case in question, to carry out the hearing officer's duties.

Article 3

1. In performing his duties, the hearing officer shall take account of the need for effective application of the competition rules in accordance with the Community legislation in force and the principles laid down by the Court of Justice and the Court of First Instance of the European Communities.

2. The hearing officer shall be kept informed by the director responsible for investigating the case (hereinafter 'the director responsible') about the development of the procedure up to the stage of the draft decision to be submitted to the competent member of the Commission.

3. The hearing officer may present observations on any matter arising out of any Commission competition proceeding to the competent member of the Commission.

---

[8] OJ L8, 12.1.2001, p 1.

Article 4

1. The hearing officer shall organise and conduct the hearings provided for in the provisions implementing Articles 81 and 82 of the EC Treaty, Articles 65 and 66 of the ECSC Treaty and Regulation (EEC) No 4064/89, in accordance with Articles 5 to 13 of this Decision.

2. The provisions referred to in paragraph 1 are:
(a) the first paragraph of Article 36 of the ECSC Treaty;
(b) Regulation (EC) No 2842/98;
(c) Regulation (EC) No 447/98.

Article 5

The hearing officer shall ensure that the hearing is properly conducted and contributes to the objectivity of the hearing itself and of any decision taken subsequently. The hearing officer shall seek to ensure in particular that, in the preparation of draft Commission decisions, due account is taken of all the relevant facts, whether favourable or unfavourable to the parties concerned, including the factual elements related to the gravity of any infringement.

Article 6

1. Applications to be heard from third parties, be they persons, undertakings or associations of persons or undertakings, shall be submitted in writing, together with a written statement explaining the applicant's interest in the outcome of the procedure.

2. Decisions as to whether third parties are to be heard shall be taken after consulting the director responsible.

3. Where it is found that an application has not shown a sufficient interest to be heard, he shall be informed in writing of the reasons for such finding. A time limit shall be fixed within which he may submit any further written comments.

Article 7

1. Applications to be heard orally shall be made in the applicant's written comments on letters which the Commission has addressed to him.

2. The letters referred to in paragraph 1 are those:
(a) communicating a statement of objections;
(b) inviting the written comments of a third party having shown sufficient interest to be heard;
(c) informing a complainant that in the Commission's view there are insufficient grounds for finding an infringement and inviting him to submit any further written comments.

3. Decisions as to whether applicants are to be heard orally shall be taken after consulting the director responsible.

Article 8

1. Where a person, an undertaing or an association of persons or undertakings has received one or more of the letters listed in Article 7(2) and has reason to believe that the Commission has in its possession documents which have not been disclosed to it and that those documents are necessary for the proper exercise of the right to be heard, access to those documents may be sought by means of a reasoned request.

2. The reasoned decision on any such request shall be communicated to the person, undertaking or association that made the request and to any other person, undertaking or association concerned by the procedure.

Article 9

Where it is intended to disclose information which may constitute a business secret of an undertaking, it shall be informed in writing of this intention and the reasons for it. A time limit shall be fixed within which the undertaking concerned may submit any written comments.

Where the undertaking concerned objects to the disclosure of the information but it is found that the information is not protected and may therefore be disclosed, that finding shall be stated in a reasoned decision which shall be notified to the undertaking concerned. The decision shall specify the date after which the information will be disclosed. This date shall not be less than one week from the date of notification.

The first and second paragraphs shall apply *mutatis mutandis* to the disclosure of information by publication in the *Official Journal of the European Communities.*

Article 10

Where a person, undertaking or association of persons or undertakings considers that the time limit imposed for its reply to a letter referred to in Article 7(2) is too short, it may, within the original time limit, seek an extension of that time limit by means of a reasoned request. The applicant shall be informed in writing whether the request has been granted.

Article 11

Where appropriate, in view of the need to ensure that the hearing is properly prepared and particularly that questions of fact are clarified as far as possible, the hearing officer may, after consulting the director responsible, supply in advance to the parties invited to the hearing a list of the questions on which he wishes them to make known their views.

For this purpose, after consulting the director responsible, the hearing officer may hold a meeting with the parties invited to the hearing and, where appropriate, the Commission staff, in order to prepare for the hearing itself.

The hearing officer may also ask for prior written notification of the essential contents of the intended statement of persons whom the parties invited to the hearing have proposed for hearing.

Article 12

1. After consulting the director responsible, the hearing officer shall determine the date, the duration and the place of the hearing. Where a postponement is requested, the hearing officer shall decide whether or not to allow it.

2. The hearing officer shall be fully responsible for the conduct of the hearing.

3. The hearing officer shall decide whether fresh documents should be admitted during the hearing, what persons should be heard on behalf of a party and whether the persons concerned should be heard separately or in the presence of other persons attending the hearing.

4. Where appropriate, in view of the need to ensure the right to be heard, the hearing officer may, after consulting the Director responsible, afford persons, undertakings, and associations of persons or undertakings the opportunity of submitting further written comments after the oral hearing. The hearing officer shall fix a date by which such submissions may be made. The Commission shall not be obliged to take into account written comments received after that date.

Article 13

1. The hearing officer shall report to the competent member of the Commission on the hearing and the conclusions he draws from it, with regard to the respect of the right to be heard. The observations in this report shall concern procedural issues, including disclosure of documents and access to the file, time limits for replying to the statement of objections and the proper conduct of the oral hearing.

A copy of the report shall be given to the Director-General for Competition and to the director responsible.

2. In addition to the report referred to in paragraph 1, the hearing officer may make observations on the further progress of the proceedings. Such observations may relate among other things to

the need for further information, the withdrawal of certain objections, or the formulation of further objections.

Article 14

Where appropriate, the hearing officer may report on the objectivity of any enquiry conducted in order to assess the competition impact of commitments proposed in relation to any proceeding initiated by the Commission in application of the provisions referred to in Article 1. This shall cover in particular the selection of respondents and the methodology used.

Article 15

The hearing officer shall, on the basis of the draft decision to be submitted to the Advisory Committee in the case in question, prepare a final report in writing on the respect of the right to be heard, as referred to in Article 13(1). This report will also consider whether the draft decision deals only with objections in respect of which the parties have been afforded the opportunity of making known their views, and, where appropriate, the objectivity of any enquiry within the meaning of Article 14.

The final report shall be submitted to the competent member of the Commission, the Director-General for Competition and the director responsible. It shall be communicated to the competent authorities of the Member States and, in accordance with the provisions on cooperation laid down in Protocol 23 and Protocol 24 of the EEA Agreement, to the EFTA Surveillance Authority.

Article 16

1. The hearing officer's final report shall be attached to the draft decision submitted to the Commission, in order to ensure that, when it reaches a decision on an individual case, the Commission is fully apprised of all relevant information as regards the course of the procedure and respect of the right to be heard.

2. The final report may be modified by the hearing officer in the light of any amendments to the draft decision up to the time the decision is adopted by the Commission.

3. The Commission shall communicate the hearing officer's final report, together with the decision, to the addressees of the decision. It shall publish the hearing officer's final report in the *Official Journal of the European Communities*, together with the decision, having regard to the legitimate interest of undertakings in the protection of their business secrets.

Article 17

Decision 94/810/ECSC, EC is repealed.

Procedural steps already taken under that Decision shall continue to have effect.

Done at Brussels, 23 May 2001.

For the Commission
Mario MONTI
Member of the Commission

APPENDIX 13

Joint Statement of the Council and the Commission on the Functioning of the Network of Competition Authorities

'1. The today adopted Regulation on the implementation of the rules on competition laid down in Articles 81 and 82 of the Treaty establishes a directly applicable exception system in which the competition authorities and courts of the Member States, along with the Commission, have the power to apply not only Articles 81(1) and 82 of the Treaty, which have direct applicability by virtue of the case-law of the Court of Justice of the European Communities, but also Article 81(3) of the Treaty.

2. In order to ensure that the Community competition rules are applied effectively and consistently, the Commission and the national competition authorities designated by the Member States (hereafter NCAs) from together a network of competition authorities (hereafter the Network) for the application in close cooperation of Articles 81 and 82 of the Treaty.

3. This Joint Statement is political in nature and does therefore not create any legal rights or obligations. It is limited to setting out common political understanding shared by all Member States and the Commission on the principles of the functioning of the Network.

4. Details will be set out in a Commission notice which will be drafted and updated as necessary in close cooperation with Member States.

General principles

5. The cooperation within the Network is dedicated to the effective enforcement of EC competition rules throughout the Community.

6. Decentralization of the implementation of Community competition rules strengthens the position of the NCAs. These will be fully competent to apply Article 81 and 82 of the Treaty, actively contributing to the development of competition policy, law and practice.

7. All competition authorities within the Network are independent from one another. Cooperation between NCAs and with the Commission takes place on the basis of equality, respect and solidarity.

8. Member States accept that their enforcement systems differ but nonetheless mutually recognize the standards of each other's system as a basis for cooperation.

9. The Commission, as the guardian of the Treaty, has the ultimate but not the sole responsibility for developing policy and safeguarding efficiency and consistency. Therefore, the instruments of the Commission on the one hand and of the NCAs on the other hand are not identical. The additional powers the Commission has been granted to fulfil its responsibilities will be exercised with the utmost regard for the cooperative nature of the Network.

10. Cooperation within the Network and the management of information will be as efficient as possible. All members of the Network will minimize the administrative burden of participating in the Network on the understanding that any information exchanged under Article 11 of the Regulation will be made available and easily accessible to all Network members.

Division of work

11. Without prejudice to Article 11(6) of the Regulation, all Network members have full parallel competence to apply Articles 81 and 82 of the Treaty.

12. Case allocation will be completed as quickly as possible. An indicative time limit (up to 3 months) will be used within the Network. Normally, this allocation will remain definitive to the end of the proceedings provided that the facts known about the case remain substantially the same. If so, this implies that the competition authority which has notified the case to the Network, will normally remain the responsible competition authority if it is well placed to deal with the case and no other competition authority raises objections during the indicative time period.

13. All members of the Network will endeavour to make allocation a predictable process with business and other interested parties receiving guidance as to where to direct complaints.

14. Members of the Network will ensure that those cases which merit a detailed investigation by a competition authority are adequately allocated and assessed. This principle does not prejudice the discretion of all Network members to decide whether or not to investigate a case.

Authority (-ies) well placed to act

15. Members of the Network will ensure an effective enforcement of Articles 81 and 82 of the Treaty. Cases will be dealt with by an authority, or by authorities, able to restore or maintain competition in the market. To that effect, the members of the Network will take into account all relevant factors in particular in which markets the main anti-competitive effects are felt and which authority is most able to deal with a case successfully depending on the ability of the authority to gather evidence, to bring the infringement to an end and to apply sanctions effectively.

16. Cases will be dealt with by a single competition authority as often as possible. A single NCA will be usually well placed to act if only one Member State is substantially affected by an agreement or practice, particularly when the main anti-competitive effects appear in the same Member State and all participating companies to an agreement or an abusive behaviour have their seat in that Member State.

17. Where an agreement or practice substantially affects competition in more than one Member State, the Network members will seek to agree between them who is best placed to deal with the case successfully.

18. In cases where single action is not possible (when competition in several Member States is affected and no NCA can deal with the case alone successfully), the Network members should coordinate their action and seek to designate one competition authority as the lead institution.

19. The Commission will be particularly well placed to deal with a case if more than three Member States are substantially affected by an agreement or practice, if it is closely linked to other Community provisions which may be exclusively or more effectively applied by the Commission, if Community interest requires the adoption of a Commission decision to develop Community competition policy particularly when a new competition issue arises or to ensure effective enforcement.

Consistent application of Community competition rules

20. After the initial allocation period, when the same case (same market, same parties, same conduct/agreement) is being dealt with by more than one NCA well placed to do so, one national competition authority will take a formal decision, whilst others stay their proceedings or, if this is not possible, the NCAs will deal with the case in close co-operation.

21. After the initial allocation period, when a case is being dealt with by one or several competition authority (-ies) which is (are) well placed to do so, the Commission will normally not

open proceedings with the effects of relieving them of their competence pursuant to Article 11(6) of the Regulation unless one of the following situations arises:

(a) Network members envisage conflicting decisions in the same case;

(b) Network members envisage a decision which is obviously in conflict with consolidated case law; the standards defined in the judgements of the Community courts and in previous decisions and regulations of the Commission should serve as a yardstick; concerning facts, only a significant divergence will trigger an intervention of the Commission;

(c) Network member(s) is (are) unduly drawing out proceedings;

(d) There is a need to adopt a Commission decision to develop Community competition policy in particular when a similar competition issue arises in several Member States;

(e) The national competition authority does not object.

Should the Commission decide to open proceedings with the effects of Article 11(6) of the Regulation, it will do so as soon as possible.

22. If an NCA is already acting on a case, the Commission will explain the reasons for the application of Article 11(6) of the Regulation in writing to the NCA concerned and to the other members of the Network.

23. The Commission will normally not—and to the extent that Community interest is not at stake—adopt a decision which is in conflict with a decision of an NCA after proper information pursuant to both Article 11(3) and (4) of the Regulation has been provided and the Commission has made no use of Article 11(6) of the Regulation.

24. Network members will inform the other members of the Network about rejections of complaints and the termination of investigations on all cases which have been notified within the Network pursuant to Article 11(2) and 11(3) of the Regulation.'

STATEMENT BY THE COMMISSION

'The today adopted Regulation establishes a directly applicable exception system. It is without prejudice to the ability of the Commission to issue informal guidance to individual undertakings seeking it, where individual cases give rise to genuine uncertainty because they present novel or unresolved questions for the application of Articles 81 or 82.

The Commission is prepared to issue a Notice which sets out the circumstances under which guidance in the form of written opinions could be provided. The Commission shall have no obligation to provide guidance in any individual case.'

STATEMENT BY THE GERMAN DELEGATION ON ARTICLE 2 OF THE REGULATION

'With a view to supplementing in particular recital 5 of this Regulation, the Government of the Federal Republic of Germany confirms its view that Article 83 of the Treaty is not a sufficient legal basis for introducing or amending criminal law or criminal procedural law provisions. This applies in particular to fundamental procedural safeguards in criminal proceedings such as the presumption of innocence on the part of the defendant. The Government of the Federal Republic of Germany would point out that these procedural safeguards also apply to criminal-law-related proceedings such as monetary fine proceedings and enjoy constitutional status. It accordingly assumes that the present Regulation, and in particular Article 2 thereof, cannot amend or adversely affect such criminal law or criminal procedural law provisions applicable to criminal proceedings or criminal-law-related proceedings and legal principles of the Member States.'

APPENDIX 14

Table of Fines

The table of fines refers to the period until 15 June 2005.

Date	Commission Decision	Infringement Type and Duration	Name of the Parties	Fine (EUR)	CFI judgment	ECJ judgment
30.11.2005	Industrial bags cartel (Press Release IP/05/1508)	Art. 81(1): Price Fixing, customer allocation, bid-rigging, exchange of information, 20 YRS.	Bernay Film Plastique	0,94 million		
			Bischof + Klein GmbH & CO	29,15 million		
			Bischof + Klein France SA	3,96 million		
			Bonar Technical Fabrics NV and Low & Bonar PLC	12,24 million		
			British Polythene Industries PLC	0 million		
			Cofira-Sac SA	0,35 million		
			Fardem Packaging BV Koninklijke	34 million		
			Verpakkingsindustrie Stempher CV and Stempher BV	2,37 million		
			Nordenia International AG & Nordenia GmbH	39,10 million		
			Plásticos Españoles SA & Armando Álvarez SA	42 million		
			RKW AG Rheinische Kunststoffwerke and JM Gesellschaft für industrielle Beteiligungen mbH & Co KgaA	39 million		
			Sachsa Verpackung GmbH and Groupe Gascogne	13,2 million		
			Trioplast Wittenheim SA and Trioplast Industrier AB, FLSmidth & Co A/S and FLS Plast A/S	17,85 million		
			UPM-Kymmene OYJ	56,55 million		
			Total	**290,7 million**		

Date	Commission Decision	Infringement: Type and Duration	Name of the Parties	Fine (EUR)	CFI judgment	ECJ judgment
20.10.2005	Italian raw tobacco market (Press Release IP/05/1315)	Art. 81(1): Price Fixing, supplier allocation, bid-rigging.	Deltafina Dimon Transcatab Romana Tabacchi APTI UNITAB *Total*	30 million 10 million 14 million 2,05 million **56,05 million**		
05.10.2005	Automobiles Peugeot SA/ Peugeot Nederland N.V. (Press Release IP/05/1227)	Art. 81(1): Concerted practices designed to prevent dealers from selling cars to customers in other Member States.	Automobiles Peugeot SA & Peugeot Nederland N.V. *Total*	49,5 million **49,5 million**		
15.06.2005	AstraZeneca COMP/37.507 (IP/05/737)	Art. 82: Abuse of dominant position by misusing the patent system and procedures for marketing pharma to block/ delay market entry for generic competitors. 7 YRS.	AstraZeneca *Total*	60,000,000 **60,000,000**	No appeal.	
19.01.2005	Monochloro-acetic (MCAA) COMP/37.773 (IP/05/61) C(2004)4876	Art. 81(1): Allocation of volume quotas and customer, agreement on price increases, exchange of information on sales volume and prices to monitor cartel and agreement on compensation mechanism to ensure implementation of arrangements. 15 YRS.	Akzo Nobel Arkema (formerly Atofina) and Elf Aquitaine S.A. *(jointly and severally liable)* Arkema (formerly Atofina) Hoechst *Total*	84,380,000 45,000,000 13,500,000 74,030,000 **216,910,000**	Appeal pending. Case T-175/05 [2005] OJ C171/52 Appeal pending. Case T-174/05 [2005] OJ C171/51 Appeal pending. Case T-174/05 [2005] OJ C171/51 Appeal pending. Case T-161/05 [2005] OJ C155/53	

Date	Commission Decision	Infringement: Type and Duration	Name of the Parties	Fine (EUR)	CFI judgment	ECJ judgment
9.12.2004	PO/Choline Chloride COMP/37.533	Art. 81(1): Price fixing, market sharing and agreed actions against competitors. 5 YRS and 11 MTHS. 1 YR and 6 MTHS.	Bioproducts Incorporated	0	No appeal.	
			Chinook Group Limited	0	No appeal.	
			DuCoa, L.P.	0	No appeal.	
			Akzo Nobel	20,990,000	Appeal pending. Case T-112/05 [2005] OJ C143/70	
			BASF A.G.	34,970,000	Appeal pending. Case T-101/05 [2005] OJ C115/51	
			UCB S.A.	10,380,000	Appeal pending. Case T-111/05 [2005] OJ C115/57	
			Total	**66,340,000**		
26.10.2004	PO/Needles COMP/38.338	Article 81(1): Concerted practices and bilateral agreements on sharing and partitioning several markets. 5 YRS and 3 MTHS.	Coats Holdings Ltd and J & P Coats Ltd	30,000,000	Appeal pending. Case T-36/05 [2005] OJ C93/50	
			Entaco Ltd and Entaco Group Ltd	0	No appeal.	
			William Prym GmbH & Co. KG and Prym Consumer GmbH & Co. KG	30,000,000	Appeal pending. Case T-30/05 [2005] OJ C106/57	
			Total	**60,000,000**		
20.10.2004	Spanish Raw Tobacco COMP/38.238	Article 81(1): Agreements and/or concerted practices designed to fix the maximum average delivery price of each variety of raw tobacco and to share out the quantities of each variety of raw tobacco to be bought. 5 YRS and 4 MTHS.	CCAE	1,000	No appeal.	
			COAG	1,000	No appeal.	
			UPA	1,000	No appeal.	
			ASAJA	1,000	No appeal.	
			Taes	108,000	No appeal.	
			Agroexpansión	2,592,000	Appeal pending. Case T-38/05 [2005] OJ C82/76	
			Dimon Inc. *D39*		Appeal pending Case T-41/05 [2005] OJ C093/64	
			WWTE	1,822,500	Appeal pending. Case T-37/05 [2005] OJ C82/75	
			SCC, SCTC, TCLT *(jointly and severally liable)*		Appeal pending. Case T-24/05 [2005] OJ C82/69	
			Cetarsa	3,631,500	Appeal pending. Case T-33/05 [2005] OJ C82/74	
			Deltafina	11,880,000	Appeal pending. Case T-29/05 [2005] OJ C82/73	
			Total	**20,038,000**		

Date	Commission Decision	Infringement: Type and Duration	Name of the Parties	Fine (EUR)	CFI judgment	ECJ judgment
29.09.2004	PO/French Beer COMP/37.750	Article 81: Agreement introducing a temporary freeze on acquisitions of wholesalers and establishment of equilibrium between the respective distribution networks of the groups in the French sector for consumption of beer on the premises. Not put into effect: no need to determine duration.	Heineken N.V. and Heineken France S.A.	1,000,000	No appeal.	
			Groupe Danone and Brasseries Kronenbourg S.A.	1,500,000	No appeal.	
			Total	**2,500,000**		
24.06.2004	Belgian Architects COMP/38.549	Article 81(1): Adopting and making available a minimum fee scale known as Ethical Standard No.2. 35 YRS and 3 MTHS.	Belgian Architects Association	100,000	No appeal.	
			Total	**100,000**		
26.05.2004	Souris Bleue/ TOPPS + Nintendo COMP/37.980	Article 81(1): Restriction of parallel imports. 10 MTHS.	The Topps Company, Inc. Topps Europe Ltd Topps UK Ltd Topps International Ltd Topps Italia SRL _(jointly and severally liable)_	1,590,000	No appeal.	
			Total	**1,590,000**		

Date	Commission Decision	Infringement: Type and Duration	Name of the Parties	Fine (EUR)	CFI judgment	ECJ judgment
24.03.04	Microsoft / W 2000 COMP/37.792	Article 82(d) EC: Abuse of a dominant position by refusing to supply and tying. 5 YRS and 5 MTHS.	Microsoft Corporation	497,196,304	Appeal pending Case T-201/04 R [2005] OJ C179/36	
			Total	**497,196,304**		
16.12.03	Industrial tubes COMP/38.240 [2004] OJ L125/50 (2004/421/EC)	Article 81(1): Price fixing and horizontal market sharing. 12 YRS and 10 MTHS.	Outokumpu Oyi and Outokumpu Copper Products Oy *(jointly and severally liable)*	18,130,000	Appeal pending, Case T-122/04 [2004] OJ C118/104	
			Wieland Werke AG	20,790,000	Appeal pending, Case T-116/04 [2004] OJ C118/99	
			KM Europa Metal AG, Tréfimétaux SA and Europa Metalli SpA *(jointly and severally liable)*	18,990,000	Appeal pending, Case T-127/04 [2004] OJ C146/07	
			KM Europa Metal AG	10,410,000	Appeal pending, Case T-109/04 [2004] OJ C146/06	
			Europa Metalli SpA and Tréfimétaux SA +D62	10,410,000	No appeal.	
			Total	**78,730,000**		
10.12.03	PO/Organic Peroxides COMP/37.857 [2005] OJ L110/44 (2005/349/EC)	Article 81(1): Price fixing and horizontal market sharing. 1971–1999.	Atofina S.A.	43,470,000	No appeal.	
			Peroxid Chemie GmbH & Co KG.	8,830,000	Appeal pending, Case T-104/04 [2004] OJ C118/97	
			Degussa UK Holdings Ltd., and Peroxid Chemie GmbH & Co KG.	16,730,000	No appeal.	
			Peroxidos Organicos S.A.	500,000	Appeal pending, Case T-120/04 [2004] OJ C118/102	
			AC-Treuhand AG	1,000	Appeal pending, Case T-99/04 [2004] OJ C118/96	
			Akzo	0	No appeal.	
			Total	**69,531,000**		

Date	Commission Decision	Infringement: Type and Duration	Name of the Parties	Fine (EUR)	CFI judgment	ECJ judgment
03.12.03	Electrical and mechanical carbon and graphite products COMP/38.359 [2004] OJ L125/45 (2004/420/EC)	Article 81(1): Price fixing and horizontal market sharing; 11 YRS and 2 MTHS /10 YRS and 8 MTHS5 YRS and 1 MTH.	C. Conradty Nurnberg	1,060,000	No appeal.	
			Hoffmann & Co. Elektrokohle AG	2,820,000	No appeal.	
			Le Carbone Lorraine S.A.	43,050,000	Appeal pending, Case T-73/04 [2004] OJ C106/144	
			The Morgan Crucible Company plc	0	No appeal.	
			Schunk GmbH and Schunk Kohlenstofftechnik GmbH	30,870,000	Appeal pending, Case T-69/04 [2004] OJ C106/143	
			SGL Carbon AG.	23,640,000	Appeal pending, Case T-68/04 [2004] OJ C106/142	
			Total	**101,440,000**		
01.10.03	PO/Sorbates COMP/37.370 OJ 2005 L182/20 (2005/493/EC)	Article 81(1): Agreement to fix target prices and to allocate volume quotas, to define a reporting and monitoring system. 1979–1996.	Hoechst AG	99,000,000	Appeal pending, Case T-410/03 [2004] OJ C59/39	
			Chisso Corporation	0	No appeal.	
			Daicel Chemical Industries, Ltd	16,600,000	No appeal.	
			Ueno Fine Chemicals Industry, Ltd	12,300,000	No appeal.	
			The Nippon Synthetic Chemical Industry Co, Ltd	10,500,000	No appeal.	
			Total	**138,400,000**		

Date	Commission Decision	Infringement: Type and Duration	Name of the Parties	Fine (EUR)	CFI judgment	ECJ judgment
16.07.03	PO / Yamaha COMP/37.975	Article 81(1): Price fixing and market sharing with authorised dealers. 1977–2002.	Yamaha Corporation Japan	2,560,000	No appeal.	
			Yamaha Europa GmbH			
			Yamaha Musica Italia S.p.A.			
			Yamaha Musique France S.A.			
			Yamaha Scandinavia AB *(jointly and severally liable)*			
			Total	**2,560,000**		
21.05.03	Deutsche Telekom AG COMP/37.451; 37.578; 37.579 [2003] OJ L263/9 (2003/707/EC)	Article 82(a): Abuse of a dominant position by charging its competitors and end-users unfair charges for access to the local network. 5 YRS.	Deutsche Telekom AG	12,600,000	Appeal pending. Case T-271/03 [2003] OJ C264/51	
			Total	**12,600,000**		
02.04.03	French Beef COMP/38.279 [2003] OJ L209/12 (2003/600/CE)	Article 81(1): Minimum price agreement and a commitment to limit imports. 2–3 MTHS.	FNSEA	12,000,000	Appeal pending. Case T-245/03 [2003] OJ C200/59	
			FNB	1,440,000		
			FNPL	1,440,000		
			JA	600,000		
			FNICGV	720,000	Appeal pending. Case T-252/03 [2003] OJ C213/78	
			FNCBV	480,000	Appeal pending. Case T-217/03 [2003] OJ C200/55	
			Total	**16,680,000**		

Date	Commission Decision	Infringement: Type and Duration	Name of the Parties	Fine (EUR)	CFI judgment	ECJ judgment
17.12.02	Speciality Graphites COMP/37.667 (IP/02/1906)	Article 81(1): Horizontal price fixing and market sharing. 3 YRS and 6 MTHS / 4 YRS and 6 MTHS.	Tokai Carbon Co. Ltd.	6,970,000	Appeal dismissed. Case T-71/03 [2005] OJ C205/31	
			Intech EDM B.V.	980,000	Appeal dismissed. Case T-74/03 [2005] OJ C205/31	
			Intech EDM A.G.	980,000	Fine reduced to 420,000. Case T-87/03 [2005] OJ C205/31	
			SGL Carbon AG.	27,750,000	Fine reduced to 9,641,970. Case T-91/03 [2005] OJ C205/31	
			Toyo Tanso Co. Ltd.	10,790,000	Appeal pending. Case T-72/03 [2003] OJ C112/66	
			Carbone-Lorraine S.A.	6,970,000	No appeal.	
			Ibiden Co. Ltd.	3,580,000	No appeal.	
			Nippon Steel Chemical Co. Ltd.	3,580,000	No appeal.	
			Graftech International, Ltd.	0	No appeal.	
			Total	**52,670,000**		

Date	Commission Decision	Infringement: Type and Duration	Name of the Parties	Fine (EUR)	CFI judgment	ECJ judgment
17.12.02	PO/Rond à béton COMP/37.956 (IP/02/1908)	Article 81(1): Horizontal price fixing and limitation of production on the Italian market of concrete reinforcing bars. 10–11 YRS.	Riva Acciaio SpA	26,900,000	Appeal pending. Case T-45/03 [2003] OJ C101/74	
			Lucchini SpA and Siderpotenza SpA	16,140,000	Appeal pending. Case T-80/03 [2003] OJ C124/45	
			Feralpi Siderurgica SpA	10,250,000	Appeal pending. Case T-77/03 [2003] OJ C112/68	
			Valsabbia Investimenti SpA and Ferriera Valsabbia SpA	10,250,000	Appeal pending. Case T-97/03 [2003] OJ C112/83	
			Alfa Acciai SpA	7,175,000	Appeal pending. Case T-98/03 [2003] OJ C112/84	
			Leali SpA and	7,175,000	Appeal pending. Case T-46/03 [2003] OJ C83/57	
			Acciaierie e Ferriere Leali Luigi SpA in liquidazione		Case T-58/03 [2003] OJ C112/84	
			IRO Industrie Riunite Odolesi SpA	3,580,000	Appeal pending. Case T-79/03 [2003] OJ C112/70	
			Ferriere Nord SpA	3,570,000	Appeal pending. Case T-94/03 [2003] OJ C112/80	
			Total	**85,040,000**		
17.12.02	Food flavour enhancers COMP/37.671 [2004] OJ L075/1 (2004/206/EC)	Article 81(1): Horizontal price fixing, implementation of concerted price increases, allocation of customers and exchange of information on sales figures: 8–10 YRS	Ajinomoto Co. Inc.	15,540,000	No appeal.	
			Cheil Jedang Corp.	2,736,000	No appeal.	
			Daesang Corp.	2,280,000	No appeal.	
			Takeda Chemical Industries Ltd	0	No appeal.	
			Total	**20,556,000**		

Date	Commission Decision	Infringement: Type and Duration	Name of the Parties	Fine (EUR)	CFI judgment	ECJ judgment
27.11.02	PO/ Plasterboard COMP/37.152 [2005] OJ L166/8 (2005/471/EC)	Article 81(1):Horizontal cartel exchanging information on sales volumes and price increases: 6–7 YRS.	Lafarge S.A.	249,600,000	Appeal pending, Case T-54/03 [2003] OJ C101/81	
			BPB plc	138,600,000	Appeal pending, Case T-53/03 [2003] OJ C101/80	
			Knauf Westdeutsche Gipswerke KG	85,800,000	Appeal pending, Case T-52/03 [2003] OJ C124/40	
			Gyproc Benelux NV	4,320,000	Appeal pending, Case T-50/03 [2003] OJ C101/78	
			Total	**478,320,000**		
27.11.02	Methyl-glucamine COMP/37.978 [2004] OJ L038/18 (2004/104/EC)	Article 81(1): Horizontal duopoly, price fixing and market sharing. 9 YRS.	Aventis Pharma SA and Rhône-Poulenc Biochimie SA	2,850,000	No appeal.	
			Merck KgaA	0	No appeal.	
			Total	**2,850,000**		
30.10.02	Fine Art Auction Houses COMP/ 37.784 [2005] OJ L200/92 (2005/590/EC)	Article 81(1): Horizontal collusive cartel by fixing prices, limiting production and sharing their markets. 6 YRS and 9 MTHS.	Christie's International plc	0	No appeal.	
			Sotheby's Holding Inc.	20,400,000	No appeal.	
			Total	**20,400,000**		

Date	Commission Decision	Infringement: Type and Duration	Name of the Parties	Fine (EUR)	CFI judgment	ECJ judgment
30.10.02	Omega-Nintendo COMP/35.587, COMP/35.706 and COMP/36.321 [2003] OJ L255/33 (2003/675/EC)	Article 81(1): Vertical restricted parallel exports in Nintendo game consoles and cartridges. 2 MTHS–6 YRS.	Nintendo Corporation Ltd / Nintendo of Europe GmbH	149,128,000	Appeal pending. Case T-13/03 [2003] OJ C70/44	
			John Menzies plc	8,640,000	No appeal.	
			Concentra SA	825,000	No appeal.	
			Linea GIG SpA	1,500,000	Appeal removed. Case T-398/02 [2005] OJ C171/57	
			Nortec AE	1,000,000	No appeal.	
			Bergsala AB	1,250,000	No appeal.	
			Itochu Corporation	4,500,000	Appeal pending. Case T-12/03 [2003] OJ C55/97	
			CD-Contact Data GmbH	1,000,000	Appeal pending. Case T18/03- [2003] OJ C70/46	
			Total	**167,843,000**		
24.07.02	Industrial and medical gases COMP/36.700 [2003] OJ L84/1 (2003/207/EC) Modified by [2003] OJ L123/49 (2003/355/EC)	Article 81(1): Agreement on price increases; moratoria to implement these price increases; minimum prices and agreeing other trade conditions in the sector of industrial and medical gases in the Netherlands. 1–4 YRS.	AGA AB	4,150,000	No appeal.	
			Air Liquide BV	3,640,000	No appeal.	
			Air Products Nederland BV	2,730,000	No appeal.	
			BOC Group Plc	1,170,000	No appeal.	
			Messer Nederland BV	1,000,000	No appeal.	
			NV Hoek Loos	12,600,000	Appeal pending. Case T-304/02 [2002] OJ C305/55	
			Westfalen Gassen Nederland BV	410,000	Appeal pending. Case T-303/02 [2002] OJ C305/54	
			Total	**25,700,000**		

Date	Commission Decision	Infringement: Type and Duration	Name of the Parties	Fine (EUR)	CFI judgment	ECJ judgment
02.07.02	Methionine COMP/37.519 [2003] OJ L255/1 (2003/674/EC)	Article 81(1): Price-fixing cartel, implementation of price increases, exchange of information on sales volumes and market sharing. 12 YRS and 10 MTHS.	Aventis SA	0	No appeal.	
			Aventis Animal Nutrition SA	0	No appeal.	
			Nippon Soda Company Ltd	9,000,000	No appeal.	
			Degussa AG	118,125,000	Appeal pending. Case T-279/02 [2002] OJ C274/62	
			Total	**127,125,000**		
11.06.02	Austrian Banks ("Lombard Club") COMP/36.571 [2004] OJ L056/1 (2004/138/EC)	Article 81(1): Horizontal price-fixing cartel, fixing of interest rates, transfers and export financing. 3–4 YRS.	Erste Bank der österreichischen Sparkassen AG ("Erste")	37,690,000	Appeal pending. Case T-264/02 [2002] OJ C274/55	
			Bank Austria Aktiengesellschaft ("BA")	30,380,000	Appeal pending. Case T-260/02 2002 OJ C274/51	
			Raiffeisen Zentralbank Österreich AG ("RZB")	30,380,000	Appeal pending. Case T-259/02 [2002] OJ C274/50	
			Bank für Arbeit und Wirtschaft Aktiengesellschaft ("BAWAG")	7,590,000	Appeal pending. Case T-261/02 [2002] OJ C274/52	
			Österreichische Postsparkasse Aktiengesellschaft ("PSK")	7,590,000	Appeal pending. Case T-263/02 [2002] OJ C274/54	
			Österreichische Volksbanken AG ("ÖVAG")	7,590,000		
			NÖ Landesbank-Hypothekenbank AG ("NÖ Hypo")	1,520,000	Appeal pending. Case 271/02 [2002] OJ C274/59	
			Raiffeisenlandesbank Niederösterreich-Wien reg Gen mbH (("RLB")	1,520,000	Appeal pending. Case 262/02 [2002] OJ C274/53	
			Total	**124,260,000**		

Date	Commission Decision	Infringement: Type and Duration	Name of the Parties	Fine (EUR)	CFI judgment	ECJ judgment
20.12.01	Carbonless paper (CLP) COMP/36.212 [2004] OJ L115/1 (2004/337/EC)	Article 81(1):Horizontal price fixing and market sharing agreements in the carbonless paper industry. 1–4 YRS.	Arjo Wiggins Appleton Limited	184,270,000	Appeal pending, Case T-118/02 [2002] OJ C169/61	
			Bolloré SA	22,680,000	Appeal pending, Case T-109/02 [2002] OJ C131/46	
			Carrs Paper Ltd	1,570,000	Appeal pending, Case T-123/02 [2002] OJ C169/64	
			Distribuidora Vizcaina de Papeles S.L.	1,750,000	Appeal pending, Case T-132/02 [2002] OJ C144/120	
			Mitsubishi HiTech Paper Bielefeld GmbH	21,240,000	Appeal pending, Case T-122/02 [2002] OJ C169/63	
			Papelera Guipozcoana de Zicuñaga SA	1,540,000	Appeal pending, Case T-136/02 [2002] OJ C156/68	
			Papeteries Mougeot SA	3,640,000	Appeal pending, Case T-128/02 [2002] OJ C144/119	
			Papierfabrik August Koehler AG	33,070,000	Appeal pending, Case T-125/02 [2002] OJ C144/116	
			Sappi Limited	0	No appeal.	
			Torraspapel SA	14,170,000	Appeal pending, Case T-129/02 [2002] OJ C169/65	
			Zanders Feninpapiere AG	29,760,000	Appeal pending, Case T-126/02 [2002] OJ C144/117	
			Total	**313,690,000**		

Date	Commission Decision	Infringement: Type and Duration	Name of the Parties	Fine (EUR)	CFI judgment	ECJ judgment
11.12.01	Bank charges for exchanging euro-zone currencies- Germany COMP/37.919 [2003] OJ L15/1 (2003/25/EC)	Article 81(1): Agreement on fixing the way of charging for the exchange of in-currency banknotes, and a target price level of about 3%. 4 YRS.	Commerzbank AG	28,000,000	Decision annulled. Case T-61/02 [2004] OJ C314/37	
			Dresdner Bank AG	28,000,000	Decision annulled. Case T-44/02 [2004] OJ C314/33	
			Bayerische Hypo- und Vereinsbank AG	28,000,000	Decision annulled. Case T-56/02 [2004] OJ C314/35	
			Deutsche VerkehrsBank AG	14,000,000	Decision annulled. Case T-60/02 [2004] OJ C314/36	
			Vereins- und Westbank AG	2,800,000	Decision annulled. Case T-54/02 [2004] OJ C314/34	
			Total	**100,800,000**		
11.12.01	Zinc Phosphate COMP/37.027 [2003] OJ L153/1 (2003/437/EC)	Article 81(1): Horizontal price fixing and market sharing cartel in zinc phosphate. 1–4 YRS.	Britannia Alloys and Chemicals Limited	3,370,000	Appeal dismissed. Case T-33/02 (Judgement 29.11.2005)	
			Dr Hans Heubach GmbH & Co. KG	3,780,000	Appeal dismissed. Case T-64/02 (Judgement 29.11.2005)	
			James M. Brown Limited	940,000	No appeal.	
			Société Nouvelle des Couleurs Zinciques SA	1,530,000	Appeal dismissed. Case T-52/02 (Judgement 29.11.2005)	
			Trident Alloys Limited	1,980,000	No appeal.	
			Waardals Kjemiske Fabrikker A/S	350,000	Appeal dismissed. Case T-62/02 (Judgement 29.11.2005)	
			Total	**11,950,000**		

Date	Commission Decision	Infringement: Type and Duration	Name of the Parties	Fine (EUR)	CFI judgment	ECJ judgment
05.12.01	Interbrew and Alken-Maes COMP/37.614 [2003] OJ L200/1 (2003/569/EC)	Article 81(1): General non-aggression pact, prices and promotions in the off-trade, customer sharing in the on-trade, restriction of investment and advertising, new pricing structure and exchange of information about sales. 5 YRS.	Interbrew NV Groupe Danone _Total_	45,675,000 44,043,000 **89,718,000**	No appeal. Fine reduced to 42,412,500. Case T-38/02 (Judgement 25.10.2005)	
		Article 81(1): Concerted practice concerning prices, customer sharing and exchange of information with regard to private-label beer in Belgium. 9 MTHS.	Interbrew NV Brouwerijen Alken-Maes NV NV Brouwerij Haacht NV Brouwerij Martens _Total_	812,000 585,000 270,000 270,000 **1,937,000**	No appeal. No appeal. Appeal dismissed. Case T-48/02 (Judgement 06.12.2005) No appeal.	
05.12.01	Luxembourg Brewers COMP/37.800 [2002] OJ L253/21 (2002/759/EC)	Article 81(1):Horizontal collusion maintaining respective clienteles in the Luxembourg on-trade and impeding penetration of that sector by foreign brewers. 14–15 YRS.	Brasserie de Luxembourg Mousel-Diekirch SA Brasserie Nationale-Bofferding Brasserie Jules Simon et Cie SCS (Wiltz) Brasserie Battin SNC _Total_	0 400,000 24,000 24,000 **448,000**	No appeal. Appeal dismissed. Case T-49/02 Judgment 27 July 2005 (not yet published) Appeal dismissed. Case T-50/02 Judgment 27 July 2005 (not yet published) Appeal dismissed. Case T-51/02 Judgment 27 July 2005 (not yet published)	

Date	Commission Decision	Infringement: Type and Duration	Name of the Parties	Fine (EUR)	CFI judgment	ECJ judgment
05.12.01	De Post-La Poste COMP/37.859 [2002] OJ L61/32 (2002/180/EC)	Article 82: Abuse of dominant position by making an agreement granting the preferential tariff for business-to private mail covered by the monopoly subject to the acceptance, by recipients of that benefit, of supplementary obligations as regards to business-to-business mail. 2–3 YRS.	De Post-La Poste	2,500,000	No appeal.	
			Total	**2,500,000**		
05.12.01	Citric acid COMP/36.604 [2002] OJ L239/18 (2002/742/EC)	Article 81(1): Price-fixing and market-sharing cartel in citric acid. 3–4 YRS.	Archer Daniels Midland Company Inc.	39,690,000	Appeal pending, Case T-59/02 [2002] OJ C144/99	
			Cerestar Bioproducts BV	170,000	No appeal.	
			F. Hoffmann-La Roche AG	63,500,000	No appeal.	
			Haarmann & Reimer Corporation	14,220,000	No appeal.	
			Jungbunzlaver AG	17,640,000	Appeal pending, Case T-43/02 [2002] OJ C97/30	
			Total	**135,220,000**		

Date	Commission Decision	Infringement: Type and Duration	Name of the Parties	Fine (EUR)	CFI judgment	ECJ judgment
21.11.01	Vitamins COMP/37.512 [2003] OJ L6/1 (2003/2/EC)	Article 81(1): Price-fixing and market-sharing affecting vitamin products. 3–9 YRS.	F. Hoffmann-La Roche AG	462,000,000	No appeal.	
			BASF AG	296,160,000	Appeal pending. Case T-15/02 [2002] OJ C109/97	
			Aventis SA	5,040,000	No appeal.	
			Takeda Chemical Industries Ltd	37,060,000	No appeal.	
			Merck KgaA	9,240,000	No appeal.	
			Daiichi Pharmaceutical Co. Ltd	23,400,000	Appeal pending. Case T-26/02 [2002] OJ C97/27	
			Lonza AG	0	No appeal.	
			Solvay Pharmaceuticals BV	9,100,000	No appeal.	
			Eisai Co. Ltd	13,230,000	No appeal.	
			Kongo Chemical Co. Ltd	0	No appeal.	
			Sumitomo Chemical Co. Ltd	0	Anulment of Commission Decision in so far as it concerns the applicant. Case T-22/02 OJ C 296/05.	
			Sumika Fine Chemicals Ltd	0	Anulment of Commission Decision in so far as it concerns the applicants. Case T-23/02 OJ C 296/05.	
			Tanabe Seiyaku Co. Ltd	0	No appeal.	
			Total	855,230,000		

Date	Commission Decision	Infringement: Type and Duration	Name of the Parties	Fine (EUR)	CFI judgment	ECJ judgment
10.10.01	Mercedes-Benz COMP/36.264	Article 81(1): Restriction of parallel trade	Mercedes Benz	71,825,000	Fine reduced to 9,800,000. Case T-325/01 (Judgement 15.09.2005).	
			Total	71,825,000		
02.10.01	Sodium Gluconate COMP/ 36.756 (IP/01/1355)	Article 81(1): Price-fixing and market-sharing for sodium gluconate. 1987–1995.	Archer Daniels Midland Company Inc.	10,130,000	Appeal pending. Case T-329/01 [2002] OJ C84/115	
			Akzo Nobel N.V.	9,000,000	Appeal pending. Case T-330/01 [2002] OJ C68/28	
			Avebe B.A.	3,600,000	Appeal pending. Case T-314/01 [2002] OJ C68/23	
			Fujisawa Pharmaceutical Company Ltd.	3,600,000	No appeal.	
			Roquette Frères S.A.	10,800,000	Appeal pending. Case T-322/01 [2002] OJ C68/25	
			Total	37,130,000		
25.07.01	Deutsche Post AG–Interception of cross-border mail COMP/36.915 [2001] OJ L331/40 (2001/892/EC)	Article 82:Abusive dominant position by intercepting, surcharging and delaying incoming cross-border letter mailings from the UK sent by senders outside Germany but containing a reference in its contents to an entity residing in Germany. 1996–1999.	Deutsche Post AG	1,000	No appeal.	
			Total	1,000		
18.07.01	SAS Maersk Air and Sun-Air versus SAS and Maersk Air COMP/37.444 and 37.386 [2001] OJ L265/15 (2001/716/EC)	Article 81(1): Overall market-sharing agreement -according to which SAS would not operate on Maersk Air's routes-, and specific market-sharing agreements regarding individual international routes. 2 YRS and 5 MTHS.	SAS, Scandinavian Airlines System	39,375,000	Appeal dismissed. Case T-241/01 Judgment 18 July 2005 (not yet published)	
			Maersk Air A/S	13,125,000	No appeal.	
			Total	52,500,000		

Date	Commission Decision	Infringement: Type and Duration	Name of the Parties	Fine (EUR)	CFI judgment	ECJ judgment
18.07.01	Graphite electrodes COMP/36.490 [2002] OJ L100/1 (2002/271/EC)	Article 81(1): Horizontal fixing price and marker-sharing in the graphite electrodes sector. 3–5 YRS.	SGL Carbon AG.	80,200,000	Fine reduced to 69,114,000. Case T-239/01 [2004] OJ C251/24	SGL Appeal pending. Case C-308/04 P [2004] OJ C262/26 Commission appeal pending Case C-301/04 P [2004] OJ C262/25
			GrafTech International (ex-UCAR)	50,400,000	Fine Reduced to 42,050,000. Case T-246/01 [2004] OJ C251/24 Removal from the Register [2004] OJ C118/115	
			VAW Aluminium AG	11,600,000	No appeal.	
			Showa Denko K.K.	17,400,000	Fine Reduced to 10,440,000. Case T-245/01 [2004] OJ C251/24	Appeal pending. Case C-289/04 P [2004] OJ C239/01
			Tokai Carbon Co. Ltd.	24,500,000	Fine Reduced to 12,276,000. Case T-236/01 [2004] OJ C251/24	
			Nippon Carbon Co. Ltd.	12,200,000	Fine Reduced to 6,274,400. Case T-244/01 [2004] OJ C251/24	
			SEC Corporation	12,200,000	Fine Reduced to 6,138,000. Case T-251/01 [2004] OJ C251/24	Appeal pending. Case C-307/04 P [2004] OJ C239/02
			The Carbide Graphite Group Inc.	10,300,000	Fine Reduced to 6,480,000. Case T-252/01 [2004] OJ C251/24	
			Total	**218,800,000**		

Date	Commission Decision	Infringement: Type and Duration	Name of the Parties	Fine (EUR)		CFI judgment	ECJ judgment
29.06.01	Volkswagen COMP/36.693 [2001] OJ L262/14 (2001/711/EC)	Article 81(1): Fixing retail prices of the VW Passat on the German market. 3 YRS.	Volkswagen AG		30,960,000	Decision annulled. Case T-208/01 [2003] ECR II-05141	Appeal pending. Case C-74/04 P [2004] OJ C94/51
				Total	30,960,000		
20.06.01	Michelin COMP/36.041 [2001] OJ L143/1 (2002/405/EC)	Article 82: Abusive dominant position by applying a system of loyalty-inducing rebates to dealers in replacement tyres for heavy vehicles in France. 9 YRS.	Michelin		19,760,000	Appeal dismissed. Case T-203/01 [2003] ECR II-04071	No appeal.
				Total	19,760,000		
20.03.01	Deutsche Post AG COMP/35.141 [2001] OJ L125/27 (2001/354/EC)	Article 82: Abuse of dominant position by granting a special price to customers for mail-order parcel services. 1974–2000.	Deutsche Post AG		24,000,000	No appeal.	
				Total	24,000,000		

Date	Commission Decision	Infringement: Type and Duration	Name of the Parties	Fine (EUR)	CFI judgment	ECJ judgment
13.12.00	Soda ash–Solvay COMP/39.004 (ex 33.133 C) [2003] OJ L10/10 (2003/6/EC)	Article 82: Abuse of dominant position through rebates and tying. 1983–1990.	Solvay SA	20,000,000	Appeal pending. Case T-57/01 [2001] OJ C161/45	
			Total	**20,000,000**		
13.12.00	Soda ash–ICI COMP/39.046 (ex 33.133D) [2003] OJ L10/33 (2003/7/EC)	Article 82: Abuse of dominant position in the market for soda ash (in the United Kingdom) through rebates and tying. 1983–1990.	Imperial Chemical Industries	10,000,000	Appeal pending. Case T-66/01. [2001] OJ C150/64	
			Total	**10,000,000**		
13.12.00	Soda ash–Solvay-CFK COMP/39.003 (ex 33.133 B) [2003] OJ L10/1 (2003/5/EC)	Article 81(1): Market-sharing agreement by which Solvay guaranteed to CFK a minimum annual sales tonnage of soda ash in Germany. 1987–1990.	Solvay SA	3,000,000	Appeal pending. Case T-58/01. [2001] OJ C161/46	
			Total	**3,000,000**		
20.09.00	Opel COMP/36.653 [2001] OJ L59/1 (2001/146/EC)	Article 81(1): Vertical agreements with dealers in the Opel distribution network in the Netherlands, in order to restrict or prohibit exports of new cars to other Member States. 17 MTHS.	Opel Nederland BV General Motors Nederland BV	43,000,000	Fine reduced to 35,475,000. Case T-368/00 [2003] ECR II-04491	Appeal pending. C-551/03 P [2004] OJ C71/12
			Total	**43,000,000**		

Date	Commission Decision	Infringement: Type and Duration	Name of the Parties	Fine (EUR)	CFI judgment	ECJ judgment
05.07.00	Nathan–Bricolux COMP/36.516 [2001] OJ L54/1 2001/135/EC	Article 81(1): Restrictions concerning passive sales, the freedom to fix prices and commercial resale conditions. 1993–1998.	Editions Nathan Bricolux SA	60,000 1,000	No appeal. No appeal.	
			Total	**61,000**		
07.06.00	Amino Acids COMP/36.545 [2001] OJ L152/24 (2001/418/EC)	Article 81(1): Participation in agreements on prices, sales volumes and the exchange of individual information on sales volumes of synthetic lysine, covering the whole of the EEA. 1990–1995.	Archer Daniels Midland Company and Archer Daniels Midland Ingredients Limited	47,300,000	Fine reduced to 43,875,000. Case T-224/00 [2003] ECR II-02597	Appeal pending. Case C-397/03 P [2003] OJ C275/50
			Ajinomoto Company, Incorporated and Eurolysine SA	28,300,000	No appeal.	
			Kyowa Hakko Kogyo Company Limited and Kyowa Hakko Europe GmbH	13,200,000	Appeal dismissed. Case T-223/00 [2003] ECR II-02553	No appeal.
			Daesang Corporation and Sewon Europe GmbH	8,900,000	Fine reduced to 7,128,240. Case T-230/00 [2003] ECR II-02733	No appeal.
			Cheil Jedang Corporation	12,200,000	Fine reduced to 10,080,000. Case T-220/00 [2003] ECR II-02473	No appeal.
			Total	**109,900,000**		

Date	Commission Decision	Infringement: Type and Duration	Name of the Parties	Fine (EUR)	CFI judgment	ECJ judgment
16.05.00	Far East Trade Tariff Charges and Surcharges Agreement (FETTCSA) COMP/ 34.018 [2000] OJ L268/1 (2000/ 627/ EC)	Article 81(1): Agreement not to discount from published tariffs for charges and surcharges entered into between the former members of the FETTCSA. 3 MTHS.	CMA CGM SA	134,000		
			Hapag-Lloyd Container Linie GmbH	368,000		
			Kawasaki Kisen Kaisha Limited	620,000		
			A.P. Møller–Maersk Sealand	836,000		
			Malaysia International Shipping Corporation Berhad	134,000		
			Mitsui OSK Lines Ltd	620,000		
			Neptune Orient Lines Ltd	368,000		
			Nippon Yusen Kaisha	620,000	Case T-213/00 Annulled Article 4 (Fines) of Commission Decision [2003] ECR II-00913	Appeal pending. Case C-236/03 P. [2003] OJ C184/39
			Orient Overseas Container Line Ltd	134,000		
			P & O Nedlloyd Container Line Ltd	1,240,000		
			Cho Yang Shipping Co. Ltd	134,000		
			DSR-Senator Lines GmbH	368,000		
			Evergreen Marine Corp. (Taiwan) Ltd	368,000		
			Hanjin Shipping Co. Ltd	620,000		
			Yangming Marine Transport Corp.	368,000		
			Total	**6,932,000**		

Date	Commission Decision	Infringement: Type and Duration	Name of the Parties	Fine (EUR)	CFI judgment	ECJ judgment
14.12.99	Anheuser-Busch Incorporated–Scottish and Newcastle COMP/34.237 [2000] OJ L49/37 (2000/146/EC)	Article 15(1) of Council Regulation No 17: Supplying negligently incorrect information to the Commission in response to a request made pursuant to Article 11 of Reg. 17.	Anheuser-Busch Incorporated	3,000	No appeal.	
			Anheuser-Busch European Trade Limited	0	No appeal.	
			Scottish & Newcastle plc.	3,000	No appeal.	
			Total	**6,000**		
08.12.99	Seamless steel tubes COMP/35.860 [2003] OJ L140/1 (2003/382/EC)	Article 81(1): Agreement for the observance of the respective domestic markets for seamless standard threaded OCTG pipes and tubes and project line pipe. 1990–1999.	Mannesmannröhren-Werke AG	13,500,000	Fine reduced to 12,600,000. Case T-44/00 [2004] OJ C239/24	Appeal pending Case C-411/04 P [2004] OJ C273/45
			Corus UK Ltd (formerly British Steel Ltd)	12,600,000	Fine reduced to 11,700,000. Case T-48/00 [2004] OJ C239/25	No appeal.
			JFE Engineering Corp. (formerly NKK Corporation)	13,500,000	Fine reduced to 10,935,000. Case T-67/00 [2004] OJ C239/27	No appeal.
			Nippon Steel Corporation	13,500,000	Fine reduced to 10,935,000. Case T-68/00 [2004] OJ C239/27	Appeal pending Case C-405/04 P [2004] OJ C284/20
			Kawasaki Steel Corporation	13,500,000	Fine reduced to 10,935,000. Case T-71/00 [2004] OJ C239/27	No appeal.
			Sumitomo Metal Industries Limited	13,500,000	Fine reduced to 10,935,000. Case T-78/00 [2004] OJ C239/27	Appeal pending Case C-403/04 P [2004] OJ C284/19
			Vallourec SA	8,100,000	No appeal.	
			Dalmine SpA	10,800,000	Fine reduced to 10,080,000. Case T-50/00 [2004] OJ C239/26	Appeal pending Case C-407/04 P [2004] OJ C300/51
			Total	**99,000,000**		

Date	Commission Decision	Infringement: Type and Duration	Name of the Parties	Fine (EUR)	CFI judgment	ECJ judgment
26.10.99	FEG & TU COMP/33.884 [2000] OJ L39/1 (2000/117/EC)	Article 81(1): Collective exclusive dealing agreement intended to prevent supplies to non-members of the FEG, on the basis of an agreement with NAVEG, and of practices concerted with suppliers not represented in NAVEG-; restriction of the freedom of the members to determine their selling prices independently. 4 – 15 YRS.	De Nederlandse Federatieve Vereniging voor de Groothandel op Elektrotechnisch Gebied (FEG) De Technische Unie BV (TU)	4,400,000 2,150,000	Appeal dismissed. Cases T-5/00 & T-6/00 [2003] ECR II-05761 Appeal dismissed. Cases T-5/00 & T-6/00 [2003] ECR II-05761	Appeal pending. Case C-105/04 P [2004] OJ C106/44 Appeal pending. Case C-113/04 P [2004] OJ C106/49
			Total	6,550,000		
20.07.99	1998 Football World Cup COMP/36.888 [2000] OJ L5/55 (2000/12/EC)	Article 82: Abuse of dominant position by applying discriminatory arrangements relating to sales to the general public of entry tickets for World Cup finals matches. 1996–1997.	Comité Français d'Organisation de la Coupe du Monde de Football 1998 (CFO)	1,000	No appeal.	
			Total	1,000		

Date	Commission Decision	Infringement: Type and Duration	Name of the Parties	Fine (EUR)	CFI judgment	ECJ judgment
14.07.99	Virgin/British Airways COMP/34.780 [2000] OJ L30/1 (2000/74/EC)	Article 82: Abuse of dominant position by operating systems incentives with the travel agents in the United Kingdom. 7 YRS.	British Airways plc.	6,800,000	Appeal dismissed. Case T-219/99. [2003] ECR II-05917	Appeal pending. Case C-95/04 P [2004] OJ C106/40
			Total	**6,800,000**		
			Minoan Lines	3,260,000	Appeal dismissed. Case T-66/99 [2003] ECR II-05515	Appeal pending. Case C-121/04 P [2004] OJ C106/56
			Strintzis Lines	1,500,000	Appeal dismissed. Case T-65/99. [2003] ECR II-05433	Appeal pending. Case C-110/04 P [2004] OJ C106/46
09.12.98	Greek Ferries COMP/34.466 [1999] OJ L109/24 (1999/271/EC)	Article 85(1) – (now Art. 81(1)):Horizontal price fixing cartel. 1987–1994.	Anek Lines	1,110,000	No appeal.	Appeal pending. Case C-112/04 P [2004] OJ C106/48
			Marlines SA	260,000	Appeal dismissed. Case T-56/99 [2003] ECR II-05225	
			Karageorgis Lines	1,000,000	No appeal.	No appeal.
			Ventouris Group Enterprises SA	1,010,000	Fine reduced to 252,500 Case T-59/99 [2003] ECR II-05257	
			Adriatica di Navigazione SpA	980,000	Fine reduced to 245,000 Case T-61/99. [2003] ECR II-05349	Appeal pending. Case C-111/04 P [2004] OJ C106/47
			Total	**9,120,000**		

Date	Commission Decision	Infringement: Type and Duration	Name of the Parties	Fine (EUR)	CFI judgment	ECJ judgment
			ABB Asea Brown Boveri Ltd	70,000,000	Fine reduced to 65.000.000 Case T-31/99 [2002] ECR II-01881	Appeal dismissed. Case C-213/02 P [2005] OJ C205/01
			Brugg Rohrsysteme GmbH	925,000	Appeal dismissed and fine upheld. Case T-15/99 [2002] ECR II-01613	Appeal dismissed. Case C-207/02 P [2005] OJ C205/01
			Dansk Rørindustri A/S	1,475,000	Annuls Art. 1 of Commission Decision but upholds fine. Case T-21/99 [2002] ECR II-01681	Appeal dismissed. Case C-189/02 P [2005] OJ C205/01
		Article 85(1)– (now Art. 81(1)):	Henss/Isoplus Group	4,950,000	Annuls Article 3(d) (fine) of Commission Decision. Case T-9/99 [2002] ECR II-01487	Appeal dismissed Case C-202/02 P [2005] OJ C205/01
21.10.98	Pre-Insulated Pipe Cartel COMP/35.691 [1999] OJ L24/1	Horizontal cartel dividing national markets; allocating national markets to particular producers; agreeing on prices. 1990–1996.	Ke-Kelit Kunststoffwerk GmbH	360,000	Appeal dismissed. Case T-17/99 [2002] ECR II-01647	Appeal dismissed. Case C-205/02 P [2005] OJ C205/01
	(1999)/60/EC)		Oy KWH Tech AB	700,000	No appeal.	
			LR AF 1998 A/S (formerly Løgstør Rør A/S)	8,900,000	Appeal dismissed. Case T-23/99 [2002] ECR II-01705	Appeal dismissed. Case C-206/02 P [2005] OJ C205/01
			LR AF 1998 GmbH (formerly Lögstör Rör A/S)		Case T-16/99 [2002] ECR II-01633	Appeal dismissed. Case C-208/02 P [2005] OJ C205/01
			Pan-Isovit GmbH	1,500,000	No appeal.	
			Sigma Tecnologie Di Rivestimento S.r.l.	400,000	Fine reduced to 300,000. Case T-28/99 [2002] ECR II-01845	No appeal.
			Tarco Energi A/S	3,000,000	No appeal.	
			Total	**92,210,000**		

Date	Commission Decision	Infringement: Type and Duration	Name of the Parties	Fine (EUR)	CFI judgment	ECJ judgment
14.10.98	British Sugar COMP/ 33.708; 33.709; 33.710; 33.711 [1999] OJ L76/ 1 (1999/210/EC)	Article 85(1)– (now Art. 81(1)): Horizontal cartel on prices for industrial sugar in Great Britain. 1986–1990.	British Sugar plc	39,600,000	Appeal dismissed and fine upheld. Case T-204/98. [2001] ECR II-02035	Appeal dismissed. Case C-359/01 P [2004] ECR I-04933
			Tate & Lyle plc	7,000,000	Fine reduced to 5,600,000. Case T-202/98 [2001] ECR II-02035	Appeal dismissed and fine upheld. Case C-359/01 P [2004] ECR I-04933
			Napier Brown & Company Ltd	1,800,000	Appeal dismissed and fine upheld. Case T-207/98. [2001] ECR II-02035	Appeal dismissed. Case C-359/01 P [2004] ECR I-04933
			James Budgett Sugars Ltd	1,800,000	No appeal.	
			Total	50,200,000		

Date	Commission Decision	Infringement: Type and Duration	Name of the Parties	Fine (EUR)	CFI judgment	ECJ judgment
16.09.98	Trans-Atlantic Conference Agreement - TACA COMP/35.134 [1999] OJ L95/1 (1999/243/EC)	Article 85(1)–(now Art. 81(1)): Horizontal cartel on prices and in terms and conditions on and under which they may enter into service contracts with shippers; and by fixing the amounts, levels or rates of brokerage and freight-forwarder remuneration.Article 86–(now Article 82):Abuse of dominant position by placing restrictions on the availability and contents of service contracts. 2–3YRS.	A.P. Møller–Maersk Sealand	27,500,000		
			Atlantic Container Line AB	6,880,000		
			Hapag-Lloyd Container Linie GmbH	20,630,000		
			P&O Nedlloyd Container Line Limited	41,260,000		
			Sea-Land Service, Inc.	27,500,000		
			Mediterranean Shipping Co. SA	13,750,000		
			Orient Overseas Container Line (UK) Ltd	20,630,000	Fine upheld for one abuse and annulled the imposition of fines for the other abuse. Joined Cases T-191/98, T-212/98, T-213/98 and T-214/98. [2003] ECR II-03275	No appeal.
			Polish Ocean Lines	6,880,000		
			DSR/Senator Lines GmbH	13,750,000		
			Cho Yang Shipping Co., Ltd	13,750,000		
			Neptune Orient Lines Ltd	13,750,000		
			Nippon Yusen Kaisha	20,630,000		
			Transportación Marítima Mexicana S.A. de CV/ Tecomar S.A. de CV	6,880,000		
			Hanjin Shipping Co., Ltd	20,630,000		
			Hyundai Merchant Marine Co., Ltd	18,560,000		
			Total	**272,980,000**		

Date	Commission Decision	Infringement: Type and Duration	Name of the Parties	Fine (EUR)	CFI judgment	ECJ judgment
17.06.98	AAMS COMP/36.010 [1998] OJ L252/47 (1998/538/EC)	Article 86–(now Art. 82): Abuse of dominant position on the Italian market for cigarettes through distribution contracts and through unilateral practices. 7 – 13 YRS.	Amministrazione Autonoma dei Monopoli di Stato	6,000,000	Appeal dismissed. Case T-139/98. [2001] ECR II-03413	No appeal.
			Total	6,000,000		
28.01.98	VW-Audi COMP/35.733 [1998] OJ L124/60 (1998/273/EC)	Article 85(1)–(now Art. 81(1)): Vertical agreements with the Italian dealers in order to prohibit or restrict sales to final customers coming from another Member State. 10 YRS.	Volkswagen AG	102,000,000	Fine reduced to 90,000,000 Case T-62/98 [2000] ECR II-02707	Main and cross-appeal dismissed. Case C-338/00 P [2003] ECR I-09189
			Total	102,000,000		

Date	Commission Decision	Infringement: Type and Duration	Name of the Parties	Fine (EUR)	CFI judgment	ECJ judgment
21.01.98	Alloy surcharge COMP/ 35.814 [1998] OJ L100/55 (98/247/ ECSC)	Article 85(1)—(now Art. 81(1)): Agreement on reference values to calculate the alloy surcharge, having both the object and the effect of restricting and distorting competition within the common market. 3 – 5 YRS.	Acenirox SA	3,530,000	Fine reduced to 3,136,000. Case T-48/98 [2001] ECR II-03859	Fine upheld. Case C-57/02 Judgment 14 July 2005 (not yet published)
			ALZ NV	4,540,000	Appeal removed from the register. CaseT-49/98 [1998] OJ C299/72	
			ThyssenKrupp Acciai speciali Terni SpA (formerly Acciai Speciali Terni SpA)	4,540,000	Fine reduced to 4,032,000. Case T-47/98 [2001] ECR II-03757	Appeals and cross-appeal dismissed. Case C-73/02 Judgment 14 July 2005 (not yet published)
			ThyssenKrupp Stainless GmbH (formerly Krupp Thyssen Nirosta GmbH)	8,100,000	Fine reduced to 4,032,000. Case T-45/98 [2001] ECR II-03757	Appeals and cross-appeal dismissed. Case C-65/02 Judgment 14 July 2005 (not yet published)
			Avesta Sheffield AB	2,810,000	No appeal.	
			Usinor SA	3,860,000	No appeal.	
			Total	**27,380,000**		
26.11.97	Wirtschaft-svereinigung Stahl COMP/ 36.069 [1998] OJ L1/ 10 (98/4ECSC)	Article 65 ECSC Treaty: Information exchange agreement. 1996.	Wirtschaftsvereinigung Stahl	0		
			AG der Dillinger Hüttenwerke	0		
			EKO Stahl GmbH	0		
			Krupp Hoesch Stahl AG	0		
			Krupp Thyssen Nirosta GmbH	0	Commission decision annulled. Case T-16/98 [2001] ECR II-01217	No appeal.
			Preussag Stahl AG	0		
			Stahlwerke Bremen GmbH	0		
			Thyssen Stahl AG	0		
			Total	**0**		

Date	Commission Decision	Infringement: Type and Duration	Name of the Parties	Fine (EUR)	CFI judgment	ECJ judgment
14.05.97	Irish Sugar COMP/ 34.621, 35.059 [1997] OJ L258/1 (97/624/EC)	Article 86: Abuse of dominant position on the granulated sugar market for retail and industrial sale in Ireland. 1985–1995.	Irish Sugar plc	8,800,000	Fine reduced to 7,883,326. Case T-228/97 [1999] ECR II-02969 Annulment of the decision of 11.02.02, by which the Commission refused to grant the applicant's request for default interest to be paid to Irish Sugar plc on the principal sum repaid to comply with the judgement in Case T-228/97. Case T-135/02 (Judgement 14.12.05).	Appeal dismissed. Case C-497/99 [2001] ECR I-05333
			Total	**8,800,000**		
04.12.96	Novalliance/ Systemform COMP/35.679 [1997] OJ L47/11 (97/123/EC)	Article 85(1)– (now Art. 81(1)): Vertical export ban and restrictions on resale prices in its contracts with distributors. 1983–1986.	Systemform GmbH	100,000	No appeal.	
			Total	**100,000**		
30.10.96	Ferry Operators COMP/34.503 [1997] OJ L26/23 (97/84/EC)	Article 85(1)– (now Art. 81(1)): Concerted practice by which the leading roll-on roll-off ferry operators in the UK-Continent freight market contacted each other secretly so as to discuss and determine their reaction to the devaluation of sterling. 3 MTHS.	P&O European Ferries Stena Line UK (Stena Sealink) Sea France (SNAT) Brittany Ferries North Sea Ferries	400,000 100,000 60,000 60,000 25,000	No appeal. No appeal. No appeal. No appeal. No appeal.	
			Total	**645,000**		

Date	Commission Decision	Infringement: Type and Duration	Name of the Parties	Fine (EUR)	CFI judgment	ECJ judgment
05.06.96	Fenex COMP/34.983 [1996] OJ L181/28 (96/438/EC)	Article 85(1)–(now Art. 81(1)): Drawing up and circulating recommended forwarding tariffs to members of association. 4 YRS and 6 MTHS.	Nederlandse Organisatie voor Expeditie en Logistiek (Fenex)	1,000	No appeal.	
			Total	**1,000**		
10.01.96	ADALAT COMP/34.279 [1996] OJ L201/1 (96/478/EC)	Article 85(1)–(now Art. 81(1)): Vertical export ban, and restrictions on parallel exports of the products ADALATE 20 mg LP from France and on that of the products ADALAT and ADALAT-Retard from Spain. 1989–1992.	Bayer AG	3,000,000	Commission Decision annulled. Case T-41/96 [2000] ECR II-03383	Appeal dismissed. Cases C-2/01 P and C-3/01 P [2004] ECR I-00023
			Total	**3,000,000**		
29.11.95	SCK/FNK COMP/34.179; 34.202, 216 [1995] OJ L312/79 (95/551/EC)	Article 85(1)–(now Art. 81(1)): FNK by applying a system of recommended and internal rates; SCK by prohibiting its affiliated firms from hiring cranes not affiliated to SCK. FNK: 1979–1992. SCK: 1991–1993.	Stichting Certificatie Kraanverhuurbedrijf (SCK) Federatie van Nederlandse Kraanverhuurbedrijven (FNK)	300,000 11,500,000	Fine reduced to 100,000. Case T-213/95 [1997] ECR II-01739 Appeal dismissed and fine upheld. Case T-18/96 [1997] ECR II-01739	No appeal. No appeal.
			Total	**11,800,000**		

Part II

MERGER CONTROL
(REGULATION (EC) 139/2004)

APPENDIX 15

Council Regulation (EC) No 139/2004 of 20 January 2004 on the control of concentrations between undertakings (the EC Merger Regulation)

(Text with EEA relevance)

THE COUNCIL OF THE EUROPEAN UNION,

Having regard to the Treaty establishing the European Community, and in particular Articles 83 and 308 thereof,

Having regard to the proposal from the Commission,[1]

Having regard to the opinion of the European Parliament,[2]

Having regard to the opinion of the European Economic and Social Committee,[3]

Whereas:

(1) Council Regulation (EEC) No 4064/89 of 21 December 1989 on the control of concentrations between undertakings[4] has been substantially amended. Since further amendments are to be made, it should be recast in the interest of clarity.

(2) For the achievement of the aims of the Treaty, Article 3(1)(g) gives the Community the objective of instituting a system ensuring that competition in the internal market is not distorted. Article 4(1) of the Treaty provides that the activities of the Member States and the Community are to be conducted in accordance with the principle of an open market economy with free competition. These principles are essential for the further development of the internal market.

(3) The completion of the internal market and of economic and monetary union, the enlargement of the European Union and the lowering of international barriers to trade and investment will continue to result in major corporate reorganisations, particularly in the form of concentrations.

(4) Such reorganisations are to be welcomed to the extent that they are in line with the requirements of dynamic competition and capable of increasing the competitiveness of European industry, improving the conditions of growth and raising the standard of living in the Community.

(5) However, it should be ensured that the process of reorganisation does not result in lasting damage to competition; Community law must therefore include provisions governing those concentrations which may significantly impede effective competition in the common market or in a substantial part of it.

(6) A specific legal instrument is therefore necessary to permit effective control of all concentrations in terms of their effect on the structure of competition in the Community and to be

---

[1] OJ C20, 28.1.2003, p 4.

[2] Opinion delivered on 9.10.2003 (not yet published in the Official Journal).

[3] Opinion delivered on 24.10.2003 (not yet published in the Official Journal).

[4] OJ L395, 30.12.1989, p 1. Corrected version in OJ L257, 21.9.1990, p 13. Regulation as last amended by Regulation (EC) No 1310/97 (O) L180, 9.7.1997, p 1). Corrigendum in OJ L40, 13.2.1998, p 17.

the only instrument applicable to such concentrations. Regulation (EEC) No 4064/89 has allowed a Community policy to develop in this field. In the light of experience, however, that Regulation should now be recast into legislation designed to meet the challenges of a more integrated market and the future enlargement of the European Union. In accordance with the principles of subsidiarity and of proportionality as set out in Article 5 of the Treaty, this Regulation does not go beyond what is necessary in order to achieve the objective of ensuring that competition in the common market is not distorted, in accordance with the principle of an open market economy with free competition.

(7) Articles 81 and 82, while applicable, according to the case-law of the Court of Justice, to certain concentrations, are not sufficient to control all operations which may prove to be incompatible with the system of undistorted competition envisaged in the Treaty. This regulation should therefore be based not only on Article 83 but, principally, on Article 308 of the Treaty, under which the Community may give itself the additional powers of action necessary for the attainment of its objectives, and also powers of action with regard to concentrations on the markets for agricultural products listed in Annex I to the Treaty.

(8) The provisions to be adopted in this Regulation should apply to significant structural changes, the impact of which on the market goes beyond the national borders of any one Member State. Such concentrations should, as a general rule, be reviewed exclusively at Community level, in application of a 'one-stop shop' system and in compliance with the principle of subsidiarity. Concentrations not covered by this Regulation come, in principle, within the jurisdiction of the Member States.

(9) The scope of application of this Regulation should be defined according to the geographical area of activity of the undertakings concerned and be limited by quantitative thresholds in order to cover those concentrations which have a Community dimension. The Commission should report to the Council on the implementation of the applicable thresholds and criteria so that the Council, acting in accordance with Article 202 of the Treaty, is in a position to review them regularly, as well as the rules regarding pre-notification referral, in the light of the experience gained; this requires statistical data to be provided by the Member States to the Commission to enable it to prepare such reports and possible proposals for amendments. The Commission's reports and proposals should be based on relevant information regularly provided by the Member States.

(10) A concentration with a Community dimension should be deemed to exist where the aggregate turnover of the undertakings concerned exceeds given thresholds; that is the case irrespective of whether or not the undertakings effecting the concentration have their seat or their principal fields of activity in the Community, provided they have substantial operations there.

(11) The rules governing the referral of concentrations from the Commission to Member States and from Member States to the Commission should operate as an effective corrective mechanism in the light of the principle of subsidiarity; these rules protect the competition interests of the Member States in an adequate manner and take due account of legal certainty and the 'one-stop shop' principle.

(12) Concentrations may qualify for examination under a number of national merger control systems if they fall below the turnover thresholds referred to in this Regulation. Multiple notification of the same transaction increases legal uncertainty, effort and cost for undertakings and may lead to conflicting assessments. The system whereby concentrations may be referred to the Commission by the Member States concerned should therefore be further developed.

(13) The Commission should act in close and constant liaison with the competent authorities of the Member States from which it obtains comments and information.

(14) The Commission and the competent authorities of the Member States should together form a network of public authorities, applying their respective competences in close cooperation,

using efficient arrangements for information-sharing and consultation, with a view to ensuring that a case is dealt with by the most appropriate authority, in the light of the principle of subsidiarity and with a view to ensuring that multiple notifications of a given concentration are avoided to the greatest extent possible. Referrals of concentrations from the Commission to Member States and from Member States to the Commission should be made in an efficient manner avoiding, to the greatest extent possible, situations where a concentration is subject to a referral both before and after its notification.

(15) The Commission should be able to refer to a Member State notified concentrations with a Community dimension which threaten significantly to affect competition in a market within that Member State presenting all the characteristics of a distinct market. Where the concentration affects competition on such a market, which does not constitute a substantial part of the common market, the Commission should be obliged, upon request, to refer the whole or part of the case to the Member State concerned. A Member State should be able to refer to the Commission a concentration which does not have a Community dimension but which affects trade between Member States and threatens to significantly affect competition within its territory. Other Member States which are also competent to review the concentration should be able to join the request. In such a situation, in order to ensure the efficiency and predictability of the system, national time limits should be suspended until a decision has been reached as to the referral of the case. The Commission should have the power to examine and deal with a concentration on behalf of a requesting Member State or requesting Member States.

(16) The undertakings concerned should be granted the possibility of requesting referrals to or from the Commission before a concentration is notified so as to further improve the efficiency of the system for the control of concentrations within the Community. In such situations, the Commission and national competition authorities should decide within short, clearly defined time limits whether a referral to or from the Commission ought to be made, thereby ensuring the efficiency of the system. Upon request by the undertakings concerned, the Commission should be able to refer to a Member State a concentration with a Community dimension which may significantly affect competition in a market within that Member State presenting all the characteristics of a distinct market; the undertakings concerned should not, however, be required to demonstrate that the effects of the concentration would be detrimental to competition. A concentration should not be referred from the Commission to a Member State which has expressed its disagreement to such a referral. Before notification to national authorities, the undertakings concerned should also be able to request that a concentration without a Community dimension which is capable of being reviewed under the national competition laws of at least three Member States be referred to the Commission. Such requests for pre-notification referrals to the Commission would be particularly pertinent in situations where the concentration would affect competition beyond the territory of one Member State. Where a concentration capable of being reviewed under the competition laws of three or more Member States is referred to the Commission prior to any national notification and no Member State competent to review the case expresses its disagreement, the Commission should acquire exclusive competence to review the concentration and such a concentration should be deemed to have a Community dimension. Such pre-notification referrals from Member States to the Commission should not, however, be made where at least one Member State competent to review the case has expressed its disagreement with such a referral.

(17) The Commission should be given exclusive competence to apply this Regulation, subject to review by the Court of Justice.

(18) The Member States should not be permitted to apply their national legislation on competition to concentrations with a Community dimension, unless this Regulation makes provision therefor. The relevant powers of national authorities should be limited to cases

where, failing intervention by the Commission, effective competition is likely to be significantly impeded within the territory of a Member State and where the competition interests of that Member State cannot be sufficiently protected otherwise by this Regulation. The Member States concerned must act promptly in such cases; this Regulation cannot, because of the diversity of national law, fix a single time limit for the adoption of final decisions under national law.

(19) Furthermore, the exclusive application of this Regulation to concentrations with a Community dimension is without prejudice to Article 296 of the Treaty, and does not prevent the Member States from taking appropriate measures to protect legitimate interests other than those pursued by this Regulation, provided that such measures are compatible with the general principles and other provisions of Community law.

(20) It is expedient to define the concept of concentration in such a manner as to cover operations bringing about a lasting change in the control of the undertakings concerned and therefore in the structure of the market. It is therefore appropriate to include, within the scope of this Regulation, all joint ventures performing on a lasting basis all the functions of an autonomous economic entity. It is moreover appropriate to treat as a single concentration transactions that are closely connected in that they are linked by condition or take the form of a series of transactions in securities taking place within a reasonably short period of time.

(21) This Regulation should also apply where the undertakings concerned accept restrictions directly related to, and necessary for, the implementation of the concentration. Commission decisions declaring concentrations compatible with the common market in application of this Regulation should automatically cover such restrictions, without the Commission having to assess such restrictions in individual cases. At the request of the undertakings concerned, however, the Commission should, in cases presenting novel or unresolved questions giving rise to genuine uncertainty, expressly assess whether or not any restriction is directly related to, and necessary for, the implementation of the concentration. A case presents a novel or unresolved question giving rise to genuine uncertainty if the question is not covered by the relevant Commission notice in force or a published Commission decision.

(22) The arrangements to be introduced for the control of concentrations should, without prejudice to Article 86(2) of the Treaty, respect the principle of non-discrimination between the public and the private sectors. In the public sector, calculation of the turnover of an undertaking concerned in a concentration needs, therefore, to take account of undertakings making up an economic unit with an independent power of decision, irrespective of the way in which their capital is held or of the rules of administrative supervision applicable to them.

(23) It is necessary to establish whether or not concentrations with a Community dimension are compatible with the common market in terms of the need to maintain and develop effective competition in the common market. In so doing, the Commission must place its appraisal within the general framework of the achievement of the fundamental objectives referred to in Article 2 of the Treaty establishing the European Community and Article 2 of the Treaty on European Union.

(24) In order to ensure a system of undistorted competition in the common market, in furtherance of a policy conducted in accordance with the principle of an open market economy with free competition, this Regulation must permit effective control of all concentrations from the point of view of their effect on competition in the Community. Accordingly, Regulation (EEC) No 4064/89 established the principle that a concentration with a Community dimension which creates or strengthens a dominant position as a result of which effective competition in the common market or in a substantial part of it would be significantly impeded should be declared incompatible with the common market.

(25) In view of the consequences that concentrations in oligopolistic market structures may have, it is all the more necessary to maintain effective competition in such markets. Many oligopolistic markets exhibit a healthy degree of competition. However, under certain

circumstances, concentrations involving the elimination of important competitive constraints that the merging parties had exerted upon each other, as well as a reduction of competitive pressure on the remaining competitors, may, even in the absence of a likelihood of co-ordination between the members of the oligopoly, result in a significant impediment to effective competition. The Community courts have, however, not to date expressly inter-preted Regulation (EEC) No 4064/89 as requiring concentrations giving rise to such non-coordinated effects to be declared incompatible with the common market. Therefore, in the interests of legal certainty, it should be made clear that this Regulation permits effective control of all such concentrations by providing that any concentration which would signifi-cantly impede effective competition, in the common market or in a substantial part of it, should be declared incompatible with the common market. The notion of 'significant impediment to effective competition' in Article 2(2) and (3) should be interpreted as extending, beyond the concept of dominance, only to the anti-competitive effects of a con-centration resulting from the non-coordinated behaviour of undertakings which would not have a dominant position on the market concerned.

(26) A significant impediment to effective competition generally results from the creation or strengthening of a dominant position. With a view to preserving the guidance that may be drawn from past judgments of the European courts and Commission decisions pursuant to Regulation (EEC) No 4064/89, while at the same time maintaining consistency with the standards of competitive harm which have been applied by the Commission and the Com-munity courts regarding the compatibility of a concentration with the common market, this Regulation should accordingly establish the principle that a concentration with a Com-munity dimension which would significantly impede effective competition, in the common market or in a substantial part thereof, in particular as a result of the creation or strengthening of a dominant position, is to be declared incompatible with the common market.

(27) In addition, the criteria of Article 81(1) and (3) of the Treaty should be applied to joint ventures performing, on a lasting basis, all the functions of autonomous economic entities, to the extent that their creation has as its consequence an appreciable restriction of competition between undertakings that remain independent.

(28) In order to clarify and explain the Commission's appraisal of concentrations under this Regulation, it is appropriate for the Commission to publish guidance which should provide a sound economic framework for the assessment of concentrations with a view to determining whether or not they may be declared compatible with the common market.

(29) In order to determine the impact of a concentration on competition in the common market, it is appropriate to take account of any substantiated and likely efficiencies put forward by the undertakings concerned. It is possible that the efficiencies brought about by the concen-tration counteract the effects on competition, and in particular the potential harm to con-sumers, that it might otherwise have and that, as a consequence, the concentration would not significantly impede effective competition, in the common market or in a substantial part of it, in particular as a result of the creation or strengthening of a dominant position. The Commission should publish guidance on the conditions under which it may take efficiencies into account in the assessment of a concentration.

(30) Where the undertakings concerned modify a notified concentration, in particular by offering commitments with a view to rendering the concentration compatible with the common market, the Commission should be able to declare the concentration, as modified, compatible with the common market. Such commitments should be proportionate to the competition problem and entirely eliminate it. It is also appropriate to accept commitments before the initiation of proceedings where the competition problem is readily identifiable and can easily be remedied. It should be expressly provided that the Commission may attach to its decision conditions and obligations in order to ensure that the undertakings concerned comply with their commitments in a timely and effective manner so as to render the

concentration compatible with the common market. Transparency and effective consultation of Member States as well as of interested third parties should be ensured throughout the procedure.

(31) The Commission should have at its disposal appropriate instruments to ensure the enforcement of commitments and to deal with situations where they are not fulfilled. In cases of failure to fulfil a condition attached to the decision declaring a concentration compatible with the common market, the situation rendering the concentration compatible with the common market does not materialise and the concentration, as implemented, is therefore not authorised by the Commission. As a consequence, if the concentration is implemented, it should be treated in the same way as a non-notified concentration implemented without authorisation. Furthermore, where the Commission has already found that, in the absence of the condition, the concentration would be incompatible with the common market, it should have the power to directly order the dissolution of the concentration, so as to restore the situation prevailing prior to the implementation of the concentration. Where an obligation attached to a decision declaring the concentration compatible with the common market is not fulfilled, the Commission should be able to revoke its decision. Moreover, the Commission should be able to impose appropriate financial sanctions where conditions or obligations are not fulfilled.

(32) Concentrations which, by reason of the limited market share of the undertakings concerned, are not liable to impede effective competition may be presumed to be compatible with the common market. Without prejudice to Articles 81 and 82 of the Treaty, an indication to this effect exists, in particular, where the market share of the undertakings concerned does not exceed 25% either in the common market or in a substantial part of it.

(33) The Commission should have the task of taking all the decisions necessary to establish whether or not concentrations with a Community dimension are compatible with the common market, as well as decisions designed to restore the situation prevailing prior to the implementation of a concentration which has been declared incompatible with the common market.

(34) To ensure effective control, undertakings should be obliged to give prior notification of concentrations with a Community dimension following the conclusion of the agreement, the announcement of the public bid or the acquisition of a controlling interest. Notification should also be possible where the undertakings concerned satisfy the Commission of their intention to enter into an agreement for a proposed concentration and demonstrate to the Commission that their plan for that proposed concentration is sufficiently concrete, for example on the basis of an agreement in principle, a memorandum of understanding, or a letter of intent signed by all undertakings concerned, or, in the case of a public bid, where they have publicly announced an intention to make such a bid, provided that the intended agreement or bid would result in a concentration with a Community dimension. The implementation of concentrations should be suspended until a final decision of the Commission has been taken. However, it should be possible to derogate from this suspension at the request of the undertakings concerned, where appropriate. In deciding whether or not to grant a derogation, the Commission should take account of all pertinent factors, such as the nature and gravity of damage to the undertakings concerned or to third parties, and the threat to competition posed by the concentration. In the interest of legal certainty, the validity of transactions must nevertheless be protected as much as necessary.

(35) A period within which the Commission must initiate proceedings in respect of a notified concentration and a period within which it must take a final decision on the compatibility or incompatibility with the common market of that concentration should be laid down. These periods should be extended whenever the undertakings concerned offer commitments with a view to rendering the concentration compatible with the common market, in order to allow for sufficient time for the analysis and market testing of such commitment offers and for the

consultation of Member States as well as interested third parties. A limited extension of the period within which the Commission must take a final decision should also be possible in order to allow sufficient time for the investigation of the case and the verification of the facts and arguments submitted to the Commission.

(36) The Community respects the fundamental rights and observes the principles recognised in particular by the Charter of Fundamental Rights of the European Union.[5] Accordingly, this Regulation should be interpreted and applied with respect to those rights and principles.

(37) The undertakings concerned must be afforded the right to be heard by the Commission when proceedings have been initiated; the members of the management and supervisory bodies and the recognised representatives of the employees of the undertakings concerned, and interested third parties, must also be given the opportunity to be heard.

(38) In order properly to appraise concentrations, the Commission should have the right to request all necessary information and to conduct all necessary inspections throughout the Community. To that end, and with a view to protecting competition effectively, the Commission's powers of investigation need to be expanded. The Commission should, in particular, have the right to interview any persons who may be in possession of useful information and to record the statements made.

(39) In the course of an inspection, officials authorised by the Commission should have the right to ask for any information relevant to the subject matter and purpose of the inspection; they should also have the right to affix seals during inspections, particularly in circumstances where there are reasonable grounds to suspect that a concentration has been implemented without being notified; that incorrect, incomplete or misleading information has been supplied to the Commission; or that the undertakings or persons concerned have failed to comply with a condition or obligation imposed by decision of the Commission. In any event, seals should only be used in exceptional circumstances, for the period of time strictly necessary for the inspection, normally not for more than 48 hours.

(40) Without prejudice to the case-law of the Court of Justice, it is also useful to set out the scope of the control that the national judicial authority may exercise when it authorises, as provided by national law and as a precautionary measure, assistance from law enforcement authorities in order to overcome possible opposition on the part of the undertaking against an inspection, including the affixing of seals, ordered by Commission decision. It results from the case-law that the national judicial authority may in particular ask of the Commission further information which it needs to carry out its control and in the absence of which it could refuse the authorisation. The case-law also confirms the competence of the national courts to control the application of national rules governing the implementation of coercive measures. The competent authorities of the Member States should cooperate actively in the exercise of the Commission's investigative powers.

(41) When complying with decisions of the Commission, the undertakings and persons concerned cannot be forced to admit that they have committed infringements, but they are in any event obliged to answer factual questions and to provide documents, even if this information may be used to establish against themselves or against others the existence of such infringements.

(42) For the sake of transparency, all decisions of the Commission which are not of a merely procedural nature should be widely publicised. While ensuring preservation of the rights of defence of the undertakings concerned, in particular the right of access to the file, it is essential that business secrets be protected. The confidentiality of information exchanged in the network and with the competent authorities of third countries should likewise be safeguarded.

---

[5] OJ C364, 18.12.2000, p 1.

(43) Compliance with this Regulation should be enforceable, as appropriate, by means of fines and periodic penalty payments. The Court of Justice should be given unlimited jurisdiction in that regard pursuant to Article 229 of the Treaty.

(44) The conditions in which concentrations, involving undertakings having their seat or their principal fields of activity in the Community, are carried out in third countries should be observed, and provision should be made for the possibility of the Council giving the Commission an appropriate mandate for negotiation with a view to obtaining non-discriminatory treatment for such undertakings.

(45) This Regulation in no way detracts from the collective rights of employees, as recognised in the undertakings concerned, notably with regard to any obligation to inform or consult their recognised representatives under Community and national law.

(46) The Commission should be able to lay down detailed rules concerning the implementation of this Regulation in accordance with the procedures for the exercise of implementing powers conferred on the Commission. For the adoption of such implementing provisions, the Commission should be assisted by an Advisory Committee composed of the representatives of the Member States as specified in Article 23,

HAS ADOPTED THIS REGULATION:

Article 1
Scope

1. Without prejudice to Article 4(5) and Article 22, this Regulation shall apply to all concentrations with a Community dimension as defined in this Article.

2. A concentration has a Community dimension where:
(a) the combined aggregate worldwide turnover of all the undertakings concerned is more than EUR 5 000 million: and
(b) the aggregate Community-wide turnover of each of at least two of the undertakings concerned is more than EUR 250 million,
unless each of the undertakings concerned achieves more than two-thirds of its aggregate Community-wide turnover within one and the same Member State.

3. A concentration that does not meet the thresholds laid down in paragraph 2 has a Community dimension where:
(a) the combined aggregate worldwide turnover of all the undertakings concerned is more than EUR 2 500 million;
(b) in each of at least three Member States, the combined aggregate turnover of all the undertakings concerned is more than EUR 100 million;
(c) in each of at least three Member States included for the purpose of point (b), the aggregate turnover of each of at least two of the undertakings concerned is more than EUR 25 million; and
(d) the aggregate Community-wide turnover of each of at least two of the undertakings concerned is more than EUR 100 million,
unless each of the undertakings concerned achieves more than two-thirds of its aggregate Community-wide turnover within one and the same Member State.

4. On the basis of statistical data that may be regularly provided by the Member States, the Commission shall report to the Council on the operation of the thresholds and criteria set out in paragraphs 2 and 3 by 1 July 2009 and may present proposals pursuant to paragraph 5.

5. Following the report referred to in paragraph 4 and on a proposal from the Commission, the Council, acting by a qualified majority, may revise the thresholds and criteria mentioned in paragraph 3.

Article 2
Appraisal of concentrations

1. Concentrations within the scope of this Regulation shall be appraised in accordance with the objectives of this Regulation and the following provisions with a view to establishing whether or not they are compatible with the common market.

In making this appraisal, the Commission shall take into account:

(a) the need to maintain and develop effective competition within the common market in view of, among other things, the structure of all the markets concerned and the actual or potential competition from undertakings located either within or outwith the Community;

(b) the market position of the undertakings concerned and their economic and financial power, the alternatives available to suppliers and users, their access to supplies or markets, any legal or other barriers to entry, supply and demand trends for the relevant goods and services, the interests of the intermediate and ultimate consumers, and the development of technical and economic progress provided that it is to consumers' advantage and does not form an obstacle to competition.

2. A concentration which would not significantly impede effective competition in the common market or in a substantial part of it, in particular as a result of the creation or strengthening of a dominant position, shall be declared compatible with the common market.

3. A concentration which would significantly impede effective competition, in the common market or in a substantial part of it, in particular as a result of the creation or strengthening of a dominant position, shall be declared incompatible with the common market.

4. To the extent that the creation of a joint venture constituting a concentration pursuant to Article 3 has as its object or effect the coordination of the competitive behaviour of undertakings that remain independent, such coordination shall be appraised in accordance with the criteria of Article 81(1) and (3) of the Treaty, with a view to establishing whether or not the operation is compatible with the common market.

5. In making this appraisal, the Commission shall take into account in particular:

— whether two or more parent companies retain, to a significant extent, activities in the same market as the joint venture or in a market which is downstream or upstream from that of the joint venture or in a neighbouring market closely related to this market,

— whether the coordination which is the direct consequence of the creation of the joint venture affords the undertakings concerned the possibility of eliminating competition in respect of a substantial part of the products or services in question.

Article 3
Definition of concentration

1. A concentration shall be deemed to arise where a change of control on a lasting basis results from:

(a) the merger of two or more previously independent undertakings or parts of undertakings, or

(b) the acquisition, by one or more persons already controlling at least one undertaking, or by one or more undertakings, whether by purchase of securities or assets, by contract or by any other means, of direct or indirect control of the whole or parts of one or more other undertakings.

2. Control shall be constituted by rights, contracts or any other means which, either separately or in combination and having regard to the considerations of fact or law involved, confer the possibility of exercising decisive influence on an undertaking, in particular by:

(a) ownership or the right to use all or part of the assets of an undertaking;

(b) rights or contracts which confer decisive influence on the composition, voting or decisions of the organs of an undertaking.

3. Control is acquired by persons or undertakings which:

(a) are holders of the rights or entitled to rights under the contracts concerned; or

(b) while not being holders of such rights or entitled to rights under such contracts, have the power to exercise the rights deriving therefrom.

4. The creation of a joint venture performing on a lasting basis all the functions of an autonomous economic entity shall constitute a concentration within the meaning of paragraph 1(b).

5. A concentration shall not be deemed to arise where:

(a) credit institutions or other financial institutions or insurance companies, the normal activities of which include transactions and dealing in securities for their own account or for the account of others, hold on a temporary basis securities which they have acquired in an undertaking with a view to reselling them, provided that they do not exercise voting rights in respect of those securities with a view to determining the competitive behaviour of that undertaking or provided that they exercise such voting rights only with a view to preparing the disposal of all or part of that undertaking or of its assets or the disposal of those securities and that any such disposal takes place within one year of the date of acquisition; that period may be extended by the Commission on request where such institutions or companies can show that the disposal was not reasonably possible within the period set;

(b) control is acquired by an office-holder according to the law of a Member State relating to liquidation, winding up, insolvency, cessation of payments, compositions or analogous proceedings;

(c) the operations referred to in paragraph 1(b) are carried out by the financial holding companies referred to in Article 5(3) of Fourth Council Directive 78/660/EEC of 25 July 1978 based on Article 54(3)(g) of the Treaty on the annual accounts of certain types of companies[6] provided however that the voting rights in respect of the holding are exercised, in particular in relation to the appointment of members of the management and supervisory bodies of the undertakings in which they have holdings, only to maintain the full value of those investments and not to determine directly or indirectly the competitive conduct of those undertakings.

Article 4
Prior notification of concentrations and pre-notification referral at the request of the notifying parties

1. Concentrations with a Community dimension defined in this Regulation shall be notified to the Commission prior to their implementation and following the conclusion of the agreement, the announcement of the public bid, or the acquisition of a controlling interest.

Notification may also be made where the undertakings concerned demonstrate to the Commission a good faith intention to conclude an agreement or, in the case of a public bid, where they have publicly announced an intention to make such a bid, provided that the intended agreement or bid would result in a concentration with a Community dimension.

For the purposes of this Regulation, the term 'notified concentration' shall also cover intended concentrations notified pursuant to the second subparagraph. For the purposes of paragraphs 4 and 5 of this Article, the term 'concentration' includes intended concentrations within the meaning of the second subparagraph.

2. A concentration which consists of a merger within the meaning of Article 3(1)(a) or in the acquisition of joint control within the meaning of Article 3(1)(b) shall be notified jointly by the parties to the merger or by those acquiring joint control as the case may be. In all other cases,

---

[6] OJ L222, 14.8.1978, p 11. Directive as last amended by Dir 2003/51/EC of the European Parliament and of the Council (O) L178, 17.7.2003, p 16).

the notification shall be effected by the person or undertaking acquiring control of the whole or parts of one or more undertakings.

3. Where the Commission finds that a notified concentration falls within the scope of this Regulation, it shall publish the fact of the notification, at the same time indicating the names of the undertakings concerned, their country of origin, the nature of the concentration and the economic sectors involved. The Commission shall take account of the legitimate interest of undertakings in the protection of their business secrets.

4. Prior to the notification of a concentration within the meaning of paragraph 1, the persons or undertakings referred to in paragraph 2 may inform the Commission, by means of a reasoned submission, that the concentration may significantly affect competition in a market within a Member State which presents all the characteristics of a distinct market and should therefore be examined, in whole or in part, by that Member State.

The Commission shall transmit this submission to all Member States without delay. The Member State referred to in the reasoned submission shall, within 15 working days of receiving the submission, express its agreement or disagreement as regards the request to refer the case. Where that Member State takes no such decision within this period, it shall be deemed to have agreed.

Unless that Member State disagrees, the Commission, where it considers that such a distinct market exists, and that competition in that market may be significantly affected by the concentration, may decide to refer the whole or part of the case to the competent authorities of that Member State with a view to the application of that State's national competition law.

The decision whether or not to refer the case in accordance with the third subparagraph shall be taken within 25 working days starting from the receipt of the reasoned submission by the Commission. The Commission shall inform the other Member States and the persons or undertakings concerned of its decision. If the Commission does not take a decision within this period, it shall be deemed to have adopted a decision to refer the case in accordance with the submission made by the persons or undertakings concerned.

If the Commission decides, or is deemed to have decided, pursuant to the third and fourth subparagraphs, to refer the whole of the case, no notification shall be made pursuant to paragraph 1 and national competition law shall apply. Article 9(6) to (9) shall apply *mutatis mutandis.*

5. With regard to a concentration as defined in Article 3 which does not have a Community dimension within the meaning of Article 1 and which is capable of being reviewed under the national competition laws of at least three Member States, the persons or undertakings referred to in paragraph 2 may, before any notification to the competent authorities, inform the Commission by means of a reasoned submission that the concentration should be examined by the Commission.

The Commission shall transmit this submission to all Member States without delay.

Any Member State competent to examine the concentration under its national competition law may, within 15 working days of receiving the reasoned submission, express its disagreement as regards the request to refer the case.

Where at least one such Member State has expressed its disagreement in accordance with the third subparagraph within the period of 15 working days, the case shall not be referred. The Commission shall, without delay, inform all Member States and the persons or undertakings concerned of any such expression of disagreement.

Where no Member State has expressed its disagreement in accordance with the third subparagraph within the period of 15 working days, the concentration shall be deemed to have a Community dimension and shall be notified to the Commission in accordance with paragraphs 1 and 2. In such situations, no Member State shall apply its national competition law to the concentration.

6. The Commission shall report to the Council on the operation of paragraphs 4 and 5 by 1 July 2009. Following this report and on a proposal from the Commission, the Council, acting by a qualified majority, may revise paragraphs 4 and 5.

Article 5
Calculation of turnover

1. Aggregate turnover within the meaning of this Regulation shall comprise the amounts derived by the undertakings concerned in the preceding financial year from the sale of products and the provision of services falling within the undertakings ordinary activities after deduction of sales rebates and of value added tax and other taxes directly related to turnover. The aggregate turnover of an undertaking concerned shall not include the sale of products or the provision of services between any of the undertakings referred to in paragraph 4.

Turnover, in the Community or in a Member State, shall comprise products sold and services provided to undertakings or consumers, in the Community or in that Member State as the case may be.

2. By way of derogation from paragraph 1, where the concentration consists of the acquisition of parts, whether or not constituted as legal entities, of one or more undertakings, only the turnover relating to the parts which are the subject of the concentration shall be taken into account with regard to the seller or sellers.

However, two or more transactions within the meaning of the first subparagraph which take place within a two-year period between the same persons or undertakings shall be treated as one and the same concentration arising on the date of the last transaction.

3. In place of turnover the following shall be used:
(a) for credit institutions and other financial institutions, the sum of the following income items as defined in Council Directive 86/635/EEC,[7] after deduction of value added tax and other taxes directly related to those items, where appropriate;
    (i)   interest income and similar income;
    (ii) income from securities;
         — income from shares and other variable yield securities,
         — income from participating interests,
         — income from shares in affiliated undertakings;
    (iii) commissions receivable;
    (iv) net profit on financial operations;
    (v)   other operating income.
The turnover of a credit or financial institution in the Community or in a Member State shall comprise the income items, as defined above, which are received by the branch or division of that institution established in the Community or in the Member State in question, as the case may be;
(b) for insurance undertakings, the value of gross premiums written which shall comprise all amounts received and receivable in respect of insurance contracts issued by or on behalf of the insurance undertakings, including also outgoing reinsurance premiums, and after deduction of taxes and parafiscal contributions or levies charged by reference to the amounts of individual premiums or the total volume of premiums; as regards Article 1(2)(b) and (3)(b), (c) and (d) and the final part of Article 1(2) and (3), gross premiums received from Community residents and from residents of one Member State respectively shall be taken into account.

---

[7] OJ L372, 31. 12. 1986, p 1. Directive as last amended by Dir 2003/51/EC of the European Parliament and of the Council.

4. Without prejudice to paragraph 2, the aggregate turnover of an undertaking concerned within the meaning of this Regulation shall be calculated by adding together the respective turnovers of the following:

(a) the undertaking concerned;

(b) those undertakings in which the undertaking concerned, directly or indirectly:

    (i) owns more than half the capital or business assets, or

    (ii) has the power to exercise more than half the voting rights, or

    (iii) has the power to appoint more than half the members of the supervisory board, the administrative board or bodies legally representing the undertakings, or

    (iv) has the right to manage the undertakings' affairs;

(c) those undertakings which have in the undertaking concerned the rights or powers listed in (b);

(d) those undertakings in which an undertaking as referred to in (c) has the rights or powers listed in (b);

(e) those undertakings in which two or more undertakings as referred to in (a) to (d) jointly have the rights or powers listed in (b).

5. Where undertakings concerned by the concentration jointly have the rights or powers listed in paragraph 4(b), in calculating the aggregate turnover of the undertakings concerned for the purposes of this Regulation:

(a) no account shall be taken of the turnover resulting from the sale of products or the provision of services between the joint undertaking and each of the undertakings concerned or any other undertaking connected with any one of them, as set out in paragraph 4(b) to (e);

(b) account shall be taken of the turnover resulting from the sale of products and the provision of services between the joint undertaking and any third undertakings. This turnover shall be apportioned equally amongst the undertakings concerned.

Article 6
Examination of the notification and initiation of proceedings

1. The Commission shall examine the notification as soon as it is received.

(a) Where it concludes that the concentration notified does not fall within the scope of this Regulation, it shall record that finding by means of a decision.

(b) Where it finds that the concentration notified, although falling within the scope of this Regulation, does not raise serious doubts as to its compatibility with the common market, it shall decide not to oppose it and shall declare that it is compatible with the common market. A decision declaring a concentration compatible shall be deemed to cover restrictions directly related and necessary to the implementation of the concentration.

(c) Without prejudice to paragraph 2, where the Commission finds that the concentration notified falls within the scope of this Regulation and raises serious doubts as to its compatibility with the common market, it shall decide to initiate proceedings. Without prejudice to Article 9, such proceedings shall be closed by means of a decision as provided for in Article 8(1) to (4), unless the undertakings concerned have demonstrated to the satisfaction of the Commission that they have abandoned the concentration.

2. Where the Commission finds that, following modification by the undertakings concerned, a notified concentration no longer raises serious doubts within the meaning of paragraph 1(c), it shall declare the concentration compatible with the common market pursuant to paragraph 1(b).

The Commission may attach to its decision under paragraph 1(b) conditions and obligations intended to ensure that the undertakings concerned comply with the commitments they have entered into vis-à-vis the Commission with a view to rendering the concentration compatible with the common market.

3. The Commission may revoke the decision it took pursuant to paragraph 1(a) or (b) where:

(a) the decision is based on incorrect information for which one of the undertakings is responsible or where it has been obtained by deceit,

or

(b) the undertakings concerned commit a breach of an obligation attached to the decision.

4. In the cases referred to in paragraph 3, the Commission may take a decision under paragraph 1, without being bound by the time limits referred to in Article 10(1).

5. The Commission shall notify its decision to the undertakings concerned and the competent authorities of the Member States without delay.

Article 7
Suspension of concentrations

1. A concentration with a Community dimension as defined in Article 1, or which is to be examined by the Commission pursuant to Article 4(5), shall not be implemented either before its notification or until it has been declared compatible with the common market pursuant to a decision under Articles 6(1)(b), 8(1) or 8(2), or on the basis of a presumption according to Article 10(6).

2. Paragraph 1 shall not prevent the implementation of a public bid or of a series of transactions in securities including those convertible into other securities admitted to trading on a market such as a stock exchange, by which control within the meaning of Article 3 is acquired from various sellers, provided that:

(a) the concentration is notified to the Commission pursuant to Article 4 without delay; and

(b) the acquirer does not exercise the voting rights attached to the securities in question or does so only to maintain the full value of its investments based on a derogation granted by the Commission under paragraph 3.

3. The Commission may, on request, grant a derogation from the obligations imposed in paragraphs 1 or 2. The request to grant a derogation must be reasoned. In deciding on the request, the Commission shall take into account *inter alia* the effects of the suspension on one or more undertakings concerned by the concentration or on a third party and the threat to competition posed by the concentration. Such a derogation may be made subject to conditions and obligations in order to ensure conditions of effective competition. A derogation may be applied for and granted at any time, be it before notification or after the transaction.

4. The validity of any transaction carried out in contravention of paragraph 1 shall be dependent on a decision pursuant to Article 6(1)(b) or Article 8(1), (2) or (3) or on a presumption pursuant to Article 10(6).

This Article shall, however, have no effect on the validity of transactions in securities including those convertible into other securities admitted to trading on a market such as a stock exchange, unless the buyer and seller knew or ought to have known that the transaction was carried out in contravention of paragraph 1.

Article 8
Powers of decision of the Commission

1. Where the Commission finds that a notified concentration fulfils the criterion laid down in Article 2(2) and, in the cases referred to in Article 2(4), the criteria laid down in Article 81(3) of the Treaty, it shall issue a decision declaring the concentration compatible with the common market.

A decision declaring a concentration compatible shall be deemed to cover restrictions directly related and necessary to the implementation of the concentration.

2. Where the Commission finds that, following modification by the undertakings concerned, a notified concentration fulfils the criterion laid down in Article 2(2) and, in the cases referred to in Article 2(4), the criteria laid down in Article 81(3) of the Treaty, it shall issue a decision declaring the concentration compatible with the common market.

The Commission may attach to its decision conditions and obligations intended to ensure that the undertakings concerned comply with the commitments they have entered into vis-à-vis the Commission with a view to rendering the concentration compatible with the common market.

A decision declaring a concentration compatible shall be deemed to cover restrictions directly related and necessary to the implementation of the concentration.

3. Where the Commission finds that a concentration fulfils the criterion defined in Article 2(3) or, in the cases referred to in Article 2(4), does not fulfil the criteria laid down in Article 81(3) of the Treaty, it shall issue a decision declaring that the concentration is incompatible with the common market.

4. Where the Commission finds that a concentration:

(a) has already been implemented and that concentration has been declared incompatible with the common market, or

(b) has been implemented in contravention of a condition attached to a decision taken under paragraph 2, which has found that, in the absence of the condition, the concentration would fulfil the criterion laid down in Article 2(3) or, in the cases referred to in Article 2(4), would not fulfil the criteria laid down in Article 81(3) of the Treaty,

the Commission may:

— require the undertakings concerned to dissolve the concentration, in particular through the dissolution of the merger or the disposal of all the shares or assets acquired, so as to restore the situation prevailing prior to the implementation of the concentration; in circumstances where restoration of the situation prevailing before the implementation of the concentration is not possible through dissolution of the concentration, the Commission may take any other measure appropriate to achieve such restoration as far as possible,

— order any other appropriate measure to ensure that the undertakings concerned dissolve the concentration or take other restorative measures as required in its decision.

In cases falling within point (a) of the first subparagraph, the measures referred to in that subparagraph may be imposed either in a decision pursuant to paragraph 3 or by separate decision.

5. The Commission may take interim measures appropriate to restore or maintain conditions of effective competition where a concentration:

(a) has been implemented in contravention of Article 7, and a decision as to the compatibility of the concentration with the common market has not yet been taken;

(b) has been implemented in contravention of a condition attached to a decision under Article 6(1)(b) or paragraph 2 of this Article;

(c) has already been implemented and is declared incompatible with the common market.

6. The Commission may revoke the decision it has taken pursuant to paragraphs 1 or 2 where:

(a) the declaration of compatibility is based on incorrect information for which one of the undertakings is responsible or where it has been obtained by deceit; or

(b) the undertakings concerned commit a breach of an obligation attached to the decision.

7. The Commission may take a decision pursuant to paragraphs 1 to 3 without being bound by the time limits referred to in Article 10(3), in cases where:

(a) it finds that a concentration has been implemented

   (i) in contravention of a condition attached to a decision under Article 6(1)(b), or

   (ii) in contravention of a condition attached to a decision taken under paragraph 2 and in accordance with Article 10(2), which has found that, in the absence of the condition, the concentration would raise serious doubts as to its compatibility with the common market; or

(b) a decision has been revoked pursuant to paragraph 6.

8. The Commission shall notify its decision to the undertakings concerned and the competent authorities of the Member States without delay.

Article 9
Referral to the competent authorities of the Member States

1. The Commission may, by means of a decision notified without delay to the undertakings concerned and the competent authorities of the other Member States, refer a notified concentration to the competent authorities of the Member State concerned in the following circumstances.

2. Within 15 working days of the date of receipt of the copy of the notification, a Member State, on its own initiative or upon the invitation of the Commission, may inform the Commission, which shall inform the undertakings concerned, that:

(a) a concentration threatens to affect significantly competition in a market within that Member State, which presents all the characteristics of a distinct market, or

(b) a concentration affects competition in a market within that Member State, which presents all the characteristics of a distinct market and which does not constitute a substantial part of the common market.

3. If the Commission considers that, having regard to the market for the products or services in question and the geographical reference market within the meaning of paragraph 7, there is such a distinct market and that such a threat exists, either:

(a) it shall itself deal with the case in accordance with this Regulation; or

(b) it shall refer the whole or part of the case to the competent authorities of the Member State concerned with a view to the application of that State's national competition law.

If, however, the Commission considers that such a distinct market or threat does not exist, it shall adopt a decision to that effect which it shall address to the Member State concerned, and shall itself deal with the case in accordance with this Regulation.

In cases where a Member State informs the Commission pursuant to paragraph 2(b) that a concentration affects competition in a distinct market within its territory that does not form a substantial part of the common market, the Commission shall refer the whole or part of the case relating to the distinct market concerned, if it considers that such a distinct market is affected.

4. A decision to refer or not to refer pursuant to paragraph 3 shall be taken:

(a) as a general rule within the period provided for in Article 10(1), second subparagraph, where the Commission, pursuant to Article 6(1)(b), has not initiated proceedings; or

(b) within 65 working days at most of the notification of the concentration concerned where the Commission has initiated proceedings under Article 6(1)(c), without taking the preparatory steps in order to adopt the necessary measures under Article 8(2), (3) or (4) to maintain or restore effective competition on the market concerned.

5. If within the 65 working days referred to in paragraph 4(b) the Commission, despite a reminder from the Member State concerned, has not taken a decision on referral in accordance with paragraph 3 nor has taken the preparatory steps referred to in paragraph 4(b), it shall be deemed to have taken a decision to refer the case to the Member State concerned in accordance with paragraph 3(b).

6. The competent authority of the Member State concerned shall decide upon the case without undue delay.

Within 45 working days after the Commission's referral, the competent authority of the Member State concerned shall inform the undertakings concerned of the result of the preliminary competition assessment and what further action, if any, it proposes to take. The Member State concerned may exceptionally suspend this time limit where necessary information has not been provided to it by the undertakings concerned as provided for by its national competition law.

Where a notification is requested under national law, the period of 45 working days shall begin on the working day following that of the receipt of a complete notification by the competent authority of that Member State.

7. The geographical reference market shall consist of the area in which the undertakings concerned are involved in the supply and demand of products or services, in which the conditions of competition are sufficiently homogeneous and which can be distinguished from neighbouring areas because, in particular, conditions of competition are appreciably different in those areas. This assessment should take account in particular of the nature and characteristics of the products or services concerned, of the existence of entry barriers or of consumer preferences, of appreciable differences of the undertakings' market shares between the area concerned and neighbouring areas or of substantial price differences.

8. In applying the provisions of this Article, the Member State concerned may take only the measures strictly necessary to safeguard or restore effective competition on the market concerned.

9. In accordance with the relevant provisions of the Treaty, any Member State may appeal to the Court of Justice, and in particular request the application of Article 243 of the Treaty, for the purpose of applying its national competition law.

Article 10
Time-limits for initiating proceedings and for decisions

1. Without prejudice to Article 6(4), the decisions referred to in Article 6(1) shall be taken within 25 working days at most. That period shall begin on the working day following that of the receipt of a notification or, if the information to be supplied with the notification is incomplete, on the working day following that of the receipt of the complete information.

That period shall be increased to 35 working days where the Commission receives a request from a Member State in accordance with Article 9(2) or where, the undertakings concerned offer commitments pursuant to Article 6(2) with a view to rendering the concentration compatible with the common market.

2. Decisions pursuant to Article 8(1) or (2) concerning notified concentrations shall be taken as soon as it appears that the serious doubts referred to in Article 6(1)(c) have been removed, particularly as a result of modifications made by the undertakings concerned, and at the latest by the time limit laid down in paragraph 3.

3. Without prejudice to Article 8(7), decisions pursuant to Article 8(1) to (3) concerning notified concentrations shall be taken within not more than 90 working days of the date on which the proceedings are initiated. That period shall be increased to 105 working days where the undertakings concerned offer commitments pursuant to Article 8(2), second subparagraph, with a view to rendering the concentration compatible with the common market, unless these commitments have been offered less than 55 working days after the initiation of proceedings.

The periods set by the first subparagraph shall likewise be extended if the notifying parties make a request to that effect not later than 15 working days after the initiation of proceedings pursuant to Article 6(1)(c). The notifying parties may make only one such request. Likewise, at any time following the initiation of proceedings, the periods set by the first sub-paragraph may be extended by the Commission with the agreement of the notifying parties. The total duration of any extension or extensions effected pursuant to this subparagraph shall not exceed 20 working days.

4. The periods set by paragraphs 1 and 3 shall exceptionally be suspended where, owing to circumstances for which one of the undertakings involved in the concentration is responsible, the Commission has had to request information by decision pursuant to Article 11 or to order an inspection by decision pursuant to Article 13.

The first subparagraph shall also apply to the period referred to in Article 9(4)(b).

5. Where the Court of Justice gives a judgment which annuls the whole or part of a Commission decision which is subject to a time limit set by this Article, the concentration shall be re-examined by the Commission with a view to adopting a decision pursuant to Article 6(1).

The concentration shall be re-examined in the light of current market conditions.

The notifying parties shall submit a new notification or supplement the original notification, without delay, where the original notification becomes incomplete by reason of intervening changes in market conditions or in the information provided. Where there are no such changes, the parties shall certify this fact without delay.

The periods laid down in paragraph 1 shall start on the working day following that of the receipt of complete information in a new notification, a supplemented notification, or a certification within the meaning of the third subparagraph.

The second and third subparagraphs shall also apply in the cases referred to in Article 6(4) and Article 8(7).

6. Where the Commission has not taken a decision in accordance with Article 6(1)(b), (c), 8(1), (2) or (3) within the time limits set in paragraphs 1 and 3 respectively, the concentration shall be deemed to have been declared compatible with the common market, without prejudice to Article 9.

Article 11
Requests for information

1. In order to carry out the duties assigned to it by this Regulation, the Commission may, by simple request or by decision, require the persons referred to in Article 3(1)(b), as well as undertakings and associations of undertakings, to provide all necessary information.

2. When sending a simple request for information to a person, an undertaking or an association of undertakings, the Commission shall state the legal basis and the purpose of the request, specify what information is required and fix the time limit within which the information is to be provided, as well as the penalties provided for in Article 14 for supplying incorrect or misleading information.

3. Where the Commission requires a person, an undertaking or an association of undertakings to supply information by decision, it shall state the legal basis and the purpose of the request, specify what information is required and fix the time limit within which it is to be provided. It shall also indicate the penalties provided for in Article 14 and indicate or impose the penalties provided for in Article 15. It shall further indicate the right to have the decision reviewed by the Court of Justice.

4. The owners of the undertakings or their representatives and, in the case of legal persons, companies or firms, or associations having no legal personality, the persons authorised to represent them by law or by their constitution, shall supply the information requested on behalf of the undertaking concerned. Persons duly authorized to act may supply the information on behalf of their clients. The latter shall remain fully responsible if the information supplied is incomplete, incorrect or misleading.

5. The Commission shall without delay forward a copy of any decision taken pursuant to paragraph 3 to the competent authorities of the Member State in whose territory the residence of the person or the seat of the undertaking or association of undertakings is situated, and to the competent authority of the Member State whose territory is affected. At the specific request of the competent authority of a Member State, the Commission shall also forward to that authority copies of simple requests for information relating to a notified concentration.

6. At the request of the Commission, the governments and competent authorities of the Member States shall provide the Commission with all necessary information to carry out the duties assigned to it by this Regulation.

7. In order to carry out the duties assigned to it by this Regulation, the Commission may interview any natural or legal person who consents to be interviewed for the purpose of collecting information relating to the subject matter of an investigation. At the beginning of the interview, which may be conducted by telephone or other electronic means, the Commission shall state the legal basis and the purpose of the interview.

Where an interview is not conducted on the premises of the Commission or by telephone or other electronic means, the Commission shall inform in advance the competent authority of the Member State in whose territory the interview takes place. If the competent authority of that Member State so requests, officials of that authority may assist the officials and other persons authorized by the Commission to conduct the interview.

Article 12
Inspections by the authorities of the Member States

1. At the request of the Commission, the competent authorities of the Member States shall undertake the inspections which the Commission considers to be necessary under Article 13(1), or which it has ordered by decision pursuant to Article 13(4). The officials of the competent authorities of the Member States who are responsible for conducting these inspections as well as those authorised or appointed by them shall exercise their powers in accordance with their national law.

2. If so requested by the Commission or by the competent authority of the Member State within whose territory the inspection is to be conducted, officials and other accompanying persons authorised by the Commission may assist the officials of the authority concerned.

Article 13
The Commission's powers of inspection

1. In order to carry out the duties assigned to it by this Regulation, the Commission may conduct all necessary inspections of undertakings and associations of undertakings.

2. The officials and other accompanying persons authorised by the Commission to conduct an inspection shall have the power:
(a) to enter any premises, land and means of transport of undertakings and associations of undertakings;
(b) to examine the books and other records related to the business, irrespective of the medium on which they are stored;
(c) to take or obtain in any form copies of or extracts from such books or records;
(d) to seal any business premises and books or records for the period and to the extent necessary for the inspection;
(e) to ask any representative or member of staff of the undertaking or association of undertakings for explanations on facts or documents relating to the subject matter and purpose of the inspection and to record the answers.

3. Officials and other accompanying persons authorized by the Commission to conduct an inspection shall exercise their powers upon production of a written authorisation specifying the subject matter and purpose of the inspection and the penalties provided for in Article 14, in the production of the required books or other records related to the business which is incomplete or where answers to questions asked under paragraph 2 of this Article are incorrect or misleading. In good time before the inspection, the Commission shall give notice of the inspection to the competent authority of the Member State in whose territory the inspection is to be conducted.

4. Undertakings and associations of undertakings are required to submit to inspections ordered by decision of the Commission. The decision shall specify the subject matter and purpose of the inspection, appoint the date on which it is to begin and indicate the penalties provided for in Articles 14 and 15 and the right to have the decision reviewed by the Court of Justice. The Commission shall take such decisions after consulting the competent authority of the Member State in whose territory the inspection is to be conducted.

5. Officials of, and those authorized or appointed by, the competent authority of the Member State in whose territory the inspection is to be conducted shall, at the request of that authority or of the Commission, actively assist the officials and other accompanying persons authorised by the Commission. To this end, they shall enjoy the powers specified in paragraph 2.

6. Where the officials and other accompanying persons authorised by the Commission find that an undertaking opposes an inspection, including the sealing of business premises, books or records, ordered pursuant to this Article, the Member State concerned shall afford them the necessary assistance, requesting where appropriate the assistance of the police or of an equivalent enforcement authority, so as to enable them to conduct their inspection.

7. If the assistance provided for in paragraph 6 requires authorisation from a judicial authority according to national rules, such authorisation shall be applied for. Such authorisation may also be applied for as a precautionary measure.

8. Where authorisation as referred to in paragraph 7 is applied for, the national judicial authority shall ensure that the Commission decision is authentic and that the coercive measures envisaged are neither arbitrary nor excessive having regard to the subject matter of the inspection. In its control of proportionality of the coercive measures, the national judicial authority may ask the Commission, directly or through the competent authority of that Member State, for detailed explanations relating to the subject matter of the inspection. However, the national judicial authority may not call into question the necessity for the inspection nor demand that it be provided with the information in the Commission's file. The lawfulness of the Commission's decision shall be subject to review only by the Court of Justice.

Article 14
Fines

1. The Commission may by decision impose on the persons referred to in Article 3(1)b, undertakings or associations of undertakings, fines not exceeding 1% of the aggregate turnover of the undertaking or association of undertakings concerned within the meaning of Article 5 where, intentionally or negligently:
(a) they supply incorrect or misleading information in a submission, certification, notification or supplement thereto, pursuant to Article 4, Article 10(5) or Article 22(3);
(b) they supply incorrect or misleading information in response to a request made pursuant to Article 11(2);
(c) in response to a request made by decision adopted pursuant to Article 11(3), they supply incorrect, incomplete or misleading information or do not supply information within the required time limit;
(d) they produce the required books or other records related to the business in incomplete form during inspections under Article 13, or refuse to submit to an inspection ordered by decision taken pursuant to Article 13(4);
(e) in response to a question asked in accordance with Article 13(2)(e),
 — they give an incorrect or misleading answer,
 — they fail to rectify within a time limit set by the Commission an incorrect, incomplete or misleading answer given by a member of staff, or
 — they fail or refuse to provide a complete answer on facts relating to the subject matter and purpose of an inspection ordered by a decision adopted pursuant to Article 13(4);

(f) seals affixed by officials or other accompanying persons authorized by the Commission in accordance with Article 13(2)(d) have been broken.

2. The Commission may be decision impose fines not exceeding 10% of the aggregate turnover of the undertaking concerned within the meaning of Article 5 on the persons referred to in Article 3(1)b or the undertakings concerned where, either intentionally or negligently, they:

(a) fail to notify a concentration in accordance with Articles 4 or 22(3) prior to its implementation, unless they are expressly authorized to do so by Article 7(2) or by a decision taken pursuant to Article 7(3);

(b) implement a concentration in breach of Article 7;

(c) implement a concentration declared incompatible with the common market by decision pursuant to Article 8(3) or do not comply with any measure ordered by decision pursuant to Article 8(4) or (5);

(d) fail to comply with a condition or an obligation imposed by decision pursuant to Articles 6(1)(b), Article 7(3) or Article 8(2), second subparagraph.

3. In fixing the amount of the fine, regard shall be had to the nature, gravity and duration of the infringement.

4. Decisions taken pursuant to paragraphs 1, 2 and 3 shall not be of a criminal law nature.

Article 15
Periodic penalty payments

1. The Commission may by decision impose on the persons referred to in Article 3(1)b, undertakings or associations of undertakings, periodic penalty payments not exceeding 5% of the average daily aggregate turnover of the undertaking or association of undertakings concerned within the meaning of Article 5 for each working day of delay, calculated from the date set in the decision, in order to compel them:

(a) to supply complete and correct information which it has requested by decision taken pursuant to Article 11(3);

(b) to submit to an inspection which it has ordered by decision taken pursuant to Article 13(4);

(c) to comply with an obligation imposed by decision pursuant to Article 6(1)(b), Article 7(3) or Article 8(2), second subparagraph; or

(d) to comply with any measures ordered by decision pursuant to Article 8(4) or (5).

2. Where the persons referred to in Article 3(1)(b), undertakings or associations of undertakings have satisfied the obligation which the periodic penalty payment was intended to enforce, the Commission may fix the definitive amount of the periodic penalty payments at a figure lower than that which would arise under the original decision.

Article 16
Review by the Court of Justice

The Court of Justice shall have unlimited jurisdiction within the meaning of Article 229 of the Treaty to review decisions whereby the Commission has fixed a fine or periodic penalty payments; it may cancel, reduce or increase the fine or periodic penalty payment imposed.

Article 17
Professional secrecy

1. Information acquired as a result of the application of this Regulation shall be used only for the purposes of the relevant request, investigation or hearing.

2. Without prejudice to Article 4(3), Articles 18 and 20, the Commission and the competent authorities of the Member States, their officials and other servants and other persons working under the supervision of these authorities as well as officials and civil servants of other authorities

of the Member States shall not disclose information they have acquired through the application of this Regulation of the kind covered by the obligation of professional secrecy.

3. Paragraphs 1 and 2 shall not prevent publication of general information or of surveys which do not contain information relating to particular undertakings or associations of undertakings.

Article 18
Hearing of the parties and of third persons

1. Before taking any decision provided for in Article 6(3), Article 7(3), Article 8(2) to (6), and Articles 14 and 15, the Commission shall give the persons, undertakings and associations of undertakings concerned the opportunity, at every stage of the procedure up to the consultation of the Advisory Committee, of making known their views on the objections against them.

2. By way of derogation from paragraph 1, a decision pursuant to Articles 7(3) and 8(5) may be taken provisionally, without the persons, undertakings or associations of undertakings concerned being given the opportunity to make known their views beforehand, provided that the Commission gives them that opportunity as soon as possible after having taken its decision.

3. The Commission shall base its decision only on objections on which the parties have been able to submit their observations. The rights of the defence shall be fully respected in the proceedings. Access to the file shall be open at least to the parties directly involved, subject to the legitimate interest of undertakings in the protection of their business secrets.

4. In so far as the Commission or the competent authorities of the Member States deem it necessary, they may also hear other natural or legal persons. Natural or legal persons showing a sufficient interest and especially members of the administrative or management bodies of the undertakings concerned or the recognised representatives of their employees shall be entitled, upon application, to be heard.

Article 19
Liaison with the authorities of the Member States

1. The Commission shall transmit to the competent authorities of the Member States copies of notifications within three working days and, as soon as possible, copies of the most important documents lodged with or issued by the Commission pursuant to this Regulation. Such documents shall include commitments offered by the undertakings concerned vis-à-vis the Commission with a view to rendering the concentration compatible with the common market pursuant to Article 6(2) or Article 8(2), second subparagraph.

2. The Commission shall carry out the procedures set out in this Regulation in close and constant liaison with the competent authorities of the Member States, which may express their views upon those procedures. For the purposes of Article 9 it shall obtain information from the competent authority of the Member State as referred to in paragraph 2 of that Article and give it the opportunity to make known its views at every stage of the procedure up to the adoption of a decision pursuant to paragraph 3 of that Article; to that end it shall give it access to the file.

3. An Advisory Committee on concentrations shall be consulted before any decision is taken pursuant to Article 8(1) to (6), Articles 14 or 15 with the exception of provisional decisions taken in accordance with Article 18(2).

4. The Advisory Committee shall consist of representatives of the competent authorities of the Member States. Each Member State shall appoint one or two representatives; if unable to attend, they may be replaced by other representatives. At least one of the representatives of a Member State shall be competent in matters of restrictive practices and dominant positions.

5. Consultation shall take place at a joint meeting convened at the invitation of and chaired by the Commission. A summary of the case, together with an indication of the most important documents and a preliminary draft of the decision to be taken for each case considered, shall be

sent with the invitation. The meeting shall take place not less than 10 working days after the invitation has been sent. The Commission may in exceptional cases shorten that period as appropriate in order to avoid serious harm to one or more of the undertakings concerned by a concentration.

6. The Advisory Committee shall deliver an opinion on the Commission's draft decision, if necessary by taking a vote. The Advisory Committee may deliver an opinion even if some members are absent and unrepresented. The opinion shall be delivered in writing and appended to the draft decision. The Commission shall take the utmost account of the opinion delivered by the Committee. It shall inform the Committee of the manner in which its opinion has been taken into account.

7. The Commission shall communicate the opinion of the Advisory Committee, together with the decision, to the addressees of the decision. It shall make the opinion public together with the decision, having regard to the legitimate interest of undertakings in the protection of their business secrets.

Article 20
Publication of decisions

1. The Commission shall publish the decisions which it takes pursuant to Article 8(1) to (6), Articles 14 and 15 with the exception of provisional decisions taken in accordance with Article 18(2) together with the opinion of the Advisory Committee in the *Official Journal of the European Union*.

2. The publication shall state the names of the parties and the main content of the decision; it shall have regard to the legitimate interest of undertakings in the protection of their business secrets.

Article 21
Application of the Regulation and jurisdiction

1. This Regulation alone shall apply to concentrations as defined in Article 3, and Council Regulations (EC) No 1/2003,[8] (EEC) No 1017/68,[9] (EEC) No 4056/86[10] and (EEC) No 3975/87[11] shall not apply, except in relation to joint ventures that do not have a Community dimension and which have as their object or effect the coordination of the competitive behaviour of undertakings that remain independent.

2. Subject to review by the Court of Justice, the Commission shall have sole jurisdiction to take the decisions provided for in this Regulation.

3. No Member State shall apply its national legislation on competition to any concentration that has a Community dimension.

The first subparagraph shall be without prejudice to any Member State's power to carry out any enquiries necessary for the application of Articles 4(4), 9(2) or after referral, pursuant to Article 9(3), first subparagraph, indent (b), or Article 9(5), to take the measures strictly necessary for the application of Article 9(8).

4. Notwithstanding paragraphs 2 and 3, Member States may take appropriate measures to protect legitimate interests other than those taken into consideration by this Regulation and compatible with the general principles and other provisions of Community law.

---

[8] OJ L1, 4.1.2003, p 1.
[9] OJ L175, 23. 7, 1968, p 1. Regulation as last amended by Reg (EC) No 1/2003 (OJ L1, 4.1.2003, p 1).
[10] OJ L378, 31. 12. 1986, p 4. Regulation as last amended by Reg (EC) No 1/2003.
[11] OJ L374, 31, 12. 1987, p 1. Regulation as last amended by Reg (EC) No 1/2003.

Public security, plurality of the media and prudential rules shall be regarded as legitimate interests within the meaning of the first subparagraph.

Any other public interest must be communicated to the Commission by the Member State concerned and shall be recognized by the Commission after an assessment of its compatibility with the general principles and other provisions of Community law before the measures referred to above may be taken. The Commission shall inform the Member State concerned of its decision within 25 working days of that communication.

Article 22
Referral to the Commission

1. One or more Member States may request the Commission to examine any concentration as defined in Article 3 that does not have a Community dimension within the meaning of Article 1 but affects trade between Member States and threatens to significantly affect competition within the territory of the Member State or States making the request.

Such a request shall be made at most within 15 working days of the date on which the concentration was notified, or if no notification is required, otherwise made known to the Member State concerned.

2. The Commission shall inform the competent authorities of the Member States and the undertakings concerned of any request received pursuant to paragraph 1 without delay.

Any other Member State shall have the right to join the initial request within a period of 15 working days of being informed by the Commission of the initial request.

All national time limits relating to the concentration shall be suspended until, in accordance with the procedure set out in this Article, it has been decided where the concentration shall be examined. As soon as a Member State has informed the Commission and the undertakings concerned that it does not wish to join the request, the suspension of its national time limits shall end.

3. The Commission may, at the latest 10 working days after the expiry of the period set in paragraph 2, decide to examine, the concentration where it considers that it affects trade between Member States and threatens to significantly affect competition within the territory of the Member State or States making the request. If the Commission does not take a decision within this period, it shall be deemed to have adopted a decision to examine the concentration in accordance with the request.

The Commission shall inform all Member States and the undertakings concerned of its decision. It may request the submission of a notification pursuant to Article 4.

The Member State or States having made the request shall no longer apply their national legislation on competition to the concentration.

4. Article 2, Article 4(2) to (3), Articles 5, 6, and 8 to 21 shall apply where the Commission examines a concentration pursuant to paragraph 3. Article 7 shall apply to the extent that the concentration has not been implemented on the date on which the Commission informs the undertakings concerned that a request has been made.

Where a notification pursuant to Article 4 is not required, the period set in Article 10(1) within which proceedings may be initiated shall begin on the working day following that on which the Commission informs the undertakings concerned that it has decided to examine the concentration pursuant to paragraph 3.

5. The Commission may inform one or several Member States that it considers a concentration fulfils the criteria in paragraph 1. In such cases, the Commission may invite that Member State or those Member States to make a request pursuant to paragraph 1.

Article 23
Implementing provisions

1. The Commission shall have the power to lay down in accordance with the procedure referred to in paragraph 2:

(a) implementing provisions concerning the form, content and other details of notifications and submissions pursuant to Article 4;

(b) implementing provisions concerning time limits pursuant to Article 4(4), (5) Articles 7, 9, 10 and 22;

(c) the procedure and time limits for the submission and implementation of commitments pursuant to Article 6(2) and Article 8(2);

(d) implementing provisions concerning hearings pursuant to Article 18.

2. The Commission shall be assisted by an Advisory Committee, composed of representatives of the Member States.

(a) Before publishing draft implementing provisions and before adopting such provisions, the Commission shall consult the Advisory Committee.

(b) Consultation shall take place at a meeting convened at the invitation of and chaired by the Commission. A draft of the implementing provisions to be taken shall be sent with the invitation. The meeting shall take place not less than 10 working days after the invitation has been sent.

(c) The Advisory Committee shall deliver an opinion on the draft implementing provisions, if necessary by taking a vote. The Commission shall take the utmost account of the opinion delivered by the Committee.

Article 24
Relations with third countries

1. The Member States shall inform the Commission of any general difficulties encountered by their undertakings with concentrations as defined in Article 3 in a third country.

2. Initially not more than one year after the entry into force of this Regulation and, thereafter periodically, the Commission shall draw up a report examining the treatment accorded to undertakings having their seat or their principal fields of activity in the Community, in the terms referred to in paragraphs 3 and 4, as regards concentrations in third countries. The Commission shall submit those reports to the Council, together with any recommendations.

3. Whenever it appears to the Commission, either on the basis of the reports referred to in paragraph 2 or on the basis of other information, that a third country does not grant undertakings having their seat or their principal fields of activity in the Community, treatment comparable to that granted by the Community to undertakings from that country, the Commission may submit proposals to the Council for an appropriate mandate for negotiation with a view to obtaining comparable treatment for undertakings having their seat or their principal fields of activity in the Community.

4. Measures taken under this Article shall comply with the obligations of the Community or of the Member States, without prejudice to Article 307 of the Treaty, under international agreements, whether bilateral or multilateral.

Article 25
Repeal

1. Without prejudice to Article 26(2), Regulations (EEC) No 4064/89 and (EC) No 1310/97 shall be repealed with effect from 1 May 2004.

2. References to the repealed Regulations shall be construed as references to this Regulation and shall be read in accordance with the correlation table in the Annex.

Article 26
Entry into force and transitional provisions

1. This Regulation shall enter into force on the 20th day following that of its publication in the *Official Journal of the European Union*.

It shall apply from 1 May 2004.

2. Regulation (EEC) No 4064/89 shall continue to apply to any concentration which was the subject of an agreement or announcement or where control was acquired within the meaning of Article 4(1) of that Regulation before the date of application of this Regulation, subject, in particular, to the provisions governing applicability set out in Article 25(2) and (3) of Regulation (EEC) No 4064/89 and Article 2 of Regulation (EEC) No 1310/97.

3. As regards concentrations to which this Regulation applies by virtue of accession, the date of accession shall be substituted for the date of application of this Regulation.

This Regulation shall be binding in its entirety and directly applicable in all Member States.

Done at Brussels, 20 January 2004.

For the Council
The President
C. McCREEVY

ANNEX CORRELATION TABLE

Regulation (EEC) No 4064/89	This Regulation
Article 1(1), (2) and (3)	Article 1(1), (2) and (3)
Article 1(4)	Article 1(4)
Article 1(5)	Article 1(5)
Article 2(1)	Article 2(1)
—	Article 2(2)
Article 2(2)	Article 2(3)
Article 2(3)	Article 2(4)
Article 2(4)	Article 2(5)
Article 3(1)	Article 3(1)
Article 3(2)	Article 3(4)
Article 3(3)	Article 3(2)
Article 3(4)	Article 3(3)
—	Article 3(4)
Article 3(5)	Article 3(5)
Article 4(1) first sentence	Article 4(1) first subparagraph
Article 4(1) second sentence	—
—	Article 4(1) second and third subparagraphs
Article 4(2) and (3)	Article 4(2) and (3)
—	Article 4(4) to (6)
Article 5(1) to (3)	Article 5(1) to (3)
Article 5(4), introductory words	Article 5(4), introductory words
Article 5(4) point (a)	Article 5(4) point (a)
Article 5(4) point (b), introductory words	Article 5(4) point (b), introductory words
Article 5(4) point (b), first indent	Article 5(4) point (b)(i)
Article 5(4) point (b), second indent	Article 5(4) point (b)(ii)
Article 5(4) point (b), third indent	Article 5(4) point (b)(iii)
Article 5(4) point (b), fourth indent	Article 5(4) point (b)(iv)

Regulation (EEC) No 4064/89	This Regulation
Article 5(4) points (c), (d) and (e)	Article 5(4) points (c), (d) and (e)
Article 5(5)	Article 5(5)
Article 6(1), introductory words	Article 6(1), introductory words
Article 6(1) points (a) and (b)	Article 6(1) points (a) and (b)
Article 6(1) point (c)	Article 6(1) point (c), first sentence
Article 6(2) to (5)	Article 6(2) to (5)
Article 7(1)	Article 7(1)
Article 7(3)	Article 7(2)
Article 7(4)	Article 7(3)
Article 7(5)	Article 7(4)
Article 8(1)	Article 6(1) point (c), second sentence
Article 8(2)	Article 8(1) and (2)
Article 8(3)	Article 8(3)
Article 8(4)	Article 8(4)
–	Article 8(5)
Article 8(5)	Article 8(6)
Article 8(6)	Article 8(7)
–	Article 8(8)
Article 9(1) to (9)	Article 9(1) to (9)
Article 9(10)	–
Article 10(1) and (2)	Article 10(1) and (2)
Article 10(3)	Article 10(3) first subparagraph, first sentence
–	Article 10(3) first subparagraph, second sentence
–	Article 10(3) second subparagraph
Article 10(4)	Article 10(4) first subparagraph
–	Article 10(4), second subparagraph
Article 10(5)	Article 10(5), first and fourth subparagraphs
–	Article 10(5), second, third and fifth subparagraphs
Article 10(6)	Article 10(6)
Article 11(1)	Article 11(1)
Article 11(2)	–
Article 11(3)	Article 11(2)
Article 11(4)	Article 11(4) first sentence
–	Article 11(4) second and third sentences
Article 11(5) first sentence	–
Article 11(5) second sentence	Article 11(3)
Article 11(6)	Article 11(5)
–	Article 11(6) and (7)
Article 12	Article 12
Article 13(1) first subparagraph	Article 13(1)
Article 13(1) second subparagraph, introductory words	Article 13(2) introductory words
Article 13(1) second subparagraph, point (a)	Article 13(2) point (b)
Article 13(1) second subparagraph, point (b)	Article 13(2) point (c)
Article 13(1) second subparagraph, point (c)	Article 13(2) point (e)
Article 13(1) second subparagraph, point (d)	Article 13(2) point (a)
–	Article 13(2) point (d)
Article 13(2)	Article 13(3)
Article 13(3)	Article 13(4) first and second sentences
Article 13(4)	Article 13(4) third sentence

Regulation (EEC) No 4064/89	This Regulation
Article 13(5)	Article 13(5), first sentence
–	Article 13(5), second sentence
Article 13(6) first sentence	Article 13(6)
Article 13(6) second sentence	–
–	Article 13(7) and (8)
Article 14(1) introductory words	Article 14(1) introductory words
Article 14(1) point (a)	Article 14(2) point (a)
Article 14(1) point (b)	Article 14(1) point (a)
Article 14(1) point (c)	Article 14(1) points (b) and (c)
Article 14(1) point (d)	Article 14(1) point (d)
–	Article 14(1) points (e) and (f)
Article 14(2) introductory words	Article 14(2) introductory words
Article 14(2) point (a)	Article 14(2) point (d)
Article 14(2) points (b) and (c)	Article 14(2) points (b) and (c)
Article 14(3)	Article 14(3)
Article 14(4)	Article 14(4)
Article 15(1) introductory words	Article 15(1) introductory words
Article 15(1) points (a) and (b)	Article 15(1) points (a) and (b)
Article 15(2) introductory words	Article 15(1) introductory words
Article 15(2) point (a)	Article 15(1) point (c)
Article 15(2) point (b)	Article 15(1) point (d)
Article 15(3)	Article 15(2)
Articles 16 to 20	Articles 16 to 20
Article 21(1)	Article 21(2)
Article 21(2)	Article 21(3)
Article 21(3)	Article 21(4)
Article 22(1)	Article 21(1)
Article 22(3)	–
–	Article 22(1) to (3)
Article 22(4)	Article 22(4)
Article 22(5)	–
–	Article 22(5)
Article 23	Article 23(1)
–	Article 23(2)
Article 24	Article 24
–	Article 25
Article 25(1)	Article 26(1), first subparagraph
–	Article 26(1), second subparagraph
Article 25(2)	Article 26(2)
Article 25(3)	Article 26(3)
–	Annex

APPENDIX 16

Commission Regulation (EC) No 802/2004 of 7 April 2004 implementing Council Regulation (EC) No 139/2004 on the control of concentrations between undertakings

(Text with EEA relevance)

THE COMMISSION OF THE EUROPEAN COMMUNITIES,

Having regard to the Treaty establishing the European Community,

Having regard to the Agreement on the European Economic Area,

Having regard to Council Regulation (EC) No 139/2004 of 20 January 2004 on the control of concentrations between undertakings (EC Merger Regulation),[1] and in particular Article 23(1) thereof,

Having regard to Council Regulation (EEC) No 4064/89 of 21 December 1989 on the control of concentrations between undertakings,[2] as last amended by Regulation (EC) No 1310/97,[3] and in particular Article 23 thereof,

Having consulted the Advisory Committee,

Whereas:

(1) Council Regulation (EEC) No 4064/89 of 21 December 1989 on the control of concentrations between undertakings has been recast, with substantial amendments to various provisions of that Regulation.

(2) Commission Regulation (EC) No 447/98[4] of 1 March 1998 on the notifications, time-limits and hearings provided for in Council Regulation (EEC) No 4064/89 must be modified in order to take account of those amendments. For the sake of clarity it should therefore be repealed and replaced by a new regulation.

(3) The Commission has adopted measures concerning the terms of reference of hearing officers in certain competition proceedings.

(4) Regulation (EC) No 139/2004 is based on the principle of compulsory notification of concentrations before they are put into effect. On the one hand, a notification has important legal consequences which are favourable to the parties to the proposed concentration, while, on the other hand, failure to comply with the obligation to notify renders the parties liable to fines and may also entail civil law disadvantages for them. It is therefore necessary in the interests of legal certainty to define precisely the subject matter and content of the information to be provided in the notification.

(5) It is for the notifying parties to make a full and honest disclosure to the Commission of the facts and circumstances which are relevant for taking a decision on the notified concentration.

[1] OJ L24, 29.1.2004, p 1.
[2] OJ L395, 30.12.1989, p 1.
[3] OJ L180, 9.7.1997, p 1.
[4] OJ L61, 2.3.1998, p 1. Reg as amended by the 2003 Act of Accession.

(6) Regulation (EC) No 139/2004 also allows the undertakings concerned to request, in a reasoned submission, prior to notification, that a concentration fulfilling the requirements of that Regulation be referred to the Commission by one or more Member States, or referred by the Commission to one or more Member States, as the case may be. It is important to provide the Commission and the competent authorities of the Member States concerned with sufficient information, in order to enable them to assess, within a short period of time, whether or not a referral ought to be made. To that end, the reasoned submission requesting the referral should contain certain specific information.

(7) In order to simplify and expedite examination of notifications and of reasoned submissions, it is desirable to prescribe that forms be used.

(8) Since notification sets in motion legal time-limits pursuant to Regulation (EC) No 139/2004, the conditions governing such time-limits and the time when they become effective should also be determined.

(9) Rules must be laid down in the interests of legal certainty for calculating the time-limits provided for in Regulation (EC) No 139/2004. In particular, the beginning and end of time periods and the circumstances suspending the running of such periods must be determined, with due regard to the requirements resulting from the exceptionally tight legal timeframe available for the proceedings.

(10) The provisions relating to the Commission's procedure must be framed in such a way as to safeguard fully the right to be heard and the rights of defence. For these purposes, the Commission should distinguish between the parties who notify the concentration, other parties involved in the proposed concentration, third parties and parties regarding whom the Commission intends to take a decision imposing a fine or periodic penalty payments.

(11) The Commission should give the notifying parties and other parties involved in the proposed concentration, if they so request, an opportunity before notification to discuss the intended concentration informally and in strict confidence. In addition, the Commission should, after notification, maintain close contact with those parties, to the extent necessary to discuss with them any practical or legal problems which it discovers on a first examination of the case, with a view, if possible, to resolving such problems by mutual agreement.

(12) In accordance with the principle of respect for the rights of defence, the notifying parties must be given the opportunity to submit their comments on all the objections which the Commission proposes to take into account in its decisions. The other parties involved in the proposed concentration should also be informed of the Commission's objections and should be granted the opportunity to express their views.

(13) Third parties demonstrating a sufficient interest must also be given the opportunity of expressing their views, if they make a written application to that effect.

(14) The various persons entitled to submit comments should do so in writing, both in their own interests and in the interests of sound administration, without prejudice to their right to request a formal oral hearing, where appropriate, to supplement the written procedure. In urgent cases, however, the Commission must be enabled to proceed immediately to formal oral hearings of the notifying parties, of other parties involved or of third parties.

(15) It is necessary to define the rights of persons who are to be heard, to what extent they should be granted access to the Commission's file and on what conditions they may be represented or assisted.

(16) When granting access to the file, the Commission should ensure the protection of business secrets and other confidential information. The Commission should be able to ask undertakings that have submitted documents or statements to identify confidential information.

(17) In order to enable the Commission to carry out a proper assessment of commitments offered by the notifying parties with a view to rendering the concentration compatible with the common market, and to ensure due consultation with other parties involved, with third parties and with the authorities of the Member States as provided for in Regulation (EC)

No 139/2004, in particular Article 18(1), 18(4), Article 19(1), 19(2), 19(3) and 19(5) thereof, the procedure and time-limits for submitting the commitments referred to in Article 6(2) and Article 8(2) of that Regulation should be laid down.

(18) It is also necessary to define the rules applicable to certain time limits set by the Commission.

(19) The Advisory Committee on Concentrations must deliver its opinion on the basis of a preliminary draft decision. It must therefore be consulted on a case after the inquiry in to that case has been completed. Such consultation does not, however, prevent the Commission from reopening an inquiry if need be.

HAS ADOPTED THIS REGULATION:

CHAPTER I. SCOPE

Article 1

Scope

This Regulation shall apply to the control of concentrations conducted pursuant to Regulation (EC) No 139/2004.

CHAPTER II. NOTIFICATIONS AND OTHER SUBMISSIONS

Article 2

Persons entitled to submit notifications

1. Notifications shall be submitted by the persons or undertakings referred to in Article 4(2) of Regulation (EC) No 139/2004.

2. Where notifications are signed by representatives of persons or of undertakings, such representatives shall produce written proof that they are authorised to act.

3. Joint notifications shall be submitted by a joint representative who is authorised to transmit and to receive documents on behalf of all notifying parties.

Article 3

Submission of notifications

1. Notifications shall be submitted in the manner prescribed by Form CO as set out in Annex I. Under the conditions set out in Annex II, notifications may be submitted in Short Form as defined therein. Joint notifications shall be submitted on a single form.

2. One original and 35 copies of the Form CO and the supporting documents shall be submitted to the Commission. The notification shall be delivered to the address referred to in Article 23(1) and in the format specified by the Commission.

3. The supporting documents shall be either originals or copies of the originals; in the latter case the notifying parties shall confirm that they are true and complete.

4. Notifications shall be one of the official languages of the Community. For the notifying parties, this language shall also be the language of the proceeding, as well as that of any subsequent proceedings relating to the same concentration. Supporting documents shall be submitted in their original language. Where the original language is not one of the official languages of the Community, a translation into the language of the proceeding shall be attached.

5. Where notifications are made pursuant to Article 57 of the Agreement on the European Economic Area, they may also be submitted in one of the official languages of the EFTA States or the working language of the EFTA Surveillance Authority. If the language chosen for the notifications is not an official language of the Community, the notifying parties shall simultaneously

supplement all documentation with a translation into an official language of the Community. The language which is chosen for the translation shall determine the language used by the Commission as the language of the proceeding for the notifying parties.

Article 4
Information and documents to be provided

1. Notifications shall contain the information, including documents, requested in the applicable forms set out in the Annexes. The information shall be correct and complete.

2. The Commission may dispense with the obligation to provide any particular information in the notification, including documents, or with any other requirement specified in Annexes I and II where the Commission considers that compliance with those obligations or requirements is not necessary for the examination of the case.

3. The Commission shall without delay acknowledge in writing to the notifying parties or their representatives receipt of the notification and of any reply to a letter sent by the Commission pursuant to Article 5(2) and 5(3).

Article 5
Effective date of notification

1. Subject to paragraphs 2, 3 and 4, notifications shall become effective on the date on which they are received by the Commission.

2. Where the information, including documents, contained in the notification is incomplete in any material respect, the Commission shall inform the notifying parties or their representatives in writing without delay. In such cases, the notification shall become effective on the date on which the complete information is received by the Commission.

3. Material changes in the facts contained in the notification coming to light subsequent to the notification which the notifying parties know or ought to know, or any new information coming to light subsequent to the notification which the parties know or ought to know and which would have had to be notified if known at the time of notification, shall be communicated to the Commission without delay. In such cases, when these material changes or new information could have a significant effect on the appraisal of the concentration, the notification may be considered by the Commission as becoming effective on the date on which the relevant information is received by the Commission; the Commission shall inform the notifying parties or their representatives of this in writing and without delay.

4. Incorrect or misleading information shall be considered to be incomplete information.

5. When the Commission publishes the fact of the notification pursuant to Article 4(3) of Regulation (EC) No 139/2004, it shall specify the date upon which the notification has been received. Where, further to the application of paragraphs 2, 3 and 4 of this Article, the effective date of notification is later than the date specified in that publication, the Commission shall issue a further publication in which it shall state the later date.

Article 6
Specific provisions relating to reasoned submissions, supplements and certifications

1. Reasoned submissions within the meaning of Article 4(4) and 4(5) of Regulation (EC) No 139/2004 shall contain the information, including documents, requested in accordance with Annex III to this Regulation.

2. Article 2, Article 3(1), third sentence, 3(2) to (5), Article 4, Article 5(1), 5(2) first sentence, 5(3), 5(4), Article 21 and Article 23 of this Regulation shall apply *mutatis mutandis* to reasoned submissions within the meaning of Article 4(4) and 4(5) of Regulation (EC) No 139/2004.

Article 2, Article 3(1), third sentence, 3(2) to (5), Article 4, Article 5(1) to (4), Article 21 and Article 23 of this Regulation shall apply *mutatis mutandis* to supplements to notifications and certifications within the meaning of Article 10(5) of Regulation (EC) No 139/2004.

CHAPTER III. TIME-LIMITS

Article 7
Beginning of time periods

Time periods shall begin on the working day, as defined in Article 24 of this Regulation, following the event to which the relevant provision of Regulation (EC) No 139/2004 refers.

Article 8
Expiry of time periods

A time period calculated in working days shall expire at the end of its last working day.

A time period set by the Commission in terms of a calendar date shall expire at the end of that day.

Article 9
Suspension of time-limit

1. The time-limits referred to in Articles 9(4), Article 10(1) and 10(3) of Regulation (EC) No 139/2004 shall be suspended where the Commission has to take a decision pursuant to Article 11(3) or Article 13(4) of that Regulation, on any of the following grounds:

(a) information which the Commission has requested pursuant to Article 11(2) of Regulation (EC) No 139/2004 from one of the notifying parties or another involved party, as defined in Article 11 of this Regulation, is not provided or not provided in full within the time-limit fixed by the Commission;

(b) information which the Commission has requested pursuant to Article 11(2) of Regulation (EC) No 139/2004 from a third party, as defined in Article 11 of this Regulation, is not provided or not provided in full within the time-limit fixed by the Commission owing to circumstances for which one of the notifying parties or another involved party, as defined in Article 11 of this Regulation, is responsible;

(c) one of the notifying parties or another involved party, as defined in Article 11 of this Regulation, has refused to submit to an inspection deemed necessary by the Commission on the basis of Article 13(1) of Regulation (EC) No 139/2004 or to cooperate in the carrying out of such an inspection in accordance with Article 13(2) of that Regulation;

(d) the notifying parties have failed to inform the Commission of material changes in the facts contained in the notification, or of any new information of the kind referred to in Article 5(3) of this Regulation.

2. The time-limits referred to in Articles 9(4), Article 10(1) and 10(3) of Regulation (EC) No 139/2004 shall be suspended where the Commission has to take a decision pursuant to Article 11(3) of that Regulation, without proceeding first by way of simple request for information, owing to circumstances for which one of the undertakings involved in the concentration is responsible.

3. The time-limits referred to in Article 9(4), Article 10(1) and (3) of Regulation (EC) No 139/2004 shall be suspended:

(a) in the cases referred to in points (a) and (b) of paragraph 1, for the period between the expiry of the time limit set in the simple request for information, and the receipt of the complete and correct information required by decision;

(b) in the cases referred to in point (c) of paragraph 1, for the period between the unsuccessful attempt to carry out the inspection and the completion of the inspection ordered by decision;

1205

(c) in the cases referred to in point (d) of paragraph 1, for the period between the occurrence of the change in the facts referred to therein and the receipt of the complete and correct information.

(d) in the cases referred to in paragraph 2 for the period between the expiry of the time limit set in the decision and the receipt of the complete and correct information required by decision.

4. The suspension of the time-limit shall begin on the working day following the date on which the event causing the suspension occurred. It shall expire with the end of the day on which the reason for suspension is removed. Where such a day is not a working day, the suspension of the time-limit shall expire with the end of the following working day.

Article 10
Compliance with the time-limits

1. The time-limits referred to in Article 4(4), fourth subparagraph, Article 9(4), Article 10(1) and (3), and Article 22(3) of Regulation (EC) No 139/2004 shall be met where the Commission has taken the relevant decision before the end of the period.

2. The time-limits referred to in Article 4(4), second subparagraph, Article 4(5), third subparagraph, Article 9(2), Article 22(1), second subparagraph, and 22(2), second subparagraph, of Regulation (EC) No 139/2004 shall be met by a Member State concerned where that Member State, before the end of the period, informs the Commission in writing or makes or joins the request in writing, as the case may be.

3. The time-limit referred to in Article 9(6) of Regulation (EC) No 139/2004 shall be met where the competent authority of a Member State concerned informs the undertakings concerned in the manner set out in that provision before the end of the period.

CHAPTER IV. EXERCISE OF THE RIGHT TO BE HEARD; HEARINGS

Article 11
Parties to be heard

For the purposes of the rights to be heard pursuant to Article 18 of Regulation (EC) No 139/2004, the following parties are distinguished:

(a) notifying parties, that is, persons or undertakings submitting a notification pursuant to Article 4(2) of Regulation (EC) No 139/2004;

(b) other involved parties, that is, parties to the proposed concentration other than the notifying parties, such as the seller and the undertaking which is the target of the concentration;

(c) third persons, that is natural or legal persons, including customers, suppliers and competitors, provided they demonstrate a sufficient interest within the meaning of Article 18(4), second sentence, of Regulation (EC) No 139/2004, which is the case in particular
   — for members of the administrative or management bodies of the undertakings concerned or the recognised representatives of their employees;
   — for consumer associations, where the proposed concentration concerns products or services used by final consumers.

(d) parties regarding whom the Commission intends to take a decision pursuant to Article 14 or Article 15 of Regulation (EC) No 139/2004.

Article 12
Decisions on the suspension of concentrations

1. Where the Commission intends to take a decision pursuant to Article 7(3) of Regulation (EC) No 139/2004 which adversely affects one or more of the parties, it shall, pursuant to

Article 18(1) of that Regulation, inform the notifying parties and other involved parties in writing of its objections and shall set a time limit within which they may make known their views in writing.

2. Where the Commission, pursuant to Article 18(2) of Regulation (EC) No 139/2004, has taken a decision referred to in paragraph 1 of this Article provisionally without having given the notifying parties and other involved parties the opportunity to make known their views, it shall without delay send them the text of the provisional decision and shall set a time limit within which they may make known their views in writing.

Once the notifying parties and other involved parties have made known their views, the Commission shall take a final decision annulling, amending or confirming the provisional decision. Where they have not made known their views in writing within the time limit set, the Commission's provisional decision shall become final with the expiry of that period.

Article 13
Decisions on the substance of the case

1. Where the Commission intends to take a decision pursuant to Article 6(3) or Article 8(2) to (6) of Regulation (EC) No 139/2004, it shall, before consulting the Advisory Committee on Concentrations, hear the parties pursuant to Article 18(1) and (3) of that Regulation.

Article 12(2) of this Regulation shall apply *mutatis mutandis* where, in application of Article 18(2) of Regulation (EC) No 139/2004, the Commission has taken a decision pursuant to Article 8(5) of that Regulation provisionally.

2. The Commission shall address its objections in writing to the notifying parties.

The Commission shall, when giving notice of objections, set a time limit within which the notifying parties may inform the Commission of their comments in writing.

The Commission shall inform other involved parties in writing of these objections.

The Commission shall also set a time limit within which those other involved parties may inform the Commission of their comments in writing.

The Commission shall not be obliged to take into account comments received after the expiry of a time limit which it has set.

3. The parties to whom the Commission's objections have been addressed or who have been informed of those objections shall, within the time limit set, submit in writing their comments on the objections. In their written comments, they may set out all facts and matters known to them which are relevant to their defence, and shall attach any relevant documents as proof of the facts set out. They may also propose that the Commission hear persons who may corroborate those facts. They shall submit one original and 10 copies of their comments to the Commission to the address of the Commission's Directorate General for Competition. An electronic copy shall also be submitted at the same address and in the format specified by the Commission. The Commission shall forward copies of such written comments without delay to the competent authorities of the Member States.

4. Where the Commission intends to take a decision pursuant to Article 14 or Article 15 of Regulation (EC) No 139/2004, it shall, before consulting the Advisory Committee on Concentrations, hear pursuant to Article 18(1) and (3) of that Regulation the parties regarding whom the Commission intends to take such a decision.

The procedure provided for in paragraph 2, first and second subparagraphs, and paragraph 3 shall apply, *mutatis mutandis*.

Article 14
Oral hearings

1. Where the Commission intends to take a decision pursuant to Article 6(3) or Article 8(2) to (6) of Regulation (EC) No 139/2004, it shall afford the notifying parties who have so requested in their written comments the opportunity to develop their arguments in a formal oral hearing. It may also, at other stages in the proceedings, afford the notifying parties the opportunity of expressing their views orally.

2. Where the Commission intends to take a decision pursuant to Article 6(3) or Article 8(2) to (6) of Regulation (EC) No 139/2004, it shall also afford other involved parties who have so requested in their written comments the opportunity to develop their arguments in a formal oral hearing. It may also, at other stages in the proceedings, afford other involved parties the opportunity of expressing their views orally.

3. Where the Commission intends to take a decision pursuant to Article 14 or Article 15 of Regulation (EC) No 139/2004, it shall afford parties on whom it proposes to impose a fine or periodic penalty payment the opportunity to develop their arguments in a formal oral hearing, if so requested in their written comments. It may also, at other stages in the proceedings, afford such parties the opportunity of expressing their views orally.

Article 15
Conduct of formal oral hearings

1. Formal oral hearings shall be conducted by the Hearing Officer in full independence.

2. The Commission shall invite the persons to be heard to attend the formal oral hearing on such date as it shall determine.

3. The Commission shall invite the competent authorities of the Member States to take part in any formal oral hearing.

4. Persons invited to attend shall either appear in person or be represented by legal representatives or by representatives authorised by their constitution as appropriate. Undertakings and associations of undertakings may also be represented by a duly authorised agent appointed from among their permanent staff.

5. Persons heard by the Commission may be assisted by their lawyers or other qualified and duly authorised persons admitted by the Hearing Officer.

6. Formal oral hearings shall not be public. Each person may be heard separately or in the presence of other persons invited to attend, having regard to the legitimate interest of the undertakings in the protection of their business secrets and other confidential information.

7. The Hearing Officer may allow all parties within the meaning of Article 11, the Commission services and the competent authorities of the Member States to ask questions during the formal oral hearing.

The Hearing Officer may hold a preparatory meeting with the parties and the Commission services, so as to facilitate the efficient organisation of the formal oral hearing.

8. The statements made by each person heard shall be recorded. Upon request, the recording of the formal oral hearing shall be made available to the persons who attended that hearing. Regard shall be had to the legitimate interest of the undertakings in the protection of their business secrets and other confidential information.

Article 16
Hearing of third persons

1. If third persons apply in writing to be heard pursuant to Article 18(4), second sentence, of Regulation (EC) No 139/2004, the Commission shall inform them in writing of the nature and subject matter of the procedure and shall set a time limit within which they may make known their views.

2. The third persons referred to in paragraph 1 shall make known their views in writing within the time limit set. The Commission may, where appropriate, afford such third parties who have so requested in their written comments the opportunity to participate in a formal hearing. It may also in other cases afford such third parties the opportunity of expressing their views orally.

3. The Commission may likewise invite any other natural or legal person to express its views, in writing as well as orally, including at a formal oral hearing.

CHAPTER V. ACCESS TO THE FILE AND TREATMENT OF CONFIDENTIAL INFORMATION

Article 17
Access to the file and use of documents

1. If so requested, the Commission shall grant access to the file to the parties to whom it has addressed a statement of objections, for the purpose of enabling them to exercise their rights of defence. Access shall be granted after the notification of the statement of objections.

2. The Commission shall, upon request, also give the other involved parties who have been informed of the objections access to the file in so far as this is necessary for the purposes of preparing their comments.

3. The right of access to the file shall not extend to confidential information, or to internal documents of the Commission or of the competent authorities of the Member States. The right of access to the file shall equally not extend to correspondence between the Commission and the competent authorities of the Member States or between the latter.

4. Documents obtained through access to the file pursuant to this Article may only be used for the purposes of the relevant proceeding pursuant to Regulation (EC) No 139/2004.

Article 18
Confidential information

1. Information, including documents, shall not be communicated or made accessible by the Commission in so far as it contains business secrets or other confidential information the disclosure of which is not considered necessary by the Commission for the purpose of the procedure.

2. Any person which makes known its views or comments pursuant to Article 12, Article 13 and Article 16 of this Regulation, or supplies information pursuant to Article 11 of Regulation (EC) No 139/2004, or subsequently submits further information to the Commission in the course of the same procedure, shall clearly identify any material which it considers to be confidential, giving reasons, and provide a separate non-confidential version by the date set by the Commission.

3. Without prejudice to paragraph 2, the Commission may require persons referred to in Article 3 of Regulation (EC) No 139/2004, undertakings and associations of undertakings in all cases where they produce or have produced documents or statements pursuant to Regulation (EC) No 139/2004 to identify the documents or parts of documents which they consider to contain business secrets or other confidential information belonging to them and to identify the undertakings with regard to which such documents are to be considered confidential.

The Commission may also require persons referred to in Article 3 of Regulation (EC) No 139/2004, undertakings or associations of undertakings to identify any part of a statement of objections, case summary or a decision adopted by the Commission which in their view contains business secrets.

Where business secrets or other confidential information are identified, the persons, undertakings and associations of undertakings shall give reasons and provide a separate non-confidential version by the date set by the Commission.

CHAPTER VI. COMMITMENTS OFFERED BY THE UNDERTAKINGS CONCERNED

Article 19
Time-limits for submission of commitments

1. Commitments offered by the undertakings concerned pursuant to Article 6(2) of Regulation (EC) No 139/2004 shall be submitted to the Commission within not more than 20 working days from the date of receipt of the notification.

2. Commitments offered by the undertakings concerned pursuant to Article 8(2) of Regulation (EC) No 139/2004 shall be submitted to the Commission within not more than 65 working days from the date on which proceedings were initiated.

Where pursuant to Article 10(3), second subparagraph, of Regulation (EC) No 139/2004 the period for the adoption of a decision pursuant to Article 8(1), (2) and (3) is extended, the period of 65 working days for the submission of commitments shall automatically be extended by the same number of working days.

In exceptional circumstances, the Commission may accept commitments offered after the expiry of the time limit for their submission within the meaning of this paragraph provided that the procedure provided for in Article 19(5) of Regulation (EC) No 139/2004 is complied with.

3. Article 7, 8 and 9 shall apply *mutatis mutandis.*

Article 20
Procedure for the submission of commitments

1. One original and 10 copies of commitments offered by the undertakings concerned pursuant to Article 6(2) or Article 8(2) of Regulation (EC) No 139/2004 shall be submitted to the Commission at the address of the Commission's Directorate General for Competition. An electronic copy shall also be submitted at the same address and in the format specified by the Commission. The Commission shall forward copies of such commitments without delay to the competent authorities of the Member States.

2. When offering commitments pursuant to Articles 6(2) or Article 8(2) of Regulation (EC) No 139/2004, the undertakings concerned shall at the same time clearly identify any information which they consider to be confidential, giving reasons, and shall provide a separate non-confidential version.

CHAPTER VII. MISCELLANEOUS PROVISIONS

Article 21
Transmission of documents

1. Transmission of documents and invitations from the Commission to the addresses may be effected in any of the following ways:
(a) delivery by hand against receipt;
(b) registered letter with acknowledgement of receipt;

(c) fax with a request for acknowledgement of receipt;

(d) telex;

(e) electronic mail with a request for acknowledgement of receipt.

2. Unless otherwise provided in this Regulation, paragraph 1 also applies to the transmission of documents from the notifying parties, from other involved parties or from third parties to the Commission.

3. Where a document is sent by telex, by fax or by electronic mail, it shall be presumed that it has been received by the addressee on the day on which it was sent.

Article 22
Setting of time-limits

In setting the time limits provided for pursuant to Article 12(1) and (2), Article 13(2) and Article 16(1), the Commission shall have regard to the time required for the preparation of statements and to the urgency of the case. It shall also take account of working days as well as public holidays in the country of receipt of the Commission's communication.

Time-limits shall be set in terms of a precise calendar date.

Article 23
Receipt of documents by the Commission

1. In accordance with the provisions of Article 5(1) of this Regulation, notifications shall be delivered to the Commission at the address of the Commission's Directorate General for Competition as published by the Commission in the *Official Journal of the European Union*.

2. Additional information requested to complete notifications must reach the Commission at the address referred to in paragraph 1.

3. Written comments on Commission communications pursuant to Article 12(1) and (2), Article 13(2) and Article 16(1) of this Regulation must have reached the Commission at the address referred to in paragraph I before the expiry of the time-limit set in each case.

Article 24
Definition of working days

The expression working days in Regulation (EC) No 139/2004 and in this Regulation means all days other than Saturdays, Sundays, and Commission holidays as published in the *Official Journal of the European Union* before the beginning of each year.

Article 25
Repeal and transitional provision

1. Without prejudice to paragraphs 2 and 3, Regulation (EC) No 447/98 is repealed with effect from 1 May 2004.

References to the repealed Regulation shall be construed as references to this Regulation.

2. Regulation (EC) No 447/98 shall continue to apply to any concentration falling within the scope of Regulation (EEC) No 4064/89.

3. For the purposes of paragraph 2, Sections 1 to 12 of the Annex to Regulation (EC) No 447/98 shall be replaced by Sections 1 to 11 of Annex 1 to this Regulation. In such cases references in those sections to the 'EC Merger Regulation' and to the 'Implementing Regulation' shall be read as referring to the corresponding provisions of Regulation (EEC) No 4064/89 and Regulation (EC) No 447/98, respectively,

Article 26
Entry into force

This Regulation shall enter into force on 1 May 2004.

This Regulation shall be binding in its entirety and directly applicable in all Member States.

Done at Brussels, 7 April 2004.

> For the Commission
> Franz FISCHLER
> *Member of the Commission*

ANNEX 1. FORM CO RELATING TO THE NOTIFICATION OF A CONCENTRATION PURSUANT TO REGULATION (EC) NO 139/2004

1 Introduction

1.1 The purpose of this Form

This Form specifies the information that must be provided by notifying parties when submitting a notification to the European Commission of a proposed merger, acquisition or other concentration. The merger control system of the European Union is laid down in Council Regulation (EC) No 139/2004 (hereinafter referred to as 'the EC Merger Regulation'), and in Commission Regulation (EC) No xx/2004 (hereinafter referred to as 'the Implementing Regulation'), to which this Form CO is annexed.[5] The text of these regulations, as well as other relevant documents, can be found on the Competition page of the Commission's Europa web site.

In order to limit the time and expense involved in complying with various merger control procedures in several individual countries, the European Union has put in place a system of merger control by which concentrations having a Community dimension (normally, where the parties to the concentration fulfil certain turnover thresholds)[6] are assessed by the European Commission in a single procedure (the 'one stop shop' principle). Mergers which do not meet the turnover thresholds may fall within the competence of the Member States' authorities in charge of merger control.

The EC Merger Regulation requires the Commission to reach a decision within a legal deadline. In an initial phase the Commission normally has 25 working days to decide whether to clear the concentration or to 'initiate proceedings', i.e., to undertake an in-depth investigation[7] If the Commission decides to initiate proceedings, it normally has to take a final decision on the operation within no more than 90 working days of the date when proceedings are initiated.[8]

---

[5] Council Reg (EC) No 139/2004 of 20 January 2004, OJ L24, 29.01.2004, p 1. Your attention is drawn to the corresponding provisions of the Agreement on the European Economic Area (hereinafter referred to as 'the EEA Agreement'). See in particular Art 57 of the EEA Agreement, point 1 of Annex XIV to the EEA Agreement and Protocol 4 to the Agreement between the EFTA States on the establishment of a Surveillance Authority and a Court of Justice, as well as Protocols 21 and 24 to the EEA Agreement and Art 1 and the Agreed Minutes of the Protocol adjusting the EEA Agreement. Any reference to EFTA States shall be understood to mean those EFTA States which are Contracting Parties to the EEA Agreement. As of 1 May 2004, these States are Iceland, Liechtenstein and Norway.

[6] The term 'concentration' is defined in Art 3 of the EC Merger Reg and the term 'Community dimension' in Art 1 thereof. Furthermore, Art 4(5) provides that in certain circumstances where the Community turnover thresholds are not met, notifying parties may request that the Commission treat their proposed concentration as having a Community dimension.

[7] See Art 10(1) of the EC Merger Reg.

[8] See Art 10(3) of the EC Merger Reg.

In view of these deadlines, and for the 'one stop shop' principle to work, it is essential that the Commission is provided, in a timely fashion, with the information required to carry out the necessary investigation and to assess the impact of the concentration on the markets concerned. This requires that a certain amount of information be provided at the time of notification.

It is recognised that the information requested in this Form is substantial. However, experience has shown that, depending on the specific characteristics of the case, not all information is always necessary for an adequate examination of the proposed concentration. Accordingly, if you consider that any particular information requested by this Form may not be necessary for the Commission's examination of the case, you are encouraged to ask the Commission to dispense with the obligation to provide certain information ('waiver'). See Section 1.3(g) for more details.

Pre-notification contacts are extremely valuable to both the notifying parties and the Commission in determining the precise amount of information required in a notification and, in the majority of cases, will result in a significant reduction of the information required. Notifying parties may refer to the Commission's Best Practices on the Conduct of EC Merger Control Proceedings, which provides guidance on pre-notification contacts and the preparation of notifications.

In addition, it should be noted that certain concentrations, which are unlikely to pose any competition concerns, can be notified using a Short Form, which is attached to the Implementing Regulation, as Annex II.

1.2 Who must notify

In the case of a merger within the meaning of Article 3(1)(a) of the EC Merger Regulation or the acquisition of joint control of an undertaking within the meaning of Article 3(1)(b) of the EC Merger Regulation, the notification shall be completed jointly by the parties to the merger or by those acquiring joint control, as the case may be.[9]

In case of the acquisition of a controlling interest in one undertaking by another, the acquirer must complete the notification.

In the case of a public bid to acquire an undertaking, the bidder must complete the notification.

Each party completing the notification is responsible for the accuracy of the information which it provides.

1.3 The requirement for a correct and complete notification

All information required by this Form must be correct and complete. The information required must be supplied in the appropriate Section of this Form.

In particular you should note that:

(a) In accordance with Article 10(1) of the EC Merger Regulation and Article 5(2) and (4) of the implementing Regulation, the time-limits of the EC Merger Regulation linked to the notification will not begin to run until all the information that has to be supplied with the notification has been received by the Commission. This requirement is to ensure that the Commission is able to assess the notified concentration within the strict time-limits provided by the EC Merger Regulation.

(b) The notifying parties should verify, in the course of preparing their notification, that contact names and numbers, and in particular fax numbers and e-mail addresses, provided to the Commission are accurate, relevant and up-to-date.

(c) Incorrect or misleading information in the notification will be considered to be incomplete information (Article 5(4) of the Implementing Regulation).

(d) If a notification is incomplete, the Commission will inform the notifying parties or their representatives in writing and without delay. The notification will only become effective on

---

[9] See Art 4(2) of the EC Merger Reg.

the date on which the complete and accurate information is received by the Commission (Article 10(1) of the EC Merger Regulation, Articles 5(2) and (4) of the Implementing Regulation).

(e) Under Article 14(1)(a) of the EC Merger Regulation, notifying parties who, either intentionally or negligently, supply incorrect or misleading information, may be liable to fines of up to 1% of the aggregate turnover of the undertaking concerned. In addition, pursuant to Article 6(3)(a) and Article 8(6)(a) of the EC Merger Regulation the Commission may revoke its decision on the compatibility of a notified concentration where it is based on incorrect information for which one of the undertakings is responsible.

(f) You may request in writing that the Commission accept that the notification is complete notwithstanding the failure to provide information required by this Form, if such information is not reasonably available to you in part or in whole (for example, because of the unavailability of information on a target company during a contested bid).

The Commission will consider such a request, provided that you give reasons for the unavailability of that information, and provide your best estimates for missing data together with the sources for the estimates. Where possible, indications as to where any of the requested information that is unavailable to you could be obtained by the Commission should also be provided.

(g) You may request in writing that the Commission accept that the notification is complete notwithstanding the failure to provide information required by this Form, if you consider that any particular information required, in the full or short form version, may not be necessary for the Commission's examination of the case.

The Commission will consider such a request, provided that you give adequate reasons why that information is not relevant and necessary to its inquiry into the notified operation. You should explain this during your pre-notification contacts with the Commission and, submit a written request for a waiver, asking the Commission to dispense with the obligation to provide that information, pursuant to Article 4(2) of the Implementing Regulation.

1.4 How to notify

The notification must be completed in one of the official languages of the European Community. This language will thereafter be the language of the proceedings for all notifying parties. Where notifications are made in accordance with Article 12 of Protocol 24 to the EEA Agreement in an official language of an EFTA State which is not an official language of the Community, the notification must simultaneously be supplemented with a translation into an official language of the Community.

The information requested by this Form is to be set out using the sections and paragraph numbers of the Form, signing a declaration as provided in Section 11, and annexing supporting documentation. In completing Sections 7 to 9 of this Form, the notifying parties are invited to consider whether, for purposes of clarity, these sections are best presented in numerical order, or whether they can be grouped together for each individual affected market (or group of affected markets).

For the sake of clarity, certain information may be put in annexes. However, it is essential that all key substantive pieces of information, and in particular market share information for the parties and their largest competitors, are presented in the body of Form CO. Annexes to this Form shall only be used to supplement the information supplied in the Form itself.

Contact details must be provided in a format provided by the Commission's Directorate-General for Competition (DG Competition). For a proper investigatory process, it is essential that the contact details are accurate. Multiple instances of incorrect contact details may be a ground for declaring a notification incomplete.

Supporting documents are to be submitted in their original language; where this is not an official language of the Community, they must be translated into the language of the proceeding (Article 3(4) of the implementing Regulation).

Supporting documents may be originals or copies of the originals. In the latter case, the notifying party must confirm that they are true and complete.

One original and 35 copies of the Form CO and the supporting documents shall be submitted to the Commission's Directorate-General for Competition.

The notification shall be delivered to the address referred to in Article 23 (1) of the Implementing Regulation and in the format specified by the Commission from time to time. This address is published in the *Official Journal of the European Union*. The notification must be deliveredto the Commission on working days as defined by Article 24 of the Implementing Regulation. In order to enable it to be registered on the same day, it must be delivered before 17,000 hrs on Mondays to Thursdays and before 16.00 hrs on Fridays and workdays preceding public holidays and other holidays as determined by the Commission and published in the *Official Journal of the European Union*. The security instructions given on DG Competition's website must be adhered to.

1.5 Confidentiality

Article 287 of the Treaty and Article 17(2) of the EC Merger Regulation as well as the corresponding provisions of the EEA Agreement[10] require the Commission, the Member States, the EFTA Surveillance Authority and the EFTA States, their officials and other servants not to disclose information they have acquired through the application of the Regulation of the kind covered by the obligation of professional secrecy. The same principle must also apply to protect confidentiality between notifying parties.

If you believe that your interests would be harmed if any of the information you are asked to supply were to be published or otherwise divulged to other parties, submit this information separately with each page clearly marked 'Business Secrets'. You should also give reasons why this information should not be divulged or published.

In the case of mergers or joint acquisitions, or in other cases where the notification is completed by more than one of the parties, business secrets may be submitted under separate cover, and referred to in the notification as an annex. All such annexes must be included in the submission in order for a notification to be considered complete.

1.6 Definitions and instructions for purposes of this Form

Notifying party or parties: in cases where a notification is submitted by only one of the undertakings who is a party to an operation, 'notifying parties' is used to refer only to the undertaking actually submitting the notification.

Party(ies) to the concentration or parties; these terms relate to both the acquiring and acquired parties, or to the merging parties, including all undertakings in which a controlling interest is being acquired or which is the subject of a public bid.

Except where otherwise specified, the terms notifying party(ies) and party(ies) to the concentration include all the undertakings which belong to the same groups as those parties.

Affected markets: Section 6 of this Form requires the notifying parties to define the relevant product markets, and further to identify which of those relevant markets are likely to be affected by the notified operation. This definition of affected market is used as the basis for requiring information for a number of other questions contained in this Form. The definitions thus submitted by the notifying parties are referred to in this Form as the affected market(s). This term can refer to a relevant market made up either of products or of services.

---

[10] See, in particular, Art 122 of the EEA Agreement, Art 9 of Protocol 24 to the EEA. Agreement and Art 17(2) of Chapter XIII of Protocol 4 to the Agreement between the EFTA States on the establishment of a Surveillance Authority and a Court of Justice (ESA Agreement).

Year: all references to the word year in this Form should be read as meaning calendar year, unless otherwise stated. All information requested in this Form must, unless otherwise specified, relate to the year preceding that of the notification.

The financial data requested in Section 3.3 to 3.5 must be provided in euros at the average exchange rates prevailing for the years or other periods in question.

All references contained in this Form are to the relevant articles and paragraphs of the EC Merger Regulation, unless otherwise stated.

1.7 Provision of information to Employees and their representatives

The Commission would like to draw attention to the obligations to which the parties to a concentration may be subject under Community and/or national rules on information and consultation regarding transactions of a concentrative nature vis-à-vis employees and/or their representatives.

SECTION 1. DESCRIPTION OF THE CONCENTRATION

1.1 Provide an executive summary of the concentration, specifying the parties to the concentration, the nature of the concentration (for example, merger, acquisition, or joint venture), the areas of activity of the notifying parties, the markets on which the concentration will have an impact (including the main affected markets)),[11] and the strategic and economic rationale for the concentration.

1.2 Provide a summary (up to 500 words) of the information provided under Section 1.1. It is intended that this summary will be published on the Commission's website at the date of notification. The summary must be drafted so that it contains no confidential information or business secrets.

SECTION 2. INFORMATION ABOUT THE PARTIES

2.1 Information on notifying party (or parties) Give details of:

2.1.1 name and address of undertaking;

2.1.2 nature of the undertaking's business;

2.1.3 name, address, telephone number, fax number and e-mail address of, and position held by, the appropriate contact person; and

2.1.4 an address for service of the notifying party (or each of the notifying parties) to which documents and, in particular, Commission decisions may be delivered. The name, telephone number and e-mail address of a person at this address who is authorised to accept service must be provided.

2.2 Information on other parties[12] to the concentration

For each party to the concentration (except the notifying party or parties) give details of:

2.2.1 name and address of undertaking;

2.2.2 nature of undertaking's business;

2.2.3 name, address, telephone number, fax number and e-mail address of, and position held by, the appropriate contact person: and

2.2.4 an address for service of the party (or each of the parties) to which documents and, in particular, Commission Decisions may be delivered. The name, e-mail address and

---

[11] See Section 6.III for the definition of affected markets.

[12] This includes the target company in the case of a contested bid, in which case the details should be completed as far as is possible.

telephone number of a person at this address who is authorised to accept service must be provided.

2.3   Appointment of representatives

Where notifications are signed by representatives of undertakings, such representatives must produce written proof that they are authorised to act. The written proof must contain the name and position of the persons granting such authority.

Provide the following contact details of any representatives who have been authorised to act for any of the parties to the concentration, indicating whom they represent:

2.3.1 name of representative;

2.3.2 address of representative;

2.3.3 name, address, telephone number, fax number and e-mail address of person to be contacted; and

2.3.4 an address of the representative (in Brussels if available) to which correspondence may be sent and documents delivered.

Section 3. Details of the Concentration

3.1   Describe the nature of the concentration being notified. In doing so, state:

   (a) whether the proposed concentration is a full legal merger, an acquisition of sole or joint control, a full-function joint venture within the meaning of Article 3(4) of the EC Merger Regulation or a contract or other means of conferring direct or indirect control within the meaning of Article 3(2) of the EC Merger Regulation:

   (b) whether the whole or parts of parties are subject to the concentration;

   (c) a brief explanation of the economic and financial structure of the concentration;

   (d) whether any public offer for the securities of one party by another party has the support of the former's supervisory boards of management or other bodies legally representing that party;

   (e) the proposed or expected date of any major events designed to bring about the completion of the concentration;

   (f) the proposed structure of ownership and control after the completion of the concentration;

   (g) any financial or other support received from whatever source (including public authorities) by any of the parties and the nature and amount of this support; and

   (h) the economic sectors involved in the concentration.

3.2   State the value of the transaction (the purchase price or the value of all the assets involved, as the case may be).

3.3   For each of the undertakings concerned by the concentration[13] provide the following data[14] for the last financial year;

3.3.1 world-wide turnover;

3.3.2 Community-wide turnover,

3.3.3 EFTA-wide turnover;

---

[13] See Commission Notice on the concept of undertakings concerned.

[14] See, generally, the Commission Notice on calculation of turnover. Turnover of the acquiring party or parties to the concentration should include the aggregated turnover of all undertakings within the meaning of Art 5(4) of the EC Merger Reg. Turnover of the acquired party or parties should include the turnover relating to the parts subject to the transaction within the meaning of Art 5(2) of the EC Merger Reg. Special provisions are contained in Arts 5(3), (4) and 5(5) of the EC Merger Reg for credit, insurance, other financial institutions and joint undertakings.

3.3.4 turnover in each Member State;

3.3.5 turnover in each EFTA State:

3.3.6 the Member State, if any, in which more than two-thirds of Community-wide turnover is achieved; and

3.3.7 the EFTA State, if any, in which more than two-thirds of EFTA-wide turnover is achieved.

3.4 For the purposes of Article 1(3) of the EC Merger Regulation, if the operation does not meet the thresholds set out in Article 1(2), provide the following data for the last financial year;

3.4.1 the Member States, if any, in which the combined aggregate turnover of all the undertakings concerned is more than EUR 100 million; and

3.4.2 the Member States, if any, in which the aggregate turnover of each of at least two of the undertakings concerned is more than EUR 25 million.

3.5 For the purposes of determining whether the concentration qualifies as an EFTA co-operation case,[15] provide the following information with respect to the last financial year:

3.5.1 does the combined turnover of the undertakings concerned in the territory of the EFTA States equal 25% or more of their total turnover in the EEA territory?

3.5.2 does each of at least two undertakings concerned have a turnover exceeding EUR 250 million in the territory of the EFTA States?

3.6 Describe the economic rationale of the concentration.

SECTION 4. OWNERSHIP AND CONTROL[16]

4.1 For each of the parties to the concentration provide a list of all undertakings belonging to the same group.

This list must include:

4.1.1 all undertakings or persons controlling these parties, directly or indirectly;

4.1.2 all undertakings active on any affected market[17] that are controlled, directly or indirectly;
(a) by these parties;
(b) by any other undertaking identified in 4.1.1.

For each entry listed above, the nature and means of control should be specified.

The information sought in this section may be illustrated by the use of organization charts or diagrams to show the structure of ownership and control of the undertakings.

4.2 With respect to the parties to the concentration and each undertaking or person identified in response to Section 4.1, provide:

4.2.1 a list of all other undertakings which are active in affected markets (affected markets are defined in Section 6) in which the undertakings, or persons, of the group hold individually or collectively 10% or more of the voting rights, issued share capital or other securities;

in each case, identify the holder and state the percentage held;

---

[15] See Art 57 of the EEA Agreement and, in particular, Art 2(1) of Protocol 24 to the EEA Agreement. A case qualifies as a cooperation case if the combined turnover of the undertakings concerned in the territory of the EFTA States equals 25% or more of their total turnover within the territory covered by the EEA Agreement; or each of at least two undertakings concerned has a turnover exceeding EUR 250 million in the territory of the EFTA States; or the concentration is liable to create or strengthen a dominant position as a result of which effective competition would be significantly impeded in the territories of the EFTA States or a substantial part thereof.

[16] See Arts 3(3), 3(4) and 3(5) and Art 5(4) of the EC Merger Reg.

[17] See Section 6 for the definition of affected markets.

4.2.2 a list for each undertaking of the members of their boards of management who are also members of the boards of management or of the supervisory boards of any other undertaking which is active in affected markets; and (where applicable) for each undertaking a list of the members of their supervisory boards who are also members of the boards of management of any other undertaking which is active in affected markets;

in each case, identify the name of the other undertaking and the positions held;

4.2.3 details of acquisitions made during the last three years by the groups identified above (Section 4.1) of undertakings active in affected markets as defined in Section 6.

Information provided here may be illustrated by the use of organization charts or diagrams to give a better understanding.

Section 5. Supporting Documentation

Notifying parties must provide the following:

5.1 copies of the final or most recent versions of all documents bringing about the concentration, whether by agreement between the parties to the concentration, acquisition of a controlling interest or a public bid;

5.2 in a public bid, a copy of the offer document; if it is unavailable at the time of notification, it should be submitted as soon as possible and not later than when it is posted to shareholders;

5.3 copies of the most recent annual reports and accounts of all the parties to the concentration; and

5.4 copies of all analyses, reports, studies, surveys, and any comparable documents prepared by or for any member(s) of the board of directors, or the supervisory board, or the other person(s) exercising similar functions (or to whom such functions have been delegated or entrusted), or the shareholders' meeting, for the purpose of assessing or analysing the concentration with respect to market shares, competitive conditions, competitors (actual and potential), the rationale of the concentration, potential for sales growth or expansion into other product or geographic markets, and/or general market conditions.[18]

For each of these documents, indicate (if not contained in the document itself) the date of preparation, the name and title of each individual who prepared each such document.

Section 6. Market Definitions

The relevant product and geographic markets determine the scope within which the market power of the new entity resulting from the concentration must be assessed.[19]

The notifying party or parties must provide the data requested having regard to the following definitions:

I Relevant product markets

A relevant product market comprises all those products and/or services which are regarded as interchangeable or substitutable by the consumer, by reason of the products' characteristics, their prices and their intended use. A relevant product market may in some cases be composed of a number of individual products and/or services which present largely identical physical or technical characteristics and are interchangeable.

---

[18] As set out in introductory Parts 1.1 and 1.3(g), in the context of pre-notification, you may want to discuss with the Commission to what extent dispensation (waivers) to provide the requested documents would be appropriate. Where waivers are sought, the Commission may specify the documents to be provided in a particular case in a request for information under Art 11 of the EC Merger Reg.

[19] See Commission Notice on the definition of the relevant market for the purposes of Community competition law.

Factors relevant to the assessment of the relevant product market include the analysis of why the products or services in these markets are included and why others are excluded by using the above definition, and having regard to, for example, substitutability, conditions of competition, prices, cross-price elasticity of demand or other factors relevant for the definition of the product markets (for example, supply-side substitutability in appropriate cases).

II Relevant geographic markets

The relevant geographic market comprises the area in which the undertakings concerned are involved in the supply and demand of relevant products or services, in which the conditions of competition are sufficiently homogeneous and which can be distinguished from neighbouring geographic areas because, in particular, conditions of competition are appreciably different in those areas.

Factors relevant to the assessment of the relevant geographic market include *inter alia* the nature and characteristics of the products or services concerned, the existence of entry barriers, consumer preferences, appreciable differences in the undertakings' market shares between neighbouring geographic areas or substantial price differences.

III Affected markets

For purposes of information required in this Form, affected markets consist of relevant product markets where, in the EEA territory, in the Community, in the territory of the EFTA States, in any Member State or in any EFTA State:

(a) two or more of the parties to the concentration are engaged in business activities in the same product market and where the concentration will lead to a combined market share of 15% or more. These are horizontal relationships;

(b) one or more of the parties to the concentration are engaged in business activities in a product market, which is upstream or downstream of a product market in which any other party to the concentration is engaged, and any of their individual or combined market shares at either level is 25% or more, regardless of whether there is or is not any existing supplier/customer relationship between the parties to the concentration.[20] These are vertical relationships.

On the basis of the above definitions and market share thresholds, provide the following information:[21]

— Identify each affected market within the meaning of Section III, at:

— the EEA, Community or EFTA level;

— the individual Member States or EFTA States level 6.2. In addition, state and explain the parties' view regarding the scope of the relevant geographic market within the meaning of Section II that applies in relation to each affected market identified above.

IV Other markets in which the notified operation may have a significant impact

6.3 On the basis of the above definitions, describe the product and geographic scope of markets other than affected markets identified in Section 6.1 in which the notified operation may have a significant impact, for example, where:

(a) any of the parties to the concentration has a market share larger than 25% and any other party to the concentration is a potential competitor into that market. A party

---

[20] For example, if a party to the concentration holds a market share larger than 25% in a market that is upstream to a market in which the other party is active, then both the upstream and the downstream markets are affected markets. Similarly, if a vertically integrated company merges with another party which is active at the downstream level, and the merger leads to a combined market share downstream of 25% or more, then both the upstream and the downstream markets are affected markets.

[21] As set out in introductory Parts 1.1 and 1.3(g), in the context of pre-notification, you may want to discuss with the Commission to what extent dispensation (waivers) to provide the requested information would be appropriate for certain affected markets, or for certain other markets (as described under IV).

    may be considered a potential competitor, in particular, where it has plans to enter a market, or has developed or pursued such plans in the past two years;

(b) any of the parties to the concentration has a market share larger than 25% and any other party to the concentration holds important intellectual property rights for that market:

(c) any of the parties to the concentration is present in a product market, which is a neighbouring market closely related to a product market in which any other party to the concentration is engaged, and the individual or combined market shares of the parties in any one of these markets is 25% or more. Product markets are closely related neighbouring markets when the products are complementary to each other[22] or when they belong to a range of products that is generally purchased by the same set of customers for the same end use;[23]

where such markets include the whole or a part of the EEA.

In order to enable the Commission to consider, from the outset, the competitive impact of the proposed concentration in the markets identified under this Section 6.3, notifying parties are invited to submit the information under Sections 7 and 8 of this Form in relation to those markets.

SECTION 7. INFORMATION ON AFFECTED MARKETS

For each affected relevant product market, for each of the last three financial years:[24]

(a) for the EEA territory:

(b) for the Community as a whole;

(c) for the territory of the EFTA States as a whole;

(d) individually for each Member State and EFTA State where the parties to the concentration do business; and

(e) where in the opinion of the notifying parties, the relevant geographic market is different;

provide the following:

7.1   an estimate of the total size of the market in terms of sales value (in euros) and volume (units).[25] Indicate the basis and sources for the calculations and provide documents where available to confirm these calculations;

7.2   the sales in value and volume, as well as an estimate of the market shares, of each of the parties to the concentration;

7.3   an estimate of the market share in value (and where appropriate, volume) of all competitors (including importers) having at least 5% of the geographic market under consideration. On this basis, provide an estimate of the HHI index[26] pre- and post-merger, and the difference

---

[22] Products (or services) are called complementary when, for example, the use (or consumption) of one product essentially implies the use (or consumption) of the other product, such as for staple machines and staples, and printers and printer cartridges.

[23] Examples of products belonging to such a range would be whisky and gin sold to bars and restaurants, and different materials for packaging a certain category of goods sold to producers of such goods.

[24] Without prejudice to Art 4(2) of the Implementing Reg.

[25] The value and volume of a market should reflect output less exports plus imports for the geographic areas under consideration. If readily available, please provide disaggregated information on Imports and exports by country of origin and destination, respectively.

[26] HHI stands for Herfindahl-Hirschman Index, a measure of market concentration. The HHI is calculated by summing the squares of the individual market shares of all the firms in the market. For example, a market containing five firms with market shares of 40%, 20%, 15%, 15% and 10% respectively, has an HHI of 2,550 ($40^2 + 20^2 + 15^2 + 15^2 + 10^2 = 2,550$). The HHI ranges from close to zero (in an atomistic market) to 10,000 (in the case of a pure monopoly). The post-merger HHI is calculated on the working assumption that the individual market shares of the companies do not change. Although it is best to include all firms in the calculation, lack of information about very small firms may not be important because such firms do not affect the HHI significantly.

between the two (the delta).[27] Indicate the proportion of market shares used as a basis to calculate the HHI, Identify the sources used to calculate these market shares and provide documents where available to confirm the calculation;

7.4 the name, address, telephone number, fax number and e-mail address of the head of the legal department (or other person exercising similar functions; and in cases where there is no such person, then the chief executive) for the competitors identified under 7.3;

7.5 an estimate of the total value and source of imports from outside the EEA territory and identify:

(a) the proportion of such imports that are derived from the groups to which the parties to the concentration belong;

(b) an estimate of the extent to which any quotas, tarrifs or non-tariff barriers to trade, affect these imports; and

(c) an estimate of the extent to which transportation and other costs affect these imports;

7.6 the extent to which trade among States within the EEA territory is affected by:

(a) transportation and other costs; and

(b) other non-tariff barriers to trade;

7.7 the manner in which the parties to the concentration produce, price and sell the products and/or services; for example, whether they manufacture and price locally, or sell through local distribution facilities;

7.8 a comparison of price levels in each Member State and EFTA State by each party to the concentration and a similar comparison of price levels between the Community, the EFTA States and other areas where these products are produced (e.g. Russia, the United States of America, Japan, China, or other relevant areas); and

7.9 the nature and extent of vertical integration of each of the parties to the concentration compared with their largest competitors.

SECTION 8. GENERAL CONDITIONS IN AFFECTED MARKETS

8.1 Identify the five largest independent[28] suppliers to the parties to the concentration and their individual shares of purchases from each of these suppliers (of raw materials or goods used for purposes of producing the relevant products). Provide the name, address, telephone number, fax number and e-mail address of the head of the legal department (or other person exercising similar functions; and in cases where there is no such person, then the chief executive) for each of these suppliers.

STRUCTURE OF SUPPLY IN AFFECTED MARKETS

8.2 Explain the distribution channels and service networks that exist in the affected markets. In so doing, take account of the following where appropriate:

---

[27] The increase in concentration as measured by the HHI can be calculated independently of the overall market concentration by doubling the product of the market shares of the merging firms. For example, a merger of two firms with market shares of 30% and 15% respectively would increase the HHI by 900 (30 × 15 × 2 = 900). The explanation for this technique is as follows: Before the merger, the market shares of the merging firms contribute to the HHI by their squares individually: $(a)^2 + (b)^2$. After the merger, the contribution is the square of their sum: $(a + b)^2$, which equals $(a)^2 + (b)^2 + 2ab$. The increase in the HHI is therefore represented by 2ab.

[28] That is, suppliers which are not subsidiaries, agents or undertakings forming part of the group of the party in question. In addition to those five independent suppliers the notifying parties can, if they consider it necessary for a proper assessment of the case, identify the intra-group suppliers. The same will apply in 8.6 in relation to customers.

(a) the distribution systems prevailing in the market and their importance. To what extent is distribution performed by third parties and/or undertakings belonging to the same group as the parties identified in Section 4?

(b) the service networks (for example, maintenance and repair) prevailing and their importance in these markets. To what extent are such services performed by third parties and/or undertakings belonging to the same group as the parties identified in Section 4?

8.3 Provide an estimate of the total Community-wide and EFTA-wide capacity for the last three years. Over this period what proportion of this capacity is accounted for by each of the parties to the concentration, and what have been their respective rates of capacity utilization. If applicable, identify the location and capacity of the manufacturing facilities of each of the parties to the concentration in affected markets.

8.4 Specify whether any of the parties to the concentration, or any of the competitors, have 'pipeline products', products likely to be brought to market in the near term, or plans to expand (or contract) production or sales capacity. If so, provide an estimate of the projected sales and market shares of the parties to the concentration over the next three to five years.

8.5 If you consider any other supply-side considerations to be relevant, they should be specified.

STRUCTURE OF DEMAND IN AFFECTED MARKETS

8.6 Identify the five[29] largest independent customers of the parties in each affected market and their individual share of total sales for such products accounted for by each of those customers. Provide the name, address, telephone number, fax number and e-mail address of the head of the legal department (or other person exercising similar functions; and in cases where there is no such person, then the chief executive) for each of these customers.

8.7 Explain the structure of demand in terms of;

(a) the phases of the markets in terms of, for example, take-off, expansion, maturity and decline, and a forecast of the growth rate of demand;

(b) the importance of customer preferences, for example in terms of brand loyalty, the provision of pre- and after-sales services, the provision of a full range of products, or network effects;

(c) the role of product differentiation in terms of attributes or quality, and the extent to which the products of the parties to the concentration are close substitutes;

(d) the role of switching costs (in terms of time and expense) for customers when changing from one supplier to another;

(e) the degree of concentration or dispersion of customers;

(f) segmentation of customers into different groups with a description of the 'typical customer' of each group;

(g) the importance of exclusive distribution contracts and other types of long-term contracts; and

(h) the extent to which public authorities, government agencies, State enterprises or similar bodies are important participants as a source of demand.

MARKET ENTRY

8.8 Over the last five years, has there been any significant entry into any affected markets? If so, identify such entrants and provide the name, address, telephone number, fax number

---

[29] Experience has shown that the examination of complex cases often requires more customer contact details. In the course of pre-notification contacts, the Commission's services may ask for more customer contact details for certain affected markets.

and e-mail address of the head of the legal department (or other person exercising similar functions; and in cases where there is no such person, then the chief executive) and an estimate of the current market share of each such entrant. If any of the parties to the concentration entered an affected market in the past five years, provide an analysis of the barriers to entry encountered.

8.9   In the opinion of the notifying parties, are there undertakings (including those at present operating only outside the Community or the EEA) that are likely to enter the market? If so, identify such entrants and provide the name, address, telephone number, fax number and e-mail address of the head of the legal department (or other person exercising similar functions; and in cases where there is no such person, then the chief executive). Explain why such entry is likely and provide an estimate of the time within which such entry is likely to occur.

8.10 Describe the various factors influencing entry into affected markets, examining entry from both a geographical and product viewpoint. In so doing, take account of the following where appropriate:

(a)   the total costs of entry (R&D, production, establishing distribution systems, promotion, advertising, servicing, and so forth) on a scale equivalent to a significant viable competitor, indicating the market share of such a competitor;

(b)   any legal or regulatory barriers to entry, such as government authorization or standard setting in any form, as well as barriers resulting from product certification procedures, or the need to have a proven track record;

(c)   any restrictions created by the existence of patents, know-how and other intellectual property rights in these markets and any restrictions created by licensing such rights;

(d)   the extent to which each of the parties to the concentration are holders, licensees or licensors of patents, know-how and other rights in the relevant markets;

(e)   the importance of economies of scale for the production or distribution of products in the affected markets; and

(f)   access to sources of supply, such as availability of raw materials and necessary infrastructure.

RESEARCH AND DEVELOPMENT

8.11 Give an account of the importance of research and development in the ability of a firm operating the relevant market(s) to compete in the long term. Explain the nature of the research and development in affected markets carried out by the parties to the concentration.

In so doing, take account of the following, where appropriate:

(a)   trends and intensities of research and development[30] in these markets and for the parties to the concentration;

(b)   the course of technological development for these markets over an appropriate time period (including developments in products and/or services, production processes, distribution systems, and so on);

(c)   the major innovations that have been made in these markets and the undertakings responsible for these innovations; and

(d)   the cycle of innovation in these markets and where the parties are in this cycle of innovation.

---

[30] Research and development intensity is defined as research development expenditure as a proportion of turnover.

COOPERATIVE AGREEMENTS

8.12 To what extent do cooperative agreements (horizontal, vertical, or other) exist in the affected markets?

8.13 Give details of the most important cooperative agreements engaged in by the parties to the concentration in the affected markets, such as research and development, licensing, joint production, specialization, distribution, long term supply and exchange of information agreements and, where deemed useful, provide a copy of these agreements.

TRADE ASSOCIATIONS

8.14 With respect to the trade associations in the affected markets.
   (a) identify those of which the parties to the concentration are members; and
   (b) identify the most important trade associations to which the customers and suppliers of the parties to the concentration belong.

Provide the name, address, telephone number, fax number and e-mail address of the appropriate contact person for all trade associations listed above.

SECTION 9. OVERALL MARKET CONTEXT AND EFFICIENCIES

9.1 Describe the world wide context of the proposed concentration, indicating the position of each of the parties to the concentration outside of the EEA territory in terms of size and competitive strength.

9.2 Describe how the proposed concentration is likely to affect the interests of intermediate and ultimate consumers and the development of technical and economic progress.

9.3 Should you wish the Commission specifically to consider from the outset[31] whether efficiency gains generated by the concentration are likely to enhance the ability and incentive of the new entity to act pro-competitively for the benefit of consumers, please provide a description of, and supporting documents relating to, each efficiency (including cost savings, new product introductions, and service or product improvements) that the parties anticipate will result from the proposed concentration relating to any relevant product.[32]

   For each claimed efficiency, provide:
   (i)   a detailed explanation of how the proposed concentration would allow the new entity to achieve the efficiency. Specify the steps that the parties anticipate taking to achieve the efficiency, the risks involved in achieving the efficiency, and the time and costs required to achieve it:
   (ii) where reasonably possible, a quantification of the efficiency and a detailed explanation of how the quantification was calculated. Where relevant, also provide an estimate of the significance of efficiencies related to new product introductions or quality improvements. For efficiencies that involve cost savings, state separately the one-time fixed cost savings, recurring fixed cost savings, and variable cost savings (in euros per unit and euros per year);

---

[31] It should be noted that submitting information in response to Sect 9.3 is voluntary. Parties are not required to offer any justification for not completing this section. Failure to provide information on efficiencies will not be taken to imply that the proposed concentration does not create efficiencies or that the rationale for the concentration is to increase market power. Not providing the requested information on efficiencies at the notification stage does not preclude providing the information at a later stage. However, the earlier the information is provided, the better the Commission can verify the efficiency claim.

[32] For further guidance on the assessment of efficiencies, see the Commission Notice on the assessment of horizontal mergers.

(iii) the extent to which customers are likely to benefit from the efficiency and a detailed explanation of how this conclusion is arrived at; and

(iv) the reason why the party or parties could not achieve the efficiency to a similar extent by means other than through the concentration proposed, and in a manner that is not likely to raise competition concerns.

SECTION 10. COOPERATIVE EFFECTS OF A JOINT VENTURE

10 For the purpose of Article 2(4) of the EC Merger Regulation, answer the following questions:

(a) Do two or more parents retain to a significant extent activities in the same market as the joint venture or in a market which is upstream or downstream from that of the joint venture or in a neighbouring market closely related to this market?[33]

If the answer is affirmative, please indicate for each of the markets referred to here:
— the turnover of each parent company in the preceding financial year;
— the economic significance of the activities of the joint venture in relation to this turnover;
— the market share of each parent.

If the answer is negative, please justify your answer.

(b) If the answer to (a) is affirmative and in your view the creation of the joint venture does not lead to coordination between independent undertakings that restricts competition within the meaning of Article 81(1) of the EC Treaty, give your reasons.

(c) Without prejudice to the answers to (a) and (b) and in order to ensure that a complete assessment of the case can be made by the Commission, please explain how the criteria of Article 81(3) apply. Under Article 81(3), the provisions of Article 81(1) may be declared inapplicable if the operation:

(i) contributes to improving the production or distribution of goods, or to promoting technical or economic progress:

(ii) allows consumers a fair share of the resulting benefit;

(iii) does not impose on the undertakings concerned restrictions which are not indispensable to the attainment of these objectives; and

(iv) does not afford such undertakings the possibility of eliminating competition in respect of a substantial part of the products in question.

SECTION 11. DECLARATION

Article 2(2) of the Implementing Regulation states that where notifications are signed by representatives of undertakings, such representatives must produce written proof that they are authorized to act. Such written authorization must accompany the notification.

The notification must conclude with the following declaration which is to be signed by or on behalf of all the notifying parties:

The notifying party or parties declare that, to the best of their knowledge and belief, the information given in this notification is true, correct, and complete, that true and complete copies of documents required by Form CO have been supplied, that all estimates are identified as such and are their best estimates of the underlying facts, and that all the opinions expressed are sincere.

---

[33] For market definitions refer to Sect 6.

They are aware of the provisions of Article 14(1)(a) of the EC Merger Regulation.

Place and date:

Signatures:

Name/s and positions:

On behalf of:

ANNEX II. SHORT FORM FOR THE NOTIFICATION OF A CONCENTRATION PURSUANT TO REGULATION (EC) No 139/2004

1 Introduction

1.1 The purpose of the Short Form

The Short Form specifies the information that must be provided by the notifying parties when submitting a notification to the European Commission of certain proposed mergers, acquisitions or other concentrations that are unlikely to raise competition concerns.

In completing this Form, your attention is drawn to Council Regulation (EC) No 139/2004 (hereinafter referred to as 'the EC Merger Regulation'), and Commission Regulation (EC) No xx/2004 (hereinafter referred to as 'the Implementing Regulation'), to which this Form is annexed.[34] The text of these regulations, as well as other relevant documents, can be found on the Competition page of the Commission's Europa web site.

As a general rule, the Short Form may be used for the purpose of notifying concentrations, where one of the following conditions is met:

1. in the case of a joint venture, the joint venture has no, or negligible, actual or foreseen activities within the territory of the European Economic Area (EEA). Such cases occur where:
   (a) the turnover of the joint venture and/or the turnover of the contributed activities is less than EUR 100 million in the EEA territory; and
   (b) the total value of the assets transferred to the joint venture is less than EUR 100 million in the EEA territory;

2. none of the parties to the concentration are engaged in business activities in the same relevant product and geographic market (no horizontal overlap), or in a market which is upstream or downstream of a market in which another party to the concentration is engaged (no vertical relationship);

3. two or more of the parties to the concentration are engaged in business activities in the same relevant product and geographic market (horizontal relationships), provided that their combined market share is less than 15%; and/or one or more of the parties to the concentration are engaged in business activities in a product market which is upstream or downstream of a product market in which any other party to the concentration is engaged (vertical relationships), and provided that none of their individual or combined market shares at either level is 25% or more; or

---

[34] Council Reg (EC) No 139/2004 of 20 January 2004, OJ L24, 29.01.2004, p 1. Your attention is drawn to the corresponding provisions of the Agreement on the European Economic Area (hereinafter referred to as 'the EEA Agreement', See in particular Art 57 of the EEA Agreement, point 1 of Annex XIV to the EEA Agreement and Protocol 4 to the Agreement between the EFTA States on the establishment of a Surveillance Authority and a Court of Justice, as well as Protocols 21 and 24 to the EEA Agreement and Art 1, and the Agreed Minutes of the Protocol adjusting the EEA Agreement. Any reference to EFTA States shall be understood to mean those EFTA States which are Contracting Parties to the EEA Agreement. As of 1 May 2004, these States are Iceland, Liechtenstein and Norway.

4. a party is to acquire sole control of an undertaking over which it already has joint control.

The Commission may require a full form notification where it appears either that the conditions for using the Short Form are not met, or, exceptionally, where they are met, the Commission determines, nonetheless, that a notification under Form CO is necessary for an adequate investigation of possible competition concerns.

Examples of cases where a notification under Form CO may be necessary are concentrations where it is difficult to define the relevant markets (for example, in emerging markets or where there is no established case practice); where a party is a new or potential entrant, or an important patent holder, where it is not possible to adequately determine the parties' market shares; in markets with high entry barriers, with a high degree of concentration or known competition problems; where at least two parties to the concentration are present in closely related neighbouring markets;[35] and in concentrations where an issue of coordination arises, as referred to in Article 2(4) of the EC Merger Regulation. Similarly, a Form CO notification may be required in the case of a party acquiring sole control of a joint venture in which it currently holds joint control, where the acquiring party and the joint venture, together, have a strong market position, or the joint venture and the acquiring party have strong positions in vertically related markets.

1.2 Reversion to the full Form CO notification

In assessing whether a concentration may be notified under the Short Form, the Commission will ensure that all relevant circumstances are established with sufficient clarity. In this respect, the responsibility to provide correct and complete information rests with the notifying parties.

If, after the concentration has been notified, the Commission considers that the case is not appropriate for notification under the Short Form, the Commission may require full, or where appropriate partial, notification under Form CO. This may be the case where:

— it appears that the conditions for using the Short Form are not met;
— although the conditions for using the Short Form are met, a full or partial notification under Form CO appears to be necessary for an adequate investigation of possible competition concerns or to establish that the transaction is a concentration within the meaning of Article 3 of the EC Merger Regulation;
— the Short Form contains incorrect or misleading information;
— a Member State expresses substantiated competition concerns about the notified concentration within 15 working days of receipt of the copy of the notification; or
— a third party expresses substantiated competition concerns within the time-limit laid down by the Commission for such comments.

In such cases, the notification may be treated as being incomplete in a material respect pursuant to Article 5(2) of the Implementing Regulation. The Commission will inform the notifying parties or their representatives of this in writing and without delay. The notification will only become effective on the date on which all information required is received.

1.3 Importance of pre-notification contacts

Experience has shown that pre-notification contacts are extremely valuable to both the notifying parties and the Commission in determining the precise amount of information required in a notification. Also, in cases where the parties wish to submit a Short Form notification, they are advised to engage in pre-notification contacts with the Commission in order to discuss whether the case is one for which it is appropriate to use a Short Form. Notifying parties may refer to the Commission's Best Practices on the Conduct of EC Merger Control Proceedings, which provides guidance on pre-notification contacts and the preparation of notifications.

---

[35] Product markets are closely related neighbouring markets when the products are complementary to each other or when they belong to a range of products that is generally purchased by the same set of customers for the same end use.

1.4 Who must notify

In the case of a merger within the meaning of Article 3(1)(a) of the EC Merger Regulation or the acquisition of joint control of an undertaking within the meaning of Article 3(1)(b) of the EC Merger Regulation, the notification shall be completed jointly by the parties to the merger or by those acquiring joint control, as the case may be.[36]

In the case of the acquisition of a controlling interest in one undertaking by another, the acquirer must complete the notification.

In the case of a public bid to acquire an undertaking, the bidder must complete the notification.

Each party completing the notification is responsible for the accuracy of the information which it provides.

1.5 The requirement for a correct and complete notification

All information required by this Form must be correct and complete. The information required must be supplied in the appropriate Section of this Form.

In particular you should note that:

(a) In accordance with Article 10(1) of the EC Merger Regulation and Article 5(2) and (4) of the Implementing Regulation, the time-limits of the EC Merger Regulation linked to the notification will not begin to run until all the information that must be supplied with the notification has been received by the Commission. This requirement is to ensure that the Commission is able to assess the notified concentration within the strict time-limits provided by the EC Merger Regulation.

(b) The notifying parties should verify, in the course of preparing their notification, that contact names and numbers, and in particular fax numbers and e-mail addresses, provided to the Commission are accurate, relevant and up-to-date.

(c) Incorrect or misleading information in the notification will be considered to be incomplete information (Article 5(4) of the Implementing Regulation).

(d) If a notification is incomplete, the Commission will inform the notifying parties or their representatives in writing and without delay. The notification will only become effective on the date on which the complete and accurate information is received by the Commission (Article 10(1) of the EC Merger Regulation, Article 5(2) and (4) of the Implementing Regulation).

(e) Under Article 14(1)(a) of the EC Merger Regulation, notifying parties who, either intentionally or negligently, supply incorrect or misleading information, may be liable to fines of up to 1% of the aggregate turnover of the undertaking concerned. In addition, pursuant to Article 6(3)(a) and Article 8(6)(a) of the EC Merger Regulation the Commission may revoke its decision on the compatibility of a notified concentration where it is based on incorrect information for which one of the undertakings is responsible.

(f) You may request in writing that the Commission accept that the notification is complete notwithstanding the failure to provide information required by this Form, if such information is not reasonably available to you in part or in whole (for example, because of the unavailability of information on a target company during a contested bid).

The Commission will consider such a request, provided that you give reasons for the unavailability of that information, and provide your best estimates for missing data together with the sources for the estimates. Where possible, indications as to where any of the requested information that is unavailable to you could be obtained by the Commission should also be provided.

---

[36] See Art 4(2) of the EC Merger Reg.

(g) You may request in writing that the Commission accept that the notification is complete notwithstanding the failure to provide information required by this Form, if you consider that any particular information required may not be necessary for the Commission's examination of the case.

The Commission will consider such a request, provided that you give adequate reasons why that information is not relevant and necessary to its inquiry into the notified operation. You should explain this during your pre-notification contacts with the Commission and submit a written request for a waiver, asking the Commission to dispense with the obligation to provide that information, pursuant to Article 4(2) of the Implementing Regulation.

1.6 How to notify

The notification must be completed in one of the official languages of the European Community. This language will thereafter be the language of the proceedings for all notifying parties. Where notifications are made in accordance with Article 12 of Protocol 24 to the EEA Agreement in an official language of an EFTA State which is not an official language of the Community, the notification must simultaneously be supplemented with a translation into an official language of the Community.

The information requested by this Form is to be set out using the sections and paragraph numbers of the Form, signing a declaration as provided in Section 9, and annexing supporting documentation. In completing Section 7 of this Form, the notifying parties are invited to consider whether, for purposes of clarity, this section is best presented in numerical order, or whether information can be grouped together for each individual reportable market (or group of reportable markets).

For the sake of clarity, certain information may be put in annexes. However, it is essential that all key substantive pieces of information, in particular, market share information for the parties and their largest competitors, are presented in the body of this Form. Annexes to this Form shall only be used to supplement the information supplied in the Form itself.

Contact details must be provided in a format provided by the Commission's Directorate-General for Competition (DG Competition). For a proper investigatory process, it is essential that the contact details are accurate. Multiple instances of incorrect contact details may be a ground for declaring a notification incomplete.

Supporting documents are to be submitted in their original language; where this is not an official language of the Community, they must be translated into the language of the proceeding (Article 3(4) of the Implementing Regulation).

Supporting documents may be originals or copies of the originals. In the latter case, the notifying party must confirm that they are true and complete.

One original and 35 copies of the Short Form and the supporting documents shall be submitted to the Commission's Directorate-General for Competition.

The notification shall be delivered to the address referred to in Article 23(1) of the Implementing Regulation and in the format specified by the Commission from time to time. This address is published in the *Official Journal of the European Union*. The notification must be delivered to the Commission on working days as defined by Article 24 of the Implementing Regulation. In order to enable it to be registered on the same day, it must be delivered before 17.00 hrs on Mondays to Thursdays and before 16.00 hrs on Fridays and workdays preceding public holidays and other holidays as determined by the Commission and published in the *Official Journal of the European Union*. The security instructions given on DG Competition's website must be adhered to.

1.7 Confidentiality

Article 287 of the Treaty and Article 17(2) of the EC Merger Regulation as well as the corresponding provisions of the EEA Agreement[37] require the Commission, the Member States, the EFTA Surveillance Authority and the EFTA States, their officials and other servants not to disclose information they have acquired through the application of the Regulation of the kind covered by the obligation of professional secrecy. The same principle must also apply to protect confidentiality between notifying parties.

If you believe that your interests would be harmed if any of the information you are asked to supply were to be published or otherwise divulged to other parties, submit this information separately with each page clearly marked 'Business Secrets'. You should also give reasons why this information should not be divulged or published.

In the case of mergers or joint acquisitions, or in other cases where the notification is completed by more than one of the parties, business secrets may be submitted under separate cover, and referred to in the notification as an annex. All such annexes must be included in the submission in order for a notification to be considered complete.

1.8 Definitions and instructions for purposes of this Form

Notifying party or parties: in cases where a notification is submitted by only one of the undertakings who is a party to an operation, 'notifying parties' is used to refer only to the undertaking actually submitting the notification.

Party(ies) to the concentration or parties: these terms relate to both the acquiring and acquired parties, or to the merging parties, including all undertakings in which a controlling interest is being acquired or which is the subject of a public bid.

Except where otherwise specified, the terms notifying party(ies) and party(ies) to the concentration include all the undertakings which belong to the same groups as those parties.

Year: all references to the word year in this Form should be read as meaning calendar year, unless otherwise stated. All information requested in this Form must, unless otherwise specified, relate to the year preceding that of the notification.

The financial data requested in Sections 3.3 to 3.5 must be provided in euros at the average exchange rates prevailing for the years or other periods in question.

All references contained in this Form are to the relevant articles and paragraphs of the EC Merger Regulation, unless otherwise stated.

1.9 Provision of information to employees and their representatives

The Commission would like to draw attention to the obligations to which the parties to a concentration may be subject under Community and/or national rules on information and consultation regarding transactions of a concentrative nature vis-à-vis employees and/or their representatives.

SECTION 1. DESCRIPTION OF THE CONCENTRATION

1.1   Provide an executive summary of the concentration, specifying the parties to the concentration, the nature of the concentration (for example, merger, acquisition, joint venture), the areas of activity of the notifying parties, the markets on which the concentration will have

---

[37] See, in particular, Art 122 of the EEA Agreement, Art 9 of Protocol 24 to the EEA Agreement and Art 17(2) of Chapter XIII of Protocol 4 to the Agreement between the EFTA States on the establishment of a Surveillance Authority and a Court of Justice (ESA Agreement).

an impact (including the main reportable markets.[38]) and the strategic and economic rationale for the concentration.

1.2   Provide a summary (up to 500 words) of the information provided under Section 1.1. It is intended that this summary will be published on the Commission's website at the date of notification. The summary must be drafted so that it contains no confidential information or business secrets.

Section 2. Information about the Parties

2.1   Information on notifying party (or parties)

Give details of:

2.1.1 name and address of undertaking:

2.1.2 nature of the undertaking's business;

2.1.3 name, address, telephone number, fax number and e-mail address of, and position held by, the appropriate contact person; and

2.1.4 an address for service of the notifying party (or each of the notifying parties) to which documents and, in particular, Commission Decisions may be delivered. The name, e-mail address and telephone number of a person at this address who is authorised to accept service must be provided.

2.2   Information on other parties[39] to the concentration

For each party to the concentration (except the notifying party or parties) give details of:

2.2.1 name and address of undertaking;

2.2.2 nature of undertaking's business;

2.2.3 name, address, telephone number, fax number and e-mail address of, and position held by, the appropriate contact person: and

2.2.4 an address for service of the party (or each of the parties) to which documents and, in particular, Commission Decisions may be delivered. The name, e-mail address and telephone number of a person at this address who is authorised to accept service must be provided.

2.3   Appointment of representatives

Where notifications are signed by representatives of undertakings, such representatives must produce written proof that they are authorised to act. The written proof must contain the name and position of the persons granting such authority.

Provide the following contact details of information of any representatives who have been authorised to act for any of the parties to the concentration, indicating whom they represent:

2.3.1 name of representative;

2.3.2 address of representative;

2.3.3 name, address, telephone number, fax number and e-mail address of person to be contacted; and

2.3.4 an address of the representative for service (in Brussels if available) to which correspondence may be sent and documents delivered.

---

[38] See Sect 6.III for the definition of reportable markets.
[39] This includes the target company in the case of a contested bid, in which case the details should be completed as far as is possible.

Section 3. Details of the Concentration

3.1 Describe the nature of the concentration being notified. In doing so state:

(a) whether the proposed concentration is a full legal merger, an acquisition of sole or joint control, a full-function joint venture within the meaning of Article 3(4) of the EC Merger Regulation or a contract or other means of conferring direct or indirect control within the meaning of Article 3(2) of the EC Merger Regulation;

(b) whether the whole or parts of parties are subject to the concentration;

(c) a brief explanation of the economic and financial structure of the concentration;

(d) whether any public offer for the securities of one party by another party has the support of the former's supervisory boards of management or other bodies legally representing that party;

(e) the proposed or expected date of any major events designed to bring about the completion of the concentration;

(f) the proposed structure of ownership and control after the completion of the concentration;

(g) any financial or other support received from whatever source (including public authorities) by any of the parties and the nature and amount of this support; and

(h) the economic sectors involved in the concentration.

3.2 State the value of the transaction (the purchase price or the value of all the assets involved, as the case may be);

3.3 For each of the undertakings concerned by the concentration[40] provide the following data[41] for the last financial year:

3.3.1 world-wide turnover;

3.3.2 Community-wide turnover;

3.3.3 EFTA-wide turnover;

3.3.4 turnover in each Member State;

3.3.5 turnover in each EFTA State;

3.3.6 the Member State, if any, in which more than two-thirds of Community-wide turnover is achieved; and

3.3.7 the EFTA State, if any, in which more than two-thirds of EFTA-wide turnover is achieved.

3.4 For the purposes of Article 1(3) of the EC Merger Regulation, if the operation does not meet the thresholds set out in Article 1(2), provide the following data for the last financial year:

3.4.1 the Member States, if any, in which the combined aggregate turnover of all the undertakings concerned is more than EUR 100 million; and

3.4.2 the Member States, if any, in which the aggregate turnover of each of at least two of the undertakings concerned is more than EUR 25 million.

---

[40] See Commission Notice on the concept of undertakings concerned.

[41] See, generally, the Commission Notice on calculation of turnover. Turnover of the acquiring party or parties to the concentration should include the aggregated turnover of all undertakings within the meaning of Art 5(4) of the EC Merger Reg. Turnover of the acquired party or parties should include the turnover relating to the parts subject to the transaction within the meaning of Art 5(2) of the EC Merger Reg. Special provisions are contained in Arts 5(3), (4) and 5(5) of the EC Merger Reg for credit, insurance, other financial institutions and joint undertakings.

3.5   For the purposes of determining whether the concentration qualifies as an EFTA co-operation case,[42] provide the following information with respect to the last financial year;

3.5.1   does the combined turnover of the undertakings concerned in the territory of the EFTA States equal 25% or more of their total turnover in the EEA territory?

3.5.2   does each of at least two undertakings concerned have a turnover exceeding EUR 250 million in the territory of the EFTA States?

3.6   In case the transaction concerns the acquisition of joint control of a joint venture, provide the following information:

3.6.1   the turnover of the joint venture and/or the turnover of the contributed activities to the joint venture; and/or

3.6.2   the total value of assets transferred to the joint venture.

3.7   Describe the economic rationale of the concentration.

SECTION 4. OWNERSHIP AND CONTROL[43]

For each of the parties to the concentration provide a list of all undertakings belonging to the same group.

This list must include:

4.1   all undertakings or persons controlling these parties, directly or indirectly:

4.2   all undertakings active in any reportable market[44] that are controlled, directly or indirectly:
  (a)   by these parties;
  (b)   by any other undertaking identified in 4.1.

For each entry listed above, the nature and means of control should be specified.

The information sought in this section may be illustrated by the use of organisation charts or diagrams to show the structure of ownership and control of the undertakings.

SECTION 5. SUPPORTING DOCUMENTATION

Notifying parties must provide the following:

5.1   copies of the final or most recent versions of all documents bringing about the concentration, whether by agreement between the parties to the concentration, acquisition of a controlling interest or a public bid; and

5.2   copies of the most recent annual reports and accounts of all the parties to the concentration.

SECTION 6. MARKET DEFINITIONS

The relevant product and geographic markets determine the scope within which the market power of the new entity resulting from the concentration must be assessed.[45]

---

[42] See Art 57 of the EEA Agreement and, in particular, Art 2(1) of Protocol 24 to the EEA Agreement. A case qualifies to be treated as a cooperation case if the combined turnover of the undertakings concerned in the territory of the EFTA States equals 25% or more of their total turnover within the territory covered by the EEA Agreement; or each of at least two undertakings concerned has a turnover exceeding EUR 250 million in the territory of the EFTA States: or the concentration is liable to create or strengthen a dominant position as a result of which effective competition would be significantly impeded in the territories of the EFTA States or a substantial part thereof.

[43] See Arts 3(3), 3(4) and 3(5) and Art 5(4) of the EC Merger Reg.

[44] See Sect 6.III for the definition of reportable markets.

[45] See Commission Notice on the definition of the relevant market for the purposes of Community competition law.

The notifying party or parties must provide the data requested having regard to the following definitions:

I Relevant product markets

A relevant product market comprises all those products and/or services which are regarded as interchangeable or substitutable by the consumer, by reason of the products' characteristics, their prices and their intended use. A relevant product market may in some cases be composed of a number of individual products and/or services which present largely identical physical or technical characteristics and are interchangeable.

Factors relevant to the assessment of the relevant product market include the analysis of why the products or services in these markets are included and why others are excluded by using the above definition, and having regard to, for example, substitutability, conditions of competition, prices, cross-price elasticity of demand or other factors relevant for the definition of the product markets (for example, supply-side substitutability in appropriate cases).

II Relevant geographic markets

The relevant geographic market comprises the area in which the undertakings concerned are involved in the supply and demand of relevant products or services, in which the conditions of competition are sufficiently homogeneous and which can be distinguished from neighbouring geographic areas because, in particular, conditions of competition are appreciably different in those areas.

Factors relevant to the assessment of the relevant geographic market include *inter alia* the nature and characteristics of the products or services concerned, the existence of entry barriers, consumer preferences, appreciable differences in the undertakings' market shares between neighbouring geographic areas, or substantial price differences.

III Reportable markets

For purposes of information required in this Form, reportable markets consist of all relevant product and geographic markets, as well as plausible alternative relevant product and geographic market definitions, on the basis of which:

(a) two or more of the parties to the concentration are engaged in business activities in the same relevant market (horizontal relationships);

(b) one or more of the parties to the concentration are engaged in business activities in a product market, which is upstream or downstream of a market in which any other party to the concentration is engaged, regardless of whether there is or is not any existing supplier/ customer relationship between the parties to the concentration (vertical relationships).

6.1 On the basis of the above market definitions, identify all reportable markets.

Section 7. Information on Markets

For each reportable market described in Section 6, for the year preceding the operation, provide the following:[46]

7.1 an estimate of the total size of the market in terms of sales value (in euros) and volume (units).[47] Indicate the basis and sources for the calculations and provide documents where available to confirm these calculations;

---

[46] In the context of pre-notification, you may want to discuss with the Commission to what extent dispensation (waivers) to provide the requested information would be appropriate for certain reportable markets.

[47] The value and volume of a market should reflect output less exports plus imports for the geographic areas under consideration.

7.2   the sales in value and volume, as well as an estimate of the market shares, of each of the parties to the concentration. Indicate if there have been significant changes to the sales and market shares for the last three financial years; and

7.3   for horizontal and vertical relationships, an estimate of the market share in value (and where appropriate, volume) of the three largest competitors (indicating the basis for the estimates). Provide the name, address, telephone number, fax number and e-mail address of the head of the legal department (or other person exercising similar functions; and in cases where there is no such person, then the chief executive) for these competitors.

SECTION 8. COOPERATIVE EFFECTS OF A JOINT VENTURE

8   For the purpose of Article 2(4) of the EC Merger Regulation, please answer the following questions:

(a) Do two or more parents retain to a significant extent activities in the same market as the joint venture or in a market which is upstream or downstream from that of the joint venture or in a neighbouring market closely related to this market?[48]

If the answer is affirmative, please indicate for each of the markets referred to here:

— the turnover of each parent company in the preceding financial year;
— the economic significance of the activities of the joint venture in relation to this turnover;
— the market share of each parent.

If the answer is negative, please justify your answer.

(b) If the answer to (a) is affirmative and in your view the creation of the joint venture does not lead to coordination between independent undertakings that restricts competition within the meaning of Article 81(1) of the EC Treaty, give your reasons.

(c) Without prejudice to the answers to (a) and (b) and in order to ensure that a complete assessment of the case can be made by the Commission, please explain how the criteria of Article 81(3) apply. Under Article 81(3), the provisions of Article 81(1) may be declared inapplicable if the operation:

(i) contributes to improving the production or distribution of goods, or to promoting technical or economic progress;

(ii) allows consumers a fair share of the resulting benefit;

(iii) does not impose on the undertakings concerned restrictions which are not indispensable to the attainment of these objectives; and

(iv) does not afford such undertakings the possibility of eliminating competition in respect of a substantial part of the products in question.

SECTION 9. DECLARATION

Article 2(2) of the Implementing Regulation states that where notifications are signed by representatives of undertakings, such representatives must produce written proof that they are authorized to act. Such written authorization must accompany the notification.

The notification must conclude with the following declaration which is to be signed by or on behalf of all the notifying parties:

The notifying party or parties declare that, to the best of their knowledge and belief, the information given in this notification is true, correct, and complete, that true and complete copies of documents required by this Form have been supplied, that all estimates are identified as such and are their best estimates of the underlying facts, and that all the opinions expressed are sincere.

---

[48] For market definitions refer to Sect 6.

They are aware of the provisions of Article 14(1)(a) of the EC Merger Regulation.

Place and date:

Signatures:

Name/s and positions:

On behalf of:

ANNEX III FORM RS

(RS = REASONED SUBMISSION PURSUANT TO ARTICLES 4(4) AND (5)
OF COUNCIL REGULATION (EC) No 139/2004)

FORM RS RELATING TO REASONED SUBMISSIONS

PURSUANT TO ARTICLES 4(4) AND 4(5) OF
REGULATION (EC) No 139/2004

INTRODUCTION

A The purpose of this Form

This Form specifies the information that requesting parties should provide when making a reasoned submission for a pre-notification referral under Article 4(4) or (5) of Council Regulation (EC) No 139/2004 (hereinafter referred to as 'the EC Merger Regulation').

Your attention is drawn to the EC Merger Regulation and to Commission Regulation (EC) No [. . ./2004] (hereinafter referred to as 'the EC Merger Implementing Regulation'). The text of these regulations, as well as other relevant documents, can be found on the Competition page of the Commission's Europa web site.

Experience has shown that prior contacts are extremely valuable to both the parties and the relevant authorities in determining the precise amount and type of information required. Accordingly, parties are encouraged to consult the Commission and the relevant Member State/s regarding the adequacy of the scope and type of information on which they intend to base their reasoned submission.

B The requirement for a reasoned submission to be correct and complete

All information required by this Form must be correct and complete. The information required must be supplied in the appropriate section of this Form.

Incorrect or misleading information in the reasoned submission will be considered to be incomplete information (Article 5(4) of the EC Merger Implementing Regulation).

If parties submit incorrect information, the Commission will have the power to revoke any Article 6 or 8 decision it adopts following an Article 4(5) referral, pursuant to Article 6(3)(a) or 8(6)(a) of the EC Merger Regulation. Following revocation, national competition laws would once again be applicable to the transaction. In the case of referrals under Article 4(4) made on the basis of incorrect information, the Commission may require a notification pursuant to Article 4(1). In addition, the Commission will have the power to impose fines for submission of incorrect or misleading information pursuant to Article 14(1)(a) of the EC Merger Regulation. (See point d below). Finally, parties should also be aware that, if a referral is made on the basis of incorrect, misleading or incomplete information included in Form RS, the Commission and/or the Member States may consider making a post-notification referral rectifying any referral made at pre-notification.

In particular you should note that:

(a) In accordance with Articles 4(4) and (5) of the EC Merger Regulation, the Commission is obliged to transmit reasoned submissions to Member States without delay. The time-limits for considering a reasoned submission will begin upon receipt of the submission by the relevant Member State or States. The decision whether or not to accede to a reasoned submission will normally be taken on the basis of the information contained therein, without further investigation efforts being undertaken by the authorities involved.

(b) The submitting parties should therefore verify, in the course of preparing their reasoned submission, that all information and arguments relied upon are sufficiently supported by independent sources.

(c) Under Article 14(1)(a) of the EC Merger Regulation, parties making a reasoned submission who, either intentionally or negligently, provide incorrect or misleading information, may be liable to fines of up to 1% of the aggregate turnover of the undertaking concerned.

(d) You may request in writing that the Commission accept that the reasoned submission is complete notwithstanding the failure to provide information required by this Form, if such information is not reasonably available to you in part or in whole (for example, because of the unavailability of information on a target company during a contested bid).

The Commission will consider such a request, provided that you give reasons for the non-availability of that information, and provide your best estimates for missing data together with the sources for the estimates. Where possible, indications as to where any of the requested information that is unavailable to you could be obtained by the Commission or the relevant Member State/s should also be provided.

(e) You may request that the Commission accept that the reasoned submission is complete notwithstanding the failure to provide information required by this Form, if you consider that any particular information requested by this Form may not be necessary for the Commission's or the relevant Member State/s' examination of the case.

The Commission will consider such a request, provided that you give adequate reasons why that information is not relevant and necessary to dealing with your request for a pre-notification referral. You should explain this during your prior contacts with the Commission and with the relevant Member State/s, and submit a written request for a waiver asking the Commission to dispense with the obligation to provide that information, pursuant to Article 4(2) of the EC Merger Implementing Regulation. The Commission may consult with the relevant Member State authority or authorities before deciding whether to accede to such a request.

C Persons entitled to submit a reasoned submission

In the case of a merger within the meaning of Article 3(1)(a) of the EC Merger Regulation or the acquisition of joint control of an undertaking within the meaning of Article 3(1)(b) of the Merger Regulation, the reasoned submission must be completed jointly by the parties to the merger or by those acquiring joint control as the case may be.

In case of the acquisition of a controlling interest in one undertaking by another, the acquirer must complete the reasoned submission.

In the case of a public bid to acquire an undertaking, the bidder must complete the reasoned submission.

Each party completing a reasoned submission is responsible for the accuracy of the information which it provides.

D How to make a reasoned submission

The reasoned submission must be completed in one of the official languages of the European Union. This language will thereafter be the language of the proceedings for all submitting parties.

In order to facilitate treatment of Form RS by Member State authorities, parties are strongly encouraged to provide the Commission with a translation of their reasoned submission in a language or languages which will be understood by all addressees of the information. As regards requests for referral to a Member State or States, the requesting parties are strongly encouraged to include a copy of the request in the language/s of the Member State/s to which referral is being requested.

The information requested by this Form is to be set out using the sections and paragraph numbers of the Form, signing the declaration at the end, and annexing supporting documentation. For the sake of clarity, certain information may be put in annexes. However, it is essential that all key substantive pieces of information are presented in the body of Form RS. Annexes to this Form shall only be used to supplement the information supplied in the Form itself.

Supporting documents are to be submitted in their original language; where this is not an official language of the Community, they must be translated into the language of the proceeding.

Supporting documents may be originals or copies of the originals. In the latter case, the submitting party must confirm that they are true and complete.

One original and 35 copies of the Form RS and of the supporting documents must be submitted to the Commission. The reasoned submission shall be delivered to the address referred to in Article 23 (1) of the EC Merger Implementing Regulation and in the format specified by the Commission services.

The submission must be delivered to the address of the Commission's Directorate-General for Competition (DG Competition). This address is published in the *Official Journal of the European Union*. The submission must be delivered to the Commission on working days as defined by Article 24 of the EC Merger Implementing Regulation. In order to enable it to be registered on the same day, it must be delivered before 17.00 hrs on Mondays to Thursdays and before 16.00 hrs on Fridays and workdays preceding public holidays and other holidays as determined by the Commission and published in the *Official Journal of the European Union*. The security instructions given on DG Competition's website must be adhered to.

E Confidentiality

Article 287 of the Treaty and Article 17(2) of the EC Merger Regulation require the Commission and the competent authorities of the Member States, their officials and other servants and other persons working under the supervision of these authorities as well as officials and civil servants of other authorities of the Member States, not to disclose information of the kind covered by the obligation of professional secrecy and which they have acquired through the application of the Regulation. The same principle must also apply to protect confidentiality between submitting parties.

If you believe that your interests would be harmed if any of the information supplied were to be published or otherwise divulged to other parties, submit this information separately with each page clearly marked 'Business Secrets'. You should also give reasons why this information should not be divulged or published.

In the case of mergers or joint acquisitions, or in other cases where the reasoned submission is completed by more than one of the parties, business secrets may be submitted in separate annexes, and referred to in the submission as an annex. All such annexes must be included in the reasoned submission.

F Definitions and instructions for the purposes of this Form

Submitting party or parties: in cases where a reasoned submission is made by only one of the undertakings who is a party to an operation, 'submitting parties' is used to refer only to the undertaking actually making the submission.

Party(ies) to the concentration or parties: these terms relate to both the acquiring and acquired parties, or to the merging parties, including all undertakings in which a controlling interest is being acquired or which is the subject of a public bid.

Except where otherwise specified, the terms 'submitting party(ies)' and 'party(ies) to the concentration' include all the undertakings which belong to the same groups as those 'parties'.

Affected markets: Section 4 of this Form requires the submitting parties to define the relevant product markets, and further to identify which of those relevant markets are likely to be affected by the operation. This definition of affected market is used as the basis for requiring information for a number of other questions contained in this Form. The definitions thus submitted by the submitting parties are referred to in this Form as the affected market(s). This term can refer to a relevant market made up either of products or of services.

Year: all references to the word 'year' in this Form should be read as meaning calendar year, unless otherwise stated. All information requested in this Form relates, unless otherwise specified, to the year preceding that of the reasoned submission.

The financial data requested in this Form must be provided in Euros at the average exchange rates prevailing for the years or other periods in question.

All references contained in this Form are to the relevant Articles and paragraphs of the EC Merger Regulation, unless otherwise stated.

Section 1. Background Information

1.0 Indicate whether the reasoned submission is made under Article 4(4) or (5).
— Article 4(4) referral
— Article 4(5) referral

1.1 Information on the submitting party (or parties)

Give details of:

1.1.1 the name and address of undertaking;

1.1.2 the nature of the undertaking's business;

1.1.3 the name, address, telephone number, fax number and electronic address of, and position held by, the appropriate contact person; and

1.1.4 an address for service of the submitting party (or each of the submitting parties) to which documents and, in particular, Commission decisions may be delivered. The name, telephone number and e-mail address of a person at this address who is authorised to accept service must be provided.

1.2 Information on the other parties[49] to the concentration

For each party to the concentration (except the submitting party or parties) give details of:

1.2.1 the name and address of undertaking;

1.2.2 the nature of undertaking's business;

1.2.3 the name, address, telephone number, fax number and electronic address of, and position held by the appropriate contact person;

1.2.4 an address for service of the party (or each of the parties) to which documents and, in particular, Commission Decisions may be delivered. The name, e-mail address and telephone number of a person at this address who is authorised to accept service must be provided.

1.3 Appointment of representatives

Where reasoned submissions are signed by representatives of undertakings, such representatives must produce written proof that they are authorized to act. The written proof must contain the name and position of the persons granting such authority.

---

[49] This includes the target company in the case of a contested bid, in which case the details should be completed as far as is possible.

Provide the following contact details of any representatives who have been authorized to act for any of the parties to the concentration, indicating whom they represent:

1.3.1 the name of the representative;

1.3.2 the address of the representative;

1.3.3 the name, address, telephone number, fax number and e-mail address of the person to be contacted; and

1.3.4 an address of the representative (in Brussels if available) to which correspondence may be sent and documents delivered.

Section 2. General Background and Details of the Concentration

2.1 Describe the general background to the concentration. In particular, give an overview of the main reasons for the transaction, including its economic and strategic rationale.

Provide an executive summary of the concentration, specifying the parties to the concentration, the nature of the concentration (for example, merger, acquisition, or joint venture), the areas of activity of the submitting parties, the markets on which the concentration will have an impact (including the main affected markets.[50]) and the strategic and economic rationale for the concentration.

2.2 Describe the legal nature of the transaction which is the subject of the reasoned submission. In doing so, indicate:

(a) whether the whole or parts of the parties are subject to the concentration;

(b) the proposed or expected date of any major events designed to bring about the completion of the concentration;

(c) the proposed structure of ownership and control after the completion of the concentration; and

(d) whether the proposed transaction is a concentration within the meaning of Article 3 of the EC Merger Regulation.

2.3 List the economic sectors involved in the concentration.

2.3.1 State the value of the transaction (the purchase price or the value of all the assets involved, as the case may be).

2.4 Provide sufficient financial or other data to show that the concentration meets OR does not meet the jurisdictional thresholds under Article 1 of the EC Merger Regulation.

2.4.1 Provide a breakdown of the Community-wide turnover achieved by the undertakings concerned, indicating, where applicable, the Member State, if any, in which more than two-thirds of this turnover is achieved.

Section 3. Ownership and Control[51]

For each of the parties to the concentration provide a list of all undertakings belonging to the same group.

This list must include:

3.1 all undertakings or persons controlling these parties, directly or indirectly;

3.2 all undertakings active on any affected market[52] that are controlled, directly or indirectly:

(a) by these parties;

(b) by any other undertaking identified in 3.1.

For each entry listed above, the nature and means of control should be specified.

---

[50] See Sect 4 for the definition of affected markets.
[51] See Art 3(3), 3(4) and 3(5) and Art 5(4).
[52] See Sect 4 for the definition of affected markets.

The information sought in this section may be illustrated by the use of organization charts or diagrams to show the structure of ownership and control of the undertakings.

SECTION 4. MARKET DEFINITIONS

The relevant product and geographic markets determine the scope within which the market power of the new entity resulting from the concentration must be assessed.[53]

The submitting party or parties must provide the data requested having regard to the following definitions:

I Relevant product markets

A relevant product market comprises all those products and/or services which are regarded as interchangeable or substitutable by the consumer, by reason of the products' characteristics, their prices and their intended use. A relevant product market may in some cases be composed of a number of individual products and/or services which present largely identical physical or technical characteristics and are interchangeable.

Factors relevant to the assessment of the relevant product market include the analysis of why the products or services in these markets are included and why others are excluded by using the above definition, and having regard to, for example, substitutability, conditions of competition, prices, cross-price elasticity of demand or other factors relevant for the definition of the product markets (for example, supply-side substitutability in appropriate cases).

II Relevant geographic markets

The relevant geographic market comprises the area in which the undertakings concerned are involved in the supply and demand of relevant products or services, in which the conditions of competition are sufficiently homogeneous and which can be distinguished from neighbouring geographic areas because, in particular, conditions of competition are appreciably different in those areas.

Factors relevant to the assessment of the relevant geographic market include, *inter alia*, the nature and characteristics of the products or services concerned, the existence of entry barriers, consumer preferences, appreciable differences in the undertakings' market shares between neighbouring geographic areas, or substantial price differences.

III Affected markets

For the purposes of the information required in this Form, affected markets consist of relevant product markets where, in the Community, or in any Member State:

(a) two or more of the parties to the concentration are engaged in business activities in the same product market and where the concentration will lead to a combined market share of 15% or more. These are horizontal relationships;

(b) one or more of the parties to the concentration are engaged in business activities in a product market, which is upstream or downstream of a product market in which any other party to the concentration is engaged, and any of their individual or combined market shares at either level is 25% or more, regardless of whether there is or is not any existing supplier/customer relationship between the parties to the concentration.[54] These are vertical relationships.

---

[53] See Commission Notice on the definition of the relevant market for the purposes of Community competition law.

[54] For example, if a party to the concentration holds a market share larger than 25% in a market that is upstream to a market in which the other party is active, then both the upstream and the downstream markets are affected markets. Similarly, if a vertically integrated company merges with another party which is active at the downstream level, and the merger leads to a combined market share downstream of 25% or more, then both the upstream and the downstream markets are affected markets.

On the basis of the above definitions and market share thresholds, provide the following information:

4.1   Identify each affected market within the meaning of Section III:

    (a) at the Community level;

    (b) in the case of a request for referral pursuant to Article 4(4), at the level of each individual Member State;

    (c) in the case of a request for referral pursuant to Article 4(5), at the level of each Member State identified at Section 6.3.1 of this Form as capable of reviewing the concentration.

4.2   In addition, explain the submitting parties' view as to the scope of the relevant geographic market within the meaning of Section II in relation to each affected market identified at 4.1 above.

Section 5. Information on Affected Markets

For each affected relevant product market, for the last financial year,

(a) for the Community as a whole;

(b) in the case of a request for referral pursuant to Article 4(4), individually for each Member State where the parties to the concentration do business; and

(c) in the case of a request for referral pursuant to Article 4(5), individually for each Member State identified at Section 6.3.1 of this Form as capable of reviewing the concentration where the parties to the concentration do business; and

(d) where in the opinion of the submitting parties, the relevant geographic market is different;

provide the following information;

5.1   an estimate of the total size of the market in terms of sales value (in Euros) and volume (units).[55] Indicate the basis and sources for the calculations and provide documents where available to confirm these calculations;

5.2   the sales in value and volume, as well as an estimate of the market shares, of each of the parties to the concentration;

5.3   an estimate of the market share in value (and where appropriate volume) of all competitors (including importers) having at least 5% of the geographic market under consideration;

    On this basis, provide an estimate of the HHI index[56] pre- and post-merger, and the difference between the two (the delta).[57] Indicate the proportion of market shares used as a basis to calculate the HHI; Identify the sources used to calculate these market shares and provide documents where available to confirm the calculation;

---

[55] The value and volume of a market should reflect output less exports plus imports for the geographic areas under consideration.

[56] HHI stands for Herfindahl-Hirschman Index, a measure of market concentration. The HHI is calculated by summing the squares of the individual market shares of all the firms in the market. For example, a market containing five firms with market shares of 40%, 20%, 15%, 15% and 10% respectively has an HHI of 2550 ($40^2 + 20^2 + 15^2 + 10^2 = 2550$). The HHI ranges from close to zero (in an atomistic market) to 10000 (in the case of a pure monopoly). The post-merger HHI is calculated on the working assumption that the individual market shares of the companies do not change. Although it is best to include all firms in the calculation, lack of information about very small firms may not be important because such firms do not affect the HHI significantly.

[57] The increase in concentration as measured by the HHI can be calculated independently of the overall market concentration by doubling the product of the market shares of the merging firms. For example, a merger of two firms with market shares of 30% and 15% respectively would increase the HHI by 900 ($30 \times 15 \times 2 = 900$). The explanation for this technique is as follows: Before the merger, the market shares of the merging firms contribute to the HHI by their squares individually: $(a)^2 + (b)^2$. After the merger, the contribution is the square of their sum: $(a + b)^2$, which equals $(a)^2 + (b)^2 + 2ab$. The increase in the HHI is therefore represented by $2ab$.

5.4   the five largest independent customers of the parties in each affected market and their individual share of total sales for such products accounted for by each of those customers;

5.5   the nature and extent of vertical integration of each of the parties to the concentration compared with their largest competitors;

5.6   identify the five largest independent[58] suppliers to the parties;

5.7   Over the last five years, has there been any significant entry into any affected markets? In the opinion of the submitting parties are there undertakings (including those at present operating only in extra-Community markets) that are likely to enter the market? Please specify.

5.8   To what extent do cooperative agreements (horizontal or vertical) exist in the affected markets?

5.9   If the concentration is a joint venture, do two or more parents retain to a significant extent activities in the same market as the joint venture or in a market which is downstream or upstream from that of the joint venture or in a neighbouring market closely related to this market?[59]

5.10   Describe the likely impact of the proposed concentration on competition in the affected markets and how the proposed concentration is likely to affect the interests of intermediate and ultimate consumers and the development of technical and economic progress.

SECTION 6. DETAILS OF THE REFERRAL REQUEST AND REASONS WHY THE CASE SHOULD BE REFERRED

6.1   Indicate whether the reasoned submission is made pursuant to Article 4(4) or 4(5) of the EC Merger Regulation, and fill in only the relevant sub-section:
— Article 4.4, referral
— Article 4.5 referral

Sub-section 6.2
Article 4(4) Referral

6.2.1 Identify the Member State or Member States which, pursuant to Article 4(4), you submit should examine the concentration, indicating whether or not you have made informal contact with this Member State/s.

6.2.2 Specify whether you are requesting referral of the whole or part of the case.

If you are requesting referral of part of the case, specify clearly the part or parts of the case for which you request the referral.

If you are requesting referral of the whole of the case, you must confirm that there are no affected markets outside the territory of the Member State/s to which you request the referral to be made.

6.2.3 Explain in what way each of the affected markets in the Member State or States to which referral is requested presents all the characteristics of a distinct market within the meaning of Article 4(4).

6.2.4 Explain in what way competition may be significantly affected in each of the above-mentioned distinct markets within the meaning of Article 4(4).

---

[58] That is suppliers which are not subsidiaries, agents or undertakings forming part of the group of the party in question. In addition to those five independent suppliers the notifying parties can, if they consider it necessary for a proper assessment of the case, identify the intra-group suppliers. The same applies in relation to customers.

[59] For market definitions refer to Sect 4.

6.2.5 In the event of a Member State/s becoming competent to review the whole or part of the case following a referral pursuant to Article 4(4), do you consent to the information contained in this Form being relied upon by the Member State/s in question for the purpose of its/their national proceedings relating to that case or part thereof? YES or NO

Sub-section 6.3
Article 4(5) Referral

6.3.1 For each Member State, specify whether the concentration is or is not capable of being reviewed under its national competition law. You must tick one box for each and every Member State.

Is the concentration capable of being reviewed under the national competition law of each of the following Member States? You must reply for each Member State. Only indicate YES or NO for each Member State. Failure to indicate YES or NO for any Member State shall be deemed to constitute an indication of YES for that Member State.

Austria:	YES	NO
Belgium:	YES	NO
Cyprus:	YES	NO
Czech Republic:	YES	NO
Denmark:	YES	NO
Estonia:	YES	NO
Finland:	YES	NO
France:	YES	NO
Germany:	YES	NO
Greece:	YES	NO
Hungary:	YES	NO
Ireland:	YES	NO
Italy:	YES	NO
Latvia:	YES	NO
Lithuaria:	YES	NO
Luxembourg:	YES	NO
Malta:	YES	NO
Netherlands:	YES	NO
Poland:	YES	NO
Portugal:	YES	NO
Slovakia:	YES	NO
Slovenia:	YES	NO
Spain:	YES	NO
Sweden:	YES	NO
United Kingdom:	YES	NO

6.3.2 For each Member State, provide sufficient financial or other data to show that the concentration meets or does not meet the relevant jurisdictional criteria under the applicable national competition law.

6.3.4 Explain why the case should be examined by the Commission. Explain in particular whether the concentration might affect competition beyond the territory of one Member State.

Section 7. Declaration

It follows from Articles 2(2) and 6(2) of the EC Merger Implementing Regulation that where reasoned submissions are signed by representatives of undertaking, such representatives must produce written proof that they are authorized to act. Such written authorization must accompany the submission.

The reasoned submission must conclude with the following declaration which is to be signed by or on behalf of all the submitting parties:

The submitting party or parties declare that, following careful verification, the information given in this reasoned submission is to the best of their knowledge and belief true, correct, and complete, that true and complete copies of documents required by Form RS, have been supplied, and that all estimates are identified as such and are their best estimates of the underlying facts and that all the opinions expressed are sincere.

They are aware of the provisions of Article 14(1)(a) of the EC Merger Regulation.

Place and date:

Signatures:

Name/s and positions:

On behalf of:

APPENDIX 17

Commission Notice on the concept of full-function joint ventures under Council Regulation (EEC) No 4064/89 on the control of concentrations between undertakings

(98/C 66/01)

(Text with EEA relevance)

I. INTRODUCTION

II. JOINT VENTURES UNDER ARTICLE 3 OF THE MERGER REGULATION

    1. Joint control

    2. Structural change of the undertakings

III. FINAL

I. Introduction

1. The purpose of this notice is to provide guidance as to how the Commission interprets Article 3 of Council Regulation (EEC) No 4064/89[1] as last amended by Regulation (EC) No 1310/97[2] (hereinafter referred to as the Merger Regulation) in relation to joint ventures.[3]

2. This Notice replaces the Notice on the distinction between concentrative and cooperative joint ventures. Changes made in this Notice reflect the amendments made to the Merger Regulation as well as the experience gained by the Commission in applying the Merger Regulation since its entry into force on 21 September 1990. The principles set out in this Notice will be followed and further developed by the Commission's practice in individual cases.

3. Under the Community competition rules, joint ventures are undertakings which are jointly controlled by two or more other undertakings.[4] In practice joint ventures encompass a broad range of operations, from merger-like operations to cooperation for particular functions such as R & D, production or distribution.

4. Joint ventures fall within the scope of the Merger Regulation if they meet the requirements of a concentration set out in Article 3 thereof.

---

[1] OJ L395, 30.12.1989, p 1, corrected version No L257, 21.9.1990, p 13.

[2] OJ L180, 9.7.1997, p 1.

[3] The Commission intends, in due course, to provide guidance on the application of Art 2(4) of the Merger Reg. Pending the adoption of such guidance, interested parties are referred to the principles set out in paras 17 to 20 of Commission Notice on the distinction between concentrative and cooperative joint ventures, OJ C385, 31.12.1994, p 1.

[4] The concept of joint control is set out in the Notice on the concept of concentration.

5. According to recital 23 to Council Regulation (EEC) No 4064/89 it is appropriate to define the concept of concentration in such a manner as to cover only operations bringing about a lasting change in the structure of the undertakings concerned.

6. The structural changes brought about by concentrations frequently reflect a dynamic process of restructuring in the markets concerned. They are permitted under the Merger Regulation unless they result in serious damage to the structure of competition by creating or strengthening a dominant position.

7. The Merger Regulation deals with the concept of full-function joint ventures in Article 3(2) as follows:

'The creation of a joint venture performing on a lasting basis all the functions of an autonomous economic entity shall constitute a concentration within the meaning of paragraph 1(b).'

II. JOINT VENTURES UNDER ARTICLE 3 OF THE MERGER REGULATION

8. In order to be a concentration within the meaning of Article 3 of the Merger Regulation, an operation must fulfil the following requirements:

1. Joint control

9. A joint venture may fall within the scope of the Merger Regulation where there is an acquisition of joint control by two or more undertakings, that is, its parent companies (Article 3(1)(b)). The concept of control is set out in Article 3(3). This provides that control is based on the possibility of exercising decisive influence over an undertaking, which is determined by both legal and factual considerations.

10. The principles for determining joint control are set out in detail in the Commission's Notice on the concept of concentration.[5]

2. Structural change of the undertakings

11. Article 3(2) provides that the joint venture must perform, on a lasting basis, all the functions of an autonomous economic entity. Joint ventures which satisfy this requirement bring about a lasting change in the structure of the undertakings concerned. They are referred to in this Notice as 'full-function' joint ventures.

12. Essentially this means that a joint venture must operate on a market, performing the functions normally carried out by undertakings operating on the same market. In order to do so the joint venture must have a management dedicated to its day-to-day operations and access to sufficient resources including finance, staff, and assets (tangible and intangible) in order to conduct on a lasting basis its business activities within the area provided for in the joint-venture agreement.[6]

13. A joint venture is not full-function if it only takes over one specific function within the parent companies' business activities without access to the market. This is the case, for example, for

---

[5] Paras 18 to 39.

[6] Case IV/M.527—Thomson CSF/Deutsche Aerospace, of 2 December 1994 (para 10)—intellectual rights, Case IV/M.560 EDS/Lufthansa of 11 May 1995 (para 11)—outsourcing, Case IV/M.585—Voest Alpine Industrieanlagenbau GmbH/Davy International Ltd, of 7 September 1995 (para 8)—joint venture's right to demand additional expertise and staff from its parent companies, Case IV/M.686—Nokia/Autoliv, of 5 February 1996 (para 7), joint venture able to terminate 'service agreements' with parent company and to move from site retained by parent company, Case IV/M.791—British Gas Trading Ltd/Group 4 Utility Services Ltd, of 7 October 1996, (para 9) joint venture's intended assets will be transferred to leasing company and leased by joint venture.

joint ventures limited to R & D or production. Such joint ventures are auxiliary to their parent companies' business activities. This is also the case where a joint venture is essentially limited to the distribution or sales of its parent companies' products and, therefore, acts principally as a sales agency. However, the fact that a joint venture makes use of the distribution network or outlet of one or more of its parent companies normally will not disqualify it as 'full-function' as long as the parent companies are acting only as agents of the joint venture.[7]

14. The strong presence of the parent companies in upstream or downstream markets is a factor to be taken into consideration in assessing the full-function character of a joint venture where this presence leads to substantial sales or purchases between the parent companies and the joint venture. The fact that the joint venture relies almost entirely on sales to its parent companies or purchases from them only for an initial start-up period does not normally affect the full-function character of the joint venture. Such a start-up period may be necessary in order to establish the joint venture on a market. It will normally not exceed a period of three years, depending on the specific conditions of the market in question.[8]

Where sales from the joint venture to the parent companies are intended to be made on a lasting basis, the essential question is whether, regardless of these sales, the joint venture is geared to play an active role on the market. In this respect the relative proportion of these sales compared with the total production of the joint venture is an important factor. Another factor is whether sales to the parent companies are made on the basis of normal commercial conditions.[9]

In relation to purchases made by the joint venture from its parent companies, the full-function character of the joint venture is questionable in particular where little value is added to the products or services concerned at the level of the joint venture itself. In such a situation, the joint venture may be closer to a joint sales agency. However, in contrast to this situation where a joint venture is active in a trade market and performs the normal functions of a trading company in such a market, it normally will not be an auxiliary sales agency but a full-function joint venture. A trade market is characterised by the existence of companies which specialise in the selling and distribution of products without being vertically integrated in addition to those which are integrated, and where different sources of supply are available for the products in question. In addition, many trade markets may require operators to invest in specific facilities such as outlets, stockholding, warehouses, depots, transport fleets and sales personnel. In order to constitute a full-function joint venture in a trade market, an undertaking must have the necessary facilities and be likely to obtain a substantial proportion of its supplies not only from its parent companies but also from other competing sources.[10]

15. Furthermore, the joint venture must be intended to operate on a lasting basis. The fact that the parent companies commit to the joint venture the resources described above normally demonstrates that this is the case. In addition, agreements setting up a joint venture often provide for certain contingencies, for example, the failure of the joint venture or fundamental

---

[7] Case IV/M.102—TNT/Canada Post etc. of 2 December 1991 (para 14).

[8] Case IV/M.560—EDS/Lufthansa of 11 May 1995 (para 11); Case IV/M.686 Nokia/Autoliv of 5 February 1996 (para 6); to be contrasted with Case IV/M.904—RSB/Tenex/Fuel Logistics of 2 April 1997 (para 15-17) and Case IV/M.979—Preussag/Voest-Alpine of 1 October 1997 (para 9-12). A special case exists where sales by the joint venture to its parent are caused by a legal monopoly downstream of the joint venture (Case IV/M.468—Siemens/Italtel of 17 February 1995 (para 12), or where the sales to a parent company consist of by-products, which are of minor importance to the joint venture (Case IV/M.550—Union Carbide/Enichem of 13 March 1995 (para 14).

[9] Case IV/M.556—Zeneca/Vanderhave of 9 April 1996 (para 8); Case IV/M.751—Bayer/Hüls of 3 July 1996 (para 10).

[10] Case IV/M.788—AgrEVO/Marubeni of 3 September 1996 (paras 9 and 10).

disagreement as between the parent companies.[11] This may be achieved by the incorporation of provisions for the eventual dissolution of the joint venture itself or the possibility for one or more parent companies to withdraw from the joint venture. This kind of provision does not prevent the joint venture from being considered as operating on a lasting basis. The same is normally true where the agreement specifies a period for the duration of the joint venture where this period is sufficiently long in order to bring about a lasting change in the structure of the undertakings concerned,[12] or where the agreement provides for the possible continuation of the joint venture beyond this period. By contrast, the joint venture will not be considered to operate on a lasting basis where it is established for a short finite duration. This would be the case, for example, where a joint venture is established in order to construct a specific project such as a power plant, but it will not be involved in the operation of the plant once its construction has been completed.

III. FINAL

16. The creation of a full-function joint venture constitutes a concentration within the meaning of Article 3 of the Merger Regulation. Restrictions accepted by the parent companies of the joint venture that are directly related and necessary for the implementation of the concentration ('ancillary restrictions'), will be assessed together with the concentration itself.[13]

Further, the creation of a full-function joint venture may as a direct consequence lead to the coordination of the competitive behaviour of undertakings that remain independent. In such cases Article 2(4) of the Merger Regulation provides that those cooperative effects will be assessed within the same procedure as the concentration. This assessment will be made in accordance with the criteria of Article 85(1) and (3) of the Treaty with a view to establishing whether or not the operation is compatible with the common market.

The applicability of Article 85 of the Treaty to other restrictions of competition, that are neither ancillary to the concentration, nor a direct consequence of the creation of the joint venture, will normally have to be examined by means of Regulation No 17.

17. The Commission's interpretation of Article 3 of the Merger Regulation with respect to joint ventures is without prejudice to the interpretation which may be given by the Court of Justice or the Court of First Instance of the European Communities.

---

[11] Case IV/M.891—Deutsche Bank/Commerzbank/J.M. Voith of 23 April 1997 (para 7).

[12] Case IV/M.791—British Gas Trading Ltd/Group 4 Utility Services Ltd of 7 October 1996, (para 10); to be contrasted with Case IV/M.722—Teneo/Merill Lynch/Bankers Trust of 15 April 1996 (para 15).

[13] See Commission Notice regarding restrictions ancillary to concentrations, OJ No C203, 14.8.1990, p 5.

APPENDIX 18

Commission Notice on the concept of concentration under Council Regulation (EEC) No 4064/89 on the control of concentrations between undertakings

(98/C 66/02)

(Text with EEA relevance)

I. INTRODUCTION

1. The purpose of this Notice is to provide guidance as to how the Commission interprets the term 'concentration' used in Article 3 of Council Regulation (EEC) No 4064/89[1] as last amended by Regulation (EC) No 1310/97[2] (hereinafter referred to as 'the Merger Regulation'). This formal guidance on the interpretation of Article 3 should enable firms to establish more quickly, in advance of any contact with the Commission, whether and to what extent their operations may be covered by Community merger control.

---

[1] OJ L395, 30.12.1989, p 1, corrected version OJ L257, 21.9.1990, p 13.
[2] OJ L180, 9.7.1997, p 1.

This Notice replaces the Notice on the notion of a concentration.[3]

This Notice deals with paragraphs (1), (3), (4) and (5) of Article 3. The interpretation of Article 3 in relation to joint ventures, dealt with in particular under Article 3(2), is set out in the Commission's Notice on the concept of full-function joint ventures.

2. The guidance set out in this Notice reflects the Commission's experience in applying the Merger Regulation since it entered into force on 21 December 1990. The principles contained here will be applied and further developed by the Commission in individual cases.

3. According to recital 23 to Regulation (EEC) No 4064/89, the concept of concentration is defined as covering only operations which bring about a lasting change in the structure of the undertakings concerned. Article 3(1) provides that such a structural change is brought about either by a merger between two previously independent undertakings or by the acquisition of control over the whole or part of another undertaking.

4. The determination of the existence of a concentration under the Merger Regulation is based upon qualitative rather than quantitative criteria, focusing on the concept of control. These criteria include considerations of both law and fact. It follows, therefore, that a concentration may occur on a legal or a *de facto* basis.

5. Article 3(1) of the Merger Regulation defines two categories of concentration:
   — those arising from a merger between previously independent undertakings (point (a));
   — those arising from an acquisition of control (point (b)).

   These are treated respectively in Sections II and III below.

II. MERGERS BETWEEN PREVIOUSLY INDEPENDENT UNDERTAKINGS

6. A merger within the meaning of Article 3(1)(a) of the Merger Regulation occurs when two or more independent undertakings amalgamate into a new undertaking and cease to exist as separate legal entities. A merger may also occur when an undertaking is absorbed by another, the latter retaining its legal identity while the former ceases to exist as a legal entity.

7. A merger within the meaning of Article 3(1)(a) may also occur where, in the absence of a legal merger, the combining of the activities of previously independent undertakings results in the creation of a single economic unit.[4] This may arise in particular where two or more undertakings, while retaining their individual legal personalities, establish contractually a common economic management.[5] If this leads to a *de facto* amalgamation of the undertakings concerned into a genuine common economic unit, the operation is considered to be a merger. A prerequisite for the determination of a common economic unit is the existence of a permanent, single economic management. Other relevant factors may include internal profit and loss compensation as between the various undertakings within the group, and their joint liability externally. The *de facto* amalgamation may be reinforced by cross-shareholdings between the undertakings forming the economic unit.

III. ACQUISITION OF CONTROL

8. Article 3(1)(b) provides that a concentration occurs in the case of an acquisition of control.

---

[3] OJ C385, 31.12.1994, p 5.

[4] In determining the previous independence of undertakings, the issue of control may be relevant. Control is considered generally in paras 12 *et seq.* below. For this specific issue, minority shareholders are deemed to have control if they have previously obtained a majority of votes on major decisions at shareholders meetings. The reference period in this context is normally three years.

[5] This could apply for example, in the case of a 'Gleichordnungskonzern' in German law, certain 'Groupements d'Intérêt Economique' in French law, and certain partnerships.

Such control may be acquired by one undertaking acting alone or by two or more undertakings acting jointly.

Control may also be acquired by a person in circumstances where that person already controls (whether solely or jointly) at least one other undertaking or, alternatively, by a combination of persons (which controls another undertaking) and/or undertakings. The term 'person' in this context extends to public bodies[6] and private entities, as well as individuals.

As defined, a concentration within the meaning of the Merger Regulation is limited to changes in control. Internal restructuring within a group of companies, therefore, cannot constitute a concentration.

An exceptional situation exists where both the acquiring and acquired undertakings are public companies owned by the same State (or by the same public body). In this case, whether the operation is to be regarded as an internal restructuring depends in turn on the question whether both undertakings were formerly part of the same economic unit within the meaning of recital 12 to Regulation (EEC) No 4064/89. Where the undertakings were formerly part of different economic units having an independent power of decision, the operation will be deemed to constitute a concentration and not an internal restructuring.[7] Such independent power of decision does not normally exist, however, where the undertakings are within the same holding company.[8]

9. Whether an operation gives rise to an acquisition of control depends on a number of legal and/or factual elements. The acquisition of property rights and shareholders' agreements are important, but are not the only elements involved: purely economic relationships may also play a decisive role. Therefore, in exceptional circumstances, a situation of economic dependence may lead to control on a *de facto* basis where, for example, very important long-term supply agreements or credits provided by suppliers or customers, coupled with structural links, confer decisive influence.[9]

There may also be acquisition of control even if it is not the declared intention of the parties.[10] Moreover, the Merger Regulation clearly defines control as having 'the possibility of exercising decisive influence' rather than the actual exercise of such influence.

10. Control is nevertheless normally acquired by persons or undertakings which are the holders of the rights or are entitled to rights conferring control (Article 3(4)(a)). There may be exceptional situations where the formal holder of a controlling interest differs from the person or undertaking having in fact the real power to exercise the rights resulting from this interest. This may be the case, for example, where an undertaking uses another person or undertaking for the acquisition of a controlling interest and exercises the rights through this person or undertaking, even though the latter is formally the holder of the rights. In such a situation, control is acquired by the undertaking which in reality is behind the operation and in fact enjoys the power to control the target undertaking (Article 3(4)(b)). The evidence needed to establish this type of indirect control may include factors such as the source of financing or family links.

11. The object of control can be one or more undertakings which constitute legal entities, or the

---

[6] Including the State itself, e.g. Case IV/M.157—Air France/Sabena, of 5 October 1992 in relation to the Belgian State, or other public bodies such as the Treuhand in Case IV/M.308—Kali und Salz/MDK/Treuhand, of 14 December 1993.

[7] Case IV/M.097—Péchiney/Usinor, of 24 June 1991; Case IV/M.216—CEA Industrie/France Telecom/SGS-Thomson, of 22 February 1993.

[8] See para 55 of the Notice on the concept of undertakings concerned.

[9] For example, in the Usinor/Bamesa decision adopted by the Commission under the ECSC Treaty. See also Case IV/M.258—CCIE/GTE, of 25 September 1992, and Case IV/M.697—Lockheed Martin Corporation/Loral Corporation, of 27 March 1996.

[10] Case IV/M.157—Air France/Sabena, of 5 October 1992.

assets of such entities, or only some of these assets.[11] The assets in question, which could be brands or licences, must constitute a business to which a market turnover can be clearly attributed.

12. The acquisition of control may be in the form of sole or joint control. In both cases, control is defined as the possibility of exercising decisive influence on an undertaking on the basis of rights, contracts or any other means (Article 3(3)).

1. Sole control

13. Sole control is normally acquired on a legal basis where an undertaking acquires a majority of the voting rights of a company. It is not in itself significant that the acquired shareholding is 50 % of the share capital plus one share[12] or that it is 100 % of the share capital.[13] In the absence of other elements, an acquisition which does not include a majority of the voting rights does not normally confer control even if it involves the acquisition of a majority of the share capital.

14. Sole control may also be acquired in the case of a 'qualified minority'. This can be established on a legal and/or *de facto* basis.

On a legal basis it can occur where specific rights are attached to the minority shareholding. These may be preferential shares leading to a majority of the voting rights or other rights enabling the minority shareholder to determine the strategic commercial behaviour of the target company, such as the power to appoint more than half of the members of the supervisory board or the administrative board.

A minority shareholder may also be deemed to have sole control on a *de facto* basis. This is the case, for example, where the shareholder is highly likely to achieve a majority at the shareholders' meeting, given that the remaining shares are widely dispersed.[14] In such a situation it is unlikely that all the smaller shareholders will be present or represented at the shareholders' meeting. The determination of whether or not sole control exists in a particular case is based on the evidence resulting from the presence of shareholders in previous years. Where, on the basis of the number of shareholders attending the shareholders' meeting, a minority shareholder has a stable majority of the votes at this meeting, then the large minority shareholder is taken to have sole control.[15]

Sole control can also be exercised by a minority shareholder who has the right to manage the activities of the company and to determine its business policy.

15. An option to purchase or convert shares cannot in itself confer sole control unless the option will be exercised in the near future according to legally binding agreements.[16] However, the likely exercise of such an option can be taken into account as an additional element which, together with other elements, may lead to the conclusion that there is sole control.

16. A change from joint to sole control of an undertaking is deemed to be a concentration within the meaning of the Merger Regulation because decisive influence exercised alone is substantially different from decisive influence exercised jointly.[17] For the same reason, an operation involving the acquisition of joint control of one part of an undertaking and sole control of

---

[11] Case IV/M.286—Zürich/MMI, of 2 April 1993.
[12] Case IV/M.296—Crédit Lyonnais/BFG Bank, of 11 January 1993.
[13] Case IV/M.299—Sara Lee/BP Food Division, of 8 February 1993.
[14] Case IV/M.025—Arjomari/Wiggins Teape, of 10 February 1990.
[15] Case IV/M.343—Société Générale de Belgique/Générale de Banque, of 3 August 1993.
[16] Judgment in Case T 2/93, *Air France* v. *Commission* [1994] ECR II-323.
[17] This issue is dealt with in paras 30, 31 and 32 of the Notice on the concept of undertakings concerned.

another part is in principle regarded as two separate concentrations under the Merger Regulation.[18]

17. The concept of control under the Merger Regulation may be different from that applied in specific areas of legislation concerning, for example, prudential rules, taxation, air transport or the media. In addition, national legislation within a Member State may provide specific rules on the structure of bodies representing the organisation of decision-making within an undertaking, in particular, in relation to the rights of representatives of employees. While such legislation may confer some power of control upon persons other than the shareholders, the concept of control under the Merger Regulation is related only to the means of influence normally enjoyed by the owners of an undertaking. Finally, the prerogatives exercised by a State acting as a public authority rather than as a shareholder, in so far as they are limited to the protection of the public interest, do not constitute control within the meaning of the Merger Regulation to the extent that they have neither the aim nor the effect of enabling the State to exercise a decisive influence over the activity of the undertaking.[19]

2. Joint control

18. As in the case of sole control, the acquisition of joint control (which includes changes from sole control to joint control) can also be established on a legal or *de facto* basis. There is joint control if the shareholders (the parent companies) must reach agreement on major decisions concerning the controlled undertaking (the joint venture).

19. Joint control exists where two or more undertakings or persons have the possibility of exercising decisive influence over another undertaking. Decisive influence in this sense normally means the power to block actions which determine the strategic commercial behaviour of an undertaking. Unlike sole control, which confers the power upon a specific shareholder to determine the strategic decisions in an undertaking, joint control is characterized by the possibility of a deadlock situation resulting from the power of two or more parent companies to reject proposed strategic decisions. It follows, therefore, that these shareholders must reach a common understanding in determining the commercial policy of the joint venture.

2.1. Equality in voting rights or appointment to decision-making bodies

20. The clearest form of joint control exists where there are only two parent companies which share equally the voting rights in the joint venture. In this case, it is not necessary for a formal agreement to exist between them. However, where there is a formal agreement, it must be consistent with the principle of equality between the parent companies, by laying down, for example, that each is entitled to the same number of representatives in the management bodies and that none of the members has a casting vote.[20] Equality may also be achieved where both parent companies have the right to appoint an equal number of members to the decision-making bodies of the joint venture.

2.2. Veto rights

21. Joint control may exist even where there is no equality between the two parent companies in votes or in representation in decision-making bodies or where there are more than two parent companies. This is the case where minority shareholders have additional rights which allow them to veto decisions which are essential for the strategic commercial behaviour of the joint venture.[21] These veto rights may be set out in the statute of the joint venture or conferred by agreement between its parent companies. The veto rights themselves may operate by means of

---

[18] Case IV/M.409—ABB/Renault Automation, of 9 March 1994.
[19] Case IV/M.493—Tractebel/Distrigaz II, of 1 September 1994.
[20] Case IV/M.272—Matra/CAP Gemini Sogeti, of 17 March 1993.
[21] Case T 2/93—Air France v Commission (ibid). Case IV/M.010—Conagra/Idea, of 3 May 1991.

a specific quorum required for decisions taken at the shareholders' meeting or by the board of directors to the extent that the parent companies are represented on this board. It is also possible that strategic decisions are subject to approval by a body, e.g. supervisory board, where the minority shareholders are represented and form part of the quorum needed for such decisions.

22. These veto rights must be related to strategic decisions on the business policy of the joint venture. They must go beyond the veto rights normally accorded to minority shareholders in order to protect their financial interests as investors in the joint venture. This normal protection of the rights of minority shareholders is related to decisions on the essence of the joint venture, such as changes in the statute, an increase or decrease in the capital or liquidation. A veto right, for example, which prevents the sale or winding-up of the joint venture does not confer joint control on the minority shareholder concerned.[22]

23. In contrast, veto rights which confer joint control typically include decisions and issues such as the budget, the business plan, major investments or the appointment of senior management. The acquisition of joint control, however, does not require that the acquirer has the power to exercise decisive influence on the day-to-day running of an undertaking. The crucial element is that the veto rights are sufficient to enable the parent companies to exercise such influence in relation to the strategic business behaviour of the joint venture. Moreover, it is not necessary to establish that an acquirer of joint control of the joint venture will actually make use of its decisive influence. The possibility of exercising such influence and, hence, the mere existence of the veto rights, is sufficient.

24. In order to acquire joint control, it is not necessary for a minority shareholder to have all the veto rights mentioned above. It may be sufficient that only some, or even one such right, exists. Whether or not this is the case depends upon the precise content of the veto right itself and also the importance of this right in the context of the specific business of the joint venture.

Appointment of management and determination of budget

25. Normally the most important veto rights are those concerning decisions on the appointment of the management and the budget. The power to co-determine the structure of the management confers upon the holder the power to exercise decisive influence on the commercial policy of an undertaking. The same is true with respect to decisions on the budget since the budget determines the precise framework of the activities of the joint venture and, in particular, the investments it may make.

Business plan

26. The business plan normally provides details of the aims of a company together with the measures to be taken in order to achieve those aims. A veto right over this type of business plan may be sufficient to confer joint control even in the absence of any other veto right. In contrast, where the business plan contains merely general declarations concerning the business aims of the joint venture, the existence of a veto right will be only one element in the general assessment of joint control but will not, on its own, be sufficient to confer joint control.

Investments

27. In the case of a veto right on investments, the importance of this right depends, first, on the level of investments which are subject to the approval of the parent companies and, secondly, on the extent to which investments constitute an essential feature of the market in which the joint venture is active. In relation to the first criterion, where the level of investments necessitating approval of the parent companies is extremely high, this veto right may be closer to the

---

[22] Case IV/M.062—Eridania/ISI, of 30 July 1991.

normal protection of the interests of a minority shareholder than to a right conferring a power of co-determination over the commercial policy of the joint venture. With regard to the second, the investment policy of an undertaking is normally an important element in assessing whether or not there is joint control. However, there may be some markets where investment does not play a significant role in the market behaviour of an undertaking.

Market-specific rights

28. Apart from the typical veto rights mentioned above, there exist a number of other veto rights related to specific decisions which are important in the context of the particular market of the joint venture. One example is the decision on the technology to be used by the joint venture where technology is a key feature of the joint venture's activities. Another example relates to markets characterised by product differentiation and a significant degree of innovation. In such markets, a veto right over decisions relating to new product lines to be developed by the joint venture may also be an important element in establishing the existence of joint control.

Overall context

29. In assessing the relative importance of veto rights, where there are a number of them, these rights should not be evaluated in isolation. On the contrary, the determination of whether or not joint control exists is based upon an assessment of these rights as a whole. However, a veto right which does not relate either to commercial policy and strategy or to the budget or business plan cannot be regarded as giving joint control to its owner.[23]

2.3. Joint exercise of voting rights

30. Even in the absence of specific veto rights, two or more undertakings acquiring minority shareholdings in another undertaking may obtain joint control. This may be the case where the minority shareholdings together provide the means for controlling the target undertaking. This means that the minority shareholders, together, will have a majority of the voting rights; and they will act together in exercising these voting rights. This can result from a legally binding agreement to this effect, or it may be established on a *de facto* basis.

31. The legal means to ensure the joint exercise of voting rights can be in the form of a holding company to which the minority shareholders transfer their rights, or an agreement by which they undertake to act in the same way (pooling agreement).

32. Very exceptionally, collective action can occur on a *de facto* basis where strong common interests exist between the minority shareholders to the effect that they would not act against each other in exercising their rights in relation to the joint venture.

33. In the case of acquisitions of minority shareholdings, the prior existence of links between the minority shareholders or the acquisition of the shareholdings by means of concerted action will be factors indicating such a common interest.

34. In the case where a new joint venture is established, as opposed to the acquisition of minority shareholdings in a pre-existing company, there is a higher probability that the parent companies are carrying out a deliberate common policy. This is true, in particular, where each parent company provides a contribution to the joint venture which is vital for its operation (e. g. specific technologies, local know-how or supply agreements). In these circumstances, the parent companies may be able to operate the joint venture with full cooperation only with each other's agreement on the most important strategic decisions even if there is no express provision for any veto rights. The greater the number of parent companies involved in such a joint venture, however, the more remote is the likelihood of this situation occurring.

35. In the absence of strong common interests such as those outlined above, the possibility of

---

[23] Case IV/M.295—SITA-RPC/SCORI, of 19 March 1993.

changing coalitions between minority shareholders will normally exclude the assumption of joint control. Where there is no stable majority in the decision-making procedure and the majority can on each occasion be any of the various combinations possible amongst the minority shareholders, it cannot be assumed that the minority shareholders will jointly control the undertaking. In this context, it is not sufficient that there are agreements between two or more parties having an equal shareholding in the capital of an undertaking which establish identical rights and powers between the parties. For example, in the case of an undertaking where three shareholders each own one-third of the share capital and each elect one-third of the members of the Board of Directors, the shareholders do not have joint control since decisions are required to be taken on the basis of a simple majority. The same considerations also apply in more complex structures, for example, where the capital of an undertaking is equally divided between three shareholders and where the Board of Directors is composed of twelve members, each of the shareholders A, B and C electing two, another two being elected by A, B and C jointly, whilst the remaining four are chosen by the other eight members jointly. In this case also there is no joint control, and hence no control at all within the meaning of the Merger Regulation.

2.4. Other considerations related to joint control

36. Joint control is not incompatible with the fact that one of the parent companies enjoys specific knowledge of and experience in the business of the joint venture. In such a case, the other parent company can play a modest or even non-existent role in the daily management of the joint venture where its presence is motivated by considerations of a financial, long-term-strategy, brand image or general policy nature. Nevertheless, it must always retain the real possibility of contesting the decisions taken by the other parent company, without which there would be sole control.

37. For joint control to exist, there should not be a casting vote for one parent company only. However, there can be joint control when this casting vote can be exercised only after a series of stages of arbitration and attempts at reconciliation or in a very limited field.[24]

2.5. Joint control for a limited period

38. Where an operation leads to joint control for a starting-up period[25] but, according to legally binding agreements, this joint control will be converted to sole control by one of the shareholders, the whole operation will normally be considered to be an acquisition of sole control.

3. Control by a single shareholder on the basis of veto rights

39. An exceptional situation exists where only one shareholder is able to veto strategic decisions in an undertaking, but this shareholder does not have the power, on his own, to impose such decisions. This situation occurs either where one shareholder holds 50 % in an undertaking whilst the remaining 50 % is held by two or more minority shareholders, or where there is a quorum required for strategic decisions which in fact confers a veto right upon only one minority shareholder.[26] In these circumstances, a single shareholder possesses the same level of influence as that normally enjoyed by several jointly-controlling shareholders, i.e. the power to block the adoption of strategic decisions. However, this shareholder does not enjoy the powers which are normally conferred on an undertaking with sole control, i. e. the power to impose strategic decisions. Since this shareholder can produce a deadlock situation compar-

---

[24] Case IV/M.425—British Telecom/Banco Santander, of 28 March 1994.
[25] This starting-up period must not exceed three years. Case IV/M.425—British Telecom/Banco Santander, *ibid.*
[26] Case IV/M.258—CCIE/GTE, of 25 September 1992, where the veto rights of only one shareholder were exercisable through a member of the board appointed by this shareholder.

able to that in normal cases of joint control, he acquires decisive influence and therefore control within the meaning of the Merger Regulation.[27]

4. Changes in the structure of control

40. A concentration may also occur where an operation leads to a change in the structure of control. This includes the change from joint control to sole control as well as an increase in the number of shareholders exercising joint control. The principles for determining the existence of a concentration in these circumstances are set out in detail in the Notice on the concept of undertakings concerned.[28]

IV. EXCEPTIONS

41. Article 3(5) sets out three exceptional situations where the acquisition of a controlling interest does not constitute a concentration under the Merger Regulation.

42. First, the acquisition of securities by companies whose normal activities include transactions and dealing in securities for their own account or for the account of others is not deemed to constitute a concentration if such an acquisition is made in the framework of these businesses and if the securities are held on only a temporary basis (Article 3(5)(a)). In order to fall within this exception, the following requirements must be fulfilled:

— the acquiring undertaking must be a credit or other financial institution or insurance company the normal activities of which are described above,

— the securities must be acquired with a view to their resale,

— the acquiring undertaking must not exercise the voting rights with a view to determining the strategic commercial behaviour of the target company or must exercise these rights only with a view to preparing the total or partial disposal of the undertaking, its assets or securities,

— the acquiring undertaking must dispose of its controlling interest within one year of the date of the acquisition, that is, it must reduce its shareholding within this one-year period at least to a level which no longer confers control. This period, however, may be extended by the Commission where the acquiring undertaking can show that the disposal was not reasonably possible within the one-year period.

43. Secondly, there is no change of control, and hence no concentration within the meaning of the Merger Regulation, where control is acquired by an office-holder according to the law of a Member State relating to liquidation, winding-up, insolvency, cessation of payments, compositions or analogous proceedings (Article 3(5)(b));

44. Thirdly, a concentration does not arise where a financial holding company within the meaning of the Fourth Council Directive 78/660/EEC[29] acquires control, provided that this company exercises its voting rights only to maintain the full value of its investment and does not otherwise determine directly or indirectly the strategic commercial conduct of the controlled undertaking.

45. In the context of the exceptions under Article 3(5), the question may arise whether a rescue operation constitutes a concentration under the Merger Regulation. A rescue operation

---

[27] Since this shareholder is the only undertaking acquiring a controlling influence, only this shareholder is obliged to submit a notification under the Merger Reg.

[28] Paras 30 to 48.

[29] OJ L222, 14.8.1978, p 11, as last amended by the Act of Accession of Austria, Finland and Sweden. Art 5(3) of this Directive defines financial holding companies as 'those companies the sole objective of which is to acquire holdings in other undertakings, and to manage such holdings and turn them to profit, without involving themselves directly or indirectly in the management of those undertakings, the foregoing without prejudice to their rights as shareholders'.

typically involves the conversion of existing debt into a new company, through which a syndicate of banks may acquire joint control of the company concerned. Where such an operation meets the criteria for joint control, as outlined above, it will normally be considered to be a concentration.[30] Although the primary intention of the banks is to restructure the financing of the undertaking concerned for its subsequent resale, the exception set out in Article 3(5)(a) is normally not applicable to such an operation. This is because the restructuring programme normally requires the controlling banks to determine the strategic commercial behaviour of the rescued undertaking. Furthermore, it is not normally a realistic proposition to transform a rescued company into a commercially viable entity and to resell it within the permitted one-year period. Moreover, the length of time needed to achieve this aim may be so uncertain that it would be difficult to grant an extension of the disposal period.

V. Final

46. The Commission's interpretation of Article 3 as set out in this Notice is without prejudice to the interpretation which may be given by the Court of Justice or the Court of First Instance of the European Communities.

---

[30] Case IV/M.116—Kelt/American Express, of 28 August 1991.

1260

APPENDIX 19

Commission Notice on the concept of undertakings concerned under Council Regulation (EEC) No 4064/89 on the control of concentrations between undertakings

(98/C 66/03)

(Text with EEC relevance)

10. Management buy-outs

11. Acquisition of control by a state-owned company

I. INTRODUCTION

1. The purpose of this notice is to clarify the Commission's interpretation of the term 'undertakings concerned' used in Articles 1 and 5 of Council Regulation (EEC) No 4064/89[1] as last amended by Regulation (EC) No 1310/97[2] (hereinafter referred to as 'the Merger Regulation') and to help identify the undertakings concerned in the most typical situations which have arisen in cases dealt with by the Commission to date. The principles set out in this notice will be followed and further developed by the Commission's practice in individual cases.

    This Notice replaces the Notice on the notion of undertakings concerned.[3]

2. According to Article 1 of the Merger Regulation, the Regulation only applies to operations that satisfy two conditions. First, several undertakings must merge, or one or more undertakings must acquire control of the whole or part of other undertakings through the proposed operation, which must qualify as a concentration within the meaning of Article 3 of the Regulation. Secondly, those undertakings must meet the turnover thresholds set out in Article 1.

3. From the point of view of determining jurisdiction, the undertakings concerned are, broadly speaking, the actors in the transaction in so far as they are the merging, or acquiring and acquired parties; in addition, their total aggregate economic size in terms of turnover will be decisive in determining whether the thresholds are met.

4. The Commission's interpretation of Articles 1 and 5 with respect to the concept of undertakings concerned is without prejudice to the interpretation which may be given by the Court of Justice or by the Court of First Instance of the European Communities.

II. THE CONCEPT OF UNDERTAKING CONCERNED

5. Undertakings concerned are the direct participants in a merger or acquisition of control. In this respect, Article 3(1) of the Merger Regulation provides that:

    'A concentration shall be deemed to arise where:
    (a) two or more previously independent undertakings merge, or
    (b) —one or more persons already controlling at least one undertaking, or
    —one or more undertakings
    acquire, whether by purchase of securities or assets, by contract or by any other means, direct or indirect control of the whole or parts of one or more other undertakings'.

6. In the case of a merger, the undertakings concerned will be the undertakings that are merging.

7. In the remaining cases, it is the concept of 'acquiring control' that will determine which are the undertakings concerned. On the acquiring side, there can be one or more companies acquiring sole or joint control. On the acquired side, there can be one or more companies as a whole or parts thereof, when only one of their subsidiaries or some of their assets are the subject of the transaction. As a general rule, each of these companies will be an undertaking concerned within the meaning of the Merger Regulation. However, the particular features of

---

[1] OJ L395, 30.12.1989, p 1; corrected version L 257, 21.9.1990, p 13.
[2] OJ L180, 9.7.1997, p 1.
[3] OJ C385, 31.12.1994, p 12.

specific transactions require some refinement of this principle, as will be seen below when analysing different possible scenarios.

8. In concentrations other than mergers or the setting-up of new joint ventures, i. e. in cases of sole or joint acquisition of pre-existing companies or parts of them, there is an important party to the agreement that gives rise to the operation who is to be ignored when identifying the undertakings concerned: the seller. Although it is clear that the operation cannot proceed without his consent, his role ends when the transaction is completed since, by definition, from the moment the seller has relinquished all control over the company, his links with it disappear. Where the seller retains joint control with the acquiring company (or companies), it will be considered to be one of the undertakings concerned.

9. Once the undertakings concerned have been identified in a given transaction, their turnover for the purposes of determining jurisdiction should be calculated according to the rules set out in Article 5 of the Merger Regulation.[4] One of the main provisions of Article 5 is that where the undertaking concerned belongs to a group, the turnover of the whole group should be included in the calculation. All references to the turnover of the undertakings concerned in Article 1 should therefore be understood as the turnover of their entire respective groups.

10. The same can be said with respect to the substantive appraisal of the impact of a concentration in the market place. When Article 2 of the Merger Regulation provides that the Commission is to take into account 'the market position of the undertakings concerned and their economic and financial power', that includes the groups to which they belong.

11. It is important, when referring to the various undertakings which may be involved in a procedure, not to confuse the concept of 'undertakings concerned' under Articles 1 and 5 with the terminology used in the Merger Regulation and in Commission Regulation (EC) No 447/98 of 1 March 1998 on the notifications, time-limits and hearings provided for in Council Regulation (EEC) No 4064/89 (hereinafter referred to as the 'Implementing Regulation')[5] referring to the various undertakings which may be involved in a procedure. This terminology refers to the notifying parties, other involved parties, third parties and parties who may be subject to fines or periodic penalty payments, and they are defined in Chapter III of the Implementing Regulation, along with their respective rights and duties.

III. IDENTIFYING THE UNDERTAKINGS CONCERNED IN DIFFERENT TYPES OF OPERATIONS

1. Mergers

12. In a merger, several previously independent companies come together to create a new company or, while remaining separate legal entities, to create a single economic unit. As mentioned earlier, the undertakings concerned are each of the merging entities.

2. Acquisition of sole control

2.1. Acquisition of sole control of the whole company

13. Acquisition of sole control of the whole company is the most straightforward case of acquisition of control; the undertakings concerned will be the acquiring company and the acquired or target company.

---

[4] The rules for calculating turnover in accordance with Art 5 are detailed in the Commission Notice on calculation of turnover.

[5] OJ L61, 2.3.1998, p 1.

2.2. Acquisition of sole control of part of a company

14. The first subparagraph of Article 5(2) of the Merger Regulation provides that when the operation concerns the acquisition of parts of one or more undertakings, only those parts which are the subject of the transaction shall be taken into account with regard to the seller. The concept of 'parts' is to be understood as one or more separate legal entities (such as subsidiaries), internal subdivisions within the seller (such as a division or unit), or specific assets which in themselves could constitute a business (e. g. in certain cases brands or licences) to which a market turnover can be clearly attributed. In this case, the undertakings concerned will be the acquirer and the acquired part(s) of the target company.

15. The second subparagraph of Article 5(2) includes a special provision on staggered operations or follow-up deals, whereby if several acquisitions of parts by the same purchaser from the same seller occur within a two-year period, these transactions are to be treated as one and the same operation arising on the date of the last transaction. In this case, the undertakings concerned are the acquirer and the different acquired part(s) of the target company taken as a whole.

2.3. Acquisition of sole control after reduction or enlargement of the target company

16. The undertakings concerned are the acquiring company and the target company or companies, in their configuration at the date of the operation.

17. The Commission bases itself on the configuration of the undertakings concerned at the date of the event triggering the obligation to notify under Article 4(1) of the Merger Regulation, namely the conclusion of the agreement, the announcement of the public bid or the acquisition of a controlling interest. If the target company has divested an entity or closed a business prior to the date of the event triggering notification or where such a divestment or closure is a pre-condition for the operation,[6] then sales of the divested entity or closed business are not to be included when calculating turnover. Conversely, if the target company has acquired an entity prior to the date of the event triggering notification, the sales of the latter are to be added.[7]

2.4. Acquisition of sole control through a subsidiary of a group

18. Where the target company is acquired by a group through one of its subsidiaries, the undertakings concerned for the purpose of calculating turnover are the target company and the acquiring subsidiary. However, regarding the actual notification, this can be made by the subsidiary concerned or by its parent company.

19. All the companies within a group (parent companies, subsidiaries, etc.) constitute a single economic entity, and therefore there can only be one undertaking concerned within the one group—i. e. the subsidiary and the parent company cannot each be considered as separate undertakings concerned, either for the purposes of ensuring that the threshold requirements are fulfilled (for example, if the target company does not meet the ECU 250 million Community-turnover threshold), or that they are not (for example, if a group was split into two companies each with a Community turnover below ECU 250 million).

20. However, even though there can only be one undertaking concerned within a group, Article 5(4) of the Merger Regulation provides that it is the turnover of the whole group to

---

[6] See judgment of the Court of First Instance of 24 March 1994 in Case T-3/93—Air France v Commission [1994] ECR II-21.
[7] The calculation of turnover in the case of acquisitions or divestments subsequent to the date of the last audited accounts is dealt with in the Commission Notice on calculation of turnover, para 27.

which the undertaking concerned belongs that shall be included in the threshold calculations.[8]

3. Acquisition of joint control

3.1. Acquisition of joint control of a newly-created company

21. In the case of acquisition of joint control of a newly-created company, the undertakings concerned are each of the companies acquiring control of the newly set-up joint venture (which, as it does not yet exist, cannot be considered to be an undertaking concerned and moreover, as yet, has no turnover of its own).

3.2. Acquisition of joint control of a pre-existing company

22. In the case of acquisition of joint control of a pre-existing company or business,[9] the undertakings concerned are each of the companies acquiring joint control on the one hand, and the pre-existing acquired company or business on the other.

23. However, where the pre-existing company was under the sole control of one company and one or several new shareholders acquire joint control while the initial parent company remains, the undertakings concerned are each of the jointly-controlling companies (including this initial shareholder). The target company in this case is not an undertaking concerned, and its turnover is part of the turnover of the initial parent company.

3.3. Acquisition of joint control with a view to immediate partition of assets

24. Where several undertakings come together solely for the purpose of acquiring another company and agree to divide up the acquired assets according to a pre-existing plan immediately upon completion of the transaction, there is no effective concentration of economic power between the acquirers and the target company since the assets acquired are jointly held and controlled for only a 'legal instant'. This type of acquisition with a view to immediate partition of assets will in fact be considered to be several operations, whereby each of the acquiring companies acquires its relevant part of the target company. For each of these operations, the undertakings concerned will therefore be the acquiring company and that part of the target which it is acquiring (just as if there was an acquisition of sole control of part of a company).

25. This scenario is referred to in recital 24 of Regulation (EEC) No 4064/89, which states that the Regulation applies to agreements whose sole object is to divide up the assets acquired immediately after the acquisition.

4. Acquisition of control by a joint venture

26. In transactions where a joint venture acquires control of another company, the question arises whether or not, from the point of view of the acquiring party, the joint venture should be regarded as a single undertaking concerned (the turnover of which would include the turnover of its parent companies), or whether each of its parent companies should individually be regarded as undertakings concerned. In other words, the issue is whether or not to 'lift the corporate veil' of the intermediate undertaking (the vehicle). In principle, the undertaking concerned is the direct participant in the acquisition of control. However, there may be circumstances where companies set up 'shell' companies, which have little or no turnover of

---

[8] The calculation of turnover in the case of company groups is dealt with in the Commission Notice on calculation of turnover, paras 36 to 42.

[9] i. e. two or more companies (companies A, B, etc.) acquire a pre-existing company (company X). For changes in the shareholding in cases of joint control of an existing joint venture, see Sect III.6.

their own, or use an existing joint venture which is operating on a different market from that of the target company in order to carry out acquisitions on behalf of the parent companies. Where the acquired or target company has a Community turnover of less than ECU 250 million, the question of determining the undertakings concerned may be decisive for jurisdictional purposes.[10] In this type of situation, the Commission will look at the economic reality of the operation to determine which are the undertakings concerned.

27. Where the acquisition is carried out by a full-function joint venture, i. e. a joint venture which has sufficient financial and other resources to operate a business activity on a lasting basis[11] and is already operating on a market, the Commission will normally consider the joint venture itself and the target company to be the undertakings concerned (and not the joint venture's parent companies).

28. Conversely, where the joint venture can be regarded as a vehicle for an acquisition by the parent companies, the Commission will consider each of the parent companies themselves to be the undertakings concerned, rather than the joint venture, together with the target company. This is the case in particular where the joint venture is set up especially for the purpose of acquiring the target company, where the joint venture has not yet started to operate, where an existing joint venture has no legal personality or full-function character as referred to above or where the joint venture is an association of undertakings. The same applies where there are elements which demonstrate that the parent companies are in fact the real players behind the operation. These elements may include a significant involvement by the parent companies themselves in the initiation, organisation and financing of the operation. Moreover, where the acquisition leads to a substantial diversification in the nature of the joint venture's activities, this may also indicate that the parent companies are the real players in the operation. This will normally be the case when the joint venture acquires a target company operating on a different product market. In those cases, the parent companies are regarded as undertakings concerned.

29. In the TNT case,[12] joint control over a joint venture (JVC) was to be acquired by a joint venture (GD NET BV) between five postal administrations and another acquiring company (TNT Ltd). In this case, the Commission considered that the joint venture GD NET BV was simply a vehicle set up to enable the parent companies (the five postal administrations) to participate in the resulting JVC joint venture in order to facilitate decision-making amongst themselves and to ensure that the parent companies spoke and acted as one; this configuration would ensure that the parent companies could exercise a decisive influence with the other acquiring company, TNT, over the resulting joint venture JVC and would avoid the situation where that other acquirer could exercise sole control because of the postal administrations' inability to reach a unified position on any decision.

---

[10] The target company hypothetically has an aggregate Community turnover of less than ECU 250 million, and the acquiring parties are two (or more) undertakings, each with a Community turnover exceeding ECU 250 million. If the target is acquired by a 'shell' company set up between the acquiring undertakings, there would only be one company (the 'shell' company) with a Community turnover exceeding ECU 250 million, and thus one of the cumulative threshold conditions for Community jurisdiction would not be fulfilled (namely, the existence of at least two undertakings with a Community turnover exceeding ECU 250 million). Conversely, if instead of acting through a 'shell' company, the acquiring undertakings acquire the target company themselves, then the turnover threshold would be met and the Merger Reg would apply to this transaction. The same considerations apply to the national turnover thresholds referred to in Art 1(3).

[11] The criteria determining the full-function nature of a joint venture are contained in the Commission Notice on the concept of full-function joint ventures.

[12] Case IV/M.102—TNT/Canada Post, DBP Postdienst, La Poste, PTT Post and Sweden Post, of 2 December 1991.

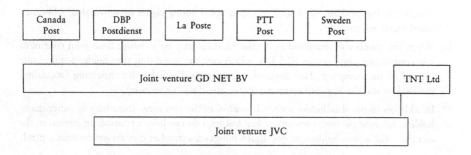

5. Change from joint control to sole control

30. In the case of a change from joint control to sole control, one shareholder acquires the stake previously held by the other shareholder(s). In the case of two shareholders, each of them has joint control over the entire joint venture, and not sole control over 50 % of it; hence the sale of all of his shares by one shareholder to the other does not lead the sole remaining shareholder to move from sole control over 50 % to sole control over 100 % of the joint venture, but rather to move from joint control to sole control of the entire company (which, subsequent to the operation, ceases to be a 'joint' venture).

31. In this situation, the undertakings concerned are the remaining (acquiring) shareholder and the joint venture. As is the case for any other seller, the 'exiting' shareholder is not an undertaking concerned.

32. The ICI/Tioxide case[13] involved such a change from joint (50/50) control to sole control. The Commission considered that '. . . decisive influence exercised solely is substantially different to decisive influence exercised jointly, since the latter has to take into account the potentially different interests of the other party or parties concerned . . . By changing the quality of decisive influence exercised by ICI on Tioxide, the transaction will bring about a durable change of the structure of the concerned parties . . .'. In this case, the undertakings concerned were held to be ICI (as acquirer) and Tioxide as a whole (as acquiree), but not the seller Cookson.

6. Change in the shareholding in cases of joint control of an existing joint venture

33. The decisive element in assessing changes in the shareholding of a company is whether the operation leads to a change in the quality of control. The Commission assesses each operation on a case-by-case basis, but under certain hypotheses, there will be a presumption that the given operation leads, or does not lead, to such a change in the quality of control, and thus constitutes, or does not constitute, a notifiable concentration.

34. A distinction must be made according to the circumstances of the change in the shareholding; firstly, one or more existing shareholders can exit; secondly, one or more new additional shareholders can enter; and thirdly, one or more existing shareholders can be replaced by one or more new shareholders.

6.1. Reduction in the number of shareholders leading to a change from joint to sole control

35. It is not the reduction in the number of shareholders *per se* which is important, but rather the fact that if some shareholders sell their stakes in a given joint venture, these stakes are then acquired by other (new or existing) shareholders, and thus the acquisition of these stakes or additional contractual rights may lead to the acquisition of control or may strengthen an

---

[13] Case IV/M.023—ICI/Tioxide, of 28 November 1990.

already existing position of control (e.g. additional voting rights or veto rights, additional board members, etc.).

36. Where the number of shareholders is reduced, there may be a change from joint control to sole control (see also Section III.5.), in which case the remaining shareholder acquires sole control of the company. The undertakings concerned will be the remaining (acquiring) shareholder and the acquired company (previously the joint venture).

37. In addition to the shareholder with sole control of the company, there may be other share-holders, for example with minority stakes, but who do not have a controlling interest in the company; these shareholders are not undertakings concerned as they do not exercise control.

6.2. *Reduction in the number of shareholders not leading to a change from joint to sole control*

38. Where the operation involves a reduction in the number of shareholders having joint control, without leading to a change from joint to sole control and without any new entry or substitution of shareholders acquiring control (see Section III.6.3.), the proposed transaction will normally be presumed not to lead to a change in the quality of control and will therefore not be a notifiable concentration. This would be the case where, for example, five shareholders initially have equal stakes of 20 % each and where, after the operation, one shareholder exits and the remaining four shareholders each have equal stakes of 25 %.

39. However, this situation would be different where there is a significant change in the quality of control, notably where the reduction in the number of shareholders gives the remaining shareholders additional veto rights or additional board members, resulting in a new acquisition of control by at least one of the shareholders, through the application of either the existing or a new shareholders' agreement. In this case, the undertakings concerned will be each of the remaining shareholders which exercise joint control and the joint venture. In Avesta II,[14] the fact that the number of major shareholders decreased from four to three led to one of the remaining shareholders acquiring negative veto rights (which it had not previously enjoyed) because of the provisions of the shareholders' agreement which remained in force.[15] This acquisition of full veto rights was considered by the Commission to represent a change in the quality of control.

6.3. *Any other changes in the composition of the shareholding*

40. Finally, in the case where, following changes in the shareholding, one or more shareholders acquire control, the operation will constitute a notifiable operation as there is a presumption that it will normally lead to a change in the quality of control.

41. Irrespective of whether the number of shareholders decreases, increases or remains the same subsequent to the operation, this acquisition of control can take any of the following forms:

— entry of one or more new shareholders (change from sole to joint control, or situation of joint control both before and after the operation),

— acquisition of a controlling interest by one or more minority shareholders (change from sole to joint control, or situation of joint control both before and after the operation),

— substitution of one or more shareholders (situation of joint control both before and after the operation).

42. The question is whether the undertakings concerned are the joint venture and the new shareholder(s) who would together acquire control of a pre-existing company, or whether all

---

[14] Case IV/M.452—Avesta II, of 9 June 1994.

[15] In this case, a shareholder who was a party to the shareholders' agreement sold its stake of approximately 7 %. As the exiting shareholder had shared veto rights with another shareholder who remained, and as the shareholders' agreement remained unchanged, the remaining shareholder now acquired full veto rights.

of the shareholders (existing and new) are to be regarded as undertakings concerned acquiring control of a new joint venture. This question is particularly relevant when there is no express agreement between one (or more) of the existing shareholders and the new shareholder(s), who might only have had an agreement with the 'exiting' shareholder(s), i.e. the seller(s).

43. A change in the shareholding through the entry or substitution of shareholders is considered to lead to a change in the quality of control. This is because the entry of a new parent company, or the substitution of one parent company for another, is not comparable to the simple acquisition of part of a business as it implies a change in the nature and quality of control of the whole joint venture, even when, both before and after the operation, joint control is exercised by a given number of shareholders.

44. The Commission therefore considers that the undertakings concerned in cases where there are changes in the shareholding are the shareholders (both existing and new) who exercise joint control and the joint venture itself. As mentioned earlier, non-controlling shareholders are not undertakings concerned.

45. An example of such a change in the shareholding is the Synthomer/Yule Catto case,[16] in which one of two parent companies with joint control over the pre-existing joint venture was replaced by a new parent company. Both parent companies with joint control (the existing one and the new one) and the joint venture were considered to be undertakings concerned.

7. 'Demergers' and the break-up of companies

46. When two undertakings merge or set up a joint venture, then subsequently demerge or break up their joint venture, and in particular the assets[17] are split between the 'demerging' parties, particularly in a configuration different from the original, there will normally be more than one acquisition of control (see the Annex).

47. For example, undertakings A and B merge and then subsequently demerge with a new asset configuration. There will be the acquisition by undertaking A of various assets (assets which may previously have been owned by itself or by undertaking B and assets jointly acquired by the entity resulting from the merger), with similar acquisitions by undertaking B. Similarly, a break-up of a joint venture can be deemed to involve a change from joint control over the joint venture's entire assets to sole control over the divided assets.[18]

48. A break-up of a company in this way is 'asymmetrical'. For such a demerger, the undertakings concerned (for each break-up operation) will be, on the one hand, the original parties to the merger and, on the other, the assets that each original party is acquiring. For the break-up of a joint venture, the undertakings concerned (for each break-up operation) will be, on the one hand, the original parties to the joint venture, each as acquirer, and, on the other, that part of the joint venture that each original party is acquiring.

8. Exchange of assets

49. In those transactions where two (or more) companies exchange assets, regardless of whether these constitute legal entities or not, each acquisition of control constitutes an independent concentration. Although it is true that both transfers of assets in a swap are usually considered by the parties to be interdependent, that they are often agreed in a single document and that they may even take place simultaneously, the purpose of the Merger Regulation is to assess the impact of the operation resulting from the acquisition of control by each of the companies.

---

[16] Case IV/M.376—Synthomer/Yule Catto, of 22 October 1993.

[17] The term 'assets' as used here means specific assets which in themselves could constitute a business (e.g. a subsidiary, a division of a company or, in some cases, brands or licences) to which a market turnover can be clearly attributed.

[18] Case IV/M.197—Solvay-Laporte/Interox, of 30 April 1997.

The legal or even economic link between those operations is not sufficient for them to qualify as a single concentration.

50. Hence the undertakings concerned will be, for each property transfer, the acquiring companies and the acquired companies or assets.

9. Acquisitions of control by individual persons

51. Article 3(1) of the Merger Regulation specifically provides that a concentration is deemed to arise, *inter alia*, where 'one or more persons already controlling at least one undertaking' acquire control of the whole or parts of one or more undertakings. This provision indicates that acquisitions of control by individuals will bring about a lasting change in the structure of the companies concerned only if those individuals carry out economic activities of their own. The Commission considers that the undertakings concerned are the target company and the individual acquirer (with the turnover of the undertaking(s) controlled by that individual being included in the calculation of the individual's turnover).

52. This was the view taken in the Commission decision in the Asko/Jacobs/Adia case,[19] where Asko, a German holding company with substantial retailing assets, and Mr Jacobs, a private Swiss investor, acquired joint control of Adia, a Swiss company active mainly in personnel services. Mr Jacobs was considered to be an undertaking concerned because of the economic interests he held in the chocolate, confectionery and coffee sectors.

10. Management buy-outs

53. An acquisition of control of a company by its own managers is also an acquisition by individuals, and what has been said above is therefore also applicable here. However, the management of the company may pool its interests through a 'vehicle company', so that it acts with a single voice and also to facilitate decision-making. Such a vehicle company may be, but is not necessarily, an undertaking concerned. The general rule on acquisitions of control by a joint venture applies here (see Section III.4.).

54. With or without a vehicle company, the management may also look for investors in order to finance the operation. Very often, the rights granted to these investors according to their shareholding may be such that control within the meaning of Article 3 of the Merger Regulation will be conferred on them and not on the management itself, which may simply enjoy minority rights. In the CWB/Goldman Sachs/Tarkett decision,[20] the two companies managing the investment funds taking part in the transaction were those acquiring joint control, and not the managers.

11. Acquisition of control by a State-owned company

55. In those situations where a State-owned company merges with or acquires control of another company controlled by the same State,[21] the question arises as to whether these transactions really constitute concentrations within the meaning of Article 3 of the Merger Regulation or rather internal restructuring operations of the 'public sector group of companies'.[22] In this respect, recital 12 of Regulation (EEC) No 4064/89 sets out the principle of non-discrimination between public and private sectors and declares that 'in the public sector, calculation of the turnover of an undertaking concerned in a concentration needs, therefore, to take account of undertakings making up an economic unit with an independent power of

---

[19] Case IV/M.082—Asko/Jacobs/Adia, of 16 May 1991.

[20] Case IV/M.395—CWB/Goldman Sachs/Tarkett, of 21 February 1994.

[21] The term 'State' as used here means any legal public entity, i.e. not only Member States, but also regional or local public entities such as provinces, departments, Länder, etc.

[22] See also Commission Notice on the concept of concentration, para 8.

decision, irrespective of the way in which their capital is held or of the rules of administrative supervision applicable to them'.

56. A merger or acquisition of control arising between two companies owned by the same State may constitute a concentration and, if so, both of them will qualify as undertakings concerned, since the mere fact that two companies are both owned by the same State does not necessarily mean that they belong to the same 'group'. Indeed, the decisive issue will be whether or not these companies are both part of the same industrial holding and are subject to a coordinated strategy. This was the approach taken in the SGS/Thomson decision.[23]

ANNEX
'DEMERGERS' AND BREAK-UP OF COMPANIES[24]

Merger scenario

Before merger

Company A		Company B

After merger

Merged company Combined assets

After breaking up the merger

Company A:
Divided assets of merged company:
— some (initial) assets of A
— some (initial) assets of B
— some (subsequent) assets of the
   merged-company
	Company B:
	Divided assets of merged company:
	— some (initial) assets of A
	— some (initial) assets of B
	— some (subsequent) assets of the
	   merged-company

Joint venture scenario (JV)

Before JV

Company A	Assets of A for the JV		Assets of B for the JV	Company B

After JV

Company A	———	Joint venture Combined assets	———	Company B

---

[23] Case IV/M.216—CEA Industrie/France Telecom/Finmeccanica/SGS-Thomson, of 22 February 1993.
[24] The term 'assets' as used here means specific assets which in themselves could constitute a business (e.g. a subsidiary, a division of a company or, in some cases, brands or licences) to which a market turnover can be clearly attributed.

After breaking up the JV

Company A	Divided assets of joint venture: — some initial (assets) of A — some initial (assets) of B — some (subsequent) assets of the JV	Divided assets of joint venture: — some initial (assets) of A — some initial (assets) of B — some (subsequent) assets of the JV	Company B

APPENDIX 20

Commission notice on calculation of turnover under Council Regulation (EEC) No 4064/89 on the control of concentrations between undertakings

(98/C 66/04)

(Text with EEA relevance)

I.   'ACCOUNTING' DETERMINATION OF TURNOVER

   1. Turnover as a reflection of business activity

     1.1. The concept of turnover
     1.2. Ordinary activities

   2. 'Net' turnover

     2.1. The deduction of rebates and taxes
     2.2. The deduction of 'internal' turnover

   3. Adjustment of turnover calculation rules for the different types of operations

     3.1. The general rule
     3.2. Acquisition of parts of companies
     3.3. Staggered operations
     3.4. Turnover of groups
     3.5. Turnover of State-owned companies

II. GEOGRAPHICAL ALLOCATION OF TURNOVER

   1. General rule

   2. Conversion of turnover into ecu

III. CREDIT AND OTHER FINANCIAL INSTITUTIONS AND INSURANCE UNDERTAKINGS

   1. Definitions

   2. Calculation of turnover

1.   The purpose of this Notice is to expand upon the text of Articles 1 and 5 of Council Regulation (EEC) No 4064/89[1] as last amended by Council Regulation (EC) No 1310/97[2] (hereinafter referred to as 'the Merger Regulation') and in so doing to elucidate certain procedural and practical questions which have caused doubt or difficulty.

---

[1] OJ L395, 30.12.1989, p 1; corrected version OJ L257, 21.9.1990, p 13.
[2] OJ L180, 9.7.1997, p 1.

2. This Notice is based on the experience gained by the Commission in applying the Merger Regulation to date. The principles it sets out will be followed and further developed by the Commission's practice in individual cases.

   This Notice replaces the Notice on calculation of turnover.[3]

3. The Merger Regulation has a two fold test for Commission jurisdiction. One test is that the transaction must be a concentration within the meaning of Article 3.[4] The second comprises the turnover thresholds contained in Article 1 and designed to identify those transactions which have an impact upon the Community and can be deemed to be of 'Community interest'. Turnover is used as a proxy for the economic resources being combined in a concentration, and is allocated geographically in order to reflect the geographic distribution of those resources.

   Two sets of thresholds are set out in Article 1, in paragraph 2 and paragraph 3 respectively. Article (2) sets out the thresholds which must first be checked in order to establish whether the transaction has a Community dimension. In this respect, the worldwide turnover threshold is intended to measure the overall dimension of the undertakings concerned; the Community turnover threshold seek to determine whether the concentration involves a minimum level of activities in the Community; and the two-thirds rule aims to exclude purely domestic transactions from Community jurisdiction.

   Article 1(3) must only be applied in the event that the thresholds set out in Article 1(2) are not met. This second set of thresholds is designed to tackle those transactions which fall short of achieving Community dimension under Article 1(2), but would need to be notified under national competition rules in at least three Member States (so called 'multiple notifications'). For this purpose, Article 1(3) provides for lower turnover thresholds, both worldwide and Community-wide, to be achieved by the undertakings concerned. A concentration has a Community dimension if these lower thresholds are fulfilled and the undertakings concerned achieve jointly and individually a minimum level of activities in at least three Member States. Article 1(3) also contains a two-thirds rule similar to that of Article 1(2), which aims to identify purely domestic transactions.

4. The thresholds as such are designed to establish jurisdiction and not to assess the market position of the parties to the concentration nor the impact of the operation. In so doing they include turnover derived from, and thus the resources devoted to, all areas of activity of the parties, and not just those directly involved in the concentration. Article 1 of the Merger Regulation sets out the thresholds to be used to determine a concentration with a 'Community dimension' while Article 5 explains how turnover should be calculated.

5. The fact that the thresholds of Article 1 of the Merger Regulation are purely quantitative, since they are only based on turnover calculation instead of market share or other criteria, shows that their aim is to provide a simple and objective mechanism that can be easily handled by the companies involved in a merger in order to determine if their transaction has a Community dimension and is therefore notifiable.

6. The decisive issue for Article 1 of the Merger Regulation is to measure the economic strength of the undertakings concerned as reflected in their respective turnover figures, regardless of the sector where such turnover was achieved and of whether those sectors will be at all affected by the transaction in question. The Merger Regulation has thereby given priority to the determination of the overall economic and financial resources that are being combined through the merger in order to decide whether the latter is of Community interest.

7. In this context, it is clear that turnover should reflect as accurately as possible the economic

---

[3] OJ C385, 31.12.1994, p 21.
[4] See the Notice on the concept of concentration.

strength of the undertakings involved in a transaction. This is the purpose of the set of rules contained in Article 5 of the Merger Regulation which are designed to ensure that the resulting figures are a true representation of economic reality.

8. The Commission's interpretation of Articles 1 and 5 with respect to calculation of turnover is without prejudice to the interpretation which may be given by the Court of Justice or the Court of First Instance of the European Communities.

I. 'Accounting' Calculation of Turnover

1. Turnover as a reflection of activity

1.1. *The concept of turnover*

9. The concept of turnover as used in Article 5 of the Merger Regulation refers explicitly to 'the amounts derived from the sale of products and the provision of services'. Sale, as a reflection of the undertaking's activity, is thus the essential criterion for calculating turnover, whether for products or the provision of services. 'Amounts derived from sale' generally appear in company accounts under the heading 'sales'.

10. In the case of products, turnover can be determined without difficulty, namely by identifying each commercial act involving a transfer of ownership.

11. In the case of services, the factors to be taken into account in calculating turnover are much more complex, since the commercial act involves a transfer of 'value'.

12. Generally speaking, the method of calculating turnover in the case of services does not differ from that used in the case of products: the Commission takes into consideration the total amount of sales. Where the service provided is sold directly by the provider to the customer, the turnover of the undertaking concerned consists of the total amount of sales for the provision of services in the last financial year.

13. Because of the complexity of the service sector, this general principle may have to be adapted to the specific conditions of the service provided. Thus, in certain sectors of activity (such as tourism and advertising), the service may be sold through the intermediary of other suppliers. Because of the diversity of such sectors, many different situations may arise. For example, the turnover of a service undertaking which acts as an intermediary may consist solely of the amount of commissions which it receives.

14. Similarly, in a number of areas such as credit, financial services and insurance, technical problems in calculating turnover arise which will be dealt with in Section III.

1.2. *Ordinary activities*

15. Article 5(1) states that the amounts to be included in the calculation of turnover must correspond to the 'ordinary activities' of the undertakings concerned.

16. With regard to aid granted to undertakings by public bodies, any aid relating to one of the ordinary activities of an undertaking concerned is liable to be included in the calculation of turnover if the undertaking is itself the recipient of the aid and if the aid is directly linked to the sale of products and the provision of services by the undertaking and is therefore reflected in the price.[5] For example, aid towards the consumption of a product allows the manufacturer to sell at a higher price than that actually paid by consumers.

---

[5] See Case IV/M.156—Cereol/Continentale Italiana of 27 November 1991. In this case, the Commission excluded Community aid from the calculation of turnover because the aid was not intended to support the sale of products manufactured by one of the undertakings involved in the merger, but the producers of the raw materials (grain) used by the undertaking, which specialized in the crushing of grain.

17. With regard to services, the Commission looks at the undertaking's ordinary activities involved in establishing the resources required for providing the service. In its Decision in the Accor/Wagons-Lits case,[6] the Commission decided to take into account the item 'other operating proceeds' included in Wagons-Lits's profit and loss account. The Commission considered that the components of this item which included certain income from its car-hire activities were derived from the sale of products and the provision of services by Wagons-Lits and were part of its ordinary activities.

2. 'Net' turnover

18. The turnover to be taken into account is 'net' turnover, after deduction of a number of components specified in the Regulation. The Commission's aim is to adjust turnover in such a way as to enable it to decide on the real economic weight of the undertaking.

2.1. *The deduction of rebates and taxes*

19. Article 5(1) provides for the 'deduction of sales rebates and of value added tax and other taxes directly related to turnover'. The deductions thus relate to business components (sales rebates) and tax components (value added tax and other taxes directly related to turnover).

20. 'Sales rebates' should be taken to mean all rebates or discounts which are granted by the undertakings during their business negotiations with their customers and which have a direct influence on the amounts of sales.

21. As regards the deduction of taxes, the Merger Regulation refers to VAT and 'other taxes directly related to turnover'. As far as VAT is concerned, its deduction does not in general pose any problem. The concept of 'taxes directly related to turnover' is a clear reference to indirect taxation since it is directly linked to turnover, such as, for example, taxes on alcoholic beverages.

2.2. *The deduction of 'internal' turnover*

22. The first subparagraph of Article 5(1) states that 'the aggregate turnover of an undertaking concerned shall not include the sale of products or the provision of services between any of the undertakings referred to in paragraph 4', i.e. those which have links with the undertaking concerned (essentially parent companies or subsidiaries).

23. The aim is to exclude the proceeds of business dealings within a group so as to take account of the real economic weight of each entity. Thus, the 'amounts' taken into account by the Merger Regulation reflect only the transactions which take place between the group of undertakings on the one hand and third parties on the other.

3. Adjustment of turnover calculation rules for the different types of operations

3.1. *The general rule*

24. According to Article 5(1) of the Merger Regulation, aggregate turnover comprises the amounts derived by the undertakings concerned in the preceding financial year from the sale of products and the provision of services. The basic principle is thus that for each undertaking concerned the turnover to be taken into account is the turnover of the closest financial year to the date of the transaction.

25. This provision shows that since there are usually no audited accounts of the year ending the day before the transaction, the closest representation of a whole year of activity of the company in question is the one given by the turnover figures of the most recent financial year.

26. The Commission seeks to base itself upon the most accurate and reliable figures available. As

---

[6] Case IV/M.126—Accor/Wagons-Lits, of 28 April 1992.

a general rule therefore, the Commission will refer to audited or other definitive accounts. However, in cases where major differences between the Community's accounting standards and those of a non-member country are observed, the Commission may consider it necessary to restate these accounts in accordance with Community standards in respect of turnover. The Commission is, in any case, reluctant to rely on management or any other form of provisional accounts in any but exceptional circumstances (see the next paragraph). Where a concentration takes place within the first months of the year and audited accounts are not yet available for the most recent financial year, the figures to be taken into account are those relating to the previous year. Where there is a major divergence between the two sets of accounts, and in particular, when the final draft figures for the most recent years are available, the Commission may decide to take those draft figures into account.

27. Notwithstanding paragraph 26, an adjustment must always be made to account for acquisitions or divestments subsequent to the date of the audited accounts. This is necessary if the true resources being concentrated are to be identified. Thus if a company disposes of part of its business at any time before the signature of the final agreement or the announcement of the public bid or the acquisition of a controlling interest bringing about a concentration, or where such a divestment or closure is a pre-condition for the operation[7] the part of the turnover to be attributed to that part of the business must be subtracted from the turnover of the notifying party as shown in its last audited accounts. Conversely, the turnover to be attributed to assets of which control has been acquired subsequent to the preparation of the most recent audited accounts must be added to a company's turnover for notification purposes.

28. Other factors that may affect turnover on a temporary basis such as a decrease in orders for the product or a slow-down in the production process within the period prior to the transaction will be ignored for the purposes of calculating turnover. No adjustment to the definitive accounts will be made to incorporate them.

29. Regarding the geographical allocation of turnover, since audited accounts often do not provide a geographical breakdown of the sort required by the Merger Regulation, the Commission will rely on the best figures available provided by the companies in accordance with the rule laid down in Article 5(1) of the Merger Regulation (see Section II.1).

3.2. Acquisitions of parts of companies

30. Article 5(2) of the Merger Regulation provides that 'where the concentration consists in the acquisition of parts, whether or not constituted as legal entities, of one or more undertakings, only the turnover relating to the parts which are the subject of the transaction shall be taken into account with regard to the seller or sellers'.

31. This provision states that when the acquirer does not purchase an entire group, but only one, or part, of its businesses, whether or not constituted as a subsidiary, only the turnover of the part acquired should be included in the turnover calculation. In fact, although in legal terms the seller as a whole (with all its subsidiaries) is an essential party to the transaction, since the sale-purchase agreement cannot be concluded without him, he plays no role once the agreement has been implemented. The possible impact of the transaction on the market will depend only on the combination of the economic and financial resources that are the subject of a property transfer with those of the acquirer and not on the remaining business of the seller who remains independent.

3.3. Staggered operations

32. Sometimes certain successive transactions are only individual steps within a wider strategy

---

[7] See Judgment of the Court of First Instance in Case T-3/93, Air France v Commission, [1994] ECR II-21.

between the same parties. Considering each transaction alone, even if only for determining jurisdiction, would imply ignoring economic reality. At the same time, whereas some of these staggered operations may be designed in this fashion because they will better meet the needs of the parties, others could be structured like this in order to circumvent the application of the Merger Regulation.

33. The Merger Regulation has foreseen these scenarios in Article 5(2), second subparagraph, which provides that 'two or more transactions within the meaning of the first subparagraph which take place within a two-year period between the same persons or undertakings shall be treated as one and the same concentration arising on the date of the last transaction'.

34. In practical terms, this provision means that if company A buys a subsidiary of company B that represents 50 % of the overall activity of B and one year later it acquires the other subsidiary (the remaining 50 % of B), both transactions will be taken as one. Assuming that each of the subsidiaries attained a turnover in the Community of only ECU 200 million, the first transaction would not be notifiable unless the operation fulfilled the conditions set out in Article 1(3). However, since the second transaction takes place within the two-year period, both have to be notified as a single transaction when the second occurs.

35. The importance of the provision is that previous transactions (within two years) become notifiable with the most recent transaction once the thresholds are cumulatively met.

3.4. Turnover of groups

36. When an undertaking concerned in a concentration within the meaning of Article 1 of the Merger Regulation[8] belongs to a group, the turnover of the group as a whole is to be taken into account in order to determine whether the thresholds are met. The aim is again to capture the total volume of the economic resources that are being combined through the operation.

37. The Merger Regulation does not define the concept of group in abstract terms but focuses on whether the companies have the right to manage the undertaking's affairs as the yardstick to determine which of the companies that have some direct or indirect links with an undertaking concerned should be regarded as part of its group.

38. Article 5(4) of the Merger Regulation provides the following:

'Without prejudice to paragraph 2 [acquisitions of parts], the aggregate turnover of an undertaking concerned within the meaning of Article 1(2) and (3) shall be calculated by adding together the respective turnovers of the following:

(a) the undertaking concerned;
(b) those undertakings in which the undertaking concerned directly or indirectly:
   — owns more than half the capital or business assets, or
   — has the power to exercise more than half the voting rights, or
   — has the power to appoint more than half the members of the supervisory board, the administrative board or bodies legally representing the undertakings, or
   — has the right to manage the undertaking's affairs;
(c) those undertakings which have in an undertaking concerned the rights or powers listed in (b);
(d) those undertakings in which an undertaking as referred to in (c) has the rights or powers listed in (b);
(e) those undertakings in which two or more undertakings as referred to in (a) to (d) jointly have the rights or powers listed in (b).'

This means that the turnover of the company directly involved in the transaction (point (a))

---

[8] See the Commission Notice on the concept of undertakings concerned.

should include its subsidiaries (point (b)), its parent companies (point (c)), the other subsidiaries of its parent companies (point (d)) and any other undertaking jointly controlled by two or more of he companies belonging to the group (point (e)). A graphic example is as follows:

The undertaking concerned and its group:

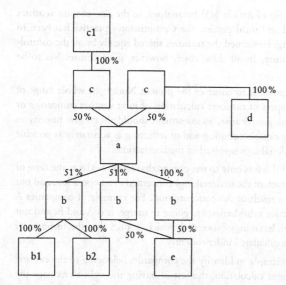

a: The undertaking concerned

b: Its subsidiaries and their own subsidiaries (b1 and b2)

c: Its parent companies and their own parent companies (c1)

d: Other subsidiaries of the parent companies of the undertaking concerned

e: Companies jointly controlled by two (or more) companies of the group

Note: these letters correspond to the relevant points of Article 5(4).

Several remarks can be made from this chart:

1. As long as the test of control of point (b) is fulfilled, the whole turnover of the subsidiary in question will be taken into account regardless of the actual shareholding of the controlling company. In the example, the whole turnover of the three subsidiaries (called b) of the undertaking concerned (a) will be included.

2. When any of the companies identified as belonging to the group also controls others, these should also be incorporated into the calculation. In the example, one of the subsidiaries of a (called b) has in turn its own subsidiaries b1 and b2.

3. When two or more companies jointly control the undertaking concerned (a) in the sense that the agreement of each and all of them is needed in order to manage the undertaking affairs, the turnover of all of them should be included.[9] In the example, the two parent companies (c) of the undertaking concerned (a) would be taken into account as well as their own parent companies (c1 in the example). Although the Merger Regulation does not explicitly mention this rule for those cases where the undertaking concerned is in fact a joint venture, it is inferred from the text of Article 5(4)(c), which uses the plural when referring to the parent companies. This interpretation has been consistently applied by the Commission.

4. Any intra-group sale should be subtracted from the turnover of the group (see paragraph 22).

39. The Merger Regulation also deals with the specific scenario that arises when two or more undertakings concerned in a transaction exercise joint control of another company. Pursuant to point (a) of Article 5(5), the turnover resulting from the sale of products or the provision of

---

[9] See Commission Notice on the concept of undertakings concerned (paras 26–29).

services between the joint venture and each of the undertakings concerned or any other company connected with any one of them in the sense of Article 5(4) should be excluded. The purpose of such a rule is to avoid double counting. With regard to the turnover of the joint venture generated from activities with third parties, point (b) of Article 5(5) provides that it should be apportioned equally amongst the undertakings concerned, to reflect the joint control.[10]

40. Following the principle of point (b) of Article 5(5) by analogy, in the case of joint ventures between undertakings concerned and third parties, the Commission's practice has been to allocate to each of the undertakings concerned the turnover shared equally by all the controlling companies in the joint venture. In all these cases, however, joint control has to be demonstrated.

   The practice shows that it is impossible to cover in the present Notice the whole range of scenarios which could arise in respect of turnover calculation of joint venture companies or joint control cases. Whenever ambiguities arise, an assessment should always give priority to the general principles of avoiding double counting and of reflecting as accurately as possible the economic strength of the undertakings involved in the transaction.[11]

41. It should be noted that Article 5(4) refers only to the groups that already exist at the time of the transaction, i.e. the group of each of the undertakings concerned in an operation, and not to the new structures created as a result of the concentration. For example, if companies A and B, together with their respective subsidiaries, are going to merge, it is A and B, and not the new entity, that qualify as undertakings concerned, which implies that the turnover of each of the two groups should be calculated independently.

42. Since the aim of this provision is simply to identify the companies belonging to the existing groups for the purposes of turnover calculation, the test of having the right to manage the undertaking's affairs in Article 5(4)[12] is somewhat different from the test of control set out in Article 3(3), which refers to the acquisition of control carried out by means of the transaction subject to examination. Whereas the former is simpler and easier to prove on the basis of factual evidence, the latter is more demanding because in the absence of an acquisition of control no concentration arises.

3.5. Turnover of State-owned companies

43. While Article 5(4) sets out the method for determining the economic grouping to which an undertaking concerned belongs for the purpose of calculating turnover, it should be read in conjunction with recital 12 to Regulation (EEC) No 4064/89 in respect of State-owned enterprises. This recital states that in order to avoid discrimination between the public and private sector, account should be taken 'of undertakings making up an economic unit with an independent power of decision, irrespective of the way in which their capital is held or of the rules of administrative supervision applicable to them'. Thus the mere fact that two companies are both State-owned should not automatically lead to the conclusion that they are part of a group for the purposes of Article 5. Rather, it should be considered whether there are grounds to consider that each company constitutes an independent economic unit.

44. Thus where a State-owned company is not part of an overall industrial holding company and is not subject to any coordination with other State-controlled holdings, it should be treated as

---

[10] For example, company A and company B set up a joint venture C. These two parent companies exercise at the same time joint control of company D, although A has 60 % and B 40 % of the capital. When calculating the turnover of A and B at the time they set up the new joint venture C, the turnover of D with third parties is attributed in equal parts to A and B.

[11] See for example Case IV/M.806—BA/TAT, of 26 August 1996.

[12] See for example Case IV/M.126—Accor/Wagons-Lits, of 28 April 1992, and Case IV/M.940—UBS/Mister Minit, of 9 July 1997.

an independent group for the purposes of Article 5, and the turnover of other companies owned by that State should not be taken into account. Where, however, a Member State's interests are grouped together in holding companies, or are managed together, or where for other reasons it is clear that State-owned companies form part of an 'economic unit with an independent power of decision', then the turnover of those businesses should be considered part of the group of the undertaking concerned's for the purposes of Article 5.

II. GEOGRAPHICAL ALLOCATION OF TURNOVER

1. General rule

45. The thresholds other than those set by Article 1(2)(a) and Article 1(3)(a) select cases which have sufficient turnover within the Community in order to be of Community interest and which are primarily cross-border in nature. They require turnover to be allocated geographically to achieve this. The second subparagraph of Article 5(1) provides that the location of turnover is determined by the location of the customer at the time of the transaction:

'Turnover, in the Community or in a Member State, shall comprise products sold and services provided to undertakings or consumers, in the Community or in that Member State as the case may be.'

46. The reference to 'products sold' and 'services provided' is not intended to discriminate between goods and services by focusing on where the sale takes place in the case of goods but the place where a service is provided (which might be different from where the service was sold) in the case of services. In both cases, turnover should be attributed to the place where the customer is located because that is, in most circumstances, where a deal was made, where the turnover for the supplier in question was generated and where competition with alternative suppliers took place.[13] The second subparagraph of Article 5(1) does not focus on where a good or service is enjoyed or the benefit of the good or service derived. In the case of a mobile good, a motor car may well be driven across Europe by its purchaser but it was purchased at only one place—Paris, Berlin or Madrid say. This is also true in the case of those services where it is possible to separate the purchase of a service from its delivery. Thus in the case of package holidays, competition for the sale of holidays through travel agents takes place locally, as with retail shopping, even though the service may be provided in a number of distant locations. This turnover is, however, earned locally and not at the site of an eventual holiday.

47. This applies even where a multinational corporation has a Community buying strategy and sources all its requirements for a good or service from one location. The fact that the components are subsequently used in ten different plants in a variety of Member States does not alter the fact that the transaction with a company outside the group occurred in only one country. The subsequent distribution to other sites is purely an internal question for the company concerned.

48. Certain sectors do, however, pose very particular problems with regard to the geographical allocation of turnover (see Section III).

2. Conversion of turnover into ecu

49. When converting turnover figures into ecu great care should be taken with the exchange rate used. The annual turnover of a company should be converted at the average rate for the twelve months concerned. This average can be obtained from the Commission. The audited annual turnover figures should not be broken down into component quarterly, monthly, or

---

[13] If the place where the customer was located when purchasing the goods or service and the place where the billing was subsequently made are different, turnover should be allocated to the former.

weekly sales figures which are converted individually at the corresponding average quarterly, monthly or weekly rates, with the ecu figures then added to give a total for the year.

50. When a company has sales in a range of currencies, the procedure is no different. The total turnover given in the consolidated audited accounts and in that company's reporting currency is converted into ecu at the average rate for the twelve months. Local currency sales should not be converted directly into ecu since these figures are not from the consolidated audited accounts of the company.

III. CREDIT AND OTHER FINANCIAL INSTITUTIONS AND INSURANCE UNDERTAKINGS

1. Definitions

51. The specific nature of banking and insurance activities is formally recognized by the Merger Regulation which includes specific provisions dealing with the calculation of turnover for these sectors.[14] Although the Merger Regulation does not provide a definition of the terms, 'credit institutions and other financial institutions' within the meaning of point (a) of Article 5(3), the Commission in its practice has consistently adopted the definitions provided in the First and Second Banking Directives:

    — 'Credit institution means an undertaking whose business is to receive deposits or other repayable funds from the public and to grant credits for its own account.[15]'
    — 'Financial institution shall mean an undertaking other than a credit institution, the principal activity of which is to acquire holdings or to carry one or more of the activities listed in points 2 to 12 in the Annex.[16]'

52. From the definition of 'financial institution' given above, it is clear that on the one hand holding companies must be regarded as financial institutions and, on the other hand, that undertakings which perform on a regular basis as a principal activity one or more activities expressly mentioned in points 2 to 12 of the abovementioned Annex must also be regarded as financial institutions within the meaning of point (a) of Article 5(3) of the Merger Regulation. These activities include:

    — lending (*inter alia*, consumer credit, mortgage credit, factoring, . . .),
    — financial leasing,
    — money transmission services,
    — issuing and managing instruments of payment (credit cards, travellers' cheques and bankers' drafts),
    — guarantees and commitments,
    — trading on own account or on account of customers in money market instruments, foreign exchange, financial futures and options, exchange and interest rate instruments, and transferable securities,
    — participation in share issues and the provision of services related to such issues,
    — advice to undertakings on capital structure, industrial strategy and related questions and advice and services relating to mergers and the purchase of undertakings,
    — money broking,

---

[14] See Art 5(3) of the Merger Regulation.

[15] Art 1 of First Council Directive 77/780/EEC of 12 December 1977 on the coordination of laws, regulations and administrative provisions relating to the taking up and pursuit of the business of credit institutions (OJ L322, 17.12.1977, p 30).

[16] Art 1(6) of Second Council Directive 89/646/EEC of 15 December 1989 on the coordination of laws, regulations and administrative provisions relating to the taking up and pursuit of the business of credit institutions (OJ L386, 30.12.1989, p 1).

— portfolio management and advice,
— safekeeping and administration of securities.

2. Calculation of turnover

53. The methods of calculation of turnover for credit and other financial institutions and for insurance undertakings are described in Article 5(3) of the Merger Regulation. The purpose of this Section is to provide an answer to supplementary questions related to turnover calculation for the abovementioned types of undertakings which were raised during the first years of the application of the Merger Regulation.

2.1. Credit and financial institutions (other than financial holding companies)

2.1.1. General

54. There are normally no particular difficulties in applying the banking income criterion for the definition of the worldwide turnover to credit institutions and other kinds of financial institutions. Difficulties may arise for determining turnover within the Community and also within individual Member States. For this purpose, the appropriate criterion is that of the residence of the branch or division, as provided by Article 5(3)(a)(v), second subparagraph, of the Merger Regulation.

2.1.2. Turnover of leasing companies

55. There is a fundamental distinction to be made between financial leases and operating leases. Basically, financial leases are made for longer periods than operating leases and ownership is generally transferred to the lessee at the end of the lease term by means of a purchase option included in the lease contract. Under an operating lease, on the contrary, ownership is not transferred to the lessee at the end of the lease term and the costs of maintenance, repair and insurance of the leased equipment are included in the lease payments. A financial lease therefore functions as a loan by the lessor to enable the lessee to purchase a given asset. A financial leasing company is thus a financial institution within the meaning of point (a) of Article 5(3) and its turnover has to be calculated by applying the specific rules related to the calculation of turnover for credit and other financial institutions. Given that operational leasing activities do not have this lending function, they are not considered as carried out by financial institutions, at least as primary activities, and therefore the general turnover calculation rules of Article 5(1) should apply.[17]

2.2. Insurance undertakings

2.2.1. Gross premiums written

56. The application of the concept of gross premiums written as a measure of turnover for insurance undertakings has raised supplementary questions notwithstanding the definition provided in point (b) of Article 5(3) of the Merger Regulation. The following clarifications are appropriate:

— 'gross' premiums written are the sum of received premiums (which may include received reinsurance premiums if the undertaking concerned has activities in the field of reinsurance). Outgoing or outward reinsurance premiums, i.e. all amounts paid and payable by the undertaking concerned to get reinsurance cover, are already included in the gross premiums written within the meaning of the Merger Regulation,

— wherever the word 'premiums' is used (gross premiums, net (earned) premiums, outgoing reinsurance premiums, etc.), these premiums are related not only to new insurance contracts made during the accounting year being considered but also to all premiums

---

[17] See Case IV/M.234—GECC/Avis Lease, 15 July 1992.

related to contracts made in previous years which remain in force during the period taken into consideration.

2.2.2. Investments of insurance undertakings

57. In order to constitute appropriate reserves allowing for the payment of claims, insurance undertakings, which are also considered as institutional investors, usually hold a huge portfolio of investments in shares, interest-bearing securities, land and property and other assets which provide an annual revenue which is not considered as turnover for insurance undertakings.

58. With regard to the application of the Merger Regulation, a major distinction should be made between pure financial investments, in which the insurance undertaking is not involved in the management of the undertakings where the investments have been made, and those investments leading to the acquisition of an interest giving control in a given undertaking thus allowing the insurance undertaking to exert a decisive influence on the business conduct of the subsidiary or affiliated company concerned. In such cases Article 5(4) of the Merger Regulation would apply, and the turnover of the subsidiary or affiliated company should be added to the turnover of the insurance undertaking for the determination of the thresholds laid down in the Merger Regulation.[18]

2.3. Financial holding companies[19]

59. A financial holding company is a financial institution and therefore the calculation of its turnover should follow the criteria established in point (a) of Article 5(3) for the calculation of turnover for credit and other financial institutions. However, since the main purpose of a financial holding is to acquire and manage participation in other undertakings, Article 5(4) also applies, (as for insurance undertakings), with regard to those participations allowing the financial holding company to exercise a decisive influence on the business conduct of the undertakings in question. Thus, the turnover of a financial holding is basically to be calculated according to Article 5(3), but it may be necessary to add turnover of undertakings falling within the categories set out in Article 5(4) ('Article 5(4) companies').

In practice, the turnover of the financial holding company (non-consolidated) must first be taken into account. Then the turnover of the Article 5(4) companies must be added, whilst taking care to deduct dividends and other income distributed by those companies to the financial holdings. The following provides an example for this kind of calculation:

		ECU million
1.	Turnover related to financial activities (from non-consolidated P&L)	3 000
2.	Turnover related to insurance Article 5(4) companies (gross premiums written)	300
3.	Turnover of industrial Article 5(4) companies	2 000
4.	Deduct dividends and other income derived from Article 5(4) companies 2 and 3	(200)
5.	Total turnover financial holding and its group	5 000

60. In such calculations different accounting rules, in particular those related to the preparation of consolidated accounts, which are to some extent harmonised but not identical within the Community, may need to be taken into consideration. Whilst this consideration applies to any type of undertaking concerned by the Merger Regulation, it is particularly important in

---

[18] See Case IV/M.018—AG/AMEV, of 21 November 1990.

[19] The principles set out in this paragraph for financial holdings may to a certain extent be applied to fund management companies.

the case of financial holding companies[20] where the number and the diversity of enterprises controlled and the degree of control the holding holds on its subsidiaries, affiliated companies and other companies in which it has shareholding requires careful examination.

61. Turnover calculation for financial holding companies as described above may in practice prove onerous. Therefore a strict and detailed application of this method will be necessary only in cases where it seems that the turnover of a financial holding company is likely to be close to the Merger Regulation thresholds; in other cases it may well be obvious that the turnover is far fro the thresholds of the Merger Regulation, and therefore the published accounts are adequate for the establishment of jurisdiction.

---

[20] See for example Case IV/M.166—Torras/Sarrió, of 24 February 1992, Case IV/M.213—Hong Kong and Shanghai Bank/Midland, of 21 May 1992, IV/M.192—Banesto/Totta, of 14 April 1992.

APPENDIX 21

Best Practices on the Conduct of EC Merger Control Proceedings

1. Scope and Purpose of the Best Practices

1. The principal aim of these Best Practices is to provide guidance for interested parties on the day-to-day conduct of EC merger control proceedings. They are intended to foster and build upon a spirit of cooperation and better understanding between DG Competition and the legal and business community. In this regard, the Best Practices seek to increase understanding of the investigation process and thereby to further enhance the efficiency of investigations and to ensure a high degree of transparency and predictability of the review process. In particular, they aim at making the short time available in EC merger procedures as productive and efficient as possible for all parties concerned.

2. The Best Practices are built on the experience to date of DG Competition in the application of Council Regulation (EEC) No 4064/89[1] (the Merger Regulation) and replace the current Best Practices of 1999. They reflect the views and practice of DG Competition at the time of publication.[2]

   The specificity of an individual case may require an adaptation of, or deviation from these Best Practices depending on the case at hand.

2. Relationship to Community Law

3. These Best Practices should not be taken as a full or comprehensive account of the relevant legislative, interpretative and administrative measures which govern Community merger control. They should be read in conjunction with such measures.

4. The Best Practices do not create or alter any rights or obligations as set out in the Treaty establishing the European Community, the Merger Regulation, its Implementing Regulation[3] as amended from time to time and as interpreted by the case-law of the Community Courts. Nor do they alter the Commission's interpretative notices. The Best Practices do not apply to proceedings under Council Regulation No 17,[4] to be replaced by Council Regulation No 1/2003[5] as of 1 May 2004, implementing Articles 81 and 82 of the Treaty.

---

[1] Council Reg No 4064/89, OJ L395, 30.12.1989 p 1; corrigendum OJ L257 of 21.9.1990, p 13; Reg as last amended by Reg (EC) No 1310/97 (OJ L180, 9.7. 1997, p 1, corrigendum OJ L40, 13.2.1998, p 17).

[2] It is to be noted that a recast Merger Reg replacing Reg 4064/89 will apply from 1 May 2004. The Best Practices are equally applicable under Reg 4064/89 and will continue to be applicable, possible with further amendments, under the recast Merger Reg. Appropriate references to the recast Merger Reg are made throughout the Best Practices by means of footnotes. Those references will only become applicable from 1 May 2004.

[3] Commission Reg (EC) No 447/98 of 1 March 1998 on the notifications, time limits and hearings provided for in the Merger Reg, OJ L61, 2.3.1998, p 1.

[4] OJ P013, 21/02/1962, p 204–211.

[5] Council Reg (EC) No 1/2003 of 16 December 2002 on the implementation of the rules on competition laid down in Arts 81 and 82 of the Treaty, OJ L1, 04.01.2003, p 1–25.

3. Pre-notification

Purpose of pre-notification contacts

5. In DG Competition's experience the pre-notification phase of the procedure is an important part of the whole review process. As a general rule, DG Competition finds it useful to have pre-notification contacts with notifying parties even in seemingly non-problematic cases. DG Competition will therefore always give notifying parties and other involved parties the opportunity, if they so request, to discuss an intended concentration informally and in confidence prior to notification (cf also Recital 10 Implementing Regulation).

6. Pre-notification contacts provide DG Competition and the notifying parties with the possibility, prior to notification, to discuss jurisdictional and other legal issues. They also serve to discuss issues such as the scope of the information to be submitted and to prepare for the upcoming investigation by identifying key issues and possible competition concerns (theories of harm) at an early stage.

7. Further, it is in the interests of DG Competition and the business and legal community to ensure that notification forms are complete from the outset so that declarations of incompleteness are avoided as far as possible. It is DG Competition's experience that in cases in which notifications have been declared incomplete, usually there were no or very limited pre-notification contacts. Accordingly, for this reason it is recommended that notifying parties contact DG Competition prior to notification.

8. Pre-notification discussions are held in strict confidence. The discussions are a voluntary part of the process and remain without prejudice to the handling and investigation of the case following formal notification. However, the mutual benefits for DG Competition and the parties of a fruitful pre-notification phase can only materialise if discussions are held in an open and co-operative atmosphere, where all potential issues are addressed in a constructive way.

9. In DG Competition's experience it is generally preferable that both legal advisers and business representatives, who have a good understanding of the relevant markets, are available for pre-notification discussions with the case-team. This normally results in more informed discussions on the business rationale for the transaction and the functioning of the markets in question.

Timing and extent of pre-notification contacts

10. Pre-notification contacts should preferably be initiated at least two weeks before the expected date of notification. The extent and format of the pre-notification contacts required is, however, linked to the complexity of the individual case in question. In more complex cases a more extended pre-notification period may be appropriate and in the interest of the notifying parties. In all cases it is advisable to make contact with DG Competition as soon as possible as this will facilitate planning of the case.

11. Pre-notification contacts should be launched with a submission that allows the selection of an appropriate DG Competition case-team.[6] This memorandum should provide a brief background to the transaction, a brief description of the relevant sector(s) and market(s) involved and the likely impact of the transaction on competition in general terms. It should also indicate the case language. In straightforward cases, the parties may chose to submit a draft Form CO as a basis for further discussions with DG Competition.

---

[6] Case teams for new cases are normally set up in weekly DG Competition's Merger Management Meetings.

12. After initial contacts have been made between the case-team and the notifying parties, it will be decided, whether it will suffice for DG Competition to make comments orally or in writing on the submissions made. This would typically be considered in straightforward cases. In more complex cases and cases that raise jurisdictional or other procedural issues, one or more pre-notification meetings are normally considered appropriate.

13. The first pre-notification meeting is normally held on the basis of a more substantial submission or a first draft Form CO. This allows for a more fruitful discussion about the proposed transaction in question or potential issue in point. Subsequent meetings may cover additional information submitted or outstanding issues.

14. Any submission sent to DG Competition should be provided sufficiently ahead of meetings or other contacts in order to allow for well prepared and fruitful discussions. In this regard, preparatory briefing memoranda/draft Form COs sent in preparation of meetings should be filed in good time before the meeting (at least three working days) unless agreed otherwise with the case team. In case of voluminous submissions and in less straightforward cases, this time may need to be extended to allow DG Competition to properly prepare for the meeting.

15. Irrespective of whether pre-notification meetings have taken place or not, it is advisable that the notifying parties systematically provide a substantially complete draft Form CO before filing a formal notification. DG Competition would thereafter normally require five working days to review the draft before being asked to comment, at a meeting or on the telephone, on the adequacy of the draft. In case of voluminous submissions, this time will normally be extended.

Information to be provided / preparation of the Form CO

16. The format and the timing of all prenotification submissions should be decided together with the case-team. Notifying parties are advised to fully and frankly disclose information relating to all potentially affected markets and possible competition concerns, even if they may ultimately consider that they are not affected and notwithstanding that they may take a particular view in relation to, for example, the issue of market definition. This will allow for an early market testing of alternative market definitions and/or the notifying parties' position on the market/s in question. In DG Competition's experience this approach minimises surprise submissions from third parties, and may avoid requests for additional information from the notifying parties at a late stage in the procedure and possible declarations of incompleteness under Article 4(2) of the Implementing Regulation or a decision under Article 11(5) of the Merger Regulation.

17. In addition, DG Competition recommends that notifying parties should, as early as possible in pre-notification, submit internal documents such as board presentations, surveys, analyses, reports and studies discussing the proposed concentration, the economic rationale for the concentration and competitive significance or the market context in which it takes place. Such documents provide DG Competition with an early and informed view of the transaction and its potential competitive impact and can thus allow for a productive discussion and finalisation of the Form CO.

18. Where appropriate, it is also recommended that notifying parties put forward, already at the pre-notification stage, any elements demonstrating that the merger leads to efficiency gains that they would like the Commission to take into account for the purposes of its competitive assessment of the proposed transaction. Such claims are likely to require extensive analysis. It is thus in the interests of the notifying parties to present these claims as early as possible to allow sufficient time for DG Competition to appropriately consider these elements in its assessment of a proposed transaction.

19. Pre-notification discussions provide the opportunity for the Commission and the notifying parties to discuss the amount of information to be provided in a notification. The notifying

parties may in pre-notification request the Commission to waive the obligation to provide certain information that is not necessary for the examination of the case. All requests to omit any part of the information specified should be discussed in detail and any waiver has to be agreed with DG Competition prior to notification.[7]

Completeness of the notification

20. Given that a notification is not considered effective until the information to be submitted in Form CO is complete in all material respects, the notifying parties and their advisers should ensure that the information contained in Form CO has been carefully prepared and verified: incorrect and misleading information is considered incomplete information.[8] In this regard, the notifying parties should take special care that the appropriate contact details are provided for customers, suppliers and competitors. If such information is not correct or provided in full it will significantly delay the investigation and therefore may lead to a declaration of incompleteness.

21. Further, to facilitate the effective and expeditious handling of their notification, notifying parties should also endeavour to provide the contact details required in Form CO electronically, at the latest on the day of notification, using the appropriate electronic form which can be provided by the case team.

22. Provided that the notifying parties follow the above described guidance, DG Competition will in principle, be prepared to confirm informally the adequacy of a draft notification at the pre-notification stage or, if appropriate, to identify in what material respects the draft Form CO is incomplete. However it has to be recognised that it will not be possible for DG Competition to exclude the fact that it may have to declare a notification incomplete in appropriate cases after notification.

23. In the event that DG Competition discovers omissions in the Form CO after formal notification, the notifying parties may be given an opportunity to urgently put right such omissions before a declaration of incompleteness is adopted. Due to the time constraints in merger procedures, the time allowed for such rectification is normally limited to 1 or 2 days. This opportunity will not be granted, however, in cases where DG Competition finds that the omissions immediately hinder the proper investigation of the proposed transaction.

Procedural questions and inter-agency cooperation

24. In addition to substantive issues, the notifying parties may in the pre-notification phase seek DG Competition's opinion on procedural matters such as jurisdictional questions.

25. Informal guidance may be provided if they are directly related to an actual, planned transaction and if sufficiently detailed background information is submitted by the notifying parties to properly assess the issue in question.[9] Further matters for prenotification discussions include the possibility of referrals to or from national EU jurisdictions,[10] parallel proceedings in other non-EU jurisdictions and the issue of waivers on information sharing

---

[7] See Art 3(2) Implementing Reg. See also Commission Notice on a simplified procedure for treatment of certain concentrations under Council Reg (EEC) No 4064/89, OJ C217, 29.07.2000, p 32.

[8] In addition, the Commission may impose fines on the notifying parties where they supply incorrect or misleading information in a notification under Art 14(1)(b) Merger Reg.

[9] Such informal guidance cannot be regarded as creating legitimate expectations regarding the proper interpretation of applicable jurisdictional or other rules.

[10] Such jurisdictional discussions will become particularly pertinent under the recast Merger Reg, which becomes applicable from 1 May 2004. Pursuant to Arts 4(4) and 4(5) of the recast Merger Reg, notifying parties may, before notification, request on the basis of a reasoned submission, referral of a case to or from the Commission. DG Competition will be ready to discuss with notifying parties informally the possibility of such pre-notification referrals and to guide them through the pre-notification referral process.

with other jurisdictions. As regards transactions likely to be reviewed in more than one jurisdiction, DG Competition invites the notifying parties to discuss the timing of the case with a view to enhance efficiency of the respective investigations, to reduce burdens on the merging parties and third parties, and to increase overall transparency of the merger review process. In this regard, notifying parties should also have regard to the EU-US Best Practices on co-operation in merger investigations.[11]

4. FACT FINDING / REQUESTS FOR INFORMATION

26. In carrying out its duties the Commission may obtain all necessary information from relevant persons, undertakings, associations of undertakings and competent authorities of Member States (see Article 11(1) Merger Regulation). That investigation normally starts after the notification of a proposed concentration. However, DG Competition may exceptionally decide that, in the interest of its investigation, market contacts could be initiated informally prior to notification. Such pre-notification contacts/enquiries would only take place if the existence of the transaction is in the public domain and once the notifying parties have had the opportunity to express their views on such measures.

27. The Commission's investigation is mainly conducted in the form of written Requests for Information (requests pursuant to Article 11 of the Merger Regulation) to customers, suppliers, competitors and other relevant parties. Such requests may also be addressed to the notifying parties. In addition to such Article 11 requests, the views of the notifying parties, other involved parties and third parties are also sought orally.

28. In the interest of an efficient investigation, DG Competition may consult the notifying parties, other involved parties or third parties on methodological issues regarding data and information gathering in the relevant economic sector. It may also seek external economic and/or industrial expertise and launch its own economic studies.

5. COMMUNICATION AND MEETINGS WITH THE NOTIFYING PARTIES, OTHER INVOLVED PARTIES AND THIRD PARTIES

29. One of the aims of these Best Practices is to enhance transparency in the day to day handling of merger cases and in particular, to ensure good communication between DG Competition, the merging parties and third parties. In this regard, DG Competition endeavours to give all parties involved in the proceeding ample opportunity for open and frank discussions and to make their points of view known throughout the procedure.

5.1. State of Play meetings with notifying parties

Aim and format of the State of Play meetings

30. The objective of the State of Play meetings is to contribute to the quality and efficiency of the decision-making process and to ensure transparency and communication between DG Competition and the notifying parties. As such these meetings should provide a forum for the mutual exchange of information between DG Competition and the notifying parties at key points in the procedure. They are entirely voluntary in nature.

31. State of Play meetings may be conducted in the form of meetings at the Commission's premises, or alternatively, if appropriate, by telephone or videoconference. In order for the meetings to operate properly they should be carefully prepared on the basis of an agenda agreed in advance. Further, senior DG Competition management will normally chair the meetings.

---

[11] http://europa.eu.int/comm/competition/mergers/others/eu_us.pdf

32. The State of Play meetings will not exclude discussions and exchanges of information between the notifying parties and DG Competition at other occasions throughout the procedure as appropriate. In this regard, notifying parties are advised to inform DG Competition, as soon as possible, about any important procedural or substantive developments that may be of relevance for the assessment of the proposed transaction. Such developments may include any remedy proposals the notifying parties are offering or are considering to offer in other jurisdictions, so as to facilitate co-ordination of the timing and substance of such remedy proposals. This also concerns matters already discussed at a State of Play meeting, in respect of which the parties consider it necessary to provide additional comments.

Timing of the State of Play meetings

33. Notifying parties will normally be offered the opportunity of attending a State of Play meeting at the following five different points in the Phase I and Phase II procedure:

a) where it appears that 'serious doubts' within the meaning of Article 6(1)(c) of the Merger Regulation are likely to be present a meeting will be offered *before the expiry of 3 weeks*[12] into *Phase I*. In addition to informing the notifying parties of the preliminary result of the initial investigation, this meeting provides an opportunity for the notifying parties to prepare the formulation of a possible remedy proposal in Phase I before expiry of the deadline provided in Article 18 of the Implementing Regulation.

b) *normally within 2 weeks following the adoption of the Article 6(1)(c) decision.* In order to prepare for this meeting, the notifying parties should provide DG Competition with their comments on the Article 6(1)(c) decision and on any documents in the Commission's file, which they may have had the opportunity to review (see below section 7.2) by way of a written memorandum in advance of the meeting. The notifying parties should contact the case team to discuss an appropriate schedule for the filing of this memorandum.

The main purpose of the post Article 6(1)(c) meeting is to facilitate the notifying parties' understanding of the Commission's concerns at an early stage of the Phase II proceedings. The meeting also serves to assist DG Competition in deciding the appropriate framework for its further investigation by discussing with the notifying parties matters such as the market definition and competition concerns outlined in the Article 6(1)(c) decision. The meeting is also intended to serve as a forum for mutually informing each other of any planned economic or other studies. The approximate timetable of the Phase II procedure may also be discussed.[13]

c) *before the issuing of a Statement of Objections* (SO). This pre-SO meeting gives the notifying parties an opportunity to understand DG Competition's preliminary view on the outcome of the Phase II investigation and to be informed of the type of objections DG Competition may set out in the SO. The meeting may also be used by DG Competition to clarify certain issues and facts before it finalises its proposal on the issuing of a SO.

d) *following the reply to the SO and the Oral Hearing.* This post-SO State of Play meeting provides the notifying parties with an opportunity to understand DG Competition's position after it has considered their reply and heard them at an Oral Hearing. If DG Competition indicates that it is minded to maintain some or all of its objections, the meeting may also serve as an opportunity to discuss the scope and timing of possible remedy proposals.[14]

e) *before the Advisory Committee meets.* The primary purpose of this meeting is to enable the notifying parties to discuss with DG Competition its views on any proposed remedies and

---

[12] Fifteen working days under the recast Merger Reg.

[13] Once the recast Merger Reg becomes applicable, this post Art 6(1)(c) State of Play meeting will also serve to discuss the possibility of any extensions to the Phase II deadline pursuant to Art 10(3) of the recast Merger Reg.

[14] It is to be noted that, under the recast Merger Reg (Art 10(3)), the submission of remedies could lead to an automatic extension of the Phase II deadline.

where relevant, the results of the market testing of such remedies. It also provides the notifying parties where necessary, with the opportunity to formulate improvements to their remedies proposal.[15]

5.2. Involvement of third parties

34. According to Community merger control law, third parties considered as having a 'sufficient interest' in the Commission's procedure include customers, suppliers, competitors, members of the administration or management organs of the undertakings concerned or recognised workers' representatives of those undertakings.[16] Their important role in the Commission's procedure is stressed in particular in Article 18(4) of the Merger Regulation and Articles 16(1) and (2) of the Implementing Regulation. In addition, the Commission also welcomes the views of any other interested third parties including consumer organisation.[17]

35. The primary way for third parties to contribute to the Commission's investigation is by means of replies to requests for information (Article 11 Merger Regulation).[18] However, DG Competition also welcomes any individual submission apart from direct replies to question-naires, where third parties provide information and comments they consider relevant for the assessment of a given transaction. DG Competition may also invite third parties for meetings to discuss and clarify specific issues raised.

36. In addition, DG Competition may in the interest of the investigation in appropriate cases provide third parties that have shown a sufficient interest in the procedure with an edited version of the SO from which business secrets have been removed, in order to allow them to make their views known on the Commission's preliminary assessment. In such cases, the SO is provided under strict confidentiality obligations and restrictions of use, which the third parties have to accept prior to receipt.

37. If third parties wish to express competition concerns as regards the transaction in question or to put forward views on key market data or characteristics that deviate from the notifying parties' position, it is essential that they are communicated as early as possible to DG Com-petition, so that they can be considered, verified and taken into account properly. Any point raised should be substantiated and supported by examples, documents and other factual evidence. Furthermore, in accordance with Article 17(2) of the Implementing Regulation, third parties should always provide the DG Competition with a non-confidential version of their submissions at the time of filing or shortly thereafter to facilitate access to the file and other measures intended to ensure transparency for the benefit of the decision making process (see further below section 7).

5.3. 'Triangular' and other meetings

38. In addition to bilateral meetings between DG Competition and the notifying parties, other involved parties or third parties, DG Competition may decide to invite third parties and the notifying parties to a 'triangular' meeting where DG Competition believes it is desirable, in the interests of the fact-finding investigation, to hear the views of the notifying parties and such third parties in a single forum. Such triangular meetings, which will be on a voluntary basis and which are not intended to replace the formal oral hearing, would take place in

---

[15] Modifications to remedies are only possible under those conditions set out in Art 18 of the Implement-ing Reg and point 43 of the Commission's Notice on Remedies.

[16] See Art 11 of the Implementing Reg.

[17] Art 16(3) Implementing Reg. To this effect, DG Competition has appointed a Consumer Liaison Officer responsible for contacts with consumer organisations.

[18] Art 11(7) of the recast Merger Reg expressly provides for the Commission's competence to interview any natural or legal person who consents to be interviewed for the purpose of collecting information relating to the subject-matter of an investigation.

situations where two or more opposing views have been put forward as to key market data and characteristics and the effects of the concentration on competition in the markets concerned.

39. Triangular meetings should ideally be held as early in the investigation as possible in order to enable DG Competition to reach a more informed conclusion as to the relevant market characteristics and to clarify issues of substance before deciding on the issuing of an SO. Triangular meetings are normally chaired by senior DG Competition management. They are prepared in advance on the basis of an agenda established by DG Competition after consultation of all parties that agreed to attend the meeting. The preparation will normally include a mutual exchange of non-confidential submissions between the notifying parties and the third party in question sufficiently in advance of the meeting. The meeting will not require the disclosure of confidential information or business secrets, unless otherwise agreed by the parties.

6. REMEDIES DISCUSSIONS

40. As stated above, the State of Play meetings in both Phase I and Phase II, in addition to providing a forum for discussing issues related to the investigation, also serve to discuss possible remedy proposals. Detailed guidance on the requirements for such proposals is set out in the Commission Notice on remedies acceptable under Council Regulation (EEC) No 4064/89 and under Commission Regulation (EC) No 447/98[19] (the Remedies Notice). In particular, the Remedies Notice sets out the general principles applicable to remedies, the main types of commitments that have previously been accepted by the Commission, the specific requirements which proposals of remedies need to fulfil in both phases of the procedure, and guidance on the implementation of remedies. As regards the design of divestiture commitment proposals, the notifying parties are advised to take due account of the Commission's 'Best Practice Guidelines on Divestiture Commitments'.[20]

41. Although it is for the notifying parties to formulate suitable remedies proposals, DG Competition will provide guidance to the parties as to the general appropriateness of their draft proposal in advance of submission. In order to allow for such discussions, a notifying party should contact DG Competition in good time before the relevant deadline in Phase I or Phase II, in order to be able to address comments DG Competition may have on the draft proposal.[21]

7. PROVISION OF DOCUMENTS IN THE COMMISSION'S FILE / CONFIDENTIALITY

7.1. Access to the file

42. According to Community law, the notifying parties have upon request a right to access the Commission's file after the Commission has issued an SO (see Article 18(3) of the Merger Regulation and Article 13(3) of the Implementing Regulation).

43. Further, the notifying parties will be given the opportunity to have access to documents received after the issuing of the SO up until the consultation of the Advisory Committee.

44. Access to the file will be provided subject to the legitimate interest of the protection of third parties' business secrets and other confidential information.

---

[19] OJ C68, 02.03.2001, p 3–11.
[20] Available under http://europa.eu.int/comm/competition/mergers/legislation/divestiture_commitments/
[21] It is to be noted that under the recast Merger Reg (Arts 10(1) and (3)), the submission of remedies could lead to an automatic extension of the Phase I and II deadlines.

7.2. Review of key documents

45. DG Competition believes in the merits of an open exchange of views with ample opportunities for the notifying parties and third parties to make their points of view known throughout the procedure. This enables DG Competition to assess the main issues arising during the investigation with as much information at its disposal as possible. In this spirit, DG Competition's objective will be to provide the notifying parties with the opportunity of reviewing and commenting on 'key documents' obtained by the Commission. Such documents would comprise substantiated submissions of third parties running counter to the notifying parties' own contentions received during Phase I and thereafter,[22] including key submissions to which specific reference is made in the Article 6(1)(c) decision and market studies.

46. DG Competition will use its best endeavours to provide notifying parties in a timely fashion, with the opportunity to review such documents following the initiation of proceedings and thereafter on an *ad hoc* basis. DG Competition will respect justified requests by third parties for non-disclosure of their submissions prior to the issuing of the SO relating to genuine concerns regarding confidentiality, including fears of retaliation and the protection of business secrets.

7.3. Confidentiality Rules

47. In accordance with Article 287 of the EC Treaty and Article 17(1) of the Implementing Regulation, the Commission will, throughout its investigation, protect confidential information and business secrets contained in submissions provided by all parties involved in EC merger proceedings. Given the short legal deadlines of EC merger procedures, parties are encouraged to clarify as soon as possible any queries related to confidentiality claims with members of the case team. Guidance on what is considered to be business secrets or other confidential information is provided in the Commission's Notice on Access to file.[23]

8. RIGHT TO BE HEARD AND OTHER PROCEDURAL RIGHTS

48. The right of the parties concerned to be heard before a final decision affecting their interests is taken is a fundamental principle of Community law. That right is also set out in the Merger Regulation (Article 18) and the Implementing Regulation (Articles 14–16). These Best Practices do not alter any such rights under Community law.

49. Any issues related to the right to be heard and other procedural issues, including access to the file, time limits for replying to the SO and the objectivity of any enquiry conducted in order to assess the competition impact of commitments proposed in EC merger proceedings can be raised with the Hearing Officer, in accordance with Commission Decision of 23 May 2001 on the terms of reference of hearing officers in certain competition proceedings.[24]

9. FUTURE REVIEW

50. These Best Practices may be revised to reflect changes to legislative, interpretative and administrative measures or due to case law of the European Courts, which govern EC merger

---

[22] This would in particular include substantiated 'complaints' contending that the notified transaction may give rise to competition concerns. The word 'complaint' is to be understood in the non-technical sense of the term as no formal complaints procedure exists in merger cases.

[23] OJ C23, 23/01/97, p 3.

[24] Official Journal L 162, 19/06/2001 p 21–24. The text can also be found at: http://europa.eu.int/comm/competition/hearings/officers/

control or any experience gained in applying such framework. DG Competition further intends to engage, on a regular basis, in a dialogue with the business and legal community on the experience gained through the application of the Merger Regulation in general, and these Best Practices in particular.

APPENDIX 22

Key Features of the EC Notification System and Procedural Requirements

MERGER NOTIFICATION AND PROCEDURES TEMPLATE

European Community

IMPORTANT NOTE:

This template is intended to provide introductory material. Reading the template is not a substitute for consulting the referenced statutes and regulations. If you are analyzing a particular transaction, this template should be a starting point only.

The following explanations are made available for information purposes only and do not constitute an official publication of the European Commission with legally binding effects. The official versions of the applicable texts are published in the Official Journal of the European Communities.

---

1. **Merger notification and review materials (please provide title(s), popular name(s) and citation(s))**

A. Notification provisions	Article 4 of the Merger Regulation; Articles 1–5 of the Implementing Regulation
	Please note that the materials referred to here and below, as well as non-confidential versions of the Commission's decisions in merger cases and other kinds of merger-related information are available at:
	http://europa.eu.int/comm/competition/index_en.html
B. Notification forms or information requirements	From CO relating to the notification of a concentration pursuant to Regulation (EEC) No 4064/89 (Annex of the Implementing Regulation)
C. Substantive merger control provisions	Council Regulation (EC) No 139/2004 of 20 January 2004 on the control of concentrations between undertakings, 'the Merger Regulation', (OJ L 24/1, 29.1.2004)
D. Implementing regulations	Commission Regulation (EC) No 802/04 of of 7 April 2004 implementing Council Regulation (EC) No 139/04 on the control of concentrations between undertakings (OJ L 133/1, 30.4.2004 (hereinafter referred to as 'the Implementing Regulation')

E. Interpretive guidelines and notices	Commission Notices:

- Commission Notice on the concept of full-function joint ventures under Council Regulation (EEC) No 4064/89 on the control of concentrations between undertakings (OJ C 66, 2.3.1998, p. 1)
- Commission Notice on the concept of a concentration under Council Regulation (EEC) No 4064/89 on the control of concentrations between undertakings (OJ C 66, 2.3.1998, p. 5)
- Commission Notice on the concept of undertakings concerned under Council Regulation (EEC) No 4064/89 on the control of concentrations between undertakings (OJ C 66, 2.3.1998, p. 14)
- Commission Notice on calculation of turnover under Council Regulation (EEC) No 4064/89 on the control of concentrations between undertakings (OJ C 66, 2.3.1998, p. 25)
- Commission Notice on the definition of the relevant market for the purposes of Community competition law (OJ C 372, 9.12.1997, p.5)
- Commission Notice on a simplified procedure for treatment of certain concentrations under Council Regulation (EEC) No 4064/89 (OJ C 217, 29.07.2000, p. 32).
- Commission Notice on remedies acceptable under Council Regulation (EEC) No 4064/89 and under Commission Regulation (EC) No 447/98 (OJ C 68, 02.03.2001, p. 3)
- Commission Notice on restrictions directly related and necessary to concentrations (OJ C 188, 04.07.2001, p. 5)
- Commission Guidelines on the assessment of horizontal mergers under the Council Regulation on the control of concentrations between undertakings (OJ C 31/5, 5.2.2004)
- DG Competition Best Practices on the conduct of EC merger control proceedings

Please note that the above materials are in the process of being amended. At any given time the relevant materials are available at:

http://europa.eu.int/comm/competition/index_en.html

F. Annual report	Annual Report on Competition Policy—available on the internet: http://europa.eu.int/comm/competition/annual_reports/

2. Authority or authorities responsible for merger enforcement

A. Name of authority If there is more than one authority, please describe allocation of responsibilities.	European Commission, Directorate General for Competition
	The European Commission has exclusive merger control jurisdiction for concentrations with a Community dimension as defined in Article 1 of the Merger Regulation (see Article 21 of the Merger Regulation). In addition, cases may be referred to the Commission by one or several Member States pursuant to Article 22(3) of the Merger Regulation. In turn, the Commission can refer or partially refer cases to the competent authorities of Member States upon their request (see Article 9 of the Merger Regulation).

<table>
<tr>
<td></td>
<td>

In addition pursuant to Art. 4(4) and 4(5) of the Merger Regulation notifying parties may request a transfer of jurisdiction either from or to the Commission prior to notification. In the case of requests for referral from the Commission to a particular Member State, Article 4(4) provides that where the concentration may significantly affect competition in a market within a Member State which presents all the characteristics of a distinct market the notifying parties may make a reasoned submission requesting that the transaction should therefore be examined, in whole or in part, by that Member State. Requests should be made on the basis of a reasoned submission from the parties using the Form RS which is an annex to the Implementing Regulation. Article 4 (5) provides that where a concentration does not have a Community dimension within the meaning of Art. 1 and where it is capable of being reviewed under the national competition laws of at least three Member States the notifying parties may, prior to notification to the competent authorities, request that the concentration is examined by the Commission, using the above mentioned Form.

The Commission is preparing a guidance Notice on the functioning of the referral provisions, a draft of which is available at: http://europa.eu.int/comm/competition/index_en.html

</td>
</tr>
<tr>
<td>

B. Address, telephone and fax (including country code), e-mail, website address and languages available.

</td>
<td>

European Commission
DG COMP
postal address: B-1049 Brussels,
                    Belgium
office address: 70, Rue Joseph II,
                    B–1000 Brussels,
                    Belgium
Tel: +32.2.299.11.11 / Fax: +32.2.296.43.01)

E-Mail: comp-mergers@cec.eu.int (caution: this e-mail address is a contact point for external queries only; it may not be used for any specific messages relating to individual merger cases, in particular not for merger notifications)

Website: http://europa.eu.int/comm/competition/index_en.html (languages available: English, French, German, Italian, Spanish, Greek, Portuguese, Dutch, Finnish, Swedish, Danish)

</td>
</tr>
<tr>
<td>

C. Is agency staff available for prenotification consultation? If yes, please provide contact points for questions on merger filing requirements and/or consultations.

</td>
<td>

Yes. The European Commission even encourages notifying parties to enter into pre-notification contacts with the relevant service. See our best practice guidelines:

http://europa.eu.int/comm/competition/mergers/others/best_practice_gl.html

Please send a fax with your query to the European Commission, addressed to the deputy Director-General formergers (Fax No +32.2.296.43.01). You may also send an e-mail to the following address: comp-mergers@cec.eu.int

</td>
</tr>
</table>

3. Notification requirements

<table>
<tr>
<td>

A. Is notification mandatory pre-merger?

</td>
<td>

Notification is mandatory pre-merger.

</td>
</tr>
</table>

B. Is notification mandatory post-merger?	Please see section 3.A: Notification is mandatory pre-merger. This obligation to notify remains unchanged should the parties illegally implement the merger without prior notification to the Commission.
C. Can parties make a voluntary pre- or post-merger filing even if filing is not mandatory?	Not applicable. The Merger Regulation provides for a system of mandatory ex-ante merger control. Concentrations which fall within the scope of the Merger Regulation must be notified to the Commission. Concentrations which do not fall within the scope of the Merger Regulation cannot be notified to the Commission; they may, however, be notifiable in one or several EU Member States pursuant to their respective national competition laws.

4. Covered transactions

A. Definitions of potentially covered transactions	Pursuant to Article 3(1) and 3(4) of the Merger Regulation: (1) A concentration shall be deemed to arise where: (a) two or more previously independent undertakings merge, or (b) one ore more persons already controlling at least one undertaking, or—one or more undertakings acquire, whether by purchase of securities or assets, by contract or by any other means, direct or indirect control of the whole or parts of one or more other undertakings. (4) The creation of a joint venture performing on a lasting basis all the functions of an autonomous economic entity, shall constitute a concentration within the meaning of paragraph 1(b). Article 3 of the Merger Regulation contains provisions concerning control and the acquisition of control. See also the Commission Notice on the concept of a concentration under Council Regulation (EEC) No 4064/89 on the control of concentrations between undertakings (OJ C 66, 2.3.1998, p.5) and the Commission Notice on the concept of full-function joint ventures under Council Regulation (EEC) No 4064/89 on the control of concentrations between undertakings (OJ C 66, 2.3.1998, p.1)
B. If change of control is a determining factor, how is control defined?	Pursuant to Article 3(3) of the Merger Regulation: For the purpose of the Merger Regulation, control shall be constituted by rights, contracts or any other means which, either separately or in combination and having regard to the considerations of fact or law involved, confer the possibility of exercising decisive influence on an undertaking, in particular by: (a) ownership or the right to use all or part of the assets of an undertaking; (b) rights or contracts which confer decisive influence on the composition, voting or decisions of the organs of an undertaking. Article 3(5) of the Merger Regulation contains specific provisions concerning the circumstances under which a concentration shall not be deemed to arise.

	See also the Commission Notice on the concept of a concentration under Council Regulation (EEC) No 4064/89 on the control of concentrations between undertakings (OJ C 66, 2.3.1998, p.5) and the Commission Notice on the concept of full-function joint ventures under Council Regulation (EEC) No 4064/89 on the control of concentrations between undertakings (OJ C 66, 2.3.1998, p. 1)
C. Are partial (less than 100%) stock acquisitions/minority shareholdings covered? At what levels?	Yes, as long as the transaction is a concentration and has a Community dimension within the meaning of Articles 1 and 3 of the Merger Regulation.
D. Do the notification requirements cover production joint ventures or any other type of joint venture?	Yes. Article 3(4) of the Merger Regulation provides that the creation of a joint venture performing on a lasting basis all the functions of an autonomous economic entity shall constitute a concentration within the meaning of the Merger Regulation. See also the Commission Notice on the concept of a concentration under Council Regulation (EEC) No 4064/89 on the control of concentrations between undertakings (OJ C 66, 2.3.1998, p.5) and the Commission Notice on the concept of full-function joint ventures under Council Regulation (EEC) No 4064/89 on the control of concentrations between undertakings (OJ C 66, 2.3.1998, p.1)
E. Are any sectors excluded from notification requirements? If so, which sectors?	No.
F. Are transactions that do not meet merger notification thresholds subject to substantive merger control?	The Merger Regulation only applies to concentrations with a Community dimension as defined in Articles 1 and 3 thereof. The European Commission has exclusive merger control jurisdiction for concentrations with a Community dimension (see Article 21 of the Merger Regulation). Note that concentrations that do not fall within the Merger Regulation's scope may be notifiable in individual member states. In addition, Article 22(3) of the Merger Regulation provides that the Commission may, at the request of a Member State or at the joint request of two or more Member States, investigate a concentration as defined in Article 3 of the Merger Regulation that has no Community dimension within the meaning of Article 1 of the Merger Regulation, insofar as that concentration affects trade between Member States.

5. Thresholds for notification

A. What are the general thresholds? Are the thresholds subject to adjustment: (e.g. annually for inflation)? If adjusted, state on what basis and how frequently	(1) Pursuant to Article 1 of the Merger Regulation, the Merger Regulation shall apply to all concentrations with a Community dimension defined as follows: (a) the combined aggregate worldwide turnover of all the undertakings concerned is more than EUR 5 billion; and

(b) the aggregate Community-wide turnover of each of at least two of the undertakings concerned is more than EUR 250 million, unless each of the undertakings concerned achieves more than two-thirds of its aggregate Community-wide turnover within one and the same Member State.

(2) A concentration that does not meet these thresholds has a Community dimension where:

(a) the combined aggregate worldwide turnover of all the undertakings concerned is more than EUR 2.5 billion;
(b) in each of at least three Member States, the combined aggregate turnover of all the undertakings concerned is more than EUR 100 million;
(c) in each of at least three Member States included for the purpose of point (b), the aggregate turnover of each of at least two of the undertakings concerned is more than EUR 25 million; and
(d) the aggregate Community-wide turnover of each of at least two of the undertakings concerned is more than EUR 100 million;

unless each of the undertakings concerned achieves more than two-thirds of its aggregate Community-wide turnover within one and the same Member State.

B. To what period(s) of time do the thresholds relate (e.g. most recent calendar year, fiscal year; for assets-based tests, calendar year-end, fiscal year-end, other)?	Pursuant to Article 5(1), first subparagraph, of the Merger Regulation, aggregate turnover within the meaning of the Merger Regulation shall comprise the amounts derived by the undertakings concerned in the preceding financial year from the sale of products and the provision of services falling within the undertakings' ordinary activities after deduction of sales rebates and of value added tax and other taxes directly related to turnover.
C. Describe methodology for identifying and calculating any values necessary to determine if notification is required, including:	
i. The methodology for identifying and calculating the value of the transaction, if applicable.	According to point 3.2 of the Form CO, the notifying parties must state the value of the transaction (the purchase price or the value of all the assets involved, as the case may be).
ii. The methodology for identifying and calculating relevant sales or turnover, if applicable.	Pursuant to Article 5(1), second subparagraph, of the Merger Regulation, turnover, in the Community or in a Member State, shall comprise products sold and services provided to undertakings or consumers, in the Community or in that Member State as the case may be. See also the Commission Notice on calculation of turnover under Council Regulation (EEC) No 4064/89 on the control of concentrations between undertakings (OJ C 66, 2.3.1998, p. 25).
iii. The methodology for identifying and calculating the value of relevant assets, if applicable.	Pursuant to Article 5(2) of the Merger Regulation, where the concentration consists of the acquisition of parts, whether or not constituted as legal entities, of one or more undertakings, only the turnover relating to the parts which are the subject of the transaction shall be taken into account with regard to the seller or sellers.

	However, two or more such transactions which take place within a two-year period between the same persons or undertakings shall be treated as one and the same concentration arising on the date of the last transaction.
	See also the Commission Notice on calculation of turnover under Council Regulation (EEC) No 4064/89 on the control of concentrations between undertakings (OJ C 66, 2.3.1998, p. 25).
iv. Methodology for calculating exchange rates.	The European Commission suggests relying on the exchange rates published by the European Central bank, to the extent applicable.
D. Do thresholds apply to worldwide sales/assets, to sales/assets within the jurisdiction, or both?	The stated tests apply to worldwide figures, Community-wide figures and figures relating to Member States.
E. How is the nexus to the jurisdiction determined? If based on an 'effects doctrine,' please describe how this is applied.	The thresholds laid down in Article 1 of the Merger Regulation determine jurisdictional nexus as far as the obligation to notify is concerned (for details regarding these thresholds, please refer to section 5.A). See also Judgment of the Court of First Instance of the European Communities of 25 March 1999 in case T-102/96—Gencor Ltd./Commission, [1999] ECR II-879, at paragraphs 76–111. The judgment can be found at the following webpage: http://curia.eu.int/en/jurisp/index.htm
F. If national sales are relevant, how are they allocated geographically (e.g. location of customer, location of seller)?	Pursuant to Article 5(1), second subparagraph, of the Merger Regulation, turnover, in the Community or in a Member State, shall comprise products sold and services provided to undertakings or consumers, in the Community or in that Member State as the case may be. The Commission Notice on calculation of turnover under Council Regulation (EEC) No 4064/89 on the control of concentrations between undertakings (OJ C 66, 2.3.1998, p. 25) clarifies 'that the location of the turnover is determined by the location of the customer at the time of the transaction.'
G. If there are market share tests, are there guidelines for calculating market shares?	The jurisdiction of the European Commission does not depend on a market share test.
H. If there are market share tests, do they apply even if there is no horizontal overlap in the parties' activities, either in the jurisdiction or worldwide?	The jurisdiction of the European Commission does not depend on a market share test.
I. Describe the methodology for determining relevant undertaking/firms for threshold purposes	Pursuant to Article 5(4) of the Merger Regulation, and without prejudice to Article 5(2), the aggregate turnover of an undertaking concerned within the meaning of Article 1 (2) and 3 shall be calculated by adding together the respective turnovers of the following:

(e.g. group-wide? only the acquired entity? If based on control, how is control determined?).	(a) the undertaking concerned; (b) those undertakings in which the undertaking concerned, directly or indirectly; – owns more than half the capital or business assets, or – has the power to exercise more than half the voting rights, or – has the power to appoint more than half the members of the supervisory board, the administrative board or bodies legally representing the undertakings, or – has the right to manage the undertakings' affairs; (c) those undertakings which have in an undertaking concerned the rights or powers listed in (b); (d) those undertakings in which an undertaking as referred to in (c) has the rights or powers listed in (b); (e) those undertakings in which two or more undertakings as referred to in (a) to (d) jointly have the rights or powers listed in (b). Pursuant to Article 5(1), first subparagraph, second sentence, of the Merger Regulation, the aggregate turnover of an undertaking concerned shall not include the sale of products or the provision of services between any of the undertakings referred to in Article 5(4). See also the Commission Notice on the concept of undertakings concerned under Council Regulation (EEC) No 4064/89 on the control of concentrations between undertakings (OJ C 66, 2.3.1998, p. 14), the Commission Notice on calculation of turnover under Council Regulation (EEC) No 4064/89 on the control of concentrations between undertakings (OJ C 66, 2.3.1998, p. 25).
J. Are there special threshold calculations for joint ventures?	Pursuant to Article 5(5) of the Merger Regulation, where undertakings concerned by the concentration jointly have the rights or powers listed in Article 5(4)(b), in calculating the aggregate turnover of the undertakings concerned for the purposes of Article 1 (2) and (3): (a) no account shall be taken of the turnover resulting from the sale of products or the provision of services between the joint undertaking and each of the undertakings concerned or any other undertaking connected with any one of them, as set out in Article 5(4)(b) to (e); (b) account shall be taken of the turnover resulting from the sale of products and the provision of services between the joint undertaking and any third undertakings. This turnover shall be apportioned equally amongst the undertakings concerned. See also the Commission Notice on the concept of undertakings concerned under Council Regulation (EEC) No 4064/89 on the control of concentrations between undertakings (OJ C 66, 2.3.1998, p. 14), the Commission Notice on calculation of turnover under Council Regulation (EEC) No 4064/89 on the control of concentrations between undertakings (OJ C 66, 2.3.1998, p. 25).
K. Are there special threshold calculations for particular sectors (e.g. banking, airlines)	Pursuant to Article 5(3) of the Merger Regulation, in place of turnover the following shall be used: (a) for credit institutions and other financial institutions, as regards Article 1 (2) and (3) of the Merger Regulation, the

or particular types of transactions (e.g. partnerships, financial investments)?	sum of the following income items as defined in Council Directive 86/635/EEC of 8 December 1986 on the annual accounts and consolidated accounts of banks and other financial institutions, after deduction of value added tax and other taxes directly related to those items, where appropriate:

(i)   interest income and similar income

(ii) income from securities:
  – income from shares and other variable yield securities,
  – income from participating interests,
  – income from shares in affiliated undertakings;

(iii) commissions receivable;

(iv) net profit on financial operations;

(v)   other operating income.

The turnover of a credit or financial institution in the Community or in a Member State shall comprise the income items, as defined above, which are received by the branch or division of that institution established in the Community or in the Member State in question, as the case may be.

(b) for insurance undertakings, the value of gross premiums written which shall comprise all amounts received and receivable in respect of insurance contracts issued by or on behalf of the insurance undertakings, including also outgoing reinsurance premiums, and after deduction of taxes and parafiscal contributions or levies charged by reference to the amounts of individual premiums or the total volume of premiums; as regards Article 1 (2)(b) and (3)(b), (c) and (d) and the final part of Article 1(2) and (3) of the Merger Regulation, gross premiums received from Community residents and from residents of one Member State respectively shall be taken into account.

See also the Commission Notice on calculation of turnover under Council Regulation (EEC) No 4064/89 on the control of concentrations between undertakings (OJ C 66, 2.3.1998, p. 25).

6. Transactions in which the acquiring and acquired parties are foreign
Are there special rules or exemptions

A. With respect to application of jurisdictional thresholds?	No
B. With respect to information required (e.g. information submitted or document legalization)?	No
C. With respect to waiting periods?	No

7. Simplified procedures

Describe any special procedures for notifying transactions that do not	Pursuant to the Form CO and the Commission Notice on a simplified procedure for treatment of certain concentrations, the Commission may allow a short form notification and dispense

raise competition concerns (e.g. short form, simplified procedures, advanced ruling certificates, waivers, etc).

with a full-form notification on the grounds that the operation to be notified will not raise competition concerns.

If the Commission is satisfied that the concentration qualifies for the simplified procedure, it will normally issue a short form clearance decision within one month from the date of notification, pursuant to Article 10(1) and 6(1)(b) of the Merger Regulation.

The categories of concentrations eligible for simplified procedure treatment, which are laid down in Form CO and the aforementioned Commission Notice, are the following:

(a) in the case of a joint venture, the joint venture has no, or negligible, actual or foreseen activities within the territory of the European Economic Area (EEA). Such cases occur where:

the turnover of the joint venture and/or the turnover of the contributed activities is less than EUR 100 million in the EEA territory; and
the total value of the assets transferred to the joint venture is less than EUR 100 million in the EEA territory;

(b) none of the parties to the concentration are engaged in business activities in the same relevant product and geographic market (no horizontal overlap), or in a market which is upstream or downstream of a market in which another party to the concentration is engaged (no vertical relationship);

(c) two or more of the parties to the concentration are engaged in business activities in the same relevant product and geographic market (horizontal relationships), provided that their combined market share is less than 15%; and/or one or more of the parties to the concentration are engaged in business activities in a market which is upstream or downstream of a market in which any other party to the concentration is engaged (vertical relationships), and provided that none of their individual or combined market shares at either level is 25% or more; or

(d) a party is to acquire sole control of an undertaking over which it has joint control.

In order to assess in detail the applicability of the simplified procedure and of the short form notification, the Commission is available for pre-notification contacts (for details, please refer to section 2 F). It is also advisable to refer to the Commission Notice on a simplified procedure for treatment of certain concentrations.

8. Timing of notification

A. What is the earliest that a transaction can be notified (e.g. is a definitive agreement required; if so, when is an agreement considered definitive?)?

Pursuant to Article 4(1) of the Merger Regulation, concentrations with a Community dimension defined in the Merger Regulation shall be notified to the Commission prior to implementation and following the conclusion of the agreement, or the announcement of the public bid, or the acquisition of a controlling interest.

Notification is also possible where the undertakings concerned satisfy the Commission of their intention to enter into an agreement for a proposed concentration and demonstrate to the Commission that their plan for that proposed concentration is sufficiently concrete, for example on the basis of an agreement in principle, a memorandum of understanding, or a letter of intent signed by all undertakings concerned, or, in the case of a public bid, where they have publicly announced an intention to make such a bid, provided that the intended agreement or bid would result in a concentration with a Community dimension.

B. Must notification be made within a specified period following a triggering event? If so, describe the triggering event (e.g. definitive agreement) and the deadline following the event.	No

9. Documents to be submitted

A. Describe the types of documents that parties must submit with the notification (e.g. agreement, annual reports, market studies, transaction documents).	Section 5 of the notification Forms (Annexes I and II to the Implementing Regulation) specify the information and the documents that must be provided by an undertaking or undertakings when notifying a proposed concentration the Commission. At a pre-notification stage, the parties can approach the Commission in order to discuss the exact type of information and documentation which should be provided in a given case.
B. Are there any document legalization requirements (e.g. notarization or apostille)?	Pursuant to Article 2(3) of the Implementing Regulation, the supporting documents shall be either originals or copies of the originals; in the latter case, the notifying parties shall confirm that they are true and complete.

10. Translation

Describe any requirements to submit translations of documents with the initial notification, or later in response to requests for information, including the categories or types of documents for which translation is required, requirements for certification, language(s) accepted, and whether selected excerpts are accepted in lieu of complete documents.	Article 21(3) of the Treaty establishing the European Community (the EC Treaty) provides that every citizen of the Union may write to any of the institutions or bodies, referred to in this Article or in Article 7 (the European Parliament, the Council, the Commission, the Court of Justice, and the Court of Auditors) in one of the languages mentioned in Article 314 of the EC Treaty and have an answer in the same language. Pursuant to Article 3(4) of the Implementing Regulation, notifications shall be in one of the official languages of the Community. This language, which notifying parties are free to choose when submitting their notification, shall also be the language of the proceeding for the notifying parties. Where the original language is not one of the official languages of the Community, a translation into the language of the proceeding shall be attached. Article 4(2) of the Implementing Regulation provides that the Commission may dispense with the obligation to provide any particular information, including documents, requested by Form CO where the Commission considers that such information is not necessary for the examination of the case.

11. Review and waiting periods/Suspensive effects

A. Describe any applicable review and/or waiting periods following notification, including whether closing is suspended during any initial review or waiting period and/or further review periods (i.e. second-phase proceedings).	Initial waiting period during the preliminary investigation ('Phase I'): Pursuant to Article 10(1) of the Merger Regulation, the decision referred to in Article 6(1) (the 'Phase I decision') must be taken within 25 working days at most. That period shall begin on the working day following that of the receipt of a notification or, if the information to be supplied with the notification is incomplete, on the working day following that of the receipt of the complete information. That period shall be increased to 35 days if the Commission receives a request from a Member State in accordance with Article 9(2) of the Merger Regulation (request for referral of the case to that Member State), or where, after notification of a concentration, the undertakings concerned submit commitments pursuant to Article 6(2) of the Merger Regulation, which are intended by the parties to form the basis for a decision pursuant to Article 6(1)(b) ('Phase I' clearance decision). Extended waiting period after the initiation of proceedings ('Phase II'): Article 10(2) of the Merger Regulation provides that decisions taken pursuant to Article 8 ('Phase II' decisions) concerning notified concentrations must be taken as soon as it appears that the serious doubts referred to in Article 6(1)(c) have been removed, particularly as a result of modifications made by the undertakings concerned. Pursuant to Article 10(3) of the Merger Regulation, without prejudice to Article 8(7), decisions taken pursuant to Article 8(3) (prohibition decisions) concerning notified concentrations must be taken within not more than 90 working days of the date on which proceedings are initiated (date of the 'Phase I' decision based on Article 6(1)(c) of the Merger Regulation). Pursuant to Article 10 (3) that period shall be increased to 105 working days where the undertakings concerned offer commitments pursuant to Article 8(2) second sub-paragraph, with a view to rendering the concentration compatible with the common market, unless these commitments have been offered less than 55 working days after the initiation of proceedings. These periods may also be extended by up to 20 working days wat the notifying parties' request or with their agreement. Obligation to suspend closing: Article 7(1) of the Merger Regulation provides that a concentration as defined in Article 1 shall not be implemented either before its notification or until it has been declared compatible with the common market pursuant to a decision under Article 6(1)(b), 8(1) or 8(2) or on the basis of a presumption according to Article 10(6) of the Merger Regulation. As regards exceptions to this rule, please refer to sections 11 B, 11 C, and 11 F.
B. Are there different rules for public tenders (e.g. open market stock purchases or hostile bids)?	Pursuant to Article 7(2) of the Merger Regulation, the obligation to suspend the concentration laid down in Article 7(1) shall not prevent the implementation of a public bid or a series of transactions on the stock exchange, provided the concentrationis notified without delay to the Commission in accordance with

	Article 4(1), and provided that the acquirer does not exercise the voting rights attached to the securities in question or does so only to maintain the full value of those investments and on the basis of a derogation granted by the Commission under paragraph 3.
C. Are the applicable waiting periods limited to aspects of the transaction that occur within the jurisdiction (e.g. acquisition or merger of local undertakings/business units)? If not, to what extent do they apply to the parties' ability to proceed with the transaction outside the jurisdiction? Describe any procedures available to permit consummation outside the jurisdiction prior to the expiration of the local waiting period and/or clearance. (e.g. request for a derogation from the bar on closing, commitment to hold separate the local business operations.)	Territorial scope of application of the waiting periods The applicable waiting periods are not limited to aspects of the transaction that occur within the Commission's jurisdiction. They apply to the proposed concentration as a whole. Derogations from the suspensive effect Pursuant to Article 7(3) of the Merger Regulation, the Commission may, on request, grant a derogation from the obligations [to suspend the concentration] imposed in paragraph 1 or 3. The request to grant a derogation must be reasoned. In deciding on the request, the Commission shall take into account inter alia the effects of the suspension on one or more undertakings concerned by a concentration or on a third party and the threat to competition posed by the concentration. That derogation may be made subject to conditions and obligations in order to ensure conditions of effective competition. A derogation may be applied for and granted at any time, even before notification or after the transaction.
D. Describe any provisions or procedures available to the enforcement authority, the parties and/or third parties to extend the waiting period. Is there a statutory maximum for extensions of the review period by the authority.	The 'Phase-I' period of 25 working days shall be increased to 35 working days if the Commission receives a request for referral from a Member State pursuant to Article 9 of the Merger Regulation, or where, after notification of a concentration, the undertakings concerned submit commitments pursuant to Article 6(2) of the Merger Regulation, which are intended by the parties to form the basis for a 'Phase I' clearance decision (Art. 10(1), second subparagraph, of the Merger Regulation) Pursuant to Article 10(4) of the Merger Regulation, the periods set by paragraphs 1 and 3 shall exceptionally be suspended where, owing to circumstances for which one of the undertakings involved in the concentration is responsible, the Commission has had to request information by decision pursuant to Article 11 or to order an investigation by decision pursuant to Article 13
E. Describe any procedures for obtaining early termination of the applicable waiting period, and the criteria and timetable for deciding whether to grant early termination.	Article 10(2) of the Merger Regulation provides that decisions taken pursuant to Article 8(2) ('Phase II' clearance decisions) concerning notified concentrations must be taken as soon as it appears that the serious doubts referred to in Article 6(1)(c) have been removed, particularly as a result of modifications made by the undertakings concerned.

F. Describe any provisions or procedures allowing the parties to close at their own risk before waiting periods expire or clearance is granted (e.g., allowing the transaction to close if no 'irreversible measures' are taken).	The possible means of derogation from the obligation to suspend implementation are described in section 11B and C above.

12. Responsibility for notification/representation

A. Who is responsible for notifying—the acquiring person(s), acquired person(s), or both?	Article 4(2) of the Merger Regulation provides that a concentration which consists of a merger within the meaning of Article 3(1)(a) or in the acquisition of joint control within the meaning of Article 3(1)(b) shall be notified jointly by the parties to the merger or by those acquiring joint control, as the case may be. In all other cases, the notification shall be effected by the person or undertaking acquiring control of the whole or parts of one or more undertakings.
B. Do different rules apply to public tenders (e.g. open market stock purchases or hostile bids)?	No. Nonetheless, at a pre-notification stage, the parties can approach the Commission in order to discuss any issues of unavailability of information on the target company, for example in hostile bids.
C. Are the parties required to appoint a joint representative?	Article 2(3) of the Implementing Regulation provides that joint notifications shall be submitted by a joint representative who is authorised to transmit and to receive documents on behalf of all notifying parties.
D. Are there any rules as to who can represent the notifying parties (e.g., must a lawyer representing the parties be a member of a local bar)?	No
E. How does the validity of the representation need to be attested (e.g., power of attorney)? Are there special rules for foreign representative of firms? Must a power of attorney be notarized, legalized or apostilled?	Article 2(2) of the Implementing Regulation provides that where notifications are signed by representatives of persons or of undertakings, such representatives shall produce written proof that they are authorized to act. There are no special rules for foreign representatives or firms

13. Filing fees

A. Are any filing fees assessed for notification? If so, in what amount and how is the amount determined?	There are no filing fees for notifications to the European Commission.

B. Who is responsible for payment?	Not applicable
C. When is payment required?	Not applicable
D. What are the procedures for making payments (e.g. accepted forms of payment, proof of payment required, wire transfer instructions)?	Not Applicable

14. Confidentiality

A. To what extent, if any, does your agency make public the fact that a pre-merger notification filing was made or the contents of the notification?	Article 4(3) of the Merger Regulation provides that where the Commission finds that a notified concentration falls within the scope of this Regulation, it shall publish the fact of the notification, at the same time indicating the names of the parties, the nature of the concentration and the economic sectors involved. The Commission takes account of the legitimate interest of undertakings in the protection of their business secrets.
B. Do notifying parties have access to the authority's file? If so, under what circumstances can the right of access be exercised?	Art. 17 of the implementing Regulation provides that the Commission shall, upon request, give notifying parties access to the file. Access is granted when the Commission has addressed to the notifying parties a Statement of Objections, for the purpose of enabling them to exercise their rights of defence. Insofar as this is necessary for the purposes of preparing their observations, the Commission shall, upon request, also give access to the file to the 'other involved parties' (such as the seller and the company which is the target of the concentration) who have been informed of the Commission's objections.
C. Can third parties or other government agencies obtain access to notification materials? If so, under what circumstances?	Pursuant to Article 19(1) of the Merger Regulation, the Commission shall transmit to the competent authorities of the Member State copies of notifications within three working days and, as soon as possible, copies of the most important documents lodged with or issued by the Commission pursuant to the Merger Regulation. Such documents shall include commitments which are intended by the parties to form the basis for a decision pursuant to Articles 6(2) or 8(2) of the Merger Regulation (conditional 'Phase I' or 'Phase II' clearance decisions).

Article 17(1) of the Merger Regulation provides that information acquired as a result of the investigation of a merger case shall be used only for the purposes of that case.

Pursuant to Article 17(2) of the Merger Regulation, without prejudice to Articles 4(3), 18 and 20, the Commission and the competent authorities of the Member States, their officials and other servants are under an obligation of professional secrecy; they shall not disclose information they have acquired through the application of the Merger Regulation of the kind covered by the obligation of professional secrecy.

As a general rule, third parties do not have access to notification materials.

D. **Are procedures available to request confidential treatment of the fact of notification and/or notification materials? If so, please describe.**

No confidential treatment can be granted with regard to the fact of the notification. As regards notification materials, please see section B. above.

E. **Is the agency or government a party to any agreements that permit the exchange of information with foreign competition authorities? If so, with which foreign authorities? Are the agreements publicly available?**

The Agreements to which the European Community is party do not permit the exchange of case related information provided by the parties or third parties without their prior consent.

For further information, please refer to the following internet websites:

http://europa.eu.int/comm/competition/international/bilateral/

http://europa.eu.int/comm/competition/international/multi-lateral/

15. Sanctions/penalties

A. **What are the sanctions/penalties for failure to file a notification and/or failure to observe any mandatory waiting periods?**

Sanctions:

Pursuant to Article 14(1) of the Merger Regulation, the Commission may by decision impose fines not exceeding 1% of the aggregate turnover of the undertaking or association of undertakings concerned where intentionally or negligently parties:

- supply incorrect or misleading information in a submission, certification, notification or supplement thereto pursuant to Article 4, article 10(5) or Article 22(3)
- supply incorrect or misleading information in response to a request made pursuant to Art. 11 (2);
- in response to a request made by decision pursuant to Article 11 (3), supply incorrect, incomplete or misleading information or do not supply information within the required time limit;
- they produce books or records related to the business in incomplete form suring an inspection or refuse to submit to an inspection ordered by decision pursuant to Art. 13 (4);
- in reponse to a question put during an oral interview they provide an incorrect or misleading answer, fail to rectify an incorrect answer or fail or refuse to provide a complete answer in relation to information requested pursuant to Art. 13 (4).

Article 14(2) of the Merger Regulation provides that the Commission may by decision impose fines not exceeding 10% of the aggregate turnover of the undertakings concerned within the meaning of Article 5 on the persons referred to in Article 3(1)b or undertakings concerned where, intentionally or negligently, they

- fail to notify a notify a concentration in accordance with Articles 4 and 22 (3) prior to its implementation;
- implement a concentration in breach of Article 7 of the Merger Regulation;
- implement a concentation declared incompatible with the common market by decision pursuant to Article 8 (3) or do not comply with any measure ordered by decision pursuant to

Article 8 (4) or (5);

– fail to comply with a condition or an obligation imposed by decision pursuant to Articles 6(1)(b), 7(3) or 8(2) of the Merger Regulation;

Other consequences:

Pursuant to Articles 6(3) and 8(6) of the Merger Regulation, the Commission may revoke a clearance decision it has taken where this decision is based on incorrect information for which one of the undertakings is responsible or where this decision has been obtained by deceit, or where the undertakings concerned commit a breach of an obligation attached to the decision.

B. Which party/ies are potentially liable?	The persons referred to in Article 3(1)(b) of the Merger Regulation, undertakings or associations of undertakings.

16. Judicial review

Describe the provisions and timetable for judicial review or other rights of appeal/ review of agency decisions on merger notification and review.

The legality of decisions adopted by the Commission can be reviewed by the Court of First Instance and the Court of Justice of the European Communities under the conditions and within the time-limits laid down in the Treaty establishing the European Community, in particular Article 230 thereof, as well as the Statute of the Court of Justice and the Rules of Procedure of the Community courts. The Rules of Procedure of the Community courts provide, for instance, the possibility of applying an expedited procedure.

[Internet links: http://europa.eu.int/comm/competition/court/ http://www.curia.eu.int/]

Pursuant to Article 10(5) of the Merger Regulation, where the Court of Justice annuls a Commission decision taken under the Merger Regulation in whole or in part, the periods laid down in the Merger Regulation shall start again from the date of the receipt of a new complete notification, a supplement to the original notification or a certification that there have been no changes to the facts contained in the original notification.

17. Additional filings

Are any additional filings/ clearances required for some types of transactions, e.g., foreign investment or regulated sectors?

Article 21(3) of the Merger Regulation provides that Member States may take appropriate measures to protect legitimate interests other than those taken into consideration by the Merger Regulation and compatible with the general principles and other provisions of the Community law.

Public security, plurality of the media and prudential rules shall be regarded as such legitimate interests.

Any other public interest must be communicated to the Commission by the Member State concerned and shall be recognized by the Commission after an assessment of its compatibility with the general principles and other provisions of Community law before the measures referred to above may be taken. The Commission shall inform the Member State concerned of its decision within one month of that communication.

18. Closing deadlines

When a transaction is cleared or approved, is there a time period within which the parties must close for it to remain authorized?	No

APPENDIX 23

Commission Notice on remedies acceptable under Council Regulation (EEC) No 4064/89 and under Commission Regulation (EC) No 447/98

(2001/C 68/03)

(Text with EEA relevance)

1. Introduction

1. Council Regulation (EEC) No 4064/89 of 21 December 1989 on the control of concentrations between undertakings,[1] as last amended by Regulation (EC) No 1310/97[2] (hereinafter referred to as 'the Merger Regulation') expressly provides that the Commission may decide to declare a concentration compatible with the common market following modification by the parties.[3] Recital 8 of Council Regulation (EC) No 1310/97 states that 'the Commission may declare a concentration compatible with the common market in the second phase[4] of the procedure, following commitments by the parties that are proportional to and would entirely eliminate the competition problem . . .' Recital 8 also provides for 'commitments in the first phase[5] of the procedure where the competition problem is readily identifiable and can easily be remedied . . . Transparency and effective consultation of Member States and interested third parties should be ensured in both phases of the procedure'.

2. The purpose of this notice is to provide guidance on modifications to concentrations, including, in particular, commitments to modify a concentration. Such modifications are more commonly described as 'remedies' since their object is to reduce the merging parties' market power and to restore conditions for effective competition which would be distorted as a result of the merger creating or strengthening a dominant position. The guidance set out in this notice reflects the Commission's evolving experience with the assessment, acceptance and implementation of remedies under the Merger Regulation since its entry into force on 21 September 1990. The principles contained here will be applied and further developed and refined by the Commission in individual cases. The guidance provided on commitments is without prejudice to the interpretation which may be given by the Court of Justice or by the Court of First Instance of the European Communities.

3. This notice sets out the general principles applicable to remedies acceptable to the Commission, the main types of commitments that have been accepted by the Commission in cases under the Merger Regulation, the specific requirements which proposals of commitments need to fulfil in both phases of the procedure, and the main requirements for the implementation of commitments.

---

[1] OJ L395, 30.12.1989, p 1; corrected version OJ L257, 21.9.1990, p 13.
[2] OJ L180, 9.7.1997, p 1.
[3] The references to 'parties' and 'merging parties' also cover situations with one notifying party.
[4] Referred to hereinafter as 'phase II'.
[5] Referred to hereinafter as 'phase I'.

II. General Principles

4. Under the Merger Regulation, the Commission assesses the compatibility of a notified concentration with the common market on the basis of its effect on the structure of competition in the Community.[6] The test for compatibility under Article 2(2) and (3) of the Merger Regulation is whether or not a concentration would create or strengthen a dominant position as a result of which effective competition would be significantly impeded in the common market or a substantial part of it.[7] A concentration that creates or strengthens a dominant position as described above is incompatible with the common market and the Commission is required to prohibit it.

5. Where a concentration raises competition concerns in that it could lead to the creation or strengthening of a dominant position, the parties may seek to modify the concentration in order to resolve the competition concerns raised by the Commission and thereby gain clearance of their merger. Such modifications may be offered and implemented in advance of a clearance decision. However, it is more common that the parties submit commitments with a view to rendering the concentration compatible with the common market within a specific period following clearance.

6. It is the responsibility of the Commission to show that a concentration creates or strengthens market structures which are liable to impede significantly effective competition in the common market. It is the responsibility of the parties to show that the proposed remedies, once implemented, eliminate the creation or strengthening of such a dominant position identified by the Commission. To this end, the parties are required to show clearly, to the Commission's satisfaction in accordance with its obligations under the Merger Regulation, that the remedy restores conditions of effective competition in the common market on a permanent basis.

7. In assessing whether or not a remedy will restore effective competition the Commission will consider all relevant factors relating to the remedy itself, including, *inter alia*, the type, scale and scope of the remedy proposed, together with the likelihood of its successful, full and timely implementation by the parties. Moreover, these factors have to be judged by reference to the structure and particular characteristics of the market in which the competition concerns arise, including of course the position of the parties and other players on the market. It follows that it is incumbent on the parties from the outset to remove any uncertainties as to any of these factors which might cause the Commission to reject the remedy proposed.

8. More generally, the Commission will take into account the fact that any remedy, so long as it remains a commitment which is not yet fulfilled, carries with it certain uncertainties as to its eventual outcome. This general factor must also be taken into consideration by the parties when presenting a remedy to the Commission.

9. In the Gencor case,[8] the Court of First Instance established the principle that the basic aim of commitments is to ensure competitive market structures. Accordingly, commitments that would amount merely to a promise to behave in a certain way, for example a commitment not to abuse a dominant position created or strengthened by the proposed concentration, are as such not considered suitable to render the concentration compatible with the common

---

[6] Recital 7 of the Merger Reg.

[7] In the case of the creation of a joint venture, the Commission will also examine the concentration under Art 2(4) of the Merger Reg. In this respect, the Commission examines whether or not the creation of the joint venture has as its object or effect the coordination of the competitive behaviour of undertakings that remain independent. Such coordination will be appraised in accordance with the criteria of Art 81(1) and (3) of the Treaty, with a view to establishing whether or not the operation is compatible with the common market. The principles set out in this notice would normally also apply to cases dealt with under Art 2(4).

[8] Judgment of the Court of First Instance of 25 March 1999 in Case T-102/96 *Gencor v Commission* [1999] ECR II-753, at para 316.

market. According to the Court,[9] commitments which are structural in nature, such as the commitment to sell a subsidiary, are, as a rule, preferable from the point of view of the Regulation's objective, inasmuch as such a commitment prevents the creation or strengthening of a dominant position previously identified by the Commission and does not, moreover, require medium or long-term monitoring measures. Nevertheless, the possibility cannot automatically be ruled out that other types of commitments may themselves also be capable of preventing the emergence or strengthening of a dominant position. However, whether such commitments can be accepted has to be determined on a case-by-case basis.

10. Once the concentration has been implemented, despite the possibility of some interim safeguards, the desired conditions of competition on the market cannot actually be restored until the commitments have been fulfilled. Therefore, commitments must be capable of being implemented effectively and within a short period. Commitments should not require additional monitoring once they have been implemented.[10]

11. The Commission may accept commitments in either phase of the procedure. However, given the fact that an in-depth market investigation is only carried out in phase II, commitments submitted to the Commission in phase I must be sufficient to clearly rule out 'serious doubts' within the meaning of Article 6(1)(c) of the Merger Regulation.[11] Pursuant to Article 10(2) of the Merger Regulation, the Commission has to take a clearance decision as soon as the serious doubts established in the decision pursuant to Article 6(1)(c) of the Merger Regulation are removed as a result of commitments submitted by the parties. This rule applies in particular to commitments proposed at an early stage of phase II-proceedings.[12] After an in-depth investigation and where the Commission in a Statement of Objections has reached the preliminary view that the merger leads to the creation or strengthening of a dominant position within the meaning of Article 2(3) of the Merger Regulation, the commitments have to eliminate the creation or strengthening of such a dominant position.

12. Whilst commitments have to be offered by the parties, the Commission may ensure the enforceability of commitments by making its authorisation subject to compliance with them.[13] A distinction must be made between conditions and obligations. The requirement for achievement of each measure that gives rise to the structural change of the market is a condition—for example, that a business is to be divested. The implementing steps which are necessary to achieve this result are generally obligations on the parties, e.g. such as the appointment of a trustee with an irrevocable mandate to sell the business. Where the undertakings concerned commit a breach of an obligation, the Commission may revoke clearance decisions issued either under Article 6(2) or Article 8(2) of the Merger Regulation, acting pursuant to Article 6(3) or Article 8(5)(b), respectively. The parties may also be subject to fines and periodic penalty payments as provided in Article 14(2)(a) and 15(2)(a) respectively of the Merger Regulation. Where, however, the situation rendering the concentration

---

[9] *Op. cit.*, at para 319.

[10] Only in exceptional circumstances will the Commission consider commitments which require further monitoring: Commission Decision 97/816/EC (IV/M.877—*Boeing/McDonnell Douglas*; OJ L336, 8.12.1997, p 16).

[11] Commitments in phase I can only be accepted in certain types of situation. The competition problem needs to be so straightforward and the remedies so clear-cut that it is not necessary to enter into an in-depth investigation.

[12] Commission Decision of 30 March 1999 (IV/JV.15—*BT/AT & T*); Commission Decision 2000/45/EC (IV/M.1532—*BP Amoco/Arco*; OJ L18, 19.1.2001, p 1).

[13] If the Commission's final assessment of a case shows that there are no competition concerns or that the resolution of the concerns does not depend on a particular element of the submitted commitments, the parties, being informed, may withdraw them. If the parties do not withdraw them, the Commission may either take note of their proposals in the decision or ignore them. Where the Commission takes note of them, it will explain in its decision that they do not constitute a condition for clearance.

compatible with the common market does not materialise,[14] that is, where the condition is not fulfilled, the compatibility decision no longer stands. In such circumstances, the Commission may, pursuant to Article 8(4) of the Merger Regulation, order any appropriate action necessary to restore conditions of effective competition.[15] In addition, the parties may also be subject to fines as provided in Article 14(2)(c).

III. TYPES OF REMEDY ACCEPTABLE TO THE COMMISSION[16]

1. Divestiture

13. Where a proposed merger threatens to create or strengthen a dominant position which would impede effective competition, the most effective way to restore effective competition, apart from prohibition, is to create the conditions for the emergence of a new competitive entity or for the strengthening of existing competitors via divestiture.

Viable Business

14. The divested activities must consist of a **viable business** that, if operated by a suitable purchaser, can compete effectively with the merged entity on a lasting basis. Normally a viable business is an **existing** one that can operate on a **stand-alone-basis**, which means independently of the merging parties as regards the supply of input materials or other forms of cooperation other than during a transitory period.

15. In proposing a viable business for divestiture, the parties must take into account the uncertainties and risks related to the transfer of a business to a new owner. These risks may limit the competitive impact of the divested business, and, therefore, may lead to a market situation where the competition concerns of the Commission will not necessarily be eliminated.

Object of the divestiture

16. Where the competition problem results from horizontal overlap, the most appropriate business has to be divested.[17] This might be the business of the acquiring company in cases of a hostile bid where the notifying party's knowledge of the business to be acquired is more limited. A commitment to divest activities of the target company might, in such circumstances, increase the risk that this business might not result in a viable competitor which could effectively compete in the market on a lasting basis.

17. In determining which overlapping business should be divested, the ability of the business to be operated on a stand-alone-basis is an important consideration.[18] In order to assure a viable business, it might be necessary to include in a divestiture those activities which are related to markets where the Commission did not raise competition concerns because this would be the only possible way to create an effective competitor in the affected markets.[19]

---

[14] The same principle applies where the situation that originally rendered the concentration compatible is subsequently reversed; see the last sentence of para 49.

[15] These measures may also lead to periodic penalty payments as provided in Art 15(2)(b).

[16] The following overview is non-exhaustive.

[17] Where the competition problem arises in vertical integration cases, divestiture may also resolve the competition concern.

[18] Commission Decision of 29 September 1999 (IV/M.1383—*Exxom/Mobil*, at para 860); Commission Decision of 9 February 2000 (COMP/M.1641 *Linde/AGA*, at para 94).

[19] Commission Decision 1999/229/EC (IV/M.913—*Siemens/Elektrowatt*; OJ L88, 31.3.1999, p 1, at para 134); Commission Decision 2000/718/EC (COMP/M.1578—*Sanitec/Sphinx*; OJ L294, 22.11.2000, p 1, at para 255); Commission Decision of 8 March 2000 (COMP/M.1802—*Unilever/Amora Maille*); Commission Decision of 28 September 2000 (COMP/M.1990—*Unilever/Bestfoods*; OJ C311, 31.10.2000, p 6).

18. Although it has been accepted in certain specific circumstances,[20] a divestiture consisting of a combination of certain assets from both the purchaser and the target may create additional risks as to the viability and efficiency of the resulting business. It will, therefore, be assessed with great care. In exceptional cases, a divestiture package including only brands and supporting production assets may be sufficient to create the conditions for effective competition.[21] In such circumstances, the Commission would have to be convinced that the buyer could integrate these assets effectively and immediately.

Suitable purchaser

19. The condition for a clearance decision by the Commission is that the viable business will have been transferred to a suitable purchaser[22] within a specific deadline. The two elements of the viable business and the suitable purchaser are thus inter-linked. The potential of a business to attract a suitable purchaser is, therefore, an important element of the Commission's assessment of the appropriateness of the proposed commitment.[23]

20. There are cases where the viability of the divestiture package depends, in view of the assets being part of the business, to a large extent on the identity of the purchaser. In such circumstances, the Commission will not clear the merger unless the parties undertake not to complete the notified operation before having entered into a binding agreement with a purchaser for the divested business (known as the 'upfront buyer'), approved by the Commission.[24]

21. Once a divestiture of a business is made a condition of the clearance decision, it is a matter for the parties to find a suitable purchaser for this business. The parties may therefore add, on their own initiative, other assets to make the package more attractive to buyers.[25]

Alternative divestiture commitments

22. In certain cases, the implementation of the parties' preferred divestiture option (of a viable business solving the competition concerns) might be uncertain or difficult in view of, for instance, third parties' pre-emption rights or uncertainty as to the transferability of key contracts, intellectual property rights or employees, as the case may be. Nevertheless, the parties may consider that they would be able to divest this business within the appropriate short time period.

23. In such circumstances, the Commission cannot take the risk that, in the end, effective competition will not be restored. Accordingly, it is up to the parties to set out in the commitment an alternative proposal, which has to be at least equal if not better suited to restore effective competition, as well as a clear timetable as to how and when the other alternative will be implemented.[26]

Removal of structural links

24. Divestiture commitments may not be limited to overcoming competition problems created by horizontal overlaps. The divestiture of an existing shareholding in a joint venture may be necessary in order to sever a structural link with a major competitor.[27]

---

[20] Commission Decision 96/222/EC (IV/M.603—*Crown Cork & Seal/CarnaudMetalbox*; OJ L75, 23.3.1996, p 38).

[21] Commission Decision 96/435/EC (IV/M.623—*Kimberly-Clark/Scott Paper*, OJ L183, 23.7.1996, p 1).

[22] See para 49 for the purchaser standards.

[23] IV/M.913—*Siemens/Elektrowatt* cited above.

[24] Commission Decision of 13 December 2000 (COMP/M.2060—*Bosch/Rexroth*).

[25] IV/M.1532—*BP Amoco/Arco* (cited above) where the commitment was to divest the interests in certain gas pipelines and processing facilities in the North Sea, also the interests in the related gas fields were divested.

[26] Commission Decision of 8 April 1999 (COMP/M.1453—*AXA/GRE*; OJ C30, 2.2.2000, p 6).

[27] Commission Decision 98/455/EC (IV/M.942—*VEBA/Degussa*; OJ L201, 17.7.1998, p 102).

25. In other cases, a possible remedy could be the divestiture of minority shareholdings or the elimination of inter-locking directorates in order to increase the incentives for competing on the market.[28]

2. Other remedies

26. Whilst being the preferred remedy, divestiture is not the only remedy acceptable to the Commission. First, there may be situations where a divestiture of a business is impossible.[29] Secondly, competition problems can also result from specific features, such as the existence of exclusive agreements, the combination of networks ('network effects') or the combination of key patents. In such circumstances, the Commission has to determine whether or not other types of remedy may have a sufficient effect on the market to restore effective competition.

27. The change in the market structure resulting from a proposed concentration can cause existing contractual arrangements to be inimical to effective competition. This is in particular true for exclusive long-term supply and distribution agreements if such agreements limit the market potential available for competitors. Where the merged entity will have a considerable market share, the foreclosure effects resulting from **existing exclusive agreements** may contribute to the creation of a dominant position.[30] In such circumstances, the termination of existing exclusive agreements[31] may be considered appropriate to eliminate the competitive concerns if there is clearly no evidence that de facto exclusivity is being maintained.

28. The change in the market structure resulting from a proposed concentration can lead to major barriers or impediments to entry into the relevant market. Such barriers may arise from control over infrastructure, in particular networks, or key technology including patents, know-how or other intellectual property rights. In such circumstances, remedies may aim at facilitating market entry by ensuring that competitors will have **access to the necessary infrastructure**[32] or **key technology**.

29. Where the competition problem is created by control over key technology, a divestiture of such technology[33] is the preferable remedy as it eliminates a lasting relationship between the merged entity and its competitors. However, the Commission may accept licensing arrangements (preferably exclusive licences without any field-of-use restrictions on the licensee) as an alternative to divestiture where, for instance, a divestiture would have impeded efficient, on-going research. The Commission has pursued this approach in mergers involving, for example, the pharmaceutical industry.[34]

---

[28] Commission Decision of 9 February 2000 (COMP/M.1628—*TotalFina/Elf*); Commission Decision of 13 June 2000 (COMP/M.1673—*VEBA/ VIAG*); Commission Decision of 1 September 2000 (COMP/M.1980—*Volvo/Renault*; OJ C301, 21.10.2000, p 23).

[29] IV/M.877—*Boeing/McDonnell Douglas* (cited above). The Commission's investigations revealed that no existing aircraft manufacturer was interested in acquiring Douglas Aircraft Company (DAC, the commercial aircraft division of McDonell Douglas) from Boeing, nor was it possible to find a potential entrant to the commercial jet aircraft market who might achieve entry through the acquisition of DAC.

[30] Commission Decision 98/475/EC (IV/M. 986—*AGFA Gevaert/DuPont*; OJ L211, 29.7.1998, p 22).

[31] Commission Decision of 28 October 1999 (IV/M.1571—*New Holland/Case*: OJ C130, 11.5.2000, p 11); Commission Decision of 19 April 1999 (IV/M.1467—*Rohm and Haas/Morton*; OJ C157, 4.6.1999, p 7).

[32] Commission Decision of 5 October 1992 (IV/M.157—*Air France/Sabena*; OJ C272, 21.10.1992, p 1; Commission Decision of 27 November 1992 (IV/M.259—*British Airways/TAT*; OJ C326, 11.12.1992, p 1); Commission Decision of 20 July 1995 (IV/M.616—*Swissair/Sabena*; OJ C200, 4.8.1995, p 10); Commission Decision of 13 October 1999 (IV/M.1439—*Telia/Telenor*); Commission Decision of 12 April 2000 (COMP/M.1795 —*Vodafone/Mannesmann*).

[33] Commission Decision of 9 August 1999 (IV/M.1378—*Hoechst/Rhône-Poulenc*; OJ C254, 7.9.1999, p 5); Commission Decision of 1 December 1999 (COMP/M.1601—*Allied Signal/Honeywell*); Commission Decision of 3 May 2000 (COMP/M.1671—*Dow/UCC*).

[34] Commission Decision of 28 February 1995 (IV/M.555—*Glaxo/Wellcome*; OJ C65, 16.3.1995, p 3).

30. Owing to the specifics of the competition problems raised by a given concentration in several markets, the parties may have to offer **remedy packages** which comprise a combination of divestiture remedies and other remedies that facilitate market entry by granting network access or access to specific content.[35] Such packages may be appropriate to remedy specific foreclosure problems arising, for instance, in concentrations in the telecommunication and media sectors. In addition, there may be transactions affecting mainly one product market where, however, only a package including a variety of other commitments will be able to remedy the competitive concerns raised by the specific concentration on an overall basis.[36]

IV. SITUATIONS WHERE REMEDIES ARE DIFFICULT, IF NOT IMPOSSIBLE

31. The Commission is willing to explore solutions to the competition problems raised by a concentration, provided that these solutions are convincing and effective. There are, however, concentrations where remedies adequate to eliminate competition concerns within the common market cannot be found.[37] In such circumstances, the only possibility is prohibition.

32. Where the parties submit proposed remedies that are so extensive and complex that it is not possible for the Commission to determine with the required degree of certainty that effective competition will be restored in the market, an authorisation decision cannot be granted.[38]

V. SPECIFIC REQUIREMENTS FOR SUBMISSION OF COMMITMENTS

1. Phase I

33. Pursuant to Article 6(2) of the Merger Regulation the Commission may declare a concentration compatible with the common market, where it is confident that following modification a notified concentration no longer raises serious doubts within the meaning of paragraph 1(c). Parties can submit proposals for commitments to the Commission on an informal basis, even before notification. Where the parties submit proposals for commitments together with the notification or within three weeks from the date of receipt of the notification,[39] the deadline for the Commission's decision pursuant to Article 6(1) of the Merger Regulation is extended from one month to six weeks.

34. In order to form the basis of a decision pursuant to Article 6(2), proposals for commitments must meet the following requirements:

    (a) they shall be submitted in due time, at the latest on the last day of the three-week period;

---

[35] COMP/M.1439—*Telia/Telenor*; COMP/M.1795—*Vodafone Airtouch/Mannesmann* (cited above); Commission Decision of 13 October 2000 (COMP/M.2050—*Vivendi/Canal+*/Seagram; OJ C311, 31.10.2000, p 3).

[36] Commission Decision 97/816/EC (IV/M.877—*Boeing/McDonnell Douglas*; OJ L336, 8.12.1997, p 16); COMP/M.1673—*VEBA/VIAG*.

[37] Commission Decision 94/922/EC (*MSG Media Service*, OJ L364, 31.12.1994, p 1); Commission Decision 96/177/EC (*Nordic Satellite Distribution*, OJ L53, 2.3.1996, p 20); Commission Decision 96/342/EC (*RTL/Veronica/Endemol*, OJ L134, 5.6.1996, p 32); Commission Decision 1999/153/EC (*Bertelsmann/Kirch/Premiere*, OJ L53, 27.2.1999, p 1; Commission Decision 1999/154/EC (*Deutsche Telekom BetaResearch*; OJ L53, 27.2.1999, p 31); Commission Decision 97/610/EC (*St Gobain/Wacker Chemie/ NOM*; OJ L247, 10.9.1997, p 1); Commission Decision 91/619/EEC (*Aerospatiale/Alenia/De Havilland*, OJ L334, 5.12.1991, p 42); Commission Decision 97/26/EC *Gencor/Lonrho*, OJ L11, 14.1.1997, p 30); Commission Decision 2000/276/EC (M.1524—*Airtours/First Choice*; OJ L93, 13.4.2000, p 1).

[38] Commission Decision of 15 March 2000 (COMP/M.1672—*Volvo/Scania*); Commission Decision of 28 June 2000 (COMP/M.1741—*WorldCom/Sprint*).

[39] Art 18(1) of Commission Reg (EC) No 447/98 (Implementing Reg), OJ L61, 2.3.1998, p 1.

(b) they shall specify the commitments entered into by the parties in a sufficient degree of detail to enable a full assessment to be carried out;

(c) they shall explain how the commitments offered solve the competition concerns identified by the Commission.

At the same time as submitting the commitments, the parties need to supply a non-confidential version of the commitments, for purposes of market testing.[40]

35. Proposals submitted by the parties in accordance with these requirements will be assessed by the Commission. The Commission will consult the authorities of the Member States on the proposed commitments and, when considered appropriate, also third parties in the form of a market test. In addition, in cases involving a geographic market that is wider than the European Economic Area ('EEA') or where, for reasons related to the viability of the business, the scope of the business to be divested is wider than the EEA territory, the proposed remedies may also be discussed with non-EEA competition authorities in the framework of the Community's bilateral cooperation agreements with these countries.

36. Where the assessment confirms that the proposed commitments remove the grounds for serious doubts, the Commission clears the merger in phase 1.

37. Where the assessment shows that the commitments offered are not sufficient to remove the competitive concerns raised by the merger, the parties will be informed accordingly. Given that phase I remedies are designed to provide a straightforward answer to a readily identifiable competition concern,[41] only limited modifications can be accepted to the proposed commitments. Such modifications, presented as an immediate response to the result of the consultations, include clarifications, refinements and/or other improvements which ensure that the commitments are workable and effective.

38. If the parties have not removed the serious doubts, the Commission will issue an Article 6(1)(c) decision and open proceedings.

2. Phase II

39. Pursuant to Article 8(2) of the Merger Regulation, the Commission must declare a concentration compatible with the common market, where following modification a notified concentration no longer creates or strengthens a dominant position within the meaning of Article 2(3) of the Merger Regulation. Commitments proposed to the Commission pursuant to Article 8(2) must be submitted to the Commission within not more than three months from the day on which proceedings were initiated. An extension, of this period shall only be taken into consideration on request by the parties setting forth the exceptional circumstances which, according to them, justify it. The request for extension must be received within the three-month-period. An extension is only possible in case of exceptional circumstances and where in the particular case there is sufficient time to make a proper assessment of the proposal by the Commission and to allow adequate consultation with Member States and third parties.[42]

40. The Commission is available to discuss suitable commitments prior to the end of the three-month period. The parties are encouraged to submit draft proposals dealing with both substantive and procedural aspects which are necessary to ensure that the commitments are fully workable.

---

[40] By way of a market test, customers, competitors, suppliers and other companies which might be affected or have specific expertise are requested to indicate to the Commission their reasoned opinion as to the effectiveness of the commitment.

[41] See recital 8 of Council Reg (EC) No 1310/97 referred to in para 1.

[42] M.1439—*Telia/Telenor*, and in Commission Decision 98/335/EC (M.754—*Anglo American/Lonrho*; OJ L149, 20.5.1998, p 21).

41. Proposals for commitments submitted in order to form the basis for a decision pursuant to Article 8(2) must meet the following requirements:

    (a) they shall be submitted in due time, at the latest on the last day of the three-month period;

    (b) they shall address all competition problems raised in the Statement of Objections and not subsequently abandoned. In this respect, they must specify the substantive and implementing terms entered into by the parties in sufficient detail to enable a full assessment to be carried out;

    (c) they shall explain how the commitments offered solve the competition concerns.

    At the same time as submitting the commitments, the parties shall supply a non-confidential version of the commitments, for purposes of market testing.

42. Proposals submitted by the parties in accordance with these requirements will be assessed by the Commission. If the assessment confirms that the proposed commitments remove the competition concerns, following consultation with the authorities of the Member States, discussions with non-Member States authorities[43] and, when considered appropriate, with third parties in the form of a market test, a clearance decision will be submitted for Commission approval.

43. Conversely, where the assessment leads to the conclusion that the proposed commitments appear not to be sufficient to resolve the competition concerns raised by the concentration, the parties will be informed accordingly. Where the parties subsequently modify the proposed commitments, the Commission may only accept these modified commitments[44] where it can clearly determine—on the basis of its assessment of information already received in the course of the investigation, including the results of prior market testing, and without the need for any other market test—that such commitments, once implemented, resolve the competition problems identified and allow sufficient time for proper consultation of Member States.

VI. Requirements for Implementation of Commitments

44. Commitments are offered as a means of securing a clearance, with the implementation normally taking place after the decision. These commitments require safeguards to ensure their successful and timely implementation. These implementing provisions will form part of the commitments entered into by the parties *vis-à-vis* the Commission. They have to be considered on a case-by-case basis. This is in particular true for the fixed time periods laid down for the implementation, which should in general be as short as is feasible. Consequently, it is not possible to standardise these requirements totally.

45. The following guidance is intended to assist the parties in framing commitment proposals. The principles are based on the framework of a divestiture commitment, which, as was seen above, is the most typical commitment. However, many of the principles discussed below are equally applicable to other types of commitments.

1. Essential features of divestment commitments

46. In a typical divestment commitment, the business to be divested normally consists of a combination of tangible and intangible assets, which could take the form of a pre-existing company or group of companies, or of a business activity which was not previously incorporated in its own right. Thus the parties,[45] when submitting a divestiture commitment, have

---

[43] See para 35.
[44] COMP/M.1628—*TotalFina/Elf*, LPG, cited above, at para 345.
[45] Commitments must be signed by a person duly authorised to do so.

to give a precise and exhaustive definition of the intended subject of divestment (hereafter referred to as 'the description of the business' or 'the description'). The description has to contain all the elements of the business that are necessary for the business to act as a viable competitor in the market: tangible (such as R & D, production, distribution, sales and marketing activities) and intangible (such as intellectual property rights, goodwill) assets, personnel, supply and sales agreements (with appropriate guarantees about the transferability of these), customer lists, third party service agreements, technical assistance (scope, duration, cost, quality) and so forth. In order to avoid any misunderstanding about the business to be divested, assets that are used within the business but that should not, according to the parties, be divested, have to be identified separately.

47. The description has to provide for a mechanism whereby the acquirer of the business can retain and select the appropriate personnel. Such a mechanism is required both for the personnel that are currently working in the business unit as it is operated and for the personnel that provide essential functions for the business such as, for instance, group R & D and information technology staff even where such personnel are currently employed by another business unit of the parties. This mechanism is without prejudice to the application of the Council Directives on collective redundancies;[46] on safeguarding employees rights in the event of transfers of undertakings;[47] and on informing and consulting employees[48] as well as national provisions implementing those Directives.

48. The divestment has to be completed within a fixed time period agreed between the parties and the Commission, which takes account of all relevant circumstances. The package will specify what kind of agreement—binding letter of intent, final agreement, transfer of legal title—is required by what date. The deadline for the divestment should start on the day of the adoption of the Commission decision.

49. In order to ensure the effectiveness of the commitment, the sale to a proposed purchaser is subject to prior approval by the Commission. The purchaser is normally required to be a viable existing or potential competitor, independent of and unconnected to the parties, possessing the financial resources,[49] proven expertise and having the incentive to maintain and develop the divested business as an active competitive force in competition with the parties. In addition, the acquisition of the business by a particular proposed purchaser must neither be likely to create new competition problems nor give rise to a risk that the implementation of the commitment will be delayed. These conditions are hereinafter referred to as 'the purchaser standards'. In order to maintain the structural effect of a remedy, the merged entity cannot, even in the absence of an explicit clause in the commitments, subsequently acquire influence over the whole or parts of the divested business unless the Commission has previously found that the structure of the market has changed to such an extent that the absence of influence over the divested business is no longer necessary to render the concentration compatible with the common market.

---

[46] Council Directive 98/59/EC of 20 July 1998 on the approximation of the laws of the Member States relating to collective redundancies (OJ L225, 12.8.1998, p 16).

[47] Council Directive 77/187/EEC of 14 February 1977 on the approximation of the laws of the Member States relating to the safeguarding of employees rights in the event of transfers of undertakings, business or parts of a business (OJ L61, 5.3.1977, p 26) as amended by Council Directive 98/50/EC (OJ L201, 17.7.1998, p 88).

[48] Council Directive 94/45/EC of 22 September 1994 on the establishment of a European Works Council or a procedure in Community-scale undertakings and Community-scale groups of undertakings for the purposes of informing and consulting employees (OJ L254, 30.9.1994, p 64), as amended by Directive 97/74/EC (OJ L10, 16.1.1998, p 22).

[49] The Commission does not accept seller-financed divestitures because of the impact this has on the divested company's independence.

2. Interim preservation of the business to be divested—the hold-separate trustee

50. It is the parties' responsibility to reduce to the minimum any possible risk of loss of competitive potential of the business to be divested resulting from the uncertainties inherent to the transfer of a business. Pending divestment, the Commission will require the parties to offer commitments to maintain the independence, economic viability, marketability and competitiveness of the business.

51. These commitments will be designed to keep the business separate from the business retained by the parties, and to ensure that it is managed as a distinct and saleable business. The parties will be required to ensure that all relevant tangible and intangible assets of the divestiture package are maintained, pursuant to good business practice and in the ordinary course of business. This relates in particular to the maintenance of fixed assets, know-how or commercial information of a confidential or proprietary nature, the customer base and the technical and commercial competence of the employees. Furthermore, the parties must maintain the same conditions of competition as regards the divestiture package as those applied before the merger, so as to continue the business as it is currently conducted. This includes providing relevant administrative and management functions, sufficient capital, and a line of credit, and it may include other conditions specific to maintaining competition in an industry.

52. As the Commission cannot, on a daily basis, be directly involved in overseeing compliance with these interim preservation measures, it therefore approves the appointment of a trustee to oversee the parties' compliance with such preservation measures (a so-called 'hold-separate trustee'). The hold-separate trustee will act in the best interests of the business to be divested. The commitment will set out the specific details of the trustee's mandate. The trustee's mandate, to be approved by the Commission, together with the trustee appointment, will include for example, responsibilities for supervision, which include the right to propose, and, if deemed necessary, impose, all measures which the trustee considers necessary to ensure compliance with any of the commitments, and periodic compliance reports.

3. Implementation of the commitments—the divestiture trustee

53. The commitment will also set out the specific details and procedures relating to the Commission's oversight of the implementation of the divestiture: for example, criteria for approval of the purchaser, periodic reporting requirements, and approval of the prospectus or advertising material. Here, too, it is noted that the Commission cannot, on a daily basis, be directly involved in managing the divestment. Consequently, in most cases, the Commission considers it appropriate to approve the appointment a trustee with responsibilities for overseeing the implementation of the commitments (the 'divestiture trustee').

54. The divestiture trustee's role will vary on a case-by-case basis, but will generally include supervision which includes the right to propose, and if deemed necessary, impose, all measures which the trustee requires to ensure compliance with any of the commitments, and reporting at regular intervals. Where appropriate, the trustee's role will span two phases: in the first phase, he or she will be responsible for overseeing the parties' efforts to find a potential purchaser. If the parties do not succeed in finding an acceptable purchaser within the time frame set out in their commitments, then in the second phase, the trustee will be given an irrevocable mandate to dispose of the business within a specific deadline at any price, subject to the prior approval of the Commission.

4. Approval of the trustee and the trustee mandate

55. Depending on the types of commitments involved and the facts of the case, the divestiture trustee may or may not be the same person or institution as the hold-separate trustee. The

trustee will normally be an investment bank, management consulting or accounting company or similar institution. The parties shall suggest the trustee (or a number of trustees) to the Commission. The trustee shall be independent of the parties, possess the necessary qualifications to carry out the job and shall not be, or become, exposed to a conflict of interests. It is the parties' responsibility to supply the Commission with adequate information for it to verify that the trustee fulfils these requirements. The Commission will review and approve the terms of the trustee's appointment, which should be irrevocable unless 'good cause' is shown to the Commission for the appointment of a new trustee.

56. The parties are responsible for remuneration of each trustee for all services rendered in the execution of their responsibilities, and the remuneration structure must be such as to not impede the trustee's independence and effectiveness in fulfilling his mandate. The trustee will assume specified duties designed to ensure compliance in good faith with the commitments on behalf of the Commission, and these duties will be defined in the trustee's mandate. The mandate must include all provisions necessary to enable the trustee to fulfil its duties under the commitments accepted by the Commission. It is subject to Commission's approval.

57. When the specific commitments with which the trustee has been entrusted have been implemented—that is to say, when legal title for the divestiture package to be divested has passed or at the end of some specific obligations which continue post-divestiture—the mandate will provide for the trustee to request the Commission for a discharge from further responsibilities. Even after the discharge has been given, the Commission has the discretion to require the reappointment of the trustee, if subsequently it appears to the Commission that the relevant commitments might not have been fully and properly implemented.

5. Approval of the purchaser and the purchase agreement

58. The parties or the trustee can only proceed with the sale if the Commission approves a proposed purchaser and the purchase agreement on the basis of the arrangements set out in the commitment. The parties or the trustee will be required to demonstrate satisfactorily to the Commission that the proposed buyer meets the requirements of the commitments, which means the purchaser's standards, and that the business is sold in a manner consistent with the commitment. The Commission will formally communicate its view to the parties. Before doing so, the Commission officials may have discussed with the proposed purchaser its incentives for competing with the merged entity on the basis of its business plans. Where different purchasers are being proposed for different parts of the package, the Commission will assess whether each individual proposed purchaser is acceptable and that the total package solves the competition problem.

59. Where the Commission determines that the acquisition of the divestiture package by the proposed purchaser, in the light of the information available to the Commission, threatens to create *prima facie* competition problems[50] or other difficulties, which may delay the timely implementation of the commitment or indicate the lack of appropriate incentives for the purchaser to compete with the merged entity, the proposed purchaser will not be considered acceptable. In this case, the Commission will formally communicate its view that the buyer does not satisfy the purchaser's standards.[51]

60. Where the purchase results in a concentration that has a Community dimension, this new operation will have to be notified under the Merger Regulation and cleared under normal

[50] This is most likely to arise where the market structure is already highly concentrated and where the remedy would transfer the market share to another market player.
[51] COMP/M.1628—*TotalFina/Elf*—motorway service stations.

procedures.[52] Where this is not the case, the Commission's approval of a purchaser is without prejudice to the jurisdiction of merger control of national authorities.

Non-opposition to a notified concentration
(Case COMP/M.2199—Quantum/Maxtor) (2001/C 68/04)
(Text with EEA relevance)

On 8 December 2000 the Commission decided not to oppose the above notified concentration and to declare it compatible with the common market. This decision is based on Article 6(1)(b) of Council Regulation (EEC) No 4064/89. The full text of the decision is only available in English and will be made public after it is cleared of any business secrets it may contain. It will be available:

— as a paper version through the sales offices of the Office for Official Publications of the European Communities (see list on the last page),

— in electronic form in the 'CEN' version of the CELEX database, under document No 300M2199. CELEX is the computerised documentation system of European Community law.

For more information concerning subscriptions please contact;

EUR-OP,

Information, Marketing and Public Relations (OP/A/4-B),

2, rue Mercier,

L-2985 Luxembourg.

Tel. (352) 29 29 424 55, fax (352) 29 29 427 63.

---

[52] Commission Decision of 29 September 1999 (Case M.1383—*Exxon/Mobil*) and the Commission Decisions of 2 February 2000 in the follow-up Cases M.1820—*BP/JV Dissolution* (not published) and M.1822—*Mobil/JV Dissolution* (OJ C112, 19.4.2000, p 6).

APPENDIX 24

Best Practice Guidelines: The Commission's Model Texts for Divestiture Commitments and the Trustee Mandate under the EC Merger Regulation

1. The European Commission's model texts for divestiture commitments and trustee mandates are designed to serve as best practice guidelines for notifying parties submitting commitments under the EC Merger Regulation.[1] These texts are (1) the model to be used for divestiture commitments (the '*Standard Model for Divestiture Commitments*' or the '*Standard Commitments*'; and (2) the model for the mandate of the two types of trustees referred to in the Standard Commitments, that is, the mandate appointing monitoring and divestiture trustees (the '*Standard Trustee Mandate*').

2. The model texts (the '*Standard Models*') are based upon the experience the Commission has gained to date in fashioning remedies from previous merger cases and are drafted in line with the remedies policy set out in the Commission's Notice on Remedies[2] (the '*Remedies Notice*'). The Standard Models are neither intended to provide an exhaustive coverage of all issues that may become relevant in all cases, nor are they legally binding upon parties in a merger procedure. Rather, they contain the elements for all standard provisions that should be included in commitments and trustee mandates relating to divestitures. In providing a framework for commitments and trustee mandates to be submitted in concrete cases, the Standard Models leave the flexibility to adapt the texts to the specific requirements of the case in question.

3. The Standard Models are designed to apply to all remedy proceedings in both Phase I and Phase II, therefore to all Commission decisions according to Articles 6(2) and 8(2) of the Merger Regulation. The Standard Models deal specifically with divestiture commitments inasmuch as the Commission's Remedies Notice stipulates that divestiture commitments are normally the preferred from of merger remedies; they are also the most common. However, it should be underlined that the Commission will consider the acceptability of other types of commitments in appropriate circumstances, as set out in the Remedies Notice. Individual provisions contained in the Standard Models can be used in cases involving such other types of commitments.

4. Finally, it is expected that the text of these models will evolve, based on ongoing practice, and will be regularly up-dated by the Commission, taking into consideration both the developments of the Commission's remedies policy and the experience gained from working with the merging parties and trustees in future matters.

---

[1] Council Reg (EEC) No 4064/89 of 21 December 1989 on the control of concentrations between undertakings, as amended, OJ L395, 30.12.1989, p 1; corrigendum OJ L257, 21.9.1990, p 13.

[2] See Commission Notice on remedies acceptable under Council Reg (EEC) No 4064/89 and Reg (EC) No 447/98 at *Official Journal* C 68, 02.03.2001, pp 3–11; published on http://europa.eu.int/eur-lex/pri/en/oj/dat/2001/c_068/c_06820010302en00030011.pdf.

The Purpose of the Standard Models

5. The Commission recognizes that timing is crucial when merging parties reach the remedies stage in merger review procedures, where they offer commitments in order to resolve the Commission's competition concerns in a given case. Through the use of standardized models, the merging parties and the Commission will be relieved of the heavy demands—both in terms of time and resources—that would otherwise be required to negotiate the standard terms and provisions for commitments and trustee mandates under tight time constraints. The use of standardized models will expedite the proceedings and allow the merging parties to concentrate more on the actual substance and implementation of the commitments.

6. The use of the standard models will ensure consistency across cases and will thereby contribute to increasing the level of transparency and legal certainty for the merging parties offering commitments to the Commission.

Overview of the Contents of the Standard Models

7. The *Standard Model for Divestiture Commitments* sets out all requirements for achieving full and effective compliance with divestiture commitments offered by the merging parties (the '*Parties*') to obtain a clearance decision. More specifically, this Model is designed (i) to describe clearly the business to be divested ('*Divestment Business*'), the divestiture procedure and the obligations of the parties in relation to the Divestment Business for the interim period until divestiture has been completed, (ii) to set out the various responsibilities that the merging parties will thereby have, respectively, to the Commission, the Trustee, and the Divestment Business; and (iii) to enshrine the importance which the Commission places upon requiring an acceptable purchaser for the Divestment Business in order to ensure the viability and competitiveness of the new entity in the market where the divestiture takes place.

8. The *Standard Model for Trustee Mandates* sets out the role and functions of the Trustee, as provided in the Standard Commitments, in a contractual relationship between the Parties responsible for the divestiture and the Trustee. As the Commitments set out the basis for the responsibilities of the Trustee, the Standard Trustee Mandate has been prepared in conformity with the requirements laid down for the Trustee in the Standard Model for Divestiture Commitments.

9. Although the Standard Trustee Mandate is a bilateral contract between the Parties responsible for the divestiture and the Trustee, this document forms the basis for a tri-partite relationship among the Commission, the Trustee, and the Parties. The relationship between the Parties and the Trustee is not a traditional trusteeship. The Trustee rather benefits from a status which makes it independent from the Parties and which is characterised by the role of the Trustee to monitor (Monitoring Trustee) or even to effectuate (Divestiture Trustee) the Parties' compliance with the commitments. Accordingly, the Parties are not entitled to give instructions to the Trustee, whereas the Commission is allowed to do so. This specific relationship is also confirmed by the fact that the Trustee Mandate requires the Commission's approval.

10. The Standard Trustee Mandate is designed (i) to facilitate the smooth and timely appointment of the Trustee and the approval of the Trustee Mandate; (ii) to clarify the relationship among the Commission, the Trustee, and the Parties; and (iii) to set out the tasks of the Trustee in the process in order to enable the Trustee to expedite compliance with the commitments. Whereas the Standard Trustee Mandate defines the role of a Monitoring and a Divestiture Trustee in one text, they can be assigned to different Trustee in practice.

11. In providing guidance for the interpretation of the Standard Texts, a certain hierarchy is established. The Standard Trustee Mandate should be interpreted in the light of the Standard

Commitments, as they lay the foundation for the application of the Trustee Mandate. To the extent that they are attached as conditions and obligations, the commitments are to be interpreted in the light of the respective Commission decision. Moreover, both Standard Texts should be interpreted in the general framework of Community law, in particular in the light of the EC Merger Regulation, and by reference to the Commission's Remedies Notice setting out the Commission's remedies policy.

DESCRIPTION OF THE PROVISIONS OF THE STANDARD MODELS

12. The most important provisions contained in both Standard Models are briefly set out below.

STANDARD MODEL FOR DIVESTITURE COMMITMENTS

13. The Standard Model for Commitments consists of the following main elements:

14. *Section A* contains a definitions section.

15. *Section B contains the commitment to divest and the definition of the Divestment Business.* After spelling out the general obligation to divest the Divestment Business as a going concern, paragraph 1 describes the *divestiture procedure*, which may take two phases. The Commitments provide that in the first phase (that is, the *Divestiture Period*), the Parties have the sole responsibility for finding a suitable purchaser for the Divestment Business. If the Parties do not succeed in divesting the business on their own in the Divestiture Period, then a Divestiture Trustee will be appointed with an exclusive mandate to dispose of the Divestment Business at no minimum price, in the *Extended Divestiture Period*. The individual deadlines are determined in the definitions section. The experience of the Commission has shown that short divestiture periods contribute largely to the success of the divestiture as, otherwise, the Divestment Business will be exposed to an extended period of uncertainty. The Commission will normally consider a period of around 6 months for the Divestiture Period and an additional period of 3 to 6 months for the Extended Divestiture Period as appropriate. These periods may be modified according to the particular requirements of the case in question.

16. The divestiture commitment will take a special form in those cases where the Parties propose an *up-front buyer*. The Parties commit not to implement the proposed concentration unless and until they have entered into a binding agreement with a purchaser for the Divestment Business, approved by the Commission. The qualification of the buyer are the same as in other divestiture commitments. The up-front buyer concept has been applied in several cases[3] and will be used in the specific circumstances as described in the Notice.[4] The structure of the divestiture commitment also needs to be adapted in cases of alternative divestitures, in particular 'Crown Jewels' structures, i.e. structures in which the Parties commit to divest a very attractive business if they have not divested the originally proposed business until the end of a period fixed in the commitments. The circumstances in which the Commission will accept alternative divestiture commitments are also set out in the Remedies Notice.[5]

17. The divestiture commitment includes the commitment not to re-acquire direct or indirect influence over the Divestment Business (paragraph 3). This *re-acquisition prohibition* is limited to ten years after the date of the decision and serves to maintain the structural effects of the Commitments. The Commission may grant a waiver if the structure of the market has changed to such an extent that the absence of influence over the Divestment Business is no longer necessary to render the concentration compatible with the common market.

---

[3] Cases COMP/M.2060—Bosch/Rexroth; COMP/M.1915—The Post Office/TPG/SPPL; COMP/M.2544—Masterfood/Royal Canin.
[4] Para 18 of the Remedies Notice.
[5] Paras 22, 23 of the Remedies Notice.

18. *Section B, together with the Schedule to the Commitments*, defines what is included in the *Divestment Business*. The clear identification of the Divestment Business is of great importance as thereby the scope of the divestiture and of the hold-separate obligations are defined. As set out in the Notice, the Divestment Business is considered to be an existing entity that can operate on a stand-alone-basis.[6] The Divestment Business is the minimum which is to be divested by the Parties in order to comply with the Commitments. In order to make the package more attractive to buyers, the Parties may add, on their own initiative, other assets.[7] The Divestment Business must include all the assets and personnel necessary to ensure the viability of the divested activities. Whereas this principle is set out as an undertaking of the Parties in paragraph 3 of the Standard Commitments, the Parties have to give a detailed factual description of the Divestment Business in the Schedule to the Standard Commitments.

19. The Divestment Business must comprise the *Personnel and the Key Personnel* retained by the Divestment Business as well as the personnel providing essential functions for the Divestment Business, such as the central R&D staff. The personnel (according to groups and functions performed) is to be listed in the Schedule to the Commitments, the Key Personnel is to be listed separately. The principle, indicated in paragraph 4 (d), is that the personnel should be transferred with the Divestment Business. If the Divestment Business takes the form of a company or if the transfer of undertakings legislation applies, the personnel will normally be transferred by operation of law. In other cases, the acquirer of the business can retain and select the personnel and can make offers of employment. The transfer—whichever form it takes—is without prejudice to the application of Council Directives, where applicable, on collective redundancies;[8] on safeguarding employees rights in the event of transfers of undertakings;[9] and on informing and consulting employees,[10] as well as relevant national law on these matters.

20. Furthermore, the Standard Commitments foresee that the Divestment Business shall be *entitled to benefit from products or services* provided by the Parties for a transitional period, determined on a case-by-case basis, if this is necessary to maintain the full economic viability and competitiveness of the Divestment Business (paragraph 4 (e) of the Standard Commitments referring to the products or services listed in the Schedule).

21. *Section C* contains a number of *related commitments*, which are designed to maintain, pending divestiture, the viability, marketability and competitiveness of the Divestment Business. These provisions deal with the *preservation of the divested entity's viability and independence, as well as the hold-separate and ring-fencing obligations*. The Hold Separate Manager, to be appointed by the Parties and normally the manager of the Divestment Business, is responsible for the management of the Divestment Business as a distinct entity separate from the businesses retained by the Parties, and is supervised by the Monitoring Trustee.

---

[6] cf para 14 of the Remedies Notice. The importance of the divestiture of an on-going business for the success of the remedy has also been underlined by the FTC in a published study entitled A Study of the Commission's Divestiture Process, prepared by the Staff of the Bureau of Competition of the Federal Trade Commission, p 10 ff.

[7] cf para 21 of the Remedies Notice.

[8] Council Directive 98/59/EC of 20 July 1998 on the approximation of the laws of the Member States relating to collective redundancies (OJ L225, 12.8.1998, p16).

[9] Council Directive 77/187/EEC on the approximation of the laws of the Member States relating to the safeguarding of employees rights in the event of transfers of undertakings, businesses or parts of a business (OJ L61, 5.3.1977, p 26) as amended by Council Directive 98/50/EC (OJ L201, 17.7.1998, p 88).

[10] Council Directive 94/45/EC of 22 September 1994 on the establishment of a European Works Council or a procedure in Community-scale undertakings and Community-scale groups of undertakings for the purposes of informing and consulting employees (OJ L254, 30.9.1994), p 64) as amended by Directive 97/74/EC (OJ L10, 16.1.1998, p 22).

22. In certain cases it may also be necessary for the *hold-separate obligation to apply to the corporate structure* itself. That is, in cases where the Divestment Business takes the form of a company and a strict separation of the corporate structure is necessary, the Monitoring Trustee must be given the authority to (i) exercise the Parties' rights as shareholders in the Divestment Business and (ii) to replace members of the supervisory board or non-executive directors on the board of directors who have been appointed on behalf of the Parties (cf. paragraph 8 of the Standard Commitments and paragraph 6 (d) of the Standard Trustee Mandate).

23. Of particular importance is the *ring-fencing of competitively sensitive information* of the Divestment Business. The parties are obliged to implement all necessary measures to ensure that they do not obtain such information of the Divestment Business and, in particular, to sever its participation in a central information technology network. The Monitoring Trustee may allow the disclosure of information to the divesting party if this is reasonably necessary for the divestiture of the Divestment Business or required by law (e.g. information necessary for group accounts).

24. The related commitments further contain a *non-solicitation* clause for Key Personnel of the Divestment Business. According to the experience of the Commission, the non-solicitation period, dependent on the circumstances of the case, should normally be two years. In addition, the Commission may request the inclusion of a *non-compete clause* in the commitments protecting the customers of the Divestment Business for a start-up period. This may be required to enable the Divestment Business to be active as a viable competitor in the market. The period for such customer protection clause will depend on the market in question.

25. During the Divestiture Phase, the divestiture lies in the hands of the divesting party. The Commission does not have a preference as to the method the parties use to select an acceptable purchaser as long as they meet the objective of the divestiture, to maintain or restore competition. However, as part of the *due diligence procedure*, it is foreseen that the divesting party shall provide to potential purchasers sufficient information as regards the Divestment Business and allow them access to its personnel (paragraph 11 of the Standard Commitments) in order to enable them to determine whether it will be possible to maintain and to develop the Divestment Business as active and viable competitive force in the market after the divestiture.

26. The divesting party shall further submit regular *reports* on potential purchasers and developments in the divestiture process to the Commission and the Monitoring Trustee (paragraph 12 of the Standard Commitments). This reporting mechanism gives the Monitoring Trustee the basis on which to assess the progress of the divestiture process as well as potential purchasers (for the Trustee's report, see paragraph 23 (vi) of the Standard Commitments) and keeps the Commission informed.

27. *Section D* sets out the requirements to be met by the *Purchaser*. The aim of this section is to ensure that the Divestment Business will be sold to a suitable purchaser who is independent of and unconnected to the Parties, and who possesses the financial resources, proven expertise and incentive to maintain and develop the Divestment Business as a viable and active competitive force in the marketplace. These Purchaser Requirements can generally be met by either industrial or financial investors. The latter must demonstrate the necessary management capabilities and 'proven expertise' which can in particular be met by financing a management buy-out.

28. Section D also deals with the *approval process*. After finalising the agreement(s), the divesting party shall submit a fully documented and reasoned proposal to the Commission. The Commission will verify that the purchaser will fulfil the requirements and that the Divestment Business is being sold in a manner consistent with the Commitments. One element for its assessment will be the report of the Monitoring Trustee according to paragraph

23 (vii). The Commission may approve the sale of the Divestment Business without parts of the assets or personnel of the Divestment Business if this does not affect the viability and competitiveness of the Divestment Business, in particular if the Purchaser provides for such assets or personnel itself.

29. *Section E* deals with both the *Monitoring and Divestiture Trustees*. It identifies the terms for their appointment, as well as the content of the Trustee Mandates, and conditions for replacement of the Trustee during the divestiture periods if that becomes necessary. A Monitoring Trustee must be proposed by the Parties within one week after the adoption of the decision, whereas a Divestiture Trustee must be proposed no later than one month before the end of the Divestiture Period, (paragraph 16 of the Standard Commitments). The Commission wishes to emphasise the importance it attaches to compliance with these deadlines in practise, as otherwise the Parties are in breach of the commitments and the divestiture procedure is endangered.

30. *Section E* also sets out the *duties and obligations of both types of Trustees*. The Monitoring Trustee's responsibilities (mainly set out in paragraph 23 Standard Commitments) relate to both the management of the Divestment Business during the hold-separate period and the monitoring of the divestiture process itself. The supervision of the management shall in particular ensure the viability, marketability and competitiveness of the Divestment Business and the compliance with the hold-separate and ring-fencing obligations. The Standard Commitments further assign certain monitoring tasks concerning the divestiture process to the Monitoring Trustee in the Divestiture Period. Once the Parties have proposed a purchaser for the Divestment Business, the Monitoring Trustee assesses the independence and suitability of the proposed purchaser and the viability of the Divestment Business after the sale to the purchaser, in order to assist the Commission in assessing the suitability of the proposed purchaser.

31. In the *Extended Divestiture Period*, the *Divestiture Trustee* will have an exclusive mandate to sell the Divestment Business at no minimum price and is empowered to include in the sale and purchase agreement such terms and conditions as it considers appropriate for an expedient sale. However, it is foreseen that the Trustee has to protect the legitimate financial interests of the divesting parties, subject to its unconditional obligation to divest at no minimum price. The Divestiture Trustee must report regularly on the progress of the divestiture process.

32. Also in Section E (paragraphs 26–30), the *duties and obligations of the Parties vis-à-vis the Trustee* are defined. Beside the provision of information, the Parties are in particular obliged to provide the Monitoring Trustee with all managerial and administrative support necessary for the Divestment Business and to grant to the Divestiture Trustee comprehensive powers of attorney covering all steps of the sale of the Divestment Business. An indemnification clause is included in order to reinforce the independent status of the Trustee from the Parties. Such a clause is already common practice in the trustee mandates submitted to the Commission for approval. The Trustee may further, at the expense of the Parties, retain advisors with specialised skills, in particular for corporate finance or legal advice.

33. Section E further foresees that trustees may only be removed in exceptional circumstances and with the approval of the Commission before the complete implementation of the Commitments.

34. *Section F* contains a *review clause*, which allows the Commission to extend the periods specified in the Commitments and to waive or modify the undertakings in the Commitments. The Parties must show good cause in order to be able to benefit from the exercise of the review clause. Requests for the extension of time periods shall, normally, be submitted no later than one month before the expiry of the time period in question.

STANDARD MODEL FOR TRUSTEE MANDATES

35. The *Standard Model for Trustee Mandates* sets out the duties and responsibilities of both Monitoring and Divestiture Trustee in a single text. However, the language makes clear that the Commission does not have a preference for the appointment of a single person to serve in the dual role of both Monitoring and Divestiture Trustee. Rather, the decision as to whether one or more trustees are appointed should be determined on a case-by-case basis by the Parties. If more than one trustee shall serve in these roles, only the provisions relevant for the Monitoring or Divestiture Trustee, respectively, have to be included in the individual mandate.

36. The Standard Trustee Mandate consists of the *following main elements*:

37. *Section A* contains some *definitions* and references the definitions included in the Standard Commitments.

38. *Sections B to G* contain provisions regarding the appointment of the Trustee (Section B), its general duties (Section C), the specific duties and obligations of the Monitoring and Divestiture Trustees (Sections D and E), reporting obligations identifying certain important subjects that should be discussed in each report (Section G), and duties and obligations of the Parties vis-à-vis the Trustee (Section F). These arrangements are based on the provisions established in the Standard Commitments in relation to the Trustee and described above.

39. *Sections H to J* cover additional trustee-related provisions, including provisions regarding the remuneration of the Trustee(s), procedures concerning the termination of the Mandate, and certain additional provisions, such as determination of applicable national law.

40. In particular, the independence of the trustee and the absence of *conflicts of interests of the trustee* are of great importance for the Commission in deciding on the approval of the Trustee and the respective mandate. The provisions in the Standard Trustee Mandate (paragraphs 20 to 23) ensuring the independence of the trustee from the parties and the absence of conflicts of interest foresee the following procedure: (1) The Trustee must disclose all current relationships with the Parties (paragraph 20) at the time at which the Trustee Mandate is entered into. (2) During the term of the mandate, the Trustee undertakes not to create a conflict of interest by having or accepting employment or appointment as a Member of the Board of the Parties or by having or accepting any assignments or other business relationships with, or financial interests in, the Parties. (3) As legal consequences it is foreseen that, if the Trustee becomes aware of a conflict of interest during the Mandate, the Trustee must notify the Commission and resolve the problem immediately and, if the conflict of interest cannot subsequently be resolved, the Commission may require the termination of the trustee mandate. These rules concerning conflicts of interests apply to the Trustee itself, members of the Trustee Team and the Trustee Partner Firms as members of the same organisation. (4) For a period of one year following termination of the Mandate, the members of the Trustee Team shall not provide services to the Parties without the Commission's prior approval and must establish measures to ensure the integrity of the members of the Trustee Team.

41. In addition to the rules laid down in the Standard Trustee Mandate, it is up to the Parties and the Trustee to include provisions dealing with other potential conflicts of interests, such as conflicts of interests of the Trustee with potential purchasers.

APPENDIX 25

Model Text Divestiture Commitments and Model Text Trustee Mandate

By hand and by fax: 00 32 2 296 4301

European Commission—Merger Task Force

DG Competition

Rue Joseph II 70 Jozef-II straat

B-1000 BRUSSELS

CASE M. [*No* . . .]—[*Title* . . .]
COMMITMENTS TO THE EUROPEAN COMMISSION

Pursuant to [Article 6(2), *if Phase I Commitments*] [Article 8(2), *if Phase II Commitments*] [Articles 8(2) and 10(2), *if in Phase II Commitments prior to the sending out of the Statement of Objections*] of Council Regulation (EEC) No. 4064/89 as amended (the '***Merger Regulation***'), [*Indicate the name of the Undertakings offering the Commitments*] (the '***Parties***') hereby provide the following Commitments (the '***Commitments***') in order to enable the European Commission (the '***Commission***') to declare [*Description of the operation: e.g. the acquisition of . . .; the creation of a full-function joint venture between . . .*] compatible with the common market and the EEA Agreement by its decision pursuant to [Article 6(1)(b) of the Merger Regulation, *if Phase I Commitments*] [Article 8(2), *if Phase II Commitments*] of the Merger Regulation (the '***Decision***').

The Commitments shall take effect upon the date of adoption of the Decision.

This text shall be interpreted in the light of the Decision to the extent that the Commitments are attached as conditions and obligations, in the general framework of Community law, in particular in the light of the Merger Regulation, and by reference to the Commission Notice on remedies acceptable under Council Regulation (EEC) No 4064/89 and under Commission Regulation (EC) No 447/98.

Section A. Definitions

For the purpose of the Commitments, the following terms shall have the following meaning:

Affiliated Undertakings: undertakings controlled by the Parties and/or by the ultimate parents of the Parties, including the JV [*Only in the case when the proposed operation is a creation of a JV*], whereby the notion of control shall be interpreted pursuant to Article 3 Merger Regulation and in the light of the Commission Notice on the concept of concentration under Council Regulation (EEC) No 4064/89.

Closing: the transfer of the legal title of the Divestment Business to the Purchaser.

Divestment Business: the business or businesses as defined in Section B and the Schedule that the Parties commit to divest.

Divestiture Trustee: one or more natural or legal person(s), independent from the Parties, who is approved by the Commission and appointed by [X] and who has received from [X] the exclusive Trustee Mandate to sell the Divestment Business to a Purchaser at no minimum price.

Effective Date: the date of adoption of the Decision.

First Divestiture Period: the period of [•] months from the Effective Date.

Hold Separate Manager: the person appointed by [X] for the Divestment Business to manage the day-to-day business under the supervision of the Monitoring Trustee.

Key Personnel: all personnel necessary to maintain the viability and competitiveness of the Divestment Business, as listed in the Schedule.

Monitoring Trustee: one or more natural or legal person(s), independent from the Parties, who is approved by the Commission and appointed by [X], and who has the duty to monitor [X's] compliance with the conditions and obligations attached to the Decision.

Personnel: all personnel currently employed by the Divestment Business, including Key Personnel, staff seconded to the Divestment Business, shared personnel and the additional personnel listed in the Schedule.

Purchaser: the entity approved by the Commission as acquirer of the Divestment Business in accordance with the criteria set out in Section D.

Trustee(s): the Monitoring Trustee and the Divestiture Trustee.

Trustee Divestiture Period: the period of [•] months from the end of the First Divestiture Period.

[X]: [*Indicate the short name of the Undertaking Concerned that will divest its business/es*], incorporated under the laws of [•], with its registered office at [•] and registered with the Commercial/Company Register at [•] under number [•].

Section B. The Divestment Business

Commitment to divest

1. In order to restore effective competition, [X] commits to divest, or procure the divestiture of the Divestment Business by the end of the Trustee Divestiture Period as a going concern to a purchaser and on terms of sale approved by the Commission in accordance with the procedure described in paragraph 15. To carry out the divestiture, [X] commits to find a purchaser and to enter into a final binding sale and purchase agreement for the sale of the Divestment Business within the First Divestiture Period. If [X] has not entered into such an agreement at the end of the First Divestiture Period, [X] shall grant the Divestiture Trustee an exclusive mandate to sell the Divestment Business in accordance with the procedure described in paragraph 24 in the Trustee Divestiture Period. [*The following sentence should be inserted in case of an 'up-front buyer'*: The proposed concentration shall not be implemented unless and until [X] or the Divestiture Trustee has entered into a final binding sale and purchase agreement for the sale of the Divestment Business and the Commission has approved the purchaser and the terms of sale in accordance with paragraph 15].

2. [X] shall be deemed to have complied with this commitment if, by the end of the Trustee Divestiture Period, [X] has entered into a final binding sale and purchase agreement, if the Commission approves the Purchaser and the terms in accordance with the procedure described in paragraph 15 and if the closing of the sale of the Divestment Business takes place within a period not exceeding 3 months after the approval of the purchaser and the terms of sale by the Commission.

3. In order to maintain the structural effect of the Commitments, the Parties shall, for a period of 10 years after the Effective Date, not acquire direct or indirect influence over the whole or part of the Divestment Business, unless the Commission has previously found that the structure of the market has changed to such an extent that the absence of influence over the

Divestment Business is no longer necessary to render the proposed concentration compatible with the common market.

Structure and definition of the Divestment Business

4. The Divestment Business consists of [*Provide a summary description of the Divestment Business*]. The present legal and functional structure of the Divestment Business as operated to date is described in the Schedule. The Divestment Business, described in more detail in the Schedule, includes

   (a) all tangible and intangible assets (including intellectual property rights), which contribute to the current operation or are necessary to ensure the viability and competitiveness of the Divestment Business;

   (b) all licences, permits and authorisations issued by any governmental organisation for the benefit of the Divestment Business;

   (c) all contracts, leases, commitments and customer orders of the Divestment Business; all customer, credit and other records of the Divestment Business (items referred to under (a)–(c) hereinafter collectively referred to as '*Assets*');

   (d) the Personnel; and

   (e) [*To be included in* cases *in which the Divestment Business needs an on-going relationship with the Parties in order to be fully competitive and viable:* the benefit, for a transitional period of up to [*insert*] years after Closing and on terms and conditions equivalent to those at present afforded to the Divestment Business, of all current arrangements under which [X] or Affiliated Undertakings supply products or services to the Divestment Business, as detailed in the Schedule, unless otherwise agreed with the Purchaser.]

Section C. Related commitments

Preservation of Viability, Marketability and Competitiveness

5. From the Effective Date until Closing, [X] shall preserve the economic viability, marketability and competitiveness of the Divestment Business, in accordance with good business practice, and shall minimise as far as possible any risk of loss of competitive potential of the Divestment Business. In particular [X] undertakes:

   (a) not to carry out any act upon its own authority that might have a significant adverse impact on the value, management or competitiveness of the Divestment Business or that might alter the nature and scope of activity, or the industrial or commercial strategy or the investment policy of the Divestment Business;

   (b) to make available sufficient resources for the development of the Divestment Business, on the basis and continuation of the existing business plans

   (c) to take all reasonable steps, including appropriate incentive schemes (based on industry practice), to encourage all Key Personnel to remain with the Divestment Business.

Hold-separate obligations of Parties

6. [X] commits, from the Effective Date until Closing, to keep the Divestment Business separate from the businesses it is retaining and to ensure that Key Personnel of the Divestment Business—including the Hold Separate Manager—have no involvement in any business retained and vice versa. [X] shall also ensure that the Personnel does not report to any individual outside the Divestment Business.

7. Until Closing, [X] shall assist the Monitoring Trustee in ensuring that the Divestment Business is managed as a distinct and saleable entity separate from the businesses retained by the Parties. [X] shall appoint a Hold Separate Manager who shall be responsible for the management of the Divestment Business, under the supervision of the Monitoring Trustee. The

Hold Separate Manager shall manage the Divestment Business independently and in the best interest of the business with a view to ensuring its continued economic viability, marketability and competitiveness and its independence from the businesses retained by the Parties.

8. [*The following is to be inserted in cases in which a company or a share in a company is to be divested and a strict separation of the corporate structure is necessary:* To ensure that the Divestment Business is held and managed as a separate entity the Monitoring Trustee shall exercise [*X*'s] rights as shareholder in the Divestment Business (except for its rights for dividends that are due before Closing), with the aim of acting in the best interest of the business, determined on a stand-alone basis, as an independent financial investor, and with a view to fulfilling [*X*'s] obligations under the Commitments. Furthermore, the Monitoring Trustee shall have the power to replace members of the supervisory board or non-executive directors of the board of directors, who have been appointed on behalf of [*X*]. Upon request of the Monitoring Trustee, [*X*] shall resign as member of the boards or shall cause such members of the boards to resign.]

Ring-fencing

9. [*X*] shall implement all necessary measures to ensure that it does not after the Effective Date obtain any business secrets, know-how, commercial information, or any other information of a confidential or proprietary nature relating to the Divestment Business. In particular, the participation of the Divestment Business in a central information technology network shall be severed to the extent possible, without compromising the viability of the Divestment Business. [*X*] may obtain information relating to the Divestment Business which is reasonably necessary for the divestiture of the Divestment Business or whose disclosure to [*X*] is required by law.

Non-solicitation clause

10. The Parties undertake, subject to customary limitations, not to solicit, and to procure that Affiliated Undertakings do not solicit, the Key Personnel transferred with the Divestment Business for a period of [•] after Closing.

Due Diligence

11. In order to enable potential purchasers to carry out a reasonable due diligence of the Divestment Business, [X] shall, subject to customary confidentiality assurances and dependent on the stage of the divestiture process:

    (a) provide to potential purchasers sufficient information as regards the Divestment Business;
    (b) provide to potential purchasers sufficient information relating to the Personnel and allow them reasonable access to the Personnel.

Reporting

12. [*X*] shall submit written reports in [*Indicate the language of the procedure or another language agreed with the Commission*] on potential purchasers of the Divestment Business and developments in the negotiations with such potential purchasers to the Commission and the Monitoring Trustee no later than 10 days after the end of every month following the Effective Date (or otherwise at the Commission's request).

13. The Parties shall inform the Commission and the Monitoring Trustee on the preparation of the data room documentation and the due diligence procedure and shall submit a copy of an information memorandum to the Commission and the Monitoring Trustee before sending the memorandum out to potential purchasers.

Section D. The Purchaser

14. In order to ensure the immediate restoration of effective competition, the Purchaser, in order to be approved by the Commission, must:

    (a) be independent of and unconnected to the Parties;

    (b) have the financial resources, proven expertise and incentive to maintain and develop the Divestment Business as a viable and active competitive force in competition with the Parties and other competitors;

    (c) neither be likely to create, in the light of the information available to the Commission, *prima facie* competition concerns nor give rise to a risk that the implementation of the Commitments will be delayed, and must, in particular, reasonably be expected to obtain all necessary approvals from the relevant regulatory authorities for the acquisition of the Divestment Business (the before-mentioned criteria for the purchaser hereafter the '***Purchaser Requirements***').

15. The final binding sale and purchase agreement shall be conditional on the Commission's approval. When [X] has reached an agreement with a purchaser, it shall submit a fully documented and reasoned proposal, including a copy of the final agreement(s), to the Commission and the Monitoring Trustee. [X] must be able to demonstrate to the Commission that the purchaser meets the Purchaser Requirements and that the Divestment Business is being sold in a manner consistent with the Commitments. For the approval, the Commission shall verify that the purchaser fulfils the Purchaser Requirements and that the Divestment Business is being sold in a manner consistent with the Commitments. The Commission may approve the sale of the Divestment Business without one or more Assets or parts of the Personnel, if this does not affect the viability and competitiveness of the Divestment Business after the sale, taking account of the proposed purchaser.

Section E. Trustee

I. Appointment Procedure

16. [X] shall appoint a Monitoring Trustee to carry out the functions specified in the Commitments for a Monitoring Trustee. If [X] has not entered into a binding sales and purchase agreement one month before the end of the First Divestiture Period or if the Commission has rejected a purchaser proposed by [X] at that time or thereafter, [X] shall appoint a Divestiture Trustee to carry out the functions specified in the Commitments for a Divestiture Trustee. The appointment of the Divestiture Trustee shall take effect upon the commencement of the Extended Divestment Period.

17. The Trustee shall be independent of the Parties, possess the necessary qualifications to carry out its mandate, for example as an investment bank or consultant or auditor, and shall neither have nor become exposed to a conflict of interest. The Trustee shall be remunerated by the Parties in a way that does not impede the independent and effective fulfilment of its mandate. In particular, where the remuneration package of a Divestiture Trustee includes a success premium linked to the final sale value of the Divestment Business, the fee shall also be linked to a divestiture within the Trustee Divestiture Period.

Proposal by the Parties

18. No later than one week after the Effective Date, [X] shall submit a list of one or more persons whom [X] proposes to appoint as the Monitoring Trustee to the Commission for approval. No later than one month before the end of the First Divestiture Period, [X] shall submit a list of one or more persons whom [X] proposes to appoint as Divestiture Trustee to the Commission for approval. The proposal shall contain sufficient information for the Commission to verify that the proposed Trustee fulfils the requirements set out in paragraph 17 and shall include:

(a) the full terms of the proposed mandate, which shall include all provisions necessary to enable the Trustee to fulfil its duties under these Commitments;

(b) the outline of a work plan which describes how the Trustee intends to carry out its assigned tasks;

(c) an indication whether the proposed Trustee is to act as both Monitoring Trustee and Divestiture Trustee or whether different trustees are proposed for the two functions.

Approval or rejection by the Commission

19. The Commission shall have the discretion to approve or reject the proposed Trustee(s) and to approve the proposed mandate subject to any modifications it deems necessary for the Trustee to fulfil its obligations. If only one name is approved, [X] shall appoint or cause to be appointed, the individual or institution concerned as Trustee, in accordance with the mandate approved by the Commission. If more than one name is approved, [X] shall be free to choose the Trustee to be appointed from among the names approved. The Trustee shall be appointed within one week of the Commission's approval, in accordance with the mandate approved by the Commission.

New proposal by the Parties

20. If all the proposed Trustees are rejected, [X] shall submit the names of at least two more individuals or institutions within one week of being informed of the rejection, in accordance with the requirements and the procedure set out in paragraphs 16 and 19.

Trustee nominated by the Commission

21. If all further proposed Trustees are rejected by the Commission, the Commission shall nominate a Trustee, whom [X] shall appoint, or cause to be appointed, in accordance with a trustee mandate approved by the Commission.

II. Functions of the Trustee

22. The Trustee shall assume its specified duties in order to ensure compliance with the Commitments. The Commission may, on its own initiative or at the request of the Trustee or [X], give any orders or instructions to the Trustee in order to ensure compliance with the conditions and obligations attached to the Decision.

Duties and obligations of the Monitoring Trustee

23. The Monitoring Trustee shall:

(i) propose in its first report to the Commission a detailed work plan describing how it intends to monitor compliance with the obligations and conditions attached to the Decision.

(ii) oversee the on-going management of the Divestment Business with a view to ensuring its continued economic viability, marketability and competitiveness and monitor compliance by [X] with the conditions and obligations attached to the Decision. To that end the Monitoring Trustee shall:

(a) monitor the preservation of the economic viability, marketability and competitiveness of the Divestment Business, and the keeping separate of the Divestment Business from the business retained by the Parties, in accordance with paragraphs 5 and 6 of the Commitments;

(b) supervise the management of the Divestment Business as a distinct and saleable entity, in accordance with paragraph 7 of the Commitments;

(c) (i) in consultation with [X], determine all necessary measures to ensure that [X] does not after the effective date obtain any business secrets, knowhow, commercial information, or any other information of a confidential or proprietary nature relating to the Divestment Business, in particular strive for the severing of the

1342

Divestment Business' participation in a central information technology network to the extent possible, without compromising the viability of the Divestment Business, and (ii) decide whether such information may be disclosed to [X] as the disclosure is reasonably necessary to allow [X] to carry out the divestiture or as the disclosure is required by law;

(d) monitor the splitting of assets and the allocation of Personnel between the Divestment Business and [X] or Affiliated Undertakings;

(iii) assume the other functions assigned to the Monitoring Trustee under the conditions and obligations attached to the Decision;

(iv) propose to [X] such measures as the Monitoring Trustee considers necessary to ensure [X]'s compliance with the conditions and obligations attached to the Decision, in particular the maintenance of the full economic viability, marketability or competitiveness of the Divestment Business, the holding separate of the Divestment Business and the non-disclosure of competitively sensitive information;

(v) review and assess potential purchasers as well as the progress of the divestiture process and verify that, dependent on the stage of the divestiture process, (a) potential purchasers receive sufficient information relating to the Divestment Business and the Personnel in particular by reviewing, if available, the data room documentation, the information memorandum and the due diligence process, and (b) potential purchasers are granted reasonable access to the Personnel;

(vi) provide to the Commission, sending [X] a non-confidential copy at the same time, a written report within 15 days after the end of every month. The report shall cover the operation and management of the Divestment Business so that the Commission can assess whether the business is held in a manner consistent with the Commitments and the progress of the divestiture process as well as potential purchasers. In addition to these reports, the Monitoring Trustee shall promptly report in writing to the Commission, sending [X] a non-confidential copy at the same time, if it concludes on reasonable grounds that [X] is failing to comply with these Commitments;

(vii) within one week after receipt of the documented proposal referred to in paragraph 15, submit to the Commission a reasoned opinion as to the suitability and independence of the proposed purchaser and the viability of the Divestment Business after the Sale and as to whether the Divestment Business is sold in a manner consistent with the conditions and obligations attached to the Decision, in particular, if relevant, whether the Sale of the Divestment Business without one or more Assets or not all of the Personnel affects the viability of the Divestment Business after the sale, taking account of the proposed purchaser.

Duties and obligations of the Divestiture Trustee

24. Within the Trustee Divestiture Period, the Divestiture Trustee shall sell at no minimum price the Divestment Business to a purchaser, provided that the Commission has approved both the purchaser and the final binding sale and purchase agreement in accordance with the procedure laid down in paragraph 15. The Divestiture Trustee shall include in the sale and purchase agreement such terms and conditions as it considers appropriate for an expedient sale in the Trustee Divestiture Period. In particular, the Divestiture Trustee may include in the sale and purchase agreement such customary representations and warranties and indemnities as are reasonably required to effect the sale. The Divestiture Trustee shall protect the legitimate financial interests of [X], subject to the Parties' unconditional obligation to divest at no minimum price in the Trustee Divestiture Period.

25. In the Trustee Divestiture Period (or otherwise at the Commission's request), the Divestiture Trustee shall provide the Commission with a comprehensive monthly report written in [*Please indicate the language of the procedure or a different language agreed with the Commission*]

1343

on the progress of the divestiture process. Such reports shall be submitted within 15 days after the end of every month with a simultaneous copy to the Monitoring Trustee and a non-confidential copy to the Parties.

III. Duties and obligations of the Parties

26. [X] shall provide and shall cause its advisors to provide the Trustee with all such cooperation, assistance and information as the Trustee may reasonably require to perform its tasks. The Trustee shall have full and complete access to any of [X's] or the Divestment Business' books, records, documents, management or other personnel, facilities, sites and technical information necessary for fulfilling its duties under the Commitments and [X] and the Divestment Business shall provide the Trustee upon request with copies of any document. [X] and the Divestment Business shall make available to the Trustee one or more offices on their premises and shall be available for meetings in order to provide the Trustee with all information necessary for the performance of its tasks.

27. [X] shall provide the Monitoring Trustee with all managerial and administrative support that it may reasonably request on behalf of the management of the Divestment Business. This shall include all administrative support functions relating to the Divestment Business which are currently carried out at headquarters level. [X] shall provide and shall cause its advisors to provide the Monitoring Trustee, on request, with the information submitted to potential purchasers, in particular give the Monitoring Trustee access to the data room documentation and all other information granted to potential purchasers in the due diligence procedure. [X] shall inform the Monitoring Trustee on possible purchasers, submit a list of potential purchasers, and keep the Monitoring Trustee informed of all developments in the divestiture process.

28. [X] shall grant or procure Affiliated Undertakings to grant comprehensive powers of attorney, duly executed, to the Divestiture Trustee to effect the sale, the Closing and all actions and declarations which the Divestiture Trustee considers necessary or appropriate to achieve the sale and the Closing, including the appointment of advisors to assist with the sale process. Upon request of the Divestiture Trustee, [X] shall cause the documents required for effecting the sale and the Closing to be duly executed.

29. [X] shall indemnify the Trustee and its employees and agents (each an '***Indemnified Party***') and hold each Indemnified Party harmless against, and hereby agrees that an Indemnified Party shall have no liability to [X] for any liabilities arising out of the performance of the Trustee's duties under the Commitments, except to the extent that such liabilities result from the wilful default, recklessness, gross negligence or bad faith of the Trustee, its employees, agents or advisors.

30. At the expense of [X], the Trustee may appoint advisors (in particular for corporate finance or legal advice), subject to [X's] approval (this approval not to be unreasonably withheld or delayed) if the Trustee considers the appointment of such advisors necessary or appropriate for the performance of its duties and obligations under the Mandate, provided that any fees and other expenses incurred by the Trustee are reasonable. Should [X] refuse to approve the advisors proposed by the Trustee the Commission may approve the appointment of such advisors instead, after having heard [X]. Only the Trustee shall be entitled to issue instructions to the advisors. Paragraph 29 shall apply mutatis mutandis. In the Trustee Divestiture Period, the Divestiture Trustee may use advisors who served [X] during the Divestiture Period if the Divestiture Trustee considers this in the best interest of an expedient sale.

IV. Replacement, discharge and reappointment of the Trustee

31. If the Trustee ceases to perform its functions under the Commitments or for any other good cause, including the exposure of the Trustee to a conflict of interest:

(a) the Commission may, after hearing the Trustee, require [X] to replace the Trustee; or

(b) [X], with the prior approval of the Commission, may replace the Trustee.

32. If the Trustee is removed according to paragraph 31, the Trustee may be required to continue in its function until a new Trustee is in place to whom the Trustee has effected a full hand over of all relevant information. The new Trustee shall be appointed in accordance with the procedure referred to in paragraphs 16–21.

33. Beside the removal according to paragraph 31, the Trustee shall cease to act as Trustee only after the Commission has discharged it from its duties after all the Commitments with which the Trustee has been entrusted have been implemented. However, the Commission may at any time require the reappointment of the Monitoring Trustee if it subsequently appears that the relevant remedies might not have been fully and properly implemented.

Section F. The Review Clause

34. The Commission may, where appropriate, in response to a request from [X] showing good cause and accompanied by a report from the Monitoring Trustee:

(i)   Grant an extension of the time periods foreseen in the Commitments, or

(ii) Waive, modify or substitute, in exceptional circumstances, one or more of the undertakings in these Commitments.

Where [X] seeks an extension of a time period, it shall submit a request to the Commission no later than one month before the expiry of that period, showing good cause. Only in exceptional circumstances shall [X] be entitled to request an extension within the last month of any period.

....

duly authorised for and on behalf of
[*Indicate the name of each of the Parties*]

Schedule

1. The Divestment Business as operated to date has the following legal and functional structure: [*Describe the legal and functional structure of the Divestment Business, including the organisational chart*].

2. Following paragraph [4] of these Commitments, the Divestment Business includes, but is not limited to:

(a) the following main tangible assets: [*Indicate the essential tangible assets, e.g. xyz factory/warehouse/pipelines located at abc and the real estate/property on which the factory/warehouse is located; the R&D facilities*];

(b) the following main intangible assets: [*Indicate the main intangible assets. This should in particular include (i) the brand names and (ii) all other Intellectual Property Rights used in conducting the Divestment Business.*];

(c) the following main licences, permits and authorisations: [*Indicate the main licences, permits and authorisations*];

(d) the following main contracts, agreements, leases, commitments and understandings [*Indicate the main contracts, etc.*];

(e) the following customer, credit and other records: [*Indicate the main customer, credit and other records, according to further sector specific indications, where appropriate*];

(f)   the following Personnel: [*Indicate the personnel to be transferred in general, including personnel providing essential functions for the Divestment Business, such as central R&D staff*];

(g)   the following Key Personnel: [*Indicate the names and functions of the Key Personnel, including the Hold Separate Manager, where appropriate*]; and

(h)   the arrangements for the supply with the following products or services by [*X*] or Affiliated Undertakings for a transitional period of up to [•] after Closing: [*Indicate the products or services to be provided for a transitional period in order to maintain the economic viability and competitiveness of the Divestment Business*].

3.   The Divestment Business shall not include:

(i)   . . .;

(ii)   [*It is the responsibility of the Parties to indicate clearly what the Divestment Business will not encompass*].

TRUSTEE MANDATE

BETWEEN:

1.   [*X*] [*Indicate a short name(s) of the Undertaking(s) Concerned that will divest its/their businesses*](hereafter [*X*]), a company organised under the laws of [*Indicate law of origin*], which has its registered seat at [*Indicate complete address*], represented by [*Indicate name and title of individual representing X for the Mandate*],

AND

2.   [*Insert name, address, and, as the case may be, company details of the Trustee*], (the '***Trustee***').

[*X*] and the Trustee are hereafter referred to as the '***Mandate Parties***'.

WHEREAS

In [*Indicate full case name and number*] and pursuant to [*Article 6(2)/Article 8(2)*] of Council Regulation (EEC) No. 4064/89 as amended (the '***Merger Regulation***'), [*X*] offered commitments (the '***Commitments***'), attached hereto as Annex 1, in order to enable the European Commission (the '***Commission***') to declare [*Description of the operation: e.g. the acquisition of. . .; the creation of a full-function joint venture between . . .*] compatible with the common market and the functioning of the EEA Agreement. The Commission approved the operation by its decision pursuant to [*Article 6(1)(b)/Article 8(2)*] of the Merger Regulation (the '***Decision***'), subject to full compliance with the conditions and obligations attached to the Decision (the '***Conditions and Obligations***').

According to the Conditions and Obligations, [*X*] undertakes to divest the [*Indicate the business to be divested*] and, in the meantime, to preserve the economic viability, marketability and competitiveness of this business. Therefore, [*X*] undertakes to appoint a Monitoring Trustee for the monitoring of the hold separate obligations and of the divestiture procedure, and to appoint a Divestiture Trustee for the divestiture of the said business if [X] has not succeeded in divesting it during the First Divestiture Period. In accordance with the Conditions and Obligations, [*X*] hereby engages the Trustee and this agreement forms the mandate referred to in the Commitments (hereafter the '***Mandate***').

The appointment of the Trustee and the terms of this Mandate were approved by the Commission on [*Indicate date of approval letter*].

In case of doubt or conflict, this Mandate shall be interpreted in the light of (1) the Conditions and Obligations and the Decision, (2) the general framework of Community law, in particular in the light of the Merger Regulation, and (3) the Commission Notice on remedies acceptable under Council Regulation (EEC) No 4064/89 and under Commission Regulation (EC) No 447/98.

IT HAS BEEN AGREED AS FOLLOWS:

Section A. Definitions

Terms used in this Mandate shall have the meaning set out in Section 1 of the Commitments. For the purpose of this Mandate, the following terms shall have the following meaning:

Sale: the entering into a binding sale and purchase agreement for the selling of the Divestment Business to the Purchaser.

Trustee Partner Firms: the other firms belonging to the same organisation of individual partnerships and companies as the Trustee.

Trustee Team: The key persons responsible for carrying out the tasks assigned by the Mandate and identified in paragraph [*3*] below of the Mandate.

Work-Plan: the outline of the work-plan submitted to the Commission by the Trustee before the approval of the Trustee and attached hereto as Annex [•], a more detailed version of which will be prepared by the Trustee and submitted to the Commission in its first report.

Section B. Appointment of Trustee

1. [*X*] hereby appoints the Trustee to act as its exclusive trustee for fulfilling the tasks of a [*Monitoring Trustee and/or Divestiture Trustee*] according to the Conditions and Obligations and the Trustee hereby accepts the said appointment in accordance with the terms of this Mandate.

2. The appointment and this Mandate shall become effective on the date hereof except for the provisions specifically addressing the duties and obligations of the Divestiture Trustee which shall become effective with the beginning of the Trustee Divestiture Period.

3. The Trustee Team consists of the following key persons: [*Indicate name and title of each of the key persons (partners/leading persons)*]. The Trustee shall not replace the persons of the Trustee Team without prior approval of the Commission and [*X*].

Section C. General Duties and Obligations of the Trustee

4. The Trustee shall act on behalf of the Commission to ensure [*X's*] compliance with the Conditions and Obligations and assume the duties specified in the Conditions and Obligations for a [*Monitoring and/or Divestiture Trustee*]. The Trustee shall carry out the duties under this Mandate in accordance with the Work-Plan as well as revisions of the Work-Plan, approved by the Commission. The Commission may, on its own initiative or at the request of the Trustee or [*X*], give any orders or instructions to the Trustee in order to ensure compliance with the Conditions and Obligations. [*X*] is not entitled to give instructions to the Trustee.

5. The Trustee shall propose to [*X*] such measures as the Trustee considers necessary to ensure [*X's*] compliance with the Commitments and/or the Mandate, and the Trustee shall propose necessary measures to the Commission in the event that [*X*] does not comply with the Trustee's proposals within the timeframe set by the Trustee.

Section D. Duties and Obligations of the Monitoring Trustee

Monitoring and Management of the Divestment Business

6. The Monitoring Trustee shall, in conformity with the Conditions and Obligations, oversee the on-going management of the Divestment Business with a view to ensuring its continued economic viability, marketability and competitiveness and monitor the compliance of [*X*] with the Conditions and Obligations. To that end, the Monitoring Trustee shall until Closing in particular:

(a) monitor (i) the preservation of the economic viability, marketability and competitiveness of the Divestment Business in accordance with good business practice, (ii) the minimisation, as far as possible, of any risk of loss of competitive potential of the Divestment Business; (iii) the not carrying out by [X] or Affiliated Undertakings of any act on its own authority that might have a significant adverse impact on the value, management or competitiveness of the Divestment Business or that might to alter the nature and scope of activity, or the industrial or commercial strategy or the investment policy of the Divestment Business; and (iv) the making available by [X] of sufficient resources for the Divestment Business to develop, based on the existing business plans and their continuation, and (v) the taking of all reasonable steps by [X], including appropriate incentive schemes (based on business practice), to encourage all Key Personnel to remain with the Divestment Business;

(b) monitor (i) the holding separate of the Divestment Business from the businesses retained by [X] and Affiliated Undertakings, (ii) the absence of involvement of Key Employees of the Divestment Business—including the Hold Separate Manager—in any business retained and vice versa, and (iii) the absence of reporting of the Personnel of the Divestment Business to any individual outside the Divestment Business, except where permitted in the Commitments;

(c) seek to ensure that the Divestment Business is managed as a distinct and saleable entity separate from [X's] or Affiliated Undertakings' businesses and that the Hold Separate Manager manages the Divestment Business independently and in the best interest of the business and ensuring its continued economic viability, marketability and competitiveness as well as its independence from the businesses retained by the Parties;

[(d) *the following paragraph to be inserted in cases in which the Commitments foresee the voting of shares by the Monitoring Trustee and/or the replacement of member of the supervisory board/ board of directors*: exercise [X's] rights as shareholder in the Divestment Business (except for its rights for dividends that are due before Closing), with the aim of acting in the best interest of the business, determined on a stand-alone basis, as an independent financial investor, and with a view to fulfilling [X's] obligation under the Conditions and Obligations. Consequently, [X] grants a comprehensive and duly executed proxy to the Monitoring Trustee in Annex [•] for the exercise of the voting rights attached to [X's] shares in the Divestment Business. The Monitoring Trustee shall have the power to replace members of the supervisory board or non-executive directors of the board of directors of the Divestment Business, who have been appointed on behalf of [X]. Upon request of the Monitoring Trustee, [X] shall resign as a member of the boards or shall cause such members of the boards to resign. The representatives of the Monitoring Trustee to be appointed to the board shall be one or more persons of the Trustee Team. In the event that appointments outside these named individuals are envisaged the prior approval of the Commission is required;]

(e) monitor the splitting of assets and the allocation of Personnel between the Divestment Business and [X] or Affiliated Undertakings;

(f) (i) in consultation with [X], determine all necessary measures to ensure that [X] does not after the Effective Date obtain any business secrets, know-how, commercial information, or any other information of a confidential or proprietary nature relating to the Divestment Business, in particular strive for the severing of the Divestment Business' participation in a central information technology network to the extent possible, without compromising the viability of the Divestment Business, and (ii) decide whether such information may be disclosed to [X] as the disclosure is reasonably necessary to allow [X] to carry out the divestiture or as the disclosure is required by law.

Monitoring of Divestiture

7. Until the end of the First Divestiture Period, the Monitoring Trustee shall assist the Commission in reviewing the divestiture process and assessing proposed purchasers. Therefore the Monitoring Trustee shall during the First Divestiture Period:

    (a) review and assess the progress of the divestiture process and potential purchasers;

    (b) verify that, dependent on the stage of the divestiture process, (i) potential purchasers receive sufficient information relating to the Divestment Business and the Personnel, in particular by reviewing, if available, the data room documentation, the information memorandum and the due diligence process, and (ii) potential purchasers are granted reasonable access to the Personnel;

8. Once [X] has submitted to the Commission a proposal for a purchaser, the Trustee shall, within one week after receipt of the documented proposal by the Parties, submit to the Commission a reasoned opinion as to the suitability and independence of the proposed purchaser and the viability of the Divestment Business after the Sale and as to whether the Divestment Business is sold in a manner consistent with the Conditions and Obligations, in particular, if relevant, whether the Sale of the Divestment Business without one or more Assets or not all of the Personnel affects the viability of the Divestment Business after the Sale, taking account of the proposed purchaser.

Section E. Duties and Obligations of the Divestiture Trustee

9. With the commencement of the Trustee Divestiture Period, [X] hereby gives the Trustee an exclusive mandate to sell the Divestment Business to a purchaser according to the provisions of this section of the Mandate and the Commitments.

10. The purchaser shall fulfil the Purchaser Requirements and both the purchaser and the final sale and purchase agreement shall be approved by the Commission in accordance with the procedure laid down in paragraph [15] of the Commitments.

11. The Divestiture Trustee shall sell the Divestment Business at no minimum price and at such terms and conditions as it considers appropriate for an expedient sale in the Trustee Divestiture Period. In particular, the Divestiture Trustee may include in the sale and purchase agreement such customary representations and warranties and indemnities as are reasonably required to effect the Sale. At the same time, the Divestiture Trustee shall protect the legitimate financial interests of [X], subject to the Parties' unconditional obligation to divest at no minimum price in the Trustee Divestiture Period.

12. [X] grants a comprehensive and duly executed power of attorney to the Divestiture Trustee in Annex [•] to effect the Sale of the Divestment Business, the Closing and all actions and declarations which the Trustee considers necessary or appropriate for achieving the Sale of the Divestment Business or the Closing, including the power to appoint advisors to assist with the sale process. The power of attorney shall include the authority to grant sub-powers of attorney to members of the Trustee Team. If necessary to accomplish the Sale, [X] shall grant the Divestiture Trustee further powers of attorney, duly executed, or cause the documents required for the effecting of the Sale and the Closing to be duly executed. Any power of attorney granted by [X], including any subpowers of attorney granted pursuant to them, shall expire on the earlier of the termination of this Mandate or the discharge of the Trustee.

13. The Trustee shall comply with the Commission's instructions as regards any aspects of the conduct or conclusion of the sale, in particular in ending negotiations with any prospective purchaser, if the Commission notifies the Trustee and [X] of the Commission's determination that the negotiations are being conducted with an unacceptable purchaser.

Section F. Reporting Obligations

14. Within 15 days of the end of each month or as otherwise agreed with the Commission, the Monitoring Trustee shall submit a written report to the Commission, sending [X] a non-confidential copy at the same time. The report shall cover the Monitoring Trustee's fulfilment of its obligations under the Mandate and the compliance of the Parties with the Conditions and Obligations. The reports shall cover in particular the following topics:

    • Operational and financial performance of the Divestment Business in the relevant period;
    • Any issues or problems which have arisen in the execution of the obligations as Monitoring Trustee, in particular any issues of non-compliance by [X] or the Divestment Business with the Conditions and Obligations;
    • Monitoring of the preservation of the economic viability, marketability and competitiveness of the Divestment Business and of [X's] compliance with the holdseparate and ringfencing obligations as well as monitoring of the splitting of assets and of the allocation of Personnel between the Divestment Business and the businesses retained by [X] or Affiliated Undertakings;
    • Review and assessment of the progress of the divestiture process, including reporting on potential purchasers and all other information received from [X] regarding the divestiture;
    • Any particular issues as set out in the Work-Plan;
    • Estimated future timetable, including the date of next anticipated reporting;
    • A proposal for a detailed Work-Plan in the first report as well as revisions in subsequent reports.

15. In the Trustee Divestiture Period, within 15 days after the end of every month, the Divestiture Trustee shall provide to the Commission, with a simultaneous copy to the Monitoring Trustee and a non-confidential copy to [X], a comprehensive report written in [*Indicate the language*] on the discharge of its obligations under the Mandate and the progress of the divestiture process, covering in particular the following information:

    • List of potential purchasers and a preliminary assessment of each of them;
    • State of negotiations with potential purchasers;
    • Any issues or problems regarding the sale of the Divestment Business, including any issues and problems regarding the negotiation of the necessary agreement(s);
    • Need for advisers for the sale of the Divestment Business and a list of advisers selected by the Trustee for this purpose;
    • Any particular issues as set out in the Work-Plan;
    • A proposal for a detailed Work-Plan in the first report as well as revisions in subsequent reports.

16. At any time, the Trustee will provide to the Commission, at its request (or on the Trustee's own initiative), a written or oral report on matters falling within the Trustee's Mandate. [X] shall receive simultaneously a non-confidential copy of such additional written reports and shall be informed promptly of the non-confidential content of any oral reports.

Section G. Duties and Obligations of [X]

17. [X] shall provide and shall cause its advisors to provide the Trustee with all such cooperation, assistance and information as the Trustee may reasonably require to perform its tasks. The Trustee shall have full and complete access to any of [X's] or the Divestment Business' books, records, documents, management or other personnel, facilities, sites and technical information necessary for fulfilling its duties under the Mandate and [X] and the Divestment Business shall provide the Trustee upon request with copies of any document. [X] and the Divestment Business shall make available to the Trustee one or more offices on their premises

and shall be available for meetings in order to provide the Trustee with all information necessary for the performance of its tasks.

18. [X] shall provide the Monitoring Trustee with all managerial and administrative support that it may reasonably request on behalf of the management of the Divestment Business. This shall include all administrative support functions relating to the Divestment Business which are currently carried out at headquarters level. [X] shall provide and shall cause its advisors to provide the Monitoring Trustee, on request, with access to the information submitted to potential purchasers, in particular to the data room documentation and all other information granted to potential purchasers in the due diligence procedure. [X] shall inform the Monitoring Trustee on possible purchasers, submit a list of potential purchasers, and keep the Monitoring Trustee informed of all developments in the divestiture process. Once a purchaser has been chosen, [X] shall submit the fully documented and reasoned proposal, including a copy of the final agreement(s), to the Monitoring Trustee and allow the Monitoring Trustee to have confidential contacts with the proposed purchaser in order for the Monitoring Trustee to determine whether or not, in its opinion, it meets the Purchaser Criteria.

19. At the expense of [X], the Trustee may appoint advisors (in particular for corporate finance or legal advice), subject to [X's] approval (this approval not to be unreasonably withheld or delayed) if the Trustee considers the appointment of such advisors necessary or appropriate for the performance of its duties and obligations under the Mandate, provided that any fees and other expenses incurred by the Trustee are reasonable. Should [X] refuse to approve the advisors proposed by the Trustee, the Commission may, after having heard [X], approve the appointment of such advisors instead. Only the Trustee shall be entitled to issue instructions to the advisors. Paragraph 25 of this Mandate shall apply to the advisors mutatis mutandis. In the Trustee Divestiture Period, the Divestiture Trustee may use advisors who served [X] during the First Divestiture Period if the Divestiture Trustee considers this in the best interest of an expedient sale.

Section H.   Trustee Related Provisions

Conflict of Interests

20. The Trustee's, the Trustee Team's and the Trustee Partner Firms' current relationships with [X] and Affiliated Undertakings are disclosed in Annex [•] to this Mandate. On this basis, the Trustee confirms that, as of the date of this Mandate, the Trustee and each member of the Trustee Team is independent of [X] and Affiliated Undertakings and has no conflict of interest that impairs the Trustee's objectivity and independence in discharging its duties under the Mandate ('***Conflict of Interest***').

21. The Trustee undertakes not to create a Conflict of Interest during the term of the Mandate. The Trustee, members of the Trustee Team and the Trustee Partner Firms may therefore not during the term of this Mandate:

    (a) Have or accept any employment by or be or accept any appointment as Member of the Board or member of other management bodies of the Parties or Affiliated Undertakings other than appointments pertaining to the establishment and performance of the Mandate;

    (b) Have or accept any assignments or other business relationships with or financial interests in the Parties or Affiliated Undertakings that might lead to a Conflict of Interest. This affects neither assignments or other business relationships between the Trustee or Trustee Partner Firms and the Parties or Affiliated Undertakings nor investments by the Trustee or Trustee Partner Firms in the stock or securities of the Parties or Affiliated Undertakings if such assignments, business relationships or investments are in the normal course of business and are material neither to the Trustee or the Trustee Partner Firms nor to the undertaking concerned.

1351

Should the Trustee, the Trustee Partner Firms or members of the Trustee Team wish to undertake an assignment, business relationship or investment, such a person must seek the prior approval of the Commission. Should the Trustee become aware of a Conflict of Interest, the Trustee shall promptly inform [X] and the Commission, of such Conflict of Interest. In the event that [X] becomes aware that the Trustee or the Trustee Partner Firms have or may have a Conflict of Interest, [X] shall promptly notify the Trustee and the Commission, of such Conflict of Interest. Where a Conflict of Interest occurs during the term of the Mandate the Trustee undertakes to resolve it immediately. In case the Conflict of Interest cannot be resolved or is not resolved by the Trustee in a timely manner, the Mandate may be terminated in accordance with paragraph 30 below.

22. [*It is up to the Mandate Parties to insert suitable provisions regarding conflict of interests of the Trustee and the Trustee Partner Firms with (potential) purchasers.*]

23. The Trustee undertakes that, during the term of the Mandate and for a period of one year following termination of the Mandate, members of the Trustee Team shall not provide services to the Parties or Affiliated Undertakings without first obtaining the Commission's prior approval. Moreover, the Trustee undertakes to establish measures to ensure the independence and integrity of the Trustee Team and the Trustee's employees and agents directly assigned to the Trustee Team ('*Assigned Persons*') during the term of the Mandate and for a period of one year following termination of the Mandate, from any undue influence that might interfere with or in any way compromise the Trustee Team in the performance of its duties under the Mandate. In particular:

    (a) Access to confidential information shall be limited to the Trustee Team and Assigned Persons; and

    (b) The Trustee Team and Assigned Persons shall be prohibited from communicating any information relating to this Mandate to any other of the Trustee's personnel, except for information of a general nature (e.g. Trustee's appointment, fees, etc.), and except for information whose disclosure is required by law.

Remuneration

24. [*It is up to the Mandate Parties to agree on a suitable fee structure. As set out in the Standard Commitments Text, the Trustee shall be remunerated in such a way that it does not impede its independence and effectiveness in fulfilling the Mandate. Regarding the Divestiture Trustee, the Commission is in favour of fee structures that, at least to a significant part, are contingent on the Divestiture Trustee's accomplishing a timely divestiture. In particular, if the remuneration package includes a success premium linked to the final sale value of the Divestment Business, the fee should also be linked to a divestiture within the Trustee Divestiture Period as specified in the Commitments. It should be noted that the fee structure—as well as the entire Mandate—is subject to the Commission's approval.*]

Indemnity

25. [X] shall indemnify the Trustee and its employees and agents (each an '*Indemnified Party*') and hold each Indemnified Party harmless against, and hereby agrees that an Indemnified Party shall have no liability to [X] for any liabilities arising out of the performance of the Mandate, except to the extent that such liabilities result from the wilful default, recklessness, gross negligence or bad faith of the Trustee, its employees, agents or advisors.

Confidentiality

26. [*It is up to the Mandate Parties to agree a suitable confidentiality provision prohibiting the use, or disclosure to anyone other than the Commission of any sensitive or proprietary information gained as a result of performing the Trustee role. As a matter of course, the Mandate cannot limit the disclosure of information by the Trustee vis-à-vis the Commission. However, the Trustee must not*

disclose certain information gained as a result of the Trustee role to the Parties. This in particular applies to information gained on the Divestment Business to which the ring-fencing provisions apply and to information received from (potential) purchasers of the Divestment Business.]

Section I. Termination of the Mandate

27. The Mandate may only be terminated under the conditions set out in paragraphs 28–31.

Regular Termination of the Mandate

28. The Mandate shall automatically terminate if the Commission approves the discharge in writing of the Trustee from its obligations under this Mandate. The approval of the discharge of the Trustee may be requested after the Trustee has completed the performance of its obligations under the Mandate.

29. The Mandate Parties acknowledge that the Commission may at any time request the reappointment of the Trustee by [X] if it subsequently appears that the Conditions and Obligations might not have been fully and properly implemented. The Trustee hereby accepts such a reappointment in accordance with the terms and conditions of this Mandate.

Termination of the Mandate before the Discharge

30. [X] may only terminate the Mandate before the discharge of the Trustee in accordance with paragraph 31 of the Commitments. The Trustee may only terminate the Mandate for good cause by giving written notice to [X], with a copy to the Commission. The Trustee shall continue carrying out its functions under the Mandate until it has effected a full handover of all relevant information to a new trustee appointed by [X] pursuant to the procedure laid down in the Commitments.

Surviving Provisions

31. Paragraphs [23]–[26] shall survive the termination of the Mandate.

Section J. Additional Provisions

Amendments to the Mandate

32. The Mandate may only be amended in writing and with the Commission's prior approval. The Mandate Parties agree to amend this Mandate if required by the Commission, after consultation with the Mandate Parties, in order to secure compliance with the Commitments, in particular if the amendment is necessary in order to adapt the Mandate to amendments of the Commitments under the Review Clause.

Governing Law and Dispute Resolution

33. This Mandate shall be governed by, and construed in accordance with, the laws of [*Indicate the state by whose laws the Mandate shall be governed*].

34. In the event that a dispute arises concerning the Mandate Parties' obligations under the Mandate, such dispute shall be submitted to the non-exclusive jurisdiction of the [*Indicate the state whose courts shall have jurisdiction for disputes regarding the Mandate*] courts.

Severability

35. [*It is up to the Mandate Parties to agree on a suitable provision on severability, taking into account the rules under the governing law*].

Notices

36. All notices sent under this Mandate shall be made in writing and be deemed to have been duly given if served by personal delivery upon the party for whom it is intended or the

Commission or delivered by registered or certified mail; return receipt requested, or if sent by fax, upon receipt of oral confirmation that such transmission has been received, to the person at the address set forth below:

If to [X], addressed as follows:

[•]

If to the Trustee, addressed as follows:

[•]

If to the Commission, addressed as follows:

To the attention of the Director
Director of Directorate B
European Commission
Directorate General for Competition
70 rue Joseph II / Jozef II-straat 70
B-1000 Brussels
Ref: Case No COMP/M . . . .
Fax : + 32 2 296 43 01

Or to any such other address or person as the relevant party may from time to time advise by notice in writing given pursuant to this section. The date of receipt of any such notice, request, consent, agreement or approval shall be deemed to be the date of delivery thereof.

[*Indicate place and date*]

_____

By:
Title:

By:
Title:

Annex [•]

Power of Attorney, duly executed, for the exercise of [X's] rights as shareholder (pursuant to paragraph 6 (d) of the Mandate)

Annex [•]

Power of Attorney, duly executed, for the Divestiture Trustee (pursuant to paragraph 12 of the Mandate)

Annex [•]

Disclosure of current relationships between the Trustee, the Trustee Team and the Trustees Partner Firm and [X] and Affiliated Undertakings.

Commission Notice on Case Referral in respect of concentrations

(2005/C 56/02)

(Text with EEA relevance)

1. The purpose of this Notice is to describe in a general way the rationale underlying the case referral system in Article 4(4) and (5), Article 9 and Article 22 of Council Regulation (EC) No 139/2004 of 20 January 2004 on the control of concentrations between undertakings (the EC Merger Regulation)[1] (hereinafter 'the Merger Regulation'), including the recent changes made to the system, to catalogue the legal criteria that must be fulfilled in order for referrals to be possible, and to set out the factors which may be taken into consideration when referrals are decided upon. The Notice also provides practical guidance regarding the mechanics of the referral system, in particular regarding the pre-notification referral mechanism provided for in Article 4(4) and (5) of the Merger Regulation. The guidance provided in this notice applies, *mutatis mutandis*, to the referral rules contained in the EEA Agreement.[2]

1. INTRODUCTION

2. Community jurisdiction in the field of merger control is defined by the application of the turnover-related criteria contained in Articles 1(2) and 1(3) of the Merger Regulation. When dealing with concentrations, the Commission and Member States do not have concurrent jurisdiction. Rather, the Merger Regulation establishes a clear division of competence. Concentrations with a 'Community dimension', i.e. those above the turnover thresholds in Article 1 of the Merger Regulation, fall within the exclusive jurisdiction of the Commission; Member States are precluded from applying national competition law to such concentrations by virtue of Article 21 of the Merger Regulation. Concentrations falling below the thresholds remain within the competence of the Member States; the Commission has no jurisdiction to deal with them under the Merger Regulation.

3. Determining jurisdiction exclusively by reference to fixed turnover-related criteria provides legal certainty for merging companies. While the financial criteria generally serve as effective proxies for the category of transactions for which the Commission is the more appropriate authority, Regulation (EEC) No 4064/89 complemented this 'bright-line' jurisdictional scheme with a possibility for cases to be re-attributed by the Commission to Member States and vice versa, upon request and provided certain criteria were fulfilled.

4. When Regulation (EEC) No 4064/89 was first introduced, it was envisaged by the Council and Commission that case referrals would only be resorted to in 'exceptional circumstances' and where 'the interests in respect of competition of the Member State concerned could not

---

[1] OJ L24, 29.1.2004, p 1. This Reg has recast Council Reg (EEC) No 4064/89 of 21 December 1989 on the control of concentrations between undertakings (OJ L395, 30.12.1989, p 1. Corrected version in OJ L257, 21.9.1990, p 13).

[2] See EEA Joint Committee Decision No 78/2004 of 8 June 2004 (OJ L219, 8.6.2004, p 13).

be adequately protected in any other way'.[3] There have, however, been a number of developments since the adoption of Regulation (EEC) No 4064/89. First, merger control laws have been introduced in almost all Member States. Second, the Commission has exercised its discretion to refer a number of cases to Member States pursuant to Article 9 in circumstances where it was felt that the Member State in question was in a better position to carry out the investigation than the Commission.[4] Likewise, in a number of cases,[5] several Member States decided to make a joint referral of a case pursuant to Article 22 in circumstances where it was felt that the Commission was the authority in a better position to carry out the investigation.[6] Third, there has been an increase in the number of transactions not meeting the thresholds in Article 1 of the Merger Regulation which must be filed in multiple Member State jurisdictions, a trend which is likely to continue in line with the Community's growing membership. Many of these transactions affect competition beyond the territories of individual Member States.[7]

5. The revisions made to the referral system in the Merger Regulation are designed to facilitate the re-attribution of cases between the Commission and Member States, consistent with the principle of subsidiarity, so that the more appropriate authority or authorities for carrying out a particular merger investigation should in principle deal with the case. At the same time, the revisions are intended to preserve the basic features of the Community merger control system introduced in 1989, in particular the provision of a 'one-stop-shop' for the competition scrutiny of mergers with a cross-border impact and an alternative to multiple merger control notifications within the Community.[8] Such multiple filings often entail considerable cost for competition authorities and businesses alike.

6. The case re-attribution system now provides that a referral may also be triggered before a formal filing has been made in any Member State jurisdiction, thereby affording merging companies the possibility of ascertaining, at as early as possible a stage, where jurisdiction for scrutiny of their transaction will ultimately lie. Such pre-notification referrals have the advantage of alleviating the additional cost, notably in terms of time delay, associated with post-filing referral.

7. The revisions made to the referral system in Regulation (EC) No. 139/2004 were motivated by a desire that it should operate as a jurisdictional mechanism which is flexible[9] but which at the same time ensures effective protection of competition and limits the scope for 'forum shopping' to the greatest extent possible. However, having regard in particular to the importance of legal certainty, it should be stressed that referrals remain a derogation from the general rules which determine jurisdiction based upon objectively determinable turnover thresholds. Moreover, the Commission and Member States retain a considerable margin of discretion in

---

[3] See the Notes on Council Reg (EEC) No 4064/89 ['Merger Control in the European union', European Commission, Brussels-Luxembourg, 1998, at p 54]. See also Case T-119/02 *Philips v Commission* [2003] ECR II-1433 (Case M.2621 *SEB/Moulinex*) at para 354.

[4] It is a fact that some concentrations of Community dimension affect competition in national or sub-national markets within one or more Member States.

[5] M.2698 *Promatech/Sulzer*, M.2738 *GE/Unison*, M.3136 *GE/AGFA*.

[6] In the same vein, Member States' competition authorities, in the context of the European Competition Authorities' association, have issued a recommendation designed to provide guidance as to the principles upon which national competition authorities should deal with cases eligible for joint referrals under Art 22 of the Merger Reg —*Principles on the application, by National Competition Authorities within the ECA network, of Art 22 of the EC Merger Reg.*

[7] While the introduction of Art 1(3) in 1997 has brought some such cases under the jurisdiction of the Merger Reg, many are unaffected. See para 21 et seq of the Commission's Green Paper of 11 December 2001 (COM(2001) 745 final).

[8] See Recitals 11, 12 and 14 to the Merger Reg.

[9] See Recital 11 to the Merger Reg.

deciding whether to refer cases falling within their 'original jurisdiction', or whether to accept to deal with cases not failing within their 'original jurisdiction', pursuant to Article 4(4) and (5), Article 9(2)(a) and Article 22.[10] To that extent, the current Notice is intended to provide no more than general guidance regarding the appropriateness of particular cases or categories of cases for referral.

II. REFERRAL OF CASES

Guiding principles

8. The system of merger control established by the Merger Regulation, including the mechanism for re-attributing cases between the Commission and Member States contained therein, is consistent with the principle of subsidiarity enshrined in the EC Treaty.[11] Decisions taken with regard to the referral of cases should accordingly take due account of all aspects of the application of the principle of subsidiarity in this context, in particular which is the authority more appropriate for carrying out the investigation, the benefits inherent in a 'one-stop-shop' system, and the importance of legal certainty with regard to jurisdiction.[12] These factors are inter-linked and the respective weight placed upon each of them will depend upon the specificties of a particular case. Above all, in considering whether or not to exercise their discretion to make or accede to a referral, the Commission and Member States should bear in mind the need to ensure effective protection of competition in all markets affected by the transaction.[13]

More appropriate authority

9. In principle, jurisdiction should only be re-attributed to another competition authority in circumstances where the latter is the more appropriate for dealing with a merger, having regard to the specific characteristics of the case as well as the tools and expertise available to the authority. Particular regard should be had to the likely locus of any impact on competition resulting from the merger. Regard may also be had to the implications, in terms of administrative effort, of any contemplated referral.[14]

10. The case for re-attributing jurisdiction is likely to be more compelling where it appears that a particular transaction may have a significant impact on competition and thus may deserve careful scrutiny.

---

[10] See, however, *infra*, n 14. It should moreover be noted that, pursuant to Art 4(5), the Commission has no discretion as to whether or not to accept a case not falling within its original jurisdiction.

[11] See Art 5 of the EC Treaty.

[12] See Recitals 11 and 14 to the Merger Reg.

[13] See Art 9(8) of the Merger Reg; see also *Philips v Commission* (para 343) where the Court of First Instance of the European Communities states that '. . . although the first subpara of Art 9(3) of Reg (EEC) No 4064/89 confers on the Commission broad discretion as to whether or not to refer a concentration, it cannot decide to make such a referral if, when the Member State's request for referral is examined, it is clear, on the basis of a body of precise and coherent evidence, that such a referral cannot safeguard effective competition on the relevant market'; see also T-346/02 and T-347/02 *Cableuropa SA v Commission* of 30 September 2003, case not yet reported (para 215). Circumstances relevant for the purpose of the Commission assessment include, *inter alia*, the fact that a Member State: (i) has specific laws for the control of concentrations on competition grounds and specialised bodies to ensure that these laws are implemented under the supervision of the national courts; (ii) has accurately identified the competition concerns raised by the concentration on the relevant markets in that Member State (see paras 346–347 of *Philips v Commission*, cited above).

[14] This may involve consideration of the relative cost, time delay, legal uncertainty and the risk of conflicting assessment which may be associated with the investigation, or a part of the investigation, being carried out by multiple authorities.

One-stop-shop

11. Decisions on the referral of cases should also have regard to the benefits inherent in a 'one-stop-shop', which is at the core of the Merger Regulation.[15] The provision of a one-stop-shop is beneficial to competition authorities and businesses alike. The handling of a merger by a single competition authority normally increases administrative efficiency, avoiding duplication and fragmentation of enforcement effort as well as potentially incoherent treatment (regarding investigation, assessment and possible remedies) by multiple authorities. It normally also brings advantages to businesses, in particular to merging firms, by reducing the costs and burdens arising from multiple filing obligations and by eliminating the risk of conflicting decisions resulting from the concurrent assessment of the same transaction by a number of competition authorities under diverse legal regimes.

12. Fragmentation of cases through referral should therefore be avoided where possible,[16] unless it appears that multiple authorities would be in a better position to ensure that competition in all markets affected by the transaction is effectively protected. Accordingly, while partial referrals are possible under Article 4(4) and Article 9, it would normally be appropriate for the whole of a case (or at least all connected parts thereof) to be dealt with by a single authority.[17]

Legal certainty

13. Due account should also be taken of the importance of legal certainty regarding jurisdiction over a particular concentration, from the perspective of all concerned.[18] Accordingly, referral should normally only be made when there is a compelling reason for departing from 'original jurisdiction' over the case in question, particularly at the post-notification stage. Similarly, if a referral has been made prior to notification, a post-notification referral in the same case should be avoided to the greatest extent possible.[19]

14. The importance of legal certainty should also be borne in mind with regard to the legal criteria for referral, and particularly—given the tight deadlines—at the pre-notification stage. Accordingly, pre-filing referrals should in principle be confined to those cases where it is relatively straightforward to establish, from the outset, the scope of the geographic market and/or the existence of a possible competitive impact, so as to be able to promptly decide upon such requests.

Case referrals: legal requirements and other factors to be considered

Pre-notification referrals

15. The system of pre-notification referrals is triggered by a reasoned submission lodged by the parties to the concentration. When contemplating such a request, the parties to the concentration are required, first, to verify whether the relevant legal requirements set out in the

---

[15] See Recital 11 of the Merger Reg.

[16] The Court of First Instance in *Philips v Commission* took the view, *obiter dictum*, that 'fragmentation' of cases, while possible as a result of the application of Art 9, is 'undesirable in view of the "one-stop-shop" principle on which Reg (EEC) No 4064/89 is based'. Moreover, the Court, while recognising that the risk of 'inconsistent, or even irreconcilable' decisions by the Commission and Member States' is inherent in the referral system established by Art 9, made it clear that this is not, in its view, desirable. (See paras 350 and 380).

[17] This is consistent with the Commission's decision in cases M.2389 *Shell/DEA* and M.2533 *BP/E.ON* to refer to Germany all of the markets for downstream oil products. The Commission retained the parts of the cases involving upstream markets. Likewise, in M.2706 *P&O Princess/Carnival*, the Commission exercised its discretion not to refer a part of the case to the United Kingdom, because it wished to avoid a fragmentation of the case (See Commission press release of 11.4.2002, IP/02/552)

[18] See Recital 11 of the Merger Reg.

[19] See Recital 14 to the Merger Reg. This is of course subject to the parties having made a full and honest disclosure of all relevant facts in their request for a pre-filing referral.

Merger Regulation are fulfilled, and second, whether a pre-notification referral would be consistent with the guiding principles outlined above.

Referral of cases by the Commission to Member States under Article 4(4)

Legal requirements

16. In order for a referral to be made by the Commission to one or more Member States pursuant to Articles 4(4), two legal requirements must be fulfilled:

    (i)   there must be indications *that the concentration may significantly affect competition* in a market or markets;

    (ii) the market(s) in question must be within a Member State and *present all the characteristics of a distinct market.*

17. As regards the *first criterion*, the requesting parties are in essence required to demonstrate that the transaction is liable to have a potential impact on competition on a distinct market in a Member State, which may prove to be significant, thus deserving close scrutiny. Such indications may be no more than preliminary in nature, and would be without prejudice to the outcome of the investigation. While the parties are not required to demonstrate that the effect on competition is likely to be an adverse one,[20] they should point to indicators which are generally suggestive of the existence of some competitive effects stemming from the transaction.[21]

18. As regards the *second criterion*, the requesting parties are required to show that a geographic market in which competition is affected by the transaction in the manner just described (paragraph 17) is national, or narrower than national in scope.[22]

Other factors to be considered

19. Other than verification of the legal requirements, in order to anticipate to the greatest extent possible the likely outcome of a referral request, merging parties contemplating a request should also consider whether referral of the case is likely to be considered appropriate. This will involve an examination of the application of the guiding principles referred to above (paragraphs 8 to 14), and in particular whether the competition authority or authorities to which they are contemplating requesting the referral of the case is the most appropriate authority for dealing with the case. To this end, consideration should be given in turn both to the likely locus of the competitive effects of the transaction and to how appropriate the national competition authority (NCA) would be for scrutinising the operation.

20. Concentrations with a Community dimension which are likely to affect competition in markets that have a national or narrower than national scope, and the effects of which are likely to be confined to, or have their main economic impact in, a single Member State,[23] are

---

[20] See Recital 16, which states that 'the undertakings concerned should not . . . be required to demonstrate that the effects of the concentration would be detrimental to competition'.

[21] The existence of 'affected markets' within the meaning of Form RS would generally be considered sufficient to meet the requirements of Art 4(4). However, the parties can point to any factors which may be relevant for the competitive analysis of the case (market overlap, vertical integration, etc).

[22] To this end, the requesting parties should consider those factors which are typically suggestive of national or narrower than national markets, such as, primarily, the product characteristics (e.g. low value of the product as opposed to significant costs of transport), specific characteristics of demand (e.g. end consumers sourcing in proximity to their centre of activity) and supply, significant variation of prices and market shares across countries, national consumer habits, different regulatory frameworks, taxation or other legislation. Further guidance can be found in the Commission Notice on the definition of the relevant market for the purposes of Community competition law (OJ C372, 9.12.1997, p 5).

[23] See, for example, the Commission's referral of certain distinct oil storage markets for assessment by the French authorities in Cases M.1021 *Compagnie Nationale de Navigation-SOGELF*, M.1464 *Total/Petrofina*, and Case M.1628 *Totalfina/Elf Aquitaine*, Case M.1030 *Lafarge/Redland*, Case M.1220 *Alliance Unichem/Unifarma*, Case M.2760 *Nehlsen/Rethmann/SWB/Bremerhavner Energiewirtschaft*, and Case M.2154 *C3D/Rhone/Go-ahead*; Case M.2845 *Sogecable/Canal Satelite Digital/Vias Digital*.

the most appropriate candidate cases for referral to that Member State. This applies in particular to cases where the impact would occur on a distinct market which does not constitute a substantial part of the common market. To the extent that referral is made to one Member State only, the benefit of a 'one-stop-shop' is also preserved.

21. The extent to which a concentration with a Community dimension which, despite having a potentially significant impact on competition in a nation-wide market, nonetheless potentially engenders substantial cross-border effects (e.g. because the effects of the concentration in one geographic market may have significant repercussions in geographic markets in other Member States, or because it may involve potential foreclosure effects and consequent fragmentation of the common market,[24]) may be an appropriate candidate for referral will depend on the specific circumstances of the case. As both the Commission and Member States may be equally well equipped or be in an equally good position to deal with such cases, a considerable margin of discretion should be retained in deciding whether or not to refer such cases.

22. The extent to which concentrations with a Community dimension, and potentially affecting competition in a series of national or narrower than national markets in more than one Member State, may be appropriate candidates for referral to Member States will depend on factors specific to each individual case, such as the number of national markets likely to be significantly affected, the prospect of addressing any possible concerns by way of proportionate, non-conflicting remedies, and the investigative efforts that the case may require. To the extent that a case may engender competition concerns in a number of Member States, and require coordinated investigations and remedial action, this may militate in favour of the Commission retaining jurisdiction over the entirety of the case in question.[25] On the other hand, to the extent that the case gives rise to competition concerns which, despite involving national markets in more than one Member State, do not appear to require coordinated investigation and/or remedial action, a referral may be appropriate. In a limited number of cases,[26] the Commission has even found it appropriate to refer a concentration to more than one Member State, in view of the significant differences in competitive conditions that characterised the affected markets in the Member States concerned. While fragmentation of the treatment of a case deprives the merging parties of the benefit of a one-stop-shop in such cases, this consideration is less pertinent at the pre-notification stage, given that the referral is triggered by a voluntary request from the merging parties.

23. Consideration should also, to the extent possible, be given to whether the NCA(s) to which referral of the case is contemplated may possess specific expertise concerning local

---

[24] See Case M.580 *ABB/Daimler Benz*, where the Commission did not accede to Germany's request for referral of a case under Art 9 in circumstances where, while the competition concerns were confined to German markets, the operation (which would create the largest supplier of railway equipment in the world) would have significant repercussions throughout Europe. See also Case M.2434 *Hidroelectrica del Cantabrico/EnBW/Grupo Vilar Mir*, where, despite a request by Spain to have the case referred under Art 9, the Commission pursued the investigation and adopted a decision pursuant to Art 8(2).

[25] For some examples, see M.1383 *Exxon/Mobil*, where the Commission, despite the United Kingdom request to have the part of the concentration relating to the market for motor fuel retailing in North west of Scotland referred to it, pursued the investigation as the case required a single and coherent remedy package designed to address all the problematic issues in the sector concerned; see also M.2706 *P&O Princess/Carnival*, where, despite the fact that the UK authorities were assessing a rival bid by Royal Caribbean, the Commission did not accede to a request for a partial referral, so as to avoid a fragmentation of the case and secure a single investigation of the various national markets affected by the operation.

[26] See M. 2898, *Le Roy Merlin/Brico*, M.1030, *Redland/Lafarge*, M. 1684, *Carrefour/Promodes*.

26. Notice on case referral

markets,[27] or be examining, or about to examine, another transaction in the sector concerned.[28]

Referral of cases from Member States to the Commission under Article 4(5)

Legal requirements

24. Under Article 4(5), only two legal requirements must be met in order for the parties to the transaction to request the referral of the case to the Commission: the transaction must be a concentration within the meaning of Article 3 of the Merger Regulation, and the concentration must be *capable of being reviewed under the national competition laws for the control of mergers of at least three Member States* (see also paragraphs 65 *et seq* and 70 *et seq*).

Other factors to be considered

25. Other than verification of the legal requirements, in order to anticipate to the greatest extent possible the likely outcome of a referral request, merging parties contemplating a request should also consider whether referral of the case is likely to be considered appropriate. This will involve an examination of the application of the guiding principles referred to above, and in particular whether the Commission is the more appropriate authority for dealing with the case.

26. In this regard, Recital 16 to the Merger Regulation states that 'requests for pre-notification referrals to the Commission would be particularly pertinent in situations where the concentration would affect competition beyond the territory of one Member State.' Particular consideration should therefore be given to the likely locus of any competitive effects resulting from the transaction, and to how appropriate it would be for the Commission to scrutinise the operation.

27. It should in particular be assessed whether the case is genuinely cross-border in nature, having regard to elements such as its likely effects on competition and the investigative and enforcement powers likely to be required to address any such effects. In this regard, particular consideration should be given to whether the case is liable to have a potential impact on competition in one or more markets affected by the concentration. In any case, indications of possible competitive impact may be no more than preliminary in nature,[29]

---

[27] In Case M.330 *MacCormick/CPC/Rabobank/Ostmann*, the Commission referred a case to Germany, because it was better placed to investigate local conditions in 85,000 sales points in Germany; a referral to the Netherlands was made in Case M.1060 *Vendex/KBB*, because it was better placed to assess local consumer tastes and habits; See also Case M.1555 *Heineken/Cruzcampo*, Case M.2621 *SEB/Moulinex* (where consumer preferences and commercial and marketing practice swere specific to the French market); Case M.2639 *Compass/Restorama/Rail Gourmet/Gourmet*, and Case M.2662 *Danish-Crown/Steff-Houlberg*.

[28] In Case M.716 *Gehe/Lloyds Chemists*, for example, the Commission referred a case because Lloyds was also subject to another bid not falling under ECMR thresholds but being scrutinised by the UK authorities: the referral allowed both bids to be scrutinised by the same authority; in M.1001/M.1019 *Preussag/Hapag-Lloyd/TUI*, a referral was made to Germany of two transactions, which together with a third one notified in Germany, would present competition concerns: the referral ensured that all three operations were dealt with in like manner; in case M.2044 *Interbrew/Bass*, the Commission referred the case to the UK authorities, because they were at the same time assessing Interbrew's acquisition of another brewer, Whitbread, and because of their experience in recent investigations in the same markets; similarly, see also Cases M.2760 *Nehlsen/Rethmann/SWB/Bremerhavener Energiewirtschaft*, M.2234 *Metsalilitto Osuuskunta/Vapo Oy/JV* M.2495 *Haniel/Fels*, M.2881 *Koninklijke BAM NBM/HBG*, and M.2857/M.3075–3080 *ECS/IEH* and six other acquisitions by Electrabel of local distributors. In M.2706 *P&O Princess/Carnival*, however, despite the fact that the UK authorities were already assessing a rival bid by Royal Caribbean, the Commission did not accede to a request for a partial referral. The Commission had identified preliminary competition concerns in other national markets affected by the merger and thus wished to avoid a fragmentation of the case (See Commission press release of 11.4.2002, IP/02/552).

[29] The existence of 'affected markets' within the meaning of Form RS would generally be considered sufficient. However, the parties can point to any factors which may be relevant for the competitive analysis of the case (market overlap, vertical integration, etc).

and would be without prejudice to the outcome of the investigation. Nor would it be necessary for the parties to demonstrate that the effect on competition is likely to be an adverse one.

28. Cases where the market(s) in which there may be a potential impact on competition is/are wider than national in geographic scope[30] or where some of the potentially affected markets are wider than national and the main economic impact of the concentration is connected to such markets, are the most appropriate candidate cases for referral to the Commission. In such cases, as the competitive dynamics extend over territories reaching beyond national boundaries, and may consequently require investigative efforts in several countries as well as appropriate enforcement powers, the Commission is likely to be in the best position to carry out the investigation.

29. The Commission may be more appropriately placed to treat cases (including investigation, assessment and possible remedial action) that give rise to potential competition concerns in a series of national or narrower than national markets located in a number of different Member States.[31] The Commission is likely to be in the best position to carry out the investigation in such cases, given the desirability of ensuring consistent and efficient scrutiny across the different countries, of employing appropriate investigative powers, and of addressing any competition concerns by way of coherent remedies.

30. Similarly to what has been said above in relation to Article 4(4), the appropriateness of referring concentrations which, despite having a potentially significant impact on competition in a nation-wide market, nonetheless potentially engender substantial cross-border effects, will depend on the specific circumstances of the case. As both the Commission and Member States may be in an equally good position to deal with such cases, a considerable margin of discretion should be retained in deciding whether or not to refer such cases.

31. Consideration should also, to the extent possible, be given to whether the Commission is particularly well equipped to properly scrutinize the case, in particular having regard to factors such as specific expertise, or past experience in the sector concerned. The greater a merger's potential to affect competition beyond the territory of one Member State, the more likely it is that the Commission will be better equipped to conduct the investigation, particularly in terms of fact finding and enforcement powers.

32. Finally, the parties to the concentration might submit that, despite the apparent absence of an effect on competition, there is a compelling case for having the operation treated by the Commission, having regard in particular to factors such as the cost and time delay involved in submitting multiple Member State filings.[32]

Post-notification referrals

Referrals from the Commission to Member States pursuant to Article 9

33. Under Article 9 there are two options for a Member State wishing to request referral of a case following its notification to the Commission: Articles 9(2)(a) and 9(2)(b) respectively.

---

[30] See the joint referral by seven Member States to the Commission of a transaction affecting worldwide markets in M. 2738 *GE/Unison*, and the joint referral by seven Member States to the Commission of a transaction affecting a Western European market in M.2698 *Promatech/Sulzer*. See also *Principles on the application, by National Competition Authorities within the ECA network, of Art 22 of the EC Merger Reg*, a paper published by the European Competition Authorities (ECA), at para 11.

[31] This may, for example, be the case in relation to operations where the affected markets, while national (or even narrower than national in scope for the purposes of a competition assessment), are nonetheless characterised by common Europe-wide or world-wide brands, by common Europe-wide or world-wide intellectual property rights, or by centralised manufacture or distribution – at least to the extent that such centralised manufacture or distribution would be likely to impact upon any remedial measures.

[32] See Recitals 12 and 16 of the Merger Reg.

Article 9(2)(a)

Legal requirements

34. In order for a referral to be made to a Member State or States pursuant to Article 9(2)(a), the following legal requirements must be fulfilled:

    (i)   the concentration must *threaten to affect significantly competition in a market*; and

    (ii) the market in question must be *within the requesting Member State, and present all the characteristics of a distinct market.*

35. As regard the *first criterion*, in essence a requesting Member State is required to demonstrate that, based on a preliminary analysis, there is a real risk that the transaction may have a significant adverse impact on competition, and thus that it deserves close scrutiny. Such preliminary indications may be in the nature of *prima facie* evidence of such a possible significant adverse impact, but would be without prejudice to the outcome of a full investigation.

36. As regards the *second criterion*, the Member State is required to show that a geographic market(s) in which competition is affected by the transaction in the manner just described (paragraph 35) is/are national, or narrower than national in scope.[33]

Other factors to be considered

37. Other than verification of the legal requirements, other factors should also be considered in assessing whether referral of a case is likely to be considered appropriate. This will involve an examination of the application of the guiding principles referred to above, and in particular whether the competition authority or authorities requesting the referral of the case is/are in the best position to deal with the case. To this end, consideration should be given in turn both to the likely locus of the competitive effects of the transaction and to how well equipped the NCA would be to scrutinise the operation (see above at paragraphs 19–23)

Article 9(2)(b)

Legal requirements

38. In order for a referral to be made to a Member State or States pursuant to Article 9(2)(b), the following legal requirements must be fulfilled:

    (i)   the concentration *must affect competition in a market*; and

    (ii) the market in question must be *within the requesting Member State, present all the characteristics of a distinct market, and must not constitute a substantial part of the common market.*

39. As regards the *first criterion*, a requesting Member State is required to show, based on a preliminary analysis, that the concentration is liable to have an impact on competition in a market. Such preliminary indications may be in the nature of *prima facie* evidence of a possible adverse impact, but would be without prejudice to the outcome of a full investigation.

40. As to the *second criterion*, a requesting Member State is required to show not only that the market in which competition is affected by the operation in the manner just described (paragraph 38) constitutes a distinct market within a Member State, but also that the market in question does not constitute a substantial part of the common market. In this respect,

---

[33] See Commission notice on the definition of relevant market for the purposes of Community competition law (OJ C372, 9.12.1997, p 5).

based on the past practice and case-law,[34] it appears that such situations are generally limited to markets with a narrow geographic scope, within a Member State.

41. If these conditions are met, the Commission has an obligation to refer the case.

Referrals from Member States to the Commission pursuant to Article 22

Legal requirements

42. In order for a referral to be made by one or more Member States to the Commission pursuant to Article 22, two legal requirements must be fulfilled:

   (i) the concentration must *affect trade between Member States*; and

   (ii) it must *threaten to significantly affect competition within the territory of the Member State or States making the request.*

43. As to the *first criterion*, a concentration fulfils this requirement to the extent that it is liable to have some discernible influence on the pattern of trade between Member States.[35]

44. As to the *second criterion*, as under Article 9(2)(a), a referring Member State is/are required in essence to demonstrate that, based on a preliminary analysis, there is a real risk that the transaction may have a significant adverse impact on competition, and thus that it deserves close scrutiny. Such preliminary indications may be in the nature of *prima facie* evidence of such a possible significant adverse impact, but would be without prejudice to the outcome of a full investigation.

Other factors to be considered

45. As post-notification referrals to the Commission may entail additional cost and time delay for the merging parties, they should normally be limited to those cases which appear to present a real risk of negative effects on competition and trade between Member States, and where it appears that these would be best addressed at the Community level.[36] The categories

---

[34] See Commission referrals granted under Art 9(2)(b) in: M.2446, *Govia/Connex South Central*, where the operation affected competition on specific railway routes in the London/Gatwick-Brighton area in the United Kingdom; in M.2730, *Connex/DNVBVG*, where the transaction affected competition in local public transport services in the Riesa area (Saxony, Germany); and in M. 3130, *Arla Foods/Express Diaries*, where the transaction affected competition in the market for the supply of bottled milk to doorstep deliverers in the London, Yorkshire and Lancashire regions of the United Kingdom. For the purpose of defining the notion of a non-substantial part of the common market, some guidance can also be found in the case-law relating to the application of Art 82 of EC Treaty. In that context, the Court of Justice has articulated quite a broad notion of what may constitute a substantial part of the common market, resorting *inter alia* to empirical evidence. In the case-law there can be found, for instance, indications essentially based on practical criteria such as 'the pattern and volume of the production and consumption of the said product as well as the habits and economic opportunities of vendors and purchasers', see Case 40/73, *Suiker Unie v Commission*, [1975] ECR 1663. See also Case C-179/90, *Porto di Genova* [1991] ECR 5889, where the Port of Genova was considered as constituting a substantial part of the common market. In its case-law the Court has also stated that a series of separate markets may be regarded as together constituting a substantial part of the common market. See, for example, Case C-323/93, *Centre d'insémination de la Crespelle* [1994] ECR I-5077, para. 17, where the Court stated 'In this case, by making the operation of the insemination centres subject to authorization and providing that each centre should have the exclusive right to serve a defined area, the national legislation granted those centres exclusive rights. By thus establishing, in favour of those under-takings, a contiguous series of monopolies territorially limited but together covering the entire territory of a Member State, those national provisions creat a dominant position, within the meaning of Art 86 of the Treaty, in a substantial part of the common market'.

[35] See also, by analogy, the Commission Notice—Guidelines on the effect on trade concept contained in Arts 81 and 82 of the Treaty (OJ C101, 27.4.2004, p 81).

[36] See the joint referral by seven Member States to the Commission of a transaction affecting worldwide markets in M.2738 *GE/Unison*, and the joint referral by seven Member States to the Commission of a transaction affecting a Western European market in M.2698 *Promatech/Sulzer*. See also *Principles on the application, by National Competition Authorities within the ECA network, of Art 22 of the EC Merger Reg*, a paper published by the European Competition Authorities (ECA), at para 11.

of cases normally most appropriate for referral to the Commission pursuant to Article 22 are accordingly the following:

— cases which give rise to serious competition concerns in one or more markets which are wider than national in geographic scope, or where some of the potentially affected markets are wider than national, and where the main economic impact of the concentration is connected to such markets,

— cases which give rise to serious competition concerns in a series of national or narrower than national markets located in a number of Member States, in circumstances where coherent treatment of the case (regarding possible remedies, but also, in appropriate cases, the investigative efforts as such) is considered desirable, and where the main economic impact of the concentration is connected to such markets.

III. Mechanics of the Referral System

A. Overview of the Referral System

46. The Merger Regulation sets out the relevant legal rules for the functioning of the referral system. The rules contained in Article 4(4) and (5), Article 9 and Article 22 set out in detail the various steps required for a case to be referred from the Commission to Member States and vice versa.

47. Each of the four relevant referral provisions establishes a self-contained mechanism for the referral of a given category of concentration. The provisions can be categorised in the following way:

(a) Pre-notification referrals:
   (i) From the Commission to Member States (Article 4(4))
   (ii) From Member States to the Commission (Article 4(5))
(b) Post-notification referrals:
   (i) From the Commission to Member States (Article 9)
   (ii) From Member States to the Commission (Article 22).

48. The flowcharts in Annex I to this Notice describe in graphical form the various procedural steps to be followed in the referral mechanisms set out in Articles 4(4) and (5), Article 9 and Article 22.

Pre-notification referrals

49. Pre-notification referrals can only be requested by the undertakings concerned.[37] It is for the undertakings concerned to verify whether the concentration meets the criteria specified in Article 4(4) (that the concentration has a Community dimension but may significantly affect competition in a distinct market within a Member State) or Article 4(5) (that the concentration does not have a Community dimension but is capable of being reviewed under the national competition laws of at least three Member States). The undertakings concerned may then decide to request a referral to or from the Commission by submitting a reasoned request on Form RS. The request is transmitted without delay by the Commission to all Member States. The remainder of the process differs under Article 4(4) and Article 4(5).

— Under Article 4(4), the Member State or States concerned[38] have 15 working days from the date they receive the submission to express agreement or disagreement with the

---

[37] The term 'undertakings concerned' includes 'persons' within the meaning of Art 3(1)(b).
[38] The Member State or States concerned are the ones identified in Form RS to which the case will be referred if the request is granted.

request. Silence on the part of a Member State is deemed to constitute agreement.[39] If the Member State or States concerned agree to the referral, the Commission has an additional period of approximately 10 working days (25 working days from the date the Commission received Form RS) in which it may decide to refer the case. Silence on the part of the Commission is deemed to constitute assent. If the Commission assents, the case (or one or more parts thereof) is referred to the Member States or States as requested by the undertakings concerned. If the referral is made, the Member State or States concerned apply their national law to the referred part of the case.[40] Articles 9(6) to 9(9) apply.

— Under Article 4(5), the Member States concerned[41] have 15 working days from the date they receive the submission to express agreement or disagreement with the request. At the end of that period, the Commission checks whether any Member State competent to examine the concentration under its national competition law has expressed disagreement. If there is no expression of disagreement by any such competent Member State, the case is deemed to acquire a Community dimension and is thus referred to the Commission which has exclusive jurisdiction over it. It is then for the parties to notify the case to the Commission, using Form CO. On the other hand, if one or more competent Member States have expressed their disagreement, the Commission informs all Member States and the undertakings concerned without delay of any such expression of disagreement and the referral process ends. It is then for the parties to comply with any applicable national notification rules.

Post-notification referrals

50. Pursuant to Article 9(2) and Article 22(1), post-notification referrals are triggered by Member States either on their own initiative or following an invitation by the Commission pursuant to Article 9(2) and Article 22(5) respectively. The procedures differ according to whether the referral is from or to the Commission.

— Under Article 9, a Member State may request that the Commission refer to it a concentration with Community dimension, or a part thereof, which has been notified to the Commission and which threatens to significantly affect competition within a distinct market within that Member State (Article 9(2)(a)), or which affects such a distinct market not constituting a substantial part of the common market (Article 9(2)(b)). The request must be made within 15 working days from the date the Member State received a

---

[40] Art 4(4) allows merging parties to request partial or full referrals. The Commission and Member States must either accede to or refuse the request, and may not vary its scope by, for example, referring only a part of case when a referral of the whole of the case had been requested. In the case of a partial referral, the Member State concerned will apply its national competition law to the referred part of the case. For the remainder of the case, the Merger Reg will continue to apply in the normal way, that is the undertakings concerned will be obliged to make a notification of the non-referred part of the concentration on Form CO pursuant to Art 4(1) of the Merger Reg. By contrast, if the whole of the case is referred to a Member State, Art 4(4) final subpara specifies that there will be no obligation to notify the case also to the Commission. The case will thus not be examined by the Commission. The Member State concerned will apply its national law to the whole of the case; no other Member State can apply national competition law to the concentration in question.

[39] This mechanism is an essential feature of all referral procedures set out in the Merger Reg. The mechanism may be termed 'positive silence' or non-opposition: that is to say that failure to take a decision on the part of the Commission or a Member State will be deemed to constitute the taking of a positive decision. This mechanism was already a feature of Reg (EEC) No 4064/89, in Art 9(5). It is now included in Art 4(4) (second and fourth sub-paras), Art 4(5) (fourth sub-para), Art 9(5) and Art 22(3) (first sub-para, last sentence) of the Merger Reg. The positive silence mechanism is, however, not applicable with regard to decisions by Member States to join a request under Art 22(2).

[41] That is, those that would be competent to review the case under their national competition law in the absence of a referral. For the concept of 'competent to review the case', see section B5 below.

copy of Form CO. The Commission must first verify whether those legal criteria are mét. It may then decide or refer the case, or a part thereof, exercising its administrative discretion. In the case of a referral request made pursuant to Article 9(2)(b), the Commission must (i.e. has no discretion) make the referral if the legal criteria are met. The decision must be taken within 35 working days from notification or, where the Commission has initiated proceedings, within 65 working days.[42] If the referral is made, the Member State concerned applies its own national competition law, subject only to Article 9(6) and (8).

— Under Article 22, a Member State may request that the Commission examine a concentration which has no Community dimension but which affects trade between Member States and threatens to significantly affect competition within its territory. The request must be made within 15 working days from the date of national notification or, where no notification is required, the date when the concentration was 'made known'[43] to the Member State concerned. The Commission transmits the request to all Member States. Any other Member States can decide to join the request[44] within a period of 15 working days from the date they receive a copy of the initial request. All national time limits relating to the concentration are suspended a decision has been taken as to where it will be examined; a Member State can re-start the national time limits before the expiry of the 15 working day period by informing the Commission and the merging parties that it does not wish to join the request. At the latest 10 working days following the expiry of the 15 working day period, the Commission must decide whether to accept the case from the requesting Member State(s). If the Commission accepts jurisdiction, national proceedings in the referring Member State(s) are terminated and the Commission examines the case pursuant to Article 22(4) of the Merger Regulation on behalf of the requesting State(s).[45] Non-requesting States can continue to apply national law.

51. The following section of the Notice focuses on a number of detailed elements of the system with the aim in particular of providing further guidance to undertakings contemplating making requests at the pre-notification stage, or who may be party to transactions subject to the possibility of post-notification referral.

---

[42] As regards cases where the Commission takes preparatory steps within 65 working days, see Art 9(4)(b) and (5).

[43] The notion of 'made known', derived from the wording of Art 22, should in this context be interpreted as implying sufficient information to make a preliminary assessment as to the existence of the criteria for the making of a referral request pursuant to Art 22.

[44] It should be noted that Art 22 enables a Member State to join the initial request even if the concentration has not yet been notified to it. However, Member States may be unable to do so if they have not yet received the necessary information from the merging parties at the time of being informed by the Commission that a referral request has been lodged by another Member State. Notwithstanding the Member State's ability to contact the merging parties in order to verify whether they are competent to review any particular transaction, the notifying parties are therefore strongly encouraged to file, where feasible, their notification to all competent Member States simultaneously.

[45] Where the Commission examines a concentration on behalf of one or more Member States pursuant to Art 22, it can adopt all the substantive decisions provided for in Arts 6 and 8 of the Merger Reg. This is established in Art 22(4) of that Reg. It is to be noted that the Commission examines the concentration upon the request of and on behalf of the requesting Member States. This provision should therefore be interpreted as requiring the Commission to examine the impact of the concentration within the territory of those Member States. The Commission will not examine the effects of the concentration in the territory of Member States which have not joined the request unless this examination is necessary for the assessment of the effects of the concentration within the territory of the requesting Member States (for example, where the geographic market extends beyond the territory/or territories of the requesting Member State(s).

B. Details of the Referral Mechanism

52. This section of this Notice provides guidance regarding certain aspects of the functioning of the referral system set out in Article 4(4) and(5), Article 9 and Article 22 of the Merger Regulation.

1. The network of competition authorities

53. Article 19(2) of the Merger Regulation provides that the Commission is to carry out the procedures set out in that Regulation in close and constant liaison with the competent authorities of the Member States (the NCAs). Cooperation and dialogue between the Commission and the NCAs, and between the NCAs themselves, is particularly important in the case of concentrations which are subject to the referral system set out in the Merger Regulation.

54. According to Recital 14 to the Merger Regulation, 'the Commission and the NCAs should form together a network of public authorities, applying their respective competences in close cooperation using efficient arrangements for information sharing and consultation with a view to ensuring that a case is dealt with by the most appropriate authority, in the light of the principle of subsidiarity, and with a view to ensuring that multiple notifications of a given concentration are avoided to the greatest extent possible'.

55. The network should ensure the efficient re-attribution of concentrations according to the principles described in section II above. This involves facilitating the smooth operation of the pre-notification referral mechanism, as well as providing, to the extent foreseeable, a system whereby potential post-notification referral requests are identified as soon as possible.[46]

56. Pursuant to Article 4(4) and (5), the Commission must transmit reasoned requests made by the undertakings concerned 'without delay'.[47] The Commission will endeavour to transmit such documents on the working day following that on which they are received or issued. Information within the network will be exchanged by various means, depending on the circumstances: e-mail, surface mail, courier, fax, telephone. It should be noted that for sensitive information or confidential information exchanges will be carried out by secure e-mail or by any other protected means of communication between these contact points.

57. All members of the network, including the Commission and all NCAs, their officials and other servants, and other persons working under the supervision of those authorities as well as officials and civil servants of other authorities of the Member States, will be bound by the professional secrecy obligations set out in Article 17 of the Merger Regulation. They must not disclose non-public information they have acquired through the application of the Merger Regulation, unless the natural or legal person who provided that information has consented to its disclosure.

58. Consultations and exchanges within the network is a matter between public enforcement agencies and do not alter any rights or obligations arising from Community or national law for companies. Each competition authority remains fully responsible for ensuring that due process is observed in the cases it deals with.

---

[46] Advance knowledge of the possibility of a referral request might, for example, be taken into account by the Commission in deciding not to accede to a request for derogation from the suspensive effect pursuant to Art 7(3) of the Merger Reg.

[47] It should be noted that, as provided for in Art 19(1) of the Merger Reg, the Commission is also under an obligation to transmit to the NCAs copies of notifications and of the most important documents lodged with or issued by the Commission.

2. Triggering the pre-notification referral system; information to be provided by the requesting parties

59. For the referral system to work swiftly and smoothly, it is crucial that the requesting parties, provide complete and accurate information, whenever required, in a timely fashion and in the most efficient way possible. Legal requirements concerning the information to be provided and the consequences of providing incorrect, incomplete or misleading information are set out in the Merger Regulation, Regulation (EC) No 802/2004 (hereinafter 'the Merger Implementing Regulation') and Form RS.[48]

60. Form RS states that all information submitted in a reasoned submission must be correct and complete. If parties submit incorrect or incomplete information, the Commission has the power to either adopt a decision pursuant to Article 6(1)(a) of the Merger Regulation (where failure to fulfil the conditions of Article 4(5) comes to its attention during the course of the investigation), or to revoke any decision it adopts pursuant to Article 6 or Article 8, following an Article 4(5) referral, pursuant to Article 6(3)(a) or 8(6)(a) of the Merger Regulation. Following the adoption of a decision pursuant to Article 6(1)(a) or following revocation, national competition laws would once again be applicable to the transaction. In the case of referrals under Article 4(4) made on the basis of incorrect or incomplete information, the Commission may require a notification pursuant to Article 4(1). In addition, the Commission has the power to impose fines under Article 14(1)(a) of the Merger Regulation. Finally, parties should also be aware that, if a referral is made on the basis of incorrect or incomplete information included in Form RS, the Commission and/or the Member States may consider making a post-notification referral reversing a pre-notification referral based on such incorrect or incomplete information.[49]

61. When providing information on Form RS or generally in making a request for a pre-notification referral, it is not envisaged or necessary for the undertakings concerned to show that their concentration will lead to detrimental effects on competition.[50] They should, however, provide as much information as possible showing clearly in what way the concentration meets the relevant legal criteria set out in Article 4(4) and (5) and why the concentration would be most appropriately dealt with by the competition authority or authorities specified in the request. The Merger Regulation does not require publication of the fact that a Form RS has been lodged, and it is not intended to do so. A non-public transaction can consequently be the subject of a pre-notification referral request.

62. Even though, according to the Merger Implementing Regulation, the Commission will accept Form RS in any official Community language, undertakings concerned providing information which is to be distributed to the network are strongly encouraged to use a language which will be understood by all addressees of the information. This will facilitate Member State treatment of such requests. Moreover, as regards requests for referral to a Member State or States, the requesting parties are strongly encouraged to include a copy of the request in the language(s) of the Member State(s) to which the referral is being requested.

63. Beyond the legal requirements specified in Form RS, the undertakings concerned should be prepared to provide additional information, if required, and to discuss the matter with the Commission and the NCAs in a frank and open manner in order to enable the Commission

---

[48] Form RS is annexed to Commission Reg (EC) No 802/2004 of 7 April 2004 implementing Council Reg (EC) No 139/2004 on the control of concentrations between undertakings (OJ L133, 30.4.2004, p 1).

[49] This would be the appropriate 'remedy' where the requesting parties have submitted incorrect or incomplete information not affecting fulfilment of the conditions of Art 4(5), which comes to the Commission's attention during the course of the investigation.

[50] See Recital 16 to the Merger Reg.

and the NCAs to assess whether the concentration in question should be the subject of referral.

64. Informal contacts between merging parties contemplating lodging a pre-filing referral request, on the one hand, and the Commission and/or Member State authorities, on the other, are actively encouraged, even following the submission of Form RS. The Commission is committed to providing informal, early guidance to firms wishing to use the pre-notification referrals system set out in Article 4(4) and (5) of the Merger Regulation.[51]

3. Concentrations eligible for referral

65. Only concentrations within the meaning of Article 3 of the Merger Regulation are eligible for referral pursuant to Article 4(5) and Article 22. Only concentrations falling within the ambit of the relevant national competition laws for the control of mergers are eligible for referral pursuant to Article 4(4) and Article 9.[52]

66. Pre-filing referral requests pursuant to Article 4(4) and (5) of the Merger Regulation must concern concentrations the plans for which are sufficiently concrete. In that regard, there must at least exist a good faith intention to merge on the part of the undertakings concerned, or, in the case of a public bid, at least a public announcement of an intention to make such a bid.[53]

4. The concept of 'prior to notification' under Article 4(4) and (5)

67. Article 4(4) and (5) only apply at the pre-notification stage.

68. Article 4(4) specifies that the undertakings concerned may make a referral request by means of reasoned submission (Form RS), 'prior to the notification of a concentration within the meaning of paragraph 1'. This means that the request can only be made where no Form CO has been submitted pursuant to Article 4(1).

69. Likewise, Article 4(5) specifies that the request may be made 'before any notification to the competent [national] authorities'. This means that the concentration in question must not have been formally notified in any Member State jurisdiction for that provision to apply. Even one notification anywhere in the Community will preclude the undertakings concerned from triggering the mechanism of Article 4(5). In the Commission's view, no penalty should be imposed for non-notification of a transaction at the national level while a request pursuant to Article 4(5) is pending.

5. The concept of a *'concentration capable of being reviewed under national competition law'* and the concept of *'competent Member State'* in Article 4(5)

70. Article 4(5) enables the undertakings concerned to request a pre-notification referral of a concentration which does not have a Community dimension and which is 'capable of being reviewed under the national competition laws of at least Member States'.

71. 'Capable of being reviewed' or reviewable should be interpreted as meaning a concentration which falls within the jurisdiction of a Member State under its national competition law for the control of mergers. There is no need for a mandatory notification requirement, i.e. it is not necessary for the concentration to be required to be notified under national law.[54]

---

[51] A request for derogation from the suspensive effect pursuant to Art 7(3) of the Merger Reg would normally be inconsistent with an intention to make a pre-notification referral request pursuant to Art 4(4).

[52] By contrast, the reference to 'national legislation on competition' in Art 21(3) and Art 22(3) should be understood as referring to all aspects of national competition law.

[53] See Recital 34 to, and Art 4(1) of, the Merger Reg.

[54] Even in circumstances where a notification is voluntary *de jure*, the parties may in practice wish or be expected to file a notification.

72. Pursuant to the third and fourth subparagraphs of Article 4(5), where at least one Member State 'competent to examine the concentration under its national competition law' has expressed its disagreement with the referral, the case must not be referred. A 'competent' Member State is one where the concentration is reviewable and which therefore has the power to examine the concentration under its national competition law.

73. All Member States, and not only those 'competent' to review the case, receive a copy of the Form RS. However, only Member States 'competent' to review the case are counted for the purposes of the third and fourth subparagraphs of Article 4(5). Pursuant to the third subparagraph of Article 4(5), 'competent' Member States have 15 working days from the date they receive the Form RS to express their agreement or disagreement with the referral. If they all agree, the case will be deemed to acquire a Community dimension pursuant to the fifth subparagraph of Article 4(5). According to the fourth subparagraph of Article 4(5), by contrast, if even only one 'competent' Member State disagrees, no referral will take place from any Member State.

74. Given the above mechanism, it is crucial to the smooth operation of Article 4(5) that *all* Member States where the case is reviewable under national competition law, and which are hence 'competent' to examine the case under national competition law, are identified correctly. Form RS therefore requires the undertakings concerned to provide sufficient information to enable each and every Member State to identify whether or not it is competent to review the concentration pursuant to its own national competition law.

75. In situations where Form RS has been filled in correctly, no complications should arise. The undertakings concerned will have identified correctly all Member States which are competent to review the case. In situations, however, where the undertakings concerned have not filled in Form RS correctly, or where there is a genuine disagreement as to which Member States are 'competent' to review the case, complications may arise.

— Within the period of 15 working days provided for in the third subparagraph of Article 4(5), a Member State which is not identified in Form RS as being competent may inform the Commission that it is competent and may, like any other competent Member State, express its agreement or disagreement with the referral.

— Likewise, within the period of 15 working days provided for in the third subparagraph of Article 4(5), a Member State which has been identified as competent in Form RS may inform the Commission that it is not 'competent'. That Member State would then be disregarded for the purposes of Article 4(5).

76. Once the period of 15 working days has expired without any disagreement having been expressed, the referral, will be considered valid. This ensures the validity of Commission decisions taken under Articles 6 or 8 of the Merger Regulation following an Article 4(5) referral.

77. This is not to say, however, that undertakings concerned can abuse the system by negligently or intentionally providing incorrect information, including as regards the reviewability of the concentration in the Member States, on Form RS. As noted at paragraph 60 above, the Commission may take measures to rectify the situation and to deter such violations. The undertakings concerned should also be aware that, in such circumstances, where a referral has been made on the basis of incorrect or incomplete information, a Member State which believes it was competent to deal with the case but did not have the opportunity to veto the referral due to incorrect information being supplied, may request a post-notification referral.

6. Notification and Publication of Decisions

78. According to the fourth subparagraph of Article 4(4), the fourth subparagraph of Article 4(5), Article 9(1) and the second subparagraph of Article 22(3), the Commission is obliged to

inform the undertakings or persons concerned and all Member States of any decision taken pursuant to those provisions as to the referral of a concentration.

79. The information will be provided by means of a letter addressed to the undertakings concerned (or for decisions adopted pursuant to Article 9(1) or Article 22(3), a letter addressed to the Member State concerned). All Member States will receive a copy thereof.

80. There is no requirement that such decisions be published in the *Official Journal of the European Union*.[55] The Commission will, however, give adequate publicity to such decisions on DG Competition's website, subject to confidentiality requirements.

7. Article 9(6)

81. Article 9(6) provides that, when the Commission refers a notified concentration to a Member State in accordance with Article 4(4) or Article 9(3), the NCA concerned must deal with the case 'without undue delay'. Accordingly, the competent authority concerned should deal as expeditiously as possible with the case under national law.

82. In addition, Article 9(6) provides that the competent national authority must, within 45 working days after the Commission's referral or following receipt of a notification at the national level if requested inform the undertakings concerned of the result of the 'preliminary competition assessment' and what 'further action', if any, it proposes to take. Accordingly, within 45 working days after the referral or notification, as appropriate, the merging parties should be provided with sufficient information to enable them to understand the nature of any preliminary competition concerns the authority may have and be informed of the likely extent and duration of the investigation. The Member State concerned may only exceptionally suspend this time limit, where necessary information has not been provided to it by the undertakings concerned as required under its national competition law.

IV. FINAL REMARKS

83. This notice will be the subject of periodic review, in particular following any revision of the referral provisions in the Merger Regulation. In that regard, it should be noted that, according to Article 4(6) of the Merger Regulation, the Commission must report to the Council on the operation of the pre-notification referral provisions in Article 4(4) and (5), by 1 July 2009.

84. This Notice is without prejudice to any interpretation of the applicable Treaty and regulatory provisions by the Court of First Instance and the Court of Justice of the European Communities.

---

[55] Pursuant to Art 20 of the Merger Reg this is only required for decisions taken under Art 8(1)–(6) and Arts 14 and 15.

ANNEXES
REFERRAL CHARTS

Article 4(4) Concentration with Community Dimension

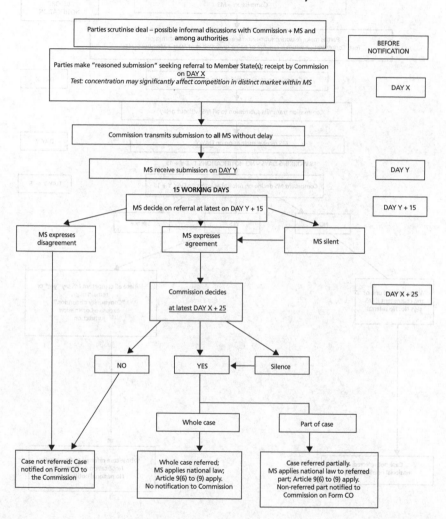

1373

Article 4(5) Concentration without Community Dimension reviewable in at least three MS under national law

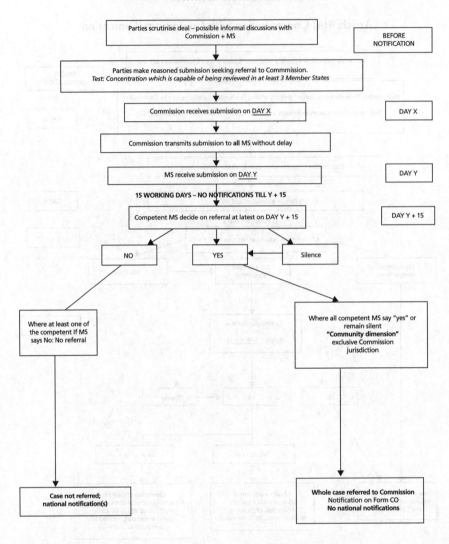

Parties scrutinise deal – possible informal discussions with Commission + MS	BEFORE NOTIFICATION
Parties make reasoned submission seeking referral to Commmission. *Test: Concentration which is capable of being reviewed in at least 3 Member States*	
Commission receives submission on <u>DAY X</u>	DAY X
Commission transmits submission to **all** MS without delay	
MS receive submission on <u>DAY Y</u>	DAY Y

15 WORKING DAYS – NO NOTIFICATIONS TILL Y + 15

Competent MS decide on referral at latest on DAY Y + 15	DAY Y + 15

NO — YES — Silence

Where at least one of the competent If MS says No: No referral

Where all competent MS say "yes" or remain silent **"Community dimension"** exclusive Commission jurisdiction

Case not referred; national notification(s)

Whole case referred to Commission Notification on Form CO **No national notifications**

Article 9 Concentration with Community Dimension

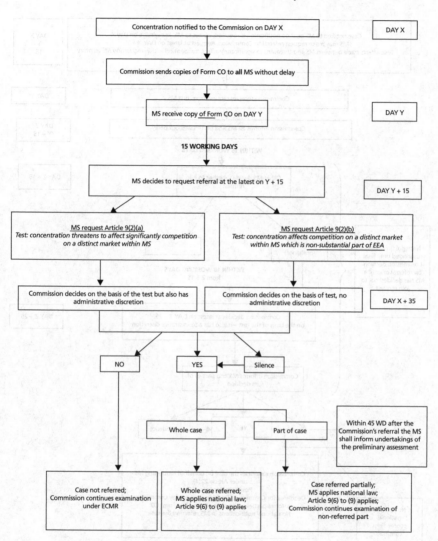

Article 22 Concentration without Community dimension

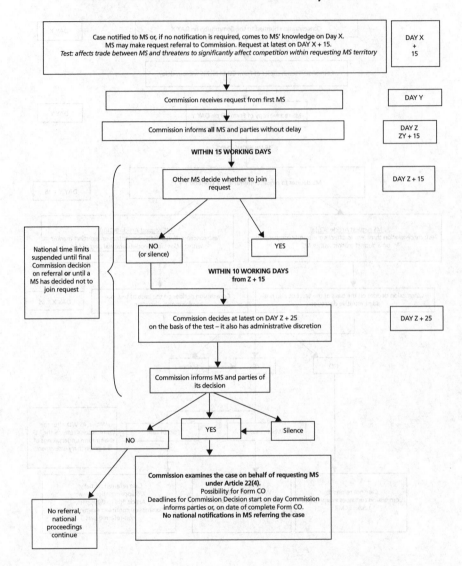

Case notified to MS or, if no notification is required, comes to MS' knowledge on Day X.
MS may make request referral to Commission. Request at latest on DAY X + 15.
Test: affects trade between MS and threatens to significantly affect competition within requesting MS territory

DAY X
+
15

Commission receives request from first MS

DAY Y

Commission informs **all** MS and parties without delay

DAY Z
ZY + 15

WITHIN 15 WORKING DAYS

Other MS decide whether to join request

DAY Z + 15

National time limits suspended until final Commission decision on referral **or** until a MS has decided not to join request

NO
(or silence)

YES

**WITHIN 10 WORKING DAYS
from Z + 15**

Commission decides at latest on DAY Z + 25
on the basis of the test – it also has administrative discretion

DAY Z + 25

Commission informs MS and parties of its decision

YES

Silence

NO

**Commission examines the case on behalf of requesting MS
under Article 22(4).**
Possibility for Form CO
Deadlines for Commission Decision start on day Commission
informs parties or, on date of complete Form CO.
No national notifications in MS referring the case

No referral, national proceedings continue

Commission Notice on a simplified procedure for treatment of certain concentrations under Council Regulation (EC) No 139/2004

(2005/C 56/04)

(Text with EEA relevance)

1. INTRODUCTION

1. This Notice sets out a simplified procedure under which the Commission intends to treat certain concentrations pursuant to Council Regulation (EC) No 139/2004 of 20 January 2004, on the control of concentrations between undertakings (the EC Merger Regulation)[1] on the basis that they do not raise competition concerns. This Notice replaces the Notice on a simplified procedure for treatment of certain concentrations under Council Regulation (EEC) No 4064/89.[2] The Commission's experience gained in applying Council Regulation (EEC) No 4064/89 of 21 December 1989 on the control of concentrations between undertakings[3] has shown that certain categories of notified concentrations are normally cleared without having raised any substantive doubts, provided that there were no special circumstances.

2. The purpose of this Notice is to set out the conditions under which the Commission usually adopts a short-form decision declaring a concentration compatible with the common market pursuant to the simplified procedure and to provide guidance in respect of the procedure itself. When all necessary conditions set forth at point 5 of this Notice are met and provided there are no special circumstances, the Commission adopts a short-form clearance decision within 25 working days from the date of notification, pursuant to Article 6(1)(b) of the EC Merger Regulation.[4]

3. However, if the safeguards or exclusions set forth at points 6 to 11 of this Notice are applicable, the Commission may launch an investigation and/or adopt a full decision under the EC Merger Regulation.

4. By following the procedure outlined in the following sections, the Commission aims to make Community merger control more focused and effective.

---

[1] OJ L24, 29.1.2004, p 1.

[2] OJ C217, 29.7.2000, p 32.

[3] OJ L395, 30.12.1989, p 1; corrected version OJ L257, 21.9.1990, p 13.

[4] The notification requirements are set out in Annexes I and II to Commission Reg (EC) No 802/2004 implementing Council Reg (EC) No 139/2004 on the control of concentrations between undertakings.

II. CATEGORIES OF CONCENTRATIONS SUITABLE FOR TREATMENT UNDER THE SIMPLIFIED PROCEDURE

Eligible concentrations

5. The Commission will apply the simplified procedure to the following categories of concentrations:

   (a) two or more undertakings acquire joint control of a joint venture, provided that the joint venture has no, or negligible, actual or foreseen activities within the territory of the European Economic Area (EEA). Such cases occur where:

      (i) the turnover[5] of the joint venture and/or the turnover of the contributed activities[6] is less than EUR 100 million in the EEA territory; and

      (ii) the total value of assets[7] transferred to the joint venture is less than EUR 100 million in the EEA territory;[8]

   (b) two or more undertakings merge, or one or more undertakings acquire sole or joint control of another undertaking, provided that none of the parties to the concentration are engaged in business activities in the same product and geographical market, or in a product market which is upstream or downstream of a product market in which any other party to the concentration is engaged;[9]

   (c) two or more undertakings merge, or one or more undertakings acquire sole or joint control of another undertaking and:

      (i) two or more of the parties to the concentration are engaged in business activities in the same product and geographical market (horizontal relationships) provided that their combined market share is less than 15 %; or

      (ii) one or more of the parties to the concentration are engaged in business activities in a product market which is upstream or downstream of a product market in which any other party to the concentration is engaged (vertical relationships),[10]

---

[5] The turnover of the joint venture should be determined according to the most recent audited accounts of the parent companies, or the joint venture itself, depending upon the availability of separate accounts for the resources combined in the joint venture.

[6] The expression 'and/or' refers to the variety of situations covered; for example:

— in the case of a joint acquisition of a target company, the turnover to be taken into account is the turnover of this target (the joint venture).

— in the case of the creation of a joint venture to which the parent companies contribute their activities, the turnover to be taken into account is that of the contributed activities,

— in the case of entry of a new controlling party into an existing joint venture, the turnover of the joint venture and the turnover of the activities contributed by the new parent company (if any) must be taken into account.

[7] The total value of assets of the joint venture should be determined according to the last prepared and approved balance sheet of each parent company. The term 'assets' includes: (1) all tangible and intangible assets that will be transferred to the joint venture (examples of tangible assets include production plants, wholesale or retail outlets, and inventory of goods; examples of intangible assets include intellectual property, goodwill, etc.), and (2) any amount of credit or any obligations of the joint venture which any parent company of the joint venture has agreed to extend or guarantee.

[8] Where the assets transferred generate turnover, then neither the value of the assets nor that of the turnover may exceed EUR 100 million.

[9] See Commission Notice on the definition of relevant market for the purposes of Community competition law (OJ C372, 9.12.1997, p 5).

[10] See n 6.

provided that none of their individual or combined market shares is at either level 25% or more;[11]

(d) a party is to acquire sole control of an undertaking over which it already has joint control.

Safeguards and exclusions

6. In assessing whether a concentration falls into one of the categories referred to in point 5, the Commission will ensure that all relevant circumstances are established with sufficient clarity. Given that market definitions are likely to be a key element in this assessment, the parties should provide information on all plausible alternative market definitions during the pre-notification phase (see point 15). Notifying parties are responsible for describing all alternative relevant product and geographic markets on which the notified concentration could have an impact and for providing data and information relating to the definition of such markets.[12] The Commission retains the discretion to take the ultimate decision on market definition, basing its decision on an analysis of the facts of the case. Where it is difficult to define the relevant markets or to determine the parties' market shares, the Commission will not apply the simplified procedure. In addition, to the extent that concentrations involve novel legal issues of a general interest, the Commission would normally abstain from adopting short-form decisions, and would normally revert to a normal first phase merger procedure.

7. While it can normally be assumed that concentrations falling into the categories referred to in point 5 will not raise serious doubts as to their compatibility with the common market, there may nonetheless be certain situations, which exceptionally require a closer investigation and/or a full decision. In such cases, the Commission may revert to a normal first phase merger procedure.

8. The following are indicative examples of types of cases which may be excluded from the simplified procedure. Certain types of concentrations may increase the parties' market power, for instance by combining technological, financial or other resources, even if the parties to the concentration do not operate in the same market. Concentrations where at least two parties to the concentration are present in closely related neighbouring markets[13] may also be unsuitable for the simplified procedure, in particular, where one or more of the parties to the concentration holds individually a market share of 25% or more in any product market in which there is no horizontal or vertical relationship between the parties but which is a neighbouring market to a market where another party is active. In other cases, it may not be possible to determine the parties' precise market shares. This is often the case when the parties operate in new or little developed markets. Concentrations in markets with high entry barriers, with a high degree of concentration[14] or other known competition problems may also be unsuitable.

---

[11] This means that only concentrations, which do not lead to affected markets, as defined in Section 6 III of Form CO, fall into this category. The thresholds for horizontal and vertical relationships apply to market shares both at national and at EEA levels and to any plausible alternative product market definition that may have to be considered in a given case. It is important that the underlying market definitions set out in the notification are precise enough to justify the assessment that these thresholds are not met, and that all plausible alternative market definitions are mentioned (including geographic markets narrower than national).

[12] As with all other notifications, the Commission may revoke the short-form decision if it is based on incorrect information for which one of the undertakings concerned is responsible (Art 6(3)(a), of the EC Merger Reg).

[13] Product markets are closely related neighbouring markets when the products are complementary to each other or when they belong to a range of products that is generally purchased by the same set of customers for the same end use.

[14] See Guidelines on the assessment of horizontal mergers under the Council Reg on the control of concentrations between undertakings OJ C31, 5.2.2004, p 5, points 14–21.

9. The Commission's experience to date has shown that a change from joint to sole control may exceptionally require closer investigation and/or a full decision. A particular competition concern could arise in circumstances where the former joint venture is integrated into the group or network of its remaining single controlling shareholder, whereby the disciplining constraints exercised by the potentially diverging incentives of the different controlling shareholders are removed and its strategic market position could be strengthened. For example, in a scenario in which undertaking A and undertaking B jointly control a joint venture C, a concentration pursuant to which A acquires sole control of C may give rise to competition concerns in circumstances in which C is a direct competitor of A and where C and A will hold a substantial combined market position and where this removes a degree of independence previously held by C.[15] In cases where such scenarios require a closer analysis, the Commission may revert to a normal first phase merger procedure.[16]

10. The Commission may also revert to a normal first phase merger procedure where neither the Commission nor the competent authorities of Member States have reviewed the prior acquisition of joint control of the joint venture in question.

11. Furthermore, the Commission may revert to a normal first phase merger procedure where an issue of coordination as referred to in Article 2(4) of the EC Merger Regulation arises.

12. If a Member State expresses substantiated concerns about the notified concentration within 15 working days of receipt of the copy of the notification, or if a third party expresses substantiated concerns within the time-limit laid down for such comments, the Commission will adopt a full decision. The time-limits set out in Article 10(1) of the EC Merger Regulation apply.

Referral requests

13. The simplified procedure will not be applied if a Member State requests the referral of a notified concentration pursuant to Article 9 of the EC Merger Regulation or if the Commission accepts a request from one or more Member States for referral of a notified concentration pursuant to Article 22 of the EC Merger Regulation.

Pre-notification referrals at the request of the notifying parties

14. Subject to the safeguards and exclusions set out in this Notice, the Commission may apply the simplified procedure to concentrations where:

   (i) following a reasoned submission pursuant to Article 4(4) of the EC Merger Regulation, the Commission decides not to refer the case to a Member State; or
   following a reasoned submission pursuant to Article 4(5) of the EC Merger Regulation the case is referred to the Commission.

III. PROCEDURAL PROVISIONS

Pre-notification contacts

15. The Commission has found pre-notification contacts between notifying parties and the Commission beneficial even in seemingly unproblematic cases.[17] The Commission's experience of the simplified procedure has shown that candidate cases for the simplified procedure may raise complex issues for instance, of market definition (see point 6) which should preferably be resolved prior to notification. Such contacts allow the Commission and

---

[15] Case No. IV/M.1328 *KLM/Martinair*, XXIXth Report on Competition Policy 1999 – SEC(2000) 720 final, points 165–166.

[16] Case No COMP/M.2908 *Deutsche Post/DHL. (II)*, Decision of 18.9.2002.

[17] See DG Competition Best Practices on the conduct of EC merger control proceedings available at: http://europa.eu.int/comm/competition/mergers/legislation/regulation/best_practices.pdf.

the notifying parties to determine the precise amount of information to be provided in a notification. Pre-notification contacts should be initiated at least two weeks prior to the expected date of notification. Notifying parties are therefore advised to engage in pre-notification contacts, particularly where they request the Commission to waive full-form notification in accordance with Article 3(1) of Commission Regulation (EC) No 802/2004 of 7 April 2004 implementing Council Regulation (EC) No 139/ 2004 on the control of concentrations between undertakings[18] on the grounds that the operation to be notified will not raise competition concerns.

Publication of the fact of notification

16. The information to be published in the *Official Journal of the European Union* upon receipt of a notification[19] will include the names of the parties to the concentration, their country of origin, the nature of the concentration and the economic sectors involved, as well as an indication that, on the basis of the information provided by the notifying party, the concentration may qualify for a simplified procedure. Interested parties will then have the opportunity to submit observations, in particular on circumstances which might require an investigation.

Short-form decision

17. If the Commission is satisfied that the concentration fulfils the criteria for the simplified procedure (see point 5), it will normally issue a short-form decision. This includes appropriate cases not giving rise to any competition concerns where it receives a full form notification. The concentration will thus be declared compatible with the common market, within 25 working days from the date of notification, pursuant to Article 10(1) and (6) of the EC Merger Regulation. The Commission will endeavour to issue a short-form decision as soon as practicable following expiry of the 15 working day period during which Member States may request referral of a notified concentration pursuant to Article 9 of the EC Merger Regulation. However, in the period leading up to the 25 working day deadline, the option of reverting to a normal first phase merger procedure and thus launching investigations and/or adopting a full decision remains open to the Commission, should it judge such action appropriate in the case in question.

Publication of the short-form decision

18. The Commission will publish a notice of the fact of the decision in the *Official Journal of the European Union* as it does for full clearance decisions. The public version of the decision will be made available on DG Competition's Internet website for a limited period. The short-form decision will contain the information about the notified concentration published in the Official Journal at the time of notification (names of the parties, their country of origin, nature of the concentration and economic sectors concerned) and a statement that the concentration is declared compatible with the common market because it falls within one or more of the categories described in this Notice, with the applicable category(ies) being explicitly identified.

IV. ANCILLARY RESTRICTIONS

19. The simplified procedure is not suited to cases in which the undertakings concerned request an express assessment of restrictions which are directly related to, and necessary for, the implementation of the concentration.

---

[18] OJ L133, 30.4.2004, p 1.
[19] Art 4(3) of the EC Merger Reg.

APPENDIX 28

DG Competition Information Note on Art. 6(1)(c) 2nd sentence of Regulation 139/2004 (abandonment of concentrations)

The revised EC Merger Regulation[1] introduced a new provision related to the closure of merger control procedures without a final decision after the Commission has initiated proceedings under Art. 6 (1) c 1st sentence. That sentence reads as follows: 'Without prejudice to Article 9, such proceedings shall be closed by means of a decision as provided for in Article 8(1) to (4), unless the undertakings concerned have demonstrated to the satisfaction of the Commission that they have abandoned the concentration'. Prior to the initiation of proceedings, such requirements do not apply.

This note sets out the requirements for this satisfaction to be achieved.

As a general principle, the requirements for the proof of the abandonment must correspond in terms of legal form, format, intensity etc. to the initial act that was considered sufficient to make the concentration notifiable. In case the parties proceed from that initial act to a strengthening of their contractual links during the procedure, for example by concluding a binding agreement after the transaction was notified on the basis of a good faith intention, the requirements for the proof of the abandonment must correspond also to the latest act.

In line with this principle, in case of implementation of the concentration prior to a Commission decision, the re-establishment of the *status quo ante* has to be shown.

In other cases, the mere withdrawal of the notification is not considered as sufficient proof that the concentration has been abandoned in the sense of Article 6(1)c. Likewise, minor modifications of a concentration, for example as regards the agreed time of implementation or minor changes in the shareholding percentages which do not affect the change in control or the quality of that change, cannot be considered as an abandonment of the original concentration.[2]

- *Binding agreement:* proof of the legally binding cancellation of the agreement in the form envisaged by the initial agreement (i.e. usually a document signed by all the parties) will be required. Expressions of intention to cancel the agreement or not to implement the notified concentration, as well as unilateral declarations by the parties will not be considered sufficient.
- *Good faith intention to conclude an agreement:* In case of a letter of intent or memorandum of understanding reflecting such good faith intention, documents proving that this basis for the good faith intention has been cancelled will be required. As for possible other forms that indicated the good faith intention, the abandonment must reverse this good faith intention and correspond in terms of form and intensity to the initial expression of intent.
- *Public announcement of a public bid or of the intention to make a public bid:* a public

---

[1] Council Reg No 139/2004 of 20 January 2004 on the control of concentrations between undertakings; OJ L24/1, 29.1.2004.

[2] The qualification of a modification as 'minor' in the sense of this paragraph does not prejudge the assessment whether the modification requires to submit additional information to the Commission under Art 5 (3) Reg 802/2004.

announcement terminating the bidding procedure will be required. The format and public reach of this announcement must be comparable to the initial announcement.

- *Implemented concentrations:* In case the concentration has been implemented prior to a Commission decision, the parties will be required to show that the situation prevailing before the implementation of the concentration has been re-established.

It is for the parties to submit the necessary documentation to meet these requirements.

This information is without prejudice to the interpretation of Community law which may be given by the Court of Justice or the Court of First Instance of the European Communities.

Part III

PUBLIC UNDERTAKINGS
(ARTICLE 86 EC)

APPENDIX 29

European Commission XXVth Report on Competition Policy 1995 (Published in conjunction with the 'General Report on the Activities of the European Union—1995')

II. STATE MONOPOLIES AND MONOPOLY RIGHTS: ARTICLES 37 AND 90

A. Introduction

1. Services of general economic interest at the heart of the Commission's liberalization policy

99. The Commission has pursued its policy of liberalizing and opening up to competition certain sectors traditionally subject to monopoly such as telecommunications, energy, postal services or transport. As these sectors are essential to individual consumers, competitiveness, growth and job creation in the European economy as a whole, the gains in efficiency resulting from the introduction of some competition will have generally positive results for the citizens of Europe. Otherwise, we will not have a true internal market while these essential sectors continue to be organized on a purely national and monopolistic basis.

Because of the importance of these sectors to our society and because of their specific characteristics, e.g. their network structure, Member States have in the past granted exclusive or special rights to public or private operators or allowed other restrictions of competition in exchange for the operation of services of general economic interest such as the supply of a universal service to all citizens on specific terms and at affordable prices.

The Commission has always acknowledged that these general economic interest objectives are legitimate but considers that the means traditionally used to provide them are no longer always justified, particularly in view of technological developments and the new needs of consumers, and also in view of European integration itself. This is particularly true for the information society, a source of growth, new services and new jobs in the years ahead.

A thorough review is therefore needed, in the light of these new realities, of the instruments most likely to provide the public with the quality services it requires. The Commission considers that the introduction of competition can, in many cases, improve service quality, allow innovation and the creation of employment and help to cut consumer prices. The removal of obstacles to free competition is, however, only one aspect of the Commission's liberalization policy. On the one hand, the adoption of a new regulatory framework will frequently be necessary to ensure that universal service is provided in a competitive environment. On the other hand, where certain restrictions of competition prove essential in maintaining a universal service, the Commission recognizes the legitimacy of these restrictions under Community law (as in the case of state aid).

The Commission therefore considers that the development of competition policy is fully compatible with public service. It should also be noted that the liberalization of a sector is different from the privatization of public enterprises operating in the sector. Whilst the introduction of competition can in certain cases stem from Community rules, the latter are neutral as regards the public or private nature of enterprises.

1387

2. Article 90(3) Directives

100. In order to achieve the objective of introducing competition, Article 90(3) gives the Commission the power to adopt decisions or directives that are binding on the Member States. This latter possibility is occasionally objected to by certain parties.

In practice, even if Article 90(3) allows the Commission to adopt directives, the Court of Justice has stipulated that the provision empowers it only to establish general rules defining the obligations already imposed on Member States by the Treaty with regard to public undertakings or undertakings granted special or exclusive rights, or to take the necessary preventive measures to allow it to carry out its monitoring function.

The limited power conferred on the Commission by Article 90(3) is thus different from and more specific than the power of the European Parliament or the Council to adopt directives. The Commission may not impose new obligations on Member States; it may only determine, with regard to all the Member States, the specific obligations imposed on them by the Treaty. The extent of the Commission's duties and powers consequently depends on the scope of the rules that are to be complied with.

The Commission has always used this instrument with caution. Directives under Article 90(3) have been used only in situations where the existence of many infringements of the fundamental rules of the EC Treaty made them necessary to avoid a multiplicity of infringement proceedings and to give operators a minimum amount of legal certainty.[1] These initiatives have generally been taken in response to concerns expressed by the Council or Parliament. The Commission has always attached the greatest importance to the need for this instrument to be used as part of a transparent procedure involving the broadest possible dialogue with the other Union institutions, Member States and interested parties.

This is the approach normally adopted in the initial assessment stages, through the publication by the Commission of Green Papers or discussion papers intended to stimulate debate at the public consultation stage. On the basis of the results of the consultations, studies by experts and information obtained by it, the Commission adopts a draft directive which is presented for comments to Parliament, the Economic and Social Committee, the Committee of the Regions and the Member States. The draft text is also published in the Official Journal of the European Communities to enable other interested parties to submit their comments.

The adoption by the Commission of the final Article 90(3) directive is in any event preceded by careful scrutiny of comments received, especially any comments from the European Parliament, the Economic and Social Committee and the Committee of the Regions.

The discussions held during the year on the directives on cable television networks, mobile communications and the full liberalization of telecommunications are good illustrations of this approach.

---

[1] Commission Directive 80/723/EEC of 25 June 1980 on the transparency of financial relations between Member States and public undertakings (OJ L195, 29.7.1980, p 35), as amended by Commission Directive 85/413/EEC of 24 July 1985 (OJ L229, 28.8.198(,p 20) and Commission Directive 93/84/EEC of 30 September 1993 (OJ L254, 12.10.1993, p 16); Commission Directive 88/301/EEC of 16 May 1988 on competition in the markets in telecommunications terminal equipment (OJ L131, 27.5.1988, p 73); Commission Directive 90/388/EEC of 28 June 1990 on competition in the markets for telecommunications services (OJ L192, 24.7.1990, p 10), as amended by Commission Directives 94/46/EC of 13 October 1994 on satellite communications (OJ L268, 19.10.1994, p 15) and 95/51/EC of 18 October 1995 on the abolition of the restrictions on the use of cable television networks for the provision of already liberalized telecommunications services (OJ L256, 26.10.1995, p 49).

Part IV

STATE AID
(ARTICLES 87 AND 88 EC)

Council Regulation (EC) No 659/1999 of 22 March 1999 laying down detailed rules for the application of Article 93 of the EC Treaty

THE COUNCIL OF THE EUROPEAN UNION,

Having regard to the Treaty establishing the European Community, and in particular Article 94 thereof,

Having regard to the proposal from the Commission,[1]

Having regard to the opinion of the European Parliament,[2]

Having regard to the opinion of the Economic and Social Committee,[3]

(1) Whereas, without prejudice to special procedural rules laid down in regulations for certain sectors, this Regulation should apply to aid in all sectors; whereas, for the purpose of applying Articles 77 and 92 of the Treaty, the Commission has specific competence under Article 93 thereof to decide on the compatibility of State aid with the common market when reviewing existing aid, when taking decisions on new or altered aid and when taking action regarding non-compliance with its decisions or with the requirement as to notification;

(2) Whereas the Commission, in accordance with the case-law of the Court of Justice of the European Communities, has developed and established a consistent practice for the application of Article 93 of the Treaty and has laid down certain procedural rules and principles in a number of communications; whereas it is appropriate, with a view to ensuring effective and efficient procedures pursuant to Article 93 of the Treaty, to codify and reinforce this practice by means of a regulation;

(3) Whereas a procedural regulation on the application of Article 93 of the Treaty will increase transparency and legal certainty;

(4) Whereas, in order to ensure legal certainty, it is appropriate to define the circumstances under which aid is to be considered as existing aid; whereas the completion and enhancement of the internal market is a gradual process, reflected in the permanent development of State aid policy; whereas, following these developments, certain measures, which at the moment they were put into effect did not constitute State aid, may since have become aid;

(5) Whereas, in accordance with Article 93(3) of the Treaty, any plans to grant new aid are to be notified to the Commission and should not be put into effect before the Commission has authorised it;

(6) Whereas, in accordance with Article 5 of the Treaty, Member States are under an obligation to cooperate with the Commission and to provide it with all information required to allow the Commission to carry out its duties under this Regulation;

(7) Whereas the period within which the Commission is to conclude the preliminary examination of notified aid should be set at two months from the receipt of a complete notification or from the receipt of a duly reasoned statement of the Member State concerned that it

---

[1] OJ C116, 16. 4. 1998, p 13.
[2] Opinion delivered on 14 January 1999 (not yet published in the Official Journal).
[3] OJ C284, 14. 9. 1998, p 10.

considers the notification to be complete because the additional information requested by the Commission is not available or has already been provided; whereas, for reasons of legal certainty, that examination should be brought to an end by a decision;

(8) Whereas in all cases where, as a result of the preliminary examination, the Commission cannot find that the aid is compatible with the common market, the formal investigation procedure should be opened in order to enable the Commission to gather all the information it needs to assess the compatibility of the aid and to allow the interested parties to submit their comments; whereas the rights of the interested parties can best be safeguarded within the framework of the formal investigation procedure provided for under Article 93(2) of the Treaty;

(9) Whereas, after having considered the comments submitted by the interested parties, the Commission should conclude its examination by means of a final decision as soon as the doubts have been removed; whereas it is appropriate, should this examination not be concluded after a period of 18 months from the opening of the procedure, that the Member State concerned has the opportunity to request a decision, which the Commission should take within two months;

(10) Whereas, in order to ensure that the State aid rules are applied correctly and effectively, the Commission should have the opportunity of revoking a decision which was based on incorrect information;

(11) Whereas, in order to ensure compliance with Article 93 of the Treaty, and in particular with the notification obligation and the standstill clause in Article 93(3), the Commission should examine all cases of unlawful aid; whereas, in the interests of transparency and legal certainty, the procedures to be followed in such cases should be laid down; whereas when a Member State has not respected the notification obligation or the standstill clause, the Commission should not be bound by time limits;

(12) Whereas in cases of unlawful aid, the Commission should have the right to obtain all necessary information enabling it to take a decision and to restore immediately, where appropriate, undistorted competition; whereas it is therefore appropriate to enable the Commission to adopt interim measures addressed to the Member State concerned; whereas the interim measures may take the form of information injunctions, suspension injunctions and recovery injunctions; whereas the Commission should be enabled in the event of non-compliance with an information injunction, to decide on the basis of the information available and, in the event of non-compliance with suspension and recovery injunctions, to refer the matter to the Court of Justice direct, in accordance with the second subparagraph of Article 93(2) of the Treaty;

(13) Whereas in cases of unlawful aid which is not compatible with the common market, effective competition should be restored; whereas for this purpose it is necessary that the aid, including interest, be recovered without delay; whereas it is appropriate that recovery be effected in accordance with the procedures of national law; whereas the application of those procedures should not, by preventing the immediate and effective execution of the Commission decision, impede the restoration of effective competition; whereas to achieve this result, Member States should take all necessary measures ensuring the effectiveness of the Commission decision;

(14) Whereas for reasons of legal certainty it is appropriate to establish a period of limitation of 10 years with regard to unlawful aid, after the expiry of which no recovery can be ordered;

(15) Whereas misuse of aid may have effects on the functioning of the internal market which are similar to those of unlawful aid and should thus be treated according to similar procedures; whereas unlike unlawful aid, aid which has possibly been misused is aid which has been previously approved by the Commission; whereas therefore the Commission should not be allowed to use a recovery injunction with regard to misuse of aid;

(16) Whereas it is appropriate to define all the possibilities in which third parties have to defend their interests in State aid procedures;

(17) Whereas in accordance with Article 93(1) of the Treaty, the Commission is under an obligation, in cooperation with Member States, to keep under constant review all systems of existing aid; whereas in the interests of transparency and legal certainty, it is appropriate to specify the scope of cooperation under that Article;

(18) Whereas, in order to ensure compatibility of existing aid schemes with the common market and in accordance with Article 93(1) of the Treaty, the Commission should propose appropriate measures where an existing aid scheme is not, or is no longer, compatible with the common market and should initiate the procedure provided for in Article 93(2) of the Treaty if the Member State concerned declines to implement the proposed measures;

(19) Whereas, in order to allow the Commision to monitor effectively compliance with Commission decisions and to facilitate cooperation between the Commission and Member States for the purpose of the constant review of all existing aid schemes in the Member States in accordance with Article 93(1) of the Treaty, it is necessary to introduce a general reporting obligation with regard to all existing aid schemes;

(20) Whereas, where the Commission has serious doubts as to whether its decisions are being complied with, it should have at its disposal additional instruments allowing it to obtain the information necessary to verify that its decisions are being effectively complied with; whereas for this purpose on-site monitoring visits are an appropriate and useful instrument, in particular for cases where and might have been misused; whereas therefore the Commission must be empowered to undertake on-site monitoring visits and must obtain the cooperation of the competent authorities of the Member States where an undertaking opposes such a visit;

(21) Whereas, in the interests of transparency and legal certainty, it is appropriate to give public information on Commission decisions while, at the same time, maintaining the principle that decisions in State aid cases are addressed to the Member State concerned; whereas it is therefore appropriate to publish all decisions which might affect the interests of interested parties either in full or in a summary form or to make copies of such decisions available to interested parties, where they have not been published or where they have not been published in full; whereas the Commission, when giving public information on its decisions, should respect the rules on professional secrecy, in accordance with Article 214 of the Treaty;

(22) Whereas the Commission, in close liaison with the Member States, should be able to adopt implementing provisions laying down detailed rules concerning the procedures under this Regulation; whereas, in order to provide for cooperation between the Commission and the competent authorities of the Member States, it is appropriate to create an Advisory Committee on State aid to be consulted before the Commission adopts provisions pursuant to this Regulation,

HAS ADOPTED THIS REGULATION:

Chapter I. General

Article 1
Definitions

For the purpose of this Regulation:

(a) 'aid' shall mean any measure fulfilling all the criteria laid down in Article 92(1) of the Treaty;

(b) 'existing aid' shall mean:

(i) without prejudice to Articles 144 and 172 of the Act of Accession of Austria, Finland and Sweden, all aid which existed prior to the entry into force of the Treaty in the respective Member States, that is to say, aid schemes and individual aid which were put into effect before, and are still applicable after, the entry into force of the Treaty;

(ii) authorised aid, that is to say, aid schemes and individual aid which have been authorised by the Commission or by the Council;

1393

(iii) aid which is deemed to have been authorised pursuant to Article 4(6) of this Regulation or prior to this Regulation but in accordance with this procedure;

(iv) aid which is deemed to be existing aid pursuant to Article 15;

(v) aid which is deemed to be an existing aid because it can be established that at the time it was put into effect it did not constitute an aid, and subsequently became an aid due to the evolution of the common market and without having been altered by the Member State. Where certain measures become aid following the liberalisation of an activity by Community law, such measures shall not be considered as existing aid after the date fixed for liberalization;

(c) 'new aid' shall mean all aid, that is to say, aid schemes and individual aid, which is not existing aid, including alterations to existing aid;

(d) 'aid scheme' shall mean any act on the basis of which, without further implementing measures being required, individual aid awards may be made to undertakings defined within the act in a general and abstract manner and any act on the basis of which aid which is not linked to a specific project may be awarded to one or several undertakings for an indefinite period of time and/or for an indefinite amount;

(e) 'individual aid' shall mean aid that is not awarded on the basis of an aid scheme and notifiable awards of aid on the basis of an aid scheme;

(f) 'unlawful aid' shall mean new aid put into effect in contravention of Article 93(3) of the Treaty;

(g) 'misuse of aid' shall mean aid used by the beneficiary in contravention of a decision taken pursuant to Article 4(3) or Article 7(3) or (4) of this Regulation;

(h) 'interested party' shall mean any Member State and any person, undertaking or association of undertakings whose interests might be affected by the granting of aid, in particular the beneficiary of the aid, competing undertakings and trade associations.

CHAPTER II. PROCEDURE REGARDING NOTIFIED AID

Article 2
Notification of New Aid

1. Save as otherwise provided in regulations made pursuant to Article 94 of the Treaty or to other relevant provisions thereof, any plans to grant new aid shall be notified to the Commission in sufficient time by the Member State concerned. The Commission shall inform the Member State concerned without delay of the receipt of a notification.

2. In a notification, the Member State concerned shall provide all necessary information in order to enable the Commission to take a decision pursuant to Articles 4 and 7 (hereinafter referred to as 'complete notification').

Article 3
Standstill Clause

Aid notifiable pursuant to Article 2(1) shall not be put into effect before the Commission has taken, or is deemed to have taken, a decision authorizing such aid.

Article 4
Preliminary Examination of the Notification and Decisions of the Commission

1. The Commission shall examine the notification as soon as it is received. Without prejudice to Article 8, the Commission shall take a decision pursuant to paragraphs 2, 3 or 4.

2. Where the Commission, after a preliminary examination, finds that the notified measure does not constitute aid, it shall record that finding by way of a decision.

3. Where the Commission, after a preliminary examination, finds that no doubts are raised as to the compatibility with the common market of a notified measure, in so far as it falls within the scope of Article 92(1) of the Treaty, it shall decide that the measure is compatible with the common market (hereinafter referred to as a 'decision not to raise objections'). The decision shall specify which exception under the Treaty has been applied.

4. Where the Commission, after a preliminary examination, finds that doubts are raised as to the compatibility with the common market of a notified measure, it shall decide to initiate proceedings pursuant to Article 93(2) of the Treaty (hereinafter referred to as a 'decision to initiate the formal investigation procedure').

5. The decisions referred to in paragraphs 2, 3 and 4 shall be taken within two months. That period shall begin on the day following the receipt of a complete notification. The notification will be considered as complete if, within two months from its receipt, or from the receipt of any additional information requested, the Commission does not request any further information. The period can be extended with the consent of both the Commission and the Member State concerned. Where appropriate, the Commission may fix shorter time limits.

6. Where the Commission has not taken a decision in accordance with paragraphs 2, 3 or 4 within the period laid down in paragraph 5, the aid shall be deemed to have been authorised by the Commission. The Member State concerned may thereupon implement the measures in question after giving the Commission prior notice thereof, unless the Commission takes a decision pursuant to this Article within a period of 15 working days following receipt of the notice.

Article 5
Request for Information

1. Where the Commission considers that information provided by the Member State concerned with regard to a measure notified pursuant to Article 2 is incomplete, it shall request all necessary additional information. Where a Member State responds to such a request, the Commission shall inform the Member State of the receipt of the response.

2. Where the Member State concerned does not provide the information requested within the period prescribed by the Commission or provides incomplete information, the Commission shall send a reminder, allowing an appropriate additional period within which the information shall be provided.

3. The notification shall be deemed to be withdrawn if the requested information is not provided within the prescribed period, unless before the expiry of that period, either the period has been extended with the consent of both the Commission and the Member State concerned, or the Member State concerned, in a duly reasoned statement, informs the Commission that it considers the notification to be complete because the additional information requested is not available or has already been provided. In that case, the period referred to in Article 4(5) shall begin on the day following receipt of the statement. If the notification is deemed to be withdrawn, the Commission shall inform the Member State thereof.

Article 6
Formal Investigation Procedure

1. The decision to initiate the formal investigation procedure shall summarise the relevant issues of fact and law, shall include a preliminary assessment of the Commission as to the aid character of the proposed measure and shall set out the doubts as to its compatibility with the common market. The decision shall call upon the Member State concerned and upon other interested parties to submit comments within a prescribed period which shall normally not exceed one month. In duly justified cases, the Commission may extend the prescribed period.

2. The comments received shall be submitted to the Member State concerned. If an interested party so requests, on grounds of potential damage, its identity shall be withheld from the Member State concerned. The Member State concerned may reply to the comments submitted within a prescribed period which shall normally not exceed one month. In duly justified cases, the Commission may extend the prescribed period.

Article 7
Decisions of the Commission to Close the Formal Investigation Procedure

1. Without prejudice to Article 8, the formal investigation procedure shall be closed by means of a decision as provided for in paragraphs 2 to 5 of this Article.

2. Where the Commission finds that, where appropriate following modification by the Member State concerned, the notified measure does not constitute aid, it shall record that finding by way of a decision.

3. Where the Commission finds that, where appropriate following modification by the Member State concerned, the doubts as to the compatibility of the notified measure with the common market have been removed, it shall decide that the aid is compatible with the common market (hereinafter referred to as a 'positive decision'). That decision shall specify which exception under the Treaty has been applied.

4. The Commission may attach to a positive decision conditions subject to which an aid may be considered compatible with the common market and may lay down obligations to enable compliance with the decision to be monitored (hereinafter referred to as a 'conditional decision').

5. Where the Commission finds that the notified aid is not compatible with the common market, it shall decide that the aid shall not be put into effect (hereinafter referred to as a 'negative decision').

6. Decisions taken pursuant to paragraphs 2, 3, 4 and 5 shall be taken as soon as the doubts referred to in Article 4(4) have been removed. The Commission shall as far as possible endeavour to adopt a decision within a period of 18 months from the opening of the procedure. This time limit may be extended by common agreement between the Commission and the Member State concerned.

7. Once the time limit referred to in paragraph 6 has expired, and should the Member State concerned so request, the Commission shall, within two months, take a decision on the basis of the information available to it. If appropriate, where the information provided is not sufficient to establish compatibility, the Commission shall take a negative decision.

Article 8
Withdrawal of Notification

1. The Member State concerned may withdraw the notification within the meaning of Article 2 in due time before the Commission has taken a decision pursuant to Article 4 or 7.

2. In cases where the Commission initiated the formal investigation procedure, the Commission shall close that procedure.

Article 9
Revocation of a Decision

The Commission may revoke a decision taken pursuant to Article 4(2) or (3), or Article 7(2), (3), (4), after having given the Member State concerned the opportunity to submit its comments, where the decision was based on incorrect information provided during the procedure which was a determining factor for the decision. Before revoking a decision and taking a new decision, the Commission shall open the formal investigation procedure pursuant to Article 4(4). Articles 6, 7 and 10, Article 11(1), Articles 13, 14 and 15 shall apply *mutatis mutandis*.

CHAPTER III. PROCEDURE REGARDING UNLAWFUL AID

Article 10
Examination, Request for Information and Information Injunction

1. Where the Commission has in its possession information from whatever source regarding alleged unlawful aid, it shall examine that information without delay.

2. If necessary, it shall request information from the Member State concerned. Article 2(2) and Article 5(1) and (2) shall apply *mutatis mutandis*.

3. Where, despite a reminder pursuant to Article 5(2), the Member State concerned does not provide the information requested within the period prescribed by the Commission, or where it provides incomplete information, the Commission shall by decision require the information to be provided (hereinafter referred to as an 'information injunction'). The decision shall specify what information is required and prescribe an appropriate period within which it is to be supplied.

Article 11
Injunction to Suspend or Provisionally Recover Aid

1. The Commission may, after giving the Member State concerned the opportunity to submit its comments, adopt a decision requiring the Member State to suspend any unlawful aid until the Commission has taken a decision on the compatibility of the aid with the common market (hereinafter referred to as a 'suspension injunction').

2. The Commission may, after giving the Member State concerned the opportunity to submit its comments, adopt a decision requiring the Member State provisionally to recover any unlawful aid until the Commission has taken a decision on the compatibility of the aid with the common market (hereinafter referred to as a 'recovery injunction'), if the following criteria are fulfilled:

— according to an established practice there are no doubts about the aid character of the measure concerned and

— there is an urgency to act and

— there is a serious risk of substantial and irreparable damage to a competitor.

Recovery shall be effected in accordance with the procedure set out in Article 14(2) and (3). After the aid has been effectively recovered, the Commission shall take a decision within the time limits applicable to notified aid.

The Commission may authorise the Member State to couple the refunding of the aid with the payment of rescue aid to the firm concerned.

The provisions of this paragraph shall be applicable only to unlawful aid implemented after the entry into force of this Regulation.

Article 12
Non-compliance with an Injunction Decision

If the Member State fails to comply with a suspension injunction or a recovery injunction, the Commission shall be entitled, while carrying out the examination on the substance of the matter on the basis of the information available, to refer the matter to the Court of Justice of the European Communities direct and apply for a declaration that the failure to comply constitutes an infringement of the Treaty.

Article 13
Decisions of the Commission

1. The examination of possible unlawful aid shall result in a decision pursuant to Article 4(2), (3) or (4). In the case of decisions to initiate the formal investigation procedure, proceedings shall

be closed by means of a decision pursuant to Article 7. If a Member State fails to comply with an information injunction, that decision shall be taken on the basis of the information available.

2. In cases of possible unlawful aid and without prejudice to Article 11(2), the Commission shall not be bound by the time-limit set out in Articles 4(5), 7(6) and 7(7).

3. Article 9 shall apply *mutatis mutandis*.

Article 14
Recovery of Aid

1. Where negative decisions are taken in cases of unlawful aid, the Commission shall decide that the Member State concerned shall take all necessary measures to recover the aid from the beneficiary (hereinafter referred to as a 'recovery decision'). The Commission shall not require recovery of the aid if this would be contrary to a general principle of Community law.

2. The aid to be recovered pursuant to a recovery decision shall include interest at an appropriate rate fixed by the Commission. Interest shall be payable from the date on which the unlawful aid was at the disposal of the beneficiary until the date of its recovery.

3. Without prejudice to any order of the Court of Justice of the European Communities pursuant to Article 185 of the Treaty, recovery shall be effected without delay and in accordance with the procedures under the national law of the Member State concerned, provided that they allow the immediate and effective execution of the Commission's decision. To this effect and in the event of a procedure before national courts, the Member States concerned shall take all necessary steps which are available in their respective legal systems, including provisional measures, without prejudice to Community law.

Article 15
Limitation Period

1. The powers of the Commission to recover aid shall be subject to a limitation period of ten years.

2. The limitation period shall begin on the day on which the unlawful aid is awarded to the beneficiary either as individual aid or as aid under an aid scheme. Any action taken by the Commission or by a Member State, acting at the request of the Commission, with regard to the unlawful aid shall interrupt the limitation period. Each interruption shall start time running afresh. The limitation period shall be suspended for as long as the decision of the Commission is the subject of proceedings pending before the Court of Justice of the European Communities.

3. Any aid with regard to which the limitation period has expired, shall be deemed to be existing aid.

CHAPTER IV. PROCEDURE REGARDING MISUSE OF AID

Article 16
Misuse of Aid

Without prejudice to Article 23, the Commission may in cases of misuse of aid open the formal investigation procedure pursuant to Article 4(4). Articles 6, 7, 9 and 10, Article 11(1), Articles 12, 13, 14 and 15 shall apply *mutatis mutandis*.

Chapter V. Procedure Regarding Existing Aid Schemes

Article 17
Cooperation Pursuant to Article 93(1) of the Treaty

1. The Commission shall obtain from the Member State concerned all necessary information for the review, in cooperation with the Member State, of existing aid schemes pursuant to Article 93(1) of the Treaty.

2. Where the Commission considers that an existing aid scheme is not, or is no longer, compatible with the common market, it shall inform the Member State concerned of its preliminary view and give the Member State concerned the opportunity to submit its comments within a period of one month. In duly justified cases, the Commission may extend this period.

Article 18
Proposal for Appropriate Measures

Where the Commission, in the light of the information submitted by the Member State pursuant to Article 17, concludes that the existing aid scheme is not, or is no longer, compatible with the common market, it shall issue a recommendation proposing appropriate measures to the Member State concerned. The recommendation may propose, in particular:
(a) substantive amendment of the aid scheme, or
(b) introduction of procedural requirements, or
(c) abolition of the aid scheme.

Article 19
Legal consequences of a Proposal for Appropriate Measures

1. Where the Member State concerned accepts the proposed measures and informs the Commission thereof, the Commission shall record that finding and inform the Member State thereof. The Member State shall be bound by its acceptance to implement the appropriate measures.

2. Where the Member State concerned does not accept the proposed measures and the Commission, having taken into account the arguments of the Member State concerned, still considers that those measures are necessary, it shall initiate proceedings pursuant to Article 4(4). Articles 6, 7 and 9 shall apply *mutatis mutandis.*

Chapter VI. Interested Parties

Article 20
Rights of Interested Parties

1. Any interested party may submit comments pursuant to Article 6 following a Commission decision to initiate the formal investigation procedure. Any interested party which has submitted such comments and any beneficiary of individual aid shall be sent a copy of the decision taken by the Commission pursuant to Article 7.

2. Any interested party may inform the Commission of any alleged unlawful aid and any alleged misuse of aid. Where the Commission considers that on the basis of the information in its possession there are insufficient grounds for taking a view on the case, it shall inform the interested party thereof. Where the Commission takes a decision on a case concerning the subject matter of the information supplied, it shall send a copy of that decision to the interested party.

3. At its request, any interested party shall obtain a copy of any decision pursuant to Articles 4 and 7, Article 10(3) and Article 11.

CHAPTER VII. MONITORING

Article 21
Annual Reports

1. Member States shall submit to the Commission annual reports on all existing aid schemes with regard to which no specific reporting obligations have been imposed in a conditional decision pursuant to Article 7(4).

2. Where, despite a reminder, the Member State concerned fails to submit an annual report, the Commission may proceed in accordance with Article 18 with regard to the aid scheme concerned.

Article 22
On-site Monitoring

1. Where the Commission has serious doubts as to whether decisions not to raise objections, positive decisions or conditional decisions with regard to individual aid are being complied with, the Member State concerned, after having been given the opportunity to submit its comments, shall allow the Commission to undertake on-site monitoring visits.

2. The officials authorised by the Commission shall be empowered, in order to verify compliance with the decision concerned:
(a) to enter any premises and land of the undertaking concerned;
(b) to ask for oral explanations on the spot;
(c) to examine books and other business records and take, or demand, copies.

The Commission may be assisted if necessary by independent experts.

3. The Commission shall inform the Member State concerned, in good time and in writing, of the on-site monitoring visit and of the identities of the authorised officials and experts. If the Member State has duly justified objections to the Commission's choice of experts, the experts shall be appointed in common agreement with the Member State. The officials of the Commission and the experts authorised to carry out the on-site monitoring shall produce an authorisation in writing specifying the subject-matter and purpose of the visit.

4. Officials authorised by the Member State in whose territory the monitoring visit is to be made may be present at the monitoring visit.

5. The Commission shall provide the Member State with a copy of any report produced as a result of the monitoring visit.

6. Where an undertaking opposes a monitoring visit ordered by a Commission decision pursuant to this Article, the Member State concerned shall afford the necessary assistance to the officials and experts authorised by the Commission to enable them to carry out the monitoring visit. To this end the Member States shall, after consulting the Commission, take the necessary measures within eighteen months after the entry into force of this Regulation.

Article 23
Non-compliance with Decisions and Judgments

1. Where the Member State concerned does not comply with conditional or negative decisions, in particular in cases referred to in Article 14, the Commission may refer the matter to the Court of Justice of the European Communities direct in accordance with Article 93(2) of the Treaty.

2. If the Commission considers that the Member State concerned has not complied with a judgment of the Court of Justice of the European Communities, the Commission may pursue the matter in accordance with Article 171 of the Treaty.

CHAPTER VIII. COMMON PROVISIONS

Article 24
Professional Secrecy

The Commission and the Member States, their officials and other servants, including independent experts appointed by the Commission, shall not disclose information which they have acquired through the application of this Regulation and which is covered by the obligation of professional secrecy.

Article 25
Addressee of Decisions

Decisions taken pursuant to Chapters II, III, IV, V and VII shall be addressed to the Member State concerned. The Commission shall notify them to the Member State concerned without delay and give the latter the opportunity to indicate the Commission which information it considers to be covered by the obligation of professional secrecy.

Article 26
Publication of Decisions

1. The Commission shall publish in the *Official Journal of the European Communities* a summary notice of the decisions which it takes pursuant to Article 4(2) and (3) and Article 18 in conjunction with Article 19(1). The summary notice shall state that a copy of the decision may be obtained in the authentic language version or versions.

2. The Commission shall publish in the *Official Journal of the European Communities* the decisions which it takes pursuant to Article 4(4) in their authentic language version. In the Official Journal published in languages other than the authentic language version, the authentic language version will be accompanied by a meaningful summary in the language of that Official Journal.

3. The Commission shall publish in the *Official Journal of the European Communities* the decisions which it takes pursuant to Article 7.

4. In cases where Article 4(6) or Article 8(2) applies, a short notice shall be published in the *Official Journal of the European Communities.*

5. The Council, acting unanimously, may decide to publish decisions pursuant to the third subparagraph of Article 93(2) of the Treaty in the *Official Journal of the European Communities.*

Article 27
Implementing Provisions

The Commission, acting in accordance with the procedure laid down in Article 29, shall have the power to adopt implementing provisions concerning the form, content and other details of notifications, the form, content and other details of annual reports, details of time-limits and the calculation of time-limits, and the interest rate referred to in Article 14(2).

Article 28
Advisory Committee on State Aid

An Advisory Committee on State aid (hereinafter referred to as the 'Committee') shall be set up. It shall be composed of representatives of the Member States and chaired by the representative of the Commission.

Article 29
Consultation of the Committee

1. The Commission shall consult the Committee before adopting any implementing provision pursuant to Article 27.

2. Consultation of the Committee shall take place at a meeting called by the Commission. The drafts and documents to be examined shall be annexed to the notification. The meeting shall take place no earlier than two months after notification has been sent. This period may be reduced in the case of urgency.

3. The Commission representative shall submit to the Committee a draft of the measures to be taken. The Committee shall deliver an opinion on the draft, within a time-limit which the chairman may lay down according to the urgency of the matter, if necessary by taking a vote.

4. The opinion shall be recorded in the minutes; in addition, each Member State shall have the right to ask to have its position recorded in the minutes. The Committee may recommend the publication of this opinion in the *Official Journal of the European Communities*.

5. The Commission shall take the utmost account of the opinion delivered by the Committee. It shall inform the Committee on the manner in which its opinion has been taken into account.

Article 30
Entry into Force

This Regulation shall enter into force on the twentieth day following that of its publication in the *Official Journal of the European Communities*.

This Regulation shall be binding in its entirety and directly applicable in all Member States.

Done at Brussels, 22 March 1999.

For the Council
The President
G. VERHEUGEN

EXTRACT FROM THE ANNEX II OF THE ACT OF ACCESSION OF
CZECH REPUBLIC, ESTONIA, CYPRUS, LATVIA, LITHUANIA,
HUNGARY, MALTA, POLAND, SLOVENIA AND SLOVAKIA

5. Competition Policy

[. . .]

6. 31999 R 0659: Council Regulation (EC) No 659/1999 of 22 March 1999 laying down detailed rules for the application of Article 93 of the EC Treaty (OJ L 83, 27.3.1999, p. 1).

Article 1(b)(i) is replaced by the following:

'(i) without prejudice to Articles 144 and 172 of the Act of Accession of Austria, Finland and Sweden and to Annex IV, point 3 and the Appendix to said Annex of the Act of Accession of the Czech Republic, Estonia, Cyprus, Latvia, Lithuania, Hungary, Malta, Poland, Slovenia and Slovakia, all aid which existed prior to the entry into force of the Treaty in the respective Member States, that is to say, aid schemes and individual aid which were put into effect before, and are still applicable after, the entry into force of the Treaty'.

[. . .]

APPENDIX 31

Commission Regulation (EC) No 794/2004 of 21 April 2004 implementing Council Regulation (EC) No 659/1999 laying down detailed rules for the application of Article 93 of the EC Treaty

THE COMMISSION OF THE EUROPEAN COMMUNITIES,

Having regard to the Treaty establishing the European Community,

Having regard to Council Regulation (EC) No 659/1999 of 22 March 1999 laying down detailed rules for the application of Article 93 of the EC Treaty,[1] and in particular Article 27 thereof,

After consulting the Advisory Committee on State Aid,

Whereas:

(1) In order to facilitate the preparation of State aid notifications by Member States, and their assessment by the Commission, it is desirable to establish a compulsory notification form. That form should be as comprehensive as possible.

(2) The standard notification form as well as the summary information sheet and the supplementary information sheets should cover all existing guidelines and frameworks in the state aid field. They should be subject to modification or replacement in accordance with the further development of those texts.

(3) Provision should be made for a simplified system of notification for certain alterations to existing aid. Such simplified arrangements should only be accepted if the Commission has been regularly informed on the implementation of the existing aid concerned.

(4) In the interests of legal certainty it is appropriate to make it clear that small increases of up to 20% of the original budget of an aid scheme, in particular to take account of the effects of inflation, should not need to be notified to the Commission as they are unlikely to affect the Commission's original assessment of the compatibility of the scheme, provided that the other conditions of the aid scheme remain unchanged.

(5) Article 21 of Regulation (EC) No 659/1999 requires Member States to submit annual reports to the Commission on all existing aid schemes or individual aid granted outside an approved aid scheme in respect of which no specific reporting obligations have been imposed in a conditional decision.

(6) For the Commission to be able to discharge its responsibilities for the monitoring of aid, it needs to receive accurate information from Member States about the types and amounts of aid being granted by them under existing aid schemes. It is possible to simplify and improve the arrangements for the reporting of State aid to the Commission which are currently described in the joint procedure for reporting and notification under the EC Treaty and under the World Trade Organisation (WTO) Agreement set out in the Commission's letter to Member States of 2 August 1995. The part of that joint procedure relating to Member States reporting obligations for subsidy notifications under Article 25 of the WTO

---

[1] OJ L83, 27.3.1999, p 1. Reg as amended by the 2003 Act of Accession.

Agreement on Subsidies and Countervailing measures and under Article XVI of GATT 1994, adopted on 21 July 1995 is not covered by this Regulation.

(7) The information required in the annual reports is intended to enable the Commission to monitor overall aid levels and to form a general view of the effects of different types of aid on competition. To this end, the Commission may also request Member States to provide, on an ad hoc basis, additional data for selected topics. The choice of subject matter should be discussed in advance with Member States.

(8) The annual reporting exercise does not cover the information, which may be necessary in order to verify that particular aid measures respect Community law. The Commission should therefore retain the right to seek undertakings from Member States, or to attach to decisions conditions requiring the provision of additional information.

(9) It should be specified that time-limits for the purposes of Regulation (EC) No 659/1999 should be calculated in accordance with Regulation (EEC, Euratom) No 1182/71 of the Council of 3 June 1971 determining the rules applicable to periods, dates and time limits,[2] as supplemented by the specific rules set out in this Regulation. In particular, it is necessary to identify the events, which determine the starting point for time-limits applicable in State aid procedures. The rules set out in this Regulation should apply to pre-existing time-limits which will continue to run after the entry into force of this Regulation.

(10) The purpose of recovery is to re-establish the situation existing before aid was unlawfully granted. To ensure equal treatment, the advantage should be measured objectively from the moment when the aid is available to the beneficiary undertaking, independently of the outcome of any commercial decisions subsequently made by that undertaking.

(11) In accordance with general financial practice it is appropriate to fix the recovery interest rate as an annual percentage rate.

(12) The volume and frequency of transactions between banks results in an interest rate that is consistently measurable and statistically significant, and should therefore form the basis of the recovery interest rate. The inter-bank swap rate should, however, be adjusted in order to reflect general levels of increased commercial risk outside the banking sector. On the basis of the information on inter-bank swap rates the Commission should establish a single recovery interest rate for each Member State. In the interest of legal certainty and equal treatment, it is appropriate to fix the precise method by which the interest rate should be calculated, and to provide for the publication of the recovery interest rate applicable at any given moment, as well as relevant previously applicable rates.

(13) A State aid grant may be deemed to reduce a beneficiary undertaking's medium-term financing requirements. For these purposes, and in line with general financial practice, the medium-term may be defined as five years. The recovery interest rate should therefore correspond to an annual percentage rate fixed for five years.

(14) Given the objective of restoring the situation existing before the aid was unlawfully granted, and in accordance with general financial practice, the recovery interest rate to be fixed by the Commission should be annually compounded. For the same reasons, the recovery interest rate applicable in the first year of the recovery period should be applied for the first five years of the recovery period, and the recovery interest rate applicable in the sixth year of the recovery period for the following five years.

(15) This Regulation should apply to recovery decisions notified after the date of entry into force of this Regulation,

HAS ADOPTED THIS REGULATION:

---

[2] OJ L124, 8.6.1971, p 1.

CHAPTER I. SUBJECT MATTER AND SCOPE

Article 1
Subject Matter and Scope

1. This Regulation sets out detailed provisions concerning the form, content and other details of notifications and annual reports referred to in Regulation (EC) No 659/1999. It also sets out provisions for the calculation of time-limits in all procedures concerning State aid and of the interest rate for the recovery of unlawful aid.

2. This Regulation shall apply to aid in all sectors.

CHAPTER II. NOTIFICATIONS

Article 2
Notification Forms

Without prejudice to Member States' obligations to notify state aids in the coal sector under Commission Decision 2002/871/CE,[3] notifications of new aid pursuant to Article 2(1) of Regulation (EC) No 659/1999, other than those referred to in Article 4(2), shall be made on the notification form set out in Part I of Annex I to this Regulation.

Supplementary information needed for the assessment of the measure in accordance with regulations, guidelines, frameworks and other texts applicable to State aid shall be provided on the supplementary information sheets set out in Part III of Annex I.

Whenever the relevant guidelines or frameworks are modified or replaced, the Commission shall adapt the corresponding forms and information sheets.

Article 3
Transmission of Notifications

1. The notification shall be transmitted to the Commission by the Permanent Representative of the Member State concerned. It shall be addressed to the Secretary—General of the Commission.

If the Member State intends to avail itself of a specific procedure laid down in any regulations, guidelines, frameworks and other texts applicable to State aid, a copy of the notification shall be addressed to the Director-General responsible. The Secretary—General and the Directors—General may designate contact points for the receipt of notifications.

2. All subsequent correspondence shall be addressed to the Director—General responsible or to the contact point designated by the Director—General.

3. The Commission shall address its correspondence to the Permanent Representative of the Member State concerned, or to any other address designated by that Member State.

4. Until 31 December 2005 notifications shall be transmitted by the Member State on paper. Whenever possible an electronic copy of the notification shall also be transmitted.

With effect from 1 January 2006 notifications shall be transmitted electronically, unless otherwise agreed by the Commission and the notifying Member State.

All correspondence in connection with a notification which has been submitted after 1 January 2006 shall be transmitted electronically.

5. The date of transmission by fax to the number designated by the receiving party shall be considered to be the date of transmission on paper, if the signed original is received no later than ten days thereafter.

---

[3] OJ L300, 5.11.2002, p 42.

6. By 30 September 2005 at the latest, after consulting Member States, the Commission shall publish in the *Official Journal of the European Union* details of the arrangements for the electronic transmission of notifications, including addresses together with any necessary arrangements for the protection of confidential information.

Article 4
Simplified Notification Procedure for Certain Alterations to Existing Aid

1. For the purposes of Article 1(c) of Regulation (EC) No 659/1999, an alteration to existing aid shall mean any change, other than modifications of a purely formal or administrative nature which cannot affect the evaluation of the compatibility of the aid measure with the common market. However an increase in the original budget of an existing aid scheme by up to 20% shall not be considered an alteration to existing aid.

2. The following alterations to existing aid shall be notified on the simplified notification form set out in Annex II:
(a) increases in the budget of an authorized aid scheme exceeding 20%;
(b) prolongation of an existing authorized aid scheme by up to six years, with or without an increase in the budget;
(c) tightening of the criteria for the application of an authorized aid scheme, a reduction of aid intensity or a reduction of eligible expenses:

The Commission shall use its best endeavours to take a decision on any aid notified on the simplified notification form within a period of one month.

3. The simplified notification procedure shall not be used to notify alterations to aid schemes in respect of which Member States have not submitted annual reports in accordance with Article 5, 6, and 7, unless the annual reports for the years in which the aid has been granted are submitted at the same time as the notification.

CHAPTER III. ANNUAL REPORTS

Article 5
Form and Content of Annual Reports

1. Without prejudice to the second and third subparagraphs of this Article and to any additional specific reporting requirements laid down in a conditional decision adopted pursuant to Article 7(4) of Regulation (EC) No 659/1999, or to the observance of any undertakings provided by the Member State concerned in connection with a decision to approve aid, Member States shall compile the annual reports on existing aid schemes referred to in Article 21(1) of Regulation (EC) No 659/1999 in respect of each whole or part calendar year during which the scheme applies in accordance with the standardised reporting format set out in Annex IIIA.

Annex IIIB sets out the format for annual reports on existing aid schemes relating to the production, processing and marketing of agricultural products listed in Annex I of the Treaty.

Annex IIIC sets out the format for annual reports on existing aid schemes for state aid relating to the production, processing or marketing of fisheries products listed in Annex I of the Treaty.

2. The Commission may ask Member States to provide additional data for selected topics, to be discussed in advance with Member States.

Article 6
Transmission and Publication of Annual Reports

1. Each Member State shall transmit its annual reports to the Commission in electronic form no later than 30 June of the year following the year to which the report relates.

In justified cases Member States may submit estimates, provided that the actual figures are transmitted at the very latest with the following year's data.

2. Each year the Commission shall publish a State aid synopsis containing a synthesis of the information contained in the annual reports submitted during the previous year.

Article 7
Status of Annual Reports

The transmission of annual reports shall not be considered to constitute compliance with the obligation to notify aid measures before they are put into effect pursuant to Article 88(3) of the Treaty, nor shall such transmission in any way prejudice the outcome of an investigation into allegedly unlawful aid in accordance with the procedure laid down in Chapter III of Regulation (EC) No 659/1999.

CHAPTER IV. TIME-LIMITS

Article 8
Calculation of Time-limits

1. Time-limits provided for in Regulation (EC) No 659/1999 and in this Regulation or fixed by the Commission pursuant to Article 88 of the Treaty shall be calculated in accordance with Regulation (EEC, Euratom) No 1182/71, and the specific rules set out in paragraphs 2 to 5 of this Article. In case of conflict, the provisions of this regulation shall prevail.

2. Time limits shall be specified in months or in working days.

3. With regard to time-limits for action by the Commission, the receipt of the notification or subsequent correspondence in accordance with Article 3(1) and Article 3(2) of this Regulation shall be the relevant event for the purpose of Article 3(1) of Regulation (EEC, Euratom) No 1182/71.

As far as notifications transmitted after 31 December 2005, and correspondence relating to them are concerned, the receipt of the electronic notification or communication at the relevant address published in the *Official Journal of the European Union* shall be the relevant event.

4. With regard to time-limits for action by Member States, the receipt of the relevant notification or correspondence from the Commission in accordance with Art. 3(3) of this Regulation shall be the relevant event for the purposes of Article 3(1) of Regulation (EEC, Euratom) No 1182/71.

5. With regard to the time-limit for the submission of comments following initiation of the formal investigation procedure referred to in Art. 6(1) of Regulation (EC) No 659/1999 by third parties and those Member States which are not directly concerned by the procedure, the publication of the notice of initiation in the *Official Journal of the European Union* shall be the relevant event for the purposes of Article 3(1) of Regulation (EEC, Euratom) No 1182/71.

6. Any request for the extension of a time-limit shall be duly substantiated, and shall be submitted in writing to the address designated by the party fixing the time-limit at least two working days before expiry.

CHAPTER V. INTEREST RATE FOR THE RECOVERY OF UNLAWFUL AID

Article 9
Method for Fixing the Interest Rate

1. Unless otherwise provided for in a specific decision the interest rate to be used for recovering State aid granted in breach of Article 88(3) of the Treaty shall be an annual percentage rate fixed for each calendar year.

It shall be calculated on the basis of the average of the five-year inter-bank swap rates for September, October and November of the previous year, plus 75 basis points. In duly justified cases, the Commission may increase the rate by more than 75 basis points in respect of one or more Member States.

2. If the latest three-month average of the five-year inter-bank swap rates available, plus 75 basis points, differs, by more than 15% from the State aid recovery interest rate in force, the Commission shall recalculate the latter.

The new rate shall apply from the first day of the month following the recalculation by the Commission. The Commission shall inform Member States by letter of the recalculation and the date from which it applies.

3. The interest rate shall be fixed for each Member State individually, or for two or more Member States together.

4. In the absence of reliable or equivalent data or in exceptional circumstances the Commission may, in close co-operation with the Member State(s) concerned, fix a State aid recovery interest rate, for one or more Member States, on the basis of a different method and on the basis of the information available to it.

Article 10
Publication

The Commission shall publish current and relevant historical State aid recovery interest rates in the *Official Journal of the European Union* and for information on the Internet.

Article 11
Method for Applying Interest

1. The interest rate to be applied shall be the rate applicable on the date on which unlawful aid was first put at the disposal of the beneficiary.

2. The interest rate shall be applied on a compound basis until the date of the recovery of the aid. The interest accruing in the previous year shall be subject to interest in each subsequent year.

3. The interest rate referred to in paragraph 1 shall be applied throughout the whole period until the date of recovery. However, if more than five years have elapsed between the date on which the unlawful aid was first put at the disposal of the beneficiary and the date of the recovery of the aid, the interest rate shall be recalculated at five yearly intervals, taking as a basis the rate in force at the time of recalculation.

CHAPTER VI. FINAL PROVISIONS

Article 12
Review

The Commission shall in consultation with the Member States, review the application of this Regulation within four years after its entry into force.

Article 13
Entry into Force

This Regulation shall enter into force on the twentieth day following that of its publication in the *Official Journal of the European Union.*

Chapter II shall apply only to those notifications transmitted to the Commission more than five months after the entry into force of this Regulation.

Chapter III shall apply to annual reports covering aid granted from 1 January 2003 onwards.

Chapter IV shall apply to any time-limit, which has been fixed but which has not yet expired on the date of entry into force of this Regulation.

Articles 9 and 11 shall apply in relation to any recovery decision notified after the date of entry into force of this Regulation.

This Regulation shall be binding in its entirety and be directly applicable in all Member States.

Done at Brussels, 21 April 2004.

For the Commission
Mario MONTI
Member of the Commission

ANNEX I. STANDARD FORM FOR NOTIFICATION OF STATE AIDS PURSUANT TO ARTICLE 88 (3) EC TREATY AND FOR THE PROVISIONS OF INFORMATION ON UNLAWFUL AID

This form shall be used by Member States for the notification pursuant to Article 88(3) EC Treaty of new aid schemes and individual aid it shall also be used when a non-aid measure is notified to the Commission for reasons of legal certainty.

Member States are also requested to use this form when the Commission requests comprehensive information on alleged unlawful aid.

The present form consists of three parts:

I   **General Information**: to be completed in all cases
II **Summary Information for publication in the Official Journal**
III **Supplementary Information Sheet depending on the type of aid**

Please note that failure to complete this form correctly may result in the notification being returned as incomplete. The completed form shall be transmitted on paper to the Commission by the Permanent Representative of the Member State concerned. It shall be addressed to the Secretary General of the Commission.

If the Member State intends to avail itself of a specific procedure laid down in any regulations, guidelines, frameworks and other texts applicable to State aid, a copy of the notification shall be as well addressed to the Director-General of the Commission department responsible.

PART I. GENERAL INFORMATION
STATUS OF THE NOTIFICATION

Does the information transmitted on this form concern:

☐ **notification pursuant to Article 88(3) EC Treaty?**

☐ **possible unlawful aid?**[4]

If yes, please specify the date of putting into effect of the aid. Please complete this form, as well as the relevant supplementary forms.

☐ **non-aid measure which is notified to the Commission for reasons of legal certainty?**

---

[4] According to Art 1 (f) of Council Reg (EC) N° 659/1999 of 22 March 1999 laying down detailed rules for the application of Art 93 of the EC Treaty (OJ L83, 27.3.1999, p 1) (hereinafter 'Procedural Regulation'), unlawful aid shall mean new aid put into effect in contravention of Art 88(3) of the EC-Treaty.

Please indicate below the reasons why the notifying Member State considers that the measure does not constitute State aid in the meaning of Article 87(1) EC Treaty. Please complete the relevant parts of this form and provide all necessary supporting documentation.

A measure will not constitute State aid if one of the conditions laid down in Article 87(1) EC Treaty is not fulfilled. Please provide a full assessment of the measure in the light of the following criteria focusing in particular on the criterion which you consider not to be met:

— No transfer of public resources (For example, if you consider the measure is not imputable to the State or where you consider that regulatory measures without transfer of public resources will be put in place).

— No advantage (For example, where the private market investor principle is respected)

— No selectivity/specificity (For example, where the measure is available to all enterprises, in all sectors of the economy and without any territorial limitation and without discretion).

— No distortion of competition/no affectation of intra-community trade (For example, where the activity is not of an economic nature or where the economic activity is purely local)

1   Identification of the aid grantor

1.1   Member State concerned

....

1.2   Region(s) concerned (if applicable)

....

1.3   ....

Responsible contact person:

Name	:	....
Address	:	....
Telephone	:	....
Fax	:	....
E-mail	:	....

1.4   Responsible contact person at the Permanent Representation:

Name	:	....
Telephone	:	....
Fax	:	....
E-mail	:	....

1.5   If you wish that a *copy* of the official correspondence sent by the Commission to the Member State should be forward to other national authorities, please indicate here their name and address:

Name	:	....
Address	:	....
		....
		....

1.6   Indicate Member State reference you wish to be included in the correspondence from the Commission

2   **Identification of the aid**

2.1   Title of the aid (or name of company beneficiary in case of individual aid)

....

2.2   Brief description of the objective of the aid.

Please indicate primary objective and, if applicable, secondary objective(s):

	Primary objective (please tick *one* only)	**Secondary objective**[5]
Regional development	☐	☐
Research and development	☐	☐
Environmental protection	☐	☐
Rescuing firms in difficulty	☐	☐
Restructuring firms in difficulty	☐	☐
SMEs	☐	☐
Employment	☐	☐
Training	☐	☐
Risk capital	☐	☐
Promotion of export and internationalisation	☐	☐
Services of general economic interest	☐	☐
Sectoral development[6]	☐	☐
Social support to individual consumers	☐	☐
Compensation of damage caused by natural disasters or exceptional occurrences	☐	☐
Execution of an important project of common European interest	☐	☐
Remedy for a serious disturbance in the economy	☐	☐
Heritage conservation	☐	☐
Culture	☐	☐

2.3   Scheme—Individual aid[7]

2.3.1 Does the notification relate to an aid scheme?

☐ yes   ☐ no

— If yes, does the scheme amend an existing aid scheme?

☐ yes   ☐ no

---

[5] A secondary objective is one for which, in addition to the primary objective, the aid will be exclusively earmarked. For example, a scheme for which the primary objective is research and development may have as a secondary objective and medium-sized enterprises (SMEs) if the aid is earmarked exclusively for SMEs. The secondary objective may also be sectoral, in the case for example of a research and development scheme in the steel sector.

[6] Please specify sector in point 4.2.

[7] According to Art 1(e) of Council Reg (EC) N° 659/1999 of 22 March 1999 laying down detailed rules for the application of Art 93 of the EC Treaty (O) L 83, 27.3.1999, p 1), individual aid shall mean aid that is not awarded on the basis of an aid scheme and notifiable award of aid on the basis of a scheme.

— If yes, are the conditions laid down for the simplified notification procedure pursuant to Article 4(2) of the Implementation Regulation (EC) N° (. . .) of (. . .) fulfilled?

☐   yes   ☐   no

— If yes, please use and complete the information requested by the simplified notification form (see Annex II).
— If no, please continue with this form and specify whether the original scheme which is being amended was notified to the Commission.

☐   yes   ☐   no

— If yes, please specify

Aid number:

....

Date of Commission approval (reference of the letter of the Commission (SG(. . .)D/. . .):
. . /. . ./...

Duration of the original scheme:...

Please specify which conditions are being amended in relation to the original scheme and why:

....

2.3.2 Does the notification relate to individual aid?

☐   yes   ☐   no

— If yes, please tick the following appropriate box
☐ aid based on a scheme which should be individually notified
Reference of the authorized scheme:

Title   : ....
Aid number   : ....
Letter of Commission approval   : ....

☐ individual aid not based on a scheme

2.3.3 Does the notification relate to an individual aidor scheme notified pursuant to an exemption regulation? If yes, please tick the following appropriate box:

☐ Commission Regulation (EC) N° 70/2001 on the application of Article 87 and 88 EC Treaty to State aid to small and medium-sized enterprises.[8] Please use the supplementary information sheet under part III, 1
☐ Commission Regulation N° 68/2001 on the application fo Articles 87 and 88 EC Treaty to training aid.[9] Please use the supplementary information sheet under part III, 2
☐ Commission Regulation (EC) N° 2204/2002 on the application of Articles 87 and 88 EC Treaty to State aid for employment.[10] Please use the supplementary information sheet under part III, 3.

---

[8] Commission Reg (EC) N° 70/2001 of 12 January 2001 on the application of Arts 87 and 88 of the EC Treaty to State aid to small and medium sized enterprises, OJ L10, 13.1.2001, p 33.
[9] Commission Reg (EC) N° 68/200 of 12 January 2001 on the application of Arts 87 and 88 of the EC Treaty to State aid to training aid, OJ L10, 13.1.2001, p 20.
[10] Commission Reg (EC) N° 2204/2002 of 12 December 2002 on the application of Arts 87 and 88 of the EC Treaty to State aid for employment, OJ L337, 13.12.2002, p 3 and OJ L349, 24.12.2002, p 126.

☐ Commission Regulation (EC) N° 1/2004 on the application of Articles 87 and 88 EC Treaty to State aid to small and medium-sized enterprises active in the production, processing and marketing of agricultural products (OJL 1 of 03.01.2004).

3 **National legal basis**

3.1 Please list the national legal basis including the implementing provisions and their respective sources of references:

Title: ....

....

....

....

Reference (where applicable): ....

....

....

3.2 Please indicate the document(s) enclosed with this notification:

☐ A copy of the relevant extracts of the final text(s) of the legal basis (and a web link, if possible)

☐ A copy of the relevant extracts of the draft text(s) of the legal basis (and a web link, if existing)

3.3 In case of a final text, does the final text contain a clause whereby the aid granting body can only grant after the Commission has cleared the aid (stand still clause)?

☐   yes   ☐   no

4 **Beneficiaries**

4.1 Location of the beneficiary(ies)

☐ in (an) unassisted region(s)

☐ in (a) region(s) eligible for assistance under Article 87(3)(c) EC Treaty (specify at NUTS-level 3 or lower)

☐ in (a) region(s) eligible for assistance under Article 87(3)(a) EC Treaty (specify at NUTS-level 2 or lower)

☐ mixed: specify ....

4.2 Sector(s) of the beneficiary(ies):

☐		Not sector specific
☐ .... A		Agriculture
☐ .... B		Fisheries
☐ C		Mining and Quarrying
☐ 10.1		Coal
☐ .... D		Manufacturing industry
	☐ 17	Textiles
	☐ 21	Pulp and paper
	☐ 24	Chemical and pharmaceutical industry
	☐ 24.7	Man-made fibres
	☐ 27.1	Steel[11]

---

[11] Annex B to the Communication from the Commission: 'Multisectoral framework on regional aid for large investment projects', OJ C70, 19.3.2002, p 8.

☐	29	Industrial machinery
☐	..............................DL	Electrical and optical equipment
☐	..............................34.1	Motor vehicles
☐	..............................35.1	Shipbuilding
☐	....	Other Manufacturing sector, please specify:...........
☐	..............................E	Electricity, gas and water supply
☐	..............................F	Construction
☐	52	Retail Services
☐	..............................H	Hotels and restaurants (Tourism)
☐	I	Transport
☐	60	Land transport and transport via pipelines
☐	..............................60.1	Railways
☐	..............................60.2	Other land transport
☐	..............................61.1	Sea and coastal water transport
☐	..............................61.2	Inland water transport
☐	62	Air transport
☐	64	Post and telecommunications
☐	..............................J	Financial intermediation
☐	72	Computer and related activities
☐	92	Recreational, cultural and sporting activities
☐	....	Other, please specify according to NACE rev. 1.1 classification[12]

....

4.3   In case of an individual aid: ....

Name of the beneficiary   : ....
Type of beneficiary   : ....

☐ SME

Number of employees   : ....
Annual turnover   : ....
Annual balance-sheet   : ....
Independence   : ....

(please attach a solemn declaration in line with the Commission Recommendation on SME[13] or provide any other evidence to demonstrate the above criteria):

....

☐ large enterprise
☐ firm in difficulties[14]

4.4   In case of an aid scheme:

Type of beneficiaries:

☐ all firms (large firms and small and medium-sized enterprises)
☐ only large enterprises

---

[12] NACE Rev. 1.1 is the Statistical classification of economic activities in the European Community.
[13] Commission Recommendation of 6 May 2003 concerning the definition of micro, small end medium-sized, OJ L124, 20.5.2003, p 36 and Draft commission Reg (EC) N° . . ./of amending Reg (EC) N° 70/2001 as regards the extension of its scope to include aid for research and development.
[14] As defined in the Community Guidelines for rescuing and restructuring firms in difficulties, OJCE C288 of 9.10.1999, p 218.

☐ small and medium-sized enterprises
    ☐ medium-sized enterprises
    ☐ small enterprises
    ☐ micro enterprises
☐ the following beneficiaries: ....

Estimated number of beneficiaries:

☐ under 10 ....
☐ from 11 to 50 ....
☐ from 51 to 100 ....
☐ from 101 to 500 ....
☐ from 501 to 1000 ....
☐ over 1000 ....

5   Amount of aid/annual expenditure

In case of an individual aid, indicate the overall amount of each measure concerned:

....

In case of a scheme, indicate the annual amount of the budget planned and the overall amount (in national currency):

....

For tax measures, please indicate the estimated annual and overall revenue losses due to tax concessions for the period covered by the notification:

....

If the budget is not adopted annually, please specify what period it covers:

....

If the notification concerns changes to an existing scheme, please give the budgetary effects of the notified changes to the scheme:

....

6   Form of the aid and means of funding

Specify the form of the aid made available to the beneficiary (where appropriate, for each measure):

☐ Direct grant
☐ Soft loan (including details of how the loan is secured)
☐ Interest subsidy
☐ Tax advantage (e.g. tax allowance, tax base reduction, tax rate reduction, tax defer-ment). Please specify:

....

☐ Reduction of social security contributions
☐ Provision of risk capital
☐ Debt write-off
☐ Guarantee (including amongst others information on the loan or other financial trans-action covered by the guarantee, the security required and the premium to be paid)
☐ Other. Please specify: ....

For each instrument of aid, please give a precise description of its rules and conditions of application, including in particular the rate of award, its tax treatment and whether the aid is accorded automatically once certain objective criteria are fulfilled (if so, please mention the criteria) or whether there is an element of discretion by the awarding authorities.

....

Specify the financing of the aid: if the aid is not financed through the general budget of the State/region/municipality, please explain its way of financing:

☐ Through parafiscal charges or taxes affected to a beneficiary, which is not the State. Please provide full details of the charges and the products/activities on which they are levied. Specify in particular whether products imported from other Member States are liable to the charges. Annex a copy of the legal basis for the imposition of the charges

☐ Accumulated reserves

☐ Public enterprises

☐ Other (please specify) ....

7   Duration

7.1   In the case of an individual aid:

Indicate the date when the aid will be put into effect (If the aid will be granted in tranches, indicate the date of each tranche)

....

Specify the duration of the measure for *which* the aid is granted, if applicable

....

7.2   In the case of a scheme:

Indicate the date from which on the aid may be granted

....

Indicate the last date until which aid may be granted

....

If the duration exceeds six years, please demonstrate that a longer time period is indispensable to achieve the objective(s) of the scheme:

....

8   Cumulation of different types of aid

Can the aid be cumulated with aid received from other local, regional, national or Community schemes to cover the same eligible costs?

                        ☐   yes   ☐   no

If so, describe the mechanisms put in place in order to ensure that the cumulation rules are respected:

....

9   Professional confidentiality

Does the notification contain confidential information which should not be disclosed to third parties?

                        ☐   yes   ☐   no

If so, please indicate which parts are confidential and explain why:

....

....

If no, the Commission will publish its decision without asking the Member State.

10   **Compatibility of the aid**

Please identify which of the existing Regulations, frameworks, guidelines and other texts applicable to State aid provide an explicit legal basis for the authorisation of the aid (where appropriate please specify for each measure) and complete the relevant supplementary information sheet(s) in part III

☐ SME aid
  ☐ Notification of an individual aid pursuant to Article 6 of Regulation (EC) N° 70/2001
  ☐ Notification for legal certainty
  ☐ Aid for SMEs in the agricultural sector
☐ Training aid
  ☐ Notification of an individual aid pursuant to Article 5 of Regulation (EC) N° 68/2001
  ☐ Notification for legal certainty
☐ Employment aid
  ☐ Notification of an individual aid pursuant to Article 9 of Regulation (EC) N° 2204/2002
  ☐ Notification of a scheme pursuant to Article 9 of Regulation (EC) N° 2204/2002
  ☐ Notification for legal certainty
☐ Regional aid
☐ Aid coming under the multisectoral framework on regional aid for large investment projects
☐ Research and development aid
☐ Aid for rescuing firms in difficulty
☐ Aid for restructuring firms in difficulty
☐ Aid for audio-visual production
☐ Environmental protection aid
☐ Risk capital aid
☐ Aid in the agricultural sector
☐ Aid in the transport sector
☐ Shipbuilding aid

Where the existing Regulations, frameworks, guidelines or other texts applicable to State aid do not provide an explicit basis for the approval of any of the aid covered by this form, please provide a fully reasoned justification as to why the aid could be considered as compatible with the EC Treaty, referring to the applicable exemption clause of the EC Treaty (Article 86(2), Article 87(2) (a) or (b), Article 87(3) (a), (b), (c) or (d)) as well as other specific provisions relating to Agriculture and Transport

11   **Outstanding recovery orders**

In the case of individual aid has any potential beneficiary of the measure received state aid which is the subject of an outstanding recovery order by the Commission?

☐   yes   ☐   no

If yes, please provide complete details: ....
....
....
....
....

12 **Other information**

Please indicate here any other information you consider relevant to the assessment of the measure(s) concerned under State aid rules.

13 **Attachments**

Please list here all documents which are attached to the notification and provide paper copies or direct internet links to the documents concerned.

14 **Declaration**

I certify that to the best of my knowledge the information provided on this form, its annexes and its attachments is accurate and complete.

Date and place of signature: ....

Signature: ....

Name and position of person signing: ....

PART II. SUMMARY INFORMATION FOR PUBLICATION IN THE OFFICIAL JOURNAL

Number of aid:	(to be completed by the Commission)		
Member State:			
Region:			
Title and objective of aid schemes or name of company beneficiary of an individual aid (aid based on a scheme which should however be notified individually and aid not based on a scheme):			
Legal basis:			
Annual expenditure planned or overall amount of individual aid granted: (In national currency)	Aid scheme	Annual expenditure planned:	Euro ... million
		Overall amount:	Euro ... million
	Individual aid	Overall amount of each measure:	Euro ... million
Duration:			
Maximum aid intensity of the individual aid or the aid scheme:			
Economic sectors:	All sectors:		
	— or Limited to specific sectors as mentioned in 'the 'General information', (Part I, par. 4.2.)		
Name and address of the granting authority	Name:		

Part III. Supplementary Information Sheets

To be completed as necessary depending on the type of aid concerned:

1. SME aid

2. Training aid

3. Employment aid

4. Regional aid

5. Aid coming under the multisectoral framework

6. Research and development aid
   a) in the case of a scheme
   b) in the case of individual aid

7. Aid for rescuing firms in difficulty
   a) in the case of a scheme
   b) n the case of individual aid

8. Aid for restructuring firms in difficulty
   a) in the case of a scheme
   b) in the case of individual aid

9. Aid for audio-visual production

10. Environmental protection aid

11. Risk capital aid

12. Aid in the agricultural sector
    a) Aid for agriculture
       i. Aid for investment in agricultural holdings
       ii. Aid for investments in connection with the processing and marketing of agricultural products
    b) Agri-environmental aid
    c) Aid to compensate for handicaps in the less favoured areas
    d) Aid for the setting up of young farmers
    e) Aid for early retirement or for the cessation of farming activities
    f) Aid for closing production, processing and marketing capacity
    g) Aid for producer groups
    h) Aid to compensate for damage to agricultural production or the means of agricultural production
    i) Aid for land reparcelling
    j) Aid for the production and marketing of quality agricultural products
    k) Aid for the provision of technical support in the agricultural sector
    l) Aid for the livestock sector
    m) Aid for the outermost regions and the Aegean Islands
    n) Aid in the form of subsidised short-term loans
    o) Aid for the promotion and advertising of agricultural and certain non-agricultural products
    p) Aid for rescue and restructuring firms in difficulty
    q) Aid for TSE tests; fallen stock and slaughterhouse waste

13. Aid in the transport sector
    a) Individual aid for restructuring firms in difficulty in the aviation sector
    b) Aid for transport infrastructure
    c) Aid for maritime transport
    d) Aid for combined transport

14. Shipbuilding aid (to be completed)

PART III.1. SUPPLEMENTARY INFORMATION SHEET ON SME AID

This supplementary information sheet must be used for the notification of any individual aid pursuant to Article 6 of Regulation (EC) 70/2001[15] in its modified form.[16] It must also be used in the case of any individual aid or scheme, which is notified to the Commission for reasons of legal certainty.

1   **Type of individual aid or scheme**

Does the individual aid or scheme relate to:

1.1   ☐ investment aid

1.2   ☐ consultancy and other services and activities including participation in fairs

1.3   ☐ R&D expenditure

  ☐ yes:

  — for notifications of R&D aid to SMEs please complete:
  — supplementary information sheet for R&D 6 a for aid schemes
  — supplementary incormation sheet for R&D 6 b for individual aid

2   **Initial investment aid**

2.1   Does the aid cover investment in fixed capital relating to:

  ☐ the setting-up of a new establishment?

  ☐ the extension of an existing establishment?

  ☐ the starting-up of a new activity involving a fundamental change in the product or production process of an existing establishment (through rationalisation, diversification or modernisation)?

  ☐ the purchase of an establishment, which has closed, or which would have closed had it not been purchased?

  Is replacement investment excluded?

  ☐   yes   ☐   no

2.2   Is the aid calculated as percentage of:

  ☐ the investment's eligible costs

  ☐ the wage costs of employment created by the investment (aid to job creation)

2.3   a) ☐ investment in tangible assets: ....

  Is the value of the investment established as a percentage on the basis of:

  ☐ land?

  ☐ buildings?

  ☐ plant/machinery (equipment)?

  Please provide a short description:

  ....

  If the undertaking has its main economic activity in the transport sector, are transport means and transport equipment excluded from the eligible costs (except for railway rolling stock)?

  ☐   yes   ☐   no

---

[15] Commission Reg (EC) N° 70/2001 of 12 January 2001 on the application of Arts 87 and 88 of the EC Treaty to State aid to small and medium sized enterprises, OJ L10, 13.1.2001, p 33.
[16] OJ L63, 28.2.2004, p 22.

If no, please specify the transport means or equipment that are eligible:

....

....

b) ☐ purchasing price for the take over of an establishment which has closed or which would have closed had it not been purchased

c) ☐ intangible investment

The eligible costs of intangible investment shall be the costs of acquisition of the technology:

☐ patents' rights

☐ operating or patented know-how licences

☐ unpatented know-how (technical knowledge)

Please provide a short description[17] ....

d) ☐ wage costs:

Is the amount of the aid expressed as a percentage of the wage costs over a period of two years relating to the employment created?

☐ yes ☐ no

2.4 Intensity of the aid

2.4.1 Investment projects situated outside of assisted regions under Article 87(3)(c) and under Article 87(3)(a) for:

small enterprises ☐ medium sized enterprises ☐

2.4.2 What are the intensities of the aid for investment projects expressed in gross terms?

Please specify: ....

....

Investment projects situated inside of assisted regions under Article 87(3)(c) and under Article 87(3)(a):

small enterprises ☐ medium sized enterprises ☐

What are the intensities of the aid for investment projects expressed in gross terms? Please specify:

....

....

3 **Cumulation of the aid**

3.1 What is the maximum ceiling for cumulated aid?

Please specify: ....

....

4 **Specific conditions for aid for job creation**

4.1 Does the aid provide for guarantees that the aid for job creation is linked to the carrying-out of an initial investment project in tangible or intangible assets?

☐ yes ☐ no

---

[17] This description should reflect how the authorities intend to ensure consistency with point 4,6 of the Guidelines of National Regional Aid, OJ 74, 10.3.1998, p 9, as amended by the community Guidelines on State aid for Rescuring and Restructuring Firms in Difficulty, OJ C288, 9.10.1999, p 2, and the subsequent Amendments to the Guidelines on National Regional Aid, OJ C258, 9.9.2000, p.5.

4.2   Does the aid provide for guarantees that the aid for job creation is created within three years of the investment's completion?

☐   yes   ☐   no

Should one of the two previous questions be answered in the negative, please explain how the authorities intend to comply with these requirements:

....

4.3   Does the employment created represent a net increase in the number of employees in the establishment concerned, compared with the average over the past 12 months?

☐   yes   ☐   no

4.4   Does the aid provide for guarantees that the employment within the qualified region will be maintained for a minimum period of five years?

☐   yes   ☐   no

If yes, what are the guarantees for that? ....

4.5   Does the aid provide for guarantees that the jobs lost during the period of reference are being deducted form the apparent number of jobs created during the same period?

☐   yes   ☐   no

5   Specific conditions for investment project in assisted areas with higher regional aid

5.1   Does the aid include a clause stipulating that the recipient has made a minimum contribution of at least 25% of the total investment and that this contribution will be exempted of any aid?

☐   yes   ☐   no

5.2   What are the guarantees that the aid for initial investment (both material and intangible investment) is made conditional on the maintenance of the investment for a minimum period of five years?

....

....

6   Aid to consultancy and other service activities

6.1   Are eligible costs limited to:

☐ costs for services provided by outside consultants and other services providers?

Please specify if such services are not a continuous or periodic activity nor relate nor relate to the enterprise's usual operating expenditure, such as routine tax consultancy services, regular legal service or advertising

....

....

☐ costs of firms participating in fairs and exhibitions? Please specify if the aid is related to the additional costs incurred for renting, setting up and running the stand:

Is the participation limited to the first participation in a fair or exhibition?

☐   yes   ☐   no

☐ Other costs (in particular cases where aid is awarded directly to the service(s) provider or consultant(s). Please specify under which conditions: ....

1422

6.2 Please indicate the maximum aid intensity expressed in gross terms:

If the aid intensity exceeds 50% gross please indicate in detail why this aid intensity should be necessary:

....

6.3 Please indicate the maximum ceiling for cumulated aid:

....

....

7 **Necessity of the aid**

7.1 Does the aid foresee that any application for aid must be submitted before work on the project is started?

☐   yes   ☐   no

7.2 If not has the Member State adopted legal provisions establishing a legal right to aid according to objective criteria, and without further exercise of discretion by the Member States?

☐   yes   ☐   no

8 **Other information**

Please indicate here any other information you consider relevant to the assessment of the measure(s) concerned under the Regulation (EC) 70/2001.

PART III.2. SUPPLEMENTARY INFORMATION SHEET ON TRAINING AID

This supplementary information sheet must be used for the notification of individual aid pursuant to Article 5 of the Regulation (EC) 68/2001[18] in its modified form.[19] It must also be used in the case of any individual aid or scheme, which is notified to the Commission for reasons of legal certainty.

1 **Scope of the individual aid or scheme**

1.1 Does the measure apply to the production and/or processing and/or marketing of the agricultural products listed in Annex I to the EC Treaty?

☐   yes   ☐   no

1.12 Does the measure apply to the production, processing and/or marketing of the fisheries and/or aquaculture products listed in Annex I to the EC Treaty?

☐   yes   ☐   no

1.13 Is the aid foreseen for the maritime transport sector?

☐   yes   ☐   no

If yes, please answer the following questions:

Is the trainee not an active member of the crew but a supernumerary on board?

☐   yes   ☐   no

Shall the training be carried out on board ships entered on Community registers?

☐   yes   ☐   no

---

[18] Commission Reg (EC) No 68/2001 of 12 January 2001 on the application of Arts 87 and 88 to training aid, OJ L10, 13.1.2001, p 20.

[19] OJ L63, 28.2.2004, p 20.

1.4   What are the intensities of the aid expressed in gross terms? Please specify:

....

....

....

2   Type of scheme or individual aid

Does the scheme or the individual aid relate to:

2.1   Specific training:

☐   yes   ☐   no

If yes, please give a description of the measure related to specific training:

....

....

2.2   General training:

☐   yes   ☐   no

If yes, please give a description of the measure related to general training:

....

....

2.3   Training aid given to disadvantaged workers:

☐   yes   ☐   no

If yes, please give a description of the measure related to disadvantaged workers:

....

....

2.4   Intensity of the aid

2.4.1   Aid for general training

2.4.1.1   ☐   granted outside of assisted regions under to Article 87.(3)(a) EC Treaty and 87 3(c) EC Treaty:

If yes, please specify what are the intensities expressed in gross terms for:
— large enterprises: ....
— small or medium-sized enterprises: ....

If yes, please specify what are the intensities in case that the training is given to disadvantaged workers:

....

2.4.1.2   ☐   granted in assisted regions under Article 87(3)(a) EC Treaty and under Article 87 (3)(c) EC Treaty

If yes, please specify what are the intensities expressed in gross terms for:
— large enterprises: ....
— small or medium-sized enterprises: ....

If yes, please specify what are the intensities in case that the training is given to disadvantaged workers:

....

2.4.2　Aid for specific training

2.4.2.1　□　granted outside of assisted regions under Article 87(3)(a) EC Treaty and under Article 87 (3)(c) EC Treaty:

□　yes　　　　　□　no

If yes, please specify what are the intensities expressed in gross terms for:
— large enterprises: ....
— small or medium-sized enterprises: ....

If yes, please specify what are the intensities in case that the training is given to disadvantaged workers:

....

2.4.2.2　□　granted in assisted regions under Article 87(3)(a) EC Treaty and under Article 87 (3)(c) EC Treaty

If yes, please specify what are the intensities expressed in gross terms for:
— large enterprises: ....
— small or medium-sized enterprises: ....

If yes, please specify what are the intensities in case that the training is given to disadvantaged workers:

....

3　**Eligible costs**

Which are the eligible costs foreseen under the scheme or for the individual aid?

□　trainers personnel costs
□　trainers and trainees travel expenses
□　other current expenses such as materials and supplies

□　depreciation of tools and equipment, to the extent that they are used exclusively for the training project
□　cost of guidance and counselling services with regard to the training project
□　trainees personnel
□　indirect costs (administrative, rent, overheads, transport and tuition costs for participants)

In the case of ad hoc individual aid under a scheme, please provide for each of the eligible costs documentary evidence, which shall be transparent and itemized ....

4　**Cumulation**

Can the aid foreseen in the scheme or in the individual aid be cumulated?

□　yes　　　　　□　no

If yes, can the aid intensities as stipulated in Art. 4 of the Regulation No 68/2001 be exceeded by this cumulation?

□　yes　　　　　□　no

5　**Other information**

Please indicate here any other information you consider relevant to the assessment of the measure(s) concerned under the Regulation (EC) 68/2001.

1425

PART III.3 SUPPLEMENTARY INFORMATION SHEET ON EMPLOYMENT AID

This supplementary information sheet must be used for the notification of any individual aid or any scheme pursuant to Article 9 of Regulation (EC) 2204/2002.[20] It must also be used in the case of an individual aid or scheme, which is notified to the Commission for reasons of legal certainty. This supplementary information sheet must as well be used for the notification of any employment aid in the transport sector (granted pursuant to Art. 4(6) of the SME Regulation or pursuant to the Regional Guidelines).

1   **Scope of the individual aid or scheme**

1.1   Does the measure apply to the production and/or processing and/or marketing of the agricultural products listed in Annex I to the EC Treaty?

☐   yes   ☐   no

1.2   Does the measure apply to the production, processing and/or marketing of the fisheries and/or aquaculture products listed in Annex I to the EC Treaty?

☐   yes   ☐   no

2   **Creation of employment**

2.1   Are the aid intensities calculated with regard to the wage costs over a period of two years relating to the employment created? ....

☐   yes   ☐   no

2.2   Is the creation of employment for SMEs outside of assited areas under the Article 87.(3).(a) EC Treaty and under Article 87 (3), (c) EC, Treaty or sectors?

☐   yes   ☐   no

if yes please specify what are the intensities expressed in gross terms

....

Is the creation of employment in assisted areas according to Article 87(3)(a) EC Treaty and 87(3)(c) EC Treaty or sectors?

☐   yes   ☐   no

2.2.1 Is the aid defined in terms of intensity compared to standard reference cost?

☐   yes   ☐   no

Is the aid subject to taxes?

☐   yes   ☐   no

What are the intensities expressed in net terms?

....

Shall the ceiling be increased because the scheme or the aid is applicable also to SMEs?

☐   yes   ☐   no

....

---

[20] Commission Reg (EC) No 2204/2002 of 12 December 2002 on the application of Arts 87 and 88 of the EC Treaty to State aid for employment, OJ L337, 13.12.2002, p 3 and OJ L349, 24.12.2002, p 126.

If yes please specify what increases are foreseen, expressed in gross terms ....
....

2.2.2 Has the recipient to make a minimum contribution, exempted of any aid, of at least 25% of the eligible costs?

☐   yes   ☐   no

2.2.3 Does the aid provide that the employment is maintained for a minimum period of three years in the case of large enterprises?

☐   yes   ☐   no

Does the aid provide that the employment in the regions or sectors which qualify for regional aid is maintained for a minimum period of two years in the case of SMEs?

☐   yes   ☐   no

If yes, what are the guarantees that the aid linked or not linked to the initial investment is made conditional on the maintenance of the employment for a minimum period of two or three years?

2.2.4 Does the employment created represent a net increase in the number of employees, both in the establishment and in the enterprise concerned, compared with the average over the past 12 months?

☐   yes   ☐   no

2.2.5 Have the new workers employed never had a job or have lost or are in the process of losing their previous job?

☐   yes   ☐   no

2.2.6 Does the scheme provide that any application for aid must be submitted before the employment concerned is created?

☐   yes   ☐   no

If not has the Member State adopted legal provisions establishing a legal right to aid according to objective criteria, and without further exercise of discretion by the Member States?

☐   yes   ☐   no

2.2.7 Does the aid provide that in cases where the employment created is linked to the carrying-out of a project of investment in tangible and intangible assets and the employment is created within three years of the investment's completion for a minimum period of three years in the case of SMEs, the application for aid must be submitted before work is started on the investment projects?

☐   yes   ☐   no

2.3 In case of creation of employment in the production, processing and marketing of products listed in Annex 1 to the EC Treaty in areas which quality as less favoured areas under Council Regulation (EC) No 1257/1999,[21] will the aid be granted according to the higher regional aid ceilings mentioned in article 4, paragraph 3, fourth subparagraph of Regulation (EC) No 2204/2002 or, where applicable, according to the higher aid ceilings of Regulation (EC) No 1257/1999. Please indicate which will be the intensity of the aid granted.

---

[21] Council Reg (EC) 1257/1999 on support for rural development from the European Agricultural Guidance and Guarantee Fund (EAGGf) and amending and repealing certain Regulations, OJ L160, 26.6.1999, p 80.

3   Recruitment of disadvantaged and disabled workers

3.1   Are the aid intensities calculated with regard to the wage costs over a period of one year relating to the employment created?

☐   yes   ☐   no

Do the gross aid intensities of all aid relating to the employment of the disadvantaged or disabled workers exceed respectively 50% or 60%?

☐   yes   ☐   no

3.2   Does the recruitment represent a net increase in the number of employees in the establishment concerned?

☐   yes   ☐   no

If not, have the post or posts fallen vacant following voluntary departure, retirement on grounds of age, voluntary reduction of working time or lawful dismissal for misconduct and not as a result of redundancy?

☐   yes   ☐   no

3.3   Is the aid limited to disadvantaged workers in the meaning of Article 2 (f)?

☐   yes   ☐   no

3.4   Is the aid limited to disabled workers in the meaning of Article 2 (g)?

☐   yes   ☐   no

If the aid is not limited to disadvantaged or disabled workers in the meaning of Article 2 (f) and (g) please explain in detail why you consider that targeted categories of workers should be considered as disadvantaged

....

4   Additional costs of employment of disabled workers

4.1   Does the aid refer to the recruitment of individual disabled workers and ancillary costs?

☐   yes   ☐   no

If yes please demonstrate that the conditions of Article 6.2 are fulfilled

4.2   Does the aid refer to sheltered employment?

☐   yes   ☐   no

If yes, please demonstrate that the aid does not exceed the costs of constructing, installing or expanding the establishment concerned, and any costs of administration and transport which result from employment of disabled workers: ....

5   Cumulation

5.1   Does the aid ceiling fixed in Article 4, 5 and 6 apply regardless of whether the support is financed entirely from state resources or is partly financed by the Community?

☐   yes   ☐   no

5.2   Can the notified aid for the creation of new jobs be cumulated with other State aid within the meaning of Article 87 (1) EC Treaty or with other Community funding in relation to the same wage costs?

☐   yes   ☐   no

If yes can the cumulation lead to a result where the aid intensity as fixed in Article 4(2) and (3) is exceeded (aid for disadvantaged and disabled workers excluded)?

☐ yes   ☐ no

5.3   Can the notified aid for the creation of employment under Article 4 of this regulation be cumulated with any other State aid within the meaning of Article 87(1) EC Treaty in relation to the costs of any investment to which the created employment is linked and which has not yet been completed at the time the employment is created or which was completed in the three years before the employment was created?

☐ yes   ☐ no

If yes can the cumulated aid result in an aid intensity exceeding the relevant ceiling of regional investment aid determined in the guidelines in regional investment aid and in the map approved by the Commission for each member State or the ceiling in Exemption Regulation (EC) N 70/2001?

☐ yes   ☐ no

5.4   Can the aid for the recruitment of disadvantaged or disabled workers under Article 5 and 6 be cumulated with aid and/or Community funding for the creation of employment under Article 4 in relation with the same wage costs?

☐ yes   ☐ no

If yes, is it ensured that such cumulation does not result in a gross aid intensity exceeding 100% of the wage costs over any period for which the worker or workers are employed?

5.5   Can the aid for the recruitment of disadvantaged or disabled workers under Article 5 and 6 of the Regulation be cumulated with other State aid and/or with other Community funding for other purposes than the creation of employment under Article 4 of the Regulation in relation to the same wage costs?

☐ yes   ☐ no

If yes, please explain the 'other purposes': ....

If yes is it ensured that such cumulation does not result in a gross aid intensity exceeding 100% of the wage costs over any period for which the worker or workers are employed?

☐ yes   ☐ no

6   **Other information**

Please indicate here any other information you consider relevant to the assessment of the measure(s) concerned under the Regulation (EC) 2204/2002.

PART III.4 SUPPLEMENTARY INFORMATION SHEET ON REGIONAL AID

This supplementary information sheet must be used for the notification of any aid scheme or individual aid covered by the guidelines on national regional aid.[22]

However, the present annex cannot be used for the particular purpose of notification of new regional aid maps. Of course, individual aid or schemes falling under the scope of the exemption regulations, both

---

[22] Guidelines on National Regional Aid, OJ C74, 10.3.1998, p 9, as amended by the Community Guidelines on State aid for Rescuing and Restructuring Firms in Difficulty, OJ C28, 9.10.1999, p.2 and the subsequent Amendments to the Guidelines on National Regional Aid, OJ C258, 9.9.2000, p.5.

the SME and the employment regulation,[23] *are exempted from notification. In this regard, Member States are invited to clarify the scope of their notification; in the particular case that their notification covers both aid to large firms and SMEs, then, they may request approval only concerning the first category.*

As stated in the guidelines, regional aid is a specific form of aid since it is reserved for particular regions. It is designed to develop the less favoured regions by supporting investment and job creation in a sustainable context.

Derogation from the incompatibility principle established in the Treaty can only be granted in respect of regional aid if the equilibrium between the resulting distortions of competition and the advantages of aid in terms of development can be guaranteed.

1   **Type of scheme or individual aid**

The scheme or the individual aid relates to

1.1   ☐ initial investment
☐ The aid is calculated as a percentage of the investment's value
☐ The aid is calculated as a percentage of the wage costs of the persons hired

1.2   ☐ operating aid

1.3   ☐ both

1.4   ☐ The aid is granted:
☐ automatically, should the conditions of the scheme be fulfilled
☐ discretionary, following a decision of the authorities

Should the aid be granted on a case basis, please provide a short description of the criteria followed and attach a copy of the administrative provisions applicable for the awarding of aid:

....

....

....

1.5   Does the aid respect the regional ceilings of the regional aid map applicable at the time of awarding the aid-including those resulting from the appropriate measures to be adopted in the framework of the 2002 Multisectoral Framework?[24]

☐   yes   ☐   no

Does the scheme include a reference to the regional aid maps applicable?

☐   yes   ☐   no

---

[23] Commission Reg (EC) N° 70/2001 of 12 January 2001 on the application of Arts 87 and 88 of the EC Treaty to small end medium-sized enterprises, OJ L10, 13.1.2001 p 33, and Commission Reg (EC) N° 2204/2002 of 12 December 2002 on the application of Art 87 and 88 of the EC Treaty to State aid for employment, OJ L337, 13.12.2002, p.3, and OJ L349, 24.12.2002, p 126.

[24] Commission letter to the Member States of 8.03.2002 on appropriate measures pursuant to Art 88(1) EC Treaty under the Multisectoral Framework SG(2002) D/228828, and Commission letter to the Member States of 8.03.2002 on appropriate measures pursuant to Art 88(1) EC Treaty as regards to the Code on aid to synthetic fibres industry and Community framework for State aid to the motor vehicle industry SG (2002) D/228829.

If yes, please specify: ....
....

2 Initial investment aid[25]

2.1 Does the scheme cover investment in fixed capital or job creation relating to:
☐ the setting-up of a new establishment?

☐ the extension of an existing establishment?

☐ the starting-up of a new activity involving a fundamental change in the product or production process of an existing establishment (through rationalisation, diversification or modernisation)?

☐ the purchase of an establishment which has closed or which would have closed had it not been purcha-sed?

2.2 Does the aid include a clause stipulating that the recipient has made a minimum contribution of at least 25% of the total investment and that this contribution will be exempted of any aid?

☐ yes ☐ no

2.3 Does the aid provide that any application for aid must be submitted before work is started on the projects?

☐ yes ☐ no

If any of the points above are not fulfilled, please explain why and how the authorities intend to comply with these necessary conditions:

....

2.4 Does the scheme define the aid in terms of intensity compared to standard reference cost?

☐ yes ☐ no

Is the aid subject to taxes?

☐ yes ☐ no

What are the intensities expressed in gross terms?

....

What are the parameters enabling calculation of aid intensities?

2.4.1 ☐ Grants:

Depreciation arrangements in force?:

....

Tax rate reduction on benefits of the firm:

....

2.4.2 ☐ Low-interest loans and interest rebate:

maximum amount of the rebate:

....

---

[25] This should be understood in the sense of point 4.1 of the Guidelines on National Regional Aid, OJ C74, 10.3.1998, p 9, according to which, 'the object of regional aid is to secure either productive investment (initial investment) or job creation, which is linked to the investment. Thus this method favours neither the capital factor nor the labour factor.'

maximum period of the loan:

....

maximum proportion:[26]

....

maximum length of the grace period:

....

In the case of low-interest loans, please specify the minimum interest rate:

....

In case of a state-loan:
— Is it covered by ordinary securities?

....

— What is the expected default rate?

....

— Is the reference rate being increased in situations involving a particular risk?

....

2.4.3 ☐ Guarantee schemes:

Please indicate the types of loans for which guarantees may be granted and specification of the fees (cf. previous point):

....
....
....

What is the expected default rate?

....

Please submit information allowing the aid intensity of guarantees to be calculated, including duration, proportion and amount:

....
....
....

2.5 Is replacement investment excluded from the scheme?:[27]

☐   yes   ☐   no

In case it is not, the authorities are requested to fill in the part on operating aid.

2.6 Is assistance for firms in difficulty[28] and/or for the financial restructuring of firms in difficulty excluded from the scheme?

☐   yes   ☐   no

---

[26] Amount of the loan as a percentage or proportion of the eligible investment.

[27] Replacing investment falls within the category of operating aid and thus it is excluded from initial investment.

[28] As defined in the Community guidelines on state aid for Rescuing and Restructuring firms in difficulty OJ C288, 9.10.1999, p 2.

Should this question be answered in the negative, will aid to investment granted to a large enterprise during the restructuring period, be notified individually?

☐   yes   ☐   no

2.7   Does the eligible expenditure under the scheme relate to:

2.7.1 ☐ Material investment:

The value of the investment is established as a percentage on the basis of:[29]

☐ land
☐ buildings
☐ plant/machinery (equipment)?

Please provide a short description:[30]

....

....

....

In the context of purchasing an establishment of the type, for which the investment aid is intended, are there any guarantees that the establishment concerned does not belong to a firm in difficulty?

☐   yes   ☐   no

Are there enough guarantees that any aid awarded in the past for the acquisition of assets has been taken into account/deducted as provided for in point 4.5 of the RAG prior to the purchase?

☐   yes   ☐   no

Are there enough guarantees that the transactions would take place under market conditions?

☐   yes   ☐   no

Should one of the three previous questions be answered in the negative, please explain how the authorities intend to comply with the necessary conditions:

....

....

....

2.7.2 ☐ Intangible investment:

The value of the investment is established on the basis of expenditure entailed by the transfer of technology through the acquisition of:

☐ patents
☐ operating or patented know-how licences
☐ unpatented know-how

Please provide a short description[31]

....

---

[29] In the transport sector, expenditure on the purchase of transport equipment cannot be included in the uniform set of items of expenditure. Such expenditure is not eligible for initial investment.

[30] The description should reflect how the authorities intend to ensure consistency with point 4.4 and point 4.5 of the Guidelines on Regional Aid, OJ C74, 10.3.1998, p 9.

[31] This description should reflect how the authorities intend to ensure consistency with point 4.6 of the Guidelines of Regional Aid. OJ C74, 10.3.1998, p 9.

....

....

Does the scheme include a clause stipulating that the expenditure on eligible intangible investment must not exceed 25% of the standard base in the case of large firms?

        ☐   yes   ☐   no

If not, explain why and how the authorities intend to respect this requirement:

....

....

In the case of large firms, does the scheme provide for guarantees that eligible assets:

2.7.2.1   ☐ will be used exclusively in the establishment receiving the aid?

2.7.2.2   ☐ must be regarded as amortisable assets?

2.7.2.3   ☐ are purchased from third parties under market conditions?

Should one of these conditions not be explicitly reflected in the scheme, please explain the reasons, as well as how the authorities intend to ensure that the eligible intangible assets will remain associated within the recipient region and will not be subject to a transfer benefiting other regions:

....

....

....

What are the guarantees that aid for initial investment (both material and intangible investment) is made conditional on the maintenance of the investment for a minimum period of five years?:

....

....

....

2.8   In case that aid to initial investment is linked to aid to employment, can the authorities provide guarantees that the cumulation rules would be respected?

....

2.9   Aid to job creation linked to initial investment

2.9.1   Does the measure provide for guarantees that the aid for job creation is linked to the carrying-out of an initial investment project?

        ☐   yes   ☐   no

Does the measure provide for guarantees that the jobs will be created within three years of the investment completion?

        ☐   yes   ☐   no

Should one of the previous questions be answered in the negative, please explain how the authorities intend to comply with these requirements:

....

....

....

In case that the investment does not relate to the setting up of a new establishment, please explain the reference period for calculating the number of jobs created:

....

....

....

2.9.2 Does the measure provide for guarantees that job creation means a net increase in the number of jobs in a particular establishment compared with the average over a period of time?

☐   yes   ☐   no

Does the measure provide for guarantees that the jobs lost during the period of reference are being deducted from the apparent number of jobs created during the same period?:[32]

☐   yes   ☐   no

Should one of the above points be answered in the negative, please explain how the authorities intend to comply with these requirements: ....

....

....

....

2.9.3 Is the aid calculated on the basis of:

☐ a percentage of the wage cost per job created?
☐ a flat-rate amount per job created?
☐ other (e.g. a progressive rate per job created). Please specify:

....

Please explain the parameters used in order to calculate the aid intensity:

....

....

....

2.9.4 Does the measure provide for guarantees that the employment created will be maintained for a minimum period of five years?:

....

....

3. Operating aid

3.1 What is the direct link between the awarding of operating aid and the contribution to regional development?

....

....

....

---

[32] The number of jobs corresponds to the number of annual labour units (ALU), i.e. the number of persons employed full-time in one year, part-time and seasonal work being ALU fractions.

3.2   What are the structural handicaps that the operating aid is seeking to redress?

   ....
   ....
   ....

3.3   Which are the guarantees that the nature and the level of the aid are proportional to the handicaps it seeks to alleviate?

   ....
   ....
   ....

3.4   What arrangements have been made to ensure that the aid is progressively reduced and limited in time?:

   ....
   ....
   ....

4   **Specific questions relating to the ultrapheric regions or to regions with low population density**

4.1   Should aid not be progressively reduced and not be limited in time, please specify whether the following conditions are met:

4.1.1   Does the aid benefit an outermost region or a region with low population density?

   □   yes   □   no

4.1.2   Is this aid intended to offset in part additional transport costs?

   □   yes   □   no

   Please provide proof of the existence of these additional costs and the method of calculation used to determine their amount:[33]

   ....
   ....

   Indicate what will be the maximum amount of aid (on the basis of an aid-per-kilometre ratio or on the basis of an aidper-kilometre and aid-per-unit-weight ratio) and the percentage of the additional costs covered by the aid:

   ....
   ....

4.1.3   Is the aid intended to offset the additional costs arising in the pursuit of economic activity from the factors identified in Article 299(2) of the EC Treaty?

   □   yes   □   no

---

[33] The description should reflect how the authorities intend to ensure that the aid is given only in respect of the extra cost of transport of goods inside national borders, is calculated on the basis of the most economical form of transport and the shortest route between the place of production or processing and commercial outlets, and cannot be given towards the transport of the products of businesses without an alternative location.

Please determine the amount of the additional cost and the method of calculation:

....

....

....

How can the authorities establish the link between the additional costs and the factors identified in Article 299(2) of the EC Treaty?

....

....

....

5   Scope of the scheme

5.1   Does the scheme apply to the production of the agricultural products listed in Annex I to the Treaty?:

☐   yes   ☐   no

For investment aid, tan the authorities confirm that the following criteria are met?
— Economic viability of beneficiaries guaranteed:

☐   yes   ☐   no

— Compliance with minimum EU standards on environment, hygiene and animal welfare:

☐   yes   ☐   no

— Availability of market outlets in compliance with applicable CMO (in accordance with point 4.2.5 of the agricultural guidelines):[34]

☐   yes   ☐   no

Please provide information about the fulfilment of these criteria?

....

....

....

What is the nature of the eligible expenses?

....

....

....

Can the authorities provide information regarding respect of maximum aid intensities?[35]

....

....

....

5.2   Does it apply to the processing and/or marketing of the agricultural products listed in Annex I to the EC Treaty?

☐   yes   ☐   no

---

[34] JOCE C 232/24 of 12.8.2000 in connexion with C 28/7 of 1.2.2000
[35] Maximum aid intensity of 40% (50% in LFA).

For investment aid, can the authorities confirm that the following criteria are met?
— Economic viability of beneficiaries guaranteed:

☐   yes   ☐   no

— Compliance with minimum EU standards on environment, hygiene and animal welfare:

☐   yes   ☐   no

— Availability of market outlets in compliance with applicable CMO (in accordance with point 4.2.5 of the agricultural guidelines):[36]

☐   yes   ☐   no

Can the authorities provide information about the fulfilment of these criteria?

....
....
....

Does the measure include a clause stipulating that an annual report should be provided containing information on the fact that the scheme takes into account the restrictions referred to in point 4.2.5 of the Guidelines for State aid in the agricultural sector?

☐   yes   ☐   no

Does the measure include a clause providing that any aid towards investment in that sector for which the eligible expenditure exceeds € 25 million or the aid amount exceeds € 12 million must be notified in accordance with Article 88(3) of the Treaty?

☐   yes   ☐   no

Should one of the two questions be answered in the negative, please explain how the authorities intend to comply with the necessary conditions:

....
....
....

Does the measure apply to the production, processing and/or marketing of the fisheries and/or aquaculture products listed in Annex I to the Treaty?

☐   yes   ☐   no

Can the authorities provide information about compliance with the specific rules applicable?

....
....
....

5.3   Does the scheme apply to the transport sector?

☐   yes   ☐   no

Should this question be answered in the positive, is there a provision in the scheme stating that transport equipment (movable assets) are excluded from the eligible investment expenditure?[37]

☐   yes   ☐   no

---

[36] See n 13
[37] Excepting the railway rolling stock in the sense provided by Art 4(5) of the Commission Reg (EC) N°70/2001, OJ L10; 13.1.2001, p 33.

6   **Respect of the relevant provisions of sectoral and multisectoral frameworks**

6.1   Does the scheme respect the specific provisions, such as the prohibition to grant aid to the steel sector[38] and/or synthetic fibres?[39]

☐   yes   ☐   no

6.2   Concerning aid awarded after the 1 January 2003: Does the scheme provide for respect of individual notification obligations foreseen in points 24 of the 2002 Multisectoral Framework.[40]

☐   yes   ☐   no

6.3   Concerning aid awarded before 1 January 2004: Does the scheme include a provision stating that any aid for large investment projects will be notified individually?

☐   yes   ☐   no

Should one of these questions be answered in the negative, please explain how the authorities intend to comply with the necessary conditions:

....

7   **Other information**

Please indicate here any other information you consider relevant to the assessment of the measure(s) concerned under the guidelines on national regional aid.

PART III.5. SUPPLEMENTARY INFORMATION SHEET ON AID
COMING UNDER THE MULTISECTORAL FRAMEWORK[41]

This supplementary information sheet must be used for the notification of any aid covered by the Multisectorial framework on regional aid for large investment projects.[42]

1   **Additional information on beneficiaries**

1.1   Structure of the company or companies investing in the project:

1.1.1 Identity of aid recipient

1.1.2 If the legal identity of the aid recipient is different from the undertaking(s) that finance(s) the project or from the actual beneficiary(s) of the aid, describe also these differences.

....
....
....

---

[38] In the sense of the Annex B of the Communication from the Commission: 'Multisectorial framework on regional aid for large investment projects', OJ C70.19. 3.2002, p 8.

[39] In the sense of Annex D of the C of the Communication from the Commission: 'Multisectorial framework on regional aid for large investment projects', OJ C70, 19.3.2002, p 8.

[40] According to this provision, 'Member States are required to notify every case of regional investment aid if the aid proposed is more than the maximum allowable aid that an investment can obtain under the scale and the rules laid down in para 21', OJ C70, 19.3.2002, p 8.

[41] For aid granted outside authorised schemes, the Member State must provide information detatiling the beneficial effects of the aid on the assisted area concerned.

[42] Communication from the Commission: 'Multisectorial framework on regional aid for large investment project', OJ C70, 19.3.2002, p 8.

1.1.2 Identify the parent group of the aid recipient, describe the group structure and ownership structure of each parent company:

....

....

....

1.2 For a company or companies investing in the project, provide the following data for the last three financial years

1.2.1 Worldwide turnover, EEA turnover, turnover in Member State concerned:

....

1.2.2 Profit after tax and cash flow (on a consolidated basis):

....

1.2.3 Employment worldwide, at EEA level and in Member State concerned:

....

1.2.4 Market breakdown of sales in the Member State concerned, in the rest of the EEA and outside the EEA:

....

1.2.5 Audited financial statements and annual report for the last three years:

....

1.3 If the investment takes place in an existing industrial location, provide the following data for the last three financial years of that entity:

1.3.1 Total turnover:

....

1.3.2 Profit after tax and cash flow:

....

1.3.3 Employment:

....

1.3.4 Market breakdown of sales: in the Member State concerned, in the rest of the EEA and outside the EEA:

....

2 **Aid**

For each aid, provide the following information:

2.1 Amount

2.1.1 Nominal amount of support and its gross and net grant equivalent:

....

2.1.2 Is the assistance measure subject to corporate tax (or other direct taxation)? If only partially, to what extent?

....

2.1.3 Provide a complete schedule of the payment of the proposed assistance. For the package of proposed public assistance, provide the following:

....

2.2 Characteristics:

2.2.1 Are any of the assistance measures of the overall package not yet defined?

☐   yes   ☐   no

If yes, please specify:

....

2.2.2 Indicate which of the abovementioned measures does not constitute State aid and for what reason(s):

....

....

....

2.3 Financing from Community sources (EIB, ECSC instruments, Social Fund, Regional Fund, other):

2.3.1 Are some of the abovementioned measures to be co-financed by Community funds? Please Explain.

....

....

....

2.3.2 Is some additional support for the same project to be requested from any other European or international financing institutions?

☐   yes   ☐   no

If so, for what amounts?

....

....

3 **Assisted project**

3.1 Duration of the project: (specify the planned start date of the new production and the year by which full production may be reached):

....

3.2 Description of the project:

3.2.1 Specify the type of the project and whether it is a new establishment or a capacity expansion or other:

....

....

....

3.2.2 Provide a short general description of the project:

....

....

....

....

....

3.3 Breakdown of the project costs:

3.3.1 Specify the total cost of capital expenditure to be invested and depreciated over the lifetime of the project:

....

....

....

3.3.2 Provide a detailed breakdown of the capital and non-capital (2) expenditure associated with the investment project:

....

....

....

3.4 Financing of total project costs:

....

....

....

4 **Product and market characteristic**

4.1 Characterisation of product(s) envisaged by the project:

4.1.1 Specify the product(s) that will be produced in the aided facility upon the completion of the investment and the relevant (sub-)sector(s) to which the product(s) belong(s) (indicate the Prodcom code or CPA nomenclature for projects in the service sectors:

....

....

....

4.1.2 What product(s) will it replace? If these replaced products are not produced at the same location, indicate where they are currently produced.

....

....

....

4.1.3 What other product(s) can be produced with the same new facilities at little or no additional cost?

....

....

....

4.2 Capacity considerations:

4.2.1 Quantify the impact of the project on the aid recipient's total viable capacity in the EEA (including at group level) for each of the product(s) concerned (in units per year in the year preceding the start year and on completion of the project).

....

....

....

4.2.2 Provide an estimate of the total capacity of all EEA producers for each of the products concerned.

....

....

....

4.3 Market data:

4.3.1 Provide for each of the last six financial years data on apparent consumption of the product(s) concerned. If available, include statistics prepared by other sources to illustrate the answer.

....

....

....

4.3.2 Provide for the next three financial years a forecast of the evolution of apparent consumption of the product(s) concerned. If available, include statistics prepared by independent sources to illustrate the answer.

....

....

....

4.3.3 Is the relevant market in decline and for what reasons?

....

....

....

4.3.4 An estimate of the market shares (in value) of the aid recipient or of the group to which the aid recipient belongs in the year preceding the start year and on completion of the project.

....

....

....

5 **Other Information**

Please indicate here any other information you consider relevant to the assessment of the measure(s) concerned under the multisectoral framework.

PART III.6.A. SUPPLEMENTARY INFORMATION SHEET FOR RESEARCH AND DEVELOPMENT AID: AID SCHEMES

This supplementary information sheet must be used for the notification of any aid scheme covered by the Community framework for State aid for research and development.[43] *It must also be used for aid schemes for Research and Development aid to SMEs which do not fall under the Block Exemption Regulation for SMEs*[44] *as well as for aid intended for the production, processing and marketing of agricultural products.*

1   **Research stage**

     Research and development stages qualifying for aid

1.1   Feasibility studies:

                              ☐   yes   ☐   no

      If yes, to which stage of research does the study refer?
      ☐ fundamental research
      ☐ industrial research
      ☐ precompetitive development

      If yes, give examples of major projects:
      ....

1.2   Fundamental research:

                              ☐   yes   ☐   no

      If yes, give examples of major projects:
      ....

1.3   Industrial research:

                              ☐   yes   ☐   no

      If yes, give examples of major projects:
      ....

1.4   Precompetitive development:

                              ☐   yes   ☐   no

      If yes, give examples of major projects:
      ....

1.5   Patent applications and renewals by SMEs:

                              ☐   yes   ☐   no

      If yes, which stage of research is concerned?:
      ☐ fundamental research

---

[43] Community framework for State aid for research and development (OJ C45, 17.2.1996, p 5) and subsequent amendments (OJ C48, 13.2.1998, p 2) and the Commission communication on the prolongation of the framework (OJ C111, 8.5.2002, p 3).

[44] Reg 70/2001 as amended, OJ L63, 28.2.2004, p 22.

☐ industrial research
☐ precompetitive development

2   **Additional information on the recipient of the aid**

2.1   Higher-education or research establishments

                       ☐   yes   ☐   no

If yes, give an estimate of the number of establishments involved:

....

If yes, state whether other firms receive aid:

                       ☐   yes   ☐   no

Are these higher-education or research establishments in the public sector?

                       ☐   yes   ☐   no

2.2   Other (please specify) ....

3   **Cooperative research**

To enable the Commission to check whether contributions from public research establishments to an R&D project constitute aid, please answer the following questions:[45]

3.1   Do the projects provide that public, non-profit-making research or higher-education establishments carry out research on behalf of or in collaboration with industry?

                       ☐   yes   ☐   no

If yes, please clarify:

— Do the public, non-profit-making research or higher-education establishments receive payment at the market rate for the services they provide?

                       ☐   yes   ☐   no

or

— Do the industrial participants bear the full cost of the project?

                       ☐   yes   ☐   no

or

— Where results which do not give rise to intellectual property rights may be widely disseminated, are any intellectual property rights fully allocated to the public, non-profit-making establishments?

                       ☐   yes   ☐   no

or

— Do the public, non-profit-making establishments receive from the industrial participants (holders of intellectual property rights resulting from the research project) compensation equivalent to the market price for those rights and for the results that do not give rise to intellectual property rights but may be widely disseminated to interested third parties?

                       ☐   yes   ☐   no

---

[45] See para 5.8 of the Community framework for State aid for research and development (OJ C45, 17.2.1996, p 5).

3.2 **Are the projects carried out in collaboration with several firms?**

☐ yes   ☐ no

If yes, what are the conditions governing such collaboration?

....

4 **Research acquired by the state**

4.1 Do projects stipulate that the public authorities may commission R&D from firms?

☐ yes   ☐ no

If yes, is there an open tender procedure?

☐ yes   ☐ no

4.2 Do projects stipulate that the public authorities may buy the results of R&D from firms?

☐ yes   ☐ no

If yes, is there an open tender procedure?

☐ yes   ☐ no

5 **Type of aid**

☐ Aid linked to an R&D contract signed with industrial firms (please specify):

....

☐ Advance repayable if the project is successful (please specify the amount and procedures for repayment; in particular, give the criteria for measuring 'success'):

....

☐ Other (please specify):

....

6 **Eligible expenditure**

☐ Costs of personnel employed solely on the research activity:

....

☐ Costs of durable assets used solely and on a continual basis for the research activity (equipment and instruments): ....

....

☐ Costs of land and premises used solely and on a continual basis (except where transferred commercially) for the research activity: ....

....

☐ Costs of consultancy and equivalent services used exclusively for the research activity, including the research, technical knowledge and patents, etc. bought from outside sources:

....

☐ Additional overheads incurred directly as a result of the research activity:

....

....

If appropriate, give a breakdown of research costs by aided and non-aided R&D:

....

Give a breakdown of the budget between firms, research centres and universities:

....

☐ Other operating expenses (costs of materials, supplies and similar products incurred directly as a result of the research activity)

7   **Aid intensity**

7.1   Gross aid intensity:

Definition stage or feasibility studies   : ....

Fundamental research   : ....

Industrial research   : ....

Precompetitive development   : ....

7.2   For aid in support of patent applications and renewals by SMEs, specify the research activities which first led to the patents concerned: ....

Planned intensity: ....

7.3   Does the same R&D activity cover several stages of research?

                                 ☐   yes   ☐   no

If yes, which? ....

Specify the aid intensity applied: ....

7.4   Bonuses applicable, if any:

7.4.1   For aid granted to SMEs, give the bonus applicable, if any:

....

7.4.2   Are the research activities in accordance with a specific project or programme undertaken as part of the Community's current framework programme for research and technological development (R&TD)?

                                 ☐   yes   ☐   no

If yes, what is the bonus applicable? ....

Please give also the exact title of the specific project or programme undertaken as part of the Community's current framework programme for R&TD, if possible using the 'call identifier' or the CORDIS web site: www.cordis.lu.

Does the project in accordance with a specific project or programme undertaken as part of the Community's current framework programme for R&TD involve cross-border cooperation between firms and public research bodies or between at least two independent partners in two Member States, where its results are widely disseminated and published?

                                 ☐   yes   ☐   no

If yes, what is the bonus applicable? ....

                                 ☐   yes   ☐   no

7.4.3   Are the aided R&D activities located in a region eligible under Article 87(3)(a) or (c) of the EC Treaty at the time the aid is granted?

                                 ☐   yes   ☐   no

Give the bonus applicable: ....

7.4.4 If the research activities are not in accordance with a specific project or programme under-taken as part of the Community's current framework programme for R&TD, clarify whether at least one of the following conditions is met:

— the project involves effective cross-border cooperation between at least two inde-pendent partners in two Member States, particularly in the context of coordinating national R&TD policies

☐ yes   ☐ no

— the project involves effective cooperation between firms and public research bodies, particularly in the context of coordination of national R&TD policies

☐ yes   ☐ no

— the project's results are widely disseminated and published, patent licences are granted or other appropriate steps are taken under conditions similar to those for the dissemination of Community R&TD results

☐ yes   ☐ no

Where at least one of the above conditions is met, give any bonus applicable:

....

7.5 Where there is a combination of bonuses and aid intensities, give the maximum aid intensity applicable for each stage of research: ....

8 Incentive effect of the aid

8.1 Provide information that will enable us to assess the incentive effect of the aid for large firms

....

8.2 Does the scheme stipulate that the annual report on implementation should, in the case of large firms, contain a description of the incentive effect for each individual application of the scheme?

☐ yes   ☐ no

9 Multinational aspects

9.1 Do the projects (scheme/programme) have any multinational aspects (e.g. Esprit or Eureka projects)?

☐ yes   ☐ no

If yes, specify:...

9.2 Do the R&D projects involve cooperation with partners in other countries?
If so, state:
(a) which other Member State(s) ....
(b) which other third country or countries ....
(c) which firm(s) in other countries ....

9.3 Give a breakdown of the total cost by partner:

....

....

....

10 **Access to results**

10.1 Who will own the R&D results in question?

10.2 Are any conditions attached to the granting of licences in respect of the results?

....

10.3 Are there any rules governing the general publication/dissemination of the R&D results?

☐   yes   ☐   no

10.4 Indicate the measures planned for the subsequent use/development of the results:

....

10.5 Is there provision for the results of publicly financed R&D projects to be made available to Community industry on a non-discriminatory basis?

☐   yes   ☐   no

11 **Information and control measures**

11.1 Give the information/control measures used to ensure that the aided projects are in line with the objectives laid down by the relevant legislation:

....

11.2 Specify the arrangements for informing the Commission about implementation of the scheme:

....

11.3 Other useful information, including an estimate of the number of jobs created or safeguarded:

....

12 **Provisions applicable to the agricultural sector**

12.1 Can you confirm that the following four conditions are met in all cases?

☐ The aid is of general interest to the sector (or subsector) concerned, without causing undue distortion of competition in other sectors (or subsectors).

☐ Information must be published in suitable newspapers, scientific periodicals with at least national circulation or on the Internet and not limited to the members of individual organisations, so as to guarantee that any operator potentially interested in the research activity can easily find out that it is planned or has started and that the results are being or will be provided, on request, to any interested party. This information should be published on a date not later than any information given directly to members of individual organisations.

☐ The results of this research activity will be provided for exploitation to all parties involved, including the beneficiary of the aid, on an equal basis in terms of both cost and timing.

☐ The aid satisfies the conditions in Annex II—internal support, i.e. the basis for exemption from the state aid reduction commitments in the Agreement on Agriculture concluded at the end of the Uruguay Round of Multilateral Trade Negotiations.[46]

---

[46] Agreement on Agriculture concluded at the end of the Uruguay Round of Multilateral Trade Negotiations (OJ L336, 23.12.1994, p 31).

☐   yes   ☐   no

If all the above conditions combined are not met, the general rules (questions 1–11) will apply.

12.2   What is the planned aid intensity?:

....

13   **Other information**

Please give any other information you consider necessary to assess the measure(s) in question under the Community framework for state aid for research and development.

PART III.6.B. SUPPLEMENTARY INFORMATION SHEET FOR RESEARCH AND DEVELOPMENT AID: INDIVIDUAL AID

This supplementary information sheet must be used for the notification of any aid scheme covered by the Community framework for State aid for research and development.[47] It must also be used for aid schemes for Research and Development aid to SMEs which do not fall under the Block Exemption Regulation for SMEs[48] as well as for aid intended for the production, processing and marketing of agricultural products.

1   **Research stage**

Research and development stages qualifying for aid

1.1   Feasibility studies:

☐   yes   ☐   no

If yes, to which stage of research does the study refer?
☐ fundamental research
☐ industrial research
☐ precompetitive development

If yes, give examples of major projects:

....

1.2   Fundamental research:

☐   yes   ☐   no

If yes, give examples of major projects:

....

1.3   Industrial research:

☐   yes   ☐   no

If yes, give examples of major projects:

....

---

[47] Community framework for State aid for research and development (OJ C45, 17.2.1996, p 5) and subsequent amendments (OJ C48, 13.2.1998, p 2) and the Commission communication on the prolongation of the framework (OJ C111, 8.5.2002, p 3).
[48] Regulation 70/2001 as amended, OJ L63, 28.2.2004, p 20.

1.4   Precompetitive development:

☐   yes   ☐   no

If yes, give examples of major projects:

....

1.5   Patent applications and renewals by SMEs:

☐   yes   ☐   no

If yes, which stage of research is concerned?:

☐ fundamental research
☐ industrial research
☐ precompetitive development

2   Additional information on the recipient of the aid

2.1   Higher-education or research establishments

☐   yes   ☐   no

If yes, give an estimate of the number of establishments involved:

....

If yes, state whether other firms receive aid:

☐   yes   ☐   no

Are these higher-education or research establishments in the public sector?

☐   yes   ☐   no

2.2   Other (please specify) ....

3   Cooperative Research

To enable the Commission to check whether contributions from public research establishments to an R&D project constitute aid, please answer the following questions:[49]

3.1   Do the projects provide that public, non-profit-making research or higher-education establishments carry out research on behalf of or in collaboration with industry?

☐   yes   ☐   no

If yes, please clarify:

—   Do the public, non-profit-making research or higher-education establishments receive payment at the market rate for the services they provide?

☐   yes   ☐   no

or

—   Do the industrial participants bear the full cost of the project?

☐   yes   ☐   no

or

—   Where results which do not give rise to intellectual property rights may be widely disseminated, are any intellectual property rights fully allocated to the public, non-profit-making establishments?

☐   yes   ☐   no

---

[49] See para 5.8 of the Community framework for State aid for research and development (OJ C45, 17.2.1996, p 5).

or

— Do the public, non-profit-making establishments receive from the industrial participants (holders of intellectual property rights resulting from the research project) compensation equivalent to the market price for those rights and for the results that do not give rise to intellectual property rights but may be widely disseminated to interested third parties?

      ☐   yes   ☐   no

3.2   Are the projects carried out in collaboration with several firms?

      ☐   yes   ☐   no

If yes, what are the conditions governing such collaboration?

....

4   Research acquired by the state

4.1   Do projects stipulate that the public authorities may commission R&D from firms?

      ☐   yes   ☐   no

If yes, is there an open tender procedure?

      ☐   yes   ☐   no

4.2   Do projects stipulate that the public authorities may buy the results of R&D from firms?

      ☐   yes   ☐   no

If yes, is there an open tender procedure?

      ☐   yes   ☐   no

5   Type of aid

☐ Aid linked to an R&D contract signed with industrial firms (please specify):

....

☐ Advance repayable if the project is successful (please specify the amount and procedures for repayment; in particular, give the criteria for measuring 'success'):

....

☐ Other (please specify):

....

6   Eligible expenditure

☐ Costs of personnel employed solely on the research activity:

....

☐ Costs of durable assets used solely and on a continual basis for the research activity (equipment and instruments): ....

☐ Costs of land and premises used solely and on a continual basis (except where transferred commercially) for the research activity: ....

☐ Costs of consultancy and equivalent services used exclusively for the research activity, including the research, technical knowledge and patents, etc. bought from outside sources:

....

☐ Additional overheads incurred directly as a result of the research activity:

....
....

If appropriate, give a breakdown of research costs by aided and non-aided R&D:

....

Give a breakdown of the budget between firms, research centres and universities:

....

7 Aid intensity

7.1 Gross aid intensity:

Definition stage or feasibility studies : ....
Fundamental research : ....
Industrial research : ....
Precompetitive development : ....

7.2 For aid in support of patent applications and renewals by SMEs, specify the research activities which first led to the patents concerned: ....
Planned intensity: ....

7.3 Does the same R&D activity cover several stages of research?

☐ yes   ☐ no

If yes, which? ....
Specify the aid intensity applied: ....

7.4 Bonuses applicable, if any:

7.4.1 For aid granted to SMEs, give the bonus applicable, if any:

....

7.4.2 Are the research activities in accordance with a specific project or programme undertaken as part of the Community's current framework programme for research and technological development (R&TD)?

☐ yes   ☐ no

If yes, what is the bonus applicable? ....

Please give also the exact title of the specific project or programme undertaken as part of the Community's current framework programme for R&TD, if possible using the 'call identifier' or the CORDIS web site: www.cordis.lu.

Does the project in accordance with a specific project or programme undertaken as part of the Community's current framework programme for R&TD involve cross-border cooperation between firms and public research bodies or between at least two independent partners in two Member States, where its results are widely disseminated and published?

☐ yes   ☐ no

If yes, what is the bonus applicable? ....

7.4.3 Are the aided R&D activities located in a region eligible under Article 87(3)(a) or (c) of the EC Treaty at the time the aid is granted?

☐   87(3)(a)   ☐   87(3)(c)

Give the bonus applicable: ....

7.4.4 If the research activities are not in accordance with a specific project or programme undertaken as part of the Community's current framework programme for R&TD, clarify whether at least one of the following conditions is met:

— the project involves effective cross-border cooperation between at least two independent partners in two Member States, particularly in the context of coordinating national R&TD policies

☐   yes   ☐   no

— the project involves effective cooperation between firms and public research bodies, particularly in the context of coordination of national R&TD policies

☐   yes   ☐   no

— the project's results are widely disseminated and published, patent licences are granted or other appropriate steps are taken under conditions similar to those for the dissemination of Community R&TD results

☐   yes   ☐   no

Where at least one of the above conditions is met, give any bonus applicable:

....

Where there is a combination of bonuses and aid intensities, give the maximum aid intensity applicable for each stage of research:

....

8   Incentive effect of the aid

8.1   How has expenditure on research and development increased or decreased?

....

8.2   Is the aid used for R&D activities over and above the recipient's traditional activities?

☐   yes   ☐   no

8.3   Is R&D-linked scientific and/or technological activity being created?

☐   yes   ☐   no

8.4   How has the number of people engaged in R&D activities evolved?

....

8.5   Has there been job creation linked to R&D activities?

☐   yes   ☐   no

If yes, give the estimated number of jobs created:...

8.6   Have jobs been safeguarded as a result of R&D activities?

☐   yes   ☐   no

8.7   What is the firm's turnover? ....

8.8   Are there additional costs linked to cross-border cooperation?

☐   yes   ☐   no

8.9   Indicate the measures planned for exploiting in part or in full the results of the research

....

8.10 Are measures planned to enable SMEs to participate?

☐   yes   ☐   no

If yes, indicate what they are: ....

8.11 Other incentive factors, such as commercial and technological risk:

....

8.12 In the case of individual, close-to-the-market research projects to be undertaken by large firms, what factors have been taken into account to ensure that the aid has an incentive effect on R&D?

....

8.13 Demonstrate that the application for aid was made before the R&D activities started:

....
....

9   **Multinational aspects**

9.1   Do the projects (scheme/programme) have any multinational aspects (e.g. Esprit or Eureka projects)?

☐   yes   ☐   no

If yes, specify:...

9.2   Do the R&D projects involve cooperation with partners in other countries?
      If so, state:
      (a) which other Member State(s) ....
      (b) which other third country or countries ....
      (c) which firm(s) in other countries ....

9.3   Give a breakdown of the total cost by partner:

....
....
....

10   **Access to results**

10.1 Who will own the R&D results in question?

10.2 Are any conditions attached to the granting of licences in respect of the results?

....

10.3 Are there any rules governing the general publication/dissemination of the R&D results?

☐   yes   ☐   no

10.4 Indicate the measures planned for the subsequent use/development of the results:

....

10.5 Is there provision for the results of publicly financed R&D projects to be made available to Community industry on a non-discriminatory basis?

☐   yes   ☐   no

11   Information and control measures

11.1 Give the information/control measures used to ensure that the aided projects are in line with the objectives laid down by the relevant legislation: ....

11.2 Specify the arrangements for informing the Commission about implementation of the scheme:

....

11.3 Other useful information, including an estimate of the number of jobs created or safeguarded:

....

12   Provisions applicable to the agricultural sector

12.1 Can you confirm that the following four conditions are met in all cases?

☐ The aid is of general interest to the sector (or subsector) concerned, without causing undue distortion of competition in other sectors (or subsectors).

☐ Information must be published in suitable newspapers, scientific periodicals with at least national circulation or on the Internet and not limited to the members of individual organisations, so as to guarantee that any operator potentially interested in the research activity can easily find out that it is planned or has started and that the results are being or will be provided, on request, to any interested party. This information should be published on a date not later than any information given directly to members of individual organisations.

☐ The results of this research activity will be provided for exploitation to all parties involved, including the beneficiary of the aid, on an equal basis in terms of both cost and timing.

☐ The aid satisfies the conditions in Annex II—internal support, i.e. the basis for exemption from the State aid reduction commitments in the Agreement on Agriculture concluded at the end of the Uruguay Round of Multilateral Trade Negotiations.[50]

☐   yes   ☐   no

If all the above conditions combined are not met, the general rules (questions 1–11) will apply.

12.2 What is the planned aid intensity?: ....

13   Other information

Please give any other information you consider necessary to assess the measure(s) in question under the Community framework for state aid for research and development.

---

[50] Agreement on Agriculture concluded at the end of the Uruguay Round of Multilateral Trade Negotiations (OJ L336, 23.12.1994, p 31).

PART III.7A. SUPPLEMENTARY INFORMATION SHEET ON AID
FOR RESCUING FIRMS IN DIFFICULTY: AID SCHEMES

This supplementary information sheet must be used for the notification of rescue aid schemes covered by the Community guidelines on State aid for rescuing and restructuring firms in difficulty.[51]

1   **Eligibility**

1.1   Is the scheme limited to firms that fulfil at least one of the eligibility criteria below:

1.1.1 Is the scheme limited to firms, where more than half their registered capital has disappeared and more than one quarter of that capital has been lost over the preceding 12 months?

☐   yes   ☐   no

1.1.2 Are the firms unlimited companies, where more than half of their capital as shown in the company accounts has disappeared and more than one quarter of that capital has been lost over the preceding 12 months?

☐   yes   ☐   no

1.1.3 Do the firms fulfil the criteria under domestic law for being the subject of collective insolvency proceedings?

☐   yes   ☐   no

1.2   Is the scheme limited to rescuing small or medium-sized enterprises in difficulty which correspond to the Community definition of SMEs?

☐   yes   ☐   no

2   **Form of aid**

2.1   Is the aid granted under the scheme in the form of a loan guarantee or loans?

☐   yes   ☐   no

2.2   If yes, will the loan be granted at an interest rate at least comparable to those observed for loans to healthy firms, and in particular the reference rate adopted by the Commission?

☐   yes   ☐   no

Please provide detailed information.

2.3   Will the aid under the scheme be linked to loans that are to be reimbursed over a period of not more than 12 months after disbursement of the last instalment to the firm?

☐   yes   ☐   no

3   **Other elements**

3.1   Will aid under the scheme be warranted on the grounds of serious social difficulties? Please justify.

3.2   Will aid under the scheme have no unduly adverse spillover effects on other Member States? Please justify.

---

[51] Community guidelines on State aid for rescuing and restructuring firms in difficulty, OJ C288, 9.10.1999, p 2.

3.3 Please explain why you think that the aid scheme is limited to the minimum necessary (i.e. is restricted to the amount needed to keep the firm in business for the period during which the aid is authorized. This should not go beyond a period of 6 months).

3.4 Do you undertake, within six months after granted the aid, to either approve a restructuring plan or a liquidation plan, or demand reimbursement of the loan and the aid corresponding to the risk premium from the beneficiary?

☐   yes   ☐   no

Please specify the maximum amount of the aid that can be awarded to any one firm as part of the rescue operation:

....

3.5 Provide all relevant information on aid of any kind which may be granted to the firms eligible for receiving rescue aid during the same period of time.

4   Annual report

4.1 Do you undertake to provide reports, at least on an annual basis, on the scheme's operation, containing the information specified in the Commission's instructions on standardized reports?

☐   yes   ☐   no

4.2 Do you undertake in such a report to include a list of beneficiary firms with at least the following information:

(a) the company name;
(b) its sectoral code, using the NACE[52] two-digit sectoral classification codes;
(c) the number of employees;
(d) annual turnover and balance sheet value;
(e) the amount of aid granted;
(f) where appropriate, any restructuring aid, or other support treated as such, which it has received in the past;
(g) whether or not the beneficiary company has been wound up or subject to collective insolvency proceedings before the end of the restructuring period.

☐   yes   ☐   no

5   Other information

Please indicate here any other information you consider relevant to the assessment of the measure(s) concerned under the guidelines on aid for rescuing and restructuring firms in difficulty.

PART III.7B. SUPPLEMENTARY INFORMATION SHEET ON AID FOR RESCUING FIRMS IN DIFFICULTY: INDIVIDUAL AID

This supplementary information sheet must be used for the notification of individual rescue aid covered by the Community guidelines on State aid for rescuing and restructuring firms in difficulty.[53]

---

[52] Statistical classification of economic activities in the European Community, published by the Statistical Office of the European Communities.
[53] Community guidelines on State aid for rescuing and restructuring firms in difficulty, OJ C288, 9.10.1999, p 2.

1   **Eligibility**

1.1   Is the firm a limited company, where more than half of its registered capital has disappeared and more than one quarter of that capital has been lost over the preceding 12 months?

☐   yes   ☐   no

1.2   Is the firm an unlimited company, where more than half of its capital as shown in the company accounts has disappeared and more than one quarter of that capital has been lost over the preceding months?

☐   yes   ☐   no

1.3   Does the firm fulfil the criteria under domestic law for being the subject of collective insolvency proceedings?

☐   yes   ☐   no

If you have answered yes to any of the above questions, please attach the relevant documents (latest profit and loss account with balance sheet, or court decision opening an investigation into the company under national company law)

If you have answered no to all of the above questions, please submit evidence supporting that the firm is in difficulties, for it to be eligible for rescue aid.

1.4   When has the firm been created?..

1.5   Since when is the firm operating?..

1.6   Does the company belong to a larger business group?

☐   yes   ☐   no

If you have answered yes, please submit full details about the group (organization chart, showing the links between the group's members with details on capital and voting rights) and attach proof that the company's difficulties are its own and are not the result of an arbitrary allocation of costs within the group and that the difficulties are too serious to be dealt with by the group itself.

1.7   Has the firm (or the group to which it belongs) in the past received any rescue aid?

☐   yes   ☐   no

If yes, please provide full details (date, amount, reference to previous Commission decision if applicable, etc.)

2   **Form of aid**

2.1   Is the aid in the form of a loan guarantee or loans? Copies of the relevant documents should be provided.

☐   yes   ☐   no

2.2   If yes, is the loan granted at an interest rate at least comparable to those observed for loans to healthy firms, and in particular the reference rate adopted by the Commission?

☐   yes   ☐   no

Please provide detailed information.

2.3   Is the aid linked to loans that are to be reimbursed over a period of not more than 12
months after disbursement of the last instalment to the firm?

☐   yes   ☐   no

3   Other elements

3.1   Is the aid warranted on the grounds of serious social difficulties? Please justify.

3.2   Does the aid have no unduly adverse spillover effects on other Member States? Please justify.

3.3   Please explain why you think that the aid is limited to the minimum necessary (i.e. is
restricted to the amount needed to keep the firm in business for the period during which
the aid is authorized). This should be done on the basis of a liquidity plan for the 6 months
ahead and on the basis of a comparison with operating costs and financial charges over the
previous 12 months.

3.4   Do you undertake, not later than six months after the rescue aid measure has been
authorized, to communicate to the Commission a restructuring plan or a liquidation plan
or proof that the loan has been reimbursed in full and/or that the guarantee has been
terminated?

☐   yes   ☐   no

4   Other Information

Please indicate here any other information you consider relevant to the assessment of the
measure(s) concerned under the guidelines on aid for rescuing and restructuring firms in
difficulty.

PART III.8.A. SUPPLEMENTARY INFORMATION SHEET ON AID FOR
RESTRUCTURING FIRMS IN DIFFICULTY: AID SCHEMES

*This supplementary information sheet must be used for the notification of restructuring aid schemes
covered by the Community Guidelines on State aid for rescuing and restructuring firms in difficulty.*[54]

1   Eligibility

1.1   Is the scheme limited to firms that fulfil at least one of the eligibility criteria below:

1.1.1 Is the scheme limited to firms, where more than half their registered capital has disappeared
and more than one quarter of that capital has been lost over the preceding 12 months?

☐   yes   ☐   no

1.1.2 Are the firms unlimited companies, where more than half of their capital as shown in the
company accounts has disappeared and more than one quarter of that capital has been lost
over the preceding months?

☐   yes   ☐   no

1.1.3 Do the firms fulfil the criteria under domestic law for being the subject to collective
insolvency proceedings?

☐   yes   ☐   no

---

[54] Community Guidelines on State aid for rescuing and restructuring firms in difficulty, OJ C288,
9.10.1999, p.2.

1.2   Is the scheme limited to restructuring small or medium-sized enterprises in difficulty which correspond to the Community definition of SMEs?

                          ☐   yes   ☐   no

2   **Return to viability**

A restructuring plan must be implemented which must assure restoration of viability. At least the following information should be included:

2.1   Presentation of the different market assumptions arising from the market survey.

2.2   Analysis of the reason(s) why the firm has run into difficulty.

2.3   Presentation of the proposed future strategy for the firm and how this will lead to viability.

2.4   Complete description and overview of the different restructuring measures planned and their cost.

2.5   Timetable for implementing the different measures and the final deadline for implementing the restructuring plan in its entirety.

2.6   Information on the production capacity of the company, and in particular on utilisation of this capacity, capacity reductions.

2.7   Full description of the financial arrangements for the restructuring, including:
— Use of capital still available;
— Sale of assets or subsidiaries to help finance the restructuring;
— Financial commitment by the different shareholders and third parties (like creditors, banks);
— Amount of public assistance and demonstration of the need for that amount;

2.8   Projected profit and loss accounts for the next five years with estimated return on capital and sensitivity study based on several scenarios;

2.9   Name(s) of the author(s) of the restructuring plan and date on which it was drawn up.

3   **Avoidance of undue distortion of competition**

Does the scheme provide that recipient firms must not increase their capacity during the restructuring plan?

                          ☐   yes   ☐   no

4   **Aid limited to the minimum necessary**

Describe how it will be assured that the aid granted under the scheme is limited to the minimum necessary.

5   **One time, last time**

Is it excluded that recipient firms receive restructuring aid more than once over a period of ten years?

                          ☐   yes   ☐   no

All cases where this principle is not respected must be notified individually

6   Amount of aid

6.1   Please specify the maximum amount of the aid that can be awarded to any one firm as part of the restructuring operation: ....

6.2   Provide all relevant information on aid of any kind which may be granted to the firms eligible for receiving restructuring aid.

7   Annual report

7.1   Do you undertake to provide reports, at least on an annual basis, on the scheme's operation, containing the information specified in the Commission's instructions on standardized reports?

☐   yes   ☐   no

7.2   Do you undertake in such report to include a list of beneficiary firms with at least the following information:

(a) the company name;
(b) its sectoral code, using the NACE[55] two-digit sectoral classification codes;
(c) the number of employees;
(d) annual turnover and balance sheet value;
(e) the amount of aid granted;
(f) where appropriate, any restructuring aid, or other support treated as such, which it has received in the past;
(g) whether or not the beneficiary company has been wound up or subject to collective insolvency proceedings before the end of the restructuring period.

☐   yes   ☐   no

8   Other Information

Please indicate here any other information you consider relevant to the assessment of the measure(s) concerned under the guidelines on aid for rescuing and restructuring firms in difficulty.

PART III.8.B. SUPPLEMENTARY INFORMATION SHEET ON AID FOR
RESTRUCTURING FIRMS IN DIFFICULTY: INDIVIDUAL AID

This supplementary information sheet must be used for the notification of individual restructuring aid covered by the Community Guidelines on State aid for rescuing and restructuring firms in difficulty.[56]

1   Eligibility

1.1   Is the firm a limited company, where more than half of its registered capital has disappeared and more than one quarter of that capital has been lost over the preceding 12 months?

☐   yes   ☐   no

---

[55] Statistical classification of economic activities in the European Community, published by the Statistical Office of the European Communities.

[56] Community Guidelines on State aid for rescuing and restructuring firms in difficulty, JO C 288, 9.10.1999, p 2. Please note that a specific form shall be used in case of aid for restructuring firms in the aviation sector (Part III.13.a) as well as in the agricultural sector (Part III. 12.p).

1.2   Is the firm an unlimited company, where more than half of its capital as shown in the company accounts has disappeared and more than one quarter of that capital has been lost over the preceding 12 months?

☐   yes   ☐   no

1.3   Does the firm fulfil the criteria under domestic law for being the subject of collective insolvency proceedings?

☐   yes   ☐   no

If you have answered yes on any of the above questions, please attach the relevant documents (latest profit and loss account with balance sheet, or court decision opening an investigation into the company under national company law)

If you have answered no to all of the above questions, please submit evidence supporting that the firm is in difficulties, for it to be eligible for restructuring aid.

1.4   When has the firm been created?..

1.5   Since when is the firm operating?...

1.6   Does the company belong to a larger business group?

☐   yes   ☐   no

If you have answered yes, please submit full details about the group (organisation chart, showing the links between the group's members with details on capital and voting rights) and attach proof that the company's difficulties are its own and are not the result of an arbitrary allocation of costs within the group and that the difficulties are too serious to be dealt with by the group itself.

1.7   Has the firm (or the group to which it belongs) in the past received any restructuring aid?

☐   yes   ☐   no

If yes, please provide full details (date, amount, reference to previous Commission decision if applicable, etc.)

2   **Restructuring plan**

2.1   Please supply a copy of the survey of the market(s) served by the firm in difficulty, with the name of the organisation which carried it out. The market survey must give in particular:

2.1.1 A precise definition of the product and geographical market(s).

2.1.2 The names of the company's main competitors with their shares of the world, Community or domestic market, as appropriate.

2.1.3 The evolution of the company's market share in recent years.

2.1.4 An assessment of total production capacity and demand at Community level, concluding whether or not there is excess capacity on the market.

2.1.5 Community-wide forecasts for trends in demand, aggregate capacity and prices on the market over the five years ahead.

2.2   Please attach the restructuring plan. At least the following information should be included:

2.2.1 Presentation of the different market assumptions arising from the market survey.

2.2.2 Analysis of the reason(s) why the firm has run into difficulty.

2.2.3 Presentation of the proposed future strategy for the firm and how this will lead to viability.

2.2.4 Complete description and overview of the different restructuring measures planned and their cost.

2.2.5 Timetable for implementing the different measures and the final deadline for implementing the restructuring plan in its entirety.

2.2.6 Information on the production capacity of the company, and in particular on utilisation of this capacity, capacity reductions.

2.2.7 Full description of the financial arrangements for the restructuring, including:
  — Use of capital still available;
  — Sale of assets or subsidiaries to help finance the restructuring;
  — Financial commitment by the different shareholders and third parties (like creditors, banks);
  — Amount of public assistance and demonstration of the need for that amount;

2.2.8 Projected profit and loss accounts for the next five years with estimated return on capital and sensitivity study based on several scenarios;

2.2.9 Name(s) of the author(s) of the restructuring plan and date on which it was drawn up.

2.3   Describe the compensatory measures proposed with a view to mitigating the distortive effects on competition at Community level.

2.4   Provide all relevant information on aid of any kind granted to the firm receiving restructuring aid, whether under a scheme or not, until the restructuring period comes to an end.

3   **Other information**

Please indicate here any other information you consider relevant to the assessment of the measure(s) concerned under the guidelines on aid for rescuing and restructuring firms in difficulty.

PART III.9. SUPPLEMENTARY INFORMATION SHEET ON
AID FOR AUDIOVISUAL PRODUCTION

This supplementary information sheet must be used for notifications of aid covered by the Commission Communication on certain legal aspects relating to cinematographic and other audiovisual works.[57]

1   **The aid scheme**

1.1   Please describe as accurately as possible the purpose of the aid and its scope, where appropriate, for each measure.

---

[57] Communication from the Commission to the Council, the European Parlament, the Economic and Social Committee and Committee of the Regions on certain legal aspects relating to cinematographic and other audiovisual works, OJ C43, 16.2.2002, p 6.

1.2 Does the aid directly benefit the creation of a cultural work (for cinema or television)?

1.3 Please indicate what provisions exist to guarantee the cultural objective of the aid:

....

....

1.4 Does the aid have the effect of supporting industrial investment?

2 **Conditions for eligibility**

Please indicate the conditions for eligibility for the planned aid:

....

....

2.2 Beneficiaries:

2.2.1 Does the scheme distinguish between specific categories of beneficiary (e.g. natural/legal person, dependent/independent producer/broadcaster, etc.)? ....

....

2.2.2 Does the scheme differentiate on grounds of nationality or place of residence?

....

....

2.2.3 In the case of establishment in the territory of a Member State, are beneficiaries obliged to fulfil any conditions other than that of being represented by a permanent agency? Note that the conditions of establishment must be defined with respect to the territory of the Member State and not to a subdivision of that State.

2.2.4 If the aid has a tax component, must the beneficiary fulfil any obligations or conditions other than that of having taxable revenue in the territory of the Member State?

3 **Territorial coverage**

3.1 Please indicate if there is provision for any form of obligation to spend in the territory of the Member State or in one of its subdivisions.

3.2 Is it necessary to comply with a minimum degree of territorial coverage in order to be eligible for the aid?

3.3 Is the required territorial coverage calculated with regard to the overall budget of the film or to the amount of aid?

3.4 Does the condition of territorial coverage apply to certain specific items of the production budget?

3.5 Is the absolute amount of aid adjustable in proportion to the expenditure carried out in the territory of the Member State?

3.6 Is the aid intensity directly proportional to the effective degree of territorial coverage?

3.7 Is the aid adjustable in proportion to the degree of territorial coverage required?

4   Eligible costs

4.1   Please specify the costs which may be taken into account to determine the amount of aid.

4.2   Do the eligible costs all relate directly to the creation of a cinematographic or audiovisual work?

5   Aid intensity

5.1   Please indicate whether the scheme provides for use of the concept of difficult, low-budget film in order to obtain an aid intensity of over 50% of the production budget.

5.2   If so, please indicate the categories of film covered by this concept.

5.3   Please indicate whether the aid can be combined with other aid schemes ('cumulation of aid') or other provisions for aid and, if so, what arrangements are made to limit such cumulation or to ensure that, in the case of cumulation, the maximum aid intensity for the work is not exceeded.

6   Compatibility

6.1   Please provide a reasoned justification in support of compatibility of the aid in the light of the principles set out in the Commission Communication on certain legal aspects relating to cinematographic and other audiovisual works.

7   Other information

Please indicate here any other information you consider relevant to the assessment of the measure(s) concerned under the Communication on certain legal aspects relating to cinematographic and other audiovisual works.

PART III.10. SUPPLEMENTARY INFORMATION SHEET ON ENVIRONMENTAL PROTECTION AID

This supplementary information sheet must be used for the notification of any aid covered by the Community Guidelines on State aid for environmental protection.[58]

1   Objective of the aid

1.1   Which are the objectives aimed at in terms of environmental protection? Please submit a detailed description for each part of the scheme

....

If the measure in question has already been applied in the past, what have been the results in terms of environmental protection?..

....

1.2   If the measure is a new one, what environmental results are anticipated, and over what period?

....

....

---

[58] Community Guidelines on State aid for environmental protection, JOC 37, 3.2.2001, p. 3.

2   **Investment aid aimed at the adaptation to new standards or aimed at going beyond existing standards**

2.1   Aid for adaptation to new Community standards

2.1.1   Will aid be granted for reaching Community standards already adopted at the time of notification?

           ☐   yes   ☐   no

In the affirmative which are the Community standards in question?

....

....

Date at which they have been formally adopted by the competent Community Institutions?

....

Please confirm that no aid will be granted to large enterprises for reaching Community standards already adopted but not yet in force

           ☐   yes   ☐   no

If Community Standards are set in a directive, which deadlines are set for the transposition?

....

2.1.2   Which are the eligible costs?

....

Please explain how it will be ensured that the eligible costs are only the extra costs necessary to meet the environmental objective, and how any cost savings engendered over the first 5 years of the life of the investment will be taken into account

....

To what extent are advantages deriving from a possible capacity increase and from accessory additional productions taken into account?..

....

2.1.3   What is the maximum aid intensity expressed as a gross amount of the planned aid?

....

2.2   State aids aimed at going beyond Community standards or planned in case no Community standard exists.

2.2.1   If Community standards exist, please describe

....

If there are no Community standards, are there national standards?

           ☐   yes   ☐   no

If yes, please attach copies of the relevant texts.

Please confirm that an enterprise will only be granted aid for reaching national standards which are more stringent than Community standards or where no Community standards exist, if it complies with the relevant standard on the final date laid down in the national measure:

....

Please give examples of eligible investments: ....

In the case of national standards, are they stricter than Community standards?

□   yes   □   no

If yes, please specify, ...

....

2.2.2 What are the eligible costs?

Please explain in what way it will be ensured that the eligible costs are only the extra costs necessary to meet the environmental objective, and how any cost savings engendered over the first 5 years of the life of the investment will be taken into account.

....

....

To what extent have possible advantage deriving from a capacity increase and additional accessory productions been taken into account?

2.2.3 Please state the maximum gross aid intensity of the planned measure

What is the standard maximum gross aid intensity of the planned measure?

Does the aid scheme provide for a bonus for undertakings situated in regions eligible for national regional aid?

□   yes   □   no

If yes, which bonuses are foreseen? ....

Does the aid scheme provide for a bonus for SMEs?

□   yes   □   no

If yes, please give details? ....

Can the bonus be cumulated with the bonus for undertakings situated in assisted regions?

□   yes   □   no

If yes, please describe the modalities:

....

3   **Investment aid in the energy sector**

3.1   Aids for investments aimed at energy saving

3.1.1 What are the energy savings expected as a result of the ad hoc aid or aid scheme?

Is the amount of the expected savings assessed by an independent expert? Please give examples of eligible investments

....

3.1.2 What are the CO^2 savings expected as a result of the ad hoc aid or aid scheme?

3.1.3 What are the eligible costs?

Please explain in what way it will be ensured that the eligible costs are only the extra costs necessary to meet the environmental objective, and how any cost savings engendered over the first 5 years of the life of the investment will be taken into account.

To what extent have possible advantages deriving from a capacity increase and additional accessory productions been taken into account?

What is the maximum gross aid intensity of the planned aid?

Does the project provide for a bonus for undertakings in areas eligible for national regional aid schemes?

☐   yes   ☐   no

If yes, which bonuses are foreseen?

Does the planned scheme provide for a bonus for SMEs?

☐   yes   ☐   no

If yes, which bonus?

Can this bonus be cumulated with the bonus applicable to undertakings in assisted areas?

☐   yes   ☐   no

If yes, what are the conditions? ....

3.2   Aids in favour of the combined production of electricity and heat

3.2.1   Which primary source of energy will be used in the production process?

3.2.2   What will be the environmental benefit of the measure in question?

If the conversion efficiency is particularly high, give the comparative average.

What will be the minimum conversion efficiency of the eligible CHP plants?

If the measures allow energy consumption to decrease, in what proportion?

Have the provisions been elaborated by an independent expert?

In what respect and to what extent is the production process less damaging for the environment, if at all?

....

3.2.3   What are the eligible costs?

What would be the investment costs for the installation of a production entity for electricity (or heat) for the same capacity in terms of effective energy production?

To what extent is the sale of heat (if the installation is primarily destined for the production of energy) or the sale of electricity (in the opposite case) taken into account in order to decrease the higher investment costs?

In the case of the replacement of an existing installation, is there an advantage deriving from the increase of capacity or from cost saving?

How are those advantages calculated?

3.2.4   What is the maximum gross aid intensity of the planned aid?

What is the standard maximum gross intensity of the aid?

Does the planned scheme provide for a bonus for undertakings in assisted areas?

☐   yes   ☐   no

If yes, which bonuses are foreseen? ....

Is a bonus foreseen for SMEs?

☐   yes   ☐   no

If yes, please give details

Can this bonus be cumulated with the bonus for undertakings in assisted areas?

☐   yes   ☐   no

If yes, under what conditions?

3.3   Aids for investment in renewable energies

3.3.1 Which are the types of energy in question? Do they fall under the definition of renewable energies described in Art. 2 of Directive 2001/77/CE of the European Parliament and of the Council of 27 September 2001?[59]

In case the investments are meant to provide energy for a whole Community, describe the limits of this community and the types of energy used before for that purpose.

3.3.2 What are the eligible costs?

What would be the investment costs for the installation of a production entity for electricity for the same capacity in terms of effective energy production?

3.3.3 What is the maximum gross aid intensity of the planned aid?

If the aid may cover the total eligible costs, why is such an aid rate indispensable?

In similar circumstances, how would the produced energy be traded, through which distributors and at what tariffs? ....

Does the planned aid scheme provide for a bonus for undertakings situated in regions eligible for national regional aid?

☐   yes   ☐   no

If so, what is the size of the bonus?...

Is a bonus foreseen for SMEs?

☐   yes   ☐   no

If yes, please give details: ....

Can this bonus be cumulated with the bonus provided for undertakings in assisted regions?

☐   yes   ☐   no

If yes, under which conditions? ....

Can the notified investment aid be combined with other State aid within the meaning of Article 87(1) of the Treaty, or with other forms of Community financing?

☐   yes   ☐   no

If yes, please undertake to respect the maximum aid intensities stipulated in the environmental aid guidelines, or, where aid serving different purposes and involving the same eligible costs is granted, the most favourable aid ceiling: ....

4   **Aid in favour of the rehabilitation of polluted industrial areas**

4.1   What is the site in question (description of the site) and what is the nature of the pollution?

---

[59] Directive 2001/77/CE of the European Parliament and of the Council of 27 September 2001, OJ L283, 27.10.2001, p 3.

Has the nature, extent and risk to human health and the environment of the pollution been subject to an independent expert assessment?

☐   yes   ☐   no

Which ones? Attach copies of the reports.

4.2   In the case of ad hoc aid, please answer the following questions:

Is the current ownership of the site public or private?

If the current ownership of the site is public, has this site been purchased by the public administration in order to carry out the remediation/rehabilitation actions?

☐   yes   ☐   no

Has the person responsible for the pollution of the site been identified?

☐   yes   ☐   no

If not, please describe briefly the exemption circumstances that render the polluter not liable

Has the value of the polluted site (before rehabilitation) been evaluated through an independent expert analysis?

☐   yes   ☐   no

What is the market value of the site before the rehabilitation action?

....

What are the costs calculated for the rehabilitation work? ....

What are the primary costs in the sense of the Commission Communication on State aid elements in sales of land and buildings by public authorities?

....

Has the value of the site after rehabilitation been estimated by an independent expert assessment?

☐   yes   ☐   no

What is the estimated market value of the rehabilitated site?

....

Has the public administration the intention of selling the land within three years after the date of acquisition?

What land use will be given to the polluted site after its rehabilitation?

What is the scope of the envisaged aid?

What is the maximum gross aid intensity of the planned aid?

4.3   In case of an aid scheme, please explain

What is the scope of the envisaged aid?

What is the maximum gross aid intensity of the planned aid?

Have similar aid schemes been given to fund the rehabilitation of other polluted sites in your Member State? Please explain how many sites have been remediated under similar schemes and what were the amounts allocated to such schemes? ....

....

5   **Aid in favour of relocalization of an Undertaking**

5.1 Where is the undertaking which should benefit from the relocation aid situated?

If the location is in a Zone Natura 2000, which legislative text provides for that qualification?

5.2 Why does the relocation takes place?

Please provide a thorough description of the environmental, social or public health circumstances that render the relocation necessary. Is the owner of the undertaking liable (under national or Community legislation) for the pollution/environmental problem?

5.3 Is there an administrative or judicial decision ordering the relocation of the undertaking?

☐   yes   ☐   no

If yes, attach a copy of the relevant decision.

Please confirm that the beneficiary will comply with the strictest environmental standards applicable in the new region where it is located.

5.4 What profits can the undertaking expect from the sale, the expropriation, or rent of the abandoned territories or installations?

5.5 What costs will have to be assumed in relation with the new installation with equal production capacity as the one abandoned?

Will the relocation cause penalties for the anticipated termination of the contract regarding the rent of the territory or of the buildings?

Will there be any benefits from the new technology used following the relocation?

Are there accounting gains from the better use of the installations following the relocation?

What is the maximum gross aid intensity of the planned aid? ....

6   **Aid to SMES for advisory/consultancy services in the environmental field**

6.1 Who are the potential beneficiaries of the aid?

Do they fulfil all the conditions of Annex 1 of Regulation (CE) No 70/2001 of the Commission of 12 January 2001, concerning the application of Articles 87 and 88 of the Treaty CE to state aids for SMEs[60]

6.2 Will the consultancy services be provided by external companies?

☐   yes   ☐   no

Do the external companies have financial links with the undertakings beneficiaries of the aid?

☐   yes   ☐   no

Please state the exact nature of the consultancy services:...

7   **Operating aid to promote waste management and energy saving**

7.1 What are the extra production costs and what share is covered by the aid?

If the aid is degressive please state the modalities?

---

[60] Regulation (EC) N° 70/2001 of the Commission of 12 January 2001 concerning the application of Art 87 and 88 EC Treaty to State aids to small and medium-sized enterprises, OL L 10, 13.10.2001, p 33.

7.2 What is the foreseen duration for the application of the notified aid scheme?

7.3 Specific questions in case of aid to promote waste management:

How is it ensured that a beneficiary finances the service provided in proportion to the amount of waste produced and/or the cost of treatment?

In case of an aid for industrial waste management are there Community rules applicable?

□   yes   □   no

If yes, please describe: ....

In the absence of Community rules, are there national rules? ....

□   yes   □   no

If yes, please describe: ....

If, yes, are these national rules stricter than Community rules?

□   yes   □   no

If yes, please describe: ....

8 **Operating aids in form of tax reductions or exemptions**

8.1 Introduction of a new tax as a result of a Community obligation

8.1.1 The Member State grants exemptions which lead to a rate lower than the minimum Community rate

From which tax will a reduction or exemption be granted?

How does the levying of the tax contribute to environmental protection?

What results have been obtained as a direct consequence of the tax, or are expected to be obtained?

Have these exemptions been authorized by the Council applying Community fiscal rules?

Why is it necessary to apply lower rates than the minimum Community rates?

Are the sectors benefiting from the tax reductions subject to strong intra-community and/or international competition?

How many undertakings may benefit from this measure?

Are those undertakings subject to other charges concerning environmental protection?

8.1.2 The Member State grants tax reductions at a rate lower than the minimum Community rate

From which tax will a reduction or exemption be granted?

How does the levying of the tax contribute to environmental protection?

What results have been obtained as a direct consequence of the tax, or are expected to be obtained? . . .

Are the derogations conditional on the conclusion of agreements between the recipient firms and the Member State in order to improve environmental protection?

□   yes   □   no

What is the nature of these agreements? ....

Are the agreements open to all sectors of the economy which can benefit from the tax measure?

....

If the signing up to an agreement is voluntary and not a condition for receiving the tax benefit, what is the (expected) rate of accession to agreements among the beneficiaries of the tax benefit?

....

Who ensures the monitoring of the agreements entered into by the firms?

Which sanctions are foreseen in case of non-compliance of the obligations undertaken in the agreements?

....

Attach a copy of such agreements or describe them in detail.

If national rules have the same effects as the above-mentioned agreements, please attach a copy of the rules.

In the absence of agreements between firms and the Member State, what will be the rate effectively paid by the firms after application of the reduction and what will be the difference between this amount and the minimum Community rate?

8.1.3 Derogation applicable for the introduction of a new tax imposed in the absence of a Community obligation

Are the derogations conditional on the voluntary or obligatory conclusion of agreements between the firms and the Member State aiming at an improvement of the environment?

        ☐   yes   ☐   no

What is the nature of such agreements?

        ☐   yes   ☐   no

Are they open to all sectors of the economy which can benefit from the tax measure?

        ☐   yes   ☐   no

If the signing up to an agreement is voluntary and not a condition for receiving the tax benefit, what is the rate of accession to agreements among the beneficiaries of the tax benefit?

Who ensures the respect of the commitments entered into by the firms?

What are the sanctions in case of non-compliance with the commitments foreseen in the agreements?

....

Attach a copy of the draft agreements if available or describe their content.

If there are national rules having the same effect as the aforementioned agreements, attach a copy of these national rules.

In the absence of agreements between firms and the Member State which rate will be effectively paid by the firms after application of the reduction and which will be the difference to the 'normal' national rate?

....

Please submit figures which enable the Commission to assess the share of the tax actually paid.

Which duration is foreseen for the application of the notified planned aid scheme?

....

8.1.4 Derogations applicable to existing taxes

What is the environmental effect of the tax concerned by the measure?

When was the tax introduced?

For which beneficiaries?

Was the decision to grant a tax reduction for the beneficiaries concerned by this notification made in connection with a significant increase of the tax?

☐   yes   ☐   no

If yes, please show the development of the relevant tax rate over time in absolute terms.

Have the derogations become necessary following a significant change in the economic conditions?

Describe the change

....

Is this change specific to one Member State or does it exist in all Member States?

....

Which increase of charges is due to the change of economic conditions?

....

What is the duration of the application of the notified planned aid scheme?

8.1.5 Tax exemption necessary for the modernization of production of energy in order to obtain a higher energy efficiency.

What traditional energy sources will be used for the production of energy?

....

What will be the difference in energy efficiency as compared to traditional methods of production?

....

What additional costs will be caused by the envisaged production?

....

9   **Operating aids in favour of renewable energies**

9.1   Which are the categories of energy in question?

Do these types of energy fall within the definition of renewable energies as set out in Art. 2 of Directive 2001/77/CE of the European Parliament and of the Council of 27 September 2001?

9.2   Aids for compensating the difference between the production costs for renewable energies and the market prices for such energy: ....

Are these new plants?

☐   yes   ☐   no

What are the average production costs and the difference to the average market price for every source of renewable energy? ....

Please describe the precise support mechanism and in particular the method for calculating the amount of aid:

....

What is the foreseen duration for amortizing the plants?..

Please show that the net present value of the aid will not exceed the net present value of the total investment costs for the power plant or the type of power plant benefiting from the aid

....

If the aid is foreseen for several years, what are the modalities for the revision of production costs and market prices?

Are the plants for the production of renewable energy sources as well eligible for investment aids?

☐   yes   ☐   no

If yes, how much?

How will the investment aid be taken into account when determining the need for operating aid?

Does the aid include an element of return on capital?

☐   yes   ☐   no

If yes, how much? Please explain why this is considered to be necessary. For the biomass sector, can the aid go beyond the coverage of the investments?

9.3   Aids in the form of market mechanisms

Are these new plants?

☐   yes   ☐   no

What are the average costs for the production of the renewable energy in question and the difference to the average market price for energy?

How will the mechanism function?

How is it ensured that the mechanism does not dissuade renewable energy producers from becoming more competitive?

How does the mechanism take imports and exports of electricity into account?

In the case of green certificates will the Member State intervene directly or indirectly in the price-setting?

Can the Member State, if it so wishes, put new certificates on the market or can it buy them?

☐   yes   ☐   no

Will the system include a charge to be paid in case of non-fulfilment of an obligation?

☐   yes   ☐   no

If yes, how will this money be collected, administered and used?

How will the control be ensured in order to avoid an overall overcompensation of the participating firms?

9.4   Operating aid on the basis of the external costs avoided

Are these new plants?

☐   yes   ☐   no

How and by whom have the external costs avoided been calculated? Please submit a reasoned and quantified comparative cost analysis together with an assessment of external costs caused by competing energy producers

....

What is the maximum amount of aid per kWh?

....

How is control ensured that the amounts of aid going beyond the amount resulting from option 1 is in fact re-invested in the sector or renewable energies?

....

10   Operating aid for the combined production of heat and electricity

10.1   Which primary energy source will be utilised in the production process?

What is the benefit of the planned measure for the environment?

If the conversion efficiency is particularly high, what is the comparative average?

What will be the minimum conversion efficiency of the eligible CHP plants?

In which proportion, if at all, does the measure allow for the reduction of energy consumption?

Have the measures been assessed by an independent expert?

In which aspects and to what extent, if at all, does the production process damage less the environment?

What are the modalities of the planned aid?

What are the average production costs and the average market prices of the produced energies?

What is the average market price of a traditional energy unit?

In case of industrial use of the combined production of heat and electricity, which are the possible benefits from the production of heat?

If the aid is foreseen for several years, which are the conditions for the adjustment of production costs and market prices?

11   Other information

Please indicate here any other information you consider relevant to the assessment of the measure(s) concerned under the guidelines on aid for environmental protection.

PART III.11. SUPPLEMENTARY INFORMATION SHEET ON RISK CAPITAL AID

This supplementary information sheet must be used for the notification of any aid scheme covered by the Communication on State aid and risk capital.[61] *Please note that if the scheme is covered by another framework or guidelines, the corresponding standard notification form for the relevant framework or guidelines should be used instead.*

1   Beneficiary of aid

Who is/are the beneficiary/ies of the scheme (please tick one or more boxes as appropriate):

1.1   ☐ investors setting up a fund or providing equity in a company or a set of companies. Please specify selection criteria:

....

....

....

---

[61] Commission Communication on State aid and Risk Capital, OJ, C 235 of 21.08.2001, p 3.

1.2 ☐ investment fund or other intermediary vehicle. Please specify selection criteria:

....

....

....

1.3 ☐ enterprises invested in. Please specify selection criteria:

....

....

....

2 Form of aid

2.1 The scheme envisages the following measure(s) and/or instrument(s) (please tick one or more boxes as appropriate):

☐ constitution of an investment fund (i.e. venture capital fund) in which public authorities are a partner, investor, or participant. Please specify:

....

....

....

☐ grants to an investment fund (i.e. venture capital fund) to cover part of its administrative and management costs. Please specify:

....

....

....

☐ guarantees to risk capital investors or to risk capital funds against a proportion of investment losses, or guarantees in respect of loans to investors or funds for investment in risk capital. Please specify:

....

....

....

☐ other financial instruments in favour of risk capital investors or of venture capital funds to provide extra capital for investment. Please specify:

....

....

....

☐ fiscal incentives to investors to undertake risk capital investments. Please specify:

....

....

....

2.2 The combination of the above measure(s) and/or instrument(s) does not lead to the provision of capital to (an) enterprise(s) invested in solely in the form of loans (including subordinated loans and 'equity' loans) or other instruments which provide the investor/lender with a fixed minimum return. Please specify:

1478

....
....
....
....

3 Existence of market failure

3.1 ☐ The maximum tranche of finance for target enterprises financed under the aid scheme does not exceed:

☐ EUR 500,000;

☐ EUR 750,000 for enterprises located in regions qualifying for assistance under Article 87(3)(c) of the EC Treaty;

☐ EUR 1 million for enterprises located in regions qualifying for assistance under Article 87(3)(a) of the EC Treaty.

3.2 ☐ If the maximum tranches of finance for target enterprises financed under the aid scheme exceeds the above thresholds, the scheme must be justified by the presence of a 'market failure' in the relevant area(s) of investment. Please specify by adducing supporting evidence:

....

....

4 Main features of aid

4.1 The State funds are restricted exclusively or prevalently to effect equity investments into:

☐ enterprises located in assisted regions qualifying under Article 87(3)(a) of the EC Treaty and/or under Article 87 (3)(c) of the EC Treaty.

☐ micro or small enterprises;

☐ medium-sized enterprises in their start-up or other early stages, or located in assisted areas.

☐ for medium-sized enterprises beyond their start-up or other early stages, or not located in assisted areas, there is a limit per enterprise on total funding through the measure. Please specify:

....

....

4.2 The scheme is focused on risk capital market failure and provides for delivery of finance to enterprises principally in the form of equity or quasi-equity. Please specify if necessary:

....

....

....

4.3 Decisions to invest are profit-driven and there is a link between investment performance and those responsible for investment decisions, demonstrated by the following:

☐ All the capital invested in the target enterprises is provided by market economy investors or

☐ There is a significant involvement of market economy investors' in the target enterprises. Please specify:

....

....

....

4.3.1 In the case of *investment funds*, the profit-driven character of investments is demonstrated by (please tick one or more as appropriate):

☐ At least 50% of the fund's capital is provided by private investors;

☐ At least 30% of the fund's capital is provided by private investors in the case of measures operating in regions qualifying under Article 87(3)(a) of the EC Treaty or under Article 87(3)(c) of the EC Treaty;

☐ Other factors justifying a different level of private capital. Please describe

....

☐ There is an agreement between a professional fund manager and participants in the fund providing that the manager's remuneration is linked to the performance of the fund and that clearly sets out the objectives of the fund and the timing of investments;

☐ private investors are represented in decision-making;

☐ there is application of best practice and regulatory supervision in the management of the fund.

4.4 ☐ Distortion of competition between investors and investment funds is minimised, as demonstrated by:

☐ a call for tender setting out any preferential terms accorded to private investors;

☐ in case of an investment fund, a public invitation to investors at its launch;

☐ in case of a scheme (e.g. a guarantee scheme), it will remain open to all new entrants.

4.5 ☐ Each investment will be based on the existence of a detailed business plan to establish the viability of each project.

4.6 ☐ A clear 'exit mechanism' is provided under the scheme. Please specify:

....

....

....

4.7 ☐ Is the possibility to recycle funds within a scheme foreseen?

4.8 ☐ Sectoral focus. Target enterprises are active in (a) certain sector(s) of the economy only. Please specify the sector(s) and the underlying commercial as well as public policy logic:

....

....

....

5   Cumulation of the aid

5.1 ☐ If the scheme provides for aid to enterprises invested in, are they already recipients of aid under another framework,[62] including under other authorised schemes? Please specify:

---

[62] The information to be provided does not cover de minimis aid pursuant to Commission Reg (EC) No 69/2001 of 12 January 2001 on the application of Arts 87 and 88 to de minimis aid, OJ L10, 13.1.2001, p 30, granted to the same enterprises, which needs not be reported.

....

....

....

5.2 ☐ If equity provided under the risk capital scheme to enterprises is used to finance initial investment, research and development costs or other costs eligible under other frameworks, is the relevant aid ceiling complied with also taking into account the aid element of the risk capital scheme? Please specify.

....

....

....

6   **Other information**

Please indicate here any other information you consider relevant to the assessment of the measure(s) concerned under the communication on aid and risk capital.

PART III.12.A SUPPLEMENTARY INFORMATION SHEET FOR AGRICULTURE

Please note that Part III.12 of the State aid notification form only applies to activities related to the production, processing and marketing of agricultural products, that is, products included in Annex 1 to the EC Treaty. However, concerning the promotion of agricultural products, exceptionally, agricultural State aid rules also apply to a certain number of non-Annex I products. Please note that the specific State aid rules for agriculture do not apply to measures related to the processing of Annex I products into non-Annex I products. For such measures you should complete the relevant section of the general notification form.

1   **Products covered**

1.1   Does the measure apply to any of the following products which are not yet subject to a common market organization:

☐ potatoes other than starch potatoes
☐ horsemeat
☐ honey
☐ coffee
☐ cork
☐ The measure does not apply to any of these products

2   **Incentive effect**

2.1   Can you confirm that no aid will be granted in respect of work begun or activities undertaken before an application for aid has been properly submitted to the competent authorities, and accepted by them with binding effect?

☐ yes   ☐ no

If no, please note that; under points 3.5 and 3.6 of the Agricultural Guidelines, aid which is granted retrospectively in respect of activities already undertaken by the beneficiary cannot be considered to contain the necessary incentive element, and must be considered operating aid (in principle prohibited by State aid legislation).

3   **Type of aid**

3.1   What type(s) of aid does the planned measure include?

3.1.1 ☐ Aid for investment in agricultural holdings (point 4.1 of the Agricultural Guidelines.[63] Please complete Part III.12.a.i of this notification form).

3.1.2 ☐ Aid for investments in connection with the processing and marketing of agricultural products (points 4.2 of the Agricultural Guidelines). Please proceed to Part III.12.a.ii of this notification form.

3.1.3 ☐ Aid for investments to promote the diversification of farm activities (points 4.3, 4.1 or 4.2 of the Agricultural Guidelines). Please proceed to Part III.12.a.i, section 10 of this notification form.

3.1.4 ☐ Aid for additional costs or income forgone because of agri-environmental commitments (point 5.3 of the Agricultural Guidelines). Please complete Part III.12.b of this notification form.

3.1.5 ☐ Operating aid related to environmental protection (point 5.5 of the Agricultural Guidelines). Please complete Part III.12.b.

3.1.6 ☐ Aid (other than investment aid) to compensate for handicaps in the less favoured areas (point 6 of the Agricultural Guidelines). Please complete Part III.12.c.

3.1.7 ☐ Aid for the setting up of young farmers (point 7 of the Agricultural Guidelines). Please complete Part III.12.d.

3.1.8 ☐ Aid for early retirement or for the cessation of farming activities (point 8 of the Agricultural Guidelines). Please complete Part III.12.e.

3.1.9 ☐ Aid for closing production, processing and marketing capacity (point 9 of the Agricultural Guidelines). Please complete Part III.12.f.

3.1.10 ☐ Aid for producer groups (point 10 of the Agricultural Guidelines). Please complete Part III.12.g.

3.1.11 ☐ Aid to compensate for damage to agricultural production or the means of agricultural production (point 11 of the Agricultural Guidelines). Please complete Part III.12.h.

3.1.12 ☐ Aid for land reparcelling (point 12 of the Agricultural Guidelines). Please complete Part III.12.i.

3.1.13 ☐ Aid to encourage the production and marketing of quality agricultural products (point 13 of the Agricultural Guidelines). Please complete Part III.12.j.

3.1.14 ☐ Aid for the provision of technical support in the agricultural sector (point 14 of the Agricultural Guidelines). Please complete Part III.12.k.

3.1.15 ☐ Aid for the livestock sector (point 15 of the Agricultural Guidelines). Please complete Part III.12.l.

---

[63] Community Guidelines for State Aid in the Agriculture Sector, OJ C232, 12.8.2000, p 17.

3.1.16 ☐ Aid for the outermost regions and the Aegean Islands (point 16 of the Agricultural Guidelines). Please complete Part III.12.m.

3.1.17 ☐ Aid for research and development (point 17 of the Agricultural Guidelines). Please complete Part III.6.a.

3.1.18 ☐ Aid for the (promotion and) advertising of agricultural products (point 18 of the Agricultural Guidelines). Please complete Part III.12.o.

3.1.19 ☐ Aid in the form of subsidised short-term loans (point 19 of the Agricultural Guidelines). Please complete Part III.12.n.

3.1.20 ☐ Aid for rescue and restructuring firms in difficulty (point 20 of the Agricultural Guidelines). Please complete Part III.12.p.

3.1.21 ☐ Aid concerning TSE tests, fallen stock and slaughterhouse waste. Please complete part III.12.q.

3.1.22 ☐ Aid for employment. Please complete the relevant section of the general notification form and part III.3.

3.1.23 ☐ Aid for training. Please complete part III.2.

PART III.12.A1. SUPPLEMENTARY INFORMATION SHEET FOR AID TO INVESTMENTS IN AGRICULTURAL HOLDINGS

This notification form applies to investments in agricultural holdings, which are dealt with in points 4.1, 4.1.2.2, 4.1.2.3, 4.1.2.4 and 4.3 of the Guidelines

This form must also be used by Member States for the notification of any aid for individual investments, with eligible expenses in excess of EUR 12,5 million, or where the actual amount of aid exceeds EUR 6 million (Article 1§3 of Regulation (EC) N° 1/2004).

1   **Objectives of the aid**

1.1   Which of the following objectives does the investment pursue:
☐ reduce production costs;
☐ improve and re-deploy production;
☐ increase quality;
☐ preserve and improve the natural environment, hygiene conditions and animal welfare standards;
☐ promote the diversification of farm activities

If the investment pursues other aims, please note that point 4.1.1.1 of the Agricultural Guidelines does not allow for aid for investments which do not pursue any of the objectives listed above.

1.2   Does the aid concern simple replacement investments?

☐   yes   ☐   no

If yes, please note that point 4.1.1.1 of the Agricultural Guidelines does not allow for aids for simple replacement investments.

2   Beneficiaries

2.1   Who are the beneficiaries of the aid?

☐ farmers
☐ producer groups
☐ other (please specify)

....

3   Aid intensity

3.1   Please state the maximum rate of public support, expressed as a volume of eligible investment:

.... in less favoured areas (max. 50%);
.... in other areas (max. 40%);
.... for young farmers in less-favoured areas (max. 55%);
.... for young farmers in other areas (max. 45%).

If aid rates are higher, please note that, under point 4.1.1.2 of the Agricultural Guidelines, aid intensity cannot exceed the ceilings set out above.

4   Eligibility criteria

4.1   Does the aid provide that aid for investment may only be granted to:

— agricultural holdings the economic viability of which can be demonstrated by an assessment of its prospects?

☐   yes   ☐   no

— agricultural holdings where the farmer possesses adequate occupational skill and competence?

☐   yes   ☐   no

— agricultural holdings complying with minimum Community standard regarding the environment, hygiene and animal welfare?

☐   yes   ☐   no

If you have answered no to any of the questions under point 4.1, please note that, under point 4.1.1.3 of the Agricultural Guidelines, all the above eligibility criteria must be met for a measure to be eligible for aid.

4.2   Is the aid intended to finance investments made in order to comply with newly introduced minimum standards[64] regarding the environment, hygiene and animal welfare?

☐   yes   ☐   no

If yes, please specify which standards are involved and indicate their legal basis

....
....

4.3   In the case of young farmers, does the measure lay down that the higher aid intensities can only be granted within five years of setting up?

☐   yes   ☐   no

---

[64] Newly introduced minimum standards are standards to be made compulsory vis-à-vis economic operators not more than 2 years before the investment is actually undertaken in the case of legislation which does not provide for any transitional period, or standards which will become compulsory after the investment is actually undertaken, on the basis of transitional periods provided for in legislation introducing such standards.

If no, please note that point 4.1.1.2 of the Agricultural Guidelines lays down that maximum aid rates of 45% or 55% can be granted to young farmers only within five years after setting up.

5   Market outlets

5.1   Does the investment entail an increase in production capacity of the holding?

☐   yes   ☐   no

5.1.1   If yes, has the existence of market outlets been assessed at the appropriate level, in terms of the products concerned, the types of investments and existing and expected capacities?

☐   yes   ☐   no

If no, please note that point 4.1.1.4 of the Agricultural Guidelines lays down that no aid may be granted for investments having as their objective increased production for which normal market outlets cannot be found.

5.2   Does the aid concern a product subject to restrictions on production or limitations of Community support at the level of individual undertakings?

☐   yes   ☐   no

5.2.1   If yes, will the investments increase production beyond these restrictions or limitations?

☐   yes   ☐   no

If yes, please note that point 4.1.1.4 of the Agricultural Guidelines lays down that no aid can be granted for investments which would increase production beyond the restrictions or limitations established under the common market organisations.

6   Expenses

6.1   Do eligible expenses include?

☐ construction, acquisition or improvement of immovable property;
☐ new machinery and equipment, including computer software;
☐ general costs (such as architects, engineers and consultation fees, feasibility studies, the acquisition of patents and licences, up to 12% of eligible expenditure)
☐ land purchase, including legal fees, taxes and land registration costs.

If eligible expenses include other items, please note that point 4.1.1.5 of the Agricultural Guidelines only allows investment aid to cover the eligible expenses listed above.

6.2   Do eligible expenses also include the purchase of second-hand equipment?

☐   yes   ☐   no

6.2.1   If yes, are all the following conditions met?

— the seller of the equipment has confirmed its exact origin in a written declaration;
— the equipment has not already been the subject of national or Community assistance;
— the purchase of the equipment represents a particular advantage for the programme or project, or is made necessary by exceptional circumstances (e.g. no new equipment available on time);
— the purchase entails a cost reduction compared with the cost of the same equipment purchased new, while maintaining a good cost–benefit ratio;

— the equipment must have the necessary technical and/or technological characteristics consistent with the requirements of the project.

☐ yes   ☐ no

If no, please note that, according to point 4.1.1.5, footnote 13 of the Agricultural Guidelines, the Commission will only authorise aid for second-hand equipment if the above conditions are met.

6.3   Will aid be granted for the purchase of production rights?

☐ yes   ☐ no

If yes, please explain how you intend to comply with the requirements of point 4.1.1.6 of the Agricultural Guidelines.

....

6.4   As regards the purchase of animals, what does the aid cover?

☐ the first purchase of livestock
☐ investments intended to improve the genetic quality of the stock through the purchase of high-quality breeding animals (male or female) registered in herd books or their equivalent.

If other expenses are covered, please note that, under point 4.1.1.7 of the Agricultural Guidelines, aid may be given only for the above eligible costs.

6.5   Do maximum expenses eligible for support exceed the limit for total investment eligible for support set by the Member State in accordance with Article 7 of the Rural Development Regulation?

☐ yes   ☐ no

If yes, please note that point 4.1.1.8 of the Agricultural Guidelines sets the above overall limit to costs eligible for support.

7   Aid for the conservation of traditional landscapes

7.1   Does the aid concern investments or capital works intended for the conservation of *non-productive* heritage features located on agricultural holdings?

☐ yes   ☐ no

7.1.1 If yes, what is the maximum aid rate? (please specify)

Maximum aid rate: ....

7.2   Does the aid concern investments or capital works intended to conserve the heritage features of *productive assets* on farms?

☐ yes   ☐ no

7.2.1 If yes, does the investment entail any increase in the production capacity of the farm?

☐ yes   ☐ no

7.2.2 What are the maximum aid rates for this type of investment? (please specify)

☐ Investments without increase in capacity:

Max. aid rate (less-favoured areas) ....

Max. aid rate (other areas):..

If aid rates exceed 75% for less-favoured areas and 60% for other areas, please note that the measure would not be in line with point 4.1.1.2, third paragraph, of the Agricultural Guidelines.

☐ Investments with increase in capacity:

Max. aid rate (contemporary materials)/ ....

Max. aid rate (extra costs of traditional materials) ....

If the aid rate exceeds normal investment aid rates (40% or 50% for less-favoured areas) for the use of contemporary materials, please note that the measure would not be in line with the ceilings set out in point 4.1.1.2, fourth paragraph, of the Agricultural Guidelines.

8   Relocation of farm buildings in the public interest

8.1   Does the need to relocate the building(s) result from an expropriation which, in accordance with national legislation, gives right to compensation?

☐   yes   ☐   no

8.2   Does relocation simply consist of the dismantling, removal and re-erection of existing facilities?

☐   yes   ☐   no

8.2.1 If yes, what is the intensity of the aid? (max. 100%)

....

8.3   Does relocation result in the farmer benefiting from more modern facilities?

☐   yes   ☐   no

8.3.1 If yes, what is the farmer's own contribution? (please specify)

☐ In less favoured areas (min. 50%) ....
☐ In other areas (min 60%)..
☐ Young farmers in less-favoured areas (min 45%) ....
☐ Young farmers in other areas (min 55%) ....

If the farmer's own contribution is lower than the thresholds above, please note that this provision would not be in line with point 4.1.2.3, fourth paragraph, of the Agricultural Guidelines.

8.4   Does relocation result in an increase of production capacity?

8.4.1 If yes, what is the farmer's own contribution? (please specify)

☐ In less favoured areas (min. 50%) ....
☐ In other areas (min 60%) ....
☐ Young farmers in less-favoured areas (min 45%) ....
☐ Young farmers in other areas (min 55%) ....

If the farmer's own contribution is lower than the thresholds above, please note that the measure would not comply with point 4.1.2.3, fifth paragraph, of the Agricultural Guidelines.

1487

9   **Investments relating to the protection and improvement of the environment, the improvement of hygiene conditions and the welfare of animals**

9.1 Does the investment result in extra costs relating to the protection and improvement of the environment, the improvement of hygiene conditions of livestock enterprises or the welfare of farm animals?

☐   yes   ☐   no

9.2 Does the investment go beyond the minimum Community requirements in force?

☐   yes   ☐   no

If yes, specify which requirements are exceeded:

....

If no, please note that point 4.1.2.4, second paragraph of the Agricultural Guidelines lays down that the higher aid intensities may only be granted for investments which go beyond the minimum Community requirements in force.

9.3 Is the investment made to comply with newly introduced minimum standards, subject to the conditions laid down in Article 1(2) of the Implementing Regulation (EC) N° 445/2002?

☐   yes   ☐   no

9.4 Does the investment result in an increase in production capacity?

☐   yes   ☐   no

If yes, please note that point 4.1.2.4 of the Agricultural Guidelines lays down that the higher aid intensities may not be granted in the case of investments which result in an increase in production capacity.

9.5 What is the maximum aid intensity? (please specify)

☐ For investments in less-favoured areas (max. 75%)

....

☐ For investments in other areas (max. 60%)

....

If the maximum aid rate exceeds the thresholds above, please note that the measure would not be in line with point 4.1.2.4 of the Agricultural Guidelines.

9.6 Is the increase strictly confined to the extra eligible costs necessary to meet the objective referred to?

☐   yes   ☐   no

If no, please note that, under point 4.1.2.4 of the Agricultural Guidelines, the higher aid intensity may be granted exclusively in respect of the extra costs necessary to meet the objective.

10   **Aids for investments to promote the diversification of farm activities**

10.1 Does the aid concern the diversification of farm activities

☐ into activities not connected to the production, processing and marketing of Annex I products (ex: rural tourism)?

In this case, note that the specific state aid rules for Annex I products are not applicable. Please refer to the relevant section of the general notification form.

☐ into activities connected to the production, processing and marketing of Annex I products (e.g., the construction of a point of sale for own farm products)?

10.2 Does the aid concern on-farm processing and marketing activities?

☐ yes   ☐ no

If no, please complete (and enclose) a copy of Part III.12.a.ii of this notification form (Aid for investments in processing and marketing activities).

10.3 If the aid concerns on-farm processing and/or marketing activities, do total eligible expenses exceed the limit for total investment eligible for support set by the Member State in accordance with Article 7 of the Rural Development Regulation?

☐ yes   ☐ no

If no, please note that the measure will be assessed as aid for investment in agricultural holdings. You should complete and enclose a copy of Part III.12.a.i of this notification form.

If yes, please note that the measure will be assessed as aid for investment in processing and marketing of agricultural products. You should complete and enclose a copy of Part III.12.a.ii of this notification form.

PART III.12A.II. SUPPLEMENTARY INFORMATION SHEET FOR AID FOR INVESTMENTS IN CONNECTION WITH THE PROCESSING AND MARKETING OF AGRICULTURAL PRODUCTS

This notification form applies to aid investments in the processing and marketing of agricultural products, as dealt with in points 4.2 and 4.3 of the Agricultural Guidelines.

This form must also be used by Member States for the notification of an aid for individual investments with eligible expenses in excess of EUR 12,5 million, or where the actual amount of aid exceeds EUR 6 million (Article 1§3 of Regulation (EC) N° 1/2004).

1   **Scope of the aid**
1.1 Is the aid for investments in connection with the processing and marketing of agricultural products granted within the framework of a regional aid scheme?

☐ yes   ☐ no

If yes, note that the assessment of such aid is to be carried out on the basis of the Guidelines on National Regional aid (OJEU C74 of 10 March 1998, p. 06). Please refer to the relevant part of the general notification form.

1.2 Does the aid concern investments to promote the diversification of farm activities?

☐ yes   ☐ no

2   **Beneficiaries**
2.1 Who are the beneficiaries of the aid?
☐ agricultural undertakings;
☐ other (please specify)

....

....

3   Aid intensity

3.1   Please state the maximum rate of public support, expressed as a volume of eligible investment:

.... in Objective 1 regions (max. 50%);

.... in other regions (max. 40%).

If aid rates are higher than the above ceilings, please note that the measure would not be in line with point 4.2.3 of the Agricultural Guidelines.

4   Eligibility criteria

4.1   Does the aid provide that aid for investment may only be granted to:

—   enterprises the economic viability of which can be demonstrated by an assessment of its prospects?

      ☐   yes   ☐   no

—   undertakings complying with minimum Community standard regarding the environment, hygiene and animal welfare?

      ☐   yes   ☐   no

If you have answered no to any of the questions under point 4.1, please note that, under point 4.2.3 of the Agricultural Guidelines, all the above eligibility criteria must be met.

4.2   Is the aid intended to finance investments made in order to comply with newly introduced minimum standards regarding the environment, hygiene and animal welfare?

      ☐   yes   ☐   no

5   Eligible expenses

5.1   Do eligible expenses include?

☐   construction, acquisition or improvement of immovable property;

☐   new machinery and equipment, including computer software;

☐   general costs (such as architects, engineers and consultation fees, feasibility studies, the acquisition of patents and licences, up to 12% of eligible expenditure)

If eligible expenses include other items, please note that point 4.2.3 of the Agricultural Guidelines only allows investment aid to cover the eligible expenses listed above.

6   Market outlets

6.1   Has the existence of market outlets been assessed at the appropriate level, in terms of the products concerned, the types of investments and existing and expected capacities?

      ☐   yes   ☐   no

If no, please note that point 4.2.5 of the Agricultural Guidelines lays down that no aid may be granted unless sufficient evidence can be produced that normal market outlets for the products concerned can be found.

6.2   Does the aid concern a product subject to restrictions on production or limitations of Community support at the level of individual undertakings, with particular reference to the rules laid down in the common organisations of the market?

      ☐   yes   ☐   no

6.2.1 If yes, explain how these restrictions have been taken into account. ....

....

....

....

6.3   Does the aid concern:

6.3.1 The manufacture and marketing of products which imitate or substitute for milk and milk products?

☐   yes   ☐   no

If yes, please note that point 4.2.5 of the Agricultural Guidelines does not allow aid to be granted for such products.

6.3.2 The processing and marketing of products in the sugar sector?

☐   yes   ☐   no

If yes, please note that, as specified in footnote 18 to the Agricultural Guidelines, aids for investments in processing and marketing activities in the sugar sector are in general prohibited by the provision of the common organisation of the market.

7   Does the aid concern investments with eligible expenses in excess of €25 million or where the actual amount of aid will exceed €12 million?

☐   yes   ☐   no

If yes, please note that such aid must be specifically notified to the Commission in accordance with article 88(3) of the EC Treaty.

Part III.12.B. Supplementary Information Sheet on Agri-Environmental Aid

This form must be used for the notification of any State aid measure to support agricultural production methods designed to protect the environment and to maintain the countryside (agri-environment) covered by point 5 of the Community Guidelines on State aid in the agricultural sector.[65]

— Does the measure concern compensation to farmers who voluntarily give agri-environmental commitments (point 5.3 of the guidelines)?

☐   yes   ☐   no

If yes, please refer to SIS relating to 'aid for agri-environmental commitments'.

— Does the measure concern a support for farmers to compensate for costs incurred and income foregone resulting from restrictions on agricultural use in areas with environmental restrictions as a result of the implementation of compulsory limitations based on Community environmental protection rules (point 5.4 of the guidelines)?

☐   yes   ☐   no

If yes, please refer to Supplementary Information Sheet (SIS) relating to 'aid for farmers in areas subject to environmental restrictions under Community legislation'.

— Does the aid only concern environmental investments (point 5.2 of the guidelines)?

☐   yes   ☐   no

If yes, please refer to SIS relating to 'Investment aids in the agricultural sector'.

— Is the measure an operating aid that relieves firms, including agricultural producers, of costs resulting from the pollution or nuisance they cause (point 5.5 of the guidelines)?

☐   yes   ☐   no

---

[65] Community Guidelines on State aid in the agricultural sector, OJ C232, 12.8.2000, p 17.

If yes, please refer to SIS relating to 'operating aids'.

— Does the environmental aid pursue other objectives such as training and advisory services to help agricultural producers (point 5.6 of the guidelines)?

☐   yes   ☐   no

If yes, please refer to SIS relating to points *13 ands 14* of the guidelines.

— Others?

Please provide a complete description of the measure(s) ....

AID FOR AGRI-ENVIRONMENTAL COMMITMENTS
(POINT 5.3 OF THE GUIDELINES)

1   **Objective of the measure**

1.1   Which one of the following specific objectives does the support measure promotes?

     ☐   ways of using agricultural land which are compatible with the protection and improvement of the environment, the landscape and its features, natural resources, the soil and genetic diversity, reduce production costs;

     ☐   an environmentally-favourable extensification of farming and management of low-intensity pasture systems, improve and re-deploy production;

     ☐   the conservation of high nature-value farmed environments, which are under threat increase quality; the upkeep of the landscape and historical features on agricultural land;

     ☐   the use of environmental planning in farming practice

If the measure does not pursue any of the above objectives, please indicate which are the objectives aimed at in terms of environmental protection? (Please submit a detailed description)

....

1.1.1   If the measure in question has already been applied in the past, what have been the results in terms of environmental protection?

....

....

2   **Eligibility criteria**

2.1   Will the aid be exclusively granted to farmers who give agri-environmental commitments for at least five years?

☐   yes   ☐   no

2.2   Will a shorter or a longer period be necessary for all or particular types of commitments?

☐   yes   ☐   no

2.2.1   In the affirmative please provide the reasons justifying that period

....

....

2.3   Please confirm that no aid will be granted to compensate for agri-environmental commitments that do not involve more than the application of usual good farming practice

☐   yes   ☐   no

If no, please note that point 5.3 of the Agricultural Guidelines does not allow for aid for agri-environmental commitments that do not involve more than the application of usual good farming practice

2.3.1 Please describe what are the relevant(s) usual good farming practice(s) and explain how the agri-environmental commitments involve more than their application.

....

....

3 **Aid amount**

3.1 Please specify what is the maximum amount of aid to be granted based on the area of the holding to which agri-environmental commitments apply:
- ☐ for specialised perennial crops ....(maximum payment of 900/ha)
- ☐ for annual crops ....(maximum payment of 600€/ha)
- ☐ for other land uses ....(maximum payment of 450 €/ha)?
- ☐ other? ....

3.1.1 If other, please justify its compatibility with the provisions of point 5.3.2 of the Guidelines and 24§2 of the Regulation EC N° 1257/1999[66]

3.2 Is the support measure granted annually? ☐ yes ☐ no

3.2.1 In the negative please provide the reasons justifying other period

....

....

3.3 Is the amount of annual support calculated on the basis of:
- — income foregone,
- — additional costs resulting from the commitment given, and
- — the need to provide an incentive of a maximum of 20% of the income foregone and eventually
- — the cost of any non-remunerative capital works necessary for the fulfilment of the commitments?

3.3.1 Explain the calculation method used in fixing the amount of support

3.4 Is the reference level for calculating income foregone and additional cost resulting from the commitments given, the usual good farming practice?

☐ yes ☐ no

3.4.1 If no, please explain the reference level taken into consideration

3.5 Payments are they made per unit of production?

☐ yes ☐ no

---

[66] Council Reg (EC) 1257/1999 on support for rural development from the European Agricultural Guidance and Guarantee Fund (EAGGf) and amending and repealing certain Regulations (OJ L160, 26.6.1999, p 80).

3.5.1 If yes please explain the reasons justifying that method and the initiatives undertaken to assure that the maximum amounts per year eligible for Community support as set out in the Annex to Regulation (EC) N°1257/1999 are complied with.

....
....

AID FOR FARMERS IN AREAS SUBJECT TO ENVIRONMENTAL RESTRICTIONS UNDER COMMUNITY LEGISLATION (POINT 5.4 OF THE GUIDELINES)

1   **Objective of the measure**

1.1 Is the measure aimed to compensate farmers for costs incurred and income foregone resulting from restrictions on agricultural use in areas with environmental restrictions as a result of the implementation of limitations based on Community environmental protection rules?

☐   yes   ☐   no

If no, please note that point 5.4 of the Agricultural Guidelines does not allow for aid to compensate for other costs that those resulting from compulsory restrictions based on Community environmental rules.

2   **Eligibility criteria**

2.1 Are costs incurred and income foregone resulting from restrictions on agricultural use in areas with environmental restrictions imposed to farmers as a result of the implementation of limitations based on Community environmental protection rules?

☐   yes   ☐   no

2.1.1 If yes please provide all the details concerning the relevant Community environmental protections rules

....

2.1.2 If no, please note that point 5.4 of the Agricultural Guidelines does not allow for aid to compensate for other costs that those resulting from compulsory restrictions based on Community environmental rules.

2.2 Are the planned compensation payments necessary to solve the specific problems arising from those rules?

☐   yes   ☐   no

2.2.1 If yes please explain why this measure is necessary

....

2.2.2 If no, please note that according to point 5.4.1 only payments that are necessary to solve the specific problems arising from those rules can be authorised.

2.3 Does the support be granted only for obligations going beyond good farming practice?

☐   yes   ☐   no

2.3.1 If no, please justify its compatibility with the provisions of point 5.4 of the guidelines

....

2.4   Is the aid granted aid in breach of the polluter pays principle?

☐   yes   ☐   no

2.4.1 If yes, please provide all the elements justifying that the aid can be justified and that it is temporary and degressive

....

....

....

3   **Aid amount**

3.1   Please specify what is the maximum amount of aid to be granted based on the area of the holding to which the restrictions apply:

☐   .... to a maximum payment of 200 EUR/ha?

☐   .... other amount?

3.1.1 If other amount, please justify its compatibility with the provisions of point 5.4.1 of the Guidelines and 16 of the Regulation EC N° 1257/1999.[67]

3.2   Please explain the measures taken to assure that payments are fixed at a level which avoids overcompensation

....

3.3   Does the compensation payment apply in less favoured areas?

☐   yes   ☐   no

3.3.1 If yes, does the total surface of these areas, combined with other areas which may be assimilated to less favoured areas by virtue of Article 20 of the Regulation (EC) N° 1257/1999, exceed 10% of the surface area of the Member State?

☐   yes   ☐   no

3.3.1.1 If yes, please justify its compatibility with the provisions of point 5.4.1 of the guidelines

....

OPERATING AID (POINT 5.5 OF THE GUIDELINES)

1   **Objective of the measure**

1.1   Which are the objectives aimed at in terms of environmental protection,

☐   to offset the costs of new mandatory national environmental requirements which go beyond existing Community rules?

☐   to offset the additional costs arising from the use of environmentally friendly inputs in comparison with conventional production processes (such as aids for the development of biofuels)?

☐   to offset a loss of international competitiveness?

☐   other? Please specify ....

---

[67] Council Reg (EC) 1257/1999 on support for rural development from the European Agricultural Guidance and Guarantee Fund (EAGGf) (OJ L214, 13.8.1999, p 31

2   **Aid to offset cost of new mandatory national environmental requirements**

2.1   Will aid be granted for reaching national environmental requirements that go beyond existing Community rules?

                        ☐   yes   ☐   no

2.1.1   In the affirmative, please describe which are the Community standards in question and how the national standards go beyond them?

....

2.1.2   In the negative, please note that according to point 5.5.2 of the guidelines no aid can be granted.

2.2   Is the aid necessary to offset a loss of competitiveness at the international level?
        Please explain why/how this measure is necessary to that aim ....

2.3   Is the aid granted for no more than 5 years and digressive?
                        ☐   yes   ☐   no

2.3.1   If yes, please describe the modalities of the payment of the aid

....

....

2.3.2   If no, please justify its compatibility with the provisions of point 5.5.2 of the guidelines

....

....

2.4   What is the maximum amount of aid planned for the measure?

....

2.5   Which guarantees are foreseen in order to assure that the initial amount of aid will not exceed the amount necessary to compensate the producer for the additional cost of compliance with the relevant national provisions in comparison with the cost of compliance with the relevant Community provisions? Please specify)

....

....

3   **Aid to offset the additional costs from the use of environmentally friendly inputs**

3.1   Please describe and provide all the elements justifying that the aid is necessary to offset the additional costs arising from the use of environmentally friendly inputs in comparison with conventional production processes.

....

....

....

3.2   To what extend the use of the new input is more environmentally friendly in comparison with the conventional production processes? Please justify

....

....
....

3.3   Will the amount of the aid be limited to neutralizing the effects of the additional costs?

3.3.1 Please explain how this limitation of the amount of the aid can be verified and is assured
....
....

3.4   Does the project provides the guaranty that the amount of the aid is going to be submitted
       to a periodic review of at least every five years, to take account of changes in the relative
       costs of the different inputs and the commercial benefits which may result from the use of
       more environmentally friendly inputs?

....

            ☐   yes   ☐   no

3.4.1 If yes, please describe how this guaranty should apply in practice.
....
....

3.4.2 If no, please justify the absence of guaranty and its compatibility with the provisions of
       point 5.5.3 of the guidelines
....
....

PART III.12.C. SUPPLEMENTARY INFORMATION SHEET ON AID TO COMPENSATE FOR HANDICAPS IN THE LESS-FAVOURED AREAS

This form must be used for the notification of aid aiming to compensate for natural handicaps in less-favoured areas, which is dealt with in point 6 of the Agricultural Guidelines.

1   Is the aid measure combined with support under the Rural Development Regulation?

            ☐   yes   ☐   no

2   Can you confirm that the total support granted to the farmer will not exceed the amounts
       determined in accordance with Article 15 of the Regulation?

            ☐   yes   ☐   no

(Specify the amount)..

If no, please note that, according to point 6.2 of the Agricultural Guidelines, the maximum
aid that can be granted in the form of compensatory allowance cannot exceed the above
amount.

3   Does the measure provide that the following eligibility criteria must be fulfilled?

       ☐ Farmers are required to farm a minimum area of land (please specify the minimum area)

       ....

       ☐ Farmers must undertake to pursue their farming activity in a less-favoured area for at
         least five years from the first payment of a compensatory allowance;

☐ Farmers must apply usual good farming practices compatible with the need to safeguard the environment and maintain the countryside, in particular by sustainable farming.

☐ yes ☐ no

4 Does the measure provide that, where residues of substances prohibited under Directive 96/22/EC or residues of substances authorized under that Directive but used illegally, are detected pursuant to the relevant provisions of Council Directive 96/23/EC in an animal belonging to the bovine herd of a producer, or where an unauthorized substance or product, or a substance or product authorized under Directive 96/22/EC but held illegally is found on the producer's holding in any form, the producer shall be excluded from receiving compensatory allowances for the calendar year of that discovery?

☐ yes ☐ no

5 Does the measure provide that, in the event of a repeated infringement, the length of the exclusion period may, depending on the seriousness of the offence, be extended to 5 years from the year in which the repeated infringement was discovered?

☐ yes ☐ no

6 Does the measure provide that, in the event of obstruction on the part of the owner or holder of the animals when inspections are being carried out and the necessary samples are being taken in application of national residue-monitoring plans, or when the investigations and checks provided for under Directive 96/23/EC are being carried out, the penalties provided for under question 4 shall apply?

☐ yes ☐ no

PART III.12.D. SUPPLEMENTARY INFORMATION SHEET ON AID FOR THE SETTING UP OF YOUNG FARMERS

This notification form applies to aid granted for the setting up of young farmers, as dealt with in point 7 of the Agricultural Guidelines.

1 **Eligibility criteria**

Please note that state aid for the setting up of young farmers may only be granted if it fulfils the same conditions set out in the Rural Development Regulation for co-financed aid, and in particular the eligibility criteria of Article 8 thereof.

1.1 Are the following conditions fulfilled?

— the farmer is under 40 years of age;
— the farmer possesses adequate occupational skill and competence;
— the farmer is setting up on an agricultural holding for the first time;
— the farmer's holding is demonstrably viable;
— the farmer's holding complies with minimum standard regarding the environment, hygiene and animal welfare.

☐ yes ☐ no

If you answered no to any of these questions, please note that the measure would not be in line with the requirements of Article 8 of the Rural Development Regulation and could not be authorized under the Guidelines.

1.2 Does the measure provide that the above eligibility requirements must be met at the time the individual decision to grant support is taken?

☐ yes ☐ no

1.3 Does the measure provide for a period not exceeding three years after starting up in order to meet the requirements relating to occupational skills and competence, economic viability and minimum standards regarding the environment, hygiene and animal welfare?

☐ yes ☐ no

1.4 Does the measure provide that the farmer must be established as head of the holding?

☐ yes ☐ no

1.4.1 If not, what conditions apply to the situation where a young farmer is not established as sole head of the holding? (please describe)

....
....

Please note that, according to article 8 of the Rural Development Regulation, these conditions must be equivalent to those required for a young farmer setting up as sole head of a holding.

2 Maximum allowable aid

2.1 Is the aid combined with support granted under the Rural Development Regulation?

☐ yes ☐ no

2.2 Does the setting up aid comprise?

☐ a single premium? (max. 25.000 EUR)

.... (please specify the amount)

and/or

☐ an interest subsidy on loans taken on with a view to covering the costs arising from setting up? (max. capitalised value of 25.000 EUR)

If yes, please describe the conditions of the loan—interest rate, duration, period of grace, etc.).

....
....

2.3 Can you confirm that the combined total of support granted under the Rural Development Regulation and support granted in the form of State aids will not exceed the amounts laid down for either form of aid (25.000 EUR for single premium; 25.000 EUR for subsidized loan)?

☐ yes ☐ no

2.4 Is it envisaged to grant additional State aid exceeding these limits?

☐ yes ☐ no

2.4.1 If yes, what is the amount of additional State aid envisaged? (max. 25.000 EUR)

....

2.4.2 Please provide evidence that the additional State aid is justified by the very high costs of setting up in the region concerned.

....

....

PART III.12.E. SUPPLEMENTARY INFORMATION SHEET FOR AID TO ON AID FOR EARLY RETIREMENT OR FOR THE CESSATION OF FARMING ACTIVITIES

This form must be used for the notification of any State aid schemes which are designed to encourage older farmers to take early retirement as described by point 8 of the Community Guidelines on State aid in the agricultural sector[68] *and articles 10–12 of Council Regulation (EC) No 1257/1999.*[69]

1   **Objective of the measure**

1.1   Which of the following specific objectives does the support measure pursue:

☐ to provide an income for elderly farmers who decide to stop farming?

☐ to encourage the replacement of such elderly farmers by farmers able to improve, where necessary, the economic viability of the remaining agricultural holdings?

☐ to reassign agricultural land to non-agricultural uses where it cannot be farmed under satisfactory conditions of economic viability?

Please note that according to point 8 of the guidelines and 10 of Regulation (EC) N° 1257/1999, no aid for early retirement can be authorized if the planned measure does not contribute to those objectives.

1.2   Does the early retirement support include measures to provide an income for farm workers?

☐   yes   ☐   no

If yes, please describe ....

2   **Eligibility criteria**

2.1   Will the aid be exclusively granted when the *transferor* of the farm,

— stops all commercial farming activity definitively; he may, however, continue non-commercial farming and retain the use of the buildings,

— is not less than 55 years old but not yet of normal retirement age at the time of transfer, and

— have practised farming for the 10 years preceding transfer?

☐   yes   ☐   no

If no please note that according to point 8 of the Guidelines combined with article 11 of Council Regulation N° 1257/1999, no aid can be authorised if the transferor do not fulfil all those conditions

2.2   Will the aid be exclusively granted when the *transferee* of the farm:

— succeed the transferor as the head of the agricultural holding or take over all or part of the land released. The economic viability of the transferee's holding must be improved within a period and in compliance with conditions to be defined in terms of, in

---

[68] Community Guidelines on State aid in the agricultural sector, J.O.N C 232 of 12.8.2000, p 17.
[69] Council Reg (EC) 1257/1999 on support for rural development from the European Agricultural Guidance and Guarantee Fund (EAGGf) and amending and repealing certain Regulations (OJ L160, 26.6.1999, p 80.

particular, the transferee's occupational skill and competence and the surface area and volume of work or income, according to the region and type of production,
— possess adequate occupational skill and competence, and
— undertake to practice farming on the agricultural holding for not less than
— five years?

☐   yes   ☐   no

If no, please note that according to point 8 of the Guidelines combined with article 11 of Council Regulation N° 1257/1999, no aid can be authorised if the transferor do not fulfil all those conditions.

2.3   When the aid planned for early retirement support include measures to provide an income for *farm workers*, please confirm that no aid will be granted if the worker does not fulfil all the following conditions:
— stop all farm work definitively,
— be not less than 55 years old but not yet of normal retirement age,
— have devoted at least half of his working time as a family helper or farm worker to farm work during the preceding five years,
— have worked on the transferor's agricultural holding for at least the equivalent of two years full-time during the four-year period preceding the early retirement of the transferor, and
— belong to a social security scheme.

☐   yes   ☐   no

Please note that according to point 8 of the Guidelines and article 11 of Council Regulation N° 1257/1999, no aid can be authorised to provide an income for farm workers if they do not fulfil all those conditions

2.4   Please described whether the transferee of the farm is in fact a 'non-farming transferee' in the sense of any other person or body who takes over released land to use it for non-agricultural purposes, such as forestry or the creation of ecological reserves, in a manner compatible with protection or improvement of the quality of the environment of the countryside.

....

2.5   Can it be assured that all the eligibility requirements imposed on the transferor of the farm, on the farming or not-farming transferee and when appropriate, on the farm worker, will be applied throughout the period during which the transferor receives the planned early retirement support?

☐   yes   ☐   no

If no, please note that point 8 of the Guidelines combined with point 11 of Council Regulation N° 1257/1999 does not allow for aid if all those requirements are not assured during that period.

3   **Aid amount**

3.1   Is the aid measure combined with support under the Rural Development Regulation?

☐   yes   ☐   no

3.1.1   If yes, please provide a brief description of the modalities and amount of such co-financed support

....

....

3.2   Please specify what is the maximum amount of aid to be granted per transferor:

☐ .... per transferor and year (maximum annual amount of 15.000 EUR/ transferor and maximum total amount of EUR 150.000 EUR/transferor)

If the maximum amounts are not respected please justify its compatibility with the provisions of point 8 of the Guidelines and 12 of the Regulation EC N° 1257/1999.

3.3   Please specify what is the maximum amount of aid to be granted per worker:

☐ .... per worker and year (maximum annual amount of 3500 EUR/worker and maximum total amount of EUR 35.000 EUR/worker)

If the maximum amounts are not respected please justify its compatibility with the provisions of point 8 of the Guidelines and 12 of the Regulation EC N° 1257/199.

3.4   Does the transferor receive a normal retirement pension paid by the Member State?

☐   yes   ☐   no

3.4.1 If yes, is the planned early retirement support granted as a supplement taking into account the amount of the national retirement pension?

☐   yes   ☐   no

If no, please note that point 8 of the Guidelines combined with point 12 of Council Regulation N° 1257/1999 requires that the amount paid as a normal retirement pension is taken into account in the calculation of the maximum amounts to be granted under the early retirement schemes.

4   Duration

4.1   Can it be assured that duration of planned early retirement support shall not exceed a total period of 15 years for the transferor and 10 years for the farm worker and that, at the same time, it shall not go beyond the 75th birthday of a transferor and not go beyond the normal retirement age of a worker?

☐   yes   ☐   no

If no, please note that point 8 of the Guidelines combined with point 12 of Council Regulation N° 1257/1999 does not allow for aid if all those requirements are not assured in the planned scheme.

PART III.12.F. SUPPLEMENTARY INFORMATION SHEET FOR AID TO ON AID SCHEMES FOR CLOSING PRODUCTION, PROCESSING AND MARKETING CAPACITY

This form must be used for the notification of any State aid schemes designed to promote the abandonment of capacity as described by point 9 of the Community Guidelines on State aid in the agricultural sector.[70]

1   Requirements

1.3   Does the planned scheme provides that,

— the aid must be in the general interest of the sector concerned
— there must be a counterpart on the part of the beneficiary

---

[70] Community Guidelines on State aid in the agricultural sector, OJ C232 of 12.08.2000, p 17.

— the possibility of the aid being for rescue and restructuring must be excluded and that
— there must be no over-compensation of loss of capital value and of future income?

☐   yes   ☐   no

If no, please note that according to point 9 of the Guidelines no aid can be granted if those conditions are not fulfilled.

'THE AID MUST BE IN THE GENERAL INTEREST OF
THE SECTOR CONCERNED'

1.2   What is the sector or sectors covered by the scheme?

....

....

1.3   Are those sectors subject to production limits or quota?

☐   yes   ☐   no

If yes, please describe ....

....

1.4   Can that sector(s) be considered to be in excess of capacity either at regional or national level?

☐   yes   ☐   no

1.4.1   If yes:

1.4.1.1   Is the planned aid scheme coherent with any Community arrangements to reduce production capacity?

☐   yes   ☐   no

Please describe this arrangements and the measures taken to assure the coherence

....

1.4.1.2   Is the planned aid scheme part of a programme for the restructuring of the sector which has defined objectives and a specific timetable?

☐   yes   ☐   no

If yes, please describe the programme ....

1.4.1.3   What is the duration of the planned aid scheme?...
Please note that according to point 9.2 of the guidelines the Commission can only authorize this type of aid when they provide for a limited duration.

1.4.2   If no, is the capacity being closed for sanitary or environmental reasons?

☐   yes   ☐   no

If yes, please describe ....

1.5   Can it be assured that no aid may be paid which would interfere with the mechanisms of the common organisations of the market (OCM) concerned?

☐   yes   ☐   no

If no, please note that according to point 9.3 of the any aid interfering with the mechanisms of the OCM concerned can be authorized.

1503

1.6 Is the aid scheme accessible to all economic operators in the sector concerned on the same conditions?

☐ yes ☐ no

If no, please note that according to point 9.6 of the Guidelines, to be authorised by the Commission the aid scheme must assure the respect of this condition.

'There must be a Counterpart on the Part of the Beneficiary'

1.7 What is the nature of the counterpart required to be beneficiary by the planned scheme?

....

....

....

1.8 Does it consist of a definitive and irrevocable decision to scrap or irrevocably close the production capacity concerned?

☐ yes ☐ no

1.8.1 If yes,

— can it be proved that this commitments are legally binding for the beneficiary?

☐ yes ☐ no

Please justify ....

— can it be assured that these commitments must also bind any future purchaser of the facility concerned?

☐ yes ☐ no

Please justify ....

1.8.2 If no, please describe the nature of the counterpart on the part of the beneficiary

....

Please note that according to point 9.4 of the guidelines where the production capacity has already closed definitively, or where such closure appears inevitable, there is *no* counterpart on the part of the beneficiary, and aid may not be paid.

'The Possibility of the Aid Being for Rescue and Restructuring must be Excluded'

1.9 Does the planned scheme provides that, when beneficiary of the aid is in financial difficulty, the aid will be assessed in accordance with the Community guidelines on rescue and restructuring of firms in difficulty?

☐ yes ☐ no

If no, please note that according to point 9.5 of the Guidelines, the Commission can not authorized an aid for the abandonment of capacity of a company in difficulties and that the aid must be evaluated under the rescue and/or restructuring aid.

'THERE MUST BE NO OVER-COMPENSATION OF LOSS OF CAPITAL VALUE AND OF FUTURE INCOME'

1.10 Please specify what is the maximum amount of aid, if any, to be granted per beneficiary?

....
....

1.11 Is the amount of aid calculated on the basis of the loss of value of the assets plus an incentive payment which may not exceed 20% of the value of the assets, and eventually, the obligatory social costs resulting from the implementation of the scheme?

☐   yes   ☐   no

If no, please note that according to point 9.6 of the Guidelines, the amount of aid should be strictly limited to compensation for those items.

1.12 Does the planned aid scheme provides that, where capacity is closed for other reasons than health or environmental, at least 50% of the costs of these aids should be met by a contribution from the sector, either through voluntary contributions or by means of compulsory levies?

☐   yes   ☐   no

If no, please note that according to point 9.7 of the Guidelines, the Commission cannot authorize the aid.

1.13 Does the planned scheme provide for the submission of an annual report on the implementation of the scheme?

☐   yes   ☐   no

PART III.12.G. SUPPLEMENTARY INFORMATION SHEET ON AID TO PRODUCER GROUPS

This form must be used for the notification of any State aid measures meant to provide aid to producers groups as described by point 10 of the Community Guidelines on State aid in the agricultural sector.[71]

1   Type of aid

1.1   Does the aid concern start-up aid to newly established producers groups?

☐   yes   ☐   no

1.2   Does the aid concern start-up aid to newly established producers associations (i.e. a producer association consists of recognised producer groups and pursues the same objectives on a larger scale)?

☐   yes   ☐   no

1.3   Does the aid cover costs linked to a new start-up of a producers group or association granted in the case of a significant extension of the activities, for example to cover new products or new sectors?

☐   yes   ☐   no

Please note that a significant extension of the activities of the group means a quantitative expansion of the activities of at least 30%.

---

[71] Community Guidelines on State aid in the agricultural sector, OJ C232 of 12.8.2000, p 17.

1.3.1 If the answer is yes, are the expenses eligible for the new aid limited to those arising from the additional tasks undertaken by the producer group or association?

☐ yes   ☐ no

If no, please note that, under point 10.6 of the agriculture Guidelines new start-up aid to producers group or associations can only be granted to cover the expenses arising from the additional tasks due to the extension, if all the other conditions set in section 10 of the agriculture Guidelines are respected.

1.4 Is aid granted to cover the start-up costs of associations of producers, which are responsible for the supervision of the use of denominations of origin or quality marks?

☐ yes   ☐ no

1.5 Is the aid granted to other producers groups or associations, which undertake tasks at the level of agricultural production, such as mutual support and farm relief and farm management services, in the members' holdings without being involved in the joint adaptation of supply to the market?

☐ yes   ☐ no

1.5.1 If the answer is yes, are the producers groups or associations performing activities related to the production, processing or marketing of annexe I products?

☐ yes   ☐ no

If not, please note that aid to these groups or associations is not covered by the agriculture Guidelines, please refer to the general notification form.

If yes, please refer to the relevant legal basis.

....

1.6 Is aid granted to producer groups or associations to cover expenses, which are not linked to setting-up costs, such as investments or promotion activities?

☐ yes   ☐ no

If yes, the aid will be assessed in accordance with the specific rules governing such aids. Please refer to the relevant sections of the notification form.

1.7. Is aid granted directly to producers to offset their contributions to the cost of running the groups during the first years following the formation of the group or association?

☐ yes   ☐ no

1.8 Doe producers groups or associations receive aid under a programme financed by the common market organisation in the sector concerned?

☐ yes   ☐ no

If yes, please specify what kind of aid is granted under the common organisation programme

....

....

2 **Beneficiary**

2.1 Is start-up aid granted to producer groups or producer associations which are entitled to assistance under the legislation of the Member State concerned?

☐   yes   ☐   no

If the answer is no, please refer to point 10.2 of the agriculture Guidelines.

2.2   Is the aid granted only if all the following rules are respected:

— The obligation on members to market production in accordance with the rules on supply and placing on the market, drawn up by the group (the rules may permit a proportion of the production to be marketed directly by the producer);

☐   yes   ☐   no

— the obligation for producers joining the group to remain members for at least three years and give at least 12 months notice of withdrawal;

☐   yes   ☐   no

— common rules on production, in particular relating to product quality, or use of organic practices, common rules for placing goods on the market and rules on product information, with particular regard to harvesting and availability;

☐   yes   ☐   no

If any of the answers to section 2.2 above is no, please refer to point 10.3 for the list of eligibility criteria for support to producers groups or associations.

2.3   Does the aid measure/scheme clearly exclude production organizations such as companies or co-operatives the objective of which is, the management of one or more agricultural holdings and which are therefore in effect single producers?

☐   yes   ☐   no

If no, please note that, according to point 10.3 of the agriculture guidelines, producers should remain responsible for managing their holdings.

2.4   Do the producer organizations respect competition rules?

☐   yes   ☐   no

2.5   Does the aid measure/scheme, clearly exclude any aid to producer groups or associations the objectives of which are incompatible with a Council Regulation setting up a common market organization?

☐   yes   ☐   no

If no, please note that, under point 3.2 of the agriculture guidelines, under no circumstances can the Commission approve an aid which is incompatible with the provisions governing a common organization of the market or which would interfere with the proper functioning of the common organisation

3   **Aid intensity and eligible costs**

3.1   Is the aid granted on a temporary and degressive basis to cover administrative start-up costs of the group or association?

☐   yes   ☐   no

3.2   Is the aid limited to 100% of costs incurred in the first year and is it then reduced by 20 percentage points for each year of operation so that in the fifth year the amount of aid is limited to 20% of actual costs in that year?

☐   yes   ☐   no

3.3 Does the aid measure/scheme clearly exclude that aid is paid in respect of costs incurred after the fifth year?

☐   yes   ☐   no

3.4 Does the aid measure/scheme clearly exclude that aid is paid following the seventh year after recognition of the producer organisation?

☐   yes   ☐   no

If the answer to any of the questions of point 3.3 and 3.4 above is no, unless aid is granted in case of a significant extension of the activities of the group or association (see point 1.3 above), please note that point 10.5 of the agriculture guidelines clearly exclude aid for costs incurred after the fifth year and aid paid after the seventh year after recognition of the producer organisation.

3.5 Do the eligible expenses, both in case of aid granted to producers groups or associations and in case of aid granted directly to producers, include only:

— the rental of suitable premises;
— the purchase of suitable premises (the eligible expenses are limited to rental costs at market rates);
— the acquisition of office equipment, including computer hardware and software, administrative staff costs, overheads and legal and administrative fees?

☐   yes   ☐   no

If the answer is no, please refer to the list of eligible expenses set in point 10.5 of the agriculture guidelines.

PART III.12.H. SUPPLEMENTARY INFORMATION SHEET ON AID TO COMPENSATE FOR DAMAGE TO AGRICULTURAL PRODUCTION OR THE MEANS OF AGRICULTURAL PRODUCTION

This form must be used by Member states for the notification of any State aid measures which are designed to compensate for damage to agricultural production as described by point 11 of the Community Guidelines on State aid in the agricultural sector.[72]

1 **Aid to make good the damage caused by natural disasters or exceptional occurrences (point 11.2 of the guidelines)**

1.1 Which disaster or exceptional occurrence caused the damage for which the compensation is foreseen?

....

....

....

1.2 What kind of physical damage was caused?

....

....

....

---

[72] Community Guidelines on State aid in the agricultural sector, OJ C232 of 12.8.2000, p 17.

1.3   What level of compensation is contemplated?

....

....

....

1.4   Is compensation planned for losses of income? If yes, what level of compensation is contemplated and how will income losses be calculated?

....

....

....

1.5   Is the compensation to be calculated for each individual recipient?

....

....

....

1.6   Are payments received under insurance policies to be deducted from the aid? How is it intended to check whether money has or has not been paid by insurance companies?

....

....

....

2   **Aid to compensate farmers[73] for losses caused by bad weather (point 11.3 of the guidelines)**

2.1   What weather event has justified the aid?

....

....

....

2.2   Weather data demonstrating the exceptional nature of the event:

....

....

....

2.3   What is the threshold of loss, in relation to gross production of the relevant crop[74] in a normal year, above which farmers will qualify for aid?

....

....

....

---

[73] In other words, farmers to the exclusion of processing and marketing undertakings.

[74] The reference to crops does not mean that livestock are excluded from aid. The principles set out in point 11.3 of the Guidelines will apply *mutatis mutandis* to aid intended to compensate for losses involving livestock due to adverse weather.

2.4 Give a figure for gross production per hectare in a normal year for each of the crops affected by the weather event. Describe the method by which this figure has been arrived at.[75]

....

....

....

2.5 In the case of damage to the means of production (e.g. destruction of trees), explain how the threshold of loss to qualify for the aid has been calculated.

....

....

....

2.5.1 If it appears, after several years, that the loss of the means of production referred to above does not reach the threshold to qualify for aid, will the amounts that may have been paid to farmers in advance be recovered? Explain what system of checks and what recovery mechanism will be set up.

....

....

....

2.6 Is the amount of aid calculated as follows: (mean level of production in a given normal period x average price for the same period)—(actual production during the year of the event x average price for that year)?

....

....

....

2.7 Are losses calculated for each individual holding or for a whole area? In the latter case, show that the averages used is representative and not likely to lead to considerable over-compensation for some beneficiaries.

....

....

....

2.8 Will any sums received from insurance be deducted from the aid, as well as any amount received as direct aid?

....

....

....

2.9 Will the normal costs no longer faced by the farmer (e.g. because there was no actual harvest) be taken into account in calculating the aid?

---

[75] The gross production of a normal year is to be calculated by reference to average gross production in the three previous years, excluding years in which compensation was paid as a result of adverse weather. Other methods of calculating normal production (including regional reference figures) may however be accepted, provided that they are representative and not based on abnormally high production figures.

....

....

....

2.10   If such normal costs go up because of the effects of the weather event, is it intended to grant additional aid to cover the extra costs? If yes, what percentage of the extra costs will the aid cover?

....

....

2.11   Will aid be paid to compensate for damage caused by the weather event to buildings and equipment? If yes, what percentage of the damage will it cover?

....

....

2.12   Will aid be paid directly to farmers or will it be paid in some circumstances to the producer organizations to which those farmers belong? In the latter case, what mechanisms will be used to check that the amount of aid collected by a farmer will not be more than the losses suffered?

....

....

....

3   **Aid for combating animal and plant diseases (point 11.4 of the guidelines)**

3.1   What disease is involved?

....

....

....

If the disease has been caused by adverse weather

3.2   Please answer the questions in point 2 above, providing any relevant information for making the cause-and-effect link between the weather even and the disease.

....

....

....

If the disease has not been caused by adverse weather

3.3   Show that there are Community-level or national legislative, regulatory or administrative provisions empowering the authorities to act against the disease, either by adopting measures to eradicate it (in particular mandatory measures giving entitlement to financial compensation) or by establishing an early-warning system combined, where necessary, with aid to encourage private individuals to participate in prevention schemes on a voluntary basis.

1511

....

....

....

3.4 Tick the applicable purpose of the aid scheme:

prevention, involving screening and/or laboratory tests, destruction of the disease vectors, vaccination of livestock/treatment of crops, and slaughtering of livestock or destruction of crops on a preventive basis.

compensation, because the infected animals have to be slaughtered or the crops destroyed by order of, or on the recommendation of, the public authorities or because animals die as a result of vaccination or any other measure recommended or ordered by the competent authorities.

combined prevention and compensation, because a programme to deal with losses resulting from the disease is subject to the condition that the beneficiaries must make a commitment to take subsequent appropriate preventive measures as ordered by the official authorities.

3.5 Show that the aid intended for controlling the disease is compatible with the specific aims and provisions of the European Union's veterinary or plant health legislation.

....

....

....

3.6 Give a detailed description of the proposed control measures.

....

....

....

3.7 What costs or losses and what percentage of these costs or losses will the aid cover?

....

....

....

3.8 Is aid proposed to compensate for losses of income caused by the difficulties involved in rebuilding herds or replanting crops, or by any period of quarantine or waiting period ordered or recommended by the competent authorities to allow eradication of the disease before herd rebuilding or crop replanting? If yes, detail all the factors making it possible to ascertain the absence of a risk of over-compensating for the income losses.

....

....

....

3.9 Has Community aid been envisaged for the same purpose? If yes, indicate the date and references of the Commission decision approving it.

....

....

....

4   **Aid towards the payment of insurance premiums (point 11.5 of the guidelines)**

4.1   Does the proposed aid involve partial financing of premiums under an insurance policy which provides for compensating:

only for losses ascribable to natural disasters and exceptional occurrences within the meaning of point 11.2 of the Guidelines or to weather events comparable to natural disasters within the meaning of point 11.3 of the Guidelines

both for the losses referred to above *and* for other losses resulting from adverse weather?

4.2   What is the level of aid proposed (please note that, in the first case in point 4.1 above, the permitted maximum aid rate is 80%, and in the second case 50%)?

....

....

....

4.3   Does the aid cover a re-insurance programme? If yes, provide all necessary information to enable the Commission to check the levels of different components of the aid and the compatibility of the proposed aid with the common market.

....

....

....

4.4   Is the possibility of covering the risk linked to only one insurance company or to a group of companies?

....

....

....

4.5   Is the aid conditional on the insurance contract being concluded with a company established in the Member State concerned (if yes, please note that under point 11.5.3 of the Guidelines the Commission cannot authorize aid towards insurance premiums which constitute an obstacle to the operation of the internal market in insurance services)?

....

....

....

PART III.12.1 SUPPLEMENTARY INFORMATION SHEET ON
AID FOR LAND REPARCELLING

This form must be used for the notification of any State aid schemes designed to cover the legal and administrative costs, including survey costs, of reparcelling as described by point 12 of the Community Guidelines on State aid in the agricultural sector.[76]

1   Is the aid measure part of a general programme of land reparcelling operations undertaken in accordance with the procedures laid down by the legislation of the concerned Member State?

            ☐   yes   ☐   no

---

[76] Community Guidelines on State aid in the agricultural sector, OJ C232 of 12.8.2000, p 17.

2   Do the eligible expenses include

☐ the legal and administrative costs, including survey costs, of reparcelling?

☐ investments including aids for land purchase?

If eligible expenses cover other items, please note that point 12 of the Guidelines only allows aid for the listed eligible expenses.

3   Please specify the maximum rate of public support expressed as a volume of eligible expenses:

.... for legal and administative costs of reparcelling, including survey costs; (max of 100%)

.... for investments including aids for land purchase (max 40% or 50% in less-favoured areas + 5% for young farmers—idem point 4.1 of guidelines)?

4   What are the measures taken to avoid overcompensation and to verify that the above mentioned aid intensities are respected?

....

PART III.12.J SUPPLEMENTARY INFORMATION SHEET ON AID FOR THE PRODUCTION AND MARKETING OF QUALITY AGRICULTURAL PRODUCTS

This form must be used for the notification of any State aid measures which are designed to encourage the production and marketing of quality agricultural products as described by point 13 of the Community Guidelines on State aid in the agricultural sector.[77]

1   **Type of products**

1.1   Does the aid only refer to quality products?

☐   yes   ☐   no

If yes, please specify what are the quality elements for the products concerned, for example, products which are of clearly higher quality, with respect to at least one criterion, than required by compulsory standards (this clearly higher quality may relate to the product or to the production process, and must be verified by independent, external control) or which meet the quality standards set out in Community legislation for specific quality products,

....

If the aid does not concern quality products please note that, under section 13 of the Agricultural Guidelines, aid is limited to quality agricultural products.

2   **Type of aids**

2.1   Which of the following types of aid can be financed by the aid scheme/individual measure?

☐ market research activities, product conception and design;

☐ aids granted for the preparation of applications for recognition of denominations of origin or certificates of specific character in accordance with the relevant Community regulations:

☐ consultancy and similar support for the introduction of quality assurance schemes such as the ISO 9000 or 14000 series, systems based on hazard analysis and critical control points (HACCP) or environmental audit systems;

☐ the costs of training personnel to apply quality assurance and HACCP-type systems;

---

[77] Community Guidelines on State aid in the agricultural sector, OJ C232 of 12.8.2000, p 17.

☐ the cost of the charges levied by recognised certifying bodies for the initial certification of quality assurance and similar systems;

☐ aid toward the costs of non—routine in-process quality controls and non-routine product controls undertaken by third bodies;

☐ aid to cover the cost of control measures undertaken to ensure the authenticity of denominations of origin, or certificates of specific character in the framework of Council Regulations (EEC) Nos 2081/92 and 2082/92;

☐ aid to cover the cost of controls carried out by other bodies responsible for supervising the use of quality marks and labels under recognised quality assurance schemes;

☐ aid to cover the cost of controls of organic production methods conducted within the framework of Council Regulation (EEC) No 2092/91.

2.2 Does the aid measure include investments, which are necessary to upgrade production facilities?

        ☐   yes   ☐   no

If yes, please refer to point 4.1 and /or point 4.2 of the Agricultural Guidelines.

2.3 Does Community legislation provide that the cost of control is to be met by producers?

        ☐   yes   ☐   no

If yes, is the aid to be paid as part of a system financed by parafiscal taxes?

        ☐   yes   ☐   no

If no, please refer to point 13.4 of the Agriculture Guidelines.

2.4 Are the controls undertaken by or on behalf of third parties, such as:

☐ the competent regulatory authorities or bodies acting on their behalf;

☐ independent organisms responsible for the control and supervision of the use of denominations of origin, organic labels, or quality labels;

☐ others (please specify, indicating how the independence of the control body is assured)

....

....

3   Beneficiaries

3.1 Who are the beneficiaries of the aid?

☐ farmers

☐ producer groups

☐ other (please specify)

....

3.2 If farmers are not the direct beneficiaries of the aid:

3.2.1 Is the aid available to all the farmers eligible in the area concerned based on objectively defined conditions?

        ☐   yes   ☐   no

3.2.2 Does the aid measure exclude compulsory membership of the producers group/ organization or intermediate entity managing the aid in order to benefit from aid?

        ☐   yes   ☐   no

3.2.3   Is the contribution towards the administrative costs of the group or organization concerned limited to the costs of providing the service?

☐   yes   ☐   no

3.2.4   Can farmers freely choose the service provider?

☐   yes   ☐   no

3.2.4.1 If no, is the provider chosen and remunerated according to market principles, in a non-discriminatory way, using a degree of advertising sufficient to enable the services market to be opened up to competition and the impartiality of procurement rules to be reviewed?

☐   yes   ☐   no

If the answer to one or more of the questions of section 3.2 above is no, please note that the end beneficiary of the aid being the farmer, aid can only be granted through an intermediate body if free access to all eligible farmers and transparency in the selection procedure of the service provider are assured.

4   Aid intensity

4.1   Please state the maximum rate of public support of the following measures:

(a)   ....; market research activities, product conception and design (max 100%)

(b)   ....; aids granted for the preparation of applications for recognition of denominations of origin or certificates of specific character in accordance with the relevant Community regulations (max 100%);

(c)   ....; consultancy and similar support for the introduction of quality assurance schemes such as the ISO 9000 or 14000 series, systems based on hazard analysis and critical control points (HACCP) or environmental audit systems (max 100%);

(d)..................................; the costs of training personnel to apply quality assurance and HACCP-type systems (max 100%);

(e)   ....; the cost of the charges levied by recognised certifying bodies for the initial certification of quality assurance and similar systems (max 100%).

4.2   Is the total amount of aid which may be granted under points from a) to e) above in section 4.1:

— limited to 100 000 EUR per beneficiary over any three-year period?

☐   yes   ☐   no

— or is the aid limited to undertakings falling within the scope of the Commission definition of small and medium-sized enterprises, up to 50% of the eligible costs, whichever is greater?

☐   yes   ☐   no

If the answer to both questions is no, please refer to the maximum aid threshold provided for in section 13.2 of the Agriculture Guidelines.

4.3   Can the same beneficiary receive aid under different measures listed in point 4.1 a) to e)?

☐   yes   ☐   no

If yes, please indicate how the respect of the 100 000 EUR threshold per beneficiary over any three-year period will be guaranteed.

....

....

4.4   Is aid toward the costs of routine in-process quality controls and routine product controls undertaken by the manufacturer clearly excluded?

☐   yes   ☐   no

If no, please refer to point 13.3 of the Agriculture Guidelines.

4.5   Is aid to cover the cost of control measures undertaken to ensure the authenticity of denominations of origin, or certificates of specific character in the framework of Council Regulations (EEC) Nos 2081/92 and 2082/92 granted on temporary and degressive basis the cost of the controls during the first six years following the establishment of the control system?

☐   yes   ☐   no

4.6   Are aids to cover the cost of controls carried out by other bodies responsible for supervising the use of quality marks and labels under recognized quality assurance schemes reduced progressively, so that by the seventh year following its establishment, they are eliminated?

☐   yes   ☐   no

4.7   Is aid for controls of organic production methods, granted up to the rate of up to 100% of actual costs incurred, granted only for organic production methods conducted within the framework of Council Regulation (EEC) No 2092/91?

☐   yes   ☐   no

PART III.12.K. SUPPLEMENTARY INFORMATION SHEET ON AID FOR THE PROVISION OF TECHNICAL SUPPORT IN THE AGRICULTURE SECTOR

This form must be used for the notification of any State aid measure whose aim is the provision of technical support in the agricultural sector as described by point 14 of the Community Guidelines on State aid in the agricultural sector.[78]

1   **Type of aids**

1.1   Which of the following types of aid can be financed by the aid scheme/individual measure:

☐ education and training;
☐ the provision of farm management services and farm replacement services;
☐ consultant's fees;
☐ the organization of competitions, exhibitions and fairs, including support for the costs incurred by participating in such events;
☐ other activities for the dissemination of knowledge relating to new techniques, (please specify

....

....

2   **Eligible costs**

2.1   Concerning the training programmes, do the eligible costs include other costs than the actual cost of organising the training programme, travel and subsistence expenses and the cost of the provision of replacement services during the absence of the farmer or the farm worker?

---

[78] Community Guidelines on State aid in the agricultural sector, OJ C232 of 12.8.2000, p 17.

☐   yes   ☐   no

If yes, please refer to point 14.1 for the list of eligible expenses.

2.2   Do the activities related to the dissemination of knowledge only include reasonable small scale pilot projects or demonstration projects?

☐   yes   ☐   no

If no, please note that under point 14.1 only small scale pilot projects or demonstration projects can be financed.

2.3   Are the fees for consultancy services which constitute a continuous or periodic activity related to the enterprise's usual operating expenditure clearly excluded from the aid measure?

☐   yes   ☐   no

If no, please note that point 3.5 of the Agriculture Guidelines provide that, unless exceptions are expressly provided for in Community legislation or in the guidelines, unilateral State aid measures which are simply intended to improve the financial situation of producers, but which in no way contribute to the development of the sector, are considered to constitute operating aids which are incompatible with the common market

2.4   In the case of participation to fairs, do the eligible costs only include: participation fees, travel costs, costs of publications, the rent of exhibition premises?

☐   yes   ☐   no

If no, please list all the additional eligible costs, giving a thorough justification of such expenses.

....

....

3   **Beneficiaries**

3.1   Who are the beneficiaries of the aid?

☐ farmers
☐ producer groups
☐ other (please specify)

....

3.2   If farmers are not the direct beneficiaries of the aid:

3.2.1 Is the aid available to all the farmers eligible in the area concerned based on objectively defined conditions?

☐   yes   ☐   no

3.2.2 Does the aid measure exclude compulsory membership of the producer's group/ organization or intermediate entity managing the aid in order to benefit from aid?

☐   yes   ☐   no

3.2.3 Is the contribution towards the administrative costs of the group or organization concerned limited to the costs of providing the service?

☐ yes   ☐ no

3.2.4 Can farmers freely choose the service provider?

☐ yes   ☐ no

3.2.4.1 If no, is the provider chosen and remunerated according to market principles, in a non-discriminatory way, using a degree of advertising sufficient to enable the services market to be opened up to competition and the impartiality of procurement rules to be reviewed?

☐ yes   ☐ no

If the answer to one or more of the questions above is no, please note that the end beneficiary of the aid being the farmer, aid can only be granted through an intermediate body if free access to all eligible farmers and transparency in the selection procedure of the service provider are assured.

4 Aid intensity

4.1 Is the cumulative total amount of aid which may be granted under this section:

— limited to 100 000 EUR per beneficiary over any three-year period?

☐ yes   ☐ no

— or is the aid limited to undertakings falling within the scope of the Commission definition of small and medium-sized enterprises, up to 50% of the eligible costs, whichever is greater?

☐ yes   ☐ no

If the answer to both questions is no, please refer to the maximum aid threshold provided for in section 14.3 of the Agriculture Guidelines.

4.2 Can the same beneficiary receive aid under different measures of point 14 of the Agriculture Guidelines?

☐ yes   ☐ no

If yes, please indicate how the respect of the 100 000 EUR threshold per beneficiary over any three-year period will be guaranteed.

....

....

4.3 Is the aid threshold calculated at the level of the beneficiary, the beneficiary being the person receiving the services?

☐ yes   ☐ no

If no, please refer to point 14.3 of the Agriculture Guidelines.

PART III.12.L1 SUPPLEMENTARY INFORMATION SHEET ON AID FOR THE LIVESTOCK SECTOR

This form must be used for the notification of any State aid schemes which are designed to support the maintenance and improvement of the genetic quality of Community livestock as described by point 15 of the Community Guidelines on State aid in the agricultural sector[79] and articles 10–12 of Council Regulation (EC) No 1257/1999.[80]

Please note that according to point 15 of the guidelines, aid for the preservation of endangered species or breeds will be assessed in accordance with the provisions of Chapter VI of Title II of the Rural Development Regulation dealing with agri-environmental measures. Thus, for this measures please refer to SIS form on agri-environmental aids.

1 Eligible expenses

1.1 Which of the following eligible expenses does the support measure cover:

□ the administrative costs of the establishment and maintenance of herd books?

□ tests to determine the genetic quality or yield of livestock?

□ the eligible costs for investments in animal reproduction centres and for the introduction at farm level of innovatory animal breeding techniques or practices?

□ the cost of keeping individual male breeding animals of high genetic quality registered in herd books?

If the planned measure includes other eligible expenses, please note that point 15 of the Guidelines only allows for this aid to cover the eligible expenses listed above.

2 Aid amout

2.1 Please specify the maximum rate of public support expressed as a volume of eligible expenses:

— .... to cover the administrative costs of the establishment and maintenance of herd books (max of 100%)

— .... for costs of tests to determine the genetic quality or yield of livestock (max of 70%)

— .... to cover the costs for investments in animal reproduction centres and for the introduction at farm level of innovatory animal breeding techniques or practices (max of 40%)

— .... to cover the cost of keeping individual male breeding animals of high genetic quality registered in herd books (max of 30%)

2.2 What are the measures taken to avoid overcompensation and to verify that the above mentioned aid intensities are respected?

....

....

---

[79] Community Guidelines on State aid in the agricultural sector, OJ C232 of 12.8.2000, p 17.

[80] Council Reg (EC) N° 1257/1999 on support for rural development from the European Agricultural Guidance and Guarantee Fund (EAGGf) and amending and repealing certain Regulations (OJ L160, 26.6.1999, p 80.

PART III.12.M. SUPPLEMENTARY INFORMATION SHEET ON AID FOR THE OUTERMOST REGIONS AND THE AEGEAN ISLANDS

This form must be used by Member State to notify aids for the outermost regions and the Aegean islands, as dealt with in point 16 of the Agricultural Guidelines.

1   Does the proposed aid for the outermost regions and the Aegean Islands depart from the provisions set out in the Guidelines?

☐   yes   ☐   no

— if no, please complete the notification form relevant to the type of aid (investment aid, technical support, etc).
— If yes, please continue to complete this form.

2   Does the measure involve the granting of operating aid?

☐   yes   ☐   no

3   What are the structural handicaps that the operating aid is seeking to redress?

....
....
....

4   Which are the guarantees that the nature and the level of the aid are proportional to the handicaps it seeks to alleviate?

....
....
....

5   Is this aid intended to offset in part additional transport costs?

☐   yes   ☐   no

5.1   If yes, please provide proof of the existence of these additional costs and the method of calculation used to determine their amount:[81]

....
....

5.2   If yes, indicate what will be the maximum amount of aid (on the basis of an aid-per-kilometre ratio or on the basis of an aid-per-kilometre and aid-per-unit-weight ratio) and the percentage of the additional costs covered by the aid:

....
....

[81] The description should reflect how the authorities intend to ensure that the aid is given only in respect of the extra cost of transport of goods inside national borders, is calculated on the basis of the most economical form of transport and the shortest route between the place of production or processing and commercial outlets, and cannot be given towards the transport of the products of businesses without an alternative location.

6   Is the aid intended to offset the additional costs arising in the pursuit of economic activity
     from the factors identified in Article 299(2) of the EC Treaty (remoteness, insularity, small
     size, difficult topography and climate, economic dependence on a few products)?

☐   yes   ☐   no

Please determine the amount of the additional cost and the method of calculation:

....

....

....

....

How can the authorities establish the link between the additional costs and the factors
identified in Article 299 (2) of the EC Treaty?

....

....

PART III.12.N. SUPPLEMENTARY INFORMATION SHEET ON SUBSIDIZED SHORT-TERM LOANS IN AGRICULTURE (CREDITS DE GESTION)

*This form must be used for the notification of any State aid scheme concerning subsidized short-term
loans in agriculture as described in the Commission Communication on State aids: subsidized
short-term loans in agriculture (crédits de gestion).*[82]

1   Please indicate who are the beneficiaries of the aid (Point B and D of the Communication):

     (a) primary producers of agricultural products as defined in Annex I to the EC Treaty.
     (b) operators marketing exclusively agricultural products as defined in Annex I to the EC
         Treaty.
     (c) operators involved in processing exclusively agricultural products as defined in Annex I
         to the EC Treaty.

....

2   Please specify if the beneficiaries are individual operators, companies, cooperatives, produ-
     cers associations, other

....

3   With regard to each type of beneficiary indicated above at point 1 and 2, please specify, the
     reasons why the beneficiary of the aid is at a relative disadvantage to operators elsewhere in
     the economy both in terms of their need for, and ability to finance, short-term loans (point
     A of the Communication).

....

....

....

4   Will the subsidized loans be used to aid selectively specific sectors or operators in
     agriculture on grounds not solely related to the difficulties of financing short-term loans
     which are linked to reasons inherent in the nature of farming and related activities,

---

[82] OJ C44, 16.2.1996, p 2.

in particular seasonality of production and structure of farm businesses? (Points A and B of the Communication).

☐ yes   ☐ no

If your answer is yes, please specify ....

5   Please specify the administrative region where the aid measure will apply.

....

6   Will the aid be made available within the administrative region of the authority granting the aid to all operators in agriculture on a non-discriminatory basis irrespective of the agricultural activity (or activities) for which the operator needs short-term loans? (Point B of the Communication).

☐ yes   ☐ no

If your answer is no, please specify ....

7   If, within the administrative region of the authority granting the aid, you wish to exclude certain activities and/or certain operators from the aid measure, please demonstrate that all such instances of exclusion are justified on the grounds that the problems of obtaining short-term loans faced by those excluded are inherently less significant than in the rest of the agricultural economy. (Point B of the Communication).

....

....

....

8   Is the duration of the subsidized short-term loan maximum one year (Point D of the Communication)?

☐ yes   ☐ no

9   Do the competent authorities envisage to renew the one year subsidized short-term loan?

☐ yes   ☐ no

If your answer is yes, please indicate for how many years ....

10   Please indicate to which agriculture campaign(s) the aid measure is designed to apply.

....

11   Is the aid linked to particular marketing or production operations?

☐ yes   ☐ no

If your answer is yes, please specify ....

12   Is the aid limited to particular products?

☐ yes   ☐ no

If your answer is yes, please specify ....

13   Please demonstrate that the element of aid under this programme is limited to that which is strictly necessary to compensate for the disadvantages referred to in the Commission

Communication under point A. With regard to each type of beneficiary indicated above at point 1 and 2, please quantify the financing disadvantages indicated at the said point A, by using the method which you consider appropriate but always remaining within the limits of the gap between the interest rate paid by a typical agricultural operator and the interest rate paid in the rest of the economy of the Member State concerned for short-term loans of a similar amount per operator, not linked with investments (Point C of the Communication). Please indicate the qualification that you have reached and describe the methodology that you have used. Please provide official documentation (e.g. statistics, etc.) to support your demonstration.

....

....

....

....

....

....

14   With regard to each type of beneficiary indicated above at point 1 and 2, please indicate whether the amount of subsidized loans to any beneficiary may exceed the cash flow requirements arising from the fact that production costs are incurred before income from output sales is received. If so please provide an explanation.

....

....

....

15   Please indicate the overall budget allocated to this aid measure on a yearly basis.

....

PART III.12.O SUPPLEMENTARY INFORMATION SHEET ON AID FOR THE PROMOTION AND ADVERTISING OF AGRICULTURAL AND CERTAIN NON-AGRICULTURAL PRODUCTS

This notification form must be used for State aid for advertising of products listed in Annex I to the EC-Treaty and certain non-Annex I products.

Please note that promotion operations as defined as the dissemination to the general public of scientific knowledge, the organisation of trade fairs or exhibitions, participation in these and similar public relations exercises, including surveys and market research, are not considered as advertising. State aid for such promotion in the broader sense is subject to points 13 and 14 of the Community Guidelines for State aid in the agriculture sector[83] or, as far as fishery products are concerned, point 2.1.4 of the guidelines for the examination of State aid to fisheries and aquaculture.[84]

For the clarification of other terms and definitions please see chapter 2 of the Community Guidelines for State aid for advertising of products listed in Annex 1 to the EC-Treaty and certain non-Annex 1 products (2001/C 252/03).

---

[83] OJ C232, 12.8.2000, p 17.
[84] OJ C19, 20.1.2001, p 7.

1   **Products covered**

1.1   Does the measure concern the following products (please check off)?

☐ products listed in Annex 1 to the Treaty

☐ non-Annex I products, which consist preponderantly of products listed in Annex 1 (in particular milk products, cereals, sugar and ethyl alcohol) in a processed form (e.g. fruit yoghurt, milk powder preparations with cocoa, butter/vegetable fat mixtures, pastry products, confectionary, and spirituous beverages)

☐ fishery products

Please note that the specific State aid rules for the advertising of agricultural and certain non-agricultural products apply exclusively to the products mentioned above. If the measure concerns other products please refer to the relevant section of the general notification form.

1.2   The measure covers the following products/product categories (e.g. fruits and vegetables, pigmeat, wine . . .):

....

2   **General information**

2.1   Where will the measure be carried out?

☐ On third country markets;

☐ On the market of another Member State;

☐ On the home market;

☐ Outside the Member State or region in which the agricultural and other products are produced;

☐ Within the Member State or region in which the agricultural and other products are produced;

2.2   The measure is aimed at the following target groups:

☐ At consumers in general;

☐ At visitors to the Member State or region in which the agricultural and other products are produced;

☐ At economic operators (e.g. food processors, wholesale or retail distributors, restaurants, hotels and catering establishments);

☐ Other target groups (to be specified);

....

2.3   Which media/means of communication will be used?

☐ Communication via the mass media (such as press, radio, TV or posters);

☐ Point of sale activities (such as leaflets, posters, free samples, tastings);

☐ Other means (please specify);

....

2.4   Does the measure provide for the promotion of labels or logos?

☐   yes   ☐   no

2.5   Can your authorities submit samples or mock-ups of the advertising material to the Commission?

☐   yes   ☐   no

If not, please explain why.

....

3   **Eligible expenses**

3.1   Please provide an exhaustive list of the eligible expenses.

....

4   **Beneficiaries**

4.1   Who are the beneficiaries of the aid?

   ☐ farmers;
   ☐ producer groups and/or producer organizations;
   ☐ enterprises active in the processing and marketing of agricultural products;
   ☐ others (please specify)

....

4.2   Can your authorities give the assurance that all producers of the products concerned are able to benefit from the aid in the same manner (with reference to marginal numbers 53 and 56 of the advertising guidelines)?

     ☐ yes   ☐ no

4.3   Will the conduct of advertising activities be entrusted to private firms or other third parties?

     ☐ yes   ☐ no

4.4   If yes, can your authorities give the assurance that the choice of the private firm/third parties concerned has been made on market principles, in a non-discriminative way, where necessary using tendering procedures which are in accordance with Community law, and in particular with case-law using a degree of advertising sufficient to enable the services market to be opened up to competition and the impartiality of procurement procedures to be reviewed?

     ☐ yes   ☐ no

If not, please refer to marginal number 30 of the advertising guidelines.

5   **Negative criteria**

5.1   National aid for an advertising campaign, which infringes Article 28 of the Treaty prohibiting quantitative restrictions on imports and all measures having equivalent effect between Member States, cannot in any circumstances be considered compatible with the common market. Can your authorities therefore give the assurance that the principles as described in point 19 of the advertising guidelines and as derived from the jurisprudence of the Court of Justice of the European Community will be respected?

     ☐ yes   ☐ no

5.2   Does the measure make any reference to the national origin of the products concerned?

     ☐ yes   ☐ no

5.3   If yes, can your authorities give the assurance that the reference to national origin is subsidiary to the main message put over to consumers by the campaign and does not constitute the principal reason why consumers are being advised to buy the product?

☐   yes   ☐   no

5.4   If the measure is undertaken inside the Member State or region in which the products are produced, can your authorities give the assurance that these measures are aimed exclusively at visitors to the Member State or region, in order to encourage them to try local products and/or to visit local production facilities?

☐   yes   ☐   no

5.5   Can your authorities give the assurance that the measure does not contravene secondary Community legislation, and in particular

— the specific labelling rules which have been laid down for the wine, dairy products, egg and poultry sectors,

— the provisions of Article 2 of Directive 2000/13/EC of the European Parliament and the Council of 20 March 2000 on the approximation of the laws of the Member States relating to labelling, presentation and advertising of foodstuffs.

— are compatible with co-financed advertising campaigns which are being undertaken at Community level?

☐   yes   ☐   no

5.6   Is the measure related directly to the products of one or more particular firm or firms?

☐   yes   ☐   no

6   Positive criteria

6.1   For which of the following reasons can be measure be considered to be in the common interest within the meaning of Article 87(3)(c) EC-Treaty?
The measure concerns

☐ surplus agricultural products or underexploited species;

☐ new products or replacement products not yet in surplus;

☐ high-quality products, including products produced or obtained using environmentally friendly production or catchment methods, such as products from organic farming;

☐ the development of certain regions;

☐ the development of small and medium sized undertakings (SMEs) as defined by Commission Regulation (EC) N° 70/2001 of 12 January 2001 on the application of Articles 87 and 88 of the EC-Treaty to State aid to small and medium-sized enterprises;

☐ projects that are implemented by organizations officially recognised within the meaning of Council Regulations (EC) No 104/2000 of 17 December 1999 on the common organization of the markets in fishery and aquaculture products;

☐ projects that are jointly implemented by producer organizations or other organizations of the fishery sector recognised by national authorities.

7   Quality products

7.1   Does the measure provide for the advertising of products covered by one of the following Regulations/provisions (please check off)?

☐ Council Regulation (EEC) No 2081/92 of 14 July 1992 on the protection of geographical indications and designations of origin for agricultural products and foodstuffs;

☐ Council Regulation (EEC) No 2082/92 of 14 July 1992 on certificates of specific character for agricultural products and foodstuffs;

☐ Council Regulation (EEC) No 2092/91 of 24 June 1991 on organic production of agricultural products and indications referring thereto on agricultural products and foodstuffs;

☐ Articles 54 to 58 of Council Regulation (EC) No 1493/1999 of 17 May 1999 on the common organization of the market in wine (concerning wines produced in specific regions).

☐ Article 24 *ter* paragraph 3, of Council Regulation (EC) 1783/2003 of 29 September 2003 amending Regulation (EC) N° 1257/1999 on support for rural development from the European Agricultural Guidance and Guarantie Fund (EAGGf).

7.2 Does the measure also provide for the advertising of other products meeting particular quality requirements?

☐   yes   ☐   no

If yes, please explain clearly and in detail why the products concerned meet standards or specifications, which are clearly higher or more specific than those laid down in the relevant Community or national legislation (with reference to marginal number 47 of the advertising guidelines). It is advisable to submit e.g. a table to the Commission, in which the different product categories, the relevant Community and/or national standards or specifications for these product categories and the quality criteria are indicated.

....

7.3 How is the constant control of the compliance with the specific quality criteria being maintained (with reference to marginal number 47 of the advertising guidelines)?

....

7.4 Can your authorities give the assurance that access to the quality control scheme will be granted to all products produced in the Community, irrespective of their origin, provided that they meet the conditions laid down?

☐   yes   ☐   no

7.5 Can your authorities give the assurance that, in the operation of the measure, the results of comparable controls, which have been carried out in other Member States, will be recognised?

☐   yes   ☐   no

8 **Aid intensity**

8.1 Please state the maximum rate of direct aid, from a general purpose government budget, expressed as a volume of eligible costs:

....%

If the aid rates for agricultural and certain non-agricultural products are higher than 50%, please refer to marginal number 60 of the advertising guidelines. If the aid rates for fishery products exceed the scales and rates of assistance as contained in Annex III and IV of Regulation (EC) No 2792/1999, please refer to these provisions.

8.2 Please state the contribution of the sector, expressed as a volume of eligible costs:

....%

8.3 The undertakings from the sector contribute through

☐ voluntary contributions;
☐ the collection of parafiscal levies or compulsory contributions.

In the latter case, please explain how the collection is organised.

....

PART III.12.P. SUPPLEMENTARY INFORMATION SHEET ON
RESTRUCTURING AID FOR FIRMS IN DIFFICULTY:
OPERATORS IN THE AGRICULTURAL SECTOR

This form must be used for the notification of restructuring aid in the agricultural sector, covering all operators involved in the production of, and/or trade in, products of Annex I to the Treaty, including fisheries and aquaculture, but having due regard to the specific features of the sector and the Community rules governing it. Please note that the Community Guidelines on State aid for rescuing and restructuring firms in difficulty[85] apply to the agricultural sector.

1 **Eligibility**

1.1 Is the measure limited to firms that fulfil at least one of the eligibility criteria below:

1.1.1 Is the measure limited to firms, where more than half their registered capital has disappeared and more than one quarter of that capital has been lost over the preceding 12 months?

☐ yes ☐ no

1.1.2 Are the firms unlimited companies, where more than half of their capital as shown in the company accounts has disappeared and more than one quarter of that capital has been lost over the preceding months?

☐ yes ☐ no

1.1.3 Do the firms fulfil the criteria under domestic law for being the subject of collective insolvency proceedings?

☐ yes ☐ no

1.2 Is the measure limited to rescuing small or medium-sized enterprises in difficulty, which correspond to the Community definition of SMEs?

☐ yes ☐ no

1.3 Please indicate if the measure concerns firms operating in the

☐ primary production and/or
☐ processing and/or
☐ marketing of Annex I-products or the
☐ fishery sector?

1.4 Please indicate if the measure is limited to small agricultural enterprises within the meaning of marginal number 76 (enterprises with not more than 10 annual work units).

☐ yes ☐ no

1.5 Please indicate if the measure applies to enterprises located in

☐ assisted areas as defined under marginal number 54 of the restructuring guidelines or

---

[85] OJ C288, 9.10.1999, p 2.

1529

□ less favoured areas as defined in Council Regulation (EC) No 1257/1999 on support for rural development from the European Agricultural Guidance and Guarantee Fund (EAGGf) and amending and repealing certain Regulations.[86]

2   **Return to viability**

A restructuring plan must be implemented which must assure restoration of viability. At least the following information should be included:

2.1   Presentation of the different market assumptions arising from the market survey.

2.2   Analysis of the reason(s) why the firm has run into difficulty.

2.3   Presentation of the proposed future strategy for the firm and how this will lead to viability.

2.4   Complete description and overview of the different restructuring measures planned and their cost.

2.5   Timetable for implementing the different measures and the final deadline for implementing the restructuring plan in its entirety.

2.6   Information on the production capacity of the company, and in particular on utilisation of this capacity.

2.7   Please provide information about the extent and trend for the relevant product category over the past three years of market stabilisation measures, especially export refunds and withdrawals from the market, development of world market prices, and the presence of sector limits in Community legislation. Primary products subject to production quotas shall be deemed not to have excess capacity. As regards fisheries and aquaculture, please provide information about the specific features of the sector and the Community rules governing it, in particular the Guidelines for the examination of State aid to fisheries and aquaculture[87] and Council Regulation (EC) No 2792/99.[88]

2.8   Full description of the financial arrangements for the restructuring, including:

— use of capital still available;
— sale of assets or subsidiaries to help finance the restructuring;
— financial commitment by the different shareholders and third parties (like creditors, banks);
— amount of public assistance and demonstration of the need for that amount;

2.9   Projected profit and loss accounts for the next five years with estimated return on capital and sensitivity study based on several scenarios;

2.10 Name(s) of the author(s) of the restructuring plan and date on which it was drawn up.

---

[86] OJ L160, 26.6.1999, p 80.
[87] OJ C19, 20.1.2001, p 7.
[88] OJ L337 of 30.12.1999, p 10.

3   **Avoidance of undue distortion of competition**

3.1   Please refer to marginal numbers 35 to 39 of the restructuring guidelines and describe which compensatory measures will be taken in order to avoid undue distortion of competition.

....

3.2   According to marginal number 70 of the restructuring guidelines, the special rules set out in points 73 to 82 may alternatively be applied (as an alternative to points 35 to 39). Do your authorities request to apply these special rules for agriculture?

☐   yes   ☐   no

3.2.1   If yes, please indicate whether one of the following conditions can be met:
☐   For measures aimed at any particular category of products or operators: The totality of decisions taken in favour of all beneficiaries over any consecutive twelve-month period does not involve a quantity of products which exceeds 3% of the total annual production of such products in that country;
☐   For other measures not so aimed: The totality of decisions taken in favour of all beneficiaries over any consecutive twelve-month period does not involve a value of product which exceeds 1, 5% of the total annual value of agricultural production in that country. Please provide the statistical information, and in particular figures about the total annual production and total annual value of agricultural production, which is necessary for the assessment of the conditions set out above.

According to marginal number 80 of the restructuring guidelines, the geographic references may be determined at a regional level. In all cases, measurement of the production of a country (or a region) shall be based on normal production levels (in general, the average of the previous three years), and, as regards the quantity or the value of production of beneficiaries, be representative of that of their enterprises prior to the decision to grant aid.

3.2.2   If the measure does not fulfill any of the conditions mentioned in point 3.2.1 please refer to marginal numbers 74 to 76 of the restructuring guidelines and describe, which compensatory measures will be taken in order to avoid undue distortion of competition.

....

3.3   Does the measure provide that recipient firms must not increase their capacity during the restructuring plan?

☐   yes   ☐   no

4   **Aid limited to the minimum necessary**

Describe how it will be assured that the aid granted is limited to the minimum necessary.

....

5   **One time, last time**

Is it excluded that recipient firms receive restructuring aid more than once over a period of ten years?

☐   yes   ☐   no

Please note that all cases where this principle is not respected must be notified individually (in the case of aid schemes). However, according to marginal number 83 of the restructuring guidelines, as regards individual awards of aid and rescue and restructuring schemes concerning primary agricultural production, the period during which further aid may not be granted except in exceptional and unforeseeable circumstances for which the company is not responsible is reduced to five years.

6   **Amount of aid**

Please specify the maximum amount of the aid that can be awarded to any one firm as part of the restructuring operation:

....

Provide all relevant information on aid of any kind, which may be granted to the firms eligible for receiving restructuring aid.

7   **Annual report**

7.1   Do you undertake to provide reports, at least on an annual basis, on the operation of the measure, containing the information specified in the Commission's instructions on standardised reports?

□   yes   □   no

7.2   Do you undertake in such report to include a list of beneficiary firms with at least the following information:

    (a) the company name;
    (b) its sectoral code, using the NACE[89] two-digit sectoral classification codes;
    (c) the number of employees;
    (d) annual turnover and balance sheet value;
    (e) the amount of aid granted;
    (f) where appropriate, any restructuring aid, or other support treated as such, which it has received in the past;
    (g) whether or not the beneficiary company has been wound up or subject to collective insolvency proceedings before the end of the restructuring period.

□   yes   □   no

Please note that point 7.2 does not apply in case of small agricultural enterprises.

Where recourse has been had to the provisions of points 73 to 82 of the restructuring guidelines, the report must also include data showing either:

    (a) the quantity (or value) of production which has effectively benefited from the restructuring aid, and data on capacity reduction achieved pursuant to those points; or
    (b) that the conditions for exemption from capacity reduction according to points 79, 80 and 81 of the restructuring guidelines have been fulfilled.

PART III.12.Q. SUPPLEMENTARY INFORMATION SHEET FOR AID CONCERNING TSE TESTS, FALLEN STOCK AND SLAUGHTERHOUSE WASTE

This notification form must be used for State aid towards the costs of TSE tests, fallen stock and slaughterhouse waste granted to operators active in the production, processing and marketing of animals and animal products falling within the scope of Annex I to the Treaty and insofar as Articles 87, 88 and 89 of the Treaty have been declared applicable to such products.

For the clarification of terms and definitions please see Chapter II of the Community Guidelines for State aid concerning TSE tests, fallen stock and slaughterhouse waste (2002/C324/02).

---

[89] Statistical classification of economic activities in the European Community, published by the Statistical Office of the European Communities.

1   **TSE tests**

1.1   Is the measure part of an appropriate programme at Community, national or regional level
      for the prevention, control or eradication of the disease?

                      ☐   yes   ☐   no

      If not, please refer to point 11.4.2 of the Community Guidelines for State aid in the
      agriculture sector.

1.2   Please indicate, which Community or national provisions exist to the effect that the com-
      petent national authorities should deal with the disease, either by organising measure to
      eradicate it, in particular through binding measures giving rise to compensation, or initially
      by setting up an alert system combined, where appropriate, with aid to encourage
      individuals to take part in preventative measures on a voluntary basis. Please enclose a copy
      of the national provisions concerned.
      ....

1.3   Please refer to point 11.4.3 of the Guidelines for State aid in the agriculture sector and
      explain, whether the measure is
      ☐ preventative,
      ☐ compensatory, or
      ☐ a combination of these two.

      ....

1.4   Is the measure compatible with both the objectives and the specific provision laid down in
      Community veterinary legislation?

                      ☐   yes   ☐   no

      If not, please refer to point 11.4.4 of the Community Guidelines for State aid in the
      agriculture sector.

1.5   Please provide an exhaustive list of the eligible expenses (e.g. the costs of the test kit, the
      taking, transporting, testing, storing and destruction of the sample . . .)?

1.6   Please state the maximum aid intensity expressed as a percentage of the eligible costs.
      According to point 11.4.5 of the Guidelines for State aid in the agriculture sector, the aid
      intensity should be a maximum of 100% of the costs incurred. Please note that any
      Community payments for TSE tests have to be included.
      .... %

1.7   Does the measure concern compulsory BSE testing of bovine animals slaughtered for
      human consumption?

                      ☐   yes   ☐   no

      Please note that the testing obligation may be based on Community or national
      legislation.

1.8   If yes, does the total direct and indirect support for these tests exceed EUR 40 per test
      (including Community payments)?

                      ☐   yes   ☐   no

      If yes, please refer to marginal number 24 of the TSE Guidelines.

1.9 Will the aid be paid to the operator where the samples for the tests have to be taken?

☐   yes   ☐   no

1.10 If not, will the aid be paid out to laboratories?

☐   yes   ☐   no

If not, please refer to marginal number 25 of the TSE guidelines.

1.11 If yes, please explain in detail how the full amount of State aid paid is passed on to the operator where the samples for the tests have to be taken.

....

Please note, that the selection of the laboratories normally has to be made on market principles, in a non-discriminative way, where necessary using tendering procedures which are in accordance with Community law, and in particular with case-law using a degree of advertising sufficient to enable the services market to be opened up to competition and the impartiality of procurement procedures to be reviewed.

1.12 Has the selection of the provider of the test-kits been made on market principles, in a non-discriminative way, where necessary using tendering procedures which are in accordance with Community law, and in particular with case-law, using a degree of advertising sufficient to enable the services market to be opened up to competition and the impartiality of procurement procedures to be reviewed?

☐   yes   ☐   no

If not, please explain how the full amount of State aid paid is passed on to the operator where the samples for the tests have to be taken and how the possibility of an aid element in favour of the provider of the test-kits can be excluded.

....

2 Fallen stock

2.1 Is the measure linked up with a consistent programme monitoring and ensuring the safe disposal of all fallen stock in the Member State?

☐   yes   ☐   no

If not, please refer to point 32 of the TSE guidelines.

2.2 Is the aid granted exclusively to farmers?

☐   yes   ☐   no

2.3 If not, will the payment of the aid be made to economic operators active downstream from the farmer, providing services linked to the removal and/or destruction of fallen stock?

☐   yes   ☐   no

If not, please refer to point 32 of the TSE guidelines.

2.4 If yes, please demonstrate properly that the full amount of State aid paid is passed on to the farmer.

....

2.5 Is the choice of the provider mentioned in point 2.3 freely left to the farmer?

☐   yes   ☐   no

2.6 If not, has the provider been chosen and remunerated according to market principles, in a non-discriminatory way, where necessary using tendering procedures which are in accordance with Community law, and in any event using a degree of advertising sufficient to enable the services market to be opened up to competition and the impartiallity of procurement rules to be reviewed?

☐   yes   ☐   no

2.7 If not, please demonstrate properly that there is only one possible provider due to the nature or the legal basis for the provision of a service given.

....

2.8 Please state the maximum aid intensity, expressed as a percentage of eligible costs.

.... % of the costs of removal (collection and transport)
.... % of the costs of destruction (storage, transformation, destruction and final disposal)

Please note that until 31 December 2003, State aid of up to 100% of the costs of removal and destruction of fallen stock may be granted. From 1 January 2004 onwards, Member States may grant State aid of up to 100% of costs of removal of fallen stock, which has to be removed of, and 75% of the costs of destruction of such carcasses. (Exceptions see points 2.10 and 2.11).

2.9 According to marginal numbers 28 and 29 of the TSE guidelines, aid up to an equivalent amount may *alternatively* be granted towards the costs of premia paid by farmers for insurance covering the costs of removal and destruction of fallen stock. Does the notified measure provide for such payments?

☐   yes   ☐   no

2.10 According to marginal number 30 of the TSE guidelines, Member States may *alternatively* grant aid of up to 100% for costs of removal and destruction of carcasses where the aid is financed through fees or through compulsory contributions destined for the financing of the destruction of such carcasses, provided that such fees or contributions are limited to and directly imposed on the meat sector. Does the notified measure provide for such payments?

☐   yes   ☐   no

2.11 Member States may grant State aid of 100% for the costs of removal and destruction, where there is an obligation to perform TSE tests on the fallen stock concerned. Does such an obligation exist?

☐   yes   ☐   no

2.12 Is the measure directly linked up with conservation measures, for instance where the feeding of endangered or protected species of necrophagous birds with fallen stock is allowed in accordance with Community rules?

☐   yes   ☐   no

2.13 If yes, has the Member State made the necessary provisions to ensure that the conservation objectives are still met?

☐   yes   ☐   no

If not, please refer to marginal number 35 of the TSE guidelines.

3   **Slaughterhouse waste**

According to marginal number 38 of the TSE guidelines, the Commission will not authorise State aid towards the costs of the disposal of slaughterhouse waste produced after the date of application of these guidelines (1 January 2003).

3.1 Exceptionally, and in order to allow the meat sector to gradually integrate the higher costs resulting from the introduction of legislation related to TSEs, the Commission will authorise State aid of up to 50% towards costs occurred for the safe disposal of specified risk material and meat and bone-meal having no further commercial use, produced in the year 2003. If the notified measure provides for such payments, please indicate

— What measures have been taken in order to ensure that the measure exclusively concerns the meat and bonemeal described above.

....

— What are the eligible costs?

....

— What is the maximum aid intensity, expressed as a percentage of the eligible costs?

....

3.2 According to marginal number 40 of the TSE guidelines, the Commission will authorise State aid of 100% for the disposal of specified risk material and meat and bone-meal having no further commercial use produced before the date of application of these guidelines. If the notified measure provides for such payments, please indicate

— What measures have been taken in order to ensure that the measure exclusively concerns the meat and bonemeal described above.

....

— What are the eligible costs?

....

— What is the maximum aid intensity, expressed as a percentage of the eligible costs?
....%

3.3 According to marginal number 41 of the TSE guidelines, the Commission will authorise State aid of up to 100 % towards the costs of safe and proper storage of specified risk material and meat and bonemeal waiting for safe disposal, until the end of 2004. If the notified measure provides for such payments, please indicate

— What measures have been taken in order to ensure that the measure exclusively concerns the specified risk material and meat and bonemeal described above.

....

— What are the eligible costs?

....

— What is the maximum aid intensity, expressed as a percentage of the eligible costs?
....%

PART III.13.A. SIS ON AID FOR RESTRUCTURING FIRMS IN
DIFFICULTY IN THE AVIATION SECTOR

This annex must be used for the notification of individual restructuring aid for airlines covered by the Community Guidelines on State aid for rescuing and restructuring firms in difficulty[90] and those on State aid in the aviation sector.[91]

1   **Eligibility**

1.1   Is the firm a limited company, where more than half of its registered capital has disappeared and more than one quarter of that capital has been lost over the preceding 12 months?

☐   yes   ☐   no

1.2   Is the firm an unlimited company, where more than half of its capital as shown in the company accounts has disappeared and more than one quarter of that capital has been lost over the preceding months?

☐   yes   ☐   no

1.3   Does the firm fulfil the criteria under domestic law for being the subject of collective insolvency proceedings?

☐   yes   ☐   no

If you have answered yes on any of the above questions, please attach the relevant documents (latest profit and loss account with balance sheet, or court decision opening an investigation into the company under national company law)

If you have answered no to all of the above questions, please submit evidence supporting that the firm is in difficulties and thus eligible for rescue aid.

1.4   When has the firm been created?..

1.5   Since when is the firm operating?...

1.6   Does the company belong to a larger business group?

☐   yes   ☐   no

If you have answered yes, please submit full details about the group (organization chart, showing the links between the group's members with details on capital and voting rights) and attach proof that the company's difficulties are its own and are not the result of an arbitrary allocation of costs within the group and that the difficulties are too serious to be dealt with by the group itself.

1.7   Has the firm (or the group to which it belongs) in the past received any restructuring aid?

☐   yes   ☐   no

If yes, please provide full details (date, amount, reference to previous Commission decision if applicable, etc.)

---

[90] Community Guidelines on State aid for rescuing and restructuring firms in difficulty, OJ C288, 9.10.1999, p 2.
[91] Community guidelines on the application of Arts 92 and 93 of the EC Treaty and Art 61 of the EEA Agreement to State aids in the aviation sector, OJ C350, 10.12.1994, p.5.

2   Restructuring plan

2.1   Please supply a copy of the survey of the market(s) served by the firm in difficulty, with the name of the organization which carried it out. The market survey must give in particular:

2.1.1   A precise definition of the product and geographical market(s).

2.1.2   The names of the company's main competitors with their shares of the world, Community or domestic market, as appropriate.

2.1.3   The evolution of the company's market share in recent years.

2.1.4   An assessment of total production capacity and demand at Community level, concluding whether or not there is excess capacity on the market.

2.1.5   Community-wide forecasts for trends in demand, aggregate capacity and prices on the market over the five years ahead.

2.2   Please attach the restructuring plan. As aid must form part of a comprehensive restructuring programme, at least the following information should be included:

2.2.1   Presentation of the different market assumptions arising from the market survey.

2.2.2   Analysis of the reason(s) why the firm has run into difficulty.

2.2.3   Presentation of the proposed future strategy for the firm and how this will lead to viability.

2.2.4   Complete description and overview of the different restructuring measures planned and their cost.

2.2.5   Timetable for implementing the different measures and the final deadline for implementing the restructuring plan in its entirety.

2.2.6   Information on the production capacity of the company, and in particular on utilisation of this capacity and capacity reductions, especially when needed by the restoration of the financial viability of the firm and/or the situation of the market.

2.2.7   Full description of the financial arrangements for the restructuring, including:
— Use of capital still available;
— Sale of assets or subsidiaries to help finance the restructuring:
— Financial commitment by the different shareholders and third parties (like creditors, banks);
— Amount of public assistance and demonstration of the need for that amount.

2.2.8   Projected profit and loss accounts for the next five years with estimated return on capital and sensitivity study based on several scenarios.

2.2.9   Commitment of the Member State authorities not to grant any further aid to the firm.

2.2.10 Commitment of the Member State authorities not to interfere in the management of the company other than due to ownership rights and allowing the company to be run according to commercial principles.

2.2.11 Commitments taken by the Member State authorities in order to limit the aid to the purposes of the restructuring programme and to prevent the firm to acquire shareholdings in other air carriers during the restructuring period.

2.2.12 Name(s) of the author(s) of the restructuring plan and date on which it was drawn up.

2.3 Describe the compensatory measures proposed with a view to mitigating the distortive effects on competition at Community level and especially the impact of the capacity and offer reduction contained in the restructuring plan of the firm on its competitors.

2.4 Provide all relevant information on aid of any kind granted to the firm receiving restructuring aid, whether under a scheme or not, until the restructuring period comes to an end.

2.5 Provide all relevant information to describe the modalities of transparency and control scheduled for the notified measure.

Part III.13.B. SIS on Transport Infrastructure Aid

This SIS must be used for the notification of any individual aid or any scheme in favour of transport infrastructure. It should also be used in the case of individual aid or scheme, which is notified to the Commission for reasons of legal certainty.

1 **Type of infrastructure**

1.1 Please specify the kind of infrastructure eligible under the measure.

1.2 Is the infrastructure in question open and accessible to all potential users on non-discriminatory terms or is it dedicated to one or more particular undertakings?

1.3 Is the infrastructure part of the public domain and operated as such or is it operated/managed by an entity separated from the public administration?

1.4 Please specify the conditions under which the infrastructure will be operated.

1.5 Does the scheme or individual measure relate to new infrastructure or the extension/upgrading of existing infrastructure?

2 **Eligible costs and aid intensity**

2.1 Does the scheme or the individual measure relate to:

☐ investment costs
☐ operating costs
☐ other (please specify)

2.2 What are the total costs for the project in question and to what extent will the beneficiary contribute to these costs.

2.3 By what means have the amount of aid been established, e.g. a tendering procedure, market studies, etc.?

2.4 Please justify the necessity of the public contributions and explain how it has been ensured that the public participation has is kept at the minimum necessary.

3 **Beneficiary**

3.1 By what means have the beneficiary been choosen.

3.2 Will the beneficiary also operate the infrastructure?

☐   yes   ☐   no

If, no, please explain how the operator has been selected.

PART III.13.C. SIS ON AID FOR MARITIME TRANSPORT

This SIS must be used for the notification of any aid scheme covered by the Community guidelines on State aid to maritime transport.[92]

1 **Types of scheme**

Does the scheme constitute or include:

(a) ☐ a Tonnage Tax

(b) ☐ a reduction in social contributions

(c) ☐ a reduction in the income tax applicable to seafarers

(d) ☐ a reduction in local taxes

(e) ☐ a reduction in registration fees

(f) ☐ aids for training

(g) ☐ aids for transferring lorries from roads to sea ways

(h) ☐ a public service contract or award procedure thereof

(i) ☐ aids of social character?

(j) ☐ other, please describe:

2 **Eligibility**

For (a) (b) (c) (d) (e) (f) (g)

2.1 What are the eligibility criteria for companies?

2.2 What are the eligibility criteria for boats, in particular is there an obligation on the flag?

2.3 Where appropriate, what are the eligibility criteria for seafarers?

2.4 Describe the list of eligible activities. In particular, does the regime concern

☐ tug activities?   ☐ dredging activities?

2.5 What are the ring-fence measures to avoid spill-over into after activities of the same company?

2.6 For (h): What are the public services obligations, the method for calculating the compensations, the different offers submitted in the tender and the reasons for the choice of the designated company?

2.7 For (i): What are the routes concerned, the populations of users concerned and the conditions attached to the award of individual grants?

---

[92] Community guidelines on State aid to maritime transport, OJ C205, 5.7.1997, p 5.

3   **Aid intensity**
    For (a):

3.1   What are the rates used to calculate the taxable income per 100 NT?
      Up to 1 000 NT
      Between 1 001 and 10 000 NT
      Between 10 001 and 20 000 NT
      More than 20 001 NT

3.2   Are companies obliged to set up separate accountings when operating both eligible and non eligible activities?

3.3   How should be treated groups of companies and intra-group transactions?

      For (b) (c) (d) (e):

3.4   What is the aid intensity in terms of percentage of the social/fiscal contributions or of the tax or fees that the seafarer or the shipowner should have normally been subject to? ....%

3.5   Or to what level in absolute terms these contributions, fees or taxes have been limited?

3.6   For (f): What is the aid intensity in terms of the cost of the training or the salary of the trainee?

3.7   For (g): What is the amount of aid per tonne kilometer transferred?

3.8   For (i): What is the amount of individual grants?

PART III.13.D. SIS ON AID FOR COMBINED TRANSPORT

This SIS must be used for the notification of any individual aid or any scheme for combined transport purposes. It should also be used in the case of individual aid or scheme, which is notified to the Commission for reasons of legal certainty.

1   **Type of scheme or measure**
    Does the scheme or the individual measure relate to:
    Acquisition of combined transport equipment
    $\square$ yes $\square$ no
    If yes, please give a description of the eligible assets:
    ....
    ....

    Construction of infrastructure related to combined transport
    $\square$ yes $\square$ no
    If yes, please give a description of the measure:
    ....
    ....

Granting of non-remboursable subsidies to reduce the costs of access to combined transport services

☐   yes   ☐   no

If yes, please provide a study justifying such a measure: ....

Other:

....

....

....

2   Eligible costs

Are maritime containers (ISO 1) eligible under the scheme?

☐   yes   ☐   no

Are wagons and locomotives eligible under the scheme?

☐   yes   ☐   no

If yes, please specify the beneficiaries:

....

....

Will the eligible items be exclusively used for combined transport operations?

☐   yes   ☐   no

....

Other eligible costs under the individual aid or scheme:

....

3   Aid intensity

Is the aid intensity for combined transport equipment higher than 30% of the eligible costs?

☐   yes   ☐   no

Is the aid intensity for combined transport infrastructure higher than 50% of the eligible costs?

☐   yes   ☐   no

If yes, please provide documentary evidence justifying it:

....

....

For subsidies to reduce the costs of access to combined transport services, please provide a study justifying the planned aid intensity

ANNEX II. SIMPLIFIED NOTIFICATION FORM

This form may be used for the simplified notification pursuant to Article 4(2) of the Commission Implementation Regulation N° present reglement of (...) implementing Council Regulation (EC) N° 659/1999.[93]

1   Prior approved aid scheme[94]
1.1   Aid number allocated by the Commission:

1.2   Title:

1.3   Date of approval [by reference to the letter of the Commission SG (..) D/ ...]:

1.4   Publication in the Official Journal of the European Union:

1.5   Primary objective (please specify one):

1.6   Legal basis:

1.7   Overall budget:

1.8   Duration:

2   Instrument subject to notification

☐ new budget (please specify the overall as well as the annual budget in the respective national currency);

☐ new duration (please specify the starting date from which the aid may be granted and the last date until which the aid may be granted):

☐ tightening of criteria (please indicate if the amendment concerns a reduction of aid intensity or eligible expenses and specify details):

Please attach a copy (or a web link) of the relevant extracts of the final text(s) of the legal basis.

ANNEX III A. STANDARDIZED REPORTING FORMAT FOR
EXISTING STATE AID

(This format covers all sectors except agriculture)

With a view to simplifying, streamlining and improving the overall reporting system for State aid, the existing Standardized Reporting Procedure shall be replaced by an annual updating exercise. The Commission shall send a pre-formatted spreadsheet, containing detailed information on all existing aid schemes and individual aid, to the Member States by 1 March each year. Member States shall return the spreadsheet in an electronic format to the Commission by 30 June of the year in question. This will enable the Commission to publish State aid data in year t for the reporting period t-1.[95]

---

[93] Council Reg (EC) No 659/1999 laying down detailed rules for the application of Art 93 of the EC Treaty, OJ L83, 27.3.1999, p.1.
[94] If the aid scheme has been notified to the Commission on more than one occasion, please provide details for the latest complete notification that has been approved by the Commission
[95] t is the year in which the data are requested.

The bulk of the information in the pre-formatted spreadsheet shall be pre-completed by the Commission on the basis of data provided at the time of approval of the aid. Member States shall be required to check and, where necessary, modify the details for each scheme or individual aid, and to add the annual expenditure for the latest year (t-1). In addition, Member States shall indicate which schemes have expired or for which all payments have stopped and whether or not a scheme is co-financed by Community Funds.

Information such as the objective of the aid, the sector to which the aid is directed, etc shall refer to the time at which the aid is approved and not to the final beneficiaries of the aid. For example, the primary objective of a scheme which, at the time the aid is approved, is exclusively earmarked for small and medium-sized enterprises shall be aid for small and medium-sized enterprises. However, another scheme for which all aid is ultimately awarded to small and medium-sized enterprises shall not be regarded as such if, at the time the aid is approved, the scheme is open to all enterprises.

The following parameters shall be included in the spreadsheet. Parameters 1–3 and 6–12 shall be pre-completed by the Commission and checked by the Member States. Parameters 4, 5 and 13 shall be completed by the Member States.

1. Title

2. Aid number

3. All previous aid numbers (e.g. following the renewal of a scheme)

4. Expiry

    Member States should indicate those schemes which have expired or for which all payments have stopped.

5. Co-financing

    Although Community funding itself is excluded, total State aid for each Member State shall include aid measures that are co-financed by Community funding. In order to identify which schemes are co-financed and estimate how much such aid represents in relation to overall State aid, Member States are required to indicate whether or not the scheme is co-financed and if so the percentage of aid that is co-financed. If this is not possible, an estimate of the total amount of aid that is co-financed shall be provided.

6. Sector

    The sectoral classification shall be based largely on NACE[96] at the [three-digit level].

7. Primary objective

8. Secondary objective

    A secondary objective is one for which, in addition to the primary objective, the aid (or a distinct part of it) was exclusively earmarked at the time the aid was approved. For example, a scheme for which the primary objective is research and development may have as a secondary objective small and medium-sized enterprises (SMEs) if the aid is earmarked exclusively for SMEs. Another scheme for which the primary objective is SMEs may have as secondary objectives training and employment if, at the time the aid was approved, the aid is earmarked for x% training and y% employment.

---

[96] NACE Rev. 1.1 is the statistical classification of economic activities in the European Community.

9. Region(s)

   Aid may, at the time of approval, be exclusively earmarked for a specific region or group of regions. Where appropriate, a distinction should be made between the Article 87(3)a regions and the Article 87(3)c regions. If the aid is earmarked for one particular region, this should be specified at NUTS[97] level II.

10. Category of aid instrument(s)

    A distinction shall be made between six categories (Grant, Tax reduction/exemption, Equity participation, Soft loan, Tax deferral, Guarantee).

11. Description of aid instrument in national language

12. Type of aid

    A distinction shall be made between three categories: Scheme, Individual application of a scheme, Individual aid awarded outside of a scheme (ad hoc aid).

13. Expenditure

    As a general rule, figures should be expressed in terms of actual expenditure (or actual revenue foregone in the case of tax expenditure). Where payments are not available, commitments or budget appropriations shall be provided and flagged accordingly. Separate figures shall be provided for each aid instrument within a scheme or individual aid (e.g. grant, soft loans, etc.). Figures shall be expressed in the national currency in application at the time of the reporting period. Expenditure shall be provided for t-1, t-2, t-3, t-4, t-5.

ANNEX III B. STANDARDIZED REPORTING FORMAT FOR EXISTING STATE AID

(This format covers the agricultural sector)

With a view to simplifying, streamlining and improving the overall reporting system for State aid, the existing Standardized Reporting Procedure shall be replaced by an annual updating exercise. The Commission shall send a pre-formatted spreadsheet, containing detailed information on all existing aid schemes and individual aid, to the Member States by 1 March each year. Member States shall return the spreadsheet in an electronic format to the Commission by 30 June of the year in question. This will enable the Commission to publish State aid data in year t for the reporting period t-1.[98]

The bulk of the information in the pre-formatted spreadsheet shall be pre-completed by the Commission on the basis of data provided at the time of approval of the aid. Member States shall be required to check and, where necessary, modify the details for each scheme or individual aid, and to add the annual expenditure for the latest year (t-1). In addition, Member States shall indicate which schemes have expired or for which all payments have stopped and whether or not a scheme is co-financed by Community Funds.

Information such as the objective of the aid, the sector to which the aid is directed, etc shall refer to the time at which the aid is approved and not to the final beneficiaries of the aid. For example, the primary objective of a scheme which, at the time the aid is approved, is exclusively earmarked for small and medium-sized enterprises shall be aid for small and medium-sized enterprises. However, another scheme for which all aid is ultimately awarded to small and medium-sized enterprises shall not be regarded as such if, at the time the aid is approved, the scheme is open to all enterprises.

---

[97] NUTS is the nomenclature of territorial units for statistical purposes in the Community.

[98] t is the year in which the data are requested

The following parameters shall be included in the spreadsheet. Parameters 1–3 and 6–12 shall be pre-completed by the Commission and checked by the Member States. Parameters 4, 5, 13 and 14 shall be completed by the Member States.

1. Title

2. Aid number

3. All previous aid numbers (e.g. following the renewal of a scheme)

4. Expiry

   Member States should indicate those schemes which have expired or for which all payments have stopped.

5. Co-financing

   Although Community funding itself is excluded, total State aid for each Member State shall include aid measures that are co-financed by Community funding. In order to identify which schemes are co-financed and estimate how much such aid represents in relation to overall State aid, Member States are required to indicate whether or not the scheme is co-financed and if so the percentage of aid that is co-financed. If this is not possible, an estimate of the total amount of aid that is co-financed shall be provided.

6. Sector

   The sectoral classification shall be based largely on NACE[99] at the [three-digit level].

7. Primary objective

8. Secondary objective

   A secondary objective is one for which, in addition to the primary objective, the aid (or a distinct part of it) was exclusively earmarked at the time the aid was approved. For example, a scheme for which the primary objective is research and development may have as a secondary objective small and medium-sized enterprises (SMEs) if the aid is earmarked exclusively for SMEs. Another scheme for which the primary objective is SMEs may have as secondary objectives training and employment aid if, at the time the aid was approved the aid is earmarked for x% training and y% employment.

9. Region(s)

   Aid may, at the time of approval, be exclusively earmarked for a specific region or group of regions. Where appropriate, a distinction should be made between Objective 1 regions and less-favoured areas.

10. Category of aid instrument(s)

    A distinction shall be made between six categories (Grant, Tax reduction/exemption, Equity participation. Soft loan, Tax deferral, Guarantee).

11. Description of aid instrument in national language

12. Type of aid

    A distinction shall be made between three categories: Scheme, Individual application of a scheme, Individual aid awarded outside of a scheme (ad hoc aid).

---

[99] NACE Rev. 1.1 is the statistical classification of economic activities in the European Community.

13. Expenditure

As a general rule, figures should be expressed in terms of actual expenditure (or actual revenue foregone in the case of tax expenditure). Where payments are not available, commitments or budget appropriations shall be provided and flagged accordingly. Separate figures shall be provided for each aid instrument within a scheme or individual aid (e.g. grant, soft loans, etc). Figures shall be expressed in the national currency in application at the time of the reporting period. Expenditure shall be provided for t-1, t-2, t-3, t-4, t-5.

14. Aid intensity and beneficiaries

Member States should indicate:

— the effective aid intensity of the support actually granted per type of aid and of region
— the number of beneficiaries
— the average amount of aid per beneficiary.

Annex III C. Information to be Contained in the Annual Report to be Provided to the Commission

The reports shall be provided in computerized form. They shall contain the following information:

1   Title of aid scheme, Commission aid number and reference of the Commission decision

2   Expenditure. The figures have to be expressed in euros or, if applicable, national currency. In the case of tax expenditure, annual tax losses have to be reported. If precise figures are not available, such losses may be estimated. For the year under review indicate separately for each aid instrument within the scheme (e.g. grant, soft loan, guarantee, etc):

2.1   amounts committed, (estimated) tax losses or other revenue forgone, data on guarantees, etc for new assisted projects. In the case of guarantee schemes, the total amount of new guarantees handed out should be provided;

2.2   actual payments, (estimated) tax losses or other revenue forgone, data on guarantees, etc for new and current projects. In the case of guarantee schemes, the following should be provided: total amount of outstanding guarantees, premium income, recoveries, indemnities paid out, operating result of the scheme under the year under review;

2.3   number of assisted projects and/or enterprises;

2.4   estimated overall amount of:

— aid granted for the permanent withdrawal of fishing vessels through their transfer to third countries;
— aid granted for the temporary cessation of fishing activities;
— aid granted for the renewal of fishing vessels;
— aid granted for modernisation of fishing vessels;
— aid granted for the purchase of used vessels;
— aid granted for socio-economic measures;
— aid granted to make good damage caused by natural disasters or exceptional occurences;
— aid granted to outermost regions;
— aid granted through parafiscal charges;

2.5   regional breakdown of amounts under point 2.1. by regions defined as Objective 1 regions and other areas;

3   Other information and remarks.

Form for the Submission of Complaints Concerning Alleged Unlawful State Aid

(2003/C 116/03)

Article 88(3) of the EC Treaty provides that the Commission shall be informed, in sufficient time to enable it to submit its comments, of any plans to grant or alter aid. Member States shall not put its proposed measures into effect until this procedure has resulted in a final decision.

Aid that has been put into effect in contravention of Article 88(3) of the Treaty constitutes 'unlawful aid'.

In accordance with Article 10(1) of Council Regulation (EC) No 659/1999,[1] where the Commission has in its possession information from whatever source regarding alleged unlawful aid, it shall examine that information without delay.

Furthermore, according to Article 20(2) of the abovementioned Regulation, any interested party may inform the Commission of any alleged unlawful aid and any alleged misuse of aid (hereinafter referred to as a complaint).

Any person or company may submit a complaint to the Commission. The procedure is free. However, when investigating complaints the Commission is obliged to respect the procedural rules set out in Regulation (EC) No 659/1999, and in particular the rights of defence of the Member State.

Moreover, as an alternative, or as well as submitting a complaint to the Commission, it is usually possible for third parties whose interests have been adversely affected by the grant of an unlawful aid to pursue the matter before the national courts. A report on the application of State aid rules by the national courts is available on

http://europa.eu.int/comm/competition/state_aid/legislation/app_by_member_states/

However, the Commission cannot offer advice about the national procedures available in individual cases.

The annexed form sets out the information the Commission needs in order to be able to follow-up a complaint about alleged unlawful aid. If you are not able to complete all the sections of the form, please give the reasons.

The form is accessible in all Community languages on the Internet server of the European Commission at the following addresses: http://europa.eu.int/comm/competition/index_en.html and http://europa.eu.int/comm/secretariat_general/index_en.htm. The Europa web site also contains much useful information about the Community's State aid rules which may help you or your adviser to complete the form.

You can send this form to the following addresses:

For complaints relating to possible unlawful State aid in the sector of the production, processing and marketing of Annex 1 agricultural products:

---

[1] OJ L83, 27.3.1999, p 1.

European Commission
Directorate-General for Agriculture
Directorate H
Office: Loi 130 5–128
B-1049 Brussels
Fax (32–2) 296 76 72
e-mail: Agri-State-Aids@cec.eu.int

For complaints relating to possible unlawful State aid in the sector of the production, processing and marketing of fisheries and aquaculture products:

European Commission
Directorate-General for Fisheries
Directorate D
Rue Joseph II 99
B-1049 Brussels
Fax (32–2) 295 19 42
e-mail: fish-aidesdetat@cec.eu.int

For complaints relating to possible unlawful State aid in the transport sector or the coal sector:

European Commission
Directorate-General for Energy and Transport
Directorate A
Unit 4—Internal Market, Public Service, Competition and Users' Rights
B-1049 Brussels
Fax (32–2) 296 41 04
e-mail: stateaid.transport@cec.eu.int

For complaints relating to possible unlawful State aid in other sectors:
European Commission
Directorate-General for Competition
State aid Greffe
J-70, (4/136)
B-1049 Brussels
Fax (32–2) 295 36 10
e-mail: Stateaidgreffe@cec.eu.int

If you are not sure which department is responsible, you may address your complaint to the

Secretary General
European Commission
B-1049 Brussels
e-mail: Aidesdetat@cec.eu.int

I.A. Information regarding the complainant

I.1 Surname and forename of complainant, or corporate name:

I.2 Address or Registered Office:

I.3 Telephone, fax, e-mail address:

I.4 Name, address, telephone, fax, e-mail address of a contact person:

I.5 If the complainant is an enterprise, a brief description of the complainant and its field(s) and place(s) of activity:

I.6   Please summarize briefly how the award of the alleged aid affects the complainant's interests.

I.B. Information regarding the representative of the complainant

I.7.   If the complaint is submitted on behalf of someone else (a person or a firm), please also provide the name, address, fax, e-mail address of the representative and attach written proof that the representative is authorized to act.

II. Information regarding the Member State

II.1.   Member State:

II.2.   Level at which the alleged unlawful State aid has been granted:
— central government
— region (please specify)
— other (please specify)

III. Information regarding the alleged aid measures complained of

III.1. Are you complaining about an alleged aid scheme, or an alleged individual aid?

III.2. When was the alleged aid given or the alleged aid scheme implemented? What is the duration of the alleged aid scheme (if known)?

III.3. In which economic sector(s) does this alleged aid apply?

III.4. What is the amount of the alleged aid? In what form is it given (loans, grants, guarantees, tax incentives or exemptions etc)?

III.5. Who is the beneficiary? In the case of a scheme, who is eligible for the alleged aid?

Please give as much information as possible, including a description of the main activities of the firm(s) concerned.

III.6. For what purpose was the alleged aid given (if known)?

IV. Grounds of complaint

Please explain in detail the grounds for your complaint, including the reasons why you have complained, what rules of community law you think have been infringed by the granting of the alleged aid in question and how this has affected conditions of competition in the common market and trade between Member States.

If the alleged aid has damaged your own commercial interests, please explain how.

V. Information on other procedures

V.1.   Details of any approaches already made to the Commission's services (if possible, attach copies of correspondence):

V.2.   Approaches already made to national authorities (e.g. central, regional or local government bodies, ombudsman, etc; if possible, attach copies of correspondence):

V.3.   Recourse to national courts or other procedures (e.g. arbitration or conciliation). (Indicate whether there has already been a decision or award and attach a copy if appropriate):

VI. Supporting documents

List any documents or evidence which is submitted in support of the complaint, and attach copies.

Whenever possible, a copy of the national law or other measure which provides the legal basis for the payment of the alleged aid should be provided.

VII. Confidentiality

You should be aware that in order to protect the rights of defence of the Member State concerned, the Commission may have to disclose your identity and any supporting documents, or their contents, to the Member State. If you do not wish your identity or certain documents or information to be disclosed, please indicate this clearly, clearly identify the confidential parts of any documents and give your reasons.

Place, date and signature of complainant

Notice concerning the anti-dumping measures in force in respect of imports into the Community of polyester staple fibres originating, *inter alia*, in India: modification of the name of a company with an individual duty rate
(2003/C 116/04)

Imports of polyester staple fibres originating, *inter alia*, in India are subject to a definitive anti-dumping duty imposed by Council Regulation (EC) No 2852/2000.[2]

Indian Organic Chemicals Limited, a company located in India, whose exports to the Community of polyester staple fibres are subject to an individual anti-dumping duty rate of 14,7% by the abovementioned Regulation, has informed the Commission that it has changed its name, as from 15 November 2002, into Futura Polyesters Limited. The company has asked the Commission to confirm that the change of name does not affect the right of the company to benefit from the individual duty rate applied to the company under its previous name of Indian Organic Chemicals Limited.

The Commission has examined the information supplied, which demonstrates that all the company's activities linked to the manufacturing, sales and exports of polyester staple fibres are unaffected by the change of name. The Commission therefore concludes that the change of name in no way affects the findings of Regulation (EC) No 2852/2000. In view of the absence of any substantive change of circumstances, the reference to Indian Organic Chemicals Limited should be read as Futura Polyesters Limited, with registered office at 13 Mathew Road, Mumbai, in Article 1(2) of Regulation (EC) No 2852/2000.

The TARIC additional code A148 previously attributed to Indian Organic Chemicals Limited shall apply to Futura Polyesters Limited.

---

[2] OJ L332, 28.12.2000, p 17.

APPENDIX 33

Commission Communication C(2003) 4582 of 1 December 2003 on professional secrecy in State aid decisions

(2003/C 297/03)

1. INTRODUCTION

(1) This Communication sets out how the Commission intends to deal with requests by Member States, as addresses of State aid decisions, to consider parts of such decisions as covered by the obligation of professional secrecy and thus not to be disclosed when the decision is published.

(2) This involves two aspects, namely:
   (a) the identification of the information which might be covered by the obligation of professional secrecy; and
   (b) the procedure to be followed for dealing with such requests.

2. LEGAL FRAMEWORK

(3) Article 287 of the Treaty states that: 'The members of the institutions of the Community, the members of committees, and the officials and other servants of the Community shall be required, even after their duties have ceased, not to disclose information of the kind covered by the obligation of professional secrecy, in particular information about undertakings, their business relations or their cost components'.

(4) This is also reflected in Articles 24 and 25 of Council Regulation (EC) No 659/1999 of 22 March 1999 laying down detailed rules for the application of Article 93 of the EC Treaty.[1]

(5) Article 253 of the Treaty states: 'Regulations, directives and decisions adopted jointly by the European Parliament and the Council, and such acts adopted by the Council or the Commission, shall state the reasons on which they are based and shall refer to any proposals or opinions which were required to be obtained pursuant to this Treaty'.

(6) Article 6(1), first sentence of Regulation (EC) No 659/1999 further stipulates with regard to decisions to initiate the formal investigation procedures: 'The decision to initiate the formal investigation procedure shall summarise the relevant issues of fact and law, shall include a preliminary assessment of the Commission as to the aid character of the proposed measure and shall set out the doubts as to its compatibility with the common market [. . .]'.

3. IDENTIFICATION OF INFORMATION WHICH CAN BE COVERED BY PROFESSIONAL SECRECY

(7) The Court of Justice has established that although Article 287 of the Treaty primarily refers to information gathered from undertakings, the expression 'in particular' shows that the principle in question is a general one which applies also to other confidential information.[2]

---

[1] OJ L83, 27.3.1999, p 1.
[2] Case 145/83 Adams v Commission [1985] ECR 3539, para 34, and Case T-353/94 Postbank v Commission [1996] ECR II-921, para 86.

(8) It follows that professional secrecy covers both business secrets and other confidential information.

(9) There is no reason why the notions of business secret and other confidential information should be interpreted differently from the meaning given to these terms in the context of antitrust and merger procedures. The fact that in antitrust and merger procedures the addresses of the Commission decision are undertakings, while in State aid procedures the addresses are Member States, does not constitute an obstacle to a uniform approach as to the identification of what can constitute business secrets or other confidential information.

3.1. Business secrets

(10) Business secrets can only concern information relating to a business which has actual or potential economic value, the disclosure or use of which could result in economic benefits for other companies. Typical examples are methods of assessing manufacturing and distribution costs, production secrets (that is to say, a secret, commercially valuable plan, formula, process or device that is used for the making, preparing, compounding, or processing of trade commodities and that can be said to be the end product of either innovation or substantial effort) and processes, supply sources, quantities produced and sold, market shares, customer and distributor lists, marketing plans, cost price structure, sales policy, and information on the internal organisation of the undertaking.

(11) It would appear that in principle business secrets can only relate to the beneficiary of the aid (or other third party) and can only concern information submitted by the Member State (or third party). Hence, statements from the Commission itself (for example, expressing doubts about feasibility of a restructuring plan) cannot be covered by the obligation of professional secrecy.

(12) The simple fact that disclosure of information might cause harm to the company is not of itself sufficient grounds to consider that such information should be considered as business secret. For example, a Commission decision to initiate the formal investigation procedure in the case of a restructuring aid may cast doubt on certain aspects of the restructuring plan in the light of information the Commission has received. Such a decision could (further) affect the credit-position of that company. However, that would not necessarily lead to the conclusion that the information on which that decision was based must be considered as business secrets.

(13) In general, the Commission will apply the following non-exhaustive list of criteria to determine whether information can be deemed to constitute business secrets:
    (a) the extent to which the information is known outside the company;
    (b) the extent to which measures have been taken to protect the information within the company, for example, through non compete clauses or non-disclosure agreements imposed on employees or agents, etc;
    (c) the value of the information for the company and its competitors;
    (d) the effort or investment which the undertaking had to undertake to acquire the information;
    (e) the effort which others would need to undertake to acquire or copy the information;
    (f) the degree of protection offered to such information under the legislation of the Member State concerned.

(14) In principle, the Commission considers that the following information would not normally be covered by the obligation of professional secrecy:
    (a) information which is publicly available, including information available only upon payment through specialised information services or information which is common knowledge among specialists in the field (for example common knowledge among engineers or medical doctors). Likewise, turnover is not normally considered as a business secret, as it is a figure published in the annual accounts or otherwise known to the

1554

market. Reasons must be given for requests for confidentiality concerning turnover figures which are not in the public domain and the requests must be evaluated on a case-by-case basis. The fact that information is not publicly available does not necessarily mean that the information can be regarded as a business secret;

(b) historical information, in particular information at least five years old;

(c) statistical or aggregate information;

(d) names of aid recipients, sector of activity, purpose and amount of the aid, etc.

(15) Detailed reasons must be given for any request to derogate from these principles in exceptional cases.

3.2. Other confidential information

(16) In antitrust and merger cases, confidential information includes certain types of information communicated to the Commission on condition that confidentiality is observed (for example a market study commissioned by an undertaking which is party to the procedure and forming part of its property). It seems that a similar approach could be retained for State aid decisions.

(17) In the field of State aid, there may, however, be some forms of confidential information, which would not necessarily be present in antitrust and merger procedures, referring specifically to secrets of the State or other confidential information relating to its organisational activity. Generally, in view of the Commission's obligation to state the reasons for its decisions and the transparency requirement, such information can only in very exceptional circumstances be covered by the obligation of professional secrecy. For example, information regarding the organisation and costs of public services will not normally be considered 'other confidential information' (although it may constitute a business secret, if the criteria laid down in section 3.1 are met).

4. APPLICABLE PROCEDURE

4.1. General principles

(18) The Commission's main task is to reconcile two opposing obligations, namely the requirement to state the reasons for its decisions under Article 253 of the Treaty and therefore ensure that its decisions contain all the essential elements on which they are based, and that of safeguarding the obligation of professional secrecy.

(19) Besides the basic obligation to state the reasons for its decisions, the Commission has to take into account the need for effective application of the State aid rules (*inter alia*, by giving Member States, beneficiaries and interested parties the possibility to comment on or challenge its decisions) and for transparency of its policy. There is therefore an overriding interest in making public the full substance of its decisions. As a general principle, requests for confidential treatment can only be granted where strictly necessary to protect business secrets or other confidential information meriting similar protection.

(20) Business secrets and other confidential information do not enjoy an absolute protection: this means for example that they could be divulged when they are essential for the Commission's statement of the reasons for its decisions. This means that information necessary for the identification of an aid measure and its beneficiary cannot normally be covered by the obligation of professional secrecy. Similarly, information necessary to demonstrate that the conditions of Article 87(1) of the Treaty are met, cannot normally be covered by the obligation of professional secrecy. However, the Commission will have to consider carefully whether the need for publication is more important, given the specific circumstances of a case, than the prejudice that might be generated for that Member State or undertaking involved.

(21) The public version of a Commission decision can only feature deletions from the adopted version for reasons of professional secrecy. Paragraphs cannot be moved, and no sentence can

be added or altered. Where the Commission considers that certain information cannot be disclosed, a footnote may be added, paraphrasing the non-disclosed information or indicating a range of magnitude or size, if useful to assure the comprehensibility and coherence of the decision.

(22) Requests not to disclose the full text of a decision or substantial parts of it which would undermine the understanding of the Commission's statement of reasons cannot be accepted.

(23) If there is a complainant involved, the Commission will take into account the complainant's interest in ascertaining the reasons why the Commission adopted a certain decision, without the need to have recourse to Court proceedings.[3] Hence, requests by Member States for parts of the decision which address concerns of complainants to be covered by the obligation of professional secrecy will need to be particularly well reasoned and persuasive. On the other hand, the Commission will not normally be inclined to disclose information alleged to be of the kind covered by the obligation of professional secrecy where there is a suspicion that the complaint has been lodged primarily to obtain access to the information.

(24) Member States cannot invoke professional secrecy to refuse to provide information to the Commission which the Commission considers necessary for the examination of aid measures. In this respect, reference is made to the procedure set out in Regulation (EC) No 659/1999 (in particular Articles 2(2), 5, 10 and 16).

4.2. Procedure

(25) The Commission currently notifies its decisions to the Member State concerned without delay and gives the latter the opportunity to indicate, normally within a time period of 15 working days, which information it considers to be covered by the obligation of professional secrecy. This time period may be extended by agreement between the Commission and the Member State concerned.

(26) Where the Member State concerned does not indicate which information it considers to be covered by the obligation of professional secrecy within the period prescribed by the Commission, the decision will normally be disclosed in full.

(27) Where the Member State concerned wishes certain information to be covered by the obligation of professional secrecy, it must indicate the parts it considers to be covered and provide a justification in respect of each part for which non-disclosure is requested.

(28) The Commission will then examine the request from the Member State without delay. If the Commission does not accept that certain parts of the decision are covered by the obligation of professional secrecy, it will state the reasons why in its view those parts cannot be left out of the public version of the decision. In the absence of an acceptable justification by the Member State for its request (i.e. reasoning which is not manifestly irrelevant or manifestly wrong), the Commission need not further specify the reasons why those parts cannot be left out of the public version of the decision other than by referring to the absence of justification.

(29) If the Commission decides to accept that certain parts are covered by the obligation of professional secrecy without agreeing in full with the Member State's request, it will notify its decision with a new draft to the Member State indicating the parts which have been omitted. If the Commission accepts that the parts indicated by the Member State are covered by the obligation of professional secrecy, the text of the decision will be published pursuant to Article 26 of Regulation (EC) No 659/1999, with the omission of the parts covered by the obligation of professional secrecy. Such omissions will be indicated in the text.[4]

---

[3] Case C-367/95 P Commission v Sytraval [ECR] 1998 I-1719, para 64.

[4] Using square brackets [. . .] and indicating in a footnote 'covered by the obligation of professional secrecy'.

(30) The Member State will have 15 working days following receipt of the Commission's decision stating the reasons for its refusal to accept the non-disclosure of certain parts, to react and provide additional elements to justify its request.

(31) If the Member State concerned does not react further within the period prescribed by the Commission, the Commission will normally publish the decision as indicated in its reply to the original request made by the Member State.

(32) If the Member State concerned does submit any additional elements within the prescribed period, those elements will be examined by the Commission without delay. If the Commission accepts that the parts indicated by the Member State are covered by the obligation of professional secrecy, the text of the decision will be published as set out in paragraph (29).

(33) In the event that it is not possible to reach agreement, the Commission will proceed with the publication of its decision to initiate the formal investigation procedure forthwith. Such decisions must summarise the relevant issues of fact and law, include a preliminary assessment of the aid character of the proposed measure and set out the doubts as to its compatibility with the common market. Clearly certain essential information must be included in order to enable third parties and the other Member States to comment usefully: The duty of the Commission to provide such essential information will normally prevail over any claim to the protection of business secrets or other confidential information. Furthermore, it is in the interest of the beneficiary as well as interested parties to have access to such a decision as quickly as possible. Permitting any delay in this respect would jeopardise the process of State aid control.

(34) In the event that it is not possible to reach agreement on requests for certain information in decisions not to raise objections and decisions to close the formal investigation procedure to be covered by the obligation of professional secrecy, the Commission will notify its final decision to the Member State together with the text it intends to publish, giving the Member State another 15 working days to react. In the absence of an answer which the Commission considers pertinent, the Commission will normally proceed with the publication of the text.

(35) The Commission is currently reviewing its State aid notification forms. In order to avoid unnecessary correspondence with Member States and delay in the publication of decisions, it intends, in the future, to include in the form a question asking whether the notification contains information which should not be published, and the reasons for non-publication. Only if that question is answered in the affirmative will the Commission enter into correspondence with the Member State in respect of specific cases. Similarly, if additional information is required by the Commission, the Member State will have to indicate at the moment it provides the information requested whether such information should not be published, and the reasons for non-publication. If the Commission uses the information thus identified by the Member State in its decision, it will communicate the adopted decision to the Member State, stating the reasons why in its view these parts cannot be left out from the public version of the decision as laid down in paragraph (28).

(36) Once the Commission has decided what text it will publish and notified the Member State of its final decision, it is for the Member State to decide whether or not to make use of any judicial procedures available to it, including any interim measures, within the time limits provided for in Article 230 of the EC Treaty.

4.3. Third parties

(37) Where third parties other than the Member State concerned (for example, complainants, other Member States or the beneficiary) submit information in the context of State aid procedures, these guidelines will be applied *mutatis mutandis*.

4.4. Application in time

(38) These guidelines cannot establish binding legal rules and do not purport to do so. They merely set out in advance, in the interests of sound administration, the manner in which the Commission intends to address the issue of confidentiality in State aid procedures. As a rule, if agreement cannot be reached, the Commission's decision to publish may be the subject of specific judicial review proceedings. As these guidelines merely pertain to procedural matters (and to a large extent set out existing practice), they will be applied with immediate effect, including for decisions not to raise objections[5] adopted before the entry into force of Regulation (EC) No 659/1999 to which third parties seek access.

---

[5] Decisions to initiate the formal investigation procedure and final decisions adopted before that date were already published in full in the *Official Journal of the European Communities*. Prior to publication, Member States could indicate whether any information was covered by the obligation of professional secrecy.

APPENDIX 34

Commission Notice on the determination of the applicable rules for the assessment of unlawful State aid

(notified under document number C(2002) 458)
(2002/C 119/12)
(Text with EEA relevance)

A number of instruments approved by the Commission over the years contain a provision to the effect that unlawful State aid, i.e. aid put into effect in contravention of Article 88(3) of the EC Treaty, shall be assessed in accordance with the texts in force at the time when the aid was granted. This is for example the case for the Community guidelines on State aid for environmental protection[1] and the multisectoral framework on regional aid for large investment projects[2]

For the purpose of transparency and legal certainty, the Commission informs Member States and third parties that it has decided to apply the same rule in respect of all instruments indicating how the Commission will exercise its discretion in order to assess the compatibility of State aid with the common market (frameworks, guidelines, communications, notices). Therefore, the Commission shall always assess the compatibility of unlawful State aid with the common market in accordance with the substantive criteria set out in any instrument in force at the time when the aid was granted.

The present notice is without prejudice to the more specific rules contained in the Community guidelines on State aid for rescuing and restructuring firms in difficulty.[3]

The present notice is without prejudice to the interpretation of Council and Commission regulations in the field of State aid.

---

[1] OJ C37, 3.2.2001, p 3.
[2] OJ C70, 19.3.2002, p 8.
[3] OJ C288, 9.10.1999, p 2.

APPENDIX 35

Notice on cooperation between national courts and the Commission in the State aid field

Notice on cooperation between national courts and the Commission in the State aid field (95/C 312/07)

The purpose of this notice is to offer guidance on cooperation between national courts and the Commission in the State aid field. The notice does not in any way limit the rights conferred on Member States, individuals or undertakings by Community law. It is without prejudice to any interpretation of Community law which may be given by the Court of Justice and the Court of First Instance of the European Communities. Finally, it does not seek to interfere in any way with the fulfilment by national courts of their duties.

I. INTRODUCTION

1. The elimination of internal frontiers between Member States enables undertakings in the Community to expand their activities throughout the internal market and consumers to benefit from increased competition. These advantages must not be jeopardized by distortions of competition caused by aid granted unjustifiably to undertakings. The completion of the internal market thus reaffirms the importance of enforcement of the Community's competition policy.

2. The Court of Justice has delivered a number of important judgments on the interpretation and application of Articles 92 and 93 of the EC Treaty. The Court of First Instance now has jurisdiction over actions by private parties against the Commission's State aid decisions and will thus also contribute to the development of case-law in this field. The Commission is responsible for the day-to-day application of the competition rules under the supervision of the Court of First Instance and the Court of Justice. Public authorities and courts in the Member States, together with the Community's courts and the Commission each assume their own tasks and responsibilities for the enforcement of the EC Treaty's State aid rules, in accordance with the principles laid down by the case-law of the Court of Justice.

3. The proper application of competition policy in the internal market may require effective cooperation between the Commission and national courts. This notice explains how the Commission intends to assist national courts by instituting closer cooperation in the application of Articles 92 and 93 in individual cases. Concern is frequently expressed that the Commission's final decisions in State aid cases are reached some time after the distortions of competition have damaged the interests of third parties. While the Commission is not always in a position to act promptly to safeguard the interests of third parties in State aid matters, national courts may be better placed to ensure that breaches of the last sentence of Article 93(3) are dealt with and remedied.

II. Powers[1]

4. The Commission is the administrative authority responsible for the implementation and development of competition policy in the Community's public interest. National courts are responsible for the protection of rights and the enforcement of duties, usually at the behest of private parties. The Commission must examine all aid measures which fall under Article 92 (1) in order to assess their compatibility with the common market. National courts must make sure that Member States comply with their procedural obligations.

5. The last sentence of Article 93 (3) (in bold below) has direct effect in the legal order of the Member States.

'The Commission shall be informed, in sufficient time to enable it to submit its comments, of any plans to grant or alter aid. If it considers that any such plan is not compatible with the common market having regard to Article 92, it shall without delay initiate the procedure provided for in paragraph 2. **The Member State concerned shall not put its proposed measures into effect until this procedure has resulted in a final decision.**'

6. The prohibition on implementation referred to in the last sentence of Article 93 (3) extends to all aid which has been implemented without being notified[2] and, in the event of notification, operates during the preliminary period and, if the Commission sets in motion the contentious procedure, until the final decision.[3]

---

[1] The Court of Justice has described the roles of the Commission and the national courts in the following way:

'9. As far as the role of the Commission is concerned, the Court pointed out in its judgment in Case 78/96, *Steinlike and Weinlig v Germany* (1977) ECR 595, at para 9, that the intention of the Treaty, in providing through Art 93 for aid to be kept under constant review and supervised by the Commission, is that the finding that aid may be incompatible with the common market is to be arrived at, subject to review by the Court, by means of an appropriate procedure which it is the Commission's responsibility to set in motion.

10. As far as the role of national courts is concerned, the Court held in the same judgment that proceedings may be commenced before national courts requiring those courts to interpret and apply the concept of aid contained in Art 92 in order to determine whether State aid introduced without observance of the preliminary examination procedure provided for in Art 93(3) ought to have been subject to this procedure.

11. The involvement of national courts is the result of the direct effect which the last sentence of Art 93(3) of the Treaty has been held to have. In this respect, the Court stated in its judgment of 11 December 1973 in Case 120/73, *Lorenz v Germany*, (1973) ECR p 1471 that the immediate enforceability of the prohibition on implementation referred to in that Art extends to all aid which has been implemented without being notified and, in the event of notification, operates during the preliminary period, and if the Commission sets in motion the contentious procedure, until the final decision.

14. . . . The principal and exclusive role conferred on the Commission by Arts 92 and 93 of the Treaty, which is to hold aid to be incompatible with the common market where this is appropriate, is fundamentally different from the role of national courts in safeguarding rights which individuals enjoy as a result of the direct effect of the prohibition laid down in the last sentence of Art 93 (3) of the Treaty. Whilst the Commission must examine the compatibility of the proposed aid with the common market, even where the Member State has acted in breach of the prohibition on giving effect to aid, national courts do no more than preserve, until the final decision of the Commission, the rights of individuals faced with a possible breach by State authorities of the prohibition laid down by the last sentence of Art 93 (3).'

Case C-354/90, Fédération nationale du commerce extérieur des produits alimentaires and Syndicat national des négociants et transformateurs de saumon v France (1991) ECR I-5505, paras 9, 10, 11 and 14, at pp 5527 and 5528.

[2] With the exception of 'existing' aid. Such aid may be implemented until the Commission has decided that it is incompatible with the common market: see Case C-387/92, *Banco de Crédito Industrial, now Banco Exterior de Espana v Ayuntamiento de Valencia* (1994) ECR I-877 and Case C-44/93, *Namur—Les Assurances du Crédit v Office National du Ducroire and Belgium* (1994) ECR I-3829.

[3] Case C-354/90, cited at n 1, para 11 at p 5527.

7. Of course a court will have to consider whether the 'proposed measures' constitute State aid within the meaning of Article 92 (1)[4] before reaching a decision under the last sentence of Article 93 (3). The Commission's Decisions and the Court's case-law devote considerable attention to this important question. Accordingly, the notion of State aid must be interpreted widely to encompass not only subsidies, but also tax concessions and investments from public funds made in circumstances in which a private investor would have withheld support.[5] The aid must come from the 'State', which includes all levels, manifestations and emanations of public authority.[6] The aid must favour certain undertakings or the production of certain goods: this serves to distinguish State aid to which Article 92 (1) applies from general measures to which it does not.[7] For example, measures which have neither as their object nor as their effect the favouring of certain undertakings or the production of certain goods, or which apply to persons in accordance with objective criteria without regard to the location, sector or undertaking in which the beneficiary may be employed, are not considered to be State aid.

8. Only the Commission can decide that State aid is 'compatible with the common market', i.e. authorized.

9. In applying Article 92 (1), national courts may of course refer preliminary questions to the Court of Justice pursuant to Article 177 of the EC Treaty and indeed must do so in certain circumstances. They must also request assistance from the Commission by asking it for 'legal or economic information' by analogy with the Court's Delimits[8] judgment in respect of Article 85 of the EC Treaty.

10. The national court's role is to safeguard rights which individuals enjoy as a result of the direct effect of the prohibition laid down in the last sentence of Article 93 (3). The court should use all appropriate devices and remedies and apply all relevant provisions of national law to implement the direct effect of this obligation placed by the Treaty on Member States.[9] A national court must, in a case within its jurisdiction, apply Community law in its entirety and

---

[4] See the Court of Justice's judgment in Case 78/76, *Steinlike and Weinlig v Germany* (1977) ECR 595, para 14: '. . . a national court may have cause to interpret and apply the concept of aid contained in Art 92 in order to determine whether State aid introduced without observance of the preliminary examination procedure provided for in Art 93 (3) ought to have been subject to this procedure'.

[5] For a recent formulation, see Advocate-General Jacob's opinion in Joined Cases C-278/92, C-278/92 and C-280/92, *Spain v Commission* para 28: '. . . State aid is granted whenever a Member State makes available to an undertaking funds which in the normal course of events would not be provided by a private investor applying normal commercial criteria and disregarding other considerations of a social, political or philanthropic nature'.

[6] The Court of Justice held in Case 290/83, *Commission v France* (1985), ECR p 439, that '. . . The prohibition contained in Art 92 covers all aid granted by a Member State or through State resources and there is no necessity to draw any distinction according to whether the aid is granted directly by the State or by public or private bodies established or appointed by it to administer the aid' (para 14 at p 449).

[7] A clear statement of this distinction is to be found in Advocate-General Darmon's opinion in Joined Cases C-72 and C-73/91, *Sloman Neptun*, (1993) ECR I-887.

[8] Case C-234/89, *Delimitis v Henninger Bräu* (1991) ECR I-935; Commission notice on cooperation between national courts and the Commission in applying Arts 85 and 86 of the EC Treaty (OJ No C 39, 13. 12. 1993, p 6). See Advocate-General Lenz's opinion in Case C-44/93, cited at n 2 (para 106). See also Case C-2/88, *Imm, Zwartveld* (1990) ECR I-3365 and I-4405: 'the Community institutions are under a duty of sincere cooperation with the judicial authorities of the Member States, which are responsible for ensuring that Community law is applied and respected in the national legal system' (para 1 at p I-3366 and para 10 at pp 4410 and 4411, respectively).

[9] As the Court of Justice held in Case C-354/90, cited at n 1, para 12 at p 5528: '. . . the validity of measures giving effect to aid is affected if national authorities act in breach of the last sentence of Art 93 (3) of the Treaty. National courts must offer to individuals in a position to rely on such breach the certain prospect that all the necessary inferences will be drawn, in accordance with their national law, as regards the validity of measures giving effect to the aid, the recovery of financial support granted in disregard of that provision and possible interim measures.'

protect rights which that law confers on individuals; it must therefore set aside any provision of national law which may conflict with it, whether prior or subsequent to the Community rule.[10] The judge may, as appropriate and in accordance with applicable rules of national law and the developing case-law of the Court of Justice,[11] grant interim relief, for example by ordering the freezing or return of monies illegally paid, and award damages to parties whose interests are harmed.

11. The Court of Justice has held that the full effectiveness of Community rules would be impaired and the protection of the rights which they grant would be weakened if individuals were unable to obtain redress when their rights are infringed by a breach of Community law for which a Member State can be held responsible:[12] the principle whereby a State must be liable for loss and damage caused to individuals as a result of breaches of Community law for which the State can be held responsible is inherent in the system of the Treaty;[13] a national court which considers, in a case concerning Community law, that the sole obstacle precluding it from granting interim relief is a rule of national law, must set aside that rule.[14]

12. These principles apply in the event of a breach of the Community's competition rules. Individuals and undertakings must have access to all procedural rules and remedies provided for by national law on the same conditions as would apply if a comparable breach of national law were involved. This equality of treatment concerns not only the definitive finding of a breach of directly effective Community law, but extends also to all legal means capable of contributing to effective legal protection.

III. THE COMMISSION'S LIMITED POWERS

13. The application of Community competition law by the national courts has considerable advantages for individuals and undertakings. The Commission cannot award damages for loss suffered as a result of an infringement of Article 93(3). Such claims may be brought only before the national courts. National courts can usually adopt interim measures and order the termination of infringements quickly. Before national courts, it is possible to combine a claim under Community law with a claim under national law. This is not possible in a procedure before the Commission. In addition, courts may award costs to the successful applicant. This is never possible in the administrative procedure before the Commission.

IV. APPLICATION OF ARTICLE 93 (3)

14. Member States are required to notify to the Commission all plans to grant aid or to alter aid plans already approved. This also applies to aid that may qualify for automatic approval under Article 92 (2), because the Commission has to check that the requisite conditions are met. The only exception to the notification obligation is for aid classed as de minimis because

---

[10] Case 106/77, *Amministrazione delle Finanze dello Stato v Simmenthal*, (1978) ECR 629, (para 21 at p 644). See also Case C-213/89, *The Queen v Secretary of State for Transport, ex parte: Factortame Ltd et al*, (1990) ECR I-2433, at p 2475.

[11] Joined Cases C-6/90 and C-9/90, *Andrea Francovich et al v Italy*, (1991) ECR I-5357. Other important cases are pending before the Court concerning the responsibilities of national courts in the application of Community law: Case C-48/93, *The Queen v Secretary of State for Transport, ex parte: Factortame Ltd. and others* (OJ No C 94, 3. 4. 1993, p 13); Case C-46/93, *Brasserie du Pêcheur SA v Germany* (OJ No C 92, 2. 4. 1993, p 4); Case C-312/93, *SCS Peterbroeck, Van Campenhout & Cie v Belgian State* (OJ No C 189, 13. 7. 1993, p 9); Cases C-430 and C-431/93, *J Van Schindel and J N C Van Veen v Stichting Pensioenfonds voor Fysiotherapeuten* (OJ No C 338, 15. 12. 1993, p 10).

[12] Francovich, cited at n 11, para 33 at p 5414.

[13] Francovich, cited at n 11, para 35 at p 5414.

[14] *The Queen v Secretary of State for Transport, ex parte: Factortame Ltd. et al*, cited at n 10.

it does not affect trade between Member States significantly and thus does not fall within Article 92 (1).[15]

15. The Commission receives notification of general schemes or programmes of aid, as well as of plans to grant aid to individual firms. Once a scheme has been authorized by the Commission, individual awards of aid under the scheme do not normally have to be notified. However, under some of the aid codes or frameworks for particular industries or particular types of aid, individual notification is required of all awards of aid or of awards exceeding a certain amount. Individual notification may also be required in some cases by the terms of the Commission's authorization of a given scheme. Member States must notify aid which they wish to grant outside the framework of an authorized scheme. Notification is required in respect of planned measures, including plans to make financial transfers from public funds to public or private sector enterprises, which may involve aid within the meaning of Article 92 (1).

16. The first question which national courts have to consider in an action under the last sentence of Article 93 (3) is whether the measure constitutes new or existing State aid within the meaning aid of Article 92 (1). The second question to be answered is whether the measure has been notified either individually or under a scheme and if so, whether the Commission has had sufficient time to come to a decision.[16]

17. With respect to aid schemes, a period of two months is considered by the Court of Justice to be 'sufficient time', after which the Member State concerned may, after giving the Commission prior notice, implement the notified measure.[17] This period is reduced by the Commission voluntarily to 30 working days for individual cases and 20 working days under the 'accelerated' procedure. The periods run from the time the Commission is satisfied that the information provided by the Member State is sufficient to enable it to reach a decision.[18]

18. If the Commission has decided to initiate the procedure provided for in Article 93 (2), the period during which the implementation of an aid measure is prohibited runs until the Commission has reached a positive decision. For non-notified aid measures, no deadline exists for the Commission's decision-making process, although the Commission will act as speedily as possible. Aid may not be awarded before the Commission's final decision.

19. If the Commission has not ruled on an aid measure, national courts can always be guided, in interpreting Community law, by the case-law of the Court of First Instance and the Court of Justice, as well as by decisions issued by the Commission. The Commission has published a number of general notices which may be of assistance in this regard.[19]

20. National courts should thus be able to decide whether or not the measure at issue is illegal under Article 93 (3). Where national courts have doubts, they may and in some cases must request a preliminary ruling from the Court of Justice in accordance with Article 77.

21. Where national courts give judgment finding that Article 93 (3) has not been complied with, they must rule that the measure at issue infringes Community law and take the appropriate measures to safeguard the rights enjoyed by individuals and undertakings.

---

[15] See point 3.2 of the Community Guidelines on State aid for SMEs (OJ No C 213, 19. 8. 1992, p 2) and the letter to the Member States ref. IV/D/06878 of 23 March 1993, Competition Law in the European Communities, Volume II.

[16] Case 120/73, *Lorenz v Germany*, (1973) ECR 1471.

[17] Case 120/73, *Lorenz v Germany*, cited at n 16, para 4 at p 1481; see also Case 84/42, Germany v Commission, (1984) ECR 1451, para 11 at p 1488.

[18] The Commission has issued a guide to its procedures in State aid cases: see Competition Law in the European Communities, Volume II.

[19] The Commission publishes and updates from time to time a compendium of State aid rules (Competition Law in the European Communities, Volume II).

V. Effects of Commission Decisions

22. The Court of Justice has held[20] that a national court is bound by a Commission Decision addressed to a Member State under Article 93 (2) where the beneficiary of the aid in question seeks to question the validity of the decision of which it had been informed in writing by the Member State concerned and where it had failed to bring an action for annulment of the decision within the time limits prescribed by Article 173 of the EC Treaty.

VI. Cooperation between National Courts and the Commission

23. The Commission realizes that the principles set out above for the application of Articles 92 and 93 by national courts are complex and may sometimes be insufficiently developed to enable them to carry out their judicial duties properly. National courts may therefore ask the Commission for assistance.

24. Article 5 of the EC Treaty establishes the principle of loyal and constant cooperation between the Community institutions and the Member States with a view to attaining the objectives of the Treaty, including implementation of Article 3 (g), which provides for the establishment of a system ensuring that competition in the internal market is not distorted. This principle involves obligations and duties of mutual assistance, both for the Member States and for the Community institutions. Under Article 5, the Commission has a duty of cooperation with the judicial authorities of the Member States which are responsible for ensuring that Community law is applied and respected in the national legal order.

25. The Commission considers that such cooperation is essential in order to guarantee the strict, effective and consistent application of Community competition law. In addition, participation by the national courts in the application of competition law in the field of State aid is necessary to give effect to Article 93 (3). The Treaty obliges the Commission to follow the procedure laid down in Article 93 (2) before it can order reimbursement of aid which is incompatible with the common market.[21] The Court has ruled that Article 93 (3) has direct effect and that the illegality of an aid measure, and the consequences that flow therefrom, can never be validated retroactively by a positive decision of the Commission on an aid measure. Application of the rules on notification in the field of State aid therefore constitutes an essential link in the chain of possible legal action by individuals and undertakings.

26. In the light of these considerations, the Commission intends to work towards closer cooperation with national courts in the following manner.

27. The Commission is committed to a policy of openness and transparency. The Commission conducts its policy so as to give the parties concerned useful information on the application of competition rules. To this end, it will continue to publish as much information as possible about State aid cases and policy. The case-law of the Court of Justice and Court of First Instance, general texts on State aid published by the Commission, decisions taken by the Commission, the Commission's annual reports on competition policy and the monthly. Bulletin of the European Union may assist national courts in examining individual cases.

---

[20] Case C-188/92, *TWD Textilwerke Deggendorf GmbH v Germany*, (1994) ECR I-833; see also Case 77/72, *Capolongo v Maya*, (1973) ECR 611.

[21] The Commission has informed the Member States that '. . . in appropriate cases it may—after giving the Member State concerned the opportunity to comment and to consider alternatively the granting of rescue aid, as defined by the Community guidelines—adopt a provisional decision ordering the Member State to recover any monies which have been disbursed in infringement of the procedural requirements. The aid would have to be recovered in accordance with the requirements of domestic law; the sum repayable would carry interest running from the time the aid was paid out.' (Commission communication to the Member States supplementing the Commission's letter No SG(91) D/4577 of 4 March 1991 concerning the procedures for the notification of aid plans and procedures applicable when aid is provided in breach of the rules of Art 93 (3) of the EC Treaty), not yet published.

28. If these general pointers are insufficient, national courts may, within the limits of their national procedural law, ask the Commission for information of a procedural nature to enable them to discover whether a certain case is pending before the Commission, whether a case has been the subject of a notification or whether the Commission has officially initiated a procedure or taken any other decision.

29. National courts may also consult the Commission where the application of Article 92 (1) or Article 93 (3) causes particular difficulties. As far as Article 92 (1) is concerned, these difficulties may relate in particular to the characterization of the measure as State aid, the possible distortion of competition to which it may give rise and the effect on trade between Member States. Courts may therefore consult the Commission on its customary practice in relation to these issues. They may obtain information from the Commission regarding factual data, statistics, market studies and economic analyses. Where possible, the Commission will communicate these data or will indicate the source from which they can be obtained.

30. In its answer, the Commission will not go into the substance of the individual case or the compatibility of the measure with the common market. The answer given by the Commission will not be binding on the requesting court. The Commission will make it clear that its view is not definitive and that the court's right to request a preliminary ruling from the Court of Justice pursuant to Article 177 is unaffected.

31. It is in the interests of the proper administration of justice that the Commission should answer requests for legal and factual information in the shortest possible time. Nevertheless, the Commission cannot accede to such requests unless several conditions are met. The requisite data must actually be at its disposal and the Commission may communicate only non-confidential information.

32. Article 214 of the EC Treaty requires the Commission not to disclose information of a confidential nature. In addition, the duty of loyal cooperation under Article 5 applies to the relationship between courts and the Commission, and does not concern the parties to the dispute pending before those courts. The Commission is obliged to respect legal neutrality and objectivity. Consequently, it will not accede to requests for information unless they come from a national court, either directly, or indirectly through parties which have been ordered by the court concerned to request certain information.

VII. FINAL REMARKS

33. This notice applies *mutatis mutandis* to relevant State aid rules, in so far as they have direct effect in the legal order of Member States, of:
— the Treaty establishing the European Coal and Steel Community and provisions adopted thereunder, and
— the Agreement on the European Economic Area.

34. This notice is issued for guidance and does not in any way limit the rights conferred on Member States, individuals or undertakings by Community law.

35. This notice is without prejudice to any interpretation of Community law which may be given by the Court of Justice and Court of First Instance of the European Communities.

36. A summary of the answers given by the Commission pursuant to this notice will be published annually in the Report on Competition Policy.

Council Regulation (EC) No 994/98 of 7 May 1998 on the application of Articles 92 and 93 of the Treaty establishing the European Community to certain categories of horizontal State aid

THE COUNCIL OF THE EUROPEAN UNION,

Having regard to the Treaty establishing the European Community, and in particular Article 94 thereof,

Having regard to the proposal from the Commission,[1]

After consulting the European Parliament,[2]

Having regard to the opinion of the Economic and Social Committee,[3]

(1) Whereas, pursuant to Article 94 of the Treaty, the Council may make any appropriate regulations for the application of Articles 92 and 93 and may, in particular, determine the conditions in which Article 93(3) shall apply and the categories of aid exempted from this procedure;

(2) Whereas, under the Treaty, the assessment of compatibility of aid with the common market essentially rests with the Commission;

(3) Whereas the proper functioning of the internal market requires strict and efficient application of the rules of competition with regard to State aids;

(4) Whereas the Commission has applied Articles 92 and 93 of the Treaty in numerous decisions and has also stated its policy in a number of communications; whereas, in the light of the Commission's considerable experience in applying Articles 92 and 93 of the Treaty and the general texts issued by the Commission on the basis of those provisions, it is appropriate, with a view to ensuring efficient supervision and simplifying administration, without weakening Commission monitoring, that the Commission should be enabled to declare by means of regulations, in areas where the Commission has sufficient experience to define general compatibility criteria, that certain categories of aid are compatible with the common market pursuant to one or more of the provisions of Article 92(2) and (3) of the Treaty and are exempted from the procedure provided for in Article 93(3) thereof;

(5) Whereas group exemption regulations will increase transparency and legal certainty; whereas they can be directly applied by national courts, without prejudice to Articles 5 and 177 of the Treaty;

(6) Whereas it is appropriate that the Commission, when it adopts regulations exempting categories of aid from the obligation to notify provided for in Article 93(3) of the Treaty, specifies the purpose of the aid, the categories of beneficiaries and thresholds limiting the exempted aid, the conditions governing the cumulation of aid and the conditions of monitoring, in order to ensure the compatibility with the common market of aid covered by this Regulation;

---

[1] OJ C262, 28.8.1997, p 6.
[2] OJ C138, 4.5.1998.
[3] OJ C129, 27.4.1998, p 70.

(7) Whereas it is appropriate to enable the Commission, when it adopts regulations exempting certain categories of aid from the obligation to notify in Article 93(3) of the Treaty, to attach further detailed conditions in order to ensure the compatibility with the common market of aid covered by this Regulation;

(8) Whereas it may be useful to set thresholds of other appropriate conditions requiring the notification of awards of aid in order to allow the Commission to examine individually the effect of certain aid on competition and trade between Member States and its compatibility with the common market;

(9) Whereas the Commission, having regard to the development and the functioning of the common market, should be enabled to establish by means of a regulation that certain aid does not fullfil all the criteria of Article 92(1) of the Treaty and is therefore exempted from the notification procedure laid down in Article 93(3), provided that aid granted to the same undertaking over a given period of time does not exceed a certain fixed amount;

(10) Whereas in accordance with Article 93(1) of the Treaty the Commission is under an obligation, in cooperation with Member States, to keep under constant review all systems of existing aid; whereas for this purpose and in order to ensure the largest possible degree of transparency and adequate control it is desirable that the Commission ensures the establishment of a reliable system of recording and storing information about the application of the regulations it adopts, to which all Member States have access, and that it receives all necessary information from the Member States on the implementation of aid exempted from notification to fulfil this obligation, which may be examined and evaluated with the Member States within the Advisory Committee; whereas for this purpose it is also desirable that the Commission may require such information to be supplied as is necessary to ensure the efficiency of such review;

(11) Whereas the control of the granting of aid involves factual, legal and economic issues of a very complex nature and great variety in a constantly evolving environment; whereas the Commission should therefore regularly review the categories of aid which should be exempted from notification; whereas the Commission should be able to repeal or amend regulations it has adopted pursuant to this Regulation where circumstances have changed with respect to any important element which constituted grounds for their adoption or where the progressive development or the functioning of the common market so requires;

(12) Whereas the Commission, in close and constant liaison with the Member States, should be able to define precisely the scope of these regulations and the conditions attached to them; whereas, in order to provide for cooperation between the Commission and the competent authorities of the Member States, it is appropriate to set up an advisory committee on State aid to be consulted before the Commission adopts regulations pursuant to this Regulation,

HAS ADOPTED THIS REGULATION:

Article 1

Group exemptions

1. The Commission may, by means of regulations adopted in accordance with the procedures laid down in Article 8 of this Regulation and in accordance with Article 92 of the Treaty, declare that the following categories of aid should be compatible with the common market and shall not be subject to the notification requirements of Article 93(3) of the Treaty:

(a) aid in favour of:

    (i)   small and medium-sized enterprises;

    (ii) research and development;

    (iii) environmental protection;

    (iv) employment and training;

(b) aid that complies with the map approved by the Commission for each Member State for the grant of regional aid.

2. The Regulations referred to in paragraph 1 shall specify for each category of aid:

(a) the purpose of the aid;

(b) the categories of beneficiaries;

(c) thresholds expressed either in terms of aid intensities in relation to a set of eligible costs or in terms of maximum aid amounts;

(d) the conditions governing the cumulation of aid;

(e) the conditions of monitoring as specified in Article 3.

3. In addition, the regulations referred to in paragraph 1 may, in particular:

(a) set thresholds or other conditions for the notification of awards of individual aid;

(b) exclude certain sectors from their scope;

(c) attach further conditions for the compatibility of aid exempted under such regulations.

Article 2
De minimis

1. The Commission may, by means of a Regulation adopted in accordance with the procedure laid down in Article 8 of this Regulation, decide that, having regard to the development and functioning of the common market, certain aids do not meet all the criteria of Article 92(1) and that they are therefore exempted from the notification procedure provided for in Article 93(3), provided that aid granted to the same undertaking over a given period of time does not exceed a certain fixed amount.

2. At the Commission's request, Member States shall, at any time, communicate to it any additional information relating to aid exempted under paragraph 1.

Article 3
Transparency and monitoring

1. When adopting regulations pursuant to Article 1, the Commission shall impose detailed rules upon Member States to ensure transparency and monitoring of the aid exempted from notification in accordance with those regulations. Such rules shall consist, in particular, of the requirements laid down in paragraphs 2, 3 and 4.

2. On implementation of aid systems or individual aids granted outside any system, which have been exempted pursuant to such regulations, Member States shall forward to the Commission, with a view to publication in the *Official Journal of the European Communities*, summaries of the information regarding such systems of aid or such individual aids as are not covered by exempted aid systems.

3. Member States shall record and compile all the information regarding the application of the group exemptions. If the Commission has information which leads it to doubt that an exemption regulation is being applied properly, the Member States shall forward to it any information it considers necessary to assess whether an aid complies with that regulation.

4. At least once a year, Member States shall supply the Commission with a report on the application of group exemptions, in accordance with the Commission's specific requirements, preferably in computerised form. The Commission shall make access to those reports available to all the Member States. The Advisory Committee referred to in Article 7 shall examine and evaluate those reports once a year.

Article 4
Period of validity and amendment of regulations

1. Regulations adopted pursuant to Articles 1 and 2 shall apply for a specific period. Aid exempted by a regulation adopted pursuant to Articles 1 and 2 shall be exempted for the period of validity of that regulation and for the adjustment period provided for in paragraphs 2 and 3.

2. Regulations adopted pursuant to Articles 1 and 2 may be repeated or amended where circumstances have changed with respect to any important element that constituted grounds for their adoption or where the progressive development or the functioning of the common market so requires. In that case the new regulation shall set a period of adjustment of six months for the adjustment of aid covered by the previous regulation.

3. Regulations adopted pursuant to Articles 1 and 2 shall provide for a period as referred to in paragraph 2, should their application not be extended when they expire.

Article 5
Evaluation report

Every five years the Commission shall submit a report to the European Parliament and to the Council on the application of this Regulation. It shall submit a draft report for consideration by the Advisory Committee referred to in Article 7.

Article 6
Hearing of interested parties

Where the Commission intends to adopt a regulation, it shall publish a draft thereof to enable all interested persons and organisations to submit their comments to it within a reasonable time limit to be fixed by the Commission and which may not under any circumstances be less than one month.

Article 7
Advisory committee

An advisory committee, hereinafter referred to as the Advisory Committee on State Aid, shall be set up. It shall be composed of representatives of the Member States and chaired by the representative of the Commission.

Article 8
Consultation of the Advisory Committee

1. The Commission shall consult the Advisory Committee on State Aid:

(a) before publishing any draft regulation;
(b) before adopting any regulation;

2. Consultation of the Committee shall take place at a meeting called by the Commission. The drafts and documents to be examined shall be annexed to the notification. The meeting shall take place no earlier than two months after notification has been sent.

This period may be reduced in the case of the consultations referred to in paragraph 1(b), when urgent or for simple extension of a regulation.

3. The representative of the Commission shall submit to the Committee a draft of the measures to be taken. The Committee shall deliver its opinion on the draft, within a time limit which the Chairman may lay down according to the urgency of the matter, if necessary by taking a vote.

4. The opinion shall be recorded in the minutes; in addition, each Member State shall have the right to ask to have its position recorded in the minutes. The Advisory Committee may recommend publication of the opinion in the *Official Journal of the European Communities*.

5. The Commission shall take the utmost account of the opinion delivered by the Committee. It shall inform the Committee of the manner in which its opinion has been taken into account.

Article 9

Final provisions

This Regulation shall enter into force on the day following its publication in the *Official Journal of the European Communities.*

This Regulation shall be binding in its entirety and directly applicable in all Member States.

Done at Brussels, 7 May 1998.

For the Council
The President
M. BECKETT

EUROPEAN ECONOMIC AREA COMPETITION PROCEDURE

Part V

EUROPEAN ECONOMIC AREA
COMPETITION PROCEDURE

APPENDIX 37

EEA Agreement as amended by the EEA Enlargement Agreement

PART IV COMPETITION AND OTHER COMMON RULES

CHAPTER 1. RULES APPLICABLE TO UNDERTAKINGS

Article 53

1. The following shall be prohibited as incompatible with the functioning of this Agreement: all agreements between undertakings, decisions by associations of undertakings and concerted practices which may affect trade between Contracting Parties and which have as their object or effect the prevention, restriction or distortion of competition within the territory covered by this Agreement, and in particular those which:

    (a) directly or indirectly fix purchase or selling prices or any other trading conditions;
    (b) limit or control production, markets, technical development, or investment;
    (c) share markets or sources of supply;
    (d) apply dissimilar conditions to equivalent transactions with other trading parties, thereby placing them at a competitive disadvantage;
    (e) make the conclusion of contracts subject to acceptance by the other parties of supplementary obligations which, by their nature or according to commercial usage, have no connection with the subject of such contracts.

2. Any agreements or decisions prohibited pursuant to this Article shall be automatically void.

3. The provisions of paragraph 1 may, however, be declared inapplicable in the case of:

    — any agreement or category of agreements between undertakings;
    — any decision or category of decisions by associations of undertakings;
    — any concerted practice or category of concerted practices;

    which contributes to improving the production or distribution of goods or to promoting technical or economic progress, while allowing consumers a fair share of the resulting benefit, and which does not:

    (a) impose on the undertakings concerned restrictions which are not indispensable to the attainment of these objectives;
    (b) afford such undertakings the possibility of eliminating competition in respect of a substantial part of the products in question.

Article 54

Any abuse by one or more undertakings of a dominant position within the territory covered by this Agreement or in a substantial part of it shall be prohibited as incompatible with the functioning of this Agreement in so far as it may affect trade between Contracting Parties.

Such abuse may, in particular, consist in:

(a) directly or indirectly imposing unfair purchase or selling prices or other unfair trading conditions;

(b) limiting production, markets or technical development to the prejudice of consumers;

(c) applying dissimilar conditions to equivalent transactions with other trading parties, thereby placing them at a competitive disadvantage;

(d) making the conclusion of contracts subject to acceptance by the other parties of supplementary obligations which, by their nature or according to commercial usage, have no connection with the subject of such contracts.

Article 55

1. Without prejudice to the provisions giving effect to Articles 53 and 54 as contained in Protocol 21 and Annex XIV of this Agreement, the EC Commission and the EFTA Surveillance Authority provided for in Article 108(1) shall ensure the application of the principles laid down in Articles 53 and 54.

   The competent surveillance authority, as provided for in Article 56, shall investigate cases of suspected infringement of these principles, on its own initiative, or on application by a State within the respective territory or by the other surveillance authority. The competent surveillance authority shall carry out these investigations in cooperation with the competent national authorities in the respective territory and in cooperation with the other surveillance authority, which shall give it its assistance in accordance with its internal rules.

   If it finds that there has been an infringement, it shall propose appropriate measures to bring it to an end.

2. If the infringement is not brought to an end, the competent surveillance authority shall record such infringement of the principles in a reasoned decision.

   The competent surveillance authority may publish its decision and authorize States within the respective territory to take the measures, the conditions and details of which it shall determine, needed to remedy the situation. It may also request the other surveillance authority to authorize States within the respective territory to take such measures.

Article 56

1. Individual cases falling under Article 53 shall be decided upon by the surveillance authorities in accordance with the following provisions:

   (a) individual cases where only trade between EFTA States is affected shall be decided upon by the EFTA Surveillance Authority;

   (b) without prejudice to subparagraph (c), the EFTA Surveillance Authority decides, as provided for in the provisions set out in Article 58, Protocol 21 and the rules adopted for its implementation, Protocol 23 and Annex XIV, on cases where the turnover of the undertakings concerned in the territory of the EFTA States equals 33 per cent or more of their turnover in the territory covered by this Agreement;

   (c) the EC Commission decides on the other cases as well as on cases under (b) where trade between EC Member States is affected, taking into account the provisions set out in Article 58, Protocol 21, Protocol 23 and Annex XIV.

2. Individual cases falling under Article 54 shall be decided upon by the surveillance authority in the territory of which a dominant position is found to exist. The rules set out in paragraph 1(b) and (c) shall apply only if dominance exists within the territories of both surveillance authorities.

3. Individual cases falling under subparagraph (c) of paragraph 1, whose effects on trade between EC Member States or on competition within the Community are not appreciable, shall be decided upon by the EFTA Surveillance Authority.

4. The terms 'undertaking' and 'turnover' are, for the purposes of this Article, defined in Protocol 22.

Article 57

1. Concentrations the control of which is provided for in paragraph 2 and which create or strengthen a dominant position as a result of which effective competition would be significantly impeded within the territory covered by this Agreement or a substantial part of it, shall be declared incompatible with this Agreement.

2. The control of concentrations falling under paragraph 1 shall be carried out by:

    (a) the EC Commission in cases falling under Regulation (EEC) No 4064/89 in accordance with that Regulation and in accordance with Protocols 21 and 24 and Annex XIV to this Agreement. The EC Commission shall, subject to the review of the EC Court of Justice, have sole competence to take decisions on these cases;

    (b) the EFTA Surveillance Authority in cases not falling under subparagraph (a) where the relevant thresholds set out in Annex XIV are fulfilled in the territory of the EFTA States in accordance with Protocols 21 and 24 and Annex XIV. This is without prejudice to the competence of EC Member States.

Article 58

With a view to developing and maintaining a uniform surveillance throughout the European Economic Area in the field of competition and to promoting a homogeneous implementation, application and interpretation of the provisions of this Agreement to this end, the competent authorities shall cooperate in accordance with the provisions set out in Protocols 23 and 24.

Article 59

1. In the case of public undertakings and undertakings to which EC Member States or EFTA States grant special or exclusive rights, the Contracting Parties shall ensure that there is neither enacted nor maintained in force any measure contrary to the rules contained in this Agreement, in particular to those rules provided for in Articles 4 and 53 to 63.

2. Undertakings entrusted with the operation of services of general economic interest or having the character of a revenue-producing monopoly shall be subject to the rules contained in this Agreement, in particular to the rules on competition, in so far as the application of such rules does not obstruct the performance, in law or in fact, of the particular tasks assigned to them. The development of trade must not be affected to such an extent as would be contrary to the interests of the Contracting Parties.

3. The EC Commission as well as the EFTA Surveillance Authority shall ensure within their respective competence the application of the provisions of this Article and shall, where necessary, address appropriate measures to the States falling within their respective territory.

Article 60

Annex XIV contains specific provisions giving effect to the principles set out in Articles 53, 54, 57 and 59.

APPENDIX ON THE AGREEMENT ON THE EUROPEAN ECONOMIC AREA:

SECTION I: INTRODUCTION TO THE AGREEMENT ON THE EUROPEAN ECONOMIC AREA

This Appendix seeks to set out the general structure of the competition provisions and procedure applicable under the Agreement on the European Economic Area ('EEA Agreement'). It will briefly set out the background to the EEA Agreement, before describing its substantive competition rules, the procedure to be followed in their application and the allocation of jurisdiction between the EC Commission and the EFTA Surveillance Authority in that application. In practical terms, the scope of application of the EEA provisions is relatively limited. Nonetheless, undertakings situated in Iceland, Liechtenstein and Norway, or undertakings doing business with those countries will need to take heed of the EEA provisions. This Appendix is therefore intended to provide only a brief overview of some of the key procedural aspects and differences in EEA competition law. Practitioners in this area are referred to more detailed practitioners' texts for further information.[1] The EEA provisions corresponding to EC Merger control, State Monopolies and State Aids (Articles 90 and 92–93 EC) and those mirroring the ECSC Articles will not be dealt with, in keeping with the main body of this work.

A. Formation and general Institutional Framework

The European Free Trade Association (EFTA) was established in 1960 by Austria, Denmark, Norway, Portugal, Sweden, Switzerland and the United Kingdom. Its goal was to reduce or remove import duties, quotas and other obstacles to trade in Western Europe and to uphold liberal, non-discriminatory practices in world trade. Iceland joined EFTA in 1970 while Finland became an associate member in 1961 and a full member in 1986. Liechtenstein became a member in 1991. Six members have since left EFTA to join the European Union ('EU'): the United Kingdom and Denmark in 1973; Portugal in 1986; and Austria, Finland and Sweden in 1995. Norway completed negotiations for accession to the EU, but decided against membership in a referendum in November 1994. The present members of EFTA are therefore Iceland, Liechtenstein, Norway and Switzerland.[2]

EFTA membership served as a platform for EFTA members to negotiate a specific agreement with Member States of the European Community for an extension of the internal market to those countries. The resultant EEA Agreement came into force on 1 January 1994.[3] It was first signed on 2 May 1992 at Oporto, Portugal, between the European Community, its then twelve Member States and the seven other countries[4] of EFTA. Since that date, Austria, Finland and Sweden have joined the EU. Switzerland is no longer a contracting party to the EEA Agreement.[5] Liechtenstein

---

[1] See, *inter alia*, Norberg, S, Hökborg, K, Johansson, M, Eliasson, D, and Dedichen, L, *The European Economic Area, EEA Law: A Commentary on the EEA Agreement*, Kluwer, Deventer, 1993 and Blanchet, T, Piipponen, R, and Westman-Clément, M, *The Agreement on the European Economic Area (EEA). A Guide to the free Movement of Goods and Competition Rules*, Clarendon Press, Oxford, 1994.

[2] See the Model Yearbook entry for EFTA found in the EFTA Secretariat's web site at www.secretariat.efta.int/Web/EFTAAtAGlance/.

[3] See Decision 94/1/ECSC, EC of the Council and Commission of 13 December 1993 on the conclusion of the Agreement on the European Economic Area, together with the Final Act, 1994 OJ L1, p 1; and Decision 94/2/ECSC, EC of the Council and Commission of 13 December 1993 on the conclusion of the Protocol adjusting the Agreement on the European Economic Area together with the Protocol, 1994 OJ L1, p 571. A special edition of the *Common Market Law Reports* contains the original EEA Treaty and EFTA Surveillance Agreement, together with the relevant Notices and Guidelines. See [1994] 5 CMLR Parts 2 and 3. See also Charlton, H, 'EC Competition Law: The New Regime under the EEA Agreement', *European Competition Law Review*, Vol 15, No 2, March 1994, pp 55–59; Diem, A, 'EEA Competition Law' *European Competition Law Review*, Vol 15, No 5, November-December 1994, p 263–271; Broberg, M, 'The Delimitation of Jurisdiction with regard to Concentration Control under the EEA Agreement' *European Competition Law Review*, Vol 16, No 1, January-February 1995, pp 30–39.

[4] Austria, Finland, Iceland, Liechtenstein, Norway, Sweden and Switzerland.

[5] In a referendum on 6 December 1992, a majority of both the Cantons and citizens voted against membership. A Protocol to the Agreement was signed on 17 March 1993, recognizing this change. Switzerland remains a party to the EFTA Convention, originally signed in 1960 in Stockholm. The original Stockholm Convention was replaced and updated in Vaduz in 2001. Art 18 of the Vaduz Convention (i.e. the updated EFTA Convention) requires Member States to recognise that conduct equivalent to that prohibited by Arts 81 and 82 EC is incompatible with the Convention.

became a full member of the EEA on 1 May 1995.[6] Further, the enlargement of the EU on 1 May 2004 has been reflected in the EEA Agreement.[7]

In December 2002, the ten countries acceding to the EU applied for EEA membership. Negotiations for their admission were successful. The EEA Enlargement Agreement was signed on 14 October 2003.[8] There was therefore a parallel enlargement of the EEA and EU on 1 May 2004.[9] Thus, after various modifications,[10] the EEA now encompasses the newly enlarged European Union, together with Iceland, Liechtenstein and Norway.

The EEA Agreement is an international treaty that is considered to be *sui generis* and which contains a distinct legal order of its own.[11] The Agreement, whilst falling short of a customs union, has created the world's largest integrated economic area.[12] The 28 EEA countries now represent a single market in services, capital, and manufactured goods for over 400 million people. The EEA Agreement reiterates the '*acquis communautaire*' in seeking to establish the 'four freedoms' of the EC Treaty in the EEA territory, as well as covering a wide range of areas linked to the achievement of the four freedoms, such as social policy, consumer protection, the environment, and competition.[13]

The EEA Enlargement Agreement consists of a main agreement listing the amendments to be made to the previous text of the EEA Agreement. The Protocols and Annexes to the EEA Agreement have also been amended to take into account the changes made to the Community *acquis* by the EU Treaty of Accession. This has been done by a simple cross-referencing technique.[14] A consolidated version of the EEA Agreement can be found on the EFTA Secretariat website.[15]

---

[6] Liechtenstein was obliged initially to wait for an EEA Council resolution confirming that its custom union with Switzerland would not adversely affect the functioning of the EEA before fully taking part.

[7] Art 128 of the EEA Agreement provides that any European country becoming a member of the European Community shall also apply for membership of the EEA. Applications are submitted to the EEA Council and subject to ratification by all parties to the EEA Agreement.

[8] The Agreement on the participation of the Czech Republic, the Republic of Estonia, the Republic of Cyprus, the Republic of Latvia, the Republic of Lithuania, the Republic of Hungary, the Republic of Malta, the Republic of Poland, the Republic of Slovenia and the Slovak Republic in the European Economic Area signed on 14 October 2003 in Luxembourg, OJ L130, 29.4.2004, p 3. See also Decision of the EEA Joint Committee No 68/2004 of 4 May 2004 extending the application of certain Decisions of the EEA Joint Committee to the New Contracting Parties and amending certain Annexes to the EEA Agreement following the enlargement of the European Union, 2004 OJ L277, p 187, 26.08.04.

[9] The national parliaments of all 28 contracting parties to the EEA Enlargement Agreement were expected to ratify the Instruments by the end of 2004. In the meantime, the EEA/EFTA states and the EU signed an agreement (constituted by an exchange of letters) that permitted the EEA Enlargement Agreement to enter into force provisionally on 1 May 2004. See OJ 2004 L No. 130, 29.4.2004, p 1.

[10] Some of these, as above, were brought about by the political process. Others, such as changes to the institutional structure, came as a response to a European Court of Justice ('ECJ') opinion, Opinion 1/91 of 14 December 1991, [1991] ECR I–6079 which held that the judicial system as initially established by the EEA Agreement was incompatible with the Treaty of Rome. An amended Agreement received the blessing of the ECJ in Opinion 1/92 [1992] ECR I–282 and was signed in its revised form by the parties on 2 May 1992.

[11] See the Advisory Opinion of the EFTA Court of 10 December 1998, Case E-9/97 *Erla María Sveinbjörnsdóttir v Iceland* [1999] 1 C.M.L.R. 884, at para 59.

[12] See the Advisory Opinion of the EFTA Court in Case E-2/97 *Mag Instrument Inc v California Trading Company Norway* [1997] EFTA Court Report 127, at para 25.

[13] For general information on the EEA Competition provisions, see the website of the EFTA Surveillance Authority (www.eftasurv.int/about/) and the overview provided on the European Commission's website at http://europa.eu.int/comm/external relations/eea/.

[14] See OJ 2004 L No. 130, 29.4.2004, p 3 and EEA Supplement No 23, 29.4.2004, p 1. Art 3 of the Enlargement Agreement states that all amendments made to the Community *acquis* by the EU Act of Accession are hereby "incorporated into and made part" of the EEA Agreement. Annex A to the Enlargement Agreement lists all the acts referred to in the Annexes of the EEA Agreement that have been amended by the EU Act of Accession and indicates where these acts are to be found in the EEA Agreement.

[15] http://secretariat.efta.int/Web/LegalCorner/.

The EEA Agreement is founded on a 'two-pillar' approach, with each 'pillar', the EC side and the EFTA[16] side, responsible for its own share of the work. The Agreement sets up several joint institutions.[17] The EEA Council is the highest political body. The EEA Joint Parliamentary Committee and the EEA Consultative Committee are intended to coordinate at a political level with their EU counterparts. The EEA Joint Committee takes decisions and administers the Agreement. All decisions made by these institutions must meet with unanimous agreement from the relevant EU institutions.

The EFTA States, through two Agreements signed on 2 May 1992,[18] have created three additional institutions to ensure the proper functioning of the EEA Agreement, which are of particular relevance to the EEA competition provisions.

First, the EFTA Surveillance Authority ('ESA'),[19] an independent body with powers similar to those of the EC Commission, which is in charge of ensuring that the EFTA States fulfill their obligations. It is also responsible for ensuring the application of the competition rules. Based in Brussels, the ESA is led by a College of three Members, one from each EFTA State participating in the EEA.[20] College Members are appointed by common agreement of the governments of the EFTA/EEA States for a period of four years. A President is appointed from among the College Members for a period of two years. The College is completely independent of other institutions, as well as of the EFTA States. It takes decisions according to the majority vote of its Members. Its working language is English.

Secondly, the EFTA Court[21] which mainly deals with: (i) infringement actions brought by the ESA against an EFTA State with regard to the implementation, application or interpretation of an EEA rule; (ii) the settlement of disputes between two or more EFTA States; (iii) appeals concerning decisions taken by the ESA; and (iv) giving advisory opinions to courts in EFTA States on the interpretation of EEA rules. It only has jurisdiction with regard to EFTA States which are parties to the EEA Agreement. The EFTA Court consists of three Judges, one nominated by each of the EFTA States party to the EEA Agreement. The Judges are appointed by common accord of the Governments for a period of six years. The Judges elect their President for a term of three years.[22] All proceedings are in English except in cases where an advisory opinion is sought by a national court of an EFTA State party to the EEA, where the opinion of the Court will be both in English and in the national language of the requesting court.

---

[16] The term EFTA is used here, even though, as has been seen, only three participating countries are 'true' EFTA states for the purposes of the EEA Agreement. This terminology is sanctioned by the Protocol adjusting the Agreement on the European Economic Area, cited above (note 3).

[17] See generally Reymond, C, 'Institutions, decision-making procedure and settlement of disputes in the European Economic Area', *Common Market Law Review*, Vol. 30, No. 3, 1993, pp 449–480.

[18] The Agreement between the EFTA States on the Establishment of a Surveillance Authority and a Court of Justice ('the Surveillance and Court Agreement') (OJ 1994 No L 344, p 1, 31.12.1994), adjusted by the Protocol Adjusting the Agreement between the EFTA States on the Establishment of a Surveillance Authority and a Court of Justice signed in Brussels on 17 March 1993 and subsequently by the Agreement Adjusting certain Agreements between the EFTA States signed in Brussels on 29 December 1994; The Agreement on a Standing Committee of the EFTA States ('the Standing Committee Agreement'), amended by the Protocol Adjusting the Agreement on a Standing Committee of the EFTA States signed in Brussels on 17 March 1993, by the Decision No 2/94/SC of the Standing Committee of the EFTA States of 10 January 1994 (OJ 1994 No L 85, p 76, 30.3.1994, and EEA Supplement No 1, 30.3.1994, p 14) and subsequently by the Agreement Adjusting certain Agreements between the EFTA States signed in Brussels on 29 December 1994.

[19] See Art 108(1) of the EEA Agreement.

[20] The current College members are: Hannes Hafstein (Iceland), President; Einar M. Bull (Norway); and Bernd Hammermann (Liechtenstein). The College heads a Competition and State Aid Directorate.

[21] See Art 108(2) of the EEA Agreement.

[22] The current full-time judges are Carl Baudenbacher (Liechtenstein), President; Per Tresselt (Norway); and Thorgeir Örlygsson (Iceland). A system of *ad hoc* judges has also been created in case one of the full-time judges is unable to sit.

Thirdly, the EFTA Standing Committee, composed of the EFTA States' representatives.[23] The Committee provides a forum in which the EEA/EFTA States may consult one another and arrive at a common position before meeting with the EU side in the EEA Joint Committee. It consists of representatives from Iceland, Liechtenstein and Norway and observers from Switzerland and the ESA. Chairmanship of the Committee rotates between the EEA/EFTA States. The EFTA Standing Committee formally liases with the EC Commission under the auspices of the EEA Joint Committee. The main function of the EEA Joint Committee is to adopt decisions extending Community Regulations and Directives to the EEA/EFTA States. The EEA is thus managed on a day-to-day basis by the EEA Joint Committee, with political direction given by the EEA Council. The EEA Council meets twice a year at ministerial level and twice a month at the level of heads of the permanent national delegations.

The institutional structure is represented diagrammatically as follows:[24]

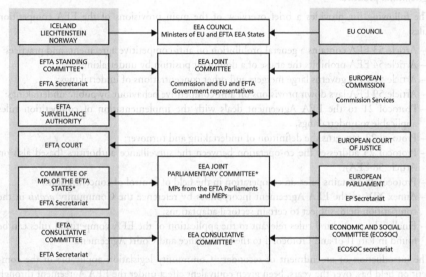

*Switzerland is an observer in these bodies

B. An overview of the competition provisions of the EEA agreement

The general aim of the EEA Agreement, as laid down in Article 1(1) EEA, is to promote a continuous and balanced strengthening of trade and economic relations between the Contracting Parties with equal conditions of competition and the respect of the same rules, with a view to creating a homogenous European Economic Area.[25] To this end, Article 1(2)(e) EEA provides for the creation and maintenance of a system ensuring that competition is not distorted and that the corresponding rules are equally respected.

---

[23] Andreas Diem notes that 'while the EFTA institutions apply EEA law only, the Commission, the ECJ and the CFI will act partly as EC institutions and partly as EEA institutions and will apply different law in each case.' 'EEA Competition Law' *op.cit.* note 3 at page 264. However he also notes that given the substantial similarity between EEA and EC provisions and the duty to interpret in the same way, any differences will have little significance.

[24] Diagram taken from the helpful website maintained by the Principality of Liechtenstein: www.liechtenstein.li/en/eliechtenstein_main_sites/portal/_fuerstentum_liechtenstein/fl-staat-staat/fl-staat-ewr/fl-staat-ewr-instutitionelleaspekte.htm

[25] See also the fourth and fifteenth recitals to the Preamble of the Agreement and Case E-9/97 *Erla María Sveinbjörnsdóttir v Iceland* (*supra* note 11) at paras 47 to 51.

The EEA competition rules may be found in Articles 53 to 60, Annex XIV and Protocols 21 to 24 of the Agreement. To all intents and purposes, these provisions adapt in their entirety the substantive rules on competition found in the original EC Treaty. They also include identical provisions to the Merger Regulation, most of the block exemptions and many of the Commission notices applicable to competition policy.

One important difference relates to the range of products falling within the scope of the competition provisions. Article 8(3) of the EEA Agreement defines the products covered by the rules of the EEA by reference to the Harmonised Commodity Description and Coding System. The EEA provisions do not apply to products described in Chapters 1 to 24 of that System, save to the extent that they are brought within the remit of the Agreement by Tables I and II attached to Protocol 3 to the Agreement. In practical terms, the EEA competition provisions will not generally apply to agricultural and fisheries products, except for a limited number of processed agricultural products.

The following list provides a brief overview of the main provisions of the EEA competition rules:

— Article 53 EEA contains a general prohibition on anti-competitive agreements and practices;
— Article 54 EEA prohibits the abuse of a dominant position by undertakings;
— Article 57 EEA governs large mergers and other concentrations of undertakings;
— Article 59 EEA lays down provisions on anti-competitive behaviour by public undertakings;
— Protocol 21 to the EEA Agreement deals with the implementation of competition rules applicable to undertakings;
— Protocol 22 concerns the definition of undertaking and turnover;
— Protocol 23 addresses the co-operation between the surveillance authorities (based also on Article 58 EEA);
— Protocol 24 contains rules on co-operation in the field of control of concentrations;
— Annex XIV to the EEA Agreement incorporates by reference the Community *acquis* in the competition field, subject to certain sectoral adaptations;
— Finally, the procedural rules relevant to the application of the EEA competition rules can be found in Part II of and Protocol 4 to the Surveillance and Court Agreement.

The introduction or amendment of secondary Community legislation applicable in the competition field has, over the years, been given equivalent effect under the EEA Agreement through decisions of the EEA Joint Committee.[26] The EEA Joint Committee is obliged to ensure the effective implementation and operation of the EEA Agreement. Its decisions insert new pieces of Community legislation into the EEA Agreement through amendment of the 22 Annexes to the EEA Agreement.[27] In this way, the parallel application of EU and EEA law in parallel fields is maintained, achieving the homogeneity across the entire EEA that the EEA Agreement mandates. New pieces of Community legislation with relevance to the EEA countries are marked 'text with EEA relevance' in any Official Journal publication. Non-binding acts in the competition area, such as notices adopted by the EC Commission, have been promulgated for the EFTA/EEA States by the ESA.

Under Article 6 of the EEA Treaty, the provisions of the EEA Agreement shall, in so far as they are identical in substance to corresponding provisions of the EC Treaty, be interpreted in conformity with the relevant rulings of the Court of Justice of the European Communities given prior to the date of signature of the EEA Agreement. Article 3(2) of the Surveillance and Court Agreement

---

[26] In accordance with the provisions of Chapter II, Part VII of the EEA Agreement, which sets out the decision-making procedure.
[27] Art 7 EEA establishes the legally binding nature of secondary EC legislation incorporated into the EEA Agreement in this manner.

also provides that 'due account' shall be paid to the relevant rulings of the ECJ given after the date of signature of the EEA Agreement. Where the EEA substantive rules are identical to the Community law rules from which they are drawn, the legal result should in practice be the same regardless of which set of rules is applied to the given facts.[28]

Subject to the process of decentralisation of enforcement of competition law, the competition rules in the EEA will be enforced by the EC Commission and the ESA.[29] However in accordance with a 'one-stop-shop' principle, cases are attributed either to the EC Commission or the ESA. In cases falling within the responsibility of the EC Commission,[30] the implementation of the EEA competition rules will be based on the existing Community competences, supplemented by the provisions contained in the EEA Agreement.

SECTION II: THE SUBSTANTIVE COMPETITION RULES OF THE
EEA AGREEMENT: A BRIEF DESCRIPTION

A. The basic rules

1. Article 53 (Article 85)

The substantive EEA competition rules are essentially identical to the corresponding EC competition rules. The only major difference is in their geographical scope. This is widened in the EEA rules to include the EFTA States. Thus Article 53(1) EEA prohibits, as incompatible with the functioning of the EEA Agreement, agreements between undertakings, decisions by associations of undertakings and concerted practices which have as their object or effect, the prevention, restriction or distortion of competition within the territory of the contracting parties to the EEA. This provision is the exact counterpart to Article 81 EC, except that trade between the EC and one or more EFTA States or between EFTA States must be affected, if the prohibition is to apply. Article 53(1) lists five paradigmatic practices which are caught by the prohibition, Articles 53(2) and 53(3) follow Articles 85(2) and 85(3) word for word.[31]

2. Article 54 (Article 86)

Similarly, Article 54 EEA prohibits, as incompatible with the functioning of the EEA Agreement, any abuse by undertakings of a dominant position within the territory covered by the Agreement or a substantial part of it. As with Article 53, the only major divergence from Article 82 EC is that trade between the EC and one or more EFTA States or between EFTA States must be affected. A list of the main abusive practices specified in Article 82 EC is repeated in Article 54.

3. Article 57 (The Merger Regulation)

Article 57(1) EEA renders incompatible with the EEA Agreement, concentrations which create or strengthen a dominant position as a result of which effective competition would be significantly impeded within the territory covered by the EEA Agreement or a substantial part of it. The original EC Merger Control Regulation[32] was applied to EEA law by Article 57(2) of and Protocol

---

[28] Art 111 and *ff* of the EEA Agreement sets up a dispute settlement procedure for differences in interpretation of the EEA rules between EC and EFTA institutions. The dispute is first referred by either side to the EEA Joint Committee which attempts to reconcile the conflicting interpretations. If the provision in dispute is identical in substance to an EC provision, the question may after three months be referred with the consent of both sides to the CJEC for a definitive ruling.

[29] Art 55(1) of the EEA Agreement.

[30] For details of how jurisdiction is allocated between the EC Commission and the ESA, see below at Section III.B.

[31] The full text of Art 53 and all the other major provisions of the EEA competition rules are reprinted at the end of this Appendix.

[32] Council Reg (EEC) No 4064/89 of 21 December 1989 on the Control of Concentrations between Undertakings (OJ L395, p 1 of 30/12/1989—as amended by OJ L257, p 13 of 21/09/1990).

24 to the EEA Agreement. The original Merger Control Regulation was replaced with a new EC Merger Regulation at Community level in early 2004, following a comprehensive review of merger control.[33] While the wording of Article 57(2) has not been up-dated, two EEA Joint Committee decisions now set out the applicability of the EC Merger Regulation to the entire EEA area.[34] The new text of Protocol 24 when read with Article 57 EEA and Article 1 of the EC Merger Regulation establishes that the EC Commission retains sole competence to rule on concentrations with a 'Community dimension.' The ESA only has competence to deal with applications to approve mergers if there is no Community dimension and an EFTA dimension is established.[35] No concentrations falling within its competence have yet been notified to the ESA. The EEA rules on merger control will not be considered further, in keeping with the main work.

4. Article 3 EEA (cf Article 10 EC)

Finally, Article 3 of the EEA Agreement corresponds to Article 10 EC and imposes a duty on the contracting parties to take appropriate measures to ensure the fulfilment of obligations arising from the Agreement.

B. 'Acts' giving effect to the basic rules

1. Block exemptions

The implementation of Article 53 is also subject to various block exemptions, which were either in force when the EEA Agreement was signed, or as have been updated from time to time.[36]

---

[33] Council Reg (EC) No 139/2004 of 20 January 2004 on the control of concentrations between undertakings ('the EC Merger Reg') OJ 2004 L No. 24, p 1, 29.01.2004. The EC Merger Reg is accompanied by Commission Reg (EC) No 802/2004 of 7 April 2004 implementing Council Reg (EC) No 139/2004 on the control of concentrations between undertakings ('the Implementing Reg').

[34] The EEA Joint Committee adopted Decision No 78/2004 (OJ 2004, L No. 219, p 1, 19.06.04) and Decision No 79/2004 (OJ 2004, L No. 219, p 24, 19.06.04) on 8 June 2004. The first decision, 78/2004 entered into force on 9 June 2004. The second decision has not yet entered into force, as notification under Art 103(1) EEA is still required from Iceland and Norway. Each has filed a notification of delay in the meantime. Decision 78/2004 establishes a new Protocol 24 which takes into account the promulgation of the new EC Merger Reg and the Implementing Reg.

[35] An EFTA dimension is established if the turnover thresholds set out in the EC Merger Reg are met within the EFTA pillar. That is, the combined aggregate worldwide turnover of all the undertakings involved is more than €5 billion and the aggregate EFTA-wide turnover of each of at least two of the undertakings is greater than €250 million. If, however, all the undertakings involved achieve more than two-thirds of their turnover within one and the same EFTA State, the requisite EFTA dimension would be lacking. The proposed merger would then be dealt with at a national level. Alternatively, a concentration which does not meet these thresholds will still have an EFTA dimension where: (a) the combined aggregate worldwide turnover of all of the undertakings concerned is more than €2.5 billion; (b) in each of at least three EFTA states, the combined aggregate turnover of all of the undertakings concerned is more than €100 million; (c) in each of at least three EFTA states included for the purpose of point (b), the aggregate turnover of each of at least two of the undertakings concerned is more than €25 million; and (d) the aggregate EFTA-wide turnover of each of at least two of the undertakings concerned is more than €100 million. This is subject to the same exception for each of the undertakings achieving more than two-thirds of its aggregate EFTA-wide turnover in one and the same EFTA state. See Art 57(1) and (2); Annex XIV, Section A *Merger Control*; and Protocols 21 and 24 to the Agreement.

[36] Art 60 and Annex XIV, Sections B to F and J, of the EEA Agreement. The block exemptions listed in Annex XIV to the EEA Agreement are currently:

— Commission Reg (EC) No. 2790/1999 of 22 December 1999 on the application of Art 81(3) of the Treaty to categories of vertical agreements and concerted practices – **the Vertical Agreements Block Exemption** (OJ 1999 L No. 336, p 21, 29.12.1999), as amended by the Act concerning the conditions of Accession of the Czech Republic, the Republic of Estonia, the Republic of Cyprus, the Republic of Latvia, the Republic of Lithuania, the Republic of Hungary, the Republic of Malta, the Republic of Poland, the Republic of Slovenia and the Slovak Republic and the adjustments to the Treaties on which the European Union is founded, adopted on 16 April 2003 ('the 2003 Act of Accession', OJ 2002 L No. 236, p 33, 23.9.2003)

New block exemption regulations have to be implemented under the rather complicated scheme contained in Articles 102 to 104 of the EEA Agreement. Annex XIV to the EEA Agreement also transposes into an EEA context two Commission Regulations applying the competition rules to the transport sector.[37]

The block exemptions have been supplemented and modified by the provisions of Protocol 1 to the EEA Agreement ('horizontal adaptations') and by Annex XIV of the EEA Agreement ('sectoral and specific adaptations'). The original text of the EC block exemptions must therefore be read subject to these adaptations. The block exemptions thus adapted will be automatically applied by the EC Commission and the ESA when dealing with EEA competition cases within their respective jurisdictions. They will also fall to be applied directly by national courts and national competition authorities acting in accordance with the Modernisation Regulation (as described below), once it comes fully into effect.

Two important differences should be noted. First, the scope for withdrawing the benefit of the exemption is expanded. Both the Commission and the ESA may now withdraw the exemption not only on their own initiative or at the request of a State or of a natural or legal person claiming a legitimate interest, but furthermore at the request of the other surveillance authority. Secondly, the provisions in any given block exemption are applied in an EEA context only through the prism of specific provisions in Protocol 21 to the EEA Agreement.[38]

— Commission Reg (EC) No. 1400/2002 of 31 July 2002 on the application of Art 81(3) of the Treaty to categories of vertical agreements and concerted practices in the motor vehicle sector – **the Motor Vehicle Block Exemption** (OJ 2002 L No. 203, p 30, 1.8.2002, as amended by the 2003 Act of Accession)

— Commission Reg (EC) No. 240/96 of 31 January 1996 on the application of Art 85(3) of the Treaty to certain categories of technology transfer agreements – **the Technology Transfer Block Exemption** (OJ 1996 L No. 31, p 2, 9.2.1996, as amended by the 2003 Act of Accession)

— Commission Reg (EC) No. 2658/2000 of 29 November 2000 on the application of Art 81(3) of the Treaty to categories of specialisation agreements – **the Specialisation Agreements Block Exemption** (OJ 2000 L No. 304, p 3, 5.12.2000, as amended by the 2003 Act of Accession)

— Commission Reg (EC) No. 2659/2000 of 29 November 2000 on the application of Art 81(3) of the Treaty to categories of research and development agreements – **the Research and Development Block Exemption** (OJ 2000 L No. 304, p 7, 5.12.2000, as amended by the 2003 Act of Accession)

— Commission Reg (EEC) No. 1617/93 of 25 June 1993 on the application of Art 85(3) of the Treaty to certain categories of agreements and concerted practices concerning joint planning and co-ordination of schedules – **IATA passenger tariff conferences block exemption** (OJ 1993 L No. 155, p 18, 26.6.93, as amended by Commission Regs Nos. 1523/96; 1083/1999; 1324/2001; 1105/2002 and the 2003 Act of Accession)

— Commission Reg (EC) No. 823/2000 of 19 April 2000 on the application of Art 81(3) of the Treaty to certain categories of agreements, decisions and concerted practices between liner shipping conferences (consortia) – **Liner conferences block exemption** (OJ 2000 L No. 100, p 24, 20.4.2000, as amended by the 2003 Act of Accession)

— Commission Reg (EC) No. 358/2003 of 27 February 2003 on the application of Art 81(3) of the Treaty to certain categories of agreements, decisions and concerted practices in the insurance sector – **Insurance agreements block exemption** (OJ 2003 L No. 53, p 8, 28.2.2003).

[37] See Council Reg (EEC) No 1017/68 of 19 July 1968 applying rules of competition to transport by rail, road and inland waterway – **Transport by rail, road and inland waterways** (OJ 1968 L 175 p 1, 23.7.1968, as amended by the Modernization Reg, Council Reg (EC) No. 1/2003 of 16 December 2002, OJ 2003 L No. 1, p 1, 4.1.2003); Council Reg (EEC) No 4056/86 of 22 December 1986 laying down detailed rules for the application of Arts 85 and 86 of the Treaty to maritime transport – **Maritime transport** (OJ 1986 L 378 p 4, 31.12.1986, as amended by the 2003 Act of Accession and the Modernization Reg).

[38] Protocol 21 on the implementation of competition rules applicable to undertakings. See Part IV.B. below. Annex XIV to the EEA Agreement makes clear that where the proper application of the above block exemptions will now be subject to the application of the Modernization Reg, in the EEA context this will be subject to the application of the provisions 'envisaged' under Protocol 21.

2. Commission Notices and Guidelines

The Commission and the ESA are obliged, when applying the EEA competition rules, to take into account pertinent, existing Commission Notices and Guidelines. The list of notices to be taken into account is set out in Annex XIV.[39] These Notices and Guidelines have not been adapted for EEA purposes. Instead the ESA is simply obliged to take due account of the principles and rules contained in them, when applying Articles 53 to 60 of the Agreement.[40] The existing Notices and Guidelines are read in light of their 'effet utile' for the application of the EEA competition provisions. It is worth noting, therefore, that a number of notices are included in the list which relate to Community measures that are no longer in force. These notices will be of largely historical interest only. They represent measures adopted by the EC Commission up to 31 July 1991.

More modern notices are not included in an amended version of Annex XIV but are instead adopted by the ESA under its own competence. From the date of entry into force of the EEA Agreement, acts corresponding to measures taken by the EC Commission are adopted by the ESA under Articles 5(2)(b) and 25 of the Surveillance and Court Agreement. They are

---

[39] The Notices and Guidelines listed in Annex XIV are:

— Commission Notice regarding restrictions ancillary to concentrations (OJ 1990 C No. 203, p 5, 14.8.1990)
— Commission Notice regarding the concentrative and cooperative operations under Council Reg (EEC) No 4064/89 of 21 December 1989 on the control of concentrations between undertakings (OJ 1990 C No. 203, p 10, 14.8.1990).
— Commission Notice concerning Commission Regs (EEC) No 1983/83 and (EEC) No 1984/83 of 22 June 1983 on the application of Art 85(3) of the Treaty to categories of exclusive distribution and exclusive purchasing agreements (OJ 1984 C No 101, p 2, 13.4.1984)
— Commission Notice concerning Reg (EEC) No 123/85 of 12 December 1984 on the application of Art 85(3) of the Treaty to certain categories of motor vehicle distribution and servicing agreements (OJ 1985 C No. 17, p 4, 18.1.1985)
— Commission Notice on exclusive dealing contracts with commercial agents (OJ No 139, p 2921/62, 24.12.1962)
— Commission Notice concerning agreements, decisions and concerted practices in the field of cooperation between enterprises (OJ 1968 C No. 75, p 3, 24.12.1962, as corrected by OJ No C 84, 28.8.1968, p 14)
— Commission Notice concerning imports into the Community of Japanese goods falling within the scope of the Rome Treaty (OJ 1972 C No. 111, p 13, 21.10.1972)
— Commission Notice of 18 December 1978 concerning its assessment of certain subcontracting agreements in relation to Art 85(1) of the EEC Treaty (OJ 1979 C No. 1, p 2, 3.1.1979).
— Commission Notice on agreements of minor importance which do not fall under Art 85(1) of the Treaty establishing the European Economic Community (OJ 1986 C No. 231, p 2, 12.9.1986)
— Guidelines on the application of EEC competition rules in the telecommunication sector (OJ 1991 C No 233, p 2, 6.9.1991).
— Commission Notice concerning Reg (EEC) No 123/85 (OJ 1985 C No. 17, p 4);
— Commission Notice on exclusive dealing contracts with commercial agents (OJ 1962 139 at 2921/62);
— Commission Notice concerning agreements, decisions and concerted practices in the field of co-operation between enterprises (OJ 1968 C75, p 3 as corrected by OJ 1968 C84, p 14);
— Commission Notice concerning imports into the Community of Japanese goods falling within the scope of the Rome Treaty (OJ 1972 C111, p 13);
— Commission Notice concerning its assessment of certain subcontracting agreements in relation to Art 85(1) of the EEC Treaty (OJ 1979 C 1, p 2);
— Commission Notice on agreements of minor importance which do not fall under Art 85(1) of the EEC Treaty (OJ 1986 C 231, p 2, updated in OJ 1994 C 386, p 20); and
— Commission's Guidelines on the application of EEC competition rules in the telecommunication sector (OJ 1991 C 233, p 2).

[40] See preamble to the section headed 'Acts of which the EC Commission and the EFTA Surveillance Authority shall take due account' in Annex XIV to the Agreement.

published in accordance with the exchange of letters on publication of EEA relevant information.[41] Thus, for example, a series of ten Annexes to a Decision of the ESA adopted in January 1994 contained the equivalent text of ten Commission Notices and Guidelines to be applied by the ESA in an EEA context.[42] Both surveillance authorities shall take due account of these measures in cases where they have jurisdiction under the EEA Agreement.[43] The scope for divergence in application is further reduced by the obligation imposed on the EC Commission to ensure that equal conditions of competition are met in the EEA as in the Community itself.

Section III: The Procedure for the Application of the EEA Competition Rules

A. The Modernization of Community Competition Law

Article 55 of the EEA Agreement entrusts the enforcement of the EEA Competition provisions to both the EC Commission and the ESA. Article 55(1) requires the 'competent surveillance authority' to investigate cases of suspected infringement of the EEA competition rules and to take appropriate measures to bring them to an end. It may launch an investigation of its own initiative, on the application of an EEA state within its respective territory, or on the application of the other surveillance authority. Investigations are required to be carried out in cooperation with the national authorities in the respective territory and with the other surveillance authority. Article 55 imposes an obligation on a surveillance authority to assist its counterpart in accordance with its own internal rules. Under Article 55(2), findings in relations to infringements must be set out in a reasoned decision, which may be published. The competent surveillance authority is also empowered to authorize States within its territory to 'take the measures, the conditions and details of which it shall determine, needed to remedy the situation.' It may also request the other surveillance authority to authorize States within the other respective territory to take such measures.

While the terms of Article 55 EEA are silent as to the detailed measures needed to ensure the enforcement of the EEA competition rules, the implicit emphasis is upon a system of centralized enforcement by the competent surveillance authorities. Such a system is no longer applied in the EC context. The Community has reformed the centralized system of enforcement provided for by Regulation 17/62. It has implemented a system of decentralized enforcement of the competition provisions, leaving the EC Commission free to focus its resources on a limited number of significant cases. The 'Modernization Regulation'—Council Regulation 1/2003—was adopted on 16 December 2002 and entered into force on 1 May 2004.[44] It brings with it a radical shake up of

---

[41] The acts adopted by the Commission will not be integrated into Annex XIV but a reference to their publication in the Official Journal of the European Communities will be made in the EEA Supplement to the Official Journal. The corresponding acts adopted by the ESA are to be published in the EEA Supplement to, and the EEA Section of, the Official Journal.

[42] Decision of the EFTA Surveillance Authority No. 3/94/COL of 12 January 1994 on the issuing of 10 notices and guidelines in the field of competition, OJ 1994 L No. 153, p 1, 18.06.1994.

[43] Examples of such measures include Notice on Co-operation between national courts and the EFTA Surveillance Authority in applying Arts 53 and 54 of the EEA Agreement (OJ 1995 C No. 112, p 7, 04.05.1995); EFTA Surveillance Authority Notice on co-operation between national competition authorities and the EFTA Surveillance Authority in handling cases falling within the scope of Arts 53 or 54 of the EEA Agreement (OJ 2000 C No. 307, p 6, 26.10.2000); EFTA Surveillance Authority Guidelines on the applicability of Art 53 of the EEA Agreement to Horizontal Co-operation Agreements (OJ 2002 C No. 266, p 1, 31.10.2002); and EFTA Surveillance Authority Guidelines on Vertical Restraints (OJ 2002 C No. 122, p 1, 23.05.2002).

[44] Council Reg (EC) No 1/2003 of 16 December 2002 on the implementation of the rules on competition laid down in Arts 81 and 82 of the Treaty (OJ 2003 L No. 1, p 1, 4.1.2003).

the enforcement of the competition rules in the Community. Its scope and effect are examined in detail in the main body of this work. The Modernization Regulation has been accompanied by a Commission Regulation ('the Implementing Regulation') that sets out the provisions governing the exercise by the Commission of its powers in the wake of the decentralization of enforcement of EC competition law.[45]

The cross application of the Modernization Regulation to undertakings established in, or conducting business with, the EEA/EFTA States is not without difficulty. By EEA Joint Committee Decision 130/2004, the text of the Modernization Regulation has, in principle, been brought within the EEA competition regime. Further, by EEA Joint Committee Decision 178/2004, the Implementing Regulation No. 773/2004 was also brought within the scope of the EEA rules. Necessary amendments to Annex XIV and Protocols 21 and 23 of the EEA Agreement have been drafted. Indeed, the implementation of Joint Decisions 130/2004 and 178/2004 will see Protocol 23 replaced in its entirety. In addition, changes will have to be made to Protocol 4 to the Surveillance and Court Agreement, which contains the procedural rules applied by the ESA for the purposes of implementing Articles 53 and 54 EEA. These changes will need to incorporate the terms of the Modernization Regulation and the Implementing Regulation. The ESA will also need to adopt, in due course, notices similar to those issued by the EC Commission under the modernisation programme.

The Joint Committee decision 130/2004 was adopted on 24 September 2004. Decision 178/2004 was adopted on 3 December 2004. Both will enter into force on the first day following the last notification under Article 103 of the EEA Agreement. At the time of writing, Norway submitted its Article 103 notification on 26 November 2004 and Liechtenstein followed suit on 17 January 2005. Notification is still awaited from Iceland. As matters stand, therefore, Decisions 130/2004 and 178/2004 have not yet entered into force. Nor has their text been published in either the Official Journal or in the EEA Supplement.

Nonetheless, Article 103(2) of the EEA Agreement provides that, if, upon the expiry of a period of six months after the decision of the EEA Joint Committee such a notification has not taken place, the decision of the EEA Joint Committee shall be applied provisionally pending the fulfilment of the constitutional requirements unless a Contracting Party notifies that such a provisional application cannot take place. As no such reservation has yet been lodged by Iceland, the modernization regime will provisionally apply in EEA competition law with effect from 24 March 2005. In any event, the ESA has updated the text of Annex XIV and Protocol 21, while entirely replacing the text of Protocol 23 to the EEA Agreement on its web site, as if the Joint EEA Committee decision were in force. It will be treated *as if* it were in force for the purposes of this Section.

The ESA will no longer receive notifications concerning the application of Articles 53 and 54 EEA. Instead, it will focus upon investigations conducted of its own initiative and complaints made to it by members of the public. The ESA will retain enforcement powers equivalent to those of the EC Commission. It will therefore be able to:

— Issue decisions finding that an agreement or practice does not infringe Articles 53 or 54 EEA;
— Close proceedings subject to commitments assumed by undertakings which will be binding upon them;
— Impose structural remedies to deal with competition concerns;
— Enjoy increased powers while on inspections; and
— Impose higher fines when procedural rules have not been complied with.[46]

---

[45] Commission Reg (EC) No. 773/2004 of 7 April 2004 relating to the conduct of proceedings by the Commission pursuant to Arts 81 and 82 of the EC Treaty (OJ 2004 L No. 123, p 18, 27.04.2004).
[46] EFTA Surveillance Authority, *Annual Report*, 2003, p 46.

In keeping with the spirit of the Modernization Regulation, the ESA has indicated that it will in the future seek to give priority (in terms of its in-depth investigations) to cases where one or more of the following conditions are met:

— The ESA has sole jurisdiction (notably in competition cases involving the potential application of Article 59 EEA to an EFTA state);
— Articles 53 and 54 may resolve a competition concern where national rules differ from EEA provisions to such an extent that they could not achieve a similar result;
— A hardcore infringement of the EEA competition rules can be established;
— The economic impact of a violation is significant in the relevant market;
— A case raises new points of law which will benefit from clarification.[47]

B. Division of Responsibility between the EC Commission and the EFTA Surveillance Authority

The ESA has been (or shortly will be) granted equivalent powers and similar functions to those of the Commission, to enable it to carry out the implementation of the EEA competition rules. It will apply procedural rules similar to those applied in the Community itself.[48] The EC Commission meanwhile, will 'continue to use its own procedural rules even when dealing with EEA cases. But the Community is obliged, under Article 1 of Protocol 21 to the EEA Agreement, to adopt any necessary provisions to ensure that the Commission is granted the necessary powers to enforce EEA competition rules under the EC pillar. This position is maintained over time by virtue of Article 2 of Protocol 21. This requires corresponding amendments to be made to the ESA's powers so that it is 'entrusted simultaneously with equivalent powers and similar functions to those of the EC Commission.'

The EEA Agreement envisages close cooperation between the EC Commission and the ESA in order to achieve a uniform application of the competition rules throughout the EEA. The two authorities are obliged to exchange information and consult one another on general policy issues and in connection with individual cases.[49] A high degree of cooperation has been achieved in practice.[50]

Given the dual enforcement policy, it is essential that some method of allocating cases to the respective authorities is established. This has been achieved through Articles 56 and 57 of the EEA Agreement. These provisions remain unchanged by the Modernization Regulation. Article 56 caters for allocation of cases concerning restrictive agreements and abuses of dominant positions. Article 57 deals with allocation for merger control cases. Whilst the EEA competition system is based on 'two pillars', a 'one-stop shop' approach has been adopted for the convenience of undertakings involved.[51] This means that undertakings should deal either solely with the Commission or solely with the ESA in relation to any given agreement or practice.

The following rules are important in practice, as they represent the only significant point of departure from the otherwise very similar substantive and procedural rules already found in EC competition law.

---

[47] EFTA Surveillance Authority, *Annual Report*, 2003, p 55.
[48] See generally Arts 1 and 2 of Protocol 21. The powers and functions of the EC Commission for the application of the EC competition rules are reflected in the acts which are listed in Art 3 of Protocol 21 to the EEA Agreement. This refers principally to the Modernisation Reg and the Implementing Reg, but also refers back to the various acts listed in Annex XIV (mentioned above). Cross-references are also made to other procedural regulations in the field of merger control, transport and coal and steel.
[49] See Art 1 of Protocol 23 to the EEA Agreement.
[50] See the *Annual Reports* prepared by the ESA for the years 2001 to 2003, available on its web site.
[51] Art 55 of the EEA Agreement mandates the 'competent surveillance authority' to ensure the application of Arts 53 and 54.

C. Allocation of cases[52]

1. Article 53 cases

Where a case raises issues of agreements, decisions or concerted practices caught by Article 53, Article 56 of the Agreement attributes competence between the EC Commission and the ESA as follows:

(a) 'EC Pure Cases':

These cases involve only trade between EC Member States. They are decided by the EC Commission on the basis of Article 81 EC. As a matter of law, these cases do not fall within the ambit of the EEA Competition rules at all.

(b) 'EFTA Pure Cases':

Where only trade between EFTA States is implicated, the case is dealt with by the ESA. Article 53 of the EEA Agreement is then the controlling, substantive provision.[53]

(c) 'Mixed Cases':

So-called 'mixed cases' involve two situations which must be distinguished if the rules on attribution of competence are to be understood. 'Mixed Cases' in the broad sense are those cases where trade between the Community and one or more EFTA States is affected by the Agreement or practice in question, regardless of whether trade between the EC Member States themselves is also affected or not. In addition there is a sub-category of 'mixed cases' which has been referred to as '1 + 1 cases'.[54] These are cases where trade between EC Member States is not affected, only trade between the Community and one or more EFTA States. The first question to ask therefore, when considering the rules governing the attribution of cases between the two authorities, is whether trade between EC Member States is affected or not.

Mixed cases where both trade between EC Member States and trade between the EC and one or more EFTA/EEA States is involved will almost always be handled by the Commission.[55] An exception is where the agreements or practices concerned, whilst formally affecting inter-EC trade or competition within the Community, do so only to a limited extent. That is, if the effect on trade between EC Member States or on competition within the Community is not appreciable, the ESA assumes jurisdiction. It has been accepted by the contracting parties to the Agreement that for these purposes, the phrase 'appreciable' shall correlate to the definition of '*de minimis*' agreements found already in EC Competition law.[56]

The allocation of '1 + 1 cases', where trade between EC Member States is not affected, is slightly more complicated. In such cases, jurisdiction is determined by a threshold criterion. Article 56(1)(b) of the EEA Agreement provides that if the turnover of the undertakings concerned in EFTA territories is equal to or greater than 33% of their turnover in the EEA as a whole,

---

[52] For a commentary on the origin of the allocation provisions, together with an explanation of their resulting nature and reasons why they are quite complicated, see Blanchet *et al*, 'The Agreement on the European Economic Area (EEA). A Guide to the free Movement of Goods and Competition Rules', *op. cit.* note 1 at pp 184–186. See also Bellamy, C and Child, G, *European Community Law of Competition*, 5th edn, Sweet & Maxwell, 2001

[53] See Art 56(1)(a) EEA.

[54] The phrase and definition comes from Blanchet *et al*, 'The Agreement on the European Economic Area (EEA). A Guide to the free Movement of Goods and Competition Rules', *op. cit.* note 1 at pp 186 *et seq*.

[55] Art 56(1)(c) of the EEA Agreement. See, for example, Case T-44/00 *Mannesmanröhren-Werke AG v Commission* [2004] ECR II-0000, CFI, at para 5.

[56] Art 56(3) of the Agreement.

then the ESA will handle the matter.[57] The Commission decides on all other cases where the threshold criterion is not met, regardless of the existence of any effect on competition in the EC or not. The fact that the undertakings achieve 67% of their turnover within the Community will be sufficient to ground the Commission's jurisdiction. In practice though, the ESA will decide the case if the effect on *competition*[58] within the EC is not an appreciable one, under Article 56(3).

Two particular situations deserve clarification:

• Article 56(1)(c) refers only to an effect on *trade* between EC Member States, not on *competition* more generally within the Community. Provided therefore that the matter qualifies as a '1 + 1 case' (trade between EC Member States not being affected) and the turnover threshold is met, the ESA will handle the case even if competition in the Community is affected to an appreciable extent.
• The ESA will also have jurisdiction over cases where the undertakings involved generate less than 33% of their turnover in EFTA States, but the effect on either trade or competition within the Community is not appreciable.[59]

The allocation of jurisdiction in 'mixed cases' can therefore be seen to be based essentially on a two-step test; a determination of whether trade between EC Member States is affected and a threshold determination of turnover, both subject to a residual 'appreciable effect' consideration. As a rough guide, it would seem that the Commission will deal with a case if either greater than two-thirds of the undertakings' turnover is achieved in the Community, or if trade between Member States or competition generally in the Community is affected to an appreciable extent. The overall process is demonstrated in Figure 1.

2. Article 54 cases

Article 56(2) provides that '[i]ndividual cases falling under Article 54 shall be decided upon by the surveillance authority in the territory of which a dominant position is found to exist.'

The only exception is where a dominant position exists within the territories of both the EC Member States and the EFTA States. Then identical rules to those for Article 53 cases apply. That is, the relevant case will be attributed to the ESA where: (i) either trade or competition within the Community is not affected to an appreciable extent; or (ii) there being no effect on trade between EC Member States and the turnover of the undertaking(s) concerned in the territory of the EFTA States equals 33 per cent or more of its (their) turnover in the territory of the EEA, even if there is an appreciable effect on competition within the Community. The Commission is competent for all other cases.

The overall process can be seen in Figure 2.

The appreciable effect criterion used in both Article 53 and 54 cases, may be equated with the notion of '*de minimis*' thresholds already encountered in EC Competition law. The ESA's 'Notice on agreements of minor importance which do not appreciably restrict competition under Article 53(1) of the EEA Agreement (*de minimis*)'[60] quantifies, with the help of market share

---

[57] This would technically encompass mixed cases generally and not just '1 + 1 cases'. Art 56(1)(b) is, however, expressed to be without prejudice to sub-para (c). Therefore, even if this threshold is met, the EC Commission retains an element of 'residual' competence. Provided that trade between EC Member States is affected to some extent, then the Commission assumes jurisdiction, relinquishing it only if the effect is not appreciable pursuant to Art 56(3). This is, in reality, simply the application of the mixed case attribution described immediately above.

[58] The effect must be on competition, not trade, since *ex hypothesi*, in a '1 + 1 case', trade between Member States is not affected.

[59] See Art 56(3) of the EEA Agreement.

[60] OJ 2003 C No. 67, p 20, 20.3.2003; and EEA Supplement No 15, p 11, 20.3.2003. The ESA's Notice follows the terms of the Commission's Notice entitled 'Agreements of minor importance which do not appreciably restrict competition under Art 81(1) of the Treaty establishing the European Community (*de minimis*)' (OJ 2001 C No. 368, p 13, 22.12.2001).

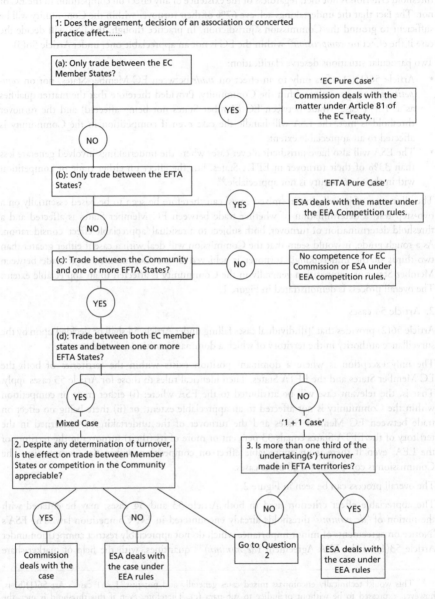

Figure 1 Allocation of Jurisdiction between the Commission and the ESA in EEA Competition Cases falling under Article 53.

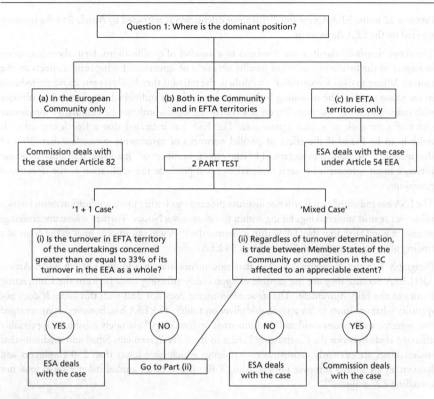

Figure 2 The Allocation of Jurisdiction in Article 54 cases.

thresholds, a negative test for determining what is not an appreciable restriction of competition for the purposes of Article 53 EEA. Paragraph 7 of the Notice sets out the ESA's view that agreements between undertakings[61] which affect trade between the Contracting Parties to the EEA Agreement do not appreciably restrict competition within the meaning of Article 53(1) EEA:

(a) If the aggregate market share held by the parties to the agreement does not exceed 10% on any of the relevant markets affected by the agreement, where the agreement is made between undertakings which are actual or potential competitors on any of these markets (agreements between competitors);

(b) If the market share held by each of the parties to the agreement does not exceed 15% on any of the relevant markets affected by the agreement, where the agreement is made between undertakings which are not actual or potential competitors on any of these markets (agreements between non-competitors).

In cases where it is difficult to classify the agreement as either an agreement between competitors or an agreement between non-competitors, the 10% threshold is applicable. Paragraph 9 permits undertakings a 'leeway' to exceed the above thresholds by 2% points, limited to a duration of two successive calendar years. Definitions of the terms 'undertaking' and 'turnover' are contained in

---

[61] An undertaking is defined in Art 1 of Protocol 22 as 'any entity carrying out activities of a commercial or economic nature.'

Protocol 22 to the EEA Agreement.[62] Turnover calculation is restricted by Article 2 to the territory covered by the EEA Agreement.

The above threshold classification is subject to a number of qualifications. First, there is a saving in respect of the foreclosure effect of parallel networks of agreement having similar effects on the market. Where market foreclosure is established, the relevant thresholds set out above are reduced in each case to 5%. The reasoning is that it is assumed that individual suppliers or distributors with market shares of less than 5% do not contribute significantly to the cumulative foreclosure effect of a network of similar agreements. The ESA has indicated that a foreclosure effect is unlikely to be found if the effect of parallel networks of agreements covers less than 30% of the market.[63] Secondly, paragraph 11 sets out a number of 'hardcore restrictions' whose presence in an agreement between undertakings will preclude the application of the *de minimis* provisions.

The ESA has indicated that it will not institute proceedings (either upon application or on its own initiative) against undertakings falling within the *de minimis* Notice. Further, where undertakings assume in good faith that they fall within its terms, the ESA will not impose fines in the event of a finding of an infringement of Articles 53 or 54 EEA.

Paragraph 3 to the Notice makes clear that agreements may in addition not fall under Article 53(1) EEA because they are not capable of appreciably affecting trade between the Contracting Parties to the EEA Agreement. The *de minimis* notice does not deal with this issue. It does not quantify what amounts to 'an appreciable effect on trade'. The ESA has, however, acknowledged that agreements between small and medium-sized undertakings[64] are rarely capable of appreciably affecting trade between the Contracting Parties to the EEA Agreement. Small and medium-sized undertakings are currently defined as undertakings which have fewer than 250 employees and have either an annual turnover not exceeding €40 million or an annual balance-sheet total not exceeding €27 million.[65]

D. Cooperation between the EC Commission and the ESA

Article 58 states that through the functioning of the EEA Agreement, it is intended to develop and maintain a uniform surveillance on competition throughout the European Economic Area and 'to promote a homogeneous implementation, application and interpretation of the relevant rules.'[66] To this end, the Article further stipulates that 'the competent authorities shall cooperate in accordance with the provisions . . . [of] Protocols 23 and 24.'[67]

The cooperation extends to general policy issues as well as involvement in particular cases.[68] The aim is to coordinate the method of and the policy behind the application of EEA Competition rules for both the Commission and the ESA. Thus, for example, the ESA participated in discussions with the EC Commission 'concerning the review of competition rules relating to vertical

---

[62] Specific rules will be used for the banking and insurance sectors (Art 3 of Protocol 22) as well as for distribution and supply arrangements and transfers of technology (Art 4 of Protocol 22). Specific rules are also included to calculate the turnover of ECSC undertakings for a mixture of ECSC and EEC products (Art 5 of Protocol 22).

[63] See para 8 of the *De minimis* Notice.

[64] As defined in the EFTA Surveillance Authority Decision No. 112/96/COL of 11 September 1996, (OJ 1996 L No. 42, p 33, 13.2.1997, and EEA Supplement No. 7, p 1, 13.2.1997). This decision corresponds to European Commission Recommendation 96/280/EC OJ 1996 No. L 107, p 4, 30.4.1996.

[65] The ESA Notice anticipates that the European Commission will revise its recommendation to increase the annual turnover threshold from €40 million to €50 million and the annual balance-sheet total threshold from €27 million to €43 million

[66] See also Case E-1/94 *Ravintoloitsijain Liiton Kustannus Oy Restamark* [1994–1995] EFTA Court Report 15, at paras 32 to 35.

[67] Protocol 23 applies to Art 53 and 54 cases and Protocol 24 relates to merger cases.

[68] See Art 109(2) EEA and Art 1 of Protocol 23 to the EEA Agreement.

restraints; the review of leniency policy; the re-drafting of the *de minimis* notice; and more recently on the need for modernisation of the Community competition regime, to name but a few.

The duty of cooperation between the surveillance authorities applies, as regards Articles 53 and 54 of the EEA Agreement, only in 'mixed cases'. In such cases, both surveillance authorities have historically supplied one another with copies of notifications, complaints and information about the opening of *ex officio* procedures. For Article 53 and 54 cases, the key aspects of cooperation are as follows:

- The EC Commission and the ESA regularly consult and inform each other at different stages of proceedings.[69] Each of the surveillance authorities and the States within the respective territories are entitled to attend any hearings or Advisory Committees held by their counter-parts. Furthermore, each surveillance authority may, before the other surveillance authority takes a final decision, make any observations it considers appropriate. To this end, each surveillance authority is entitled to see copies of the important documents held by the other.
- In addition to the above exchange of information, the Commission and ESA grant each other more tangible, administrative assistance,[70] if the need arises in individual cases. For instance, each competent surveillance authority may request the other surveillance authority to under-take investigations within its territory, and may take an active part in such investigations. Thus in 1994, the ESA asked the EC Commission to carry out investigations at the premises of a number of Community undertakings as part of the ESA investigation into the supply of steel tubes to the Norwegian offshore industry. Conversely, in 1998, the ESA carried out investigations at the Commission's request into undertakings in its territory operating in the zinc phosphate industry. Parallel investigations have also occurred, for example, into the telecommunications sector.[71] In practice, cooperation has tended to involve the ESA assisting the EC Commission with the latter's case load. Between 1994 and 2001, the ESA was involved in assisting with or commenting on over 400 cases managed by the EC Commission. During the same period, the ESA took only two formal decisions finding infringements in competition matters.[72]

E. Judicial review

The Court of First Instance ('CFI') and the Court of Justice ('ECJ') hear appeals concerning decisions taken by the EC Commission in the competition field. The EFTA Court entertains appeals against competition appeals adopted by the ESA.[73] The two court systems operate in parallel and exchange information with each other on the development of their case law.

F. Rights of lawyers

Individuals and undertakings have the right to be represented, before the CFI and ECJ as well as before the EFTA Court, by lawyers entitled to practice either before the EC or EFTA national courts. Lawyers of EC Member States and EFTA/EEA States further enjoy rights as to legal privilege, whether the proceeding is conducted by the EC Commission or the ESA, meaning that special protection is granted as regards their relationship with their clients.

---

[69] See below at Section IV.B.1.
[70] For further details, see also below at Section IV.B.1.
[71] Commission Press Release, IP/99/786; ESA Press Release PR(99)19.
[72] Both concerning the markets for round wood in Norway. See the summary given by the ESA on its web site.
[73] See Diem, 'EEA Competition Law', *op. cit.* note 3, at page 270.

SECTION IV: PRACTICAL PROCEDURAL ASPECTS IN ARTICLE 53 AND 54 CASES

A. The former system of Notifications, Applications and Complaints

Formerly, undertakings that wished to obtain a negative clearance or an individual exemption or partake in the 'opposition procedure' under various block exemption regulations had to notify their agreements or practices to the competent surveillance authority.[74] The ESA would be required to examine a case where an agreement was notified to it, an application was made for an individual exemption or where a complaint was received from another undertaking. It might also decide to investigate a matter on its own initiative. In fact, the ESA found that the majority of its cases were opened either as a result of complaints received or on the authority's own initiative. The ESA on average opened between 10 and 12 new competition cases a year between 1994 and 2003. By the end of 2003, it had 25 pending cases awaiting resolution. Of these, 18 had arisen from complaints.[75]

B. The new decentralized enforcement of the EEA Competition Rules

Neither Article 81(3) EC nor Article 53(3) EEA stated who should (or could) actually grant exemptions from the provisions of Articles 81(1) and 53(1) respectively. The former regime[76] provided that only the competent surveillance authority, be it the Commission or the ESA, could grant individual exemptions. By 2003, however, it was considered that the centralised scheme no longer secured a proper balance between effective supervision of the competition provisions and, as far as possible, a simplified administration. The centralised scheme for enforcement was felt to hamper the application of competition law by the courts and national competition authorities of the Member States. Further, the administrative burden of the notification scheme prevented the Commission from concentrating its resources on the most serious infringements.

The Community therefore decided to decentralize the enforcement of competition law. It put in place a directly applicable 'exception system.' This permits both the national authorities and the courts of the Member States to consider Article 53 in its entirety and grant exemptions where they consider the relevant conditions are met. The system of notifications and applications for negative clearance and/or exemption has now been swept away.

C. The main features of the decentralized regime

Although the relevant provisions have yet to be brought into force by the EFTA/EEA States, it is possible to anticipate the main features of the new system by reference to the Modernisation Regulation and the Implementing Regulation. The key features will be:

- The enforcement of Articles 53 and 54 in their entirety is now permitted by the national competition authorities and national courts of the EFTA/EEA States. Indeed, national authorities and national courts will be obliged to apply these provisions to cases before them which may affect trade between EEA States when they apply national competition law. Further, they should also apply Article 54 EEA whenever they apply national competition law to any abuse prohibited by that Article. In order to ensure a level-playing field, national competition law can no longer prohibit agreements, decisions or concerted practices which are not also prohibited by the EEA competition rules. Nonetheless, EFTA/EEA States will not be prevented from applying on their own territory stricter national laws which prohibit or sanction unilateral conduct engaged in by undertakings. Nor will EFTA/EEA States be

---

[74] The relevant rules were contained in the previous version of Protocol 23 to the EEA Agreement.
[75] See the Annual Report for 2003 (supra note 46). 88% of the ESA's cases between 1994 and 2003 related to Norway.
[76] Under Reg 17/62 as transposed to the EEA context.

precluded by these provisions from applying national laws which predominantly pursue an objective different from that of Articles 53 or 54 EEA.[77]

- Despite this decentralisation, the Commission and the ESA retain a key role in the enforcement of the competition provisions. They will each be empowered to make a finding that there has been an infringement of the competition provisions. They may then take steps to terminate that infringement. The competent surveillance authorities are now empowered to impose both structural and behavioural remedies where they find an infringement. Each is also empowered to impose interim measures and to accept binding commitments from an undertaking to cease its infringing behaviour. In addition, where the public interest so requires it, the competent surveillance authority may, acting on its own initiative, make a finding that Articles 53 and/or 54 EEA are inapplicable to an agreement, decision and concerted practice or to the actions or omissions of an undertaking in a dominant position.[78]

- The Commission, ESA and national competition authorities of the EFTA/EEA States will form a network of public authorities applying the Community competition rules. This will provide for close co-operation between the different bodies and for the exchange of information. The Regulation makes provision for the Commission to assume sole responsibility for the proceedings in a given case. Provision is also made for determining which national competition authority should deal with a case where two or more are interested. The Advisory Committee on Restrictive Practices and Dominant Positions is retained. A network of co-operation is also envisaged between different national courts.[79]

- The Commission and ESA are permitted to carry out investigations into sectors of the economy or to specific types of agreement. They retain powers to require undertakings to supply them with all necessary information. In addition, they are empowered to take statements from the personnel of undertakings, carry out inspections and seek assistance from national competition authorities. This now expressly encompasses a power to carry out a search in the private homes of directors, subject to prior sanction from a national judicial authority. Officials from the competent surveillance authority may also assist with investigations conducted by national competition authorities.[80]

- The competent surveillance authority retains the power to impose fines for breach of procedural requirements and for infringements of the substantive provisions of Articles 53 and 54 EEA. They are also authorised to impose periodic penalty payments on defaulters.[81]

- Provision is made for limitation periods both within the context of powers exercised by the competent surveillance authority and for the imposition of penalties under the Regulation.[82]

- The Modernization Regulation also provides for the rights of the defence in hearings involving parties, complainants and others. Protection is afforded for documents which are covered by obligations of professional secrecy.[83]

- The recitals to the Preamble of the Modernization Regulation envisage the use of guidance letters by the competent surveillance authorities to ease uncertainty; and the application to the competition field of the principles contained in the Charter of Fundamental Rights of the European Union.[84]

---

[77] See Art 3 of the Modernisation Reg, read together with recitals (6) to (9) of the Preamble to the Reg.
[78] See Arts 7 to 10 of the Modernisation Reg, read together with recitals (10) to (14) of the Preamble.
[79] See Arts 11 to 16 of the Modernisation Reg and recitals (15) to (22) of the Preamble.
[80] See Arts 17 to 22 and recitals (23) to (28) to the Preamble.
[81] Arts 23 and 24 of the Modernisation Reg and recitals (29) and (30) to the Preamble.
[82] Arts 25 and 26 and recital (31) to the Preamble.
[83] Art 27 and 28 of the Modernisation Reg and recital (32).
[84] Recitals (38) and (37) respectively.

1. Powers of the competition authorities of EFTA/EEA States

Complaints remain a feature of the new competition regime. They may be addressed to either surveillance authority.[85] The address of the ESA for such complaints is 'EFTA Surveillance Authority, Competition Directorate, Rue Belliard 35, B-1040 Brussels, Belgium' and their telephone number is (+32)(0)2 286 18 11.

A transfer system operates between the Commission and ESA so that any complaint should end up in the right hands even if it is technically addressed to the wrong authority.[86] Complaints are not subject to particular formal requirements,[87] but it is important that the behaviour which is challenged is described in as much detail as possible and that supporting proof is supplied. In practice, Form C[88] caters for complaints under the EEA competition rules and its completion will ensure that the ESA has all the information necessary effectively to pursue the complaint.

3. Language

In their complaints, undertakings or individuals are free to use any official language of the European Community or the EFTA States when addressing the Commission or the ESA.[89] The language they chose shall also be the language of the proceedings. It will therefore be the language in which any further communication between the ESA and the parties involved takes place[90] and the one in which they have the right to be addressed by the surveillance authorities. If the language chosen is not one of the official languages of the Community, all documentation must be supplemented with a translation into one of the official languages of the Community. Any supporting documents (which must be submitted in their original language) must be similarly translated, if the original language of the document(s) is not an official language.[91] This principle shall also be valid as regards proceedings which are opened upon the surveillance authorities' own initiative.[92]

However, in order to ensure a rapid and efficient procedure, companies are encouraged to use one of the official or working languages of the respective surveillance authority who is responsible. It should be noted that English (an official language of the Community) is the working language of the ESA, in addition to the official languages of the EFTA States. In practice, therefore, it may be easier for undertakings (if not to choose English as the language of the proceedings) at least to submit a translation of all documentation into English, which satisfies the requirements of both the Commission and the ESA.

4. Transmission of cases

What happens if the notifications or applications are addressed to the wrong surveillance authority by mistake? Or if a surveillance authority discovers in the course of proceedings launched on its own initiative that the case should be dealt with by the other surveillance authority? In such situations, the EEA system envisages the transmission of cases between the authorities.[93] Undertakings will be duly informed of any such transfer of their file.

---

[85] See Art 10(1) of Protocol 23 to the Agreement.

[86] See Section IV.A.4 of this Appendix, below.

[87] Although specific forms for complaints are foreseen in Protocol 4 to the ESA Agreement, the use of this form is not compulsory.

[88] Ibid.

[89] See Art 12 of Protocol 23 and Art 2(5) of Reg 3385/94 which also states that an applicant or notifying party under the EEA rules may also use the working language of the ESA.

[90] Except if the Commission or ESA proceeds to send a statement of objections or initiate infringement proceedings.

[91] See Art 2(4) of Reg 3385/94.

[92] Art 11 of Protocol 23 provides that '[t]his [choice of language by a formal applicant or complainant] shall also cover all instances of a proceeding, whether it be opened on notification, application or complaint or *ex officio* by the competent surveillance authority.'

[93] See Art 10(2) and 10(3) of Protocol 23 to the Agreement.

In order to avoid cases being transmitted several times between the authorities, such individual cases may not be re-transmitted to the initial surveillance authority once a transfer of the file has taken place.[94]

Further, a transmission may not take place after proceedings have reached a certain stage, namely after:

- the publication of the intention to give negative clearance or exemption; or
- the addressing of a statement of objections to the undertaking(s) concerned; or
- the sending of a letter informing an applicant that there are insufficient grounds for pursuing his complaint.[95]

The mistaken initial seizure of the authority which is not competent to deal with a given case will not usually be detrimental for the applicants. An example is the time limits within which certain decisions must be taken in opposition procedures in the context of several group exemptions.[96] Under these procedures an agreement is considered to be exempted unless the responsible surveillance authority has opposed it within six months of notification. Such periods will continue to run regardless of whether the case is transmitted to the other authority.

(e) Complaints and Proceedings Initiated by the Commission on its own initiative.

Where such proceedings, although commenced before the entry into force of the Agreement, implicate the EEA rules, such rules will be considered and the scope of the procedure extended automatically, unless the procedure has already reached an advanced stage. This applies only where the alleged infringements to which the procedure relates are ongoing. If the actions on which any decision will be based have already terminated before the entry into force of the Agreement, no reference will be made to the EEA rules. New proceedings (instigated either on the basis of complaints or on the Commission's own initiative) will take into account the EEA competition provisions where appropriate. In either event, the decision should refer to the relevant provisions. A limited exception to this exists: if a complainant has not mentioned the EEA provisions, there is no need to refer to them where the Commission intends to reject the complaint.

B. The Different Procedural Steps

As indicated above, the EC Commission and the ESA will follow the same procedural rules,[97] namely those which are in use in the EC (listed in Article 3 of Protocol 21 to the EEA Agreement). In the context of the EEA, some more particular aspects should be observed.

1. Mutual information and consultation of the other surveillance authority

In order to make the cooperation between the surveillance authorities effective, exchange of information and consultation between the surveillance authorities takes place at different stages of the proceeding.[98] A task force consisting of representatives from the Commission and from the ESA has prepared pro-forma letters which are used in this consultation process and this should ensure an uncomplicated implementation of the cooperation procedure. Each surveillance authority generally only has a right to be consulted or informed in 'mixed cases'. In practice, however, the two authorities liaise very closely with each other all the time.

Once undertakings (or individuals in the case of complaints) have submitted their notification, application, or complaint, the surveillance authority with responsibility for the conduct of the

---

[94] See Art 10(4) of Protocol 23.
[95] Ibid.
[96] See Chapter 11.II.A. above.
[97] See Art 1 of Protocol 21. Protocol 4 to the ESA/Court Agreement reproduces (with adaptations for the EEA context) the procedural rules applied by the Commission in competition cases.
[98] See Art 58 of the EEA Agreement and Protocol 23 attached thereto.

case first examines whether the case appears to have a 'mixed' nature. That is whether it is likely to produce effects both within the common market and within the EFTA territory.[99]

If such is the case, this surveillance authority transmits, without delay, a copy of the notification, application or complaint to the other surveillance authority which then has 40 working days to make any comments.[100] In practice, this means that the dispatching surveillance authority will refrain from taking any definitive measures[101] within those 40 days which might pre-empt any observations that are received.

In case of initiation of proceedings commenced on their own initiative, the responsible surveillance authority informs its counterpart as soon as possible.[102]

Further consultation takes place when a surveillance authority is:
• publishing its intention to grant a negative clearance; or
• publishing its intention to grant an individual exemption; or
• addressing to undertakings a statement of objections.[103]

The surveillance authority which is consulted makes its comments within the same time limits as set out in the publication or in the statement of objections. Observations received from the undertakings involved or comments received from third parties as a result of the communications mentioned above are similarly transmitted between the two authorities.[104]

The surveillance authorities inform each other if an individual case is settled by a formal decision. Transmission of copies of the administrative letters by which a file is closed or a complaint is rejected is also provided for.[105]

More generally, in 'mixed cases', the surveillance authority not in charge of the matter may request at any stage of proceedings copies of the most important documents lodged and filed with their counterpart.[106] This is provided, however, that these documents are aimed at establishing infringements of Articles 53 or 54 EEA or are related to an application for negative clearance or notification for an individual exemption under the same Articles. Each surveillance authority does not have an automatic right to documents relating to matters within the other's exclusive domain. The authorities may also, at any stage before a final decision is made, submit any observations it considers appropriate.[107]

Cooperation between the two authorities also takes place with regard to requests for information, investigations and inspections; hearings; and advisory committee meetings, as described more fully in the following sections.

2. Requests for information and investigations

It may occur in the context of notifications or applications, but also when examining a complaint and more particularly in the context of investigations instigated on their own initiative, that the responsible surveillance authority needs to receive information from the undertakings. To this end, the Commission and ESA have two main powers at their disposal.

The first option is the written request for information. A two step procedure is followed.[108] The first step consists of a letter requesting the information and calling attention to the legal consequences of supplying incorrect information. Where an undertaking does not supply the

---

[99] A practical indication to be considered is, in particular, whether turnover is apparent in both territories.
[100] See Art 2 of Protocol 23 to the Agreement. This time period may be shortened where time is of the essence. For example, where the authority is working under a restricted deadline, as in the case of applications under the accelerated process available for structural cooperative joint ventures. See Chapter 2 above.
[101] Conversely, this means that urgent or provisional measures could be taken.
[102] See Art 2 of Protocol 23.   [103] See Art 3 to Protocol 23.   [104] Ibid.
[105] See Art 4 of Protocol 23.   [106] See Art 7 of Protocol 23.   [107] Ibid.
[108] See generally Chapters 4 of the main book.

information requested by such letter, or supplies incomplete information, the second step then may take the form of a formal decision in which the information is once more requested and appropriate sanctions (fines or periodic penalty payments) are indicated. The final amount of the periodic penalty payments may, where necessary, be fixed at a later date.

Where such requests for information (by simple letter or by decision) are addressed to undertakings located in the territory of the other surveillance authority, a copy of the request for information is at the same time transmitted to the other surveillance authority.[109]

The second possibility for the Commission or ESA is to organize on-the-spot investigations in the premises of the relevant undertakings.[110] Two sorts of such investigations may be chosen: those made in agreement with the undertaking concerned and those made pursuant to a decision which is legally binding on the undertaking. This latter option allows both the Commission and ESA to make unannounced 'dawn raids' if there is a danger that evidence will be tampered with otherwise. On the spot investigations are undertaken in the territory of the responsible surveillance authority, in accordance with its internal rules (for example Regulation No 17 or the corresponding ESA rules) and in cooperation with the national authorities of the States concerned. Each surveillance authority informs the other of the fact that such investigations have taken place and will receive upon request a note of the outcome of these investigations.[111]

The Commission or ESA may consider that investigations in the territory of the other surveillance authority are necessary. If so, these must be organized and carried out by their counterpart. Each may therefore request the other surveillance authority to undertake such investigation. The latter is then obliged to do so, in accordance with its own internal rules, and in cooperation with the competent national authorities of the States concerned.[112] This obligation extends to adopting a formal decision if one is needed.

If this 'cross-border' investigation is planned, the requesting authority will give the other authority all the requisite information and reasons for an investigation, as well as an indication of whether and why a prior formal decision is advisable. Officials of the requesting surveillance authority are entitled to be present at these investigations and may even participate actively in them.[113] If officials from the other authority do participate, they must get prior authorization from the authority in charge of the inspection. The information obtained during these investigations shall, if such a request is made, immediately be transmitted to the requesting surveillance authority once the investigations are completed.[114] It is possible for coordinated inspections to be instigated simultaneously in both the EC and EFTA territories.

3. Hearings

Undertakings involved in competition procedures have the right to be heard in a certain number of instances, including the right to make written observations.[115] Such written observations – as well as observations from third parties shall be transmitted to the other surveillance authority for information. Where an oral hearing is organized in a 'mixed case', the competent surveillance authority must invite its counterpart to be represented and extend the invitation to representatives of States of the other territory, who both have the right to attend such hearings.[116]

---

[109] See Art 8(1) of Protocol 23.
[110] See generally Chapter 5 above.
[111] See Art 8(6) of Protocol 23.
[112] See Art 8(3) of Protocol 23.
[113] See Art 8(4) of Protocol 23.
[114] See Art 8(5) of Protocol 23. If officials from the other surveillance authority take part, they may well have already taken copies of any documents uncovered, in which case such communication is obviously unnecessary.
[115] See generally Chapter 7 above.
[116] See Art 5 of Protocol 23.

4. Advisory Committees

Whenever an Advisory Committee is to be convened before a final decision is taken by one of the surveillance authorities, the latter is obliged to inform the other authority of the date of the Advisory Committee meeting and transmit any relevant documentation.[117] The other surveillance authority as well as representatives of the States of its territory have the right to attend the meetings and to express their views at it. They have, however, no right to vote at such meetings.[118]

5. Professional secrecy and restricted use of information

Strict rules on professional secrecy apply to the authorities in competition proceedings under the EEA Agreement.

The provisions guaranteeing professional secrecy and ensuring restricted use of information apply both to information received by the surveillance authorities on the basis of their own internal rules and to the information that is received in the context of cooperation and administrative assistance between the surveillance authorities. Thus any information acquired as a result of the coordination provisions of Protocol 23 can only be used for the purpose of procedures under Articles 53 and 54.[119] Furthermore, the relevant surveillance and national authorities, as well as the competent authorities of Member and EFTA States, may not disclose any information covered by the obligation of professional secrecy and obtained in the course of EEA competition procedures. This limitation applies equally to officials and employees of any such authority.[120]

Article 9(3) of Protocol 23 does, nonetheless, state that these restrictions do not prevent the exchange of information envisaged by the Protocol itself.

Section V: Adaptation Periods

A. Article 53

Articles 5 and following of Protocol 21 to the EEA Agreement provided for certain transitional arrangements to apply to agreements, decisions and concerted practices in existence at the date of entry into force of the EEA Agreement.

1. New agreements

The EEA Agreement does not provide for transition periods for agreements between enterprises which are concluded after its entry into force (Article 4 of Protocol 21).[121]

2. Existing agreements

An adaptation period was provided for existing agreements which, by virtue of the entry into force of the EEA Agreement, fell under the prohibition contained in Article 53(1).[122]

a. General

Undertakings were allowed a period of 6 months as from the entry into force of the EEA Agreement to adapt such arrangements to or take any other steps necessary to bring them into line with the new provisions of the EEA. This period has now passed. Undertakings should either have:

---

[117] See Art 6(1) of Protocol 23. On the Advisory Committee, see generally Chapter 1 above.
[118] Ibid.
[119] See Art 9(1) of Protocol 23
[120] See Art 9(2) of Protocol 23.
[121] This requirement mirrors the rules contained in Art 4 of Reg 17/62.
[122] See Arts 5 and 7 of Protocol 21, which reflect the rules contained in Arts 5 and 7 of Reg 17/62, respectively.

- modified their agreements or practices so that they now comply with existing block exemptions, taking into account the ESA dimension. (See Article 11 of Protocol 21);[123]
- notified such agreements etc. in order to obtain a negative clearance or an individual exemption;
- modified them in such a way that they are no longer caught by the prohibition of Article 53(1) of the EEA Agreement (see Article 12 of Protocol 21).

It is advisable for undertakings which have not verified their agreements but suspect that Article 53 may be applicable to them, to carry out compliance programmes to ensure that their agreements are not at risk.

b. Already notified agreements

Agreements already notified to the Commission before the entry into force of the EEA Agreement but not yet finally decided upon do not lose the benefit of notification with respect to the new EEA dimension. However, they will be treated in a manner that takes into account the new substantive aspects.[124]

c. Already exempted agreements

Agreements which at the date of entry into force of the EEA Agreement already enjoy a formal individual exemption granted by the EC Commission will continue to benefit from this even in relation to EEA aspects for the duration stipulated in the exemption decision, unless the Commission decides to withdraw the exemption (Article 13 of Protocol 21).[125]

d. Agreements having been granted a negative clearance

Agreements already covered by an individual decision of the Commission granting negative clearance before the entry into force of the EEA Agreement should however be reviewed by enterprises as to their compatibility with the EEA rules, and possibly brought in line with them as described above.

e. Administrative letters

Finally, agreements already the subject of an administrative letter from the Commission before the entry into force of the EEA Agreement should be brought into conformity with the new EEA provisions.

f. Other

It should be noted that, pursuant to Article 9 of Protocol 21 existing agreements which were notified within six months of the date of entry into force of the EEA Agreement, will be granted immunity from fines for the period preceding the notification, it being understood that such immunity may be withdrawn by the competent surveillance authority in accordance with its internal procedural rules.[126]

Section VI: Conclusion

The EFTA competition rules should not pose any particular problems for undertakings already used to the enforcement of competition policy in the EC. The substantive provisions are, to all intents and purposes, identical and the procedures involved in their application should be very familiar. Agreements may be checked for compatibility with the EEA competition rules at the same time as for the EC competition rules, without a great deal of additional effort. The two most

---

[123] The corresponding rules in the EC context are contained in different block exemptions.
[124] See Art 8 of Protocol 21 and Section IV.A.5 above.
[125] On withdrawing individual exemptions, see generally Chapter 11.
[126] For instance Art 15(6) of Reg 17/62 and the corresponding provision in Protocol 4 to the ESA Agreement. See generally Chapter 11 above.

significant differences are to be found in the wider geographical scope of the rules and the introduction of a system of attribution of cases and cooperation between the two surveillance authorities.

The establishment of a parallel system may even have some advantages for undertakings. Their agreements and other arrangements can now be assessed and approved for the whole European Economic Area at once. The close and constant cooperation instituted between the EC Commission and the ESA and the judicial control exercised, as appropriate, by the CFI, the CJEC and the EFTA Court should lead to a 'homogeneous application' of the EEA competition rules throughout the area. It is hoped that such cooperation will not exacerbate delays in procedures. This in turn will serve the macroeconomic goal of establishing equal conditions of competition, necessary for the achievement of the four freedoms.

The entry into force of the EEA Agreement may pose more difficulties for undertakings in either the EFTA States or newly joined Member States which retain strong trade links with EFTA States. The provisions of the EEA Agreement are directly applicable before the national courts of such states. This means that restrictive agreements falling within Article 53(1) (and not exemptable under Article 53(3)) will be void and unenforceable. Similarly, infringements of Article 53 or 54 may give rise to a claim for damages for those who suffer loss occasioned by such infringements. This decentralized enforcement may prove to be as significant as the ESA enforcement of the EEA competition rules. Undertakings which are concerned about the potential applicability of the EEA competition provisions to their agreements or practices should not hesitate, given the practical significance of any infringement, to contact the Commission or ESA. Both authorities have indicated that they are prepared informally to advise undertakings uncertain as to the application of this new body of law.

ANNEX 14 to the EEA Agreement

COMPETITION

List provided for in Article 60.

INTRODUCTION

When the acts referred to in this Annex contain notions or refer to procedures which are specific to the Community legal order, such as:

— preambles;
— the addresses of the Community acts;
— references to territories or languages of the EC;
— references to rights and obligations of EC Member States, their public entities, undertakings or individuals in relation to each other; and
— references to information and notification procedures;

Protocol 1 on horizontal adaptations shall apply, unless otherwise provided for in this Annex.

SECTORAL ADAPTATIONS

Unless otherwise provided for, the provisions of this Annex shall, for the purposes of the present Agreement, be read with the following adaptations:

I.   the term 'Commission' shall read 'competent surveillance authority';
II.   the term 'common market' shall read 'the territory covered by the EEA Agreement';
III. the term 'trade between Member States' shall read 'trade between Contracting Parties';
IV. the term 'the Commission and the authorities of the Member States' shall read 'the EC Commission, the EFTA Surveillance Authority, the authorities of the EC Member States and of the EFTA States';
V.   References to Articles of the Treaty establishing the European Economic Community (EEC) or the Treaty establishing the European Coal and Steel Community (ECSC) shall be read as references to the EEA Agreement (EEA) as follows:
    Article 85 (EEC)—Article 53 (EEA),
    Article 86 (EEC)—Article 54 (EEA),
    Article 90 (EEC)—Article 59 (EEA),
    Article 66 (ECSC)—Article 2 of Protocol 25 to the EEA Agreement,
    Article 80 (ECSC)—Article 3 of Protocol 25 to the EEA Agreement.
VI. the term 'this Regulation' shall read 'this Act';
VII. the term 'the competition rules of the Treaty' shall read 'the competition rules of the EEA Agreement';
VIII. the term 'High Authority' shall read 'competent surveillance authority'.

Without prejudice to the rules on control of concentrations, the term 'competent surveillance authority' as referred to in the rules below shall read 'the surveillance authority which is competent to decide on a case in accordance with Article 56 of the EEA Agreement'.

ACTS REFERRED TO

A. MERGER CONTROL

1. [1] **32004 R 0139:** Council Regulation (EC) No 139/2004 of 20 January 2004 on the control of concentrations between undertakings (the EC Merger Regulation) (OJ L 24, 29.1.2004, p. 1).

The provisions of the Regulation shall, for the purposes of the Agreement, be read with the following adaptations:

(a)[2] In Article 1 (1), the phrase 'or the corresponding provisions in Protocol 21 and Protocol 24 to the EEA Agreement' shall be inserted after the words 'Without prejudice to Article 4(5) and Article 22';

furthermore, the term 'Community dimension' shall read 'Community or EFTA dimension';

(b) In Article 1(2), the term 'Community dimension' shall read 'Community or EFTA dimension respectively';

furthermore, the term 'Community-wide turnover' shall read 'Community-wide turnover or EFTA wide turnover';

in the last subparagraph, the term 'Member State' shall read 'EC Member State or EFTA State';

(c) In Article 1(3), the 'Community dimension' shall read 'Community or EFTA dimension respectively';

furthermore, the term 'Community-wide turnover' shall read 'Community-wide turnover or EFTA-wide turnover';

in Article 1(3)(b) and (c), the term 'Member States' shall read 'EC Member States or in each of at least three EFTA States;

in the last subparagraph, the term 'Member States' shall read 'EC Member State or EFTA State';

(d) Article 1(4) and (5) shall not apply;

(e) In Article 2(1), first subparagraph, the term 'common market' shall read 'functioning of the EEA Agreement';

(f) In Article 2(2), at the end, the term 'common market' shall read 'functioning of the EEA Agreement';

(g) In Article 2(3), at the end, the term 'common market' shall read 'functioning of the EEA Agreement';

(h) In Article 2(4), at the end, the term 'common market' shall read 'functioning of the EEA Agreement';

(i) In Article 3(5)(b), the term 'Member State' shall read 'EC Member State or EFTA State';

(j) In Article 4 (1), first subparagraph, the term 'Community dimension' shall read 'Community or EFTA dimension';

furthermore, in the first sentence, the phrase 'in accordance with Article 57 of the EEA Agreement' shall be inserted after the words 'shall be notified to the Commission';

in Article 4(1), second subparagraph, the term 'Community dimension' shall read 'Community or EFTA dimension';

(k) In Article 5(1), the last subparagraph shall read:

'Turnover, in the Community or in an EC Member State, shall comprise products sold and services provided to undertakings or consumers, in the Community or in

---

[1] Text of point 1 (Council Reg (EEC) No 4064/89) replaced by Decision No 78/2004 (OJ No L 219, 19.6.2004, p 13 and EEA Supplement No 32, 19.6.2004, p 1), e.i.f. 9.6.2004.

[2] The Text of adaptation (a) replaced by Decision No 79/2004 (OJ No L 219, 19.6.2004, p 24 and EEA Supplement No 32, 19.6.2004, p 10), e.i.f. pending.

that EC Member State as the case may be. The same shall apply as regards turnover in the territory of the EFTA States as a whole or in an EFTA State.';

(l) In Article 5(3)(a), the last subparagraph shall read:

'The turnover of a credit or financial institution in the Community or in an EC Member State shall comprise the income items, as defined above, which are received by the branch or division of that institution established in the Community or the EC Member State in question as the case may be. The same shall apply as regards turnover of a credit or financial institution in the territory of the EFTA States as a whole or in an EFTA State.';

(m) In Article 5(3)(b), the last phrase ', . . . gross premiums received from Community residents and from residents of one Member State respectively shall be taken into account.' shall read:

', . . . gross premiums received from Community residents and from residents of one EC Member State respectively shall be taken into account. The same shall apply as regards gross premiums received from residents in the territory of the EFTA States as a whole and from residents in one EFTA State, respectively.'

B. Vertical Agreements and Concerted Practices[3]

2.[4] **399 R 2790**: Commission Regulation (EC) No 2790/1999 of 22 December 1999 on the application of Article 81(3) of the Treaty to categories of vertical agreements and concerted practices (OJ L 336, 29.12.1999, p. 21), as amended by:

—[5] **1 03 T**: Act concerning the conditions of accession of the Czech Republic, the Republic of Estonia, the Republic of Cyprus, the Republic of Latvia, the Republic of Lithuania, the Republic of Hungary, the Republic of Malta, the Republic of Poland, the Republic of Slovenia and the Slovak Republic and the adjustments to the Treaties on which the European Union is founded adopted on 16 April 2003 (OJ L 236, 23.9.2003, p. 33).

The provisions of the Regulation shall, for the purpose of the Agreement, be read with the following adaptations:

(a) in Article 6, the phrase 'pursuant to Article 7(1) of Regulation No 19/65/EEC' shall read 'either on its own initiative or at the request of the other surveillance authority or a State falling within its competence or of natural or legal persons claiming a legitimate interest';

(b)[6] the following paragraph shall be added at the end of Article 6: 'The competent surveillance authority may in such cases issue a decision in accordance with Article 10 of Regulation (EC) No 1/2003, or the corresponding provisions envisaged in Protocol 21 to the EEA Agreement'.

3. [ ][7]

4. [ ][8]

4a. [ ][9]

---

[3] Title of Chapter B replaced by Decision No 18/2000 (OJ L103, 12.4.2001, p 36 and EEA Supplement No 20, 12.4.2001p. 179) e.i.f. 29.1.2000.

[4] Text of point 2 replaced by Decision No 18/2000 (OJ No L 103, 12.4.2001, p 36 and EEA Supplement No 20, 12.4.2001p. 179), e.i.f. 29.1.2000.

[5] Indent and words 'as amended by:' added by the EEA Enlargement Agreement (OJ L130, 29.4.2004, p 3 and EEA Supplement No 23, 29.4.2004, p 1), e.i.f. 1.5.2004.

[6] Words 'Arts 6 and 8 of Reg (EEC) No 17/62' replaced by the words 'Art 10 of Reg (EC) No 1/2003' and words 'without any notification from the undertakings concerned being required' deleted by Decision 130/2004 (OJ L[to be published]), e.i.f. pending.

[7] Text of point 3 deleted by Decision No 18/2000 (OJ No L 103, 12.4.2001, p 36 and EEA Supplement No 20, 12.4.2001p. 179), e.i.f. 29.1.2000.

[8] Point deleted by Decision 130/2004 (OJ L[to be published]), e.i.f. pending.

[9] Point deleted by Decision 130/2004 (OJ L[to be published]), e.i.f. pending.

4b.[10] **32002 R 1400**: Commission Regulation (EC) No 1400/2002 of 31 July 2002 on the application of Article 81(3) of the Treaty to categories of vertical agreements and concerted practices in the motor vehicle sector (OJ L 203, 1.8.2002, p. 30), as amended by:

—[11] **1 03 T**: Act concerning the conditions of accession of the Czech Republic, the Republic of Estonia, the Republic of Cyprus, the Republic of Latvia, the Republic of Lithuania, the Republic of Hungary, the Republic of Malta, the Republic of Poland, 'the Republic of Slovenia and the Slovak Republic and the adjustments to the Treaties on which the European Union is founded adopted on 16 April 2003 (OJ L 236, 23.9.2003, p. 33).

The provisions of the Regulation shall, for the purposes of the Agreement, be read with the following adaptations:

(a) In Article 6(1), the phrase 'pursuant to Article 7(1) of Regulation No 19/65/EEC' shall read 'either on its own initiative or at the request of the other surveillance authority or a State falling within its competence or of natural or legal persons claiming legitimate interest';

(b)[12] The following shall be added at the end of Article 6(1):

'The competent surveillance authority may in such cases issue a decision in accordance with Article 10 of Regulation (EC) No 1/2003, or the corresponding provisions in Protocol 21 to the EEA Agreement.'

C. Technology Transfer Agreements[13]

5.[14] **396 R 0240**: Commission Regulation (EC) No 240/96 of 31 January 1996 on the application of Article 85(3) of the Treaty to certain categories of technology transfer agreements (OJ No L 31, 9.2.1996, p. 2), as amended by:

—[15] **1 03 T**: Act concerning the conditions of accession of the Czech Republic, the Republic of Estonia, the Republic of Cyprus, the Republic of Latvia, the Republic of Lithuania, the Republic of Hungary, the Republic of Malta, the Republic of Poland, the Republic of Slovenia and the Slovak Republic and the adjustments to the Treaties on which the European Union is founded adopted on 16 April 2003 (OJ L 236, 23.9.2003, p. 33).

The provisions of the Regulation shall, for the purposes of the Agreement, be read with the following adaptations:

(a) In Article 1(4) the term 'Member States' shall read 'EC Member States or EFTA States';

(b) in Article 4(1), the phrase 'on condition that the agreements in question are notified to the Commission in accordance with the provisions of Articles 1, 2 and 3 of Regulation (EC) No 3385/94 and that the Commission does not oppose such exemption within a period of four months' shall read 'on condition that agreements in question are notified to the EC Commission or the EFTA Surveillance Authority in accordance with Articles 1, 2 and 3 of Regulation (EC) No 3385/94, and the corresponding provisions envisaged

---

[10] Point inserted by Decision 136/2002 (OJ No L 336, 12.12.2002, p 38 and EEA Supplement No 61, 12.12.2002, p 31), e.i.f. 28.9.2002.

[11] Indent and words ', as amended by:' added by the EEA Enlargement Agreement (OJ L130, 29.4.2004, p 3 and EEA Supplement No 23, 29.4.2004, p 1), e.i.f. 1.5.2004.

[12] Words 'Arts 6 and 8 of Reg (EEC) No 17/62' replaced by the words 'Art 10 of Reg (EC) No 1/2003' and words 'without any notification from the undertakings concerned being required' deleted by Decision 130/2004 (OJ L[to be published]), e.i.f. pending.

[13] Title 'Patent licensing agreement' replaced by 'Technology transfer agreements' by Decision No 12/97 (OJ No L 182, 10.7.1997, p 42 and EEA Supplement No 29, 10.7.1997, p 46), e.i.f. 1.4.1997.

[14] Text of point 5 replaced by Decision No 12/97 (OJ No L 182, 10.7.1997, p 42 and EEA Supplement No 29, 10.7.1997, p 46), e.i.f. 1.4.1997.

[15] Indent and words ', as amended by:' added by the EEA Enlargement Agreement (OJ L130, 29.4.2004, p 3 and EEA Supplement No 23, 29.4.2004, p 1), e.i.f. 1.5.2004.

in Protocol 21 to the EEA Agreement and Chapter III of Protocol 4 to the Agreement on the Establishment of a Surveillance Authority and a Court of Justice, and that the competent surveillance authority does not oppose such exemption within a period of four months.';

(c) In Article 4(3), the phrase 'in accordance with Article 4 of Regulation (EC) No 3385/94' shall read 'in accordance with Article 4 of Regulation (EC) No 3385/94, and the corresponding provisions envisaged in Protocol 21 to the EEA Agreement and Chapter III of Protocol 4 to the Agreement on the Establishment of a Surveillance Authority and a Court of Justice.';

(d) In Article 4(5), the second sentence shall be replaced by the following:

'It shall oppose exemption if it receives a request to do so from a State falling within its competence within two months of the transmission to the States of the notification referred to in paragraph 1 or of the communication referred to in paragraph 4.';

(e) In Article 4(6) the second sentence shall be replaced by the following:

'However, where the opposition was raised at the request of a State falling within its competence and this request is maintained, it may be withdrawn only after consultation of its Advisory Committee on Restrictive Practices and Dominant Position.';

(f) The following shall be added at the end of Article 4(9):

', or the corresponding provisions in Protocol 21 to the EEA Agreement and Chapter II of Protocol 4 to the Agreement on the Establishment of a Surveillance Authority and a Court of Justice.';

(g) In Article 7, introductory paragraph, the phrase 'pursuant to Article 7 of Regulation No 19/65/EEC' shall read 'either on its own initiative or at the request of the other surveillance authority or a State falling within its competence or of natural or legal persons claiming a legitimate interest';

(h)[16] The following paragraph shall be added at the end of Article 7:

'The competent authority may in such cases issue a decision in accordance with Article 10 of Regulation (EC) No 1/2003, or the corresponding provisions in Protocol 21 to the EEA Agreement and Chapter II of Protocol 4 to the Agreement on the Establishment of a Surveillance Authority and a Court of Justice';

(i) In Article 10(13), the term 'Member States' shall read 'EC Member State or EFTA State'.

D. Specialization and Research and Development Agreements

6.[17] **32000 R 2658**: Commission Regulation (EC) No 2658/2000 of 29 November 2000 on the application of Article 81(3) of the Treaty to categories of specialisation agreements (OJ L 304, 5.12.2000, p. 3), as amended by:

—[18] **1 03 T**: Act concerning the conditions of accession of the Czech Republic, the Republic of Estonia, the Republic of Cyprus, the Republic of Latvia, the Republic of Lithuania, the Republic of Hungary, the Republic of Malta, the Republic of Poland, the Republic of Slovenia and the Slovak Republic and the adjustments to the Treaties on which the European Union is founded adopted on 16 April 2003 (OJ L 236, 23.9.2003, p. 33).

---

[16] Words 'Arts 6 and 8 of Reg (EEC) No 17/62' replaced by the words 'Art 10 of Reg (EC) No 1/2003' and words 'without any prior notification being required' deleted by Decision 130/2004 (OJ L[to be published]), e.i.f. pending.

[17] Text of point 6 replaced by Decision No 113/2000 (OJ No L 52, 22.2.2001, p 38 and EEA Supplement No 9, 22.2.2001, p 5)), e.i.f. 1.1.2001.

[18] Indent and words ', as amended by:' added by the EEA Enlargement Agreement (OJ L130, 29.4.2004, p 3 and EEA Supplement No 23, 29.4.2004, p 1), e.i.f. 1.5.2004.

The provisions of the Regulation shall, for the purposes of the Agreement, be read with the following adaptations:

(a) in Article 7, introductory paragraph, the phrase 'pursuant to Article 7 of Regulation (EEC) No 2821/71, where, either on its own initiative or at the request of a Member State or of a natural or legal person claiming a legitimate interest' shall read ', where, either on its own initiative or at the request of the other surveillance authority or a State falling within its competence or of a natural or legal person claiming a legitimate interest';

(b)[19]the following paragraph shall be added at the end of Article 7:

> 'The competent surveillance authority may in such cases issue a decision in accordance with Article 10 of Regulation (EC) No 1/2003, or the corresponding provisions envisaged in Protocol 21 to the EEA Agreement.'

7.[20] **32000 R 2659**: Commission Regulation (EC) No 2659/2000 of 29 November 2000 on the application of Article 81(3) of the Treaty to categories of research and development agreements (OJ L 304, 5.12.2000, p. 7), as amended by:

—[21] **1 03 T**: Act concerning the conditions of accession of the Czech Republic, the Republic of Estonia, the Republic of Cyprus, the Republic of Latvia, the Republic of Lithuania, the Republic of Hungary, the Republic of Malta, the Republic of Poland, the Republic of Slovenia and the Slovak Republic and the adjustments to the Treaties on which the European Union is founded adopted on 16 April 2003 (OJ L 236, 23.9.2003, p. 33).

The provisions of the Regulation shall, for the purposes of the Agreement, be read with the following adaptations:

(a) in Article 7, introductory paragraph, the phrase 'pursuant to Article 7 of Regulation (EEC) No 2821/71, where, either on its own initiative or at the request of a Member State or of a natural or legal person claiming a legitimate interest' shall read, 'where, either on its own initiative or at the request of the other surveillance authority or a State falling within its competence or of a natural or legal person claiming a legitimate interest';

(b)[22]the following paragraph shall be added at the end of Article 7:

> 'The competent surveillance authority may in such cases issue a decision in accordance with Article 10 of Regulation (EC) No 1/2003, or the corresponding provisions envisaged in Protocol 21 to the EEA Agreement.'

E. [ ][23]

8. [ ][24]

---

[19] Words 'Arts 6 and 8 of Reg (EEC) No 17/62' replaced by the words 'Art 10 of Reg (EC) No 1/2003' and words 'without any notification from the undertakings concerned being required' deleted by Decision 130/2004 (OJ L[to be published]), e.i.f. pending.

[20] Text of point 7 replaced by Decision No 113/2000 (OJ No L 52, 22.2.2001, p 38 and EEA Supplement No 9, 22.2.2001, p 5)), e.i.f. 1.1.2001.

[21] Indent and words ', as amended by:' added by the EEA Enlargement Agreement (OJ L130, 29.4.2004, p 3 and EEA Supplement No 23, 29.4.2004, p 1), e.i.f. 1.5.2004.

[22] Words 'Arts 6 and 8 of Reg (EEC) No 17/62' replaced by the words 'Art 10 of Reg (EC) No 1/2003' and words 'without any notification from the undertakings concerned being required' deleted by Decision 130/2004 (OJ L[to be published]), e.i.f. pending.

[23] Title 'Franchising agreements' deleted by Decision No 18/2000 (OJ No L 103, 12.4.2001, p 36 and EEA Supplement No 20, 12.4.2001p. 179), e.i.f. 29.1.2000.

[24] Text of point 8 deleted by Decision No 18/2000 (OJ No L 103, 12.4.2001, p 36 and EEA Supplement No 20, 12.4.2001 p 179), e.i.f. 29.1.2000.

F. [ ]²⁵

9. [ ]²⁶

G. Transport

10.²⁷ **368 R 1017**: Council Regulation (EC) No 1017/68 of 19 July 1968 applying rules of competition to transport by rail, road and inland waterway (OJ No L 175, 23.7.1968, p. 1), as amended by:

—**32003 R 0001**: Council Regulation (EC) No 1/2003 of 16 December 2002 (OJ L 1, 4.1.2003, p. 1).

The provisions of the Regulation shall, for the purposes of the Agreement, be read with the following adaptation:

Article 3 (2) shall not apply.

11. **386 R 4056**: Council Regulation (EEC) No 4056/86 of 22 December 1986 laying down detailed rules for the application of Articles 85 and 86 of the Treaty to maritime transport (OJ No L 378, 31.12.1986, p. 4), as amended by:

—²⁸ **1 03 T**: Act concerning the conditions of accession of the Czech Republic, the Republic of Estonia, the Republic of Cyprus, the Republic of Latvia, the Republic of Lithuania, the Republic of Hungary, the Republic of Malta, the Republic of Poland, the Republic of Slovenia and the Slovak Republic and the adjustments to the Treaties on which the European Union is founded adopted on 16 April 2003 (OJ L 236, 23.9.2003, p. 33),

—²⁹ **32003 R 0001**: Council Regulation (EC) No 1/2003 of 16 December 2002 (OJ L 1, 4.1.2003, p. 1).

The provisions of Section I of the Regulation shall, for the purposes of the Agreement, be read with the following adaptations:

(a) in Article 1 (2), the term 'Community ports' shall read 'ports in the territory covered by the EEA Agreement';

(b) Article 2 (2) shall not apply;

(c)³⁰in Article 7(1), introductory paragraph, the term 'Council Regulation (EC) No 1/2003 of 16 December 2002 on the implementation of the rules on competition laid down in Articles 81 and 82 of the Treaty' shall read 'Council Regulation (EC) No 1/2003 of 16 December 2002 on the implementation of the rules on competition laid down in Articles 81 and 82 of the Treaty or the corresponding provisions envisaged in Protocol 21 to the Agreement;

(d)³¹in Article 7(2)(a), the term 'Council Regulation (EC) No 1/2003' shall read 'Council Regulation (EC) No 1/2003 or the corresponding provisions envisaged in Protocol 21 to the Agreement';

---

²⁵ Title 'Know-how licensing agreements' deleted by Decision No 12/97 (OJ No L 182, 10.7.1997, p 42 and EEA Supplement No 29, 10.7.1997, p 46), e.i.f. 1.4.1997.
²⁶ Text of point 9 (Commission Reg (EEC) No 556/89) deleted by Decision No 12/97 (OJ No L 182, 10.7.1997, p 42 and EEA Supplement No 29, 10.7.1997, p 46), e.i.f. 1.4.1997.
²⁷ Text of point 10 (Council Reg (EEC) 1917/68) replaced by Decision 130/2004 (OJ L[to be published]), e.i.f. pending.
²⁸ Indent and words ', as amended by:' added by the EEA Enlargement Agreement (OJ L130, 29.4.2004, p 3 and EEA Supplement No 23, 29.4.2004, p 1), e.i.f. 1.5.2004.
²⁹ Indent added by Decision 130/2004 (OJ L[to be published]), e.i.f. pending.
³⁰ Text of adaptation (c) replaced by Decision 130/2004 (OJ L[to be published]), e.i.f. pending.
³¹ Text of adaptation (d) replaced by Decision 130/2004 (OJ L[to be published]), e.i.f. pending.

(e)[32]in Article 7(2)(c)(i), second sentence of the second subparagraph, the term 'Article 9 of Regulation (EC) No 1/2003' shall read 'Article 9 of Regulation (EC) No 1/2003 or the corresponding provisions envisaged in Protocol 21 to the Agreement';

(f) the following subparagraphs shall be added to Article 7 (2) (c) (i):

'If any of the Contracting Parties intends to undertake consultations with a third country in accordance with this Regulation, it shall inform the EEA Joint Committee.

Whenever appropriate, the Contracting Party initiating the procedure may request the other Contracting Parties to cooperate in these procedures.

If one or more of the other Contracting Parties object to the intended action, a satisfactory solution will be sought within the EEA Joint Committee. If the Contracting Parties do not reach agreement, appropriate measures may be taken to remedy subsequent distortions of competition.';

(g)[33]in Article 8, the term 'at the request of a Member State' shall read 'at the request of a State falling within its competence'. Furthermore, the term 'Regulation (EC) No 1/2003' shall read 'Regulation (EC) No 1/2003 or the corresponding provisions envisaged in Protocol 21 to the Agreement';

(h) in Article 9 (1), the term 'Community trading and shipping interests' shall read the 'trading and shipping interests of the Contracting Parties';

(i) the following paragraph shall be added to Article 9:

'4. If any of the Contracting Parties intends to undertake consultations with a third country in accordance with this Regulation, it shall inform the EEA Joint Committee.

Whenever appropriate, the Contracting Party initiating the procedure may request the other Contracting Parties to cooperate in these procedures.

If one or more of the other Contracting Parties object to the intended action, a satisfactory solution will be sought within the EEA Joint Committee. If the Contracting Parties do not reach agreement, appropriate measures may be taken to remedy subsequent distortions of competition.'

11a. [ ][34]

11b. [35] **393 R 1617**: Commission Regulation (EEC) No 1617/93 of 25 June 1993 on the application of Article 85 (3) of the Treaty to certain categories of agreements and concerted practices concerning joint planning and co-ordination of schedules, joint operations, consultations on passenger and cargo tariffs on schedules air services and slot allocation at airports (OJ No L 155, 26.6.1993, p. 18),[36] as amended by:

—[37] **396 R 1523**: Commission Regulation (EC) No 1523/96 of 24 July 1996 amending Regulation (EEC) No 1617/93 (OJ No L 190, 31.7.1996, p. 11),

—[38] **399 R 1083**: Commission Regulation (EC) No 1083/1999 of 26 May 1999 (OJ L 131, 27.5.1999, p. 27),

---

[32] Adaptation text added and previous adaptations (e), (f), (g) and (h) renamed as adaptations (f), (g), (h) and (i) respectively by Decision 130/2004 (OJ L[to be published]), e.i.f. pending.

[33] Text of adaptation replaced by Decision 130/2004 (OJ L[to be published]), e.i.f. pending.

[34] Text of point 11a (Commission Reg (EEC) No 3652/93) deleted by Decision 130/2004 (OJ L[to be published]), e.i.f. pending.

[35] Point inserted by Decision No 7/94.

[36] The text of this Directive was corrected by a Corrigendum published in OJ No L 71, 15.3.1994, p 26. The Corrigendum was taken note of by the EEA Joint Committee (fifteenth meeting of 27.1.1995).

[37] Indent, and words ', as amended by:' above, added by Decision No 65/96 (OJ No L 71, 13.3.1997, p 38 and EEA Supplement No 11, 13.3.1997, p 41), e.i.f. 1.12.1996.

[38] Indent added by Decision No 87/1999 (OJ No L 296, 23.11.2000, p 47 and EEA Supplement No 54, 23.11.2000, p 268 (Icelandic) and Del 2, p 232 (Norwegian)), e.i.f. 26.6.1999.

—[39] **32001 R 1324**: Commission Regulation (EC) No 1324/2001 of 29 June 2001 (OJ L 177, 30.6.2001, p. 56),

—[40] **32002 R 1105**: Commission Regulation (EC) No 1105/2002 of 25 June 2001 (OJ L 167, 26.6.2002, p. 6),

—[41] **1 03 T**: Act concerning the conditions of accession of the Czech Republic, the Republic of Estonia, the Republic of Cyprus, the Republic of Latvia, the Republic of Lithuania, the Republic of Hungary, the Republic of Malta, the Republic of Poland, the Republic of Slovenia and the Slovak Republic and the adjustments to the Treaties on which the European Union is founded adopted on 16 April 2003 (OJ L 236, 23.9.2003, p. 33).

The provisions of the Regulation shall, for the purposes of the Agreement, be read with the following adaptations:

(a) in Article 1, the term 'Community airports' shall read 'airports in the territory covered by the EEA Agreement';

(b) in Article 6, introductory paragraph, the phrase 'pursuant to Article 7 of Regulation (EEC) No 3976/87' shall read 'either on its own initiative or at the request of the other surveillance authority or a State falling within its competence or of natural or legal persons claiming a legitimate interest';

(c)[42] the following shall be added at the end of Article 6: 'The competent surveillance authority may in such cases take, pursuant to Article 24 of Regulation (EC) No 1/2003, or the corresponding provisions envisaged in Protocol 21 to the EEA Agreement, all appropriate measures for the purpose of bringing these infringements to an end. Before taking such decision, the competent surveillance authority may address recommendations for termination of the infringement to the persons concerned.';

(d) The last paragraph of Article 7 shall read:

'This act shall apply with retroactive effect to agreements, decisions and concerted practices in existence at the date of entry into force of the EEA Agreement, from the time when the conditions of application of this act were fulfilled'.

11c.[43] **32000 R 0823**: Commission Regulation (EC) No 823/2000 of 19 April 2000 on the application of Article 81(3) of the Treaty to certain categories of agreements, decisions and concerted practices between liner shipping companies (consortia) (OJ L 100, 20.4.2000, p. 24), as amended by:

—[44] **1 03 T**: Act concerning the conditions of accession of the Czech Republic, the Republic of Estonia, the Republic of Cyprus, the Republic of Latvia, the Republic of Lithuania, the Republic of Hungary, the Republic of Malta, the Republic of Poland, the Republic of Slovenia and the Slovak Republic and the adjustments to the Treaties on which the European Union is founded adopted on 16 April 2003 (OJ L 236, 23.9.2003, p. 33),

---

[39] Indent added by Decision No 96/2001 (OJ L251, 20.9.2001, p 23 and EEA Supplement No 47, 20.9.2001, p 10), e.i.f. 1.7.2001.

[40] Indent added by Decision No 137/2002 (OJ No L 336, 12.12.2002, p 40 and EEA Supplement No 61, 12.12.2002, p 32), e.i.f. 28.9.2002.

[41] Indent and words ',as amended by:' added by the EEA Enlargement Agreement (OJ L130, 29.4.2004, p 3 and EEA Supplement No 23, 29.4.2004, p 1), e.i.f. 1.5.2004.

[42] Words 'Art 13 of Reg (EEC) No 3975/87' replaced by the words 'Art 24 of Reg (EC) No 1/2003' by Decision 130/2004 (OJ L[to be published]), e.i.f. pending.

[43] Point inserted by Decision No 12/96 (OJ No L 124, 23.5.1996, p 13 and EEA Supplement No 22, 23.5.1996, p 54), e.i.f. 1.4.1996. Text replaced by Decision No 49/2000 (OJ No L 237, 21.9.2000, p 60 and EEA Supplement No 42, 21.9.2000, p 3), e.i.f. 1.6.2000.

[44] Indent and words ', as amended by:' added by the EEA Enlargement Agreement (OJ L130, 29.4.2004, p 3 and EEA Supplement No 23, 29.4.2004, p 1), e.i.f. 1.5.2004.

—[45] **32004 R 0463**: Commission Regulation (EC) No 463/2004 of 12 March 2004 (OJ L 77, 13.3.2004, p. 23).

The provisions of the Regulation shall, for the purposes of the Agreement, be read with the following adaptations:

(a) In Article 1 the words 'Community ports' shall read 'ports in the territory covered by the EEA Agreement';

(b)[46]In Article 12, paragraph 1, the following shall be added after the words 'in accordance with Article 29(1) of Council Regulation (EC) No 1/2003': 'or the corresponding provision in Article 29(1) of Chapter II of Part I of Protocol 4 to the Agreement between the EFTA States on the Establishment of a Surveillance Authority and a Court of Justice.'

(c)[47]In Article 13, paragraph 2, the words 'as from 1 May 2004' shall be deleted.

H. PUBLIC UNDERTAKINGS

12. **388 L 0301**: Commission Directive 88/301/EEC of 16 May 1988 on competition in the markets in telecommunications terminal equipment (OJ No L 131, 27.5.1988, p. 73), as amended by:

—[48] 394 L 0046: Commission Directive 94/46/EC of 13 October 1994 (OJ No L 268, 19.10.1994, p. 15).

The provisions of the Directive shall, for the purposes of the Agreement, be read with the following adaptations:

(a) in the second subparagraph of Article 2, the phrase 'notification of this Directive' shall be replaced by 'entry into force of the EEA Agreement';

(b) Article 10 shall not apply;

(c) in addition, the following shall apply:

> as regards EFTA States, it is understood that the EFTA Surveillance Authority shall be the addressee of all the information, communications, reports and notifications which according to this Directive are, within the Community, addressed to the EC Commission.

> As regards the different transition periods provided for in this act, a general transition period of six months as from the entry into force of the EEA Agreement shall apply.

13.[49]

13a.[50] **32002 L 0077**: Commission Directive 2002/77/EC of 16 September 2002 on competition in the markets for electronic communications networks and services (OJ L 249, 17.9.2002, p. 21).

The provisions of the Directive shall, for the purposes of the present Agreement, be read with the following adaptation:

In Article 7(2), the words 'competition rules of the EC Treaty' shall read 'the competition rules of the EEA Agreement'.

---

[45] Indent added by Decision No 17/2005 (OJ No L 130 [to be published]), e.i.f. 9.2.2005 or on the day of e.i.f. of Decision No 130/2004, whichever is the later.

[46] Former adaptations (b) to (g) replaced by adaptations (b) and (c) by Decision No 17/2005 (OJ No L 130 [to be published]), e.i.f. 9.2.2005 or on the day of e.i.f. of Decision No 130/2004, whichever is the later.

[47] Former adaptations (b) to (g) replaced by adaptations (b) and (c) by Decision No 17/2005 (OJ No L 130 [to be published]), e.i.f. 9.2.2005 or on the day of e.i.f. of Decision No 130/2004, whichever is the later.

[48] Indent added by Decision No 25/95 (OJ No L 251, 19.10.1995, p 31 and EEA Supplement No 39, 19.10.1995, p 1), e.i.f. 1.9.1995.

[49] Point deleted with effect from 25 July 2003 by Decision No 153/2003 (OJ No L 41, 12.02.2004, p 45 and EEA Supplement No 7, 12.02.2004, p 32), e.i.f. 1.11.2004.

[50] Point inserted by Decision No 153/2003 (OJ No L 41, 12.02.2004, p 45 and EEA Supplement No 7, 12.02.2004, p 32), e.i.f. 1.11.2004.

I. Coal and steel

14. **354 D 7024**: High Authority Decision No 24/54 of 6 May 1954 laying down in implementation of Article 66 (1) of the Treaty a regulation on what constitutes control of an undertaking (OJ of the ECSC No 9, 11.5.1954, p. 345/54).

The provisions of the Decision shall, for the purposes of the Agreement, be read with the following adaptation:

Article 4 shall not apply.

15. **367 D 7025**: High Authority Decision No 25/67 of 22 June 1967 laying down in implementation of Article 66 (3) of the Treaty a regulation concerning exemption from prior authorization (OJ No 154, 14.7.1967, p. 11), as amended by:

—**378 S 2495**: Commission Decision No 2495/78/ECSC of 20 October 1978 (OJ No L 300, 27.10.1978, p. 21),

—[51] **391 S 3654**: Commission Decision No 3654/91/ECSC of 13 December 1991 (OJ No L 348, 17.12.1991, p. 12).

The provisions of the Decision shall, for the purposes of the Agreement, be read with the following adaptations:

(a) in Article 1 (2), the phrase 'and within the EFTA States' shall be inserted after '. . . within the Community';

(b) in the heading of Article 2, the phrase 'the scope of the Treaty' shall read 'the scope of Protocol 25 to the EEA Agreement';

(c) in the heading of Article 3, the phrase 'the scope of the Treaty' shall read 'the scope of Protocol 25 to the EEA Agreement';

(d) Article 11 shall not apply.

J. Insurance sector[52]

15a.[ ][53]

15b.[54] **32003 R 0358**: Commission Regulation (EC) No 358/2003 of 27 February 2003 on the application of Article 81(3) of the Treaty to certain categories of agreements, decisions and concerted practices in the insurance sector (OJ L 53, 28.2.2003, p. 8).

The provisions of the Regulation shall, for the purposes of the present Agreement, be read with the following adaptations:

(a) In Article 10, introductory paragraph, the phrase 'pursuant to Article 7 of Regulation (EEC) No 1534/91,' shall read 'either on its own initiative or at the request of the other surveillance authority or a State falling within its competence or of a natural or legal person claiming a legitimate interest';

(b)[55]the following paragraph shall be added at the end of the Article 10: 'The competent surveillance authority may in such cases issue a decision in accordance with Article 10 of Regulation (EC) No 1/2003, or the corresponding provisions envisaged in Protocol 21 to the EEA Agreement'.

---

[51] Indent added by Decision No 7/94.

[52] Chapter and point 15a inserted by Decision No 7/94.

[53] Text of point 15a (Commission Reg (EEC) No 3932/92) deleted by Decision 130/2004 (OJ L [to be published]), e.i.f. pending.

[54] Point inserted by Decision No 82/2003 (OJ No L257, 9.10.2003, p 37 and EEA Supplement No 51, 9.10.2003, p 24), e.i.f. 21.6.2003.

[55] Words 'Arts 6 and 8 of Reg (EEC) No 17/62' replaced by the words 'Art 10 of Reg (EC) No 1/2003' and words 'without any notification from the undertakings being required' deleted by Decision 130/2004 (OJ L[to be published]), e.i.f. pending.

ACTS OF WHICH THE EC COMMISSION AND THE EFTA SURVEILLANCE AUTHORITY SHALL TAKE DUE ACCOUNT

In the application of Articles 53 to 60 of the Agreement and the provisions referred to in this Annex, the EC Commission and the EFTA Surveillance Authority shall take due account of the principles and rules contained in the following acts:

Control of concentrations

16. **C/203/90/p. 5**: Commission Notice regarding restrictions ancillary to concentrations (OJ No C 203, 14.8.1990, p. 5).

17. **C/203/90/p. 10**: Commission Notice regarding the concentrative and cooperative operations under Council Regulation (EEC) No 4064/89 of 21 December 1989 on the control of concentrations between undertakings (OJ No C 203, 14.8.1990, p. 10).

Exclusive dealing agreements

18. **C/101/84/p. 2**: Commission Notice concerning Commission Regulations (EEC) No 1983/83 and (EEC) No 1984/83 of 22 June 1983 on the application of Article 85 (3) of the Treaty to categories of exclusive distribution and exclusive purchasing agreements (OJ No C 101, 13.4.1984, p. 2).

19. **C/17/85/p. 4**: Commission Notice concerning Regulation (EEC) No 123/85 of 12 December 1984 on the application of Article 85 (3) of the Treaty to certain categories of motor vehicle distribution and servicing agreements (OJ No C 17, 18.1.1985, p. 4).

Other

20. **362 X 1224(01)**: Commission Notice on exclusive dealing contracts with commercial agents (OJ No 139, 24.12.1962, p. 2921/62).

21. **C/75/68/p. 3**: Commission Notice concerning agreements, decisions and concerted practices in the field of cooperation between enterprises (OJ No C 75, 29.7.1968, p. 3) as corrected by OJ No C 84, 28.8.1968, p. 14.

22. **C/111/72/p. 13**: Commission Notice concerning imports into the Community of Japanese goods falling within the scope of the Rome Treaty (OJ No C 111, 21.10.1972, p. 13).

23. **C/1/79/p. 2**: Commission Notice of 18 December 1978 concerning its assessment of certain subcontracting agreements in relation to Article 85 (1) of the EEC Treaty (OJ No C 1, 3.1.1979, p. 2).

24. **C/231/86/p. 2**: Commission Notice on agreements of minor importance which do not fall under Article 85 (1) of the Treaty establishing the European Economic Community (OJ No C 231, 12.9.1986, p. 2).

25. **C/233/91/p. 2**: Guidelines on the application of EEC competition rules in the telecommunication sector (OJ No C 233, 6.9.1991, p. 2).

General[56]

I. The above acts were adopted by the EC Commission up to 31 July 1991. Upon entry into force of the Agreement, corresponding acts are to be adopted by the EFTA Surveillance Authority under Articles 5 (2) (b) and 25 of the Agreement between the EFTA States on the Establishment of a Surveillance Authority and a Court of Justice. They are to be published in accordance with the exchange of letters on publication of EEA relevant information.

II. As regards EEA relevant acts adopted by the EC Commission after 31 July 1991, the EFTA Surveillance Authority, in accordance with the powers vested in it under the Agreement between

---

[56] Section added by Decision No 7/94.

the EFTA States on the Establishment of a Surveillance Authority and a Court of Justice, is to adopt, after consultations with the EC Commission, corresponding acts in order to maintain equal conditions of competition. The acts adopted by the Commission will not be integrated into this Annex but a reference to their publication in the Official Journal of the European Communities will be made in the EEA Supplement to the Official Journal. The corresponding acts adopted by the EFTA Surveillance Authority are to be published in the EEA Supplement to, and the EEA Section of, the Official Journal. Both surveillance authorities shall take due account of these acts in cases where they are competent under the Agreement.

APPENDIX 39

Protocol 21 to the EEA Agreement

PROTOCOL 21 ON THE IMPLEMENTATION OF COMPETITION
RULES APPLICABLE TO UNDERTAKINGS

Article 1

The EFTA Surveillance Authority shall, in an agreement between the EFTA States, be entrusted with equivalent powers and similar functions to those of the EC Commission, at the time of the signature of the Agreement, for the application of the competition rules of the Treaty establishing the European Economic Community and the Treaty establishing the European Coal and Steel Community, enabling the EFTA Surveillance Authority to give effect to the principles laid down in Articles 1(2)(e) and 53 to 60 of the Agreement, and in Protocol 25.

The Community shall, where necessary, adopt the provisions giving effect to the principles laid down in Articles 1(2)(e) and 53 to 60 of the Agreement, and in Protocol 25, in order to ensure that the EC Commission has equivalent powers and similar functions under this Agreement to those which it has, at the time of the signature of the Agreement, for the application of the competition rules of the Treaty establishing the European Economic Community and the Treaty establishing the European Coal and Steel Community.

Article 2

If, following the procedures set out in Part VII of the Agreement, new acts for the implementation of Articles 1(2)(e) and 53 to 60 and of Protocol 25, or on amendments of the acts listed in Article 3 of this Protocol are adopted, corresponding amendments shall be made in the agreement setting up the EFTA Surveillance Authority so as to ensure that the EFTA Surveillance Authority will be entrusted simultaneously with equivalent powers and similar functions to those of the EC Commission.

Article 3

1. In addition to the acts listed in Annex XIV, the following acts reflect the powers and functions of the EC Commission for the application of the competition rules of the Treaty establishing the European Economic Community:

Control of concentrations

1. [1] **32004 R 0139**: Article 4(4) and (5) and Articles 6 to 26 of Council Regulation (EC) No 139/2004 of 20 January 2004 on the control of concentrations between undertakings (the EC Merger Regulation) (OJ L 24, 29.1.2004, p. 1).

2. [2] **398 R 0447**: Commission Regulation (EC) No 447/98 of 1 March 1998 on the notifications, time limits and hearings provided for in Council Regulation (EEC) No 4064/89

---

[1] Text of point 1 (Council Reg (EEC) No 4064/89) replaced by Decision No 78/2004 (OJ No L [to be published]), e.i.f. 9.6.2004, and subsequently replaced by Decision No 79/2004 (OJ No L [to be published]), e.i.f. pending.

[2] This point, introduced by Decision No 77/98 (OJ No L172, 8.7.1999, p 56 and EEA Supplement No 30, 8.7.1999, p 153), e.i.f. 1.9.1998, replaces former point 2. See also Decision No 13/97 (OJ No L182, 10.7.1997, p 44 and EEA Supplement No 29, 10.7.1997, p 59), e.i.f. 1.4.1997.

on the control of concentrations between undertakings (OJ L 61, 2.3.1998, p. 1), as amended by:

—³ **1 03 T**: Act concerning the conditions of accession of the Czech Republic, the Republic of Estonia, the Republic of Cyprus, the Republic of Latvia, the Republic of Lithuania, the Republic of Hungary, the Republic of Malta, the Republic of Poland, the Republic of Slovenia and the Slovak Republic and the adjustments to the Treaties on which the European Union is founded adopted on 16 April 2003 (OJ L 236, 23.9.2003, p. 33).

General procedural rules

3. ⁴ **32003 R 0001**: Council Regulation (EC) No 1/2003 of 16 December 2002 on the implementation of the rules on competition laid down in Articles 81 and 82 of the Treaty (OJ L 1, 4.1.2003, p. 1).

4. ⁵ **32004 R 0773**: Commission Regulation (EC) No 773/2004 of 7 April 2004 relating to the conduct of proceedings by the Commission pursuant to Articles 81 and 82 of the EC Treaty (OJ L 123, 27.4.2004, p. 18).

5. [ ]⁶

Transport

6. [ ]⁷

7. [ ]⁸

8. [ ]⁹

9. [ ]¹⁰

10. **374 R 2988**: Council Regulation (EEC) No 2988/74 of 26 November 1974 concerning limitation periods in proceedings and the enforcement of sanctions under the rules of the European Economic Community relating to transport and competition (OJ No L 319, 29.11.1974, p. 1), as amended by:

—¹¹**32003 R 0001**: Council Regulation (EC) No 1/2003 of 16 December 2002 (OJ L 1, 4.1.2003, p. 1).

11. [ ]¹²

12. [ ]¹³

---

³ Indent and words ',as amended by:' added by the EEA Enlargement Agreement (OJ No L130, 29.4.2004, p 3 and EEA Supplement No 23, 29.4.2004, p 1), e.i.f. 1.5.2004.
⁴ Text replaced by Decision No 130/2004 (OJ No L [to be published]), e.i.f. pending.
⁵ Text of point 4 (Commission Regulation (EC) No 3385/94) replaced by Decision No 178/2004 (OJ No L [to be published]), e.i.f. pending.
⁶ Text of point 5 (Commission Regulation (EC) No 2842/98) deleted by Decision No 178/2004 (OJ No L [to be published]), e.i.f. pending.
⁷ Text of point 6 (Council Regulation (EEC) No 141/62) deleted by Decision No 130/2004 (OJ No L [to be published]), e.i.f. pending.
⁸ Text of point 7 (Article 6 and articles 10 to 31 of Council Regulation (EEC) No 1017/68) deleted by Decision No 130/2004 (OJ No L [to be published]), e.i.f. pending.
⁹ Text of point 8 deleted by Decision No 60/1999 (OJ No L 284, 9.11.2000, p 38 and EEA Supplement No 50, 9.11.2000, p 118), e.i.f. 1.5.1999.
¹⁰ Text of point 9 deleted by Decision No 60/1999 (OJ No L 284, 9.11.2000, p 38 and EEA Supplement No 50, 9.11.2000, p 118), e.i.f. 1.5.1999.
¹¹ Indent and words 'as amended by:' above added by Decision No 130/2004 (OJ No L) [to be published]), e.i.f. pending.
¹² Text of point 11 (Section II of Council Regulation (EEC) No 4056/86) deleted by Decision No 130/2004 (OJ No L [to be published]), e.i.f. pending.
¹³ Text of point 12 deleted by Decision No 60/1999 (OJ No L 284, 9.11.2000, p 38 and EEA Supplement No 50, 9.11.2000, p 118), e.i.f. 1.5.1999.

13. **387 R 3975**: Council Regulation (EEC) No 3975/87 of 14 December 1987 laying down the procedure for the application of the rules on competition to undertakings in the air transport sector (OJ No L 374, 31.12.1987, p. 1), as amended by:

    —**391 R 1284**: Council Regulation (EEC) No 1284/91 of 14 May 1991 (OJ No L 122, 17.5.1991, p. 2),

    —[14] **392 R 2410**: Council Regulation (EEC) No 2410/92 of 23 July 1992 (OJ No L 240, 24.8.1992, p. 18),

    —[15] **32003 R 0001**: Council Regulation (EC) No 1/2003 of 16 December 2002 (OJ L 1, 4.1.2003, p. 1).

14. [16]

15. [ ][17]

16. [ ][18]

2. In addition to the acts listed in Annex XIV, the following acts reflect the powers and functions of the EC Commission for the application of the competition rules of the Treaty establishing the European Coal and Steel Community (ECSC):

    1. Article (ECSC) 65(2), subparagraphs 3 to 5, (3), (4), subparagraph 2, and (5).

    2. Article (ECSC) 66(2), subparagraphs 2 to 4, and (4) to (6).

    3. **354 D 7026**: High Authority Decision No 26/54 of 6 May 1954 laying down in implementation of Article 66(4) of the Treaty a regulation concerning information to be furnished (OJ of the European Coal and Steel Community No 9, 11.5.1954, p. 350/54).

    4. **378 S 0715**: Commission Decision No 715/78/ECSC of 6 April 1978 concerning limitation periods in proceedings and the enforcement of sanctions under the Treaty establishing the European Coal and Steel Community (OJ No L 94, 8.4.1978, p. 22).

    5. **384 S 0379**: Commission Decision No 379/84/ECSC of 15 February 1984 defining the powers of officials and agents of the Commission instructed to carry out the checks provided for in the ECSC Treaty and decisions taken in application thereof (OJ No L 46, 16.2.1984, p. 23).

Article 4[19]

Article 5[20]

Article 6[21]

Article 7[22]

---

[14] Indent added by Decision No 3/94 (OJ No L 85, 30.3.1994, p 65 and EEA Supplement No 1, 30.3.1994, p 5), e.i.f. 1.7.1994.

[15] Indent and words ', as amended by:' above added by Decision No 130/2004 (OJ No L [to be published]), e.i.f. pending.

[16] Text deleted by Decision No 60/1999 (OJ No L 284, 9.11.2000, p 38 and EEA Supplement No 50, 9.11.2000, p 118), e.i.f. 1.5.1999.

[17] Text of point 15 (Commission Regulation (EC) No 2842/98) deleted by Decision No 178/2004 (OJ No L [to be published]), e.i.f. pending.

[18] Text of point 16 (Commission Regulation (EC) No 2843/98) deleted by Decision No 178/2004 (OJ No L [to be published]), e.i.f. pending.

[19] Text of article 4 deleted by Decision No 130/2004 (OJ No L [to be published]), e.i.f. pending.

[20] Text of article 5 deleted by Decision No 130/2004 (OJ No L [to be published]), e.i.f. pending.

[21] Text of article 6 deleted by Decision No 130/2004 (OJ No L [to be published]), e.i.f. pending.

[22] Text of article 7 deleted by Decision No 130/2004 (OJ No L [to be published]), e.i.f. pending.

Article 8[23]

Applications submitted to the EC Commission prior to the date of entry into force of the Agreement shall be deemed to comply with the provisions on application under the Agreement. The competent surveillance authority pursuant to Article 56 of the Agreement and Article 10 of Protocol 23 may require a duly completed form as prescribed for the implementation of the Agreement to be submitted to it within such time as it shall appoint. In that event, applications shall be treated as properly made only if the forms are submitted within the prescribed period and in accordance with the provisions of the Agreement.

Article 9[24]

Article 10

The Contracting Parties shall ensure that the measures affording the necessary assistance to officials of the EFTA Surveillance Authority and the EC Commission, in order to enable them to make their investigations as foreseen under the Agreement, are taken within six months of the entry into force of the Agreement.

Article 11

As regards agreements, decisions and concerted practices already in existence at the date of entry into force of the Agreement which fall under Article 53(1), the prohibition in Article 53(1) shall not apply where the agreements, decisions or practices are modified within six months from the date of entry into force of the Agreement so as to fulfil the conditions contained in the block exemptions provided for in Annex XIV.

Article 12

As regards agreements, decisions of associations of undertakings and concerted practices already in existence at the date of entry into force of the Agreement which fall under Article 53(1), the prohibition in Article 53(1) shall not apply, from the date of entry into force of the Agreement, where the agreements, decisions or practices are modified within six months from the date of entry into force of the Agreement so as not to fall under the prohibition of Article 53(1) any more.

Article 13

Agreements, decisions of associations of undertakings and concerted practices which benefit from an individual exemption granted under Article 85(3) of the Treaty establishing the European Economic Community before the entry into force of the Agreement shall continue to be exempted as regards the provisions of the Agreement, until their date of expiry as provided for in the decisions granting these exemptions or until the EC Commission otherwise decides, whichever date is the earlier.

Review clause[25]

By the end of 2005 and at the request of one of the Contracting Parties, the Parties shall review the mechanisms for the enforcement of Articles 53 and 54 of the Agreement as well as the co-operation mechanisms of Protocol 23 to the Agreement, with a view to ensuring the homogenous and effective application of those Articles. The Parties shall in particular review the decision of the EEA Joint Committee No 130/2004 of 24 September 2004 in light of the Parties' experiences

---

[23] Words 'and notifications' deleted by Decision No 130/2004 (OJ No L [to be published]), e.i.f. pending.
[24] Text of article 9 deleted by Decision No 130/2004 (OJ No L [to be published]), e.i.f. pending.
[25] Review clause added by Decision No 130/2004 (OJ No L [to be published]), e.i.f. pending.

with the new system of enforcing the competition rules and explore the possibility of mirroring in the EEA the system established in the EU by Council Regulation (EC) No 1/2003 as regards the application of Articles 81 and 82 of the Treaty by national competition authorities, the horizontal cooperation between national competition authorities and the mechanism for ensuring uniform application of the competition rules by national authorities.

APPENDIX 40

Protocol 22 to the EEA Agreement

Concerning the Definition of 'Undertaking' and 'Turnover' (Article 56)

Article 1

For the purposes of the attribution of individual cases pursuant to Article 56 of the Agreement, an 'undertaking' shall be any entity carrying out activities of a commercial or economic nature.

Article 2

'Turnover' within the meaning of Article 56 of the Agreement shall comprise the amounts derived by the undertakings concerned, in the territory covered by the Agreement, in the preceding financial year from the sale of products and the provision of services falling within the undertaking's ordinary scope of activities after deduction of sales rebates and of value-added tax and other taxes directly related to turnover.

Article 3[1]

In place of turnover the following shall be used:

(a) for credit institutions and other financial institutions, the sum of the following income items as defined in Council Directive 86/635/EEC, after deduction of value added tax and other taxes directly related to those items, where appropriate:

   (i) interest income and similar income;

   (ii) income from securities:
     — income from shares and other variable yield securities,
     — income from participating interests,
     — income from shares in affiliated undertakings;

   (iii) commissions receivable;

   (iv) net profit on financial operations;

   (v) other operating income.

   The turnover of a credit or financial institution in the territory covered by the Agreement shall comprise the income items, as defined above, which are received by the branch or division of that institution established in the territory covered by the Agreement;

(b) for insurance undertakings, the value of gross premiums written which shall comprise all amounts received and receivable in respect of insurance contracts issued by or on behalf of the insurance undertakings, including also outgoing reinsurance premiums, and after deduction of taxes and parafiscal contributions or levies charged by reference to the amounts of individual premiums or the total volume of premiums; as regards Article 1(2)(b) and (3)(b), (c) and (d) and the final part of Article 1(2) and (3) of Council Regulation (EC) No 139/2004, gross premiums received from residents in the territory covered by the Agreement shall be taken into account.

---

[1] Text of Article 3 replaced by Decision No 78/2004 (OJ No L [to be published]), e.i.f. 9.6.2004.

Article 4

1. In derogation from the definition of the turnover relevant for the application of Article 56 of the Agreement, as contained in Article 2 of this Protocol, the relevant turnover shall be constituted:

(a) as regards agreements, decisions of associations of undertakings and concerted practices related to distribution and supply arrangements between non-competing undertakings, of the amounts derived from the sale of goods or the provision of services which are the subject matter of the agreements, decisions or concerted practices, and from the other goods or services which are considered by users to be equivalent in view of their characteristics, price and intended use;

(b) as regards agreements, decisions of associations of undertakings and concerted practices related to arrangements on transfer of technology between non-competing undertakings, of the amounts derived from the sale of goods or the provision of services which result from the technology which is the subject matter of the agreements, decisions or concerted practices, and of the amounts derived from the sale of those goods or the provision of those services which that technology is designed to improve or replace.

2. However, where at the time of the coming into existence of arrangements as described in paragraph 1(a) and (b) turnover as regards the sale of goods or the provision of services is not in evidence, the general provision as contained in Article 2 shall apply.

Article 5

1. Where individual cases concern products falling within the scope of application of Protocol 25, the relevant turnover for the attribution of those cases shall be the turnover achieved in these products.

2. Where individual cases concern products falling within the scope of application of Protocol 25 as well as products or services falling within the scope of application of Articles 53 and 54 of the Agreement, the relevant turnover is determined by taking into account all the products and services as provided for in Article 2.

APPENDIX 41

Protocol 23 to the EEA Agreement

PROTOCOL 23[1] CONCERNING THE COOPERATION BETWEEN
THE SURVEILLANCE AUTHORITIES (ARTICLE 58)

GENERAL PRINCIPLES

Article 1

1. The EFTA Surveillance Authority and the EC Commission shall exchange information and consult each other on general policy issues at the request of either of the surveillance authorities.

2. The EFTA Surveillance Authority and the EC Commission, in accordance with their internal rules, respecting Article 56 of the Agreement and Protocol 22 and the autonomy of both sides in their decisions, shall cooperate in the handling of individual cases falling under Article 56(1)(b) and (c), (2), second sentence and (3), as provided for in the provisions below.

3. For the purposes of this Protocol, the term 'territory of a surveillance authority' shall mean for the EC Commission the territory of the EC Member States to which the Treaty establishing the European Community applies, upon the terms laid down in that Treaty, and for the EFTA Surveillance Authority the territories of the EFTA States to which the Agreement applies.

THE INITIAL PHASE OF THE PROCEEDINGS

Article 2

1. In cases falling under Article 56(1)(b) and (c), (2), second sentence and (3) of the Agreement, the EFTA Surveillance Authority and the EC Commission shall without undue delay forward to each other complaints to the extent that it is not apparent that these have been addressed to both surveillance authorities. They shall also inform each other when opening *ex officio* procedures.

2. The EFTA Surveillance Authority and the EC Commission shall without undue delay forward to each other information received from the national competition authorities within their respective territories concerning the commencement of the first formal investigative measure in cases falling under Article 56 (1)(b) and (c), (2), second sentence and (3) of the Agreement.

3. The surveillance authority which has received information as provided for in the first paragraph may present its comments thereon within 30 working days of its receipt.

Article 3

1. The competent surveillance authority shall, in cases falling under Article 56(1)(b) and (c), (2), second sentence and (3) of the Agreement, consult the other surveillance authority when:
— addressing to the undertakings or associations of undertakings concerned its statement of objections,
— publishing its intention to adopt a decision declaring Article 53 or 54 of the Agreement not applicable, or
— publishing its intention to adopt a decision making commitments offered by the undertakings binding on the undertakings.

---

[1] Text of protocol 23 replaced by Decision No 130/2004 (OJ L [to be published]), e.i.f. pending.

2. The other surveillance authority may deliver its comments within the time limits set out in the abovementioned publication or statement of objections.

3. Observations received from the undertakings concerned or third parties shall be transmitted to the other surveillance authority.

Article 4

In cases falling under Article 56(1)(b) and (c), (2), second sentence and (3) of the Agreement, the competent surveillance authority shall transmit to the other surveillance authority the administrative letters by which a file is closed or a complaint rejected.

Article 5

In cases falling under Article 56(1)(b) and (c), (2), second sentence and (3) of the Agreement, the competent surveillance authority shall invite the other surveillance authority to be represented at hearings of the undertakings concerned. The invitation shall also extend to the States falling within the competence of the other surveillance authority.

ADVISORY COMMITTEES

Article 6

1. In cases falling under Article 56(1)(b) and (c), (2), second sentence and (3) of, the Agreement, the competent surveillance authority shall, in due time, inform the other surveillance authority of the date of the meeting of the Advisory Committee and transmit the relevant documentation.

2. All documents forwarded for that purpose from the other surveillance authority shall be presented to the Advisory Committee of the surveillance authority which is competent to decide on a case in accordance with Article 56 together with the material sent out by that surveillance authority.

3. Each surveillance authority and the States falling within its competence shall be entitled to be present in the Advisory Committees of the other surveillance authority and to express their views therein; they shall not have, however, the right to vote.

4. Consultations may also take place by written procedure. However, if the surveillance authority which is not competent to decide on a case in accordance with Article 56 so requests, the competent surveillance authority shall convene a meeting.

REQUEST FOR DOCUMENTS AND THE RIGHT TO MAKE OBSERVATIONS

Article 7

The surveillance authority which is not competent to decide on a case in accordance with Article 56 of the Agreement may request from the other surveillance authority at all stages of the proceedings copies of the most important documents concerning cases falling under Article 56(1)(b) and (c), (2) second sentence and (3) of the Agreement, and may furthermore, before a final decision is taken, make any observations it considers appropriate.

ADMINISTRATIVE ASSISTANCE

Article 8

1. When the competent surveillance authority, as defined in Article 56 of the Agreement, by simple request or by decision requires an undertaking or association of undertakings located within the territory of the other surveillance authority to supply information, it shall at the same time forward a copy of the request or decision to the other surveillance authority.

2. At the request of the competent surveillance authority, as defined in Article 56 of the Agreement, the other surveillance authority shall, in accordance with its internal rules, undertake inspections within its territory in cases where the competent surveillance authority so requesting considers it to be necessary.

3. The competent surveillance authority is entitled to be represented and take an active part in inspections carried out by the other surveillance authority in respect of paragraph 2.

4. All information obtained during such inspections on request shall be transmitted to the surveillance authority which requested the inspections immediately after their finalization.

5. Where the competent surveillance authority, in cases falling under Article 56(1)(b) and (c), (2), second sentence and (3) of the Agreement, carries out inspections within its territory, it shall inform the other surveillance authority of the fact that such inspections have taken place and, on request, transmit to that authority the relevant results of the inspections.

6. When the competent surveillance authority as defined in Article 56 of the Agreement interviews a consenting natural or legal person in the territory of the other surveillance authority, the latter shall be informed thereof. The surveillance authority which is not competent may be present during such an interview, as well as officials from the competition authority on whose territory the interviews are conducted.

EXCHANGE AND USE OF INFORMATION

Article 9

1. For the purpose of applying Articles 53 and 54 of the Agreement, the EFTA Surveillance Authority and the EC Commission shall have the power to provide one another with and use in evidence any matter of fact or of law, including confidential information.

2. Information acquired or exchanged pursuant to this Protocol shall only be used in evidence for the purpose of procedures under Articles 53 and 54 of the Agreement and in respect of the subject matter for which it was collected.

3. Where the information referred to in Article 2(1) and (2) concerns a case which has been initiated as a result of an application for leniency, that information cannot be used by the receiving surveillance authority as the basis for starting an inspection on its own behalf. This is without prejudice to any power of the surveillance authority to open an inspection on the basis of information received from other sources.

4. Save as provided under paragraph 5, information voluntarily submitted by a leniency applicant will only be transmitted to the other surveillance authority with the consent of the applicant. Similarly other information that has been obtained during or following an inspection or by means of or following any other fact-finding measures which, in each case, could not have been carried out except as a result of the leniency application will only be transmitted to the other surveillance authority if the applicant has consented to the transmission to that authority of information it has voluntarily submitted in its application for leniency. Once the leniency applicant has given consent to the transmission of information to the other surveillance authority, that consent may not be withdrawn. This paragraph is without prejudice, however, to the responsibility of each applicant to file leniency applications to whichever authorities it may consider appropriate.

5. Notwithstanding paragraph 4, the consent of the applicant for the transmission of information to the other surveillance authority is not required in any of the following circumstances:
a) no consent is required where the receiving surveillance authority has also received a leniency application relating to the same infringement from the same applicant as the transmitting surveillance authority, provided that at the time the information is transmitted it is not open to the applicant to withdraw the information which it has submitted to that receiving surveillance authority;

b) no consent is required where the receiving surveillance authority has provided a written commitment that neither the information transmitted to it nor any other information it may obtain following the date and time of transmission as noted by the transmitting surveillance authority, will be used by it or by any other authority to which the information is subsequently transmitted to impose sanctions on the leniency applicant or on any other legal or natural person covered by the favourable treatment offered by the transmitting authority as a result of the application made by the applicant under its leniency programme or on any employee or former employee of the leniency applicant or of any of the aforementioned persons. A copy of the receiving authority's written commitment will be provided to the applicant.

c) in the case of information collected by a surveillance authority under Article 8(2) at the request of the surveillance authority to whom the leniency application was made, no consent is required for the transmission of such information to, and its use by, the surveillance authority to whom the application was made.

PROFESSIONAL SECRECY

Article 10

1. For the purpose of carrying out the tasks entrusted to it by this Protocol, the EC Commission and the EFTA Surveillance Authority can forward to the States falling within their respective territories all information acquired or exchanged by them pursuant to this Protocol.

2. The EC Commission, the EFTA Surveillance Authority, the competent authorities of the EC Member States and the EFTA States, their officials, servants and other persons working under the supervision of these authorities as well as officials and servants of other authorities of the States shall not disclose information acquired or exchanged by them as a result of the application of this Protocol and of the kind covered by the obligation of professional secrecy.

3. Rules on professional secrecy and restricted use of information provided for in the Agreement or in the legislation of the Contracting Parties shall not prevent exchange of information as set out in this Protocol.

ACCESS TO THE FILE[2]

Article 10A

When a surveillance authority grants access to the file to the parties to whom it has addressed a statement of objections, the right of access to the file shall not extend to internal documents of the other surveillance authority or of the competition authorities of the EC Member States and the EFTA States. The right of access to the file shall also not extend to correspondence between the surveillance authorities, between a surveillance authority and the competition authorities of the EC Member States or EFTA States or between the competition authorities of the EC Member States or EFTA States where such correspondence is contained in the file of the competent surveillance authority.

COMPLAINTS AND TRANSFERRAL OF CASES

Article 11

1. Complaints may be addressed to either surveillance authority. Complaints addressed to the surveillance authority which, pursuant to Article 56, is not competent to decide on a given case shall be transferred without delay to the competent surveillance authority.

---

[2] Heading and article 10A inserted by Decision No 178/2004 (OJ No L [to be published]), e.i.f. pending.

2. If, in the preparation or initiation of *ex officio* proceedings, it becomes apparent that the other surveillance authority is competent to decide on a case in accordance with Article 56 of the Agreement, this case shall be transferred to the competent surveillance authority.

3. Once a case is transferred to the other surveillance authority as provided as provided for in paragraphs 1 and 2, the case may not be transferred back. A case may not be transferred after

— the statement of objections has been sent to the undertakings or associations of undertakings concerned,

— a letter has been sent to the complainant informing him that there are insufficient grounds for pursuing the complaint,

— the publication of the intention to adopt a decision declaring Article 53 or 54 not applicable, or the publication of the intention to adopt a decision making commitments offered by the undertakings binding on the undertakings.

LANGUAGES

Article 12

Any natural or legal person shall be entitled to address and be addressed by the EFTA Surveillance Authority and the EC Commission in an official language of an EFTA State or the European Community which they choose as regards complaints. This shall also cover all instances of a proceeding, whether it be opened following a complaint or *ex officio* by the competent surveillance authority.

INDEX